Tolley's
VAT Cases
2012

Twenty-seventh Edition

by Alan Dolton MA (Oxon)

David Rudling CTA AIIT

Members of the LexisNexis Group worldwide

United Kingdom	LexisNexis, a Division of Reed Elsevier (UK) Ltd, Halsbury House, 35 Chancery Lane, London, WC2A 1EL, and London House, 20-22 East London Street, Edinburgh EH7 4BQ 3AF
Australia	LexisNexis Butterworths, Chatswood, New South Wales
Austria	LexisNexis Verlag ARD Orac GmbH & Co KG, Vienna
Benelux	LexisNexis Benelux, Amsterdam
Canada	LexisNexis Canada, Markham, Ontario
China	LexisNexis China, Beijing and Shanghai
France	LexisNexis SA, Paris
Germany	LexisNexis GmbH, Dusseldorf
Hong Kong	LexisNexis Hong Kong, Hong Kong
India	LexisNexis India, New Delhi
Italy	Giuffrè Editore, Milan
Japan	LexisNexis Japan, Tokyo
Malaysia	Malayan Law Journal Sdn Bhd, Kuala Lumpur
New Zealand	LexisNexis NZ Ltd, Wellington
Poland	Wydawnictwo Prawnicze LexisNexis Sp, Warsaw
Singapore	LexisNexis Singapore, Singapore
South Africa	LexisNexis, Durban
USA	LexisNexis, Dayton, Ohio

First published in 1982

© Reed Elsevier (UK) Ltd 2012

Published by LexisNexis

ISBN: 9780754542414

Printed and bound by CPI Group (UK) Ltd, Croydon, CR0 4YY

Visit LexisNexis at www.lexisnexis.co.uk

About This Book

VAT was introduced in the UK in 1973. The thousands of appeal decisions form an essential commentary on many aspects of the legislation. They also show the impact of the tax on an increasing range of business and private circumstances.

This twenty-seventh edition of Tolley's VAT Cases contains entries for more than 4,000 cases, comprising public court and tribunal decisions, decided up to 1 January 2012, which are relevant to current VAT legislation. The book is one of the Tolley annuals and is updated to 1 January each year. Where possible, 'postscripts' have been added where later decisions bear directly on relevant entries.

The digest of decisions is in 69 chapters arranged alphabetically by subject, together with an introductory survey of the leading decisions reached in 2011. Tables of cases, statutes, statutory instruments and European Community Directives and a detailed subject index are provided.

Many of the cases in this edition relate to periods before *Value Added Tax Act 1994* came into force. References marked with an asterisk (*) are to legislation which has replaced that involved in the case summarised.

If it is desired to refer to a particular case, the parties to which are not known, or to cases dealing with a particular subject, the book provides three ways of obtaining the information required. Firstly, there is the Contents list at the beginning of the book, which lists the chapters and the main headings in them. The longer chapters are also headed by their own contents lists, which contain any subheadings as well as the main headings. Secondly, there is a table of statutes. In accordance with the method of citing legislation described at the head of the Abbreviations and References (to which particular attention is drawn), the cases are listed by reference to current legislation where the legislation in force at the time of the case has been replaced. Thirdly, there is an extensive general subject index at the end of the book.

Transcripts of tribunal decisions are available from the Tribunals Service (Tax), 2nd Floor, 54 Hagley Road, Birmingham, B16 8PE.

The summaries of cases are published with kind permission of the Tribunals Service.

Whilst reasonable care has been taken to ensure the accuracy of the text at the time it was written, no responsibility for loss or damage occasioned to any person acting or refraining from action as a result of any statement in it can be accepted by the authors, editors or publishers.

LEXISNEXIS

Contents

About This Book		iii
Abbreviations and References		xix
Glossary of Latin & Old French Phrases		xxiv
Survey of Leading Decisions in 2011		xxvii
Table of Statutes		xxxv
Table of Statutory Instruments		xli
Table of European Community Directives		xlv
Table of Cases		xlix
Chapter		
1	**Agents**	
Definition of agent		**1.1**
Whether acting as agent or principal		**1.2**
Supplies through agents acting in own name (*VATA 1994, s 47(3)*)		**1.72**
Disbursements		**1.81**
Estate agents		**1.86**
Nursing agencies		**1.88**
'Party plan' and direct selling		**1.91**
2	**Appeals**	
The making of the appeal		**2.1**
Matters within the discretion of the Commissioners		**2.83**
Estoppel and allied matters		**2.109**
The requirements of *VATA 1994, s 84(3)*		**2.128**
Allocation of cases to categories (*SI 2009/273, rule 23*)		**2.148**
Statements of case, etc. (*SI 1986/590, rules 7–9; SI 2009/273, rule 25*)		**2.150**
Applications for the admission of late appeals		**2.172**
Settlement of appeals by agreement (*VATA 1994, s 85*)		**2.200**
Applications for adjournments		**2.211**
The hearing of the appeal before the tribunal (*SI 2009/273, rules 29–33*)		**2.234**
The tribunal decision (*SI 2009/273, rules 34–42*)		**2.309**
Applications for reinstatement of appeals (*SI 2009/273, rule 17(3)*)		**2.315**

Contents

Applications for judicial review **2.328**

The award of costs (*SI 1986/590, rule 29; SI 2009/273, rule 10*) **2.350**

The award of interest (*VATA 1994, s 84(8)*) **2.512**

3   Assessment

Whether assessment made to best of Commissioners' judgment (*VATA 1994, s 73(1)*) **3.1**

Time limit for assessment (*VATA 1994, s 73(6)*) **3.40**

Assessment where purchases cannot be reconciled with sales (*VATA 1994, s 73(7)*) **3.113**

The validity of the assessment **3.114**

The amount of the assessment **3.146**

Miscellaneous **3.170**

4   Bad debts

The 'outstanding amount' (*VATA 1994, s 36(2,3)*) **4.1**

Miscellaneous **4.16**

5   Books, etc.

Books and booklets (*VATA 1994, Sch 8, Group 3, Item 1*) **5.1**

Brochures, pamphlets and leaflets (*VATA 1994, Sch 8, Group 3, Item 1*) **5.54**

Newspapers, journals and periodicals (*VATA 1994, Sch 8, Group 3, Item 2*) **5.93**

Music (*VATA 1994, Sch 8, Group 3, Item 4*) **5.109**

Maps, charts etc. (*VATA 1994, Sch 8, Group 3, Item 5*) **5.110**

6   Buildings and land

The option to tax land (*VATA 1994, Sch 10, paras 1–34**) **6.1**

Beneficial interests (*VATA 1994, Sch 10, para 40**) **6.51**

Supplies between landlord and tenant **6.53**

7   Business

Court decisions **7.1**

Tribunal decisions **7.17**

8   Business entertainment

Cases held to constitute 'business entertainment' **8.1**

Cases where the input tax was apportioned **8.28**

Cases held not to constitute 'business entertainment' **8.35**

9   Capital goods scheme

10   Cash accounting scheme

Termination of authorisation **10.1**

Other matters | **10.11**

11   **Charities**

Supplies to charities—whether zero-rated (*VATA 1994, Sch 8, Group 15*) | **11.1**

Fund-raising events by charities—whether exempt (*VATA 1994, Sch 9, Group 12*) | **11.32**

Apportionment of input tax | **11.39**

Miscellaneous | **11.60**

12   **Clothing and footwear**

Whether a supply of articles 'designed as clothing' | **12.1**

Whether articles 'not suitable for older persons' | **12.10**

Miscellaneous | **12.25**

13   **Clubs, associations and organisations**

Whether *VATA 1994, s 94(2)(a)* applicable | **13.1**

The taxation of the receipts of a club, etc. | **13.17**

Other matters | **13.43**

14   **Collection and enforcement**

Power to require security (*VATA 1994, Sch 11 para 4*) | **14.1**

Recovery of VAT (*VATA 1994, Sch 11 para 5(1) (3)*) | **14.69**

Distraint (*VATA 1994, Sch 11 para 5(4)*) | **14.77**

Furnishing of information (*VATA 1994, Sch 11 para 7*) | **14.86**

Entry and search of premises (*VATA 1994, Sch 11 para 10*) | **14.93**

Order for access to recorded information (*VATA 1994, Sch 11 para 11*) | **14.97**

Restraint orders | **14.101**

Miscellaneous | **14.103**

15   **Construction of buildings, etc.**

Definition of 'person constructing a building' (*VATA 1994, Sch 8, Group 5, Item 1(a); VATA 1994, s 35(1)(1A)*) | **15.1**

Definition of 'building designed as a dwelling' (*VATA 1994, Sch 8, Group 5, Items 1(a), 2(a); VATA 1994, s 35(1A)(a)*) | **15.35**

Definition of 'relevant residential purpose' (*VATA 1994, Sch 8, Group 5, Items 1, 2(a); VATA 1994, s 35(1A)(b)*) | **15.70**

Definition of 'relevant charitable purpose' (*VATA 1994, Sch 8, Group 5, Items 1, 2(a); VATA 1994, s 35(1A)(b)*) | **15.82**

Residential conversions (*VATA 1994, Sch 8, Group 5, Item 1(b); VATA 1994, s 35(1A)(c) (1D)*) | **15.120**

Definition of 'major interest in building, dwelling or site' (*VATA 1994, Sch 8, Group 5, Item 1*) | **15.148**

Whether services supplied 'in the course of construction' (*VATA 1994, Sch 8, Group 5, Item 2*) **15.154**

Supplies to relevant housing associations (*VATA 1994, Sch 8, Group 5, Item 3*) **15.215**

Construction of garages (*VATA 1994, Sch 8, Group 5, Note 3*) **15.218**

Building materials, etc. (*VATA 1994, Sch 8, Group 5, Item 4*) **15.221**

Miscellaneous **15.261**

16   Cultural Services

Eligible bodies (*VATA 1994, Sch 9, Group 13, Note 2*) **16.1**

Miscellaneous **16.10**

17   Default interest

Appeals (*VATA 1994, s 84(6)*) **17.1**

Calculation of interest **17.6**

Miscellaneous **17.13**

18   Default surcharge

The surcharge liability notice (*VATA 1994, s 59(2, 3)*) **18.1**

Computation of the surcharge (*VATA 1994, s 59(4, 5)*) **18.18**

Despatch of return and payment to the Commissioners (*VATA 1994, s 59(7)(a)*) **18.42**

Whether a 'reasonable excuse' (*VATA 1994, s 59(7)(b)*) **18.70**

Material defaults (*VATA 1994, s 59(8)*) **18.614**

Validity of the surcharge **18.616**

19   Drugs, medicines, aids for the handicapped, etc.

Supplies of goods by registered practitioner (*VATA 1994, Sch 8, Group 12, Item 1*) **19.1**

Supplies to handicapped people (*VATA 1994, Sch 8, Group 12, Items 2, 2A, 3*) **19.9**

Supplies of widening doorways, etc. (*VATA 1994, Sch 8, Group 12, Items 8, 9*) **19.76**

Supplies of bathrooms, washrooms, etc. (*VATA 1994, Sch 8, Group 12, Items 10, 11*) **19.86**

Supplies of lifts (*VATA 1994, Sch 8, Group 12, Items 16–18*) **19.95**

20   EC Directive 2006/112/EC

Scope of the Directive (*Articles 1–4*) **20.1**

Taxable persons (*Articles 9–13*) **20.5**

Taxable transactions (*Articles 14–30*) **20.11**

Place of taxable transactions (*Articles 31–61*) **20.24**

Chargeable event (*Articles 62–71*)   **20.43**

Taxable amount (*Articles 72–92*)   **20.45**

Rates (*Articles 93–130*)   **20.52**

Exemptions (*Articles 131–166*)   **20.63**

Deductions (*Articles 167–192*)   **20.104**

Obligations of taxable persons, etc. (*Articles 193–280*)   **20.120**

Special schemes (*Articles 281–343*)   **20.125**

Derogations (*Articles 370–396*)   **20.134**

Miscellaneous (*Articles 397–401*)   **20.137**

21   Education

Provision of education by an 'eligible body' (*VATA 1994, Sch 9, Group 6, Item 1(a)*)   **21.1**

The provision of research (*VATA 1994, Sch 9, Group 6, Item 1(b)*)   **21.21**

Vocational training (*VATA 1994, Sch 9, Group 6, Items 1(c), 5, 5A*)   **21.23**

Private tuition (*VATA 1994, Sch 9, Group 6, Item 2*)   **21.30**

Examination services (*VATA 1994, Sch 9, Group 6, Item 3*)   **21.43**

Incidental goods and services (*VATA 1994, Sch 9, Group 6, Item 4*)   **21.44**

Youth club facilities (*VATA 1994, Sch 9, Group 6, Item 6*)   **21.49**

22   European Community law

EC Treaty   **22.1**

EC Directives—general principles   **22.12**

Status of ECJ decisions   **22.39**

Time limits   **22.43**

The principle of 'abuse'   **22.58**

EC Sixth VAT Directive (*77/388/EEC*)   **22.78**

EC Eighth VAT Directive (*79/1072/EEC*)   **22.531**

EC Thirteenth VAT Directive (*86/560/EEC*)   **22.545**

Miscellaneous   **22.548**

23   European Union: single market

Zero-rating of specified exports (*VATA 1994, s 30(8)*)   **23.1**

Miscellaneous   **23.23**

24   Exemptions: miscellaneous (*VATA 1994, Sch 9*)

Group 3—Postal services   **24.1**

Group 4—Betting, gaming and lotteries   **24.10**

Group 8—Burial and cremation   **24.26**

Contents

Group 10—Sport, sports competitions and physical education   **24.31**

25   **Exports**

Notice No 703   **25.1**

Retail export schemes (*Notice No 704*)   **25.16**

Miscellaneous   **25.27**

26   **Farming**

Flat-rate scheme for farmers (*VATA 1994, s 54*)   **26.1**

Miscellaneous   **26.3**

27   **Finance**

Dealings with money (*VATA 1994, Sch 9, Group 5, Item 1*)   **27.1**

Granting of credit (*VATA 1994, Sch 9, Group 5, Item 2*)   **27.10**

The provision of instalment credit finance (*VATA 1994, Sch 9, Group 5, Items 3, 4*)   **27.15**

Intermediary services (*VATA 1994, Sch 9, Group 5, Item 5*)   **27.18**

Dealings with securities (*VATA 1994, Sch 9, Group 5, Item 6*)   **27.46**

Arrangements for dealings with securities (*VATA 1994, Sch 9, Group 5, Item 7*)   **27.56**

Operation of current, deposit or savings accounts (*VATA 1994, Sch 9, Group 5, Item 8*)   **27.58**

Management of authorised unit trust scheme (*VATA 1994, Sch 9, Group 5, Item 9*)   **27.59**

Management of scheme property of open-ended investment company (*VATA 1994, Sch 9, Group 5, Item 10*)   **27.60**

Supplies relating to credit or charge cards (*VATA 1994, Sch 9, Group 5, Note 4*)   **27.61**

Miscellaneous   **27.65**

28   **Flat-rate scheme (*VATA 1994, s 26B*)**

Relevant supplies and turnover (*VATA 1994, s 26B(2)*)   **28.1**

Regulatory provisions (*VAT Regulations, regs 55A-55V*)   **28.3**

Miscellaneous   **28.21**

29   **Food**

Supplies in the course of catering (*VATA 1994, Sch 8, Group 1(a)*)   **29.1**

Whether 'food of a kind used for human consumption' (*VATA 1994, Sch 8, Group 1, General Item 1*)   **29.81**

Animal feeding stuffs (*VATA 1994, Sch 8, Group 1, General Item 2*)   **29.106**

Means of propagation of plants (*VATA 1994, Sch 8, Group 1, General Item 3*)   **29.119**

Live animals (*VATA 1994, Sch 8, Group 1, General Item 4*)   **29.120**

Ice cream, etc. (*VATA 1994, Sch 8, Group 1, Excepted Item 1*) **29.125**

Confectionery, etc. (*VATA 1994, Sch 8, Group 1, Excepted Item 2*) **29.128**

Beverages (*VATA 1994, Sch 8, Group 1, Excepted Item 4*) **29.165**

Potato crisps, etc. (*VATA 1994, Sch 8, Group 1, Excepted Item 5*) **29.181**

Pet food, etc. (*VATA 1994, Sch 8, Group 1, Excepted Item 6*) **29.187**

30 Fuel and power

Standard-rated supplies **30.1**

Supplies qualifying for reduced rate (*VATA 1994, Sch 7A, Group 1*) **30.12**

31 Gold

32 Groups of companies

Group registration **32.1**

Avoidance schemes **32.17**

Miscellaneous **32.21**

33 Health and welfare

Supplies of services by registered practitioners, etc. (*VATA 1994, Sch 9, Group 7, Item 1*) **33.1**

Dental services (*VATA 1994, Sch 9, Group 7, Item 2*) **33.32**

Provision of care, etc. in hospital or similar institution (*VATA 1994, Sch 9, Group 7, Item 4*) **33.39**

Human blood, organs and tissue (*VATA 1994, Sch 9, Group 7, Items 6–8*) **33.61**

Supplies of welfare services (*VATA 1994, Sch 9, Group 7, Item 9*) **33.62**

Supplies of transport services (*VATA 1994, Sch 9, Group 7, Item 11*) **33.76**

Imported goods (*VAT (Imported Goods) Relief Order (SI 1984/746), Sch 2 Group 5*) **33.77**

34 Human rights

35 Imports

Imports from outside EU (*VATA 1994, ss 15-17*) **35.1**

Value of imported goods (*VATA 1994, s 21*) **35.20**

Miscellaneous **35.23**

36 Input tax

Whether supplies made to the appellant **36.1**

Whether supplies used for the purposes of the business **36.169**

Whether supplies intended for use in future business **36.554**

Pre-registration input tax **36.589**

Advance payments, etc. **36.620**

Contents

Compensation and damages payments   **36.637**

Post-cessation input tax   **36.643**

Disputed repayment claims   **36.648**

Other matters   **36.662**

37   **Insolvency**

Company liquidation and receivership   **37.1**

Bankruptcy and personal insolvency   **37.21**

38   **Insurance**

The provision of insurance and reinsurance (*VATA 1994, Sch 9, Group 2, Item 1*)   **38.1**

Services of an insurance intermediary (*VATA 1994, Sch 9, Group 2, Item 4*)   **38.13**

Superseded legislation   **38.34**

39   **International services**

Zero-rating (*VATA 1994, Sch 8, Group 7*)   **39.1**

Reverse charge on services received from abroad (*VATA 1994, s 8, Sch 5*)   **39.4**

40   **Invoices and credit notes**

Whether documents to be treated as VAT invoices (*VAT Regulations 1995, reg 14*)   **40.1**

Input tax reclaimed without invoices (*VAT Regulations 1995, reg 29*)   **40.62**

Rounding of VAT on invoices   **40.82**

Credit notes   **40.85**

41   **Land**

Whether a licence to occupy land (*VATA 1994, Sch 9, Group 1, Item 1*)   **41.1**

Hotel accommodation, etc. (*VATA 1994, Sch 9, Group 1, Item 1(d)*)   **41.96**

Holiday accommodation (*VATA 1994, Sch 9, Group 1, Item 1(e)*)   **41.116**

Caravan facilities (*VATA 1994, Sch 9, Group 1, Item 1(f)*)   **41.128**

Parking facilities (*VATA 1994, Sch 9, Group 1, Item 1(h)*)   **41.136**

Mooring facilities (*VATA 1994, Sch 9, Group 1, Item 1(k)*)   **41.149**

Sports grounds, etc. (*VATA 1994, Sch 9, Group 1, Item 1(l)*)   **41.153**

Facilities for playing sport (*VATA 1994, Sch 9, Group 1, Item 1(m)*)   **41.156**

Miscellaneous   **41.163**

42   **Local authorities and statutory bodies**

Refunds of VAT (*VATA 1994, s 33)*)   **42.1**

Miscellaneous   **42.11**

43   **Management services**

44   **Motor cars**

The definition of 'motor car' (*Cars Order, Article 2*)   **44.1**

Treatment of specific transactions (*Cars Order, Article 4*)   **44.53**

Self-supplies (*Cars Order, Article 5*)   **44.55**

Relief for second-hand motor cars (*Cars Order, Article 8*)   **44.60**

Disallowance of input tax (*Input Tax Order, Article 7*)   **44.97**

Fuel for private use (*VATA 1994, ss 56, 57*)   **44.140**

Miscellaneous   **44.154**

45   **Overseas traders**

Repayments of VAT (*VATA 1994, s 39*)   **45.1**

Other cases   **45.9**

46   **Partial exemption**

Non-business input tax (*VAT Regulations 1995, reg 100*)   **46.1**

Attribution of input tax to taxable supplies (*VAT Regulations 1995, reg 101*)   **46.2**

Special methods (*VAT Regulations 1995, reg 102*)   **46.102**

Attribution of input tax to foreign and specified supplies (*VAT Regulations 1995, reg 103*)   **46.173**

Attribution of input tax on self-supplies (*VAT Regulations 1995, reg 104*)   **46.182**

Treatment of input tax attributable to exempt supplies as being attributable to taxable supplies (*VAT Regulations 1995, regs 105, 106*)   **46.183**

Adjustments of attributions (*VAT Regulations 1995, regs 107—110*)   **46.194**

Exceptional claims for VAT relief (*VAT Regulations 1995, reg 111*)   **46.221**

47   **Partnership**

Partnership assessments   **47.1**

Partnership appeals   **47.12**

Partnership registration   **47.13**

Whether a partnership exists   **47.17**

Associated partnerships   **47.65**

Miscellaneous   **47.69**

48   **Payment of tax**

Payment of VAT and credit for input tax (*VATA 1994, s 25*)   **48.1**

Repayment of tax (*VATA 1994, s 80*)   **48.16**

Repayment supplement (*VATA 1994, s 79*)   **48.82**

Contents

Interest payable in cases of official error (*VATA 1994, s 78*)   **48.114**

Miscellaneous   **48.148**

49   Penalties: criminal offences

Offences under *VATA 1994, s 72*   **49.1**

Offences under *Proceeds of Crime Act 2002*   **49.18**

Common law offences   **49.25**

50   Penalties: evasion of tax

Computation of the penalty   **50.1**

The assessment of the penalty (*VATA 1994, s 76*)   **50.3**

Liability of directors (*VATA 1994, s 61*)   **50.13**

Other cases   **50.67**

Miscellaneous   **50.156**

51   Penalties: failure to notify, etc.

Definition of 'relevant tax' (*VATA 1994, s 67(1)*)   **51.1**

Date from which penalty commences (*VATA 1994, s 67(3)*)   **51.5**

Date on which penalty ceases (*VATA 1994, s 67(3)*)   **51.9**

Whether a reasonable excuse (*VATA 1994, s 67(8)*; *FA 2008, Sch 41 para 20*)   **51.13**

Unauthorised issue of invoices (*VATA 1994, s 67(1)(c)*; *FA 2008, Sch 41 para 2*)   **51.139**

Mitigation of penalties (*VATA 1994, s 70*; *FA 2008, Sch 41 paras 12, 13*)   **51.146**

52   Penalties: misdeclaration and errors

Definition of 'prescribed accounting period' (*VATA 1994, s 63(1)*)   **52.1**

Whether a return has been 'made' (*VATA 1994, s 63(1)(a)*)   **52.2**

Inadequate estimated assessment (*VATA 1994, s 63(1)(b)*; *FA 2007, Sch 24 para 2*)   **52.5**

Definition of 'tax which would have been lost' (*VATA 1994, s 63(2)*)   **52.24**

Whether return corrected by subsequent return (*VATA 1994, s 63(8)*)   **52.27**

Whether a 'reasonable excuse' (*VATA 1994, s 63(10)(a)*)   **52.31**

Whether error 'voluntarily disclosed' (*VATA 1994, s 63(10)(b)*)   **52.377**

Mitigation of penalties (*VATA 1994, s 70*)   **52.392**

Penalties for errors: amount of penalty (*FA 2007, Sch 24 paras 4–12*)   **52.449**

Validity of the penalty   **52.452**

53   Penalties: sales statements and regulatory provisions

Failure to submit EC sales statement (*VATA 1994, s 66*)   **53.1**

Breaches of regulatory provisions (*VATA 1994, s 69*) **53.18**

54   Pension funds

Input tax cases **54.1**

Output tax cases **54.11**

55   Protected buildings

Definition of 'protected building' (*VATA 1994, Sch 8, Group 6, Note 1*) **55.1**

Whether a 'substantial reconstruction' (*VATA 1994, Sch 8, Group 6, Item 1, Note 3*) **55.19**

Whether an 'approved alteration' (*VATA 1994, Sch 8, Group 6, Item 2, Note 4*) **55.27**

Whether a supply of services (*VATA 1994, Sch 8, Group 6, Item 2*) **55.83**

Miscellaneous **55.88**

56   Reduced-rate supplies: miscellaneous

Group 2—Energy-saving materials **56.1**

Group 5—Children's car seats **56.2**

Group 6—Residential conversions **56.3**

Group 7—Residential renovations and alterations **56.8**

57   Registration

Liability to be registered (*VATA 1994, Sch 1 para 1*) **57.1**

Registration of associated persons as a single taxable person (*VATA 1994, Sch 1 para 2*) **57.35**

Notification of liability and registration (*VATA 1994, Sch 1 para 5*) **57.82**

Entitlement to be registered (*VATA 1994, Sch 1 para 9*) **57.101**

Cancellation of registration (*VATA 1994, Sch 1 para 13*) **57.120**

Exemption from registration (*VATA 1994, Sch 1 para 14*) **57.167**

The person by whom the business is carried on **57.170**

Miscellaneous **57.218**

58   Retailers' special schemes

What supplies are within the schemes **58.1**

Retrospective changes of scheme **58.13**

Transitional matters **58.25**

Gross takings **58.36**

Expected selling prices **58.48**

Point of Sale Scheme **58.50**

Apportionment Schemes **58.53**

Direct Calculation Schemes **58.55**

Contents

Miscellaneous   **58.60**

59   **Returns**

Accounting periods   **59.1**

Making of returns (*VAT Regulations 1995, reg 25*)   **59.8**

Correction of errors (*VAT Regulations 1995, regs 34, 35*)   **59.23**

Miscellaneous   **59.34**

60   **Second-hand goods**

Records and accounts   **60.1**

Works of art, etc.   **60.7**

Miscellaneous   **60.16**

61   **Self-supply**

Self-supplies of goods (*VATA 1994, s 5(5)*)   **61.1**

Self-supplies of services (*VATA 1994, s 5(6)*)   **61.8**

62   **Supply**

Whether there has been a supply   **62.1**

By whom the supply was made   **62.223**

The time of the supply (*VATA 1994, s 6*)   **62.382**

The place of the supply (*VATA 1994, s 7*)   **62.476**

Single or multiple supplies   **62.548**

Miscellaneous matters   **62.557**

63   **Tour operators and travel agents**

Definition of 'tour operator' (*VATA 1994, s 53(3)*)   **63.1**

Tour Operators' Margin Scheme   **63.9**

64   **Trade unions, professional and public interest bodies**

Associations held to be within *VATA 1994, Sch 9, Group 9*   **64.1**

Associations held not to be within *VATA 1994, Sch 9, Group 9*   **64.12**

Miscellaneous   **64.37**

65   **Transfers of going concerns**

Cases held to fall within *Special Provisions Order, Article 5*   **65.1**

Cases held not to fall within *Special Provisions Order, Article 5*   **65.38**

Land and buildings (*Special Provisions Order, Article 5(2)*)   **65.86**

Liability to register (*VATA 1994, Sch 1 para 1(2)*)   **65.90**

Liability to account for tax (*VAT Regulations 1995, reg 6*)   **65.108**

Miscellaneous   **65.118**

66   Transport

Supply and maintenance of ships (*VATA 1994, Sch 8, Group 8, Item 1*)   **66.1**

Transport of passengers (*VATA 1994, Sch 8, Group 8, Item 4*)   **66.2**

Transport of goods (*VATA 1994, Sch 8, Group 8, Item 5*)   **66.40**

Handling services (*VATA 1994, Sch 8, Group 8, Item 6*)   **66.41**

The 'making of arrangements' (*VATA 1994, Sch 8, Group 8, Item 10*)   **66.44**

Handling or storage of goods (*VATA 1994, Sch 8, Group 8, Item 11*)   **66.50**

67   Valuation

Transactions between connected persons (*VATA 1994, Sch 6 paras 1, 1A*)   **67.1**

Whether agreed price to be treated as exclusive or inclusive of VAT   **67.4**

Supplies of goods   **67.11**

Supplies of services   **67.88**

Face value vouchers (*VATA 1994, Sch 10A*)   **67.151**

68   Warehoused goods and free zones

69   Zero-rating: miscellaneous (*VATA 1994, Sch 8*)

Group 2—Sewerage services and water   **69.1**

Group 9—Caravans and houseboats   **69.5**

Index

Abbreviations and References

References throughout the book to numbered sections and schedules are to the Value Added Tax Act 1994 unless otherwise stated. An asterisk (*) added to a statutory reference indicates that it has replaced, but is similar or identical to, the relevant legislation involved in the case. References to VAT Tribunals Rules, VAT Regulations and Special Provisions Order are respectively to The Value Added Tax Tribunals Rules 1986 (SI 1986/590), The Value Added Tax Regulations 1995 (SI 1995/2518) and The Value Added Tax (Special Provisions) Order 1995 (SI 1995/1268). A reference to Notice No 700 is to HM Revenue & Customs Notice No 700 and similarly for other numbered Notices. Some of these Notices, or parts of them, have statutory force.

Abbreviations

Adm Ct	Administrative Court
Art	Article
C & E	Customs & Excise
CA	Court of Appeal
Ch D	Chancery Division
CIR	Commissioners of Inland Revenue
CJEC	Court of Justice of the European Communities
CJEU	Court of Justice of the European Union
col.	column
Comm Ct	Commercial Court
Commissioners	Commissioners of C & E, or Her Majesty's Revenue & Customs
Commrs	Commissioners of C & E, or Her Majesty's Revenue & Customs
CS	Court of Session (Scotland)
DC	Divisional Court
EC	European Community
ECHR	European Court of Human Rights
EEC	European Economic Community

ex p.	ex parte
FA	Finance Act
F(No 2) A	Finance (No 2) Act
FC(A)	Federal Court (Australia)
FTC	Finance and Tax Chamber (of the First-Tier Tribunal)
FTT	First-Tier Tribunal
HCJ (S)	High Court of Justiciary (Scotland)
HL	House of Lords
HMRC	Commissioners of Her Majesty's Revenue & Customs
ICAEW	Institute of Chartered Accountants in England and Wales
ICTA	Income and Corporation Taxes Act
KB	King's Bench Division
NI	Northern Ireland
NIQB	Northern Ireland Queen's Beech
NSW	New South Wales
oao	on the application of
p	page
PC	Privy Council
PCC	Parochial Church Council
PCTA	Provisional Collection of Taxes Act 1968
QB	Queen's Bench Division
r	rule
Reg	Regulation
RSC	Rules of the Supreme Court
s	section
SC	Supreme Court
Sch	Schedule
SI	Statutory Instrument
t/a	trading as
TC	Tax Chamber (First-Tier Tribunal)
TCC	Tax & Chancery Chamber (Upper Tribunal)
UKSC	United Kingdom Supreme Court

UKUT   United Kingdom Upper Tribunal

UT   Upper Tribunal

VATA   Value Added Tax Act

REFERENCES (*denotes a series accredited for citation in court)

AC   *Law Reports, Appeal Cases, (Incorporated Council of Law Reporting for England and Wales, 3, Stone Buildings, Lincoln's Inn, WC2A 3XN)

All ER   *All England Law Reports, (LexisNexis, Halsbury House, 35 Chancery Lane, London WC2A 1EL).

All ER (Comm)   *All England Law Reports (Commercial Cases), (Lexis Nexis, as above).

All ER (D)   All England Reporter Direct, (LexisNexis, as above).

All ER (EC)   *All England Law Reports: European Cases, (LexisNexis, as above).

ALR   Argus Law Reports, Victoria.

BCLC   Butterworths' Company Law Cases, (LexisNexis, as above).

BMLR   Butterworths' Medico-Legal Reports, (LexisNexis, as above).

BPIR   Bankruptcy and Personal Insolvency Reports (Jordan Publishing Ltd, 21 St Thomas Street, Bristol BS1 6JS).

BTC   British Tax Cases, (CCH Editions Ltd, Telford Road, Bicester, Oxon OX6 OXD).

BVC   British Value Added Tax Cases, (CCH Editions Ltd, as above).

CBNS   Common Bench New Series Reports.

Ch   *Law Reports, Chancery Division.

CMLR   Common Market Law Reports (European Law Centre, South Quay Plaza, 183 Marsh Wall, London E14 9FT).

Cr AR   Criminal Appeal Reports.

CSIH   *Court of Session, Inner House Cases.

CSOH   *Court of Session, Outer House Cases.

D	Session Cases, 2nd Series (Dunlop).
DLR	Dominion Law Reports.
E & E	Ellis & Ellis's Reports.
ECCD	European Commission Collection of Decisions.
ECDR	European Commission Decisions and Reports.
ECHR	European Court of Human Rights Reports.
ECR	European Community Reports.
EG	Estates Gazette.
EHRR	European Human Rights Reports.
EWCA Civ	*England & Wales Court of Appeal Civil Cases.
EWCA Crim	*England & Wales Court of Appeal Criminal Cases.
EWHC Admin	*England & Wales High Court (Administrative Court).
FCR	Federal Court Reports (Australia).
H & N	*Hurlstone & Norman's Reports.
ICR	Industrial Cases Reports.
IEHC	Irish High Court Decisions.
IESC	Supreme Court of Ireland Decisions.
ITLR	International Tax Law Reports, (LexisNexis, as above).
LR Ind App	*Law Reports, Indian Appeals.
LTR	*Law Times Reports.
OJ	Official Journal of the European Communities.
QBD	Queen's Bench Decisions.
SC	Court of Session Cases.
SCLR	Scottish Civil Law Reports.
SFTD	Simon's First-Tier Tax Decisions, (Lexis Nexis, as above).
SR (NSW)	Session Reports (New South Wales).
STC	*Simon's Tax Cases, (LexisNexis, as above).
STI	Simon's Tax Intelligence, (LexisNexis, as above).
SWTI	Simon's Weekly Tax Intelligence, (LexisNexis, as above).
TC	*Official Reports of Tax Cases, (The Stationery Office, 49 High Holborn, WC1V 6HB).
TTC	Tolley's Tax Cases, (LexisNexis, as above).
UKHL	*UK House of Lords Cases.

VATDR	Value Added Tax and Duties Reports, (HM Stationery Office, as above).
VATTR	Value Added Tax Tribunal Reports, (HM Stationery Office, as above).
VTD	VAT Tribunal Decision, (Tribunals Service (Tax), 2nd Floor, 54 Hagley Road, Birmingham, B16 8PE).
WLR	*Weekly Law Reports, (Incorporated Council of Law Reporting, as above).

Court cases. The first number in the citation refers to the volume, and the second to the page, so that [1985] 1 All ER 15 means that the report is to be found on page fifteen of the first volume of the All England Law Reports for 1985. Where no volume number is given, only one volume was produced in that year.

In English cases, Scottish and Northern Irish decisions (unless there is a difference of law between the countries) are generally followed but are not binding.

In the text, citation where appropriate is of Simon's Tax Cases, the official court judgment number (either the Law Reports or the Weekly Law Reports for cases before 2001), and the All England Reports. For ECJ cases, the official case reference is given together with citations for the Common Market Law Reports, the European Community Reports, and (where appropriate) Simon's Tax Cases and the All England Reports. Only in default of these are other series referred to. The citation is preceded by the Court and the month and year of the decision.

Tribunal cases. Where a decision is reported in the Value Added Tax Tribunals Reports (VATTR) or Value Added Tax and Duties Reports (VATDR) published by HM Stationery Office by the direction of the President of the VAT and Duties Tribunals, the citation is the VATTR or VATDR reference followed by the number assigned to the decision by the VAT Tribunals Headquarters [e.g. [1989] VATTR 199 (VTD 4137)]. In other VAT Tribunal cases, the citation is the tribunal centre reference followed by the number assigned to the decision by the VAT and Duties Tribunals Headquarters [e.g. MAN/77/247 (VTD 537)]. The letters in the tribunal centre reference are the first three letters of the tribunal [e.g. EDN = Edinburgh, LON = London, MAN = Manchester]. In all tribunal cases only the appellant or applicant is named.

For decisions of the Upper Tribunal, the citation is to Simon's Tax Cases followed by the official citation of the Upper Tribunal, e.g. UT [2009] STC 2485; [2009] UKUT 175 (TCC).

For decisions of the First–Tier Tribunal, the citation is to Simon's First–Tier Decisions (where available), followed by the official citations of the First-Tier Tribunal and of the Tax Chamber, e.g. [2009] SFTD 590; [2009] UKFTT 184 (TC), TC00139.

Where legal decisions are very recent and in the lower courts or the tribunals, it must be remembered that they may be reversed on appeal.

Glossary of Latin & Old French Phrases

acte claire	so obvious as to leave no scope for any reasonable doubt.
causa causans	the immediate cause; the last link in the chain of causation.
causa sine qua non	an essential link in the chain of causation, but not the immediate cause.
certiorari	a writ commanding a lower court to certify a matter to the High Court.
eiusdem generis	of the same type.
estoppel	rule of evidence which stops a person from denying the truth of a statement previously made by him to, and relied on by, another person.
estoppel per rem judicatum	rule of evidence which stops a person from contesting an issue decided by the Court in previous litigation between the same parties.
ex gratia	voluntarily, without accepting legal liability.
ex parte	an application made to the court by one party without giving notice to the other party.
in re	in the matter of, concerning.
inter alia	among other things.
mandamus	a writ ordering the performance of a specific duty.
obiter dictum / obiter dicta	opinion(s) expressed by a judge in passing, on issues which do not form part of the essential reasoning of the decision in the case (and thus carry little authority as precedents).
per incuriam	where a court overlooks relevant authorities (so that the decision may be considered doubtful or unreliable).
prima facie	at first sight.

ratio decidendi	reason for deciding; the principle of law on which a case is decided.
re	in the matter of; concerning.
res judicata	an issue which a court has decided in an action between parties and cannot be questioned in a later action between the same parties.
sic	thus (used, for example, to show that a grammatical mistake was that of the original authority being cited, and is not a mistake made by the editor or typesetter).
sine die	indefinitely.
sub nomine	under the name of.
sui generis	of its own type.
ultra vires	outside the powers recognised by law as belonging to the person or body in question; without authority.

Survey of Leading Decisions in 2011

There follows a numerical analysis of the court decisions reached in 2011 and included in this book, and an outline narrative survey of the leading decisions. The numerical analysis is confined to decisions in UK courts, and thus excludes decisions of the ECJ and ECHR. 'Other' decisions which were not wholly or substantially in favour of either party, or those in which HMRC were not a party and neutral as to the outcome. The figures in brackets are the averages of the corresponding figures for the years 2001–2010 inclusive (unfortunately, the corresponding figures for the VAT tribunal are not available, and the figures for the First-Tier Tribunal are for 2010 only).

Court	Number of decisions			
	TOTAL	For HMRC	For taxpayer	Others
First-Tier Tribunal	239 (245)	159 (177)	52 (47)	28 (21)
Upper Tribunal, High Court and Court of Session (Outer House)	22 (24.5)	11 (14.4)	8 (7.2)	3 (2.9)
Court of Appeal, CA(NI) and Court of Session (Inner House)	7 (13.0)	6 (7.3)	1 (3.9)	– (1.8)
Supreme Court (including House of Lords 2001-2009)	– (2.1)	– (1.1)	– (0.7)	– (0.3)
Total for all courts and tribunals	268 (284.6)	176 (199.8)	61 (58.8)	31 (26.0)

As usual, most of the decisions reached by the courts and tribunals during 2011 appear to be of somewhat limited interest. In the interests of space, only the most significant decisions will be referred to in this summary.

The case of *Agurdino Srl v Moldova*, **34.23** HUMAN RIGHTS, is an interesting illustration of the fact that the legal principles which we take for granted in the UK do not necessarily apply in Eastern Europe. When HMRC lose an important case, they sometimes persuade Parliament to change the law in their favour, but they do not make such changes retrospective and they have never petitioned the House of Lords or the Supreme Court to reopen a previous decision to as to give effect to a subsequent change in the law. Sadly, taxpayers in Moldova cannot be sure of the same protection. In 2002 the Moldovan Supreme Court had allowed an appeal by a company, holding that the relevant supplies were exempt under the legislation then in force. In October 2005 the Moldovan Parliament amended the relevant legislation, and in November 2005 the Moldovan Tax Inspectorate applied for a review of the 2002

Supreme Court decision, contending that the amendment to the legislation should have retrospective effect. Later that month the Moldovan Supreme Court accepted the Inspectorate's application and quashed its previous judgment. Not surprisingly, the ECHR held that this was a breach of the European Convention on Human Rights.

In *HMRC v The Rank Group plc*, **22.375** EUROPEAN COMMUNITY LAW, the ECJ delivered a typically lengthy decision on the interpretation of the last eleven words of *Article 13B(f)* of the *Sixth Directive*, which provides exemption for 'betting, lotteries, and other forms of gambling, subject to conditions and limitations laid down by each Member State'. The decision suggests that the 'conditions and limitations' which the UK had imposed breached the principle of 'fiscal neutrality'. HMRC have accepted this interpretation with regard to the companies' supplies of bingo, but are continuing to contest the case with regard to gaming machines: see HMRC Brief 39/11.

The ECJ delivered an interesting judgment on the scope of the 'reverse charge' principle in *Finanzamt Deggendorf v Stoppelkamp (Raab's Administrator)*, **22.462** EUROPEAN COMMUNITY LAW, holding that the definition of a "taxable person who is not established within the territory of the country" should be considered solely by reference to the place from which the relevant economic activities were carried out. Accordingly, the ECJ held that a trader who lived in Germany, but whose business was based in Austria, qualified as a taxable person who was not established in Germany for the purposes of the 'reverse charge' procedure.

In *Finanzamt Burgdorf v Bog*, **22.155** EUROPEAN COMMUNITY LAW, the ECJ held that the supply of hot food such as sausages and chips from mobile snack bars was a supply of goods rather than services. The effect of this is that such supplies appear to qualify for a reduced rate of VAT under German law. However, the decision does not appear to have any direct effect in the UK, where such supplies are standard-rated whereas supplies of cold food which are not 'in the course of catering' may qualify for zero-rating under a derogation which is not dependent on the distinction between a supply of goods and a supply of services.

Advocate-General Jääskinen delivered an interesting Opinion in *Lebara Ltd v HMRC*, **22.190** EUROPEAN COMMUNITY LAW, concerning the VAT treatment of sales of phonecards. He expressed the view that that 'Article 6(4) of the Sixth VAT Directive creates the legal fiction of two identical supplies of services provided consecutively', and that that legal fiction was 'the key to resolving this case'. It seems likely that the ECJ will follow his Opinion.

The Court of Appeal heard fewer cases concerning VAT in 2011 than it has done in most previous years. Last year's edition of this survey recorded the ECJ decision in *HMRC v Axa UK plc*, **22.362** EUROPEAN COMMUNITY LAW. The ECJ sometimes cloaks its decisions in somewhat Delphic language, but most observers felt that the *Axa* decision was sufficiently clear-cut to make it apparent that the company's supplies failed to qualify for exemption, Somewhat optimistically, the company decided to seek a further hearing of the case by the CA, which duly delivered a unanimous judgment in favour of HMRC.

HMRC were relieved to win the case of *HMRC v Rochdale Drinks Distributors Ltd*, 37.6 INSOLVENCY, where the CA unanimously approved the appointment of a provisional liquidator, finding that there was substantial evidence that the company had been involved in VAT fraud. In *HMRC v Chamberlin*, 37.24 INSOLVENCY, the CA unanimously upheld a bankruptcy order against a solicitor who had failed to account for VAT.

The CA had to consider the consequences of VAT fraud in *R v Takkar*, 49.21 PENALTIES: CRIMINAL OFFENCES, and *R v McIntosh*, 49.22 PENALTIES: CRIMINAL OFFENCES, in both of which it upheld very substantial confiscation orders against company directors.

The CA upheld the validity of a floor-based 'partial exemption' method of attributing input tax in *HMRC v London Clubs Management Ltd*, 46.136 PARTIAL EXEMPTION. The most surprising feature of this case is that HMRC, which had lost at both the First-Tier Tribunal and the Upper Tribunal, thought it worth taking the case to the CA.

The case of *Europeans Ltd v HMRC (No 3)*, 2.371 APPEALS, is noteworthy as it is the first case involving MTIC fraud in which HMRC have sought a third party costs order against a company's director. The Ch D granted the order. Proudman J observed that the Tribunal had found that M had given dishonest evidence and that he 'had actual knowledge of the chain of fraudulent transactions', had 'masterminded a serious VAT fraud', and had 'lied in evidence to the Tribunal and failed to cooperate with either HMRC or the joint liquidators of the company'. Accordingly HMRC were entitled to costs against M. It is understood that HMRC intend making similar applications in other such cases.

The Upper Tribunal held that the case of *HMRC v Grattan plc (No 6)*, 2.523 APPEALS, should be referred to the ECJ for a further ruling on the question of whether interest should be compounded. Interestingly, Judge Bishopp specifically declined to follow the earlier CA decision in *John Wilkins (Motor Engineers) Ltd v HMRC*, 2.520 APPEALS, where the CA had ordered that similar proceedings should be stayed pending the ECJ decision in *Littlewoods Retail Ltd v HMRC*, 2.522 APPEALS (which the ECJ began hearing in November 2011).

The Upper Tribunal allowed an appeal by HMRC in *HMRC v BAA Ltd*, 32.30 GROUPS OF COMPANIES, holding that the company was not entitled to reclaim a substantial amount of input tax relating to a successful 'takeover bid' for another company, on the grounds that there was 'no direct and immediate link' between the supplies to which the input tax related and any onward taxable supplies. For a discussion of the case, see the article by Greg Sinfield and Lee Squires in Tax Journal, 15 July 2011. (Greg Sinfield's comments are particularly noteworthy, as he has subsequently been appointed as an Upper Tribunal judge.) At first sight, this seems to be a somewhat harsh decision; but it is worth noting that the European Commission is taking infraction proceedings against the UK for allowing 'mere holding companies' to join a VAT group, which presumably explains why the company, which had succeeded at the First-Tier Tribunal, has apparently not sought to appeal against the Upper Tribunal decision.

The First-Tier Tribunal reached an interesting decision in *Wakefield College v HMRC*, **15.100** CONSTRUCTION OF BUILDINGS, where Judge Barlow was forced to consider the apparent conflict between the Court of Session decision in *Edinburgh Telford College v HMRC*, **22.149** EUROPEAN COMMUNITY LAW (where the CS had held that a college was a 'body governed by public law'), and the subsequent High Court decision in *University of Cambridge v HMRC*, **61.5** SELF-SUPPLY (where counsel for the university apparently did not refer to the *Edinburgh Telford* case, and the court held that a university was not a 'body governed by public law'). Judge Barlow applied the *University of Cambridge* decision, and declined to follow the decision in *Edinburgh Telford College* on the grounds that it had been based on a concession by HMRC which was incorrect in law. Judge Barlow held that the CS decision was 'authority for the proposition that a public body is acting as such when it carries out its core activities', but was 'not authority for the proposition that a further education college is a public body in the sense required'.

Another particularly interesting decision was reached in *The British Disabled Flying Association v HMRC*, **19.33** DRUGS, MEDICINES, AIDS FOR THE HANDICAPPED, ETC. Judge Geraint Jones held that the fact that the aircraft had not originally been manufactured for the use of handicapped people did not prevent their supply from qualifying for zero-rating, since *Item 2(g)* applied 'to equipment designed solely for the use by a handicapped person regardless of when it became so designed'. There was 'no good reason, either as a matter of statutory construction or common sense, for an item not to be designed solely for use by a handicapped person simply because a factory manufactured item, not so designed, has then been subject to modifications to make it designed for use by handicapped person'.

In *Bridport & West Dorset Golf Club Ltd v HMRC*, **20.74** EC DIRECTIVE 2006/112/EC, the tribunal accepted the club's contention that it should not be required to account for VAT on 'green fees' from non-members. Judge Bishopp held that the exclusion of supplies to non-members from the scope of the exemption in *VATA 1994, Sch 9, Group 10, Item 3* contravened *Article 133* of *Directive 2006/112/EC*. The decision was particularly interesting because Judge Bishopp specifically declined to follow his own previous decision in *Keswick Golf Club v C & E Commrs*, [1998] VATDR 267 (VTD 15493), which HMRC had for many years cited as an authority. Not surprisingly, HMRC have appealed to the Upper Tribunal against Judge Bishopp's decision.

In *Paymex Ltd v HMRC*, **20.81** EC DIRECTIVE 2006/112/EC, the tribunal accepted a company's contention that supplies relating to the establishment and supervision of individual voluntary arrangements qualified for exemption under EC law. HMRC have reportedly accepted the decision, which does of course mean that small insolvency practitioners will now have to face the complexities of the partial exemption regime.

The tribunal reached an important decision in *Noor v HMRC*, **22.553** EUROPEAN COMMUNITY LAW, where a trader had reclaimed input tax on services which he had received more than six months before the date of registration, and gave evidence that he had previously telephoned HMRC's National Advice Service and had been told that that there was a three-year period for reclaiming input tax. The tribunal held that the National

Advice Service had given the appellant a 'legitimate expectation' that he could reclaim the tax in question. The case is an important victory for the taxpayer on the subject of 'legitimate expectation'. The principle had previously been aired in the 2010 case of *Hanover Company Services Ltd*, **22.552** EUROPEAN COMMUNITY LAW, where the tribunal upheld HMRC's view that, on the facts of that case, the company did not have a 'legitimate expectation' that it could treat certain supplies as zero-rated. However, in the *Hanover* case, the appellant company seemed to be on rather weak ground, in that it was not relying on a specific individual assurance, but simply on a passage in HMRC's VAT Manual which had not been updated promptly. (Experienced readers of tax encyclopaedias, whether in electronic or looseleaf format, should be well aware that such encyclopaedias are not always updated as promptly as the reader may wish, and it is dangerous to rely on guidance in such an encyclopaedia without considering whether it may have been over-taken by subsequent developments.) In the *Noor* case, however, the appellant was relying on a specific individual assurance in a telephone conversation, and Judge Brooks held that this conversation had given the appellant a 'legitimate expectation' that he would be entitled to reclaim the tax.

The decision in *Cumbria County Council v HMRC*, **40.112** INVOICES AND CREDIT NOTES, is notable for Judge Demack's unusually strong criticisms of the HMRC officer who had rejected the council's claim. Judge Demack found that the officer's witness statement had contained an allegation 'without any evidence whatsoever to support such a statement', and which had been 'totally unjustified'. The council seems to have been given a difficult time by two different arms of Her Majesty's Government. Firstly, the Department of Environment, Food and Rural Affairs failed to pay the full amount which the council had invoiced, forcing the council to begin High Court proceedings; and secondly, HMRC persisted in rejecting the council's claim for repayment of VAT. The tribunal duly allowed the council's appeal, holding that there had been a 'decrease in consideration', within *VAT Regulations (SI 1995/2518), reg 38(1)(b)*.

The tribunal reached an interesting decision in *Firstpoint (Europe) Ltd v HMRC*, **62.518** SUPPLY. A Scottish company had been formed to provide guidance and advice to students pursuing sports scholarships in the USA. HMRC issued a ruling that the place of supply was in the UK, where the company was incorporated and where its clients lived. However, the tribunal allowed the company's appeal, holding that it was an intermediary and that its supplies fell within *VATA 1994, Sch 4A para 10(2)*, so that its supplies should be 'treated as made in the same country as the supply to which it relates', which was the USA.

Table of Statutes

1882 Bills of Exchange Act
.... 18.28–18.30

1890 Partnership Act
s 10 .... 50.99
s 12 .... 50.11
s 16 .... 50.11

1925 Law of Property Act
s 109(8) 37.11

1958 Recreational Charities Act
s 1 .... 15.82, 15.86, 15.108

1968 Theft Act
s 32(1) 49.25, 49.26

1972 European Communities Act
.... 22.24
article 28 .... 22.564

1975 Litigants in Person (Costs & Expenses) Act ... 2.388, 2.389, 2.400, 2.404, 2.455, 2.456, 2.470, 2.471

1979 Customs and Excise Management Act
s 6 .... 3.123
s 68 .... 36.203
s 147(3) 14.119
s 152 .... 2.206
s 170 .... 36.231
s 171 .... 14.67

1980 Limitation Act
s 32 .... 48.146

1981 Contempt of Court Act
ss 9, 19 .... 2.294

1981 Supreme Court Act
s 35A 2.531, 2.532

1985 Companies Act
s 196 .... 37.9
s 458 .... 36.242

1986 Insolvency Act
s 135 .... 37.5, 37.6
s 175 .... 37.9
s 267 .... 47.69
s 271(3) 37.21
s 375(1) 37.22
s 423 .... 37.13
Sch 6 .... 32.33

1988 Income and Corporation Taxes Act
s 402 .... 43.8

1989 Finance Act
s 182 .... 2.418

1992 Tribunals and Inquiries Act
s 11 .... 2.172, 2.334

1994 Value Added Tax Act
s 4(1) 62.150–62.162, 62.456
s 5(2) 11.55, 54.11, 62.137, 62.186
s 6 .... 62.382–62.475
s 6(2) 62.382–62.395

1994 Value Added Tax Act – cont.
s 6(2)(a) 62.393
s 6(2)(c) 62.389, 62.393, 62.395
s 6(3) 62.396–62.410
s 6(4) 32.17, 62.89, 62.92, 62.411–62.464
s 6(6) 62.170
s 6(14) 67.3
s 7 .... 62.476–62.546
s 7(3) 23.33
s 7(7) 62.476
s 7(10) 62.480–62.499
s 8 .... 39.4–39.19
s 9(2) 62.480–62.499
s 9(3) 62.502, 62.503
s 9(4) 62.505, 62.506
s 9(5) 62.507, 62.536
s 10 .... 23.23–23.26
s 13 .... 23.28
s 15 .... 35.18, 35.19
s 18 .... 68.1, 68.2
s 19 .... 44.86
s 19(2) 13.50, 65.97, 67.5, 67.103
s 19(3) 41.82, 67.38
s 21 .... 35.20
s 21(5) 35.21
s 24 .... 36.612
s 24(1) . 35.14, 36.186, 36.321, 36.662
s 24(3) 36.330–36.340
s 24(5) .. 11.51, 32.19, 36.400, 46.197, 48.134
s 24(6) 52.172
s 25 .... 48.1, 59.23
s 25(6) 36.558, 36.578
s 25(7) 42.9
s 26 .... 36.84, 46.28
s 26(2) 11.55, 62.526
s 26(3) 46.122
s 26A 36.672, 36.673
s 26B 28.1, 28.2, 28.11
s 26B(5) 28.22
s 28 .... 18.463, 18.548
s 30 .... 23.9, 55.88
s 30(5) 11.55
s 30(6) ... 25.27, 25.28, 52.204–52.210
s 30(8) 22.518, 23.1–23.21, 23.35, 23.36, 50.82
s 33 .... 42.1–42.5, 46.156, 48.53
s 33(1) 42.1, 42.4, 42.9
s 33(3) 42.7, 42.8
s 33(6) 42.9
s 33A 48.83
s 35 .... 15.1–15.147, 15.210, 15.263–15.280
s 35(1) 15.1–15.34
s 35(1)(b) 15.263–15.271
s 35(1)(c) 15.279, 15.280

1994 Value Added Tax Act – *cont.*

s 35(1A)(a) 15.35–15.66
s 35(1A)(b) 15.70–15.119
s 35(1B) 15.221–15.260
s 35(1C) 15.276
s 35(1D) 15.128–15.147
s 36 .... 4.1–4.24
s 36(1) 4.24, 4.32
s 36(2)(3) 4.1–4.15
s 36(4) 4.33
s 39 .... 45.1–45.8
s 41(2) 33.52
s 42 .... 42.11, 62.207
s 43 .. 32.9–32.21, 32.28, 32.31, 43.12,
54.7, 62.505
s 43(1) 32.17, 32.18, 32.22, 46.153
s 43B 32.13
s 43C 32.14
s 45 .... 47.1–47.6, 47.13
s 45(2) 47.70, 50.11
s 45(3) 50.11
s 47(2A), (3) 1.72–1.79
s 49(3) 65.119
s 53(3) 22.487, 63.1–63.8
s 54 .... 26.1, 26.2
s 55 .... 31.1
s 56 .... 44.140–44.153
s 56(1) 44.143
s 57 .... 44.140–44.153
s 59(2) 18.1–18.17, 18.460
s 59(3) 18.1, 18.9, 18.17
s 59(4) 18.18–18.40, 18.458
s 59(5) 18.18–18.40
s 59(7) 18.8–18.15
s 59(7)(a) 18.42–18.69
s 59(7)(b) 18.70–18.613
s 59(8) 18.614, 18.615
s 60 .... 50.1–50.152
s 60(1) 3.101, 50.1, 50.129
s 60(3) 50.1
s 60(7) 50.137
s 61 .... 50.3–50.66
s 63(1) 52.1–52.21
s 63(1)(a) 52.2–52.4
s 63(1)(b) 52.5–52.21, 52.430
s 63(2) 52.24–52.26
s 63(8) 52.27–52.30
s 63(10)(a) 52.31–52.376
s 63(10)(b) 52.377–52.391
s 66 .... 53.1–53.17
s 66(2) 53.15
s 66(3) 53.15
s 67(1) 51.1–51.4
s 67(1)(c) 51.139–51.145
s 67(3) 51.5–51.12
s 67(8) 51.13–51.138
s 69 .... 53.18–53.22
s 70 .... 50.67–50.152, 51.146–51.185,
52.392–52.448
s 70(2) 50.44
s 70(4) 52.447

1994 Value Added Tax Act – *cont.*

s 71(1)(a) 18.312–18.383
s 71(1)(b) 18.84, 18.273, 18.275,
18.393, 18.589, 51.83–51.102,
52.57–52.70, 52.275
s 72 .... 49.1–49.17
s 73(1) 3.1–3.39, 3.140, 57.45
s 73(2) 3.44, 3.176
s 73(6) 3.179
s 73(6)(a) 3.40–3.46, 3.110
s 73(6)(b) 3.47–3.85, 3.110
s 73(7) 3.113
s 73(9) 2.193, 37.2
s 74 .... 17.1–17.17
s 74(3) 17.16
s 76 .... 18.19, 18.622, 50.3–50.12,
52.456
s 76(3) 50.3
s 76(9) 18.4, 18.38
s 77(1) 3.86–3.100
s 77(4) 3.101–3.109
s 77(6) 3.110
s 77A 22.466
s 78 ...... 2.526–2.528, 48.114–48.146
s 78(1) 48.114–48.122, 48.129
s 78(1A) 48.144
s 78(2) 48.132, 48.145
s 78(5) 48.142
s 78(11) 48.118, 48.125
s 78A 48.90
s 78A(2) 3.111
s 79 .... 48.50, 48.82–48.113
s 79(1) 59.10
s 79(2)(a) 48.98
s 79(2)(b) 48.82, 48.83, 48.94
s 79(2)(c) 48.84
s 79(2A) 48.94
s 79(3)(a) 48.85–48.108
s 79(4) 48.97–48.108
s 80 .... 48.16–48.81
s 80(1) 48.16–48.27
s 80(2) 48.76, 48.77
s 80(3) 48.28–48.49
s 80(4) . 2.30, 22.55, 48.2, 48.50–48.75
s 80(4ZA) 48.75
s 80(4A) 3.44, 3.111, 48.76–48.80
s 80(4B) 48.51
s 80(6) 48.81
s 81(3) 48.53, 48.152
s 81(3A) 48.153, 48.154
s 82(2) 2.1–2.51
s 83 ..... 2.1–2.51, 2.83, 2.146, 18.622
s 83(1)(a) 57.103, 59.2, 59.3
s 83(1)(b) 2.9, 2.10, 2.94
s 83(1)(c) . 2.12–2.13, 2.15, 2.134, 48.1
s 83(1)(p) 2.20–2.26, 2.50, 2.118,
2.132–2.134, 2.196
s 83(1)(q) 2.27
s 83(1)(s) 2.28
s 83(1)(t) 2.29–2.32
s 84(3) 2.128–2.148

1994 Value Added Tax Act – *cont.*
s 84(3A) 2.128–2.135
s 84(3B) 2.136–2.148
s 84(3C) 2.137
s 84(4) 36.169–36.172, 36.485
s 84(4ZA) 28.3, 28.4, 28.12
s 84(5) 3.17, 3.168, 3.169
s 84(6) 17.1–17.4
s 84(8) 2.512–2.533
s 84(10) . 2.85–2.94, 2.118, 25.34, 60.2
s 85 .... 2.200–2.210, 2.434, 57.146
s 89 .... 18.445
s 94(1) 7.1–7.122
s 94(2) 13.1–13.16
s 94(4) 62.163–62.166
s 94(6) 62.150
s 95(3) 23.23, 23.25
s 96 .... 15.148
s 98 .... 47.2
Sch A1 .... 30.1–30.13
Item 5(b) 30.8
Sch 1
para 1(1)(a) 57.1–57.11
para 1(1)(b) 57.12–57.16
para 1(2) 65.90–65.107
para 1(3) 57.20–57.32, 65.97
para 1(4) 57.33
para 1(7) 57.34
para 1A 57.81
para 2 .... 52.303, 57.35–57.81
para 4 .... 65.97
para 5 .... 57.82–57.100
para 9 . 32.7, 57.101–57.118, 57.132
para 10 .... 8.41, 45.9
para 10(2) 57.111
para 13(1) 7.97, 57.120–57.143
para 13(2) 57.144–57.166
para 14 .... 57.167–57.169
Sch 4
para 1 .... 62.87–62.94
para 2 .... 12.8
para 5 .... 58.1, 62.95–62.115,
67.11–67.17
para 5(1) 62.97, 62.98, 62.101,
62.112–62.115, 67.11
para 5(2) 62.99, 62.100, 62.115,
67.154
para 5(4) 67.18
para 5(4A) 2.487
para 6(1) 23.33
para 7 .... 14.114, 62.329
para 8 .... 52.291, 62.116,
67.20–67.25, 67.140
Sch 4A ....
para 10 .... 62.518
Sch 5 .... 39.4–39.19
para 2 .... 39.4, 62.497, 62.514,
62.526, 62.527

1994 Value Added Tax Act – *cont.*
para 3 .... 39.7, 39.8, 39.11,
62.485–62.488, 62.499, 62.500,
62.510–62.513, 62.532, 62.533,
62.536
para 5 .... 62.538, 62.539
para 6 .... 62.482, 62.541
para 7 .... 62.543
para 7A 67.172
para 7C 62.545
Sch 6
para 1 .... 67.1, 67.2
para 1A 67.3
para 2 .... 22.469, 67.27–67.36
para 4 .... 67.88
para 5 .... 67.157–67.162
para 6 .... 67.14, 67.17
para 7 .... 67.18
para 9 .... 67.90–67.93
para 10 .... 62.13
Sch 7A
Group 1 .... 30.1–30.8
Item 5 .... 30.8
Group 2 .... 56.1
Group 5 .... 56.2
Group 6 .... 56.3–56.7
Item 1 .... 56.6
Note 2 .... 56.3, 56.4
Note 3 .... 56.5
Note 6 .... 56.4
Group 7 .... 56.8–56.10
Sch 8
Group 1(a) 29.1–29.72
General Item 1 .... 29.81–29.105
General Item 2 .... 29.106–29.118
General Item 3 .... 29.119
General Item 4 .... 29.120–29.124
Excepted Item 1 ...... 29.125–29.127
Excepted Item 2 ...... 29.128–29.164
Excepted Item 4 ...... 29.165–29.180
Excepted Item 5 ...... 29.181–29.186
Excepted Item 6 ...... 29.187–29.196
Overriding Item 1 .... 29.126, 29.127
Overriding Item 4 .... 29.84,
29.175–29.177
Overriding Item 6 .... 29.178–29.180
Note 1 .... 29.91
Note 3(a) 29.20–29.54
Note 3(b) 29.55–29.80
Note 5 .... 29.136, 29.153
Group 2 .... 69.1–69.4
Group 3
Item 1 .... 5.1–5.92
Item 2 .... 5.93–5.108
Item 4 .... 5.109
Item 5 .... 5.110
Group 5
Item 1 .... 15.1–15.153
Item 1(a) 15.1–15.66

1994 Value Added Tax Act – *cont.*
Item 1(b) 15.130–15.147
Item 2 .... 15.35–15.214
Item 2(a) 15.35–15.119
Item 3 .... 15.215–15.217
Item 4 .. 15.221–15.242, 55.83–55.87
Note 2 .... 15.36, 15.131–15.133
Note 2(a) 6.4, 15.37
Note 2(c) . 15.38–15.40, 15.44, 15.45,
15.50–15.59
Note 2(d) 15.61–15.64
Note 3 .... 15.218, 15.220
Note 4 .... 15.70–15.76, 15.81
Note 6 .... 15.83–15.118
Note 6(a) 15.91, 15.95, 15.99, 15.108,
15.111, 15.113, 15.115, 15.118
Note 6(b) 15.83–15.87, 15.102–15.106,
15.113, 15.117, 55.16
Note 7 .... 15.130–15.139, 15.215
Note 7A 15.122, 15.141
Note 8 .... 15.123, 15.146
Note 9 .... 15.132, 15.143
Note 10 .... 15.102
Note 11 .... 15.181
Note 13 .... 15.42, 15.67, 15.68
Note 16 ..... 15.155, 15.158, 15.165,
15.169, 15.181, 15.183, 15.199,
15.200
Note 17 ..... 15.155, 15.183, 15.184,
15.201–15.205
Note 18 ..... 15.171, 15.172, 15.207
Note 22 .... 15.221–15.260
Note 22(a) 15.221–15.233
Note 22(b) 15.224
Note 22(c) 15.234–15.240
Group 6 .... 55.1–55.90
Item 1 .... 55.19–55.26
Item 2 .... 55.27–55.87
Item 3 .... 55.89
Note 1 .... 55.1–55.18
Note 2(c) 55.3–55.12
Note 4 .... 55.19–55.26
Note 6 .... 55.27–55.82
Note 10 .. 55.39, 55.48, 55.50, 55.51
Group 7 .... 39.1–39.3
Item 1 .... 39.1
Item 2 .... 39.2, 39.3
Group 8
Item 1 .... 66.1–66.10
Item 4 .... 66.12–66.38
Item 5 .... 66.40
Item 6 .... 66.41–66.43
Item 10 .... 66.44–66.49
Item 11 .... 66.42
Note A1 .... 66.3–66.7
Note 1 .... 66.10
Note 4A 66.22, 66.36, 66.39
Group 9 .... 69.5–69.13
Item 3 .... 69.13
Note (a) 22.507
Note (b) 69.13

1994 Value Added Tax Act – *cont.*
Group 12
Item 1 .... 19.1–19.6
Item 1A 19.7, 19.8
Item 2
Item 2(a) 19.10–19.12
Item 2(b) 19.13–19.15
Item 2(f) 19.16–19.22
Item 2(g) 19.24–19.69
Item 2(h) 19.70–19.73
Item 2A 19.23
Item 3 .... 19.74, 19.75
Item 7 .... 19.12
Items 8, 9 .... 19.76–19.85
Item 10 .... 19.78, 19.86–19.94
Item 11 .... 19.86–19.94
Item 12 .... 19.92
Item 13 .... 19.82
Item 17 .... 19.97–19.99
Note 3 .... 19.27, 19.29, 19.58
Note 5B 19.68
Note 5D 19.68
Group 13 .... 25.29
Group 15 .... 11.1–11.29
Item 1 .... 11.1, 11.2
Item 4 .... 11.3–11.23
Item 5 .... 11.3–11.23
Item 8 .... 11.24–11.29
Item 9 .... 11.30, 11.31
Note 3 .... 11.3–11.14
Note 4 .... 11.15–11.20
Note 5 .... 11.21–11.23
Note 9 .... 11.16
Note 11 .... 11.30
Group 16 .... 12.1–12.23
Item 1 .... 12.4
Note 1 .... 12.5
Sch 9
Group 1
Item 1 .... 15.261, 41.1–41.95
Item 1(d) 41.96–41.115
Item 1(e) 41.116–41.127
Item 1(f) 41.128–41.135
Item 1(h) 41.136–41.148
Item 1(k) 41.149–41.152
Item 1(l) 41.153–41.155
Item 1(m) 41.156–41.162
Note 4 .... 41.122, 62.116
Note 9 .... 41.97, 41.98
Note 11 .... 41.127
Note 12 .... 41.122
Note 14 .... 41.130–41.134
Note 16 .... 41.160–41.162
Group 2
Item 1 .... 38.1–38.12
Item 4 .... 38.13–38.33
Note 1 .... 38.26, 38.28
Notes 4, 5 .... 38.22
Group 3 .... 24.1–24.9
Group 4 .... 24.10–24.26
Note 1(b) 24.10, 24.12–24.15

1994 Value Added Tax Act – *cont.*
  Note 1(d) . 24.18, 24.20, 24.23, 49.29
  Note 3 . . . . 24.19
  Group 5
  Item 1 . . . . 27.1–27.9
  Item 2 . . . . 27.10
  Item 3 . . . . 27.15–27.17
  Item 5 . . . . 27.18–27.45
  Item 6 . . . . 27.46–27.55
  Item 7 . . . . 22.360, 27.57
  Item 8 . . . . 27.58
  Item 9 . . . . 27.59
  Item 10 . . . . 22.368
  Note 4 . . . . 27.61, 27.62
  Group 6
  Item 1(a) 21.1–21.20
  Item 1(b) 21.21
  Item 1(c) 21.23–21.28
  Item 2 . . . . 21.30–21.41
  Item 3 . . . . 21.43
  Item 4 . . . . 21.19, 21.44–21.48
  Item 5 . . . . 21.23–21.28
  Item 5A 21.29
  Item 6 . . . . 21.49–21.53
  Note 1 . . . . 21.9–21.19
  Note 2 . . . . 21.20
  Group 7
  Item 1 . . . . 33.1–33.31
  Item 1(c) 33.1
  Item 1(d)33.2, 33.3, 33.4, 33.17, 33.23
  Item 2 . . . . 33.32–33.38
  Item 2(c) 33.33
  Item 4 . . . . 33.39–33.60
  Items 6–8 . . . . 33.61
  Item 9 . . . . 33.59, 33.62–33.75
  Item 11 . . . . 33.76
  Note 1 . . . . 33.18
  Note 2 . . . . 33.6, 33.25–33.30
  Note 6 . . . . 33.67–33.69, 33.73
  Note 7 . . . . 33.63, 33.70, 33.71
  Group 8 . . . . 24.26–24.30
  Item 1 . . . . 24.26
  Item 2 . . . . 24.27–24.30
  Group 9
  Item 1 . . . . 64.1–64.36
  Item 1(b) 64.1, 64.2, 64.12, 64.22
  Item 1(c) 64.3–64.7, 64.12, 64.27
  Item 1(d) 64.8
  Item 1(e) . . . 64.9–64.11, 64.26, 64.31
  Note 4 . . . . 64.12, 64.36
  Note 5 . . . . 64.8
  Group 10 . . . . 24.31–24.52
  Item 3 . . . . 24.32–24.50, 41.161
  Note 2A 24.52
  Group 12 . . . . 11.32–11.38
  Note 3 . . . . 11.38
  Group 13 . . . . 16.1–16.12
  Item 2(a) 16.10
  Item 2(b) 16.11
  Note 2 . . . . 16.1–16.9
  Group 15 . . . . 31.2

1994 Value Added Tax Act – *cont.*
  Sch 10
  para 6 . . . . 6.1–6.4
  para 7 . . . . 6.5
  para 10 . . . . 6.6
  para 12 . . . . 6.7–6.11
  para 14 . . . . 6.7
  para 15 . . . . 6.9, 6.10
  para 18(1) 6.12–6.15
  para 18(2) 6.16
  para 19 . . . . 6.18–6.41
  para 28 . . . . 6.44
  para 40 . . . . 6.51
  Sch 10A 67.151–67.175
  para 3 . . . . 62.546, 67.172
  Sch 11
  para 1 . . . . 14.103, 46.179
  para 2(1) 3.175, 52.2
  para 2(12) 14.114
  para 4 . . . . 2.47, 14.1–14.68
  para 5 . . . . 14.69
  para 5(2) 14.71–14.76
  para 5(3) 14.75
  para 5(4) 14.77–14.85
  para 7 . . . 14.86–14.92, 14.96, 53.18,
                        53.19
  para 10 . . . . 14.93–14.96
  para 11 . . . . 14.96–14.100
  Sch 12
  para 5(2) 2.309, 2.310
  para 10 . . . . 2.157–2.160
1995 Pensions Act
  s 25(6) 54.8
1996 Finance Act
  s 197 . . . . 2.515
1997 Finance Act
  s 39 . . . . 4.33
  s 47 . . . . 2.30, 22.55, 48.51
1998 Data Protection Act
  . . . . 14.103
1998 Human Rights Act
  . . . . 34.10
2000 Care Standards Act
  . . . . 33.56
2002 Proceeds of Crime Act
  . . . . 49.18–49.21
  s 6 . . . . 49.19
2005 Commissioners for Revenue and Customs Act 49.18–49.20
  s 17(1) 14.103
2007 Finance Act
  Sch 24 . 52.23, 52.291, 52.321, 52.449,
                        52.450
  Sch 24 para 2 . . . . 52.23
  Sch 24 para 10 . . . . 52.450
  Sch 24 para 11 . . . . 52.450
2008 Finance Act . . . .
  Sch 41 para 2 . . . 51.139–51.145
  Sch 41 paras 12, 13
  . . . . 51.146–51.185

2008 Finance Act – *cont.*
  Sch 41 para 20 .... 51.13–51.138

2009 Finance Act ....
  s 108 .... 18.350

Table of Statutory Instruments

1984/746 VAT (Imported Goods) Relief
Order
Sch 2 Group 5 .... 33.77, 35.24
1986/590 VAT Tribunals Rules
r 3(2) 2.65
r 7 .... 2.150–2.169
r 8 .... 2.151–2.169, 2.277
r 9 .... 2.67, 2.168
r 11 .... 2.66, 2.136–2.148
r 13 .... 2.73, 2.297, 2.298
r 14 .... 2.73
r 18(1) 2.14, 2.15
r 18(2) 2.238
r 19(1) 2.194–2.198
r 19(3) 2.75, 2.78, 2.122
r 19(4) 2.152, 2.157, 2.245–2.248,
2.271, 2.276
r 20(2) 2.150
r 20(3) 2.257–2.265
r 21 .... 2.266–2.276
r 21(4) 2.276
r 22 .... 2.300, 2.301
r 23 .... 2.304
r 25 .... 2.450
r 26 .... 2.194
r 26(1) 2.318
r 26(2) 2.138, 2.139, 2.317
r 27 .... 2.305
r 28 .... 2.277–2.291
r 29 .... 2.372, 2.400, 2.435, 2.450
r 29(1) 2.446
r 29(5) 2.389
1986/1925 Insolvency Rules
r 4.218 .... 37.1
1987/1427 VAT (Cash Accounting)
Regulations 10.1–10.12
1987/1806 VAT (Tour Operators) Order
.... 63.1–63.12
Article 2 .... 63.5
Article 3 .... 63.5, 63.9, 63.10
Article 3(1) 63.2, 63.3
Article 7 .... 22.493, 63.11
1989/2248 VAT (Accounting & Records)
Regulations
r 57 .... 59.28
1992/3121 VAT (Place of Supply of
Services) Order
Article 5 .... 62.510–62.515
Article 13 .... 62.516, 62.518
Article 14 .... 62.519
Article 15 .... 62.521–62.525
Article 16 .... 2.488, 41.52, 46.174,
62.495, 62.497, 62.499, 62.514,
62.526–62.546
Article 21 .... 62.546, 67.173

1992/3122 VAT (Cars) Order
Article 2 .... 44.1–44.52
Article 2(b) 44.11, 44.16, 44.27,
44.40, 44.46
Article 2(i) 44.49
Article 2(iv) 44.50
Article 2(vi) 44.37, 44.39, 44.46,
44.51
Article 4(1) 44.53, 44.54
Article 5 .... 44.55–44.59
Article 5(3) 44.59
Article 8(1) 44.60–44.67
Article 8(2) 44.68–44.76
Article 8(5) 44.77–44.96
1992/3131 VAT (Tax-Free Shops) Order
.... 2.337
1992/3193 Customs & Excise Duties
(Personal Reliefs for Goods
Permanently Imported) Order
Article 11 .... 35.23
1992/3220 VAT (Flat-Rate Scheme for
Farmers) (Designated Activities) Order
.... 26.1
1992/3222 VAT (Input Tax) Order
Article 5 .... 8.1–8.48
Article 6 ...... 15.220, 15.225, 15.226,
15.229, 15.246, 15.248, 15.255,
15.259
Article 7 .... 22.424, 44.97–44.139
Article 7(1) 46.98
Article 7(2) 44.17
Article 7(2A) 44.104
Article 7(2C) 44.104
Article 7(2E) 44.106–44.139
Article 7(2G) 44.106–44.139
1993/1507 VAT (Supply of Services) Order
Article 3 .... 62.15, 62.16
1994/686 VAT (Tax-Free Shops) Order
.... 2.337
1994/687 VAT (Sport, Physical Education
and Fund-Raising Events) Order
.... 13.50
1995/1268 VAT (Special Provisions) Order
Article 4 .... 60.20
Article 5(1) .. 58.31, 62.83, 65.1–65.84
Article 5(2) 65.86–65.89
Article 5(3) 65.88
Article 12 ..... 2.84, 22.98, 60.1, 60.18
Article 12(2) 60.8
Article 13 .... 60.3, 60.4
1995/2518 VAT Regulations
r 4 .... 47.1
r 5 .... 57.118
r 5(2) 47.8
r 6 .... 65.108–65.117, 65.119
r 13 .... 40.4, 62.470

1995/2518 VAT Regulations – *cont.*

r 14 .... 36.104, 40.1–40.61
r 14(1)(e) 40.50
r 14(1)(g) 36.104, 40.51, 40.53
r 14(1)(h) 36.104
r 24 .... 37.12, 40.108, 40.109, 40.116
r 25 .... 18.446, 52.1, 52.2, 57.93, 59.8–59.22
r 25(1) 3.117, 3.144, 59.1, 59.3, 59.13–59.19
r 25(1)(b) 59.14
r 25(1)(c) 3.117, 3.144, 59.3, 59.15–59.19
r 25(5) 59.21
r 29 .... 18.252, 40.62–40.81, 48.2
r 29(1A) 48.3–48.10
r 29(2) 35.12
r 31A 31.2
r 34 .... 11.53, 46.197, 59.23–59.29
r 34(1A) 59.29, 59.30
r 35 .... 46.197, 59.21
r 38 ..... 3.176, 37.12, 40.107–40.112, 40.116, 48.42, 59.28
r 38(1A) 40.114, 59.33
r 38(6) 37.12
r 40(3) 18.446, 18.448
r 55B 28.3–28.8
r 55E 28.9
r 55H 28.10
r 55JB 28.11
r 55K 28.12–28.16
r 55L 28.1, 28.17, 28.18
r 55P 28.17, 28.18
r 55Q 28.17, 28.18, 28.19, 28.20
r 60(1) 10.10
r 63(2) 10.13
r 64 .... 10.6
r 67 .... 58.32, 58.36, 58.37
r 68 .... 58.38, 58.56
r 81(1) 67.3
r 86 .... 62.465
r 90 .... 37.18, 43.20, 62.456, 62.466–62.471
r 90(1) 43.2, 43.8, 52.113, 62.468
r 90(2) 52.96
r 91 .... 62.472, 62.473
r 92 .... 62.474
r 93 .... 62.475
r 99 .... 46.188–46.190
r 99(1) ... 46.184, 46.190, 46.191, 46.196, 46.198
r 100 .... 46.1
r 101 .... 46.2–46.101, 46.109
r 101(2) 32.18, 46.2–46.96
r 101(2)(b) 46.2–46.12
r 101(2)(c) 46.13–46.39
r 101(2)(d) 46.40–46.96, 46.174
r 101(3)(a) 46.97, 46.98
r 101(3)(b) 46.99–46.101
r 102 .... 46.102–46.169
r 102(1) 46.102–46.112

1995/2518 VAT Regulations – *cont.*

r 102(3) 46.113–46.127
r 102(4) 46.128–46.130
r 102A 46.131
r 102B 46.132, 46.133
r 102C 46.132, 46.133
r 103 .... 46.173–46.181
r 104 .... 46.182
r 106 .... 46.183–46.193
r 107 .... 43.20, 46.194–46.200
r 107(1) 3.97, 46.198
r 107B .. 2.481, 46.140, 46.201–46.203
r 107C 46.201
r 108 .... 46.194, 46.205–46.211
r 109 .... 46.212–46.220
r 111 . 36.614, 36.615, 46.221–46.234, 52.101
r 111(1) 36.614, 36.615
r 111(2) 36.591–36.602
r 111(3) 46.233
r 111(5) 46.234
r 112 .... 9.5
r 112(2) 6.8
r 113(b) 9.3
r 113(e) 6.8
r 114(4) 6.8
r 115 .... 9.9, 22.459
r 117 .... 25.18
r 121A 35.26–35.28
r 129 .... 25.5, 25.6, 25.14, 25.30
r 131 .... 25.16, 25.23
r 134 ... 23.1, 23.3–23.5, 23.16, 23.18, 23.21
r 158 .... 4.16
r 165A 4.25, 4.26
r 166A 4.27, 52.242, 52.429
r 167 .... 4.29
r 170 .... 4.30
r 172D 4.31
r 179(1) 23.30–23.32
r 186 .... 45.2
r 192 .... 25.32, 25.33, 45.4
r 201 .... 15.23

1998/1461 Air Passenger Duty and Other Indirect Taxes (Interest) Rate Regulations 2.515
r 5 .... 2.531

1998/3132 Civil Procedure Rules
.... 2.173
r 25.1 .... 36.651
r 25.12 .... 2.369
Part 36 .... 2.483

1999/3121 VAT (Input Tax) (Specified Supplies) Order 46.178
Article 3 .... 25.37, 36.678

2009/273 Tribunal Procedure (First-Tier Tribunal) (Tax Chamber) Rules
r 10 .... 2.372, 2.447
r 17(1) 2.72
r 17(3) 2.315–2.327

2009/273 Tribunal Procedure (First-Tier
  Tribunal) (Tax Chamber) Rules – *cont.*
  r 23 .... 2.148
  r 25 .... 2.150–2.171

2009/273 Tribunal Procedure (First-Tier
  Tribunal) (Tax Chamber) Rules – *cont.*
  r 32 .... 2.249–2.255
  r 35 .... 2.269

Table of European Community Directives

EC Sixth VAT Directive (77/388/EEC)
Article 2 .... 22.78–22.102, 62.77
Article 2(1) 22.78–22.98
Article 2(2) 22.99–22.102
Article 4 .... 22.103–22.150
Article 4(1) 1.48, 22.103–22.108,
36.554
Article 4(2) 22.109–22.119, 42.11,
62.207
Article 4(3) 22.121–22.123
Article 4(4) 22.124, 32.15, 57.39,
62.505
Article 4(5) 22.127–22.150, 42.11,
55.15, 62.495
Article 5 .... 22.151–22.170
Article 5(1) 22.152
Article 5(3) 22.156
Article 5(4) 1.78
Article 5(6) ... 22.158, 22.159, 22.163,
67.156
Article 5(7) 6.1
Article 5(8) 15.20, 22.166–22.169,
22.419, 65.88
Article 6(1) 22.171–22.175, 27.51
Article 6(2) 22.114, 22.179–22.187
Article 6(3) 22.165
Article 6(4) 22.189, 22.190
Article 7(1) 22.191
Article 7(3) 22.192
Article 8 .... 22.193, 44.19
Article 8(1) 22.174, 22.195, 23.33,
62.479
Article 9 ...... 22.198–22.228, 62.490,
62.511
Article 9(1) 22.174, 22.198–22.205,
62.489, 62.490
Article 9(2) 22.205–22.227, 62.489,
62.491, 62.495, 62.511
Article 9(2)(a) 22.206–22.208
Article 9(2)(b) 22.209–22.212
Article 9(2)(c) . 22.214–22.216, 62.523,
62.524
Article 9(2)(e) . 22.218–22.227, 62.495,
62.536
Article 9(3) 22.228
Article 10 .... 22.229–22.231
Article 10(2) 22.229, 22.230
Article 10(3) 22.231
Article 11 ..... 22.232–22.258, 22.496,
22.498, 58.39
Article 11 A1 ... 22.232–22.250, 62.36,
62.134
Article 11 A1(a) . 22.232–22.247, 67.73
Article 11 A1(c) 22.114, 22.249
Article 11 A2(b) 44.99
Article 11 A3(b) 22.158, 22.251,
22.253, 67.58

EC Sixth VAT Directive (77/388/EEC) – cont.
Article 11 A3(c) . 22.255, 22.256, 62.36
Article 11 B1 .... 22.69
Article 11 C1 .... 3.176, 22.253,
22.258–22.260, 40.116,
59.33, 67.58, 67.127
Article 12 .... 22.262–22.269
Article 13 A1 .... 22.270–22.323
Article 13 A1(a) 22.272
Article 13 A1(b) 22.273–22.277,
22.298, 33.57
Article 13 A1(c) 22.279–22.285
Article 13 A1(d) 22.287
Article 13 A1(e) 22.288, 22.289
Article 13 A1(f) 22.290, 22.292
Article 13 A1(g) . 22.293–22.301, 33.70
Article 13 A1(h) 22.300, 22.301,
33.59, 33.73
Article 13 A1(i) . 21.45, 22.303, 22.304
Article 13 A1(j) 22.306–22.308
Article 13 A1(l) .. 22.311, 64.18, 64.20,
64.21
Article 13 A1(m) 22.295,
22.313–22.315, 24.48,
24.50, 48.40
Article 13 A1(n) 22.318, 22.319
Article 13 A1(o) 11.32
Article 13 A2 .... 22.321, 24.32
Article 13 B 22.324–22.379, 62.195
Article 13 B(a) .. 22.324–22.327, 38.34
Article 13 B(b) . 22.332–22.340, 41.61,
41.66, 41.127, 41.132
Article 13 B(c) . 22.349, 22.350, 44.168
Article 13 B(d) ... 22.352–22.364, 27.5,
27.57, 27.59
Article 13 B(f) .. 22.371–22.375, 24.20,
49.29
Article 13 B(g) 22.379
Article 13 B(h) 22.123, 22.511
Article 13 C . 6.7, 6.18, 22.380–22.383,
22.457
Article 14 .... 22.384–22.386
Article 15 ...... 22.387–22.396, 25.14,
63.21
Article 15(2) 22.388
Article 15(4) 22.389, 22.390
Article 15(5) 22.391, 22.392
Article 15(6) 22.393
Article 15(7) 22.393
Article 15(8) 22.394
Article 15(9) 66.45
Article 15(10) 62.499
Article 17 .... 6.23, 22.397–22.433,
22.501, 36.273, 36.307, 46.15,
46.205, 48.134
Article 17(2) 22.402–22.416, 32.18,
36.40, 36.662

EC Sixth VAT Directive (77/388/EEC) – *cont.*
Article 17(3) 22.417
Article 17(5) ... 11.53, 22.419, 22.420,
46.103, 46.174
Article 17(6) ... 22.409, 22.422–22.431
Article 17(7) 22.432–22.434
Article 18 ..... 22.435–22.442, 46.222,
46.224
Article 18(1) 22.435, 40.66
Article 18(2) 22.437
Article 18(3) 46.222, 48.5
Article 18(4) 22.439–22.442
Article 19 ..... 22.443–22.448, 46.115
Article 19(1) 22.443, 22.444
Article 19(2) .. 22.446, 22.448, 22.451,
22.452
Article 20 ..... 22.383, 22.454–22.459,
46.212
Article 20(1) ... 22.160, 22.454, 46.210
Article 20(2) 22.456, 22.457
Article 20(3) 22.459
Article 21(1) 22.460–22.465
Article 21(1)(c) 22.465
Article 21(3) 22.466, 22.467
Article 22 .... 22.469, 22.470
Article 22(3) 22.471–22.473
Article 22(4) 22.53
Article 22(5) 22.476
Article 22(8) 2.23, 57.89
Article 24 .... 22.479, 46.224
Article 24(6) 32.7
Article 25 .... 22.482–22.484
Article 26 .. 22.485–22.492, 63.2, 63.3,
63.18
Article 26(1) 63.3
Article 26(2) 22.492, 22.493
Article 26(3) 63.21
Article 26a 22.494, 44.68, 44.73,
44.168
Article 27 ...... 22.496–22.504, 58.29,
58.43, 67.2
Article 27(1) 22.497, 58.29
Article 27(5) 22.498
Article 28 .... 22.505
Article 28(2) 22.506–22.509
Article 28(3) 22.511, 22.512
Article 28a(1) 23.25
Article 28a(5) 23.33
Article 28b 22.411, 22.515, 44.69
Article 28c 22.517–22.522, 23.1,
23.33–23.36
Article 28k 22.524
Article 29 .... 22.433, 22.434
Article 33 .... 22.526–22.530
Annex F2 .... 22.509, 62.500
Annex H 22.268
EC Eighth VAT Directive (79/1072/EEC)
Article 1 .... 22.193, 22.531
Article 2 .... 22.532–22.534
Article 3 .... 22.537–22.539
Article 5 .... 22.532, 22.535

EC Eighth VAT Directive (79/1072/EEC) –
cont.
Article 7(1) 23.30, 45.5
Article 7(4) 22.60, 22.542
Annex A 22.544
EC Thirteenth VAT Directive (86/560/EEC)
.... 25.20, 45.1
Article 1 .... 22.546
Article 2 .... 22.545
Directive 77/799/EEC
.... 22.564

Directive 2006/112/EC
Article 2 .... 22.78–22.102, 23.25
Article 9 .... 22.91, 22.103–22.116
Article 11 .... 32.15, 57.39, 62.505
Article 12 .... 22.121–22.123
Article 13 . 20.9, 22.127–22.150, 30.11
Article 14 .... 22.151, 22.152
Article 15 .... 22.156
Article 16 .... 22.158–22.163
Article 17 .... 23.33
Article 18 .... 22.165
Article 19 .... 22.166–22.169
Article 20 .... 20.18
Article 24 .... 22.171–22.173
Article 26 ...... 20.20, 22.179–22.186
Article 27 .... 22.165
Article 30 .... 22.191
Articles 32–36 .... 22.193
Article 37 .... 22.195
Article 43 .... 22.203–22.207
Article 44 .... 22.515
Article 45 .... 22.206, 22.207
Article 46 .... 22.209–22.212
Article 52 .... 22.214–22.216
Article 56 .... 20.34, 20.36,
22.218–22.227
Article 61 .... 22.192
Article 66 .... 22.229, 22.230
Article 70 .... 22.231
Article 73 .... 22.232–22.248
Article 75 .... 22.249
Article 78 .... 20.48
Article 79 .... 22.251–22.253
Article 90 .... 22.258–22.260
Article 96 .... 20.52, 20.53
Articles 98–101 .... 20.52–20.54,
22.262–22.266
Article 102 .... 22.269
Article 110 .... 22.505–22.507
Article 118 .... 22.509
Article 131 .... 22.270, 22.271
Article 132 .... 20.65, 20.74,
22.273–22.319
Article 133 ..... 20.74, 22.321, 22.322
Article 134 .... 20.74
Article 135 .... 20.81, 20.84, 20.86,
22.324–22.346,
22.352–22.374, 38.32
Article 136 .... 22.349, 22.350
Article 137 .... 22.380–22.382

Directive 2006/112/EC – *cont.*
Article 138 .... 22.517–22.521
Article 140 .... 22.384–22.386
Article 146 .... 22.387
Article 148 ...... 20.98, 22.389–22.394
Article 151 .... 20.102
Article 158 .... 22.524
Articles 167–172 ...... 20.104, 20.105,
22.397–22.415
Article 173 .... 22.405, 22.407, 22.419
Article 174 .... 22.443–22.450
Article 176 .... 22.409, 22.422–22.424
Article 177 .... 22.432–22.434
Article 179 .... 22.437
Article 180 .... 46.222, 48.5
Article 183 .... 20.114, 20.115, 22.439,
22.442
Article 184 .... 22.454
Article 187 .... 22.456–22.458
Article 188 .... 22.459

Directive 2006/112/EC – *cont.*
Articles 193–205 .... 22.460–22.466
Articles 206–212 .... 22.476
Articles 217–240 .... 22.469, 22.472
Article 252 .... 3.118, 45.5
Article 281 .... 22.479
Article 283 .... 20.126
Article 290 .... 32.7
Articles 295–305 .... 22.482–22.484
Article 306 .... 22.485–22.489
Article 307 .... 22.492
Article 308 .... 22.493
Articles 311–343 .... 22.494
Article 314 .... 20.132
Article 320 .... 20.132
Article 371 .... 22.511, 22.512
Article 394 .... 22.496–22.500
Article 395 .... 22.501
Article 398 .... 22.433, 22.434
Article 401 .... 22.526–22.529

Table of Cases — A to J

The table is referenced to the paragraph number.

A

A & B Motors (Newton-le-Willows) Ltd, [1981] VATTR 29 (VTD 1024) 44.56
A & D Stevenson (Trading) Ltd, [2003] VATDR 82 (VTD 17979) 44.156
A & E Mechanical Services Ltd (VTD 1069) 36.347
A & M Insulations Ltd (VTD 7498) 52.39
A & S Services (VTD 16025) 33.25
A & T Barr (Electrical) Ltd (VTD 13848) 2.228
A Better Choice Ltd (VTD 9048) 18.436
A Russell Heating (VTD 20681) 48.63
A1 Construction (Derby) Ltd, [2011] UKFTT 178 (TC), TC01047 .... 40.52
A1 Distribution (UK) Ltd, [2010] UKFTT 439 (TC), TC00704 .... 36.121
A1 Lofts Ltd, [2010] UKFTT 581 (TC), TC00831 .... 1.69
A1 Rushmoor Radio Taxis Ltd (VTD 17634) 27.10
A2B Radio Cars (VTD 15145) 67.122
A5 Television Ltd (VTD 12181) 67.47
AA Insurance Services Ltd, [1999] VATDR 361 (VTD 16117) 41.67
Aardvark Excavations Ltd (VTD 20468) 18.614
AB Gee of Ripley Ltd, [1991] VATTR 217 (VTD 5948) 52.30
AB SKF, Skatteverket v, ECJ Case C-29/08; [2010] STC 419 .... 22.366
AB Transport (VTD 12481) 52.69
Abassi (Mrs J) (VTD 10411) 52.457
ABB Power Ltd, [1992] VATTR 491 (VTD 9373) 62.414
Abbarchi (R) (VTD 17444) 59.16
Abbasford Ltd (t/a Watford Electronics) (VTD 10229) 52.315
Abbey Life Japan Trust (VTD 11205) 2.325
Abbey (Manchester) Ltd, [2011] UKFTT 90 (TC), TC00967 .... 36.113
Abbey National plc, ECJ Case C-408/98, [2001] STC 297; [2001] 1 WLR 769;
     [2001] All ER (EC) 385 .... 22.419
Abbey National plc (No 2), ECJ Case C-169/04; [2006] STC 1136 .... 22.368
Abbey National plc (No 3), Ch D 2005, [2006] STC 1; [2005] EWHC 1187 (Ch) 4.30
Abbey National plc (No 4), CA [2006] STC 1961; [2006] EWCA Civ 886 .... 41.19
Abbeygate Holdings Ltd (VTD 17046) 52.315
Abbeytrust Homes Ltd, [2011] UKFTT 150 (TC), TC01024 .... 15.63
Abbeyview Bowling Club (VTD 20661) 46.201
Abbotsley Golf & Squash Club Ltd, [1997] VATDR 355 (VTD 15042) 41.159
Abbott v Philbin, HL 1960, 39 TC 82; [1961] AC 352; [1960] 2 All ER 763 .... 3.23
Abdullah (AA) (t/a Aladdin's Cave Kebab House) (VTD 16774) 51.156
Abedin (KJ) (VTD 19149) 50.59
Abedin (Z), QB 1978, [1979] STC 426 .... 2.214
Abel (G) (t/a Abel Guest House) (VTD 17409) 51.147
Abenheim, Re, LT 1913, 109 LT 219 .... 7.7
Abercromby Motor Group Ltd (No 1) (VTD 19015) 48.24
Abercromby Motor Group Ltd (No 2) (VTD 20092) 48.25
Abercych Village Association (VTD 20746) 15.203
Abercynon Rugby Football Club, [1982] VATTR 166 (VTD 1286) 13.39
Aberdeen (CW) (VTD 7027) 18.586
Aberdeen (CW) (t/a Smithfield Electronics) (VTD 9944) 18.429
Aberdeen Chamber of Commerce (VTD 3622) 36.129

Aberdeen Estates Ltd (VTD 13622) 48.18
Aberystwyth Cliff Railway Co Ltd (VTD 6449) 67.117
Able Foods Ltd (VTD 11317) 8.4
Able UK Ltd, UT [2011] STC 1110 .... 20.102
Ablefame Ltd (VTD 5560) 62.331
Abrook (PB) (VTD 11473) 51.60
AC Newline Cabs (VTD 19343) 62.33
AC Tours, [2010] UKFTT 363 (TC), TC00645 .... 62.498
ACC American Car Centre Ltd (VTD 5883) 52.26
Accenture Services Ltd, oao, R v HMRC, QB [2009] STC 1503; [2009] EWHC 857
  (Admin) 2.347
Accountancy Executive Appointments (VTD 5891) 18.71
Accounting Alliance Ltd (VTD 17741) 18.295
Ace Estates Ltd (VTD 6216) 46.47
Ace Telecom Ltd (VTD 19214) 57.16
Acer Engineering Ltd (VTD 7536) 18.13
ACH Transport Ltd (VTD 6006) 52.125
ACL Engineering Ltd (VTD 18788) 18.547
ACL Leasing & Finance Ltd (VTD 18808) 44.122
Acorn Management Services Ltd (VTD 17338) 41.98
Acorn Origination Ltd (VTD 5517) 18.286
Acorne Sports Ltd (VTD 18009) 62.458
Acoustiolox Suspended Ceilings (VTD 9049) 52.136
ACP Technical Services Ltd (VTD 10332) 52.21
Acquisitions (Fireplaces) Ltd (VTD 10097) 52.9
Acre Friendly Society, [1992] VATTR 308 (VTD 7649) 6.19
Acrefirst Ltd, [1985] VATTR 133 (VTD 1857) 65.15
Acrejean Ltd (VTD 12262) 36.414
Acrol UK Ltd (VTD 20338) 53.10
Acrylux Ltd, [2009] SFTD 763; UKFTT 223 (TC), TC00173 .... 41.114
ACT Construction Ltd, HL 1981, [1982] STC 25; [1981] 1 WLR 1542; [1982] 1 All ER
  84 .... 56.9
Actel Group Ltd (VTD 3301) 18.456
Actinic plc (VTD 18044) 27.52
Active Clothing Ltd (VTD 11363) 40.42
Active Handling (UK) Ltd (VTD 5273) 18.83
Active Infotech Ltd, [2011] UKFTT 328 (TC), TC01188 .... 36.121
Activ8 Alarms Ltd, [2010] UKFTT 48 (TC), TC00361 .... 50.80
AD High & Sons Ltd (VTD 13399) 18.377
AD Motors (Woodford) (VTD 1449) 44.63
Adam v Administration de l'enregistrement et des domaines, ECJ Case C-267/99; [2003]
  BTC 5240 .... 22.509
Adam Geoffrey & Co (Management) Ltd (VTD 16074) 3.103
Adam Smith Ltd (VTD 16282) 52.422
Adams (AW) (Mrs) (VTD 18054) 55.49
Adams (J), Woskett (AC) & Partners (VTD 9647) 30.12
Adams (PC) (VTD 5665) 18.563
Adams (RW) (VTD 175) 7.88
Adams (SE) (t/a Windows by Wise) (VTD 19218) 40.105
Adams Foods Ltd, [1983] VATTR 280 (VTD 1514) 29.146
Adath Yisroel Synagogue (VTD 20809) 15.209
Adcon Holdings Ltd (VTD 10324) 52.257
ADI Driving School (VTD 11469) 62.231
ADI Driving School 'A' (VTD 11469) 62.231
ADI School of Motoring (VTD 11469) 62.231
Adkin (JM) (VTD 18645) 18.543
Adland Group Co Ltd (VTD 10397) 5.87
Adler Properties Ltd (VTD 4088) 57.88
Adley (A) (t/a Jean Wenham) (VTD 4798) 2.424
ADM Glass Ltd, [2011] UKFTT 339 (TC), TC01199 .... 18.543
ADM (North East) Ltd (VTD 12640) 18.368

Administración del Estado, Campsa Estaciones de Servicio SA v, ECJ Case C-285/10; [2011] STC 1603 .... 22.503
Administración del Estado, Navicon SA v, ECJ Case C-97/06; [2008] STC 2693 .... 22.391
Administration de l'Enregistrement et des Domaines v Eurodental SARL, ECJ Case C-240/05; [2007] STC 275 .... 22.288
Administration de l'Enregistrement et des Domaines v Feltgen, ECJ Case C-116/10; [2011] STC 994 .... 22.392
Administration de l'Enregistrement et des Domaines v Vermietungsgesellschaft Objekt Kirchberg SARL, ECJ Case C-269/03; [2005] STC 1345 .... 22.381
Administration de l'Enregistrement et des Domaines, Adam v, ECJ Case C-267/99; [2003] BTC 5240 .... 22.509
Administration de l'Enregistrement et des Domaines, Zita Modes SARL v, ECJ Case C-497/01; [2005] STC 1059 .... 22.167
Administration des Douanes v Société Anonyme Gondrand Freres, ECJ Case 169/80; [1981] ECR 1931 .... 22.548
Administration des Impôts, Deville v, ECJ Case 240/87; [1988] ECR 3513; [1989] 3 CMLR 611 .... 22.44
Adó-és Pénzügyi Ellenőrzési Hivatal Hatósági Főosztály Észak-magyarországi Kihelyezett Hatósági Osztály, Parat Automotive Cabrio Textiltetőket Gyártó Kft v, ECJ Case C-74/08; 23 April 2009 unreported 22.410
Adplates Offset Ltd, QB [1989] STC 346 .... 18.2
Adrian Laflin Estate Agents (VTD 3811) 18.156
Adstock Ltd (VTD 10034) 7.113
ADV Allround Vermittlungs AG v Finanzamt Hamburg-Bergedorf, ECJ Case C-218/10; 28 June 2011 unreported 22.225
Advanced Business Technology Ltd (VTD 1488) 65.8
Advanced Medical Solutions Group plc (VTD 19925) 2.178
Advanced Security Installations Ltd (VTD 14297) 18.617
Advansys plc (VTD 4427) 36.679
AE Hamlin & Co, Ch D [1983] STC 780; [1983] 3 All ER 654 .... 14.87
AE Pipework Services Ltd (VTD 10724) 52.255
AE Technical Services (VTD 5931) 18.79
AE Walker Ltd, [1973] VATTR 8 (VTD 3) 5.1
AEG (UK) Ltd (VTD 10944) 67.127
AEG (UK) Ltd, [1993] VATTR 379 (VTD 11428) 4.10
Aegis Technology Ltd (VTD 13588) 36.602
Aer Lingus plc, [1992] VATTR 438 (VTD 8893) 36.678, 63.2
Aeresta Ltd & C & E Commrs, Schwarz and Others v, QB 1988, [1989] STC 230 .... 2.73
AF Ross & Sons (VTD 17525) 44.134
Afro-Caribbean Housing Association Ltd (The), [2006] VATDR 124 (VTD 19450) 67.92
Age Concern Leicestershire & Rutland (VTD 20762) 33.65
Agencia Estatal de Administracion Tributaria, Gabalfrisa SL & Others v, ECJ Cases C-110/98 to C-147/98; [2002] STC 535 .... 22.401
Agentevent Ltd (VTD 17764) 38.30
Agentmode Ltd (VTD 18024, VTD 18101) 40.41
Agenzia delle Entrate Ufficio di Roma 2, EGN BV Filiale Italiana v, ECJ Case C-377/08; [2009] STC 2544 .... 22.417
Agenzia delle Entrate Ufficio di Trento, Stradasfalti Srl v, ECJ Case C-228/05; [2007] STC 508 .... 22.434
Agenzia Entrate Ufficio Genova 3, Ecotrade SpA v, ECJ Cases C-95/07 and C-96/07; [2008] STC 2626 .... 22.435
AGP (2001) Ltd (VTD 20020) 62.473
Agrichem International Holdings Ltd, Hammond Suddard Solicitors v, CA [2001] All ER (D) 258 (Dec) 2.369
Agudas Israel Housing Association Ltd (VTD 18798) 15.37
Agurdino Srl v Moldova, ECHR Case 7359/06; 27 September 2011 unreported 34.23
Ahluwalia (HS & KK) (t/a Kings Headlines) (VTD 15258) 50.138
Ahmad (SK), [1976] VATTR 128 (VTD 266) 2.398
Ahmed (G) (t/a Lister Fisheries), QB [1999] STC 468 .... 3.7

Ahmed (M) (VTD 15399) 65.97
Ahmed (M) (t/a New Touch) (VTD 20119) 40.37
Ahmed (S & C) (VTD 16998) 57.38
Ahmed (SZ) (VTD 20187) 51.172
Ahmed (N) & Akhtar (K) (t/a The Albany Fish Bar), [1993] VATTR 262 (VTD
  11509) 2.356
Ahmed (S) & Haque (SA) (t/a Taj Tandoori Restaurant) (VTD 16262) 50.71
Ahmed (JU) & Wahab (JA) (VTD 10120) 50.46
Ahsan v Ward, HL [2007] UKHL 51 .... 2.123
Aikman v White, CS 1985, [1986] STC 1 .... 59.8
Ainsleys of Leeds Ltd (VTD 19694) 29.61
Aircall Export Ltd (VTD 19185) 36.81
Airdre Ltd v Isle of Man Treasury (VTD 20591) 57.149
Airline Computer Services Ltd (VTD 4311) 18.173
Airmaster Southern Ltd (VTD 20335) 18.542
Airspeed Aviation Ltd (VTD 11544) 50.148
Airtours Holiday Transport Ltd, [2010] UKUT 404 (TCC); [2011] STC 239 .... 36.163
Airtours plc, ECJ Case C-291/03; [2005] STC 1617 .... 22.488
Aisereigh Investments Ltd (VTD 15988) 62.329
Akar (C) (t/a Akar Kebabs), [1994] VATTR 176 (VTD 11873) 2.318
Akbar (GK, RK, GK, M, F & K) (t/a Mumtaz Paan House), [1998] VATDR 52 (VTD
  15386) 50.7
Akbar (GK, RK, GK, M, F & K) (t/a Mumtaz Paan House), QB [2000] STC 237 .... 50.72
Aken, CIR v, CA [1990] STC 497 .... 2.196
Akhtar (M & ZP) (t/a Ruwaz Knitwear) (VTD 17824) 50.98
Akritidis, Finanzamt Herne-West v, ECJ Case C-462/02; [2008] STC 1069 .... 22.373
Aktiebolaget NN v Skatteverket, ECJ Case C-111/05; [2008] STC 3203 .... 22.196
AL Currie & Brown (VTD 14678) 18.540
AL Davis & Co (VTD 17802) 44.164
Al Faham (NA) (t/a Express Food Supplies), [2010] UKFTT 466 (TC), TC00728 ... 52.449
AL Yeoman Ltd (VTD 4470) 44.44
Aladdin Window Co (VTD 3026) 2.423
Alam (SS) & Ahmed (SU) (t/a Anarkali Tandoori Restaurant) (VTD 14584) 50.107
Alan Davison (Construction) Ltd (VTD 14531) 18.286
Alan Franks Group (VTD 10146) 52.41
Alan Franks Group (VTD 13731) 18.118
Alan Glaves International Ltd (VTD 16151) 48.124
Alan Roper & Sons Ltd (VTD 15260) 55.80
Alan Wright & Partners (VTD 6114) 52.216
Alarmond Ltd (VTD 19324) 4.27
Alba Motor Homes Ltd (VTD 12853) 48.120
Albany Building Services Ltd (VTD 10531) 2.64
Albany Building Services Ltd (VTD 11294) 52.375
Alberni String Quartet, [1990] VATTR 166 (VTD 5024) 21.2
Albert (Mr & Mrs JG & Mr SJ) (t/a The Groves Hotel) (VTD 11651) 62.301
Albert Guest House (VTD 5524) 18.53
Albion Taxis Ltd, [2010] UKFTT 389 (TC), TC00671 .... 62.239
Alcatel Business Systems Ltd (VTD 11411) 52.296
Aldam (JC) (t/a John Charles Associates) (VTD 15851) 44.129
Alden (GJ) (VTD 461) 25.18
Aldford Aluminium Products (VTD 2190) 62.427
Aldon Engineering (Yorkshire) Ltd (VTD 743) 4.5
Aleena Electronics Ltd, [2010] UKFTT 608 (TC), TC01451 .... 36.658
Aleris Recycling (Swansea) Ltd, [2010] UKFTT 341 (TC), TC00623 .... 17.18
Alert Security Supplies Ltd (VTD 12677) 18.71
Alexander (EM), [1976] VATTR 107 (VTD 251) 36.184
Alexander (MW) (VTD 7208) 36.468
Alexander (RAS) (VTD 4560) 15.263
Alexander (Mrs SM) (VTD 12810) 57.19
Alexander Designs Ltd (VTD 3325) 18.71
Alexander MacRobert (Sir) Memorial Trust, [1990] VATTR 56 (VTD 5125) 36.159

Alexander (LWM) Oliver Bennett Partnership (VTD 9153) 18.425
Alexandrou (P) (VTD 2944) 51.107
Alexis Modes Ltd (VTD 4780) 18.371
Alfred Crompton Amusement Machines Ltd (No 2), HL 1972, [1974] AC 405; [1972]
  2 All ER 353 .... 2.282
ALH Interiors Ltd, [2009] UKFTT 234 (TC), TC00183 .... 51.152
Ali (A) (VTD 17565) 51.164
Ali (A & A) (t/a Dos Tandoori & Balti House Restaurant) (VTD 16803) 52.448
Ali (L) (t/a Vakas Balti), CA 2006, [2007] STC 618; [2006] EWCA Civ 1572 .... 50.12
Ali (M) (t/a The Candy Bar) (VTD 3441) 51.104
Ali (S) (t/a The Bengal Brasserie) (VTD 16952) 3.63
Ali (Y) (t/a HAR Fashions) (VTD 17814) 40.40
Ali (N) & Begum (S) (t/a Shapla Tandoori Restaurant), [2002] VATDR 71 (VTD
  17681) 34.16
Ali (J) & Rahman (F) (VTD 16277) 52.448
Ali Baba Tex Ltd, QB [1992] STC 590 .... 12.4
Align Technology UK Ltd (VTD 18426) 2.7
Alito Colour Ltd (VTD 7504) 36.359
Alkhatib (MS) (t/a Roxana Takeaway) (VTD 18514) 65.109
All England Film Caterers Ltd (VTD 20183) 18.307
All Saints Church (Tilsworth) Parochial Church Council (VTD 10490) 55.30
All Saints Commercial Ltd (VTD 5798) 18.113
All Saints Garage Ltd (VTD 5798) 18.113
All Saints with St Nicholas Church Icklesham (VTD 16321) 55.35
Allan Water Developments Ltd (VTD 19131) 15.169
Allard (M) [1984] VATTR 157 (VTD 1566) 36.589
Allclean Cleaning Services (VTD 9885) 18.206
Allegra Strategies Ltd (VTD 20539) 18.455
Allen (CJ) (VTD 17342) 15.274
Allen (LC & P) (VTD 12547) 18.226
Allen (P, C & J) (VTD 12209) 57.76
Allen (SH, HA, BP & D) (t/a The Shovel) (VTD 16906) 62.299
Allen (WD) (VTD 11000) 57.7
Allen Carr's Easyway (International) Ltd, [2009] SFTD 523; [2009] UKFTT 181 (TC);
  TC00136 .... 33.7
Allen-Fletcher (J) (VTD 12898) 50.116
Allergycare (Testing) Ltd (VTD 18026) 33.29
Allerton Motors (VTD 9427) 57.58
Alliance & Leicester plc [2007] VATDR 240 (VTD 20094) 48.105
Allied Carpets Group plc, QB [1998] STC 894 .... 58.44
Allied Dancing Association Ltd, [1993] VATTR 405 (VTD 10777) 21.33, 64.1
Allied Domecq plc, ECJ Case C-305/97; [1999] STC 998; [2000] 1 WLR 1151;
  [1999] All ER (EC) 908 .... 22.424
Allied Lyons plc [1994] VATTR 361 (VTD 11731) 62.4
Allied Medicare Nursing Services Ltd (VTD 5485) 33.2
Allied Schools Agency Ltd, [1973] VATTR 155 (VTD 36) 7.83
Allied Windows (South Wales) Ltd, [1973] VATTR 3; QB 1973 (unreported) 2.1
Allman Holdings Ltd (VTD 11285) 52.39
Allseal Gasket & Engineering Services Ltd (VTD 17358) 53.16
Allt-Yr-Yn & Caerleon Enterprises & Services Ltd, [1997] VATDR 417 (VTD 15280)
  .... 11.1
Allum (BC) (VTD 12646) 36.5
Alm (GE) (VTD 15863) 2.46, 51.141
Almond (K), [2009] UKFTT 177 (TC), TC00132 .... 15.173
Alpha Engineering Services Ltd (VTD 5775) 52.275
Alpha International Coal Ltd (VTD 9795) 1.81
Alpha International Coal Ltd (VTD 11441) 2.451
Alpha Leisure (Scotland) Ltd (VTD 18199) 4.11
Alpha Numeric Ltd (VTD 5519) 18.588
Alpro Ltd (VTD 19911) 29.180

Alstom Power Hydro *v* Valsts ieņēmumu dienests, ECJ Case C-472/08; [2010] STC 777 .... 22.441
Alsuna Ltd (VTD 3845) 18.404
Altman Blane & Co (VTD 12381) 41.8
Alucast (Diecastings) Ltd (VTD 10291) 18.367
Alvabond Ltd (VTD 10598) 36.633
Alzheimer's Society (The) (VTD 18318) 15.203
AM Autos (VTD 3698) 51.25
Amana Books Ltd (VTD 19541) 36.528
Ambrose (CH) (VTD 2303) 51.137
Ambrose (EW) Ltd (VTD 5766) 36.380
Ambulanter Pflegedienst Kügler GmbH *v* Finanzamt fur Körperschaften, ECJ Case C-141/00; [2002] All ER (D) 40 (Sept) 22.299
Ambu-Medics Ltd (VTD 5697) 67.21
Amengual Far (J) *v* Amengual Far (M), ECJ Case C-12/98; [2002] STC 382 .... 22.339
Americana Europe Ltd (VTD 6712) 52.69
American Express Bank Ltd (VTD 9748) 48.114
American Express Services Europe Ltd, Ch D [2010] STC 1023; [2010] EWHC 120 (Ch) 62.484
American Institute of Foreign Study (UK) Ltd (VTD 13886) 62.541
American Real Estate (Scotland) Ltd, [1980] VATTR 80 (VTD 947) 41.118
Amesbury Motor Co (VTD 9644) 18.352
Amicus Group Ltd (VTD 17693) 15.216
Amiji (MS) (VTD 16552) 50.120
Amministrazione delle Finanze dello Stato *v* San Giorgio SpA, ECJ Case C-199/82; [1983] ECR 3513; [1985] 2 CMLR 658 .... 22.556
Amministrazione delle Finanze dello Stato *v* Simmenthal SpA, ECJ Case 106/77; [1978] ECR 629; [1978] 3 CMLR 263 .... 22.22
Amministrazione delle Finanze dello Stato, Aprile Srl *v*, ECJ Case C-228/96, 17 November 1998 unreported 22.51
Amministrazione delle Finanze dello Stato, Dilexport Srl *v*, ECJ Case C-343/96, 9 February 1999 unreported 22.557
Amministrazione dell'Economia e delle Finanze *v* Fallimento Olimpiclub Srl, ECJ Case C-2/08; 3 September 2009 unreported 22.555
Ampafrance SA *v* Directeur des Services Fiscaux de Maine-et-Loire, ECJ Case C-177/99; [2002] BTC 5520 .... 22.501
Ampleforth Abbey Trust (VTD 15763) 46.106
Ampliscientifica Srl & Amplifin SpA *v* Ministero dell'Economia e delle Finanze, ECJ Case C-162/07; [2011] STC 566 .... 22.125
Amsbury (FJ) (VTD 5999) 18.56
Amspray Ltd (t/a Champion Tools & Supplies) (VTD 10888) 52.73
Amsterdam Bulb *v* Produktsckap voor Sietegewassen, ECJ [1977] ECR 137 .... 52.452
Amusement Solutions Ltd (VTD 20838) 24.52
Anacomp Ltd (VTD 7824) 52.263
Analog & Numeric Devices Ltd (VTD 9340) 52.165
Anchor Foods Ltd, QB 1998, [1999] VATDR 425 .... 22.6
Anchor Foods Ltd, Ch D [1999] 1 WLR 1139; [1999] 3 All ER 268 .... 14.109
Anchor Foods Ltd, CA [2000] BTC 8035 .... 14.109
Anderson (CAM), [2010] UKFTT 432 (TC), TC00701 .... 15.278
Anderson (CJ), [2007] VATDR 137 (VTD 20255) 28.3
Anderson (IT) (VTD 13226) 2.327
Anderson (J) (t/a R Boa Ironmonger) (VTD 15717) 44.97
Anderson (RNM) (VTD 11776) 44.141
Anderson, Mullan *v*, CS [1993] SLT 835 .... 50.77
Andreucci (G, A & C) (t/a Joe's Chip Shop) (VTD 11223) 50.144
Andrew Hillas Ltd (VTD 18671) 67.65
Andrew S Campbell Associates (VTD 7262) 18.206
Andrews (GA & P) (VTD 1310) 65.93
Andrews Kent & Stone (VTD 7753) 18.442
Andy Smith Bloodstock Ltd (VTD 1663) 7.62
Angel Foundation Ltd (The) (VTD 18818) 5.98

Anglia Building & Decorating Contractors (VTD 16852) 52.343
Anglia Energy Conservation Ltd (VTD 14216) 2.5
Anglia Energy Conservation Ltd (VTD 14620) 67.110
Anglia Regional Co-Operative Society Ltd, [2005] VATDR 100 (VTD 18991) 48.73
Anglian Farming Contracts Ltd (VTD 7928) 18.432
Anglo-German Breweries Ltd, Ch D [2002] EWHC 2458(Ch) 37.2
Anglo-German Breweries Ltd, re, Forrester (N) v Hooper (RAJ) (VTD 18008) 2.510
Anglo Persian Emporium Trading Co Ltd, [2010] UKFTT 296 (TC), TC00584 ..... 52.167
Anglodent Company (The) (VTD 16891) 11.4
Angus MacKinnon Ltd (VTD 18015) 44.73
Angus Modelmakers Ltd (VTD 10655) 18.83
Anholt (A) (VTD 4215) 36.507
Animal Virus Research Institute, [1988] VATTR 56 (VTD 2692) 2.118
Anker, Arthur v, CA 1996, [1997] QB 564; [1996] 3 All ER 783 .... 1.27
Annabel's Casino Ltd, QB 1994, [1995] STC 225 .... 24.21, 46.75
Annova Ltd, [2011] UKFTT 742 (TC), TC01579 .... 36.120
Anozinc Ltd (VTD 12695) 18.558
Anrich North West Ltd (VTD 18996) 18.543
Ansari (Dr A) (t/a Northside House Hotel) (VTD 11093) 52.21
Anti-Sonics Ltd (VTD 7196) 52.39
Anti-Static Technology Ltd (VTD 5065) 18.299
António Jorge Lda v Fazenda Pública, ECJ Case C-536/03; [2008] STC 2533 .... 22.444
Antoniou (C) (t/a Cosmos Patisserie) (VTD 15781) 50.71
Antoniou (K & D) (t/a Sackville Fisheries) (VTD 17165) 59.13
Antoniou-Savva (TC) (t/a Game Atronics) (VTD 11982) 67.72
Antrobus Farm Ltd (VTD 16029) 52.283
Anwar (R) (VTD 12748) 36.226
Anycom Ltd, [2011] UKFTT 654 (TC), TC01496 .... 28.6
AOC International Ltd (VTD 11139) 52.39
AP, MP & TP v Switzerland, ECHR Case 19958/92, 26 EHRR 541 .... 34.5
APD Insulations (Group) Ltd, [1987] VATTR 26 (VTD 2292) 62.402
APEH Kozponti Hivatal Hatósági Foosztály, Uszodaépíto Kft v, ECJ Case C-392/09;
    30 September 2010 unreported 20.105
APEH Központi Hivatal Hatósági Főosztály Dél-dunántúli Kihelyezett Hatósági Osztály,
    Pannon Gép Centrum v, ECJ Case C-368/09; [2010] STC 2400 .... 20.104
Apex Denim & Fabric Finishers (VTD 10989) 52.21
Aplin (CJ, JD & EN) (VTD 14660) 36.305
Apple & Pear Development Council (The), ECJ Case 102/86; [1988] STC 221;
    [1988] ECR 1443; [1988] 2 CMLR 394; [1988] 2 All ER 922 .... 22.80
Apple Contractors (Northern) Ltd (VTD 7853) 52.58
Appleby (D) (VTD 14580) 44.33
Appleby Bowers, Ch D 2000, [2001] STC 185 .... 5.64
Appleyard Lees & Co (VTD 2928) 18.251
Appleyard Vehicle Contracts Ltd (VTD 20891) 23.21
Applied Cutting Technology (VTD 6489) 18.427
Applied Software Control Ltd (VTD 17675) 52.347
Appropriate Technology Ltd, [1991] VATTR 226 (VTD 5696) 52.31
Aprile Srl v Amministrazione delle Finanze dello Stato, ECJ Case C-228/96,
    17 November 1998 unreported 22.51
APS-Centriline Ltd, [2009] UKFTT 149 (TC), TC00117 .... 36.28
APUK Ltd (VTD 15796) 18.26, 18.232
Apuzzo (Ms F) (t/a Casamia Restaurant) (VTD 19962) 18.496
Aquability Partnership (VTD 10635) 18.358
Aquakraft Ltd (VTD 2215) 19.10
Aquarium Entertainments Ltd, [1994] VATTR 61 (VTD 11845) 22.345
AR Communications & Electronics Ltd, [2011] UKFTT 637 (TC), TC01479 .... 36.113
Arachchige (PKS), CA [2010] EWCA Civ 1255; [2011] STC 33 .... 62.546
Aramark Ltd (VTD 20515) 1.39
Arbib (M), QB [1995] STC 490 .... 55.39
Arbroath Herald Ltd (VTD 182) 5.72

Archdiocese of Southwark Commission for Schools and Colleges (The) (VTD 18883)
.... 15.203
Archer (RA) (No 2), [1975] VATTR 1 (VTD 134) 62.6
Archibald & Co Ltd, [2010] UKFTT 21 (TC), TC00336 .... 28.10
Archway (Shoes) Ltd (VTD 4250) 18.436
Arco British Ltd (VTD 7041, 7806) 52.32
Arctrend Ltd (VTD 10011) 52.169
Ardenglen Developments Ltd (VTD 19906) 15.96
Ardmore Direct (VTD 7055) 52.256
Arena Corporation Ltd, Ch D [2003] EWHC 3032 (Ch) 37.3
Arendal Smelterwork AS (VTD 11427) 52.158
Areva T & D Protection et Controle, FTT [2010] UKFTT 134 (TC), TC00443 .... 45.5
Argents Nurseries Ltd (VTD 20045) 41.61
Argos Distributors Ltd, ECJ Case C-288/94; [1996] STC 1359; [1996] 1 ECR 5311;
[1996] 3 CMLR 569; [1997] 2 WLR 477 .... 22.236
Argosy Co Ltd v Guyana Commissioner of Inland Revenue, PC [1971] 1 WLR 514
.... 3.1, 58.42
Argyle Park Taxis Ltd (VTD 20277) 62.243
Argyll Developments Ltd, CS [2009] STC 2698; [2009] CSOH 131 .... 46.226
Aries (DM) (VTD 12172) 15.274
Arif (M) (t/a Trinity Fisheries) (VTD 19296) 2.305
Arif (M) (t/a Trinity Fisheries), Ch D [2006] STC 1989; [2006] EWHC 1262 (Ch)
.... 50.100
Arm Inc (VTD 20238) 25.31
Armbrecht, Finanzamt Ülzen v, ECJ Case C-291/92; [1995] STC 997; [1995] 1 ECR
2775; [1995] All ER (EC) 882 .... 22.93
Armsarmah (A) (VTD 19988) 50.20
Armstrong (JA) (VTD 5262) 18.610
Armstrong (M), [1984] VATTR 53 (VTD 1609) 29.22
Armstrong (W) (t/a Armstrong Stone Quarries) (VTD 17072) 52.417
Armstrongs Transport (Wigan) Ltd (VTD 7464) 18.83
Arnaoutis (P & F) (t/a Trafford Chip Shop) (VTD 13829) 57.84
Arnold (A) (VTD 19511) 19.69
Arnold (SH), QB [1996] STC 1271 .... 2.91
Arnold Clark Automobiles Ltd (VTD 1058) 44.57
Arnold Clark Automobiles Ltd (No 2), [1985] VATTR 90 (VTD 1858) 67.44
ARO Lease BV v Inspecteur der Belastingdienst Grote Ondernemingen Amsterdam, ECJ
Case C-190/95; [1997] STC 1272; [1997] 1 ECR 4383 .... 22.199
Arora (RM) & Others (t/a Angela), [1976] VATTR 53 (VTD 244) 3.146
Around the Clock Ltd (VTD 7157) 18.388
Arrowfinch (VTD 10413) 52.140
Arrowin Ltd (VTD 10575) 52.283
Arsenal Football Club plc (The), [1996] VATDR 5 (VTD 14011) 67.141
Art Store (British Isles) Ltd (The) (VTD 6938) 52.72
Artful Dodger (Kilmarnock) Ltd, CS [1993] STC 330 .... 18.351
Arthritis Care (VTD 13974) 19.63
Arthro Vite Ltd (VTD 14836) 29.90
Arthur v Anker, CA 1996, [1997] QB 564; [1996] 3 All ER 783 .... 1.27
Arthur Andersen & Co, Staatssecretaris van Financiën v , ECJ Case C-472/03; [2005]
STC 508 .... 22.327
Arthur's (VTD 13650) 57.97
Artic Shield Ltd (VTD 3789) 18.396
Artinville Ltd (VTD 5515) 18.43
Artistic Ironworkers Supplies Ltd (VTD 11228) 52.39
Arts Council of Great Britain (The), [1994] VATTR 313 (VTD 11991) 7.80
Asda Stores Ltd, FTT 2009, [2010] SFTD 175; [2009] UKFTT 267 (TC), TC00211
.... 29.161
Ash Fibre Processors Ltd (VTD 12201) 36.209
Ashbolt Ltd (VTD 11019) 52.344
Ashby Catering Ltd (VTD 4220) 29.29
Ashcroft (JNE & SA) (VTD 17476) 47.27

Ashe Construction Southern Ltd (VTD 7075) 52.217
Ashfield District Council, Ch D [2001] STC 1706 .... 42.3
Ashmall & Parkinson Ltd (VTD 1387) 44.67
Ashmore (P) (VTD 6910) 62.268
Ashton (GL) (t/a Country Hotel Narrowboats) (VTD 14197) 66.18
Ashtree Holdings Ltd, QB [1979] STC 818 .... 36.366
Ashvail Services Ltd (VTD 14440) 18.150
Ashwell House (St Albans) Ltd (VTD 12483) 46.23
Ashworth (Mrs B), [1994] VATTR 275 (VTD 12924) 41.127
ASI Glass Processing Ltd (VTD 12631) 18.441
Asif, R v, CA Criminal Division 1985, 82 Cr AR 123; [1985] CLR 679 .... 49.3
Asif & Others, ex p., R v City of London Magistrates, QB [1996] STC 611 .... 14.98
Asington Ltd (VTD 18171) 41.104
ASJ Manufacturing Ltd (VTD 2832) 18.433
Asker (G) (VTD 16753) 18.120
Aslam (M) (VTD 18775) 50.25
Aslan Imaging Ltd, [1989] VATTR 54 (VTD 3286) 33.18
Aslanbeigi (A) & Kanani (M) (t/a Cuccina) (VTD 18382) 51.131
Aspen Advisory Services Ltd (VTD 13489) 62.513
Aspex Visual Arts Trust (VTD 16419) 19.98
Aspinall's Club Ltd (VTD 17797) 46.135
Aspley Caterers Ltd (VTD 12235) 2.201
Aspro Travel Ltd, QB 1996, [1997] STC 151 .... 63.21
ASR Consultants Ltd (VTD 18600) 36.20
Assets Recovery Agency (Director) v Creaven, QB [2005] EWHC 2726 (Admin); Times
    4.10.2006 .... 49.17
Associated Cab Co Ltd (VTD 3394) 44.88
Associated Concrete Repairs Ltd (VTD 15963) 36.146
Associated Nursing Services plc (VTD 11203) 15.164
Associated Provincial Picture Houses v Wednesbury Corporation, CA 1947, [1948] 1 KB
    223; [1947] 2 All ER 680 . 3.30, 14.22, 14.30, 14.54, 14.55, 47.41, 52.454, 52.455, 57.147,
                                                                                     57.157
Association of Payroll & Superannuation Administrators (VTD 7009) 64.22
Association of Reflexologists (The) (VTD 13078) 64.27
Assurandør-Societetet (on behalf of Taksatorringen) v Skatteministeriet, ECJ Case
    C-8/01; [2006] STC 1842 .... 22.326
Astim Ltd (VTD 19521) 6.30
Aston (AA) [1991] VATTR 170 (VTD 5955) 48.82
Astor (Sir John) [1981] VATTR 174 (VTD 1030) 62.361
Astra Zeneca UK Ltd, ECJ Case C-40/09; [2010] STC 2298 .... 22.92
Astral Print Ltd (VTD 12837) 14.47
AT & T Rentals Ltd (VTD 10790) 18.352
AT Warner & Sons Ltd (VTD 19605) 18.118
ATEC Associates Ltd, UT [2010] STC 1882 .... 2.321
Athenaeum Club (The), [2010] UKFTT 583 (TC), TC00833 .... 52.321
Athesia Druck Srl v Ministero dell'Economia e delle Finanze, ECJ Case C-1/08; [2009]
    STC 1334 .... 22.228
Athol Street Auctioneers Ltd v Isle of Man Treasury (VTD 12478) 1.43
Atkins (Mrs PJ) (VTD 4142) 18.484
Atkins Macreadie & Co (VTD 2381) 29.42
Atkinson (Ms JR) (VTD 309) 57.84
Atkinson (MR) (VTD 12763) 62.78
Atkinson (S) (VTD 6989) 52.378
Atlantic Electronics Ltd (No 1) (VTD 19256) 23.36
Atlantic Electronics Ltd (No 2), [2011] UKFTT 314 (TC), TC01175 .... 2.270
Atlantic Electronics Ltd (No 3), UT [2012] UKUT 45 (TCC) 2.373
Atlantic Holidays Ltd (VTD 20011) 63.17
Atlas Economy Hire Ltd (VTD 20472) 44.63
Atlas Interlates Ltd (VTD 7904) 52.1
Atlas Marketing (VTD 1905) 36.410
Atrium Club Ltd (The), Ch D [2010] STC 1493; [2010] EWHC 970 (Ch) 22.73

Attorney-General *v* Milliwatt Ltd, KB [1948] 1 All ER 331 .... 19.9
Attorney-General's Reference No 7 of 2000, CA [2001] EWCA Crim 888 .... 2.283
Attwater (A) (VTD 15496) 57.113
Auchterarder Golf Club (VTD 19907) 46.141
Auchtertyre Farmers (VTD 2822) 65.60
Audiostore Ltd (t/a Stagestruck) (VTD 11827) 17.4
Augusta Extrusions Ltd (VTD 8892) 65.24
Auld (SR) (VTD 11956) 2.45
Auldbrook Ltd (VTD 11717) 14.4
Aura Trading Ltd (VTD 16534) 52.21
Austin (J) (VTD 7668) 18.404
Austin Company of UK Ltd (The) (VTD 7981) 52.82
Austin (F) (Leyton) Ltd, Ch D [1968] 2 All ER 13; [1968] Ch D 529 .... 15.221
Australian Federal Commissioners of Tax, Saffron *v*, (No 2), FC(A) [1991] FCR 578
.... 2.207
Austria, Meidl *v*, ECHR Case 33951/05; 12 April 2011 unreported 34.30
Austrian National Tourist Office (VTD 15561) 36.499, 62.497
Austrian Republic, EC Commission *v*, ECJ Case C-128/05; [2008] STC 2610 ...... 22.479
Austrian Republic, T-Mobile Austria GmbH and Others *v*, ECJ Case C-284/04; [2008]
STC 184 .... 22.118
Auto Bodies (Hemel) Ltd (VTD 4184) 18.239
Auto-Factors Ltd (VTD 3055) 18.502
Auto Lease Holland BV v Bundesamt für Finanzen, ECJ Case C-185/01; [2005] STC
598 .... 22.152
Auto Nikolovi OOD, Direktsia Obzhalvane I upralenie na izpalnenieto Varna *v*, ECJ
Case C-203/10; [2011] STC 1294 .... 20.133
Auto-Plas (International) Ltd (VTD 8860) 52.78
Autocraft Motor Body Repairs (VTD 15077) 4.2
Autolease (UK) Ltd (VTD 19136) 44.94
Automobile Association (The), QB [1974] STC 192; [1974] 1 WLR 1447; [1974]
1 All ER 1257 .... 13.17
Automotive Parts Distributions Ltd (VTD 17261) 18.541
Autotag Ltd (VTD 17126) 53.2
Ava Knit Ltd (VTD 1461) 36.477
Avantgo Ltd (VTD 17363) 2.440
Avco Trust plc (VTD 16251) 48.122
Avery's of Bristol Ltd (VTD 1252) 3.151
Avis (DJ) (t/a Property Alterations) (VTD 10664) 19.78
Aviss Holdings Ltd (VTD 3982) 18.586
Avondale Management Ltd (VTD 18144) 5.70
Avonline Communications (Bristol) Ltd (VTD 9204) 52.105
Avonwave Ltd (t/a Gatewood Joinery) (VTD 17509) 18.529
AW Mills Engineering Ltd (VTD 13196) 36.513
Awnhail Ltd (VTD 11465) 18.392
AWTS Transportation International Ltd (VTD 11089) 17.3
Axa UK plc (No 1), ECJ Case C-175/09; [2010] STC 2825 .... 22.362
Axa UK plc (No 2), CA [2011] EWCA Civ 1607 .... 22.362
Ayr Pavilion Ltd (VTD 19119) 52.419
Ayrton (WM) & Co (Holdings) Ltd (VTD 9195) 52.281
Ayuntamiento de Sevilla *v* Recaudadores de las Zonas Primera y Segunda, ECJ Case
C-202/90; [1991] 1 ECR 4247; [1993] STC 659; [1994] 1 CMLR 424 .... 22.131
Ayurveda Ltd (VTD 3860) 29.83
AZ Cleaning Services (South West) Ltd (VTD 182008) 18.542
A-Z Electrical (VTD 10718) 10.12
Azo-Maschinenfabrik Adolf Zimmerman (No 2), [1987] VATTR 25 (VTD 2296) ... 22.193
Aztec Computer Products Ltd (VTD 7127) 18.417

B

B & B Packaging (VTD 18792) 40.36

B & H Carpentry & Joinery (VTD 12791) 4.3
B Fairall Ltd (in liquidation), [2010] UKFTT 305(TC), TC00592 .... 2.198
BAA Ltd, UT [2011] UKUT 258 (TCC); [2011] STC 1791 .... 32.30
BAA plc, CA 2002, [2003] STC 35; [2002] EWCA Civ 1814 .... 27.20
Baba Cash & Carry Ltd (VTD 20416) 40.50
Babber (HR) (t/a Ram Parkash Sunderdass & Sons) [1992] VATTR 268 (VTD 5958)
.... 3.62, 67.60
Babergh District Council, [2011] UKFTT 341 (TC); [2011] SFTD 709, TC01201 .... 2.149
Babytec Ltd (VTD 12391) 65.52
Back (LR) (VTD 1306) 2.195
Back In Health Ltd (VTD 10003) 19.53
Bacon Empire (Publishing) Ltd (The) (VTD 1688) 36.535
Baden (T) Hardstaff Ltd (VTD 7230) 52.294
Badge Sales (VTD 17388) 53.8
Badman (R) (t/a Gardener & Badman) (VTD 15938) 18.94
BAG Building Contractors (VTD 18638) 56.1
Bagshawe (JNS) & Walker (CAE) (VTD 1762) 1.2
Bagshawe (WN) (t/a Bagshawes) (VTD 14103) 62.406
Bahd (PS) (t/a Kingsbury Liquor Mart) (VTD 11688) 17.3
Baildon Rugby Union Football Club (VTD 3239) 13.42
Bailes (P) (VTD 12459) 11.38
Bailey (P) (VTD 2851) 51.27
Bailey (R) (VTD 9677) 18.120
Bailey (RF) (t/a Llancillo Hall Farm) (VTD 18719) 36.523
Bailey (TN) (VTD 1587) 36.377
Bailiwick Ltd (VTD 7802) 7.68
Baines & Ernst Ltd (VTD 18516) 2.160
Baines & Ernst Ltd (No 2), CA [2006] STC 1632; [2006] EWCA Civ 1040 .... 48.48
Baines (PF) & McDonough (J) (VTD 4921) 18.361
Baird (PA) (t/a Baird Motors), QB April 1976 unreported 2.136
Bairstow & Harrison, Edwards v, HL 1955, 36 TC 207 . 3.6, 36.97, 62.109, 62.325, 67.61
Baker (R) (VTD 11634) 52.285
Baker (R & M) Ltd (t/a Castle Designs) (VTD 1695) 36.437
Bakcsi v Finanzamt Fürstenfeldbruck, ECJ Case C-415/98; [2002] STC 802; [2002] 2
   WLR 1188 .... 22.94
Ball (B) (VTD 18708) 22.322
Ball (I & L) (VTD 9251) 1.100
Ball (W) (VTD 3865) 36.261
Ball (W) (VTD 17648) 52.174
Ballygrant Inn (VTD 15683) 18.125
Balma Time Ltd (VTD 3585) 18.175
Balmain (J) (t/a Glenrothes Motor Factors) (VTD 16678) 65.82
Balmoral Ltd (No 1) (VTD 19233) 14.65
Balmoral Ltd (No 2) (VTD 20677) 40.74
Balocchi (M) v Ministero delle Finanze dello Stato, ECJ Case C-10/92; [1993] 1 ECR
   5105; [1997] STC 640; [1995] 1 CMLR 486 .... 22.476
Baltex Clothing Manufacturers (VTD 12606) 50.140
Baltex Clothing Manufacturers (VTD 13777) 3.88
Baltic Leasing Ltd, [1986] VATTR 98 (VTD 2088) 65.17
Balton Ltd (VTD 5980) 18.216
Bambers Frozen Meats Ltd (VTD 17626) 29.193
Bamford (Mr & Mrs FJ) (t/a FJ Hardy Tilers) (VTD 11584) 18.149
Bammi (SC) & Dhir (BK) (t/a The Last Viceroy) (VTD 17660) 34.7
Banbridge District Enterprises Ltd (VTD 6406) 52.85
Banbury (RN) (t/a Creative Impressions) (VTD 15047) 52.363
Banbury Visionplus Ltd (and related appeals), Ch D [2006] STC 1568; [2006] EWHC
   1024 (Ch) 46.126
Banco Antoniana Popolare Veneta SpA v Ministero dell' Economia e delle Finanze, ECJ
   Case C-427/10; 15 December 2011 unreported 22.54
Bank Austria Trade Services Gesellschaft mbH (VTD 16918) 2.528
Bank of Ireland (Governor & Company of), [2008] VATDR 352 (VTD 20824) 38.25

Bank of Scotland (Governor & Company of) (VTD 13854) 46.158
Banks (Mrs E) (VTD 12004) 15.274
Banner Management Ltd [1991] VATTR 254 (VTD 5678) 46.40
Bannon (S) (VTD 4877) 18.488
Banque Bruxelles Lambert SA *v* Belgian State, ECJ Case C-8/03; [2004] STC 1643
.... 22.107
Banstead Downs Golf Club, [1974] VATTR 219 (VTD 229) 41.70
Banstead Manor Stud Ltd, [1979] VATTR 154 (VTD 816) 29.113, 39.1
Banwell (DJ & Mrs SA) (VTD 13944) 44.30
BAPP Industrial Supplies Ltd (VTD 10632) 18.235
Barar (S & Mrs S) (t/a Turret House Rest Home) (VTD 12707) 2.12
Barber (JH), [1992] VATTR 144 (VTD 7727) 3.37
Barber *v* Guardian Royal Exchange Assurance Group, ECJ Case 262/88; [1990] 1 ECR
   1889; [1990] 2 CMLR 513; [1990] 2 All ER 660 .... 22.40
Barber (DE) & Bayly (PA) (t/a The Pitts Head) (VTD 17856) 47.2
Barbour (K) (VTD 2651) 44.22
Barclays Bank Ltd *v* Quistclose Investments Ltd, HL [1970] AC 567 .... 37.8
Barclays Bank plc (No 1), [1988] VATTR 23 (VTD 2622) 27.25
Barclays Bank plc (No 2), [1991] VATTR 115 (VTD 5616) 46.80
Barclays Bank plc (No 3), [1991] VATTR 466 (VTD 6469) 38.45
Barclays Bank plc (No 4), CA [2001] STC 1558; [2001] EWCA Civ 1513 .... 32.15
Barclays Bank plc (No 5) (VTD 18410) 48.27
Barclays Bank plc (No 6), HL [2006] UKHL 28; [2006] 3 WLR 1; [2006] 4 All ER
   256 .... 14.112
Barclays Bank plc (No 7) (VTD 19302) 25.37
Barclays Bank plc (No 8), [2008] VATDR 107 (VTD 20528) 27.45
Barclays Bank plc *v* Visa International Service Association [1992] VATTR 229 (VTD
   7911, 9059) 2.75, 2.495
Barclays Bank Trust Ltd, Bartlett *v*, [1982] 2 All ER 92 .... 2.513
Barclays Bros Ltd (VTD 17507) 18.27
Bardetti (R & A) (t/a Obertelli Quality Sandwiches) (VTD 16758) 29.8, 58.36
Bardon Environmental Services Ltd (VTD 6504) 18.425
Bardsley (GP, D & A) (t/a Bardsley Car Sale), [1984] VATTR 171 (VTD 1718) 44.64
Barhale Construction plc, [1992] VATTR 409 (VTD 9137) 52.194
Barker (Mr & Mrs E) (VTD 4589) 62.12
Barker (Mrs JG), [1984] VATTR 147 (VTD 1671) 21.4
Barker (RJ & Mrs GD) (VTD 7952) 18.148
Barking Vehicle Rentals Ltd (VTD 4934) 18.610
Barkworth (JR), QB [1988] STC 771 .... 33.24
Barmor Engineering Ltd (VTD 2214) 51.122
Barnard (IM) (VTD 3741) 18.91
Barnard (J) (t/a Baron Security) (VTD 14206) 51.167
Barnard (KV) (VTD 13865) 44.51
Barnes (D) (t/a The Haven) (VTD 16371) 65.91
Barnes (RG) (VTD 14463) 52.342
Barnes (KC & HM) (t/a Sidlesham Common Carriage Co) (VTD 14090) 36.46
Barnes (Mr & Mrs) (VTD 19407) 40.23
Barnett (E) (t/a Barnett Motor Services) (VTD 6868) 44.79
Barnett (LA) (VTD 3245) 36.34
Barnett (PG) & Larsen (TB) (VTD 11056) 52.303
Barnett (Mrs P) & Read (Mrs L) (T/a Burghill Valley Golf Club), FTT 2009, TC00087
.... 24.45
Barnett Gray Ltd (VTD 11155) 52.170
Barnett Lawson (Trimmings) Ltd (VTD 4400) 18.190
Barney & Freeman [1990] VATTR 119 (VTD 4849) 18.451
Barnfinds Ltd (C198) 60.11
Baronshire Engineering Ltd (VTD 5027) 18.338
Barr (LE) (VTD 14529) 29.113
Barraclough (BD) (VTD 2529) 55.21
Barras (Garages) Ltd (VTD 6913) 40.97
Barratt (DR), QB [1995] STC 661 .... 69.8

Barratt Construction Ltd [1989] VATTR 204 (VTD 4230) 3.86
Barratt Goff & Tomlinson, [2011] UKFTT 71 (TC); [2011] SFTD 334, TC00949 .... 62.61
Barratt Homes Ltd (and associated appeals) (VTD 16533) 48.133
Barrett (AJ) (as provisional liquidator for Rafidain Bank) (VTD 11016) 46.129
Barrett (D) (t/a The Carib Takeaway) (VTD 15389) 51.4
Barrie (GC) (VTD 11470) 51.60
Barron (P) (VTD 6370) 62.59
Barrowcliffe (P) (VTD 18855) 50.36
Barrs (W & J) Ltd (VTD 2564) 36.434
Barry (J) (VTD 11281) 18.483
Bartlett v Barclays Bank Trust Ltd, Ch D [1982] 2 All ER 92 .... 2.513
Barton, QB [1974] STC 200; [1974] 1 WLR 1447; [1974] 3 All ER 337 .... 13.18
Barton (M) Consultancy Ltd (VTD 18233) 44.120
Bartram Planned Preventative Maintenance Ltd (VTD 12418) 52.252
Barugh (R) (VTD 18725) 55.85
Basdring Ltd (VTD 13263) 62.175
Base Interactive Ltd, [2007] VATDR 463 (VTD 20437) 40.41
Basebuy Ltd (VTD 12088) 24.6
Bashir (T) (VTD 19295) 57.186
Bashir Mohamed Ltd (VTD 16762) 1.76, 52.211
Basicflex Ltd (t/a Proline Engineering) (VTD 13370) 18.309
Basingstoke & District Sports Trust Ltd [1995] VATDR 405 (VTD 13347) 24.32
Basnet (EP) (t/a EB Roofing Services) (VTD 3795) 18.507
Basran (N & M) (VTD 1312) 57.7
Bass plc, QB 1992, [1993] STC 42 .... 62.93
Bassi (VP) (t/a Imperial Wines) (VTD 16449) 17.3
Bassimeh (N), CA 1996, [1997] STC 33 .... 50.3
Batchwood Hall Bowling Club (VTD 19797) 19.93
Bateman (GF) (VTD 9344) 52.75
Bates (P & M) (VTD 20948) 15.281
Bates (TR) (VTD 2925) 55.22
Bath Festivals Trust Ltd (VTD 20840) 42.19
Bath Taxis (UK) Ltd (VTD 20974) 62.243
Battersea Leisure Ltd, QB [1992] STC 213 .... 67.136
Batty (KM) (VTD 2199) 44.38
Baxi Group Ltd, ECJ Case C-55/09; 7 September 2010 unreported 22.154
Baxter (GW) (VTD 9152) 51.60
Baxter Healthcare Ltd (VTD 14670) 33.61
Baylis Baxter v Sabath, CA [1958] 1 WLR 529; [1958] 2 All ER 209 .... 2.376
Baysouth Ltd (VTD 17597) 60.4
Baytrust Holdings Ltd v CIR, Ch D [1971] 3 All ER 76 .... 65.40
BAZ Bausystem AG v Finanzamt München für Körperschaften, ECJ Case 222/81;
    [1982] ECR 2527; [1982] 3 CMLR 688 .... 22.232
BC Shutters & Doors Ltd (VTD 20404) 53.14
BCC (Building Services) Ltd (VTD 13211) 18.286
Beaches Ltd (VTD 16448) 53.6
Beagley (JR) (VTD 15107) 36.133, 65.28
Bean (DC) (VTD 339) 36.259
Bear (P) & Hill (S) (VTD 17215) 51.65, 57.197
Beardshaw (MB) (VTD 9245) 51.44
Beast in the Heart Films (UK) Ltd, [2009] UKFTT 230 (TC), TC00180 .... 48.94
Beaton, Snelling & Co (VTD 2206) 51.126
Beattie (W) (VTD 18979) 44.112
Beatwood Ltd (t/a Royals of London) (VTD 13229) 18.588
Beaublade Ltd (VTD 3066) 51.111
Beaumont (G & BM) (t/a Beaumont Home Improvements) (VTD 6063) 18.303
Beaumont English Language Centre (VTD 4907) 51.89
Beauty Direct Ltd (VTD 18353) 18.462
Beaver Oil Services Ltd (VTD 5786) 18.214
Beaverbank Properties Ltd [2003] VATDR 538 (VTD 18099) 36.556
Beckbell Ltd [1993] VATTR 212 (VTD 9847) 67.34

Beckenham Constitutional Club Ltd (VTD 10041) 62.319
Becker (U) *v* Finanzamt Münster-Innenstadt, ECJ Case 8/81; [1982] ECR 53; [1982] 1 CMLR 499 .... 22.352
Beckett (C) (VTD 4766) 18.609
Beckett & Graham Ltd (VTD 6878) 36.362
Beckley (C) (t/a The College of Meditation) (VTD 19860) 21.34
Beckley (JR) (VTD 114) 2.55
Beco Products Ltd (VTD 18638) 56.1
Bedford (P) (VTD 17085) 57.130
Bedward (W & D) (VTD 698) 3.158
Bedworth Car Centre Ltd (VTD 10706) 18.157
Bedworth Commercials Ltd (VTD 7585) 62.321
Begum (N), Ch D [2010] EWHC 1799 (Ch) 37.13
Begum Eastern Ocean Ltd (VTD 19633) 65.91
Beheersmaatschappij Van Ginkel Waddinxveen BV & Others *v* Inspecteur der Omzetbelasting Utrecht, ECJ Case C-163/91; [1992] 1 ECR 5723; [1996] STC 825
.... 22.485
Bekelect Ltd (VTD 7779) ....: 52.385
Belastingdienst Grote Ondernemingen, Gemeente Emmen *v*, ECJ Case C-468/93; [1996] STC 496; [1996] 1 ECR 1721; [1996] All ER (EC) 372 .... 22.123
Belgian Ministry of Finance, Chaussures Bally SA *v*, ECJ Case C-18/92; [1993] 1 ECR 2871; [1997] STC 209 .... 22.238
Belgian State *v* De Fruytier, ECJ Case C-237/09; [2010] STC 1792 .... 22.287
Belgian State *v* Henfling & Others (administrators of Tiercé Franco-Belge SA), ECJ Case C-464/10; [2011] STC 1851 .... 22.189
Belgian State *v* Recolta Recycling SPRL, ECJ Case C-440/04; 6 July 2006 unreported
.... 22.415
Belgian State *v* Temco Europe SA, ECJ Case C-284/03; [2005] STC 1451 .... 22.341
Belgian State, Banque Bruxelles Lambert SA *v*, ECJ Case C-8/03; [2004] STC 1643
.... 22.107
Belgian State, Berginvest SA *v*, ECJ Case C-142/99; [2000] STC 1044; [2001] All ER (EC) 37 .... 22.447
Belgian State, British American Tobacco International Ltd *v*, ECJ Case C-435/03; [2006] STC 158 .... 22.88
Belgian State, Floridienne SA *v*, ECJ Case C-142/99; [2000] STC 1044; [2001] All ER (EC) 37 .... 22.447
Belgian State, Garage Molenheide BVBA & Others *v*, ECJ Case C-286/94; [1998] STC 126; [1998] 1 CMLR 1186; [1998] All ER (EC) 61 .... 22.439
Belgian State, Intercommunale voor Zeewaterontzilting *v*, ECJ Case C-110/94; [1996] STC 569; [1996] 1 ECR 857 .... 22.110
Belgian State, Jeunehomme (L) & Société Anonyme d'Etude et de Gestion Immobilière 'EGI' *v*, ECJ Case 123/87; [1988] ECR 4517 .... 22.471
Belgian State, Kittel *v*, ECJ Case C-439/04; [2008] STC 1537 .... 22.415
Belgian State, Newman Shipping & AgencyCo NV *v* , ECJ Case C-435/03; [2006] STC 158 .... 22.88
Belgian State, Société Financière d'Investissements SPRL (SFI) *v*, ECJ Case C-85/97; [2000] STC 164 .... 22.53
Belgian State, Tiercé Ladbroke SA *v*, ECJ Case C-231/07; 14 May 2008 unreported
.... 22.359
Belgian Trading Co (VTD 12644) 18.261
Belgische Staat, Erotic Center BVBA *v*, ECJ Case C-3/09; [2010] STC 1018 .... 22.268
Belgische Staat, Vandoorne NV *v*, ECJ Case C-489/09; 27 January 2011 unreported
.... 22.499
Belgium (Kingdom of) *v* Ghent Coal Terminal NV, ECJ Case C-37/95; [1998] STC 260; [1998] All ER (EC) 223 .... 22.406
Belgium (Kingdom of), Belgocodex SA *v*, ECJ Case C-381/97; [2000] STC 351 ..... 22.380
Belgium (Kingdom of), EC Commission *v*, ECJ Case 324/82; [1984] ECR 1861; [1985] 1 CMLR 364 .... 22.498
Belgium (Kingdom of), Idéal Tourisme SA *v*, ECJ Case C-36/99; [2001] STC 1386
.... 22.512

Belgium (Kingdom of), Lease Plan Luxembourg SA *v*, ECJ Case C-390/96; [1998] STC 628 .... 22.542

Belgium (Kingdom of), Office des Produits Wallons ASBL *v*, ECJ Case C-184/00; [2003] STC 1100; [2003] All ER (EC) 747 .... 22.246

Belgium (Kingdom of), SCS Peterbroeck Van Campenhout & Cie *v*, ECJ Case C-312/93; [1995] 1 ECR 4599; [1996] 1 CMLR 793; [1996] All ER (EC) 242 .... 22.48

Belgocodex SA *v* Kingdom of Belgium, ECJ Case C-381/97; [2000] STC 351 .... 22.380

Bell & Another (ex p.), R *v* Epsom Justices, QB 1988, [1989] STC 169 .... 14.97

Bell (D) (VTD 1480) 19.42

Bell (IK), [2009] UKFTT 270 (TC), TC00216 .... 22.29

Bell (JA) (VTD 7411) 51.44

Bell (JS & L) (VTD 13448) 15.8

Bell (RE) [1979] VATTR 115 (VTD 761) 3.136

Bell Concord Educational Trust Ltd, CA [1989] STC 264; [1989] 2 All ER 217; [1989] 1 CMLR 845 .... 21.9

Bellevue Roofing Supplies Ltd (VTD 17121) 2.27

Bells of Lazonby Ltd (VTD 20490) 29.155

Belmore (Earl of) (VTD 9775) 36.254

Belvedere & Calder Vale Sports Club (VTD 931) 13.40

Belvedere Properties (Cheltenham) Ltd (VTD 18851) 15.135

Bendenoun *v* France, ECHR 1994, 18 EHRR 54 .... 34.5

Benefoot UK Ltd (VTD 17022) 19.67

Benenden School Trust [2007] VATDR 55 (VTD 20140) 22.70

Bengal Brasserie (The) [1991] VATTR 210 (VTD 5925) 47.1

Benjamin Clowes Ltd (VTD 19164) 18.524

Bennachie Leisure Centre Association (VTD 14276) 15.85

Bennett (A), QB [1999] STC 248 .... 3.21, 57.13

Bennett (A) (No 2), Ch D [2001] STC 137 .... 2.127, 34.14

Bennett (JA) (VTD 865) 33.33

Bennett (L) (VTD 19305) 57.191

Bennett (P) & Marshall (I) (t/a Enerco) (VTD 17520) 40.78

Bennetts of Sheffield Ltd [1986] VATTR 253 (VTD 2219) 67.134

Benning (P) (t/a PB Cars) (VTD 19557) 44.164

Benridge Care Homes Ltd [2010] UKFTT 493 (TC), TC00751 .... 48.32

Benrose Ltd (t/a Multi-Stock Ltd) (VTD 15783) 12.24

Bent (R) (t/a Bay Tree Trading Co) (VTD 17139) 3.67

Bentley & Bentley Ltd (VTD 18917) 19.20

Bentley Restaurant Ltd (VTD 4327) 2.140

Benton (G) [1975] VATTR 138 (VTD 185) 62.382

Berbrooke Fashions [1977] VATTR 168 (VTD 426) 36.1

Berck Ltd (VTD 20051) 4.12

Bercor Ribbon Co Ltd (VTD 14025) 18.286

Beresford (B) (VTD 9673) 29.194

Beresfors (SCS) (t/a Elidaprint) (VTD 11555) 62.30

Bergandi *v* Directeur Général des Impôts, ECJ Case 252/86; [1988] ECR 1343; [1991] STC 529; [1989] 2 CMLR 933 .... 22.526

Bergen Transport Ltd (VTD 4481) 18.200

Berginvest SA *v* Belgian State, ECJ Case C-142/99; [2000] STC 1044; [2001] All ER (EC) 37 .... 22.447

Bergonzi (GME) (t/a Beppi's Buffet Service) (VTD 12122) 29.53

Berkholz (G) *v* Finanzamt Hamburg-Mitte-Altstadt, ECJ Case C-168/84; [1985] 3 CMLR 667; [1985] ECR 2251 .... 22.198, 22.394

Berkley *v* Poulett, [1976] 241 EG 911 .... 15.247

Bernard & Smith (VTD 2607) 18.566

Bernstein (R) (VTD 4816) 18.473

Berry (DC) (VTD 13380) 18.24

Berry (J) (t/a Automotive Management Services) (VTD 16664) 44.131

Berry *v* St Marylebone Borough Council, CA 1957, [1958] Ch 406; [1957] 3 All ER 677 .... 22.293

Bertelsmann AG v Finanzamt Wiedenbrück, ECJ Case C-380/99; [2001] STC 1153 .... 22.243

Bertram & Co, QB [1974] STC 142; [1975] QB 465; [1974] 1 All ER 1041 .... 57.1
Berwick (M & C) (VTD 17686) 7.45
BES Holdings Ltd (VTD 6405) 52.26
Best Electrical Factors Ltd (VTD 15508) 50.51
Best Images Ltd, [2010] UKFTT 175 (TC), TC00480 .... 41.59
Best Selling Ltd (VTD 17766) 23.12
Best Travel Ltd (VTD 15753) 63.22
Bestuur van de Bedriffsvereniging voor Detailhandel, Ambachten en
    Huisvrouwen, Steenhorst-Neerings v, ECJ Case C-338/91; [1993] 1 ECR 5475;
    [1995] 3 CMLR 323 .... 22.46
Betar Aluminium Fixings Ltd (VTD 9432) 51.10
Beth Johnson Housing Association Ltd (The) [2001] VATDR 167 (VTD 17095) 15.114
Bethway & Moss Ltd (VTD 2667) 62.444
Betterware Products Ltd, QB [1985] STC 648 .... 1.96
Betterweigh Leicester (VTD 19551) 18.543
Betty Foster (Fashion Sewing) Ltd [1976] VATTR 229 (VTD 299) 5.55
Bevan (RM) (VTD 14016) 44.141
Beveridge (W) (VTD 16205) 52.426
Beverley Properties Ltd (VTD 18232) 57.162
Beverley Video (VTD 3550) 51.104
Bevington (JD) (VTD 282) 66.40
Beynon (Doctor) & Partners, HL 2004, [2005] STC 55; [2004] UKHL 53; [2004]
    4 All ER 1091 .... 19.8
BG Supplies (Birmingham) Ltd (VTD 11633) 12.7
BGM Ltd (VTD 11793) 15.234
Bhalla (GS & DS) (t/a Pinehurst Hotel) (VTD 11284) 18.83
Bhambra (BS) (VTD 15503) 50.20
Bhanderi (H), Ch D [2004] EWHC 1765(Ch); [2005] 1 BCLC 388 .... 37.4
Bhanderi (H) (E814) 2.74
Bhetcha, Jefferson Ltd v, CA [1979] 1 WLR 898; [1979] 2 All ER 1108 .... 2.217
Biburtry Ltd (VTD 10615) 41.82
BICC plc [1998] VATDR 224 (VTD 15324) 48.59
Bidco Impex Ltd (VTD 7406) 52.69
Big Pit (Blaenafon) Trust Ltd (VTD 6705) 66.37
Bill Hennessy Associates Ltd (VTD 2656) 3.161, 18.18
Bills (B & SA) (VTD 14715) 57.36
Bilton (PF) (VTD 2324) 36.251
Binder Hamlyn [1983] VATTR 171 (VTD 1439) 62.480
Bindman (SL) (VTD 7340) 18.83
Bing Transport & Trading (VTD 9688) 18.157
Bingley (AJ) Ltd (VTD 1597) 36.354
Binof Construction Ltd (VTD 5113) 36.13
Binof Construction Ltd (VTD 7404) 52.347
Bio Oil Research Ltd (VTD 12252) 19.4
Bioconcepts Ltd (VTD 11287) 29.166
Birch (DV) (t/a Robert Gibbons & Son) (VTD 15762) 44.141
Birchall Blackburn (VTD 9547) 18.447
Birchforest Ltd (VTD 6046) 41.7
Birchview Ltd (VTD 15275) 36.628
Birchwatt Productions Ltd (VTD 4182) 18.586
Bird (RJ) (VTD 6715) 52.75
Bird, Lancaster v, CA 19 November 1998 unreported 67.4
Bird Racing (Management) Ltd (VTD 11630) 7.97
Bird Semple & Crawford Herron [1986] VATTR 218 (VTD 2171) 36.30
Birkdale School Sheffield, Ch D [2008] STC 2002; [2008] EWHC 409 (Ch) 21.8
Birketts [2002] VATDR 100 (VTD 17515) 62.165
Birkin (PM) (VTD 6113) 52.342
Birkinshaw (JK) (t/a JB Plant) (VTD 10648) 18.160
Birks (B) (VTD 2201) 51.104
Birmingham & Solihull Learning Exchange Ltd (The) (VTD 19310) 7.111
Birmingham City Football Club plc [2007] VATDR 149 (VTD 20151) 36.139

Birmingham Council for Old People (VTD 15437) 15.231
Birmingham Hippodrome Theatre Trust, [2011] UKFTT 117 (TC); [2011] SFTD 473;
  TC00993 .... 48.154
Birmingham Royal Institution for the Blind (VTD 16386) 57.104
Bishop (A) (VTD 17267) 57.7
Bishop (J) & Elcocks (P) (VTD 17620) 29.36
Bishop & Knight Ltd (VTD 9315) 43.3
Bissell Homecare (Overseas) Inc (VTD 18217) 48.65
Bissmire (RR) (VTD 7303) 51.2, 57.128
Bistro Inns Ltd (VTD 15613) 51.129
BJ Executive Services (VTD 2048) 62.171
BJ Group Ltd (VTD 18234) 41.109
BJ Kershaw Transport Ltd (VTD 1785) 36.478
BJ Rice & Associates, CA [1996] STC 581 .... 62.456
BJ Rice & Associates (VTD 14659) 2.456
Bjellica (V), CA [1995] STC 329 .... 51.3, 57.89
Black (A) (VTD 7919) 52.332
Black Eagle Ltd (VTD 7682) 52.225
Black Pearl Entertainments Ltd, [2011] UKFTT 368 (TC), TC01223 .... 2.187
Blackburn (G) (VTD 8845) 18.186
Blackburn (RC) (VTD 13798) 62.83
Blackburn & District Group Training Association Ltd (VTD 2735) 18.563
Blackie & Sons Ltd (VTD 7632) 62.85
Blacklock (RD) [2007] VATDR 225 (VTD 20171) 15.124
Blackmoor Golf Club (VTD 2027) 13.35
Blackpool Pleasure Beach Co, QB [1974] STC 138; [1974] 1 WLR 540; [1974] 1 All ER
  1011 .... 66.34
Blackpool Pleasure Beach (Holdings) Ltd (VTD 19014) 67.168
Blackqueen Ltd (VTD 17680) 22.65
Blackwell (J) (VTD 18523) 50.88
Blada Ltd, [2010] UKFTT 131 (TC), TC00440 .... 36.121
Blair (J) (VTD 16767) 62.519
Blake (DB & Mrs JP) (VTD 3515) 51.18
Blake Paper Ltd (VTD 9829) 52.281
Bland (G) (VTD 17395) 50.32
Blandy (Mrs G) (VTD 13123) 7.28
Blanks (RJ & CA) (VTD 14099) 67.121
Blasi v Finanzamt München I, ECJ Case C-346/95; [1998] STC 336; [1998] All ER (EC)
  211 .... 22.338
Blaydon Rugby Football Club, [1996] VATDR 1 (VTD 13901) 11.35
Blendhome Ltd (t/a Stanhill Court Hotel) (VTD 16048) 41.113
Bleyer Hair Clinic Ltd (VTD 1947) 36.146
Bliss Trading Ltd, [2011] UKFTT 740 (TC), TC01577 .... 36.121
Blom-Cooper (Lady), CA [2003] STC 669; [2003] EWCA Civ 493 .... 15.132
Blomfield (RJ) (VTD 5759) 36.248
Blomfield (T) (VTD 1177) 47.51
Bloxwich Engineering Ltd (VTD 3396) 18.79
BLP Group plc, ECJ Case C-4/94; [1995] STC 424; [1995] 1 ECR 983; [1996] 1 WLR
  174; [1995] All ER (EC) 401 .... 22.399
BLP Group plc, ex p., R v C & E Commrs, QB 1993, [1994] STC 41 .... 2.333
Blue Boar Computers Ltd (VTD 6416) 52.26
Blue Boar Property & Investment Co Ltd [1984] VATTR 12 (VTD 1579) 32.5
Blue Sphere Global Ltd (No 1) (VTD 20694) 2.165
Blue Sphere Global Ltd (No 2), CA [2010] STC 1436; [2010] EWCA Civ 517 .... 36.87
Blue Sphere Global Ltd (No 3), CA [2010] EWCA Civ 1448; [2011] STC 547 .... 2.483
Blue Sphere Global Ltd (No 4), QB [2011] EWHC 90217 (Costs) 2.483
Blusins Ltd (VTD 15119) 57.172
Blyth Elfords [1985] VATTR 204 (VTD 1939) 2.232
Blyth-Palk (E & S) (t/a John Baxter Hair Fashions) (VTD 718) 36.174
Blyth Valley Borough Council (VTD 6417) 52.58
Blythe Limited Partnership [1999] VATDR 112 (VTD 16011) 6.13

Blythswood Motors Ltd (VTD 14203) 36.132
BMS Medical Manufacturer & Supplies Ltd (VTD 7836) 18.216
BMW AG, oao, R v HMRC, CA [2009] STC 963; [2009] EWCA Civ 77 .... 59.4
BMW (GB) Ltd, QB [1997] STC 824 .... 8.33
BMW (GB) Ltd (No 2) (VTD 14823) 46.123
BMW Finance (GB) Ltd (VTD 13131) 46.121
BMW Financial Services (GB) Ltd (VTD 17913) 36.182
BNR Company Services Ltd (VTD 13783) 5.90
Board of Governors of the Robert Gordon University (The), CS [2008] CSIH 22 ...... 21.7
Boardmans (J) (1980) Ltd, QB [1986] STC 10 .... 58.38
Boardmans (J) (1980) Ltd (VTD 2025) 36.356
Bobacre Ltd (t/a Geary Drive Hire) (VTD 12829) 52.299
BOC International Ltd [1982] VATTR 84 (VTD 1248) 54.7
Bockemühl, Finanzamt Gummersbach v, ECJ Case C-90/01; [2005] STC 934 .... 22.461
Boden (VTD 377) 58.15
Body Shop Supply Services Ltd [1984] VATTR 233 (VTD 1752) 67.153
Bodyguard Workwear Ltd (VTD 20949) 62.51
Boffey (A) [2008] VATDR 395 (VTD 20865) 52.388
Bog, Finanzamt Burgdorf v, ECJ Case C-497/09; [2011] STC 1221 .... 22.155
Boggeln (J) (t/a Divine Fireplaces) (VTD 18965) 51.55
Bokor (A), [2009] UKFTT 322 (TC), TC00265 .... 19.48
Bolinge Hill Farm (VTD 4217) 44.43
Boltgate Ltd [1982] VATTR 120 (VTD 1246) 2.129
Bolton Consultants Ltd (VTD 6611) 52.217
Bolukbasi (M & F) (VTD 11293) 50.48
Bomanite (Southeast) (VTD 13745) 52.192
Bonanni (Mr & Mrs P) (VTD 11823) 48.118
Bond (ACH) (VTD 4722) 36.271
Bond (S) & Baxter (Ms S), [2010] UKFTT 242 (TC), TC00539 .... 15.264
Bond House Systems Ltd [2003] VATDR 210 (VTD 18100) 36.101
Bondcloak Ltd (VTD 4858) 18.352
Bondi (F) (VTD 173) 41.137
Boni Faccenda Ltd [1975] VATTR 155 (VTD 196) 29.129
Boniface (Ms C) (VTD 9954) 18.247
Bonnet to Boot Ltd (VTD 13466) 65.42
Bonusclass Ltd (VTD 17528) 44.72
Boodle & Dunthorne Ltd (VTD 18429) 67.17
Book Club Associates [1983] VATTR 34 (VTD 1363) 5.22
Book People Ltd (The) (VTD 18240) 5.12
Bookmakers' Protection Association (Southern Area) Ltd (The) [1979] VATTR 215
  (VTD 849) 64.13
Bookit Ltd, CA [2006] STC 1367; [2006] EWCA Civ 550 .... 27.23
Boon (A) (t/a Allan Boon Haulage) (VTD 9952) 18.387
Booth (AL) [1977] VATTR 133 (VTD 385) 40.6
Booth (R) (t/a Discovery Trading Co) (VTD 12778) 18.579
Bootle Transfer Station Ltd (VTD 17051) 65.91
Boots Co plc (The), ECJ Case 126/88; [1990] STC 387; [1990] 1 ECR 1235;
  [1990] 2 CMLR 731 .... 22.251
Boots Co plc (No 2), CA 2009, [2010] STC 637; [2009] EWCA Civ 1396 .... 58.12
Bophutatswana National Commercial Corporation Ltd, CA [1993] STC 702 .... 39.2
Bord (MD) (VTD 7946) 2.266
Bord (MD) (VTD 9824) 60.5
Border Flying Co [1976] VATTR 132 (VTD 300) 7.48
Bordergem Ltd (VTD 2887) 44.63
Bornfleet Forwarding Ltd (VTD 9704) 52.72
Bornoosh (M) (VTD 18493) 50.155
Boscawen, Mason v, Ch D 2008, [2009] STC 624; [2008] EWHC 3100 (Ch) 6.49
Botanical Catering Ltd, [2009] UKFTT 265 (TC), TC00212 .... 48.63
Bott (Mrs M) (t/a Clothesline) (VTD 10267) 52.75
Bourne (SA) (VTD 16023) 52.215
Bourne (W) (TC00582) 15.269

Bourne Vehicle Hire (VTD 15267) 50.74
Bournemouth Indoor Bowls Centre Ltd (VTD 14335B) 52.112
Bournemouth Symphony Orchestra, CA 2006, [2007] STC 198; [2006] EWCA Civ
1281 .... 16.7
Bowcombe Shoot, [2011] UKFTT 64 (TC), TC00942 .... 2.491
Bowden Associates Ltd (VTD 7449) 18.389
Bowe (J) (VTD 6748) 52.313
Bowen (J) (VTD 11167) 52.186
Bowen (M) [1987] VATTR 255 (VTD 2535) 18.103
Bowen-Jones v Bowen-Jones, [1968] All ER 163 .... 2.446
Bower (JF) (t/a Bean Bower & Co) [1995] VATDR 294 (VTD 13224) 18.617
Bowles (JA) (t/a Oakey Bros Butchers) (VTD 12422) 44.141
Bowles (P), RCPO v, Oxford Crown Court 7 December 2009, Times 9.12.2009 ..... 49.32
Bowthorpe Community Trust (Trustees of the) (VTD 12978) 42.18
Boyd (G & G) (t/a Boyd Motors) (VTD 20034) 53.10
Boyd (GA) Building Services Ltd [1993] VATTR 26 (VTD 9788) 2.470
Boys' and Girls' Welfare Society (VTD 15274) 19.35, 19.89
Boz Ltd (VTD 9353) 52.69
Bozdaq (M) (VTD 17787) 57.179
BP Stone & Brickwork Contractors Ltd (VTD 11722) 14.6
BP Supergas Anonimos Etairia Geniki Emporiki-Viomichaniki kai Antiprossopeion v
Greece, ECJ Case C-62/93; [1995] STC 805; [1995] 1 ECR 1883; [1995] All ER (EC)
684 .... 22.558
BPH Equipment Ltd (VTD 13914) 62.543
Bracegirdle (MJ) (VTD 20889) 15.60
Bradbury (M) (VTD 17596) 3.141
Bradfield (JH) [1991] VATTR 22 (VTD 5339) 55.71
Bradley (S) (VTD 18735) 2.265
Bradshaw (K) (VTD 20498) 40.24
Bradshaw & Others (as Trustees for Taylor Dyne Ltd Pension Fund) [1992] VATTR 315
(VTD 6964) 6.19
Braes (J) (t/a Aquarius) (VTD 11951) 51.117
Brailsford (Mrs LJ) (VTD 13472) 19.47
Braine (ME) (Boatbuilders) Ltd (VTD 3881) 40.91
Brainstormers Web Factory Ltd (VTD 15761) 18.425
Brakel Ltd (VTD 9685) 18.83
Brambletye School Trust Ltd [2002] VATDR 265 (VTD 17688) 6.9
Bramley (DR) & Bradley (MA) [1987] VATTR 72 (VTD 2349) 57.160
Bramley Caterers (VTD 6385) 29.54
Brammer (G) (t/a Talking Heads) (VTD 17761) 62.262
Brammer plc (VTD 6420) 41.25
Brand (Mrs DM) (Racket Sports for Children with Special Needs) (VTD 14080) 19.83
Brandenstein, Finanzamt Düsseldorf-Mettman v, ECJ Case C-323/99, [2001] STC 1356;
[2002] 2 WLR 1207 .... 22.161
Brannan (GA) (t/a G Brannan Builders) (VTD 5939) 51.99
Brasserie du Pêcheur SA v Federal Republic of Germany, ECJ Case C-46/93; [1996]
1 ECR 1029; [1996] 1 CMLR 889; [1996] 2 WLR 506; [1996] All ER (EC) 301 .... 22.31
Brasplern (Group Services) Ltd (VTD 1558) 46.13
Bray (DB) (VTD 5538) 36.269
Bray Walker (VTD 18339) 62.166
Brayfal Ltd, Ch D 4 March 2008 unreported 2.285
Brayfal Ltd (No 4), UT [2011] STC 1338 .... 36.85
Brayfal Ltd (No 5), Ch D [2011] EWHC 407 (Ch); [2011] STC 1482 .... 2.416
Brayfal Ltd, oao, R v HMRC, QB [2007] EWHC 521 (Admin) 36.653
Brayfal Ltd, oao, R v HMRC (No 2), QB [2009] EWHC 3354 (Admin) 59.5
Brays of Glastonbury Ltd (VTD 650) 12.13
Breach (DV) (t/a Neath Mailing Services) (VTD 17279) 5.51
Brearley Townsend Painters Ltd (VTD 3126) 18.201
Brechin Motor Co Ltd (VTD 9525) 52.125
Brecon Brewery Ltd (VTD 3053) 18.605
Breese Brick Ltd (VTD 6009) 52.121

Breezes Patisserie (VTD 10081) 29.49
Breitsohl, Finanzamt Goslar v, ECJ Case C-400/98; [2001] STC 355 .... 22.122
Bremen Fitted Furniture (VTD 17676) 48.77
Bremner (AB) (VTD 6112) 18.120
Brennan (J) (VTD 11657) 51.106
Brennan (TA) (VTD 19982) 2.327
Brentwood Construction & Development Ltd (VTD 16073) 50.56
Brewhurst Health Food Supplies (VTD 8928) 29.104
Brian Gubby Ltd [1985] VATTR 59 (VTD 1961) 2.130, 7.64
Brian Perkins & Co Ltd (VTD 3885) 19.96
Brian Yeardley Continental Ltd (VTD 2035) 36.357
Briana Electronics Ltd (VTD 4629) 18.183
Briararch Ltd, QB [1992] STC 732 .... 46.212
Brice (N) (VTD 6376) 55.56
Brice (V) (VTD 9721) 52.105
Bridge Book Co Ltd (The) (VTD 935) 36.373
Bridge Metal Services (Thurrock) Ltd (VTD 7971) 18.332
Bridgeman (JP) (VTD 1206) 47.52
Bridgeman (RM) (t/a Bridgeman Building & Public Works Contractors) (VTD 6563)
.... 52.107
Bridges (JR) (t/a Plastering Contractors Ltd) (VTD 9653) 52.21
Bridgewater (PJ) (VTD 10491) 29.71
Bridgnorth Golf Club, [2009] UKFTT 126 (TC), TC00094 .... 46.67
Bridport & West Dorset Golf Club Ltd, [2011] UKFTT 354 (TC), TC01214 .... 20.74
Briggs (I) [1995] VATDR 386 (VTD 13603) 3.34
Briggs 'Palm Shoes' Ltd (VTD 9840) 18.563
Bright (BH) (VTD 3924, 4577) 67.119
Bright (BH) (VTD 4339) 2.383
Bright (BH) (VTD 5022) 2.403
Brind, ex p., R v Secretary of State for the Home Department, HL [1991] 2 WLR 588;
[1991] 1 All ER 720 .... 52.452
Brisbane (GT) (VTD 16691) 50.58
Bristol Bathroom Co (VTD 5340) 62.447
Bristol Bloodstock Ltd (VTD 11955) 36.601
Bristol Cathedral (Dean & Chapter) (VTD 14591) 36.552
Bristol Churches Housing Association (VTD 10515) 46.51
Bristol City Council (VTD 17665) 62.214
Bristol City Football Supporters Club [1975] VATTR 93 (VTD 164) 29.37
Bristol Engineering & Hydraulics Ltd (VTD 15431) 65.45
Bristol Street Motors (Bromley) Ltd (VTD 6381) 52.58
Bristow & Darlington Ltd (VTD 6961) 52.347
Britannia Building Society (VTD 14886) 46.76
Britannia Steel Ltd (VTD 11675) 52.380
British & Foreign Bible Society (VTD 10149) 11.43
British Airports Authority (No 1), CA 1976, [1977] STC 36; [1977] 1WLR 302; [1977]
1 All ER 497 .... 41.1
British Airports Authority (No 2) [1975] VATTR 43 (VTD 146) 41.32, 66.47
British Airports Authority (No 3) (VTD 147) 41.33
British Airports Authority (No 4) (VTD 148) 66.41
British Airports Authority (No 5) (VTD 447) 15.241
British Airways Board (VTD 663) 62.23
British Airways Board (VTD 846) 32.3
British Airways Housing Trust Ltd (VTD 663) 62.23
British Airways plc (No 1), CA [1990] STC 643 .... 66.13
British Airways plc (No 2), QB [1996] STC 1127 .... 36.155
British Airways plc (No 3), [2000] VATDR 74 (VTD 16446) 36.131
British American Tobacco International Ltd v Belgian State, ECJ Case C-435/03; [2006]
STC 158 .... 22.88
British Association for Counselling (The) (VTD 11855) 64.4
British Association for Shooting & Conservation Ltd (The) (No 2), [2010] SFTD 993;
[2010] UKFTT 258 (TC), TC00562 .... 24.38

British Association of Leisure Parks, Piers & Attractions Ltd (The), [2011] UKFTT 662
(TC), TC01504 .... 64.35
British Broadcasting Corporation, [1974] VATTR 100 (VTD 73) 36.311
British Car Auctions Ltd, [1978] VATTR 56 (VTD 522) 36.367
British Dental Association, [2010] UKFTT 176 (TC); [2010] SFTD 757, TC00481
.... 46.3
British Disabled Flying Association (The), [2011] UKFTT 743 (TC), TC01580 .... 19.33
British European Breeders Fund (The Trustees of), [1985] VATTR 12 (VTD 1808)
.... 7.77
British Eventing Ltd, [2010] UKFTT 382 (TC); [2011] SFTD 18, TC00664 .... 6.48
British Field Sports Society, CA [1998] STC 315; [1998] 1 WLR 962; [1998] 2 All ER
1003 .... 13.10
British Gas plc, Foster & Others v, ECJ Case C-188/89; [1990] ECR 3313; [1990]
3 All ER 897 .... 22.16
British Hardware Federation [1975] VATTR 172 (VTD 216) 27.18
British Horse Society Ltd (VTD 16204) 38.50
British Iberian International Transport Ltd (VTD 2101) 36.665
British Institute of Cleaning Science Ltd (The) (VTD 1981) 64.16
British Institute of Management (No 1) [1978] VATTR 101 (VTD 565) 57.202
British Institute of Management (No 2) [1980] VATTR 42 (VTD 900) 2.444
British Jewellery & Giftware Federation Ltd (VTD 12194) 65.79
British Nursing Co-operation Ltd (VTD 8816) 33.20
British Olympic Association [1979] VATTR 122 (VTD 779) 13.13
British Organic Farmers [1988] VATTR 64 (VTD 2700) 64.14
British Railways Board, CA [1976] STC 359; [1976] 1 WLR 1036; [1976] 3 All ER
100 .... 54.1
British Railways Board (No 2), CA [1977] STC 221; [1977] 1 WLR 588; [1977]
2 All ER 873 .... 66.12
British Shoe Corporation (ex p. Coopers & Lybrand) [1998] VATDR 348 (C00086)
.... 2.300
British Sky Broadcasting Group plc [1999] VATDR 283 (VTD 16220) 5.97
British Sky Broadcasting Group plc (oao), R v C & E, CA [2001] STC 437; [2001]
EWHC Admin 127 .... 2.341
British Sky Broadcasting Ltd [1994] VATTR 1 (VTD 12394) 62.489
British Steel Exports Ltd (VTD 7562) 48.109
British Telecommunications plc, CA [1996] STC 818; [1996] 1 WLR 1309 .... 62.457
British Telecommunications plc (No 2), HL [1999] STC 758; [1999] 1 WLR 1376;
[1999] 3 All ER 961 .... 44.99
British Telecommunications plc (No 3) (VTD 14669) 40.116
British Telecommunications plc (No 4) (VTD 14830) 62.200
British Telecommunications plc (No 5) (VTD 16244) 41.12
British Telecommunications plc, ex p., R v HM Treasury, ECJ Case C-392/93; [1996]
1 ECR 1631; [1996] 2 CMLR 217; [1996] 3 WLR 303; [1996] All ER (EC) 401 .... 22.34
British Telecommunications plc, oao, R v HMRC, QB [2005] STC 1148; [2005] EWHC
1043(Admin) 48.52
British Teleflower Service Ltd [1995] VATDR 356 (VTD 13756) 3.56, 40.57
British Tenpin Bowling Association [1989] VATTR 101 (VTD 3213, 3552) 64.20
British United Provident Association Ltd, CA [1997] STC 445 .... 19.12
British United Provident Association Ltd (No 2) (VTD 17286) 62.496
British United Shoe Machinery Co Ltd [1977] VATTR 187 (VTD 463) 40.85
British Vita Co Ltd (VTD 322) 12.3
Britton (RTG) (VTD 445) 36.263
Britton (VJ) [1986] VATTR 209 (VTD 2173) 47.46
Britwood Toys Ltd (VTD 2263) 36.239
Broadbent (CM) (VTD 15809) 51.154
Broadgate Software Ltd (VTD 5662) 18.357
Broadhead Peel & Co [1984] VATTR 195 (VTD 1737) 36.176
Broadhurst (Mr & Mrs) (t/a RMS Heating) (VTD 2007) 62.101
Broadley (LW & A) (t/a Professional Haircare) (VTD 16643) 41.88
Broadley (LW & A) (t/a Professional Haircare) (No 2) [2001] VATDR 271 (VTD
17153) 2.125

Broadside Colours & Chemicals Ltd (VTD 6994) 52.69
Broadway Video (Wholesale) Ltd [1994] VATTR 271 (VTD 11935, 12446) ... 2.390, 2.533
Broadwell Land plc [1993] VATTR 346 (VTD 10521) 36.636
Brockholes Electrics Co Ltd (VTD 6519) 18.608
Brodrick Wright & Strong Ltd (VTD 2347) 62.510
Brogden (M) (VTD 19827) 7.107
Broomfield (PE & WA) (t/a Rockingham Arms) (VTD 18139) 18.347
Brollies Ltd (VTD 11966) 6.27
Brook Leisure Holdings Ltd (VTD 19156) 67.171
Brooker (RD) (VTD 15164) 3.109
Brookes (A) [1994] VATTR 35 (VTD 11752) 2.49
Brookfields (VTD 577) 58.15
Brooks (LVJ) (VTD 1722) 36.180
Brooks (N) (VTD 4784) 18.145
Brooks (SR) (VTD 12754) 36.231
Brooks Histograph Ltd [1984] VATTR 46 (VTD 1570) 5.110
Brough (W & B) (t/a Chaddy Cars) (VTD 16700) 47.28
Brough, Smith v, CA [2005] EWCA Civ 261 .... 2.175
Brough Bros (Kitchens & Bathrooms) Ltd (VTD 7915) 18.212
Brown (BJ) (VTD 6552) 36.186
Brown (G) (VTD 7718) 2.121
Brown (G & C) (VTD 7430) 36.645
Brown (J) (VTD 7747) 10.5
Brown (J & J) (t/a Shaw's Bar) [1977] VATTR 253 (VTD 393) 2.399
Brown (JW), [2009] UKFTT 359 (TC), TC00297 .... 65.91
Brown (KS) (VTD 9614) 51.44
Brown (LP & CG) (VTD 16109) 44.107
Brown (ME) (VTD 11429) 62.297
Brown (S) (VTD 19884) 15.212
Brown (T) (VTD 1020) 3.159
Brown & Frewer Ltd (VTD 15209) 50.146
Brown & Rochester (VTD 9751) 44.148
Browne (Dr NDF) (VTD 11388) 55.53
Browsers Bookshop (VTD 2837) 44.23
BRS Automotive Ltd, CA [1998] STC 1210 .... 44.104
Bruce (AC) & Hull (ML) (VTD 2248) 19.43
Bruce (CS) (VTD 11861) 51.75
Bruce (ED), [1991] VATTR 280 (VTD 6326) 15.7
Bruce (M) (VTD 16660) 18.32
Bruce (PS) (VTD 12484) 57.95
Bruce Banks Sails Ltd, [1990] VATTR 175 (VTD 4896) 62.446
Bruce Miller & Co (VTD 9402) 52.58
Bruce Weir & Co (VTD 7620) 18.157
Brucegate Ltd (VTD 4903) 36.51
Brundrit (DB) (VTD 17952) 50.4
Brunel Motor Co Ltd, [2011] UKFTT 589 (TC), TC01432 .... 37.12
Brunswick (Mr & Mrs) (t/a The Bull Inn) (VTD 20357) 18.125
Brunt (WJ), QB 10 November 1998 unreported 14.119
Bryan Keenan & Co (VTD 17407) 18.27
Bryan Markwell & Co Ltd (VTD 4358) 58.23
Bryant (J) (VTD 11212) 36.255
Bryant Glass Ltd (VTD 3431) 18.71
Bryce (D) (t/a The Barn), UT [2011] STC 903; [2010] UKUT 26 (TCC) 41.60
Brydon (WW) (VTD 20740) 51.163
Brytahomes Window Company (VTD 9379) 18.445
BS Electrical (VTD 9199) 18.180
BSN (Import & Export) Ltd [1980] VATTR 177 (VTD 998) 24.5
BTR Industries Ltd (VTD 11828) 8.46
Buck (L) (t/a Idealogic) (VTD 20082) 18.528
Buckley (Mr & Mrs) (t/a Wheelcraft Centre & Original Homes) (VTD 7150) 46.48
Buckley (JR) (VTD 7644) 58.23

Buckley Jewellery Ltd (VTD 18178) 65.53
Bugeja (A), CA [2001] EWCA Civ 1542; [2001] STC 1568 .... 67.76
Bugg (AA) (VTD 15123) 15.15
Bugmile Ltd (VTD 12574) 50.26
Building Societies Ombudsman Co Ltd, ex p., R *v* C & E, CA [2000] STC 892 ...... 48.51
Bulgaria, Bulves AD *v* , ECHR Case 3991/03; [2009] STC 1161 .... 34.27
Bulgaria, Business Support Centre *v* , ECHR Case 6689/03; 18 March 2010
   unreported 34.28
Bulgin Powersource plc (VTD 13915) 18.506
Bulkhaul Ltd (VTD 5725) 52.118
Bulkliner Intermodal Ltd [2010] UKFTT 395 (TC), TC00677 .... 2.447
Bullimore (M) (VTD 2626) 41.74
Bulthuis-Griffioen *v* Inspector der Omzetbelasting, ECJ Case C-453/93; [1995] STC 954;
   [1995] 1 ECR 2341 .... 22.297
Bulves AD*v* Bulgaria, ECHR Case 3991/03; [2009] STC 1161 .... 34.27
Bundesamt für Finanzen, Auto Lease Holland BV *v* ECJ Case C-185/01; [2005] STC
   598 .... 22.152
Bundesamt für Finanzen, Denkavit International BV & Others *v*, ECJ Case C-283/94;
   [1996] STC 1445; [1996] 1 ECR 5063 .... 22.35
Bundesamt für Finanzen, Řízení Letového Provozu ČR sp *v*, ECJ Case C-335/05; [2007]
   STC 1509 .... 22.545
Bundesamt für Finanzen, Société Générale des Grandes Sources d'Eaux Minérales
   Françaises *v*, ECJ Case C-361/96; [1998] STC 981 .... 22.538
Bundeszentralamt für Steuern, Planzer Luxembourg Sàrl *v*, ECJ Case C-73/06; [2008]
   STC 1113 .... 22.539
Bundeszentralamt für Steuern, Yaesu Europe BV *v*, ECJ Case C-433/08; [2010] STC
   809 .... 22.544
BUPA Nursing Services Ltd (VTD 10010) 62.316
BUPA Hospitals Ltd, ECJ Case C-419/02; [2006] STC 967; [2006] 2 WLR 96 ...... 22.230
BUPA Purchasing Ltd, Ch D [2003] STC 1203; [2003] EWHC 1957(Ch) 32.19
BUPA Purchasing Ltd (No 2), CA 2007, [2008] STC 101; [2007] EWCA Civ 542 ... 3.179
Burdett (DC) (VTD 9695) 52.136
Burford *v* Durkin, CA 1990, [1991] STC 75 .... 3.94
Burgess (MEJ) & Holmes (AP) (t/a Cards'N Cuddles) (VTD 14475) 36.591
Burgess Detective Agency Ltd (VTD 2685) 44.41
Burgess *v* Stafford Hotels Ltd, [1990] 3 All ER 222 .... 2.474
Burghill Valley Golf Club (VTD 18876) 14.91
Burgin (R) Ltd (VTD 5916) 18.166
Burke (DE), Ch D [2009] EWHC 2587 (Ch); [2011] STC 625 .... 28.4
Burke (Ms J), [2009] UKFTT 87 (TC), TC00055 .... 33.55
Burley Estates Ltd (VTD 7937) 52.41
Burmese Cat Benevolent Fund (The) (VTD 20015) 11.31
Burnham Logistics Ltd (VTD 18005) 40.114
Burnham Radio Recreational & Welfare Club (VTD 518) 29.40
Burns (Dr KP & Mrs LM) (t/a Sheffield Clinic of Complementary Medicine) (VTD
   12046) 51.36
Burns (Dr KP & P) (t/a North Ferriby Chiropractic Clinic) (VTD 12046) 51.36
Burns (PE) (VTD 3151) 18.467
Burntisland Golf Club (VTD 6340) 36.511
Burr (M & EJ) (t/a Penny's Place) (VTD 16866) 57.26
Burrell (RJ) (t/a The Firm), QB [1997] STC 1413 .... 47.41
Burridge (RT) (VTD 3723) 18.478
Burrows (S), [2007] VATDR 478 (VTD 20454) 62.523
Burton Group plc (The) (VTD 15046) 58.35
Bushby (DW & MJ), QB 1978, [1979] STC 9 .... 29.112
Bushell (BCW) (VTD 15094) 36.275
Business Enterprises (UK) Ltd, [1988] VATTR 160 (VTD 3161) 41.6
Business Management Concepts Ltd, [2011] UKFTT 520 (TC), TC01367 .... 36.113
Business Post Holdings Ltd (VTD 5002) 18.441
Business Support Centre *v* Bulgaria, ECHR Case 6689/03; 18 March 2010 unreported
   .... 34.28

Butcher (PC) (t/a Ashley Motor Services) (VTD 17423) 44.75
Butchwick (AJ) (VTD 12782) 18.392
Butland (P) (t/a Harrogate Site Services) (VTD 6531) 55.1
Butler (S) (VTD 3067) 51.44
Butler & Tanner Ltd [1974] VATTR 72 (VTD 68) 5.28
Butler Newall Ltd (VTD 12292) 52.210
Butler Question Method School of Languages Ltd (VTD 5677) 36.154
Butler Question Method School of Languages Ltd (VTD 7178) 67.98
Butler School of Languages (VTD 7067) 18.259
Butterfield (J) [1977] VATTR 152 (VTD 404) 2.230
Butterworth (CR) (VTD 1395) 36.266
Button Eventures Ltd (VTD 5995) 18.200
Buxhall Ltd (VTD 20075) 18.580
Buxton (MP) (VTD 10108) 3.177
Buxton & District Civic Association Ltd (VTD 3380) 21.5
Buy As You View Ltd, [2010] UKFTT 182 (TC), TC00486 .... 60.20
Buyagift Ltd (VTD 19856) 1.58
Buyagift Ltd (No 2) (VTD 20774) 1.58
Buyco Ltd, [2006] VATDR 57 (VTD 19752) 2.144
By Storm Ltd (VTD 17249) 18.443
Byrd (GN) (t/a GN Byrd & Co) (VTD 12675) 46.224
Byrne (JC) (VTD 4202) 18.485
Byrt (AG), [2011] UKFTT 600 (TC), TC01443 .... 48.63
Byrom, Kane & Kane (t/a Salon 24), Ch D [2006] STC 992; [2006] EWHC 111 (Ch)
.... 41.95

C

C & C Engineering (WGC) Ltd (VTD 6605) 18.551
C & G Developments Ltd (VTD 2384) 2.117
C & P Building & Welding (Wantage) Ltd (VTD 2062) 36.350
C & S Cladding Ltd (VTD 11102) 18.558
C & S Glaziers (North Wales) Ltd (VTD 6247) 52.277
C & V (Advice Line) Services Ltd [2001] VATDR 446 (VTD 17310) 38.17
C & W Clothiers Ltd (VTD 1756) 36.438
C Bond Ltd (VTD 15515) 57.130
C Cohen (Furriers) Ltd (VTD 4933) 65.47
C Hesketh & Sons Ltd (VTD 16963) 44.93
C, V v, CA [2001] EWCA Civ 1509 .... 2.220
Cabinet Diot (SA) v France, ECHR Case 49217/99; 22 July 2003 unreported 34.25
Cable (F) (VTD 13845) 36.37
Cable & Wireless plc, [2009] VATDR 538; [2009] UKFTT 32 (TC); TC00004 .... 48.10
Cadbury Ireland Trust Ltd v Revenue Commrs (Ireland), HC(I) [2007] IEHC 179 ... 54.12
Caddey (RJ) (C154) 35.21
Cadogan Club Ltd (The) (VTD 548) 2.494
Caernarfonshire Fatstock Group Ltd (VTD 5033) 4.3
Café Da Vinci & Da Vinci Too (VTD 7298) 50.102
Café Da Vinci & Da Vinci Too (VTD 7634) 2.409
Caine (MH & ST) (VTD 2398) 62.441
Caira (R) (t/a The Ambassador Leisure Club) (VTD 7625) 52.69
Cairngorm Mountain (VTD 17679) 66.27
Cake (BD) (VTD 10272) 52.97
CAL Ingot Manufacturers (VTD 12298, 13069) 52.367
Calabar Developments Ltd [1976] VATTR 1 (VTD 218) 62.20
Calam Vale Ltd (VTD 16869) 15.133
Calderprint (VTD 4541) 18.563
Caledonia Motor Group Ltd (VTD 20021) 67.18
Caledonian Paper plc (VTD 6139) 52.253
Calibre Tas Ltd (VTD 20508) 28.15
Callaghan (LF) (VTD 6445) 57.7

Calland (J) (VTD 2627) 62.400
Callaway (C) (VTD 12039) 3.30
Callison (BR) (VTD 810) 66.1
Calltell Telecom Ltd (No 1), Ch D [2008] STC 3246; [2008] EWHC 2107 (Ch) 2.369
Calltell Telecom Ltd (No 2), CA [2010] STC 1436; [2010] EWCA Civ 517 .... 36.105
Calor Gas Ltd [1973] VATTR 205 (VTD 47) 30.1
Calpeel Ltd (VTD 4194) 18.100
Calscot Stocktaking (VTD 15573) 18.118
Calver Weir Restoration Project, [2011] UKFTT 460 (TC); [2011] SFTD 1001;
  TC01310 .... 55.13
Câmara Municipal do Porto, Fazenda Pública v, ECJ Case C-446/98; [2001] STC 560
  .... 22.137
Camberwell Cars Ltd (VTD 10178) 62.249
Camberwell Cars Ltd (No 2) (VTD 17376) 67.124
Camberwell Cars Ltd (No 3) (VTD 17566) 2.503
Cambridge (JV) (VTD 5104) 25.14
Cambridge Connectivity Ltd (VTD 13046) 18.421
Cambridge University (Chancellor, Masters & Scholars), Ch D [2009] EWHC 434
  (Ch) 30.11
Cambridge University Local Examination Syndicate (VTD 15015) 61.5
Cambuslang Athletic Club (VTD 1592) 13.44
Camden (Hardchrome) Ltd (VTD 3724) 18.607
Camden (London Borough of) (VTD 6123) 52.58
Camden (London Borough of) [1993] VATTR 73 (VTD 10476) 17.6
Camden Motors (Holdings) Ltd, [2008] VATDR 245 (VTD 20674) 46.202
Camelot Cars Couriers Ltd (VTD 1474) 62.62
Cameron (Dr AJ) [1973] VATTR 177 (VTD 41) 33.52
Cameron (CJ) (VTD 15779) 14.25
Cameron (R) (t/a RC Bookmakers) (E00096) 3.23
Cameron New Homes Ltd (VTD 17309) 15.18
Camford Ltd (t/a The Cotswold Collection) (VTD 13339) 37.32
Camilla Enterprises Ltd (VTD 10426) 41.108
Camp (BR) (VTD 3605) 18.272
Campbell (D) (VTD 14410) 62.84
Campbell (DC) (VTD 14723) 18.483
Campbell (DS) (VTD 15051) 62.67
Campbell (M) (VTD 6269) 18.158
Campbell (MJ) (VTD 17425) 50.38
Campbell (SC) (Plastics) Ltd (VTD 6086) 18.588
Camping & Caravanning Club (The) (VTD 20679) 64.33
Campsa Estaciones de Servicio SA v Administración del Estado, ECJ Case C-285/10;
  [2011] STC 1603 .... 22.503
Campus Martius Ltd (VTD 7199) 52.58
Canadian Airlines International Ltd, QB [1995] STC 341 .... 66.15
Canaltime Developments Ltd (VTD 18561) 69.13
Canary Wharf Ltd, [1996] VATDR 323 (14513) 43.12
Candy Maid Confections Ltd, Ch D [1968] 3 All ER 773 .... 29.128
Cannings-Knight (BH) (VTD 11291) 19.81
Cannon (DE) (VTD 2486) 57.21
Cannon Express & Logistics Ltd, [2009] UKFTT 116 (TC), TC00084 .... 28.16
Canotec Ltd, [2011] UKFTT 661 (TC), TC01503 .... 36.32
Cant (CI) [1976] VATTR 237 (VTD 317) 21.1
Canterbury Amateur Operatic Society (VTD 5709) 51.97
Canterbury Hockey Club (VTD 19086) 2.56
Canterbury Hockey Club (No 2), ECJ Case C-253/07; [2008] STC 3351 .... 22.316
Canterbury Ladies Hockey Club (VTD 19086) 2.56
Canton (A) (VTD 11485) 50.62
Cantor Fitzgerald International, ECJ Case C-108/99; [2001] STC 1453 .... 22.334
Cantors plc [1993] VATTR 367 (10834) 3.175
Cantrell & Cantrell (t/a Foxearth Lodge Nursing Home), Ch D [2003] STC 486; [2003]
  EWHC 404 (Ch) 15.165

Capaldi & Company (VTD 18330) 17.3
Capewell, HL [2007] UKHL 2; [2007] 2 All ER 370 .... 14.102
Capital Air Services Ltd (No 1), UT [2010] UKUT 373 (TCC); [2010] STC 2726 .... 2.148
Capital Air Services Ltd (No 2), UT [2011] STC 617 .... 2.148
Capital Computers Ltd (VTD 9095) 52.268
Capital Cranfield Trustees Ltd [2008] VATDR 123 (VTD 20532) 54.8
Capital One Bank (Europe) plc (VTD 19238, VTD 19556) 46.159
Capital One Developments Ltd (No 1), Ch D [2002] STC 479; [2002] EWHC 197
  (Ch) 36.651
Capital One Developments Ltd (No 2) (VTD 18642) 22.67
Capper (RMO & RCO) (VTD 18116) 52.414
Car Factors Ltd, [2011] UKFTT 465 (TC), TC01315 .... 57.111
Capricorn Business Services Ltd (VTD 4802) 18.261
Card Protection Plan Ltd, ECJ Case C-349/96; [1999] STC 270; [1999] 3 WLR 203;
  [1999] All ER (EC) 339 .... 22.324
Card Protection Plan Ltd, HL [2001] STC 174; [2001] UKHL 4; [2001] 2 WLR 329;
  [2001] 2 All ER 143 .... 38.44
Cardholder Services Ltd, CA [1989] STC 407; [1989] 2 All ER 385 .... 27.61
Cardiff City Council, oao, R v C & E, CA 2003, [2004] STC 356; [2003] EWCA Civ
  1456 .... 48.53
Cardiff Community Housing Association Ltd [2000] VATDR 346 (VTD 16841) 15.95
Care @ Ltd (VTD 20316) 33.66
Carew (MM) & Son Marble Co Ltd (VTD 11681) 18.317
Carey (D) (VTD 7619) 52.69
Cargill (A) & McWilliams (K) (t/a Pende Café), [2009] UKFTT 381 (TC), TC00316
  .... 65.106
Cargo Express (UK) Ltd (VTD 9779) 52.257
Carless (FG), QB [1993] STC 632 .... 62.245
Carlton Clubs Ltd, [2011] UKFTT 542 (TC); [2011] SFTD 1209, TC01389 .... 40.111
Carlton Lodge Club Ltd, QB [1974] STC 507; [1975] 1 WLR 66; [1974] 3 All ER
  798 .... 13.29
Carmichael Jennifer May Ltd (VTD 3159) 18.502
Caro (D) (VTD 3284) 18.446
Caroline General Services Ltd (VTD 12048) 52.307
Carpenter (AP) (VTD 15253) 5.62
Carpenter (A) & Hayles (S) (t/a Carpenter Catering) (VTD 17851) 29.15
Carpenter (A) & Hayles (S) (t/a Carpenter Catering) (No 2) (VTD 18148) 29.30
Carr v CIR, CA [1944] 2 All ER 163 .... 64.14, 64.22
Carr (DH) (VTD 19267) 55.36
Carr (PM) (t/a P & L Packaging) (VTD 6726) 52.5
Carr (R) (VTD 15411) 36.48
Carr (RA) (VTD 20690) 52.436
Carr (T) (t/a The Princess Royal Public House) (VTD 20507) 65.99
Carrick (J) (VTD 7664) 18.104
Carrophil Ltd (VTD 10190) 15.154
Cartagena (G) (VTD 19454) 15.52
Carter (AR) (VTD 13828) 15.261
Carter (AR) (VTD 14217) 50.129
Carter (NCD) (VTD 17288) 29.124
Carter (RH) (t/a Protheroe Carter & Eason Ltd) (VTD 12047) 41.50
Carter Morris Roofing Ltd (VTD 7229) 52.136
Cartlidge (QJ) (VTD 7152) 62.100
Carville (R), [2011] UKFTT 763 (TC), TC01600 .... 62.504
Casa Frattini Ltd (VTD 20645) 57.180
Casban (MJ & Mrs G) (t/a Lounge) (VTD 20469) 57.143
Casey Flooring (Contracts) Ltd (VTD 10205) 14.47
Casselson (RV) (VTD 17164) 50.37
Cassidy (Mrs V) (t/a Balou) (VTD 5760) 12.5
Casson (J) (VTD 16535) 7.115
Castle (LD) (t/a Langford Building Supplies) (VTD 12813) 36.582
Castle Caereinion Recreation Association (VTD 18303) 15.183

Castlegate Holdings Ltd (VTD 11579) 3.54
Castrue Ltd (VTD 12681) 2.45
Caswell (SP) (VTD 4176) 18.402
Catchlord Ltd, [1985] VATTR 238 (VTD 1966) 40.82
Cater Clark Ltd (VTD 20546) 52.113
Catholic Care Consortium Ltd (VTD 17315) 33.45
Cauillez (UK) Ltd (VTD 11031) 52.160
Caunt (EJ) (t/a Edward James Confectionery) (VTD 1561) 65.39
Cave (N) (VTD 13346) 2.180
Cavenco Ltd (VTD 11700) 35.14
Cavendish Aviation Ltd (VTD 1471) 7.49
Cavendish Constructors plc (VTD 6957) 52.63
Cavner (SB & JM) (VTD 7714) 36.561
Cawley Hotels & Leisure Ltd (VTD 5812) 52.119
Cawthorne (TR) (VTD 7877) 52.21
CB Group Ltd (VTD 5841) 18.216
CBA Enterprises Ltd (VTD 4741) 18.586
CBR Systems Ltd (VTD 5871) 18.420
CDA Fasteners Ltd (VTD 6389) 18.272
CDN Property Services Ltd (VTD 12275) 18.443
CE Kinsella Traction (VTD 10130) 3.70
CEB Ltd (VTD 17054) 46.196
Cedac Structures Ltd (VTD 3307) 65.61
Cedar Court Business Centre Ltd (VTD 6976) 41.69
Cedar House Hotel Co Ltd (The) (VTD 20012) 18.348
Ceiling Services (VTD 6289) 18.207
Celahurst Ltd (VTD 13502) 46.16
Celikyay (C) (VTD 11491) 50.49
Cell Ltd (VTD 13942) 18.541
Cell Trading (UK) Ltd, TC00936 .... 36.113
Cellcom Ltd, Ch D [2010] EWHC 1799 (Ch) 37.13
Cellular Solutions (T Wells) Ltd (VTD 19903) 48.93
Celtic Football & Athletic Club Ltd, CS [1983] STC 470 .... 8.35
Celtic Football & Athletic Co Ltd (No 2) (VTD 14898) 27.49
Celtic plc, [1997] VATDR 111 (VTD 14762) 62.436
Celtic plc (No 2) (VTD 14898) 27.49
Celtic Trading (Midlands) (VTD 2194) 51.104
CEM Computers (VTD 3647) 18.308
Center Parcs (UK) Group plc (VTD 19848) 56.2
Central Blasting & Painting Ltd (VTD 18294) 50.128
Central Capital Corporation Ltd (VTD 13319) 41.66
Central Catering Equipment Ltd (VTD 14605) 14.15
Central Cleaning Contractors Ltd (VTD 20869) 18.615
Central Council of Physical Recreation (The) (VTD 17803) 62.47
Central Roadways Ltd (VTD 3576) 18.132
Central Trains Ltd (VTD 17475) 29.19
Central YMCA [1994] VATTR 146 (VTD 12425) 22.295
Central Young Men's Christian Association (The) (VTD 9318) 18.616
Centralan Property Ltd, ECJ Case C-63/04; [2006] STC 1542 .... 22.459
Centrax Ltd [1998] VATDR 369 (VTD 15743) 23.33
Century Life plc, CA 2000, [2001] STC 38 .... 38.13
Century Supplies Ltd (VTD 14375) 14.20
CF Dale Ltd (VTD 7385) 18.92
CF Leisure Mobility Ltd (VTD 16790) 19.60
CGI Group (Europe) Ltd (No 1), [2010] SFTD 1001; [2010] UKFTT 224 (TC),
    TC00525 .... 2.296
CGI Group (Europe) Ltd (No 2), [2010] SFTD 1178; [2010] UKFTT 396 (TC),
    TC00678 .... 62.39
CGI Pension Trust Ltd (VTD 15926) 48.135
CH Beazer (Holdings) plc, QB [1989] STC 549 .... 46.99
CHA Ltd (VTD 6618) 52.125

Chacombe Park Development Services Ltd (VTD 19414) 15.166
Chalk Springs Fisheries (VTD 2518) 29.122
Chalegrove Properties Ltd [2001] VATDR 316 (VTD 17151) 65.89
Chalmers (JR) (VTD 1433) 29.120
Chalmers (JW & MW) (VTD 1354) 62.224
Chamberlain (JO), QB [1989] STC 505 .... 57.35
Chamberlain Domestic Services Ltd (VTD 12492) 62.193
Chamberlin (M), CA [2011] EWCA Civ 271; [2011] STC 1237 .... 37.24
Chambers (Homefield Sandpit) Ltd (VTD 9012) 36.421, 52.356
Chamelon Mirrors Ltd (VTD 20640) 55.34
Champion (MB) (VTD 13307) 48.121
Chance (JF) (VTD 17623) 2.301
Chancellor (D) (VTD 9051) 18.485
Chancellor, Masters & Scholars of the University of Cambridge, Ch D [2009] EWHC
    434 (Ch) 30.11
Chandler (MJ) (Treasurer of the Bee Farmers' Association) (VTD 1565) 64.15
Chandler Forest Products Ltd (VTD 2612) 18.564
Chandlers Garage Holdings Ltd (VTD 16610) 44.164
Chantrey Vellacott [1992] VATTR 138 (VTD 7311) 62.481
Chapeltown Baths Community Business Ltd (VTD 18142) 57.130
Chapman (B) (VTD 17932) 44.159
Chapman (GW) [1992] VATTR 402 (VTD 7843) 51.87
Chapman (K & D) (VTD 1209) 36.283
Chapman & Frearson Ltd (VTD 4428) 29.106
Chapman Roofing Co (VTD 4186) 18.157
Chappel & Co Ltd v Nestlé Co Ltd, HL 1959, [1960] AC 87; [1959] 2 All ER 701
    .... 67.154
Chappell (DE) [1977] VATTR 94 (VTD 352) 44.61
Chappell v United Kingdom, ECHR 1989, 12 EHRR 1 .... 14.87
Characters (Hairdressers) Ltd (VTD 15351) 41.81
Chard Bowling Club (VTD 13575) 24.34
Chard Bowling Club (No 2) [1997] VATDR 375 (VTD 15114) 46.65, 46.130
Charity People Ltd (VTD 18283) 18.295
Charles (EWA) (VTD 596) 58.15
Charles (JA & SL) (VTD 17922) 21.39
Charles & Charles-Tijmens v Staatssecretaris van Financiën, ECJ Case C-434/03; [2006]
    STC 1429 .... 22.183
Charles Bell (BD) Ltd (VTD 4887) 18.79
Charles Church Spitfires Ltd (VTD 9512) 52.347
Charles Dominic Ltd (VTD 17830) 46.64
Charles F Hunter Ltd (VTD 11619) 2.158
Charles Forrington & Partners Ltd (VTD 5540) 62.191
Charles Gray (Builders) Ltd, CS [1990] STC 650 .... 15.191
Charles-Greed (P) (VTD 7790) 36.608
Charles Oliver Enterprises Ltd (VTD 268) 44.63
Charles Osenton & Co v Johnston, HL [1941] 2 All ER 245 .... 32.5
Charles Owen & Co (Bow) Ltd [1993] VATTR 514 (VTD 11267) 12.23
Charlesworth (G) (t/a Centurions) (VTD 9015) 38.36
Charlton (NP) (VTD 18268) 15.136
Charman (BJ) (VTD 2270) 62.427
Charnwood Holdings Ltd (VTD 7099) 52.43
Chartcliff Ltd (VTD 302) 2.461
Chartcliff Ltd [1976] VATTR 165 (VTD 262) 44.1, 44.36
Chartercoach Holidays Ltd (VTD 11193) 52.83
Chartered Institute of Bankers (The) (VTD 15648) 48.131
Chartered Society of Physiotherapy (The) (VTD 15108) 46.118
Charterhall Marketing Ltd (VTD 19050) 5.71
Charterhouse Mercantile Properties Ltd (VTD 17835) 6.15
Chartridge Construction Ltd (VTD 9449) 52.125
Chasekey Personnel Ltd (VTD 9101) 18.508
Chaseside Shopfitters Ltd (VTD 2023) 14.47

Chasney (C) Ltd [1989] VATTR 152 (VTD 4136) 29.3
Chatfield Applied Research Laboratories Ltd (VTD 11117) 3.54
Chatha (S & Mrs R) (VTD 20135) 51.145
Chattin (FW) (VTD 1226) 44.7
Chau (SY) (t/a Oriental Fry) (VTD 17263) 65.91
Chau (TTM) (VTD 7244) 18.231
Chaudhry (EA) v RCPO, QB 2007, [2008] STC 2357; [2007] EWHC 1805 (Admin)
.... 14.67
Chauhan (N & S) (VTD 17160) 36.502
Chaussures Bally SA v Ministry of Finance (Belgium), ECJ Case C-18/92; [1993] 1 ECR
2871; [1997] STC 209 .... 22.238
Chavda (GN) (t/a Hare Wines) (VTD 9895) 40.10
Chea (Mrs MM) (VTD 6357) 18.429
Checkstatus Ltd [1996] VATDR 81 (VTD 13168) 50.53
Cheek (AJP) (t/a Swanley Contractors) (VTD 13456) 51.20
Cheeseman (B) (VTD 5133) 55.55
Cheeseman (G) (t/a Well In Tune), Ch D [2000] STC 1119 .... 3.85
Cheesman (DL & Mrs LE) (t/a Kraft E) (VTD 10347) 52.351
Chef de Service Interregional des Douanes, Bergeres-Becque v, ECJ [1986] 2 CMLR
143 .... 22.258
Chelms (S) (t/a Central Consultancy & Training Services) (VTD 10489) 18.94
Cheltenham & Gloucester College of Higher Education Students Union (VTD 15727)
.... 11.36
Cheltenham College Enterprises Ltd, [2010] SFTD 696; [2010] UKFTT 118 (TC),
TC00429 .... 55.20
Cheltenham Countryside Race Day (The) (VTD 12460) 1.42
Cheltenham Old People's Housing Society Ltd (VTD 18795) 19.57
Chemical Corporation (UK) Ltd (VTD 2750) 18.181
Chequepoint (UK) Ltd (VTD 16754) 46.164
Cherry (CA) (VTD 13861) 62.302
Cheshire (C & G) (t/a Jeeves of Hampshire) (VTD 15624) 18.83
Cheshire Mushroom Farm [1974] VATTR 87 (VTD 71) 29.119
Cheshire Racing Ltd [2007] VATDR 345 (VTD 20283) 46.91
Cheshire Securities Ltd (VTD 3240) 8.17
Cheshire Trafford Estates Ltd (VTD 15495) 27.40
Chester Rural District Council, North of England Zoological Society v, CA [1959] 1
WLR 773; [1959] 3 All ER 116 .... 21.6
Chester Swimming Association (VTD 10969) 46.187
Chesterfield Borough Council (VTD 7104) 52.259
Chestergage Ltd (VTD 6179) 18.114
Cheung (D) (VTD 18276) 50.25
Cheung (KL) (t/a K Yuen Chinese Takeaway) (VTD 17635) 50.104
Cheung (TS) (t/a May Wah Takeaway) (VTD 16670) 2.303
Cheverton Construction Ltd (VTD 3254) 19.46
Chewton Glen Hotels Ltd (VTD 20686) 41.59
Cheyne Motors Ltd (VTD 5854) 52.58
Chicago Board of Trade (The City of) (VTD 9114) 8.41
Chichester Cinema at New Park Ltd (VTD 19344) 16.11
Chichester Plant Contractors Ltd (VTD 6575) 44.42
Chief Adjudication Officer, Johnson v (No 2), ECJ Case C-410/92; [1994] 1 ECR 5483;
[1994] 1 CMLR 725; [1995] All ER (EC) 258 .... 22.47
Chief Constable of South Wales Police, O'Brien v, HL [2005] 2 WLR 1038 .... 2.270
Chief Constable of Warwickshire Constabulary, R v (ex p. Fitzpatrick & Others), QB
[1998] 1 All ER 65 .... 14.94
Child (GM) (t/a Child & Co) (VTD 6827) 44.140, 36.236
Childs (D) (VTD 1373) 15.27
Childs (D) (VTD 7328) 18.473
Childs (RP) (VTD 6120) 62.108
Chilli Club Restaurant Ltd (VTD 20043) 36.596
Chilly Wizard Ice Cream Co Ltd (The) (VTD 19977) 28.13
Chiltern Windows Ltd (VTD 12208) 62.405

Chinese Channel (Hong Kong) Ltd (The), QB [1998] STC 347 .... 62.490
Ching (KH), Yi (HB) & Yong (HC) (t/a Chef Peking-on-Thames) (VTD 14079) 18.244
Chiplen (DLR & Mrs LM) (VTD 12280) 36.281
Chipping Sodbury Town Trust (VTD 16641) 15.218
Chitolie (DL), CA 30 November 1999 unreported 2.441
Chitolie (DL), Ch D [2002] STC 1532; [2002] EWHC 2323(Ch) 68.1
Chiverton (EA) (VTD 6130) 52.60
Chobham Golf Club [1997] VATDR 36 (VTD 14867) 24.33
Cholerton Ltd v The Isle of Man Treasury (VTD 13387) 66.8
Chorley, London Scottish Benefit Society v, QB 1884, 13 QBD 872 .... 2.460
Choudhary Trading Co Ltd (VTD 20251) 23.5
Choudhury (BA) (VTD 2490) 65.110
Choudhury (SM) (t/a Eastcheap Tandoori) (VTD 15003) 52.443
Choudhury, R v, CA Criminal Division [1996] STC 1163 .... 49.4
Chowdhury (SA), CS 1997, [1998] STC 293 .... 50.28
Christian Art Ltd (VTD 5940) 5.84
Christofi (A) (VTD 550) 3.135
Christon (CJ) (t/a Christon Davies Advertising) (VTD 17953) 50.121
Christoph-Dornier-Stiftung für Klinische Psychologie v Finanzamt Gießen, ECJ Case
    C-45/01; [2005] STC 228 .... 22.280
Christopher Gibbs Ltd [1992] VATTR 376 (VTD 8981) 2.85, 60.2
Christ's Hospital [2005] VATDR 442 (VTD 19126) 15.232
CHS Publications Ltd (VTD 15191) 18.186
Chubb Cars Ltd (VTD 20368) 62.236
Church (NB) (t/a Milton Antique Restoration) (VTD 12427) 55.25
Church of Christ the King (VTD 12783) 2.4
Church of England Children's Society, Ch D [2005] STC 1644; [2005] EWHC
    1692(Ch) 11.45
Church of Scientology of California (No 1), CA [1980] 3 CMLR 114, [1981] STC 65;
    [1981] 1 All ER 1035 .... 7.4
Church of Scientology of California (No 2) [1981] VATTR 130 (VTD 1134) 7.4
Church of Scientology Religious Education College Inc (VTD 19673) 48.61
Church of Scientology Religious Education College Inc (No 2), Ch D [2007] STC 1196;
    [2007] EWHC 1329(Ch) 2.175
Church Schools Foundation Ltd, CA [2001] STC 1661; [2001] EWCA Civ 1745 .... 62.46
Churchill Express (London) Ltd (VTD 9726) 18.563
Churchill Radio Cars Ltd (VTD 11658) 52.281
Churchview Ltd (VTD 17919) 65.87
Churchway Crafts Ltd (No 1) (VTD 782) 1.92
Churchway Crafts Ltd (No 2) (VTD 1186) 67.39
CI Cruises International SA, [2011] UKFTT 761 (TC), TC01598 .... 8.12
Cibenze Services plc (VTD 20637) 18.541
Cibo Participations SA v Directeur régional des impôts du Nord-Pas-de-Calais, ECJ Case
    C-16/00, [2002] STC 160 .... 22.113
Cicero Languages International (VTD 4286) 62.285
Cicero Languages International (No 2) (VTD 15246) 63.16
Cilfaoglu (T) (VTD 18409) 2.264
Cimber Air A/S v Skatteministeriet, ECJ Case C-382/02; [2005] STC 547 .... 22.393
Cindason (VTD 6749) 52.136
CIR v Aken, CA [1990] STC 497 .... 2.196
CIR v Pearlberg, [1953] 1 All ER 388 .... 2.196
CIR, R v (ex p. Preston), HL [1985] STC 282 .... 2.344
CIR v Sempra Metals Ltd, HL [2007] STC 1559 .... 2.520
CIR v Soul, CA 1976, 51 TC 86 .... 2.196
CIR v Williamson, CS 1928, 14 TC 335 .... 57.105
CIR, Carr v, CA [1944] 2 All ER 163 .... 64.14, 64.22
Circa Ltd (VTD 9908) 46.49
Circare Ltd (VTD 6903) 18.166
Cirdan Sailing Trust, Ch D 2005, [2006] STC 185; [2005] EWHC 2999 (Ch) 66.19
Cirencester Rugby Football Club, [2010] UKFTT 453 (TC), TC00718 .... 46.69
Ciro Citterio Menswear plc (VTD 16336) 18.83

Cirrus Reynolds & Co Ltd (VTD 4951) 18.551
Ciss Ltd (VTD 18839) 4.23
Citistar (UK) Ltd (VTD 18967) 52.431
Citroen UK Ltd, Ch D [2003] STC 1438; [2003] EWHC 2304 (Ch) 38.51
Citrone (C & J), R v, CA 1998, [1999] STC 29 .... 49.12
Citrone (GM & CW) (VTD 15702) 2.207
City Cabs (Edinburgh) Ltd (VTD 928) 64.14
City Centre Commercials Ltd (VTD 20166) 36.585
City Centre Ticketline Ltd (VTD 7553) 52.326
City College of Higher Education Ltd (VTD 2500) 62.367
City Cycles (VTD 5699) 52.57
City Fine Wine plc (VTD 12947) 2.430
City Industries Ltd (VTD 6097) 18.558
City of Belfast Warehousing Ltd (VTD 20196) 36.207
City of London Corporation [2003] VATDR 504 (VTD 17892) 22.148
City of London Magistrates, R v (ex p. Asif & Others), QB [1996] STC 611 .... 14.98
City of London Magistrates' Court, C & E v, QB [2000] STC 447; [2000] 1 WLR 2020;
 [2000] 4 All ER 763 .... 14.100
City of London Magistrates Court, R v (ex p. Peters), QB 1996, [1997] STC 141 .... 14.99
City of Sunderland College Supplies Ltd (VTD 15701) 2.65
City Rentals Ltd (VTD 4806) 18.83
City Research Associates Ltd [1984] VATTR 189 (VTD 1745) 5.14
City Shredding Services Ltd (VTD 9329) 18.610
Civil Service Motoring Association, CA 1997, [1998] STC 111 .... 27.19
Civil Service Pensioners' Alliance [1995] VATDR 228 (VTD 13024) 64.24
Civil Service Pensioners' Alliance (No 2) (VTD 18911) 64.25
Civilscent Ltd, [2009] SFTD 233; [2009] UKFTT 102 (TC), TC00070 .... 41.147
CJ Williams' Funeral Service of Telford [1999] VATDR 318 (VTD 16261) 24.27
CJW Manufacturing Ltd (VTD 16417) 53.7
CK Formwork Ltd (VTD 17791) 18.521
CL Dyer & Co (VTD 16053) 48.21
Claim 13 plc (VTD 19122) 46.105
Clamp (D & L) [1999] VATDR 520 (VTD 16422) 55.4
Clamp & Son, MacGregor v, KB [1914] 1 KB 288 .... 14.78
Claremont Construction (London) Ltd (VTD 7016) 52.293
Clarina Live-In Care Service (VTD 16434) 1.48
Clark (D), [2011] UKFTT 256 (TC), TC01120 .... 18.533
Clark (D) (t/a Clark Electrical Services) (VTD 15927) 36.201
Clark (J) (No 1), [2010] UKFTT 258 (TC), TC00552 .... 15.128
Clark (J) (No 2), [2010] UKFTT 458 (TC), TC00723 .... 15.129
Clark (R) (t/a Norblast) (VTD 7043) 52.373
Clark (RD), QB 1995, [1996] STC 263 .... 62.254
Clark (TR) (VTD 1370) 62.293
Clarke (A & H) (VTD 15201) 21.40
Clarke (C & E) (VTD 15201) 21.40
Clarke (LO) (VTD 457) 41.137
Clarke (LJB) (t/a Snips & Snips Hair & Beauty Salon) (VTD 14227) 62.261
Clarke (PC) (VTD 13728) 18.553
Clarke (PC) (No 2) (VTD 17154) 2.310
Clarke (S & H) (VTD 18859) 57.19
Clarke Street Joinery (t/a Clarke Street Building Services) (VTD 16805) 57.5
Clark's Cereal Products Ltd, QB 1965, [1968] 3 All ER 778 .... 29.144
Clarkson (WH) & Son (VTD 7479) 52.54
Classic Driveways (UK) Ltd (VTD 15521) 67.50
Classic Furniture (Newport) Ltd (VTD 16977) 6.35
Classicmoor Ltd [1995] VATDR 1 (VTD 13336) 3.64
Clayton (JH & M) (VTD 6207) 65.77
Claytons Upholstery Ltd (VTD 18253) 38.18
Clean Car Company Ltd (The) [1991] VATTR 234 (VTD 5695) 52.84
Cleary & Cleary (t/a Mobile X-Rays) (VTD 7305) 33.1
Cleco Ltd (VTD 7084) 52.142

Clees (U) v Hauptzollamt Wuppertal, ECJ Case C-259/97, 3 December 1998 unreported ... 60.9
Clements (MJ) (VTD 19216) ... 57.31
Cleshar Contract Services Ltd (VTD 7621) ... 18.400
Cleshar Contract Services Ltd (VTD 8803) ... 52.281
Cliff College (VTD 12000) ... 46.61
Cliff College Outreach (VTD 17301) ... 46.125
Clifford Construction Ltd (VTD 3929) ... 18.22
Clinkscale Radio & Musical Ltd (VTD 4279) ... 18.277
Clive White Chartered Surveyors (VTD 3989) ... 18.308
Close (NP) (VTD 20801) ... 2.322
Cloth Development Co Ltd (The) (VTD 5985) ... 18.425
Cloudmead Ltd (VTD 3290) ... 18.506
Clovelly Estate Co Ltd [1991] VATTR 351 (VTD 6353) ... 46.46
Clover Asphalte (IOM) Ltd v The Isle of Man Treasury (VTD 6645) ... 52.276
Clowance Holdings Ltd (VTD 17289) ... 22.256
Clowance Owners Club Ltd (VTD 18787) ... 62.71
Clowance plc (VTD 2541) ... 62.432
Club Centre of Leeds Ltd [1980] VATTR 135 (VTD 985) ... 14.58
Club Taxis (VTD 20179) ... 44.169
Clwb Rygbi Nant Conwy (VTD 16376) ... 13.8
Clycan Management Ltd (VTD 16651) ... 52.395
Clycol Precious Metals Ltd [1993] VATTR 425 (VTD 11543) ... 40.13
CMC (Preston) Ltd (VTD 3858) ... 30.7
CMS Peripherals Ltd (No 1) (VTD 19234) ... 18.314
CMS Peripherals Ltd (No 2), Ch D 2007, [2008] STC 985; [2007] EWHC 1128(Ch) ... 18.500
Coach House Property Management Ltd (VTD 7564) ... 6.26
Coastal Design (VTD 9001) ... 52.127
Coastrider Holidays Ltd (VTD 5289) ... 63.1
Coates (IG) (VTD 20682) ... 24.3
Cobb McCallum & Co (VTD 19668) ... 18.421
Cobb's Croft Service Station Ltd [1976] VATTR 170 (VTD 269) ... 36.568
Cobojo Ltd (VTD 4055) ... 40.94
Cobol Ltd (VTD 20976) ... 6.40
Cobra Consultancy Ltd (VTD 17615) ... 51.161
Cobrabrook Ltd (VTD 3185) ... 51.104
Cockroft (RW) & Co (Travel) Ltd (VTD 11800) ... 8.18
Coe (DJ & Mrs PA) (VTD 10911) ... 57.49
Coe (NG & BE) (VTD 165) ... 58.2
Coffee Republic plc (VTD 20150) ... 29.79
Coffeeshop Siberië vof, Staatssecretaris van Financiën v, ECJ Case C-158/98; [1999] STC 742; [1999] All ER (EC) 560 ... 22.83
COGEP Srl, Ministero delle Finanze v, ECJ Case C-174/06; [2008] STC 2744 ... 22.344
Cohen (DG) (VTD 16074) ... 50.14
Cohen (M) [2010] UKFT 631 (TC), TC00870 ... 25.11
Cohen (MB) [1994] VATTR 290 (VTD 12732) ... 51.148
Cohen, ex p., R v C & E, QB 3 December 1998 unreported ... 2.331
Cohen and others (ex p.), R v VAT Tribunal, QB [1984] STC 361 ... 2.328
Colaingrove Ltd, CA [2004] STC 712; [2004] EWCA Civ 146 ... 41.132
Colaingrove Ltd (No 2) (VTD 16981) ... 2.33
Colby (K) (VTD 16387) ... 57.194
Colchester School of Gymnastics (VTD 15370) ... 41.161
Colchester Sixth Form College (VTD 16252) ... 15.203
Colegate (TK) (t/a Shrewsbury English School) (VTD 10329) ... 18.563
Coleman (BM) (t/a D & A Newsagents) (VTD 1013) ... 58.3
Coleman (KG) [1976] VATTR 24 (VTD 242) ... 7.29
Coleman (MJ) (VTD 10512) ... 33.53
Coleman (PW) [1999] VATDR 133 (VTD 15906, VTD 16178) ... 2.23
Coleman Machines Ltd (VTD 3196) ... 18.7
Colin Maynard Builders (VTD 10895) ... 52.196

Colette (Ltd) [1992] VATTR 240 (VTD 6975) 14.55
Collard (T & H) Ltd (VTD 2654) 18.567
Collection Guns GmbH v Hauptzollamt Koblenz, ECJ [1985] ECR 3387 .... 60.8
Collée v Finanzamt Limburg an der Lahn, ECJ Case C-146/05; [2008] STC 757 .... 22.519
College of Estate Management (The), HL [2005] STC 1597; [2005] UKHL 62; [2005]
   4 All ER 933 .... 5.36
College Street Market Gardens (VTD 14115) 36.485
Coller Paper Co Ltd (VTD 7890) 52.69
Collie (JM) (VTD 6144) 36.192
Collier, R v, CA Criminal Division 1997 STI 474 .... 49.11
Collins (A) (t/a Inta Colour Brochures) (VTD 6491) 40.25
Collins (AC) (VTD 19564) 15.49
Collins (WA) (VTD 13579) 3.80
Collins (WJ) (t/a Triangle TVs) (VTD 6804) 62.80
Collins, Uratemp Ventures Ltd v, HL [2001] 3 WLR 806 .... 15.216
Collins & Beckett Ltd (VTD 19212) 55.51
Collinson (MA & DJ) (t/a Megazone) (VTD 15942) 50.122
Collyer (R) (VTD 2628) 18.550
Colorlam Ltd (VTD 9412) 52.99
Colour Offset Ltd, QB 1994, [1995] STC 85 .... 5.44
Colson & Kay Ltd (VTD 6148) 52.110
Columbia Veneering Co Ltd (VTD 5907) 18.468
Commercial Union Assurance Co plc (VTD 14195) 36.67
Commercials Trading Co Ltd (The) (VTD 3962) 18.506
Commission of the European Communities, see EC Commission
Commissioners for Local Administration, R v (ex p. Croydon London
   Borough Council), CA [1989] 1 All ER 1033 .... 2.341
Committee of Directors of Polytechnics, QB [1992] STC 873 .... 64.21
Commonwealth Telecommunications Bureau (VTD 189) 62.43
Communication Consultants Ltd (VTD 8973) 52.43
Communications & Leisure Group of Companies Ltd (The) (VTD 7788) 52.315
Community Housing Association Ltd, Ch D [2009] STC 1324; [2009] EWHC 455
   (Ch) 46.219
Company Registrations Online Ltd (VTD 19461) 5.41
Compaq Computer Manufacturing Ltd (VTD 10354) 35.12
Compass Contract Services UK Ltd, CA [2006] STC 1999; [2006] EWCA Civ 730
   .... 29.31
Compassion in World Farming Ltd [1997] VATDR 281 (VTD 15204) 13.16
Complete Maintenance Ltd (VTD 4669) 18.201
Composite Technics Ltd (VTD 4683) 18.563
Compton (S) (t/a Stan Compton Electrical Engineers & Contractors) (VTD 10259)
   .... 44.21
Compton & Woodhouse Ltd (VTD 20551) 62.463
Computeach International Ltd [1994] VATTR 237 (VTD 12115) 67.120
Computech Development Ltd (VTD 9798) 65.44
Computer Aided Systems (UK) Ltd (VTD 3729) 18.352
Computer Cave Ltd (VTD 15212) 14.29
Computer Equipment Investors Ltd (VTD 10092) 59.36
Computer Minicabs Ltd (VTD 15614) 67.123
Computer Presentations Ltd (VTD 3039) 18.558
Computer Technology Solutions Ltd (VTD 12721) 18.389
Comune di Carpaneto Piacentino & Others v Ufficio Provinciale Imposta sul Valore
   Aggiunto di Piacenza, ECJ Case C-4/89; [1990] 1 ECR 1869; [1990] 3 CMLR 153
   .... 22.130
Comune di Carpaneto Piacentino, Ufficio Distrettuale delle Imposte Dirette di
   Fiorenzuola d'Arda v, ECJ Case 231/87; [1989] ECR 3233; [1991] STC 205 .... 22.129
Comune di Rivergaro & Others, Ufficio Provinciale Imposta sul Valore Aggiunto di
   Piacenza v, ECJ Case 231/87; [1989] ECR 3222; [1991] STC 205 .... 22.129
Concept Direct Ltd (VTD 19721) 27.3
Conde Nast Publications Ltd, HL [2008] STC 324; [2008] UKHL 2; [2008] 1 All ER
   1061 .... 48.7

Condon (SLE) (VTD 19837) 51.178
Conference Staging Ltd (VTD 11434) 18.21
Conlin (J) (t/a Cottage Art & Frames) (VTD 17550) 62.156
Conlon (JA) (VTD 2343) 7.93
Conlon (P) (VTD 20877) 50.88
Connect Global Ltd, UT [2010] UKUT 372 (TCC); [2011] STC 51 .... 2.289
Connell (J), [2009] UKFTT 34 (TC), TC00003 .... 52.402
Connors (B) (VTD 17666) 44.76
Conoco Ltd, CA July 1995 unreported 2.172
Conoco Ltd, QB [1995] STC 1022 .... 2.313
Conoco Ltd [1997] VATDR 47 (VTD 14679) 67.155
Conoco Ltd [1997] VATDR 47 (VTD 14814) 2.413
Conoco Ltd, ex p., R v VAT Tribunal, CA July 1995 unreported 2.334
Conroy (KA) (VTD 1916) 19.95
Conroy, Woodworth v, CA [1996] 1 All ER 107 .... 40.75
Conservators of Ashdown Forest (VTD 18796) 42.7
Consolidated Holdings Ltd (VTD 13483) 18.61
Consolidated Holdings Ltd (VTD 13875, 14352) 18.541
Consortium Communications International Club (VTD 824) 2.252
Consortium International Ltd (VTD 824) 2.252
Constructive Solutions (Contracts) Ltd (VTD 18930) 48.4
Constantgreen Ltd (VTD 20303) 2.516
Constantine (P) (t/a The Red Lion Inn) (VTD 15792) 57.129
Continuum (Europe) Ltd, ECJ Case C-235/00, [2002] STC 57; [2002] 1 WLR 2200;
    [2002] All ER (EC) 289 .... 22.360
Contrast Graphic Supplies Ltd, [2010] UKFTT 289 (TC), TC00578 .... 28.22
Control Computers & Telecommunications Ltd (VTD 3461) 18.213
Control Ltd (VTD 16973) 14.42
Conway (ME) (VTD 11725) 44.141
Cook (LG) (t/a Ellon Plant Hire) (VTD 12302) 36.257
Cook (P & J) (t/a Blacksmiths Arms) (VTD 16770) 18.304
Cook (PW) (VTD 12571) 55.87
Cooke (JE) (t/a Surrey Language Centre) [2002] VATDR 357 (VTD 17691) 21.13
Cooke (WJ) (VTD 1844) 62.399
Cookies World Vertriebsgesellschaft mbH iL v Finanzlandesdirektion für Tirol, ECJ Case
    C-155/01; [2004] STC 1386 .... 22.203
Coolbreeze Ltd (VTD 18933) 3.105
Coombe (RS) (VTD 11154) 18.274
Coombes (K) (VTD 9417) 18.443
Coombes Transport (VTD 11275) 52.287
Cooper (DG & LM) (VTD 19179) 27.31
Cooper (GAG) (VTD 9719) 52.315
Cooper (M) (VTD 2665) 29.27
Cooper (PA) (t/a Bits of PCs) (VTD 17927) 52.429
Cooper & Chapman (Builders) Ltd, QB 1992, [1993] STC 1 .... 46.205
Cooper Chasney Ltd (VTD 4898) 62.137
Cooper-Cocks (T) (VTD 9062) 18.443
Cooperatieve Vereniging 'Cooperatieve Aardappelenbewaarplaats GA', Staatssecretaris
    van Financiën v, ECJ [1981] ECR 445; [1981] 3 CMLR 337 .... 22.78
Co-Operative Insurance Society Ltd [1992] VATTR 44 (VTD 7109) 62.5
Co-Operative Insurance Society Ltd [1997] VATDR 65 (VTD 14862) 36.17
Co-Operative Retail Services Ltd [1992] VATTR 60 (VTD 7527) 22.252
Co-Operative Wholesale Society Ltd, QB [1995] STC 983 .... 58.31
Co-Operative Wholesale Society Ltd (No 2) (VTD 15633) 46.111
Co-Operative Wholesale Society Ltd (No 3), CA [2000] STC 727 .... 24.29
Coopers & Lybrand, ex p., British Shoe Corporation, [1998] VATDR 348 (C00086)
    .... 2.300
Cope (BH), QB [1981] STC 532 .... 29.45
Copeland (CL) (VTD 13325) 50.136
Copes Service Station Ltd (VTD 17934) 67.159

Coppard (EJ), CA [2003] EWCA Civ 511; [2003] 2 WLR 1618; [2003] 3 All ER 351 .... 37.28
Copson (J) (t/a Compressors & Air Equipment) (VTD 13335) 59.28
Copthorne Village Golf Club (VTD 17426) 24.48
CopyGene A/S v Skatteministeriet, ECJ Case C-262/08; [2010] STC 1799 .... 22.277
Coracle Ventures Ltd, [2011] UKFTT 630 (TC), TC01472 .... 36.121
Corbitt (JH) (Numismatists) Ltd, HL [1980] STC 231; [1981] AC 22; [1980] 2 All ER 72 .... 60.1
Corke (NR) (VTD 16832) 46.233
Corkteck Ltd, oao, R v HMRC, QB [2009] STC 1681; [2009] EWHC 785 (Admin) 2.346
Corn Exchange Newbury (The) (VTD 20268) 16.12
Cornforth (RB) (VTD 4532) 14.24
Cornhill Management Ltd, [1991] VATTR 1 (VTD 5444) 1.8
Cornwall Training Ltd (VTD 17745) 21.14
Corporate Risk Associates Ltd (VTD 17872) 18.447
Corps of Commissionaires Management Ltd (VTD 14593) 18.590
Corriegour Lodge Hotel (VTD 11536) 18.337
Corriform Ltd, [2010] UKFTT 52 (TC), TC00365 .... 53.10
Corston (A) (VTD 19991) 3.129
Cortellesa (F & M) (VTD 16333) 62.306
Corthine (WJ), [1988] VATTR 90 (VTD 3012) 51.1
Corton Bashforth Screenprint Ltd (VTD 3232) 18.403
Corvi (B) (t/a Corvi Seaside Cafe), [2011] UKFTT 758 (TC), TC01595 .... 48.63
Cosalt Coolair Ltd (VTD 1908) 65.16
Cosmogen Ltd (VTD 3347) 51.102
Costa (D) (VTD 10761) 50.18
Costa v ENEL, ECJ Case 6/64; [1964] ECR 585; [1964] CMLR 425 .... 22.21
Coster (ME) (VTD 1057) 36.70
Costello (G) (VTD 16680) 2.156
Costello v Somerset County Council, CA [1993] 1 WLR 256 .... 2.181, 2.182, 2.183
Cotel Developments Ltd (VTD 9149) 52.227
Cotswold Computer Components Ltd (No 1) (VTD 19833) 2.18
Cotswold Computer Components Ltd (No 2) [2006] VATDR 202 (VTD 19909) 2.298
Cottage Holiday Associates Ltd, QB 1982, [1983] STC 278 .... 15.149
Cottam (S) (VTD 20036) 15.123
Cotterell (WH) (VTD 4573) 29.151
Coudrat, CA [2005] STC 1006; [2005] EWCA Civ 616 .... 49.16
Cough & Candy Ltd (VTD 5952) 36.544
Coughlan, ex p., R v North & East Devon Health Authority, CA [2001] 1 QB 213 .... 22.552
Coules (E) & Son Ltd (VTD 9608) 52.179
Countgold Ltd (VTD 2894) 51.139
Country Manor Manufacturing Ltd (VTD 6518) 51.10
Country Wide Property Investments Ltd, ECJ Case C-255/02; [2006] STC 919; [2006] 2 WLR 90 .... 22.60
Countrywide Insurance Marketing Ltd [1993] VATTR 277 (VTD 11443) 38.47
County Telecommunications Systems Ltd (VTD 10224) 44.8
Courage Ltd (VTD 8808) 58.41
Court Barton Property plc [1985] VATTR 148 (VTD 1903) 41.120
Courtlands Car Services Ltd (VTD 1778) 66.39
Courts plc, CA 2004, [2005] STC 27; [2004] EWCA Civ 1527 .... 3.46
Courts plc (No 2) [2004] VATDR 316 (VTD 18746) 67.70
Coventry (PV) (t/a Vincent James of Bath) (VTD 9617) 44.84
Coventry City Council, Hytec Information Systems Ltd v, CA [1997] 1 WLR 1666 .... 2.245
Coventry Motors & Sundries Co Ltd (VTD 7378) 52.85
Covercraft Ltd (VTD 3558) 18.28
Coward (G) (VTD 13542) 65.93
Cowdy (PA) (t/a Berriewood Farm) (VTD 18599) 48.36
Cowley (A) (VTD 16073) 50.56

Co-Work Camphill Ltd (VTD 17636) 15.116
Cowx (W) (VTD 10037) 17.3
Cox (BE) (VTD 18709, VTD 18990) 48.63
Coxhill Electronics Ltd (VTD 6433) 52.42
Cox's Cars Ltd (VTD 19855) 3.54
Coxshall (A) (VTD 14317) 25.25
Cozens (JA), CA [1999] BPIR 252 .... 2.193
Cozens (JA) (VTD 16545) 2.193
CP Textiles (VTD 11031) 52.160
CPA Environmental Control Associates Ltd (VTD 2953) 18.186
CPG Logistics Ltd [2010] UKFTT 345 (TC), TC00627 .... 4.15
CR Construction (VTD 7737) 67.11
CR Investments SRO (VTD 15474) 45.1
CR King & Partners (Holdings) Ltd (VTD 6695) 7.41
CR Smith Glaziers (Dunfermline) Ltd, HL [2003] STC 419; [2003] UKHL 7; [2003] 1
    WLR 656; [2003] 1 All ER 801 .... 38.22
Crabb (RG) (VTD 9091) 18.429
Craddock (GM) & Walker (BM) (t/a Warwick Garages) (VTD 16513) 38.28
Craig Security Services Ltd (VTD 11484) 14.47
Craiglands Hotel Ltd (The) (VTD 17931) 18.530
Crane & Manpower Ltd (VTD 2807) 18.165
Cranmer (SV) (VTD 17037) 41.89
Crayford & Bexleyheath (Motors) Ltd (VTD 13620) 67.99
Crayford Tandoori [2000] VATDR 340 (VTD 16749) 2.295
Crazy Farm Golf Course Ltd, [2010] UKFTT 307 (TC), TC00594 .... 36.600
Creasey (T) (VTD 5116) 18.477
Creating Careers [2006] VATDR 46 (VTD 19509) 21.29
Creative Facility Ltd (VTD 10891) 48.28
Creaven (D), Director of Assets Recovery Agency v, QB [2005] EWHC 2726 (Admin);
    Times 4.10.2006 .... 49.17
Creber (RG) (VTD 2623) 7.65
Credit Ancillary Services Ltd [1986] VATTR 204 (VTD 2172) 40.56
Credit Risk Management Ltd (VTD 12971) 46.82
Credit Suisse, Trendtex Trading Corporation v, CA [1981] QB 629 .... 2.445
Creditgrade Ltd [1991] VATTR 87 (VTD 5390) 62.92
Creflo Dollar Ministries (VTD 17705) 11.44
Creighton Griffiths (Investments) Ltd [1983] VATTR 175 (VTD 1442) 15.246
Creighton (RJN) Ltd (VTD 12395) 48.125
Cresta Holidays Ltd (VTD 16857) 2.79
Crestar Global Ltd (VTD 20258) 23.11
Crestbond Ltd (VTD 15728) 52.420
Cresthaven Contractors Ltd (VTD 12845) 18.558
Cresthaven Contractors Ltd (VTD 13010) 18.172
Cretney (P & V) [1983] VATTR 271 (VTD 1503) 41.119
Crewlyn (WB) (Electrical Contractors) Ltd (VTD 10027) 52.378
Crichton (CMM) & Another (VTD 2748) 36.303
Cricket St Thomas, Milk Marketing Board v, ECJ Case C-372/88; [1990] 1 ECR 1345
    .... 22.310
Crimpers Ltd (VTD 5466) 18.43
Cringan (W) & Watson (T) (VTD 7519) 57.71
Croall Bryson & Co Ltd, [2011] UKFTT 494 (TC), TC01341 .... 19.18
Croft Fuels Ltd (VTD 6644) 52.90
Crolla (M) (VTD 4701) 18.233
Cromford Hill Motor Sales (VTD 16152) 44.92
Crompton (R) (VTD 12033) 50.151
Crompton Enterprises Ltd, [1992] VATTR 321 (VTD 7866) 36.41
Cronin (J) (t/a Cronin's Driving School), QB [1991] STC 333 .... 62.228
Cronsvale Ltd [1983] VATTR 313 (VTD 1552) 5.56
Crooks (E & J) (VTD 1602) 29.187
Cropper (KJ) (t/a KJC Games) (VTD 13679) 62.550
Cross Border Lease Management Ltd (VTD 19853) 62.453

Cross Electrical & Building Services Ltd (VTD 16954) 19.75
Cross Levels Developments Ltd [2004] VATDR 248 (VTD 18689) 62.475
Crosstyle plc (VTD 7169) 52.85
Crothall & Co Ltd [1973] VATTR 20 (VTD 6) 33.46
Crowborough Rugby Football Club Ltd (VTD 6023) 18.596
Crown & Cushion Hotel (Chipping Norton) Ltd, CA [2004] STC 1212; [2004] EWCA
    Civ 516 .... 44.121
Crown Treatment Centre (VTD 15564) 11.11
Crownlion (Seafood) Ltd, [1985] VATTR 188 (VTD 1924) 29.48
Crowther Print Ltd (VTD 10241) 18.235
Croydon Architectural Ltd (VTD 7823) 14.47
Croydon Hotel & Leisure Co Ltd (The), CA [1996] STC 1105 .... 3.43
Croydon Hotel & Leisure Co Ltd, [1997] VATDR 245 (VTD 14920) 36.641
Croydon London Borough Council, ex p., R v Commissioners for Local
    Administration, CA [1989] 1 All ER 1033 .... 2.341
Croydon Power & Light Ltd (VTD 13296) 18.561
Crucial Components Ltd, [2011] UKFTT 690 (TC), TC01532 .... 36.78
Crusader Line Ltd (t/a Spaghetti Western) (VTD 12439) 18.23
Cruse (Mrs PK) (VTD 5975) 51.57
Crux Engineering Ltd (VTD 7706) 52.338
CSC Electrix Ltd (VTD 15956) 18.557
CSC Financial Services Ltd, ECJ Case C-235/00, [2002] STC 57; [2002] 1 WLR 2200;
    [2002] All ER (EC) 289 .... 22.360
CSL Building Services Ltd (VTD 14193) 14.11
CT Finance Ltd (VTD 9286) 52.342
Cudworth (M) (t/a Cudworth of Norden), [2011] UKFTT 312 (TC), TC01173 ...... 23.22
Cullen (C) (VTD 17169) 2.327
Cullens Holdings plc (VTD 12376) 41.29
Culverhouse (RJ) (VTD 2130) 57.175
Culverpalm Ltd, [1984] VATTR 199 (VTD 1727) 62.539
Culverwell (MR), [2009] UKFTT 276 (TC), TC00222 .... 15.274
Cumarasany, Ratnam v, PC 1964, [1965] 1 WLR 8; [1964] 3 All ER 933 .... 2.180
Cumbernauld Development Corporation (VTD 14630) 67.81
Cumbernauld Development Corporation (No 2), CS [2002] STC 226 .... 62.391
Cumbershourne Ltd (t/a Hockley Enterprises), [1977] VATTR 110 (VTD 369) 2.139
Cumbrae Properties (1963) Ltd, QB [1981] STC 799 .... 62.24
Cumbria County Council, [2011] UKFTT 621 (TC), TC01463 .... 40.112
Cummings (C) (VTD 14870) 2.206
Cummings (Mr & Mrs M) (t/a Inn On The Lake) (VTD 8891) 36.296
Cummins (WD) (VTD 1985) 62.293
Cun (SQ) (t/a Kung Fung Takeaway) (VTD 19491) 52.305
Cunningham (JP), Ch D [2001] STC 736 .... 3.11
Cupboard Love Ltd (VTD 267) 2.110
Cupit (W) & Sons (VTD 5403) 36.285
Curia (G) v Ministero dell'Economia e delle Finanze, ECJ Case C-381/09; 7 July 2010
    unreported 22.358
Curley (RL) (t/a Scan Print Services) (VTD 10691) 52.38
Currall (IPS) (t/a Ian Currall & Partners) (VTD 11652) 14.58
Currie (AL) & Brown (VTD 14678) 18.590
Curry (MP) (VTD 20077) 15.267
Curry Garden Tandoori Restaurant (The) (VTD 10766) 2.227
Curry Mahal Restaurant Manchester Ltd (VTD 4244) 18.233
Curtain Clearance (VTD 10683) 65.13
Curtis (CA) (t/a Green Baize Snooker) (VTD 11128) 65.90
Curtis (DH) (Builders) Ltd, Re, [1978] 2 All ER 183 .... 37.16
Curtis (DJ) (VTD 20330) 62.53
Curtis Edington & Say Ltd (VTD 11699) 38.48
Curtis Henderson Ltd, QB [1992] STC 732 .... 46.213
Curwood (C) (VTD 5915) 18.483
Cusdin (R) (VTD 19739) 15.236
Cushla Ltd, Re, Ch D [1979] STC 615; [1979] 2 All ER 415 .... 37.16

Cussins (P) (VTD 20541) 15.54
Cuthbert (J & Mrs A) (VTD 20466) 62.533
Cuthbert (R) (VTD 16518) 51.129
Cutler (BV) (VTD 17149) 51.62
Cutting (SJ) (VTD 3433) 51.107
Cutts (OAS), QB 1988, [1989] STC 201 .... 3.52
CV Staff Services Ltd, [2011] UKFTT 384 (TC), TC01239 .... 18.543

D

D v W, ECJ Case C-384/98; [2002] STC 1200 .... 22.279
D & D Marketing, Ch D [2002] EWHC 660(Ch) 37.1
D & D Marketing (UK) Ltd, Ch D [2002] EWHC 660 (Ch) 37.1
D & K Builders & Sons (Ampthill) Ltd (VTD 4287) 36.71
D & M Builders (Hamilton) Ltd (VTD 6713) 52.137
D & M Electro Plating Ltd (VTD 10966) 52.72
D Brown Scaffolding Ltd (VTD 20685) 52.448
D Gillespie Ltd (VTD 17492) 44.164
D Gregorio & Sons (VTD 9105) 57.55
Da Conti International Ltd (VTD 6215) 36.670
Dada Records Ltd, [2009] UKFTT 251 (TC), TC00199 .... 14.14
Daiber (E) v Hauptzollamt Reutlingen, ECJ Case 200/84; [1985] ECR 3363 .... 60.8
Dajani (NS) (t/a Lancashire Marketing Consultants) (VTD 10861) 52.58
Dale (IW) (VTD 3385) 51.84
Dale (IW) (VTD 4353) 2.384
Dalesid Ltd (VTD 9147) 40.22
Dallas (L) (VTD 3620) 36.423
Dallas Knitwear (Manchester) Ltd (VTD 14653) 52.205
Daltry (Mr & Mrs J) (VTD 2277) 51.110
D'Ambrosio (Dr J) (VTD 15) 33.50
d'Ambrumenil (PL), ECJ Case C-307/01; [2005] STC 650; [2004] 3 WLR 174 ..... 22.282
d'Ambrumenil (PL) (No 2) [2004] VATDR 134 (VTD 18551; VTD 18581) 22.283
Danebridge Group Practice (VTD 18610) 67.145
Danfoss A/S v Skatteministeriet, ECJ Case C-371/07; [2009] STC 701 .... 22.186
Dangeville (SA) v France, ECHR Case 36677/97; [2003] STC 771; 5 ITLR 604 ...... 34.24
Dangol (t/a The Great Kathmandu Tandoori), ex p., R v C & E, QB 1999, [2000] STC
  107 .... 2.329
Danielon (F) (VTD 19244) 65.102
Daniels (GG & Mrs HK) (t/a Group Montage) (VTD 12014) 41.75
Daniels (S) & Stevenson (S) (t/a Homeforce) [2003] VATDR 591 (VTD 17948) 57.135
Danish Firma Center plc (VTD 6196) 52.46
Dankowski v Dyrektor Izby Skarbowej w Lodzi, ECJ Case C-438/09; 22 December 2010
  unreported 22.473
Dankroy Ltd (VTD 7743) 18.178
Daňové riaditeľstvo Slovenskej republiky, Tanoarch sro v, ECJ Case C-504/10;
  27 October 2011 unreported 22.63
Daòový úrad Košice V, Mihal (K) v, ECJ Case C-456/07; 21 May 2008 unreported
  .... 22.128
Dansk Denkavit ApS & Others v Skatteministeriet, ECJ Case C-200/90; [1992] 1 ECR
  2217; [1994] 2 CMLR 377; [1994] STC 482 .... 22.41, 22.527
Dant (MJ) (VTD 16043) 36.476
Darci Shoes Ltd (VTD 13228) 18.36
Darker (F) (VTD 15771) 50.34
Darker (TE) (t/a Fig Tree Coffee Shop) (VTD 16620) 57.123
Darlington Borough Council, [1980] VATTR 120 (VTD 961) 29.96
Darlington Finance Ltd, [1982] VATTR 233 (VTD 1337) 44.80
Daron Motors Ltd (VTD 11695) 44.81
Dart (JL) (VTD 9066) 3.69, 52.362
Dart Major Works Ltd (VTD 18781) 15.159
Dartford Borough Council (VTD 20423) 65.35

Dartford Golf Club Ltd (VTD 1576) 13.46
Darvill (JT) (VTD 9299) 52.370
Dashmore Clothing Ltd (VTD 17776) 3.68
Datapoint Global Services Ltd (VTD 20971) 18.545
Datoo (R) & Others (t/a The Datoo Partnership), [2011] UKFTT 595 (TC), TC01438
  .... 18.586
Daunter (KR) (VTD 20120) 62.515
Dauntgate Ltd (VTD 11663) 12.7, 12.19
Dave (M), Ch D [2002] STC 900; [2002] EWHC 969 (Ch) 2.439
Davencroft Brickwork Ltd (VTD 10692) 55.32
Davey (AP) (VTD 17427) 2.327
Davey (EG) (t/a EG Davey & Co) (VTD 13538) 36.49
Davey (TE) Photo-Service Ltd, QB 1995, [1997] STC 889 .... 18.346
David Baxendale Ltd, CA [2009] STC 2578; [2009] EWCA Civ 831 .... 62.553
David Geddes (Commodities) Ltd (VTD 2664) 67.52
David Graham & Associates (VTD 11068) 5.15
David Jacobs UK Ltd (in liquidation), [2009] UKFTT 106 (TC), TC00074 .... 36.474
David John (Papers) Ltd (VTD 10084) 52.234
David Leslie (Hairfashions) Ltd (VTD 3446) 18.282
David Lewis Centre (The), QB [1995] STC 485 .... 11.8, 19.34
David Morris Homes Ltd (VTD 7081) 52.190
David Taylor Tool Hire Ltd (VTD 4969) 18.335
David Wickens Properties Ltd [1982] VATTR 143 (VTD 1284) 7.55
Davidson (AD) (VTD 9537) 57.130
Davidson (DR) (VTD 18721) 48.145
Davidson (M) (VTD 16207) 18.354
Davidson (M & R) (VTD 12908) 48.119
Davidsons (VTD 12120) 18.163
Davies (B) (VTD 12023) 62.298
Davies (BJ) (VTD 10676) 18.495
Davies (G) (VTD 2126) 51.35
Davies (GS) (VTD 5182) 51.91
Davies (JJ), QB 1974, [1975] STC 28; [1975] 1 WLR 204; [1975] 1 All ER 309 .... 67.151
Davies (KP) (VTD 831) 44.37
Davies (Dr M) (VTD 219) 36.258
Davies (PG) (VTD 11456) 18.600
Davies (PJ) [1979] VATTR 162 (VTD 791) 2.197
Davies (PR & Mrs HK) (t/a Lymington Power Boat Charter) (VTD 20032) 7.33
Davies & Davies Ltd (VTD 9692) 52.21
Davis (IJ) (VTD 15508) 50.51
Davis (R & M) (t/a El Shaddai Private Nursing Home) (VTD 16275) 57.114
Davis Advertising Service Ltd [1973] VATTR 16 (VTD 5) 2.83
Davison (AI) (VTD 17130) 15.61
Daws (NS) (VTD 7643) 36.681
Dawson (BW) (VTD 5216) 51.54
Dawson, Furniss v, HL [1984] STC 153 .... 36.495
Dawson Strange Photography Ltd (VTD 15967) 18.436
Day (DC) (VTD 7764) 52.262
Dayani (J) (VTD 3491) 36.371
Daynes (P & Mrs E) (VTD 10988) 48.29
Dayrich Bookmakers (VTD 14638) 52.346
Dayrich Bookmakers (VTD 13503) 46.186
Daytona Surf Ltd, [2011] UKFTT 383 (TC), TC01238 .... 36.673
DCA Industries Ltd [1983] VATTR 317 (VTD 1544) 29.20
DCB Mouldings (VTD 7522) 52.152
DCM Leisure Ltd (VTD 16966) 57.147, 67.24
DCM (Optical Holdings) Ltd (No 2), [2010] UKFTT 393 (TC), TC00675, TC00675A
  .... 46.138
DD Group Ltd (VTD 19405) 52.307
DDR Distribution Ltd (VTD 20694) 2.165

De Danske Bilimportører v Skatteministeriet, ECJ Case C-98/05; [2006] 1 ECR 4945 .... 22.255
De Ferranti (MZ), [2011] UKFTT 435 (TC), TC01288 .... 36.514
De Fruytier, Belgian State v, ECJ Case C-237/09; [2010] STC 1792 .... 22.287
De Jong (P) v Staatssecretaris van Financiën, ECJ Case C-20/91; [1992] 1 ECR 2847; [1992] 3 CMLR 260; [1995] STC 727 .... 22.163
De Montfort University Students' Union (VTD 18434) 62.552
DE Siviter (Motors) Ltd (VTD 3556) 44.91
De Vere Golf & Leisure Ltd (VTD 18078) 24.41
De Vere Group plc (VTD 18078) 24.41
Dealy, R v, CA Criminal Division 1994, [1995] STC 217 .... 49.10
Dean (Mr & Mrs AF) (VTD 1455) 36.531
Dean (MP & Mrs EM) (t/a Hartlebury Store) (VTD 12116) 58.18
Dean (PS) (VTD 4314) 51.9
Dean & Canons of Windsor (VTD 15703) 16.6
Dean & Chapter of the Cathedral Church of Christ (VTD 15068) 46.110
Dean & Chapter of the Cathedral Church of St Peter (VTD 3591) 46.115
Deandrake Ltd, [2011] UKFTT 250 (TC), TC01114 .... 36.121
Deans Ltd (VTD 13935) 44.153
Dear (I), [2010] UKFTT 111 (TC), TC00422 .... 48.63
Dearwood Ltd, QB [1986] STC 327 .... 65.12
Debenhams Retail plc, CA [2005] STC 1155; [2005] EWCA Civ 892 .... 27.11
Debenhams Retail plc v Sun Alliance & London Assurance Co Ltd, CA [2005] STC 1443; [2005] EWCA Civ 868 .... 67.9
Debouche v Inspecteur der Invoerrechten en Accijnzen Rijswijk, ECJ Case C-302/93; [1996] STC 1406; [1996] 1 ECR 4495; [1997] 2 CMLR 511 .... 22.537
Debt Management Associates Ltd (VTD 17880) 27.30
Debtor, re (No 8 of 1997), Ch D 1998 .... 37.22
Decal Co Ltd (The) (VTD 16274) 53.11
Dedman v British Building and Engineering Appliances Ltd, [1974] 1 All ER 520 .... 2.138
Deeds Ltd (VTD 1500) 40.17
Deepblue Ltd (VTD 4126) 18.413
Deeside Welding Co (VTD 9238) 52.283
Defrenne v SA Belge de Navigation Aerienne Sabena, ECJ Case 43/75; [1976] ECR 455; [1976] 2 CMLR 98; [1981] 1 All ER 122 .... 22.39
DEKA Getreideprodukte GmbH & Co KG iL v EEC, ECJ Case 250/78; [1983] ECR 421 .... 22.39
Delaney (PA) (VTD 6105) 18.428
Deliverance Ltd, [2011] UKUT 58 (TCC); [2011] STC 1049 .... 29.68
Dellastreet Systems Ltd (VTD 11965) 18.411
Delta House Installations Ltd (VTD 12151) 36.391
Delta Newsagents Ltd [1986] VATTR 260 (VTD 2220) 65.76
Deltaview Ltd (VTD 1832, 1876) 14.18
Delton Central Services Ltd (VTD 3904) 18.79
Delton Electric Ltd (VTD 3904) 18.79
Deluni Mobile Ltd (VTD 19205) 2.479
Deluni Mobile Ltd (No 2) (VTD 19301) 36.96
Delves (JF) (No 2) (VTD 157) 57.121
Demack (H) (VTD 5534) 57.212
Demor Investments Ltd [1981] VATTR 66 (VTD 1091) 36.348
Dempster (N) (t/a Boulevard), Ch D [2008] STC 2079; [2008] EWHC 63 (Ch) 36.124
Dempster (WM) (VTD 1316) 2.367
Denbrae Ltd, [2010] UKFTT 195 (TC), TC00497 .... 36.208
Denby (C) (VTD 9668) 36.405
Denholmegate Engineering Ltd (VTD 17350) 51.130
Denimode Ltd (VTD 11952) 14.47
Denizil (I) & Karaca (N) (VTD 14644) 50.142
Denkavit International BV & Others v Bundesamt für Finanzen, ECJ Case C-283/94; [1996] STC 1445; [1996] 1 ECR 5063 .... 22.35
Denman College [1998] VATDR 399 (VTD 15513) 15.71
Dennett (MP) (VTD 18763) 57.130

Dennis (V) (t/a Lynden Property Co) (VTD 11299) 6.22
Dennis Rye Ltd (VTD 4545) 36.240
Dennis Rye Ltd, QB 1995, [1996] STC 27 .... 46.83
Dennis Rye Ltd (VTD 15848) 46.112
Dennison (LA) (VTD 18619) 19.79
Dennison (LA) (No 2) (VTD 18733) 19.80
Dennison Commercials Ltd (VTD 20334) 23.7
Dent (CD & JMR) (VTD 18500) 19.36
Dental IT Ltd, [2011] UKFTT 128 (TC), TC01002 .... 18.441
Dentith *v* The Treasury of the Isle of Man Government (VTD 4272) 18.441
Denton (CJW) (t/a Denton Auto Repairs) (VTD 20627) 44.167
Denyer (CJ), Ch D 2007, [2008] STC 633; [2007] EWHC 2750 (Ch) 41.90
Denyer (CJ) (No 2) (VTD 20691) 51.33
Depot Corner Car Sales (VTD 16907) 44.96
Depot (The) Ltd, FTT [2009] UKFTT 51 (TC); TC00030 .... 18.545
Derby Plating Services Ltd (VTD 11352, 12018) 18.506
Derby YMCA (VTD 16914) 15.217
Derbyshire (CB) (VTD 12963) 52.445
Derbyshire Building Society (VTD 14026) 46.96
Derbyshire Security Services (VTD 14809) 65.81
Derrick A Knightley & Associates (VTD 4972) 18.164
Derry Brothers (VTD 17701) 62.494
Desai (M) (t/a Regency Garments) (VTD 16036) 3.18
Design Concept SA *v* Flanders Expo SA, ECJ Case C-438/01; [2003] STC 912 ..... 22.221
Designspeedy Ltd (VTD 18309) 2.184
Desouza (R) (VTD 11819) 44.141
Deutsche Olivetti GmbH, Hauptzollamt Frankfurt am Main-Ost *v*, ECJ Case C-17/89;
    [1990] 1 ECR 2301; [1992] 2 CMLR 859 .... 22.226
Deutsche Ruck UK Reinsurance Co Ltd, QB [1995] STC 495 .... 46.5
Deva Trading Co Ltd (The) (VTD 3421) 18.279
Devereux (KW) & Sons (VTD 11187) 38.43
Deville *v* Administration des Impôts, ECJ Case 240/87; [1988] ECR 3513;
    [1989] 3 CMLR 611 .... 22.44
Devine (J) (VTD 15312) 41.56
Devoirs Properties Ltd (VTD 6646) 6.24
Devonshire Hotel (Torquay) Ltd (The) (VTD 14448) 63.13
Devoti (DP) (t/a Belmont Associates) (VTD 11868) 27.28
Devro Ltd (VTD 7570) 29.89
Dewar (L) (VTD 7899) 52.354
Dewar Associates Ltd (VTD 18748) 18.516
Dewhirst (JP) (VTD 13793) 57.106
Dewsbury Road Social Club (VTD 17168) 3.91
Dexter Brent & Patterson Ltd (VTD 3136) 18.201
DFDS A/S, ECJ Case C-260/95; [1997] STC 384; [1997] 1 ECR 1005; [1997] 1 WLR
    1037; [1997] All ER (EC) 342 .... 22.492
DFS Furniture Co Ltd (No 3), [2010] SFTD 195; [2009] UKFTT 204 (TC), TC00157
    .... 46.107
DFS Furniture Co plc (No 1), CA 2002, [2003] STC 1; [2002] EWCA Civ 1708 ..... 48.76
DFS Furniture Co plc (No 2), CA [2004] STC 559; [2004] EWCA Civ 243; [2004] 1
    WLR 2159 .... 3.111
DH Commercials (Leasing) Ltd (VTD 14115) 41.143
Di Resta (F & D) (t/a Bottoms Up) (VTD 18641) 62.282
Di Rienzo (F) (t/a Franco's Fish Bar) (VTD 15599B) 62.305
Di Tondo (L) (t/a Partners Associates) (VTD 18858) 17.18
Diacutt Concrete Drilling Services Ltd (VTD 9728) 52.257
Diaform Ltd (VTD 11069) 62.389
Diagnostiko & Therapeftiko Kentro Athinon-Ygeia AE *v* Ipourgos Ikonomikon, ECJ
    Case C-394/04; [2006] STC 1349 .... 22.275
Dial-a-Phone Ltd, CA [2004] STC 987; [2004] EWCA Civ 603 .... 46.85
Dialrace Ltd [1991] VATTR 505 (VTD 6328) 14.54

Diamond GoGo Bar v Fylkesskattesjefen, Lagmannsrett 6 December 2006; Times
7.12.2006 .... 22.319
Diamond Investigations Ltd (VTD 15176) 18.508
Dickins Ltd (VTD 1477) 36.353
Dickinson (R) (VTD 6309) 50.150
Dickinson (WF) (Dorset) Ltd (VTD 2778) 1.3
Dicksmith Properties Ltd (VTD 13136) 52.19
Dickson (JAJ) (VTD 2560) 51.45
Diesel Generating (Tetbury) Ltd (VTD 2702) 36.537
Different Kettle Ltd, [2011] UKFTT 540 (TC), TC01387 .... 36.517
Digbeth Cash & Carry Ltd (VTD 13180) 52.305
Diggor Gaylord Ltd (VTD 11380) 62.466
Digi Systems (Ireland) Ltd, [2009] UKFTT 183 (TC), TC00138 .... 23.32
Digi Trade Ltd, [2011] UKFTT 566 (TC), TC01411 .... 36.121
Digit Digital Experience Ltd (VTD 17553) 18.546
Digital Albums Ltd (VTD 20783) 5.30
Digital Intelligence Systems Ltd (VTD 6500) 18.286
Digva (SS & Mrs GRK) (t/a International Marketing) (VTD 17684) 52.428
Digwa (TS) [1978] VATTR 119 (VTD 612) 2.194
Dilawri (VK & Mrs U) (t/a East & West Textiles) (VTD 11409) 40.76
Dilexport Srl v Amministrazione delle Finanze dello Stato, ECJ Case C-343/96,
9 February 1999 unreported 22.557
Dillenkofer & Others v Federal Republic of Germany, ECJ Case C-178/94; [1996]
1 ECR 4845; [1996] 3 CMLR 469; [1996] All ER (EC) 917 .... 22.33
Dilley (JC) (VTD 12617) 2.433
Dillon (C) (VTD 10681) 52.273
Din (AK & AR) (t/a Indus Restaurant) [1984] VATTR 228 (VTD 1746) 3.120
Dinaro Ltd (t/a Fairway Lodge) (VTD 17148) 41.102
Diners Club Ltd (The), CA [1989] STC 407; [1989] 2 All ER 385 .... 27.61
Dinglis Property Services Ltd (VTD 15159) 52.347
Diputacion Foral de Alava v EC Commission, ECJ Case T-346/99; [2002] All ER(D)
338(Oct) 22.10
Diputacion Foral de Guipuzcoa v EC Commission, ECJ Case T-269/99;
[2002] All ER(D) 337(Oct) 22.9
Direct Cosmetics Ltd (No 1), ECJ Case 5/84; [1985] STC 479; [1985] ECR 617;
[1985] 2 CMLR 145 .... 22.496
Direct Cosmetics Ltd (No 2), ECJ Case 138/86; [1988] STC 540; [1988] ECR 3937
.... 22.497
Direct Drilling (VTD 11071) 40.35
Direct Link Couriers (Bristol) Ltd (VTD 2105) 44.7
Direct Marketing Bureau (VTD 16696) 5.63
Direct Valeting Ltd (VTD 7118) 18.565
Directeur des Services Fiscaux de Maine-et-Loire, Ampafrance SA v, ECJ Case C-177/99;
[2002] BTC 5520 .... 22.501
Directeur des Services Fiscaux du Val-de-Marne, Sanofi Synthelabo v, ECJ Case
C-181/99; [2002] BTC 5520 .... 22.501
Directeur Général des Douanes et droits indirects, Société Comateb & Others v, ECJ
Case C-192/95; [1997] STC 1006; [1997] 1 ECR 165; [1997] 2 CMLR 649 .... 22.559
Directeur Général des Impôts, Bergandi v, ECJ Case 252/86; [1988] ECR 1343; [1991]
STC 259; [1989] 2 CMLR 933 .... 22.526
Directeur régional des impôts du Nord-Pas-de-Calais, Cibo Participations SA v, ECJ
Case C-16/00; [2002] STC 160 .... 22.113
Direction des Services Fiscaux du Pas-de-Calais, Roquette Frères SA v, ECJ Case
C-88/99; [2000] All ER (D) 2008 .... 22.52
Director of Assets Recovery Agency v Creaven, QB [2005] EWHC 2726 (Admin); Times
4.10.2006 .... 49.17
Director of Border Revenue, System Fabricators Ltd v, [2011] UKFTT 436 (TC),
TC01289 .... 57.154
Direktor Obzhalvane i upravlenie na izpalnenieto NAP, Enel Maritsa Iztok 3AD v, ECJ
Case C-107/10; 12 May 2011 unreported 20.114

Direktsia Obzhalvane I upravlenie na izpalnenieto Varna *v* Auto Nikolovi OOD, ECJ
    Case C-203/10; [2011] STC 1294 .... 20.133
Discount Window Systems Ltd (VTD 10159) 18.293
Discover Travel & Tours International Ltd (VTD 18665) 2.204
Discovery Housing Association Ltd (VTD 8847) 52.344
Dispute Resolution Services Ltd, ECJ Case C-307/01; [2003] All ER (D) 281 (Nov)
    .... 22.282
Dispute Resolution Services Ltd (No 2) (VTD 18551) 22.283
Ditchfield (TJ) *v* The Isle of Man Treasury (VTD 6533) 52.134
Divers (J) (VTD 12525) 51.82
Diversified Agency Services Ltd, QB 1995, [1996] STC 398 .... 62.495
Dixon (J & J), [2010] UKFTT 281 (TC), TC00570 .... 48.13
Dixons (VTD 4053) 18.413
Dixons Group plc (VTD 9604) 67.126
DIY Conservatory Centre Ltd (VTD 19290) 36.62
DJ Electrical Contractors (VTD 3916) 18.474
D'Jan (H) (VTD 19045) 50.20
DJI Electrical Services Ltd (VTD 3671) 51.123
DK Wright & Associates Ltd [1975] VATTR 168 (VTD 203) 59.22
DL Marketing (Direct Link) Ltd (VTD 17006) 5.65
DM Builders (Chichester) Ltd (VTD 7618) 55.18
Docutex Business Solutions Ltd (VTD 18138) 53.13
Dodd (RJ) (t/a Able Machines) (VTD 12856) 51.150
Dodds (GK) [1989] VATTR 98 (VTD 3383) 44.82
Dodson Bros (Thatchers) Ltd (VTD 13734) 55.28
Dogbreeders Associates [1989] VATTR 317 (VTD 4295) 38.41
Doherty (J) (VTD 6609) 52.75
Doherty (K) (VTD 13075) 51.174
Dollar Land (Feltham) Ltd, QB [1995] STC 414 .... 18.622
Dollard (S) (VTD 18656) 65.91
Dollond & Aitchison Ltd, ECJ Case C-491/04; 23 February 2006 unreported 35.24
Dolmetsch Foundation Inc (VTD 5876) 52.358
Dolomite Double Glazing Ltd [1985] VATTR 184 (VTD 1922) 62.422
Dolphin Fish Bar Ltd (VTD 18993) 65.91
Dom Buckley IRS Ltd [2011] UKFTT 5 (TC), TC00882 .... 23.3
Domestic Service Care Ltd (VTD 11869) 38.49
Domino's Pizza Group Ltd (No 1) (VTD 18010) 29.75
Domino's Pizza Group Ltd (No 2) (VTD 18866) 29.76
Don Aldridge Associates (VTD 11452) 52.143
Don Bosco Onroerend Goed BV *v* Staatssecretaris van Financiën, ECJ Case C-461/08;
    [2010] STC 476 .... 22.378
Don Pasquale, CA [1990] STC 556 .... 2.141
Donaghy (R) (VTD 19802) 15.46
Donald (GD & AY) (VTD 17894) 18.541
Donaldson (JW) (VTD 3668) 44.65
Donaldson (P) (VTD 1082) 2.225
Donaldson's College (VTD 19258) 7.84
Doncaster Borough Council (VTD 12458) 42.2
Doncaster Skillshop Ltd (VTD 17433) 21.27
Donnison & Smith Engineering Ltd (VTD 5651) 18.397
Dorfman (S) (VTD 18816) 1.53
Dori (F) *v* Recreb Srl, ECJ Case C-91/92; [1994] 1 ECR 3325; [1994] 1 CMLR 665;
    [1995] All ER (EC) 1 .... 22.20
Doris (D) (t/a Gardiners of Denny), [2011] UKFTT 142 (TC), TC01016 .... 67.85
Dormers Builders (London) Ltd, CA [1989] STC 539; [1989] 2 All ER 938 .... 62.430
Dos Santos Tavares (A) (VTD 4956) 18.278
Dotter *v* Willimaier, ECJ Case C-384/98; [2002] STC 1200 .... 22.279
Double D Freight Services Ltd (VTD 3987) 18.374
Double Luck Restaurant Ltd (VTD 578) 3.157
Double Shield Window Co Ltd (VTD 1771) 62.421
Dougall, Ch D 2000, [2001] BPIR 269 .... 37.21

Douros (T) (t/a Olympic Financial Services) (VTD 12454) 46.222
Dove Services (Manchester) Ltd (VTD 5510) 18.313
Doveton (RM) (VTD 4164) 18.485
Dow Chemical Co Ltd [1996] VATDR 52 (VTD 13954) 18.38
Dow Engineering (VTD 5771) 18.12
Dow-Nell Construction Co Ltd (VTD 16871) 36.46
Downes Crediton Golf Club Ltd (VTD 868) 13.23
Downey Ltd (VTD 11862) 52.158
Dowse (AJ) (VTD 46) 41.136
Doyle (JPS) (VTD 13742) 44.79
Doyle (PJ) (VTD 8811) 51.38
DPA (Market Research) Ltd (VTD 14751) 8.48
DPC European Transport (VTD 16177) 18.328
DR Auto Repair Tech (VTD 7489) 52.323
Dragon Futures Ltd (No 2) (VTD 19186) 36.95
Dragon Futures Ltd (No 3) [2006] VATDR 348 (VTD 19831) 36.115
Dragon Futures Ltd (No 4) (VTD 20868) 36.116
Draper (DA) (VTD 1107) 5.29
Draxtech Ltd (VTD 6432) 52.40
Dreestone Ltd (VTD 1900) 14.45
Drennan (J) Partnership (VTD 15190) 18.278
Dresswell (Newtownards) Ltd (VTD 3568) 18.79
Drexlodge Ltd (VTD 5614) 1.50
Drillfact Ltd (VTD 3009) 18.240
Drosden Plantruck Ltd, [2009] UKFTT 115 (TC), TC00083 .... 57.114
Drummond (P) (VTD 13100) 19.55
Drury (Mrs J) (VTD 6030) 19.90
Drury (NP), [2009] UKFTT 50 (TC), TC00029 .... 57.29
DS Supplies Ltd (VTD 13559) 7.43
DS Talafair & Sons (VTD 16144) 6.14
D'Souza, Ch D 27 February 2001 unreported. 2.212
DT Engineering Ltd (VTD 7912) 18.286
DTA Ross & Son (VTD 10755) 17.3
DTC (CTC) Ltd v Gary Sargent & Co, Ch D [1996] BCC 290 .... 40.75
Du Beau Ltd (VTD 7667) 52.314
Du Vergier (E) & Co Ltd [1973] VATTR 11 (VTD 4) 32.1
Dudda v Finanzamt Bergisch Gladbach, ECJ Case C-327/94; [1996] STC 1290; [1996]
    1 ECR 4595; [1996] 3 CMLR 1063 .... 22.214
Dudman Group Ltd, FTT [2009] UKFTT 52 (TC), TC00031 .... 18.547
Duffree (MG) (VTD 15793) 57.141
Duffy (JJ) (VTD 15343) 57.7
Duffy & Carr Group plc (VTD 11728) 36.667
Dugdale (L) & Son (VTD 5431) 51.28
Duke v GEC Reliance Ltd, HL [1988] 1 AC 718; [1988] 1 All ER 626 .... 22.24
Dulay (Mr & Mrs) (t/a Star Fisheries) (VTD 16443) 65.96
Dullaghan (M) [2000] VATDR 188 (VTD 16407) 35.2
Duncan (G) (t/a G Duncan Motor Services) [2007] VATDR 114 (VTD 20100) 44.165
Dundee & Angus Dyslexic Association (Mrs J Smith for) (VTD 12909) 11.23
Dunelm (Castle Homes) Ltd (VTD 16052) 52.410
Dunham (IF) (VTD 13359) 36.618
Dunhill (J) (VTD 13313) 57.130
Dunholme Decorators Ltd (VTD 16484) 14.34
Dunkirk Panel Services Ltd (VTD 12834) 18.153
Dunn (Dr) & Others (VTD 14788) 46.191
Dunning (TL) (VTD 12739) 2.327
Dunster (WR) [2010] UKFTT 462 (TC), TC00727 .... 15.32
Dunston (C) (VTD 5705) 18.485
Dunwood Travel Ltd, CA [2008] STC 959; [2008] EWCA Civ 174 .... 3.98
Dureau (CB) (VTD 9355) 52.140
Dureau (CB) (No 2) (VTD 14643) 36.223
Durham Aged Mineworkers' Homes Association, QB [1994] STC 553 .... 62.45

Durham City Car Co Ltd (VTD 3604) 18.83
Durham River Trips Ltd (VTD 17328) 66.24
Durkin, Burford *v*, CA 1990, [1991] STC 7 .... 3.94
Durnell Marketing Ltd (VTD 17813) 36.321
Durrant (P) (VTD 17430) 51.170
Durwin Banks (No 1) (VTD 18904) 29.98
Durwin Banks (No 2) [2008] VATDR 429 (VTD 20695) 29.93
Dust Extraction (International) Ltd (VTD 3175) 18.262
Duval (F) (t/a L'Ecluse Restaurant) (VTD 12082) 18.563
Duvan Estates Ltd (VTD 7040) 52.72
Duwel (D) (VTD 3483) 57.187
DVK Executive Hotels (VTD 4786) 18.377
Dwek (M & N) & Co Ltd (VTD 7082) 52.281
Dwyer Property Ltd, QB [1995] STC 1035 .... 46.58
Dyball (D) & Son (VTD 4863) 36.278
Dyer (P & G) (VTD 390) 57.84
Dyer (T) (VTD 5356) 36.379
Dyer (T) (VTD 16359) 53.21
Dyer (T) (No 3), CS [2005] STC 715 .... 57.33
Dynamic Construction Ltd (VTD 12079) 40.43
Dynic (UK) Ltd (VTD 7412) 52.204
Dyrektor Izby Skarbowej w Bialymstoku *v* Profaktor Kulesza Frankowski Józwiak
    Orlowski sp j, ECJ Case 188/09; 29 July 2010 unreported 22.477
Dyrektor Izby Skarbowej w Krakowie, Magoora sp zoo *v*, ECJ Case C-414/07;
    22 December 2008 unreported 22.426
Dyrektor Izby Skarbowej w Lodzi, Dankowski *v*, ECJ Case C-438/09; 22 December
    2010 unreported 22.473
Dyrektor Izby Skarbowej w Rzeszowie, Kronospan Mielec sp zoo *v*, ECJ Case C-222/09;
    [2011] STC 80 .... 22.222
Dyrektor Izby Skarbowej w Warszawie, Kuc *v*, ECJ Case C-181/10; [2011] STC 2230
    .... 20.5
Dyrektor Izby Skarbowej we Wroclawiu Osrodek Zamiejscowy w Walbrzychu,
    Sosnowska *v*, ECJ Case C-25/07; 10 July 2008 unreported 22.440
Dyrham Park Country Club Ltd, [1978] VATTR 244 (VTD 700) 13.31
Dysart Developments Ltd (VTD 17333) 36.512
Dyslexia Institute Ltd (The) (VTD 12654) 11.22

E

E & G Catering Services Ltd (VTD 15552) 29.16
E Goozeberry Ltd (VTD 20088) 18.543
E Moss Ltd (VTD 19510) 33.16
E Stringer (Paints) Ltd (VTD 16319) 62.323
Eadon (Mr & Mrs) (t/a Motaelectrics) (VTD 1692) 36.436
Eagle Capital Corporation Ltd (VTD 7447) 52.347
Eagle Trust plc (VTD 12871) 36.161
EAP Ltd (VTD 12089) 18.436
Earlswood Environmental Systems Ltd (VTD 2605) 51.98
Earthshine Ltd (No 1), [2010] UKFTT 67 (TC), TC00379 .... 2.286
Earthshine Ltd (No 2), [2010] UKFTT 314 (TC), TC00601 .... 2.490
Earthshine Ltd (No 3), [2011] UKFTT 667 (TC), TC01509 .... 36.113
Easden Manufacturing Co Ltd (VTD 10116) 4.16
East India Devonshire Sports & Public Schools Club Ltd, [2010] UKFTT 627 (TC),
    TC00866 .... 18.425
East Kent Medical Services Ltd (VTD 16095) 6.8
East Kilbride Golf Club (VTD 5503) 62.420
East London Fancy Goods Ltd (VTD 5542) 25.23
East Norfolk Sixth Form College (VTD 20816) 15.203
Eastbourne Borough Council, Wren *v*, ECJ [1993] 3 CMLR 166 .... 22.27

Eastbourne Town Radio Cars Association, HL [2001] STC 606; [2001] UKHL 19; [2001] 1 WLR 794; [2001] 2 All ER 597 .... 62.32
Eastbridge Joiners & Shopfitters (VTD 4229) 18.206
Eastgate Christian Bookshop Ltd (VTD 16766) 59.14
Eastwell Manor Ltd, [2011] UKFTT 293 (TC), TC01155 .... 18.619
Eastwood (dec'd), Re, CA [1974] 3 All ER 603 .... 2.356, 2.452
Eastwood Care Homes (Ilkeston) Ltd, CA [2001] STC 1629 .... 32.7
Eastwood Care Homes (Ilkeston) Ltd, QB 18 January 2000, Times 7.3.2000 .... 2.173
EasyJet plc, [2003] VATDR 559 (VTD 18230) 46.175
Easyway Productions Ltd (VTD 14938) 33.27
Eaton (Dr CJ) (VTD 2315) 11.7
Eaton (SM) & Grove (SL) (VTD 16575) 18.208
EB Central Services Ltd, CA [2008] STC 2209; [2008] EWCA Civ 486 .... 66.42
EBA Systems Ltd (VTD 4770) 18.200
EC Commission v Austria (Republic of), ECJ Case C-128/05; [2008] STC 2610 ... 22.479
EC Commission v Belgium (Kingdom of), ECJ Case 324/82; [1984] ECR 1861; [1985] 1 CMLR 364 .... 22.498
EC Commission v EU Council, ECJ Case C-533/03; [2007] STC 1121 .... 22.565
EC Commission v Finland, ECJ Case C-169/00; [2004] STC 1232 .... 22.96
EC Commission v Finland, ECJ Case C-495/01; [2004] All ER (D) 265 (Jul) 22.248
EC Commission v Finland, ECJ Case C-246/08; 29 October 2009 unreported 22.132
EC Commission v French Republic (No 1), ECJ Case 50/87; [1988] ECR 4797; [1989] 1 CMLR 505 .... 22.397
EC Commission v French Republic (No 2), ECJ Case C-30/89; [1990] 1 ECR 691 .... 22.210
EC Commission v French Republic (No 3), ECJ Case C-68/92; [1993] 1 ECR 5881; [1997] STC 684; [1995] 2 CMLR 1 .... 22.218
EC Commission v French Republic (No 4), ECJ Case C-43/96; [1998] STC 805; [1998] All ER (EC) 951 .... 22.422
EC Commission v French Republic (No 5), ECJ Case C-60/96; [1997] 1 ECR 3827; [1999] STC 480 .... 22.336
EC Commission v French Republic (No 6), ECJ Case C-276/97; 12 September 2000 unreported 22.135
EC Commission v French Republic (No 7), ECJ Case C-429/97; [2001] STC 156 ... 22.533
EC Commission v French Republic (No 8), ECJ Case C-481/98; [2001] STC 919 ... 22.506
EC Commission v French Republic (No 9), ECJ Case C-76/99; 11 January 2001 unreported 22.273
EC Commission v French Republic (No 10), ECJ Case C-345/99; [2003] STC 372 .... 22.423
EC Commission v French Republic (No 11), ECJ Case C-404/99; 29 March 2001 unreported 22.241
EC Commission v French Republic (No 12), ECJ Case C-40/00; [2003] STC 390 ... 22.409
EC Commission v French Republic (No 13), ECJ Case C-384/01; 8 May 2003 unreported 22.269
EC Commission v French Republic (No 14), ECJ Case C-243/03; [2006] STC 1098 .... 22.450
EC Commission v French Republic (No 15), ECJ Case C-492/08; 17 June 2010 unreported 20.52
EC Commission v French Republic (No 16), ECJ Case C-94/09; 6 May 2010 unreported 20.53
EC Commission v Germany (Federal Republic of) (No 1), ECJ Case C-74/91; [1992] 1 ECR 5437; [1996] STC 843 .... 22.486
EC Commission v Germany (Federal Republic of) (No 2), ECJ Case C-427/98; [2003] STC 301 .... 22.237
EC Commission v Germany (Federal Republic of) (No 3), ECJ Case C-287/00; [2002] STC 982 .... 22.303
EC Commission v Germany (Federal Republic of) (No 4), ECJ Case C-109/02; [2006] STC 1587 .... 22.265
EC Commission v Germany (Federal Republic of) (No 5), ECJ Case C-144/02; [2004] All ER(D) 264(Jul) 22.248

EC Commission *v* Germany (Federal Republic of) (No 6), ECJ Case C-401/06; [2008] STC 2906 ... 22.224
EC Commission *v* Hellenic Republic, ECJ Case C-331/94; [1996] STC 1168; [1996] 1 ECR 2675 ... 22.211
EC Commission *v* Hellenic Republic, ECJ Case C-260/98; 12 September 2000 unreported ... 22.136
EC Commission *v* Hellenic Republic, ECJ Case C-13/06; [2007] STC 194 ... 22.329
EC Commission *v* Hungary (Republic of), ECJ Case C-274/10; 28 July 2011 unreported ... 20.115
EC Commission *v* Ireland (Republic of), ECJ Case C-358/97; 12 September 2000 unreported ... 22.135
EC Commission *v* Ireland (Republic of), ECJ Case C-554/07; 16 July 2009 unreported ... 20.9
EC Commission *v* Italian Republic, ECJ Case 3/86; [1988] ECR 3369, [1989] 3 CMLR 748 ... 22.482
EC Commission *v* Italian Republic (No 2), ECJ Case 257/86; [1988] ECR 3249; [1990] 3 CMLR 718; [1991] BTC 5104 ... 22.386
EC Commission *v* Italian Republic (No 3), ECJ Case 122/87; [1988] ECR 2919; [1989] BVC 232; [1989] 3 CMLR 844 ... 22.270
EC Commission *v* Italian Republic (No 4), ECJ Case C-45/95; [1997] STC 1062; [1997] 1 ECR 3605 ... 22.349
EC Commission *v* Italian Republic (No 5), ECJ Case C-78/00; [2003] BTC 5255 ... 22.442
EC Commission *v* Italian Republic (No 6), ECJ Case C-381/01; [2004] All ER (D) 271 (Jul) ... 22.248
EC Commission *v* Italian Republic (No 7), ECJ Case C-132/06; 17 July 2008 unreported ... 22.469
EC Commission *v* Italian Republic (No 8), ECJ Case C-174/07; 11 December 2008 unreported ... 22.470
EC Commission *v* Italian Republic (No 9), ECJ Case C-244/08; 16 July 2009 unreported ... 22.531
EC Commission *v* Luxembourg (Grand Duchy of), ECJ Case C-69/92; [1993] 1 ECR 5907; [1997] STC 712; [1995] 2 CMLR 1 ... 22.219
EC Commission *v* Netherlands (Kingdom of), ECJ Case 235/85; [1987] ECR 1471; [1988] 2 CMLR 921 ... 22.127
EC Commission *v* Netherlands (Kingdom of), ECJ Case C-408/97; 12 September 2000 unreported ... 22.136
EC Commission *v* Netherlands (Kingdom of), ECJ Case C-338/98; [2003] STC 1506; [2004] 1 WLR 35 ... 22.403
EC Commission *v* Netherlands (Kingdom of), ECJ Case C-41/09; 3 March 2011 unreported ... 20.54
EC Commission *v* Poland (Kingdom of), ECJ Case C-49/09; 28 October 2010 unreported ... 20.55
EC Commission *v* Portuguese Republic, ECJ Case C-276/98; [2001] BTC 5135 ... 22.264
EC Commission *v* Portuguese Republic, ECJ Case C-462/05; 12 June 2008 unreported ... 22.263
EC Commission *v* Republic of Ireland, ECJ Case C-358/97; 12 September 2000 unreported ... 22.135
EC Commission *v* Republic of Ireland, ECJ Case C-554/07; 16 July 2009 unreported ... 20.9
EC Commission *v* Spain (Kingdom of), ECJ Case C-73/92; [1993] 1 ECR 5997; [1997] STC 700; [1995] 2 CMLR 1 ... 22.219
EC Commission *v* Spain (Kingdom of), ECJ Case C-124/96; [1998] STC 1237 ... 22.313
EC Commission *v* Spain (Kingdom of), ECJ Case C-414/97; 16 September 1999 unreported ... 22.102
EC Commission *v* Spain (Kingdom of), ECJ Case C-83/99; 18 January 2001 unreported ... 22.262
EC Commission *v* Spain (Kingdom of), ECJ Case C-204/03; [2006] STC 1087 ... 22.449
EC Commission *v* Spain (Kingdom of), ECJ Case C-154/08; 12 November 2009 unreported ... 22.98
EC Commission *v* Sweden, ECJ Case C-463/02; [2004] All ER (D) 267 (Jul) ... 22.248

EC Commission *v* United Kingdom, ECJ Case C-353/85; [1988] STC 251; [1988] ECR
817 .... 22.271
EC Commission *v* United Kingdom (No 2), ECJ Case C-416/85; [1988] STC 456;
[1988] ECR 3127 .... 22.505
EC Commission *v* United Kingdom (No 3), ECJ Case C-359/97; [2000] STC 777 ... 22.134
EC Commission *v* United Kingdom (No 4), ECJ Case C-33/03; [2005] STC 582 .... 22.404
EC Commission *v* United Kingdom (No 5), ECJ Case C-305/03; [2007] STC 1211
.... 22.98
EC Commission *v* United Kingdom (No 6), ECJ Case C-349/03; [2006] STC 1944
.... 22.564
EC Commission *v* United Kingdom (No 7), ECJ Case C-582/08; [2010] STC 2364
.... 22.546
EC Commission, Diputacion Foral de Alava *v*, ECJ Case T-346/99; [2002] All ER (D)
338 (Oct) 22.10
EC Commission, Diputacion Foral de Guipuzcoa *v*, ECJ Case T-269/99; [2002] All ER
(D) 337 (Oct) 22.9
EC Commission, Germany (Federal Republic of) *v*, ECJ Case 332/85; [1985] ECR
5143 .... 22.549
EC Commission, Territorio Historico de Alava *v*, ECJ Case T-346/99; [2002] All ER (D)
338 (Oct) 22.10
EC Commission, Territorio Historico de Guipuzcoa *v*, ECJ Case T-269/99;
[2002] All ER (D) 337 (Oct) 22.9
Eccles (ACS) & Co (VTD 2057) 36.291
Eccles (PC) (VTD 13372) 3.124
Eccleston (PAJ) (VTD 16037) 44.30
Eckels (AD & JR) (VTD 15593) 58.3
Eco-Hygiene Ltd, [2011] UKFTT 754 (TC), TC01591 .... 18.619
Ecotrade SpA *v* Agenzia Entrate Ufficio Genova 3, ECJ Cases C-95/07 and C-96/07;
[2008] STC 2626 .... 22.435
ECU Group plc (The), [2010] SFTD 1108; [2010] UKFTT 297 (TC), TC00585 .... 27.9
Eddie Stobart Group Ltd (VTD 18873) 5.23
Eddystone Computers Ltd (VTD 11018) 36.465
Eden District Council (VTD 10245) 52.261
Edgecox (AGH) (VTD 5334) 18.43
Edgemond Group Ltd (VTD 11620) 46.41
Edgeskill Ltd, [2011] UKFTT 393 (TC), TC01248 .... 36.113
Edgewater Motel Ltd *v* New Zealand Commissioner of Inland Revenue, PC [2004] STC
1382; [2004] UKPC 44 .... 14.114
Edgley Management Ltd (VTD 17410) 36.146
Edilizia Industriale Siderurgica Srl *v* Ministero delle Finanze, ECJ Case C-231/96; [1998]
1 ECR 4951 .... 22.50
Edinburgh Leisure, [2004] VATDR 394 (VTD 18784) 42.20
Edinburgh Piano Co Ltd (The) (VTD 16132) 52.415
Edinburgh University (VTD 6569) 46.145
Edinburgh University (No 2) (VTD 10936) 21.10
Edinburgh Telford College, CS [2006] STC 1291; [2006] CSIH 13 .... 22.149
Edmond Homes Ltd (VTD 11567) 15.229
Education & Jobs Fairs Ltd (VTD 15231) 7.118
Edwards (A) (VTD 16849) 51.34
Edwards (CW) (VTD 16245) 50.17
Edwards (PJ & ML) (VTD 15533) 57.114
Edwards *v* Bairstow & Harrison, HL 1955, 36 TC 207 . 3.6, 36.97, 62.109, 62.325, 67.61
Edwards, Metford *v*, KB [1915] 1 KB 172 .... 13.29
Edwick (DC) (VTD 10962) 18.83
Eftekhari (J) (VTD 10271) 52.21
Egan (JT) (VTD 7528) 50.95
Egerton Transplant Ltd (VTD 6505) 18.295
Eggleton (M) (VTD 18287) 50.94
Eggleton (R) (VTD 7932) 52.69
Egleton & Others, Ch D [2006] EWHC 2313 (Ch); [2007] 1 All ER 606 .... 14.110
Eglington DIY Ltd (VTD 9858) 18.421

EGN BV Filiale Italiana *v* Agenzia delle Entrate Ufficio di Roma 2, ECJ Case C-377/08; [2009] STC 2544 .... 22.417
Eidographics Ltd [1991] VATTR 449 (VTD 6788) 18.13
Einberger *v* Hauptzollamt Freiburg (No 2), ECJ Case 294/84; [1984] ECR 1177; [1985] 1 CMLR 765 .... 22.99
Einfuhr- und Vorratstelle für Getriede und Futtermittel, Internationale Handelsgesellschaft mbH *v*, ECJ [1970] ECR 1145; [1972] CMLR 255 .... 18.616
El Al Israel Airlines Ltd (VTD 12750) 66.38
EL Davis & Co Ltd (VTD 1477) 36.352
Eland (Mr & Mrs G) (VTD 5716) 18.125
Elanders (UK) Ltd (VTD 6137) 52.69
Elcomatic Ltd (VTD 14456) 18.112
Elder (RD & SM) (VTD 15881,15882) 57.80
Elder (RD & SM) (VTD 17653) 2.359
Elder Home Care Ltd (VTD 11185) 33.4
Eleanor Cleaning Services (VTD 11353) 47.2
Electric Tool Repair Ltd [1986] VATTR 257 (VTD 2208) 51.109
Electricity Commission (Balmain Electric Light Co), NSW CA [1957] SR(NSW) 100 .... 65.46
Electritec Ltd (VTD 12423) 18.341
Electronic Data Systems Ltd, CA [2003] STC 688; [2003] EWCA Civ 492 .... 22.361
Eleftheriou (L & A) (t/a Picnic Kebab House) (VTD 16659) 57.183
Elegant Clothing (Blackburn) Ltd (VTD 14739) 40.78
Elesa Ltd (VTD 10308) 17.2
Elga & Askar Co Ltd and Another, QB [1983] STC 628 .... 67.90
Elgar Hotel Worcester Ltd (VTD 19579) 51.129
Elgindata, Re (No 2), CA [1992] 1 WLR 1207; [1993] 1 All ER 232 .... 2.413
Elias Gale Racing, QB 1998, [1999] STC 66 .... 3.168
Elida Gibbs Ltd, ECJ Case C-317/94; [1996] STC 1387; [1996] 1 ECR 5339; [1997] 2 WLR 477; [1997] All ER (EC) 53 .... 22.235
Elim Church Tamworth (Trustees) (VTD 19190) 15.206
Elite Mobile plc, oao, R *v* C & E, QB 2004, [2005] STC 275; [2004] EWHC 2923 (Admin) 2.531
Elizabethan Banquets (VTD 1795) 8.29
Ellen Garage (Oldham) Ltd [1994] VATTR 392 (VTD 12407) 40.11
Ellicott (Mrs V) (VTD 11472) 21.36
Ellinas (CT, C & P) (t/a Hunts Cross Supper Bar) (VTD 15346) 2.282
Ellinas (CT, C & P) (t/a Hunts Cross Supper Bar) (VTD 16105) 50.127
Ellinas (PA) (VTD 16576) 50.73
Elliniko Dimosio (Greek State) v Karageorgou & Others, ECJ Cases C-78/02 to C-80/02; [2006] STC 1654 .... 22.464
Elliott (AJ & A) (VTD 4926) 15.279
Elliott (K) (t/a Harbourne Engineering) (VTD 16010) 18.585
Elliott (Mr & Mrs), QB [1993] STC 369 .... 15.195
Elliott (S) (VTD 13432) 14.40
Ellis (CK) (VTD 18279) 50.154
Ellis (N, J & N) (VTD 18460) 52.440
Elm Milk Ltd, CA [2006] STC 792; [2006] EWCA Civ 164 .... 44.138
Elmec (Blackburn) Ltd (VTD 9222) 52.378
Elmeka NE *v* Ipourgos Ikonomikon, ECJ Case C-181/04; 14 September 2006 unreported 22.390
Elscint (GB) Ltd (VTD 1654) 69.5
Elsham Golf Club Ltd (VTD 18107) 46.66
Elstead (Thursley Road) Recreational Trust (VTD 18852) 2.6
Eltham Park Insurance Brokers Ltd (VTD 14306) 46.189
Elton (RD) (VTD 11590) 36.262
Eltraco (UK) Ltd (VTD 9089) 52.155
Elvington Ltd (VTD 14537) 63.23
EMAG Handel Eder OHG *v* Finanzlandesdirektion für Kärnten, ECJ Case C-245/04; [2007] STC 1461 .... 22.517
EMAP Consumer Magazines Ltd (VTD 13322) 5.95

EMAP MacLaren Ltd, QB [1997] STC 490 .... 67.105
Emberson (Mr & Mrs R) (VTD 17604) 15.139
Emblaze Mobility Solutions Ltd [2010] UKFTT 410 (TC), TC00680 .... 36.88
Embleton Ltd (VTD 12897) 52.225
Emery (DJ) (VTD 187) 5.54
EMI Group plc, ECJ Case C-581/08; [2010] STC 2609 .... 22.164
EMI Records v Spillane and Others, Ch D [1986] STC 374 .... 14.88
Emir 8 Petroleum plc (VTD 17400) 68.2
EMIS National User Group (VTD 19645) 64.6
Emmabee Fashions Ltd (VTD 5077) 18.216
Emmanuel Church Northwood Parochial Church Council (DC Morgan) [1973] VATTR
    76 (VTD 21) 2.2
Emmaus Ltd (VTD 11679) 36.497
Emmott v Minister for Social Welfare & Another, ECJ Case C-208/90; [1991] 1 ECR
    4269; [1991] 3 CMLR 894 .... 22.45
Emperor Enterprises Ltd (VTD 11038) 19.21
Emphasis Ltd [1995] VATDR 419 (VTD 13759) 29.14
Empire Contracts Ltd (VTD 7200) 36.479
Empire Stores Ltd, ECJ Case C-33/93; [1994] STC 623; [1994] 1 ECR 2329;
    [1994] 1 CMLR 751; [1994] 2 All ER 90 .... 22.234
Empowerment Enterprises Ltd, CS 2006, [2008] STC 1835; [2006] CSIH 46 .... 22.306
Empresa de Desenvolvimento Mineiro SGPS v Fazenda Publica, ECJ Case C-77/01;
    [2005] STC 65 .... 22.448
Empress Car Company (Abertillery) Ltd (VTD 4832) 14.120
Empress of India Restaurant [1997] VATDR 242 (VTD 15087) 2.319
Emsland-Stärke GmbH v Hauptzollamt Hamburg-Jonas, ECJ Case C-110/99,
    [2001] All ER (D) 34 (Jan) 22.59
Enderby Transport Ltd (VTD 1607) 4.1
Endersby (Mrs B) (VTD 5754) 51.89
ENEL, Costa v, ECJ Case 6/64; [1964] ECR 585; [1964] CMLR 425 .... 22.21
Enel Maritsa Iztok 3AD v Direktor Obzhalvane i upravlenie na izpalnenieto NAP, ECJ
    Case C-107/10; 12 May 2011 unreported 20.114
Enersys Holdings UK Ltd, FTT [2010] SFTD 387; [2010] UKFTT 20 (TC), TC00335
    .... 18.620
Enever (Mrs WB) (VTD 1537) 41.45
Engineering Building Services Ltd (VTD 10875) 52.251
Engineering Quality Consultants (VTD 16634) 36.486
Engineering Services (Bridgend) Ltd (VTD 17556) 4.7
England (BA) (VTD 5292) 18.198
English (J) (VTD 15879) 36.577
English-Speaking Union of the Commonwealth (The) [1980] VATTR 184 (VTD 1023)
    .... 13.5
Enkler v Finanzamt Homburg, ECJ Case C-230/94; [1996] STC 1316; [1996] 1 ECR
    4517; [1997] 1 CMLR 881 .... 22.114
Enron Europe Ltd (No 1), Ch D [2006] STC 1339; [2006] EWHC 824 (Ch) 62.465
Enron Europe Ltd (No 2) (VTD 20436) 3.82
Entertainment Group of Companies Ltd (The) [2000] VATDR 447 (VTD 16639) 8.26
Enterprise Safety Coaches Ltd [1991] VATTR 74 (VTD 5391) 52.81
Enviroengineering Ltd (No 2), [2011] UKFTT 366 (TC), TC01221 .... 2.26
EP Mooney Ltd (VTD 6418) 52.322
Epsom Justices, R v (ex p. Bell & Another), QB 1988, [1989] STC 169 .... 14.97
Equal Opportunities Commission, ex p., R v Secretary of State for Employment, HL
    [1994] 1 All ER 910 .... 22.36
Equiname Ltd (VTD 7592) 52.87
Equitable Life Assurance Society [2003] VATDR 523 (VTD 18072) 38.26
ERF Ltd [2010] UKFTT 238 (TC), TC00537 .... 50.86
Eric Ladbroke (Holbeach) Ltd (VTD 1557) 65.54
Eric Taylor Testimonial Match Committee (The) [1975] VATTR 8 (VTD 139) 7.87
Ericsons Fashions Ltd (VTD 6241) 52.163
Erinmore Homes Ltd (VTD 17233) 15.235
Ernest George Ltd (VTD 1760) 36.444

Ernest Lee (Electrical Services) Ltd (VTD 3584) 18.570
Ernest Platt (Bury) Ltd (VTD 13208) 18.185
Ernest William (Drums) Ltd (VTD 4278) 18.553
Ernst & Young, [1997] VATDR 183 (VTD 15100) 8.23, 8.43
Erotic Center BVBA, Belgische Staat v, ECJ Case C-3/09; [2010] STC 1018 .... 22.268
Errey's Furnishing Ltd (VTD 4110) 18.352
Erskine (Messrs WB) (VTD 6310) 52.74
Erskine (A) Electrical Co Ltd (VTD 10139) 18.436
Esporta Ltd, [2011] UKFTT 633 (TC), TC01475 .... 62.149
ESS International Ltd, [1992] VATTR 336 (VTD 7771) 62.90
Essex (A & S) (t/a Essex Associates) (VTD 15072) 57.60
État Belge v Henfling & Others (administrators of Tiercé Franco-Belge SA), ECJ Case
    C-464/10; [2011] STC 1851 .... 22.189
Ethical Trading Initiative, [2010] UKFTT 423 (TC), TC00690 .... 64.11
ETS (Scotland) Ltd (VTD 6987) 52.344
EU Council, EC Commission v, ECJ Case C-533/03; [2007] STC 1121 .... 22.565
Euphony Communications Ltd, Ch D 2003, [2004] STC 301; [2003] EWHC 3008
    (Ch) 67.58
Eureka! The Children's Museum (VTD 15710) 5.59
Euro Catering Equipment Ltd (VTD 14375) 14.20
Euro Properties (Scotland) Ltd (VTD 15291) 6.39
Euro Quest Trading Ltd, [2011] UKFTT 145 (TC), TC01019 .... 36.113
Euro Stock Shop Ltd, UT [2010] SFTD 2454; [2010] UKUT 259 (TCC) 36.117
Euro Tyre Holding BV v Staatssecretaris van Financiën, ECJ Case C-430/09; [2011] STC
    798 .... 22.522
Eurobait Ltd (VTD 17252) 29.109
Eurocare Impex Trading Ltd (VTD 17516) 52.396
Eurodental Sàrl, Administration de l'Enregistrement et des Domaines v, ECJ Case
    C-240/05; [2007] STC 275 .... 22.288
Euromech Ltd (VTD 17429) 18.586
Euromer Stevedores Ltd (VTD 11755) 52.283
Euromove International Movers Ltd (VTD 1710) 65.56
Europa Plaza Developments Ltd (VTD 19196) 52.441
European Computer Centre Ltd (VTD 7220) 52.151
European Independent Purchasing Co Ltd (VTD 20697) 29.80
European Lift Services Ltd (VTD 15551) 52.448
European Publishing Consultants Ltd (VTD 13841) 5.96
European Tour Operators Association, [2011] UKFTT 88 (TC), TC00965 .... 64.8
Europeans Ltd (No 1) (VTD 20796) 2.272
Europeans Ltd (No 2) (VTD 20883) 36.106
Europeans Ltd (No 3), Ch D [2011] EWHC 948 (Ch); [2011] STC 1449 .... 2.371
Europhone International Ltd v Frontel Communications Ltd, Ch D [2001] STC 1399
    .... 62.470
Europlex Technologies (UK) Ltd (VTD 18042) 18.590
Eurosel Ltd [2010] UKFTT 451 (TC), TC00716 .... 36.121
Eurospray Midlands Ltd (VTD 16775) 53.12
Eurostar Telecom Ltd, [2011] UKFTT 75 (TC), TC00953 .... 36.113
Eurotunnel plc & Others, ex p., R v HM Customs & Excise, QB 1995 unreported
    .... 2.337
Eurotunnel SA & Others v SeaFrance, ECJ Case C-408/95; [1996] BTC 5200 ...... 22.524
Euroware Fashions Ltd (VTD 3600, 4012) 18.374
Euroweb Ltd (VTD 6843) 52.281
Evangelical Movement of Wales [2004] VATDR 138 (VTD 18556) 33.69
Evans (AG) (VTD 1453) 7.37
Evans (AL) (VTD 7639) 18.391
Evans (Dr AR), [1976] VATTR 175 (VTD 285) 33.17
Evans (CE, EM & PC) (t/a Coney Leasing) (VTD 17510) 10.10
Evans (CN) (VTD 4415) 55.27
Evans (CP) (VTD 4717) 18.280
Evans (DR) (VTD 13290) 57.188
Evans (EM, PG & CP) (VTD 10532) 57.59

Evans (MJ) (t/a ATC) (VTD 14665) 52.425
Evans (P) (VTD 17264) 15.207
Evans (RV) (t/a Britannia Services), [2011] UKFTT 439 (TC), TC01292 .... 57.29
Evans (S), [1979] VATTR 194 (VTD 836) 14.22
Evans (S) (t/a EPS Plant & Safety Services) (VTD 18644) 52.342
Evans (Mrs S), [2011] UKFTT 464 (TC), TC01314 .... 51.173
Evans (VW) (VTD 14662) 36.237
Evans (WB) (t/a BSEC) (VTD 18432) 19.92
Evans & Marland Ltd (t/a Greyform Publications) [1988] VATTR 125 (VTD 3158)
.... 5.94
Evans & Others, QB 1981, [1982] STC 342 .... 47.1, 50.7
Evans (DR) & Rees (GL) (t/a L & R Building Contractors) (VTD 15738) 52.393
Evans Brothers (Glass & Glazing) Ltd (VTD 14333) 50.124
Evans Transport (VTD 2974) 18.70
Evensis Ltd (VTD 17218) 8.25
Eventful Management Ltd (VTD 20300) 28.9
Everest Ltd, [2010] UKFTT 621 (TC); [2011] SFTD 217, TC00863 .... 67.147
Everett (A & A) (VTD 3669) 18.96
Everett (DF & A) (VTD 1606) 36.301
Everett (Mrs DG) (VTD 11736) 66.3
Everitt (A) (t/a Reading Lasses) (VTD 17408) 15.143
Eversleigh Investments & Property Co Ltd (VTD 9646) 52.69
Everything Everywhere Ltd, ECJ Case C-276/09; [2011] STC 316 .... 22.363
Evolink Ltd (VTD 18207) 2.13
Evolution Export Trading Ltd, oao, R v HMRC, QB [2007] EWHC 521 (Admin) .. 36.653
EW (Computer Training) Ltd (VTD 5453) 5.35
Exact Electronics Ltd (VTD 11391) 14.2
Excel RTI Solutions Ltd, [2010] UKFTT 519 (TC), TC00774 .... 36.113
Excel Shopfitting Ltd (VTD 16270) 18.425
Excell Consumer Industries Ltd, [1985] VATTR 94 (VTD 1865) 36.680
Exchange Car Hire, [1992] VATTR 430 (VTD 9343) 18.30
Exchange Club Ltd (VTD 3031) 18.71
Executive Security (Wentworth) Ltd (VTD 15052) 18.359
Exeter Golf and Country Club Ltd, CA [1981] STC 211 .... 13.32
Expert Systems Design Ltd (VTD 7974) 2.43
Expert Witness Institute (The), CA 2001, [2002] STC 42; [2001] EWCA Civ 1882;
  [2002] 1 WLR 1674 .... 22.311
Express Computers UK Ltd, [2011] UKFTT 572 (TC), TC01415 .... 36.80
Express Medicare Ltd, [2000] VATDR 377 (VTD 16969) 1.78
Express Pipework Co (VTD 12108) 2.327
Express Vending Ltd (VTD 13252) 18.295
Extrastable Services Ltd (VTD 13911) 14.32
Eydmann (JL), [2011] UKFTT 732 (TC), TC01569 .... 52.405
Eye Gee Co Ltd (The) (VTD 1269) 2.368
Eye-Tech Opticians, [2001] VATDR 468 (VTD 17498) 33.9
Eyears Ltd (VTD 20167) 1.46
Eyre (K) (VTD 5200) 18.502

F

F & I Services Ltd, CA [2001] STC 939 .... 2.338, 67.162
F Machin & Sons Ltd (VTD 17906) 36.548
F Options Ltd (No 1) (VTD 18521) 2.14
F Options Ltd (No 2) (VTD 19033) 2.222
F Troop & Son (VTD 18957) 48.70
F1 Promotions Ltd, [2010] UKFTT 159 (TC), TC00464 .... 40.52
F2 Leisure Ltd (VTD 19253) 2.80
Faaborg-Gelting Linien A/S v Finanzamt Flensburg, ECJ Case C-231/94; [1996] STC
  774; [1996] 1 ECR 2395; [1996] 3 CMLR 535; [1996] All ER (EC) 656 .... 22.174
Fabbri & Partners Ltd [1973] VATTR 49 (VTD 9) 5.25

Fabco Ltd (VTD 9739) 53.18
Faccenda Chicken Ltd [1992] VATTR 395 (VTD 9570) 2.157
Facet Holding BV, Staatssecretaris van Financiën *v*, ECJ Case C-539/08; [2010] STC 1701 .... 22.411
Facthaven Incentive Marketing Ltd (VTD 6443) 66.48
Facthaven Incentive Marketing Ltd, QB [1992] STC 839 .... 2.174
Factortame Ltd & Others *v* Secretary of State for Transport (No 2), ECJ Case C-213/89; [1990] 1 ECR 2433; [1990] 3 CMLR 375; [1991] 1 All ER 70 .... 22.26
Factortame Ltd & Others, ex p., R *v* Secretary of State for Transport, R *v* (No 3), ECJ Case C-48/93; [1996] 1 ECR 1029; [1996] 1 CMLR 889; [1996] 2 WLR 506; [1996] All ER (EC) 301 .... 22.31
Faimana Properties Ltd (VTD 14600) 57.134
Fairbairn (P) (VTD 18538) 2.25
Fairbairn (SP & A) (t/a Ruffles) (VTD 12825) 3.130
Fairclough, R *v*, CA Criminal Division (unreported) 49.2
Fairhome Ltd (VTD 11314) 52.226
Fairmatch Ltd (VTD 14194) 65.27
Fairpay Ltd (VTD 20455) 62.486
Fairview Windows Ltd (VTD 3619) 18.425
Fairway Lubricants Ltd (VTD 1577) 36.3
Faith Clothing Ltd [2008] VATDR 379 (VTD 29854) 52.365
Faith Construction Ltd, CA [1989] STC 539; [1990] 1 QB 905; [1989] 2 All ER 938 .... 62.423
Fallimento Olimpiclub Srl, Amministrazione dell'Economia e delle Finanze *v*, ECJ Case C-2/08; 3 September 2009 unreported 22.555
Fakenham Conservative Association Bingo Club (VTD 76) 24.10
Falcon Plastics Ltd (VTD 13050) 18.244
Falcon Sportswear Ltd (VTD 2019) 12.18
Families for Children (No 2) (VTD 19857) 33.73
Family Car Centre Ltd (VTD 16141) 44.95
Fanfield Ltd, [2011] UKFTT 42 (TC); [2011] SFTD 324, TC00919 .... 28.2
Fantasia (Knutsford) (VTD 12515) 36.141
Fantask A/S & Others *v* Industriministeriet, ECJ Case C-188/95; [1998] 1 CMLR 473; [1998] All ER (EC) 1 .... 22.49
Farley (J) (VTD 6558) 18.59
Farley (PA) (VTD 2567) 36.244
Farm Facilities (Fork Lift) Ltd [1987] VATTR 80 (VTD 2366) 65.18
Farm Services (Gillingham) Ltd (VTD 9514) 17.2
Farnglobe Ltd (t/a Tooto's The Club) (VTD 6582) 52.125
Farnham Physiotherapy & Sports Clinic (VTD 20004) 46.142
Farnocchia (A & B), CS [1994] STC 881 .... 3.5
Farrey (M) (VTD 6709) 52.89
Farrimond (RJ & JM) (VTD 10831) 1.101
Farrington (JA) (VTD 5456) 51.101
Farrington (K) (VTD 2177) 36.268
Farrow (D) (VTD 6410) 51.74
Farrow (R) (VTD 10612) 25.34
Fashanu (JA) (VTD 13137) 25.2, 40.43
Fast Technology Ltd (VTD 9974) 52.72
Faststar Ltd (VTD 4707) 18.508
Fat Sam's American Food & Beverage Co Ltd (VTD 5785) 18.341
Fattal *v* Walbrook Trustee (Jersey) Ltd, CA [2008] EWCA Civ 427 .... 2.287
Fawson (R) (VTD 9724) 57.22
Faxlink Communications (VTD 7766) 18.367
Faxworld Vorgründungsgesellschaft Peter Hünninghausen und Wolfgang Klein GbR, Finanzamt Offenbach am Main-Land *v*, ECJ Case C-137/02; [2005] STC 1192 ..... 22.168
Fazenda Pública *v* Câmara Municipal do Porto, ECJ Case C-446/98; [2001] STC 560 .... 22.137
Fazenda Pública, António Jorge Lda *v* , ECJ Case C-536/03; [2008] STC 2533 ..... 22.444
Fazenda Pública, Empresa de Desenvolvimento Mineiro SGPS *v*, ECJ Case C-77/01; [2005] STC 65 .... 22.448

Fazenda Pública, Lidl & Companhia v, ECJ Case C-106/10; [2011] STC 1979 .... 20.48
FC Milnes (Bradford) Ltd (VTD 478) 3.116
FCE Bank plc, Ministero dell'Economia e delle Finanze v, ECJ Case C-210/04; [2007]
   STC 165 .... 22.201
FD Todd & Sons Ltd (VTD 14731) 36.331
FDR Ltd, CA [2000] STC 672 .... 27.5
FEA Briggs Ltd (VTD 12804) 23.1
Feal & Oats (VTD 6706) 52.136
Federal Republic of Germany v EC Commission, ECJ Case 332/85; [1985] ECR 5143
   .... 22.549
Federal Republic of Germany, Brasserie du Pêcheur SA v, ECJ Case C-46/93; [1996]
   1 ECR 1029; [1996] 1 CMLR 889; [1996] 2 WLR 506; [1996] All ER (EC) 301 .... 22.31
Federal Republic of Germany, Dillenkofer & Others v, ECJ Case C-178/94; [1996]
   1 ECR 4845; [1996] 3 CMLR 469; [1996] All ER (EC) 917 .... 22.33
Federal Republic of Germany, EC Commission v (No 1), ECJ Case C-74/91; [1992]
   1 ECR 5437; [1996] STC 843 .... 22.486
Federal Republic of Germany, EC Commission v (No 2), ECJ Case C-427/98; [2003]
   STC 301 .... 22.237
Federal Republic of Germany, EC Commission v (No 3), ECJ Case C-287/00; [2002]
   STC 982 .... 22.303
Federal Republic of Germany, EC Commission v (No 4), ECJ Case C-109/02; [2006]
   STC 1587 .... 22.265
Federal Republic of Germany, EC Commission v (No 5), ECJ Case C-144/02;
   [2004] All ER(D) 264(Jul) 22.248
Federal Republic of Germany, EC Commission v (No 6), ECJ Case C-401/06; [2008]
   STC 2906 .... 22.224
Federated Pensions Services Ltd, [1992] VATTR 358 (VTD 8932) 38.46
Federation of Technological Industries & Others, ECJ Case C-384/04; [2006] STC
   1483 .... 22.466
Fee (RJ) (t/a Swiftcraft Boats) (VTD 20489) 66.7
Feehan (MJ), QB 1994, [1995] STC 75 .... 24.20
Felicitations Ltd (VTD 12409) 14.56
Felix Quinn Enterprises Ltd (VTD 12411) 36.483
Feltgen, Administration de l'Enregistrement et des Domaines v, ECJ Case C-116/10;
   [2011] STC 994 .... 22.392
Feltham (I), [2011] UKFTT 612 (TC), TC01455 .... 23.26
Femco Engineering Co Ltd (VTD 7454) 18.286
Fencing Supplies Ltd, [1993] VATTR 302 (VTD 10451) 6.33
Fengate Developments, CA 2004, [2005] STC 191; [2004] EWCA Civ 1591 .... 62.342
Fenning (LH) (VTD 19297) 57.134
Fenstone (Quarries) Ltd (VTD 7236) 36.363
Fenwick Builders Ltd (VTD 5801) 36.425
Fenwood Developments Ltd, Ch D 2005, [2006] STC 644; [2005] EWHC 2954(Ch)
   .... 15.74
Ferguson (RJ) (VTD 1578) 36.250
Ferrazzini v Italy, ECHR Case 44759/88; [2001] STC 1314 .... 34.16
Ferrero UK Ltd, CA [1997] STC 881 .... 29.137
Ferris & Budd (t/a Z Cars) (VTD 412) 41.36
Feuerbestattungsverein Halle eV, Finanzamt Eisleben v, ECJ Case C-430/04; [2006] STC
   2043 .... 22.139
Fforestfach Medical Centre (VTD 16587) 6.31
Fibreglass Direct (Ireland) Ltd (VTD 20751) 17.3
Fida Interiors Ltd (VTD 8907) 52.217
Fidelity International Management Holdings Ltd (VTD 7323) 46.153
Fidler (RW & JR) (t/a Holt Manor Farm Partners) (VTD 12892) 29.115
Field (PM & Mrs P) (t/a Paul Field Hair and Beauty Salon) (VTD 2047) 41.78
Field Fisher Waterhouse Llp, [2011] UKFTT 524 (TC); [2011] SFTD 1015; TC01371
   .... 22.347
Fielder & Sons (Enfield) Ltd (VTD 7017) 52.85
Fiesta Fashions Ltd (VTD 1975) 14.47
Finance Board (The) (Isle of Man), Castle Wines Ltd v (VTD 1271) 40.91

Financial & General Print Ltd (VTD 13795) 36.640
Finanční ředitelství v Ústí nad Labem, RLRE Tellmer Property sro v, ECJ Case C-572/07; [2009] STC 2006 .... 22.346
Finanzamt Arnberg v Stadt Sundern, ECJ Case C-43/04; 26 May 2005 unreported
.... 22.484
Finanzamt Augsburg-Land, Maierhofer v, ECJ Case C-315/00; [2003] STC 564 .... 22.337
Finanzamt Augsburg-Stadt v Marktgemeinde Welden, ECJ Case C-247/95; [1997] STC 531; [1997] 1 ECR 779; [1997] All ER (EC) 665 .... 22.133
Finanzamt Bad Segeberg, Mohr v, ECJ Case C-215/94; STC 328; [1996] 1 ECR 959; [1996] All ER (EC) 450 .... 22.172
Finanzamt Bergisch Gladbach v HE, ECJ Case C-25/03; [2007] STC 128 .... 22.407
Finanzamt Bergisch Gladbach v Skripalle, ECJ Case C-63/96; [1997] STC 1035; [1997] 1 ECR 2847 .... 22.500
Finanzamt Bergisch Gladbach, Dudda v, ECJ Case C-327/94; [1996] STC 1290; [1996] 1 ECR 4595; [1996] 3 CMLR 1063 .... 22.214
Finanzamt Bochum-Mitte, L.u.P GmbH v, ECJ Case C-106/05; [2008] STC 1742 .. 22.276
Finanzamt Borken, Schmeink & Cofreth AG & Co KG v, ECJ Case C-454/98; [2000] STC 810 .... 22.414
Finanzamt Buchholz in der Nordheide, Leo Libera GmbH v, ECJ Case C-58/09; [2010] STC 1950 .... 20.86
Finanzamt Burgdorf v Bog, ECJ Case C-497/09; [2011] STC 1221 .... 22.155
Finanzamt Burgdorf v Fischer, ECJ Case C-322/99, [2001] STC 1356; [2002] 2 WLR 1207 .... 22.160
Finanzamt Calau, Landboden-Agrardienste GmbH & Co KG v, ECJ Case C-384/95; [1998] STC 171 .... 22.173
Finanzamt Charlottenburg, KapHag Renditefonds 35 Spreecenter Berlin-Hellersdorf 3 Tanche GbR v, ECJ Case C-442/01; [2005] STC 1500 .... 22.90
Finanzamt Deggendorf v Stoppelkamp (Raab's Administrator), ECJ Case C-421/10; [2011] STC 2358 .... 22.462
Finanzamt Detmold, Fleischerei Nier GmbH & Co KG v, ECJ Case C-502/09; [2011] STC 1221 .... 22.175
Finanzamt Donaueschingen, Fischer v, ECJ Case C-283/95; [1998] STC 708; [1998] All ER (EC) 567 .... 22.371
Finanzamt Dresden I, Ingenieurbüro Eulitz GbR Thomas und Marion Eulitz v, ECJ Case C-473/08; 28 January 2010 unreported 22.308
Finanzamt Düsseldorf-Mettman v Brandenstein, ECJ Case C-323/99, [2001] STC 1356; [2002] 2 WLR 1207 .... 22.161
Finanzamt Düsseldorf-Nord, Köhler v, ECJ Case C-58/04; [2006] STC 469 .... 22.195
Finanzamt Düsseldorf-Süd v SALIX Grundstücks-Vermietungsgesellschaft mbH & Co. Objekt Offenbach KG, ECJ Case C-102/08; [2009] STC 1607 .... 22.141
Finanzamt Eisleben v Feuerbestattungsverein Halle eV, ECJ Case C-430/04; [2006] STC 2043 .... 22.139
Finanzamt Essen Nord-Ost v GFKL Financial Services AG, ECJ Case C-93/10; 27 October 2011 unreported 22.95
Finanzamt Esslingen, Strobel v, ECJ Case C-454/98; [2000] STC 810 .... 22.414
Finanzamt Flensburg, Faaborg-Gelting Linien A/S v, ECJ Case C-231/94; [1996] STC 774; [1996] 1 ECR 2395; [1996] 3 CMLR 535; [1996] All ER (EC) 656 .... 22.174
Finanzamt Freital, Minerva Kulturreisen GmbH v, ECJ Case C-31/10; [2011] STC 532 .... 22.490
Finanzamt fur Körperschaften, Ambulanter Pflegedienst Kügler GmbH v, ECJ Case C-141/00; [2002] All ER(D) 40 (Sept) 22.299
Finanzamt für Körperschaften Hamburg, RA Grendel GmbH v, ECJ Case 255/81; [1982] ECR 2301; [1983] 1 CMLR 379 .... 22.353
Finanzamt Fürstenfeldbruck, Bakcsi v, ECJ Case C-415/98, [2002] STC 802; [2002] 2 WLR 1188 .... 22.94
Finanzamt Fürstenfeldbruck, Lange v, ECJ Case C-111/92; [1993] 1 ECR 4677; [1994] 1 CMLR 573; [1997] STC 564 .... 22.387
Finanzamt Gießen, Christoph-Dornier-Stiftung für Klinische Psychologie v, ECJ Case C-45/01; [2005] STC 228 .... 22.280
Finanzamt Gladbeck v Linneweber, ECJ Case C-453/02; [2008] STC 1069 .... 22.372
Finanzamt Goslar v Breitsohl, ECJ Case C-400/98; [2001] STC 355 .... 22.122

Finanzamt Göttingen, Securenta Göttinger Immobilienanlagen und Vermögensmanagement AG *v*, ECJ Case C-437/06; [2008] STC 3473 .... 22.420

Finanzamt Groß-Gerau *v* MKG-Kraftfahrzeuge-Factoring GmbH, ECJ Case C-305/01; [2003] STC 951; [2004] All ER (EC) 454 .... 22.364

Finanzamt Graz-Stadt, Heger Rudi GmbH *v*, ECJ Case C-166/05; [2008] STC 2679 .... 22.206

Finanzamt Gummersbach *v* Bockemühl, ECJ Case C-90/01; [2005] STC 934 .... 22.461

Finanzamt Hamburg-Barmbek-Uhlenhorst, HJ Glawe Spiel und Unterhaltungsgeräte Aufstellungsgesellschaft mbH & Co KG *v*, ECJ Case C-38/93; [1994] STC 543; [1994] 1 ECR 1679; [1995] 1 CMLR 70 .... 22.239

Finanzamt Hamburg-Bergedorf, ADV Allround Vermittlungs AG *v*, ECJ Case C-218/10; 28 June 2011 unreported 22.225

Finanzamt Hamburg-Eimsbüttel, Hamann *v*, ECJ Case C-51/88; [1989] ECR 767; [1990] 2 CMLR 377; [1991] STC 193 .... 22.202

Finanzamt Hamburg-Eimsbüttel, Velvet & Steel Immobilien und Handels GmbH *v*, ECJ Case C-455/05; [2008] STC 922 .... 22.356

Finanzamt Hamburg-Mitte-Altstadt, Berkholz *v*, ECJ Case C-168/84; [1985] 3 CMLR 667; [1985] ECR 2251 .... 22.198, 22.394

Finanzamt Heidelberg *v* IST Internationale Sprach- und Studienreisen GmbH, ECJ Case C-200/04; [2006] STC 52 .... 22.489

Finanzamt Herne-West *v* Akritidis, ECJ Case C-462/02; [2008] STC 1069 .... 22.373

Finanzamt Homburg, Enkler *v*, ECJ Case C-230/94; [1996] STC 1316; [1996] 1 ECR 4517; [1997] 1 CMLR 881 .... 22.114

Finanzamt Innsbruck, Heiser *v*, ECJ Case C-172/03; [2005] All ER (D) 66 (Mar) 22.11

Finanzamt Klagenfurt, Sozialdemokratische Partei Österreichs Landesorganisation Kärnten *v*, ECJ Case C-267/08; [2010] STC 287 .... 22.120

Finanzamt Köln-West, Reisdorf *v*, ECJ 1996, [1997] STC 180 .... 22.472

Finanzamt Landshut, Wollny (J & S) *v*, ECJ Case C-72/05; [2008] STC 1618 .... 22.249

Finanzamt Leer, Kloppenburg *v*, ECJ Case 70/83; [1984] ECR 1075; [1985] 1 CMLR 205 .... 22.353

Finanzamt Lenz, Kretztechnik AG *v* , ECJ Case C-465/03; [2005] STC 1118; [2005] 1 WLR 3755 .... 22.91

Finanzamt Leverkusen *v* Verigen Transplantation Service International AG, ECJ Case C-156/09; [2011] STC 255 .... 22.285

Finanzamt Limburg an der Lahn, Collée *v*, ECJ Case C-146/05; [2008] STC 757 ... 22.519

Finanzamt Luckenwalde, Ludwig (V) *v*, ECJ Case C-453/05; [2008] STC 1640 ..... 22.355

Finanzamt Lüdenscheid *v* Schriever, ECJ Case C-444/10; 10 November 2011 unreported 22.169

Finanzamt Malchin, Netto Supermarkt GmbH & Co OHG *v*, ECJ Case C-271/06; [2008] STC 3280 .... 22.388

Finanzamt Mönchengladbach-Mitte, Kerrutt & Another *v*, ECJ Case 73/85; [1986] ECR 2219; [1987] BTC 5015; [1987] 2 CMLR 221 .... 22.121

Finanzamt München I, Blasi *v*, ECJ Case C-346/95; [1998] STC 336; [1998] All ER (EC) 211 .... 22.338

Finanzamt München III *v* Mohsche, ECJ Case C-193/91; [1993] 1 ECR 2615; [1997] STC 195 .... 22.181

Finanzamt München III, Kühne *v*, ECJ Case 50/88; [1989] ECR 1925; [1990] STC 749; [1990] 3 CMLR 287 .... 22.179

Finanzamt München III, Lennartz *v*, ECJ Case C-97/90; [1991] 1 ECR 3795; [1993] 3 CMLR 689; [1995] STC 514 .... 22.456

Finanzamt München für Körperschaften, BAZ Bausystem AG *v*, ECJ Case C-222/81; [1982] 3 CMLR 688 .... 22.232

Finanzamt München für Körperschaften, Swiss Re Germany Holding GmbH*v*, ECJ Case C-242/08; [2010] STC 189 .... 22.330

Finanzamt Münster-Innenstadt, Becker *v*, ECJ Case 8/81; [1982] ECR 53; [1982] 1 CMLR 499 .... 22.352

Finanzamt Neustadt, Julius Fillibeck Söhne GmbH & Co KG *v*, ECJ Case C-258/95; [1998] STC 513; [1998] 1 WLR 697; [1998] All ER (EC) 466 .... 22.184

Finanzamt Neustadt en der Weinstraße, ECJ Case 207/87; [1988] ECR 4433; [1991] STC 589 .... 22.353

Finanzamt Offenbach am Main-Land *v* Faxworld Vorgründungsgesellschaft Peter Hünninghausen und Wolfgang Klein GbR, ECJ Case C-137/02; [2005] STC 1192 .. 22.168

Finanzamt Oschatz *v* Zweckverband zur Trinkwasserversorgung und Abwasserbeseitigung Torgau-Westelbien, ECJ Case C-442/05; [2009] STC 1 .... 22.267

Finanzamt Osnabrück-Land *v* Langhorst, ECJ Case C-141/96; [1997] STC 1357; [1997] 1 ECR 5073; [1998] 1 WLR 52; [1998] All ER (EC) 178 .... 22.460

Finanzamt Osterholz-Scharmbeck, Terra Baubedarf-Handel GmbH *v*, ECJ Case C-152/02; [2005] STC 525 .... 22.437

Finanzamt Paderborn, Grundstückgemeinschaft Schloßstraße GbR *v*, ECJ Case C-396/98; 8 June 2000 unreported 22.398

Finanzamt Rendsburg *v* Harbs, ECJ Case C-321/02; [2006] STC 340 .... 22.483

Finanzamt Starnberg, Seeling *v*, ECJ Case C-269/00; [2003] STC 805 .... 22.182

Finanzamt Stuttgart-Körperschaften, Reisebüro Binder GmbH *v*, ECJ Case C-116/96; [1998] STC 604 .... 22.212

Finanzamt Sulingen *v* Sudholz, ECJ Case C-17/01; [2005] STC 747 .... 22.502

Finanzamt Trier, Von Hoffmann *v*, ECJ Case C-145/96; [1997] STC 1321; [1997] All ER (EC) 852 .... 22.223

Finanzamt Ülzen *v* Armbrecht, ECJ Case C-291/92; [1995] STC 997; [1995] 1 ECR 2775; [1995] All ER (EC) 882 .... 22.93

Finanzamt Waldviertel, Schmelz (I) *v*, ECJ Case C-97/09; [2011] STC 88 .... 20.126

Finanzamt Waldviertel, Walderdorff (G) *v*, ECJ Case C-451/06; [2008] STC 3079 .. 22.343

Finanzamt Wiedenbrück, Bertelsmann AG *v*, ECJ Case C-380/99; [2001] STC 1153 .... 22.243

Finanzamt Wilmersdorf, Haderer (W) *v*, ECJ Case C-445/05; [2008] STC 2171 ..... 22.307

Finanzlandesdirektion für Kärnten, EMAG Handel Eder OHG *v*, ECJ Case C-245/04; [2007] STC 1461 .... 22.517

Finanzlandesdirektion für Oberösterreich, Turn-und Sportunion Waldburg *v*, ECJ Case C-246/04; [2006] STC 1506 .... 22.382

Finanzlandesdirektion für Steinmark, Metropol Treuhand WirtschaftstreuhandgmbH *v*, ECJ Case C-409/99; [2002] All ER (D) 15 (Jan) 22.433

Finanzlandesdirektion für Tirol, Cookies World Vertriebsgesellschaft mbH iL *v*, ECJ Case C-155/01; [2003] All ER (D) 91 (Sep) 22.203

Finanzlandesdirektion für Vorarlberg, Stadler *v*, ECJ Case C-409/99; [2002] All ER(D) 15(Jan) 22.433

Finaplan Ltd (VTD 13224) 18.617

Finch (SR) (VTD 10948) 62.415

Finch (WL) (VTD 15826) 18.319

Findel Ltd, [2011] UKFTT 723 (TC), TC01560 .... 67.74

Findhelp Ltd, [1991] VATTR 341 (VTD 6431, 7015) 46.214

Fine (AG) (VTD 4977) 36.541

Fine Art Developments plc, HL [1989] STC 85; [1989] 2 WLR 369; [1989] 1 All ER 502; [1989] 2 CMLR 185 .... 2.138, 59.23

Fine Art Developments plc, HL [1996] STC 246; [1996] 1 WLR 1054; [1996] 1 All ER 888 .... 67.33

Fineline Bedrooms & Kitchens Ltd (VTD 20049) 62.335

Finest Golf Clubs of the World Ltd (The) (VTD 19347) 62.516

Finglands Travel Agency Ltd (VTD 1447) 44.67

Finishfavour Ltd (VTD 7053) 18.79

Finland, EC Commission *v*, ECJ Case C-169/00; [2004] STC 1232 .... 22.96

Finland, EC Commission *v*, ECJ Case C-495/01; [2004] All ER (D) 265 (Jul) 22.248

Finland, EC Commission *v*, ECJ Case C-246/08; 29 October 2009 unreported 22.132

Finland, Jussila *v*, ECHR Case 73053/01; [2009] STC 29; 9 ITLR 662 .... 34.12

Finland, Nordea Pankki Suomi Oyi *v*, ECJ Case C-350/10; [2011] STC 1956 .... 22.365

Finnamore (D) (t/a Hanbridge Storage Services), [2011] UKFTT 216 (TC); [2011] SFTD 551, TC01081 .... 41.23

Firepoint Scotland Ltd (VTD 18187) 18.425

Firepower Builders Ltd (VTD 3358) 14.19

Firm of Brandy's (VTD 17250) 18.553

First Base Properties Ltd (VTD 11598) 41.27

First Choice Holidays plc, ECJ Case C-149/01; [2003] STC 934; [2003] All ER (EC) 705 .... 22.493

First Choice Holidays plc, CA [2004] STC 1407; [2004] EWCA Civ 1044 .... 63.11
First Class Communications Ltd (VTD 20779) 2.18
First Class Communications (Sales) Ltd (VTD 19950) 43.4
First County Garages Ltd (VTD 14417) 40.91
First de Parys (Dry Cleaners) Ltd (VTD 12178) 18.104
First Indian Cavalry Club Ltd, CS 1997, [1998] STC 293 .... 50.70
First International Conference on Emergency Medicine (VTD 2881) 51.52
First Medical Ltd (VTD 17847) 19.68
First National Bank of Chicago, ECJ Case C-172/96; [1998] STC 850; [1998] All ER
    (EC) 744; [1999] 2 WLR 230 .... 22.89
First National Telecom Services Ltd (VTD 19681) 36.660
First Talk Mobile Ltd, [2011] UKFTT 423 (TC), TC01276 .... 2.81
First-Tier Tribunal, R v (oao Totel Ltd), QB [2011] EWHC 652 (Admin) 2.137
Firstpoint (Europe) Ltd, [2011] UKFTT 708 (TC), TC01545 .... 62.518
Fiscale eenheid Koninklijke Ahold NV v Staatssecretaris van Financiën, ECJ Case
    C-484/06; [2009] STC 45 .... 22.562
Fischer v Finanzamt Donaueschingen, ECJ Case C-283/95; [1998] STC 708;
    [1998] All ER (EC) 567 .... 22.371
Fischer, Finanzamt Burgdorf v, ECJ Case C-322/99, [2001] STC 1356; [2002] 2 WLR
    1207 .... 22.160
Fisher (DC) (VTD 12356) 15.275
Fisher (JW) (VTD 179) 41.149
Fisher (NJ) (VTD 11238) 18.583
Fisher (Lord), QB [1981] STC 238; [1981] 2 All ER 147 .... 7.6
Fisher & Others, R v, CA Criminal Division, [1989] STI 269 .... 49.28
Fisher Educational Ltd (VTD 17902) 5.49
Fishguard Bay Developments Ltd (VTD 3225, 4549) 46.15
Fishwick (AG) (VTD 3642) 18.584
Fitch (KC) [2006] VATDR 196 (VTD 19914) 2.267
Fitch (MW) & Slade (B) (t/a Michael W Fitch Antiques) (VTD 16880) 53.4
Fitton (K) (VTD 13844) 57.7
Fitzgerald (S) (VTD 18662) 18.122
Fitzgerald (SN) & Robinson (DP) (t/a Autozone) (VTD 18168) 36.486
Fitzpatrick (A) (VTD 10282) 18.269
Fitzpatrick (E) (VTD 5247) 18.353
Fitzpatrick (PJ) [1996] VATDR 81 (VTD 13168) 50.53
Fitzpatrick & Others, ex p., R v Chief Constable of Warwickshire Constabulary, QB
    [1998] 1 All ER 65 .... 14.94
Five Oaks Properties Ltd (VTD 6085) 48.89
Five Steps Community Nursery (VTD 16684) 52.312
Fivegrange Ltd (VTD 5338) 47.56
FJ Chalke Ltd, CA [2010] STC 1640; [2010] EWCA Civ 313 .... 48.146
FJ Meaden Ltd (VTD 13215) 36.335
Flame Cheater International Ltd (VTD 14288) 18.118
Flame Cheater Ltd (VTD 5685) 18.43
Flan-Form Ltd (VTD 9415) 18.367
Flanaghan (GJ & GM) (VTD 4648) 51.107
Flanders Expo SA, Design Concept SA v, ECJ Case C-438/01; [2003] STC 912 ..... 22.221
Flashlight Photography Ltd (VTD 9088) 67.53
Flashpoint Technology Ltd, [2011] UKFTT 353 (TC), TC01213 .... 36.121
Flashshine Ltd (VTD 11433) 65.32
Flather (G) (VTD 11960) 19.82
Flax Bourton Magistrates' Court, R v (ex p. C & E Commrs), QB 1996 unreported
    .... 49.9
Fleet School of Motoring (VTD 7299) 62.230
Fleischerei Nier GmbH & Co KGv Finanzamt Detmold, ECJ Case C-502/09; [2011]
    STC 1221 .... 22.175
Fleming (M) (t/a Bodycraft), HL [2008] STC 324; [2008] UKHL 2; [2008] 1 All ER
    1061 .... 48.6
Fletcher (JE & JB) (VTD 2356) 51.132
Flinders (SG) (VTD 6349) 18.438

Flip Cards (Marine) Ltd (VTD 14483) 5.109
Flipcards Ltd (VTD 13916) 5.47
Flitcroft (D) (VTD 2328) 1.32
Floridienne SA v Belgian State, ECJ Case C-142/99; [2000] STC 1044; [2001] All ER
(EC) 37 .... 22.447
Floris Merchandise Ltd (VTD 7437) 52.123
Flowers (GM & EA) (VTD 13889) 3.81
Floyde Brothers (VTD 6765) 40.70
Fluff Ltd (t/a Mag-It), QB 2000, [2001] STC 674 .... 29.108
Flynn (HW) (VTD 16930) 15.265
FMCG Home Services Ltd (VTD 18377) 65.82
FOD Financiën, Vlaamse Oliemaatschappij NV v, ECJ Case C-499/10; 21 December
2011 unreported 22.467
Foley (CN) (VTD 13496) 55.40
Folknoll Ltd (VTD 4022) 51.114
Fondbane Motors (VTD 2813) 65.21
Fonden Marselisborg Lystbådehavn v Skatteministeriet, ECJ Case C-428/02; [2006] STC
1467 .... 22.342
Fong (TK), [1978] VATTR 75 (VTD 590) 57.167
Food Concepts International Ltd (VTD 19484) 18.579
Food Engineering Ltd, [1992] VATTR 327 (VTD 7787) 52.454
Food-Wrap Ltd (VTD 10817) 18.224
Football Association Ltd (The) (VTD 1845) 2.163
Football Association Ltd (The), [1985] VATTR 106 (VTD 1860) 8.36
Force One Training Ltd (VTD 13619) 5.7
Ford (C & A) (VTD 837) 3.150
Ford (D) (t/a Donald Ford Financial Services), [1987] VATTR 130 (VTD 2432) 38.34
Ford (DS) (VTD 16271) 55.3
Ford (Mrs P) (t/a Children's Riding Stables) (VTD 6855) 51.17
Ford Fuels Ltd (VTD 7213) 52.82
Ford Motor Company Ltd (No 1) [2006] VATDR 114 (VTD 19424) 2.8
Ford Motor Company Ltd (No 2), CA 2007, [2008] STC 1016; [2007] EWCA Civ
1730 .... 38.29
Ford Motor Company Ltd (No 3) (VTD 20028) 44.155
Ford Motor Company Ltd (No 4), [2007] VATDR 475 (VTD 20315) 52.413
Foreman (FC) & Partners (VTD 11894) 18.125
Forestmead Ltd (VTD 15852) 47.57
Forever Living Products Ltd (VTD 16263) 29.103
Forexia (UK) Ltd (VTD 16041) 5.107
Forman Hardy (N), [1994] VATTR 302 (VTD 12776) 55.37
Formstone (TE) (VTD 3693) 2.327
Formtax Plastics Ltd (VTD 11605) 18.199
Forrest (FFJ & FK) (VTD 10576) 52.317
Forrester (N) v Hooper (RAJ) (re Anglo-Breweries Ltd) (VTD 18008) 2.510
Försäkringsaktiebolaget Skandia, ECJ Case C-240/99; [2001] STC 754; [2001] 1 WLR
1617; [2001] All ER (EC) 822 .... 22.325
Forster (A, D & J), [2011] UKFTT 469 (TC), TC01319 .... 57.75
Forster (P) (VTD 9367) 52.295
Forsters School & Leisurewear Ltd (VTD 20758) 12.21
Fort Vale Engineering Ltd (VTD 17456) 52.242
Forth Dry Dock & Engineering Co Ltd, Litster v, HL 1989, [1990] 1 AC 546; [1989]
1 All ER 1134 .... 63.11
Forth Skips Ltd (VTD 5016) 18.287
Förvaltnings AB Stenholmen v Riksskatteverket, ECJ Case C-320/02; [2004] STC 104;
[2004] All ER (EC) 870 .... 22.494
Fosberry (KAJ & Mrs BM) (VTD 19189) 2.486
Foster (D & J) (t/a David Foster Associates) (VTD 14820) 5.80
Foster (Mr & Mrs I) (VTD 6787) 52.111
Foster (N & T) (t/a Foster Leisure) (VTD 16617) 52.416
Foster (RA & Mrs JC) (t/a The Watersplash Hotel) (VTD 12723) 3.123
Foster (SR) (VTD 17241) 47.71

Foster & Others *v* British Gas plc, ECJ Case C-188/89; [1990] ECR 3313; [1990] 3 All ER 897 .... 22.16
Foster Cars (Rotherham) Ltd (VTD 3586) 18.563
Foster Penny Ltd (VTD 7716) 52.369
FourDistribution Ltd (No 1) (VTD 20931) 36.108
FourDistribution Ltd (No 2), [2009] UKFTT 242 (TC), TC00191 .... .36.109
Fourth Road Consultants Ltd (VTD 13626) 18.421
Fowle (F) (VTD 9174) 10.5
Fox, Ch D 11 May 2006 unreported 50.20
Foxer Industries (VTD 13817) 19.59
Foxer Industries (No 2) (VTD 14469) 19.74
Foxmead Services (Northern) Ltd (VTD 1625) 36.145
Fox-Pitt Kelton Ltd (VTD 11556) 46.52
FPS (UK) Ltd (VTD 15716) 18.61
FPV Ltd (VTD 15666) 40.48
Frambeck Ltd, CA [1989] STC 395 .... 46.17
Framesouth Ltd (VTD 15270) 5.89
Frampton (SJ & CA) (t/a Framptons) (VTD 14065) 48.41
France, Bendenoun *v*, ECHR 1994, 18 EHRR 54 .... 34.5
France, SA Cabinet Diot *v*, ECHR Case 49217/99; 22 July 2003 unreported 34.25
France, SA Dangeville *v*, ECHR Case 36677/97; [2003] STC 771; 5 ITLR 604 ...... 34.24
France, SA Gras Savoye *v*, ECHR Case 49218/99; 22 July 2003 unreported 34.25
France, *see also* French Republic
Franchise Development Services Ltd (VTD 14295) 5.38
Francis (G & Mrs H) [2006] VATDR 487 (VTD 19919) 57.72
Francis (RG) (VTD 9063) 52.69
Francis Jackson Homes Ltd (VTD 6352) 36.52
Francis John (VTD 3447) 62.256
Francis John Hair Studio (VTD 3447) 62.256
Francis John (Saltcoats) Ltd (VTD 3447) 62.256
Franco F'Lli Ltd (VTD 13153) 46.206
Francovich *v* Italian State, ECJ Case C-6/90; [1991] 1 ECR 5357; [1993] 2 CMLR 66
.... 22.30
Frank Coleman (Luton) Ltd (VTD 6653) 18.286
Frank Galliers Ltd, QB 1992, [1993] STC 284 .... 52.66
Frank Haslam Milan & Co Ltd (VTD 3857) 15.248
Frankenberg *v* Famous Lasky Film Service, [1931] 1 Ch 428 .... 2.426
Fraser (AE & Mrs ME) (VTD 16761) 47.27
Fraser (TW) (VTD 18753) 18.483
Fraser Bruce Group Ltd (The) (VTD 17763) 2.44
Fraserburgh Harbour Commissioners (VTD 15797) 8.11
Fred's Newsagents Ltd (VTD 2815) 18.197
Freelance Door Services Ltd (VTD 1384) 36.441
Freeland (DJ) (VTD 11358) 3.128
Freeman & Another (re Margaretta Ltd), Ch D [2005] STC 610 .... 37.8
Freeman Box & Co (VTD 3524) 18.79
Freemans plc, ECJ Case C-86/99; [2001] STC 960; [2001] 1 WLR 1713 .... 22.253
Freemans plc (No 2) (VTD 17019) 48.138
Freer (DJ & Mrs AP) (t/a Shooting & Fishing) (VTD 18921) 62.79
Freer (DL) (VTD 7648) 52.265
Freeserve.com plc, oao, R *v* C & E, QB 2003, [2004] STC 187; [2003] EWHC 2736(Admin) 2.342
Freeway Marketing Ltd (VTD 5905) 18.425
Freewheeler Co Ltd (VTD 4544) 18.20
Freezerman (UK) Ltd (VTD 2061) 29.188
Freight Transport Leasing Ltd [1991] VATTR 142 (VTD 5578) 27.15
Freight Transport Leasing Ltd [1992] VATTR 120 (VTD 7000, 7515) 2.396
Freight Transport Leasing Ltd (VTD 7500) 2.385
French (DA) (t/a Adept Architectural Aluminium) (VTD 9706) 14.46
French Republic, EC Commission *v* (No 1), ECJ Case 50/87; [1988] ECR 4797; [1989] 1 CMLR 505 .... 22.397

French Republic, EC Commission *v* (No 2), ECJ Case C-30/89; [1990] 1 ECR 691 .... 22.210
French Republic, EC Commission *v* (No 3), ECJ Case C-68/92; [1993] 1 ECR 5881; [1997] STC 684; [1995] 2 CMLR 1 .... 22.218
French Republic, EC Commission *v* (No 4), ECJ Case C-43/96; [1998] STC 805; [1998] All ER (EC) 951 .... 22.422
French Republic, EC Commission *v* (No 5), ECJ Case C-60/96; [1997] 1 ECR 3827; [1999] STC 480 .... 22.336
French Republic, EC Commission *v* (No 6), ECJ Case C-276/97; 12 September 2000 unreported 22.135
French Republic, EC Commission *v* (No 7), ECJ Case C-429/97; [2001] STC 156 .. 22.533
French Republic, EC Commission *v* (No 8), ECJ Case C-481/98; [2001] STC 919 .. 22.506
French Republic, EC Commission *v* (No 9), ECJ Case C-76/99; 11 January 2001 unreported 22.273
French Republic, EC Commission *v* (No 10), ECJ Case C-345/99; 14 June 2001 unreported 22.423
French Republic, EC Commission *v* (No 11), ECJ Case C-404/99; 29 March 2001 unreported 22.241
French Republic, EC Commission *v* (No 12), ECJ Case C-40/00; 14 June 2001 unreported 22.409
French Republic, EC Commission *v* (No 13), ECJ Case C-384/01; 8 May 2003 unreported 22.269
French Republic, EC Commission *v* (No 14), ECJ Case C-243/03; [2006] STC 1098 .... 22.450
French Republic, EC Commission *v* (No 15), ECJ Case C-492/08; 17 June 2010 unreported 20.52
French Republic (No 16), EC Commission *v*, ECJ Case C-94/09; 6 May 2010 unreported 20.53
Fresh Pasta Products [1993] VATTR 238 (VTD 9781) 3.29
Fresh Sea Foods (Barry) Ltd [1991] VATTR 388 (VTD 6658) 29.33
Freshgro (Bicester) Ltd (VTD 7250, 7832) 36.400
Friary Electrical Co Ltd (The) (VTD 7554) 40.98
Friary Leasing Ltd (VTD 3893) 36.491
Frid, Secretary of State for Trade & Industry *v*, HL [2004] UKHL 24; [2004] All ER (D) 180 (May) 37.17
Friel (P) [1977] VATTR 147 (VTD 396) 3.26
Friendly Loans Ltd, FTT 2009, [2010] SFTD 96; [2009] UKFTT 247 (TC), TC00196 .... 27.33
Friends of the Elderly [2008] VATDR 169 (VTD 20597) 19.99
Friends of the Ironbridge Gorge Museum [1991] VATTR 97 (VTD 5639) 13.14
Fritz Bender Metals (UK) Ltd [1991] VATTR 80 (VTD 5426) 52.24, 52.34
Frizzell, Kenmir Ltd *v*, QB [1968] 1 WLR 329; [1968] 1 All ER 414 .... 65.10, 65.11
Froelich (JW) (UK) Ltd (VTD 10193) 52.209
From (Miss CDA) (VTD 5605) 51.19
Frontel Communications Ltd, Europhone International Ltd *v*, Ch D [2001] STC 1399 .... 62.470
Frost (A) (VTD 5813) 52.75
Frost (J) [2010] UKFTT 344 (TC), TC00626 .... 15.278
Frost (Dr & Mrs P) (VTD 13045) 36.546
Fryer (L & P) (VTD 14265) 58.21
Fu (JHK) (VTD 11718) 50.115
Fulcrum Electronics Ltd, ECJ Case C-355/03; [2006] STC 419; [2006] 2 WLR 456 .... 22.115
Full Force Marketing Ltd (VTD 15270) 5.89
Funding Corporation Ltd (The) (VTD 19525) 2.481
Fundmain Ltd (VTD 1493) 36.435
Funeral Planning Services Ltd (VTD 19975) 24.30
Funky End (The), [2009] UKFTT 110 (TC), TC00078 .... 24.30
Furby (AJ) (VTD 622) 62.383
Furness Vale Yacht Hire Ltd (VTD 12628) 36.562
Furniss (RJ & JW) (t/a Newspoint) (VTD 14758) 3.54

Furniss v Dawson, HL [1984] STC 153 .... 36.495
Furniture Finders of Winsford Ltd, [2010] UKFTT 426 (TC), TC00691 .... 11.68
Fusion Electronics Ltd, [2011] UKFTT 529 (TC), TC01376 .... 36.120
Future Components Ltd, [2010] UKFTT 101 (TC), TC00412 .... 48.106
Future Health Technologies Ltd, ECJ Case C-86/09; [2010] STC 1836 .... 20.65
Futures Restaurants Ltd (VTD 5717) 18.193
Fyfe & Fyfe Ltd (VTD 1199) 3.160
Fyffe (RLO) (VTD 9686) 52.127
Fylkesskattesjefen, Diamond GoGo Bar v, Lagmannsrett 6 December 2006; Times
  7.12.2006 .... 22.319

G

G, re, QB 2001, [2002] STC 391; [2001] EWHC Admin 606 .... 14.101
G Comms Ltd [2010] UKFTT 605 (TC), TC00846 .... 36.113
G Draper (Marlow) Ltd (VTD 2079) 65.3
G Wilson (Glaziers) Ltd, [2011] UKFTT 731 (TC), TC01568 .... 18.447
GA Security Systems Ltd (VTD 1527) 44.7
Gabalfrisa SL & Others v Agencia Estatal de Administracion Tributaria, ECJ Cases
  C-110/98 to C-147/98; [2002] STC 535 .... 22.401
Gabbitas Educational Consultants Ltd, [2009] UKFTT 325 (TC), TC00268 .... 62.487
Gableglade Ltd (VTD 9597) 18.367
Gables Nursing Home (The) (VTD 15456) 57.118
Gables Farm Dogs & Cats Home (VTD 20519) 11.2
Gabrielson (PS) (VTD 606) 44.63
Gagliardi (KJ) (VTD 667) 2.444
Galaxy Equipment (Europe) Ltd (VTD 11415) 40.55
Gale (JF) [1986] VATTR 185 (VTD 2138) 51.5
Gale & Daws Ltd (VTD 11126) 4.3
Gallagher (JJ & Mrs BM) (VTD 12140) 46.55
Gallaher Ltd (VTD 14827, 16395) 67.156
Gallo (B) (VTD 7686) 50.135
Gallo (R) (t/a The Fun Pub) (VTD 11502) 52.267
Gallucci (AP) (VTD 19830) 50.20
Gambro Hospital Ltd [2004] VATDR 21 (VTD 18588) 33.44
Game Conservancy Trust (The) [2001] VATDR 422 (VTD 17394) 64.10
Gamefishing Publications Ltd (VTD 12553) 18.558
Games Workshop Ltd (VTD 16975) 5.39
Gandesha (P) (VTD 5111) 25.21
Gandhi Tandoori Restaurant [1989] VATTR 39 (VTD 3303) 50.68
Gandhum (SS) (VTD 18848) 48.63
Gandy (AS) (VTD 1029) 58.25
Garage Door Co (The) (VTD 11144) 18.261
Garage Molenheide BVBA & Others v Belgian State, ECJ Case C-286/94; [1998] STC
  126; [1998] 1 CMLR 1186; [1998] All ER (EC) 61 .... 22.439
Garavand (A) (t/a Caspian Kebab & Pizza) (VTD 11847) 3.63
Garcha Group (VTD 13130) 58.23
Gardens Entertainments Ltd (The) (VTD 8972) 18.366
Gardith Construction Ltd (VTD 6959) 52.281
Gardner (JJ), [1989] VATTR 132 (VTD 3687) 62.163
Gardner (M) (t/a Gardner & Co), [2011] UKFTT 470 (TC), TC01320 .... 57.157
Gardner (MC) (VTD 588) 44.6
Gardner Lohman Ltd, [1981] VATTR 76 (VTD 1081) 62.538
Garlick (MJG) (t/a John Moreton Photography) (VTD 17672) 48.4
Garner (CW & JA) (VTD 1476) 41.38
Garnham (Mr & Mrs) (t/a Pro-Mac Surfacing) (VTD 15918) 62.136
Garrard (TJD) (VTD 5447) 18.441
Garraway (PA) (VTD 6479) 18.485
Garret (PT) & Sons (Contractors) Ltd (VTD 7073) 52.105
Garrett (A) (VTD 10798) 51.22

Garsington Opera Ltd, [2009] UKFTT 77 (TC), TC00045 .... 46.88
Gartland (JJ) (VTD 7331) 36.253
Garton (S) & Davies (J) (t/a The Dolly Tub) (VTD 16260) 57.8
Gary Sargent & Co, DTC (CTC) Ltd *v*, Ch D [1996] BCC 290 .... 40.75
Gas & Chemicals Ltd (VTD 18160) 29.105
Gasus Dosier und Fördertechnik GmbH *v* Netherlands, ECHR Case 15375/89; 20 EHRR 403 .... 18.618, 34.1
Gateacre Park Motor Co Ltd (VTD 17921) 57.199
Gateshead Talmudical College, [2011] UKUT 131 (TCC); [2011] STC 1593 .... 9.9
Gateway Leisure (Caravan Sales) (VTD 7943) 52.335
Gateway Leisure (Caravan Sales) (VTD 9689) 17.3
Gatherchoice Holdings Ltd (VTD 5804) 3.50
Gauntlett (MV) [1996] VATDR 138 (VTD 13921) 3.16
Gavacan (JW) (VTD 13670) 40.26
Gayle (NN) (VTD 20982) 57.152
GB Capital Ltd (VTD 6138) 52.344
GB Express Ltd (VTD 6822) 52.109
GB Techniques Ltd [1988] VATTR 95 (VTD 3121) 18.19
GC Parts Ltd (VTD 7545) 52.52
GD Searle & Co Ltd (VTD 13439) 19.58
GDI Game Domain International plc (VTD 20962) 36.619
Gean House Hotel Ltd (VTD 6687) 52.383
Geary (SJ) (VTD 2314) 51.43
GEC Reliance Ltd, Duke *v*, [1988] 1 AC 718; [1988] 1 All ER 626 .... 22.24
Geddes (HB & DD) (VTD 3378) 38.35
Gee (NSR) (VTD 5687) 18.563
Gee (SA) (VTD 5656) 18.402
Geistlich Sons Ltd (VTD 11468) 25.28
Gemeente Emmen *v* Belastingsdienst Grote Ondernemingen, ECJ Case C-468/93; [1996] STC 496; [1996] 1 ECR 1721; [1996] All ER (EC) 372 .... 22.123
Gemeente Leusden *v* Staatssecretaris van Financien, ECJ Case C-487/01; [2004] STC 776 .... 22.457
Gemini Cars (Egham) Ltd (VTD 20035) 62.244
Gemini Fashion Accessories Ltd (VTD 3262) 18.79
Genc (M) [1988] VATTR 16 (VTD 2595) 41.79
General Healthcare Group Ltd [2001] VATDR 328 (VTD 17129) 15.73
General Metals (Glasgow) Ltd (VTD 9399) 52.277
General Mills UK Ltd (VTD 20905) 29.156
General Motors Acceptance Corporation (UK) plc [1999] VATDR 456 (VTD 16137) 27.16
General Motors Acceptance Corporation (UK) plc (No 2), Ch D [2004] STC 577; [2004] EWHC 192 (Ch) 40.109, 44.53
General Motors Acceptance Corporation (UK) plc (No 3) (VTD 19989) 48.64
General Trading Stores Ltd (VTD 17591) 60.19
Generalbundesanwalt beim Bundesgerichtshof, R *v*, ECJ Case C-285/09; [2011] STC 138 .... 22.520
Genesis Hair & Beauty Ltd (VTD 17177) 57.123
Genie Financial Services Europe Ltd (VTD 20367) 3.176
Genius Holding BV *v* Staatssecretaris van Financiën, ECJ Case 342/87; [1989] ECR 4227; [1991] STC 239 .... 22.413
Genrey (PT) VTD 20929) 28.8
Gent (Mrs E) (t/a Elizabeth Corke Catering) (VTD 14438) 36.274
Gent (Mrs L) (VTD 13227) 51.160
Genuine Car Services (VTD 18141) 44.164
Geoffrey Clarke Grain Co Ltd (VTD 7142) 52.72
Geoffrey Davis (Menswear) Ltd (VTD 12576) 18.571
Geomatrix Ltd (VTD 10701) 10.5
Georgalakis Partnership (VTD 10083) 3.89
George (G) (t/a Top Six Hairdressing) (VTD 16971) 57.91
George (PS) (VTD 20400) 15.230
George (TW) (VTD 3974) 18.111

George (VD) (VTD 5072) 2.404
George & George (VTD 4562) 18.286
George Hammond plc [2007] VATDR 383 (VTD 20353) 66.43
George Hamshaw (Golf Services) Ltd [1979] VATTR 51 (VTD 722) 62.418
George Kerr Enterprises Ltd (VTD 18079) 57.206
George Kuikka Ltd [1990] VATTR 185 (VTD 5037) 62.476
Georghiou (K) (VTD 14970) 50.29
Georgiou (M & A) (t/a Mario's Chippery), CA [1996] STC 463 .... 3.6
Georgiou (M & A) v United Kingdom, ECHR 2000; [2001] STC 80; 3 ITLR 145 ..... 34.1
Germany (Federal Republic of) v EC Commission, ECJ Case 332/85; [1985] ECR
   5143 .... 22.549
Germany (Federal Republic of), Brasserie du Pêcheur SA v, ECJ Case C-46/93; [1996]
   1 ECR 1029; [1996] 1 CMLR 889; [1996] 2 WLR 506; [1996] All ER (EC) 301 .... 22.31
Germany (Federal Republic of), Dillenkofer & Others v, ECJ Case C-178/94; [1996]
   1 ECR 4845; [1996] 3 CMLR 469; [1996] All ER (EC) 917 .... 22.33
Germany (Federal Republic of), EC Commission v (No 1), ECJ Case C-74/91; [1992]
   1 ECR 5437; [1996] STC 843 .... 22.486
Germany (Federal Republic of), EC Commission v (No 2), ECJ Case C-427/98; [2003]
   STC 301 .... 22.237
Germany (Federal Republic of), EC Commission v (No 3), ECJ Case C-287/00; [2002]
   STC 982 .... 22.303
Germany (Federal Republic of), EC Commission v (No 4), ECJ Case C-109/02; [2006]
   STC 1587 .... 22.265
Germany (Federal Republic of), EC Commission v (No 5), ECJ Case C-144/02;
   [2004] All ER (D) 264 (Jul) 22.248
Germany (Federal Republic of), EC Commission v (No 6), ECJ Case C-401/06;
   6 December 2007 unreported 22.224
Gevroeders Benedik Abattoir CV, Spijkers v, ECJ Case C-24/85; [1986] ECR 1119;
   [1986] 2 CMLR 296 .... 22.133
GF Mercer Ltd, [2011] UKFTT 539 (TC), TC01386 .... 48.63
GFKL Financial Services AG, Finanzamt Essen Nord-Ost v, ECJ Case C-93/10;
   27 October 2011 unreported 22.95
GGN Builders Ltd, [2010] UKFTT 184 (TC), TC00488 .... 55.58
Ghafoor (B) (VTD 13329) 57.204
Ghaidan v Godin-Mendoza, HL [2004] 2 AC 557 .... 67.172
Ghaus (MR) (t/a Ghaus & Co) (VTD 4999) 62.454
Ghaus (MR) (t/a Ghaus & Co) (No 2) (VTD 10419) 62.455
Ghent Coal Terminal NV, Belgium (Kingdom of) v, ECJ Case C-37/95; [1998] STC 260;
   [1998] All ER (EC) 223 .... 22.406
Ghosh, R v, CA [1982] 3 WLR 110; [1982] 2 All ER 689 .... 50.29
Gibb (A) (t/a Business Post Fife) (VTD 11166) 18.585
Gibbs (A) (VTD 18270) 50.20
Gibbs (RW) (VTD 5596) 55.66
Gibbs Travel (VTD 18472) 62.237
Giblin (MJ) (VTD 20352) 15.56
Gibson (Mrs S) (t/a Miss Toner) (VTD 13293) 57.46
Giddian Ltd [1984] VATTR 161 (VTD 1706) 14.44
Giffenbond Ltd (VTD 13481) 36.338
GIL Insurance Ltd, ECJ Case C-308/01; [2004] STC 961 .... 22.529
Gilberts Motors Ltd (VTD 3424) 18.506
Gilbourne (B) [1974] VATTR 209 (VTD 109) 2.53
Gilder (GD) (VTD 18143) 15.16
Giles (G), [2009] UKFTT 109 (TC), TC00077 .... 62.267
Giles (JT) (VTD 6789) 62.66
Giles (Mr & Mrs) (VTD 5449) 62.267
Giles v Thompson, HL 1993, [1994] 1 AC 142; [1993] 3 All ER 321 .... 2.297
Gill (MS) (VTD 4904) 15.170
Gillamoor Ltd v Isle of Man Treasury (VTD 20591) 57.149
Gillan (J & M) (t/a Gracehill Golf Course), [2010] UKFTT 8 (TC), TC00327 .... 41.34
Gillan Beach Ltd, Ministre de l'Économie, des Finances et de l'Industrie v, ECJ Case
   C-114/05; [2006] STC 1080 .... 22.216

Gillard (WJS) (VTD 5040) 51.44
Gillaroo Ltd (VTD 8889) 18.101
Gillespie (G) (VTD 11504) 51.28
Gillex (UK) Ltd [2010] UKFTT 517 (TC), TC00772 .... 36.121
Gilmour (S) (VTD 5305) 57.127
Gingell (KAG) (VTD 5168) 18.475
GJ Bennett & Co (Builders) Ltd (VTD 6457) 52.245
GK Electrical UK Ltd (VTD 2861) 25.22
GL Motor Services Ltd (VTD 2413) 36.446
Glamorgan Prestige Developments Ltd, [2010] UKFTT 237 (TC), TC00536 .... 36.599
Glasgow City Council [1998] VATDR 407 (VTD 15491) 42.6
Glasgow City Council (No 2) (VTD 16613) 48.55
Glasgow Indoor Bowling Club (VTD 14889) 46.124
Glasgow Vending Services (VTD 943) 62.386
Glasgow's Miles Better Mid-Summer 5th Anniversary Ball (VTD 4460) 67.135
Glassborow & Another, QB [1974] STC 142; [1975] QB 465; [1974] 1 All ER 1041
.... 57.1
Glasse Brothers [1989] VATTR 143 (VTD 3716) 36.40
Glassiron Ltd [1989] VATTR 245 (VTD 4592) 62.64
Glastonbury Abbey (VTD 14579) 16.1
Glawe (HJ) Spiel und Unterhaltungsgeräte Aufstellungsgesellschaft mbH & Co KG v
   Finanzamt Hamburg-Barmbek-Uhlenhorst, ECJ Case C-38/93; [1994] STC 543;
   [1994] 1 ECR 1679; [1995] 1 CMLR 70 .... 22.239
GlaxoSmithKline Services Unlimited, [2010] UKFTT 418 (TC); [2011] SFTD 98,
   TC00688 .... 29.173
Gleeds Chartered Quantity Surveyors (VTD 9770, VTD 10069) 52.69
Glen-Jones (Ms A), [2011] UKFTT 141 (TC), TC01015 .... 41.93
Glen & Padden (t/a Shieldfield Processors and Refiners) (VTD 917) 2.195
Glendale Social Club [1994] VATTR 372 (VTD 12869) 62.110
Glendinning (R) (VTD 5245) 57.7
Glendower Cutting Tools Ltd (VTD 3564) 18.361
Gleneagles Hotel plc [1986] VATTR 196 (VTD 2152) 62.125
Glenfall House Trust (VTD 16657) 21.45
Glengate KG Properties Ltd (VTD 14236) 43.18
Glenshane Construction Services Ltd (VTD 14160) 37.18
Glenshee Chairlift Co Ltd (VTD 18162) 66.31
Glinski (C) (t/a Redcliffe Precious Metals) (VTD 11300) 40.72
Global Active Holdings Ltd [2006] VATDR 190 (VTD 19715) 2.219
Global Active Technologies Ltd (VTD 19715) 2.219
Global Games International Ltd [2005] VATDR 246 (18912) 5.48
Global Marketing (WM) Ltd (VTD 20377) 2.248
Global Master Ltd (VTD 20476) 57.110
Global Security Services Ltd (VTD 4035) 18.591
Global Self Drive Ltd [2005] VATDR 284 (VTD 19162) 38.3
Global Trade Centre Ltd (VTD 14866) 51.143
Global Vehicle Imports (UK) Ltd (VTD 18546) 18.462
Globalbis Distribution Ltd [2010] UKFTT 567 (TC), TC00808 .... 2.269
Globe Equities Ltd [1995] VATDR 472 (VTD 13105) 38.40
Glossop Sectional Buildings Ltd (VTD 4100) 18.285
GM Supplies (VTD 12983) 18.75
GMAC UK plc, UT [2011] UKUT 112 (TCC) 4.33
GNP Booth Ltd (VTD 17555) 5.58
Goddard (A & A) (VTD 11983) 55.84
Goddard & Phillips Ltd (VTD 3218) 18.470
Godfrey (AS) (VTD 14648) 65.43
Godin-Mendoza, Ghaidan v, HL [2004] 2 AC 557 .... 67.172
Godiva Bearings (Southern) Ltd (VTD 9778) 52.32
Godlin Ltd (VTD 4416) 7.20
Gohil (Mr & Mrs M) (t/a Gohil Fashions) (VTD 15435) 44.14
Gold (K) (VTD 11939) 50.50
Gold Star Publications Ltd, QB [1992] STC 365 .... 67.31

Goldcrest Transport Services Ltd (VTD 18722) 57.130
Golden Cloud Solarium (VTD 6761) 52.69
Golden Echo Productions (VTD 11747) 52.354
Golden Oak Partnership (The) (VTD 7212) 36.555
Golden Pyramid Ltd (VTD 9133) 57.102
Golden Wonder Ltd (VTD 18650) 29.163
Goldenberg (J) (VTD 11591) 2.50
Goldfinch Blinds Ltd (VTD 2671) 18.502
Goldfinch Transport Ltd [1996] VATDR 484 (VTD 14145) 18.9
Goldhaven Ltd (VTD 14675) 14.60
Goldmax Resources Ltd (VTD 18219) 46.27
Goldsborough Developments Ltd, ECJ Case C-419/02; [2006] STC 967; [2006] 2 WLR
  96 22.199
Goldsmith Foundation for European Affairs, [2000] VATDR 97 (VTD 16544) 62.530
Goldsmiths (Jewellers) Ltd, ECJ Case C-330/95; [1997] STC 1073; [1997] 1 ECR 3801;
  [1997] 3 CMLR 520 .... 22.258
Goldstar Distribution Ltd (VTD 20467) 57.109
Goliath International (Tools) Ltd (VTD 4737) 18.200
Goni (A) & Ali (A) (t/a Curry Centre Tandoori Restaurant) (VTD 15840) 57.90
Good (FVE) [1974] VATTR 256 (VTD 119) 62.211
Good Marriott & Hursthouse Ltd (VTD 6633) 52.33
Good Roofing (Devon) (VTD 7845) 52.74
Goodfellow (RW & MJ) [1986] VATTR 119 (VTD 2107) 62.13
Goodfellow & Steven Ltd (VTD 2453) 29.133
Goodhew (KWG) & Others [1975] VATTR 111 (VTD 170) 3.155
Goodluck Employment Services Ltd (VTD 19766) 40.43
Goodpass Ltd (VTD 14088) 36.146
Goodrich (N) (t/a Uye Tours) (VTD 17707) 57.133
Goodshelter Holdings Ltd (VTD 19219) 62.48
Goodwin & Unstead, R v, ECJ Case C-3/97; [1998] STC 699; [1998] 3 WLR 565;
  [1998] All ER (EC) 500 .... 22.82
Gorringe Pine (VTD 14036) 44.12
Götz, Landesanstalt für Landwirtschaft v, ECJ Case C-408/06; 13 December 2007
  unreported 22.140
Gould & Co (VTD 4773) 59.11
Gould & Cullen [1993] VATTR 209 (VTD 10156) 65.78
Goulds of Glasgow (VTD 14264) 2.526
Gourmet Sandwich Ltd (The) (VTD 5505) 36.542
Gow (CD & MD) (VTD 16272) 47.19
Gow (JW) (t/a Falkirk Building Company) (VTD 2983) 19.46
GPC Properties Ltd (VTD 7044) 52.125
Grace (I) [1998] VATDR 86 (VTD 15323) 44.128
Grace Baptist Church (VTD 16093) 15.155
Gracechurch Management Services Ltd, Ch D 2007, [2008] STC 795; [2007] EWHC
  755(Ch) 32.20
Graden Builders Ltd (VTD 12637) 15.194
Graham (B) (t/a Excel Tutoring Services) (VTD 16814) 21.38
Graham (KJ) (VTD 4350) 51.89
Graham (W) (t/a Sunlover Sunbeds) (VTD 10148) 52.374
Graham (SP) Ltd & Others (VTD 14789) 57.105
Graham Fredericks Ltd (VTD 3304) 18.5
Graham Leisure Ltd (VTD 1304) 5.31
Granada plc [1993] VATTR 94 (VTD 9782) 38.8
Granada Group plc [1991] VATTR 104 (VTD 5565) 62.194
Granada Group plc (No 2) (VTD 14803) 66.36
Grange Builders (Quainton) Ltd [2005] VATDR 147 (VTD 18905) 55.6
Grange (S) (VTD 15706) 36.143
Grange Farm (The) (VTD 2344) 36.290
Granmore Ltd (VTD 5253) 18.200
Grant Melrose & Tennant Ltd [1985] VATTR 90 (VTD 1858) 67.44
Grantham (W & D) (VTD 853) 24.16

Grantham Cricket Club (VTD 12287, 12863) 41.68
Grantham Cricket Club (No 2) (VTD 15527) 48.33
Granton Marketing Ltd, CA [1996] STC 1049 .... 67.166
Granton Marketing Ltd (No 2) [1999] VATDR 383 (VTD 16118) 62.409
Grants of St James's Ltd (VTD 427) 62.10
Graphic Eye Ltd (VTD 6249) 18.106
Graphic Procédé v Ministère du Budget, des Comptes publics et de la Fonction
  publique, ECJ Case C-88/09; [2010] STC 918 .... 22.177
Graphicad Ltd (VTD 6503) 18.425
Gras Savoye (SA) v France, ECHR Case 49218/99; 22 July 2003 unreported 34.25
Grattan plc (No 1), QB [1995] STC 651 .... 58.29
Grattan plc (No 2) (VTD 19515) 62.462
Grattan plc (No 3), Ch D [2009] STC 882; [2009] EWHC 364 (Ch) 2.304
Grattan plc (No 4), [2009] SFTD 590; [2009] UKFTT 184 (TC), TC00139 .... 2.28
Grattan plc (No 5), [2011] UKFTT 31 (TC); [2011] SFTD 297, TC00908 .... 67.56
Grattan plc (No 6), UT [2011] UKUT 399 (TCC); [2011] STC 2342 .... 2.523
Gravity Productions Ltd (VTD 7068) 18.214
Gray (JG) (t/a William Gray & Son), Ch D [2000] STC 880 .... 57.28
Gray (RN) (t/a RN Gray & Co) (VTD 12661) 40.36
Gray Dunn & Co Ltd (VTD 16839) 18.437
Great American Bagel Factory Ltd (The) (VTD 17018) 29.59
Great Central Railway (1976) plc (VTD 11402) 66.16
Greater London Council [1982] VATTR 94 (VTD 1224) 41.43
Greater London Red Cross Blood Transfusion Service [1983] VATTR 241 (VTD 1495)
  .... 7.102
Greater Manchester Police Authority ex p., R v C & E, CA [2001] STC 406 .... 42.9
Greater World Association Trust, (Trustees for the) [1989] VATTR 91 (VTD 3401)
  .... 62.401
Greece, BP Supergas Anonimos Etairia Geniki Emporiki-Viomichaniki kai
  Antiprossopeion v, ECJ Case C-62/93; [1995] STC 805; [1995] 1 ECR 1883;
  [1995] All ER (EC) 684 .... 22.558
Greece, Louloudakis v, ECJ Case C-262/99, 12 July 2001 unreported 18.620
Greece, see also Hellenic Republic and Elliniko Dimosio
Green (GW & Mrs JA) (VTD 9016) 7.25
Green (J) (t/a CMOS) (VTD 19265) 36.579
Green (MWJ) (VTD 14844) 48.19
Green Business Co Ltd (VTD 10523) 18.447
Green Cook Ltd (VTD 5781) 18.406
Greenall (DN) (VTD 2362, 2520) 36.625
Greener Solutions Ltd [2010] UKFTT 412 (TC), TC00682 .... 36.89
Greengate Furniture Ltd [2003] VATDR 178 (VTD 18280) 18.618
Greenhalgh's Craft Bakery Ltd (VTD 10955) 3.42, 29.56
Greenhouse Stirton & Co (VTD 5481) 18.223
Greenpeace Ltd (VTD 16681) 46.197
Greenspear Products Ltd (VTD 2124) 59.25
Greenwich Property Ltd (oao), R v C & E, Ch D [2001] STC 618; [2001] EWHC Admin
  230 .... 2.94
Greenwood (GE, PI & DL) (t/a Blinkers of South Lane) (VTD 12534) 18.206
Greer (FW) (VTD 6070) 51.100
Gregg (J & M), ECJ Case C-216/97; [1999] STC 934; [1999] All ER (EC) 775 ..... 22.298
Gregorio (D) & Sons (VTD 9105) 57.55
Gregory (JMG) (VTD 7979) 18.389
Greig (WJ & L) & Son (VTD 2918) 36.292
Grenane Properties Ltd, [2010] UKFTT 192 (TC), TC00494 .... 6.32
Grendel (RA) GmbH v Finanzamt fur Körperschaften Hamburg, ECJ Case 255/81;
  [1982] ECR 2301; [1983] 1 CMLR 379 .... 22.353
Greves (JE) & Son [1993] VATTR 127 (VTD 9777) 41.13
Grey Marlin, re, Ch D [1999] 3 All ER 429 .... 37.5
Greyhound Transport (UK) Ltd (VTD 13216) 14.9
Greystone Export Trading Ltd, oao, R v HMRC, QB [2007] EWHC 521 (Admin)
  .... 36.653

Greystone International Ltd, [2011] UKFTT 321 (TC), TC01181 .... 36.113
Grieco (S) (t/a Globetrotters Fish Bar) (VTD 13194) 65.91
Grieve (J) (VTD 20149) 66.4
Griffin (RP) & Griffin (DM), [2010] UKFTT 220 (TC), TC00521 .... 18.615
Griffin-Woodhouse Ltd (VTD 8942) 36.389
Griffiths (RT) (t/a Action for Business) (VTD 17404) 5.67
Griffiths & Another, Hayman v, QB [1987] STC 649 .... 59.9
Griffiths & Goddard Restorations Ltd (VTD 6523) 18.230
Grimsby College Enterprises Ltd, UT [2010] SFTD 2009 .... 36.74
Grisdale (G & Mrs W) [1989] VATTR 162 (VTD 4069) 57.65
Grogan (N & A) (t/a Valet Plus) (VTD 16084) 57.130
Groom (CR) (VTD 1630) 36.267
Gross (MI) (VTD 14454) 44.141
Grosvenor Commodities Ltd (VTD 7221) 29.99
Group Topek Holdings Ltd (VTD 13146) 18.192
Groupment des Hauts Fourneaux et Acieres Belges v High Authority of the
  European Coal and Steel Community, ECJ [1958] ECSC 245 .... 41.127
Grove Fresh Ltd (VTD 19241) 29.168
Groves Garage (VTD 5895) 18.187
Grovewood (1988) Ltd (VTD 17125) 41.7
Grundstückgemeinschaft Schloßstraße GbR v Finanzamt Paderborn, ECJ Case
  C-396/98; 8 June 2000 unreported 22.398
Grundig Italiana SpA v Ministero delle Finanze, ECJ Case C-255/00; [2003] All ER (EC)
  176 .... 22.57
Grunwick Processing Laboratories Ltd, CA [1987] STC 357 .... 2.234, 3.61
GT Collins & Son (VTD 3738) 44.89
GT Marketing (Clacton) Ltd (VTD 18167) 18.66
GT Scaffolding Ltd (VTD 18226) 15.177
Guardian Building Services (VTD 11050) 52.39
Guardian Royal Exchange Assurance Group, Barber v, ECJ Case 262/88; [1990] 1 ECR
  1889; [1990] 2 CMLR 513; [1990] 2 All ER 660 .... 22.40
Guernsey Leasing Co (VTD 19974) 2.145
Guest Leasing & Bloodstock Co Ltd (VTD 1277) 7.60
Guinea Grill Stakes Ltd (VTD 1291) 7.61
Gulf Trading & Management Ltd (VTD 16847) 46.208
Gulland Properties Ltd (VTD 13955) 46.228
Gulliver's Travel Agency Ltd [1994] VATTR 210 (VTD 12494) 63.5
Gundy Harris & Co Ltd (VTD 5172) 18.54
Gunlab Ltd (VTD 19026) 18.543
Gunn (R) & Davies (MJ) (VTD 16927) 18.83
Guntert (PJ) (t/a Abingdon Scaffolding Co) (VTD 10604) 52.195
Guntert (PJ) (t/a Abingdon Scaffolding Co) (VTD 12127) 2.419
Gura (NA) (t/a Vincent Footwear) (VTD 18416) 12.14
GUS Catalogue Order Ltd (VTD 2958) 5.10
GUS Merchandise Corporation Ltd [1978] VATTR 28 (VTD 553) 2.113
GUS Merchandise Corporation Ltd, QB [1992] STC 776 .... 2.284
GUS Merchandise Corporation Ltd, CA [1981] STC 569; [1981] 1 WLR 1309 .... 58.1
GUS Merchandise Corporation Ltd (No 2), CA 1994, [1995] STC 279 .... 58.53
GUS Merchandise Corporation Ltd (VTD 2958) 5.10
Gutherie (P) [1980] VATTR 152 (VTD 986) 3.113
Guttenburg & Sons (VTD 3392) 14.47
Guy Butler (International) Ltd (No 1) [1974] VATTR 199 (VTD 106A) 2.249
Guyana Commissioner of Inland Revenue, Argosy Co Ltd v, PC [1971] 1 WLR 514
  .... 3.1, 58.42
Gwent County Council (VTD 6153) 52.2
Gwent Technical Mouldings Ltd (VTD 7939) 18.170
Gymer (JC) (VTD 16007) 50.35
Gynn (RJ) (VTD 15360) 48.129
Gyte (AC & PS) [1999] VATDR 241 (VTD 16031) 58.22

H

H & B Motors (Dorchester) (VTD 11209) 2.474
H & M Hennes Ltd, Ch D [2005] STC 1749; [2005] EWHC 1383 (Ch) 12.22
H & V Commissioning Services (VTD 17461) 18.541
H Griffiths Engineering Ltd (VTD 19098) 18.523
H James Builders (Wolverhampton) Ltd (VTD 7102) 52.105
H Tempest (Cardiff) Ltd [1993] VATTR 482 (VTD 11210) 67.28, 67.54
H Tempest Ltd [1975] VATTR 161 (VTD 201) 67.27
H Tempest Ltd (No 2) [1993] VATTR 482 (VTD 11210) 67.28, 67.54
H5 Ltd (t/a High Five) (VTD 20821) 29.158
Haden & Son (VTD 2209) 15.254
Haderer (W) v Finanzamt Wilmersdorf, ECJ Case C-445/05; [2008] STC 2171 ..... 22.307
Hadfield (GI) & Son Ltd (VTD 6421) 36.328
Hadi (F) (t/a Avionics Maintenance) (VTD 14677) 67.23
Hadjigeorgiou (I) (VTD 18246) 50.20
Hadley (C) (VTD 10663) 51.89
Haggs Castle Golf Club (VTD 13653) 21.53
Hague (Mrs J) (VTD 1159) 36.175
Hague Farms Ltd (VTD 13722) 44.30
Hague Shaw (Marketing) Ltd (VTD 11445, 11474) 5.19
Hagyard (P) & Gardiner (A) (VTD 5240) 18.206
Haigh (Dr DT) (VTD 20934) 55.81
Haigh (JB & PA) (VTD 15835) 48.60
Haines (H) (VTD 13986) 51.176
Haines (PJ & AL) (VTD 13834) 33.47
Hair by John Oliver [1987] VATTR 239 (VTD 2532) 18.373
Håkansson & Sturesson v Sweden, ECHR 1991, 13 EHRR 1 .... 2.251
Halcove Ltd (VTD 6935) 18.83
Halcro-Johnston (J) [2001] VATDR 335 (VTD 17147) 15.137
Halifax plc (No 1) (VTD 16697) 46.218
Halifax plc (No 2), ECJ Case C-255/02; [2006] STC 919; [2006] 2 WLR 90 .... 22.60
Halil (E) [1992] VATTR 432 (VTD 9590) 2.235
Hall (C) (VTD 14131) 52.197
Hall (G & I) (VTD 623) 2.195
Hall (PJ) (VTD 6722) 52.58
Hall (R), [2009] UKFTT 58 (TC), TC00037 .... 15.208
Hall (WM) (VTD 16989) 19.32
Hall of Names Ltd (The) (VTD 8806) 5.43
Hall Park Garage Ltd (VTD 1185) 44.58
Halladale Group plc [2003] VATDR 551 (VTD 18218) 46.44
Hallam (B) (t/a APX Car Sales) [1977] VATTR 105 (VTD 394) 2.138
Hallam (WR) (VTD 683) 2.176
Hallborough Properties Ltd (VTD 10849) 65.25
Halliwell (MJA) (VTD 17743) 66.6
Halloran (P) & Hollingsworth (M) (VTD 14412) 18.205
Halls Dry Cleaning Co Ltd (VTD 15069) 57.36
Halpern & Woolf (VTD 10072) 62.468
Halroy Products Ltd (VTD 1010) 1.72
Halsall Riding & Livery Centre (VTD 19342) 48.74
Halsey (JH) [1996] VATDR 508 (VTD 14313) 36.565
Halstead Motor Company [1995] VATDR 201 (VTD 13373) 18.47
Halt Garage (VTD 3749) 18.586
Ham Enterprises Ltd (VTD 19908) 52.95
Hamann v Finanzamt Hamburg-Eimsbuttel, ECJ Case 51/88; [1989] ECR 767;
    [1990] 2 CMLR 377; [1991] STC 193 .... 22.202
Hamer (DG & SE) (VTD 17669) 48.63
Hamid (A) (VTD 18802) 51.131
Hamiltax (VTD 8948) 62.233
Hamilton (BH) (VTD 2460) 7.94
Hamilton (I & J) (VTD 15556) 58.23

Hamilton (LR) (VTD 16020) 15.48
Hamilton (W) & Son (VTD 14812) 44.49
Hamilton Golf Club (VTD 1150) 13.34
Hamlet's (Radio & TV) Ltd (VTD 12716) 36.472
Hammersmith & West London College (VTD 17540) 6.28
Hammond Suddard Solicitors *v* Agrichem International Holdings Ltd, CA [2001] All ER
    (D) 258 (Dec) 2.369
Hamore Ltd (VTD 15061) 50.27
Hampden-Smith (MR) (VTD 7468) 52.93
Hamperbay Ltd (VTD 3048) 18.423
Hampson (S) (VTD 3402) 18.506
Hampton (JPR) (VTD 2196) 36.243
Hampton (RA & BD) (t/a Tongue Electrics) (VTD 15171) 62.50
Hamptons (VTD 3883) 36.404
Hamstead Holdings Ltd (VTD 19867) 1.30
Han (GK) & Yau (D) (t/a Murdishaw Supper Bar), CA [2001] STC 1188; 3 ITLR 873;
    [2001] 1 WLR 2253; [2001] 4 All ER 687 .... 34.5
Han Ali Ltd [2010] UKFTT 351 (TC), TC00633 .... 36.121
Hanbury Charity (VTD 20126) 15.89
Hanby, Walker *v*, QB [1987] STC 649 .... 59.9
Hancock *v* Austin, 1863, 14 CBNS 634 .... 14.80
Hancock & Wood Ltd (VTD 6691) 52.58
Hands (T) (VTD 20788) 52.309
Handyside (AJ) (t/a Stratagem International) (VTD 13182) 36.211
Hangleton Farm Education Ltd (VTD 19001) 21.16
Hanif (M) (VTD 6430, 7815) 2.279, 2.355
Hannah Auto Electronics Ltd (VTD 15429) 18.441
Hannan (WE) & Associates Ltd (VTD 5343) 18.79
Hanover Company Services Ltd, [2010] SFTD 1047; [2010] UKFTT 256 (TC),
    TC00550 .... 22.552
Hansen (P) (VTD 1154) 36.621
Happy Place Ltd (t/a The Munch Box) (VTD 17654) 29.6
Haque (M) (VTD 20296) 51.129
Haque (S) [1999] VATDR 219 (VTD 16047) 2.183
Haque (M) & Company (VTD 4517) 18.203
Harber (AT) (VTD 12979) 65.92
Harbig Leasing Two Ltd [2000] VATDR 469 (VTD 16843) 57.34
Harbs, Finanzamt Rendsburg *v*, ECJ Case C-321/02; [2006] STC 340 .... 22.483
Harbury Estates Ltd (VTD 8851) 18.502
Hardlife Ladder Co Ltd (VTD 2715) 65.46
Harding (RC & R) (t/a Tolcarne Motors) (VTD 11809) 17.15
Hardman (Ms DA) (VTD 14045) 48.44
Hardwick (RL) (VTD 5961) 18.142
Hardwill (PH) (VTD 13958) 52.108
Hardy (S) (VTD 289) 15.9
Hardy (Dr TSR) (VTD 5521) 18.133
Hardys of Telford (VTD 6791) 52.342
Hare (A) (t/a Imperial Dry Cleaners) (VTD 14202) 57.23
Hare (S) (t/a Ican Finance), [2011] UKFTT 81 (TC), TC00958 .... 57.7
Hare Wines Ltd (VTD 6721) 52.32
Haresfield Court Tenants Association (VTD 20133) 55.58
Hargreaves Lansdown Asset Management Ltd (VTD 12030) 27.41
Hargreaves (UK) plc (VTD 20382) 36.661
Haringey Borough Council, QB [1995] STC 830 .... 42.1
Harlech Estates Ltd (VTD 9548) 40.44
Harley (JD & J) (t/a The Treasure Chest) (VTD 13533) 57.7
Harley Engineering Ltd (VTD 3271) 18.435
Harleyford Estate Ltd (VTD 7741) 18.51
Harleyford Golf Club Ltd (No 1) (VTD 14466) 67.142
Harleyford Golf Club Ltd (No 2), [2011] UKFTT 634 (TC), TC01476 .... 27.53
Harman (JH) (VTD 18415) 18.439

Harmer (DJ) (VTD 9581) 18.88
Harnas & Helm CV v Staatssecretaris van Financiën, ECJ Case C-80/95; [1997] STC
   364; [1997] 1 ECR 745; [1997] 1 CMLR 649; [1997] All ER (EC) 267 .... 22.112
Haroun (M) (t/a Prince of Bengal Restaurant) (VTD 14232) 65.96
Harpcombe Ltd, QB [1996] STC 726 .... 46.24
Harper (D & KL) (t/a Tee Time Catering) (VTD 20176) 65.91
Harper Collins Publishers Ltd (VTD 12040) 46.54
Harpur (JR) (VTD 2930) 18.482
Harpur Group Ltd, [1994] VATTR 180 (VTD 12001) 27.36
Harrid (GN & Mrs AV) (VTD 18132) 18.585
Harrier Llc, [2011] UKFTT 725 (TC), TC01562 .... 5.24
Harrier Shoes Ltd (VTD 3814) 18.280
Harriet's House Ltd (VTD 16315) 23.13
Harrild (D) (VTD 19604) 65.99
Harrington (M) & Jones (M) (t/a The Station) (VTD 20336) 18.542
Harrington Construction Ltd (VTD 3470) 15.225
Harris (A & J) (t/a Gribbens Taxis & Wedding Cars) (VTD 4882) 57.54
Harris (AE & Mrs JM) (VTD 18822) 15.53
Harris (AW, JE & AO) (t/a the Marcia Inn) (VTD 19221) 18.154
Harris (D) (t/a Fellows Sandwich Bar) (VTD 20235) 47.23
Harris (D) & Harris (DA), QB [1989] STC 907 .... 51.88
Harris (EVW) (VTD 11925) 3.90
Harris (GM) (VTD 9069) 52.75
Harris (J & E) (VTD 373) 57.2
Harris (JLH) (VTD 6019) 51.94
Harris (Mrs M) (t/a Fellows Bistro) (VTD 20235) 47.23
Harris, ex p., R v C & E, QB [1999] STC 1016 .... 14.94
Harrison (EG), [2011] UKFTT 345 (TC), TC01025 .... 7.114
Harrison (GA), [1981] VATTR 164 (VTD 1125) 3.27
Harrison (GA), [1982] VATTR 7 (VTD 1182) 2.458
Harrison (L & R) (VTD 13544) 58.3
Harrison (LS) (VTD 20392) 65.99
Harrison (Mrs B) (VTD 12351) 51.32
Harrison (RJ) (VTD 4908) 51.96
Harrison (T) (VTD 3078) 18.260
Harrison-Devereux (S), [2010] UKFTT 267 (TC), TC00561 .... 15.275
Harrison Meillam Construction Ltd (VTD 5875) 52.125
Harrison Priddey & Co (VTD 14089) 6.12
Harrod (ML) (t/a Roadcraft UK) (VTD 19644) 1.35
Harrods (UK) Ltd (VTD 19318) 2.480
Harrogate Business Development Centre Ltd [1998] VATDR 466 (VTD 15565) 21.26
Harry (D) (t/a Principal Financial Associates) (VTD 15747) 57.26
Harry B Litherland & Co Ltd [1978] VATTR 226 (VTD 701) 62.167
Harry Friar Partnership (VTD 9395) 44.148
Hartley Engineering Ltd (VTD 12385) 65.51
Hartridge (P) (t/a Hartridge Consultancy) (VTD 15553) 36.566
Hartwell plc, CA [2003] STC 396; [2003] EWCA Civ 130 .... 44.86, 67.167
Harvey (N) (t/a Green Express Railtours) (VTD 15608) 63.10
Harvey (RE & EM) (VTD 4899) 57.126
Harz & Power, HL 1966, [1967] 1 All ER 177 .... 14.86
Hashash, R v, CA Criminal Division 2006, [2008] STC 1158; [2006] EWCA Crim
   2518 .... 49.13
Hassan (MK) (VTD 17949) 59.17
Hastings & Rother YMCA (VTD 2329) 21.50
Hastings Borough Council (VTD 8934) 52.140
Hatfield (R & Mrs MR) (VTD 11677) 18.569
Hatt (WJ) Ltd (VTD 10762) 18.214
Hatton Garden Agency Ltd (VTD 13285) 18.71
Haugh (D) (VTD 15055) 36.604
Haulfryn Estates Co Ltd (VTD 16145) 69.9

Hauptzollamt Emmerich, Wiener SI GmbH *v*, ECJ Case C-338/95; [1997] 1 ECR 6495; [1998] 1 CMLR 1110 .... 22.5

Hauptzollamt Frankfurt am Main-Ost *v* Deutsche Olivetti GmbH, ECJ Case C-17/89; [1990] 1 ECR 2301; [1992] 2 CMLR 859 .... 22.226

Hauptzollamt Freiburg, Einberger *v* (No 2), ECJ Case 294/82; [1984] ECR 1177; [1985] 1 CMLR 765 .... 22.99

Hauptzollamt Hamburg-Jonas, Emsland-Stärke GmbH *v*, ECJ Case C-110/99, [2001] All ER (D) 34 (Jan) 22.59

Hauptzollamt Koblenz, Collection Guns GmbH *v*, ECJ [1985] ECR 3387 .... 60.8

Hauptzollamt München-Mitte, Witzemann *v*, ECJ Case C-343/89; [1993] STC 108; [1991] 1 ECR 4477 .... 22.101

Hauptzollamt Reutlingen, Daiber (E) *v*, ECJ Case 200/84; [1985] ECR 3363 .... 60.8

Hauptzollamt Wuppertal, Clees (U) *v*, ECJ Case C-259/97, 3 December 1998 unreported 60.9

Havant Borough Council (VTD 6080) 52.65

Hawkeye Communications Ltd (No 1), [2010] UKFTT 636 (TC); [2011] SFTD 250, TC00875 .... 2.372

Hawkeye Communications Ltd (No 2), [2011] UKFTT 720 (TC), TC01557 .... 2.275

Hawthorn *v* Smallcorn, Ch D [1998] STC 591 .... 47.72

Haycock (T) (VTD 6850) 51.77

Haydn Welch Jewellers (VTD 14428) 18.130

Haydon-Baillie (WG) [1986] VATTR 79 (VTD 2072) 36.560

Hayes (S & SJ) (VTD 4693) 51.10

Hayhoe (AG) (for Watchet Bowling Club and Watchet Indoor Bowling Club) (VTD 1026) 13.43

Hayhoe (PD) (VTD 568) 58.3

Hayman *v* Griffiths & Another, QB [1987] STC 649 .... 59.9

Haynes (RC) (VTD 2948) 29.123

Hays Personnel Services Ltd (VTD 14882) 1.45

Hayter Brothers Ltd (VTD 9378) 52.35

Hayward Gill & Associates Ltd [1998] VATDR 352 (VTD 15635) 48.20

Hazel Grove Timber & Building Supplies Ltd (VTD 13801) 18.352

Hazel Street Ltd (VTD 6229) 52.355

Hazell (M) (VTD 5574) 51.136

Hazelwood Caravans & Chalets Ltd [1985] VATTR 179 (VTD 1923) 30.6

HBOS plc, CS 2008, [2009] STC 486; [2008] CSIH 69 .... 27.44

HC Motors Ltd , [2011] UKFTT 129 (TC), TC01003 .... 48.63

HDG Harbour Development Group Ltd (VTD 9386) 46.29

HE, Finanzamt Bergisch Gladbach *v* , ECJ Case C-25/03; [2007] STC 128 .... 22.407

Head (AD) (VTD 4828) 57.53

Head (M) (VTD 1119) 3.73

Headlam (Floorcovering Distributor) Ltd (t/a Florco) (VTD 16478) 18.64

Headley Enterprises (VTD 1295) 62.362

Headline & Just Hair (VTD 4089) 62.257

Headway Commercial Ltd (VTD 15535) 6.5

Healan (AT) (VTD 9351) 18.447

Health Response UK Ltd, [2010] UKFTT 123 (TC), TC00434 .... 33.31

Healthcare at Home Ltd, [2007] VATDR 511 (VTD 20379) 19.6

Healthcare Leasing Ltd, [2007] VATDR 494 (VTD 20260) 62.493

Heard (RA) (VTD 20102) 18.543

Heart of Variety [1975] VATTR 103 (VTD 168) 62.19

Heath (JA) (t/a Heath Private & Commercial Vehicles) (VTD 16212) 44.108

Heath House Charter Ltd, [2010] SFTD 245; [2009] UKFTT 305 (TC), TC00249 .... 7.44

Heath Plastering Co Ltd (VTD 10680) 62.560

Heather (AP) Ltd (VTD 4376) 18.50

Heathill Developments Ltd (VTD 2412) 19.86

Heating & Management Services Ltd (VTD 4200) 18.84

Heating & Ventilating Contractors' Association (VTD 20887) 64.34

Heatley (AG) (t/a AGH Shopfitting) (VTD 18836) 4.29

Heaton (B & A) (t/a Freshmaid Sandwiches Take Away) (VTD 16661) 50.138

Hedges & Mercer [1976] VATTR 146 (VTD 271) 27.35
Hedley (Mrs BD) (t/a Birtle Riding Centre) 48.63
Hedley Lomas (Ireland) Ltd, ex p., R v Ministry of Agriculture, Fisheries & Food, ECJ
  Case C-5/94; [1996] 1 ECR 2553; [1996] 2 CMLR 391; [1996] All ER (EC) 493 .... 22.32
Heerma, Staatssecretaris van Financiën v, ECJ Case C-23/98; [2001] STC 1437 ..... 22.108
Heffernan (DRM) (VTD 10735) 18.273
Heger Rudi GmbH v Finanzamt Graz-Stadt, ECJ Case C-166/05; [2008] STC 2679
  .... 22.206
Heights of Abraham (Matlock Bath) Ltd (VTD 1914) 66.32
Heijn (Dr A) (VTD 15562) 55.78
Heiser v Finanzamt Innsbruck, ECJ Case C-172/03; [2005] All ER(D) 66(Mar) 22.11
Helgor Furs Ltd (VTD 728) 25.19
Hellaby (MJ) (VTD 4790) 29.51
Hellenic Republic, EC Commission v, ECJ Case C-331/94; [1996] STC 1168; [1996]
  1 ECR 2675 .... 22.211
Hellenic Republic, EC Commission v, ECJ Case C-260/98; 12 September 2000
  unreported 22.136
Hellenic Republic, EC Commission v, ECJ Case C-13/06; [2007] STC 194 .... 22.329
Hellenic Republic, see also Elliniko Dimosio
Hellesdon Developments Ltd (VTD 16833) 46.62
Hellewell (M & A) (VTD 1274) 3.153
Help the Aged, QB [1997] STC 406 .... 11.17
Helping Hand Asset Management Ltd (VTD 20408) 1.47
Helsby (Mrs S) (VTD 6066) 18.233
HEM Construction Ltd (VTD 12449) 53.19
HEM Construction Ltd (No 2) (VTD 13203) 53.20
Hempsons [1977] VATTR 73 (VTD 361) 14.71
Hemsworth Town Council (VTD 14985) 62.345
Henderson (GJ) (VTD 17294) 44.132
Henderson (MA & JS) (t/a Tony's Fish and Chip Shop), Ch D 2000, [2001] STC 47
  .... 3.10
Henderson (RG) (t/a La Coupe) (VTD 13469) 57.129
Henderson v Henderson, 1843, 3 Hare 100 .... 2.125
Henfling & Others (administrators of Tiercé Franco-Belge SA), État Belge v, ECJ Case
  C-464/10; [2011] STC 1851 .... 22.189
Henley Glass Centre Ltd (VTD 5236) 18.211
Henley Picture House Ltd (VTD 895) 41.139
Henn & Darby, R v, HL 1980, [1981] AC 850; [1980] 2 All ER 166 .... 22.2
Henriksen, Skatteministeriet v, ECJ Case 173/88; [1989] ECR 2763; [1990] STC 768;
  [1990] 3 CMLR 558 .... 22.332
Henry Moss of London Ltd & Another, CA 1980, [1981] STC 139; [1981] 2 All ER
  86 .... 25.1
Henshaws Society for Blind People (VTD 19373) 15.203
Herbert (PM) (VTD 2350) 36.147
Herbert Berry Associates Ltd v CIR, HL 1977, 52 TC 113 .... 14.84
Herbert of Liverpool (Hair Design) Ltd (VTD 15949) 41.86
Hereford Cathedral (The Dean and Chapter of) (VTD 11737) 36.320
Heritage of London Trust Operations Ltd (VTD 18545) 62.161
Heritage Venture Enterprises Ltd (VTD 10741) 36.72
Herling Ltd, [2009] UKFTT 257 (TC), TC00205 .... 15.68
Herman (R & R) (t/a Retell) (VTD 16591) 18.427
Hermolis & Co Ltd, [1989] VATTR 199 (VTD 4137) 29.165
Heron (PA) (VTD 13529B) 51.123
Herrod-Taylor & Co (VTD 1475) 36.284
Hesketh (C) & Sons Ltd (VTD 16963) 44.93
Heslop (AA) (VTD 3862) 15.5
Hetherington (D) (VTD 15647) 7.123
Hewitt (JE) (VTD 9910) 52.21
Hewitt (JE) (t/a James E Hewitt Associates) (VTD 11177) 18.248
Hewitt (K), [2011] UKFTT 571 (TC), TC01414 .... 15.275
Hewitt (N) (VTD 1149) 2.195

Hewitt Overall Associates (VTD 9374) 19.45
Hexham Steeplechase Co Ltd (VTD 10481) 52.346
Heyfordian Travel Ltd, [1979] VATTR 139 (VTD 774) 3.115
Heyrod Construction Ltd (VTD 7882) 36.381
H5 Hotels Ltd (VTD 20662) 18.619
HHT Ltd (VTD 19169) 18.525
Hi-Wire Ltd (VTD 6204) 6.21
HIBT Ltd (t/a Hertfordshire International College of Business and Technology) (VTD
    19978) 21.17
Hickey (KG) (VTD 18711) 2.35
Hickford (D) (VTD 6290) 18.600
Hicking (N & J) (VTD 17117) 15.140
Hickling & Squires Ltd (VTD 2287) 36.358
Hicks (BA) (VTD 11215) 44.141
Hicks (TF & H) (t/a Parc Golf Centre) (VTD 18121) 3.95
Hickson (C) & Others (t/a Flury's) (VTD 11455) 14.28
Higgins (A) (VTD 6205) 41.11
Higgins (MJ) (VTD 18354) 18.64
High Peak Theatre Trust Ltd (VTD 13678) 67.104
High Range Developments Ltd (VTD 8989) 18.83
High Street Vouchers Ltd, QB [1990] STC 575 .... 67.160
Highacre (Cambridge) Ltd (VTD 12060) 2.327
Higher Education Statistics Agency Ltd, QB [2000] STC 332 .... 65.88
Highfire Ltd (t/a School Dinners) (VTD 2399) 14.47
Highland Council (The), CS 2007, [2008] STC 1280; [2007] CSIH 36 .... 42.24
Highsize Ltd (VTD 7098) 40.103
Highview Ltd (VTD 9564) 52.241
Higson (P) (VTD 6826) 7.70
Hi-Life Promotions Ltd (VTD 13033) 18.506
Hill (A) (VTD 4973) 51.112
Hill (AG) (VTD 3809) 18.413
Hill (Dr A) (VTD 5658) 33.41
Hill (Dr J) (VTD 15543) 57.115
Hill (Mrs E) (VTD 17307) 18.343
Hill (ER) (VTD 5001) 18.92
Hill (JE) (VTD 10967) 18.421
Hill (MRK) (t/a Marcus Builders) (VTD 13235) 18.88
Hill (TJ) [1982] VATTR 134 (VTD 1225) 15.4
Hill (JK) & Mansell (SJ) (t/a JK Hill & Co), QB [1988] STC 424 .... 1.6, 36.187
Hill & Son (Manor Park) Ltd (VTD 1629) 36.443
Hill Ash Developments [2000] VATDR 366 (VTD 16747) 55.38
Hill Welsh (VTD 6828) 52.108
Hillas (S) (VTD 12630) 50.21
Hillfoots Drystone Dyking (VTD 8966) 18.129
Hillingdon Legal Resources Centre Ltd [1991] VATTR 39 (VTD 5210) 11.47
Hillingdon Shirt Co Ltd (VTD 678) 36.342
Hills Diecasting Co Ltd (VTD 4399) 18.214
Hilltop Assistance Ltd, [2009] UKFTT 200 (TC), TC00153 .... 62.49
Hinckley Golf Club Ltd [1992] VATTR 259 (VTD 9527) 13.15
Hindi Picture Ltd (VTD 4490) 18.283
Hindforce Ltd (VTD 18920) 36.94
Hindle (D & A) (t/a DJ Baker Bar), Ch D 2003, [2004] STC 412; [2003] EWHC 1665
    (Ch) 3.12
Hipisol Ltd, [2010] UKFTT 392 (TC), TC00388 .... 18.440
Hira Co Ltd, [2011] UKFTT 450 (TC), TC01302 .... 36.90
Hiross Ltd (VTD 10630) 18.133
Hislop (MP) (t/a Dorchester Productions) (VTD 2258) 51.104
Historic Motorsport Ltd (VTD 19048) 25.10
Hitchcock v Post Office, EAT [1980] ICR 100 .... 7.104
Hitron Ltd [1989] VATTR 148 (VTD 3755) 14.53
HJ Banks & Co Ltd, [2010] UKFTT 33 (TC), TC00347 .... 46.203

HJ Berry & Sons Ltd (VTD 1324) 44.17
HJ Glawe Spiel und Unterhaltungsgeräte Aufstellungsgesellschaft mbH & Co KG *v*
Finanzamt Hamburg-Barmbek-Uhlenhorst, ECJ Case C-38/93; [1994] STC 543;
[1994] 1 ECR 1679; [1995] 1 CMLR 70 .... 22.239
HJF Enterprises Ltd (VTD 13788) 25.24
HKS Coachworks Ltd (VTD 1124) 44.16
HM Advocate, Singh (M & J) *v*, HCJ(S) [2001] STC 790 .... 14.96
HM Treasury, R *v* (ex p. British Telecommunications plc), ECJ Case C-392/93; [1996]
1 ECR 1631; [1996] 2 CMLR 217; [1996] 3 WLR 303; [1996] All ER (EC) 401 .... 22.34
HM Treasury & Another, R *v* (ex p. Service Authority for the National Crime Squad and
Others), QB [2000] STC 638 .... 42.8
HMG Europe BV (VTD 9814) 51.48
Ho (CK) (t/a New Lucky Ho) (VTD 15605) 62.310
Ho (PN) (VTD 18315) 14.41
Ho (R & YL) (t/a Robert's Golden Cod Fish Bar) [1996] VATDR 423 (VTD 14252)
.... 3.17
Hobson (WHD, PM & AD) (VTD 14671) 52.439
Hodge (AC & Y) (t/a Priory Kitchen) (VTD 16185) 29.13
Hodge Servicing Ltd (VTD 11561) 17.3
Hodges (EL, CM, KC & E) (VTD 16983) 57.209
Hodges (RJ & AS), QB [2000] STC 262 .... 62.325
Hodgkins (JR) (t/a Clifton Books) (VTD 6496) 36.270
Hodgkiss (P) (VTD 6825) 18.425
Hodgson (KJ) (VTD 7138, 7159) 52.342
Hodgson (RA & E) (VTD 5052) 18.404
Hodgson (RW & J) (VTD 15165) 50.74
Hodgson Martin Ltd (VTD 9108) 18.184
Hodson (D & Mrs C) (t/a Bordercraft Workshops) (VTD 13897) 15.253
Hodson (K) (VTD 4709) 62.192
Hoffmann, ECJ Case C-144/00; [2004] STC 740 .... 22.318
Hoi Shan Chinese Restaurant (VTD 2368) 47.6
Holborn Commrs, R *v* (ex p. Rind Settlement Trustees), QB [1974] STC 567 . 52.24, 52.25
Holden Plant Hire Ltd (VTD 10685) 52.378
Holder (C) & Holder (GP), QB [1989] STC 327 .... 3.3
Holder (P) (VTD 6446) 36.361
Holding (GR & JM) (VTD 19573) 41.104
Holdproud Ltd (VTD 15589) 18.235
Holdsworth & Co *v* Isle of Man Treasury (VTD 12480) 17.14
Holiday Inns (UK) Ltd [1993] VATTR 321 (VTD 10609) 62.142
Holin Groep BV cs *v* Staatssecretaris van Financiën, ECJ Case C-7/02; [2004] STC
776 .... 22.457
Holland (A) (t/a The Studio Hair Company), Ch D 2008, [2009] STC 150; [2008]
EWHC 2621 (Ch) 41.91
Holland (ME) [1978] VATTR 108 (VTD 580) 62.212
Holland (P) (VTD 15996) 65.91
Holland Studio Craft Ltd (VTD 3771) 18.401
Hollick (DP) (VTD 3956) 18.241
Hollier (J) (VTD 3758) 55.52
Hollies Discount Furniture Centre Ltd (VTD 5243) 51.107
Hollingworth (GJ) (VTD 672) 2.378
Hollosi (M & TEJ) (VTD 13757) 57.7
Holloway (RJ) (VTD 7493) 52.341
Hollybourne Hotels Ltd (VTD 17486) 62.451
Holman Kelly Paper Co Ltd (VTD 6899) 52.69
Holmen Paper AB (VTD 7628) 52.32
Holmes (NM) (t/a The Chicken Shop) (VTD 16264) 29.66
Holmes (Mrs R), [2011] UKFTT 347 (TC), TC01207 .... 21.35
Holmwood House School Developments (VTD 18130) 41.10
Holt (M) (Manchester) Ltd (VTD 6312) 52.71
Holvey, QB 1977, [1978] STC 187; [1978] QB 310; [1978] 1 All ER 1249 .... 2.192
Holy Spirit Association for the Unification of World Christianity (VTD 1777) 7.92

Holy Trinity Church (Heath Town Wolverhampton) PCC (VTD 13652) 55.45
Holywell International (Engineering) Ltd (VTD 1470) 36.2
Home Or Away Ltd (VTD 17623) 2.301
Home Or Away Ltd (No 2) (VTD 18195) 62.250
Homecraft Manufacturing Ltd (VTD 9300) 32.6
Hometex Trading Ltd (VTD 13012) 36.638
Honeyfone Ltd (VTD 20667) 36.118
Hong Kong Trade Development Council, Staatssecretaris van Financiën v, ECJ Case
  89/81; [1982] ECR 1277; [1983] 1 CMLR 73 .... 22.79
Hood (AG) (VTD 7994) 18.485
Honourable Society of Middle Temple (The), [2011] UKFTT 390 (TC); [2011] SFTD
  1088, TC01245 .... 69.2
Hood & Others, Silversafe Ltd v, Ch D 2006, [2007] STC 871; [2006] EWHC 1849
  (Ch) 22.566
Hookcroft Ltd (VTD 8870) 52.136
Hooper (C) (VTD 19276) 36.470
Hooper (D & S) (t/a Masterclass) (VTD 16764) 62.270
Hooper (RAJ), Forrester (N) v (re Anglo-Breweries Ltd) (VTD 18008) 2.510
Hooton (Mr & Mrs BJ) (t/a BJH Supplies & Services) (VTD 10118) 36.390
Hopcraft (B) (VTD 18590) 41.144
Hopcraft (B) (No 2) (VTD 19220) 59.19
Hope Barton Owners Association Ltd (VTD 20410) 18.532
Hopewell-Smith (N) (VTD 16725) 55.7
Hopkins (GD & M) (t/a Marianne's Hair Salon) (VTD 11587) 51.69
Hopkins (I) (VTD 18572) 39.8
Hopkins (KJ) (VTD 8890) 51.75
Hopkins (J) (Contractors) Ltd [1989] VATTR 107 (VTD 3511) 62.173
Hordern (ACS) [1992] VATTR 382 (VTD 8941) 36.558
Horizon College (Stichting Regionaal Opleidingen Centrum Noord-Kennemerland/West-
  Friesland t/a) v Staatssecretaris van Financiën, ECJ Case C-434/05; 13 June 2007
  unreported 22.304
Horlick (Mr & Mrs T) (VTD 17977) 55.70
Horn (BS) (VTD 1250) 15.26
Hornby (WW & JH) (VTD 155, 227) 2.191
Horrox (N) (VTD 6270) 18.483
Horsman (D & Mrs LM) [1990] VATTR 151 (VTD 5401) 57.73
Horstead (AM) (VTD 19697) 19.17
Horton (JC) (VTD 7258) 40.79
Hosepower Ltd (VTD 12594) 14.47
Hoskin (PR & NA) (t/a Parsons & Son) (VTD 5306) 18.574
Hosmer (ME) (VTD 7313) 62.258
Hospital of St John & St Elizabeth (VTD 19141) 15.75
Hospitality Resource Ltd (VTD 16526) 67.93
Hospitality Training Foundation (VTD 18359) 11.50
Hossain (H) (t/a Balti House Tandoori), Ch D [2004] STC 1672; [2004] EWHC
  1898(Ch) 3.13
Hostgilt Ltd v Megahart Ltd, Ch D 1998, [1999] STC 141 .... 67.5
Hotchkiss (RH) (t/a Roger Herbert Hotchkiss Car Sales) (VTD 17207) 44.96
Hotel Booking Service Ltd (VTD 10606) 62.408
Hotel Scandic Gasaback AB v Rikksskatteverket, ECJ Case C-412/03; [2005] STC 1311
  .... 22.185
Hotels Abroad Ltd (VTD 13026) 63.6
Hough (R) (VTD 488) 36.505
Hounslow Sweet Centre (VTD 10026) 52.214
Housden (Mrs AL) [1981] VATTR 217 (VTD 1178) 58.30
House (PJ) (t/a P & J Autos), CA 1995, [1996] STC 154 .... 3.127
House (AE) & Son (VTD 2620) 36.343
House of Goodness Ltd (VTD 19880) 36.634
Housiaux & Housiaux, CA [2003] EWCA Civ 257; [2003] BPR 858 .... 37.27
Houston Stewart (VTD 9526) 2.496

Hout van Eijnsbergen v Staatssecretaris van Financiën, ECJ Case C-444/04; [2007] STC 71 .... 22.284
Hovan (T), [2010] UKFTT 260 (TC), TC00554 .... 62.501
Howard (L) (VTD 19838) 57.96
Howard (P) (VTD 1106) 36.630
Howard-Williams (RB) (VTD 14474) 23.24
Howards Way Cleaning (VTD 10458) 10.5
Howarth (CL) (VTD 2363) 44.63
Howarth (R) (VTD 632) 44.7
Howe (M), [2009] UKFTT 73 (TC), TC00041 .... 51.70
Howe-Davies (AJ) (t/a D & B Contracts) (VTD 5609) 18.600
Howells (FWK) (t/a Buckingham Commercial Motor Co) (VTD 16488) 44.31
Howes (KR) [2001] VATDR 263 (VTD 17196) 36.642
Howletts (Autocare) Ltd (VTD 14467) 40.90
Howroyd (PG) (VTD 5582) 50.13
Hoylake Cottage Hospital Charitable Trust, [2011] UKFTT 48 (TC), TC00925 ...... 50.13
HP Bulmer Ltd & Another v J Bollinger SA & Others, CA [1974] Ch 401; [1974] 2 All ER 1226 .... 22.1
HP Lansdown (Linguistickers) Ltd (VTD 14714) 5.73
HPAS Ltd (t/a Safestyle UK) (VTD 18701) 27.12
Hua (Dr X) (VTD 13811) 29.84
Hubbard (WG) (VTD 2913) 51.28
Hubbard & Houghton Ltd (VTD 1028) 36.424
Hubbard Foundation Scotland, CS [1981] STC 593 .... 2.128
Hubbard Foundation Scotland (VTD 1194) 2.323
Huckridge (R) (VTD 1969) 4.2
Huczek (EJ) (VTD 8850) 29.157
Hudson (D) (VTD 15618) 40.77
Hudson (R) (t/a 21st Century Demolition & Plant Hire) (VTD 9666) 36.664
Hughes (A & J) (t/a Pennine Boat Trips of Skipton) (VTD 15680) 66.21
Hughes (A) & Son (Skellingthorpe) Ltd (VTD 1301) 36.385
Hughes (A) & Sons Ltd (t/a The Derby House) (VTD 13504) 36.164
Hughes (DP & C) (VTD 17700) 47.22
Hughes (JE) (VTD 552) 62.73
Hughes (NCJ) (VTD 8916) 62.404
Hughes (NG) (t/a Lightning Couriers) (VTD 11685) 18.275
Hughes (PG) (VTD 5223) 51.44
Hughes Bros (VTD 450) 44.63
Hulme Trust Educational Foundation [1978] VATTR 179 (VTD 625) 15.19
Hulse (A) (VTD 13896) 65.98
Hulsta Furniture (UK) Ltd (VTD 16289) 19.15
Humatt Holdings Ltd (VTD 10236) 52.312
Humphrey (J) & Smith (AG) (t/a Abacus Jewellery & Antiques) (VTD 13561) 57.78
Humphreys (CAM & P) (t/a Wilmington Trading Co) (VTD 13007) 57.3
Hundsdoerfer (HD & Mrs DM) [1990] VATTR 158 (VTD 5450) 57.74
Hungary (Republic of), EC Commission v , ECJ Case C-274/10; 28 July 2011 unreported 20.115
Hunmanby Bowling Club (VTD 12136) 15.108
Hunt (DT) [1992] VATTR 255 (VTD 10147) 37.29
Hunt (RC & CH) (VTD 9135) 52.283
Hunt v RM Douglas (Roofing) Ltd, HL [1990] 1 AC 398 .... 48.143
Hunter (J) (VTD 4566) 18.88
Hunter (JK) (VTD 13099) 18.506
Hunter (C), Kiernan (A), Wigglesworth (M) & Wright (LA) (VTD 16558) 47.59
Hunter Ridgeley Ltd (VTD 13662) 29.101
Hunter Saphir plc (VTD 10770) 52.387
Hunters Hereditaments Ltd (VTD 14748) 52.448
Huntley (CJ) & Brookes (RJ) (t/a Brimar Guest House) (VTD 5847) 62.383
Huntley Hair Transplants Ltd (VTD 823) 33.54
Hurd (WD) [1995] VATDR 128 (VTD 12985) 36.273
Hurley (F) & Sons Ltd (VTD 6719) 52.33

Hurley (GA) Ltd (VTD 3510) 36.644
Hurley Robinson Partnership (VTD 750) 62.135
Hurlingham Club, QB [1976] STC 122; [1976] 1 WLR 932; [1976] 2 All ER 199
.... 41.71
Hurlstone (AG) (VTD 6167) 18.316
Hurst (A & Mrs K) (VTD 9756) 62.290
Hurst (Mr & Mrs M) (t/a Park Fisheries) (VTD 19546) 2.308
Hurstbourne Properties Ltd, [2010] UKFTT 38 (TC), TC00352 .... 40.38
Hussain (A) (t/a Crossleys Private Hire Cars) (VTD 16194) 62.242
Hussain (A) (t/a Villa Bombay) (VTD 11961) 40.36
Hussain (AT) (t/a Al Ameer) (VTD 15668) 41.107
Hussain (K) (VTD 15830) 67.69
Hussain (M) (VTD 17217) 57.215
Hussain (Z) (t/a Zabar Hosiery) (VTD 6895) 52.91
Hussain (M) & Ghazenfer (M) (t/a Central Taxis) (VTD 17526, 17559) 3.143
Hussein (TAZ) & Asim (M) (t/a Pressing Dry Cleaners) [2003] VATDR 440 (VTD
   18341) 47.7
Hutchings (PHV) & Liggett (JH) (t/a Cashlandoo Inn) [1987] VATTR 58 (VTD 2313)
.... 51.121
Hutchinson (M) (t/a Clifton Fisheries), [2009] UKFTT 252 (TC), TC00200 .... 48.63
Hutchinson (PA) (VTD 20898) 18.413
Hutchinson Locke & Monk (VTD 5212) 62.128
Hutchison 3G UK Ltd, ECJ Case C-369/04; [2008] STC 218 .... 22.119
Hutchvision Hong Kong Ltd (VTD 10509) 62.488
Hydewood Ltd (VTD 14828) 18.541
Hydrabell Ltd (VTD 3519) 18.384
Hydril UK Ltd (VTD 16508) 18.515
Hylands (Q) (VTD 18560) 19.23
Hytec Information Systems Ltd v Coventry City Council, CA [1997] 1 WLR 1666
.... 2.245
Hytex Clothing (VTD 10700) 50.139

I

Ian Flockton Developments Ltd, QB [1987] STC 394 .... 36.341
Ian Fraser & Partners Ltd (VTD 6931) 52.181
IB Construction Ltd (VTD 17702) 15.113
Ibstock Building Products Ltd [1987] VATTR 1 (2304) 36.14
IC Blue Ltd, FTT [2009] UKFTT 40 (TC); TC00018 .... 35.28
ICB Ltd (VTD 1796) 65.59
Iceland Foodstores Ltd [1998] VATDR 498 (VTD 15833) 58.34
Icon Construction Services Ltd (VTD 16416) 36.629
Iconeyewear Distribution Ltd (VTD 20213) 18.543
Iconeywear Distributions Ltd (VTD 19566) 18.280
Ideal Shopping Direct plc, [2009] UKFTT 136 (TC), TC00104 .... 18.39
Idéal Tourisme SA v Belgium, ECJ Case C-36/99; [2001] STC 1386 .... 22.512
IDS Aircraft Ltd (VTD 12452) 62.492
IDT Card Services Ireland Ltd, CA [2006] STC 1252; [2006] EWCA Civ 29 .... 67.172
IG Farbenindustrie AG Agreement, In re, CA [1943] 2 All ER 525 .... 2.55
IHD Security Ltd (VTD 12359) 65.68
Ike, R v, CA Criminal Division 1995, [1996] STC 391 .... 49.5
Il Pozzo Restaurant (VTD 5195) 18.128
Iliffe (M & J) (t/a Otterton Post Office) (VTD 18446) 36.308
Iliffe (N) & Holloway (DC) [1993] VATTR 439 (VTD 10922) 62.133
Ilott (TJ) (VTD 10942) 57.50
Imagebase Technology Ltd (VTD 6720) 52.69
Imperial War Museum [1992] VATTR 346 (VTD 9097) 46.2
Impetus Engineering (International) Ltd (VTD 10596) 18.617
IMO Precision Controls Ltd (VTD 7948) 36.621
Impress Music Ltd (VTD 18086) 4.25

In Good Taste (VTD 2956) 29.149
In Health Group SA [2006] VATDR 281 (VTD 19593) 33.19
In Style Pleaters (VTD 7700) 18.16
Inchcape Management Services Ltd [1999] VATDR 397 (VTD 16256) 59.21
Independent Coach Travel (Wholesaling) Ltd [1993] VATTR 357 (VTD 11037) 63.3
Independent Community Care Ltd (VTD 7735) 4.3
Independent Thinking Ltd (VTD 20884) 36.447
Indigo Global Trading Ltd, QB [2009] EWHC 3126 (Admin) 2.493
Industcool Engineering Ltd (VTD 15196) 18.359
Industrial Doors (Scotland) Ltd (VTD 12656) 36.480
Industrial Fabrication Systems Ltd (VTD 4219) 18.298
Industriministeriet, Fantask A/S & Others v, ECJ Case C-188/95; [1998] 1 CMLR 473;
    [1998] All ER (EC) 1 .... 22.49
Industry Northwest Publications (1983) Ltd (VTD 9425) 10.5
Infinite Mind Ltd (VTD 16980) 46.211
Infinity Distribution Ltd, Ch D [2010] STC 2258; [2010] EWHC 1393 (Ch) 36.657
Infocall Universal Ltd (t/a The Psychic Centre) (VTD 16909) 62.346
Infocard (VTD 5732) 5.82
Ingenieurbüro Eulitz GbR Thomas und Marion Eulitz v Finanzamt Dresden I, ECJ Case
    C-473/08; 28 January 2010 unreported 22.308
Inger (M) (VTD 9522) 52.184
Ingram (GG) (t/a Ingram & Co) (VTD 4605) 36.54
Innings Telecom Europe Ltd (VTD 17335) 62.416
Innocent Ltd (No 1), [2010] UKFTT 516 (TC); [2011] SFTD 111, TC00771 .... 29.170
Innocent Ltd (No 2), [2011] UKFTT 607 (TC); [2011] SFTD 1253, TC01450 .... 2.358
Innova Inc (UK) Ltd (VTD 18989) 57.148
Inscape Investment Fund, ECJ Case C-169/04; 4 May 2006 unreported 22.368
Insite Associates Ltd (VTD 19102) 18.506
Insley (SR) & Clayton (Ms L) (t/a S & L Caterers) (VTD 13677) 62.309
Inspecteur der Belastingdienst Grote Ondernemingen Amsterdam, ARO Lease BV v, ECJ
    Case C-190/95; [1997] STC 1272; [1997] 1 ECR 4383 .... 22.199
Inspecteur der Belastingdienst/Ondernemingen Roermond, Maatschap MJM Linthorst
    & Others v, ECJ Case C-167/95; [1997] STC 1287 .... 22.205
Inspecteur der Invoerrechten en Accijnzen, Debouche v, ECJ Case C-302/93; [1996] STC
    1406; [1996] 1 ECR 4495; [1997] 2 CMLR 511 .... 22.537
Inspecteur der Invoerrechten en Accijnzen, Mol v, ECJ Case 269/86; [1988] ECR 3627;
    [1989] BVC 205; [1989] 3 CMLR 729 .... 22.81
Inspecteur der Invoerrechten en Accijnzen, Polysar Investments Netherlands BV v, ECJ
    Case C-60/90; [1991] 1 ECR 3111; [1993] STC 222 .... 22.106
Inspecteur der Invoerrechten en Accijnzen, Roders BV & Others v, ECJ Case C-367/93;
    [1995] 1 ECR 2229 .... 22.42
Inspecteur der Invoerrechten en Accijnzen, Verbond van Nederlandse Ondernemingen
    v, ECJ Case 51/76; [1977] ECR 113; [1977] 1 CMLR 413 .... 22.432
Inspecteur der Omzetbelasting, Vereniging Happy Family Rustenburgerstrat v, ECJ Case
    289/86; [1988] ECR 3655; [1989] BVC 216; [1989] 3 CMLR 743 .... 22.81
Inspecteur der Omzetbelasting Leeuwarden, Tolsma v, ECJ Case C-16/93; [1994] STC
    509; [1994] 1 ECR 743; [1994] 2 CMLR 908 .... 22.84
Inspecteur der Omzetbelasting Utrecht, Beheersmaatschappij Van Ginkel
    Waddinxveen BV & Others v, ECJ Case C-163/91; [1992] 1 ECR 5723; [1996] STC
    825 .... 22.485
Inspecteur van de Belastingdienst, Van der Steen v, ECJ Case C-355/06; [2008] STC
    2379 .... 22.124
Inspecteur van de Belastingdienst Utrecht-Gooi, Oracle Nederland v, ECJ Case C-33/09;
    [2010] STC 1221 .... 22.429
Inspection Equipment Ltd (VTD 10237) 52.111
Inspector der Omzetbelasting, Bulthuis-Griffioen v, ECJ Case C-453/93; [1995] STC
    954 .... 22.297
Instamech Ltd (VTD 20596) 48.63
Institute of Biomedical Science (VTD 20609) 46.93
Institute of Chartered Accountants in England & Wales (The), HL [1999] STC 398;
    [1999] 1 WLR 701; [1999] 2 All ER 449 .... 62.159

Institute of Chartered Foresters (VTD 16884) 13.19
Institute of Chartered Shipbrokers (VTD 15033) 64.2
Institute of Directors, CA 2002, [2003] STC 35; [2002] EWCA Civ 1814 .... 27.22
Institute of EAV and Bio-Energetic Medicine (The) (VTD 1667) 11.3
Institute of Employment Consultants Ltd (The) (VTD 2309) 64.19
Institute of Information Security Professionals, [2009] UKFTT 365 (TC), TC00303
.... 64.7
Institute of Legal Cashiers and Administrators (VTD 12383) 64.23
Institute of Leisure & Amenity Management, QB [1988] STC 602; [1988] 3 CMLR
380 .... 64.18
Institute of Purchasing & Supply, [1987] VATTR 207 (VTD 2533) 36.15
Institute of the Motor Industry, ECJ Case C-149/97; [1998] STC 1219 .... 22.310
Institute of the Motor Industry (No 2), [2000] VATDR 62 (VTD 16586) 64.30
Insurancewide.com Services Ltd, CA [2010] STC 1572; [2010] EWCA Civ 422 ...... 38.23
Insured Vehicle Coatings Ltd, [2009] UKFTT 97 (TC), TC00065 .... 46.34
Integral Resources (UK) Ltd, [2010] UKFTT 167 (TC), TC00472 .... 23.15
Integrated Allied Industries (VTD 7947) 14.47
Integrated Furniture Systems (VTD 6549) 52.72
Inter City Motor Auctions Ltd (VTD 2319) 41.140
Inter-Mark Group sp. z o.o. sp. komandytowa v Minister Finansów, ECJ Case C-530/09;
27 October 2011 unreported 20.34
Interbet Trading Ltd (No 2) [1978] VATTR 235 (VTD 696) 62.507
Interchem (Chemists Wholesale) Ltd (VTD 13952) 18.147
Intercommunale voor Zeewaterontzilting v Belgian State, ECJ Case C-110/94; [1996]
STC 569; [1996] 1 ECR 857 .... 22.110
Intercraft UK Romania (VTD 13707) 44.32
Interflex Data Systems Ltd (VTD 9578) 18.216
Interglow Ltd (VTD 15200) 67.111
Interhouse Ltd (VTD 4782) 18.586
Interior Design & Construction Ltd (VTD 3484) 18.449
Interleasing Ltd [2002] VATDR 372 (VTD 17819) 14.90
Interleisure Club Ltd (VTD 7458) 5.32
Interlude Houses Ltd (VTD 12877) 41.123
International Advisory Co Ltd (VTD 12186) 62.26
International Bible Students Association, QB 1987, [1988] STC 412; [1988] 1 CMLR
491 .... 22.294
International Corporate Restructuring & Insolvency Ltd (VTD 20331) 10.8
International Correspondence Schools Ltd (VTD 17662) 5.4
International Gymnastic School Ltd (VTD 6550) 21.52
International Institute for Strategic Studies [1992] VATTR 245 (VTD 6673) 3.173
International Institute for Strategic Studies (VTD 13551) 5.52
International Language Centres Ltd, QB [1983] STC 394 .... 3.41
International Language Centres Ltd (No 2), QB [1986] STC 279 .... 14.69
International Life Leisure Ltd (VTD 19649) 63.8
International Master Publishers Ltd (VTD 8807) 5.27, 5.85
International Masters Publishers Ltd (No 2), CA 2006, [2007] STC 153; [2006] EWCA
Civ 1455 .... 5.40
International News Syndicate Ltd (VTD 14425) 5.3
International Planned Parenthood Federation [2000] VATDR 396 (VTD 16922) 11.55
International Student House (VTD 14420) 41.97
International Supplier Auditing Ltd (t/a MNGP Food Technology) (VTD 18111) 65.74
International Trade & Exhibitions J/V Ltd [1996] VATDR 165 (VTD 14212) 62.526
Internationale Handelsgesellschaft mbH v Einfuhr- und Vorratstelle für Getreide und
Futtermittel, ECJ [1970] ECR 1145; [1972] CMLR 255 .... 18.616
Internet for Business Ltd (VTD 16266) 18.79
Internoms Ltd (VTD 16527) 41.141
Intersport Manchester Ltd (VTD 3625) 18.263
Intertrade (GB) Ltd (VTD 9610) 18.335
Inter Trading Sports Associates Ltd (VTD 12344) 18.152
Introbond Ltd (VTD 19976) 53.10
Investment Chartwork Ltd [1981] VATTR 114 (VTD 1093) 2.466

Investrand BV v Staatsecretaris van Financiën, ECJ Case C-435/05; [2008] STC 518 .... 22.408
Inward Treasure (UK) Ltd (VTD 19047) 57.134
IP Chemical & Petroleum Services Ltd (VTD 15530) 14.21
IPMC Ltd (VTD 2797) 18.292
Ipourgos Ikonomikon, Diagnostiko & Therapeftiko Kentro Athinon-Ygeia AE v, ECJ Case C-394/04; [2006] STC 1349 .... 22.275
Ipourgos Ikonomikon, Elmeka NE v, ECJ Case C-181/04; 14 September 2006 unreported 22.390
Iqbal Jaurah & Sons (VTD 12501) 62.339
Ireland, Republic of, EC Commission v, ECJ Case C-358/97; 12 September 2000 unreported 22.135
Ireland, Republic of, EC Commission v, ECJ Case C-554/07; 16 July 2009 unreported 20.9
Irish Roofing Felts Ltd (VTD 11425) 52.283
Irrepressible Records Ltd (VTD 2947) 4.3
Irving (R) (t/a Rosemary Irving Contracts) (VTD 15188) 55.69
I/S Fini H v Skatteministeriet, ECJ Case C-32/03; [2005] STC 903 .... 22.105
Isaac (CS & JM) (VTD 14656) 15.148
Isabel Medical Charity (VTD 18209) 11.20
Isfa Management Ltd (VTD 14999) 50.23
Isis Specialist Office Supplies Ltd (VTD 13389) 18.393
Island Trading Co Ltd (The) [1996] VATDR 245 (VTD 13838) 46.194
Islam (N) & Others (t/a India Garden Tandoori Restaurant) (VTD 17834) 50.9
Isle of Wight Council (No 2), ECJ Case C-288/07; [2008] STC 2964 .... 22.138
Isle of Wight Council (No 3), Ch D [2009] STC 1098; [2009] EWHC 592 (Ch) 22.144
Isle of Wight Council (No 4), [2010] UKFTT 264 (TC), TC00558 .... 22.144
Ismail (ME) (VTD 16423) 50.71
Ismay (DB) [1980] VATTR 19 (VTD 877) 7.58
IST Internationale Sprach- und Studienreisen GmbH, Finanzamt Heidelberg v, ECJ Case C-200/04; 13 October 2005 unreported 22.489
Italian Republic, EC Commission v, ECJ 1988, [1989] 3 CMLR 748 .... 22.482
Italian Republic, EC Commission v (No 2), ECJ Case 257/86; [1988] ECR 3249; [1990] 3 CMLR 718; [1991] BTC 5104 .... 22.386
Italian Republic, EC Commission v (No 3), ECJ Case 122/87; [1988] ECR 2919; [1989] BVC 232; [1989] 3 CMLR 844 .... 22.270
Italian Republic, EC Commission v (No 4), ECJ Case C-45/95; [1997] STC 1062; [1997] 1 ECR 3605 .... 22.349
Italian Republic, EC Commission v (No 5), ECJ Case C-78/00; [2003] BTC 5255 .. 22.442
Italian Republic, EC Commission v (No 6), ECJ Case C-381/01; [2004] All ER (D) 271 (Jul) 22.248
Italian Republic, EC Commission v (No 7), ECJ Case C-132/06; 17 July 2008 unreported 22.469
Italian Republic, EC Commission v (No 8), ECJ Case C-174/07; 11 December 2008 unreported 22.470
Italian Republic, EC Commission v (No 9), ECJ Case C-244/08; 16 July 2009 unreported 22.531
Italian State, Francovich v, ECJ Case C-6/90; [1991] 1 ECR 5357; [1993] 2 CMLR 66 .... 22.30
Italittica SpA, Ufficio IVA di Trapani v, ECJ Case C-144/94; [1995] STC 1059; [1995] 1 ECR 3653 .... 22.229
Italpaving Ltd (VTD 7807) 52.217
Italy, Ferrazzini v, ECHR Case 44759/88; [2001] STC 1314 .... 34.16
Ivory & Sime Trustlink Ltd, CS [1998] STC 597 .... 27.55
Ivy Cafe Ltd (VTD 288) 29.39
Ivychain Ltd (VTD 5627) 62.315
Ixes UK Ltd, [2011] UKFTT 586 (TC), TC01429 .... 36.121

J

J & B Properties (Yorkshire) Ltd (VTD 9912) 2.380
J & G Associates (VTD 13471) 18.79
J & S Glass & Mirror Centre (VTD 6117) 18.425
J & S Joiners & Builders (Paisley) Ltd (VTD 16892) 18.541
J & T Blacksmith Ltd (VTD 16710) 18.102
J & V Printing Services Ltd (VTD 6136) 52.33
J & W Plant & Tool Hire Ltd, [2003] VATDR 350 (VTD 18069) 32.9
J & W Waste Management Ltd, [2003] VATDR 350 (VTD 18069) 32.9
J Boardmans Ltd (VTD 2025) 36.356
J Bollinger SA & Others, HP Bulmer Ltd & Another v, CA [1974] Ch 401; [1974]
  2 All ER 1226 .... 22.1
J Drennan Partnership (VTD 15190) 18.278
J McArdle (Haulage) Ltd (VTD 5779) 18.220
J Walter Thompson UK Holdings Ltd [1996] VATDR 145 (VTD 14058) 2.181
Jabat Ltd (VTD 18752) 57.29
Jack Camp Productions (VTD 6261) 25.32
Jackson (B) (t/a Suite Sixe) (VTD 469) 57.124
Jackson (G) (VTD 2314) 51.43
Jackson (I & H) (VTD 16001) 57.37
Jackson (RD & Mrs SL) (VTD 1959) 47.43
Jackson (TF), Ch D 2003, [2004] STC 164; [2003] EWHC 3219 (Ch) 2.151
Jackson (TF) (No 2) (VTD 19225) 50.20
Jackson & Padgett Ltd (VTD 3435) 18.402
Jacobs (E) (Batchwood Hall Bowling Club) (VTD 19797) 19.93
Jacobs (I), CA [2005] STC 1518; [2005] EWCA Civ 930 .... 15.120
Jacobs (RE) (VTD 18367) 15.31
Jag Communications (Plymouth) Ltd, [2007] VATDR 251 (VTD 20002) 67.77
Jahansouz (AK), [2010] UKFTT 355 (TC), TC00637 .... 15.127
Jalf (KK) (VTD 5767) 40.30
Jalota (HR) (VTD 2684) 40.75
James (AC & GC) (VTD 16988) 57.211
James (BF) (VTD 5078) 51.46
James (Ms C) (t/a Ilkley Dress Agency), [2011] UKFTT 693 (TC), TC01535 .... 57.130
James (GA) (VTD 2207) 51.128
James (MP) (VTD 10474) 52.161
James (Mr & Mrs) (VTD 20426) 15.179
James A Laidlaw (Dunfermline) Ltd (VTD 1376) 44.83
James A Laidlaw (Edinburgh) Ltd (VTD 1376) 44.83
James Ashworth Waterfoot (Successors) Ltd (VTD 13851) 50.84
James Paget Industries Ltd (VTD 18436) 48.4
James Pringle Ltd (VTD 3945) 18.214
James Trevor Ltd (VTD 1425) 36.3
James Watt College (VTD 15916) 46.119
James Watts Transport Southwark Ltd (VTD 11067) 18.79
James Yorke (Holdings) Ltd (VTD 9583) 52.233
Jamestown Concrete Co Ltd (VTD 5722) 52.102
Jamie plc (VTD 11962) 17.3
Jamieson (H) (VTD 16476) 52.407
Jamieson (MP) (t/a Martin Jamieson Motor Repairs) (VTD 20269) 44.166
Jamieson (Mrs), Ch D 2001, [2002] STC 1418 .... 47.70
Jamil (K) (VTD 16795) 58.23
Jandu (D) (VTD 4475) 14.23
Jane Montgomery (Hair Stylists) Ltd, CS [1994] STC 256 .... 62.255
Janice Traders Ltd, [2010] UKFTT 513 (TC), TC00768 .... 2.327
Janwear Ltd (VTD 15460) 14.29
Japan Executive Chauffeur (VTD 11836) 52.298
Japan Racing Association (VTD 11489) 46.173
Jardin Trim Ltd (VTD 7695) 18.398
Jarmain (MH) [1979] VATTR 41 (VTD 723) 5.68

Jarman (S & DE) (VTD 11637) 48.141
Jarrett (RM & DJ) [1991] VATTR 435 (VTD 6670) 2.426
JARS (VTD 13451) 62.236
Jayhard Ltd (VTD 15306) 18.541
Jaymarke Developments Ltd v Elinacre Ltd (in liquidation) and others, CS [1992] STC
575 .... 6.42
Jaymix (VTD 1526) 65.5
JC Lewis Partnership (VTD 7368) 52.105
JCB Electronics Ltd (VTD 5004) 18.402
JCM Beheer BV v Staatssecretaris van Financiën, ECJ Case C-124/07; [2008] STC
3360 .... 22.328
JD Classics Holdings Ltd, [2010] UKFTT 259 (TC), TC00553 .... 60.12
JD Fox Ltd (VTD 1012) 62.440
JD Wetherspoon plc, ECJ Case C-302/07; [2009] STC 1022 .... 22.563
JDL Ltd, Ch D 2001, [2002] STC 1 .... 46.98
JDs (VTD 13703) 65.91
JE Beale plc (VTD 15920) 36.134
Jeancharm Ltd (t/a Beaver International), Ch D [2005] STC 918; [2005] EWHC
839(Ch) 36.43
Jeanfield Swifts Football Club (VTD 20689) 15.84
Jebb (SC) (VTD 17811) 53.13
Jefferby Ltd (VTD 11057) 18.169
Jefferson Ltd v Bhetcha, CA [1979] 1 WLR 898; [1979] 2 All ER 1108 .... 2.217
Jeffrey Green & Co Ltd [1974] VATTR 94 (VTD 69) 12.10
Jeffries (SJ) (t/a Stu's Fruit & Convenience Store), [2011] UKFTT 724 (TC), TC01561
.... 44.141
Jeffs (MD & RW) (t/a J & J Joinery), QB [1995] STC 759 .... 15.252
Jelley (GJ) (VTD 6790) 57.84
Jenkins (M) (t/a Lifetime Financial Services) (VTD 14784) 46.223
Jenkinson (KE), [1988] VATTR 45 (VTD 2688) 51.83
Jenks (RJ) (VTD 10196) 7.75
Jennings (Mrs IS) (No 1), [2010] UKFTT 49 (TC), TC00362 .... 15.42
Jennings (Mrs IS) (No 2), [2010] UKFTT 298 (TC), TC01160 .... 15.42
Jennings (S) (VTD 14372) 4.3
Jenny Braden Holidays Ltd (ex p.), R v VAT Tribunal, QB March 1994 unreported
.... 2.330
Jenny Braden Holidays Ltd (VTD 10892, 12860) 63.9
Jepp (AJ & R) (VTD 19065) 50.123
Jersey Telecoms (VTD 13940) 45.4
Jervis (P & RJ) (VTD 3920) 57.48
Jerzynek (D) (VTD 18767) 36.614
Jet Across Ltd (VTD 12541, 13526) 36.551
Jet Rod (Franchising) Ltd (VTD 4502) 18.176
Jeudwine (WRH) [1977] VATTR 115 (VTD 376) 3.134
Jeunehomme (L) & Société Anonyme d'Etude et de Gestion Immobilière 'EGI' v
Belgian State, ECJ Case 123/87; [1988] ECR 4517 .... 22.471
Jeyes Ltd (VTD 10513) 52.269
Jeynes (t/a Midland International (Hire) Caterers), QB [1984] STC 30 ...... 44.18
JFD Cartons Ltd (VTD 10293) 18.586
JG Brolly & Bros Ltd (VTD 13762) 18.46
JH Corbitt (Numismatists) Ltd, HL [1980] STC 231; [1981] AC 22; [1980] 2 All ER
72 .... 60.1
Jin-Xu (H) (t/a Wong Kok Fish & Chips) (VTD 16520) 52.305
Jivelynn Ltd (VTD 1092) 62.247
JJ Foggon Ltd (VTD 789) 57.85
JJ Manpower Services (VTD 9405) 4.3
JJH (Building Developments) Ltd (VTD 6651) 52.32
JLG Industries (UK) Ltd (VTD 5814) 52.339
JM Associates (VTD 18624) 15.188
JMD Group plc (VTD 9129) 52.58
JN Electrical Units (VTD 3346) 18.81

JND Ltd (VTD 13719) 18.61
Joannides (JR) (VTD 11373) 36.433, 62.478
Job Creation (UK) Ltd (VTD 12186) 62.26
Jocelyn Feilding Fine Arts Ltd [1978] VATTR 164 (VTD 652) 60.7
Jocelyn Feilding Fine Arts Ltd (VTD 749) 2.463
Joe Pole Construction Co (VTD 7101) 52.82
Joel (GE) (VTD 3925) 15.260
Johanson Ltd (VTD 1730) 36.11
John Beharrell Ltd [1991] VATTR 497 (VTD 6530) 44.47
John Clark (Holdings) Ltd (VTD 19327) 48.56
John Compass Ltd (VTD 3163) 15.160
John Dee Ltd, CA [1995] STC 941 .... 14.31
John E Buck & Co Ltd (VTD 1525) 38.7
John F Stott Ltd (VTD 19406) 67.83
John Harrison (Gatesby) Ltd (VTD 5581) 5.60
John Hilditch Plant Hire (VTD 4151) 18.603
John Lanham Watts (Carpets) Ltd (VTD 8846) 52.154
John McMillan & Son Ltd (VTD 1610) 36.431
John Martin Group (The) (VTD 19257) 2.32
John Martin Holdings Ltd (VTD 14264) 2.526
John Mills Ltd (VTD 20526) 18.464
John Oliver Haircutters [1987] VATTR 239 (VTD 2532) 18.373
John Oliver Haircutters (Colchester) [1987] VATTR 239 (VTD 2532) 18.373
John Page Empowerment Enterprises Ltd (VTD 18820) 21.15
John Pargeter & Sons Ltd (VTD 3318) 18.578
John Pimblett & Sons Ltd, CA 1987, [1988] STC 358 .... 29.55
John Price Business Courses Ltd [1995] VATDR 106 (VTD 13135) 36.169
John Slough of London (VTD 1427) 44.19
John Turner & Smith Ltd (VTD 124) 15.251
John Village Automotive Ltd [1998] VATDR 340 (VTD 15540) 62.527
John Wilkins (Motor Engineers) Ltd, CA [2011] EWCA Civ 429; [2011] STC 1371
.... 2.520
John Willment (Ashford) Ltd, Re, Ch D 1978, [1979] STC 286 .... 37.10
John Wilson Cars Ltd (VTD 16655) 44.92
Johnson (A & T) (VTD 20506) 15.141
Johnson (E), QB [1980] STC 624 .... 1.1
Johnson (GV) (VTD 16672) 19.84
Johnson (J) (t/a London Angling Supplies) (VTD 9898) 52.361
Johnson (LH) (VTD 14955) 41.158
Johnson (R) (Chairman of Shalden Millennium Committee) (VTD 17897, VTD
18670) 19.85
Johnson (RK) (VTD 15868) 50.126
Johnson (SJ) (VTD 1367) 36.264
Johnson v Chief Adjudication Officer (No 2), ECJ Case C-410/92; [1994] 1 ECR 5483;
[1994] 1 CMLR 725; [1995] All ER (EC) 258 .... 22.47
Johnson v Walden, CA 1995, [1996] STC 382 .... 2.78
Johnson, Lord Advocate v, CS [1985] STC 527 .... 14.118
Johnstone, Charles Osenton & Co v, HL [1941] 2 All ER 245 .... 32.5
Johnstone (P) (VTD 211) 25.17
Joiner Cummings, [2010] UKFTT 606 (TC), TC00847 .... 27.34
Joint Post Ltd (The) (VTD 20089) 18.543
Jointstock Ltd (VTD 4236) 14.47
Jolly Tots Ltd (VTD 13087) 46.225
Jomast Trading and Developments Ltd, [1984] VATTR 219 (VTD 1735) 36.152
Jonathan Alexander Ltd v Proctor, CA 1995, [1996] 1 WLR 518; [1996] 2 All ER
334 .... 2.388
Jonathan Berry Ltd, [2011] UKFTT 652 (TC), TC01494 .... 15.16
Jones (A) (t/a Jones Motors of Ynysybwl) (VTD 15861) 52.274
Jones (ATB & Mrs SDL) (VTD 11410) 36.289, 36.392
Jones (B) (t/a Beejay Enterprises) (VTD 17036) 1.28
Jones (BO) (VTD 6141) 65.22

Jones (DB) (VTD 16796) 57.40
Jones (DJ) (VTD 19570) 36.46
Jones (DL) (VTD 11430) 36.532, 52.202
Jones (EH) (VTD 17558) 57.108
Jones (EN) (VTD 5023) 36.487
Jones (F) & Sons (Cheltenham) Ltd (VTD 4511) 36.573
Jones (GDG) (t/a Jones & Son) (VTD 14535) 44.106
Jones (HG) & Associates (VTD 10399) 52.8
Jones (I) (VTD 232) 44.63
Jones (JE, JH & AG) (t/a S Jones & Son) (VTD 13308) 47.3
Jones (L) (Mr & Mrs) (VTD 15595) 46.234
Jones (Mrs M) (VTD 13313) 57.130
Jones (MF) (VTD 17512) 23.26
Jones (PT) (VTD 1401) 44.20
Jones (R) (VTD 5753) 59.11
Jones (RA) (VTD 4664) 18.225
Jones (RJ) (VTD 5701) 36.42
Jones (TDO) (t/a Evan Jones & Son) (VTD 365) 36.260
Jones (WG) & Son (VTD 117) 12.12
Jones & Attwood Ltd (VTD 7046) 52.378
Jones Executive Coaches Ltd (VTD 6870) 52.91
Jong (P de) v Staatssecretaris van Financiën, ECJ [1992] STI 763 .... 22.163
Joppa Enterprises Ltd, CS [2009] STC 1279; [2009] CSIH 17 .... 62.277
Jordan (E) (t/a Eddie Jordan Racing) (VTD 11310) 62.390
Jordan (SD) (VTD 5071) 36.213
Jordan (TR) [1994] VATTR 286 (VTD 12616) 51.149
Jordans (W) (Cereals) Ltd (VTD 3275) 29.153
Jordans Plumbing Merchants Ltd (VTD 7822) 52.58
Jorion (L) & Société Anonyme d'Etude et de Gestion Immobilière 'EGI' v
  Belgian State, ECJ Case 123/87; [1988] ECR 4517 .... 22.471
Joseph Nelson Investment Planning Ltd (VTD 10964) 32.31
Joseph Rowntree Foundation (VTD 12913, 14534) 21.21
Joulesave Emes Ltd (VTD 17115) 19.30
Joy (KUR) & Rao (PB) (VTD 19568) 46.89
Joyce (JD) (VTD 14573) 67.108
Joyce (KVJ) (VTD 3224) 18.252
JP Commodities Ltd (No 1), Ch D 2007, [2008] STC 816; [2007] EWHC 2474 (Ch)
  .... 23.4
JP Commodities Ltd (No 2), [2011] UKFTT 622 (TC), TC01464 .... 36.121
JP Company Registrations Ltd (VTD 2249) 5.41
JP Morgan Fleming Claverhouse Investment Trust plc, ECJ Case C-363/05; [2008] STC
  1180 .... 22.369
JP Morgan Trading & Finance [1998] VATDR 161 (VTD 15373) 32.18
JRL Newsletters Ltd (VTD 14394) 43.19
Jubilee Fashions Ltd (VTD 15046) 58.56
Jubilee Hall Recreation Centre Ltd, CA [1999] STC 381 .... 55.16
Judd (C) (t/a CJ Plant Hire) (VTD 813) 3.48
Julian (A & H) (VTD 16532) 26.1
Julian Hodge Bank Ltd (VTD 10197) 46.108
Julius Fillibeck Söhne GmbH & Co KG v Finanzamt Neustadt, ECJ Case C-258/95;
  [1998] STC 513; [1998] 1 WLR 697; [1998] All ER (EC) 466 .... 22.184
Jumpers (VTD 4052) 18.498
Juppon Trading Ltd, [2009] UKFTT 98 (TC), TC00066 .... 18.41
Jussila v Finland, ECHR Case 73053/01; [2009] STC 29; 9 ITLR 662 .... 34.12
Just Fabulous (UK) Ltd, oao, R v HMRC, QB 2007, [2008] STC 2123; [2007] EWHC
  521 (Admin) 36.653
Justrading Ltd, [2009] UKFTT 105 (TC), TC00073 .... 40.41
Jutla (SS & JK) (VTD 15446) 58.23
Jyske Finans A/S v Skatteministeriet, ECJ Case C-280/04; [2006] STC 1744 .... 22.350

Table of Cases — K to Z

The table is referenced to the paragraph number.

K

K & L Childcare Services Ltd, Ch D 2005, [2006] STC 18; [2005] EWHC 2414 (Ch) 33.74
Kahal Imrei Chaim Ltd (VTD 19625) 15.157
Kain (SH & VS) (VTD 12331) 55.60
Kalron Foods Ltd, Ch D [2007] STC 1100; [2007] EWHC 695 (Ch) 29.169
Kam (Stationery) Ltd (VTD 5897) 18.23
Kampelmann & Others v Landschaftsverband Westfalen-Lippe & Others, ECJ Cases C-253/96 & C-258/96; [1997] 1 ECR 2771 .... 22.17
Kane (A) (VTD 9784) 52.108
KapHag Renditefonds 35 Spreecenter Berlin-Hellersdorf 3 Tanche GbR v Finanzamt Charlottenburg; ECJ Case C-442/01; [2005] STC 1500 .... 22.90
Karageorgou & Others, Elliniko Dimosio (Greek State) v, ECJ Cases C-78/02 to C-80/02; [2006] STC 1654 .... 22.464
Karakusevic Carson LLP (VTD 20550) 18.543
Kardi Car & Van Hire Ltd (VTD 19299) 53.10
Karim (F), Ali (M) & Majid (t/a Dhaka Tandoori Restaurant) (VTD 10987) 2.70
Karl Joh (UK) Ltd (VTD 5537) 18.457
Kashmir Tandoori, [1998] VATDR 104 (VTD 15363) 2.168
Kathy's Kones Ltd (VTD 11705) 29.162
Kathy's Kones Ltd (No 2) (VTD 14880) 29.130
Kaul (P) (t/a Alpha Care Services), [1996] VATDR 360 (VTD 14028) 33.57
Kaur (G) (t/a GK Trading) (VTD 15366) 14.76
Kaur (Mrs G) (VTD 13537) 23.9
Kaur (K) & Singh (N) (t/a Andy's Fish Bar) (VTD 14857) 52.448
Kavanagh (K) (VTD 6409) 51.28
Kay (NJR) (VTD 2373) 51.78
Kay & Co Ltd and Others (VTD 14557) 2.29
Kay & Co Ltd and Others, ex p., R v C & E Commrs, QB [1996] STC 1500 .... 48.50
Kay Quality Management Ltd (VTD 18373) 44.113
Kaymac Fashions Ltd (VTD 1945) 14.47
KBC Tent & Marquee Hire Ltd (VTD 4765) 18.426
KCP Computer Services Ltd (VTD 8877) 18.558
KCS Management Systems (VTD 9013) 18.387
KCT Holdings Ltd (VTD 18734B) 52.103
KDP (UK) Ltd (VTD 20659) 36.525
Keam (ML) (VTD 16685) 36.212
Keane (BB) (VTD 9131) 18.13
Kear (A) (VTD 9896) 51.116
Kearns (GA & AE) (t/a Victoria Cars) (VTD 11655) 62.248
Kedington (NI) Ltd (VTD 18544) 53.13
Keele University Student Union, [2009] UKFTT 114 (TC), TC00082 .... 16.9
Keeley (MJ) (VTD 16219) 15.197
Keen (A & D) (VTD 11824) 48.119
Keeping Newcastle Warm, ECJ Case C-353/00; [2002] STC 943; [2002] All ER (EC) 769 .... 22.247
Keesing (UK) Ltd (VTD 16840) 5.103
Keith Motors (Christchurch) Ltd (VTD 17592) 50.153

Kellpak Ltd (VTD 14018) 40.36
Kelly (DA) (VTD 7941) 17.1
Kelly (D & D) (VTD 2452) 1.97
Kelly (GWH) (VTD 598) 7.51
Kelly (J) (VTD 18220) 18.485
Kelly (JJ) (VTD 15637) 50.31
Kelly (JM & MC) (VTD 4139) 58.58
Kelly (R) (VTD 5026) 51.107
Kelly (RM) (VTD 11347) 18.454
Kelvingold Ltd (VTD 2110) 51.6
Ken Reid Ltd (VTD 20494) 28.14
Kenealy (P) (VTD 466) 67.106
Kenkay Ltd (VTD 6923) 52.39
Kenmir Ltd v Frizzell, QB [1968] 1 WLR 329; [1968] 1 All ER 414 .... 65.10
Kennedy (CB) (VTD 16068) 4.14
Kennedy (T & D), [1991] VATTR 157 (VTD 5880) 52.368
Kennell (KB), [1977] VATTR 265 (VTD 487) 15.2
Kennemer Golf & Country Club v Staatsecretaris van Financiën, ECJ Case C-174/00;
    [2002] STC 502; [2002] 3 WLR 829; [2002] All ER (EC) 480 .... 22.315
Kenney (RC) & Stiles (BJ) (t/a AD Fine Art) (VTD 14969) 44.13
Kenny (WE) (t/a Scruples) (VTD 2039) 47.25, 47.58
Kent (CJ) (t/a Market Integration) (VTD 13214) 36.516
Kenwood Appliances Ltd, [1996] VATDR 127 (VTD 13876) 36.38
Kenwyn Management Services Ltd (VTD 13765) 17.3
Kernahan (AJ & L) (VTD 15203) 55.76
Kernot Cases & Cartons Ltd (VTD 11564) 52.241
Kerr (J), Lloyd (E) and Flatman (R) (VTD 2193) 62.103
Kerrutt & Another v Finanzamt Monchengladbach-Mitte, ECJ Case 73/85; [1986] ECR
    2219; [1987] BTC 5015; [1987] 2 CMLR 221 .... 22.121
Keswick Golf Club [1998] VATDR 267 (VTD 15493) 20.74
Keswick Motor Co Ltd (VTD 18831) 44.164
Kewpost Ltd (VTD 14664) 18.174
Key (WEH) (VTD 15354, 15794) 46.21
Key Finance Ltd (VTD 19148) 52.418
Key Kitchens Ltd (VTD 2261) 62.428
Key Personnel (Midlands) Ltd (VTD 9833) 18.443
Key Properties Ltd (VTD 11778) 36.466, 41.122, 52.281
Keydon Estates Ltd (VTD 4471) 47.55
Khan (AU) (VTD 6450) 50.97
Khan (K) (VTD 17790) 47.34
Khan (M) (t/a Jesmond Tandoori Takeaway Ltd) (VTD 12336) 50.24
Khan (MR), CA 3 May 2000 unreported 37.23
Khan (MS) (t/a Greyhound Dry Cleaners), CA [2006] STC 1167; [2006] EWCA Civ
    89 .... 50.89
Khan (MT) (VTD 6860) 18.120
Khan (P) & Parvez (M) (t/a On Time Cars) (VTD 14293) 51.183
Khan (SN) (VTD 19513) 47.49
Khawaja v Secretary of State for the Home Department, HL 1983, [1984] AC 74; [1983]
    1 All ER 765 .... 50.62, 50.68
Kiddicare Ltd (VTD 17349) 46.195
Kidease Ltd (VTD 20793) 52.344
Kids Church (VTD 18145) 15.203
Kids of Wilmslow Ltd (VTD 12341) 33.62
Kidz R Us Children Centre Ltd (VTD 20882) 3.58
Kieran Mullin Ltd, Ch D [2003] STC 274; [2003] EWHC 4 (Ch) 62.266
Kiff (CJ) Ltd [1981] VATTR 88 (VTD 1084) 38.1
Kilburn (EA) (VTD 3937) 36.506, 62.190
Kilburn (EA) (VTD 4866) 2.401
Killingbeck (Mr & Mrs MAR) (VTD 14592) 58.21
Kilroy Television Co Ltd (The), QB [1997] STC 901 .... 8.47
Kimber (M) (VTD 10469) 44.143

Kimberley-Clark Ltd, Ch D 2003, [2004] STC 473; [2003] EWHC 1623 (Ch) 12.25
King (E) (VTD 19208) 55.11
King (GD) (Mr & Mrs) (VTD 15961) 15.138
King (J) (Mr & Mrs) (t/a Barbury Shooting School) (VTD 17822) 48.45
King (J) (Mr & Mrs) (t/a Barbury Shooting School) (No 2) [2003] VATDR 471 (VTD
   18313) 2.391
King (JA) [1980] VATTR 60 (VTD 933) 41.41
King (R) (VTD 7201) 62.332
King Engineering Ltd (VTD 19432) 62.139
Kingdom Amusements (VTD 8872) 18.43
Kingdom Sports Ltd [1991] VATTR 55 (VTD 5442) 25.9
Kingfisher Events Ltd, [2011] UKFTT 140 (TC), TC01014 .... 67.132
Kingfisher plc, QB 1993, [1994] STC 63 .... 32.28
Kingfisher plc, Ch D [2000] STC 992 .... 67.152
Kingfisher plc (No 3) [2004] VATDR 206 (VTD 18668) 67.164
Kingpin European Ltd (VTD 18695) 2.271
Kingpin European Ltd (No 2) (VTD 19293) 2.259
Kings Lynn Motor Co Ltd (VTD 5312) 38.2
Kings Norton Carpet Centre Ltd (VTD 4749) 14.47
Kingscastle Ltd (VTD 17777) 15.134
Kingscrest Associates Ltd & Montecello Ltd (t/a Kingcrest Residential Care Homes),
   Ch D [2002] STC 490; [2002] EWHC 410 (Ch) 33.60
Kingscrest Associates Ltd & Montecello Ltd (t/a Kingcrest Residential Care Homes)
   (No 2), ECJ Case C-498/03; [2005] STC 1547 .... 22.300
Kingsley Holidays Ltd (VTD 13487) 36.365
Kingsley-Smith (B) (VTD 13787) 2.61
Kingsnorth Developments Ltd (VTD 12544) 36.242
Kingston Craftsmen (1981) Ltd (VTD 3838) 18.558
Kingston Craftsmen (1981) Ltd (VTD 5409) 18.322
Kingston Hospital (League of Friends of) (VTD 12764) 15.110
Kinnell (I) (t/a Berkshire Diet Clinic) (VTD 18073) 33.14
Kinney (G), [2009] UKFTT 273 (TC), TC00219 .... 62.525
Kinnon (DH) (t/a Henderson Associates) (VTD 14461) 18.483
Kinsella (CE) Traction (VTD 10130) 3.70
Kirbas (H) (VTD 12329) 50.20
Kirby (RW) (VTD 5092) 47.53
Kircher (JR) (VTD 7352) 52.140
Kirk (D) (VTD 14042) 57.84
Kirkby (BJ) (VTD 6545) 51.29
Kirkcroft Skips Ltd (VTD 7560) 18.390
Kirkham (MJ) (VTD 18640) 50.33
Kirklees Developments Ltd (VTD 6785) 52.123
Kirkman (DR) (VTD 17651) 41.89
Kirkton Investment Ltd (VTD 15096) 18.110
Kirkwood (LW & PE) (VTD 564) 44.63
Kirsopp (HN) (VTD 1236) 15.11
Kirtley (MJ) (t/a Encore International) (VTD 12471) 62.450
Kirton Designs Ltd (VTD 2374) 19.24
Kirton Healthcare Group Ltd (The) (VTD 17062) 19.37
Kitchen (H) (VTD 397) 44.63
Kitchens For You Ltd (VTD 10802) 18.286
Kitchin (HA & DB) Ltd (VTD 9513) 52.41
Kitsfern Ltd [1989] VATTR 312 (VTD 4472) 48.85
Kitson (A) (VTD 2030) 36.518
Kittel v Belgian State, ECJ Case C-439/04; [2008] STC 1537 .... 22.415
Kleanthous (A) (t/a AK Building Services) (VTD 9504) 55.88
Kleen Technologies International Ltd (VTD 970) 40.63
Kleen Technologies International Ltd (VTD 1005) 2.465
Klockner Ferromatik Desma Ltd (VTD 7061) 36.8
Kloppenburg (G) v Finanzamt Leer, ECJ Case 70/83; [1984] ECR 1075; [1985] 1 CMLR
   205 .... 22.353

Klub Ltd (VTD 18352) 18.461
Knapp (TW) (VTD 778) 44.11
Knight v CIR, CA [1974] STC 156 .... 52.24
Knight (R) (VTD 13769) 57.7
Knight Guard Security Ltd (VTD 5788) 18.551
Knights (RJ) & Wendon (WC) (VTD 5165) 57.70
Knittex Ltd (VTD 3541) 18.258
Knockhatch Leisure Ltd (VTD 10518) 52.386
Knowles (AD) (VTD 3393) 21.23
Knowles (J) (t/a Rainbow Taxis) (VTD 13913) 62.234
Knowles Food Services Ltd (VTD 17674) 48.4
Knowsley Associates Ltd (VTD 18180) 15.203
Koca (V & S), QB 1995, [1996] STC 58 .... 3.31
Kocaman (A) (VTD 11730) 50.19
Kohanzad (A), QB [1994] STC 967 .... 40.71
Kohanzad (R & N) (VTD 19013) 48.132
Köhler v Finanzamt Düsseldorf-Nord, ECJ Case C-58/04; [2006] STC 469 .... 22.195
Kollektivavtalsstiftelsen TRR Trygghetsrådet v Skatteverket, ECJ Case C-291/07; [2009]
   STC 526 .... 20.36
Korberg (BTG) (VTD 2966) 51.47
Korner (J) and Others (VTD 2008) 36.287
Koundakjian (J), [2009] UKFTT 89 (TC), TC00057 .... 48.63
Kpack (UK) Ltd (VTD 20109) 18.67
KPL Contracts Ltd (VTD 19629) 36.417
KPMG Peat Marwick McLintock [1993] VATTR 118 (VTD 10135) 8.42
KPMG (No 2) [1997] VATDR 192 (VTD 14962) 8.34
Kretztechnik AG v Finanzamt Lenz, ECJ Case C-465/03; [2005] STC 1118; [2005] 1
   WLR 3755 .... 22.91
KRG Designs Ltd (VTD 11348) 52.21
KRG Precision Ltd (VTD 17414) 18.517
Kronospan Mielec sp zoo v Dyrektor Izby Skarbowej w Rzeszowie, ECJ Case C-222/09;
   [2011] STC 80 .... 22.222
KS & P (VTD 17548) 52.173
KTS Fashions Ltd (VTD 6782) 2.473
Kubota (UK) Ltd (VTD 6960) 52.58
Kuchick Trading (VTD 12131) 36.225
Kuc v Dyrektor Izby Skarbowej w Warszawie, ECJ Case C-181/10; [2011] STC 2230
   .... 20.5
Kudhail (VS) (VTD 18161) 50.104
Kudmany (H) (t/a The Kasbah) (VTD 17198) 50.136
Kuhne v Finanzamt München III, ECJ Case 50/88; [1989] ECR 1925; [1990] STC 749;
   [1990] 3 CMLR 287 .... 22.179
Kulka (A) (t/a Kulka Models) (VTD 9753) 51.142
Kumar (R) (VTD 16893) 23.12
Kunz (BC) (VTD 13514) 44.29
Kushoom Koly Ltd [1998] VATDR 363 (VTD 15591) 14.61
Kuwait Petroleum (GB) Ltd, ECJ Case C-48/97; [1999] STC 488; [1999] All ER (EC)
   450 .... 22.158
Kuwait Petroleum (GB) Ltd (No 2), Ch D 2000, [2001] STC 62 .... 22.159
Kuwait Petroleum (GB) Ltd (No 3), CA [2001] EWCA Civ 1542; [2001] STC 1568
   .... 22.259
Kwiatkowski (FJ) (VTD 5457) 51.10
Kwik Fit (GB) Ltd [1992] VATTR 427 (VTD 9383) 40.96
Kwik-Fit (GB) Ltd, CS 1997, [1998] STC 159 .... 32.32
Kwik Move UK Ltd (VTD 20842) 18.78
Kwik Save Group plc [1994] VATTR 457 (VTD 12749) 65.80
Kyffin (R) [1978] VATTR 175 (VTD 617) 2.190
Kyriacou (JO) (t/a Niki Taverna) (VTD 11537) 50.114
Kyriacou (JO) (VTD 12003) 2.412

L

L & B Scaffolding Ltd (VTD 4543) 18.107
L & N Tiles (VTD 5120) 18.124
La Comercial Internacional de Alimentacion SA, Marleasing SA v, ECJ Case C-106/89;
  [1990] 1 ECR 4135 .... 22.15
La Cucaracha (VTD 9988) 18.125
LA Leisure Ltd (VTD 20648) 48.75
La Reine (Limoges Porcelain) Ltd (VTD 10468) 18.45
Labelwise Ltd (VTD 1499) 14.48
Labour Party (The) [2001] VATDR 39 (VTD 17034) 46.168
Lacara Ltd, ex p., R v C & E Commrs, QB [1998] STI 576 .... 36.650
Lacy Simmons Ltd (VTD 11211) 52.187
Ladbroke (Palace Gate) Property Services Ltd (VTD 16666) 7.119
Lady & Kid A/S v Skatteministeriet, ECJ Case C-398/09; 6 September 2011
  unreported 22.560
Lady Blom-Cooper, CA [2003] STC 669; [2003] EWCA Civ 493 .... 15.132
Lady Di (London) Ltd (VTD 17618) 36.27
Lady Jane (London) Ltd (VTD 7143) 18.417
Lady Nuffield Home (VTD 19123) 19.91
Lafferty (WE) (t/a Bell Transport), [2010] UKFTT 12 (TC), TC00331 .... 62.63
Lagumina (S) & Bottiglieri (A) (t/a La Piazza) (VTD 15542) 65.93
Lai (K & M) (t/a The Rice Bowl) (VTD 20531) 36.596
Lai (YL & MY) [2003] VATDR 570 (VTD 17739) 2.257
Laing The Jeweller Ltd (VTD 18841) 48.153
Lait (TH & PG) (t/a The Lait Dance Club) [2001] VATDR 159 (VTD 17038) 62.347
Lake (M) (VTD 1388) 36.386
Lal Jewellers Ltd [2010] UKFTT 594 (TC), TC00844 .... 31.2
Lam (KW) (t/a Dragon Inn Chinese Restaurant) (VTD 14974) 50.136
Lam Cash & Carry Ltd (VTD 3400) 18.146
Lam Watson & Woods (VTD 7307) 52.69
Lamb (DJF & PE) (t/a D & R Services) (VTD 13802) 44.30
Lamb (PJ) (t/a Footloose) (VTD 15136) 41.53
Lamb (S), RCPO v, CA [2010] EWCA Civ 285 .... 49.24
Lambert (AS), [2009] UKFTT 208 (TC), TC00151 .... 52.444
Lamberts Construction Ltd (VTD 8882) 15.180
Lambourne (RP) (VTD 4771) 51.10
Lamdec Ltd [1991] VATTR 296 (VTD 6078) 2.200
Lamming (K), [2009] UKFTT 44 (TC); TC00022 .... 15.46
Lamming (S) (VTD 6635) 52.212
Lancashire County Council [1996] VATDR 550 (VTD 14655) 62.368
Lancashire County Cricket Club (VTD 1244) 8.7
Lancaster (M) (t/a Airport Cars) (No 1), [2009] UKFTT 155 (TC), TC00121 .... 62.251
Lancaster (M) (t/a Airport Cars) (No 2), [2010] UKFTT 559 (TC), TC00810 .... 48.152
Lancaster (S) (VTD 9261) 52.37
Lancaster v Bird, CA 19 November 1998 unreported 67.4
Lancaster Fabrications Ltd (VTD 1317) 14.73
Lancaster Insurance Services Ltd (VTD 5455) 38.6
Lancer UK Ltd [1986] VATTR 112 (VTD 2070) 11.6
Land (AJ) (t/a Crown Optical Centre) (VTD 15547) 33.6
Land Nordrhein-Westfalen, Von Colson v, ECJ Case 14/83; [1984] ECR 1891 .... 22.13
Landau (L) (VTD 13644) 57.103
Landboden-Agrardienste GmbH & Co KG v Finanzamt Calau, ECJ Case C-384/95;
  [1998] STC 171 .... 22.173
Landels (TA) & Sons Ltd (VTD 521) 62.559
Landene Investments Ltd (VTD 9510) 52.345
Landesanstalt für Landwirtschaft v Götz, ECJ Case C-408/06; 13 December 2007
  unreported 22.140
Landmark Cash and Carry Group Ltd (The) [1980] VATTR 1 (VTD 883) 62.186
Landowner Liquid Fertilisers Ltd (VTD 6692) 52.72
Landscape Management Construction Ltd (VTD 17131) 62.439

Landschaftsverband Westfalen-Lippe & Others, Kampelmann & Others v, ECJ Cases C-253/96 & C-258/96; [1997] 1 ECR 2771 .... 22.17
Landseer Film & Television Productions Ltd (VTD 10812) 18.194
Landwirtschaftskammer für das Saarland, Rewe-Zentralfinanz eG & Rewe-Zentral AG v, ECJ Case 33/76; [1976] ECR 1989; [1977] 1 CMLR 533 .... 22.43
Lane (PJI) (VTD 13583) 23.23
Lane (RM) (VTD 5038) 44.65
Lange v Finanzamt Fürstenfeldbruck, ECJ Case C-111/92; [1993] 1 ECR 4677; [1994] 1 CMLR 573; [1997] STC 564 .... 22.387
Langhorst, Finanzamt Osnabrück-Land v, ECJ Case C-141/96; [1997] STC 1357; [1997] 1 ECR 5073; [1998] 1 WLR 52; [1998] All ER (EC) 178 .... 22.460
Langley House Trust (VTD 19749) 51.42
Langran (G) (VTD 20969) 36.60
Langrick (G) & Coe (DG) (VTD 18205) 48.22
Langstane Housing Association Ltd (VTD 19111) 6.6
Largs Golf Club, Lord Advocate v, CS [1985] STC 226 .... 13.6
Larkfield Ltd v RCPO, CA [2010] STC 1506; [2010] EWCA Civ 521 .... 49.23
Lasrado (AF) (VTD 10656) 18.575
Latchmere Properties Ltd, Ch D [2005] STC 731; [2005] EWHC 133 (Ch) 41.21
Late Editions Ltd, [2009] SFTD 488; [2009] UKFTT 166 (TC), TC00128 .... 36.111
Latimer (B & Mrs E) (VTD 6486) 33.58
Laughlin (JF) (VTD 10499) 18.289
Laughtons Photographs Ltd, ECJ Case 138/86; [1988] STC 540; [1988] ECR 3937 .... 22.497
Launderette Investments Ltd (VTD 2360) 62.27
Laura Anderson Ltd (VTD 20743) 46.143
Laura Ashley, Ch D 2003, [2004] STC 635; [2003] EWHC 2832(Ch) 3.44
Laurels Nursing Home Ltd (The) (VTD 15259) 46.59
Laurels Nursing Home Ltd (The) (VTD 16092) 52.312
Laurence Scott Ltd [1986] VATTR 1 (VTD 2004) 40.93
Laurentian Management Services Ltd (VTD 16447) 62.532
Laurie (AD) (t/a Betterwater Systems) (VTD 7889) 62.526
Laurie (J & H) (t/a The Peacock Montessori Nursery) (VTD 17219) 62.160
Lavelle (JF) (VTD 18023) 50.88
Law (SK & KN) (t/a Happy Valley) 3.163
Lawrence (P) (t/a PLC) (VTD 13092) 39.4
Lawson (PJ and LJ) (t/a Country Fayre) (VTD 14903) 29.9
Lawson (WA) (VTD 5823) 18.432
Lawson Mardon Group Pension Scheme (VTD 10231) 6.23
Lawson-Tancred (RT), QB [1988] STC 326 .... 29.121
Lawton (D) (VTD 576) 2.442
Laycock (JL) (VTD 1887) 36.623
Lazard Brothers & Co Ltd (VTD 13476) 3.79
Le Rififi Ltd, CA [1994] STC 383 .... 2.500
Le Rififi Ltd, CA 1994, [1995] STC 103 .... 3.87
Lea (J & L) (VTD 2018) 62.57
Leach (A) (t/a Carlton Catering) (VTD 17767) 29.67
Lead Asset Strategies (Liverpool) Ltd, [2009] UKFTT 122 (TC), TC00090 .... 57.114
Leaders (North East) Ltd (VTD 9004) 52.336
Leadstar Ltd (VTD 7153) 36.545
Leadx (VTD 20904) 38.32
Lea-Francis Cars Ltd (VTD 1166) 44.59
League of Friends of Kingston Hospital (VTD 12764) 15.110
Lean & Rose, [1974] VATTR 7 (VTD 54) 62.360
Leander International Pet Foods Ltd (t/a Arden Grange) (VTD 18870) 41.42
Leander Shellfish Ltd (VTD 18227) 53.9
Leapmagic Ltd (VTD 6441) 62.281
Lease Plan Luxembourg SA v Belgium, ECJ Case C-390/96; [1998] STC 628 .... 22.542
Leather Fashions Ltd (VTD 15016) 35.10
Leavesley (JD) (VTD 2987) 36.539
Lebara Ltd, ECJ Case C-520/10; 8 December 2011 unreported 22.190

Leberl Advertising Ltd (VTD 10599) 52.235
LEBS Services Ltd (VTD 15550) 14.17
Lecht Ski Co Ltd (The) (No 1) (VTD 18163) 66.31
Lecht Ski Co Ltd (The) (No 2) (VTD 20886) 66.33
Leckwith Engineering Ltd (VTD 7702) 52.16
Ledamaster Ltd (VTD 344) 36.312
Ledbury Amateur Dramatic Society (VTD 16845) 15.87
Ledger (JM & CE) (t/a Lewis Carpets) (VTD 18756) 62.337
Ledoux, Ministère Public & Ministre des Finances du Royaume de Belgique *v*, ECJ Case
    127/86; [1988] ECR 3741; [1991] STC 553 .... 22.385
Lee (AA) (VTD 15205) 38.11
Lee (ADJ) (VTD 5887) 55.23
Lee (CM) (VTD 10662) 55.75
Lee (EM) (VTD 16750) 62.69
Lee (FJ) (t/a Gladrags) (VTD 16028) 18.483
Lee (I & AJ) (VTD 2640) 57.43
Lee (K) (t/a Euro Impex) (VTD 15427) 50.93
Lee (P), [2010] UKFTT 520 (TC), TC00775 .... 57.155
Lee (PDJ) (VTD 14127) 52.446
Lee (WG) & Sarrafan (N) (t/a The Regal Sporting Club) (VTD 15563) 24.15
Lee *v* Lee's Air Farm Ltd, PC [1961] AC 12 .... 44.138
Leeds & Holbeck Building Society (VTD 15356) 46.182
Leeds Kashrut Commission & Beth Din Administration Committee (VTD 465) 7.91
Leeds Permanent Development Services Ltd, ECJ Case C-255/02; [2006] STC 919;
    [2006] 2 WLR 90 .... 22.60
Lee-Kemp (PW) & O'Brien (PM) (t/a Sevenoaks Hi-Fi & Video) (VTD 7772) 65.40
Lee's Air Farm Ltd, Lee *v*, PC [1961] AC 12 .... 44.138
Lees Heginbotham & Sons Ltd (VTD 4533) 18.140
Leeside Leisure Ltd (VTD 18688) 46.68
Leesportfeuille 'Intiem' CV *v* Staatssecretaris van Financiën, ECJ Case 165/86;
    [1988] ECR 1471; [1989] 2 CMLR 856; [1989] 4 BVC 180 .... 22.402
Leez Priory (VTD 18185) 41.58
Legal & Contractual Services Ltd, [1984] VATTR 85 (VTD 1649) 43.1
Legge (C) (VTD 20964) 56.7
Leicester City Council (VTD 18108) 42.23
Leigh (JG) (t/a Moor Lane Video), [1990] VATTR 59 (VTD 5098) 67.137
Leighton (PH) & Henry (JP) (t/a Lacy's Wine Bar) (VTD 9793) 51.123
Leighton-Jones & Craig (t/a Saddletramps) (VTD 597) 47.17
Leighton Park School (VTD 9392) 15.99
Leightons Ltd, QB [1995] STC 458 .... 33.8
Leightons Ltd (No 2), [2001] VATDR 468 (VTD 17498) 33.9
Leisure Circle Ltd (The) (VTD 1362) 5.21
Leisure Contracts Ltd (VTD 19392) 15.239
Leisure Karts (UK) Ltd (VTD 19403) 19.61
Leisure Pass Group Ltd (No 1), Ch D [2008] STC 3340; [2008] EWHC 2158 (Ch)
    .... 67.169
Leisure Pass Group Ltd (No 2) (VTD 20910) 67.170
Leisure West Clothing Ltd (VTD 5930) 18.214
Lenihan (MA), QB [1992] STC 478 .... 36.397, 62.75
Lennartz *v* Finanzamt München III, ECJ Case C-97/90; [1991] 1 ECR 3795;
    [1993] 3 CMLR 689; [1995] STC 514 .... 22.456
Lennick Precision Engineering Ltd (VTD 3342) 18.360
Leo Libera GmbH*v* Finanzamt Buchholz in der Nordheide, ECJ Case C-58/09; [2010]
    STC 1950 .... 20.86
Leofabs Ltd (VTD 6632) 52.166
Leogem Ltd (VTD 19829) 36.91
Leon (S) (t/a Custom Bedrooms) (VTD 13200) 15.224
Leonidas (PC & VL), [2000] VATDR 207 (VTD 16588) 47.21, 59.15
LEP Luma Ltd (VTD 11490) 52.283
Leslie (DC & LM) (VTD 3294) 50.67
Leslie Wise Ltd (VTD 13354) 18.61

Lester Aldridge, [2004] VATDR 292 (VTD 18864) 36.31
Letchworth Polishing & Plating Co Ltd (VTD 13675) 18.588
Leukaemic Disorders Trust (VTD 16783) 11.29
Leung (CS) (t/a Driffield Tasty House) (VTD 13862) 50.138
Levell (K & G) (VTD 6202) 55.74
Levi Solicitors Llp, [2011] UKFTT 727 (TC), TC01564 .... 18.350
Levob Verzekeringen BV v Staatssecretaris van Financiën, ECJ Case C-41/04; [2006]
    STC 766 .... 22.176
Lewis (Mr & Mrs AA) (VTD 11596) 62.383
Lewis (AS) (VTD 3329) 57.44
Lewis (GD & Mrs D) (t/a Russell Francis Interiors), [2011] UKFTT 107 (TC),
    TC00983 .... 52.450
Lewis (L & J) [1996] VATDR 541 (VTD 14085) 58.20
Lewis (MJ) (VTD 4150) 51.120
Lewis (NL) (t/a Care Design) (VTD 19210) 44.145
Lewis (RA) (VTD 9845) 36.475
Lewis-Cox (FL) (t/a The Hair Emporium) (VTD 14349) 57.133
Lewis's Group Ltd (The) (VTD 4931) 29.64
Lewsey (P) (VTD 10784) 52.180
Lex Services plc, HL 2003, [2004] STC 73; [2003] UKHL 67; [2004] 1 WLR 1; [2004]
    1 All ER 434 .... 44.85
LHA Ltd (VTD 11911) 36.241, 36.563
LHA-Asra Group Ltd, [2010] UKFTT 177 (TC), TC00482 .... 42.22
Li (SW & XM) (t/a Summer Palace Restaurant) (VTD 15133) 50.138
Liakat (SH) (t/a Banaras Tandoori Restaurant) (VTD 3300) 51.127
Liam Findlay Architects (VTD 15568) 52.344
Libdale Ltd [1993] VATTR 425 (VTD 11543) 40.13
Liberexim BV v Staatssecretaris van Financiën, ECJ Case C-371/99; [2002] All ER(D)
    178 (Jul) 22.192
Licensed Establishments Management Services Ltd (VTD 11777) 18.77
Lidl & Companhia v Fazenda Pública, ECJ Case C-106/10; [2011] STC 1979 .... 20.48
Lieder (ND) (VTD 10400) 52.296
Life Education Centre (Nottinghamshire) Ltd (VTD 16499) 62.35
Life Enterprises Ltd, [2009] UKFTT 340 (TC), TC00281 .... 36.121
Lifestyles Healthcare (Europe) Ltd (VTD 19300) 33.30
Light Wire Ltd (VTD 7967) 18.568
Lilac Property Services Ltd (VTD 17876) 2.506
Lilley, Morris Motors Ltd v, [1959] All ER 737 .... 44.66
L'Image Ltd (VTD 12028) 65.91
Lime Avenue Sales & Services Ltd [2007] VATDR 55 (VTD 20140) 22.70
Lincars Radio Taxis (VTD 1118) 2.121
Lincoln Assurance Ltd (No 1) (VTD 16447) 62.532
Lincoln Assurance Ltd (No 2) (VTD 20619) 46.178
Lincoln Oak Co Ltd (VTD 18503) 56.6
Lincoln Street Motors (Birmingham) Ltd [1981] VATTR 120 (VTD 1100) 44.66
Lindley (D) (VTD 12037) 62.169
Lindsay (HA) (VTD 9530) 18.341
Lindsay (JT) (t/a Galloway Design & Inspection Services) (VTD 9151) 18.161
Lindsay Cars Ltd [2005] VATDR 21 (VTD 18970) 38.19
Lindum Resources Ltd (VTD 12445) 27.29
Lineham (MG) (t/a MG Lineham Homes & Improvements) (VTD 7410) 52.217
Lineham, Ward-Lee v, CA [1993] 1 WLR 754, [1993] 2 All ER 1006 .... 2.181, 2.182
Lineplan Ltd (VTD 9369) 18.329
Ling (SR) (VTD 3099) 51.28
Linguarama Ltd (VTD 4011) 18.200
Linham (MC) (VTD 11359) 1.41
Link Housing Association Ltd, CS [1992] STC 718 .... 15.1
Link Industrial Services Ltd (VTD 5663) 18.214
Linn Motor Group Ltd (No 1) (VTD 19015) 48.24
Linn Motor Group Ltd (No 2) (VTD 20092) 48.25
Linneweber, Finanzamt Gladbeck v , ECJ Case C-453/02; [2008] STC 1069 .... 22.372

Linotype & Machinery Ltd [1978] VATTR 123 (VTD 594) 54.2
Linward (AI) (VTD 20942) 36.276
Linzi Dresses, Samuels v, CA [1980] 2 WLR 836; [1980] 1 All ER 803 .... 2.319
Lipjes, Staatssecretaris van Financiën v, ECJ Case C-68/03; [2004] STC 1592 .... 22.515
Liquatek Ltd (VTD 17912) 18.547
Lister (K) (VTD 13044) 36.206
Lister (M & RJ) (VTD 9972) 36.18
Lister (H) (Slippers) Ltd (VTD 1747) 36.378
Lite Ltd (VTD 15223) 21.25
Litster v Forth Dry Dock & Engineering Co Ltd, HL 1989, [1990] 1 AC 546; [1989]
   1 All ER 1134 .... 63.11
Little Bradley Farm Partnership (VTD 18420) 46.192
Little Rock Ltd (VTD 424) 12.2
Little Spain Club Ltd, QB 1978, [1979] STC 170 .... 41.72
Littlejohn (A) (t/a Carpet Trades) (VTD 1716) 4.6
Littlemoss Preservation Ltd, [2011] UKFTT 692 (TC), TC01534 .... 18.349
Littler Machinery Ltd, [2009] UKFTT 131 (TC), TC00099 .... 23.8
Littlewoods Home Shopping Group Ltd, ex p., R v C & E, CA [1998] STC 445 ..... 58.39
Littlewoods Organisation plc [1997] VATDR 408 (VTD 14977) 62.393
Littlewoods Organisation plc (No 2), CA [2001] EWCA Civ 1542; [2001] STC 1568
   .... 67.42
Littlewoods Retail Ltd (No 1), QB 2008, [2009] STC 22; [2008] EWHC 2622 (QB)
   .... 2.213
Littlewoods Retail Ltd (No 2), Ch D [2010] STC 2072; [2010] EWHC 1071 .... 2.522
Littlewoods Retail Ltd (No 3), Ch D [2010] EWHC 2771 (Ch); [2011] STC 171 .... 2.522
Littley (R), [2010] UKFTT 616 (TC), TC00858 .... 50.36
Livebrace Ltd (VTD 5957) 52.26
Liverpool Commercial Vehicles Ltd (Re), Ch D [1984] BCLC 587 .... 36.675
Liverpool Institute for Performing Arts, HL [2001] STC 891; [2001] UKHL 28; [2001]
   1 WLR 1187 .... 46.174
Livewire Telecom Ltd, Ch D [2009] STC 643; [2009] EWHC 15 (Ch) 36.83
Living Design (Home Improvements) Ltd (VTD 17874) 46.139
Livingstone (A) (VTD 17642) 19.64
Livingstone Homes UK Ltd (VTD 16649) 15.41
LJ Harvey & Associates (Bournemouth) Ltd (VTD 10389) 18.588
Llandaff Athletic Rugby Club (VTD 4143) 18.242
Llandudno Cabinlift Co Ltd [1973] VATTR 1 (VTD 1) 66.30
Llanfyllin Group Practice (VTD 16156) 57.169
Lledo (London) Ltd (VTD 3590) 18.79
Lloyd (HW) (VTD 11307) 51.107
Lloyd (PK & Mrs PM) (VTD 13562) 58.4
Lloyd (RN & BA) (VTD 15786) 57.140
Lloyd Scotter Electrical Ltd (VTD 4482) 18.283
Lloyds Bank plc (VTD 14181) 62.143
Lloyds TSB Group Ltd, QB [1998] STC 528 .... 27.26
Lloyds TSB Group plc (No 2) [2005] VATDR 405 (VTD 19330) 14.92
LM & R Food Stores (VTD 1936) 58.23
LMB Holdings Ltd (VTD 15739) 36.29
Loach (R & D) (t/a Micronet Showroom) (VTD 19560) 36.669
Loadstone Ltd (VTD 7878) 18.177
Local Authorities Mutual Investment Trust, Ch D 2003, [2004] STC 246; [2003] EWHC
   2766(Ch) 48.5
Loch Tay Highland Lodges Ltd (VTD 18785) 15.67
Lock (AW) (VTD 6768) 18.494
Lock (Dr) & Partners (VTD 10946) 51.24
Lock (JC) (VTD 9720) 50.45
Lock (MA) (t/a MAL Carpenters & Joiners) (VTD 14427) 44.28
Lockerbie Meat Packers Ltd (VTD 13826B) 18.235
Lockwood (B & SE) (t/a Northern Carpet Group) (VTD 18235) 62.336
Lockwood (SE) (t/a Cash & Carry Carpets) (VTD 18235) 62.336
Lofthouse (J), QB [1997] STC 800 .... 50.6

Loftus (I) & Son Ltd (VTD 12678) 52.283
Loftus (ME) (VTD 18435) 51.158
Logic Ltd (VTD 13934) 24.22
Logmoor Ltd (VTD 14733) 55.43
Lois Engineering Ltd (VTD 7327) 18.421
Lombard Guildhouse plc (VTD 12974) 1.25
Lombardelli (AP) (t/a Century 21 Lombard Estates) (VTD 17016) 51.157
Lomond Services Ltd (VTD 15451) 14.61
London & Exmoor Estates Ltd (VTD 16707) 46.28
London & Newcastle Holdings plc (VTD 16042) 52.283
London & Quadrant Housing Trust (VTD 19206) 62.37
London & West Riding Investments Ltd, Snook v, CA [1967] 2 QB 786; [1967] 1 All ER
    518 .... 10.6
London Art College (VTD 20657) 5.37
London Board for Shechita (The), [1974] VATTR 24 (VTD 52) 29.81
London Borough of Camden (VTD 6123) 52.58
London Borough of Camden (No 2), [1993] VATTR 73 (VTD 10476) 17.6
London Borough of Camden (No 3) (VTD 17211) 42.5
London Borough of Haringey (Mayor & Burgesses of), QB [1995] STC 830 .... 42.1
London Brick Company King's Dyke Social Club (VTD 10387) 51.123
London Bridge Cycles (VTD 2550) 18.370
London Building Co plc (VTD 9971) 18.233
London Clubs Management Ltd, CA [2011] EWCA Civ 1323 .... 46.136
London Cyrenians Housing (VTD 14426) 5.16
London Express Ltd (VTD 12375) 2.432
London Federation of Clubs for Young People (The) (VTD 16477) 2.507
London Federation of Clubs for Young People (The), [2001] VATDR 501 (VTD
    17079) 15.105
London International College (VTD 10886) 52.230
London International Financial Futures Exchange (Administration & Management),
    [1993] VATTR 474 (VTD 11611) 40.117
London Mob (Great Portland Street) Ltd (The), CA 1980, [1981] STC 139; [1981]
    2 All ER 86 .... 25.1
London Regeneration Project Services Ltd (VTD 12062) 43.17
London Scottish Benefit Society v Chorley, QB 1884, 13 QBD 872 .... 2.460
London Tideway Harbour Co Ltd (The) (VTD 11736) 66.3
London Wiper Co Ltd, [2011] UKFTT 445 (TC), TC01298 .... 40.19
Lonergan (MP) (VTD 13305) 40.59
Long v Clark, QB [1894] 1 QB 119 .... 14.82
Longborough Festival Opera, Ch D [2006] STC 818; [2006] EWHC 40 (Ch) 16.8
Longbow (VTD 551) 7.30
Longparish Church of England Primary School (VTD 20464) 15.184
Long's Supermarket Ltd (VTD 9309) 52.336
Longstone Ltd, [2001] VATDR 213 (VTD 17132) 18.324
Lonie (SR) (VTD 19901) 19.66
Lonsdale Travel Ltd (VTD 12113) 1.67
Look Ahead Housing & Care Ltd (VTD 17613) 33.71
Look Ahead Housing Association (VTD 16816) 15.215
Lookers Ellesmere Port Ltd (VTD 18770) 50.81
Lookers Motor Group Ltd, [2009] UKFTT 215 (TC), TC00165 .... 67.3
Lord (V) (t/a Lords Electrical and Fancy Goods) (VTD 320) 3.71
Lord Advocate v Johnson, CS [1985] STC 527 .... 14.118
Lord Advocate v Largs Golf Club, CS [1985] STC 226 .... 13.6
Lord Advocate v McKenna, CS [1989] STC 485 .... 3.145
Lord Advocate v Meiklam, 1860, 22 D 1427 .... 2.120
Lord Advocate v Shanks, Sheriff Court, CS [1992] STC 928 .... 2.196
Lord and Lady Watson of Richmond (VTD 18903) 55.10
Lord Fisher, QB [1981] STC 238; [1981] 2 All ER 147 .... 7.6
Lord Mayor & Citizens of the City of Westminster [1989] VATTR 71 (VTD 3367)
    .... 22.143
Lordsregal Ltd (VTD 18535) 55.19

Louca (L) (t/a Gardner's Cafe) (VTD 13186) 65.26
Loucaides (M) (VTD 7707) 18.120
Loucaides (M) (VTD 9307) 18.122
Loughborough University, [2009] SFTD 200; [2009] UKFTT 91 (TC), TC00059 .... 46.132
Louis Dreyfus & Co Ltd (VTD 10795) 46.155
Louloudakis v Greece, ECJ Case C-262/99, 12 July 2001 unreported 18.620
Lounais-Suomen Verovirasto, Uudenkaupungin kaupunki v, ECJ Case C-184/04; [2008]
   STC 2329 .... 22.458
Lounds (MH) (t/a Lounds Associates) (VTD 13999) 6.16
Lovejoy (H) (t/a HRS Recoveries) (VTD 2488) 44.39
Lovejoy (HA) (t/a HRS Recoveries) (VTD 12835) 36.526, 41.14
Lovejoy (JD) (t/a Crumbs) (VTD 14370) 57.7
Low (JE) (VTD 5586) 58.23
Low (WM) & Co plc (VTD 7162) 3.28
Lowe (BA) (t/a BA Lowe Construction) (VTD 6806) 52.177
Lowe (SF) (VTD 15124) 44.126
Lower (KJ & Mrs SJ), [2008] VATDR 199 (VTD 20567) 44.167
Lower Mill Estate Ltd, UT [2011] STC 636 .... 22.75
Lower Mill Estate Ltd, oao, R v HMRC, QB [2008] EWHC 2409 (Admin) 15.282
Lowrie (T) (VTD 5965) 51.80
Loyalty Management UK Ltd, ECJ Case C-53/09; [2010] STC 2651 .... 22.153
LS & A International Ltd (VTD 3717) 1.14
LSA (Full Time Courses) Ltd [1983] VATTR 256 (VTD 1507) 5.6
LTE Network Communications Ltd (VTD 19643) 18.425
Lubbock Fine & Co, ECJ Case C-63/92; [1993] 1 ECR 6665; [1994] STC 101; [1994] 3
   WLR 261; [1994] 3 All ER 7 .... 22.333
Lucas (M) & Jones (G) (t/a Mayfair Building & Roofing Services) (VTD 10715) 57.87
Lucia (RC) (VTD 5776) 44.4
Lucky (Y) & Another (t/a Le Bistenoo) (VTD 2701) 51.107
Ludovico (N) & De Martiis (M) (t/a Paradiso Italian Restaurant) (VTD 18620) 57.96
Ludwig (V) v Finanzamt Luckenwalde, ECJ Case C-453/05; [2008] STC 1640 ...... 22.355
Lumar Developments Ltd (VTD 19729) 52.231
Lumby (D) (VTD 12972) 8.32
Lumsden v Burnett, QB [1898] 2 QB 177 .... 14.83
Lunkowsky (B) (VTD 19572) 23.31
Lunn (GA & DM) (VTD 1518) 58.23
Lunn (S), UT 2009, [2010] STC 486; [2009] UKUT 244 (TCC) 55.12
Lunn Poly Ltd, ex p., R v C & E, CA [1999] STC 350 .... 22.8
Luong (Mr & Mrs Y) [1994] VATTR 349 (VTD 12234) 57.132
L.u.P GmbH v Finanzamt Bochum-Mitte, ECJ Case C-106/05; [2008] STC 1742 ... 22.276
Lurgan Cash and Carry Ltd (VTD 1738) 36.422
Lutron Ltd (VTD 3686) 29.58
Luxembourg (Grand Duchy of), EC Commission v, ECJ Case C-69/92; [1993] 1 ECR
   5907; [1997] STC 712; [1995] 2 CMLR 1 .... 22.219
LVG Ltd (VTD 20938) 18.549
Lycett Industries Ltd (VTD 11672) 18.434
Lyezeal Ltd (VTD 3823) 18.280
Lygate (Dr JF) (VTD 19552) 18.155
Lyham Property Services (VTD 6874) 18.201
Lylybet Dishwashers (UK) Ltd (VTD 915) 62.549
Lynam (T) (t/a Victoria Road Carpets) (VTD 15585) 67.55
Lynben Ltd (VTD 7291) 18.610
Lynch (JB) (VTD 7392) 18.473
Lynton Group Ltd (VTD 11049) 18.104
Lynton Tool & Die Ltd (VTD 11288) 52.222
Lyons (C) (t/a Wayne Anthony's) (VTD 16791) 62.273
Lyons (I) [1987] VATTR 187 (VTD 2451) 57.36
Lyons (MF) (t/a Trendz Jewellery) (VTD 12243) 62.104
Lysander Systems Ltd (VTD 13672) 18.413
Lythgoe (R & LJ) (t/a Utopia) (VTD 18201) 52.342

M

M & E Sports Ltd (VTD 16051) 62.551
M & J Investment Co Ltd (VTD 16996) 52.432
M & M Wholesale (NE) Ltd (VTD 18055) 62.384
M & S London Ltd (VTD 19149) 50.59
M & S Services Ltd [1995] VATDR 512 (VTD 13610) 2.167
MA Shad (Newsagents) (VTD 13145) 57.189
Maatschap MJM Linthorst & Others v Inspecteur der Belastingdienst/Ondernemingen
    Roermond, ECJ Case C-167/95; [1997] STC 1287 .... 22.205
MBNA Europe Bank plc, Ch D [2006] STC 2089; [2006] EWHC 2326 (Ch) 46.181
McAdam (B) (t/a Brian McAdam Plumbing & Heating), [2011] UKFTT 22 (TC),
    TC00899 .... 51.180
McAdam (W) (VTD 13286) 44.27
Macaire (RF & Mrs RJ) (VTD 10471) 36.304
McAleer (M) (t/a McAleer Projects) (VTD 18365) 18.510
McAlister (A) (VTD 3148) 15.258
McAlister (C) (VTD 18011) 15.24
McAulay (H) (VTD 4372) 18.492
Macaulay (W) (VTD 14429) 15.29
McBurney, Clelland & Boyd Ltd (VTD 20701) 67.84
McCafferty (HE) (VTD 483) 3.47
McCaig (J) (VTD 6362) 18.362
McCalden (WG) (VTD 4216) 44.65
McCall (JA) (VTD 1588) 36.621
McCallum (BP) [1980] VATTR 79 (VTD 945) 36.198
McCann (G) (t/a Ulster Video Amusements) [1987] VATTR 101 (VTD 2401) 24.18
McCarthy, R v, CA Criminal Division, [1981] STC 298 .... 49.1
McCarthy (M & G) (t/a Croft Homes) (VTD 16789) 15.238
McCarthy (ST) (t/a Autoelec) (VTD 18166) 44.72
McCarthy & Stone plc [1992] VATTR 198 (VTD 7014, 7752) 15.227, 15.255
McClymont (J & E) (VTD 1253) 2.121
McCord (I) & Alford (M) (VTD 17189) 60.3
McCormick (A) [1991] VATTR 196 (VTD 5724) 67.22
McCormick (UK) plc (VTD 15202) 29.174
McCourt (P) (t/a The Millstone Inn) (VTD 14452) 36.398
McCourtie (CA) (VTD 12239) 3.15
McCree Music Ltd (VTD 19009) 18.283
McCrindle (S & M) (t/a Frisco Hair) (VTD 17134) 57.221
McCulloch (V) (VTD 5949) 2.2
McDivitt (R) (VTD 5203) 50.133
McDonald (MD) (VTD 12153) 18.392
MacDonald (PE) (VTD 17326) 57.133
McDonald (SD) (VTD 5313) 62.58
McDonald (SJ & CM) (VTD 19473) 7.46
MacDonald & Muir Ltd (VTD 10497) 8.28
MacDonald of Sleat (Sir Ian) [1981] VATTR 223 (VTD 1179) 36.247
Macdonald Resorts Ltd, ECJ Case C-270/09; [2011] STC 412 .... 22.208
McDonald's Restaurants Ltd (VTD 3884) 67.154
McDove (D & A) (VTD 19501) 15.59
McElroy (Mrs S) (t/a Boundary Café) (VTD 10540) 46.50
McElroy (VW) (VTD 490) 15.3
McEwan (K) (t/a Scotpoint) (VTD 17554) 62.60
Macey (DR) & Atkins (DJ) (t/a Sandwich Cars) (VTD 20257) 62.241
McFarlane Roofing Ltd (VTD 10845) 18.246
McGarry (KJ & Mrs BM) (VTD 10385) 18.206
McGeoghan Plant Hire & Excavations Ltd (VTD 3246) 18.79
McGinty (JJ) (t/a Alton Transport) (VTD 12671) 2.434
McGinty (JJ) (t/a Alton Transport) [1995] VATDR 193 (VTD 13463) 2.435
McGleish (SRJ) (VTD 5318) 14.47
McGowan (J) (VTD 11967) 40.36

McGowan-Kemp (Printing Machines) Ltd (VTD 16553) 3.172
McGrath (Mrs RI), QB [1992] STC 371 .... 41.106
McGrath Brothers (Engineering) Ltd (VTD 5551) 18.502
McGready (Mrs J) (t/a Abbey Flowers) (VTD 13993) 18.138
McGreevy Construction Ltd (VTD 19877) 48.103
MacGregor (AS) (VTD 7840) 52.320
MacGregor v Clamp & Son, KB [1914] 1 KB 288 .... 14.78
MacGregor Nash & Co (VTD 7873) 18.473
McGuckin (M) (VTD 12659) 57.217
McGuire (APG) (VTD 1305) 57.171
McHarg (RJ) (VTD 7254) 62.104
MacHenrys (Hairdressers) Ltd, QB [1993] STC 170 .... 62.265
MacHenrys II, QB [1993] STC 170 .... 62.265
Machin (F) & Sons Ltd (VTD 17906) 36.548
McInroy & Wood Ltd (VTD 20780) 46.144
McIntosh, R v, CA [2011] EWCA Crim 1501; [2011] STC 2349 .... 49.22
McIver (Mr & Mrs ABC) (t/a Alan's School of Motoring) (VTD 5315) 62.229
McKay (EP) (VTD 3406) 51.133
Mackay (GA) (VTD 5547) 18.608
Mackay (PRC) & Correll (SJ) (t/a The Black Horse) (VTD 20928) 52.305
McKean Smith & Co Ltd (VTD 10334) 52.108
McKenna, Lord Advocate v, CS [1989] STC 485 .... 3.145
MacKenzie (D) (VTD 11597) 17.8
McKenzie Bain Ltd (VTD 5994) 18.245
Macklin Services (Vending) West Ltd [1979] VATTR 31 (VTD 688) 3.40, 29.41
McLaren (RV) (VTD 4117) 51.11
McLaughlin (JG) (t/a The Hip Flask) (VTD 10920) 65.63
McLaughlin (R) (VTD 7514) 52.77
McLean (Mrs LD) (VTD 6920) 18.198
MacLean (Linda) (VTD 5350) 65.113
McLean & Gibson (Engineers) Ltd (VTD 17500) 62.512
McLean Homes East Anglia Ltd [1992] VATTR 460 (VTD 7748) 15.259
McLean Homes Midland Ltd (No 1) (VTD 5010) 36.7
McLean Homes Midland Ltd (No 2), QB [1993] STC 335 .... 15.226
McLean Homes Midland Ltd (No 3) (VTD 6447) 2.406
McLeod (S) (t/a Sally McLeod Associates) (VTD 12886) 36.216
McLintock (RK) (VTD 2102) 36.572
MacMahon (B) (t/a Irish Cottage Trading Co), [2009] UKFTT 304 (TC), TC00248
.... 23.18
McMahon (NB) (VTD 12904) 18.432
McMahon (PJ) (VTD 11308) 18.563
McMaster (WR) (t/a Delta Bar) (VTD 12109) 18.233
McMaster Stores Scotland Ltd (in receivership), CS [1995] STC 846 .... 48.42
McMenemy (G) (VTD 13878) 57.134
Macmillan Cancer Trust [1998] VATDR 289 (VTD 15603) 33.70
McMullan (MK) (VTD 4917) 18.585
McMullen Holdings Ltd, [2011] UKFTT 327 (TC), TC01187 .... 51.12
McMurray (J) (a Governor of Allen Hall) [1973] VATTR 161 (VTD 39) 41.96
McNally & Waite (t/a Macray Motor Bodies) (VTD 1109) 44.63
Macnamara (BT) [1999] VATDR 171 (VTD 16039) 15.202
McNaughton (M & P) (VTD 7438) 52.312
McNeil Consumer Nutritionals Ltd (VTD 17736) 29.154
McNicholas Construction Co Ltd [1997] VATDR 73 (VTD 14975) 2.217
McNicholas Construction Co Ltd (No 2) [1998] VATDR 220 (VTD 15575) 2.250
McNicholas Construction Co Ltd (No 3), QB [2000] STC 553 .... 3.102
McNicholas Construction Co Ltd & Others, ex p., R v C & E, QB [1997] STC 1197
.... 14.93
MacNiven v Westmoreland Investments Ltd, HL [2001] STC 237 .... 46.151
McNulty (E), [2009] UKFTT 111 (TC), TC00079 .... 23.16
McNulty Offshore Services Ltd (VTD 14824) 2.203
McPhee (J) (VTD 15606) 14.26

McPhee (J) (t/a K2 Interiors) (VTD 16158) 14.38
McPherson (JV) & Weather (N) (VTD 4800) 18.196
McPherson (N) (VTD 9580) 51.14
MacPhie & Co (Glenbervie) Ltd, CS [1992] STC 886 .... 29.88
MacQueen (A) (VTD 20386) 18.443
Macrae (PA) (VTD 7849) 19.76
McRandal (T) (VTD 9860) 52.183
Macris (DF) (t/a Helena's Unisex Beauty Centre) (VTD 15073) 18.302
McSorley (F) (VTD 1938) 36.621
Maddermarket Theatre Trust Ltd (VTD 10393) 18.265
Made To Measure, [2011] UKFTT 154 (TC), TC01028 .... 19.54
Made To Order Ltd (VTD 20959) 29.24
Maden (AJ) [1996] VATDR 449 (VTD 14603) 35.20
Madgett (TP) & Baldwin (RM) (t/a Howden Court Hotel), ECJ Cases C-308/96 &
  C-94/97; [1998] STC 1189 .... 22.487
Madgett, Baldwin & Madgett (t/a Howden Court Hotel) (No 2) [2006] VATDR 214
  (VTD 19719) 63.15
Madisons (VTD 2516) 62.400
Madysen Ltd, 21st Century Logistic Solutions Ltd (in liquidation) v, QB [2004] STC
  1535; [2004] EWHC 231 (QB) 62.176
Magill Business Associates Ltd (VTD 7855) 18.586
Magma Bars Ltd (VTD 20329) 18.526
Magna Kansei Ltd (VTD 19905) 18.543
Magnum Craft Ltd (VTD 11316) 52.363
Magnumcraft Technology Ltd (VTD 20733) 18.421
Magoora sp zoo v Dyrektor Izby Skarbowej w Krakowie, ECJ Case C-414/07;
  22 December 2008 unreported 22.426
Magor Products Engineering Ltd (VTD 6532) 44.149
Magpie Court Ltd (VTD 6166) 18.429
Magright Ltd (VTD 6925) 52.238
Magstack Ltd (t/a Brixton Academy) (VTD 12009) 18.79
Maguire (C) (t/a TC Autos) (VTD 7056) 52.46
Maguire (S) (t/a Skian Mhor) [2004] VATDR 288 (VTD 18667) 53.17
Maharani Restaurant (VTD 15088) 2.322
Maharani Restaurant, QB [1999] STC 295 .... 2.78
Maharani Restaurant (No 3) (VTD 16537) 50.74
Mahmood (MF) (t/a Mahmood Mobile Service), [2010] UKFTT 166 (TC), TC00471
  .... 52.308
Mahon (W & B) (VTD 5335) 18.206
Mahoney (M) (VTD 12063) 52.305
Mahoney (WJM) [1976] VATTR 241 (VTD 258) 2.512
Maidstone Sailing Club (DG Oliver) (VTD 511) 57.93
Maierhofer v Finanzamt Augsburg-Land, ECJ Case C-315/00; [2003] STC 564 ..... 22.337
Mail Brokers International (VTD 14188) 1.44
Main Pine Company (The) (VTD 6384) 52.74
Maine Distribution Ltd (Nos 1 & 2) (VTD 20284, VTD 20823) 23.6
Mainline Fabrications (VTD 7010) 10.4
Mainstream Productions Ltd (VTD 5301) 18.473
Majid & Partners, QB 1998, [1999] STC 585 .... 3.14
Major Micros Ltd, [2010] UKFTT 105 (TC), TC00417 .... 48.95
Makebrite Ltd (VTD 5490) 18.586
Maliha Group Ltd, [2011] UKFTT 10 (TC), TC00887 .... 40.15
Malik (MA), QB [1998] STC 537 .... 29.72
Malik (MTR & MKR) (t/a Attractions) (VTD 17021) 23.12
Malik (PA) (VTD 15711) 65.91
Malik (SA) (VTD 18091) 50.30
Malik (T) (VTD 18891) 57.29
Malin (J & E) (VTD 10085) 51.30
Malin (Mrs K) (VTD 7623) 52.36
Mallalieu v Drummond, HL [1983] STC 665 .... 36.341
Mallinson (WE) & Woodbridge (M) (t/a The Hair Team) (VTD 19087) 41.89

Malloch (D) (VTD 5811) 52.75
Mallon (GE) (t/a Phoenix Agency Services) (VTD 18222) 44.72
Maloney (JD) (VTD 14754) 40.77
Maltby Motors Ltd (VTD 7026) 18.588
Management Consult Ltd (VTD 9228) 18.216
Management Facilities (Northern) Ltd (VTD 18191) 10.7
Management Services Ltd (VTD 2503) 36.388
Managerial Problem Solving Ltd (VTD 2826) 51.57
Manatlantic Ltd, [2011] UKFTT 527 (TC), TC01374 .... 36.120
Manchester Corporation, Twyford v, Ch D [1946] Ch 236; [1946] 1 All ER 621 ..... 2.58
Manchester Scaffolding Ltd (VTD 2855) 18.168
Manchester Ship Canal Co, QB [1982] STC 351 .... 54.6
Manchester United plc (VTD 17234) 5.77
Manchester Young Men's Christian Association (VTD 9215) 52.55
Mancumi & Sons Ltd (VTD 1213) 40.46
Mander Laundries Ltd [1973] VATTR 136 (VTD 31) 69.1
Mandelberg (CA) (t/a Andrew Mandelberg & Co) (VTD 7114) 18.286
Mann (CC) (VTD 15182) 50.145
Mann (CW) (VTD 14004) 55.50
Mann (E) (t/a Black & Gold Taxis) (VTD 204) 62.232
Mann (SS & MK) (t/a Chaucer Fish Bar) (VTD 16442) 50.112
Mannesmann Demag Hamilton Ltd [1983] VATTR 156 (VTD 1437) 40.87
Mannin Shipping Ltd [1979] VATTR 83 (VTD 738) 32.2
Manor Forstal Residents Society Ltd [1976] VATTR 63 (VTD 245) 13.1
Mantio (S) (t/a Zazzera Hair Salon) (VTD 17190) 51.70
Manvik Plant & Hire Ltd, [2009] UKFTT 144 (TC), TC00112 .... 18.317
Manx International Rally Ltd v The Isle of Man Treasury (VTD 6711) 46.73
Maple Network Consultancy Ltd (VTD 11488) 52.342
Maplefine Ltd (VTD 15499) 52.318
Maranello Concessionaires Ltd (VTD 14211) 18.210
Marbourne Ltd (VTD 12670) 41.65
Marcantonio Foods Ltd (VTD 15486) 29.131
March (S), [2009] UKFTT 94 (TC), TC00062 .... 28.19
Marchant (J) (VTD 11026) 51.107
Marchday Holdings Ltd [1992] VATTR 484 (VTD 8964) 2.62
Marcus Webb Golf Professional, [2009] UKFTT 388 (TC), TC00323 .... 21.41
Marczak (S & J) (t/a Suzanne's Riding School) (VTD 13141) 29.116
Marfleet Refining Co Ltd [1974] VATTR 289 (VTD 129) 29.97
Margaretta Ltd, re, Ch D [2005] STC 610 .... 37.8
Margrie Holdings Ltd (EDN/85/69 unreported) 2.517
Marguerita Hoare School of Dancing (VTD 18906) 48.69
Marine & General Print Holdings Ltd (VTD 2120) 32.8
Marine Caravan Park (VTD 12342) 52.115
Marine Confectioners & Tobacconists Ltd (VTD 5435) 58.15
Marine Electronic Services Ltd (VTD 15172) 52.412
Marinello (PE) (VTD 15915) 36.489
Maritime Housing Association Ltd (VTD 16232) 41.18
Markdome Ltd (VTD 6007) 52.133
Market & Opinion Research International Ltd (VTD 18422) 18.619
Marketing Middle East Ltd (VTD 15666) 10.6
Marks (A) (t/a Marks Cameron Davies & Co) (VTD 15541) 62.481
Marks (HD) (VTD 11381) 36.221
Marks (PE) (VTD 4515) 18.159
Marks & Spencer plc (No 1) (VTD 4510) 29.134
Marks & Spencer plc (No 2) [1998] VATDR 93 (VTD 15302) 2.30
Marks & Spencer plc (No 3), CA 1999, [2000] STC 16 .... 48.38
Marks & Spencer plc (No 4), ECJ Case C-62/00; [2002] STC 1036; [2003] 1 WLR
    665 .... 22.55
Marks & Spencer plc (No 5), ECJ Case C-309/06; [2008] STC 1408 .... 22.56
Marks & Spencer plc (No 6), HL [2009] STC 452; [2009] UKHL 8; [2009] 1 All ER
    939 .... 22.56

Marktgemeinde Welden, Finanzamt Augsburg-Stadt v, ECJ Case C-247/95; [1997] STC 531; [1997] 1 ECR 779; [1997] All ER (EC) 665 .... 22.133

Marleasing SA v La Comercial Internacional de Alimentacion SA, ECJ Case C-106/89; [1990] 1 ECR 4135 .... 22.15

Marlow & Hind (VTD 407) 62.278

Marlow Gardner & Cooke Ltd Directors' Pension Scheme, Ch D [2006] STC 2014; [2006] EWHC 1612 (Ch) 6.37

Marner (P & V) (VTD 443) 47.42

Marquez (J) (t/a Kwick Chick Barbecue) (VTD 15767) 50.117

Marquiss of Scotland (VTD 7161) 52.144

Marsden, R v, CA [2011] EWCA Crim 1501; [2011] STC 2349 .... 49.22

Marsh (LP) (VTD 9810) 51.68

Marsh (PR) (VTD 20091) 18.327

Marshall (AJD), [1975] VATTR 98 (VTD 166) 62.81

Marshall (GL) (VTD 9321) 18.62

Marshall (PA) (t/a Harry Ramsbottom's) (VTD 13766) 29.73

Marshall v Southampton & South-West Hampshire Health Authority, ECJ Case 152/84; [1986] 1 CMLR 688; [1986] ECR 723; [1986] 2 All ER 584 .... 22.14

Marshall Brown Aluminium Ltd (VTD 6853) 52.136

Marshall Cavendish Ltd, [1973] VATTR 65 (VTD 16) 5.26

Marshall Motor Group Ltd (VTD 19828) 48.72

Mart Play Ltd (VTD 9046) 52.283

Martem Ltd, [2011] UKFTT 641 (TC), TC01483 .... 36.121

Martin (JH) (VTD 5543) 50.134

Martin (PJ) (t/a Martin Motors) (VTD 17809) 44.71

Martin (SL) (VTD 2224) 51.123

Martin (I & N) (t/a Beechwood Studios) (VTD 13805) 52.394

Martin Engineers (Wishaw) Ltd (VTD 6667) 36.346

Martin Gibson Ltd (VTD 5473) 10.11

Martin Groundland & Co Ltd (VTD 15696) 18.434

Martin-Jenkins (TD), [2009] SFTD 192; [2009] UKFTT 99 (TC); TC00067 .... 25.30

Martin Weitz Associates Ltd (VTD 17941) 18.586

Martin Yaffe International Ltd, [2005] VATDR 495 (C197) 35.26

Martinez (L), [1999] VATDR 267 (VTD 16320) 44.109

Martins & Martins, CA [2001] STC 1188; [2001] 4 All ER 687 .... 34.5

Martins Properties (Chelsea) Ltd (VTD 14092) 46.220

Martorana (J) (t/a Mr Unique Tyre and Exhaust Centre) (VTD 2557) 18.79

Marvelle Bras (London) Ltd (VTD 9350) 62.29

Maryam (T), [2010] UKFTT 528 (TC), TC00782 .... 57.219

Marylebone Cricket Club (VTD 1074) 5.78

Masa Invest Group plc v Ukraine, ECHR Case 3540/03; 8 ITLR 262 .... 34.26

Mashood (S), [1999] VATDR 133 (VTD 15896, VTD 16178) 2.24

Mason (C) (VTD 16250) 55.48

Mason (CW) (VTD 3517) 51.115

Mason (I) (VTD 12406) 55.90

Mason (MJ) (t/a Bramble Lodge) (VTD 17405) 15.200

Mason v Boscawen, Ch D 2008, [2009] STC 624; [2008] EWHC 3100 (Ch) 6.49

Masson (AK) (VTD 6542) 18.402

Masstech Corporation Ltd, [2011] UKFTT 649 (TC), TC01491 .... 2.274

Masstech Ltd, [2010] UKFTT 386 (TC), TC00668 .... 36.92

Masstype Properties Ltd (VTD 11124) 52.347

Masterguard Security Services Ltd (VTD 18631) 44.136

Masterlease Ltd, [2010] SFTD 1243; [2010] UKFTT 339 (TC), TC00621 .... 44.54

Masterscore Ltd (VTD 5611) 52.27

Maston (Property Holdings) Ltd (VTD 6564) 52.382

Matcroft Ltd (VTD 14715) 57.36

Mates Vending Ltd, [1995] VATDR 266 (VTD 13429) 25.36

Mather (TG) (t/a Economy Appliances) (VTD 3829) 18.29

Mathieson (ID), CS [1999] STC 835 .... 48.136

Matilot Ltd (t/a Hardlife Ladder Co) (VTD 4847) 18.60

Matin (MA) (VTD 17441) 50.136

Matrec Ltd (VTD 6693) 52.217
Matrix Europe Ltd, [2011] UKFTT 792 (TC), TC01628 .... 36.121
Matthews (CR) (VTD 15935) 50.63
Matthews (E), R v, CA Criminal Division [2008] STC 1999; [2008] EWCA Crim 423
.... 49.27
Matthews (N) (t/a Tradewinds Restaurant) (VTD 5189) 18.472
Matthias (E) & Goode (S) (t/a The Music Warehouse) (VTD 17692) 2.326
Mattia (HB) Ltd [1976] VATTR 33 (VTD 243) 62.72
Mauritius National Transport Authority v Mauritius Secondary Industry Ltd, PC [2010]
  UKPC 31 .... 67.8
Mauritius Secondary Industry Ltd, Mauritius National Transport Authority v, PC
  [2010] UKPC 31 .... 67.8
Mavji, R v, CA Criminal Division [1986] STC 508 .... 49.25
Mawer (AW) & Co, [1986] VATTR 87 (VTD 2100) 4.8
Mawhinney (DN) (VTD 10475) 51.60
Mawji (AW, UK & HK) (VTD 7769, VTD 10829) 65.49
Max Security Ltd (VTD 20892) 18.210
Maximum Networks Ltd, [2011] UKFTT 93 (TC), TC00970 .... 36.113
Maxwell (P) & Hodges (B) (VTD 8887) 2.428
May, R v, HL 2008, [2009] STC 852; [2008] UKHL 28 .... 49.19
May, RCPO v, CA [2010] STC 1506; [2010] EWCA Civ 521 .... 49.23
Mayariya (D & S) (t/a Oaktree Lane Selly Oak Post Office & Stores) (VTD 19049, VTD
  19078) 52.331
Maybeck Llp (VTD 19898) 36.196
Maybourne & Russell (VTD 11289) 17.7
Mayfair Executive Ltd, [2011] UKFTT 148 (TC), TC01022 .... 36.121
Mayflower Theatre Trust Ltd (The), CA [2007] STC 880; [2007] EWCA Civ 116 .... 46.87
Mayne-Flower (Mrs W) (VTD 6513) 52.69
Mayor Fashions Ltd (VTD 4429) 14.1
Mayspark Ltd (VTD 13152) 36.383
Maystore Ltd (VTD 2096) 58.23
MB Metals Ltd (VTD 666) 62.11
MBC Trading Ltd, [2009] UKFTT 372 (TC), TC00310 .... 36.121
MBL Services Ltd (VTD 20488) 18.352
MBS plc (VTD 7542) 27.48
MBS Rüter Fassadenbau GmbH (VTD 10472) 52.69
McGee Associates, [2010] UKFTT 144 (TC), TC00450 .... 48.63
MD Design Group Ltd (VTD 10070) 10.5
MD Foods plc (VTD 17080) 29.95
ME Smith (Electrical Engineers) Ltd (VTD 13594) 15.213
Meadow Contracts Group plc (VTD 9431) 52.250
Meadows (R) (VTD 11817) 15.82
Meads (KR) (VTD 7283) 52.6
Meanwell Construction Co Ltd (VTD 10726) 55.57
Mearns (AB) (VTD 16947) 52.405
Mears (D), [1981] VATTR 99 (VTD 1095) 36.246
Mecca Ltd, QB 1978, [1979] STC 406 .... 56.8
Mechanical Engineering Consultants Ltd (VTD 13287) 62.511
Med Trading Ltd (VTD 19355) 36.79
Medcross Ltd (VTD 13080) 18.217
Mediaid Training Services Ltd (VTD 20902) 18.440
Medialift Ltd (t/a Pitman Training Centre) (VTD 18468) 52.312
Medical & Dental Staff Training Ltd (VTD 17031) 11.5
Medical Aviation Services Ltd (VTD 15308) 11.16
Medical Care Foundation, [1991] VATTR 28 (VTD 5411) 11.21
Medical Centre Developments Ltd (VTD 15601) 62.134
Medical Protection Society Ltd, oao, R v HMRC, QB 2009, [2010] STC 555; [2009]
  EWHC 2780 (Admin) 39.11
Medical Services & Equipment (ME) Ltd (VTD 13077) 62.65
Medicare Français (VTD 13929) 11.15
Medicare Research Ltd (VTD 1045) 8.6

Medivac Healthcare Ltd (VTD 16829) 19.29
Medlam (POH) (VTD 545) 2.112
Medway Draughting & Technical Services Ltd, QB [1989] STC 346 .... 18.1
Megahart Ltd, Hostgilt Ltd v, Ch D 1998, [1999] STC 141 .... 67.5
Megaink Sro, [2010] UKFTT 257 (TC), TC00551 .... 23.31
Megalith Ltd (VTD 15207) 25.3
Megantic Services Ltd (No 1), QB [2006] EWHC 3232 (Admin) 36.655
Megantic Services Ltd (No 2), UT [2011] STC 1000 .... 2.287
Megantic Services Ltd (No 3), [2010] UKFTT 125 (TC), TC00436 .... 48.107
Megatron Ltd (VTD 9207) 18.407
Megtian Ltd (No 1), Ch D [2010] STC 840; [2010] EWHC 18 (Ch) 36.107
Megtian Ltd (No 2), Ch D 5 November 2009 unreported 2.370
Mehmet (AY) (VTD 16189) 62.263
Mehmet (T & L) (t/a Leyla Dry Cleaners) (VTD 14473) 51.155
Meidl v Austria, ECHR Case 33951/05; 12 April 2011 unreported 34.30
Meiklam, Lord Advocate v, 1860, 22 D 1427 .... 2.120
Meldreth Construction Ltd (VTD 9418) 52.140
Mellerstain Trust (The Trustees of the), [1989] VATTR 223 (VTD 4256) 7.106
Mellor (GN) (VTD 10703) 52.108, 62.102
Melroad Ltd (t/a Pipework Fabrications) (VTD 9438) 18.367
Melville (EQ) (VTD 10548) 52.270
Memco Engineering Ltd, Ch D [1985] 3 All ER 267 .... 14.84
Mendes (B) (VTD 1192) 67.20
Menendez (C) (t/a La Casona) (VTD 15784) 65.91
Menheneott (BG & Mrs PL) (VTD 10542) 36.295
Mentford Ltd (VTD 16724) 3.81
Menzies (DS) (VTD 15733) 15.167
MEP Research Services Ltd (VTD 16044) 62.499
Mercantile Contracts Ltd (VTD 4357) 62.407
Mercantile Contracts Ltd (VTD 5266) 67.139
Mercedes-Benz Financial Services Ltd [2010] UKFTT 332 (TC), TC00617 .... 46.171
Mercer Associates Ltd (VTD 18779) 52.208
Merchant Navy Officers Pension Fund Trustees Ltd (VTD 14262) 46.122
Merchant Navy Ratings Pension Fund Trustees Ltd (VTD 14262) 46.122
Mercuri Urval Ltd (VTD 4438) 18.256
Merlewood Estates Ltd (VTD 20810) 15.126
Merley Bird Gardens (VTD 12426) 29.196
Merlin HC Ltd (VTD 9251) 1.100
Merrett (JC) (Builders) Ltd (VTD 10279) 52.33
Merrifield (BL & N) (VTD 10563) 7.24
Merriman White (VTD 16045) 18.425
Merseyside Cablevision Ltd [1987] VATTR 134 (VTD 2419) 36.554
Merseyside Police Authority [1991] VATTR 152 (VTD 5654) 52.64
Merseyside Trailer Hire (VTD 10136) 18.367
Merton College Oxford [2007] VATDR 177 (VTD 20233) 46.149
Mervyn Conn Organisation Ltd (VTD 5205) 3.54
Meschia's Frozen Foods, Ch D 2000, [2001] STC 1 .... 29.126
Meshberry Ltd (VTD 835) 2.464
Messenger & Co (VTD 12413) 18.334
Messenger Leisure Developments Ltd, CA [2005] STC 1078; [2005] EWCA Civ 648
      .... 24.42
Metallic Wool Co Ltd (The) (VTD 13495) 35.9
Metal Woods Ltd (VTD 1473) 36.375
Metford v Edwards, KB [1915] 1 KB 172 .... 13.29
Metravision (GB) Ltd [1977] VATTR 26 (VTD 340) 62.21
Metro College of English (VTD 11312) 51.73
Metrogold Ltd (VTD 12002) 50.74
Metrogold (Building Contractors) Ltd (VTD 16911) 62.383
Metroland Ltd (VTD 14550) 66.35
Metropol Treuhand WirtschaftstreuhandgmbH v Finanzlandesdirektion
      für Steinmark, ECJ Case C-409/99; [2002] All ER (D) 15 (Jan) 22.433

Metropole (Folkestone) Ltd (VTD 19917) 55.63
Metropolitan Borough of Wirral, QB [1995] STC 597 .... 1.73
Metropolitan Borough of Wirral (No 2) (VTD 14674) 22.145
Metropolitan Police Commissioner, Reynolds v, CA [1984] 3 All ER 649 .... 14.94
Metson (DR) & Partners (VTD 11218) 44.26
Metzger (KA) (VTD 5304) 51.60
Mevagissey Harbour Trustees (VTD 111) 41.31
Mexcom Ltd, [2010] UKFTT 163 (TC), TC00468 .... 23.28
Meyer (JW) (VTD 10899) 18.473
MF Printers (VTD 5770) 18.55
MG Rover Group Ltd (in liquidation) (VTD 20871) 2.489
MHC (Michael Hammond Partnership) [2004] VATDR 1 (VTD 18504) 18.443
Miah (A, A, A & R) (t/a The Raj Restaurant) (No 1) (VTD 19465) 47.24
Miah (A, A, A & R) (t/a The Raj Restaurant) (No 2), CS 2008, [2009] STC 729; [2008]
    CSIH 68 .... 3.144
Miah (D) (VTD 17920) 2.258
Miah (D) (VTD 18387) 47.8
Miah (D) (t/a Village Tandoori) (VTD 19084, VTD 19085) 50.104
Miah (J) (VTD 20684) 57.150
Miah (S) (t/a Agra Indian Restaurant) (VTD 17450) 52.21
Michael Cooney & Co Ltd (VTD 9627) 52.281
Michael Jackson Bloodstock Ltd (VTD 7863) 7.72
Michael Nightingale & Co Ltd (VTD 4873) 18.216
Michael Rogers Ltd (VTD 9157) 52.284
Michael Sellers & Co Ltd (LON/92/574X unreported) 36.339
Michaelis (JR) (VTD 5734) 36.158
Michaels (HJ) (VTD 4958) 18.506
Midda (RK) (VTD 8951) 18.608
Mid-Derbyshire Cheshire Home (VTD 4512) 19.88
Middle Temple (The Honourable Society of), [2011] UKFTT 390 (TC); [2011] SFTD
    1088, TC01245 .... 69.2
Middlesbrough & District Motor Club (VTD 4728) 18.134
Middlesbrough Football and Athletic Co (1986) Ltd (VTD 3836) 18.280
Middlesex Textiles Ltd, [1979] VATTR 239 (VTD 866) 25.7
Middleton (BJ) (VTD 17985) 36.557, 44.84
Middleton (Dr SGP) (VTD 6034) 1.40
Middleton (Dr SGP) (VTD 11208) 1.40
Middleton (ED & M) (VTD 6208) 52.47
Middleton (IJ) (t/a Freshfields), [2011] UKFTT 316 (TC), TC01177 .... 57.114
Midgley (R & SL) (VTD 15379) 15.171
Midland Bank plc, [1991] VATTR 525 (VTD 6129) 32.22
Midland Bank plc, ECJ Case C-98/98, [2000] STC 501; [2000] All ER (EC) 673 ... 22.400
Midland Mortgages Ltd, [2011] UKFTT 631 (TC), TC01473 .... 36.120
Midland Plant & Scaffolding Ltd (VTD 11603) 40.58
Midland Repetition Co Ltd (The) (VTD 6869) 52.33
Midland Wheel Club Ltd (The) (VTD 1770) 62.44
Midlands Co-Operative Society Ltd, Ch D 2001, [2002] STC 198 .... 58.33
Midlands Co-Operative Society Ltd (No 2), CA [2008] STC 1803; [2008] EWCA Civ
    305 .... 65.119
Mid-Rhondda Central Workmen's Institute Ltd (VTD 6770) 18.319
Migliore (L) (VTD 18692) 57.136
Mihal (K) v Daòový úrad Košice V, ECJ Case C-456/07; 21 May 2008 unreported
    .... 22.128
Mike Kiernan's Beer Tent Co Ltd (t/a Fish & Duck) (VTD 17794, VTD 18310) 57.66
Mike Parker Productions Ltd, [1976] VATTR 115 (VTD 275) 62.330
Mild Seven Chinese Takeaway (The) (VTD 16962) 50.136
Miles (PT) (VTD 33) 36.643
Milhench Brothers (VTD 3375) 18.186
Miliam (EL & HN) (VTD 4876) 18.203
Milk Marketing Board (VTD 3389) 62.172

Milk Marketing Board v Cricket St Thomas, ECJ Case C-372/88; [1990] 1 ECR 1345 .... 22.310
Mill House Management UK Ltd, [2011] UKFTT 83 (TC), TC00960 .... 6.36
Millennium Catering & Pub Co Ltd (VTD 14275) 14.12
Millennium Nails Ltd (VTD 19900) 53.10
Miller v Tebb, QB 1893, 9 TLR 515 .... 14.81
Miller (G, J & B) (VTD 18630) 36.592
Miller (GK) & Turner (JD) (t/a Britannia Wine Bar) (VTD 2389) 51.107
Miller (JA & Mrs IA) (t/a Miller Transport) (VTD 2041) 36.419
Miller Freeman Worldwide plc (VTD 15439) 8.24
Miller Freeman Worldwide plc (No 2) [1998] VATDR 435 (VTD 15452) 62.514
Milligan (Mrs D) (VTD 19224) 15.45
Milligan (W) & Sons (VTD 4297) 44.84
Milliner (DJ) & Burt (RF) [1995] VATDR 255 (VTD 13438) 3.32
Milliwatt Ltd, Attorney-General v, KB [1948] 1 All ER 331 .... 19.9
Mills (AD) (VTD 12312) 3.78
Mills (BL) (VTD 1686) 41.103
Mills (C) (VTD 4864) 36.205
Mills (I) (VTD 1893) 19.71
Mills (S) (t/a Steve Mills Advertising) (VTD 18292) 57.133
Mills Marketing Services Ltd (VTD 4861) 35.8
Milnathort Golf Club Ltd (VTD 15816) 24.49
Milnathort Golf Club Ltd (No 2) (VTD 17889) 46.9
Milne & Mackintosh (t/a Jack and Jill), [1981] VATTR 61 (VTD 1063) 2.120, 2.121
Milner (KJ) (VTD 13648) 36.583
Milward (W) (VTD 18442) 44.141
Minder Music Ltd (VTD 2678) 18.257
Minerva Kulturreisen GmbH v Finanzamt Freital, ECJ Case C-31/10; [2011] STC 532 .... 22.490
Minister Finansów, Inter-Mark Group sp. z o.o. sp. komandytowa v, ECJ Case C-530/09; 27 October 2011 unreported 20.34
Minister Finansów, Oasis East sp zoo v, ECJ Case C-395/09; 30 September 2010 unreported 22.430
Minister Finansów, Slaby v, ECJ Case C-180/10; [2011] STC 2230 .... 20.5
Minister for Social Welfare & Another, Emmott v, ECJ Case C-208/90; [1991] 1 ECR 4269; [1991] 3 CMLR 894 .... 22.45
Minister van Financiën, Rompelman & Rompelman-van-Deelen v, ECJ Case 268/83; [1985] 3 CMLR 202; [1985] ECR 655 .... 22.103
Ministère de l'Économie, des Finances et de l'Industrie, Société Thermale d'Eugénie-les-Bains v, ECJ Case C-277/05; [2008] STC 2470 .... 22.86
Ministère de l'Économie, des Finances et de l'Industrie, Syndicat des Producteurs Indépendants v, ECJ Case C-108/00, [2001] STC 523; [2001] All ER (EC) 564. .... 22.220
Ministère du Budget, des Comptes publics et de la Fonction publique, Graphic Procédé v, ECJ Case C-88/09; [2010] STC 918 .... 22.177
Ministère Public & Ministry of Finance v Profant (V), ECJ Case 249/84; [1985] ECR 3237; [1986] 2 CMLR 378 .... 22.384
Ministère Public & Ministre des Finances du Royaume de Belgique v Ledoux, ECJ Case 127/86; [1988] ECR 3741; [1991] STC 553 .... 22.385
Ministero dell'Economia e delle Finanze v FCE Bank plc, ECJ Case C-210/04; [2007] STC 165 .... 22.201
Ministero dell'Economia e delle Finanze v Part Service Srl, ECJ Case C-425/06; [2008] STC 3132 .... 22.62
Ministero dell'Economia e delle Finanze, Ampliscientifica Srl & Amplifin SpA v, ECJ Case C-162/07; [2011] STC 566 .... 22.125
Ministero dell'Economia e delle Finanze, Athesia Druck v, ECJ Case C-1/08; [2009] STC 1334 .... 22.228
Ministero dell' Economia e delle Finanze, Banco Antoniana Popolare Veneta SpA v, ECJ Case C-427/10; 15 December 2011 unreported 22.54
Ministero dell'Economia e delle Finanze, Curia (G) v, ECJ Case C-381/09; 7 July 2010 unreported 22.358
Ministero delle Finanze v COGEP Srl, ECJ Case C-174/06; [2008] STC 2744 .... 22.344

Ministero delle Finanze, Edilizia Industriale Siderurgica Srl *v*, ECJ Case C-231/96; [1998] 1 ECR 4951 .... 22.50
Ministero delle Finanze, Grundig Italiana SpA *v*, ECJ Case C-255/00; [2003] All ER (EC) 176 .... 22.57
Ministero delle Finanze, Pezzullo Molini Pastifici Mangimifici SpA *v*, ECJ Case C-166/94; [1996] STC 1236; [1996] 1 ECR 331 .... 22.231
Ministero delle Finanze, Reemtsma Cigarettenfabriken GmbH *v*, ECJ Case C-35/05; [2008] STC 3448 .... 22.535
Ministero delle Finanze dello Stato, Balocchi (M) *v*, ECJ Case C-10/92; [1993] 1 ECR 5105, [1997] STC 640; [1995] 1 CMLR 486 .... 22.476
Ministre de l'Économie, des Finances et de l'Industrie *v* Gillan Beach Ltd, ECJ Case C-114/05; [2006] STC 1080 .... 22.216
Ministre du Budget *v* Société Monte Dei Paschi Di Siena, ECJ Case C-136/99; [2001] STC 1029 .... 22.532
Ministre du Budget, Régie Dauphinoise-Cabinet A Forest Sarl *v*, ECJ Case C-306/94; STC 1176; [1996] 1 ECR 3695; [1996] 3 CMLR 193 .... 22.446
Ministre du Budget, Satam SA *v*, ECJ Case C-333/91; [1993] 1 ECR 3513; [1997] STC 226 .... 22.443
Ministro della Sanita, Srl CILFIT and Lanificio di Gavardo SpA *v*, ECJ [1982] ECR 3415 .... 22.3
Ministry of Agriculture, Fisheries & Food, R *v* (ex p. Hedley Lomas (Ireland) Ltd), ECJ Case C-5/94; [1996] 1 ECR 2553; [1996] 2 CMLR 391; [1996] All ER (EC) 493 .... 22.32
Ministry of Defence, R *v* (ex p. Smith), CA 1995, [1996] QB 517; [1996] 1 All ER 257 .... 42.8
Ministry of Finance (Belgium), Chaussures Bally SA *v*, ECJ 1993, [1997] STC 209 .... 22.238
Minstead House Care Management Ltd (VTD 9506) 52.281
Minster Associates, QB 1992 (unreported) 27.38
Mirror Group Newspapers Ltd (VTD 3876) 5.79
Mirror Group Newspapers Ltd, CA [2001] STC 192; [2001] EWCA Civ 65 .... 27.51
Mirror Group plc, ECJ Case C-409/98; [2001] STC 1453; [2002] 2 WLR 288 .... 22.335
Miss Charlie Ltd (VTD 9301) 40.72
Miss Mary of Sweden Cosmetics Ltd [1985] VATTR 159 (VTD 1921) 67.40
Miss Worth Ltd (VTD 1623) 25.20
Missionfine Ltd (t/a GT Air Services) (VTD 10331) 43.5
Mistry (G) (VTD 11624) 18.120
Mitchell (HD) (t/a Mitchell & Co) (VTD 16547) 57.40
Mitchell Haselhurst Ltd [1979] VATTR 166 (VTD 812) 62.3
Mitchells of Hailsham Ltd (VTD 9862) 52.85
Mithras (Wine Bars) Ltd, [2010] UKFTT 622 (TC), TC00864 .... 3.165
Mitrolone Ltd (VTD 4301) 62.98
Mittu (JS) (VTD 1275) 62.76
MJ Foster Ltd (VTD 75) 32.6
MJ Gleeson plc (VTD 13332) 40.57
MKG-Kraftfahrzeuge-Factoring GmbH, Finanzamt Groß-Gerau *v*, ECJ Case C-305/01; [2003] STC 951; [2004] All ER (EC) 454 .... 22.364
MKM Builders (VTD 10511) 55.2
MM Skip Hire Ltd (VTD 12528) 18.551
MML Systems (VTD 18677) 59.30
MMO2 plc [2006[VATDR 108 (VTD 19514) 2.263
Mobile Export 365 Ltd (No 2), Ch D [2007] STC 1794; [2007] EWHC 1737 (Ch) 2.276
Mobile Export 365 Ltd (No 3), Ch D [2009] EWHC 797 (Ch) 2.291
Mobile Export 365 Ltd (No 4), [2010] UKFTT 367 (TC), TC00649 .... 36.113
Mobile Export 365 Ltd (oao), R *v* HMRC, QB [2006] STC 1069; [2006] EWHC 311 (Admin) 2.532
Mobile Motoring Maintenance Ltd, [2011] UKFTT 6 (TC), TC00883 .... 48.63
Mobile Radio Ltd (VTD 3994) 18.553
Mobilx Ltd (No 1), Ch D 2007, [2008] STC 3071; [2007] EWHC 1769 (Ch) 2.17
Mobilx Ltd (No 2), CA [2010] STC 1436; [2010] EWCA Civ 517 .... 36.119
Moda Ltd (VTD 10761) 50.18

Modified Gumball Rally Ltd (t/a Modball Ltd), [2009] UKFTT 250 (TC), TC00198 .... 57.138
Mohammed (A) (VTD 15438) 52.21
Mohammed (AQ) (VTD 14999) 50.23
Mohammed (D) (t/a Aglow Fashions) (VTD 10246) 3.83
Mohammed (N) (t/a The Indian Palmist) (VTD 18397) 62.500
Mohawk (Contract Hire & Leasing) Ltd (VTD 10998) 65.66
Moher (S) (t/a Premier Dental Agency), [2011] UKFTT 286 (TC); [2011] SFTD 917, TC01148 .... 33.37
Mohr v Finanzamt Bad Segeberg, ECJ Case C-215/94; [1996] STC 328; [1996] 1 ECR 959; [1996] All ER (EC) 450 .... 22.172
Mohsche, Finanzamt München III v, ECJ Case C–193/91; [1993] 1 ECR 2615, [1997] STC 195 .... 22.181
Moir, Wallensteiner v (No 2), QB [1975] QB 373 .... 2.445
Mol v Inspecteur der Invoerrechten en Accijnzen, ECJ Case 269/86; [1988] ECR 3627; [1989] BVC 205; [1989] 3 CMLR 729 .... 22.81
Moldova, Agurdino Srl v, ECHR Case 7359/06; 27 September 2011 unreported 34.23
Molino (Miss R) (VTD 9056) 18.481
Moll (AD) (VTD 17302) 53.15
Mollan & Co Ltd [2010] UKFTT 578 (TC), TC00828 .... 52.291
Moloney (S) (VTD 14873) 57.130
Molyneux (D) (VTD 9265) 18.563
Molyneux (GC) (VTD 3322) 51.123
Monevate Services Ltd (VTD 19965) 52.129
Money (AJ) (VTD 5655) 2.425
Monks & Sons (VTD 10401) 36.623
Mono Global Ltd (VTD 18559) 36.136
Monoprio (P) (VTD 17806) 56.3
Monsell Youell Developments Ltd [1978] VATTR 1 (VTD 538) 15.17
Monster Worldwide Holdings Ltd (VTD 20085) 18.468
Montague Burton Developments Ltd (VTD 10090) 46.18
Montalbano (S) (VTD 2113) 40.69
Montessori Teachers Supplies Ltd (VTD 8825) 67.68
Montreux Fabrics Ltd [1988] VATTR 71 (VTD 2673) 18.4
Montrose DIY Ltd (VTD 2652) 65.20
Moody (PJ) (t/a PMS Telecom) (VTD 13234) 18.263
Moon (A) (t/a Craft Master Construction) (VTD 14855) 3.35
Moon Fashions Ltd (VTD 14324) 14.47
Mooney (EJ) (t/a Company Moves) [1990] VATTR 50 (VTD 4667) 38.42
Moonraker's Guest House Ltd, QB [1992] STC 544 .... 62.443
Moor Lodge Developments Ltd (VTD 7285) 52.384
Moorbury Ltd, UT [2010] STC 2715 .... 22.77
Moore (B) (VTD 18653) 55.65
Moore (DM) (VTD 5244) 18.281
Moore (JA) (VTD 15972) 15.144
Moore (JK) [1989] VATTR 276 (VTD 4474) 67.32
Moores Furniture Group Ltd (VTD 15044) 15.228
Moorim UK Ltd (VTD 19794) 18.283
Moorthorpe Empire Working Men's Club (VTD 1127) 3.152
Morga (MAG & G) (VTD 4905) 50.132
Morgan (DH) (VTD 6805) 40.70
Morgan (HE) (t/a Hayden Trading Co) (VTD 15177) 36.611
Morgan (JE) (t/a Wishmore Morgan Investments) (VTD 2150) 40.7
Morgan (MW) (VTD 16968) 2.327
Morgan (VWS) (VTD 633) 41.117
Morgan (Mr & Mrs) (t/a The Harrow Inn) (VTD 19671) 28.12
Morgan Automation Ltd (VTD 5539) 36.218
Morgan Brothers (Mid-Wales) Ltd (VTD 8913) 52.72
Morgan-Jones (DT) (VTD 1340) 36.265
Morgan Stanley UK Group (VTD 20424) 46.172
Morganash Ltd (VTD 19777) 38.21

Morland & Co plc [1992] VATTR 411 (VTD 8869) 65.62
Morley v Pincombe, Ex D 1848, 2 Ex D 101 .... 14.77
Morley Electronic Fire Systems Ltd (VTD 10957) 40.107
Morley Retreat and Conference House (VTD 17265) 15.118
Morpheus 2002 Ltd [2006] VATDR 428 (VTD 19854) 27.43
Morrell (JL) (t/a Morrell Middleton) (VTD 13970) 14.63
Morris (AD) (VTD 3456) 51.67
Morris (B) (VTD 18741) 1.34
Morris (GM) (VTD 17860) 15.23
Morris (K) & Others [2006] VATDR 263 (E894) 34.15
Morris (L) (t/a DV8) (VTD 19492) 14.27
Morris (M) (t/a Reward) (VTD 16846) 62.213
Morris (RBF & NJ) (t/a Roundstone Caravan Depot) (VTD 11092) 46.74
Morris (SR) (t/a Two Plus Two) (VTD 18621) 24.7
Morris Amusements Ltd (VTD 15829) 48.81
Morris Motors Ltd v Lilley [1959] All ER 737 .... 44.66
Morrish (CR), QB [1998] STC 954 .... 55.61
Morrison (PG) (VTD 15244) 52.427
Morrison Bowmore Distillers Ltd [2010] UKFTT 394 (TC), TC00676 .... 8.44
Morrison Dunbar Ltd, QB 1978, [1979] STC 406 .... 56.8
Morrison's Academy Boarding Houses Association, CS 1977, [1978] STC 1 .... 7.1
Morrow (KEG) & Wells (AE) (VTD 2424) 36.520
Morshan Contractors Ltd (VTD 1861) 40.9
Morston Properties Ltd (VTD 15004) 65.73
Morston Properties Ltd (No 2) (VTD 15444) 36.25
Mortimer (JD) (VTD 381) 5.74
Mortimer (MHD) (VTD 4235) 18.88
Morton (HC) (VTD 438) 15.12
Morton (R & J) (VTD 17179) 52.398
Morton Hotels Ltd (VTD 20039) 65.34
Moss (A) (VTD 919, 953) 2.327
Moss (GE) (t/a The Red House) (VTD 14633) 62.293
Motcombe Bakeries (VTD 2216) 36.406
Mote v Secretary of State for Work & Pensions, CA [2007] EWCA Civ 1324 .... 2.220
Mothercare Ltd (VTD 323) 12.1
Mothercare (UK) Ltd [1993] VATTR 391 (VTD 10751) 58.8
Moti Mahal Indian Restaurant [1992] VATTR 188 (VTD 9375) 50.137
Motor & Legal Group Ltd (VTD 12036) 62.469
Motor Vehicle Protection Association (VTD 20673) 64.32
Motorways Auto Spares (VTD 4045) 18.555
Mould (LJ) (t/a Leon Jaimes Hair Fashions) (VTD 19087) 41.89
Moulding (R) (Contractors Plant) Ltd (VTD 15102) 52.411
Mount Edgcumbe Hospice Ltd (VTD 14807) 11.54
Mountfield Software Ltd (VTD 12816) 18.34
Mountford, Street v, HL [1985] 1 AC 809; [1985] 2 All ER 289 .... 41.159
Mounty (F & M) & Sons [1995] VATDR 128 (VTD 12985) 36.307
Mowbray (K) [1986] VATTR 266 (VTD 2239) 29.50
Mowbray (K) (t/a Maypole Self-Service Station) (VTD 20620) 48.63
Mowbray Properties Ltd (VTD 6033) 7.69
Mowco Ltd (VTD 15657) 36.146
Mower (SJ) (VTD 17210) 44.141
MPH Leisure Ltd (VTD 19778) 65.91
Mr Builder (1987) Ltd (VTD 6265) 52.280
Mr Francis Ltd (VTD 16804) 41.89
Mr Wishmore Ltd, QB [1988] STC 723 .... 14.52
MSK (Insulation Services) Ltd (VTD 4198) 18.502
MSS (North West) Ltd [1980] VATTR 29 (VTD 882) 36.372
Mu (KH & CB) (VTD 17504) 34.2
Muir (KM) (t/a Ken Muir Nurseries) (VTD 6830) 52.69
Muir (B) & Edwards (Ms G) (t/a Muir-McGill Associates) (VTD 7469) 36.297
Muirtown Motel (VTD 7431) 52.13

Mullan *v* Anderson, CS [1993] SLT 835 .... 50.77
Mullan (B) & Son (Contractors) Ltd (VTD 6833) 52.125
Mullen (WJ) (VTD 3374) 18.563
Mulligan (GA) (VTD 17895) 57.7
Mullis (R) (VTD 18501) 57.80
Mulhearn (LJ) (t/a Sandancer Amusements) (VTD 19188) 46.70
Multiform Printing Ltd [1996] VATDR 580 (VTD 13931) 5.57
Multiprime Cuisine Ltd (VTD 17399) 6.38
Munir (K) (t/a Favourite Chicken) (VTD 18612) 65.91
Munn (MS) [1989] VATTR 11 (VTD 3296) 36.631
Munnery (JC) (VTD 17903) 15.50
Munster (IM & PA) (t/a M & M Heating Services) (VTD 7961) 36.464
Murat (MYH) (VTD 14759) 51.184
Murat (MYH), QB [1998] STC 923 .... 3.164
Murden (MB) (VTD 207) 36.128
Murden (NE & RWH) (VTD 9192) 18.126
Murdie Partnership Ltd (The) (VTD 17786) 18.519
Murdoch UK Ltd, [2011] UKFT 62 (TC), TC00940 .... 28.6
Murphy (JJ) (VTD 5475) 18.120
Murray (B) (t/a Benco Taxis) (VTD 17334) 62.236
Murray (DE) (VTD 3692) 18.486
Murray (Mrs MA) (VTD 13907) 36.245
Murray (N) (VTD 15149) 35.1
Murrayfield Indoor Sports Club (VTD 6613) 52.312
Murrell (VTD 16878) 34.10
Musashi Autoparts Europe Ltd, CA 2003, [2004] STC 220; [2003] EWCA Civ 1738
.... 17.17
Musgrave & Larkin (Solicitors) (VTD 10885) 2.497
Mushtaq's Food Factory Ltd (VTD 20496) 14.39
Music & Video Exchange Ltd, QB [1992] STC 220 .... 1.7
Music Shop (Romford) Ltd (The) (VTD 4696) 18.85
Music View Ltd (VTD 9122) 36.515
Mutch (DG) (VTD 2559) 36.536
Muys en De Winters's Bouw-en Aannemingsbedriff BV *v* Staatssecretaris van
Financiën, ECJ Case C-281/91; [1997] STC 665; [1993] 1 ECR 5405; [1995] 1 CMLR
126 .... 22.354
MW Helicopters Ltd (VTD 16888) 52.207
MW Plant (Contracts) Ltd (E1074) 2.280
My Secrets Ltd, [2011] UKFTT 72 (TC), TC00950 .... 36.100
Myatt & Leason [1995] VATDR 440 (VTD 13780) 36.171
Myers (JT & Mrs SM) (VTD 3951) 57.64
Myerscough (M) (t/a Summerleaze Beach Hotel) (VTD 17583) 63.14
Mylos of Reading (Catering & Ices) Ltd (VTD 2538) 29.52
Mynt Ltd, [2011] UKFTT 162 (TC), TC01031 .... 36.113
MyTravel Group plc (VTD 18940) 63.25
MyTravel plc (No 1), ECJ Case C-291/03; [2005] STC 1617 .... 22.488

N

Nader (R) (t/a Try Us) (VTD 4927) 1.4
Nader (R) (t/a Try Us), CA [1993] STC 806 .... 2.389
Nader & Associated Manufacturing Co (VTD 4746) 18.127
Nadler Enterprises Ltd, Re, Ch D [1980] STC 457; [1981] 1 WLR 23; [1980] 3 All ER
350 .... 32.10
Nagra (SS & AK) (VTD 19849) 52.21
Namecourt Ltd [1984] VATTR 22 (VTD 1560) 41.100
Nandera (KS) (VTD 7880) 50.149
Nara Manufacturers (VTD 603, 894) 2.422
Nares International Ltd (VTD 20018) 18.214
Narogauge Ltd (VTD 14680) 66.22

Nash (RJ & J) (VTD 14944) 57.24
Nasim (TS & Y) (t/a Yasmine Restaurant), QB [1987] STC 387 .... 57.203
Nathaniel & Co Solicitors [2010] UKFTT 472 (TC), TC00734 .... 48.63
Nathoo (t/a Kamona Enterprises) (VTD 6551) 2.407
National & Provincial Building Society [1991] VATTR 540 (6293) 46.72
National & Provincial Building Society [1996] VATDR 153 (14017) 48.43
National Association of Funeral Directors (VTD 1989) 64.17
National Bus Company (VTD 2530) 1.38
National Business Register plc (VTD 20262) 5.42
National Coal Board, QB [1982] STC 863 .... 54.11
National Council of YMCAs Inc [1990] VATTR 68 (VTD 5160) 21.51
National Council of YMCAs Inc [1993] VATTR 299 (VTD 10537) 48.140
National Council of YMCAs (No 3) (VTD 15247) 48.144
National Federation of Post Office and British Telecom Pensioners (VTD 17980) 64.26
National Galleries of Scotland (No 1) (VTD 18413) 48.83
National Galleries of Scotland (No 2) (VTD 19372) 48.12
National Galleries of Scotland (No 3) [2007] VATDR 234 (VTD 20253) 48.9
National House Building Council [2010] UKFTT 326 (TC), TC00611 .... 46.31
National Provident Institution [2005] VATDR 297 (VTD 18944) 46.177
National Safety Associates of America (UK) Ltd (VTD 14241) 29.102
National Society for the Prevention of Cruelty to Children [1992] VATTR 417 (VTD
    9325) 11.49
National Transit Insurance Co Ltd, QB 1974, [1975] STC 35; [1975] 1 WLR 552;
    [1975] 1 All ER 303 .... 1.83
National Water Council, QB 1978, [1979] STC 157 .... 7.2
National Westminster Bank plc (No 2) [2000] VATDR 484 (VTD 17000) 61.3
National Westminster Bank plc (No 3) [2002] VATDR 414 (VTD 17687) 27.58
National Westminster Bank plc (No 4), Ch D [2002] EWHC 2204(Ch); [2003] 1 All ER
    (Comm) 327 .... 48.148
National Westminster Bank plc (No 5), Ch D [2003] STC 1072; [2003] EWHC 1822
    (Ch) 48.35
Nationwide Anglia Building Society [1994] VATTR 30 (VTD 11826) 27.2
Nationwide Building Society [1993] VATTR 205 (VTD 10117) 61.1
Nationwide Hygiene Supplies Ltd (VTD 5389) 18.31
Nationwide Leisure Ltd (VTD 16482) 18.226
Nationwide Roofing Co (VTD 9861) 52.217
Natt (SS) (VTD 6999) 44.90
Natural Stone Co (The) (VTD 15272) 14.29
Natural World Products Ltd (VTD 11064) 65.67
Naturally Yours Cosmetics Ltd (No 1) [1985] VATTR 159 (VTD 1921) 67.40
Naturally Yours Cosmetics Ltd (No 2), ECJ Case 230/87; [1988] STC 879; [1988] ECR
    6365; [1989] 1 CMLR 797 .... 22.233
Nature's Balance Ltd (VTD 12295) 29.100
Nature's Larder (VTD 4856) 18.432
Naughton (T) (VTD 7854) 62.74
Navicon SA v Administración del Estado, ECJ Case C-97/06; [2008] STC 2693 .... 22.391
Navydock Ltd (VTD 18281) 62.215
Nawab Tandoori Restaurant (The) (VTD 6636) 50.106
Nawaz (M) (t/a Elvis Private Hire) (VTD 16017) 57.14
Nawaz (T), QB [1986] STC 484 .... 2.324
Nawrot (JK) (VTD 11775) 62.59
Naylor (R & J) (VTD 17305) 15.172
Nazif (MK & ME) (VTD 13616) 50.5
NCC Construction Danmark A/S v Skatteministeriet, ECJ Case C-174/08; [2010] STC
    532 .... 22.452
NCC Developments Ltd (VTD 7388) 52.85
NCJ Electrical Ltd (VTD 6383) 52.244
NCS Associates Ltd (VTD 16007) 50.35
NCS Northern Communication Systems Ltd (VTD 4242) 36.418
NDF Administration Ltd (VTD 18301) 46.176
NDP Co Ltd [1988] VATTR 40 (VTD 2653) 67.107

Neal (Miss J), QB 1987, [1988] STC 131 .... 51.50
Nealeplan (VTD 3457) 18.599
Needham (A) (VTD 5150) 18.263
Needles Chairlift Co Ltd (VTD 90) 66.31
Neen Design Ltd (VTD 11782) 19.11
Neil MacLeod (Prints & Enterprises) Ltd (VTD 17144) 44.124
Neilson (O) (t/a The News Shop) (VTD 15197) 58.23
Nell Gwynn House Maintenance Fund (Trustees of), HL 1998, [1999] STC 79; [1999] 1
  WLR 174; [1999] 1 All ER 385 .... 62.36
Nelsons of Newark Ltd (VTD 1751) 44.63
Nelson Stokes Ltd (VTD 7690) 18.473
Nene Packaging Ltd [2001] VATDR 286 (VTD 17365) 2.170
Neocli (A & T) (VTD 15771) 50.34
NEP Group Ltd (VTD 6751) 52.348
Neruby Computing Services Ltd (VTD 15874) 18.179
Ness (JR) (VTD 11559) 2.501
Nestlé Co Ltd, Chappel & Co Ltd v, HL 1959, [1960] AC 87; [1959] 2 All ER 701
  .... 67.154
Netherlands (Kingdom of), EC Commission v, ECJ Case 235/85; [1987] ECR 1471;
  [1988] 2 CMLR 921 .... 22.127
Netherlands (Kingdom of), EC Commission v, ECJ Case C-408/97; 12 September 2000
  unreported 22.136
Netherlands (Kingdom of), EC Commission v, ECJ Case C-338/98; [2003] STC 1506;
  [2004] 1 WLR 35 .... 22.403
Netherlands (Kingdom of), EC Commission v, ECJ Case C-41/09; 3 March 2011
  unreported 20.54
Netherlands (Kingdom of), Gasus Dosier - und Fördertechnik GmbH
  Netherlands, ECHR Case 15375/89; 20 EHRR 403 v 18.618, 34.1
Netherlands Board of Tourism (VTD 12935) 36.498
Netto Supermarkt GmbH & Co OHG v Finanzamt Malchin, ECJ Case C-271/06;
  [2008] STC 3280 .... 22.388
Network Data Ltd (VTD 4393) 18.586
Network Euro Ltd, [2011] UKFTT 255 (TC), TC01119 .... 36.113
Network Insurance Brokers Ltd (VTD 14755) 24.28
Network International Group Ltd (VTD 16554) 8.4
Neurotech International Ltd (VTD 18812) 33.28
Neuvale Ltd, CA [1989] STC 395 .... 46.17
Neville (GM) & Clark (MR) (t/a Trueline Interiors) (VTD 10350) 51.38
Neville (JP) (t/a Neville Engineering) (VTD 10128) 65.64
Neville Russell (a firm) [1987] VATTR 194 (VTD 2484) 62.127
Nevisbrook Ltd, CA [1989] STC 539; [1989] 2 All ER 938 .... 62.431
New Ash Green Village Association Ltd [1976] VATTR 63 (VTD 245) 13.11
New Bengal Tandoori Restaurant (VTD 5211) 18.244
New Concept Ltd (VTD 15174) 18.612
New Forest Agricultural Show Society (VTD 17631) 11.37
New Mansion Pension Managers Ltd (VTD 13527) 36.473
New Way School of Motoring Ltd [1979] VATTR 57 (VTD 724) 62.223
New Western (Panels) Ltd (VTD 6990) 52.12
New World Payphones Ltd (VTD 15964) 67.138
New Zealand Commissioner of Inland Revenue, Edgewater Motel Ltd v, PC [2004] STC
  1382; [2004] UKPC 44 .... 14.114
Newall (A & A) (VTD 18074) 41.144
Newall (RJ) (VTD 14109) 62.253
Neways International (UK) Ltd, Ch D [2003] STC 795; [2003] EWHC 934 (Ch) 2.154
Newby (P) (t/a Peter Newby & Co) (VTD 10395) 51.60
Newcastle Double Glazing Ltd (VTD 3026) 2.468
Newcastle Theatre Royal Trust Ltd (VTD 18952) 48.46
Newcastle United plc, Ch D [2007] STC 1330; [2007] EWHC 612 (Ch) 36.138
Newcourt Property Fund (VTD 5825) 6.18
Newett (D & JE) (t/a Stirling Investments), [2010] UKFTT 61 (TC), TC00374 .... 40.99
Newey (P) (t/a Ocean Finance), [2010] SFTD 836; UKFTT 183 (TC), TC00487 ..... 22.74

Newland Technical Services Ltd (VTD 9294) 36.330, 40.80
Newman (BE) (VTD 191) 3.156
Newman (JJ) (VTD 781, 903) 40.62
Newman (NA & Mrs FAF) [2007] VATDR 276 (VTD 20006) 18.543
Newman Shipping & Agency Co NV v Belgian State, ECJ Case C-435/03; [2006] STC 158 .... 22.88
Newmir plc [1993] VATTR 55 (VTD 10102) 7.116
Newnham College in the University of Cambridge (Principal & Fellows), HL [2008] STC 1225; [2008] UKHL 23; [2008] 2 All ER 863 .... 6.10
Newport County AFC Social Club Ltd (VTD 19807) 62.123
News Trade Supplies Ltd (VTD 17339) 5.104
Newstar Jeans Co Ltd (C264) 35.27
Newsvendors Benevolent Institution (VTD 14343) 11.33
Newton (RE & RL) (t/a RE Newton) (VTD 17222) 62.369
Newton (SP) (VTD 5367) 18.485
Newton Newton (VTD 11372) 48.116
Newtownbutler Playgroup Ltd (VTD 13741) 15.90
Next Generation International Ltd, [2010] UKFTT 46 (TC), TC00359 .... 36.121
Next Group plc, [2011] UKFTT 122 (TC); [2011] SFTD 511; TC00998 .... 5.34
Next plc, QB [1995] STC 651 .... 58.28
NG International Ltd, [2010] UKFTT 417 (TC), TC00687 .... 36.111
Ng Yuet Sar Restaurant Ltd (VTD 319) 3.147
NGF 90 (Gateshead) Ltd (VTD 9816) 52.167
NGS (Coatbridge) Ltd (VTD 15970) 4.17
Niagara Holdings Ltd [1993] VATTR 503 (VTD 11400) 19.14
Nicholas (PJ & AJ) (t/a A & P Scaffolding) (VTD 15898) 40.72
Nicholls (DT) (VTD 7960) 18.43
Nicholls (PVR) (VTD 11115) 55.73
Nichols (JA) (VTD 14521) 36.68
Nichols (P) (VTD 9304) 51.21
Nicholson (JR) (VTD 6707) 62.191
Nicholson (Dr RW) (VTD 19412) 55.12
Nicol (EG) (VTD 571) 44.55
Nicolaides (K & H) (VTD 15355) 50.138
Nidderdale Building Ltd (VTD 13158) 15.196
Nidderdale Building Ltd, QB [1997] STC 800 .... 50.6
Nield (Mrs M) (t/a Soft Options) (VTD 10677) 51.23
Nielsen (J) (VTD 11852) 36.567
Nigel Lowe Consulting Ltd, [2009] UKFTT 130 (TC), TC00098 .... 18.516
Nigel Mansell Sports Co Ltd [1991] VATTR 491 (VTD 6116) 62.452
Nigel Sullivan Fibres Ltd (VTD 9842) 52.342
Nightfreight plc (VTD 15479) 27.57
Nightingale (Mrs ACS) (t/a Arrowe Rental) (VTD 17750) 44.119
Nightingale Holdings (VTD 16721) 52.400
Nightingale Music Ltd (VTD 5060) 18.413
Nightingale Partnership (The) (VTD 10219) 18.203
Nightingales Motors (Exmouth) Ltd (VTD 6842) 52.342
Nike (SF), [2009] UKFTT 349 (TC), TC00287 .... 15.276
Nimmock (MA) (VTD 13857) 18.88
Nissan Motor Manufacturing (UK) Ltd, [2007] VATDR 1 (C236) 22.69
Nissan UK Ltd (ex p.), R v C & E, CA 1987, [1988] BTC 8003 .... 44.40
Nivek Holdings Ltd (VTD 7383) 52.132
Niven (Y) (VTD 2591) 67.95
Nixon v Freeman, QB 1860, 5 H & N 647 .... 14.79
Nixon (GMB) (VTD 233) 7.50
Nixon (H), [1980] VATTR 66 (VTD 973) 44.62
Noades (VA) (VTD 17152) 57.198
Noble (ME) (VTD 12346) 62.197
Nock (PC) (VTD 10169) 52.337
Nolan (DS) (VTD 2283) 51.107
Nomura Properties Management Services Ltd, QB [1994] STC 461 .... 52.4

Noor (A), [2011] UKFTT 349 (TC), TC01209 .... 22.553
Nor-Clean Ltd, [1991] VATTR 239 (VTD 5954) 52.175
Norbury Developments Ltd, ECJ Case C-136/97; [1999] STC 511; [1999] All ER (EC) 436 .... 22.511
Nordania Finans A/S v Skatteministeriet, ECJ Case C-98/07; [2008] STC 3314 ..... 22.451
Nordea Pankki Suomi Oyi v Finland, ECJ Case C-350/10; [2011] STC 1956 .... 22.365
Nordic Subscription Service UK Ltd (VTD 10705) 5.105
Norfolk & Suffolk Finance Ltd (VTD 15288) 36.635
Norgate (LJ & H) (t/a Dog's Dinner) (VTD 5241) 29.191
Norglen Ltd v Reeds Rains Prudential Ltd, HL [1999] 2 AC 14 .... 2.297
Normaco Ltd (VTD 11821) 18.588
Normal Films Ltd (VTD 15558) 36.666
Normal Motor Factors Ltd, [1978] VATTR 20 (VTD 499) 62.184
Norman (T) (VTD 3257) 18.505
Norman Adams Artists & Potters (VTD 9964) 51.60
Norman Allen Group Travel Ltd, [1996] VATDR 405 (VTD 14156) 63.4
Norman Lavelle Ltd (VTD 1330) 58.26
Norman Riding Poultry Farm Ltd [1989] VATTR 124 (VTD 3726) 29.190
Norman Wood & Sons (VTD 10558) 50.77
Norpak Engineering Ltd (VTD 7462) 18.238
North & East Devon Health Authority, R v (ex p. Coughlan), CA [2001] 1 QB 213 .... 22.552
North Anderson Cars Ltd, CS [1999] STC 902 .... 44.154
North Birmingham & Aldridge Motor Co Ltd (VTD 4014) 18.374
North British Housing Association Ltd (VTD 7195) 46.128
North Cheshire Foods Ltd (VTD 2709) 29.147
North East Direct Access Ltd (VTD 18267) 41.101
North East Garages Ltd (VTD 15734) 38.38
North East Garages Ltd, QB [1999] STC 1057 .... 2.376
North East Media Development Trust Ltd (VTD 13104) 48.134
North East Media Development Trust Ltd (No 2) [1995] VATDR 240 (VTD 13425) 48.142
North East Media Development Trust Ltd (No 3) [1996] VATDR 396 (VTD 14416) 48.143
North East Worcestershire College (VTD 16665) 46.1
North Isles Shellfish Ltd [1995] VATDR 415 (VTD 13083) 29.118
North Kent Motor Company (VTD 3735) 67.45
North Lanarkshire CCTV Ltd (VTD 18031) 7.98
North London Business Development Agency Ltd (VTD 17092) 8.27
North London College of Accountancy Ltd (VTD 14054) 21.12
North of England Zoological Society, QB [1999] STC 1027 .... 21.6
North of England Zoological Society v Chester Rural District Council, CA [1959] 1 WLR 773; [1959] 3 All ER 116 .... 21.6
North Scene Video Ltd (VTD 7136) 52.136
North West Business Centres Ltd (VTD 4594) 46.19
North West Cash & Carry Ltd (VTD 18177) 23.11
North West Freighters Ltd (VTD 3341) 18.166
North West Leicestershire Youth Training Scheme Ltd [1989] VATTR 321 (VTD 4476) 21.24
North West Leicestershire Youth Training Scheme Ltd (VTD 4929) 2.402
North Wiltshire District Council [2010] UKFTT 449 (TC), TC00714 .... 2.179
Northampton Magistrates' Court, R v (ex p. C & E Commrs), QB [1994] BVC 111 .... 49.8
Northampton Theatres Trust Ltd [2006] VATDR 27 (VTD 19485) 48.47
Northamptonshire Football Association (VTD 12936) 13.7
Northern Clubs Federation Brewery Ltd (VTD 8881) 8.20
Northern Counties Co-operative Enterprises Ltd [1986] VATTR 250 (VTD 2238) .. 36.624
Northern 4 x 4 Centre Ltd (VTD 19811) 40.44
Northern Ireland Council for Voluntary Action [1991] VATTR 32 (VTD 5451) 11.32
Northern Lawn Tennis Club [1989] VATTR 1 (VTD 3528) 36.16
Northern Software Consultants Ltd (VTD 9027) 18.367

Northumbria & Cumbria Estates Ltd (VTD 10366) 52.347
Northwood Garage (Whitstable) Ltd (VTD 4352) 18.300
Norton (EF & Mrs K) (VTD 151) 57.13
Norwich & Peterborough Building Society v Steed, CA [1991] 1 WLR 449; [1991]
  2 All ER 880 .... 2.182, 2.184
Norwich Camera Centre Ltd (VTD 11629) 11.10
Norwich City Council (VTD 11822) 42.11
Norwich Union Life Insurance Society (VTD 7205) 36.632
Nose Cash and Carry Ltd (VTD 3763) 2.354
Nottingham Fire Service Messing Club [1977] VATTR 1 (VTD 348) 13.12
Nottinghamshire Wildlife Trust (VTD 19540) 11.56
Noudoost-Beni (B) (VTD 17625) 57.178
Nova Group (London) Ltd (VTD 10252) 18.295
Nova Roofing Co Ltd (VTD 10252, 10409) 18.295
Nova Stamps AB (VTD 15304) 23.30
Novakovic (M) (t/a Novakovic & Co) (VTD 18462) 10.14
Novelminster Ltd (VTD 10314) 18.138
N2J Ltd, Ch D [2009] STC 2193; [2009] EWHC 1596 (Ch) 23.14
Nuffield Nursing Homes Trust [1989] VATTR 62 (VTD 3327) 33.40
Nulmay Ltd (VTD 6627) 2.469
Nuniv Developments Ltd (VTD 17424) 59.3
Nutley Hall Ltd (VTD 18242) 15.117
Nuttall (D & J) (VTD 6343) 52.106
Nuttall (SH) (VTD 5892) 18.483
Nye Saunders & Partners (VTD 11384) 36.47

O

Oaks Pavilion Ltd, TC00145 .... 36.615
Oasis East sp zoo v Minister Finansów, ECJ Case C-395/09; 30 September 2010
  unreported 22.430
Oasis Technologies (UK) Ltd, [2010] UKFTT 292 (TC), TC00581 .... 24.23
Oathplan Ltd [1982] VATTR 195 (VTD 1299) 41.121
Oblique Press Ltd (VTD 10891) 48.28
O'Brien (B), Ch D 2007, [2008] STC 487; [2007] EWHC 3121 (Ch) 2.135
O'Brien (B) (t/a Poster Sites Southern) (No 2), [2009] UKFTT 262 (TC), TC00209
  .... 2.36
O'Brien v Chief Constable of South Wales Police, HL [2005] 2 WLR 1038 ...... 2.270
O'Callaghan (TM) (VTD 5981) 18.562
Ocean Grown Ltd (VTD 20562) 29.172
Ocean Leisure International Ltd (VTD 13169) 40.5
Oceana Holdings plc (VTD 9961) 52.140
Oceanteam Power & Umbilical ASA, [2009] UKFTT 361 (TC), TC00299 .... 25.33
O'Connor (JJ, BB & S) (VTD 1170) 47.50
Oddbins Ltd (VTD 9011) 52.29
Oddonetto (P) (VTD 5208) 44.45
Odell (A) & Ogden (M) (VTD 13512) 57.133
O'Dell (CP & EA) (t/a CP Motors) (VTD 13802) 44.30
Odhams Distribution Pergamon Holdings Ltd (VTD 6295) 5.102
Odhams Leisure Group Ltd, QB [1992] STC 332 .... 2.3, 5.81
ODM Ltd (VTD 17484) 46.84
O'Donnell (M), [2010] UKFTT 236 (TC), TC00535 .... 15.275
O'Driscoll (N) (VTD 16941) 40.74
O'Driscoll (TR) (t/a Kitchenfit) (VTD 14350) 57.130
Office des Produits Wallons ASBL v Belgium, ECJ Case C-184/00; [2003] STC 1100;
  [2003] All ER (EC) 747 .... 22.246
Offshore Hydrocarbon Mapping plc (VTD 19438) 2.529
Offshore Marine Engineering Ltd (VTD 6840) 52.246
Ogilvie (JD) (t/a O & D Consultants) (VTD 14536) 40.43
Oglethorpe Sturton & Gillibrand (VTD 17491) 62.164

Ojeh (D) (VTD 15369) 65.91
Old Chelsea Properties Ltd *v* Isle of Man Treasury (VTD 15230) 46.207
Old Chigwellians' Club (The) [1987] VATTR 66 (VTD 2332) 62.419
Old Farm Service Station Ltd (VTD 4261) 57.52
Old Parkinsonians Association (VTD 10908) 13.45
Old Red Lion Restaurant (The) (VTD 1446) 65.2
Oldbus Ltd (VTD 5119) 27.47
Oldershaw (G & D) (t/a Oldershaw Brewery) (VTD 19011) 28.1
Oldfield (P) (VTD 12233) 36.222
Oldfield (Mrs S) (t/a Merchant's Bistro) (VTD 17352) 57.19
Oldham (J) (VTD 1113) 62.292
Oldrings Development Kingsclere Ltd (VTD 17769) 15.36
Olivant (M) (VTD 15422) 36.46
Olive Tree Press Ltd (VTD 5349) 48.86
Oliver (A) & Sons (VTD 5953) 52.25
Oliver (DG) (Maidstone Sailing Club) (VTD 511) 57.93
Oliver (JG) (VTD 10579) 19.16
Oliver (JRR), QB 1979, [1980] STC 73; [1980] 1 All ER 353 .... 62.168
Olivers of Hull Ltd (VTD 17434) 48.66
Olivieri (Q & M) (VTD 16991) 41.89
Ollerton Hotel (Kirkcaldy) Ltd (VTD 10530) 18.447
Oloyede (WA) (VTD 11944) 40.78
Oluwatyi (J & E) (t/a Lizjohn & Associates) (VTD 18089) 36.660
Olympia Technology Ltd (No 1) (VTD 19145) 2.515
Olympia Technology Ltd (No 2) (VTD 19647) 48.92
Olympia Technology Ltd (No 3) (VTD 19984) 2.15
Olympia Technology Ltd (No 4), Ch D [2009] STC 643; [2009] EWHC 15 (Ch) 36.98
Olympia Technology Ltd (No 5), [2010] UKFTT 45 (TC), TC00358 .... 36.99
Olympia Testing (East Anglia) Ltd (VTD 9260) 18.220
Olympiad Signs Ltd (VTD 14566) 18.590
Olympian Automotive Ltd (VTD 7141) 52.92
OM Properties Investment Co Ltd, [2010] UKFTT 494 (TC), TC00752 .... 38.12
Omega Cars Ltd (VTD 1528) 36.442
Omega Design & Marketing Ltd (VTD 10004) 52.281
100 Per Cent (VTD 6238) 18.83
One For All Ltd, [2010] UKFTT 91 (TC), TC00402 .... 36.167
Onemli (M, B & A) & Karadal (R) (t/a West Kebab) (VTD 13983) 65.95
Ong (LC) (VTD 7460) 62.259
Opal Carleton Ltd, [2010] UKFTT 353 (TC), TC00635 .... 56.4
Open Rule Ltd (VTD 4130) 18.186
Open University (The), [1982] VATTR 29 (VTD 1196) 21.3
O-Pro Ltd (VTD 16780) 33.35
Optigen Ltd, ECJ Case C-354/03; [2006] STC 419; [2006] 2 WLR 456 .... 22.115
Optika Ltd (VTD 18627) 46.137
Optimum Personnel Evaluation (Operations) Ltd (VTD 2334) 57.12
Option NTC Ltd, [2011] UKFTT 768 (TC), TC01605 .... 36.113
Opto Telelinks (Europe) Ltd (No 1), Ch D [2008] STC 3246; [2008] EWHC 2107 (Ch) 2.369
Opto Telelinks (Europe) Ltd (No 2), CA [2010] STC 1436; [2010] EWCA Civ 517 .... 36.105
Oracle Nederland *v* Inspecteur van de Belastingdienst Utrecht-Gooi, ECJ Case C-33/09; [2010] STC 1221 .... 22.429
Orange Rooms (The) (VTD 19133) 40.14
Orbit Housing Association (VTD 1783) 2.454
Orbvent Ltd (VTD 6602) 52.334
Orchard Associates Ltd (VTD 11576) 52.378
Orchid Drinks Co Ltd (VTD 14222) 29.177
O'Reilly (D) (VTD 20945) 15.210
O'Reilly Transport (Newry) Ltd (VTD 2434) 62.366
Organix Brands plc (VTD 19134) 29.139
Oriel Support Ltd (VTD 20930) 1.79

Oriental Delicacy Ltd (VTD 19129) 36.595
Oriental Kitchen (VTD 13736) 50.118
Orin Engineering (UK) Ltd (VTD 15254) 44.118
Ormac (No 49) Ltd (VTD 6537) 36.200
Orme (CA) (VTD 9975) 55.72
Ormesby St Michael Parochial Council (VTD 17375) 5.46
Ormiston Charitable Trust, [1995] VATDR 180 (VTD 13187) 15.102
Ornamental Design plc (VTD 15364) 23.11
Osborn (GA) (VTD 13254) 51.153
Osborne's Big Man Shop, Ch D 2006, [2007] STC 586; [2006] EWHC 3172 (Ch)
.... 24.4
Oshitola (ST) (VTD 15487) 57.134
Osman (AB), QB [1989] STC 596 .... 57.39
Osteria Romana Ltd (VTD 20635) 18.430
Ottoman Textiles Ltd (VTD 12795) 17.3
Oughtred & Harrison Ltd, [1988] VATTR 140 (VTD 3174) 67.1
Our Communications Ltd (VTD 20903) 36.86
Out To Lunch (VTD 13031) 29.7
Outis Ltd (VTD 14864) 40.57
Oval (717) Ltd, [2003] VATDR 581 (VTD 17875) 30.10
Oval (1742) Ltd, re, C & E v Royal Bank of Scotland plc, CA [2007] EWCA Civ
   1262 .... 37.9
Overburn Properties Ltd (VTD 9966) 52.277
Owan Bebb A'I Gwmni (VTD 18047) 18.541
Owen (EC) (VTD 18660) 55.33
Owen (GL) (t/a New Product Research & Development) (VTD 5363) 18.558
Owen (KJ) (VTD 17970) 18.558
Owen (T) (VTD 741) 15.13
Owen (R) & Freeman (D) (t/a Worcester Flooring) (VTD 18539) 65.105
Owners Abroad Group plc (VTD 9354) 52.371
Oxfam, Ch D 2009, [2010] STC 586; [2009] EWHC 3078 (Ch) 11.51
Oxford Film Foundation (VTD 5031) 62.121
Oxford Open Learning (Systems) Ltd (VTD 16160) 21.28
Oxford Open Learning (Systems) Ltd (No 2) (VTD 16890) 5.66
Oxford, Swindon & Gloucester Co-Operative Society Ltd, QB [1995] STC 583 .... 58.9
Oysters Fish Bar (VTD 16203) 47.3

P

P & A Fencing & Sheds Ltd (VTD 6089) 18.588
P & C Morris Catering Group Ltd (VTD 19245) 44.50
P & H Pipework Ltd (VTD 4092) 18.238
P & M Marketing (UK) Ltd (VTD 1385) 67.43
P & O European Ferries (Dover) Ltd, [1992] VATTR 221 (VTD 7846) 36.230
P & O Ferries, QB [1992] STC 809 .... 52.453
P & R Fabrics Ltd (VTD 17776) 3.104
P & S Catering (VTD 6382) 29.70
P Burke Construction Ltd (VTD 7222) 52.136
P Jennings & Sons Ltd (VTD 6696) 18.290
Pace Group (Communications) Ltd (VTD 510) 5.75
Pacey Rogers & Co (VTD 2308) 51.123
Pacitti (G) (VTD 16759) 62.307
Pack & Moore Builders Co Ltd (VTD 9130) 52.344
Packford (S) (VTD 11626) 41.110
Packwell Cartons Ltd (VTD 14314) 18.307
Paddon (Mrs HD) (VTD 1987) 41.105
Padglade Ltd, QB [1995] STC 602 .... 65.50
Padmore (M) (VTD 345) 57.6
Page (DJ) (VTD 17142) 19.56
Page (J) (t/a Upledger Institute) (VTD 16650) 21.37

Page Motors (Ferndown) Ltd (VTD 7517) 52.342
Paget (PLA), QB [1989] STC 773 .... 1.64
Paice (PM & JB) (VTD 9649) 36.288
Paine Leisure Products Ltd (VTD 1836) 8.13
Painter (G) (VTD 17530) 33.77
Pal, Pal, Quillen Alonso & El Bouacheri (t/a Tapas Bar Cerveceria), Ch D 2006, [2008]
    STC 2442; [2006] EWHC 2016(Ch) 47.5
Palatine Hotel Ltd v The Isle of Man Treasury (VTD 6534) 52.344
Palco Industry Co Ltd, QB [1990] STC 594 .... 18.414
Palfry (J) & Rodzian (JD) (VTD 18465) 57.163
Palliser (P) (VTD 6262) 51.38
Palmer (RC) (t/a R & K Engineering) (VTD 11739) 4.4
Palmer (JH) & Sons (VTD 10230) 52.39
Palmers of Oakham Ltd, [2011] UKFTT 82 (TC), TC00959 .... 15.219
Palmun Ltd, [2011] UKFTT 738 (TC), TC01575 .... 18.537
Palotai (E & B) (VTD 656) 62.396
Pan Graphics Industrial Ltd (VTD 13126) 18.541
Panesar (KWS & BK) (t/a KSP Builders and Panesar Building & Plumbers' Merchants)
    (VTD 16143) 19.46
Pang (CY) & Kong (SY) (t/a The Peking House) (VTD 17361) 3.96
Pang (P) (t/a Lafite's) (VTD 7065) 50.113
Panini Publishing Ltd (VTD 3876) 5.79
Pank (JF & SD) (VTD 4930) 36.279
Pannon Gép Centrum v APEH Központi Hivatal Hatósági Főosztály Dél-dunántúli
    Kihelyezett Hatósági Osztály, ECJ Case C-368/09; [2010] STC 2400 .... 20.104
Pantekoek (EM) (VTD 17765) 19.19
Papachristoforou (C & K) (t/a Norton Fisheries) (VTD 17113) 2.418
Paradise Forum Ltd (VTD 8885) 52.125
Paragon Business Products Ltd (VTD 14263) 18.459
Parat Automotive Cabrio Textiltetőket Gyártó Kft v Adó-és Pénzügyi Ellenőrzési Hivatal
    Hatósági Főosztály Észak-magyarországi Kihelyezett Hatósági Osztály, ECJ Case
    C-74/08; 23 April 2009 unreported 22.410
Parcare International Ltd (VTD 9773) 18.195
Parekh (B & N), QB [1984] STC 284 .... 3.75
Parents and Children Together (VTD 17283) 33.67, 39.3
Parfitt (AJ) (t/a Parfitt & Craig Hall) (VTD 5623) 18.186
Parfitt (DA) (VTD 10184) 18.341
Parish (EJ) (VTD 474) 44.63
Park Avenue Methodist Church Trustees (VTD 17443) 36.598
Park Commercial Developments plc [1990] VATTR 99 (VTD 4892) 27.46
Park Hotel (The) (VTD 16959) 18.514
Park Industrial & Commercial Holdings Ltd (VTD 17882) 52.400
Parker (t/a The Roker Park Suite) (VTD 956) 29.38
Parker (B & C) (VTD 2454) 57.125
Parker (BR & JG) (t/a Sea Breeze Café) (VTD 16350) 57.207
Parker (C) (VTD 292) 44.63
Parker (IW) [1989] VATTR 258 (VTD 4473) 50.131
Parker (J) (VTD 18853) 48.63
Parker (PAF) (VTD 3810) 51.86
Parker (H) & Hornsby (M) (t/a Water Two) (VTD 16225) 36.603
Parker Bond Ltd (VTD 13160) 36.538
Parker Car Services, [2010] UKFTT 227 (TC), TC00528 .... 67.125
Parker Hale Ltd, QB [2000] STC 388 .... 62.145
Parker Radio Cars (Sutton Coldfield) Ltd (VTD 2504) 41.37
Parker-Smith (VTD 18497) 3.92
Parkers Motorist Discount (VTD 9545) 18.125
Parkgate Quarries Ltd (VTD 3712) 18.551
Parkhouse (Mrs LA), [2011] UKFTT 677 (TC), TC01519 .... 46.35
Parkinson (Dr J) (VTD 17257) 15.30
Parkinson (Mrs MG) (VTD 6017) 33.3
Paro Ltd (VTD 9414) 17.2

Parochial Church Council of St Andrew's Church Bedford (VTD 19061) 15.206
Parochial Church Council of St Andrew's Church Eakring (VTD 15320) 55.29
Parr (TE, M & IJ), [1985] VATTR 250 (VTD 1967) 58.6
Parr Partnership (The) (VTD 6733) 52.105
Pars Technology Ltd, [2011] UKFTT 9 (TC), TC00886 .... 36.121
Parson (R & GA) (VTD 17137) 62.295
Parsons (CP) (VTD 20033) 51.171
Parsons Green Ltd, [1990] VATTR 194 (VTD 5044) 19.1
Part Service Srl, Ministero dell'Economia e delle Finanze v, ECJ Case C-425/06; [2008]
    STC 3132 .... 22.62
Partridge Homes Ltd (VTD 15289) 52.188
Party Paragon The Shop Ltd (VTD 7242) 18.409
Pasante Healthcare Ltd (VTD 19724) 11.30
Patel (A) (t/a Swami Stores) (VTD 4912) 51.10
Patel (ACK) (VTD 17248) 2.150
Patel (AR) (VTD 1252) 3.149
Patel (BG) (VTD 19634) 48.63
Patel (H & V) (VTD 14956) 7.104
Patel (H & V) (VTD 15328) 36.501
Patel (JM) (t/a Magsons) (VTD 936) 58.16
Patel (K, J & M) (t/a Dhruva Newsagents) (VTD 14843) 58.23
Patel (NG & MG) (VTD 2463) 58.57
Patel (NM & HN) (VTD 11635) 50.136
Patel (R) (t/a AF Fashions) (VTD 19246) 40.36
Patel (RB & MR) (t/a Rama Stores) (VTD 1392) 58.17
Patel (YY & MV) (t/a Rumi Clothing) (VTD 15268) 2.502
Paterson (C & S) (VTD 17323) 44.133
Paterson (KW) (VTD 7423) 51.75
Paterson Arran Ltd (VTD 15041) 29.86
Patrick (E), [1994] VATTR 247 (VTD 12354) 67.73
Patrick Eddery Ltd, [1986] VATTR 30 (VTD 2009) 62.521
Patterson (RM) (VTD 13669) 23.25
Paul (JS) (C210) 60.13
Paul da Costa & Co, oao, R v Thames Magistrates Court, DC [2002] STC 267; [2002]
    EWHC Admin 40 .... 14.95
Paul Hoskins Ltd, [2011] UKFTT 538 (TC), TC01385 .... 18.104
Pauline (JD) (VTD 11029) 52.76
Pavigres-Wich Ltd (VTD 13414) 18.558
Paymex Ltd, [2011] UKFTT 350 (TC); [2011] SFTD 1028, TC01210 .... 20.81
Payne (RB) (VTD 9211) 7.74, 36.576
Payton (M), [1974] VATTR 140 (VTD 89) 2.58, 33.39
PBK Catering Ltd (VTD 11426) 1.5
PCC Agriculture (VTD 9034) 52.28
PCCI Ltd, [2010] UKFTT 65 (TC), TC00377 .... 36.121
PD Concepts Ltd, [2009] SFTD 353; [2009] UKFTT 127 (TC), TC00095 .... 36.110
PDS (Gold Plating) Co Ltd (VTD 5468) 18.441
Peach (FM) (VTD 6499) 51.89
Peachman Building Services (Croydon) Ltd (VTD 5041) 18.82
Peachtree Enterprises Ltd, QB [1994] STC 747 .... 14.59
Pearce (J) (VTD 7860) 36.190, 36.549
Pearl Assurance plc (VTD 15960) 46.103
Pearl Top Services Ltd (VTD 2888) 14.47
Pearlberg, CIR v, [1953] 1 All ER 388 .... 2.196
Pearson & Sons (E) (Teesside) Ltd (VTD 11187) 38.43
Pearson (RH) & Sons (VTD 7287) 36.432
Peart (JL & PA) (t/a The Border Reiver) (VTD 14672) 48.126
Pecheries (SA) Ostendaises v Merchants Marine Insurance Co CA, [1928] 1 KB 757
    .... 2.426
Peddars Way Housing Association Ltd (VTD 12663) 15.20
Pedersen Caterers (VTD 10818) 18.421
Peek Catering Ltd (VTD 10628) 29.23

Pegasus Birds Ltd, CA [2000] STC 91 .... 3.57
Pegasus Birds Ltd (No 2), CA [2004] STC 1509; [2004] EWCA Civ 1015 .... 3.20
Pegasus Flooring Co Ltd (VTD 17708) 18.518
Pegasus Holdings (Malvern) Ltd (VTD 12539) 14.47
Peking Inn (Cookham) Ltd (VTD 14079) 18.244
Pelzl & Others v Steiermärkische Landesregierung & Others, ECJ Cases C-338/97,
    C-344/97 & C-390/97; 8 June 1999 unreported 22.528
Pemberton (KL) (t/a The Sandwich Box Plus) (VTD 19307) 57.68
Pemberton (KL & EM) (t/a Desmond's) (VTD 19307) 57.68
Pembridge Estates Ltd (VTD 9606) 46.4
Pemsel, Special Commissioners v, HL 1891, 3 TC 53 .... 15.82
Pendleton (J & C) Ltd (VTD 6092) 18.469
Pendragon plc, [2009] UKFTT 192 (TC); [2010] SFTD 1, TC00147 .... 22.72
Penfold (TL) (VTD 524) 44.63
Peninsular & Oriental Steam Navigation Co plc (t/a P & O Ferries), QB [1992] STC
    809 .... 52.453
Peninsular & Oriental Steam Navigation Co (The) (No 2), QB [1996] STC 698 ..... 66.20
Peninsular & Oriental Steam Navigation Co (The) (No 3), QB [2000] STC 488 .... 62.479
Penjen Ltd (VTD 5882) 36.575
Pennine Carpets Ltd (VTD 5894) 36.649, 65.48
Pennine Industrial Equipment Ltd (VTD 6512) 52.147
Pennington Lee Ltd (VTD 6625) 18.15, 18.551
Penny (DJW) (VTD 20813) 18.619
Penny (F) (t/a FMS Management Services) (VTD 10398) 62.141
Pennystar Ltd, QB 1995, [1996] STC 163 .... 36.627
Pensionsversicherungsanstalt der Arbeiter, Unterpertinger v, ECJ Case C-212/01; [2005]
    STC 678 .... 22.281
Pentex Oil Ltd (VTD 7989, VTD 7991) 43.2
People Products Ltd (VTD 7379) 52.53
Peoples Bathgate & Livingston Ltd (VTD 14264) 2.526
Peoples Liverpool Ltd (VTD 14264) 2.526
Pepis (Marina) Ltd (VTD 5879) 52.120
Pepper v Hart, HL [1992] STC 898 .... 6.7
Pepper Personnel Ltd (VTD 2175) 51.124
Pereira (A) (VTD 5835) 18.280
Perez (JA & GL) (VTD 6758) 36.280
Performance Print Ltd (VTD 15810) 18.369
Perks (M) (VTD 1556) 40.21
Permacross Ltd (VTD 13521) 15.151
Permanent Way Institution (VTD 17746) 64.5
Perna (V), [1990] VATTR 106 (VTD 5017) 46.79
Perranporth Rugby Football Club (VTD 17422) 36.597
Perry (RC), QB [1983] STC 383 .... 15.28
Perry (T) (VTD 19428) 15.249
Perryman Motor Factors (Greenford) Ltd (VTD 2793) 18.144
Perryman Motor Factors (Greenford) Ltd (VTD 7173) 18.157
Personal Assistance UK Ltd (VTD 17649) 33.15
Perth Junior Chamber Conferences (1994) Ltd (VTD 13450) 36.610
Pet Street Ltd, [2010] UKFTT 149 (TC), TC00455 .... 36.607
Peter Anthony Estates Ltd (VTD 13250) 41.55
Peter Boizot (Franchises) Ltd (VTD 10773) 18.267
Peter Cripwell & Associates (VTD 660) 40.86
Peter Jackson (Jewellers) Ltd (VTD 19474) 44.137
Peter Jones & Son (VTD 2990) 51.118
Peter Oates Ltd (VTD 2576) 44.79
Peter Scott (Printers) Ltd (VTD 6356) 52.36
Peter Turner Associates (VTD 6896) 52.33
Peterborough Diocesan Conference & Retreat House (VTD 14081) 33.68
Peters (B & J), ex p., R v City of London Magistrates Court, QB 1996, [1997] STC
    141 .... 14.99
Peters (KV) (VTD 14328) 38.9

Peters (P) & Riddles (KP) (t/a Mill Lane Farm Shop) (VTD 12937) 29.192
Peters (SR) (VTD 19876) 62.204
Pethericks & Gillard Ltd (VTD 20564) 41.47
Pet-Reks Southern Ltd (No 1) (VTD 9070) 52.69
Pet-Reks Southern Ltd (No 2) (VTD 9347) 52.281
Petroline Wireline Services Ltd (VTD 9200) 36.412
Petros Leasing Ltd (VTD 4056) 7.40
Pets Place (UK) Ltd [1996] VATDR 418 (VTD 14642) 65.114
Peugeot-Citroen Automobiles Ltd [2004] VATDR 157 (VTD 18681) 62.187
Peugeot Motor Co plc [1998] VATDR 1 (VTD 15314) 44.68
Peugeot Motor Co plc (No 2), Ch D [2003] STC 1438; [2003] EWHC 2304(Ch) 38.51
Peugeot Motor Co plc (No 3) (VTD 16731) 62.16
Peugeot Motor Co plc (No 4) (VTD 18059) 48.78
Peugeot Motor Co plc (No 5) (VTD 19260) 67.48
Peverley (M) (t/a Lifeline Medical Transport Services) (VTD 15353) 33.76
Pexum Ltd (VTD 20083) 40.51
Pezzullo Molini Pastifici Mangimifici SpA v Ministero delle Finanze, ECJ Case C-166/94;
  [1996] STC 1236; [1996] 1 ECR 331 .... 22.231
Pharmaquim Ltd, [2010] UKFTT 279 (TC), TC00568 .... 36.113
Pharoah Scaffolding (VTD 20741) 15.186
Pharro (K) (t/a KP Building Services) (VTD 17041) 40.74
Phelps (KR & EM) (VTD 4486) 18.206
PHH Europe plc (VTD 12027) 62.28
Philbin, Abbott v, HL 1960, 39 TC 82; [1961] AC 352; [1960] 2 All ER 763 .... 3.23
Philbor Motors Ltd (VTD 5388) 18.10
Philip Drakard Trading Ltd, QB [1992] STC 568 .... 62.107
Philip Green Education Ltd (VTD 15669) 5.86
Philip Law Ltd (VTD 3466) 18.552
Philip Maddison Haulage Ltd (VTD 6428) 18.356
Philips Exports Ltd, QB [1990] STC 508 .... 25.27
Philipson Studios Ltd (VTD 10488) 18.359
Philips (D) (VTD 7883) 36.488, 52.327
Phillips (E & E) (VTD 1130) 65.1
Phillips (G) (VTD 12184) 44.142
Phillips (I) (VTD 19519) 28.11
Phillips (I), [2011] UKFTT 372 (TC), TC01227 .... 15.40
Phillips (SL), [2010] UKFTT 262 (TC), TC00556 .... 62.349
Phillips (TK) (t/a Bristol Motorcycle Training Centre) [1992] VATTR 77 (VTD 7444)
  .... 21.30
Phillips (RFS) & Another (VTD 2829) 51.71
Phipps (L) (VTD 19352) 44.71
Phipps (MF) [1996] VATDR 241 (VTD 13839) 36.519
Phoenix Safe Co Ltd, [2011] UKFTT 27 (TC), TC00904 .... 18.210
Phonepoint Communications Ltd, [2010] UKFTT 452 (TC), TC00717 .... 36.120
Photographics (VTD 3407) 18.284
Physical Distribution Services Ltd (VTD 12069) 52.11
Picken & Son Ltd (VTD 10952) 18.222
Pier Aquatics (VTD 7063) 29.107
Piero's Restaurant and Pizzeria (VTD 17711) 3.45
Pierre Leon Ltd (VTD 9794) 52.125
Pigott, RCPO v, CA [2010] STC 1190; [2010] EWCA Civ 285 .... 49.24
Pilgrims Languages Courses Ltd, CA [1999] STC 874 .... 21.20
Pillars Property Cleaning & Maintenance Ltd, [2009] UKFTT 235 (TC), TC00184
  .... 18.186
Pilling House Properties Ltd (VTD 12965) 52.455
Pinchdean Ltd (VTD 9796) 6.20
Pinder (SG) (VTD 3582) 51.68
Pine-Coffin (Lt Col TJ & Mrs ST) (VTD 1620) 30.5
Pinetree Housing Association (VTD 1487) 57.101
Ping (Europe) Ltd, CA [2002] STC 1186; [2002] EWCA Civ 1115 .... 67.78
Pinnacle Tooling Ltd (VTD 18271) 36.587

Pinnock (KS) & Lambden (KJ) (t/a TNT Printed Leisurewear) (VTD 11263) 18.162
Pip Systems (VTD 3413) 18.202
Pipeline Protection Ltd (VTD 10336) 18.235
Pippa-Dee Parties Ltd, QB [1981] STC 495 .... 67.37
Pittam (C) (VTD 13268) 33.26
Pizza Express Ltd (VTD 3340) 18.201
PJG Developments Ltd, [2005] VATDR 215 (VTD 19097) 6.3
PL Schofield Ltd (VTD 7736) 46.116
Placeware Ltd (VTD 17363) 2.440
Plant Repair & Services (South Wales) Ltd, QB [1994] STC 232 .... 8.30
Plantasia Ltd (VTD 3291) 18.109
Plantation Wharf Management Ltd (VTD 12755) 52.257
Plantiflor Ltd, HL [2002] STC 1132; [2002] UKHL 33; [2002] 1 WLR 2287 ...... 24.2
Planzer Luxembourg Sàrl v Bundeszentralamt für Steuern, ECJ Case C-73/06; [2008]
    STC 1113 .... 22.539
Plasma Trading Ltd (No 1) (VTD 18908) 2.134
Plasma Trading Ltd (No 2) (VTD 19499) 36.123
Plastic Developments Ltd (VTD 17416) 48.3
Plastic Protection Ltd (VTD 9259) 52.156, 52.240
Plat Ror Och vets Service i Norden AB & Others v Sweden, ECHR Case 12637/05;
    [2009] ECHR 1015 .... 34.13
Platinum Acquisitions Ltd (VTD 20514) 36.496
Platinum Clothing Ltd (VTD 19144) 40.41
Playden Oasts Hotel (VTD 6468) 44.147
Playford & Pope (VTD 13989) 18.25
Plazadome Ltd, [2009] UKFTT 229 (TC), TC00179 .... 40.53
Pleasurama Casinos Ltd (VTD 357) 62.22
Plessey Co Ltd (The) (VTD 12814) 54.10
PLR Ltd (VTD 9501) 36.429
Plumb (MD) (VTD 13621) 55.79
Plummer (DJ, J & S) (VTD 16976) 3.140, 57.205
Plymouth Marine Laboratory, [2009] UKFTT 179 (TC), TC00134 .... 66.10
PNC Telecom plc (VTD 19754) 2.18
PNW Computer Services Ltd (VTD 17731) 18.541
Podbury (MD) (t/a Moordown Graphics) (VTD 1906) 57.7
Podium Investments Ltd [1977] VATTR 121 (VTD 314) 36.662
Podolsky (J), [2009] UKFTT 387 (TC), TC00322 .... 15.146
Pody (DA) (VTD 217) 44.60
Pokrivka v Slovakia, ECHR Case C-35933/06; 26 October 2010 unreported 34.29
Poladon Ltd (VTD 16825) 36.73
Poland (BC) (t/a Cameron Electrical Contractors) (VTD 10536) 18.123
Poland (Kingdom of), EC Commission v, ECJ Case C-49/09; 28 October 2010
    unreported 20.55
Polarstar Ltd (VTD 14445) 18.593
Polash Tandoori Restaurant (VTD 10903) 8.21
Pole (AG) (VTD 13225) 47.47
Pollitt (Mr & Mrs A) (VTD 4463) 58.23
Pollock (C) (VTD 6638) 36.272
Pollock (D) & Heath (D) (VTD 20380) 15.208
Pollok Golf Club (VTD 1044) 13.33
Polo Farm Sports Club (No 1) (VTD 11386) 46.188
Polo Farm Sports Club (No 2) [2007] VATDR 44 (VTD 20105) 41.160
Poloco SA (VTD 6565) 52.26
Polok (R & J), Ch D [2002] STC 361 .... 62.279
Polysar Investments Netherlands BV v Inspecteur der Invoerrechten en Accijnzen, ECJ
    Case C-60/90; [1991] 1 ECR 3111; [1993] STC 222 .... 22.106
Ponsonby & Ponsonby, QB 1987, [1988] STC 28 .... 65.108
Ponting (F & A) Ltd (VTD 12595) 18.83
Pook (C) (VTD 2314) 51.43
Poole (GH) (t/a Glenwood Polishing & Manufacturing 1992) (VTD 16339) 18.402
Poole Borough Council [1992] VATTR 88 (VTD 7180) 41.126

Poole General Hospital League of Friends (VTD 10621) 33.48
Poole Shopmobility (VTD 16290) 11.18, 19.73
Popat (DK) (VTD 10452) 52.302
Popcorn House Ltd, QB 1965, [1968] 3 All ER 782 .... 29.145
Popely, ex p., R v C & E, QB [1999] STC 1016 .... 14.94
Popes Lane Pet Food Supplies Ltd [1986] VATTR 221 (VTD 2186) 29.189
Port (GF) (VTD 3772) 14.47
Port Erin Hotels v Isle of Man Treasury (VTD 5045) 62.130
Portal Contracting Ltd (VTD 10234) 52.247
Porters End Estates Ltd (VTD 15872) 52.399
Portland College (VTD 9815) 19.52, 19.77
Portman Escort Agency (VTD 19728) 62.280
Portnacraig Inn & Restaurant (VTD 11528) 36.594
Portsmouth City Football Club Ltd, Ch D [2010] EWHC 75 (Ch); [2011] STC 683
    .... 48.37
Portswood Haulage Contractors (VTD 6556) 18.425
Portuguese Republic, EC Commission v, ECJ Case C-276/98; [2001] BTC 5135 .... 22.264
Portuguese Republic, EC Commission v, ECJ Case C-462/05; 12 June 2008
    unreported 22.263
Post Form Products (VTD 9767) 52.241
Post Office (The), QB [1995] STC 749 .... 3.55
Post Office (The) (VTD 14075) 62.112
Post Office, Hitchcock v, EAT [1980] ICR 100 .... 7.104
Post Office, Tanna v, EAT [1981] ICR 374 .... 7.104
Postlethwaite (T) (t/a TP Transport) (VTD 14925) 40.18
Postproof Ltd (VTD 18547) 50.65
Posturite (UK) Ltd (VTD 7848) 19.51
Potter (P & R), CA 1984, [1985] STC 45 .... 1.91
Potter (R & Mrs PA) [1985] VATTR 255 (VTD 1982) 2.524
Potterburn Ltd (VTD 15912) 18.99
Potters Lodge Restaurant Ltd (VTD 905) 67.128
Pottie (AD) (VTD 5460) 67.109
Potton (JG & MU) (VTD 2882) 36.44
Potts (G) (t/a Landmark) (VTD 18467) 50.81
Potts (KM) (VTD 17390) 62.296
Pouladdej (A), [2010] UKFTT 592 (TC), TC00842 .... 52.305
Poulett, Berkley v, [1976] 241 EG 911 .... 15.247
Poullais (A & A) (t/a Nightingale Café) (VTD 14140) 65.91
Poulton Park Golf Club Ltd (VTD 4653) 18.595
Poultries Al Hilal Ltd (VTD 20381) 15.270
Powa (Jersey) Ltd, [2009] UKFTT 360 (TC), TC00298 .... 36.121
Powell (DL) (VTD 7933) 18.402
Powell (GP) (VTD 17380) 2.92, 35.23
Powell (J) (VTD 5261) 51.89
Powell (R & A) (VTD 601) 58.23
Powell (RG) (t/a Anwick Agricultural Engineers) (VTD 14520) 55.47
Power (JW) [2000] VATDR 175 (VTD 16748) 2.238
Power (PM) & Clark (DG) (VTD 6120) 18.559
Power Leasing Ltd [1984] VATTR 104 (VTD 1661) 36.322
Power Rod (UK) Ltd [1983] VATTR 334 (VTD 1550) 14.49
Power TV Ltd (VTD 20565) 36.672
Poyser & Holmes (VTD 7059) 52.136
PPG Publishing Ltd (VTD 3047) 44.79
PR Mitchell Ltd (VTD 9394) 52.281
PR Promotions (VTD 2122) 8.16
Practitioner (A) (VTD 18459) 2.251
Pratt (TJ) (VTD 17718) 51.144
Pre-School Learning Alliance (The) (VTD 17737) 11.42
Prebble (C & H) (t/a Monks Kitchen) (VTD 16631, VTD 19331) 50.130
Precious Metal Industries (Wales) Ltd (VTD 7750) 52.282
Premiair Charter Ltd (VTD 15129) 52.404

Premier Aluminium & Glass Ltd (VTD 6831) 52.217
Premier Despatch Ltd (VTD 20231) 18.463
Premier Foods (Holdings) Ltd, Ch D 2007, [2008] STC 176 .... 29.160
Premier Joint Ventures Ltd, [2010] UKFTT 135 (TC), TC00444 .... 40.54
Premier Leisure (Events) Ltd (VTD 19320) 18.443
Premier Motor Yacht Charters Ltd (VTD 15506) 7.44
Premier Roofing Systems Ltd (VTD 6388) 18.321
Prenn (DD) (VTD 793) 7.57
Prescott (J) (VTD 529) 7.18
Presentway Ltd (VTD 17383) 51.129
Pressland (D) [1995] VATDR 432 (VTD 13059) 60.10
Prestige Freight (VTD 17614) 4.24
Preston (R), Ch D 15 December 1999 unreported 2.186
Preston (R) (VTD 5702) 62.320
Preston (R) (VTD 17826) 2.186
Preston, ex p., R v CIR, HL [1985] STC 282 .... 2.344
Prestonfield Golf Club Ltd (VTD 14841) 18.216
Pret A Manger (Europe) Ltd (No 1) (VTD 16246) 29.77
Pret A Manger (Europe) Ltd (No 2) (VTD 19755) 29.32
Price (AJ & K) (VTD 20700) 15.280
Price (AK) (VTD 5927) 18.59
Price (AJ & K) (VTD 20700) 15.280
Price (J) [2010] UKFTT 634 (TC), TC00873 .... 15.250
Price (WJ) [1978] VATTR 115 (VTD 559) 2.182
Price (M & D) Bros Ltd (VTD 713) 62.561
Price Legand Offset International Ltd (VTD 7066) 18.71
Pride & Leisure Ltd (VTD 6911) 40.28
Primback Ltd, ECJ Case C-34/99, [2001] STC 803; [2001] 1 WLR 1693; [2001] All ER
  (EC) 735 .... 22.242
Primboon Ltd (VTD 7757) 18.313
Prime Agency Recruitment Ltd (VTD 18043) 18.332
Princess Louise Scottish Hospital (The) [1983] VATTR 191 (VTD 1412) 19.39
Princess Royal Sports Club (VTD 16227) 15.103
Print On Time (Pontefract) Ltd (VTD 11458) 52.201
Prior (MJ & Mrs KE) (VTD 7978) 51.40
Prior Diesel Ltd (VTD 10306) 52.220
Pritchard (P & B) (VTD 18019) 41.162
Private & Confidential Ltd, [2009] UKFTT 59 (TC), TC00038 .... 47.57
Probelook Ltd [1989] VATTR 303 (VTD 4538) 62.286
Probyn (T) (VTD 10679) 17.2
Processed Vegetable Growers Association Ltd [1973] VATTR 87 (VTD 25) 2.52, 62.42
Procter & Gamble UK (No 1) (VTD 18381) 29.185
Procomm Consultancy Ltd, [2010] UKFTT 561 (TC), TC00812 .... 36.113
Procter & Gamble UK (No 2), CA [2009] STC 1990; [2009] EWCA Civ 407 .... 29.185
Proctor, Jonathan Alexander v, CA 1995, [1996] 1 WLR 518; [1996] 2 All ER 334
  .... 2.388
Profaktor Kulesza Frankowski Józwiak Orlowski sp j, Dyrektor Izby Skarbowej w
  Bialymstoku v, ECJ Case 188/09; 29 July 2010 unreported 22.477
Profant, Ministère Public & Ministry of Finance v, ECJ Case 249/84; [1985] ECR 3237;
  [1986] 2 CMLR 378 .... 22.384
Professional Footballers Association (Enterprises) Ltd, HL [1993] STC 86 .... 67.12
Professional Testing Services Ltd (VTD 6689) 18.399
Profile Security Services Ltd, QB [1996] STC 808 .... 18.589
Progenitive Chemicals Ltd (VTD 6591) 52.69
Project Research & Evaluation Ltd (VTD 13183) 18.342
Promanex Group Ltd (VTD 19500) 18.536
Prontobikes Ltd (VTD 13213) 1.26
Proops (J) (t/a JP Antiques) (VTD 16409) 53.5
Proos (AM) & Sons Ltd (VTD 7717, 7734) 52.257
Propaganda Pictures Ltd (VTD 20613) 52.442
Property Enterprise Managers Ltd (VTD 7711) 36.493

Property & Investment Centre Ltd (VTD 11686) 52.293
Prospects Care Services Ltd, [1997] VATDR 209 (VTD 14810) 33.59
Prosser (SJ) (VTD 15461) 44.144
Proto Glazing Ltd (VTD 13410) 4.20
Prottey (GM) (t/a The Lord Nelson) & Brampton (MW) (VTD 16730) 47.60
Provident Direct Sales (Holdings) Ltd (VTD 3952) 18.263
Provident Financial plc (VTD 10215) 67.46
Prudential Assurance Co Ltd (VTD 17030) 27.59
Prudential Assurance Co Ltd (No 2) (VTD 19364) 27.21
Prudential Assurance Co Ltd (No 3), [2006] VATDR 301 (VTD 19607) 32.13
Prudential Assurance Co Ltd (No 4) (VTD 19675) 2.260
Prudential Assurance Co Ltd (No 5), [2008] VATDR 439 (VTD 20957) 3.118
Pryce (RWJB & GH) (VTD 6398) 52.74
PSI Engineering Ltd, [2011] UKFTT 765 (TC), TC01602 .... 2.417
PSL Freight Ltd, Ch D [2001] BTC 5437 .... 35.18
PT Garrett & Sons (Contractors) Ltd (VTD 7073) 52.105
PTE plc (t/a Physique) (VTD 20722) 18.295
Pubblico Ministero v Ratti, ECJ Case 148/78; [1979] ECR 1629; [1980] 1 CMLR 96
.... 22.19
Public & Commercial Services Union, Ch D 2003. [2004] STC 376; [2003] EWHC
2845(Ch) 3.166
Public Relations Co Ltd (VTD 20676) 18.547
Puffer v Unabhängiger Finanzsenat Außenstelle Linz, ECJ Case 460/07; [2009] STC
1693 .... 22.427
Pugh (A) (VTD 17202) 62.291
Pugh (C) (VTD 17093) 18.249
Pugh (JH & H) (VTD 16034) 36.502
Punchwell Ltd, [1981] VATTR 93 (VTD 1085) 59.2
Purcell (J) (t/a John Purcell Paper) (VTD 10925) 18.268
Purdue (Dr BN) (VTD 13430) 2.90
Purdue (JR & S), [1994] VATTR 387 (VTD 11779) 36.494
Pure Atma Ltd (VTD 18716) 29.60
Pure Independence (UK) Ltd, [2011] UKFTT 611 (TC), TC01454 .... 19.28
Purewal (AS) and Others (VTD 2055) 36.293
Purite Ltd (VTD 16161) 18.389
Purple International Ltd (VTD 18243) 48.101
Purple Parking Ltd, [2009] SFTD 445; [2009] UKFTT 152 (TC), TC00118 .... 66.39
Purshotam M Pattni & Sons, QB 1986, [1987] STC 1 .... 62.387
Pursol Ltd (VTD 5721) 52.26

Q

Q-Com Maintenance Ltd (VTD 12918) 18.380
Q Inns Ltd (VTD 8929) 29.46
Q & B Motor Accessories Ltd (VTD 6037) 18.447
Qaisar (MS) (VTD 18098) 2.283
Qaisar (MS), Ch D 2004, [2005] STC 119; [2004] EWHC 506 (Ch) 50.55
Qcom Maintenance Ltd (VTD 13933) 14.37
QED Marine [2001] VATDR 534 (VTD 17336) 66.9
QSR Ltd (t/a First Taste) (VTD 19528) 29.26
Quad (Civil Engineering) Ltd (VTD 6093) 18.355
Quadrant Stationers Ltd (VTD 1599) 2.353, 65.9
Quaife (R) (VTD 1394) 41.73
Quaker Trading Ltd (VTD 20604) 29.182
Quality Care Homes Ltd (VTD 7391) 36.480
Quality Embryo Transfer Co Ltd (VTD 7538) 18.425
Quality Import Export Ltd, [2010] UKFTT 47 (TC), TC00360 .... 36.113
Quantum Learning Curve (VTD 19181) 5.8
Quarriers (No 1), [2008] VATDR 290 (VTD 20660) 15.97
Quarriers (No 2), [2008] VATDR 192 (VTD 20670) 7.85

Quarterman (AD) (VTD 6200) 52.104
Quay Marine Ltd (VTD 9054) 52.164
Quaysiders Club Ltd (VTD 17204) 24.51
Qubit (UK) Ltd (VTD 9073) 18.443
Queen Mary University of London (No 1) (VTD 20960) 2.487
Queen Mary University of London (No 2), [2011] UKFTT 229 (TC), TC01094 .... 62.554
Queens Park Football Club Ltd [1988] VATTR 76 (VTD 2776) 41.156
Queensborough Motors (VTD 1139) 44.67
Queenspice Ltd, UT [2011] UKUT 111 (TCC); [2011] STC 1457 .... 3.106
Queghan Construction Co Ltd (VTD 1538) 36.351
Quest Trading Co Ltd (in liquidation) [2006] VATDR 202 (VTD 19909) 2.298
Quex Park Estates Ltd, [2010] UKFTT 126 (TC), TC00437 .... 36.334
Quicks plc [1998] VATDR 491 (VTD 15836) 2.63
Quigley, R v, CA Criminal Division, [2002] BTC 5518; [2002] EWCA Crim 2148
.... 49.14
Quintain Estates Development plc [2005] VATDR 123 (VTD 18877) 48.11
Quintiles (Scotland) Ltd (VTD 18790) 8.39
Quinton (I & L) (VTD 19117) 50.54
Quistclose Investments Ltd, Barclays Bank Ltd v , HL [1970] AC 567 .... 37.8

R

R v Asif, CA Criminal Division 1985, 82 Cr AR 123, [1985] CLR 679 .... 49.3
R v C & E (ex p. BLP Group plc), CA 1993, [1994] STC 41 .... 2.333
R v C & E (ex p. Building Societies Ombudsman Co Ltd), CA [2000] STC 892 ...... 48.51
R v C & E (ex p. Cohen), QB 3 December 1998 unreported 2.331
R v C & E (ex p. Dangol t/a The Great Kathmandu Tandoori), QB 1999, [2000] STC
107 .... 2.329
R v C & E (ex p. Eurotunnel plc & Others), QB 17 February 1995 unreported 2.337
R v C & E (ex p. Greater Manchester Police Authority), CA [2001] STC 406; [2001]
EWCA Civ 213 .... 42.9
R v C & E (ex p. Harris), QB [1999] STC 1016 .... 14.94
R v C & E (ex p. Kay & Co Ltd and Others), QB [1996] STC 1500 .... 48.50
R v C & E (ex p. Lacara Ltd), QB [1998] STI 576 .... 36.650
R v C & E (ex p. Littlewoods Home Shopping Group Ltd), CA [1998] STC 445 .... 58.39
R v C & E (ex p. Lunn Poly Ltd & Another), CA [1999] STC 350 .... 22.8
R v C & E (ex p. McNicholas Construction Co Ltd & Others), QB [1997] STC 1197
.... 14.93
R v C & E (ex p. Nissan UK Ltd), CA 1987, [1988] BTC 8003 .... 44.40
R v C & E (ex p. Popely), QB [1999] STC 1016 .... 14.94
R v C & E (ex p. Richmond & another), QB 1988, [1989] STC 429 .... 36.676
R v C & E (ex p. Sims), QB 1987, [1988] STC 210 .... 29.25
R v C & E (ex p. Strangewood), QB [1987] STC 502 .... 36.648
R v C & E (ex p. X Ltd), QB [1997] STC 1197 .... 14.93
R v Chief Constable of Warwickshire Constabulary (ex p. Fitzpatrick & Others), QB
[1998] 1 All ER 65 .... 14.94
R v Choudhury, CA Criminal Division [1996] STC 1163 .... 49.4
R v CIR (ex p. Preston), HL [1985] STC 282 .... 2.344
R v Citrone (C & J), CA 1998, [1999] STC 29 .... 49.12
R v City of London Magistrates (ex p. Asif & Others), QB [1996] STC 611 .... 14.98
R v City of London Magistrates' Court (ex p. Peters), QB 1996, [1997] STC 141 .... 14.99
R v Collier, CA Criminal Division 1997 STI 474 .... 49.11
R v Dealy, CA Criminal Division 1994, [1995] STC 217 .... 49.10
R v Eleftheriou & Another, CCA [1993] BTC 257 .... 49.7
R v Epsom Justices (ex p. Bell and Another), QB 1988, [1989] STC 169 .... 14.97
R v Fairclough, CA Criminal Division 1982 (unreported) 49.2
R v Fisher & Others, CA Criminal Division, [1989] STI 269 .... 49.28
R v Flax Bourton Magistrates' Court (ex p. C & E Commrs), QB 1996 unreported
.... 49.9

R v Generalbundesanwalt beim Bundesgerichtshof, ECJ Case C-285/09; [2011] STC 1387 .... 22.520
R v Ghosh, CA [1982] 3 WLR 110; [1982] 2 All ER 689 .... 50.29
R v Goodwin & Unstead, ECJ Case C-3/97; [1998] STC 699; [1998] 3 WLR 565; [1998] All ER (EC) 500 .... 22.82
R v Hashash, CA Criminal Division 2006, [2008] STC 1158; [2006] EWCA Crim 2518 .... 49.13
R v Henn & Darby, HL 1980, [1981] AC 850; [1980] 2 All ER 166 .... 22.2
R v HM Treasury (ex p. British Telecommunications plc), ECJ Case C-392/93; [1996] 1 ECR 1631; [1996] 2 CMLR 217; [1996] 3 WLR 303; [1996] All ER (EC) 401 .... 22.34
R v HM Treasury & Another (ex p. Service Authority for the National Crime Squad and Others), QB [2000] STC 638 .... 42.8
R v Holborn Commrs (ex p. Rind Settlement Trustees), QB [1974] STC 567 .. 52.24, 52.25
R v Ike, CA Criminal Division 1995, [1996] STC 391 .... 49.5
R v Kelsey, 1981, 74 Cr App R 213 .... 49.7
R v McCarthy, CA Criminal Division, [1981] STC 298 .... 49.1
R v McIntosh, CA [2011] EWCA Crim 1501; [2011] STC 2349 .... 49.22
R v Manchester VAT Tribunal (ex p. C & E Commrs), QB 1982 (unreported) 2.254
R v Marsden, CA [2011] EWCA Crim 1501; [2011] STC 2349 .... 49.22
R v Matthews, CA Criminal Division [2008] EWCA Crim 423 .... 49.27
R v Mavji, CA Criminal Division, [1986] STC 508 .... 49.25
R v May, HL 2008, [2009] STC 852; [2008] UKHL 28 .... 49.19
R v Ministry of Agriculture, Fisheries & Food (ex p. Hedley Lomas (Ireland) Ltd), ECJ Case C-5/94; [1996] 1 ECR 2553; [1996] 2 CMLR 391; [1996] All ER (EC) 493 .... 22.32
R v Ministry of Defence (ex p. Smith), CA 1995, [1996] QB 517; [1996] 1 All ER 257 .... 42.8
R v North & East Devon Health Authority (ex p. Coughlan), CA [2001] 1 QB 213 .... 22.552
R v Northampton Magistrates' Court (ex p. C & E Commrs), QB [1994] BVC 111 .... 49.8
R v Quigley, CA Criminal Division, [2002] BTC 5518; [2002] EWCA Crim 2148 .... 49.14
R v Redford, CA Criminal Division, [1988] STC 845 .... 49.26
R v Ryan and Others, CA Criminal Division, [1994] STC 446 .... 49.29
R v Sangha & Others, CA Criminal Division 2008, [2009] STC 570; [2008] EWCA Crim 2562 .... 49.20
R v Secretary of State for Employment (ex p. Equal Opportunities Commission), HL [1994] 1 All ER 910 .... 22.36
R v Secretary of State for the Home Department (ex p. Brind), HL [1991] 2 WLR 588; [1991] 1 All ER 720 .... 52.452
R v Secretary of State for Transport (ex p. Factortame Ltd & Others) (No 3), ECJ Case C-48/93; [1996] 1 ECR 1029; [1996] 1 CMLR 889; [1996] 2 WLR 506; [1996] All ER (EC) 301 .... 22.31
R v Stanley, CA 17 September 1998, Times 8 December 1998 .... 49.6
R v Takkar, CA Criminal Division [2011] EWCA Crim 646; [2011] 3 All ER 340 ... 49.21
R v Tower Hamlets London Borough Council (ex p. Chetnik Developments Ltd), HL [1988] AC 858 .... 48.1
R v Uddin, CA Criminal Division [1996] STC 1163 .... 49.4
R v Unstead, CA 1996, [1997] STC 22 .... 62.177
R v VAT Tribunal (ex p. Cohen and others), QB [1984] STC 361 .... 2.328
R v VAT Tribunal (ex p. Conoco Ltd), CA July 1995 unreported 2.334
R v VAT Tribunal (ex p. Jenny Braden Holidays Ltd), QB March 1994 unreported 2.330
R (Criminal Proceedings), ECJ Case C-285/09; 7 December 2010 unreported 22.520
R (oao Accenture Services Ltd) v HMRC, QB [2009] STC 1503; [2009] EWHC 857 (Admin) 2.347
R (oao BMW AG) v HMRC, CA [2009] STC 963; [2009] EWCA Civ 77 .... 59.4
R (oao Brayfal Ltd) v HMRC, QB [2007] EWHC 521 (Admin) 36.653
R (oao Brayfal Ltd) v HMRC (No 2), QB [2009] EWHC 3354 (Admin) 59.5
R (oao British Sky Broadcasting Group plc) v C & E, QB [2001] STC 437; [2001] EWHC Admin 127 .... 2.341

R (oao British Telecommunications plc) v HMRC, QB [2005] STC 1148; [2005] EWHC
1043 (Admin) 48.52
R (oao Cardiff County Council) v C & E, CA 2003, [2004] STC 356; [2003] EWCA Civ
1456 .... 48.53
R (oao Corkteck Ltd) v HMRC, QB [2009] STC 1681; [2009] EWHC 785 (Admin)
.... 2.346
R (oao Elite Mobile plc) v C & E, QB 2004, [2005] STC 275; [2004] EWHC 2923
(Admin) 2.531
R (oao Evolution Export Trading Ltd) v HMRC, QB [2007] EWHC 521 (Admin)
.... 36.653
R (oao Federation of Technological Industries & Others) v C & E, CA [2004] EWCA
Civ 1020; [2004] All ER (D) 612 (Jul) 22.466
R (oao Freeserve.com plc) v C & E, QB 2003, [2004] STC 187; [2003] EWHC 2736
(Admin) 2.342
R (oao Greenwich Property Ltd) v C & E, Ch D [2001] STC 618; [2001] EWHC Admin
230 .... 2.94
R (oao Greystone Export Trading Ltd) v HMRC, QB [2007] EWHC 521 (Admin)
.... 36.653
R (oao IDT Card Services Ireland Ltd) v C & E, CA [2006] STC 1252; [2006] EWCA
Civ 29 .... 67.172
R (oao Indigo Global Trading Ltd) v HMRC, QB [2009] EWHC 3126 (Admin) 2.493
R (oao Just Fabulous (UK) Ltd) v HMRC, QB 2007, [2008] STC 2123; [2007] EWHC
521 (Admin) 36.653
R (oao Lower Mill Estate Ltd) v HMRC, QB [2008] EWHC 2409 (Admin) 15.282
R (oao Medical Protection Society Ltd) v HMRC, QB 2009, [2010] STC 555; [2009]
EWHC 2780 (Admin) 39.11
R (oao Mobile Export 365 Ltd) v HMRC, QB [2006] STC 1069; [2006] EWHC 311
(Admin) 2.532
R (oao Paul da Costa & Co) v Thames Magistrates Court, DC [2002] STC 267; [2002]
EWHC Admin 40 .... 14.95
R (oao Sagemaster plc) v C & E, CA [2004] STC 813; [2004] EWCA Civ 25 .... 2.344
R (oao Silicon Graphics Finance SA) v HMRC, QB 2006, [2008] STC 1928; [2006]
EWHC 1889 (Admin) 2.95
R (oao Teleos plc & Others) v C & E, ECJ Case C-409/04; [2008] STC 706 .... 22.518
R (oao Teleos plc & Others) v C & E (No 2), CA [2005] STC 1471; [2005] EWCA Civ
200; [2005] 1 WLR 3007 .... 36.654
R (oao TNT Post UK Ltd) v HMRC, ECJ Case C-357/07; [2009] STC 1438 .... 22.272
R (oao Totel Ltd) v First-Tier Tribunal, QB [2011] EWHC 652 (Admin); [2011] STC
1485 .... 2.137
R (oao UK Tradecorp Ltd) v C & E, QB 2004, [2005] STC 138; [2004] EWHC 2515
(Admin) 36.652
R & F Building Services (VTD 11083) 52.217
R & M International Engineering Ltd (VTD 17278) 65.72
R & M Scaffolding Ltd (VTD 18954, VTD 18955) 15.185
R & N Miller Ltd (VTD 13236) 17.10
R & R Pension Fund, Trustees for, QB [1996] STC 889 .... 18.166
R Burgin Ltd (VTD 5916) 18.166
R Moulding (Contractors Plant) Ltd (VTD 15102) 52.411
R Twining & Co Ltd (VTD 20230) 29.179
R Walia Opticians (London) Ltd (VTD 5085) 18.42
R Walia Opticians Ltd (VTD 15050) 6.46
RA Grendel GmbH v Finanzamt für Körperschaften Hamburg, ECJ Case 255/81;
[1982] ECR 2301; [1983] 1 CMLR 379 .... 22.353
RAAR Associates Ltd (VTD 3365) 18.276
Raceshine Ltd (VTD 7688) 36.495
Radarbeam Ltd, [2010] UKFTT 431 (TC), TC00699 .... 36.113
Radford (M) (t/a Atlantis Trading Co) (VTD 16243) 53.3
Radio Authority (The) [1992] VATTR 155 (VTD 7826) 7.79
RAF Aldergrove Service Institute Fund (VTD 8812) 52.342
Rafferty (ST) (VTD 8911) 52.315
Rahman (MH) (t/a Khayam Restaurant), QB [1998] STC 826 .... 2.309, 3.8

Rahman (MH) (t/a Khayam Restaurant) (No 2), CA 2002, [2003] STC 150; [2002] EWCA Civ 1881 .... 3.9
Rainbow Pools London Ltd (VTD 20800) 15.240
Rainford (JA) (VTD 11011) 18.506
Rainheath Ltd (VTD 1249) 7.35
RAL (Channel Islands) Ltd, ECJ Case C-452/03; [2005] STC 1025 .... 22.215
Ram Computercare (Sales) Ltd (VTD 16102) 14.36
Rambla Properties (VTD 13030) 54.3
Ramm (L) (t/a Ramm Louis & Co) (VTD 11242) 36.550
Ramm Contract Furnishing (Northern) Ltd (VTD 9098) 52.239
Rampling (MH) [1986] VATTR 62 (VTD 2067) 62.426
Ramsay (I & Mrs PA) (t/a Kitchen Format) (VTD 12393) 62.333
Ramsey (G & A) (t/a George's Kitchen), [1995] VATDR 484 (VTD 13582) 3.33
Ramsey (MS) (VTD 14280) 18.381
Ramzan (M) (VTD 7725) 52.344
Rana (JD) (VTD 11842) 57.18
Randall Bros (Furs) Ltd (VTD 210) 25.16
Randall Orchard Holdings Ltd (VTD 18046) 55.42
Randhawa (GS & H) (VTD 7704) 52.350
Randhawa (HK) (t/a Mill Hill Food Store) (VTD 16692) 3.139
Randle (Dr MEC) (VTD 9000) 18.585
Rangers Football Club plc (VTD 19159) 2.437
Rank Group plc (The), ECJ Case C-259/10; 10 November 2011 unreported 22.375
Rankin (S) (t/a RDR Construction) (VTD 3623) 62.429
Rannoch School Ltd, CS [1993] STC 389 .... 15.174
RAP Group plc, Ch D [2000] STC 980 .... 46.42
Rapid Results College Ltd (The), [1973] VATTR 197 (VTD 48) 5.2
Rapide Security & Surveillance Ltd (VTD 20198) 44.150
Raptor Commerce Ltd, [2010] UKFTT 620 (TC), TC00620 .... 48.108
Rashid (Mr & Mrs) (t/a Handy Store) (VTD 13321) 62.105
Rashmi Knitwear & Leisurewear (VTD 20497) 53.10
Rastegar (MR) (t/a Mo's Restaurant), [2010] UKFTT 471 (TC), TC00733 .... 3.107
Ratcliffe (TA) (VTD 12396) 18.485
Rathbone Community Industry (VTD 18200) 6.29
Rating Report Ltd, [2011] UKFTT 721 (TC), TC01558 .... 24.25
Ratnam v Cumarasany, PC 1964, [1965] 1 WLR 8; [1964] 3 All ER 933 .... 2.180
Ratti, Pubblico Ministero v, ECJ Case 148/78; [1979] ECR 1629; [1980] 1 CMLR 96 .... 22.19
Ravanfar (Mrs C) (VTD 14159) 65.91
Ravenfield Ltd, [2010] UKFTT 359 (TC), TC00641 .... 44.105
Rawlings Bros (GS) Ltd (VTD 7533) 52.257
Rawlings & Lucas (Builders) Ltd (VTD 10252, 10409) 18.295
Ray (Dr KC) (VTD 20516) 36.148
Rayner & Keeler Ltd, QB [1994] STC 724 .... 36.590
Raywood (Mr & Mrs F) (VTD 11945) 51.123
Raza (Mrs N) (VTD 17084) 57.27
Razaq (M) & Bashir (M) (t/a Streamline Taxis) [2002] VATDR 92 (VTD 17537) 47.16
Razaq (M), Mushtaq (M) & Azam (M) (t/a Liberty Cars) (VTD 14949) 2.327
Razzak (SA) & Mishari (MA) [1997] VATDR 392 (VTD 15240) 62.503
RBS Deutschland GmbH [2004] VATDR 447 (VTD 18840) 2.306
RBS Deutschland GmbH (No 2) (VTD 19055) 2.262
RBS Deutschland GmbH (No 3), CS 2006, [2007] STC 814; [2006] CSIH 10 .... 2.223
RBS Deutschland Holdings GmbH (No 4), ECJ Case C-277/09; [2011] STC 345 ... 22.418
RBS Leasing & Services (No 1) Ltd (VTD 15643) 2.51
RBS Leasing & Services (No 1) Ltd (and related appeals), [2000] VATDR 33 (VTD 16569) 67.2
RBS Property Developments (VTD 17789) 22.68
RC Frame Erectors Ltd (VTD 7042) 52.254
RCI Europe, ECJ Case C-37/08; [2009] STC 2407 .... 22.207
RCPO v Bowles (P), Oxford Crown Court 7 December 2009, Times 9.12.2009 ...... 49.32

RCPO v Chaudhry (EA), QB 2007, [2008] STC 2357; [2007] EWHC 1805 (Admin) 14.67
RCPO v May, CA [2010] STC 1506; [2010] EWCA Civ 521 .... 49.23
RCPO v Pigott, CA [2010] STC 1190; [2010] EWCA Civ 285 .... 49.24
RCPO v Wilmot, Southwark Crown Court 1 July 2008 unreported 49.15
RCPO, Lamb (S) v, CA [2010] EWCA Civ 285 .... 49.24
RCPO, Larkfield Ltd v, CA [2010] EWCA Civ 521 .... 49.23
RDF Management Services Ltd, [2010] UKFTT 74 (TC), TC00387 .... 28.18
Read (C) & Smith (D) [1982] VATTR 12 (VTD 1188) 40.64
Reading (R) & Crabtree (R) (t/a Mostyn Lodge Hotel) (VTD 12756) 46.227
Reading Cricket & Hockey Club (VTD 13656) 11.34
Reading Industrial Therapy Organisation Ltd (VTD 15132) 46.78
Readings & Headley Ltd (VTD 1535) 44.10
Readman (M) (VTD 18862) 18.504
Readon Holdings Ltd (VTD 3705) 18.424
Realm Defence Industries Ltd (VTD 16831) 36.19
Really Useful Group (The) plc (VTD 6578) 46.20
Reay (MA) (VTD 20378) 15.57
Reayner (I), Colegate (J) & Reayner (A) (VTD 15396) 57.77
Rebba Construction Ltd, [2009] UKFTT 296 (TC), TC00240 .... 15.199
Rebel Fashions (VTD 15057) 18.429
Recaudadores de las Zonas Primera y Segunda, ECJ Case C-202/90; [1991] 1 ECR 4247; [1993] STC 659; [1994] 1 CMLR 424 .... 22.131
Recolta Recycling SPRL, Belgian State v, ECJ Case C-440/04; 6 July 2006 unreported 22.415
Recreb Srl, Dori (F) v, ECJ Case C-91/92; [1994] 1 ECR 3325; [1994] 1 CMLR 665; [1995] All ER (EC) 1 .... 22.20
Red Barn Contracting Ltd (VTD 6294) 52.277
Red Contractors Ltd, [2011] UKFTT 788 (TC), TC01622 .... 18.535
Red Developments (London) Ltd, [2005] VATDR 215 (VTD 19097) 6.3
Red Giant Promotions Ltd (VTD 15667) 23.2
Red 12 Trading Ltd, Ch D 2009, [2010] STC 589; [2009] EWHC 2563 (Ch) 36.97
Redcats (Brands) Ltd (VTD 19648) 5.33
Redford, R v, CA Criminal Division, [1988] STC 845 .... 49.26
Redgrove (R) (VTD 16817) 36.212
Redhead (Mrs WD) (VTD 3201) 29.69
Redington Design Co Ltd (The) (VTD 12656) 36.480
Redland Auto Service Centre Ltd (VTD 15691) 50.44
Redland Timber Co Ltd (VTD 7558) 52.378
Redrow Group plc, HL [1999] STC 161; [1999] 1 WLR 408; [1999] 2 All ER 1 ... 36.130
Reece (MG) (t/a Mako Consultants) (VTD 13980) 5.18
Reed Employment plc (No 1), [2010] UKFTT 222 (TC), TC00523 .... 2.166
Reed Employment plc (No 3), [2011] UKFTT 200 (TC); [2011] SFTD 720, TC01069 .... 48.39
Reed Personnel Services Ltd, QB [1995] STC 588 .... 33.21
Reeds (E) (VTD 4578) 62.226
Reeds Rains Prudential Ltd, Norglen Ltd v, HL [1999] 2 AC 14 .... 2.297
Reeds School of Motoring (Nottingham) Ltd (VTD 4578) 62.226
Reeds School of Motoring (Sheffield) Ltd (VTD 13404) 62.227
Reemtsma Cigarettenfabriken GmbH v Ministero delle Finanze, ECJ Case C-35/05; [2008] STC 3448 .... 22.535
Rees (C) (VTD 4440) 18.408
Rees (DLG) Partner (t/a Sayes Court Farm) (VTD 6809) 52.67
Reflex Synthesisers Controllers Ltd (VTD 8815) 18.313
Reflexions Market Research Ltd (VTD 4850) 18.209
Refrigeration Spares (Manchester) Ltd (VTD 17603) 48.98
Refrigeration Spares (Manchester) Ltd (VTD 17852) 2.471
Regalstar Enterprises (VTD 3102) 62.445
Regency Villas Owners Club (The) (VTD 16525) 13.2
Regent Commodities Ltd, UT [2011] UKUT 259 (TCC); [2011] STC 1964 .... 36.113
Regent Investment Fund Ltd (VTD 12152) 52.344

Régie Dauphinoise-Cabinet A Forest Sarl v Ministre du Budget, ECJ Case C-306/94; [1996] STC 1176; [1996] 1 ECR 3695; [1996] 3 CMLR 193 .... 22.446
Regis Commercial Property (VTD 6617) 52.136
Regular Music Ltd (VTD 15571) 52.145
Reich (L) (VTD 9548) 62.138
Reich (L) & Sons Ltd (VTD 97) 57.218
Reichel Magrath, 1889, 14 AC 665 .... 2.122
Reid (A) (VTD 10403) 52.75
Reid (A) (VTD 10406) 18.83
Reid (BC) (VTD 11625) 62.154
Reid (C) (t/a Glynfield Cleaning Contractors) (VTD 1543) 36.376
Reid (C) (VTD 4103) 18.139
Reisdorf v Finanzamt Köln-West, ECJ Case C-85/95; [1996] 1 ECR 6257; [1997] STC 180; [1997] 1 CMLR 536 .... 22.472
Reisebüro Binder GmbH v Finanzamt Stuttgart-Körperschaften, ECJ Case C-116/96; [1998] STC 604 .... 22.212
Relay Couriers Ltd (VTD 7990) 18.364
Remlock Design Ltd (VTD 9145) 18.214
Remlock Design Ltd (VTD 9146) 2.410, 36.524, 36.570
Renaissance Bronzes Ltd (VTD 6849) 52.139
Renco Aviation Ltd (VTD 1646) 36.426
Rendle (JE) (t/a Coventry International English Studies Centre) (VTD 1389) 5.5
Renlon Ltd [2000] VATDR 442 (VTD 16987) 18.520
Renshall (AP & P) (t/a Kingsway Convenience Store) (VTD 16273) 52.302
Rental Concepts Ltd (VTD 20692) 36.22
Rentexit Ltd (t/a Leadair Technical & Refrigeration) (VTD 10335) 18.506
Renton (WA) (VTD 870) 57.11
Rentorn Ltd (VTD 3334) 46.14
Renwalk Ltd (VTD 1255) 2.316
Republic National Bank of New York [1992] VATTR 299 (VTD 7894) 62.195
Republic of Austria, EC Commission v, ECJ Case C-128/05; 28 September 2006 unreported 22.479
Republic of Austria, T-Mobile Austria GmbH and Others v, ECJ Case C-284/04; [2008] STC 184 .... 22.118
Republic of Ireland, EC Commission v, ECJ Case C-358/97; 12 September 2000 unreported 22.135
Republic of Ireland, EC Commission v, ECJ Case C-554/07; 16 July 2009 unreported 20.9
Research Establishment (VTD 19095) 11.9
Resincrest Ltd (VTD 7310) 52.69
Resource Maintenance Ltd (VTD 13204) 6.25
Restaurant Portfolio Ltd (t/a L'Escargot) (VTD 15245) 14.64
Resteel Trading Ltd [2009] UKFTT 236 (TC), TC00185 .... 4.26
Restorex Ltd [1997] VATDR 402 (VTD 15014) 14.16
Retainco (51) Ltd (t/a The Royal Hotel) (VTD 11265) 2.411
Retro (Scotland) Ltd (VTD 19529) 40.41
Revelstar Ltd (VTD 6734) 51.75
Reverse Osmosis Systems Ltd (VTD 10436) 52.136
Rewe-Zentralfinanz eG & Rewe-Zentral AG v Landwirtschaftskammer für das Saarland, ECJ Case 33/76; [1976] ECR 1989; [1977] 1 CMLR 533 .... 22.43
Rey (BE & Mrs CS) (t/a Wood Hall Hotel & Country Club) (VTD 5676) 67.91
Reynolds (B), [2010] UKFTT 40 (TC), TC00354 .... 28.20
Reynolds v Commissioner of the Metropolitan Police, CA [1984] 3 All ER 649 ...... 14.94
RGB Contractors (VTD 133) 36.299
RHM Bakeries (Northern) Ltd, QB 1978, [1979] STC 72 .... 62.9
Rhodes (DL) (VTD 2883) 62.431
Rhodes (NF) (VTD 14533) 55.41
Rhondda Cynon Taff County Borough Council [2000] VATDR 149 (VTD 16496) 22.146
RHS Structural Engineering Ltd (VTD 7354) 51.15
Rhymney Valley District Council (VTD 6939) 52.378

Rialto Homes plc [1999] VATDR 477 (VTD 16340) 15.257
RIBA Publications [1999] VATDR 230 (VTD 15983) 48.34
Ribbans (HV) (VTD 346) 2.111
Rice (BJ) & Associates, CA [1996] STC 581 .... 62.456
Rice (BJ) & Associates (VTD 14659) 2.456
Richard Drewitt Productions Ltd (VTD 11999) 36.413
Richard Haynes Associates (VTD 10068) 2.133
Richard Haynes Associates (VTD 12300) 46.56
Richard Salmon Ltd (VTD 12126) 5.17
Richards (W) (VTD 11674) 36.189
Richards (WG) (VTD 2355) 62.188
Richards & Goldsworthy (Wales) Ltd (VTD 10346) 65.65
Richardson (D) (VTD 8849) 57.7
Richardson (K) (VTD 18617) 1.33
Richardson (MRW) (VTD 6937) 52.150
Richardson (RG) (t/a Castle Mouldings) (VTD 3898) 18.320
Riches (MS) [1994] VATTR 401 (VTD 12210) 36.249
Richford Designs Ltd (VTD 18639) 17.19
Richmond Cars Ltd [2000] VATDR 388 (VTD 16942) 44.69
Richmond Design Interiors Ltd (VTD 13549) 50.82
Richmond Resources Ltd (VTD 13435) 40.73
Richmond Theatre Management Ltd, QB [1995] STC 257 .... 62.434
Richmond & Another, ex p., R v C & E, QB 1988, [1989] STC 429 .... 36.676
Rickarby (R) [1973] VATTR 186 (VTD 44) 7.103
Ricocrest Ltd (VTD 5179) 18.551
Ridal (Mrs S) (C149) 29.92
Ridgeon (GF) (VTD 17749) 19.65
Ridgeons Bulk Ltd [1992] VATTR 169 (VTD 7655) 62.131
Ridgeons Bulk Ltd, QB [1994] STC 427 .... 3.179
Ridgeway (PJ) (VTD 6140) 52.88
Ridley (A) [1983] VATTR 81 (VTD 1406) 62.150
Ridsdill-Smith (Dr GP) & Partners (VTD 16992) 2.436
Riftmain Ltd (VTD 2819) 36.324
Rightacres Ltd (VTD 19140) 46.100
Riksskatteverket, Förvaltnings AB Stenholmen v, ECJ Case C-320/02; [2004] STC 1041;
  [2004] All ER (EC) 870 .... 22.494
Riksskatteverket, Hotel Scandic Gasaback AB v, ECJ Case C-412/03; [2005] STC
  1311 .... 22.185
Rimland Ltd, QB 1992 (unreported) 2.211
Rimmer (Mrs MA) (VTD 11397) 52.304
Ringer (L) (VTD 20060) 51.151
Ringside Refreshments, Ch D 2003, [2004] STC 426; [2003] EWHC 3043 (Ch) 62.303
Rioni Ltd, QB 7 June 2007, Tax Journal 25.6.2007 .... 36.656
Risbey's Photography Ltd (VTD 20783) 5.30
Risby (BC & ME) (VTD 6544) 46.183
Rivella (UK) Ltd (VTD 16382) 29.178
River Barge Holidays Ltd (VTD 572) 67.114
Rivers Machinery Ltd (VTD 7505) 62.449
Riverside Housing Association Ltd, Ch D [2006] STC 2072; [2006] EWHC 2383 (Ch)
  .... 15.115
Riverside School (Whassett) Ltd [1995] VATDR 186 (VTD 13170) 15.79
Riverside Sports & Leisure Ltd [2008] VATDR 326 (VTD 20848) 67.146
Riverward Ltd (VTD 13094) 65.69
Řízení Letového Provozu ČR sp v Bundesamt für Finanzen, ECJ Case C-335/05; [2007]
  STC 1509 .... 22.545
RJN Creighton Ltd (VTD 12395) 48.125
RK Enterprises (VTD 17440) 18.286
RK Transport Ltd (VTD 6358) 18.74
RLRE Tellmer Property sro v Finanční ředitelství v Ústí nad Labem, ECJ Case C-572/07;
  [2009] STC 2006 .... 22.346
RM Douglas (Roofing) Ltd, Hunt v, HL [1990] 1 AC 398 .... 48.143

RM Education plc (VTD 20911) 21.43
RM Joinery & Double Glazing (VTD 3658) 51.90
RMSG [1994] VATTR 167 (VTD 11920) 17.5
RMSG [1994] VATTR 167 (VTD 11921) 2.255
RMSG (VTD 12520) 52.353
RNIB Properties Ltd (VTD 15748) 11.26
RO Somerton Ltd (VTD 18809) 18.503
Robbie (Mr & Mrs D) (t/a Dunlaw House Hotel), [2009] UKFTT 82 (TC), TC00050
.... 57.30
Robbins (PJ), Ch D 2004, [2005] STC 1103; [2004] EWHC 3373 (Ch) 44.115
Robbins of Putney Ltd (VTD 610) 25.5
Robeda Ltd (VTD 7781) 52.41
Robert Gordon University (Board of Governors), CS [2008] STC 1890; [2008] CSIH
22 .... 21.7
Robert Gordon's College, HL [1995] STC 1093; [1996] 1 WLR 201 .... 22.165
Robert Matthews Ltd (VTD 9801) 52.257
Robert Mullis Restoration Services Ltd (VTD 18501) 57.80
Robert S Monk Ltd (VTD 14346) 52.409
Robert Smith & Sons Ltd (VTD 19010) 48.74
Roberts (AW) (VTD 353) 33.32
Roberts (DM & Mrs PJ) [1992] VATTR 30 (VTD 7516) 41.152
Roberts (J) (VTD 2555) 44.63
Roberts (L) (VTD 15759) 3.110
Roberts (P) & Brooke (D) (VTD 2153) 51.123
Robertson (I), [2010] UKFTT 102 (TC), TC00413 .... 15.277
Robertson (J) (VTD 1797) 44.78
Robertson Robertson Construction Co (VTD 2071) 36.370
Robertson's Electrical Ltd, CS 2005, [2007] STC 612; [2005] CSIH 75 .... 62.464
Robey (DW) & Sons Ltd (VTD 6967) 18.57
Robin Ellis Contracts Ltd (VTD 18500) 19.36
Robinson (B) (VTD 634) 3.148
Robinson (D) (VTD 12667) 18.120
Robinson (G) (t/a Swallow Motor Co) (VTD 11120) 18.86
Robinson (P) (VTD 4063) 55.83
Robinson (P) (VTD 4530) 2.317
Robinson (P) (VTD 12325) 50.22
Robinson (PJ) (VTD 7145) 52.168
Robinson (PJ) (VTD 13102) 52.312
Robinson (S), [1991] VATTR 440 (VTD 6267) 18.14, 18.465
Robinson Cooke (VTD 4040) 18.402
Robinson Group of Companies Ltd (The) (VTD 16081) 40.108
Robinsons Removals (Cleveland) Ltd (VTD 11187) 38.43
Robotham (KN & DJ) (t/a North Walsham Insurance Services) (VTD 15325) 3.54
Rocco Mana Ltd (t/a Spearmint Rhino Rouge), [2011] UKFTT 153 (TC), TC01027
.... 18.476
Rochdale Drinks Distributors Ltd, CA [2011] EWCA Civ 1116 .... 37.6
Rochdale Hornets Football Club Co Ltd, [1975] VATTR 71 (VTD 161) 41.153
Rock Lambert (VTD 6637) 36.55
Rodcom Europe Ltd (VTD 20874) 18.527
Rodeo Catering Ltd (VTD 11870) 36.621
Roderick Gunkel & Associates Ltd, [2009] UKFT 308 (TC), TC00252 .... 36.340
Roders BV & Others v Inspecteur der Invoerrechten en Accijnzen, ECJ Case C-367/93;
[1995] 1 ECR 2229 .... 22.42
Roebuck (JB) (VTD 10171) 51.92
Rogers Torbay Ltd (VTD 11389) 48.117
Rok Crete Units Co Ltd (VTD 2660) 18.501
Roma II Ltd, [2010] UKFTT 243 (TC), TC00540 .... 36.121
Roman Catholic Diocese of Shrewsbury (VTD 17900) 15.205
Romill Engineering (VTD 3109) 18.58
Rompelman & Rompelman-van-Deelen v Minister van Financiën, ECJ Case 268/83;
[1985] 3 CMLR 202; [1985] ECR 655 .... 22.103

Ron Miller Ltd (VTD 5827) 36.183, 62.472
Ronald D Rawcliffe Ltd (VTD 17118) 18.541
Ronton Haulage Ltd (VTD 2234) 36.621
Rooke (MJ) (VTD 9819) 69.11
Roopers Export Sales Ltd (VTD 10801) 52.200
Roose (BE) (VTD 12350) 52.217
Root 89 Ltd, [2011] UKFTT 94 (TC), TC00971 .... 36.113
Rootes (TD) (t/a The Shutford Stud) (VTD 6808) 36.252
Roquette Frères SA v Direction des Services Fiscaux du Pas-de-Calais, ECJ Case
  C-88/99; [2000] All ER(D) 2008 .... 22.52
Rose (K) (t/a KJ Rose Building Services) (VTD 7694) 52.136
Rose Household Textiles Ltd (VTD 7105) 52.153
Rosebronze Ltd (VTD 1668) 14.50
Rosedew Ltd (VTD 9619) 52.157
Rosemoor Holdings Ltd (VTD 4068) 38.39
Rosenberg (DS) (t/a Crusade) (VTD 14049) 18.341
Rosgill Group Ltd, CA [1997] STC 811; [1997] 3 All ER 1012 .... 67.38
Rosignoli (P & J) [1983] VATTR 266 (VTD 1502) 2.142
Rosner (FW) (t/a London School of International Business), QB 1993, [1994] STC 228
  .... 36.232
Ross (DW and Others), QB [1990] STC 353; [1990] 2 All ER 65 .... 2.400
Ross (G) (VTD 18672) 2.360
Ross & Liddell Ltd (VTD 19559) 46.10
Ross (G) & Metcalfe (S) (VTD 4835) 18.581
Ross Pharmacy Ltd (VTD 20634) 36.74D
Ross Young Holdings Ltd [1996] VATDR 230 (VTD 13972) 29.125
Rossiter (K & C) (VTD 1452) 7.32
Rotary International [1991] VATTR 177 (VTD 5946) 64.9
Rotherham Borough Council Employees Sports & Social Club (VTD 3543) 18.80
Rotherham Golf Academy, [2009] UKFTT 57 (TC), TC00036 .... 41.39
Rothley Park Golf Club (VTD 2074) 13.36
Round (E) & Son Ltd (VTD 2069) 29.150
Round (K) (t/a Circle Interiors) (VTD 10844) 52.75
Roundhouse Work Ltd (VTD 18595) 52.283
Roundstar Ltd (VTD 15471) 14.10
Rourke (M) (t/a The Market Pantry) (VTD 16671) 29.74
Rouse Kent Ltd (VTD 8862) 52.125
Routledge (KT) (VTD 18395) 41.146
Rowan (JP) (VTD 16357) 1.75
Rowan Timber Supplies (Scotland) Ltd (VTD 16305) 18.513
Rowe (B) (t/a Cheshire Hearing Centre) [2002] VATDR 156 (VTD 17600) 33.12
Rowe & Maw, QB [1975] STC 340; [1975] 1 WLR 1291; [1975] 2 All ER 444 ..... 62.52
Rowland (L) & Co (Retail) Ltd, QB [1992] STC 647 .... 48.87
Rowlands (Messrs) (VTD 2752) 18.229
Rowledge (TP) (VTD 12590) 67.140
Rowley (MD) (VTD 5089) 18.585
Roxburghe Hotel Ltd (VTD 456) 2.421
Roy (J) (VTD 9384) 57.57
Roy Conway Industrial Services Ltd (VTD 9439) 18.235
Royal Academy of Music [1994] VATTR 105 (VTD 11871) 55.15
Royal Agricultural College (VTD 17508) 46.33
Royal & Sun Alliance Insurance Group plc, HL [2003] STC 832; [2003] UKHL 29;
  [2003] 1 WLR 1387; [2003] 2 All ER 1073 .... 46.216
Royal & Sun Alliance plc (VTD 18842) 46.179
Royal Bank of Canada Trust Corporation Ltd (VTD 20520) 36.647
Royal Bank of Scotland Group plc (No 1) [1999] VATDR 122 (VTD 16035) 48.54
Royal Bank of Scotland Group plc (No 2) (VTD 16418) 3.84
Royal Bank of Scotland Group plc (No 3), CS [2002] STC 575 .... 27.4
Royal Bank of Scotland Group plc (No 4) (VTD 17637) 65.33
Royal Bank of Scotland Group plc (No 5) (VTD 17789) 22.68
Royal Bank of Scotland Group plc (No 6), ECJ Case C-488/07; [2009] STC 461 ... 22.445

Royal Bank of Scotland Group plc (No 7), CS [2008] STC 3301; [2008] CSIH 49 .... 46.165
Royal Bank of Scotland Group plc (No 8) [2008] VATDR 336 (VTD 20856) 38.33
Royal Bank of Scotland plc, re Oval 1742 Ltd, CA [2007] EWCA Civ 1262 .... 37.9
Royal British Legion Drumnadrochit Branch (VTD 16957) 57.130
Royal College of Anaesthetists (VTD 18632) 13.20
Royal College of Obstetricians & Gynaecologists (VTD 14558) 48.1
Royal Exchange Theatre Trust, QB [1979] STC 728; [1979] 3 All ER 797 .... 7.5
Royal Incorporation of Architects in Scotland (VTD 20252) 38.20
Royal Midland Counties Home for Disabled People, Ch D 2001, [2002] STC 395 .... 11.12
Royal Midland Counties Home for Incurables at Leamington Spa (General Committee), Minister of Health v, CA [1954] 1 Ch 530 .... 15.74
Royal National LIfeboat Institution, [2009] SFTD 55; [2009] UKFTT 39 (TC); TC00017 .... 20.98
Royal Photographic Society [1978] VATTR 191 (VTD 647) 64.12
Royal Pigeon Racing Association (VTD 14006) 24.50
Royal Scottish Automobile Club (The) (VTD 257) 13.30
Royal Society for the Encouragement of Arts, Manufacture & Commerce (The), QB 1996, [1997] STC 437 .... 11.24
Royal Society for the Prevention of Cruelty to Animals (No 1) [1991] VATTR 407 (VTD 6218) 7.95
Royal Society for the Prevention of Cruelty to Animals (No 2), Ch D 2007, [2008] STC 885; [2007] EWHC 422(Ch) 2.518
Royal Thames Yacht Club (VTD 14046) 24.40
Royal Ulster Constabulary Athletic Association Ltd [1989] VATTR 17 (VTD 3529) 13.25
Royscot Leasing Ltd, ECJ Case C-305/97; [1999] STC 998; [2000] 1 WLR 1151; [1999] All ER (EC) 908 .... 22.424
RP Ltd [2004] VATDR 452 (VTD 18935) 2.76
RSH Associates Ltd (VTD 19912) 5.37
RSK Newsagents Ltd (VTD 15750) 58.23
RSM Industries Ltd (VTD 2810) 18.271
RSPCA (No 1) [1991] VATTR 407 (VTD 6218) 7.95
RSPCA (No 2) Ch D 2007, [2008] STC 885; [2007] EWHC 422(Ch) 2.518
RTI Services Ltd (VTD 18512) 10.15
Rubie (S) (VTD 20666) 18.462
Rudd (SP) (t/a Duo's Spa & Sauna) (VTD 16844) 62.274
Rugby Football Union [2003] VATDR 45 (VTD 18075) 27.54
Rum Runner Casino Ltd (VTD 1036) 24.14
Rumline Ltd (VTD 20406) 18.296
Rumney Rugby Football Club (VTD 19480) 62.122
Rupert Page Developments Ltd (VTD 379) 2.462
Rupert Page Developments Ltd (No 2) [1993] VATTR 152 (VTD 9823) 2.388
Ruse (MH) (VTD 18522) 18.543
Rushcombe Ltd (VTD 14727) 36.219
Rushfern Ltd (VTD 1509) 2.327
Rushgreen Builders Ltd (VTD 2470) 36.150
Ruskin College (VTD 16726) 46.198
Rusland Education & Training Ltd (t/a Rusland College) (VTD 19806) 5.37
Russell (A) Heating (VTD 20681) 48.63
Russell (T & GA) (VTD 7534) 52.217
Russguild Ltd (VTD 3321) 51.107
Rustem (EK) (t/a The Dry Cleaners) (VTD 15206) 3.22
Ruttle Plant (Midlands) Ltd (VTD 18048) 65.112
RW Construction (Stockport) Ltd (VTD 3761) 18.8
RW Joinery (Stockport) Ltd (VTD 3761) 18.8
Ryan, R v, CA [1994] STC 446 .... 49.29
Ryan (M) & Townsend (M) (t/a Reliables Fuel Plus) (VTD 12806) 65.41
Ryan Evans Ltd (VTD 5682) 51.10
Rye (D) (VTD 7578) 57.165

Rye Mill Garage Ltd (VTD 19060) 48.74
Ryebank Heating Ltd (VTD 7405) 52.105
Ryebank Ltd (VTD 20212) 51.168
Rykneld Thoroughbred Co Ltd (VTD 6894) 7.71

S

S & I Electronics Ltd (VTD 20078) 48.104
S & I Electronics plc, [2009] SFTD 241; [2009] UKFTT 108 (TC), TC00076 .... 36.120
S & J Property Centres (VTD 16985) 62.400
S & U Stores Ltd (VTD 726) 36.2
S & U Stores plc, QB [1985] STC 506 .... 46.102
S Taylor (Machine Tools) Ltd (VTD 11171) 52.297
SA Belge de Navigation Aerienne Sabena, Defrenne v, ECJ Case 43/75; [1976] ECR 455;
   [1976] 2 CMLR 98; [1981] 1 All ER 122 .... 22.39
SA Cabinet Diot v France, ECHR Case 49217/99; 22 July 2003 unreported 34.25
SA Dangeville v France, ECHR Case 36677/97; [2003] STC 771; 5 ITLR 604 .... 34.24
SA Gras Savoye v France, ECHR Case 49218/99; 22 July 2003 unreported 34.25
Saab Great Britain Ltd (VTD 20046) 2.482
Sabath, Baylis Baxter v, CA [1958] 1 WLR 529; [1958] 2 All ER 209 .... 2.376
Sadiq (MK) (VTD 2160) 44.63
Sadler (R) (t/a Warmfield Group) (VTD 20893) 52.289
Sadri (AA) (t/a Hutosh Commercial) (VTD 694) 25.6
Saeed (M) & Arabian (P) (VTD 1859) 2.195
Safdar (M) (VTD 13646) 53.21
Safegold Fashions Ltd [1992] VATTR 105 (VTD 7343) 2.132
Safety Boat Services Ltd (VTD 6487) 65.19
Safeway Stores plc, QB 1996, [1997] STC 163 .... 29.5
Saffron v Australian Federal Commissioners of Tax (No 2), FC(A) [1991] FCR 578
   .... 2.207
Saga Holidays plc [2004] VATDR 94 (VTD 18591) 67.88
Sagar (HS & HK) (t/a AMR Pipeline Products Co) (VTD 12692) 18.563
Sagemaster plc (oao), R v C & E, CA [2004] STC 813; [2004] EWCA Civ 25 .... 2.344
Sageworth Ltd (t/a Anton Hammes) (VTD 11151) 18.460
Sahib Restaurant Ltd (VTD 20264) 50.96
Sahota (RS) (VTD 14986) 57.192
SAI Jewellers, QB [1996] STC 269 .... 67.61
Saint (WH) (VTD 1147) 21.44
St Andrew's Church Eakring Parochial Church Council (VTD 15320) 55.29
St Andrew's Motor Homes Ltd (VTD 14100) 19.22
St Andrew's Property Management Ltd (VTD 20499) 15.76
St Anne's Catholic Church [1994] VATTR 102 (VTD 11783) 55.68
St Anne's Distributors Ltd [2010] UKUT 458 (TCC); [2011] STC 708 .... 2.72
St Anne's-on-Sea Lawn Tennis Club Ltd [1977] VATTR 229 (VTD 434) 30.4
St Benedict Trading Ltd [1994] VATTR 376 (VTD 12915) 29.34
St Benedict's School (VTD 7235) 51.39
St Dunstan's [2003] VATDR 634 (VTD 17896) 55.17
St Dunstan's Educational Foundation, CA [1999] STC 381 .... 15.104
St Dunstan's Roman Catholic Church Southborough [1998] VATDR 264 (VTD
   15472) 15.98
St George's Home Co Ltd (VTD 10213) 46.221
Saint Gobain Building Distribution Ltd, [2011] UKFTT 461 (TC), TC01311 .... 18.619
St Helens School Northwood Ltd, Ch D 2006, [2007] STC 633; [2006] EWHC 3306
   (Ch) 46.140
St Honore Mailles (Scotland) Ltd (VTD 18901) 53.10
St James Court Hotel Ltd (VTD 17487) 46.20
St John's College Oxford, [2010] UKFTT 113 (TC), TC00424 .... 46.133
St Luke's (Great Crosby PCC), QB [1982] STC 856 .... 2.513
St Martin's Healthcare Ltd (VTD 20778) 3.81
St Martin's Hospital, CA [1997] STC 445 .... 19.3

St Martin's Medical Services Ltd (VTD 20778) 3.81
St Mary Magdalene College Cambridge (Master & Fellows), [2011] UKFTT 680 (TC), TC01522 .... 46.150
St Marylebone Borough Council, Berry v, CA 1957, [1958] Ch 406; [1957] 3 All ER 677 .... 22.293
St Mary's Roman Catholic High School, QB [1996] STC 1091 .... 15.189
St Paul's Community Project Ltd, Ch D 2004, [2005] STC 95; [2004] EWHC 2490 (Ch) 15.92
St Petroc Minor Vicar and Parochial Church Council (VTD 16450) 55.54
Sajawal (S) (VTD 10971) 57.181
Saleem (FA) (VTD 12995) 33.42
Saleh (E) (VTD 20288) 58.21
Salevon Ltd, QB [1989] STC 907 .... 18.312
Salina Ltd (VTD 6287) 2.405
SALIX Grundstücks-Vermietungsgesellschaft mbH & Co. Objekt Offenbach KG, Finanzamt Düsseldorf-Süd v, ECJ Case C-102/08; [2009] STC 1607 .... 22.141
Saltaire Private Hire Ltd (VTD 17596) 3.141
Salumets & Others, Tullihallitus v, ECJ Case C-455/98; [2000] All ER (D) 891 ..... 22.100
Samrosa Ltd (VTD 3984) 14.47
Samuel (J) (t/a Joseph Samuel Developments) [1992] VATTR 1 (VTD 7177) 15.162, 15.192
Samuel (M) [2010] UKFTT 633 (TC), TC00872 .... 15.208
Samuels v Linzi Dresses, CA [1980] 2 WLR 836; [1980] 1 All ER 803 .... 2.319
Samzou Ltd (VTD 11013) 18.326
Samzou Ltd (VTD 11483) 18.116
San Giorgio SpA, Amministrazione delle Finanze dello Stato v, ECJ Case C-199/82; [1983] ECR 3513; [1985] 2 CMLR 658 .... 22.556
Sandell (VTD 9665) 62.174
Sanders (AF) (VTD 13423) 44.141
Sandley (BJ) (t/a Bemba Sandley Management Co) QB [1995] STC 230 .... 62.109
Sandmar Technologies Ltd (VTD 11326) 18.563
Sandwell Scaffold Company Ltd (VTD 12823) 18.333
Sangha & Others, R v, CA Criminal Division, [2008] EWCA Crim 2562 .... 49.20
Sangster Group Ltd (VTD 15544) 36.337
Sanleo Ltd, [2010] UKFTT 266 (TC), TC00560 .... 14.43
Sanofi Synthelabo v Directeur des Services Fiscaux du Val-de-Marne, ECJ Case C-181/99; [2002] BTC 5520 .... 22.501
Sansom (PJ) (VTD 7121) 18.283
Santi (VTD 954) 2.351
Santi Bag Restaurant (VTD 13114) 50.99
Sapphire Retail Fund Ltd (VTD 20232) 18.548
Sargent, CA [1995] STC 399; [1995] 1 WLR 821 .... 37.11
Sargeson (MN) (VTD 4480) 18.120
Sarwar (M) (VTD 7120) 18.473
SAS Fashions Ltd (VTD 9426) 3.138
Sassi (P), [2009] UKFTT 280 (TC), TC00224 .... 15.268
Sassoon Bury Ltd, [2011] UKFTT 797 (TC), TC01633 .... 36.593
Satam SA v Ministre du Budget, ECJ Case C-333/91; [1993] 1 ECR 3513; [1997] STC 226 .... 22.443
Satchwell Grant Ltd (VTD 14577) 18.138
Satnam Investments Ltd (VTD 6746) 52.224
Satis Italsempione SA (VTD 19683) 57.159
Saturn Leisure Ltd (VTD 20185) 52.228
Saunders (H), [1980] VATTR 53 (VTD 913) 47.15
Saunders v United Kingdom, ECHR 1996, 23 EHRR 313 .... 2.283
Saunders-Pederson (J) (t/a Advanced Information Systems UK) (VTD 15675) 52.430
Savannah Landscapes & Building Services (VTD 17883) 51.177
Save & Prosper Group Ltd, QB 1978, [1979] STC 205 .... 32.4
Savidge (K) (t/a KCS Car Spa) (VTD 20972) 57.130
Savin (HS) (VTD 12104, VTD 12873) 52.307
Savva (Mr & Mrs K) (t/a Venus Restaurant) (VTD 127) 57.120

Savva (Z & C) (VTD 2561) 51.104
Sawadee Restaurant (VTD 15933) 65.101
Sawley Security Ltd (VTD 20282) 18.530
Sawyer (D) (VTD 19035) 50.60
Sawyer (J) (VTD 18872) 7.52
Sawyer & Another, CA 7 November 2001 unreported 14.111
Saxton (BT) (VTD 17191) 62.236
SC Campbell (Plastics) Ltd (VTD 6086) 18.588
SC Driver (Opticians) Ltd (VTD 12410) 18.588
Scally (JE), [1989] VATTR 245 (VTD 4592) 37.30
Scandinavian Village Ltd (VTD 16961) 13.3
Scanes (R) (VTD 347) 57.7
Scanland Agencies Ltd (VTD 6648) 52.62
Scarfe (V) & Cowley (J) (VTD 703) 3.135
Scargill (LS) (VTD 1420) 44.7
Sceptre Services Ltd (No 1), [2010] UKFTT 247 (TC), TC00542 .... 2.268
Sceptre Services Ltd (No 2), [2010] UKFTT 315 (TC), TC00602 .... 2.288
Sceptre Services Ltd (No 3), [2011] UKFTT 265 (TC), TC01127 .... 36.121
Schemepanel Trading Ltd, QB [1996] STC 871 .... 36.612
Schlumberger Inland Services Inc, QB 1986, [1987] STC 228 .... 3.51
Schmeink & Cofreth AG & Co KG v Finanzamt Borken, ECJ Case C-454/98, [2000]
  STC 810 .... 22.414
Schmelz (I), Re, ECJ Case C-97/09; [2011] STC 88 .... 20.126
Schoemann ISR (UK) Ltd (VTD 11713) 5.50
Schofield (PL) Ltd (VTD 7736) 46.116
Scholastic Publications Ltd (VTD 14213) 5.13
School Book Fairs (GB) Ltd (VTD 10553) 52.72
School of Finance and Management (London) Ltd, Ch D [2001] STC 1690 .... 21.11
Schooler (Mrs VGM), CA 1995 (unreported) 47.69
Schriever, Finanzamt Lüdenscheid v, ECJ Case C-444/10; 10 November 2011
  unreported 22.169
Schusman (SP), [1994] VATTR 120 (VTD 11835) 5.61
Schwarz & Others v Aeresta Ltd & C & E Commrs, QB 1988, [1989] STC 230 ...... 2.73
Scomark Engineering Ltd (VTD 9104) 52.250
Scorpio Marine Enterprises Ltd (VTD 9121) 52.257
Scotford-Smith (S) (VTD 14609) 65.19
Scotia Homes Ltd (VTD 6044) 52.311
Scott v Scott, HL [1913] AC 417 .... 2.255
Scott (AJ) (VTD 2926) 57.184
Scott (DD), QB 1977, [1978] STC 191 .... 29.111
Scott (GHJA) (t/a Chancellor & Sons) (VTD 6922) 36.66
Scott (MJ) (VTD 4257) 36.540
Scott (R) (VTD 517) 3.135
Scott (RN) (VTD 2302) 36.235
Scott (RN) (No 2) (VTD 11574) 36.234
Scott (WA) (2938) (VTD 4208) 51.28
Scott-Dickinson (NP) & Nunn (AF) (VTD 11859) 51.60
Scott-Martin (J) (t/a SM Harris) (VTD 8954) 51.140
Scott-Morley (AJ) (VTD 1097) 69.4
Scottish Eastern Investment Trust plc (VTD 16882) 46.167
Scottish Equitable plc, CS 2 July 2009 unreported 48.57
Scottish Exhibition Centre Ltd, CS 2006, [2008] STC 967; [2006] CSIH 42 ...... 27.24
Scottish Football Association Ltd (VTD 14895) 67.13
Scottish Highland Hotels Group Ltd [1981] VATTR 146 (VTD 1115) 62.397
Scottish Homes (VTD 13292) 46.156
Scottish Homes (No 2) (VTD 16644) 46.53
Scottish Investment Trust plc (VTD 9368) 2.88
Scottish Solicitors' Discipline Tribunal (The) [1989] VATTR 138 (VTD 3539) 7.108
Scottish Tourist Board (VTD 16883) 46.8
Scotts Group Ltd (VTD 20924) 36.166

Scout Association Trust Corporation and Others *v* Secretary of State for the Environment, CA [2005] STC 1808; [2005] EWCA Civ 980 .... 67.10
Scrace (C) & Keeshan (E), Ch D 2006, [2007] STC 269; [2006] EWHC 2646(Ch) 47.4
SCS Peterbroeck Van Campenhout & Cie *v* Belgium, ECJ Case C-312/93; [1995] 1 ECR 4599; [1996] 1 CMLR 793; [1996] All ER (EC) 242 .... 22.48
SCSI-Com Ltd (VTD 17644) 23.12
SD Solutions Ltd, [2010] UKFTT 228 (TC), TC00529 .... 28.6
Sea-Change Ltd (VTD 11759) 18.365
Sea Containers Services Ltd, QB [2000] STC 82 .... 66.26
SeaFrance, Eurotunnel SA & Others *v*, ECJ Case C-408/95; [1996] BTC 5200 ...... 22.524
Seagar Enterprises Ltd (t/a Ace Security Services) (VTD 15432) 1.27
Seal (JD) (VTD 4586) 62.474
Sealine International Ltd (VTD 10061) 8.4
Sealjet UK Ltd (VTD 6683) 52.148
Seamill Hydro (VAT Tribunal, unreported) 41.111
Searle (D) (VTD 5900) 51.66
Searle (Mrs SA), [2011] UKFTT 679 (TC), TC01521 .... 15.64
Seatechs Ltd, [2009] UKFTT 146 (TC), TC00114 .... 18.310
Seaton Parochial Church Council (VTD 18742) 55.89
Seaton Sands Ltd & Others (No 1) (VTD 13879) 67.75
Seaton Sands Ltd & Others (No 2) (VTD 15381) 2.527
Secret Hotels2 Ltd, UT [2011] UKUT 308 (TCC); [2011] STC 1750 .... 1.29
Secretary of State for Employment, R *v* (ex p. Equal Opportunities Commission), HL [1994] 1 All ER 910 .... 22.36
Secretary of State for the Environment, Scout Association Trust Corporation and Others *v*, CA [2005] STC 1808; [2005] EWCA Civ 980 .... 67.10
Secretary of State for the Home Department, Khawaja *v*, HL 1983, [1984] AC 74; [1983] 1 All ER 765 .... 50.62, 50.68
Secretary of State for the Home Department, R *v*, (ex p. Brind), HL [1991] 2 WLR 588; [1991] 1 All ER 720 .... 52.452
Secretary of State for Trade & Industry *v* Frid, HL [2004] UKHL 24; [2004] All ER (D) 180 (May) 37.17
Secretary of State for Transport, Factortame Ltd & Others *v* (No 2), ECJ Case C-213/89; [1990] 1 ECR 2433; [1990] 3 CMLR 375; [1991] 1 All ER 70 .... 22.26
Secretary of State for Transport, R *v* (ex p. Factortame Ltd & Others) (No 3), ECJ Case C-48/93; [1996] 1 ECR 1029; [1996] 1 CMLR 889; [1996] 2 WLR 506; [1996] All ER (EC) 301 .... 22.31
Secretary of State for Work & Pensions, Mote *v*, CA [2007] EWCA Civ 1324 .... 2.220
Secure Areas Ltd (VTD 7969) 18.450
Securenta Göttinger Immobilienanlagen und Vermögensmanagement AG *v* Finanzamt Göttingen, ECJ Case C-437/06; [2008] STC 3473 .... 22.420
Securicor Granley Systems Ltd [1990] VATTR 9 (VTD 4575) 40.95
Security Despatch Ltd [2001] VATDR 392 (VTD 17313) 2.478
Sedat (K) (t/a Sherry's Kebab & Burger Bar) (VTD 9566) 50.103
Seddon Investments (VTD 15679) 44.148
See Europe Ltd (VTD 6926) 18.563
Seeling *v* Finanzamt Starnberg, ECJ Case C-269/00; [2003] STC 805 .... 22.182
Sefton I-Tec Ltd (VTD 7813) 52.344
Segger (Mrs GA) (VTD 18673) 50.10
SEH Holdings Ltd [2000] VATDR 324 (VTD 16771) 6.2
Selbix Ltd (VTD 20473) 36.21
Selected Growers Ltd (VTD 10) 59.1
Selfridges Retail Ltd [2007] VATDR 264 (VTD 20314) 58.11
Sellco Ltd [2006] VATDR 57 (VTD 19752) 2.144
Sellhire Autos Ltd (VTD 10568) 44.65
Selmar Burglar Alarms Co Ltd (VTD 7740) 18.421
Selwyn (L) [1986] VATTR 142 (VTD 2135) 51.103
Semec (Engineering) Ltd (VTD 5963) 18.191
Sempra Metals Ltd, CIR *v*, HL [2007] STC 1559 .... 2.518
Senator Marketing Ltd (VTD 5598) 40.89

Senergy (UK) Ltd (VTD 19727) 36.122
Senes Sportswear Ltd (VTD 5930) 18.214
Senit Steels Ltd (VTD 6898) 52.149
Sergeant (BK) (VTD 9039) 52.178
Serpes (M) (VTD 20906) 2.460
Servewell Site Services Ltd (VTD 3291) 18.109
Service Authority for the National Crime Squad and Others, ex p., R v HM Treasury &
  Another, QB [2000] STC 638 .... 42.8
Sessions (DG & Mrs C) (VTD 13162) 52.392
SET (Services) Ltd (VTD 7420) 52.116
Setar Lines Ltd (VTD 316) 36.137
Setlode Ltd (VTD 7765) 36.329
Seto (SY), CS 1980, [1981] STC 698 .... 3.2
Seven (J) Ltd [1986] VATTR 42 (VTD 2024) 24.17
Severnside Machinery Ltd (VTD 10828) 52.151
Severnside Siren Trust Ltd [2000] VATDR 497 (VTD 16640) 11.14
Seward (D) (VTD 14706) 67.80
Sewards (Electrical) Ltd (VTD 9709) 18.307
Seymour Caravan Sales Ltd, Ch D [2007] STC 309; [2007] EWHC 442 (Ch) 48.8
Seymour Hunter Ltd (VTD 18284) 18.543
Seymour Limousines Ltd (VTD 20966) 2.488
SFU Barbers Ltd (VTD 19851) 57.195
SGS Holding UK Ltd (VTD 13018) 17.9
Shabani (AR) (E482) 34.3
Shad (MA) (t/a MA Shad Newsagents) (VTD 13145) 57.189
Shadow Photographic Ltd, [2010] UKFTT 467 (TC), TC00729 .... 57.153
Shafiq (M) (VTD 18815) 57.216
Shaft Sports Ltd [1983] VATTR 180 (VTD 1451) 2.20
Shaklee International & Another, CA [1981] STC 776 .... 8.3
Shalden Millennium Committee (VTD 17897) 19.85
Shalloe (M) (VTD 6234) 18.600
Shamrock Leasing Ltd [1998] VATDR 323 (VTD 15719) 62.505
Shamrock Sports & Social Club (VTD 12767) 18.250
Shan Trading Ltd (VTD 15726) 18.83
Shanahan (MJ) (t/a MJS Haulage) (VTD 12634) 18.447
Shani Fashion Industries Ltd (VTD 9789) 40.57
Shanks (Mrs F) (VTD 11015) 57.213
Shanks, Lord Advocate v, CS [1992] STC 928 .... 2.196
Sharif (M) (VTD 1701, 1886) 2.195
Sharland (W & B) (t/a Sharlands Fir Tree Café) (VTD 17387) 2.290
Sharp (Mrs JP) (VTD 6795) 62.383
Sharp (S) & Lockwood (B) (t/a Northern Carpet Group) (VTD 18235) 62.336
Sharpe (CG) (VTD 7679) 18.186
Sharpe (K) (VTD 8914) 51.38
Sharples (DY) (VTD 16234) 57.61
Sharples (JFB & FR) [2008] VATDR 618 (VTD 20775) 15.39
Sharuna Jewellers [1979] VATTR 14 (VTD 709) 67.59
Shatliff (Mrs A) (VTD 17431) 2.189
Shaw (GT) & Whilock (MA) (VTD 3530) 18.325
Shaw (MJ) (t/a Shaw Associates) (VTD 15099) 36.469
Shaw (PJR), Ch D 2006, [2007] STC 1525; [2006] EWHC 3699 (Ch) 44.116
Shaw Lane Estates (VTD 4420) 36.204
Shazia Fashion Fabrics (VTD 7184) 2.327
Shazia Fashion Fabrics (VTD 11020) 50.143
Sheard (J) (VTD 6318) 18.51
Shearer (EC) (VTD 10608) 62.561
Shearer Holdings Ltd (VTD 7088) 18.395
Shearing (HT) (VTD 16723) 7.26
Sheepcote Commercial (Vehicles) Ltd (VTD 2378) 40.88
Sheet & Roll Convertors Ltd (VTD 7991B) 36.382
Sheffield & Rotherham Nursing Agency (VTD 11279) 33.22

Sheffield Co-Operative Society Ltd [1987] VATTR 216 (VTD 2549) 46.22
Sheftz (Mrs S), [2009] UKFTT 316 (TC), TC00260 .... 35.19
Sheikh (R) (VTD 15684) 51.123
Sheiling Trust (Ringwood Waldorf School) [2006] VATDR 1(VTD 19472) 15.93
Shek (CY & TY) (t/a The Golden Bowl Café) (VTD 16509) 2.302
Shek (WS & CK) (t/a Wing Lee Carry Out) (VTD 17047) 34.6
Shek (WS & CK) (t/a Wing Lee Carry Out) (No 2) (VTD 17247) 50.101
Sheldon (P) (t/a Nova Gold) (VTD 16551) 31.1
Sheldon School (VTD 15300) 15.233
Sheldrake (JM) (VTD 16119) 18.585
Shelford IT Ltd [2010] UKFTT 367 (TC), TC00649 .... 36.113
Shell International Petroleum Co Ltd [2005] VATDR 503 (VTD 19345) 36.24
Shelston (Construction) Ltd (VTD 6616) 52.176
Shendish Manor Ltd [2004] VATDR 64 (VTD 18474) 65.118
Shephard (WF) (VTD 2232) 51.56
Shepherd (RW) [1994] VATTR 47 (VTD 11753) 25.35
Sheppard (RW & B) [1977] VATTR 272 (VTD 481) 41.116
Sheppard (TH) (VTD 13815) 44.46
Sheraton (Blythswood) Ltd, Villaswan Ltd v, CS 9 November 1998, Times 7.1.1999
.... 32.33
Sherburn Aero Club Ltd (VTD 18540) 24.37
Sherlock & Neal Ltd (VTD 18793) 55.72
Sherman (J) & Perilly (S), Ch D [2001] STC 733 .... 36.58
Sherratt (D & Mrs E), [2011] UKFTT 320 (TC), TC01180; [2011] UKFTT 381 (TC),
TC01236 .... 15.58
Sherriff (KJ) (VTD 10820) 18.485
Sherwin (DE) (VTD 3299) 7.19
Sherwin (JS) & Green (RK) (VTD 16396) 15.38
Shields (JW) (VTD 15154) 15.13
Shinewater Association Football Club (VTD 12938) 15.83
Shingler Risdon Associates (VTD 2981) 62.189
Shingleton, Ch D [1988] STC 190 .... 51.7
Shipping & Forwarding Enterprise (SAFE) BV, Staatssecretaris van Financiën v, ECJ
Case 320/88; [1990] 1 ECR 285; [1991] STC 627; [1993] 3 CMLR 547 .... 22.151
Shipquay Enterprises Ltd (VTD 6741) 52.378
Shire Equip Ltd (VTD 1464) 65.4
Shiri Guru Nanaka Sikh Temple (VTD 14972) 15.201
Shirlaw Allan & Co (VTD 2596) 18.412
Shokar (MS) (t/a Manor Fish Bar) [1998] VATDR 301 (VTD 15674) 17.16
Shokrollahi (B) (t/a BS Mondial) (VTD 13781) 35.15
Shomdul (MSI) (VTD 6348) 18.120
Shoot Super Soccer Ltd (VTD 6882) 52.69
Shore (A) (VTD 5799) 52.130
Short (B) (VTD 6694) 18.402
Short (HR) [1983] VATTR 94 (VTD 1408) 57.94
Short (RK) (VTD 4296) 62.56
Shorter (MJ) (t/a Ideal Scaffolding) (VTD 17277) 65.71
Showmarch Marketing Ltd, QB 1993, [1994] STC 19 .... 67.161
Showtry Ltd (VTD 10028) 30.9
Shroufi (S & H) (t/a Morris Grange Nursing Home) (VTD 14852) 15.197
Shrowder (W) (VTD 20912) 14.103
Shurgard Storage Centres UK Ltd (VTD 20797) 6.11
Shute (JW & YE) (VTD 11303) 18.458
Shutt (AJ) (VTD 9817) 1.74
Shuttleworth & Co, [1994] VATTR 355 (VTD 12805) 62.340
Siberian Trading Co Ltd (VTD 14229) 8.4
Siddique (M) (VTD 9244) 52.213
Siddiquee (SH) (VTD 20295) 3.54
Sidgwick (R), [2010] UKFTT 421 (TC), TC00695 .... 15.237
Sig Video Gems Ltd (VTD 12486) 18.13
Sign Specialists Ltd (VTD 4477) 18.425

Silicon Graphics Finance SA, oao, R *v* HMRC, QB [2006] EWHC 1889 (Admin); [2006] All ER (D) 311 (Jul) 2.95
Silicon Valley Estates Ltd (VTD 11017) 7.42
Silver (G), [2011] UKFTT 644 (TC), TC01486 .... 15.52
Silver Knight Exhibitions Ltd (VTD 10569) 52.264
Silver Software Consultants Ltd (VTD 19236) 18.216
Silverdale Transport Ltd (VTD 5192) 18.44
Silvermere Golf and Equestrian Centre Ltd, [1981] VATTR 106 (VTD 1122) 40.102
Silversafe Ltd *v* Hood & Others, Ch D 2006, [2007] STC 871; [2006] EWHC 1849 (Ch) 22.566
Sim (JP) & Co (VTD 2543) 18.376
Simister (AG & Mrs W) (VTD 12715) 15.21
Simkins Partnership (The) (VTD 9705) 52.96
Simmenthal SpA, Amministrazione delle Finanze dello Stato *v*, ECJ Case 106/77; [1978] ECR 629; [1978] 3 CMLR 263 .... 22.22
Simmons (B & PD) (VTD 7996) 4.3
Simmons (E) (VTD 6622) 19.49
Simon Harris Hair Design Ltd [1996] VATDR 177 (VTD 13939) 41.85
Simon Macczak Transport (VTD 10887) 52.125
Simplelink Ltd (t/a Homecare Exteriors) (VTD 11593) 52.111
Simply Cross-stitch [1985] VATTR 241 (VTD 1968) 1.94
Simply Travel Ltd, Ch D 2001, [2002] STC 194 .... 63.24
Simpson & Marwick [2010] UKFTT 380 (TC); [2011] SFTD 1, TC00662 .... 4.9
Simpson (M) & Scoffin (G) (VTD 7390) 18.394
Sims (CJ), [2010] SFTD 674; [2010] UKFTT 73 (TC), TC00386 .... 28.7
Sims (Mrs DA) (t/a Supersonic Snacks), (R *v* C & E, ex p.), QB 1987, [1988] STC 210 .... 29.25
Sims (MJC) (VTD 5928) 18.491
Sinclair (A) (t/a The Magpie Bar) (VTD 6589) 18.425
Sinclair (B) (VTD 18079) 57.206
Sinclair (D & J) (VTD 17961) 3.65
Sinclair (IC) (t/a Ian Sinclair & Son) (VTD 12842) 3.122
Sinclair Collis Ltd, ECJ Case C-275/01; [2003] STC 898 .... 22.340
Sinclair Developments Ltd (1466) 36.349
Singer & Friedlander Ltd [1989] VATTR 27 (VTD 3274) 62.481
Singh (B) (VTD 7584) 52.329
Singh (B) (t/a BS Construction), [2009] UKFTT 245 (TC), TC00194 .... 57.91
Singh (D & J) (t/a Sandhu Brothers) (VTD 9387) 50.79
Singh (J) & Kaur (G) (t/a Denim House Clothing Co) (VTD 14532) 65.91
Singh (KA) (t/a Borealis) (VTD 20956) 57.151
Singh (M) (VTD 18179) 57.123
Singh (M & N) (t/a The Food Palace & Wine King) (VTD 16378) 47.32
Singh (R) (t/a Best Buy Conventional Store) (VTD 13011) 58.10
Singh (RK) (VTD 2433) 12.16
Singh (M & J) *v* HM Advocate, HCJ(S) [2001] STC 790 .... 14.96
Singh & Choudry (VTD 7654) 18.404
Sinnett (AT) (VTD 14201) 36.646
Sir Christopher Wren's House Ltd [2006] VATDR 399 (VTD 19504) 18.344
Sir John Astor [1981] VATTR 174 (VTD 1030) 62.361
Siri Behavioural Health (VTD 19016) 11.52
Sirpal Trading Co Ltd (VTD 13288) 3.101
SIS (Science in Sport) Ltd [2000] VATDR 194 (VTD 16555) 29.91
SIS (Science in Sport) Ltd (No 2) (VTD 17116) 29.138
Sisson (RA) (VTD 1056) 36.185
Sitar Tandoori Restaurant *v* C & E Commrs, QB [1993] STC 591 .... 2.66
Sitta *v* Slovakia, ECHR Case C-48144/06; 26 October 2010 unreported 34.29
Sittingbourne, Milton & District Chamber of Commerce (341) 36.504
Sixth Gear Experience Ltd (VTD 20890) 44.52
SJ Grange Ltd, CA 1978, [1979] STC 183; [1979] 1 WLR 239 .... 3.114
SJ Grange Ltd (VTD 884) 3.49
SJ Phillips Ltd (VTD 17717) 40.101

Skandinaviska Enskilda Banken AB Momsgrupp *v* Skatteverket, ECJ Case C-540/09; [2011] STC 1125 .... 22.367
Skatteministeriet *v* Henriksen, ECJ Case 173/88; [1989] ECR 2763, [1990] STC 768; [1990] 3 CMLR 558 .... 22.332
Skatteministeriet, Assurandør-Societetet (on behalf of Taksatorringen) *v*, ECJ Case C-8/01; [2006] STC 1842 .... 22.326
Skatteministeriet, Cimber Air A/S *v*, ECJ Case C-382/02; [2005] STC 547 .... 22.393
Skatteministeriet, CopyGene A/S *v*, ECJ Case C-262/08; [2010] STC 1799 .... 22.277
Skatteministeriet, Danfoss A/S *v*, ECJ Case C-371/07; 11 December 2008 unreported 22.186
Skatteministeriet, Dansk Denkavit ApS & Others *v*, ECJ Case C-200/90; [1992] 1 ECR 2217; [1994] 2 CMLR 377; [1994] STC 482 .... 22.41, 22.527
Skatteministeriet, De Danske Bilimportører *v*, ECJ Case C-98/05; [2006] 1 ECR 4945 .... 22.255
Skatteministeriet, Fonden Marselisborg Lystbådehavn *v*, ECJ Case C-428/02; [2006] STC 1467 .... 22.342
Skatteministeriet, I/S Fini H *v* , ECJ Case C-32/03; [2005] STC 903 .... 22.105
Skatteministeriet, Jyske Finans A/S *v*, ECJ Case C-280/04; [2006] STC 1744 .... 22.350
Skatteministeriet, Lady & Kid A/S *v*, ECJ Case C-398/09; 6 September 2011 unreported 22.560
Skatteministeriet, NCC Construction Danmark A/S *v*, ECJ Case C-174/08; [2010] STC 532 .... 22.452
Skatteministeriet, Nordania Finans A/S *v*, ECJ Case C-98/07; [2008] STC 3314 .... 22.451
Skatteministeriet, Sparekassernes Datacenter *v*, ECJ Case C-2/95; [1997] STC 932; [1997] 1 ECR 3017; [1997] 3 CMLR 999; [1997] All ER (EC) 610 .... 22.357
Skatteverket *v* AB SKF, ECJ Case C-29/08; [2010] STC 419 .... 22.366
Skatteverket, Aktiebolaget NN *v*, ECJ Case C-111/05; [2008] STC 3203 .... 22.196
Skatteverket, Kollektivavtalsstiftelsen TRR Trygghetsrådet *v*, ECJ Case C-291/07; [2009] STC 526 .... 20.36
Skatteverket, Skandinaviska Enskilda Banken AB Momsgrupp *v*, ECJ Case C-540/09; [2011] STC 1125 .... 22.367
Skatteverket, X *v*, ECJ Case C-84/09; [2011] STC 189 .... 20.18
Skellett (CH) (t/a Vidcom Computer Services), CS 2003, [2004] STC 201 .... 44.111
Skelmersdale Centre Ltd (The) (VTD 18813) 62.384
Skelton Waste Disposal (VTD 17351) 62.370
Skeltools Ltd (VTD 968) 36.344
Skilton & Gregory (VTD 11723) 29.47
Skingrade Ltd (VTD 4377) 18.214
Skinner (DL), [2010] UKFTT 64 (TC), TC00376 .... 28.5
Skipton Building Society (TC00146) 46.77
SKN Electronics Ltd (VTD 10210) 2.429
Skripalle, Finanzamt Bergisch Gladbach *v*, ECJ Case C-63/96; [1997] STC 1035; [1997] 1 ECR 2847 .... 22.500
Skytech Aluminium Stockholding & Distribution Ltd (VTD 14023) 4.22
Slaby *v* Minister Finansów, ECJ Case C-180/10; [2011] STC 2230 .... 20.5
Slack (O) & Taylor (M) (t/a Olives) (VTD 537) 2.350
Slater (D) (VTD 12020) 18.120
Slater (N) (VTD 9865) 51.60
Sleaford Rugby Football Club (VTD 9844) 13.41
Slee Blackwell Solicitors (VTD 7263) 18.436
Sloan Electronics Ltd (VTD 16062) 53.1
Slot (AC) (VTD 15076) 36.50, 41.144
Slouand Ltd (VTD 11701) 52.281
Slough Motor Co (VTD 11818) 18.538
Slovakia, Pokrivka *v*, ECHR Case C-35933/06; 26 October 2010 unreported 34.29
Slovakia, Sitta *v*, ECHR Case C-4814/06; 26 October 2010 unreported 34.29
SM & E Properties Ltd (VTD 7140) 52.136
Small & Co Ltd (VTD 9642) 2.387
Smallcorn, Hawthorn *v*, Ch D [1998] STC 591 .... 47.72
Smalley (JH) (No 1) (VTD 3894) 36.203
Smalley (JH) (No 2), [2011] UKFTT 134 (TC), TC01008 .... 36.228

Smallman (JE) (VTD 7228) 52.69
Smallman (R) (VTD 11538) 18.410
Smart (TL) (t/a On Tour Catering) (VTD 10303) 18.608
Smart Alec Ltd (VTD 17832) 12.20
Smart County Personnel Ltd (VTD 3751) 18.138
Smart Voucher Ltd, [2009] UKFTT 169 (TC), TC00131 .... 62.545
Smarter Money Ltd, [2006] VATDR 296 (VTD 19632) 27.27
Smartone Connect Ltd (VTD 12789) 14.8
Smith (A & IA) (VTD 4995) 2.322
Smith (AD) (VTD 2164) 15.78
Smith (AR & A) (t/a Ginger's Fish & Chip Shop) (VTD 5694) 50.105
Smith (ARM) (VTD 2954) 29.117
Smith (AW) (VTD 19113) 52.424
Smith (Dr DA) (VTD 6598) 51.76
Smith (DA) (VTD 1830) 36.569
Smith (DA) (t/a Varcom Sailplane Computers) (VTD 14196) 67.79
Smith (DB) (VTD 5561) 51.85
Smith (DC) (VTD 11382) 52.347
Smith (DE) (VTD 6668) 10.3
Smith (J) (t/a Morecambe Used Car Centre) (VTD 554) 44.63
Smith (JG) (VTD 2917) 51.58
Smith (JH) (LON/x, 23 June 1999 unreported) 2.218
Smith (JMC) (t/a Qualified School of Motoring) (VTD 20275) 21.31
Smith (J & A) (t/a Ty Gwyn Hotel) (VTD 17406) 47.27
Smith (J & SF) (VTD 16190) 47.26
Smith (M) (VTD 18393) 57.91
Smith (M, G & N), [2001] VATDR 323 (VTD 17035) 15.181
Smith (Mrs ME) (VTD 6921) 51.81
Smith (N) (Mr & Mrs) (VTD 5579) 15.35
Smith (N) (t/a The Chippy) (VTD 11806) 57.122
Smith (NP) (VTD 19064) 55.5
Smith (P) & Ashton (AR) (VTD 3317) 62.412
Smith (R) (t/a Ray Smith Associates) (VTD 6624) 10.3
Smith (RH) (t/a Robert H Smith Investments & Consulting), [2011] UKFTT 576 (TC),
    TC01419 .... 45.6
Smith (RM) (t/a Smiths Auto Services) (VTD 19702) 44.164
Smith (T) (VTD 1155) 36.621
Smith (T & M) (VTD 13052) 41.130
Smith v Brough, CA [2005] EWCA Civ 261 .... 2.175
Smith, ex p., R v Ministry of Defence, CA 1995, [1996] QB 517; [1996] 1 All ER 257
    .... 42.8
Smith & Byford Ltd, [1996] VATDR 386 (VTD 14512) 50.141
Smith & Choyce Ltd (VTD 7817) 18.511
Smith & Williamson [1976] VATTR 215 (VTD 281) 43.14
Smith Kline Beecham plc [1993] VATTR 219 (VTD 10222) 29.136
Smith Kline Beecham plc (No 2) (VTD 13674) 29.167
Smith Parkinson (EH) (Motors) Ltd (VTD 4289) 18.182
Smith Wheeler and Hay (VTD 1208) 36.140
Smithers (MJ) (VTD 16100) 18.484
Smiths Foods Ltd [1983] VATTR 21 (VTD 1346) 29.141
Smitmit Design Centre Ltd, QB [1982] STC 525 .... 15.222
SMS Stores Ltd (VTD 17226) 40.47
Smyth (BA) (VTD 5039) 18.141
Snaddon (J) (VTD 19964) 51.179
Snaith (R) (t/a English Rose Collection) (VTD 16997) 62.235
Snape (CJ & K) (t/a The Homelea Hotel) (VTD 13465) 50.152
Snapple Beverage Corporation (VTD 13690) 29.175
Sneller (HK) (VTD 2556) 3.171
Snook v London & West Riding Investments Ltd, CA [1967] 2 QB 786; [1967] 1 All ER
    518 .... 10.6
Snow (FD) (VTD 13283) 51.181

Snow & Rock Sports Ltd (VTD 3223) 18.297
Snushall Dalby & Robinson QB, [1982] STC 537 .... 5.93
SOC Private Capital Ltd [2002] VATDR 179 (VTD 17747) 38.15
Social Surveys (Gallup Poll) Ltd (VTD 3775) 18.255
Social Workline Ltd (VTD 10351) 52.18
Société Anonyme Gondrand Freres, Administration des Douanes v, ECJ Case 169/80;
  [1981] ECR 1931 .... 22.548
Société Comateb & Others v Directeur Général des Douanes et droits indirects, ECJ
  Case C-192/95; [1997] STC 1006; [1997] 1 ECR 165; [1997] 2 CMLR 649 .... 22.559
Société Financière d'Investissements SPRL (SFI) v Belgian State, ECJ Case C-85/97;
  [2000] STC 164 .... 22.53
Société Générale des Grandes Sources d'Eaux Minérales Françaises v Bundesamt
  für Finanzen, ECJ Case C-361/96; [1998] STC 981 .... 22.538
Société Internationale de Télécommunications Aeronautiques (No 1) (VTD 19) 66.44
Société Internationale de Télécommunications Aeronautiques (No 2), [2003] VATDR
  131 (VTD 17991) 2.124
Société Internationale de Télécommunications Aeronautiques (No 3), Ch D 2003, [2004]
  STC 950; [2003] EWHC 3039(Ch) 66.45
Société Monte Dei Paschi Di Siena, Ministre du Budget v, ECJ Case C-136/99; [2001]
  STC 1029 .... 22.531
Société Thermale d'Eugénie-les-Bains v Ministère de l'Économie, des Finances et de
  l'Industrie, ECJ Case C-277/05; [2008] STC 2470 .... 22.86
Sofitam SA v Ministre chargé du Budget, ECJ Case C-333/91; [1993] 1 ECR 3513;
  [1997] STC 226 .... 22.443
Soft Solutions Ltd (VTD 4793) 18.506
Softley Ltd (t/a Softley Kitchens) (VTD 15034) 19.26
Software One Ltd (VTD 11090) 52.146
Soka Gakkai International UK (VTD 14175) 41.99
Solihull Sports Services Ltd (VTD 2713) 36.360
Sollac SA (VTD 13688) 18.85
Solleveld v Staatssecretaris van Financiën, ECJ Case C-443/04; [2007] STC 71 ..... 22.284
Solomon's Kebab House (VTD 13560) 3.126
Solution Seekers Ltd (VTD 20817) 18.143
Somerset Car Sales Ltd (VTD 11986) 23.19
Somerset County Council, Costello v, CA [1993] 1 WLR 256 .... 2.181, 2.182, 2.183
Somji (AF) (t/a Akber & Co) (VTD 18443) 18.531
Sonat Offshore (UK) Inc (VTD 14021) 2.153
Soni (A & M) (VTD 9919) 52.74
Soni (GR) [1980] VATTR 9 (VTD 897) 29.82
Sonnat Ltd (VTD 5436) 18.43
Sood (BK & Mrs U) (t/a Good News) (VTD 9950) 52.301
Sooner Foods Ltd, QB [1983] STC 376 .... 62.363
Sophia Ltd (VTD 7261) 18.417
Sophie Holdings Ltd, [2009] UKFTT 88 (TC), TC00056 .... 3.81
Sorisi (P) (VTD 15453) 62.272
Sorrell (TG) [1980] VATTR 53 (VTD 913) 47.15
Sosnowska v Dyrektor Izby Skarbowej we Wrocɜawiu Oœrodek Zamiejscowy w
  Waɜbrzychu, ECJ Case C-25/07; 10 July 2008 unreported 22.440
Soul, CIR v, CA 1976, 51 TC 86 .... 2.196
Soul Jazz Records (VTD 11066) 51.123
Soundmethods Ltd (VTD 14523) 14.13
Soundvision Ltd (VTD 12977) 18.586
Source Enterprise Ltd (The) (VTD 7881) 45.9
Souter (DJ) (t/a Brodie Duncan Marketing) (VTD 18515) 52.448
South Aston Community Association (VTD 17702) 15.113
South Caernarvon Creameries Ltd (VTD 6230) 52.122
South Hams Nursing Agency (VTD 13027) 62.317
South Herefordshire Golf Club (No 1) (VTD 19653) 24.44
South Herefordshire Golf Club (No 2) (VTD 19767) 2.365
South Liverpool Housing Ltd (VTD 18750) 42.21
South Molton Swimming Pool Trustees (VTD 16495) 15.106

South Tyne Chalets Ltd (VTD 7377) 52.347
South Wales Home Care Ltd (VTD 19170) 36.588
South Wales Industrial Valve Services Ltd (VTD 5222) 18.506
South West Launderettes Ltd (VTD 2608) 57.36
South Yorkshire Style Tile (VTD 20175) 14.74
Southampton & South-West Hampshire Health Authority, Marshall v, ECJ Case 152/84;
   [1986] 1 CMLR 688; [1986] ECR 723; [1986] 2 All ER 584 .... 22.14
Southampton Leisure Holdings plc [2002] VATDR 235 (VTD 17716) 46.43
Southchurch Workingmen's Club & Institute Ltd (VTD 613) 13.4
Southcombe Brothers Ltd (VTD 10151) 52.39
Southend United Football Club (VTD 11919) 62.155
Southend United Football Club (No 2) [1997] VATDR 202 (VTD 15109) 41.155
Southern Counties Lighting Ltd (VTD 11438) 62.322
Southern County Taverns Ltd (VTD 18306) 18.186
Southern Fabrics Ltd (VTD 4781) 18.286
Southern Girl Ltd (VTD 1803) 2.352
Southern Groundworks (VTD 5970) 18.563
Southern Primary Housing Ltd, CA 2003. [2004] STC 209; [2003] EWCA Civ 1662
   .... 46.26
Southern Ski Enterprises Ltd (VTD 13797) 18.108
Southern UK Breeders (VTD 15303) 44.127
Southill Sawmills Ltd (VTD 17337) 52.128
Southlong East Midlands Ltd (VTD 18943) 55.26
Southwest Blasting Ltd (VTD 9657) 52.7
Southwick Community Association [2002] VATDR 288 (VTD 17601) 15.88
Sovereign Finance plc (VTD 16237) 46.163
Sovereign Street Workplace Ltd (VTD 9550) 41.26
Sozialdemokratische Partei Österreichs Landesorganisation Kärnten v Finanzamt
   Klagenfurt, ECJ Case C-267/08; [2010] STC 287 .... 22.120
SP Graham Ltd & Others (VTD 14789) 57.105
SP Wound Components Ltd (VTD 19836) 18.543
Spa & Resort Operations Ltd (VTD 20979) 67.174
Spain (FP) (VTD 1555) 40.27
Spain (Kingdom of), EC Commission v, ECJ Case C-73/92; [1993] 1 ECR 5997; [1997]
   STC 700; [1995] 2 CMLR 1 .... 22.219
Spain (Kingdom of), EC Commission v, ECJ Case C-124/96; [1998] STC 1237 ..... 22.313
Spain (Kingdom of), EC Commission v, ECJ Case C-414/97; 16 September 1999
   unreported 22.102
Spain (Kingdom of), EC Commission v, ECJ Case C-83/99; 18 January 2001
   unreported 22.262
Spain (Kingdom of), EC Commission v, ECJ Case C-204/03; [2006] STC 1087 ..... 22.449
Spain (Kingdom of), EC Commission v, ECJ Case C-154/08; 12 November 2009
   unreported 22.98
Span Computer Contracts Ltd (VTD 6323, 6461) 18.79
Sparekassernes Datacenter v Skatteministeriet, ECJ Case C-2/95; [1997] STC 932;
   [1997] 1 ECR 3017; [1997] 3 CMLR 999; [1997] All ER (EC) 610 .... 22.357
Spargo [1873] Ch 407 .... 10.12
Sparkholme Ltd (t/a Top Class Sauna) (VTD 19187) 62.275
Sparrow (UK) Ltd (VTD 16642) 40.74
Spearing (QEN) (VTD 16314) 18.261
Spearmint Rhino Ventures (UK) Ltd, Ch D [2007] STC 1252; [2007] EWHC 613(Ch)
   .... 62.283
Special Commissioners v Pemsel, HL 1891, 3 TC 53 .... 15.82
Specialised Cars Ltd (VTD 11123) 44.25
Specialist Computer Holdings Ltd, [2007] VATDR 396 (VTD 20440) 18.444
Specialist Rainwater Services Ltd (VTD 7732) 52.277
Speciality Restaurants plc (VTD 10310) 18.33
Specsavers Optical Group [2003] VATDR 268 (VTD 18025) 48.127
Specsavers Optical Group (No 2) [2003] VATDR 268 (VTD 18186) 48.128
Speedy Products Ltd (VTD 6754) 18.386
Spellar (JD) (t/a Allied Satellite Systems) (VTD 6829) 52.237

Spelthorne Borough Council (VTD 6958) 52.58
Spence (N) (VTD 20563) 65.103
Spence (WP & Mrs DKM) (VTD 5698) 57.51
Spencer & Harrison (VTD 10697) 52.271
Spencer (D) (VTD 19416) 40.59
Spiby (JE & K) (t/a Spymore Wall Coverings) (VTD 1812) 2.195
Spicer (RD & EC) (VTD 13858) 44.148
Spicer Kilpatrick Ltd (VTD 18384) 52.347
Spigot Lodge Ltd, QB [1985] STC 255 .... 62.365
Spijkers (JMA) v Gevroeders Benedik Abattoir CV, ECJ Case 24/85; [1986] ECR 1119;
  [1986] 2 CMLR 296 .... 22.166
Spillane (M), QB 1989, [1990] STC 212 .... 3.4, 36.233
Spillane and Others, EMI Records v, Ch D [1986] STC 374 .... 14.88
Spinnaker MDC Ltd (VTD 7841) 52.17
Spoils Kitchen Reject Shops Ltd (VTD 2200) 36.463
Spokes (JF) (VTD 10191) 51.89
Sport in Desford (VTD 18914) 15.86
Sportswords Ltd (VTD 11178) 36.364
Sprake (A) (t/a Sprake & Tyrell) (VTD 10391) 2.459
Springback Investments Ltd (VTD 11849) 18.305
Springfield China Ltd (VTD 4546) 59.26
Springvale EPS Ltd (VTD 7421) 52.125
Sprintman Ltd (VTD 5810) 18.475
Sprosson (GAW) (VTD 12073) 18.577
Sprowston Hall Hotel Ltd (VTD 7253) 52.85
Spurtrade Ltd (VTD 2290) 51.57
Square Moves Ltd (VTD 5050) 18.264
Squibb & Davies (Demolition) Ltd (VTD 17829) 44.135
Squire (A) (VTD 5821) 18.480
Squires (Miss D) (VTD 1436) 36.374
SRI International, UT [2011] UKUT 240 (TCC); [2011] STC 1614 .... 45.2
Srl CILFIT and Lanificio di Gavardo SpA v Ministro della Sanita, ECJ Case 283/81;
  [1982] ECR 3415; [1983] 1 CMLR 472 .... 22.3
SSAFA Forces Help (VTD 19832) 19.62
SSL Ltd (VTD 2478) 36.323
SSR Group Services Ltd (VTD 16033) 18.40
SSY Research Services Ltd (VTD 7306) 52.127
Staatssecretaris van Financiën v Arthur Andersen & Co, ECJ Case C-472/03; [2005]
  STC 508 .... 22.327
Staatssecretaris van Financiën v Coffeeshop Siberië vof, ECJ Case C-158/98; [1999] STC
  742; [1999] All ER (EC) 560 .... 22.83
Staatssecretaris van Financiën v Cooperatieve Vereniging 'Cooperatieve
  Aardappelenbewaarplaats GA', ECJ Case 154/80; [1981] ECR 445; [1981] 3 CMLR
  337 .... 22.78
Staatssecretaris van Financiën v Facet Holding BV, ECJ Case C-539/08; [2010] STC
  1701 .... 22.411
Staatssecretaris van Financiën v Heerma, ECJ Case C-23/98; [2001] STC 1437 ..... 22.108
Staatssecretaris van Financiën v Hong Kong Trade Development Council, ECJ Case
  89/81; [1982] ECR 1277; [1983] 1 CMLR 73 .... 22.79
Staatssecretaris van Financiën v Lipjes, ECJ Case C-68/03; [2004] STC 1592 .... 22.515
Staatssecretaris van Financiën v Shipping & Forwarding Enterprises (SAFE) BV, ECJ
  Case 320/88; [1990] 1 ECR 285; [1991] STC 627; [1993] 3 CMLR 547 .... 22.151
Staatssecretaris van Financiën v Stadeco BV, ECJ Case C-566/07; [2009] STC 1639
  .... 22.465
Staatssecretaris van Financiën v Stichting Kinderopvang Enschede, ECJ Case C-415/04;
  [2007] STC 294 .... 22.301
Staatssecretaris van Financiën v VDP Dental Laboratory NV, ECJ Case C-401/05; [2007]
  STC 474 .... 22.289
Staatssecretaris van Financiën v Velker International Oil Co Ltd NV, ECJ Case
  C-185/89; [1990] 1 ECR 2561; [1991] STC 640 .... 22.389
Staatssecretaris van Financiën v X, ECJ Case C-536/08; [2010] STC 1701 .... 22.411

Staatssecretaris van Financiën, Charles & Charles-Tijmens *v*, ECJ Case C-434/03; [2006]
STC 1429 .... 22.183
Staatssecretaris van Financiën, de Jong (P) *v*, ECJ Case C-20/91; [1992] 1 ECR 2847;
[1992] 3 CMLR 260; [1995] STC 727 .... 22.163
Staatssecretaris van Financiën, Don Bosco Onroerend Goed BV *v*, ECJ Case C-461/08;
[2010] STC 476 .... 22.378
Staatssecretaris van Financiën, Euro Tyre Holding BV *v*, ECJ Case C-430/09; [2011]
STC 798 .... 22.522
Staatssecretaris van Financiën, Fiscale eenheid Koninklijke Ahold NV *v*, ECJ Case
C-484/06; [2009] STC 45 .... 22.562
Staatssecretaris van Financiën, Gemeente Leusden *v*, ECJ Case C-487/01; [2004] All ER
(D) 351 (Apr) 22.459
Staatssecretaris van Financiën, Genius Holding BV *v*, ECJ Case 342/87; [1989] ECR
4227; [1991] STC 239 .... 22.413
Staatssecretaris van Financiën, Harnas & Helm CV *v*, ECJ Case C-80/95; [1997] STC
364; [1997] 1 ECR 745, [1997] 1 CMLR 649; [1997] All ER (EC) 267 .... 22.112
Staatssecretaris van Financiën, Holin Groep BV cs *v*, ECJ Case C-7/02; [2004] All ER
(D) 351 (Apr) 22.459
Staatssecretaris van Financiën, Hout van Eijnsbergen *v*, ECJ Case C-444/04; [2007] STC
71 .... 22.284
Staatsecretaris van Financiën, Investrand BV *v*, ECJ Case C-435/05; [2008] STC 518
.... 22.408
Staatsecretaris van Financiën, JCM Beheer BV *v*, ECJ Case C-124/07; [2008] STC
3360 .... 22.328
Staatsecretaris van Financiën, Kennemer Golf & Country Club *v*, ECJ Case C-174/00;
[2002] STC 502; [2002] 3 WLR 829; [2002] All ER (EC) 480 .... 22.315
Staatssecretaris van Financiën, Leesportfeuille 'Intiem' CV *v*, ECJ Case 165/86;
[1988] ECR 1471; [1989] 2 CMLR 856; [1989] 4 BVC 180 .... 22.402
Staatssecretaris van Financiën, Levob Verzekeringen BV *v*, ECJ Case C-41/04; [2006]
STC 766 .... 22.176
Staatssecretaris van Financiën, Liberexim BV *v*, ECJ Case C-371/99; [2002] All ER(D)
178(Jul) 22.192
Staatssecretaris van Financiën, Muys en De Winters's Bouw-en Aannemingsbedriff BV
v, ECJ Case C-281/91; [1997] STC 665; [1993] 1 ECR 5405; [1995] 1 CMLR 126
.... 22.354
Staatssecretaris van Financiën, Solleveld *v*, ECJ Case C-443/04; [2007] STC 71 ..... 22.284
Staatssecretaris van Financiën, Stichting Centraal Begeleidingsorgaan voor de
Intercollegiale Toetsing *v*, ECJ Case C-407/07; [2009] STC 869 .... 22.292
Staatssecretaris van Financiën, Stichting Goed Wonen *v*, ECJ Case C-326/99; [2003]
STC 1137 .... 22.156
Staatssecretaris van Financiën, Stichting Goed Wonen *v* (No 2), ECJ Case C-376/02;
[2006] STC 833 .... 22.550
Staatssecretaris van Financiën, Stichting Regionaal Opleidingen Centrum Noord-
Kennemerland/West-Friesland (Horizon College) *v*, ECJ Case C-434/05; [2008] STC
2145 .... 22.304
Staatssecretaris van Financiën, Stichting Uitvoering Financiële Acties *v*, ECJ Case
348/87; [1989] ECR 1737; [1991] 2 CMLR 429 .... 22.290
Staatssecretaris van Financiën, Twoh International BV *v*, ECJ Case C-184/05; [2008]
STC 740 .... 22.521
Staatssecretaris van Financiën, Van der Kooy *v*, ECJ Case C-181/97; 28 January 1999
unreported 22.191
Staatssecretaris van Financiën, Van Dijk's Boekhuis BV *v*, ECJ Case 139/84; [1985] ECR
1405; [1986] 2 CMLR 575 .... 22.171
Staatssecretaris van Financiën, Vereniging Noordelijke Land-en Tuinbouw Organisatie
v, ECJ Case C-515/07; 12 February 2009 unreported 22.187
Staatssecretaris van Financiën, Waterschap Zeeuws Vlaanderen *v*, ECJ Case C-378/02;
[2005] STC 1298 .... 22.454
Staatssecretaris van Financiën, X Holding BV *v*, ECJ Case C-538/08; [2010] STC
1221 .... 22.428
Stacey (L) (t/a LJ Motors) (VTD 17538) 36.427

Stadeco BV, Staatssecretaris van Financiën v , ECJ Case C-566/07; [2009] STC 1639 .... 22.465
Stadler v Finanzlandesdirektion für Vorarlberg, ECJ Case C-409/99; [2002] All ER (D) 15 (Jan) 22.433
Stadt Sundern, Finanzamt Arnberg v, ECJ Case C-43/04; 26 May 2005 unreported 22.484
Stafford (RH) (Lt Col) (VTD 3472) 51.93
Stafford & Worcester Property Co Ltd (VTD 16302) 18.623
Stafford Land Rover [1999] VATDR 471 (VTD 16388) 44.168
Staffordian Travel Ltd (VTD 15135) 50.125
Staffquest Group Holdings Ltd (VTD 17632) 3.94
Stagg (AJW) (General Builders) Ltd (VTD 6283) 18.151
Staimer Productions Ltd (VTD 1605) 65.55
Stalwart Environmental Services Ltd (VTD 7179) 52.50
Standard Flat Roofing Co Ltd (VTD 13151) 65.70
Standard Life Assurance Co [2007] VATDR 356 (VTD 20355) 46.180
Standard Tandoori Nepalese Restaurant (VTD 16458) 50.8
Standard Tandoori Nepalese Restaurant [2000] VATDR 105 (VTD 16597) 2.420
Standen Ltd (VTD 10785) 52.45
Standing Conference of Voluntary Organisations for People with a Learning Disability in Wales (VTD 17827) 51.41
Standoak Ltd (VTD 2250) 51.113
Standridge Farm Ltd (VTD 16850) 52.342
Stanhope Properties plc (VTD 6971) 52.44
Stanley (NC) (VTD 10857) 17.12
Stanley, R v, CA 17 September 1998 .... 49.6
Stanley Long & Partners (VTD 17812) 18.560
Stanton-Precious (A) & Hunt (MZ) (t/a Hogs Back Brewery) (VTD 14791) 18.206
Stanwix (J & B) & Son (VTD 6347) 36.286
Stapenhill Developments Ltd [1984] VATTR 1 (VTD 1593) 15.150
Star Automatics (VTD 311) 41.3
Stardust Leisure Ltd (VTD 9740) 36.481
Starglaze Windows & Consrvatories Ltd, [2010] UKFTT 119 (TC), TC00430 ...... 40.110
Starline & Wessex Taxis Ltd (VTD 20294) 62.238
Starlite (Chandeliers) Ltd [1999] VATDR 313 (VTD 16188) 18.448
Starmill UK Ltd (VTD 18720) 23.35
Starplex Ltd (VTD 2552) 18.186
Starr (D) (VTD 19176) 55.31
Starwest Investment Holdings Ltd (VTD 6547) 18.71
Status Cards Ltd (VTD 128) 5.9
Stave-Con Ltd (VTD 5808) 18.228
Stavrinou (Mrs RD) (VTD 12546) 52.305
Stead (T) (VTD 6650) 44.24
Steed, Norwich & Peterborough Building Society v, CA [1991] 1 WLR 449; [1991] 2 All ER 880 .... 2.182, 2.184
Steel Direct Ltd (VTD 15272) 14.29
Steel Services (Great Yarmouth) Ltd (VTD 19575) 18.619
Steel Windows Co Ltd (VTD 19158) 40.41
Steele (Mrs AM) (VTD 9017) 57.7
Steenhorst-Neerings v Bestuur van de Bedrijfsvereniging voor Detailhandel, Ambachten en Huisvrouwen, ECJ Case C-338/91; [1993] 1 ECR 5475; [1995] 3 CMLR 323 .... 22.46
Steiermärkische Landesregierung & Others, Pelzl & Others v, ECJ Cases C-338/97, C-344/97 & C-390/97; 8 June 1999 unreported 22.528
Steliana's and Saphos Ltd, MAN/07/036 (VTD 20387) 65.96
Stella Products Ltd (VTD 5494) 18.82
Stephens (MD) (VTD 3963) 18.89
Stephens Catering Equipment Co Ltd (VTD 10150) 18.233
Stephenson (DP) (t/a Sutton Chauffeuring) (VTD 9914) 18.429
Steptoe (JB), CA [1992] STC 757 .... 18.330
Sterling (Mr & Mrs) (t/a Sally's Sandwich Bar) (VTD 19057) 57.42
Stern (WG) (VTD 1970) 36.199

Steve Hill (Plant Hire) Ltd (VTD 5507) 36.416
Steven (F) (t/a City Ceramic Dental Laboratory) (VTD 16083) 33.34
Stevenson (A & JE) (t/a Prime & Co) (VTD 17166) 18.340
Stevenson (A & JE) (t/a Prime & Co) (VTD 17392) 2.485
Stevenson (C) (VTD 7598) 52.14
Stevenson (CS), CA [1996] STC 1096 .... 50.1
Stevenson, Havering London Borough Council v, [1970] 3 All ER 609 .... 62.21
Steventon & Co Ltd (E) (VTD 11250) 18.367
Stevie's Restaurant Ltd (VTD 12349) 50.115
Stewart (G) & Hammond (T) (t/a GT Shooting), CA 2001, [2002] STC 255; [2001]
    EWCA Civ 1988 .... 62.146
Stewart (MW) (t/a Sodisk) (VTD 6013) 18.90
Stewart Ward (Coins) Ltd [1986] VATTR 129 (VTD 2108) 2.224
Stewart Ward (Coins) Ltd (No 2) (VTD 2134) 40.12
Stewarts Supermarkets Ltd (VTD 13338) 29.65
Stichting Centraal Begeleidingsorgaan voor de Intercollegiale Toetsing v Staatssecretaris
    van Financiën, ECJ Case C-407/07; [2009] STC 869 .... 22.292
Stichting Goed Wonen v Staatssecretaris van Financiën, ECJ Case C-326/99; [2003] STC
    1137 .... 22.156
Stichting Goed Wonen v Staatssecretaris van Financiën (No 2), ECJ Case C-376/02;
    [2006] STC 833 .... 22.550
Stichting Kinderopvang Enschede, Staatssecretaris van Financiën v, ECJ Case C-415/04;
    [2007] STC 294 .... 22.301
Stichting Regionaal Opleidingen Centrum Noord-Kennemerland/West-Friesland
    (Horizon College) v Staatssecretaris van Financiën, ECJ Case C-434/05; [2008] STC
    2145 .... 22.304
Stichting Uitvoering Financiële Acties (SUFA) v Staatssecretaris van Financiën, ECJ Case
    348/87; [1989] ECR 1737; [1991] 2 CMLR 429 .... 22.290
Stickland (J) (VTD 5971) 18.556
Stikatak Ltd (VTD 20471) 18.543
Stirling (RWK) [1985] VATTR 232 (VTD 1963) 62.77
Stirling Council (VTD 17480) 22.147
Stirlings (Glasgow) Ltd, [1982] VATTR 116 (VTD 1232) 36.6
Stockdale (TBV) (t/a Compass Charters) (VTD 18757) 7.44
Stocken & Lambert (VTD 10527) 18.76, 18.315
Stockham (JF) (VTD 5178) 18.43
Stockholm Lindöpark AB v Sweden, ECJ Case C-150/99; [2001] STC 103 .... 22.314
Stockler (WT) (VTD 15350) 52.292
Stockton Park (Leisure) Ltd (VTD 14548) 36.574
Stockton Plant & Equipment Ltd, [1986] VATTR 94 (VTD 2093) 25.8
Stockwell Carpets Ltd (VTD 7782) 52.360
Stoke-on-Trent Citizens Advice Bureau (VTD 17296) 52.330
Stone (B) (VTD 12442) 36.57
Stone (Lt-Cmdr C), Ch D [2008] STC 2501; [2008] EWHC 1249 (Ch) 66.5
Stone (M & GA) (VTD 7798) 51.44
Stone (PJ) Ltd (VTD 2241) 36.191
Stonecliff Caravan Park, [1993] VATTR 464 (VTD 11097) 15.153, 69.6
Stonehills Television Ltd (VTD 8993) 52.124
Stoppelkamp (Raab's Administrator), Finanzamt Deggendorf v, ECJ Case C-421/10;
    [2011] STC 2358 .... 22.462
Storey (G) (VTD 17793) 50.87
Stormseal (UPVC) Window Company Ltd, [1989] VATTR 303 (VTD 4538) 62.286
Storrie (GM & JA) (VTD 14543) 36.282
Stosic (M & P) (t/a Dave & Sidas Fish Bar) (VTD 10728) 57.131
Stott (A) (VTD 15622) 2.5
Stott (JA) (VTD 15061) 50.27
Stourbridge Golf Club Ltd (VTD 3359) 18.601
Strachan (Dr AN) (VTD 2165) 19.44
Strachan (Mr & Mrs JC) (VTD 9568) 7.96
Stradasfalti Srl v Agenzia delle Entrate Ufficio di Trento, ECJ Case C-228/05; [2007]
    STC 508 .... 22.434

Strand Ship Building Co Ltd (VTD 1651) 41.150
Strangewood Ltd (R *v* C & E Commrs, ex p.), QB [1987] STC 502 .... 36.648
Strangewood Ltd (No 2), [1988] VATTR 35 (VTD 2599) 2.47
Stratford (DM) (VTD 9621) 52.185
Strathearn Gordon Associates Ltd, [1985] VATTR 79 (VTD 1884) 47.54
Stratton (B) (VTD 13185) 57.7
Stratton (R) (t/a SRG Hire) (VTD 16879) 38.2
Stream International Ltd (VTD 15602) 18.453
Streamline Taxis (Southampton) Ltd (VTD 2016) 29.44
Street *v* Mountford, HL [1995] 1 AC 809; [1985] 2 All ER 289 .... 41.159
Street Magazine Ltd (VTD 10991) 18.11
Strobel *v* Finanzamt Esslingen, ECJ Case C-454/98; [2000] STC 810 .... 22.414
Strollmoor Ltd (VTD 5454, 12765) 62.482, 62.483
Strong (UK) Ltd (VTD 10799) 52.171
Strong & Co of Romsey Ltd *v* Woodifield, HL 1906, 5 TC 215 .... 36.536
Strowbridge (JMB) (VTD 16521) 15.168
Stuttard (B & D) (t/a De Wynns Coffee House), QB [2000] STC 342 .... 50.111
Stuart & Co (Motors) Ltd [1984] VATTR 207 (VTD 1753) 44.84
Sub One (t/a Subway) (No 1), [2009] UKFTT 385 (TC), TC00320 .... 2.10
Sub One (t/a Subway) (No 2), [2010] UKFTT 487 (TC), TC00747 .... 29.80
Subhan (A), Uddin (M) & Mustak (M) (VTD 17110) 3.66
Sudholz, Finanzamt Sulingen *v*, ECJ Case C-17/01; [2005] STC 747 .... 22.502
Sue Ryder Care (VTD 18826) 46.169
Suffolk Heritage Housing Association Ltd (VTD 13713) 30.13
Sugar and Spice On Tour Catering (VTD 17698) 62.524
Suhail (A) (VTD 19448) 50.66
Suitmart (UK) Ltd (VTD 10392) 52.364
Suleyman (H, H & M) (t/a Red Rose Dry Cleaners) (VTD 13753) 53.21
Sullivan (J) (VTD 5881) 57.185
Sullivan (P) [1995] VATDR 85 (VTD 13245) 18.37
Sullivan (PT) (t/a Property Trade Services) (VTD 10349) 57.168
Sumitomo Mitsui Banking Corporation Europe Ltd (No 1), [2009] UKFTT 121 (TC),
    TC00089 .... 62.485
Sumitomo Mitsui Banking Corporation Europe Ltd (No 2), [2010] UKFTT 203 (TC),
    TC00505 .... 2.504
Summer Institute of Linguistics Ltd (VTD 16159) 15.111
Summer Palace Ltd, Ch D 2004, [2005] STC 564; [2004] EWHC 2804 (Ch) 2.414
Summerfield (P & M) (VTD 108) 58.13
Summers (M, J & P) (VTD 3498) 57.45
Sumner (TJ) & Kiddle (PS) (t/a The Extravaganza Hair Workshop) (VTD 17784) 51.63
Sun Alliance & London Assurance Co Ltd, Debenhams Retail plc *v*, CA [2005] STC
    1443; [2005] EWCA Civ 868 .... 67.9
Sundeck plc (VTD 14051) 8.19
Sunderland City Council, Thoburn *v*, QB [2002] EWHC 195 (Admin) 22.28
Sundial International plc (VTD 16698) 40.36
Sunfine Developments Ltd (VTD 6124) 32.11
Sunner & Sons (VTD 8857) 36.471
Sunningdale Golf Club [1997] VATDR 79 (VTD 14899) 48.31
Supanet Ltd (VTD 17682) 67.16
Supercook UK Llp, [2010] UKFTT 13 (TC), TC00332 .... 29.87
Superstore Discount Tile Warehouse Ltd (VTD 13393) 14.35
Supplier Ltd (VTD 18247) 11.13
Supreme Petfoods Ltd, [2011] UKFTT 19 (TC), TC00896 .... 29.195
Surecliff Ltd (VTD 8922) 18.604
Suregrove Ltd (VTD 10740) 36.332
Surgenor (HJ) (VTD 7223) 52.125
Surma News Group Ltd (VTD 17170) 2.22
Surma News Group Ltd (VTD 17585) 11.27
Surrey College Ltd [1992] VATTR 181 (VTD 9087) 2.427
Survey & Marketing Services (VTD 4455) 18.83
Sussex County Association of Change Ringers (VTD 14116) 11.25

Sussex Police Authority, [2009] UKFTT 188 (TC), TC00143 .... 62.38
Sutherland Commercial Cleaning Services Ltd (VTD 20551) 18.429
Sutton (SA) (t/a Dunchurch Motor Co) (VTD 9987) 65.58
Sutton Housing Trust (The) (No 1) (VTD 1148, 1198) 2.452
Sutton Housing Trust (The) (No 2) (VTD 1279, 1296) 2.453
Sutton Kitchens (VTD 7432) 52.74
Svenska International plc, HL [1999] STC 406; [1999] 1 WLR 769; [1999] 2 All ER
   906 .... 43.20
SW Haulage Ltd (VTD 4108) 18.59
Swaffer Truscott Ltd (VTD 7780) 52.217
Swailes (R & HM) (VTD 16069) 44.130
Swain (R) (VTD 5286) 18.600
Swaine (GT) (VTD 6451) 2.226
Swallowfield plc [1992] VATTR 212 (VTD 8865) 27.50
Swan Plant Ltd (VTD 20759) 36.165
Swanlion Ltd (VTD 3399) 18.405
Swansea Yacht & Sub Aqua Club [1996] VATDR 89 (VTD 13938) 24.36
Swanson (RS & DE) (VTD 959) 44.63
Sweden, EC Commission v, ECJ Case C-463/02; [2004] All ER(D) 267(Jul) 22.248
Sweden, Håkansson & Sturesson v, ECHR 1991, 13 EHRR 1 .... 2.251
Sweden, Plat Ror Och vets Service i Norden AB & Others v, ECHR Case 12637/05;
   [2009] ECHR 1015 .... 34.13
Sweden, Stockholm Lindöpark AB v, ECJ Case C-150/99; [2001] STC 103 .... 22.314
Swedish Snowball Production Ltd (VTD 2311) 29.152
Sweetmate Ltd (VTD 6676) 52.26
Swift Catering Services (VTD 6740) 18.318
Swinbank (GA) (VTD 18192) 36.217
Swindon Masonic Association Ltd [1978] VATTR 200 (VTD 682) 62.119
Swinger (Mr & Mrs WHG) (VTD 414) 24.1
Swiss National Tourist Office (VTD 13192) 41.51
Swiss Re Germany Holding GmbH v Finanzamt München für Körperschaften, ECJ Case
   C-242/08; [2010] STC 189 .... 22.330
Swithland Motors plc (VTD 6125) 52.26
Switzerland, AP, MP & TP v, ECHR Case 19958/92, 26 EHRR 541 .... 34.5
Switzerland Tourism (VTD 17068) 48.115
Sydenham Commercial Property Ltd (VTD 20742) 65.85
Syed (MA) (VTD 3534) 51.59
Symonds (R) (VTD 9050) 15.193
Symons (B) (VTD 19174) 19.31
Symons (BO) (VTD 18534) 19.50
Syndicat des Producteurs Indépendants v Ministère de l'Économie, des Finances et de
   l'Industrie, ECJ Case C-108/00, [2001] STC 523; [2001] All ER (EC) 564. .... 22.220
Synectiv Ltd [2006] VATDR 183 (VTD 19698) 2.164
Synopsys Ltd (VTD 7207) 2.253
System Fabricators Ltd v Director of Border Revenue, [2011] UKFTT 436 (TC),
   TC01289 .... 57.154
Systemplay Ltd (VTD 11030) 52.21
Syston Tooling & Design Ltd (VTD 4553) 40.67

T

T & B Garages (Wimbledon) (VTD 4613) 38.5
T & D Services (Timber Preservation and Damp Proofing Contractors) Ltd (VTD
   1157) 15.25
T Clark & Son Ltd (VTD 8933) 46.117
T Mobile Austria GmbH and Others v Republic of Austria, ECJ Case C-284/04; [2008]
   STC 184 .... 22.118
T Mobile (UK) Ltd, ECJ Case C-276/09; [2011] STC 316 .... 22.363
T Naughton Ltd (VTD 16702) 23.20
Tabner (RA) (VTD 16155) 50.85

Tahmassebi (H) (t/a Sale Pepe) (VTD 13177) 65.94
Tai (Mrs M) (t/a North Bersted Chinese Takeaway) (VTD 16451) 50.110
Taito (Europe) Corporation Ltd (VTD 7758) 52.159
Take Care (Agency Services) Ltd (VTD 18041) 2.9
Takkar, R v, CA Criminal Division [2011] EWCA Crim 646; [2011] 3 All ER 340
.... 49.21
Taksatorringen v Skatteministeriet, ECJ Case C-8/01; [2006] STC 1842 .... 22.326
Tal Ltd (VTD 6397) 52.105
Talacre Beach Caravan Sales Ltd, ECJ Case C-251/05; [2006] STC 1671 .... 22.507
Talbot (CJ) (VTD 4807) 51.134
Talbot (MD) (VTD 20665) 7.99
Talbot (SR) (t/a SRT Labels) (VTD 15774) 23.11
Talbot Motor Co Ltd (VTD 1728) 54.3
Talent & Production Services Ltd (VTD 18654) 62.531
Talking Point (Europe) Ltd (VTD 7698) 18.59
Tall Pines Golf & Leisure Co Ltd (VTD 16538) 41.9
Tallington Lakes Ltd, Ch D 2007, [2008] STC 2734; [2007] EWHC 1955 (Ch) 41.134
Tallishire Ltd [1979] VATTR 180 (VTD 834) 36.368
Talon Holdings Ltd (VTD 6897) 52.131
Tamburello Ltd [1996] VATDR 268 (VTD 14305) 44.139
Tamdown Ltd (VTD 10180) 52.456
Tameplace Ltd (VTD 16736) 18.311
Tameside Metropolitan Borough Council [1979] VATTR 93 (VTD 733) 41.5
Tang (W & J) (t/a Ziploc) (VTD 15426) 47.31
Tang (SN) & Coong (ND) (t/a Man Ying) (VTD 18524) 3.54
Tann (AF) Ltd (VTD 5012) 18.83
Tanna v Post Office, EAT [1981] ICR 374 .... 7.104
Tanner (WA) (VTD 15691) 50.44
Tannington Growers (1984) Ltd [1992] VATTR 135 (VTD 6877) 52.3
Tanoarch sro v Daňové riaditeľstvo Slovenskej republiky, ECJ Case C-504/10;
    27 October 2011 unreported 22.63
Tantol Ltd (VTD 10013) 36.39
Tape Recorder Hi-fi Centre (VTD 3221) 18.352
Tarmac Roadstone Holdings Ltd, CA [1987] STC 610 .... 62.25
Tarrakarn Ltd [1996] VATDR 516 (VTD 14279) 36.564
Tarvet Electronics Ltd (VTD 17463) 18.541
Tary Cash & Carry Ltd (VTD 11850) 48.99
Tas-Stage Ltd QB, [1988] STC 436 .... 62.89
Taste of Raj (VTD 17243) 3.81
Taunton Deane Borough Council (VTD 5545) 52.59, 52.377
Tax Briefs Ltd (VTD 9258) 5.83
Taylor (AP) (VTD 7893) 18.88
Taylor (BD & Mrs MA) (VTD 10980) 2.71
Taylor (BH) (VTD 12061) 50.140
Taylor (C & E) (t/a Sandwich Heaven) (VTD 16211) 29.10
Taylor (D) (VTD 20099) 51.151
Taylor (DW) (VTD 454) 15.10
Taylor (FA) (VTD 3882) 14.47
Taylor (I) (VTD 15566) 15.22
Taylor (JCNT) (VTD 3408) 18.582
Taylor (K) (t/a Jeans) [1975] VATTR 86 (VTD 163) 3.25
Taylor (K) (t/a Jeans) [1975] VATTR 147 (VTD 163A) 2.67
Taylor (K) (t/a Jeans) (VTD 163B) 2.450
Taylor (K & G) (VTD 13475) 57.4
Taylor (KW) (VTD 14244) 36.56
Taylor (PD & G) (t/a Riverside Sports & Leisure Club) (VTD 18056) 50.83
Taylor (PD & G) (t/a Riverside Sports & Leisure Club) (No 2) (VTD 19354) 27.13
Taylor (R & ME) (t/a Chew Magna Post Office) (VTD 19740) 36.503
Taylor (RF) (VTD 2841) 44.84
Taylor (S & L) (VTD 9125) 57.56
Taylor (W) (VTD 18298) 50.40

Taylor *v* Taylor & Another (re Colebrook's Conveyances), Ch D 1972, [1973] 1 All ER
132 .... 15.148
Taylor & Fraser Ltd (VTD 8977) 52.182
Taylor & Taylor (VTD 7187) 18.79
Taylor Construction (VTD 13269) 18.586
Taylor Tunnicliffe Ltd (VTD 18378) 4.26
Taylor's Executors & Taylor (Mrs P) (VTD 20323) 41.76
Tayside Aviation Ltd (VTD 18241) 62.459
Tayside Numbers Ltd [1992] VATTR 406 (VTD 8874) 48.40
TBC Catering Ltd (VTD 12235) 2.201
TBS (South Wales) Ltd [1981] VATTR 183 (VTD 1144) 62.7
TC Harrison Group Ltd, ECJ Case C-305/97; [1999] STC 998; [2000] 1 WLR 1151;
[1999] All ER (EC) 908 .... 22.424
TC Plastics (Manchester) Ltd (VTD 7684) 52.199
TD Reid (Braids) Ltd (VTD 4638) 36.420
TDA (School) Ltd (VTD 4900) 62.225
TE Davey Photo-Service Ltd, QB 1995, [1997] STC 889 .... 18.346
TE Penny & Co Ltd (VTD 15329) 11.28
Teamspirit Holdings Ltd (VTD 20337) 18.526
Tecfacs Ltd (VTD 19868) 18.65
Technicolor Ltd (VTD 14871) 25.29
Technip Coflexip Offshore Ltd (VTD 19298) 3.181
Tecnomare (UK) Ltd (VTD 6329) 52.35
Teknequip Ltd, QB [1987] STC 664 .... 67.131
Telecential Communications Ltd (VTD 15361) 62.15
Telemed Ltd, QB [1992] STC 89 .... 67.14
Telement Ltd, [2010] UKFTT 470 (TC), TC00732 .... 36.113
Telent plc [2007] VATDR 81 (VTD 19967) 36.63
Teleos plc *v* C & E, ECJ Case C-409/04; [2008] STC 706 .... 22.518
Teleos plc & Others, oao, R *v* C & E (No 2), CA [2005] STC 1471; [2005] EWCA Civ
200; [2005] 1 WLR 3007 .... 36.654
Telequick Ltd (VTD 5319) 36.12
Teletech UK Ltd [2004] VATDR 44 (VTD 18080) 38.16
Televideo (VTD 10052) 18.71
Television Information Network Ltd (VTD 3403) 18.73
Telewest Communications Group Ltd [1996] VATDR 566 (VTD 14383) 67.144
Telewest Communications plc, CA [2005] STC 481; [2005] EWCA Civ 102 .... 62.371
Telewest Communications (Publications) Ltd, CA [2005] STC 481; [2005] EWCA Civ
102 .... 62.371
Tel-Ka Talk Ltd, HC [2010] EWHC 90175 (Costs); [2011] STC 497 .... 2.445
Telstar Leisure Ltd (VTD 9126) 2.386
Temco Europe SA, Belgian State *v*, ECJ Case C-284/03; [2005] STC 1451 .... 22.341
Tempest (H) (Cardiff) Ltd [1993] VATTR 482 (VTD 11210) 67.28, 67.54
Tempest (H) Ltd [1975] VATTR 161 (VTD 201) 67.27
Tempest (H) Ltd (No 2) [1993] VATTR 482 (VTD 11210) 67.28, 67.54
Temple Avenue Finance Ltd (VTD 9965) 52.281
Temple House Developments Ltd (VTD 15583) 15.121
Templegate Accounting Services Ltd (VTD 14446) 40.72
Tempur Pedic (UK) Ltd (VTD 13744) 19.27
Tennessee Secret (UK) Ltd (VTD 16945) 29.127
Terard Ltd (VTD 16949) 52.315
Terra Baubedarf-Handel GmbH *v* Finanzamt Osterholz-Scharmbeck, ECJ Case
C-152/02; [2005] STC 525 .... 22.437
Terracopia Ltd (VTD 11341) 17.13
Territorio Historico de Alava *v* EC Commission, ECJ Case T-346/99; [2002] All ER(D)
338 (Oct) 22.10
Territorio Historico de Guipuzcoa *v* EC Commission, ECJ Case T-269/99;
[2002] All ER(D) 337 (Oct) 22.9
Terropol Ltd (VTD 3021) 36.411
Terry (KA) (t/a Advanced Laboratory Techniques) (VTD 9803) 52.75
Terry (WJ) (t/a Wealden Properties), [2009] UKFTT 202 (TC), TC00155 .... 15.271

Terry Cohn Ltd (VTD 15962) 36.178
Terry Shaw Holdings (VTD 11613) 2.327
Tesco plc [1994] VATTR 425 (VTD 12740) 58.59
Tesco plc (No 2), CA [2003] STC 1561; [2003] EWCA Civ 1367 .... 67.157
Tetra International Ltd (VTD 15820) 18.233
Tewkesbury Borough Council (VTD 5773) 52.381
Tex Holdings plc (VTD 10416) 52.69
Texas Touch Dallas Diet Ltd [1984] VATTR 115 (VTD 1664) 29.132
Tezgel (A) (t/a Master Chef) (VTD 20462) 65.84
TF Mechanical Engineering Ltd (VTD 12975) 2.202
TFA Box Company Ltd (VTD 19771) 53.10
Thames Magistrates Court, R (oao Paul da Costa & Co) v, DC [2002] STC 267; [2002]
    EWHC Admin 40 .... 14.95
Thamesdown Engineering Systems Ltd (VTD 5341) 18.216
Thamesdown Transport Ltd (VTD 19386) 66.49
Thamesview Estate Agents Ltd (VTD 20572) 18.547
Thanet District Council (VTD 9308) 52.32
Thayer (WS) (VTD 14382) 44.141
Thayers Ltd (VTD 7541) 27.62
THC Fabricators (UK) Ltd (VTD 11414) 62.438
The Corner Café (Tooting) Ltd (VTD 19057) 57.42
The Wine Portfolio Company Ltd (VTD 19058) 48.4
Theatres Consolidated Ltd, [1975] VATTR 13 (VTD 141) 41.2
Themis FTSE Fledgling Index Trust (VTD 17039) 62.144
Theotrue Holdings Ltd, [1983] VATTR 88 (VTD 1358) 36.622
THI Leisure Two Partnership (VTD 16876) 48.90
Thimbleby Farms Ltd, [2010] SFTD 1216; [2010] UKFTT 320 (TC), TC00607 ..... 67.133
Third Generation Communication Ltd, [2010] UKFTT 486 (TC), TC00746 .... 36.113
Thoburn v Sunderland City Council, QB [2002] EWHC 195 (Admin) 22.28
Thomas (C), [2001] VATDR 307 (VTD 17127) 37.31
Thomas (DN & Mrs JF) (VTD 11040) 52.10
Thomas (HW) (VTD 18680) 57.7
Thomas (IC), [1985] VATTR 67 (VTD 1862) 5.69, 67.118
Thomas Holdings Ltd, [2011] UKFTT 656 (TC), TC01498 .... 2.448
Thomas M Devon & Co (VTD 13098) 48.121
Thomas Moriarty Associates Ltd (VTD 10668) 18.490
Thompson (A) (t/a AY Cars) (VTD 1043) 36.430
Thompson (G) (VTD 2666) 62.442
Thompson (HAS) (No 1) (VTD 14777) 44.125
Thompson (HAS) (No 2), Ch D [2005] STC 1777; [2005] EWHC 342 (Ch) 44.114
Thompson (P), [1998] VATDR 524 (VTD 15834) 15.44
Thompson (A) & Sons Ltd (VTD 7833) 44.101
Thompson, Thompson & Giblin (VTD 4196) 57.69
Thompson, Giles v, HL 1993, [1994] 1 AC 142; [1993] 3 All ER 321 .... 2.297
Thomson (JT) (VTD 1300) 44.7
Thomson (TAN) (VTD 17489) 50.39
Thorn EMI plc, CA [1995] STC 674 .... 8.30
Thorn EMI plc, [1993] VATTR 94 (VTD 9782) 38.8
Thorn Materials Supply Ltd, HL [1998] STC 725; [1998] 1 WLR 1106; [1998] 3 All ER
    384 .... 32.17
Thorn plc, [1998] VATDR 80 (VTD 15283) 32.23
Thorn plc, [1998] VATDR 383 (VTD 15284) 67.15
Thorn Resources Ltd, HL [1998] STC 725; [1998] 1 WLR 1106; [1998] 3 All ER 384
    .... 32.17
Thornber (F) (VTD 16235) 50.57
Thorncroft Ltd, [2011] UKFTT 694 (TC), TC01536 .... 29.176
Thorne (LR) (VTD 10175) 51.57
Thorne (TN) (VTD 6231) 18.266
Thornfield Redditch Limited Partnership (The) (VTD 17997) 48.100
Thornhill (A) (t/a Motormill) (VTD 20858) 44.63
Thornpark Maintenance Services Ltd (VTD 20263) 17.3

Thornsett Structures Ltd (VTD 15934) 52.397
Thornton (EM) (t/a Forum Stud Farm) (VTD 4711) 7.66
Thornton (J) (VTD 20719) 50.41
Thorogood (K & K) Ltd (VTD 1595) 36.571
Thorpe Architecture Ltd (VTD 6955) 36.510
Thorstone Developments Ltd (VTD 17821) 47.57
Thousand Yard Store (VTD 12006) 18.425
Three Cooks Ltd (VTD 13352) 29.57
3D Micro Ltd (VTD 18907) 23.12
Three H Aircraft Hire, QB [1982] STC 653 .... 7.7
Threshfield Motors Ltd (VTD 16699) 41.151
Throston Ltd (VTD 11770) 52.277
Thruxton Parachute Club (VTD 1816) 65.7
Thurley (JL) (VTD 9509) 18.491
Tia (GB) Ltd (VTD 20861) 53.10
Tibbs (G & J) (t/a Joanne Yacht Services) (VTD 1098) 7.34
Ticklock Ltd, [2010] UKFTT 284 (TC), TC00573 .... 41.131
Tidesave Ltd (t/a Yu Chinese Restaurant) (VTD 15418) 14.5
Tidy (RE) (VTD 11957) 18.341
Tiercé Ladbroke SA v Belgian State, ECJ Case C-231/07; 14 May 2008 unreported
.... 22.359
Tiffin Developments Ltd (VTD 4462) 14.47
Tilbury (JW) (VTD 1102) 15.256
Tilley (R & A) (VTD 15097) 15.130
Tilling Management Services Ltd, QB 1978, [1979] STC 365 .... 43.8
Timark Warehousing Ltd (VTD 10360) 52.35
Time (Ancient & Modern) Ltd (VTD 8814) 52.316
Timeplas Ltd (VTD 2570) 51.104
Times of Wigan Ltd (VTD 1917) 7.63
Times Right Marketing Ltd (in liquidation) (VTD 20611) 4.32
Timewade Ltd (VTD 12786) 44.152
Timms (RJ) (VTD 18760) 62.348
Timms (W) & Son (Builders) Ltd, QB [1992] STC 374 .... 59.10
Timur (B & J) (t/a Istanbul Kebab House) (VTD 15305) 57.25
Tindsley (I & G) (t/a Padway Nurseries) (VTD 18571) 57.130
Tingdene Developments Ltd (VTD 16546) 46.25
Tingley (D) (t/a Homecare Exteriors) (VTD 11592) 62.413
Tinker (M) (VTD 18033) 15.13
Tinsley (AC), Ch D [2005] STC 1612; [2005] EWHC 1508 (Ch) 55.62
Tipton Non-Ferrous Foundry Ltd (VTD 10328) 18.367
Tiravie Entertainments LLP (VTD 19018) 18.235
Tisdall (AG) & Co Ltd (VTD 11521) 52.72
Tiwana (KS) (VTD 16202) 58.23
TJ Tiling (Contractors) Ltd (VTD 6194) 18.200
TL Smith Properties Ltd, [2011] UKFTT 528 (TC), TC01375 .... 15.197
TLC Incentives Ltd, [2011] UKFTT 617 (TC), TC01459 .... 18.286
TLV (Manufacturing) Ltd (VTD 2058) 36.439
TM Technology Ltd (VTD 14509) 18.441
TNT Post UK Ltd, oao, R v HMRC, ECJ Case C-357/07; [2009] STC 1438 .... 22.272
Tobell (G) (VTD 16646) 15.131
Tobin (JC) [1991] VATTR 165 (VTD 5740) 57.86
Todd (CG) (VTD 130) 44.77
Todd (CV) (t/a Sweeney Todd's Plumbing Squad) (VTD 14341) 65.111
Todd (FD) & Sons Ltd (VTD 14731) 36.331
Toga Freight Services (UK) Ltd (VTD 9906) 52.236
Tolley (J) (t/a WH Tolley & Son) (VTD 11627) 52.136
Tolsma v Inspecteur der Omzetbelasting Leeuwarden, ECJ Case C-16/93; [1994] STC
509; [1994] 1 ECR 743; [1994] 2 CMLR 908 .... 22.84
Tom Wilson (Tobacco) Ltd (VTD 16437) 36.626
Tomkins (CD) (t/a Options) (VTD 11738) 51.16
Tomlinson (B & S) (VTD 4351) 51.89

Tomlinson (PW) (VTD 20059) 19.5
Tong Garden Centre plc (VTD 12103) 52.60
Top Grade Cars Ltd (VTD 7602) 52.324
Top Quality Seconds Prescot Ltd (VTD 5096) 18.341
Topps Tiles plc [2006] VATDR 480 (VTD 19751) 40.83
Topzone Ltd (VTD 14782) 14.33
Torfaen Voluntary Alliance (VTD 18797) 15.156
Tork (K) (t/a KT Motors) (VTD 7013) 44.63
Torq Ltd (VTD 19389) 29.159
Tortoise Factory Units Ltd (VTD 4932) 40.26
Total Network SL, HL [2008] STC 644; [2008] UKHL 19; [2008] 2 All ER 413 ..... 49.30
Total Technology (Engineering) Ltd, [2011] UKFTT 473 (TC), TC01323 .... 18.621
Total UK Ltd, CA 2007, [2008] STC 19; [2007] EWCA Civ 987 .... 22.260
Totel Distribution Ltd (No 1) (VTD 18956) 36.93
Totel Distribution Ltd (No 2), [2011] UKFTT 217 (TC), TC01082 .... 36.121
Totel Ltd, Ch D 2007, [2008] STC 885; [2007] EWHC 422 (Ch) 2.519
Totel Ltd, oao, R v First-Tier Tribunal, QB [2011] EWHC 652 (Admin); [2011] STC 1485 .... 2.137
Tottey (AJF) (VTD 12149) 50.52
Touchwood Services Ltd, Ch D [2007] STC 1425; [2007] EWHC 105 (Ch) 2.16
Tourick (RM) (t/a RM Tourick & Co) (VTD 7712) 57.166
Tower Cleaners (VTD 20333) 43.11
Tower Hamlets Housing Action Trust (VTD 17308) 41.28
Tower Steel (Holdings) Ltd (VTD 5029) 36.445
Town & City Parking Ltd (VTD 15730) 62.202
Town & County Factors Ltd, ECJ Case C-498/99, [2002] STC 1263; [2003] All ER (EC) 33 .... 22.85, 22.240
Town & County Factors Ltd (No 2) (VTD 18569) 5.76
Town & County Factors Ltd (No 3) (VTD 19616) 46.90
Townsend (AJ) (VTD 18327) 19.41
Townsend (D & M) (VTD 17081) 47.48
Townville (Wheldale) Miners Sports and Recreational Club and Institute (VTD 719) 62.383
TP Activity Toys Ltd (VTD 14377) 67.35
TR Fastenings Ltd (VTD 1016) 62.97
TR Shop Ltd (VTD 20776) 53.10
Trade Development Associates (VTD 12699) 36.179
Trade Direct Ltd (VTD 10142) 52.241
Trade Only Plant Sales Ltd (VTD 18847) 62.116
Trademarque Tools Ltd (VTD 20308) 48.4
Tradeplan Ltd (VTD 4033) 18.216
Trader Media Group Ltd, CA [2010] STC 1572; [2010] EWCA Civ 422 .... 38.24
Traderco Ltd, [2010] UKFTT 632 (TC), TC00871 .... 2.220
Trafalgar Tours Ltd, CA 1989, [1990] STC 127 .... 67.97
Traidcraft plc [2003] VATDR 583 (VTD 18189) 67.36
Training Technology International Ltd (VTD 6727) 52.126
Trans Medium Ltd (t/a Connectivity), [2009] UKFTT 243 (TC), TC00192 .... 21.18
Trans Tirreno Express SpA v Ufficio Provinciale IVA, ECJ Case 283/84; [1986] ECR 231; [1986] 2 CMLR 100 .... 22.209
Transam Ltd (VTD 13987) 18.512
Transtrek Ltd (t/a Thropton Motor Co) (VTD 9749) 52.342
Trathern (D) & Goode (V), [2011] UKFTT 21 (TC), TC00898 .... 15.69
Travellers Fare Ltd (VTD 13482) 29.35
Travers (Mrs S) (VTD 7942) 52.342
Trebah Garden Trust (VTD 16598) 16.10
Treetops Hospice Trust, [2011] UKFTT 503 (TC), TC01350 .... 15.203
Tregarn Developments Ltd (VTD 7358) 52.347
Tregenza (WG) (VTD 1907) 36.177
Tremerton Ltd, QB [1999] STC 1039 .... 46.210
Trenchard Management Ltd (VTD 17517) 36.668
Trendadd Ltd (VTD 3222) 18.441

Trendtex Trading Corporation v Credit Suisse, CA [1981] QB 629 .... 2.445
Trent Manor Farms (VTD 11216) 48.84
Trevalyn Estates Ltd (VTD 6749) 52.136
Trevor Toys Ltd (VTD 7805) 46.185
Trevor Toys Ltd (VTD 9352) 2.525
Trewby (on behalf of members of Hurlingham Club), QB [1976] STC 122; [1976] 1
   WLR 932; [1976] 2 All ER 199 .... 41.71
Trexagrove Ltd [1984] VATTR 222 (VTD 1758) 7.39
Triad Timber Components Ltd [1993] VATTR 384 (VTD 10694) 4.19
Triangle Press Ltd (VTD 9648) 29.44
Triangle Thoroughbreds Ltd (VTD 5404) 7.67
Tricell UK Ltd [2003] VATDR 333 (VTD 18127) 2.13
Trident Exhibitions Ltd (VTD 6028) 52.33
Trident Housing Association (VTD 10642) 15.163
Trigg's Plumbing & Heating (VTD 14142) 36.527
Trimming (DJ) Ltd (VTD 7733) 52.193, 52.218
Trina Ltd (VTD 7713) 52.281
Trinity Factoring Services Ltd, CS [1994] STC 504 .... 41.142
Trinity Methodist Church (Royton)(Building Committee) (807) 7.54
Trinity Mirror plc, CA [2001] STC 192; [2001] EWCA Civ 65 .... 27.51
Trinity Mirror plc, Ch D [2003] STC 518; [2003] EWHC 480(Ch) 62.129
Trioport Ltd (VTD 4923) 51.89
Triple Crown Securities Holdings Ltd (VTD 13154) 4.3
Trippett (D) [1978] VATTR 260 (VTD 686) 2.177
Trippitt (S & AJ) (VTD 17340) 57.67
Tritin Ltd (VTD 10354) 52.125
Triton Properties Ltd (VTD 7492) 52.123
Triumph & Albany Car Service (VTD 977, 1004) 62.240
Tron Theatre Ltd (The), CS 1993, [1994] STC 177 .... 67.103
Troop (F) & Son (VTD 18957) 48.70
Trowbridge Trades & Labour Club & Institute Ltd (VTD 6640) 18.286
TRS Cabinet Co Ltd (VTD 11750) 52.285
True Engineers Ltd (VTD 4032) 18.588
Tru-Form Sheet Metal Ltd (VTD 9240) 62.88
Trust Securities Holdings Ltd [1990] VATTR 1 (VTD 4550) 2.131
Trustcorp Ltd (VTD 13779) 46.109
Trustees for the Macmillan Cancer Trust (VTD 15603) 33.70
Trustee of Sir Robert Geffery's School Charity (VTD 17667) 15.190
Trustees of The Langley House Trust (VTD 19749) 51.42
Trustees of The Lyndon David Hollinshead SIPP (and related appeals), [2009] UKFTT
   92 (TC), TC00060 .... 41.7
Trustees of The Nell Gwynn House Maintenance Fund, HL 1998, [1999] STC 79;
   [1999] 1 WLR 174; [1999] 1 All ER 385 .... 62.36
Trustees of The Whitbread Harrowden Settlement (and related appeals) (VTD 16781)
   .... 46.97, 52.423
TS Harrison & Sons Ltd (VTD 11043) 43.16
TS International Freight Forwarders Ltd (VTD 7080) 52.86
Tse (M) (VTD 18362) 3.97
Tucker (AM) (t/a Montgomery Canal Cruises) (VTD 17329) 66.25
Tudor Hotel & Restaurant (VTD 9683) 52.74
Tudor Print & Design Ltd (VTD 17848) 5.45
Tulip (N and Mrs M) (VTD 3243) 18.306
Tullihallitus v Salumets & Others, ECJ Case C-455/98; [2000] All ER (D) 891 ..... 22.100
Tulsidas (K) & Bhatt (MK) (t/a Amazon International) (VTD 16335) 36.49
Tumble Tots UK Ltd, Ch D [2007] STC 1171; [2007] EWHC 103 (Ch) 12.26
Tuppen (I) (t/a Kingswood Trading Services) (VTD 18950) 2.243
Turbine Motor Works Ltd, [2011] UKFTT 706 (TC), TC01543 .... 9.6
Turespaña (VTD 14568) 36.500
Turmeau (AC) (VTD 1135) 44.100
Turmeaus Ltd (VTD 6052) 52.72
Turnbull (I) (VTD 9903) 50.15

Turner (AJ) (VTD 1965) 38.2
Turner (K & E) (VTD 19076) 57.81
Turner (Mrs LV) (VTD 12839) 18.402
Turner (M) (VTD 12028) 65.91
Turner (NO) (t/a Turner Agricultural), QB [1992] STC 621 .... 36.45
Turner (P) (t/a Turner Hire & Sales) (VTD 4610) 18.120
Turner Stroud & Burley Construction Ltd (VTD 15454) 15.176
Turnstem Ltd, Re, Ch D [2004] EWHC 1765(Ch); [2005] 1 BCLC 388 .... 37.4
Turn-und Sportunion Waldburg v Finanzlandesdirektion für Oberösterreich, ECJ Case
   C-246/04; [2006] STC 1506 .... 22.382
Tuscan Food Ltd (VTD 18716) 29.60
Twentieth Century Cleaning and Maintenance Co Ltd (VTD 838) 36.403
21st Century Logistic Solutions Ltd (in liquidation) v Madysen Ltd, QB [2004] STC
   1535; [2004] EWHC 231(QB) 62.176
22A Property Investments Ltd (VTD 14544) 62.199
24/7 Fuels Ltd, [2009] UKFTT 274 (TC), TC00220 .... 2.327
Twigg (AC) [1983] VATTR 17 (VTD 1329) 67.130
Twin Cleaning Contractors Ltd (VTD 20624) 44.34
Two Oaks Leisure Ltd (t/a The Hyde) (VTD 17276) 4.31
Twoh International BV v Staatssecretaris van Financiën, ECJ Case C-184/05; [2008]
   STC 740 .... 22.521
2S Airchangers Ltd (VTD 12495) 15.243
Twycross Zoo East Midland Zoological Society (No 1) (VTD 19548) 16.4
Twycross Zoo East Midland Zoological Society (No 2), [2007] VATDR 425 (VTD
   20439) 16.5
Twyford v Manchester Corporation, Ch D [1946] Ch 236; [1946] 1 All ER 621 ...... 2.58
TY McGuirk Sports Ltd [2003] VATDR 472 (VTD 17599) 3.38
Tynewydd Labour Working Men's Club & Institute Ltd, QB [1979] STC 570 .... 24.11
Tynewydd Labour Working Men's Club & Institute Ltd [1980] VATTR 165 (VTD
   1089) 67.115
Typeflow Ltd (VTD 3264) 51.8
Tyre Team Ltd (VTD 6407) 52.378
Tyrrel (JFE) (VTD 11984) 51.22

U

UBAF Bank Ltd, CA [1996] STC 372 .... 46.7
UBU Projex (VTD 4820) 18.204
Uddin (J), R v, CA Criminal Division [1996] STC 1163 .... 49.4
Uddin (K & A) (t/a Sangam Balti House) (VTD 16337) 52.21
Uddin (MA) & Bari (A) (t/a Ringmer Tandoori Restaurant) (VTD 19043) 50.74
UDL Construction plc, [1995] VATDR 396 (VTD 13714) 40.3
UDS Group Ltd, [1977] VATTR 16 (VTD 333) 62.8
UDS Tailoring Ltd, [1977] VATTR 16 (VTD 333) 62.8
UFD Ltd, [1981] VATTR 199 (VTD 1172) 24.26
Ufficio Distrettuale delle Imposte Dirette di Fiorenzuola d'Arda v Comune di Carpaneto
   Piacentino, ECJ Case 231/87; [1989] ECR 3233; [1991] STC 205 .... 22.129
Ufficio IVA di Trapani v Italittica Sp A, ECJ Case C-144/94; [1995] STC 1059; [1995]
   1 ECR 3653 .... 22.229
Ufficio Provinciale Imposta sul Valore Aggiunto di Piacenza, Comune di Carpaneto
   Piacentino & Others v, ECJ Case C-4/89; [1990] 1 ECR 1869; [1990] 3 CMLR 153
   .... 22.130
Ufficio Provinciale Imposta sul Valore Aggiunto di Piacenza v Comune di Rivergaro and
   Others, ECJ Case 231/87; [1989] ECR 3233; [1991] STC 205 .... 22.129
Ufficio Provinciale IVA, Trans Tirreno Express SpA v, ECJ Case 283/84; [1986] ECR
   231; [1986] 2 CMLR 100 .... 22.209
UK Carpets Ltd (VTD 11526) 14.3
UK Digital Ltd (VTD 17096) 52.458
UK Inspection Ltd (VTD 11467) 18.216

UK Storage Company (SW) Ltd, [2011] UKFTT 549 (TC); [2011] SFTD 1233, TC01394 .... 41.24
UK Tradecorp Ltd (No 1), [2004] VATDR 195 (VTD 18714) 2.514
UK Tradecorp Ltd (No 2), [2004] VATDR 438 (VTD 18879) 2.155
UK Tradecorp Ltd (No 3), [2005] VATDR 82 (VTD 18992) 2.245
UK Tradecorp Ltd, oao, R v C & E, QB 2004, [2005] STC 138; [2004] EWHC 2515 (Admin) 36.652
Ukraine, Masa Invest Group plc v, ECHR Case 3540/03; 8 ITLR 262 .... 34.26
UK Travel Agent Ltd (The) (VTD 12861) 66.17
Ulster Independent Clinic Ltd, [2004] VATDR 32 (VTD 18517) 22.274
Ultimate Advisory Services Ltd (No 1) (VTD 9523) 41.46
Ultimate Advisory Services Ltd (No 2) (VTD 17610) 54.5
Ultimate Hair & Beauty Suppliers Ltd (VTD 20209) 18.319
Ultimate Leisure (Scotland) Ltd (VTD 18573) 18.43
Ultra Sport Europe Ltd Directors Retirement Benefits Scheme (VTD 20194) 52.403
Ultracell (UK) Ltd (VTD 19508) 36.82
Ultracolour Ltd (VTD 3278) 18.215
Ultralase Medical Aesthetics Ltd, [2009] SFTD 541; [2009] UKFTT 187 (TC), TC00142 .... 33.56
Ultratone Ltd (VTD 5536) 2.446
Unabhängiger Finanzsenat Außenstelle Linz, Puffer v, ECJ Case 460/07; [2009] STC 1693 .... 22.427
Uncles the Original Pawnbrokers Ltd (VTD 4437) 51.89
Unibev Ltd (VTD 18437) 29.164
Unilever Bestfoods UK Ltd, [2007] VATDR 119 (VTD 20016) 29.171
Union Bank of Switzerland, [1987] VATTR 221 (VTD 2551) 46.157
Union Club Seaford (The) (VTD 17442) 48.62
Union of Students of the University of Warwick, [1995] VATDR 219 (VTD 13821) 19.97
Uniq Group plc (VTD 19125) 29.143
Unique Film Company (The) (VTD 12214) 18.125
Unique Sealed Units Ltd (VTD 10235) 18.436
United Biscuits (UK) Ltd (t/a Simmers), CS [1992] STC 325 .... 29.85
United Biscuits (UK) Ltd (VTD 6344) 29.135
United Biscuits (UK) Ltd (No 3) (VTD 17391) 29.181
United Biscuits (UK) Ltd (No 4) (VTD 18090) 29.148
United Biscuits (UK) Ltd (No 5), [2004] VATDR 201 (VTD 18596) 29.140
United Biscuits (UK) Ltd (No 6) (VTD 18947) 29.183
United Biscuits (UK) Ltd (No 7) (VTD 19319) 29.184
United Biscuits (UK) Ltd (No 8), [2011] UKFTT 673 (TC), TC01515 .... 29.186
United Cutlers Ltd (VTD 3116) 18.294
United Kingdom, Chappell v, ECHR 1989, 12 EHRR 1 .... 14.87
United Kingdom, EC Commission v, ECJ Case 353/85; [1988] STC 251; [1988] ECR 817 .... 22.271
United Kingdom, EC Commission v (No 2), ECJ Case 416/85; [1988] STC 456 .... 22.505
United Kingdom, EC Commission v (No 3), ECJ Case C-359/97; [2000] STC 777 .... 22.134
United Kingdom, EC Commission v (No 4), ECJ Case C-33/03; [2005] STC 582 ... 22.404
United Kingdom, EC Commission v (No 5), ECJ Case C-305/03; [2007] STC 1211 .... 22.266
United Kingdom, EC Commission v (No 6), ECJ Case C-349/03; [2006] STC 1944 .... 22.564
United Kingdom, EC Commission v (No 7), ECJ Case C-582/08; [2010] STC 2364 .... 22.546
United Kingdom, Georgiou (M & A) v, ECHR 2000; [2001] STC 80; 3 ITLR 145 .... 34.1
United Kingdom, Saunders v, ECHR 1996, 23 EHRR 313 .... 2.283
United News Shops (Holdings) Ltd (VTD 12321) 52.258
United Norwest Co-Operatives Ltd, CA [1999] STC 686 .... 58.32
United Norwest Food Markets Ltd (VTD 14923) 58.55
United Photographic Laboratories Ltd (VTD 10071) 62.99

United Refining Co (Precious Metals) Ltd (VTD 1019) 62.170
United Society of Poets Ltd (VTD 15772) 36.26
United Utilities plc, ECJ Case C-89/05; [2006] STC 1423 .... 22.374
Unity Farm Holiday Centre Ltd (VTD 2620) 41.129
Universal Display Fittings Co Ltd (VTD 15838) 18.617
University College London [2008] VATDR 409 (VTD 20664) 46.151
University Court of the University of Dundee (VTD 20728) 11.39
University Court of the University of Glasgow, CS [2003] STC 495 .... 3.132
University Court of the University of Glasgow (No 2) (VTD 17744) 14.89
University Court of the University of Glasgow (No 3) [2005] VATDR 198 (VTD
    19052) 46.86
University Court of the University of Glasgow (No 4) (VTD 19885) 46.148
University Court of the University of St Andrews (VTD 15243) 15.66
University Court of the University of St Andrews (No 2) (VTD 19054) 15.77
University of Bath (VTD 14235) 15.65
University of Bristol (VTD 17316) 46.147
University of Cambridge (Chancellor, Masters & Scholars), Ch D [2009] EWHC 434
    (Ch) 61.5
University of Cambridge Local Examination Syndicate, [1997] VATDR 245 (VTD
    15015) 61.5
University of Edinburgh (VTD 6569) 46.145
University of Edinburgh (No 2) (VTD 10936) 21.10
University of Essex, [2010] SFTD 893; [2010] UKFTT 162 (TC), TC00467 .... 9.7
University of Exeter (VTD 18117) 46.113
University of Huddersfield (VTD 17159) 3.93
University of Huddersfield Higher Education Corporation, ECJ Case C-223/03; [2006]
    STC 980 .... 22.116
University of Hull (VTD 180) 15.187
University of Kent, [2004] VATDR 372 (VTD 18625) 69.7
University of Leicester Students Union, CA 2001, [2002] STC 147; [2001] EWCA Civ
    1972 .... 21.19
University of Liverpool (VTD 16769) 48.63
University of Reading (VTD 4209) 15.247
University of Reading, [1998] VATDR 27 (VTD 15387) 2.357
University of Sheffield (VTD 20174) 11.41
University of Southampton, Ch D [2006] STC 1389; [2006] EWHC 528(Ch) 11.40
University of Sussex (VTD 16221) 46.146
University of Sussex, CA 2003, [2004] STC 1; [2003] EWCA Civ 1448 .... 48.2
University of Wales College Cardiff, QB [1995] STC 611 .... 46.215
University of Wales College Newport [1997] VATDR 417 (VTD 15280) 11.1
UNO Upholstery Superstores Ltd (VTD 13036) 62.448
Unstead, R v, CA 1996, [1997] STC 22 .... 62.177
Unterpertinger v Pensionsversicherungsanstalt der Arbeiter, ECJ Case C-212/01; [2005]
    STC 678 .... 22.281
Unwin Estates Ltd (VTD 7955) 52.347
Uppal (DS) (t/a Mr Chips) (VTD 14074) 57.177
Upper Don Walk Trust (VTD 19476) 15.33
Upson (JS) (VTD 13350) 51.182
Upton (CM) (t/a Fagomatic), CA [2002] EWCA Civ 520; [2002] STC 640 .... 44.110
Uratemp Ventures Ltd v Collins, HL [2001] 3 WLR 806 .... 15.216
Urdd Gobaith Cymru [1997] VATDR 273 (VTD 14881) 15.70
USAA Ltd (VTD 10369) 62.502
Uszodaépíto Kft v APEH Kozponti Hivatal Hatósági Foosztály, ECJ Case C-392/09;
    30 September 2010 unreported 20.105
Utilicom Ltd (VTD 4200) 18.84
UU Bibliotech Ltd [2006] VATDR 501 (VTD 19764) 5.53
Uudenkaupungin kaupunki v Lounais-Suomen Verovirasto, ECJ Case C-184/04; [2008]
    STC 2329 .... 22.458

V

V v C, CA [2001] EWCA Civ 1509 .... 2.220
V Tech Electronics Ltd (VTD 6677) 52.249
V & P Midlands Ltd (VTD 7589) 36.492
Vaghela (JD) & Unadkat (NR) (t/a Vaghela Unadkat & Co) (VTD 17331) 10.13
Vale of White Horse District Council (VTD 6924) 52.56
Valewood Furniture Ltd (VTD 12447) 18.374
Valley Chemical Co Ltd (VTD 17989) 59.29
Valley Industrial Services Ltd (VTD 9302) 18.417
Valsts ieņēmumu dienests, Alstom Power Hydro v, ECJ Case C-472/08; [2010] STC
777 .... 22.441
Value Catering Ltd, [2011] UKFTT 329 (TC); [2011] SFTD 868, TC01189 .... 29.11
Van Boeckel, QB 1980, [1981] STC 290; [1981] 2 All ER 505 .... 3.1
Van Colle (I & CJ) (t/a GVC Optometrists) (VTD 20332) 48.63
Van der Kooy v Staatssecretaris van Financiën, ECJ Case C-181/97; 28 January 1999
unreported 22.191
Van der Steen (JA) v Inspecteur van de Belastingdienst, ECJ Case C-355/06; [2008] STC
2379 .... 22.124
Van Dijk's Boekhuis BV v Staatssecretaris van Financiën, ECJ Case 139/84;
[1986] 2 CMLR 575; [1985] ECR 1405 .... 22.171
Van Heyningen Brothers Ltd (VTD 1675) 36.387
Van Tiem (WM) v Staatssecretaris van Financiën, ECJ Case C-186/89; [1990] 1 ECR
4363; [1993] STC 91 .... 22.109
Vandoorne NV v Belgische Staat, ECJ Case C-489/09; 27 January 2011 unreported
.... 22.499
Vane Ltd (VTD 19786) 18.265
Vann (EM) (VTD 13581) 51.175
Vasiljevic (G) (t/a Geneve) (VTD 17820) 62.272
Vass (P), [2010] UKFTT 208 (TC), TC00510 .... 57.130
Vassall Centre Trust (VTD 17891) 19.38
VAT Tribunal (ex p. Cohen and others), R v, QB [1984] STC 361 .... 2.328
Vaughan (AM) (VTD 20547) 57.32
Vaughan (MS) [1996] VATDR 95 (VTD 14050) 40.66
Vaughans of Dudley Ltd (VTD 11374) 52.252
Vauxhall Motors Ltd (VTD 19425) 44.48
Vauxhall Motors Ltd (No 2) (VTD 20046) 2.482
Vaz (VR), QB 1994, [1995] STC 14 .... 2.397
VDP Dental Laboratory NV, Staatssecretaris van Financiën v, ECJ Case C-401/05;
[2007] STC 474 .... 22.289
Veale (D & DA) (VTD 14637) 62.341
Veda Products Ltd (VTD 13685) 18.138
Vedilux Ltd (VTD 7252) 52.125
Vehicle Control Services Ltd, [2011] UKFTT 125 (TC), TC00999 .... 62.203
Veitch (A) (t/a Pine Products) (VTD 11963) 51.135
Velker International Oil Co Ltd NV, Staatssecretaris van Financiën v, ECJ Case
C-185/89; [1990] 1 ECR 2561; [1991] STC 640 .... 22.389
Velvet & Steel Immobilien und Handels GmbH v Finanzamt Hamburg-Eimsbüttel, ECJ
Case C-455/05; [2008] STC 922 .... 22.356
Ventnor Towers Hotel (VTD 4537) 51.108
Venton (DF) (VTD 10526) 52.272
Ventrolla Ltd (VTD 12045) 55.64
Venture Capital Ltd (VTD 6794) 52.378
Venuebest Ltd, Ch D 2002, [2003] STC 433; [2002] EWHC 2870 (Ch) 41.145
Venuebest Ltd (No 2) [2005] VATDR 92 (VTD 18863) 57.62
Verbond van Nederlandse Ondernemingen v Inspecteur der Invoerrechten en
Accijnzen, ECJ Case 51/76; [1977] 1 CMLR 413; [1977] ECR 113 .... 22.432
Vereniging Happy Family Rustenburgerstrat v Inspecteur der Omzetbelasting, ECJ Case
289/86; [1988] ECR 3627; [1989] BVC 216; [1989] 3 CMLR 743 .... 22.81
Vereniging Noordelijke Land-en Tuinbouw Organisatie v Staatssecretaris van
Financiën, ECJ Case 515/07; 12 February 2009 unreported 22.187

Verigen Transplantation Service International AG, Finanzamt Leverkusen *v*, ECJ Case C-156/09; [2011] STC 255 ...... 22.285

Vermietungsgesellschaft Objekt Kirchberg SARL, Administration de l'Enregistrement et des Domaines *v*, ECJ Case C-269/03; [2005] STC 1345 ...... 22.381

Vernitron Ltd [1978] VATTR 157 (VTD 615) 62.87

Vernon Packaging Ltd (VTD 6360) 52.379

Vetplus Ltd (VTD 19850) 2.117

VF Corporation (UK) Ltd (VTD 898) 12.16

Vicar and Parochial Church Council of St Petroc Minor (VTD 16450) 55.54

Vickers Reynolds & Co (Lye) Ltd (VTD 16965) 40.36

Victoria Alloys (UK) Ltd [1991] VATTR 163 (VTD 5608) 52.61

Victoria & Albert Museum Trustees, QB [1996] STC 1016 ...... 11.53

Victoria Gardens Nursing Home (VTD 10547) 15.198

Vidhani Brothers Ltd (VTD 18997) 12.6

Viewpoint Housing Association Ltd (VTD 13148) 33.63

Vig (AR) (t/a One by One Fashions) (VTD 14504) 23.10

Vig (AR) (t/a One by One Fashions) (No 2) (VTD 14837) 52.206

Vigdor Ltd (t/a Michael Jane), Ch D 2008, [2009] STC 150; [2008] EWHC 2621 (Ch) 41.92

Village Collection Interiors Ltd (VTD 6146) 65.23

Village Surgery Ltd (The) (VTD 17939) 9.3

Villaswan Ltd *v* Sheraton (Blythswood) Ltd, CS 9 November 1998, Times 7.1.1999 ...... 32.33

Villiers Group plc *v* Isle of Man Treasury (VTD 15230) 46.207

Vinalith Ltd (VTD 20696) 18.544

Vincent Consultants Ltd [1988] VATTR 152 (VTD 3091) 62.481

Vincett (RJ) (VTD 10932) 15.273

Vin-Dotco (UK) Ltd (VTD 11346) 52.172

Vine (Mrs CA) (t/a Cornish Car Hire) (VTD 7467) 38.2

Vinetay Ltd (VTD 2230) 51.95

Vinhispania Ltd (VTD 14939) 18.506

VIP (Scotland) Ltd, [2010] UKFTT 63 (TC), TC00375 ...... 36.113

Virgin Atlantic Airways Ltd, [1993] VATTR 136 (VTD 11096) 63.7

Virgin Atlantic Airways Ltd, QB [1995] STC 341 ...... 63.7, 66.14

Virgin Atlantic Airways Ltd (No 2) (VTD 13840) 66.23

Virgo Plant Hire Ltd [1990] VATTR 113 (VTD 5046) 4.13

Virtual Leisure Ltd (VTD 19253) 2.80

Virtue (D & S) (t/a Lammermuir Game Services), [2007] VATDR 308 (VTD 20259) 41.22

Visa International Service Association, Barclays Bank plc *v*, [1992] VATTR 229 (VTD 7911) 2.75

Visa International Service Association, Barclays Bank plc *v* (No 2), [1992] VATTR 229 (VTD 9059) 2.495

Viscount Reinsurance Co Ltd, CA [2007] STC 1695; [2007] EWCA Civ 728 ...... 22.71

Vision Aid Centre (VTD 17298) 46.32

Vision Computer Products Ltd (VTD 7072) 52.232

Vision Express Ltd (VTD 16848) 39.7

Vision Express (UK) Ltd, Ch D 2009, [2010] STC 742; [2009] EWHC 3245 (Ch) 46.131

Visionplus Southport Ltd (VTD 17502) 33.10

Vital Touch Ltd (VTD 20409) 18.543

Vitalia Ltd (VTD 11682) 18.436

Vitech Engineering Ltd (VTD 5154) 10.2

Vitouladitis (D) (VTD 18547) 50.65

Vitzthum (Mr & Mrs G) (t/a Leeds Wine Services) (VTD 11076) 36.302

Viva Gas Appliances Ltd, HL [1983] STC 819; [1983] 1 WLR 1445 ...... 56.10

Vivat Holdings plc, [1995] VATDR 348 (VTD 13568) 36.36

Vivodean Ltd (VTD 6538) 55.24

Vlaamse Oliemaatschappij NV *v* FOD Financiën, ECJ Case C-499/10; 21 December 2011 unreported 22.467

Vodden (RU) (VTD 1842) 29.2

Vogue Holdings Inc, Wynn Realisations Ltd *v*, CA [1999] STC 524 ...... 67.6

Voland Asphalt Co Ltd (VTD 14553) 18.116
Volkswagen Financial Services (UK) Ltd (No 1), QB [1998] STC 528 .... 27.26
Volkswagen Financial Services (UK) Ltd (No 2), [2011] UKFTT 556 (TC), TC01401
  .... 46.166
Volvo Trucks (GB) Ltd, [1988] VATTR 11 (VTD 2579) 62.388
Von Colson *v* Land Nordrhein-Westfalen, ECJ Case 14/83; [1984] ECR 1891 .... 22.13
Von Hoffmann *v* Finanzamt Trier, ECJ Case C-145/96; [1997] STC 1321; [1997] All ER
  (EC) 852 .... 22.223
Vorngrove Ltd (VTD 1733) 2.162
Vojtisek (M) (t/a TV & Hi Fi Studio) (VTD 12905) 25.21
VSP Marketing Ltd (VTD 12636) 14.7
VSP Marketing Ltd (No 2) (VTD 13167) 2.476
VSP Marketing Ltd (No 3), [1995] VATDR 328 (VTD 13587) 2.477
Vulgar (RJ), [1976] VATTR 197 (VTD 304) 58.14

W

W, D *v*, ECJ Case C-384/98; [2002] STC 1200 .... 22.279
W & JR Watson Ltd [1974] VATTR 83 (VTD 67) 62.1
W Hamilton & Son (VTD 14812) 44.49
W Puddifer (Junior) Ltd [1996] VATDR 237 (VTD 13898) 36.623
Waddell (R & L) (t/a LCD Plant Hire), [2009] UKFTT 185 (TC), TC00140 .... 52.325
Wade (Ms J), [2011] UKFTT 504 (TC), TC01351 .... 15.125
Wade (JM & MC) (VTD 2022) 47.18
Wade (SH) (VTD 13164) 48.16
Wadham College Oxford [2007] VATDR 177 (VTD 20233) 46.149
Wadlewski (A & C) (VTD 13340) 58.24
Wadsworth (RG) (VTD 16128) 57.142
Wagon Finance Ltd (VTD 16288) 27.17
Wagstaffe Ellis & Associates (VTD 5115) 18.558
Wainbody Estates (VTD 18732) 36.59
Wainwright (RS) (VTD 3150) 18.413
Wakefield College, [2011] UKFTT 70 (TC), TC00948 .... 15.100
Walbrook Trustee (Jersey) Ltd, Fattal *v*, CA [2008] EWCA Civ 427 .... 2.287
Walden, Johnson *v*, CA 1995, [1996] STC 382 .... 2.78
Walderdorff (G) *v* Finanzamt Waldviertel, ECJ Case C-451/06; [2008] STC 3079 ... 22.343
Wales (KA) (VTD 12561) 51.75
Walia (R) Opticians (London) Ltd (VTD 5085) 18.42
Walia (R) Opticians Ltd (VTD 15050) 46.63
Walk The Walk In Action Ltd, [2009] UKFTT 186 (TC), TC00141 .... 48.130
Walker *v* Hanby, QB [1987] STC 649 .... 59.9
Walker (A) (VTD 12421) 35.17
Walker (DA) [1976] VATTR 10 (VTD 240) 7.17
Walker (DR) (VTD 20937) 18.382
Walker (W) (t/a Ziska) (VTD 11825) 41.84
Walker Navigation (VTD 7775) 52.125
Wall (VJ) (VTD 4795) 18.307
Wall Colmonoy Ltd (VTD 13210) 52.378
Wallace (E) (VTD 16281) 58.23
Wallace (J) (t/a the Cornish Pasty) (VTD 19793) 29.78
Wallace (JG) (VTD 7487) 51.28
Wallace (R) (t/a Inn House) (VTD 17109) 62.294
Wallace King plc (VTD 6498) 18.434
Waller (AR) & Associates (VTD 10297) 52.140
Waller (AR) & Associates [1993] VATTR 408 (VTD 10712) 17.11
Wallensteiner *v* Moir (No 2), QB [1975] QB 373 .... 2.445
Walley (NAJ), [2011] UKFTT 120 (TC), TC00996 .... 36.227
Wallis Ltd, [2003] VATDR 151 (VTD 18012) 15.81
Wallman Foods Ltd (VTD 1411) 36.238
Walnut Tree at Yalding Ltd (The) (VTD 14551, 15082) 65.91

Walsh (JS) (VTD 3706) 18.416
Walsh Brothers (Tunnelling) Ltd (VTD 7186) 52.191
Walsingham College (Yorkshire Properties) Ltd [1995] VATDR 141 (VTD 13223) ... 55.46
Walter E Sturgess & Sons Ltd (VTD 9009) 36.394
Walter Stewart Ltd [1974] VATTR 131 (VTD 83) 12.11
Walters (H) (t/a St George's Secretarial College) (VTD 602) 62.417
Walthall (DM) & Crisp (LD) (VTD 15979) 36.306
Wan (WC & LT) (VTD 10107) 50.109
Wan (WY & YS) (t/a Wan's Chinese Takeaway) (VTD 14829) 2.182
Wanklin (A) (Haresfield Court Tenants Association) (VTD 20133) 55.58
Ward (MA) (t/a Acorn Garage) (VTD 15875) 44.162
Ward (P) (VTD 11406) 18.226
Ward (WJ) (VTD 15713) 50.64
Ward, Ahsan v, HL [2007] UKHL 51 .... 2.123
Ward-Lee v Lineham, CA [1993] 1 WLR 754; [1993] 2 All ER 1006 .... 2.181, 2.182
Ward Meadows (Plant) Ltd (VTD 5752) 18.83
Wardhire Ltd (VTD 5622) 18.425
Warehouse & Interior Design Ltd (VTD 5893) 52.33
Waring (P & E) (VTD 15864) 58.23
Warley Denim Services (VTD 10396) 12.8
Warmfield Developments Ltd (VTD 16953) 43.10
Warner (MP & CM) (VTD 2409) 41.128
Warner (GWM) & Others (VTD 1402) 36.530
Warnock (J) (VTD 5396) 51.13
Warren (F) (t/a Sports Network Europe) (VTD 19213) 8.31
Warren (RJ) (t/a WTY Warren & Son) (VTD 19902) 29.63
Warren Bradley Estates (VTD 20672) 48.67
Warren Garage Ltd (VTD 5798) 18.113
Warren Park Hotel (VTD 3508) 18.97
Warriors Social Club (VTD 11146) 18.135
Wartsila NSD Sweden AB (VTD 16921) 52.433
Warwest Holdings Ltd (VTD 14114) 36.584
Warwick Masonic Rooms Ltd (VTD 839) 62.120
Warwick Students Union Services Ltd (VTD 12166) 18.235
Warwick University Union of Students [1995] VATDR 219 (VTD 13821) 19.97
Warwickshire Private Hospital (VTD 3531) 51.72
Washwood Heath & Ward End Conservative and Unionist Club Ltd (VTD 50) 30.3
Wat (EYS) (t/a Kam Tong Restaurant) (VTD 494, 642) 2.69
Watchet Bowling Club and Watchet Indoor Bowling Club (VTD 1026) 13.43
Watco Design Ltd (VTD 14136) 18.307
Water Hall Group plc [2003] VATDR 257 (VTD 18007) 36.678
Waterfields (Leigh) Ltd (VTD 20761) 29.62
Waterford Galleries (VTD 3448) 36.294
Waterhouse Coaches Ltd (VTD 1417) 67.116
Waterhouse Ltd (VTD 17483) 44.163
Waterlink Distribution Ltd (VTD 7913) 52.60
Waterschap Zeeuws Vlaanderen v Staatssecretaris van Financien, ECJ Case C-378/02;
    [2005] STC 1298 .... 22.454
Waterside (Wakefield) Ltd (VTD 20723) 52.438
Waterways Services [1990] VATTR 37 (VTD 4643) 15.6
Waterwynch House Ltd (VTD 2734) 57.176
Watford & District Old People's Housing Association Ltd (t/a Watford Help in The
    Home Service) [1998] VATDR 477 (VTD 15660) 33.64
Watford Timber Co Ltd (VTD 14756) 48.97
Watkins (AL) (t/a Fence-Tech) (VTD 12819) 18.263
Watkins (BS) (VTD 4668) 51.123
Watkinson (DJ) (VTD 5794) 18.280
Watson (G) (t/a Watson Cleaning Contractors) (VTD 18811) 50.92
Watson (MJ) [2010] UKFTT 526 (TC), TC01024 .... 15.62
Watson (R & L) [2004] VATDR 408 (VTD 18675) 15.266
Watson (RA) (VTD 758) 44.63

Watson Norrie Ltd (VTD 6248) 52.105
Watson of Richmond (Lord and Lady) (VTD 18903) 55.10
Watt (Mrs S) (VTD 15800) 65.100
Watters (J) (VTD 13337) 6.1
Watts (AP) (VTD 4535) 18.93
Waugh (JD) (VTD 5344, 6206) 51.37
Waverley Housing Management Ltd (VTD 11765) 43.6
Wayfarer Leisure Ltd [1985] VATTR 174 (VTD 1898) 4.18
Wayment (C) (VTD 4846) 2.59
Wayne Farley Ltd, QB [1986] STC 487 .... 2.277
WBL Ltd (VTD 6606) 18.336
Weakley (KN) (VTD 56) 57.144
Weald Leasing Ltd, ECJ Case C-103/09; [2011] STC 596 .... 22.61
Weale (KW) (VTD 14654) 57.133
Weatherproof Flat Roofing (VTD 1240) 44.5
Webb (H) (VTD 3788) 18.71
Webbro Ltd (VTD 8999) 18.611
Webster Communications International Ltd [1997] VATDR 173 (VTD 14753) 8.38
Wednesbury Corporation, Associated Provincial Picture Houses v, CA 1947, [1948]
  1 KB 223; [1947] 2 All ER 680 . 3.30, 14.22, 14.30, 14.54, 52.454, 52.455, 57.147, 57.157
Weedon (CV) (VTD 10181) 18.600
Weight Watchers (UK) Ltd, CA [2008] STC 2313; [2008] EWCA Civ 715 .... 5.91
Weight Watchers (UK) Ltd (No 2) [2010] UKFTT 384 (TC), TC00666 .... 3.59
Weissgerber (G) v Finanzamt Neustadt an der Weinstraße, ECJ Case 207/87;
  [1988] ECR 4433; [1991] STC 589 .... 22.353
Welbeck Video plc (VTD 11383) 36.482
Weldon-Hollingworth (AM) (VTD 13248) 51.49
Weldons (West One) Ltd (VTD 984) 36.620
Weldstruct Ltd [1977] VATTR 101 (VTD 374) 40.4
Weldwork Ltd (VTD 12953) 18.188
Wellcome Trust Ltd (The), ECJ Case C-155/94; [1996] STC 945; [1996] 1 ECR 3013;
  [1996] 2 CMLR 909; [1996] All ER (EC) 589 .... 22.111
Wellcome Trust Ltd [1997] VATDR 1 (VTD 14813) 7.117
Wellcome Trust (No 3) [2003] VATDR 572 (VTD 18417) 56.5
Wellcome Trust (No 4) [2008] VATDR 509 (VTD 20731) 46.217
Wellesley-Miller (TCT) (VTD 7691) 18.483
Wellington Private Hospital Ltd (The) [1993] VATTR 86 (VTD 10627B) 46.120
Wellington Private Hospital Ltd, CA [1997] STC 445 .... 19.2
Wellman (R & P) (VTD 4383) 15.161
Wellright Ltd (VTD 14646) 36.336
Wells (MF), QB [1981] STC 588; [1982] 1 All ER 920 .... 14.72
Wells (MP) (Mr & Mrs) (VTD 15169) 55.44
Welsh's Coaches Ltd (VTD 20193) 63.18
Welshback Exercise Ltd (VTD 20310) 28.17
Wendels (Mrs ME), [2010] UKFTT 476 (TC), TC00737 .... 15.272
Wendy Fair Market Club (No 1) (VTD 679, VTD 833) 2.455, 41.4
Wendy's Kitchen (VTD 15531) 29.12
Wenlock Building Centre Ltd (VTD 10893) 36.351
Wentwalk Ltd, CA [1996] STC 1049 .... 67.166
Wentwalk Ltd (No 2) [1999] VATDR 383 (16118) 62.409
Weru (UK) Ltd (VTD 12738) 18.254
Wesley (AC) (VTD 9074) 19.72
Wesley Barrell (Witney) Ltd (VTD 1087) 58.27
Wessex Continental Travel Co Ltd, [2010] UKFTT 36 (TC), TC00350 .... 57.130
West (JB) (t/a West One) (VTD 19677) 28.21
West (P), Ch D [2008] EWHC 2277 (Ch) 60.14
West (SJ) (t/a Stallard News) (VTD 5802) 58.23
West Central Halifax Partnership Ltd (VTD 16570) 7.110
West Country Vending Service Ltd, [2010] UKFTT 124 (TC), TC00435 .... 29.44
West Devon District Council, Ch D [2001] STC 1282 .... 42.4
West End Health and Fitness Club (VTD 4070) 57.47

West Essex Golf Club [1992] VATTR 35 (VTD 7321) 13.24
West Heat (Eltra) Ltd (VTD 4742) 18.278
West Herts College, Ch D 2000, [2001] STC 1245 .... 62.114
West Midlands Motors Ltd (VTD 16512) 52.447
West London Air Conditioning Ltd (VTD 10797) 52.281
West Lothian College SPV Ltd (VTD 18133) 46.60
West Way Garage (Bournemouth) Ltd (VTD 2151) 62.383
West Yorkshire Independent Hospital (Contract Services) Ltd, CA [1989] STC 539;
 [1990] 1 QB 905; [1989] 2 All ER 938 .... 62.424
Westbourne Domestic Care Agency Ltd (VTD 20947) 1.49
Westbourne Hotel (The) (VTD 1652) 7.38
Westbury (BL) (VTD 1168) 62.55
Western Road Properties Ltd (VTD 7304) 52.135
Western Waste Management Ltd (VTD 17428) 44.15
Westland Horticulture Ltd (VTD 18686) 48.4
Westminster, The Lord Mayor and Citizens of the City of [1989] VATTR 71 (VTD
 3367) 22.143
Westmoreland Investments Ltd, MacNiven v, HL [2001] STC 237 .... 46.151
Westmorland Motorway Services Ltd, CA [1998] STC 431 .... 67.143
Weston (M) (VTD 18190) 59.18
Westone Wholesale Ltd (No 1), Ch D 2007, [2008] STC 828; [2007] EWHC 2676
 (Ch) 3.133
Westone Wholesale Ltd (No 2), [2009] UKFTT 218 (TC), TC00168 .... 23.17
Westpark Interiors Ltd [1983] VATTR 289 (VTD 1534) 65.38
WF Electrical plc (VTD 17083) 18.307
WF Graham (Northampton) Ltd (VTD 908) 5.11
WF Marston & Son Ltd (VTD 15208) 62.31
WFS Metals Ltd (VTD 12293) 40.72
WG Beynon & Sons Ltd (VTD 10043) 18.452
WGM Decorating (VTD 12401) 18.389
WGM Decorating (No 2) (VTD 13344) 18.359
WH Blatch Investments Ltd (VTD 13727) 36.151
WH Payne & Co [1995] VATDR 490 (VTD 13668) 62.536
WH Smith Ltd, [2000] VATDR 1 (VTD 16505) 58.42
WH Trace & Sons Ltd (VTD 2306) 67.66
WHA Ltd, CA [2007] STC 1695; [2007] EWCA Civ 728 .... 22.71
Wharmby (CA) (VTD 16436) 67.101
Whatling (PRG) (VTD 9322) 52.21
Whatton (GM), QB [1996] STC 519 .... 2.215
Wheeled Sports 4 Hereford Ltd, [2011] UKFTT 190 (TC), TC01059 .... 15.119
Wheeler (AD) (t/a Wheeler Motor Co) (VTD 13617) 48.123
Wheeler (RJ) (VTD 7366) 52.140
Wheels Common Investment Fund Trustees Ltd, [2011] UKFTT 534 (TC); [2011] SFTD
 1025; TC01381 .... 20.84
Whereat (SJ) (VTD 16751) 51.169
Whiffen (FP) (t/a FP Whiffen Opticians) (VTD 18951) 67.82
Whiffen (FP) (t/a FP Whiffen Opticians) (No 2) (VTD 18969) 2.415
Whirlpool UK Ltd (VTD 18427) 18.307
Whiston Hall Golf Club Ltd (VTD 20361) 2.247
Whitbread Group plc, Ch D [2005] STC 539; [2005] EWHC 418 (Ch) 29.17
Whitbread Harrowden Settlement Trustees (and related appeals) (VTD 16781) 46.97,
 52.423
White (AJ) (VTD 15388) 65.86
White (D) (VTD 4254) 15.14
White (GB) (t/a Chiffon Couture) (VTD 4785) 18.6
White (MJ) (VTD 12360) 36.142
White, Aikman v, CS 1985, [1986] STC 1 .... 59.8
White (Mr & Mrs) (t/a The Kings Arms) (VTD 20859) 18.499
White & Sons (VTD 11680) 8.22
White Row Cottages Bewerley (1–4), in re, Ch D [1991] Ch 441; [1991] 4 All ER 50
 .... 15.137

Whitechapel Art Gallery, QB [1986] STC 156; [1986] 1 CMLR 79 .... 11.46
Whitechapel Art Gallery (No 2) [2008] VATDR 530 (VTD 20720) 20.20
Whitefield (JW & MJ) & Osbourne (AJ & JA) (VTD 10926) 52.74
Whitefield & Sons (Builders) Ltd (VTD 11286) 17.3
Whitehall Chase Foundation Trust (VTD 5134) 7.21
Whitehead (AJ) (VTD 10696) 52.70
Whitehead (SJ) [1975] VATTR 152 (VTD 202) 57.83
Whitehead & Wood Ltd (VTD 6341) 52.60
Whitehouse (FP) (VTD 11114) 2.60
Whitehouse (SP) (VTD 6763) 10.1
Whitelaw (J) (t/a Law Property & Leisure Group) (VTD 17640) 52.401
Whitelaw (JG) (VTD 4299) 46.134
Whiteley (SA) [1993] VATTR 248 (VTD 11292) 15.43
Whites Metal Company (VTD 2400) 36.637
Whitfield (CSJ & Mrs DJ) (VTD 3506) 36.277
Whitley (DJ) (VTD 2435) 62.225
Whitney v CIR, HL 1925, 10 TC 88 .... 32.23
Whitport plc (VTD 14337) 18.63
Whittaker (DJ) (t/a Cheslyn Hay Fish Bar) (VTD 14585) 65.91
Whittaker (M & H) & Son Ltd (VTD 3554) 36.508
Whittle (RA, DL & GA) (t/a Go Whittle) [1994] VATTR 202 (VTD 12164) 63.12
Whyte (A) (VTD 914) 2.366
Whyte (AA) (VTD 5829) 10.3
Widnes Spastic Fellowship (VTD 455) 7.53
Wiener SI GmbH v Hauptzollamt Emmerich, ECJ Case C-338/95; [1997] 1 ECR 6495;
    [1998] 1 CMLR 1110 .... 22.5
Wigan Metropolitan Development Co (Investment) Ltd (VTD 4993) 46.20
Wiggett Construction Ltd, Ch D [2001] STC 933 .... 46.209
Wigley (NCF) (VTD 7300) 44.2
Wigmore (CH) [1991] VATTR 290 (VTD 6040) 15.242
Wigmore Hall Trust (The) (VTD 13773) 18.171
Wilcock (SP) (t/a The Hi-Fi People) (VTD 9737) 18.485
Wilcox (JW) [1978] VATTR 79 (VTD 546) 7.22
Wild (MA & AJ) (t/a Audrey's Pianos), Ch D 2008, [2009] STC 566; [2008] EWHC
    3401 (Ch) 47.35
Wilf Gilbert (Staffs) Ltd (VTD 20170) 46.228
Wilkes (S) (t/a Dipton Chippy) (VTD 16652) 57.123
Wilkinson (JDG) (VTD 583, 649) 2.315
Willan (PNDC) (VTD 12563) 18.235
Willcox & Co (VTD 8813) 36.521
Willerby Manor Hotels Ltd (VTD 16673) 41.112
Willert (PW) (VTD 4970) 51.89
William Cowan & Son Ltd (VTD 1792) 36.355
William Johnson & Sons (Contractors) Ltd (VTD 11028) 52.140
William Matthew Mechanical Services Ltd [1982] VATTR 63 (VTD 1210) 8.8
William O'Hanlon & Co Ltd (VTD 12309) 18.558
William Peto & Co Ltd (VTD 736) 62.2
William Youngs & Son (Farms) Ltd (VTD 9660) 52.283
Williams (Mr & Mrs AJ) (t/a Bridge St Snack Bar) (VTD 513, 593) 2.377
Williams (BD) (VTD 15163) 52.342
Williams (E) (t/a Memories on Video) (VTD 14960) 52.435
Williams (Mrs E) (t/a Premier Flowers) (VTD 20639) 57.200
Williams (G), [2009] UKFTT 96 (TC), TC00064 .... 15.275
Williams (GD) (VTD 4810) 18.489
Williams (JO) (VTD 14240) 62.151
Williams (K & D) (VTD 7078) 4.3
Williams (L) (VTD 4261) 57.52
Williams (NM) (VTD 12876) 4.3
Williams (NR) (VTD 11361) 58.7
Williams (TSD & Mrs ME) (VTD 2445) 57.41
Williams & Glyn's Bank Ltd [1974] VATTR 262 (VTD 118) 27.1

Williams (JR) & Wallis (RJS) (VTD 7286) 46.184
Williams & Williams (t/a A Williams & Son) (VTD 4191) 18.431
Williams Grand Prix Engineering Ltd [2010] UKFTT 607 (TC), TC00848 .... 62.522
Williamson (J) [2010] UKFTT 254 (TC), TC00548 .... 15.13
Williamson (RW & AAW) [1978] VATTR 90 (VTD 555) 7.23
Williamson, CIR *v*, CS 1928, 14 TC 335 .... 57.105
Willimaier, Dotter *v*, ECJ Case C-384/98; [2002] STC 1200 .... 22.279
Willingale (J) (VTD 12029) 36.256
Willis Pension Trustees Ltd [2005] VATDR 418 (VTD 19183) 62.196
Willpower Garage Ltd (VTD 12114) 36.467
Wilmot, RCPO *v*, Southwark Crown Court 1 July 2008 unreported 49.15
Wilson (DJ) (VTD 15919) 18.509
Wilson (DL) (VTD 15803) 55.72
Wilson (GG) [1977] VATTR 225 (VTD 428) 41.138
Wilson (K) (VTD 12042) 36.578
Wilson (M) (t/a M & S Interiors) (VTD 17494) 62.334
Wilson (R & Mrs J) (t/a Mountain View Hotel) (VTD 16404) 47.20
Wilson Boyle (Development) Ltd (VTD 17029) 52.21
Wilsons of Rathkenny Ltd, [2011] UKFTT 406 (TC), TC01261 .... 48.63
Wilsons Transport Ltd (VTD 1468) 8.10
Wiltshire & Gloucestershire Draining Co Ltd (VTD 6559) 18.417
Wimborne Rugby Football Club (VTD 4547) 24.31
Wimpey Construction UK Ltd [1979] VATTR 174 (VTD 808) 44.98
Wimpey Group Services Ltd, CA [1988] STC 625 .... 15.158
Windeatt (RL) (VTD 6571) 36.605
Winder (A) (t/a Anthony & Patricia) (VTD 11784) 41.83, 62.271
Windflower Housing Association, QB [1995] STC 860 .... 55.59
Window (J) [2001] VATDR 252 (VTD 17186) 41.15
Window Glazing Consultancy (The) (VTD 6892) 52.136
Windowmaker UPVC Ltd (VTD 9939) 52.363
Windows Direct Ltd (VTD 4762) 18.243
Windsor (AT) (t/a ATW Transport) (VTD 11241) 52.349
Windsor (M) (VTD 14185) 36.195
Windsor House Investments Ltd (VTD 19666) 6.26
Wine Warehouses Europe Ltd [1993] VATTR 307 (VTD 11525) 2.159
Winfield *v* Stowmarket Golf Club Ltd, 1995 (unreported) 13.50
Wing Wah Restaurant (Birmingham) Ltd (VTD 17399) 6.38
Wingate Electrical plc (VTD 14078) 18.539
Winser (JDJ) (VTD 19366) 69.3
Winslade Electrical Ltd (VTD 10943) 14.57
Winstone (JH) (VTD 11948) 17.3
Winterthur Life UK Ltd (VTD 14935) 38.10
Winterthur Life UK Ltd (No 2) (VTD 15785) 6.7
Winterthur Life UK Ltd (No 3) (VTD 17572) 38.14
Winterthur Swiss Insurance Company [2006] VATDR 375 (VTD 19411) 22.534
Winturn Ltd (VTD 10699) 3.77
Wiper (C) (VTD 152) 57.9
Wirral, Metropolitan Borough of, QB [1995] STC 597 .... 1.73
Wirral, Metropolitan Borough of (No 2) (VTD 14674) 42.12
Wisebeck Construction Ltd (VTD 6612) 52.89
Wiseman (PH) (VTD 17374) 15.51
Wiseman (R) & Sons [1984] VATTR 168 (VTD 1691) 36.4
Wisker (G) (VTD 9716) 51.57
Witherow (GR) (VTD 20040) 15.122
Withers (RJ) & Gibbs (S) (t/a The General Stores) [1983] VATTR 323 (VTD 1553)
    .... 58.19
Withers of Winsford Ltd, QB [1988] STC 431 .... 44.3
Withies Inn Ltd (The) (VTD 14257) 43.9
Witney Golf Club [2002] VATDR 397 (VTD 17706) 9.5
Witzemann *v* Hauptzollamt München-Mitte, ECJ Case C-343/89; [1993] STC 108;
    [1991] 1 ECR 4477 .... 22.101

Wizard Accounting Solutions Ltd (VTD 12304) 18.200
WJ Brown Toys Ltd (VTD 1684) 36.33
WM Management & Marketing Ltd [2005] VATDR 242 (VTD 19075) 2.320
WMT Entertainments Ltd (VTD 9385) 24.12
WN Heaton & Son Ltd (VTD 2397) 19.25
Wold Construction Co Ltd (VTD 11704) 14.30
Wolf Management Services Ltd (VTD 1270) 8.9
Wolfe (M) (t/a Arrow Coach Services) (VTD 171) 62.82
Wolfe Ware Ltd (VTD 20941, VTD 20954) 18.543
Wollny (J & S) v Finanzamt Landshut, ECJ Case C-72/05; [2008] STC 1618 .... 22.249
Wolverhampton & Dudley Breweries plc (The) [1990] VATTR 131 (VTD 5351) 41.48
Wolverhampton Citizens Advice Bureau (VTD 16411) 11.48
Wong (B) (t/a the Four Seasons) (VTD 18931) 2.143
Wong (WY) (VTD 17348) 3.56
Wong (YY) (VTD 7591) 52.15
Wong's Chinese Takeaway (VTD 18766) 62.311
Wood (AJ) (VTD 17518) 36.10
Wood (Mrs EJ) (VTD 17256) 44.70
Wood (Mrs PD) (VTD 1037) 57.170
Wood (Mrs PD) (No 2) (VTD 4644) 36.440
Wood (Mrs SM) (t/a Moulton Auto Hire) (VTD 9565) 10.5
Wood (T) (VTD 6992) 2.115
Wood (T) (t/a Thomas Wood Associates) (VTD 15028) 18.485
Wood (J) & Riley (P) (VTD 18743) 50.47
Wood Auto Supplies Ltd (VTD 17356) 18.522
Woodcock (B) (VTD 7459) 36.606
Woodger (M) (VTD 5402) 3.76
Woodifield, Strong & Co of Romsey Ltd v, HL 1906, 5 TC 215 .... 36.536
Woodings, Rees, Crossthwaite & Jones (Drs) [1999] VATDR 294 (VTD 16175) 19.7
Woodley Baptist Church (VTD 17833) 15.204
Woods (E) (VTD 15485) 65.104
Woods (PJ) (VTD 6134) 18.441
Woods (S) (Mrs) (VTD 19024) 51.162
Woods (TE) (VTD 18049) 50.36
Woods Place Management Ltd (VTD 12812) 52.347
Woodstock Timber Products (VTD 11693) 18.473
Woodward (JJ) (VTD 569) 44.63
Woodward & Stalder Ltd (VTD 10378) 52.347
Woodworth v Conroy, CA [1996] 1 All ER 107 .... 40.75
Woolf (Mrs S) (t/a Sally Woolf Interiors) (VTD 10415) 8.2
Woolfold Motor Co Ltd, QB [1983] STC 715 .... 62.411
Woolwich Equitable Building Society v CIR, HL [1992] STC 657 .... 17.10
Worboys (AS) (VTD 3866) 51.68
Word (UK) Ltd (VTD 5224) 18.79
World Association of Girl Guides and Girl Scouts [1984] VATTR 28 (VTD 1611) ... 21.49
World Chief Ltd (VTD 2582) 1.13
Worldstill Ltd (VTD 3796) 18.307
Worldwide Surplus Supplies Ltd (VTD 16198) 36.547
Worsfold (P) (VTD 19968) 44.146
Worshipful Company of Painter-Stainers (The) (VTD 20668) 64.31
Worthington (T, EC, PT & A) (t/a Conochies) (VTD 16228) 36.300
WP Holdings plc (VTD 15134) 4.2
WR Davies Motor Group (VTD 19374) 2.31
WR Ltd (VTD 6968) 8.40
Wrag Barn Golf & Club Country Club, [2010] UKFTT 30 (TC), TC00344 .... 6.26
Wragg (JA) (t/a Take 5 Hair Design) (VTD 10574) 62.269
Wren (S) (t/a Blue & White Car Service) 67.100
Wren v Eastbourne Borough Council, ECJ [1993] 3 CMLR 166 .... 22.27
Wren Group Ltd (The) (VTD 5998) 48.88
Wrencon Ltd (VTD 13968) 55.67
Wrenshall (A) (VTD 10963) 65.31

Wright (A & Mrs M), [2011] UKFTT 681 (TC), TC01523 .... 57.107
Wright (Mrs AE) (VTD 10408) 21.32
Wright (D) (VTD 12451) 40.65
Wright (DI) (VTD 9254) 18.286
Wright (DJ & MA) (VTD 14570) 3.108
Wright (F) (VTD 7465) 52.312
Wright (GG) (VTD 5691) 18.121
Wright (JA & Mrs J) (t/a Euro Dec) (VTD 3540) 51.119
Wright (MH) (VTD 10760) 50.78
Wright (MV) (VTD 12701) 57.161
Wright (R) (t/a Gotterson's Fish Bar) (VTD 6732) 18.117
Wright (RS & EM) Ltd (VTD 12984) 36.333
Wright & Partners (VTD 10295) 27.39
Wright & Son (Building Contractors) Ltd (VTD 10055) 52.39
Wright Manley Ltd (VTD 10295) 27.39
Wrights International Leather Ltd (VTD 6399) 52.100
WS Atkins (Services) Ltd (VTD 10131) 36.35
WS Parsons Ltd (VTD 10693) 4.3
WSJ (Contractors) Ltd (VTD 11602) 52.136
Wyatt (WB) (VTD 263) 8.1
Wyck (DW) (VTD 6619) 52.101
Wydale Hall (VTD 14273) 48.137
Wyld (Mr & Mrs J) (t/a Wyldwood Coppice) (VTD 12420) 30.8
Wynd Consulting (VTD 14773) 18.600
Wyndley Nurseries Ltd (VTD 10269) 52.87
Wynn Realisations Ltd v Vogue Holdings Inc, CA [1999] STC 524 .... 67.6
Wyre Borough Council (VTD 8880) 52.260
Wythe (JC) (VTD 15054) 18.485
Wyvern Shipping Co Ltd, QB 1978, [1979] STC 91 .... 60.18

X

X v Skatteverket, ECJ Case C-84/09; [2011] STC 189 .... 20.18
X, Staatssecretaris van Financiën v, ECJ Case C-536/08; [2010] STC 1701 .... 22.411
X Ltd, ex p., R v C & E, QB [1997] STC 1197 .... 14.93
X Holding BV v Staatssecretaris van Financiën, ECJ Case C-538/08; [2010] STC 1221
.... 22.428
Xansa Barclaycard Partnership Ltd [2004] VATDR 457 (VTD 18780) 32.14
Xentric Ltd (No 1), [2010] UKFTT 249 (TC), TC00544 .... 2.273
Xentric Ltd (No 2), [2010] UKFTT 620 (TC), TC00862 .... 36.121
Xicom Systems Ltd, Ch D [2008] STC 3492; [2008] EWHC 1945 (Ch) 2.509
XL Refrigerators Ltd (VTD 9763) 18.115

Y

Yaesu Europe BV v Bundeszentralamt für Steuern, ECJ Case C-433/08; [2010] STC
809 .... 22.544
Yang Sing Chinese Restaurant (VTD 1693, VTD 1757) 2.379
Yarburgh Children's Trust, Ch D 2001, [2002] STC 207 .... 15.91
Yarl Wines (VTD 17846) 50.11
Yarlett (D) (VTD 1490) 44.9
Yarlett (J), [2011] UKFTT 253 (TC), TC01117 .... 51.55
Yasin (M) & Hussain (M) (VTD 15804) 57.43
Yate (S) (t/a Yummies) (VTD 16943) 18.189
Yavuz (N) (t/a Fosters Off Licence / Supermarket) (VTD 18593) 2.239
Yazaki (UK) Ltd (VTD 7128) 52.277
Yelland (ED) [2010] UKFTT 340 (TC), TC00622 .... 48.63
Yeung (HC) (t/a Yeung's Garden) (VTD 17574) 50.104

Yeung (YM) (t/a Golden House) (VTD 18017) 57.137
Yip (KH) (t/a Manie Takeaway) (VTD 17163) 52.305
Yoga for Health Foundation, QB [1984] STC 630; [1985] 1 CMLR 340 .... 22.293
York Avenue Garage (VTD 3252) 18.137
Yorkhurst Ltd (VTD 14458) 46.190
Yorkshire & Humberside Tourist Board (VTD 4744) 18.236
Yorkshire Co-Operatives Ltd, ECJ Case C-398/99; [2003] STC 234; [2003] 1 WLR
   2821 .... 22.244
Yorkshire Rural Investments Ltd (VTD 15083) 52.20
Young (C), CS [1993] STC 394 .... 2.152
Young (L) (VTD 14987) 62.293
Young (Professor RM) (VTD 7922) 57.130
Young (RV) Ltd (VTD 12123) 52.352
Young Construction (London) Ltd (VTD 14565) 18.590
Young Street Management Services Ltd (VTD 5711) 18.586
Younger (AL) (VTD 1173) 1.93
Younghusband (PR) (VTD 7443) 36.188
Younis (M) (t/a Heaton Private Hire) (VTD 11908) 3.137
Yuen Tung Restaurant Ltd (t/a The Far East Restaurant) [1993] VATTR 226 (VTD
   11008) 3.121
Yung (P & A) (t/a Chilli Restaurant & Hong Kong Food) (VTD 16695) 47.33
Yusupoff (L) (VTD 18152) 33.24

Z

Zaman (T) (VTD 18647) 36.619
Zanex Ltd (VTD 17460) 67.25
Zargari (S) (VTD 17138) 65.96
Zaveri (S) (t/a The Paper Shop) [1986] VATTR 133 (VTD 2121) 51.105
Zeldaline Ltd [1989] VATTR 191 (VTD 4388) 29.28
Zemmel (H) (VTD 498) 57.10
Zen Internet Ltd (VTD 18563) 50.119
Zenith Holdings Ltd (VTD 6032) 52.48
Zenith Publishing Ltd (VTD 20973) 36.61
Zetland Garage (Southport) Ltd (VTD 4676) 18.283
Zhiren (J) (t/a Captain's Catch Restaurant) (VTD 17785) 57.19
Zielinski Baker & Partners, HL [2004] STC 456; [2004] UKHL 7; [2004] 1 WLR 707;
   [2004] 2 All ER 141 .... 55.9
Zimmatore (P) (VTD 10376) 52.105
Zita Modes Sàrl v Administration de l'enregistrement et des domaines, ECJ Case
   C-497/01; [2005] STC 1059 .... 22.167
Zonner Industries Ltd (VTD 6031) 52.32
Zoo Clothing Ltd (VTD 9161) 62.14
Zoological Society of London (The), ECJ Case C-267/00; [2002] STC 521;
   [2002] All ER (EC) 465 .... 22.321
Zoological Society of Wales (The) (VTD 18786) 16.2
Zoungrou (L & E) (t/a Highlands Steak House), QB 1988, [1989] STC 313 .... 2.375
Zurich Insurance Company, CA [2007] STC 1756; [2007] EWCA Civ 218 .... 62.506
Zweckverband zur Trinkwasserversorgung und Abwasserbeseitigung Torgau-Westelbien,
   Finanzamt Oschatz v, ECJ Case C-442/05; [2009] STC 1 .... 22.267

1

Agents

The cases in this chapter are arranged under the following headings.

Definition of agent	**1.1**
Whether acting as agent or principal	
Cases held to constitute an agency	**1.2**
Cases held not to constitute an agency	**1.32**
Supplies through agents acting in own name (VATA 1994, s 47(2A), (3))	**1.72**
'Disbursements'	**1.81**
Estate agents	**1.86**
Nursing agencies	**1.88**
'Party plan' and direct selling	**1.91**

Definition of agent

[1.1] In a case concerning zero-rating provisions in *FA 1972*, which have since been superseded, the Commissioners issued an assessment on a woman who had organised educational holidays. She appealed, contending that she was acting as an agent of overseas organisations, so that she was not required to account for VAT under the law then in force. The tribunal accepted this contention but the QB remitted the case to the tribunal for rehearing. Woolf J held that the tribunal had erred in law, and defined agency as 'the relationship which exists between two persons, one of whom expressly or impliedly consents that the other should represent him or act on his behalf and the other of whom similarly consents to represent the former or so to act'. *C & E Commrs v E Johnson*, QB [1980] STC 624. (*Note.* There was no further public hearing of the appeal.)

Whether acting as agent or principal

NOTE

VATA 1994, s 47(2A), introduced by *FA 1995, s 23* with effect from 1 June 1995, provides that where an agent acts in his or her own name in relation to a supply of goods, the goods are treated as having been supplied to and by the agent. If the goods are eligible second-hand goods, the 'margin scheme' may be used provided that the conditions of the scheme are met. Cases relating to periods before 1 June 1995 should be read in the light of the subsequent change in the law.

Cases held to constitute an agency

Art dealers

[1.2] A partnership which carried on business as art dealers was approached by a potential customer who wished to purchase an oil painting. They sought advice from a specialist dealer who recommended a painting which he had in stock, which he suggested that they could sell for between £3,000 and £5,000. The partners agreed a price with their customer of £3,300, and received this sum in cash before they had actually purchased the painting from the specialist dealer. They subsequently paid him £2,700 for the painting. The Commissioners issued an assessment on the partners, charging output tax on the full price of £3,300 paid by the customer. They appealed, contending that they had undertaken the transaction as agents for the specialist dealer, and that they should only be required to account for tax on their profit of £600. The tribunal accepted this contention and allowed their appeal. *JNS Bagshawe & CAE Walker*, LON/84/163 (VTD 1762).

Building company

[1.3] A building contractor (D) was also the controlling shareholder of a company carrying on a similar business. D recruited subcontractors to work for the company when required. The Commissioners assessed the company on the basis that it had supplied the services of some of these subcontractors to D for work which he had undertaken as a contractor. The company appealed, contending that it had merely acted as an agent for D and had not made any supplies to D as an independent principal. The tribunal accepted this contention and allowed the company's appeal. *WF Dickinson (Dorset) Ltd*, LON/87/327 (VTD 2778).

Meals delivered by taxi—whether proprietor acting as agent or principal

[1.4] A trader (N) operated a delivery service, whereby food was delivered from restaurants to consumers by taxi. Customers contacted N with orders for food, following which N contacted the restaurant and a taxi driver, and the taxi driver collected the meal and paid for it either by cash or by a voucher debiting the cost to N. The driver received payment from the customer, including a delivery charge, and N received a payment described as an 'agency fee' from the restaurant. N only accounted for output tax on the 'agency fees'. The Commissioners issued an assessment charging output tax on the full amounts paid by the consumers, including the prices of the meals and the delivery charges paid to the drivers. The tribunal allowed N's appeal, holding that the meals were purchased by the taxi drivers rather than by N, and that N was acting as an agent rather than as a principal. *Dr R Nader (t/a Try Us)*, LON/89/1395Y (VTD 4927). (*Note.* For a subsequent application for costs, see **2.389** APPEALS.)

Company providing catering services for charity at residential homes

[1.5] A charity which operated a number of residential homes engaged a company (P) to provide catering services. P was paid a management fee, and also retained discounts which it obtained on the bulk purchase of food. It accounted for VAT on the management fee, but did not account for VAT on the discounts. The Commissioners issued an assessment charging output tax on the discounts, on the basis that P was acting as an agent of the charity and that the discounts were part of the consideration for P's services. The tribunal dismissed P's appeal, holding that there was a single supply of catering services, and that P was acting as an agent of the charity when it made its purchases of food. Accordingly, the discounts which P retained constituted consideration for P's services, and P was required to account for output tax on them. *PBK Catering Ltd*, LON/91/2688Y (VTD 11426).

Sales of craft pottery

[1.6] A partnership sold craft pottery from a retail shop. The partners purchased some items for resale, but other items were deposited with them by individual potters. In such cases, the partners considered that they were acting as agents for the potters, and only accounted for VAT on their agreed commission. The Commissioners issued an assessment on the basis that the partners were selling the pottery as principals, and should account for VAT on the full sale price. The QB allowed the partners' appeal, holding that the partnership was selling the pottery as agents of the individual potters. *JK Hill & SJ Mansell (t/a JK Hill & Co) v C & E Commrs*, QB [1988] STC 424. (*Note.* For another issue in this case, not taken to the QB, see **36.187** INPUT TAX.)

Second-hand musical equipment

[1.7] A company owned seven shops trading in second-hand musical equipment. It accepted and paid for goods brought into its shops by members of the public, but in such cases it gave the vendors a notice stating that 'these goods are accepted for sale on your behalf by the company acting as your agent' and 'the goods will remain your property until sold'. The Commissioners issued an assessment to the company, charging output tax on the full sale price of the goods. The company appealed, contending that it was acting as an agent and should only be assessed on its margin. The tribunal accepted this contention and allowed the appeal, and the QB upheld this decision, holding that the terms of the contract agreed between the company and the vendors made it clear that the company was acting as an agent rather than as a principal. *C & E Commrs v Music & Video Exchange Ltd*, QB [1992] STC 220.

Company investing money deposited by clients

[1.8] A company received money from members of the public and invested it in options and futures, dealing through brokers. The Commissioners assessed the company on the basis that it was acting as a principal when buying and selling options and futures. The company appealed, contending that it was acting as the agent of its clients. The tribunal allowed the company's appeal, holding on the evidence that the company was acting as the agent of its investors and not as a principal on its own account. *Cornhill Management Ltd*, [1991] VATTR 1 (VTD 5444).

'Party plan' hostesses

[1.9] See the cases noted at **1.92** to **1.94** below.

Musical tuition at universities

[1.10] See *Alberni String Quartet*, 21.2 EDUCATION.

Export of goods

[1.11] See *Geistlich Sons Ltd*, 25.28 EXPORTS.

Import of goods

[1.12] See *Angela Walker*, 35.17 IMPORTS.

Input tax reclaimed by company managing pop group

[1.13] A company carried on the business of managing the affairs of performers in the entertainment industry. In 1983 it managed a European tour by an Australian pop group. In the course of arranging the tour, the company entered into various contracts, some of which were in its own name and some in the name of the group. It reclaimed input tax in respect of the supplies made under these contracts. The Commissioners rejected the claim and the tribunal dismissed the company's appeal, holding that the company was acting as an agent for the group rather than as a principal, and that the supplies under the contracts were made to the group rather than to the company. *World Chief Ltd*, LON/87/350 (VTD 2582).

Input tax claimed on purchase of paper

[1.14] A company (L), which carried on business as an advertising agency, reclaimed input tax in respect of the purchase of a large quantity of paper. The Commissioners rejected the claim, considering that L had acquired the paper as agent for a US company, rather than as a principal. The tribunal upheld the Commissioners' contentions and dismissed L's appeal. *LS & A International Ltd*, LON/88/598X (VTD 3717).

Supplies of employees' services

[1.15] See *British United Shoe Machinery Co Ltd*, 40.85 INVOICES, and *Hilltop Assistance Ltd*, 62.49 SUPPLY.

Nursing agency

[1.16] See *British Nursing Co-Operation Ltd*, 33.20 HEALTH AND WELFARE; *Reed Personnel Services Ltd*, 33.21 HEALTH AND WELFARE; *Sheffield & Rotherham Nursing Agency*, 33.22 HEALTH AND WELFARE; *BUPA Nursing Services Ltd*, 62.316 SUPPLY, and *South Hams Nursing Agency*, 62.317 SUPPLY.

Employment agency

[1.17] See *Wood*, 36.10 INPUT TAX, and *Reed Employment Ltd (No 3)*, 48.39 PAYMENT OF TAX.

Company dealing in vehicle registration numberplates

[1.18] See *Tayside Numbers Ltd*, 48.40 PAYMENT OF TAX.

Auctioneers

[**1.19**] See *Jocelyn Feilding Fine Arts Ltd*, 60.7 SECOND-HAND GOODS.

Charity sharing office accommodation with associated company

[**1.20**] See *Durham Aged Mineworkers' Homes Association*, 62.45 SUPPLY.

Driving instructors

[**1.21**] See the cases noted at **62.223** to **62.231** SUPPLY.

Taxi and car hire businesses

[**1.22**] See *Triumph & Albany Car Service*, **62.240** SUPPLY; *Hussain*, **62.242** SUPPLY, and the cases noted at **62.243** to **62.245** SUPPLY.

Taxi drivers

[**1.23**] See *Hamiltax*, **62.233** SUPPLY; *Knowles*, **62.234** SUPPLY, and *Snaith*, **62.235** SUPPLY.

Escort agency

[**1.24**] See *Polok*, **62.279** SUPPLY, and *Portman Escort Agency*, **62.280** SUPPLY.

Company trading as pawnbroker

[**1.25**] A company which traded as a pawnbroker sold quantities of gold coins. The Commissioners formed the opinion that it had sold the coins as a principal and should have accounted for output tax on the full sale price. They issued an assessment accordingly. The company appealed, contending that it had sold the coins as an agent of the members of the public who provided the coins, rather than as an independent principal, and was therefore only required to account for output tax on its profit. The tribunal allowed the company's appeal, holding on the evidence that 'on the true construction of the contract notes the appellant acted as the seller's agent in the transactions in question'. *Lombard Guildhouse plc*, MAN/93/1417 (VTD 12974).

Motorcycle courier service

[**1.26**] A company operated a motorcycle courier service. It had about 150 accounts customers. Where work was carried out for such customers, the company retained 40% of the receipts and paid the other 60% to the couriers. The company also received occasional requests from people other than accounts customers. In such cases, it allowed the riders who worked for it to accept the work and retain the whole of the payments which they received. It did not account for output tax on such payments. The Commissioners issued an assessment to recover the tax and the tribunal dismissed the company's appeal, holding that the couriers were acting as agents of the company, even though the company made no profit from the cash customers. The tribunal observed that the company had an interest in allowing the couriers to keep sums received for cash work, since 'this meant that the riders could rely on immediate cash receipts to meet their cash needs for such items as petrol and personal expenses'. *Prontobikes Ltd*, LON/94/1198A (VTD 13213).

Company providing parking control services—whether agent of landowner

[1.27] A company provided parking control services, under an agreement with a landowner. The landowner paid the company a fixed fee of £200 pa plus VAT, and the company placed a notice on the site, warning that vehicles parked without authority would be clamped and that the charge for removing the clamp was £58.75. The company retained such fees and did not account for tax on them. The Commissioners issued an assessment charging output tax. The company appealed, contending that the charges represented damages for trespass which were paid to it as an independent principal and were outside the scope of VAT. The tribunal rejected this contention and dismissed the appeal, holding on the evidence that the company was acting an agent of the landowner, applying *Arthur v Anker*, CA 1996, [1997] QB 564; [1996] 3 All ER 783. By allowing the company to retain the fees, the landowner had effectively paid the fees back to the company 'as a fee for carrying out its services to the landowner of carrying out parking control'. The fees were therefore consideration for a standard-rated supply of services. *Seagar Enterprises Ltd (t/a Ace Security Services)*, LON/97/1190 (VTD 15432).

Commission for collecting royalties

[1.28] An individual (J) agreed to collect levies for a group of film-makers, retaining 25% of the fees he collected as his commission. The Commissioners issued an assessment charging tax on this commission. The tribunal upheld the assessment and dismissed J's appeal. *B Jones (t/a Beejay Enterprises)*, MAN/00/181 (VTD 17036).

Supplies of hotel accommodation

[1.29] A company (S) operated a website through which it marketed hotel accommodation outside the UK. About 94% of its sales were to travel agents and about 6% for holidaymakers. It failed to account for VAT on its supplies. HMRC issued assessments charging output tax of more than £7,000,000. S appealed, contending that it was acting as an agent for the owners of the hotels, and should not be required to account for UK VAT. The Upper Tribunal accepted this contention and allowed the appeal (reversing the First-Tier decision). Morgan J held that 'the question as to the identity of the supplier of holiday accommodation is to be answered by considering the contracts entered into between the relevant parties and determining their effect as a matter of contract'. In this case, the contracts for the provision of hotel accommodation were 'between the hotel operator and the holidaymaker'. Accordingly, the supplies of hotel accommodation were made by the owners of the hotels, and S was only supplying agency services. *Secret Hotels2 Ltd v HMRC*, UT [2011] UKUT 308 (TCC); [2011] STC 1750. (*Note.* HMRC have applied for permission to appeal to the CA against this decision.)

Input tax reclaimed on supplies for property development

[1.30] A company (H) purchased a property. It engaged another company (B) to develop the property. B arranged for a firm (D) to provide services relating to a planning appeal. D invoiced B for its services. Although the invoices were addressed to B, H reclaimed the input tax. Customs issued an assessment to recover the tax and H appealed, contending that it had paid the invoices even though they had been addressed to B, that B had been acting as its agent, and that it should be treated as the recipient of D's supplies. The tribunal accepted these contentions and allowed the appeal. *Hamstead Holdings Ltd*, LON/06/132 (VTD 19867). (*Note*. No other cases were cited in the decision. Compare *Barnes*, 40.23 INVOICES AND CREDIT NOTES.)

[**1.31**] See also *Rental Concepts Ltd*, 36.22 INPUT TAX.

Cases held not to constitute an agency

Sale of vehicles—whether supplier acting as agent

[**1.32**] A trader obtained black taxicabs from London to sell in Blackpool and accounted for tax only on his profit. Customs assessed him on the full sale price and he appealed, contending that he was acting as agent for the purchasers of the vehicles and that tax should be payable only on his commission. The tribunal rejected this contention and dismissed his appeal. *D Flitcroft*, MAN/86/328 (VTD 2328).

[**1.33**] The Commissioners discovered that an unregistered trader (R) was selling vehicles from a garage forecourt. They issued a notice of compulsory registration. R appealed, contending that he was acting as an agent, so that his turnover was below the registration threshold. The tribunal rejected this contention and dismissed his appeal, holding that he was acting as an independent principal. *K Richardson*, MAN/03/448 (VTD 18617).

[**1.34**] A similar decision was reached in *B Morris*, MAN/03/682 (VTD 18741).

Trader providing services to trainee driving instructors

[**1.35**] A trader provided services to customers who wished to train as driving instructors, including arranging for tuition by experienced instructors and tutors. Customs issued a ruling that he was required to account for VAT on the full amount of his fees (except for the DSA examination and registration fees). He appealed, contending that where he arranged for other instructors to give tuition, he was acting as an agent and should not be required to account for VAT on the amounts which he passed on to those instructors. The tribunal rejected this contention and dismissed his appeal, holding that he was acting as an independent principal. *ML Harrod (t/a Roadcraft UK)*, LON/05/778 (VTD 19644).

Proprietor of taxi business

[**1.36**] See *Hussain*, 62.242 SUPPLY.

Taxi drivers

[**1.37**] See *Jivelynn Ltd*, 62.247 SUPPLY, and *Kearns*, 62.248 SUPPLY.

Food sold by hostesses on buses

[**1.38**] A company (N) operated long-distance coach services. It arranged for 'hostesses' to sell food to passengers during the journeys. The hostesses were responsible for purchasing the food, and were entitled to retain any profits made. Customs assessed N on the basis that the hostesses were acting as agents, and that N was required to account for tax on the full amounts paid by the passengers. N appealed, contending that the hostesses were acting as independent principals. The tribunal accepted this contention and allowed the appeal. *National Bus Company*, LON/86/622 (VTD 2530).

Catering services

[1.39] A company supplied food and catering services at the US embassy. It accounted for tax on the basis that it was supplying the food as an independent principal but was supplying the catering services as an agent. Customs issued assessments on the basis that company was supplying the catering services as an independent principal. The tribunal dismissed the company's appeal. *Aramark Ltd*, MAN/05/605 (VTD 20515).

Chiropractor

[1.40] A chiropractor (M) entered into an agreement with another chiropractor (C), whereby C provided chiropractic services at M's premises, using M's equipment. The fees from the patients treated by C were divided equally between C and M. Customs issued an assessment on the basis that the effect of the agreement was that C was treating patients as an agent of M, so that M was accountable for VAT on the whole of the fees charged, and not merely on the 50% which he retained. The tribunal allowed M's appeal, finding that 'none of the provisions in the agreement points conclusively towards the relationship of principal and agent', and holding that C was supplying services to the patients as a principal, rather than as M's agent. Accordingly, M was only required to account for output tax on the amounts which he actually received from C. *Dr SGP Middleton (No 2)*, MAN/90/588 (VTD 11208).

Dealer in industrial mouldings

[1.41] A trader acted as exclusive distributor of a type of polyurethane mouldings manufactured by a German company. The Commissioners issued a ruling that he was acting as an agent of the German company, so that his commission was standard-rated. He appealed, contending that he was an independent principal and that the amounts which he received from the manufacturer were zero-rated under the legislation then in force. The tribunal accepted his evidence and allowed his appeal, applying *dicta* in *Potter*, 1.89 below. *MC Linham*, LON/92/1651A (VTD 11359).

Goods sold at auction organised by fund-raising committee

[1.42] A committee was established to raise funds to aid blood sports, such as stag-hunting and fox-hunting. It organised an auction in connection with a horse-race meeting, at which it sold goods which had been donated to it by supporters of its activities. It did not account for output tax on the sales made at the auction. The Commissioners issued an assessment charging tax on the sales, and the committee appealed, contending that it was selling the goods as agents for the donors. The tribunal rejected this contention and dismissed the appeal, holding that the committee was selling the goods as independent principals rather than as agents. *The Cheltenham Countryside Race Day*, LON/93/2877A (VTD 12460).

Auctioneers

[**1.43**] A company (L) traded as auctioneers. In cases where a successful bidder failed to pay the amount promised, L paid the vendor as if it had received the amount in question, and subsequently offered the goods for sale again, but did not account for output tax on the proceeds of this sale. Customs issued an assessment charging tax on the proceeds, and L appealed, contending that it was selling such goods as agents for the original vendor. The tribunal rejected this contention and dismissed the appeal, holding that L was selling the goods as an independent principal, and was obliged to account for output tax. *Athol Street Auctioneers Ltd*, MAN/93/375 (VTD 12478).

Mail broker

[**1.44**] A company (M) carried on business as a mail broker. It only accounted for output tax on 20% of the payments which it received from two major clients, treating the remaining 80% as disbursements and as outside the scope of VAT. Customs issued an assessment charging tax on the payments, and M appealed, contending that it was acting as an agent. The tribunal rejected this contention and dismissed the appeal, holding that M was trading as an independent principal and was required to account for output tax on the full amounts which it received. *Mail Brokers International Ltd*, LON/94/1939A (VTD 14188).

Company providing staff for clients

[**1.45**] A company (H) provided temporary accountancy and banking staff for client companies. It accounted for PAYE, and until 1994 it accounted for VAT on the basis that it was acting as an independent principal. In 1995 its accountants formed the opinion that it should only have accounted for VAT on its commission, and not on the amounts which it passed to the temps as wages. They wrote to Customs requesting permission to issue credit notes on this basis. Customs rejected the claim, and H appealed. The tribunal dismissed the appeal, holding that H had been acting as an independent principal and had been supplying temporary staff for 'a unitary charge', rather than merely introducing staff in return for commission. *Hays Personnel Services Ltd*, LON/95/2610 (VTD 14882).

[**1.46**] A similar decision was reached in a case where a company provided nursery staff. The tribunal held that the company was acting as a principal and was required to account for VAT on the full amount of its consideration. *Eyears Ltd*, MAN/06/559 (VTD 20167). (*Note*. The tribunal also held that the supplies failed to qualify for exemption—see **33.75** HEALTH AND WELFARE.)

[**1.47**] A company was registered as a 'recruitment agency' and helped clients to find temporary staff. The tribunal held that for VAT purposes, it was acting as an independent principal rather than as an agent. *Helping Hand Asset Management Ltd*, LON/07/775 (VTD 20408).

Partnership providing domestic care workers

[**1.48**] A partnership provided domestic care workers. The Commissioners issued an assessment charging tax on the charges which the partnership made to its clients. The partnership appealed, contending that it was acting as an agent rather than as a principal, and should only be required to account for tax on the commission which it retained. The tribunal rejected this contention and dismissed the appeal. *Clarina Live-In Care Service*, LON/99/96 (VTD 16434).

[1.49] The decision in *Clarina Live-In Care Service*, 1.48 above, was applied in the similar subsequent case of *Westbourne Domestic Care Agency Ltd*, LON/07/733 (VTD 20947).

Property development

[1.50] A company (D) carried on a property development business. It became aware of two sites which were suitable for development, but did not have the resources to finance this. It entered into arrangements with a larger company (C) whereby C acquired the freehold interest in one site and the leasehold interest in the other (the freehold of the latter being retained by the local County Council). D was to build large office buildings on the sites and to receive payment from C to meet the costs of the work. At the completion of the work, C was to pay D the excess of the value of the buildings over their cost. D reclaimed input tax on the expenditure incurred on the work, and Customs issued assessments to recover the tax, considering that D was acting as an agent for C, rather than as an independent principal. The tribunal allowed D's appeal, holding that the work was a joint venture which was intended to result in an investment for C and a profit for D, which was acting as an independent principal. *Drexlodge Ltd*, MAN/88/705 (VTD 5614).

Magazine distribution company

[1.51] See *Odhams Distribution Pergamon Holdings Ltd*, 5.102 BOOKS, ETC and *Keesing (UK) Ltd*, 5.103 BOOKS, ETC.

Company placing orders for magazines with publishers

[1.52] See *Nordic Subscription Service UK Ltd*, 5.105 BOOKS, ETC.

Group of musicians

[1.53] Customs registered the leader of a group of musicians. He appealed, contending that he should be treated as an agent for the other musicians in the group, so that the amounts paid to the other musicians did not form part of his turnover, and he should not be required to register. The tribunal rejected this contention and dismissed his appeal, holding that he was the sole proprietor of the group, trading as an independent principal rather than as an agent, and was required to register and account for VAT accordingly. *S Dorfman*, MAN/03/578 (VTD 18816).

[1.54] See also *Kirkby*, 51.29 PENALTIES: FAILURE TO NOTIFY.

Nursing agency

[1.55] See *Allied Medicare Nursing Services Ltd*, 33.2 HEALTH AND WELFARE, and *Parkinson*, 33.3 HEALTH AND WELFARE.

Tupperware sub-distributors

[1.56] See *Potter*, 1.91 below.

'Door-to-door' salesmen

[**1.57**] See *Betterware Products Ltd*, 1.96 below, and *Kelly*, 1.97 below.

Company selling vouchers for services

[**1.58**] A company (B) sold vouchers entitling the purchasers to certain services (such as a flight in a biplane or a drive in a Ferrari). Customs issued a ruling that it was liable to account for tax on the full amounts it received from its customers. B appealed, contending that it was acting as an agent for the service providers and was only required to account for tax on its commission. The tribunal rejected this contention and dismissed the appeal. *Buyagift Ltd*, LON/05/602 (VTD 19856). (*Note.* A subsequent appeal by the same company was also dismissed, with costs being awarded to Customs (*VTD 20774*).)

Property conveyancing business

[**1.59**] See *Culverhouse*, 57.175 REGISTRATION.

Association of taxi drivers

[**1.60**] See *Eastbourne Town Radio Cars Association*, 62.32 SUPPLY.

Hairstylists at salon

[**1.61**] See *Ashmore*, 62.268 SUPPLY.

Hostesses at night club

[**1.62**] See *Leapmagic Ltd*, 62.281 SUPPLY.

Launderette staff providing 'service washes'

[**1.63**] See *Ivychain Ltd*, 62.315 SUPPLY.

School photographs supplied to school for resale to parents

[**1.64**] A photographer supplied school photographs to schools which resold the photographs to parents at prices recommended by the photographer. The school retained an agreed percentage of the payments and paid the balance to the photographer. The Commissioners issued an assessment on the basis that the school was acting as an agent and that the photographer was liable to account for VAT on the amounts paid by the parents to the school, rather than just the amounts received by him from the school. The tribunal allowed the photographer's appeal, holding that the schools had not entered into an agency agreement and that the photographer's customers were the schools rather than the parents. The QB upheld the tribunal decision, holding that the schools had not been authorised to create contractual agreements between the photographer and the parents. *C & E Commrs v PLA Paget*, QB [1989] STC 773.

Supply of facilities for taking school photographs

[**1.65**] See *Lancashire County Council*, 62.368 SUPPLY.

Council playground including miniature railway operated independently

[**1.66**] See *Hemsworth Town Council*, 62.345 SUPPLY.

Whether building company acting as agent for development company

[1.67] A company (L), which traded as a travel agent, agreed to purchase a freehold property for £100,000 from a development company (D), and to pay a construction company (B) £145,000 plus VAT for the renovation of the property. B and D were associated companies. L reclaimed the input tax on the renovation, and the Commissioners issued an assessment to recover the tax, on the basis that there was in reality a single exempt supply of a renovated building. L appealed, contending that there were two separate supplies. The tribunal accepted this contention and allowed L's appeal. On the evidence, the transactions were genuine and were not a sham. B had supplied its services to L as an independent principal, rather than as an agent for D, and L was entitled to credit for the input tax. *Lonsdale Travel Ltd*, MAN/90/535 (VTD 12113).

Tenant of bomb-damaged building arranging for repairs

[1.68] See *Commercial Union Assurance Co plc*, 36.67 INPUT TAX.

Companies advertising loft conversion services

[1.69] Two associated companies advertised loft conversion services. They failed to account for VAT on the full amounts charged to their customers. Customs issued assessments charging tax on the full amounts paid by the customers. The companies appealed, contending that they were acting as agents for the self-employed contractors who carried out the conversion, and that they should only be required to account for tax on their net takings. The tribunal rejected this contention and dismissed the appeals, but the Ch D remitted the case for rehearing. The tribunal duly reheard the case and upheld its previous decision, holding that the agreement was 'not compatible with agency'. *A1 Lofts Ltd v HMRC (and related appeal)*, [2010] UKFTT 581 (TC), TC00831.

Company operating travel club

[1.70] See *The UK Travel Agent Ltd*, 66.17 TRANSPORT.

Amount paid to finance company under sales promotion scheme

[1.71] See *Classic Driveways (UK) Ltd*, 67.50 VALUATION.

Supplies through agents acting in own name (VATA 1994, s 47(2A), (3))

[1.72] In a case where the facts were complex and unusual, the Commissioners issued an assessment on the basis that a company had purchased goods as an agent for another company, within what is now *VATA 1994, s 47(3)*, and should therefore have accounted for output tax. The tribunal allowed the company's appeal, holding that the goods had been purchased as an independent principal. As a result, *s 47(3)* was not applicable and the basis of the assessment was untenable. (The tribunal declined to consider the alternative argument that the amount of the assessment would have been the same if the Commissioners had based their assessment on the company having acted as an independent principal.) *Halroy Products Ltd*, MAN/79/80 (VTD 1010).

[**1.73**] A borough council had engaged contractors to carry out building and engineering work. Subsequently the council entered into an agreement with a finance company, whereby the finance company became the contractor and appointed the council as its agent. The subcontractors who performed the work were paid by the council, which was reimbursed by the finance company. (Additionally, the finance company agreed to pay the contractors amounts outstanding under the contracts and the council agreed to reimburse the company for this.) The council reclaimed the input tax charged to it by the contractors, but did not account for output tax on its deemed supplies of building services to the company. The Commissioners issued an assessment on the basis that, by virtue of what is now *VATA 1994, s 47(3)*, the council should have accounted for output tax. The council appealed, contending that it should have been permitted to delay accounting for output tax until it received reimbursement from the finance company (which in some cases was a year after it had reclaimed input tax on its payments to the subcontractors). The tribunal rejected this contention and dismissed the appeal, and the QB upheld this decision. Potts J held that the tax points for the input tax and output tax must be the same, that the tax point was not fixed by the date of reimbursement since these were deemed supplies, and that the only sensible time when the deemed output could take place was simultaneously with the deemed input. *Metropolitan Borough of Wirral v C & E Commrs*, QB [1995] STC 597.

[**1.74**] A trader (S) acted as a franchisee for a company (M) which provided finance for the leasing of commercial vehicles. S sold a vehicle which he had acquired in a part-exchange transaction, and paid the proceeds of the sale to M. He then reclaimed input tax on the payment. The Commissioners issued an assessment to recover the tax, considering that S had sold the vehicle as a principal, so that there was no justification for the reclaim of input tax. S appealed, contending that he had sold the vehicle as an agent of M, and was therefore entitled to reclaim the tax by virtue of what is now *VATA 1994, s 47(2A)*. The tribunal rejected this contention and dismissed the appeal, holding on the evidence that S had made the sale as a principal, rather than as an agent, and was not entitled to reclaim the VAT as input tax. *AJ Shutt*, MAN/92/219 (VTD 9817).

[**1.75**] In July 1997 a woman (R) began a used car business. Because she did not have sufficient capital to purchase used cars, she allowed other vendors to display cars on her premises on the basis that, when a purchaser was found, R would purchase the car from the vendor, resell it to the purchaser and recover a commission from the vendor by deducting this from the sale price. R did not register for VAT until September 1998. The Commissioners discovered that she had become liable to register from September 1997, and issued a notice of compulsory registration, backdated accordingly. R appealed, contending that the commission which she retained had been below the registration threshold. The tribunal dismissed her appeal, holding that *VATA 1994, s 47(2A)* applied. R had supplied the cars as an agent acting in her own name, so that the gross sale price of the cars should be treated as her turnover for VAT purposes. *JP Rowan*, MAN/99/92 (VTD 16357).

[**1.76**] A company which dealt in antiques arranged for an antique locket to be sold at auction. It was purchased by a Kuwaiti who exported it. The company did not account for output tax on the sale of the locket. The Commissioners issued an assessment and imposed a misdeclaration penalty. The company appealed, contending that the sale should be treated as a zero-rated export. The tribunal rejected this contention and dismissed the appeal, holding that the locket was sold through the auctioneers who were agents acting in their own name. Accordingly, by virtue of *VATA 1994, s 47(2A)*, there was a supply of goods by the company to the auctioneers and a supply by the auctioneers to the Kuwaiti purchaser. Although the sale by the auctioneers was an export which qualified for zero-rating, the supply by the company to the auctioneers was standard-rated. *Bashir Mohamed Ltd*, LON/99/188 (VTD 16762). (*Note*. The appeal against the penalty was also dismissed—see **52.211** PENALTIES: MISDECLARATION.)

[1.77] See also *Tomlinson*, **19.5** DRUGS, MEDICINES, AIDS FOR THE HANDICAPPED, ETC.

Nursing homes ordering incontinence pads for specific residents

[1.78] A company supplied incontinence pads to various nursing homes, on behalf of specific named residents. The supplies were billed to the nursing homes, which obtained payment from the residents. The company treated the supplies as zero-rated under *VATA 1994, Sch 8, Group 12, Item 2(g)*. The Commissioners issued an assessment on the basis that the nursing homes were agents acting in their own names, within *VATA 1994, s 47(2A)*, so that the supplies were not made to the residents but to the nursing homes, and the company was obliged to account for output tax. The company appealed. The tribunal allowed the appeal, holding that 'if an agent signs a contract "for and on behalf of" his principal we consider that he is not acting in his own name, but in that of his principal. In the present case the declarations which were clearly contractual documents expressly stated that the nursing home was acting "on behalf of" its handicapped residents and was using their funds'. The tribunal observed that *s 47(2A)* was apparently intended to implement *Article 5(4)(c)* of the *EC Sixth Directive*, but observed that 'the English version of *Article 5(4)(c)* differs radically from the French version' and that *s 47(2A)* appeared to be 'a very poor rendition'. Since the UK legislation failed 'to implement the *Directive* properly', the Commissioners could not 'rely on the direct effect of *Article 5(4)(c)*'. The tribunal concluded that 'the words "acts in his own name" in *section 47(2A)* do not cover an agent who is expressly acting on behalf of named principals. The wording of *section 47(2A)* cannot be reconciled with *Article 5(4)(c)* in the English version. The English version is wholly different from the French version. *Section 47(2A)* treats goods in the same way as services, whereas they are covered by different articles of the *Directive* with totally different wording. *Section 47(2A)* did not apply to the supplies.' *Express Medicare Ltd*, [2000] VATDR 377 (VTD 16969). (*Note*. The relevant supplies took place in 1996. With regard to the rating of the supplies, see now *VATA 1994, Sch 8, Group 12, Note 5B*, introduced by *VAT (Drugs, Medicines and Aids for the Handicapped) Order 1997 (SI 1997/2744)*, with effect from 1 January 1998. This provision is designed to ensure that supplies to individuals who are patients in, or attending at the premises of, a relevant institution are excluded from zero-rating, and that it is not possible to arrange for third parties to make zero-rated supplies. For the Commissioners' interpretation of this provision, see Business Brief 29/97, issued on 16 December 1997. For a case where it was held to apply, see *First Medical Ltd*, **19.68** DRUGS, MEDICINES, AIDS FOR THE HANDICAPPED, ETC.)

'Outsourcing service'—whether within VATA 1994, s 47(3)

[1.79] A company (OS) provided an 'administrative and financial outsourcing service' for various employment agencies. It registered for VAT, and subsequently issued the employment agencies with invoices, enabling them to reclaim input tax. Customs formed the opinion that OS and the agencies were accounting for VAT incorrectly. They issued a ruling that OS was not making supplies of staff to its customers. OS appealed, contending firstly that it should be treated as making supplies of staff, and alternatively that it was making supplies which fell within *VATA 1994, s 47(3)*. The tribunal reviewed the evidence in detail, rejected these contentions, and dismissed the appeal, distinguishing the earlier decision in *Helping Hand Asset Management Ltd*, **1.47** above. The tribunal held that it was the employment agencies, rather than OS, which was providing the services of suitable workers for the agencies' customers. The economic purpose of the contract between the agencies and OS was to provide payroll and invoicing services. It also improved the agencies' cash-flow 'by payment (or set-off against other amounts due) in advance of the time of actual payment by the customer'. The tribunal held that the employment agencies were acting as independent principals. They were entitled to input tax for the amounts which they paid OS for outsourcing services, but were still required to account for output tax in the normal way. Furthermore, OS was not supplying the services of the workers, either as a principal or as an agent, for the purposes of *s 47(3)*. VAT was not chargeable on the 'payroll invoices' which OS issued, and accordingly the employment agencies were not entitled to reclaim input tax on these invoices. *Oriel Support Ltd*, LON/07/001 (VTD 20930).

Article 6(4) of EC Sixth Directive—agents acting in own name

[1.80] See *État Belge v Henfling & Others*, **22.189** EUROPEAN COMMUNITY LAW.

'Disbursements'

Reimbursement of director's expenses—whether made as agent

[1.81] Two companies (C and F) formed a third company (E) as a joint venture. C had a 25% shareholding in E, and F had a 75% shareholding. One of C's directors was appointed as a director of E. His travelling expenses were reimbursed by C. The Commissioners issued an assessment to C on the basis that the reimbursement of his expenses constituted consideration for a supply, on which output tax was chargeable. C appealed, contending that it had been acting as an agent of E when it made the reimbursements, so that no VAT was chargeable. The tribunal accepted this contention and allowed the appeal. *Alpha International Coal Ltd*, LON/92/79Y3 (VTD 9795). (*Note*. For a subsequent application for costs, see **2.441** APPEALS.)

Reimbursements of expenses—other cases

[1.82] See the cases noted at **62.52** SUPPLY to **62.71** SUPPLY.

Fee for handling insurance claim—whether a disbursement

[1.83] A company failed to account for fees which it received for handling insurance claims. The Commissioners issued an assessment charging output tax on the fees, and the company appealed, contending that the fees were disbursements and that output tax was not chargeable. The tribunal rejected this contention and dismissed the appeal, and the QB upheld this decision. *National Transit Insurance Co Ltd v C & E Commrs*, QB 1974, [1975] STC 35; [1975] 1 WLR 552; [1975] 1 All ER 303.

Company trading as 'mail broker'

[1.84] See *Mail Brokers International Ltd*, **1.44** above.

Fees for arranging MoT vehicle tests—whether disbursements

[1.85] See *Ward*, **44.162** MOTOR CARS; *Waterhouse Ltd*, **44.163** MOTOR CARS, and the cases noted at **44.164** MOTOR CARS.

Estate agents

Estate agents—expenses charged to clients

[1.86] See *Lea*, **62.57** SUPPLY.

Estate agents—time of supply

[1.87] See *Cooke*, **62.399** SUPPLY, and the cases noted at **62.400** and **62.401** SUPPLY.

Nursing agencies

Nursing agency—whether acting as independent principal

[1.88] See *Allied Medicare Nursing Services Ltd*, **33.2** HEALTH AND WELFARE; *Parkinson*, **33.3** HEALTH AND WELFARE; *British Nursing Co-Operation Ltd*, **33.20** HEALTH AND WELFARE; *Reed Personnel Services Ltd*, **33.21** HEALTH AND

WELFARE; *Sheffield & Rotherham Nursing Agency*, 33.22 HEALTH AND WELFARE; *BUPA Nursing Services Ltd*, 62.316 SUPPLY, and *South Hams Nursing Agency*, 62.317 SUPPLY.

Employment agency supplying care workers

[1.89] See *Wood*, 36.10 INPUT TAX.

Nursing services partly provided by unqualified staff

[1.90] See *Elder Home Care Ltd*, 33.4 HEALTH AND WELFARE.

'Party plan' and direct selling

'Party plan' sales—whether hostess acting as agent or principal

[1.91] A company (D) established a 'party plan' system for the sale of tupperware to the public. Under the system, D appointed a number of distributors. The distributors purchased the tupperware from D, which fixed a recommended retail price for it. Each distributor then appointed a number of 'sub-distributors', who persuaded friends or acquaintances to act as 'hostesses', arranging parties at their homes, at which the 'sub-distributor' displayed tupperware and obtained orders from the guests. The sub-distributors passed these orders to the distributors, who delivered the goods to the sub-distributors for onward supply to the customers. The sub-distributor paid the distributor 70% of the recommended retail price of the goods, retaining the remaining 30% as commission. The Commissioners assessed the distributors on the full amount paid by the customers, considering that the sub-distributors were acting as agents of the distributor. A married couple acting as distributors appealed, contending that they had sold the goods to the sub-distributors, who in turn had acted as a principal rather than as an agent in selling them to the customers, so that the distributors were only liable to account for tax on the price paid to them by the sub-distributor. The CA accepted this contention and allowed the appeal. *P & R Potter v C & E Commrs*, CA 1984, [1985] STC 45. (*Note*. For subsequent proceedings in this case, see 2.524 APPEALS.)

[1.92] A company (C) sold wickerwork goods, etc., using the 'party plan' system. Through its agents, it found individuals, usually housewives, to act as hostesses at parties held in private houses at which the company's goods were displayed and orders taken. In return for her services, the hostess was given a 'reward' dependent on the value of the goods ordered. This 'reward' could be taken either in cash or goods. The Commissioners issued an assessment on the basis that the company was liable to account for tax on the full value of all the goods ordered at the party. The company appealed, contending that the amount of the reward paid to the hostess should be deducted in computing the consideration. The tribunal rejected this contention and dismissed the appeal, holding that the hostess was acting as an agent rather than as an independent principal. *Churchway Crafts Ltd (No 1)*, LON/78/143 (VTD 782).

[1.93] A similar decision was reached in *AL Younger*, LON/81/278 (VTD 1173).

[1.94] A similar decision was reached in a case concerning the sale of embroidery kits under a 'party plan'. The tribunal held that the distributors were liable to account for tax on the full amount paid by the ultimate customer, with no deduction for the commission retained by the hostess. *Simply Cross-stitch*, [1985] VATTR 241 (VTD 1968).

Value of consideration for goods supplied to hostess

[1.95] See *Pippa-Dee Parties Ltd*, **67.37** VALUATION, and *Churchway Crafts Ltd (No 2)*, **67.39** VALUATION.

Whether salesmen agents or independent contractors

[1.96] A company manufactured household goods, which it sold through catalogues distributed by self-employed part-time salesmen. The salesmen obtained orders from customers and passed these orders to the company, paying the company 80% of the catalogue price for the products. The Commissioners issued an assessment on the basis that the company should account for VAT on the full amount paid to the salesman by the customer, rather than on the amount paid to the company by the salesman. The tribunal allowed the company's appeal, holding that the salesmen were acting as independent contractors. *Betterware Products Ltd*, LON/83/384 (VTD 1951).

[1.97] The decision in *Betterware Products Ltd*, **1.96** above, was applied in the similar subsequent case of *D & D Kelly*, LON/87/173 (VTD 2452).

Mail order goods supplied to agents for promotional purposes

[1.98] See *GUS Merchandise Corporation Ltd*, **58.1** RETAILERS' SPECIAL SCHEMES.

Mail order goods sold to agents—application of Retail Scheme

[1.99] See *GUS Merchandise Corporation Ltd (No 2)*, **58.53** RETAILERS' SPECIAL SCHEMES.

Commission received by agents

[1.100] Appeals against assessments charging tax on commission received by agents were dismissed in *I & L Ball*, MAN/91/985 (VTD 9251) and *Merlin HC Ltd*, MAN/92/743 (VTD 9251).

[1.101] A couple sold second-hand children's clothing as agents. They did not account for output tax on their commission. The Commissioners issued an assessment and the tribunal dismissed the couple's appeal, holding that tax remained due on the commission even though the sales of clothing were zero-rated. *RJ & JM Farrimond*, MAN/92/278 (VTD 10831).

2

Appeals

The cases in this chapter are arranged under the following headings.

The making of the appeal

The tribunal's jurisdiction (*VATA 1994, s 82(2), 83*)	**2.1**
Miscellaneous	
Whether the recipient of a supply may appeal	**2.52**
The notice of appeal	**2.62**
Miscellaneous	**2.67**
Matters within the discretion of the Commissioners	**2.83**
Estoppel and allied matters	**2.109**
The requirements of VATA 1994, s 84(3)	
Payment of assessed tax	**2.128**
Hardship applications (*VATA 1994, s 84(3B)*)	**2.136**
Allocation of cases to categories (SI 2009/273, rule 23)	**2.148**
Statements of case, etc. (SI 1986/590, rules 7–9; SI 2009/273, rule 25)	**2.150**
Applications for the admission of late appeals, etc.	**2.172**
Settlement of appeals by agreement (VATA 1994, s 85)	**2.200**
Applications for adjournments	**2.211**
The hearing of the appeal before the tribunal (SI 2009/273, rules 29–33)	
Onus of proof	**2.234**
Tribunal powers	**2.237**
Whether appeal to be heard in private (*SI 2009/273, rule 32*)	**2.249**
Disclosure of documents	**2.256**
Witness statements	**2.266**
Evidence at hearing	**2.277**
Miscellaneous	**2.293**
The tribunal decision (SI 2009/273, rules 34–42)	**2.309**
Applications for reinstatement of appeals (SI 2009/273, rule 17(3))	
Cases where the application was successful	**2.315**
Cases where the application was unsuccessful	**2.323**
Applications for judicial review	**2.328**
The award of costs (SI 1986/590, rule 29; SI 2009/273, rule 10)	
Applications by the Commissioners	**2.350**
Costs where the appellant was successful: general principles	**2.375**
Costs where the appellant was partly successful	**2.398**
Costs where Commissioners' decision or assessment is withdrawn	**2.421**
Costs where the appellant was not legally represented	**2.449**
Costs where company appellant represented by director	**2.461**
Application for costs on indemnity basis	**2.473**
Miscellaneous	**2.494**
The award of interest (VATA 1994, s 84(8))	
General principles	**2.512**

Whether interest may be compounded	**2.517**
Whether interest claimable on tax overdeclared	**2.524**
Whether interest claimable where assessment withdrawn	**2.525**
Whether interest payable under *VATA 1994, s 78* or *s 84*	**2.526**
Claim to interest under *Supreme Court Act 1981, s 35A*	**2.531**
Whether interest to be included in award of costs	**2.533**

CROSS-REFERENCE

For appeals by partnerships see **47.1** PARTNERSHIP *et seq.*

The making of the appeal

The tribunal's jurisdiction (VATA 1994, s 82(2), 83)

NOTE

For appeals against decisions on matters within the discretion of the Commissioners, including those involving *VATA 1994, s 84(10)*, see **2.83** *et seq.* below.

Future supplies

[2.1] In a case where the substantive issue is no longer relevant, a company appealed to the QB against a tribunal decision. The tribunal hearing had related to supplies under contracts which had already been made but not yet executed. The QB struck out the appeal, holding that the tribunal had no jurisdiction in relation to future supplies. *Allied Windows (South Wales) Ltd v C & E Commrs*, QB April 1973 unreported.

[2.2] Tribunals struck out appeals, applying the QB decision in *Allied Windows (South Wales) Ltd*, 2.1 above, in *DC Morgan (for Emmanuel Church, Northwood Parochial Church Council)*, [1973] VATTR 76 (VTD 21) and *V McCulloch*, LON/90/1512Y (VTD 5949).

[2.3] The decision in *Allied Windows (South Wales) Ltd*, 2.1 above, was applied by the QB in another case where an appeal was struck out on the grounds that it related to a supply that had not taken place at the time of the appeal. *Odhams Leisure Group Ltd v C & E Commrs*, QB [1992] STC 332. (*Note.* For another issue in this case, see **5.81** BOOKS, ETC.)

[2.4] The QB decision in *Odhams Leisure Group Ltd*, 2.3 above, was applied in a subsequent case in which an appeal was adjourned indefinitely on the grounds that it related to future supplies. *Church of Christ the King*, LON/93/2029A (VTD 12783).

[2.5] Similar decisions, also applying *Odhams Leisure Group Ltd*, 2.3 above, were reached in *Anglia Energy Conservation Ltd*, LON/95/2862 (VTD 14216) and *A Stott*, LON/98/352 (VTD 15622).

[2.6] A recreational trust was formed in 1999 to build a pavilion for two village sports clubs. The Commissioners issued a ruling that the construction would not qualify for zero-rating, as the pavilion would be used for commercial purposes as well as for charitable purposes. The VAT office responsible for the decision advised the trust that it had the right of appeal to the VAT tribunal. The trust appealed. The Commissioners applied for the appeal to be struck out on the grounds that the tribunal had no jurisdiction, since construction had not commenced and the tribunal had no jurisdiction in relation to future supplies. The tribunal granted the Commissioners' application and struck the appeal out, holding that 'there is no right of appeal in the present circumstances under the framework of the *VATA*'. The tribunal observed that the trust could apply for judicial review of the Commissioners' decision, and held that 'whilst the Commissioners have undoubtedly acted in such a way as to cause the appellant hardship both in terms of time wasted and money spent', it was 'not possible to construe the primary legislation in such a way as to give the appellant a right of appeal to the Tribunal'. The tribunal awarded costs to the trust, and noted that the trust had the right to apply to the Adjudicator. *Elstead (Thursley Road) Recreational Trust*, LON/04/828 (VTD 18852).

[2.7] A US company supplied dental prostheses to orthodontists in the UK. The Commissioners treated such supplies as standard-rated. It incorporated a UK company to act as an intermediary. The UK company requested the Commissioners to give a ruling as to whether supplies via the UK company would qualify for exemption. The Commissioners advised the company that the supplies would still be standard-rated if the prostheses were manufactured outside the UK. The UK company lodged a notice of appeal. The tribunal struck out the appeal, observing that the UK company had not yet made any supplies and holding that it had no jurisdiction with regard to future supplies. *Align Technology UK Ltd*, LON/02/1109 (VTD 18426).

[2.8] A company (F) wrote to Customs asking for a ruling as to the VAT liability of a promotion scheme which it was hoping to introduce. A Customs officer sent a reply indicating that output tax would be payable. F lodged an appeal against this letter. Customs applied for the appeal to be struck out as it related to supplies which had not yet taken place, applying the QB decision in *Odhams Leisure Group Ltd v C & E Commrs*, 2.3 above. The tribunal dismissed Customs' application, distinguishing *Allied Windows (South Wales) Ltd*, 2.1 above, and *Odhams Leisure Group Ltd*, 2.3 above, on the grounds that in those cases there had been no supply at the time of the appeal hearing. In the present case, however, F had made supplies between the original decision letter and the date of the hearing. The chairman (Dr. Avery Jones) held that 'a tribunal could not rule on a hypothetical supply, but if Customs were willing to give a decision I see no reason in principle why such a decision could not be appealed so long as by the time of the tribunal hearing there had been a supply'. *Ford Motor Company Ltd (No 1)*, [2006] VATDR 114 (VTD 19424). (*Note.* For subsequent developments in this case, see **44.155** MOTOR CARS.)

Appealable matters (VATA 1994, s 83)

VATA 1994, s 83—whether any appealable decision

[2.9] A company provided nursing staff to local authorities. It registered for VAT in 1997 and charged VAT on its supplies, but did not make any VAT returns until 1999. Customs subsequently imposed default surcharges, and the company appealed to the tribunal, contending that its supplies should have been treated as exempt. The tribunal dismissed the appeal, finding that Customs had never issued a ruling as to whether the supplies were taxable or exempt, so that there was no appealable matter within *VATA 1994, s 83(1)(b)*. *Take Care (Agency Services) Ltd*, LON/00/510 (VTD 18041).

[2.10] In *European Independent Purchasing Co Ltd*, **29.80** FOOD, the tribunal held that the sale of toasted sandwiches was standard-rated. Following this decision, an HMRC officer wrote to a large number of franchisees making similar supplies, stating that they were 'failing to declare the correct rate of VAT on some of their sales' and that the toasted sandwiches 'have always been standard-rated supplies'. The franchisees appealed. HMRC applied for the appeals to be struck out, contending that the officer's letter was not an appealable decision. The tribunal rejected this contention and dismissed HMRC's application. Judge Tildesley held that the officer's letter was an appealable decision, within *VATA 1994, s 83(1)(b)*. Judge Tildesley also directed that one of the appeals should be treated as a 'lead appeal' under *Tribunal Procedure (First-Tier Tribunal) (Tax Chamber) Rules 2009 (SI 2009/273), rule 18(2)*. *Sub One Ltd (t/a Subway) v HMRC (No 1) (and related appeals)*, [2009] UKFTT 385 (TC), TC00320. (*Note*. The lead appeal was subsequently dismissed—see **29.80** FOOD.)

Assessment to recover input tax—whether appeal within VATA 1994, s 83

[2.11] See *R v C & E Commrs (oao Greenwich Property Ltd)*, **2.94** below.

VATA 1994, s 83(1)(c)*—claim for repayment of input tax

[2.12] The proprietors of a rest home claimed input tax on supplies made to them before registration. Customs rejected the claim and the proprietors appealed. Customs applied for the appeal to be struck out on the grounds that the decision on whether to allow pre-registration input tax under what is now *VAT Regulations 1995 (SI 1995/2518), reg 111* was outside the tribunal's jurisdiction. The tribunal dismissed the application, holding that it had jurisdiction to review the decision. The tribunal held that 'the appeal relates to input tax even though the Commissioners have decided not to authorise the appellants to treat the amounts as if they were input tax'. Accordingly, the appeal related to an appealable matter within what is now *VATA 1994, s 83(1)(c)*. *S & Mrs S Barar (t/a Turret House Rest Home)*, LON/93/2021A & 2224A (VTD 12707).

[2.13] A company (E) submitted a return requesting a VAT repayment of more than £1,500,000. Customs made a repayment of £270,000, but declined to repay the balance pending an investigation into the activities of E's suppliers. E appealed to the tribunal. Customs applied for a direction that the appeal should be struck out on the grounds that they had not made any appealable decision. The tribunal granted the application, specifically declining to follow the previous tribunal decision in *Tricell UK Ltd*, [2003] VATDR 333 (VTD 18127). The tribunal chairman (Dr. Avery Jones) held that 'the sole issue here is whether on the facts there is a carousel fraud, which the Commissioners are still investigating' and that 'until the Commissioners finish their investigations of the facts, there is no decision that can be appealed'. *Evolink Ltd*, LON/03/419 (VTD 18207).

[2.14] A company's first VAT return claimed a VAT repayment of more than £200,000. The Commissioners requested further information. The company lodged a notice of appeal. The Commissioners applied for the appeal to be struck out by virtue of *VAT Tribunals Rules (SI 1986 No 590), rule 18(1)(a)*, on the basis that they had not made any appealable decision. The tribunal accepted the Commissioners' application and struck out the appeal, applying the reasoning in *Evolink Ltd*, 2.13 above. *F Options Ltd (No 1)*, LON/03/945 (VTD 18521). (*Note.* For a subsequent appeal by the same company, see **2.222** below.)

[2.15] A company submitted two VAT returns claiming substantial repayments in relation to the purchase of large quantities of mobile telephones, which it claimed to have exported to Spain. Customs requested further information. The company lodged a notice of appeal. Customs applied for the appeal to be struck out on the basis that they had not made any appealable decision. The tribunal accepted Customs' application and struck out the appeal. The tribunal chairman (Mr. Wallace) observed that 'the tribunal is not in the position of an umpire in a game of cricket to whom a bowler appeals for a catch. The tribunal exists to adjudicate on a dispute following a ruling or determination by Customs'. In order for the tribunal to have jurisdiction, 'there must be an issue between the parties which has been sufficiently crystallised to constitute a decision falling within one of the paragraphs of *section 83*'. *Olympia Technology Ltd (No 3)*, LON/06/1092 (VTD 19984).

[2.16] A company (T) submitted a VAT return claiming a repayment of more than £715,000. Customs requested further information. T lodged a notice of appeal. Customs applied for the appeal to be struck out on the basis that they had not made any appealable decision. The tribunal accepted Customs' application and struck out the appeal. T appealed to the Ch D, which upheld the tribunal decision. Lindsay J held that there had been no appealable decision, and that, if Customs were unduly slow in making an appealable decision, the appropriate remedy was judicial review. *Touchwood Services Ltd v HMRC*, Ch D [2007] STC 1425; [2007] EWHC 105(Ch).

[2.17] A company submitted two VAT returns claiming substantial repayments. Customs requested further information. The company lodged a notice of appeal. Customs applied for the appeal to be struck out the basis that they had not made any appealable decision. The tribunal rejected the application but the Ch D reversed this decision, applying the principles laid down in *Touchwood Services Ltd v HMRC*, 2.16 above. *HMRC v Mobilx Ltd*, Ch D 2007, [2008] STC 3071; [2007] EWHC 1769 (Ch). (*Note.* For a subsequent appeal by the same company, see **36.119** INPUT TAX.)

[2.18] Similar decisions were reached in *PNC Telecom plc*, LON/06/685 (VTD 19754); *Cotswold Computer Components Ltd*, LON/06/557 (VTD 19833), and *First Class Communications Ltd*, LON/08/1073 (VTD 20779).

[2.19] See also *Royal College of Obstetricians and Gynaecologists*, 48.1
PAYMENT OF TAX.

Application by Customs to strike out appeal—VATA 1994, s 83(1)(p)

[2.20] A company appealed against an assessment covering nine prescribed
periods, for five of which it had not submitted returns. The tribunal struck out
the appeals against the five periods for which returns had not been made,
holding that it had no jurisdiction to hear them. (The appeals against the
remaining four were dismissed.) *Shaft Sports Ltd*, [1983] VATTR 180 (VTD
1451).

[2.21] In the case noted at 25.15 EXPORTS, a company (M) failed to account
for output tax on supplies of silver to Bangladesh. In the export documentation, the silver was described as lead solder. Customs issued an assessment
charging output tax on the supplies, on the basis that they did not qualify for
zero-rating since the documentation did not clearly identify the goods in
question. M appealed, and Customs applied for the appeal to be struck out on
the grounds that it was outside the tribunal's jurisdiction. The tribunal rejected
the application, holding that although it had 'no jurisdiction to consider the
validity of the conditions laid down for zero-rating', the assessment as such
was an appealable matter. *G McKenzie & Co Ltd*, LON/92/2015A (VTD
11992).

[2.22] A similar decision was reached in *Surma News Group Ltd*,
LON/00/275 (VTD 17170). (*Note.* For the substantive appeal, see 11.27
CHARITIES.)

[2.23] A trader (C) appealed against ten assessments. Customs lodged an
application for the appeals to be struck out on the grounds that C had not
made returns for the relevant periods, so that the appeals were not authorised
by *VATA 1994, s 83(1)p)(i)**. The tribunal accepted this contention, holding
that the requirements of *VATA 1994, s 83(1)(p)(i)** were authorised by *Article
22(8)* of the *Sixth Directive. PW Coleman*, [1999] VATDR 133 (VTD 15906,
VTD 16178).

[2.24] An accountant appealed against three assessments. The Commissioners lodged an application for the appeal to be struck out on the grounds that
the accountant had not made returns for the relevant periods, so that the
appeals were not authorised by *VATA 1994, s 83(1)(p)(i)**. The tribunal
accepted this contention and struck out the appeals, observing that the
accountant had 'quite simply decided not to comply with the system'. *S
Mashood*, [1999] VATDR 133 (VTD 15896, VTD 16178). (*Note.* The
substantive appeal was heard with *Coleman*, 2.23 above.)

[2.25] The decision in *Coleman*, 2.23 above, was applied in the subsequent
Scottish case of *P Fairbairn*, EDN/03/130 (VTD 18538).

[2.26] A company (E) submitted VAT returns for the periods from February
to October 2000, showing substantial VAT liability. In 2010 E sought to adjust
the returns, contending that they overstated its liability. HMRC rejected the
claim and E appealed to the tribunal. HMRC applied for the appeal to be
struck out on the grounds that it had no reasonable prospect of success. Judge
Brooks accepted this contention and struck out E's appeal, observing that *VAT*

Regulations, reg 34 'limits the period during which any overstatement in a return may be corrected to four years from the end of the prescribed accounting period for which the return was made'. *Enviroengineering Ltd v HMRC (No 2)*, [2011] UKFTT 366 (TC), TC01221.

Appeal against interest charge—effect of VATA 1994, s 83(1)(q)

[2.27] A company had claimed bad debt relief without giving the notice required by *VAT Regulations 1995, reg 166A*. The Commissioners issued an assessment to recover the tax, and also imposed an interest charge. The company appealed against the interest charge. The tribunal struck out the appeal, holding that *VATA 1994, s 83(1)(q)** only gave it the right to hear an appeal against the amount of an interest charge, and that it had 'no jurisdiction to deal with a decision by the Commissioners to impose interest'. *Bellevue Roofing Supplies Ltd*, MAN/00/814 (VTD 17121).

VATA 1994, s 83(1)(s)—appeal against rejection of claim to interest

[2.28] Following the CA decision in *Littlewoods Organisation plc v C & E Commrs*, **67.42** VALUATION, a company (G) applied for a repayment of tax, with interest under *VATA 1994, s 78*, covering the periods from January 1999 to November 2001. Following the ECJ decision in *Marks & Spencer plc v C & E Commrs (No 4)*, **22.55** EUROPEAN COMMUNITY LAW, it made a similar claim for the periods from April 1973 to November 1998. In October 2004 it made a further claim for the periods from December 2001 to August 2004. In January 2005 HMRC made the repayment for the periods from January 1999 to August 2004, and in April 2005 they made a payment of interest for these periods. However HMRC rejected G's claim for the earlier periods. In 2008 G applied for an award of compound interest, covering the entire period from April 1973 to August 2004. HMRC rejected this application and G appealed. HMRC applied to the tribunal for the appeal to be struck out on the grounds that it had been made out of time. The tribunal reviewed the evidence in detail and accepted HMRC's application with regard to the periods from January 1999 to August 2004, finding that these claims had been made almost three years after the expiry of the statutory time limit. However the tribunal rejected HMRC's application with regard to the periods from April 1973 to November 1998, observing that HMRC's substantive decision not to make a repayment of the tax for those periods was still under appeal. The tribunal directed that that appeal should be listed for hearing. *Grattan plc v HMRC (No 4)*, [2009] SFTD 590; [2009] UKFTT 184 (TC), TC00139. (*Note.* For subsequent developments in this case, see **67.56** VALUATION.)

Application of VATA 1994, s 83(1)(t)

[2.29] In the case noted at **48.50** PAYMENT OF TAX, two associated companies lodged substantial repayment claims under *VATA 1994, s 80*. On 18 July 1996 the Paymaster-General stated in Parliament that legislation was to be included in the 1997 Finance Bill to introduce a three-year limit for retrospective repayment claims, and to amend the law on unjust enrichment, with retrospective effect from 18 July 1996. Following this announcement, Customs rejected the claims, and the companies appealed. Customs applied for the appeals to be struck out, contending that the tribunal had no jurisdiction. The tribunal rejected this application, holding that there was a dispute concerning 'a claim for the repayment of an amount under *s 80*', within *VATA 1994, s 83(1)(t)**. *Kay & Co Ltd and Others*, MAN/96/859 (VTD 14557).

[2.30] A similar decision was reached in *Marks & Spencer plc*, [1998] VATDR 93 (VTD 15302). (*Note*. For the substantive appeal, see **22.55** EUROPEAN COMMUNITY LAW.)

[2.31] A group of companies submitted a repayment claim, backdated to 1973, relating to sales of demonstration cars, which should have been treated as exempt from VAT, applying the ECJ decision in *EC Commission v Italian Republic*, **22.349** EUROPEAN COMMUNITY LAW. Customs rejected the claim on the basis that it was outside the three-year time limit laid down by *VATA 1994, s 80(4)*. The companies appealed. Customs applied for the appeal to be struck out, contending that their decision was not an appealable matter within *VATA 1994, s 83*. The tribunal dismissed Customs' application, holding that 'the subject matter of the appeal is the overpayment of tax which falls within the tribunal's jurisdiction by reason of *section 83(t)* and so it follows that the tribunal has jurisdiction'. *WR Davies Motor Group*, MAN/04/728 (VTD 19374).

[2.32] A company made a repayment claim in 2003. After correspondence, a Customs officer sent the company an email in August 2004, agreeing to repay some of the tax in question, but stating that most of the tax was not repayable. After further emails, the company's accountants sent Customs a letter in February 2005 reiterating that the company considered that it was entitled to a larger repayment. Customs rejected this on the grounds that the email sent in August 2004 had been an appealable decision, and that the letter of February 2005 was a new claim which was outside the statutory time limits. The company appealed to the tribunal, contending that the letter of February 2005 was an amendment to the original claim rather than a new claim. The tribunal accepted this contention, holding that the email which Customs had sent in August 2004 was 'not a decision letter' since 'it contains no reference to the matter of finality or of appeal'. Furthermore, 'no letter from the respondents in this case purported to be either final or to comply with the internal guidelines for officers of the respondents in relation to decisions or reconsiderations'. The tribunal observed that HMRC Internal Guidance, V1-29, para 12.1 stated that a letter from HMRC 'must be issued within the appropriate time' and must 'contain a statement that if the appellant wishes to appeal it has 30 days from the date of the letter to appeal to an independent VAT and Duties Tribunal. Nowhere in that guidance is it contemplated that a letter could properly be issued which could be asserted by HMRC to be a decision which did not contain intimation of the right to appeal nor, even, that a decision could be communicated other than by letter. This tribunal does not consider that email chat can constitute such a significant communication as will contain intimation of the need to appeal and as a consequence be significant in relation to time limits and capping provisions.' Accordingly, the company's letter of February 2005 was 'not a new claim but an adjustment of an existing claim'. *The John Martin Group*, EDN/05/44 (VTD 19257).

Rejection of repayment claim—whether an appealable decision

[2.33] A company (C) submitted a return claiming a repayment of more than £2,000,000. Customs formed the opinion that C had wrongly treated certain supplies as zero-rated, and requested further information. C did not provide the information, but lodged an appeal with the Tribunal Centre. Customs lodged an application for the appeal to be struck out on the grounds that there had been no appealable decision. The tribunal rejected the application, holding that Customs had made a decision not to make a repayment until they had received further information, and that this was 'an appealable decision'. With regard to the substantive appeal, the tribunal observed that the burden of proof was on C, and that C 'would have been much wiser' to have given 'reasonable particulars of the claims'. *Colaingrove Ltd (No 2)*, LON/00/765 (VTD 16981).

[2.34] See also *City of Sunderland College Supplies Ltd*, 2.65 below.

'Statement of Account' issued by Customs

[2.35] A trader formed the opinion that he had overpaid VAT. Customs issued a 'Statement of Account', indicating that he had underpaid. The trader lodged a Notice of Appeal. Customs applied for the appeal to be struck out on the grounds that there was no appealable decision within *VATA 1994, s 83*. The tribunal accepted this contention and struck out the appeal. The chairman observed that 'the correct analysis of (the trader's) position is that he is trying to assert a money claim against the Commissioners'. The tribunal had 'no jurisdiction over such money claims (save where they raise issues specifically covered by one or other of the heads in *section 73*). The right venue for such a claim may be the civil courts, eg the "county court".' *KG Hickey*, LON/04/815 (VTD 18711).

[2.36] A similar decision was reached in *B O'Brien (t/a Poster Sites Southern) v HMRC (No 2)*, [2009] UKFTT 262 (TC), TC00209.

Miscellaneous

Extra-statutory concessions

[2.37] See the cases noted at 2.83 to 2.96 below.

VATA 1994, s 33—whether tribunal has jurisdiction to hear appeal

[2.38] See *Conservators of Ashdown Forest*, 42.7 LOCAL AUTHORITIES AND STATUTORY BODIES.

Special Provisions Order 1995, Article 12—whether tribunal has jurisdiction

[2.39] See *JH Corbitt (Numismatists) Ltd*, 60.1 SECOND-HAND GOODS, and *Christopher Gibbs Ltd*, 60.2 SECOND-HAND GOODS.

Special Provisions Order 1995, Article 13—whether tribunal has jurisdiction

[2.40] See *McCord & Alford*, 60.3 SECOND-HAND GOODS.

Decision of Commissioners as to period of returns—whether appealable

[2.41] See *Selected Growers Ltd*, 59.1 RETURNS; *Punchwell Ltd*, 59.2 RETURNS, and *Nuniv Developments Ltd*, 59.3 RETURNS.

Appeal against default interest—effect of VATA 1994, s 84(6)*

[2.42] See the cases noted at **17.1** to **17.3** DEFAULT INTEREST.

Appeal against surcharge liability notice before any surcharge incurred

[2.43] A company which had been served with a surcharge liability notice lodged an appeal to the tribunal. The Commissioners applied for the appeal to be struck out, contending that it was premature and that no appeal could be lodged until a default surcharge had been imposed. The tribunal granted the Commissioners' application, holding that it had no jurisdiction to entertain an appeal against the issue of a surcharge liability notice. *Expert Systems Design Ltd*, MAN/92/367 (VTD 7974).

[2.44] The decision in *Expert Systems Design Ltd*, **2.43** above, was applied in the similar subsequent case of *The Fraser Bruce Group Ltd*, EDN/02/48 (VTD 17763).

[2.45] Similar decisions were reached in *SR Auld*, LON/93/108P (VTD 11956) and *Castrue Ltd*, LON/94/712P (VTD 12681).

VATA 1994, Sch 11 para 5(2)(3)—whether tribunal has jurisdiction

[2.46] In the case noted at **51.141** PENALTIES: FAILURE TO NOTIFY, a deregistered builder had issued eleven invoices purporting to charge VAT, although he was no longer registered. The Commissioners sought to recover the amount in question under *VATA 1994, Sch 11 para 5(2)(3)*. The trader appealed. The Commissioners applied for the appeal to be struck out, on the grounds that the tribunal had no jurisdiction to hear the appeal under *VATA 1994, s 83*. The tribunal granted the Commissioners' application, observing that, since the facts of the case had been fully explored in the appeal against the penalty (where the tribunal had jurisdiction under *VATA 1994, s 83(q)*), 'the lack of jurisdiction to hear an appeal against the amount due has not, in this appeal, meant that the appellant has been unable to put forward all his arguments'. *GE Alm*, LON/98/961 (VTD 15863).

VATA 1994, Sch 11 para 4(1)*—whether appealable decision

[2.47] The Commissioners had served a notice requiring a company to give security under what is now *VATA 1994, Sch 11 para 4(1)* in the sum of £170,801.89 in a case where approximately £80,000 of input tax had been reclaimed by the company. The company sought to appeal against this requirement. The Commissioners applied to strike out the appeal on the grounds that no such appeal lay under *VATA 1994, s 83*. The tribunal allowed the Commissioners' application, holding that it had no jurisdiction to entertain the appeal, on the grounds that no express right of appeal lay against a notice requiring security under *Sch 11 para 4(1)*. *Strangewood Ltd (No 2)*, [1988] VATTR 35 (VTD 2599). (*Note. VATA 1994, s 83(l)* only allows an appeal against a requirement to give security under *Sch 11 para 4(2)*.)

[2.48] See also *Ali & Begum*, **34.16** HUMAN RIGHTS.

Retrospective cancellation of registration—jurisdiction of tribunal

[2.49] A woman had registered for VAT in 1982 as a breeder of racehorses. She regularly made claims for repayment of VAT. In 1991 a VAT officer formed the opinion that she was not carrying on a business. The Commissioners issued a ruling that her registration should be cancelled with retrospective effect, and issued an assessment to recover input tax which she had reclaimed in the years 1986 to 1991 inclusive. She appealed, contending that the Commissioners' decision to backdate the cancellation of her registration was unreasonable. The Commissioners applied for a direction that the appeal should be struck out as it did not relate to an appealable matter within what is now *VATA 1994, s 83*, and thus was outside the jurisdiction of the tribunal. The tribunal dismissed the Commissioners' application, holding that the tribunal had 'a supervisory jurisdiction to review any decision to deregister'. *Anne Brookes*, [1994] VATTR 35 (VTD 11752).

Appellant contending that assessment invalid because tax already paid

[2.50] The Commissioners issued an assessment on an individual (G), including £10,260 in respect of tax unpaid for the period ending 31 March 1985. G did not pay the tax charged by the assessment, and the Commissioners presented a bankruptcy petition. G appealed, contending that he had paid the tax by cheque in March 1985. The tribunal observed that it was doubtful whether it 'had jurisdiction to enquire into a matter which seemed to involve no issue of liability but to be concerned essentially with debt recovery', but agreed to hear the appeal on the basis 'that if the tax had originally been paid by (G) as he contended the assessment subsequently made under (*VATA 1994, s 73*) to recover it would have been bad; and that assessment was itself clearly appealable by virtue of (*VATA 1994, s 83(p)*)'. The Commissioners gave evidence that they had never received the £10,260. G produced a copy of his VAT return for the period in question, but did not produce a copy of the cheque which he claimed to have sent, or a bank statement showing that the cheque had been debited. The tribunal dismissed G's appeal, finding on the evidence that G had submitted the return and the cheque but that there was no evidence that the return had ever been received or that the cheque had been presented. G 'had not discharged the burden of proving on the balance of probabilities that the tax due for March 1985 was received by the Commissioners'. *J Goldenberg*, LON/92/3294A (11591).

Application to transfer appeals from Scottish tribunal to English tribunal

[2.51] A Scottish company had four English subsidiaries. The VAT affairs of all five companies were dealt with in Scotland. The English subsidiaries appealed to the Edinburgh VAT Tribunal against directions issued by the Commissioners. The companies subsequently applied for the appeals to be heard by the London Tribunal Centre, contending that since the appeals involved the application of English law to English contracts, they should be heard by an English tribunal. The Edinburgh Tribunal granted the application, holding that it had jurisdiction to hear the appeals, since 'delivery to any Tribunal Centre should be sufficient to instigate proceedings, particularly when there is one UK respondent'. However, 'in the present case where the companies are registered in England, where the contracts with which the application is concerned concern matters of English law, it is plain that the matter should be appropriately dealt with under the control of an English Tribunal Centre, from which there is an English appeal route'. *RBS Leasing & Services (No 1) Ltd (and related appeals)*, EDN/98/58-61 (VTD 15643). (*Note*. For the substantive appeal, see **67.2** VALUATION.)

Whether the recipient of a supply may appeal

Cases where the recipient was permitted to appeal

[2.52] In the case noted at **62.42** SUPPLY, a company which was the recipient of a supply appealed against the Commissioners' decision that tax was payable on the supply. The Commissioners did not object to the hearing of the appeal but the tribunal considered as a preliminary matter whether the appellant had any *locus standi*. It concluded that what is now *VATA 1994, s 83* does not require the appellant to be the taxable person accountable for the tax in dispute, but that the appellant must have a sufficient legal interest in maintaining the appeal. This was clearly so in the case in question but might not apply to, for example, a member of the public buying an article from a retailer. The tribunal held that, where the appellant was the recipient of a supply, he should 'wherever possible seek the consent of the supplier to the appeal being brought by them jointly, upon such terms as to costs as they may agree'. *Processed Vegetable Growers Association Ltd*, [1973] VATTR 87 (VTD 25).

[2.53] In the case noted at **15.244** CONSTRUCTION OF DWELLINGS, ETC., where the appellant was the recipient of the relevant supply, the tribunal held that he had sufficient interest to maintain the appeal. The decision in *Payton*, 2.58 below, was distinguished, on the grounds that the appellant had deposited with the Commissioners an amount equal to the tax in dispute, on condition that it would be refunded if the appeal succeeded. *B Gilbourne*, [1974] VATTR 209 (VTD 109).

[2.54] In a case noted at **27.1** FINANCE, the tribunal held that the appellant company, which was the recipient of the relevant supplies, had sufficient interest to maintain the appeal. The decision in *Payton*, 2.58 below, was not followed (and was implicitly disapproved). The tribunal observed that if the appeal succeeded, and was not reversed by the courts, the Commissioners would be bound to observe it and repay or credit to the supplier the tax which he had accounted for. *Williams & Glyn's Bank Ltd*, [1974] VATTR 262 (VTD 118).

[2.55] An individual (B) had been invoiced by contractors who had carried out work on his house. The amount invoiced included VAT of £106.50. B considered that no tax was chargeable under the legislation then in force. He paid the contractor for the amount exclusive of the VAT, sent the Commissioners a cheque for £106.50 and appealed. The Commissioners refused to accept the cheque and contended at the hearing that the appellant did not have a sufficient financial interest to maintain the appeal, relying on *In re IG Farbenindustrie AG Agreement*, CA [1943] 2 All ER 525. The tribunal rejected the Commissioners' contention, distinguishing *IG Farbenindustrie* because the appellant had a statutory right of appeal. The appellant also had a sufficient financial interest in the matter as he had not paid the contractors the whole of the amount invoiced. *JR Beckley*, LON/74/68 (VTD 114). (*Note*. Compare *Wade*, **48.16** PAYMENT OF TAX, in which the facts were broadly similar but the appellant did not query the rating of the relevant supply until after he had paid the tax to the supplier, and his appeal was dismissed by the tribunal.)

[2.56] Customs issued a ruling that VAT was chargeable on affiliation fees to the English Hockey Association (EH). EH initially appealed against this ruling, but subsequently withdrew its appeal. However, two affiliated clubs lodged appeals, contending that the fees qualified for exemption under *VATA 1994, Sch 9, Group 10, Item 3*. Customs applied for the appeals to be struck out on the grounds that the clubs did not have 'sufficient interest'. The tribunal rejected this contention and dismissed Customs' application. The tribunal chairman (Mr. Oliver) held that 'the words of *section 83(b)* are equally applicable to the recipient of a supply as they are to the supplier; the fact that a decision that supplies are to be standard-rated has been issued to the supplier does not disqualify the recipient, who has to bear the tax, from appealing'. *Canterbury Hockey Club; Canterbury Ladies Hockey Club*, LON/04/823 (VTD 19086). (*Note*. For the substantive appeal, see **22.316** EUROPEAN COMMUNITY LAW.)

[2.57] There have been a very large number of other cases in which the tribunal has entertained an appeal by the recipient of a supply. In the interests of space, the cases are not listed individually in this book. For a list of such cases decided up to and including 31 December 2000, see Tolley's VAT Cases 2001.

Cases where the appeal was struck out

[2.58] A woman had been supplied with a surgical belt for an amount which included VAT of 96p. She paid the amount 'under protest' and lodged an appeal. The tribunal held that she did not have sufficient interest to maintain the appeal, applying the principles laid down by Romer J in *Twyford v Manchester Corporation*, Ch D [1946] 1 All ER 621. Although she had paid 'under protest', she had paid the tax voluntarily without compulsion or threats and accordingly had no right to recover the tax should her appeal succeed. The tribunal observed that the appeal would have succeeded (see **33.39** HEALTH AND WELFARE). *M Payton*, [1974] VATTR 140 (VTD 89). (*Note*. The decision here was distinguished in *Gilbourne*, **2.53** above, and not followed in *Williams & Glyn's Bank Ltd*, **2.54** above. Romer J's decision in *Twyford v Manchester Corporation* was subsequently disapproved by Lord Goff of Chieveley in *Woolwich Equitable Building Society v CIR*, HL [1992] STC 657. Lord Goff observed that Romer J had overlooked that 'in cases of compulsion, a threat which constitutes the compulsion may be expressed or implied'.)

[2.59] An individual (W) booked a holiday with a large company which was registered for VAT and accounted for tax under a Retail Scheme. W considered that the VAT included in the cost of the holiday was excessive, and appealed to a tribunal. The tribunal directed that the appeal be struck out, holding that the appeal was outside the scope of what is now *VATA 1994, s 83*, since W was the recipient of the supply and was not a taxable person. Previous decisions in which appeals by recipients of supplies had been entertained were distinguished, as in those cases the rating of the supply had been in issue, whereas in the present case it was accepted by all parties that the supply of the holiday was standard-rated. *C Wayment*, LON/89/1854Y (VTD 4846).

[2.60] An individual (W), who was not registered for VAT, received tuition in flying in order to qualify as a commercial pilot. The cost of the courses included VAT. W appealed to the tribunal, contending that VAT should not have been charged. The tribunal dismissed his appeal, holding that W was not entitled to credit for any input tax since he was not a taxable person. (The tribunal also observed that the VAT was correctly chargeable, since the tuition was neither exempt nor zero-rated.) *FP Whitehouse*, LON/92/404A (VTD 11114).

[2.61] The Commissioners issued a ruling that a property management company was supplying its services to the owners of the relevant premises, rather than to the subtenants who occupied the premises. The owners were property investors who were not registered for VAT and were therefore unable to reclaim input tax on the management services. One of them sought to lodge an appeal against the Commissioners' ruling, on the basis that if the services were deemed to be supplied to the occupiers, they would be able to recover input tax, so that the owners could charge a higher rent without making the premises more difficult to let. The tribunal struck out the appeal, holding that he did not have sufficient legal interest in the disputed decision. *B Kingsley-Smith*, LON/95/1563A (VTD 13787).

The Notice of Appeal

[2.62] In a case where the substantive issue has been superseded by changes to the legislation, the Commissioners issued an assessment on a company after discovering that it had reclaimed input tax which the Commissioners considered was attributable to an exempt supply. The company lodged an appeal against the assessment, describing its reason for appealing as being that the assessment was out of time. Subsequently the company applied to amend its Notice of Appeal to include an alternative contention that the input tax was attributable to a zero-rated supply, rather than to an exempt supply. The tribunal allowed the company's application, holding that it 'would be reluctant in the extreme to prevent a taxpayer from raising a *bona fide* defence'. *Marchday Holdings Ltd*, [1992] VATTR 484 (VTD 8964).

[2.63] In 1994 a company submitted a claim for a substantial VAT repayment, contending that *Input Tax Order, Article 7* was invalid. The Commissioners rejected the claim and the company appealed. The appeal was stood over pending the ECJ decision in *Royscot Leasing Ltd*, **22.424** EUROPEAN COMMUNITY LAW. In 1998, following the CA decision in *British Telecommunications plc*, **44.99** MOTOR CARS, the company applied to amend its Notice of Appeal to include an alternative contention that part of the tax in question related to delivery charges which were outside the scope of *Input Tax Order, Article 7*. The tribunal granted the application, applying *Marchday Holdings Ltd*, 2.62 above, and holding that 'the tribunal should be reluctant to prevent a taxpayer from raising a *bona fide* defence'. *Quicks plc*, [1998] VATDR 491 (VTD 15836).

[2.64] A company appealed against an assessment and a misdeclaration penalty, contending in its Notice of Appeal that it had been misdirected by a VAT officer. The Commissioners made a preliminary application for the appeal to be struck out or for the company to give further particulars of the ground of appeal. The tribunal rejected the Commissioners' application, observing that while the doctrine of personal bar could not prevent the Customs from recovering any tax due, an alleged misdirection could constitute a reasonable excuse for a misdeclaration and justify the discharging of a penalty. *Albany Building Services Ltd*, EDN/92/335 (VTD 10531). (*Notes*. (1) For cases concerning the doctrine of personal bar, see **2.120** *et seq*. below. (2) The appeal was subsequently dismissed—see **52.375** PENALTIES: MISDECLARATION. The tribunal found that the VAT officer had not misdirected the company. (3) The *Rules of the Supreme Court 1965 (SI 1965/1776)* referred to 'particulars'. With effect from 26 April 1999, these rules were largely replaced by the *Civil Procedure Rules 1998 (SI 1998/3132)*, which refer instead to 'information'.)

[2.65] A company (S) submitted a return claiming a repayment of more than £149,000. Following a visit by a VAT officer, Customs informed S that they were 'of the opinion that the supplies amount to tax avoidance' and needed 'to be satisfied that the terms of the leasing agreement are consistent with the supply being at open market value'. They therefore requested 'confirmation from a duly authorised representative of the board of directors' that the purchase of computer equipment and its proposed onward leasing 'is not part of some wider tax avoidance motive which involves the leases being terminated prior to the expiry of its five-year term'. S did not provide this confirmation, but lodged an appeal with the Tribunal Centre. Prior to the hearing of the appeal, Customs sent S four letters requesting further information, which S refused to provide. Customs lodged an application for the appeal to be struck out on the grounds that there had 'been no appealable decision'. The tribunal held that Customs had 'made a decision not to make a repayment to the appellant at least unless and until certain information is provided', but that S's Notice of Appeal did not comply with *VAT Tribunals Rules (SI 1986/590), rule 3(2)*. The tribunal directed that S should 'provide particulars whether in an amended Notice of Appeal or otherwise, in accordance with *rule 3(2)* of the VAT Tribunals Rules*, of the decision with respect to which the appeal is made'. *City of Sunderland College Supplies Ltd*, MAN/98/252 (VTD 15701).

Appeal procedure where assessment reduced by Commissioners

[2.66] A partnership which operated a restaurant appealed against an estimated assessment, but did not pay the tax of £35,000 charged by the assessment. The partnership lodged a hardship application under *VAT Tribunals Rules (SI 1986/590), rule 11*. The application was heard in April 1991, and the partnership was given three months to pay the tax charged. Meanwhile, in May 1991 the Commissioners reduced the assessment to £25,000. In July 1991 the partnership submitted a further notice of appeal. The Tribunal Centre allocated a new reference number to this notice of appeal, and the Commissioners applied for the appeals to be consolidated. In September 1991 the tribunal consolidated the appeals, finding that the grant of a second reference number had been an administrative error, and dismissed the appeals on the grounds that the tax charged had not been paid. The partnership appealed to the QB, contending that the appeals should not have been consolidated and that the time for paying the tax charged by the amended assessment should therefore have been extended. The QB dismissed the appeal, holding that where an assessment, against which an appeal had been lodged, was reduced, there was no need for any further appeal, nor was there any statutory provision for such an appeal. The grant of a separate reference number was of no significance and did not mean that the appeal should be treated as two separate appeals. Since the partnership had not paid the sum charged by the assessment, the tribunal had been entitled to dismiss the appeal. *Sitar Tandoori Restaurant v C & E Commrs*, QB [1993] STC 591.

Miscellaneous

Whether appellant may require production of Commissioners' papers

[2.67] In the case noted at 3.25 ASSESSMENT, a trader had appealed against some estimated assessments on her and made an application for further and better particulars of the Commissioners' case. It became apparent during the hearing of the application that she wanted to see the Commissioners' working papers leading to the amount of the assessments. The tribunal rejected the application. *K Taylor (t/a Jeans)*, [1975] VATTR 147 (VTD 163A). (*Note.* The *Rules of the Supreme Court 1965 (SI 1965/1776)* referred to 'particulars'. With effect from 26 April 1999, these rules were largely replaced by the *Civil Procedure Rules 1998 (SI 1998/3132)*, which refer instead to 'information'.)

[2.68] See also *Lai & Lai*, 2.257 below.

Whether notebooks of investigating VAT officer privileged

[2.69] A trader, whose VAT affairs were under investigation, applied to a tribunal for notes of interviews made by a VAT officer to be made available to his solicitors. The tribunal rejected the application, holding that the notes were privileged. *E YS Wat (t/a Kam Tong Restaurant)*, LON/76/82 (VTD 494).

[2.70] The proprietors of a restaurant applied for records made by VAT officers carrying out observations at the restaurant to be made available to them. The tribunal granted the application, applying *dicta* in *Moti Mahal Indian Restaurant*, 50.137 PENALTIES: EVASION OF TAX, and observing that there was 'no basis upon which contemporaneous records of the kind with which this case is concerned and which are central to the assessment in question should be protected from disclosure in the ordinary way'. *F Karim, M Ali & A Majid (t/a Dhaka Tandoori Restaurant)*, MAN/92/1642 (VTD 10987).

Solicitor withdrawing appeal—whether binding on clients

[2.71] A married couple had lodged an appeal against an assessment, and in October 1992 their solicitor met VAT officers to discuss the appeal. Three weeks later the solicitor wrote to the VAT office withdrawing the appeal. Subsequently the couple submitted a further Notice of Appeal relating to the same assessment. The Commissioners applied for the appeal to be struck out. The tribunal granted the Commissioners' application, finding that the couple had authorised the solicitor to act on their behalf, and holding that, by virtue of what is now *VATA 1994, s 85*, the assessment was now *res judicata*. *BD & Mrs MA Taylor*, MAN/93/78 (VTD 10980).

Whether appeal may be withdrawn by email

[2.72] A company (S) appealed against an assessment charging VAT, and against the rejection of a substantial claim for repayment of input tax. On 7 September 2009 it sent an email to the Tribunal Centre purporting to withdraw the appeals. On 24 September 2009 it sent a message to the Tribunal Centre stating that, despite its previous email, it wished to proceed with the appeals. The First-Tier Tribunal treated this as an application to reinstate the appeals, and dismissed it, but the Upper Tribunal allowed S's appeal against this decision. Sir Stephen Oliver QC held that the email of 7 September had simply been a 'proposal', and had not been a 'written notice of withdrawal', as required by *Tribunal Procedure (First-Tier Tribunal) (Tax Chamber) Rules 2009 (SI 2009/273), rule 17(1)*. Accordingly S's subsequent message should not have been treated as an application for reinstatement. He observed that 'the scheme of *rule 17(1)* and *(2)* is to give an appellant the unilateral right to withdraw the appeal without permission of the tribunal and without the intervention of HMRC. The formalities for withdrawal are required to enable the tribunal and anyone with an interest in the outcome of the proceedings to satisfy themselves that a notice describing itself as a "notice of withdrawal" means what it says. *Rule 17(3)* and *(4)* are there to protect the appellant who for some reason has, deliberately and in good faith, withdrawn his appeal but, for an acceptable reason (e.g. because he has insufficient funds to continue the fight or has come to see the implications of withdrawal), has applied to reinstate the appeal within the 28-day cooling-off period. *Rule 17* is not a weapon to enable the tribunal to cull unmeritorious appeals of non-cooperative traders.' *St Anne's Distributors Ltd v HMRC*, UT [2010] UKUT 458 (TCC); [2011] STC 708.

Whether former shareholders of company can be enjoined in appeal

[2.73] Following the sale of a company, the new shareholders discovered, and informed the Commissioners, that some cash receipts and other transactions had not previously been reported. The Commissioners issued an estimated assessment and the company appealed. The vendors, who were liable to indemnify the company for any tax liabilities relating to the time before the sale, deposited the tax demanded but did not provide the new owners of the company with information to enable them to pursue the appeal, and lodged an application to be enjoined in the appeal. The tribunal rejected the application and the QB dismissed the vendors' appeal against this decision, holding that there would be no injustice if they were excluded because they could in the future dispute any liability under the indemnity. If the necessary information was provided to the company, the tribunal could allow the applicants to join in the appeal at a later date under *VAT Tribunals Rules (SI 1986/590), rules 13, 14* and *19*. *Schwarcz & Others v Aeresta Ltd & C & E Commrs*, QB 1988, [1989] STC 230.

Company in liquidation—whether former director has right of appeal

[2.74] In the case noted at 37.4 INSOLVENCY, the Commissioners had presented a petition for the winding-up of a company which owed substantial amounts of VAT and excise duty. The company went into liquidation (and the liquidator began legal proceedings against the company's controlling director, alleging that he had been involved in the fraudulent evasion of the payment of VAT and excise duties). The director subsequently lodged a purported appeal against the assessments. The tribunal struck out the appeal, holding that since the company was in liquidation, the director had no *locus standi*. *H Bhanderi*, LON/03/8066 (E814).

Whether appeals by supplier and recipient should be heard together

[2.75] A company (V) issued credit cards and made related supplies to banks. Its supplies had been treated as exempt, but it considered that they should be standard-rated. In November 1990 the Commissioners accepted V's contention, and issued a ruling accordingly. A bank (B), to which V supplied services, objected to the ruling, since it was partly exempt and would be unable to recover much of the input tax which it would have to pay in respect of the supplies it received from V. In June 1991 B lodged a formal appeal against the ruling. V applied for a direction under *VAT Tribunals Rules (SI 1986/590), rule 19(3)* that it should be joined as a party to the appeal. The Commissioners supported the application, but B objected to it. The tribunal granted the application, holding that it had power to grant the application, applying *dicta* in *Schwarcz & Others v Aeresta Ltd*, 2.73 above, and that 'it would be much better equipped to do justice to the matter if (V) were joined as a party'. It was 'both necessary and expedient to have (V) as a party to the appeal'. *Barclays Bank plc v C & E Commrs and Visa International Service Association*, [1992] VATTR 229 (VTD 7911). (*Note.* For a direction as to costs, see **2.495** below.)

[2.76] Three companies reclaimed substantial amounts of input tax. The Commissioners rejected the claims, on the basis that the relevant transactions formed part of a 'carousel fraud', of the type at issue in *Optigen Ltd (and related appeals)*, 22.115 EUROPEAN COMMUNITY LAW. The companies appealed. The Commissioners applied for the appeals to be heard together. The tribunal rejected this application, holding that 'the facts in each appeal will have to be considered separately. There is no allegation by Customs that there was a common ringmaster.' The tribunal chairman (Mr. Wallace) held that 'while there may be cases where the objective of a just determination will outweigh delay, it is impossible to say that individual appeals will be expedited by a joint hearing unless added to a hearing the date for which has already fixed (*sic*). That is not the case here.' *RP Ltd (and associated appeals)*, [2004] VATDR 452 (VTD 18935).

[2.77] See also *RBS Deutschland Holdings GmbH*, 2.306 below.

Whether appeals by associated partnerships should be heard together

[2.78] The Commissioners issued estimated assessments on two partnerships which operated restaurants. Three of the four members of each partnership were the same. Both partnerships appealed. The Commissioners applied for a direction that the appeals should be heard together. The tribunal made a direction accordingly, under *VAT Tribunals Rules (SI 1986/590), rule 19(3)*, applying the CA decision in *Johnson v Walden*, CA 1995, [1996] STC 382. One of the partnerships appealed to the QB, contending that the appeals should not be heard together. Turner J rejected this contention and dismissed the appeal, holding on the evidence that the tribunal had been entitled to make the direction in question. The tribunal's decision was 'entirely rational', and it would 'have been a mischievous result if there had been two separate hearings and witnesses whose evidence was believed in one case in relation to the same evidential matters were not believed in the other, or the other way about'. *Maharani Restaurant v C & E Commrs*, QB [1999] STC 295. (*Note*. At a subsequent hearing, the appeals were dismissed and penalties under *VATA 1994, s 60* were upheld—see **50.79** PENALTIES: EVASION OF TAX.)

Whether appeals by related companies should be heard together

[2.79] The decision in *Maharani Restaurant*, 2.78 above, was applied in an insurance premium tax case where the tribunal held that appeals by six related companies should be heard together. *Cresta Holidays Ltd (and related appeals)*, LON/00/9000-4 (VTD 16857). (*Note*. For subsequent developments in this case, concerning the interpretation of *FA 1994, s 59*, see the CA decision reported at [2001] STC 386.)

[2.80] A similar decision was reached in a case where two associated companies had appealed against notices requiring security. *F2 Leisure Ltd*, MAN/05/228 (VTD 19253); *Virtual Leisure Ltd*, MAN/05/303 (VTD 19253).

[2.81] A similar decision was reached in a case where two associated companies had reclaimed substantial amounts of input tax, and HMRC formed the opinion that the transactions were connected to MTIC fraud. *First Talk Mobile Ltd v HMRC (and related appeal)*, [2011] UKFTT 423 (TC), TC01276.

Group registration—right of appeal

[2.82] See *J & W Waste Management Ltd*, **32.9** GROUPS OF COMPANIES.

Matters within the discretion of the Commissioners

Whether a concession can be the subject of an appeal

[2.83] A company (D) applied to the Commissioners for a concession that services which it supplied under long-term contracts made before January 1973 should not be chargeable to VAT. The Commissioners rejected the claim, notifying D by letter. D and two associated companies appealed. The tribunal struck out the appeals, holding that the question of whether a concession should be made was not a subject of appeal within what is now *VATA 1994, s 83*. *Davis Advertising Service Ltd*, [1973] VATTR 16 (VTD 5). (*Note*. The tribunal also held that the associated companies had no *locus standi* as the decision was not communicated to them. The decision on this point was disapproved by a subsequent tribunal in *J & W Waste Management Ltd*, **32.9** GROUPS OF COMPANIES.)

Special Provisions Order 1995—tribunal jurisdiction

[2.84] In the case noted at **60.1** SECOND-HAND GOODS, the HL held that a tribunal's jurisdiction was restricted to considering whether a trader's records complied with the statutory requirements, and that where the records did not meet those requirements, the tribunal could not consider whether the Commissioners should have used their discretion to permit the use of the scheme. *C & E Commrs v JH Corbitt (Numismatists) Ltd*, HL [1980] STC 231; [1981] AC 22; [1980] 2 All ER 72. (*Note.* This case was decided before the introduction of what is now *VATA 1994, s 84(10)* by *FA 1981*. The decision should be read in the light of *s 84(10)* — see *Christopher Gibbs Ltd*, 60.2 SECOND-HAND GOODS — but is still frequently cited as an authority.)

[2.85] In the case noted at **60.2** SECOND-HAND GOODS, the tribunal considered that it had jurisdiction to overrule a Commissioners' decision that a company was not entitled to use the margin scheme for sales of antiques, since its records did not comply with the scheme requirements. The tribunal declined to follow *JH Corbitt (Numismatists) Ltd*, 60.1 SECOND-HAND GOODS, since that case had been decided before the enactment of what is now *VATA 1994, s 84(10)*. *Christopher Gibbs Ltd*, [1992] VATTR 376 (VTD 8981).

[2.86] See also *McCord & Alford*, 60.3 SECOND-HAND GOODS.

Customs refusing to operate 'Sheldon statement'

[2.87] See *Animal Virus Research Institute*, 2.118 below.

Customs refusing to backdate extra-statutory concession

[2.88] Before 1 April 1983, the VAT liability on the sale of a security depended on the 'place of belonging' of the purchaser. The Commissioners agreed with the Investment and Unit Trust Associations that, with effect from 1 April 1983, members of the Associations should have the option of treating the country in which the sale took place as the 'place of belonging' of the purchaser, in any case where the identity (and thus the place of belonging) of the purchaser was unknown, and also in any case where it was not known where the sale took place. An investment trust submitted a claim that the concession should be backdated to 1 April 1978. The Commissioners rejected this claim and the investment trust lodged an appeal. The tribunal struck out the appeal, holding that it had no jurisdiction and that there had been no decision within what is now *VATA 1994, s 84(10)*. *Scottish Investment Trust plc*, EDN/92/77 (VTD 9368).

Extra-statutory concession—whether within VATA 1994, s 84(10)

[2.89] In the case noted at **25.35** EXPORTS, the tribunal held that it could consider the application of an extra-statutory concession, since the effect of what is now *VATA 1994, s 84(10)* was 'to allow the tribunal to review whether, as a matter of fact, the taxpayer has acted in accordance with guidelines prescribed by the Commissioners in the exercise of a discretion conferred on them, but not to review the laying down of the guidelines or requirements themselves'. *RW Shepherd*, [1994] VATTR 47 (VTD 11753). (*Note*. Compare now, however, the subsequent cases noted at **2.90** to **2.92** below.)

[2.90] An individual who had converted an old church into a dwelling appealed against the Commissioners' refusal to apply an extra-statutory concession which would have entitled him to reclaim input tax. (The concession took effect from 21 April 1994, and the Commissioners refused to apply it to the appellant since the work in question had been completed before that date.) The tribunal dismissed the appeal, holding that it had 'no jurisdiction in regard to the operation of extra-statutory concessions'. *Dr BN Purdue*, EDN/94/511 (VTD 13430). (*Notes*. (1) The decision here was approved by the QB in *Arnold*, **2.91** below. (2) An alternative contention by the appellant, that the work had not been completed until after 21 April 1994, was also rejected by the tribunal — see **15.147** CONSTRUCTION OF BUILDINGS.)

[2.91] In a subsequent case in which the application of the same concession was in dispute, the QB held that the tribunal had no jurisdiction in relation to the concession, which was a matter for the Commissioners. Hidden J held that the provisions of *VATA 1994, s 84(10)* only applied to a case where there were two separate decisions (as had been the case in *JH Corbitt (Numismatists) Ltd*, **60.1** SECOND-HAND GOODS) and did not apply in the present case where there had only been one decision. He approved the decisions in *G McKenzie & Co*, **2.21** above, and *Purdue*, **2.90** above, and disapproved *obiter dicta* of the tribunal chairman in *British Teleflower Service Ltd*, **40.57** INVOICES AND CREDIT NOTES. *C & E Commrs v SH Arnold*, QB [1996] STC 1271.

[2.92] The decision in *Arnold*, **2.91** above, was applied by the tribunal in the case noted at **35.23** EXPORTS, where the tribunal held that it had no jurisdiction to consider the Commissioners' refusal to apply Extra-Statutory Concession 5.6. The tribunal held that 'an extra-statutory concession creates no legal right and therefore its application or non-application raises questions about the exercise by the Commissioners of their powers that go beyond the particular interests of a particular taxpayer. Such questions may be apt for decision by means of a judicial review because any relevant third party interests may be represented there. They are not apt for decision by the tribunal which is concerned only with the legal relationship between a particular taxpayer and the Commissioners.' *GP Powell*, MAN/00/134 (VTD 17380).

[2.93] The decision in *Arnold*, **2.91** above, was also applied in *Lady Nuffield Home*, **19.91** DRUGS, MEDICINES, AIDS FOR THE HANDICAPPED, ETC.

Commissioners refusing to apply extra-statutory concession

[2.94] The decision in *Arnold*, **2.91** above, was distinguished in a subsequent case in which a university owned all the shares in a property company (G). G constructed certain buildings for the university, and granted the university an underlease of these buildings. The university gave G a certificate that it would use the buildings for relevant residential purposes (see **15.70** *et seq* CONSTRUCTION OF BUILDINGS, ETC). On 6 July 1999 the Commissioners issued a ruling that the certificate should not have been issued. On 14 July they issued an assessment to recover the input tax which G had reclaimed. G appealed. The Commissioners applied for the appeal to be struck out, contending that the question of whether the certificate should have been issued depended on the application of an extra-statutory concession, over which the tribunal had no jurisdiction. The tribunal rejected the Commissioners' application, holding that *VATA 1994, s 83(b)* enabled it to hear the appeal, but proceeded to dismiss the appeal, holding that it had no jurisdiction to review the application of the concession. G applied for judicial review. The QB granted the application. Collins J observed that the purpose behind the relevant concession 'was to enable the universities to make profitable use of their student accommodation in vacations and still get the benefit of zero-rating'. The concession 'contained guidelines which had been approved by the Commissioners who must be taken to have known and intended that the higher education establishments would act upon them'. Accordingly, 'it would be unfair and so unlawful' for the Commissioners not to apply the concession, 'provided that the taxpayer has complied with its terms'. On the evidence, the language of the concession was 'unambiguous and the university clearly complied with it'. While the Commissioners 'may not like the concession being used in this way to reduce the amount of VAT otherwise payable by increasing input against a zero-rated supply', there was 'nothing in the language of the concession that prevents it being done. The Commissioners could have made it clear, if they had wished, that the university must make the arrangements itself and not as a third party. They did not. There is no overriding public interest that prevents a person taking advantage of a concession to maximise the benefits he can legitimately expect from its terms.' Accordingly, 'the Commissioners were not entitled to raise the assessment' and G was 'entitled to rely on the concession'. *R (oao Greenwich Property Ltd) v C & E Commrs*, Ch D [2001] STC 618; [2001] EWHC Admin 230.

[2.95] In 1997 Customs issued a concession stating that they would not apply the statutory three-year time limit to repayment claims where the claim related to 'claims or adjustments which cover tax appearing on both sides of a VAT return and therefore cancel each other out (such as those in respect of acquisition tax or the reverse charge), correction of tax point errors and simple duplications of output tax'. (The concession was subsequently withdrawn with effect from 1 July 2005.) In its return for the period ending December 1999, a company made two errors, as a result of which it made an overpayment of VAT. It did not discover this until after the expiry of the three-year time limit. Customs refused to apply the published extra-statutory concession on the grounds that the company's errors were more than a 'simple duplication of output tax'. The QB dismissed the company's application for judicial review. On the evidence, there had been both a bookkeeping error (the failure to process a credit note correctly) and a separate transposition error, with the result that the company had declared output tax relating to an associated company. This was more than 'simple duplication of output tax', and the concession did not apply. *R (oao Silicon Graphics Finance SA) v HMRC*, QB 2006, [2008] STC 1928; [2006] EWHC 1889 (Admin).

Concessions, etc.—other cases

[**2.96**] For the jurisdiction of the tribunal in relation to a published non-statutory arrangement, see also *McLean Homes Midland Ltd*, 36.7 INPUT TAX. For a case where an application for judicial review has been referred to the CJEC, see *R (oao British Telecommunications plc) v HMRC*, 48.52 PAYMENT OF TAX. There have been a large number of cases in which a tribunal has dismissed an appeal because it had no jurisdiction in non-statutory matters or because the appellant has failed to disclose a ground of appeal, but which raise no point of general interest. In the interests of space, such cases are not summarised individually in this book.

Cancellation of registration under VATA 1994, Sch 1 para 13

[**2.97**] See *The Source Enterprise Ltd*, 45.1 OVERSEAS TRADERS.

Penalty under VATA 1994, s 63*—whether unreasonable

[**2.98**] See *Food Engineering Ltd*, 52.454 PENALTIES: MISDECLARATION.

Retrospective group registration—nature of tribunal's jurisdiction

[**2.99**] In the case noted at 32.4 GROUPS OF COMPANIES, the QB held that the Commissioners have power under what is now *VATA 1994, s 43(7)* to admit group registration retrospectively. However the discretion to admit retrospective treatment was that of the Commissioners and could not be exercised by the tribunal. *C & E Commrs v Save and Prosper Group Ltd*, QB 1978, [1979] STC 205.

VATA 1994, Sch 11 para 4*—nature of tribunal's jurisdiction

[**2.100**] See *Mr Wishmore Ltd*, 14.52 COLLECTION AND ENFORCEMENT.

Cash accounting scheme—nature of tribunal's jurisdiction

[**2.101**] See *Mainline Fabrications*, 10.4 CASH ACCOUNTING SCHEME.

VATA 1994, Sch 1 para 1(3)—nature of tribunal's jurisdiction

[**2.102**] See *Hare*, 57.23 REGISTRATION, and *Timur & Timur*, 57.25 REGISTRATION.

VATA 1994, Sch 1 para 2*—nature of tribunal's jurisdiction

[**2.103**] See *Chamberlain*, 57.35 REGISTRATION, and *Gregorio & Sons*, 57.55 REGISTRATION.

VATA 1994, Sch 1 para 9*—nature of tribunal's jurisdiction

[2.104] See *Golden Pyramid Ltd*, 57.101 REGISTRATION.

VAT Regulations 1995, reg 29*—nature of tribunal's jurisdiction

[2.105] See *Vaughan*, 40.66 INVOICES AND CREDIT NOTES.

Definition of 'tax year' for partial exemption calculations

[2.106] See *Yorkhurst Ltd*, 46.190 PARTIAL EXEMPTION.

Pre-registration input tax—jurisdiction of tribunal

[2.107] See *Tricell UK Ltd*, 2.13 above.

VAT Regulations 1995, regs 185–197—jurisdiction of tribunal

[2.108] In the case noted at 45.4 OVERSEAS TRADERS, the tribunal held that it had no 'jurisdiction to review the exercise by Customs & Excise of any discretion it may have in its management of the collection and refund of VAT'. *Jersey Telecoms*, LON/95/1965 (VTD 13940).

Estoppel and allied matters

Commissioners' practice where taxpayer misled by VAT officer

[2.109] In a Parliamentary question and answer on 21 July 1978, the then Financial Secretary to the Treasury, Mr Robert Sheldon stated: 'When it is established that an officer of Customs and Excise, with the full facts before him, has given a clear and unequivocal ruling on VAT in writing; or it is established that an officer knowing the full facts has misled a trader to his detriment, the Commissioners of Customs and Excise would only raise an assessment based on the correct ruling from the date the error was brought to the attention of the registered person concerned.' (*Hansard Vol. 161, col. 426; C & E Notice No 48, Extra-Statutory Concession 3.5.*)

[2.110] In December 1973 a company which manufactured and installed built-in wardrobes for new houses was informed by the Commissioners that its supply of such wardrobes was zero-rated under the legislation then in force. In May 1975 the Commissioners informed the company that they had changed their view, and now considered that such supplies were standard-rated. The company accepted this ruling but appealed against an assessment charging tax on supplies made before May 1975. The tribunal dismissed the company's appeal, holding that there was no question of estoppel against the Commissioners. *Cupboard Love Ltd*, LON/76/40 (VTD 267).

[2.111] A similar decision was reached in *HV Ribbans*, LON/76/200 (VTD 346).

[2.112] In a similar case, the tribunal held that 'on the existing state of the authorities we are bound to hold that no estoppel can arise against the mandatory provisions of a taxing statute'. *POH Medlam*, LON/77/304 (VTD 545).

[2.113] In the case noted at **58.1** RETAILERS' SPECIAL SCHEMES, the tribunal held that an inspection of a trader's records, and a general assurance that they were in order, was insufficient to form the basis of an estoppel. *GUS Merchandise Corporation Ltd*, [1978] VATTR 28 (VTD 553).

[2.114] In the case noted at **65.18** TRANSFERS OF GOING CONCERNS, Lord Grantchester held that 'there can be no estoppel against the Crown in the person of the Commissioners of Customs & Excise which prevents them from recovering tax which is lawfully due under the provisions of an Act of Parliament and Regulations made thereunder'. *Farm Facilities (Fork Lift) Ltd*, [1987] VATTR 80 (VTD 2366).

[2.115] A builder had carried out work on a protected building which did not qualify as an 'approved alteration' and was therefore not eligible for zero-rating. However he did not charge VAT on the work and appealed against a subsequent assessment, contending that he had been told by a VAT officer that tax would not be chargeable. The tribunal dismissed his appeal. Applying *dicta* of Finlay J in *Williams v Grundy's Trustees*, KB 1933, 18 TC 271, 'nothing is better settled than the principle that there is no estoppel as against the Crown'. *PT Wood*, MAN/91/513 (VTD 6992).

[2.116] There are a large number of other cases in which tribunals have held, applying one or more of the preceding decisions, that the Commissioners cannot be estopped from collecting VAT. Such cases appear to raise no point of general importance, and in the interests of space, are not reported individually in this book. For a list of such cases decided up to and including 31 December 1993, see Tolley's VAT Cases 1994. For a case in which costs were awarded to the appellant, see *Ness*, **2.501** below.

[2.117] A company, which had wrongly treated certain animal feeding stuffs as zero-rated rather than standard-rated, appealed to the tribunal, contending that Customs should have applied Extra-Statutory Concession 3.5, applying the principles laid down in *C & G Developments Ltd*, LON/86/682 (VTD 2384). The tribunal rejected this contention and dismissed the appeal, observing that *C & G Developments Ltd* 'was decided in 1987. There is now a fully fledged official complaints procedure which there was not then and the appropriate avenue to the appellant would be to take his case to the Adjudicator. This option was not open to *C & G*.' The tribunal held that it had 'no jurisdiction to consider the issue of misdirection and it would not be an appropriate course of action for the tribunal to act as an unofficial arbitrator'. *Vetplus Ltd*, MAN/04/312 (VTD 19850).

[2.118] The Commissioners made an application for an appeal to be struck out on the grounds that it pertained to what is now Extra-Statutory Concession 3.5 (see **2.109** above) and that estoppel was not one of the grounds of appeal under what is now *VATA 1994, s 83*. The tribunal dismissed the application, holding that the grounds of the appeal made it clear that the appeal was brought under what is now *VATA 1994, s 84(10)* and that, in the alternative, the appeal was against a decision of the Commissioners relating to the assessment, such appeal being under *s 83(p)*. While an appeal was unlikely to succeed under either *subsection*, that was insufficient to justify a conclusion that no appeal lay to the tribunal. *Animal Virus Research Institute*, [1988] VATTR 56 (VTD 2692).

Whether Customs estopped from treating return as valid

[2.119] See *AB Gee of Ripley Ltd*, 52.30 PENALTIES: MISDECLARATION.

Scottish appeals—whether Commissioners personally barred

[2.120] In a Scottish case, a partnership contended that it had been misled by VAT officers and that the Commissioners were personally barred (the Scottish equivalent of estoppel) from demanding the assessed tax. The tribunal accepted that the partners had been wrongly advised, but dismissed the appeal, holding that in Scotland the plea of personal bar does not operate against the Crown in taxation matters, applying *Lord Advocate v Meiklam* 1860, 22 D 1427 and other authorities. *Milne & Mackintosh (t/a Jack and Jill)*, [1981] VATTR 61 (VTD 1063).

[2.121] The decision in *Milne & Mackintosh*, 2.120 above, was applied in the similar subsequent cases of *Lincars Radio Taxis*, EDN/81/17 (VTD 1118); *J & E McClymont*, EDN/82/15 (VTD 1253); *G Brown*, EDN/92/76 (VTD 7718) and *St. Andrew's Motor Homes Ltd*, 19.22 DRUGS, MEDICINES, AIDS FOR THE HANDICAPPED, ETC.

Issue estoppel per rem judicatum

[2.122] A trader (F) had been convicted at a Crown Court under *Criminal Law Act 1977, s 1(1)*, for conspiracy to cheat the public revenue by failing to account for VAT on takings from gaming machines. The Commissioners issued assessments on him, charging tax on the takings from the machines. He appealed, contending that, notwithstanding the conviction in the Crown Court, he had not been the operator of the machines in question. The Commissioners applied for a direction under *rule 19(3)* of the *VAT Tribunals Rules* that the appellant should not be permitted to reopen issues which had been determined against him in the Crown Court. The tribunal granted the application sought by the Commissioners. The tribunal held that it had inherent jurisdiction to prevent abuse of process. The present case fell within the doctrine of '*issue estoppel per rem judicatum*'. Applying *dicta* of Lord Halsbury LC in *Reichel Magrath*, HL 1889, 14 AC 665, 'it would be a scandal to the administration of justice if, the same question having been disposed of by one case, the litigant were to be permitted by changing the form of the proceedings to set up the same case again'. The tribunal chairman (Mr. Potter) held that the issue had been 'effectively covered by the criminal proceedings'. Furthermore, the fact that 'neither the learned judge nor either counsel appears to have considered those parts of the law relating to VAT' and that the judge had appeared 'sometimes to take it for granted that VAT should have been charged' was not sufficient to alter this conclusion, since 'it was open to the defence, if it saw fit, to raise all relevant matters of law; and the defence did not do so'. The criminal proceedings had found as a fact that the appellant had made the supplies in question, and the tribunal had no discretion to reach a different conclusion. *MJ Feehan*, [1993] VATTR 266 (VTD 10154). (*Note.* For the substantive appeal, see **24.20** EXEMPTIONS: MISCELLANEOUS.)

[2.123] In a subsequent (non-tax) case, Lord Hoffmann held that 'the whole point of an issue estoppel on a question of law is that the parties remain bound by an erroneous decision'. *Ahsan v Ward*, HL [2007] UKHL 51.

Whether tribunal bound by decision reached several years earlier

[2.124] In the case noted at **66.45** TRANSPORT, the Commissioners issued a ruling to a company in 1997. The company appealed, contending that the issue had been decided by a previous tribunal decision in 1973. The tribunal rejected this contention and dismissed the appeal, holding that the 1973 decision did not give rise to any estoppel, and observing that 'the public policy behind the general application of issue estoppel is to ensure the finality of litigation. In taxation and rating cases, however, that aspect of public policy has been overridden by a different element of public policy. Recurring business transactions, which fall to be assessed period by period, as is the case of supplies of a VAT-registered trader, are involved here. Administrative flexibility is needed to enable the even-handed management of the revenue. To impose on a trader the unalterable privilege or disadvantage of a particular tax treatment of his supplies as the result of a decision of a tribunal or court might lead to inequity as between him and other traders making similar supplies the liability of which had been determined at a later date. The principle of public policy that applies in that situation, and in particular through the taxation of business transactions, is that of ensuring that the tax operates uniformly.' *Société Internationale de Télécommunications Aeronautiques (No 2)*, [2003] VATDR 131 (VTD 17991). (*Note.* For a subsequent case in which this decision was distinguished, see *University College London*. **46.151** PARTIAL EXEMPTION.)

'Res judicata'

[2.125] In the case noted at **41.88** LAND, the tribunal held that supplies by the owners of a hairdressing salon failed to qualify for exemption, and that the owners had been required to register for VAT from 1996. The proprietors subsequently sought to lodge a further appeal against the date of registration. The tribunal struck out the second appeal, applying *dicta* of Lord Bingham in *Johnson v Gore Wood*, HL 2000, [2001] 1 All ER 481, and holding that the issue was *res judicata*. *LW & A Broadley (t/a Professional Haircare)*, [2001] VATDR 271 (VTD 17153).

[2.126] See also *BD & Mrs MA Taylor*, **2.71** above.

Whether Customs estopped from issuing replacement assessment

[2.127] Following the tribunal decision in the case noted at **3.21** ASSESSMENT, the Commissioners issued a replacement assessment in 1998. The trader applied for the assessment to be struck out, contending that the principle of '*res judicata*' estopped the Commissioners from issuing a replacement assessment. The tribunal rejected this contention and dismissed the trader's application. The tribunal observed that another issue in the case had been considered by the High Court (for which see **57.13** REGISTRATION) and had been remitted to a new tribunal for reconsideration. The tribunal reviewed the evidence and held that 'the interests of justice require that this appeal should be determined on its merits bearing in mind the views of the High Court'. Although the tribunal could not 'now consider the original assessment and the supplementary assessment (as they have been withdrawn), the interests of justice would best be served by referring all the outstanding issues (including the new assessment) to a newly constituted tribunal for a decision on the merits'. The trader appealed to the Ch D, which upheld the tribunal decision. Patten J held that the assessment was valid. There was 'no good reason in principle or of policy why Parliament should have intended to prevent Customs & Excise from waiting until after a determination by the tribunal so as to be able to base a new corrective assessment on the tribunal's own finding of what is due'. The doctrine of '*res judicata*' did not apply here, since 'the only determination made by the tribunal in respect of the central assessment was that it was not made to best judgment. The Commissioners accepted that and have withdrawn the assessment. The tribunal did not decide that £9,853 of (the trader's) alleged tax liability was not due.' The trader had 'lost nothing by the withdrawal of the 1996 assessments other than the ability to take advantage of a technical defect in the central assessment. All the points about registrability, the transfer of his business and quantum which he wished to be able to raise at the new tribunal hearing ordered by Carnwath J will be open to him on the appeal from the 1998 assessment.' *A Bennett v C & E Commrs (No 2)*, Ch D [2001] STC 137. (*Note.* The Ch D also held that the delays in determining the trader's liability did not involve any breach of *Article 6* of the *European Convention on Human Rights* — see **34.14** HUMAN RIGHTS.)

The requirements of VATA 1994, s 84(3)

Payment of assessed tax

Date from which appeal 'entertained'

[2.128] A Foundation was established with the main object of furthering the instruction and study of Scientology. It appealed against ten assessments without paying the tax charged. The Commissioners applied to the tribunal for the appeals to be dismissed under what is now *VATA 1994, s 84(3)(a)*. The tribunal initially rejected the application, considering that an appeal was not entertained until it was heard on the merits, but the CS overruled this decision and remitted the case to the tribunal with a direction to it to order the Foundation to pay the tax within 14 days. The CS held that there was a distinction between an appeal being 'entertained' and an appeal being 'heard'. An appeal begins to be entertained when the tribunal sets in motion the requisite procedure for its determination. *C & E Commrs v Hubbard Foundation Scotland*, CS [1981] STC 593. (*Note*. For subsequent proceedings in this case, see **2.323** below.)

Assessment to recover input tax—application of VATA 1994, s 84(3)

[2.129] A company appealed against an assessment to recover input tax which it had deducted in its returns. The Commissioners applied for a direction that the appeal should be struck out, since the company had not paid the tax charged by the assessment. The company applied for an extension of the time in which to apply for a direction excusing it from paying or depositing the tax on account of hardship. The tribunal allowed the company's application. *Boltgate Ltd*, [1982] VATTR 120 (VTD 1246). (*Note*. The decision in this case was distinguished in *Safegold Fashions Ltd*, **2.132** below.)

[2.130] The decision in *Boltgate Ltd*, **2.129** above, was applied in a subsequent case where the tax assessed had not been paid. The tribunal held that it could entertain the appeal since the question at issue was an amount of input tax. *Brian Gubby Ltd*, [1985] VATTR 59 (VTD 1961). (*Notes*. (1) The decision in this case was distinguished in *Safegold Fashions Ltd*, **2.132** below. (2) For the substantive appeal, see **7.64** BUSINESS.)

[2.131] A company which was partly exempt appealed against an assessment issued by the Commissioners to recover input tax which it had claimed. The Commissioners applied for a direction that the appeal should be struck out as the company had not paid the tax assessed. The tribunal allowed the company's application, observing that the appeal concerned a dispute over input tax within what is now *VATA 1994, s 83(c)* or *(e)*. Applying *dicta* of Lord Grantchester in *Boltgate Ltd*, **2.129** above, Parliament had intended disputes as to registration and input tax to be entertained by tribunals without payment or deposit of the disputed tax. *Trust Securities Holdings Ltd*, [1990] VATTR 1 (VTD 4550). (*Note*. The decision in this case was disapproved by a subsequent tribunal in *Safegold Fashions Ltd*, **2.132** below.)

[2.132] The Commissioners formed the opinion that a company had re-claimed input tax on the basis of false invoices. They therefore issued an assessment to recover the tax in question. The company appealed against the assessment but did not pay the tax assessed. The Commissioners applied for a direction that the appeal should be dismissed since the company had not complied with what is now *VATA 1994, s 84(3)*. The tribunal accepted the Commissioners' application and dismissed the appeal. Because the appeal was against an assessment, it was made under what is now *VATA 1994, s 83(p)* as well as under *s 83(c)*, and thus could not be entertained unless the tax was deposited. *Boltgate Ltd*, **2.129** above, was distinguished since it had been decided before the enactment of what is now *VATA 1994, s 73(2)*; *Brian Gubby Ltd*, **2.130** above, was distinguished since it had been decided before the amendment of that provision by *FA 1988*. The tribunal specifically disapproved the decision in *Trust Securities Holdings Ltd*, **2.131** above. Applying *R v C & E Commrs (ex p. Strangewood Ltd)*, **36.648** INPUT TAX, the Commissioners were not required to allow credit for all input tax claimed in a return. Where more input tax was credited or repaid than was allowable, the excess was properly assessable under *s 73(2)*. *Safegold Fashions Ltd*, [1992] VATTR 105 (VTD 7343).

[2.133] The Commissioners formed the opinion that a company had re-claimed input tax which was attributable to an exempt supply, and issued an assessment to recover the tax. The company appealed against the assessment but did not pay the tax assessed. The Commissioners applied for a direction that the appeal should be struck out as the company had not complied with what is now *VATA 1994, s 84(3)*. The tribunal accepted the application and struck out the appeal, applying the principles laid down in *Safegold Fashions Ltd*, **2.132** above. The assessment had been properly made under what is now *VATA 1994, s 73*, and *VATA 1994, s 83(p)* therefore provided that the appeal could not be heard unless the tax was deposited. *Boltgate Ltd*, **2.129** above, was distinguished since it had been decided before the enactment of *VATA 1994, s 73(2)*; *Brian Gubby Ltd*, **2.130** above, was distinguished because it had been decided before the amendment of that provision by *FA 1988*. *Richard Haynes Associates*, LON/92/2597 (VTD 10068).

[2.134] A company had submitted a VAT return for the period ending January 2004 claiming a VAT repayment of £58,000, which Customs repaid. It submitted a return for the period ending March 2004, claiming a repayment of more than £700,000, in respect of purported purchases of platinum, which it claimed to have exported to China. Customs formed the opinion that the claimed exports were fictitious, and that the company appeared to have participated in a fraud. They rejected the March repayment claim, and issued an assessment to recover the January repayment. The company appealed, and applied for a direction that the appeal should be heard without payment of the tax. The tribunal rejected the application with regard to the January assess-ment, applying the principles laid down in *Safegold Fashions Ltd*, **2.132** above. (The tribunal also observed that the appeal had actually been lodged following receipt of a letter from the Commissioners and before the date on which the assessment was actually made. The tribunal held that this did not circumvent the requirements of *VATA 1994, s 83(p)* and *s 84(3)*, and commented that 'it would be most unfortunate if a taxpayer's appeal foundered procedurally because he or his professional advisers had been too quick off the mark and had appealed on the basis of a communicated intention to make an assessment but before the assessment was actually made'.) However, the tribunal accepted the application with regard to the March repayment claim, distinguishing *Safegold*, on the basis that there had been no assessment for the relevant period. Accordingly, the appeal for that period fell within *VATA 1994, s 83(c)* rather than *s 83(p)*. *Plasma Trading Ltd (No 1)*, LON/04/1187 (VTD 18908). (*Note*. The tribunal subsequently dismissed the substantive appeal—see **36.123** INPUT TAX.)

Assessment charging output tax—application of VATA 1994, s 84(3)

[2.135] A trader failed to account for output tax on his supplies. Customs issued an assessment charging tax on them, and he appealed. The tribunal struck out his appeal on the grounds that he had not complied with *VATA 1994, s 84(3)*. He appealed to the Ch D, contending that the provisions of *s 84(3)* contravened the *European Convention on Human Rights*. The Ch D rejected this contention and dismissed his appeal. *B O'Brien v HMRC*, Ch D 2007, [2008] STC 487; [2007] EWHC 3121 (Ch).

Hardship applications (VATA 1994, s 84(3B))

[2.136] Assessments charging tax of over £27,000 were made on a car dealer, following his conviction for having submitted fraudulent returns. He applied under *Tribunals Rules (SI 1986/590), rule 11* for the appeal to be entertained without payment or deposit of the tax. After one adjournment the application was set down for hearing in September 1975. The dealer was represented at the hearing by counsel but did not attend. He was believed to be in Spain and the reason for his non-attendance was not known. The tribunal refused a further adjournment and dismissed the *rule 11* application. The QB upheld the tribunal decision. *PA Baird (t/a Baird Motors) v C & E Commrs*, QB April 1976 unreported.

[2.137] A company appealed against two assessments to recover input tax, and applied under *VATA 1984, s 84(3B)* for the appeals to be entertained without paying or depositing the tax. The First-Tier Tribunal rejected the applications, finding that T had not submitted sufficient evidence to show that payment of the tax would cause hardship. T applied for judicial review. The QB dismissed the application, holding that the tribunal's decision had not been unreasonable. Simon J observed that T's accountants had asserted that they 'had been "too busy" to prepare relevant and up-to-date material'. He also held that 'the abolition of a right of appeal to the Upper Tribunal against the tribunal's refusal to give a hardship direction was lawful', and that the provisions of *VATA 1994 s 84(3B) (3C)* did not contravene European law. *R (oao Totel Ltd) v First-Tier Tribunal (and related application)*, QB [2011] EWHC 652 (Admin); [2011] STC 1485.

[2.138] A trader had appealed against two assessments and applied under *Tribunals Rules, rule 11* for the appeals to be entertained notwithstanding that he had not paid or deposited the tax. The notices of appeal had indicated that the trader's accountant would deal with the appeal, but neither the trader nor the accountant attended at the time fixed for the hearing of the application. The trader then applied under *rule 26(2)* for the decision to be set aside, appearing in person and contending that, because of his accountant's negligence, he had not been notified of the time fixed for hearing the *rule 11* application. The tribunal set aside its initial decision on the *rule 11* application, which it then proceeded to hear in private. *B Hallam (t/a APX Car Sales)*, [1977] VATTR 105 (VTD 394). (*Note.* The appeals were subsequently dismissed.)

[2.139] A company appealed against an assessment and at the same time applied under *Tribunals Rules, rule 11* for the appeal to be entertained notwithstanding that the tax had not been paid or deposited. The company was not represented at the hearing of the application but six days previously its accountants had written to the tribunal, sending a copy of a letter from the company's bank manager refusing it an overdraft. The tribunal dismissed the application, considering that the evidence before it did not establish that payment of the tax would result in hardship. The company then applied under *rule 26(2)* for the decision to be set aside. Its accountant attended the hearing and stated that he had assumed that the letter which he had submitted would be sufficient to support the *rule 11* application, being more familiar with the informal procedures of General Commissioners with regard to income tax, etc. The tribunal decided in the circumstances to set aside its decision on the *rule 11* application which it then proceeded to rehear in private. *Cumbershourne Ltd (t/a Hockley Enterprises)*, [1977] VATTR 110 (VTD 369).

[2.140] A company applied for an appeal to be entertained by the tribunal without the tax in dispute being paid or deposited. The company had been prosecuted under what is now *VATA 1994, s 72*, and the proceedings had been compounded by the payment of a penalty. The company had recently purchased a freehold restaurant for more than £900,000. It had a bank overdraft of slightly under £80,000. The tax assessed was almost £115,000. The tribunal held that, in view of the company's existing overdraft, the payment of the tax would cause hardship, and therefore allowed the application. *Bentley Restaurant Ltd*, LON/88/620 (VTD 4327).

[2.141] A partnership failed to pay any VAT, or make any VAT returns, for 25 successive prescribed accounting periods between 1 June 1981 and 31 August 1987. The Commissioners issued an estimated assessment covering the whole of the period, charging tax of more than £56,000. The partnership appealed and applied for the appeal to be heard without payment of the tax assessed, on the grounds that payment would cause it hardship. The tribunal was satisfied that payment of the full amount would cause hardship, but held that, as the assessment was a composite one covering several accounting periods, each period should be considered separately. On the evidence, the tribunal held that the partnership had not established that payment of the tax assessed for the last five accounting periods of the assessment (totalling slightly more than £10,000) would cause hardship, and ordered that the partnership should pay this amount. The partnership appealed to the QB, which held that the assessment had to be considered as a whole and that the appeal against the assessment should be heard without any tax being paid. The CA upheld this decision. *Don Pasquale v C & E Commrs*, CA [1990] STC 556. (*Note.* The decision in this case was unanimously disapproved by the CA in the subsequent case of *Le Rififi Ltd*, 3.87 ASSESSMENT. Millett LJ observed that 'the case has no *ratio decidendi* (and) Dillon LJ appears to have treated the question as one of first impression'. The effect of the decision in *Le Rififi Ltd* is that the notice of assessment would be deemed to comprise 25 separate assessments. *Dicta* of Dillon LJ were also disapproved by Jonathan Parker LJ in the subsequent case of *Courts plc*, 3.46 ASSESSMENT.)

[2.142] The Commissioners issued an assessment charging tax of more than £56,000 on a married couple who operated a restaurant, and also instigated criminal proceedings against the couple for fraudulent evasion of tax. The couple appealed against the assessment and applied for the appeal to be heard without payment of the tax. The Commissioners opposed this application and in turn applied for a direction that the appeal and all proceedings other than the hardship application should be stood over pending the result of the criminal proceedings. The couple admitted fraudulent evasion of tax but disputed the quantum, admitting that they had underpaid £17,000, of which £10,000 had already been deposited with the Commissioners. The tribunal held that it would be unfair to the appellants to require them to proceed with their *rule 11* application under the threat of possible or actual criminal proceedings, and adjourned all the proceedings, including the *rule 11* application, until the completion of the criminal proceedings. *P & J Rosignoli*, [1983] VATTR 266 (VTD 1502).

[2.143] The tribunal allowed an application under *Tribunals Rules, rule 11* by the former proprietor of a Chinese restaurant, observing that the restaurant had ceased to trade and finding that 'there would be considerable hardship if the appellant had to pay or deposit the tax'. *B Wong (t/a The Four Seasons)*, LON/04/1091 (VTD 18931).

[2.144] In an anonymised decision, two companies applied for appeals to be heard without payment of the assessed tax, contending that payment would cause them hardship. The tribunal accepted the applications, holding that 'a business may need to borrow in order to pay VAT in dispute if the business had existing unused borrowing facilities' but that a business should not 'be expected to pursue other sources of finance purely for the purpose of paying the tax in dispute'. *Buyco Ltd, Sellco Ltd*; [2006] VATDR 57 (VTD 19752).

[2.145] The tribunal also granted a 'hardship' application in a case where the chairman (Mr. Wallace) expressed concern at 'the difference in treatment of a payment trader who can keep the tax pending the appeal if hardship is established and the repayment trader who must await the appeal'. *Guernsey Leasing Co*, LON/x (VTD 19974).

[2.146] See also WM *Management & Marketing Ltd*, 2.313 below.

[2.147] There have been a number of cases, which appear to raise no point of general interest, in which hardship applications have been dismissed. In the interests of space, such cases have not been included in this book.

Allocation of cases to categories (SI 2009/273, rule 23)

[2.148] A company claimed input tax on the purchase and chartering of a helicopter. HMRC rejected the claim, and the company appealed. The company made a preliminary application for the appeal to be categorised as a 'complex case', within *Tribunal Procedure (First-Tier Tribunal) (Tax Chamber) Rules (SI 2009/273), rule 23(2)(d)*. The First-Tier Tribunal rejected this contention but the Upper Tribunal allowed the company's appeal against this decision, observing that the case required 'a full analysis of the fiduciary and contractual relationships embodied in the documents that were created for the purposes of the arrangements'. On the evidence, 'the entity seeking registration is holding the equipment as trustee for at least one beneficiary and leasing it to that beneficiary and to itself as non-trustee'. Accordingly, the case should be categorised as complex. *Capital Air Services Ltd v HMRC*, UT [2010] UKUT 373 (TCC); [2010] STC 2726. (*Note.* The company subsequently applied for the costs of this application, but the Upper Tribunal rejected its application, holding that 'applications of this sort' should not normally 'carry any adverse costs consequences'—UT [2011] STC 617.)

[2.149] The principles laid down in *Capital Air Services Ltd v HMRC*, 2.148 above, were applied in a subsequent case where the First-Tier Tribunal agreed that a case should be categorised as 'complex', and directed that it should referred to the President of the Tax Chamber with a request that the case be considered for transfer to the Upper Tribunal. *Babergh District Council v HMRC*, [2011] UKFTT 341 (TC); [2011] SFTD 709, TC01201.

Statements of Case, etc. (SI 1986/590, rr 7–9; SI 2009/273, rule 25)

SI 1986/590, rule 7(1)

[2.150] In an appeal against penalties under *VATA 1994, s 60*, the tribunal held that *VAT Tribunals Rules (SI 1986/590), rule 7(1)(b)* was incompatible with the *Human Rights Act 1998*. The tribunal stated that 'we do not see how the requirements of *rule 7(1)(b)* can be reconciled with *Article 6(1)* (of the *European Convention on Human Rights*) and the implicit right to silence except on the footing that the appellant is not obliged to state any matters or facts which do not advance his case. We do not consider that admissions obtained without any reference to the right to silence can be utilised. Nor can we reconcile the unqualified obligation on an appellant to serve a List of Documents pursuant to *rule 20(1)* and *rule 20(2)(a)* with the right to silence'. The tribunal therefore held that certain evidence submitted by Customs was inadmissible. (However, on the admissible evidence, the tribunal held that the only reasonable conclusion was that the appellant had 'deliberately and regularly understated his sales', and upheld the penalties with regard to 16 of the 17 periods in question.) *ACK Patel*, LON/99/1144 (VTD 17248).

Application for extension of time to serve Statement of Case

[2.151] A company director lodged an appeal against a penalty which had been apportioned to him under *VATA 1994, s 61*. Customs applied for an extension of time to serve their Statement of Case. The tribunal chairman granted 'Customs' application, observing that 'this seems to me to be a case of some complexity and importance for which the time taken to prepare the statement of case seems entirely reasonable'. The director appealed to the Ch D, contending that the tribunal decision was unreasonable. The Ch D rejected this contention, holding that the tribunal had been entitled to grant Customs an extension of time. *TF Jackson v C & E Commrs*, Ch D 2003, [2004] STC 164; [2003] EWHC 3219 (Ch). (*Note*. The tribunal subsequently dismissed the director's appeal against the penalty—see 50.20 PENALTIES: EVASION OF TAX.)

Customs' failure to submit Statement of Case

[2.152] Customs rejected a claim for a refund of tax under what is now *VATA 1994, s 35*. The claimant lodged an appeal on 26 March 1992. The appeal was listed for hearing on 29 May 1992, but Customs applied for an extension of time to serve their Statement of Case. The tribunal directed that Customs should serve their Statement of Case by 26 June 1992. However, they did not do so until 8 July. At the hearing of the appeal, the claimant's accountant applied for the appeal to be allowed under *rule 19(4)* of the *Tribunals Rules*, since the Customs had not complied with the tribunal's direction. The tribunal accepted this application and formally allowed the appeal, holding that there were 'no unusual circumstances and no reasonable excuses in this case'. The CS upheld the tribunal decision, holding that it could only overturn the tribunal decision if the tribunal had acted unreasonably. In the absence of any mitigating circumstances, the tribunal had been entitled to exercise its discretion to allow the appeal. *C & E Commrs v C Young*, CS [1993] STC 394.

[2.153] The CS decision in *Young*, 2.152 above, was applied in the similar subsequent cases of *Sonat Offshore (UK) Inc*, EDN/95/189 (VTD 14021), and *G Costello*, MAN/99/890 (VTD 16680).

[2.154] On 23 May 2002 Customs had applied for an extension of time to submit their statement of case. The tribunal granted an extension to 23 August 2002. On 16 August 2002 Customs applied for a further extension to 23 September 2002. The appellant company did not receive notice of this, and the tribunal did not grant the application. Nevertheless, Customs failed to submit their statement of case until 8 October. The tribunal allowed the company's appeal, applying the principles laid down by the CS in *Young*, 2.152 above. The Ch D upheld the tribunal decision. Lloyd J held that he could only 'overturn the tribunal's decision if, on the material before it, its decision was erroneous in law and the result of either an apparent or a latent misdirection'. That was not the case here, and the tribunal had been entitled to exercise its discretion to allow the appeal. *C & E Commrs v Neways International (UK) Ltd*, Ch D [2003] STC 795; [2003] EWHC 934(Ch).

[2.155] The decision in *Neways International (UK) Ltd*, 2.154 above, was applied in the similar subsequent cases of *UK Tradecorp Ltd (No 2)*, [2004] VATDR 438 (VTD 18879) and *Deluni Mobile Ltd (No 1)*, 2.479 below.

[2.156] A partnership had claimed a substantial repayment of input tax. Customs rejected the claim and the partnership appealed. In May 2000, Customs asked the tribunal to postpone the appeal on the grounds that they were considering criminal proceedings against the partnership. At a subsequent hearing on 3 July, Customs informed the tribunal that they 'withdrew the allegation of fraud', and the tribunal directed that Customs should serve a Statement of Case by 1 August. On 31 July Customs made a written application that they should 'be permitted to assert' that the transactions in question were not genuine. The partnership made a cross-application that Customs' application should be struck out and that the appeal should be allowed. The tribunal the partnership's appeal, observing that 'the tribunal expected the Commissioners strictly to comply with directions as to time limits, and there was put forward no explanation or excuse for non-compliance'. Customs appealed to the Ch D, which upheld the tribunal decision,. applying the principles laid down in *Young*, 2.153 above, and holding the tribunal had 'exercised its discretion reasonably and in a judicial way'. *C & E Commrs v A & D Goddard*, Ch D [2001] STC 725.

[2.157] A company appealed against an assessment and a misdeclaration penalty. On 10 June 1992 Customs applied for an extension of time to serve their Statement of Case. The tribunal directed that Customs should serve their Statement of Case by 8 August. Customs did not comply with this direction, and were granted a further extension of time until 8 October. Again Customs failed to comply, and on 9 October they applied for a further extension to 8 December. On 19 October the company lodged an application for the appeal to be allowed, since Customs had not complied with the tribunal's direction to serve their Statement of Case. The tribunal heard the company's application on 17 November, by which time the Commissioners had (on 2 November) served their Statement of Case. The tribunal held that it had jurisdiction under *rule 19(4)* of the *Tribunals Rules* to allow the appeal on the grounds of 'Customs' late service of their Statement of Case, applying *Young*, 2.152 above. However, the tribunal declined to exercise its jurisdiction in such a way, observing that 'the approach of the Scottish courts to delays and failure to comply with directions is not necessarily the same as in England and Wales'. *Faccenda Chicken Ltd*, [1992] VATTR 395 (VTD 9570).

[2.158] A similar decision was reached in *Charles F Hunter Ltd*, MAN/93/231 (VTD 11619).

[2.159] In a similar case, an appeal was lodged in February 1993, and Customs applied for an extension of time until 16 May to serve their Statement of Case. The tribunal allowed the application, which the appellant company did not oppose. However, Customs failed to submit their Statement of Case, and in August they applied for a further extension of time until 16 September. The tribunal again allowed the application, and the case was set down for hearing on 23 November. At the date of the hearing, Customs had still not submitted their Statement of Case. The tribunal observed that there were 'no mitigating circumstances' for the long delays, and that it had 'become standard practice to apply for extensions of time for the Statement of Case and too often the Commissioners fail to observe extended time limits'. The tribunal awarded a penalty of £200 against Customs under what is now *VATA 1994, Sch 12 para 10*, and directed that Customs should serve their Statement of Case within twelve days. *Wine Warehouses Europe Ltd*, [1993] VATTR 307 (VTD 11525).

[2.160] In the case noted at **48.48** PAYMENT OF TAX, a company lodged an appeal in September 2003. Customs were granted an extension of time until 28 January 2004 to serve their Statement of Case. They did not serve the Statement of Case until 29 January. The company applied for a direction that its appeal should be allowed. The tribunal dismissed this application but awarded a penalty of £500 against Customs under *VATA 1994, Sch 12 para 10*. *Baines & Ernst Ltd*, MAN/03/661 (VTD 18516).

[2.161] See also *Vaz*, 2.397 below.

Whether Customs may amend their Statement of Case

[2.162] At the start of an appeal hearing the Commissioners applied to amend their Statement of Case. The amendment raised a new alternative ground for the assessment, and required the admission in evidence of two further documents. The appellant company objected, contending that it had been taken by surprise. The tribunal rejected the Commissioners' application, finding that the material facts and documents had been known to the Commissioners at the date on which the assessment was issued, and holding that the application was unfair to the appellant company. *Vorngrove Ltd*, MAN/84/55 (VTD 1733).

[2.163] However, in the case noted at **62.284** SUPPLY, Customs were allowed to amend a Statement of Case by introducing an alternative contention. The tribunal held that the appellant company was not prejudiced by this, since there was no rule prohibiting a party to an action from raising alternative contentions. Lord Grantchester observed that 'an assessment for a net amount of tax payable will normally involve a consideration both of output tax and input tax'. *The Football Association Ltd*, LON/83/484 (VTD 1845).

[2.164] A company claimed a substantial repayment of input tax. Customs rejected the claim on the grounds that they believed that the relevant transactions formed part of a carousel fraud. The company appealed. While the appeal was pending, Customs applied to amend their Statement of Case to take account of the CJEC decisions in *Optigen Ltd v C & E Commrs*, **22.115** EUROPEAN COMMUNITY LAW, and *Kittel v Belgian State*, **22.415** EUROPEAN COMMUNITY LAW. The tribunal granted Customs' application, finding that 'Customs have sufficiently pleaded the facts and matters on which Customs intend to rely to establish that the appellant knew or had the means to know that the transaction so identified was vitiated by fraud'. *Synectiv Ltd*, [2006] VATDR 183 (VTD 19698).

[2.165] Two associated companies claimed substantial repayments of input tax in relation to transactions in mobile telephones. Customs rejected the claims, and the companies appealed. Customs subsequently applied for leave to amend their Statement of Case to make a specific allegation of fraud against one of the companies (B). They also applied for the appeals to be consolidated. The tribunal chairman (Mr. Wallace) rejected Customs' applications, and directed that 'all allegations in the Statement of Case that the appellant "knew" that the purchases on which input tax is in dispute formed part of transaction chains in which one or more of the transactions was connected with the fraudulent evasion of VAT should be disregarded so that the sole issue is whether the appellant "should have known" of that fact'. *Blue Sphere Global Ltd (No 1)*, LON/07/934; *DDR Distribution Ltd*, LON/08/349 (VTD 20694). (*Note*. The Ch D subsequently allowed the substantive appeal by one of the companies—see **36.87** INPUT TAX. There has been no public hearing of the other company's substantive appeal.)

[2.166] In the case noted at **48.39** PAYMENT OF TAX, a company which operated an employment agency had claimed a substantial repayment of VAT. HMRC rejected the claim and the company appealed. While the appeal was pending, HMRC applied to amend their Statement of Case to include a contention that, notwithstanding the QB decision in the related case of *C & E Commrs v Reed Personnel Services Ltd*, **33.21** HEALTH AND WELFARE, the company had in some instances been acting as an independent principal rather than as an agent. The company opposed HMRC's application but the tribunal accepted it, observing that the company had substantially increased the amount of its claim in March 2009, while the appeal was pending, and holding that HMRC had been entitled to review the case in response to the company's introduction of 'a further significant claim'. *Reed Employment plc v HMRC (No 1)*, [2010] UKFTT 222 (TC), TC00523.

Contents of Statement of Case

[2.167] In a case in which an appeal against a requirement for security was dismissed, Customs' representative made allegations about the company which had not been included in Customs' Statement of Case. The tribunal chairman observed that the drafting of the Case was 'hardly satisfactory' and that any relevant factors 'should be included in the Statement of Case, and not either left unsaid or left to be deduced by the inclusion of certain documents in their List of Documents'. *M & S Services Ltd*, [1995] VATDR 512 (VTD 13610).

Application for 'further and better particulars'

[2.168] Customs imposed a penalty on a partnership which operated a restaurant. The partnership appealed, stating that its grounds of appeal were 'basis of assessment unsafe'. Customs submitted an application under *Tribunals Rules, rule 9* for the partnership to serve 'further and better particulars of the grounds of appeal', requesting 'the precise grounds of appeal and the basis on which the Commissioners' decision is disputed'. The tribunal dismissed Customs' application, observing that 'given that the matters and facts relied on must be pleaded in the defence, it is difficult to see what is to be gained from asking for precise grounds at this stage. The main effect of the request is to delay the procedure and to involve paperwork which will be duplicated in the defence.' *Kashmir Tandoori*, [1998] VATDR 104 (VTD 15363).

[2.169] See also *Albany Building Services Ltd*, **2.64** above, and *Taylor*, **2.67** above.

Premature application for disclosure of documents

[2.170] In six cases heard together, concerning appeals against penalties under *VATA 1994, s 60*, the appellants applied to the tribunal for a ruling that the Commissioners should disclose, *inter alia*, 'copies of all statements, exhibits and records of interview to be used in evidence' and 'copies of, or access to, all unused material relating to the appellants and/or relevant to the appeal'. The tribunal rejected the applications, holding that they were 'premature' and 'may well prove to be completely unnecessary'. The tribunal observed that the effect of the *Tribunals Rules* was that the Commissioners had to serve a List of Documents within 78 days of the service of a Statement of Case. *Nene Packaging Ltd (and related appeals)*, [2001] VATDR 286 (VTD 17365).

[2.171] See also *Lai*, **2.257** below, and *Miah*, **2.258** below.

Applications for the admission of late appeals, etc.

Application for late appeal granted by Court of Appeal

[2.172] In the case noted at 67.155 VALUATION, the tribunal referred the case to the CJEC for a ruling. The appellant company applied for judicial review of the terms of reference, but this application was rejected by the QB and the CA. Following the QB decision dismissing this application, the company applied for an extension of time to appeal against the tribunal decision under *Tribunals and Inquiries Act 1992, s 11*. The CA granted the application. Sir Thomas Bingham MR observed that 'it seems to me quite clear that (the company) intended to do all it could to challenge the tribunal's decision on this point. It has not been in any sense playing the system or behaving in a mischievous manner. It has merely adopted an understandable (though in my view incorrect) means of seeking to mount the challenge.' Schiemann LJ observed that 'it is, as has been recognised by the Law Commission in its paper on judicial review, one of the defects of our law at the moment that there can be situations in which there is some doubt as to which procedural route should be adopted'. *Conoco Ltd v C & E Commrs*, CA 19 July 1995 unreported. (*Note.* For subsequent developments in this case, see 2.313 below.)

Customs' application for late appeal granted by High Court

[2.173] Customs applied to the High Court for an extension of time to appeal against the tribunal decision noted at 32.6 GROUPS OF COMPANIES. Lightman J granted the application, holding that, under the *Civil Procedure Rules 1998 (SI 1998/3132)*, it was no longer sufficient to apply a rigid formula in deciding whether an extension was to be granted, and that each application had to be viewed by reference to the criterion of justice. In the case in question, an extension of time should be granted since the delay had been short, there had been no prejudice to the company, the subject matter of the appeal was important, and there were strong arguments in support of Customs' case. *C & E Commrs v Eastwood Care Homes (Ilkeston) Ltd and Others*, QB 18 January 2000, Times 7.3.2000. (*Note.* The Ch D subsequently allowed the substantive appeal.)

Customs' application for late appeal rejected by High Court

[2.174] In the case noted at 66.48 TRANSPORT, the tribunal decision was released on 18 September 1991. On 13 March 1992 the successful appellant company went into voluntary liquidation. On 18 March Customs made an application to lodge a late appeal to the High Court against the tribunal decision. The QB rejected the application, observing that tribunal decisions were not binding precedents, and that since the company had gone into liquidation, Customs were unlikely to receive any money even if a late appeal was successful. *C & E Commrs v Facthaven Incentive Marketing Ltd*, QB [1992] STC 839.

[2.175] The Ch D rejected an application by Customs to lodge a late appeal against the decision noted at 48.61 PAYMENT OF TAX. Morgan J held that there was no justification for the delay in appealing, applying the principles laid down in *Smith v Brough*, CA [2005] EWCA Civ 261. *HMRC v Church of Scientology Religious Education College Inc*, Ch D [2007] STC 1196; [2007] EWHC 1329 (Ch).

Application for late appeal—general principles

[2.176] A trader applied for an extension of the period in which to appeal, contending that he had been under the impression that his accountants were dealing with the matter. The tribunal allowed the application on condition that the trader paid £40 towards the Commissioners' costs. *WR Hallam*, MAN/78/187 (VTD 683).

[2.177] The Commissioners had begun proceedings to recover unpaid tax from a partnership. They sought to recover some of the tax from an individual (T) who had been registered as one of the partners. T disputed liability, and in 1976 the Commissioners issued a ruling that T had been a partner in the business. In 1978 T applied for leave to lodge a late appeal against this decision. The tribunal granted the application, holding that it would not prejudice the Commissioners. *D Trippett*, [1978] VATTR 260 (VTD 686). (*Note*. See now, however, the subsequent decision in *Wan & Wan*, 2.182 below.)

[2.178] A company reclaimed input tax relating to share issues. In 2001 Customs issued an assessment to recover the tax on the basis that it was attributable to exempt supplies. In 2004 the company applied to lodge a late appeal. The tribunal granted the application. *Advanced Medical Solutions Group plc*, MAN/05/417 (VTD 19925).

[2.179] A district council had accounted for VAT on its receipts from car parks. It claimed a repayment on the basis that it should have treated these receipts as outside the scope of VAT. HMRC rejected the claim, The council failed to appeal within the statutory time limit, but subsequently applied for an extension of time in which to appeal against the decision. The First-Tier Tribunal granted the application, observing that the council's appeal appeared to have a strong chance of success, applying the ECJ decision in *HMRC v Isle of Wight Council (No 2)*, **22.138** EUROPEAN COMMUNITY LAW. Although the council had been 'seriously culpable' in failing to appeal within the statutory time limit, the appeal here was 'additional to the appeals of other local authorities which raise the same general issue'. The fact that many similar appeals were still open significantly reduced 'the prejudice to HMRC in terms of the public interest in good administration and legal certainty'. *North Wiltshire District Council v HMRC*, [2010] UKFTT 449 (TC), TC00714. (*Note*. For further developments in the *Isle of Wight* case, see *HMRC v Isle of Wight Council (No 4)*, **22.144** EUROPEAN COMMUNITY LAW.)

[2.180] An application for a late appeal by an appellant who appeared in person was dismissed in a case where the tribunal applied *dicta* of Lord Guest in *Ratnam v Cumarasany*, PC 1964, [1965] 1 WLR 8; [1964] 3 All ER 933. *N Cave*, LON/95/582P (VTD 13346).

[2.181] A similar decision was reached in a case in which a company applied in February 1996 for leave to appeal against assessments which had been issued in January 1993. The tribunal held that the company had failed to give a satisfactory explanation for its failure to act within the time limit, applying the principles laid down in *Costello v Somerset County Council*, CA [1993] 1 WLR 256 and *Ward-Lee v Lineham*, CA [1993] 1 WLR 754; [1993] 2 All ER 1006. *J Walter Thompson UK Holdings Ltd*, [1996] VATDR 145 (VTD 14058).

[2.182] The decision in *J Walter Thompson UK Holdings Ltd*, 2.181 above, was applied in a subsequent case in which a partnership applied in January 1997 for leave to appeal against assessments which had been issued in May 1993. The tribunal specifically declined to follow the decision in *WJ Price*, [1978] VATTR 115 (VTD 559), on the grounds that the tribunal's reasoning in that case was inconsistent with the subsequent CA decisions in *Norwich & Peterborough Building Society v Steed*, CA [1991] 1 WLR 449; [1991] 2 All ER 880; *Costello v Somerset County Council*, CA [1993] 1 WLR 256 and *Ward-Lee v Lineham*, CA [1993] 1 WLR 754; [1993] 2 All ER 1006. The tribunal observed that the decision in *Price* 'concentrated on one issue, namely where the balance of prejudice lay, whereas the more recent decisions emphasise the importance of carrying out a discretionary balancing exercise where the balance of prejudice is only one factor to be taken into account'. *WY & YS Wan (t/a Wan's Chinese Takeaway)*, LON/97/160 (VTD 14829).

[2.183] A similar decision, also applying *Costello v Somerset County Council*, CA [1993] 1 WLR 256, was reached in *S Haque*, [1999] VATDR 219 (VTD 16047).

[2.184] A similar decision, applying *dicta* of Lord Donaldson in *Norwich & Peterborough Building Society v Steed*, CA [1991] 1 WLR 449; [1991] 2 All ER 880. and of the tribunal chairman in *Wan & Wan*, 2.182 above, was reached in *Designspeedy Ltd*, LON/03/361 (VTD 18309).

[2.185] In 1992 the Commissioners issued an assessment, charging tax of more than £1,300,000, on a university. In March 1997 the university applied for leave to appeal against the assessment. The tribunal dismissed the application, applying *J Walter Thompson UK Holdings Ltd*, 2.181 above, and *Norwich & Peterborough Building Society v Steed*, CA [1991] 1 WLR 449; [1991] 2 All ER 880. *University of Reading*, LON/x (VTD 15387). (*Note*. Costs were awarded to the Commissioners—see 2.357 below.)

[2.186] The Ch D dismissed an application to make a late appeal against the tribunal decision noted at 62.320 SUPPLY. Richards J reviewed the evidence in detail, and held that a further appeal would 'be doomed to failure' and that 'the delay as a whole was inexcusable'. *R Preston v C & E Commrs*, Ch D 15 December 1999 unreported. (*Note*. Despite the Ch D decision, the appellant lodged a further notice of appeal with the Tribunal Centre, which was also dismissed—LON/01/1172 (VTD 17826).)

[2.187] In December 2006 a company (B) submitted a repayment claim relating to output tax on income from gaming machines, claiming that it should have treated this income as exempt by virtue of the ECJ decision in *Finanzamt Gladbeck v Linneweber*, 22.372 EUROPEAN COMMUNITY LAW. In January 2007 HMRC rejected the claim. B did not appeal against this decision, but in May 2010 it wrote to HMRC requesting that its claim should be reconsidered in the light of the Ch D decision in *HMRC v The Rank Group plc*, 22.375 EUROPEAN COMMUNITY LAW. In June 2010 HMRC replied stating that B's claim 'would not be processed' because B had not appealed against the original refusal of its claim in January 2007. In August 2010 B appealed to the tribunal for permission to lodge a late appeal. The tribunal dismissed the application. Judge Connell observed that B's 'failure to lodge or pursue an appeal was entirely intentional'. *Black Pearl Entertainments Ltd v HMRC*, [2011] UKFTT 368 (TC), TC01223.

[2.188] There are a very large number of cases in which tribunals have dismissed applications for late appeals, and where the decision appears to raise no point of general interest. In the interests of space, such cases are not reported in this book. For a list of such cases decided up to and including 30 September 1989, see Tolley's VAT Cases 1990.

Late appeal against penalty—effect of Human Rights Act 1998

[2.189] The decision in *University of Reading*, 2.186 above, was not followed in a subsequent case where the tribunal chairman (Mr. Johnson, sitting alone) allowed an application for a late appeal against a penalty under *VATA 1994, s 60*, although the appeal had not been lodged until 15 months after the issue of the relevant assessment. The chairman criticised the trader's adviser for not having lodged an appeal in time, but held that, since the CA had held that such penalties involved a 'criminal charge' within *Article 6* of the *European Convention on Human Rights* (see *Han & Yau*, 34.5 HUMAN RIGHTS), to reject the application would risk breaching the trader's right to a fair trial under *Article 6*. *Mrs A Shatliff*, MAN/99/981 (VTD 17431).

Late appeal following tribunal decision in similar case

[2.190] A trader had reclaimed input tax relating to the training of a racehorse. In July 1977 the Commissioners issued an assessment to recover the tax, on the basis that the expenditure had not been incurred for the purposes of the trader's business. The trader paid the tax charged by the assessment. In March 1978, following the tribunal decision in *British Car Auctions Ltd*, 36.367 INPUT TAX, the trader applied to the tribunal for an extension of time in which to appeal against the assessment. The tribunal rejected the application. *R Kyffin*, [1978] VATTR 175 (VTD 617).

Partnership appeal delayed by illness of one partner

[2.191] A husband and wife carried on a hotel in partnership. They failed to appeal against an estimated assessment until, five months after it was issued, the Commissioners threatened distraint proceedings. They then paid the tax and applied for an extension of the time in which to make an appeal. The tribunal granted the application, holding that the Commissioners would not be prejudiced as the tax had already been paid. *WW & JH Hornby*, MAN/74/28A (VTD 155).

Late appeals during collection proceedings

[2.192] A trader failed to make returns and the Commissioners issued assessments charging tax of £2,106 under what is now *VATA 1994, s 73(1)*. She did not appeal and the Commissioners applied for summary judgment. She sought leave to defend, contending that the tax was not due. The QB held that it was not open to the trader to raise this defence in the High Court and that the Commissioners were entitled to summary judgment. *C & E Commrs v J Holvey*, QB 1977, [1978] STC 187; [1978] QB 310; [1978] 1 All ER 1249.

[2.193] A similar decision was reached in a case where an accountant had failed to pay a VAT assessment, and the Commissioners had issued a statutory demand. The CA held that there were no grounds for setting aside the statutory demand. Mummery LJ held that the effect of *VATA 1994, s 73(9)* was that the amount assessed was 'recoverable as a debt due to the Crown. The sum mentioned in the assessment remains a debt due, until that assessment is successfully appealed to the Tribunal.' *JA Cozens v C & E Commrs*, CA [1999] BPIR 252. (*Note*. At a subsequent hearing, the tribunal dismissed a late appeal and ordered the accountant to pay costs to the Commissioners—see LON/99/94 (VTD 16545).)

[2.194] The Commissioners obtained a final judgment with costs, for the tax charged by an assessment against which no appeal had been made. The defendant then applied under *Tribunals Rules, rule 19* for an extension of the period in which he could appeal against the assessment. The tribunal dismissed this application. The defendant subsequently applied under *rule 26* for the *rule 19* application to be reinstated. The tribunal dismissed this application, holding that, in view of the High Court judgment, it had no jurisdiction to entertain the appeal. *TS Digwa*, [1978] VATTR 119 (VTD 612).

[2.195] The decision in *Digwa*, 2.194 above, was applied in *G & I Hall*, MAN/78/55 (VTD 623); *Glen & Padden (t/a Shieldfield Processors & Refiners)*, MAN/79/140 (VTD 917); *N Hewitt*, MAN/81/93 (VTD 1149); *LR Back*, MAN/82/154 (VTD 1306); *M Sharif*, MAN/84/188 (VTD 1701, 1886); *JE & K Spiby (t/a Spymore Wall Coverings)*, MAN/83/72 (VTD 1812) and *M Saeed & P Arabian*, MAN/85/143 (VTD 1859).

[2.196] In a Scottish case, the Lord Advocate took proceedings, on behalf of the Commissioners, in the Sheriff Court in respect of three assessments against which no appeal had been made to a tribunal. The defendant contended that one of the assessments had been made outside the time limit of what is now *VATA 1994, s 73*. The Sheriff Court allowed the defendant's appeal in respect of the disputed assessment, holding that although the amount of the assessment was (applying *Holvey*, **2.192** above), exclusively a matter for the tribunal, the question of whether the assessment had been made out of time was a matter of law which could be raised in collection proceedings. The CS upheld this decision, holding that, since the assessment had been made out of time, it was a nullity and did not fall within what is now *VATA 1994, s 83(p)*. The defence that the assessment was a nullity could be taken before the court even though the point had not been taken before a tribunal. *Lord Advocate v J Shanks (t/a Shanks & Co)*, CS [1992] STC 928. (*Note*. The decision here appears to conflict with the established case law relating to direct tax, where it has consistently been held that the validity of assessments cannot be disputed in collection proceedings. See *CIR v Pearlberg*, CA [1953] 1 All ER 388; *CIR v Soul*, CA 1976, 51 TC 86 and *CIR v Aken*, CA [1990] STC 497. None of these three cases were cited in *Shanks*. In the subsequent case of *Bennett*, **57.13** REGISTRATION, the tribunal chairman expressed the view that the principle laid down in *Shanks* should be confined to cases where the issue was whether the assessment had been issued within the statutory time limit, and did not extend to cases where the point at issue was whether the assessment had been made to the best of the Commissioners' judgment.)

[2.197] On 3 November 1978 the Commissioners issued assessments charging tax of £2,153. The trader paid £153 and the Commissioners agreed to accept payment of the balance in two instalments. The trader did not keep the agreement and in January 1979 the Commissioners levied distraint on 9 January 1979, entering into a form of 'Walking Possession Agreement'. The trader then applied to lodge a late appeal. The tribunal dismissed the application and awarded costs of £100 to the Commissioners. *PJ Davies*, [1979] VATTR 162 (VTD 791).

Company in liquidation—late appeal permitted

[2.198] In February 2007 HMRC issued a substantial assessment on a company. Six months later the company went into liquidation, without having appealed against the assessment. In 2009 the company's former directors applied to lodge a late appeal, contending that they had been under the impression that the company's former accountant had lodged an appeal. The tribunal granted the application. Judge Berner observed that 'there has been a very considerable delay' but the company had been 'under a reasonable and mistaken misapprehension that its accountant had appealed', that the company had a 'prima facie case' and that there would be 'demonstrable injustice if the appeal is not heard'. *B Fairall Ltd (in liquidation) v HMRC*, [2010] UKFTT 305 (TC), TC00592.

Application for reinstatement of appeal

[2.199] See the cases noted at 2.315 *et seq.* below.

Settlement of appeals by agreement (VATA 1994, s 85)

[2.200] A company (L) carried out construction work for a manufacturing company (P). P withheld payment of some of the invoices issued by L, considering that the work in question should have been zero-rated, and L did not account for output tax on the disputed invoices. Subsequently L issued a credit note to P in respect of the invoices which remained unpaid. L later went into receivership. The receiver formed the opinion that all the work done for P should have been zero-rated, and issued a credit note in respect of the invoices which P had paid. The receiver submitted a VAT return on behalf of L claiming a repayment of more than £1.5 million, being the amount of VAT which L had charged to P and had accounted for to the Commissioners.

The Commissioners refused to repay the VAT in question, considering that the credit note should be disallowed since it had been issued for an improper purpose and that repayment would result in the 'unjust enrichment' of L. (Since L was by now in liquidation, the amount in question would have been divided between all its creditors rather than being returned to P, which had actually suffered the tax.) The Commissioners offered to repay the money directly to P, rather than to the liquidator of L. The liquidator rejected this proposal and lodged an appeal against the refusal to make the repayment. A VAT officer wrote to the liquidator on 3 January 1991 to inform him that 'the Commissioners have reconsidered their decision on the validity of the credit note issued by L' and that 'it is now agreed that L are entitled to a refund of the VAT overpaid in error'. A few days later another officer reviewed the case. He considered that his colleague had acted incorrectly, and that the money in question should be paid to P, as the Commissioners had originally intended, rather than to L, as his colleague had subsequently promised. He wrote to the liquidator on 14 January, informing him that his colleague's letter was 'hereby withdrawn' and that the money should be repaid to P rather than to L. The liquidator refused to agree to this and his appeal against the original refusal was heard by the tribunal. The tribunal held that the letter dated 3 January 1991 constituted the settlement of the appeal by agreement, within what is now *VATA 1994, s 85(1)*. Under what is now *VATA 1994, s 85(2)*, an appellant could resile from such an agreement within 30 days, but there was no such provision whereby the Commissioners could resile from such an agreement. The letter dated 14 January, whereby the Commissioners purported to withdraw from the agreement, was therefore ineffective. *Lamdec Ltd (in receivership and liquidation)*, [1991] VATTR 296 (VTD 6078). (*Notes*. (1) The tribunal chairman also considered that, since L was in liquidation, the repayment of the tax would not result in 'unjust enrichment'. However, the chairman's *obiter dicta* with regard to 'unjust enrichment' were not followed, and were implicitly disapproved, in the subsequent case of *Creative Facility Ltd*, 48.28 PAYMENT OF TAX. (2) For a subsequent case where this decision was distinguished, see *Discover Travel & Tours International Ltd*, **2.204** below.)

[2.201] The Commissioners issued assessments charging output tax on two companies which they considered had underdeclared tax. In December 1992 the Commissioners wrote to the companies offering them compounded settlements under *CEMA 1979, s 152*, as an alternative to criminal prosecution. On 13 January 1993 solicitors acting on behalf of the companies wrote to the Commissioners purporting to accept the offers to compound. However, in the letter the solicitors stated that the companies and their directors 'expressly deny any dishonesty or deliberate misdeclaration and reserve all their rights to challenge on appeal the quantum and the legal and/or factual basis of all or any of the assessments to which this agreement relates. It is intended to take these appeals before the tribunal'. On the same date, the solicitors lodged notices of appeal against the assessments. On 22 January the Commissioners wrote to the solicitors rejecting the proposals set out in their letter of 13 January. On 28 January the solicitors replied to the Commissioners, informing them that the companies 'do not now insist on the reservation of their rights of appeal'. On 4 February the Commissioners replied to the solicitors, accepting their proposals for settlement subject to the companies completing an undertaking to inform the tribunal that the appeals had been settled by agreement. The companies' signatories completed this undertaking on 12 February. However, they did not inform the tribunal that the appeals had been settled, and the Commissioners subsequently lodged applications for the appeals to be struck out. The tribunal accepted the Commissioners' applications, holding that the parties had entered into agreements within what is now *VATA 1994, s 85(1)* and that the appellants had not resiled from the agreements within the time limits laid down by what is now *VATA 1994, s 85(2)*. The compounding agreement was authorised by *CEMA 1979, s 152. Aspley Caterers Ltd*, MAN/93/65; *TBC Catering Ltd*, MAN/93/67 (VTD 12235).

[2.202] An engineering company reclaimed substantial amounts of input tax. The Commissioners rejected the claim, considering that the relevant supplies had not been made to the claimant company, but to one of its associated companies. The company appealed, and the case was set down for hearing by the tribunal in January 1994. After its counsel had made a long opening statement the case was adjourned for lunch, and during the adjournment the company's counsel and Customs' solicitor came to a provisional agreement, as a result of which they jointly asked the tribunal to adjourn the case indefinitely. The company's counsel formed the opinion that Customs' solicitor had agreed that £53,000 could be repaid to the company. In February 1994 the company's solicitors wrote to the Commissioners formally requesting the repayment. The Commissioners responded in May, rejecting the claim and stating that while the solicitor had agreed in principle that the company might be entitled to bad debt relief, this would only be possible if output tax had previously been accounted for on the transactions in question. The company's counsel replied disputing the terms of this letter, and in June the solicitor with whom he had originally discussed the case replied stating *inter alia* that 'I am happy to confirm that we agreed that (the company) would be allowed the credit for input tax calculated at £53,000 odd' and concluding 'that appears to me to dispose of the appeal. The question of (the company's) entitlement to bad debt relief is a separate matter.' In the interval between these two letters, the Customs' officer responsible for the original assessment had formed the opinion that, if the company had genuinely received the supplies in question and thus been entitled to reclaim input tax, it had also made an onward supply on which it was required to account for output tax. He therefore arranged for the issue of an assessment charging output tax of £53,000. The company applied to the tribunal for a direction that the original appeal be recorded as having been settled by agreement under what is now *VATA 1994, s 85*. The case was relisted for hearing in January 1995. The tribunal dismissed the company's application, finding that the provisions of what is now *s 85(3)(a)* had not been complied with, since the agreement had not been confirmed in writing. (The tribunal observed that the assessment to output tax which had been issued in June 1994 was apparently not under appeal, but expressed the opinion on the available evidence that it had been made outside the one-year time limit of what is now *VATA 1994, s 73(6)(b)*.) *TF Mechanical Engineering Ltd*, MAN/93/718 (VTD 12975).

[2.203] In July and October 1992 a company (M) submitted returns claiming credit for substantial amounts which it had previously accounted for as output tax. It had originally treated the relevant supplies as standard-rated and had issued invoices to the recipients of the supplies, which had reclaimed the amounts in question as input tax. One of M's directors subsequently formed the opinion that, notwithstanding the invoices which M had issued, the supplies in question should have been treated as zero-rated under the law then in force. However, M failed to issue credit notes to the recipients. In November 1992 the Commissioners issued an assessment to recover £829,726 from M (this being the amount reclaimed in the return submitted in July 1992). M appealed. The appeal was settled by agreement under *VATA 1994, s 85* in May 1995. Under the agreement, M was required to issue a credit note in respect of the tax of £829,726 to the recipients of the supplies. However, although M issued a document, described as a credit note, to one of the recipients (C), it failed to refund the tax which it had charged C in respect of the supplies in question. (It had previously threatened to take legal proceedings against C in relation to another dispute concerning the contract in question.) In October 1995, having discovered that M had not made a refund to C, the Commissioners issued a further assessment to collect the tax of £829,726 from M. M appealed, contending firstly that the note it had issued to C was not a credit note and that it was under no obligation to make a refund to C, and secondly that the assessment was invalid. The tribunal rejected these contentions, upheld the October 1995 assessment, and dismissed M's appeal. The effect of the *s 85* agreement had been to uphold the November 1992 assessment. Under the agreement, M had been required to adjust its VAT account under what is now *reg 38* of the *VAT Regulations 1995*. That adjustment 'required the issue of a *bona fide* credit note, and the giving of value to (C)'. For a credit note 'to give value to the customer, it must represent a genuine entitlement by the recipient either to a refund or to some type of offset'. Such a refund or offset was 'a mandatory requirement of a person issuing a credit note'. On the evidence, the tribunal was 'quite satisfied that (M) intended neither to refund to (C) the sum for which the note was issued nor to offset such sum'. Consequently, 'the credit note issued to (C) was not valid for VAT purposes'. Furthermore, the October assessment was a valid assessment under *VATA 1994, s 73(2)*. (The tribunal also held that M had been required to give credit to C in its accounting period ending 31 May 1995, and the assessment was issued within two years of that accounting period.) *McNulty Offshore Services Ltd*, MAN/96/119 (VTD 14824).

[2.204] The Commissioners issued an assessment on a company in May 2002. The company appealed. On 19 November 2002 the Commissioners sent a notice to the Tribunal Centre stating that they were withdrawing the assessment. On 22 November they sent a fax to the Tribunal Centre stating that this notice had been issued in error and that the appeal should proceed. However the Tribunal Centre ignored this fax, and on 28 November the Tribunal Centre informed the company that the assessment had been withdrawn. In the meantime, on 21 November, the Commissioners had written to the company requesting copies of certain documents in connection with the appeal. The company claimed that the notice issued on 19 November 2002 was binding and that the appeal had been settled by agreement, within *VATA*

1994, s 85. The tribunal reviewed the evidence and rejected this contention, distinguishing *Lamdec Ltd,* **2.200** above. The tribunal observed that 'the language of the 19 November Notice is not that of withdrawal; it is at best that of notification'. Accordingly 'the assessment under appeal was not withdrawn; it remains extant as does (the company's) appeal against it'. *Discover Travel & Tours International Ltd,* MAN/02/411 (VTD 18665).

[2.205] See also *The Mayflower Theatre Trust Ltd,* **46.87** PARTIAL EXEMP-TION; *C & E Commrs v DFS Furniture Co plc (No 1),* **48.76** PAYMENT OF TAX, and *Tourick,* **57.166** REGISTRATION.

Compounding agreement—whether within VATA 1994, s 85

[2.206] The Commissioners investigated the proprietor of a taxi business, whom they considered had been evading VAT. In June 1994 they issued an assessment on him, charging VAT of more than £350,000. The proprietor appealed. In January 1995 the proprietor signed an agreement with the Commissioners, under *CEMA 1979, s 152.* Under the agreement, the proprietor undertook to pay £500,000 by instalments, to include 'all arrears, interest and penalties'. The Commissioners undertook not to institute criminal proceedings against the proprietor provided that he paid the £500,000 by July 1997. When the appeal was first listed for hearing, the Commissioners applied for it to be struck out on the grounds that it had been settled by the compounding agreement. The tribunal chairman (Dr. Brice) dismissed this application and directed that the appeal should be heard in the usual way. The appeal was subsequently heard by a different chairman (Mr. Palmer), who dismissed the appeal, holding that the effect of the compounding agreement was that the appeal had been settled by agreement, within *VATA 1994, s 85.* The chairman observed that the agreement was 'clearly intended to be an agreement affecting the assessment and finally resolving any dispute between the parties relating to it'. The purpose of *s 85* was 'to encourage settlement by agreement of disputes between Customs & Excise and taxpayers'. Those agreements were 'intended to be given finality', so that 'the assessment is therefore effectively treated as discharged by the agreement'. *C Cummings,* LON/94/1128 (VTD 14870).

Appeals following criminal proceedings—whether any agreement

[2.207] In December 1997 two individuals pleaded guilty at a Crown Court to charges of fraudulent evasion of VAT. The Crown Court adjourned sentencing, thus giving the defendants the opportunity to pay the evaded tax. Following negotiations, the Commissioners formed the opinion that they had reached agreement with the defendants' accountants, and issued a notice purporting to be a confirmation of the agreement under *VATA 1994, s 85(3).* The defendants' solicitors issued a notice under *VATA 1994, s 85(2)* resiling from the agreement (and contending alternatively that the Commissioners' notice was void as there had never been a formal agreement of the appeals). The appeals in question were then set down for hearing by the tribunal, and the Commissioners applied for the appeals to be struck out on the grounds that they had already been settled by agreement under *s 85.* The tribunal observed that the defendants' position appeared to be 'particularly unmeritorious', but held on the evidence that the appeals had not been settled by agreement and directed that the Commissioners' application be struck out. The tribunal also directed that the appeals would be dismissed unless the appellants registered for VAT and rendered returns to the Commissioners in respect of the periods covered by the assessments under appeal. *GM & CW Citrone*, MAN/97/1187 & MAN/98/215 (VTD 15702). (*Note.* The assessments were subsequently reduced—(VTD 16662).)

Appeal settled by agreement—subsequent application for costs

[2.208] See *McGinty*, 2.434 below.

Solicitor agreeing to withdraw appeal on behalf of clients

[2.209] See *Taylor*, 2.71 above.

Agreement of appeal concerning 'partial exemption'

[2.210] See *University College London*, **46.151** PARTIAL EXEMPTION.

Applications for adjournments

Application for adjournment of High Court hearing

[2.211] The tribunal dismissed a company's appeal against an estimated assessment and the company appealed to the High Court against the tribunal decision. The case was listed for a High Court hearing in March 1992, but the hearing was adjourned because the controlling director of the company was in prison. The case was relisted for hearing in July 1992. The company's solicitors applied for a further adjournment, contending that the company needed time to obtain sufficient funds to proceed with the appeal. The QB rejected the application, holding that lack of funds was not a proper basis for an adjournment. Counsel for the company was unable to proceed with the appeal, which was dismissed with costs. *Rimland Ltd v C & E Commrs*, QB 10 July 1992 unreported.

[2.212] A defendant, who had been charged with fraud, applied for an adjournment of the High Court hearing, contending that he was suffering from ill-health. The Ch D dismissed his application, holding that the medical reports which his solicitors had submitted did not contain sufficient information to justify an adjournment. *C & E Commrs v D'Souza*, Ch D 27 February 2001 unreported.

Customs applying for stay of High Court proceedings

[2.213] In the case noted at 22.563A, several retail companies had claimed repayments of VAT. HMRC applied for the proceedings to be stayed pending a decision in a similar case brought by a group of car dealers (see *John Wilkins*

(Motor Engineers) Ltd v HMRC, **2.520** below). The QB rejected HM-RC's application, holding that the proposed stay would be unfair to the retail companies, and directed HMRC to serve their substantive defences to the claims. *Littlewoods Retail Ltd v HMRC (and related applications) (No 1)*, QB 2008, [2009] STC 22; [2008] EWHC 2622 (QB).

Adjournment refused by tribunal—whether courts should interfere

[2.214] The Commissioners issued an assessment on a partnership which operated a restaurant, covering the period from April 1973 to January 1975. When the appeal was set down for hearing, the partnership requested an adjournment. The tribunal rejected this request and held that it could not entertain the appeal as the tax had not been paid or deposited, and a return for one of the periods covered by the assessment had not been made. The partnership appealed to the QB, which upheld the tribunal's decision. Neill J held that a court should interfere with a tribunal's refusal to grant an adjournment only if the refusal would cause an injustice. *Abedin & Abedin v C & E Commrs*, QB 1978, [1979] STC 426.

[2.215] In April 1989 the Commissioners issued a 'global' assessment on a builder (W), covering the period from June 1985 to 1988. In October 1989 W was convicted of two charges of fraudulent evasion of VAT, and received a sentence of imprisonment. In April 1991 W lodged a late appeal against the assessment. The hearing of the appeal was eventually fixed for December 1993, but, at W's request, was delayed until April 1994. W did not attend the hearing but was represented by an accountant who requested a further adjournment until September 1994, stating that W was outside the UK. The tribunal rejected this application and confirmed the assessment. W appealed to the QB, contending that the tribunal had been wrong to refuse a further adjournment. The QB rejected this contention and dismissed the appeal, observing that in view of the history of the case, the tribunal had been 'perfectly entitled to say that enough is enough' and to exercise its discretion to refuse a further adjournment. *GM Whatton v C & E Commrs*, QB [1996] STC 519.

[2.216] See also *R v VAT Tribunal (ex p. Cohen & Others)*, **2.328** below.

Application for standover pending criminal prosecution

[2.217] A company appealed against an assessment covering six years and charging tax of more than £1,000,000. The Commissioners applied for the hearing of the appeal to be stood over for six months on the grounds that they were considering criminal proceedings against the company. The tribunal chairman (Mr. Oliver, sitting alone) rejected the application, observing that the company wished the appeal to be heard and stating 'I fully recognise that there is a public interest in bringing perceived criminals to trial. I am not, however, persuaded that the hearing of a civil VAT appeal, before criminal proceedings based on a similar subject-matter take place, can frustrate that public interest.' Mr. Oliver held that the Commissioners had not 'shown that there would be any real risk of serious prejudice leading to injustice — either to the Commissioners or to (the company) — as the result of holding the VAT tribunal appeal before any criminal proceedings are concluded'. *McNicholas Construction Co Ltd*, [1997] VATDR 73 (VTD 14975). (*Notes*. (1) For subsequent developments in this case, see **2.250** below, **3.102** ASSESSMENT, and **14.93** COLLECTION AND ENFORCEMENT. (2) Despite Mr. Oliver's decision that the hearing of the appeal would not jeopardise the criminal proceedings, the Harrow Crown Court subsequently determined that 'the evidence disclosed in public at the VAT tribunal and later published was an abuse of process, and the various defendants could not receive a fair trial'. See Taxation, 22 April 1999, p 103.)

[2.218] The decision in *McNicholas Construction Co Ltd*, 2.217 above, was not followed, and was implicitly disapproved, in a subsequent case in which the tribunal held that the hearing of the appeal should await the outcome of the related criminal prosecution. *JH Smith*, LON/x, 23 June 1999 unreported.

[2.219] The decision in *McNicholas Construction Co Ltd*, 2.217 above, was also not followed in a subsequent case where a company (T) had reclaimed substantial input tax on the purchase of a large quantity of mobile telephones. Customs rejected the claim on the basis that the transaction formed part of a 'carousel fraud'. T appealed. Customs applied for the hearing of the appeal to be adjourned as it was taking criminal proceedings against both T's directors, relating to transactions in computer processing units (in which T was not involved). The tribunal observed that although there were 'factual differences' between the cases, it was 'clear that both relate to alleged carousel frauds. It is possible therefore that for example a finding in this appeal (should such finding be made) that the appellants knew that they were engaged in carousel frauds could prejudice their criminal trial even though the criminal trial relates to an earlier period.' Accordingly the tribunal granted Customs' application for the appeal to be stood over for nine months (or until the conclusion of the criminal proceedings if earlier). *Global Active Holdings Ltd; Global Active Technologies Ltd*, [2006] VATDR 190 (VTD 19715). (*Note*. For another issue in this case, see **2.297** below.)

[2.220] A company (T) treated several supplies as zero-rated exports. HMRC formed the opinion that the supplies failed to qualify for zero-rating, and issued assessments charging tax on them. T appealed. HMRC applied for the hearing of the appeal to be stood over pending the outcome of criminal proceedings against a former director of T. The tribunal rejected this application, applying the CA decisions in *V v C*, CA [2001] EWCA Civ 1509, and *Mote v Secretary of State for Work & Pensions*, CA [2007] EWCA Civ 1324. (The tribunal proceeded to dismiss the substantive appeal.) *Traderco Ltd v HMRC*, [2010] UKFTT 632 (TC), TC00871.

[2.221] See also *Rosignoli*, 2.142 above.

Application for standover pending CJEC decision

[2.222] A company claimed repayment of a substantial amount of input tax. Customs applied for the appeal to be stood over for six months pending the CJEC decision in *Optigen Ltd*, **22.115** EUROPEAN COMMUNITY LAW. The tribunal dismissed Customs' application, observing that the Advocate-General's Opinion had already been delivered, and that it would be wrong to deny the company an 'early hearing'. The tribunal directed both parties to serve witness statements. *F Options Ltd (No 2)*, LON/04/830 (VTD 19033).

[2.223] A company submitted a claim for a substantial repayment of input tax (taking advantage of the different treatment of certain transactions in Germany and the UK). Customs rejected the claim, considering firstly that the transactions in question had not been entered into for business purposes, and alternatively that the company had 'artificially created conditions in order to obtain a tax advantage against the spirit and purpose of the value added tax legislation, amounting to an abuse of rights'. The company appealed. Customs applied for the appeal to be stood over pending the CJEC decision on 'abuse of rights' in *Halifax plc*, **22.60** EUROPEAN COMMUNITY LAW. The tribunal rejected Customs' application but the CS reversed this decision. Lord Osborne observed that the tribunal chairman appeared to have reached 'a firm conclusion about the abuse of rights element in the appellants' case, without holding a full hearing on that matter'. He had 'prejudged that issue on an unsound basis'. The CS directed that the proceedings should be halted pending the *Halifax* decision, and remitted to a different tribunal chairman. *HMRC v RBS Deutschland Holdings GmbH (No 3)*, CS 2006, [2007] STC 814; [2006] CSIH 10. (*Note*. For preliminary issues in this case, see **2.262** and **2.306** below.)

Application by Customs to consider granting immunity to witness

[2.224] In the case noted at **40.12** INVOICES AND CREDIT NOTES, the Commissioners produced as a witness a trader (C) who had been convicted of registering in a false name. The Commissioners' case rested on the assumption that there had been collusion between C and the appellant company, and the company's solicitor submitted that C should be cautioned that he need not answer incriminating questions. C then asked for an opportunity to consult a solicitor, and the Commissioners requested an adjournment to consider whether they should grant C immunity from prosecution. The tribunal refused the Commissioners' request, holding that the Commissioners should have foreseen the course of events and that the adjournment requested would be unfair to the company. *Stewart Ward (Coins) Ltd*, [1986] VATTR 129 (VTD 2108).

Application for adjournment for medical reasons

[2.225] A trader did not attend the hearing of an appeal. Prior to the hearing, he had sent in an unsatisfactory doctor's statement which the tribunal decided to treat as an application for an adjournment. The Commissioners opposed this, having regard to the previous history of the case, and the tribunal dismissed the application and the appeal. *P Donaldson*, LON/80/345 (VTD 1082).

[2.226] A chartered accountant (S) who also owned an estate agency failed to account for VAT on fees and commission he had received. The Commissioners issued assessments in September 1988 charging tax on this income. S appealed, and the hearing of the appeal was delayed from November 1990 to March 1991 at his request because of his ill-health. It was then postponed again, for the same reason, and relisted for August 1991. Two weeks before the hearing was due, S requested a further postponement, enclosing a doctor's letter to confirm that he was suffering from Parkinson's disease. The Commissioners objected to the application, which was heard by the tribunal in S's absence. The Commissioners gave evidence that S had been regularly seen at business premises, including several sightings in August 1991. The tribunal rejected the application for postponement of the hearing, and proceeded to hear the appeal, which it dismissed. The tribunal observed that S was a Fellow of the Institute of Chartered Accountants, and expressed surprise at his 'conduct with regard to avoiding attendance at this hearing'. Costs of £200 were awarded to the Commissioners. *GT Swaine*, MAN/90/543 (VTD 6451).

[2.227] A partnership which operated a restaurant appealed against an estimated assessment. The appeal was listed for hearing in October 1992, but was adjourned since the principal partner was suffering from angina. The case was relisted for hearing in June 1993. The partnership's accountant requested a further adjournment, since the partner was still suffering from angina and unable to attend the hearing. The tribunal rejected the application, observing that the accountant was unlikely to give any indication as to when the partner might be able to attend a hearing, and that the partnership had failed to submit information in support of its appeal. (The tribunal also dismissed the appeal.) *The Curry Garden Tandoori Restaurant*, LON/91/12 (VTD 10766).

[2.228] A company appealed against three default surcharge assessments. The hearing was originally arranged for February 1994, but was postponed on five occasions on account of the prolonged illness of one of the company's two directors. In October 1995 the company requested a further postponement for the same reasons. The tribunal rejected the application, observing that the company had continued to trade despite the illness of the director in question and holding that 'the ends of justice would be better served by the hearing proceeding as called'. *A & T Barr (Electrical) Ltd*, EDN/93/200 (VTD 13848). (*Note.* The tribunal also dismissed the company's appeals against the surcharges.)

[2.229] See also *Baird v C & E Commrs*, 2.136 above.

Accountant not ready to present appeal

[2.230] On the morning of the day fixed for hearing an adjourned appeal, the appellant telephoned to say that he had recently appointed an accountant who had not had time to prepare the appeal and accordingly he would not attend or be represented. The tribunal treated the telephone call as an application for a further adjournment, and in view of the circumstances, it dismissed both the application and the appeal. *J Butterfield*, [1977] VATTR 152 (VTD 404).

[2.231] In the case noted at 52.214 PENALTIES: MISDECLARATION, the partnership's accountant applied for an adjournment on the grounds that he had only been instructed two days before the hearing and had not had time to prepare his case. The tribunal rejected the application, observing that the hearing had previously been adjourned because one of the partners had been ill, and stating that 'it is clearly unreasonable to instruct a new adviser two days before the second hearing date which had been fixed and expect the tribunal to grant an adjournment because the appellants did nothing earlier'. *Hounslow Sweet Centre*, LON/92/271X (VTD 10026).

Application by former partners

[2.232] In an appeal by a firm of solicitors which was in receivership, the tribunal allowed an application for an adjournment made on behalf of former partners in the firm so that they could serve concurrent notice of appeal. *Blyth Elfords*, [1985] VATTR 204 (VTD 1939).

Other cases

[2.233] There have been a large number of other cases involving applications for adjournments, in which the decision appears to raise no point of general interest. In the interests of space, such cases are not summarised individually in this book.

The hearing of the appeal before the tribunal (SI 2009/273, rules 29–33)

Onus of proof

[2.234] In the case noted at **3.61** ASSESSMENT, the QB and CA held that, in the hearing of an appeal against an assessment to VAT, the burden of proof was on the appellant to show, on the balance of probabilities, that the assessment was wrong, rather than on the Commissioners to show that it was correct. Macpherson J held that 'at no time do the Commissioners have any burden to prove anything before the tribunal'. It was 'up to the taxpayer company, if it can, to attack the assessment in whole or in part'. *Grunwick Processing Laboratories v C & E Commrs*, CA [1987] STC 357.

[2.235] The decision in *Grunwick Processing Laboratories Ltd*, 2.234 above, was applied in a subsequent case in which the proprietor of a pizza restaurant appealed against an estimated assessment. The tribunal held that the burden of proof remained on the appellant notwithstanding the fact that the assessment under appeal had been computed on the assumption that the appellant had deliberately underdeclared takings. While an allegation of fraud or dishonesty should be included in the Statement of Case and should be supported by evidence, the Commissioners were not required to prove that the appellant had acted dishonestly. *Dicta* of the tribunal in *Stewart Ward (Coins) Ltd*, **40.12** INVOICES AND CREDIT NOTES, were specifically disapproved. *E Halil*, [1992] VATTR 432 (VTD 9590)

[2.236] The decision in *Grunwick Processing Laboratories Ltd*, 2.234 above, has been applied in a very large number of subsequent cases in which tribunals have held that the burden of proof is on the appellant. In the interests of space, such cases are not reported individually in this book.

Tribunal powers

SI 1986/590, rule 18(1)—appeal struck out by tribunal

[2.237] See *F Options Ltd*, 2.14 above.

SI 1986/590, rule 18(2)—appeal dismissed 'for want of prosecution'

[2.238] In 1998 a publican appealed against a ruling that he had acquired his business as a going concern. Subsequently he left the premises, and the Commissioners were unable to trace him. They applied, under *VAT Tribunals Rules (SI 1986/590), rule 18(2)*, for his appeal to be dismissed 'for want of prosecution'. The tribunal dismissed the appeal, holding on the evidence that the appellant had 'wilfully refused to correspond with the tribunal' and had 'deliberately made it impossible for the tribunal to communicate with him'. *JW Power*, [2000] VATDR 175 (VTD 16748).

[2.239] An appeal was also dismissed 'for want of prosecution' in *N Yavuz (t/a Fosters Off Licence/Supermarket)*, LON/03/219 (VTD 18593).

SI 1986/590, rule 19(1)—application for extension of time

[2.240] See the cases noted at 2.176 to 2.198 above.

SI 1986/590, rule 19(3)—recipient of supply joined as party to appeal

[2.241] See *Barclays Bank plc v C & E Commrs and Visa International Service Association*, 2.75 above.

SI 1986/590, rule 19(3)—related appeals to be heard together

[2.242] See *Maharani Restaurant*, 2.78 above.

SI 1986/590, rule 19(3)—application for appeal to be allowed

[2.243] A trader submitted a return claiming a substantial repayment of input tax. The Commissioners formed the opinion that the relevant transactions formed part of a 'carousel fraud', of the type at issue in *Optigen Ltd (and related appeals)*, 22.115 EUROPEAN COMMUNITY LAW. The trader appealed. The Commissioners failed to lodge their Statement of Case three months later. The trader lodged an application for the appeal to be allowed under *VAT Tribunals Rules (SI 1986/590), rule 19(3)* on the grounds that the Commissioners had not lodged the Statement of Case within the 30-day time limit laid down by *VAT Tribunals Rules (SI 1986/590), rule 8*. The tribunal rejected the application, holding that 'there is nothing in that subrule which empowers the tribunal to allow an appeal for a failure by the Commissioners simply to comply with the Rules, in the absence of a direction'. The tribunal also observed that this was 'a complicated appeal', and that there were 'some hundreds of documents involved'. In a case of this nature, a time limit of 30 days was 'inadequate for drafting the Statement of Case'. The Commissioners had needed 'to liaise with foreign tax authorities', which was clearly 'a time-consuming exercise'. Accordingly, the Commissioners' delay in submitting their Statement of Case had not been excessive. *I Tuppen (t/a Kingswood Trading Services)*, LON/03/1245 (VTD 18950).

SI 1986/590, rule 19(3)— 'issue estoppel' direction

[2.244] See *Feehan*, 2.122 above.

SI 1986/590, rule 19(4)—failure to comply with direction

[2.245] A company appealed against the rejection of a claim to repayment of input tax. The tribunal directed that the Commissioners should serve witness statements and provide the company with copies of documents which were included in the Commissioners' Statement of Case. The Commissioners failed to comply with the tribunal direction and the tribunal allowed the company's appeal, applying the principles laid down by Ward LJ in *Hytec Information Systems Ltd v Coventry City Council*, CA [1997] 1 WLR 1666. *UK Tradecorp Ltd (No 3)*, [2005] VATDR 82 (VTD 18992).

[2.246] See also *Young*, 2.152 above; *Neways International (UK) Ltd*, 2.154 above; *Faccenda Chicken Ltd*, 2.157 above, and *Kingpin European Ltd (No 1)*, 2.271 below.

[2.247] An appeal was dismissed in a case where the appellant company had persistently failed to comply with directions by the tribunal. The tribunal observed that the company appeared 'to have shown wholesale disregard of whatever directions the tribunal has made with a view to progressing the appellant's appeal'. *Whiston Hall Golf Club Ltd*, LON/04/1255; LON/05/356 (VTD 20361).

[2.248] A similar decision was reached in *Global Marketing (WM) Ltd*, MAN/06/647 (VTD 20377).

Whether appeal to be heard in private (SI 2009/273, rule 32)

Application dismissed

[2.249] In a case where the substantive issue has been overtaken by subsequent changes in the legislation, the tribunal rejected a company's application that its appeal should be heard in private, holding that 'whenever possible, decisions of these tribunals should be given in public so that they could be published for general guidance'. The tribunal observed that an appeal should be heard in private 'when a hearing in public would defeat the ends of justice, or would be likely to harm the appellant in the course of his business'. *Guy Butler (International) Ltd (No 1)*, [1974] VATTR 199 (VTD 106A).

[2.250] A company applied for the hearing of an appeal to be heard in private, contending that, since the Commissioners had alleged that it had been involved in fraudulent conduct, a public hearing would be damaging to its business. The tribunal dismissed the application, observing that 'the assessments and the allegations on which they are based must be assumed to be made seriously and in good faith by the Commissioners through their own professional lawyers'. Furthermore, dishonesty had to be alleged in all civil penalty cases and in all extended time limit cases, so that 'harm to reputation is a risk that inevitably follows from all assessments based on alleged dishonesty on the part of an appellant'. *McNicholas Construction Co Ltd (No 2)*, [1998] VATDR 220 (VTD 15575). (*Notes.* (1) For preliminary issues in this case, see

2.217 above and **14.93** COLLECTION AND ENFORCEMENT. For the substantive appeal, see **3.102** ASSESSMENT. (2) Despite the tribunal's decision that the hearing of the appeal in public would not jeopardise criminal proceedings against some of the company's employees, the Harrow Crown Court subsequently determined that 'the evidence disclosed in public at the VAT tribunal and later published was an abuse of process, and the various defendants could not receive a fair trial'. See Taxation, 22 April 1999, p 103.)

[2.251] The Commissioners formed the opinion that a solicitor had over-claimed input tax, and issued an assessment accordingly. The solicitor appealed against the assessment, and made a preliminary application for the appeal to be heard in private, contending that to hear the appeal in public might damage his reputation. The tribunal dismissed his application, observing that in *Håkansson & Sturesson v Sweden*, ECHR 1991, 13 EHRR 1, the ECHR had held that 'the public character of court hearings constitutes a fundamental principle'. The tribunal also observed that 'other citizens are entitled to know that the tribunal is applying the law correctly and fairly. That entitlement is not compatible with holding hearings in private'. *A Practitioner*, MAN/x (VTD 18459).

Application granted

[2.252] Two companies applied for their appeals to be heard in private. The Commissioners had no objection to the applications. The tribunal granted the applications, but observed that appeals should if possible be heard in public, and that 'a direction to the contrary should be made only in exceptional circumstances. In our judgment exceptional circumstances would arise where the disclosure of confidential information would harm an appellant in his business, or where the evidence to be given would involve the disclosure of a process, where such disclosure would prejudice his competitive position.' *Consortium International Ltd; Consortium Communications International Club*, LON/79/93, 94 (VTD 824).

[2.253] Similar decisions were reached in *Synopsys Ltd*, LON/91/2309Z (VTD 7207) and *Lonsdale Travel Ltd*, **1.67** AGENTS.

Hearing in private—whether expert witness may be excluded

[2.254] A company which had reclaimed input tax on the purchase of a yacht applied for its appeal to be heard in private, on the grounds that it was carrying out work of a 'highly sensitive' nature. The tribunal granted the application, and the Commissioners sought leave to produce an expert witness. The tribunal directed that the Commissioners' expert witness should not be present when the company's evidence was given, and the Commissioners applied by way of judicial review for an order to quash this direction. Forbes J granted the Commissioners' application. If the Commissioners satisfied the tribunal that their expert witness was a properly qualified expert in the particular field, he should be entitled to attend the tribunal throughout the hearing of the company's expert witness. It would be contrary to natural justice to prevent an expert witness listening to sensitive evidence given by the other side, even at a hearing in private, if the tribunal were satisfied that the expert witness was qualified as an expert on the matter to which the sensitive evidence related. *R v Manchester VAT Tribunal (ex p. C & E Commrs)*, QB February 1982 unreported.

Application to strike out appeal—whether decision to be made public

[2.255] In the case noted at **17.5** DEFAULT INTEREST, the Commissioners had applied for an appeal to be struck out on the grounds that it was outside the tribunal's jurisdiction. The tribunal chairman rejected this contention and advised the parties that, although the hearing had been in private, she proposed to publish her decision. The Commissioners objected to this proposal, stating that the decision was 'based on an inaccurate appreciation of the facts', was 'wrong in law' and 'would not be useful to the public as a helpful precedent'. The tribunal rejected the application, applying *Guy Butler (International) Ltd (No 1)*, **2.249** above, and *dicta* of Lord Halsbury in *Scott v Scott*, HL [1913] AC 417. The tribunal observed that the publication of the decision would not prejudice the appellant partnership, and that the partnership had no objection to publication. *RMSG*, [1994] VATTR 167 (VTD 11921).

Disclosure of documents

SI 1986/590, rule 20(2)—European Convention on Human Rights

[2.256] See *Patel*, **2.150** above.

SI 1986/590, rule 20(3)—application for disclosure of documents

[2.257] Customs took penalty proceedings against a couple who operated a restaurant. The couple appealed, and Customs served their Statement of Case and List of Documents. The couple applied for disclosure of various documents from Customs. Customs objected to the application, contending that it was a 'fishing expedition'. The tribunal upheld Customs' objection and dismissed the couple's application, holding that Customs 'have disclosed everything that they are obliged to disclose in the nature of the proceedings' and observing that 'training and/or instructions given to Customs officers' were 'properly to be kept confidential in any event, rather than disclosed'. *YL & Mrs MY Lai*, [2003] VATDR 570 (VTD 17739).

[2.258] The decision in *Lai*, **2.257** above, was applied in the similar subsequent case of *D Miah*, MAN/01/675 (VTD 17920). (*Note.* For the substantive appeal, see **47.8** PARTNERSHIP.)

[2.259] Following the decision noted at **2.271** below, the company applied for a direction under *VAT Tribunals Rules (SI 1986/590), rule 20(3)* requiring Customs to disclose their records of a related criminal investigation. The tribunal rejected the application, holding that the company had not shown 'that the information requested was necessary for a fair trial' and that it was 'akin to a fishing expedition'. *Kingpin European Ltd (No 2)*, LON/01/712 (VTD 19293).

[2.260] An insurance company applied for a company to be admitted to its VAT group. Customs rejected the claim on the basis that the refusal was 'necessary for the protection of the revenue'. The company appealed, and applied for Customs to disclose parts of volume 6 of the HMCE Manual. Customs refused to disclose certain sections of the Manual on the grounds that they were subject to public interest immunity. The tribunal dismissed the company's application, observing that 'the unpublished parts of the version of the Manual existing at the relevant time' contained 'the operational criteria the Commissioners use when an application is made'. Although the information was procedural, 'publication could cause serious harm if taxpayers knew what Customs were looking out for by taxpayers presenting relevant facts in a way that avoidance would be unlikely to be detected'. *Prudential Insurance Co Ltd (No 4)*, LON/04/2392 (VTD 19675).

[2.261] See also *Wat*, 2.69 above; *Karim, Ali & Majid*, 2.70 above, and *Nene Packaging Ltd*, 2.170 APPEALS.

[2.262] A German company (G) agreed to purchase a number of vehicles from a UK company (V), and reclaimed input tax. Customs issued assessments on G to recover the input tax, and G appealed. Customs applied to the tribunal for an order that G disclose certain documents. The tribunal rejected Customs' application. The tribunal chairman (Mr. Coutts) held that 'the documents asked for have no obvious relevance. They are an attempt to find something which might show some subjective consideration in relation to tax in the arrangements.' He observed that 'if documents are thought to be essential by HM Revenue & Customs in order to form a view about a transaction they have ample powers to require the production of such documents prior to the making of any assessment and the matter coming before the Tribunal on appeal. The Tribunal is not to be used as a means of attempting to acquire information.' *RBS Deutschland GmbH (No 2)*, EDN/04/77 (VTD 19055). (*Notes.* (1) For a preliminary issue in this case, see **2.306** below. (2) The CS subsequently reversed Mr.Coutts' decision on another point at issue in this case: see **2.223** above.)

[2.263] Customs formed the opinion that a large company had engaged in a tax avoidance scheme, involving the creation of an associated Irish company, which constituted an 'abusive practice', within the scope of the CJEC decision in *Halifax plc v C & E Commrs*, **22.60** EUROPEAN COMMUNITY LAW. They applied to the tribunal for an order that the companies should disclose various documents including 'all external advice from tax and other advisors relating to the adoption and/or operation and/or implications of the scheme' and 'all internal advice and presentations to senior management, staff and contractors relating to the adopting and/or operation and/or implications of the scheme.' The tribunal granted the order, observing that it was required 'to examine the evidence and assess the purpose of the transaction. If the purpose can be characterized, in the light of the evidence, as having the essential aim of securing a tax advantage, then the requirements of the second limb of the abuse test (see paragraph 75 of the *Halifax* decision) will be satisfied.' The tribunal held that 'the tax advice, if any, given to the management' was 'relevant to the above issue'. *MMO2 plc (and related appeals)*, [2006] VATDR 108 (VTD 19514).

Commissioners failing to comply with direction under SI 1986/590, rule 20(3)

[2.264] The Commissioners issued assessments on a company which operated a catering business, and imposed penalties on its directors under *VATA 1994, s 61*. The company and the directors appealed, contending that most of the assessments had been issued outside the statutory time limit. In March 2003 the tribunal issued a direction under *VAT Tribunals Rules (SI 1986/590), rule 20(3)* requiring the Commissioners to disclose all documentation 'concerning the time of raising and notifying of the assessments', within 28 days. The Commissioners did not comply with this direction within the time limit. In May 2003 they disclosed copies of two internal faxes, but failed to include the relevant form VAT 641. In July 2003 they produced a copy of the relevant form. At a subsequent hearing in October 2003, the Commissioners informed the tribunal that 'the original Form 641 could not be produced since it had been destroyed after being scanned onto a computer'. The tribunal allowed the company's appeal, applying the principles laid down by the CS in *Young*, 2.152 above, and by the Ch D in *Neways International (UK) Ltd*, 2.154 above. The tribunal observed that 'the only excuse advanced for the failure to comply with the Direction was the volume of work in the Solicitors' Office'. The fact that the Commissioners had not made sufficient resources available to cope with the volume of work was no excuse for non-compliance. *T Cilfaoglu (and related appeals)*, LON/01/730-732 (VTD 18409).

[2.265] The Commissioners issued an estimated assessment on the proprietor of a restaurant. He appealed. The tribunal issued a direction under *VAT Tribunals Rules (SI 1986/590), rule 20(3)* requiring the Commissioners to disclose certain observation records on which the assessment was based. The Commissioners failed to comply with the direction, and subsequently informed the tribunal that they could not produce the records, which had 'probably been destroyed'. The tribunal allowed the proprietor's appeal, criticising the VAT officer who had been responsible for conducting the appeal, and observing that 'without the missing evidence, Customs' case is an extremely flimsy one'. *S Bradley*, MAN/03/321 (VTD 18735).

Witness statements

Notice of objection to Witness Statements

[2.266] A gold coin dealer accounted for VAT under the margin scheme in respect of a large proportion of his takings. The Commissioners formed the impression that he had acted fraudulently, in that he had falsely attributed takings to purported second-hand transactions which had not in fact taken place, so that the conditions for the margin scheme were not satisfied and output tax was chargeable on the full amount of the takings. The dealer provided the Commissioners with the names of two people—one a Canadian and the other a resident of the USA—to whom he claimed he had made substantial supplies of gold coins under the margin scheme. The two people in question gave the Commissioners written statements denying that they had received such supplies. The Commissioners included these statements as Witness Statements with their Statement of Case. The dealer objected to the Statements being put in evidence and served a notice of objection, applying for directions, under *rule 21(4)* of the *VAT Tribunals Rules*. The tribunal rejected the dealer's application, holding that whether the statements should be given any weight as evidence was 'entirely a matter for the tribunal that hears the appeal'. *MD Bord*, LON/91/2595Y (VTD 7946). (*Note*. For the substantive appeal, see **60.5** SECOND-HAND GOODS.)

[2.267] Customs formed the opinion that a trader had failed to account for VAT on cash receipts. They imposed penalties under *VATA 1994, s 60*. The trader applied. After having served their Statement of Case, Customs applied for an extension to serve witness statements from seven customers. The trader objected and applied for the statements to be excluded and for the witnesses to be required to attend the hearing so that they could be cross-examined. The tribunal granted the trader's application, holding that 'it would be wrong in principle for the tribunal to allow such statements to be read as evidence of the truth of their contents without the witnesses attending in the face of objections by the appellant'. *KC Fitch*, [2006] VATDR 196 (VTD 19914).

[2.268] In one of the cases noted at **36.121** INPUT TAX, a company claimed repayments of VAT relating to alleged transactions in electronic components. HMRC rejected the claim on the basis that the transactions were connected with MTIC fraud. The company appealed. HMRC applied to serve a witness statement from a consultant with specialist knowledge of the electronic components industry. The company objected to the statement but the tribunal overruled the company's objection. Applying the principles laid down by Lightman J in *Mobile Export 365 Ltd v HMRC*, **2.276** below, 'the presumption must be that all relevant evidence should be admitted unless there is a compelling reason to the contrary'. *Sceptre Services Ltd v HMRC (No 1)*, [2010] UKFTT 247 (TC), TC00542.

[2.269] A company (G) claimed substantial repayments of input tax. HMRC rejected the claims on the grounds that it appeared that the transactions were connected with MTIC fraud. G appealed, and HMRC served several witness statements. G applied for one of the witness statements to be struck out, on the grounds that it was a lengthy generic statement on MTIC fraud. The tribunal accepted this contention and directed that the statement should be excluded under *Tribunal Procedure (First-Tier Tribunal) (Tax Chamber) Rules (SI 2009/273), rule 35*. Judge Wallace held that the statement contained 'very limited potential evidential value and a considerable amount of material which is potentially prejudicial'. *Globalbis Distribution Ltd v HMRC*, [2010] UKFTT 557 (TC), TC00808.

[2.270] A company reclaimed input tax of more than £1,000,000 on the purchase of a large number of mobile telephones. HMRC rejected the claim on the basis that the transactions formed part of an MTIC fraud, and the company appealed. HMRC applied for several witness statements to be admitted in evidence. The company objected to ten of the statements. Judge Wallace applied the principles laid down in *O'Brien v Chief Constable of South Wales Police*, HL [2005] 2 WLR 1038, and his own previous decision in *Globalbis Distribution Ltd v HMRC*, **2.269** above, and admitted three of the disputed statements but directed that the other seven should be excluded. *Atlantic Electronics Ltd v HMRC*, [2011] UKFTT 314 (TC), TC01175. (*Note*.

HMRC have appealed to the Upper Tribunal against this decision. The Upper Tribunal is scheduled to begin hearing the appeal on 11 November 2011.)

Delay in Customs lodging witness statements

[2.271] A company submitted a VAT return claiming a substantial repayment of VAT. Customs requested further information concerning the claim. The company failed to provide the requested information, and Customs rejected the claim on the basis that 'no evidence had been adduced to support the claim for input tax'. The company appealed. The tribunal issued a direction for the company to provide 'further and better particulars of the appeal'. The company produced photocopies of invoices. Customs formed the opinion that these invoices did not relate to 'genuine onward supplies' to customers in other Member States of the EU. In November 2002 the tribunal issued a direction for Customs to serve witness statements. Customs subsequently made three successive applications for an extension of time for the service of these statements. In January 2004 the company lodged an application for its appeal to be allowed in view of the delays by Customs. The tribunal reviewed the evidence and dismissed the application, observing that the company had been slow in providing information and had not been prejudiced by Customs' delay in producing witness statements. The tribunal observed that the company 'now has the Commissioners' amended Statement of Case and witness statements' and 'should now be in a position to proceed with the appeal'. *Kingpin European Ltd*, LON/01/712 (VTD 18695). (*Note.* For subsequent developments in this case, see **2.259** above.)

[2.272] In the case noted at **36.106** INPUT TAX, Customs applied for leave to serve six late witness statements. The tribunal granted leave in respect of four of the statements, but refused leave in respect of the other two, applying the principles laid down by Lewison J in *HMRC v Brayfal Ltd*, **2.285** below. *Europeans Ltd*, LON/07/811 (VTD 20796). (*Note.* For subsequent developments in this case, see **2.371** below.)

[2.273] In one of the cases noted at **36.121** INPUT TAX, HMRC applied for leave to serve nine late witness statements. The tribunal granted leave in respect of one of the statements, but refused leave in respect of the other eight. *Xentric Ltd v HMRC (No 1)*, [2010] UKFTT 249 (TC), TC00544.

[2.274] HMRC rejected a claim to input tax on the grounds that it appeared that the relevant transactions were connected with MTIC fraud. The company (M) appealed, and HMRC applied to submit seven late witness statements, four of which related to a information about the appellant company which had been discovered on the server of a Curacao bank, which had been the subject of a investigation by the UK and Netherlands authorities (see *Megantic Services Ltd v HMRC (No 2)*, **2.287** below). Judge Mosedale held that the evidence obtained from the bank 'was likely to be of important probative value. It is alleged to show that the movement of money on a significant proportion of a sample of alleged deal chains in this case was circular. A judge is likely to draw the conclusion from this (if proved) that the deal chains (if proved) were orchestrated for the purposes of fraud.' After reviewing conflicting earlier decisions, she observed that 'each case is decided on its own particular facts and in this case the crucial distinction is the potentially highly probative nature of the evidence sought to be admitted.' She directed that the four statements relating to the Curacao bank should be admitted on condition that HMRC gave an undertaking to make good the extra costs arising out of the late admission of this evidence', and that if the case were to be adjourned to enable M to consider this evidence, one of the other three statements should also be admitted. However, the other two statements 'did not contain new evidence', and should be excluded. *Masstech Corporation Ltd v HMRC*, [2011] UKFTT 649 (TC), TC01491.

[**2.275**] In the case noted at **2.372** above, the tribunal admitted seven late witness statements by Customs, but excluded two other statements (including a generic statement concerning MTIC fraud). *Hawkeye Communications Ltd v HMRC (No 2)*, [2011] UKFTT 720 (TC), TC01557.

Delays by both parties

[**2.276**] A company (M) reclaimed input tax of more than £5,000,000 in respect of purported supplies of mobile telephones. M's major shareholder had twice been convicted for VAT fraud, and Customs rejected the claim on the basis that it appeared that the transactions formed part of a 'carousel fraud'. M appealed. M did not serve two witness statements until three weeks after the date set by the tribunal. However, at the hearing of the appeal, M's barrister (P) applied as a preliminary point for the appeal to be allowed under *rule 19(4)* of the *Tribunals Rules* on the grounds that Customs had not served 'a further list of documents listing the documents exhibited to the three late served witness statements'. The tribunal rejected this application and the Ch D dismissed M's appeal against this decision. Lightman J strongly criticised P for his conduct of the case. He held that an appeal would only be allowed under *rule 19(4)* of the *Tribunals Rules* as 'a last resort where a party's misconduct is of a serious nature and the prejudice to the applicant is not otherwise remediable'. He criticised P for 'springing surprises' on Customs and the tribunal, and commented that 'such tactics are not acceptable conduct today in any civil proceedings. They are clearly repugnant to the Overriding Objective laid down in CPR 1.1' and to 'the duty of the parties and their legal representatives to help the court to further that objective'. *Mobile Export 365 Ltd v HMRC (and related appeal)*, Ch D [2007] STC 1794; [2007] EWHC 1737 (Ch). (*Note.* For subsequent proceedings in this case, see **2.291** below.)

Evidence at hearing

Admissibility of hearsay evidence

[**2.277**] In a case where no witness statements had been served, the QB held that it was permissible for a tribunal to admit hearsay evidence provided that there was no objection to the admission of such evidence and that the tribunal did not decide of its own volition that such evidence should be excluded. *Wayne Farley Ltd & Another v C & E Commrs*, QB [1986] STC 487. (*Note.* With regard to the use of hearsay evidence, see now *Civil Procedure Rules 1998 (SI 1998/3132), rule 33.*)

[2.278] Hearsay evidence concerning the alleged dishonesty of an employee of the appellant company was ruled inadmissible in *Deeds Ltd*, **40.17** INVOICES AND CREDIT NOTES.

Record book found at premises—whether admissible as evidence

[2.279] In an appeal against an estimated assessment on a clothing manufacturer, the Commissioners introduced as evidence a record book which had been found by VAT officers at the manufacturer's premises. The manufacturer's solicitor objected to the production of the book, contending that it was hearsay evidence and should not be admitted. The tribunal ruled that the book was admissible as evidence. The tribunal was not satisfied that the book was hearsay evidence, and observed that 'if any part of the evidence offered to link the book and the appellant is hearsay, we can deal with that evidence as it is tendered'. *M Hanif*, MAN/89/747 (VTD 6430). (*Notes.* (1) The appeal was subsequently dismissed. The tribunal held that it was 'not satisfied on the balance of probabilities that the book does not relate to the appellant's business'. For the award of costs to the Commissioners, see **2.355** below. (2) With regard to the use of hearsay evidence, see now the note following *Wayne Farley Ltd*, **2.277** above.)

Definition of 'expert witness'

[2.280] In a Scottish excise duty case, the tribunal held that a representative of the appellant company did not qualify as an 'expert witness'. *MW Plant (Contracts) Ltd*, EDN/05/8007 (E1074). (*Note.* Although the case concerned excise duty, the principles also seem to be relevant to VAT. See also the income tax case of *Liverpool Roman Catholic Archdiocesan Trustees Incorporated v Goldberg (No 2)*, Ch D [2001] 1 WLR 2337; [2001] 4 All ER 950.)

Hearing in private—whether expert witness may be excluded

[2.281] See *R v Manchester VAT Tribunal (ex p. C & E Commrs)*, **2.254** above.

Exclusion of evidence—public interest immunity

[2.282] The Commissioners issued estimated assessments on a partnership, and imposed a penalty under *VATA 1994, s 60(1)*. The partnership appealed. During the hearing of the appeal, the Commissioners applied for a direction that witnesses should not be required to answer questions in cross-examination which might serve to identify an informant, claiming public interest immunity. The tribunal granted the application, observing that 'in the case of public prosecutions, it has been settled since the eighteenth century that witnesses cannot be asked questions tending to disclose the identity of an informant. In civil cases, the rule has been applied to a range of situations where the effective functioning of an organisation established under Act of Parliament might be adversely affected by allowing the identity of informants to be disclosed.' Applying *dicta* of Lord Cross in *Alfred Crompton Amusement Machines Ltd v C & E Commrs (No 2)*, HL 1972, [1974] AC 405; [1972] 2 All ER 353 (a purchase tax case), 'in a case where the considerations for and against disclosure appear to be fairly evenly balanced', the courts should 'uphold a claim to privilege on the ground of public interest and trust to the head of the department concerned to do whatever he can to mitigate the ill-effects of non-disclosure'. On the evidence, the partnership had not shown that 'the withheld evidence is at all likely to be relevant to its determination of the issues in the appeals in this case'. The tribunal was obliged to observe 'the legitimate public interest of protecting the identity of informers and the contents of information obtained from them'. *CT, C & P Ellinas (t/a Hunts Cross Supper Bar)*, MAN/96/692 (VTD 15346). (*Note*. For subsequent developments in this case, see **50.127** PENALTIES: EVASION OF TAX.)

Evidence obtained from Insolvency Service—whether admissible

[**2.283**] In the case noted at **50.55** PENALTIES: EVASION OF TAX, the Commissioners sought to introduce as evidence various documents provided by the Insolvency Service, including a statement which the appellant (Q) had made to the Insolvency Service under compulsion. The tribunal held that the statement which Q had made under compulsion was not admissible as evidence. Applying the decisions in *Saunders v United Kingdom*, ECHR 1996, 23 EHRR 313 and *Attorney-General's Reference No 7 of 2000*, CA [2001] EWCA Crim 888, there was a distinction 'between statements made under coercion in defiance of the will of the accused and other material obtained through the use of compulsory powers which has an existence independent of the will of the suspect (for example documents acquired pursuant to a warrant)'. To admit statements made under coercion would infringe *Article 6 of the European Convention on Human Rights*, whereas 'admitting into evidence material so obtained which has an existence independent of the will of the suspect' would not. *MS Qaisar*, LON/00/400 (VTD 18098).

Whether tribunal should admit late evidence

[**2.284**] In the case noted at **58.53** RETAILERS' SPECIAL SCHEMES, the tribunal refused to admit as evidence certain correspondence which the Commissioners had sought to introduce on the third day of the hearing. The Commissioners appealed to the QB, contending as a preliminary point that the tribunal should have considered the correspondence. The QB accepted this contention and remitted the case to the tribunal. The tribunal had acted unreasonably and had been wrong in law in refusing to consider the correspondence as evidence. *C & E Commrs v GUS Merchandise Ltd*, QB [1992] STC 776.

[**2.285**] However, in a subsequent case concerning a claim to input tax in relation to transactions in mobile telephones, Lewison J held that the tribunal had been entitled to exclude evidence which Customs had sought to admit at a late stage. He strongly criticised one of Customs' officers, observing that she had indicated that she wished to correct her evidence, and had indicated that 'the evidence that she gave to the tribunal in chief was wrong'. To allow the officer to submit new evidence under cross-examination would be unfair to the appellant company. *HMRC v Brayfal Ltd*, Ch D 4 March 2008 unreported. (*Note*. For the substantive appeal, see **36.85** INPUT TAX.)

[**2.286**] During the hearing of an appeal, HMRC applied to admit further evidence (consisting of copies of emails sent to and from the company's principal director, which had been contained in a file of documents which HMRC had temporarily mislaid). The company opposed the application but the tribunal granted it. Applying *dicta* of Lightman J in *Mobile Export 365 Ltd v HMRC*, **2.276** above, 'the presumption must be that all relevant evidence should be admitted unless there is a compelling reason to the contrary'. Since the company had sent or received the emails in question, this was 'not new evidence as far as the appellant is concerned', and there was no question of the company being taken by surprise. The tribunal distinguished the Ch D decision in *HMRC v Brayfal Ltd*, **2.285** above, observing that 'the facts were distinctly different'. *Earthshine Ltd v HMRC (No 1)*, [2010] UKFTT 67 (TC), TC00379. (*Notes*. (1) For a subsequent application for costs, see **2.490** below. (2) The appeal was subsequently dismissed —see **36.113** INPUT TAX.)

[2.287] A company (M) claimed a substantial repayment of VAT. HMRC rejected the claim on the basis that it appeared that the relevant transactions formed part of a MTIC fraud. M appealed. HMRC made an application to admit evidence relating to certain transactions with a Curacao bank (F). M opposed the application but the tribunal granted it. Judge Berner observed that F's business had been 'effectively closed down' following an investigation by the UK and Netherlands authorities, and a raid on its premises. The delay in reviewing and processing the evidence obtained as a result of this investigation had not been unreasonable. The transactions at issue in this case were complex, and the time taken in analysing the evidence was not disproportionate. The Upper Tribunal upheld this decision. Applying the principles laid down by Lawrence Collins LJ in *Fattal v Walbrook Trustee (Jersey) Ltd*, CA [2008] EWCA Civ 427, 'an appellate court should not interfere with case management decisions by a judge who has applied the correct principles and who has taken into account matters which should be taken into account and left out of account matters which are irrelevant'. *Megantic Services Ltd v HMRC (No 2)*, UT, [2011] STC 1000. (*Note*. For a preliminary issue in this case, see **36.655** INPUT TAX.)

[2.288] In another case where HMRC made a late application to admit new evidence, the tribunal rejected the application, applying the principles laid down by Lewison J in *HMRC v Brayfal Ltd*, **2.285** above, and specifically distinguishing the tribunal decision in *Earthshine Ltd v HMRC (No 1)*, **2.286** above. *Sceptre Services Ltd v HMRC (No 2)*, [2010] UKFTT 315 (TC), TC00602.

[2.289] In another case involving MTIC fraud, where HMRC made a late application to admit new evidence, the First-Tier Tribunal granted the application and the company appealed to the Upper Tribunal. The Upper Tribunal upheld the First-Tier Tribunal decision, applying the principles laid down by Lightman J in *Mobile Export 365 Ltd v HMRC*, **2.276** above, and distinguishing *C & E Commrs v GUS Merchandise Ltd*, **2.284** above, and *HMRC v Brayfal Ltd*, **2.285** above. *Connect Global Ltd v HMRC*, UT [2010] UKUT 372 (TCC); [2011] STC 51.

Whether tape-recorded interviews admissible as evidence

[2.290] A married couple who operated a café appealed against a penalty under *VATA 1994, s 60*. The couple's solicitor contended, as a preliminary point, that the effect of the *Human Rights Act 1998* was that tape-recorded interviews between the couple and a VAT officer should not be admitted in evidence. The tribunal rejected this contention, holding that the interviews had been 'properly conducted in accordance with *Notice 730*' and were admissible.

Dicta of Potter LJ in *Han & Yau,* 34.5 HUMAN RIGHTS, applied. *W & B Sharland (t/a Sharlands Fir Tree Café),* LON/99/1361 (VTD 17387). (*Note.* The tribunal dismissed the couple's appeal against the penalty.)

Whether evidence of French law admissible

[2.291] Two companies reclaimed substantial amounts of input tax relating to purported transactions in mobile telephones. HMRC rejected the claims on the basis that the transactions formed part of a 'missing trader intra-Community fraud'. The companies appealed to the tribunal. At the hearing of their appeals, HMRC applied to introduce a witness statement from an accountant who was employed by a major accountancy firm. The companies objected to this witness statement, and applied to introduce evidence of French law, with regard to the French interpretation of the CJEC decision in *Kittel v Belgian State,* 22.415 EUROPEAN COMMUNITY LAW. The tribunal chairman (Dr. Williams) rejected this application and admitted the witness statement from the accountant. The companies lodged an interlocutory application in the Ch D, objecting to both of the relevant decisions. The Ch D rejected this application and upheld Dr. Williams' decisions. Sir Andrew Park held that the tribunal had been entitled to treat the accountant as an expert witness, and to decline to admit the evidence of French law. He observed that it was clear that the companies 'wished to use the French law in support of arguments presented to the Tribunal in the United Kingdom that the French approach to the interpretation of *Kittel* is correct and that the approach of HMRC is wrong'. He held that 'where a tribunal in the United Kingdom is concerned to determine the ambit of the *Kittel* decision it should do so on the basis of the decision of the ECJ taking account, if it wishes to do so and if it is invited to do so, of the text of that decision not just in English but in other languages'. However, 'an opinion of the VAT administrative authority in another member state about the meaning of an ECJ decision is not material which can be legitimately prayed in aid where the issue is one for the United Kingdom tribunal or court and concerns the meaning of the decision'. *Mobile Export 365 Ltd v HMRC (No 3) (and related appeal),* Ch D [2009] EWHC 797 (Ch). (*Notes.* (1) For another issue in this case, see **2.276** above. (2) At a subsequent hearing, the tribunal dismissed the appeals, finding that the companies' witnesses 'were less than open and honest in their evidence to the tribunal' and 'should have known' that the transactions in question 'were connected directly with fraud'—[2010] UKFTT 367 (TC), TC00649.)

Appeal against penalty under VATA 1994, s 60—admissibility of evidence

[2.292] See *Bammi & Dhir (t/a The Last Viceroy),* 34.7 HUMAN RIGHTS.

Miscellaneous

Application of European Convention on Human Rights

[2.293] See *Ali & Begum,* 34.16 HUMAN RIGHTS.

Unauthorised use of tape recorder by appellant during hearing

[2.294] In the case noted at 22.234 EUROPEAN COMMUNITY LAW, a shorthand writer engaged by the appellant company recorded part of the proceedings without the permission of the tribunal. The tribunal imposed restrictions on the use of the recorder, and warned that its unauthorised use had been a breach of *Contempt of Court Act 1981, ss 9, 19*, and that such contempts could be punished. *Empire Stores Ltd*, [1992] VATTR 271 (VTD 8859).

Appellant applying for separate preliminary hearing

[2.295] The Commissioners issued an estimated assessment on a partnership which operated a restaurant business. The partnership appealed, contending firstly that the assessment was excessive, and secondly that it had been raised outside the statutory time limit. At the hearing of the appeal, the partnership was represented by counsel, who contended that the question with regard to the time limit should be considered at a separate preliminary hearing. The tribunal rejected this contention, observing that 'as the facts which will be relevant to the issue of the time limit will be many of the same facts as will be relevant to the other issues in the appeal, no time would be saved by hearing the time limit issue as a separate issue. Indeed, such a proceeding could lengthen the overall time of the hearing of the appeal.' *Crayford Tandoori*, [2000] VATDR 340 (VTD 16749).

Application to introduce alternative grounds of appeal

[2.296] In the case noted at 62.39 SUPPLY, the appellant company applied to amend its 'grounds of appeal' to include an alternative contention that the principle of 'legitimate expectation', as set out by Sales J in *Oxfam v HMRC*, 11.51 CHARITIES, should be applied. HMRC opposed the application but the tribunal granted it. Judge Hellier held that 'given the possible uncertainty surrounding the issue of legitimate expectation, it would be fairer and more expedient for the FTT to hear the relevant evidence and make its findings of fact at the same time as it considers the other issues, rather than for the issue to be left in abeyance pending the possibility that a higher court may resolve the issue in a way which requires further findings of fact by the tribunal'. *CGI Group (Europe) Ltd v HMRC (No 1)*, [2010] SFTD 1001; [2010] UKFTT 224 (TC), TC00525.

Assignment of appeal

[2.297] In the case noted at 2.219 above, the tribunal noted that the appellant company (T) had been struck off the Register of Companies for not filing the returns required by the *Companies Act*. The tribunal directed that an associated company (H) which had funded the appeal could be substituted as the appellant, rejecting Customs' contention that this 'assignment' of the appeal was 'champertous and accordingly illegal as being contrary to public policy'. *Global Active Holdings Ltd; Global Active Technologies Ltd*, [2006] VATDR 190 (VTD 19715). (*Note*. For the principle of 'champerty', see the judgment of Lord Mustill in *Giles v Thompson*, HL 1993, [1994] 1 AC 142; [1993] 3 All ER 321 and the judgment of Lord Hoffmann in *Norglen Ltd v Reeds Rains Prudential Ltd*, HL [1999] 2 AC 1.)

[2.298] A company (Q) claimed a substantial repayment of input tax. Customs rejected the claim on the grounds that 'the invoices represented part of a circular chain of transactions which did not in their view constitute an economic activity'. Q appealed, but subsequently went into creditors' voluntary liquidation. Q's liquidator entered into a deed of assignment, purporting to assign its interest in the appeal to another company (C). C applied to the tribunal to be substituted as the appellant. The tribunal granted the application, observing that the deed of assignment was badly drafted but holding that there was 'no reason why the assignment should be treated as void or unenforceable'. *Quest Trading Co Ltd (in liquidation); Cotswold Computers Components Ltd (No 2)*, [2006] VATDR 202 (VTD 19909).

[2.298A] In a case where a company had claimed an award of compound interest, Judge Kempster agreed that the appeal could be assigned to one of its creditors under SI 2009/273, rule 9. B *Hilton-Foster v HMRC (re New Miles Ltd)*, [2012] UKFTT 33 (TC), TC01731.

SI 1986/590, rule 21(4)

[2.299] See *Murrell*, 34.10 HUMAN RIGHTS.

SI 1986/590, rule 22—summons to third party

[2.300] A company issued a summons, under *VAT Tribunals Rules (SI 1986/590), rule 22*, to a firm of accountants, seeking to inspect certain documents. The firm applied to have the summons set aside, contending that the summons was defective as it was directed to the firm and not to any named individual. The tribunal accepted this contention, granted the application and set the summons aside, holding that the summons was invalid since the *Tribunals Rules* 'did not provide for the service of a summons on a partnership as such'. The tribunal observed that a partnership was not a legal entity, and held that the effect of *rule 22(4)* was that 'the third party to whom the summons was issued must be either an individual or a body corporate'. *British Shoe Corporation Ltd v C & E Commrs (ex p. Coopers & Lybrand)*, [1998] VATDR 348 (C86).

SI 1986/590, rule 22—summons to company's accountant

[2.301] A company, which operated a car hire and taxi business, appealed against an assessment. The Commissioners applied for a witness summons, under *VAT Tribunals Rules (SI 1986/590), rule 22*, to require the company's accountant to attend the hearing. The Tribunal Registrar granted the application. The accountant applied for a direction to set the summons aside, contending that to compel him to give evidence would breach his duty of confidentiality to his client and would contravene the *European Convention on Human Rights*. The tribunal rejected these contentions, dismissed the accountant's application, and upheld the summons. The chairman observed that, while *Notice 700/47/93* 'contemplates the duty of confidentiality which a tax adviser has to his client, the circumstances in this appeal are such that it appears to me to be reasonable that that duty should be over-ridden by the requirement to place before the tribunal the unusual evidential situation that has come about'. Furthermore, there was no breach of *Article 6* of the

European Convention on Human Rights. Home Or Away Ltd; JF Chance, LON/99/1133 (VTD 17623). (*Note.* For subsequent developments in this case, see **62.250** SUPPLY.)

Attendance of interpreter

[2.302] In an appeal by a partnership which operated a Chinese restaurant, the appellants presented as an interpreter an accountant who was a partner in the firm dealing with the restaurant's affairs. The Commissioners objected to the use of the accountant as an interpreter on the basis that he 'could not be seen to be independent'. The tribunal accepted this contention and ruled that the hearing should be adjourned 'so that the name of an independent linguistic interpreter can be submitted'. *CY & TY Shek (t/a The Golden Bowl Café),* EDN/99/89 & 113 (VTD 16509).

[2.303] A similar decision was reached in *TS Cheung (t/a May Wah Takeaway),* EDN/99/123 (VTD 16670).

Failure to comply with SI 1986/590, rule 23

[2.304] A company (G) applied for an award of compound interest. HMRC rejected the application and G appealed. HMRC applied to the tribunal for the appeal to be struck out on the grounds that it had been made out of time and the tribunal had no jurisdiction to hear it. In May 2008 the tribunal informed G that this application would be heard in July 2008. However, there was no evidence that the tribunal informed HMRC of this. The tribunal allowed G's application and HMRC appealed to the Ch D, contending that the decision should be set aside as the tribunal had failed to comply with *VAT Tribunals Rules (SI 1986/590), rule 23.* The Ch D accepted this contention and set aside the tribunal decision. Lewison J held that there had been 'a serious procedural irregularity' in the tribunal's proceedings. *HMRC v Grattan plc (No 3),* Ch D [2009] STC 882; [2009] EWHC 364 (Ch). (*Note.* For subsequent developments in this case, see **2.28** above.)

SI 1986/590, rule 27—procedure at hearing

[2.305] In the case noted at **50.100** PENALTIES: EVASION OF TAX, counsel for the Commissioners claimed the right to make the closing submission, in accordance with *VAT Tribunals Rules (SI 1986/590), rule 27(2)(a).* The tribunal rejected this contention, holding that notwithstanding the provisions of *rule 27(2)(a),* there was a 'convention that has developed in our civil courts and tribunals whereby, when the advocate who should be last to address the tribunal has raised matters not dealt with in the closing address of the advocate who has previously made his closing address, the previous advocate is permitted a *limited* right of reply to deal with any points that he has not previously dealt with. This practice is not provided for in *rule 27,* but it is a useful one, and can be extremely helpful to the tribunal, which otherwise might not have heard full argument.' The reality was that 'an appellant in an evasion penalty appeal is in the position of a defendant to a quasi-criminal charge, because in practice the element of dishonesty, or the lack of it, tends to be decisive. In a criminal jury trial, he or his advocate would address the jury last. There is a danger that, in his closing address, if given first in order, an appellant or his advocate might omit to deal with matters raised by HMRC in their closing address, simply because, speaking first, he would not know precisely what HMRC will say. That could create an adverse impression, because it may look as though those matters were deliberately not dealt with. It is moreover not in the interests of a fair trial that submissions which fully cover the ground might not have been presented. For those reasons we feel that, generally speaking, an appellant ought to make the second closing address in civil evasion appeals, despite what the *Tribunal Rules* provide.' Counsel for HMRC should then have 'a final limited right of reply by way of amplification of his previous address'. *M Arif (t/a Trinity Fisheries)*, MAN/00/162 (VTD 19296).

Whether appeal should be transferred from Scotland to England

[2.306] A German company (G) agreed to purchase a number of vehicles from a UK company (V), and reclaimed input tax. The Commissioners issued assessments on G to recover the input tax, and also issued alternative assessments on V charging output tax. G lodged an appeal with the Edinburgh tribunal, and V lodged an appeal with the London tribunal. The Commissioners applied to the Edinburgh tribunal for G's appeal to be transferred to the London tribunal, so that the appeals could be heard together, contending that 'it is in the interests of justice for the same tribunal to consider both appeals to ensure legal certainty and also to reduce the cost to the public purse'. The tribunal rejected this application, observing that V did not want the appeals to be heard together, and that there were issues of confidentiality. *RBS Deutschland Holdings GmbH*, [2004] VATDR 447 (VTD 18840). (*Notes.* (1) For subsequent developments in this case, see **2.223** above and **22.418** EUROPEAN COMMUNITY LAW. (2) For an English case where the tribunal ruled that appeals by a supplier and recipient should be heard together, even though one of the parties objected, see *Barclays Bank plc v C & E Commrs and Visa International Service Association*, **2.75** above.)

Appellant not legally represented—whether any unfairness

[2.307] See *Qaisar*, **50.55** PENALTIES: EVASION OF TAX.

Counsel for appellant also acting as tribunal chairman in separate appeal

[2.308] A partnership appealed against assessments. At the hearing of their appeal, the partners were represented by a barrister (B) who also sometimes acted as a VAT tribunal chairman. The tribunal hearing their appeal comprised a chairman and two other members. The hearing of the appeal was adjourned at the end of the second day. Before the third day of the hearing, one of the tribunal members (W) sat with B at the hearing of another tribunal appeal. The tribunal held that the effect of W and B having sat together as tribunal members, and of B then continuing to represent the partnership, was that W was disqualified from continuing to hear the partnership appeal. The remaining two tribunal members proceeded to hear the remainder of the appeal (which was dismissed). *Mr & Mrs M Hurst (t/a Park Fisheries)*, MAN/01/796 (VTD 19546).

The tribunal decision (SI 2009/273, rules 34–42

Difference of opinion between tribunal members

[2.309] A restaurant proprietor appealed against estimated assessments. His appeal was heard by a tribunal consisting of a chairman and one other member. The chairman concluded that the assessments had been made to the best of the Commissioners' judgment, and should be upheld. However, the lay member formed the opinion that the assessments had not been made to the best of the Commissioners' judgment, as required by *VATA 1994, s 73(1)*, and should be discharged. The tribunal held that, by virtue of *VATA 1994, Sch 12 para 5(2)*, which provides for the chairman to have a casting vote, 'the chairman's conclusion determines the outcome of this appeal', and dismissed the appeal. The proprietor appealed to the QB, which directed that the case should be remitted to a new tribunal for re-hearing. Carnwath J held that a tribunal should not treat an assessment as invalid merely because it disagreed as to how the Commissioners' judgment should have been exercised. An assessment should only be held to fail the 'best judgment' test of *s 73(1)* where it had been made 'dishonestly or vindictively or capriciously', or was a 'spurious estimate or guess in which all elements of judgment are missing', or was 'wholly unreasonable'. Short of such a finding, there was no justification for setting aside an assessment. Carnwath J observed that 'it is only in a very exceptional case that an assessment will be upset because of a failure by the Commissioners to exercise best judgment. In the normal case the important issue will be the amount of the assessment.' On the evidence, the approach of the lay member had been wrong, and the tribunal chairman had been entitled to conclude that the assessment had been issued to the best of the Commissioners' judgment. His reasoning on this point was 'clearly set out' and 'impeccable'. However, having concluded by virtue of *Sch 12 para 5(2)* that the assessment had been made to the best of the Commissioners' judgment, both the chairman and the lay member should then have given further consideration, acting jointly, to the amount of the assessment. It appeared that the lay member had 'taken no part in the decision on the amount of the assessment', having 'regarded his function as discharged when he had expressed his view on the best judgment issue'. There was 'at least a possibility that, if he had taken part, the decision would have been more favourable to the appellant'. *MH Rahman (t/a Khayam Restaurant) v C & E Commrs*, QB [1998] STC 826. (*Note.* For subsequent developments, see 3.9 ASSESSMENT.)

[2.310] A racehorse trainer, who was registered for VAT, received payments totalling more than £500,000 from a woman (L) who owned some horses which he trained for her. The Commissioners issued assessments on the basis that some of these payments represented consideration for supplies of services. The trainer appealed. The appeal was heard by a chairman and a lay member, who disagreed. The lay member considered that the appeal should be dismissed, but the chairman held that the appeal should be allowed. By virtue of *VATA 1994, Sch 12 para 5(2)*, the chairman's views prevailed and the appeal was allowed. *PC Clarke*, LON/94/1703 (VTD 17154).

Tribunal delaying release of decision

[2.311] See *R v C & E Commrs (ex p. Dangol)*, **2.329** below.

Failure by Commissioners to comply with direction of tribunal

[2.312] See *Young*, **2.152** above; *Vaz*, **2.397** below, and *AR Waller & Associates*, **17.11** DEFAULT INTEREST.

Appeal against tribunal refusal to refer question to ECJ

[2.313] In the case noted at **67.155** VALUATION, the tribunal referred the case to the ECJ for a ruling, but rejected a request by the appellant company to refer an additional question to the ECJ seeking a ruling on whether the company was entitled to reclaim input tax. The company obtained leave from the CA to lodge a late appeal against this refusal (see **2.172** above) and, at a subsequent hearing, the QB held that the input tax question was not '*acte claire*' and that the tribunal should have referred the input tax question to the ECJ. Applying *dicta* of the ECJ in *Srl CILFIT and Lanificio di Gavardo SpA v Ministro della Sanita*, **22.3** EUROPEAN COMMUNITY LAW (the leading authority on the legal principle of '*acte claire*'), the point in dispute was not 'so obvious as to leave no scope for any reasonable doubt as to the manner in which the question raised is to be resolved'. The QB remitted the case to the tribunal to make the reference in question. *Conoco Ltd v C & E Commrs*, QB [1995] STC 1022.

Appeal referred to ECJ—late attempt to raise alternative contention

[2.314] See *Kuwait Petroleum (GB) Ltd v C & E Commrs*, **22.259** EUROPEAN COMMUNITY LAW.

Applications for reinstatement of appeals (SI 2009/273, rule 17(3))

Cases where the application was successful

[2.315] An appellant, who had failed to attend a hearing at which his appeal was dismissed, subsequently applied for the appeal to be reinstated, contending that he had been under the impression that his solicitors were dealing with the appeal. The tribunal directed that the appeal should be reinstated on condition that the appellant paid costs of £300 to the Commissioners. *JDG Wilkinson*, MAN/77/303 (VTD 583, VTD 649).

[2.316] In a case where a company's managing director had suffered from illness, the tribunal allowed an application for the reinstatement of an appeal on condition that the company paid £5,000 on account of the tax and £75 on account of the Commissioners' costs. *Renwalk Ltd*, MAN/80/119 (VTD 1255).

[2.317] The unsuccessful appellant in the case noted at 55.83 PROTECTED BUILDINGS subsequently applied under *rule 26(2)* of the *Tribunals Rules* to have the decision set aside, on the grounds that he had been let down by accountants who had not attended the hearing. The tribunal stated that it was 'reluctant to deny anyone a chance to argue his rights especially when problems have existed about representation', and reinstated the appeal on condition that the appellant should pay costs of £300 to the Commissioners. *P Robinson*, MAN/89/131 (VTD 4530).

[2.318] The Commissioners issued an assessment on the proprietor of a kebab shop, covering a period of four years. The proprietor appealed but did not pay the tax charged by the assessment. On 25 November 1993 the Commissioners made an application for the appeal to be struck out, and the application was set down for hearing on 13 January 1994. On receiving notification of the hearing, the proprietor applied under *rule 11* of the *Tribunals Rules* for the appeal to be heard without payment of the tax assessed, on the grounds that payment would cause him hardship. On 31 December 1993 the Commissioners served a notice opposing the hardship application. The appellant did not attend the hearing on 13 January, and in his absence the tribunal chairman gave a direction that the appeal be dismissed in accordance with *rule 19(4)*. This direction was notified to the appellant, who served a notice of application for the appeal to be reinstated under *rule 26(1)* of the *Tribunals Rules*, contending that on 11 January a member of the tribunal staff had told him by telephone that the hearing scheduled for 13 January had been adjourned and that he need not attend. The tribunal chairman accepted the appellant's evidence, set aside the previous direction, and reinstated the appeal. The chairman awarded costs against the Commissioners, observing that the notice which the Commissioners had served on 31 December had been accompanied by a letter stating that the hardship application would not be listed for 30 days, and commenting that it was 'the duty of the advocate of HM Customs and Excise' to ensure that 'any direction dismissing an appeal by virtue of (*VATA 1994, s 82**) is validly given and that the tribunal is aware of any potential problem'. *C Akar (t/a Akar Kebabs)*, [1994] VATTR 176 (VTD 11873).

[2.319] An application for reinstatement of an appeal was allowed in a case in which the tribunal applied *dicta* of Roskill LJ in *Samuels v Linzi Dresses*, CA [1980] 2 WLR 836; [1980] 1 All ER 803 and observed that the Commissioners had not 'suffered any substantial prejudice through the delay'. *Empress of India Restaurant*, [1997] VATDR 242 (VTD 15087). (*Note.* Costs of £300 were awarded to the Commissioners.)

[2.320] A company made an application under *Tribunals Rules, rule 11* for an appeal to be entertained without payment of the assessed tax, on the grounds that payment would cause it hardship. It was not represented at the hearing of this application. The tribunal dismissed the application and struck out the substantive appeal. The company subsequently applied for its 'hardship' application to be reinstated. Customs opposed this application but the tribunal allowed it. The chairman (Mr. Wallace) observed that there was 'considerable doubt as to whether an immediate dismissal of the appeal without time to pay was compatible with Community law'. *WM Management & Marketing Ltd*, [2005] VATDR 242 (VTD 19075).

[2.321] A company which traded in computer components and mobile telephones claimed repayments of input tax. HMRC rejected the claims on the grounds that the transactions appeared to be connected with MTIC fraud. The company appealed, but failed to comply with a direction by the VAT tribunal. In November 2008 the VAT tribunal dismissed the appeals. The company subsequently applied for the appeals to be reinstated, contending that its directors had been badly let down by the company's accountant, who had not informed them that the appeals had been heard and dismissed. The First-Tier Tribunal rejected the application but the Upper Tribunal granted it. Briggs J observed that there had been 'an extraordinary level of incompetence' on the part of the accountant, and the company had subsequently dispensed with his services. The company's directors had been 'entirely unaware of what had previously been done or omitted in the company's name'. If the company were 'permanently disabled from pursuing the appeals', it would 'have no realistic remedy for a very large financial loss, or be able to clear its or its directors' names, from an allegation of, and administrative action based on, alleged tax fraud'. *ATEC Associates Ltd v HMRC*, UT [2010] STC 1882.

[2.322] Applications for the reinstatement of an appeal were also allowed in *A & IA Smith*, LON/87/588X (VTD 4995); *Maharani Restaurant*, LON/x (VTD 15088); *W Rankin*, EDN/00/149 (VTD 17059); *BP Davis*, LON/99/684 (VTD 17245); *NP Close*, MAN/07/1333 (VTD 20801), and *Harleyford Golf Club Ltd (No 2)*, **27.53** FINANCE.

Cases where the application was unsuccessful

[2.323] An appeal by an unincorporated association was dismissed on the grounds that the association had failed to pay the tax in dispute. (It had sent a cheque for the amount in question, but the cheque had been dishonoured.) Subsequently the association paid the tax and applied for the appeal to be reinstated. The tribunal rejected the application, observing that the association had a history of dilatory tactics and that a letter it had sent indicated that it desired to change its grounds of appeal. *Hubbard Foundation Scotland*, EDN/81/23 (VTD 1194). (*Note.* For other proceedings involving this association, see **2.128** above.)

[2.324] In a case where the tribunal had dismissed appeals by an accountancy partnership against assessments, the partners failed to pay the tax charged and the Commissioners issued writs against the partners. One of the partners obtained a stay of proceedings by order of a Master of the Queen's Bench, conditional upon his entering a fresh appeal. He did so but the tribunal dismissed his appeal, holding that there were no grounds for reinstatement. The accountant appealed to the QB, which upheld the tribunal decision, holding that there was no matter of principle involved and observing that the accountant's only real purpose in seeking to reinstate the appeal appeared to be to delay the enforcement proceedings. *T Nawaz v C & E Commrs*, QB [1986] STC 484.

[2.325] In a case where an appeal had been settled by agreement under what is now *VATA 1994, s 85*, the tribunal dismissed a subsequent application for reinstatement, holding that it had no jurisdiction to reinstate the appeal. *Abbey Life Japan Trust*, LON/91/1889 (VTD 11205).

[2.326] A partnership appealed against an assessment. In June 2000, less than four weeks later, it withdrew the appeal. In July 2001 it applied for the appeal to be reinstated. The tribunal rejected the application, applying the HL decision in *Johnson v Gore Wood*, HL 2000, [2001] 1 All ER 481, and observing that 'there is a public interest in the finality of litigation'. *E Matthias & S Goode (t/a The Music Warehouse)*, LON/01/877 (VTD 17692).

[2.327] Applications for the reinstatement of appeals were dismissed in *A Moss*, MAN/79/91 (VTD 919, VTD 953); *Rushfern Ltd*, MAN/83/35 (VTD 1509); *TE Formstone*, MAN/88/559 (VTD 3693); *Shazia Fashions Fabrics*, LON/91/627 (VTD 7184); *Terry Shaw Holdings*, MAN/92/671 (VTD 11613); *Highacre (Cambridge) Ltd*, LON/93/819A (VTD 12060); *Express Pipework Co*, EDN/93/261 (VTD 12108); *TL Dunning*, LON/93/2027 & LON/94/784 (VTD 12739); *IT Anderson*, LON/94/1006P (VTD 13226); *M Razaq, M Mushtaq & M Azam (t/a Liberty Cars)*, MAN/94/877 (VTD 14949); *MW Morgan*, LON/95/2893 (VTD 16968); *C Cullen*, LON/00/446 (VTD 17169); *AP Davey*, LON/00/1319 (VTD 17427); *TA Brennan*, MAN/05/426 (VTD 19982); *24/7 Fuels Ltd*, [2009] UKFTT 274 (TC), TC00220, and *Janice Traders Ltd*, [2010] UKFTT 513 (TC), TC00768.

Applications for judicial review

Application for judicial review of tribunal decision

[2.328] Customs issued estimated assessments on two companies which had not submitted VAT returns, and which were the subject of an investigation by VAT officers. Customs had begun criminal proceedings against the companies' directors, alleging conspiracy to defraud. The companies appealed against the assessments and applied for the appeals to be adjourned until the criminal proceedings had been completed. The tribunal granted an adjournment of the appeals for one month only, to enable the companies to submit the outstanding returns. The directors applied for judicial review of the tribunal decision. The QB rejected the application. McCullough J held that the company should have appealed under the *Tribunals and Inquiries Act*. *R v VAT Tribunal (ex p. Cohen & Others)*, QB 1983, [1984] STC 361.

[2.329] A restaurant proprietor appealed against estimated assessments. The tribunal began hearing the appeals for three days in September 1996. It then adjourned until April 1997, when it sat for a further three days, and did not conclude the hearing until August 1997. The tribunal then did not release its decision until May 1998. It held that the assessments had been made to the best of the Commissioners' judgment, but were excessive, and reduced them by one-third. The proprietor applied for judicial review, contending that the effect of the delay was that the tribunal would have forgotten parts of the evidence and that its decision was unsafe. The QB criticised the tribunal for the delays, but dismissed the proprietor's application. Moses J held that the delay in releasing the decision was 'unjustified and unjustifiable'. However, 'unless an unsuccessful party can show that the delay has tainted the conclusion and the findings, it would be wrong to say that he is entitled as of right to have the case remitted to be heard again depriving the other side, who after all is equally not responsible for the delay, of the fruits of victory'. *R v C & E Commrs (ex p. Dangol)*, QB 1999, [2000] STC 107.

[2.330] The appellant company in the case noted at **63**.9 TOUR OPERATORS AND TRAVEL AGENTS applied for judicial review of the tribunal decision. The QB rejected the application. Popplewell J held that the company should have appealed under the *Tribunals and Inquiries Act. R v VAT Tribunals (ex p. Jenny Braden Holdings Ltd)*, QB 10 March 1994 unreported.

[2.331] A similar decision was reached in *R v C & E Commrs and VAT Tribunal (ex p. Cohen)*, QB 3 December 1998 unreported.

[2.332] For a case where the QB granted judicial review of a tribunal decision, see *R v C & E Commrs (ex p. Sims)*, **29**.25 FOOD.

Application for reference to ECJ

[2.333] In the case noted at **22**.399 EUROPEAN COMMUNITY LAW, the QB rejected an application by the company for a reference to the ECJ. The company appealed to the CA, which reversed the QB decision and directed that the case should be referred to the ECJ. *R v C & E Commrs (ex p. BLP Group plc)*, CA 1993, [1994] STC 41.

Application for judicial review of terms of reference to ECJ

[2.334] See *R v VAT Tribunal (ex p. Conoco Ltd)*, **2**.172 above.

Application for judicial review of validity of legislation

[2.335] See *C & E Commrs v Federation of Technological Industries & Others*, **22**.466 EUROPEAN COMMUNITY LAW, and *Teleos plc & Others v C & E Commrs*, **22**.518 EUROPEAN COMMUNITY LAW.

Application for judicial review of VATA 1994, s 80(4)

[2.336] See *R (oao British Telecommunications plc) v HMRC*, **48**.74 PAYMENT OF TAX.

Application for judicial review of validity of Statutory Instruments

[2.337] In June 1994 a group of companies (E) which operated the Channel Tunnel terminals lodged an application for leave to apply for judicial review of the *VAT (Tax-Free Shops) Order 1992 (SI 1992/3131)* and the *VAT (Tax-Free Shops) Order 1994 (SI 1994/686)*, contending that the Statutory Instruments in question failed to implement *Article 28K* of the *EC Directive* (and the similar *Directive* relating to excise duty) correctly, and failed to prevent evasion or avoidance. Customs did not oppose the application, and Tucker J granted leave. Several companies which operated tax-free shops at airports and seaports and on ferries, and which would have been adversely affected if the application were successful, subsequently issued notices of motion, applying for orders that the grant of leave to apply for judicial review should be set aside. At a subsequent hearing the QB upheld the objectors' contentions and revoked the grant of leave, observing that the original grant of leave had been made outside the normal time limits and had been made *ex parte*, and holding that the objectors had sufficient *locus standi*. E 'could not, by choosing to give informal notice of its intention to apply for judicial review to some only of the persons directly affected, viz. the Commissioners, thereby affect the right of other persons directly affected, viz. the objectors, to apply to set aside the leave granted'. While a grant of leave should be set aside only in exceptional circumstances, this was 'an exceptional case in its size, complexity and ramifications'. Although the form of the original application was an attack, by way of judicial review, on the validity of the Statutory Instruments, in its substance it was an attack on the validity of the *Directives* themselves. It was accepted that E did not have the necessary *locus standi* to challenge the validity of the *Directives* under *Article 173* of the *EC Treaty*. The objectors had shown that to uphold E's original application would 'cause severe prejudice to the objectors and to other persons not only in the UK but throughout the European Community'. Furthermore, 'the fact that the present case concerns the validity of Community measures provides no reason to disregard or modify the provisions of English domestic law concerning time limits'. *R v HM Customs & Excise (ex p. Eurotunnel plc & Others)*, QB 17 February 1995 unreported. (*Notes.* (1) See also the subsequent case of *Eurotunnel SA & Others v SeaFrance*, **22.524** EUROPEAN COMMUNITY LAW. (2) The zero-rating of sales from 'tax-free shops' was subsequently abolished, with effect from 1 July 1999, by the *VAT (Abolition of Zero-Rating for Tax-Free Shops) Order 1999 (SI 1999/1642)*.)

Customs withdrawing previous ruling

[2.338] In the case noted at **67.162** VALUATION, a company (F) sold books of vouchers to car dealers, who then passed the books of vouchers to the purchasers of second-hand cars. F accounted for output tax on the amounts which it received from the car dealers for the vouchers, but the car dealers did not account for tax on their onward supply of the vouchers to their customers. In March 1998 a local VAT officer ruled that no tax was chargeable on these onward supplies, on the basis that they fell within *VATA 1994, Sch 6 para 5*. However, the scheme came to the attention of a regional office, and in June 1998 the Commissioners withdrew the first ruling and ruled that the sale of the vouchers was not within *Sch 6 para 5*, so that VAT was chargeable. F applied for judicial review of the Commissioners' decision to withdraw their original ruling. The QB held that there was no legal basis for any claim for compensation, and F appealed to the CA, which upheld the QB decision. Robert Walker LJ held that the Commissioners were 'bound (both by Community law and by domestic law) to administer the VAT system correctly and to collect all tax which is properly due. They have no general dispensing power, and taxpayers cannot have any legitimate expectation that they will administer VAT in any way which is contrary to law'. F's 'only legitimate expectation was that it would not be asked to pay tax in respect of past transactions'. The

30-day breathing space which the Commissioners allowed for existing customers was 'reasonable in all the circumstances'. Sedley LJ observed that a public authority could not 'create a legitimate expectation which defeats the law'. The *Bill of Rights 1688* confirmed that the Crown did not have a 'dispensing power'. *F & I Services Ltd v C & E Commrs*, CA [2001] STC 939.

[2.339] In the case noted at 22.75 EUROPEAN COMMUNITY LAW, HMRC issued assessments on two companies on the basis that they were supplying grants of a major interest in leasehold holiday accommodation, which was chargeable to VAT at the standard rate. The companies applied for judicial review, contending that in 1998 a VAT officer had agreed that such supplies would be zero-rated. The QB directed that the application for judicial review should be adjourned until the First-Tier Tribunal had heard appeals against the disputed assessments. *R (oao Lower Mill Estate Ltd) v HMRC (and related application)*, QB [2008] EWHC 2409 (Admin).

[2.340] See also *R (oao Medical Protection Society Ltd) v HMRC*, 39.11 INTERNATIONAL SERVICES.

Claim that Customs treating taxpayers unequally

[2.341] In the case noted at 5.97 BOOKS, ETC., the tribunal held that a company (S) which supplied satellite broadcasting services was not entitled to treat part of the subscriptions which it received as attributable to the zero-rated supply of magazines. S subsequently applied for judicial review, contending that Customs had acted unfairly because it had to account for tax in this way from June 1998, but the Commissioners had not issued similar rulings to suppliers of cable broadcasting services until July 1999 (after the tribunal decision). The QB dismissed the application. Elias J held that Customs were entitled to have formed the opinion that there were material differences between S and the suppliers of cable services. The fact that Customs had subsequently decided that the cable suppliers should be treated in the same way as S did not mean that their previous policy was unfair or unreasonable. *R (oao British Sky Broadcasting Group plc) v C & E Commrs*, QB [2001] STC 437; [2001] EWHC Admin 127.

[2.342] A company (F) carried on business as an internet service provider in the UK, and was required to account for VAT accordingly. Its directors formed the opinion that it was at a disadvantage by comparison with a competitor (AOL) which was based in the USA and which, under the legislation in force prior to 1 July 2003, was not required to account for VAT on supplies to UK customers. It applied for judicial review of Customs' decision not to require AOL to account for VAT on such supplies. The QB dismissed the application. Evans-Lombe J held that Customs had not acted unreasonably in not requiring AOL to account for UK VAT before 1 July 2003 (when *EC Directive 2002/38/EC*, under which AOL was required to account for VAT, came into force). He also observed that F had no standing to bring its complaint, since there was a general principle that 'one taxpayer has no right to bring judicial review proceedings against the taxing authorities with relation to the tax affairs of another'. *R (oao Freeserve.com plc) v C & E Commrs*, QB 2003, [2004] STC 187; [2003] EWHC 2736 (Admin).

Delay in repayment of input tax pending enquiries

[2.343] See *R v C & E Commrs (ex p. Strangewood Ltd)*, 36.648 INPUT TAX, and the cases noted at 36.650 to 36.655 INPUT TAX.

Assessments to recover input tax—application for judicial review

[2.344] Customs formed the opinion that a company had reclaimed input tax to which it was not entitled. They issued two assessments to recover the tax. The company applied for judicial review, contending *inter alia* that a VAT officer had given it a legitimate expectation that it was entitled to reclaim input tax. The QB dismissed the application, holding that the company should have appealed to the tribunal, but the CA allowed the company's appeal against this decision. Tuckey LJ (sitting alone) held that the question of 'legitimate expectation' should be considered on judicial review, rather than by a VAT tribunal. *R (oao Sagemaster plc) v C & E Commrs*, CA [2004] STC 813; [2004] EWCA Civ 25. (*Notes*. (1) There was no further public hearing of the case. (2) Customs were not represented at the hearing. Compare the HL decision in *R v CIR (ex p. Preston)*, HL [1985] STC 282, where Lord Scarman held that 'a remedy by way of judicial review is not to be made available where an alternative remedy exists' and that 'where Parliament has provided by statute appeal procedures, as in the taxing statutes, it will only be very rarely that the courts will allow the collateral process of judicial review to be used to attack an appealable decision'. This case was not referred to in Tuckey LJ's decision. Tuckey LJ's judgment also does not discuss the principle of estoppel, under which (in the words of Lord Grantchester) 'there can be no estoppel against the Crown in the person of the Commissioners of Customs & Excise which prevents them from recovering tax which is lawfully due under the provisions of an Act of Parliament and Regulations made thereunder'. For cases concerning this principle, see **2.109** *et seq.* above.)

Failure to make repayments for previous accounting periods

[2.345] See *R v C & E Commrs (ex p. Kay & Co Ltd and Others)*, 48.50 PAYMENT OF TAX.

Application for judicial review of assessment

[2.346] A UK company (C) sold a large quantity of beverages to a Belize company (S) which had an office in Poland. S then sold the beverages to a Polish company (K). C failed to account for VAT on its supplies to S, treating them as zero-rated. HMRC issued an assessment charging tax on them, and C applied for judicial review, contending firstly that the transactions should be treated as a 'standard triangulation procedure' and that no VAT should be due, and alternatively that it had been misled by a VAT officer when its director (M) had telephoned HMRC's National Advice Service. The QB rejected these contentions and dismissed the application for judicial review. Sales J held that the transactions could not benefit from the triangulation arrangements because the supplies had been to S, which was not registered for VAT. Furthermore, it appeared that the VAT officer to whom M had spoken by telephone had specifically drawn M's attention to the requirements of *Notice 725, section 3*. Sales J observed that M appeared to have shown 'a degree of wishful thinking' in interpreting what had been said to him on the telephone, and had not 'put all his cards face upwards on the table'. *R (oao Corkteck Ltd) v HMRC*, QB [2009] STC 1681; [2009] EWHC 785 (Admin).

[2.347] A company (AS) failed to account for VAT on supplies of staff to a bank. HMRC issued an assessment charging tax on the supplies. AS and the bank applied for judicial review, contending that the effect of *Leaflet 700/34/94* was that no VAT was due. The QB rejected this contention and dismissed the applications for judicial review. Sales J observed that the concession set out in *Leaflet 700/34/94* had been significantly amended by Business Brief 07/97 with effect from 1 April 1997. Furthermore, there was a 'need for HMRC to avoid departing too far from the requirements of EU law on VAT, according to which VAT should be charged on the full amount of consideration in relation to the supply of staff, since departure from those requirements would tend to undermine the need for equal application of EU law throughout the EU Member States and could give rise to difficulties with the EU Commission'. On the evidence, the arrangements between AS and the bank were 'a considerable distance from any situation likely to be regarded as deserving to benefit from the policy underlying the concession'. AS 'retained predominant control over its employees', and HMRC had been entitled to conclude that its supplies did not fall within the scope of the concession. *R (oao Accenture Services Ltd) v HMRC (and related application)*, QB [2009] STC 1503; [2009] EWHC 857 (Admin).

[2.348] See also *R (oao DFS Furniture Co plc) v C & E Commrs*, 48.76 PAYMENT OF TAX.

Customs directing companies to make quarterly returns

[2.349] See *R (oao BMW AG) v HMRC*, 59.4 RETURNS, and *R (oao Brayfal Ltd) v HMRC (No 2)*, 59.5 RETURNS.

The award of costs (SI 1986/590, rule 29; SI 2009/273, rule 10)

NOTE

The cases under this heading are those which appear to raise points of general interest and are mainly separate applications for costs after the hearing of the appeal. In general a decision as to costs at the conclusion of the hearing is not referred to either here or in the note on the hearing, unless it raises a point of general interest in relation to costs.

Applications by the Commissioners

[2.350] A partnership's appeal was listed for hearing on 13 March 1978. The partners did not attend and were not represented. A tribunal officer telephoned the partnership's accountant, and was told that a letter withdrawing the appeal had been posted on 9 March. The letter had not been received and the tribunal dismissed the appeal and awarded costs of £50 to the Commissioners. (The letter of withdrawal did in fact reach the Tribunal Centre on the following day, having been posted on 10 March by second-class post. The tribunal, in its decision, severely criticised the accountant's behaviour and regretted that it had no power to ensure that the accountant should pay the costs awarded.) *Slack & Taylor (t/a Olives)*, MAN/77/247 (VTD 537).

[2.351] In a case where an appellant failed to appear at the hearing of the appeal, the tribunal awarded costs of £100 to the Commissioners. The chairman observed that 'appellants who abandon appeals to these tribunals at the last moment or who do not attend to pursue their appeals or applications without reasonable explanation should be aware that an order for costs may be made against them'. *R Santi*, MAN/80/38 (VTD 954).

[2.352] At the hearing of a company's appeal, the Commissioners were represented by three officers who gave evidence. The company was not represented and, during the hearing of the evidence, the tribunal received a letter from the company, stating that the appeal had been withdrawn. The tribunal awarded the Commissioners costs of £1,500. *Southern Girl Ltd*, LON/84/160 (VTD 1803).

[2.353] In the case noted at **65.9** TRANSFERS OF GOING CONCERNS, where a company had purchased a business as a going concern, and had appealed against the disallowance of input tax, the tribunal held that the appeal was frivolous and an abuse of process, and awarded costs of £200 to the Commissioners. *Quadrant Stationers Ltd*, LON/83/32 (VTD 1599).

[2.354] In a case where the tribunal upheld an estimated assessment charging tax of more than £1,700,000, the Commissioners applied for costs. The tribunal quoted from a statement by the then Financial Secretary to the Treasury, Mr Robert Sheldon in the House of Commons on 13 November 1978 (reproduced at [1978] VATTR 266), in which he stated that the Commissioners 'have concluded that, as a general rule, they should continue their policy of not seeking costs against unsuccessful appellants; however they will ask for costs in certain cases so as to provide protection for public funds and the general body of taxpayers. For instance, they will seek costs at those exceptional tribunal hearings of substantial and complex cases where large sums are involved and which are comparable with High Court cases, unless the appeal involves an important general point of law requiring clarification. The Commissioners will also consider seeking costs where the appellant has misused the tribunal procedure — for example, in frivolous or vexatious cases, or where the appellant has first produced at a hearing relevant evidence which ought properly to have been disclosed at an earlier stage and which could have saved public funds had it been produced timeously.' On the facts of the case, the Commissioners were awarded their costs. *Nose Cash & Carry Ltd*, LON/87/311 (VTD 3763).

[2.355] In the case noted at **2.279** above, where an appeal against an estimated assessment was dismissed after a hearing lasting five days, the tribunal awarded costs of £5,657 to the Commissioners. *M Hanif*, MAN/89/747 (VTD 7815).

[2.356] In a case where the tribunal had upheld a penalty on a partnership under what is now *VATA 1994, s 60*, computed at the rate of 90% of the evaded tax, but had reduced the quantum of the assessment in respect of which the penalty was imposed, the Commissioners applied for costs of £6,390. The partnership contended that the costs claimed (most of which related to solicitors employed by the Commissioners) were excessive. The tribunal assessed the costs at £5,251, applying *dicta* in *Re Eastwood (decd)*, CA [1974] 3 All ER 603, and directed that the partnership should pay two-thirds of this amount. *N Ahmed & K Akhtar (t/a The Albany Fish Bar)*, [1993] VATTR 262 (VTD 11509).

[2.357] Following the decision in the case noted at **2.185** above, the Commissioners applied for costs. The tribunal granted the Commissioners' application, observing that the Parliamentary Statement reproduced at [1978] VATTR 266 had indicated that the Commissioners would seek costs following 'tribunal hearings of substantial and complex cases where large sums are involved and which are comparable with High Court cases, unless the appeal involves an important general point of law'. Since the assessment in question charged tax of more than £1,300,000, this was clearly a case where 'large sums are involved' and there was nothing in the Parliamentary Statement to displace 'the general rule that costs should follow the event'. *University of Reading*, [1998] VATDR 27 (VTD 15387).

[2.358] Following the decision in the case noted at **29.170** FOOD, HMRC applied for costs. The tribunal granted the application. Judge Mosedale observed that the company had claimed a repayment of £27,000.000, and that the hearing had lasted for six days. The Parliamentary Statement reproduced at [1978] VATTR 266 had made it clear that HMRC would apply for costs in such cases. *Innocent Ltd v HMRC (No 2)*, [2011] UKFTT 607 (TC); [2011] SFTD 1253, TC01450.

[2.359] Following the decision noted at **57.80** REGISTRATION, on 24 October 2000 the Commissioners issued a further direction under *VATA 1994, Sch 1 para 2*, requiring the couple to register for VAT from 25 November. The couple's accountants lodged a notice of appeal, stating that the couple had divorced. The Commissioners had received information that the couple were continuing to trade from the same café, and in view of previous correspondence from the couple's accountants, the appeal was set down for hearing. The accountants subsequently ceased to act for the couple, and they instructed a solicitor and counsel. At a procedural hearing in November 2001 the case was adjourned until April 2002. At the subsequent hearing, counsel for the appellants informed the tribunal that the wife had ceased to trade in November 2000 (after the issue of the direction in question), and that from that date the business had been split between the husband and his son, but that from April 2002 the business had been transferred to a company. The Commissioners accepted that the wife had ceased to trade, but applied for costs in view of the fact that the couple had withheld information until the date of the hearing. The tribunal awarded costs to the Commissioners, against each of the appellants jointly and severally. The tribunal noted that it appeared that the couple had been 'led into a confrontational situation by advisers' and that counsel acting for them had been 'inadequately instructed' and 'placed in a position of considerable embarrassment on the day of the hearing'. *RD & SM Elder (t/a Riverside Snack Bar)*, EDN/00/161 (VTD 17653).

[2.360] In a case where the tribunal found that a solicitor had reclaimed excessive amounts of input tax, and failed to attend the hearing of his appeal, the Commissioners applied for costs. The tribunal held that the appeal was 'frivolous', and awarded costs of £2,300 to the Commissioners. *G Ross*, MAN/01/454 (VTD 18672).

[2.361] In *Isfa Management Ltd*, 50.23 PENALTIES: EVASION OF TAX, the tribunal awarded costs of £1,000 to the Commissioners.

[2.362] In *Potts*, 50.81 PENALTIES: EVASION OF TAX, the tribunal awarded costs of £2,500 to the Commissioners.

[2.363] Costs were also awarded to the Commissioners in *Ali*, 3.63 ASSESSMENT; *United Society of Poets Ltd*, 36.26 INPUT TAX; *LMB Holdings Ltd*, 36.29 INPUT TAX; *Power TV Ltd*, 36.672 INPUT TAX; *Capital One Bank (Europe) plc (No 2)*, 46.159 PARTIAL EXEMPTION, and *CAL Ingot Manufacturers*, 52.367 PENALTIES: MISDECLARATION.

[2.364] There have been a number of other cases in which costs have been awarded to the Commissioners, where the tribunal has held that the appeal was 'frivolous and vexatious', and which appear to raise no point of general importance. In the interests of space, such cases are not reported individually in this book. For a list of such cases up to and including 30 September 1989, see Tolley's VAT Cases 1990.

[2.365] In the case noted at **24.44** EXEMPTIONS: MISCELLANEOUS, Customs applied for costs. The tribunal dismissed the application, observing that it was Customs' stated practice not to apply for costs unless an appeal 'was exceptional in terms of its complexity and involved large sums of money' or was 'frivolous or vexatious'. The tribunal held that the appeal had not been 'frivolous or vexatious', so that it would not be appropriate to award costs to Customs. *South Herefordshire Golf Club (No 2)*, LON/02/131 (VTD 19767).

Customs' representatives travelling from London to Scotland

[2.366] An appeal was listed for hearing in Edinburgh. The appellant did not attend and was not represented. The tribunal therefore dismissed the appeal. The Commissioners applied for costs in respect of two officers, one of whom was legally qualified, who had travelled from London to present their case. The tribunal held that the appellant should not be made 'liable for more than these services would cost locally, as both are available locally', and awarded total costs of £150. *A Whyte*, EDN/79/4 (VTD 914).

[2.367] A similar decision was reached in another Scottish case, where the appellant had telephoned on the morning of the hearing to state that he would not be attending. The Commissioners, who were represented by a member of their Solicitor's Office, were awarded costs of £320, but the expenses of travelling from London were not awarded, since the Commissioners could have obtained local legal representation. *WM Dempster*, EDN/82/7 (VTD 1316).

Customs' representative engaged in other cases on same day

[2.368] In a Manchester case at which the appellant did not attend, the Commissioners were represented by a member of their Solicitor's Office, who had also been engaged in two other cases on the same day. The Commissioners applied for costs of £126. The tribunal took the view that the officer's expenses should be apportioned equally between the three cases in which he had been engaged, and awarded costs of £42. *The Eye Gee Co Ltd*, MAN/81/154 (VTD 1269).

Customs applying for security for costs of appeal

[2.369] In the case noted at **36.105** INPUT TAX, the tribunal found that two companies, which had reclaimed substantial amounts of input tax, had been involved in 'carousel fraud'. The tribunal dismissed the companies' appeals and awarded costs to Customs. The companies appealed to the Ch D. Customs applied, under *Civil Procedure Rules 1998 (SI 1998/3132), rule 25.12*, for security for the costs of the pending appeal and for security in respect of the order for costs made by the tribunal. The Ch D granted the application, applying the principles laid down in *Hammond Suddard Solicitors v Agrichem International Holdings Ltd*, CA [2001] All ER (D) 258 (Dec). Briggs J held that the evidence showed that it was 'probable that the appellants will not be able to pay the Revenue's costs if they lose the appeal'. He observed that the companies' appeals to the tribunal had been 'funded at very large expense', and that they had 'retained leading tax counsel and a new firm of solicitors to prosecute the appeal'. The evidence indicated that the companies' controlling shareholder had 'both the means and the motive to provide the necessary security if necessary as the price of being able to pursue this appeal'. *Calltell Telecom Ltd v HMRC; Opto Telelinks (Europe) Ltd v HMRC (No 1)*, Ch D [2008] STC 3246; [2008] EWHC 2107 (Ch).

[2.370] A similar decision was reached in the case noted at **36.107** INPUT TAX. *Megtian Ltd v HMRC (No 2)*, Ch D 5 November 2009 unreported.

HMRC applying for costs against third party

[2.371] In the case noted at **36.106** INPUT TAX, the Ch D had struck out an appeal by a company (E) and awarded costs to HMRC. Six days after the Ch D decision, E went into liquidation. HMRC applied for a third party costs order against E's controlling director (M). The Ch D granted the order. Proudman J observed that the tribunal had found that M had given dishonest evidence 'and that he had actual knowledge of the chain of fraudulent transactions. Those findings impacted directly on his personal reputation. He had a clear incentive of his own to clear his name by reversing the effect of the tribunal's findings that he had masterminded a serious VAT fraud'. Applying the principles laid down by Briggs J in *Calltell Telecom Ltd v HMRC*, 2.369 above, 'it is hard to escape the conclusion that the appeal was brought on a speculative "heads I win, tails the Revenue get no cost recovery" basis'. M had treated E as his 'cypher', and had carried on its business for his personal benefit. He had 'lied in evidence to the tribunal and failed to cooperate with either HMRC or the joint liquidators of the company'. Accordingly HMRC were entitled to costs against M. *Europeans Ltd v HMRC (No 3)*, Ch D [2011] EWHC 948 (Ch); [2011] STC 1449.

HMRC applying for 1986 Rules to continue to apply to appeal

[2.372] A company (H) reclaimed input tax. HMRC rejected the claim on the basis that the relevant transactions were connected to MTIC fraud. H appealed in June 2008. While the appeal was pending, HMRC applied to the First-Tier Tribunal for a direction that the *VAT Tribunal Rules 1986 (SI 1986/590), rule 29* should apply to the proceedings rather than the *Tribunal Procedure (First-Tier Tribunal) (Tax Chamber) Rules 2009 (SI 2009/273), rule 10*. Judge Berner rejected the application, finding that H had 'a reasonable and legitimate expectation' that the 2009 rules would apply. He observed that 'there is no explanation for the failure of HMRC to seek a direction of the tribunal to apply the 1986 Rules at an earlier stage. The longer the period from 1 April 2009 during which no application is made, and no other indication is given that the tribunal will be asked to make a direction, the greater the weight that must be attached to the reasonable expectation that the other party will have as to the applicability of the 2009 Rules to the entire appeal.' *Hawkeye Communications Ltd v HMRC (No 1)*, [2010] UKFTT 636 (TC); [2011] SFTD 250, TC00875. (*Note.* For subsequent developments in this case, see 2.275 above.)

[2.373] The decision in *Hawkeye Communications Ltd v HMRC (No 1)*, 2.372 above, was applied in the similar subsequent case of *Atlantic Electronics Ltd v HMRC (No 2)*, [2011] UKFTT 276 (TC); [2011] SFTD 700, TC01138.

Tribunal awarding costs to Commissioners without application

[2.374] See the cases noted at 2.496 to 2.499 below.

Costs where the appellant was successful: general principles

[2.375] Following a successful appeal against an estimated assessment, the appellant partnership made an application for costs. The tribunal found that the aggressive tone of a letter which the partnership's accountants had sent to the Commissioners had led to a degree of animosity which was not conducive to a settlement between the parties, and made a deduction for this in computing the award of costs. The partnership appealed to the QB, which reversed the tribunal's decision on this point and awarded the partnership its costs in full (including costs relating to correspondence preceding the issue of the assessment). Rose J held that a settlement had been inhibited by the contentions of the Commissioners, rather than by those of the partnership. *L & E Zoungrou (t/a Highlands Steak House) v C & E Commrs*, QB 1988, [1989] STC 313. (*Note.* The decision here was not followed, and was implicitly disapproved, by Burton J in the subsequent case of *Dave*, 2.439 below.)

[2.376] In the case noted at 38.38 INSURANCE, the tribunal allowed a company's appeals against two assessments, holding on the evidence that the officer responsible for the assessments had not acted to the best of his judgment. However, the tribunal refused to award costs to the company, on the grounds that the company had given evidence which was untruthful. The QB dismissed the company's appeal against this decision. Lightman J held that it was clear, as a matter of principle and authority, that where a party had given false evidence on an issue relevant to the court's decision, the court could take that into account when deciding the question of costs. On the evidence, the tribunal was entitled to refuse to award the company the costs of its appeal. *Dicta* of Parker LJ in *Baylis Baxter Ltd v Sabath*, CA [1958] 1 WLR 529; [1958] 2 All ER 209 applied. *North East Garages Ltd v C & E Commrs*, QB [1999] STC 1057.

[2.377] A couple who owned a snack bar, and had successfully appealed against an estimated assessment, applied for costs. The tribunal refused the application, holding that an award of costs would be inappropriate in view of the appellants' uncooperative attitude to the Commissioners' officers. *Mr & Mrs AJ Williams (t/a Bridge St Snack Bar)*, CAR/77/191 (VTD 593).

[2.378] In a case where an assessment was reduced to £56, the tribunal awarded the appellant costs of £300. The appellant had also claimed tribunal costs of £916 in respect of his own time in relation to the appeal. The tribunal rejected this claim, holding that 'an appellant in a fiscal matter is not entitled to charge at profit costs for his attempts, even though successful, to avoid the effect of an assessment'. *GJ Hollingworth*, MAN/77/278 (VTD 672).

[2.379] Following a successful appeal by a partnership which operated a restaurant, the tribunal awarded the appellants only half of their costs, holding that they were the architects of their own misfortune because of the unsatisfactory nature of their accounts and the late stage at which they had supplied essential information. *Yang Sing Chinese Restaurant*, MAN/83/1 (VTD 1757).

[2.380] A similar decision was reached in a successful appeal against a misdeclaration penalty. *J & B Properties (Yorkshire) Ltd*, MAN/92/988 (VTD 9912).

[2.381] In the case noted at **44.52** MOTOR CARS, the tribunal awarded the successful appellant company only 75% of its costs, finding that the company had not made sufficient evidence available to the Commissioners before the hearing. *Sixth Gear Experience Ltd*, MAN/08/234 (VTD 20890).

[2.382] In the case noted at **7.43** BUSINESS, the tribunal rejected an application for costs by the successful appellant company, finding that the company had not made sufficient evidence available to the Commissioners before the hearing. *DS Supplies Ltd*, MAN/95/884 (VTD 13559).

[2.383] In the case noted at **67.118** VALUATION, the appellant applied for costs after the initial hearing. The Commissioners opposed the claim as the decision in the appellant's favour had been a decision in principle only, against which they had lodged an appeal to the QB, and they considered that the application was premature. The tribunal accepted the Commissioners' contention that it would be premature to award costs. *BH Bright*, LON/88/1393X (VTD 4339). (*Note.* For a further subsequent application by the appellant, see 2.403 below.)

[2.384] The successful appellant in the case noted at **51.84** PENALTIES: FAILURE TO NOTIFY applied for costs of more than £4,300, including more than £3,600 in respect of his accountant's services. The tribunal held that the accountant's claim to have written 41 letters and spent 63 hours on the case was excessive, and awarded costs of £2,300, representing £2,000 in respect of the accountant and £300 in respect of the appellant. *IW Dale*, LON/87/562Z (VTD 4353).

[2.385] In the case noted at **27.48** FINANCE, where the tax in dispute was £166,000, the tribunal awarded costs on the standard basis. The company claimed costs of more than £42,000, which the Commissioners objected to as excessive. The company had been represented by a leading firm of accountants, which had charged hourly rates of £186.30 for a tax partner, £117.35 for a tax senior manager and £91.10 for a tax manager. The tribunal held that these rates were reasonable, but held that the firm had spent excessive time both on the case itself and in preparing its analysis of, and claim for, costs. The tribunal awarded total costs of £30,941 (including £20,000 in respect of the accountants' charges and £8,500 in respect of counsel's fees). *Freight Transport Leasing Ltd*, MAN/89/862 (VTD 7500). (*Note.* For another issue in this case, see **2.396** below.)

[2.386] A company which had successfully appealed against a misdeclaration penalty applied for costs of £2,510, including £1,500 in respect of its accountants' fees (calculated on the basis of 12.5 hours at £120 per hour). The Commissioners objected to the claim, contending that since the appeal had not involved any complex points of law, the amount of time claimed for was excessive. The tribunal rejected this contention, observing that the penalty imposed had been more than £57,000, and that the bill had only covered preparatory advice, since the accountants had not attended the hearing, at which the company had been represented by two of its officers. The tribunal upheld the claim of £1,500 in respect of the accountants, but reduced the claim in respect of the company's officers by £90, making a total award of £2,420. *Telstar Leisure Ltd*, LON/91/2071X (VTD 9126).

[2.387] A successful appellant company applied for costs of more than £7,500, including £3,375 in respect of its accountants; £3,028 in respect of a firm of VAT consultants whom the accountants had engaged to conduct the appeal; and £1,123 in respect of its own employees. The tribunal observed that the fee charged by the VAT consultants should not have exceeded £1,000, and awarded total costs of £3,500. *Small & Co Ltd*, LON/91/255Y (VTD 9642).

[2.388] A company, which had successfully appealed against a misdeclaration penalty, applied for costs of more than £5,000. £2,137 of the claim related to its solicitors; £2,000 to its accountants, and £1,002 to the company's own expenses, including 14 hours of the chairman's time. The tribunal accepted that the claim in respect of the solicitors was reasonable, but held that the claim in respect of the accountants should be reduced to £750, and that the claim for the company's own expenses was not allowable (except with regard to travelling expenses). The tribunal held that 'there was no logical distinction between a company and a litigant in person', so that the company was not entitled to claim costs in respect of the time expended by its chairman. *Rupert Page Developments Ltd*, [1993] VATTR 152 (VTD 9823). (*Note.* In the subsequent case of *Jonathan Alexander Ltd v Proctor*, CA 1995, [1996] 1 WLR 518; [1996] 2 All ER 334, the CA held that the term 'litigant in person' did not apply to a company represented by one of its directors. Despite this, however, the effect of the CA decision in *Nader*, **2.389** below, appears to be that a company is not entitled to be awarded costs in respect of time spent by its directors in preparing for an appeal. See also the subsequent tribunal decision in *Refrigeration Spares (Manchester) Ltd*, **2.471** below.)

[2.389] The successful appellant in the case noted at **1.4** AGENTS applied for costs, and the tribunal directed that the award be assessed by a Taxing Master. The appellant submitted claims for £67,827 in respect of loss of income from his business (which he had temporarily closed pending the hearing of the appeal) and for £17,172 in respect of loss of profit for the time he had spent on the case, together with interest. The Taxing Master rejected these claims and the CA upheld the Master's decision. The *Litigants in Person (Costs and Expenses) Act 1975* did not apply to VAT tribunals. Accordingly, an award of costs to a successful litigant in person could not exceed those costs recoverable at common law. The appellant could only recover out-of-pocket expenses and was not entitled to remuneration for the time he had spent in conducting the appeal. Since the costs were (by virtue of *Tribunals Rules, rule 29(5)*) a civil debt rather than a judgment debt, the appellant was also not entitled to interest on costs. *R Nader (t/a Try Us) v C & E Commrs*, CA [1993] STC 806. (*Note. The Rules of the Supreme Court 1965 (SI 1965/1776)*, and their precursors, refer to the 'taxation of costs', and to a 'Taxing Master'. With effect from 26 April 1999, these rules have largely been replaced by the *Civil Procedure Rules 1998 (SI 1998/3132)*, which refer instead to the 'assessment of costs', and to a 'costs judge'.)

[2.390] A successful appellant company applied for costs of more than £18,000 (including £6,400 attributable to its solicitors, £3,600 attributable to its accountants, £5,000 attributable to one of its directors, and £3,500 attributable to counsel). The Commissioners agreed to pay costs attributable to counsel's fees, but refused to agree the remainder of the claim, considering that it was excessive. The tribunal reviewed the claim in detail and awarded £2,500 in respect of the solicitors' fees and £1,000 in respect of its accountants' fees, observing that the remainder of the amounts claimed related to work done before the appeal had been lodged. The tribunal rejected the company's claim for £5,000 attributable to work done by its director, observing that although the director was a qualified valuer, the bill in question did not relate to work 'done by him as a professional adviser'. *Broadway Video (Wholesale) Ltd*, [1994] VATTR 271 (VTD 11935, 12446). (*Note. The tribunal also held that the company was not entitled to interest on the costs—see 2.533 below.*)

[2.391] The partnership which was successful in the case noted at **48.45** PAYMENT OF TAX subsequently applied for costs of more than £22,000. This included an hourly rate of £375 for a partner in an accountancy firm, and an hourly rate of £225 for a chartered tax advisor employed by the firm. The Commissioners objected to the claim on the grounds that these hourly rates were excessive. The tribunal awarded costs on the basis that the appropriate hourly rate was £280 for the partner and £160 for the advisor. *Mr & Mrs J King (t/a Barbury Shooting School)*, [2003] VATDR 471 (VTD 18313).

[2.392] In *Constantgreen Ltd*, 2.516 below, the successful appellant company was represented by a solicitor. The tribunal awarded costs of £100 per hour in respect of the solicitor's time.

Award of costs where appellant not legally represented

[2.393] See the cases noted at 2.449 *et seq.* below.

Award of costs where company appellant represented by director

[2.394] See the cases noted at 2.461 *et seq.* below.

Application for costs on indemnity basis

[2.395] See the cases noted at 2.473 *et seq.* below.

Failure by Commissioners to comply with award of costs

[2.396] In the case noted at 27.15 FINANCE, the tribunal made an interim award of costs of £10,000 to the appellant company pending the hearing of the application noted at 2.385 above. The Commissioners were ordered to pay this amount within one month. However, the Commissioners did not pay the sum in question until ten weeks after the date of the award. The tribunal met again to consider the award of a penalty against the Commissioners under what is now *VATA 1994, Sch 12 para 10*. The £10,000 had been paid by the time of this hearing, and the tribunal chose not to award any penalty. However, the tribunal rejected the Commissioners' contention that the provisions of *Sch 12 para 10* did not apply to the Commissioners, and commented that 'we strongly disapprove of the lack of efficiency which has led to the appellant's being deprived for over a month of a substantial sum of money to which it was entitled'. *Freight Transport Leasing Ltd*, [1992] VATTR 120 (VTD 7000, VTD 7515).

Appellant represented by VAT consultant working on contingency basis

[2.397] In a case where an appeal had been allowed on the grounds that the Commissioners had failed to serve their Statement of Case within the prescribed time limits, the appellant applied for an award of the costs incurred by a VAT consultant who had represented him. The Commissioners objected to the claim on the grounds that the consultant had been working for the appellant on a contingency basis, and that if no award of costs were made, the appellant would have no liability to pay the consultant. The QB upheld the Commissioners' contentions and held that the amount claimed was not allowable. Macpherson J held that 'where a successful party has no liability to pay those acting for him, he has incurred no expense in respect of which an order for costs can be made in his favour'. In the absence of an award of costs, the appellant had no liability to pay the consultant for his services. Accordingly, no award could be made. *C & E Commrs v VR Vaz*, QB 1994, [1995] STC 14. (*Notes.* (1) The tribunal had not issued a public report of its decision to allow the substantive appeal. Compare, however, *Young*, 2.152 above, and *Faccenda Chicken Ltd*, 2.157 above. (2) Compare the subsequent decision in *Tel-Ka Talk Ltd v HMRC*, 2.445 below.)

Costs where the appellant was partly successful

[2.398] In a case where an assessment had been reduced from £991 to £290, the appellant applied for costs of £756, the bulk of which were those of his accountants who represented him at the appeal. The tribunal awarded 70% of the admissible costs, based on the proportion by which the tax was reduced. In arriving at the admissible costs, it deducted £300 in respect of work which ought to have been done in relation to the rendering of the applicant's returns. (The tribunal also held that VAT should not be added to costs awarded to a taxable person and costs should be on a party to party basis.) *SK Ahmad*, [1976] VATTR 128 (VTD 266).

[2.399] The Commissioners issued an estimated assessment on a partnership, charging tax of £2,769. On appeal, the assessment was reduced to £1,175. There had been an abortive first hearing of the appeal, and in the interval between the first and the second hearing the Commissioners had offered to reduce the assessment to £1,568, to which the partners did not respond. The partners applied for an award of costs. The tribunal observed that the need for an estimated assessment had arisen because the partners' records were defective, and the Commissioners could not be called on to bear the partners' costs because the estimate turned out to be excessive. *J & J Brown (t/a Shaw's Bar)*, [1977] VATTR 253 (VTD 393).

[2.400] In a case where two assessments on a family partnership had been reduced to an agreed amount before the hearing, the partnership applied for costs. The senior partner, who was blind, had had to memorise details of the case, and the partnership applied for £670 in respect of his time, as well as for lesser amounts in respect of other staff. The QB held that a litigant in person was not entitled to an order for costs in respect of time expended in preparing a case to be heard by a VAT tribunal. The *Litigants in Person (Costs and Expenses) Act 1975* did not apply to VAT tribunals, and accordingly the tribunal's power under *rule 29* of the *Tribunals Rules* was confined to costs recoverable at common law. *C & E Commrs v D W Ross & Others*, QB [1990] STC 353; [1990] 2 All ER 65. (*Note*. The decision in this case was approved by the CA in *Nader*, 2.389 above.)

[2.401] The appellant in the case noted at **36.506** INPUT TAX and **62.190** SUPPLY applied for costs. He had succeeded in one of the two issues in the appeal, but had been unsuccessful in the other. The Commissioners contended that in the circumstances there should be no award of costs. The tribunal rejected this contention and awarded the appellant one half of the costs of his appeal and the whole of the costs of the application. *EA Kilburn*, MAN/87/277 (VTD 4866).

[2.402] The appellant company in the case noted at **21.24** EDUCATION subsequently applied for costs. The tribunal awarded costs of £340, including £250 in respect of the services of an accountant (representing five hours at £50 per hour). *North West Leicestershire Youth Training Scheme Ltd*, MAN/88/548 (VTD 4929).

[2.403] The appellant in the case noted at **67.119** VALUATION applied for costs. The tribunal dismissed her application, holding that as her appeal had only succeeded with regard to 33.5% of her supplies, there should be no order as to costs. *BH Bright*, LON/88/393 (VTD 5022).

[2.404] In a case where an estimated assessment had been reduced from £5,051 to £2,469, the appellant applied for costs. The tribunal held that the appellant was partly responsible for the assessment being raised as she had been dilatory in supplying information to the Commissioners, but awarded costs of £300 in respect of her accountant's services. The tribunal rejected a claim for costs in respect of the appellant's own time, applying the QB decision in *Ross*, 2.400 above, and holding that the *Litigants in Person (Costs and Expenses) Act 1975* had no application to VAT tribunals. *VD George*, LON/89/1014Z (VTD 5072).

[2.405] In a case where an estimated assessment had been reduced from £46,000 to £28,060, the company applied for costs of more than £16,000. The Commissioners opposed the application, considering that the case had been prolonged by the behaviour of the company's accountant. The tribunal criticised the accountant for his lack of co-operation, but awarded the company one-half of the costs incurred after the date on which it lodged its appeal. (The company's application had included costs incurred before that date, which the tribunal held to be irrecoverable.) *Salina Ltd*, LON/89/1823Y (VTD 6287).

[2.406] Following the decision in the case noted at **36.7** INPUT TAX, the appellant company applied for costs. The tribunal had dismissed the appeal in question, but the Commissioners had subsequently reduced the assessment under appeal by agreement, to take account of the view which the tribunal had expressed on an alternative issue. The tribunal rejected the application. It had dismissed the company's appeal after specifically finding that the supplies in dispute had not been made to the company. The views it had expressed on the alternative issue were *obiter dicta*. The Commissioners had been under no obligation to reduce the assessment, which they had done 'entirely within their discretion' and 'independently of the appeal'. In the circumstances, each party should pay its own costs with regard to the substantive appeal. The company was ordered to pay costs to the Commissioners in respect of the hearing of the application. *McLean Homes Midland Ltd (No 3)*, MAN/89/363 (VTD 6447).

[2.407] In a case where an estimated assessment had been reduced from £4,082 to £20, the tribunal refused the appellant's application for an award of costs. The reduction in the assessment had been the result of the production by the appellant, at a late stage, of records which had not been available at the time of the control visits which resulted in the assessment. In the circumstances an award of costs was not appropriate. *Nathoo (t/a Kamona Enterprises)*, LON/91/1692 (VTD 6551).

[2.408] A similar decision was reached in a case where an estimated assessment was reduced from £83,000 to £32,000. The tribunal held that, as the appellant had 'systematically concealed sales' and 'wilfully concealed relevant material', his conduct had 'disqualified him from any award of costs'. *A Kocak (t/a Mediterranean Fish Bar)*, LON/98/605 (VTD 17282).

[2.409] In the case noted at **50.103** PENALTIES: EVASION OF TAX, the tribunal awarded costs to the appellant partnership, but declined to sanction an award requested by the partnership in regard to a barrister and solicitor who had both represented it, holding that the case could have been conducted by a solicitor alone. *Café Da Vinci & Da Vinci Too*, EDN/90/132 (VTD 7634).

[2.410] In the case noted at **36.524** and **36.570** INPUT TAX, where the appellant company had been partly successful, the tribunal strongly criticised the company's controlling director for having failed to co-operate with the Commissioners through not providing any information in support of the claims to input tax. On the evidence, the appeal had 'taken place mainly because of (the director's) refusal to give any reasons, until the hearing, as to why the two items might have been purchased for business purposes'. In the circumstances, the company was ordered to pay 75% of the Commissioners' total costs. *Remlock Design Ltd*, LON/92/1124Y (VTD 9146).

[2.411] A company appealed against a default surcharge, contending firstly that the amount of the surcharge was excessive since it had paid part of the tax before the due date, and secondly that it had a reasonable excuse for non-payment of the balance. Shortly before the hearing of the appeal the Commissioners accepted the company's first contention, admitting that the amount of the surcharge was excessive. At the hearing of the appeal, the tribunal rejected the company's second contention and upheld the reduced surcharge. However, the tribunal awarded costs to the company in respect of the time spent by its accountant in disputing the amount of the surcharge. *Retainco (51) Ltd (t/a The Royal Hotel)*, MAN/93/589 (VTD 11265).

[2.412] Following the case noted at **50.114** PENALTIES: EVASION OF TAX, the appellant applied for costs. The tribunal rejected his application, observing that the validity of the assessment and penalty had been upheld and that the appellant had been found to have acted dishonestly. Therefore, despite the mitigation of the penalty, an award of costs was not appropriate. *JO Kyriacou*, LON/92/2098A (VTD 12003).

[2.413] In the case noted at **67.155** VALUATION, the appellant company applied for costs. The Commissioners opposed the application, contending firstly that there should be no award of costs since the appeal should have been stood over pending the CJEC decision in *Elida Gibbs Ltd*, **22.235** EUROPEAN COMMUNITY LAW, and alternatively that the award of costs should be restricted since, although the company had been successful on the issue relating to its output tax, it had been unsuccessful on an alternative contention relating to input tax (which had been the subject of the Court decisions noted at **2.172** above and **2.313** above). The tribunal rejected the Commissioners' first contention, observing that the facts in *Elida Gibbs Ltd* were distinguishable and might not have been determinative of the case. However, the tribunal accepted the Commissioners' second contention and awarded only 75% of the company's costs. The tribunal held that the input tax issue had been 'a separate issue' on which the appellant company had failed. Applying the principles laid down by Nourse LJ in *Re Elgindata (No 2)*, CA [1992] 1 WLR 1207; [1993] 1 All ER 232, the company should therefore 'be deprived of that part of its costs which related to the time spent in arguing (that) issue'. *Conoco Ltd*, [1997] VATDR 47 (VTD 14814).

[2.414] The Commissioners issued an estimated assessment on a company which operated a restaurant. The tribunal reduced the amount of the assessment, finding that the company had suppressed some of its takings but that the amount of the assessment was excessive. The tribunal made no award of costs to either side. The company appealed, contending that it should have been awarded 50% of its costs. The Ch D rejected this contention and dismissed the appeal. Lawrence Collins J held that, since the tribunal had found that the company had suppressed some of its takings, there was 'an entirely rational basis for the decision not to award the appellant part of its costs'. *Summer Palace Ltd v C & E Commrs*, Ch D 2004, [2005] STC 564; [2004] EWHC 2804 (Ch).

[2.415] In the case noted at **67.82** VALUATION, where an assessment was substantially reduced, the tribunal held that the appellant was entitled to an award of the costs, but that the award should be restricted because of time wasted by his adviser. The chairman (Mr. Oliver) held that 'litigation demands a focused and disciplined approach by both parties. This is not evident from the correspondence originating from the appellant's adviser.' Accordingly, the costs should be 'restricted to the costs attributable to two days in court, the cost of the time spent agreeing and preparing the bundle, the cost of (the appellant's) attendance and the costs of complying with any directions given by this Tribunal'. On the evidence, the chairman held that 'the costs incurred in corresponding with the Commissioners can properly be described as costs of and incidental to and consequent on the hearing'. *FP Whiffen (t/a FP Whiffen Opticians) (No 2)*, LON/01/1351 (VTD 18969).

[2.416] In the case noted at **36.85** INPUT TAX, the First-Tier Tribunal awarded the company 90% of its costs. The company appealed to the Ch D, which upheld the tribunal decision. Lewison J observed that 'a tribunal is entitled to make a partial costs order when a party has not been wholly successful; and it is equally well-known that a party who exaggerates his case or who gives false evidence may be deprived of part of his costs'. *Brayfal Ltd v HMRC (No 5)*, Ch D [2011] EWHC 407 (Ch); [2011] STC 1482.

[2.417] A company, which had been represented by a VAT consultant, applied for costs of £12,779. The tribunal awarded costs of £7,000. Judge Nowlan observed that 'there were some unsatisfactory aspects to the claim'. *PSI Engineering Ltd v HMRC*, [2011] UKFTT 765 (TC), TC01602.

Customs refusing to give trader details of suppliers' records

[2.418] The Commissioners issued an assessment on the proprietors of a fish and chip shop, after discovering that their purchase records did not include a number of transactions indicated in the records of the relevant suppliers. The tribunal reviewed the evidence in detail and upheld the assessment in principle, but reduced it in the case of two of the suppliers, holding that the relevant suppliers' records were unreliable. The tribunal expressed concern that the Commissioners had 'failed to deal with the appellants' requests for information about supplies made to them', and observed that there appeared to be 'an assumption by the Commissioners that all suppliers whose sales records differed from their customers' purchase records were trading honestly, whilst all their customers were doing just the opposite'. The tribunal held that the effect of *FA 1989, s 182* was that the Commissioners should authorise the disclosure of information to one taxpayer about another 'where a supplier claims to have made more supplies to a taxpayer than the taxpayer admits to having received. If disclosure is restricted to the suppliers' sales record, there can surely be no objection to it for the suppliers' sales record should simply mirror the taxpayer's purchase record.' In such cases, 'disclosure by the Commissioners of their evidence is an absolute requirement in best judgment cases where the assessment is based on undisclosed purchases. Only in that way can the person supplied hope to obtain justice; in human rights terms, there must be equality of arms.' The tribunal directed that the Commissioners should pay 'those expenses which were necessarily incurred on behalf of the appellants to obtain that information which the Commissioners held but refused to disclose', and which 'ought to have been disclosed'. *C & K Papachristoforou (t/a Norton Fisheries)*, MAN/96/209 (VTD 17113). (*Note.* For other cases where suppliers' records were held to be unreliable, see *Qaisar*, 50.55 PENALTIES: EVASION OF TAX; *Andreucci*, 50.144 PENALTIES: EVASION OF TAX, and *Mann*, 50.145 PENALTIES: EVASION OF TAX.)

Appeal against assessment dismissed but appeal against penalty allowed

[2.419] In the case noted at 52.195 PENALTIES: MISDECLARATION, a trader had appealed against an assessment charging output tax and a misdeclaration penalty. The tribunal dismissed his appeal against the assessment in principle, but reduced the amount of the assessment, and allowed his appeal against the penalty on the grounds that he had a 'reasonable excuse' for the misdeclaration. The trader applied for costs of £3,700. The Commissioners opposed the application, firstly on the grounds that the appeal had only succeeded in part, and alternatively on the grounds that the trader's accountants had agreed that, if the appeal was unsuccessful, they would only charge him a total fee of £1,000. The tribunal rejected the Commissioners' contentions and allowed the trader's application in full, holding that it was 'irrelevant that only a short amount of time was spent arguing the issue of a serious misdeclaration penalty'. The fact that the accountants had agreed to reduce their fee if the appeal was unsuccessful was not relevant, since the appeal had been partly successful and they had therefore charged a fee of £3,700. *PJ Guntert (t/a Abingdon Scaffolding Co)*, LON/92/2183A (VTD 12127). (*Note.* Compare, however, the subsequent QB decision in *Vaz*, 2.397 above.)

Assessment reduced but penalty upheld

[2.420] In the case noted at 50.8 PENALTIES: EVASION OF TAX, a partnership which operated a restaurant appealed against an assessment and a penalty under *VATA 1994, s 60*. The tribunal directed that the assessment should be reduced, but upheld the penalty. The Commissioners applied for costs. The tribunal observed that much of the evidence given by Customs' officers 'was of little or no use to us in coming to our decision', and directed that the appellants should only pay 85% of the Commissioners' costs. *Standard Tandoori Nepalese Restaurant*, [2000] VATDR 105 (VTD 16597).

Costs where Commissioners' decision or assessment is withdrawn

[2.421] In order to arrive at its employees' emoluments for income tax, a hotel company entered in its pay sheets the value of any meals or accommodation it provided its employees without charge. The Commissioners assessed it on the basis that the amounts entered were the consideration for taxable supplies to the employees. The company appealed and the Commissioners subsequently withdrew the assessment. The tribunal awarded the company costs of £50. *Roxburghe Hotel Ltd*, EDN/77/18 (VTD 456).

[2.422] In a case where a partnership had applied for costs of £4,090, the tribunal awarded costs of £626. *Nara Manufacturers*, MAN/76/146 (VTD 603, VTD 894).

[2.423] In a case where the Commissioners had withdrawn a default surcharge before the hearing, the appellant partnership sought costs in respect of bank interest which it had paid, contending that it would not have incurred the interest had it not had to pay the surcharge. The tribunal refused the partnership's claim, as the partnership had been at fault by not lodging an appeal against the surcharge at the appropriate time, but had lodged a late appeal after receiving a demand for payment. *Aladdin Window Co*, MAN/88/12 (VTD 3026). (*Note.* The case was heard with *Newcastle Double Glazing Ltd*, 2.468 below.)

[2.424] In a similar case, a trader applied for costs of £840. The tribunal awarded costs of £50 only, and awarded £30 to the Commissioners in respect of a summons the appellant had issued to a VAT officer, whose 'testimony could have no relevance to the issues'. *A Adley (t/a Jean Wenham)*, LON/89/1039 (VTD 4798).

[2.425] The Commissioners had attempted to deregister a trader as they had considered that he was not carrying on a business. The trader consulted a chartered accountant who made representations on his behalf, and the Commissioners subsequently accepted that his registration was valid. The trader applied for costs of £767, comprising £392 for the services of the accountant and £375 for the services of another adviser who had recommended the accountant. The tribunal allowed the £392 in respect of the accountant but only awarded £100 in respect of the adviser. The tribunal also awarded £75 in respect of the hearing of the application, making a total award of £567. *AJ Money*, LON/90/669X (VTD 5655).

[2.426] The Commissioners issued an assessment on a partnership on 13 November 1990. On receipt of the assessment, the partnership telephoned its local VAT office to arrange a meeting to discuss the matter. The meeting was arranged for 23 November. On 20 November the partnership submitted a formal appeal against the assessment. At the meeting the partnership satisfied the VAT officers that the assessment was incorrect, and it was withdrawn. The partnership applied for costs in respect of its accountant's time in preparing for and attending the meeting. The Commissioners opposed any award, but the tribunal awarded costs of £309.70. The appeal had not been premature and costs incurred prior to proceedings were allowable, applying *dicta* of Lord Hanworth MR in *SA Pecheries Ostendaises v Merchants Marine Insurance Co*, CA [1928] 1 KB 757 and *Frankenberg v Famous Lasky Film Service*,

[1931] 1 Ch 428. *RM & DJ Jarrett*, [1991] VATTR 435 (VTD 6670). (*Note.* See now, however, the subsequent Ch D decision in *Dave*, **2.439** below.)

[2.427] The decision in *Jarrett*, **2.426** above, was applied in a case where the Commissioners had sought to register a college on the basis that it was conducted on a profit-making basis and was therefore ineligible for exemption under the legislation then in force, but had subsequently accepted that the college's supplies were exempt from VAT. The Commissioners contended that an award of costs was inappropriate since draft accounts which they had inspected indicated that the college was making substantial profits, and that the college had not initially indicated that the profits would be reinvested rather than distributed to its shareholders. The tribunal rejected this contention, holding that the college had not acted unreasonably and was entitled to an award of costs. Since the college had not submitted a quantified claim, the amount of the award was left to be determined by a Taxing Master of the Supreme Court. *Surrey College Ltd*, [1992] VATTR 181 (VTD 9087). (*Notes.* (1) The relevant supplies would now qualify for exemption under *VATA 1994, Sch 9, Group 6.* (2) The *Rules of the Supreme Court 1965 (SI 1965/1776)*, and their precursors, referred to the 'taxation of costs', and to a 'Taxing Master'. With effect from 26 April 1999, these rules were largely replaced by the *Civil Procedure Rules 1998 (SI 1998/3132)*, which refer instead to the 'assessment of costs', and to a 'costs judge'.)

[2.428] In a case where three assessments had been withdrawn, the appellants claimed costs totalling £6,300. £1,500 of this was attributable to the appellants' usual accountants, and £4,800 was attributable to a major firm of accountants who had been requested to assist with the case. The Commissioners contended that the claim was excessive, and that there had been a duplication of costs because of the use of two different firms of accountants. The tribunal awarded total costs of £4,500. *P Maxwell & B Hodges*, LON/91/920, LON/91/1402 & LON/91/1436 (VTD 8887).

[2.429] In a case where a default surcharge had been withdrawn, the tribunal rejected an application by the appellant company for costs, observing that the company had been dilatory in providing evidence in support of its contentions. *SKN Electronics Ltd*, MAN/92/1667 (VTD 10210).

[2.430] A similar decision was reached in a case where the tribunal found that a company had been dilatory in providing evidence in support of its claim to bad debt relief. *City Fine Wine plc*, LON/93/1600A (VTD 12947).

[2.431] A similar decision was reached in *Compound Semiconductor Technologies Ltd*, EDN/99/165 (VTD 17088).

[2.432] In a case where the Commissioners had withdrawn a requirement for a company to provide security under what is now *VATA 1994, Sch 11 para 4*, the company applied for costs, and the tribunal awarded it costs of £750. *London Express Ltd*, LON/93/1213A (VTD 12375).

[2.433] In a case where costs were awarded to a sole trader following the withdrawal of an assessment, the tribunal chairman observed that the accountant's charges of £120 per hour were not 'unreasonable for an experienced practitioner in this highly specialised and contentious field'. *JC Dilley*, LON/92/761 (VTD 12617).

[2.434] The Commissioners issued an assessment on a trader who operated a removals business. He appealed, and the assessment was subsequently withdrawn by the Commissioners. The trader applied for costs. The Commissioners refused to pay his costs and the trader appealed to the tribunal. The tribunal dismissed his application, holding that the appeal had been settled by an agreement within what is now *VATA 1994, s 85*, and observing that 'if agreements are reached before any appeal is heard, then costs, if appropriate, would normally form part of any concluded agreement'. The tribunal chairman (Miss Plumptre, sitting alone) observed that she could 'find nothing in (*VATA 1994, s 83**) which would give this tribunal jurisdiction to hear this appeal'. *JJJ McGinty (t/a Alton Transport)*, LON/94/912A (VTD 12671). (*Note*. No cases were cited in the decision. Compare *Jarrett*, **2.426** above, and *Surrey College Ltd*, **2.427** above.)

[2.435] In a subsequent appeal by the same trader, the tribunal again refused to make an award of costs. The tribunal held that, although it had jurisdiction under *Tribunals Rules, rule 29* to make an order for costs when an appeal had been determined under *VATA 1994, s 85*, any agreement to conclude an appeal should have the effect of disposing of the dispute between the parties. Accordingly, any application for costs should either have been incorporated in the agreement, or brought to the attention of the tribunal at the time the agreement was recorded, or dealt with within the 30-day 'cooling-off' period provided by *s 85(2)*. *JJJ McGinty (t/a Alton Transport)*, [1995] VATDR 193 (VTD 13463). (*Note*. The decision here discusses the decision in *Taylor*, **2.71** above, but does not refer to *Jarrett*, **2.426** above, or *Surrey College Ltd*, **2.427** above.)

[2.436] A medical partnership appealed against a ruling by the Commissioners. After correspondence, the Commissioners withdrew the ruling. The partnership's accountant claimed costs of £7,500 plus VAT. The Commissioners considered that the claim was excessive, and offered to pay £2,864 plus VAT. The tribunal awarded costs of £4,250 plus VAT. The accountant also claimed further costs of £5,235 plus VAT in respect of the hearing. The tribunal held that this was 'excessive', and awarded £1,500 plus VAT. *Dr GP Ridsdill-Smith & Partners*, LON/99/1250 (VTD 16992).

[2.437] In a Scottish case where Customs withdrew an assessment shortly before the hearing of the appeal, the tribunal held that 'Customs' conduct in belatedly withdrawing the assessment, and failing to provide any rational explanation to justify doing so, falls well below the standard the Tribunal has come to expect of Customs. We mark our disapproval by finding Customs liable in expenses on an agent client basis.' *Rangers Football Club plc*, EDN/04/155 (VTD 19159).

[2.438] See also *Serpes*, **2.460** below.

Costs relating to correspondence prior to issue of assessment

[2.439] In an excise duty case, the Commissioners informed a garage proprietor in June 1998 that they were considering issuing an assessment. Following further enquiries, they issued assessments in October 1998 and confirmed them (on review) in December 1998. The proprietor appealed in January 1999. Following prolonged correspondence, the Commissioners withdrew the assessments before the hearing of the appeal. They agreed to pay the proprietor's costs from the date of their review in December 1998, but refused to pay costs of £9,975, incurred between June and December 1998. The tribunal allowed the proprietor's appeal but the Ch D reversed this decision. Burton J held that costs incurred prior to the date of the review were not allowable. *C & E Commrs v M Dave*, Ch D [2002] STC 900; [2002] EWHC 969(Ch). (*Note.* Although this is an excise duty case, the principles are clearly also relevant to VAT.)

Accountant's time charged at £695.75 per hour—whether unreasonable

[2.440] In two cases which were heard together, two companies appealed against decisions by the Commissioners. After correspondence, the Commissioners withdrew the decisions and each of the companies applied for costs of £7,312, relating to work carried out by a major accountancy firm. The claim included an hourly rate of £695.75 for a partner in the firm and £561.20 for a senior employee, while an 'assistant consultant' was charged at £126.50 per hour. The Commissioners considered that the claim was excessive, and offered to pay £3,334. The Commissioners contended that the maximum allowable rate would be £375 per hour in respect of a partner and £95 per hour in respect of an assistant consultant. The Commissioners also considered that the number of hours claimed was excessive, and that some of the work need not have been done by a partner but could have been done by 'somebody less senior'. The tribunal reviewed the evidence in detail and held that the fees charged by the firm were not 'excessive or disproportionate' but disallowed some elements of the claim, holding that 'the amount of time spent in relation to the costs claim is disproportionate'. *Avantgo Ltd*, LON/00/1006; *Placeware Ltd*, LON/00/1007 (VTD 17363).

Award of costs to sole trader—appropriate hourly rate

[2.441] The Commissioners withdrew a statutory demand which had been issued to a sole trader (C). The registrar held that there should be no award of costs. C appealed to the CA, claiming costs of £8,000 (computed as 8 hours at £1,000 per hour). The CA held that C was entitled to costs, but that the sum which he had claimed was excessive. Robert Walker LJ observed that the effect of the *Civil Procedure Rules* was that 'a litigant in person is entitled to whichever is the lowest of, first, his actual loss of earnings or wages, as proved by his evidence; second, two-thirds of what lawyers of appropriate standing would have charged; and, third, the sum of £9.25 per hour'. Sedley LJ observed that 'not even the most overpaid partner, in the most prestigious firm of City solicitors, would be allowed to claim £1,000 an hour for his services'. The CA awarded costs of £160 (computed as 17.3 hours at £9.25 per hour). *DL Chitolie v C & E Commrs*, CA 30 November 1999 unreported. (*Note.* For a subsequent appeal involving the same appellant, where costs were awarded to the Commissioners, see **68.1** WAREHOUSED GOODS AND FREE ZONES.)

Assessment issued because of misleading information

[2.442] In a case where the Commissioners withdrew an assessment under appeal, the tribunal refused the appellant's application for costs, finding that the need for an assessment had arisen because the appellant had given inaccurate information to VAT officers. *D Lawton*, MAN/77/237 (VTD 576).

[2.443] A similar decision was reached in *KJ Gagliardi*, CAR/78/29 (VTD 667).

Further proceedings stayed, subject to the award of costs

[2.444] In May 1979 the Commissioners issued a ruling that certain supplies by the British Institute of Management (BIM) were exempt. Because of BIM's input tax position, it was in its interest for the supplies to be treated as standard-rated. BIM therefore appealed and the appeal was fixed for hearing on 30 October 1979. Shortly before that date, the Commissioners informed BIM that they were withdrawing their decision and agreed that the supplies were still standard-rated. The tribunal awarded BIM costs of £1,720 (but rejected BIM's application for costs incurred prior to receipt of the Commissioners' ruling in May 1979). *British Institute of Management (No 2)*, [1980] VATTR 42 (VTD 900). (*Note*. The decision was subsequently approved by the Ch D in *Dave*, 2.439 above.)

Company represented by solicitor working on contingency basis

[2.445] A company (T), which traded in mobile telephones, claimed a repayment of input tax. HMRC initially rejected the claim and T appealed. Following the ECJ decision in *Optigen Ltd*, 22.115 EUROPEAN COMMUNITY LAW, HMRC withdrew their decision and made the repayment. T applied for costs. HMRC rejected the claim on the grounds that the solicitor who had represented T had being doing so on a contingency basis, and that 'contingency fees are not enforceable in the VAT and Duties Tribunal and indeed are illegal on the grounds of champerty'. Judge Hurst rejected this contention, holding that the VAT Tribunal was not a 'court' for the purposes of *Solicitors Act 1974*, and that the contingency fee agreement was lawful. Judge Hurst specifically declined to follow the principles laid down by Buckley LJ in *Wallersteiner v Moir (No 2)*, QB [1975] QB 373 and Oliver LJ in *Trendtex Trading Corporation v Credit Suisse*, CA [1981] QB 629 (which HMRC had cited as authorities). *Tel-Ka Talk Ltd v HMRC*, HC [2010] EWHC 90175 (Costs); [2011] STC 497. (*Notes*. (1) Judge Hurst's decision fails to refer to the QB decision in *C & E Commrs v VR Vaz*, 2.397 above. (2) For the principle of 'champerty', see the judgment of Lord Mustill in *Giles v Thompson*, HL 1993, [1994] 1 AC 142; [1993] 3 All ER 321 and the judgment of Lord Hoffmann in *Norglen Ltd v Reeds Rains Prudential Ltd*, HL [1999] 2 AC 1.)

Costs claimed on indemnity basis

[2.446] The Commissioners issued an assessment charging tax of more than £650,000 on a company which supplied and fitted hearing aids. The Commissioners subsequently accepted the company's contention that the fitting of hearing aids was an exempt supply at the relevant time, and withdrew the assessment. The company applied for costs on the indemnity basis. The tribunal rejected this contention, applying *Bowen-Jones v Bowen-Jones*, [1986] 3 All ER 163, and holding that 'an award of costs on the indemnity basis will only be made in exceptional circumstances'. The tribunal approved an award of costs on the standard basis, to be taxed by a district registrar under *VAT Tribunals Rules 1986, rule 29(1)(b)*. *Ultratone Ltd*, MAN/90/299 (VTD 5536). (*Notes*. (1) The supply of hearing aids is no longer exempt following changes to what is now *VATA 1994, Sch 9, Group 7* by *FA 1988*. Compare *Coleman*, 33.53 HEALTH AND WELFARE. (2) For cases where costs were awarded on the indemnity basis, see 2.473 *et seq*. below.)

Tribunal Procedure (First-Tier Tribunal) (Tax Chamber) Rules (SI 2009/273)

[2.447] A company (B) discovered that another company had been using its VAT registration number. It informed HMRC of this, and took court proceedings against the other company. However HMRC issued assessments charging output tax in respect of invoices which the other company had issued. B appealed, and HMRC subsequently withdrew the assessments. B applied to the First-Tier Tribunal for costs, contending that HMRC had acted unreasonably in issuing the assessments. The tribunal dismissed the application. Judge Berner held that the effect of *Tribunal Procedure (First-Tier Tribunal) (Tax Chamber) Rules (SI 2009/273), rule 10* was that the tribunal's jurisdiction was 'limited to considering actions of a party in the course of "the proceedings", that is to say proceedings before the Tribunal whilst it has jurisdiction over the appeal. It is not possible under the 2009 Rules, any more than it was under the Special Commissioners' regulations, for a party to rely upon the unreasonable behaviour of the other party prior to the commencement of the appeal, at some earlier stage in the history of the tax affairs of the taxpayer, nor, even if unreasonable behaviour were established for a period over which the tribunal does have jurisdiction, can costs incurred before that period be ordered.' On the evidence here, while it was arguable that HMRC had acted unreasonably in issuing the assessments, they had not acted unreasonably in defending or conducting the proceedings, and 'the decision to withdraw the assessment was taken and notified in a timely fashion in the context of the commencement of the appeal process'. *Bulkliner Intermodal Ltd v HMRC*, [2010] SFTD 1198; [2010] UKFTT 395 (TC), TC00677.

[2.448] A company (T) claimed a substantial repayment of VAT, relating to supplies which had been treated as taxable under UK law, but should have been treated as exempt under *Article 13B(f)* of the *EC Sixth Directive* (see HMRC Business Brief 20/06). HMRC initially rejected the claim on the basis that the relevant supplies had been made by one of T's subsidiaries, rather than by T itself. T appealed, contending that as the representative member of the relevant VAT group, it was entitled to the repayment. Shortly before the hearing of the appeal, HMRC withdrew the disputed decision. T applied for costs. The tribunal granted the application. Judge Clark held that 'HMRC had acted unreasonably in defending and conducting the proceedings'. *Thomas Holdings Ltd v HMRC*, [2011] UKFTT 656 (TC), TC01498.

Costs where the appellant was not legally represented

Company appellant represented by director

[2.449] See the cases noted at 2.461 *et seq*. below.

Appellant represented by chartered accountant

[2.450] In the case noted at **3.25** ASSESSMENT, the trader, who had success-fully appealed against an estimated assessment, applied for costs of £2,201, comprising the costs of the services of the chartered accountant who had conducted the matter on her behalf, plus the costs of the application itself. The Commissioners opposed the application, contending that 'costs' in *Tribunals Rules, rule 29* should be confined to 'legal costs', i.e. costs recoverable in the High Court and amounts charged by solicitors. The tribunal rejected this. Under *Tribunals Rules, rule 25* 'any person' may represent an appellant and it would be 'contrary to natural justice and to the construction of *rules 25* and *29* to hold that a party is entitled to recover the taxed costs of his solicitor for conducting an appeal on his behalf whereas he is precluded from recovering the taxed costs of his accountant for performing precisely the same task, and possibly with more expertise so far as figures are concerned.' Accordingly the tribunal awarded the amount claimed (except for the costs relating to the unsuccessful interlocutory application noted at **2.67** above). *K Taylor (t/a Jeans)*, MAN/75/5 (VTD 163B).

[2.451] The successful appellant company in the case noted at **1.81** AGENTS applied for costs of £944. The company had been represented at the hearing by its company secretary, a certified accountant who was not a shareholder in the company. The Commissioners opposed the application, contending that since the accountant held the post of company secretary, the company should be treated as a litigant in person, so that, applying *Rupert Page Develop-ments Ltd*, **2.388** above, costs should only be awarded in respect of out-of-pocket expenses. The tribunal rejected this contention, holding that the accountant was acting as an 'independent adviser', so that the company was not subject to the restrictions imposed upon a litigant in person. The tribunal awarded the company costs of £944 in accordance with its claim, together with a further £318 in respect of the hearing of the application. *Alpha International Coal Ltd*, LON/92/79 (VTD 11441).

Housing Association represented by one of its officers

[2.452] A Housing Association, which was a registered charity, provided rented accommodation for people on low incomes. The Commissioners issued a ruling that tax was chargeable on certain work done on houses owned by the Association. The Association appealed, contending that the work was zero-rated under the legislation then in force. The Association was represented by its Deputy Surveyor (K), who was an Associate of the Royal Institute of Chartered Surveyors but otherwise had no professional qualifications. The appeal was successful and the Association applied for costs, made up mainly of amounts for the time spent by K in preparing and presenting the appeal. The hours and hourly rates were not disputed, but the Commissioners contended that K's costs were not allowable as he was not a qualified solicitor. The tribunal rejected this contention and allowed the claim in full, applying the principles laid down in *Re Eastwood (decd)*, CA [1974] 3 All ER 603, and *K Taylor*, **2.450** above. *The Sutton Housing Trust (No 1)*, LON/81/160 (VTD 1198).

[2.453] The applicant in the case noted at 2.452 above later made a similar application (for costs of £829) following its success in a subsequent appeal. The Commissioners again contended that K's time in preparing (as distinct from presenting) the appeal was not allowable. The tribunal again rejected this and awarded costs of £763, applying *British Institute of Management (No 2)*, 2.444 above. *The Sutton Housing Trust (No 2)*, LON/82/149 (VTD 1296).

[2.454] A similar decision was reached in *Orbit Housing Association*, LON/84/73 (VTD 1783).

Club represented by committee member

[2.455] In the case noted at **41.4** LAND, a club had successfully appealed against the disallowance of input tax. The club's appeal had been conducted by one of its committee members (H). The club applied for costs of £1,643, of which £1,600 represented H's 'remuneration' for preparing and attending the appeal at £10 per hour. The tribunal rejected this claim, holding that in the circumstances of the case H should be treated as a litigant in person and could only recover his out-of-pocket expenses. The tribunal noted that the *Litigants in Person (Costs and Expenses) Act 1975* did not apply to appeals to a VAT tribunal. *Wendy Fair Market Club (No 1)*, LON/77/400 (VTD 679; VTD 833). (*Note*. The decision here was approved by the QB in *C & E Commrs v DW Ross & Others*, 2.400 above.)

Partnership appellant represented by partner

[2.456] In the case noted at **62.456** SUPPLY, the appellant partnership was unsuccessful at the tribunal but was successful in the Court of Appeal. The partnership, which had been represented by the senior partner (R), applied for costs. The tribunal directed that the determination of the partnership's costs should be referred to the Taxing Master. The chairman observed that 'normally this tribunal would treat a partner as a litigant in person and award him his out-of-pocket expenses. This is because the *Litigants in Person (Costs and Expenses) Act 1975, s 1(1)*, which might otherwise authorise an award of a sum in respect of work done and expenses or losses incurred, does not apply to tribunal proceedings'. The chairman noted that R now claimed that he had not conducted the appeal in his capacity as a partner, but in the capacity of an employee of one of the other partners, although R had produced no written evidence to support his claim. The chairman observed that 'a thorough investigation was needed' into 'the basis of and *bona fides* of (R's) assertions. The hearing before the Taxing Master might be an appropriate occasion to conduct the enquiry.' *BJ Rice & Associates*, LON/91/1370 (VTD 14659). (*Note*. The *Rules of the Supreme Court 1965 (SI 1965/1776)*, and their precursors, referred to the 'taxation of costs', and to a 'Taxing Master'. With effect from 26 April 1999, these rules were largely replaced by the *Civil Procedure Rules 1998 (SI 1998/3132)*, which refer instead to the 'assessment of costs', and to a 'costs judge'.)

[2.457] See also *DW Ross & Others*, 2.400 above.

Appellant represented by person with no professional qualifications

[2.458] In the case noted at **3.27** ASSESSMENT, the successful appellant (H) was represented by K, who was a law graduate and practised as a consultant, but had no professional or accountancy qualifications. H claimed costs of £2,594 represented mainly by the time of K, his clerk and his typist, which were charged at £40, £20 and £9 per hour for each respectively. The tribunal considered the hourly rates charged excessive and substituted £15, £10 and £6 for K, his clerk and his typist respectively. After examining the itemised bill in detail, it awarded total costs of £582. Items wholly disallowed included those incurred because of H's neglect or because of a postponement of the appeal made to suit his convenience. *GA Harrison*, [1982] VATTR 7 (VTD 1182).

Application for costs by litigant in person

[2.459] The tribunal allowed an appeal against a misdeclaration penalty after finding that the penalty assessments had been computed incorrectly. The successful appellant applied for costs. The tribunal held that, applying the QB decision in *Ross*, **2.400** above, no award could be made in respect of the time of a litigant in person, and awarded £50 to cover the appellant's expenses. *A Sprake (t/a Sprake & Tyrell)*, LON/92/1300P (VTD 10391).

[2.460] After protracted correspondence, Customs withdrew several assessments on a woman. She subsequently applied for costs of more than £240,000 (on the basis that she had spent more than 1,000 hours on the case and that her time should be charged at £202 per hour). The tribunal dismissed her application, applying the principles laid down in *London Scottish Benefit Society v Chorley*, QB 1884, 13 QBD 872 and *Nader*, **2.389** above. The tribunal held that a litigant in person was not entitled to recover costs except in respect of specific out-of-pocket expenses 'and, specifically, not in respect of the time which she, as a litigant in person, spent on preparing the case and carrying it on'. *M Serpes*, LON/00/1392 (VTD 20906).

Costs where company appellant represented by director

[2.461] In the case noted at **44.1** MOTOR CARS, the company claimed costs of £116.60 including £60 for the time spent by its director in preparing for and conducting the appeal and £15 for his travelling expenses, in addition to those already awarded, because he had travelled by Rolls Royce. The tribunal disallowed the £60 because it was not an expense incurred by the company and the £15 because the Commissioners cannot be expected to bear the extra cost of travelling by Rolls Royce. The remaining items claimed were disallowed as not being expenses of the appeal. *Chartcliff Ltd*, LON/76/73 (VTD 302).

[2.462] A company had appealed against an assessment of £1,864 made in March 1976. In September 1976 the Commissioners notified it that the assessment would be withdrawn. The company then applied to the tribunal for an award of costs, including £3 per hour for the time of one of its directors. The tribunal disallowed this, applying *Chartcliff Ltd*, **2.461** above, but awarded costs in respect of the remaining items on a party to party basis. *Rupert Page Developments Ltd*, LON/76/64 (VTD 379). (*Note.* For a subsequent appeal by the same company, see **2.388** above.)

[2.463] In the case noted at **60.7** SECOND-HAND GOODS, the appellant company had been represented by its managing director and claimed costs including £100 for its estimated loss of earnings because of the director's absence from its business for the day of appeal. The tribunal held that, as the director had been present as advocate as well as witness, the company was entitled to the cost of his services. As his average daily remuneration was £34, it considered £50 a day as reasonable for his services and allowed £100 to cover the day of the hearing plus half a day in preparing for the appeal and half a day for the hearing of the application for costs. *Jocelyn Feilding Fine Arts Ltd*, LON/78/81 (VTD 749).

[2.464] The Commissioners had issued a ruling that a company was required to register for VAT, and the company appealed, contending that its supplies were exempt. Following the decision against them in *Tameside Metropolitan Borough Council*, 41.5 LAND, the Commissioners withdrew their ruling and the company applied for an award of £1,234 for costs incurred in preparing for the appeal. This included £400 for the work done by one of its directors (at £10 an hour) in preparing the appeal and an amount representing the director's expenses in attending (apparently as an onlooker) the *Tameside* appeal. The tribunal awarded total costs of £400, comprising £300 for legal expenses and £100 for the work done by the company director. The tribunal held that the costs incurred in attending the *Tameside* appeal were not allowable. *Meshberry Ltd*, LON/78/384 (VTD 835).

[2.465] The successful appellant company in the case noted at **40.63** IN-VOICES AND CREDIT NOTES was represented by one of its directors. It applied for an award of costs including £360 (£60 a day) for the work done by the director and £132 for the services of two other employees who assisted him in preparing the appeal. The Commissioners opposed the claim, contending that it was excessive. The director's salary was £15,000 per annum. The tribunal held that the amounts were reasonable and, applying *Jocelyn Feilding Fine Arts Ltd*, 2.463 above, were allowable except in so far as they related to the period prior to the Notice of Appeal. The tribunal awarded costs of £390 (£300 for the director and £90 for the other employees). *Kleen Technologies International Ltd*, LON/80/66 (VTD 1005).

[2.466] A private company had appealed against an assessment relating to certain transactions in silver bars, contending that it had acted as an agent in the transactions and not as an independent principal. In the event, the Commissioners accepted the company's view and agreed to limit the assessment to tax on the company's commission. The company claimed costs of £420 for the time spent by the directors in preparing for the appeal (representing 42 hours at £10 per hour). The tribunal rejected this claim, applying *Rupert Page Developments Ltd*, 2.462 above, but awarded £50 in respect of the costs incurred by the director and his wife at the hearing. *Investment Chartwork Ltd*, [1981] VATTR 114 (VTD 1093).

[2.467] In the appeal noted at **36.345** INPUT TAX, the successful appellant company was represented by its managing director (GW). It subsequently applied for costs of £2,845. This included £1,120 for the time spent by GW in preparing for and attending the appeal, a similar amount of £540 for another director (R), £961 for the work carried out by a third director (GP) who was a practising chartered accountant, and disbursements of £224. The tribunal reviewed the evidence in detail and awarded costs of £1,024 (comprising £280 in respect of GW, £520 in respect of GP, nothing in respect of R, and the disbursements of £224). The awards in respect of GW and GP were calculated on the basis of an hourly rate of £20. The claim in respect of R was disallowed on the grounds that he had attended the appeal as a witness and his preparation time was mostly spent in preparing the proof of his evidence. *GW Martin & Co Ltd*, LON/83/263 (VTD 1448). (*Note.* Compare, however, the subsequent tribunal decision in *Refrigeration Spares (Manchester) Ltd*, **2.471** below, where the tribunal held that the effect of the CA decision in *Nader*, **2.389** above, was that it had no jurisdiction to make such an award.)

[2.468] Following a successful appeal in one of the cases noted at **18.105** DEFAULT SURCHARGE, the company applied for costs in respect of wages or salaries for its employees when attending the hearing. The tribunal refused the application, holding that the amounts sought were not properly recoverable. The company was, however, awarded costs of £275 in respect of its accountant's services. *Newcastle Double Glazing Ltd*, MAN/88/13 (VTD 3026). (*Note.* The case was heard with *Aladdin Window Co*, **2.423** above.)

[2.469] Following a successful appeal in one of the cases noted at **18.98** DEFAULT SURCHARGE, the company applied for costs totalling £633.50. The Commissioners offered to pay £255, but the company rejected this offer and appealed to the tribunal. The tribunal held that the company should be awarded costs at the rate of £35 per hour for a period of nine hours (four hours for preparing the appeal and five hours for attending the hearing), together with travelling expenses of £31.50, making a total award of £346.50 in respect of the appeal against the surcharge. In addition, the company was awarded a further £271.50 in respect of the hearing of the application. *Nulmay Ltd*, MAN/90/52 (VTD 6627).

[2.470] Following a successful appeal in one of the cases noted at **52.51** PENALTIES: MISDECLARATION, the appellant company, which had been represented by its director, applied for costs of £426.40, including £280 in respect of time spent by its director in preparing for the appeal (computed on the basis of 6 hours at £35 per hour). The Commissioners opposed the application, contending that it was not appropriate to make any award in respect of the time spent by the director in preparing for the hearing. The tribunal granted the application in full, holding that the amount claimed was reasonable. (The tribunal awarded a further £146.40 in respect of the hearing of the application.) *GA Boyd Building Services Ltd*, [1993] VATTR 26 (VTD 9788). (*Note.* Compare, however, the subsequent tribunal decision in *Refrigeration Spares (Manchester) Ltd*, **2.471** below, where the tribunal held that the effect of the CA decision in *Nader*, **2.389** above, was that it had no jurisdiction to make such an award.)

[2.471] The successful appellant company in the case noted at **48.98** PARTIAL EXEMPTION applied for costs. The company had been represented by its managing director. The Commissioners agreed to pay the entire costs charged by the company's accountants, plus the director's travelling expenses, plus £480 (representing 16 hours at £30 per hour) for the director's time when attending the tribunal. The company claimed a further £4,490, representing 131 hours of its director's time at £30 per hour and 56 hours of an employee's time at £10 per hour. The tribunal rejected this claim, holding that the company should be treated as a litigant in person, that the effect of the decision in *Nader*, 2.389 above, was that the *Litigants in Person (Costs and Expenses) Act 1975* did not apply to VAT tribunals, and that it had no jurisdiction to award the amount claimed. *Refrigeration Spares (Manchester) Ltd*, LON/01/276 (VTD 17852).

[2.472] See also *Broadway Video (Wholesale) Ltd*, 2.390 above.

Application for costs on indemnity basis

Application granted

[2.473] A company which carried on a retail clothing business successfully appealed against an estimated assessment. The tribunal awarded costs to the company on the indemnity basis. The VAT officer responsible for the assessment had suggested that there had been large-scale defalcations, but the tribunal considered that this allegation was 'without foundation and not reasonably capable of belief'. The company's records were good, and the assessment had not been made to the best of the Commissioners' judgment. There had been 'a level of competence in the investigation and assessment below that which the taxpaying public has a right to expect'. *KTS Fashions Ltd*, LON/90/505 (VTD 6782).

[2.474] In March 1988 the Commissioners issued an assessment, charging VAT of more than £104,000, on a partnership which had operated five garages. The assessment was based on allegations made by a former member of the partnership, who had not taken any active part in the running of the business, and had taken High Court proceedings against his former colleagues. The partnership appealed against the assessment, contending that it was excessive and had not been made to the best of the Commissioners' judgment. In March 1992, after prolonged correspondence and several meetings, the Commissioners reduced the assessment to £3,152. The partnership accepted this liability and withdrew the appeal. However, the partnership applied to the tribunal for an award of costs on the indemnity basis, contending that the Commissioners' conduct 'had throughout been so unreasonable and exceptional that an order for costs on an indemnity basis was appropriate'. The tribunal reviewed the evidence and held that the assessment had not been made to the best of the Commissioners' judgment, applying *dicta* of Woolf J in *Van Boeckel*, 3.1 ASSESSMENT. The officer responsible for the assessment 'had not fairly considered' information supplied by the partnership's accountants. On the evidence, 'if he had fairly considered the material put before him he would have realised that the assessment was for an amount in excess of any that could possibly be due'. Medd J held, applying *dicta* of Glidewell LJ in *Burgess v Stafford Hotel Ltd*, CA [1990] 3 All ER 222, that costs should only be awarded on an indemnity basis if the Commissioners had 'acted disgracefully to such an extent as to make this a wholly exceptional case'. In this case, the officer responsible for the assessment had not fairly considered information supplied by the partnership, either before the issue of the assessment or on a number of subsequent occasions 'both in writing and at meetings'. It appeared 'that he had convinced himself that a massive fraud had taken place and that any argument put forward which suggested to the contrary could not be sound and therefore need not be considered with care'. The officer who succeeded him was not trained in investigation work, and had 'adopted the same approach'. As a result, the partnership had incurred costs which were 'enormous' and 'very much larger than they need have been'. The conduct of the two VAT officers had been 'so exceptional that an order for costs on an indemnity basis was appropriate'. *H & B Motors (Dorchester)*, LON/88/821 (VTD 11209).

[2.475] In the case noted at **14.7** COLLECTION AND ENFORCEMENT, where the tribunal had allowed an appeal against a notice requiring security, the tribunal awarded costs to the appellant company on the indemnity basis. The tribunal chairman held, on the evidence, that the Commissioners 'did not take reasonable steps to ascertain the full and correct facts before issuing the notice'. The Commissioners' Statement of Case had contained factual inaccuracies, and had not 'set out accurately and fully all the grounds on which the decision was taken'. On the evidence, it appeared that the notice had been issued 'for an unauthorised purpose', namely to recover money owed by a company in a different ownership, the trade of which had been taken over by the appellant company. The tribunal observed that 'if Customs and Excise have used the power for an unauthorised purpose, they must bear all the financial costs borne by the taxpayer in getting the decision set aside'. *VSP Marketing Ltd*, LON/94/794A (VTD 12636).

[2.476] Following the decision noted at **2.475** above, the Commissioners paid the appellant company costs of £30,000 relating to work done by its accountants. The company applied for further costs relating to work done by its solicitors. The Commissioners opposed the application on the grounds that the company had been represented by its accountants and that the costs sought in respect to the solicitors related to periods before the issue of the notice which was the subject of the appeal. The company applied to the tribunal for a ruling that the Commissioners should pay the costs sought in respect of its solicitors. The tribunal dismissed the application, holding that, if the parties were unable to agree on the amount of costs to be awarded, the matter should be the subject of a further hearing before the tribunal chairman who had determined the original appeal, and that it would not be proper to make any such preliminary ruling as the company had sought. *VSP Marketing Ltd (No 2)*, LON/94/794A (VTD 13167).

[2.477] Following the decision noted at **2.476** above, the appellant company applied for costs of more than £26,000 relating to work done by its solicitors and more than £38,900 in relation to work done by its accountants. The solicitors' costs were based on 58 hours at £450 per hour. The accountants' costs were based on £200 per hour for work done by an employed barrister, £250 per hour for an employed solicitor, and £469 per hour for a partner. Some of the costs which the company claimed related to work done before the date on which the disputed notice requiring security was issued. The Commissioners objected to the claim, contending that it was unreasonable to have incurred the costs of three lawyers and that the hourly charging rates of the solicitors' firm, and the partner in the accountancy firm, were unreasonable. They also contended that no costs should be awarded in respect of work done before the notice requiring security was issued. The tribunal upheld this contention, holding that its 'only jurisdiction is to award a sum of costs of and incidental to and consequent on the appeal'. Until the Commissioners had made a decision against which an appeal could be lodged, there was no appealable matter so that costs incurred before then could not be costs of the appeal. The tribunal also held on the evidence that this was not 'a case which at any stage warranted the services of lawyers from two different firms', and observed that 'by the time the security notice was issued the accountancy firm were so firmly in charge of the proceedings that the services of the law firm partner were not reasonably warranted save and so far as specific research was required in order to assist the accountancy firm in the presentation of the case'. With regard to the charging rates, the tribunal held that the rate charged for the partner in the accountancy firm should not have exceeded £320 per hour (i.e. a basic rate of £200 per hour with a 60% mark-up), and that the rate charged by the solicitors' firm should not have exceeded £300 per hour. The result was that the tribunal awarded costs of £26,834 in respect of the work done by the accountancy firm and £3,600 in respect of the work done by the solicitors' firm. *VSP Marketing Ltd (No 3)*, [1995] VATDR 328 (VTD 13587).

[**2.478**] In May 1999 the Commissioners issued an assessment on a company, charging tax of £31,709. In February 2000 they issued an amended notice of assessment, purporting to increase the assessment to £292,784. In April 2000 a VAT officer informed the company that the February 2000 assessment was being withdrawn because it had not taken account of information which the company had supplied in October 1999, and thus was not 'made in best judgment (*sic*)'. The company subsequently submitted a claim for costs of £21,207 in respect of work done by its accountants. In August 2000 the Commissioners requested a detailed analysis of the claim. In March 2001 their Solicitor's Office rejected the claim. The company appealed to the tribunal. The tribunal reviewed the evidence in detail and awarded costs on the indemnity basis in respect of the work done after August 2000, holding that the Commissioners had acted unreasonably in seeking a detailed analysis of the claim to costs. *Security Despatch Ltd*, [2001] VATDR 392 (VTD 17313).

[**2.479**] A company (D) reclaimed significant amounts of input tax. Customs rejected the claims on the basis that the transactions were part of a 'carousel fraud'. D appealed. At the hearing of the appeal, Customs accepted that D 'was not itself a fraudulent trader, so that its involvement in the carousels, if such they were, was innocent'. The tribunal allowed D's appeal. The tribunal also noted that D had to cease trading and make its employees redundant, and that Customs had persistently failed to agree convenient dates for the hearing of the appeal. Furthermore, Customs had made 'an untrue statement as the basis of an application to these tribunals to vary a direction with which, when the application was made, they could not possibly have complied'. The tribunal chairman observed that 'it is essential that these tribunals, including the supporting administrative staff, be able to rely on the word of those representing Customs in all matters concerned with taxpayers' appeals. If they cannot do so, and that would now appear to be in doubt, it bodes ill for the future professional relationship between Customs and the tribunals'. The tribunal concluded that Customs had failed 'throughout the appeal to deal with matters in accordance with the tribunal rules and its directions'. Accordingly the tribunal awarded costs to D on the indemnity basis. *Deluni Mobile Ltd (No 1)*, MAN/04/149 (VTD 19205). (*Note.* For a subsequent appeal by the same company, see **36.96** INPUT TAX.)

[2.480] Following a CA decision in April 1996, a company submitted a repayment claim on the basis that it should not have accounted for output tax. (The CA decision in question was subsequently overruled by the CJEC and HL—see *Primback Ltd*, **22.242** EUROPEAN COMMUNITY LAW.) Customs made the repayment, but subsequently issued an assessment under *VATA 1994, s 80(4A)* to recover the tax. The company paid the sum assessed. However, following the CA decision in *DFS Furniture Co plc (No 2)*, **3.111** ASSESSMENT, the company claimed a repayment on the basis that the assessments were invalid. Customs rejected the claim and the company lodged a late appeal with the tribunal. Following further correspondence, Customs eventually decided not to oppose the appeal, and to make the repayment claimed. The company applied to the tribunal for costs to be awarded on the indemnity basis. The tribunal granted the application, holding that there had been 'no justification' for Customs' delay in conceding the appeal. The company had incurred substantial costs as a result of Customs having 'unjustifiably dragged out' the litigation. *Harrods (UK) Ltd*, LON/05/355 (VTD 19318).

[2.481] A finance company used the standard partial exemption method to calculate its recoverable input tax. Customs issued an assessment on the basis that the company should have made a 'standard method override' adjustment under *VAT Regulations 1995 (SI 1995/2518), reg 107B*. The company appealed, accepting that an adjustment was required but contending that the assessment was excessive. On the second day of the hearing, the VAT officer responsible for the assessment was taken ill while being cross-examined, and the appeal was adjourned. Customs subsequently accepted that the assessment was excessive. The tribunal awarded costs to the company on the indemnity basis, finding that 'admissions made by (the VAT officer) under cross-examination had undermined his calculations' and holding that 'in the administration of VAT it is incumbent on the Commissioners to facilitate so far as they reasonably can achievement of finality and certainty for a trader in the disputed area giving rise to an appeal to the tribunal'. In this case, 'more ought to have been done by the Commissioners to ensure that, however the instant litigation was decided, it would afford some certainty for the future VAT treatment of the appellant. As it is, having effectively won this litigation, the appellant is no further forward in respect of further potential standard method override disputes. This is an avoidable and unfair aspect of the outcome for the appellant and, in the tribunal's view, justifies the award of costs against the Commissioners on the indemnity basis.' *The Funding Corporation Ltd*, LON/04/932 (VTD 19525).

[2.482] In 2004 two companies made repayment claims under *VATA 1994, s 80* relating to overpayments of output tax on demonstrator cars. Customs rejected the claims and the companies appealed. After substantial delays, the appeals were set down for hearing by the tribunal in February 2007. On 31 January, shortly before the hearing, Customs agreed to accept the claims. The companies applied to the tribunal for costs to be awarded on the indemnity basis. The tribunal granted the applications, finding that there had been 'no apparent justification for the delay by the Commissioners settling this matter'. *Vauxhall Motors Ltd (No 2)*, LON/04/1618; *Saab Great Britain Ltd*, LON/04/1619 (VTD 20046).

[2.483] Following the CA decision noted at **36.87** INPUT TAX, the company applied for indemnity costs. The CA directed that the company should receive its costs on the indemnity basis with effect from 23 July 2009 (the date on which the company had made an offer under *Part 36* of the *Civil Procedure Rules*). Moses LJ observed that 'where a claimant's Part 36 offer is refused the claimant is compelled to continue in order to recover at least the sum for which the claimant is prepared to settle. In those circumstances it is to be expected that the Rule would acknowledge the predicament of a claimant whose only choice is either to abandon the appeal or to press on.' He held that 'the fact that HMRC was pursuing the appeal for the public good does not mean that (B), having maintained its success both before the Chancellor and this Court, should be regarded as an appropriate sacrificial lamb. If anyone should suffer as a result of HMRC's laudable persistence, it is the taxpayer at large, on whose behalf HMRC fought this particular appeal. It lost, and it is difficult to see why, in those circumstances, a particular trader which vindicated its rights to repayment of input tax should be deprived of the effect of its Part 36 offer.' He observed that 'the purpose of awarding costs on an indemnity basis and interest at an enhanced rate is not in order to penalise the claimant but is part of the culture of the CPR to encourage parties to avoid proceedings unless it is unreasonable for them to do otherwise'. *HMRC v Blue Sphere Global Ltd (No 3)*, CA [2010] EWCA Civ 1448; [2011] STC 547. (*Note*. For a further hearing with regard to the amount of the company's costs, see [2011] EWHC 90217 (Costs).)

Application rejected

[2.484] An application for costs to be awarded on the indemnity basis was rejected in *Ultratone Ltd*, **2.446** above, where an assessment had been withdrawn before the hearing and the tribunal observed that 'an award of costs on the indemnity basis will only be made in exceptional circumstances'.

[2.485] The appellant partnership in the case noted at **18.340** APPEALS applied for an award of costs on the indemnity basis. The tribunal rejected the application, holding that 'the circumstances were not exceptional or so unusual as to warrant an award of costs on the indemnity basis'. *A & JE Stevenson (t/a Prime & Co)*, MAN/99/163 (VTD 17392).

[2.486] Customs refused to register a couple who provided fostering services, on the basis that they were not making any taxable supplies. The couple appealed. Customs subsequently withdrew their decision and agreed to pay the couple's costs. However, the couple applied to the tribunal for a ruling that Customs should pay their costs on the indemnity basis. The tribunal dismissed this application, holding that Customs had not acted unreasonably. The tribunal also ordered the couple to pay Customs' costs of £1,050 in respect of the hearing of the application. *KAJ & Mrs BM Fosberry*, LON/02/530 (VTD 19189).

[2.487] A university claimed a VAT repayment of more than £2,000,000, relating to the building of a laboratory. Customs rejected the claim on the grounds that the effect of *VATA 1994, Sch 4 para 5(4A)* (which was subsequently repealed by *FA 2007*) was that the tax was not reclaimable. The university appealed, contending that *Sch 4 para 5(4A)* was invalid under EC law. Shortly before the hearing of the appeal, Customs accepted the university's claim. The university applied for costs on the indemnity basis. The tribunal rejected this application, holding that Customs' conduct of the case had not been 'so unreasonable as to warrant a direction for indemnity costs'. Accordingly costs should be awarded on the standard basis. *Queen Mary University of London*, LON/07/794 (VTD 20960).

[2.488] A company (S) provided security personnel to the Saudi Arabian military attaché. In 2003 Customs issued an assessment charging tax on the supplies. S appealed, contending that the supplies were within *VAT (Place of Supply of Services) Order 1992 (SI 1992/3121), article 16*, so that for VAT purposes, they were made where the recipient belonged, and no UK VAT was due. Customs did not accept this contention until 2006, when they withdrew the assessment shortly before the hearing of the appeal. S applied for costs on the indemnity basis, contending that there had been a 'significant level of unreasonableness' in Customs' conduct, and that it had been 'objectively hopeless to resist the appeal'. The tribunal chairman observed that Customs' stance had been 'clearly wrong and it is surprising to put it at its lowest that it was maintained for so long'. However although Customs' stance had been 'unreasonable in that it was lacking in common sense', it had not been 'unreasonable to such a high degree as to justify an order for indemnity costs'. *Seymour Limousines Ltd*, LON/04/1217 (VTD 20966).

[2.489] The liquidator of a company (M) claimed an input tax credit of more than £900,000. Customs rejected the claim and M appealed. After the appeal had been set down for hearing, Customs lodged their skeleton argument, contending that the effect of *VAT Regulations 1995 (SI 1995/2518), reg 25(3)* was that the tax was not reclaimable. M accepted this argument and withdrew its appeal. However M lodged an application for indemnity costs, contending that Customs had acted unreasonably by not putting this argument forward when they initially rejected the claim. The tribunal rejected this contention and dismissed the application. The tribunal observed that the claim had been 'improbable and unlikely', and that allowing the claim would have violated 'the principle of neutrality'. M's liquidator had spent money in pursuit of a claim that should have been 'dropped earlier had the strength of HMRC's case been revealed at that earlier date. The other side of the coin is that the liquidator chose to pursue the dud claim and to run up the fees because he had failed to spot that the claim was flawed. The skeleton argument from HMRC alerted the liquidator at the last minute to something he should have known all along. But the skeleton did not cause additional costs.' M's professional advisers 'should have recognised the weakness of their case at a much earlier time'. Accordingly M was not entitled to any costs, 'let alone indemnity costs'. *MG Rover Group Ltd (in liquidation)*, LON/06/997 (VTD 20871).

[2.490] In the case noted at 2.286 above, where HMRC had successfully applied to admit late evidence, the company applied for indemnity costs. The tribunal rejected this application, holding that there was no reason to award indemnity costs, and made an interim award of £5,000. *Earthshine Ltd v HMRC (No 2)*, [2010] UKFTT 314 (TC), TC00601.

[2.491] HMRC issued rulings that two shooting syndicates were required to register for VAT. They also issued assessments and imposed penalties. The syndicates appealed. HMRC subsequently accepted that the supplies by the syndicates qualified for exemption under *VATA 1994, Sch 9, Group 10*. The syndicates applied for costs on the indemnity basis. The tribunal rejected the applications. Judge Berner held that 'nothing in HMRC's conduct both before the taking of proceedings nor during the proceedings' had been 'unreasonable enough to merit an award of costs on the indemnity basis'. *Bowcombe Shoot v HMRC (and related appeal)*, [2011] UKFTT 64 (TC), TC00942.

High Court awarding costs to HMRC on indemnity basis

[2.492] In the case noted at 48.74 PAYMENT OF TAX, where a company had made an application for judicial review, Lightman J awarded costs to Customs on the indemnity basis, finding that the company had failed 'to lend proper attention to the factual basis on which the application was made', and had involved the court in a 'futile exercise'. *R (oao British Telecommunications plc) v HMRC*, QB [2005] STC 1148; [2005] EWHC 1043 (Admin).

[2.493] A company applied for a repayment of input tax of more than £2,000,000. HMRC rejected the claim on the grounds that it appeared that the transactions were connected with MTIC fraud. The company applied for judicial review, but withdrew its application during the course of the hearing. The QB awarded HMRC costs on the indemnity basis. Stadlen J observed that the company had pursued 'a claim for judicial review which the claimant accepts has no real prospect of success, and the fact that that was only openly acknowledged in the context of a late, and, in my judgment, hopeless application to amend and adjourn, does not alter the fact that it is a matter that was there on the documents for all to see'. *R (oao Indigo Global Trading Ltd) v HMRC*, QB [2009] EWHC 3126 (Admin).

Miscellaneous

Costs when parties compromise

[2.494] After the hearing of a company's appeals had begun, there was an adjournment, during which the company and the Commissioners came to a compromise agreement. On the resumption of the hearing, the company's solicitor applied for an award of costs. The tribunal rejected the application, holding that if a party to an appeal wholly concedes his case, the tribunal can consider an award of costs, but where the parties reach a compromise agreement, the tribunal cannot continue the hearing purely in relation to costs. If one side is to be recompensed for costs, the compromise agreement must provide for this. *The Cadogan Club Ltd*, LON/76/202, LON/77/194 (VTD 548).

Costs where third party joined in appeal

[2.495] In the case noted at 2.75 above, the tribunal granted an application that a third party should be joined in an appeal. (The appeal was by the recipient of the services in dispute, and the third party was the supplier of those services.) The appellant company (B) applied for a direction that the third party (V) should not seek costs. The tribunal granted the application, holding that to put an appellant 'at risk for the costs of one or more other parties who subsequently establish their right to be joined could be a serious disincentive to his freedom to exercise the right of appeal'. *Barclays Bank plc v C & E Commrs and Visa International Service Association*, LON/91/1159Y (VTD 9059).

Tribunal awarding costs to Customs without application

[2.496] In a case where an appeal by a firm of solicitors was dismissed, the Commissioners did not apply for costs but the tribunal nevertheless made an award of costs to the Commissioners, as a mark of 'concern at the ignorance of law and the function and procedures of the tribunal which the appellants have displayed, which is aggravated by the fact that they are a firm of practising solicitors and should know better'. *Houston Stewart*, EDN/91/236 (VTD 9526).

[2.497] A VAT officer on a control visit discovered that a two-partner firm of solicitors had failed to account for VAT on receipts of more than £16,000. The solicitors were unable to provide a satisfactory explanation of this, and the Commissioners issued an assessment. The firm appealed, but neither of the solicitors attended the hearing. Six minutes before the hearing was due to start, the tribunal clerk received a faxed letter from the firm requesting an adjournment. The tribunal refused the application, dismissed the appeal, and awarded costs of £400 to the Commissioners, observing that this was 'a case where the two solicitors have no excuse for their lack of co-operation both with Customs and with this tribunal'. *Musgrave & Larkin (Solicitors)*, LON/92/2119A (VTD 10885).

[2.498] In the cases noted at 10.6 CASH ACCOUNTING SCHEME and 40.48 INVOICES AND CREDIT NOTES, where an invoice issued between associated companies was held to be a sham, the tribunal held that the companies had pursued their appeals 'on a vexatious and frivolous basis', and awarded costs of £1,000 to the Commissioners. *FPV Ltd*, MAN/97/828; *Marketing Middle East Ltd*, MAN/97/1110 (VTD 15666).

[2.499] In the case noted at 36.19 INPUT TAX, where the tribunal found that a company had reclaimed input tax in respect of false invoices, the tribunal awarded costs of £2,000 to the Commissioners. *Realm Defence Industries Ltd*, LON/98/799 (VTD 16831).

Court of Appeal imposing restrictions as to costs

[2.500] In the case noted at 3.87 ASSESSMENT, the QB found in favour of the appellant company, and the Commissioners appealed to the CA. The company applied to the CA for a ruling that the QB award of costs to the company should not be disturbed, and that the Commissioners should bear the costs of both parties in the CA. The CA rejected the application, holding that the costs of the appeal to the QB should follow the result of the appeal to the CA, in accordance with normal principles. Sir Thomas Bingham MR observed that the CA 'would not wish to countenance a general rule that tax-collecting bodies can only collect small sums of revenue at their own expense'. However, in the circumstances of the case the CA imposed a condition that the Commissioners should not seek to disturb the award of costs to the company in respect of the tribunal hearing, and that, if the Commissioners' appeal to the CA was successful, each side should pay its own costs in respect of that appeal. *C & E Commrs v Le Rififi Ltd*, CA [1994] STC 383. (*Note*. The CA subsequently allowed the Commissioners' appeal on the substantive issue.)

Appeal dismissed but costs awarded to appellant

[2.501] In a case where an appeal was dismissed, the tribunal found that the appellant had been misdirected by a VAT officer and directed that he should be awarded his costs. *JR Ness*, EDN/93/116 (VTD 11559).

[2.502] In a case where an appeal against the disallowance of input tax was dismissed after a hearing lasting for five days (with an interval of six months between the second and third days), the tribunal found that the appeal had been prolonged by the conduct of the Commissioners' Solicitors' Office, and directed that the appellant should be awarded 40% of his costs. The tribunal found that the Solicitors' Office had been dilatory in disclosing documents to the appellant's agent, and that this had caused the agent additional work. On the evidence, the agent had been 'dealt with in a most unhelpful manner by the Solicitors' Office when he quite properly attempted to have rectified, for the reconvened hearing, matters which should have been before the tribunal at the outset'. The tribunal observed that 'had everything been conducted as it should have been by the Commissioners, the case would not have lasted five days.' *YY & MV Patel (t/a Rumi Clothing)*, MAN/96/489 (VTD 15268).

[2.503] In the case noted at **67.124** VALUATION, the tribunal awarded costs to the unsuccessful appellant company, observing that the company had been acting in accordance with a previous tribunal decision (see **62.249** SUPPLY) and that a VAT officer had advised the company that she would not seek to assess for periods before 1998, but that despite this assurance, the Commissioners had in fact issued assessments dating back to 1995. The chairman observed that the VAT officer who had decided not to issue retrospective assessments had been 'absolutely correct', and criticised her 'superior officers' for having 'reneged on the deal'. *Camberwell Cars Ltd (No 3)*, LON/00/303 (VTD 17566).

[2.504] In the case noted at **62.485** SUPPLY, the unsuccessful appellant company applied for costs of more than £300,000, contending that HMRC had acted unreasonably in that the reasons given in their Skeleton Argument were significantly different from those given in their Statement of Case, and that it had only received HMRC's Skeleton Argument three days before the hearing of the appeal. The tribunal found that 'there was a material and substantive difference between HMRC's skeleton argument and its statement of case', but held that the amount claimed by the company was excessive. The tribunal ordered that HMRC should pay the company costs of £20,000 plus VAT. *Sumitomo Mitsui Banking Corporation Europe Ltd v HMRC (No 2)*, [2010] UKFTT 203 (TC), TC00505.

[2.505] See also *Elstead (Thursley Road) Recreational Trust*, **2.6** above, and *Law*, **3.163** ASSESSMENT.

Commissioners verifying repayment claim before making repayment

[2.506] A company submitted a claim for a repayment of £1,979,000. The Commissioners wrote to the company on 5 June, requesting clarification of its entitlement to the repayment. The company provided the information which the Commissioners had requested. On 12 July the Commissioners agreed to repay £1,970,000 (ie £9,000 less than the company had originally claimed). The company subsequently applied for costs. The tribunal rejected the application, holding that there had been no 'appealable decision' and that the Commissioners had been entitled to make enquiries before making the repayment. The tribunal observed that 'if the Commissioners need to know certain facts without which they would not be justified in making the repayment, it is only reasonable that they should be permitted to pursue them without finding that they have made an appealable decision not to repay'. *Lilac Property Services Ltd*, LON/01/1245 (VTD 17876).

Commissioners failing to comply with directions by tribunal

[2.507] The Commissioners had issued a ruling that certain building work undertaken by a charity failed to qualify for zero-rating. The charity appealed, and the appeal was stood over pending a CA decision (see *Jubilee Hall Recreation Centre Ltd*, 55.16 PROTECTED BUILDINGS). In September 1999 the tribunal issued a direction requiring the Commissioners to serve a Statement of Case by 8 October. The Commissioners served the Statement of Case on 25 October. On 26 October the tribunal made several directions, which the charity complied with but the Commissioners did not. On 25 November the tribunal sent a form T19 to both parties. The charity responded but, despite a subsequent reminder, the Commissioners failed to do so. In January 2000 the case was listed for hearing by the tribunal chairman (Mr. Oliver), who awarded costs against the Commissioners, observing that 'the tribunal is concerned with the repeated failures of the Solicitors' Office (of the Commissioners) to respond to T19 letters. The matter has been taken up with the office on several occasions in the past. Moreover, in this case the Solicitors' Office had been out of time in providing the Statement of Case and had only done so in the teeth of a coercive direction from the tribunal. The Statement of Case, when it arrived, had been exiguous in the extreme and has been the subject of an application by the appellant for further and better particulars which I have allowed. The excuse offered by the solicitor for the Commissioners was that the T19 letter had been misfiled. That would have been unfortunate if it had happened only once. As it is two T19 letters went unanswered and I do not accept that both were misfiled. Taxpayers must not be prejudiced by official delays. The problems of a charity seeking to reclaim input tax are more acute than most and a proper standard of efficiency is demanded from the Commissioners in dealing with these.' *London Federation of Clubs for Young People*, LON/97/283 (VTD 16477). (*Note.* For the substantive appeal, see 15.105 CONSTRUCTION OF BUILDINGS, ETC.)

[2.508] See also *Faccenda Chicken Ltd*, 2.157 above.

HMRC applying for set-off of costs against unpaid tax

[2.509] The tribunal awarded costs to a successful appellant company. HMRC had obtained a county court judgment against the company for unpaid

PAYE and NIC. They applied for the costs payable by them to be set against the tax payable to them. The company opposed the application, contending that the court had no jurisdiction to make such a set-off. The Ch D rejected this contention and granted the application. *HMRC v Xicom Systems Ltd*, Ch D [2008] STC 3492; [2008] EWHC 1945 (Ch).

Former company director applying for costs against provisional liquidator

[2.510] In May 2002 a company was placed in provisional liquidation. The Commissioners issued three VAT assessments on the basis that the company had been involved in substantial evasion of VAT and excise duty. The company appealed. In November 2002 a winding-up order was made (see **37.2** INSOLVENCY). The liquidator decided not to proceed with the appeals, and obtained a 'freezing order' under *Civil Procedure Rules 1998 (SI 1998/3132)* against the company's former director (F). F applied to the tribunal for a direction that the provisional liquidator should pay costs which the company had incurred between May and November in relation to the appeals. The tribunal rejected this contention and dismissed the director's application, holding that he had no power to make an application for costs. The tribunal also observed that 'the position in a VAT appeal when a provisional liquidator is appointed is confused and unsatisfactory. Once a winding-up order is made, the assets including rights of appeal pass to the liquidator. Before then the rights do not automatically pass.' *N Forrester v RAJ Hooper (formerly provisional liquidator of Anglo-Breweries Ltd)*, LON/02/966 (VTD 18008).

Allocation of cases to categories—application for costs

[2.511] See *Capital Air Services Ltd v HMRC*, **2.148** above.

The award of interest (VATA 1994, s 84(8))

General principles

[2.512] A company had supplied certain goods to an individual (M) in connection with work on his house. The Commissioners considered that the supply was standard-rated. The company accepted this, accounting for the relevant tax of £65 and charging it to the customer. M did not accept the Commissioners' view and, after paying the amount to the company 'without prejudice', appealed on the ground that the supply was zero-rated under the legislation then in force. The tribunal allowed the appeal and M applied for interest on the amount repayable to him. The Commissioners opposed the application, contending that the amount repayable had not been paid or deposited with them, within the meaning of what is now *VATA 1994, s 84(8)*. The tribunal rejected this contention and allowed interest at 10% per annum (the rate which M had applied for). *WJM Mahoney*, [1976] VATTR 241 (VTD 258).

[2.513] In a case where the substantive issue has been overtaken by subsequent changes in the legislation, the QB allowed an appeal by a parish church council. The tax in dispute was refunded to the council, which then applied for interest under what is now *VATA 1994, s 84(8)*. The council had paid the tax in paying the contractors' bills for the relevant work, and the Commissioners accepted that, applying *Mahoney*, **2.512** above, the council was entitled to interest. However, the parties were unable to agree the calculation of the interest, and the appeal was referred to the tribunal, which held that the rate should be that allowed from time to time on the courts' short-term investment account, applying *dicta* in *Bartlett v Barclays Bank Trust Ltd*, Ch D [1980] 2 All ER 92. *St Luke Great Crosby PCC*, MAN/78/59 (VTD 1463).

[2.514] A company appealed against the rejection of a repayment claim. The Commissioners subsequently agreed that a repayment was due, and made the repayment, together with repayment supplement under *VATA 1994, s 79*. The company applied for interest under *VATA 1994, s 84(8)* to be paid at 8%. The Commissioners considered that the rate claimed was excessive. The tribunal directed that interest should be paid at 6.25%, in line with the rates of interest under *VATA 1994, s 74*. *UK Tradecorp Ltd*, [2004] VATDR 195 (VTD 18714).

[2.515] In a subsequent case where the facts were similar, the tribunal directed that interest under *VATA 1994, s 84(8)* should be paid at 7.5%, in accordance with the rate prescribed by *Air Passenger Duty and other Indirect Taxes (Interest) Rate Regulations 1998 (SI 1998/1461)* for the purposes of *FA 1996, s 197*. *Olympia Technology Ltd (No 1)*, LON/04/271 (VTD 19145). (*Note*. For subsequent developments in this case, see **48.92** PAYMENT OF TAX. For a subsequent appeal by the same company, see **2.15** above.)

[2.516] During 2004 and 2005 a company (C) claimed five repayments of VAT, relating to the reconstruction of a protected building. Customs rejected the claims, and C appealed to the tribunal, which allowed its appeals. The tribunal directed that interest under *VATA 1994, s 84(8)* should be paid at base rate plus 2.75%, this being the rate which C's bank charged on its overdraft. The tribunal observed that C had been 'deprived of its input tax for a period in excess of two years which it could have applied as working capital'. With regard to the first repayment claim, the tribunal found that Customs had been given sufficient information to justify the repayment on 31 August 2004, and directed that interest should run from 9 September 2004. With regard to the subsequent claims, the tribunal directed that interest should run from 16 days after the dates on which the claims were received. *Constantgreen Ltd*, LON/04/1868 (VTD 20303). (*Note*. C was represented by a solicitor, and the tribunal also awarded costs of £100 per hour in respect of her time.)

Whether interest may be compounded

[2.517] In a case where the substantive issue has been overtaken by changes in the legislation, the successful appellant company applied for interest to be awarded at 2.5% over the base rate of the Bank of Scotland, compounded quarterly. The Commissioners accepted the rate as reasonable, but objected to the compounding of the interest. The tribunal allowed the company's application, observing that 'where the taxpayer can show the specific amount which it has cost him in interest due to the non-payment of input tax by (the Commissioners) he is entitled to an award at least approximating to that loss'. The compounding of the interest was reasonable and appropriate. *Margrie Holdings Ltd*, EDN/85/69, February 1992 unreported. (*Note*. See now, however, the subsequent Ch D decisions in *HMRC v Royal Society for the Prevention of Cruelty to Animals*, **2.518** below, and *HMRC v Totel Ltd*, **2.519** below.)

[2.518] A charity appealed against the rejection of a repayment claim. Customs subsequently agreed that a repayment was due, and made the repayment, together with repayment supplement under *VATA 1994, s 79*. The charity applied for interest under *VATA 1994, s 84(8)*. The tribunal directed that interest under *s 84(8)* should be paid at 4.3%. Customs appealed to the Ch D. Lawrence Collins LJ held that, in awarding interest, 'the overriding principle is that interest should be awarded to the claimant not as compensation for the damage done but for being kept out of money which ought to have been paid to him'. The conventional practice in commercial cases was 'to award simple interest at base rate plus 1%'. *VATA 1994, s 84(8)* 'should not be judicially interpreted to include the power to award compound interest'. On the evidence, the tribunal appeared to have sought 'to achieve the same effect as an award of compound interest by increasing the rate of simple interest payable to reflect compound rates'. This had been 'an error of principle'. *HMRC v Royal Society for the Prevention of Cruelty to Animals (No 2)*, Ch D 2007, [2008] STC 885; [2007] EWHC 422 (Ch).

[2.519] A company submitted VAT returns which claimed substantial repayments. Customs delayed repayment in order to investigate the possibility that the relevant transactions had formed part of a 'carousel fraud'. Subsequently they accepted that repayment was due. The tribunal ordered Customs to pay compound interest at 3% above base rate, from 30 days after the date on which they received the relevant return. Customs appealed to the Ch D, contending that the tribunal had been wrong to award compound interest. The Ch D accepted this contention and allowed Customs' appeal. Lawrence Collins LJ held that *VATA 1994, s 84(8)* 'should not be judicially interpreted to include the power to award compound interest' and that 'Community law does not require the award of compound interest'. *HMRC v Totel Ltd*, Ch D 2007, [2008] STC 885; [2007] EWHC 422 (Ch). (*Note*. The Ch D heard the case with *HMRC v Royal Society for the Prevention of Cruelty to Animals*, **2.518** above.)

[2.520] Five companies which traded as car dealers had accounted for output tax on sales of 'demonstrator cars' on which input tax had been 'blocked' and which should have been treated as exempt (applying the ECJ decision in *EC Commission v Italian Republic*, **22.349** EUROPEAN COMMUNITY LAW) and on payments from manufacturers which should have been treated as discounts on the sale price of the cars (applying the ECJ decision in *Elida Gibbs Ltd*, **22.235** EUROPEAN COMMUNITY LAW). HMRC made the repayments, together with simple interest under *VATA 1994, s 78*. The companies appealed to the Upper Tribunal, contending that the effect of the HL decision in *CIR v Sempra Metals Ltd*, HL [2007] STC 1559 was they were entitled to compound interest. The Upper Tribunal dismissed the appeals, holding that they were out of time, and that there were insufficient grounds for extending the statutory time limit. The CA allowed the companies' appeal against this decision (by a 2-1 majority, Etherton LJ dissenting), but without deciding the substantive question of whether the companies were entitled to compound interest. At a subsequent hearing, the CA accepted HMRC's contention that the proceedings should be stayed pending the ECJ decision in *Littlewoods Retail Ltd v HMRC (and related applications) (No 2)*, **22.563A** below. *John Wilkins (Motor Engineers) Ltd v HMRC (and related appeals)*, CA [2011] EWCA Civ 429; [2011] STC 1371.

[2.521] See also *Littlewoods Retail Ltd v HMRC (and related applications) (No 2)*, at **2.563A** below, and *FJ Chalke Ltd v HMRC*, **48.146** PAYMENT OF TAX.

[2.523] In the case noted at **67.56** VALUATION, the First-Tier Tribunal directed that there should be a reference to the ECJ, expressing the view that the fourth question posed in *Littlewoods Retail Ltd v HMRC*, **2.563A** above, was 'too limited to be relied upon as an aid to our decision on the arguments' which the appellant company had raised. The Upper Tribunal dismissed HMRC's appeal against this decision, and specifically declined to follow the CA decision in *John Wilkins (Motor Engineers) Ltd v HMRC*, **2.520** above, where the CA had ordered a stay of similar proceedings. Judge Bishopp observed that it was 'open to the CJEU to decline to accept the reference'. *HMRC v Grattan plc (No 6)*, [2011] UKUT 399 (TCC); [2011] STC 2342. (*Note*. For the wording of the question referred, see [2011] UKFTT 691 (TC), TC01533.)

Whether interest claimable on tax overdeclared

[2.524] In the case noted at **1.91** AGENTS, a couple trading as Tupperware distributors successfully appealed against a decision by the Commissioners that they were liable to account for tax on amounts which their agents retained as commission. Following the CA decision that the tax paid was not due, the distributors applied for a direction that it be repaid with interest under what is now *VATA 1994, s 84(8)*. The tribunal dismissed the application, holding that its jurisdiction was restricted to matters specified in what is now *VATA 1994, s 83*, and that the omission of any reference to a claim for an overdeclaration or overpayment of tax suggested that the tribunals were not intended to hear and determine such matters. *R & P A Potter*, [1985] VATTR 255 (VTD 1982). (*Note*. The Commissioners eventually made repayments to the distributors following the HL decision in *Fine Art Developments plc*, **59.23** RETURNS.)

Whether interest claimable where assessment withdrawn

[2.525] A company appealed against an assessment and paid the tax charged. Subsequently the Commissioners withdrew the assessment and repaid the tax. The company lodged a claim for interest, which the Commissioners refused to pay. The tribunal rejected the company's claim. The tribunal chairman observed that the potential right to interest could not 'be defeated simply by a withdrawal of an assessment before hearing'. However, the withdrawal of the assessment in question had been concessionary. Accordingly the application was outside the scope of what is now *VATA 1994, s 84* and the tribunal had no jurisdiction to make an award of interest in such circumstances. *Trevor Toys Ltd*, LON/91/1294X (VTD 9352).

Whether interest payable under VATA 1994, s 78 or s 84

[2.526] Until 1993, the Commissioners required car dealers, in accounting for VAT, to reduce the purchase price of cars which they had purchased by the amount of any refund of the relevant road fund licence. They subsequently accepted that this requirement had been incorrect, and made repayments to four dealers with interest under *VATA 1994, s 78*. The dealers appealed to the Edinburgh tribunal, contending that they should have been entitled to compound interest under *VATA 1994, s 84(8)* rather than to simple interest under *VATA 1994, s 78*. The tribunal rejected this contention and dismissed the appeals, holding that *VATA 1994, s 84(8)* was inapplicable. The tribunal observed that 'the purpose of *s 84(8)* was to empower the tribunal, on proof of the exceptional circumstances in *s 84(8)(b)* or if consequently upon a determination that a payment or deposit had to be made before the appeal could be entertained and the taxpayer had to either borrow money or incur costs or lose the benefit of funds which he should not have lost, that the tribunal had a very wide discretion in the interests of justice to make such an award by way of interest as was appropriate in the circumstances'. The tribunal also held that 'compounding interest unless specifically sanctioned by Statute would be a most unusual course to follow'. The fact that the appellants had incurred overdraft interest was not conclusive. *Peoples Bathgate & Livingston Ltd*, EDN/93/260; *John Martin Holdings Ltd*, EDN/93/262; *Goulds of Glasgow*, EDN/94/22; *Peoples Liverpool Ltd*, EDN/96/20 (VTD 14264).

[2.527] The decision in *Peoples Bathgate & Livingston Ltd*, 2.526 above, was applied in the similar subsequent case of *Seaton Sands Ltd & Others*, LON/95/2609 (VTD 15381).

[2.528] The decision in *Peoples Bathgate & Livingston Ltd*, 2.526 above, was not followed in a subsequent case in which a company had submitted a repayment claim in December 1996 and the Commissioners had not made the repayment until July 1997. The Commissioners subsequently made a payment of repayment supplement under *VATA 1994, s 79*. The company claimed a further payment of interest under *VATA 1994, s 84(8)*. The Commissioners rejected this claim on the basis that the effect of *VATA 1994, s 78(2)* was that no further payment of interest was due. The tribunal allowed the company's appeal, holding that 'the words of *s 78* make it clear that it is subordinated to claims for interest under other sections' and that 'interest claimed under *s 84* prevails over an interest claim under *s 78*'. The tribunal observed that repayment supplement was 'not a payment in lieu of interest' but was 'a penalty on Customs for refusing to pay that which was due'. The tribunal directed that the company should be paid simple interest at 8% for the period from January to March 1997 and at 6% from April to July 1997 (the rates applied for). *Bank Austria Trade Services Gesellschaft mbH*, EDN/97/39 (VTD 16918).

[2.529] The decision in *Bank Austria Trade Services Gesellschaft mbH*, 2.528 above, was applied in the similar subsequent case of *Offshore Hydrocarbon Mapping plc*, EDN/05/24 (VTD 19438).

[2.530] See also *National Galleries of Scotland*, 48.83 PAYMENT OF TAX.

Claim to interest under Supreme Court Act 1981, s 35A

[2.531] A company (E) claimed a VAT repayment of more than £5,000,000. The Commissioners initially informed E that they intended to set this amount against an assessment, against which E had appealed. Following correspondence, they agreed to make the repayment claimed, together with interest under *VATA 1994, s 78* (the rate of which, at the relevant period, ranged from 2% to 3%, in accordance with *Air Passenger Duty and other Indirect Taxes (Interest) Rate Regulations 1998 (SI 1998/1461), reg 5*). E applied for judicial review, contending that it was entitled to interest under *Supreme Court Act 1981, s 35A*, and that the rate of interest should be 8%. The QB held that in principle E was entitled to interest under *Supreme Court Act 1981, s 35A(3)*, but that there was no justification for awarding interest at 8%. The rates of interest laid down by *VATA 1994, s 78* were not 'so materially out of step with current commercial rates' as to be unjust, and the interest to be awarded under *Supreme Court Act 1981, s 35A(3)* should be at the same rates as would have been awarded under *s 78*. *R (oao Elite Mobile plc) v C & E Commrs*, QB 2004, [2005] STC 275; [2004] EWHC 2923 (Admin).

[2.532] A company submitted VAT returns for May 2005 and June 2005, claiming substantial repayments. Customs delayed repayment in order to investigate the possibility that the relevant transactions had formed part of a 'carousel fraud'. Subsequently they accepted that a repayment was due. The QB held that the company was entitled to interest under *Supreme Court Act 1981, s 35A* at 7% (ie 2.5% above base rate). Collins J held that since the transactions in question were commercial transactions, the award of interest should 'reflect the cost of borrowing the sums which have not been paid'. With regard to the date from which interest should run, a reasonable period was needed to enable Customs to investigate the claims. That would amount to 30 days in respect of these two returns, and 16 days for subsequent returns. *R (oao Mobile Export 365 Ltd) v HMRC*, QB [2006] STC 1069; [2006] EWHC 311 (Admin). (*Note.* For a subsequent appeal involving the same company, see 2.165 above.)

Whether interest to be included in award of costs

[2.533] In the case noted at 2.390 above, the tribunal held that it had no jurisdiction, in awarding costs, to take interest into account. (The tribunal chairman commented that 'although the lack of any jurisdiction in the tribunal to reflect the liability to interest, or to offer compensation for the loss of the use of money, can unquestionably produce an unjust result', the effect of the law was that 'it is not competent to the tribunal to provide any remedy'.) *Broadway Video (Wholesale) Ltd*, [1994] VATTR 271 (VTD 12446).

3

Assessment

The cases in this chapter are arranged under the following headings.

Whether assessment made to best of Commissioners' judgment (VATA 1994, s 73(1))
Cases where the assessment was upheld | **3.1**
Cases where the appellant was partly successful | **3.20**
Cases where the appellant was successful | **3.25**
Time limit for assessment (VATA 1994, s 73(6))
Whether assessment made within two years of end of accounting period (*VATA 1994, s 73(6)(a)*) | **3.40**
Whether assessment made within one year of 'evidence of facts' (*VATA 1994, s 73(6)(b)*) | **3.47**
Whether assessment issued within three-year time limit (*VATA 1994, s 77(1)*) | **3.86**
Whether twenty-year time limit applicable (*VATA 1994, s 77(4)*) | **3.101**
Supplementary assessments (*VATA 1994, s 77(6)*) | **3.110**
Assessments for overpayments (*VATA 1994, s 78A(2)*) | **3.111**
Assessment where purchases cannot be reconciled with sales (VATA 1994, s 73(7)) | **3.113**
The validity of the assessment
Cases where the assessment was upheld | **3.114**
Cases where the appellant was successful | **3.134**
The amount of the assessment | **3.146**
Miscellaneous | **3.170**

CROSS-REFERENCE

For partnership assessments see **47.1** PARTNERSHIP *et seq.*

Whether assessment made to best of Commissioners' judgment (VATA 1994, s 73(1))

Cases where the assessment was upheld

Court decisions

[3.1] The Commissioners issued an estimated assessment, covering a three-year period, on a publican. The publican appealed, contending that the assessment had not been made to the best of the Commissioners' judgment, because it was based on a sample period of only five weeks. The tribunal rejected this contention and upheld the assessment in principle, but reduced the amount of the assessment to allow for pilferage of stock. The QB upheld the tribunal decision. Woolf J held that the Commissioners should 'fairly consider all material placed before them and, on that material, come to a decision which is one which is reasonable and not arbitrary as to the amount of tax which is due. As long as there is some material on which the Commissioners can reasonably act, then they are not required to carry out investigations which may or may not result in further material being placed before them'. Applying *dicta* of Lord Donovan in *Argosy Co Ltd v Guyana Commissioner of Inland Revenue*, PC [1971] 1 WLR 514, 'once a reasonable opinion that liability exists is formed, there must necessarily be guess-work at times as to the quantum of liability'. Furthermore, the fact that the original assessment had not made any allowance for pilferage did not render it invalid or unreasonable. *CPM Van Boeckel v C & E Commrs*, QB 1980, [1981] STC 290; [1981] 2 All ER 505.

[3.2] The Commissioners issued an estimated assessment on the proprietor of two Chinese restaurants. The assessment had been computed by assuming that the average mark-up on sales of drinks was 130%, and that takings from sales of drinks were 12% of total takings. The proprietor appealed, contending that the assessment had not been made to the best of the Commissioners' judgment. The tribunal rejected this contention and dismissed the appeal, and the CS upheld the tribunal decision. *SY Seto v C & E Commrs*, CS 1980, [1981] STC 698.

[3.3] The Commissioners issued an estimated assessment on two publicans, computed on the basis of an average mark-up of 67% on drink and 100% on sales of food. The publicans' accountant had informed a VAT officer that the publicans had made supplies of accommodation, and an estimated figure of receipts from accommodation was also included in the assessment. The publicans appealed, contending that the mark-up used in the assessment was excessive and that they had ceased to make supplies of accommodation before the start of the period covered by the assessment. The tribunal allowed their appeal in part, accepting the mark-up of 100% on sales of food but directing that the assessment be recomputed on the basis that the average mark-up on sales of drink was 62%, and that the estimate for supplies of accommodation should be reduced to nil. The result was that the tax charged by the assessment was reduced from £25,372 to £19,345. The QB upheld the tribunal decision, holding that the assessment had been made to the best of the Commissioners' judgment. *C & GP Holder v C & E Commrs*, QB [1989] STC 327.

[3.4] A trader carried on a clandestine business of manufacturing and selling counterfeit recording tapes. He did not register for VAT and kept no accounting records. The Commissioners issued assessments, and he appealed, contending that they were not to the best of the Commissioners' judgment. The tribunal rejected this contention and the QB dismissed the trader's appeal. Simon Brown J observed that 'in a case of this sort where the taxpayer's dishonesty deprives the Commissioners of most of the critical information needed for a proper assessment', there was 'a wide bracket represented at the top end by the very most which could possibly be payable'. There was 'no possible reason why the Commissioners should decide on some figure beneath the upper end of the bracket'. *M Spillane v C & E Commrs*, QB 1989, [1990] STC 212. (*Note.* For another issue in this case, see 3.53 below.)

[3.5] The Commissioners issued an estimated assessment on the proprietors of an Italian restaurant, covering a five-year period. The assessment was based on a review of the restaurant's records for a period of three months, and computed by applying a weighted mark-up (of 163.07%) to sales of drinks and treating sales of drinks as 30.95% of total sales. The tribunal dismissed the proprietors' appeal and the CS upheld this decision, holding that the assessment had been made to the best of the Commissioners' judgment. *A & B Farnocchia v C & E Commrs*, CS [1994] STC 881.

[3.6] The Commissioners issued an estimated assessment on a couple who operated a fish and chip shop. The couple appealed, admitting that they had suppressed some of their takings but contending that the assessment was excessive and had not been made to the best of the Commissioners' judgment. The tribunal reviewed the evidence in detail and upheld the validity of the assessment but directed that the amount of the assessment should be reduced. The CA upheld this decision, holding that the tribunal had been entitled to find that the assessment had been made to the best of the Commissioners' judgment, notwithstanding that the amount of the assessment had been reduced. The tribunal had not misdirected itself and its decision was a finding of fact with which the court could not interfere. *M & A Georgiou (t/a Mario's Chippery) v C & E Commrs*, CA [1996] STC 463. (*Note*. An appeal against a penalty was also dismissed—see **50.108** PENALTIES: EVASION OF TAX and **34.1** HUMAN RIGHTS.)

[3.7] The Commissioners issued estimated assessments on the proprietor of a fish and chip shop, covering accounting periods from December 1993 to August 1995. In computing the last of these assessments, the officer responsible for the assessment inadvertently included purchase invoices from the period from 1 September 1995 to 11 September 1995. The proprietor appealed, contending *inter alia* that this error meant that the assessment had not been made to the best of the Commissioners' judgment. The tribunal rejected this contention and upheld the validity of the assessment while reducing it in amount. The proprietor appealed to the QB, which upheld the tribunal decision. Burton J observed that 'the only legitimate grievance that the appellant could have had was that 11 days' worth of purchases were included which should not have been, and that grievance was removed by the tribunal'. *G Ahmed (t/a Lister Fisheries) v C & E Commrs*, QB [1999] STC 468. (*Note*. The appellant also contended that the tribunal chairman had been biased. The QB rejected this contention, holding that there was not 'any evidence of bias'.)

[3.8] In the case noted at **2.309** APPEALS, Carnwath J held that a tribunal should not treat an assessment as invalid merely because it disagreed as to how the Commissioners' judgment should have been exercised. An assessment should only be held to fail the 'best judgment' test of *s 73(1)* where it had been made 'dishonestly or vindictively or capriciously', or was a 'spurious estimate or guess in which all elements of judgment are missing', or was 'wholly unreasonable'. Short of such a finding, there was no justification for setting aside an assessment. Carnwath J observed that 'it is only in a very exceptional case that an assessment will be upset because of a failure by the Commissioners to exercise best judgment. In the normal case the important issue will be the amount of the assessment.' *MH Rahman (t/a Khayam Restaurant) v C & E Commrs (No 1)*, QB [1998] STC 826. (*Note*. For subsequent developments in this case, see **3.9** below.)

[3.9] Following the decision noted at **3.8** above, a new tribunal reheard the appeal and reduced the assessment from £17,249 to £7,683. The trader lodged a further appeal to the Ch D and the CA, contending that the tribunal decision was unreasonable, and that the reduction in the amount of the assessment indicated that the original assessment had not been made to the best of the Commissioners' judgment. The Ch D and CA unanimously rejected this contention and dismissed the trader's appeal. Chadwick LJ held that, although there had been errors in the computation of the assessment, it had been 'an honest and genuine attempt to make a reasoned assessment of the VAT payable'. Accordingly, it had still been made to the best of the Commissioners' judgment. *MH Rahman (t/a Khayam Restaurant) v C & E Commrs (No 2)*, CA 2002, [2003] STC 150; [2002] EWCA Civ 1881.

[3.10] The Commissioners issued an estimated assessment on a couple who operated a fish and chip shop. They appealed, contending that the assessment had not been made to the best of the Commissioners' judgment. The tribunal rejected this contention and dismissed their appeal, holding *inter alia* that the wife had acted dishonestly. The Ch D upheld this decision as one of fact (and held that the Commissioners had been entitled to register the couple from 1 October 1991). *MA & JS Henderson (t/a Tony's Fish and Chip Shop) v C & E Commrs*, Ch D 2000, [2001] STC 47.

[3.11] The Commissioners issued an estimated assessment on a retailer. The tribunal upheld the assessment, and the Ch D upheld this decision as one of fact. *JP Cunningham v C & E Commrs*, Ch D [2001] STC 736.

[3.12] A married couple began to operate a café in September 1994. They subsequently divorced, and with effect from October 1996, the husband operated the café as a sole trader. Neither the couple, nor the husband, registered for VAT. The Commissioners subsequently issued an assessment on the partnership covering the period from December 1995 to September 1996; a notice of compulsory registration to the husband from October 1996, and an assessment on the husband covering the period from October 1996 to July 1999. They also imposed a penalty on the husband under *VATA 1994, s 60*. The partnership and the husband appealed. The tribunal reviewed the evidence in detail and dismissed the appeals, and the Ch D upheld this decision. Neuberger J held that the tribunal had been entitled to accept the Commissioners' estimates of the turnover of the café, and to hold that the assessments had been made to the best of the Commissioners' judgment. *D & A Hindle (t/a DJ Baker Bar) v C & E Commrs*, Ch D 2003, [2004] STC 426; [2003] EWHC 1665 (Ch). (*Note.* For another issue in this case, see **3.117** below.)

[3.13] The Commissioners issued an estimated assessment on a restaurant proprietor. The tribunal upheld the assessment in principle, but reduced the amount of the assessment by 10%. The proprietor appealed to the Ch D, contending that the assessment had not been made to the best of the Commissioners' judgment. The Ch D rejected this contention and upheld the tribunal decision. *H Hossain (t/a Balti House Tandoori) v C & E Commrs*, Ch D [2004] STC 1572; [2004] EWHC 1898 (Ch).

[3.14] The Commissioners issued an assessment on a partnership which operated a fish and chip shop. The assessment was computed on the basis that

40% of takings had been suppressed. The tribunal upheld the assessment, holding that it had been made to the best of the Commissioners' judgment and had been made within the statutory one-year time limit of *VATA 1994, s 73(6)(b)*. The partners appealed to the QB, contending that the tribunal should have also considered the amount of the assessment. The QB dismissed the appeal. As a matter of principle, a tribunal should consider the amount of an assessment as well as deciding that it had been made to the best of the Commissioners' judgment. However, in the case in question, the partners had denied that there had been any suppression of takings whatsoever. As the partners had not challenged the amount of the assessment before the tribunal, there was nothing which would have enabled the tribunal to reach a different conclusion with regard to the percentage of takings that had been suppressed. Accordingly, there would be no purpose in remitting the case to the tribunal to consider the amount of the assessment. *Majid & Partners v C & E Commrs*, QB 1998, [1999] STC 585.

Tribunal decisions

[3.15] The Commissioners issued an estimated assessment on a publican. He appealed, contending that the assessment had not been made to the best of the Commissioners' judgment. The tribunal rejected this contention and dismissed the appeal, applying the principles laid down in *Van Boeckel v C & E Commrs*, 3.1 above. The tribunal chairman (Dr. Brice) also held that 'in addition to the conclusions drawn by Woolf J in *Van Boeckel*, earlier tribunal decisions identified three further propositions of relevance in determining whether an assessment is reasonable. These are, first that the facts should be objectively gathered and intelligently interpreted; secondly, that the calculations should be arithmetically sound; and, finally, that any sampling technique should be representative and free from bias.' CA McCourtie, LON/92/191 (VTD 12239). (*Note*. An appeal against a misdeclaration penalty was also dismissed.)

[3.16] The Commissioners issued a 'global' assessment on a company director who had bought and sold a number of cars. The assessment covered the period from July 1988 to April 1993, but the officer responsible for computing the assessment mistakenly included some outputs relating to previous periods. The director appealed, contending as a preliminary point that the assessment was invalid as it had not been made to the best of the Commissioners' judgment. The tribunal chairman (Mr. de Voil) rejected this contention, holding that although the officer responsible for the assessment had undoubtedly made an error, the error was not one of 'judgment', since 'judgment' connoted a deliberate choice between possible alternatives. The fact that, in computing the assessment, the officer had 'showed a want of care' was not sufficient to render the assessment invalid. Mr. de Voil observed that 'the purpose of the "best judgment" provision is to prevent an unfair onus from being placed on an appellant—to prevent the perpetuation of an injustice which cannot be properly remedied on appeal. There is no unfair onus here; there is no irremediable injustice; there is a simple error.' *MV Gauntlett*, [1996] VATDR 138 (VTD 13921).

[3.17] The proprietors of a fish and chip shop appealed against an estimated assessment. The tribunal reviewed the evidence in detail and found that, owing to an arithmetical error by the officer responsible for the assessment, the assessment had in fact understated the amount of underdeclared tax. The tribunal observed that 'it would offend against the obvious mischief at which *s 73* is aimed, and would be offensive to common sense, if a trader should be able to escape the consequences of his misdeclarations by reason of an arithmetical mistake on the Commissioners' part resulting in an underdeclaration of the tax properly due from him'. The tribunal directed that the assessment be increased in accordance with *VATA 1994, s 84(5)*. *R & YL Ho (t/a Robert's Golden Cod Fish Bar)*, [1996] VATDR 423 (VTD 14252). (*Note.* An appeal against a penalty under *VATA 1994, s 60* was also dismissed.)

[3.18] A clothing manufacturer appealed against an estimated assessment, contending that it had not been made to the best of the Commissioners' judgment. The tribunal rejected this contention and upheld the validity of the assessment while reducing it in amount. The tribunal observed that the officer responsible for the assessment had erred in failing to analyse a sample of goods obtained from the manufacturer. However, applying *dicta* of Carnwath J in *Rahman*, 3.8 above, 'the tribunal should not treat an assessment as invalid merely because it disagrees as to how the judgment should have been exercised. A much stronger finding is required.' Accordingly, the fact that the Commissioners had not fully considered all the material put before them did not invalidate the assessment. The tribunal observed that 'it cannot be right that a trader can escape his liabilities because an officer did not take into account something that may well not have influenced his decision in any event'. *M Desai (t/a Regency Garments)*, MAN/97/455 (VTD 16036).

Other cases

[3.19] There have been a very large number of other cases in which the tribunal has held that an assessment has been made to the best of the Commissioners' judgment, and has dismissed the appeal. In the interests of space, such cases are not summarised individually in this book.

Cases where the appellant was partly successful

[3.20] The Commissioners had issued assessments charging VAT of more than £650,000 on a company (P) which imported and sold tropical birds. The company's controlling director (H) had been convicted of evasion of VAT and sentenced to 12 months' imprisonment. Following the conclusion of the criminal proceedings, the tribunal heard the appeal against the assessments, observing that 'the assessments assumed undeclared tax-inclusive sales of £4,050,000'. The tribunal reviewed the evidence in detail and held that the assessments had not been made to the best of the Commissioners' judgment, finding on the evidence that 'the tax evaded was only a small fraction of that assessed'. The Commissioners appealed to the Ch D, contending that the fact that the tribunal considered the assessment to be excessive did not justify a conclusion that it had not been made to the best of their judgment. The Ch D accepted this contention, allowed the Commissioners' appeal, and remitted the case to the tribunal to determine the amount of the assessment. Patten J held that the tribunal had 'misdirected itself and misapplied the law on best judgment'. There was no evidence that the officer responsible for the assessment 'did anything but his honest and genuine best, however mistaken he may have been'. The CA unanimously upheld this decision. Carnwath LJ held that 'this was not an appropriate case for the assessments to be set aside. The background was a serious fraud on the Customs, to which (H) had pleaded guilty. There was no doubt that an assessment to VAT was appropriate. The burden was on (P) to show what was the correct amount. The Commissioners were entitled to be highly sceptical of any information coming from a convicted fraudster. They took the view that the fraud was on a much larger scale than (H) had admitted. They had plenty of material on which they could reasonably do so.' Against that background, 'it was wrong for the tribunal to allow the "best of their judgment" issue to dominate the proceedings'. Carnwath LJ observed that 'the hearing would have been much more manageable if attention had been directed to the admissible evidence relevant to fixing the correct amount of tax.' *Pegasus Birds Ltd v C & E Commrs (No 2)*, CA [2004] STC 1509; [2004] EWCA Civ 1015. (*Note*. For a preliminary issue in this case, see **3.57** below.)

Estimated initial assessment followed by further assessment

[3.21] The proprietor of a dry-cleaning business was registered for VAT in March 1996 after the Commissioners had formed the opinion that his turnover exceeded the registration threshold. In July 1996 an estimated assessment was issued by the VAT Central Unit at Southend, covering the period to May 1996. The officer who was investigating the trader's liability considered that the assessment was inadequate, and arranged for the issue of a further assessment two months later. The tribunal held that the initial assessment had not been made to the best of the Commissioners' judgment. The chairman (Mr. Wallace) observed that 'it is not clear to us that the Commissioners are empowered to exercise their best judgment under *s 73(1)* through the agency of a computer or to authorise a computer programmer coupled with persons feeding information into a computer to assess to best judgment on their behalf'. The assessment was 'wholly inconsistent' with the details which the Commissioners had already obtained. The fact that the assessment was too low rather than too high was 'irrelevant', and the Commissioners should have withdrawn the initial assessment and substituted a new assessment for the correct figure. However, the further assessment had been made to the best of the Commissioners' judgment and was valid, since it 'was independent and did not depend on the validity of the (initial) assessment'. The proprietor appealed to the QB, which upheld the validity of the supplementary assessment. Carnwath J observed that there was 'no reason in principle or common sense why the Commissioners' conclusion on the Central Assessment, assuming it to have been correct, should deprive the Customs of the right to pursue the supplementary assessment'. *A Bennett v C & E Commrs*, QB [1999] STC 248. (*Notes*. (1) The Commissioners did not cross-appeal against the tribunal's decision that the initial assessment was not made to the best of their judgment. They subsequently issued a replacement assessment, for which see **2.127** APPEALS. (2) For other issues in this case, see **57.13** REGISTRATION and **34.14** HUMAN RIGHTS.)

[3.22] The decision in *Bennett*, **3.21** above, was applied in the similar subsequent case of *EK Rustem (t/a The Dry Cleaners)*, LON/96/821 (VTD 15206).

Scottish tribunals—whether 'Rahman' principles applicable in Scotland

[3.23] In a Scottish excise duty case, the tribunal chairman (Mr. Coutts, sitting alone) specifically questioned the application in Scotland of the principles laid down by Carnwath J in *Rahman*, **3.8** above. Mr. Coutts expressed the view that the *dicta* of Carnwath J were not 'necessarily binding' in Scotland, and stated that 'the entire discussion of *Van Boeckel* (see **3.1** above) in *Rahman* was *obiter* and it should not be assumed that the observations therein would necessarily be followed in Scotland'. Mr. Coutts directed that the assessment under appeal should be substantially reduced. *R Cameron (t/a RC Bookmakers)*, EDN/98/8001 (E96). (*Notes.* (1) Although this was an excise duty case, Mr. Coutts' observations are clearly also relevant to VAT. (2) The decision in *Rahman* has been approved and applied in a large number of subsequent English cases. With regard to the inter-relationship between English and Scottish courts in tax cases, see the judgment of Lord Reid in *Abbott v Philbin*, HL 1960, 39 TC 82; [1961] AC 352; [1960] 2 All ER 763. Mr. Coutts' decision in *Cameron* fails to refer to the guidelines laid down by Lord Reid.)

Other cases

[3.24] There have been a number of other cases in which the tribunal has held, on the particular facts, that an assessment has been excessive, and has allowed the appeal in part, reducing the amount of the assessment. In the interests of space, such cases are not summarised individually in this book. For summaries of such cases decided up to 31 December 1993, see Tolley's VAT Cases 1994.

Cases where the appellant was successful

[3.25] The Commissioners issued an estimated assessment on the proprietor of a retail shop selling women's clothing. The trader's accounts had showed a gross profit rate of 34%. The assessment charged tax of £441 and was based on a gross profit rate of 47%. The tribunal reviewed the evidence in detail and allowed the appeal, finding that the trader had 'discharged the onus of proof' that her records and accounts were accurate. *Mrs K Taylor (t/a Jeans)*, [1975] VATTR 86 (VTD 163). (*Note.* For a preliminary issue in this case, see **2.67** APPEALS, and for the award of costs, see **2.450** APPEALS.)

[3.26] An appeal against an estimated assessment was allowed in a case where the officer responsible for the assessment agreed that he had wrongly used tax-inclusive figures for purchases and tax-exclusive figures for takings. The tribunal held that the assessment had not been made to the best of the Commissioners' judgment. *P Friel*, [1977] VATTR 147 (VTD 396).

[3.27] The Commissioners issued an estimated assessment, covering a period of more than four years, on the proprietor of a café. The proprietor had treated 30% of his sales as zero-rated. The assessment, which was issued after two days' observation of the café by VAT officers, was computed on the basis that only 15% of the sales were zero-rated. The tribunal allowed the proprietor's appeal, holding on the evidence that it was unreasonable to issue an assessment covering more than four years on the basis of two years' observations, and that the assessment had not been made to the best of the Commissioners' judgment. *GA Harrison*, [1981] VATTR 164 (VTD 1125). (*Note.* For the award of costs, see **2.458** APPEALS.)

[3.28] A VAT officer conducting a control visit discovered that, through a clerical error, a company had overclaimed input tax by £119. She issued an estimated assessment charging tax of more than £22,000, computed on the assumption that there had been a large number of similar errors. The company appealed, contending that the error of £119 was the only large error of its type and that the total of overclaimed input tax for the relevant period was £153. The tribunal accepted the company's evidence and reduced the assessment to this amount. The officer had not made the assessment to the best of her judgment, as it was not reasonable to suppose that the error of £119 which she had discovered was typical of other errors. There was 'no element whatsoever of evasion'. *WM Low & Co plc*, EDN/91/78 (VTD 7162).

[3.29] An appeal was allowed in a case where the tribunal found that the officer responsible for an assessment had failed to apply the rules relating to tax points correctly, and had charged tax twice in respect of continuous supplies of services (firstly when invoices were raised and again when payments were made in respect of those invoices). The tribunal held that the assessment must be viewed as a whole, and that the result of these errors was that the whole assessment was invalid as it had not been made to the best of the Commissioners' judgment. *Fresh Pasta Products*, [1993] VATTR 238 (VTD 9781). (*Note. Dicta* of the tribunal were disapproved by the QB in the subsequent case of *Dollar Land (Feltham) Ltd*, **18.622** DEFAULT SURCHARGE.)

[3.30] A builder made supplies to a brewery company, and issued three invoices in respect of these services. He accounted for output tax in his return for December 1990. Subsequently the brewery company questioned the invoices, and requested the builder to cancel the three original invoices and issue six replacement invoices, with more details of the work which he had carried out. He issued the replacement invoices in January 1991. In June 1992 a VAT officer discovered that the builder had issued two sets of invoices and had not issued a credit note to cancel the original set. The officer formed the opinion that the builder should have accounted for output tax on the January 1991 invoices, and should issue a credit note to recover the output tax on the original invoices, which he had accounted for in December 1990. He issued an assessment, including a charge to default interest for the period from January 1991 to June 1992. The tribunal allowed the builder's appeal, holding that the assessment had not been issued to the best of the Commissioners' judgment. Furthermore, in raising the interest charge, the Commissioners had not acted 'reasonably', applying *Associated Provincial Picture Houses v Wednesbury Corporation*, CA 1947, [1948] 1 KB 223; [1947] 2 All ER 680. The tribunal chairman commented that 'the tax liability arising on the replacement invoices, and the lack of any credit note in respect of the original invoices, did not alter the fact that the amount of tax due was already in the hands of the Commissioners'. *C Callaway*, LON/92/2978A (VTD 12039).

[3.31] The Commissioners issued an estimated assessment on the proprietors of a kebab and pizza shop. The assessment was computed on the basis of an average rate of suppression of takings. The tribunal upheld the assessment and the proprietors appealed to the QB. Latham J held that the tribunal had erred in its reasoning by failing to appreciate that the proprietors had not sold pizzas for the whole of the period assessed, and by taking purchases of pizza boxes into account without making allowances for the closing stock of such boxes. On the evidence, the tribunal had 'misdirected itself or misunderstood the true nature of the issue'. Its reasoning was fundamentally flawed and the case should be remitted to a new tribunal for rehearing. *V & S Koca v C & E Commrs*, QB 1995, [1996] STC 58. (*Note.* There was no further public hearing of the appeal.)

[3.32] An appeal was allowed in a case involving an upholstery business, where the tribunal found that the VAT officer responsible for the assessment had failed to take account of wastage. The chairman observed that 'it is not enough to go through the motions of a mark-up exercise, however faultless one's arithmetic, merely on the basis of what one is told; one should apply some common-sense to the analysis of the situation'. To assess an upholsterer without taking wastage into account 'does not constitute the exercise of best judgment'. *DJ Milliner & RF Burt*, [1995] VATDR 255 (VTD 13438).

[3.33] A partnership operated a sandwich bar which provided hot and cold food for consumption on and off the premises, so that some of its supplies were standard-rated whereas others were zero-rated. From July 1989 to September 1994 the partnership treated 60% of its sales as zero-rated. Following a control visit in September 1994, the partners agreed that this figure should be reduced to 50%. The Commissioners issued an assessment on the basis that the figure of 50% should be backdated to October 1989. The tribunal allowed the partnership's appeal, holding that the assessment was based on 'wholly inadequate material' and was not to the best judgment of the Commissioners. *G & M Ramsey (t/a George's Kitchen)*, [1995] VATDR 484 (VTD 13582).

[3.34] The Commissioners issued an estimated assessment on a retail shop-keeper selling newspapers, confectionery and tobacco. The shopkeeper had been using a Retail Scheme (Scheme B2, which has subsequently been withdrawn) but the assessment had not been based on a Retail Scheme calculation. The tribunal allowed the shopkeeper's appeal, holding that the assessment had not been made to the best of the Commissioners' judgment, since the Commissioners had entered into a legally binding agreement to permit the shopkeeper to use a Retail Scheme. Applying *dicta* in *Tesco plc*, 58.59 RETAILERS' SPECIAL SCHEMES, 'a scheme which has been agreed cannot be altered retrospectively'. The effect of the agreement was that any estimated assessment must be based on the agreed Retail Scheme calculation. *I Briggs*, [1995] VATDR 386 (VTD 13603).

[3.35] The Commissioners issued estimated assessments on a builder (M) who used the same bank account for business and private transactions. In the assessment, lodgments into M's bank account were treated as business receipts. M appealed, contending that his business records were accurate and that the lodgments in question were not business takings. The tribunal accepted M's evidence and allowed his appeal, finding that M had shown on the balance of probabilities that the relevant lodgments were non-business items. The tribunal observed that 'there is no statutory obligation on a taxable person to keep a separate business bank account' and held that 'the appellant is not required to provide written evidence that each and every one of the items which go to make up the appealed assessment are private receipts rather than business receipts'. *A Moon (t/a Craft Master Construction)*, LON/96/1435 (VTD 14855).

[3.36] See also *University Court of the University of Dundee*, **11.39** CHARITIES; *Moti Mahal Indian Restaurant*, **50.137** PENALTIES: EVASION OF TAX, and *Li (t/a Summer Palace Restaurant)*, **50.138** PENALTIES: EVASION OF TAX.

Assessment partly duplicating previous assessment

[3.37] Following a control visit in 1988, the Commissioners issued a 'global' assessment covering the twelve months ending 29 February 1988. In 1990 another VAT officer made a control visit to the same trader, and arranged for the issue of another 'global' assessment covering three years, and including the tax which had already been assessed in 1988. The trader appealed, contending that the assessment was invalid since it had not been made to the best of the Commissioners' judgment. The Commissioners accepted that the assessment should be reduced to take account of the duplication of the previous assessment, but contended that the assessment should still be treated as valid with regard to the periods beginning on 1 March 1988, which had not been included in the previous assessment. The tribunal allowed the trader's appeal. The officer responsible for issuing the second assessment should have considered whether she was duplicating the previous assessment. Her failure to do this meant that the assessment had not been made to the best of the Commissioners' judgment. Since the assessment had not been made to the best of the Commissioners' judgment, it was invalid and void, and could not be corrected by any subsequent amendment to it. Applying *dicta* of Woolf J in *International Language Centres Ltd*, **3.41** below, an assessment had to be considered as a whole and treated as either wholly valid or wholly void; if part of the assessment was invalid it followed that the whole assessment was a nullity. *JH Barber*, [1992] VATTR 144 (VTD 7727). (*Note. Dicta* of Woolf J in *International Language Centres Ltd* were subsequently disapproved by the CA in *House*, **3.127** below.)

[3.38] The decision in *Barber*, **3.37** above, was applied in a subsequent case where the facts were broadly similar, and the tribunal held that 'fresh interpretation of already known facts is not sufficient'. *TY McGuirk Sports Ltd*, [2003] VATDR 472 (VTD 17599).

Other cases

[3.39] There have been a number of other cases in which the tribunal has held, on the particular facts, that an assessment has not been made to the best of the Commissioners' judgment, and has allowed the appeal. In the interests of space, such cases are not summarised individually in this book. For summaries of such cases decided up to 31 December 1993, see Tolley's VAT Cases 1994. Where the cases in question were decided before the QB and CA decisions in *Rahman*, **3.8** and **3.9** above, they should be read in the light of that case.

Time limit for assessment (VATA 1994, s 73(6))

Whether assessment made within two years of end of accounting period (VATA 1994, s 73(6)(a))

[3.40] In the case noted at 29.41 FOOD, the tribunal held that an assessment covering a period of three and a half years was invalid to the extent that it covered accounting periods ending more than two years before the date on which it was issued. *Macklin Services (Vending) West Ltd*, [1979] VATTR 31 (VTD 688).

[3.41] A company which supplied educational courses to students visiting the UK formed the opinion that it should have treated some of its supplies as zero-rated under *FA 1972*, and had thereby overpaid tax of £40,560. It deducted this amount, in two stages, in computing its tax liability for the periods ending February 1979 and November 1979. In January 1982 the Commissioners issued an assessment to recover the £40,560, together with an unrelated underdeclaration of £1,436. The company appealed, contending that the assessment was out of time. The QB accepted this contention and allowed the appeal, holding that the assessment was a 'global' assessment and could not be separated into its two component parts. *International Language Centres Ltd v C & E Commrs*, QB [1983] STC 394. (*Notes*. (1) The disputed supplies were subsequently held to be standard-rated, and would be standard-rated under the law as now in force. (2) For subsequent developments in this case, see **14.69** COLLECTION AND ENFORCEMENT. (3) *Obiter dicta* of Woolf J were disapproved by the CA in the subsequent case of *House*, **3.127** below.)

[3.42] The decision in *International Language Centres Ltd*, **3.41** above, was applied in a subsequent case where the Commissioners issued an assessment, covering the period from January 1988 to March 1990, in January 1991. The tribunal held that the assessment was out of time. *Greenhalgh's Craft Bakery Ltd*, MAN/91/626 (VTD 10955). (*Note*. For another issue in this case, see **29.56** FOOD.)

[3.43] A company (C) made a payment of £2,000,000 to another company (H) in February 1991. C considered that this payment should be treated as inclusive of VAT. However, H considered that the payment was outside the scope of VAT, and did not issue a VAT invoice. C reclaimed input tax in respect of the payment in its return for the period ending June 1991. The Commissioners initially accepted C's claim, and issued an assessment on H charging output tax on the payment, but H's appeal was allowed by a tribunal (see **62.142** SUPPLY). In June 1993 the Commissioners issued an assessment on C to recover the input tax which C had claimed. C appealed, contending that the assessment was outside the time limit of what is now *VATA 1994, s 73(6)(a)*, on the basis that the 'prescribed accounting period' referred to in *s 73(6)(a)* should be treated as the period in which the payment was made (i.e. the period ending March 1991), rather than the period in which the input tax was claimed. The CA rejected this contention and upheld the assessment. The 'prescribed accounting period' was the period in which the input tax had been claimed. Accordingly the assessment had been made within the statutory time limit. Thorpe LJ held that 'as a matter of practicality and good sense any limitation period to run against the Commissioners would not naturally be expected to run earlier than the date upon which they first receive notice by way of account' and observed that there could not be any injustice to taxpayers in holding that 'certainty is deferred until 24 months after the end of the prescribed accounting period covered by the return within which the transaction was included'. *C & E Commrs v The Croydon Hotel & Leisure Co Ltd*, CA [1996] STC 1105. (*Note*. For the hearing of the substantive appeal, see **36.641** INPUT TAX.)

[3.44] A company sold clothing and arranged interest-free credit for customers. Initially, it accounted for VAT on the full purchase price. In October 1999, it submitted a repayment claim on the basis that the effect of a CA decision was that it should not have accounted for output tax on the commission which it paid to the finance company. (The CA decision in question was subsequently overruled by the CJEC and HL—see *Primback Ltd*, **22.242** EUROPEAN COMMUNITY LAW.) The Commissioners accepted that, on the basis of the CA decision, the company was entitled to a repayment, which they made in March 2000. In October 2000 (before the CJEC overruled the CA decision in *Primback*), the Commissioners issued assessments to recover the amounts which they had repaid. The assessments for most of the periods were made under the provisions of *VATA 1994, s 80(4A)*. However, the assessments relating to the periods ending in October 1996 and October 1997 (where the company's input tax had exceeded its output tax, because of substantial purchases of stock) were made under the provisions of *VATA 1994, s 73(2)*. The company appealed, contending that these two assessments had been made outside the statutory two-year time limit. The tribunal accepted this contention and allowed the appeal, holding that the assessments had to be treated as being for the periods ending October 1996 and October 1997, rather than for the period ending October 1999 in which the company had made its repayment claim. Accordingly the assessments were outside the statutory two-year time limit. The Ch D upheld this decision. David Richards J held that the correct accounting period for the purposes of *VATA 1994, s 73(2)* was 'the period to which the relevant VAT credit related'. He distinguished the CA decision in *The Croydon Hotel & Leisure Co Ltd*, **3.43** above, holding that the decision there did not compel 'the conclusion that where a claim is properly made by way of correction or adjustment to the return for an earlier period, the ensuing repayment or credit is paid or given not for that period but for the period for which the claim is made'. *C & E Commrs v Laura Ashley Ltd*, Ch D 2003, [2004] STC 635; [2003] EWHC 2832 (Ch). (*Note*. Customs announced that they were appealing to the CA against this decision: see Business Brief 25/2004, issued on 14 September 2004. However, there was no further public hearing of the appeal.)

Letter within time limit but form VAT 641 outside limit

[3.45] On 20 September 1999 a VAT officer wrote to a partnership which operated a restaurant, to advise the partnership that he had issued an assessment covering the accounting periods from October 1997 to April 1999. The partnership appealed. The appeal was not heard until July 2002. At the hearing, the partnership contended as a preliminary issue that the letter did not constitute an assessment, and that the relevant assessment had not been made until July 2001, when the relevant form VAT 641 was completed. The tribunal rejected this contention, holding that the assessment had been made within the statutory time limit. The tribunal chairman (Mr. Oliver) observed that the reason for the delay in completing the VAT 641 was that the Commissioners had been considering penalty proceedings, and that it was 'the Commissioners' practice not to prepare a from VAT 641 until the decision to assess for such penalties has been made'. The VAT 641 had eventually been issued 'to enable the central computer to make interest calculations'. There were 'no statutory provisions which govern either the manner in which assessments should be "made" by the Commissioners or the manner in which such assessments should be notified. These matters are left to the discretion and administrative practice of the Commissioners'. Accordingly, 'so long as there is a properly evidenced decision to assess which is based on a properly calculated quantification of arrears, there will be an effective assessment. The form 641 procedure coupled with the issue of a notification on from 655 is of course desirable, but it is not essential.' Accordingly, the letter constituted an assessment and the assessment had been made within the statutory time limit. *Piero's Restaurant and Pizzeria*, LON/01/927 (VTD 17711).

Letter within time limit but form VAT 655 not issued until after time limit

[3.46] In 1999 the Commissioners sent a letter to a company (C), informing it that they had made a 'protective assessment', which would not be enforced pending the forthcoming CJEC decision in *C & E Commrs v Primback Ltd*, 22.242 EUROPEAN COMMUNITY LAW. The CJEC did not deliver judgment until 2001, when it found in favour of the Commissioners. The relevant form VAT 641 had been completed in 1999, but the Commissioners did not issue a form VAT 655 until after the CJEC decision. C appealed, contending that the assessment was invalid because the form VAT 655 had not been issued within the statutory two-year time limit. The tribunal, Ch D and CA unanimously rejected this contention and dismissed C's appeal. Jonathan Parker LJ held that 'a "protective" assessment, in the sense of an assessment which is made in order to protect the Commissioners' position in the event of a subsequent appeal being decided in their favour' was still an assessment. In this case, 'the assessment was complete on the signing off of the VAT 641 dated 16 December 1999'. Jonathan Parker LJ also observed that 'this case illustrates the risks the revenue authorities may run when attempting to deal fairly and straightforwardly with a taxpayer'. There were 'no merits in this appeal'. C had 'attempted to construct a case based purely on technicalities', in circumstances where the Commissioners 'were doing their best to deal fairly and straightforwardly with (C), and where (C) can have been in no doubt as to what the Commissioners were attempting to achieve'. *Courts plc v C & E Commrs*, CA 2004, [2005] STC 27; [2004] EWCA Civ 1527.

Whether assessment made within one year of 'evidence of facts' (VATA 1994, s 73(6)(b))

Cases where the assessment was upheld

Date on which evidence received

[3.47] In May 1977 Customs issued an assessment covering the period from 1 April 1973 to 30 April 1976. The trader appealed, contending that the assessment was invalid as it had been made outside the statutory time limit. The tribunal rejected this contention and dismissed the appeal, finding that Customs had not received the information necessary to issue the assessment until June 1976. *HE McCafferty*, LON/77/224 (VTD 483).

[3.48] Following a control visit, Customs issued an assessment covering a period of 28 months. The officer responsible for the assessment also discovered that the trader had treated the sale of an excavator as a zero-rated export, although he was unable to produce the necessary proof of export. The trader assured the officer that the excavator had been exported, and undertook to submit evidence of this. Accordingly the liability was not included in the assessment. However, the trader subsequently failed to submit the evidence in question, and thus Customs issued a further assessment charging tax of £70 on the sale of the excavator. The tribunal dismissed the trader's appeal, holding that the assessment had been made within the one-year time limit of what is now *VATA 1994, s 73(6)(b)*. *C Judd (t/a CJ Plant Hire)*, LON/79/9 (VTD 813).

[3.49] In July 1976 Customs issued an estimated assessment on a company trading as jewellers, covering the 21 months ending 31 December 1974. The company appealed, contending as a preliminary point that the assessment was invalid as it covered more than one accounting period. The tribunal rejected this contention and the company appealed to the CA, which upheld the tribunal decision (see **3.114** below) and remitted the case to the tribunal to hear the substantive appeal. The tribunal upheld the assessment, finding that Customs had been unable to quantify the assessment until December 1975, when they received details of the company's turnover. Accordingly the assessment had been made within the one-year time limit of what is now *VATA 1994, s 73(6)(b)*. *SJ Grange Ltd*, CAR/77/120 (VTD 884).

[3.50] The decision in *SJ Grange Ltd*, **3.49** above, was applied in the similar case of *Gatherchoice Holdings Ltd*, LON/90/1339Y (VTD 5804).

[3.51] A company failed to account for output tax on certain supplies which it made, treating them as exempt from VAT under the legislation then in force. In 1981 Customs discovered that the supplies had taken place and appeared to be taxable. In February 1982 Customs asked the company to provide details of the amounts of the supplies in question. The company did not provide these details until February 1984, and Customs issued an assessment in April 1984. The company appealed, contending that the assessment was outside the statutory time limit. The tribunal rejected this contention and dismissed the appeal, and the QB upheld this decision. On the evidence, Customs had not had sufficient information to raise an assessment until February 1984, so that the assessment was within the one-year time limit of what is now *VATA 1994, s 73(6)(b)*. *Schlumberger Inland Services Inc v C & E Commrs*, QB 1986, [1987] STC 228.

[3.52] A farmer (C) registered for VAT in 1973, and also obtained a second registration in respect of a restaurant of which he was the proprietor. This separate registration was cancelled in 1976, on the basis that an individual was only entitled to one registration for all his business activities (see the cases at 57.1 *et seq.* REGISTRATION). Following this, C failed to account for output tax on his takings from the restaurant. On 22 August 1983 a VAT officer made a routine control visit to the farm. He was told of the existence of the restaurant, and was told that it was run by a limited company. In May 1984 he made a further visit, and was told that the restaurant was run by C as sole proprietor. Customs issued estimated assessments in respect of the restaurant on 21 June and 3 August 1984. C appealed, contending that the assessments were out of time and invalid. The tribunal dismissed the appeal, holding that the necessary evidence of facts did not come to Customs' knowledge until 22 August 1983. The fact that Customs knew that C had operated a restaurant from 1973 to 1976 did not justify an inference that they were aware of the subsequent underdeclarations. The Commissioners were entitled to assume either that the restaurant had closed, or that the tax due in respect of it was being correctly accounted for under C's existing registration number. The QB upheld the tribunal decision, holding that there was no basis for inferring that Customs knew of any underpayment of tax before 22 August 1983, and it followed that the assessments were within the statutory time limit. *OAS Cutts v C & E Commrs*, QB 1988, [1989] STC 201.

[3.53] In the case noted at 3.4 above, where a trader who carried on a clandestine business of manufacturing and selling counterfeit recording tapes did not register for VAT and kept no accounting records, the QB held that the assessments had been issued within the statutory time limit. Simon Brown J held that the reference to 'evidence of facts coming to the Commissioners' "knowledge", in my judgment, means what it says; the word does not encompass constructive knowledge'. *M Spillane v C & E Commrs*, QB 1989, [1990] STC 212.

[3.54] Similar decisions were reached in *Mervyn Conn Organisation Ltd*, LON/89/67Z (VTD 5205); *Chatfield Applied Research Laboratories Ltd*, LON/92/3393A (VTD 11117); *Castlegate Holdings Ltd*, MAN/92/1120 (VTD 11579); *RJ & JW Furniss (t/a Newspoint)*, LON/96/486 (VTD 14758); *KN & DJ Robotham (t/a North Walsham Insurance Services)*, LON/97/879 (VTD 15325); *SN Tang & ND Coong (t/a Man Ying)*, MAN/01/363 (VTD 18524); *Cox's Cars Ltd*, MAN/06/137 (VTD 19855), and *SH Siddiquee*, LON/06/1025 (VTD 20295).

[3.55] In April 1992 a VAT officer discovered errors in the way in which the Post Office had accounted for output tax on self-supplies of stationery. In September 1992 and March 1993 Customs issued assessments to the Post Office, charging output tax on self-supplies of stationery made in the periods from September 1986 to March 1992. The Post Office appealed, contending that the assessments were outside the one-year time limit of what is now *VATA 1994, s 73(6)(b)*, since Customs had had all the information necessary to issue the assessments more than a year before they were actually issued. The tribunal accepted this contention but the QB remitted the case to the tribunal for rehearing, holding that the tribunal chairman had erred in law, and had wrongly treated *VATA 1994, s 73(6)(b)* as encompassing constructive knowledge. Potts J held that the words 'evidence of facts' should be construed as 'evidence of facts giving rise to a particular assessment. This is not the same as the date on which the Customs should have been aware that there was an under declaration of tax, i.e. the date on which the Customs could be said to be fixed with constructive knowledge of an error in the taxpayer's returns.' Applying *dicta* of Simon Brown J in *Spillane*, 3.53 above, 'evidence of facts' did not encompass 'constructive knowledge'. *C & E Commrs v The Post Office*, QB [1995] STC 749.

[3.56] The QB decision in *The Post Office*, 3.55 above, was applied in *WY Wong*, MAN/98/546 (VTD 17348) and in *British Teleflower Service Ltd*, [1995] VATDR 356 (VTD 13756).

[3.57] Customs began criminal proceedings against the controlling director of a company which sold exotic birds. The trial was adjourned in an attempt to quantify the amount of evaded VAT. On 30 April 1996 an accountant, employed by Customs, calculated an appropriate mark-up of 159% for sales to the public and 104% for sales to other retailers. On 30 September 1996 an accountant representing the company put forward a lower mark-up of 80%. A meeting took place on 30 January 1997, and on 16 April 1997 the Commissioners issued ten quarterly assessments charging VAT. The company appealed, contending as a preliminary point that the assessments had been issued outside the one-year time limit of *VATA 1994, s 73(6)(b)*. The tribunal rejected this contention and upheld the assessments in principle, and the QB and CA upheld this decision. Aldous LJ observed that the purpose of *s 73(6)* 'is to protect the taxpayer from tardy assessment, not to penalise Customs for failing to spot some fact which, for example, may have become available to them in a document obtained during a raid'. On the evidence, Customs had needed to establish the appropriate mark-up figure, which had occurred at the meeting on 30 January 1997. The one-year time limit therefore ran from that date, and the assessments had been made within the statutory time limit. *Pegasus Birds Ltd v C & E Commrs (No 1)*, CA [2000] STC 91. (*Notes*. (1) At a separate hearing, the director was convicted of evasion of VAT and sentenced to 12 months' imprisonment. (2) For subsequent developments in this case, see **3.20** above.)

[3.58] The CA decision in *Pegasus Birds Ltd v C & E Commrs (No 1)*, 3.57 above, was applied in a similar subsequent case where Customs made an assessment in February 2007 and the tribunal held that they had not obtained the necessary 'evidence of facts' until October 2006, so that the assessment was within the statutory time limit. *Kidz R Us Children Centre Ltd*, MAN/07/814 (VTD 20882).

[3.59] A similar decision, also applying the principles laid down in *Pegasus Birds Ltd v C & E Commrs (No 1)*, 3.57 above, was reached in *Weight Watchers (UK) Ltd v HMRC (No 2)*, [2010] UKFTT 384 (TC), TC00666.

[3.60] There are a large number of other cases in which tribunals have upheld the validity of assessments and have rejected appellants' contentions that

Customs had the necessary 'evidence of facts' more than a year before the issue of the assessment in question. In the interests of space, such cases are not reported individually in this book. For a list of such cases decided up to and including 31 December 1993, see Tolley's VAT Cases 1994.

Date on which assessment issued

[3.61] Customs formed the opinion that a company had failed to account for tax on sales of silver to metal dealers, and issued an assessment which was dated within the one-year time limit but was not notified to the company until after the expiry of the time limit. The company appealed, contending that the assessment was invalid. The tribunal dismissed the appeal, holding that an assessment which had not been properly notified was unenforceable until it had been notified, but was not rendered invalid by a delay in notification. The CA upheld the tribunal decision. *Grunwick Processing Laboratories Ltd v C & E Commrs*, CA [1987] STC 357. (*Notes*. (1) For another issue in this case, see **2.234** APPEALS. (2) For Customs' current policy with regard to time limits, see Business Brief 5/01, issued on 13 March 2001, and *Notice No 915*, issued on 1 March 2001.)

[3.62] The decision in *Grunwick Processing Laboratories Ltd*, **3.61** above, was applied in a subsequent case where an assessment had been completed and signed within the one-year time limit but was not notified to the person assessed until after the expiry of the time limit. The tribunal held that 'the date on which the assessment was made is the date on which the decision to assess is recorded together with the amount of the assessment and on which this record is countersigned and dated'. *HR Babber (t/a Ram Parkash Sunderdass & Sons)*, [1992] VATTR 268 (VTD 5958). (*Note*. The decision in this case was approved by the QB in *The Post Office*, **3.55** above. For another issue in this case, see **67.60** VALUATION.)

[3.63] The decision in *Grunwick Processing Laboratories Ltd*, **3.61** above, was also applied in the subsequent cases of *A Garavand (t/a Caspian Kebab & Pizza)*, LON/93/217A (VTD 11847); *S Ali (t/a The Bengal Brasserie)*, MAN/98/644 (VTD 16952) and *Yuen Tung Restaurant Ltd*, **3.121** below.

[3.64] A similar decision was reached in a case where Customs had withdrawn an assessment following the QB decision in *Ridgeons Bulk Ltd* (see **3.179** below), and had subsequently issued a replacement assessment which was not notified to the company until more than a year after Customs had received the necessary 'evidence of facts'. The company appealed, contending that the assessment was out of time and invalid. The tribunal rejected this contention and dismissed the appeal, applying *dicta* of Balcombe LJ in *Le Rififi Ltd*, **3.87** below, and holding that 'the assessment of the amount of tax considered to be due and the notification to the taxpayer were separate operations'. Accordingly the assessment under appeal had been 'made' when the form VAT 641 was countersigned by the appropriate officer, which was within the relevant one-year time limit, and was valid even though the notice of assessment (form VAT 655) had not been sent to the company until after the expiry of the one-year limit. *Classicmoor Ltd*, [1995] VATDR 1 (VTD 13336).

[3.65] The decision in *Classicmoor Ltd*, **3.64** above, was applied in the similar subsequent case of *D & J Sinclair*, LON/99/703 (VTD 17961).

[3.66] A similar decision was reached in a case where a form VAT 641 was completed in January 2000, but the relevant form VAT 655 was not issued until May 2000. The tribunal specifically declined to follow the decision in *Royal Bank of Scotland Group plc*, **3.84** below, observing that it 'appears to us to be contrary to the weight of authority'. *A Subhan, M Uddin & M Mustak*, LON/00/643 (VTD 17110).

[3.67] A similar decision was reached in a case where a form VAT 641 was completed in October 1999 but the form VAT 655 was not issued until February 2000. *R Bent (t/a Bay Tree Trading Co)*, LON/00/398 (VTD 17139).

[3.68] An assessment was upheld in a case where the tribunal accepted Customs' evidence that the relevant form VAT 642 was date-stamped 5 December 1997 (which was within the one-year time limit), although it was not posted to the appellant company until 23 December (which was outside the time limit). *Dashmore Clothing Ltd*, MAN/98/347 & 348 (VTD 17776). (*Note.* The case was heard with *P & R Fabrics Ltd*, **3.104** below.)

[3.69] In the case noted at **52.362** PENALTIES: MISDECLARATION, the assessment imposing the penalty was posted on 20 March 1991. The rate of such penalties was reduced from that date by *FA 1991*, but the penalty in question was imposed at the old rate. Customs submitted evidence showing that the penalty had been computed, and the assessment prepared, on 15 March, before the reduction of the rate. The tribunal held that 'an assessment is made when the Commissioners reach a decision to make the assessment and calculate the amount due', and that 'the act of assessing and the act of notifying are two different acts that can occur on different dates'. Accordingly, the assessment here had been made on 15 March. *JL Dart*, LON/91/2033 (VTD 9066).

[3.70] A similar decision, applying *Babber*, **3.62** above, was reached in *CE Kinsella Traction*, LON/92/1461 (VTD 10130).

Cases where the appellant was partly successful

[3.71] The supplies made by a trader included exempt supplies, necessitating an apportionment of his input tax. He used a method approved by the Commissioners for his accounting periods up to 28 February 1974, but thereafter switched to an alternative method without obtaining the Commissioners' approval as required by the regulations then in force, although the change was apparent from his returns. The alternative method was inappropriate for his circumstances and gave him a greater credit for input tax than the method which he had originally used. In June 1976 the Commissioners issued an assessment covering the period from 1 April 1973 to 31 March 1975. The tribunal held that as the returns were in the possession of the Commissioners, the assessment was out of date with regard to the periods up to 28 February 1974, having been made outside the two years of what is now *VATA 1994, s 73(6)(a)* and no evidence of new facts having reached the Commissioners to bring the case within *VATA 1994, s 73(6)(b)*. *V Lord (t/a Lords Electrical and Fancy Goods)*, MAN/76/113 (VTD 320).

[3.72] In the case noted at **62.24** SUPPLY, the Commissioners issued an assessment in March 1980, covering the accounting periods from April 1974 to December 1979 inclusive. The company appealed, contending that the assessment had been issued outside the one-year time limit of what is now *VATA 1994, s 73(6)(b)*. The tribunal allowed the appeal in part, holding that the assessment was out of time with regard to the accounting periods ending in 1974 and 1975, since the Commissioners had received full information for these years before the end of 1976, but that the assessment was valid with regard to the periods from 1976 to 1979 inclusive, since the Commissioners did not have sufficient information to quantify the assessment until 1980. The company appealed to the QB, which upheld the tribunal decision as one of fact. Sir Douglas Frank QC observed that 'the tribunal cannot substitute its own view of what facts justify the making of an assessment but can only decide when the last of those facts was communicated or came to the knowledge of the officer'. *Cumbrae Properties (1963) Ltd v C & E Commrs*, QB [1981] STC 799.

[3.73] A trader (H) had been registered for VAT when carrying on a business of retailing and wholesaling poultry. In about 1975 he and his wife decided that she should start up a business of dealing in second-hand furniture. This business was duly started but, because of illness, H's wife was unable to take any part in it and it was carried on by the appellant. H did not disclose the existence of this business in his returns, and in December 1980 the Commissioners issued an assessment covering the period from 25 April 1977 to 27 September 1980, on the basis that H was liable to account for the tax on the takings of the furniture-dealing business. The tribunal found that a VAT officer was informed of the existence of the business on 28 June 1979, and held that in view of this, the assessment was out of date as regards periods ending more than two years before it was made. *M Head*, MAN/80/242 (VTD 1119). (*Note.* Compare the subsequent QB decision in *Cutts*, **3.52** above.)

[3.74] See also *Hospitality Training Foundation*, **11.50** CHARITIES.

Cases where the appellant was successful

[3.75] Two relatives, B and N, carried on business as goldsmiths from 1975 to March 1976, when N left the business leaving B as the sole proprietor. They did not apply for registration for VAT, but were registered by the Commissioners in February 1979. In May 1979 the Commissioners issued assessments, against which they appealed. They subsequently submitted returns showing no tax due. The Commissioners were not satisfied by the returns, and in December 1981 they withdrew the original assessments and issued new assessments for the same periods. B and N appealed against the replacement assessments, contending that they were out of time. The QB accepted this contention and allowed the appeals. Woolf J held that the submission of returns showing no tax due did not constitute 'evidence of facts' within *s 73(6)(b)*, so that the assessments had been made outside the time limits of *s 73(6)*. Woolf J observed that 'the Commissioners were not obliged to withdraw the previous assessments which were made prior to the making of the returns, and they should have continued to rely on them'. Woolf J also observed that where the two-year period had not elapsed, 'the language of the section does not appear to prevent an assessment being withdrawn and replaced by another assessment'. *B & N Parekh v C & E Commrs*, QB [1984] STC 284.

[**3.76**] The proprietor of a fish and chip shop was deregistered in June 1985 on the basis that his turnover had declined. However, the Commissioners received information that his turnover continued to exceed the registration threshold, and made control visits in June and July 1987. In July 1988 the proprietor was informed that he was being re-registered for VAT with retrospective effect. In August 1988 the Commissioners sent the proprietor a schedule of estimated sales and tax due. In January 1990 the Commissioners issued an estimated assessment, based on the figures in this schedule, covering the period from June 1985 to January 1990. The proprietor appealed, contending that the assessment was out of time, as the Commissioners had had all the information necessary for the issue of the assessment in August 1988 but had not issued the assessment until after the expiry of the one-year time limit laid down by *s 73(6)(b)*. The tribunal accepted this contention and allowed the appeal. *M Woodger*, MAN/90/127 (VTD 5402).

[**3.77**] In December 1989 a company (W) purchased a property from another company (M), which had made an election to waive exemption. W paid a deposit of £36,000, and M issued a completion statement requesting payment of £378,000, and a VAT invoice stating the sale price as £414,000 (i.e. £360,000 plus VAT of £54,000). However, in January 1990 M issued a revised completion statement (for reasons that are not fully set out in the decision) showing a sale price of £326,400 plus VAT of £48,960. In its return for the period ending 31 January 1990, W reclaimed input tax of £48,960. At a control visit in May 1990 a VAT officer saw the earlier completion statement and the VAT invoice, and pointed out that W appeared to have underclaimed input tax by £5,040. He arranged for this amount to be repaid to W in June 1990. In May 1992 a different VAT officer saw the subsequent completion statement and formed the opinion that the £5,040 should not have been repaid to W, and in June 1992 the Commissioners issued an assessment to recover this amount. The company appealed, contending that the assessment was out of time. The tribunal allowed the appeal, finding that the VAT officer who had made the May 1990 control visit had been presented with all the relevant information concerning the transaction, so that no further facts had come to the Commissioners' knowledge after that control visit and the assessment issued in June 1992 was outside the statutory time limit. *Winturn Ltd*, MAN/92/1128 (VTD 10699). (*Notes.* (1) An appeal against a subsequent assessment was dismissed. (2) *Dicta* of the tribunal chairman were disapproved by a subsequent tribunal in *Strollmoor Ltd*, **62.483** SUPPLY.)

[**3.78**] A trader (M) borrowed money from a partnership. He entered into an arrangement whereby, instead of repaying the loan, he would meet leasing payments on equipment which the partnership had leased. He reclaimed input tax on these payments. A VAT officer made a control visit to M in April 1991 and formed the opinion that M had entered into a sale and leaseback arrangement with the effect that M was entitled to credit for the input tax but was required to account for output tax on the purported sale. M wrote to the VAT office explaining the true nature of the transaction, but the officer did not accept M's explanation and arranged for the issue of an assessment in October 1991. M appealed, but the appeal was not set down for hearing. A subsequent control visit took place in April 1993, and on this occasion the officer realised the true nature of the transaction. He withdrew the original assessment charging output tax, and arranged for the issue of an assessment to recover the input tax on the basis that the relevant supplies of leasing equipment had not been made to M. The assessment was dated May 1993, and covered periods from 1990 to October 1992 inclusive. The tribunal allowed M's appeal, holding that the assessment was a global assessment, and was out of time since the necessary evidence of facts had been in the Commissioners' possession for more than a year before the assessment was issued. *AD Mills*, MAN/93/1263 (VTD 12312). (*Note.* For whether an assessment is a 'global' assessment, see now the CA decision in *Le Rififi Ltd*, 3.87 below.)

[3.79] In August 1992 a VAT officer formed the opinion that a company which was partially exempt, and operated a special method of calculating its deductible input tax, had overclaimed input tax by treating too much tax as attributable to taxable supplies. Following correspondence, an assessment covering the period from January 1991 to March 1992 was issued in May 1994. The company appealed, contending that all the relevant information had been in the hands of the Commissioners since September 1992, so that the assessment was outside the twelve-month time limit of what is now *VATA 1994, s 73(6)(b)*. The tribunal accepted this contention and allowed the appeal. The tribunal held that 'in judging what evidence is sufficient', the Commissioners 'may not neglect the consideration that they can assess without exhaustive enquiries and on the material which is before them'. Furthermore, 'the desire to reach an agreement with the taxpayer, though laudable, is not one which should of itself be taken to interrupt the running of the time limits imposed by statute'. *Lazard Brothers & Co Ltd*, LON/94/943 (VTD 13476).

[3.80] An appeal was allowed in a case where assessments were issued in January 1995 and the tribunal found that the Commissioners had held all the necessary information since a control visit in June 1992. *WA Collins*, LON/95/594A (VTD 13579).

[3.81] Similar decisions were reached in *GM & EA Flowers (t/a Soar Valley Construction)*, MAN/95/1805 (VTD 13889); *Mentford Ltd*, LON/99/535 (VTD 16724); *Taste of Raj*, LON/00/507 (VTD 17243); *St Martin's Healthcare Ltd*, LON/01/090 (VTD 20778); *St Martin's Medical Services Ltd*, LON/01/600 (VTD 20778) and *Sophie Holdings Ltd*, [2009] UKFTT 88 (TC), TC00056.

[3.82] In the case noted at **62.465** SUPPLY, Customs had issued an assessment for the period ending 30 September 2002, charging tax of more than £6,000,000. In March 2005 they raised an alternative assessment for the period ending 31 March 2002. The company appealed to the tribunal, contending that this assessment had been raised outside the time limit of *VATA 1994, s 73(6)(b)*. The tribunal accepted this contention and allowed the appeal, holding that Customs had had all the necessary information more than twelve months before they issued the alternative assessment. The only additional information which they had received after March 2004 was the 'skeleton argument' prepared by counsel (H) acting for the appellant company, arguing that the original assessment had been made for the wrong period because the 'tax point' had taken place before March 2002. Applying *dicta* of Jonathan Parker LJ in *C & E Commrs v DFS Furniture Co plc (No 2)*, **3.111**

below, an 'expression of an opinion as to the current state of the law' by 'leading counsel or a distinguished academic' was not a 'fact'. Accordingly H's 'skeleton argument' was not 'evidence of facts'. *Enron Europe Ltd (in administration) (No 2)*, LON/05/435 (VTD 20436).

Date on which assessment issued

[3.83] At a control visit in June 1990, a VAT officer discovered that a clothing manufacturer had apparently been treating clothing suitable for adult women as zero-rated rather than standard-rated. He issued an assessment in July 1990 charging tax on the supplies in question. However, the notice of assessment did not specify the accounting periods to which it related, and the Commissioners formed the opinion that the assessment could therefore have been considered invalid. Accordingly, on 21 May 1991 the Commissioners formally withdrew the defective assessment. A second assessment was issued, dated 30 May, to replace the original assessment. The manufacturer appealed, contending that the second assessment was out of time and invalid as he had not received it until July 1991, which was outside the one-year time limit of *s 73(6)(b)*. The tribunal chairman (Mr. Hilton, sitting alone) accepted this contention and allowed the appeal, rejecting the Commissioners' evidence that the date of issue of the assessment had been 30 May 1991, and holding that the assessment was invalid since 'the date of notification was more than one year after the Commissioners had knowledge of the evidence of the facts which justified the assessment'. *D Mohammed (t/a Aglow Fashions)*, MAN/91/1044 (VTD 10246). (*Notes*. (1) Compare *Grunwick Processing Laboratories Ltd*, **3.61** above, and the cases noted at **3.62** to **3.70** above, in all of which it was held that an assessment had been 'made' on a date prior to that on which it was notified to the appellant. None of these cases is referred to in Mr. Hilton's decision in *Mohammed*. (2) For the Commissioners' current policy with regard to time limits, see Business Brief 5/01, issued on 13 March 2001, and *Notice No 915*, issued on 1 March 2001.)

[3.84] In a Scottish case, the Commissioners issued an assessment on a bank. The notification was dated 5 January 1999. The bank appealed, contending that the assessment was outside the statutory time limit, because the Commissioners had all the information necessary to raise the assessment not later than December 1997. The Commissioners produced an internal form VAT 641, dated 14 December 1998. The tribunal accepted the company's contention and allowed the appeal, holding that 'in the light of the evidence before us that an assessment whether by way of administrative action or on the merits could be stopped or altered at any time prior to the notice going out', there was 'insufficient evidence to establish that an assessment was made prior to 5 January 1999'. The tribunal observed that 'it would be manifestly unsatisfactory if, say, eleven months after an officer made some calculation, which he then dignifies with the title "assessment", it was then issued to the taxpayer'. The tribunal declined to follow the English decisions in *Babber*, **3.62** above, or *Classicmoor Ltd*, **3.64** above. *Royal Bank of Scotland Group plc (No 2)*, EDN/99/22 (VTD 16418). (*Notes*. (1) The decision refers to *dicta* of Potts J in *The Post Office*, **3.55** above, and to *dicta* of Millett LJ in *Le Rififi Ltd*, **3.87** below, but fails to refer to the CA decision in *Grunwick Processing Ltd*, **3.61** above. (2) A subsequent tribunal specifically declined to follow this decision in

Ali, 3.63 above, on the grounds that it was inconsistent with the CA decision in *Grunwick Processing Ltd*, 3.61 above. The decision was also specifically not followed in *Subhan, Uddin & Mustak*, 3.66 above; *University of Huddersfield*, 3.93 below; *Staffquest Group Holdings Ltd*, 3.94 below, and *Hicks & Hicks*, 3.95 below.)

[3.85] The Commissioners issued a notice of assessment on a trader, covering the periods from January 1991 to January 1995. The trader appealed, contending that the Commissioners had had all the necessary facts in July 1995, but had not made the assessments until September 1996, so that 15 of them had been made outside the statutory time limit. The Commissioners gave evidence that the assessments had actually been made in March 1996, although they had not been notified until September. The tribunal accepted this evidence but the Ch D allowed the trader's appeal. Lawrence Collins J observed that 'assessment of VAT is an important step, and it is unsatisfactory that the process is not transparent, and not defined by legislation or even by clear administrative practice'. On the evidence in this case, although a form VAT 641 had been prepared in March 1996, it had not been signed by a 'check officer'. A further form VAT 641 had been prepared in September 1996. The relevant notification (form VAT 655) was based on the form VAT 641 which had not been completed until September 1996, rather than on the one which had been completed in March. Accordingly the assessments were outside the one-year time limit of *s 73(6)(b)*, so that only those assessments which had been issued within the normal two-year time limit were valid. *G Cheeseman (t/a Well In Tune) v C & E Commrs*, Ch D [2000] STC 1119. (*Note*. For the Commissioners' practice following this decision, see *Notice No 915*, issued on 1 March 2001.)

Whether assessment issued within three-year time limit (VATA 1994, s 77(1))

NOTE

VATA 1994, s 77, as amended by *FA 1997, s 47*, provides that the normal time limit for assessment is three years after the end of the relevant accounting period. Before the enactment of *FA 1997*, the time limit was six years. (The extended time limit under *s 77(4)* continued to be twenty years.) The cases in this section should be read in the light of this change.

[3.86] In March 1987 the Commissioners issued an assessment on a company covering the period from 1 January 1980 to 31 December 1986. The company appealed, contending that the assessment was invalid because it was made more than six years after the start of the period assessed. The tribunal accepted this contention and allowed the company's appeal, holding that the assessment was a nullity. *Barratt Construction Ltd*, [1989] VATTR 204 (VTD 4230).

[3.87] In August 1989 the Commissioners issued three forms VAT 191 to a company, assessing the periods from 1 May 1983 to 30 April 1989 inclusive. The tax due for each quarterly period was separately stated. The company appealed, contending as a preliminary point that the assessment was a single global assessment and was wholly invalid because it was made more than six years after the start of the period assessed. The tribunal accepted this contention but the CA reversed this decision, holding that the notice comprised 24 separate quarterly assessments and that only the earliest period was out of time. The decision in *Don Pasquale*, **2.141** APPEALS, was unanimously disapproved. Millett LJ observed that 'the case has no *ratio decidendi* (and) Dillon LJ appears to have treated the question as one of first impression'. Balcombe LJ observed that 'the assessment of the amount of tax considered to be due, and the notification to the taxpayer, are two separate operations'. *C & E Commrs v Le Rififi Ltd*, CA 1994, [1995] STC 103. (*Note*. For a preliminary issue in this case, see **2.500** APPEALS.)

[3.88] The CA decision in *Le Rififi Ltd*, **3.87** above, was applied in the subsequent cases of *Baltex Clothing Manufacturers*, MAN/92/108 (VTD 13777); *SCM Parker-Smith*, LON/03/273 (VTD 18497) and *Copeland*, **50.136** PENALTIES: EVASION OF TAX.

[3.89] In July 1992 the Commissioners issued a notice of assessment on a partnership which carried on business as architects. The notice of assessment covered the period from May 1985 to May 1990. Accompanying schedules indicated that the assessment comprised three distinct elements of underdeclaration. One schedule covered the period from May 1985 to April 1988. A second schedule covered the period from June 1987 to February 1990, and fifteen further schedules covered the quarterly accounting periods from May 1988 to January 1992. The partnership appealed, contending that the assessment was a global assessment and had been issued outside the statutory time limit. The Commissioners agreed to withdraw the schedule covering the period from May 1985 to April 1988, as the start of this period was clearly outside the six-year time limit, but refused to withdraw the remainder of the assessment, considering that the original assessment was a composite assessment rather than a single 'global' assessment, and that the assessments for the periods from June 1987 to January 1992 had been issued within the statutory time limit. The tribunal dismissed the partnership's appeal, holding that the original notice of appeal represented seventeen separate assessments rather than a single global assessment. Only the assessment covering the period from May 1985 to April 1988, which the Commissioners had already withdrawn, had been issued outside the statutory time limit. *Georgalakis Partnership*, LON/92/1692 (VTD 10083).

[3.90] The Commissioners issued a 'global' assessment, dated 13 January 1992 and covering the period from 1 October 1985 to 31 March 1990, to a builder. The builder appealed, contending that the assessment was out of time and invalid. The Commissioners submitted that the assessment had actually been made on 13 December 1991, when the officer responsible for the assessment had completed a form VAT 641. The tribunal rejected this contention and allowed the appeal, observing that the form VAT 641 had not been countersigned in accordance with the Commissioners' usual practice, and holding that the date on which the assessment was made was 8 January 1992, when the form was processed by a computer operator. The chairman observed that 'the assessment has not been made until it is at the stage when it simply requires clerical processing. That must be after supervisory consideration. Until then the Commissioners have not made a decision and the assessed amount has not been finally determined.' *EVW Harris*, MAN/93/346 (VTD

11925). (*Note.* The decision here was not followed, and was implicitly disapproved, in the subsequent case of *University of Huddersfield*, **3.93** below.)

[3.91] A similar decision was reached in a case where an assessment for the period ending 31 January 1997 was processed by a computer operator on 8 February 2000, but the Commissioners gave evidence that it had actually been prepared on 4 January 2000. The tribunal held that the Commissioners had produced 'insufficient evidence . . . to show why there was a five week delay' and held that the assessment was out of time. *Dewsbury Road Social Club*, MAN/00/545 (VTD 17168). (*Note.* Appeals against subsequent assessments were dismissed.)

[3.92] The Commissioners issued a notice of assessment, covering the periods from 1 March 1996 to 28 February 1999, to a company which operated a restaurant. The relevant form VAT 641 was dated 31 January 2000, and the form VAT 655 was dated 3 February 2000. The tribunal held that the assessment was 'made' on 31 January 2000, when the form VAT 641 was completed. Accordingly, the assessments for the periods from 1 March 1996 to 30 November 1996 had been issued outside the statutory three-year time limit and were therefore invalid. *Nemonthron Restaurants Ltd*, LON/00/633 (VTD 18123). (*Note.* Appeals against the subsequent assessments, and against misdeclaration penalties, were dismissed.)

Assessment dated within time limit but not notified until after limit

[3.93] The Commissioners issued an assessment to a university, to recover input tax which the university had claimed in its accounting period ending 31 January 1997. The form VAT 641 was completed on 26 January 2000 and a letter was sent to the university on that date, but the relevant form VAT 655 was not issued until 18 February 2000. The university appealed, contending as a preliminary point that the assessment had not been issued within the three-year time limit. The tribunal rejected this contention, holding that the assessment had been made on 26 January 2000 and was therefore valid. The tribunal accepted the Commissioners' evidence that the relevant form VAT 641 did not require a counter-signature, declining to follow the decisions in *Royal Bank of Scotland Group plc*, **3.84** above, and *Harris*, **3.90** above. *University of Huddersfield*, MAN/00/263 (VTD 17159). (*Note.* For subsequent developments in this case, see **22.116** EUROPEAN COMMUNITY LAW.)

[3.94] A similar decision was reached in a case where a form VAT 641 was completed on 23 December 1999 but the relevant form VAT 655 was not posted until 5 January 2000. The tribunal held that the assessment had been made on 23 December 1999, applying the CA decisions in *Grunwick Processing Ltd*, **3.61** above, and *Burford v Durkin*, CA 1990, [1991] STC 7, and specifically declining to follow the decision in *Royal Bank of Scotland Group plc*, **3.84** above. *Staffquest Group Holdings Ltd*, LON/01/944 (VTD 17632).

[3.95] A similar decision was reached in a case where a form VAT 641 was completed on 24 December 1997 but the relevant form VAT 655 was not posted until 13 January 1998. The tribunal held that the assessment had been made on 24 December 1997, and was therefore within the three-year time limit, applying the tribunal decision in *Classicmoor Ltd*, 3.64 above, and *dicta* of Millett LJ in *Le Rififi Ltd*, 3.87 above, and specifically declining to follow the decision in *Royal Bank of Scotland Group plc*, 3.84 above. *TF & H Hicks (t/a Parc Golf Centre)*, LON/98/809 (VTD 18121).

Assessment dated within time limit but form VAT 641 outside limit

[3.96] The Commissioners issued an assessment, covering the period from 1 November 1995 to 31 July 1998, on a partnership which operated a restaurant. In a letter dated 28 January 1999, a VAT officer informed the partnership that the Commissioners had 'assessed the tax due as £35,611.80'. The method of calculation was set out in appendices to the letter. However, the officer did not complete the relevant form VAT 641 until 15 March. The partnership appealed, contending that the assessment had not been issued within the three-year time limit. The tribunal rejected this contention, observing that 'no particular form is required for notifying an assessment' and that 'an assessment by letter is by no means impossible. For there to be an assessment, there is no need for there to be a Form 641, though it would be very unusual for that form not to be completed at some stage of the process.' On the evidence, 'the letter of 28 January 1999 contained the decision of the assessing officer to assess, the four schedules accompanying the letter set out in considerable detail how the amount assessed has been calculated, and the five documents together leave the appellants in no doubt whatsoever that they are required to pay that amount to the Commissioners as arrears of tax'. Accordingly, the assessment here had been made within the statutory time limit. *CY Pang & SY Kong (t/a The Peking House)*, LON/99/1012 (VTD 17361).

VAT Regulations 1995, reg 107(1)(c)—failure to make annual adjustment

[3.97] A partly exempt trader failed to make his annual adjustment, as required by *VAT Regulations 1995, reg 107(1)(c)*, for the year ending 31 March 1999. The Commissioners did not discover this until 2001. In April 2002 they issued an assessment to recover the input tax which the trader had overclaimed. He appealed, contending that the assessment was outside the three-year time limit of *VATA 1994, s 77*. The tribunal rejected this contention and dismissed his appeal, observing that *reg 107(1)(c)* had required him to make the adjustment in April 1999, and holding that the three-year time limit did not therefore expire until 30 April 2002, so that the assessment had been issued within the time limit. *M Tse*, MAN/02/297 (VTD 18362).

Tour Operators' Margin Scheme—failure to make annual adjustment

[3.98] A company operated the Tour Operators' Margin Scheme. It failed to make its prescribed annual adjustment for the year ending 31 March 2001. Customs discovered this in 2004. In June 2004 Customs issued a notice of assessment, expressed to be for the two years ending 31 March 2003, but including an annual adjustment for the year ending 31 March 2001. The company appealed, contending that since the assessment for the period ending 30 June 2001 included the annual adjustment for the year ending 31 March 2001, it had been made outside the statutory three-year time limit and was invalid. The CA unanimously rejected this contention and upheld the assessment. Rix LJ observed that the 'difference between what is due and what had been previously paid has to be adjusted on the VAT return "for the first prescribed accounting period ending after the end of the financial year during which the supplies were made"'. The company should have made such a calculation in the period ending 30 June 2001 but had failed to do so. Accordingly its return for that period had been incorrect, and the assessment to correct this had been within the statutory time limit. *HMRC v Dunwood Travel Ltd*, CA [2008] STC 959; [2008] EWCA Civ 174.

Whether assessment authorised by VAT Regulations, reg 25(1)

[3.99] See *Hindle*, 3.117 below; *Antoniou*, 59.13 RETURNS, and the cases noted at 59.14 to 59.19 RETURNS.

Whether assessment authorised by VAT Regulations, reg 25(5)

[3.100] See *Inchcape Management Services Ltd*, 59.21 RETURNS.

Whether twenty-year time limit applicable (VATA 1994, s 77(4))

Cases held to be within s 77(4)

[3.101] In December 1991 the Commissioners issued a 'global' assessment on a company covering the period from 1 August 1985 to 31 January 1990, together with assessments for the five subsequent three-month periods, charging tax of more than £90,000. The company appealed, contending that the global assessment was invalid since the start of the period was outside the six-year time limit of what is now *VATA 1994, s 77*. The Commissioners defended the assessment on the basis that the company's conduct fell within *VATA 1994, s 60(1)*, so that the extended 20-year time limit of *VATA 1994, s 77(4)* applied. (The Commissioners had not in fact imposed a penalty under what is now *VATA 1994, s 60*, and explained this in correspondence as 'an oversight on the part of the case officer'. The hearing of the appeal against the assessment was delayed pending criminal proceedings against some of the company's suppliers.) The tribunal chairman observed that, since there was nothing in *VATA 1994, s 77(4)* which required the Commissioners to have made a penalty assessment in order to bring the 20-year limitation period into operation, 'it follows that there need be no such penalty assessment to extend the limitation period'. The chairman also observed that the Customs officer dealing with the case seemed to have been under the misapprehension that the time limit for imposing a penalty had expired, and commented that the officer 'appeared to have little or no knowledge of the limitation period applicable to penalty assessments'. Accordingly, the tribunal held that the Commissioners were entitled to rely on the 20-year time limit for the making of assessments 'subject to their proving fraud or dishonesty to a high degree of probability on the part of (the company) at the substantive hearing'. (The tribunal also rejected a contention by the company that the assessments were invalid since the period assessed was not stated on a notice of amendment—see 3.131 below.) *Sirpal Trading Co Ltd*, MAN/92/37 (VTD 13288).

[3.102] In March 1997 the Commissioners issued 24 assessments, covering the period from April 1990 to March 1996, on a company (M) in the construction industry. The assessments were issued to recover input tax which

M had claimed on the basis of invoices issued in the names of 12 VAT-registered nominal subcontractors, for services which the purported subcontractors had not in fact supplied, and on the basis that the circumstances fell within *VATA 1994, s 77(4)*, since certain senior employees of M had acted fraudulently and that fraudulent conduct could be attributed to M. M appealed, contending firstly that the assessments had not been made to the best of the Commissioners' judgment, and additionally that the conditions of *s 73(6)(b)* and *s 77(4)* were not satisfied and that the pre-1995 assessments had been made outside the statutory time limit. The tribunal reviewed the evidence in detail and upheld the assessments with regard to nine of the twelve subcontractors in question, finding that M had wrongly obtained credit for input tax, under *VATA 1994, s 26(1)*, for the purpose of evading VAT. (The tribunal accepted that the invoices issued by one of the subcontractors represented genuine supplies, and found that there was insufficient evidence that M's conduct with regard to the other two subcontractors fell within *VATA 1994, s 60(1)*, as required by *VATA 1994, s 77(4)(a)*.) It followed from the fact that the alleged subcontractors did not make genuine supplies to M that M 'had no right to deduct, as its input VAT, the amounts purporting to be VAT in the VAT invoices'. M had 'through its employees provided its self-employed workforce with the facility of payment without proper deduction of income tax'. The means by which the facility was provided were 'fraudulent and dishonest, and (M's) acts of claiming relief for input tax for the amounts shown as VAT on the VAT-only invoices issued in the names of the bogus subcontractors in respect of non-existent supplies were equally fraudulent and dishonest.' Although M had not actually benefited from the fraud in terms of cash, 'it achieved the commercial advantage of satisfied gangmasters and a contented workforce who regarded themselves as entitled to expect that lump fraud facilities would be available to them'. The company appealed to the QB, which upheld the tribunal decision (except that the amount of the assessments for 1992 and 1993 was slightly reduced to take account of the tribunal's finding that there was insufficient proof of dishonest conduct with regard to one of the subcontractors, deleting sums relating to that subcontractor from the assessments). Dyson J held that the tribunal had been entitled to find that there was dishonest conduct on the part of two site managers and of a contract manager who reported directly to M's chief executive, that the organisers of the fraud were not acting as agents of the nominal subcontractors, and the nominal subcontractors had not in fact supplied any labour to M. The transactions were 'shams'. Furthermore, the tribunal was correct to hold that the relevant statutory provisions required 'the attribution to (M) of the knowledge, acts and omissions of site managers and site agents', and that the conditions of *s 77(4)(a)* were satisfied. The fact that some of M's directors may have been unaware of the fraud was not conclusive. Dyson J observed that failing to attribute the site agents' knowledge to M 'would encourage those prepared to engage in fraud or turn a blind eye to fraud to set up separate VAT accounts departments for that purpose' and 'would discriminate against small companies that do not have separate accounts departments insulated from what happens on site or in contracts departments'. Additionally, the assessments had been made to the best of the Commissioners' judgment, as required by *s 73(1)*, and the Commissioners had not had sufficient 'evidence of facts' to justify an assessment until March 1996, less than twelve months before the actual issue of the assessments, so that the conditions of *s 73(6)(b)* were also satisfied. *McNicholas Construction Co Ltd v C & E Commrs*, QB [2000] STC 553. (*Note*. For preliminary issues in this case, see **2.217** and **2.228** APPEALS and **14.93** COLLECTION AND ENFORCEMENT.)

[3.103] In November 1997 the Commissioners issued an assessment on a company for the period ending 31 May 1991, charging tax on a sale of property which had not been declared in the company's return. The company appealed, contending that the assessment was invalid since the start of the period was outside the three-year time limit of what is now *VATA 1994, s 77*. The Commissioners defended the assessment on the basis that the company's conduct fell within *VATA 1994, s 60(1)*, so that the extended 20-year time limit of *VATA 1994, s 77(4)* applied. The tribunal accepted the Commissioners' contentions and dismissed the company's appeal, finding that the company's return for the relevant period had wrongly stated that it had no VAT liability, that the company's accountants had acted 'irresponsibly', and that the company's controlling director had signed the return 'without checking its contents and ensuring that they were complete and correct'. Applying *Howroyd*, **50.13** PENALTIES: EVASION OF TAX, it was dishonest if a company officer signed 'a return containing a mis-statement and he has no honest belief in the truth of the statement he has made, and in particular if he makes the statement recklessly, not caring whether it is true or false'. *Adam Geoffrey & Co (Management) Ltd*, MAN/98/324 (VTD 16074). (*Note*. The tribunal also upheld a penalty imposed on the director under *VATA 1994, s 61*—see **50.14** PENALTIES: EVASION OF TAX.)

[3.104] In February 2001 a company's financial controller was convicted of fraud. After his conviction, the Commissioners issued two assessments on the company under the extended 20-year time limit of *VATA 1994, s 77(4)*. The tribunal upheld the assessments. *P & R Fabrics Ltd*, MAN/02/156 (VTD 17776). (*Note*. The case was heard with *Dashmore Clothing Ltd*, **3.68** above.)

[3.105] In 1999 the Commissioners issued an assessment, covering the period from 1993 to 1998, on a company which operated a night club and restaurant. They also took criminal proceedings against one of the directors, the bookkeeper, and a consultant. All three were subsequently convicted of 'conspiracy to fraudulently evade VAT, contrary to *Criminal Law Act 1977, s 1*'. The tribunal upheld the assessment, finding that there had been a substantial underdeclaration of the company's takings. On the evidence, the company had acted dishonestly, so that the assessment was within the extended 20-year time limit of *VATA 1994, s 77(4)*. *Coolbreeze Ltd*, MAN/99/0288 (VTD 18933).

[3.106] HMRC formed the opinion that a company which operated a restaurant had substantially underdeclared its takings. They issued additional assessments covering the period from March 2002 to May 2008, under the extended 20-year time limit of *VATA 1994, s 77(4)*. The First-Tier Tribunal upheld the assessments and dismissed the company's appeal, finding that there had been 'systematic suppression of the correct turnover'.The Upper Tribunal upheld this decision, applying the principles laid down by the CA in *Pegasus Birds Ltd v C & E Commrs (No 2)*, **3.20** above. *Queenspice Ltd v HMRC*, [2011] UKUT 111 (TCC); [2011] STC 1457.

[3.107] A restaurant proprietor (R) failed to register for VAT. HMRC issued assessments covering a period of nine years. R appealed, contending as a preliminary issue that the assessments were invalid. The tribunal rejected this contention, holding that the assessment was within the extended 20-year time limit of *VATA 1994, s 77(4)*. *MR Rastegar (t/a Mo's Restaurant) v HMRC*, [2010] UKFTT 471 (TC), TC00733.

Cases held not to be within s 77(4)

[3.108] In July 1995 the Commissioners issued an assessment on a married couple who operated a launderette. The assessment covered the period from 21 July 1985 to 28 February 1995. The couple appealed, contending that the extended time limit imposed by *VATA 1994, s 77(4)* was inapplicable. The tribunal accepted this contention and allowed the appeal. The assessment in question was a single 'global' assessment. The couple did not fall within *VATA 1994, s 77(4)(a)* as they had not been guilty of dishonest conduct within *VATA 1994, s 60(1)*. The assessment could not be validated under *VATA 1994, s 77(4)(b)* because the assessment had been backdated to 21 July 1985, whereas *VATA 1994, s 67* derived from provisions in *FA 1985* which had not come into force until 25 July 1985. For the purposes of *VATA 1994, s 77(1)*, the prescribed accounting period was a three-month period beginning in July 1985, rather than the whole of the extended period covered by the assessment. The Commissioners had not issued a direction under *VAT Regulations 1995, reg 25(1)(c)*, and in any event it would not 'be a proper exercise of the power to give such a direction to use it to get round the time limit in *s 77(1)*'. The officer responsible for the assessment had misunderstood the law and had not given 'proper consideration' to her power to backdate the assessment. Furthermore, applying *dicta* in *Van Boeckel*, 3.1 above, the assessment had not been issued to the best of the Commissioners' judgment. *DJ & MA Wright*, MAN/95/135 (VTD 14570).

[3.109] The Commissioners were investigating the proprietor of a road haulage business. In January 1996 they issued an assessment covering more than six years. The trader appealed, contending that the assessment was invalid because the conditions of *VATA 1994, s 77(4)* were not satisfied. The tribunal allowed the appeal in part. With regard to *VATA 1994, s 77(4)(a)*, the tribunal held on the evidence that there was 'no question of a *s 60* civil penalty' because the trader's affairs had been handled by his wife, who was not herself a taxable person. (The wife had stated at interview that she 'did everything but drive the lorries'. The Commissioners had begun criminal proceedings against the trader's wife for furnishing false documents, but had not taken proceedings against the trader himself.) Furthermore, at the time the assessment was raised, the trader's wife had not been convicted of fraud. The fact that a fraud trial may be 'in prospect' did not meet the requirements of *s 77(4)(a)*, which referred to a person who 'has been convicted of fraud'. It followed that the assessment was invalid in so far as it related to accounting periods ending before January 1990. (The appeal was dismissed with regard to the six years for which the assessment was within the normal time limit of *s 77(1)* as then in force.) *RD Brooker*, LON/x (VTD 15164).

Supplementary assessments (VATA 1994, s 77(6))

[3.110] On 4 September 1996 the Commissioners issued an assessment on a building contractor, covering the periods from May 1994 to July 1996. On 10 October 1996 they issued a further assessment covering the period from 1 May 1994 to 31 July 1994. It was accepted that the Commissioners had obtained no further evidence since the issue of the September assessment, and the assessment was issued on the basis that items had been omitted from the September assessment. The contractor appealed, contending that the October 1996 assessment was invalid on the grounds that it was not authorised by *VATA 1994, s 73(6)(b)*, since the Commissioners had obtained no further evidence since the issue of the September assessment, and that the effect of *VATA 1994, s 77(6)* was that the assessment could only be issued within the two-year time limit of *VATA 1994, s 73(6)(a)*. The tribunal chairman (Mr. Heim) accepted this contention and allowed the appeal, holding that the September 1996 assessment was valid and that the result of its issue was that the Commissioners could not issue an additional assessment under *VATA 1994, s 73(6)* unless further evidence came to their knowledge after it had been made. As the Commissioners had obtained no 'further such evidence', the assessment could only be treated as a supplementary assessment under *VATA 1994, s 77(6)* and could only be made 'within the period of two years after the end of the prescribed accounting period specified in *s 73(6)(a)*'. *L Roberts*, LON/98/31 (VTD 15759).

Assessments for overpayments (VATA 1994, s 78A(2))

Assessment under VATA 1994, s 80(4A)

[3.111] A company (D) sold furniture and arranged interest-free credit for customers. Initially, it accounted for VAT on the full purchase price. However, following a CA decision in April 1996, it submitted a repayment claim on the basis that it should not have accounted for output tax on the commission which it paid to the finance company. (The CA decision in question was subsequently overruled by the CJEC and HL—see *Primback Ltd*, 22.242 EUROPEAN COMMUNITY LAW.) The Commissioners accepted that, on the basis of the CA decision, D was entitled to a repayment, which they made in September 1996. In January 1997 they also paid interest on the repayment. However, in 2001, following the CJEC decision in *Primback*, the Commissioners issued assessments to recover the tax relating to the periods from April 1993 to June 1996. The company appealed, contending that the assessments were invalid as they had been made outside the two-year time limit laid down by *VATA 1994, s 78A(2), 80(4B)*. The Ch D rejected this contention and held that the assessments were valid, since they had been made within two years of the CJEC decision in *Primback*. However, the CA reversed this decision and allowed the company's appeal. Jonathan Parker LJ held that *s 78A(2)* 'does not extend to the effect of a subsequent judicial decision'. *C & E Commrs v DFS Furniture Co plc (No 2)*, CA [2004] STC 559; [2004] EWCA Civ 243; [2004] 1 WLR 2159. (*Notes.* (1) The HL rejected an application by Customs to lodge an appeal against this decision: see Business Brief 25/2004, issued on 14 September 2004. See now, however, the amendments introduced by *FA 2008*, *s 120*. (2) For an application for judicial review, relating to the periods prior to April 1993, see **48.76** PAYMENT OF TAX.)

[3.112] For cases where assessments under *VATA 1994, s 80(4A)* were held to be valid, see *Laura Ashley*, **3.44** above; *Bremen Fitted Furniture Ltd*, **48.77** PAYMENT OF TAX, and *Peugeot Motor Co plc (No 4)*, **48.78** PAYMENT OF TAX.

Assessment where purchases cannot be reconciled with sales (VATA 1994, s 73(7))

[3.113] A trader (G) based in England carried on a business of dealing in second-hand agricultural machinery. He made his purchases in the UK but sent most of the machinery to premises he owned in the Irish Republic, and sold the machinery in the Irish Republic. The Commissioners issued an assessment under what is now *VATA 1994, s 73(7)* in relation to some 300 of his purchases over the three years to 31 March 1979. G appealed, contending that the 'missing' 300 items had been resold in the Irish Republic and that the Commissioners were estopped from assessing because his records had been inspected at a control visit in 1975. The tribunal rejected this contention and dismissed the appeal (except for one item of machinery), finding that G had not produced an adequate record of the actual machinery alleged to have been sold in the Irish Republic. *P Gutherie*, [1980] VATTR 152 (VTD 986).

The validity of the assessment

Cases where the assessment was upheld

Validity of assessment covering more than one accounting period

[3.114] In the case noted at **3.49** above, the company contended as a preliminary point that the assessment was invalid as it covered more than one accounting period. The tribunal rejected this contention and the CA dismissed the company's appeal. *SJ Grange Ltd v C & E Commrs*, CA 1978, [1979] STC 183; [1979] 1 WLR 239.

[3.115] The CA decision in *SJ Grange Ltd v C & E Commrs*, **3.114** above, was applied in a similar subsequent case in which the tribunal held that the judgments in that case should not be construed 'as limiting the powers of the Commissioners to make an assessment for more than one prescribed accounting period to those cases where the facts known to them are insufficient to enable them to split up the assessment into the prescribed accounting periods'. *Heyfordian Travel Ltd*, [1979] VATTR 139 (VTD 774).

[3.116] A company which was partly exempt reclaimed the whole of its input tax. Customs issued an assessment, covering a period of 20 months, to recover the overclaimed tax. The company appealed, contending that the assessment should only cover a period of 12 months. The tribunal rejected this contention and dismissed the appeal. *FC Milnes (Bradford) Ltd*, MAN/77/62 (VTD 478).

[3.117] In the case noted at **3.12** above, the Commissioners issued an assessment on a partnership covering a period of ten months. The partnership contended that the assessment was invalid. The Ch D rejected this contention and dismissed the appeal. Neuberger J held that the Commissioners were entitled to form the opinion that the partnership had become liable to VAT from 1 December 1995, and were entitled to issue an estimated assessment covering the period from that date to the cessation of the partnership on 30 September 1996. The issue of returns and assessments covering more than one accounting period was authorised by *VAT Regulations 1995 (SI 1995/2518), reg 25(1)(c)*. The fact that the partnership had not submitted a return was not conclusive, since it would be 'unreal to treat *reg 25(1)(c)* as only applicable where there has been a return'. *D & A Hindle (t/a DJ Baker Bar) v C & E Commrs*, Ch D 2003, [2004] STC 426; [2003] EWHC 1665 (Ch).

[3.118] In January 2007 Customs formed the opinion that a company (E) should have registered for VAT from 1 June 2004 (by virtue of *VATA 1994, Sch 1 para 1(1)(b)*). They issued a notice of compulsory registration, and in June 2007 they issued an assessment covering the period from 1 June 2004 to 30 April 2007. The representative company of E's VAT group appealed, contending as a preliminary point that an assessment could not be made for a period exceeding twelve months. The tribunal rejected this contention, applying the CA decision in *Bjellica (t/a Eddy's Domestic Appliances) v C & E Commrs*, **57.89** REGISTRATION, and holding that in view of E's late registration, 'the Commissioners could lawfully require a VAT return to be made for a period of 34 months'. *Prudential Assurance Co Ltd (No 5)*, [2008] VATDR 439 (VTD 20957). (*Note*. The hearing of the substantive appeal has been stood over pending a ECJ decision in another case.)

[3.119] See also *Hopcraft*, **59.19** RETURNS.

Undated assessment—whether valid

[3.120] A partnership appealed against an assessment which had been delivered by hand by a VAT officer, contending that the assessment was invalid since it had not been dated. The tribunal dismissed the appeal, holding that although it was advisable for an assessment to be dated, there was no statutory requirement for this. *AK & AR Din (t/a Indus Restaurant)*, [1984] VATTR 228 (VTD 1746).

Assessment to rectify error in previous assessment—whether valid

[3.121] In April 1991 the Commissioners issued four estimated assessments to a company which operated a restaurant. The first assessment covered the period from 1 December 1987 to 31 March 1990, and the other three assessments covered the three succeeding quarters. Through a clerical error, the period covered by the first assessment was not stated on the Notice of Assessment. The company appealed, and following the appeal the case was reviewed by a VAT officer who formed the opinion that the omission of the dates covered by the first assessment rendered it invalid. The Commissioners wrote to the company stating that the first assessment was being withdrawn, and issued a replacement assessment dated 31 May 1991. The company appealed against the replacement assessment, contending as a preliminary point that it was invalid since no new facts had come to the Commissioners' knowledge since the issue of the first assessment. The tribunal rejected this contention, holding that the effect of the withdrawal of an assessment was 'that the Commissioners are entitled to proceed as if the assessment had not been made' and that they were 'entitled, until the expiration of the time limit which applied to the withdrawn assessment, to make another assessment on the same basis'. *Jeudwine*, **3.134** below, was distinguished on the basis that, in that case, the first assessment had not been withdrawn at the time when the second assessment was issued. *Yuen Tung Restaurant Ltd (t/a The Far East Restaurant)*, [1993] VATTR 226 (VTD 11008). (*Note*. It was agreed by the appellant company and the Commissioners that the first assessment could have been considered valid since the period assessed was stated on accompanying schedules. Compare *House*, **3.127** below.)

[3.122] The decision in *Yuen Tung Restaurant Ltd*, **3.121** above, was applied in the similar case of *IC Sinclair (t/a Ian Sinclair & Son)*, EDN/94/55 (VTD 12842).

[3.123] A VAT officer visited a hotel in August 1993, and formed the opinion that the hotel records were incomplete and incorrect. Following his visit the Commissioners issued an assessment to the hotel proprietors in January 1994. In February 1994 the officer responsible for the assessment wrote to the proprietors to inform them that the assessment contained an error and would be withdrawn and replaced by a corrected assessment. A replacement assessment was issued in March 1994. The proprietors appealed, contending that the assessment was invalid. The tribunal rejected this contention and dismissed the appeal, applying *dicta* in *Parekh*, **3.75** above, and *Yuen Tung Restaurant Ltd*, **3.121** above, and holding that 'the result of the withdrawal of an assessment is that it has no further effect. It does not therefore limit the Commissioners' powers or their duties under *CEMA 1979, s 6* to continue to exercise those powers and to carry out those duties.' The tribunal specifically declined to follow *Jeudwine*, **3.134** below, on the grounds that that case had been decided before the enactment of what is now *VATA 1994, s 77* by *FA 1985*. *RA & Mrs JC Foster (t/a The Watersplash Hotel)*, LON/94/582A (VTD 12723).

[3.124] Similar decisions were reached in *PC Eccles*, LON/93/2503A (VTD 13372) and *Classicmoor Ltd*, **3.64** above.

Assessment to rectify omission from previous assessment

[3.125] See *Judd*, **3.48** above.

Error in notice of assessment—start of period incorrectly stated

[3.126] A partnership which operated a restaurant became liable to register in October 1989 but failed to do so. One of the partners left the partnership in December 1990. The remaining partners continued to operate the restaurant and belatedly registered for VAT in January 1992. Subsequently the Commissioners issued an assessment which covered the period from 8 December 1990 (the date of the partnership change) to 31 March 1992. Because of an error in programming the VAT Central Unit computer at Southend, the form VAT 655 described the assessment as covering the period from 9 October 1989 (the date when the original partnership had become liable to register) to 31 March 1992. The partnership appealed, contending as a preliminary issue that the effect of the error on the form VAT 655 was that the assessment was invalid. The tribunal rejected this contention and held that the assessment was valid. The result of the error was that the assessment had not been validly notified. However, applying *Grunwick Processing Laboratories Ltd*, **3.61** above, a delay in notification did not render the assessment invalid, but merely rendered it unenforceable until it was notified properly. Applying *dicta* of Balcombe LJ in *Le Rififi Ltd*, **3.87** above, 'the assessment of the amount of tax considered to be due, and the notification to the taxpayer, are separate operations'. The tribunal decisions in *Younis*, **3.137** below, and *SAS Fashions Ltd*, **3.138** below, were not followed, and were specifically disapproved on the grounds that they had been decided without reference to the High Court decision in *Grunwick Processing Laboratories Ltd*, **3.61** above, and were inconsistent with the subsequent CA decision in *Le Rififi Ltd*, **3.87** above. *Solomon's Kebab House*, MAN/94/2107 (VTD 13560).

Period assessed stated on accompanying schedules

[3.127] The Commissioners issued an assessment on a car dealer, covering the period from 1 November 1984 to 31 January 1990. On the formal notice of assessment (form VAT 655), the dates covered by the assessment were left blank, but the period assessed was indicated by accompanying schedules. The trader appealed, contending that the assessment was invalid since the period assessed was not stated on the form VAT 655. The tribunal rejected this contention and dismissed the appeal, distinguishing *Bell*, **3.136** below, because in that case the notice of assessment and the schedules were inconsistent with each other, whereas in the present case there was no inconsistency. The CA upheld this decision. Applying *SJ Grange Ltd*, **3.49** above, and *Le Rififi Ltd*, **3.87** above, the fact that the assessment was a 'global' assessment did not render it invalid. The CA specifically disapproved *obiter dicta* of Woolf J in *International Language Centres Ltd*, **3.41** above. The CA also held that a notification could be contained in more than one document provided that it was clear which document or documents were intended to contain the notification and that document or documents contained the necessary details. In the present case, the schedules contained with the assessment showed with complete clarity how the assessment had been computed. The notification in question was valid and gave rise to an enforceable obligation to pay the agreed amount of tax. *PJ House (t/a P & J Autos) v C & E Commrs*, CA 1995, [1996] STC 154.

[3.128] The tribunal decision in *House*, **3.127** above, was applied in a similar subsequent case in which *SAS Fashions Ltd*, **3.138** below, was distinguished. *DJ Freeland*, LON/92/2349 (VTD 11358).

[3.129] The CA decision in *House*, **3.127** above, was also applied in a case in which the tribunal chairman (Mr. Bishopp) observed that 'the assessment process is not a kind of challenge in which, regardless of the merits, the Commissioners have to comply with rigid but inconsequential matters of form, and run the risk that if they make a mistake, however unimportant and however obvious to the taxpayer, he secures an adventitious escape from his liability'. *A Corston*, MAN/04/273 (VTD 19991). (*Note.* The tribunal also dismissed an appeal against a penalty under *VATA 1994, s 60*.)

Period assessed not stated on notice of amendment

[3.130] In July 1991 the Commissioners issued an assessment, covering more than one return period, on a partnership, charging output tax of £15,344. In July 1993 they issued a notice of amendment of assessment, indicating that the assessments had been reduced to £8,586. This notice did not specifically state the period covered by the assessments. The partnership appealed, contending as a preliminary issue that the amended assessment was invalid, and applying for a direction that the appeal should be allowed on this basis. The tribunal rejected this contention and dismissed the application, applying *House*, **3.127** above, and holding that the assessment contained the necessary minimum requirements 'in unambiguous and reasonably clear terms'. *SP & A Fairbairn (t/a Ruffles)*, MAN/92/1475 (VTD 12825).

[3.131] A similar decision, also applying *House*, **3.127** above, was reached in *Sirpal Trading Co Ltd*, **3.101** above.

Validity of alternative assessments

[3.132] A university entered into a leasing arrangement and reclaimed input tax relating to these transactions. The Commissioners issued an assessment to recover part of the tax, on the basis that the transactions were partly attributable to exempt supplies. They also issued an alternative assessment on the basis that the transactions had no commercial purpose and were not in the course or furtherance of any business. The university appealed, contending as a preliminary point that the assessments were invalid. The tribunal rejected this contention, holding that 'the intimation of alternative assessments is little more than appropriate pleading given an appropriate situation. The taxpayer is put on notice as to possible analyses of the trading situation which can result in different sums being considered as the "correct amount" of tax.' It would be unreasonable 'so to construe legislation and the concept of "best judgment" as to force the Commissioners to opt for a situation which may turn out to result from an inappropriate legal analysis.' The CS unanimously upheld this decision. Lord Hamilton held that 'alternative assessments for VAT provide in appropriate cases a practical and workable machinery for the ultimate recovery of the tax properly due. In the present case, where the preferred assessment and the alternative assessment in each case proceeded on different calculations with different results, the use of distinct but alternative assessments' was within the power of assessment conferred on the Commissioners and was to the best of their judgment. *University Court of the University of Glasgow v C & E Commrs*, CS [2003] STC 495. (*Note.* For subsequent developments in this case, see **14.89** COLLECTION AND ENFORCEMENT.)

[3.133] A company (W) claimed substantial repayments of VAT on the basis that it had purchased goods from a registered UK trader and sold them to a Spanish customer. Customs received information indicating that the goods had never been delivered to Spain. They issued assessments charging tax on the basis that W's supplies did not qualify for zero-rating. Subsequently Customs formed the opinion that W's alleged purchases were fictitious, and issued alternative assessments to recover the input tax which W had claimed. W appealed, contending that the assessments were invalid. The tribunal rejected this contention and the Ch D dismissed W's appeal, applying the principles laid down by the CS in *University Court of the University of Glasgow v C & E Commrs*, **3.132** above. Patten J observed that the assessments related to different transactions. The original assessments related to supplies which W claimed to have made, while the subsequent assessments related to supplies which W claimed to have received. The facts of what had happened were disputed, and Customs were entitled to raise alternative assessments in order to 'recover unpaid tax and prevent fraud'. *Westone Wholesale Ltd v HMRC (No 1)*, Ch D 2007, [2008] STC 828; [2007] EWHC 2676 (Ch). (*Note*. For subsequent developments in this case, see **23.17** EUROPEAN COMMUNITY: SINGLE MARKET.)

Cases where the appellant was successful

Assessment to rectify error in previous assessment—whether valid

[3.134] A trader (J) failed to account for tax on sales of 168 prints at auction sales in 1974–1976, treating them as zero-rated. A VAT officer, on examining his records in September 1976, considered that there was no proof of export. J then obtained and forwarded to the VAT officer a letter from the auctioneers, identifying certain prints which had been sold to foreign buyers, and another letter from a New York gallery stating that certain prints, which its director had purchased at one of the auctions, were for export to New York. An assessment was thereupon issued on 24 November 1976 charging tax of £187, covering the only three items sold which were not referred to in the two letters. However, the Commissioners subsequently considered that the letters were not adequate proof of export, and a further assessment was issued on 9 December 1976 in respect of all the items sold, charging tax of £1,605 with a set-off for the £187 assessed in the first assessment. J appealed against the second assessment, contending that it was invalid as no further evidence to justify it had come to light since the first assessment. The tribunal accepted this contention and allowed the appeal, holding that a further assessment could only be raised where new evidence had come to the knowledge of the Commissioners since the previous one. *WRH Jeudwine*, [1977] VATTR 115 (VTD 376). (*Notes*. (1) *Dicta* of the tribunal chairman were implicitly disapproved by the QB in the subsequent case of *Parekh*, **3.75** above. Woolf J observed that 'the language of the section does not appear to prevent an assessment being withdrawn and replaced by another assessment'. (2) In *Foster & Foster*, **3.123** below, the tribunal declined to follow the decision in *Jeudwine* on the grounds that it had been decided before the enactment of what is now *VATA 1994, s 77* by *FA 1985*.)

[3.135] The decision in *Jeudwine*, **3.134** above, was applied in the similar subsequent cases of *R Scott*, MAN/76/181 (VTD 517); *A Christofi*, LON/77/258 (VTD 550); and *V Scarfe & J Cowley*, LON/77/28 (VTD 703).

Assessment not showing start of period covered—whether valid.

[3.136] The Commissioners issued an estimated assessment which was intended to cover a period of 33 months ending on 30 April 1978. However, the Notice of Assessment (form VAT 191) described the period assessed as 'period 61 ended 30 April 1978'. The tribunal held that the assessment was only valid for the three months ending on that date, found that there had been no underdeclaration for those three months, and allowed the appeal. *RE Bell*, [1979] VATTR 115 (VTD 761). (*Notes.* (1) Form VAT 191 has subsequently been superseded by form VAT 655. (2) *Obiter dicta* of the tribunal chairman (Mr. Shirley) were disapproved by the CA in the subsequent case of *House*, **3.127** above. Sir John Balcombe observed that Mr. Shirley's decision gave to the form VAT 191 'an importance which it cannot properly bear'.)

Start of period incorrectly stated on notice of assessment.

[3.137] The Commissioners issued an assessment which was intended to cover the period from 1 March 1986 to 30 November 1990. However, the notice of assessment was incorrectly typed, and stated that the assessment was for the period from 1 March 1985 to 30 November 1990. The tribunal allowed the trader's appeal, holding that the effect of the typing error was that the assessment was invalid. *M Younis (t/a Heaton Private Hire)*, MAN/92/739 (VTD 11908). (*Note.* The decision in this case was disapproved in the subsequent case of *Solomon's Kebab House*, **3.126** above, on the grounds that it had been decided without reference to the High Court decision in *Grunwick Processing Laboratories Ltd*, **3.61** above, and was inconsistent with the subsequent CA decision in *Le Rififi Ltd*, **3.87** above.)

Assessment not stating period assessed—whether valid

[3.138] The Commissioners issued a 'global' assessment to a company. Through a clerical error, the period intended to be covered by the assessment was not specified. The company appealed, contending that the assessment was invalid. The tribunal accepted this contention and allowed the appeal. The tribunal decision in *House*, **3.127** above, was distinguished because in that case the period covered by the assessment had been indicated in accompanying schedules, whereas that was not so in the instant case. *SAS Fashions Ltd*, MAN/90/1024 (VTD 9426). (*Note.* The decision in this case was made after the tribunal decision in *House*, **3.127** above, but before the CA decision, and was subsequently specifically disapproved by the CA. Sir John Balcombe observed that the case had been decided without reference to the High Court decision in *Grunwick Processing Laboratories Ltd*, **3.61** above, and was inconsistent with the subsequent CA decision in *Le Rififi Ltd*, **3.87** above.)

Amendment of assessment—whether properly notified

[3.139] In October 1998 the Commissioners issued an assessment of a penalty to a couple who traded as shopkeepers. The couple appealed. In December 1998 the Commissioners sent a letter advising the couple's accountant that the assessment had been reduced, and stating that 'the revised Notice of Assessment will be issued to your client direct as soon as possible'. When the appeal was set down for hearing, the tribunal found that the amount of the revised assessment had not been validly notified. Applying *dicta* of Woolf J in *International Language Centres Ltd*, **3.41** above, 'the taxpayer is entitled to be informed in reasonably clear terms of the effect of the assessment'. On the evidence, the letter dated December 1998 did not inform the couple's accountants 'in reasonably clear terms of the amount of the amended assessment. It clearly leaves some further computation to be carried out.' Additionally, it appeared that the letter had not been intended to be a notice of assessment, because 'it contemplates that a revised notice of assessment is to be issued in the near future'. *Mr & Mrs HK Randhawa (t/a Mill Hill Food Store)*, MAN/97/944 (VTD 16692).

Assessment not complying with certificate of registration—whether valid

[3.140] The proprietors of a fish-and-chip shop registered for VAT from 1 November 1998. The Commissioners formed the opinion that they should have registered for VAT from 1 November 1996. On 8 June 1999 they issued a certificate of registration requiring the proprietors to make a return covering the period from 1 November 1996 to 31 August 1999. On the following day a VAT officer issued a letter requiring them to make a return for the period from 1 November 1996 to 31 October 1998. In July 1999 the Commissioners issued an assessment covering this latter period. The proprietors appealed, contending as a preliminary point that the assessment was invalid, since the effect of *VATA 1994, s 73(1)* was that 'the only valid period for which the Commissioners could assess the appellants to tax was that from 1 November 1996 to 31 August 1999'. The tribunal accepted this contention and allowed the appeal. *DJ, J & S Plummer*, MAN/99/589 (VTD 16976). (*Note.* For another issue in this case, see **57.205** REGISTRATION.)

[3.141] A similar decision was reached in *M Bradbury and Saltaire Private Hire Ltd*, MAN/00/268 (VTD 17596).

[3.142] See also *Weston*, **59.18** RETURNS.

Assessment but no certificate of registration—whether assessment valid

[3.143] The Commissioners formed the opinion that a partnership which operated a taxi business should have registered for VAT. In August 1998 they issued a notice of compulsory registration from July 1993 to the partnership. The notice stated that a certificate of registration would be forwarded 'in due course'. Subsequently an estimated assessment, charging VAT of £7,103, was issued by the VAT Central Unit at Southend, covering the period from July 1993 to August 1998. In February 1999 the Commissioners wrote to the partnership, directing it to forward a return covering the period from 1 March 1992 to 30 June 1993. In August 1999 the Commissioners issued a global estimated assessment, charging £104,957, for the period from 1 March 1992 to 31 October 1998. The partnership appealed. In October 2000, before the hearing of the appeal, a VAT officer wrote to the partnership, stating that 'in order to regularise the position', the original centrally issued assessment of £7,103 was to be increased to £112,060 and the officer's assessment of £104,957 was to be withdrawn. The tribunal held that both assessments were invalid. The tribunal observed that the Commissioners had failed to produce a copy of a certificate of registration, or any evidence that one had been issued to the partnership. The chairman observed that 'if a party to proceedings before these tribunals intends to rely on a document, it is for that party to produce the document, or otherwise properly prove its contents both to confirm that it was in fact issued or that it exists, and to show that it contains the information it is said to contain'. In view of the direction contained in their letter of February 1999, the Commissioners could issue a global assessment covering the period from 1 March 1992 to 30 June 1993. However, in the absence of any direction contained in a certificate of registration, the Commissioners 'could assess quarter by quarter for the remainder of the period between 1 July 1993 and 31 October 1998, but in no other way'. *M Hussain & M Ghazenfer (t/a Central Taxis)*, MAN/99/22, >AN/00/171, MAN/01/61 (VTD 17526, VTD 17559). (*Note*. The decision here was not followed, and was implicitly disapproved, by the Ch D in the subsequent case of *Hindle*, **3.117** above.)

[3.144] In July 2002 Customs issued a notice of compulsory registration to four members of the same family, on the basis that they were operating a partnership in partnership. The notice stated that the partnership registration had retrospective effect from 18 September 1995. In September 2002 Customs issued an assessment covering the period from 18 September 1995 to 31 July 2002. The partners appealed against both the notice of registration and the assessment. The tribunal heard the appeal against the notice of registration in 2005 and found that the appellants were trading in partnership (see **47.24** PARTNERSHIP). The partners' appeal against the assessment was heard by a different tribunal in 2007. At the hearing, the partnership contended that the assessment was invalid because although Customs had issued a notice of registration in July 2002, they had not issued a certificate of registration until January 2007, and the assessment did not correspond to a prescribed accounting period. The tribunal accepted this contention and allowed the appeal, and the CS unanimously upheld this decision. Lord Reed observed that 'where a person is registered late for VAT, it is open to the Commissioners to make a "long period" direction under *regulation 25(1)(c)*, directing that the first return should cover the entire period from the date when the person ought to have been registered until a point in time after the date of registration'. However, in this case, Customs had failed to make such a direction. Since the assessment did not relate to a prescribed accounting period, it was invalid. *HMRC v A, A, A & R Miah (t/a the Raj Restaurant) (No 2)*, CS 2008, [2009] STC 729; [2008] CSIH 68.

Partnership name wrongly recorded on registration certificate

[3.145] See *Razaq & Bashir (t/a Streamline Taxis)*, **47.16** PARTNERSHIP.

The amount of the assessment

NOTE

For cases concerning the question of whether an assessment was made to the best of the Commissioners' judgment, as required by *VATA 1994, s 73(1)*, see **3.1** *et seq.* above.

Estimated assessment

[3.146] Customs formed the opinion that a partnership which sold clothing had underdeclared its takings. They issued an assessment on the basis of a mark-up of 20%. The partnership appealed, contending that the assessment should be reduced to take account of an increase in stock. The tribunal rejected this contention and dismissed the appeal, holding that 'in order to make such an adjustment it is necessary that there should be available evidence to establish what is the opening and closing stock', and finding that there was 'no material in evidence before us to enable us to embark upon a reasonable calculation of quantum'. *RM Arora & Others (t/a Angela)*, [1976] VATTR 53 (VTD 244).

[3.147] Customs issued an estimated assessment on a company which operated a Chinese restaurant, computed on the basis of an overall mark-up of 100%. The company appealed, admitting that it had wrongly deducted staff wages in computing takings, but contending that its overall mark-up was only 70%. The tribunal reviewed the evidence in detail and dismissed the appeal, finding that the company's records were unreliable because a 'test meal' taken by Customs officers had not been included. *Ng Yuet Sar Restaurant Ltd*, BIR/76/22 (VTD 319).

[3.148] Customs issued an estimated assessment on a grocer, charging additional tax of £164, computed on the basis of an overall mark-up of 17%. The tribunal reviewed the evidence in detail and reduced the assessment to £125 (on the basis of an overall mark-up of 14%). The tribunal observed that 'the method of obtaining a hypothetical mark-up over a test period in order that it may then be applied to the whole period of assessment is one which has frequently been approved by these tribunals. Of necessity there are imponderable factors inherent in its adoption, and in every case its use requires careful scrutiny.' However, 'where the books and accounts are themselves suspect it is difficult to see what other method can be employed for the purposes of an assessment.' *B Robinson*, MAN/76/48 (VTD 634).

[3.149] Customs issued an estimated assessment on a grocer, based on a mark-up computation. The tribunal upheld the assessment in principle but reduced it by £57 to make allowance for thefts of stock. *AR Patel*, MAN/77/84 (VTD 692).

[3.150] Customs issued an estimated assessment on an elderly couple who had operated a public house. The assessment charged additional tax of £948, computed on the basis of an overall mark-up of 38%. The tribunal reviewed the evidence in detail and reduced the assessment to £500 (on the basis of an overall mark-up of 27%). *C & A Ford*, MAN/79/12 (VTD 837).

[3.151] A company which sold alcoholic drinks appealed against an estimated assessment, contending that it had failed to achieve the intended mark-up because of substantial thefts of stock. The tribunal upheld the assessment in principle but reduced it in amount. *Avery's of Bristol Ltd*, LON/81/85 (VTD 1252).

[3.152] A club failed to account for VAT on takings from two gaming machines. Customs officers visited the premises on two occasions and formed the opinion that on each occasion the machine takings were not less than 6.9% of the bar takings. They issued an assessment on this basis. The tribunal upheld the assessment, finding that the assumption of a relation between the machine takings and the bar takings was reasonable, and there was no realistic alternative method of estimating the takings. *Moorthorpe Empire Working Men's Club*, MAN/80/84 (VTD 1127).

[3.153] A partnership which carried on business as market traders failed to keep proper records. They did not keep records of purchases and recorded takings weekly in round sums (multiples of £100). Customs issued an estimated assessment in which they estimated the partners' personal expenditure by reference to the annual Family Expenditure Survey issued by the Department of Employment. The tribunal upheld the assessment. *M & A Hellewell*, MAN/81/166 (VTD 1274).

[3.154] There have been a very large number of appeals against estimated assessments, in which the decision turns entirely on the facts of the particular case. In the interests of space, such decisions are not normally summarised in this book. For summaries of such cases decided up to and including 31 December 1993, see Tolley's VAT Cases 1994. For an analysis of the principles underlying the making of an estimated assessment, see De Voil Indirect Tax Service, para V5.251 et seq.

Assessment reduced by tribunal—mark-up computations criticised

[3.155] The Commissioners issued six estimated assessments on a partnership which operated a snack bar. The assessments charged tax of £723, and were computed on the basis that the partnership had underdeclared its takings and had also wrongly treated certain sales as zero-rated when they should have been standard-rated. The tribunal reviewed the evidence in detail and reduced the assessments to £248. The tribunal observed that mark-up computations 'may give rise to a suspicion that a trader may not have disclosed all the receipts of his business, but cannot establish with any degree of precision the actual amount of such receipts. A mark-up computation is made on a number of assumptions so that a small inaccuracy in a basic assumption may produce a large error in the result. Very few, if any traders sell only one line at a constant mark-up year after year so that for other circumstances a mark-up calculation had to be weighted and allowances made for estimated losses, wastage and sales at a discount. All such factors are matters of guesswork. No trader can always, day after day, estimate his demand so accurately that he never has any loss or wastage, or run his business so efficiently that he suffers no shrinkage.' *KWG Goodhew & Others*, [1975] VATTR 111 (VTD 170).

Appeal allowed by tribunal—mark-up computations criticised

[3.156] A publican's returns showed an overall mark-up of 41.5%. Customs issued an estimated assessment on the basis that the mark-up should have been 54%. The tribunal allowed the publican's appeal, finding that the records were accurate and that Customs had failed to make adequate allowance for wastage. *BE Newman*, LON/75/50A (VTD 191).

[3.157] Customs issued an estimated assessment on a company which operated a Chinese restaurant. The assessment was based on a mark-up calculation by reference to the amount of rice which the company had purchased. The company appealed, contending that the assessment was incorrect because it underestimated wastage and underestimated the weight of rice served in each portion. The tribunal accepted the company's evidence and allowed the appeal. *Double Luck Restaurant Ltd*, MAN/77/282 (VTD 578).

[3.158] Customs issued an estimated assessment on a partnership which operated a restaurant, based on a mark-up calculation. The partnership appealed, contending that the returns were correct and that the assessment made insufficient allowance for wastage and underestimated the weight of steaks served in the restaurant. The tribunal accepted the partnership's evidence and allowed the appeal. *W & D Bedward*, LON/78/246 (VTD 698).

[3.159] Customs issued an estimated assessment on a florist (B), based on a mark-up of 20% and allowing 5% for wastage. The tribunal allowed B's appeal, finding that his records were accurate and that Customs had significantly underestimated the degree of wastage. The tribunal observed that the low gross profit rate was attributable to 'unwise purchases'. *T Brown*, LON/80/109 (VTD 1020).

[3.160] A company operated a restaurant. Its accounts for 1979 indicated an overall mark-up of 37%. Customs issued an estimated assessment on the basis of an overall mark-up of 100%. The tribunal allowed the company's appeal, holding that Customs 'had failed to establish that a 100% mark-up was appropriate'. *Fyfe & Fyfe Ltd*, EDN/81/34 (VTD 1199).

Whether amount of assessment may be altered after issue

[3.161] In the case noted at **18.18** DEFAULT SURCHARGE, the appellant company contended that the amount charged by an assessment could not be amended after the assessment had been issued. The tribunal rejected this contention, holding that what is now *VATA 1994, s 73* enabled Customs to withdraw or reduce an assessment if they discovered that the amount of the assessment was incorrect. *Bill Hennessy Associates Ltd*, LON/87/640 & 709 (VTD 2656).

[3.162] The decision in *Bill Hennessy Associates Ltd*, **3.161** above, was applied in the subsequent case of *Yuen Tung Restaurant Ltd*, **3.121** above.

Form 656 issued in error—whether binding on Customs

[3.163] Customs issued an assessment, charging VAT of £29,250, to a partnership. The partnership appealed. In May 2000, as a result of a clerical error by a Customs officer, the VAT Central Unit issued a Notice of Amendment (form 656), indicating that the assessment had been reduced to nil. In June 2000 Customs wrote to the partnership's accountants, stating that the form 656 was incorrect and that the assessment was 'still extant'. The appeal was referred to the tribunal to consider whether the form 656 was binding on Customs. The tribunal held that the form 656 did not constitute a 'clear and unequivocal ruling'. On the evidence, its issue had been 'a patent mistake, immediately rectified and notified to the appellants upon discovery'. *SK & KN Law (t/a Happy Valley)*, MAN/00/13 (VTD 17612). (*Note.* Customs were ordered to pay costs of £750 to the appellants.)

Assessment remitted to tribunal to consider amount

[3.164] Customs issued estimated assessments on an accountant who had failed to submit VAT returns. The tribunal dismissed the accountant's appeals, holding that the assessments had been made to the best of Customs' judgment.

The accountant appealed to the QB, which directed that the case should be remitted to a new tribunal to consider the amount of the assessment. Collins J observed that it was important to distinguish between the issue of whether an assessment had been made to the best of Customs' judgment (as required by *VATA 1994, s 73(1)*) and the amount of the assessment. In deciding whether an assessment had been made to the best of Customs' judgment, the tribunal had a supervisory role, but once a tribunal had accepted that Customs were entitled to make that assessment, the amount of the assessment was for the tribunal to decide. On the evidence, the tribunal had correctly held that the assessment had been made to the best of Customs' judgment. However, the language used in the decision made it clear that the tribunal had then misdirected itself, since it had failed to consider the amount of the assessment. The tribunal 'should have considered the material put before it by the appellant and decided for itself whether the assessments should be changed'. *MYH Murat v C & E Commrs*, QB [1998] STC 923. (*Notes.* (1) For another issue in this case, not taken to the QB, see **51.184** PENALTIES: FAILURE TO NOTIFY. (2) Compare the subsequent decision, also by Collins J, in *Majid & Partners*, 3.14 above, where he declined to remit a case to the tribunal, since the appellant had failed to challenge the amount of the assessment at the initial hearing.)

[3.165] HMRC issued assessments on a company (M) which operated two wine bars and six delicatessens. The First-Tier Tribunal upheld the assessments, holding inter alia that 30% of the sales from the delicatessens were standard-rated and that 70% qualified for zero-rating. M appealed to the Upper Tribunal, contending that the First-Tier Tribunal had erred in holding that its jurisdiction was supervisory rather than appellate, and that it should have given more detailed consideration to the quantum of the assessments. The Upper Tribunal remitted the case to the First-Tier Tribunal for rehearing, holding that the First-Tier Tribunal 'should have exercised a full appellate jurisdiction and decided for itself the correct amount of the tax due'. *Mithras (Wine Bars) Ltd v HMRC*, UT [2010] STC 1370; [2010] UKUT 115 (TCC). (*Note.* The First-Tier Tribunal subsequently reheard the company's appeal and dismissed it—[2010] UKFTT 622 (TC), TC00864.)

Assessments to adjust 'partial exemption' computation

[3.166] A trade union, which was partly exempt, produced an in-house magazine ten times a year, which it distributed to its members free of charge. In apportioning its residual input tax between taxable and exempt supplies, it treated the distribution of the magazine as a taxable supply of £1.80 per issue to each of its members, giving a total taxable supply of £1,234,395 per quarter. Customs accepted that the distribution of the magazine was a taxable supply, but considered that the magazines should be valued at cost, and that the total taxable supply should be treated as £493,578 per quarter. They issued assessments to adjust the attribution of input tax on this basis. The tribunal upheld the assessments, and the union appealed, contending that the assessments were excessive. The Ch D accepted this contention and allowed the union's appeal. Lindsay J held that the tribunal had been entitled to reject the union's computation. However, the officer responsible for the assessment had made a significant error in his treatment of the union's overheads, since 'given the scheme of the audited accounts', it was an error of law 'to exclude from the computation of the denominator all £7,540,000 of the annual employment costs '. The available evidence pointed 'on a balance of probabilities', to employment costs of more than £56,124 per quarter being fairly attributable to the composition, production and distribution of the magazines. He directed that the case should be remitted to a new tribunal for reconsideration. *Public & Commercial Services Union v C & E Commrs*, Ch D 2003, [2004] STC 376; [2003] EWHC 2845 (Ch).

[3.167] See also *Rahman*, 2.309 APPEALS.

VATA 1994, s 84(5)—assessment increased by tribunal

[3.168] Customs issued estimated assessments, covering the periods from July 1993 to September 1994, on a partnership which traded as racehorse dealers. The partnership appealed. The tribunal allowed the appeals with regard to the periods up to and including January 1994, holding on the evidence that these assessments had not been made to the best of Customs' judgment. However, the tribunal increased the assessments for the periods from February to September 1994, finding that the assessments were inadequate and holding that it had power to increase the assessments under *VATA 1994, s 84(5)*. The partnership appealed to the QB, contending that the tribunal had acted unreasonably in increasing the assessments. The QB accepted this contention and allowed the appeal. Carnwath J held that the tribunal could exercise its power to increase assessments in order to correct arithmetical errors, or where the Commissioners had argued at the hearing that the assessments should be increased. However, the tribunal did not have 'a free-standing power to increase the assessment entirely of its own initiative'. Furthermore, if a tribunal was contemplating increasing an assessment, the appellant should be given 'a fair opportunity (by adjournment, if necessary)' to consider the position. On the evidence, the tribunal here had not given the partnership adequate notice of its intention to increase the assessments. *Elias Gale Racing v C & E Commrs*, QB 1998, [1999] STC 66.

[3.169] For a case in which the tribunal increased an assessment under *VATA 1994, s 84(5)*, see *Ho*, 3.17 above.

Miscellaneous

Business taken over as going concern—assessment on transferee.

[3.170] See *Bjellica*, 57.89 REGISTRATION; *Ponsonby*, 65.108 TRANSFERS OF GOING CONCERNS, and the cases noted at **65.110** to **65.112** TRANSFERS OF GOING CONCERNS.

Whether assessment issued for wrong period

[3.171] The Commissioners issued an assessment for the period from 27 October 1983 to 31 May 1985. However, the tribunal found that the supplies to which the assessment related had taken place between 1 June and 31 August 1985. The tribunal allowed the trader's appeal, holding that the assessment was invalid since it had been made for the wrong period. *HK Sneller*, LON/87/124 (VTD 2556).

[3.172] A similar decision was reached in *McGowan-Kemp (Printing Machines) Ltd*, MAN/98/745 (VTD 16553).

[3.173] The Commissioners issued an assessment which purported to cover the period from 1 May 1984 to 30 April 1989. However, it also included supplies made in the period from 1 February 1984 to 30 April 1984. The company appealed, contending that the assessment was invalid for this reason. The tribunal accepted this contention and allowed the appeal, applying *dicta* of Lord Grantchester in *Sneller*, 3.171 above. *International Institute for Strategic Studies*, [1992] VATTR 245 (VTD 6673).

[3.174] See also *Garnham*, 62.136 SUPPLY, and *Enron Europe Ltd v HMRC (No 1)*, 62.465 SUPPLY.

[3.175] The Commissioners discovered that a company had failed to account for tax on deposits at the time of receipt. They instructed the company to include any such amounts on which tax had not been accounted for in its return for the period ending January 1991. The company failed to comply with this and the Commissioners issued an assessment for that period charging tax on the receipts in question. The company appealed, contending that the assessment was invalid because most of the deposits in question had been received before the start of the relevant return period, so that the assessment had been issued for the wrong period. The tribunal dismissed the appeal, holding that what is now *VATA 1994, Sch 11 para 2(1)* empowered the Commissioners to direct that the receipts in question should be accounted for in the return for the period ending January 1991. *Cantors plc*, [1993] VATTR 367 (VTD 10834).

[3.176] A company (G) reclaimed input tax of £980,500 in its return for the period ending September 1999, in respect of the purported purchase of some equipment from an associated company. However, it never took delivery of the equipment, and the transaction was cancelled in the following quarter. The vendor adjusted its accounting records, but did not issue a credit note to G. When Customs discovered what had happened, they issued an assessment for the period ending September 1999, to recover the input tax which G had claimed. G appealed, accepting that it was not entitled to credit for the £980,500 but contending that the assessment was invalid because it should have been raised for the period ending December 1999 rather than for the period ending September 1999. The tribunal rejected this contention and dismissed G's appeal, holding that the effect of *VATA 1994, s 73(2)* was that the assessment had been issued for the correct period. The tribunal observed that *Article 11C1* of the *EC Sixth Directive* provided that 'in the case of cancellation, it is the taxable amount which is to be reduced'. This implied that there was 'not a separate balancing exercise in a later period but an adjustment to the original output tax liability and corresponding input tax claim, an adjustment which could take place only by reference to the period in which the liability and claim arose'. *VATA 1994, s 73(2)* implemented *Article 11C1* and made it clear that 'a retrospective adjustment is not merely possible but appropriate'. The tribunal also held that *VAT Regulations, reg 38* 'does not apply to a case in which the consideration is not reduced, but cancelled altogether because the underlying supply has itself been cancelled. The wording of the regulation clearly contemplates the continuing existence of the supply.' *Genie Financial Services Europe Ltd*, MAN/02/417 (VTD 20367).

Change of basis of assessment

[3.177] The Commissioners issued an assessment on a manufacturer of steel shelving, after discovering that his records indicated an unusually low gross profit rate. The assessment was originally issued to recover output tax, on the basis that the manufacturer had failed to record some sales. Subsequently, the Commissioners discovered that the discrepancy was attributable to the fact that the manufacturer had reclaimed input tax on the basis of false invoices, issued in the name of a company which had ceased trading 13 years previously. They recomputed the assessment accordingly, changing the basis of the assessment from undeclared output tax to overclaimed input tax. The manufacturer appealed, contending that an assessment issued to charge output tax could not be treated as an assessment to recover input tax. The tribunal rejected this contention and dismissed the appeal, applying *dicta* of Lord Grantchester in *The Football Association Ltd*, **62.284** SUPPLY. *MP Buxton*, MAN/90/993 (VTD 10108).

[3.178] In the case noted at **62.363** SUPPLY, where the Commissioners had issued assessments on a company (S) to charge output tax, the QB upheld the tribunal's decision that S was not liable to account for output tax, but also held that S had not been entitled to reclaim input tax on the supplies, and directed that the assessments should be amended accordingly. *C & E Commrs v Sooner Foods Ltd*, QB [1983] STC 376.

[3.179] In the case noted at **32.19** GROUPS OF COMPANIES, the tribunal held that certain assessments which had originally been issued to recover overclaimed input tax could also be treated as assessments to charge underdeclared output tax, applying the principles laid down by Forbes J in *Sooner Foods Ltd*, **3.178** above. The CA unanimously upheld the tribunal decision, and specifically disapproved the decision of Popplewell J in *Ridgeons Bulk Ltd v C & E Commrs*, QB [1994] STC 427. Arden LJ held that if, after making an assessment under *VATA 1994, s 73(1)*, Customs subsequently accepted that additional input tax was deductible, they were not prevented from charging 'underdeclared output tax in respect of the same transactions as formed the basis of the assessment which has not previously been taken into account'. It was 'an essential part of an assessment for the purposes of *s 73(1)* that it determines the net amount due by way of VAT'. Customs had power to reduce an assessment, and 'it must thus follow that when they reduce an assessment they have power under *VATA* to change the calculation as to input tax or output tax on which the assessment was based. To hold that Customs 'could only make adjustments to input and output tax if they were exercising their power to reduce an assessment' would be 'inconsistent with the intention of Parliament appearing from the power to make assessments to the best of their judgment'. *HMRC v BUPA Purchasing Ltd (No 2)*, CA 2007, [2008] STC 101; [2007] EWCA Civ 542.

Assessment covering period before date of registration

[3.180] See *Adler Properties Ltd*, 57.88 REGISTRATION; *Bjelica*, 57.89 REGISTRATION, and *Short*, 57.94 REGISTRATION.

Whether Customs should have issued assessment

[3.181] A company had mistakenly accounted for tax on certain supplies which should have been treated as outside the scope of VAT. It subsequently claimed bad debt relief in respect of some of these supplies. Customs issued an assessment to recover the tax in question on the grounds that the bad debt relief claim had been made outside the statutory time limit. The tribunal allowed the company's appeal against the assessment, holding that Customs had 'a discretion in the matter of making an assessment', but that it was 'apparent from the correspondence in the present dispute that the Commissioners took the view that they had no discretion at all and never considered the particular circumstances'. The tribunal held that 'the effect of what the Commissioners have done is to attempt to secure to themselves a sum of money which never was due in reality and always fell outwith the scope of the tax. There never was a taxable transaction. There could be no tax point.' Customs had failed 'to consider whether they are justified in seeking, obtaining or retaining this windfall which in our view would be a matter of unjust enrichment, before making an assessment like the present. As a public body they have to consider the appropriateness of the whole circumstances, and not to seek a manifestly unfair advantage.' *Technip Coflexip Offshore Ltd*, EDN/01/165 (VTD 19298).

4

Bad Debts

The cases in this chapter are arranged under the following headings.

The 'outstanding amount' (VATA 1994, s 36(2)(3))   4.1
Miscellaneous   4.16

NOTE

There have been substantial changes in the rules governing bad debt relief. The current provisions are contained in *VATA 1994, s 36*. Cases relating to the earlier provisions of *FA 1978* and *VATA 1983* should be read in the light of the changes in the legislation.

The 'outstanding amount' (VATA 1994, s 36(2)(3))

Customer paying contract price exclusive of VAT

[4.1] A company sold goods for £10,200 plus VAT of £816. The customer only paid £10,200 and the company claimed bad debt relief of £816. The tribunal held that the outstanding debt of £816 should be treated as a gross debt and that only the VAT element of ³/₂₃rds of the debt (i.e. £106.43) was eligible for bad debt relief. *Enderby Transport Ltd*, MAN/83/304 (VTD 1607).

[4.2] The decision in *Enderby Transport Ltd*, 4.1 above, was applied in the similar cases of *R Huckridge*, LON/85/141 (VTD 1969); *Autocraft Motor Body Repairs*, MAN/96/1362 (VTD 15077); *WP Holdings plc*, MAN/96/995 (VTD 15134) and *Empire Contracts Ltd*, 36.479 INPUT TAX.

[4.3] Similar decisions were reached in *Irrepressible Records Ltd*, LON/87/615 (VTD 2947); *Caernarfonshire Fatstock Group Ltd*, MAN/89/748 (VTD 5033); *K & D Williams*, LON/91/285Y (VTD 7078); *Independent Community Care Ltd*, LON/91/1971Z (VTD 7735); *B & PD Simmons*, LON/91/947Y (VTD 7996); *JJ Manpower Services*, LON/92/729Y (VTD 9405); *WS Parsons Ltd*, LON/92/3427 (VTD 10693); *Gale & Daws Ltd*, LON/92/2613A (VTD 11126); *B & H Carpentry & Joinery*, LON/94/296A (VTD 12791); *NM Williams*, LON/94/1076A (VTD 12876); *Triple Crown Securities Holdings Ltd*, LON/94/433A (VTD 13154) and *S Jennings*, MAN/96/68 (VTD 14372).

[4.4] The decision in *Caernarfonshire Fatstock Group*, 4.3 above, was distinguished in a subsequent case in which a trader had been registered for VAT in January 1990 with retrospective effect from August 1989. Between August and December 1989 he had made supplies to an engineering company (G) on which he had not charged VAT. In February 1990 he issued an invoice to G charging VAT on these supplies. G did not pay the VAT, and went into receivership later in 1990. The trader claimed bad debt relief in respect of the whole of the amount charged by the February invoice, but the Commissioners only allowed relief of the VAT fraction of $^3/_{23}$. The tribunal allowed the trader's appeal, observing that he had contacted his local VAT office in July 1989 to enquire about registration, and the VAT office had been dilatory in dealing with his enquiry. The tribunal chairman observed that the February invoice had been issued in respect of 'a sum the entirety of which was value added tax which the appellant was attempting to recover for the Commissioners' benefit. The position might be different in the case of a trader who, culpably registering late, was attempting, belatedly, to recover from his customer sums which he should have charged at an earlier date but which, because of his own default, he has failed to charge.' In the circumstances of this case, 'the amount of tax chargeable by reference to the outstanding amount is the whole of the VAT-only invoice and the appellant is entitled to bad debt relief for the entirety of that sum'. *RC Palmer (t/a R & K Engineering)*, MAN/92/724 (VTD 11739). (*Note*. An appeal against a misdeclaration penalty was also allowed.)

Insurance company declining to pay VAT

[4.5] A company repaired a vehicle for an insurance company. The contract price was £11,300 plus VAT of £904. The insurance company paid £11,250 only, contending that the VAT of £904 and the balance of £50 should be paid by its client. The company which had carried out the repair invoiced the client but failed to obtain payment, and claimed bad debt relief. The tribunal dismissed its appeal, holding that the only remedy open to it was civil proceedings. *Aldon Engineering (Yorkshire) Ltd*, MAN/78/235 (VTD 743).

[4.6] A similar decision was reached in a case where an insurance company withheld the VAT element of the price paid to a trader who had replaced water-damaged carpets. *A Littlejohn (t/a Carpet Trades)*, EDN/83/72 (VTD 1716).

[4.7] A similar decision was reached in *Engineering Services (Bridgend) Ltd*, LON/01/161 (VTD 17556).

[4.8] A firm of solicitors acted for a company in an action to recover damages following a fire at its premises. The company was awarded costs of £7,127 plus VAT of £709. The defendants' insurers only paid £7,127. The solicitors then applied to their client company for payment of the VAT, but that company did not pay the bill and subsequently went into liquidation. The solicitors therefore claimed bad debt relief, but the Commissioners only allowed relief of $^3/_{23}$rds of the outstanding debt, i.e. £92. The tribunal upheld the Commissioners' decision. The £709 was a debt owed to the solicitors by the client, and relief could only be given on the VAT element of the gross debt. *AW Mawer & Co*, [1986] VATTR 87 (VTD 2100). (Note. See now, however, the subsequent Upper Tribunal decision in *Simpson & Marwick v HMRC*, 4.9 below.)

[4.9] The decision in *AW Mawer & Co* above was not followed in a subsequent Scottish case where the Upper Tribunal allowed an appeal by a firm of solicitors which provided legal services in respect of insurance claims. Lord Drummond Young observed that 'the specialty in the present case is that the unpaid amount consists entirely of VAT and, importantly, is clearly identifiable as consisting entirely of VAT. That is because the unpaid amount is contained in invoices that are for VAT only, as it is only the VAT component that is payable by the policyholders; the net price of the appellants' services is paid by the insurance companies.' He held that VATA 1994, s 36 'permits "a refund of the amount of VAT chargeable by reference to [an amount equal to the amount of the consideration so written off]". The amount written off is, demonstrably, all VAT. The compound preposition "by reference to" indicates that in determining the amount of the refund reference must be had to the consideration that is written off. If that amount is only VAT, that fact must in my opinion be taken into account in determining how reference is to be made to the consideration written off. If that is done, it is clear that the consideration so written off is all VAT, and the refund should be calculated accordingly.' *Simpson & Marwick v HMRC*, UT [2011] UKUT 498 (TCC).

Shares received as consideration under voluntary arrangement

[4.10] A company (U) had made supplies to another company (H), which was in financial difficulties. At a meeting of H's creditors, a voluntary arrangement was proposed whereby the creditors would receive ten redeemable preference shares for every £8 owed by H. A majority of H's creditors voted in favour of this proposal, although U's company secretary voted against it. Following the meeting, U received a share certificate from H in accordance with the voluntary arrangement. Subsequently U claimed bad debt relief in respect of the amounts it was owed by H. The Commissioners issued an assessment to recover the tax, considering that the share certificate issued by H to U constituted consideration for the debt, so that no bad debt relief was due. U appealed, contending that the share certificate was worthless and did not amount to satisfaction of the debt. The tribunal dismissed the appeal, holding that U was bound by the decision reached at the creditors' meeting, and that the share certificate represented full consideration for the debt. Consequently there was no longer any 'outstanding amount' within what is now *VATA 1994, s 36(2)*, and bad debt relief was not due. *AEG (UK) Ltd*, [1993] VATTR 379 (VTD 11428).

Associated companies—partial change in ownership

[4.11] A company (L) had four directors, one of whom (B) was also the managing director of another company (P). The other three directors (G, E and H) were directors and minority shareholders in P. L made various supplies to P, which did not pay for the supplies. G, E and H decided that they wished to sever their connections with B and P. In March 2001 B purchased their shares in P for the nominal price of £1 per share. They resigned as directors of P, and B resigned as a director of L. L wrote off the amounts which it was owed by P, and claimed bad debt relief. Subsequently the Commissioners issued an assessment on L to recover the relief in question, on the basis that the agreed change in ownership of the companies represented consideration for the debts in question. L appealed. The tribunal allowed L's appeal, holding that 'formally discharging a valueless claim' against P did not prevent L from claiming bad debt relief. The tribunal chairman (Mr. Reid) held that 'Parliament did not intend to defeat a *bona fide* claim by a trader who has recognised the inevitable and formally discharged a claim for payment which had no value'. *Alpha Leisure (Scotland) Ltd*, EDN/03/14 (VTD 18199).

Debt written off as part of management buyout

[4.12] A company (B) owned 41.5% of the shares in another company (F), which was in financial difficulties and owed B significant sums of money. As part of a management buyout of F, B agreed to write off some of the debt which it was owed by F. In return, F entered into an 'exclusive supply agreement' with B for a period of four years. B subsequently claimed bad debt relief in respect of the amounts it had written off. Customs rejected the claim on the basis that the exclusivity agreement represented consideration for the debt. The tribunal upheld Customs' ruling and dismissed B's appeal. *Berck Ltd*, MAN/06/386 (VTD 20051).

Relief claimed but debt already paid

[4.13] A company (J) had made both standard-rated and zero-rated supplies to another company (V). J went into liquidation in July 1985, owing V £32,000. All its supplies to V between May and July 1985 had been zero-rated, and the total amount of these zero-rated supplies exceeded £32,000. However V claimed bad debt relief, contending that payments which J had made before going into liquidation should be allocated to the most recent zero-rated supplies, and that the outstanding £32,000 should be treated as including standard-rated supplies made before May 1985. The Commissioners rejected V's claim and the tribunal dismissed V's appeal. It was an established legal principle that payments should be allocated to earlier debts before later debts. It followed that the debt in respect of which V had claimed relief had already been paid by J, and the £32,000 outstanding at July 1985 related entirely to zero-rated supplies in respect of which relief was not due. *Virgo Plant Hire Ltd*, [1990] VATTR 113 (VTD 5046).

[4.14] A similar decision was reached in *CB Kennedy*, MAN/96/151 (VTD 16068). (*Note.* Costs were awarded to the Commissioners.)

Apportionment of payment between taxable supplies and other debt

[4.15] A company (T) went into administration. It owed another company (C) £576,494 in respect of taxable supplies, on which C had accounted for output tax. It also owed C £680,000 under an 'investment amortisation agreement' which was outside the scope of VAT. C subsequently reached an agreement with T's administrators, under which it received £1,000,000 in respect of both debts, leaving an unpaid balance of £256,494. C submitted a claim for bad debt relief on the basis that the payment of £1,000,000 should be apportioned equally between the taxable supplies and the amount due under the investment amortisation agreement, so that bad debt relief was due on the proportion of the taxable supplies which remained unpaid. HMRC rejected the claim and issued an assessment to recover the relief, on the basis that the £1,000,000 should be attributed firstly to the taxable supplies and that no bad debt relief was due. The tribunal allowed C's appeal against this decision. Judge Berner held that it was 'just and reasonable to apportion the total amount received on a pro rata basis', and that this was 'the only proper approach that can be adopted'. *CPG Logistics Ltd*, [2010] UKFTT 345 (TC), TC00627.

Miscellaneous

Relief claimed—records inadequate

[4.16] In its return for the period ending 31 March 1991, a company (E) claimed bad debt relief of £7,047 in respect of money allegedly owed to it by a company which had gone into liquidation in 1987. A VAT officer discovered that E did not have the documents required by what is now *VAT Regulations 1995 (SI 1995/2518), reg 168*, and issued an assessment to recover the tax in question. The tribunal dismissed the company's appeal against this decision, holding that its jurisdiction was supervisory rather than appellate, applying *dicta* of Farquharson J in *Mr Wishmore Ltd*, **14.52** COLLECTION AND ENFORCEMENT. *Easden Manufacturing Co Ltd*, LON/92/1772A (VTD 10116).

[4.17] A similar decision was reached in *NGS (Coatbridge) Ltd*, EDN/98/68 (VTD 15970).

Intermediary becoming insolvent

[4.18] A retail company traded within a large store under a concession. It dealt with the public in the normal way, but at the close of trading each day it handed its payments to the store for banking. At the end of each week the store repaid the company its receipts for that week after deducting 10% commission. The store went into liquidation owing a substantial amount to the company, and the company claimed bad debt relief. The Commissioners rejected the claim and the tribunal dismissed the company's appeal, holding that the company was in a similar position to a trader who was robbed of his weekly takings on the way to the bank. The company's contracts were with its customers, and the customers had paid it for the goods which it sold. The store was not a customer of the company, but was in the position of a person to whom the company had lent its takings for safe keeping. *Wayfarer Leisure Ltd*, [1985] VATTR 174 (VTD 1898).

Company leaving group

[4.19] In 1990 a company (T) made some supplies in respect of which it was never paid. At the time T was a member of a group of companies, the representative member of which was a public company (P). In March 1991 P sold its interest in T, which continued trading. In November 1991 T wrote off the amount it was owed, and claimed bad debt relief under what is now *VATA 1994, s 36*. The Commissioners rejected the claim, on the grounds that the relief should have been claimed by P rather than by T, since it was P which had accounted for output tax on the supplies in question. The tribunal allowed T's appeal, observing that P had sold its shareholding in T at a valuation which treated the outstanding debts as good, and that, since T was no longer a member of the group of which P was the representative member, the intention of the legislation was that T should be entitled to the relief. The tribunal held that the fact that T had had a different VAT registration number since its departure from the group was 'irrelevant to the claim'. *Triad Timber Components Ltd*, [1993] VATTR 384 (VTD 10694).

[4.20] The decision in *Triad Timber Components Ltd*, **4.19** above, was applied in the similar case of *Proto Glazing Ltd*, LON/95/573A (VTD 13410).

Barter transactions—whether bad debt relief due

[4.21] See *Goldsmiths (Jewellers) Ltd*, **22.258** EUROPEAN COMMUNITY LAW.

Debt assigned under factoring agreement

[4.22] A company assigned some of its bad debts to a factoring company. It received some of the debts in question from the factoring company, and claimed bad debt relief in respect of the remainder. The Commissioners rejected the claim and the tribunal dismissed the company's claim. Since the company had assigned the debts, it was not entitled to relief under what is now *VATA 1994, s 36*. *Skytech Aluminium Stockholding & Distribution Ltd*, MAN/94/667 (VTD 14023).

[4.23] A company, which had assigned some of its debts to a factoring company, claimed bad debt relief in respect of the difference between the face value of the debts and the amounts which it received from the factoring company. The Commissioners rejected the claim and the tribunal dismissed the company's appeal, observing that the factors might recover the full amount of the debts, and holding that 'it would be quite wrong for the full amount of VAT shown on the invoices not to be accounted for, simply because, in purchasing the debts, the factors paid the appellant a "discounted" amount. The fact remains that the appellant made supplies at an agreed price for which it has invoiced its customers.' The discounted price paid by the factors to the appellant was irrelevant. *Ciss Ltd*, MAN/01/973 (VTD 18839).

Import agent claiming bad debt relief due to importer

[4.24] A partnership (P) traded as an import agent. It paid VAT as agent for an importer (S). S claimed input tax credit, but became insolvent before paying P. P claimed bad debt relief. The Commissioners rejected the claim on the grounds that P was not the 'person who has supplied goods or services', within *VATA 1994, s 36(1)*. The tribunal dismissed P's appeal against this decision. *Prestige Freight*, LON/01/0440 (VTD 17614).

VAT Regulations, reg 165A—time limit for claims

[4.25] A company claimed bad debt relief outside the 3½ year time limit laid down by *VAT Regulations 1995 (SI 1995/2518), reg 165A*. The Commissioners rejected the claim and the tribunal dismissed the company's appeal. *Impress Music Ltd*, LON/02/845 (VTD 18086).

[4.26] Similar decisions were reached in *Taylor Tunnicliffe Ltd*, MAN/03/043 (VTD 18378) and *Resteel Trading Ltd*, [2009] UKFTT 236 (TC), TC00185.

Failure to comply with VAT Regulations, reg 166A

[4.27] A company claimed bad debt relief without notifying the relevant customer, as required by *VAT Regulations 1995 (SI 1995/2518), reg 166A*. Customs rejected the claim and the tribunal dismissed the company's appeal, observing that 'to satisfy *regulation 166A* the notice must be issued within seven days of the claim being made', and holding that a subsequent duplicate claim 'cannot enable a belated notice to be served timeously'. *Alarmond Ltd*, EDN/05/43 (VTD 19324).

[4.28] See also *Fort Vale Engineering Ltd*, 52.242 PENALTIES: MISDECLARATION, and *Cooper*, 52.429 PENALTIES: MISDECLARATION.

Failure to comply with VAT Regulations, reg 167

[4.29] A claim to bad debt relief was dismissed in a case where the tribunal found that the claimant had failed to produce the evidence required by *VAT Regulations 1995 (SI 1995/2518), reg 167*. *AG Heatley (t/a AGH Shopfitting)*, MAN/02/062 (VTD 18836).

VAT Regulations, reg 170—conditional sale agreement

[4.30] A company (W) provided finance for the purchase of cars under conditional sale agreements. Some of W's customers defaulted on the agreements. In such cases, W claimed bad debt relief under *VATA 1994, s 36*. In making its claim, W did not follow the method of apportionment laid down by *VAT Regulations 1995 (SI 1995/2518), reg 170*, but allocated a greater proportion of the payments which it had received to the credit charge, and a smaller proportion of the payments to the goods, thus increasing its claim to bad debt relief. Customs issued an assessment on the basis that W's claim to bad debt relief contravened the requirements of *VAT Regulations 1995 (SI 1995/2518), reg 170*, and that the amount of relief should be computed by using a 'straightline' method of apportionment. The representative member of W's VAT group appealed, contending that the provisions of *reg 170* were unreasonable and should be treated as invalid. The tribunal rejected this contention and dismissed the appeal, and the Ch D upheld this decision. Lindsay J held that *reg 170* was within 'the Commissioners' rule-making powers' and was 'not irrational'. He also observed that 'were there to be a conflict between the accepted principles of commercial accountancy and the requirements of VAT law, it would be the statutory requirements of VAT law that would hold sway'. *Abbey National plc v C & E Commrs (No 3)*, Ch D

2005, [2006] STC 1; [2005] EWHC 1187 (Ch). (*Note.* See also now *VAT Regulations 1995, reg 170A*, introduced with effect from 1 January 2003. The assessment in this case covered the period ending 30 June 2000, so that *reg 170A* was not directly relevant.)

Repayment of input tax where bad debt relief claimed

[4.31] A company (T) operated a social club. It arranged for an associated company (R) to carry out construction work at its premises. R issued an invoice in November 1997, charging VAT of £21,000. T claimed this amount as input tax in its return for the period ending November 1997. In May 1999 R claimed bad debt relief in respect of the £21,000. The Commissioners discovered that T had failed to correct its claim for input tax, as required by *VAT Regulations 1995 (SI 1995/2518), reg 172D*. In May 2000 they issued an assessment, for the period ending 31 May 1999, to recover the £21,000 from T. T appealed, contending that the assessment should have been for the period ending November 1997, when it had made the original claim. The tribunal rejected this contention and dismissed the appeal, observing that *reg 172D(2)* required that T should have corrected its accounts 'for the period in which the claim for bad debt relief had been claimed. The *regulation* makes it entirely clear that the crucial date is the date when the claim for bad debt relief is made, not the date upon which the bad debt is incurred. That is logical enough, since the refund of tax does not become payable until after the claim has been made, and that has to be at least six months after the date on which the invoice is issued and output tax paid in respect of what later becomes the bad debt.' *Two Oaks Leisure Ltd (t/a The Hyde)*, LON/00/783 (VTD 17276).

Claims relating to input tax credit

[4.32] During 2004 a company (T) suffered several bad debts. In November 2004 it went into voluntary liquidation. In January 2006 its liquidators claimed bad debt relief. Customs accepted the claim relating to supplies made before April 2004, but rejected the claim for the three subsequent periods on the grounds that T had not paid its output tax liability for those periods. T appealed, contending that it was only claiming a refund where it had effectively paid the tax because it had valid claims for input tax, which exceeded the amounts of output tax due after excluding the bad debts. (For example, T's return for its final period of trading showed output tax of £46,563 and input tax of £40,311. The output tax claimed on its bad debts for that period totalled £20,600. It contended that its input tax should be treated as covering its actual output tax liability of £25,963, leaving a balance of £14,348 which could be attributed to the bad debts.) The tribunal accepted this contention and allowed T's appeal, holding that the phrase "accounted for and paid VAT" (in *VATA 1994, s 36(1)*) included payment by way of a valid claim for input tax credit. The tribunal held that it was 'the intention of *Article 11C1* (of the *EC Sixth Directive*) that, where invoices are not paid, the price (or taxable amount) on which tax is charged is reduced accordingly. *Article 11C1* also applies where invoices are only partly paid and provides that in those cases the price (or taxable amount) on which tax is charged is reduced accordingly.' On the evidence, T had 'made a number of supplies of goods and services, each for a consideration in money, and has accounted for and paid tax (by way of input tax credit) up to the amount in respect of which a claim was made. All of the consideration has been written off as a bad debt and the period of six months from the date of each supply has elapsed. (T) should therefore receive a refund of the amount of tax it has paid.' *Times Right Marketing Ltd (in liquidation)*, LON/06/1376 (VTD 20611). (*Note.* For HMRC's practice following this decision, see HMRC Brief 18/09, issued on 31 March 2009.)

Pre-1997 rules—whether compatible with EC law

[4.33] A company (G) claimed bad debt relief of more than £2,000,000, covering the period from 1978 to 1997, in relation to hire purchase contracts for motor vehicles terminated early on default without full payment and without the buyer becoming owner. HMRC rejected the claim on the basis that the effect of *VATA 1994, s 36(4)(b)*, as originally enacted and prior to its amendment by *FA 1997*, was that no relief was due. G appealed, contending that the relevant conditions contravened EC law and should be treated as invalid and ineffective. The tribunal accepted this contention and allowed the appeal. Judge Wallace held that the 'property requirement' of *s 36(4)(b)* had been 'incompatible with EC law', and that the time limit imposed by *FA 1997, s 39(5)* was also invalid as it failed to allow for transitional relief. HMRC appealed to the Upper Tribunal and made a preliminary application for the case to be referred to the ECJ. The Upper Tribunal adjourned this application, holding that there was 'a real prospect of being able to resolve the issue' without a reference, and directed that the case should be relisted for the hearing of the substantive appeal. *HMRC v GMAC UK plc*, UT [2011] UKUT 112 (TCC).

Cross-references

[4.34] For cases where credit notes were issued to cancel a debt, see **40.85** *et seq.* INVOICES AND CREDIT NOTES. See also *Vernitron Ltd*, **62.87** SUPPLY (goods sold conditionally and resold by purchaser without vendor's permission) and *Hurley Robinson Partnership*, **62.135** SUPPLY (goods invoiced—amount disputed by customer company which later went into liquidation).

5

Books, etc

The cases in this chapter are arranged under the following headings.

Books and booklets (VATA 1994, Sch 8, Group 3, Item 1)

Goods held to qualify for zero-rating	5.1
Cases where the consideration was apportioned	5.23
Goods held not to qualify for zero-rating	5.25

Brochures, pamphlets and leaflets (VATA 1994, Sch 8, Group 3, Item 1)

Goods held to qualify for zero-rating	5.54
Cases where the consideration was apportioned	5.68
Goods held not to qualify for zero-rating	5.72

Newspapers, journals and periodicals (VATA 1994, Sch 8, Group 3, Item 2)	5.93
Music (VATA 1994, Sch 8, Group 3, Item 4)	5.109
Maps, charts, etc. (VATA 1994, Sch 8, Group 3, Item 5)	5.110

Books and booklets (VATA 1994, Sch 8, Group 3, Item 1)

Goods held to qualify for zero-rating

Ring binders for workshop manuals

[5.1] A company supplied ring binders for workshop manuals. It did not account for VAT on these supplies, treating them as zero-rated. Customs issued a ruling that, since the binders were supplied separately from their intended contents, they were standard-rated. The tribunal allowed the company's appeal, holding that the supplies of the binders were zero-rated. *AE Walker Ltd*, [1973] VATTR 8 (VTD 3). (*Note.* The decision in this case was regarded as doubtful, and as 'extremely limited' in application, by a subsequent tribunal in *International Master Publishers Ltd (No 1)*, 5.27 below.)

Textbooks supplied with correspondence course

[5.2] A company which provided correspondence courses treated 80% of the fees which it charged students as being for the supply of textbooks and zero-rated. Customs issued an assessment to charge VAT on the whole of the fees, considering that there was a single supply of tuition. The tribunal allowed the company's appeal, holding that there was a separate zero-rated supply of the textbooks. *The Rapid Results College Ltd*, [1973] VATTR 197 (VTD 48).

[5.3] A publishing company supplied correspondence courses in journalism, including printed course notes and manuals. It treated part of its fees as attributable to the course notes and manuals and as zero-rated. Customs issued an assessment on the basis that the company was making a single supply of tuition services and that the whole of the consideration should be standard-rated. The company appealed, contending firstly that it was making two separate supplies and had accounted for tax on the correct basis, and alternatively that if it were deemed to be making a single supply, it was making a single supply of goods which qualified for zero-rating. The tribunal accepted the company's second contention and allowed the appeal, holding that, in view of 'the small element of external tuition', the company was making a single supply of manuals to which the tuition was incidental. Accordingly, the whole supply was zero-rated. *International News Syndicate Ltd*, LON/96/1306 (VTD 14425).

[5.4] A similar decision was reached in *International Correspondence Schools Ltd*, EDN/01/180 (VTD 17662).

'Course books' supplied to students of English

[5.5] The proprietor of a business which provided tuition in English charged an inclusive fee, part of which he treated as being for the supply of course books and as zero-rated. Customs issued an assessment on the basis that there was a single standard-rated supply of tuition. The tribunal allowed the proprietor's appeal, holding that the course books qualified for zero-rating and that the proprietor was entitled to apportion the fees. *JE Rendle (t/a Coventry International English Studies Centre)*, MAN/82/120 (VTD 1389).

Course manuals supplied to accountancy students

[5.6] A company (L) which provided accountancy tuition treated part of its fees as being for the supply of course manuals and as zero-rated. Customs issued an assessment on the basis that there was a single standard-rated supply of tuition. The tribunal allowed L's appeal, holding that the manuals constituted a separate supply and qualified for zero-rating. *LSA (Full Time Courses) Ltd*, [1983] VATTR 256 (VTD 1507).

Course books supplied with vocational retraining courses

[5.7] A company (F) supplied residential training courses for army personnel who were about to return to civilian life. The courses available included computer tuition and driving instruction. It supplied course books to the students, and treated part of the consideration as being for the supply of these course books, and as zero-rated. Customs issued an assessment on the basis that the company was making a single supply of tuition, so that the whole of the consideration was taxable at the standard rate. F appealed. The tribunal allowed the appeal, holding that F was making separate supplies of tuition and books. *Force One Training Ltd*, LON/95/1594A (VTD 13619).

Loose-leaf binder containing printed matter and CD-ROMs

[5.8] A partnership marketed an 'educational learning programme' for children. It supplied a loose-leaf binder containing about 350 pages and 24 CD-ROMs. Customs issued a ruling that the supplies were standard-rated. The partnership appealed, contending that it should be treated as supplying loose-leaf books, which qualified for zero-rating. The tribunal accepted this contention and allowed the appeal. *Quantum Learning Curve*, LON/04/011 (VTD 19181).

Directory supplied as part of discount scheme

[5.9] A company operated a discount scheme under which subscribers were provided with a 'Status Card' to enable them to obtain discounts from specified retailers, and a 'Status Directory' listing the retailers within the scheme and the discounts they would offer to Status Card holders. Customs issued a ruling that the payments by subscribers were wholly standard-rated. The tribunal allowed the company's appeal in part, holding that the major part of the consideration was paid for the right to receive discounts, which was a standard-rated supply of services, but that part of the consideration was attributable to the supply of the Directory, which was a booklet which qualified for zero-rating. *Status Cards Ltd*, LON/74/102 (VTD 128).

Mail order catalogues

[5.10] Two associated companies sold goods by mail order, under a number of different trading names. They produced catalogues twice a year for distribution to agents or potential agents. The catalogues had different covers for each of the trading names which the companies used, but apart from these covers, the contents of the catalogues were identical. The catalogues were printed overseas. Most of them arrived in the UK in their finished condition. However, in case of a shortage of any particular version of the catalogue, they also had printed extra copies (known as 'float copies') of the body of the catalogue. These float copies had temporary protective covers, consisting of a sheet of white card, and the pages had not been trimmed. Customs issued a ruling that the 'float copies' were not 'books' and not eligible for zero-rating, on the grounds that they would need further processing after they had been imported. The tribunal allowed the companies' appeals, holding that, even though further work would be carried out on them, the 'float copies' were 'books' when they were imported, and qualified for zero-rating. *GUS Catalogue Order Ltd; GUS Merchandise Corporation Ltd*, MAN/87/532 (VTD 2958).

Children's cut-out books

[5.11] A company published children's books, and also manufactured and sold plastic toys. It sold a sixteen-page cut-out book entitled 'The Twins on Holiday'. The narrative story was on the four inside pages. The remaining pages were designed to be cut out to form figures of two girls and of their clothing, intended to illustrate the story. Customs issued a ruling that the product was not eligible for zero-rating, on the grounds that it was a toy rather than a book. The tribunal allowed the company's appeal against this decision, holding that the product was a book at the time of supply even though the reader might subsequently cut out the figures. *WF Graham (Northampton) Ltd*, LON/79/332 (VTD 908).

[5.12] A similar decision was reached in a subsequent case involving a children's book called 'The House That Jack Built', the parts of which were designed to be cut out and assembled into a model house. The tribunal held that the product was a book at the time of supply even though the reader might subsequently assemble the parts into a model house. *The Book People Ltd*, LON/02/1053 (VTD 18240).

Young children's publication containing yearplanner

[5.13] A company (S) marketed a 66-page publication, priced at £2.99 and aimed at young children, which included a 24-page 'yearplanner' and a 4-page section for names, addresses and telephone numbers. The remaining 38 pages contained a number of quizzes and jokes as well as a section about money. S did not account for output tax on sales of the product, treating it as a zero-rated book. Customs issued an assessment charging tax on the basis that it was akin to a diary and did not qualify for zero-rating. The tribunal allowed S's appeal, holding that the product was 'much more than a diary and address book' and was 'designed to be read as entertainment'. *Scholastic Publications Ltd*, MAN/95/2087 (VTD 14213).

Market research reports

[5.14] A company which carried on a market research business produced reports, which it treated as zero-rated. Customs issued an assessment charging tax on them, on the basis that the company was supplying services rather than goods. The tribunal allowed the company's appeal, holding that it was supplying zero-rated booklets. *City Research Associates Ltd*, [1984] VATTR 189 (VTD 1745).

Booklet containing audience viewing figures for TV programmes

[5.15] A company (D) supplied reports, comprising details of audience viewing figures for TV programmes. It did not account for VAT on its receipts from these supplies, considering that the reports were booklets which qualified for zero-rating. Customs issued assessments charging tax on the basis that D was making standard-rated supplies of services, to which the reports were incidental. The tribunal allowed D's appeal, holding that it was supplying zero-rated booklets. *David Graham & Associates*, LON/92/3394A (VTD 11068).

Charity annual report

[5.16] A charity published its annual report for 1995 in a ring-bound format whereby the back of 12 of the 15 pages contained a monthly calendar with a photograph illustrating the charity's work. The back page comprised stiff card and contained a flap intended to enable the calendar to be stood upright on a desk. Customs issued a ruling that the charity was obliged to account for output tax on the cost of producing the report. The charity appealed, contending that the report was a booklet which qualified for zero-rating. The tribunal accepted this contention and allowed the appeal. *London Cyrenians Housing*, LON/95/3173A (VTD 14426).

Illustrated diary

[5.17] A company traded as a dealer in second-hand works of art. It produced a book (in a limited edition of 1,000) entitled 'Today And Tomorrow', which contained 17 illustrations of paintings by a well-known film director. Opposite each illustrated painting were pages headed with the 12 months of the year and lines ending with a printed number for each day of the month. The company did not account for tax on sales of the book, treating it as zero-rated. Customs issued an assessment charging tax, on the basis that it was a diary for completion and was not within the definition of a 'book'. The tribunal allowed the company's appeal, holding that the book qualified for zero-rating. *Richard Salmon Ltd*, LON/92/2893A (VTD 12126).

Payments to trader advertising 'money-making scheme'

[5.18] A trader advertised a 'money-making scheme', inviting potential customers to send him an initial monthly 'subscription fee' of £49.95. On receipt of an initial payment, he sent his customers a 'start-up information pack', and on receipt of subsequent payments, he sent books on subjects such as 'grants and sources of free money', 'venture capital', 'loan finance', 'marketing', 'leasing finance', etc. He did not account for output tax on the payments which he received. Customs issued a ruling that the payments were liable to VAT, and he appealed, contending that the payments were wholly attributable to the supply of books which qualified for zero-rating. The tribunal accepted this contention and allowed his appeal, observing that 'it is true that each book was not worth £49.95 or anything like it, but at the end of the day that is all that was actually supplied, other than items to which no value can be attributed'. *MG Reece (t/a Mako Consultants)*, LON/94/3388 (VTD 13980)

Publication supplied to members of unincorporated association

[5.19] A company (H) produced the annual members' handbook of the Professional Association of Teachers. It treated its supplies of the handbook as zero-rated. Customs formed the opinion that, since the handbook contained details of benefits available to members of the PAT, including a 'Spend and Save' scheme which H organised, part of the consideration should be treated as attributable to this scheme and as paid for a standard-rated supply of services. They issued an assessment. The tribunal allowed H's appeal, holding that the whole of the consideration was attributable to the zero-rated supply of the handbooks, and that no part of the consideration was attributable to the supply of benefits to members of the PAT. *Hague Shaw (Marketing) Ltd*, MAN/92/338 (VTD 11445, VTD 11474).

[5.20] See also *Automobile Association*, 13.17 CLUBS, ASSOCIATIONS AND ORGANISATIONS; *Barton*, 13.18 CLUBS, ASSOCIATIONS AND ORGANISATIONS, and *Institute of Chartered Foresters*, 13.19 CLUBS, ASSOCIATIONS AND OR-GANISATIONS.

Books supplied to club members by mail order

[5.21] A company supplied books by post to members of a club which it organised. It charged a reduced price for the books, plus a contribution to the cost of postage and packing. Customs issued a ruling that there were two separate supplies, one of the books and one of their delivery, and that the delivery charges were standard-rated. The tribunal allowed the company's appeal, holding that there was a single zero-rated supply. *The Leisure Circle Ltd*, LON/82/198 (VTD 1362).

[5.22] A similar decision was reached in *Book Club Associates*, [1983] VATTR 34 (VTD 1363).

Cases where the consideration was apportioned

Printed matter supplied to members of proprietary club

[5.23] A company operated a proprietary club. Members had to pay subscriptions to the company, and received in return a booklet giving details of vehicles used in the haulage industry, a booklet for members to record when they had seen such vehicles, a quarterly magazine, a catalogue of goods (with discounts to club members), a calendar, a membership card and badge, and access to a website. The company did not account for VAT on the subscriptions which it received, treating them as zero-rated. The Commissioners issued a ruling that the subscriptions were only partly attributable to supplies of zero-rated printed matter, and were partly attributable to standard-rated supplies of services. The tribunal upheld the Commissioners' ruling and dismissed the company's appeal. The tribunal also held that the booklet provided to club members to record when they had seen various vehicles did not qualify for zero-rating, applying the principles laid down by May J in *Colour Offset Ltd*, **5.44** below. *Eddie Stobart Group Ltd*, MAN/04/52 (VTD 18873).

Photobooks

[5.24] A company (H) supplied various types of 'photobooks', produced by processing digital photographs. Initially it accounted for VAT on its supplies, but subsequently it submitted a repayment claim on the basis that it was making supplies of books or booklets which qualified for zero-rating. HMRC rejected the claim on the basis that H was making supplies of photographic services which did not qualify for zero-rating. H appealed. The tribunal allowed the appeal in part. Judge Berner held that 'looking at the objective characteristics of the supplies that (H) makes, the principal supply is clearly that of the photobooks themselves, a supply of goods. The services that surround that supply, including the making available of the production process, are ancillary to the supply of the goods. Those supplies are so closely linked that, viewed objectively, they form a single, indivisible supply, and that is, in this case, a supply of goods.. On the evidence, most of H's 'photobooks' qualified for zero-rating, but two types of 'photobook' failed to qualify on the basis that they did not 'satisfy the minimum characteristics for the external appearance of a book or booklet', and that their leaves had 'the quality and appearance of individual photographic prints, and not pages of a book'. *Harrier Llc v HMRC*, [2011] UKFTT 725 (TC), TC01562.

Goods held not to qualify for zero-rating

Binders

[5.25] A company published an encyclopaedia, which was issued in weekly parts. It also supplied special binders for the encyclopaedia. The tribunal held that the binders were not a component part of a book, and that the supply of the binders was standard-rated. *Fabbri & Partners Ltd*, [1973] VATTR 49 (VTD 9).

[5.26] The decision in *Fabbri & Partners Ltd*, 5.25 above, was applied in the similar case of *Marshall Cavendish Ltd*, [1973] VATTR 65 (VTD 16).

[5.27] A company supplied binders intended to be filled with cards providing pictures of, and information about, wildlife. The tribunal held that the binders were not eligible for zero-rating. *International Master Publishers Ltd (No 1)*, LON/91/2534Y (VTD 8807).

Component parts of book

[5.28] A company carried on business as printers and bookbinders. It supplied publishers with all the component parts of books for publication, including the covers, the endpapers, and the unfolded and uncut printed sheets of the pages. Customs issued a ruling that these supplies were standard-rated. The tribunal dismissed the company's appeal, holding that the component parts of a book were not themselves a book and were not eligible for zero-rating. *Butler & Tanner Ltd*, [1974] VATTR 72 (VTD 68).

Wedding photograph albums

[5.29] A trader (D) supplied wedding photograph albums. An independent photographer took the photographs, while D supplied the film and produced the photographs. D failed to account for VAT on his supplies, and Customs issued an assessment charging tax on them. The tribunal dismissed D's appeal, holding that the albums were not books. *DA Draper*, MAN/80/197 (VTD 1107).

[5.30] The decision in *Draper*, 5.29 above, was applied in the similar subsequent cases of *Risbey's Photography Ltd*, MAN/07/1114 (VTD 20783) and *Digital Albums Ltd*, MAN/07/1115 (VTD 20783).

Booklet of vouchers for admission to entertainments

[5.31] A company (G) trading in a holiday area supplied hoteliers and tourists with booklets containing twelve leaves, each of which comprised or included a detachable voucher entitling the holder to admission, either free or at a discount, to an entertainment in the area. It did not account for VAT on its supplies of these booklets. Customs issued a ruling that they were not eligible for zero-rating, and the tribunal dismissed G's appeal, holding that it was making a standard-rated supply of services. *Graham Leisure Ltd*, LON/81/329 (VTD 1304).

'Leisure guides' containing vouchers

[5.32] A company published 'leisure guides', which consisted largely of vouchers enabling customers to obtain accommodation at hotels or guest houses, and meals at restaurants, for less than the normal price. It did not account for VAT on the sales of these guides. Customs issued a ruling that the guides were not eligible for zero-rating. The tribunal dismissed the company's appeal, holding that it was making a supply of standard-rated services. *Interleisure Club Ltd*, LON/91/1681X (VTD 7458).

Sales of catalogue goods—supplies of catalogues

[5.33] A group of companies sold goods by mail order. In accounting for tax, it treated part of the consideration as attributable to the supplies of its catalogues, and as zero-rated. Customs issued assessments on the basis that the whole of the consideration was attributable to the standard-rated supplies of goods. The tribunal upheld the assessments and dismissed the group's appeal, holding that there was 'no commercial justification' for the charge. *Redcats (Brands) Ltd*, MAN/02/275 (VTD 19648).

[5.34] In a subsequent case in which the facts were broadly similar to *Redcats (Brands) Ltd*, 5.33 above, the tribunal held that the whole of the consideration paid by the company's customers was attributable to the standard-rated supplies of goods, rather than to the supply of the company's catalogues. (However, the tribunal allowed appeals against some of the assessments on the grounds that they had been made outside the statutory time limit.) *Next Group plc v HMRC*, [2011] UKFTT 122 (TC); [2011] SFTD 511; TC00998.

Computer manuals supplied with computer tuition

[5.35] A company provided courses of computer training, for which it charged a fee of £150. In accounting for VAT, it treated part of these fees as attributable to the supply of a manual, and as zero-rated. Customs issued an assessment on the basis that there was a single standard-rated supply. The tribunal dismissed the company's appeal. *EW (Computer Training) Ltd*, LON/90/484X (VTD 5453).

Study materials supplied with educational services

[5.36] A college reclaimed input tax on the cost of producing study materials which it distributed to students. Customs rejected the claim on the basis that the college was making exempt supplies of educational services, and the supplies of printed matter were merely ancillary. The college appealed, contending that it was making separate supplies and that its supplies of study materials qualified for zero-rating. The tribunal rejected this contention and dismissed the appeal, holding that 'the supply of printed materials' was 'a means of better enjoying the provision of education'. The HL unanimously upheld the tribunal decision as one of fact. Lord Walker of Gestingthorpe observed that 'it is customary for an appellate court to show some circum-spection before interfering with the decision of the tribunal'. He also observed that 'it is inappropriate to analyse the transaction in terms of what is "principal" and "ancillary", and it is unhelpful to strain the natural meaning of "ancillary" in an attempt to do so'. *HMRC v The College of Estate Management*, HL [2005] STC 1597; [2005] UKHL 62; [2005] 4 All ER 933. (*Note.* For Customs' practice following this decision, see Business Brief 20/2005, issued on 28 October 2005.)

[5.37] The HL decision in *College of Estate Management*, 5.36 above, was applied in the similar subsequent cases of *Rusland Education & Training Ltd (t/a Rusland College)*, LON/03/1016 (VTD 19806); *RSH Associates Ltd*, MAN/05/582 (VTD 19912), *London Art College*, MAN/07/104 (VTD 20657).

Instruction manuals supplied with franchising advice

[5.38] A company (F) provided advisory services to clients with regard to franchising. It provided its clients with a prospectus, an instruction manual and other printed materials. Customs issued a ruling that F's supplies were entirely standard-rated. F appealed, contending that part of the consideration which it received should be attributed to the prospectuses, instruction manuals and other printed materials. The tribunal rejected this contention and dismissed the appeal, holding that F was making a single composite supply which did not qualify for zero-rating. *Franchise Development Services Ltd*, LON/95/2530A (VTD 14295).

Books supplied with boxed games

[5.39] A company supplied boxed sets of 'fantasy war games'. The boxes included a rulebook, and a second book giving information about the game. In accounting for tax, the company treated part of the price of the games as attributable to the books and as zero-rated. Customs issued assessments on the basis that the supplies were entirely standard-rated. The tribunal dismissed the company's appeal, holding that 'the essential feature of the transaction is the supply of a war game' and that the books did not have 'a distinct and separate identity'. *Games Workshop Ltd*, MAN/98/1073 (VTD 16975).

Booklets supplied with CDs

[5.40] A company supplied CDs of music by 'classic composers', including a 12-page booklet. Customs issued a ruling that the supplies were standard-rated, and the company appealed. The tribunal dismissed the appeal, holding that the CDs were 'the principal supply' and that the booklets were 'ancillary'. The CA unanimously upheld this decision. *International Masters Publishers Ltd v HMRC (No 2)*, CA 2006, [2007] STC 153; [2006] EWCA Civ 1455.

Memorandum and Articles of Association supplied for new companies

[5.41] A company carried on business as company formation agents. It charged customers £80 for its services, and treated £40 of this as attributable to supplying five copies of the companies' Memorandum and Articles of Association, and thus as zero-rated. Customs issued a ruling that there was a single supply which did not qualify for zero-rating. The tribunal dismissed the company's appeal, holding that the provision of the Memorandum & Articles was 'one ancillary element of a single service and it is artificial to attempt to split it and treat it in its own right as a principal supply'. The tribunal specifically declined to follow the 1986 decision of Lord Grantchester in *JP Company Registrations Ltd*, LON/86/302 (VTD 2249). *Company Registrations Online Ltd*, MAN/05/232 (VTD 19461).

[5.42] The decision in *Company Registrations Online Ltd*, 5.41 above, was applied in the similar subsequent cases of *National Business Register plc*, MAN/06/678 (VTD 20262) and *Hanover Company Services Ltd*, **22.552** EUROPEAN COMMUNITY LAW.

Surname histories supplied as scroll

[5.43] A company supplied scrolls, measuring 17 ins by 11 ins, each of which gave a history of a particular surname, derived from a computer database. Customs issued a ruling that the scrolls were standard-rated. The tribunal dismissed the company's appeal, holding that the scrolls were not eligible for zero-rating. *The Hall of Names Ltd*, LON/91/1256 (VTD 8806).

Diaries and address books

[5.44] A printing company did not account for VAT on sales of diaries and address books which it produced. Customs issued an assessment charging tax on these supplies, and the company appealed, contending that they were zero-rated. The QB rejected this contention and upheld the assessment. May J held that a book was something to be read or looked at. A completed diary of historical or literary interest may be a book, but a blank diary was not. Similarly, a blank address book was not a book. *C & E Commrs v Colour Offset Ltd*, QB 1994, [1995] STC 85.

[5.45] A company (T) produced diaries for customers of betting-shops. The diaries included 20 pages of information about various sporting events (mainly horse-racing), while the diary pages included, for each day of the year, the names of racecourses at which race meetings were scheduled for that day. T did not account for VAT on its supplies of the diaries. Customs issued an assessment charging tax on them, and the tribunal dismissed the company's appeal. *Tudor Print & Design Ltd*, MAN/01/1771 (VTD 17848).

Memorial Book purchased by church

[5.46] A parochial church council commissioned a leather-bound A4 book. It was intended to be used as a Memorial Book, recording the dates of death of parishioners. The parish name was inscribed in gold lettering on the front of the book, but the inside of the book was blank. Customs issued a ruling that VAT was chargeable on the book, and the church appealed. The tribunal dismissed the appeal. Applying the QB decision in *Colour Offset Ltd*, **5.44** above, the fact that the pages of the book were blank at the time of purchase meant that it failed to qualify for zero-rating. *Ormesby St Michael Parochial Church Council*, LON/01/69 (VTD 17375).

Sets of cards for learner drivers

[5.47] A company (F) sold packs of cards which were intended to be used by learner drivers. They measured 9cm by 5.7cm, and resembled small playing cards. One side of each card contained a question about road signs or the Highway Code, with the answer to the question being printed on the reverse of the card. F did not account for output tax on sales of the cards. Customs issued a ruling that they did not qualify for zero-rating. The tribunal dismissed F's appeal, applying the QB decision in *Colour Offset Ltd*, **5.44** above. *Flipcards Ltd*, MAN/95/2210 (VTD 13916).

[5.48] The decision in *Flipcards Ltd*, 5.47 above, was applied in the similar subsequent case of *Global Games International Ltd*, [2005] VATDR 246 (VTD 18912).

Mathematical worksheets supplied on CD-ROM

[5.49] A company supplied mathematical worksheets on CD-ROM. Customs issued a ruling that it was required to account for output tax on these supplies. The company appealed, contending that since the worksheets would be printed by its customers, they should be treated as zero-rated. The tribunal rejected this contention and dismissed the appeal. *Fisher Educational Ltd*, MAN/02/109 (VTD 17902).

Payments in response to advertisements

[5.50] A company (S) advertised in certain publications inviting readers to send it £47.50. It informed readers that, in return for such a payment, they would be entitled to give a name of their choice to a star. (The names in question were not recognised by NASA or the International Astronomical Union, and a leading astronomer described the services which S offered as 'quite valueless and unofficial', and 'a complete waste of money'.) On receipt of such a payment, S sent the customer an acknowledgement, together with a five-page booklet giving some information about stars, and two charts showing details of constellations. Customs issued a ruling that the receipts were liable to VAT. The tribunal dismissed S's appeal, holding that the booklet was 'economically indissociable' from the advertised supply of services and there was 'no rational basis for apportionment'. *Schoemann ISR (UK) Ltd*, LON/93/1792A (VTD 11713).

[5.51] A similar decision was reached in a case where a trader (B) placed advertisements in local newspapers, inviting readers to send a registration fee of £9.99, in return for which he would provide details of how they could work from home and 'earn money obtaining and mailing envelopes'. On receipt of such fees, B sent the readers a small booklet, inviting them to place similar advertisements. The tribunal held that 'what the appellant was offering to supply was a system for working from home'. The supply of the booklet was 'not an independent or separate supply'. *DV Breach (t/a Neath Mailing Services)*, LON/00/764 (VTD 17279).

Charity supplying 'camera-ready copy' to publishing company

[5.52] A registered charity (S) entered into an agreement with a publishing company (B), whereby it submitted material to B as camera-ready copy, B arranged for printing and marketing, and S granted B 'the sole and exclusive right to publish and sell' the publications in question. S did not account for output tax on the amounts which it received from B. Customs issued an assessment charging tax on them, and S appealed, contending that it had entered into a joint venture and was making zero-rated supplies of books and journals. The tribunal dismissed the appeal, holding on the evidence that the production and publication of the books and journals was the sole responsibility of B, and that there was 'no common property in the publications'. B was acting as an independent principal, rather than as an agent of S. S was supplying standard-rated services to B. *International Institute for Strategic Studies*, LON/95/1533A (VTD 13551).

Supplies by libraries to university

[5.53] A university incorporated a subsidiary company (U) to operate five libraries. U charged the university for its services. At first it accounted for VAT on its supplies, but it subsequently submitted a repayment claim on the basis that it was lending its books to the university and that this was a zero-rated supply. Customs rejected the claim and the tribunal dismissed U's appeal, holding that U was 'making a single overarching supply of learning resources to the university'. *UU Bibliotech Ltd*, [2006] VATDR 501 (VTD 19764).

Brochures, pamphlets and leaflets (VATA 1994, Sch 8, Group 3, Item 1)

Goods held to qualify for zero-rating

Stapled pamphlets supplied with geological kits

[5.54] A trader supplied a product called 'British Geology', which was primarily a collection of geological specimens, but which included four printed sheets, stapled together, containing relevant information. The stapled sheets could be supplied separately for 10p (wholesale). The Commissioners issued a ruling that his supplies were wholly standard-rated, and he appealed, contending that part of the consideration was attributable to the printed sheets which were a pamphlet and should be zero-rated. The tribunal accepted this contention and allowed his appeal to this extent. (However, printed pieces of card containing instructions for polishing specimens were held to be standard-rated.) *DJ Emery*, MAN/75/2 (VTD 187).

Dress designing kits—whether 'brochures'

[5.55] A company supplied courses in dress designing and pattern construction. The course consisted of a folder containing an instruction booklet and instruction sheets, a teaching strip of fabric, some miniature patterns and a fabric requirement planner (a sheet of paper marked in such a way as to achieve the best use of material when cutting out). The Commissioners issued a ruling that the supply of the teaching strip, miniature patterns and fabric planner were standard-rated, and that 54% of the purchase price was attributable to these items. The company appealed, contending that the whole supply was zero-rated. The tribunal accepted this contention and allowed the appeal, holding that there was a single composite supply which, although it had some unusual features, was of a brochure and was zero-rated under what is now *VATA 1994, Sch 8, Group 3, Item 1*. *Betty Foster (Fashion Sewing) Ltd*, [1976] VATTR 229 (VTD 299). (*Note.* The Commissioners regard this as 'an exceptional decision' and instruct VAT officers 'to resist its application to any other such other cases'—see Customs' VAT Manual, Part 7, chapter 3, paras 2.18(d) and 3.8.)

Advertising materials—whether 'leaflets'

[5.56] A company which carried on a printing business produced advertising material, most of which was slightly larger than standard A4 size, and was intended to be delivered by door-to-door canvassers. The Commissioners issued a ruling that output tax was chargeable on the supplies in question. The company appealed, contending that the materials were 'leaflets' and should be zero-rated. The tribunal allowed the company's appeal in part, holding that 38 of the 40 items in question were suitably sized to be described as leaflets and were therefore zero-rated, but that the remaining two items (which measured 20 ins by 15 ins) were too large to be described as leaflets, and were therefore standard-rated. *Cronsvale Ltd*, [1983] VATTR 313 (VTD 1552).

[5.57] A company produced printed sheets advertising products for people who were hard of hearing. The sheets were on thick paper, weighing about

150g per square metre, and included a tear-off slip at the bottom of each sheet. They were distributed with newspapers and magazines. The company did not account for output tax on its supplies of these sheets, treating them as zero-rated. The Commissioners issued an assessment charging tax on the supplies, and the company appealed, contending that the printed sheets were within the definition of 'leaflets'. The tribunal accepted this contention and allowed the appeal. The chairman (Mr. Lightman, sitting alone) disapproved *dicta* of Lord Grantchester in *Marylebone Cricket Club*, 5.78 below, and held that 'there is no need for a leaflet to be flimsy'. *Multiform Printing Ltd*, [1996] VATDR 580 (VTD 13931).

[5.58] The decision in *Multiform Printing Ltd*, 5.57 above, was applied in a subsequent Scottish case where the tribunal held that a number of advertisements, printed on 'reasonably sturdy' paper, qualified as 'leaflets'. The tribunal considered that the weight of the paper did not prevent the items from constituting 'leaflets', and that 'the proper distinction to be drawn is one which has particular attention to purpose and ephemeral nature and the reasonable size'. *GNP Booth Ltd*, EDN/01/129 (VTD 17555).

A4 publication supplied at children's museum—whether 'leaflets'

[5.59] A company operated a children's museum. It accounted for output tax on its admission charges. Subsequently its accountants submitted a repayment claim on the basis that part of the admission charges should be attributed to the supply of two publications which were given to visiting children, and these information sheets were leaflets which qualified for zero-rating. The Commissioners accepted that one of the publications was a leaflet, but issued a ruling that the second publication—a folded A4 sheet entitled 'Me and My Body' —was not a leaflet. This publication contained some information about the museum, and a number of questions with spaces for the children to insert the appropriate answer, and the Commissioners considered that it was a worksheet or activity sheet, rather than a leaflet. The tribunal allowed the company's appeal, distinguishing *Marylebone Cricket Club*, 5.78 below, and holding that the publication was within the definition of a 'leaflet'. It was flimsy, designed to be held in the hand, and the area for completion was less than 25% of the total area. *Eureka! The Children's Museum*, MAN/97/1143 (VTD 15710).

Telecommunications instruction manuals—whether 'brochures'

[5.60] A company sold telecommunications equipment, including instruction manuals which it supplied to potential distributors of its equipment. It did not account for VAT on the supply of the instruction manuals, considering that they were zero-rated. The Commissioners issued an assessment on the basis that the manuals were part of a standard-rated supply of items of equipment. The tribunal allowed the company's appeal, holding that the manuals were brochures and were zero-rated. *John Harrison (Gatesby) Ltd*, MAN/89/510 & MAN/89/911 (VTD 5581).

Folders containing postage stamps—whether 'brochures'

[5.61] A stamp dealer did not account for tax on sales of certain collector's items, originally sold by the Post Office, which consisted of documents made of stout paper or card, measuring about 17 ins by 4 ins, and folded twice so as to produce folders measuring about 7 ins by 4 ins. The folders illustrated particular themes, and included mounted postage stamps relating to that theme. The Commissioners issued a ruling that these supplies did not qualify for zero-rating, and the dealer appealed. The tribunal allowed the appeal, holding that the items were within the definition of 'brochures', so that their sale was zero-rated under what is now *VATA 1994, Sch 8, Group 3, Item 1*. (However, the tribunal also held that old books of stamps, sold by the dealer to collectors, did not qualify for zero-rating, so that tax was chargeable on the excess of the sale price over the face value) *SP Schusman*, [1994] VATTR 120 (VTD 11835).

Graphic designer—whether supplying brochures

[5.62] A graphic designer (C) agreed to produce a brochure for a building firm. He did not account for output tax on this supply, treating it as zero-rated. The Commissioners issued an assessment on the basis that C was only supplying design services, which did not qualify for zero-rating, and that the actual brochures were supplied by the printer whom C had employed. C appealed, contending that, under the relevant contract, he was wholly responsible for the production of the brochure. The tribunal accepted this contention and allowed C's appeal, holding that he was supplying brochures which qualified for zero-rating. The fact that the printer rendered a separate invoice to the customer 'did not of itself create a separate contract between the printer and the customer'. *AP Carpenter*, LON/96/430 (VTD 15253).

Partnership preparing marketing mailshots for insurance company

[5.63] A partnership traded as a marketing agency. It agreed to prepare mailshot packages for an insurance company. The Commissioners issued a ruling that the partnership was making standard-rated supplies of advertising services. The partnership appealed, contending that it was supplying brochures which qualified for zero-rating. The tribunal accepted this contention and allowed the appeal, holding that the partnership was supplying brochures. The supply of the brochures was separate from any previous supply of design services. *Direct Marketing Bureau*, MAN/99/581 (VTD 16696).

Brochures supplied with promotional services

[5.64] A partnership supplied promotional services, including advertising brochures, to an insurance company. The Commissioners issued a ruling that it was required to account for output tax on the whole of its receipts. The partnership appealed, contending that part of the consideration should be attributed to the supplies of brochures, which qualified for zero-rating. The Ch D accepted this contention and allowed the appeal. On the evidence, the insurance company ordered the brochures when they were needed. The partnership had invoiced and itemised the brochures separately from its promotional services. Accordingly, as a matter of commercial reality, the partnership had made separate supplies and its supplies of brochures qualified for zero-rating. *Appleby Bowers v C & E Commrs*, Ch D 2000, [2001] STC 185.

[5.65] A similar decision was reached in *DL Marketing (Direct Link) Ltd*, LON/00/54 (VTD 17006).

Supplies of study packs to students

[5.66] A company advertised GCSE and A level courses in collaboration with colleges of further education. Under the scheme, the company advertised for students, who enrolled with one of the colleges and worked from home with materials supplied by the company, under the supervision of a tutor provided by the company. The company provided the students with 'study packs'. The Commissioners issued an assessment on the basis that the study packs were part of a supply of educational services (which did not qualify for exemption—see **21.28** EDUCATION). The company appealed, contending that the study packs were a separate supply of printed materials which qualified for zero-rating under *VATA 1994, Sch 8, Group 3, Item 1*. The tribunal accepted this contention and allowed the appeal, observing that 'the company does not supply the student with instruction, tuition or schooling. The most it does is to counsel the prospective student and to facilitate his enrolment application at the relevant college.' On the evidence, 'the students' fees relates (*sic*) to what the company provides to the students, that is the course packs coupled with the service of facilitating access to the college'. *Oxford Open Learning (Systems) Ltd (No 2)*, LON/99/1041 (VTD 16890).

Monthly publication listing planning applications—whether a 'brochure'

[5.67] A trader produced a monthly publication, available on subscription, listing planning applications and related information, within a particular area (usually a specific county). The publication was intended to be read by small and medium-sized businesses in the building industry, to enable them to monitor what was happening in the area. The trader did not account for VAT on the publications, considering that they were brochures which qualified for zero-rating under *VATA 1994, Sch 8, Group 3, Item 1*. The Commissioners issued an assessment charging output tax on the basis that the trader should be treated as making standard-rated supplies of information services. The trader appealed. The tribunal allowed the appeal, observing that some of the trader's advertising material indicated that he was supplying information services, but holding that what he actually supplied was within the definition of a 'brochure'. Accordingly his supplies were zero-rated. *RT Griffiths (t/a Action for Business)*, MAN/99/352 (VTD 17404). (*Note.* The tribunal held that, in view of the misleading statements in the trader's advertising material, he should only receive 50% of his costs.)

Cases where the consideration was apportioned

Programmes sold at stamp fairs

[5.68] A stamp dealer organised stamp fairs. He prepared for each fair a programme, with details of the exhibitors, which was sold to those attending the fair. There was no admission charge as such. He did not account for VAT on his receipts from programme sales. The Commissioners issued an assessment on the basis that only 25% of the consideration was zero-rated, the remaining 75% being standard-rated as being for admission to the fair. The dealer appealed, contending that the whole of the consideration should be zero-rated. The tribunal upheld the assessment in principle and held on the evidence that two-thirds of the consideration was standard-rated. *MH Jarmain*, [1979] VATTR 41 (VTD 723).

Programmes included with admission charge to greyhound stadium

[5.69] The decision in *Jarmain*, 5.68 above, was applied in a similar case where admission to a greyhound stadium included the provision of a programme. The tribunal held that 15% of the admission fee was zero-rated as being attributable to the supply of the programme, the remaining 85% being standard-rated (see **67.118** VALUATION). *IC Thomas*, [1985] VATTR 67 (VTD 1862). (*Note*. The decision here was not followed in the subsequent case of *Town & County Factors Ltd*, 5.76 below.)

Programmes included with admission charge to motorcycle championship

[5.70] A company organised an annual motorcycle championship. It charged adults between £19.50 and £22 for admission to the championship, which included the provision of a programme. In accounting for VAT, it treated £9 of the admission charge as attributable to the zero-rated supply of a programme. The Commissioners issued an assessment on the basis that only £5 should be attributed to the supply of the programme. The tribunal reviewed the evidence and allowed the company's appeal in part, holding that £7 should be attributed to the supply of the programme. *Avondale Management Ltd*, MAN/02/494 (VTD 18144).

'Mail packs' including leaflets supplied by marketing company to bank

[5.71] A marketing company supplied 'mail packs', including leaflets, to a bank. It treated its supplies as zero-rated. Customs issued a ruling that the supplies did not qualify for zero-rating. The tribunal reviewed the evidence in detail and allowed the appeal in part, holding that the company was making multiple supplies and that the consideration had to be apportioned. The part of the consideration which related to the leaflets qualified for zero-rating, while the part of the consideration which related to the accompanying letters was standard-rated. *Charterhall Marketing Ltd*, EDN/04/127 (VTD 19050).

Goods held not to qualify for zero-rating

Car stickers—whether 'leaflets'

[5.72] A company supplied car stickers for advertising forthcoming events, and did not account for VAT on these supplies. The Commissioners issued a ruling that the car stickers were liable to VAT, and the company appealed, contending that they were 'leaflets' and should be zero-rated. The tribunal dismissed the company's appeal, holding that a leaflet was something produced and designed to be read by one person at a time. The car stickers were not leaflets, since they were posters or notices designed to be read by the public at large. *Arbroath Herald Ltd*, EDN/75/9 (VTD 182).

Adhesive labels in foreign languages—whether 'leaflets'

[5.73] A company published sheets of adhesive labels, bearing the names of household objects in a foreign language. They were designed as an aid to the learning of languages. The Commissioners issued a ruling that the company was required to account for output tax on its supplies. The company appealed, contending that the labels should be treated as leaflets and should be zero-rated. The tribunal rejected this contention and dismissed the appeal, holding that the labels were not within the definition of 'leaflets'. *HP Lansdown (Linguistickers) Ltd*, LON/96/518 (VTD 14714).

Boards for displaying hairdressing charges—whether 'leaflets'

[5.74] A trader supplied black plastic boards, measuring 23 ins by 11 ins, to hairdressers, together with a book of peelable stickers to be placed on the board, to be used for displaying charges to customers. He did not account for VAT on these supplies, and the Commissioners issued an assessment charging tax on them. He appealed, contending that he was supplying leaflets which should be zero-rated. The tribunal dismissed his appeal, holding that the articles were not leaflets. *JD Mortimer*, MAN/76/184 (VTD 381).

Advertising materials—whether 'pamphlets'

[5.75] A company carried on an advertising consultancy business. It supplied a client with quantities of window banners, door stickers and posters, together with folded 'pamphlets' comprising a single sheet of paper measuring 40 ins by 14 ins and printed on one side. These 'pamphlets' were intended to be used by the client's representatives for showing to retailers who might be interested in the client's products. The tribunal held that these 'pamphlets' qualified for zero-rating, but that the window banners, door stickers and posters were neither pamphlets nor leaflets and were standard-rated. *Pace Group (Communications) Ltd*, MAN/77/210 (VTD 510).

Programmes included with admission charge to greyhound stadium

[5.76] A company operated a greyhound stadium. It charged customers £5 for admission to race meetings, and provided them with a programme. In accounting for VAT, it treated £1.50 of the admission price as attributable to a zero-rated supply of a programme. The Commissioners issued a ruling that the whole of the £5 was standard-rated. The tribunal upheld the Commissioners' ruling and dismissed the company's appeal, holding that the whole of the £5 was attributable to a single standard-rated supply of admission to the meeting. *Town & County Factors Ltd (No 2)*, LON/02/322 (VTD 18569).

Programmes included as part of 'hospitality package' at football stadium

[5.77] A football club offered 'hospitality packages', including meals and alcoholic drinks, at its home matches. It provided match programmes as part of the 'packages'. Initially it accounted for VAT on the full price of the packages, but in 1999 it submitted a repayment claim, contending that part of the tax was attributable to its supplies of programmes, which it should have treated as zero-rated. The Commissioners rejected the claim and the club appealed. The tribunal dismissed the appeal, applying the CJEC decision in *Card Protection Plan Ltd*, **22.324** EUROPEAN COMMUNITY LAW, and holding that 'the essential feature' of the hospitality package was 'the right to attend and watch a football match'. The programmes formed 'part of a single supply' of the hospitality packages. *Manchester United plc*, MAN/00/371 (VTD 17234).

Scorecards at cricket matches—whether 'leaflets'

[5.78] A cricket club sold scorecards at its home matches. These scorecards consisted of a single sheet of card or stiff paper on which were printed the teams and certain other information relating to the match, together with a list of forthcoming fixtures and an advertisement. In 1980 the Commissioners issued a ruling that the scorecards were not eligible for zero-rating. The club appealed, contending that the scorecards were leaflets. The tribunal dismissed the appeal, holding that a leaflet was 'a flimsy piece of paper containing propaganda, advertisement or similar information in writing which is distributed gratuitously or for a nominal consideration', and that the scorecards were not within the definition of 'leaflets'. *Marylebone Cricket Club*, LON/81/88 (VTD 1074). (*Note*. *Dicta* of Lord Grantchester were disapproved by a subsequent tribunal in *Multiform Printing Ltd*, 5.57 above.)

Adhesive-backed photographs for insertion into albums—whether leaflets

[5.79] Two companies in the same group distributed adhesive-backed reproductions of photographs. A description of the subject of each photograph was printed on the protective cover for the adhesive back. Each photograph formed part of a series designed to be collected and inserted into an album. The photographs were retailed by newsagents. The companies did not account for VAT on its supplies of the photographs, and the Commissioners issued a ruling that they were standard-rated. The companies appealed, contending that the photographs were leaflets and should be zero-rated. The tribunal dismissed the companies' appeals, holding that 'a leaflet must be limp, and generally if not inevitably on unlaminated paper'. The photographs were not leaflets and were therefore standard-rated. *Panini Publishing Ltd*, LON/88/166Y; *Mirror Group Newspapers Ltd*, LON/88/887X (VTD 3876).

Pictures of sports personalities

[5.80] A partnership sold pictures of sports personalities. It failed to account for output tax on its sales. The Commissioners issued an assessment charging tax on them, and the partnership appealed, contending that they should be treated as zero-rated. The tribunal rejected this contention and dismissed the appeal. *D & J Foster (t/a David Foster Associates)*, MAN/95/2552 (VTD 14820).

Illustrated children's story sheets—whether 'leaflets'

[5.81] A company sold packs designed for pre-school children. The packs included play mats and jigsaw puzzles, which were accepted as standard-rated, and leaflets for parents, which were accepted as zero-rated. They also contained illustrated story sheets and dictionary cards. The story sheets were printed on one side of the paper, and some words were printed in red so as to correspond with the words in the dictionary cards. There were eight dictionary cards in each pack, which were held together by an elastic band. The Commissioners issued a ruling that neither of these items qualified for zero-rating. The company appealed, contending that the items were leaflets. The tribunal rejected this contention and dismissed the appeal, and the QB upheld this decision. *Odhams Leisure Group Ltd v C & E Commrs*, QB [1992] STC 332. (*Note*. For another issue in this case, see 2.3 APPEALS.)

Information sheets—whether 'brochures' or 'leaflets'

[5.82] A partnership produced and distributed information sheets providing information about company law, tax and insolvency. The sheets were made of stiff plastic and measured about 9 ins by 12 ins. The Commissioners issued a ruling that the sheets were standard-rated and the partnership appealed, contending that the sheets were brochures or pamphlets, and should be zero-rated. The tribunal rejected this contention and dismissed the appeal, holding that the sheets could not be described either as brochures or as pamphlets. *Infocard*, LON/90/1314Z (VTD 5732).

Tax cards—whether 'brochures' or 'leaflets'

[5.83] A company published glossy cards, which it described as 'tax cards', containing various items of information relating to tax. The cards measured 21.5 centimetres by 10.25 centimetres, and were scored in such a way that they could be folded into three, enabling them to be kept in a jacket pocket. The company did not account for VAT on the supply of these cards. The Commissioners issued a ruling that the cards were standard-rated, and the company appealed, contending that the cards were brochures or leaflets. The tribunal rejected this contention and dismissed the appeal, holding that the cards were not brochures since they consisted of a single sheet, and were not leaflets since they were printed on stiff card whereas a leaflet must be limp. *Tax Briefs Ltd*, LON/91/2541Z (VTD 9258).

Cards containing religious verse—whether 'leaflets'

[5.84] A company carried on business as wholesale suppliers of religious articles. It sold laminated cards, measuring 9.5cm by 6cm, containing a prayer or religious verses. It did not account for VAT on sales of these cards. The Commissioners issued an assessment charging tax on them, and the company appealed, contending that they were 'leaflets' and should be zero-rated. The tribunal rejected this contention and dismissed the company's appeal, holding that the cards did not qualify as 'leaflets' and were not eligible for zero-rating. *Christian Art Ltd*, LON/90/414Z (VTD 5940).

Laminated recipe cards—whether 'leaflets'

[5.85] A company produced laminated cards, on which were printed recipes. The Commissioners issued a ruling that the cards were not eligible for zero-rating, and the company appealed, contending that they were leaflets and should be zero-rated. The tribunal rejected this contention and dismissed the appeal, holding that the cards did not qualify as leaflets. *International Master Publishers Ltd*, LON/91/2534Y (VTD 8807). (*Note.* For another issue in this case, see **5.27** above.)

Illustrated A4 cards—whether 'leaflets'

[5.86] A company produced packs of A4 cards. The front of each card contained a copy of a painting or drawing, and the back of the card contained information about the painting or drawing in question. The Commissioners issued a ruling that output tax was chargeable on the supplies, and the company appealed, contending that the cards should be treated as leaflets and as zero-rated. The tribunal rejected this contention and dismissed the appeal. *Philip Green Education Ltd*, MAN/97/1202 (VTD 15669).

Inserts for telephone directories—whether leaflets

[5.87] A printing company supplied inserts for 'Yellow Pages' telephone directories. The inserts were printed on shiny paper which was substantially heavier than the rest of the directory, so that the volume would naturally fall open at the insert and provide publicity to the advertiser. The company did not account for VAT on the inserts, and the Commissioners issued an assessment charging tax on the consideration. The company appealed, contending that the inserts were leaflets and should be zero-rated. The tribunal rejected this contention and dismissed the appeal, holding that, in view of the weight of the paper in question, the inserts did not qualify as leaflets and were not eligible for zero-rating. *Adland Group Co Ltd*, LON/92/1871A (VTD 10397).

Broadsheet containing information about greyhound racing

[5.88] See *Evans & Marland Ltd*, 5.94 below.

'Discount cards'—whether brochures

[5.89] Two companies issued documents incorporating 'discount cards', with a face value of £14.99, entitling the holder to obtain a free course on up to twelve occasions at a stated restaurant. The Commissioners issued a ruling that output tax was payable on the supplies of the cards, and the companies appealed, contending that the cards should be treated as brochures and as zero-rated under *Sch 8, Group 3, Item 1*. The tribunal rejected this contention and dismissed the appeal. The tribunal declined to follow *obiter dicta* of Waite LJ in *Granton Ltd*, **67.166** VALUATION, on the grounds that that case had been concerned with whether the cards were within what is now *VATA 1994, Sch 6 para 5*. Although Waite LJ had stated that the cards were 'incorporated in a three-page brochure', the question of whether the cards were brochures was not an issue which the CA had been asked to determine, so that 'the use of that word by Waite LJ can therefore not have been a part of the *ratio decidendi* of that judgment'. Furthermore, Waite LJ had only stated that the card was incorporated in a 'brochure', rather than that it was a brochure. The document was perforated so that the part which entitled the bearer to a discount could be torn off. The tribunal held that this was 'the essential part of the whole A4 document' and that it was not within the definition of a 'brochure'. The discount cards were sold because they gave rise to an 'expectation of benefit', and it followed that their sale was a supply of services, rather than of goods, and was standard-rated. *Full Force Marketing Ltd; Framesouth Ltd*, LON/93/783 (VTD 15270).

Business registration certificates

[5.90] A company provided a service of registering business names, in accordance with the *Business Names Act 1985*. It treated part of its fees as attributable to the issue of certificates, and as zero-rated. The Commissioners issued an assessment to recover the tax, and the tribunal dismissed the company's appeal. Firstly, the company was making a single composite supply of registration services, which were standard-rated, and the supply of a certificate was incidental. Secondly, the supply of a certificate did not qualify for zero-rating under *VATA 1994, Sch 8, Group 3, Item 1*, since a certificate was not within the definition of a 'leaflet' or 'pamphlet'. *BNR Company Services Ltd*, MAN/94/1618 (VTD 13783).

Leaflets and magazines supplied with 'weight loss' programme

[5.91] A company (W) marketed a 'weight loss' programme. Customers were asked to attend weekly meetings, where they were weighed. They were also given an initial handbook, monthly magazines and weekly leaflets. In 2005 Customs issued a ruling that W was making a single supply of a weight-loss programme, so that it was required to account for VAT on the whole of its takings. The CA unanimously upheld Customs' ruling. Sir Andrew Morritt held that the only reasonable conclusion was that W was making a single supply, and that none of the consideration qualified for zero-rating. *HMRC v Weight Watchers (UK) Ltd*, CA [2008] STC 2313; [2008] EWCA Civ 715.

Postal games—whether a separate supply of printed matter

[5.92] See *Cropper*, 62.550 SUPPLY, and *M & E Sports Ltd*, 62.551 SUPPLY.

Newspapers, journals and periodicals (VATA 1994, Sch 8, Group 3, Item 2)

Property guides

[5.93] A firm of chartered surveyors and estate agents published a monthly property guide, consisting almost entirely of advertisements for houses. It was sold to other estate agents, rather than to members of the public. The firm did not account for VAT on supplies of this guide, and the Commissioners issued an assessment charging tax on them. The firm appealed, contending that the guide should be zero-rated as a 'newspaper, journal or periodical'. The tribunal rejected this contention and dismissed the appeal, and the QB upheld this decision. The guide contained nothing which could be regarded as news and thus was not a newspaper or journal. Since it was not sold to the public, it was not within the ordinary meaning of 'periodical'. *Snushall Dalby & Robinson v C & E Commrs*, QB [1982] STC 537.

Broadsheet containing information about greyhound racing

[5.94] A company produced a publication which gave information concerning greyhound races. It was printed on one side of the paper only, and was designed to be displayed in betting shops. 95% of its subscribers were proprietors of betting shops. It was produced on most weekdays throughout the year. The Commissioners issued a ruling that the publication did not qualify for zero-rating, and the company appealed, contending firstly that it was a 'newspaper or journal', and alternatively that it was a pamphlet. The tribunal rejected these contentions and dismissed the appeal, holding that it was not a newspaper or journal, since its predominant function was to act as a guide to betting rather than to publish new information about recent or imminent events, and its format disqualified it from being a pamphlet. *Evans & Marland Ltd (t/a Greyform Publications)*, [1988] VATTR 115 (VTD 3158).

Quarterly pictorial magazine—whether a 'periodical'

[5.95] A publishing company produced a quarterly 32-page magazine called 'Just Seventeen Posters', which consisted almost entirely of large poster-sized photographs. It treated its sales of the magazine as zero-rated under *VATA 1994, Sch 8, Group 3, Item 2*. The Commissioners issued a ruling that the publication did not qualify for zero-rating, and the company appealed, contending that the publication was a 'periodical'. The tribunal allowed the appeal, holding that the publication was within the ordinary meaning of the word 'periodical' notwithstanding the fact that it had very little text, and that some readers would probably unstaple it to extract some of the posters. *EMAP Consumer Magazines Ltd*, LON/94/1710 (VTD 13322).

Bi-monthly publication with poster-sized photographs of musicians

[5.96] In August and October 1993 a company published two issues of a bi-monthly publication devoted to a group of musicians. In 1994 it published a third issue of the publication in a somewhat different format. It did not account for output tax on its sales of the publication, treating it as a zero-rated periodical. The Commissioners issued a ruling that the publication did not qualify for zero-rating, and the company appealed. The tribunal allowed the appeal. Applying *EMAP Consumer Magazines Ltd*, 5.95 above, the fact that much of the publication consisted of poster-sized photographs did not prevent it from qualifying as a 'periodical'. The tribunal was satisfied on the evidence that it had been the company's intention 'at the relevant time to continue with regular publication, although it later decided to cease or suspend further publication'. *European Publishing Consultants Ltd*, LON/94/698A (VTD 13841).

Broadcasting services—provision of magazine

[5.97] A company supplied satellite broadcasting services to subscribers. It provided the subscribers with a magazine providing details of the programmes which it broadcast. The Commissioners ruled that the whole of the subscriptions were for standard-rated supplies of broadcasting services. The company appealed, contending that part of the subscription should be attributed to zero-rated supplies of the magazines. The tribunal rejected this contention and dismissed the appeal, holding that the 'true nature of the contract' between the company and the subscribers was that the company was making single supplies of broadcasting services. *British Sky Broadcasting Group plc*, [1999] VATDR 283 (VTD 16220). (*Note.* For subsequent developments in this case, see **2.341** APPEALS.)

[5.98] A company broadcasted programmes of a religious nature. It issued its subscribers with a magazine giving details of the programmes. The Commissioners issued a ruling that the company was required to account for tax on the full amounts which it charged its subscribers. The company appealed, contending that part of the consideration should be attributed to zero-rated supplies of the magazines. The tribunal rejected this contention and dismissed the appeal, holding that the magazine was 'merely ancillary' to the supply of 'television services'. *The Angel Foundation Ltd*, MAN/03/482 (VTD 18818).

[5.99] See also *Telewest Communications plc*, 62.371 SUPPLY.

Quarterly magazine supplied to members of Institute

[5.100] See *Institute of Chartered Foresters*, 13.19 CLUBS, ASSOCIATIONS AND ORGANISATIONS.

Journals supplied to graduates of Royal College of Anaesthetists

[5.101] See *Royal College of Anaesthetists*, 13.20 CLUBS, ASSOCIATIONS AND ORGANISATIONS.

Magazine distribution company—supplies of magazines

[5.102] A company carried on business as a distributor of magazines. The Commissioners issued assessments on the basis that the company supplied the magazines as an agent of the publishers, and that since it never took possession of the magazines, the consideration which it received was for making supplies of marketing and distribution services to the publishers, which were standard-rated. The company appealed, contending that, under its contracts, it purchased the magazines from the publishers for an agreed percentage of the cover price and sold them to wholesalers. Its supplies were supplies of the magazines to wholesalers, and were zero-rated under what is now *VATA 1994, Sch 8, Group 3, Item 2*. The tribunal accepted this contention and allowed the company's appeal. Although the company did not take physical possession of the magazines, on the evidence it clearly purchased the magazines from the publishers, and supplied them to wholesalers as principal. It incurred the costs of transporting the magazines, and also incurred the risk of their loss in transit. The sale of the magazines was, therefore, within the zero-rating provisions of *Group 3, Item 2*. *Odhams Distribution Pergamon Holdings Ltd*, LON/90/1546Y (VTD 6295).

Free gifts supplied with magazines

[5.103] A company (K) published magazines for children. It supplied free gifts with the magazines. The magazines were distributed by another company (C), which paid K 55% of the cover price of the magazines. The Commissioners issued an assessment on the basis that the free gifts were a separate supply which did not qualify for zero-rating. K appealed, contending that the free gifts cost less than 20% of the cover price of the magazines, and therefore qualified as a linked supply under what is now Extra-Statutory Concession 3.7. The tribunal rejected this contention and dismissed K's appeal, finding that the 'total cost' for the purposes of Extra-Statutory Concession 3.7 was the 55% which K received from C. C was an independent principal rather than an agent of K. Accordingly, the cost of the free gifts exceeded 20% of the total cost of the magazines, and they were a separate supply which could not be treated as zero-rated. *Keesing (UK) Ltd*, LON/98/898 (VTD 16840).

Videotapes supplied with magazines

[5.104] A company sold pornographic magazines. It included videotapes with some of the magazines. It did not account for VAT on these supplies. The Commissioners issued an assessment on the basis that one-third of the consideration related to the supplies of the videotapes, which did not qualify for zero-rating. The company appealed, contending that the whole of the consideration should be attributed to the zero-rated supplies of magazines, and that the videotapes were supplied free of charge. The tribunal rejected this contention and dismissed the appeal, observing that the Commissioners had 'acted generously' in assessing the apportionment of the videotape at one-third. *News Trade Supplies Ltd*, MAN/x (VTD 17339).

Company placing orders for magazines with publishers

[5.105] A company (N) obtained orders for magazines from students and staff at universities and schools, and placed these orders with the publishers. The subscribers paid their subscriptions to N, which paid lesser amounts to the publishers, retaining part of the amounts paid. The publishers sent the magazines directly to the subscribers. N did not account for VAT, considering that it was supplying the magazines, which were zero-rated goods within what is now *VATA 1994, Sch 8, Group 3*, to the subscribers. The Commissioners issued an assessment on the basis that the magazines were supplied by the publishers to the subscribers, that N was dealing with the subscribers' orders merely as an agent of the publishers, and that N was making a standard-rated supply of services to the publishers. The tribunal allowed N's appeal, holding that N was acting as a principal and that the magazines were supplied by the publishers to N and by N to the subscribers. Accordingly, N's supplies were zero-rated. *Nordic Subscription Service UK Ltd*, MAN/90/892 (VTD 10705).

In-house magazines distributed to employees—whether zero-rated

[5.106] See *The Post Office*, 62.112 SUPPLY.

News digest supplied by fax, e-mail or internet

[5.107] A company (F) supplied a regular digest of financial news to customers by fax, e-mail or internet. The Commissioners issued a ruling that F's supplies failed to qualify for zero-rating, since the paper which produced the printed matter was provided by F's customers, rather than by F. The tribunal dismissed F's appeal, holding that 'exemptions and zero-ratings must be strictly construed' and observing that *Group 3* 'clearly refers to goods, or in the language of *Article 5* of the *Sixth Directive*, to tangible property'. F was supplying information 'in the form of electrical impulses' and it 'would be stretching the language of the statute beyond reasonable limits' to hold that F's supplies qualified for zero-rating. The tribunal observed that 'it may be that the European Court of Justice will eventually have to tackle the whole problem of electronic commerce, but we do not think that this case would be a proper one to refer on our own initiative'. *Forexia (UK) Ltd*, LON/98/879 (VTD 16041).

Delivery charges by newsagents

[5.108] See *Coe*, 58.2 RETAILERS' SPECIAL SCHEMES, and the cases noted at 58.3 RETAILERS' SPECIAL SCHEMES.

Music (VATA 1994, Sch 8, Group 3, Item 4)

Flipcards containing information about music

[5.109] A company sold packs of cards which measured 9cm by 5.7cm, resembled small playing cards in appearance, and were printed on glossy cardboard. They were sold in packs of about 100. One side of each card contained a question about music, with the answer to the question being printed on the reverse of the card. The company did not account for output tax on sales of the cards, treating them as zero-rated. The Commissioners issued a ruling that the cards did not qualify for zero-rating. The company appealed, contending that each set of cards should be treated as zero-rated under *VATA 1994, Sch 8, Group 3, Item 4*. The tribunal rejected this contention and dismissed the appeal, holding that 'music' should be defined as 'the written or printed score or set of parts of a musical composition' and that the cards in question were outside this definition. *Flip Cards (Marine) Ltd*, MAN/96/248 (VTD 14483).

Maps, charts, etc. (VATA 1994, Sch 8, Group 3, Item 5)

Histographs

[5.110] A company sold sets of 'histographs', which set out the family trees of the Kings and Queens of England in tabular form as historical charts. It did not account for VAT on these supplies. The Commissioners issued a ruling that they were standard-rated, and the company appealed, contending that they were zero-rated under what is now *VATA 1994, Sch 8, Group 3, Item 5*. The tribunal rejected this contention and dismissed the appeal, holding that, under the '*eiusdem generis*' principle, the reference to 'charts' in *Item 5* had to be construed in the context of the entire *Item*, and referred to geographical charts only and not to historical charts. Accordingly, the supply of historical charts was standard-rated. *Brooks Histograph Ltd*, [1984] VATTR 46 (VTD 1570).

6

Buildings and Land

The cases in this chapter are arranged under the following headings.

The option to tax land (VATA 1994, Sch 10, paras 1–34*)

Grants to which the option does not apply (*VATA 1994, Sch 10 paras 5–12*) — 6.1

The scope of the option (*VATA 1994, Sch 10 para 18**) — 6.12

The day from which the option has effect (*VATA 1994, Sch 10 para 19(1)**) — 6.18

Miscellaneous — 6.42

Beneficial interests (VATA 1994, Sch 10, para 40*) — 6.51

Supplies between landlord and tenant — 6.53

CROSS-REFERENCES

For cases concerning the reduced-rate provisions of *VATA 1994, Sch 7A, Groups 6 and 7*, see 56 REDUCED-RATE SUPPLIES: MISCELLANEOUS. For cases concerning the zero-rating provisions of *VATA 1994, Sch 8, Group 5*, see 15 CONSTRUCTION OF BUILDINGS, ETC. For cases concerning the zero-rating provisions of *VATA 1994, Sch 8, Group 6*, see 55 PROTECTED BUILDINGS. For cases concerning exemption under *VATA 1994, Sch 9, Group 1*, see 41 LAND. *VATA 1994, Sch 10* was substantially amended by the *VAT (Buildings and Land) Order 2008 (SI 2008/1146)* with effect from 1 June 2008. Among the changes are that the 'election to waive exemption' was renamed as the 'option to tax'. The cases in this chapter should be read in the light of these changes.

The option to tax land (VATA 1994, Sch 10, paras 1–34)

Grants to which the option does not apply (VATA 1994, Sch 10 para 5–12*)

Sale of public house—whether within Sch 10 para 6*

[6.1] A brewery sold a disused public house, which it had opted to tax. It charged output tax on the sale. The purchaser lodged an appeal, contending that the effect of what is now *Sch 10 para 6* was that output tax should not have been charged, since he intended to use the building as a dwelling. The tribunal accepted this contention and allowed his appeal, holding on the evidence that he had always intended to use the building as a dwelling and that he had communicated this intention to the brewery, so that the effect of what is now *Sch 10 para 6(1)* was that the sale was exempt from VAT. *J Watters*, LON/94/2980A (VTD 13337).

[6.2] A company (P) sold a disused public house, which it had opted to tax, to an unrelated company (S) in the construction industry. On the same day S sold the property to two purchasers, and contracted with the purchasers to build residential units on the site. P accounted for output tax on its sale to S. S appealed to the tribunal, contending that despite P's option, the sale should have been treated as exempt by virtue of what is now *VATA 1994, Sch 10 para 6*. The tribunal rejected this contention and dismissed the appeal, holding that what is now *Sch 10 para 6* only applied where the purchaser intended to use the building as a dwelling, which was not the case here. The tribunal observed that 'normally the rate of value added tax applicable to any transaction is determinable by the application of objective criteria. However, in this appeal the rate depends, unusually, on the intention of someone other than the supplier.' Accordingly 'the legislation which refers to such intention should be narrowly construed', since 'any move away from the contractual link between the vendor and the purchaser would create many difficulties'. The tribunal also held that it was necessary for the vendor to be aware of the purchaser's intention at the time of the sale and, on the evidence, S had not shown that P was aware of the intended use of the property at the time of the sale. *SEH Holdings Ltd*, [2000] VATDR 324 (VTD 16771). (*Note*. For Customs' practice following this decision, see Business Brief 8/01, issued on 2 July 2001.)

[6.3] A company (R) owned a disused public house, which it had opted to tax. It obtained planning permission to convert the building into two semi-detached houses, and then sold the building to another company (P). R charged output tax on the sale. P lodged an appeal, contending that the effect of what is now *VATA 1994, Sch 10 para 6* was that output tax should not have been charged, since the building was intended for use 'as a dwelling or a number of dwellings'. The tribunal accepted this contention and allowed P's appeal. The tribunal distinguished the earlier decision in *SEH Holdings Ltd*, 6.2 above, observing that R had advertised the building as 'a delightful residential opportunity', and finding that R 'was aware of the intention that the whole building was to be used as dwellings'. *PJG Developments Ltd; Red Developments (London) Ltd*, [2005] VATDR 215 (VTD 19097).

[6.4] In the case noted at 65.86 TRANSFERS OF GOING CONCERNS, the tribunal held that an option to tax extended to the whole of a public house. On the evidence, none of the building was 'intended for use as a dwelling', since no part of it consisted of 'self-contained living accommodation', within *VATA 1994, Sch 8, Group 5, Note 2(a)*. Accordingly what is now *VATA 1994, Sch 10 para 6* did not apply and the whole of the building was covered by the option. *AJ White*, LON/96/1964 (VTD 15388).

Building leased to charity—application of Sch 10 para 7*

[6.5] A company reclaimed input tax on the refurbishment of a building (consisting of a shop and three flats), which it had opted to tax. Customs issued an assessment to recover the tax, on the basis that the ground floor of the building (the shop) was leased to a charity, so that the effect of what is now *Sch 10 para 7* was that the option was ineffective. The tribunal upheld the assessment and dismissed the company's appeal. *Headway Commercial Ltd*, EDN/97/179 (VTD 15535).

VATA 1994, Sch 10 para 10*—whether certificate may be retrospective

[6.6] A housing association purchased a commercial property. The vendor had opted to tax the property several years previously, and charged VAT on the purchase. The association subsequently sought repayment of the VAT. Customs rejected the claim on the grounds that the association had not given the vendor the certificate as to intended use required by what is now *VATA 1994, Sch 10 para 10*. The association appealed, contending that it should be permitted to issue such a certificate retrospectively. The tribunal rejected this contention and dismissed the appeal, holding that 'the certificate seeking disapplication of the "option to tax" cannot be issued retrospectively'. *Langstane Housing Association Ltd*, EDN/04/144 (VTD 19111).

VATA 1994, Sch 10 para 12*—whether option ineffective

[6.7] A company (P), which was the trustee of a number of personal pension schemes and was a member of a VAT group, purchased a property which the vendor had opted to tax. P granted a lease of the property to three pension scheme members, who occupied the property for an exempt insurance business, and whose contributions had been used to fund the acquisition of the property. P wished to recover input tax on the purchase of the property, and opted to tax it. Customs issued a ruling that the effect of what is now *VATA 1994, Sch 10 para 12* was that P's option was ineffective and that the lease to the pension scheme members remained exempt. The representative member of P's VAT group appealed, contending that Parliamentary statements by the then Exchequer Secretary in 1997, when what is now *Sch 10 para 12* was introduced, had shown that it was intended to counter tax avoidance, whereas the transaction here was a legitimate commercial transaction. The tribunal dismissed the appeal and upheld Customs' ruling. The pension scheme members had provided finance for the acquisition of the land, within what is now *Sch 10 para 14*. Accordingly, the conditions of what is now *Sch 10 para 12* were satisfied and the option was ineffective. The facts that the transactions 'were not for the avoidance of taxation', and that 'the terms of the lease were fully commercial', were not conclusive. There was no ambiguity in the legislation, so that the decision in *Pepper v Hart*, HL [1992] STC 898 did not apply. The provisions of what is now *Sch 10 para 12* were authorised by *Article 13C* of the *EC Sixth Directive*. (The tribunal observed that, unlike *Articles 13A* and *13B, Article 13C* made no reference to the prevention of 'possible evasion, avoidance or abuse', but simply provided that 'Member States may restrict the scope of this right of option and shall fix the details of its use'.) *Winterthur Life UK Ltd (No 2)*, LON/98/127 (VTD 15785).

[6.8] A company (E) and an NHS trust entered into a development agreement whereby E agreed to construct a building for the trust, the trust agreed to grant E a 99-year lease of the building, E agreed to grant an underlease of the building back to the trust (for 99 years less 3 days), and the trust agreed to grant E a sub-underlease of about 70% of the building. E opted to tax the underlease, with the intention of recovering the input tax on the construction of the building. Customs issued a ruling that the effect of what is now *VATA 1994, Sch 10 para 12* was that P's option was ineffective and that the underlease to the trust remained exempt. The tribunal upheld Customs' ruling and dismissed E's appeal, holding that E was a 'developer of the land' within what is now *Sch 10 para 12*. The land was a capital item within *VAT Regulations 1995 (SI 1995/2518), regs 112(2), 113(e)*. The grant of a lease of an uncompleted building was within the definition of 'use' for the purposes of *reg 113(e)* and *114(4)(e)*. The fact that the building was incomplete did not prevent it from constituting a 'building' for the purposes of *reg 113(e)*. *East Kent Medical Services Ltd*, LON/98/935 (VTD 16095).

[6.9] A registered charity (B) operated a preparatory school. In January 2000 it opted to tax a new sports hall. In May 2000 it granted a lease of the hall to a subsidiary company (S). It reclaimed input tax on the construction of the hall. Customs issued an assessment to recover the tax, on the basis that the hall was 'exempt land' within what is now *VATA 1994, Sch 10 paras 12*, since B was 'in occupation of the land' within what is now *Sch 10 para 15*. B appealed, contending that the hall was occupied solely by S. The tribunal rejected this contention and dismissed the appeal, holding that B occupied the hall since 'at all times when the hall is being used by the pupils, the control of the use of the hall, through the supervision of the staff, rests with the appellant'. Accordingly B had 'a physical presence in the hall, at the very least through the members of staff'. *Brambletye School Trust Ltd*, [2002] VATDR 265 (VTD 17688).

[6.10] A college wished to renovate its library. It formed a wholly-owned subsidiary company (N), and opted to tax the library. It granted a lease to N, and reclaimed input tax on the costs of renovating the library. HMRC issued a ruling that the effect of what is now *VATA 1994, Sch 10 para 12* was that the college's option was ineffective and that the lease to N remained exempt, so that the college was unable to recover the input tax. The CA allowed the college's appeal, and the HL upheld this decision (by a 3-2 majority, Lord Walker of Gestingthorpe and Lord Neuberger of Abbotsbury dissenting). Lord Hoffmann held that 'occupation' for the purposes of what is now *Sch 10 para 15* should be defined as 'the right to occupy property as if that person were the owner and to exclude any other person from enjoyment of such a right'. In this case, 'the essence of the right conferred on the college is the right to the use of the books', and this did not amount to 'occupation' of the library by the college. Lord Hoffmann distinguished the earlier decision in *Brambletye School Trust Ltd*, **6.9** above, holding that 'a decision as to whether acts attributable to a body like the school or college amount to occupation of premises is a question of degree, sensitive to the particular constellation of facts'. Lord Mance observed that 'there is an important distinction between occupation of land and merely using it'. *HMRC v The Principal & Fellows of Newnham College in the University of Cambridge*, HL [2008] STC 1225; [2008] UKHL 23; [2008] 2 All ER 863. (*Note*. For HMRC's practice following this decision, see HMRC Brief 33/09, issued on 8 June 2009.)

[6.11] In 1995 a partnership purchased a property to use for its business. The partnership opted to tax the property and reclaimed input tax on the purchase. In 2004 the partnership agreed to sell its business to a company (S) which did not wish to tax the site. S and the partnership entered into a complex series of transactions with the aim of utilising what is now *VATA 1994, Sch 10 para 12* to make the option to tax ineffective and avoiding VAT on the sale. Customs issued an assessment charging VAT on the sale. S and the partnership appealed. The tribunal dismissed the appeals, holding that the sale of the property was a taxable supply. It was neither exempt, nor within the capital goods scheme, nor was it a transfer of a going concern. *Shurgard Storage Centres UK Ltd (and related appeal)*, LON/06/192 (VTD 20797).

The scope of the option (VATA 1994, Sch 10 para 18*)

VATA 1994, Sch 10 para 18(1)*—land covered by option

[6.12] An accountancy partnership owned property in Droitwich, Worcester and Barnstaple. The partners occupied parts of the Worcester and Barnstaple properties as their offices, the remainder of those properties being let. The whole of the Droitwich property was let to tenants. In July 1989 the partnership wrote to its local VAT office, stating that it intended to opt to tax three properties. Subsequently the partners formed the opinion that it would be to their advantage to opt to tax the Droitwich property (as renovation work was to be carried out on that property) but not to opt to tax the other two properties. In October the partnership submitted a formal option to tax in respect of the Droitwich property only. Customs treated the July letter as an option relating to all three properties and, following a control visit, issued assessments charging tax on the rental income from the Worcester and Barnstaple properties. The partnership appealed, contending that that income was not covered by the option and was therefore exempt from VAT. The tribunal accepted this contention and allowed the appeal, holding that 'an election and its notification are different processes'. The tribunal concluded 'on the balance of probabilities that the partners elected in relation to the Droitwich property alone'. *Harrison Priddey & Co*, MAN/95/2291 (VTD 14089).

[6.13] Two companies, which were members of separate groups, formed a limited partnership by a deed dated 25 September 1997. The partnership acquired 16 properties which had previously been owned by a different partnership comprising a company from each of the two groups. Of the 16 properties, four were subject of options to tax, while the remaining 12 were not. Solicitors acting for the partnership sent the local VAT office a notification that it had opted to tax all 16 properties. However, this notification was dated 22 September 1997, three days before the formation of the partnership, was only signed by a representative of the general partner, and was not authorised by the partnership deed. Subsequently Customs issued an assessment on the basis that the partnership had opted to tax all 16 properties. The partnership appealed, contending that the notification was inaccurate and did not bind the partnership. The tribunal accepted this contention and allowed the appeal. The tribunal observed that 'an election has a separate existence from the notification and must be made on a particular date, take effect on a specified date, if different, and relate to specified land'. On the evidence, the actual option was made in respect of four properties only. To the extent that the notification purported to relate to the other 12 properties, it had no effect. Furthermore, the signature of the representative of the general partner was binding on that partner only. The signatory had no authority to bind the limited partner, because the partnership was not in existence at the time of the notification. *Blythe Limited Partnership*, [1999] VATDR 112 (VTD 16011). (*Note.* For Customs' practice following this decision, see Business Brief 16/99, issued on 20 July 1999, and Business Brief 17/99, issued on 6 August 1999. Customs stated that they 'fully agree with the tribunal's approach and will not be appealing'.)

[6.14] The decision in *Blythe Limited Partnership*, 6.13 above, was applied in a subsequent case in which the tribunal found on the evidence that a family partnership had only opted to tax one of three properties which it owned, and that a letter purporting to opt to tax the other two properties had been sent by a member of the family who was not in fact a partner, and was not binding on the partnership. *DS Talafair & Sons*, MAN/98/956 (VTD 16144).

[6.15] An 'industrial village' included 68 small business units, and an undeveloped area, described as 'the yard', which comprised about 25% of the total area. In 1989 the company which owned the village made an option to tax. Subsequently Customs issued a ruling that the option covered the whole of the 'industrial village', including the yard. The company appealed, contending that the option only applied to the area covered by the 68 business units, and did not extend to the yard. The tribunal accepted this contention and allowed the appeal, holding that the 'industrial village' was not a 'complex' for the purposes of what is now *VATA 1994, Sch 10 para 18*, since it was not 'developed or redeveloped as a whole' and that 'as a matter of impression' a large undeveloped area did not appear to be part of a complex. The tribunal also held that the undeveloped area was 'a site separate from the already developed part' of the 'industrial village', and was not land specified in the election, within what is now *para 18(1)*. *Charterhouse Mercantile Properties Ltd*, LON/02/169 (VTD 17835).

Sch 10 para 18(2)*—option intended to apply only to part of building

[6.16] A consultant (L), who was registered for VAT, owned the freehold of a three-storey building. The ground floor was occupied by two shops. The first and second floors were also divided into two independent units. One of these was used by L as his business premises. The other unit (67A) had been used as a flat, but was in need of refurbishment. In March 1990 L wrote to his local VAT office stating that he wished to opt to tax unit 67A. The VAT office replied, informing L that the option covered all his 'transactions for the land and buildings concerned' and was irrevocable. L converted 67A into office premises, and reclaimed input tax on the work. However, he was unable to find a suitable tenant, and subsequently reconverted it into a flat which he occupied himself. At a control visit in 1994, a VAT officer discovered that, although L had reclaimed input tax relating to 67A, he had not accounted for output tax on his income from the two shops. She arranged for the issue of an assessment, against which L appealed, contending that the option should be treated as only covering 67A and not as covering the whole building. The tribunal rejected this contention and dismissed the appeal, holding that the effect of what is now *VATA 1994, Sch 10 para 18(2)* was that the option had effect in relation to the whole of the building. Furthermore, the option was irrevocable. The fact that L had not been able to let 67A, and had subsequently reconverted it into a flat, did not alter the effect of the option. *MH Lounds (t/a Lounds Associates)*, MAN/95/1794 (VTD 13999).

[6.17] See also *White*, 6.4 above, and *Finanzamt Goslar v Breitsohl*, 22.122 EUROPEAN COMMUNITY LAW.

The day from which the option has effect (VATA 1994, Sch 10 para 19(1)*)

Whether option may be retrospective

[6.18] A unit trust owned the freehold of a building which was leased to the Law Society until August 1988. From September 1988 to March 1990 the building was unoccupied while refurbishments took place. In March 1990 it was let to a firm of solicitors. In September the trustees of the unit trust notified Customs that they wished to opt to tax the property with effect from 1 August 1989. Subsequently they reclaimed input tax which they had incurred between August 1988 and August 1989. The Customs refused to repay the tax incurred prior to 1 August 1989. The trustees appealed, contending that the provisions of what is now *VATA 1994, Sch 10* were inconsistent with *Article 13C* of the *EC Sixth Directive*. The tribunal rejected this contention and dismissed the trustees' appeal, holding that *Article 13C* of the *Directive* gave member states the right to restrict the scope of the option to tax such supplies. *Newcourt Property Fund*, LON/90/1029X (VTD 5825).

[6.19] The decision in *Newcourt Property Fund*, 6.18 above, was applied in the similar subsequent cases of *Bradshaw & Others (as Trustees for Taylor Dyne Ltd Pension Fund)*, [1992] VATTR 315 (VTD 6964) and *Acre Friendly Society*, [1992] VATTR 308 (VTD 7649).

[6.20] A similar decision was reached in *Pinchdean Ltd*, LON/91/1678Z (VTD 9796).

[6.21] A company built an extension to its premises, which it let to an associated company. It reclaimed input tax in respect of the extension in its returns for August and November 1989. Customs issued an assessment to recover the tax, considering that it was not reclaimable since it related to an exempt supply. The company appealed, contending that it had intended to opt to tax the building in question, and had sent a written option to the local VAT office on 14 September 1990. The tribunal dismissed the company's appeal, holding that, by virtue of what is now *VATA 1994, Sch 10 para 19(1)*, the option to tax the building was only effective from 14 September 1990 and could not be backdated. Input tax could not be reclaimed in respect of a supply which had taken place before the effective date of the option. *Hi-Wire Ltd*, MAN/90/990 (VTD 6204).

[6.22] Similar decisions were reached in *V Dennis (t/a Lynden Property Co)*, LON/92/641Y (VTD 11299); *Hellesdon Developments Ltd*, **46.62** PARTIAL EXEMPTION, and *22A Property Investments Ltd*, **62.199** SUPPLY.

[6.23] In December 1991 the trustees of a pension fund (L) purchased a leasehold property which comprised office accommodation with a residential flat. The vendor had opted to tax the property, and issued an invoice including VAT. L reclaimed the VAT as input tax in its return for the period ending 31 December 1991. However, Customs did not repay the tax, as L had not notified them that it was opting to tax the property in question. In February 1992 L submitted an option in respect of its ownership of the property. The option was backdated to the date of purchase. Customs took the view that the input tax on the purchase of the property should be treated as deductible on the date of the option, when it became clear that it had been incurred for the purpose of making a taxable supply, so that it was only repayable following receipt of L's return for the period ending 31 March 1992. L submitted a claim for repayment supplement on the basis that the input tax should have been treated as deductible in December 1991 and repaid accordingly. Customs rejected the claim and the tribunal dismissed L's appeal, holding that, until L had opted to tax the property, there were no grounds for treating the input tax as attributable to an intended taxable supply. *Lawson Mardon Group Pension Scheme*, LON/92/492 (VTD 10231).

Whether letter constituted an option—whether option irrevocable

[6.24] In November 1989 a company wrote to its local VAT office stating that 'as from our rental quarter commencing 25 December 1989 we wish to charge VAT on our rental invoices'. The VAT office treated this as an option to tax under what is now *VATA 1994, Sch 10*. At a control visit in July 1990, a VAT officer discovered that, despite the letter, the company had not accounted for VAT. Customs issued an assessment charging tax on the rents received after 25 December. The tribunal dismissed the company's appeal, holding that the letter constituted an option to tax and that such an option was irrevocable. *Devoirs Properties Ltd*, MAN/90/1061 (VTD 6646).

[6.25] In July 1989 a property development company (R) wrote to its local VAT office concerning a building which it had purchased, and stating 'it is our intention, as owners of the above building, to elect that as from now the building is to be treated as taxable under the commercial property regulations'. The VAT office replied, stating 'we acknowledge that you will exercise your option to tax at the standard rate supplies in respect of the above building'. In 1994 R went into receivership, and the receivers sold the building in question. Customs issued a ruling that, in view of the option to tax the property, output tax was payable on the sale. R appealed, contending that its letter of July 1989 'was a letter expressing intention' and that 'at no time did we write to make the formal election'. The tribunal rejected this contention and dismissed the appeal, holding that R had made an irrevocable option to tax the property. *Resource Maintenance Ltd*, LON/95/137A (VTD 13204).

[6.26] Options to tax property were also held to be irrevocable in *Coach House Property Management Ltd*, LON/91/1709Z (VTD 7564); *Windsor House Investments Ltd*, LON/05/610 (VTD 19666) and *Wrag Barn Golf & Country Club*, [2010] UKFTT 30 (TC), TC00344.

[6.27] The decision in *Coach House Property Management Ltd*, **6.26** above, was applied in the similar subsequent case of *Brollies Ltd*, MAN/93/556 (VTD 11966).

[6.28] A college owned three properties. In 1993 it sent a letter, signed by its assistant principal, to the VAT Registration Unit, stating that it was 'opting to tax' all three properties. In 1999 it sold the freehold of one of its properties. It did not account for tax on the sale proceeds. Customs issued an assessment on the basis that, since the college had opted to tax the property, the sale was a standard-rated supply and it was obliged to account for VAT. The college appealed, contending that its governing body had not authorised its assistant principal to write the letter in question, and that the letter should not be treated as formal option. The tribunal rejected this contention and dismissed the appeal, holding on the evidence that it was 'not tenable' to suggest that the assistant principal had been 'engaged on some frolic of his own and did not know what he was doing'. The evidence showed that he, and the college's finance director, had acted 'in the confident and justified belief that they had authority to make the election on behalf of the college'. *Hammersmith & West London College*, LON/00/907 (VTD 17540).

[6.29] The decision in *Hammersmith & West London College*, 6.28 above, was applied in the similar subsequent case of *Rathbone Community Industry*, MAN/x (VTD 18200).

[6.30] A company (L) which owned a hotel leased it to another company, and opted to tax the property. However L did not account for output tax on the payments which it received. Customs issued an assessment charging tax on them, and L appealed, contending firstly that the option should be disregarded because it had not received any acknowledgment from Customs, and alternatively that the lease was illegal and the payments were outside the scope of VAT. The tribunal rejected these contentions and dismissed the appeal, holding that L had given a valid written notification of the option to Customs and was required to account for output tax on the payments which it received. *Astim Ltd*, MAN/05/498 (VTD 19521). (*Note.* Costs of £750 were awarded to Customs.)

Letter held not to constitute option

[6.31] A medical partnership entered into a contract to develop some land as a new medical centre. The partnership registered for VAT in 1993, and the centre was let to tenants in 1995. In April 1996 the partnership's accountants wrote to Customs, asking them to treat the letter as a 'retrospective election' to tax the property. Customs informed the accountants that, if the partnership had 'previously made exempt supplies (since 1989) on the above property, this option cannot take effect until you have written to Customs & Excise with full details'. Subsequently the partnership reclaimed input tax on the development. In February 1998, after further correspondence, Customs issued an assessment in accordance with the provisions of *FA 1989*, which imposed a self-supply charge on developers of non-residential buildings put to exempt use within a ten-year period. (This charge was phased out over the period to 1 March 1997 and was abolished for all new developments beginning after 28 February 1995.) The partnership appealed, contending that the letter which its accountants had sent in April 1996 should be treated as an option to tax the property. The tribunal rejected this contention and dismissed the appeal, holding that the letter of April 1996 'was not, and was not capable of being, a valid notification of an election to tax with effect from any date'. *Fforestfach Medical Centre*, LON/98/746 (VTD 16587). (*Note.* The tribunal also held that the assessment had been made within the one-year time limit of *VATA 1994, s 73(6)(b)*.)

Form VAT1614 held not to constitute option

[6.32] In a Northern Ireland case, a company (G) purchased a property in February 2006. It registered for VAT from 1 June 2006. On 30 June 2006 one of the company's three directors (M), who was a chartered accountant, signed a form VAT1614, opting to tax the property. In November 2006 G sold the property without charging VAT. HMRC discovered this at a control visit in 2007, and issued an assessment charging tax on the sale. G appealed, contending that the VAT1614 had not been authorised by the company's other directors and should not be treated as a valid election. The tribunal accepted this contention and allowed the appeal, finding that M 'did not take time to consider the import of the actual forms' and that 'the forms did not receive more than a cursory glance'. On the evidence, the election 'made no commercial sense'. The tribunal held that 'the concept of an "election" – to give it its natural meaning – requires positive intent; and 'there was no such intent' in this case. Accordingly, the form VAT1614 should not be treated as a valid option. *Grenane Properties Ltd v HMRC*, [2010] UKFTT 192 (TC), TC00494.

Whether option made although not notified to Customs

[6.33] A company (F) let a property on an industrial estate to another company (G). On the advice of its accountants, F charged VAT on the rent. Subsequently F sold the property to G for £200,000. On the advice of its solicitor, F did not charge VAT on the sale. Customs issued an assessment charging tax on the basis that, by charging VAT on the rent, F had opted to tax the property, and should therefore have charged VAT on the sale. F appealed, contending that it had not made a formal option, and that the sale was therefore exempt from VAT. The tribunal rejected this contention and dismissed the appeal (with liberty to apply for a further hearing as to whether the £200,000 should be held to be inclusive or exclusive of tax). The act of opting to tax the property and the act of notifying that option were two distinct processes. Since F had no right to charge VAT on the rent except by making an option under what is now *VATA 1994, Sch 10*, its demands for VAT on the rent were an option that its supplies in relation to the property were no longer to be exempt from VAT. *Fencing Supplies Ltd*, [1993] VATTR 302 (VTD 10451). (*Note*. See now, however, *VATA 1994, Sch 10 para 20*, introduced by *SI 2008/1146* with effect from 1 June 2008.)

[6.34] A similar decision was reached in *Resource Maintenance Ltd*, **6.25** above.

[6.35] The decision in *Fencing Supplies Ltd*, **6.33** above, was applied in a subsequent case in which the tribunal upheld a company's claim that it had made an option to tax on 31 July 1999, although it had not notified the option to Customs until 10 November 1999. *Classic Furniture (Newport) Ltd*, MAN/00/34 (VTD 16977). (*Note*. See now, however, the note following *Fencing Supplies Ltd*, **6.33** above.)

[6.36] The decision in *Fencing Supplies Ltd*, **6.33** above, was not followed in a subsequent case where a company (M) had purported to charge VAT to tenants of a serviced office block from 2005 to 2008, but had neither registered for VAT nor accounted for the purported VAT. In May 2008 M submitted what it described as a 'belated notification' of an option to tax. HMRC declined to accept the notification and the tribunal dismissed M's appeal. Judge Mitting observed that 'making a legally effective election to waive exemption is a two-stage process, the first stage being to make the decision to opt to tax and the second being to notify such decision to the Commissioners'. M had not produced any 'satisfactory or clear evidence from which the tribunal could conclude that a positive decision to opt had been made. It followed that if no decision had been made there could not have been an election and the Commissioners had acted reasonably in refusing to accept the appellant's request for acceptance of a belated notification'. *Mill House Management UK Ltd v HMRC*, [2011] UKFTT 83 (TC), TC00960.

[6.37] A company (N) purchased a property in September 1998. In October 1998 it let part of the building. It charged VAT on the rent, and accounted for this to Customs, although it did not formally notify Customs of an option to tax the property. In January 2004 N sold the property to an unrelated purchaser, and charged VAT on the sale. The purchaser disputed the imposition of VAT, and in February 2004 N wrote to Customs making a belated notification that it had opted to tax the property in October 1998 when it chose to charge VAT on the rent from it. Customs accepted this belated notification. The purchaser appealed to the tribunal. The tribunal dismissed the appeal, holding that since M had no right to charge VAT on the rent except by opting to tax the property, its initial demand for VAT on the rent had been an option that its supplies in relation to the property were not to be exempt from VAT. The Ch D upheld the tribunal decision as one of fact. Mann J held that there was nothing 'which renders ineffective a notification of election made after the disposal of the land in question'. *Marlow Gardner & Cooke Ltd Directors' Pension Scheme v HMRC*, Ch D [2006] STC 2014; [2006] EWHC 1612 (Ch). (*Note.* See now, however, the note following *Fencing Supplies Ltd*, **6.33** above.)

[6.38] A company (M) registered for VAT from April 1997, declaring that it was carrying on the business of a Chinese restaurant, which it had leased from another company (Y). In its first return, M claimed a substantial repayment of input tax, attributable to the refurbishment of the restaurant. However, its next return declared no output tax liability. When Customs questioned this, M stated that it had granted an associated company (W) a licence to operate the restaurant for a period of three years. W had registered for VAT from August 1997, and had reclaimed input tax on payments of rent to Y. Customs formed the opinion that M was only making exempt supplies to W, and issued an assessment to recover the input tax which M had reclaimed. M appealed, contending that it had opted to tax the property in July 1997. Customs also issued an assessment to recover the input tax which W had reclaimed, considering that any supplies which Y had made under the lease were made to M rather than to W. W appealed against this assessment. The tribunal dismissed both appeals. The tribunal accepted Customs' evidence that they had not received the option which M purported to have made in July 1997, and found that no option had been made until July 1999. Customs were entitled to refuse to accept a retrospective option, particularly since M had failed to disclose that it was in reality a property holding company, and because both M and W had failed to account for tax correctly. Prior to July 1999, 'any supplies made by (M) of a licence to occupy the premises were therefore exempt supplies', so that M was not entitled to claim input tax in respect of supplies made to it for refurbishing the premises. W was not entitled to claim input tax on its payments of rent, since these payments were made to M rather than to

Y, and were exempt from VAT. *Multiprime Cuisine Ltd*, LON/00/1395; *Wing Wah Restaurant (Birmingham) Ltd*, LON/00/1396 (VTD 17399).

[6.39] A company (E) sold a property to another company (P) for £940,000. P reclaimed input tax on the payment. Customs rejected the claim on the grounds that the sale was exempt, as E had never opted to tax the property. P appealed, contending that E had issued it with an invoice indicating that the purchase price included VAT, and the fact that E had never informed Customs that it was opting to tax the property was inconclusive. The tribunal rejected this contention and dismissed the appeal, holding that the effect of what is now *VATA 1994, Sch 10 para 20* was that any option to tax a property had to be notified to Customs. The evidence showed that E had not given any such notification. Accordingly the supply from E to P was exempt, and P was not entitled to credit for input tax on the transaction. *Euro Properties (Scotland) Ltd*, EDN/95/306 (VTD 15291).

[6.40] In 2004 a company (C) purchased a commercial property, and reclaimed the input tax. It subsequently leased the property to an associated partnership, and did not charge VAT on the rent or notify Customs that it had opted to tax the property. When Customs discovered this, they issued an assessment to recover the tax which C had reclaimed on its purchase of the property. C appealed, contending that it should be treated as having opted to tax the property even though it had not charged VAT on the rent. The tribunal rejected this contention and dismissed C's appeal, holding on the evidence that the company's controlling director had been 'ignorant of the process of opting to tax' and observing that 'he could not make a decision to do something which he did not know he had to do'. *Cobol Ltd*, MAN/06/689 (VTD 20976).

[6.41] An option which had not been notified was also held to be ineffective in *McMaster Stores (Scotland) Ltd*, **48.42** PAYMENT OF TAX.

Miscellaneous

Amount of consideration where no option to tax property made

[6.42] A development company (J) agreed to buy some agricultural land from another company (E). In its letter of offer, J described the agreed price as 'deemed to be inclusive of VAT'. The sale of the land was exempt from VAT under what is now *VATA 1994, Sch 9, Group 1*. E could have opted to tax the land under *VATA 1994, Sch 10*, but did not make any such option. J took legal proceedings against E, contending that, since E could have opted to tax the property, and J could then have reclaimed input tax, E should repay to J the proportion of the price that would have represented VAT if an option had been made. The CS unanimously rejected this contention and dismissed the proceedings. Lord Penrose held that the contract had specified a single price, and the words 'deemed to be inclusive of VAT' merely meant that the price would be deemed to include VAT if any were payable. Since no VAT was payable, the contingency implied in the clause did not take effect, and J was not entitled to any repayment. *Jaymarke Developments Ltd v Elinacre Ltd (in liquidation) & Others*, CS [1992] STC 575.

Sch 10 para 15*—whether grantor 'in occupation of the land'

[6.43] See *Brambletye School Trust Ltd*, 6.9 above, and *HMRC v The Principal & Fellows of Newnham College in the University of Cambridge*, 6.10 above.

VATA 1994, Sch 10 para 28*—'fair and reasonable' attribution

[6.44] The trustees of a pension fund, which was registered for VAT, constructed a commercial building and reclaimed input tax. In August 1993 they granted a 15-year lease of the building. Customs issued an assessment on the deemed self-supply in accordance with the provisions of *FA 1989*, which imposed a self-supply charge on developers of non-residential buildings put to exempt use within a ten-year period. (This charge was phased out over the period to 1 March 1997 and was abolished for all new developments beginning after 28 February 1995.) In December 1994 the trustees opted to tax the building and claimed 99.1% of the input tax on the self-supply, on the basis that the exempt lease had lasted for 16 months whereas the expected life of the building was 150 years. Customs rejected the claim on the basis that they could not allow any revised initial attribution of input tax, since the building was within the capital goods scheme and, if the building continued to be used for taxable purposes, 86.67% of the relevant input tax would be recovered within ten years. The trustees appealed, contending that the application of the capital goods scheme did not amount to a 'fair and reasonable' attribution of the input tax, as required by what is now *VATA 1994, Sch 10 para 28*, since it would have to wait for several years to recover most of the input tax. The QB rejected this contention and upheld Customs' ruling, holding that if a taxpayer opted to tax a property, he was bound by the provisions of the capital goods scheme. What is now *VAT Regulations 1995 (SI 1995/2518), regs 112–116* prevented Customs from agreeing a revised initial attribution. The provisions of *reg 116(2)* only permitted a revised attribution in subsequent periods, rather than in the initial period. Buxton J observed that, if a taxpayer sought to opt to tax a property, he must be taken to have made that decision on an informed basis regarding the capital goods scheme. *C & E Commrs v Trustees for R & R Pension Fund*, QB [1996] STC 889. (*Note*. For Customs' practice following this decision, see Business Brief 17/96, issued on 16 August 1996.)

[6.45] See also *The Island Trading Co*, 46.194 PARTIAL EXEMPTION.

Effect of option to tax—attribution of input tax

[6.46] A company trading as opticians from leased premises made both taxable and exempt supplies. The landlords of three of the properties from which the company traded had opted to tax the properties. The company reclaimed the whole of the input tax on the rent. Customs rejected the claim, on the basis that the tax had to be attributed between the company's taxable and exempt supplies. The company appealed, contending that a landlord should not be permitted to exercise an option to tax where a tenant made exempt supplies and was therefore unable to reclaim the whole of the input tax. The tribunal rejected this contention and dismissed the appeal, holding that there was 'nothing in the fundamental principles of Community law' that 'in any material respect cuts down the discretion given to the Member State to enact its own "option to tax" provisions in such a way that the landlord should be precluded from exercising his option where his tenant is a partially exempt trader'. *R Walia Opticians Ltd*, [1997] VATDR 368 (VTD 15050).

[6.47] See also *Cliff College*, **46.61** PARTIAL EXEMPTION; *Hellesdon Developments Ltd.* **46.62** PARTIAL EXEMPTION, and *Royal Sun Alliance Insurance Group plc*, **46.216** PARTIAL EXEMPTION.

HMRC refusing permission for option

[6.48] In 1997 a company (B) acquired the lease of a racecourse. It arranged for another company (T) to manage the course. The racecourse needed substantial repair work, and in 2007 B decided to assign the lease to T. It was agreed that B should pay T a substantial 'reverse premium' of £340,000, while T should pay B a nominal consideration on the assignment of the lease. In October 2007 B wrote to HMRC applying for permission to opt to tax the racecourse, with the intention of reclaiming input tax. HMRC refused to grant B permission, on the grounds that B would not be making any further taxable supplies after the assignment, so that the input tax that B wished to recover was 'not attributable to any anticipated taxable supplies from the property'. B appealed. The tribunal reviewed the evidence in detail and noted that 'there was no direct right of appeal against a refusal to give permission to opt', but both parties accepted that B 'had a right of appeal against the decision as it amounted to a refusal to repay input tax'. Judge Mosedale observed that the lease was not an asset, as it had a 'negative value', and B had 'paid £340,000 to be rid of it'. On the evidence, 'the transaction should properly be viewed as an assignment with a reverse premium of £339,990'. It followed that B had not made any supply to T. Since the lease was not an asset, the assignment of that lease 'was not a supply for VAT purposes' and it was 'impossible for the input tax on the reverse premium to be attributable to it'. Since the reverse premium was not attributable to the disposal of an asset, it had to be treated as 'an overhead expense of the appellant's business as a whole'. Accordingly, since B was partly exempt, it was 'entitled to recover the VAT on the reverse premium in accordance with its partial exemption method applicable to the period in which the expense was incurred'. The tribunal held that HMRC were entitled to refuse permission 'to convert an exempt supply into a taxable one' and that HMRC were only required 'to take into account the putative opter's grants and not the grants made by anyone else'. However, the finding that no input tax was attributable to the assignment meant that as a matter of law, the tribunal had 'no jurisdiction to consider HMRC's refusal of permission on the option to tax because the recovery of the input tax did not in law depend on it'. *British Eventing Ltd v HMRC*, [2010] UKFTT 382 (TC); [2011] SFTD 18, TC00664.

Tenant objecting to option

[6.49] In 2001 the landlord of a farm opted to tax it. In 2006 the tenant failed to pay the rent. In 2007 the landlord served a notice to quit. The tenant took proceedings in the Ch D, contending that the inclusion of VAT in the rent was unfair and that the notice was invalid. The Ch D rejected this contention and gave judgment for the landlord, holding that the notice was valid. *Mason v Boscawen*, Ch D 2008, [2009] STC 624; [2008] EWHC 3100 (Ch).

Input tax on speculative land development project—land never acquired

[6.50] See *Beaverbank Properties Ltd*, 36.556 INPUT TAX.

Beneficial Interests (VATA 1994, Sch 10, para 40)

[6.51] In the case noted at 62.36 SUPPLY, where the owners of a large building arranged for employees to carry out maintenance services, the HL held that what is now *VATA 1994, Sch 10 para 40* did not apply. Lord Slynn held that *para 40** was 'aimed at the situation where the legal title is in one person, so that he can make a grant of an interest in the land, but the beneficial interest is in another person, so he receives any rent or other payment for the grant of the lease' and was 'directed to the case where trustees grant an interest in land on behalf of the beneficiary and the benefit of the consideration for the grant accrues to the beneficiary'. *C & E Commrs v Trustees of the Nell Gwynn House Maintenance Fund*, HL 1998, [1999] STC 79; [1999] 1 WLR 174; [1999] 1 All ER 385. (*Note.* For HMRC's current interpretation of what is now *VATA 1994, Sch 10 para 40*, see Business Brief 16/2005, issued on 18 August 2005, and Business Brief 23/2005, issued on 5 December 2005.)

[6.52] For a case where *VATA 1994, Sch 10 para 40** was held to apply, see *HMRC v Abbey National plc (No 4)*, 41.19 LAND.

Supplies between landlord and tenant

Leaseback transaction—effect of VAT Regulations, reg 115

[6.53] See *Centralan Property Ltd*, 22.459 EUROPEAN COMMUNITY LAW.

Reverse premium by landlord to tenant

[6.54] See *Gleneagles Hotel plc*, 62.125 SUPPLY; *Neville Russell*, 62.127 SUPPLY, and *Hutchinson Locke & Monk*, 62.128 SUPPLY.

Improvements to hotel paid for by tenant

[6.55] See *Port Erin Hotels Ltd*, 62.130 SUPPLY.

Repairs to premises paid in return for rent-free occupation

[6.56] See *Ridgeons Bulk Ltd*, 62.131 SUPPLY.

Payment by landlord for surrender of lease by tenant

[6.57] See *Lubbock Fine & Co*, 22.333 EUROPEAN COMMUNITY LAW.

Payment by tenant to landlord for surrender of onerous lease

[6.58] See *Central Capital Corporation Ltd*, 41.66 LAND, and *AA Insurance Services Ltd*, 41.67 LAND.

Compensation payment by tenant for termination of lease

[6.59] See *Lloyds Bank plc*, 62.143 SUPPLY.

Rent paid while premises unoccupied—treatment of input tax

[6.60] See *Harper Collins Publishers Ltd*, 46.54 PARTIAL EXEMPTION.

Payments under agreement capping mortgage interest

[6.61] See *Iliffe & Holloway*, 62.133 SUPPLY.

Repairs to bomb-damaged building—to whom supplies made

[6.62] See *Commercial Union Assurance Co plc*, 36.67 INPUT TAX.

7

Business

The cases are arranged under the following headings.

Court decisions	**7.1**
Tribunal decisions	
Letting of property (including lock-up garages)	**7.17**
Hiring of boats and yachts	**7.29**
Hiring of aircraft	**7.48**
Conversion, etc. of buildings	**7.50**
Ownership of horses	**7.57**
Promotion of tourism	**7.78**
Statutory bodies	**7.79**
Educational activities	**7.82**
Miscellaneous activities	**7.87**

NOTE

Cases in this chapter involve the general meaning of 'business' as defined in what is now *VATA 1994, s 94(1)*. For activities which are deemed to be businesses by virtue of *s 94(2)(a)*, see **13** CLUBS, ASSOCIATIONS AND ORGANISATIONS. For cases where the existence of a business is not disputed, and the issue is whether there has been a supply for the purposes of the business or in the course or furtherance of the business, see **36** INPUT TAX and **62** SUPPLY. For cases where the issue is whether there has been a supply for the purpose of a future business, see **36.554** et seq. INPUT TAX. For cases where the existence of a business is not disputed, and the issue is by whom the business is carried on, see **57.170** et seq. REGISTRATION. Although the UK legislation refers to 'business', the relevant EC legislation (*Article 4 of the EC Sixth Directive*) refers to an 'economic activity'. For cases concerning the definition of an 'economic activity', see **22.103** to **22.114** EUROPEAN COMMUNITY LAW. The Commissioners take the view that 'the meaning of "economic activity" is not materially different from the meaning of "business" in the UK legislation'—see Customs' VAT Manual, Part 6, para 1.7.

Court decisions

Charity providing accommodation for schoolchildren

[7.1] A company, limited by guarantee and accepted by the Inland Revenue as charitable, carried on the activity of providing boarding houses for the pupils of a school. The boarding fees were charged to the parents separately from the school fees and the company was conducted so as to achieve neither profits nor losses. The Commissioners issued a ruling that output tax was chargeable on the fees, and the company appealed, contending that it was not carrying on a 'business' for VAT purposes. The CS rejected this contention, holding that the company was carrying on a business within the scope of what is now *VATA 1994, s 94(1)*. The CS observed that the activities were predominantly concerned with making taxable supplies to consumers for a consideration. The supplies were of a kind which, subject to differences of detail, were made commercially by those who sought to profit from them, and were continued over an appreciable period of time and with such frequency as to amount to a recognisable and identifiable activity. Lord Emslie held that 'the natural meaning of the word "business" does not require that what is done must be done commercially' or with 'the object of making profits'. *C & E Commrs v Morrison's Academy Boarding Houses Association*, CS 1977, [1978] STC 1.

Statutory body—whether carrying on a business

[7.2] The *Water Act 1973* set up ten water authorities in England and Wales and established the National Water Council with a wide variety of functions. The Commissioners issued a ruling that, except with regard to certain ancillary activities, the Council was not carrying on a business (so that it was not entitled to reclaim input tax). The QB allowed the Council's appeal in part, applying *Morrison's Academy Boarding Houses Association*, 7.1 above, and holding that 'business' was not restricted to activities carried on commercially with a view to profit. The fact that services were supplied in the performance of a statutory duty did not automatically prevent them from constituting supplies in the course of business. However, certain advisory and administrative services, which the Council supplied exclusively to public bodies, were outside the definition of 'business'. *National Water Council v C & E Commrs*, QB 1978, [1979] STC 157.

[7.3] See also *Apple and Pear Development Council*, **22.80** EUROPEAN COMMUNITY LAW.

Organisation distributing religious propaganda

[7.4] The Church of Scientology, an organisation established in California, acquired premises in Sussex, at which it provided training courses and sold books and other goods. It did not account for output tax on its supplies. The Commissioners issued an assessment on the basis that the Church was carrying on a business. The Church appealed, contending that an organisation which propagated a religious philosophy should not be treated as carrying on a 'business'. The tribunal rejected this contention and dismissed the appeal, and the CA upheld this decision. *Church of Scientology of California v C & E Commrs*, CA 1980, [1981] STC 65; [1980] 3 CMLR 114; [1981] 1 All ER 1035.

Charitable trust to raise funds for construction of theatre

[7.5] A charitable trust was set up in 1972 with the primary object of constructing a theatre in a disused hall and raising funds from the public for this. The Trust reclaimed input tax on the goods and services supplied to it for the purposes of the project. The Commissioners rejected the claim, considering that the Trust was not carrying on a business. The QB upheld this decision. Neill J held that the Trust's activities 'lacked any commercial element at all' and could not 'properly be regarded as business activities'. *C & E Commrs v Royal Exchange Theatre Trust*, QB [1979] STC 728; [1979] 3 All ER 797.

Pheasant shoots—contributions by participants towards cost

[7.6] A landowner (F), who was registered for VAT, organised the shooting of pheasants on his family estate. Originally, friends and relatives had been invited to shoot on the estate as family guests. F asked those he invited to make specified contributions towards the cost. He did not advertise for guests and only invited family friends and relatives. The contributions usually met about half the cost of the shooting. Customs issued an assessment on the basis that F was making supplies for consideration. F appealed, contending that the running of the shoots did not amount to the carrying on of a business. The tribunal accepted this contention and allowed F's appeal, and the QB upheld this decision as one of fact. Gibson J held that the primary meaning of 'business' was 'an occupation by which a person earns a living'. *C & E Commrs v Lord Fisher*, QB [1981] STC 238; [1981] 2 All ER 147. (*Note.* For a subsequent case in which this decision was distinguished, see *Williams*, **62.151** SUPPLY.)

Partnership hiring aircraft from company

[7.7] Three people, who had registered as a partnership for VAT, owned an aircraft, which they hired out to a company which carried on the business of hiring aircraft to qualified pilots. Under the charter agreement, the partnership received a fee from the company based on the number of hours for which the aircraft was hired. The Commissioners issued a ruling that the partnership was not carrying on a business, and should therefore be deregistered. The tribunal dismissed the partnership's appeal and the QB upheld this decision, holding that the charter of a single asset to a single customer did not constitute a business. *Three H Aircraft Hire v C & E Commrs*, [1982] STC 653. (*Note.* Compare, however, the subsequent CJEC decision in *Staatssecretaris van Financien v Heerma*, **22.108** EUROPEAN COMMUNITY LAW.)

Hire of shed to partnership—whether an 'economic activity'

[7.8] See *Staatssecretaris van Financien v Heerma*, **22.108** EUROPEAN COMMUNITY LAW.

Playgroup—whether a business

[7.9] See *Yarburgh Children's Trust*, **15.91** CONSTRUCTION OF BUILDINGS, ETC.

Nursery—whether a business

[7.10] See *St Paul's Community Project Ltd*, **15.92** CONSTRUCTION OF BUILDINGS, ETC.

Institute of Chartered Accountants

[7.11] See *The Institute of Chartered Accountants in England and Wales v C & E Commrs*, **62.159** SUPPLY.

Holding company—whether carrying on any business

[7.12] See *Polysar Investments Netherlands BV v Inspecteur der Invoerrechten en Accijnzen*, **22.106** EUROPEAN COMMUNITY LAW, and *Cumbrae Properties (1963) Ltd*, **62.24** SUPPLY.

Investment trust

[7.13] See *The Wellcome Trust Ltd*, **22.111** EUROPEAN COMMUNITY LAW.

Investment management of pension funds

[7.14] See *Cadbury Ireland Pension Trust Ltd v Revenue Commrs (Ireland)*, **54.12** PENSION FUNDS.

Limited partnership holding investments

[7.15] See *Harnas & Helm CV v Staatssecretaris van Financien*, **22.112** EUROPEAN COMMUNITY LAW.

Grant of building rights—whether an 'economic activity'

[7.16] See *van Tiem v Staatssecretaris van Financien*, **22.109** EUROPEAN COMMUNITY LAW.

Tribunal decisions

Letting of property (including lock-up garages)

Furnished letting—whether carrying on a business

[7.17] An accountant (W) owned three houses in Bradford which were let furnished under arrangements which were agreed to amount to licences to occupy land. The Commissioners issued a ruling that the letting amounted to the carrying on of a business (with the result that W was partly exempt). The tribunal dismissed W's appeal, holding that the letting amounted to a business within the ordinary meaning of the word and that W's registration as an accountant covered the business of furnished letting. The fact that the income from the letting was accepted as investment income for income tax purposes was not conclusive. *DA Walker*, [1976] VATTR 10 (VTD 240).

Letting of houses held as investments

[7.18] A builder (P) owned about twelve houses, the letting of which was in the hands of estate agents. The rents were treated as investment income for income tax purposes. P reclaimed the whole of his input tax. The Commissioners issued an assessment to recover some of the tax, on the basis that the rental income was a business activity with the result that P was partly exempt. The tribunal upheld the assessment and dismissed P's appeal. *J Prescott*, MAN/77/239 (VTD 529).

Letting of business premises

[7.19] An estate agent (S) and his wife purchased a dilapidated building and carried on the estate agency business from its basement. The ground floor was let as a hairdressing salon, and the first floor as a residential flat. Although the property was owned jointly, the rents were paid to S and were placed in a bank account in his sole name. He reclaimed the whole of his input tax and the Commissioners issued an assessment to recover the tax, on the basis that the letting was a business activity and that S was therefore partly exempt. The tribunal upheld the assessment and dismissed S's appeal. *DE Sherwin*, MAN/86/171 (VTD 3299).

[7.20] A company, 90% of the shares in which were owned by a solicitor, applied for registration, describing its business activity as 'property owning and management'. It also reclaimed input tax incurred on the refurbishment of office premises, which it had transferred under licence to an associated company, in which the solicitor also owned 90% of the shares. There was no formal agreement concerning this transfer. The Commissioners rejected the application for registration, on the basis that the company was not carrying on any business. The tribunal dismissed the company's appeal against this decision. The onus was on the company to show that its activities constituted a business which was to include the making of taxable supplies. The owning and holding of a property was not in itself a business. *Godlin Ltd*, LON/99/912Y (VTD 4416).

[7.21] A charity, which owned two buildings which it let to another charity at a rent of £1 p.a., applied for registration for VAT. The Commissioners rejected the application on the grounds that the charity was not carrying on any business, and the tribunal dismissed the charity's appeal. *Whitehall Chase Foundation Trust*, LON/89/1378 (VTD 5134).

Letting of lock-up garages

[7.22] An architect (W) owned 24 lock-up garages, managed for him by estate agents who accounted to him quarterly for the net receipts. He took no direct part in the management of the garages and the Inland Revenue accepted that the rents were investment income for income tax purposes. The Commissioners issued an assessment charging output tax on the basis that the rents were from taxable supplies. (It was common ground that the rents were not exempt, being within what is now *VATA 1994, Sch 9, Group 1, Item 1(h)*.) The tribunal dismissed W's appeal, holding that the letting amounted to carrying on a business even though the day-to-day management of the garages was left to agents. *JW Wilcox*, [1978] VATTR 79 (VTD 546).

[7.23] A two-person partnership carried on a retail business. The partners also jointly owned some 60 lock-up garages in the area, which they let. The Commissioners issued an assessment charging output tax on the basis that the rents were taxable. (It was common ground that they were within what is now *VATA 1994, Sch 9, Group 1, Item 1(h)* and not exempt.) The partners appealed, contending that the letting should be treated as an investment and not as a business activity. The tribunal rejected this contention and dismissed the appeal, finding that the letting was conducted on business principles and involved the provision of services for consideration. Accordingly, the letting was within the definition of a 'business'. The partnership registration covered the letting of the garages as well as the retail business. *RW & AAW Williamson*, [1978] VATTR 90 (VTD 555).

[7.24] The decision in *Williamson*, 7.23 above, was applied in the similar case of *BL & N Merrifield*, LON/92/2676A (VTD 10563).

[7.25] A married couple purchased a number of garages and let them to tenants. They did not register for VAT, and the Commissioners issued a ruling that they were liable to be registered. The couple appealed, contending that the garages had been purchased as an investment and did not constitute a business. The tribunal dismissed the couple's appeal, holding that the letting of the garages was a business activity. *GW & Mrs JA Green*, LON/91/2594Y (VTD 9016).

Letting of beach chalet

[7.26] A retired accountant hired a 'beach chalet' from a District Council. The Council charged VAT on the hire. The accountant appealed to the tribunal, contending that VAT was not due because the Council should not be regarded as carrying on a business. The tribunal rejected this contention and dismissed his appeal, holding that the Council's letting of beach chalets were 'activities that might be carried out by any other landlord'. *HT Shearing*, LON/99/885 (VTD 16723).

Letting of cottages purchased with business premises

[7.27] See *Johnson*, 36.264 INPUT TAX.

Whether property let by individual to associated partnership

[7.28] A married couple owned and operated a nursing home in partnership. They built an extension to the home, and entered into an agreement whereby the wife purported to grant the partnership authority to use the extension. The wife registered for VAT and reclaimed input tax of £49,000 on the extension. The Commissioners rejected the claim and cancelled the registration, considering that the wife was not making any taxable supplies. The tribunal dismissed the wife's appeal, holding that she was not making any taxable supplies and was not entitled to be registered. The effect of *Law of Property Act 1925* was that the couple owned the whole of the nursing home as joint tenants, and the wife did 'not use or occupy the extension to the nursing home in her own right'. Accordingly, the purported agreement between the wife and the partnership was 'null and void'. *Mrs G Blandy*, MAN/94/303 (VTD 13123).

Hiring of boats and yachts

Letting of pleasure boat—whether a business

[7.29] An individual (C) acquired a pleasure boat and let it to a company carrying on the business of holiday boat hire. The charterers were to use the vessel in their business, taking reasonable steps to maximise the revenue from hiring it out, and paying C 45% of the hiring fees received. He applied for registration for VAT. The Commissioners rejected his application, considering that the hiring out of the vessel did not amount to the carrying on of a business. The tribunal dismissed C's appeal. The hiring out of the vessel for holiday use was a trade but he did not participate in this. His intention was to make an investment and his receipt of a share of the hire fees, and the activities on his behalf as a consequence of the charter, did not make the investment a business. *KG Coleman*, [1976] VATTR 24 (VTD 242). (*Note.* The decision was approved by the QB in *Three H Aircraft Hire*, 7.7 above.)

[7.30] A partnership purchased a boat from a company under an agreement whereby the company was to retain possession of the boat for use in its boat hire business and to maintain and insure it and provide fuel and stores for it. Bookings could be by either the company or the partnership. The partnership received 45% of the net hire charges, as defined, where the booking was made by the company, and 50% where the partnership made the booking. The partnership advertised for bookings and applied for registration for VAT. The Commissioners rejected the application on the basis that the partnership was not carrying on any business. The tribunal allowed the partnership's appeal, holding that, in view of the efforts which the partnership made to attract customers, it was carrying on business. *Longbow*, MAN/77/253 (VTD 551).

[7.31] See also *Purdue*, 36.494 INPUT TAX.

Motor cruiser acquired for chartering

[7.32] The purchase of a motor cruiser for chartering was held to be an investment, rather than a business activity, in *K & C Rossiter*, LON/83/104 (VTD 1452).

Purchase and charter of powerboats

[7.33] A married couple registered for VAT on the basis that they had begun a business of chartering powerboats. They purchased a boat (which they subsequently part-exchanged for a larger boat) and reclaimed substantial amounts of VAT. Customs discovered that from 2003 to 2005 the couple had used the boats themselves for 93 days, and had only chartered one boat for one day. They formed the opinion that the couple were not carrying on a business, and issued an assessment to recover the tax. The tribunal reviewed the evidence in detail and dismissed the couple's appeal, finding that 'far from being a genuine economic activity', the enterprise was simply a device to obtain relief from personal tax 'and to acquire boats without paying VAT'. *PR & Mrs HK Davies (t/a Lymington Power Boat Charter)*, LON/05/1139 (VTD 20032).

Chartering of sailing yacht

[7.34] A couple who owned a sailing yacht registered for VAT in 1977. In 1978 they chartered the yacht to a company, which became responsible for maintaining and insuring it and retained 50% of all hiring fees received. In 1980 the Commissioners cancelled the couple's registration on the ground that the charter of the yacht to a company did not constitute the carrying on of a business. The tribunal dismissed the couple's appeal against this decision. *G & J Tibbs (t/a Joanne Yacht Services)*, MAN/80/241 (VTD 1098).

[7.35] A company which carried on a pig-farming business reclaimed input tax on the purchase of a yacht, which was used by directors of the company and their families, and was also let on hire. The Commissioners issued an assessment to recover the tax and the company appealed, contending that it was carrying on a separate business of chartering. The tribunal rejected this contention and dismissed the appeal, holding that in view of the small number of lettings, the limited nature of advertising, and the company's selectivity in accepting hirers, the hiring of the yacht did not constitute a business. The chairman observed that 'evidence of performance is to be preferred to the evidence of intent where the latter is unaccompanied by performance'. *Rainheath Ltd*, MAN/81/70 (VTD 1249).

[7.36] A small private company, which carried on a business of mobile crane hire, reclaimed input tax on the purchase of a yacht. The Commissioners issued an assessment to recover the tax, considering that the yacht had been acquired for the personal purpose of the company directors, rather than for business purposes. The company appealed, contending that the yacht had been purchased to set up a new business of chartering. The tribunal allowed the appeal in part, holding on the evidence that the yacht chartering constituted a business but that the yacht had partly been purchased for personal enjoyment, and that 25% of the input tax was allowable. *RF Henfrey (Midlands) Ltd*, MAN/82/174 (VTD 1409).

[7.37] An accountant who had retired from full-time practice purchased a yacht and reclaimed the input tax thereon. The Commissioners issued an assessment to recover the tax and he appealed, contending that he had purchased the yacht to establish a new business of chartering. The tribunal accepted his evidence and allowed his appeal. *AG Evans*, LON/83/62 (VTD 1453).

[7.38] A married couple who owned a hotel reclaimed input tax on the purchase of a yacht. The Commissioners issued an assessment to recover the tax and they appealed, contending that they had purchased the yacht for the purpose of establishing a chartering business. The tribunal accepted their evidence and allowed the appeal. *The Westbourne Hotel*, EDN/84/5 (VTD 1652).

[7.39] A plant hire company reclaimed input tax on the purchase of a yacht. The Commissioners issued an assessment to recover the tax, considering that it had been acquired for the personal enjoyment of the company directors. The company appealed, contending that it had been acquired for the purpose of chartering. The tribunal dismissed the appeal, finding that there was no evidence of any steps having been taken to charter the yacht, and holding that the tax was not deductible. *Trexagrove Ltd*, [1984] VATTR 222 (VTD 1758).

[7.40] A company which carried on a leasing business reclaimed input tax on the purchase of a yacht. The yacht was entered in races and was then twice let on charter before being sold. The Commissioners issued an assessment to recover the tax, considering that the yacht had not been acquired for business purposes but for the personal pleasure of the company chairman. The company appealed, contending that the yacht had been acquired for chartering. The tribunal accepted the company's evidence and allowed the appeal. *Petros Leasing Ltd*, MAN/88/366 (VTD 4056).

[7.41] A similar decision was reached in a case where a holding company reclaimed input tax on two yachts. The Commissioners rejected the claim but the tribunal allowed the company's appeal, holding on the evidence that the yachts had been purchased for the purpose of a separate business of chartering. *CR King & Partners (Holdings) Ltd*, LON/90/1646Z (VTD 6695).

[7.42] A company which had carried on a property development business chartered a yacht, which was owned by its controlling director, for a five-year period. It reclaimed input tax on repairs to the yacht. The Commissioners rejected the claim, considering that the expenditure had not been incurred for business purposes. The company appealed, contending that it had acquired the yacht for the purpose of hiring it to customers. Two customers had agreed to hire the yacht, but in one case the customer withdrew from the agreement, and in the other case the company was unable to fulfil the agreement because the yacht had broken down. The tribunal allowed the company's appeal, holding on the evidence that 'it was at all times the appellant company's intention to engage in the business of boat chartering', and 'any expenditure which it may have incurred on the repair and maintenance of the boat was expenditure on goods or services to be used for the purpose of its business'. *Silicon Valley Estates Ltd*, LON/92/211X (VTD 11017).

[7.43] A company which had carried on a business of open-cast coal mining purchased a yacht at a cost of £336,000, and reclaimed input tax on the purchase. The Commissioners issued an assessment to recover the tax, considering that the yacht had been purchased for the personal pleasure of the company's principal director. The company appealed, contending that the yacht had been purchased with a view to chartering it to customers. The tribunal accepted the company's evidence and allowed the appeal, applying *dicta* in *Ian Flockton Developments Ltd*, **36.341** INPUT TAX. *DS Supplies Ltd*, MAN/95/884 (VTD 13559). (*Note.* The tribunal rejected the company's application for costs, finding that the company had not made sufficient evidence available to the Commissioners before the hearing.)

[7.44] The chartering of a yacht was also held to constitute a business in *Premier Motor Yacht Charters Ltd*, MAN/97/223 (VTD 15506); *TBV Stockdale (t/a Compass Charters)*, LON/03/864 (VTD 18757) and *Heath House Charter Ltd*, [2010] SFTD 245; [2009] UKFTT 305 (TC), TC00249.

[7.45] In February 2000 an individual (B) purchased a luxury yacht from a company (S) for £111,625. Under the agreement, S agreed to manage the yacht and attempt to hire it to customers for a minimum period of 12 months. In April 2000 B and his wife applied to register for VAT, describing their business as 'yacht chartering'. In their first VAT return, they claimed a repayment of £14,835. In September 2000 the Commissioners issued a ruling that B and his wife were not carrying on any business and were not entitled to be registered.

They appealed. The tribunal dismissed their appeal, holding that the letting of the yacht to S was 'an isolated transaction which was not part of a sequence of transactions amounting to economic activity. The economic activities involved in this case were those of (S).' *M & C Berwick*, LON/00/1190 (VTD 17686).

[7.46] In 2001 a family partnership (comprising a mother and her son) registered for VAT, describing their business as 'yacht charterers'. They reclaimed input tax on the purchase of a yacht. They subsequently sold that yacht and purchased a replacement, again reclaiming input tax on the purchase. Customs subsequently formed the opinion that they were not actually carrying on a business, and that the yachts had been purchased for the personal use of one of the partners. They cancelled the partnership registration. The tribunal reviewed the evidence in detail and dismissed the partners' appeal, finding that 'the partners never conducted a business on sound and recognised principles; they kept no proper financial records; and their supplies were not substantial in amount'. *SJ & CM McDonald*, MAN/05/098 (VTD 19473).

[7.46A] A company, which was controlled by an accountant (W), registered for VAT and reclaimed input tax of £85,000 on the purchase of a yacht. HMRC subsequently formed the opinion that the company was not carrying on any business. They cancelled the company's registration and issued an assessment to recover the tax. The tribunal dismissed the company's appeal. Judge Anne Scott held that W had not adopted 'the approach of a chartered accountant acting in a business environment', and appeared to have made 'a personal investment decision'. The yacht had been used by a businessman who was a close friend of W. There had been 'no substantive business plan' and 'almost no marketing of the vessel'. Accordingly it appeared that the company was not carrying on any business or economic activity. *Ocean Charters Ltd v HMRC*, [2011] UKFTT 1688 (TC), TC01688.

Whether yacht purchased for future chartering business

[7.47] See *Furness Vale Yacht Hire Ltd*, 36.562 INPUT TAX; *Milner*, 36.583 INPUT TAX, *Warwest Holdings Ltd*, 36.584 INPUT TAX, and *City Centre Commercials Ltd*, 36.585 INPUT TAX.

Hiring of aircraft

Hiring out of aircraft by partnership—hire mainly to partners

[7.48] Six people who were interested in flying acquired a four-seater aircraft and obtained permission to fly it from a hitherto disused airfield, with the intention of using it themselves and hiring it out as a commercial venture. They formed themselves into a partnership, registered the business name and were registered for VAT from September 1974. However, following an inspection of the partnership records, the Commissioners cancelled the registration on the grounds that the partnership was not carrying on any business. The tribunal allowed the partnership's appeal, finding that the hire of the aircraft was 'available to the public at large' and was so used by certain members of the public, 'albeit to a small extent in the first 12 months of operation'.

Accordingly there was 'an occupation carried on as a commercial activity' which qualified as a business. The tribunal also held that the supply of the use of the aircraft to a partner was a supply in the course of that business, applying the principles laid down in *Carlton Lodge Ltd*, **13.29** CLUBS, ASSOCIATIONS AND ORGANISATIONS. *Border Flying Co*, [1976] VATTR 132 (VTD 300).

Hire of aircraft to flying club

[7.49] A company which owned a light aircraft hired it to a flying club. The company was responsible for the maintenance, cleaning and insurance of the aircraft. The Commissioners issued a ruling that the company was not carrying on any business and was not entitled to be registered. The tribunal allowed the company's appeal, applying the principles laid down in *Walker*, **7.17** above, and distinguishing *Three H Aircraft Hire*, **7.7** above, and *Coleman*, **7.29** above. *Cavendish Aviation Ltd*, MAN/81/80 (VTD 1471).

Conversion, etc. of buildings

Conversion of building into dwelling-house

[7.50] A consultant, who was registered for VAT, bought 1½ acres of land with an old barn on it and with planning permission to convert the barn into a dwelling-house. The conversion of the barn was completed in October 1973 and he moved into it with his family, having sold his previous house in September. He reclaimed input tax on the conversion and the Commissioners issued an assessment to recover the tax. He appealed, contending that he should be treated as carrying on a business as a builder. The tribunal rejected this contention and dismissed his appeal, holding on the evidence that he had converted the barn for his personal occupation. *G Nixon*, CAR H/75/184 (VTD 233). (*Note*. Relief would now be available under *VATA 1994, s 35* as amended by *FA 1996, s 30*.)

[7.51] A civil servant and his wife purchased an old stable, coachhouse, etc. for conversion into a dwelling-house. He decided to do the work of conversion himself. He applied for and obtained registration as a builder and reclaimed input tax on the conversion. The Commissioners rejected his claim and the tribunal dismissed his appeal, holding that he and his wife had not acquired the buildings as partners, that he was not carrying on a business, and that the fact that he had been registered did not prevent the Commissioners from reviewing the registration. *GWH Kelly*, EDN/77/43 (VTD 598). (*Notes*. (1) This case was distinguished in the 1995 case of *Dewhirst*, **57.106** REGISTRATION. (2) Relief would now be available under *VATA 1994, s 35* as amended by *FA 1996, s 30*.)

Improvements to existing dwelling

[7.52] A married couple lived in a listed building. The husband (S) retired from his employment and registered for VAT as a builder. He did not account for output tax on any supplies, but reclaimed input tax in respect of various improvements to his home. The Commissioners rejected the claim on the basis that S was not carrying on any business. The tribunal dismissed S's appeal against this decision. Applying *dicta* of Gibson J in *C & E Commrs v Lord*

Fisher, 7.6 above, the primary meaning of 'business' was 'an occupation by which a person earns a living'. On the evidence, 'the building work undertaken by (S) was not an occupation by which he earned a living'. *J Sawyer*, LON/03/1199 (VTD 18872).

Charity—conversion of building for use as centre for handicapped

[7.53] A registered charity which ran a centre for the handicapped acquired two vacant shops and converted them into a new centre at the cost of some £37,000. Most of the labour was done by workmen, the charity being reimbursed their wages by the Manpower Services Commission. The charity reclaimed input tax on the work. The Commissioners rejected the claim, considering that the Fellowship was not carrying on a business. The tribunal dismissed the charity's appeal. *Widnes Spastic Fellowship*, MAN/77/132 (VTD 455).

Committee set up to enlarge church hall

[7.54] A church established a committee to enlarge the church hall. The committee appealed against the Commissioners' refusal to register it, contending that it was carrying on a business. The tribunal rejected this contention and dismissed the appeal, holding that there was not sufficient continuity in the project to bring it within the meaning of 'business'. *Trinity Methodist Church Royton (Building Committee)*, MAN/78/159 (VTD 807).

Intermittent property development—whether company still in business

[7.55] A small property development company registered for VAT in 1977 and completed a contract in 1979. In January 1981 it purchased a large house which it renovated and sold at a profit in August. (The renovation was accepted as being zero-rated under legislation which has subsequently been superseded.) In 1982 the Commissioners issued a ruling that the company was not carrying on a business and was not entitled to be registered. The company appealed. The tribunal accepted the company's evidence and allowed the appeal, observing that an activity such as property development could still constitute a business even though supplies were only made infrequently. *David Wickens Properties Ltd*, [1982] VATTR 143 (VTD 1284).

Statutory repair work carried on by City Council

[7.56] See *Glasgow City Council*, 42.6 LOCAL AUTHORITIES AND STATUTORY BODIES.

Ownership of horses

NOTE

In the 1993 Budget Statement, the then Chancellor of the Exchequer announced the introduction of arrangements to help racehorse owners to meet 'the normal business test for VAT registration'. See Customs & Excise News Release No 43/93, issued on 16 March 1993. Most of the cases below refer to periods before the introduction of the current arrangements, and should be read in that light. For cases where appellants have reclaimed input tax on the basis that the

purpose of owning racehorses has been to advertise an existing business activity, see **36.341** *et seq*.
INPUT TAX.

[7.57] An individual (P) had owned racehorses for many years, and in 1967 decided to begin breeding them. He kept his horses at stud farms (not owned by him) in England and France. He registered for VAT in 1973, and reclaimed substantial amounts of input tax. His accounts showed small amounts of income, but consistent net losses. In 1975 the Commissioners decided to cancel his registration, considering that his activities constituted a hobby rather than business. The tribunal allowed P's appeal, holding that the breeding of horses was necessarily a long-term activity and that his activities amounted to the carrying on of a business. *DD Prenn*, LON/78/406 (VTD 793).

[7.58] The proprietor of a stud farm raced four horses, three of which had been bred at her stud, and reclaimed the input tax thereon. The Commissioners issued an assessment to recover the tax, considering that the racing of horses was not a business activity. She appealed, contending that the horses had been raced to demonstrate their value for breeding purposes. The tribunal accepted her evidence and allowed her appeal. *DB Ismay*, [1980] VATTR 19 (VTD 877).

[7.59] A similar decision was reached in *GB Turnbull Ltd*, [1986] VATTR 247 (VTD 1769).

[7.60] A company was incorporated with the object of breeding horses. It reclaimed input tax in respect of the purchase of a share in a colt. The Commissioners refused to repay the tax, considering that the company's activities did not constitute a business for VAT purposes. The tribunal allowed the company's appeal against this decision, holding that the breeding of horses could constitute a business despite the fact that supplies may be intermittent. On the evidence, the company was carrying on a business and the input tax in question was deductible. *Guest Leasing & Bloodstock Co Ltd*, LON/81/133 (VTD 1227).

[7.61] A company which operated a public house and restaurant incorporated a subsidiary company (G). G purchased a number of racehorses and applied to be registered for VAT. The Commissioners rejected the application, considering that G was not carrying on a business. The tribunal dismissed G's appeal against this decision, holding that horse racing could not constitute a business since it did not involve the making of any taxable supplies. *Guinea Grill Stakes Ltd*, LON/82/129 (VTD 1291). (*Note*. See now, however, the note preceding 7.57 above.)

[7.62] A company which bought and sold horses raced some of the horses which it owned, and reclaimed input tax on their upkeep. The Commissioners issued an assessment to recover the tax, considering that the racing of horses did not constitute a business activity, and that the horses had been raced for the personal pleasure of the company's principal director. The company appealed, contending that the horses had been raced in order to advertise their value. The tribunal accepted this contention and allowed the appeal. *Andy Smith Bloodstock Ltd*, LON/83/187 (VTD 1663).

[7.63] A company which carried on a welding business reclaimed input tax on the purchase of racehorses. The Commissioners issued an assessment to recover the tax and the company appealed, contending that its horse-racing activities constituted a separate business. The tribunal rejected this contention and dismissed the appeal. *Times of Wigan Ltd*, MAN/83/33 (VTD 1917). (*Note.* See now, however, the note preceding 7.57 above.)

[7.64] A company which sold cars reclaimed input tax on the upkeep of several racehorses. The Commissioners issued an assessment to recover the tax, considering that the horses had been purchased for the enjoyment of the principal director, rather than for business purposes. The company appealed, contending that its horse-racing activities constituted a business in their own right. The tribunal rejected this contention and dismissed the appeal. *Brian Gubby Ltd*, [1985] VATTR 59 (VTD 1961). (*Notes.* (1) See now, however, the note preceding 7.57 above. (2) For a preliminary application in this case, see **2.130** APPEALS.)

[7.65] A publican purchased some horses and reclaimed the input tax thereon. The Commissioners issued an assessment to recover the tax, considering that the horses had not been purchased for business purposes. The publican appealed, contending that he had bought the horses to begin a new business of breeding them, and that this would be a full-time business activity, since he had had to close the public house which he had operated. The tribunal accepted his evidence and allowed his appeal. *RG Creber*, LON/86/450 (VTD 2623).

[7.66] A chemist, who was registered for VAT, also bought and sold horses. He had purchased two mares for breeding, but failed to make a profit on this. Subsequently he bought foals with the intention of selling them as yearlings. From 1984 to 1987 he sold five such foals at a profit. The Inland Revenue accepted that he was carrying on a trade for income tax purposes. However, the Commissioners considered that his purchase and sale of foals did not amount to a business for VAT purposes, and informed him that he could neither claim input tax on the purchase of foals, nor charge output tax on their sale as yearlings. The tribunal dismissed his appeal against this decision, holding that there was 'not sufficient frequency' in his dealing activities for them to constitute a business. *EM Thornton (t/a Forum Stud Farm)*, LON/88/945Z (VTD 4711).

[7.67] A company registered for VAT, describing its business as the breeding and selling of racehorses. It reclaimed input tax, and the Commissioners issued an assessment to recover the tax, considering that the company's activities were primarily recreational and that the company was not carrying on a business. The tribunal dismissed the company's appeal against the assessment. On the evidence, the company's predominant activity had been racing horses rather than breeding them, and the racing activities had been 'carried on primarily for the interest and enjoyment of the three directors'. *Triangle Thoroughbreds Ltd*, MAN/90/470 (VTD 5404). (*Note.* See now, however, the note preceding 7.57 above.)

[7.68] The decision in *Triangle Thoroughbreds Ltd*, 7.67 above, was applied in a subsequent case where a company which carried on a property consultancy business had also bought and sold horses. In 1985 and 1986 the company received gross income of £7,000 and £4,700 respectively from horse-trading, but there had been no such income in 1987 and only one sale of £500 in 1989. The tribunal reviewed the evidence in detail and held that for 1985 and 1986 the company's horse-trading activities had constituted a business, but that from 1987 to 1990 they had been so sporadic that they did not amount to a business and no input tax was reclaimable. *Bailiwick Ltd*, LON/91/451X (VTD 7802).

[7.69] A company which had carried on a business of property development reclaimed input tax on the purchase of some land and a brood mare. The Commissioners refused to repay the tax, considering that the expenditure had not been incurred for the purpose of any business. The company appealed, contending that it had decided to begin a new business of breeding and selling racehorses. The tribunal accepted the company's evidence and allowed the appeal. *Mowbray Properties Ltd*, MAN/90/650 (VTD 6033).

[7.70] An individual, employed by a printing company, registered for VAT in August 1988 as a breeder of racehorses. On his registration form VAT1 he estimated his taxable supplies for the following twelve months as £23,000. In fact he only made one taxable supply in that period, selling a gelding (which he had purchased in 1986) for £2,100, and made no sales in the following year. However, he bought seven other horses and reclaimed input tax on their upkeep. In 1990 the Commissioners cancelled his registration on the grounds that he was not carrying on a business. The tribunal dismissed his appeal against this decision, holding that his activities were not 'predominantly concerned with the making of taxable supplies to consumers for a consideration'. *P Higson*, LON/90/1472X (VTD 6826).

[7.71] An appeal was dismissed in a case in which the tribunal found that a company's primary purpose was to race horses, and held that 'racing horses, as such, cannot be a business since no taxable supplies are made'. *Rykneld Thoroughbred Co Ltd*, MAN/90/668 (VTD 6894). (*Note.* See now, however, the note preceding 7.57 above.)

[7.72] A company was incorporated to breed and race horses. It applied to be registered for VAT, but the Commissioners rejected its application on the grounds that it was not carrying on a business. The tribunal dismissed the company's appeal against this decision, applying *Brian Gubby Ltd*, 7.64 above, and *Triangle Thoroughbreds Ltd*, 7.67 above. *Michael Jackson Bloodstock Ltd*, LON/90/1650X (VTD 7863).

[7.73] See also *K & K Thorogood Ltd*, 36.571 INPUT TAX.

[7.74] A property developer, who was registered for VAT, reclaimed input tax on the purchase of two racehorses and two yearlings. The Commissioners issued an assessment to recover the tax and he appealed, contending that he intended to deal in horses, and that his dealing in horses constituted a business activity. Of the two racehorses in question, one had raced five times (winning once) before being sold at a loss; the other had raced 21 times (winning once) and had been offered for sale but no buyer had been found. The two yearlings had been bought for a total of £4,500 and had been sold for a total of £11,000 five months later. He had subsequently bought and sold a number of other horses, and over a four-year period had spent £134,000 on purchases and received £102,000 from sales. The Inland Revenue had accepted that he was carrying on a trade of dealing in horses. The tribunal allowed his appeal, holding that his activities constituted a business. *RB Payne*, LON/90/1476X (VTD 9211). (*Note.* For another issue in this case, see **36.576** INPUT TAX.)

[7.75] An individual (J) was registered for VAT as a breeder of horses, some of which he raced. In 1990 the Commissioners issued a ruling that he was not entitled to be registered, considering that his horse-breeding activities were not in the course or furtherance of a business. He appealed, contending that he was carrying on a business of breeding horses to be sold as potential steeplechasers, although at the time of the appeal hearing he had not yet sold any horses. The tribunal allowed the appeal, holding that J's breeding of horses was 'a serious undertaking honestly pursued' with 'reasonable or recognisable continuity'. *RJ Jenks*, LON/91/810 (VTD 10196).

Racehorse breeder—appeal against cancellation of registration

[7.76] See *Brookes*, **2.49** APPEALS.

Trust Fund publishing lists of stallions and receiving registration fees

[7.77] In 1983 the Thoroughbred Breeders' Association established a Trust to encourage the owners of thoroughbred stallions and mares to support British horse racing. Owners of stallions were required to pay a registration fee of £100 to the Trust for each of their stallions, and were requested to make additional contributions to the Trust Fund. The Trust undertook to help promote at least 200 races, to be held at the 34 British flat-racing courses, and to be restricted to the progeny of registered stallions. The Trust published lists of the registered stallions for this purpose. The Commissioners issued a ruling that the Trust was carrying on a business activity for VAT purposes, and was required to register for VAT and to account for tax on the registration fees and contributions which it received. The Trust appealed, contending that it was not carrying on a business and was not making any taxable supplies. The tribunal accepted these contentions and allowed the appeal, holding that in publishing the lists of registered stallions the Trustees were merely carrying out their duties under the Trust Deed, rather than supplying services to the owners of the stallions. *British European Breeders' Fund Trustees*, [1985] VATTR 12 (VTD 1808).

Promotion of tourism

[7.78] The promotion of tourism was held to constitute a business in *Netherlands Board of Tourism*, **36.498** INPUT TAX, and in *Austrian National Tourist Office*, **36.499** INPUT TAX, but was held not to constitute a business in *Turespaña*, **36.500** INPUT TAX.

Statutory bodies

NOTE

For court decisions concerning whether statutory bodies are carrying on a business, see *National Water Council*, **7.2** above, and *Apple & Pear Development Council*, **22.80** EUROPEAN

COMMUNITY LAW.

Radio Authority

[7.79] The Radio Authority was established by the *Broadcasting Act 1990* to take over the regulation and licensing of independent radio. It reclaimed input tax which it had incurred. The Commissioners issued a ruling that the Authority was not carrying on a business within the meaning of what is now *VATA 1994, s 4(1)*. The Authority appealed, contending that it was carrying on an economic activity within *Article 4(1)* of the *EC Sixth Directive*. The tribunal dismissed the appeal, holding that the Authority was a regulatory body which was not carrying on a business for VAT purposes. It was a body governed by public law, and accordingly *Article 4(5)* of the *Sixth Directive* directed that it was not to be considered as a taxable person. *The Radio Authority*, [1992] VATTR 155 (VTD 7826).

Arts Council

[7.80] The Arts Council was incorporated by Royal Charter in 1946. Its main activity was the distribution of an annual Parliamentary grant. It registered for VAT in 1973. Until 1989 it provided its services free of charge, but from 1989 it began to charge fees, on a sliding scale, to the recipients of grants. In 1990 the Commissioners issued a ruling that the Council's grant-making activities did not constitute a business (so that it was not entitled to reclaim input tax attributable to these activities). The Council appealed, contending that its grant-making activities were economic activities which involved the making of taxable supplies. The tribunal dismissed the appeal, holding that the Council was not making taxable supplies, either to the Department of National Heritage or to the recipients of grants. The Council was not supplying services for consideration, and was not carrying out an economic activity within *Article 4(2)* of the *EC Sixth Directive*. Furthermore, the Council was a body governed by public law, and was acting as a public authority within *Article 4(5)* of the *Directive*. Since there was no rival authority, treating the Council as a non-taxable person did not lead to any distortion of competition. *The Arts Council of Great Britain*, [1994] VATTR 313 (VTD 11991).

Conservators of Ashdown Forest

[7.81] See *Conservators of Ashdown Forest*, 42.7 LOCAL AUTHORITIES AND STATUTORY BODIES.

Educational activities

Charitable school charging fees to pupils

[7.82] See *Leighton Park School*, 15.99 CONSTRUCTION OF BUILDINGS, ETC.

Company providing services to schools

[7.83] A number of independent schools established a company to supervise the finances of the schools. The schools reimbursed the company's expenses. Customs issued a ruling that output tax was payable on the amounts reimbursed. The company appealed, contending that it was not carrying on any business. The tribunal accepted this contention and allowed the appeal. *Allied Schools Agency Ltd*, [1973] VATTR 155 (VTD 36).

Charity providing education for deaf children

[7.84] A charity had been established in the nineteenth century to provide education for deaf children, teaching them British Sign Language. Customs issued a ruling that it was carrying on a business, and was required to register for VAT. The charity appealed, contending that it should not be treated as carrying on a 'business' for VAT purposes. The tribunal reviewed the evidence in detail, accepted this contention and allowed the appeal. The tribunal noted that 60% of the charity's funding came from the Scottish Executive and 35% came from local authorities. The tribunal observed that 'the appellant is unique. There is no competition for the provision of their services nor any likelihood of any such competition. Equally there is no prospect of, or ambition for, financial independence by the appellant.' The tribunal concluded that the charity was 'not predominantly concerned with the making of taxable supplies for a consideration. It is predominantly concerned with providing a service which is required to be provided by the State: that is to say, the provision of education to deaf or partially hearing children and children with communication difficulties.' The charity was 'not a commercial concern'. *Donaldson's College*, EDN/05/12 (VTD 19258).

Charity providing education for children with 'emotional difficulties'

[7.85] A Scottish charity provided 'educational and related care services for children with serious emotional difficulties'. Customs issued a ruling that it was carrying on a business, and was required to account for VAT on its supplies. The charity appealed, contending that it should not be treated as carrying on a 'business' for VAT purposes. The tribunal accepted this contention and allowed the appeal, applying the principles laid down in *Donaldson's College*, 7.84 above, and holding that the services which the company provided were not 'taxable supplies made for a consideration'. *Quarriers (No 2)*, [2008] VATDR 192; (VTD 20670). (*Note.* For another appeal involving the same charity, see **15.97** CONSTRUCTION OF BUILDINGS, ETC.)

Catering by educational charity

[7.86] See *Summer Institute of Linguistics Ltd*, **15.111** CONSTRUCTION OF BUILDINGS, ETC.

Miscellaneous activities

Cases held to constitute a business

Committee formed to organise testimonial football match

[7.87] A committee was formed to organise a testimonial football match, to raise money for the dependants of a former player. The Commissioners issued a ruling that the committee was required to register for VAT. The committee appealed, contending that it was not carrying on a business. The tribunal dismissed the appeal, holding that the committee was deemed to be carrying on a business by virtue of what is now *VATA 1994, s 94(2)(b)*. *The Eric Taylor Testimonial Match Committee*, [1975] VATTR 8 (VTD 139).

Dealing in second-hand cars—whether a business

[7.88] A jeweller also dealt in second-hand cars, but did not account for output tax on his sales of such cars. The Commissioners issued an assessment charging tax on these sales, and he appealed, contending that he dealt in cars as a hobby and not as a business. The tribunal dismissed his appeal, holding that his dealing in cars constituted a business. *RW Adams*, BIR/75/8A (VTD 175).

Motorboat purchased for resale—whether a business

[7.89] See *Cavner*, 36.561 INPUT TAX.

Catering at public house—whether a separate business

[7.90] See *Oldham*, 62.292 SUPPLY, and the cases noted at **62.293** to **62.300** SUPPLY.

Administration of Jewish ecclesiastical court

[7.91] A committee of eight people comprised a Jewish ecclesiastical court, and also issued licences to catering firms, certifying that food had been prepared in accordance with Jewish ecclesiastical law. The Commissioners issued a ruling that the committee was carrying on a business, and was required to be registered for VAT. The tribunal upheld the ruling and dismissed the committee's appeal, applying *Morrison's Academy Boarding Houses Association*, 7.1 above. *Leeds Kashrut Commission & Beth Din Administration Committee*, MAN/77/137 (VTD 465).

Religious association

[7.92] An association which published religious books and magazines, and organised religious seminars, failed to account for output tax on its takings from such seminars. The Commissioners issued an assessment and the association appealed, contending that it was not carrying on a business. The tribunal rejected this contention and dismissed the appeal. *Holy Spirit Association for the Unification of World Christianity*, LON/84/179 (VTD 1777).

Musical entertainment at public house—whether a separate business

[7.93] A publican arranged for an individual (B) to promote music at the public house. He paid B a nightly fee to cover B's expenses and also allowed B to charge for admission and retain such takings. The Commissioners formed the opinion that B was acting as an employee or agent of the publican, and assessed the publican on the admission takings. He appealed, contending that he had entered into the arrangement with B in order to increase his bar takings, and that B was carrying on a separate business of promoting music. The tribunal accepted the publican's evidence and allowed his appeal. *JA Conlon*, LON/85/610 (VTD 2343).

Gaming machines and poolroom at premises used for selling cars

[7.94] The Commissioners discovered that a car dealer was not accounting for output tax on takings from gaming machines and a poolroom located at his premises. They issued an assessment charging tax on such takings. The dealer appealed, contending that the machines and poolroom were operated by his wife and constituted a separate business. The tribunal accepted his evidence and allowed the appeal. *BH Hamilton*, BEL/87/3 (VTD 2460). (*Note.* The Commissioners might now have recourse to a direction under *VATA 1994, Sch 1 para 2*. For cases concerning this provision, see 57.35 *et seq.* REGISTRATION.)

Royal Society for Prevention of Cruelty to Animals

[7.95] In 1990 the Commissioners formed the opinion that the RSPCA, which had been registered for VAT for many years, was not carrying on a business and thus should not be registered. They therefore issued an assessment to recover input tax which the RSPCA had reclaimed from 1988 to 1990. The RSPCA appealed, contending that its activities constituted a business and that the input tax had been correctly reclaimed. The tribunal allowed the RSPCA's appeal. The provision of veterinary services was a business activity, notwithstanding that the charges which the RSPCA levied for such services were treated as voluntary rather than obligatory, and that about 20% of the owners of animals treated by the RSPCA did not pay for such treatment. On the evidence, the RSPCA received consideration in respect of the majority of animals it treated. Applying *Morrison's Academy Boarding Houses Association*, 7.1 above, the fact that the RSPCA was a charity, and that its activities were not carried on for profit, did not prevent its activities from constituting a business. *Royal Society for Prevention of Cruelty to Animals*, [1991] VATTR 407 (VTD 6218).

Breeding of sheep—whether a business

[7.96] A married couple had registered for VAT as breeders of Wiltshire Longhorn sheep, from 24 acres of land near Chippenham. For the period from 1989 to 1992 they received income of less than £800 and incurred expenditure of more than £28,000. The Commissioners formed the opinion that their breeding of sheep was a hobby rather than a business, and sought to deregister them under what is now *VATA 1994, Sch 1 para 13(3)*. The couple appealed, contending that their breeding of sheep constituted a business from which they hoped to make profits in the future. The tribunal allowed their appeal, finding that their breeding of sheep constituted a business rather than a hobby. *Mr & Mrs JC Strachan*, LON/91/2621Y (VTD 9568).

Company formed to promote career of racing driver

[7.97] A company was incorporated with the aim of attracting sponsorship for a young motor racing driver. It registered for VAT. A VAT officer formed the opinion that the company's activities did not constitute a business, and the Commissioners cancelled the company's registration under what is now *VATA 1994, Sch 1 para 13*. The tribunal allowed the company's appeal, holding on the evidence that the company's activities 'were predominantly concerned with the making of taxable supplies to sponsors for a consideration'. Accordingly the company was carrying on a business and was entitled to be registered. *Bird Racing (Management) Ltd*, LON/93/1889A (VTD 11630).

Company operating closed circuit television for District Council

[7.98] A company was incorporated as a non-profit-making organisation, to operate a closed circuit television network for a District Council. It received grants from the Council. In its first VAT return, it claimed a substantial repayment of input tax. The Commissioners initially accepted the claim, but subsequently issued an assessment to recover the tax, on the basis that the company was not carrying on a business. The company appealed. The tribunal allowed the company's appeal, holding that the company was making 'direct supplies to those bodies with whom they had the contractual arrangements to supply surveillance cameras'. Accordingly it was carrying on a business and was entitled to reclaim input tax. *North Lanarkshire CCTV Ltd*, EDN/01/209 (VTD 18031).

Minicab driver—whether a 'taxable person' or an employee

[7.99] An individual (T) had registered for VAT as a computer consultant. However his income from this source 'dried up' when his major client cancelled its contract with him. He did not cancel his VAT registration, and made some small repayment claims. From October 2003 to January 2004 he worked as a minicab driver for a company (M) which provided him with a minicab. In March 2004 he and his wife bought a Renault which they registered as a minicab. He hired a radio from a firm (C) which operated a 'dial-a-taxi' agency to introduce minicab drivers to potential customers. T did not account for VAT on his income from minicab driving. In 2006 Customs issued an assessment covering the periods from November 2003 to April 2006. T appealed, contending that he should be treated as an employee of both M and C (and alternatively that he should be treated as having been in partnership with his wife). The tribunal reviewed the evidence and rejected these contentions, holding that T had been an employee of M from October 2003 to January 2004, but had been self-employed as a minicab driver from March 2004 onwards. He was a 'taxable person' and, because he had registered for VAT, was required to account for output tax on his gross takings from March 2004 onwards. (The tribunal observed that T's income had been below the registration threshold so that he would not have been required to account for VAT if he had applied to cancel his registration.) *MD Talbot*, LON/07/243 (VTD 20665).

Royal Academy of Music

[7.100] See *The Royal Academy of Music*, **55.15** PROTECTED BUILDINGS.

Bowling club

[7.101] See *Hunmanby Bowling Club*, **15.108** CONSTRUCTION OF BUILD-INGS, ETC.

Cases held not to constitute a business

Provision of volunteer blood donors

[7.102] An association was established to enable hospitals to contact suitable volunteer blood donors. In order to defray administrative expenses it charged a 'capitation fee', or 'transfusion fee' to hospitals which required the services of such volunteers. In 1983 the association, thinking that it might be advantageous if it could register voluntarily, approached Customs, who issued a notice of registration. The association was then advised that it would not be in its interests to register for VAT, and it appealed against the Commissioners' decision. The tribunal allowed the association's appeal, finding that the fees were a contribution towards the administrative costs of the service, and holding that this did not amount to the carrying on of a business. *Greater London Red Cross Blood Transfusion Service*, [1983] VATTR 241 (VTD 1495).

Subpostmaster

[7.103] The Commissioners issued a ruling that a subpostmaster, with no other occupation, was carrying on a business and was required to register for VAT. The subpostmaster appealed. The tribunal allowed his appeal, observing that he was treated as an employee for income tax and national insurance purposes and holding that his contract with the Post Office was a contract of service and that he was an employee. *R Rickarby*, [1973] VATTR 186 (VTD 44).

[7.104] Two brothers carried on a retail newsagency and catering business from various premises in Wiltshire. One of the brothers (P) applied to run a sub-post office from premises in Swindon. He was required to pay Post Office Counters Ltd (POCL) £88,560, including VAT of £13,189. The partnership reclaimed input tax on this payment. The Commissioners rejected the claim on the basis that P was an employee of the Post Office and that running a sub-post office did not constitute a business for VAT purposes. The partnership appealed, contending that P had applied to run the sub-post office for the purpose of expanding the partnership retail business. The contract between P and POCL stated that it was a contract for services and that P was an agent rather than an employee. The tribunal dismissed the appeal, holding that, despite the express statement to the contrary in the contract, the contract was a contract of service rather than a contract for services, and that P was an employee of Post Office Counters Ltd rather than an independent contractor. The chairman held that 'the most significant feature' was 'the ability reserved by the contract to POCL to control the subpostmaster in all aspects of his running of the sub-post office' and concluded that 'after reviewing all the contractual materials including the method of appointment', the resulting picture was 'not one of a person carrying on a business on his own account in running this sub-post office but that of a servant'. *H & V Patel (No 1)*, LON/94/2821 (VTD 14956). (*Note.* For another issue in this case, see **36.501** INPUT TAX.)

Catering at public house—whether a separate business

[**7.105**] See *Smith & Smith*, 47.26 PARTNERSHIP; the cases noted at 47.27 PARTNERSHIP, and *Allen*, 62.299 SUPPLY.

Sale of pictures by trust owning historic house

[**7.106**] The Earl of Haddington owned a large estate in Berwickshire. He decided to set up a charitable trust to preserve the house and gardens and to allow the public to have access to them. He gave the house and gardens to the trust, except for a portion which he retained as his private residence. He also gave the trust seventeen pictures to be sold at auction to raise money. The pictures were sold in July and September 1987, and the trustees took over the management of the estate in October 1987. The trustees requested, and obtained, registration for VAT from October 1987 on the grounds that their management of the estate constituted the carrying on of a business. Subsequently Customs sought to register the trustees with effect from July, and thus to charge VAT on the sale of the pictures. The trustees appealed, contending that the sale of the pictures was the realisation of an investment, and that they were not carrying on any business until they took over the management of the estate in October. The tribunal accepted this contention and allowed the appeal. *Trustees of the Mellerstain Trust*, [1989] VATTR 223 (VTD 4256).

Sale of inherited items

[**7.107**] An individual (B) registered for VAT from February 2005 on the basis that he was buying and selling 'collectables', mainly on the internet via 'eBay'. Customs subsequently discovered that he had earned significant income from such sales before the date of registration, and sought to backdate his registration. B appealed, contending that the earlier sales had been of personal items, including many items which his wife had inherited, and did not form part of any business. The tribunal accepted B's evidence and allowed his appeal, observing that 'because of the nature of the way the assets were acquired we consider that the appropriate tax to be levied in the early stages would have been capital gains tax'. *M Brogden*, LON/06/043 (VTD 19827).

Solicitors' Discipline Tribunal

[**7.108**] The Scottish Solicitors' Discipline Tribunal (SSDT) was established in 1933. It applied for registration for VAT and the Commissioners refused to register it on the grounds that it was not carrying on a business. The tribunal upheld the Commissioners' decision. The activities of the SSDT had no element of commerciality or of economic activity. *The Scottish Solicitors' Discipline Tribunal*, [1989] VATTR 138 (VTD 3539).

Activities of clubs, associations, etc

[**7.109**] In some of the cases noted in chapter 13 CLUBS, ASSOCIATIONS AND ORGANISATIONS, it was explicitly held that the club, etc. was not carrying on a business within the meaning of what is now *VATA 1994, s 94(1)*. These include *New Ash Green Village Association Ltd*, **13.11** (association providing amenities for village inhabitants); *Notts Fire Service Messing Club*, **13.12** (fire station canteen); and *British Olympic Association*, **13.13** (UK National Olympic Committee).

Company receiving grant under Housing & Planning Act 1986

[7.110] In 1995 a company was incorporated to help regenerate an urban area. It received a grant from the Secretary of State for the Environment under the *Housing & Planning Act 1986*. In 1998 it made a late claim for input tax in respect of various purchases including a computer. The Commissioners rejected the claim on the grounds that the company was not carrying on a business. The company appealed, contending that it was supplying services to its local Metropolitan Borough Council. The tribunal rejected this contention and dismissed the company's appeal, holding that it was not supplying any services and that the grant which it had received did not represent consideration for any supply. *West Central Halifax Partnership Ltd*, MAN/98/262 (VTD 16570).

Company distributing grants on behalf of Learning and Skills Council

[7.111] A company, limited by guarantee, was incorporated in 1999 to administer grants from the Learning and Skills Council for England, and to distribute the grants to local learning centres. Customs issued a ruling that in distributing the grants, the company was making taxable supplies in the course of a business, and was required to register for VAT. The company appealed, contending that it was providing non-profit-making services to a local community and that these did not amount to a 'business'. The tribunal accepted this contention and allowed the appeal, holding that the company was 'not making any supply of services to the learning centres'. *The Birmingham & Solihull Learning Exchange Ltd*, MAN/04/684 (VTD 19310).

Charitable housing associations

[7.112] See *Cardiff Community Housing Association Ltd*, 15.95 CONSTRUCTION OF BUILDINGS, ETC, and *Riverside Housing Association Ltd*, 15.115 CONSTRUCTION OF BUILDINGS, ETC.

Fishing rights—occasional lettings

[7.113] A company which operated a stud farm acquired fishing rights over part of the River Spey for two weeks in May each year. It reclaimed input tax in respect of this purchase. Customs issued an assessment to recover the tax, considering that the rights had not been purchased for the purpose of any business activity, but for the personal pleasure of the company's controlling director, who was a keen fisherman. The company appealed, contending that it had acquired the rights with the intention of letting them at market rents, and subsequently reselling them at a profit. The rights had been let to friends and relatives of the controlling director, and in one case to a business acquaintance of his. The tribunal dismissed the company's appeal, finding that the company had purchased the fishing rights as an investment and not as a business nor an 'economic activity', so that the input tax was not deductible. *Adstock Ltd*, LON/91/1866A (VTD 10034).

Shooting syndicate

[7.114] HMRC formed the opinion that an individual (H), who was a member of a farming partnership, was making supplies of shooting rights in the course or furtherance of a business. They issued a notice of compulsory registration, and assessments charging VAT. H appealed, contending that he was not carrying on any business, but was merely supplying administrative services to a shooting syndicate which was organised for the enjoyment of its members, rather than with a view to a profit. The tribunal accepted this contention and allowed his appeal, specifically distinguishing *Williams*, **62.151** SUPPLY, where the shooting syndicate had been organised by the landowner. *EG Harrison v HMRC*, [2011] UKFTT 345 (TC), TC01205.

Care of retired police horse

[7.115] A former police officer (C), who owned a stable and land, agreed to care for a retired police horse. He applied for VAT registration so that he could reclaim input tax. The Commissioners rejected the claim on the grounds that he was not making any taxable supplies. The tribunal dismissed C's appeal (while observing that, if he wished to register, he 'might consider' setting up a business of selling the horse's manure). *J Casson*, LON/99/330 (VTD 16535).

Holding company

[7.116] A holding company registered for VAT with effect from November 1987. Subsequently Customs formed the opinion that the company was not carrying on any business, and cancelled its registration. The company appealed, contending that it was carrying on an 'economic activity' of providing management services. The tribunal rejected this contention and dismissed the appeal, holding that the services 'lacked the element of regularity necessary to constitute economic activities'. *Newmir plc*, [1993] VATTR 55 (VTD 10102).

Charitable trust

[7.117] In the case noted at **22.111** EUROPEAN COMMUNITY LAW, the CJEC ruled that a company which acted as the sole trustee of a charitable trust was not carrying on a business, since an activity consisting in the purchase and sale of shares and other securities was not within the definition of an 'economic activity' for the purposes of the *EC Sixth Directive*. The case was remitted to the tribunal for the formal determination of the company's appeal. The company sought to adduce further evidence and argument. The tribunal rejected the company's application and formally dismissed the appeal. *Wellcome Trust Ltd*, [1997] VATDR 1 (VTD 14813).

Company organising 'jobs fairs' for educational institutes

[7.118] A company was incorporated to organise education and jobs fairs for universities, polytechnics and colleges of higher education. It received subscriptions from such institutions, and allowed its subscribers to occupy stands at its fairs free of charge. It reclaimed substantial amounts of input tax. Customs issued assessments to recover the tax, on the basis that the provision of free stand space was not a business activity, so that the company was not entitled to reclaim input tax relating to it. The tribunal upheld the assessments and dismissed the company's appeal, holding that the effect of *VATA 1994, s 5(2)(a)* was that the provision of free stand space was not to be treated as a supply for VAT purposes. *Education & Jobs Fairs Ltd*, MAN/96/1063 (VTD 15231).

Company carrying out refurbishment work for associated company

[7.119] A company (P) registered for VAT in 1997. It agreed to carry out some refurbishment work at a property owned by an associated company (L), which was a member of a group of companies which operated a number of casinos. (Although P and L were associated, P was not a member of L's VAT group.) P reclaimed substantial amounts of input tax relating to the refurbishment. In 1999 the Commissioners issued a ruling that P was not entitled to be registered, as it was not making any taxable supplies. (They also issued assessments to recover input tax which P had reclaimed.) The tribunal dismissed P's appeal against this decision, holding on the evidence that it was not satisfied that P 'has made, or is to make, any taxable supplies'. *Ladbroke (Palace Gate) Property Services Ltd*, LON/99/643 (VTD 16666).

Dealing in shares

[7.120] See *National Society for the Prevention of Cruelty to Children*, **11.49** CHARITIES.

Partnership—investment of surplus funds

[7.121] See *Kuchick Trading*, **36.225** INPUT TAX.

Playgroup

[7.122] See *Newtonbutler Playgroup Ltd*, **15.90** CONSTRUCTION OF BUILDINGS, ETC.

Construction of yacht

[7.123] In January 1995 an individual (H) applied to be registered for VAT, stating on form VAT1 that he had begun a business of constructing yachts. Customs duly registered him and he reclaimed input tax. A VAT officer visited him in August 1996, ascertained that he had only constructed one yacht, and formed the opinion that his activities did not constitute a business. Customs therefore issued an assessment to recover the input tax which H had claimed. The tribunal upheld the assessment and dismissed H's appeal, holding on the evidence that his construction of a single yacht was 'an isolated transaction, and one which did not amount to a recognisable and identifiable activity'. Furthermore, H 'did not conduct his activities in a regular manner on sound and recognised business principles: he did not maintain proper books and records, engaged casual labour, and seemingly made no effort to advertise or otherwise publicise his services as a boatbuilder'. *D Hetherington*, LON/96/1909 (VTD 15647).

VATA 1994, s 94(4)—whether office accepted in the course of business

[7.124] See *Gardner*, **62.163** SUPPLY, and *Oglethorpe Sturton & Gillibrand*, **62.164** SUPPLY.

8

Business Entertainment

The cases in this chapter are arranged under the following headings.

Cases held to constitute 'business entertainment'	8.1
Cases where the input tax was apportioned	8.28
Cases held not to constitute 'business entertainment'	8.35

NOTE

The effect of *Input Tax Order 1992 (SI 1992/3222), Article 5*, is that tax is not deductible on goods or services used for the purposes of 'business entertainment'.

Cases held to constitute 'business entertainment'

Expenditure in restaurants

[8.1] A surveyor reclaimed input tax in respect of expenditure on lunches in restaurants for himself and clients. Customs issued an assessment to recover the tax and the tribunal dismissed his appeal. *WB Wyatt*, CAR/76/65 (VTD 263).

[8.2] Similar decisions were reached in *Mrs S Woolf (t/a Sally Woolf Interiors)*, LON/92/2713A (VTD 10415), and in *Richards*, **36.189** INPUT TAX.

Provision of food and accommodation for trainee agents

[8.3] Two corporations sold goods through a pyramid of distributors, who were agents rather than employees. They held regular courses for the distributors, and provided food and accommodation. They reclaimed input tax on this expenditure. The Commissioners issued an assessment to recover the tax on the basis that the expenditure constituted 'business entertainment'. The QB upheld the decision and the CA dismissed the corporations' appeals, holding that the provision of free food and accommodation was within the definition of 'entertainment', so that the input tax was not deductible. *C & E Commrs v Shaklee International and Another*, CA [1981] STC 776.

[8.4] The decision in *Shaklee International*, 8.3 above, was applied in the similar cases *of Sealine International Ltd*, MAN/91/1257 (VTD 10061); *Able Foods Ltd*, LON/92/2950A (VTD 11317); *Siberian Trading Co Ltd*, EDN/96/4 (VTD 14229) and *Network International Group Ltd*, MAN/98/782 (VTD 16554).

[8.5] A similar decision, also applying *Shaklee International*, 8.3 above, was reached in a subsequent case where the tribunal specifically held that the

---

recipients of the entertainment were agents rather than employees, applying *dicta* of Cooke J in *Market Investigations Ltd v Minister of Social Security*, QB [1968] 3 All ER 732.

Food provided at business discussion meetings

[8.6] A company carried on the business of market research for manufacturers of medical goods and equipment. It arranged discussion meetings, held at hotels and attended by about ten people. It provided these people with food and drink, and reclaimed the input tax on this expenditure. Customs issued an assessment to recover the tax and the tribunal dismissed the company's appeal. *Medicare Research Ltd*, LON/80/385 (VTD 1045).

Provision of meals by cricket club for visiting teams

[8.7] A county cricket club provided lunch and tea for visiting teams and officials, including umpires and scorers, as required by the County Cricket Club Board. It engaged an outside caterer for this purpose, and reclaimed input tax on the amounts it paid to the caterer. Customs issued an assessment to recover the tax, and the tribunal dismissed the club's appeal, holding that the expenditure was within the definition of 'business entertainment'. *Lancashire County Cricket Club*, MAN/81/27 (VTD 1244).

Subscription for theatre tickets

[8.8] A club was formed to assist in financing the reconstruction of a theatre. In return for their subscriptions, members were guaranteed specified seats for an evening of their choice for each weekly performance for four years. A company which purchased a subscription to the club reclaimed input tax on this expenditure. Customs issued an assessment to recover the tax, considering that the expenditure constituted 'business entertainment'. The tribunal upheld the assessment and dismissed the company's appeal. *William Matthew Mechanical Services Ltd*, [1982] VATTR 63 (VTD 1210).

[8.9] A similar decision was reached in *Wolf Management Services Ltd*, MAN/82/7 (VTD 1270).

Launching party for new premises

[8.10] A company (W) arranged a lunch at a local hotel to mark the opening of new premises. The lunch was attended by 25 senior employees and about 130 actual or potential customers or suppliers. W reclaimed input tax on the cost of the lunch. Customs issued an assessment to recover the tax and the tribunal dismissed W's appeal, holding that the expenditure was on 'business entertainment'. The proportion of the expenditure which was attributable to the company's employees was not deductible, because its provision was 'incidental to its provision for others', within what is now *Input Tax Order, Article 5(3)*. *Wilsons Transport Ltd*, MAN/83/68 (VTD 1468).

[8.11] The Fraserburgh Harbour Commissioners opened a new inner harbour, which was significantly deeper than the previous inner harbour, and held a party to publicise its opening. The party was attended by the Prince of Wales, local dignitaries, and potential users of the harbour. Free food and drink was provided. The tribunal held that the input tax relating to this was not deductible, since it was within the definition of 'business entertainment'. *Fraserburgh Harbour Commissioners*, EDN/98/9 (VTD 15797).

Launching party for new cruise ship

[8.12] A company (C) reclaimed input tax of more than £111,000 in respect of a launch party for a new cruise ship. HMRC rejected the claim on the basis that this constituted 'business entertainment'. C appealed, contending that the party should be treated as a product demonstration, or as advertising services. The tribunal rejected these contentions and dismissed the appeal. Judge Khan observed that 'the fact that an event can be described as a product demonstration does not prevent it being treated as business entertainment since the definition of business entertainment includes "hospitality of any kind", which makes the definition very wide'. *CI Cruises International SA v HMRC*, [2011] UKFTT 761 (TC), TC01598.

Motor racing

[8.13] A company (P) carried on the business of manufacturing and selling sunbeds. Its principal director, who had been a professional racing driver, raced cars bearing the name of the company's product. Potential customers were invited to the pits and provided with entertainment. P reclaimed input tax on this expenditure. Customs issued an assessment to recover the tax. The tribunal dismissed P's appeal, holding that the expenditure constituted 'business entertainment'. *Paine Leisure Products Ltd*, LON/84/380 (VTD 1836).

Powerboat racing

[8.14] See *Denby*, 36.405 INPUT TAX.

Horse racing

[8.15] See *British Car Auctions Ltd*, 36.367 INPUT TAX, and *Dyer*, 36.379 INPUT TAX.

Hospitality at golf championship

[8.16] A partnership entertained prospective clients at the British Open Golf Championship, and reclaimed input tax on the expenditure. Customs issued an assessment to recover the tax, considering that the hospitality was within the definition of 'business entertainment'. The tribunal dismissed the partnership's appeal. *PR Promotions*, MAN/86/15 (VTD 2122).

[8.17] A similar decision was reached in *Cheshire Securities Ltd*, MAN/87/57 (VTD 3240).

Hospitality suite at sports ground

[8.18] A company leased a 'hospitality box' at a rugby league ground and reclaimed input tax on this expenditure. The Commissioners issued an assessment to recover half of the tax. The tribunal dismissed the company's appeal. (The tribunal chairman commented that, since half the input tax had been allowed, 'the assessments are unduly favourable to the appellant'.) *RW Cockroft & Co (Travel) Ltd*, MAN/93/850 (VTD 11800).

[8.19] A professional football club operated a scheme limited to 40 subscribers, who were allocated particular seats at the ground and were provided with lunch in a special suite. A company (S) which operated a property management business purchased two of the 40 subscriptions and reclaimed input tax on their cost. Customs issued an assessment to recover the tax, on the grounds that it related to a supply of business entertainment. The tribunal dismissed S's appeal, noting that S's business activities took place at a significant distance from the football ground, and concluding that 'if there was an element of advertising, as a business use, it must be considered to have been essentially fortuitous, and not significant enough to be measurable'. Furthermore, since one of the subscriptions had been used to entertain S's financial advisor, who was not an employee, the entertainment could not be treated as being outside the definition of 'business entertainment' in *Input Tax Order, Article 5(3)*. The chairman observed that 'given the nature and very small number of staff in (this) case, and the prominent role of (the financial advisor), it is impossible to say that the paramount purpose was provision for the employees and/or directors'. *Sundeck plc*, LON/95/1297A (VTD 14051).

Cabaret evenings organised by brewery

[8.20] A brewery company organised cabaret evenings at its headquarters, and gave free admission to its customers. The company reclaimed input tax on the cost of the cabaret evenings, and the Commissioners issued an assessment to recover the tax, considering that they constituted 'business entertainment'. The tribunal dismissed the company's appeal. *Northern Clubs Federation Brewery Ltd*, MAN/91/1017 (VTD 8881).

Free drinks provided to restaurant customers

[8.21] A VAT officer discovered that the gross profit rate of a restaurant was unusually low. The restaurant proprietors explained that they provided free drinks to some customers. The Commissioners issued an assessment to recover input tax attributable to such drinks, on the basis that their provision constituted 'business entertainment'. The tribunal upheld the assessment and dismissed the proprietors' appeal. *Polash Tandoori Restaurant*, LON/92/1998A (VTD 10903).

Estate agents reclaiming input tax on wine

[8.22] A firm which carried on business as estate agents stayed open late on some evenings in December, and provided wine to people who visited its offices. It also held an anniversary celebration, to which it invited local dignitaries, and provided wine to those attending. The firm reclaimed input tax on the cost of the wine, and Customs issued an assessment to recover the tax. The tribunal dismissed the firm's appeal, holding that the provision of the wine constituted 'business entertainment'. *White & Sons*, LON/93/1770 (VTD 11680).

Cabaret at conference for members of accountancy partnership

[8.23] A large accountancy partnership organised a conference which was attended by around 400 partners. The conference included a cabaret. The partnership reclaimed input tax on the whole cost of the conference, including the cabaret. The Commissioners issued an assessment to recover the tax relating to the cabaret. The partnership appealed, contending that the cabaret should be treated as an integral part of the conference. The tribunal rejected this contention and dismissed the appeal, holding on the evidence that the cabaret was 'pure entertainment' and that the expenditure on the cabaret had not been incurred for the purpose of the partnership's business. *Ernst & Young*, [1997] VATDR 183 (VTD 15100). (*Notes*. (1) For another issue in this case, see **8.43** below. (2) For the Commissioners' practice following this decision, see Business Brief 25/97, issued on 10 November 1997.)

Food and drink provided at exhibitions

[8.24] A company organised a number of exhibitions. In conjunction with some of the exhibitions it staged receptions, at which food and drinks were provided. It reclaimed input tax on this expenditure. The Commissioners issued an assessment to recover the tax, on the basis that the expenditure constituted 'business entertainment'. The tribunal upheld the assessment and dismissed the company's appeal. *Miller Freeman Worldwide plc*, LON/94/3345 (VTD 15439).

[8.25] A similar decision was reached in a subsequent case where a company organised exhibitions at which lunches were provided for customers who registered in advance. The tribunal held that the company could not reclaim input tax on the cost of the lunches. *Evensis Ltd*, MAN/00/1088 (VTD 17218).

Party for premiere of film

[8.26] A company agreed to promote a film in the UK, in exchange for a share in the film's profits. It hosted a party for the UK premiere of the film, and reclaimed input tax on the party. Customs rejected the claim on the basis that the expenditure was 'business entertainment'. The tribunal dismissed the company's appeal against this decision, applying *Shaklee International*, **8.3** above, and distinguishing *Kilroy Television Company Ltd*, **8.47** below. *The Entertainment Group of Companies Ltd*, [2000] VATDR 447 (VTD 16639).

Anniversary gala dinner

[8.27] A company which carried on business as a development agency reclaimed input tax on a gala dinner to celebrate its tenth anniversary. The Commissioners issued an assessment to recover the tax, on the basis that it was within the definition of 'business entertainment'. The tribunal upheld the assessment and dismissed the company's appeal. *North London Business Development Agency Ltd*, LON/99/1096 (VTD 17092).

Cases where the input tax was apportioned

Premises partly used for business entertainment

[8.28] A company which produced and marketed Scotch whisky reclaimed input tax relating to premises which were primarily used for business administration but were partly used as a venue for business entertainment. The Commissioners issued an assessment to recover the tax, contending that, since the premises were partly used for business entertainment, the effect of *Input Tax Order, Article 5(1)* was that the tax could not be apportioned and that none of the tax was deductible. The tribunal rejected this contention and allowed the company's appeal, holding on the evidence that 70% of the tax was deductible. *MacDonald & Muir Ltd*, EDN/92/208 (VTD 10947).

Elizabethan banquets

[8.29] A partnership carried on the business of providing Elizabethan banquets. Each banquet was attended by about 240 people. If a particular banquet failed to attract the expected number of customers, the partnership invited its employees to attend free of charge, to maintain the expected atmosphere. Most of the customers were driven to the banquet in coaches. At the banquets the customers were entertained by actors in Elizabethan costume. The partnership reclaimed input tax on the banquets. The Commissioners issued an assessment to recover the tax attributable to the food provided to the coach drivers, to the partnership's employees who attended free of charge, and to the actors. The tribunal held that the tax attributable to the food provided to the coach drivers and the employees was 'business entertainment' and was not deductible. (However, the food and drink consumed by the actors while performing was not 'business entertainment', so that the tax attributable to this was deductible.) *Elizabethan Banquets*, LON/84/455 (VTD 1795).

Hospitality chalets at air shows

[8.30] A company manufactured complex electronic systems, which it displayed and sold at air shows. At these shows it had exhibition stands and 'hospitality chalets'. It reclaimed input tax in respect of the hospitality chalets, and the Commissioners issued an assessment to recover this tax, considering that the expenditure in question was for the purpose of business entertainment. The company appealed, contending that the chalets were essential as a place in which to hold confidential discussions with potential purchasers. The CA held that the tax should be apportioned, and specifically disapproved the QB decision in *C & E Commrs v Plant & Repair Services (South Wales) Ltd*, QB [1994] STC 232. Millett LJ held that what is now *Article 5* of the *Input Tax Order* should be construed as permitting apportionment in the case of supplies used partly for business entertainment and partly for other business purposes. The exclusion of all credit for input tax in such a case would be a contravention of *Article 17* of the *EC Sixth Directive*. *Thorn EMI plc v C & E Commrs*, CA [1995] STC 674.

'Hospitality box' at football ground

[8.31] A boxing promoter (W) reclaimed input tax on the hire of a 'hospitality box' at a major football ground. Customs agreed that 25% of the tax was deductible as being attributable to the right to advertise W's business. However, they issued an assessment to recover the remainder of the tax, on the basis that W was using the box for 'business entertainment'. The tribunal upheld the assessment and dismissed W's appeal. *F Warren (t/a Sports Network Europe)*, LON/04/1250 (VTD 19213).

Provision of beer by concert promoter

[8.32] The promoter of a 'rock music' concert tour, comprising five concerts, advertised tickets at £10 each with the incentive of free beer for those attending. The tour was not a success, and only 370 tickets in total were sold for the five concerts. The promoter reclaimed input tax on the purchase of 9,600 cans of beer and lager. The Commissioners issued an assessment to recover the tax, considering that the provision of free beer and lager at concerts was within the definition of 'business entertainment', and that it was in any event unlikely that 370 customers would have drunk 9,600 cans between them. The promoter appealed, contending that the beer and lager had been provided to customers, and to his 16 employees, for the purpose of the business, and that the input tax should be treated as deductible. The tribunal allowed the appeal in part, finding that the price paid by each customer 'entitled the customer to listen to three rock bands in concert, and to drink beer and lager without paying extra for such drink'. Since the customers had paid for their tickets, the beer and lager was not within the definition of 'business entertainment', so that the input tax was deductible in principle, applying *The City of Chicago Board of Trade*, 8.41 below. However, the tribunal also found that not all of the beer purchased could have been drunk by customers. The tribunal chairman (Mr Vellins) observed that 'not all the customers who attended the rock concerts would have been male' and expressed the view that 'a female attending a rock concert would not be likely to consume the same amount of drink of beer and lager as a male' and 'it would not be credible to envisage that a female would drink some 13 cans of beer or lager'. The tribunal found on the balance of probabilities that the customers had consumed an average of eight cans each, making a total of 2,960 cans. With regard to the 16 employees, the tribunal held that the input tax was deductible in principle, but found that each employee would have consumed an average of eight cans per concert for each of the five concerts, making a total of 640 cans. Accordingly the tribunal held that the input tax on 3,600 cans was deductible but that the tax on the remaining 6,000 cans was not deductible. *D Lumby*, MAN/94/593 (VTD 12972).

Motor distributor

[8.33] A company (BMW) carried on business as an importer and distributor of motorcars and motorcycles. It sold such vehicles to independent dealers, who in turn sold them to members of the public. In the course of its promotional activities it arranged 'track days', at which dealers and potential customers could test-drive its cars. Dealers were required to make payments ranging from £25 to £85 per person attending. (For 1994, the amount reimbursed by the dealers represented 29% of BMW's total costs in arranging the 'track days'.) BMW also arranged golfing days and curling days, and reclaimed input tax on the total costs of these activities. The Commissioners issued assessments on the basis that BMW could only recover the proportion of the input tax which equated to the proportion of the costs which was reimbursed by the dealers (i.e. 29% of the input tax on the 'track days', and 17% of the input tax on the 'curling days'), but that the remainder of the input tax was not recoverable, since it was attributable to supplies of business entertainment. BMW appealed, contending that it was not making any supply of hospitality, since it was making supplies to the dealers and it was those dealers who were supplying hospitality to their customers. The tribunal rejected this contention and upheld the assessments in principle (subject to adjustment of the figures). The tribunal observed that there were 'two quite distinct elements in the track days'. Expenditure on demonstrating BMW's products, such as test drives and brake demonstrations, was not within the definition of 'business entertainment'. However, BMW had also incurred substantial expenditure on 'hospitality'. This hospitality was supplied by BMW rather than by the dealers and only the percentage of the relevant input tax which was attributable to the supplies to the dealers was recoverable. The percentage which was attributable to the supplies to the potential customers was 'business entertainment' and was not recoverable. The QB upheld the tribunal decision. On the evidence, the supply of facilities to the customers was distinguishable from the transaction between BMW and the dealers. There was a gratuitous provision of services by BMW to the customers, which was within the definition of 'business entertainment'. *BMW (GB) Ltd v C & E Commrs*, QB [1997] STC 824.

Dinner dance for employees of accountancy partnership

[8.34] An accountancy partnership reclaimed input tax in respect of dinner dances which it organised for its employees. Each employee was entitled to bring one guest. The Commissioners issued an assessment to recover 45% of the tax, considering that the proportion of the expenditure which was attributable to the employees' guests constituted 'business entertainment'. The tribunal upheld the assessment and dismissed the partnership's appeal. The decision in *KPMG Peat Marwick McLintock*, 8.42 below, was disapproved and not followed, on the basis that in that case both parties had accepted in argument that the tax could not be apportioned, so that it was either wholly allowable or wholly disallowable, whereas in the subsequent case of *Thorn EMI plc*, **8.30** above, the CA had held that *Article 5* of the *Input Tax Order* should be construed as permitting apportionment in the case of supplies used partly for business entertainment and partly for other purposes. The tribunal chairman held that the tribunal hearing the previous case noted at **8.42** below had erred in drawing a distinction between the use of goods and services for business reasons and for social reasons, and had erred in applying a test of 'predominance or paramount purpose'. The chairman observed that there was nothing in the *Input Tax Order* 'which stated or implied that the provision of entertainment for non-employees was to be treated as not being business entertainment where its provision was incidental to the provision of entertainment for employees, in contrast to the specific provision made in the converse case'. Accordingly, the partnership was only entitled to credit for the tax attributable to the entertainment of its employees as distinct from its employees' guests. *KPMG (No 2)*, [1997] VATDR 192 (VTD 14962). (*Notes.* (1) For the Commissioners' practice following this decision, see Business Brief 25/97, issued on 10 November 1997. (2) The decision here was distinguished in *Ernst & Young*, **8.43** below, where employees were required to pay £15 towards the cost of their guests' attendance at a Christmas party, whereas the employees here had not been required to make any payment towards the cost.)

Cases held not to constitute 'business entertainment'

Hotel expenses of visiting football club met by host club

[8.35] A Scottish football club (Celtic) took part in the European Cup organised by the Union of European Football Associations, and played teams from Romania and Hungary in successive rounds. Two games were played in each round on a 'home' and 'away' basis, and the rules provided that the home club was to pay the hotel expenses of the visiting club. Celtic reclaimed input tax in respect of the hotel accommodation which it provided in Glasgow for the Romanian and Hungarian teams. The Commissioners issued an assessment to recover the tax, considering that the expenditure constituted 'business entertainment'. Celtic appealed. The CS allowed Celtic's appeal, holding that 'entertainment' should be construed as meaning hospitality free to the recipient. Because of the reciprocal obligations under the competition rules, what the visiting teams enjoyed at Celtic's expenses was not free to them, since they were required to meet Celtic's hotel expenses for the other matches in the round. There was, therefore, no provision of 'business entertainment' within what is now *Input Tax Order, Article 5. Celtic Football & Athletic Club Ltd v C & E Commrs*, CS [1983] STC 470.

[8.36] The decision in *Celtic Football & Athletic Club Ltd*, **8.35** above, was applied in a subsequent case where the Football Association arranged and paid for hotel accommodation for visiting teams and reclaimed the input tax thereon. The tribunal allowed the Association's appeal against an assessment to recover the tax, holding that the provision of the accommodation did not constitute business entertainment. The hospitality provided by the Association was enforced and contractual, and there was a reciprocal element because the Association's teams had in previous years received such accommodation when playing abroad. *Football Association Ltd*, [1985] VATTR 106 (VTD 1860). (*Note.* For another issue in this case, see **62.284** SUPPLY.)

Hotel expenses of tennis players

[8.37] See *Northern Lawn Tennis Club*, **36.16** INPUT TAX.

Refreshments at conferences

[8.38] A company (W) organised conferences on financial issues. The cost of some of these conferences was met by sponsors (such as banks or other financial institutions), who were entitled to nominate up to 120 delegates (usually customers or potential customers) who could attend the conferences free of charge. Meals and refreshments were provided at the conferences, which were held at hotels. W reclaimed input tax on the cost of the meals and refreshments. The Commissioners issued an assessment to recover the proportion of the tax which related to the delegates of the sponsors, considering that the provision of meals and refreshments to these delegates was within the definition of 'business entertainment'. The tribunal allowed W's appeal, holding on the evidence that the relevant entertainment was supplied to the delegates by the sponsors, rather than by W. Since W was not the person providing business entertainment, it was entitled to reclaim input tax on the supplies which it received from the hotels, although the sponsors would not be entitled to reclaim input tax on the supplies of meals and refreshments which they received from W. *Webster Communications International Ltd*, [1997] VATDR 173 (VTD 14753). (*Note.* For a subsequent case in which this decision was distinguished, see *Evensis Ltd*, **8.25** above.)

Pharmaceutical company—food provided to doctors

[8.39] A company (Q) promoted pharmaceutical products for pharmaceutical companies. It arranged presentations to doctors at lunchtimes, at which it provided meals or refreshments. Q reclaimed input tax on the cost of these presentations. The Commissioners rejected the claim, and Q appealed, contending that the refreshments were actually supplied by the pharmaceutical companies whose goods it was promoting. The tribunal accepted this contention and allowed the appeal, applying *Webster Communications International Ltd*, **8.38** above, and distinguishing *Evensis Ltd*, **8.25** above. The tribunal observed that the contracts between Q and the pharmaceutical companies provided for the reimbursement of refreshments and held that although Q was not acting as an agent in law, it was providing refreshments on behalf of the pharmaceutical companies. *Quintiles (Scotland) Ltd*, LON/02/762 (VTD 18790).

Theatre tickets supplied to potential customers

[8.40] A company was incorporated to market the works of a well-known playwright. It supplied theatre tickets to people who might wish to see plays written by the playwright, with a view to negotiating performance rights. It reclaimed input tax on the cost of these tickets. The Commissioners issued an assessment to recover the tax, considering that the supply of the tickets constituted the provision of 'business entertainment'. The tribunal allowed the company's appeal. Generally, the provision of theatre tickets would fall within the definition of 'business entertaining'. However, in the case under appeal, the tickets were supplied in the hope that the customers to whom they were supplied would be interested in producing a film or television version of the playwright's work. They were akin to 'an industrial product buyer visiting another user of the product at the instigation of the manufacturer', and no element of hospitality or entertainment was involved. *WR Ltd*, MAN/91/116 (VTD 6968).

Conference receptions

[8.41] An association (CBOT) was established under USA law by members of the Chicago futures and options market, with the object of promoting the market. It was a member of the Futures Industry Association (FIA), which was based in the USA and which organised annual conferences in London. CBOT registered for VAT in the UK in accordance with the provisions of what is now *VATA 1994, Sch 1 para 10*. It sponsored a cocktail party and a champagne reception at the 1989 and 1990 London conferences of the FIA, and reclaimed input tax on this expenditure. The Commissioners issued an assessment to recover the tax, considering that—with the exception of the part attributable to the CBOT's own staff—it was not deductible by virtue of what is now *Input Tax Order 1992, Article 5*. The CBOT appealed, contending that the expenditure was not within the definition of 'business entertainment' since the delegates had paid to attend the conference. The tribunal accepted this contention and allowed the appeal, holding that payment was 'incompatible with the concept of entertainment or hospitality'. Since the delegates had paid to attend the conference, it followed that what they received was not 'entertainment or hospitality'. *The City of Chicago Board of Trade*, LON/92/766Y (VTD 9114).

Staff entertainment

[8.42] An accountancy partnership reclaimed input tax in respect of a dinner dance which it organised for its employees. Each employee was entitled to bring one guest. The Commissioners issued an assessment to recover the tax, considering that the function constituted 'business entertainment' and that its provision for the employees was 'incidental to its provision for others'. The tribunal allowed the partnership's appeal, finding that the attendance of the employees' guests was incidental and ancillary to the attendance of the employees themselves, and holding that this was not within the definition of 'business entertainment'. *KPMG Peat Marwick McLintock*, [1993] VATTR 118 (VTD 10135). (*Notes.* (1) For the Commissioners' practice following this

decision, see Business Brief 21/95, issued on 8 October 1995. (2) The decision
here was disapproved by a subsequent tribunal in another case involving the
same partnership—see **8.34** above—on the basis that both parties had
accepted in argument that the tax could not be apportioned, so that it was
either wholly allowable or wholly disallowable, whereas in the subsequent
case of *Thorn EMI plc*, **8.30** above, the CA had held that *Article 5* of the *Input
Tax Order* should be construed as permitting apportionment in the case of
supplies used partly for business entertainment and partly for other purposes.
The chairman in the case noted at **8.34** above observed that there was nothing
in the *Input Tax Order* 'which stated or implied that the provision of
entertainment for non-employees was to be treated as not being business
entertainment where its provision was incidental to the provision of entertainment for employees, in contrast to the specific provision made in the converse
case', and held that the tribunal hearing the case noted here had erred in
drawing a distinction between the use of goods and services for business
reasons and for social reasons, and had erred in applying a test of 'predominance or paramount purpose'.)

[8.43] An accountancy partnership reclaimed input tax in respect of a
Christmas party and a dinner dance which it organised for its employees. For
the Christmas party, each employee was required to pay £10 towards the cost,
and was entitled to bring one guest to the Christmas party but was required to
pay a further £15. (No guests attended the dinner dance, which took place
after a conference attended by partners and employees.) With regard to the
Christmas party, the Commissioners issued an assessment to recover the tax on
the amount by which the cost of the party exceeded the payments made by the
employees. With regard to the dinner dance, the Commissioners issued an
assessment to recover the whole of the tax attributable to the cost of the disco
and to the cost of alcoholic drinks which were served before and after the meal,
and 50% of the tax attributable to the cost of the dinner. The partnership
appealed, contending that its purpose in incurring the expenditure was to
reward its staff, so that the expenditure had been incurred for the purpose of
its business. The tribunal accepted this contention and allowed the appeal. The
tribunal specifically disapproved the Commissioners' practice, laid down in
Leaflet 700/55/93, of allowing only 50% of input tax attributable to entertainment of employees. With regard to the guests of the employees, the
tribunal distinguished *KPMG (No 2)*, **8.34** above, on the grounds that in that
case no charge had been made. Applying *dicta* of Keene J in *BMW (GB) Ltd*,
8.33 above, 'the crucial characteristic of "entertainment" within the phrase
"business entertainment" is that it is provided to a person or persons who
enjoy it free of charge'. Although the charge of £15 was considerably less than
the cost of the party, 'it was not so small that one can say that the meal was
effectively supplied free of charge'. The tribunal held that the expenditure was
not within *VATA 1994, s 84(4)*, since that provision had to be read in the light
of *Article 17(6)* of the *EC Sixth Directive*. Alternatively, the tribunal considered that even if the expenditure were deemed to be within *s 84(4)*, the appeal
would still be successful on the grounds that 'the Commissioners were
unreasonable in disallowing the expenditure because no reasonable body
of Commissioners understanding the law as we have found it to be could
consider that the expenditure was non-business'. *Ernst & Young*, [1997]

VATDR 183 (VTD 15100). (*Notes.* (1) For another issue in this case, see **8.23** above. (2) For the Commissioners' practice following this decision, see Business Brief 25/97, issued on 10 November 1997.)

[8.44] The decision in *Ernst & Young*, **8.43** above, was applied in the similar subsequent case of *Morrison Bowmore Distillers Ltd v HMRC*, [2010] UKFTT 394 (TC), TC00676.

Car manufacturer providing entertainment for sales staff of dealers

[8.45] See *Peugeot-Citroen Automobiles Ltd*, **62.187** SUPPLY.

Debentures providing seats at tennis tournament

[8.46] A company which manufactured sports equipment purchased ten debentures issued by the All England Lawn Tennis Club, entitling it to a total of 130 seats at the annual Wimbledon tennis tournament. It reclaimed input tax on the purchase. The Commissioners issued an assessment to recover the tax, considering that the expenditure had been incurred for the purpose of business entertainment. The company appealed, contending that the expenditure had been incurred for the purpose of promoting its products, and that the business entertainment was incidental and subsidiary. The tribunal allowed the appeal in part, holding on the evidence that 50 of the seats had been purchased for entertainment, so that the input tax relating to them was not deductible, but that 80 of the seats had been purchased for employees and their relatives, so that the input tax relating to those seats was deductible. *BTR Industries Ltd*, MAN/90/913 (VTD 11828).

Buffet meal for participants in television programme

[8.47] A company which produced television programmes provided modest buffet meals, costing less than £10 per head, for people who participated in the programmes. It reclaimed input tax on the cost of the meals. The Commissioners issued assessments to recover the tax, considering that the expenditure was within the definition of 'business entertainment', and the company appealed. The tribunal allowed the company's appeal, finding that the company had placed itself under a legal obligation to provide the meals. The QB upheld this decision as one of fact. The case was 'on the borderline', but on the evidence, the tribunal had been entitled to find that the meals did not constitute 'business entertainment'. *C & E Commrs v The Kilroy Television Company Ltd*, QB [1997] STC 901.

Market research company—product trials for alcoholic beverages

[8.48] A market research company organised 'product trials' for brewery companies. At the trials, members of the public were asked to consume a number of alcoholic beverages and to complete questionnaires on them. They were also provided with sandwiches or bread and cheese, and with a taxi journey home. The company reclaimed input tax on the cost of the 'product trials'. The Commissioners issued an assessment to recover the tax relating to the food, considering that this expenditure was within the definition of 'business entertainment'. The tribunal allowed the company's appeal. The Commissioners had accepted that the provision of the alcoholic beverages was not 'business entertainment'. On the evidence, the tribunal held that 'the provision of the simple food was a necessary part of the provision of the drinks, bearing in mind that the drinks were alcoholic, that the participants would not have eaten for some time before the product trial took place, and also bearing in mind the very simple quality of the food provided'. Accordingly, the provision of the food was 'a necessary part of the provision of the drinks'. *DPA (Market Research) Ltd*, LON/95/2837 (VTD 14751).

9

Capital Goods Scheme

The cases in this chapter are arranged under the following headings.

EC legislation   9.1
UK legislation   9.3

EC Legislation

Article 17(7) of EC Sixth Directive—definition of 'capital goods'

[9.1] See *Verbond van Nederlandse Ondernemingen v Inspecteur der Invoerrechten en Accijnzen*, **22.432** EUROPEAN COMMUNITY LAW.

Article 20(2) of EC Sixth Directive—adjustments of input tax

[9.2] See *Lennartz v Finanzamt München III*, **22.456** EUROPEAN COMMUNITY LAW.

UK Legislation

Land and buildings—whether a 'capital item'

[9.3] In 1994 a doctor transferred a surgery to a company which she controlled, for consideration of £250,000. The company subsequently leased the surgery back to the doctor. The Commissioners issued a ruling that the surgery was a 'capital item', within the capital goods scheme. The company appealed, contending that the surgery included some chattels, and therefore the building should be treated as having been valued at less than £250,000, and therefore below the threshold set out in *VAT Regulations (SI 1995/2518), reg 113(b)*. The tribunal rejected this contention and dismissed the company's appeal, finding that 'the chattels were not, on the face of the documentation, included in the sale'. *The Village Surgery Ltd*, MAN/02/0364 (VTD 17939).

[9.4] See also *East Kent Medical Services Ltd*, **6.8** BUILDINGS AND LAND; *Shurgard Storage Centres UK Ltd*, **6.11** BUILDINGS AND LAND; *Trustees for R & R Pension Fund*, **6.44** BUILDINGS AND LAND, and *Centralan Property Ltd*, **9.9** below.

Interaction with partial exemption provisions

[9.5] A company (W) owned a golf club. The club and the course were operated by associated companies, to which W made taxable supplies of management services. W arranged for work on extending its premises. This work fell within the provisions of *VAT Regulations 1995, regs 112–116* (the 'capital goods' scheme). W reclaimed input tax on the work. The Commissioners issued an assessment for the period ending 31 March 2000, on the basis that W was partly exempt for that year, and that input tax incurred in that year was partly attributable to W's exempt supplies. W appealed, contending that because the building work fell within *VAT Regulations 1995, regs 112–116*, it would be unfair to also treat it as falling within the partial exemption provisions. The tribunal rejected this contention and dismissed the appeal, accepting the Commissioners' contention that 'it is inevitable that there should be an adjustment both under the capital goods scheme and under the partial exemption rules', and observing that '*Part XV of the VAT Regulations* cannot be read apart from *Part XIV*'. *Witney Golf Club*, [2002] VATDR 397 (VTD 17706).

[9.6] A company (T), which carried on a business repairing aircraft engines, purchased the lease of a property (comprising four large aircraft hangars) in June 2004. The vendor charged VAT of £332,500, which T reclaimed as input tax. T used one of the hangars itself; two of the other hangars were used by associated companies; and the fourth hangar was used by all four companies. In October 2006 T transferred the property to an associated company. Although T had reclaimed input tax on its acquisition of the property, it had not opted to tax the property, and treated its disposal as an exempt supply. In 2008 HMRC issued an assessment charging tax of £232,750, on the basis that the disposal fell within the capital goods scheme. T appealed, accepting that it should not have reclaimed input tax on its initial acquisition, but contending that the disposal was outside the scope of the capital goods scheme, since there had been no change in the intended use of the property. The tribunal accepted this contention and allowed the appeal. Judge Radford found that, despite its initial reclaim of input tax, T had never intended to make taxable supplies of the property and had always intended to make exempt supplies to associated companies. The initial reclaim of input tax should have been corrected using a 'standard method override' under *VAT Regulations, reg 107B*. *Turbine Motor Works Ltd v HMRC*, [2011] UKFTT 706 (TC), TC01543.

Interaction with grouping provisions

[9.7] A university, which was partly exempt, was a member of a VAT group. In 2000 It arranged for a property development company (U) to build some new student accommodation. U reclaimed input tax on the construction, and made a zero-rated supply of the accommodation to the university. In June 2004 the university acquired U's share capital. In July 2004 U applied to become a member of the university's VAT group. HMRC accepted the application, and issued a ruling that the effect of the capital goods scheme was that there must be an adjustment to U's original repayment claim, and that the university was required to repay £248,000. The university appealed (and also applied for U to cease to be a member of its group—see **32.16** GROUPS OF COMPANIES). The tribunal allowed the appeal, holding on the evidence that at the time when U was a member of the university's VAT group, the university was not using the development to make exempt supplies, so that no adjustment under the capital goods scheme was required. *University of Essex v HMRC,* [2010] SFTD 893; [2010] UKFTT 162 (TC), TC00467.

Input tax—VAT Regulations, reg 101(3)(a)

[9.8] See *Trustees of the Whitbread Harrowden Settlement,* **46.97** PARTIAL EXEMPTION, and *JDL Ltd,* **46.98** PARTIAL EXEMPTION.

Leaseback transaction—effect of VAT Regulations, reg 115

[9.9] A college of religious education arranged for the construction of an extension to its premises. In September 1996 it registered for VAT, describing its business as property letting'. In November 1996 it leased the extension to a company (S), which leased it back to the college. Both S and the college opted to tax the property, and the college claimed a repayment of VAT on the construction costs. HMRC made the repayment. From November 1996 to August 1998 S and the college accounted for output tax on the rental payments under the lease and leaseback agreement. However they both failed to account for tax after August 1998. In July 1999 S was struck off the Register of Companies. In 2002 HMRC made assessments under *VAT Regulations (SI 1995/2518), reg 115,* making adjustments under the capital goods scheme to take account of the fact that the college was no longer receiving rental income from the property. The college appealed, contending that 'as the lease continued to exist as a matter of law taxable supplies continued to be made'. The First-Tier Tribunal rejected this contention and dismissed the appeal. Judge Barlow observed that 'that argument would be difficult to support where both parties to the lease had in fact stopped abiding by its terms and were behaving as if it did not exist but where one of those parties had itself also ceased to exist the argument is completely untenable'.The Upper Tribunal upheld this decision. Sir Stephen Oliver observed that 'the parties to the lease had stopped abiding by the lease, the single most important term of which, namely the payment of rent, had been abandoned completely'. *Gateshead Talmudical College v HMRC,* UT [2011] UKUT 131 (TCC); [2011] STC 1593. (*Note.* The leaseback scheme which the college had entered in order to trigger a repayment of VAT would no longer be effective. For a historical summary of the relevant legislation, see De Voil Indirect Tax Service, para V4.115.)

[9.10] See also *Centralan Property Ltd v C & E Commrs,* **22.459** EUROPEAN COMMUNITY LAW.

Motor cars—whether 'capital assets'

[9.11] See *Harbig Leasing Two Ltd,* **57.34** REGISTRATION.

10

Cash Accounting Scheme

The cases in this chapter are arranged under the following headings.

Termination of authorisation
      Cases where the appellant was successful   **10.1**
      Cases where the appellant was unsuccessful   **10.2**
Other matters   **10.11**

Termination of authorisation

Cases where the appellant was successful

[10.1] In the case noted at **18.298** DEFAULT SURCHARGE, a trader had incurred a default surcharge and, as a result, the Commissioners withdrew his authority to use the Cash Accounting Scheme. The tribunal held that the trader had a reasonable excuse for the default giving rise to the surcharge and, therefore, also allowed his appeal against the withdrawal of his authorisation to use the Scheme. *SP Whitehouse*, LON/91/1726 (VTD 6763).

Cases where the appellant was unsuccessful

[10.2] A company began to use the Cash Accounting Scheme in October 1987. Subsequently it incurred several default surcharges. In November 1989 the Commissioners withdrew the company's authorisation to use the scheme. The tribunal dismissed the company's appeal against this decision. *Vitech Engineering Ltd*, LON/90/102X (VTD 5154).

[10.3] The decision in *Vitech Engineering Ltd*, 10.2 above, was applied in the similar cases of *AA Whyte*, MAN/90/686 (VTD 5829); *R Smith (t/a Ray Smith Associates)*, LON/91/287Y (VTD 6624) and *DE Smith*, MAN/91/453 (VTD 6668).

[10.4] An appeal was dismissed in a case where the tribunal held that its jurisdiction was supervisory rather than appellate, applying *JH Corbitt (Numismatists) Ltd*, **58.1** SECOND-HAND GOODS, and *Mr Wishmore Ltd*, **14.45** COLLECTION AND ENFORCEMENT. *Mainline Fabrications*, MAN/91/435 (VTD 7010).

[10.5] Similar decisions, also applying *JH Corbitt (Numismatists) Ltd*, **58.1** SECOND-HAND GOODS, and *Mr Wishmore Ltd*, **14.45** COLLECTION AND ENFORCEMENT, were reached in *J Brown*, MAN/91/709 (VTD 7747); *F Fowle*, LON/92/962X (VTD 9174); *Industry Northwest Publications (1983) Ltd*, MAN/91/1507 (VTD 9425); *Mrs SM Wood (t/a Moulton Auto Hire)*, LON/92/600X (VTD 9565); *MD Design Group Ltd*, LON/92/2502A (VTD 10070); *Howards Way Cleaning*, MAN/92/1073 (VTD 10458) and *Geomatrix Ltd*, MAN/92/640 (VTD 10701).

[10.6] A company (M) operated the Cash Accounting Scheme. It issued an invoice to an associated company (F) in respect of future marketing services of more than £410,000. F, which did not operate the Cash Accounting Scheme, reclaimed input tax in respect of the amount charged on the invoice. The Commissioners issued a ruling withdrawing M's entitlement to operate the cash accounting scheme, and the tribunal dismissed M's appeal. By virtue of *VAT Regulations 1995 (SI 1995/2518), reg 64(1)(e)*, a taxable person was not entitled to operate the scheme where the Commissioners considered this necessary for the protection of the revenue. On the evidence, there was 'a clear threat to the revenue' that, if F's claim were allowed, 'no subsequent transactions will take place and the revenue will not recover that payment. The revenue clearly needs protecting against the misappropriation of funds due to the timing arising from the cash accounting system.' The chairman observed that there was 'no obvious or sustainable commercial justification for the business practice adopted other than the gaining of a tax advantage. The scheme for cash accounting was designed to give small businesses the option of accounting for VAT when they received payments rather than when they issued a tax invoice. This automatically gave bad debt relief. It is not designed to enable a business to structure its arrangements so that it issues an invoice before any supplies are made (or any costs incurred in relation thereto) where payment by design, in whole or in part, only occurs after a considerable period.' There was 'very serious doubt that there was any possibility' of F ever being able to pay the amount charged by the invoice. Applying *dicta* of Diplock LJ in *Snook v London & West Riding Investments Ltd*, CA [1967] 2 QB 786; [1967] 1 All ER 518, the tribunal was satisfied that the 'arrangements between (M) and (F) were no more than a sham'. *Marketing Middle East Ltd*, MAN/97/1110 (VTD 15666). (*Notes.* (1) The tribunal also rejected F's claim to input tax—see **40.48** INVOICES AND CREDIT NOTES. (2) The tribunal awarded costs of £1,000 to the Commissioners, finding that M had pursued the appeal 'on a vexatious and frivolous basis'. (3) See now *VAT Regulations 1995, reg 58(2)(f)*. With effect from 3 July 1997, the cash accounting scheme cannot be used for supplies of goods or services in respect of which a VAT invoice is issued in advance of the delivery of goods or performance of services.)

[10.7] A company (M) registered for VAT in 1999 and operated the cash accounting scheme. It issued a number of invoices with an associated company which did not operate the scheme, and thus was entitled to reclaim input tax before paying the amounts shown on the invoices. In April 2001 the Commissioners issued a ruling withdrawing M's entitlement to operate the cash accounting scheme. The tribunal dismissed M's appeal, applying the decision in *Marketing Middle East Ltd*, **10.6** above, and holding that 'the phrase "necessary for the protection of the revenue", in the context of the cash accounting scheme, comprehends or includes the situation in which a taxpayer arranges or conducts his business with the intention, or where the actual consequence is, to give rise to an unjustified tax advantage, and that "protection of the revenue" can be invoked by the Commissioners where a taxpayer attempts to arrange his business to exploit a scheme'. On the evidence, the Commissioners' decision to withdraw the scheme had not been unreasonable. *Management Facilities (Northern) Ltd*, MAN/02/347 (VTD 18191).

[10.8] A company (C) which operated the cash accounting scheme issued an invoice for £125,500 to an associated company (D) trading in mobile telephones which did not operate the scheme. Customs formed the opinion 'that the amount invoiced could not be justified by reference to the services to which the invoice purported to relate; that the invoice related in part to services to be supplied after the invoice was issued; and that the circumstances of the associated company (which accounted for VAT by the normal, invoice-based, method) could result in a VAT benefit accruing to that company notwithstanding that it might not be in a position to settle the invoice'. Accordingly Customs issued a ruling withdrawing C's entitlement to operate the cash accounting scheme. The tribunal dismissed C's appeal, finding that there was no evidence that C 'had carried out work to the value of £125,500'. Customs had been entitled to conclude that the invoice 'was both excessive in relation to the value of the services to which it refers and also in part related to future services, and therefore to that extent outside the terms of the cash accounting scheme'. *International Corporate Restructuring & Insolvency Ltd*, LON/06/1281 (VTD 20331).

[10.9] There are a large number of other cases, which appear to raise no point of general importance, in which tribunals have dismissed appeals against the termination of authorisation to use the Cash Accounting Scheme. In the interests of space, such cases are not reported individually in this book. For a list of such cases decided up to and including 31 December 1992, see Tolley's VAT Cases 1993.

Application of VAT Regulations, reg 60(1)

[10.10] A partnership operated the cash accounting scheme. In August 1997 it sold a capital asset for £680,000 plus VAT. The Commissioners therefore notified the partnership that, because its turnover had exceeded the limit of £437,500 laid down by *VAT Regulations, reg 60(1)*, it had to withdraw from the scheme. The partnership appealed, contending that sales of capital assets should be excluded from the computation of the turnover limit. The tribunal rejected this contention and dismissed the appeal. *CE, EM & PC Evans (t/a Coney Leasing)*, LON/98/217 (VTD 17510). (*Notes.* (1) The limit has subsequently been increased to £750,000. (2) See now C & E Notice 731, para 5.2. Customs may allow the business to remain in the scheme in such circumstances, provided that certain conditions are met.)

Other matters

Application of Scheme where grant received from third party

[10.11] A company carrying on a management consultancy business operated the Cash Accounting Scheme. It took advantage of a scheme run by the Scottish Development Agency whereby the Agency paid a grant of 55% of the cost of the company's services to certain qualifying clients. The Agency stipulated that VAT should be paid by the clients on the total cost of the service, including the amount covered by the grant. The company submitted invoices to its clients charging gross fees plus VAT, and deducting the amount of any grant. The company submitted invoices to the Agency on which no VAT was charged. Thus, where the clients paid the invoices in full, the VAT was recovered from them and paid to the Commissioners. However, where the invoices were not paid by the clients, but the grants relating to the invoices were paid to the company by the Agency, the company did not account for VAT on the amount thus received. The Commissioners issued an assessment charging VAT on such amounts and the company appealed, contending that if nothing was paid for the services except the grant, no VAT should be due. The tribunal dismissed the company's appeal. The amounts paid by the Agency were clearly consideration for services which the company supplied. The fact that the consideration was paid by a third party was immaterial, applying *Lord Advocate v Largs Golf Club*, 13.6 CLUBS, ASSOCIATIONS AND ORGANISATIONS. Under the Cash Accounting Scheme, VAT had to be accounted for in the accounting period in which payment for the supply was received. *Martin Gibson Ltd*, EDN/90/54 (VTD 5473).

Application of Scheme where debt discharged by payment in kind

[10.12] A partnership, which accounted for tax under the Cash Accounting Scheme, had supplied goods to a company which was in financial difficulty. The company owed the partnership £29,600. The company came to an arrangement with its creditors by which it increased its share capital and the creditors received shares as payment of the money owed to them. The partnership received shares in the company, but did not account for VAT on the £29,600. The Commissioners issued an assessment charging tax on this amount, and the partnership appealed, contending that the shares were effectively worthless and that it had never received payment. The tribunal dismissed the partnership's appeal. Applying the principles laid down in *Spargo*, Ch D [1873] Ch 407, the correct analysis of the transaction was that each shareholder should be taken to have received cash in satisfaction of the debt owed to him, and to have paid the same amount of cash for his shares. Although the two deemed payments were self-cancelling, the deemed payment in respect of the supplies which the partnership had previously made was liable to VAT. *A–Z Electrical*, LON/93/95A (VTD 10718).

Partnership dissolution—application of VAT Regulations, reg 63(2)

[10.13] Two people had carried on an accountancy business in partnership, and had operated the cash accounting scheme. In 1999 they dissolved the partnership and carried on business as sole practitioners. One of them, who was already registered as a sole practitioner, continued to practise from the premises formerly used by the partnership. The other practised from new premises. They divided the partnership clients between them, and neither of them took over the partnership registration number. At the date of dissolution, the partnership had unpaid debts of more than £210,000, for which invoices had been issued. The Commissioners issued an assessment charging tax on these amounts, in accordance with *VAT Regulations 1995, reg 63(2)*. The partners appealed, contending that they should be allowed to defer accounting for tax on these debts until they had been paid by their clients. The tribunal rejected this contention and dismissed the appeal, holding that the assessment was in accordance with the requirements of *reg 63(2)*. *JD Vaghela & NR Unadkat (t/a Vaghela Unadkat & Co)*, MAN/00/816 (VTD 17331).

Input tax credit claimed but invoices not paid

[10.14] An accountant operated the cash accounting scheme. A VAT officer discovered that he had reclaimed input tax in respect of three invoices which he appeared not to have paid. The Commissioners issued assessments to recover the tax in question. The accountant appealed, contending that he had paid the amounts in question. The tribunal reviewed the evidence in detail, rejected the accountant's contentions and dismissed his appeal, observing that the accountant had failed to produce his cheque stubs and finding that he had not produced 'convincing evidence' that he had paid the disputed amounts. *M Novakovic (t/a Novakovic & Co)*, LON/02/685 (VTD 18462). (*Note.* Costs of £500 were awarded to the Commissioners.)

Company operating cash accounting scheme—assignment of debts

[10.15] A company (R) which operated the cash accounting scheme assigned most of its debts to a factoring company. The Commissioners issued an assessment on the basis that R was required to account for output tax on the full value of the debt in the tax period in which the debt was assigned. R appealed, contending that all the factored debts were reassignable, and that it should be allowed to delay accounting for VAT until the tax period in which the factor received payment from the debtor. The tribunal rejected this contention and dismissed R's appeal, holding that 'the fact that the debt might revert back to the trader under a recourse agreement' did not 'alter the trader's obligation to account for output tax in the period in which the debt is sold or assigned to the factor'. *RTI Services Ltd*, LON/02/776 (VTD 18512).

11

Charities

The cases in this chapter are arranged under the following headings.

Supplies to charities—whether zero-rated (VATA 1994, Sch 8, Group 15)

Supplies of goods donated for sale (*VATA 1994, Sch 8, Group 15, Item 1*)   **11.1**

Supplies of 'relevant goods' (*VATA 1994, Sch 8, Group 15, Items 4, 5, Note 3*)   **11.3**

Supplies to an 'eligible body' (*VATA 1994, Sch 8, Group 15, Items 4–6, Note 4*)   **11.15**

Provision of care for 'handicapped persons' (*VATA 1994, Sch 8, Group 15, Item 5, Note 5*)   **11.21**

Supplies of advertising facilities (*VATA 1994, Sch 8, Group 15, Item 8*)   **11.24**

Supplies of medicinal products (*VATA 1994, Sch 8, Group 15, Item 9, Note 11*)   **11.30**

Fund-raising events—whether exempt (VATA 1994, Sch 9, Group 12)   **11.32**

Apportionment of input tax

Educational charities   **11.39**

Religious charities   **11.43**

Other charities   **11.46**

Miscellaneous   **11.60**

Supplies to charities—whether zero-rated (VATA 1994, Sch 8, Group 15)

Supplies of goods donated for sale (VATA 1994, Sch 8, Group 15, Item 1)

Whether goods 'donated for sale'

[11.1] A college (N), which was an educational charity, arranged for the incorporation of a wholly-owned subsidiary company which had covenanted to give all its profits to its parent charity. A neighbouring college (C), which was also a charity, wished to purchase various goods (such as photocopiers and computer equipment). In an attempt to avoid output tax from being charged on the supplies, the goods in question were treated as being supplied to N, as being donated by N to its subsidiary company and as being sold to C by the subsidiary. The subsidiary charged a small commission to C. The supplies of the goods were treated as zero-rated under *VATA 1994, Sch 8, Group 15, Item 1*. The Commissioners issued a ruling that the goods had not been 'donated for sale', and thus failed to qualify for zero-rating. N and its subsidiary company appealed. The tribunal dismissed the appeals, observing that 'as a matter of commercial reality, the transactions represented a tripartite agreement' and involved 'no requirement or justification for a "donation" of the relevant equipment to (the company)'. On the evidence, the goods were never delivered to the company, and it was clear that C 'was intended to have the beneficial use and enjoyment of the goods from the moment of delivery'. Neither N nor the company ever acquired title to the goods, and the supplies failed to qualify for zero-rating. *University of Wales College Newport; Allt-Yr-Yn & Caerleon Enterprises & Services Ltd*, [1997] VATDR 417 (VTD 15280). (*Note.* See also *Group 15, Note 1* as substituted by *FA 1997, s 33*. The substituted *Note 1* was intended to block avoidance schemes of this nature.)

Abandoned dogs and cats—whether goods 'donated for sale'

[11.2] A charity had been established 'to rescue and shelter lost, unwanted and homeless dogs and cats'. It sold most of the dogs and cats to new owners, and treated such sales as zero-rated. Customs issued an assessment charging tax on the sales of abandoned dogs and cats, on the basis that animals which had been abandoned had not been 'donated for sale', within *VATA 1994, Sch 8, Group 15, Item 1*. The tribunal allowed the charity's appeal, holding that 'a gift of a stray cat or dog to the appellant by a person other than the original owner was capable of transferring ownership rights in the animal to the appellant'. This included gifts of stray dogs by local wardens under *Environmental Protection Act 1990, s 149(6)(7)*. Accordingly, such animals were within the definition of 'donated goods' and qualified for zero-rating. The tribunal observed that 'the historical analysis of the zero-rating provisions showed that animal charities were the second group of charities to benefit from this relief. They were granted this relief for the specific purpose of protecting animals.' Furthermore, Customs' policy 'of distinguishing between sales of animals directly given to the appellant by their owners and sales of animals intentionally abandoned by their owners produced an irrational result when set against the specific purpose of animal protection'. *Gables Farm Dogs & Cats Home*, LON/05/907 (VTD 20519). (*Note.* Following this decision, Customs now accept that 'charities selling animals in similar circumstances should zero-rate their supplies'. See HMRC Brief 14/08, issued on 4 March 2008.)

Whether charity making taxable supplies of abandoned dogs

[11.2A] A charity received abandoned and rescued dogs and passed them to new owners in return for a payment which it described as a donation. Following the decision in Gables Farm Dogs & Cats Home, 11.2 above, it applied to be registered for VAT, and lodged a reclaim of input tax. HMRC rejected the claim on the basis that the charity was 'merely re-homing dogs in return for a voluntary donation', and was not making any taxable supplies. The charity appealed, contending that the donations which it received from the new owners should be seen as consideration for supplies of the dogs, so that it was entitled to be registered for VAT. The tribunal accepted this contention and allowed the appeal, finding that although the charity described the payments from new owners as 'donations', they were in fact compulsory and that if a prospective owner refused to make a donation, 'the re-homing process would be terminated as it would be deemed that if the new owner was unable to afford the contribution, he would be unable to cover the future upkeep costs of owning the animal'. *Three Counties Dog Rescue v HMRC*, [2011] UKFTT 817 (TC), TC01653.

Supplies of 'relevant goods' (VATA 1994, Sch 8, Group 15, Items 4, 5, Note 3)

Equipment used by homeopathic institute

[11.3] A charity provided seminars in homeopathic and other alternative forms of medicine. Its founder and manager also ran a private practice in the field of alternative medicine, although he had no medical or scientific qualifications. The charity provided training in a technique used by its founder in his private practice, involving the use of a metal box with an electrical current flowing through it, in contact with the patient. Ampoules of various liquids, imported from Germany, were placed in the metal box, and the readings thus obtained were used for diagnosis. The Commissioners issued a ruling that the ampoules were standard-rated. The charity appealed, contending that they were zero-rated on the basis that they were 'medical or scientific equipment' and were therefore zero-rated under what is now *VATA 1994, Sch 8, Group 15, Item 5, Note 3*. The tribunal dismissed the appeal, holding on the evidence that the metal box was not 'medical or scientific equipment', and that the ampoules were used by the charity's founder in his private practice, rather than being used by the charity. *The Institute of EAV & Bio-Energetic Medicine*, LON/83/303 (VTD 1667).

Dental simulation equipment—whether within Group 15, Note 3(a)

[11.4] A company supplied dental simulation equipment, designed for training dental students, to two universities. The Commissioners issued an assessment charging tax on the supplies. The company appealed, contending that the equipment was medical equipment, within *VATA 1994, Sch 8, Group 15, Item 5, Note 3(a)*, and therefore qualified for zero-rating. The tribunal accepted this contention and allowed the appeal. *The Anglodent Company*, LON/00/271 (VTD 16891).

Artificial heads for use in training dentists

[11.5] A company supplied artificial human heads, for use in training dentists. The Commissioners issued a ruling that output tax was chargeable on these supplies. The company appealed, contending that the heads were 'medical equipment', within *VATA 1994, Sch 8, Group 15, Item 5, Note 3(a)*, and therefore qualified for zero-rating. The tribunal accepted this contention and allowed the appeal, finding that the heads 'were clearly medical equipment for use in medical training'. *Medical & Dental Staff Training Ltd*, LON/98/1442 (VTD 17031).

Washing machines for cleaning surgical equipment

[11.6] A company (L) manufactured and sold washing machines for the cleaning of surgical and laboratory equipment. It did not account for VAT on its sales of the machines, treating them as zero-rated. Customs issued an assessment charging tax on the sales, and L appealed. The tribunal dismissed

L's appeal, holding that the sales failed to qualify for zero-rating. Although the supply was to eligible bodies within the scope of what is now *VATA 1994, Sch 8, Group 15*, the washing machines could not properly be described as scientific equipment within *Group 15, Note 3*. *Lancer UK Ltd*, [1986] VATTR 112 (VTD 2070).

Forms used to describe injuries of accident victims

[11.7] A charity purchased a supply of forms, used to describe the injuries of accident victims. The vendor charged VAT on the supply and the chairman of the charity lodged an appeal to the tribunal, contending that the forms should have been treated as zero-rated. The tribunal rejected this contention and dismissed the appeal, holding that the forms failed to qualify for zero-rating, since they were not within the definition of 'medical equipment' and thus were not 'relevant goods' within *VATA 1994, Sch 8, Group 15, Note 3*. *Dr CJ Eaton*, LON/86/321 (VTD 2315).

Observation window at centre for treating epilepsy

[11.8] A registered charity, which provided residential assessment, treatment and care for sufferers from epilepsy, incurred expenditure on refurbishing and improving its facilities, installing an observation window and a special 'soft games room' with heavily padded walls, floor and ceiling. The Commissioners issued a ruling that the work was standard-rated, and the charity appealed, contending that the work should be treated as zero-rated under what is now *VATA 1994, Sch 8, Group 15, Item 5*. The QB rejected this contention, holding that the goods were not 'medical goods' within *Group 15, Note 3*, and thus the supplies failed to qualify for zero-rating. *C & E Commrs v The David Lewis Centre*, QB [1995] STC 485. (*Note.* For another issue in this case, not taken to the QB, see **19.34** DRUGS, MEDICINES, AIDS FOR THE HANDICAPPED, ETC.)

Ventilation system—whether within Group 15, Note 3(a)

[11.9] A medical research establishment (R) arranged for contractors to replace the ventilation system in its laboratories. Customs issued a ruling that the supply was standard-rated. R appealed, contending that the ventilation system was 'laboratory equipment' which qualified for zero-rating under *VATA 1994, Sch 8, Group 15, Note 3(a)*. The tribunal reviewed the evidence in detail, accepted this contention and allowed the appeal. The tribunal observed that the ventilation system had been specially designed because R needed 'to have precise control over not only temperature and humidity but also pressure'. Consequently the equipment 'went way beyond anything that could be described simply as "air conditioning"'. It allowed 'scientific experiments to take place under laboratory conditions controlled to the highest practicable levels'. *Research Establishment*, LON/03/931 (VTD 19095).

Supplies of chemicals and paper to charity for use in X-ray work

[11.10] A company supplied chemicals and photographic paper to a charity for use in X-ray work. It did not account for output tax on the supplies, considering that they should be zero-rated under what is now *VATA 1994, Sch 8, Group 15*. The Commissioners issued a ruling that the supplies were not eligible for zero-rating, since the chemicals and paper were not 'relevant goods' within what is now *Group 15, Note 3*. The company appealed, contending that the chemicals and paper should be regarded as 'parts or accessories' within *Note 3(c)*. The tribunal rejected this contention and dismissed the appeal, holding that the chemicals and paper were not within the definition of 'parts or accessories'. *Norwich Camera Centre Ltd*, LON/93/1610 (VTD 11629).

Supply of photocopier—whether 'relevant goods' within Group 15, Note 3

[11.11] A charity acquired a photocopier. The Commissioners issued a ruling that output tax was chargeable on the supply. The charity appealed, contending that the photocopier was an accessory for use with medical equipment, and therefore should be treated as zero-rated under *VATA 1994, Sch 8, Group 15, Item 5, Note 3(c)*. The tribunal rejected this contention and dismissed the appeal, holding that the supply did not qualify for zero-rating on the basis that the photocopier was not an 'accessory' and therefore was not within the definition of 'relevant goods' in *Group 15, Note 3*. *Crown Treatment Centre*, LON/97/1573 (VTD 15564).

Emergency generator—whether within Group 15, Note 3(c)

[11.12] A registered charity, which ran a nursing home for the severely disabled, purchased an emergency generator. The Commissioners issued a ruling that VAT was chargeable on the generator. The charity appealed, contending that the generator was an accessory for use with medical equipment, and therefore qualified for zero-rating under *VATA 1994, Sch 8, Group 15, Item 5, Note 3(c)*. The Ch D accepted this contention and allowed the appeal. Neuberger J held that the only reasonable conclusion on the evidence was that the generator was 'an accessory for use with medical equipment' within the meaning of *Note 3(c)*. *Royal Midland Counties Home for Disabled People v C & E Commrs*, Ch D 2001, [2002] STC 395. (*Note*. The Court of Appeal refused Customs leave to appeal against this decision—CA [2001] EWCA Civ 1548.)

Goods supplied to medical research institutions for animal experiments

[11.13] A company supplied animal bedding materials to pharmaceutical and medical research institutions which carried out experiments on animals. It treated these supplies as zero-rated under *VATA 1994, Sch 8, Group 15*. The Commissioners issued an assessment on the basis that the supplies were not 'relevant goods' within *Group 15, Note 3* and were therefore standard-rated. The company appealed, contending that the materials were accessories for use with laboratory equipment, and therefore qualified for zero-rating under *Note 3(c)*. The tribunal accepted this contention and allowed the company's appeal. *Supplier Ltd*, LON/x (VTD 18247). (*Notes*. (1) The tribunal also held that a respirator helmet was 'laboratory equipment' but that various other items including protective clothing, decontaminating agents and dispensers were not 'laboratory equipment'. (2) For the Commissioners' revised policy following this decision, see Business Brief 21/2003, issued on 11 November 2003.)

Warning sirens—whether 'relevant goods' within Group 15, Note 3(g)

[11.14] After two major fires at large industrial plants in the Avonmouth area, a charitable trust was established to provide and maintain an 'early warning system' in the area. It purchased a number of early-warning sirens. The Commissioners issued a ruling that the supply of the sirens was standard-rated. The trust appealed, contending that the sirens were aural equipment and were intended to be used for rescue services, and were therefore zero-rated 'relevant goods' within *VATA 1994, Sch 8, Group 15, Note 3(g)*. The tribunal accepted this contention and allowed the appeal. *Severnside Siren Trust Ltd,* [2000] VATDR 497 (VTD 16640).

Supplies to an 'eligible body' (VATA 1994, Sch 8, Group 15, Items 4–6, Note 4)

Registered charity providing medical facilities—whether an 'eligible body'

[11.15] A registered charity provided medical and dental facilities, primarily for French-speakers in the London area. The Commissioners issued a ruling that it was not an 'eligible body' within *VATA 1994, Sch 8, Group 15, Item 5, Note 4*. The company appealed, contending that its premises were a 'hospital', within *Note 4(d)*, or 'a charitable institution providing care or medical or surgical treatment for handicapped persons', within *Note 4(f)*. The tribunal rejected this contention and dismissed the appeal, holding that the premises were 'a medical care centre with surgical facilities', rather than a hospital. The company did not deal with serious accidents, carry out operations 'other than those of a minor nature', or employ nurses or porters. Furthermore, the company's premises were not 'an institution for the treatment of the chronically sick or disabled'. The fact that some of the company's patients were within the definition of 'handicapped persons' was not conclusive, since there was no evidence that 'that class of patients amounts to a significant part of (the company's) clientele'. *Medicare Français,* LON/95/2314A (VTD 13929).

Provision of air ambulances

[11.16] A company arranged to provide helicopters, fully fitted out for use as air ambulances, to two charitable trusts. The Commissioners issued a ruling that output tax was chargeable on the supply of the helicopters. The company appealed, contending that its supplies should be treated as zero-rated under *VATA 1994, Sch 8, Group 15, Item 5*. The tribunal held that, as a matter of principle, the company was making separate supplies of the helicopter and of the services of the pilot, and that the supply of the pilot's services failed to qualify for zero-rating, but that the hire of the helicopter was, in principle, within *Group 15, Note 9*. The tribunal directed that the case should be relisted for further argument as to whether the charitable trusts were 'eligible bodies' within *Group 15, Note 4*. *Medical Aviation Services Ltd,* LON/97/16 (VTD 15308). (*Note.* There was no further public hearing of the appeal. See now *VATA 1994, Sch 8, Group 15, Notes 4A, 4B*, introduced by *FA 1997, s 34* with effect from 26 November 1996.)

Minibuses supplied to charities for elderly

[11.17] A registered charity provided a variety of services to elderly people. It purchased a number of minibuses, arranged for them to be converted to carry wheelchairs, and supplied them to other charities for the benefit of elderly people. It treated its supplies as zero-rated under *VATA 1994, Sch 8, Group 15*. The Commissioners issued assessments on the basis that the charities to which the minibuses were supplied were not 'eligible bodies' within *Group 15, Note 4*, so that the supplies did not qualify for zero-rating. The tribunal allowed the appeal, holding that the recipient charities were within the definition of an 'eligible body' in *Group 15, Note 4(f)*. The QB upheld this decision. *C & E Commrs v Help The Aged*, QB [1997] STC 406. (*Note*. See now, however, *VATA 1994, Sch 8, Group 15, Notes 4A, 4B*, introduced by *FA 1997, s 34* with effect from 26 November 1996. The new provisions were intended to restrict the scope of the zero-rating provisions to 'charities providing personal care or treatment predominantly for the handicapped' in an 'institutional or a domiciliary setting'.)

Charity providing scooters and wheelchairs for disabled

[11.18] A registered charity provided scooters and wheelchairs for disabled people. The Commissioners issued a ruling that the scooters and wheelchairs failed to qualify for zero-rating under *VATA 1994, Sch 8, Group 15, Item 5*, as the charity was not an 'eligible body' as defined by *Note 4A*. The tribunal upheld this decision and dismissed the charity's appeal. *Poole Shopmobility*, LON/98/1486 (VTD 16290). (*Note*. For another issue in this case, see **19.73** DRUGS, MEDICINES, AIDS FOR THE HANDICAPPED, ETC.)

Charitable trust providing emergency 'early-warning' system

[11.19] In the case noted at **11.14** above, the tribunal held that a charitable trust, established to provide an 'early-warning' system in the case of an emergency, was providing rescue services within *VATA 1994, Sch 8, Group 15, Note 4(h)* and was therefore within the definition of an 'eligible body'. *Severnside Siren Trust Ltd*, LON/99/88 (VTD 16640).

Medical charity—whether an 'eligible body' within Group 15, Note 4(h)

[11.20] A medical charity had been established to operate a website to help practitioners involved in paediatric medicine to diagnose potential complications. It purchased computer equipment. The Commissioners issued a ruling that tax was chargeable on the supply. The charity appealed, contending that it should be treated as an 'eligible body' within *VATA 1994, Sch 8, Group 15, Note 4(h)*, so that the supply should be treated as zero-rated. The tribunal rejected this contention and dismissed the appeal, holding that the charity was not supplying 'rescue services' within *VATA 1994, Sch 8, Group 15, Note 4(h)*, so that it was not an eligible body and the supply of computer equipment failed to qualify for zero-rating. *Isabel Medical Charity*, LON/02/113 (VTD 18209).

Provision of care for 'handicapped persons' (VATA 1994, Sch 8, Group 15, Item 5, Note 5)

Purchase of microcomputer—whether 'the provision of care'

[11.21] A registered charity purchased a microcomputer and arranged for it to be delivered to an individual who was severely handicapped with muscular dystrophy. The Commissioners issued an assessment on the basis that the sale of the microcomputer was standard-rated. The charity appealed, contending that the provision of the microcomputer constituted the 'provision of care for a handicapped person', and was therefore zero-rated under what is now *VATA 1994, Sch 8, Group 15, Item 5*. The tribunal rejected this contention and dismissed the charity's appeal, holding that the 'provision of care' required that 'the provider himself provides, or assumes the responsibility of providing, something in the nature of protection or a continuing state of care for the handicapped person'. The 'absence of any continuing personal supervisory role' by the charity meant that the provision of the microcomputer did not constitute the provision of 'care', and did not qualify for zero-rating. *Medical Care Foundation*, [1991] VATTR 28 (VTD 5411).

Spellcheckers purchased by Dyslexia Institute

[11.22] The Dyslexia Institute purchased a number of 'spellcheckers' from a firm of electronic publishers. In accordance with advice from the Commissioners, the vendors charged VAT. The Institute appealed, contending that the goods should have been treated as zero-rated under what is now *VATA 1994, Sch 8, Group 15*. The tribunal dismissed the appeal, holding that dyslexics were not 'handicapped persons' as defined in *Note 5*, and that the Institute was not providing 'medical treatment' within *Item 5*. The chairman also observed that she was 'not satisfied that these "spellmasters" are computer equipment within the ordinary and natural meaning of those words'. *The Dyslexia Institute Ltd*, LON/94/293A (VTD 12654). (*Note.* See now, however, the December 2002 edition of Customs' VAT Manual, Part 7, Chapter 12, para 4.3.3. This states that Customs have subsequently concluded that 'where a person's dyslexia or asthma has a substantial long term adverse effect on his/her ability to carry out normal day to day activities, then he/she should be treated as being disabled for VAT purposes. This means that not everyone with dyslexia or asthma is disabled.')

[11.23] The decision in *The Dyslexia Institute*, 11.22 above, was applied in the similar case of *Mrs J Smith (for Dundee & Angus Dyslexic Association)*, EDN/94/122 (VTD 12909).

Supplies of advertising facilities (VATA 1994, Sch 8, Group 15, Item 8)

NOTE

VATA 1994, Sch 8, Group 15, Item 8 was substituted by the *VAT (Charities and Aids for the Handicapped) Order 2000 (SI 2000/805)* with effect from 1 April 2000. The cases in this section should be read in the light of this change.

Advertising posters—whether zero-rated under Group 15, Item 8

[11.24] The Royal Society for the Encouragement of Arts, Manufacture and Commerce is a registered charity and the representative member of a VAT group. Posters, advertising a special awards scheme, were designed and prepared outside the group but printed within the group. The charity treated the self-supply of the posters as zero-rated. The Commissioners issued an assessment on the basis that the supply did not qualify for zero-rating. The QB upheld the assessment. Scott-Baker J held that the purpose of *VATA 1994, Sch 8, Group 15, Item 8* was to help charities obtain supplies of advertising services from third party suppliers, and that the legislation was not intended to promote 'in-house' advertising, which did not need such assistance. *C & E Commrs v The Royal Society for the Encouragement of Arts, Manufacture & Commerce*, QB 1996, [1997] STC 437.

Advertisements in periodical—whether zero-rated under Group 15, Item 8

[11.25] An association of bell-ringers, which was a registered charity, arranged for the inclusion of two advertisements in a periodical dealing with bell-ringing. The Commissioners issued a ruling that output tax was chargeable on the advertisements. The association appealed, contending that they should be zero-rated under *VATA 1994, Sch 8, Group 15, Item 8*. The tribunal allowed the appeal in part, holding that a small classified advertisement, advertising a quarterly meeting, was standard-rated but that a large display advertisement, advertising a bell-ringing festival, was zero-rated. The tribunal observed that an advertisement could be zero-rated under *Item 8* if it was either for the purpose of raising funds for the charity, or for the purpose of making known the objects of the charity. On the evidence, neither of the advertisements had been for the purpose of making known the objects of the charity. However, the second advertisement had been for the purpose of raising funds, and therefore qualified for zero-rating. *Sussex County Association of Change Ringers*, LON/95/2266A (VTD 14116). (*Note.* The association was not registered for VAT, but the Commissioners accepted that it had sufficient *locus standi* to lodge an appeal—see **2.57** APPEALS.)

Recruitment advertising services supplied to registered charity

[11.26] A registered charity arranged for an associated company (which was not a member of the same VAT group) to supply services in connection with advertising for new staff for the charity. The company and the charity treated the supplies as zero-rated under *VATA 1994, Sch 8, Group 15, Item 8*. The Commissioners issued a ruling that the supplies did not qualify for zero-rating, on the basis that the primary purpose of the advertisements was to recruit new staff, rather than 'making known the objects or reasons' of the charity, as required by *Item 8*. The company appealed, contending that the advertisements should be treated as zero-rated, on the grounds that 'making known the objects of the charity and the raising of money for it' was a substantial purpose of the recruitment advertisements. The tribunal dismissed the appeal, holding that the primary purpose of the advertisements was the recruitment of staff, which was not a qualifying purpose within *Item 8*. The tribunal observed that 'if Parliament had intended that all charitable advertisement should be zero-rated, the preamble to (*Item 8*) would have been unnecessary', and to 'allow a test less stringent than "predominance"' would mean that 'all advertisements in any way concerned with charities would pass the test for zero-rating'. *RNIB Properties Ltd*, LON/97/982 (VTD 15748).

[11.27] A similar decision was reached in *Surma News Group Ltd*, LON/00/275 (VTD 17585). (*Note.* For a preliminary issue in this case, see 2.22 APPEALS.)

Printing company supplying collection envelopes to charities

[11.28] A printing company supplied quantities of collection envelopes to charities. It did not account for output tax on these supplies. The Commissioners issued a ruling that the supplies were standard-rated, and the company appealed, contending that the envelopes should be treated as advertisements and as qualifying for zero-rating under *VATA 1994, Sch 8, Group 15, Item 8*. The tribunal rejected this contention and dismissed the appeal, holding that, although some of the envelopes could fairly be described as 'advertisements', the company was only making a supply of printing services, and the advertisements were actually published by the charity. *TE Penny & Co Ltd*, LON/97/291 (VTD 15329).

Steel badges requesting support for charity—whether an 'advertisement'

[11.29] A registered charity (LDT) purchased a number of steel badges from a company. The badges bore the slogan 'please support LDT'. LDT gave these badges to donors. The Commissioners issued a ruling that the company's sales of the badges to LDT were standard-rated supplies. LDT appealed, contending that the sales should be treated as zero-rated under *VATA 1994, Sch 8, Group 15, Item 8*. The tribunal rejected this contention and dismissed the appeal, holding that the badges were not an 'advertisement' and did not qualify for zero-rating under the legislation then in force. *Leukaemic Disorders Trust*, EDN/99/157 (VTD 16783). (*Note.* See now *Item 8* as substituted by *VAT (Charities and Aids for the Handicapped) Order 2000 (SI 2000/805)* with effect from 1 April 2000. It appears that the badges would now qualify for zero-rating as a 'medium of communication with the public'.)

Supplies of medicinal products (VATA 1994, Sch 8, Group 15, Item 9, Note 11)

Condoms—whether 'medicinal products' within Note 11

[11.30] A company (P) supplied condoms to charities, for distribution to clients. Customs issued a ruling that VAT was chargeable on these supplies. P appealed, contending that the condoms were 'medicinal products' which qualified for zero-rating under *VATA 1994, Sch 8, Group 15, Item 9, Note 11*. The tribunal accepted this contention and allowed the appeal, holding that when a charity gave a condom to one of its clients, the condom was being administered 'for a medicinal purpose', within *Note 11(a)(i)*. *Pasante Healthcare Ltd*, LON/06/118 (VTD 19724). (*Note.* For HMRC's practice following this decision, see Business Brief 16/06, issued on 12 October 2006.)

Drugs administered by veterinary surgeon—whether zero-rated

[11.31] A registered charity arranged for veterinary surgeons to provide treatment to cats, on behalf of the cats' owners. Customs issued a ruling that VAT was chargeable on the vets' supplies. The charity appealed, contending that where the vets were administering drugs to the cats, the supplies should be treated as supplies of medicinal products and as zero-rated under *VATA 1994, Sch 8, Group 15, Item 9*. The tribunal rejected this contention and dismissed the appeal, holding that where a vet administered veterinary services or medicines to a cat, the vet was making a composite supply of services and was not making a separate supply of goods. Furthermore, *Item 9* restricted zero-rating to cases where a charity which purchased medicinal products for their own use, and did not apply where a vet supplied drugs to the owner of a cat, even if the charity paid for the drugs. *The Burmese Cat Benevolent Fund*, LON/05/1059 (VTD 20015).

Fund-raising events—whether exempt (VATA 1994, Sch 9, Group 12)

NOTE

VATA 1994, Sch 9, Group 12 was substituted by the *VAT (Fund-Raising Events by Charities and Other Qualifying Bodies) Order 2000 (SI 2000/802)* with effect from 1 April 2000. The cases in this section should be read in the light of this change.

Series of fund-raising events—whether exempt

[11.32] A registered charity arranged seven performances of a play, and a pre-release screening of a film. The Commissioners issued a ruling that the charges made for admission to these performances were chargeable to VAT at the standard rate. The charity appealed, contending firstly that the performances constituted a 'fund-raising event' and were exempt under what is now *VATA 1994, Sch 9, Group 12*. The tribunal dismissed the charity's appeal, holding that the performances constituted a 'series' and were thus excluded from exemption under the legislation then in force. The restriction of the scope of the exemption was in accordance with the provisions of *Article 13A1(o)* of the *Sixth Directive*. *Northern Ireland Council for Voluntary Action*, [1991] VATTR 32 (VTD 5451). (*Note*. See now, however, *Sch 9, Group 12, Notes 4* and *5*, introduced by *SI 2000/802*. It appears that, as the series consisted of fewer than 15 events, they would now qualify for exemption.)

[11.33] A registered charity organised a festival dinner, a race day and a carol concert. It reclaimed input tax on the expenditure related to these events. The Commissioners rejected the claim and issued a ruling that the supplies were exempt by virtue of *VATA 1994, Sch 9, Group 12*. The charity appealed, contending that the events were 'part of a series or regular run of like or similar events' and thus were excluded from exemption under the legislation then in force. The tribunal rejected this contention and dismissed the charity's appeal, holding that the events were not 'part of a series or regular run of like or similar events' on the grounds that the events were 'intrinsically dissimilar and there is no quality inherent in the nature of the events which is common to all'. *Newsvendors Benevolent Institution*, LON/96/567 (VTD 14343).

Real ale and jazz festival

[11.34] A sports club organised a real ale and jazz festival, lasting for three consecutive evenings. The Commissioners issued a ruling that the festival did not qualify for exemption under *VATA 1994, Sch 9, Group 12*, on the grounds that it comprised a 'series or regular run of like or similar events', and thus was excluded from exemption under the legislation then in force. The club appealed. The tribunal allowed the appeal, noting that different jazz bands played on each of the three days, and holding that the festival should be viewed as 'a single organic whole', rather than as a series of three separate events. *Reading Cricket & Hockey Club*, LON/95/1093A (VTD 13656).

Rugby club social events

[11.35] A rugby union club staged a number of social functions such as 'stag nights'. It did not account for output tax on its receipts from such events, treating them as exempt from VAT under *VATA 1994, Sch 9, Group 12*. The Commissioners issued an assessment on the basis that the events comprised a 'series or regular run of similar or like events', and were thus excluded from exemption under the legislation then in force. The tribunal upheld the assessment and dismissed the club's appeal. (The tribunal chairman also considered that some of the functions did not qualify as 'fund-raising events', on the grounds that the club had not shown that the main purpose of staging such events was to raise funds.) *Blaydon Rugby Football Club*, [1996] VATDR 1 (VTD 13901).

Student union balls—whether 'fund-raising events'

[11.36] A student union, which was a charity under *Charities Act 1993, Sch 2(w)*, and was registered for VAT, organised balls for students. It treated these balls as exempt from VAT. The Commissioners issued a ruling that the balls did not qualify for exemption, on the grounds that they were primarily social events rather than fund-raising events. The union appealed, contending that the balls were 'fund-raising events' within *VATA 1994, Sch 9, Group 12*. The tribunal accepted this contention and allowed the appeal, holding on the evidence that the raising of funds was 'a main purpose' of staging the events and 'not merely (an) incidental purpose'. *Cheltenham & Gloucester College of Higher Education Students Union*, LON/97/1198 (VTD 15727). (*Note.* See now, however, *Group 12, Item 1* as substituted by *SI 2000/802*. To qualify for exemption, the 'primary purpose' of an event now has to be the raising of money.)

Agricultural show—whether a 'fund-raising event'

[11.37] A charity, which was registered for VAT, organised a three-day agricultural show in the New Forest. It accounted for tax on its takings from the show, but subsequently submitted a repayment claim on the grounds that it should have treated the takings as exempt under *VATA 1994, Sch 9, Group 12, Item 1*. The Commissioners rejected the claim with regard to the periods prior to 1 April 2000, on the grounds that the show was not a 'fund-raising event' under the legislation in force prior to *SI 2000 No 802*. The tribunal dismissed the charity's appeal against this decision. *New Forest Agricultural Show Society*, LON/00/1053 (VTD 17631). (*Note*. The Commissioners accepted that the takings after 31 March 2000 qualified for exemption under *Group 12, Item 1* as substituted by *SI 2000/802*.)

Whether event staged by a 'qualifying body'

[**11.38**] An unincorporated committee was established to organise a testimonial football match to raise money for a fund. Most of the fund was to be paid to a former footballer, and the remainder was to be used to buy hospital equipment in a ward for patients suffering from cancer. The Commissioners issued a ruling that the supplies made by the committee did not qualify for exemption under what is now *VATA 1994, Sch 9, Group 12*, as the committee was not a 'qualifying body' within *Note 3*. The secretary of the committee appealed. The tribunal dismissed the appeal, holding that the committee was not within what is now *VATA 1994, Sch 9, Group 12, Item 1*, since most of the fund's proceeds were to be paid to the former footballer, rather than to the hospital. *P Bailes*, LON/93/1430 (VTD 12459).

Apportionment of input tax

Educational charities

University

[**11.39**] In 2000 a university had agreed a method of apportioning its input tax between business and non-business activities. In 2005 Customs issued an assessment disallowing some of the input tax which the university had reclaimed for the year ending 31 March 2004. The university appealed. The tribunal allowed the appeal, and strongly criticised the Customs officer responsible for the assessment, describing him as not 'capable of sensible or selective application of general principles to particular cases' and as 'a person who concentrated almost obsessively on detail making many demands for information about matters which could happily have been accommodated by a general approach'. The tribunal held that the assessment was not made to the best of the Commissioners' judgment, since it was not 'a genuine and honest attempt to ascertain the amount of tax due' and was 'made not with a view to its accuracy or appropriateness but as a measure of perceived exasperation by the officer because he thought that the University and its advisers were not complying with his demands for information within the timescale he thought they should'. *University Court of the University of Dundee*, EDN/05/102 (VTD 20728).

University—expenditure on research

[11.40] A university, which was a registered charity, reclaimed input tax on expenditure relating to research. The Commissioners rejected the claim on the basis that the expenditure was publicly funded and was not used for the purpose of the university's business. The university appealed, contending that the expenditure was incurred for the purpose of its business even though the research was publicly funded. The tribunal rejected this contention and dismissed the appeal, holding that 'publicly funded research does not result in the making of any taxable supplies and is not predominantly concerned with the making of taxable supplies to consumers for a consideration'. (The tribunal noted that several other universities had taken the view that publicly funded research was not a business, so that they could claim zero-rating for purpose-built research centres.) The Ch D upheld the tribunal decision. Warren J held that publicly funded research was 'completely distinct' from the university's other activities of education and commercial research, and was 'a separate economic activity or business'. Accordingly, the input tax on goods or services used exclusively for publicly funded research was not deductible or recoverable. Tax on goods or services used partly for publicly funded research and partly for business purposes would have to be apportioned under *VATA 1994, s 24(5)*. *University of Southampton v HMRC*, Ch D [2006] STC 1389; [2006] EWHC 528(Ch).

[11.41] The decision in *University of Southampton v HMRC*, **11.40** above, was applied in the similar subsequent case of *University of Sheffield, MAN/05/363 (VTD 20174)*.

Nursery education

[11.42] A charity (P) agreed to provide services to four councils. Customs issued rulings that the agreements did not provide for any taxable supplies, so that P was unable to reclaim any related input tax. The tribunal allowed P's appeal, holding that there was 'sufficient evidence that the local authorities sought, and obtained, properly costed and regulated services which they needed to have'. Accordingly P was entitled to reclaim the relevant input tax. *The Pre-School Learning Alliance*, LON/99/1048 (VTD 17737).

Religious charities

[11.43] In a case where the facts are not fully set out in the tribunal decision, the tribunal directed that the input tax incurred by a registered charity which was established for the promotion of religion, and which engaged in both business and non-business activities, should be apportioned. *British & Foreign Bible Society*, EDN/92/262 (VTD 10149).

[11.44] A registered UK charity had been established to promote the teachings of a preacher based in Atlanta (USA). It reclaimed input tax on the promotion of a convention in London. No entry fee was charged, but a videocassette of the convention was subsequently sold. The tribunal held that the expenditure was partly for business purposes and partly for non-business purposes. The tribunal observed that 44.5% of the charity's income (excluding bank interest) consisted of donations, and therefore directed that 55.5% of the input tax should be treated as deductible. *Creflo Dollar Ministries,* MAN/01/64 (VTD 17705).

[**11.45**] A registered charity reclaimed input tax on supplies of fund-raising services, and on supplies relating to the production and distribution of newsletters which it gave to regular donors. Customs rejected the claim on the basis that the input tax did not relate to any supply by the charity. The Ch D allowed the charity's appeal. Blackburne J held that the fund-raising activities were 'general overheads' and were thus 'cost components' of the charity's economic activities. He remitted the case to the tribunal 'to determine the extent to which the monies raised as a result of the use of the fundraising services' were used by the charity to make taxable supplies. The tribunal would have to determine what proportion of the charity's activities were 'non-business' (and thus outside the scope of VAT) and what proportion was attributable to taxable supplies. *The Church of England Children's Society v HMRC,* [2005] STC 1644; [2005] EWHC 1692(Ch). (*Note.* For Customs' practice following this decision, see Business Brief 19/05, issued on 7 October 2005.)

Other charities

[**11.46**] A charity (W) operated an art gallery. It did not charge visitors for admission, but received income from selling souvenirs, from organised tours and lectures, from the occasional hire of the gallery, and from charging admission fees to occasional exhibitions. It reclaimed the whole of its input tax. Customs issued an assessment to recover some of the tax, considering that W's entitlement to input tax should be restricted to the proportion which its taxable supplies bore to its total supplies. The tribunal upheld the assessment and the QB dismissed W's appeal. Kennedy J held that the free display of works of art was not a business activity. *Whitechapel Art Gallery v C & E Commrs,* QB [1986] STC 156; [1986] 1 CMLR 79. (*Note.* For a subsequent appeal by the same charity, see **20.20** EC DIRECTIVE 2006/112/EC.)

[**11.47**] A charity (H) provided legal aid and assistance free of charge to people on low incomes. It reclaimed the whole of the input tax which it incurred. Customs issued an assessment on the basis that the input tax relating to the services which H provided free of charge was not recoverable, so that H's total input tax should be apportioned. The tribunal dismissed H's appeal, holding that as some of its services were made for no consideration, the input tax relating to those services could not be recovered. *Hillingdon Legal Resources Centre Ltd,* [1991] VATTR 39 (VTD 5210).

[**11.48**] The decision in *Hillingdon Legal Resources Centre Ltd,* **11.47** above, was applied in the similar subsequent cases of *Wolverhampton Citizens Advice Bureau,* MAN/96/1145 (VTD 16411) and *Stoke-on-Trent Citizens Advice Bureau,* **52.330** PENALTIES: MISDECLARATION.

[**11.49**] A charity (N) had a substantial fund of investments, which produced income of more than £1,000,000 per year. Its general charitable activities were accepted as not constituting a business, but it also made a number of taxable supplies, and had regularly reclaimed about 5% of its total input tax. It submitted a claim for its investment activities to be treated as a business, with the result that a substantially greater proportion of its input tax would be treated as deductible. Customs issued a ruling that the investment activities did not amount to a business, and should therefore be left out of account in determining how much of N's input tax should be apportioned to its business activities. The tribunal dismissed N's appeal, holding that its investment activities could not be regarded as constituting a business. *National Society for the Prevention of Cruelty to Children*, [1992] VATTR 417 (VTD 9325).

[11.50] A registered charity made taxable and exempt supplies, and supplies which were outside the scope of VAT. In 1994 it agreed a special method of attributing its input tax with the Commissioners. In 2001 a VAT officer discovered that the charity had not apportioned the tax on its inputs between taxable supplies and supplies that were outside the scope of VAT. Following this visit, she issued eleven assessments on the basis that the charity had incorrectly reclaimed excessive amounts of input tax. The charity appealed, contending that its method of computation was permissible under the terms of its special method. The tribunal rejected this contention and dismissed the charity's appeal against the last seven assessments, holding that the wording of the special method did 'not concede a right to deduct input tax incurred on goods or services used wholly or partly for non-business purposes'. (However, the tribunal allowed the appeals against the first four assessments, finding that all the necessary information had been made available to a previous VAT officer, so that these assessments were outside the time limit of *VATA 1994, s 73(6)*.) *Hospitality Training Foundation*, LON/03/009 (VTD 18359).

[11.51] In 2000 a charity had agreed a formula for determining the appropriate percentage of its input tax which could be apportioned to business activities. Following the Ch D decision in *Church of England Children's Society v HMRC*, **11.45** above, the charity submitted a claim for input tax of more than £5,000,000 relating to fees charged by professional fundraisers. HMRC repaid £2,548,590, but rejected the remainder of the claim. The charity appealed, contending that the effect of the decision in *Church of England Children's Society* was not only to increase the amount of VAT which was subject to apportionment between business and non-business activities, but should also be treated as increasing the recoverable percentage (from about 75% to more than 85%). The tribunal rejected this contention and dismissed the appeal, accepting HMRC's contention that the formula agreed in 2000 no longer produced a 'fair and reasonable' attribution of input tax, and holding that the formula was not 'a binding contract'. The tribunal observed that more than 80% of the donations which the charity received were used for 'the relief of poverty', which was a non-business activity. The effect of *VATA 1994, s 24(5)* was that the charity was only entitled to reclaim input tax which was referable to its business activities. The claim which the charity had submitted did not meet the requirements of *s 24(5)*. The Ch D dismissed the charity's appeal against this decision. Sales J held that the tribunal had been entitled to conclude 'that there was no intention on the part of the parties to create a binding contract'. There had been no 'abuse of power' in HMRC's decision that it should no longer be bound by the formula agreed in 2000. *Oxfam v HMRC*, Ch D 2009, [2010] STC 686; [2009] EWHC 3078 (Ch).

[11.52] A charity reclaimed the whole of its input tax, although most of its income was 'non-business income'. Customs issued an assessment to recover 97.51% of the input tax, on the basis that only 2.49% of the charity's income was business income. The tribunal upheld the assessment and dismissed the charity's appeal. *Siri Behavioural Health*, LON/03/327 (VTD 19016).

Retrospective claim by museum trustees

[11.53] The Board of Trustees of the Victoria and Albert Museum was established under the *National Heritage Act*. They apportioned the Museum's input tax between business and non-business activities, operating the income-based method described in what is now *VAT Notice No 700, Appendix F*. However, they subsequently formed the opinion that this method led to too small an amount of input tax being apportioned to business activities. From April 1993 they adopted a revised method of apportionment which determined the residual input tax by using the ratio which the Museum's input tax directly attributable to its wholly taxable activities bore to the VAT incurred by the Museum on all the supplies made to it which could be directly attributed to either its taxable activities or its non-business activities. The Commissioners agreed to the use of this method for the period beginning on 1 April 1993. In September 1993 the Trustees submitted a retrospective claim to input tax for the period from 1 April 1990 to March 1993, based on using the method which they had adopted since April 1993 rather than the income-based method which they had actually operated during the three years in question. The Commissioners rejected the claim and the Trustees appealed. The tribunal dismissed the appeal and the QB upheld this decision. Turner J held that the *Appendix F* method which the Trustees had adopted was 'an acceptable method of apportionment', and was not inconsistent with *Article 17(5)* of the *EC Sixth Directive*. Although the Trustees could have chosen another acceptable method of apportionment, they had not made an 'error', and the case did not fall within what is now *VAT Regulations 1995 (SI 1995/2518), reg 34. Victoria & Albert Museum Trustees v C & E Commrs*, QB [1996] STC 1016.

Extension to premises owned by charity and used by subsidiaries

[11.54] A company (M), which was a registered charity, owned a hospice. It had two wholly-owned subsidiary companies which were also charities. One of these subsidiaries operated a number of charity shops which made taxable supplies, and was registered for VAT, while the other subsidiary was not registered, since its sole activity was the provision of care for the terminally ill, which was exempt from VAT. M was registered for VAT on the basis that it was making taxable supplies to its two subsidiaries. M arranged for an extension to the hospice and reclaimed 89% of the input tax on the relevant construction work. Customs rejected the claim on the basis that the expenditure was primarily attributable to non-business activities, so that only a much smaller proportion of the tax was reclaimable. The tribunal chairman (Mr. Heim, sitting alone) allowed M's appeal, holding that the licences which M had granted its two subsidiaries were taxable supplies, since they did not grant an exclusive right of occupation. Accordingly, the principal purpose of the construction work had been the making of taxable supplies. *Mount Edgcumbe Hospice Ltd*, LON/94/519 (VTD 14807). (*Notes.* (1) On the issue of whether a non-exclusive licence to occupy land is exempt from VAT, compare *Altman Blane & Co*, **41.8** LAND, which was not referred to in this decision. See also the subsequent case of *Abbotsley Golf & Squash Club Ltd*, **41.159** LAND, where the same tribunal chairman (Mr. Heim) held that a licence to occupy land did not have to be exclusive to qualify for exemption, on the grounds that exclusivity of occupation was a necessary condition for the creation of a tenancy, but was not a necessary condition for the creation of a licence. Mr. Heim's conclusion in *Abbotsley Golf & Squash Club Ltd* appears to contradict his reasoning in *Mount Edgcumbe Hospice Ltd* on the question of the taxability of the licences. The decision on this point is therefore of doubtful value as a precedent: for a fuller analysis, see the memorandum by the VAT Practitioners' Group published in the Tax Journal, 8 March 1999. (2) For Customs' practice following these decisions, see Business Brief 25/97, issued on 10 November 1997, and Business Brief 22/98, issued on 3 November 1998.)

Charity reclaiming tax relating to transactions outside UK

[11.55] A charity, which was registered for UK VAT, purchased various goods outside the UK. It stored the goods in a warehouse in the Netherlands, and gave them away for no consideration to recipients outside the EU. Although the goods never entered the UK, their distribution was arranged by the charity's London office. The charity reclaimed input tax relating to these transactions. The Commissioners issued an assessment to recover the tax, and the tribunal dismissed the charity's appeal. Because the goods had never entered the UK, they did not qualify as exports within *VATA 1994, s 30(5)*, since '"export" involves removal from the United Kingdom'. Accordingly, there was no entitlement to input tax under *s 26(2)(a)*. There was also no entitlement to input tax credit under *s 26(2)(b)*, since the goods had been distributed for no consideration, and therefore, by virtue of *s 5(2)(a)*, did not qualify as supplies. (The tribunal also held that, even if the goods were treated as supplies, they were not made in the course or furtherance of the charity's business.) *International Planned Parenthood Federation*, [2000] VATDR 396 (VTD 16922).

Charity—expenditure on farming and forestry

[11.56] A registered charity (N) was established 'to advance, promote and further the conservation, maintenance and protection of wildlife and its habitats'. It reclaimed input tax relating to the costs of maintaining a flock of sheep, and of managing an area of woodlands. Customs rejected the bulk of the claim on the basis that N's primary purpose in keeping a flock of sheep was 'to advance its charitable, non-business, object of conservation'. N appealed, contending that it was carrying on a business of sheep farming and forestry. The tribunal reviewed the evidence in detail and allowed N's appeal in part, holding that N was carrying on a business activity of sheep farming but that some of the input tax which N had claimed did not have a 'direct and immediate link' with that business activity. *Nottinghamshire Wildlife Trust*, MAN/03/130 (VTD 19540).

Input tax apportioned to take account of non-business use

[11.57] See *North East Media Development Trust Ltd*, **48.134** PAYMENT OF TAX.

Purchase of premises by partly exempt charity

[11.58] See *Bristol Churches Housing Association*, 46.51 PARTIAL EXEMP-TION.

Partly exempt charity—interpretation of special method

[11.59] See *Sue Ryder Care*, 46.169 PARTIAL EXEMPTION.

Miscellaneous

Whether charity carrying on a business

[11.60] See *Morrison's Academy Boarding Houses Association*, 7.1 BUSI-NESS; *Royal Exchange Theatre Trust*, 7.5 BUSINESS; *Widnes Spastic Fellow-ship*, 7.53 BUSINESS; *Donaldson's College*, 7.84 BUSINESS, and *The Wellcome Trust Ltd*, 22.111 EUROPEAN COMMUNITY LAW.

Supplies of welfare services—EC Sixth Directive

[11.61] See *Yoga for Health Foundation*, 22.293 EUROPEAN COMMUNITY LAW; *International Bible Students Association*, 22.294 EUROPEAN COMMUNITY LAW; *Central YMCA*, 22.295 EUROPEAN COMMUNITY LAW; *Peterborough Diocesan Conference & Retreat House*, 33.68 HEALTH AND WELFARE, and *Trustees for the Macmillan Cancer Trust*, 33.70 HEALTH AND WELFARE.

Construction of buildings—whether for relevant charitable purpose

[11.62] See *Meadows*, 15.82 CONSTRUCTION OF BUILDINGS, ETC.; *Shinewater Association Football Club*, 15.83 CONSTRUCTION OF BUILDINGS, ETC; *Bennachie Leisure Centre Association*, 15.85 CONSTRUCTION OF BUILDINGS, ETC.; *St Dunstan's Roman Catholic Church Southborough*, 15.98 CONSTRUC-TION OF BUILDINGS, ETC.; *Leighton Park School*, 15.99 CONSTRUCTION OF BUILDINGS, ETC.; *St Dunstan's Educational Foundation*, 15.104 CONSTRUC-TION OF BUILDINGS, ETC., and *League of Friends of Kingston Hospital*, 15.110 CONSTRUCTION OF BUILDINGS, ETC.

Royal Academy of Music—concert hall

[11.63] See *The Royal Academy of Music*, 55.15 PROTECTED BUILDINGS.

Fitness centre operated by charity

[11.64] See *Jubilee Hall Recreation Centre Ltd*, 55.16 PROTECTED BUILD-INGS.

Charities operating sports centres for local authorities

[11.65] See *Edinburgh Leisure*, 42.20 LOCAL AUTHORITIES AND STATUTORY BODIES.

Bowling club—whether a charity

[11.66] See *Hunmanby Bowling Club*, 15.108 CONSTRUCTION OF BUILD-INGS, ETC..

Community Amateur Sports Club—whether a charity

[11.67] See *Jacobs*, 19.93 DRUGS, MEDICINES, AIDS FOR THE HANDICAPPED, ETC.

Limited company—whether a charity

[11.68] A company (F), which was registered for VAT, appealed for dona-tions of furniture, furnishings and electrical items. It sold most, but not all, of such donated items to people who were in need. It failed to account for VAT on such sales. HMRC issued a ruling that F's supplies were liable to VAT. F appealed, contending that it should be treated as a charity (so that its sales would qualify for zero-rating under *VATA 1994, Sch 8, Group 15, Item 1*). The tribunal rejected this contention and dismissed the appeal, finding that F was not a charity. *Furniture Finders of Winsford Ltd v HMRC*, [2010] UKFTT 426 (TC), TC00691.

Payment made to charity by associated company

[11.69] See *Durham Aged Mineworkers' Homes Association*, 62.45 SUPPLY.

Payment between associated charities—whether any supply

[11.70] See *Church Schools Foundation Ltd*, 62.46 SUPPLY.

Company acting as trustee of charity

[11.71] See *The Central Council of Physical Recreation*, 62.47 SUPPLY.

Fund-raising event organised by charity—amount of consideration

[11.72] See *Glasgow's Miles Better Mid-Summer 5th Anniversary Ball*, 67.135 VALUATION.

Sponsorship received by charity in return for benefits

[11.73] See *Tron Theatre Ltd*, 67.103 VALUATION.

Local authority providing grants to charity

[11.74] See *Trustees of the Bowthorpe Community Trust*, **42.18** LOCAL AUTHORITIES AND STATUTORY BODIES.

12

Clothing and Footwear

The cases in this chapter are arranged under the following headings.

Whether a supply of articles 'designed as clothing'	**12.1**
Whether articles 'not suitable for older persons'	**12.10**
Miscellaneous	**12.25**

Whether a supply of articles 'designed as clothing'

Article for use in push-chairs

[12.1] A company supplied an article designed for protecting a child when placed in a push-chair. In appearance the article resembled a romper-suit, but a child could not readily walk in it. The company did not account for output tax on its supplies of these articles, treating them as zero-rated. The Commissioners issued a ruling that the articles were not eligible for zero-rating, on the grounds that they were not within the definition of 'clothing'. The tribunal upheld this decision and dismissed the company's appeal. *Mothercare Ltd*, LON/76/177 (VTD 323).

Article to support young child when carried

[12.2] A company manufactured an article, under the brand name of 'Easy Rider', which was designed to help a baby to be carried by its mother by providing warmth and support. It did not account for output tax on its supplies of these articles. The Commissioners issued a ruling that the articles were not eligible for zero-rating, on the grounds that they were not within the definition of 'clothing'. The tribunal upheld this decision and dismissed the company's appeal. *Little Rock Ltd*, LON/77/121 (VTD 424).

'Buoyancy vest'

[12.3] A company supplied articles described as 'buoyancy vests', designed to support young children while they were learning to swim. The Commissioners issued a ruling that supplies of the buoyancy vests did not qualify for zero-rating, on the grounds that they were not within the definition of 'clothing'. The tribunal upheld this decision and dismissed the company's appeal. *British Vita Co Ltd*, MAN/76/135 (VTD 332).

Pleating of textile material for girls' skirts

[12.4] A company carried on the business of pleating textiles for other companies which made girls' and women's clothing. It did not account for output tax on work done on material for skirts for young girls, treating such supplies as zero-rated. The Commissioners issued an assessment on the basis that the work was liable to VAT at the standard rate. The tribunal allowed the company's appeal, holding that the company was to be treated as supplying the pleated pieces of material and not merely the services of pleating. The pleated material in question was designed to be used as parts of skirts for young children and was not suitable for adult women. The pleated pieces fell within the description 'articles designed as clothing' in what is now *VATA 1994, Sch 8, Group 16, Item 1*. The QB upheld the tribunal decision. The pleated material was processed in such a way that it was only suitable to be used as clothing for young children, and the fact that further work would subsequently have to be carried out did not prevent the material from qualifying for zero-rating under *Sch 8, Group 16, Item 1*. *C & E Commrs v Ali Baba Tex Ltd*, QB [1992] STC 590. (*Note.* The Commissioners now accept that 'where an article has been processed to the extent that it cannot make anything other than children's clothing, new goods have been supplied'; see Customs' VAT Manual, Part 3, para 3.1.)

Girls' elasticated headbands

[12.5] A trader manufactured elasticated headbands, intended to be worn by girls under 14 years of age. She did not account for output tax on sales of these headbands, treating them as zero-rated. The Commissioners formed the opinion that the headbands were not within the definition of 'clothing', and issued an assessment, against which the trader appealed. The tribunal dismissed her appeal, holding that the headbands did not qualify as 'other headgear' within what is now *VATA 1994, Sch 8, Group 16, Note 1*, and were therefore not eligible for zero-rating. The tribunal considered that 'headgear must be similar or analogous to hats and must give some covering or protection to the head'. *Mrs V Cassidy (t/a Balou)*, MAN/90/884 (VTD 5760).

Wristbands

[12.6] A company sold sportswear including wristbands, made of a towelling material, designed to absorb perspiration when playing tennis and similar sports. It treated supplies of small wristbands (designed for children under 13) as zero-rated. The Commissioners issued a ruling that the wristbands did not qualify for zero-rating, as they were not within the definition of 'clothing'. The tribunal upheld the Commissioners' ruling and dismissed the company's appeal, holding that the wristbands were 'accessories' rather than 'clothing'. *Vidhani Brothers Ltd*, MAN/04/296 (VTD 18997).

Badge sashes and woggles for Girl Guides and Brownies

[12.7] Two companies manufactured and sold items designed as uniforms for Girl Guides (aged 10 to 13 inclusive) and Brownies (aged 7 to 9 inclusive). They did not account for output tax on such supplies, treating them as zero-rated. The Commissioners issued rulings that badge sashes and woggles did not qualify for zero-rating under what is now *VATA 1994, Sch 8, Group 16*, on the grounds that they were not within the definition of 'clothing'. The tribunal upheld the Commissioners' rulings and dismissed the companies' appeals. *Dauntgate Ltd*, MAN/93/144Y; *BG Supplies (Birmingham) Ltd*, MAN/93/373W (VTD 11663). (*Note*. For another issue in this case, see **12.19** below.)

Washing of children's jeans prior to sale—whether zero-rated

[12.8] A partnership carried on the business of washing denim jeans prior to sale, with the object of lightening the colour of the cloth and softening the material. It did not account for output tax on the consideration it received for washing jeans designed for children, treating such supplies as zero-rated. The Commissioners issued a ruling that the partnership was making supplies of services which did not qualify for zero-rating. The partnership appealed, contending that the washing had the effect of making the jeans more fashionable and was a 'treatment or process' within what is now *VATA 1994, Sch 4 para 2*, and thus a supply of zero-rated clothing. The tribunal dismissed the appeal, holding that, although the washing could be described as a 'treatment or process', it did not produce any goods, since 'what went into the process was a pair of jeans and that is what was there at the end of the process'. Accordingly, the partnership was making standard-rated supplies of services rather than zero-rated supplies of goods. *Warley Denim Services*, MAN/92/1668 (VTD 10396).

Sale of discount cards for purchases of clothing

[12.9] See *Mothercare (UK) Ltd*, 58.8 RETAILERS' SPECIAL SCHEMES.

Whether articles 'not suitable for older persons'

Fashion knitwear

[12.10] A company did not account for output tax on sales of eleven types of 'one-size fashion knitwear'. All, with one exception, were of approximately the same size and possessed the quality of 'stretchability'. The tribunal held that, except for one item which was significantly smaller than the others, their supply did not qualify for zero-rating. Although they were intended for the use of young children, they were also 'suitable for older persons' and were thus excluded from zero-rating. *Jeffrey Green & Co Ltd*, [1974] VATTR 94 (VTD 69).

Leather overcoats

[12.11] A company did not account for output tax on a type of overcoat, bearing no size label but advertised as a 'girl's leather coat'. The coats were 35 inches in length and measured 35 inches across the bust. The Commissioners issued a ruling that, because the coats had a three-inch bust dart, they were 'suitable for wear by older persons' and did not qualify for zero-rating. The company appealed, contending that the waist and hip measurements of the coats were such that they were not 'suitable for wear by older persons'. The tribunal rejected this contention and dismissed the appeal, observing that the length of the overcoats appeared to be 'suitable on older persons' and holding that, in view of the three-inch bust dart, the overcoats in question did not qualify for zero-rating. The tribunal observed that, in interpreting the reference to 'young children' in what is now *VATA 1994, Sch 8, Group 16, Item 1*, it was 'prepared to accept 14 years as being reasonable in the case of a girl's outer coat, having regard to the clear purpose of Parliament in relieving young children's clothing from value added tax as being to save parents' expense during the period of rapid growth, which we observe from British Standards compilation BS 3728:1970, put in evidence before us, as commencing to decelerate after the age of 13 years'. *Walter Stewart Ltd*, [1974] VATTR 131 (VTD 83).

Nursing shawls

[12.12] A partnership manufactured nursing shawls. It did not account for output tax on its supplies of these shawls, treating them as zero-rated. The Commissioners issued a ruling that the shawls were not eligible for zero-rating, on the grounds that they were 'suitable for older persons'. The tribunal accepted this contention and dismissed the firm's appeal. *WG Jones & Son*, BIR/74/12 (VTD 117).

Footwear

[12.13] A company manufactured a type of moccasin. In accounting for tax, it treated sizes up to and including 5.5 as zero-rated. The Commissioners issued a ruling that the moccasins in size 3 to size 5.5 inclusive did not qualify for zero-rating on the grounds that they were also suitable for some older women. The company which manufactured them appealed, contending that they were designed for young girls and should therefore be zero-rated. The tribunal dismissed the appeal, holding on the evidence that the moccasins in question were 'suitable for wear by older persons generally', and were therefore excluded from zero-rating. *Brays of Glastonbury Ltd*, CAR/78/95 (VTD 650).

Footwear—definition of 'young children' in Group 16, Item 1

[12.14] A trader did not account for VAT on sales of girls' shoes in size 5.5, treating them as zero-rated. The Commissioners issued an assessment on the basis that the shoes were suitable for 'older persons' and that the sales should have been standard-rated, in accordance with *Notice No 714*. The trader appealed, contending that for the purposes of *VATA 1994, Sch 8, Group 16, Item 1*, 'young children' should be construed as including all children under the age of 16, rather than only children under the age of 14. The tribunal rejected this contention and dismissed the trader's appeal, applying the principles laid down in *Walter Stewart Ltd*, **12.11** above. *NA Gura (t/a Vincent Footwear)*, LON/01/978 (VTD 18416).

Slippers—whether unisex—effect of Notice No 714

[**12.15**] A company did not account for VAT on sales of slippers which it manufactured in sizes 4 and 5. The Commissioners issued an assessment charging tax on the slippers, considering that they were designed for girls and that, by virtue of *Notice No 714*, only girls' slippers up to and including size 3 could be zero-rated. The company appealed, contending that the slippers were unisex, and that *Notice No 714* indicated (at *p 21* of the 1986 edition) that unisex slippers could be zero-rated up to and including size 5.5. The tribunal criticised the wording of *Notice No 714* as being inconsistent with the legislation, since 'sizes 4 or 5 in general fit girls of ages greater than 14 and some adult women'. Accordingly, any unisex slippers in those sizes were suitable for wear by 'older persons', and not eligible for zero-rating. The tribunal remitted the case to the parties to consider the different fabric colours, patterns and designs individually, on the principle that designs suitable for both sexes, and designs only suitable for girls, were not eligible for zero-rating; but designs which were only suitable for boys were eligible for zero-rating. *R Spencer (Cosy Comfort Slippers) Ltd*, MAN/91/1636 (VTD 7945). (*Note. Notice No 714* has subsequently been revised and reissued.)

Jeans

[**12.16**] Boys' jeans were held, on the evidence, to be designed as clothing for young children, and not to be suitable for older persons, in *VF Corporation (UK) Ltd*, BEL/79/7 (VTD 898).

[**12.17**] A similar decision was reached in *R Kaur Singh*, MAN/86/6 (VTD 2433).

Sports shorts

[**12.18**] A company did not account for output tax on supplies of elasticated white shorts designed to be worn by children under the age of 14 when playing games such as football or tennis, treating them as zero-rated. The Commissioners formed the opinion that some of the shorts, with advertised waist sizes of 28 ins, 30 ins and 32 ins, were suitable for people over the age of 14, and thus did not qualify for zero-rating. They issued an assessment charging tax on the supplies of these shorts, and the company appealed. The tribunal allowed the company's appeal, finding that because the waist-crotch-waist measurement of the shorts in question did not exceed 26 ins, they were too small to be suitable for people over the age of 14. (The tribunal noted that the waist measurements of the shorts 'at rest' were up to four inches smaller than the advertised waist measurements, which were measured at 'a position of comfortable stretch in wear', and also observed that 'we are not concerned with what an abnormally small person, but rather an average person of age groups, could wear'.) *Falcon Sportswear Ltd*, MAN/85/374 (VTD 2019). (*Note.* At the hearing, the Commissioners' representative contended that because the company had listed the shorts alongside adults' shorts in a price list, they had been held out for sale as being suitable for older persons. The tribunal rejected this contention, and the chairman observed that 'we deprecate argument for standard-rating of garments manufactured within the tolerances proposed by a Public Notice, merely on the layout of such a list'.)

Culottes and sweatpants for Girl Guides and Brownies

[12.19] Two companies manufactured and sold items designed as uniforms for Girl Guides (aged 10 to 13 inclusive) and Brownies (aged 7 to 9 inclusive). They did not account for output tax on such supplies, treating them as zero-rated. The Commissioners issued rulings that neckerchiefs, culottes in waist sizes of 30 and 32inches, and Guides' sweatpants with a 32-inch waist did not qualify for zero-rating on the grounds that they were 'suitable for older persons'. The companies appealed. The tribunal allowed the appeals in part, holding that the culottes did not qualify for zero-rating because their waist size rendered them suitable for 60% of all women and, although they were intended as uniform for Guides, their dark blue colour was 'perfectly standard and acceptable' for older persons. However, the sweatpants qualified for zero-rating because, although their waist measurement of 32 inches was in principle 'suitable for older persons', the garments had a waist–crotch–waist measurement of only 23 inches. It followed that, unlike the culottes, they were 'not sufficiently full at lower points' to be 'suitable for older persons'. The neckerchiefs also qualified for zero-rating on the grounds that they would not be worn by 'any persons other than girl guides and boy scouts'. *Daunt-gate Ltd*, MAN/93/144Y; *BG Supplies (Birmingham) Ltd*, MAN/93/373W (VTD 11663). (*Note*. For another issue in this case, see **12.7** above.)

School uniform items exceeding sizes laid down in Notice 714

[12.20] A company sold items of school uniform, including sweatshirts with school logos. The Commissioners issued a ruling that such items were standard-rated where they exceeded the size limits laid down in *Notice No 714, para 4.2*. The company appealed, contending that where the purchaser signed a declaration that the relevant garment was intended for a child aged under 14, the supply should be treated as zero-rated, even if the garment exceeded the size limits laid down in *Notice No 714, para 4.2*. The tribunal rejected this contention and dismissed the appeal, holding that 'the zero-rating of an item of clothing cannot depend on a declaration that the intended wearer of a particular garment' was aged less than 14 years. The tribunal held that 'in determining whether or not an item of uniform is "designed for young children", the size of the uniform is important. The age of the eventual wearer of the particular item of uniform actually supplied is not relevant. It is the intent of the designer that matters, not the age in fact of the wearer of a particular garment produced in accordance with that design.' The tribunal also held that the fact that a school logo had been attached to a garment did not make it 'unsuitable for older persons'. *Smart Alec Ltd*, LON/01/1307 (VTD 17832).

[12.21] The decision in *Smart Alec Ltd*, **12.20** above, was applied in the similar subsequent case of *Forsters School & Leisurewear Ltd*, LON/07/1501 (VTD 20758).

Clothing designed for children 164cm in height

[12.22] A company sold a large variety of clothing for children and teenagers. The Commissioners issued a ruling that VAT was chargeable on clothing designed for children 164cm in height (their height limits for zero-rating being 163cm for boys and 161cm for girls). The company appealed, contending that clothing designed for children 164cm in height should be zero-rated. The tribunal rejected this contention and dismissed the appeal, observing that 'the statistics we have seen show that the size limits are suitable to an average child up to his or her 14th birthday' and that 'the 14th birthday limit seems generous'. The tribunal held that 'by the nature of such a test it cannot cater for the very tall child'. The 164cm size was 'not designed for young children and is suitable in size for a 14-year-old'. The Ch D upheld this decision, Sir Donald Rattee held that the tribunal had been entitled to hold that 'a 14-year-old is not within the normal meaning of the words "young children"'. *H & M Hennes Ltd v C & E Commrs*, Ch D [2005] STC 1749; [2005] EWHC 1383 (Ch).

Riding hats

[12.23] A company manufactured riding hats. The Commissioners accepted that the hats were zero-rated up to and including size 6.5, but issued a ruling that the hats were not eligible for zero-rating above 6.5, on the grounds that they were suitable for older persons as well as for young children. The tribunal allowed the appeal, finding that, since cartoon characters were portrayed on the hats, which bore the words 'Kids Own', any adult who wore one would risk being exposed to 'ridicule or contempt'. Accordingly the hats were not 'suitable' for anyone over the age of 14, and qualified for zero-rating. *Charles Owen & Co (Bow) Ltd*, [1993] VATTR 514 (VTD 11267).

Acrylic hats with football logos

[12.24] A company imported a quantity of knitted acrylic hats, with logos referring to well-known football teams. The Commissioners issued a ruling that the sale of the hats was standard-rated. The company appealed, contending that the hats should be zero-rated as they were designed for young children and were not suitable for older persons. The tribunal accepted this contention and allowed the appeal. On the evidence, although the hats could be stretched so that it was physically possible for an adult to wear them, they were 'too close-fitting for comfortable wear over an extended period'. Furthermore, they were intended as a 'cheap imitation' of official football club hats, to be worn by young children who could not afford the official hats. The tribunal considered that the hats 'would be unlikely to be worn by any persons other than football supporters, and supporters over 14 would want the official hats'. The hats 'would not in general be acceptable headwear for adults or children over 14'. *Benrose Ltd (t/a Multi-Stock Co)*, LON/98/7048 (VTD 15783).

Miscellaneous

Disposable nappies supplied with toy box

[12.25] A company produced disposable nappies, which were accepted as zero-rated. Under a promotional scheme, it supplied some of these with a plastic toy box. It did not account for VAT on these sales, treating them as entirely zero-rated. The Commissioners issued an assessment on the basis that the company was making a separate supply of a standard-rated toy box, so that the consideration had to be apportioned. The tribunal upheld the assessment but the Ch D allowed the company's appeal. Lloyd J held that there was a single zero-rated supply of nappies, to which the toy box was ancillary. *Kimberly-Clark Ltd v C & E Commrs*, Ch D 2003, [2004] STC 473; [2003] EWHC 1623 (Ch).

Membership of playgroup including T-shirt

[12.26] A company operated a number of playgroups, on a franchise basis. It charged an initial membership fee of £19, plus subsequent fees of from £4 to £8.50 per session. New members received a T-shirt, a DVD, a CD and a magazine. Customs issued a ruling that the company was required to account for VAT on the initial membership fees. The company appealed, contending that they should be treated as attributable to the zero-rated supplies of the T-shirt and magazine. The Ch D rejected this contention and upheld Customs' ruling. Briggs J held that there was a single supply of membership of the playgroup, and that it would be artificial to treat the provision of the T-shirt as a separate zero-rated supply. *Tumble Tots (UK) Ltd v HMRC (and cross-appeal)*, Ch D [2007] STC 1171; [2007] EWHC 103 (Ch).

13

Clubs, Associations and Organisations

The cases in this chapter are arranged under the following headings.

Whether VATA 1994, s 94(2)(a) applicable

    Cases held to be within s *94(2)(a)*   **13.1**

    Cases held not to be within s *94(2)(a)*   **13.11**

The taxation of the receipts of a club, etc.

    Annual subscriptions   **13.17**

    Receipts other than annual subscriptions   **13.29**

Other matters   **13.43**

NOTE

This chapter includes cases concerning *VATA 1994, s 94(2)(a)*, under which the provision of 'facilities or advantages' by a club, association or organisation to its members is deemed to be the carrying on of a business. *VATA 1994, s 94(3)*, which previously provided that certain bodies in the public interest were not to be treated as carrying on a business, was repealed by *FA 1999* with effect from 1 December 1999. The subscriptions which, in accordance with *s 94(3)*, were previously disregarded for VAT purposes, are now exempt by virtue of *VATA 1994, Sch 9, Group 9, Item 1(e)*, introduced by the *VAT (Subscriptions to Trade Unions, Professional and Other Public Interest Bodies) Order 1999 (SI 1999/2834)*. For details, see Tolley's Value Added Tax. For cases concerning *VATA 1994, Sch 9, Group 9* (Trade unions, professional and public interest bodies) see **64** TRADE UNIONS, PROFESSIONAL AND PUBLIC INTEREST BODIES.

Whether VATA 1994, s 94(2)(a) applicable

Cases held to be within s 94(2)(a)

Association of local residents

[13.1] A new village was divided into a number of 'neighbourhood areas' and a society was established as a residents' association for each of the areas. Each society was registered under the *Industrial and Provident Societies Act 1965*, its members being the owners of houses in its area. It was financed by members' subscriptions and its main activities were the upkeep of the amenity land in its area and the periodical external redecoration of members' houses. The tribunal upheld the Commissioners' contention that it was an association providing facilities available to its members and hence carrying on a business by virtue of what is now *VATA 1994, s 94(2)(a)*. *Manor Forstal Residents Society Ltd*, [1976] VATTR 63 (VTD 245). (*Note.* The case was heard with *New Ash Green Village Association Ltd*, **13.11** below.)

Members' club operating 'timeshare' accommodation

[13.2] A members' club operated a holiday complex, comprising 26 self-contained units. It had about 1,300 members, each of which were entitled to one week's holiday at the complex each year. The members were required to pay an annual contribution to a central fund which was used to cover the cost of wages, laundry and general maintenance and management. The club registered for VAT from 1991, but applied for deregistration in 1993. The Commissioners rejected the application, on the basis that the effect of what is now *VATA 1994, s 94(2)(a)* was that the club was deemed to be carrying on a business. The tribunal dismissed the club's appeal against this decision, holding that the club was within *s 94(2)(a)*, and was making supplies for consideration. Furthermore, these supplies did not qualify for exemption under *Article 13A1(f)* of the *EC Sixth Directive. The Regency Villas Owners Club*, LON/95/305 (VTD 16525).

Company operating 'timeshare' accommodation

[13.3] The owners of a 'timeshare' holiday complex formed a limited company to maintain the accommodation at the complex. Each owner held one share in the company. The Commissioners issued a ruling that the company was carrying on a business and was required to account for VAT. The company appealed, contending that its activities were not conducted on a commercial basis. The tribunal dismissed the appeal, holding that the supplies were within *VATA 1994, s 94(2)(a). Scandinavian Village Ltd*, EDN/99/216 (VTD 16961).

Working Men's Club

[13.4] An incorporated Industrial and Provident Society provided the usual facilities of a Workmen's Club and Institute, including the provision of alcoholic drinks and recreational facilities. The facilities were available to members who were required to hold one 50p share in the Club and pay an annual subscription. The Commissioners issued a ruling that VAT was chargeable on members' subscriptions (including the payments for the shares). The tribunal dismissed the club's appeal, holding that the subscriptions were consideration for the club's provision of facilities or advantages available to members. *Southchurch Workingmen's Club & Institute Ltd*, MAN/78/40 (VTD 613). (*Note*. The tribunal also held that the club was not within what is now *VATA 1994, Sch 9, Group 9, Item 1(e)*.)

English-Speaking Union

[13.5] The English-Speaking Union (ESU) was established by Royal Charter and registered as a charity, with the principal object of promoting the 'mutual advancement of the education of the English-speaking peoples of the world'. In return for their subscription, members were entitled to take part in ESU's activities. With two exceptions, non-members had an equal right to participate in, or take advantage of, these activities. The two exceptions were that the ESU journal, published every few months, was issued free to members but non-members had to pay for it, and that members could obtain contacts and introduction to other members, when travelling away from home. The Commissioners issued a decision that ESU was deemed to be carrying on a business by virtue of what is now *VATA 1994, s 94(2)(a)*. The tribunal dismissed ESU's appeal. *The English-Speaking Union of the Commonwealth*, [1980] VATTR 184 (VTD 1023). (*Note*. The tribunal held that ESU was not within *FA 1972, s 45(3)* (which became *VATA 1994, s 94(3)*). However it is arguable that ESU would now qualify for exemption under *VATA 1994, Sch 9, Group*

9, *Item 1(e)*, which was introduced by the *VAT (Subscriptions to Trade Unions, Professional and Other Public Interest Bodies) Order 1999 (SI 1999/2834)* with effect from 1 December 1999.)

Golf club—trust established to purchase course

[13.6] A golf club, which had previously held the leasehold of its course, established a trust to purchase the freehold. The trust divided the ownership into 750 units, 200 of which were allocated to the club and 550 of which were reserved for allocation to individual members, no member being entitled to more than one unit. No member was entitled to play golf on the course unless he was the holder of a unit. The Commissioners assessed the club on the basis that it was carrying on a business by providing the facilities of the golf course for consideration. The club appealed, contending that the facilities were provided by the trust which was a separate legal entity, and that it received no consideration for the supply of the units by the trust to the members. The CS rejected this contention and upheld the assessment, holding that it was the club which provided the facilities, the consideration for which was the members' subscriptions and the payments which the members made for units in the trust. *Lord Advocate v Largs Golf Club*, CS [1985] STC 226.

County football association—income from fines

[13.7] The Northamptonshire Football Association was registered for VAT, and reclaimed the whole of its input tax. A significant proportion of its income came from fines imposed on players who had been cautioned or dismissed from the field of play. The Commissioners issued a ruling that part of the Association's input tax should be apportioned to the receipt of fines, which related to a disciplinary activity which should be treated as outside the scope of VAT, and was not deductible. The Association appealed, contending that it was carrying on a business within what is now *VATA 1994, s 94(2)(a)* and that all its input tax related to its business activities. The tribunal accepted this contention and allowed the appeal, holding that the enforcement of the rules of the game was 'an essential element of the administration of the playing of the game'. The enforcement of the rules was 'an advantage of membership' and 'an obligation of the Association undertaken in favour of each of the members' in return for their membership fees and subscriptions. It was thus deemed to be part of the carrying on of a business, within what is now *VATA 1994, s 94(2)(a)*. *Northamptonshire Football Association*, LON/94/727 (VTD 12936).

Rugby club

[13.8] A rugby club was established as a non-profit-making body, although it charged spectators 25p for admission to first-team matches, and sold match programmes. It arranged for the construction of a new changing-room block (including separate toilets for spectators), and reclaimed input tax on this. The Commissioners issued assessments to recover the tax, on the basis that the club was not carrying on any business. The tribunal allowed the club's appeal, holding that it was carrying on a business within *VATA 1994, s 94(2)(a)*, and was making taxable supplies which were 'directly referable to the construction of the building'. The fact that the club was a non-profit-making body was not conclusive, since 'it was carrying on business (*sic*) and the construction of the changing-room block was in furtherance of that deemed business'. *Clwb Rygbi Nant Conwy*, MAN/97/864 (VTD 16376). (*Note*. The tribunal also held that the club's supplies were excluded from exemption by *Sch 9, Group 1, Item 1(l)* and *(m)*.)

Association of taxi drivers

[13.9] In the case noted at **62.32** SUPPLY, the HL upheld Customs' contention that an association of taxi drivers was within *VATA 1994, s 94(2)(a)*. Lord Slynn observed that the intention of *VATA 1994, s 94* was that 'the activities of an association should not be excluded from VAT merely because it was unincorporated and not a legal person'. For VAT purposes, an unincorporated association was a legal entity, separate from its members. On the evidence, there was a direct link between the services which the association provided and the payments which its members made. The association was supplying facilities or advantages to its members for consideration, and was required to register for VAT. *Eastbourne Town Radio Cars Association v C & E Commrs*, HL [2001] STC 606; [2001] UKHL 19; [2001] 1 WLR 794; [2001] 2 All ER 597.

Society for defence of hunting

[13.10] An association was formed in 1930 to defend deer-hunting, stag-hunting, and similar 'blood sports', which some Members of Parliament had sought to outlaw. Between 1991 and 1995 it was active in opposing proposed legislation on this subject. It was registered for VAT and reclaimed input tax on its expenditure. It accounted for output tax on a proportion of members' subscriptions, the balance of the subscriptions being treated as attributable to exempt supplies of insurance or zero-rated supplies of printed matter. In 1993 the Commissioners issued assessments to recover some of the association's input tax, on the basis that much of the expenditure related to general propaganda which did not provide any 'facility or advantage' to the association's members and was not to be treated as a business activity. The association appealed, contending that, by campaigning against proposed legislation which would outlaw its members' leisure activities, it was providing its members with 'facilities or advantages', which constituted the carrying on of a business by virtue of *VATA 1994, s 94(2)(a)*. The tribunal accepted this contention and allowed the appeal, and the CA upheld this decision. The fact that the expenditure benefited people who participated in blood sports without being members of the association was not conclusive. On the evidence, the tribunal had been entitled to conclude that the association's propaganda provided its members with 'facilities or advantages', so that the association was entitled to reclaim input tax on its expenditure. The term 'facilities and advantages' should be construed widely. There was a direct link between the members' subscriptions and the association's campaigning activities. *C & E Commrs v British Field Sports Society*, CA [1998] STC 315; [1998] 1 WLR 962; [1998] 2 All ER 1003.

Cases held not to be within s 94(2)(a)

Village development association

[13.11] An association was incorporated, as a company limited by guarantee, under a scheme for developing a large village with some 2,000 houses. The association comprised 16 'consultant members' and 18 'representative members', appointed by societies established for each of the 'neighbourhood areas' into which the village was divided. Its principal activities were the upkeep of amenity land in the village, providing and maintaining street lighting, running a village sports ground and running a village hall. Its principal income consisted of payments from all houseowners in the area under covenants which formed part of the Deeds of Transfer under which they acquired their houses. The Commissioners issued a ruling that the company was an association providing facilities to its members and was carrying on a business by virtue of what is now *VATA 1994, s 94(2)(a)*. The tribunal allowed the company's appeal against this decision, holding that the houseowners to whom its services were supplied were not its 'members'. The term 'member' could not be extended to mean any person who had entered into a contractual relationship with the association. *New Ash Green Village Association Ltd*, [1976] VATTR 63 (VTD 245). (*Note.* See *Manor Forstal Residents Society Ltd*, 13.1 above, for an appeal by one of the neighbourhood area societies.)

Canteen at fire station

[13.12] Canteen facilities were provided at a fire station. The fire service provided the canteen, cooking equipment and the cooks, and paid £1 per week to an operational fireman to act as 'mess manager'. As such he signed the accounts of the canteen which, although described as a club, was in fact very loosely organised with no constitution, rules, committee or officers. Anyone at the fire station could use the canteen and prices were fixed to cover the cost of the food supplied. The Commissioners issued a ruling that the club was required to register for VAT. The tribunal allowed the club's appeal, holding on the evidence that the canteen was not run by a club or organisation within what is now *VATA 1994, s 94(2)(a)*. The canteen was run by the mess manager, who performed his duties as an employee or agent of the fire authority. *Nottingham Fire Service Messing Club*, [1977] VATTR 1 (VTD 348).

Association to raise funds for Olympics

[13.13] The British Olympic Association reclaimed input tax on the cost of supplying clothing for British competitors in the 1976 Olympics, and on fees charged by advertising agents who had helped it in fund-raising appeals. Customs issued assessmenst to recover the tax, and the Association appealed. The tribunal dismissed the appeal, holding that the British competitors at the Olympics were not, as such, members of the Association and accordingly the provision of clothing for them was not for the purpose of any deemed business of providing facilities available to the Association's members. The tribunal also held that the Association was not carrying on a business in the general sense of the term. *British Olympic Association*, [1979] VATTR 122 (VTD 779).

Fund-raising association for Ironbridge Museum

[13.14] In 1968 the Ironbridge Museum Trust was established to preserve the history of the Ironbridge area. It was incorporated as a limited company and registered as a charity. A fund-raising association was also established, and was called the Friends of the Ironbridge Gorge Museum. In 1990 Customs sought to register the Friends for VAT. The Friends appealed, contending that in law they were acting as agents of the Trust, that subscriptions from members included donations which were passed to the Trust and were not liable to VAT, and that any benefits received by members (such as free admission to sites and the receipt of a quarterly newsletter) were conferred by the Trust rather than by the Friends. The tribunal allowed the Friends' appeal, holding that the Friends were not 'quite on the same basis as a private members club'. In the case of a private members club, the subscriptions paid by members were consideration for facilities provided by the club. However, people joined the Friends not in order to receive facilities, but in order to make financial contributions to the Museum. Donations were not consideration for benefits or facilities, and were therefore outside the scope of VAT. Since any benefits received by members were supplied by the Trust rather than by the Friends, what is now *VATA 1994, s 94(2)(a)* did not apply and the Friends were not liable to be registered. *Friends of the Ironbridge Gorge Museum*, [1991] VATTR 97 (VTD 5639). (*Note.* For Customs' practice following this decision, see Customs' VAT Manual, Part 12, chapter 3, para 9.13. Customs take the view that parts of the decision are 'open to challenge' and are seeking 'a suitable test-case'.)

Golf club—free membership given to honorary members

[13.15] A limited company was established under the Business Expansion Scheme to operate a golf club. It gave honorary membership of the club to 64 of its shareholders. The Commissioners issued an assessment on the basis that the grant of honorary membership was a taxable supply by virtue of what is now *VATA 1994, s 94(2)(a)*, and that the value of the supply was the normal subscription paid by members who were not shareholders. The club appealed, contending that the only supply was the issue of shares, which was exempt from VAT. The tribunal allowed the club's appeal, holding on the evidence that the shareholders' 'paramount purpose in buying the shares was to invest in the company with a view to profit', and that the club had offered honorary membership to such shareholders as an 'incentive to invest'. *Hinckley Golf Club Ltd*, [1992] VATTR 259 (VTD 9527).

Company campaigning for welfare of farm animals

[13.16] Two companies had been established to campaign for the welfare of farm animals. They were registered as a group for VAT purposes. One of the companies (S) was limited by guarantee and received subscriptions from supporters of the companies' aims, but the actual campaigning was undertaken by the other company (C), which was the representative member of the group for VAT. S owned 50% of the shares in C, the other 50% being owned by an individual. Members of the public who paid subscriptions to S received a quarterly magazine, published by C. C reclaimed input tax in respect of campaigning expenditure. The Commissioners issued an assessment to recover the tax on the basis that the companies' campaigning activities did not constitute a business. C appealed, contending that they should be treated as a business for VAT purposes by virtue of *VATA 1994, s 94(2)(a)*. The tribunal rejected this contention, holding on the evidence that members of the public who subscribed to S were not 'members' of S, as required by *s 94(2)(a)*, and that the subscriptions which they paid did not give them any contractual rights. *Compassion in World Farming Ltd*, [1997] VATDR 281 (VTD 15204). (*Note*. The tribunal directed that some of the assessments under appeal should be discharged as they had been incorrectly computed and had not been made to the best of the Commissioners' judgment.)

The taxation of the receipts of a club, etc

Annual subscriptions

Whether subscription covers more than one supply

[13.17] The Automobile Association provided members with an annual handbook and a magazine. The Commissioners issued a ruling that the whole of members' subscriptions was chargeable at the standard rate. The Association appealed, contending that part of the subscriptions were attributable to the supply of the handbook and magazine, which were zero-rated under what is now *VATA 1994, Sch 8, Group 3*. The tribunal accepted this contention and allowed the appeal, and the QB upheld this decision as one of fact. *C & E Commrs v The Automobile Association*, QB [1974] STC 192; [1974] 1 WLR 1447; [1974] 1 All ER 1257. (*Notes*. (1) *Obiter dicta* of Lord Widgery CJ, with regard to the distinction between questions of law and questions of fact, were disapproved by Lord Denning MR in the subsequent case of *British Railways Board*, 66.12 TRANSPORT. (2) With regard to the distinction between single and multiple supplies, see now the subsequent ECJ decision in *Card Protection Plan Ltd*, 22.324 EUROPEAN COMMUNITY LAW.)

[13.18] A similar decision was reached in a case concerning a society which had been formed to further the knowledge of alpine plants. Its principal activity was the supply to members of an annual handbook and a quarterly bulletin. The QB held that part of the subscriptions was attributable to these publications, and was zero-rated under what is now *VATA 1994, Sch 8, Group 3*. *Barton v C & E Commrs*, QB [1974] STC 200; [1974] 1 WLR 1447; [1974] 3 All ER 337.

[13.19] The Institute of Chartered Foresters was established as a non-profit-making body to provide training in, and information about, forestry. In accounting for tax, it treated part of its members' subscriptions as attributable to the zero-rated supplies of a quarterly magazine (so that it could reclaim the relevant input tax). The Commissioners issued a ruling that the magazine was part of a single supply of services to the Institute's members, which failed to qualify for zero-rating but was exempt from VAT. The tribunal upheld the Commissioners' ruling and dismissed the Institute's appeal. *Institute of Chartered Foresters*, EDN/00/51 (VTD 16884).

Royal College of Anaesthetists—supply of journals to graduates

[13.20] The Royal College of Anaesthetists charged annual subscriptions of £320 pa to its graduate members. In accounting for VAT, it initially treated part of these subscriptions as attributable to the zero-rated supply of journals, and part as exempt. In 2001 it submitted a repayment claim on the basis that it should have treated the whole of the subscriptions as zero-rated. Customs rejected the claim and the tribunal dismissed the College's appeal, holding that the journals should be treated as supplied at cost (which was about £30 pa). *The Royal College of Anaesthetists*, LON/03/170 (VTD 18632).

Yacht club—whether subscriptions entirely exempt from VAT

[13.21] See *Royal Thames Yacht Club*, 24.40 EXEMPTIONS: MISCELLANEOUS.

Golf club subscription—whether exempt under Sch 9, Group 1

[13.22] See *Banstead Downs Golf Club*, 41.70 LAND.

Golf club—entrance subscriptions

[13.23] A golf club did not account for tax on the 'entrance subscriptions' which it charged new members. Customs issued an assessment charging tax on them, and the tribunal dismissed the club's appeal, holding that the subscriptions were part of the consideration for the facilities which the club supplied to its members. *Downes Crediton Golf Club*, CAR/79/203 (VTD 868).

Golf club charging reduced subscriptions to members making loans to it

[13.24] A golf club had raised finance through loans from members. In return for these loans, it charged a reduced level of annual subscription to such members. Customs considered that, in such cases, the club should account for VAT on the full subscription rate charged to members who had not made loans to the club. The club appealed, contending that the value of the supply should be the reduced subscription actually charged, plus an amount equal to the annual interest that would be paid in the open market on loans such as those made to the club. The tribunal accepted this contention and allowed the club's appeal. *West Essex Golf Club*, [1992] VATTR 35 (VTD 7321).

Sports and social club owning premises including playing fields

[13.25] A limited company, describing itself as an 'athletic association' but described by the tribunal as a sports and social club, owned premises including playing fields and pitches. It established a fund, described as a sports fund, to which its members paid subscriptions. The Commissioners issued an assessment on the basis that by providing its facilities the club was carrying on a business and that the fund subscriptions were liable to VAT. The company appealed, contending that there was no direct link between the payment of subscriptions and the provision of facilities, and that the subscriptions were in the nature of donations. The tribunal dismissed the appeal, holding that on the evidence, the link between the payment of subscriptions and the provision of facilities was clearly discernible. *Royal Ulster Constabulary Athletic Association Ltd*, [1989] VATTR 17 (VTD 3529).

Country club—whether subscriptions for licence to occupy land

[13.26] See *Trewby*, 41.71 LAND.

Holiday club—increase in subscriptions to meet special expenditure

[13.27] See *Little Spain Club*, 41.72 LAND.

Annual subscriptions—time at which VAT chargeable

[13.28] See *East Kilbride Golf Club*, 62.420 SUPPLY.

Receipts other than annual subscriptions

Club bar sales—whether supplies

[13.29] An unincorporated members' club sold alcoholic drinks to its members. It applied for its VAT registration to be cancelled. The Commissioners rejected the application on the grounds that the club's supplies exceeded the registration threshold. The club appealed, contending that, since the members were already part-owners of its stock of drinks, it should not be treated as supplying them to its members. The tribunal rejected this contention and dismissed the appeal, and the QB unanimously upheld this decision. Milmo J observed that 'the issue here is not whether there was a sale, but whether there was a supply'. Applying the principles laid down in *Metford v Edwards*, KB [1915] 1 KB 172, the club was supplying its drinks to its members, notwithstanding that the members were already part-owners of the club's stock. *Carlton Lodge Club v C & E Commrs*, QB [1974] STC 507; [1975] 1 WLR 66; [1974] 3 All ER 798.

Levy on members to meet capital expenditure

[13.30] A club which was heavily in debt foresaw capital expenditure of up to £50,000 on its premises, partly to comply with fire precaution regulations. Its rules were altered to permit levies on members to meet its special needs, to obviate an increase in the annual subscriptions. Following this it made a levy of £7.50 per member for its financial year ending 31 January 1975. The Commissioners issued an assessment on the basis that the levies were chargeable at the standard rate. The club appealed. The tribunal dismissed the appeal, holding that the levies were to meet expenditure to provide the facilities available to the members and were therefore taxable by virtue of what is now *VATA 1994, s 94(2)(a)*. *The Royal Scottish Automobile Club*, EDN/76/7A (VTD 257).

Bonds issued as a condition of membership

[13.31] A company ran a members' golf and country club, with various classes of membership. Full members and social members were required, in addition to paying the usual annual subscriptions, to subscribe for a bond in the company within 28 days of becoming members. The bond was unsecured, carried no interest, and, with regard to these classes of Members, not transferable; if for any reason the holder ceased to be a member, the Bond was cancelled after five years. The bond had a face value of £350 but the committee required members to pay more than this. The Commissioners issued a ruling that output tax was payable on the amounts which the members paid for the bonds, and the club appealed. The tribunal held that the bond was a 'security for money' within the meaning of what is now *VATA 1994, Sch 9, Group 5, Item 1* and that the real character of the transaction was a composite supply to the member comprising the bond (which was exempt) and the grant of the right to remain a member (which was standard-rated). The appeal was therefore stood over to enable the parties to arrive at a suitable apportionment under what is now *VATA 1994, s 24(5)*. *Dyrham Park Country Club Ltd*, [1978] VATTR 244 (VTD 700). (*Note.* There was no further public hearing of the appeal.)

Interest-free loans by club members

[13.32] A limited company operated a golf club. It required its members, in addition to paying subscriptions, to make interest-free loans to the club to help finance its development. The loans were repayable should the member die, cease to be a full member, or reach the age of 65. The Commissioners issued an assessment on the basis that the club was required to account for output tax on the consideration which it received from members, and that this consideration included not only the amounts of the loans but also interest at the minimum lending rate. The tribunal upheld the assessment, and the CA dismissed the club's appeal against this decision. Cumming-Bruce LJ observed that 'in connection with the market value the Commissioners have been modest in their assessment of tax on their calculation because it might be thought that the hypothetical lender would not lend his money at less than the minimum lending rate plus 2%'. *Exeter Golf & Country Club Ltd v C & E Commrs*, CA [1981] STC 211. (*Note.* With regard to the valuation of the consideration, see the subsequent case of *Harleyford Golf Club plc*, 67.142 VALUATION, in which the tribunal held that the consideration should be taken to be interest at the minimum lending rate, declining to follow the *obiter dicta* of Cumming-Bruce LJ on the grounds that they were inconsistent with the subsequent ECJ decisions in *Naturally Yours Cosmetics Ltd (No 2)*, 22.233 EUROPEAN COMMUNITY LAW, and *Empire Stores Ltd*, 22.234 EUROPEAN COMMUNITY LAW.)

[13.33] Members of a golf club were called on to make a levy or interest-free loan to meet the cost of extensive work on the clubhouse. The contributions were repayable should the member die or resign before 1 October 1980 but otherwise would then be 'deemed to be a gift to the club'. The club did not account for VAT on these contributions, and Customs issued an assessment charging tax on them. The club appealed, contending that the contributions should be treated as voluntary donations. The tribunal rejected this contention and dismissed the apeal, holding that the contributions were compulsory interest-free loans, which were part of the consideration paid by the members for the facilities of the club. Accordingly, they were chargeable to VAT. *Pollok Golf Club*, EDN/80/4 (VTD 1044).

[13.34] Members of a golf club were required to make interest-free loans as a condition of membership. The loans were primarily to enable the club to purchase the golf course of which it had hitherto held a tenancy. The Commissioners issued an assessment charging tax on the market value of the loans. The tribunal upheld the assessment and dismissed the club's appeal, holding that, since making the loan was a condition of membership, it was part of the consideration for the supplies made by the club. Although the member was given a letter of acknowledgement of his loan, this was not a 'security for money' or a 'security' such as a debenture. The function of the document was 'purely evidential and its commercial value were it to be assigned would be negligible'. *Hamilton Golf Club*, EDN/80/65 (VTD 1150). (*Note.* For a subsequent case in which the purchase of debentures in a golf club was held to be taxable consideration for supplies of services, see *Harleyford Golf Club plc*, 67.142 VALUATION.)

[13.35] A similar decision was reached in a case where all playing members of a golf club were required as a condition of membership to make a compulsory loan to the club. The tribunal held that the loan was part of the consideration for the facilities which the club supplied. *Blackmoor Golf Club*, LON/83/251 (VTD 2027).

[13.36] An unincorporated members' club provided facilities for its members, including a golf course and club building. Having previously held the course as lessee, the club acquired the freehold in 1976. A scheme was devised to raise the necessary finance by means of interest-free loans from members, or the payment of a subscription surcharge as a condition of membership if no loan was made. The club accounted for VAT on the subscription surcharges but not on the loans. The Commissioners issued an assessment charging output tax on the open market value of all loans, whether compulsory or voluntary. The tribunal upheld the assessment and dismissed the club's appeal, holding that the consideration for the loans was the continued supply of the club's facilities, and that the club's motive in raising the loans was irrelevant. *Rothley Park Golf Club*, MAN/85/231 (VTD 2074).

Golf club—sale of debentures to members

[13.37] See *Harleyford Golf Club plc*, 27.53 FINANCE and 67.142 VALUATION.

Football club—supplies of season tickets to bondholders

[13.38] See *The Arsenal Football Club plc*, 67.141 *valuation*.

Rugby club—disposal of right to apply for international match tickets

[13.39] A rugby club purchased ten interest-free debentures from the Welsh Rugby Union. Each of these gave the club the right to pay for one seat at international matches at Cardiff Arms Park. The club then informed its members that in return for a 'donation' of £250 a member could have the right to apply for a ticket for the internationals for 25 years, to be paid for at their face value in the normal way. The member also had certain rights to extend the option after the 25 years. The option was not transferable should the member die. Nine of the club's members responded to this offer. The club failed to account for VAT on the payments it received from the members, and Customs issued an assessment charging tax on them. The tribunal dismissed the club's appeal, holding that the club had made a supply of services for consideration and that each payment of £250 was consideration for a taxable supply. *Abercynon Rugby Football Club*, [1982] VATTR 166 (VTD 1286).

Sports club—match fees

[13.40] A sports club provided its members with facilities for playing cricket, rugby union and association football. Its rules provided for the payment of annual subscriptions, but in addition each of the three main sports sections fixed 'match fees' for members actually playing in a match. These fees, which were not referred to in the club rules, were intended to cover match expenses such as travel, hire of pitches and referees' fees and expenses. The team captain, or other sports section representative who collected them, defrayed petty cash expenses out of them and paid the balance to the club treasurer. The Commissioners issued an assessment charging tax on these match fees, and the club appealed, contending that they were donations. The tribunal rejected this contention and dismissed the appeal. Applying the reasoning in *British Railways Board*, **66.12** TRANSPORT, both the annual subscriptions and the match fees together constituted the consideration for the provision by the Club of the facilities available to its members. *Belvedere & Calder Vale Sports Club*, MAN/79/129 (VTD 931).

Rugby club match fees—whether donations

[13.41] A rugby club levied match fees of £2, which were collected by the team captain and were used to pay the referee's expenses and to buy refreshments (principally beer) for the visiting team. Any surplus was paid to the club treasurer. The club did not account for VAT on the amounts collected, and the Commissioners issued an assessment charging tax on them. The club appealed, contending that the fees should be regarded as voluntary donations and as outside the scope of VAT. The tribunal accepted this contention and allowed the appeal, holding that the fees did not 'represent consideration for goods or services'. The decision in *Belvedere & Calder Vale Sports Club*, **13.40** above, was distinguished, on the grounds that the match fees in that case were required and formally fixed by the relevant section of the club. The chairman also doubted the correctness of the decision in *Belvedere*, and expressed the view that *British Railways Board*, **66.12** TRANSPORT, which had been regarded as an important precedent in *Belvedere*, was not 'applicable in the case of match fees or players' donations'. The chairman observed that 'there is no nexus between a voluntary kitty to pay the referee his travelling expenses and buy refreshments for the players of both teams, and the general club charges or subscription to enable the member to enjoy the privilege thereof'. *Sleaford Rugby Football Club*, MAN/92/213 (VTD 9844).

Rugby club—bar stock acquired from cricket club using same premises

[13.42] A rugby club operated a bar from September to April each year. During the intervening months the same bar was operated by a cricket club. A loan account was operated between the clubs. The rugby club was registered for VAT but the cricket club was not. The rugby club's treasurer deducted input tax in respect of bar stock which it acquired from the cricket club. The Commissioners issued an assessment to recover the input tax and the tribunal dismissed the club's appeal. Since the cricket club was not registered for VAT, the rugby club was not entitled to claim input tax on supplies from it. *Baildon Rugby Union Football Club*, MAN/88/359 (VTD 3239).

Other matters

Whether sports clubs separate entities

[13.43] The Commissioners sought to register two bowling clubs, which had the same secretary and operated from the same premises, on the basis that they formed two branches of a single entity. The secretary lodged appeals, contending that the clubs were separate entities, with separate memberships and separate records and accounts, and that their supplies were below the registration threshold. The tribunal accepted the clubs' evidence and allowed their appeals. *AG Hayhoe (for Watchet Bowling Club & Watchet Indoor Bowling Club)*, LON/80/341 (VTD 1026).

[13.44] A sports club (C) comprised a number of 'section clubs' covering separate sports such as rugby and hockey. These section clubs used C's premises and facilities but had their own rules, annual general meetings, officers and accounts. The tribunal held that the 'section clubs' were separate entities. Accordingly, the payments they received from their own members were not liable to VAT, but the sums which C received from the 'section clubs' were liable to VAT. *Cambuslang Athletic Club*, EDN/82/39 (VTD 1592).

[13.45] An 'old boys' association' of former pupils at a high school had three affiliated sports clubs; a football club, a cricket club, and a tennis club. The Commissioners issued a ruling that the association was liable to account for tax on supplies made by the clubs, on the basis that the association and the clubs were a single legal person. The association appealed, contending that the three sports clubs were separate legal entities. The tribunal reviewed the club rules and allowed the association's appeal, holding that the three sports clubs were separate legal entities. *Old Parkinsonians Association*, LON/92/2573 (VTD 10908).

Limited company and associated unincorporated association

[13.46] A limited company had been incorporated in 1930 to hold the assets of a golf club, which had previously been an unincorporated association. The club continued to function from the same premises, which were owned by the limited company. The same people comprised the club's management committee and the company's board of directors. In 1975, when income from gaming machines became liable to VAT, there were two such machines on the premises. One of these was owned by the club and the other was owned by the limited company. The Commissioners issued an assessment on the company, charging it to tax on the takings from both machines. The company appealed, contending that it was not liable to tax on the takings from the machine which was owned by the unincorporated association. The tribunal accepted this contention and allowed the appeal, holding that the company and the association were separate legal entities. *Dartford Golf Club Ltd*, LON/83/37 (VTD 1576). (*Note.* The Commissioners might now have recourse to a direction under *VATA 1994, Sch 1 para 2*. For cases concerning this provision, see 57.35 *et seq.* REGISTRATION.)

Rugby club—donations and sponsorship payments

[13.47] See *Rumney Rugby Football Club*, **62.122** SUPPLY.

Football supporters' club—grant of 'founder membership'

[13.48] See *Newport County AFC Social Club Ltd*, **62.123** SUPPLY.13.47B

Institute of Chartered Accountants—licensing activities

[13.49] See *The Institute of Chartered Accountants in England and Wales*, **62.159** SUPPLY.

Overpaid VAT refunded to members' club

[13.50] Under the *VAT (Sport, Physical Education and Fund-Raising Events) Order 1994 (SI 1994/687)*, the scope of what is now *VATA 1994, Sch 9, Group 10* was extended with effect from 1 April 1994, to exempt services supplied by non-profit-making sports clubs to their members. (Such services had previously been standard-rated under UK law.) Clubs were allowed to backdate their exemption to January 1990, and were permitted to reclaim VAT which they had overpaid from January 1990 to April 1994. In a case where a members' golf club had received a substantial refund, a former member of the club took County Court proceedings against the club demanding repayment of the VAT which had been charged on his annual subscriptions from 1990 to 1993. The County Court rejected his claim. The club was a separate entity from its individual members. If a members' club were to fail to pay VAT to the Commissioners, the individual members would not be liable to pay the tax due. Under *VATA 1994, s 19(2)*, the consideration for membership of the club was the amount of the subscription inclusive of any VAT charged. A members' club was at liberty to vote to return overpaid VAT to those members from whom it was originally collected, but was under no obligation to do so. *Winfield v Stowmarket Golf Club Ltd*, Ipswich County Court 22 May 1995 unreported.

14

Collection and Enforcement

The cases in this chapter are arranged under the following headings.

Power to require security (VATA 1994, Sch 11 para 4)
Cases where the appellant was successful   **14.1**
Cases where the appellant was partly successful   **14.44**
Cases where the appellant was unsuccessful   **14.48**
Recovery of VAT (VATA 1994, Sch 11 para 5(1)–(3))   **14.69**
Distraint (VATA 1994, Sch 11 para 5(4))   **14.77**
Furnishing of information (VATA 1994, Sch 11 para 7)   **14.86**
Entry and search of premises (VATA 1994, Sch 11 para 10)   **14.93**
Order for access to recorded information (VATA 1994, Sch 11 para 11)   **14.97**
Restraint orders   **14.101**
Miscellaneous   **14.103**

CROSS-REFERENCE

See also **49** PENALTIES: CRIMINAL OFFENCES.

Power to require security (VATA 1994, Sch 11 para 4)

NOTE

VATA 1994, Sch 11 para 4 was amended by *FA 2003* in order to extend Customs' powers to require security. The cases in this section should be read in the light of the changes in the legislation. For an application for judicial review of the legislative changes, see *R (oao Federation of Technological Industries & Others) v C & E Commrs*, **22.466** EUROPEAN COMMUNITY LAW.

Cases where the appellant was successful

Change in active directors

[14.1] The Commissioners issued a notice requiring security of £12,900 from a company. The company's controlling director had not been involved with any other companies, but his parents had been directors of three companies which had become insolvent with substantial VAT liabilities. The tribunal allowed the company's appeal against the notice, observing that neither of the director's parents were directors or shareholders of the appellant company. *Mayor Fashions Ltd*, LON/89/440Z (VTD 4429).

[14.2] The Commissioners issued a notice requiring security of £6,500 from an electronics company. The company's managing director had been involved with two previous companies which had become insolvent. The company appealed, contending that the notice was unreasonable because its VAT payments were up to date, and the director had ceased his involvement with one of the previous companies well before it became insolvent. The tribunal accepted the company's evidence and allowed the appeal. *Exact Electronics Ltd*, LON/92/2754A (VTD 11391).

[14.3] The Commissioners issued a notice requiring security of £139,500 from a company (C) which carried on business as a dealer in imported carpets. The officer responsible for the notice acted on the basis that one of C's two directors (J) had previously been a director of another company (T) which had ceased to trade while owing unpaid VAT of £295,000. C appealed, contending that J had never been a director of T, although his father had been T's managing director. The tribunal allowed C's appeal, holding that the Commissioners' decision to require security was flawed because it was based on incorrect assumptions. *UK Carpets Ltd*, LON/93/768A (VTD 11526).

[14.4] The Commissioners issued a notice requiring security from a company which operated a restaurant. The reason of the notice was that one of the company's employees (N) had previously been a partner in a firm which had owned the same restaurant, and that the partnership owed VAT of more than £200,000. The company appealed, contending that the requirement was unreasonable since it employed N as a chef and he was no longer involved in the management of the restaurant. The tribunal accepted the company's evidence and allowed the appeal, holding that the decision to require security was unreasonable. *Auldbrook Ltd*, EDN/93/164 (VTD 11717).

[14.5] A similar decision was reached in *Tidesave Ltd (t/a Yu Chinese Restaurant)*, EDN/97/89 (VTD 15418).

[14.6] The Commissioners issued a notice requiring security of £19,600 from a company, on the grounds that its business was managed by an individual (P) who had been adjudged bankrupt owing more than £100,000 in unpaid VAT and surcharges. The company appealed, contending that the notice was unreasonable since, although P had previously been a director, he was in poor health and had resigned his directorship before the company had registered for VAT. The tribunal accepted the company's evidence and allowed the appeal. *BP Stone & Brickwork Contractors Ltd*, MAN/93/1215 (VTD 11722).

[14.7] In May 1994 the Commissioners issued a notice requiring security of more than £800,000 from a company (V), which had been incorporated as a joint venture by a Swedish company (O) and a Dutch company (P) to trade as a distributor of petroleum products. The reason given for the notice was that two of V's directors had previously been directors of another company (N) carrying on a similar business which had been deregistered in November 1993 while owing more than £1,000,000 in unpaid VAT. V appealed, contending that the notice was unreasonable, since the controlling shareholder of N was not involved in V, O had not had any connection with N, and P had merely been a supplier of N. The two directors referred to in the notice were the controlling directors of P, but had only been appointed directors of N in December 1992, at a time when N was already in serious financial difficulties. The tribunal reviewed the evidence in detail and allowed V's appeal, noting that the ownership of N had 'nothing in common' with that of V, and that V had provided guarantees from a Dutch bank, so that 'the possibility of V being a likely risk to the revenue' was 'very remote'. *VSP Marketing Ltd*, LON/94/794A (VTD 12636). (*Note.* Costs were awarded to the appellant on the indemnity basis—see **2.475** APPEALS.)

[14.8] The Commissioners issued a notice requiring security of £50,000 from a company (S) which operated a cellular telephone business, after discovering that a previous company (E) with two of the same directors had become insolvent owing more than £140,000 in unpaid VAT. S appealed, contending that the requirement was unreasonable, as its controlling director had not been involved with E. The tribunal allowed the appeal, holding that, since the officer responsible for the notice had ignored the fact that S's controlling director had not been involved with E, the requirement was unreasonable. *Smartone Connect Ltd*, LON/94/703A (VTD 12789).

[14.9] The Commissioners issued a notice requiring security of £12,500 from a company (G) which carried on a road haulage business. The company's controlling director (B) had previously been a director of another company with a similar name operating a similar business. B and his wife had had a 50% shareholding in that company. However, he had fallen out with the other directors, and that company had ceased trading and gone into voluntary liquidation. G appealed against the notice, contending that it was unreasonable, since B had not been responsible for the administrative and financial affairs of the previous company. The tribunal accepted this contention and allowed the appeal. *Greyhound Transport (UK) Ltd*, LON/94/1365A (VTD 13216).

[14.10] A similar decision was reached in *Roundstar Ltd*, LON/x (VTD 15471).

[14.11] The Commissioners issued a notice requiring security of £79,000 from a building company on the basis that two of its senior employees had been directors of previous companies which had become insolvent while owing substantial amounts of unpaid VAT. The company appealed, contending that the requirement was unreasonable because neither of the employees concerned were 'employed by it in such a role as to affect its financial viability', and its controlling director had not been involved in any of the companies in question. The tribunal accepted the company's evidence and allowed the appeal. *CSL Building Services Ltd*, LON/95/3123 (VTD 14193).

[14.12] The Commissioners issued notices requiring security from two associated companies which operated licensed premises, on the grounds that the two directors of the companies (who were sisters) had previously been directors of other businesses which had become deregistered or insolvent with substantial VAT arrears. The companies appealed, contending that although the sisters had been directors of the previous companies, they had played no part in the management of those companies, which had effectively been controlled by their parents, and that their parents were not involved in the management of the appellant companies. The tribunal accepted the companies' evidence and allowed the appeals. *Millennium Catering & Pub Co Ltd*, EDN/95/353; *Jointexit Ltd*, EDN/96/15 (VTD 14275).

[14.13] The Commissioners issued a notice requiring security of £16,400 from a company (S) operating a shopfitting business, on the grounds that the principal director of S had previously been the sales director of a company operating a similar business which had gone into liquidation owing more than £60,000 in unpaid VAT. S appealed, contending that the notice was unreasonable because the failure of the previous company was attributable to one of the other directors, who was not a director of S. The tribunal accepted this evidence and allowed the appeal. *Soundmethods Ltd*, MAN/96/353 (VTD 14523).

[14.14] A similar decision was reached in *Dada Records Ltd*, [2009] UKFTT 251 (TC), TC00199.

[14.15] The Commissioners issued a notice requiring security from a company supplying catering equipment, on the grounds that its principal director (R) had previously been involved in a company which had ceased trading while owing VAT. The company appealed, contending that the requirement was unreasonable because the failure of the previous company had been attributable to the behaviour of R's husband, who had also been a director of that company, and who had become 'very vindictive' towards R following the breakdown of their marriage. The tribunal accepted the company's evidence and allowed the appeal. *Central Catering Equipment Ltd*, MAN/96/536 (VTD 14605).

[14.16] The Commissioners issued a notice requiring security from a company carrying on business as a cleaning contractor, after discovering that one of its employees (J) had previously been a director of two companies which had traded from the same premises and had ceased to trade while owing unpaid VAT. The company appealed, contending that the notice was unreasonable because its controlling director had not been involved in either of the previous companies, and that J was merely an employee and was not involved in the management of the company. The tribunal accepted the company's evidence and allowed the appeal. The chairman observed that 'there may be occasions when the Commissioners have to react with great speed to the tell-tale signs of imminent insolvency' but that 'it is only the most extreme of circumstances that could justify the taking of the decision without giving the taxpayer the opportunity to explain his side of the picture'. *Restorex Ltd*, [1997] VATDR 402 (VTD 15014).

[14.17] The decision in *Restorex Ltd*, **14.16** above, was applied in a subsequent case where the Commissioners issued a notice requiring security from a company of which the controlling director was a married woman, whose husband was in business as a sole trader with substantial arrears. The tribunal found that the Commissioners had failed to make enquiries before issuing the notice, and observed that 'however likely a requirement may have been, it has not been shown to our satisfaction that the decision would inevitably have been the same'. *LEBS Services Ltd*, LON/97/1650 (VTD 15550).

Other cases

Previous liquidation of company in similar ownership

[14.18] Customs issued a notice requiring security from a company in the clothing trade, on the grounds that the company secretary had previously been secretary of two companies in the same business which had gone into liquidation owing unpaid VAT. The company appealed, contending that the requirement was unreasonable since the company was trading profitably and one of the previous liquidations had been the result of a fire at the company's premises. The tribunal allowed the company's appeal, holding that the requirement was unreasonable. *Deltaview Ltd*, LON/84/540 (VTD 1832, VTD 1876).

[14.19] Customs issued a notice requiring security from a company on the basis that one of its directors had previously been a director of two other companies which had became insolvent owing VAT. The company appealed, contending that the insolvency of the two previous companies had been a result of late payment by a Borough Council, and that because of the experience of the two previous companies, it was not accepting contracts with local authorities. The tribunal allowed the appeal, finding that the company had a good compliance record and that it was unreasonable for Customs to have required security. *Firepower Builders Ltd*, LON/88/301Y (VTD 3358).

[14.20] Two associated companies appealed against requirements for security, contending that the requirement was unreasonable because only one of the two companies was in arrears with its VAT, and those arrears were the result of delay in receiving payment from its major customer. The tribunal accepted the companies' evidence and allowed the appeals. *Century Supplies Ltd; Euro Catering Equipment Ltd*, MAN/95/483, 2566 & 2574 (VTD 14375).

[14.21] A company (C), which provided temporary staff to small businesses, suffered a large number of bad debts and became insolvent, owing VAT to Customs. An associated company (S) provided temporary staff to larger businesses. Following C's insolvency, Customs issued a notice requiring security from S. S appealed, contending that the notice was unreasonable because its client base was completely different from that of C, and its clients were 'large and creditworthy'. The tribunal accepted S's evidence and allowed the appeal. *IP Chemical & Petroleum Services Ltd*, LON/x (VTD 15530).

Sole trader

[14.22] Customs issued a notice requiring security of £10,000 from a scrap dealer (E), who had previously been involved in three companies which owed VAT totalling more than £26,000. The tribunal allowed E's appeal, holding that the amount demanded was excessive and unreasonable, and that Customs should restrict such demands to 'an estimate of the net tax payable by the trader over a period of six months'. *S Evans*, [1979] VATTR 194 (VTD 836).

[14.23] Customs issued a notice requiring security of £4,500 from a sole trader, who had previously been employed by a company owned by his parents. This company had gone into liquidation with arrears of VAT. The trader appealed against the notice, contending that it was unreasonable to require security from him as he had not been responsible for the finances of his parents' company. The tribunal accepted this contention and allowed the appeal. *D Jandu*, MAN/89/232 (VTD 4475).

[14.24] Customs issued a notice requiring security of £3,750 from a sole trader who had previously been a director of two companies which had gone into liquidation owing VAT totalling almost £29,000. The trader appealed, contending that the requirement was unreasonable as his turnover was less than £10,000 a year. The tribunal accepted this contention and allowed the appeal. *RB Cornforth*, LON/89/842 (VTD 4532).

[14.25] An accountant (C), who had retired from a partnership and had begun a small sole practice, failed to make VAT returns but paid the tax charged by estimated assessments. Customs issued a notice requiring security, but the tribunal allowed C's appeal. The chairman (Mr. Coutts, sitting alone) expressed the view that ' a requirement for security for tax to be collected is a measure which should be used sparingly' and was not 'an appropriate method for ensuring that returns are made'. *CJ Cameron*, EDN/97/222 (VTD 15779).

[14.26] An interior designer did a significant amount of work on listed buildings, so that some of his turnover was standard-rated and some zero-rated. He found difficulty in dividing payments for work in progress between these categories, and consistently submitted returns after the due date. Customs issued a notice requiring security. The tribunal allowed the trader's appeal, observing that the officer responsible for the notice 'has not distinguished in his mind the position of a sole trader from that of a limited company, where at the cessation of trading Customs & Excise have no means of recovering any outstanding VAT. This is not the case where a sole trader is concerned, such a person remaining personally liable.' *J McPhee*, LON/97/1564 (VTD 15606). (*Note*. For a subsequent appeal by the same appellant, see **14.38** below.)

[14.27] Customs issued a notice requiring security of £29,800 from the owner of a nightclub (M), who had failed to submit VAT returns, and had paid the tax charged by estimated assessments. M appealed, contending that the notice was unreasonable since the amount of security exceeded his annual VAT liability. The tribunal accepted this contention and allowed the appeal, holding that 'the amount of security demanded must be proportionate to the risk posed by the taxpayer to the protection of the revenue, having regard to the fact that the purpose of the security is not to collect the arrears'. *L Morris (t/a DV8)*, LON/05/656 (VTD 19492).

Current VAT liability up to date

[14.28] Customs issued a notice requiring security from a partnership which traded as locksmiths. The principal partner had previously been a director of a company which had ceased trading, owing £5,900 in unpaid VAT. The tribunal allowed the partnership's appeal, holding that, since the partnership had submitted four returns and paid all the VAT shown thereon, it was unreasonable for Customs to continue to require security. *C Hickson & Others (t/a Flury's)*, LON/93/1723A (VTD 11455).

[14.29] Similar decisions were reached in *Computer Cave Ltd*, MAN/97/370 (VTD 15212); *The Natural Stone Co*, LON/97/717 (VTD 15272); *Steel Direct Ltd*, LON/97/733 (VTD 15272) and *Janwear Ltd*, MAN/97/1013 (VTD 15460).

[14.30] Customs issued a notice requiring security of £2,800 from a company (W) in the construction industry. W's controlling director had previously been a director of two other companies which had gone into receivership, owing VAT to Customs. W appealed, contending that the requirement was unreasonable because it was financially sound and 80% of its supplies were zero-rated, so that it normally owed no VAT. The tribunal allowed the appeal, holding that Customs had acted unreasonably and had ignored the fact that most of W's supplies were zero-rated. *Wold Construction Co Ltd*, MAN/93/432 (VTD 11704).

[14.31] In January 1992 Customs issued a notice requiring security of more than £350,000 from a company (J) which had been incorporated to carry on a road haulage business. The business had previously been carried on by six associated companies in similar ownership, which had gone into receivership in January 1991, owing a total of more than £1,000,000 in unpaid VAT. J appealed, contending that Customs had acted unreasonably and should have requested further information concerning its finances, since some of its directors had not been involved with the previous companies, and it had made pre-tax profits of more than £400,000 in its first six months of trading. The tribunal upheld the notice, finding that Customs had failed to take account of J's financial status, but holding on the evidence that even if they had held additional information concerning its finances, it would still have been reasonable for them to require security. The QB allowed the company's appeal and the CA upheld this decision, holding that the tribunal had to consider whether Customs had acted reasonably and had taken account of all relevant material, but had no power to substitute its own decision for one reached on an incorrect basis (except that it could dismiss an appeal where it was shown that, even if additional material had been taken into account, the decision would *inevitably* have been the same). Neill LJ observed that the tribunal should 'consider whether Customs had acted in a way in which no reasonable panel of Commissioners could have acted or whether they had taken into account some irrelevant matter or had disregarded something to which they should have given weight'. However, the tribunal could not exercise a fresh discretion, since 'the protection of the revenue is not a responsibility of the tribunal or of a court'. In the present case the tribunal had found that Customs had failed to enquire into J's financial status. It was not inevitable that, if this material had been considered, the result would have been the same. *C & E Commrs v John Dee Ltd*, CA [1995] STC 941.

[14.32] An established construction company (D), which had had a turnover of more than £5,000,000 in 1990, suffered financial difficulties and went into receivership, owing about £74,000 in unpaid VAT. Its principal director became a director of a new company (E), which operated a joinery business. E did not pay its VAT for the periods from July 1993 to January 1995, and in May 1995 Customs issued a notice requiring security of £46,500. E appealed, contending that the notice was unreasonable because it was in a sound financial position (and had subsequently paid its VAT arrears), and D's insolvency had been caused by a major recession in the building industry. The tribunal accepted E's evidence and allowed its appeal. *Extrastable Services Ltd*, MAN/95/2059 (VTD 13911).

Notice issued following late submission of two returns

[14.33] On 15 July 1996 Customs issued a notice requiring security of £10,600 from a company (T) which had failed to submit its returns for the periods ending January 1996 and April 1996. Customs received the returns in question two days later, and issued a revised notice requiring security of £4,100. T appealed, contending that the notice was unreasonable. The tribunal accepted this contention and allowed the appeal, observing that T had been registered for VAT since 1994 and that its returns and payments were up-to-date at the time the revised notice was issued. *Topzone Ltd*, MAN/96/855 (VTD 14782).

[14.34] A similar decision was reached in *Dunholme Decorators Ltd*, MAN/99/752 (VTD 16484).

Amount of demand excessive

[14.35] Customs issued a notice requiring security of £21,800 from a retail company (S), on the grounds that its principal director had been a director of four other companies which had failed to pay VAT. The tribunal allowed S's appeal, holding that the decision to require security was reasonable in principle, but that the amount required was unreasonable, since it had been based solely on a consideration of S's projected annual turnover of £250,000 and had failed to take account of the fact that S was a retailer and was entitled to credit for significant amounts of input tax. *Superstore Discount Tile Warehouse Ltd*, LON/95/1077A (VTD 13393).

[14.36] A similar decision was reached in *Ram Computercare (Sales) Ltd*, LON/97/24 (VTD 16102).

[14.37] In 1995 Customs issued a notice requiring security of £75,500 from a company which had been registered for VAT since 1979. This sum represented the current arrears of almost £36,600 together with unpaid surcharges totalling some £7,500 and an estimated six months' future liability of £31,400. The tribunal allowed the company's appeal, holding that, while it had been reasonable for the Commissioners to require security, the amount of the unpaid default surcharges should not have been included in the requirement, and the requirement was therefore 'flawed' and incorrect. *Qcom Maintenance Ltd*, MAN/95/1399 (VTD 13933).

[14.38] An appeal against a notice requiring security was allowed in a case where the tribunal found that the relevant VAT officer 'could not have acted reasonably in deciding on what security should be paid as he is unable to identify to us not only the amounts outstanding in relation to this appeal, but to identify how any of the figures of the various other businesses and the arrears, tie in with the figures he apparently relied on'. *J McPhee (t/a K2 Interiors)*, MAN/99/69 (VTD 16158).

[14.39] An appeal against a notice requiring security was allowed in a case where the tribunal found that the company had previously informed Customs that it had ceased trading, so that it 'no longer posed a significant risk to the protection of the revenue'. *Mushtaq's Food Factory Ltd*, MAN/06/480 (VTD 20496).

Business transferred from wife to husband

[**14.40**] Customs issued a notice requiring security of £1,750 from a trader (E) who operated a catering business including a café. E's wife had previously operated the café but had been declared bankrupt owing more than £12,000 in unpaid VAT. Following her bankruptcy the café had been transferred to E. He appealed against the notice, contending that he had not been responsible for the business when it was operated by his wife, that she had been defrauded by a dishonest manager who had stolen more than £10,000, and that the notice was unreasonable. The tribunal allowed the appeal, holding on the evidence that the officer responsible for issuing the notice had failed to consider all the relevant information. *S Elliott*, LON/95/1278A (VTD 13432).

[**14.41**] A married woman was registered for VAT from June 1997 as the proprietor of a Chinese restaurant. She ceased trading in February 2001. Customs formed the opinion that there had been a substantial underdeclaration of VAT, and issued assessments on her. In July 2002 her husband (P) opened a restaurant at the same premises. The Commissioners issued a notice requiring security from him, and he appealed. The tribunal allowed his appeal, observing that he had previously been registered for VAT between 1982 and 1995 (when he ceased trading because of ill-health) and his VAT record had been 'entirely satisfactory'. The officer responsible for issuing the notice requiring security had not attached sufficient importance to P's previous good VAT record, and had been unduly influenced by the poor record of his wife. Accordingly, the decision to require security was unreasonable. *PN Ho*, EDN/03/48 (VTD 18315).

Company acquired from company formation agent

[**14.42**] A company (R) acted as a company formation agent. When R formed a new company, it became the registered company secretary until the purchasers appointed a new secretary. The Commissioners issued a notice requiring security from a company (C), of which R was the registered company secretary, on the basis that 16 other companies with R as secretary had poor compliance records. C appealed, contending that it had no connection with the other 16 companies. The tribunal accepted this contention and allowed the appeal, expressing the view that 'the function of a company secretary' had 'nothing to do with the management of the business of the company in question, unless he is specifically engaged to carry out wider functions (which was not the case here)'. On the evidence, 'there was no suggestion that (R) was in some way instrumental in causing the tax debts or poor compliance' of the other 16 companies, and the Commissioners' decision to require security was unreasonable. *Control Ltd*, LON/00/632 (VTD 16973).

HMRC officer failing to submit evidence

[**14.43**] Appeals against two notices requiring security were allowed in a case where the officer responsible for the relevant decision letters failed to give evidence (either written or oral) to the tribunal. The tribunal observed that 'without hearing from her, it is quite impossible for the tribunal to be satisfied that her decision to uphold the requirements was one which was reasonably taken.' *Sanleo Ltd v HMRC (and related appeal)*, [2010] UKFTT 266 (TC), TC00560.

Cases where the appellant was partly successful

[14.44] The Commissioners issued a notice requiring security of £5,000 from a company (G) which operated an employment agency. The principal director of the company had previously been a director of five other companies which had ceased trading, owing a total of more than £50,000 in unpaid VAT. The company appealed, contending that the notice was unreasonable because the previous five companies had all carried on businesses in the motor trade. The tribunal allowed the appeal in part, holding that the decision to require security was reasonable but that the amount required was unreasonable because the turnover of the previous companies had been taken into consideration, although G was operating in a completely different line of business and had a significantly lower turnover. The tribunal directed that the amount of security should be fixed at £4,000. *Giddian Ltd*, [1984] VATTR 161 (VTD 1706).

[14.45] The Commissioners issued a notice requiring security of £40,000 from a car hire company, on the basis that two of the company's four directors, and the company secretary, had previously been involved with other companies which had gone into liquidation owing VAT. The company appealed, contending that the requirement was unreasonable since the secretary and one of the two directors in question had resigned, and it had brought its payments up to date. The tribunal allowed the appeal in part, ordering the company to provide security of £10,000 and submit monthly returns. *Dreestone Ltd*, LON/85/119 (VTD 1900).

[14.46] The Commissioners issued a notice requiring security of £10,000 from a sole trader who had previously been a director of a company which had become insolvent owing substantial VAT. The trader appealed, contending that the amount required was unreasonable. He submitted further details of his turnover, following which the Commissioners agreed to reduce the amount required to £2,900. The tribunal reviewed the evidence in detail, applying *dicta* in *Giddian Ltd*, **14.44** above, and indicating that the requirement should not exceed 30% of the trader's projected net liability for the next 12 months. It found that in this case the projected net liability was £8,800, and reduced the requirement to £2,500. *DA French (t/a Adept Architectural Aluminium)*, LON/91/1156Y (VTD 9706).

[14.47] Requirements to give security were reduced in *Kaymac Fashions Ltd*, LON/85/267 (VTD 1945); *Fiesta Fashions Ltd*, LON/85/436 (VTD 1975); *Chaseside Shopfitters Ltd*, LON/85/497 (VTD 2023); *Highfire Ltd*, LON/87/128 (VTD 2399); *Pearl Top Services Ltd*, MAN/88/168 (VTD 2888); *Guttenberg & Sons*, MAN/88/432 (VTD 3392); *GF Port*, MAN/89/25 (VTD 3772); *FA Taylor*, LON/88/1465Y (VTD 3882); *Samrosa Ltd*, LON/88/1442X (VTD 3984); *Jointstock Ltd*, LON/89/606 (VTD 4236); *Tiffin Developments Ltd*, MAN/89/729 (VTD 4462); *Kings Norton Carpet Centre Ltd*, MAN/89/762 (VTD 4749); *SRJ McGleish*, MAN/90/261 (VTD 5318); *Croydon Architectural Ltd*, LON/91/2711Y (VTD 7823); *Integrated Allied Industries Ltd*, LON/91/2700Z (VTD 7947); *Casey Flooring (Contracts) Ltd*, MAN/92/1698 (VTD 10205); *Craig Security Services Ltd*, LON/93/853A (VTD 11484); *Denimode Ltd*, LON/93/1493A (VTD 11952); *Pegasus Holdings (Malvern) Ltd*, MAN/94/287 (VTD 12539); *Hose-*

power Ltd, LON/94/513 (VTD 12594); *Astral Print Ltd*, LON/94/1171 (VTD 12837) and *Moon Fashions Ltd*, LON/95/218 (VTD 14324).

Cases where the appellant was unsuccessful

[14.48] The Commissioners issued a notice requiring security of £15,000. The company appealed, contending that the amount required was excessive. The tribunal dismissed the appeal. Lord Grantchester held that it was reasonable for the Commissioners to require 'security to be in an amount slightly in excess of the estimated tax liability of the trader concerned over a recent six-month period'. *Labelwise Ltd*, LON/83/192 (VTD 1499).

[14.49] A company appealed against the Commissioners' requirement for security of £11,600. One of its directors had been a director of seven companies engaged in a similar business, all of which had gone into liquidation owing considerable sums of VAT to the Commissioners. The tribunal dismissed the appeal, holding that the Commissioners had not acted unreasonably. *Power Rod (UK) Ltd*, [1983] VATTR 334 (VTD 1550).

[14.50] Customs issued a notice requiring security of £22,000 from a company which manufactured clothing. The company appealed, contending that the amount of the requirement was unreasonable since it would force it to cease trading and make its 14 employees redundant. The tribunal dismissed the appeal. Lord Grantchester held that 'the decision was eminently reasonable', and that the fact that the company might have to make some of its employees redundant was not a consideration which the tribunal could take into account. The tribunal could 'only allow an appeal against a decision of the Commissioners to act thereunder if it is one that no reasonable body of Commissioners could reach'. *Rosebronze Ltd*, LON/84/154 (VTD 1668).

[14.51] The decision in *Rosebronze Ltd*, 14.50 above, has been applied in a large number of subsequent cases in which appeals against requirements for security have been dismissed. In the interests of space, such cases are not summarised individually in this book. For a list of such cases decided up to 31 December 1995, see Tolley's VAT Cases 1996.

[14.52] A company carried on business as suppliers and installers of double-glazing. Its managing director had previously been involved in two other double-glazing companies which had become insolvent with heavy liabilities, including a debt of £85,000 for VAT to the Commissioners. The company was in arrears with its VAT returns and payments, and the Commissioners issued a notice of requirement of security. The tribunal dismissed the company's appeal and the QB upheld this decision. Farquharson J held that the Commissioners were justified in requiring security in view of the conduct of the earlier companies controlled by the same director, and of the late returns of the appellant company. *Mr Wishmore Ltd v C & E Commissioners*, QB [1988] STC 723. (*Note. Obiter dicta* of Farquharson J were disapproved by the CA in the subsequent case of *John Dee Ltd*, 14.31 above.)

[14.53] The Commissioners issued a notice requiring security of £16,500 from an electronic engineering company. The directors of this company had previously been directors of two other companies which had ceased trading with substantial arrears of VAT. The company appealed against the notice, contending that the Commissioners had not given adequate consideration to the financial history of the three companies. The tribunal dismissed the company's appeal, applying the principles laid down in *Mr Wishmore Ltd*, **14.52** above. The Commissioners had a duty to consider all the relevant facts before them, but they were not obliged to make detailed enquiries. On the evidence, there was a long history of default by companies under the control of the same two directors for which no explanation had been given, and the Commissioners were entitled to assume that there had been financial mismanagement. *Hitron Ltd*, [1989] VATTR 148 (VTD 3755).

[14.54] The Commissioners issued a notice requiring security of £253,000 from a company which had fallen into arrears with its VAT liability. One of the company's directors had previously been involved with three previous companies which had ceased trading with arrears of VAT. The company appealed, contending that the notice had been unreasonable and that the Commissioners had been unduly influenced by the director's involvement with the three previous companies. The tribunal rejected this contention and dismissed the appeal. Applying the principles laid down in *Mr Wishmore Ltd*, **14.52** above, the tribunal's jurisdiction was supervisory rather than appellate. The tribunal could only intervene if the Commissioners had acted unreasonably, applying the standards laid down by Lord Greene MR in *Associated Provincial Picture Houses v Wednesbury Corporation*, CA 1947, [1948] 1 KB 223; [1947] 2 All ER 680. The Commissioners' decision here was not unreasonable on the evidence. *Dialrace Ltd*, [1991] VATTR 505 (VTD 6328).

[14.55] The Commissioners issued a notice requiring security of £23,000 from a company (C) trading as jewellers. C's controlling director had previously been the controlling director of another company which had become insolvent, owing £300,000 in unpaid VAT. The tribunal dismissed C's appeal, holding that the decision to require security was reasonable on the evidence, applying the principles laid down in *Mr Wishmore Ltd*, **14.52** above, and *dicta* of Lord Greene in *Associated Provincial Picture Houses v Wednesbury Corporation*, CA 1947, [1948] 1 KB 223; [1947] 2 All ER 680. *Colette Ltd*, [1992] VATTR 240 (VTD 6975).

[14.56] The decision in *Colette Ltd*, **14.55** above, was applied in the similar case of *Felicitations Ltd*, LON/93/2375 (VTD 12409).

[14.57] A company appealed against a notice requiring security of £10,425, contending that the notice was unreasonable. The tribunal rejected this contention and dismissed the appeal, applying the QB decision in *Mr Wishmore Ltd*, **14.52** above, and distinguishing *Dreestone Ltd*, **14.45** above. *Winslade Electrical Ltd*, LON/93/658 (VTD 10943).

[14.58] A company appealed against a notice requiring security, contending that the notice was unreasonable and was not 'necessary for the protection of the revenue'. The tribunal rejected this contention and dismissed the appeal, applying *Rosebronze Ltd*, **14.50** above. The tribunal declined to follow *dicta* in *Club Centre of Leeds Ltd*, [1980] VATTR 135 (VTD 985) (a case concerning provisions in *FA 1972* which had subsequently been amended by *FA 1981*, but which the company had cited as an authority), observing that

that case dealt with a different area of VAT law, and was 'not of direct relevance to the present case'. *IPS Currall (t/a Ian Currall & Partners)*, MAN/92/1567 (VTD 11652).

[14.59] The Commissioners issued a notice requiring security of £7,350 from a company controlled by a married couple, on the grounds that the wife had previously been a director of two other companies which had become insolvent owing substantial amounts of VAT. The company appealed, contending that the decision was unreasonable because the two previous companies had been controlled by the wife's parents, and that, although she had been a director, she had had no control over the management of those companies and had not been authorised to sign cheques. Her parents had subsequently returned to Italy, so that she was no longer under the influence of her father. The tribunal allowed the appeal but the QB reversed this decision, holding that the Commissioners' decision to require security had not been unreasonable. Dyson J observed that 'in exercising its supervisory jurisdiction the tribunal must limit itself to considering facts and matters which existed at the time the challenged decision was taken'. *C & E Commrs v Peachtree Enterprises Ltd*, QB [1994] STC 747. (*Note. Obiter dicta* of Dyson J were disapproved by the CA in the subsequent case of *John Dee Ltd*, **14.31** above.)

[14.60] The principles laid down by Dyson J in *Peachtree Enterprises Ltd*, **14.59** above, were applied in a subsequent case where the tribunal held that it 'had to limit itself to considering facts and matters which were known when the disputed decision was made by Customs & Excise'. The tribunal also observed, applying the CA decision in *John Dee Ltd*, **14.31** above, that it 'could not exercise a fresh discretion; the protection of the revenue was not a responsibility of the tribunal or the court. However, if it was shown that the decision of Customs & Excise was erroneous, because they had failed to take some relevant material into account, the tribunal could, nevertheless, dismiss the appeal if the decision would *inevitably* have been the same had account been taken of the additional material.' *Goldhaven Ltd*, LON/06/1348 (VTD 14675).

[14.61] *Dicta* of Dyson J in *Peachtree Enterprises Ltd*, **14.59** above, were also applied in a subsequent case in which a family company had taken over a restaurant which had previously been operated by members of the same family trading in partnership. The Commissioners issued a notice requiring security from the company and the tribunal dismissed the company's appeal. The tribunal chairman observed that, since 'the tribunal must limit itself to considering facts and matters which existed at the time the challenged decision was taken', subsequent events were 'irrelevant'. *Obiter dicta* of the tribunal chairman in the Scottish case of *Lomond Services Ltd*, EDN/98/3 (VTD 15451) (which the company had cited as an authority) were specifically disapproved. *Kushoom Koly Ltd*, [1998] VATDR 363 (VTD 15591).

[14.62] The QB decision in *Peachtree Enterprises Ltd*, **14.59** above, has been applied in a large number of subsequent cases in which appeals against requirements for security have been dismissed. In the interests of space, such cases are not summarised individually in this book. For a list of such cases decided up to 31 December 2000, see Tolley's VAT Cases 2001.

[14.63] The Commissioners issued a notice requiring security of £7,300 from a certified accountant who had consistently paid his VAT liability after the due date. The accountant appealed, contending that the requirement was unnecessary since, 'as he was a member of the association of certified accountants and would be deprived of membership thereof were he to be made bankrupt, the rules of that professional association would in themselves ensure that he paid all VAT due'. The tribunal rejected this contention and dismissed his appeal, holding that it was not 'in any way unreasonable' for the Commissioners to require security. *JL Morrell (t/a Morrell Middleton)*, MAN/95/1543 (VTD 13970).

[14.64] The Commissioners issued a notice requiring security from a company which operated a restaurant. The restaurant had previously been operated by another company which had suffered financial difficulties and had gone into liquidation. The same individual had been secretary of both companies. The tribunal upheld the notice and dismissed the company's appeal, holding that the Commissioners had not acted unreasonably. The tribunal chairman observed that 'the tribunal's jurisdiction in a security appeal is appellate not supervisory, and the tribunal must examine whether the Commissioners had rightly exercised their power to require security. The tribunal must consider whether the Commissioners have acted in a way in which no reasonable panel of Commissioners could have acted, whether they have taken into account some irrelevant matter or have disregarded something to which they should have given weight. It is not for the tribunal to exercise a fresh discretion, as the protection of the revenue is not the responsibility of any court or tribunal.' *Restaurant Portfolio Ltd (t/a L'Escargot)*, LON/96/1979 (VTD 15245).

[14.65] A company (B) traded in mobile telephones. Customs discovered that it appeared to have been involved in a 'carousel fraud', and issued a notice requiring security of more than £1,500,000. B appealed, admitting 'that it had been involved in a supply chain where there had been irregularity' but contending that 'the irregularity had not been caused or permitted by it'. The tribunal reviewed the evidence in detail and dismissed B's appeal, holding that it was reasonable and 'proportionate' for Customs to have required security. The tribunal also observed that the validity of *VATA 1994 Sch 11 para 4*, as amended by *FA 2003*, had been unanimously upheld by the CA in *C & E Commrs v Federation of Technological Industries & Others*, **22.466** EUROPEAN COMMUNITY LAW. *Balmoral Ltd*, MAN/04/610 (VTD 19233).

[14.66] Appeals against requirements to give security have been dismissed in a very large number of other cases, in which the decisions appear to raise no point of general interest. In the interests of space, such cases are not reported individually in this book. For a list of such cases decided up to and including 31 October 1990, see Tolley's VAT Cases 1991.

Company continuing to trade without providing security

[14.67] Customs issued a notice requiring a company to provide security under *VATA 1994, Sch 11 para 4*. The company failed to provide the security, and continued to trade. Customs took proceedings against the *de facto* director (C) under *CEMA 1979, s 171(4)*. C was convicted, and appealed to the QB.

The QB dismissed his appeal. Sedley LJ held that 'the whole point of *s 171(4)* is to place liability not only on directors, but on those who, not being directors, act as if they were, as (C) admitted doing'. *EA Chaudhry v RCPO*, QB 2007, [2008] STC 2357; [2007] EWHC 1805 (Admin).

Sch 11 para 4(1)—appeal against requirement to give security

[14.68] See *Strangewood Ltd (No 2)*, 2.47 APPEALS.

Recovery of VAT (VATA 1994, Sch 11 para 5(1)–(3))

VATA 1994, Sch 11 para 5—tax declared in returns but not paid

[14.69] In the case noted at 3.41 ASSESSMENT, a company had correctly accounted for tax of £40,560 in its returns for the periods ending May 1976. However, it subsequently formed the view that it should have treated the supplies as zero-rated, and recovered the £40,560 by unilaterally deducting it from its liability for subsequent accounting periods. The tribunal subsequently held that the disputed supplies did not qualify for zero-rating, but the Commissioners failed to issue an assessment to recover the tax within the statutory time limits. They instead sought to recover the tax by issuing a writ against the company, on the grounds that it had declared the tax in its returns for the periods to May 1976, but had failed to pay the tax to the Commissioners. The QB upheld the writ, holding that the tax had been accounted for in the company's returns and had been borne by the company's customers. The fact that it had been declared in the company's returns meant that the Commissioners were entitled to recover it as a debt due to the Crown. *C & E Commrs v International Language Centres Ltd*, QB [1986] STC 279.

[14.70] See also *Take Care (Agency Services) Ltd*, 2.9 APPEALS.

Recovery of tax under VATA 1994, Sch 11 para 5(2)

[14.71] A partner in a firm of solicitors had held the office of Clerk of the Horserace Betting Levy Board Appeal Tribunal. The firm issued three invoices in respect of services which he supplied in his capacity as Clerk, but did not account to the Commissioners for the VAT thereon. The Commissioners issued a ruling that the firm was liable to account for the VAT by virtue of what is now *VATA 1994, Sch 11 para 5(2)*. The tribunal dismissed the firm's appeal against this decision. *Hempsons*, [1977] VATTR 73 (VTD 361). (*Note.* The appeal also concerned the application of provisions in *FA 1972, s 45* which have subsequently been superseded.)

[14.72] An individual (W) acted as a management consultant. In October 1973 he incorporated a company (S) to sell his services. He had issued eight tax invoices before the incorporation of the company, and issued two further invoices after the incorporation, but did not account for VAT on any of the ten invoices. All ten invoices were issued in the name of a company which did not exist. The Commissioners brought an action against W for payment of the amount of tax shown on the invoices. The QB held that the first eight invoices had been issued by W and that he was accountable for the tax, applying *European Communities Act 1972, s 9(2)*. However, on the evidence the QB held that the last two invoices had been issued by S (which had subsequently gone into liquidation). The amounts of VAT were recoverable from W and from the liquidator of S respectively, by virtue of what is now *VATA 1994, Sch 11 para 5(2)*. *C & E Commrs v MF Wells*, QB [1981] STC 588; [1982] 1 All ER 920.

[14.73] A company (L) supplied goods to a customer, and issued a tax invoice for the sale price inclusive of VAT, but did not account for the VAT shown on the invoice. The Commissioners issued an assessment to recover the tax and the tribunal dismissed L's appeal, applying what is now *VATA 1994, Sch 11 para 5(2)*. *Lancaster Fabrications Ltd*, MAN/82/109 (VTD 1317).

[14.74] A partnership (S) began trading in 2002. It did not register for VAT, but issued invoices stating 'net plus VAT'. In 2004 it registered for VAT, and its registration was backdated to 2002 by agreement. S did not account for VAT on the invoices it had issued. When Customs discovered this, they issued assessments charging VAT on the relevant supplies. The tribunal dismissed S's appeal, holding that the effect of *VATA 1994, Sch 11 para 5(2)* was that S was required to account for VAT. *South Yorkshire Style Tile*, MAN/06/197 (VTD 20175).

[14.75] In the case noted at **2.46** APPEALS, the tribunal held that it had no jurisdiction to hear an appeal under *VATA 1994, Sch 11 para 5(2)(3)*. *GE Alm*, LON/98/961 (VTD 15863).

[14.76] On examining a trader's records, a VAT officer discovered an invoice in the trader's name for a supply of cloth, charging VAT of £3,675. The trader had not accounted for output tax on this invoice, although the company to which the invoice was addressed had reclaimed input tax on it. The Commissioners issued an assessment charging tax and the trader appealed, contending that the invoice was a 'pro-forma' and had been cancelled, and that the supply had never taken place. The tribunal accepted the trader's evidence and allowed the appeal, holding that there had been no supply and that the assessment was not authorised by *VATA 1994, s 73*. The tribunal held that the effect of *Sch 11 para 5(2)* was that 'the Commissioners are entitled to recover from the appellant the sum of £3,675, being the amount shown as VAT on the invoice, but this is recoverable as a debt to the Crown and not by way of an assessment'. *G Kaur (t/a GK Trading)*, MAN/97/688 (VTD 15366).

Distraint (VATA 1994, Sch 11 para 5(4))

NOTE

See now the *Distress for Customs & Excise Duties and Other Indirect Taxes Regulations 1997 (SI 1997/1431)*, which took effect from 1 July 1997, and which extended the Commissioners' powers of distraint.

Perishable items

[14.77] It was held that perishable items (such as food), which could not be restored in the same condition as when they were distrained upon, were exempt from distraint. *Morley v Pincombe*, Ex D 1848, 2 Ex D 101.

Tools of trade

[14.78] In a case where a Collector of Taxes had levied distraint on a piano which the debtor's wife used to give music lessons, the KB held that the tools of a debtor's trade were only exempt from distraint for rent, and were not exempt from distraint for tax. *MacGregor v Clamp & Son*, KB [1914] 1 KB 288.

Entry to premises

[14.79] The QB held that a bailiff was entitled to enter premises through an open window, and may also further open a window which was already partly open. *Nixon v Freeman*, QB 1860, 5 H & N 647.

[14.80] The QB held that a bailiff was not entitled to open a window catch in order to enter premises without a warrant authorising him to 'break open' the premises. *Hancock v Austin*, QB 1863, 14 CBNS 634.

[14.81] The QB held that a bailiff was entitled to enter premises through a partially opened skylight. *Miller v Tebb*, QB 1893, 9 TLR 515.

[14.82] The QB held that a bailiff had no right to break into premises without a warrant, but was entitled to climb over a wall or fence from adjoining premises. *Long v Clark*, QB [1894] 1 QB 119.

'Walking possession' agreement

[14.83] The QB held that entering into a 'walking possession' agreement did not constitute the abandonment of a distraint. *Lumsden v Burnett*, QB [1898] 2 QB 177.

Distraint levied on company—subsequent liquidation of company

[14.84] In October 1982 the Commissioners levied distraint on a company which owed more than £30,000 in unpaid VAT. A 'walking possession' agreement was signed on behalf of the company. In February 1983 the company went into liquidation. In May 1983 the company's plant and machinery were sold by agreement between the Commissioners and the liquidator. The Commissioners claimed the net proceeds of the sale (£27,080). The liquidator objected to the claim, and the Commissioners applied to the Ch D for a declaration that they were entitled to the proceeds. The Ch D held, applying *Herbert Berry Associates Ltd v CIR*, HL 1977, 52 TC 113, that the court had a discretion to allow the Commissioners to retain the proceeds of the distraint, and that since there had been 'no unconscionable conduct or delay' in this case, the Commissioners were entitled to the proceeds of the distraint. *Re Memco Engineering Ltd*, Ch D [1985] 3 All ER 267.

Late appeal after levy of distraint

[14.85] See *Davies*, 2.197 APPEALS.

Furnishing of information (VATA 1994, Sch 11 para 7)

Customs' power to require information

[14.86] In a purchase tax case, the HL considered the extent of Customs' power to require information. Lord Reid held that 'if a demand for information is made in the proper manner, the trader is bound to answer the demand within the time and in the form required, whether or not the answers may tend to incriminate him, and if he fails to comply with the demands, he may be prosecuted'. Although a trader was 'bound to furnish information within such time and in such form as the Commissioners require', this did not entitle Customs 'to send a representative to confront the trader, put questions to him orally and demand oral answers on the spot; and I am certainly of the opinion that it does not entitle them to send their representative to subject the trader to a prolonged interrogation in the nature of a cross-examination'. *C & E Commrs v Harz & Power*, HL [1967] 1 All ER 177.

Extent of Customs' power to inspect and copy documents

[14.87] Search orders were made against defendants in a civil action concerning the manufacture of illegally copied videocassettes. Documents belonging to two of the defendants (H and R) had been entrusted to the custody of the plaintiffs' solicitors. Customs were investigating the failure of H and R to account for VAT on the sale of the illegal cassettes, and sought to inspect and copy the documents. H had authorised this but R had not. In accordance with the undertaking which they had given to the court, the solicitors declined to allow Customs to inspect the documents without a specific Court order. Customs made an application to the High Court, which granted the order sought. Farquharson J held that, in view of the terms under which the documents were held, the solicitors were correct in refusing to allow Customs access to them except by order of the Court. However, on the facts of the case it was proper to make such an order. *C & E Commrs v AE Hamlin & Co*, Ch D [1983] STC 780; [1983] 3 All ER 654. (*Note.* The validity of such search orders was upheld by the ECHR in *Chappell v United Kingdom*, ECHR 1989, 12 EHRR 1.)

VATA 1994, Sch 11 para 7(2)—production of documents

[14.88] Search orders were made against defendants in a civil action concerning the manufacture of illegally copied audiocassettes. The orders authorised the plaintiff company to remove into the custody of their solicitors counterfeit records and documents, relating to the action, which were the property of the defendants. The action was settled and the solicitors returned the goods but retained the documents. Customs were investigating the defendants' failure to account for VAT on the sale of the illegal cassettes, and asked the solicitors for access to the documents. The solicitors refused to allow such access without the defendants' consent, which the defendants refused. Customs thereupon issued a notice to the solicitors under what is now *VATA 1994, Sch 11 para 7(2)* requiring the production of the documents. The solicitors applied to the High Court for directions. Sir Nicholas Browne-Wilkinson VC held that, in ordinary cases, Customs could not require solicitors holding documents which had been seized under search orders to produce those documents, and that the solicitors in such cases could not disclose the documents in question to Customs except by order of the Court. However, in the circumstances of this case, the Court would authorise the documents to be disclosed. *EMI Records Ltd v Spillane & Others*, Ch D [1986] STC 374. (*Notes.* (1) For subsequent proceedings in this case, see **3.53** ASSESSMENT. (2) The *Civil Procedure Rules 1998* now refer to a 'claimant' rather than to a 'plaintiff'.)

[**14.89**] A university, and three companies, entered into a series of transactions designed to minimise liability to VAT. The Commissioners issued notices under *VATA 1994, Sch 11 para 7(2)*, requiring the university and the companies to produce a large number of documents for inspection. They failed to comply with the notices, and the Commissioners issued penalty notices under *VATA 1994, s 69*. The university and the companies appealed, contending that the Commissioners had no right to see the documents in question. The tribunal allowed the appeals, holding that the wording of the notice was too vague and that it included documents which were subject to legal professional privilege. The tribunal observed that 'any person upon whom a penalty is sought to be imposed is entitled to know in what respect it is alleged they have failed to comply so that they might have an opportunity of considering their position'. It was not sufficient 'to issue a wide-ranging demand and then in effect say because everything that the Commissioners might have thought could have been produced was not produced that there has been a failure to comply'. *University Court of the University of Glasgow (No 2) (and related appeals)*, EDN/01/164 (VTD 17744). (*Note.* For another issue in this case, see **3.132** ASSESSMENT.)

[**14.90**] A group of companies carried on the business of leasing cars to members of the public. The group implemented a series of transactions which was intended to have the effect that one of the companies would be able to dispose of cars whose leases had expired under the 'margin scheme' for second-hand goods. Following the implementation of some of the transactions, one of the companies lodged a repayment claim for about £42,000,000. The Commissioners served notices under *VATA 1994, Sch 11 para 7(2)*, requiring seven of the companies to produce certain documents for inspection. The companies failed to comply with the notices, and the Commissioners issued penalty notices under *VATA 1994, s 69*. The companies appealed, contending that the notices were *ultra vires* and invalid. The tribunal rejected this contention and dismissed the appeals, observing that 'a taxpayer cannot reasonably expect to receive a repayment while refusing to produce the evidence by which his claim may be tested'. The Commissioners were entitled to request the production of documents in a case where it was unclear whether a particular transaction constituted a supply. The tribunal held that 'a claim by a trader that he has made a supply is, of itself, sufficient to make the *para 7(2)* power available'. The tribunal directed that the Commissioners were entitled to require production of the documents listed in the notices, but gave the companies leave to apply for a further hearing if the parties were unable to agree on whether any of the documents were covered by legal professional privilege. (The tribunal also declined to impose any penalties under *VATA 1994, s 69*, observing that there had been 'a genuine dispute about the validity of the notices' and holding that this appeared to constitute a 'reasonable excuse' for not producing the documents.) *Interleasing Ltd (and related appeals)*, [2002] VATDR 372 (VTD 17819).

[14.91] A partnership (BR), which was registered for VAT, owned land which was used as a golf course. It submitted a VAT return claiming a substantial repayment of input tax. The Commissioners discovered that BR had 'restructured' the operation of the golf course, involving two associated companies and an associated partnership (BG), none of which was registered for VAT, in an attempt to take advantage of the exemption for sporting activities provided by *VATA 1994, Sch 9, Group 10*. The Commissioners issued notices under *VATA 1994, Sch 11 para 7(2)*, requiring BG and the two companies to produce certain documents for inspection. BG and the companies failed to comply with the notices, and the Commissioners imposed penalties under *VATA 1994, s 69*. BG and the companies appealed. The tribunal dismissed the appeals and upheld the penalties, holding that the notices complied with *Sch 11 para 7(2)* and that there was no reasonable excuse for the appellants' failure to comply. *Burghill Valley Golf Club (and related appeals)*, LON/03/1054 (VTD 18876).

[14.92] Customs issued a notice under *VATA 1994, Sch 11 para 7(2)* to a major bank, requiring it to produce certain documents including copies of its management accounts, in order that Customs could review the operation of the bank's special 'partial exemption' method of attributing its input tax. The bank failed to comply with the notice, and Customs also imposed a penalty under *VATA 1994, s 69*. The bank appealed against the notice and the penalty. The tribunal dismissed both appeals, holding that the notice was reasonable and had been validly issued. Furthermore, there was no reasonable excuse for the bank's failure to comply with it. *Lloyds TSB Group plc (No 2)*, [2005] VATDR 405 (VTD 19330).

Entry and search of premises (VATA 1994, Sch 11 para 10)

NOTE

VATA 1994, Sch 11 para 10(3)–(6) were repealed by *FA 2007* with effect from 1 December 2007, and were superseded by the relevant provisions of the *Police and Criminal Evidence Act 1984*.

[14.93] The Commissioners were investigating a construction company and obtained search warrants authorising them to enter the company's premises and the homes of the company's two directors. The company and the directors applied for judicial review, contending firstly that *VATA 1994, Sch 11 para 10* should be held to be invalid under EC law, and alternatively that the warrants were unnecessary, since the company had offered to co-operate with the Commissioners. The QB rejected these contentions and dismissed the applications. *Article 22(8)* of the *EC Sixth Directive* authorised Member States to impose 'obligations which they deem necessary for the correct collection of tax and for the prevention of evasion'. On the evidence, the Commissioners' determination that search warrants were needed, and the magistrates' decision to grant the warrants, were entirely rational. The company had made a partial offer of co-operation, but it was an offer 'hedged around by conditions'. The Commissioners had merely been given the opportunity to inspect files and records of the company at the premises of the company's solicitors. This was 'completely unsatisfactory'. McCowan LJ observed that 'Customs require to be able themselves to search all parts of the premises in question and all cupboards, cabinets, etc. Often the evidence is found on odd sheets of paper found in the backs of cupboards, desks, etc., rather than in formal files and records.' *R v C & E Commrs (ex p. X Ltd) (aka R v C & E Commrs ex p. McNicholas Construction Co Ltd & Others)*, QB [1997] STC 1197. (*Note.* For a preliminary issue in this case, see **2.217** APPEALS. For subsequent developments, see **2.250** APPEALS and **3.102** ASSESSMENT.)

[14.94] The Commissioners obtained warrants under *Sch 11 para 10(3)*, authorising them to search, and remove materials from, the premises of a trader and his solicitor, who had been involved in a complex avoidance scheme involving the use of several companies resident outside the UK. The trader and solicitor applied for judicial review, contending that some of the items which the Commissioners had seized from the solicitor were subject to legal privilege. The QB rejected the applications, with the exception of three small classes of documents which the Commissioners were ordered to return. Applying *dicta* of Jowitt LJ in *R v Chief Constable of Warwickshire Constabulary and Another (ex p. Fitzpatrick & Others)*, QB [1998] 1 All ER 65, circumstances 'may very well require decisions to be made at speed and without time for reflection or that opportunity to assess the significance of material which only becomes possible when it can be considered in the context of other material'. Furthermore, 'judicial review is not a fact-finding exercise and it is an extremely unsatisfactory tool by which to determine, in any but the clearest of cases, whether there has been a seizure of material not permitted by the search warrant'. Accordingly, a person who 'complains of excessive seizure' should not 'seek his remedy by way of judicial review but should rely on his private law remedy when he will have a tribunal which will be able to hear evidence and make findings of fact unfettered by *Wednesbury* principles'. Applying *dicta* of Waller LJ in *Reynolds v Commissioner of the Metropolitan Police*, CA [1984] 3 All ER 649, 'to do a detailed examination in a house would no doubt have required several police officers to be there for some days, causing disturbance to the householder, and might require comparisons to be made with other documents already in the hands of the police'. Smedley J observed that 'in judicial review cases, the court's essential function is not to act as an appellate court but to look at the material available to the decision-makers, in this case the officers of Customs & Excise, and ask whether they have acted unfairly'. If, however, 'in the course of a legitimate search of a solicitor's office, particularly where the solicitor himself is alleged to be complicit in the offence being investigated, the officers seize material which includes items subject to legal privilege inadvertently, it cannot be that the seizure of those items renders the execution of the warrant unlawful.' The Commissioners had adopted a system of applying to the Attorney-General to nominate a barrister to sift through seized documents before deciding which of them should be retained. This procedure protected the interests of both the solicitor and of the Commissioners. *R v C & E Commrs (ex p. Popely); R v C & E Commrs (ex p. Harris)*, QB [1999] STC 1016.

[14.95] Customs officers formed the opinion that an accountancy firm was involved in VAT fraud. They obtained warrants from a deputy district judge, authorising them to search the firm's premises, under *VATA 1994, Sch 11 para 10(3)*. When the premises were searched, the officers conducting it took images of the two hard disks on the firm's computer server, and requested the firm's employees to complete certain questionnaires. Customs officers also searched the home of the partners (which Customs subsequently admitted was illegal). The firm applied for judicial review, contending *inter alia* that the computer imaging was unlawful and that the use of the questionnaires rendered the search unlawful. The DC rejected these contentions and dismissed the application with regard to the search of the firm's premises. Kennedy LJ held that 'no complaint can be sustained in relation to the imaging procedure which was adopted'. (The case was remitted to a district judge to assess the damages which should be awarded in respect of the search of the partner's home.) *R (oao Paul Da Costa & Co) v Thames Magistrates' Court*, DC [2002] STC 267; [2002] EWHC 40 (Admin).

[14.96] In a Scottish case, the Commissioners were investigating a married couple who owned two restaurants. One of the investigating officers obtained a warrant 'authorising any such authorised person or persons not exceeding four in number and such other persons (not being authorised persons) as appear to him or them to be necessary' to enter the couple's home. Following the issue of the warrant, eight officers searched the couple's home and removed certain documents relating to meal bills. Subsequently Customs officers also visited the couple's accountant and removed VAT books which he had prepared for the restaurants. The couple were convicted of fraudulent evasion of VAT. They appealed against their convictions, contending that the material recovered from their home was inadmissible evidence, as the relevant warrant had only authorised four officers to conduct the search whereas in fact eight officers had done so, and that the removal of the VAT books from their accountant's premises was also not authorised by what is now *VATA 1994, Sch 11*. The HCJ accepted these contentions, allowed the couple's appeals, and quashed the convictions. With regard to the search of the couple's home, Lord Cameron of Lochbroom held that *Sch 11 para 10(5)** specifically provided for restrictions in relation to the number of authorised persons who could exercise a warrant. On the evidence, only four officers were authorised by the warrant, and 'the four additional officers could not be regarded as "necessary" persons, within the terms of the warrant, for the purposes of entry or search of the premises'. Accordingly, the documents relating to meal bills had been 'unlaw-fully taken'. With regard to the removal of books from the accountants' premises, the seizure had not complied with the provisions of *Sch 11 para 11**, which was apparently intended to protect suspected offenders from 'fishing expeditions' carried out under the guise of *Sch 11 para 7**. Lord Cameron held that the structure of *Sch 11** appeared 'to draw a ready distinction' between cases within *paras 10–12** where a criminal investigation was under way, and cases within *para 7** 'where the documents are sought to be produced for the purposes of managing VAT'. On the evidence, the seizure and removal of documents from the couple's accountant had been unlawful and the evidence derived from them was inadmissible. *M & J Singh v HM Advocate,* HCJ(S) [2001] STC 790.

Order for access to recorded information (VATA 1994, Sch 11 para 11)

Conditions for issue of a search warrant

[14.97] A solicitor had been summoned to appear before magistrates to answer charges that he had knowingly been concerned in the fraudulent evasion of VAT by a company of which he was a director. He was remanded on bail, and a Customs officer made an *ex parte* ('without notice') application to a magistrate under what is now *VATA 1994, Sch 11 para 11(1)* for a warrant requiring the Midland Bank to give him access to records of six accounts held in the name of the solicitor's firm, and to take copies. The magistrate granted the warrant, but the solicitor made an immediate application to the QB for an order of *certiorari* to quash it. The QB granted the order, holding that *VATA 1994, Sch 11 para 11(1)(b)* required the magistrate who granted the application to have 'reasonable grounds' for believing that an offence had been committed and that the information required was relevant. The granting of a warrant was not a mere formality. In this case, the QB held that there was insufficient information before the magistrate which could have satisfied him that there were reasonable grounds for believing that the Midland Bank was in possession of information which might be required as evidence in respect of an offence. In certain circumstances, *ex parte* applications under *VATA 1994, Sch 11 para 11(1)* would be justified, but it was desirable that such applications should have been made on notice. In the circumstances here, the application should have been made under the *Bankers Book Evidence Act 1879* rather than under the *VATA. R v Epsom Justices (ex p. Bell & Another),* QB 1988, [1989] STC 169. (*Note.* The *Rules of the Supreme Court 1965 (SI 1965/1776)* refer to applications being made '*ex parte*' or '*inter partes*'. With effect from 26 April 1999, these rules were largely replaced by the *Civil Procedure Rules 1998 (SI 1998/3132)*, which refer instead to applications being made 'on notice' or 'without notice'.)

[14.98] The Commissioners obtained orders from a magistrates' court under *VATA 1994, Sch 11 para 11*, requiring three banks to give them access to certain certified documents relating to a company. The company's controlling directors applied for judicial review. The QB granted the applications and quashed the orders. Kennedy LJ observed that, although *VATA 1994, Sch 11 para 11* enabled the Commissioners to seek orders *ex parte* ('without notice'), it was preferable for them to proceed *inter partes* ('on notice'), unless there was 'real reason to believe that something of value to the investigation may be lost' if that course was adopted. *R v City of London Magistrates (ex p. Asif & Others)*, QB [1996] STC 611. (*Notes.* (1) Compare the subsequent decision in *R v City of London Magistrates Court & Another (ex p. Peters)*, **14.99** below, where the QB held that the Commissioners had been justified in proceeding *ex parte*, rather than *inter partes*, because there was reason to believe that the director might have transferred funds abroad if the application had been made *inter partes*. (2) See the note following *R v Epsom Justices (ex p. Bell)*, **14.97** above, with regard to the *Civil Procedure Rules 1998 (SI 1998/3132)*.)

[14.99] The Commissioners obtained an order from a magistrates' court under *VATA 1994, Sch 11 para 11*, requiring a bank to give them access to documents relating to a company which carried on a jewellery business. The company's controlling director applied for judicial review, contending firstly that the order was defective because it referred to 'reasonable grounds for suspecting' that an offence had been committed, whereas the statutory test was that there should be 'reasonable grounds for believing' that an offence had been committed, and secondly that there had been procedural irregularities. The QB dismissed the application, holding on the evidence that the officer who had applied for the order had believed that an offence had been committed, that the magistrate had believed what he was required to believe, and that the order was not defective. The officer had presented his information to the magistrates in a balanced way, and there had been no procedural irregularity. Furthermore, the Commissioners had been justified in proceeding *ex parte* ('without notice'), rather than *inter partes* ('on notice'), because there was reason to believe that the director might have transferred funds abroad if the application had been made *inter partes*. *R v City of London Magistrates Court & Another (ex p. B & J Peters)*, QB 1996, [1997] STC 141.

Applications for access orders under Sch 11 para 11

[14.100] The Commissioners applied for four access orders under *VATA 1994, Sch 11 para 11*. Half a day of court time was set aside for the hearing. Two days before the date set for the hearing, the respondents' solicitors applied for an adjournment, contending that the hearing would require a complete day. The Commissioners refused to agree to the application, but on the date fixed for the hearing, the magistrates found that insufficient time was available, and adjourned the case to be heard for a full day. At the adjourned hearing 17 days later, the magistrate granted the access orders but the respondents applied for costs, contending that the proceedings were criminal proceedings and that the Commissioners had acted unreasonably in refusing to agree to set aside a whole day for the hearing. The QB held that the proceedings were civil rather than criminal, and the magistrate had no jurisdiction to award costs. Lord Bingham CJ observed that 'although the respondents were suspected of criminal offences, no formal accusation had been made against any of them on behalf of the state or any private prosecutor and there were no proceedings in being which could have led to the conviction of the respondents of any breach of the criminal law or to their condemnation'. *C & E Commrs v City of London Magistrates' Court and Others*, QB [2000] STC 447; [2000] 1 WLR 2020; [2000] 4 All ER 763.

Restraint orders

[14.101] Customs applied for a restraint order, under *Criminal Justice Act 1988, s 77*, against a businessman (G) who had been charged with a number of offences relating to fraudulent evasion of duty and VAT. Stanley Burnton J held that an order was justified in principle, but that the draft order submitted by Customs was technically deficient and contained some inappropriate provisions, and that additional provisions should be included. He observed that the object of a restraint order was 'to set out clear and specific prohibitions affecting the defendant and the other persons affected by the order'. If the evidence raised a *prima facie* case for 'lifting the corporate veil', and treating property of a company as property of the defendant, the order 'should prohibit the company, in addition to the defendant, from dealing with its property'. However, on the evidence here, the assets which G should be restrained from dealing with were assets which he himself held, rather than assets held by a limited company. *Re G*, QB 2001, [2002] STC 391; [2001] EWHC Admin 606. (*Note. Criminal Justice Act 1988, s 77* was repealed by *Proceeds of Crime Act 2002* with effect from 24 March 2003.)

[14.102] A financial adviser (C) was charged with conspiracy to cheat the public revenue, relating to a 'carousel fraud' involving supplies of mobile telephones. Customs applied for a restraint order and the appointment of a receiver. The QB made a restraint order in October 2001 and appointed a receiver in January 2003. C was subsequently declared bankrupt in separate proceedings brought by the Inland Revenue. The receivership was discharged in October 2004. At a subsequent hearing, the CA expressed the view that the receivership could have been discharged earlier, and held that Customs should pay the receiver's remuneration from 1 June 2004. Customs appealed to the HL, which unanimously reversed the CA decision. Lord Walker of Gestingthorpe observed that 'it has always been a basic principle of receivership that the receiver is entitled to be indemnified in respect of his costs and expenses, and his remuneration if he is entitled to be remunerated, out of the assets in his hands as receiver'. He held that 'a prosecutor cannot be required to give an undertaking in damages as a condition of obtaining the appointment of a receiver' and that 'receivership expenses and remuneration are to come out of the assets subject to the receivership'. Furthermore, 'a receiver takes on heavy responsibilities when he accepts appointment, and he is entitled to the security of knowing that the terms of his appointment will not be changed retrospectively'. *HMRC v Capewell*, HL [2007] UKHL 2; [2007] 2 All ER 370.

Miscellaneous

[14.103] A trader (S) failed to register for VAT. Customs issued a notice of compulsory registration and estimated assessments, and also imposed a misdeclaration penalty. S appealed, contending that Customs had made use of information which he had submitted in his income tax returns, and that this breached the *Data Protection Act 1998*. The tribunal rejected this contention and dismissed the appeal, holding that Customs' use of S's tax returns was authorised by *CRCA 2005, s 17(1)*, and that the *Data Protection Act* did not give 'any protection against the cross-referencing of information between the VAT and the direct tax functions of the Commissioners which has occurred'. Furthermore, such cross-referencing was 'clearly necessary for the exercise of the function of collection and management of VAT conferred on the Commissioners' by *VATA 1994, Sch 11 para 1. W Shrowder*, LON/06/580 (VTD 20912).

Application of CRCA 2005, s 17

Company in receivership—whether receiver obliged to pay VAT

[14.104] See *Re John Willment (Ashford) Ltd*, 37.10 INSOLVENCY, and *Sargent v C & E Commrs*, 37.11 INSOLVENCY.

Liability of provisional liquidator under Insolvency Act 1986, s 135

[14.105] See *Re Grey Marlin Ltd*, 37.5 INSOLVENCY.

Company in liquidation—liquidators' obligation to pay VAT

[14.106] See *Freeman & Another v C & E Commrs (re Margaretta Ltd)*, 37.8 INSOLVENCY.

Set-off of Crown debts

[14.107] See *Re Cushla Ltd*, 37.16 INSOLVENCY, and *Secretary of State for Trade & Industry v Frid*, 37.17 INSOLVENCY.

Set-off of costs against unpaid tax

[14.108] See *HMRC v Xicom Systems Ltd*, 2.509 APPEALS.

Customs obtaining 'Mareva injunction'

[14.109] Customs received information that a company, which they considered owed a substantial amount in customs duty, intended transferring its business to a newly-formed company, without paying the outstanding duty. They therefore applied for an injunction (a 'Mareva injunction') to restrain the company from selling or disposing of its assets. The Ch D granted the injunction. Neuberger J observed that 'the proposed sale of the business is not an arm's length transaction or in the ordinary course of trade' and held on the evidence that 'there is a real prospect of irreversible and very substantial damage to Customs' if the injunction were not granted. *C & E Commrs v Anchor Foods Ltd*, Ch D [1999] 1 WLR 1139; [1999] 3 All ER 268. (*Notes.* (1) Although the case concerned customs duty, the principles are also relevant to VAT. (2) Under the *Civil Procedure Rules 1998 (SI 1998/3132)*, which largely took effect from 26 April 1999, '*Mareva*' injunctions are now referred as 'freezing injunctions'. (3) The injunction was subsequently discharged. For further developments in this case, see the CA decision reported at [2000] BTC 8035.)

Customs obtaining 'freezing orders'

[**14.110**] Customs formed the opinion that two companies (C and T) had been involved in a VAT fraud, as a result of which C had become insolvent while owing substantial amounts of VAT. They presented a winding-up petition against one of the companies (C). They also applied for 'freezing orders' against T and against the controlling directors of both C and T. The Ch D granted the orders. Briggs J observed that there was substantial evidence 'that each of the respondents was aware of and participated in the intended fraud on Customs' and 'thereby all incurred liabilities to (C) and its liquidator'. *HMRC v Egleton & Others*, Ch D [2006] EWHC 2313 (Ch); [2007] 1 All ER 606.

[**14.111**] Customs formed the opinion that two traders, who dealt in computer chips, had been involved in VAT fraud. They instituted proceedings against the traders and obtained a 'freezing order', which 'froze' substantial sums in the defendants' bank accounts. Two trade creditors applied to the CA for a variation in the order, to allow them to be repaid the price of certain undelivered chips. The CA granted the application, observing that the purpose of a 'freezing order' was to avoid the dissipation of assets. However, such an order should not have the effect of creating a secured debt or giving priority to the claimant over an established debtor. On the evidence, the trade creditors were entitled to repayment. *C & E Commrs v Sawyer & Another*, CA 7 November 2001 unreported.

Whether bank owed duty of care to Customs

[**14.112**] Customs obtained 'freezing injunctions' against two companies which owed substantial amounts of VAT. They served the injunctions on the companies' bank by fax. Despite the injunctions, the bank allowed the companies to withdraw substantial sums of money from their accounts. Customs took proceedings against the bank, claiming damages for negligence. The bank defended the proceedings, contending that it did not owe a duty to Customs to prevent the withdrawals. The CA gave judgment for Customs but the HL allowed the bank's appeal. Lord Hoffmann held that 'the law of negligence does not impose liability for mere omissions'. Lord Rodger of Earlsferry observed that 'if the bank had deliberately ignored the orders and set about assisting the companies to transfer their assets, that would have thwarted the court's purpose in granting the orders and the bank would have been in contempt of court, even if the companies themselves had still been unaware of the relevant order'. *Barclays Bank plc v C & E Commrs*, HL [2006] UKHL 28; [2006] 3 WLR 1; [2006] 4 All ER 256.

Cheating the revenue—amount of confiscation order

[14.113] See *R v May*, 49.19 PENALTIES: CRIMINAL OFFENCES.

VATA 1994, Sch 11 para 2(12)*—liability to account for VAT

[14.114] In a New Zealand case, a company (E) was the second mortgagee of a freehold property. The mortgagor became insolvent, and the first mortgagee (B) sold the property. This was a deemed supply under New Zealand legislation similar to *VATA 1994, Sch 4 para 7*, and B accounted for tax under legislation similar to *VATA 1994, Sch 11 para 2(12)*. E took proceedings against B and the New Zealand Revenue, contending that B had not been required to account for tax. The New Zealand CA rejected this contention and the Privy Council dismissed E's appeal, holding that B had been required to account for tax on the deemed supply. *Edgewater Motel Ltd v New Zealand Commissioner of Inland Revenue*, PC [2004] STC 1382; [2004] UKPC 44.

Company in receivership—input tax on repossessed goods

[14.115] See *Re Liverpool Commercial Vehicles Ltd*, 36.675 INPUT TAX.

Group registration—liability of members

[14.116] See *Re Nadler Enterprises Ltd*, 32.10 GROUPS OF COMPANIES.

Representative member seeking to disclaim liability

[14.117] See *Sunfine Developments Ltd*, 32.11 GROUPS OF COMPANIES.

Scottish proceedings—averment of notification of assessment

[14.118] In a Scottish case, the Lord Advocate took proceedings for the recovery of tax assessed by Customs. The defendant appealed, contending that the sum sought had not previously been claimed from him. The Crown's pleadings contained no reference to the manner in which the assessment had been notified. Counsel for the Crown accepted that he would have to prove that such notification had been given, but contended that it was not necessary specifically to aver this in the pleadings, and did not give details of the date on which the notification was made or the address to which it was made. The CS allowed the defendant's appeal, holding that the fact that the amount assessed has been notified to the person assessed in accordance with what is now *VATA 1994, s 73(1)* must be averred in the Crown's pleadings. *Lord Advocate v Johnson*, CS [1985] STC 527.

Customs' right to appeal against lenient sentence

[14.119] A defendant was convicted for fraudulent evasion of excise duty. The magistrates fined him £500. Customs considered that the sentence was unduly lenient, and appealed to the Crown Court under *CEMA 1979, s 147(3)*. The Crown Court judge held that he had no jurisdiction to entertain the appeal. Customs appealed to the QB, which reversed the Crown Court decision and remitted the case to the Crown Court to hear Customs' appeal. The QB held that, in proceedings under *CEMA 1979*, the prosecution had a right of appeal against any decision by a magistrates' court. This included the sentence imposed by the magistrates. *C & E Commrs v WJ Brunt*, QB 10 November 1998, Times 25.11.1998. (*Note.* Although the case concerned excise duty, the decision is also relevant to VAT. With regard to the appropriate sentence for fraudulent evasion of VAT, see *R v Quigley*, **49.14** PENALTIES: CRIMINAL OFFENCES, where the CA imposed a sentence of six months' imprisonment.)

Agreement for compounding criminal proceedings

[14.120] The managing director of a company was arrested on 12 March 1986. Subsequently Customs issued assessments on the company, charging VAT of more than £160,000. In November an agreement was made whereby Customs agreed to compound criminal proceedings for alleged offences committed between 1 November 1983 and 12 March 1986, and the company agreed to pay £140,000 by instalments ending on 31 October 1987. Subsequently the company submitted its return for the quarter ending 30 April 1986, amended in manuscript to indicate that it covered the period from 12 March to 30 April only, rather than the whole of the quarter. Customs issued an assessment charging VAT on sales between 1 February and 12 March 1986, and the company appealed, contending that this liability was already covered by the agreement made in November 1986. The tribunal allowed the company's appeal, holding that the compounding agreement should be construed as including all arrears for the period from 1 November 1983 to 12 March 1986. *Empress Car Company (Abertillery) Ltd*, LON/88/987 (VTD 4832).

[14.121] See also *Cummings*, **2.206** APPEALS.

Assessment not under appeal challenged in collection proceedings

[14.122] See the cases noted at **2.192** *et seq.* APPEALS.

Appellant contending that tax already paid

[14.123] See *Goldenberg*, **2.50** APPEALS.

Validity of bankruptcy order against member of partnership

[14.124] See *Schooler*, **47.69** PARTNERSHIP.

Validity of statutory demand against member of partnership

[14.125] See *Jamieson*, 47.70 PARTNERSHIP.

Trader's wife concealing statutory demand from husband

[14.126] See *Housiaux & Housiaux*, 37.27 INSOLVENCY.

Statutory demand—Insolvency Act 1986, s 375(1)

[14.127] See *Cozens*, 2.193 APPEALS, and *Re A Debtor (No 8 of 1997)*, 37.22 INSOLVENCY.

Winding-up order made although assessments under appeal

[14.128] See *C & E Commrs v D & D Marketing (UK) Ltd*, 37.1 INSOLVENCY, and *C & E Commrs v Anglo-German Breweries Ltd*, 37.2 INSOLVENCY.

Commissioners mistakenly making repayment to company's bank

[14.129] See *C & E Commrs v National Westminster Bank plc*, 48.148 PAYMENT OF TAX.

15

Construction of Buildings, etc.

The cases in this chapter are arranged under the following headings.

Definition of 'person constructing a building' (VATA 1994, Sch 8, Group 5, Item 1(a); VATA 1994, s 35(1)(1A))
    Cases held to qualify for zero-rating or refund   **15.1**
    Cases held not to qualify for zero-rating or refund   **15.9**
Definition of 'building designed as a dwelling' (VATA 1994, Sch 8, Group 5, Items 1, 2(a); VATA 1994, s 35(1A)(a))
    Cases held to qualify for zero-rating   **15.35**
    Cases held not to qualify for zero-rating   **15.43**
Definition of 'relevant residential purpose' (VATA 1994, Sch 8, Group 5, Items 1, 2(a); VATA 1994, s 35(1A)(b))
    Cases held to qualify for zero-rating   **15.70**
    Cases where the appellant was partly successful   **15.77**
    Cases held not to qualify for zero-rating   **15.78**
Definition of 'relevant charitable purpose' (VATA 1994, Sch 8, Group 5, Items 1, 2(a); VATA 1994, s 35(1A)(b))
    Cases held to qualify for zero-rating or refund   **15.82**
    Cases held not to qualify for zero-rating or refund   **15.99**
Residential conversions (VATA 1994, Sch 8, Group 5, Item 1(b); VATA 1994, s 35(1A)(c)(1D))
    Cases held to qualify for zero-rating or refund   **15.120**
    Cases where the appellant was partly successful   **15.128**
    Cases held not to qualify for zero-rating or refund   **15.130**
Definition of 'major interest in building, dwelling or site' (VATA 1994, Sch 8, Group 5, Item 1)
    Cases held to qualify for zero-rating or refund   **15.148**
    Cases held not to qualify for zero-rating or refund   **15.149**
Whether services supplied 'in the course of construction' (VATA 1994, Sch 8, Group 5, Item 2)
    Cases where the appellant was successful   **15.154**
    Cases where the appellant was partly successful   **15.180**
    Cases where the appellant was unsuccessful   **15.187**
Supplies to relevant housing associations (VATA 1994, Sch 8, Group 5, Item 3)   **15.215**
Construction of garages (VATA 1994, Sch 8, Group 5, Note 3)   **15.218**
Building materials, etc. (VATA 1994, Sch 8, Group 5, Item 4; VATA 1994, s 35(1B))
    Finished or prefabricated furniture (*Note 22(a)*)   **15.221**
    Electrical or gas appliances (*Note 22(c)*)   **15.234**
    Other items   **15.241**
Miscellaneous   **15.261**

NOTE

This chapter contains mainly cases turning on the zero-rating provisions of *VATA 1994, Sch 8, Group 5*, but also includes cases involving the application of what is now *VATA 1994, s 35* (which provides for refunds of VAT to 'persons constructing certain buildings') and *Input Tax Order, Article 6* (which disallows an input tax credit on standard-rated goods supplied to persons constructing dwellings by way of business). There have been substantial changes to the legislation in recent years. *VATA 1994, Sch 8, Group 5* was substituted by the *VAT (Construction of Buildings) Order 1995 (SI 1995/280)* with effect from 1 March 1995. The cases in this chapter should be read in the light of the changes in the legislation. For cases concerning the reduced-rate provisions of *VATA 1994, Sch 7A, Groups 6 and 7*, see 56 REDUCED-RATE SUPPLIES: MISCELLANEOUS.

Definition of 'person constructing a building' (VATA 1994, Sch 8, Group 5, Item 1(a); VATA 1994, s 35(1)(1A))

Cases held to qualify for zero-rating or refund

Interval between construction and sale—whether sale within Item 1

[15.1] A housing association had built houses and let them on short tenancies. The houses were subsequently sold to the tenants. The association did not account for output tax on the sales but reclaimed input tax on the costs associated with the disposal, considering that the sales were zero-rated by virtue of what is now *VATA 1994, Sch 8, Group 5, Item 1*. The Commissioners refused to repay the tax in question, considering that because of the lettings which had taken place between the construction and sale of the buildings, the association did not qualify as a 'person constructing a building'. The tribunal allowed the association's appeal and the CS upheld this decision. The phrase 'a person constructing a building' simply meant that only the person who had constructed a building was entitled to treat its sale as zero-rated. Zero-rating was not restricted to cases where the sale took place while the building was in the course of construction. *C & E Commrs v Link Housing Association Ltd*, CS [1992] STC 718. (*Note.* For the Commissioners' practice following this decision, see Business Brief 15/92, issued on 5 October 1992.)

House partly built by subcontractors

[15.2] An individual (K) planned and supervised the construction of a house for him to live in. He did some of the work himself (including work on the foundations and preparatory plumbing work), but much of the work was done by subcontractors. He claimed a refund, under what is now *VATA 1994, s 35*, of tax of £212 on materials which he had purchased for the work which he had carried out himself. Customs rejected the claim on the basis that K was not 'a person constructing a building', since much of the work had been carried out by subcontractors. The tribunal allowed K's appeal, finding that K had undertaken 18.29% of the work 'if only the value of materials is taken into account (and considerably more if notional labour costs were taken into account for the purposes of comparison)'. This was too great to be disregarded on 'de minimis' grounds. The tribunal held that K had constructed the dwelling, partly with his own hands and 'partly through the hands of his contractors' servants', and was entitled to the refund which he had claimed. *KB Kennell*, [1977] VATTR 265 (VTD 487).

Completion of partly-built house

[15.3] An individual (M) purchased a partly completed house from a developer for £25,000, the builder having gone bankrupt. The building was structurally complete and M completed the house himself, including the joinery work, installation of sanitary ware, central heating and electrical fittings, and internal and external decoration. He claimed a refund, under what is now *VATA 1994, s 35*, of tax on materials. The Commissioners rejected the claim, considering that the house had been completed when M acquired it. The tribunal allowed M's appeal, holding that the construction of a dwelling involved its completion to a habitable state, and observing that the use in the legislation of the indefinite article in 'a person constructing' indicated that the claimant need not be the only person constructing a dwelling. On the evidence, the work done by M could not be disregarded on *de minimis* grounds, and accordingly he was a person constructing the dwelling for the purposes of *s 35**. *VW McElroy*, LON/77/289 (VTD 490).

House added to existing house to form a pair of semi-detached dwellings

[15.4] A claimant (H) had built a house for himself in 1968, known as No 10 Rest Bay Close. Ten years later he built another house on the same plot, which became No 10A. The two dwellings formed a pair of semi-detached houses, each with its own access and services and separately owned and rated. H moved into No 10A and claimed a refund of tax under what is now *VATA 1994, s 35*. The Commissioners rejected the claim on the ground that No 10A was an enlargement of No 10. The tribunal allowed H's appeal, holding on the evidence that No 10A was clearly not an enlargement of No 10. *TJ Hill*, [1982] VATTR 134 (VTD 1225). (*Note.* The decision was approved by the QB in *Perry*, **15.28** below.)

Construction of flat adjacent to house

[15.5] An individual (H) constructed a garage and a flat adjacent to his house. The east wall of the garage was about four feet away from the west wall of the house. The flat was a single-storey building and was attached to the south wall of the garage but was not attached to the house. The only external access to the flat was by means of a passageway between the garage and the house, leading onto the drive. The passageway was covered, with a lockable door at each end. H claimed a refund of tax under what is now *VATA 1994, s 35*. The Commissioners rejected the claim, considering that the work constituted the enlargement of an existing building. The tribunal allowed H's appeal, holding that the interpolation of the passageway did not provide a sufficiently direct access to link the occupation of the flat and the house. (The tribunal also held that a refund of tax was not due in respect of the garage, as on the evidence the garage was part of the existing house rather than part of the flat.) *AA Heslop*, EDN/89/43 (VTD 3862).

Construction of house adjacent to offices

[15.6] A husband and wife partnership built a house adjacent to their business premises. The two buildings shared a common wall and were connected by a communicating door. The partnership reclaimed tax under what is now *VATA 1994, s 35*, but the Commissioners disallowed the claim as there was internal access between the two buildings. The partnership appealed and the tribunal allowed the appeal. The decision in *Perry*, 15.28 below, was distinguished because in that case both buildings were dwelling-houses so that the new dwelling had become an enlargement of the existing dwelling. In the instant case the existing building comprised offices whereas the new building was a house. The house could not be said to be an enlargement of the existing offices. *Waterways Services*, [1990] VATTR 37 (VTD 4643).

Replacement of old farmhouse by new farmhouse

[15.7] A farmer owned an old stone-built farmhouse which had been built in the late 19th century, had no foundations, and was in poor condition. He obtained planning permission for 'improvements and extension' to the build-ing. However, in view of the absence of foundations, the whole of the old building was demolished and a completely new house was erected on the site. He claimed relief under what is now *VATA 1994, s 35*. The Commissioners rejected the claim, considering that in view of the nature of the planning permission, the work had in law constituted the reconstruction of an existing building, rather than the construction of a new one. The tribunal allowed the farmer's appeal, finding that since no part of the original farmhouse remained standing, the work was the construction of a new building and was eligible for relief. Applying *dicta* in *Waterways Services Ltd*, 15.6 above, the fact that the proposed work was described in the planning permission as an 'extension' did not render it unlawful or prevent it from qualifying as the construction of a building. *ED Bruce*, [1991] VATTR 280 (VTD 6326).

Replacement of semi-detached cottages by detached house

[15.8] A married couple purchased two 18th century semi-detached cottages. They obtained planning permission to convert the cottages into a single building, and reclaimed input tax under what is now *VATA 1994, s 35*. The Commissioners rejected the claim on the grounds that the work amounted to the conversion of an existing building. The couple appealed, contending that, despite the terms of the planning permission, the cottages had been in such poor condition that they had had to demolish them and construct a new building. The tribunal accepted the couple's evidence and allowed the appeal. *JS & L Bell*, MAN/94/438 (VTD 13448).

Cases held not to qualify for zero-rating or refund

Construction of flat on top of existing building

[15.9] A three-storey house was divided into three flats. An additional flat was built on top of the existing house. The tribunal held that the work did not qualify for relief under what is now *VATA 1994, s 35*. The flat did not have a separate entrance, had no independent foundation, and was clearly an enlargement of an existing building. *S Hardy*, LON/76/46 (VTD 289).

Construction of flat as extension to bungalow

[15.10] A flat was built as an extension to a bungalow. The bungalow already had a flat-roofed extension and the flat was partly at ground level, sharing a common wall with the existing extension, and partly over the existing extension. It had separate access and services and was separately rated. The tribunal held that the flat was an enlargement of the bungalow and that its construction did not qualify for relief under what is now *VATA 1994, s 35*. *DW Taylor*, MAN/77/94 (VTD 454).

Construction of flat adjacent to house

[15.11] A self-contained flat was constructed adjacent to an existing house. The roof of the house was extended to cover the flat. The tribunal held that the flat was an enlargement of an existing building for the purposes of what is now *VATA 1994, s 35*. *HN Kirsopp*, MAN/81/203 (VTD 1236).

Reconstruction of derelict cottage

[15.12] An individual bought a 17th century cottage which was derelict and uninhabitable. He carried out extensive work to make it suitable as a dwelling-house for himself but, to comply with the terms of his planning permission, he used the old foundation and some of the old building. He reclaimed tax under what is now *VATA 1994, s 35*. The Commissioners rejected the claim and the tribunal dismissed his appeal, holding that the work was the reconstruction of an existing building. *HC Morton*, CAR/77/137 (VTD 438).

[15.13] Similar decisions were reached in *T Owen*, LON/78/345 (VTD 741); *JW Shields*, EDN/96/246 (VTD 15154); *M Tinker*, LON/01/967 (VTD 18033) and *J Williamson*, [2010] UKFTT 254 (TC), TC00548.

Reconstruction of bungalow

[15.14] An appellant (W) purchased a bungalow which was structurally unsound. He obtained planning permission to convert it into a 'dwelling and granny flat'. The existing walls were replaced but the roof structure and windows were retained. There was little change in the external appearance of the bungalow. W claimed a refund of VAT under what is now *VATA 1994, s 35*. The Commissioners rejected the claim, considering that the work was the alteration of an existing building and that no refund was therefore due. The tribunal dismissed W's appeal, holding that the work constituted the reconstruction of an existing building rather than the construction of a new one. *D White*, EDN/89/93 (VTD 4254).

[15.15] A claimant (B) obtained planning permission for extensions to a bungalow. After beginning work on the extensions, he became aware that the existing walls had been badly affected by damp. He replaced the external walls, replaced the roof, and then demolished the internal walls. The Commissioners rejected his claim for a refund of tax, on the basis that the work constituted the reconstruction of an existing building and the bungalow had never been 'demolished completely to ground level', as required by *VATA 1994, Sch 8, Group 5, Note 18*. The tribunal upheld this decision and dismissed B's appeal. *AA Bugg*, LON/97/224 (VTD 15123).

[15.16] Similar decisions were reached in *GD Gilder*, MAN/99/851 (VTD 18143) and *Jonathan Berry Ltd*, [2011] UKFTT 652 (TC), TC01494.

Sales of land on which houses built by associated company

[15.17] A company (D) was a member of a group engaged in building, for which there was no group registration. D's principal function was to acquire building land and necessary planning permission, plan the layout of the estates and see to the landscaping and the building of roads and sewers. Another group company (Y) built the houses in accordance with D's plans and specifications. D then sold the plots of land with the houses built on them. In a typical sale, D was described as the vendor and Y as the builder, and the completion statement showed separate figures for the house and the land, the former being the amount invoiced by Y to D for erecting the house. The Commissioners issued a ruling that D's sales of land were exempt. D appealed, contending that they were zero-rated and that it could therefore reclaim part of its input tax. The tribunal rejected this contention and dismissed the appeal. The functions performed by D were not those of 'a person constructing a building' for the purpose of what is now *VATA 1994, Sch 8, Group 5, Item 1*. *Monsell Youell Developments Ltd*, [1978] VATTR 1 (VTD 538).

Sale of land prepared for construction of buildings

[15.18] A building company sold some development land, on which it had undertaken some civil engineering work in preparation for the construction of buildings. The Commissioners issued an assessment to recover the input tax which the company had previously reclaimed, on the basis that the sale of the land was an exempt supply. The company appealed, contending that it had changed the condition of the land to the extent that it should be treated as a 'person constructing a building', so that the sale qualified for zero-rating under *VATA 1994, Sch 8, Group 5, Item 1*. The tribunal rejected this contention and dismissed the appeal, holding that 'at the time of the sale there was nothing on the land that was recognisably a building under construction'. Accordingly the sale of the land was an exempt supply and did not qualify for zero-rating. *Cameron New Homes Ltd*, LON/01/49 (VTD 17309).

Work carried out by lessee

[15.19] In 1965 a redevelopment scheme was begun under which land owned by an educational foundation was let for 125 years to a company (C) which was to finance the redevelopment, and sublet by C to another company (M) for a similar term. The redevelopment was completed in 1971, and the foundation reclaimed the input tax incurred. The Commissioners rejected the claim, considering that the foundation was not the 'person constructing a building', and thus was not within what is now *VATA 1994, Sch 8, Group 5, Item 1*. The tribunal dismissed the foundation's appeal, holding that the words 'person constructing a building' must be given their natural meaning. The 'construction must be physically done by the person concerned or by his servants or agents, or the person must himself directly enter into a contract or arrangement for another to do the physical construction works'. The construction work here was done under contracts to which the foundation was not a party. *Hulme Trust Educational Foundation*, [1978] VATTR 179 (VTD 625).

Sale by housing association of former council houses

[15.20] In March 1993 a housing association purchased a number of council houses from the district council which had built them. In 1994 the association sold four of the houses to sitting tenants, in accordance with the provisions introduced by the *Housing Act 1980*. The Commissioners issued a ruling that the sales did not qualify for zero-rating, since the association was not the 'person constructing' the dwellings. The association appealed, contending that the effect of *Article 5(8)* of the *EC Sixth Directive* was that it should be treated as the 'person constructing' the dwellings. The tribunal dismissed the appeal, holding that *Article 5(8)* was 'wholly permissive' and 'does not create a directly effective entitlement that United Kingdom taxpayers can rely on'. Furthermore, the purchase of the houses from the council by the association did not constitute the transfer of a business as a going concern. *Peddars Way Housing Association Ltd*, LON/93/2619A (VTD 12663).

Materials added to house after completion of contract

[15.21] A married couple purchased a newly-built house in May 1993. They also purchased a conservatory (in kit form), additional light fittings, curtain rails, a fitted wardrobe, and additional shelving and miscellaneous hardware. All these items were attached to the house after completion of the contract. The couple reclaimed input tax under what is now *VATA 1994, s 35*. The Commissioners rejected the claim, on the grounds that the couple were not 'a person constructing a building'. The couple appealed, contending that the house had not been completed at the time they purchased it. The tribunal rejected this contention and dismissed their appeal, holding on the evidence that 'on the completion of the contract the vendor handed over a completed building'. The addition of a conservatory 'amounted to the enlargement of an existing building' and none of the other items in question 'could fairly be described as constructing a building or as completing the construction of a building'. *AG & W Simister*, MAN/93/1376 (VTD 12715).

[15.22] An appeal was dismissed in a case where a claimant had purchased a fireplace for a new house before taking occupation but after the completion certificate had been issued by the local authority. The tribunal held that 'the completion of a building is a matter of fact and evidence of completion is the local authority certificate'. *I Taylor*, EDN/97/170 (VTD 15566).

[15.23] In 1999 an individual (M) arranged for a builder to construct a new bungalow. The local authority issued a certificate of completion in April 2000. In July 2001 M claimed relief under *VATA 1994, s 35* in respect of the construction of new paths and the installation of a new shower cubicle. The Commissioners rejected the claim and the tribunal dismissed M's appeal, observing that it had been made outside the time limit laid down by *VAT Regulations 1995, reg 201*. *GM Morris*, LON/01/902 (VTD 17860).

[15.24] A similar decision was reached in *C McAlister*, LON/02/408 (VTD 18011).

Sale of renovated houses

[15.25] A company sold houses which it had renovated, and did not account for output tax on the sales. The Commissioners issued an assessment charging tax on the sales, and the company appealed, contending that the sales were zero-rated under what is now *VATA 1994, Sch 8, Group 5, Item 1*. The tribunal dismissed the company's appeal, holding that the work of renovation did not amount to 'construction' and accordingly the company was not a 'person constructing a building'. *T & D Services (Timber Preservation & Damp Proofing Contractors) Ltd*, LON/80/435 (VTD 1157).

[15.26] A similar decision was reached in *BS Horn*, MAN/82/18 (VTD 1250).

Extension to existing house

[15.27] An individual (C) converted a house comprising 156 square metres into two semi-detached houses with a total area of 244 square metres. He reclaimed tax under what is now *VATA 1994, s 35*. The Commissioners rejected the claim and the tribunal dismissed C's appeal, holding that the work constituted the enlargement of an existing building. *D Childs*, LON/82/330 (VTD 1373).

Dwelling added to existing house with communicating door

[15.28] The owner of a house built a two-storey extension to be used by members of his family. The extension had a separate entrance. However, a condition of the planning permission was that the extension was to be used 'only in conjunction with the existing building'. A communicating door was built in the party wall between the existing house and the extension. The Commissioners rejected the owner's claim for a refund of tax, considering that the work did not constitute the construction of a new building. The QB upheld the Commissioners' decision. On the evidence, the extension was an enlargement of the existing dwelling, so that relief was not due. The terms of the planning permission and the existence of the communicating door dictated the conclusion that the extension was not a separate building. *C & E Commrs v RC Perry*, QB [1983] STC 383.

[15.29] The decision in *Perry*, 15.28 above, was applied in the similar subsequent case of *W Macaulay*, EDN/95/291 (VTD 14429).

Conversion of disused boat into houseboat

[15.30] A doctor converted a disused Thames lighter boat into a houseboat. He claimed a refund of tax under *VATA 1994, s 35*. The Commissioners rejected the claim on the basis that the work did not constitute the 'construction of a building'. The tribunal dismissed the doctor's appeal, observing that *VATA 1994* 'discriminates against houseboat builders'. *Dr J Parkinson*, LON/00/110 (VTD 17257).

[15.31] A similar decision was reached in *RE Jacobs*, LON/03/305 (VTD 18367).

Construction of purpose-built houseboat

[15.32] An architect reclaimed VAT on the construction of a purpose-built houseboat. HMRC rejected the claim and he appealed. The tribunal dismissed the appeal, applying the principles in *Parkinson*, 15.30 above. *WR Dunster v HMRC*, [2010] UKFTT 462 (TC), TC00727.

Construction of bridge

[15.33] A charity arranged for the construction of a bridge across the River Don, for cyclists and pedestrians. Customs issued a ruling that VAT was chargeable on the work. The charity appealed, contending that the bridge should be treated as a building and as qualifying for zero-rating. The tribunal rejected this contention and dismissed the appeal, holding that the bridge was not a 'building'. *Upper Don Walk Trust*, MAN/05/716 (VTD 19476).

Reconstruction or alteration of existing building

[15.34] There have been a large number of cases in which tribunals have found that work has constituted the reconstruction or alteration of an existing building, rather than the construction of a new building, and which appear to raise no point of general interest. In the interests of space, such cases are not summarised individually in this book. For summaries of such cases decided up to 31 December 1995, see Tolley's VAT Cases 1996.

Definition of 'building designed as a dwelling' (VATA 1994, Sch 8, Group 5, Items 1, 2(a); VATA 1994, s 35(1A)(a))

Cases held to qualify for zero-rating

Prefabricated bungalows—whether 'buildings designed as a dwelling'

[15.35] A married couple purchased a caravan site which was 'almost derelict', renovated the site, and built a number of luxury prefabricated bungalows for sale. The bungalows were erected on a brick foundation with a brick skirting. The couple considered that the sale of the bungalows qualified for zero-rating under what is now *VATA 1994, Sch 8, Group 5, Item 1*. Accordingly, they reclaimed input tax and did not account for output tax. The Commissioners issued an assessment to recover the input tax on the basis that the sale of the bungalows did not qualify for zero-rating, but was the grant of an interest over land which was exempt from VAT. The tribunal allowed the couple's appeal, holding that the bungalows were clearly 'buildings', rather than caravans. They were rated and insured as bungalows, and although they were described as 'mobile homes' in agreements between the purchasers and the site manager, it was unlikely that they would in fact be moved. The cost of removal would be prohibitive, and the homes were occupied and used as permanent dwellings. When they were erected on the site, they 'lost the physical characteristics which had made them mobile and they acquired new characteristics (such as the brickwork base) which made them buildings'. *Mr & Mrs N Smith*, MAN/89/708 (VTD 5579).

Single-storey building in grounds of large house

[15.36] The owner of a large house, set in seven acres of grounds, arranged for the construction of a single-storey self-contained building within the grounds, about 40 feet from the house. The building comprised one large room of about 300 square feet, plus a small room with a WC and washbasin (and with room for a shower unit, although no shower had been installed at the time of the appeal). It had its own central heating system, hot water system and electricity supply. The room was primarily used by the owner's wife as a studio for painting, but had also been used as sleeping accommodation for her children. The company which constructed the building did not account for tax on it, treating it as zero-rated. The Commissioners issued an assessment charging tax on the work, and the company appealed, contending that the building had been 'designed as a dwelling', even though it was not primarily used as a dwelling. The tribunal accepted this contention and allowed the appeal, holding that the building met the requirements of *VATA 1994, Sch 8, Group 5, Note 2*, so that its construction qualified for zero-rating. The tribunal found that although the building did not have a 'shower unit or bath installed, it is still capable of being used as a studio flat providing living accommodation. The provision of a shower unit or bath would add to the amenities but it is not essential when hot and cold water are available with a wash basin and sink unit installed'. *Oldrings Development Kingsclere Ltd*, LON/00/636 (VTD 17769).

Bedsitting rooms with en-suite shower room

[15.37] A housing association operated a care home, which was a two-storey building. It arranged for the construction of an additional floor, containing eight residential units, each of which consisted of a bedsitting room with an en-suite shower room. The Commissioners issued a ruling that the work was chargeable to VAT. The association appealed, contending that each of the units was 'self-contained living accommodation', within *VATA 1994, Sch 8, Group 5, Note 2(a)*, and that the work qualified for zero-rating. The tribunal accepted this contention and allowed the appeal, applying the HL decision in *Uratemp Ventures Ltd v Collins*, HL [2001] 3 WLR 806, and holding that 'premises with their own front door, en suite bathing facilities and the ability to cook with a microwave cooker and a kettle are self-contained living accommodation'. *Agudas Israel Housing Association Ltd*, LON/03/344 (VTD 18798).

Conversion of mill into residential units

[15.38] Two individuals obtained permission to convert a mill into two residential units. They each acquired one of the units, and retained joint ownership of a workshop which stood in the grounds of the mill. They signed an agreement under *Town and Country Planning Act 1990, s 10*, respectively covenanting not to sever the legal ownership of any part of either of the residential units or the workshop. They reclaimed tax on the conversion work under *VATA 1994, s 35*. The Commissioners rejected the claim on the grounds that the effect of the covenant was to prohibit the separate use or disposal of either of the residential units, so that the effect of *VATA 1994, Sch 8, Group 5, Note 2(c)* was that neither of the units qualified as a building 'designed as a dwelling'. The tribunal allowed the claimants' appeal, holding that since the covenants related 'to each of the three properties respectively', their effect was to prevent any further subdivision of either of the two residential units, but that they did not prohibit the separate disposal of either of the units 'in the sense contemplated by *Note 2(c)*'. *JS Sherwin & RK Green*, LON/98/708 (VTD 16396).

Cottages built in grounds of care home

[15.39] A family partnership arranged for the construction of seven cottages in the grounds of a large house which was used as a care home. The local planning authority required the partnership to enter into a covenant that the cottages would only be occupied by people aged 55 or over, and that the freehold of the cottages would not be disposed of separately from the care home. Customs issued a ruling that the effect of this covenant was that the construction of the cottages failed to qualify for zero-rating by virtue of *VATA 1994, Sch 8, Group 5, Note 2(c)*. The partnership appealed, contending that there was no prohibition on the separate use of the cottages and that the covenant did not amount to a prohibition on the separate disposal of the cottages, so that *Note 2(c)* did not apply. The tribunal accepted this contention and allowed the appeal. *JFB & FR Sharples*, [2008] VATDR 618 (VTD 20775).

House adjacent to holiday chalets—whether Note 2(c) applicable

[15.40] In a Scottish case, a married couple operated a number of holiday chalets. They applied for planning permission to build a house on the site, to be occupied by their son (P) in order that he could help them with the business. The planning permission included a requirement that the house should be occupied 'only by persons engaged in the management or operation of the existing holiday chalet letting business together with their family members'. P built the house and reclaimed VAT under *VATA 1994, s 35*. HMRC rejected the claim on the grounds that the effect of the planning permission was that zero-rating was precluded by *VATA 1994, Sch 8, Group 5, Note 2(c)*. The tribunal allowed P's appeal against this decision. Judge Barton held that the planning permission imposed an occupancy restriction, but did not prohibit the separate use or disposal of the dwelling, so that *Note 2(c)* did not apply. *I Phillips v HMRC*, [2011] UKFTT 372 (TC), TC01227.

Construction of farmhouse in national park—whether Note 2(c) applicable

[15.40A] A married couple constructed a farmhouse in the Exmoor National Park. Somerset County Council granted planning permission subject to a proviso that the farmhouse 'shall not be transferred, let or in any way disposed of separately' from the land. The couple reclaimed tax on the construction. HMRC rejected the claim on the basis that effect of the planning permission was that zero-rating was precluded by VATA 1994, Sch 8, Group 5, Note 2(c). The tribunal allowed the couple's appeal against this decision. Judge Cornwell-Kelly held that the effect of Town and Country Planning Act 1990, s 4A was that the relevant planning authority was the Exmoor National Park Committee, rather than Somerset County Council. It followed that the restriction which the County Council had sought to impose had no legal effect, and the farmhouse qualified as a 'building designed as a dwelling'. *TW & Mrs SM Stevens v HMRC*, FTT [2011] UKFTT 835 (TC), TC01671.

Properties described as 'holiday dwelling-houses'

[15.41] A company developed a site in Ayrshire, constructing a number of detached dwelling-houses. Under the relevant agreement with the local authority, it was a condition of the development that 'all houses on the development shall be used as holiday dwelling-houses only and for no other purpose'. The company treated its sales of the houses as zero-rated. The Commissioners issued an assessment on the basis that the effect of *VATA 1994, Sch 8, Group 5, Note 13* was that the sales failed to qualify for zero-rating. The tribunal allowed the company's appeal, expressing the opinion that 'the two states of use', namely as a holiday dwelling house or as a principal private residence, were not mutually exclusive, since the houses could be purchased by retired people 'whose time may be available on a year-round basis for 365 days as "days on which work is suspended" and "days of recreation and amusement"' (the dictionary definitions of a 'holiday'). *Livingstone Homes UK Ltd*, EDN/99/98 (VTD 16649). (*Note*. The decision here was disapproved by subsequent tribunals in *Loch Tay Highland Lodges Ltd*, **15.67** below, and *Herling Ltd*, **15.68** below. In *Loch Tay Highland Lodges Ltd*, the chairman (Mr. Coutts) observed that the tribunal in *Livingstone* had 'ignored the word "only" and the phrase "for no other purpose"', and held that the case was wrongly decided.)

Whether Group 5, Note 13 applies to VATA 1994, s 35

[15.42] A woman (J) reclaimed VAT under *VATA 1994, s 35* on materials which she had purchased for the construction of a log cabin. The relevant planning permission provided that the cabin 'shall not be occupied during the month of February in any calendar year'. HMRC rejected the claim on the basis that the effect of *VATA 1994, Sch 8, Group 5, Note 13* was that no refund was due. J appealed, contending that *Group 5, Note 13* did not apply to *VATA 1994, s 35*. The tribunal accepted this contention and allowed her appeal, holding that *Note 13* only applied to cases within *Group 5 Item 1*, ie where a building was purchased from a developer. It did not apply to cases within *Group 5 Item 2*, ie where a landowner arranged for a contractor to construct a building on his land. It should also not be treated as applying to cases within *s 35*, where a landowner purchased materials for the construction of a building. Judge Hellier observed that 'if a DIY builder agrees with a contractor for the construction of the entire building, that supply is zero-rated by *Item 2* and *Item 4* of *Group 5*, both of which are unaffected by *Note 13*. The materials used in the construction are effectively zero-rated.' HMRC were contending that 'if the DIY builder separately buys labour and materials, the labour will be zero-rated but the materials will not be'. There was 'no reason to construe *section 35* as not being intended to relieve that hardship'. *Mrs IS Jennings v HMRC (No 1)*, [2010] UKFTT 49 (TC), TC00362. (*Notes*. (1) For HMRC's practice following this decision, see HMRC Brief 29/10, issued on 15 June 2010. (2) At a subsequent hearing, the tribunal also held that a document issued by the supplier qualified as an 'invoice' for the purposes of *VATA 1994, s 35*, although it did not meet the requirements of *VAT Regulations 1995, reg 14*—[2011] UKFTT 298 (TC), TC01160.)

Cases held not to qualify for zero-rating

Independent building in grounds of existing house

[15.43] An individual purchased a house and obtained planning permission to build a new house on the same site. The structure of the new house was completed in August 1990, and the internal fitting was completed in May 1991. In October 1991 the owner applied for permission to demolish a garage block and replace it by an annexe consisting of a triple garage with office space and residential accommodation for domestic staff, and to build an indoor swimming pool. The annexe was not physically attached to the new house. Planning consent for this was granted in March 1992, and the construction of the annexe began in August 1992. The Commissioners issued a ruling that the construction of the annexe and swimming pool did not qualify for zero-rating under what is now *VATA 1994, Sch 8, Group 5, Item 2*, and the owner appealed. The tribunal dismissed the appeal, holding that the annexe did not qualify for zero-rating. The garage was not constructed at the same time as the house and thus did not fall within what is now *VATA 1994, Sch 8, Group 5, Note 3*. Although the annexe contained residential accommodation, it was not within the definition of 'a building designed as a dwelling'. *SA Whiteley*, [1993] VATTR 248 (VTD 11292).

[15.44] A married couple arranged for the construction of a new two-storey building, in the grounds of their existing house, and including two bedrooms, a kitchen, a bathroom and a shower. The Commissioners issued a ruling that the work did not qualify for zero-rating. The husband appealed, contending firstly that the new building was designed as a dwelling and alternatively that it was intended for use for a residential purpose. The tribunal rejected these contentions and dismissed the appeal. The effect of *VATA 1994, Sch 8, Group 5, Note 2(c)* was that the building did not qualify as a 'building designed as a dwelling', since its separate use was prohibited by the terms of the relevant planning permission. Furthermore, the fact that the couple's eldest child occupied the new building did not mean that it qualified as 'residential accommodation for students', since the child was 'occupying the new building as being a child of the appellant and part of the appellant's household rather than as a student or school pupil'. *P Thompson*, [1998] VATDR 524 (VTD 15834).

[15.45] A woman (M) built a bungalow at the rear of her house, for use as self-contained accommodation for her elderly mother. The relevant planning permission prohibited the separate use and independent disposal of the bungalow. M claimed a refund of the VAT incurred under *VATA 1994, s 35*. Customs rejected the claim on the grounds that the effect of *VATA 1994, Sch 8, Group 5, Note 2(c)* was that the building did not qualify as a 'building designed as a dwelling', since its separate use was prohibited by the terms of the relevant planning permission. The tribunal upheld Customs' ruling and dismissed M's appeal. *Mrs D Milligan*, MAN/04/718 (VTD 19224).

[15.46] Similar decisions were reached in *R Donaghy*, EDN/06/06 (VTD 19802) and *K Lamming*, [2009] UKFTT 44 (TC); TC00022.

[15.47] See also *Moore*, 15.144 below.

Conversion of stable block into living accommodation

[15.48] An individual (H) claimed a refund of VAT under *VATA 1994, s 35* in respect of the conversion of a stable block into an 'annexe for living accommodation'. The Commissioners rejected the claim on the basis that, in view of the relevant planning permission, the converted stable block did not qualify as a 'building designed as a dwelling'. The tribunal dismissed H's appeal against this decision. *LR Hamilton*, MAN/97/975 (VTD 16020).

[15.49] A similar decision was reached in *AC Collins*, MAN/05/506 (VTD 19564).

Conversion of cowshed into living accommodation

[15.50] An individual (M) converted an old cowshed to provide living accommodation for his mother-in-law. He claimed a refund of tax under *VATA 1994, s 35*. The Commissioners rejected the claim on the basis that the relevant planning permission prohibited the separate use or disposal of the building, so that the conditions of *VATA 1994, Sch 8, Group 5, Note 2(c)* were not satisfied. The tribunal dismissed M's appeal against this decision. *JC Munnery*, MAN/01/420 (VTD 17903).

Conversion of barn into living accommodation

[15.51] A widower lived in a two-storey house, the grounds of which contained a barn. He decided to convert the barn into living accommodation, so that his son and daughter-in-law could live near to him. He conveyed the property into the joint names of himself, his son (W) and his daughter-in-law, as tenants in common. They reclaimed tax on the work under *VATA 1994, s 35*. The Commissioners rejected the claim, on the basis that the work failed to qualify for zero-rating since the relevant planning permission prohibited the separate disposal of the barn, so that the conditions of *VATA 1994, Sch 8, Group 5, Note 2(c)* were not satisfied. W appealed, contending that *Note 2(c)* did not apply because the relevant planning permission permitted the separate use of the barn, and that, applying *dicta* of the tribunal chairman in *Hopewell-Smith*, 55.7 PROTECTED BUILDINGS, *Note 2(c)* should be read as offering two alternatives, with the condition being fulfilled if either alternative was met. The tribunal rejected this contention and dismissed the appeal, specifically disapproving the reasoning in *Hopewell-Smith*. The tribunal held that 'Parliament undoubtedly meant by *Note 2(c)* to exclude from zero-rating any residential building which was not capable of *either* separate use *or* disposal. Both conditions have to be satisfied.' *PH Wiseman*, LON/00/1040 (VTD 17374).

[15.52] The decision in *Wiseman*, 15.51 above, was applied in the similar subsequent cases of *G Cartagena*, MAN/05/530 (VTD 19454) and *G Silver*, [2011] UKFTT 644 (TC), TC01486.

[15.53] A married couple arranged for a barn, in the grounds of their existing house, to be converted into a residential building for the use of the wife's parents. The relevant planning permission stipulated that 'the new building should only be used ancillary to the main dwelling and not as a separate unit of accommodation'. The couple claimed a refund of tax under *VATA 1994, s 35*. The Commissioners rejected the claim on the grounds that the effect of *VATA 1994, Sch 8, Group 5, Note 2(c)* was that the building was not 'designed as a dwelling'. Eighteen months after the conversion had been completed, the couple obtained permission for the separate use or disposal of the new building. They appealed to the tribunal, contending that they should now be entitled to a refund under *VATA 1994, s 35*. The tribunal rejected this contention and dismissed the appeal, holding that the condition in *Note 2(c)* had to be fulfilled at 'the time of the design of the building (that is, at the date of the planning consent) and not later'. *AE & Mrs JM Harris*, LON/04/185 (VTD 18822).

[15.54] An individual (C) converted a barn to include residential accommodation, offices and a workshop. He claimed a refund of tax under *VATA 1994, s 35*. Customs rejected the claim on the basis that the relevant planning permission stipulated that the residential accommodation could only be occupied in conjunction with commercial use, so that the effect of *VATA 1994, Sch 8, Group 5, Note 2(c)* was that the building was not 'designed as a dwelling'. The tribunal upheld Customs' ruling and dismissed C's appeal, finding that 'the planners had required the majority of the property to be non-domestic' and that 'the occupation of the residential accommodation may not be separated from the commercial use of the business premises'. *P Cussins*, MAN/06/807 (VTD 20541).

[15.55] See also *Ford*, 55.3 PROTECTED BUILDINGS, and *Clamp*, 55.4 PROTECTED BUILDINGS.

Conversion of farm buildings into living accommodation

[15.56] An individual (G) obtained planning permission for the conversion of some farm buildings into living accommodation. The planning permission provided that the new accommodation could only be used 'as ancillary to the residential accommodation presently on the site as a single dwelling unit and not as a separate unit of residential accommodation in its own right'. G claimed a refund of tax under *VATA 1994, s 35*. Customs rejected the claim on the grounds that the effect of *VATA 1994, Sch 8, Group 5, Note 2(c)* was that the converted building was not 'designed as a dwelling', since it could not be used separately from the existing house. The tribunal dismissed G's appeal against this decision. *MJ Giblin*, LON/06/1286 (VTD 20352).

[15.57] A similar decision was reached in *MA Reay*, MAN/06/837 (VTD 20378).

Construction of farmhouse adjacent to existing farm buildings

[15.58] A couple arranged for the construction of a new farmhouse, adjacent to some existing farm buildings. They reclaimed input tax under *VATA 1994, s 35*. HMRC rejected the claim on the grounds that the relevant planning permission prohibited the separate disposal of the house, so that the effect of *VATA 1994, Sch 8, Group 5, Note 2(c)* was that it did not qualify as a 'building designed as a dwelling'. The tribunal dismissed the couple's appeal against this decision. *D & Mrs E Sherratt v HMRC*, [2011] UKFTT 320 (TC), TC01180; [2011] UKFTT 381 (TC), TC01236.

Addition of self-contained flat to existing house

[15.59] A married couple arranged for the construction of a self-contained flat, adjoining their existing house and incorporating a small part of the house, to be used by the wife's mother. The relevant planning permission prohibited the separate disposal of the flat. The couple claimed a refund of tax under *VATA 1994, s 35*. The Commissioners rejected the claim on the grounds that the effect of *VATA 1994, Sch 8, Group 5, Note 2(c)* was that the flat did not qualify as a building 'designed as a dwelling'. The tribunal dismissed the couple's appeal against this decision. *D & A McDove*, EDN/05/60 (VTD 19501).

[15.60] A similar decision was reached in a case where the tribunal applied the principles laid down in *Wiseman*, 15.51 above. *MJ Bracegirdle*, MAN/07/792 (VTD 20889).

Application of Note 2(d)

[15.61] An individual (D) owned a large house in 20 acres of land. He obtained planning permission for the construction of a double garage. Above the garage he built a second storey, which he furnished as a kitchen, living room and a bedroom. He claimed a refund of tax under *VATA 1994, s 35*. The Commissioners rejected the claim on the basis that the new building was not within the definition of a 'building designed as a dwelling'. D appealed. The tribunal dismissed his appeal, holding that although the building was 'self-contained living accommodation', the work did not qualify for zero-rating because it had not been carried out in accordance with statutory planning consent, so that the requirements of *Sch 8, Group 5, Note 2(d)* had not been met. *AI Davison*, LON/00/946 (VTD 17130).

[15.62] An appeal was dismissed in a case where the tribunal held that, for the purposes of *Note 2(d)*, planning permission could not be retrospective. *MJ Watson v HMRC*, [2010] UKFTT 526 (TC), TC00780.

[15.63] A similar decision was reached in *Abbeytrust Homes Ltd*, [2011] UKFTT 150 (TC), TC01024.

[15.64] A woman (S) bought a plot of land adjacent to her existing house. She wanted to build two semi-detached houses (one for each of her daughters), but the local council refused planning permission for this. The council subsequently agreed to grant planning permission for the construction of a bungalow 'to provide two residential units for two related families', subject to a covenant that the bungalow would only be occupied by S and her family. The planning permission showed an internal door between the units, but the doorway was subsequently blocked up and plastered over. S claimed a refund of VAT under *VATA 1994, s 35*. HMRC rejected the claim on the grounds that the work failed to meet the requirements of either *Group 5, Note 2(c)* or *(d)*. The tribunal dismissed S's appeal against this decision. Judge Mosedale observed that the building had not been 'constructed entirely in accordance with the planning consent', so the conditions of *Note 2(d)* were not satisfied. *Mrs SA Searle v HMRC*, [2011] UKFTT 679 (TC), TC01521.

University buildings used for vacation lettings

[15.65] A university owned a number of buildings, which had been designed and used as student accommodation but which were also partly used for vacation lettings for non-educational purposes. It arranged for the refurbishment of the buildings and leased them to an associated company. It reclaimed the relevant input tax. The Commissioners rejected the claim on the grounds that the grants of the leases were exempt supplies. The university appealed, contending that, since it had originally constructed the buildings and was granting major interests in them, the grants qualified for zero-rating under *VATA 1994, Sch 8, Group 5, Item 1*. The tribunal rejected this contention and dismissed the appeal, holding that, in view of the nature of the accommodation, the buildings were not 'designed as a dwelling or number of dwellings' and were not 'intended for use solely for a relevant residential or a relevant charitable purpose'. *University of Bath*, LON/95/2791A (VTD 14235).

[15.66] The decision in *University of Bath*, 15.65 above, was applied in a subsequent case where the facts were similar. The tribunal observed that the rooms occupied by the students were not within the definition of a 'dwelling', since they contained no cooking or toilet facilities. *University Court of the University of St Andrews*, EDN/96/182 (VTD 15243).

Holiday accommodation—effect of Sch 8, Group 5, Note 13

[15.67] A company sold a number of lodges in a holiday development. It was a condition of the relevant planning permission that these lodges should 'be used solely for holiday accommodation and shall not be occupied as the sole or main residence of any occupant'. The company treated its sales of the houses as zero-rated. The Commissioners issued assessments on the basis that the effect of *VATA 1994, Sch 8, Group 5, Note 13* was that the sales failed to qualify for zero-rating. The tribunal upheld the assessments and dismissed the company's appeal. The tribunal specifically disapproved the previous decision in *Livingstone Homes UK Ltd*, 15.41 above, observing that the tribunal in that case had 'ignored the word "only" and the phrase "for no other purpose"'. *Loch Tay Highland Lodges Ltd*, EDN/01/101 (VTD 18785).

[15.68] A company constructed 28 houses. The relevant planning permission provided that the houses should 'be used for holiday accommodation only and for no other purpose'. The company sold some of the houses, and granted long leases of others. HMRC issued a ruling that the sales and leases were standard-rated. The tribunal upheld HMRC's ruling and dismissed the company's appeal, holding that the effect of *VATA 1994, Sch 8, Group 5, Note 13* was that the houses failed to qualify for zero-rating. *Herling Ltd v HMRC*, [2009] UKFTT 257 (TC), TC00205.

[15.69] The decisions in *Loch Tay Highland Lodges Ltd*, 15.67 above, and *Herling Ltd*, 15.68 above, were applied in the similar subsequent case of *D Trathern & V Goode v HMRC*, [2011] UKFTT 21 (TC), TC00898.

Definition of 'relevant residential purpose' (VATA 1994, Sch 8, Group 5, Items 1, 2(A); VATA 1994, s 35(1a)(B))

Cases held to qualify for zero-rating

Whether building intended as 'residential accommodation for students'

[15.70] An educational establishment (G) provided courses in Welsh. It arranged for the construction of two buildings, to be used as accommodation for students on residential courses lasting for up to a week. It treated the work as zero-rated, on the basis that the buildings were intended to be used solely for a 'relevant residential purpose', namely as 'residential accommodation for students', within *VATA 1994, Sch 8, Group 5, Item 2(a)* and *Note 4(d)*. The Commissioners issued a ruling that VAT was chargeable on the work in question, considering that the accommodation did not qualify as 'residential accommodation', since no student occupied it for more than a week. The tribunal allowed G's appeal, holding that, although 'residence' (when used as a noun) 'clearly implies a building with a significant degree of permanence of occupation', the word 'loses that clear meaning when used as an adjective. In ordinary English "residential accommodation" merely signifies lodging, sleeping or overnight accommodation. It does not suggest the need for such accommodation to be for any fixed or minimum period.' *Urdd Gobaith Cymru*, [1997] VATDR 273 (VTD 14881).

[15.71] A college arranged for the construction of four accommodation blocks intended for use by short-stay students attending courses which lasted between three and six days. The accommodation did not include catering or kitchen facilities. The Commissioners issued a ruling that output tax was chargeable on the work. The college appealed, contending that the accommodation was intended for use 'solely for a relevant residential purpose'. The tribunal accepted this contention and allowed the appeal. Applying *Urdd Gobaith Cymru*, 15.70 above, the phrase 'residential accommodation' merely signified 'lodging, sleeping or overnight accommodation'. Accordingly, the fact that there were no kitchen or catering facilities within the blocks did not prevent them from qualifying as 'residential accommodation for students'. *Denman College*, [1998] VATDR 399 (VTD 15513).

[15.72] See also *R v C & E Commrs (oao Greenwich Property Ltd)*, 2.94 APPEALS.

Whether building used as 'a hospital or similar institution'

[15.73] A company owned a property which was used as a rehabilitation home for people who had suffered brain injuries. The Commissioners issued a ruling that the effect of *VATA 1994, Sch 8, Group 5, Note 4* was that certain building work at the home did not qualify for zero-rating, on the basis that the home was used as a hospital 'or similar institution'. The company appealed, contending that the property was used as 'a home or other institution providing residential accommodation', within *Note 4(b)*, and was not used as a hospital 'or similar institution'. The tribunal accepted this contention and allowed the company's appeal, observing that the home provided 'care' but did not provide medical treatment or diagnosis. The average length of stay was 700 days, which 'significantly exceeds what one would reasonably expect to find in a hospital'. Accordingly, the home was not used as a hospital 'or similar institution', and the work qualified for zero-rating. *General Healthcare Group Ltd*, [2001] VATDR 328 (VTD 17129).

[15.74] A company constructed a nursing home for people who were suffering from mental illness. Many, but not all, of the residents had been detained under the *Mental Health Act 1983*. The company treated its supplies in relation to the construction as zero-rated. Customs issued an assessment on the basis that the effect of *VATA 1994, Sch 8, Group 5, Note 4* was that the work did not qualify for zero-rating, on the basis that the home was used as a hospital 'or similar institution'. The company appealed, contending that the property was used as 'a home or other institution providing residential accommodation', within *Note 4(b)*, and was not used as a hospital 'or similar institution'. The tribunal accepted this contention and allowed the company's appeal, and the Ch D upheld this decision. Sir Andrew Morritt held that there was a distinction 'between a home or institution providing residential accommodation with personal care for those who need it' and 'an institution providing medical treatment and associated care, usually on a short-term basis'. On the evidence, the tribunal had been entitled to find that the property here was not intended for use 'as a hospital or similar institution', so that the construction work qualified for zero-rating. *C & E Commrs v Fenwood Developments Ltd*, Ch D 2005, [2006] STC 644; [2005] EWHC 2954 (Ch).

[15.75] A charity which operated a hospital arranged for the construction of a nursing home for people who were suffering from mental illness. Customs issued a ruling that the effect of *VATA 1994, Sch 8, Group 5, Note 4* was that the work did not qualify for zero-rating, on the basis that the home was used as a hospital 'or similar institution'. The charity appealed, contending that the property was used as 'a home or other institution providing residential accommodation', within *Note 4(b)*, and was not used as a hospital 'or similar institution'. The tribunal accepted this contention and allowed the charity's appeal, finding that the residents at the home were 'elderly and suffering from severe dementia'. They required 'a secure environment' but did not require 'medical intervention or treatment'. The home 'was not intended to be used as a hospital or similar institution' and its construction qualified for zero-rating. *Hospital of St John & St Elizabeth*, LON/04/780 (VTD 19141).

[15.76] A charity which provided healthcare services arranged for a subsidiary company to construct a building to be used for 'accommodating and treating young people who have both learning difficulties and challenging behaviour'. Customs issued a ruling that the construction work was standard-rated. The company appealed, contending that the property was used as 'a home or other institution providing residential accommodation', within *Note 4(b)*, and was not used as a hospital 'or similar institution'. The tribunal accepted this contention and allowed the appeal, holding that the building was not a hospital because 'the care given is mostly not medically based'. The tribunal observed that 'hospitals do not normally teach life skills and address behavioural problems'. *St Andrew's Property Management Ltd*, MAN/05/638 (VTD 20499).

Cases where the appellant was partly successful

'Facilities building' constructed for student halls of residence

[15.77] A university arranged for the construction of some halls of residence for students, located about a mile from the main university buildings. These were accepted as qualifying for zero-rating as being for a 'relevant residential purpose'. It also arranged for the construction of a 'facilities building', including a gym, music room, kitchen and dining room, conference room, projection room, bar, shop and common room. Customs issued a ruling that part of the construction of the 'facilities building' was standard-rated (accepting that the part attributable to the construction of the gym, music room, kitchen and dining room qualified for zero-rating). The university appealed. The tribunal reviewed the evidence in detail and allowed the appeal in part, holding that the first aid room, toilets, and a corridor leading to the music room and gym also qualified for zero-rating. However, the part of the construction attributable to the conference room, projection room, bar, shop and common room failed to qualify for zero-rating. *University Court of the University of St Andrews (No 2)*, EDN/03/76 (VTD 19054).

Cases held not to qualify for zero-rating

Construction of building in garden of private house

[15.78] A building constructed in the garden of a private house, and comprising a garage, games room and lavatory, was held not to be suitable for residential occupation, and therefore not to qualify for zero-rating, in *AD Smith*, MAN/86/26 (VTD 2164).

Classroom block constructed by fee-paying school

[15.79] The Commissioners issued a ruling that supplies in the course of construction of two classroom buildings at a fee-paying boarding school did not qualify for zero-rating. The company which operated the school appealed, contending that the buildings should be treated as being used for a relevant residential purpose. (It was accepted that the school was not a charity.) The tribunal dismissed the company's appeal, holding that the buildings did not qualify for zero-rating since they were 'intended for use solely as classrooms and for purposes associated with that use; they are thus intended to be used merely as part of a home or other institution and not as the home or institution itself'. *Riverside School (Whassett) Ltd*, [1995] VATDR 186 (VTD 13170).

Whether building intended as 'residential accommodation for students'

[15.80] See *Thompson*, 15.44 above, and *University of Bath*, 15.65 above.

Residential building for mentally ill

[15.81] A company agreed with a NHS Trust that it would construct a residential building for people who were mentally ill. The Commissioners issued a ruling that the work was standard-rated, since the building was used as a 'hospital or similar institution' and was therefore excluded from zero-rating by *VATA 1994, Sch 8, Group 5, Note 4*. The tribunal dismissed the company's appeal, observing that the *National Health Service Act 1977* defined a hospital as 'any institution for the reception and treatment of persons suffering from illness', and holding that the building was within this definition. *Wallis Ltd*, [2003] VATDR 151 (VTD 18012).

Definition of 'relevant charitable purpose' (VATA 1994, Sch 8, Group 5, Items 1, 2(A); VATA 1994, s 35(1a)(B))

Cases held to qualify for zero-rating or refund

Changing rooms constructed for under-16s' football club

[15.82] A builder constructed a block of changing rooms for a junior football club (whose players were all under 16 years of age), and did not account for VAT on the work. Customs issued an assessment, against which he appealed, contending that the work should be zero-rated on the grounds that it was for a 'charitable purpose'. The tribunal adjourned the appeal for further evidence, finding that the club was not a registered charity but holding that it might still qualify as a charity on the basis that it was established for 'purposes beneficial to the community' (applying *Special Commissioners v Pemsel*, HL 1891, 3 TC 53) or that it fell within *Recreational Charities Act 1958, s 1*. R Meadows, LON/93/213A (VTD 11817) (*Note*. There was no further public hearing of the appeal. It is understood that, following the tribunal decision, Customs accepted that the club was within *Recreational Charities Act 1958, s 1*.)

Football club pavilion

[15.83] A football club built a pavilion, with the aid of a loan from the National Playing Fields Association (NPFA). The pavilion was owned by the NPFA, which granted the club a licence to use it. The club was the principal user of the pavilion, but it was used by other organisations with the permission of a local committee of the NPFA. The club reclaimed input tax on the building of the pavilion. Customs rejected the claim on the grounds that the club was not a charity and that the club was carrying on a business. The club appealed, contending that the pavilion was used by the NPFA, which was a charity, and was used 'in providing social or recreational facilities for a local community', within what is now *VATA 1994, Sch 8, Group 5, Note 6(b)*. The tribunal allowed the appeal, holding on the evidence that the construction of the pavilion was 'gratuitous work done for the prime benefit of the NPFA' and was 'primarily and substantially in furtherance of the activities and ownership rights of NPFA'. The pavilion was used 'for the charitable purposes of NPFA' to the local community. Accordingly the conditions of *Note 6(b)* were satisfied and the club was entitled to a refund of the input tax. *Shinewater Association Football Club*, LON/94/732A (VTD 12938).

[15.84] A football club, which was registered as a Community Amateur Sports Club, arranged for the building of a pavilion on land which it leased from a local authority. Customs issued a ruling that VAT was chargeable on the work. The tribunal allowed the club's appeal, finding that the club 'performs and operates for purposes beneficial to the community', and holding that it did not constitute a business. The tribunal observed that the club had provided 'a commendable and desirable facility designed not for trading but for the benefit of the local community in a deprived area'. *Jeanfield Swifts Football Club*, EDN/07/104 (VTD 20689).

Leisure centre constructed by charity–whether within Note 6(b)

[15.85] An association which was a registered charity arranged for the construction of a leisure centre. Membership of the association was automatically granted to the inhabitants of ten adjoining parishes. Customs issued a ruling that the construction of the centre failed to qualify for zero-rating on the basis that the centre was operated as a business. The association appealed, contending that the construction qualified for zero-rating under what is now *VATA 1994, Sch 8, Group 5, Note 6(b)* as the centre was used similarly to a village hall, 'in providing social or recreational facilities for a local community'. The tribunal accepted this contention and allowed the appeal. The fact that the building was 'reasonably substantial' in size did not prevent it from being treated as similar to a village hall. *Bennachie Leisure Centre Association*, EDN/96/60 (VTD 14276).

Clubhouse constructed by registered charity–whether within Note 6(b)

[15.86] A village sports club, which was a registered charity, arranged for the construction of a new clubhouse. Customs issued a ruling that VAT was due on the construction. The club appealed, contending that the work qualified for zero-rating under *VATA 1994, Sch 8, Group 5, Note 6(b)* as the clubhouse was used by a charity and was used similarly to a village hall, 'in providing social or recreational facilities for a local community'. The tribunal accepted this contention and allowed the appeal, observing that the club was registered as a charity with the Charity Commission and holding that this was 'compelling evidence that it does qualify as a charity'. Its objects and activities were 'purposes beneficial to the community for the public benefit', and were within *Recreational Charities Act 1958, s 1*. The clubhouse was 'intended as a village hall', and there was 'a high degree of community and voluntary involvement in the running of the building, (and) a desire to promote the use of the facilities by members of the community'. On the evidence, 95% of the club's members lived within six miles of the clubhouse. Accordingly the work qualified for zero-rating. *Sport in Desford*, MAN/99/803 (VTD 18914).

Theatre constructed for charity–whether within Note 6(b)

[15.87] An amateur dramatic society, based in a small town with a population of 8,000 people, was a registered charity. It arranged for the construction of a theatre. Customs issued a ruling that tax was chargeable on the work. The society appealed, contending that the construction qualified for zero-rating under *VATA 1994, Sch 8, Group 5, Note 6(b)* as the theatre was used similarly to a village hall, 'in providing social or recreational facilities for a local community'. The tribunal accepted this contention and allowed the appeal. On the evidence, 90% of the society's members lived in the town where the theatre was built, so that the facilities were provided for a 'local community'. The theatre employed no full-time staff, and was used similarly to a village hall. *Ledbury Amateur Dramatic Society*, LON/99/634 (VTD 16845).

Construction of community centre—whether within Note 6

[15.88] A community association had been formed with the objects of promoting 'the benefit of the inhabitants of Southwick and its immediate neighbourhood'. It was a registered charity, and had 60 affiliated organisations. It arranged for the construction of a new building at its community centre. The new building was self-contained, with independent access, although it was connected to an existing storage room. Customs issued a ruling that output tax was chargeable on the work, and the association appealed, contending that it should be treated as zero-rated, since it was intended for use 'in providing social or recreational facilities for a local community'. The tribunal accepted this contention and allowed the appeal, observing that 'the fact that the community centre's success attracts a few members from outside the immediate area cannot prevent its being considered as providing for its local community'. Furthermore, the fact that the building was occasionally used by an adult education college and a disco for business purposes did not prevent it from being qualifying as a charitable building, since 'minimal non-qualifying use does not jeopardise zero-rating'. The charity's trustees were 'not acting with a view to making a profit' but were 'acting in order to provide a benefit to the local community'. *Southwick Community Association (No 2)*, [2002] VATDR 288 (VTD 17601).

[15.89] A charity had been established to promote education in four neighbouring parishes in Leicestershire. The charity arranged for the construction of a community hall in one of the parishes. Customs issued a ruling that VAT was chargeable on the work. The charity appealed, accepting that a specific part of the hall failed to qualify for zero-rating because it was used as a nursery (with its own access), but contending that the remainder was to be used as a village hall and qualified for zero-rating under *VATA 1994, Sch 8, Group 5*. The tribunal accepted this contention and allowed the appeal, finding that 'the predominant part of the community hall was used solely for a relevant charitable purpose'. *Hanbury Charity*, MAN/06/408 (VTD 20126).

Playgroup—whether a business

[15.90] A company, which operated a playgroup and was accepted as being a charity, reclaimed VAT under what is now *VATA 1994, s 35* on the construction of a new building. The company's turnover was less than £4,000 p.a. and, although the majority of parents made contributions to the cost of running the playgroup, such contributions were not compulsory. Customs rejected the claim on the basis that the building was used in the course or furtherance of a business of providing playgroup facilities, and was therefore not used solely for a relevant charitable purpose. The tribunal allowed the company's appeal, holding that in view of the low turnover and the voluntary nature of the contributions, the playgroup was not a 'business'. *Newtownbutler Playgroup Ltd*, LON/94/1457A (VTD 13741).

Construction of building for children's charity

[15.91] A charity was formed in 1925 to provide 'a home for the treatment and care of children under the age of five'. It owned a large Victorian building, which included a summerhouse in the grounds. It allowed a local playgroup, which was also a charity, to use the summerhouse. However, the summerhouse became unsafe and had to be closed in 1996. It arranged for the construction of a replacement building at a cost of about £100,000. Customs issued a ruling that output tax was chargeable on the construction of the new building. The charity appealed, contending that the building was intended for use solely for a relevant charitable purpose, and therefore qualified for zero-rating. The tribunal accepted this contention and allowed the appeal, holding that 'the purpose for which the building is designed is an educational one' and that the building was used 'otherwise than in the course or furtherance of a business', within *VATA 1994, Sch 8, Group 5, Note 6(a)*. The Ch D upheld this decision. Patten J held that the lease of the building to the playgroup was not within the definition of an 'economic activity'. It was 'a relatively informal arrangement between closely connected organisations in conformity with their respective aims'. The playgroup was not itself a business, since it was 'not predominantly concerned with the making of taxable supplies for a consideration'. *C & E Commrs v Yarburgh Children's Trust*, Ch D 2001, [2002] STC 207. (*Notes*. (1) Patten J also observed that the building did not fall within *Note 6(b)*, since it did not provide facilities 'for the local community at large'. (2) For Customs' practice following this decision, see Business Brief 4/2003, issued on 27 May 2003.)

Nursery operated by charity—whether a business

[15.92] A charity operated a nursery, some of the places at which were reserved for children who were referred by the local authority. The charity reclaimed VAT on the construction of a new building. Customs rejected the claim on the basis that the nursery was a business. The tribunal allowed the charity's appeal, observing that the charity was established in 'a disadvantaged part of Birmingham', and holding that the operation of the nursery was not a 'business'. Accordingly, the construction work qualified for zero-rating. The Ch D upheld this decision. Evans-Lombe J held that the tribunal was entitled to find that the nursery was not 'predominantly concerned with the making of taxable supplies to consumers for a consideration'. *C & E Commrs v St Paul's Community Project Ltd*, Ch D 2004, [2005] STC 95; [2004] EWHC 2490 (Ch). (*Note*. For Customs' practice following this decision, see Business Brief 2/2005, issued on 10 February 2005. They stated that they 'do not agree' with the decision but 'have decided not to appeal further'.)

Charity operating school—construction of classroom block

[15.93] A charity operated a school. It arranged for the construction of a new classroom block, and claimed a refund of tax under *VATA 1994, s 35*. Customs rejected the claim on the basis that the school was a business. The charity appealed, contending that the school was not a business since it was not a 'conventional fee-paying school', but was a 'contribution school', under which each child's parents were expected to contribute to the well-being of the school community not just by making financial contributions, but by making some contribution of social and practical skills. The charity asked parents to make financial contributions, and laid down a 'recommended minimum contribution', but treated these 'as gifts to the whole community'. The tribunal accepted the charity's evidence and allowed the appeal, holding on the evidence that the school was not 'predominantly concerned with the making of taxable supplies to consumers for a consideration'. *The Sheiling Trust (Ringwood Waldorf School)*, [2006] VATDR 1 (VTD 19472).

Charity providing education for deaf children—whether a business

[15.94] See *Donaldson's College*, 7.84 BUSINESS.

Building constructed for housing association

[15.95] A charitable housing association, registered under the *Industrial & Provident Societies Act 1965*, arranged for the construction of an office block. Customs issued a ruling that the work was standard-rated. The association appealed, contending that the offices were used for a 'relevant charitable purpose' within *VATA 1994, Sch 8, Group 5, Item 2(a)*. The tribunal accepted this contention and allowed the appeal, holding that the association was not carrying on a business, and its offices were used 'otherwise than in the course or furtherance of a business', within *Group 5, Note 6(a)*. *Cardiff Community Housing Association Ltd*, [2000] VATDR 346 (VTD 16841). (*Note.* The decision here was not followed, and was implicitly disapproved, by the Manchester tribunal in the subsequent case of *Riverside Housing Association Ltd*, **15.115** below.)

[15.96] A housing association incorporated a subsidiary company (D), which constructed an annexe and leased it to the association. The association let the annexe to a charity which provided care services in the local community. It was accepted that the annexe met the criteria for zero-rating laid down by *Group 5, Note 17*, in that it could be accessed separately from the original premises and could function independently from those premises. However Customs issued a ruling that the annexe failed to qualify for zero-rating, on the grounds that D's lease of the building was 'in the course or furtherance of a business'. D appealed, contending that the building was being used for a relevant charitable purpose and that the grant of the lease qualified for zero-rating. The tribunal accepted this contention and allowed the appeal, holding that since the annexe had been constructed with the intention of being used by a charity, and the fact that D was not a charity did not prevent its supply from qualifying for zero-rating. *Ardenglen Developments Ltd*, EDN/05/03 (VTD 19906).

Building for assessment of epilepsy

[15.97] A Scottish charity arranged for the construction of a building to be used as a centre for the assessment of epilepsy. Customs issued a ruling that output tax was chargeable on the work. The charity appealed, contending that the building was intended for use 'solely for a relevant charitable purpose', and therefore qualified for zero-rating. The tribunal accepted this contention and allowed the appeal, holding that the supplies which the charity made to the NHS were not 'in the course or furtherance of a business', since they were 'not in any real sense a trading or commercial activity which might justify them being described as economic'. *Quarriers (No 1)*, [2008] VATDR 290 (VTD 20660). (*Note.* For another appeal involving the same charity, see **7.85** BUSINESS.)

Garage constructed at church

[15.98] A Catholic Church arranged for the construction of a garage, within the curtilage of the church building, for parking cars which were provided by the parish and driven by priests resident at the presbytery. Customs issued a ruling that output tax was chargeable on the work. The church appealed, contending that the garage was intended for use 'solely for a relevant charitable purpose', and therefore qualified for zero-rating under *VATA 1994, Sch 8, Group 5, Item 2(a)*. The tribunal accepted this contention and allowed the appeal, observing that the cars were provided for pastoral use and holding that any private use was *de minimis* and could be disregarded. *St Dunstan's Roman Catholic Church Southborough*, [1998] VATDR 264 (VTD 15472).

Cases held not to qualify for zero-rating or refund

Classroom block constructed by fee-paying school

[15.99] A school, which was operated by a charitable company limited by guarantee, constructed a new classroom block. It applied for a certificate of zero-rating under what is now *VATA 1994, Sch 8, Group 5, Note 12(b)*. The Commissioners rejected the application, considering that the classroom block was not to be used for a relevant charitable purpose, since it was intended for use in the course of a business of providing education for a consideration. The school appealed, contending that since some of the pupils who were to be educated in the classroom block were in receipt of scholarships and bursaries, the block was partly for charitable purposes and an apportionment should be made under *Sch 8, Group 5, Note 10*. The tribunal rejected the school's contention and dismissed the appeal. None of the pupils were admitted free, so that the school was making supplies for consideration in respect of all its pupils. Applying *Morrison's Academy Boarding Houses Association*, 7.1 BUSINESS, such supplies constituted the carrying on of a business. The whole of the classroom block was to be used in the course or furtherance of that business, so that the conditions of *VATA 1994, Sch 8, Group 5, Note 6(a)* were not satisfied. Furthermore, even if many of the pupils had been educated free of charge, so that their education would not constitute a business activity, no part of the block would be used for non-business purposes unless no fee-paying pupils were educated there. *Leighton Park School*, LON/91/1673Z (VTD 9392).

Campus constructed by college

[15.100] A college, which was a registered charity, arranged for the construction of a new campus. HMRC issued a ruling that the construction was standard-rated. The college appealed, contending that the construction qualified for zero-rating. The First-Tier Tribunal rejected this contention and dismissed the appeal, holding that the building was to be used in the course of a business, so that the conditions of VATA 1994, Sch 8, Group 5, Note 6(a) were not satisfied. However, the Upper Tribunal remitted the case to the First-Tier Tribunal to consider whether the business use could be treated as de minimis. *Wakefield College v HMRC*, [2011] UKUT 495 (TCC). (Note. The First-Tier Tribunal specifically rejected the college's contention that it should be regarded as a 'body governed by public law', applying the principles laid down by the Ch D in Chancellor, Masters & Scholars of the University of Cambridge v HMRC, **30.11**. The Upper Tribunal did not pass judgment on this issue.)

University buildings used for vacation lettings

[15.101] See *University of Bath*, **15.65** above.

Sports pavilion constructed by charity—whether within Note 6(b)

[15.102] A registered charity arranged for the construction of a building, on land at the rear of a school, to be used as a sports pavilion. The Commissioners issued a ruling that the supplies made in the course of construction did not qualify for zero-rating, on the basis that the building was not intended to be used solely for a relevant charitable purpose. The charity appealed, contending that the building was intended to be used 'in providing social or recreational facilities for a local community', within what is now *VATA 1994, Sch 8, Group 5, Note 6(b)*. The tribunal dismissed the appeal, holding that the building was not within *Note 6(b)*, on the grounds that it was not used 'similarly' to a village hall. The people to whom it provided facilities were 'a particular section of the community, not a local community', and the building was not 'operated in the way in which a village hall is carried on'. *Ormiston Charitable Trust*, [1995] VATDR 180 (VTD 13187).

[15.103] A similar decision was reached in a subsequent case in which the tribunal applied the CA decision in *Jubilee Hall Recreation Centre Ltd*, 55.16 PROTECTED BUILDINGS, and distinguished *Bennachie Leisure Centre Association*, 15.85 above, on the basis that the charity's constitution here did 'not provide that the local community are *ipso facto* members nor does it provide for any defined area of membership'. *Princess Royal Sports Club*, EDN/99/43 (VTD 16227).

Sports hall constructed by charity—whether within Note 6

[15.104] A registered educational charity arranged for the construction of a sports hall, which was intended to be used by an independent fee-paying school, and to be made available for community use at specified times. The Commissioners issued a ruling that the supplies made in the course of construction did not qualify for zero-rating, on the basis that the school was charging for the use of the facilities, so that the building was not intended to be used solely for a relevant charitable purpose. The charity appealed, contending that the school was also a charity and that its use of the sports hall was within *VATA 1994, Sch 8, Group 5, Note 6*. The CA rejected this contention, holding that the building was used for the purposes of a business, and was not intended for use in providing 'recreational facilities for a local community', since the community use was secondary to the use by the school. Sir John Vinelott observed that 'insofar as pupils at the school benefited from that facility, they did so not as members of the local community, but as pupils on whose behalf fees were paid to the school'. *C & E Commrs v St Dunstan's Educational Foundation*, CA 1998, [1999] STC 381. (*Note*. The case was heard by the CA together with *Jubilee Hall Recreation Centre Ltd*, 55.16 PROTECTED BUILDINGS.)

Recreation centre constructed by charity—whether within Note 6

[15.105] A federation of youth clubs, which was a registered charity, arranged for the construction of a recreation centre, including a swimming pool and gymnasium, at premises which it owned in a small village (comprising 22 houses) in Buckinghamshire. The centre was intended for use by local community groups during the week, and by members of the youth clubs at the weekend. The Commissioners issued a ruling that output tax was chargeable on the construction. The charity appealed, contending that it should be treated as zero-rated under *VATA 1994, Sch 8, Group 5, Item 2* and *Note 6*. The tribunal rejected this contention and dismissed the appeal. The charity had a policy 'of balancing the books by making the facilities available to a wide range of local community organisations and voluntary groups'. Accordingly, the charity was carrying on a business and the work failed to qualify for zero-rating under *Note 6(a)*. Furthermore, the centre was 'a sports centre run by the appellant, not a village hall run by or predominantly for the village', so that it also failed to qualify for zero-rating under *Note 6(b)*. *The London Federation of Clubs for Young People*, [2001] VATDR 501 (VTD 17079). (*Note*. For preliminary proceedings in this case, see 2.507 APPEALS.)

Swimming pool constructed by charity—whether within Note 6

[15.106] A charity was established for the purpose of building and operating a swimming pool in a rural area of North Devon. (The area had previously been served by a pool operated by the local district council, but that pool had closed in 1991.) The Commissioners issued a ruling that output tax was chargeable on the construction of the pool. The charity appealed, contending that the pool qualified for zero-rating under *VATA 1994, Sch 8, Group 5, Note 6*. The tribunal rejected this contention and dismissed the appeal, finding that the pool was 'a well-organised commercial operation' and holding that it was not solely used 'as a village hall or similarly in providing social or recreational facilities'. The tribunal also held that the pool facilities were not provided solely for a local community, since it was used by people from up to 23 miles away, whereas for the purposes of *Note 6(b)* 'the local community being referred to is on the scale of a village'. *South Molton Swimming Pool Trustees*, LON/98/372 (VTD 16495).

Building used by charity as sports and fitness centre

[15.107] See *Jubilee Hall Recreation Centre Ltd*, 55.16 PROTECTED BUILD-INGS.

Bowling club—whether within VATA 1994, Sch 8, Group 5, Note 6(a)

[15.108] A bowling club reclaimed input tax on materials used for the construction of a pavilion. The Commissioners rejected the claim on the grounds that the club was not a charity and that the club was carrying on a business. The tribunal dismissed the club's appeal, holding that the club was a charity within the *Recreational Charities Act 1958*, but that it was also carrying on a business within what is now *VATA 1994, s 94*, so that the conditions of what is now *VATA 1994, Sch 8, Group 5, Note 6(a)* were not satisfied and no refund was due. *Hunmanby Bowling Club*, MAN/93/862 (VTD 12136). (*Note*. Despite the tribunal's decision that the club was a charity, the Commissioners consider that 'sports clubs are not usually charities' because 'the promotion of sport is not a charitable object in itself and such clubs usually exist to provide facilities for their members'. See Customs' VAT Manual, Part 9, para 5.4.)

Whether concert hall to be used for 'relevant charitable purpose'

[15.109] See *The Royal Academy of Music*, 55.15 PROTECTED BUILDINGS.

Building constructed to house scanner unit for hospital

[15.110] A registered charity arranged for the construction of a building to house a scanner unit for a hospital. The Commissioners issued a ruling that the services supplied to the charity in the course of construction of the building did not qualify for zero-rating. The charity appealed. The tribunal dismissed the appeal, holding that since the hospital itself was not a charity, the building was not being used for a relevant charitable purpose. *League of Friends of Kingston Hospital*, LON/93/1870A (VTD 12764).

Building used by charity for catering supplies

[15.111] A registered charity constructed a building which comprised a kitchen, two dining rooms and a coffee lounge. It claimed a refund of tax under *VATA 1994, s 35*. The Commissioners rejected the claim on the ground that the charity was using the building to make supplies of catering services 'in the course or furtherance of a business', so that the conditions of *VATA 1994, Sch 8, Group 5, Note 6(a)* were not satisfied. The tribunal dismissed the charity's appeal. Applying *Morrison's Academy Boarding Houses Association*, 7.1 above, 'the provision of catering for consideration does not cease to be a business by reason of the fact that it is not designed to make a profit'. *Summer Institute of Linguistics Ltd*, LON/98/1400 (VTD 16159).

Building used by charity for the blind

[15.112] See *St Dunstan's*, 55.17 PROTECTED BUILDINGS.

Community centre—whether within VATA 1994, Sch 8, Group 5, Note 6

[15.113] A community association had been formed 'to promote the health and welfare and to advance the education and training of the community of South Aston and surrounding areas'. It arranged for the construction of a community centre. The Commissioners issued a ruling that output tax was chargeable on the work. The association, and the company which had constructed the centre, appealed, contending that the work should be treated as zero-rated. The tribunal rejected this contention and dismissed the appeal. The tribunal observed that part of the centre was used by a local college for business purposes, so that the conditions of *VATA 1994, Sch 8, Group 5, Note 6(a)* were not satisfied. With regard to *Note 6(b)*, the centre was not providing facilities similarly to a village hall, since the part of the centre which was occupied by the college was open to anyone 'whether they be local or not, who may care to come and sign up for a course'. *South Aston Community Association; IB Construction Ltd*, MAN/00/797 (VTD 17702).

Day centre—whether within VATA 1994, Sch 8, Group 5, Note 6

[15.114] A company, which acted as a housing association and was a registered charity, arranged for the construction of a 'day centre', as an annexe to a residential care home. The Commissioners issued a ruling that output tax was chargeable on the work, and the company appealed, contending that it should be treated as zero-rated. The tribunal rejected this contention and dismissed the appeal. Firstly, the day centre was run as a business. Secondly, the facilities were not for a local community, since they were not 'geographically specific'. The tribunal observed that 'it may be possible to say that a hall constructed in a rural village is a facility for a local community when for reasons of geography only the villagers will be using it; the same kind of hall constructed in an urban location may not be a facility for a local community if its attractiveness is such that persons from "across town" make a trip to get to it'. *The Beth Johnson Housing Association Ltd*, [2001] VATDR 167 (VTD 17095).

Office for housing association—whether within Note 6

[15.115] A housing association (R), which was a registered charity, arranged for the construction of a new office. Customs issued a ruling that VAT was chargeable on the work. R appealed, contending that it should be treated as zero-rated. The tribunal rejected this contention and dismissed the appeal, holding that the conditions of *VATA 1994, Sch 8, Group 5, Note 6(a)* were not satisfied, since R was carrying on a business and was using the office for the purposes of its business. The Ch D upheld this decision. Lawrence Collins J observed that 'the whole of (R's) very substantial activity is concerned with letting the properties on assured tenancies to residential occupiers, selling properties to tenants in accordance with "right to buy" provisions, and selling properties which are surplus to requirements'. The tribunal was entitled to find that R's activities were in the course or furtherance of a business. *Riverside Housing Association Ltd v HMRC*, Ch D [2006] STC 2072; [2006] EWHC 2383 (Ch).

Conversion of barn into 'community hall' for use by charity

[15.116] A registered charity provided education and training to physically and mentally handicapped young adults. It arranged for a construction company to convert a barn into a 'community hall' for its use. The company did not account for tax on this work. The Commissioners issued an assessment charging tax on it and the company appealed, contending that it should be treated as zero-rated since the 'community hall' was intended for charitable use. The tribunal rejected this contention and dismissed the appeal, holding that the building was not being used for a 'relevant charitable purpose' within *VATA 1994, Sch 8, Group 5, Note 6*. It failed to qualify under *Note 6(a)* because it was being used 'in the course or furtherance of a business'; and it failed to qualify under *Note 6(b)* because it was not used to provide 'social or recreational facilities for a local community'. *Co-Work Camphill Ltd*, LON/99/1351 (VTD 17636). (*Note.* The tribunal also held that the 'community hall' was not used for a 'relevant residential purpose', within *Note 4*.)

Construction of premises for charity—whether within Note 6(b)

[15.117] A company was registered as a charity, with the aim of providing for 'the care and education of persons with learning difficulties'. It arranged for the construction of new premises. The Commissioners issued a ruling that the relevant supplies were standard-rated. The company appealed, contending that they should be treated as zero-rated under *VATA 1994, Sch 8, Group 5, Item 2(a)*. The tribunal rejected this contention and dismissed the appeal, holding that the building was 'not used as a village hall or similarly', as required by *Note 6(b)*, since 'the design of (the building) and the way it is used and managed go beyond what we would regard as characteristics of a village hall'. *Nutley Hall Ltd*, LON/02/988 (VTD 18242).

Construction of chapel—whether within Note 6(a)

[15.118] A registered charity offered facilities for retreats and conferences, in five acres of grounds. It arranged for the construction of a chapel within the grounds. The Commissioners issued a ruling that output tax was chargeable on the work. The charity appealed, contending that it should be treated as zero-rated. The tribunal dismissed the appeal, holding that the charity was carrying on a business and finding that the chapel 'was at all times intended to be used' in the course or furtherance of that business. Accordingly the effect of *VATA 1994, Sch 8, Group 5, Note 6(a)* was that the work did not qualify for zero-rating. *Morley Retreat and Conference House*, MAN/00/223 (VTD 17265).

Skate park—whether a building

[15.119] A registered charity arranged for the construction of a skate park. HMRC issued a ruling that VAT was payable on the construction. The charity appealed, contending that it should be zero-rated. The tribunal rejected this contention and dismissed the appeal, holding that the skate park was not a 'building'. *Wheeled Sports 4 Hereford Ltd v HMRC*, [2011] UKFTT 190 (TC), TC01059.

Residential conversions (VATA 1994, Sch 8, Group 5, Item 1(b); VATA 1994, s 35(1A)(c),(1D))

NOTE

The cases in this question relate to claims for zero-rating under *VATA 1994, Sch 8, Group 5* or *VATA 1994, s 35*. See **56** REDUCED-RATE SUPPLIES for claims to the reduced rate of 5% for work falling within *VATA 1994, Sch 7A, Group 6*.

Cases held to qualify for zero-rating or refund

Conversion of building formerly used as school

[15.120] A property, which had been originally constructed in about 1900 but had subsequently been substantially altered, had been used as a boarding school from 1950 to 1995. In 1996 it was sold to a private purchaser (J), who decided to convert it into a large private house, including three self-contained staff flats on the first floor. J claimed a refund of tax on the conversion work. Customs rejected the claim on the basis that the building had previously been used for residential purposes, so that the work did not qualify for zero-rating. J appealed, contending that the property had previously been 'a non-residential building', and therefore qualified for zero-rating. The tribunal accepted this contention and allowed his appeal, holding that the property was 'non-residential' since 'no boarding school child, except in the rarest of circumstances, sees school as his home or main residence'. The CA unanimously upheld the tribunal decision. Ward LJ held that the work was within *VATA 1994, Sch 8, Group 5, Note 9*. He held that *Note 9* 'has to be construed so that the result of the conversion is to create in the building an additional dwelling or dwellings. One counts the number of dwellings in the building before conversion and again after conversion. If there are more on the recount, *Note 9* is satisfied.' *C & E Commrs v I Jacobs*, CA [2005] STC 1518; [2005] EWCA Civ 930. (*Note.* For HMRC's practice following this decision, see Business Brief 22/2005, issued on 1 December 2005. HMRC state that they 'now accept that, for the purposes of the DIY Refund Scheme, the conversion of a building that contains both a residential part and a non-residential part comes within the scope of the Scheme so long as the conversion results in an additional dwelling being created. It is no longer necessary for the additional dwelling to be created exclusively from the non-residential part. However, VAT recovery is restricted to the conversion of the non-residential part.')

Public house converted into two semi-detached houses

[15.121] A company purchased a public house and obtained planning permission for its conversion into two semi-detached houses. The company elected to waive exemption on the property and reclaimed input tax on the purchase and conversion. Customs issued assessments to recover the tax. The company appealed, contending that the public house had been a 'non-residential building', within *VATA 1994, Sch 8, Group 5, Item 1(b)*, so that the subsequent sales would be zero-rated supplies and the input tax was recoverable. The tribunal accepted this contention and allowed the appeal, holding on the evidence that no part of the public house 'was designed as a dwelling' before the planning consent. The effect of *Group 5, Notes 2 and 7* was that 'there was no part of the (public house) which was not non-residential'. *Temple House Developments Ltd*, LON/97/787 (VTD 15583). (*Notes.* (1) The decision here was disapproved by a subsequent tribunal in *Tobell*, **15.131** below, on the grounds that the tribunal here had erred in law by reading *Note 2* in conjunction with *Note 7*. It was also not followed, and implicitly disapproved, by a subsequent tribunal in *Calam Vale Ltd*, **15.133** below. (2) See also the note following *Tobell*, **15.131** below.)

Conversion of unoccupied property into living accommodation

[15.122] In 2005 an individual (W) converted an unoccupied property into living accommodation. He claimed a refund of tax under *VATA 1994, s 35*. Customs rejected the claim on the basis that the property had previously been used as living accommodation. W appealed, contending that the property had been vacant since 1990, so that it qualified as a 'non-residential building' under *VATA 1994, Sch 8, Group 5, Note 7A*. The tribunal accepted W's evidence and allowed his appeal. *GR Witherow*, LON/06/116 (VTD 20040).

Conversion of outbuilding into living accommodation

[15.123] An individual (C) converted a two-storey outbuilding, the lower floor of which had been used as a garage, into a small cottage. She claimed a refund of tax under *VATA 1994, s 35*. Customs rejected the claim on the basis that the building had previously been used as a garage, so that the effect of *VATA 1994, Sch 8, Group 5, Note 8* was that the work did not qualify for zero-rating. The tribunal allowed C's appeal, finding that 'taken in its entirety' the outbuilding could not have been 'properly described as a garage'.

S Cottam, LON/06/232 (VTD 20036). (*Note.* The decision here was disapproved in the subsequent case of *Clark*, **15.128** below.)

[15.124] The decision in *Cottam*, **15.123** above, was applied in the similar subsequent case of *RD Blacklock*, [2007] VATDR 225 (VTD 20171).

Conversion of barn into living accommodation

[15.125] A woman (W) reclaimed tax under *VATA 1994, s 35* on the conversion of a barn into living accommodation. HMRC rejected the claim on the basis that the barn formed part of a property which had previously been used as living accommodation. The tribunal allowed W's appeal, finding that the barn had not previously been used as living accommodation and that 'an additional dwelling had been created'. *Ms J Wade v HMRC*, [2011] UKFTT 504 (TC), TC01351.

Construction of new flats in roof space of block of flats

[15.126] A company (M) decided to construct new flats in the roof spaces of five existing blocks of flats. It applied for registration for VAT, so that it could recover the related input tax. Customs rejected the application on the grounds that all M's supplies would be exempt from VAT. M appealed, contending that it was undertaking residential conversions and that its supplies would be zero-rated. The tribunal accepted this contention and allowed M's appeal, observing that 'before the conversion the roof spaces were not owned or occupied by the residents of the flats who had no access to them. The roof spaces were effectively empty. This is not a case where the roof space of a building used as a single household and occupied with the rest of the house was converted.' Accordingly the tribunal held that the roof spaces had previously been a non-residential part of the relevant buildings, within *VATA 1994, Sch 8, Group 5, Item 1(b)*. *Merlewood Estates Ltd*, LON/07/1979 (VTD 20810).

Construction of new flat above existing flats

[15.127] An individual (J) owned a Victorian two-storey house which was divided into two flats. He decided to construct a third flat above the two existing flats, and claimed a refund of VAT under *VATA 1994, s 35*. HMRC rejected the claim but the tribunal allowed J's appeal, finding that a two-storey building had been converted into a three-storey building and an additional dwelling had been created. The tribunal observed that this was not simply a 'loft conversion', since 'typically a loft conversion would be within the confines of the original roof', whereas J had 'completely demolished the original roof structure and created an entirely new dwelling which does not incorporate any of the original roof structure'. *AK Jahansouz v HMRC*, [2010] UKFTT 355 (TC), TC00637.

Cases where the appellant was partly successful

Conversion of garage and stable block

[15.128] An individual (C) converted a garage and stable block into a residential dwelling for the use of himself and his wife. He reclaimed VAT on the work under *VATA 1994, s 35*. HMRC rejected the claim on the basis that, before the conversion, the building had been used as a 'residential garage'. C appealed. The tribunal reviewed the evidence in detail and allowed the appeal in part, holding that *VATA 1994, s 35(1D)* 'clearly envisages a case where part of a building is non-residential and part is residential (or not non-residential). It specifically does not deny relief in those circumstances, but instead provides for works to be within the meaning of "residential conversion", and so to qualify for relief, "to the extent that" the works consist of a conversion of the relevant part of the building into, for example, a building designed as a dwelling or a number of dwellings. The use of the expression "to the extent that" itself demonstrates that relief may be only partially available, and that some allocation or apportionment may be required.' The tribunal specifically declined to follow the earlier decisions in *Cottam*, **15.123** above, and *Podolsky*, **15.146** below, disapproving the 'all or nothing' approach which had been applied in those cases. On the evidence, the tribunal held that 'the conversion of the non-residential part of the existing building in this case (ie excluding the garage area) did create an additional dwelling for the purpose of *Note 9*, and that the conversion was accordingly to that extent within *section 35(1D)* and was a residential conversion within the meaning of *section 35(1A)(c)*'. *J Clark v HMRC (No 1)*, [2010] UKFTT 258 (TC), TC00552.

[15.129] Following the decision noted at **15.128** above, the parties were unable to agree the appropriate apportionment, and the tribunal held a further hearing of the appeal. The tribunal reviewed the evidence in detail and concluded that 51.43% of the disputed work constituted a 'residential conversion', so that 51.43% of the tax was refundable. *J Clark v HMRC (No 2)*, [2010] UKFTT 458 (TC), TC00723.

Cases held not to qualify for zero-rating or refund

Conversion of building formerly used as public house

[15.130] A married couple purchased a run-down building which had been used as a public house until the 1970s, but which had been unoccupied for some time and had been deemed 'unfit for human habitation' by the local council. They converted the building into a dwelling-house, and claimed a refund of tax under *VATA 1994, s 35*. The Commissioners rejected the claim on the basis that the building had been used as a dwelling after 1 April 1973, so that it was not a 'non-residential building' as defined by the legislation then in force. The tribunal dismissed the couple's appeal against this decision. *R & A Tilley*, LON/96/1199 (VTD 15097). (*Note.* See now *VATA 1994, Sch 8, Group 5, Note 7*, as substituted by the *VAT (Conversion of Buildings) Order 2001 (SI 2001/2305)*, with effect from 1 August 2001. The revised *Note 7* was intended to provide relief for the sale of renovated houses that have not been used as a dwelling, or for a relevant residential purpose, for ten years or more.)

[15.131] An individual (T) purchased a public house, which had included residential accommodation on the upper floor, and converted it into a private dwelling-house. He claimed a refund of tax under *VATA 1994, s 35*. The Commissioners rejected the claim on the basis that the building had previously been used as a dwelling, so that it was not a 'non-residential building' as defined by *VATA 1994, Sch 8, Group 5, Note 7*, and the work was therefore not a residential conversion as defined by *VATA 1994, s 35(1D)*. The tribunal dismissed T's appeal, holding that the upper floor of the building was not 'non-residential' before the conversion. Since the building had already contained a residential part, and the conversion did not create an additional dwelling, the work was not within the definition of a 'residential conversion'. The tribunal specifically declined to follow the decision in *Temple House Developments Ltd*, **15.121** above, on the grounds that the tribunal there had erred in law by reading *Note 7* in conjunction with *Note 2*. The chairman (Mr. Lightman) held that *Note 2* was 'only intended to be relevant to the question of whether there is "a building designed as a dwelling" after the conversion', whereas the purpose of *Note 7* was to determine 'whether the building or part of the building was non-residential *before* the conversion'. *G Tobell*, LON/98/1349 (VTD 16646). (*Note. VATA 1994, Sch 8, Group 5, Note 7* was substituted by the *VAT (Conversion of Buildings) Order 2001 (SI 2001/2305)*, with effect from 1 August 2001. The revised *Note 7* was intended to provide relief for the sale of renovated houses that have not been used as a dwelling, or for a relevant residential purpose, for ten years or more. The change in the legislation does not affect the specific point at issue in this case.)

[15.132] A married couple purchased a building which had previously been used as a public house, and obtained planning permission to convert it into a family dwelling. The wife arranged for the work to be done, and reclaimed VAT under *VATA 1994, s 35*. The Commissioners rejected the claim on the basis that the first and second floors of the building had previously been used by the publican as residential accommodation, so that it was not a 'non-residential building' as defined by *VATA 1994, Sch 8, Group 5, Note 7*, and the work was therefore not a residential conversion as defined by *VATA 1994, s 35(1D)*. The CA upheld the Commissioners' rejection of the claim, holding that the effect of *VATA 1994, Sch 8, Group 5, Note 9* was that no refund was due. Chadwick LJ observed that *Note 9* applied 'to cases where the conversion is "of a non-residential part of a building which already contains a residential part"'. Its purpose was to give a restricted meaning to the conversion of 'a non-residential part of a building', in that where the building already contained a residential part, the conversion of a non-residential part would not qualify for zero-rating or refund unless the result of that conversion was to create an additional dwelling or dwellings. *VATA 1994, s 35(4)* plainly required that that same restricted meaning also applied for the purposes of *VATA 1994, s 35(1D)*. *C & E Commrs v Lady Blom-Cooper*, CA [2003] STC 669; [2003] EWCA Civ 493. (*Notes*. (1) For the Commissioners' practice following this decision, see Business Brief 11/2003, issued on 25 July 2003. See also the note following *Tobell*, **15.131** above.(2) The HL rejected an application by the claimant for leave to appeal against this decision.)

Public house converted into two semi-detached houses

[15.133] A company converted a public house into two semi-detached dwellings. The Commissioners issued a ruling that the sale of the dwellings was exempt from VAT, so that the company could not reclaim the related input tax. The company appealed, contending that the public house had been a 'non-residential building', within *VATA 1994, Sch 8, Group 5, Item 1(b)*, so that the subsequent sale was zero-rated and the input tax was recoverable. The tribunal rejected this contention and dismissed the appeal, holding that the public house was not a 'non-residential building' as defined by *VATA 1994, Sch 8, Group 5, Note 7*, and the work was therefore not a 'residential conversion'. The tribunal observed that *Sch 8, Group 5, Note 2* was 'meant to refer to a building after construction or conversion, whereas *Note 7* is meant to refer to it before its *Item 1(b)* conversion'. The tribunal also held that *Note 9* did not apply to the conversion, observing that *Note 9* was 'apparently intended not to extend *Item 1(b)* but to cut it down: conversion of a non-residential part of a building is not after all to qualify if the building contained a residential part'. The work here did not fall within *Item 1(b)*, since 'it is not the simple conversion of a non-residential part of a building but the conversion of that part plus a residential part'. *Calam Vale Ltd*, LON/99/977 (VTD 16869). (*Note.* See the note following *Tobell*, 15.131 above.)

Conversion of upper storeys of public house into flats

[15.134] A company converted the two upper floors of a large 17th-century public house into three flats. The Commissioners issued a ruling that, because part of those floors had previously been used as living accommodation, the work relating to that part was attributable to an exempt supply, so that the company was not entitled to reclaim the relevant input tax. The company appealed, contending that none of the building had been 'designed or adapted for use as a dwelling', so that the whole of the work should be treated as a 'residential conversion' within *VATA 1994, s 35(1D)*. The tribunal rejected this contention and dismissed the appeal, finding that at least one of the rooms 'had been used as living accommodation by publicans and landlords', and that 'the rooms used by the publicans/landlords (had been) designed for use as a dwelling'. Accordingly the work relating to those rooms failed to qualify for zero-rating. *Kingscastle Ltd*, LON/01/417 (VTD 17777).

Conversion of 'bedsits' into self-contained flats

[15.135] A company reclaimed input tax on the conversion of a property, which had originally been used as a commercial property but had subsequently been used as bed-sitting accommodation, into nine self-contained flats. The Commissioners rejected the claim and the company appealed, contending that the work was a residential conversion so that the sale of the property qualified for zero-rating. The tribunal rejected this contention and dismissed the appeal, holding that the property had been used as a 'dwelling' before the conversion, so that the work failed to qualify for zero-rating. *Belvedere Properties (Cheltenham) Ltd*, LON/03/1159 (VTD 18851).

Conversion of upper storey of music school into student accommodation

[15.136] A married couple owned a two-storey building, part of which was used a music school and part of which was let as student accommodation. In 1999 the husband (C) obtained permission to convert part of the upper storey, which had previously been used as teaching rooms for the music school, into residential student accommodation. He applied for a refund of VAT under *VATA 1994, s 35*. The Commissioners rejected his claim on the basis that the work had been carried out 'in the course or furtherance of any business' and therefore failed to meet the requirements of *VATA 1994, s 35(1)(b)*. C appealed. The tribunal dismissed his appeal, holding on the evidence that 'this was not work carried out for purely altruistic or charitable motives; the intention was to earn an income from the rent paid by the occupying students'. *NP Charlton*, MAN/01/553 (VTD 18268).

Conversion of croft into bungalow

[15.137] An individual (H) purchased a nineteenth-century croft which had been occupied by a couple between 1973 and 1980 but had subsequently become derelict. He converted the building into a bungalow, and claimed a refund of tax under *VATA 1994, s 35*. The Commissioners rejected the claim on the basis that the building had been used as a dwelling after 1 April 1973, so that it was not a 'non-residential building' under the legislation then in force. The tribunal dismissed H's appeal against this decision, applying the decisions in *Tilley*, **15.130** above, and *Tobell*, **15.131** above. The tribunal also observed that, applying *In re 1–4 White Row Cottages Bewerley*, Ch D [1991] Ch 441; [1991] 4 All ER 50, 'a derelict dwelling-house remains a dwelling-house and does not become something else merely for being derelict'. *J Halcro-Johnston*, [2001] VATDR 335 (VTD 17147). (*Note.* See now the note following *Tilley*, **15.130** above.)

Conversion of building formerly used as nursing home

[15.138] A married couple reclaimed input tax on the conversion of a derelict building into a dwelling-house. The Commissioners rejected the claim, on the basis that the building had been used as a nursing home between 1968 and 1992, so that the effect of *VATA 1994, Sch 8, Group 5, Note 7* was that it was not a 'non-residential' building. The tribunal dismissed the couple's appeal against this decision. *Mr & Mrs GD King*, LON/98/555 (VTD 15961). (*Note.* See the note following *Tobell*, **15.131** above.)

Conversion of building formerly used as hotel

[15.139] A large house had been built in 1898 and converted into a hotel in about 1930. The hotel closed in 1991. In 1993 the building was purchased by a married couple who used it as their private residence. In 1998 they obtained planning permission for the division of the building into two semi-detached houses. They reclaimed tax on the conversion work. The Commissioners rejected the claim, on the basis that the building had been used as a hotel until 1991, so that the effect of *VATA 1994, Sch 8, Group 5, Note 7* was that it was not a 'non-residential' building. The tribunal dismissed the couple's appeal against this decision. *Mr & Mrs R Emberson*, LON/00/963 (VTD 17604).

Conversion of dilapidated farmhouse

[15.140] A farmhouse, built in the 18th century, fell into poor condition. In 1967 the local council issued a 'closing order' under the *Housing Act*, declaring the house unfit for habitation. Despite the order, the house continued to be used as a residence until February 1999. It was then substantially renovated. The Commissioners issued a ruling that the renovation work was standard-rated. The owners appealed, contending that the effect of the 'closing order' was that the house should be treated as having been a 'non-residential building' since the date of the order, so that the work qualified for zero-rating.

The tribunal rejected this contention and dismissed the appeal, observing that the building 'was in its origin designed as a dwelling, more than two centuries ago' so that there was 'no question of converting it into a building designed as a dwelling'. *N & J Hicking*, MAN/00/532 (VTD 17117). (*Note.* See the note following *Tobell*, **15.131** above.)

Conversion of dilapidated cottage

[15.141] A couple converted and extended a dilapidated cottage, which had been used as a dwelling until 2000, but had subsequently been declared unfit for human habitation. They claimed a refund of tax under *VATA 1994, s 35*. Customs rejected the claim on the basis that *VATA 1994, Sch 8, Group 5, Note 7A* only provided relief for the sale of renovated houses that had not been used as a dwelling, or for a relevant residential purpose, for ten years or more. The tribunal dismissed the couple's appeal against this decision. *A & T Johnson*, LON/07/633 (VTD 20506).

Conversion of upper storeys of townhouse into maisonette

[15.142] A company converted the upper two storeys of a four-storey townhouse into a separate maisonette. The Commissioners issued a ruling that VAT was chargeable on the work. The company appealed, contending that the upper two storeys should be treated as having been 'non-residential' for the purposes of *VATA 1994, Sch 8, Group 5, Item 1(b)*, so that the work should be treated as zero-rated. The tribunal rejected this contention and dismissed the appeal. *Lightspace Partnership Ltd*, MAN/01/185 (VTD 17393). (*Note.* With effect from 11 May 2001, such work would now be liable to VAT at the reduced rate of 5%—see *VATA 1994, Sch A1 para 6* and *VATA 1994, Sch 7A, Group 6*, introduced by *FA 2001*.)

Conversion of disused outhouses into living accommodation

[15.143] A shopkeeper extended her business premises by converting a living-room into additional shop space. To compensate for the loss of the living-room, she converted two disused outhouses into additional living accommodation. The Commissioners issued a ruling that this work was standard-rated. She appealed, contending that the work should be treated as a residential conversion, within *VATA 1994, Sch 8, Group 5, Item 1(b)*. The tribunal rejected this contention and dismissed her appeal, observing that *Item 1(b)* only applied where there was a grant of a major interest, which was not the case here. Furthermore, even if there had been a grant of a major interest, the effect of *Note 9* was that the work would not have qualified for zero-rating. *A Everitt (t/a Reading Lasses)*, EDN/01/50 (VTD 17408).

Conversion of barns into recreational buildings—whether within s 35(1D)

[15.144] An individual (M) owned a farm which included a number of barns. He converted one of these into a dwelling-house and converted two other barns into a swimming pool and a recreation complex. He claimed a refund of VAT in respect of the conversion of all three barns. The Commissioners accepted the claim in relation to the barn which had been converted into a dwelling-house, but rejected the claim with regard to the other two barns. M appealed. The tribunal dismissed his appeal, observing that *VATA 1994,* *s 35(1D)* specifically referred to 'a building designed as a dwelling' and holding that the word 'building' could not 'be interpreted in the plural'. Accordingly, the construction of the swimming pool and recreation complex was not within *VATA 1994, s 35(1D)* and relief was not due. *JA Moore*, MAN/x (VTD 15972).

Conversion of farm buildings into living accommodation

[15.145] See the cases noted at 15.50 above to 15.57 above.

Conversion of garage into living accommodation

[15.146] An individual (P) obtained permission for the conversion of a building, which had been used as a garage and workshop, into living accommodation. He claimed a refund of VAT under *VATA 1994, s 35*. HMRC rejected the claim on the grounds that the effect of *VATA 1994, Sch 8, Group 5, Note 8* was that the work did not qualify as a 'residential conversion'. The tribunal accepted this contention and dismissed P's appeal, specifically distinguishing the earlier decisions in *Cottam*, 15.123 above, and *Blacklock*, 15.126 above. *J Podolsky v HMRC*, [2009] UKFTT 387 (TC), TC00322.

Time at which conversion completed

[15.147] In the case noted at 2.90 APPEALS, an individual who had converted an old church into a dwelling reclaimed input tax on the conversion. The Commissioners rejected the claim on the grounds that the work had been completed before 21 April 1994, before the relevant provisions came into effect. (The provisions now contained in *s 35(1D)* were applied from 21 April 1994 by extra-statutory concession. The relevant certificate of completion was dated 10 March 1994.) The tribunal dismissed the claimant's appeal, holding that the conversion was complete when the building was habitable, safe and hygienic, as evidenced by the certificate of completion. The fact that some decoration and electrical work remained to be done had no bearing on the completion of the conversion. *Dr BN Purdue*, EDN/94/511 (VTD 13430).

Definition of 'major interest in building, dwelling or site' (VATA 1994, Sch 8, Group 5, Item 1)

Cases held to qualify for zero-rating

Lease originally granted for 21-year period—Deed of Rectification

[15.148] A married couple arranged for the construction of a building comprising two residential flats. They registered for VAT and reclaimed input tax on the construction. Subsequently they granted a lease of one of the flats for a period of 21 years. When the Commissioners discovered this, they issued an assessment to recover the tax, since the lease did not exceed 21 years and was therefore not a 'major interest' as defined by *VATA 1994, s 96*. The couple appealed against the assessment. On legal advice, they and the lessees entered into a Deed of Rectification to extend the term of the lease to 22 years. The tribunal allowed the couple's appeal, applying the principles laid down in

Taylor v Taylor & Another (re Colebrook's Conveyances), Ch D 1972, [1973] 1 All ER 132, and holding that 'the mere fact that the sole purpose of the rectification is a tax advantage is not a bar to rectification'. *CS & JM Isaac*, MAN/96/254 (VTD 14656).

Cases held not to qualify for zero-rating

'Time-sharing' leases—whether a grant of a major interest

[15.149] A company had constructed cottages on a holiday site in Cornwall and let them on a time-sharing basis, under which it granted customers an 80-year lease of a cottage for a specified 'holiday period' (usually one week) in each of the 80 years. It did not account for tax on the payments it received from customers, and the Commissioners issued an assessment charging tax on the payments. The company appealed, contending that, since the tenancy lasted for more than 21 years, the supply was zero-rated under what is now *VATA 1994, Sch 8, Group 5, Item 1*. The tribunal rejected this contention and dismissed the appeal, and the QB upheld this decision. Although the lease extended for more than 21 years, the grant did not constitute the grant of a major interest because the interest was not continuous. *Cottage Holiday Associates Ltd v C & E Commrs*, QB 1982, [1983] STC 278. (*Note*. See now *VATA 1994, Sch 8, Group 5, Note 13*.)

Definition of 'site'

[15.150] A building company sold some development land, on which it had undertaken some civil engineering work including pile-driving for the foundations of buildings. The Commissioners issued an assessment to recover the input tax which the company had previously reclaimed, considering that the sale of the site was an exempt supply. The company appealed, contending that it had granted a major interest in a site, which should be treated as zero-rated under what is now *VATA 1994, Sch 8, Group 5, Item 1*. The tribunal rejected this contention and dismissed the appeal, holding that the land was not the 'site' of a specific building so that its sale did not qualify for zero-rating. *Stapenhill Developments Ltd*, [1984] VATTR 1 (VTD 1593).

[15.151] A similar decision was reached in *Permacross Ltd*, MAN/94/878 (VTD 13251).

[15.152] See also *Cameron New Homes Ltd*, **15.18** above.

Licence to occupy 'park home' erected on caravan site

[15.153] A company which owned a caravan site arranged for structures, described as 'park homes', to be erected on the site, and reclaimed the relevant input tax. The Commissioners issued an assessment to recover the tax, considering that it related to exempt supplies. The company appealed, contending that the 'park homes' were buildings, and that the pitch agreements under which they were occupied constituted the grant of a major interest in land, so that the supply was zero-rated under what is now *VATA 1994, Sch 8, Group 5, Item 1*. The tribunal held that the 'park homes' were buildings, applying *Smith*, **15.35** above, but that the pitch agreements constituted an indefinite licence to occupy land, which did not amount to the grant of a major interest in land, and did not grant any interest in the 'park homes' themselves. Accordingly the pitch fees were exempt from VAT and the supplies of the 'park homes' were not within what is now *VATA 1994, Sch 8, Group 5, Item 1. Stonecliff Caravan Park*, [1993] VATTR 464 (VTD 11097). (*Note.* For another issue in this case, see **69.6** ZERO-RATING.)

Whether services supplied 'in the course of construction' (VATA 1994, Sch 8, Group 5, Item 2)

Cases where the appellant was successful

NOTE

See *VATA 1994, Sch 8, Group 5, Note 18*, introduced by *SI 1995/280*. Several appeals which had been successful before the introduction of *Note 18* would now fall within that provision and be excluded from zero-rating. Such cases have not normally been summarised in this book, except where they illustrate a point which continues to be of importance. The cases in this section should be read in the light of the changes in the legislation.

Sunday School hall alongside church

[15.154] A church obtained planning permission for the building of a room, to be used as a Sunday School, on the site of an old vestry. The work described in the planning permission was completed in 1991, at which time there was direct access from the church to the new Sunday School room, through double doors which had formerly led to the vestry. In 1992 the doorway between the church and the Sunday School room was blocked up with plasterboard and sealant. Customs issued a ruling that the work did not qualify for zero-rating. The company which had carried out the work appealed, contending that the Sunday School room was a new building and that its construction had not been completed until 1992 when the old doorway was blocked. The tribunal accepted this contention and allowed the appeal. *Carrophil Ltd*, LON/92/1005 (VTD 10190).

Annexe to church

[15.155] A church arranged for the construction of a new annexe to replace its existing chapel house. Customs issued a ruling that the effect of *VATA 1994, Sch 8, Group 5, Note 16* was that the construction was standard-rated. The tribunal allowed the church's appeal, holding that the church had constructed a zero-rated annexe within *Note 17*, rather than an extension within *Note 16*. *Grace Baptist Church*, MAN/98/798 (VTD 16093). (*Note.* The decision in this case was distinguished, and implicitly disapproved, in the subsequent case of *Woodley Baptist Church*, **15.204** below.)

[15.156] A similar decision, applying *Grace Baptist Church*, **15.155** above, and distinguishing *Macnamara*, **15.202** below, was reached in *Torfaen Voluntary Alliance*, LON/03/756 (VTD 18797).

Synagogue

[15.157] A company arranged for the construction of a building, to be used as a synagogue, in the grounds of an existing synagogue. Customs issued a ruling that VAT was chargeable on the work on the basis that the two buildings formed 'a synagogue complex'. The tribunal allowed the company's appeal, finding that 'there was no synagogue complex' and holding that the work qualified for zero-rating. *Kahal Imrei Chaim Ltd*, LON/04/1186 (VTD 19625).

Redevelopment

[15.158] A company owned a site which it wished to redevelop. Customs issued a ruling that the relevant supplies were undertaken in the course of reconstructing an existing building, and thus were excluded from zero-rating by what is now *VATA 1994, Sch 8, Group 5, Note 16(a)*. The company appealed, contending that the supplies were zero-rated. The QB and CA accepted this contention, holding on the evidence that the work constituted the construction of a new building rather than the reconstruction of an existing building because it was 'not a replication or construction anew of what was there before'. *Wimpey Group Services Ltd v C & E Commrs*, CA [1988] STC 625. (*Note*. The services would not now qualify for zero-rating because the building was not used for a 'relevant residential or charitable purpose'—see *Item 2(a)*, originating from *FA 1989*. However, the case remains relevant with regard to the definition of 'reconstruction'.)

Demolition of old building—whether part of construction of new building

[15.159] A building was severely damaged by fire. Its owners arranged for the demolition of what remained of it, and the construction of a new building. Customs issued a ruling that VAT was chargeable on the demolition work. The company which had carried out the demolition appealed. The tribunal allowed the appeal, holding that the demolition qualified as a zero-rated supply of services in the course of construction of the new building, since 'there was no undue time lag' between the demolition and the construction, and that 'what happened was consecutive'. *Dart Major Works Ltd*, LON/03/1133 (VTD 18781).

Construction of flats

[15.160] A company constructed a block of flats, part of which was sited underneath an existing building. The foundations of the existing building were reinforced, but the access and services to the new block were entirely independent. Customs issued a ruling that the work did not qualify for zero-rating, but the tribunal allowed the company's appeal, holding that the work constituted the construction of a new building rather than the enlargement of an existing building. *John Compass Ltd*, EDN/87/35 (VTD 3163).

[15.161] A building containing four flats was built behind an existing house comprising two flats, but with a shared entrance. Customs issued a ruling that the work did not qualify for zero-rating, but the tribunal allowed the builders' appeal, holding that the new building was not an enlargement of the existing building. *R & P Wellman*, LON/89/1251Z (VTD 4383).

[15.162] A contractor built a flat at the back of an existing property. There was no internal access between the flat and the existing building. Customs issued a ruling that the work did not qualify for zero-rating, but the tribunal allowed the contractor's appeal, holding that the work constituted the construction of a new building, rather than the conversion of an existing building. *J Samuel (t/a Joseph Samuel Developments)*, LON/90/1516 (VTD 7177). (*Note.* For another issue in this case, see **15.192** below.)

[15.163] A company which owned a two-storey car park obtained planning permission to build 24 flats on top of it. Customs issued a ruling that the work was standard-rated. The tribunal allowed the company's appeal, holding that the building of the flats constituted the construction of a new building, rather than the conversion of an existing one. *Trident Housing Association Ltd*, MAN/92/387 (VTD 10642).

[15.164] A company which owned a nursing home obtained permission for the construction of a block of 15 flats, designed for elderly people in need of care, adjacent to the nursing home. The nursing home and the flats had a common party wall, with internal access which was used by nurses to visit the residents of the flats. Customs issued a ruling that, because of the internal access, the construction of the flats was standard-rated. The tribunal allowed the company's appeal, holding that despite the internal access, the block of flats was a separate building rather than an enlargement of the nursing home, and the construction qualified for zero-rating. *Associated Nursing Services plc*, LON/93/1173A (VTD 11203).

Residential unit in grounds of nursing home

[15.165] A couple operated a nursing home comprising two separate units, one for medical patients and one for mentally infirm patients. The couple arranged for building work which involved extending the unit which housed the mentally infirm patients so that it joined onto the unit comprising the medical patients. However, there was no internal access. Customs issued a ruling that the work failed to qualify for zero-rating. The Ch D allowed the couple's appeal. Sir Andrew Morritt V-C held that 'an annexe is an adjunct or accessory to something else, such as a document. When used in relation to a building it is referring to a supplementary structure, be it a room, a wing or a separate building.' On the evidence, the works 'did not constitute the construction of an annexe to any existing building', and qualified for zero-rating. *Cantrell & Cantrell (t/a Foxearth Lodge Nursing Home) v C & E Commrs*, Ch D [2003] STC 486; [2003] EWHC 404 (Ch).

[15.166] The QB decision in *Cantrell & Cantrell*, **15.165** above, was applied in the similar subsequent case of *Chacombe Park Development Services Ltd*, LON/05/110 (VTD 19414).

Residential building in grounds of study centre

[15.167] A charity operated a field centre. It arranged for the construction of a residential building in the grounds of the centre, to provide accommodation for visiting students. There was a gap of one metre between the existing building and the residential building but, 28 days after the completion of the residential building, the contractor constructed a link between the two buildings. Customs issued a ruling that the work constituted the alteration of an existing building and was standard-rated. The tribunal allowed the contractor's appeal, holding that the work constituted the construction of a new building and qualified for zero-rating. *DS Menzies*, EDN/97/114 (VTD 15733).

Residential building adjoining nursing home

[15.168] A nursing home proprietor (S) arranged for the construction of a new residential building adjoining the home, to be used for the same purposes. When the new building was completed, there was no internal access to the original building and the two homes were operated separately. However, three weeks after the new building had been completed, S arranged for an interconnecting door to be fitted so that the two homes could be operated as one unit. Customs issued an assessment on the basis that the work did not qualify for zero-rating. S appealed, contending that he had intended to operate two separate nursing homes but had been forced to merge them because five of his patients had died, which had significantly reduced his income. The tribunal accepted S's evidence and allowed his appeal. *JMB Strowbridge*, MAN/95/2449 (VTD 16521).

[15.169] A company operated a nursing home with room for 81 residents. It arranged for the construction of a further building, to be used for patients suffering from dementia and mental illness. The two buildings were linked by a corridor, which was used to transport meals from the nursing home to the new building, but was not used by residents or patients. Customs issued a ruling that the work was standard-rated, but the tribunal allowed the company's appeal, holding that the construction of the new building qualified for zero-rating. *Allan Water Developments Ltd*, EDN/04/160 (VTD 19131).

Replacement of barn by four-bedroomed house

[15.170] The owner of a derelict barn obtained planning permission for its conversion into a four-bedroomed house. The barn was totally demolished, but some of the internal timber work was used in the new house for decorative purposes. Customs issued a ruling that the work was not eligible for zero-rating as it was the conversion of an existing building. The tribunal allowed the owner's appeal, holding that the work constituted the construction of 'an entirely new building'. *MS Gill*, LON/89/1359X (VTD 4904).

Retention of wall required by statutory planning consent

[15.171] A couple obtained planning permission to build an extension to a dilapidated farmhouse. During the work, they discovered that all except one of the existing walls were unstable and had to be demolished to ground level. They obtained retrospective planning permission for the 'construction of a replacement dwelling incorporating part of an existing wall'. Customs issued a ruling that output tax was chargeable on the work. The couple appealed, contending that the effect of *VATA 1994, Sch 8, Group 5, Note 18(b)* was that the building had ceased to be 'an existing building', since all that was left of the original building was one wall and the retention of that wall was 'a condition or requirement of statutory planning consent'. The tribunal accepted this contention and allowed the appeal. *R & SL Midgley*, MAN/96/640 (VTD

15379). (*Note.* The decision here was not followed, and was implicitly disapproved, in the subsequent case of *Pollock & Heath*, **15.208** below.)

[**15.172**] The decision in *Midgley*, **15.171** above, was applied in a similar subsequent case in which *Evans*, **15.207** below, was distinguished. *R & J Naylor*, MAN/x (VTD 17305).

[**15.173**] A similar decision was reached in *K Almond*, [2009] UKFTT 177 (TC), TC00132.

Sewage treatment plant installed at boarding school

[**15.174**] A company which operated a boarding school built a new boarding house. A new sewage treatment plant was installed to serve the house, in accordance with the relevant building regulations. Customs accepted that the construction of the house was zero-rated, but ruled that the expenditure on the sewage treatment plant did not qualify for zero-rating. The tribunal allowed the company's appeal and the CS upheld this decision, holding that the sewage plant qualified for zero-rating since it was contemporaneous with the construction of the new boarding house and would not have been needed but for the new boarding house. *C & E Commrs v Rannoch School*, CS [1993] STC 389.

Kitchen and laundry block at nursing home

[**15.175**] A charity arranged for the construction of a nursing home at its premises. This was completed in 2008. In 2009 HMRC issued a ruling that VAT would be chargeable on the proposed construction of a kitchen and laundry block at the site. The charity appealed, contending that this work should be treated as having taken place in the course of construction of the nursing home. The tribunal accepted this contention and allowed the appeal, specifically distinguishing the QB decision in *C & E Commrs v St Mary's Roman Catholic High School*, **15.189** below, and holding that 'a period of 18 months between the developments' was 'not an unreasonable delay in all the circumstances'. *Hoylake Cottage Hospital Charitable Trust v HMRC*, [2011] UKFTT 48 (TC), TC00925.

Riverside house incorporating dock

[**15.176**] A company constructed a house on the River Thames. The house was built on stilts, underneath which was a dock, constructed by sheet piling to hold back the riverbank, for a boat. The lower level of the house was higher than the minimum level necessary under the relevant building regulations, so that the owner could drive a boat from the river into the dock and then enter the house by a staircase. The company did not account for tax on the sheet piling work, treating it as part of the construction of the house. Customs issued an assessment charging tax on the work, but the tribunal allowed the company's appeal, holding on the evidence that the work was 'related to the construction' of the house and qualified for zero-rating. *Turner Stroud & Burley Construction Ltd*, LON/97/1440 (VTD 15454).

Scaffolding

[**15.177**] A company (G) which supplied and erected scaffolding treated its supplies as zero-rated supplies of services. Customs issued a ruling that G was making standard-rated supplies of the hire of the scaffolding (applying the 1974 decision in *Gilbourne*, **15.244** below). The tribunal allowed G's appeal, holding that since it retained the legal possession of the scaffolding throughout the duration of the contract, its supplies qualified for zero-rating. *GT Scaffolding Ltd*, LON/02/1103 (VTD 18226). (*Note.* This decision was distinguished in the subsequent cases of *R & M Scaffolding Ltd*, **15.185** below, and *Pharaoh Scaffolding*, **15.186** below.)

Civil engineering work

[15.178] In the case noted at **41.22** LAND, the tribunal held that work supplied by a civil engineering contractor to a landowner, in preparation for the construction of buildings, was 'in the course of construction' and qualified for zero-rating. *D & S Virtue (t/a Lammermuir Game Services)*, EDN/06/104 (VTD 20259). (*Notes.* (1) For HMRC's practice following this decision, see HMRC Brief 64/07, issued on 17 October 2007. (2) Compare the earlier decisions in *Cameron New Homes Ltd*, **15.18** above, and *Stapenhill Developments Ltd*, **15.150** above.)

Replacement of defective plastering

[15.179] A married couple were building a house. They subcontracted the plastering work. The original contractor's work was defective, and they had to arrange for the defective plastering to be removed and replaced by new plastering installed by a different firm. Customs issued a ruling that the replacement of the defective plastering did not qualify for zero-rating, because the house had already been completed before this work took place, so that it constituted the reconstruction or alteration of an existing house, rather than part of the construction of a new house. The tribunal allowed the couple's appeal, finding that 'the old plasterwork was obviously inadequate and dangerous' and 'the new plastering work was supplied in the course of the construction of the building'. Accordingly it qualified for zero-rating. *Mr & Mrs James*, LON/07/328 (VTD 20426).

Cases where the appellant was partly successful

Access roads constructed in preparation for housing development

[15.180] A company (L) agreed to construct access roads for a new housing development comprising seven houses, two of which were to be new buildings and the other five of which were to be conversions of existing buildings. It treated the whole of the work as zero-rated. Customs issued an assessment on the basis that, since only two of the houses were new buildings, and only one of the houses had been sold at the relevant time, only one-seventh of the work was eligible for zero-rating. The company appealed. The tribunal allowed the company's appeal in part, holding that the fact that one of the houses had not been sold did not prevent the work attributable to that house from qualifying for zero-rating. The input tax should be apportioned between the new houses and the converted houses, so that two-sevenths of the total tax was deductible. *Lamberts Construction Ltd*, MAN/91/486 (VTD 8882).

Additional dwelling created by enlargement of existing building

[15.181] A married couple arranged for the construction of a new dwelling, to be occupied by the wife's uncle, adjacent to their existing house. The ground floor of the new dwelling was entirely new, but the house was constructed in such a way that part of the upper floor of the existing house (including a bathroom and a small bedroom) was incorporated into the new dwelling, with the internal access to the old dwelling being blocked off. The result was that the two dwellings appeared from the outside to form a pair of semi-detached houses, but part of the upper floor of the new house stood on top of part of the ground floor of the old house. The Commissioners issued a ruling that the work did not qualify for zero-rating, since the new dwelling had involved the alteration of an existing building, within *VATA 1994, Sch 8, Group 5, Note 16(a)*. The couple and their uncle appealed, contending that the work constituted the enlargement of an existing building which had created an additional dwelling, and should therefore be treated as zero-rated under *Group 5, Note 16(b)*. The tribunal allowed the appeal in part, holding that 'the natural meaning of the words used in *Note 16* is that an enlargement or extension qualifies for zero-rating if it creates an additional dwelling' and that there was 'no reason to import the notion that the additional dwelling must be incorporated wholly within that enlargement or extension'. The development consisted partly of zero-rated new building work and partly of standard-rated conversion work, so the effect of *Group 5, Note 11* was that an apportionment should be made. The tribunal adjourned the appeal in the hope that the parties could agree the apportionment. *M, G & N Smith*, [2001] VATDR 323 (VTD 17035). (*Note.* There was no further public hearing of the appeal.)

[15.182] The decision in *Smith*, 15.181 above, was applied in the subsequent case of *Wright v HMRC*, **57.107** REGISTRATION.

Construction of additional rooms at village hall

[15.183] A community association, which was a registered charity, arranged for the construction of two additional rooms at its village hall. It was accepted that the village hall was used for a 'relevant charitable purpose'. However, the Commissioners issued a ruling that the effect of *VATA 1994, Sch 8, Group 5, Note 16* was that the construction of the additional rooms did not qualify for zero-rating. The association appealed. The tribunal allowed its appeal in part, holding that the construction of one of the rooms was an independent annexe which qualified for zero-rating by virtue of *Note 17*. However, the other room was 'an extension to the hall', so that it did not qualify for zero-rating. *Castle Caereinion Recreation Association*, LON/02/87 (VTD 18303).

Construction of school classrooms, hall and playschool

[15.184] A school arranged for the construction of new classrooms, a new hall and a new room for use by a playgroup. Customs issued a ruling that VAT was chargeable on the work. The school appealed, contending that it should be treated as zero-rated. The tribunal reviewed the evidence in detail and allowed the appeal in part. The tribunal held that the construction of the new classrooms constituted the enlargement of an existing building and was therefore standard-rated. However the new hall and the room for the playgroup were 'annexes' which met the criteria for zero-rating laid down by *VATA 1994, Sch 8, Group 5, Note 17*, in that the main access was separate from the original premises and they could function 'entirely independently' from those premises. *Longparish Church of England Primary School*, LON/05/290 (VTD 20464).

Scaffolding

[15.185] A company supplied and erected scaffolding in the course of the construction of houses. It treated its supplies as zero-rated supplies of services, within *VATA 1994, Sch 8, Group 5, Item 2*. The Commissioners issued a ruling that the company was making standard-rated supplies of the hire of the scaffolding (on the basis laid down by the 1974 tribunal decision in *Gilbourne*, **15.244** below). The tribunal reviewed the evidence in detail and allowed the company's appeal in part, distinguishing the previous decision in *GT Scaffolding Ltd*, **15.177** above, and holding that 'once the scaffolding had been erected and certified as safe by the appellant, "possession" passed to its customer'. Accordingly 'there should be an apportionment of the price between the erection and dismantling on the one hand, and the use by the customer on the other.' *R & M Scaffolding Ltd*, EDN/04/89 (VTD 18954, VTD 18955).

[15.186] A similar decision, applying the principles laid down in *R & M Scaffolding Ltd*, **15.185** above, and distinguishing *GT Scaffolding Ltd*, **15.177** above, was reached in *Pharaoh Scaffolding*, MAN/07/423 (VTD 20741).

Cases where the appellant was unsuccessful

Definition of 'in the course of construction'

[15.187] In an unsuccessful appeal, where the substantive issue has subsequently been clarified by what is now *Sch 8, Group 5, Note 22*, the tribunal held that 'a building remains in the course of construction until the main structure is completed, the windows glazed and all essential services and fittings, such as plumbing and electricity, have been installed therein. Thereafter the building ceases to be in the course of construction' and 'the phase of fitting out and furnishing is ready to begin'. *University of Hull*, LEE/75/31 (VTD 180).

[15.188] The decision in *University of Hull*, **15.187** above, was applied in the subsequent cases of *JM Associates*, LON/02/114 (VTD 18624) and *Birmingham Council for Old People*, **15.231** below. See also *Simister*, **15.21** above, and *Taylor*, **15.22** above.

School playgrounds

[15.189] In 1979 work began on the building of a new school. The school opened to pupils in 1981, but two playgrounds were not completed until 1994. Customs issued a ruling that the construction of the playgrounds was standard-rated. The QB upheld Customs' ruling, holding that the work failed to qualify for zero-rating. Jowitt J held that, although zero-rating under *Group 5, Item 2* was not restricted to the services of constructing the relevant building itself, related services could only qualify for zero-rating if there was 'a temporal connection between the construction of the building and the provision of the other services'. On the evidence, the interval between the completion of the building work on the school and the construction of the playgrounds was far too long to establish the necessary temporal link. *C & E Commrs v St Mary's Roman Catholic High School*, QB [1996] STC 1091.

School classrooms

[15.190] A new school building was constructed between 1989 and 1992. In 1998 two new classrooms were added above part of the existing building. Customs issued a ruling that this work was the enlargement of an existing building. The charity which owned the school appealed, contending that the work should be viewed as part of the original construction. The tribunal rejected this contention and dismissed the appeal. *Trustee of the Sir Robert Geffery's School Charity*, LON/01/560 (VTD 17667).

Single-storey house adjoining existing house in same occupation

[15.191] The owner of a large house wished to build a separate self-contained house within its grounds. The local authority granted planning permission only on condition that the new house adjoined the old house and appeared to form a single dwelling with it, and that the new house must remain in the same ownership as the existing house and must not be separately let or occupied. Accordingly a single-storey extension was built, connected to two walls of the existing house, and appearing from outside to be an integral part of the existing house, but having no internal access. The company which built the extension failed to account for tax. Customs issued an assessment and the tribunal dismissed the company's appeal, holding that, having regard to the terms of the planning permission, and the common occupation of the two houses, the new building was an extension or enlargement of the old building despite its internal independence. The QB upheld this decision as one of fact. *Charles Gray (Builders) Ltd v C & E Commrs*, CS [1990] STC 650.

Block of flats constructed at rear of existing building

[15.192] A trader converted a Victorian house into seven flats and constructed a new block of four flats at the rear of the house. The only entrance to the new flats was through the existing building. The tribunal held that the new flats were an extension or enlargement of the existing building, so that the work was not eligible for zero-rating. *J Samuel (t/a Joseph Samuel Developments)*, LON/90/1516 (VTD 7177). (*Note*. For another issue in this case, see **15.162** above.)

Extension constructed in two stages

[15.193] The owner of a small three-bedroomed detached house obtained planning permission for the building of a two-storey extension to it. He engaged a contractor to construct the extension as a self-contained building without internal access from the existing house. He then engaged a second contractor to cut through the party wall which divided the original house from the extension, so as to provide internal access. The contractor who had constructed the initial extension did not account for VAT on the work. Customs issued an assessment on the basis that the work was not eligible for zero-rating. The tribunal dismissed the contractor's appeal, finding that 'notwithstanding the form of the planning proposals the whole of the building work was in truth and in fact a single operation with a rest or pause at a convenient stage'. The fact that the work had deliberately been entrusted to two contractors, rather than one, did not change its nature. The work carried out by the first contractor 'was the first stage, and a substantial stage, of an intended and declared enlargement of an existing dwelling'. *R Symonds*, LON/90/1836X (VTD 9050).

[15.194] A similar decision was reached in *Graden Builders Ltd*, MAN/93/1545 (VTD 12637).

Extension to nursing home

[15.195] A married couple owned a small nursing home, which had originally been a farmhouse. They obtained planning permission for an extension to the home. The two buildings were linked by an internal passageway. Customs issued a ruling that the new building was an enlargement or extension of the existing building, and was therefore not eligible for zero-rating. The QB upheld Customs' ruling. The terms of the planning permission required the construction of a connecting door and passageway. It followed that the new structure was not itself a separate nursing home, but could only function in connection with the existing building. *C & E Commrs v Mr & Mrs Elliott*, QB [1993] STC 369.

[15.196] The QB decision in *Elliott*, **15.195** above, was applied in the subsequent case of *Nidderdale Building Ltd*, MAN/94/604 (VTD 13158).

[15.197] Similar decisions were reached in *S & H Shroufi (t/a Morris Grange Nursing Home)*, MAN/95/2769 (VTD 14852); *MJ Keeley*, LON/98/679 (VTD 16219), and *TL Smith Properties Ltd (and related appeal)*, [2011] UKFTT 528 (TC), TC01375.

Conversion of buildings into nursing home

[15.198] A partnership purchased a site containing four buildings, standing in a U-shaped formation. It obtained planning permission to redevelop the site as a nursing home. During the redevelopment, two-thirds of the old buildings were demolished and the four buildings were joined together by intercommunicating doors. The partnership claimed that the work carried out should be treated as zero-rated. Customs rejected the claim and the tribunal dismissed the partnership's appeal, holding that the work constituted the conversion of existing buildings. *Victoria Gardens Nursing Home*, MAN/91/1197 (VTD 10547).

Extension to residential home

[15.199] The proprietors of a residential home arranged for a building company to construct a new wing at the home. HMRC issued a ruling that the wing was an extension to the existing building, and was standard-rated. The tribunal dismissed the company's appeal, finding that the wing was an 'integral part' of the existing building 'in both appearance and layout'. *Rebba Construction Ltd v HMRC*, [2009] UKFTT 296 (TC), TC00240.

Annexe to residential care home

[15.200] The proprietor of a residential care home arranged for the construction of a new building adjoining the home. Customs issued a ruling that the new building was an 'annexe', so that the effect of *Sch 8, Group 5, Note 16(c)* was that the work did not qualify for zero-rating. The tribunal dismissed the proprietor's appeal, holding that the new building was an annexe (and observing that *Note 17* did not apply, since the annexe was intended for use for a residential purpose, rather than a charitable purpose). *MJ Mason (t/a Bramble Lodge)*, MAN/00/881 (VTD 17405).

Construction of extension or annexe used for relevant charitable purpose

[15.201] A Sikh Temple, which was a recognised charity, arranged for the construction of an extension or annexe to its place of worship. Customs issued a ruling that the work was the extension of an existing building and that the contractor was required to account for output tax on the construction. The tribunal dismissed the charity's appeal, holding that because the main access to the extension or annexe was via the existing building, the effect of *Sch 8, Group 5, Note 17(b)* was that it failed to qualify for zero-rating. *Shiri Guru Nanaka Sikh Temple*, MAN/96/1159 (VTD 14972).

[15.202] An appeal was dismissed in a case where the tribunal held that an extension to a school building was not within the definition of an 'annexe', and did not qualify for zero-rating. The tribunal held that an annexe should be 'either not integrated with the existing building or of tenuous integration'. *BT MacNamara*, [1999] VATDR 171 (VTD 16039). (*Note.* The tribunal also observed that, even if the extension had been treated as an 'annexe', it would still not have qualified for zero-rating, since it was not 'capable of functioning independently from the existing building', as required by *VATA 1994, Sch 8, Group 5, Note 17(a)*.)

[15.203] The decision in *MacNamara*, 15.202 above, was applied in the similar subsequent cases of *Colchester Sixth Form College*, LON/98/1341 (VTD 16252); *Thomas Rotherham College*, MAN/01/874 (VTD 17841); *Kids Church*, LON/02/448 (VTD 18145); *Knowsley Associates Ltd*, MAN/02/338 (VTD 18180); *The Alzheimer's Society*, LON/03/107 (VTD 18318); *The Archdiocese of Southwark Commission for Schools and Colleges*, LON/04/013 (VTD 18883); *Henshaws Society for Blind People*, MAN/04/794 (VTD 19373); *Abercych Village Association*, LON/07/185 (VTD 20746); *East Norfolk Sixth Form College*, LON/07/1929 (VTD 20816), and *Treetops Hospice Trust*, [2011] UKFTT 503 (TC), TC01350.

[15.204] A Baptist Church arranged for the construction of a youth centre, above the church hall at the rear of the church, with a separate entrance. Customs issued a ruling that the work was standard-rated. The Church appealed, contending that it should be treated as a zero-rated annexe. The tribunal rejected this contention and dismissed the appeal, holding that the work was an extension rather than an annexe. *Woodley Baptist Church*, LON/01/112 (VTD 17833).

[15.205] A Catholic diocese arranged for the construction of a meeting room at one end of a church building. Customs issued a ruling that the work was standard-rated. The diocese appealed, contending that the work should be treated as a zero-rated annexe. The tribunal rejected this contention and dismissed the appeal, holding that the work did not qualify as an annexe, since it was integrated with the existing building, and that since the main access was via the existing building, it did not meet the requirements of *Group 5, Note 17(b)*. *Roman Catholic Diocese of Shrewsbury*, MAN/02/055 (VTD 17900).

[15.206] Similar decisions were reached in *The Parochial Church Council of Saint Andrew's Church Bedford*, LON/04/993 (VTD 19061) and *Trustees of Elim Church Tamworth*, MAN/03/177 (VTD 19190).

Retention of wall

[15.207] A householder obtained planning permission for the 'part demolition' of his bungalow and the construction of a 'replacement dwelling'. Customs issued a ruling that output tax was chargeable on the work. The builder who was carrying out the work appealed, contending that the building had ceased to be 'an existing building', since all that was left of the original building was one wall. The tribunal rejected this contention and dismissed the appeal, holding that the retention of the wall meant that the work did not qualify for zero-rating. *P Evans*, MAN/01/151 (VTD 17264).

[15.208] Similar decisions were reached in *D Pollock & D Heath*, MAN/06/622 (VTD 20380); *R Hall*, [2009] UKFTT 58 (TC), TC00037, and *M Samuel*, [2010] UKFTT 633 (TC), TC00872.

Construction of wall

[15.209] A synagogue arranged for the construction of a wall enclosing a cemetery. Customs issued a ruling that the work was standard-rated. The synagogue appealed. The tribunal dismissed the appeal, holding that the wall did not qualify as a 'building'. *Adath Yisroel Synagogue*, LON/07/1748 (VTD 20809).

Swimming pool

[15.210] An individual (D) purchased a plot of land and obtained outline planning permission to build a house on the site. He began by arranging for the construction of a swimming pool, and claimed a refund of tax under *VATA 1994, s 35*. Customs rejected the claim, on the grounds that the pool was not part of the house which D subsequently built on the site. The tribunal upheld Customs' ruling and dismissed D's appeal. *D O'Reilly*, LON/08/878 (VTD 20945).

Work on existing buildings

[15.211] There have been a large number of cases in which tribunals have found that work has constituted the conversion, reconstruction, enlargement or alteration of an existing building, rather than the construction of a new building, and which appear to raise no point of general interest. In the interests of space, such cases are not summarised individually in this book.

Demolition of old building—whether part of construction of new building

[15.212] A house was severely damaged by fire. Its owner arranged for the demolition of what remained of it, and subsequently arranged for the construction of a new building. Customs issued a ruling that VAT was chargeable on the demolition work. The owner appealed, contending that the demolition should be treated as zero-rated on the grounds that it had been undertaken in the course of construction of the new building. The tribunal rejected this contention and dismissed the appeal, finding that the demolition of the old building was not an 'integral part' of the construction of the new building. *S Brown*, MAN/06/289 (VTD 19884).

Supplies by subcontractor to contractor

[15.213] A contractor was supplying services in the course of constructing a building which was accepted as being for a 'relevant charitable purpose'. It arranged for a subcontractor to carry out the electrical installation, and told the subcontractor that the work was zero-rated, so that he need not charge VAT. Customs issued an assessment on the subcontractor, charging output tax on the basis that his supplies had been made to the contractor rather than to the customer, so that the effect of what is now *Sch 8, Group 5, Note 12* was that it did not qualify for zero-rating. The tribunal upheld the assessment. *ME Smith (Electrical Engineers) Ltd*, MAN/94/2101 (VTD 13594).

[15.214] See also *Ian Fraser & Partners Ltd*, 52.181 PENALTIES: MISDECLARATION; *Taylor & Fraser Ltd*, 52.182 PENALTIES: MISDECLARATION, and *McRandal*, 52.183 PENALTIES: MISDECLARATION.

Supplies to relevant housing associations (VATA 1994, Sch 8, Group 5, Item 3)

Conversion of 'bedsits' into self-contained flats

[15.215] A housing association arranged for the conversion of 24 'bedsits' into self-contained flats. The Commissioners issued a ruling that output tax was chargeable on the work. The association appealed, contending that the bedsits had been 'non-residential', so that the work qualified for zero-rating under *VATA 1994, Sch 8, Group 5, Item 3*. The tribunal accepted this contention and allowed the appeal, holding that, because the bedsits had had shared bathroom and kitchen facilities, they had been neither 'designed nor adapted for use as a dwelling or number of dwellings nor for a relevant residential purpose', within *Group 5, Note 7*. *Look Ahead Housing Association*, LON/99/860 (VTD 16816). (*Notes*. (1) The decision here was specifically disapproved in the subsequent case of *Amicus Group Ltd*, 15.216 below, on the grounds that it was inconsistent with the HL decision in *Uratemp Ventures Ltd v Collins*, HL [2001] 3 WLR 806. (2) *VATA 1994, Sch 8, Group 5, Note 7* was substituted by the *VAT (Conversion of Buildings) Order 2001 (SI 2001/2305)*, with effect from 1 August 2001. The revised *Note 7* was intended to provide relief for the sale of renovated houses that have not been used as a dwelling, or for a relevant residential purpose, for ten years or more. The change in the legislation does not affect the specific point at issue in this case.)

[15.216] The decision in *Look Ahead Housing Association*, **15.215** above, was specifically disapproved in a subsequent case where a housing association converted two properties from bedsitting accommodation into self-contained flats. The Commissioners issued a ruling that output tax was chargeable on the work, and the association appealed, contending that the bedsits had been 'non-residential', so that the work qualified for zero-rating under *VATA 1994, Sch 8, Group 5, Item 3*. The tribunal rejected this contention and dismissed the appeal. Applying *dicta* of Lord Irvine in *Uratemp Ventures Ltd v Collins*, HL [2001] 3 WLR 806, a 'dwelling' should be interpreted as 'a place where one lives, regarding and treating it as home'. Therefore the bedsitting accommodation had qualified as 'dwellings;' even though it had not contained separate cooking facilities. *Amicus Group Ltd*, LON/01/309 (VTD 17693).

Conversion of bedrooms in youth hostel

[15.217] A YMCA, which was a registered housing association, owned a youth hostel containing 44 hostel-type bedrooms and 9 self-catering flatlets, all of which shared bath and shower facilities. It arranged for the conversion of 15 of the hostel-type bedrooms into 10 self-catering flatlets. The Commissioners issued a ruling that VAT was chargeable on the work, and the YMCA appealed, contending that it should be treated as zero-rated under *VATA 1994, Sch 8, Group 5, Item 3*. The tribunal rejected this contention and dismissed the appeal, holding that, although the new flatlets were used as a 'sole or main residence', they were not used for a relevant residential purpose within *Note 4(g)*, as they did not constitute a 'self-sufficient institution'. *Derby YMCA*, MAN/00/473 (VTD 16914). (*Note*. The tribunal allowed an appeal against a misdeclaration penalty, holding that the complexity of the law constituted a reasonable excuse.)

Construction of garages (VATA 1994, Sch 8, Group 5, Note 3)

Whether dwelling and garage constructed 'at the same time'

[15.218] A trust arranged for the construction of two semi-detached dwelling-houses. A certificate of completion was issued in December 1997. In January 1998 the trust applied for planning permission to add two garages to the dwellings. This was granted the following month. The construction of the garages began in March 1998 and was completed within two months. The Commissioners issued a ruling that VAT was chargeable on the construction of the garages, since the dwellings and garages had not been constructed 'at the same time', as required by *VATA 1994, Sch 8, Group 5, Note 3*. The trust appealed, contending that, despite the issue of the certificate of completion, the houses should not be treated as having been completed until the construction of the garages. The tribunal rejected this contention and dismissed the appeal, finding that the evidence 'establishes that the construction of the dwellings was in fact complete at the date of the certificate of practical completion'. *Chipping Sodbury Town Trust*, LON/99/743 (VTD 16641).

[15.219] The decision in *Chipping Sodbury Town Trust*, 15.218 above, was distinguished in a subsequent case in which a couple obtained planning permission to erect a dwelling-house with an 'attached triple garage'. The building of the house was delayed by the need to fell some trees, and the company which carried out the work constructed the garage before building the house, although the completion of the house required subsequent work on the garage, including drainage and the fitting of a pressurised water supply. The company also constructed a large games room above the garage. HMRC issued an assessment charging VAT on the construction of the garage and games room, on the basis that because this work had been constructed before the house was complete, it failed to qualify for zero-rating. The company appealed, contending that the construction of the garage was part of a single project and qualified for zero-rating. The tribunal allowed the appeal with regard to the garage, holding that 'the certificate of practical completion will, when given, attach to the entire development'. However, the tribunal held that VAT was chargeable on the construction of the games room, since 'the legislation is quite clear that only a garage attracts zero-rating'. (The tribunal expressed the hope that the parties could agree an apportionment.) *Palmers of Oakham Ltd v HMRC*, [2011] UKFTT 82 (TC), TC00959.

Construction of garage in grounds of recently-built house

[15.220] See *Whiteley*, 15.43 above.

Building materials (VATA 1994, Sch 8, Group 5, Item 4; VATA 1994, s 35(1B))

NOTE

Whether there has been a supply of 'building materials', or articles ordinarily incorporated by builders, may arise under three VAT provisions, affecting respectively the zero-rating of the supply (*VATA 1994, Sch 8, Group 5, Item 4*), the input tax credit of the recipient of the supply (*Input Tax Order, Article 6*) and the amount of the 'do-it-yourself' housebuilders relief (*VATA 1994, s 35*). Where the appeal relates to *Sch 8, Group 5*, the summaries should be read in the light of subsequent changes in the legislation. The zero-rating of most alterations to buildings was removed by *FA 1984* with respect to supplies made after 31 May 1984. The provisions now in *Note 22*, excluding certain materials etc. from *Item 4*, were introduced at the same time so as to exclude prefabricated furniture, except where designed for kitchens, and electrical or gas appliances, except for appliances falling within one of the specific exceptions. See also VAT Information Sheet 5/00—'Construction and Building Materials' for Customs' interpretation of when building materials are 'ordinarily incorporated' into a building.

Finished or prefabricated furniture (Note 22(a)(b))

Built-in dressing table units

[15.221] In a purchase tax case, the Ch D held that built-in dressing table units were not 'ordinarily installed by builders', since they were not 'articles which one would expect a builder to install as fixtures in the ordinary way without any special instruction'. *F Austin (Leyton) Ltd v C & E Commrs*, Ch D [1968] Ch 529; [1968] 2 All ER 13. (*Note*. The purchase tax legislation provided that furniture was chargeable to purchase tax, but excluded builders' hardware 'and other articles of kinds ordinarily installed by builders as fixtures'. The current VAT legislation (*Sch 8, Group 5, Note 22*) refers to 'goods of a description ordinarily incorporated by builders'.)

Built-in wardrobes

[15.222] The Commissioners issued a ruling that built-in wardrobes failed to qualify for zero-rating. The company which supplied the wardrobes appealed. The tribunal allowed the appeal but the QB held that the tribunal had erred in law, and remitted the case to the tribunal for rehearing. Glidewell J held that, in order to meet the conditions of being 'ordinarily installed by builders', it was not sufficient that an article fell within a general class of items which could be regarded as 'ordinarily installed', but the tribunal should also consider whether the specific type of article in question fell within the definition of 'ordinarily installed'. *C & E Commrs v Smitmit Design Centre Ltd*, QB [1982] STC 525. (*Notes*. (1) There was no further public hearing of the appeal, which was apparently dismissed by consent following Glidewell J's rulings. (2) The legislation has subsequently been amended and the phrase 'ordinarily installed' has been replaced by the phrase 'ordinarily incorporated'.)

[15.223] In the case noted at **48.16** PAYMENT OF TAX, the tribunal held that wardrobes which were fitted in a new bungalow were furniture and were excluded from zero-rating, distinguishing *McLean Homes Midland*, **15.226** below. *SH Wade*, MAN/94/642 (VTD 13164). (*Note*. For the Commissioners' practice following this decision, see Business Brief 12/97, issued on 5 June 1997.)

[15.224] A trader who supplied bedroom furniture and fittings failed to account for output tax on his supplies. The Commissioners issued an assessment and he appealed, contending that his supplies should be treated as zero-rated. The tribunal dismissed his appeal, distinguishing *McLean Homes Midland Ltd*, **15.226** below. The tribunal observed that the trader's supplies 'would be tailor-made to the room for which they were intended, being assembled on site and carefully fitted to the room, to produce a carefully-joined and extremely smart result'. He 'produced a design on the basis that he was fitting to an ordinarily rectangular room, with featureless walls, and by fitting his units to the size of room, provided the customer with a bespoke version of storage space which the customer would otherwise have had to provide by obtaining furniture from a furniture dealer'. The fact that he commonly used two walls as part of the wardrobe did not prevent his supplies from being within what is now *Note 22(a)(b)*. *S Leon (t/a Custom Bedrooms)*, MAN/94/989 (VTD 13200).

Shelves and rails provided for use in recesses used as wardrobes

[15.225] A building company purchased prefabricated houses in kit form. The plans for the houses provided for recesses which could be used as wardrobes. The kits included shelving and lengths of railing which could be used in the recessed wardrobes. The company reclaimed input tax on the shelves and rails. The Commissioners issued an assessment to recover the tax, considering that they were 'finished or prefabricated furniture' or, alternatively, that they were 'materials for the construction of fitted furniture' within what is now *Input Tax Order, Article 6*. The tribunal allowed the company's appeal, holding that the walls, floor and ceiling of the recess could not be considered as furniture, and that the materials could not therefore be considered as used for the construction of fitted furniture. *Harrington Construction Ltd*, EDN/88/110 (VTD 3470).

[15.226] A company reclaimed input tax on items such as doors and shelves intended for installation in built-in wardrobes in houses which it had constructed. The walls of the rooms were used as the sides and backs of the wardrobes. The Commissioners issued an assessment to recover the tax, considering that it was not deductible by virtue of what is now *Input Tax Order, Article 6*. The tribunal allowed the company's appeal, applying *Harrington Construction Ltd*, 15.225 above, and holding that the materials in question were of a type ordinarily installed as fixtures, and were not materials for the construction of fitted furniture. Consequently the input tax was deductible. The QB upheld this decision as one of fact. Brooke J held that 'whether something was an item of furniture or not was very much a matter of impression. It was quite impossible to characterise an annex or closet or a cupboard either as being furniture or not being furniture'. *C & E Commrs v McLean Homes Midland Ltd*, QB [1993] STC 335. (*Notes.* (1) This case was distinguished in *Wade*, 15.223 above, and *Leon*, 15.224 above. (2) For the Commissioners' interpretation of the distinction between *Wade* and this decision, and for their interpretation of what constitutes 'furniture', see Business Brief 12/97, issued on 5 June 1997.)

[15.227] The decisions in *Harrington Construction Ltd*, 15.225 above, and *McLean Homes Midland Ltd (No 2)*, 15.226 above, were applied in a subsequent case in which the Commissioners had issued an assessment to recover input tax claimed on wardrobe doors designed to convert recesses into built-in wardrobes. The tribunal allowed the company's appeal on this point, holding that the doors were not fitted furniture, nor were they materials for the construction of fitted furniture. *McCarthy & Stone plc*, LON/91/382 (VTD 7014). (*Note.* For another issue in this case, see 15.255 below.)

[15.228] The decision in *McLean Homes Midland Ltd*, 15.226 above, was applied in a similar subsequent case in which *Wade*, 15.223 above, and *Leon*, 15.224 above, were distinguished. The tribunal held that shelves and doors qualified for zero-rating, on the basis that they were 'the very simplest of internal fittings plus a set of doors separating a natural recess from the rest of the room'. The recesses in question were 'an integral part of the room and form part of the fabric of the building'. (However, wardrobes with a melamine end panel, and wardrobes with a raised wooden floor, were held to be within the definition of 'furniture', and thus failed to qualify for zero-rating.) *Moores Furniture Group Ltd*, MAN/97/142 (VTD 15044).

Washbasin units

[15.229] A company, which built houses for sale, installed in some of these houses washbasins which were supported by basin units rather than pedestals. It reclaimed input tax on the purchase of the basin units. The Commissioners issued an assessment to recover the tax, considering that the units were 'finished or prefabricated furniture', so that, by virtue of what is now *Article 6* of the *Input Tax Order 1992*, the tax was not deductible. The company appealed, contending that the units were not within the definition of 'furniture'. The tribunal accepted this contention and allowed the appeal, holding on the evidence that the purpose of the units was simply to support the basins and to hide the piping, and that they were not intended to be used as cupboards or worktops. Accordingly they were not within the definition of 'furniture'. *Edmond Homes Ltd*, MAN/92/1502 (VTD 11567). (*Note.* For Customs' practice following this decision, see Business Brief 3/94, issued on 15 February 1994. See also the subsequent decision in *George*, **15.230** below.)

Vanity units—whether 'furniture'

[15.230] An individual (G) built a large house, and reclaimed input tax under *VATA 1994, s 35*. He reclaimed tax on the purchase of self-assembly 'vanity units', incorporating inside shelving and designed to be installed around a washbasin. Customs rejected the claim on the basis that the vanity units were 'finished or prefabricated furniture', so that the effect of *VATA 1994, Sch 8, Group 5, Note 22* was that the tax was not deductible. The tribunal upheld Customs' ruling and dismissed G's appeal. *PS George*, MAN/06/594 (VTD 20400). (*Note.* The tribunal also rejected a claim for repayment of tax which had been wrongly charged by a contractor who had fitted windows and doors. See the cases noted at **15.273** to **15.275** below.)

Staff lockers in nursing home—whether 'furniture'

[15.231] A charity arranged for the construction of a nursing home. A number of lockers, for the use of staff, were included in the building. The Commissioners issued a ruling that the construction of these lockers was standard-rated, considering firstly that the lockers were not supplied until after the construction had been completed, and secondly that they were 'finished or prefabricated furniture' and thus excluded from zero-rating in any event by *Note 22(a)*. The charity appealed, contending that the lockers were not within the definition of 'furniture', but were zero-rated building materials which had been supplied in the course of construction. The tribunal rejected this contention and dismissed the appeal, holding that the construction had been completed before the lockers were supplied. Additionally, the lockers were within the definition of 'furniture'. *Birmingham Council for Old People*, MAN/96/1062 (VTD 15437).

Study-bedrooms in boarding school

[15.232] A boarding school obtained listed buildings consent to convert some dormitories, in a protected building, into smaller study-bedrooms. Customs issued a ruling that supplies of wardrobes, bed bases, desk tops and shelves were 'finished or prefabricated furniture', within *VATA 1994, Sch 8, Group 5, Note 22*, and were therefore excluded from zero-rating. The school appealed. The tribunal reviewed the evidence in detail and dismissed the appeal with regard to the wardrobes and bed bases, holding that they were furniture and were excluded from zero-rating. However, the tribunal allowed the appeal with regard to the desk tops and shelves, holding on the evidence that they were not furniture and their supply was zero-rated. The tribunal observed that the shelves 'were not grouped as a bookcase but were single shelves: one per pupil fixed generally within reach of the desk top. Had there been several of them together, designed with sides and a top, we would have tended to view them as furniture.' The tribunal observed that the desk tops were 'unsophisticated' and 'did not have any of the normal additional items one would associate with a piece of furniture or a desk'. There were no drawers, and essentially 'they were large shelves at a convenient height for writing on'. *Christ's Hospital*, [2005] VATDR 442 (VTD 19126).

Bollards installed in school science laboratories

[15.233] A school arranged for the fitting-out of a science block containing seven laboratories. The Commissioners issued a ruling that output tax was chargeable on the installation of 42 bollards in the laboratories. The school appealed, contending that the bollards were 'building materials' within *VATA 1994, Sch 8, Group 5, Item 4*, and qualified for zero-rating. The tribunal rejected this contention and dismissed the appeal, holding that the bollards were 'finished or prefabricated furniture', within *Note 22*. *Sheldon School*, LON/97/817 (VTD 15300).

Electrical or gas appliances (Note 22(c))

Cooker hoods

[15.234] A property development company reclaimed input tax in respect of cooker hoods, which it had purchased for incorporation in a block of 14 flats which it was developing. The Commissioners issued an assessment to recover the tax, considering that it was not deductible by virtue of what is now *VATA 1994, Sch 8, Group 5, Note 22(c)*. The tribunal dismissed the company's appeal, holding that the cooker hoods were electrical appliances. *BGM Ltd*, LON/93/851A (VTD 11793).

Electric ovens and hobs

[15.235] A housebuilding company reclaimed input tax in respect of electric ovens and hobs, which it had purchased for incorporation in new houses. The Commissioners issued an assessment to recover the tax, considering that it was not deductible by virtue of what is now *VATA 1994, Sch 8, Group 5, Note 22(c)*. The company appealed, contending that the tax should be treated as deductible since the items were integrated fixtures rather than free-standing fittings. The tribunal upheld the assessment and dismissed the company's appeal, holding that the effect of *Note 22(c)* was that the tax was not deductible. *Erinmore Homes Ltd*, MAN/00/536 (VTD 17233).

Aga cooker

[15.236] An individual (C) claimed a refund of tax, under *VATA 1994, s 35*, on the purchase and installation of an Aga cooker. Customs rejected the claim and he appealed, contending that the Aga was intended as an appliance which was 'designed to heat space', within *Sch 8, Group 5, Note 22(c)(i)*, as well as simply as a cooker. The tribunal rejected this contention and dismissed the appeal, accepting that the Aga had the effect of heating space, but holding that it was not 'designed to heat space', as required by *Note 22(c)(i)*. The tribunal noted that the manufacturers regarded the heating effect of the Aga as 'an incidental consequence of the product, not as a function of it. The Aga is not offered to purchasers as a space heater, even as ancillary to its function as a cooker.' Accordingly the effect of *Note 22(c)* was that C was not entitled to a refund of tax on the Aga. *R Cusdin*, MAN/05/758 (VTD 19739).

[15.237] The decision in *Cusdin*, 15.236 above, was applied in the similar subsequent case of *R Sidgwick v HMRC*, [2010] UKFTT 421 (TC), TC00695.

Electric security gates

[15.238] A partnership constructed expensive houses, some of which included electrically operated security gates. It did not account for tax on the supplies of the gates. The Commissioners issued an assessment on the basis that the gates failed to qualify for zero-rating under *VATA 1994, Sch 8, Group 5, Note 22* since they were not 'ordinarily incorporated by builders', and also that the gates were electrical appliances and thus excluded from zero-rating by *Note 22(c)*. The tribunal upheld both the Commissioners' contentions and dismissed the partnership's appeal. *M & G McCarthy (t/a Croft Homes)*, LON/99/1253 (VTD 16789).

Electric covers for swimming pools

[15.239] A company (L) supplied and installed swimming pools in new luxury houses. Customs accepted that the installation of an indoor swimming pool, in the course of a construction of a new house, was zero-rated. L also treated the supply and installation of electric covers for the pools as zero-rated. Customs issued an assessment charging tax on the covers, on the basis that they were electrical appliances which were excluded from zero-rating by *VATA 1994, Sch 8, Group 5, Note 22(c)*. L appealed, contending that the covers should be treated as part of the pool since 'without a cover, an indoor swimming pool would cause considerable condensation problems within the building and the heat loss would increase the owner's heating bills substantially'. The tribunal held that the effect of *Note 22(c)* was that the covers had to be treated as standard-rated under UK law. However, the tribunal noted that the question of 'whether the components of a single supply may attract differing tax treatments' had been referred to the ECJ in *Talacre Beach Caravan Sales Ltd*, 22.507 EUROPEAN COMMUNITY LAW. The tribunal therefore gave L liberty to apply for a further hearing following the CJEC decision in *Talacre Beach Caravan Sales Ltd. Leisure Contracts Ltd*, MAN/05/227 (VTD 19392). (*Note.* The ECJ subsequently held that 'the fact that specific goods are counted as a single supply' did not 'prevent the Member State concerned from levying VAT at the standard rate on the supply of those excluded items'. Following this decision, L did not seek a further hearing of its appeal. See now, however, the subsequent decision in *Rainbow Pools Ltd*, 15.240 below.)

[15.240] A company (R) constructed indoor swimming pools in new luxury houses. The pools had retractable insulated covers, and some of the pools had a movable tiled floor which could be locked at varying depths. R treated the covers and floors as 'building materials' within *VATA 1994, Sch 8, Group 5, Note 22*. Customs issued a ruling that the covers and floors failed to qualify as 'building materials'. The tribunal allowed R's appeal with regard to the covers, declining to follow the earlier decision in *Leisure Contracts Ltd*, **15.239** above, where the Manchester tribunal had held that a swimming pool cover was an electrical appliance which was excluded from the definition of 'building materials' by *Note 22(c)*, and was therefore standard-rated. The tribunal chairman (Mr. Nowlan) held that swimming pool covers were not electrical appliances, since it was 'purely incidental to their description that they are electrically powered'. (However the tribunal dismissed R's appeal with regard to the floors, holding that they did not qualify as 'building materials', since they were not 'ordinarily incorporated' into buildings of any description.) *Rainbow Pools London Ltd*, LON/06/1343 (VTD 20800).

Other items

Mechanical ventilator units

[15.241] The tribunal held that mechanical ventilator units, which were installed for sound-proofing purposes in houses near to an airport, were articles 'of a kind ordinarily installed by builders'. *British Airports Authority (No 5)*, LON/77/144 (VTD 447).

Ventilating system

[15.242] An individual (W) claimed a refund of tax on the installation of a ventilating system in a bungalow which he had built. The Commissioners rejected his claim, considering that a ventilation system was not 'ordinarily incorporated' in a bungalow. The tribunal allowed W's appeal. Most houses did not have ventilating systems installed, but where there was no natural ventilation, a ventilation system was generally required by building regulations. On the evidence, a ventilation system was necessary for this particular bungalow. The system was an article of a type ordinarily incorporated in a building, when such installation was considered necessary. *CH Wigmore*, [1991] VATTR 290 (VTD 6040).

[15.243] A company manufactured mechanical ventilation systems with heat recovery, for installation in domestic buildings. The Commissioners issued a ruling that its supplies of these systems were standard-rated, and the company appealed, contending that the systems were 'articles of a kind ordinarily installed by builders', and qualified for zero-rating under what is now *VATA 1994, Sch 8, Group 5, Item 4*. The tribunal accepted this contention and allowed the appeal. *2S Airchangers Ltd*, BEL/93/1A (VTD 12495).

Scaffolding

[15.244] An individual (G) arranged for the construction of a house. Much of the work was carried out by specialist contractors. G arranged for a company (S) to erect scaffolding on site. Customs issued a ruling that VAT was chargeable on the amount which G paid S for the hire of the scaffolding. G appealed, contending that it should be treated as a zero-rated supply of building materials. The tribunal allowed the appeal in part, holding that the services of designing, erecting and dismantling the scaffolding were within what is now *Sch 8, Group 5, Item 2* and zero-rated, but that the scaffolding was not 'building materials' within *Item 4* and the hire was standard-rated.

Accordingly the consideration for the hire should be apportioned, and the appeal was adjourned for this to be agreed. *B Gilbourne*, [1974] VATTR 209 (VTD 109). (*Note.* There was no further public hearing of the appeal.)

[15.245] See also *Guntert*, 52.195 PENALTIES: MISDECLARATION.

Waste disposal units

[15.246] A company reclaimed input tax in respect of waste disposal units which it had purchased for installation in fitted kitchens. The Commissioners issued an assessment to recover the tax, considering that waste disposal units were not 'ordinarily' installed in fitted kitchens, so that the claim for input tax was prohibited by what is now *Article 6* of the *Input Tax Order*. The company appealed, contending that the flats were luxury flats and that waste disposal units were ordinarily installed in luxury flats. The tribunal dismissed the appeal, holding that 'ordinarily' implies installation in all sections of the market, not just in luxury homes. *Creighton Griffiths (Investments) Ltd*, [1983] VATTR 175 (VTD 1442).

Telephone exchange

[15.247] A university installed a new telephone exchange system. The Commissioners issued a ruling that the supply of the new telephone exchange was standard-rated. The university appealed, contending that the telephone exchange system was within what is now *VATA 1994, Sch 8, Group 5, Item 4* and was therefore zero-rated. The tribunal allowed the university's appeal, holding that the exchange was a fixture rather than a chattel, applying *dicta* of Scarman LJ in *Berkley v Poulett*, CA 1976, 241 EG 911. *University of Reading*, LON/89/235 (VTD 4209).

Venetian blinds

[15.248] A construction company built two houses designed for low energy consumption. They had south-facing windows, which incorporated Venetian blinds which opened and closed automatically so as to admit or retain heat. The company reclaimed input tax on the blinds. The Commissioners issued an assessment to recover the tax, considering that it was not deductible by virtue of what is now *Input Tax Order, Article 6*. The company appealed, contending that the blinds were items ordinarily installed by builders, and that the tax was deductible. The tribunal rejected this contention and dismissed the appeal, holding that the blinds were not items ordinarily installed by builders, so that *Article 6* applied and the tax was not deductible. *Frank Haslam Milan & Co Ltd*, MAN/87/89 (VTD 3857).

[15.249] The decision in *Frank Haslam Milan & Co Ltd*, **15.248** above, was applied in the similar subsequent case of *T Perry*, LON/05/369 (VTD 19428).

Roller blinds

[15.250] An individual (P) reclaimed tax under *VATA 1994, s 35* on nine roller blinds. HMRC rejected the claim on the grounds that the blinds were not 'items ordinarily installed by builders'. The tribunal allowed P's appeal on this point, holding that roller blinds were 'items ordinarily installed by builders'. (P's appeal in respect of certain other supplies was dismissed.) *J Price v HMRC,*

[2010] UKFTT 634 (TC), TC00873. (*Note*. For HMRC's policy following this decision, see HMRC Brief 2/2011, issued on 25 January 2011. HMRC state that they still consider that roller blinds are not 'building materials' but that, 'given the small amount of VAT at stake in this particular case', they are not appealing to the Upper Tribunal against this decision.)

Timber used for shelving

[15.251] Timber used for shelving was held to qualify as 'materials' in *John Turner & Smith Ltd*, MAN/74/23 (VTD 124).

Conservatories, roof timbers and fire doors

[15.252] A joinery partnership supplied two conservatories, some new roof windows and some fire doors to the owners of protected buildings, and did not account for output tax on the supplies, treating them as zero-rated. The Commissioners issued an assessment charging tax, on the basis that the supplies did not qualify for zero-rating under what is now *VATA 1994, Sch 8, Group 5, Item 4*, since the materials had not been supplied with any related zero-rated services. The partnership appealed, contending that it had supplied services as well as the materials, so that the materials qualified for zero-rating under what is now *VATA 1994, Sch 8, Group 5, Item 4*. The QB rejected this contention and upheld the assessment. Ognall J held that the partnership was doing no more than was necessary to supply goods. As a matter of law, the services found to have been provided were nothing more than the normal obligations imposed by law on a person selling any articles. The partnership had made a single supply of goods which did not qualify for zero-rating. *C & E Commrs v MD & RW Jeffs (t/a J & J Joinery)*, QB [1995] STC 759.

Kitchen units

[15.253] The QB decision in *Jeffs*, 15.252 above, was applied in a subsequent case in which the tribunal held that supplies of kitchen units were supplies of goods and there were no related supplies of services. Accordingly the supplies did not qualify for zero-rating. *D & Mrs C Hodson (t/a Bordercraft Workshops)*, MAN/95/1769 (VTD 13897).

Snooker table

[15.254] A partnership claimed a deduction for input tax in respect of the installation of a snooker table. The Commissioners issued an assessment to recover the tax and the partnership appealed. The tribunal dismissed the appeal, holding that snooker tables were not 'articles ordinarily installed by builders'. *Haden & Son*, LON/85/615 (VTD 2209).

Material for soundproofing concrete floors

[15.255] A company reclaimed input tax on the supply of a material for soundproofing concrete floors. The Commissioners issued an assessment to recover the tax, considering that the tax was not recoverable by virtue of what is now *Article 6* of the *Input Tax Order*. The tribunal dismissed the company's appeal. *McCarthy & Stone plc*, LON/91/382 (VTD 7014). (*Note*. For another issue in this case, see **15.227** above.)

Planting of trees and shrubs

[15.256] A landscape gardener reclaimed input tax in respect of trees and shrubs which he had planted in the grounds of a new estate. The Commissioners issued an assessment to recover the tax, considering that the trees and shrubs were not within the definition of materials 'of a kind ordinarily installed by builders'. The tribunal dismissed the gardener's appeal against this decision. (The tribunal also observed that the planting of the trees was not 'in the course of construction' of the buildings.) *JW Tilbury*, LON/80/407 (VTD 1102).

[15.257] The decision in *Tilbury*, 15.256 above, was not followed in a subsequent case involving a housing development, where the tribunal held on the evidence that 'it is now normal practice for planning authorities in the case of new housing developments to require a scheme of hard and soft landscaping to be submitted and approved before the commencement of the development'. Accordingly, the tribunal held that the trees and shrubs were 'goods ordinarily at the present time incorporated in the site of buildings of the description that are involved here'. *Rialto Homes plc*, [1999] VATDR 477 (VTD 16340). (*Note*. For the Commissioners' practice following this decision, see Business Brief 7/00, issued on 18 May 2000.)

[15.258] An individual (M) claimed a refund of tax on hedging shrubs and weedkiller. The Commissioners rejected the claim on the basis that they could not be regarded as 'building materials', and the tribunal dismissed M's appeal. *A McAlister*, BEL/87/14 (VTD 3148).

[15.259] A company reclaimed input tax in respect of trees and shrubs which it had planted in the grounds of a housing development. The Commissioners issued an assessment to recover the tax, considering that it was not deductible by virtue of what is now *Article 6* of the *Input Tax Order*. The company appealed, contending that the trees and shrubs were 'articles of a kind ordinarily installed as fixtures'. The tribunal dismissed the company's appeal. The trees and shrubs were 'not articles which one would expect a builder to install as fixtures in the ordinary way'. *McLean Homes East Anglia Ltd*, [1992] VATTR 460 (VTD 7748).

Safe

[15.260] An individual (J) claimed a refund of tax on the installation of a safe. The Commissioners rejected the claim on the basis that a safe was not 'ordinarily incorporated' in a dwelling-house. The tribunal dismissed J's appeal against this decision. *GE Joel*, LON/88/403 (VTD 3295).

Miscellaneous

Interaction of Sch 8, Group 5 and Sch 9, Group 1

[15.261] An individual (C) purchased a house in 1.8 acres of land. He carried out substantial demolition work, constructed a larger house on the site, and reclaimed input tax on the materials which he had used. The Commissioners rejected the claim, considering firstly that, because he had retained a small proportion of the walls of the existing house, the work did not qualify as the construction of a building, and contending alternatively that the input tax was not recoverable because C intended to sell the house after building it, so that the input tax had been incurred for the purpose of making an exempt supply under what is now *VATA 1994, Sch 9, Group 1, Item 1*. The tribunal allowed C's appeal. With regard to the first issue, the tribunal held that the work qualified as the 'construction of a building' under the legislation then in force. With regard to the Commissioners' second contention, the tribunal observed that this would 'have the effect that even if the fee simple of the land is sold by a person constructing a building designed as a dwelling, the grant of any interest in land is exempt. Being a taxing statute, these provisions must be construed strictly, and should be construed in favour of the taxpayer. Further, it is well settled that a statute should be construed so that it should have a sensible meaning.' The Commissioners' contentions 'would have, or be capable of having, the effect of nullifying the zero-rating of the grant of a major interest in land by a person constructing a building. It appears to me that that cannot have been the intention of Parliament.' The tribunal held that 'it would appear that the intention was that (*Sch 9**) should apply subject to (*Sch 8**). But whether that be right or not, if (*Sch 9**) is to apply to all grants of an interest in land, then it renders (*Sch 8, Group 5, Item 1**) meaningless'. Accordingly, the input tax should be deemed not to have been incurred for the purpose of an exempt supply. *AR Carter*, LON/95/1390 (VTD 13828). (*Note.* With regard to the definition of 'construction of a building', see now *VATA 1994, Sch 8, Group 5, Note 18*, introduced by *VAT (Construction of Buildings) Order 1995 (SI 1995/280)*. The work in question would not now qualify for zero-rating, but the case remains a useful authority with regard to the interaction of *VATA 1994, Sch 8, Group 5* and *VATA 1994, Sch 9, Group 1*.)

Change in law relating to construction work

[15.262] See *Martins Properties (Chelsea) Ltd*, **46.220** PARTIAL EXEMPTION.

Whether VATA 1994, s 35(1)(b) applicable

[15.263] An appellant claimed a refund of input tax incurred in building a flat adjacent to an existing house. There was no communication between the flat and the house. The flat was separately rated and was self-contained in respect of all services. However, the relevant planning permission stated that the flat was to 'remain solely for the enjoyment of the dwelling house'. The Commissioners therefore rejected the claim, considering that the work was not within what is now *VATA 1994, s 35(1)(b)*, because it was not 'lawful'. The tribunal upheld this contention and dismissed the appeal. *RAS Alexander*, EDN/89/140 (VTD 4560).

[15.264] A couple claimed a refund of tax under *VATA 1994, s 35* in respect of the conversion of part of a factory into a residential flat. HMRC rejected the claim on the basis that the work had not received planning permission, so that it was not 'lawful' and the conditions of *s 35(1)(b)* were not satisfied. The tribunal upheld HMRC's ruling and dismissed the couple's appeal. *S Bond & Ms S Baxter v HMRC*, [2010] UKFTT 242 (TC), TC00539.

[15.265] An individual (F) obtained planning permission for the erection of a 'dwelling house incorporating bed and breakfast facilities'. He claimed a refund of tax under *VATA 1994, s 35*. The Commissioners rejected the claim and the tribunal dismissed his appeal. *VATA 1994, s 35(1)(b)* provided that a refund was only due where the works were 'otherwise than in the course of any business'. On the evidence, F had undertaken the work with 'the intention to further the business of running a bed and breakfast establishment in the building'. *HW Flynn*, LON/99/1161 (VTD 16930).

[15.266] A married couple arranged for the conversion of a derelict barn into two semi-detached residential dwellings. They claimed a refund of tax under *VATA 1994, s 35*. The Commissioners rejected the claim on the basis that the dwellings were intended for letting, whereas *VATA 1994, s 35(1)(b)* provided that a refund was only due where the works were 'otherwise than in the course of any business'. The couple appealed, contending that they intended to let the dwellings for a limited period of no more than ten years, after which they would be occupied by their children (who were aged between 3 and 9 at the time of the appeal). The tribunal dismissed the couple's appeal, finding that the dwellings were being let and producing rental income totalling £2,500 per month. Accordingly the effect of *s 35(1)(b)* was that relief was not due. *R & L Watson*, [2004] VATDR 408 (VTD 18675).

[15.267] An individual (C) purchased a house which had planning permission for the construction of a second house on part of its land. He arranged for the construction of such a house, which he subsequently let to friends who needed temporary accommodation, and claimed a refund of tax under *VATA 1994, s 35*. Customs rejected the claim on the basis that C had intended to let and then sell the newly-built house, so that its construction should be treated as being 'in the course of any business' and the effect of *s 35(1)(b)* was that no refund was due. C appealed, contending that he intended to retain ownership of the newly-built house, to move into it when his friends moved out, and to sell the original house, but wished to retain ownership of both houses for a period so that if his relationship with his current partner were to break down, they could 'then each have accommodation without causing each other any problems'. The tribunal accepted C's evidence and allowed his appeal. The tribunal observed that 'the factor that is fatal to a VAT refund claim under *section 35* is not the "self-builder's" intention to sell the property, but the feature that his building work is "carried out in the course or furtherance of any business". The most obvious business that the self-builder might be conducting is of course the business of being a house-builder, which immediately means that although the self-builder will not be able to reclaim VAT under *section 35*, nevertheless precisely the same amounts of VAT will still be recovered when the self-builder grants the first major interest in the newly built house, since the sale of the house will be a zero-rated supply. It accordingly appears that where self-builders are denied refunds of VAT under *section 35*, on account of their intention to sell the property on completion, the authorities ought to be directing the claimants to ensure that they are registered for VAT purposes whereupon their sale of the house will be zero-rated, and precisely the same VAT will be refunded, as was being claimed mistakenly under *section 35.*' The tribunal held that the letting of the newly-built house was 'not a transaction in the course of the business of letting, but a short-term expedient'. And C's desire to move into that house meant that 'any possible business as regards that property never commenced, rather than that a business asset has been appropriated to private use'. *MP Curry*, LON/06/134 (VTD 20077).

[15.268] A university lecturer in architecture (S) arranged for the construction of a building comprising two flats. She intended to live in one of the flats and let the other. She claimed a refund of VAT on the construction under *VATA 1994, s 35*. HMRC refunded half of the tax claimed but rejected the remainder of the claim on the grounds that the construction of the flat which S had intended to let should be treated as being 'in the course of any business', and the effect of *s 35(1)(b)* was that no refund was due. S appealed. The tribunal allowed her appeal, holding on the evidence that the construction was not 'predominantly concerned with the making of supplies for a consideration'. For the purpose of *VATA 1994, s 35*, the construction work should be treated as 'carried out otherwise than in the course of any business'. *P Sassi v HMRC*, [2009] UKFTT 280 (TC), TC00224.

[15.269] The decision in *Sassi*, **15.268** above, was applied in the similar subsequent case of *W Bourne v HMRC*, FTT August 2010, TC00582.

[15.270] A company which owned a farm, but was not registered for VAT, built an 'agricultural dwelling', to be occupied by an employee. It claimed a refund of tax under *VATA 1994, s 35*. Customs rejected the claim and the tribunal dismissed the company's appeal, observing that *VATA 1994, s 35(1)(b)* provided that a refund was only due where the works were 'otherwise than in the course of any business'. The tribunal also commented that '*section 35* is a relieving provision and is designed to assist individuals who are not and do not wish to be registered for VAT purposes. Businesses have the opportunity to reclaim VAT on building costs if the property is to be used for the purposes of its *(sic)* businesses.' *Poultries Al Hilal Ltd*, MAN/07/447 (VTD 20381).

[15.271] A builder (T), who had ceased to be registered for VAT because his turnover was below the statutory threshold, constructed a bungalow for a friend. He reclaimed a refund of tax under *VATA 1994, s 35*. HMRC rejected the claim and the tribunal dismissed T's appeal, observing that *VATA 1994, s 35(1)(b)* provided that a refund was only due where the works were 'otherwise than in the course of any business', and finding that T had built the bungalow in the course of his business. The tribunal observed that if T wished to recover the VAT, he should consider voluntary registration. *WJ Terry (t/a Wealden Properties) v HMRC*, [2009] UKFTT 202 (TC), TC00155.

[15.272] A married couple operated a cattery business on the site of a former orchard. In 2005 they obtained planning permission for the construction of a house on the site. The relevant permission provided that 'the occupation of the dwelling shall be limited to a person solely or mainly employed or last employed in the cattery business or a widow or widower of such a person, or any resident dependants'. The couple reclaimed VAT on the construction of the house. HMRC rejected the claim on the basis that the construction of the house was in the course or furtherance of the cattery business. The wife appealed. The tribunal allowed her appeal. Judge Tildesley held that 'the condition imposed related to the category of persons occupying the property, and in no way restricted its separate use or disposal as a dwelling house'. He expressed the view that 'occupancy restrictions are not prohibitions on separate use or disposal' and that the planning conditions were 'not determinative of whether the supplies of building materials were for business or non-business use within the meaning of the VAT legislation'. *Mrs ME Wendels v HMRC*, [2010] UKFTT 476 (TC), TC00737.

Tax wrongly charged by contractor—claim for refund under s 35

[15.273] An individual (V) engaged a builder to construct a house for him. The contract excluded work on all external doors and windows. V arranged for this work to be carried out for him by a separate company. That company issued an invoice charging VAT on its services, which V paid. V applied for the tax to be refunded under what is now *VATA 1994, s 35*. The Commissioners rejected the claim on the grounds that the work was in the course of construction of the building and should have been zero-rated, so that V should have requested a refund from the company. The tribunal dismissed V's appeal against this decision, holding that *VATA 1994, s 35* only provided for refunds of tax in cases where tax was 'chargeable on the supply of goods', as in cases where articles were purchased from a builders' merchant. In the case under appeal, although the tax had been charged, it had not been properly chargeable, so that *VATA 1994, s 35* did not apply and V's remedy was against the company, rather than against the Commissioners. *RJ Vincett*, LON/93/233A (VTD 10932).

[15.274] The decision in *Vincett*, 15.273 above, was applied in the similar cases of *E Banks*, LON/93/2845 (VTD 12004); *DM Aries*, LON/93/2611A (VTD 12172); *CJ Allen*, MAN/00/752 (VTD 17342) and *MR Culverwell*, [2009] UKFTT 276 (TC), TC00222.

[15.275] Similar decisions were reached in *DC Fisher*, LON/93/2723A (VTD 12356); *G Williams*, [2009] UKFTT 96 (TC), TC 00064; *M O'Donnell*, [2010] UKFTT 236 (TC), TC00535; *S Harrison-Devereux*, [2010] UKFTT 267 (TC), TC00561; *K Hewitt*, [2011] UKFTT 571 (TC), TC01414; *O'Reilly*, 15.210 above; *George*, 15.230 above, and *Bates*, 15.281 below.

[15.276] A farmer (N) decided to convert a disused barn into a dwelling-house for her daughter. She engaged two contractors, who charged her VAT at 17.5%. She reclaimed this tax under *VATA 1994, s 35*. HMRC formed the opinion that the contractors should only have charged VAT at 5%, and repaid VAT on this basis. N appealed. The tribunal dismissed her appeal, observing that *s 35(1C)* provided that the Commissioners should 'refund to the relevant person the amount of VAT so chargeable'. The contractors' supplies qualified for the reduced rate of 5% under *VATA 1994, Sch 7A, Group 6*. HMRC was only liable 'to refund VAT which is properly chargeable'. *SF Nike v HMRC*, [2009] UKFTT 349 (TC), TC00287.

[**15.277**] The decision in *Nike v HMRC*, **15.276** above, was applied in the similar subsequent case of *I Robertson v HMRC*, [2010] UKFTT 102 (TC), TC00413.

[**15.278**] Similar decisions were reached in *J Frost v HMRC*, [2010] UKFTT 344 (TC), TC00626 and *CAM Anderson v HMRC*, [2010] UKFTT 432 (TC), TC00701.

Whether supplies within VATA 1994, s 35(1)(c)

[**15.279**] A married couple claimed relief under what is now *VATA 1994, s 35* in respect of a fence and a garden wall, built for them by contractors. The Commissioners rejected the claim and the tribunal dismissed the couple's appeal, holding that the invoices in question related to supplies of services and that the goods which were included in the supply were an 'integral and incidental part of the overall single supply of a service'. Accordingly the supplies were not within what is now *VATA 1994, s 35(1)(c)* and relief was not due. *AJ & A Elliott*, LON/89/1782X (VTD 4926).

[**15.280**] A couple, who were building a house, purchased some granite blocks as building materials. They arranged for a haulage company to transport the granite from the quarry to the site. They reclaimed input tax on the invoice from the haulage company as well as on the purchase of the granite. Customs refunded the VAT on the purchase of the granite, but rejected the claim relating to the invoice from the haulage company on the grounds that it related to a separate supply of services which was outside the scope of *VATA 1994, s 35*. The couple appealed, contending that the haulage costs should be regarded as 'an integral component of the building materials'. The tribunal rejected this contention and dismissed the couple's appeal. *AJ & K Price*, LON/07/1012 (VTD 20700).

[**15.281**] A couple were building a three-storey house. The relevant building regulations required them to install a fire sprinkler system on the ground floor. The company which installed the sprinkler system charged VAT. The couple reclaimed this from Customs. Customs rejected the claim and the tribunal dismissed the couple's appeal. The tribunal held that the supply of the sprinkler system was a supply of services rather than a supply of goods. Accordingly the supply was not within *VATA 1994, s 35 (1)(c)*. The tribunal held that the contractor should not have charged VAT on the supply, and that the couple should seek a refund of the VAT from the contractor. *P & M Bates*, MAN/08/046 (VTD 20948).

Sale of holiday homes—whether a separate supply of services

[**15.282**] See *Lower Mill Estate Ltd v HMRC (and related appeal)*, **22.75** EUROPEAN COMMUNITY LAW.

Time of supply—VAT Regulations 1995, reg 93

[**15.283**] See *Cross Levels Developments Ltd*, **62.475** SUPPLY.

16

Cultural Services

The cases in this chapter are arranged under the following headings.

Eligible bodies (VATA 1994, Sch 9, Group 13, Note 2)   16.1
Miscellaneous   16.10

Eligible bodies (VATA 1994, Sch 9, Group 13, Note 2)

Museum—whether within Group 13, Note 2(c)

[16.1] The trustees of Glastonbury Abbey did not account for output tax on admission charges to the Abbey museum, treating them as exempt. The Commissioners issued an assessment charging tax, considering that the Abbey did not qualify for exemption as the trustees had two paid employees, so that the Abbey was not 'managed and administered on a voluntary basis by persons who have no direct or indirect financial interest in its activities', as required by *Group 13, Note 2(c)*. The trustees appealed. The tribunal allowed the appeal, finding that the admission fees totalled about £125,000 p.a. and the employees' salaries totalled £19,800 p.a. Accordingly, the payments to the two employees did not mean that the Abbey was not 'managed and administered on a voluntary basis', and thus did not prevent the trustees from qualifying for exemption within *Note 2(c)*. *Glastonbury Abbey*, [1996] VATDR 307 (VTD 14579).

Zoological society—whether within Group 13, Note 2(c)

[16.2] A zoological society, which was a registered charity, was formed in 1983 to take over the operation of a zoo which had previously been run by a limited company (Z). One member of the society's management council (J) held a debenture issued by the society, and received a small pension from it. Initially the society accounted for output tax on its admission charges. Subsequently it claimed repayment of the tax on the basis that its supplies qualified for exemption under *VATA 1994, Sch 9, Group 13*. The Commissioners rejected the claim for periods up to June 2003 on the grounds that J had had a financial interest in its activities, so that the society was not 'managed and administered on a voluntary basis by persons who have no direct or indirect financial interest in its activities', as required by *Group 13, Note 2(c)*. The society appealed, contending that, even though J held a debenture issued by the society and received a small pension from it, the society was still 'managed and administered on a voluntary basis by persons who have no direct or indirect financial interest in its activities'. The tribunal accepted this contention and allowed the appeal, finding that J had earned her pension by working for Z from 1963 to 1981, and that the debenture which J held had been issued as consideration for the transfer of the shares which she had held in Z. The tribunal noted that J had not received any interest from the debenture, and commented that 'it is the appellant who has benefited from the generosity of (J) and not (J) who is benefiting from the appellant'. On the evidence, 'the contribution to the management of the appellant made by (J) did not affect the essentially voluntary character of the management and administration of the appellant'. *The Zoological Society of Wales,* LON/96/1615 (VTD 18786).

[16.3] See also *The Zoological Society of London,* **22.321** EUROPEAN COMMUNITY LAW.

Zoological society—claim for input tax

[16.4] Customs accepted that a zoological society qualified for exemption under *VATA 1994, Sch 9, Group 13,* and was not required to account for output tax on its admission charges. However, the society reclaimed significant amounts of input tax relating to the keep of the animals at the zoo. Customs rejected the claim on the basis that the relevant expenditure was attributable to exempt supplies. The society appealed, contending that the expenditure was partly attributable to taxable supplies of catering and merchandising. The tribunal rejected this contention and dismissed the appeal, holding that 'there was a direct and immediate link between the animal costs and the exempt supply of admission to view the animals exhibited'. There was no such direct link between those costs and the society's other commercial activities. *Twycross Zoo East Midland Zoological Society (No 1),* MAN/04/682 (VTD 19548).

[16.5] The zoological society in the case noted at **16.4** above charged customers an additional fee for 'close encounters' with giraffes and elephants, in addition to its normal charges for admission to the zoo. The society reclaimed input tax with regard to the upkeep of the animals in question. Customs issued a ruling that the relevant supplies were exempt. However the tribunal allowed the society's appeal, finding that 'there is in the encounter a degree of closeness and intimacy with the animals which the general public would not experience' and that the society was 'not merely supplying the right of admission to a part of the zoo to which the general public would not normally be allowed access'. *Twycross Zoo East Midland Zoological Society (No 2),* [2007] VATDR 425 (VTD 20439).

Chapel—whether within Group 13, Note 2(c)

[16.6] The Commissioners issued a ruling that the trustees of a chapel, which included a historic library, were required to account for output tax on admission charges for entry to the chapel. They appealed, contending that the charges should be treated as exempt from VAT under *VATA 1994, Sch 9, Group 13.* The tribunal rejected this contention and dismissed the appeal. The tribunal held that, in view of the chapel's collections of historic books and other items of historic or artistic interest, the chapel could be described as a 'museum', within *Group 13, Item 2(a).* However, the trustees were not an 'eligible body' within *Item 2,* since the stipends of the dean and canons who acted as the trustees were 'at least in material part, paid for the management duties and roles they perform, and have always had to perform'. Accordingly, they were 'remunerated to a material extent for their management activities', and it followed that the chapel was not 'managed and administered on a voluntary basis by persons who have no direct or indirect financial interest in its activities', as required by *Group 13, Note 2(c)*. (The tribunal also observed that the trustees had not shown that it applied any profits from the admission charges to the 'continuance or improvement of the facilities made available by means of the supplies', as required by *Note 2(b)*.) *Dean & Canons of Windsor*, LON/97/552 (VTD 15703).

Orchestra—whether within Group 13, Note 2(c)

[16.7] Customs issued a ruling that a company (B) which operated a symphony orchestra was required to account for VAT on its supplies. B appealed, contending that its supplies qualified for exemption under *VATA 1994, Sch 9, Group 13*. The tribunal rejected this contention and dismissed B's appeal, and the Ch D and the CA unanimously upheld this decision. Lloyd LJ observed that *Group 13, Note 2(c)* restricted exemption to organisations which were 'managed and administered on a voluntary basis by persons who have no direct or indirect financial interest in its activities'. However, B's managing director was a full-time employee, and was paid remuneration of more than £80,000. He held that 'for the relevant body to have a managing director who is paid for taking part in the decision-making process at the highest level' was inconsistent with the exemption 'because it does not allow the management and administration to be described as being carried out on an essentially voluntary basis'. On the evidence, 'the managing director's remuneration and his participation in the highest decision-making processes of (B) makes it impossible to say that the management and administration of (B) is conducted on an essentially voluntary basis'. Therefore B's supplies failed to qualify for exemption. *Bournemouth Symphony Orchestra v C & E Commrs*, CA 2006, [2007] STC 198; [2006] EWCA Civ 1281. (*Note.* For HMRC's practice following this decision, see HMRC Brief 27/07, issued on 22 March 2007.)

Operatic company—whether within Group 13, Note 2(c)

[16.8] A company (L) was formed in 2000 to stage operatic performances. It was limited by guarantee, and had four trustees, one of whom owned the premises which it used, and had undertaken to guarantee its losses. Customs issued a ruling that it was required to account for VAT on its supplies. L appealed, contending that its supplies qualified for exemption under *VATA 1994, Sch 9, Group 13*. The Ch D accepted this contention and allowed the appeal. Lightman J held that 'in the context of the legislation in question the crucial distinction is being made between commercial profit-making and non-commercial non-profit making bodies'. The reference in *Group 13, Note 2(c)* to 'financial interest' should be construed as being 'directed at potential enrichment', and not as 'designed to preclude participation in management by persons who for the benefit of the cultural body assumed responsibility for some one or other liability of the body and accordingly the risk of an actual impoverishment'. Furthermore, a qualifying body could enter into commercial contracts with one of its directors, provided that the contract did 'not confer any interest in the body's results or profits'. *Longborough Festival Opera v HMRC*, Ch D [2006] STC 818; [2006] EWHC 40 (Ch). (*Note*. The CA rejected an application by HMRC for leave to appeal against this decision. For HMRC's practice following the decision, see HMRC Brief 27/07, issued on 22 March 2007.)

Student union—whether within Group 13, Note 2(c)

[16.9] A university students' union organised various 'cultural entertainments', for which it charged admission. HMRC issued a ruling that the union was required to account for VAT on the admission charges. The union appealed, contending that its supplies qualified for exemption under *VATA 1994, Sch 9, Group 13*. The tribunal rejected this contention and dismissed the appeal, holding that the union met the requirements of *Group 13, Note 2(a) and (b)*, but that it did not meet the requirements of *Note 2(c)*, because it was managed by 'sabbatical officers' who were 'entitled to bursaries which in effect were annual salaries. The bursaries although below the market rate for jobs of equivalent responsibilities were significantly more than a nominal rate.' Accordingly the union was not 'managed on an essentially voluntary basis', as required by *Note 2(c)*. *Keele University Students Union v HMRC*, [2009] UKFTT 114 (TC), TC00082.

Miscellaneous

Restored Victorian garden—whether a 'museum'

[16.10] In the 1840s a large garden was established in a steep ravine by the River Helford in Cornwall. It included many plants from different parts of the world. After the Second World War the garden was substantially neglected. In 1981 the property was purchased by a couple who set about restoring the garden. In 1990 they transferred the property and garden to a trust and charged visitors for admission to the garden. They did not account for output tax on the admission charges. The Commissioners issued a ruling that they were taxable and the trust appealed, contending that the charges qualified for exemption from VAT under *VATA 1994, Sch 9, Group 13*. The tribunal rejected this contention and dismissed the appeal, holding that, 'even allowing for the great age of many of the trees', the garden could not be described as a 'museum', within *Group 13, Item 2(a)*. *Trebah Garden Trust*, LON/98/1372 (VTD 16598).

Cinema—whether supplies exempt under Item 2(b)

[16.11] A company, limited by guarantee and registered as a charity, operated a cinema. Customs issued a ruling that it was required to account for VAT on its supplies. The company appealed, contending that its supplies should be treated as exempt under *VATA 1994, Sch 9, Group 13, Item 2(b)*, as the supply of a right of admission to 'a theatrical, musical or choreographic performance'.

The tribunal rejected this contention and dismissed the appeal, holding that 'the natural interpretation of the phrase "admission to theatrical, musical and choreographic performances of a cultural nature" is that it refers to live performances of theatrical works, whether in the theatre or open air or in some other venue, live concerts and musical shows, and live ballet and dance shows'. The phrase could not be construed as including 'attendance at the cinema to watch a film'. *Chichester Cinema at New Park Ltd*, LON/04/266 (VTD 19344).

[**16.12**] The decision in *Chichester Cinema at New Park Ltd*, **16.11** above, was applied in the similar subsequent case of *The Corn Exchange Newbury*, LON/06/821 (VTD 20268).

Musical performances

[**16.13**] See *Hoffmann*, **22.318** EUROPEAN COMMUNITY LAW.

Striptease—whether a cultural service

[**16.14**] See *Fylkesskattesjefen v Diamond GoGo Bar*, **22.319** EUROPEAN COMMUNITY LAW.

17

Default Interest

The cases in this chapter are arranged under the following headings.

Appeals (VATA 1994, s 84(6))   **17.1**
Calculation of interest   **17.6**
Miscellaneous   **17.13**

Appeals (VATA 1994, s 84(6))

Appeal against interest charge—effect of VATA 1994, s 84(6)

[17.1] On 20 December 1990 the Commissioners issued an assessment charging VAT of £44,158. The trader did not pay the tax until 14 February 1991, and an interest charge was imposed. The trader appealed, contending that the interest charge should be waived because he had queried the assessment with the Commissioners, and had written to the Commissioners stating that he would not pay the tax assessed until he had received further clarification. The Commissioners applied for the appeal to be struck out. The tribunal allowed the application and struck out the appeal. The interest was lawfully payable and what is now *VATA 1994, s 84(6)* provided that the tribunal had no power to vary the amount assessed. *DA Kelly*, LON/91/1887Z (VTD 7941).

[17.2] The decision in *Kelly*, 17.1 above, was applied in the following cases in which appeals against interest charged under what is now *VATA 1994, s 74* were dismissed: *Paro Ltd*, LON/92/1921P (VTD 9414); *Farm Services (Gillingham) Ltd*, LON/92/219X (VTD 9514); *Elesa Ltd*, LON/92/1669A (VTD 10308); *T Probyn*, MAN/92/637 (VTD 10679); *Inspection Equipment Ltd*, 52.111 PENALTIES: MISDECLARATION and *Stratford*, 52.185 PENALTIES: MISDECLARATION.

[17.3] Similar decisions were reached in *Gateway Leisure (Caravan Sales)*, EDN/92/304 (VTD 9689); *W Cowx*, LON/92/1920 (VTD 10037); *DTA Ross & Son*, EDN/93/106 (VTD 10755); *AWTS Transportation International Ltd*, LON/93/560A (VTD 11089); *WM Whitefield & Sons (Builders) Ltd*, EDN/93/40 (VTD 11286); *Hodge Servicing Ltd*, MAN/93/264 (VTD 11561); *PS Bahd (t/a Kingsbury Liquor Mart)*, LON/92/1954A (VTD 11688); *JH Winstone*, LON/93/1527 (VTD 11948); *Jamie plc*, LON/93/1971A (VTD 11962); *Ottoman Textiles Ltd*, MAN/93/1566 (VTD 12795); *Kenmyn Management Services Ltd*, LON/94/1561A (VTD 13765); *VP Bassi (t/a Imperial Wines)*, LON/1321 (VTD 16449); *Capaldi & Co*, EDN/03/81 (VTD 18330), *Thornpark Maintenance Services Ltd*, MAN/06/704 (VTD 20263), and *Fibreglass Direct (Ireland) Ltd*, MAN/07/1320 (VTD 20751).

[17.4] A company appealed against a charge to interest under what is now *VATA 1994, s 74* (originally *FA 1985, s 18*). The Commissioners applied to strike out the appeal on the grounds that there was no appealable matter within what is now *VATA 1994, s 83*. The tribunal chairman (Miss Plumptre, sitting alone) rejected the application, holding that despite the wording of what is now *VATA 1994, s 84(6)*, an appellant 'may wish to take the opportunity to argue that the decision to assess to default interest is incompatible with the principles of European Community law'. *Audiostore Ltd (t/a Stagestruck)*, LON/93/2220A (VTD 11827). (*Notes.* (1) Miss Plumptre's decision discusses *obiter dicta* of the tribunal chairman in *London Borough of Camden*, **17.6** below, but does not refer to any of the cases noted at **17.1** to **17.3** above. (2) For the compatibility of the measures enacted in *FA 1985* with Community law, see the QB decision in *P & O Ferries*, **52.25** PENALTIES: MISDECLARATION, and the tribunal decisions in *The Central YMCA*, **18.616** DEFAULT SURCHARGE, *Impetus Engineering Co (International) Ltd*, **18.617** DEFAULT SURCHARGE, and *W Emmett & Son Ltd*, **52.452** PENALTIES: MISDECLARATION. Miss Plumptre's decision in *Audiostore Ltd* does not refer to any of these four decisions.)

[17.5] A similar decision was reached (again by Miss Plumptre) in a case where a partnership had paid interest under what is now *VATA 1994, s 74* in respect of an assessment which was under appeal, and had subsequently sought repayment of the interest which it had paid. *RSMG*, [1994] VATTR 167 (VTD 11920). (*Note.* For another issue in this case, see **2.256** APPEALS.)

Calculation of interest

Calculation of interest—whether set-off permissible

[17.6] A London Borough Council, which had admitted underdeclarations of tax, appealed against a default interest assessment, contending firstly that the Commissioners had acted unreasonably in raising it, and secondly that the assessment was wrongly computed because it failed to make allowance for unclaimed input tax which should have been set against the output tax on which the interest was charged, and which it had notified to the Commissioners on a form VAT 657. The tribunal rejected the Council's first contention, holding that what is now *VATA 1994, s 83* did not give it jurisdiction to review the Commissioners' decision to impose an interest charge. However, the tribunal upheld the Council's second contention, holding that since the Council had previously notified its unclaimed input tax on a form VAT 657, the input tax unclaimed for a particular accounting period should be set against the output tax assessed for that period in computing the interest charge. (The tribunal also held that only amounts relating to the same prescribed accounting periods could be aggregated, and that any surplus of input tax for a particular period could not be carried forward.) *London Borough of Camden*, [1993] VATTR 73 (VTD 10476).

[17.7] A partnership reclaimed input tax of £16,250 which was attributable to exempt supplies, and the Commissioners issued an assessment to recover the tax. They also imposed an interest charge covering the period from August 1991 to March 1992. In July 1992 the partnership lodged an election to waive exemption in respect of the property to which the input tax related. The Commissioners accepted that, following this election, the partnership was entitled to reclaim input tax of £15,200. The partnership appealed against the charge to default interest, contending that, in computing the charge, the £15,200 which was repayable should be set against the £16,250 which had been assessed, and that interest should only be charged on the balance. The tribunal dismissed the appeal, holding that the interest charge had been correctly calculated and that the subsequent repayment could not be set against the amount of the assessment. *Maybourne & Russell*, LON/93/618A (VTD 11289).

[17.8] The Commissioners discovered that a trader had underdeclared output tax, and issued an assessment, covering the period from 1 April 1989 to 30 April 1991, charging output tax of £5,901, with default interest from 1 April 1990. The trader appealed against the interest charge, contending that he had underclaimed input tax of £3,657, and that this should be set against the output tax in computing the interest charge. He had notified this underclaimed input tax in March 1992, after the issue of the assessment, and the Commissioners had accepted the claim in May 1992. The tribunal dismissed the appeal, distinguishing *London Borough of Camden*, **17.6** above, on the grounds that, in that case, the input tax had previously been notified by a voluntary disclosure on form VAT 657, so that there had been 'an earlier assessment' within what is now *VATA 1994, s 74(1)(a)(ii)*. In the present case, however, there had been no such disclosure at the time when the output tax assessment was issued, so that the effect of what is now *s 74(1)(a)(i)* was that the interest charge applied to the whole of the output tax charged by that assessment, and the input tax of £3,657 could only be set against that output tax from the date in May 1992 when the Commissioners acknowledged their acceptance of the claim to input tax. The tribunal chairman observed that 'there is no provision in the legislation whereby the amount of (an) assessment can be recalculated to take account of a subsequent claim to further credit for input tax in the same accounting periods', and that 'it is unfortunate for the taxpayer that interest is charged by (*VATA 1994, s 74**) not on the amount by which his true liability for the periods in question exceeds the tax declared on his returns but on the whole amount assessed by an assessment made under (*VATA 1994, s 73**)'. *D MacKenzie, LON/92/904X (VTD 11597)*.

[17.9] The decision in *MacKenzie*, **17.8** above, was distinguished in a subsequent case in which a company had notified an underclaim of input tax before the Commissioners issued an assessment to recover underdeclared output tax. The tribunal held that the input tax should be set against the output tax in computing the interest charge. *SGS Holding UK Ltd*, LON/93/2016A (VTD 13018).

[17.10] In January 1992 a company discovered that, for the period ending August 1990, it had underclaimed input tax of £7,235. It submitted a repayment claim, which the Commissioners accepted, and the sum in question was repaid to the company in February. In June 1992 a VAT officer discovered that the company had underdeclared output tax of £15,209 for the period ending August 1990. The Commissioners raised a default interest charge on this amount. The company appealed, contending that the input tax of £7,235 should be set against the output tax of £15,209 in calculating the interest charge. The tribunal accepted this contention and allowed the appeal, applying *London Borough of Camden*, 17.6 above, and observing that a Customs' Press Release of 7 September 1994 had stated that 'in general Customs will not in future seek to assess interest where it does not represent commercial restitution'. Furthermore, to charge default interest on the gross amount of output tax without taking account of the underclaimed input tax would be contrary to the principles enunciated by Lord Goff of Chieveley in *Woolwich Equitable Building Society v CIR*, HL [1992] STC 657. *R & N Miller Ltd*, LON/92/2297 (VTD 13236).

Calculation of interest disputed

[17.11] In an appeal against default interest, the tribunal chairman held that the Commissioners had not provided sufficient details of how the interest was calculated, and adjourned the hearing with a direction that the Commissioners should, within 28 days, provide 'full details in a form readily understood of the calculation of default interest'. The Commissioners failed to comply with the direction, and at the resumed hearing the tribunal formally allowed the appeal. *AR Waller & Associates*, [1993] VATTR 402 (VTD 10712).

Date on which interest ceases to run

[17.12] In 1991 a builder reclaimed input tax in respect of materials purchased for a house which he intended building for himself. Following a control visit in January 1992, the Commissioners issued an assessment to recover the tax. In April 1992 the builder submitted a claim for the tax to be treated as repayable under what is now *VATA 1994, s 35*. Meanwhile the Commissioners took proceedings to enforce payment of the tax charged by the assessment, and the builder paid the tax assessed in May 1992. His claim for the tax to be refunded under *s 35** was accepted, and the tax was repaid to him in June. The Commissioners demanded default interest on the tax charged by the assessment, and the builder appealed, contending that the charge was unfair since the officer who made the control visit in January 1992 had not told him that he would have to claim the tax under *s 35**, and that if the officer had told him this, he could have reclaimed the tax earlier. The tribunal allowed his appeal in part, holding that he had been 'misinformed as to the correct procedure for reclaiming input tax on the building of his own house, and that as a result, the repayment of that input tax was unreasonably delayed', and that had it not been for this, the tax could have been repaid in April. The tribunal held that, in the circumstances, the default interest should cease to run after 31 March 1992. *NC Stanley*, MAN/92/1319 (VTD 10857).

Miscellaneous

Company reclaiming input tax attributable to partnership

[17.13] A company reclaimed input tax of £11,000 in its return for the period ending November 1991 which was in fact attributable to an associated partnership. The company's accountant discovered this in March 1992, and the company notified the Commissioners accordingly on 20 March. In the meantime, the company had claimed and received a repayment of £7,500, when it should have paid output tax of £3,500 to the Commissioners. The Commissioners issued an assessment charging default interest on the company from January 1992 to 21 April 1992. The company appealed, contending that the interest charge was unjust as there had been no net loss of tax. The tribunal dismissed the appeal, observing that the company and the partnership were separate entities and that the interest had been computed in accordance with what is now *VATA 1994, s 74*. *Terracopia Ltd*, MAN/92/1283 (VTD 11341).

Partnership failing to account for tax on payments from companies

[17.14] In an Isle of Man case, an accountancy partnership failed to account for tax on payments from associated companies. The Isle of Man Treasury imposed an interest charge. The partnership appealed, contending that the charge should be waived because the companies could have reclaimed the amounts in question as input tax, so that there had been no net loss of tax. The tribunal dismissed the appeal, holding that the interest was lawfully due and that neither the Treasury nor the tribunal had discretion to waive it. *Holdsworth & Co v Isle of Man Treasury*, MAN/93/275 (VTD 12480). (*Note.* See now the Commissioners' News Release 34/94, dated 7 September 1994, indicating that Customs will no longer charge interest in such circumstances.)

Incorrect reclaim of input tax following misdirection by VAT officer

[17.15] A company which traded as car dealers reclaimed input tax on certain transactions without holding VAT invoices. It was accepted that this was largely due to incorrect advice given by a VAT officer in 1989. In the circumstances the Commissioners did not impose a penalty under what is now *VATA 1994, s 63*. However, they did issue an assessment to recover the net amount underdeclared. They also imposed an interest charge under what is now *VATA 1994, s 74*. The company appealed against the interest charge. The tribunal dismissed the appeal, holding that there had been a temporary loss of tax to the Crown, that the default interest was lawfully due, and that the Commissioners could not be estopped from collecting it. *RC & R Harding (t/a Tolcarne Motors)*, LON/92/986X (VTD 11809).

Assessment to interest covering multiple accounting periods

[17.16] In March 1996 the Commissioners issued an assessment on a trader, covering the period from August 1988 to May 1994. They subsequently issued an assessment charging interest. The trader appealed, contending firstly that the assessment to interest was invalid because it was 'global' and did not identify the separate accounting periods to which the interest related, and alternatively *VATA 1994, s 74(3)* should be interpreted as meaning that interest should be restricted to the assessments made in respect of the last three years, rather than being the interest on the whole sum outstanding calculated for the last three years. The tribunal rejected these contentions and dismissed the appeal. Applying the CA decision in *Bassimeh*, **50.3** PENALTIES: EVASION OF TAX, 'to subdivide this total figure into 18 quarterly figures and then aggregate them so as to reproduce the same figure' would be 'entirely otiose and unnecessary'. With regard to the trader's alternative contention, the effect of *VATA 1994, s 74(3)* was that the interest was chargeable on the whole debt but limited to the amount in respect of the last three years. *MS Shokar (t/a Manor Fish Bar)*, [1998] VATDR 301 (VTD 15674).

Delay in producing evidence of zero-rating

[17.17] A company made supplies of goods which qualified for zero-rating under *VATA 1994, s 30(8)*. However, initially the company failed to provide the documentary evidence of removal required by *Notice No 703*, and the Commissioners issued an assessment charging tax on the supplies, together with a charge to interest under *VATA 1994, s 74(1)*. Subsequently the Commissioners accepted that the goods had been removed from the UK, and withdrew the assessment. However, they refused to withdraw the interest charge. The company appealed. The tribunal allowed the appeal but the Ch D reversed this decision and upheld the assessment to interest. Lightman J held that 'when it is open to the taxable person to establish that his supply is zero-rated but he fails to do so, the taxable person and the Commissioners are to treat the supply as standard-rated and the Commissioners are empowered to make an assessment imposing an obligation to pay VAT and interest on this basis'. The subsequent satisfaction of the conditions for zero-rating did not have retrospective effect, and 'the satisfaction of the liability under the assessment of VAT in no way discharges or undermines the assessment for interest. The liability for interest accrued (as it could only accrue) during the period of the liability for VAT. On satisfaction of the liability for VAT, there could be no further accrual of interest, but the liability for accrued interest continues undisturbed. The satisfaction of the conditions for zero-rating gives rise to no separate credit in respect of the liability for accrued interest.' Accordingly, the assessment for interest continued to be enforceable. The CA upheld the Ch D decision. Pill LJ held that 'the Commissioners have the power to make an assessment, which carries interest, and that power was validly exercised'. Accordingly, there was 'no basis for holding that the assessment loses its validity by reason of the subsequent meeting of prescribed conditions by the taxpayer'. He also observed that there was 'an incentive to the keeping of good records; zero-rating from the start, which good records permits (*sic*), will prevent the liability to interest which arose in this case'. *Musashi Autoparts Europe Ltd v C & E Commrs*, CA 2003, [2004] STC 220; [2004] EWCA Civ 1738.

[17.18] The decision in *Musashi Autoparts Europe Ltd*, **17.17** above, was applied in the similar subsequent cases of *L Di Tondo (t/a Partners Associates)*, MAN/03/302 (VTD 18858) and *Aleris Recycling (Swansea) Ltd*, [2010] UKFTT 341 (TC), TC00623.

Assessment reduced on appeal—computation of interest

[17.19] The Commissioners issued an assessment for the period ending 31 July 1999, charging tax of £4,112. The company appealed, contending *inter alia* that one of the relevant supplies was zero-rated. The tribunal accepted this contention and reduced the assessment by £773. The Commissioners had also issued a notice of assessment to interest, and counsel representing them at the hearing contended that interest should be charged on this £773 from the original due date to the date of the hearing, contending that the effect of the decision in *Musashi Autoparts Europe Ltd*, **17.17** above, was that interest remained due until the date of the hearing 'because the evidence to justify zero-rating was not produced until the hearing'. The tribunal rejected this contention and held that no interest was due on the £773. The tribunal observed that the Commissioners had put forward a 'surprising proposition' which appeared 'difficult to reconcile with the principle of proportionality under Community law or the Human Rights Convention'. The tribunal distinguished *Musashi* on the basis that the decision in that case 'turned on the requirement in (*VATA 1994, s 30(8)(b)*) that conditions specified by the Commissioners in regulations for zero-rating exports to other Member States be met. The conditions required valid commercial documentary evidence that the goods had been removed. There is no equivalent condition for zero-rating a supply in the course of construction as in the present case. The decision in *Musashi* does not in any way affect the general principle that if an assessment is reduced or withdrawn, the interest based on the assessment must be adjusted accordingly. The interest stands or falls with the assessment'. The tribunal also observed that the Commissioners' contention contravened their statement in *Notice 700/43, para 2.9* that 'if, as a result of the reconsideration or appeal the original assessment is reduced or withdrawn, the amount of interest charged to you will be recalculated and similarly reduced or withdrawn, as appropriate'. *Richford Designs Ltd*, LON/02/1057 (VTD 18639).

Duplicate invoices—whether interest charge unreasonable

[17.20] See *Callaway*, **3.30** ASSESSMENT.

Other cases

[17.21] There have been a number of other cases, which appear to raise no point of general interest, in which appeals against assessments to default interest have been dismissed. In the interests of space, such cases are not reported individually in this book.

18

Default Surcharge

The cases in this chapter are arranged under the following headings.

The surcharge liability notice (VATA 1994, s 59(2,3))	**18.1**
Computation of the surcharge (VATA 1994, s 59(4,5))	**18.18**
Despatch of return and payment to the Commissioners (VATA 1994, s 59(7)(a))	**18.42**
Whether a 'reasonable excuse' (VATA 1994, s 59(7)(b))	
Computer problems	**18.70**
Illness or bereavement	**18.87**
Pregnancy and childbirth	**18.144**
Loss or unavailability of key personnel	**18.164**
Loss, unavailability or inadequacy of records	**18.239**
Change of accounting dates	**18.292**
Insufficiency of funds (VATA 1994, s 71(1)(a))	**18.312**
Cheque dishonoured or incorrectly made out	**18.384**
Misleading advice from Customs	**18.433**
Return form not available	**18.465**
Sole trader—absence from usual address	**18.477**
Matrimonial and domestic problems	**18.489**
Difficulty in computing liability	**18.500**
Payment by credit transfer or BACS	**18.513**
Other cases	**18.550**
Material defaults (VATA 1994, s 59(8))	**18.614**
Validity of the surcharge	**18.616**

GENERAL NOTE

There have been a very large number of appeals against default surcharges. All appeals to the Courts are summarised individually. However, unsuccessful appeals to tribunals are only summarised where the case appears to raise a point of general importance.

The surcharge liability notice (VATA 1994, s 59(2,3))

Receipt of surcharge liability notice disputed

[18.1] A company appealed against a default surcharge, contending that it had not received the relevant surcharge liability notice. The tribunal allowed the company's appeal, holding that the surcharge liability notice had not been served and thus the default surcharge was invalid. The QB upheld this decision, holding that the whole scheme of default surcharges was dependent upon service of the surcharge liability notice. *C & E Commrs v Medway Draughting & Technical Services Ltd*, QB [1989] STC 346.

[18.2] A similar decision was reached in a case heard in the QB with the preceding case. *C & E Commrs v Adplates Offset Ltd*, QB [1989] STC 346.

[18.3] There have been a large number of cases in which appellants have claimed that they have not received the relevant surcharge liability notice. Such decisions turn entirely on whether the tribunal accepts or rejects the appellant's evidence on the balance of probabilities. In the interests of space, such cases are not reported individually in this book.

Whether surcharge liability notice withdrawn

[18.4] In July 1987 a company received a surcharge liability notice indicating that its return for the period ending 30 April 1987 had not been received. It telephoned its local VAT office, to state that the return must have been received because the cheque which had accompanied it had been banked. (In fact the return had been received after the due date, so that the company had incurred a potential surcharge liability although the wording of the notice was inaccurate and misleading.) A VAT officer advised the company that there had been an industrial dispute at the VAT Central Unit which had resulted in a backlog of work, and advised the company to destroy the notice as it had been issued in error. In fact the company filed the notice. It submitted its next return late, and a surcharge was subsequently imposed. The company appealed, contending that the surcharge liability notice had been withdrawn, so that the surcharge was invalid. The tribunal accepted this contention and allowed the company's appeal. It was implicit in what is now *VATA 1994, s 76(9)* that a surcharge could be withdrawn, and it followed that a surcharge liability notice could also be withdrawn. The effect of the company's conversation with the VAT officer had been to withdraw the surcharge liability notice. *Montreux Fabrics Ltd*, [1988] VATTR 71 (VTD 2673).

[18.5] A company submitted its return for the period ending 31 August 1987 in early October. On 21 October the Commissioners issued an estimated default surcharge. The company, knowing that the return and payment were in the post, took no action. In April 1988 the Commissioners issued a revised surcharge notice based on the figures in the company's return. The company's director telephoned the local VAT office to state that he had paid the tax in October, and was told by a VAT officer that he should ignore the notice and throw it away, which he did. Subsequently the Commissioners continued to seek payment of the surcharge and the company lodged a formal appeal. The tribunal allowed the appeal, holding on the evidence that the surcharge had been withdrawn by the officer who had discussed it with the company in April 1988. *Graham Fredericks Ltd*, LON/88/201 (VTD 3304).

[18.6] A similar decision, applying *dicta* in *Montreux Fabrics Ltd*, **18.4** above, was reached in *GB White (t/a Chiffon Couture)*, LON/89/894Z (VTD 4785).

Validity of surcharge liability notice disputed

[18.7] A company's return for the period ending 31 March 1987 was submitted on 12 May 1987 and received by the VAT Central Unit on

18 May 1987. At the time the return was received there was an industrial dispute at the VAT Central Unit. On 10 July 1987 a surcharge liability notice was issued to the company. The notice stated that the return for the period ending 31 March 1987 had not been received. Subsequently the company submitted another return late and a default surcharge was imposed. The company appealed, contending that the surcharge liability notice was invalid since it had incorrectly stated that the return for the period ending 31 March 1987 had not been received, instead of stating that the return had been received late. The tribunal accepted this contention and allowed the appeal, holding that the effect of the inaccurate wording of the notice was that it could not be considered as a valid surcharge liability notice. *Coleman Machines Ltd*, MAN/88/437 (VTD 3196).

[18.8] A tribunal had held that two companies had a reasonable excuse for a first default because their bookkeeper had been ill, but held that there was no reasonable excuse for subsequent defaults. The companies appealed against the surcharges imposed in respect of these defaults, contending that, by virtue of what is now *VATA 1994, s 59(7)*, the effect of allowing the appeal against the first default was that the remaining surcharges should be held to be ineffective. The tribunal rejected this contention and upheld the surcharges, holding that 'the consequence of the deemed non-service is no more than that one of the three requirements specified' for the application of *s 59(4)* * had not been satisfied. It was not 'required to treat the surcharge period specified' in the notice as 'not having been notified' to the appellant. *RW Joinery (Stockport) Ltd*, MAN/88/830; *RW Construction (Stockport) Ltd*, MAN/88/831 (VTD 3761).

[18.9] A similar decision was reached in a subsequent case where the tribunal held that the fact that a reasonable excuse had been established for the first default did not render the subsequent form VAT 164 ineffective. The wording of the form VAT 164 was adequate to take effect either as a surcharge liability notice within *VATA 1994, s 59(2)(b)* or as an extension notice within *VATA 1994, s 59(3)*. *Goldfinch Transport Ltd*, [1996] VATDR 484 (VTD 14145).

[18.10] A company changed its name without notifying the Commissioners. It received a surcharge liability notice addressed in its former name, and appealed against a subsequent default surcharge, contending that the notice had been invalid as it had been issued in the company's former name. The tribunal dismissed the company's appeal, finding that the company's directors had not been misled and holding that the company was at fault in not having notified the Commissioners of its change of name. *Philbor Motors Ltd*, LON/90/454X (VTD 5388).

[18.11] A similar decision was reached in *Street Magazine Ltd*, MAN/93/142 (VTD 10991).

[18.12] In a case where a surcharge liability notice had not been received, but surcharge extension notices, issued subsequently, had been received, the tribunal held that the extension notices were invalid. Applying *dicta* in *RW Joinery (Stockport) Ltd*, 18.8 above, a surcharge extension notice remained valid if the original notice had been received, even if there were subsequently held to have been a reasonable excuse for the initial default. However, since a surcharge extension notice only indicated the end of a surcharge liability period, and did not state the beginning of that period, it was not valid in a case where an appellant had not actually received the initial notice, and thus had not been notified of the date on which the period in question began. *Dow Engineering*, MAN/90/657 (VTD 5771).

[18.13] Similar decisions were reached in *Eidographics Ltd*, [1991] VATTR 449 (VTD 6788); *Acer Engineering Ltd*, MAN/91/1063 (VTD 7536); *BB Keane*, LON/92/786X (VTD 9131) and *Sig Video Gems Ltd*, LON/94/236P (VTD 12486).

[18.14] A trader had submitted four successive returns late, but had satisfied the tribunal that he had a reasonable excuse for the first default, since he had never received the appropriate blank return form (see **18.465** below). He contended that, because of this, the effect of what is now *VATA 1994, s 59(7)* was that the first surcharge liability notice was deemed not to have been served, that the extension notices issued in respect of the next default were therefore invalid, and that all the surcharges should be discharged. Customs considered that the effect of *s 59(7)** was that the second default fell to be treated as the first default, the third default as the second, and the fourth default as the third, so that the trader remained liable to a 5% surcharge. The tribunal allowed the trader's appeal, holding that the effect of *s 59(7)** was to deem the notice in question never to have been received, and disapproving *dicta* of the tribunal in *RW Joinery (Stockport) Ltd*, **18.8** above. *S Robinson*, [1991] VATTR 440 (VTD 6267). (*Notes.* (1) Compare *Dow Engineering*, **18.12** above, in which *RW Joinery (Stockport) Ltd*, **18.8** above, was approved and applied. (2) Customs subsequently amended the wording of the surcharge liability notice to include a statement that 'if no surcharge period has been notified to you previously, the period beginning on the date of this notice'is 'hereby specified as a surcharge period'. (3) The decision here was not followed in the subsequent case of *Goldfinch Transport Ltd*, **18.9** above, where the tribunal held that the wording of the form VAT 164 was adequate to have effect either as a surcharge liability notice within *VATA 1994, s 59(2)(b)* or as an extension notice within *VATA 1994, s 59(3)*.)

[18.15] The decision in *Robinson*, **18.14** above, was applied in *Pennington Lee*, **18.551** below, in which there was held to be a reasonable excuse for the first default. (*Note.* The decision does not discuss the conflict between the decision reached in *Robinson*, **18.14** above, and those reached in *RW Joinery (Stockport) Ltd*, **18.8** above, and *Dow Engineering*, **18.12** above. See now the note following *Robinson*, **18.14** above.)

[18.16] An appeal was allowed in a case where a surcharge liability notice issued in July 1991 indicated that the surcharge liability period ended in May 1991 (this being a typing error for May 1992). The tribunal held that the notice was invalid. *In Style Pleaters*, LON/92/585 (VTD 7700).

Appeal against SLN before surcharge incurred

[18.17] See *Expert Systems Design Ltd*, **2.43** APPEALS; *The Fraser Bruce Group Ltd*, **2.44** APPEALS; *Auld*, **2.45** APPEALS, and *Castrue Ltd*, **2.45** APPEALS.

Computation of the surcharge (VATA 1994, s 59(4,5))

Whether surcharges to be recomputed

[18.18] A company (B) failed to submit several VAT returns. Customs issued estimated assessments and imposed surcharges computed on the basis of the tax charged by the assessments. Subsequently B submitted the returns, showing a higher liability than Customs had assessed. Customs therefore withdrew the original surcharges and replaced them with increased surcharges computed on the basis of the tax shown in the returns. B appealed, contending that the revised surcharges were invalid. The tribunal rejected this contention and dismissed the appeal, holding that the issue of the revised surcharges was authorised by what is now *VATA 1994, s 59(4)*. *Bill Hennessey Associates Ltd*, LON/87/640 & 709 (VTD 2656).

Whether cancellation equivalent to annulment

[18.19] A company (G) which had received a surcharge liability notice in July 1987 did not submit its return for the period ending 30 September 1987. In November 1987 Customs issued an estimated assessment for the period, together with a surcharge computed at the rate of 5% of the tax charged by the estimated assessment. In December 1987 G submitted the return, showing that a repayment was due to it for that period. Accordingly Customs cancelled the surcharge. G submitted its return for the period ending 31 December 1987 seven weeks late, and Customs imposed a surcharge computed at the rate of 10% of the tax shown on the return. G appealed, contending that, since the previous surcharge had been cancelled, the surcharge should have been computed at the rate of 5% rather than 10%. The tribunal rejected this contention and dismissed the appeal. The words 'may assess' in what is now *VATA 1994, s 76* gave Customs a discretion. The fact that a surcharge of the statutory minimum had not been imposed did not mean that the default should be left out of account for the purposes of what is now *VATA 1994, s 59(5)*. *GB Techniques Ltd*, [1988] VATTR 95 (VTD 3121).

[18.20] The decision in *GB Techniques Ltd*, **18.19** above, was applied in the similar case of *Freewheeler Co Ltd*, MAN/89/668 (VTD 4544).

[18.21] A similar decision was reached in *Conference Staging Ltd*, LON/93/1141P (VTD 11434).

VAT office allocating payments to previous surcharges

[18.22] A company (C) which had incurred two default surcharges made lump sum payments totalling £9,000 in December 1987 in respect of its VAT liabilities. The local VAT office allocated the payments to the surcharge arrears, and did not allocate any of the payments to C's liability for the period ending 30 November 1987. A further surcharge was consequently imposed in respect of that period. C appealed, contending that its payments should have been used to clear its current liability first, with only the excess of the payments over the current liability being set against the surcharges. The tribunal accepted this contention and allowed the appeal. *Clifford Construction Ltd*, LON/89/141X (VTD 3929). (*Note.* (1) For another issue in this case, see **18.441** below.)

[18.23] Similar decisions were reached in *Kam (Stationery) Ltd*, LON/90/1289 (VTD 5897) and *Crusader Line Ltd (t/a Spaghetti Western)*, LON/93/2871A (VTD 12439, 12568).

[18.24] A contrasting decision was reached in a case where a trader (B) had incurred arrears totalling £1,771. He paid this amount on 14 August 1990, but then failed to pay his liability for the period ending 31 July 1990 by the due date. Customs imposed a further surcharge, and B appealed, contending that the payment which he had made on 14 August should be set firstly against his liability for the period ending 31 July, and that only the balance should be set against the previous arrears. The tribunal rejected this contention and dismissed his appeal, holding that the payment made on 14 August should be set against the previous arrears, rather than against the liability for the period ending 31 July. *DC Berry*, LON/94/1163 (VTD 13380).

[18.25] An appeal was dismissed in a case where a firm of solicitors, which had incurred eight successive defaults, contended that payments which it had made should be reallocated to clear its current tax liabilities, rather than being set against the surcharges. The tribunal chairman observed that 'the appellants were a firm of solicitors and were in a position to advise themselves either to appeal against the penalties or to pay the outstanding tax first before the penalties'. On the evidence, the Commissioners had not insisted 'upon the payment of the penalties before the tax; they accepted cheques sent to them by the appellants' and applied them in 'a reasonable way in the circumstances of this case'. *Playford & Pope*, LON/95/1151P (VTD 13989).

[18.26] A company appealed against five default surcharges, contending that Customs had acted unfairly in allocating payments which it had made to its oldest arrears, rather than to its current liability. The tribunal rejected this contention and dismissed the appeal, holding that 'the Commissioners were entitled to allocate the payments towards the oldest debts'. *APUK Ltd*, MAN/98/345 (VTD 15796). (*Note.* For another issue in this case, see **18.232** below.)

[18.27] Similar decisions were reached in *Bryan Keenan & Co*, EDN/01/22 (VTD 17407) and *Barclays Bros Ltd*, EDN/01/11 (VTD 17507).

Submission of cheque with words and figures differing

[18.28] A company sent a cheque for its quarterly VAT payment on which the amount in words was correctly stated but the amount in figures was incorrect. The bank returned the cheque unpaid, endorsed 'words and figures differ'. The Commissioners imposed a default surcharge but the tribunal allowed the company's appeal, holding that the bank was wrong not to honour the cheque for the amount stated in words. Under the *Bills of Exchange Act 1882, s 9(2)*, a cheque on which the words and figures differ is valid for the amount stated in words. *Covercraft Ltd*, MAN/88/791 (VTD 3558).

[18.29] A trader had a quarterly VAT liability of £5,545.98. He submitted a cheque made out for this amount in figures, but for only £5,545.00 in words.

The cheque was dishonoured by his bank and the Commissioners imposed a default surcharge of £831.89, calculated at the appropriate rate of 15%. The trader appealed, contending that he had a reasonable excuse. The tribunal rejected this contention, holding that 'mere carelessness' could not constitute a reasonable excuse. However, the tribunal held that, under the *Bills of Exchange Act 1882, ss 9(2), 72*, where there is a discrepancy between the words and figures on a cheque, the amount in words is the amount payable. Consequently the cheque in question was a valid payment of £5,545.00, and should have been honoured by the bank accordingly. It followed that the trader was in default only to the extent of 98 pence, so that the surcharge should be reduced to the statutory minimum of £30. *TG Mather (t/a Economy Appliances)*, LON/88/581Y (VTD 3829).

Submission of cheque with amount in words missing

[18.30] A partnership submitted a cheque on which the amount in figures was correctly stated, but the amount in words was missing. Customs returned the cheque to the partnership for amendment without presenting it, and imposed a surcharge. The tribunal allowed the partnership's appeal, holding that the cheque was a valid cheque within *Bills of Exchange Act 1882, s 3(1)*, notwithstanding that the amount of the cheque was only stated in figures and not in words. *Exchange Car Hire*, [1992] VATTR 430 (VTD 9343).

Surcharge imposed but no tax due

[18.31] A company submitted a late return, showing tax payable to the Commissioners, and a default surcharge was imposed. Subsequently the company's accountant discovered that he had made a mistake in the return and that a repayment was due. The Commissioners accepted that the original return was incorrect but refused to discharge the surcharge. The tribunal allowed the company's appeal, holding that 'it cannot be appropriate to levy a surcharge on a figure which does not in truth amount to a figure for outstanding tax'. *Nationwide Hygiene Supplies Ltd*, EDN/90/128 (VTD 5389).

[18.32] A trader persistently submitted returns late. The Commissioners issued estimated assessments and imposed surcharges. Subsequently the trader submitted returns showing that his liability was less than the amounts assessed, and that, viewed as a whole, his account with the Commissioners was in credit. The tribunal allowed his appeal against the surcharges, holding that there was no 'outstanding VAT' for the purposes of *VATA 1994, s 59(4)(b)*. *M Bruce*, MAN/99/253 (VTD 16660).

Change of company name

[18.33] A company (S) changed its name in 1988. Prior to its change of name, it had submitted a return after the due date. Its next two returns were also submitted late, and Customs imposed a surcharge. S appealed, contending that, because of its change of name, the first default should not be taken into account. The tribunal rejected this contention and dismissed the appeal. *Speciality Restaurants plc*, LON/92/12Y (VTD 10310).

Return period ending on last day of surcharge period

[18.34] A company (M) submitted its return for the period ending 30 April 1992 late. Customs issued a surcharge liability notice, with the surcharge period extending until 30 April 1993. M's return for the period ending on that date was also submitted late and Customs imposed a surcharge. M appealed, contending that the surcharge was invalid because the two defaults were more than 52 weeks apart. The tribunal rejected this contention and dismissed the appeal, holding that the accounting period ending 30 April 1993 ended within the surcharge period so that the surcharge had been correctly imposed. *Mountfield Software Ltd*, LON/94/865P (VTD 12816).

[18.35] See also *Sageworth Ltd*, **18.454** below, and *Shute*, **18.452** below.

Surcharge imposed at excessive rate

[18.36] A surcharge was reduced in a case where the tribunal found that the Commissioners had levied it at 15% rather than 10%, as a result of an error in programming the computer at the VAT Central Unit at Southend. *Darci Shoes Ltd*, LON/94/2732 (VTD 13228). (*Note.* See VAT Information Sheet 7/95, issued on 10 April 1995.)

[18.37] A similar decision was reached in *P Sullivan*, [1995] VATDR 85 (VTD 13245).

Effect of invalidity of previous surcharge assessment

[18.38] Customs issued a surcharge assessment for October 1994 to a company (D) which made monthly returns and had paid its liability after the due date. The surcharge was computed at the rate of 2%, but the assessment wrongly stated that it covered the three-month period from 1 August to 31 October. D also paid its November liability after the due date, and Customs issued a surcharge assessment imposing a 5% surcharge. D appealed against the surcharges, contending that it had a reasonable excuse. In October 1995 Customs, having discovered that the October 1994 assessment was expressed to be for a three-month period instead of a one-month period, wrote to D withdrawing it and purporting to reduce the November 1995 assessment from 5% to 2%. The tribunal allowed D's appeal against the November 1994 assessment, holding that, because the October 1994 assessment was accepted by Customs as invalid, 'it followed that the Commissioners could not "determine" the November 1994 surcharge assessment as 5% and that assessment was accordingly void'. The assessment could not be reduced either through *VATA 1994, s 76(9)* or through 'the Commissioners' inherent power to reduce assessments'. The tribunal held that 'each liability occasioned by each default is separate' and that 'only properly notified defaults for a prescribed accounting period count (and they drop out of account if a reasonable excuse defence is sustained)'. The power to reduce an assessment could not 'be exercised where the assessment is ineffective and so void *ab initio*'. (The tribunal observed that 'this is different from the position that obtains where a taxable person establishes the defence of reasonable excuse under *VATA 1994, s 59(7)*; the *subsection* itself appears to contemplate that the specified percentages for subsequent defaults will be adjusted accordingly'.) *Dow Chemical Company Ltd*, [1996] VATDR 52 (VTD 13954). (*Note.* See now, however, the subsequent decision in *Juppon Trading Ltd*, 18.41 below.)

[18.39] The decision in *Dow Chemical Company Ltd*, 18.38 above, was applied in a subsequent case where a previous surcharge had been withdrawn after HMRC accepted that the appellant company had had no tax liability for the period. The tribunal held that 'assessments can be amended when information not known to HMRC at the time they made the assessment comes to light, such as a taxpayer later establishing a defence of reasonable excuse to a default which counted towards the specified percentage. But assessments which were always wrong cannot be so amended and HMRC's only course would be to issue a new assessment if time limits permitted.' *Ideal Shopping Direct plc v HMRC*, [2009] UKFTT 136 (TC), TC00104.

Rate of surcharge reduced—validity of assessment

[18.40] A company appealed against a default surcharge, contending that the surcharge was invalid because a previous surcharge had been withdrawn. The tribunal rejected this contention, holding that 'where a taxable person establishes the defence of reasonable excuse under *VATA 1994, s 59(7)*, the *subsection* itself appears to contemplate that the specified percentages for subsequent defaults will be adjusted accordingly'. *SSR Group Services Ltd*, LON/98/1506 (VTD 16033).

[18.41] The decision in *Dow Chemical Company Ltd*, 18.38 above, was distinguished in a subsequent case where the tribunal dismissed a company's appeal against a surcharge, holding that while a surcharge assessment was invalid if it was based on an incorrect specified percentage, a surcharge assessment was capable of amendment if the specified percentage was prima facie correct at the time of issue. The tribunal held that 'assessments can be amended when information not available to HMRC at the time they made the assessment comes to light, such as a taxpayer later establishing a defence of reasonable excuse to a default which counted towards the specified percentage. But assessments which were always wrong cannot be so amended and HMRC's only course would be to issue a new assessment if time limits permitted'. The tribunal also held that there was 'a general principle that an assessment using the wrong specified percentage is not wrong from the start and can be later amended to correct the specified percentage if at the time it was made, it was made on a proper count of what appeared to be actual defaults – prima facie defaults – even though the taxpayer later shows some defence to the assessment of a penalty in respect of one or more of these prima facie defaults'. On the evidence, the tribunal held that the disputed surcharge assessment 'was not wrong from the start and could be and was validly amended'. *Juppon Trading Ltd v HMRC*, [2009] UKFTT 98 (TC), TC00066.

Despatch of return and payment to the Commissioners (VATA 1994, s 59(7)(a))

Return posted one day before due date

[18.42] In a case where a return was posted on the day prior to the due date, but was not received until the following week, the tribunal dismissed the company's appeal, holding that it was not reasonable to expect the return to be received within the time limit. *R Walia Opticians (London) Ltd*, LON/90/670Y (VTD 5085). (*Note.* Customs subsequently stated in correspondence that they will accept that a return has been posted in time if it was posted at least one working day prior to the due date—see *1991 STI 389*. However, despite this apparent assurance, the tribunals have continued to uphold surcharges in such circumstances in appeals where the Commissioners' representative has not drawn this statement to the attention of the tribunal. See, for example, *Nicholls*, **18.43** below; *Kingdom Amusements*, **18.43** below; *Michelotti*, **18.43** below; *Ultimate Leisure (Scotland) Ltd*, **18.43** below, and *La Reine (Limoges Porcelain) Ltd*, **18.45** below.)

[18.43] Similar decisions were reached in *JF Stockham*, LON/89/220Z (VTD 5178); *AGH Edgecox*, MAN/90/450 (VTD 5334); *Sonnat Ltd*, MAN/90/327 (VTD 5436); *Crimpers Ltd*, LON/89/592Z (VTD 5466); *Artinville Ltd*, LON/90/729X (VTD 5515); *Flame Cheater Ltd*, LON/90/1420Y (VTD 5685); *DT Nicholls*, LON/92/616 (VTD 7960); *Kingdom Amusements*, EDN/92/40 (VTD 8872); *SL Michelotti*, LON/93/1284 (VTD 11551) and *Ultimate Leisure (Scotland) Ltd*, EDN/03/113 (VTD 18573).

[18.44] A similar decision was reached in a case where the return was posted two days before the due date (which was a Sunday). *Silverdale Transport Ltd*, LON/90/752 (VTD 5192). (*Note.* The decision here was not followed, and was implicitly disapproved, in the subsequent case of *Halstead Motor Company*, **18.47** below. The decision here was made before Customs' published statement reported at *1991 STI 389*, for which see the note following *R Walia (Opticians) Ltd*, **18.42** above.)

[18.45] An appeal was dismissed in a case where the due date was Sunday 31 May 1992 and the tribunal found that the return had been posted at Bournemouth Post Office before 7 p.m. on Friday 29 May. The tribunal chairman held that the return had not been 'posted early enough that it was reasonable to expect that it would be received by Customs on or before Sunday 31 May'. *La Reine (Limoges Porcelain) Ltd*, LON/92/2842P (VTD 10468). (*Note.* The decision here was not followed, and was implicitly disapproved, in the subsequent case of *Halstead Motor Company*, **18.47** below. The decision here fails to refer to Customs' published statement reported at *1991 STI 389*, for which see the note following *R Walia (Opticians) Ltd*, **18.42** above.)

[18.46] A similar decision was reached in *JG Brolly & Bros. Ltd*, EDN/94/83 (VTD 13762). (*Note.* Compare *Halstead Motor Company Ltd*, **18.47** below, which was not referred to in this decision.)

[18.47] An appeal was allowed in a case where the tribunal found that a return for the period ending 30 June 1994 was posted in the early afternoon of Friday 29 July. At the hearing, and despite Customs' statement reproduced at *1991 STI 389* (see the note following *R Walia Opticians (London) Ltd*, **18.42** above), the representative of Customs' Solicitor's Office contended that because the due date was Saturday 30 July, the company had not sent it 'at such a time and in such a manner that it was reasonable to expect it to be received by the Commissioners within the appropriate time limit'. The tribunal rejected this contention, declining to follow the decisions in *Silverdale Transport Ltd*, **18.44** above, and *La Reine (Limoges Porcelain) Ltd*, **18.45** above, and observing that Customs were not complying with their previous statement reproduced at *1991 STI 389*. The tribunal held that, by posting the return before the last collection on Friday 29 July, the company had 'despatched the return at such a time and in such a manner that it was reasonable to expect that it would be delivered at Southend on Saturday 30 July and be received by the Commissioners within the appropriate time limit'. *Halstead Motor Company*, [1995] VATDR 201 (VTD 13373).

Return not submitted until due date

[**18.48**] There have been a large number of cases in which tribunals have dismissed appeals against default surcharges after finding that the relevant return had not been posted until the due date, and holding that this failed to meet the requirements of what is now *VATA 1994, s 59(7)(a)*. In the interests of space, such cases are not reported individually in this book.

Date of posting disputed

[**18.49**] There have been a very large number of cases in which appellants have claimed that the relevant return was posted before the due date, although postmarked and received after the due date. Such decisions turn entirely on the particular facts of the case, and on whether the tribunal accepts or rejects the appellant's evidence on the balance of probabilities. In the interests of space, such decisions are not reported individually in this book.

Receipt of return denied by Commissioners

[**18.50**] An appeal was allowed in a case where a company's managing director gave evidence that he had personally delivered the return in question to the Woking VAT office before the due date. *AP Heather Ltd*, LON/89/1134Z (VTD 4376).

[**18.51**] Similar decisions were reached in *J Sheard*, MAN/90/783 (VTD 6318) and *Harleyford Estate Ltd*, LON/91/2487Z (VTD 7741).

Local VAT office refusing to accept hand-delivered return

[**18.52**] See *Light Wire Ltd*, **18.568** below, and *Hatfield*, **18.569** below.

Return delivered by hand—accountant claiming to have posted it

[18.53] A surcharge was imposed on a partnership which had submitted two returns after the due date. The partnership's accountant appealed and stated in evidence that one of the returns had been posted before the due date but had been delayed by a fire at the local sorting office. Customs produced evidence that both returns had been delivered by hand, rather than by post, and also submitted a letter from the Post Office confirming that there had been no fire at the sorting office in question at the relevant time. The tribunal dismissed the appeal and awarded costs to Customs. *Albert Guest House*, LON/90/239 (VTD 5524).

Accountant claiming to have delivered return by hand

[18.54] A company's return for the period ending 31 December 1989 was received by post on 17 January 1990, postmarked 16 January. The company appealed and its accountant gave evidence that he had delivered the return by hand on 22 December. In cross-examination, his description the building appeared not to correspond with the actual geography of the VAT office in question. The accountant also stated that there had been a postal strike, whereas Customs produced a letter from the GPO stating that there had been no strike or industrial action at the relevant period. The tribunal dismissed the appeal, finding that the return had in fact been delivered by post, and that the accountanthad not shown 'on the balance of probabilities' that he had actually visited the VAT office. *Gundy Harris & Co Ltd*, LON/90/638 (VTD 5172).

Partner claiming to have delivered return by hand on due date

[18.55] A similar decision was reached in a case where a partner gave evidence that he had delivered two returns by hand on the due date, but Customs produced evidence to show that the returns had been received by post and had been postmarked after the due date. The tribunal dismissed the partnership's appeal. *MF Printers*, LON/90/1526Z (VTD 5770).

Appellant claiming to have delivered return by hand on due date

[18.56] An appeal was dismissed in a case where a trader contended that his return for the period ending 31 July 1990 had been delivered by hand on 31 August, although the records kept at the local VAT office indicated that it had been delivered by hand on 19 September. The tribunal stated that it was 'unable to accept the appellant's allegation that the envelope (had) been lying around the office for 19 days before being opened and dealt with'. *FJ Amsbury*, LON/90/1933Y (VTD 5999).

Director claiming to have delivered return by hand on due date

[18.57] An appeal was dismissed in a case where a company's managing director stated in evidence that he had delivered the company's return to the local VAT office by hand on the due date. The tribunal commented that the director and his secretary 'may have been mistaken in their recollection'. *DW Robey & Sons Ltd*, LON/91/1732Z (VTD 6967).

Receipt of cheque denied by Commissioners

[18.58] An appeal against a default surcharge was allowed in a case where Customs accepted that a return had been received on time but contended that it had not contained the appropriate cheque. The tribunal found, on the balance of probabilities, that the cheque and the return were posted together, but that the cheque had been lost at the VAT Central Unit. *Romill Engineering*, LON/88/132 (VTD 3109).

[18.59] Similar decisions were reached in *SW Haulage Ltd*, MAN/89/370 (VTD 4108); *AK Price*, LON/90/885Y (VTD 5927); *J Farley*, LON/90/1678 (VTD 6558) and *Talking Point (Europe) Ltd*, LON/91/2725Z (VTD 7698).

Payment by credit transfer

[18.60] A company (M) submitted its return for the period ending 30 September 1989 before the due date (31 October). However, it paid the tax by credit transfer, and did not initiate the payment until 7 November. Customs received the payment on 9 November, and imposed a surcharge. M appealed, contending that the payment had been made within the extra seven days allowed for payments by credit transfer. The tribunal dismissed the appeal, holding that payments by credit transfer had to be received by Customs by the seventh day. As M had not initiated the payment until the seventh day, there was no chance of Customs receiving it within the extra seven days allowed. *Matilot Ltd (t/a Hardlife Ladder Co)*, MAN/89/998 & MAN/90/97 (VTD 4847).

[18.61] Similar decisions were reached in *Leslie Wise Ltd*, LON/94/3452A (VTD 13354); *Consolidated Holdings Ltd*, MAN/95/107 (VTD 13483); *JND Ltd*, LON/95/2471P (VTD 13719); *FPS (UK) Ltd*, MAN/98/537 (VTD 15716); *Paragon Business Products Ltd*, **18.459** below; *Slough Motor Co*, **18.538** below, and *Wingate Electrical plc*, **18.539** below.

[18.62] In 1987 a trader received a letter inviting him to adopt the credit transfer scheme. He did not respond to the letter, but in January 1992, having incurred several default surcharges, he decided to take advantage of the scheme. His payment for the period ending 29 February 1992 was received on 6 March. Customs imposed a further surcharge but the tribunal allowed the trader's appeal, holding that in view of the letter which Customs had sent him in 1987, he had been entitled to pay his VAT liability by credit transfer. *GL Marshall*, LON/92/1344 (VTD 9321). (*Note.* The decision here was not followed, and was implicitly disapproved, in the subsequent case of *Whitport plc*, **18.63** below.)

[18.63] A company (W) paid its VAT by credit transfer. For the period ending 30 June 1995, it initiated its payment on Friday 4 August 1995. Customs did not receive the payment until Tuesday 8 August, and imposed a surcharge. W appealed, contending that payment had been made within the seven-day extended time limit. The tribunal rejected this contention and dismissed the appeal, declining to follow the decision in *Marshall*, **18.65** above, and applying *Wingate Electrical plc*, **18.539** below. *Whitport plc*, LON/95/2782 (VTD 14337). (*Note*. The tribunal also held that the circumstances did not constitute a reasonable excuse.)

[18.64] The decision in *Whitport plc*, **18.63** above, was applied in the similar subsequent cases of *Headlam (Floorcovering Distributor) Ltd (t/a Florco)*, LON/99/416 (VTD 16478); *MJ Higgins*, LON/03/562 (VTD 18354) and *AL Currie & Brown*, **18.590** below.

[18.65] A similar decision was reached in *Tecfacs Ltd*, LON/06/766 (VTD 19868).

[18.66] A company (G) paid its VAT by bank giro transfer. For the period ending 31 March 2002, it initiated its payment on 3 May. The payment was credited to the Bank of England (acting as bankers for Customs) on 7 May, but the Bank did not credit it to Customs' account until 8 May. Customs imposed a default surcharge, and G appealed. The tribunal allowed the appeal, holding that payment had taken place on 7 May, when the money was credited to the Bank of England, within the seven-day extended time limit. *GT Marketing (Clacton) Ltd*, LON/02/487 (VTD 18167).

[18.67] See also *Rowan Timber Supplies (Scotland) Ltd*, **18.513** below, and *Clark*, **18.533** below.

Payment by BACS—application of extended time limit

[18.68] A company (K) paid its VAT liability by electronic transfer under the Bankers Automated Clearing System (BACS). Its payment for the period ending 31 May 2006 was initiated on 6 June but Customs did not receive it until 8 June. Customs imposed a surcharge and K appealed, contending that the payment should be treated as being made when it was initiated. The tribunal rejected this contention and dismissed the appeal. *Kpack (UK) Ltd*, LON/06/811 (VTD 20109).

[18.69] See also *AZ Cleaning Services (South West) Ltd*, **18.542** below, and the cases noted at **18.543** below.

Whether a 'reasonable excuse' (VATA 1994, s 59(7)(b))

Computer problems

Cases where the appellant was successful

Installation of computer

[18.70] A company which had installed a new computer found that it would be unable to complete its first return after the installation by the due date. It telephoned its local VAT office to ask whether some self-billing invoices could be entered on the following return instead. Following its conversation with the

VAT office, the company took the view that it was more important for the return to be accurate than for it to be punctual. It therefore delayed the submission of the return, and a default surcharge was imposed. The tribunal allowed the company's appeal, holding that the VAT office should have advised the company that an estimated return would be acceptable, and that the circumstances therefore constituted a reasonable excuse. *Evans Transport*, LON/87/637 (VTD 2974).

[18.71] Delay resulting from the installation of a computer was held to constitute a reasonable excuse in *Exchange Club Ltd*, MAN/88/144 (VTD 3031); *Alexander Designs Ltd*, LON/88/816 (VTD 3325); *Bryant Glass Ltd*, MAN/88/864 (VTD 3431); *H Webb*, MAN/89/235 (VTD 3788); *Accountancy Executive Appointments*, EDN/91/8 (VTD 5891); *Starwest Investment Holdings Ltd*, LON/91/541X (VTD 6547); *Price Legand Offset International Ltd*, LON/90/942Y (VTD 7066); *JJ Cumpstey Ltd*, LON/92/2542 (VTD 9883); *Televideo*, MAN/92/910 (VTD 10052); *Alert Security Supplies Ltd*, MAN/94/425 (VTD 12677) and *Hatton Garden Agency Ltd*, LON/94/2525 (VTD 13285).

Computer malfunction

[18.72] There have been a large number of cases in which tribunals have found that the malfunction of a computer has constituted a reasonable excuse for a late return. In the interests of space, such cases are not listed individually in this book. For a list of such cases decided up to 31 December 1994, see Tolley's VAT Cases 1995.

[18.73] In a case where a computer had broken down, with loss of data, following the insertion of an unauthorised program by a former employee, the tribunal held that this constituted a reasonable excuse. *Television Information Network Ltd*, LON/88/720 (VTD 3403).

[18.74] A company's computer was damaged by one of its staff in May 1987. The company found it difficult to obtain spare parts for the computer, and acquired a replacement in June. The tribunal held that this constituted a reasonable excuse for the late submission of the company's return for the period ending 30 April 1987. (There was, however, held to be no reasonable excuse for subsequent defaults.) *RK Transport Ltd*, LON/91/858Y (VTD 6358).

[18.75] Damage to a computer was also held to be a reasonable excuse in *GM Supplies*, LON/94/854 (VTD 12983).

Theft of computer

[18.76] The computer used by a firm of solicitors was stolen in October 1988. A replacement was not installed until February 1989, and the correct disk converter was not supplied until May 1989. After the disk converter had been installed, it was discovered that the back-up disks containing the firm's records for July 1988 to October 1988 had been corrupted, so that the relevant data had to be re-entered. The firm did not complete this until January 1990. In the meantime, its returns for the periods ending from 31 October 1988 to 31 October 1989 were submitted late, and default surcharges were imposed. The tribunal allowed the firm's appeal in part, holding that the disruption arising from the theft constituted a reasonable excuse for the late submission of the returns for the periods ending October 1988 and January 1989, but not for the period ending April 1989. (The tribunal also held that the firm's discovery in May 1989 that it would need to re-enter some of its old data constituted a reasonable excuse for the late submission of its returns for the periods ending July and October 1989.) *Stocken & Lambert*, LON/92/2818 (VTD 10527). (*Note.* For another issue in this case, see **18.315** below.)

[18.77] The theft of a company's computer, together with the disks containing copies of the information needed to compile its VAT returns, was also held to constitute a reasonable excuse in *Licensed Establishments Management Services Ltd*, LON/93/1908 (VTD 11777).

Problems with HMRC server

[18.78] A company submitted its VAT returns electronically. Its return for the period ending 31 March 2008 was not submitted until 8 May. Customs imposed a default surcharge. The company appealed, contending that it had a reasonable excuse because it had made three attempts to submit the return on 6 May, but had been unable to do so because of problems with the HMRC server. The tribunal accepted this contention and allowed the appeal, observing that 'there is no dispute that the three attempts were made to file on 6 May, since HMRC themselves have a record of this'. The tribunal also observed that the late filing was due to 'a fault on the part of HMRC in not having the capacity to take the volume of calls likely to be made on the days when numerous VAT filings will inevitably be made'. *Kwik Move UK Ltd*, LON/08/1382 (VTD 20842).

Cases where the appellant was unsuccessful

Installation of computer

[18.79] Pressure of work arising from the installation of a computer was held not to constitute a reasonable excuse in *J Martorana (t/a Mr Unique Tyre & Exhaust Centre)*, LON/87/591 (VTD 2557); *McGeoghan Plant Hire & Excavations Ltd*, LON/88/221 (VTD 3246); *Gemini Fashion Accessories Ltd*, MAN/88/294 (VTD 3262); *Bloxwich Engineering Ltd*, MAN/88/673 (VTD 3396); *Freeman Box & Co*, LON/88/918 (VTD 3524); *Dresswell (Newtownards) Ltd*, BEL/88/15 (VTD 3568); *Lledo (London) Ltd*, LON/89/28X (VTD 3590); *Delton Electric Ltd*, MAN/89/196 (VTD 3904); *Delton Central Services Ltd*, MAN/89/197 (VTD 3904); *Charles Bell (BD) Ltd*, MAN/90/172 (VTD 4887); *Word (UK) Ltd*, LON/90/619 (VTD 5224); *WE Hannan & Associates Ltd*, MAN/90/441 (VTD 5343); *AE Technical Services*, EDN/91/42 (VTD 5931); *Span Computer Contracts Ltd*, LON/91/327Z (VTD 6323, 6461); *Finishfavour Ltd*, LON/91/1652X (VTD 7053); *Taylor & Taylor*, LON/91/2176Y (VTD 7187); *James Watts Transport Southwark Ltd*, LON/93/770P (VTD 11067); *Magstack Ltd (t/a Brixton Academy)*, LON/93/2574P (VTD 12009); *J & G Associates*, EDN/95/27 (VTD 13471) and *Internet for Business Ltd*, EDN/99/103 (VTD 16266).

[18.80] The treasurer of a social club transferred its accounts onto a computer without maintaining a manual back-up system. Six months later he resigned from the treasurership and passed his successor a number of computer disks, which his successor had no means of processing. Consequently the club was unable to submit its next return in time and incurred a default surcharge. The tribunal found that the surcharge clearly arose from the actions of the former treasurer, but held that, as the club was responsible for its treasurer's actions, this did not constitute a reasonable excuse. *Rotherham Borough Council Employees Sports & Social Club*, MAN/88/797 (VTD 3543).

Failure to keep back-up data

[18.81] A firm appealed against a default surcharge, contending that it had a reasonable excuse because its computer had broken down. The tribunal dismissed the appeal, holding that the firm had been at fault in not keeping a back-up copy of the data fed into the computer. *JN Electrical Units*, LON/88/583 (VTD 3346).

[18.82] Similar decisions were reached in *Peachman Building Services (Croydon) Ltd*, LON/90/260 (VTD 5041) and *Stella Products Ltd*, MAN/90/234 (VTD 5494).

Computer malfunction

[18.83] The malfunction of a computer was held not to be a reasonable excuse in *Durham City Car Co Ltd*, MAN/88/723 (VTD 3604); *Survey & Marketing Services*, MAN/89/724 (VTD 4455); *City Rentals Ltd*, LON/90/81 (VTD 4806); *AF Tann Ltd*, LON/90/435Y (VTD 5012); *Active Handling (UK) Ltd*, LON/90/377 (VTD 5273); *Ward Meadows (Plant) Ltd*, MAN/90/1058 (VTD 5752); *100 Per Cent*, LON/91/690Z (VTD 6238); *JF Turkington (Engineers) Ltd*, MAN/91/380 (VTD 6484); *Halcove Ltd*, EDN/91/227 (VTD 6935); *SL Bindman*, MAN/91/1248 (VTD 7340); *Armstrongs Transport (Wigan) Ltd*, MAN/91/1253 (VTD 7464); *High Range Developments Ltd*, LON/92/355Z (VTD 8989); *Brakel Ltd*, MAN/91/1280 (VTD 9685); *A Reid*, EDN/92/353 (VTD 10406); *Angus Modelmakers Ltd*, EDN/92/316 (VTD 10655); *DC Edwick*, MAN/93/187 (VTD 10962); *GS & DS Bhalla (t/a Pinehurst Hotel)*, LON/93/1005 (VTD 11284); *F & A Ponting Ltd*, MAN/94/529 (VTD 12595); *C & G Cheshire (t/a Jeeves of Hampshire)*, LON/98/174 (VTD 15624); *Shan Trading Ltd*, LON/98/710 (VTD 15726); *Ciro Citterio Menswear plc*, MAN/99/95 (VTD 16336) and *R Gunn & MJ Davies*, LON/99/858 (VTD 16927).

[18.84] Two companies appealed against default surcharges, contending that they had a reasonable excuse for the late submission of returns in that they had installed computer programs which had failed to work. The firm which had supplied the computer programs had subsequently gone into liquidation. The tribunal dismissed the companies' appeals, holding that they had placed reliance on the firm of computer programmers to produce an accounting system, and that what is now *VATA 1994, s 71(1)(b)* precluded this from being a reasonable excuse. *Heating & Management Services Ltd*, LON/89/1191Z; *Utilicom Ltd*, LON/89/1206Z (VTD 4200).

[18.85] Similar decisions were reached in *The Music Shop (Romford) Ltd*, LON/89/980Z (VTD 4696) and *Sollac SA*, LON/95/1842P (VTD 13688).

Change in VAT rate—difficulty in reprogramming computer

[18.86] A trader appealed against a default surcharge, contending that he had a reasonable excuse because he had experienced difficulty in reprogramming his computer following the increase in the VAT rate from 15% to 17.5%. The tribunal dismissed his appeal, observing that he should have calculated his VAT manually, and holding that the circumstances did not constitute a reasonable excuse. *G Robinson (t/a Swallow Motor Co)*, LON/93/398P (VTD 11120).

Illness or bereavement

Cases where the appellant was successful

Illness or injury of appellant

[18.87] There have been a large number of cases in which tribunals have held that illness or injury suffered by an appellant has constituted a reasonable excuse for a late return. Such cases turn entirely on the particular facts and, in the interests of space, are not summarised individually in this book. For a list of such cases decided up to 31 December 1995, see Tolley's VAT Cases 1996.

Illness of trader's wife

[18.88] Illness suffered by a trader's wife was held to constitute a reasonable excuse for a late return in *MHD Mortimer*, LON/89/435Y (VTD 4235); *J Hunter*, EDN/89/191 (VTD 4566); *AP Taylor*, LON/91/1505X (VTD 7893); *DJ Harmer*, LON/92/1728P (VTD 9581); *MRK Hill (t/a Marcus Builders)*, LON/94/2031P (VTD 13235) and *MA Nimmock*, LON/95/2821P (VTD 13857).

Death of trader's wife

[18.89] In a case where a trader's wife died from cancer on 30 November 1987, the tribunal held that this constituted a reasonable excuse for the late submission of returns for the periods ending 31 October 1987 and 31 January 1988. *MD Stephens*, LON/88/746Z (VTD 3963).

Illness of trader's husband

[18.90] A married woman submitted two returns late and default surcharges were imposed. She appealed, contending that she had a reasonable excuse because her husband, who assisted her in the business, had suffered from prolonged illness and had been unable to work properly. The tribunal allowed her appeal. *Mrs MW Stewart (t/a Sodisk)*, LON/90/1832X (VTD 6013).

Death of trader's mother

[18.91] A trader's mother became very ill with cancer in October 1987, and died in March 1988. The tribunal held that this constituted a reasonable excuse for the late submission of the return for the period ending 31 January 1988. *IM Barnard*, LON/89/252Y (VTD 3741).

[18.92] Similar decisions were reached in *ER Hill*, LON/90/234 (VTD 5001) and *CF Dale Ltd*, LON/91/2198X (VTD 7385).

Death of trader's father

[18.93] The father of a sole trader was diagnosed as having cancer in April 1987. He was admitted to hospital in May and died in August. The tribunal held that this constituted a reasonable excuse for the late submission of the return for the period ending 31 May. (There was held to be no reasonable excuse for subsequent defaults.) *AP Watts*, LON/89/1204X (VTD 4535).

[18.94] Similar decisions were reached in *S Chelms (t/a Central Consultancy & Training Services)*, LON/93/16P (VTD 10489) and *R Badman (t/a Gardener & Badman)*, LON/98/342 (VTD 15938).

Illness or injury of partner

[18.95] There have been a large number of cases in which tribunals have held that illness or injury suffered by one of the members of a small partnership has constituted a reasonable excuse for a late return. Such cases turn entirely on the particular facts and, in the interests of space, are not summarised individually in this book. For a list of such cases decided up to 31 December 1995, see Tolley's VAT Cases 1996.

Illness of partner's mother

[18.96] A husband and wife traded in partnership. The wife's mother, who lived in the Netherlands, fell ill with cancer and the wife travelled to the Netherlands to be with her. The tribunal held that this constituted a reasonable excuse for the late submission of two VAT returns. *A & A Everett*, LON/88/942Y (VTD 3669).

Death of partner's mother

[18.97] A husband and wife operated a hotel in partnership. The husband had to fly to Guyana at short notice when his mother, who was resident there, became ill and died. The tribunal held that this constituted a reasonable excuse for a late return. *Warren Park Hotel*, LON/88/473Y (VTD 3508).

Illness or injury of director

[18.98] There have been a large number of cases in which tribunals have held that illness or injury suffered by a company director has constituted a reasonable excuse for a late return. Such cases turn entirely on the particular facts and, in the interests of space, are not summarised individually in this book. For a list of such cases decided up to 31 December 1995, see Tolley's VAT Cases 1996.

Illness of director's wife

[18.99] A company appealed against three default surcharges, contending that it had a reasonable excuse because the wife of its principal director had been seriously ill throughout the period in question (and had subsequently died). The tribunal allowed the appeal, holding that the circumstances constituted a reasonable excuse. *Potterburn Ltd*, EDN/98/195 (VTD 15912).

Emotional strain following trial of murderer of director's father

[18.100] The father of a company's principal director was murdered in September 1985. A man was convicted of the murder in July 1986, but appealed to the Court of Appeal, which upheld the conviction in July 1987. The tribunal held that, in view of the emotional strain on the director, the circumstances constituted a reasonable excuse for the late submission of the company's return for the period ending 31 July 1987. (There was, however, held to be no reasonable excuse for a subsequent default.) *Calpeel Ltd*, LON/88/1339Y (VTD 4194).

Illness of director's father

[18.101] A company appealed against a default surcharge, contending that it had a reasonable excuse because a director who was required to sign the relevant cheque had been called away at short notice to visit his father who was ill. The tribunal allowed the appeal, holding that the circumstances constituted a reasonable excuse. (There was, however, held to be no reasonable excuse for a subsequent default.) *Gillaroo Ltd*, LON/92/777 (VTD 8889).

Death of director's brother

[18.102] A small family company appealed against a default surcharge, contending that it had a reasonable excuse for a late return because all its administration was carried out by one of its directors, and her brother had died suddenly shortly before the return was due. The tribunal accepted this contention and allowed the appeal. *J & T Blacksmith Ltd*, EDN/00/59 (VTD 16710).

Illness of secretary

[18.103] The illness of an appellant's secretary was held to constitute a reasonable excuse for a first default in *M Bowen*, [1987] VATTR 255 (VTD 2535). (*Note.* There was, however, held to be no reasonable excuse for three subsequent defaults.)

[18.104] Illness of a secretary was also held to be a reasonable excuse in *J Carrick*, LON/91/2442Y (VTD 7664); *Lynton Group Ltd*, LON/93/1008P (VTD 11049); *First de Parys (Dry Cleaners) Ltd*, LON/93/2151P (VTD 12178), and *Paul Hoskins Ltd*, [2011] UKFTT 538 (TC), TC01385.

Illness or injury of bookkeeper

[18.105] There have been a large number of cases in which tribunals have held that illness suffered by a bookkeeper has constituted a reasonable excuse for a late return. Such cases turn entirely on the particular facts and, in the interests of space, are not summarised individually in this book. For a list of such cases decided up to 31 December 1994, see Tolley's VAT Cases 1995.

Injury to bookkeeper's husband

[18.106] On 27 December 1990 a company's bookkeeper received a telephone call advising her that her husband had been injured in a road accident in Scotland. The bookkeeper travelled to Scotland to be with her husband, and did not return to work until January 1991. In her absence, the company's return for the period ending 30 November was not submitted until 4 January 1991 and a default surcharge was imposed. The tribunal allowed the company's appeal, holding that the circumstances constituted a reasonable excuse. *Graphic Eye Ltd*, LON/91/543X (VTD 6249). (*Note.* The location of the company's office is not stated in the decision, but the case was heard in London, so presumably the company's office was somewhere in Southern England. The case appears to have been decided on the basis that the husband's accident occurred a long way away from the company's office.)

Illness of bookkeeper's father

[18.107] The father of a small company's bookkeeper suffered a heart attack on 24 February 1989. The bookkeeper left the office to visit him and to help look after her mother. She did not return to work until 6 March. The tribunal held that this constituted a reasonable excuse for the late submission of the return for the period ending 31 January 1989. *L & B Scaffolding Ltd*, LON/89/677 & 678Z (VTD 4543).

Illness of bookkeeper's mother

[18.108] A company appealed against a default surcharge for the period ending 31 March 1994, contending that it had a reasonable excuse because its bookkeeper, who had been entrusted with the posting of the relevant return, had been told on 28 April that her mother had been taken ill, and had travelled from Hampshire to London to visit her. The tribunal held that the circumstances constituted a reasonable excuse. *Southern Ski Enterprises Ltd*, LON/95/2574 (VTD 13797).

Illness of computer operator

[18.109] In a case where the only employee who could operate the computer used by two associated companies fell seriously ill, thus delaying the submission of six returns, the tribunal held that this constituted a reasonable excuse. *Servewell Site Services Ltd*, LON/88/759; *Plantasia Ltd*, LON/88/760 (VTD 3291).

[18.110] A similar decision was reached in *Kirkton Investment Ltd*, EDN/97/36 (VTD 15096).

Illness of cashier

[18.111] In a case where a trader's cashier was off work through illness for three weeks, the tribunal held that the circumstances constituted a reasonable excuse for a late return. *TW George*, LON/89/656Y (VTD 3974).

[18.112] The illness of a company's cashier was held to constitute a reasonable excuse for late payment in *Elcomatic Ltd*, EDN/96/96 (VTD 14456).

Illness of wages clerk

[18.113] The illness of the wages clerk employed by three associated companies was held to constitute a reasonable excuse in *All Saints Garage Ltd*, MAN/90/843; *All Saints Commercial Ltd*, MAN/90/941; *Warren Garage Ltd*, MAN/90/942 (VTD 5798).

Illness of shop manager

[18.114] A company owned a newsagency. During July 1990 its shop manager, who was responsible for maintaining its accounting records, suffered severe toothache and had two teeth extracted. He was unable to keep the company's records up to date, and the VAT return for the period ending 30 June 1990 was not submitted until 10 August. The Commissioners imposed a default surcharge but the tribunal allowed the company's appeal, holding that the circumstances constituted a reasonable excuse. *Chestergage Ltd*, MAN/91/134 (VTD 6179).

Illness of office manager

[18.115] A company appealed against a default surcharge, contending that it had a reasonable excuse because its office manager, who had been responsible for its returns for 18 years, had unexpectedly been absent from work at the relevant time, suffering from menopausal depression. The tribunal allowed the appeal, holding that the circumstances constituted a reasonable excuse. *XL Refrigerators Ltd*, MAN/91/1485 (VTD 9763).

[18.116] Illness of a company's office manager was also held to constitute a reasonable excuse in *Samzou Ltd*, MAN/92/1443 & MAN/93/351 (VTD 11483) and *Voland Asphalt Co Ltd*, LON/95/2649 (VTD 14553).

Illness of employee

[18.117] In a case where the only full-time employee of a fish and chip shop suffered from severe influenza in late March 1991, and was off work for two weeks, the tribunal held that the consequent disruption constituted a reasonable excuse for the late submission of the return for the period ending 28 February 1991. *R Wright (t/a Gotterson's Fish Bar)*, LON/91/1082X (VTD 6732).

[18.118] Illness suffered by an employee was also held to constitute a reasonable excuse in *Alan Franks Group*, MAN/94/1352 (VTD 13731); *Flame Cheater International Ltd*, LON/96/459 (VTD 14288); *E Collins*, LON/96/1759 (VTD 14888); *Calscot Stocktaking*, EDN/98/56 (VTD 15573) and *AT Warner & Sons Ltd*, LON/05/939 (VTD 19605).

Illness or injury of accountant

[18.119] There have been a number of cases in which tribunals have held that illness or injury suffered by an accountant has constituted a reasonable excuse for a late return. Such cases turn entirely on the particular facts and, in the interests of space, are not summarised individually in this book. For a list of such cases decided up to 31 December 1994, see Tolley's VAT Cases 1995.

Cases where the appellant was unsuccessful

Illness

[18.120] Illness suffered by the appellant was held not to constitute a reasonable excuse in *MN Sargeson*, MAN/89/686 (VTD 4480); *P Turner (t/a Turner Hire & Sales)*, MAN/89/933 (VTD 4610); *JJ Murphy*, LON/90/1066Y (VTD 5475); *AB Bremner*, EDN/91/45 (VTD 6112); *MSI Shomdul*, LON/91/787X (VTD 6348); *MT Khan*, MAN/91/663 (VTD 6860); *M Loucaides*, LON/91/2553X (VTD 7707); *R Bailey*, MAN/92/748 (VTD 9677); *G Mistry*, LON/93/1931P (VTD 11624); *D Slater*, MAN/93/1424 (VTD 12020); *D Robinson*, EDN/94/60 (VTD 12667) and *G Asker*, LON/00/362 (VTD 16753).

Depression

[**18.121**] A sole trader appealed against a default surcharge, contending that he had a reasonable excuse in that he had been suffering from depression since his relationship with a woman had ended. The tribunal dismissed his appeal, observing that he had been able to work despite his depression and 'he should have engaged someone to take on the task of keeping his records'. *GG Wright*, LON/90/1380X (VTD 5691).

[**18.122**] Similar decisions were reached in *M Loucaides*, LON/92/2553X (VTD 9307) and *S Fitzgerald*, LON/03/1206 (VTD 18662).

Single parent suffering from stress

[**18.123**] A divorced electrician appealed against six default surcharges, contending that he had a reasonable excuse because he had been suffering from stress, and was having to bring up two teenage children single-handed. The tribunal dismissed his appeals, holding that the circumstances did not constitute a reasonable excuse. *BC Poland (t/a Cameron Electrical Contractors)*, LON/92/2154P (VTD 10536).

Illness of partner

[**18.124**] In a case where one member of a partnership had suffered a prolonged illness, the tribunal held that this did not constitute a reasonable excuse for five separate defaults. *L & N Tiles*, LON/90/442Z (VTD 5120).

[**18.125**] Illness suffered by a partner was also held not to be a reasonable excuse in *Mr & Mrs G Eland*, MAN/90/862 (VTD 5716); *Parkers Motorist Discount*, MAN/91/1889 (VTD 9545); *La Cucaracha*, LON/92/2827P (VTD 9988); *FC Foreman & Partners*, LON/93/2387P (VTD 11894); *The Unique Film Company*, LON/94/126P (VTD 12214); *Ballygrant Inn*, EDN/98/107 (VTD 15683) and *Mr & Mrs Brunswick (t/a the Bull Inn)*, LON/07/765 (VTD 20357).

[**18.126**] A partnership appealed against a default surcharge, contending that it had a reasonable excuse because one of the partners had suffered from severe depression after his wife had left him, and had had to see a psychiatrist. The tribunal dismissed the appeal, holding that this was not a reasonable excuse. *NE & RWH Murden*, MAN/92/228 (VTD 9192). (Note. For another issue in this case, see **18.253** below.)

Injury to partner

[**18.127**] A partnership contended that it had a reasonable excuse for several late returns extending over more than two years, as one of the partners had suffered serious head injuries in a road accident and was unable to work regularly. The tribunal dismissed the appeals, observing that one of the other partners should have arranged for the completion of the returns. *Nader & Associated Manufacturing Co*, MAN/90/87 (VTD 4746).

[**18.128**] In a case where a husband and wife ran a restaurant, the tribunal held that chronic back pain suffered by the husband, which at times rendered him unable to work, did not constitute a reasonable excuse. *Il Pozzo Restaurant*, LON/90/279Z (VTD 5195).

[18.129] A similar decision was reached in *Hillfoots Drystone Dyking*, EDN/92/148 (VTD 8966).

Illness of partner's wife

[18.130] Illness suffered by the wife of a partner was held not to constitute a reasonable excuse in *Haydn Welch Jewellers*, LON/96/640 (VTD 14428).

Illness of director

[18.131] There have been a large number of cases in which tribunals have held that illness suffered by a director has not constituted a reasonable excuse for a late return. Such cases turn entirely on the particular facts and, in the interests of space, are not summarised individually in this book. For a list of such cases decided up to 31 December 1995, see Tolley's VAT Cases 1996.

Illness of secretary

[18.132] In a case where a company's secretary had been admitted to hospital for surgery, the tribunal dismissed the company's appeal against a default surcharge, observing that the directors should have made alternative arrangements for submitting the relevant return. *Central Roadways Ltd*, MAN/88/827 (VTD 3576).

[18.133] Illness suffered by a secretary was also held not to constitute a reasonable excuse in *Dr TSR Hardy*, LON/90/809Z (VTD 5521) and *Hiross Ltd*, LON/93/229P (VTD 10630).

Illness of club treasurer

[18.134] The tribunal held that the prolonged illness of a club treasurer, who was suffering from a tumour, did not constitute a reasonable excuse for seven successive defaults, as alternative arrangements should have been made. *Middlesbrough & District Motor Club Ltd*, MAN/90/71 (VTD 4728).

[18.135] A similar decision was reached in *Warriors Social Club*, EDN/93/78 (VTD 11146).

Illness of bookkeeper or employee

[18.136] There have been a large number of cases in which tribunals have held that illness suffered by a bookkeeper or employee has not constituted a reasonable excuse for a late return. Such cases turn entirely on the particular facts and, in the interests of space, are not summarised individually in this book. For a list of such cases decided up to 31 December 1994, see Tolley's VAT Cases 1995.

Illness of accountant

[18.137] A company appealed against a default surcharge, contending that it had a reasonable excuse because its accountant had only recently returned to work after four months' absence following a heart operation, and could only work for sixteen hours a week. The tribunal dismissed the appeal, observing that the company should have made alternative arrangements for completion of the returns. *York Avenue Garage*, MAN/88/310 (VTD 3252).

[18.138] Similar decisions were reached in *Smart County Personnel Ltd*, LON/88/704 (VTD 3751); *Novelminster Ltd*, LON/91/2301Z &

LON/91/2489Z (VTD 10314); *Veda Products Ltd*, LON/95/2402P (VTD 13685); *Mrs J McGready (t/a Abbey Flowers)*, EDN/95/365 (VTD 13993) and *Satchwell Grant Ltd*, LON/96/970 (VTD 14577).

[18.139] The tribunal held that the prolonged illness of an accountant was not a reasonable excuse for the late submission of five successive late returns, as the trader should have engaged another accountant. *C Reid*, MAN/89/552 (VTD 4103).

[18.140] In a case where a company's accountant had a history of angina and subsequently suffered two heart attacks, the tribunal held that this did not constitute a reasonable excuse for five successive defaults, as the company directors had 'let the situation continue when it was unlikely to improve'. *Lees Heginbotham & Sons Ltd*, MAN/89/754 (VTD 4533).

Death of trader's mother

[18.141] A trader appealed against a default surcharge for the period ending 31 December 1988, contending that he had a reasonable excuse because he had been upset by the death of his mother in August 1988. The tribunal dismissed his appeal, finding that his turnover in the relevant quarter had not been adversely affected by his bereavement, and that he had failed to give sufficient priority to fulfilling his basic statutory obligations. *BA Smyth*, LON/90/439Y (VTD 5039).

Death of son-in-law

[18.142] A trader appealed against a default surcharge, contending that he had a reasonable excuse because his son-in-law had died four months before the due date of the return in question, and he had therefore needed to spend more time with his daughter. The tribunal dismissed his appeal, holding that the circumstances did not constitute a reasonable excuse. *RL Hardwick*, MAN/91/7 (VTD 5961).

Death of director's father.

[18.143] A company appealed against a default surcharge for the period ending January 2008, contending that it had a reasonable excuse because the father of one of its two directors had died on 1 October 2007. The tribunal dismissed the appeal, observing that there had been almost five months between the death and the due date of the return, and that this had been 'sufficient time to make alternative arrangements to ensure that the return and payment were made on time'. *Solution Seekers Ltd*, LON/08/1483 (VTD 20817).

Pregnancy and childbirth

Cases where the appellant was successful

Secretary suffering miscarriage

[18.144] In a case where a company's secretary had suffered a miscarriage, the tribunal held that this constituted a reasonable excuse for a late return. *Perryman Motor Factors (Greenford) Ltd*, LON/87/841 (VTD 2793). (*Notes.*

(1) There was held to be no reasonable excuse for subsequent defaults. (2) For a subsequent appeal by the same company, see **18.157** below.)

Bookkeeper suffering miscarriage

[18.145] An electrician's bookkeeper became pregnant. She continued to keep his books but developed complications and had to go to hospital on several occasions. She eventually suffered a miscarriage. The tribunal held that the circumstances constituted a reasonable excuse for the late submission of two returns. *N Brooks*, LON/89/1269Y (VTD 4784).

Director's wife developing complications during pregnancy

[18.146] The wife of the principal director of a small company became pregnant early in 1987. She had a history of gynaecological problems. During her pregnancy she developed placenta previa, and had to be admitted to hospital. She remained in hospital until after the birth of the child in October. During her time in hospital, her husband visited her each day. The tribunal held that this constituted a reasonable excuse for the late submission of a VAT return. *Lam Cash & Carry Ltd*, LON/88/991 (VTD 3400).

[18.147] A similar decision was reached in *Interchem (Chemists Wholesale) Ltd*, MAN/95/2486 (VTD 13952). (*Note*. There was held to be no reasonable excuse for other defaults.)

Partner suffering complications in pregnancy

[18.148] A married couple appealed against two default surcharges, contending that they had a reasonable excuse because the wife had suffered difficulties in pregnancy. The tribunal accepted their evidence and allowed the appeal. *RJ & Mrs GD Barker*, LON/92/327Z (VTD 7952).

Partner giving birth

[18.149] A married couple who traded in partnership submitted their return for the period ending 31 May 1991 after the due date, and a default surcharge was imposed. They appealed, contending that they had a reasonable excuse because the wife had given birth to a child in April 1991. The tribunal allowed their appeal, holding that the circumstances constituted a reasonable excuse. *Mr & Mrs FJ Bamford (t/a FJ Hardy Tilers)*, LON/93/1286 (VTD 11584). (*Note*. Compare *Pinnock & Lambden*, **18.160** below, where similar circumstances were held not to constitute a reasonable excuse.)

Director giving birth

[18.150] A company submitted its return for the period ending 31 August 1995 after the due date and a default surcharge was imposed. The company appealed, contending that it had a reasonable excuse because one of its two directors had given birth in early September 1995 and it had been unable to transfer money from a deposit account to its current account until both directors could visit its bank. The tribunal accepted the company's evidence and allowed the appeal. *Ashvail Services Ltd*, MAN/96/457 (VTD 14440).

Company secretary on maternity leave—clerical error by employee

[18.151] The company secretary of a building company gave birth on 14 November 1990. The company's return for the period ending 31 October

1990 was submitted by another employee, who accidentally postdated the accompanying cheque. The Commissioners imposed a default surcharge but the tribunal allowed the company's appeal. Applying *Reddish Electronics Ltd* and *Dabchicks Sailing Club*, **18.419** below, the accidental postdating of a cheque was not a reasonable excuse. However, the absence on maternity leave of the company secretary, who had arranged for another employee to carry out her duties, did constitute a reasonable excuse. *AJW Stagg (General Builders) Ltd*, LON/91/280X (VTD 6283). (*Note.* Compare the cases noted at **18.423** to **18.425** below, in which errors by employees or bookkeepers were held not to constitute a reasonable excuse.)

Pregnancy of secretary

[18.152] A company appealed against a default surcharge, contending that it had a reasonable excuse because its secretary had been pregnant and had been absent from work with morning sickness, and that the secretary had not told the principal director that she was pregnant, so that he had not realised that it might be necessary to make other arrangements for submitting the return. The tribunal accepted the company's evidence and allowed the appeal, observing that 'it is common for young ladies to keep secret their condition in the early weeks of pregnancy'. *Inter Trading Sports Associates Ltd*, MAN/93/1527 (VTD 12344).

[18.153] An appeal was allowed in a case where a company's secretary had gone into labour prematurely. *Dunkirk Panel Services Ltd*, LON/94/1182P (VTD 12834).

Pregnancy of bookkeeper

[18.154] An appeal was allowed in a case where a partnership's bookkeeper had gone into labour prematurely. *AW, JE & AO Harris (t/a The Marcia Inn)*, MAN/05/234 (VTD 19221).

Pregnancy of wife

[18.155] A doctor paid his VAT by credit transfer. The payment due on 31 October 2005 was not received by Customs until 8 November 2005 (ie one day outside the extended time limit for electronic payments). Customs imposed a default surcharge. The doctor appealed, contending that he had a reasonable excuse because at the time the payment was due, his wife had been in hospital in the late stages of pregnancy, and he had been visiting her in hospital. The tribunal accepted the doctor's evidence and allowed the appeal. *Dr JF Lygate*, EDN/05/104 (VTD 19552).

Cases where the appellant was unsuccessful

Pregnancy of bookkeeper

[18.156] A firm of estate agents did not submit its return for the period ending 30 June 1988 until 12 August. A default surcharge was imposed and the firm appealed, contending that it had a reasonable excuse because its bookkeeper had been pregnant and had given birth to a son on 17 August. The tribunal dismissed the appeal, observing that 'the appellants must have known for a considerable period of time that their only bookkeeper was going to have a baby'. *Adrian Laflin Estate Agents*, LON/89/71 (VTD 3811).

[18.157] Similar decisions were reached in *Chapman Roofing Co*, LON/88/1052 (VTD 4186); *Perryman Motor Factors (Greenford) Ltd*, LON/90/1290, LON/91/1493 (VTD 7173); *Bruce Weir & Co*, LON/91/962Z (VTD 7620); *Bing Transport & Trading*, EDN/92/285 (VTD 9688) and *Bedworth Car Centre Ltd*, MAN/91/952 (VTD 10706).

[18.158] A trader appealed against a default surcharge, contending that he had a reasonable excuse because his bookkeeper had been four months pregnant, and had been off work suffering from morning sickness. The tribunal dismissed the appeal, observing that the trader should have realised that the bookkeeper's pregnancy might impair her ability to work, and should have made alternative arrangements for submitting the return. *M Campbell*, MAN/91/424 (VTD 6269).

Wife giving birth

[18.159] A trader appealed against a default surcharge, contending that he had a reasonable excuse for the late submission of a return because his wife had given birth to a daughter less than four weeks before the return was due. The tribunal dismissed his appeal, observing that the daughter's birth 'was an event which must have been anticipated for a considerable period'. *PE Marks*, LON/88/106Z (VTD 4515).

[18.160] A similar decision was reached in *JK Birkinshaw (t/a JB Plant)*, MAN/93/94 (VTD 10648).

Pregnancy of wife

[18.161] A trader appealed against a default surcharge, contending that he had a reasonable excuse because his wife had been heavily pregnant at the relevant time and had been 'having problems with bleeding'. The tribunal dismissed the appeal, holding that this did not constitute a reasonable excuse. *JT Lindsay (t/a Galloway Design & Inspection Services)*, EDN/92/32 (VTD 9151).

Partner giving birth

[18.162] A two-person partnership submitted their returns for the periods ending 31 October 1991 and 31 January 1992 after the due date, and Customs imposed default surcharges. The partners appealed, contending that they had a reasonable excuse because one of the partners had been pregnant and had given birth on 7 February 1992. The tribunal dismissed the appeal, holding that this was not a reasonable excuse for submitting the return late. *KS Pinnock & KJ Lambden (t/a TNT Printed Leisurewear)*, LON/93/45P (VTD 11263).

Cashier on maternity leave

[18.163] A firm of solicitors appealed against a default surcharge, contending that it had a reasonable excuse because its cashier had been on maternity leave. The tribunal dismissed the appeal, holding that this was not a reasonable excuse. *Davidsons*, LON/93/2852 (VTD 12120).

Loss or unavailability of key personnel

Cases where the appellant was successful

Partner abroad on business

[18.164] A partnership had arranged a meeting with a VAT officer, because the senior partner was not sure how to account for VAT on car fuel and did not have a copy of *Notice No 700* dealing with the car fuel scale charges. The partner delayed completing the return for the period ending 31 March 1989, intending to complete it after the meeting, which took place on 28 April. He had to travel to France on business on 29 April, and did not submit the return until after his return at the beginning of May. Customs imposed a surcharge but the tribunal allowed the partnership's appeal. *Derrick A Knightley & Associates*, MAN/89/897 (VTD 4972).

Death of director

[18.165] A company was run by two directors, one of whom controlled the administration and was the sole signatory. The tribunal held that the death of the administrative director constituted a reasonable excuse for the late submission of a return. *Crane & Manpower Ltd*, MAN/88/82 (VTD 2807).

[18.166] The death of a company's managing director was held to be a reasonable excuse in *North West Freighters Ltd*, MAN/88/584 (VTD 3341); *R Burgin Ltd*, LON/90/1779X (VTD 5916) and *Circare Ltd*, LON/91/1770Z (VTD 6903).

Cash-flow problems following death of director

[18.167] See *WBL Ltd*, 18.334 below.

Resignation of managing director

[18.168] The wife of a company's managing director kept the company's books. Her husband resigned from the company and left almost immediately, and she ceased to act as the company's bookkeeper with effect from her husband's departure. The tribunal held that this constituted a reasonable excuse for the late submission of a return. *Manchester Scaffolding Ltd*, MAN/88/96 (VTD 2855).

[18.169] The resignation of a company's managing director, who had been personally responsible for its VAT returns, was also held to constitute a reasonable excuse for a late return in *Jefferby Ltd*, MAN/92/1425 (VTD 11057).

Loss of director

[18.170] The sudden resignation of a company's finance director was held to constitute a reasonable excuse in *Gwent Technical Mouldings Ltd*, LON/92/302X (VTD 7939).

[18.171] The resignation of a company's director was also held to constitute a reasonable excuse for a late return in *The Wigmore Hall Trust*, LON/95/2225P (VTD 13773). (*Note.* There was held to be no reasonable excuse for a subsequent default.)

[18.172] The disappearance of one of a company's two directors was held to constitute a reasonable excuse for two late returns in *Cresthaven Contractors Ltd*, LON/94/1308 (VTD 13010). (*Note*. There was held to be no reasonable excuse for subsequent defaults.)

Dismissal of director

[18.173] In a case where a company had dismissed its finance director for incompetence, the tribunal held that this constituted a reasonable excuse for the late submission of a return. *Airline Computer Services Ltd*, MAN/89/520 (VTD 4311).

Imprisonment of director

[18.174] A company appealed against a surcharge, contending that it had a reasonable excuse because one of its two directors had been imprisoned shortly before the start of the accounting period in question, leaving his co-director in sole charge of the company. The tribunal accepted this contention and allowed the appeal. *Kewpost Ltd*, LON/96/1300 (VTD 14664). (*Note*. Compare *Brough Bros (Kitchens & Bathrooms) Ltd*, 18.212 below, where the imprisonment of a company's controlling director was held not to constitute a reasonable excuse.)

Director called away to deal with family problems

[18.175] The principal director of a small company (B) received an urgent telephone call from his sister in October 1988, asking him to stay with her in Scotland to ease relations between her and her husband, which had become strained. He left for Scotland two days later and stayed for two weeks. As a result he failed to submit B's VAT return for the period ending 30 September 1988 in time. Customs imposed a surcharge but the tribunal allowed B's appeal, holding that the circumstances constituted a reasonable excuse. *Balma Time Ltd*, MAN/89/71 (VTD 3585).

Director abroad on business

[18.176] A company (J) had entered into an agreement with a US company whereby the US company would take over J's business. The deal was due to be completed on 1 August 1989. On 13 July J's managing director was told that the US company was withdrawing from the deal. He flew to the USA on 23 July in an attempt to persuade the US company to proceed with the transaction. He did not return until 31 July. As he was the sole signatory of J's cheques, J did not pay its VAT for the quarter ending 30 June until after the due date. Customs imposed a surcharge but the tribunal allowed J's appeal, holding that the circumstances constituted a reasonable excuse. *Jet Rod (Franchising) Ltd*, MAN/89/846 (VTD 4502).

[18.177] An appeal was allowed in a case where a company's controlling director had had to visit Los Angeles on business shortly before the due date of a return. *Loadstone Ltd*, LON/91/1774 (VTD 7878).

Director called away on business

[18.178] An appeal was allowed in a case where the controlling director of a company based in Finchley, with no other employees, had to travel to

Yorkshire on urgent business three days before a return was due, and did not return to Finchley in time to post the return before the due date. *Dankroy Ltd*, LON/91/2738 (VTD 7743).

[18.179] A similar decision was reached in *Neruby Computing Services Ltd*, LON/98/1221 (VTD 15874).

[18.180] A company (B) did not submit its return for the period ending 31 January 1992 until 2 March. Customs imposed a surcharge . B appealed, contending that it had a reasonable excuse because both its directors, who were its only full-time employees, were away on business when the return was due. B had only one office employee, a young woman who worked part-time on two days a week (Mondays and Wednesdays). She had been instructed to complete and post the form before leaving the office on Wednesday 25 February, but had left the completed form in her desk instead of posting it. The tribunal allowed the appeal, holding that the circumstances constituted a reasonable excuse. *BS Electrical Ltd*, EDN/92/145 (VTD 9199).

Loss of company secretary

[18.181] In a case where a company secretary had left the company at short notice following serious disputes which had become the subject of a High Court action, the tribunal held that this constituted a reasonable excuse for the late submission of a return. *Chemical Corporation (UK) Ltd*, LON/87/842 (VTD 2750).

[18.182] A company secretary left his employment at short notice in May 1989, without completing the VAT return for the period ending 30 April. The tribunal held that the circumstances constituted a reasonable excuse for the late submission of the return. *EH Smith Parkinson (Motors) Ltd*, MAN/89/648 (VTD 4289).

[18.183] The wife of the managing director of a small engineering company (B) acted as the company secretary. She began a liaison with B's only other engineer. They eloped together, and she subsequently sought and obtained a divorce. Because of the loss of his company secretary and of his only qualified colleague, the managing director was unable to complete B's principal contract. The tribunal held that the circumstances constituted a reasonable excuse for the late submission of two VAT returns. (There was, however, held to be no excuse for four subsequent defaults.) *Briana Electronics Ltd*, LON/89/1429Y (VTD 4629).

[18.184] The loss of a company secretary was also held to constitute a reasonable excuse in *Hodgson Martin Ltd*, EDN/92/100 (VTD 9108).

Death of bookkeeper

[18.185] The death of a company's bookkeeper was held to constitute a reasonable excuse for a late return in *Ernest Platt (Bury) Ltd*, MAN/94/1779 (VTD 13208).

Loss of bookkeeper

[18.186] The resignation of a bookkeeper at short notice was held to constitute a reasonable excuse for a late return in *Starplex Ltd*, LON/87/632

(VTD 2552); *CPA Environmental Control Associates Ltd*, LON/88/417 (VTD 2953); *Milhench Brothers*, BEL/88/13 (VTD 3375); *Open Rule Ltd*, LON/88/311 & 312X (VTD 4130); *AJ Parfitt (t/a Parfitt & Craig Hall)*, LON/90/1268X (VTD 5623); *CG Sharpe*, MAN/91/1376 (VTD 7679); *G Blackburn*, MAN/92/355 (VTD 8845); *CHS Publications Ltd*, LON/97/440 (VTD 15191); *Southern County Taverns Ltd*, LON/02/1042 (VTD 18306) and *Pillars Property Cleaning & Maintenance Ltd*, [2009] UKFTT 235 (TC), TC00184.

Temporary absence of bookkeeper

[18.187] A partnership (G) submitted its return for the period ending 31 August 1990 late, and Customs imposed a surcharge. G appealed, contending that it had a reasonable excuse because its bookkeeper had been on jury service from 17 to 26 September. She had only been notified of the jury service in August and had only expected it to last for a week. The tribunal allowed the appeal, holding that this constituted a reasonable excuse. *Groves Garage*, LON/91/55X (VTD 5895).

[18.188] A similar decision was reached in *Weldwork Ltd*, LON/94/1057P (VTD 12953).

[18.189] A trader (Y), based in Maidenhead, submitted his return for the period ending 29 February 2000 late. Customs imposed a surcharge, and Y appealed, contending that he had a reasonable excuse because his bookkeeper had travelled to Cornwall on 16 March because her father was seriously ill. She had expected to return within a week, but had stayed in Cornwall for the rest of the month. The tribunal allowed the appeal, holding that the circumstances constituted a reasonable excuse. *S Yate (t/a Yummies)*, LON/00/750 (VTD 16943).

Resignation of computer operator

[18.190] In a case where a company's computer clerk, who was responsible for the preparation of the VAT return, left at short notice sixteen days before the due date of the return, the tribunal held that this constituted a reasonable excuse. *Barnett Lawson (Trimmings) Ltd*, LON/89/1316Z (VTD 4400).

Death of employee

[18.191] The death of a company's office manager, sixteen days before the due date of a return, was held to be a reasonable excuse in *Semec (Engineering) Ltd*, LON/91/182X (VTD 5963).

[18.192] The death of an employee was also held to constitute a reasonable excuse for a late return in *Group Topek Holdings Ltd*, EDN/94/137 (VTD 13146).

Resignation of manager

[18.193] The manager of a restaurant resigned at short notice in June 1990, following the unexpected death of his stepmother. The tribunal held that this constituted a reasonable excuse for the late submission of the return for the period ending 31 May 1990. *Futures Restaurants Ltd*, LON/90/1440X (VTD 5717).

[18.194] The resignation of a company's manager, a month before the due date of a return, was held to constitute a reasonable excuse in *Landseer Film & Television Productions Ltd*, LON/93/622 (VTD 10812).

Manager away on business

[18.195] An appeal was allowed in a case where a company's general manager, who was required to sign the company's cheque in payment of its VAT, was unexpectedly called away on business shortly before the due date of a return. *Parcare International Ltd*, LON/92/2196P (VTD 9773).

Dismissal of accounts clerk

[18.196] In a case where a firm of solicitors had been obliged to dismiss their accounts clerk, the tribunal held that this constituted a reasonable excuse for the late submission of the first return following the dismissal. *JV McPherson & N Weather*, LON/89/1442X (VTD 4800).

Death of accountant

[18.197] The sudden death of a company's accountant was held to constitute a reasonable excuse for a first default in *Fred's Newsagents Ltd*, LON/88/191 (VTD 2815).

[18.198] The sudden death of an accountant employed by a sole trader was held to constitute a reasonable excuse for a late return in *BA England*, LON/90/731Y (VTD 5292) and *Mrs LD McLean*, LON/91/865 (VTD 6920).

Dismissal of accountant

[18.199] In a case where a company had been obliged to dismiss a newly-appointed accountant for unsatisfactory work, the tribunal held that this constituted a reasonable excuse for the late submission of the first return following the dismissal. *Formtax Plastics Ltd*, LON/93/1767P (VTD 11605).

Loss of accountant

[18.200] The resignation of a company's accountant was held to constitute a reasonable excuse in *Linguarama Ltd*, LON/89/312Z (VTD 4011); *Bergen Transport Ltd*, MAN/89/842 (VTD 4481); *Goliath International (Tools) Ltd*, MAN/89/1048 (VTD 4737); *EBA Systems Ltd*, LON/89/1381 (VTD 4770); *Granmore Ltd*, MAN/90/448 (VTD 5253); *Button Eventures Ltd*, LON/90/1948 (VTD 5995); *TJ Tiling (Contractors) Ltd*, MAN/90/851 (VTD 5664, 6194) and *Wizard Accounting Solutions Ltd*, LON/94/163P (VTD 12304).

Staff turnover

[18.201] Exceptional staff turnover was held to constitute a reasonable excuse in *Brearly Townsend Painters Ltd*, MAN/84/419 (VTD 3126); *Dexter Brent & Patterson Ltd*, LON/88/489 (VTD 3136); *Pizza Express Ltd*, LON/88/868 (VTD 3340); *Complete Maintenance Ltd*, LON/89/989X (VTD 4669) and *Lyham Property Services*, LON/90/1936Y (VTD 6874).

Cases where the appellant was unsuccessful

Partners away from office on business

[18.202] In a case where the three members of a partnership were all working away from their office at the time when a return was due, and had not delegated the completion of the return to any of their employees, the tribunal held that this did not constitute a reasonable excuse for a late return. *Pip Systems*, MAN/88/551 (VTD 3413).

[18.203] Similar decisions were reached in *M Haque & Co*, LON/89/1622X (VTD 4517); *EL & HN Miliam*, LON/90/296Z (VTD 4876) and *The Nightingale Partnership*, LON/92/3028P (VTD 10219).

Partners abroad on business

[18.204] A partnership of musicians appealed against a surcharge, contending that the partners and their manager had been on business in the USA when the return was due. The tribunal held that the circumstances did not constitute a reasonable excuse. *UBU Projex*, LON/89/1835Z (VTD 4820).

[18.205] A similar decision was reached in *P Halloran & M Hollingsworth*, LON/96/465 (VTD 14412).

Partner on holiday

[18.206] The absence on holiday of a partner was held not to be a reasonable excuse in *Eastbridge Joiners & Shopfitters*, EDN/89/130 (VTD 4229); *KR & EM Phelps*, LON/89/486Y (VTD 4486); *P Hagyard & A Gardiner*, MAN/90/374 (VTD 5240); *W & B Mahon*, MAN/90/546 (VTD 5335); *Andrew S Campbell Associates*, LON/91/2326Y (VTD 7262); *Allclean Cleaning Services*, LON/92/2642 (VTD 9885); *KJ & Mrs BM McGarry*, LON/93/184P (VTD 10385); *GE, PI & DL Greenwood (t/a Blinkers of South Cave)*, MAN/93/1620 (VTD 12534) and *A Stanton-Precious & MZ Hunt (t/a Hogs Back Brewery)*, LON/96/1867 (VTD 14791).

Partner on honeymoon

[18.207] A partnership appealed against a default surcharge, contending that it had a reasonable excuse because one of the two partners had married during the week before the due date of the return and had then gone on a honeymoon. The tribunal dismissed the appeal, observing that the wedding was 'not unforeseen' and that alternative arrangements should have been made for the submission of the return. *Ceiling Services*, EDN/91/77 (VTD 6289).

[18.208] A similar decision was reached in *SM Eaton & SL Grove*, LON/x (VTD 16575).

Resignation of director

[18.209] A company's finance director gave notice of leaving on 14 August and left on 4 September. His replacement did not take up duty until 3 October. During the intervening period the company did not submit its return for the period ending 31 August. The tribunal held that the circumstances did not constitute a reasonable excuse, as the managing director should have made alternative arrangements for the completion of the return. *Reflexions Market Research Ltd*, LON/90/208X (VTD 4850).

[18.210] Similar decisions were reached in *Maranello Concessionaires Ltd*, LON/96/297 & 298 (VTD 14211); *Max Security Ltd*, LON/08/935 (VTD 20892), and *Phoenix Safe Co Ltd*, [2011] UKFTT 27 (TC), TC00904.

Director in Court

[18.211] A company did not submit its return for the period ending 31 August 1989 until November, and Customs imposed a surcharge. The company appealed, contending that its director had been on trial for a criminal offence from early September until 5 October. At the end of the trial the director was sentenced to a term of imprisonment. The tribunal dismissed the company's appeal, holding that the company had not established a reasonable excuse. *Henley Glass Centre Ltd*, LON/90/445Z (VTD 5236, 5921).

Director in prison

[18.212] A company (B) submitted its return for the period ending 31 July 1991 after the due date, and Customs imposed a surcharge. B appealed, contending that it had a reasonable excuse because its controlling director had been committed to prison in May 1991, and his wife had had to take over its management during his imprisonment. The tribunal dismissed the appeal, holding that the circumstances did not constitute a reasonable excuse. *Brough Bros (Kitchens & Bathrooms) Ltd*, LON/92/82Z (VTD 7915).

Director away from office on business

[18.213] In a case where the principal director of a small company had to work away from the company's office for two weeks, and did not submit a VAT return until after the due date, the tribunal held that the circumstances did not constitute a reasonable excuse. *Control Computers & Telecommunications Ltd*, LON/88/1438Z (VTD 3461).

[18.214] Similar decisions were reached in *James Pringle Ltd*, EDN/89/85 (VTD 3945); *Skingrade Ltd*, EDN/89/138 (VTD 4377); *Hills Diecasting Co Ltd*, LON/89/1406Z (VTD 4399); *Link Industrial Services Ltd*, MAN/90/850 (VTD 5663); *Beaver Oil Services Ltd*, LON/90/1445X (VTD 5786); *Leisure West Clothing Ltd*, LON/91/42Y (VTD 5930); *Senes Sportswear Ltd*, LON/91/43Y (VTD 5930); *Gravity Productions Ltd*, LON/91/1987X (VTD 7068); *Remlock Design Ltd*, LON/92/1180Y (VTD 9145); *WJ Hatt Ltd*, LON/93/662P (VTD 10762) and *Nares International Ltd*, LON/06/115 (VTD 20018).

Director abroad on business

[18.215] A company appealed against a surcharge, contending that its principal director had been abroad for three weeks on business at the time the return was due. The tribunal dismissed the appeal, holding that the director should have delegated the return. *Ultracolour Ltd*, LON/88/1241 (VTD 3278).

[18.216] Similar decisions were reached in *Tradeplan Ltd*, LON/89/719Z (VTD 4033); *Michael Nightingale & Co Ltd*, LON/89/1722Y (VTD 4873);

Emmabee Fashions Ltd, LON/88/1074 (VTD 5077); *Thamesdown Engineering Systems Ltd*, LON/90/1008Y (VTD 5341); *CB Group Ltd*, LON/91/65 (VTD 5841); *Balton Ltd*, LON/90/359Z (VTD 5980); *BMS Medical Manufacturer & Supplies Ltd*, MAN/91/767 (VTD 7836); *Management Consult Ltd*, MAN/92/420 (VTD 9228); *Interflex Data Systems Ltd*, LON/92/1983P (VTD 9578); *UK Inspection Ltd*, MAN/93/803 (VTD 11467) and *Silver Software Consultants Ltd*, LON/04/2322 (VTD 19236).

Director contesting Parliamentary election

[18.217] A company (M) submitted a return late, and Customs imposed a surcharge. M appealed, contending that its controlling director had been standing for election to the European Parliament, and had been too busy to complete the return. The tribunal dismissed the appeal, holding that this was not a reasonable excuse, since 'the date of these elections is known far in advance so that a taxpayer has every possibility of arranging his affairs in advance to comply with his statutory obligations'. *Medcross Ltd*, LON/94/1515P (VTD 13080).

Director on holiday

[18.218] There have been a very large number of cases in which companies have contended that they have had a reasonable excuse because a company director has been on holiday at the relevant time, and where the tribunal has dismissed the appeal, holding that this does not constitute a reasonable excuse. In the interests of space, such cases are not reported individually in this book. For a list of such cases decided up to 31 December 1993, see Tolley's VAT Cases 1994.

Resignation of employee

[18.219] There have been a large number of cases in which tribunals have held that the resignation of the employee who had been responsible for VAT returns has not constituted a reasonable excuse for a late return. In the interests of space, such cases are not summarised individually in this book. For a list of such cases decided up to 31 December 1995, see Tolley's VAT Cases 1996.

Company secretary on holiday

[18.220] The absence on holiday of a company secretary was held not to be a reasonable excuse in *J McArdle (Haulage) Ltd*, LON/90/1891X (VTD 5779) and *Olympia Testing (East Anglia) Ltd*, LON/92/1710P (VTD 9260).

Club treasurer on holiday

[18.221] A golf club appealed against a default surcharge, contending that it had a reasonable excuse because its treasurer had been on holiday at the relevant time. The tribunal dismissed the appeal, holding that this was not a reasonable excuse. *Prestonfield Golf Club Ltd*, EDN/96/244 (VTD 14841).

Financial controller on holiday

[18.222] The absence on holiday of a company's financial controller was held not to be a reasonable excuse in *Picken & Son Ltd*, MAN/92/1587 (VTD 10952).

Redundancy of bookkeeper

[18.223] A firm of solicitors made its bookkeeper redundant in December 1989. Its VAT return for the period ending 31 March 1990 was submitted late and Customs imposed a surcharge. The tribunal dismissed the solicitors' appeal, observing that the loss of a bookkeeper could constitute a reasonable excuse in certain circumstances, but not where the firm itself had made the decision to discharge the bookkeeper. *Greenhouse Stirton & Co,* LON/90/1336Y (VTD 5481). (*Note.* For another issue in this case, see **18.606** below.)

[18.224] A similar decision was reached in *Food-Wrap Ltd,* LON/93/961P (VTD 10817).

Loss of bookkeeper

[18.225] A sole trader contended that he had a reasonable excuse for the late submission of several returns because his fiancée, who acted as his bookkeeper, had left him. The tribunal dismissed his appeal, holding that this did not constitute a reasonable excuse. *RA Jones,* MAN/89/776 (VTD 4664).

[18.226] The loss of a bookkeeper was also held not to constitute a reasonable excuse in *P Ward,* MAN/93/874 (VTD 11406); *LC & P Allen,* LON/94/802P (VTD 12547) and *Nationwide Leisure Ltd,* MAN/99/913 (VTD 16482).

Bookkeeper on holiday

[18.227] There have been a number of cases in which traders have contended that they have had a reasonable excuse because their bookkeeper has been on holiday at the relevant time, and where the tribunal has dismissed the appeal, holding that this does not constitute a reasonable excuse. In the interests of space, such cases are not reported individually in this book. For a list of such cases decided up to 31 December 2004, see Tolley's VAT Cases 2005.

Computer operator on holiday

[18.228] The absence on holiday of a company's computer operator was held not to be a reasonable excuse in *Stave-Con Ltd,* MAN/90/915 (VTD 5808).

Dismissal of manager

[18.229] A firm of solicitors dismissed its office manager after discovering financial irregularities. The manager had submitted two VAT returns late, and the next return was also submitted late. Customs imposed a surcharge and the tribunal dismissed the firm's appeal, holding that the partners should have been aware that the returns were being submitted late and the circumstances did not constitute a reasonable excuse. *Messrs Rowlands,* MAN/88/15 (VTD 2752).

Office manager on holiday

[18.230] The absence on holiday of a company's office manager was held not to constitute a reasonable excuse in *Griffiths & Goddard Restorations Ltd,* LON/91/1857Y (VTD 6523).

Loss of accountant

[18.231] In a case where a trader's accountant had emigrated unexpectedly and without warning, the tribunal held that this was not a reasonable excuse. *TTM Chau*, LON/91/2323 (VTD 7244).

[18.232] A company appealed against five default surcharges, contending that it had a reasonable excuse because its accountant and his assistant had resigned within two months of each other. The tribunal dismissed the appeal, observing that it was the company's responsibility 'to obtain trained staff and, if there was difficulty in doing so, to employ professional accountants'. *APUK Ltd*, MAN/98/345 (VTD 15796). (*Note.* For another issue in this case, see **18.26** above.)

Accountant on holiday

[18.233] The absence on holiday of the accountant responsible for submitting the relevant return was held not to be a reasonable excuse in *Curry Mahal Restaurant Manchester Ltd*, MAN/89/323 (VTD 4244); *M Crolla*, EDN/90/17 (VTD 4701); *Mrs S Helsby*, MAN/91/50 (VTD 6066); *London Building Co plc*, LON/92/2767 (VTD 9971); *Stephens Catering Equipment Co Ltd*, BEL/92/72 (VTD 10150); *WR McMaster (t/a Delta Bar)*, EDN/93/233 (VTD 12109) and *Tetra International Ltd*, LON/98/847 (VTD 15820).

Staff shortages

[18.234] There have been a number of cases in which tribunals have held that staff shortages have not constituted a reasonable excuse for a late return. In the interests of space, such cases are not summarised individually in this book. For a list of such cases decided up to 31 December 2009, see Tolley's VAT Cases 2010.

Staff holidays

[18.235] Staff holidays were held not to constitute a reasonable excuse in *Roy Conway Industrial Services Ltd*, MAN/92/94 (VTD 9439); *Crowther Print Ltd*, EDN/92/319 (VTD 10241); *Pipeline Protection Ltd*, MAN/92/1559 (VTD 10336); *BAPP Industrial Supplies Ltd*, MAN/92/1787 (VTD 10632); *Warwick Students Union Services Ltd*, MAN/93/1618 (VTD 12166); *PNDC Willan*, MAN/93/1575 (VTD 12563); *Lockerbie Meat Packers Ltd*, EDN/95/296 (VTD 13826B); *Holdproud Ltd*, LON/98/383 (VTD 15589) and *Tiravie Entertainments LLP*, EDN/04/159 (VTD 19018).

Industrial action

[18.236] Industrial action by staff was held not to be a reasonable excuse in *Yorkshire & Humberside Tourist Board*, MAN/89/1007 (VTD 4744).

Christmas holidays

[18.237] There have been a large number of cases in which tribunals have held that Christmas holidays have not constituted a reasonable excuse for a late return. In the interests of space, such cases are not summarised individually in this book. For a list of such cases decided up to 31 December 1995, see Tolley's VAT Cases 1996.

Easter holiday

[**18.238**] The closure of a business for an Easter holiday was held not to be a reasonable excuse in *P & H Pipework Ltd*, LON/89/816Y (VTD 4092) and *Norpak Engineering Ltd*, MAN/91/1175 (VTD 7462).

Loss, unavailability or inadequacy of records

Cases where the appellant was successful

Dismissal of bookkeeper—records missing

[**18.239**] A company dismissed its bookkeeper in June 1987 for fraud and embezzlement. After the bookkeeper's departure, it was discovered that sales invoices were missing, and that both the purchases ledger and the cash book were incomplete. The tribunal held that this constituted a reasonable excuse for the late submission of the return for the period ending 31 July 1987. (There was, however, held to be no reasonable excuse for subsequent defaults.) *Auto Bodies (Hemel) Ltd*, LON/89/110Y (VTD 4184).

Records temporarily unavailable

[**18.240**] A company's return for the period ending 30 September 1987 was submitted late, and a default surcharge was imposed. The company appealed, contending that it had a reasonable excuse because a Canadian company had offered to take over its business and, as 30 September was the end of its financial year, its books and records had been sent to a firm of accountants, who were not responsible for the firm's VAT return. The accountants had retained the books for longer than had been anticipated. The tribunal allowed the appeal, holding that the circumstances constituted a reasonable excuse. *Drillfact Ltd*, MAN/88/181 (VTD 3009). (*Note.* Compare *Heffernan*, 18.271 below, where similar circumstances were held not to constitute a reasonable excuse.)

[**18.241**] A trader had lent his books to his accountant to prepare accounts for income tax. On 22 December 1988 he visited his accountant to retrieve the books so that he could complete his VAT return for the period ending 30 November 1988. The accountant was not in his office and his secretary refused to hand over the books. The trader did not succeed in obtaining the books until 5 January, so that his return was submitted late. The tribunal allowed his appeal, holding that the circumstances constituted a reasonable excuse. *DP Hollick*, LON/89/499X (VTD 3956).

[**18.242**] A similar decision was reached in a case where a rugby club dispensed with the services of a firm of accountants whose work had been 'inadequate', but was unable to recover its records from the firm for three weeks. *Llandaff Athletic Rugby Club*, LON/89/945Z (VTD 4143).

[**18.243**] A company took over the business of an associated company as a going concern, and wrongly reclaimed input tax on the stock taken over. The Commissioners discovered this at a control visit in October 1987, and a further visit was made on 1 December 1987, at which the company's VAT records were taken away by two VAT officers for detailed inspection. In July

1988 the documents were released to the company's accountants. The tribunal held that the retention of the company's records constituted a reasonable excuse for the late submission of the returns due from February 1988 to November 1988 inclusive. (There was, however, held to be no excuse for the late submission of the returns due in February and May 1989.) *Windows Direct Ltd*, MAN/90/16 (VTD 4762).

[18.244] Similar decisions were reached in *New Bengal Tandoori Restaurant*, LON/89/171Y, 174Y & 177Y (VTD 5211); *Falcon Plastics Ltd*, MAN/93/1582 (VTD 13050); *Peking Inn (Cookham) Ltd*, LON/95/3106 (VTD 14079) and *KH Ching, HB Yi & HC Yong (t/a Chef Peking-on-Thames)*, LON/95/3068P (VTD 14079).

[18.245] A company's return for the period ending 31 December 1990 was not submitted until 7 January and a default surcharge was imposed. The company appealed, contending that it had a reasonable excuse because its books had been in the hands of its accountants from late November until 6 January. The company had been suffering cash-flow problems and had an overdraft of more than £70,000. On 26 November its bank had insisted that audited accounts should be submitted if the overdraft facility was to be continued. The tribunal allowed the appeal, holding that the circumstances constituted a reasonable excuse. *McKenzie Bain Ltd*, LON/91/360 (VTD 5994).

[18.246] A similar decision was reached in *McFarlane Roofing Ltd*, MAN/92/1586 (VTD 10845).

[18.247] An appeal was allowed in a case where the proprietor of a restaurant had posted the relevant records to her accountant for him to complete the VAT return, and the records had been delayed for ten days in the post. *C Boniface*, LON/92/1184Y (VTD 9954).

[18.248] A trader appealed against several default surcharges, contending that he had a reasonable excuse because the Inland Revenue had taken possession of his records in October 1989, and had retained them for 21 months. The tribunal allowed his appeal in part, holding that this was a reasonable excuse for the late submission of the return for the period ending September 1991, but that there was no reasonable excuse for subsequent defaults. *JE Hewitt (t/a James E Hewitt Associates)*, MAN/93/543 (VTD 11177).

[18.249] A similar decision was reached in a case where the Inland Revenue had held a trader's records for four months. *C Pugh*, LON/00/890 (VTD 17093). (*Note.* There was held to be no excuse for subsequent defaults.)

[18.250] In a Northern Ireland case, a social club appealed against a surcharge, contending that it had a reasonable excuse because its records had been held by the Royal Ulster Constabulary. The tribunal accepted this evidence and allowed the appeal. *Shamrock Sports & Social Club*, LON/94/307P (VTD 12767).

Details of input tax not available

[18.251] An appeal was allowed in a case where a company had submitted returns late because of delays in receiving invoices in respect of imported goods. *Appleyard Lees & Co*, MAN/88/145 (VTD 2928).

[18.252] An agricultural contractor had not received all his invoices from his suppliers for the period ending 31 October 1987. He telephoned his local VAT office to ask whether he could submit a return on the basis of the figures actually available, but was told that he could not submit an incomplete return. He therefore delayed the submission of the return, and a default surcharge was imposed. The tribunal allowed his appeal, holding that he should have been advised that he could estimate part of his input tax in accordance with what is now *VAT Regulations 1995 (SI 1995/2518), reg 29(3)*, and that the circumstances constituted a reasonable excuse. *KVJ Joyce*, LON/88/394 (VTD 3224).

[18.253] The decisions in *Appleyard Lees & Co*, 18.251 above, and *Joyce*, 18.252 above, were applied in the similar case of *NE & RWH Murden*, MAN/92/228 (VTD 9192). (*Note.* For another issue in this case, see **18.126** above.)

[18.254] A similar decision was reached in *Weru (UK) Ltd*, LON/94/862 (VTD 12738).

Industrial action by Post Office staff—delay in receiving invoices

[18.255] In a case where industrial action by Post Office staff led to a company receiving many invoices much later than usual, the tribunal held that this constituted a reasonable excuse for the late submission of a return. *Social Surveys (Gallup Poll) Ltd*, LON/89/321Z (VTD 3775).

[18.256] A similar decision was reached in *Mercuri Urval Ltd*, LON/89/821Y (VTD 4438).

Details of income not available

[18.257] A company which published music obtained royalties from record sales and from the performance of songs on radio and television. In respect of the latter, a payment was made by the Performing Rights Society Ltd and, for the purposes of calculating its income, the company relied on a quarterly statement from the society. For the period ending 30 June 1987 the figures were seriously understated in the statement, and so the company contacted its local VAT office to explain that it could not furnish a correct return until the true figures were available. The Commissioners imposed a default surcharge but the tribunal allowed the company's appeal, holding that the VAT office should have advised the company to submit an estimated return, and that the circumstances therefore constituted a reasonable excuse. *Minder Music Ltd*, LON/87/838 (VTD 2678).

[18.258] A company which operated a knitting business sent fabric to dyers according to customers' requirements. The dyers despatched the dyed fabric directly to the customers. However the dying process involved a loss in weight through evaporation and shrinkage. Thus the weight and length of cloth delivered to customers was about 5% less than its weight and length when it left the factory. The company made out blank invoices when the fabric left the factory, and completed the invoices when the customers notified it of the weight of the cloth they had received. This procedure led to delay in completing quarterly returns, and the company later abandoned it, but not before it had incurred a default surcharge. The tribunal allowed the company's appeal, holding that the unusual circumstances constituted a reasonable excuse. *Knittex Ltd*, MAN/89/42 (VTD 3541).

[18.259] An appeal was allowed in a case where invoices were issued in Italy on behalf of a UK company which supplied English-language tuition to Italian students. The tribunal found that a VAT officer had given the company's director the impression that he should delay the company's returns until he had received confirmation of the issue of such invoices, even if this meant that the return would have to be delayed until after the due date, and held that this misunderstanding constituted a reasonable excuse. *Butler School of Languages*, LON/91/700 (VTD 7067). (*Note.* There was held to be no reasonable excuse for other defaults.)

Return delayed while records verified

[18.260] A trader appealed against a default surcharge, contending that he had a reasonable excuse because his accountant had discovered errors in previous returns, and had advised him to delay submitting the return until a control visit by a VAT officer. The tribunal allowed the appeal, holding that the circumstances constituted a reasonable excuse. *T Harrison*, MAN/88/307 (VTD 3078).

[18.261] Similar decisions were reached in *Capricorn Business Services Ltd*, LON/89/1815X (VTD 4802); *The Garage Door Co*, EDN/93/87 (VTD 11144); *Belgian Trading Co*, LON/94/817P (VTD 12644) and *QEN Spearing*, LON/98/370 (VTD 16314).

[18.262] An appeal was allowed in a case where a company's directors discovered errors in the company's records, and delayed submitting a return until they had verified the figures. *Dust Extraction (International) Ltd (VTD 3175)*.

[18.263] Similar decisions were reached in *Intersport Manchester Ltd*, MAN/89/16 (VTD 3625); *Provident Direct Sales (Holdings) Ltd*, MAN/89/233 (VTD 3952); *A Needham*, MAN/90/257 (VTD 5150); *AL Watkins (t/a Fence-Tech)*, MAN/94/818 (VTD 12819) and *PJ Moody (t/a PMS Telecom)*, LON/94/3128P (VTD 13234).

[18.264] In October 1989 a company's accountant discovered that the company's bookkeeper had failed to pay cash takings into the company's bank account, and had apparently pocketed the cash in question. The accountant spent the whole of the next week examining the company's records, with the result that the company's return for the period ending 30 September was submitted late and a default surcharge was imposed. The tribunal allowed the company's appeal, holding that the circumstances constituted a reasonable excuse. *Square Moves Ltd*, LON/90/395 (VTD 5050).

[18.265] Similar decisions were reached in *Maddermarket Theatre Trust Ltd*, LON/92/3332 (VTD 10393) and *Vane Ltd*, LON/06/559 (VTD 19786).

[18.266] In a case where some of a hotelier's invoices were accidentally damaged by water, requiring an additional ten hours' work in summarising them for the quarterly return, the tribunal held that the circumstances constituted a reasonable excuse. *TN Thorne*, MAN/91/82 (VTD 6231).

[18.267] An appeal was allowed in a case where a company's bookkeeper gave evidence that he had been surprised by the unusually high amount of input tax shown on the return, and had therefore delayed submission of the return for four days while she checked the relevant figures. *Peter Boizot (Franchises) Ltd*, LON/93/456P (VTD 10773).

[18.268] A paper merchant, who imported quantities of paper and paid for this by direct debit, habitually awaited receipt of his monthly bank statement before completing his VAT return. Normally he received his bank statement before the end of the month and was therefore able to submit his return before the due date. However, his September bank statement had not arrived by 30 October. He therefore telephoned his bank to obtain details of the payments he had made, but was told that the statement was in the post and that the figures were not available. He received the statement on 5 November, and submitted the return on 6 November. The Commissioners imposed a default surcharge but the tribunal allowed his appeal, holding that the circumstances constituted a reasonable excuse. *J Purcell (t/a John Purcell Paper)*, LON/93/752P (VTD 10925).

Imported goods—delay in receiving C79 certificate from Customs

[18.269] A trader imported flowers from outside the UK, using the services of an import agent. In preparing his VAT returns, he relied on the monthly issue of forms C79 from Customs to ascertain how much tax he could reclaim in respect of the goods which he had imported. On two occasions in 1992, Customs did not send him the C79 in time for him to complete his VAT return. The trader delayed submitting the returns until he had received the C79, and the Commissioners imposed a default surcharge. The tribunal allowed the trader's appeal, holding that the delays by Customs in sending the forms C79 constituted a reasonable excuse. *A Fitzpatrick*, MAN/92/1180 (VTD 10282).

[18.270] See also *Chandler Forest Products Ltd*, **18.564** below.

Cases where the appellant was unsuccessful

Omission in records

[18.271] A company's accountants found that the bookkeeper had failed to enter an invoice in the company's books, and delayed the VAT return. The tribunal dismissed the appeal, holding that this was not a reasonable excuse. *RSM Industries Ltd*, MAN/88/55 (VTD 2810).

[18.272] Similar decisions were reached in *BR Camp*, MAN/88/927 (VTD 3605) and *CDA Fasteners Ltd*, MAN/91/511 (VTD 6389).

Records temporarily unavailable

[18.273] A sole trader appealed against a default surcharge, contending that he had a reasonable excuse because his accountants had kept his records so that they could prepare his annual accounts, and had delayed returning them to him. The tribunal dismissed his appeal, observing that what is now *VATA 1994, s 71(1)(b)* precluded delay by the accountants from constituting a reasonable excuse. *DRM Heffernan*, LON/93/454 (VTD 10735).

[18.274] A similar decision was reached in *RS Coombe*, LON/93/323P (VTD 11154).

[18.275] A trader appealed against four default surcharges, contending that he had a reasonable excuse because his records had been held by his solicitors. The tribunal dismissed his appeal, observing that the trader should have demanded the return of his records from his solicitors, and that what is now *VATA 1994, s 71(1)(b)* precluded reliance on a third party from constituting a reasonable excuse. *NG Hughes (t/a Lightning Couriers)*, MAN/92/519 (VTD 11685).

Details of input tax not available

[18.276] A company which imported raw materials required certificates from Customs detailing the amount of input tax paid at the port when the goods were imported. Its certificate relating to the period ending 30 November 1987 was not available until 8 December. The company did not submit its return until 10 January 1988, and a default surcharge was imposed. The company appealed, contending that it was unfair for the Commissioners to require it to submit a return within only 22 days of receiving the certificate. The tribunal dismissed the appeal, holding that the circumstances did not constitute a reasonable excuse. *RAAR Associates Ltd*, LON/88/437Y (VTD 3365).

[18.277] The late arrival of import certificates from import agents was held not to be a reasonable excuse, on the grounds that the company should have submitted estimated returns. *Clinkscale Radio & Musical Ltd*, EDN/89/76 (VTD 4279).

[18.278] Similar decisions were reached in *West Heat (Eltra) Ltd*, LON/89/1430Z (VTD 4772); *A dos Santos Tavares*, LON/90/270 (VTD 4956) and *J Drennan Partnership*, LON/97/117 (VTD 15190).

[18.279] A company appealed against a default surcharge, contending that it had a reasonable excuse because there had been a delay in receiving invoices, in respect of which it wished to claim input tax, from suppliers. The tribunal dismissed the appeal, holding that this was not a reasonable excuse. *The Deva Trading Co Ltd*, MAN/88/714 (VTD 3421).

[18.280] Similar decisions were reached in *Harrier Shoes Ltd*, LON/89/310X (VTD 3814); *Lyezeal Ltd*, LON/89/127 (VTD 3823); *Middlesbrough Football & Athletic Co (1986) Ltd*, MAN/89/14 (VTD 3836); *AV Turner & Sons Ltd*, LON/88/1463Z (VTD 3877); *CP Evans*, MAN/89/955 (VTD 4717); *DJ Watkinson*, MAN/91/40 (VTD 5794); *A Pereira*, LON/90/1856Z (VTD 5835) and *Iconeywear Distributions Ltd*, MAN/05/797 (VTD 19566).

[18.281] A barrister did not submit his return for the period ending 28 February 1988 until April, and the Commissioners imposed a default surcharge. The barrister appealed, contending that he had a reasonable excuse because he had been unable to find certain receipts for expenses on which he wished to reclaim input tax. He had eventually found the receipts in a box in the playroom used by his two-year-old daughter. The tribunal dismissed his appeal, observing that it was the barrister's responsibility to keep the papers necessary for completion of the return in a safe place. *DM Moore*, LON/88/1095 (VTD 5244).

Details of income not available

[18.282] Delays in obtaining details of income from departmental branches of a business were held not to be a reasonable excuse in *David Leslie (Hairfashions) Ltd*, LON/88/1091 (VTD 3446).

[18.283] Delays in obtaining details of income were also held not to be a reasonable excuse in *Lloyd Scotter Electrical Ltd*, MAN/89/803 (VTD 4482); *Hindi Picture Ltd*, LON/89/1495Z (VTD 4490); *Zetland Garage (Southport) Ltd*, MAN/89/936 (VTD 4676); *PJ Sansom*, MAN/91/937 (VTD 7121); *McCree Music Ltd*, LON/04/1888 (VTD 19009) and *Moorim UK Ltd*, LON/06/558 (VTD 19794).

Cessation of business—firm wishing to check final VAT return

[18.284] A firm which had ceased to trade delayed submitting its final VAT return so that it could reconcile the figures with its final accounts. The tribunal held that this did not constitute a reasonable excuse. *Photographics*, LON/88/1246X (VTD 3407).

Return delayed while figures verified

[18.285] In a case where a company's accountant delayed the submission of a VAT return so that he could reconcile the figures with the accounts, the tribunal held that this was not a reasonable excuse. *Glossop Sectional Buildings Ltd*, MAN/89/466 (VTD 4100).

[18.286] Similar decisions were reached in *George & George*, LON/89/1402Z (VTD 4562); *Southern Fabrics Ltd*, LON/88/791Z (VTD 4781); *Acorn Origination Ltd*, LON/90/1257 (VTD 5517); *Digital Intelligence Systems Ltd*, MAN/90/696 (VTD 6500); *Trowbridge Trades & Labour Club & Institute Ltd*, LON/91/1313 (VTD 6640); *Frank Coleman (Luton) Ltd*, LON/91/1598X (VTD 6653); *CA Mandelberg (t/a Andrew Mandelberg & Co)*, MAN/91/701 (VTD 7114); *Femco Engineering Co Ltd*, LON/91/2101X (VTD 7454); *DT Engineering Ltd*, LON/92/598Y (VTD 7912); *DI Wright*, MAN/92/464 (VTD 9254); *Kitchens For You Ltd*, LON/93/828P (VTD 10802); *BCC (Building Services) Ltd*, LON/X (VTD 13211); *Bercor Ribbon Co Ltd*, MAN/95/2198 (VTD 14025); *Alan Davison (Construction) Ltd*, MAN/96/426 (VTD 14531); *RK Enterprises*, LON/00/1167 (VTD 17440), and *TLC Incentives Ltd*, [2011] UKFTT 617 (TC), TC01459.

Integration of company's records with those of parent company

[18.287] The shares of a company (F) were purchased by another company in January 1989. The new parent company decided to integrate F's records with its own. However, the companies remained separate entities and F's return for the quarter ending 31 December 1989 was submitted late. The tribunal dismissed F's appeal, holding that the extra work required by the integration of the companies' records did not amount to a reasonable excuse. *Forth Skips Ltd*, EDN/90/55 (VTD 5016).

Records under investigation with Commissioners

[18.288] In June 1987 two VAT officers made a control visit to a company. They formed the opinion that some purchase invoices, in respect of which the company had reclaimed input tax, were fictitious. In July they interviewed the company's directors and removed a large number of documents. They informed the directors that they would provide photocopies of the documents on request, but the company did not request copies. In the meantime the company did not submit its returns for the periods ending 30 June and 30 September 1987, and a default surcharge was imposed. The company appealed, contending that the circumstances constituted a reasonable excuse. The tribunal dismissed the appeal, holding that the company should have requested copies and that it was not reasonable for the directors to have decided to withhold the company's returns. 'A person in the appellant's position, who knows that improper conduct of some sort is alleged against him, is not entitled to sit back and postpone his returns'. *G & J Spencer Ltd*, MAN/89/50 (VTD 5428).

[18.289] A similar decision was reached in *JF Laughlin*, EDN/92/338 (VTD 10499).

Company's records in Chinese

[18.290] A company appealed against a default surcharge, contending that it had a reasonable excuse because its accounts clerk for the relevant period had kept its records in Chinese. He had subsequently left the company and his successor could not read Chinese. The tribunal dismissed the appeal, holding that the circumstances did not constitute a reasonable excuse. *P Jennings & Sons Ltd*, LON/91/1533 (VTD 6696).

Change of address

[18.291] See *Fishwick*, 18.584 below.

Change of accounting dates

Cases where the appellant was successful

[18.292] A company appealed against a default surcharge, contending that it had a reasonable excuse for the late submission of a return because, at a control visit, it had requested that its accounting periods for VAT (which ended in February, May, August and November) should be changed to end on 31 March, 30 June, 30 September and 31 December, so that they would coincide with its annual accounting date for corporation tax. It had followed this with a request in writing, to which the Commissioners had not replied. Subsequently the Commissioners issued an estimated assessment, and imposed a surcharge, for a period of one month ending on 30 June. However, as the company's previous period had ended on 31 May, its accountant wrote to the Commissioners stating that he had assumed that the next return should be for a period ending on either 31 August (if the existing dates were continued) or 30 September. The tribunal allowed the company's appeal, holding that, in view of the Commissioners' failure to reply to correspondence, there was a reasonable excuse for the company's failure to make a return for June. *IPMC Ltd*, LON/88/5 (VTD 2797).

[18.293] A similar decision was reached in *Discount Window Systems Ltd*, BEL/92/58 (VTD 10159).

[18.294] A company, whose accounting periods had ended in January, April, July and October, applied to change its quarterly periods so that they ended in February, May, August and November. The Commissioners approved this change, and the company anticipated that its next return would cover the four-month period from 1 November 1987 to 29 February 1988. In mid-January 1988 the company received a return form expressed to be for the period from 1 November 1987 to 31 January 1988. In mid-February 1988 it received a further return form covering the period from 1 February to 29 February. The company submitted both returns together in late March, and a default surcharge was imposed in respect of the first return. The tribunal allowed the company's appeal, holding that the circumstances constituted a reasonable excuse. *United Cutlers Ltd*, MAN/88/324 (VTD 3116).

[18.295] Similar decisions were reached in *Egerton Transport Ltd*, MAN/91/227 (VTD 6505); *Nova Group (London) Ltd*, LON/92/2923P (VTD 10252, 10409); *Nova Roofing Co Ltd*, LON/92/2924P (VTD 10252, 10409); *Rawlings & Lucas (Builders) Ltd*, LON/92/2925P (VTD 10252, 10409); *Express Vending Ltd*, LON/95/323P (VTD 13252); *Accounting Alliance Ltd*, LON/01/688 (VTD 17741); *Charity People Ltd*, LON/03/366 (VTD 18283) and *PTE plc (t/a Physique)*, MAN/08/265 (VTD 20722).

[18.296] In October 2006 a company, whose accounting periods had ended in March, June, September and December, applied to change its quarterly periods so that they ended in January, April, July and October. Customs accepted the request. The next return form that the company received was expressed to be for the month ending 31 October 2006. Realising that it had not yet accounted for VAT for the three months ending September 2006, the company completed this return with details of the four months ending 31 October 2006. However Customs imposed a default surcharge on the basis that the company should have submitted an earlier return for the three months ending 30 September 2006. The company appealed, contending that it had a reasonable excuse because it had never received a form requiring such a return, and had not specifically requested a form because it had assumed that it was being allowed to submit a single return covering the four months ending 31 October. The tribunal accepted the company's evidence and allowed the appeal. *Rumline Ltd*, LON/07/937 (VTD 20406).

[18.297] On 6 April 1987 a company, which had previously submitted returns for the quarterly periods ending in March, June, September and December, applied to change its quarterly periods so that they would end in January, April, July and October. This request was accepted, but on 14 May the company applied for a further change so that its periods would end in February, May, August and November. The Commissioners replied on 27 May, accepting this request but asking for a return for the one-month period ending 30 April to be submitted by 31 May. The company did not comply and a surcharge was subsequently imposed. The tribunal allowed the company's appeal, holding that it was unreasonable for the Commissioners to expect a one-month return at such short notice. *Snow & Rock Sports Ltd*, LON/88/596 (VTD 3223).

[18.298] A company whose accounting periods had ended in December, March, June and September applied to change its accounting dates so that its future accounting periods would end in February, May, August and November. In February 1988 the Commissioners issued an amended certificate of registration stating 'returns to be made in respect of period ending 31 May 1988 and three-monthly thereafter' and including the words 'recipients of amended certificates are required to furnish by the due dates previously notified any returns outstanding in respect of periods ending prior to that shown above'. The company took the view that it could submit a return covering the five months to 31 May 1988, and need not submit a separate return for the period ending 31 March. The Commissioners imposed a surcharge for the late payment of the tax due for those three months and the company appealed, contending that the amended certificate had been ambiguous and had not made it clear that the Commissioners would still require a separate return for the period ending 31 March. The tribunal allowed the company's appeal, holding that the wording of the certificate was 'extremely ambiguous' and that the circumstances constituted a reasonable excuse. *Industrial Fabrication Systems Ltd*, LON/89/881Y (VTD 4219).

[18.299] The decision in *Industrial Fabrication Systems Ltd*, **18.298** above, was applied in a subsequent case where a company applied to change its accounting periods and submitted its first subsequent return after the due date. *Anti-Static Technology Ltd*, LON/90/327Z (VTD 5065).

[18.300] In a case where a small company applied to change its accounting dates in March 1989, but was not allowed to implement the change until the following quarter, the tribunal held that the circumstances constituted a reasonable excuse for the late submission of the return for the period ending 30 April 1989, because the company had not been given adequate warning that it would still need to submit a return for that period. *Northwood Garage (Whitstable) Ltd*, LON/89/1364Y (VTD 4352).

[18.301] A similar decision was reached in *SP Whitehouse*, LON/91/1726 (VTD 6763). (*Note.* For another issue in this case, see **10.1** CASH ACCOUNTING SCHEME.)

[18.302] A sole trader's accounting periods had ended in February, May, August and November. She decided to transfer the business to a limited company with effect from 1 January 1997. Her accountant visited the local VAT office in November 1996 to make the necessary arrangements. Following this conversation, he assumed that his client would be permitted to submit a final return for the four methods ending 31 December 1996 instead of the normal quarterly return for the three months ending 30 November 1996. On 22 January 1997 he submitted a return covering the final four months of trading. The Commissioners imposed a default surcharge for the late submission of the return for the three months ending 30 November, but the tribunal allowed the trader's appeal, holding that the circumstances constituted a reasonable excuse. *DF Macris (t/a Helena's Unisex Beauty Centre)*, LON/97/550 (VTD 15073).

[18.303] A married couple carried on a home improvement business and were registered for VAT with accounting periods ending in March, June, September and December. Subsequently they began a second business with a separate trading name and obtained a separate registration with accounting periods ending in February, May, August and November. In August 1990 they also purchased a public house, and applied for a third registration number. The Commissioners informed the couple that they could only have one registration, in accordance with the QB decision in *Glassborow*, 57.1 REGISTRATION, and that the input tax and output tax relating to all three businesses should be aggregated and included on the same return form. The couple included the figures for all three businesses in a single return for the period ending 30 September 1990 as requested, but because of the extra work, the return was submitted late. The Commissioners imposed a default surcharge, against which the couple appealed. The tribunal allowed the couple's appeal, holding that the extra work caused by having to alter the accounting period of one of the businesses, and include all three businesses on the same return for the first time, constituted a reasonable excuse. *G & BM Beaumont (t/a Beaumont Home Improvements)*, MAN/91/112 (VTD 6063).

Cases where the appellant was partly successful

[18.304] A partnership's quarterly return periods had ended in February, May, August and November. It applied for these to be changed so that they ended in March, June, September and December. The Commissioners issued a return covering the single month of March 1999 and a return covering the three months ending June 1999. The partnership submitted both returns after the due date, and the Commissioners imposed a default surcharge. The partnership appealed, contending that the change of accounting dates constituted a reasonable excuse. The tribunal allowed the appeal in part, holding that the circumstances constituted a reasonable excuse for the late submission of the return for March 1999 but that there was no reasonable excuse for the return for the period ending June 1999. *P & J Cook (t/a Blacksmiths Arms)*, MAN/00/54 (VTD 16770).

Cash-flow problems following change of accounting dates

[18.305] A company's return periods ended in February, May, August and November. It was suffering cash-flow problems, and in 1992 it applied for its return periods to be changed so that they ended in March, June, September and December. The Commissioners accepted the application and requested the company to submit a three-month return for the period ending 30 November 1992 followed by a one-month return for the period ending 31 December 1992. The company was unable to pay these liabilities by the due dates, and default surcharges were imposed. The company appealed, contending that it had a reasonable excuse because it had anticipated that it would be granted a four-month period ending in December 1992, so that the effect of the change would have been to enable it to defer its payment for the three months ending November 1992 by one month, but that the actual effect of the change was that it was still required to pay its liability for those three months by 31 December 1992 and was also required to pay its liability for December by 31 January 1993. The tribunal allowed the appeal in part, holding that there could be no reasonable excuse for failing to pay any VAT for the periods in question, but since the company had suffered 'an acceleration of its tax liabilities', there was a reasonable excuse for the late payment of the VAT for the month ending 31 December. *Springback Investments Ltd*, LON/93/1090P (VTD 11849).

Cases where the appellant was unsuccessful

[18.306] In a case where a partnership had applied to change its accounting periods, and had then overlooked the effect of the change, the tribunal held that this did not constitute a reasonable excuse. *N & Mrs M Tulip*, MAN/88/402 (VTD 3243).

[18.307] Similar decisions were reached in *Worldstill Ltd*, MAN/89/142 (VTD 3796); *VJ Wall*, LON/89/1027Y (VTD 4795); *Sewards (Electrical) Ltd*, LON/92/2356P (VTD 9709); *Watco Design Ltd*, EDN/95/351 (VTD 14136); *Packwell Cartons Ltd*, LON/96/478 (VTD 14314); *WF Electrical plc*, LON/00/1044 (VTD 17083); *Whirlpool UK Ltd*, LON/03/228 (VTD 18427) and *All England Film Caterers Ltd*, LON/07/121 (VTD 20183).

[18.308] Extra work caused by a change of accounting date was held not to constitute a reasonable excuse in *CEM Computers*, BEL/88/42 (VTD 3647) and *Clive White Chartered Surveyors*, LON/88/963Z (VTD 3989).

[18.309] A company's financial year ended on 31 August, but its quarterly return periods ended on 31 January, 30 April, 31 July and 31 October. It did not submit its return for the period ending 31 July 1994 by the due date, but on 1 September 1994 it submitted a request for its return periods to be changed so that they ended on 28 February, 31 May, 31 August and 30 November. The Commissioners accepted this request, but refused to apply it retrospectively, and imposed a default surcharge for the three-month period ending on 31 July 1994. The company appealed, contending that the circumstances constituted a reasonable excuse. The tribunal dismissed the appeal, observing that the company was already in default at the time it submitted its request to change its accounting periods, and holding that the circumstances did not constitute a reasonable excuse. *Basicflex Ltd (t/a Proline Engineering)*, LON/94/3125 (VTD 13370).

[18.310] A similar decision was reached in *Seatechs Ltd v HMRC*, [2009] UKFTT 146 (TC), TC00114.

[18.311] A company's financial year ended on 31 December, but its quarterly return periods had ended in February, May, August and November. In July 1998 it applied to change its accounting dates so as to coincide with its financial year. The Commissioners issued a one-month return covering September 1998, followed by a three-month return ending on 31 December 1998. The company submitted both of these returns late. The Commissioners accepted that the change constituted a reasonable excuse for the late delivery of the September return, but imposed a default surcharge for the quarterly period ending in December. The tribunal dismissed the company's appeal, holding that there was no reasonable excuse for the late submission of this return. *Tameplace Ltd*, LON/00/360 (VTD 16736).

Insufficiency of funds (VATA 1994, s 71(1)(a))

Cases where the appellant was successful

Dishonesty of former company secretary

[18.312] The shareholders of a company (S) sold their shares without telling the purchaser that it owed £24,000 unpaid tax. S subsequently made arrangements to pay this by instalments, but suffered cash-flow problems and its current VAT fell into arrears. Customs imposed a surcharge but the tribunal allowed S's appeal, holding that although an insufficiency of funds was not of itself a reasonable excuse, the dishonesty of S's former secretary did constitute a reasonable excuse. The QB upheld the tribunal decision. S's explanation for non-payment was not simply a temporary cash shortage, but was that the dishonesty of its former secretary had deprived it of the means to pay. The tribunal was entitled to find that this constituted a reasonable excuse. *C & E Commrs v Salevon Ltd*, QB [1989] STC 907.

Dishonesty of former director

[18.313] The dishonesty of a company's former managing director was held to constitute a reasonable excuse in *Dove Services (Manchester) Ltd*, MAN/90/695 (VTD 5510); *Primboon Ltd*, LON/91/2053Y (VTD 7757); *Reflex Synthesisers Controllers Ltd*, LON/92/1044 (VTD 8815), and *Prime Agency Recruitment Ltd*, LON/02/654 (VTD 18043).

[18.314] The dishonesty of a company's former finance director was held to constitute a reasonable excuse in *CMS Peripherals Ltd (No 1)*, LON/04/067 (VTD 19234). (*Note.* For a subsequent appeal by the same company, see **18.500** below.)

Dishonesty of former partner

[18.315] The dishonesty of a former partner in a firm of solicitors was held to constitute a reasonable excuse in *Stocken & Lambert*, LON/92/2818 (VTD 10527). (*Note.* For another issue in this case, see **18.76** above.)

Dishonesty of bookkeeper

[18.316] In a case where a trader had dismissed his bookkeeper for stealing from him, the tribunal held that this constituted a reasonable excuse for non-payment. *AG Hurlstone*, LON/90/1746 (VTD 6167).

[18.317] Similar decisions were reached in *MM Carew & Son Marble Co Ltd*, LON/93/1888P (VTD 11681) and *Manvik Plant & Hire Ltd*, [2009] UKFTT 144 (TC), TC00112.

Dishonesty of employee

[18.318] In a case where an employee of a partnership had stolen £25,000 from the partnership while the partners were on holiday, the tribunal held that this constituted a reasonable excuse for non-payment. *Swift Catering Services*, LON/91/1400Y (VTD 6740).

[18.319] The theft of funds by employees was also held to constitute a reasonable excuse in *Mid-Rhondda Central Workmen's Institute Ltd*,

LON/91/1206X (VTD 6770); *WL Finch*, LON/98/1066 (VTD 15826), and *Ultimate Hair & Beauty Suppliers Ltd*, LON/07/476 (VTD 20209).

Account frozen by bank

[18.320] A sole trader sold a large quantity of goods for £55,000. His bank initially cleared the purchaser's cheque for this amount, but subsequently informed him that the cheque was a forgery, and froze his account. Consequently he was unable to send a quarterly VAT payment, and Customs imposed a surcharge. The tribunal allowed his appeal, observing that he had sufficient funds to pay the VAT, but had been denied access to them by the bank's action in freezing his account. *RG Richardson (t/a Castle Mouldings)*, LON/89/525Y (VTD 3898).

[18.321] A company (P) issued a cheque for £2,220.50. However, when the cheque was presented, its bank wrongly debited its account with £22,205.50. This substantially increased P's overdraft, and the bank froze its account. The bank did not admit its error until the following month, so that P was unable to pay its quarterly VAT liability. The tribunal held that the bank's error constituted a reasonable excuse. *Premier Roofing Systems Ltd*, MAN/91/246 (VTD 6338).

Overdraft limit reduced by bank

[18.322] In a case where a company's bank unexpectedly reduced its overdraft limit from £470,000 to £220,000, the tribunal held that this constituted a reasonable excuse for the company's inability to pay its VAT liability by the due date. *Kingston Craftsmen (1981) Ltd*, MAN/90/603 (VTD 5409).

[18.323] Similar decisions have been reached in a considerable number of subsequent cases. In the interests of space, such cases are not summarised individually in this book.

Overdraft limit withdrawn by bank

[18.324] In December 1998 a company's bank unexpectedly withdrew its overdraft facility. The tribunal held that the financial problems which this caused constituted a reasonable excuse for the company's inability to pay its VAT liability for the periods ending December 1998 to March 2000 inclusive. *Longstone Ltd*, [2001] VATDR 213 (VTD 17132).

Tax repayment not received

[18.325] A partnership could not pay its VAT liability because it had not received a repayment due from Customs in respect of an earlier period. The tribunal held that this constituted a reasonable excuse. *GT Shaw & MA Whilock*, MAN/88/616 (VTD 3530).

[18.326] A similar decision was reached in *Samzou Ltd*, MAN/93/351 (VTD 11013).

[18.327] A trader (M) paid his VAT liability four days after the due date, and HMRC imposed a surcharge. M appealed, contending that he had a reasonable excuse because he had been awaiting a repayment from HMRC of tax that had been deducted under the Construction Industry Scheme. The tribunal accepted M's evidence and allowed his appeal. *PR Marsh*, LON/06/1099 (VTD 20091).

[**18.328**] A company appealed against a surcharge, contending that it had a reasonable excuse because it was owed almost £9,000 in VAT by the Luxembourg Government. The tribunal accepted this contention and allowed the appeal. *DPC European Transport*, LON/98/850 (VTD 16177).

Excessive balancing payment under Annual Accounting Scheme

[**18.329**] A company (L) had been allowed to adopt the Annual Accounting Scheme from August 1988, and was required to pay £956 per month. In May 1989 its payments were reduced to £10 per month, but in October 1990 they were increased to £1,200 per month. For the year ending July 1991 it was required to make a balancing payment of £15,200. It was unable to pay this, and Customs imposed a surcharge imposed. L appealed, contending that it had a reasonable excuse because of the dramatic fluctuations in the amount of the payments required by Customs. The tribunal allowed the appeal, observing that 'the whole purpose of the Annual Accounting Scheme is to reduce the possibility of a cash-flow crisis for the taxpayer by enabling him to make regular payments of a reasonably consistent amount throughout the year towards his tax liability' and holding that Customs 'had a duty of care to respond effectively to notified changes in circumstances by setting revised realistic monthly payments'. Their failure to do so constituted a reasonable excuse. *Lineplan Ltd*, EDN/92/173 (VTD 9369).

Late payment from Council

[**18.330**] A contractor worked almost exclusively for a London borough council, which persistently paid him late, so that he incurred two surcharges. The tribunal allowed his appeal and the CA upheld this decision (by a 2-1 majority, Scott LJ dissenting). Lord Donaldson of Lymington held that, despite what is now *VATA 1994, s 71(1)(a)*, an insufficiency of funds could constitute a reasonable excuse 'if the exercise of reasonable foresight and of due diligence and a proper regard for the fact that the tax would become due on a particular date would not have avoided the insufficiency'. On the evidence here, if the trader had brought further pressure to bear on the council, 'he would probably have received no further orders and the bulk of his livelihood would have disappeared'. (Nolan LJ commented that 'as a general rule a small trader dealing with larger organisations and having difficulty in securing the prompt payment of his bills should elect to account for his Value Added Tax on the cash basis and would have no reasonable excuse for failing to do so'.) *C & E Commrs v JB Steptoe*, CA [1992] STC 757.

Late payment by major client

[**18.331**] The decision in *Steptoe*, 18.330 above, has been applied in a large number of subsequent cases in which late payment, or non-payment, by a major client has been held to constitute a reasonable excuse for non-payment of VAT. In the interests of space, such cases are not reported individually in this book.

Delay in receiving compensation following compulsory purchase order

[18.332] In a case where a company's premises had been the subject of a compulsory purchase order, and the payment of compensation to the company had been delayed, the tribunal held that this constituted a reasonable excuse for non-payment. *Bridge Metal Services (Thurrock) Ltd*, LON/92/325Z (VTD 7921).

[18.333] A similar decision was reached in *Sandwell Scaffold Co Ltd*, MAN/94/713 (VTD 12823).

Industrial action by Post Office staff

[18.334] As a result of industrial action by Post Office staff, a company failed to receive payment from some of its customers and could only pay part of its VAT liability. Customs imposed a surcharge but the tribunal allowed the company's appeal, holding that the circumstances constituted a reasonable excuse. *A Lockett & Co Ltd*, MAN/89/28 (VTD 3546).

[18.335] Similar decisions were reached in *David Taylor Tool Hire Ltd*, MAN/89/355 (VTD 4969) and *Intertrade (GB) Ltd*, LON/92/1491P (VTD 9610).

Death of director

[18.336] One of the three directors of a building company was killed in a car accident. This led to a sharp drop in the company's income, and it subsequently incurred a surcharge. The tribunal allowed the company's appeal, holding that the circumstances constituted a reasonable excuse. *WBL Ltd*, LON/91/985Z (VTD 6606).

Death of employee

[18.337] The proprietors of a hotel had to cancel an annual dance at two days' notice following the death of one of their employees in a road accident. The loss of the expected income from this dance prevented them from paying their VAT liability, and Customs imposed a surcharge. The tribunal allowed the proprietors' appeal, holding that the circumstances constituted a reasonable excuse. *Corriegour Lodge Hotel*, EDN/93/92 (VTD 11536).

Cash-flow problems following fire

[18.338] A company suffered a fire at its factory, which stopped production for three weeks. This caused cash-flow problems, and it was unable to pay the full amount of its VAT liability. Customs imposed a surcharge but the tribunal allowed the company's appeal, applying the decision in *Salevon Ltd*, **18.312** above. *Baronshire Engineering Ltd*, EDN/90/56 (VTD 5027).

[18.339] A similar decision was reached in *Forgeville Ltd*, LON/96/433 (VTD 14298).

Cash-flow problems following burglary and vandalism

[18.340] A solicitors' firm suffered a burglary. The burglars damaged or destroyed a large quantity of the firm's records. Following the burglary the firm suffered cash-flow problems and Customs imposed a number of surcharges.

The tribunal allowed the firm's appeal, finding that the insufficiency of funds was attributable to the burglary and holding that this constituted a reasonable excuse. *A & JE Stevenson (t/a Prime & Co)*, MAN/99/163 (VTD 17166). (*Note*. For a subsequent application for costs, see **2.485** APPEALS.)

Theft of cash

[18.341] Theft of cash was held to constitute a reasonable excuse for non-payment of VAT in *Top Quality Seconds Prescot Ltd*, MAN/90/207 (VTD 5096); *Fat Sam's American Food & Beverage Co Ltd*, LON/90/1408Z (VTD 5785); *HA Lindsay*, MAN/91/946 & MAN/92/1130 (VTD 9530); *DA Parfitt*, LON/92/3172 (VTD 10184); *RE Tidy*, LON/93/660P (VTD 11957); *Electritec Ltd*, LON/94/392A (VTD 12423) and *DS Rosenberg (t/a Crusade)*, LON/95/3166 (VTD 14049).

Increase in loan repayments

[18.342] A company had obtained a loan from Barclays Bank, which it was repaying by monthly payments of £530. A new branch manager insisted that the payments should be increased to £1,488 per month. This caused the company financial problems, and it incurred a surcharge. The tribunal allowed the company's appeal, holding that the 'unexpected' conduct of the bank constituted a reasonable excuse. *Project Research & Evaluation Ltd*, LON/94/2097P (VTD 13183).

'Civil disturbances'

[18.343] In a Northern Ireland case, the tribunal found that a trader's cash-flow difficulties were 'directly linked to civil disturbances' and held that the circumstances constituted a reasonable excuse. *Mrs E Hill*, LON/00/1223 (VTD 17307).

'Foot and mouth' epidemic

[18.344] A company which operated six hotels suffered cash-flow problems following the 'foot and mouth disease epidemic' of 2001. The tribunal held that this constituted a reasonable excuse for three successive defaults in 2002. *Sir Christopher Wren's House Ltd*, [2006] VATDR 399 (VTD 19504).

Other cases

[18.345] There have been a number of other cases in which tribunals have held that, despite the provisions of *VATA 1994, s 71(1)(a)*, an insufficiency of funds has been attributable to exceptional and unavoidable circumstances which have amounted to a reasonable excuse, but where the nature of the case is such that it is of little value as a precedent. In the interests of space, such cases are not summarised individually in this book.

Cases where the appellant was partly successful

Application of 'Steptoe' principles

[18.346] A company failed to pay its VAT liabilities for five accounting periods by the due dates, and the Commissioners imposed default surcharges. The company appealed, contending that its failure to pay was attributable to non-payment by some of its customers. The tribunal reviewed the evidence in detail and found, applying the principles laid down in *Steptoe*, **18.330** above, that there was no reasonable excuse for the first three defaults in question, but that there was a reasonable excuse for the last two defaults. The company appealed to the QB, which upheld the tribunal decision as one of fact. On the evidence, the tribunal had been entitled to draw a distinction between the first three defaults and the last two defaults. *TE Davey Photo-Service Ltd v C & E Commrs*, QB 1995, [1997] STC 889.

Effect of 'foot and mouth' epidemic—whether a reasonable excuse

[18.347] A couple operated a public house on the edge of the New Forest. They failed to pay their VAT liability for the periods ending 31 October 2001 and 31 January 2002 by the due date, and the Commissioners imposed default surcharges. The tribunal allowed the appeal against the first surcharge, holding that there was a reasonable excuse 'because the national foot and mouth disease epidemic had only officially finished in June 2001 and, as the appellant's licensed premises are on the edge of the New Forest, their business was seriously affected by the cancellation of summer holiday bookings at the critical time when the VAT was due'. However, there was no reasonable excuse for the subsequent default because 'the effect of the foot and mouth disease epidemic had diminished to a great extent and the minimal loss of revenue in the appellants' business, amounting to no more than 10% or thereabouts, did not amount to a *Steptoe* situation'. *PE & WA Broomfield (t/a The Rockingham Arms)*, LON/02/1055 (VTD 18139).

Cash-flow problems following flood

[18.348] A company which operated a hotel suffered cash-flow problems following a flood at the hotel in September 2004. It failed to pay its VAT for the periods ending December 2004 to December 2005 by the due date, and Customs imposed default surcharges. The tribunal allowed the company's appeal in part, holding that the flood constituted a reasonable excuse for the first three periods, but that there was no reasonable excuse for the two later periods. *The Cedar House Hotel Co Ltd*, LON/06/582 (VTD 20012).

Bank withdrawing offer of overdraft

[18.349] A company (L) appealed against seven default surcharges, contending that its bank had verbally agreed to grant it an overdraft of £10,000, but had not honoured the offer. The First-Tier Tribunal held that this constituted a reasonable excuse for the first default, but not for subsequent defaults, and directed that the surcharges should be reduced accordingly. Lady Mitting observed that 'this is not a reason which can just continue open-endedly to constitute a reasonable excuse' and that 'the company continued to trade, receiving VAT from its customers but applying it elsewhere to enable it to continue to trade'. *Littlemoss Preservation Ltd v HMRC*, [2011] UKFTT 692 (TC), TC01534. (*Note.* Appeals against penalties under *FA 2007, Sch 24* were dismissed—see **52.23** PENALTIES: MISDECLARATION AND ERRORS.)

Solicitors' firm suffering financial problems—whether FA 2009,
s 108 applicable

[**18.350**] In December 2008 a solicitors' firm telephoned HMRC to state that it was suffering cash-flow problems and wished to pay its VAT liability for the period ending October 2008 by instalments. HMRC accepted this request and did not impose a default surcharge for that period. However, the firm failed to pay the instalments as agreed, and entered further negotiations with HMRC. After prolonged discussions, in January 2010 it agreed an instalment agreement to cover the periods up to October 2009. The firm began making payments in February 2010. In the meantime, HMRC had imposed a default surcharge for the period ending January 2009, and they subsequently imposed a further surcharge for the period ending October 2009. The firm appealed, contending that the effect of *FA 2009, s 108* was that the surcharges should be withdrawn. (HMRC accepted that *s 108* applied to the periods ending April and July 2009, but considered that it did not apply to the preceding and succeeding periods.) The tribunal allowed the firm's appeal against the surcharge for January 2009, but dismissed the appeal against the surcharge for October 2009 (subject to a reduction in the percentage). Judge Connell found that 'on 28 January 2009 there was an agreement by HMRC to defer further action regarding VAT (and PAYE) owed by the appellant and that the agreement was intended to include both the VAT then outstanding and the VAT for the quarter 01/09.' *Levi Solicitors Llp v HMRC*, [2011] UKFTT 727 (TC), TC01564.

Cases where the appellant was unsuccessful

Repayment claimed to be due to associated company

[**18.351**] A company appealed against 13 surcharges, contending that it had a reasonable excuse for some of the defaults because Customs had taken eight months to make a repayment of VAT to an associated company. The tribunal dismissed the appeals and the CS upheld this decision, holding that the tribunal was entitled to conclude that the only reason for the company's non-payment was insufficiency of funds. Furthermore, the company had taken no steps to register itself or any associated company as a group, and could not claim that non-payment to a separate legal entity was a reason for its own non-payment. *Artful Dodger (Kilmarnock) Ltd v C & E Commrs*, CS [1993] STC 330.

[**18.352**] Similar decisions were reached in *Tape Recorder Hi-Fi Centre*, LON/88/387 (VTD 3221); *Computer Aided Systems (UK) Ltd*, LON/88/657X (VTD 3729); *Errey's Furnishing Ltd*, MAN/89/630X (VTD 4110); *Bondcloak Ltd*, MAN/90/201 (VTD 4858); *Amesbury Motor Co*, LON/92/1448 (VTD 9644); *AT & T Rentals Ltd*, BEL/92/16P (VTD 10790); *Hazel Grove Timber & Building Supplies Ltd*, MAN/95/1409 (VTD 13801) and *MBL Services Ltd*, MAN/07/715 (VTD 20488).

Repayment claimed to be due to associated partnership

[**18.353**] A sole trader appealed against a default surcharge, contending that she had a reasonable excuse because the Commissioners had delayed making a repayment to a family partnership of which she was a member. The tribunal dismissed her appeal, holding that this was not a reasonable excuse. *E Fitzpatrick*, BEL/90/7 (VTD 5427).

[18.354] A similar decision was reached in *M Davidson*, EDN/99/79 (VTD 16207).

[18.355] A company appealed against a default surcharge, contending that it had a reasonable excuse for non-payment because the Commissioners owed money to an associated partnership. The tribunal dismissed the appeal, holding that this was not a reasonable excuse. *Quad (Civil Engineering) Ltd*, MAN/91/119 (VTD 6093).

[18.356] A similar decision was reached in *Philip Maddison Haulage Ltd*, MAN/90/931 (VTD 6428).

Cash-flow problems following withdrawal from Cash Accounting Scheme

[18.357] A company (B) which had adopted the Cash Accounting Scheme found that its turnover had almost reached the statutory maximum, and therefore applied to revert to the normal rules for VAT accounting. Its first return under the normal rules showed an increased VAT liability, and was submitted late. Customs imposed a surcharge and B appealed, contending that its withdrawal from the Cash Accounting Scheme had caused cash-flow problems. The tribunal dismissed the appeal, holding that the insufficiency of funds was foreseeable and did not constitute a reasonable excuse. *Broadgate Software Ltd*, MAN/90/778 (VTD 5662).

[18.358] A similar decision was reached in *Aquability Partnership*, MAN/92/1105 (VTD 10635).

Overdraft limit reduced by bank

[18.359] The reduction of a company's overdraft limit was held not to constitute a reasonable excuse in *Philipson Studios Ltd*, MAN/92/1629 (VTD 10488); *WGM Decorating*, LON/95/445P (VTD 13344); *Executive Security (Wentworth) Ltd*, LON/97/469 (VTD 15052) and *Industcool Engineering Ltd*, LON/97/850 (VTD 15196). (*Note.* Compare, however, *Kingston Craftsmen (1981) Ltd*, **18.322** above, and the note at **18.323** above.)

Cheque from customer delayed in post

[18.360] A company (L) which was suffering cash-flow problems had to pay VAT of about £21,000 for its period ending February 1988. It was expecting a cheque of about £20,000 from a customer. This cheque was posted on or about 24 March but was delayed in the post by an industrial dispute. On 5 April, as the cheque had still not arrived, L's managing director visited the customer and obtained a duplicate cheque which he banked on the same day. He then drew a cheque for the VAT due and delivered it personally to the VAT Central Unit on 6 April. Customs imposed a surcharge and L appealed. The tribunal dismissed the appeal, holding that the case was therefore governed by what is now *VATA 1994, s 71(1)(a)* and the circumstances did not constitute a reasonable excuse. *Lennick Precision Engineering Ltd*, LON/88/1085 (VTD 3342).

[18.361] Similar decisions were reached in *Glendower Cutting Tools Ltd*, MAN/88/917 (VTD 3564) and *PF Baines & J McDonough (t/a Still Visual)*, LON/89/1551X (VTD 4921).

Cash-flow problems following late payment by principal customer

[**18.362**] A trader was unable to pay his VAT liability for the period ending February 1991, and a surcharge was imposed. The trader appealed, contending that he had a reasonable excuse because 80% of his work was carried out for one customer, who owed him more than £200,000. The tribunal dismissed his appeal, finding that the problems were 'relatively short-term', and the business was not solely dependent on the defaulting customer. The decision in *Steptoe*, **18.330** above, was distinguished because the trader there 'was totally dependent on one customer for the continued existence of his business and because of the identity of the customer was unable to exert normal business pressures to induce payment'. *J McCaig*, EDN/91/142 (VTD 6362).

[**18.363**] The decision in *Steptoe*, **18.330** above, has also been distinguished in several subsequent cases where defaulting customers accounted for less than 75% of the appellant's turnover. In the interests of space, such cases are not reported individually in this book.

Cash-flow problems following personal bankruptcy of financial director

[**18.364**] A company had an overdraft facility of £60,000, supported by a personal guarantee given by one of its directors. In 1991 the director became bankrupt, and the bank withdrew the overdraft facility. The company was unable to pay its next VAT liability, and a surcharge was imposed. The tribunal dismissed the company's appeal, holding that the circumstances did not constitute a reasonable excuse. *Relay Couriers Ltd*, LON/91/2098Z (VTD 7990).

Cash-flow problems following receivership of major shareholder

[**18.365**] A company (S) failed to pay its VAT liability for the period ending July 1991 by the due date, and a surcharge was imposed. S appealed, contending that 33% of its share capital was owned by another company (R), which had gone into receivership in June 1991. The tribunal dismissed the appeal, holding that the circumstances did not constitute a reasonable excuse. *Sea-Change Ltd*, MAN/93/1268 (VTD 11759).

Cash-flow problems attributed to economic recession

[**18.366**] A company which had been unable to pay its VAT liability appealed against a default surcharge, contending that its cash-flow problems were caused by the 'severe effects of the recession', rather than by any culpable default. The tribunal dismissed the appeal, holding that 'the general state of the economy cannot in itself be a satisfactory excuse for late payment' and that the case was governed by what is now *VATA 1994, s 71(1)(a)*. *The Gardens Entertainments Ltd*, LON/92/136Z (VTD 8972).

[**18.367**] Similar decisions were reached in *Faxlink Communications*, LON/91/2747Y (VTD 7766); *Northern Software Consultants Ltd*, MAN/91/1021 (VTD 9027); *Flan-Form Ltd*, LON/92/1444P (VTD 9415); *Melroad Ltd (t/a UK Pipework Fabrications)*, MAN/92/102 (VTD 9438); *Gableglade Ltd*, LON/92/2006 (VTD 9597); *Merseyside Trailer Hire*, MAN/92/801 (VTD 10136); *Alucast (Diecastings) Ltd*, MAN/92/912 (VTD 10291); *Tipton Non-Ferrous Foundry Ltd*, MAN/92/913 (VTD 10328) and *E Steventon & Co Ltd*, LON/93/1449P (VTD 11250).

Cash-flow problems attributed to labour costs

[**18.368**] A company appealed against a default surcharge, contending that it had needed to make some of its employees redundant in order to reduce its labour costs, but that the statutory redundancy payments had increased its short-term cash-flow problems. The tribunal dismissed the appeal, holding that the circumstances did not constitute a reasonable excuse. *ADM (North East) Ltd*, MAN/93/1473 (VTD 12640).

Cash-flow problems attributed to change of premises

[**18.369**] A company appealed against a default surcharge, contending that it had a reasonable excuse because of the cost of changing premises. The tribunal dismissed the appeal, holding that the circumstances did not constitute a reasonable excuse. *Performance Print Ltd*, MAN/98/572 (VTD 15810).

Payment by instalments

[**18.370**] A partnership was unable to pay the whole of its quarterly VAT liability by the due date. It submitted a valid cheque for part of the amount due, and a postdated cheque for the remainder. Customs imposed a surcharge and the tribunal dismissed the partnership's appeal. *London Bridge Cycles*, LON/87/593 (VTD 2550).

[**18.371**] A company was unable to pay its quarterly liability due on 31 October 1989. It posted a letter to Customs on 26 October 1989, offering payment by instalments. The director concluded the letter with the words 'I hope that this arrangement is acceptable to you, if it is not please contact me by return post'. Customs did not reply to the letter but imposed a surcharge. The tribunal dismissed the company's appeal, holding that an offer to pay tax by instalments without Customs' approval or consent could not be a reasonable excuse for not making such payments at the time and in the manner laid down by Parliament. The fact that the Commissioners had not sent an immediate reply to the company's letter could not be taken as implying either approval or consent. *Alexis Modes Ltd*, LON/90/27Z (VTD 4780).

[**18.372**] Similar decisions have been reached in a considerable number of subsequent cases. In the interests of space, such cases are not summarised individually in this book. For a list of such cases decided up to 31 December 2009, see Tolley's VAT Cases 2010.

Payment by postdated cheque

[**18.373**] Three associated partnerships paid their VAT liability for the period ending 30 April 1987 with cheques postdated to 1 June. Customs imposed surcharges and the tribunal dismissed the partnerships' appeals, observing that the obligation to effect payment by the due date was not satisfied by the delivery of a cheque dated after the due date had expired, and holding that there was no reasonable excuse for the defaults. *John Oliver Haircutters (Colchester); Hair by John Oliver; John Oliver Haircutters*, [1987] VATTR 239 (VTD 2532).

[**18.374**] The decision in *John Oliver Haircutters (Colchester)*, **18.373** above, was applied in the similar cases of *Double D Freight Services Ltd*,

MAN/89/333 (VTD 3987); *Eurowear Fashions Ltd*, LON/88/654 (VTD 3600, 4012); *North Birmingham & Aldridge Motor Co Ltd*, MAN/89/108 (VTD 4014); *Valewood Furniture Ltd*, LON/93/1203 (VTD 12447) and *Southern Ski Enterprises Ltd*, 18.108 above.

[18.375] There have been a very large number of other cases in which tribunals have held that the submission of postdated cheques has not constituted a reasonable excuse for the late payment of the VAT due. In the interests of space, such cases are not summarised individually in this book. For a list of such cases decided up to 31 December 1995, see Tolley's VAT Cases 1996.

Postdated cheques previously accepted by Commissioners

[18.376] A partnership which had submitted a postdated cheque in payment of its liability appealed against a default surcharge, contending that the Commissioners had always accepted postdated cheques in the past. The tribunal dismissed the appeal, holding that this did not constitute a reasonable excuse. *JP Sim & Co*, EDN/87/78 (VTD 2543).

[18.377] Similar decisions were reached in *DVK Executive Hotels*, LON/90/68X (VTD 4786) and *AD High & Sons Ltd*, LON/95/1306 (VTD 13399).

Temporary insufficiency of funds

[18.378] See *Palco Industry Co Ltd*, 18.414 below.

Cash-flow problems attributed to absence of financial controller on holiday

[18.379] See *Picken & Son Ltd*, 18.222 above.

Cash-flow problems following loss of credit controller

[18.380] A company's credit controller gave one month's notice on 6 June 1991, and left her employment on 6 July 1991. Following her departure, the company's cash-flow deteriorated, and the company was unable to pay its liability for the periods ending 31 July and 31 October by the due date. The Commissioners accepted that there was a reasonable excuse for the non-payment of the tax for the period ending 31 July, but imposed a surcharge in respect of the following period. The tribunal dismissed the company's appeal, holding that the circumstances did not constitute a reasonable excuse. *Q-Com Maintenance Ltd*, MAN/92/1834 (VTD 12918).

Cash-flow problems attributed to divorce

[18.381] An accountant appealed against two default surcharges, contending that he had a reasonable excuse for non-payment since his wife had left him and he had suffered cash-flow problems as a result of the divorce settlement. The tribunal dismissed his appeal, holding that this did not constitute a reasonable excuse. *MS Ramsey*, LON/95/2783 (VTD 14280).

Income tax repayment not received

[18.382] A solicitor appealed against a default surcharge, contending that he had a reasonable excuse for non-payment because he had been expecting a repayment of income tax relating to an investment in a film partnership which had made losses. The tribunal dismissed his appeal, holding that this did not constitute a reasonable excuse. The tribunal observed that 'the investment made by the appellant in the film partnership was, in terms of business, unrelated to his business as a solicitor in private practice – the only relationship was that he anticipated that the investment would provide relief in the form of losses which could be set against the taxable profits of his solicitor's practice thereby reducing the amount of income tax payable on those profits. It is clear from the case law that where a business suffers a cashflow difficulty which could not reasonably have been expected, then that might constitute a reasonable excuse for the late payment of the VAT due in relation to that business, but that must be a difficulty resulting from the vicissitudes of the business itself. In this case the appellant chose to invest funds otherwise available to his business (together with a substantial borrowing) to make a very sizeable investment in an unrelated business less than three months before his VAT was due. The detriment he suffered (or, rather, which we are prepared to assume he suffered) was in respect of that investment, not his solicitor's practice. He would have been fully able to pay his VAT on time in relation to his solicitor's practice had he not made the investment in the unrelated business. A taxable person is expected to make proper provision for the payment of VAT due from his business, and it is not reasonable that losses or other detriment suffered as a result of other ventures which he embarks upon should excuse him from making such proper provision.' *DR Walker*, LON/08/549 (VTD 20937).

Other cases

[18.383] There have been a very large number of other cases in which appellants have contended that they could not pay the tax due because of cash-flow problems, and in which the appeals have been dismissed. In the interests of space, such cases are not summarised individually in this book.

Cheque dishonoured or incorrectly made out

Cases where the appellant was successful

Cheque wrongly dishonoured by bank

[18.384] A company paid its quarterly liability by a cheque drawn on the Royal Bank of Scotland. The bank failed to honour the cheque. The company protested to the bank, which apologised and confirmed that the cheque should have been met, but had been dishonoured through a 'clerical error'. The company subsequently paid the VAT with a banker's draft, but this was not sent until after the due date and Customs imposed a surcharge. The tribunal allowed the company's appeal, holding that the bank's error constituted a reasonable excuse for the late payment. *Hydrabell Ltd*, LON/88/1256 (VTD 3519).

[18.385] Similar decisions have been reached in a considerable number of subsequent cases. in the interests of space, such cases are not summarised individually in this book. For a list of such cases reported up to 31 December 1996, see Tolley's VAT Cases 1997.

[18.386] An appeal was allowed in a case where a bank had failed to honour an agreement that it would telephone a company before dishonouring a cheque in payment of VAT. *Speedy Products Ltd*, MAN/91/406 (VTD 6754).

[18.387] Similar decisions were reached in *KCS Management Systems*, LON/91/2703 (VTD 9013) and *A Boon (t/a Allan Boon Haulage)*, LON/92/2257P (VTD 9952).

[18.388] A similar decision was reached in a case where a bank dishonoured a cheque although the company in question had adequate funds in another account, and the bank had previously checked the state of the other account before dishonouring a cheque. *Around the Clock Ltd*, LON/91/1304Y (VTD 7157).

[18.389] Similar decisions were reached in *Bowden Associates Ltd*, MAN/91/133 (VTD 7449); *JMG Gregory*, LON/92/738Y (VTD 7979); *Mikelyjos Process Automation Ltd*, LON/93/894 (VTD 11305); *WGM Decorating*, LON/93/2850P (VTD 12401); *Computer Technology Solutions Ltd*, LON/94/1007 (VTD 12721) and *Purite Ltd*, LON/99/84 (VTD 16161).

[18.390] An appeal was allowed in a case where a bank had returned a cheque to Customs endorsed 'signature differs', and the company's managing director gave evidence that he had signed the cheque and was an authorised signatory. *Kirkcroft Skips Ltd*, MAN/91/1226 (VTD 7560).

[18.391] An appeal was allowed in a case where the appellant had paid sufficient funds into his account two days before Customs presented his cheque, but the bank had dishonoured the cheque and returned it endorsed 'effects uncleared'. *AL Evans*, MAN/91/1498 (VTD 7639).

[18.392] Similar decisions were reached in *Awnhail Ltd*, MAN/93/911 (VTD 11465); *MD McDonald*, MAN/93/655 (VTD 12153) and *AJ Buthwick*, LON/94/1300P (VTD 12782).

[18.393] An appeal was allowed in a case where a bank cashier had failed to process a cheque which had been submitted for payment by bank giro. The tribunal held that the cashier's error constituted a reasonable excuse. *Isis Specialist Office Supplies Ltd*, LON/95/987 (VTD 13389).

Bank returning cheque unpaid endorsed 'refer to drawer please represent'

[18.394] A partnership's cheque was dishonoured by its bank, being returned endorsed 'refer to drawer please represent'. Customs imposed a surcharge and the partnership appealed, contending that the cheque would have been honoured if it had been represented, and producing a letter from the bank to confirm this. The tribunal allowed the appeal, finding that the bank would have honoured the cheque if it had known that Customs adopted a policy of not representing cheques, and holding that the circumstances constituted a reasonable excuse. *M Simpson & G Scoffin*, MAN/91/1130 (VTD 7390). (*Note.* No other cases were referred to in the decision. Compare *Palco Industry Co Ltd*, **18.414** below, *Walsh*, **18.416** below, and the cases noted at **18.417** below.)

Commissioners delaying presentation of cheque

[18.395] A company (S) delivered its return and cheque for the period ending 31 March 1991 to its local VAT office by hand on 30 April. In mid-May S received an estimated assessment for the relevant period, with a covering letter stating that its return and payment had not been received. S's director assumed that the cheque had been lost in transit. He therefore cancelled the original cheque and issued a replacement. In the meantime, Customs belatedly presented the original cheque, which was returned unpaid by S's bank. Customs imposed a surcharge but the tribunal allowed S's appeal. In assuming that the original cheque had been lost in transit, and consequently cancelling it, S had not acted unreasonably and there was no justification for a surcharge. *Shearer Holdings Ltd*, EDN/91/214 (VTD 7088).

Cheque dishonoured following change of bank account

[18.396] A company submitted a return shortly before moving its bank account from Barclays to National Westminster. The return was delayed in the post and the cheque which accompanied it was not presented until after the closure of the Barclays account. In the meantime Barclays had already returned a number of cheques, unpaid, to the company instead of forwarding them to National Westminster in accordance with normal banking practice. When the director realised that the return had been delayed, he personally gave a cheque drawn on the National Westminster account to a VAT officer. The tribunal held that the circumstances constituted a reasonable excuse. *Artic Shield Ltd*, MAN/89/248 (VTD 3789).

[18.397] A similar decision was reached in another unrelated case where a company's accountant had submitted a return while in the process of transferring the relevant bank account from Barclays to National Westminster. Although there were adequate funds in the account for the cheque to be cleared, Barclays dishonoured the cheque instead of forwarding it to National Westminster in accordance with normal banking practice. The tribunal allowed the company's appeal, holding that the circumstances constituted a reasonable excuse. *Donnison & Smith Engineering Ltd*, MAN/90/770 (VTD 5651).

[18.398] A similar decision was reached in *Jardin Trim Ltd*, LON/92/288 (VTD 7695).

Cheques previously represented by Customs

[18.399] A company's cheque for the period ending 31 March 1991 was returned unpaid by its bank, endorsed 'refer to drawer—please represent'. However, Customs did not represent the cheque, and imposed a surcharge. The company appealed, contending that the cheque would have been honoured on representation, and that its cheque for the period ending 30 September 1990 had been similarly dishonoured when first presented but had subsequently been represented and honoured without a surcharge being imposed. The company's accountant referred the tribunal to a statement by Customs Press Office, reproduced in *Tolley's Practical Tax 1986* at p 120, which stated that 'provided that a cheque, which is subsequently honoured, is received by the Commissioners on or before the due date, a default will not be recorded'. The tribunal allowed the appeal. The company was clearly in default and its insufficiency of funds could not constitute a reasonable excuse. However, the fact that Customs had previously represented dishonoured cheques, and had publicly stated that they would do so without imposing surcharges, and had not advised the company of their change of policy, meant that the company had a reasonable excuse for its late payment. *Professional Testing Services Ltd*, EDN/91/166 (VTD 6689). (*Note.* Compare *Palco Industry Ltd*, **18.414** below; *Walsh*, **18.416** below, and the cases noted at **18.417** below.

[18.400] The decision in *Professional Testing Services Ltd*, **18.399** above, was applied in the similar case of *Cleshar Contract Services Ltd*, LON/91/1066 (VTD 7621).

Cheque accidentally postdated

[18.401] In a case where a cheque was inadvertently dated 31 November 1988 rather than 31 October 1988, the tribunal held that this error was a reasonable excuse. *Holland Studio Craft Ltd*, MAN/89/34 (VTD 3771).

[18.402] The accidental postdating of a cheque was also held to constitute a reasonable excuse in *Jackson & Padgett Ltd*, MAN/88/795 (VTD 3435); *Robinson Cooke*, LON/88/806Y (VTD 4040); *SP Caswell*, LON/89/1172X (VTD 4176); *JCB Electronics Ltd*, LON/89/1360Y (VTD 5004); *SA Gee*, MAN/90/832 (VTD 5656); *AK Masson*, LON/91/1298Z (VTD 6542); *B Short*, MAN/91/769 (VTD 6694); *DL Powell*, LON/92/447Z (VTD 7933); *LV Turner*, MAN/94/777 (VTD 12839) and *GH Poole (t/a Glenwood Polishing & Manufacturing 1992)*, MAN/99/573 (VTD 16339). (Note. There have, however, been many more cases where accidentally postdating a cheque has been held not to constitute a reasonable excuse—see **18.419** below.)

Cheque out of date

[18.403] An appeal was allowed in a case where a company had inadvertently dated a cheque 1986 instead of 1988. *Corton Bashforth Screenprint Ltd*, MAN/88/491 (VTD 3232).

[18.404] Similar decisions were reached in *Alsuna Ltd*, MAN/89/278 (VTD 3845); *RA & E Hodgson*, MAN/90/92 (VTD 5052); *Singh & Choudry*, LON/92/201 (VTD 7654); *J Austin*, LON/91/1442X (VTD 7668) and *Guy Engraving & Engineering Co*, LON/92/2003P (VTD 9337).

Cheque not signed in accordance with bank mandate

[18.405] An appeal was allowed in a case where a company had submitted a cheque signed by two signatories who were not directors, but had overlooked the fact that, as the cheque was for more than £2,000, it should have been signed by a director in accordance with the bank mandate. *Swanlion Ltd*, MAN/88/341 (VTD 3399). (*Note.* Compare the cases noted at **18.423** to **18.425** below, where similar circumstances were held not to constitute a reasonable excuse.)

[18.406] An appeal was allowed in a case where a company had submitted a cheque signed by only one director, when its bank mandate required the signature of two directors, and gave evidence that the omission was accidental. *Green Cook Ltd*, LON/90/1749X (VTD 5781).

[18.407] A similar decision was reached in *Megatron Ltd*, LON/92/1369 (VTD 9207).

Alteration to cheque not initialled

[18.408] A trader submitted a VAT return with a cheque on which the date had been altered in manuscript, but the alteration had not been initialled. (The alteration in question amended the date by one calendar month, and the cheque had not been postdated.) The bank did not honour the cheque but returned it unpaid, endorsed 'alteration required drawer's signature'. Customs imposed a surcharge, and the trader appealed. The tribunal allowed the appeal, applying a statement in *Halsbury's Laws of England vol. 3(1) para 180*, and holding that it was unreasonable for the bank not have honoured the cheque, since the cheque was neither postdated nor out of date, regardless of whether the original date or the altered date was taken as the date of issue. *C Rees*, LON/89/734 (VTD 4440).

[18.409] A similar decision was reached in a case where the date on a cheque had been altered from 1931 to 1991, and the alteration had not been initialled. The tribunal commented that the bank were 'not justified' in failing to honour the cheque. *Party Paragon The Shop Ltd*, LON/91/1886 (VTD 7242).

[18.410] An appeal was allowed in a case where the appellant had failed to initial an alteration to a cheque, and the Commissioners had returned the cheque to him for amendment without presenting it. *R Smallman*, LON/93/1990 (VTD 11538).

[18.411] A similar decision was reached in *Dellastreet Systems Ltd*, MAN/92/330 (VTD 11965).

Cheque submitted for incorrect amount

[18.412] The tribunal allowed an appeal against a default surcharge in a case where a firm had sent a cheque in the sum of £6,322.22 in respect of a payment due, as shown on the return, of £6,332.22. *Shirlaw Allan & Co*, EDN/87/111 (VTD 2596).

[18.413] Similar decisions were reached in *RS Wainwright*, BEL/88/14 (VTD 3150); *AG Hill*, MAN/89/276 (VTD 3809); *Dixons*, LON/89/802Z (VTD 4053); *Deepblue Ltd*, LON/89/448Y (VTD 4126); *Nightingale Music Ltd*, LON/90/630X (VTD 5060); *Lysander Systems Ltd*, LON/95/222P (VTD 13672) and *PA Hutchinson*, LON/08/1893 (VTD 20898).

Cases where the appellant was unsuccessful

Cheque delayed in post

[18.414] A company (P), which had an overdraft facility of £1 million, posted its return for the period ending 31 October 1988 by recorded delivery on 28 November. A cheque for the tax due was sent with the return. The return was not delivered until 7 December. However, because the cheque was for more than £10,000, it was presented by the Commissioners on the day of receipt. The cheque was dishonoured and a default surcharge was imposed. The company appealed, contending that the cheque would have been cleared if it had been delivered promptly by the Post Office. The QB upheld the surcharge, holding that it was the responsibility of the drawer of a cheque to ensure that there were adequate funds available to meet that cheque. A cheque was only valid as payment if it was honoured on due presentation, which did not require immediate presentation or presentation on some precisely calculated day. A payer could not dictate when a cheque was to be paid. What is now *VATA 1994, s 71(1)(a)* specifically excluded an 'insufficiency of funds' as a reasonable excuse for the failure to pay any tax due. The despatch of a worthless cheque could not amount to the despatch of tax. *C & E Commrs v Palco Industry Co Ltd*, QB [1990] STC 594.

[18.415] The decision in *Palco Industry Co Ltd*, **18.414** above, has been applied in a very large number of subsequent cases. In the interests of space, such cases are not summarised individually in this book. For a list of such cases decided up to 31 December 2009, see Tolley's VAT Cases 2010.

Cheque not represented by Customs

[18.416] A trader's contention that a dishonoured cheque should have been represented by Customs, since it might have been honoured if represented, was rejected by the tribunal in *JS Walsh*, MAN/89/81 (VTD 3706).

[18.417] The decision in *Walsh*, **18.416** above, was applied in *Wiltshire & Gloucestershire Draining Co Ltd*, LON/91/1102 (VTD 6559); *Aztec Computer Products Ltd*, LON/91/1753Y (VTD 7127); *Lady Jane (London) Ltd*, LON/91/2263Y (VTD 7143); *Sophia Ltd*, LON/91/1243Y (VTD 7261) and *Valley Industrial Services Ltd*, LON/91/2231Y (VTD 9302).

[18.418] Similar decisions have been reached in a large number of other cases. In the interests of space, such cases are not summarised individually in this book. For a list of such cases decided up to 31 December 2009, see Tolley's VAT Cases 2010.

Cheque accidentally postdated

[18.419] There have been a very large number of cases in which the tribunal has held that accidentally postdating the cheque tendered in payment of the VAT due does not constitute a reasonable excuse for non-payment. In the interests of space, such cases are not summarised individually in this book. For a list of such cases decided up to 31 December 2009, see Tolley's VAT Cases 2010.

Cheque out of date

[18.420] A company submitted a cheque dated 1989 instead of 1990. The cheque was not honoured by its bank and a default surcharge was imposed. The tribunal dismissed the company's appeal, holding that the circumstances did not constitute a reasonable excuse. *CBR System Ltd*, LON/90/1905Y (VTD 5871).

[18.421] Similar decisions were reached in *Lois Engineering Ltd*, MAN/91/783 (VTD 7327); *Selmar Burglar Alarms Co Ltd*, LON/92/347Y (VTD 7740); *Eglington DIY Ltd*, BEL/92/56 (VTD 9858); *Pedersen Caterers*, LON/93/193P & 523P (VTD 10818); *JE Hill*, MAN/93/83 (VTD 10967); *Cambridge Connectivity Ltd*, LON/94/1694P (VTD 13046); *Fourth Road Consultants Ltd*, EDN/95/22 (VTD 13626); *Cobb McCallum & Co*, EDN/06/32 (VTD 19668) and *Magnumcraft Technology Ltd*, LON/07/892 (VTD 20733).

Unsigned cheque

[18.422] There have been a very large number of cases in which the tribunal has held that the accidental failure to sign the cheque tendered in payment of the VAT due does not constitute a reasonable excuse for non-payment. In the interests of space, such cases are not summarised individually in this book. For a list of such cases decided up to 31 December 1994, see Tolley's VAT Cases 1995.

Cheque not signed in accordance with bank mandate

[18.423] A company submitted a cheque for its quarterly VAT payment with only one signature, although its bank mandate required two signatures. The bank did not honour the cheque and the tribunal held that the oversight did not constitute a reasonable excuse. *Hamperbay Ltd*, LON/88/547 (VTD 3048).

[18.424] The decision in *Hamperbay Ltd*, **18.423** above, was applied in *Readon Holdings Ltd*, MAN/89/183 (VTD 3705).

[18.425] Similar decisions were reached in *Fairview Windows Ltd*, MAN/88/788 (VTD 3619); *Sign Specialists Ltd*, MAN/89/681 (VTD 4477); *Wardhire Ltd*, LON/90/136Y (VTD 5622); *Freeway Marketing Ltd*, LON/90/1751Y (VTD 5905); *The Cloth Development Co Ltd*, LON/90/1854Z (VTD 5985); *J & S Glass Mirror Centre*, LON/91/64Y (VTD 6117); *Graphicad Ltd*, MAN/91/228 (VTD 6503); *Bardon Environmental Services Ltd*, MAN/91/651 (VTD 6504); *Portswood Haulage Contractors*, LON/91/965X (VTD 6556); *A Sinclair (t/a The Magpie Bar)*, EDN/91/98 (VTD 6589); *P Hodgkiss*, EDN/91/144 (VTD 6825); *Quality Embryo Transfer Co Ltd*, MAN/91/324 (VTD 7538); *LWM Alexander Oliver Bennett Partnership*, EDN/92/151 (VTD 9153); *Thousand Yard Store*, LON/93/1676P (VTD 12006); *Brainstormers Web Factory Ltd*, LON/98/730 (VTD 15761); *Merriman White*, LON/97/516 & LON/98/1449 (VTD 16045); *Excel Shopfitting Ltd*, LON/98/1265 (VTD 16270); *Firepoint Scotland Ltd*, EDN/02/192 (VTD 18187); *LTE Network Communications Ltd*, LON/06/374 (VTD 19643), and *East India Devonshire Sports & Public Schools Club Ltd*, [2010] UKFTT 627 (TC), TC00866.

Alterations to cheque not initialled

[18.426] A company's cheque was dishonoured by its bank because the date on the cheque had been altered but the alteration had not been initialled. The tribunal held that the failure to initial the alteration was not a reasonable excuse. *KBC Tent & Marquee Hire Ltd*, MAN/90/26 (VTD 4765).

[18.427] Similar decisions were reached in *Applied Cutting Technology*, LON/91/1138Z (VTD 6489) and *R & R Herman (t/a Retell)*, LON/99/241 (VTD 16591).

Words and figures on cheque differing

[18.428] An appeal was dismissed in a case where a trader had submitted a cheque on which the amount shown in words differed from that shown in figures, and the VAT Central Unit returned the cheque to the trader for amendment without presenting it. *PA Delaney*, LON/91/438Y (VTD 6105). (*Note.* For the validity of such a cheque, see *Covercraft Ltd*, 18.28 above, and *Mather*, 18.29 above. Neither of these cases were referred to in the decision.)

[18.429] Similar decisions were reached in *Magpie Court Ltd*, LON/91/473Z (VTD 6166); *MM Chea*, LON/91/1127Y (VTD 6357); *RG Crabb*, LON/91/1546Y (VTD 9091); *DP Stephenson (t/a Sutton Chauffeuring)*, MAN/92/527 (VTD 9914); *CW Aberdeen (t/a Smithfield Electronics)*, MAN/91/801 & MAN/92/1437 (VTD 9944); *Rebel Fashions*, MAN/97/112 (VTD 15057) and *Sutherland Commercial Cleaning Services Ltd*, EDN/07/145 (VTD 20651).

Amount in words not included on cheque.

[18.430] A company sent Customs a cheque on which the amount due was correctly stated in figures, but which did not include the payee's name or the amount in words. The bank did not honour the cheque and Customs imposed a surcharge. The tribunal dismissed the company's appeal, holding that there was no reasonable excuse for the error. *Osteria Romana Ltd*, LON/08/203 (VTD 20635).

Cheque made out for incorrect amount

[18.431] An appeal was dismissed in a case where the company had submitted a cheque for a lesser amount than the liability shown on its return, and contended that the error was accidental. *A Williams & Son*, LON/89/801Z (VTD 4191).

[18.432] Similar decisions were reached in *Nature's Larder*, EDN/90/44 (VTD 4856); *WA Lawson*, LON/90/506X (VTD 5823); *Anglian Farming Contracts Ltd*, LON/92/635X (VTD 7928) and *NB McMahon*, LON/94/1306P (VTD 12904).

Misleading advice from Customs

Cases where the appellant was successful

Telephone conversation with VAT office

[18.433] A company had obtained permission from the Commissioners to submit returns covering twelve-week periods rather than quarterly periods. It was sent a return covering a period from 15 August 1987 to 7 November 1987. The due date for this return was stated on the return form to be 7 December 1987. However, one of the company's directors telephoned the Halifax VAT office and was informed by that office that the due date was 31 December 1987. The return was actually sent on 29 December and received on 31 December. The Commissioners imposed a default surcharge, but the tribunal allowed the company's appeal. The date by which the return was legally due remained 7 December 1987, as stated on the return form. However, the Halifax VAT office had incorrectly informed the company that the due date was 31 December, and the company therefore had a reasonable excuse for believing that that was the due date. *ASJ Manufacturing Ltd*, MAN/88/156 (VTD 2832).

[18.434] Similar decisions were reached in *Wallace King plc*, LON/91/566Z (VTD 6498); *Lycett Industries Ltd*, MAN/91/1563 (VTD 11672) and *Martin Groundland & Co Ltd*, EDN/98/82 (VTD 15696).

[18.435] A company did not have sufficient funds to pay its VAT liability for the period ending 30 April 1988. Its managing director telephoned the local VAT office in mid-May and asked whether it would be acceptable to pay by three postdated cheques, the last cheque to be dated 21 June. The conversation that followed was disputed, but the tribunal found that the VAT officer who took the call had led the director to believe that the submission of such cheques would be acceptable. Accordingly the circumstances constituted a reasonable excuse. *Harley Engineering Ltd*, LON/88/768 (VTD 3271).

[18.436] Similar decisions were reached in *Archway (Shoes) Ltd*, LON/89/1147Y (VTD 4250); *Slee Blackwell Solicitors*, LON/91/1312Z (VTD 7263); *A Better Choice Ltd*, LON/92/1501P (VTD 9048); *EJ Scarlett (t/a Spectrum Building Services)*, LON/92/2173P (VTD 9618); *Mo's Music Machine Ltd*, LON/92/2843 (VTD 10032); *Wentworth Sawmills Ltd*, MAN/92/640 (VTD 10105); *A Erskine Electrical Co Ltd*, MAN/92/1536 (VTD 10139); *Unique Sealed Units Ltd*, LON/92/2904 (VTD 10235); *Vitalia Ltd*, LON/93/1900P (VTD 11682); *EAP Ltd*, LON/93/2193P (VTD 12089) and *Dawson Strange Photography Ltd*, LON/98/1411 (VTD 15967).

[18.437] A company which was suffering cash-flow problems did not send its payment for the period ending 31 March 1999 until 30 April. The Commissioners imposed a surcharge but the tribunal allowed the company's appeal, finding that a VAT officer had agreed to allow the late payment in a telephone conversation with the company's accountants. *Gray Dunn & Co Ltd*, EDN/00/71 (VTD 16839).

[18.438] A video producer had arranged to be abroad on business from 15 January 1991 to 2 March 1991. In December 1990 she telephoned her local VAT office to ask whether she could delay her return for the period ending 31 January 1991 until after she returned to the UK. The officer to whom she spoke asked her to write to the office with details. She wrote to the office on 3 January, stating that she would submit the return as soon as possible after 2 March. She received no reply, and a default surcharge was imposed, against which she appealed. The tribunal allowed her appeal, holding that, when she telephoned her local VAT office, she should have been advised to submit an estimated return. She had been given misleading advice by the VAT office and, in view of this, her absence abroad constituted a reasonable excuse. *SG Flinders*, LON/91/1022X (VTD 6349).

[18.439] A trader was unable to pay the full amount of his VAT liability for the period ending 31 August 2002. He telephoned his local VAT office to ask if he could make a payment on account and pay the balance at a later date. The officer to whom he spoke told him that part payment was not acceptable. Subsequently the Commissioners imposed a default surcharge, against which the trader appealed. The tribunal allowed the appeal against 50% of the surcharge, finding that the trader would have paid this amount before the due date if it had not been for the misleading advice given by his local VAT office, and holding that this constituted a reasonable excuse with regard to 50% of the surcharge. *JH Harman*, LON/03/029 (VTD 18415).

[**18.440**] The decision in *Harman*, **18.439** above, was applied in the similar subsequent cases of *Mediaid Training Services Ltd*, LON/07/1298 (VTD 20902) and *Hipisol Ltd*, [2010] UKFTT 392 (TC), TC00388.

[**18.441**] Misleading advice by a VAT officer was also held to constitute a reasonable excuse in *Trendadd Ltd*, LON/88/479 (VTD 3222); *RA Dentith v The Treasury of the Isle of Man Government* , MAN/x (VTD 4272); *Business Post Holdings Ltd*, LON/89/879 & LON/90/69Y (VTD 5002); *TJD Garrard*, LON/90/1061Y (VTD 5447); *PDS (Gold Plating) Co Ltd*, LON/90/328Z (VTD 5468); *PJ Woods*, MAN/91/202 (VTD 6134); *ASI Glass Processing Ltd*, MAN/94/441 (VTD 12631); *TM Technology Ltd*, MAN/96/480 (VTD 14509); *Hannah Auto Electronics Ltd*, EDN/97/231 (VTD 15429) ; *Dental IT Ltd*, [2011] UKFTT 128 (TC), TC01002, and *Clifford Construction Ltd*, **18.22** above.

[**18.442**] An appeal was allowed in a case where a VAT officer had agreed to accept payment of a partnership's quarterly liability by instalments, and had not informed the partnership that this agreement would not prevent a default surcharge from being imposed. The tribunal held that the circumstances constituted a reasonable excuse for the late payment. *Andrews Kent & Stone*, LON/92/309X (VTD 7753).

[**18.443**] Similar decisions were reached in *T Cooper-Cocks*, LON/92/1380 (VTD 9062); *Qubit UK Ltd*, LON/92/1685 & 1847 (VTD 9073); *K Coombes*, LON/92/1068Y (VTD 9417); *Key Personnel (Midlands) Ltd*, MAN/92/668 (VTD 9833); *CDN Property Services Ltd*, LON/94/301 (VTD 12275);*By Storm Ltd*, EDN/01/19 (VTD 17249); *MHC (Michael Hammond Partnership)*, [2004] VATDR 1 (VTD 18504); *Premier Leisure (Events) Ltd*, MAN/05/406 (VTD 19320) and *A MacQueen*, EDN/07/89 (VTD 20386).

[**18.444**] A company paid its VAT liability by the due date, but did not submit the return until three days after the due date. Customs imposed a surcharge and the company appealed, contending that a VAT officer had informed it that provided that the relevant payments were made on time, the late submission of the return 'would not be a problem'. The tribunal accepted the company's evidence and allowed its appeal. *Specialist Computer Holdings Ltd*, [2007] VATDR 396 (VTD 20440).

[**18.445**] In the March 1991 Budget, the Chancellor of the Exchequer announced that the standard rate of VAT would be increased from 15% to 17.5% with effect from 1 April 1991. A partnership which supplied windows had already taken a large number of provisional orders, in respect of which it had quoted prices on the basis that the rate of VAT would be 15%. It consulted the Balham VAT office as to the effect of the change, and was told that it must charge VAT at 17.5% unless the tax point was before 1 April. In order to create a tax point before the increase in the rate, it issued invoices in respect of these provisional orders dated March 1991. Because of the increased work which this caused, its return for the period ending 31 March was not submitted until after the due date, and a default surcharge was imposed. The partnership appealed, contending that the increased workload constituted a reasonable excuse. The tribunal accepted this contention and allowed the appeal, observing that the Balham VAT office should have informed the partnership of the effect of what is now *VATA 1994, s 89*, under which VAT could have been charged at 15% in respect of contracts made before 1 April, even if the tax point was not until 1 April. *Brytahomes Window Company*, LON/91/1599X (VTD 9379).

Misunderstanding between appellant and VAT officer

[18.446] An appeal was allowed in a case where the appellant contended that he had been given permission by a VAT officer to delay payment until the following period. The tribunal accepted his evidence in respect of the conversation that had taken place between him and the officer. The Commissioners could 'otherwise allow or direct', within what is now *VAT Regulations 1995 (SI 1995/2518), reg 40(3)*, for payment of tax and submission of returns at a time different from that laid down by *SI 1995/2518, reg 25*. It appeared that the officer was not authorised to make such a concession, but the conversation had given the appellant the impression that additional time had been granted, and the circumstances therefore constituted a reasonable excuse. *D Caro*, MAN/88/34 (VTD 3284).

[18.447] Similar decisions were reached in *Q & B Motor Accessories Ltd*, LON/91/83Z (VTD 6037); *AT Healan*, LON/92/1565P (VTD 9351); *Birchall Blackburn*, MAN/91/1444 (VTD 9547); *Green Business Co Ltd*, LON/93/196P & 197P (VTD 10523); *Ollerton Hotel (Kirkcaldy) Ltd*, EDN/92/269 (VTD 10530); *MJ Shanahan (t/a MJS Haulage)*, LON/94/279 (VTD 12634); *Corporate Risk Associates Ltd*, LON/02/573 (VTD 17872), and *G Wilson (Glaziers) Ltd*, [2011] UKFTT 731 (TC), TC01568.

[18.448] In a case where the facts were similar, the tribunal held that a VAT officer, who had agreed to accept payment of a company's VAT liability by 25 April rather than 31 March, had effectively allowed an extension of the due date under *VAT Regulations 1995 (SI 1995/2518), reg 40(3)*. *Starlite (Chandeliers) Ltd*, [1999] VATDR 313 (VTD 16188).

[18.449] A company had failed to submit returns for the three quarters ending 31 March 1986, although it had submitted subsequent returns. A VAT officer made a control visit in July 1988 and agreed to collect the outstanding returns a month later. Following the visit, the company did not submit its return for the quarter ending 30 June 1988, but gave it to the VAT officer on 23 August with the earlier returns. A surcharge was subsequently imposed and the company appealed, contending that it had a reasonable excuse because its director had believed that the agreement for collection of the earlier returns also applied to the current return. The tribunal found that there had been a genuine misunderstanding and allowed the company's appeal. *Interior Design & Construction Ltd*, LON/89/192Y (VTD 3484).

[18.450] A similar decision was reached in *Secure Areas Ltd*, MAN/91/1006 (VTD 7969).

Misleading letter from local VAT office

[18.451] A partnership elected to pay its VAT liabilities by credit transfer. It had received a letter signed by a senior VAT officer, stating that 'if you do elect to pay via a credit transfer system the Commissioners will allow you a further 7 days in which to pay the tax due and furnish the VAT return'. It paid its liability for the quarter ending 31 January 1989 by a bank giro credit dated 6 March, and its liability for the quarter ending 31 July by a bank giro credit dated 7 August. The Commissioners imposed a default surcharge and the partnership appealed, contending that the payments had been made within the time limit as extended by the letter from the VAT officer. The tribunal found that the partners had misunderstood the terms of the officer's letter. The VAT return explicitly stated that taxpayers must ensure that returns and payments were received by the due date, and this advice was repeated in the *VAT Guide*. It was not sufficient to submit a return or a payment on the due date; returns and payments must be submitted in time to arrive on or before the due date. However, as the officer's letter was not clear on this matter, and as the Commissioners had not informed the partnership that its practice was incorrect until October 1989, seven months after the first default, the partners had a reasonable excuse for their incorrect belief that their system of making payments on the final or penultimate day satisfied the Commissioners. *Barney & Freeman*, [1990] VATTR 119 (VTD 4849). (*Note.* A subsequent tribunal specifically declined to follow this decision in *Wingate Electrical plc*, **18.539** below. In *Slough Motor Co*, **18.538** below, the tribunal held that a 'reasonable competent businessman using the bank giro credit system and seeking to effect payment within a shorter period than two days should make sure that this is possible under the particular banking procedures used by him'. See also *Paragon Business Products Ltd*, **18.459** below, and the cases noted at **18.541** below.)

[18.452] A similar decision was reached in *WG Beynon & Sons Ltd*, LON/92/2368P (VTD 10043).

[18.453] An appeal was allowed in a subsequent case where the tribunal held that a letter from a VAT office had been misleading, and had given the recipient company the incorrect impression that its VAT liability could be paid by direct debit. *Stream International Ltd*, EDN/97/164 (VTD 15602).

[18.454] A trader had fallen into arrears with his VAT liability. He visited the Coventry VAT office to ascertain how much he owed, and was told that he owed £1,222, which he paid. Two weeks later he received a letter from the VAT office, not referring to his visit, and informing him that he owed £817. He formed the opinion that his payment of £1,222 had not been taken into account, and that he had overpaid £405. He therefore withheld this amount from his next payment, and the Commissioners imposed a default surcharge. The tribunal allowed his appeal, finding that the letter sent to him by the VAT office had been incorrect and had misled the trader into believing that he had overpaid, and holding that this constituted a reasonable excuse. *RM Kelly*, MAN/93/553 (VTD 11347).

[18.455] A company was unable to pay its full VAT liability for the period ending 30 September 2006. It wrote to Customs on 19 October 2006, asking for an extra 30 days 'to pay the outstanding amount without a surcharge liability'. Customs replied on 26 October with a letter which was ambiguous, and could have been construed as stating that a surcharge would only be imposed if the company defaulted on the arrangement to pay within 30 days. Despite this letter, Customs subsequently imposed a surcharge, but the tribunal allowed the company's appeal, holding that the ambiguous wording of Customs' letter constituted a reasonable excuse. *Allegra Strategies Ltd*, LON/07/1357 (VTD 20539).

Cases where the appellant was unsuccessful

Notice of security—whether misleading

[18.456] A company was served with a notice of requirement to give security of £7,500, but was unable to pay this amount. It continued to trade, but did not issue further VAT invoices or submit its next VAT return. It appealed against a default surcharge, contending that it had been misled by the wording of the notice of requirement to give security, which neither its accountant nor its solicitor could understand. The tribunal dismissed the appeal, stating that it might be understandable for a layman not to understand the notice, 'but it is astonishing that neither a chartered accountant nor a solicitor of the Supreme Court could understand it. It is equally astonishing that neither of them was able to or did seek advice on the matter.' *Actel Group Ltd*, LON/88/591 (VTD 3301).

VAT Guide—whether misleading

[18.457] A company appealed against a default surcharge, contending that it had been misled by the Commissioners' *VAT Guide* into believing that the late submission of two returns showing repayments due would not count as defaults. The tribunal dismissed the appeal. *Karl Joh (UK) Ltd*, EDN/90/156 (VTD 5537).

Surcharge liability notice—whether misleading

[18.458] A company had been served with a surcharge liability notice covering the period to 31 December 1992. However, it submitted its return for the period ending 31 December 1992 after the due date, and a default surcharge was imposed. The company appealed, contending that it had a reasonable excuse because the due date for the return in question was 31 January 1993, and it had assumed that no surcharge would be imposed because the surcharge liability period had ended before the due date. The tribunal dismissed the appeal, holding that the surcharge had been in accordance with what is now *VATA 1994, s 59(4)*, and that the circumstances did not constitute a reasonable excuse. *JW & YE Shute*, LON/93/559 (VTD 11303).

Form VAT 597—whether misleading

[18.459] A company paid its VAT liability by credit transfer. It appealed against a default surcharge, contending that it had a reasonable excuse because the wording of the form VAT 597 which it had received when it joined the scheme in 1991 was misleading in that it implied that a trader only had to initiate a payment within the seven-day extension and did not make it clear that the payment had to be received by the Commissioners within the extra seven days. The tribunal dismissed the appeal, accepting that the form had been potentially misleading and had subsequently been revised in 1992, but holding that the circumstances did not amount to a reasonable excuse since a 'reasonably conscientious businessman' would have 'been aware that payment had to be effected at least two banking days before the due date, given that this warning appears on the bank giro credit book'. (The tribunal also observed that the bank through which the payments were made was acting as the agent of the company rather than as the agent of the Commissioners.) *Paragon Business Products Ltd*, LON/95/2570P (VTD 14263). (*Note.* Since 1992 the form VAT 597 has contained the words 'you must allow at least two banking days for the bank to complete the transaction. The amount due must be in the department's account on the seventh day; if the seventh day falls on the weekend, the amount due must be received by the Friday.')

Whether appellant misled by VAT officer

[18.460] A company appealed against a default surcharge, contending that it had a reasonable excuse because the defaults in question occurred exactly twelve months apart, and its director had been told by a VAT officer that no surcharge would be imposed unless the company defaulted more than once in a twelve-month period. The tribunal dismissed the appeal, observing that the imposition of the surcharge was in accordance with what is now *VATA 1994, s 59(2)*, finding that the trader had not specifically questioned a VAT officer about the position since receiving a surcharge liability notice, and holding that the circumstances did not constitute a reasonable excuse. *Sageworth Ltd (t/a Anton Hammes)*, LON/93/1030P (VTD 11151).

[18.461] A company had fallen into arrears with its VAT liability, and arranged with a VAT officer that it could pay its arrears by instalments. However it failed to keep its current liability up to date, and the Commissioners imposed a default surcharge. The company appealed against the surcharge, contending that it had been misled by the officer with whom it had negotiated its instalment arrangement, because he had not specifically warned it that failure to pay its current liability would lead to the imposition of a surcharge. The tribunal reviewed the evidence and dismissed the company's appeal, finding that the letters which the company had received from Customs' Debt Management Unit clearly stated that 'acceptance of this arrangement does not prevent or cancel the recording of defaults, liability to surcharge, and interest where applicable'. Accordingly the circumstances did not constitute a reasonable excuse. *Klub Ltd*, LON/03/341 (VTD 18352).

[18.462] Similar decisions were reached in *Beauty Direct Ltd*, LON/03/353 (VTD 18353); *Global Vehicle Imports (UK) Ltd*, LON/03/899 (VTD 18546), and *S Rubie*, LON/08/389 (VTD 20666).

Whether company misled by HMRC National Advice Helpline

[18.463] A company had an annual VAT liability of more than £2,000,000, and was therefore required to operate the Payments on Account Scheme under *VATA 1994, s 28*. However its finance director telephoned the HMRC National Advice Helpline to ask for a seven-day extension in making one of its payments. He failed to disclose that the company was required to operate the Payments on Account Scheme. HMRC imposed a default surcharge. The company appealed, contending that it had a reasonable excuse because the HMRC National Advice Helpline had agreed that it could submit its payment a week late. The tribunal dismissed the appeal, finding that HMRC had previously advised the company that, because it was a 'large payer' subject to the Payments on Account Scheme, it was required to make all its payments by the due dates. HMRC had also advised the company that it should direct any queries regarding payments to the HMRC Large Payers Unit in Liverpool rather than the National Advice Helpline. The tribunal found that the company was not suffering cash-flow difficulties, and had ignored HMRC's previous advice by telephoning the HMRC National Advice Helpline rather than the HMRC Large Payers Unit. Accordingly there was no reasonable excuse for the late payment. *Premier Despatch Ltd*, LON/07/1301 (VTD 20231).

[18.464] A similar decision was reached in *John Mills Ltd*, LON/07/1646 (VTD 20526).

Return form not available

Cases where the appellant was successful

Non-receipt of blank VAT return form

[18.465] A trader appealed against a default surcharge, contending that he had a reasonable excuse because he had not received a blank return form despite having telephoned his local VAT office to request one. The tribunal allowed his appeal, holding that the failure to receive a blank return form could only be accepted as a reasonable excuse if the trader took steps to obtain a duplicate form, but also holding that one telephone call was sufficient for this purpose. *S Robinson*, [1991] VATTR 440 (VTD 6267). (*Note.* For another issue in this case, see **18.14** above.)

[18.466] Similar decisions have been reached in a considerable number of subsequent cases. In the interests of space, such cases are not summarised individually in this book. For a list of such cases decided up to 31 December 1995, see Tolley's VAT Cases 1996.

VAT return form mislaid

[18.467] A trader appealed against a default surcharge, contending that he had a reasonable excuse because he had mislaid the blank VAT return form, but had requested a replacement form as he had realised that he had lost the original, and submitted the return as soon as he received the replacement form. The tribunal allowed the appeal, holding that the circumstances constituted a reasonable excuse. *PE Burns*, BEL/88/10 (VTD 3151).

[18.468] Similar decisions were reached in *Brown's Boathouse Ltd*, MAN/89/1047 (VTD 4726) and *Monster Worldwide Holdings Ltd*, LON/06/1252 (VTD 20085).

[18.469] An appeal was allowed in a case where a company, which had mislaid its return form, submitted its quarterly details in manuscript instead, and enclosed a cheque for the VAT due. On receiving the manuscript details, the Commissioners sent the company a duplicate return, but this was not completed and returned until after the due date. The tribunal held that, since the company had not realised that it could be issued with a duplicate return form, the circumstances constituted a reasonable excuse. *J & C Pendleton Ltd*, MAN/91/122 (VTD 6092).

Cases where the appellant was unsuccessful

Non-receipt of blank VAT return form

[18.470] A company did not receive a blank VAT return form for the period ending 31 October 1987. It did not request a duplicate form until January 1988. The Commissioners imposed a default surcharge and the tribunal dismissed the company's appeal, holding that the delay in requesting a duplicate form was unreasonable and that the circumstances did not constitute a reasonable excuse. *Goddard & Phillips Ltd*, LON/88/566 (VTD 3218).

[18.471] There have been a very large number of other cases in which the tribunal has found that the appellant did not receive the appropriate blank VAT return form, but did not request a form until after the due date, and has held that the delay in requesting a duplicate form did not constitute a reasonable excuse. In the interests of space, such cases are not reported individually in this book. For a list of such cases decided up to 31 December 1993, see Tolley's VAT Cases 1994.

VAT return form mislaid

[18.472] In a case where a trader lost her VAT return form, and did not request another form until after the due date, the tribunal held that this did not constitute a reasonable excuse. *N Matthews (t/a Tradewinds Restaurant)*, LON/90/237Z (VTD 5189).

[18.473] Similar decisions were reached in *R Bernstein QC*, LON/88/1056X (VTD 4816); *Mainstream Productions Ltd*, LON/90/696 (VTD 5301); *M Sarwar*, MAN/91/1039 (VTD 7120); *D Childs*, MAN/91/1172 (VTD 7328); *JB Lynch*, LON/91/2670Z (VTD 7392); *Nelson Stokes Ltd*, LON/92/241X (VTD 7690); *MacGregor Nash & Co*, LON/91/2540 (VTD 7873); *JW Meyer*, LON/93/778P (VTD 10899) and *Woodstock Timber Products*, LON/93/1460 (VTD 11693).

Receipt of return form disputed

[18.474] A partnership appealed against a default surcharge, contending that it had a reasonable excuse for the late submission of two returns as it had not received return forms and had had to request duplicates. The Commissioners produced the completed return forms in evidence, showing that these were the original forms and were not duplicates, and gave evidence that no request for duplicates had been received and no duplicates had been sent. The tribunal dismissed the appeal, finding that it was satisfied that the partnership's evidence was untruthful. *DJ Electrical Contractors*, LON/89/100X (VTD 3916).

[18.475] Similar decisions were reached in *RW Dodds (Marlow) Ltd*, LON/89/155Z (VTD 4016); *KAG Gingell*, LON/88/922Z (VTD 5168) and *Sprintman Ltd*, MAN/90/607 (VTD 5810).

No letterbox at company's business address

[18.476] A company which operated a night club submitted several VAT returns after the due date. HMRC imposed default surcharges, and the company appealed, contending that it had a reasonable excuse because its business premises had no letterbox, and it had not received many of the returns which HMRC had sent. The tribunal dismissed the appeal, holding that the circumstances did not constitute a reasonable excuse. Judge Mosedale observed that 'the company ought to have known its VAT liability and the date on which it was due to be paid'. Furthermore, 'the receipt of a blank VAT return is not a prerequisite to liability to pay the VAT. In any event, even if it were, the company should put in place an effective system for receiving its post.' It should have arranged for its mail to be redirected to an appropriate address. *Rocco Mana Ltd (t/a Spearmint Rhino Rouge) v HMRC*, [2011] UKFTT 153 (TC), TC01027.

Sole trader—absence from usual address

Cases where the appellant was successful

Appellant in prison

[18.477] A trader was imprisoned on 13 March 1988, after a criminal trial lasting two months. The tribunal held that this constituted a reasonable excuse for the late submission of the return for the period ending 31 March 1988. (There was, however, held to be no excuse for a subsequent default, the tribunal holding that the trader should have delegated subsequent returns to his wife or son who carried on his business during his imprisonment.) *T Creasey*, LON/90/308X (VTD 5116). (*Note.* Compare *Squire*, 18.480 below.)

Appellant abroad on business

[18.478] In a case where the appellant was abroad on business at the time a return was due, the tribunal held that this constituted a reasonable excuse. *RT Burridge*, MAN/89/151 (VTD 3723).

[18.479] See also *Flinders*, 18.438 above.

Cases where the appellant was unsuccessful

Appellant in prison

[18.480] In December 1987 an accountant and tax adviser was imprisoned for six weeks after being convicted of defrauding the Inland Revenue. He appealed against six successive default surcharges covering the periods ending 28 February 1987 to 31 May 1988, contending that he had a reasonable excuse because of the worry of preparing for the trial and the trauma of being sent to prison. The tribunal dismissed his appeal, holding that the circumstances did not constitute a reasonable excuse. On the evidence, the accountant's business had continued to operate 'with a substantial turnover', and his wife had previously submitted most of his VAT returns. *A Squire*, MAN/90/715 (VTD 5821).

[18.481] In a case where a sole trader had been in prison for three months beginning on 14 April 1989, the tribunal held that this did not constitute a reasonable excuse for the late submission of her returns for the periods ending 28 February 1989 and 31 May 1989. *R Molino*, LON/91/1997Y (VTD 9056).

Appellant abroad on business

[18.482] An appellant's claim that he had a reasonable excuse for the late submission of a return, because he had been abroad on business when the return was due, was rejected in *JR Harpur*, LON/88/41 (VTD 2930).

[18.483] Similar decisions were reached in *SH Nuttall*, MAN/90/789 (VTD 5892); *C Curwood*, LON/90/935X (VTD 5915); *N Horrox*, MAN/91/313 (VTD 6270); *TCT Wellesley-Miller*, LON/91/2564Y (VTD 7691); *J Barry*, MAN/91/536 (VTD 11281); *DH Kinnon (t/a Henderson Associates)*, EDN/96/80 (VTD 14461); *DC Campbell*, EDN/96/183 (VTD 14723); *FJ Lee (t/a Gladrags)*, LON/98/1570 (VTD 16028) and *TW Fraser*, LON/04/21 (VTD 18753).

Frequent business travel

[18.484] A dancer appealed against a default surcharge, contending that her work involved frequent travel and that this constituted a reasonable excuse for late submission of VAT returns. The tribunal dismissed her appeal, holding that the circumstances did not constitute a reasonable excuse. *PJ Atkins*, MAN/89/460 (VTD 4142).

[18.485] Business travel was also held not to be a reasonable excuse in *RM Doveton*, LON/89/967 (VTD 4164); *JC Byrne*, LON/88/1145Z (VTD 4202); *SP Newton*, LON/90/633X (VTD 5367); *C Dunstan*, MAN/90/791 (VTD 5705); *PA Garraway*, LON/91/1242Y (VTD 6479); *AG Hood*, LON/92/418Z (VTD 7994); *D Chancellor*, LON/92/1015Z (VTD 9051); *SP Wilcock (t/a The Hi-Fi People)*, LON/92/2062P (VTD 9737); *KJ Sherriff*, LON/93/915P (VTD 10820); *TA Ratcliffe*, MAN/93/1502 (VTD 12396); *T Wood (t/a Thomas Wood Associates)*, MAN/97/69 (VTD 15028); *JC Wythe*, LON/97/528 (VTD 15054); *MJ Smithers*, LON/98/512 (VTD 16100) and *J Kelly*, EDN/02/165 (VTD 18220).

Appellant on holiday

[18.486] A trader contended that he had a reasonable excuse for the late submission of a return because he had been abroad on holiday. The tribunal dismissed his appeal, holding that this was not a reasonable excuse. *DE Murray*, EDN/89/37 (VTD 3692).

[18.487] There have been a very large number of other cases in which tribunals have held that the absence on holiday of the appellant has not constituted a reasonable excuse for the late payment of the VAT due. In the interests of space, such cases are not summarised individually in this book. For a list of such cases decided up to 31 December 1995, see Tolley's VAT Cases 1996.

Appellant on honeymoon

[18.488] A hairdresser was married on 23 September 1989 and went to Jamaica for a fortnight's honeymoon immediately after the wedding. She did not submit her return for the quarter ending 31 August until after the honeymoon. The tribunal held that, as the honeymoon had been arranged four months in advance, this was not a reasonable excuse. *S Bannon*, LON/90/203Z (VTD 4877).

Matrimonial and domestic problems

Cases where the appellant was successful

Divorce

[18.489] A trader was divorced in July 1989 after nineteen years of marriage. The tribunal held that this constituted a reasonable excuse for the late submission of the return for the period ending 31 July 1989. *GD Williams*, MAN/90/17 (VTD 4810).

[18.490] A company appealed against a default surcharge, contending that it had a reasonable excuse for the late submission of two successive returns because its principal director had been in the process of divorcing his wife. The tribunal accepted the company's evidence and allowed the appeal. *Thomas Moriarty Associates Ltd*, LON/92/1841 (VTD 10668).

Matrimonial difficulties

[18.491] Matrimonial difficulties were held to constitute a reasonable excuse for the late submission of two successive returns in *MJC Sims*, LON/90/1599X (VTD 5928) and *JL Thurley*, LON/92/1095Y (VTD 9509).

Domestic problems

[18.492] A trader appealed against a default surcharge, contending that he had a reasonable excuse because his daughter had been served with a notice to quit the accommodation where she was living, and he had had to help her find new accommodation. The tribunal accepted this contention and allowed his appeal. *H McAulay*, LON/89/682Y (VTD 4372). (*Note.* There was, however, held to be no reasonable excuse for subsequent defaults.)

[18.493] See also *PM Power & DG Clark*, **18.559** below.

Cases where the appellant was unsuccessful

Marriage breakdown

[18.494] A trader appealed against a series of default surcharges, contending that he had a reasonable excuse because he had been badly affected by the breakdown of his marriage in October 1987. The Commissioners accepted that this was a reasonable excuse for the late submission of the return for the period ending 30 November 1987, but considered that it did not constitute a reasonable excuse for the late submission of subsequent returns. The tribunal dismissed the trader's appeal. *AW Lock*, LON/90/1141 (VTD 6768).

Divorce

[18.495] A trader appealed against four successive default surcharges, contending that he had a reasonable excuse because he had been 'going through a somewhat traumatic divorce'. The tribunal dismissed his appeal, holding that this was not a reasonable excuse. *BJ Davies*, MAN/92/1297 (VTD 10676).

[18.496] A similar decision was reached in *Ms F Apuzzo (t/a Casamia Restaurant)*, LON/06/566 (VTD 19962).

Cash-flow problems following divorce

[18.497] See *Ramsey*, 18.381 above.

Matrimonial difficulties

[18.498] A husband and wife traded in partnership as retailers. In 1986 the wife began having an affair with one of their employees. This led to matrimonial difficulties, and they subsequently separated. In the meantime the partnership submitted three returns late. The tribunal dismissed the appeal, holding that the circumstances did not constitute a reasonable excuse. *Jumpers*, LON/88/708Z (VTD 4052).

[18.499] A married couple operated a public house in partnership. They experienced matrimonial difficulties, separated in August 2008, and surrendered the tenancy of the public house in October 2008. Their returns for the periods ending 31 January and 30 April 2008 were submitted late, and Customs imposed default surcharges. Customs subsequently accepted that the couple's marital difficulties constituted a reasonable excuse for the period ending 31 January 2008, but considered that they did not constitute a reasonable excuse for the late submission of the April return. The tribunal dismissed the couple's appeal, holding that 'a prudent business person exercising reasonable foresight and due diligence would have taken steps to ensure that the return was made on time'. *Mr & Mrs M White (t/a the Kings Arms)*, MAN/08/1052 (VTD 20859).

Difficulty in computing liability

Cases where the appellant was successful

Clerical error by company employee

[18.500] A company prepared a VAT return showing net VAT payable (in box 5) of £2,213,095. Before the return was submitted, the employee responsible for the return realised that that figure was incorrect. She made a deduction of £1,029,536 in respect of import VAT, which she entered in manuscript immediately below box 5 on the return. After also deducting two payments on account, she computed the net liability as £690,943, and arranged for that amount to be paid to Customs. Customs considered that the deduction in respect of import VAT was excessive, and imposed a default surcharge (rather than a misdeclaration penalty) on the basis that the company had not paid the amount shown as due on box 5 of the return. The tribunal upheld the surcharge, holding that 'taxpayers are rightly regarded as being under a duty to declare the correct amount of tax (and are required by law to do so). To adopt the attitude that they would make a hasty correction to avoid overpaying when that gave rise to a significant underpayment' was not reasonable. The company appealed to the Ch D. Kitchin J allowed the appeal, holding that the tribunal had erred in law by forming the view 'that the correction was made in haste and without adequate consideration as to whether it would result in a considerable underpayment'. The employee had genuinely believed that she was entitled to make a deduction of £1,029,536, and her belief constituted a reasonable excuse. *CMS Peripherals Ltd v HMRC (No 2)*, Ch D 2007, [2008] STC 985; [2007] EWHC 1128 (Ch).

VAT officer directing change in accounting methods

[**18.501**] An appeal was allowed in a case where a VAT officer on a control visit had instructed a company to change its system of claiming input tax. The tribunal held that, in view of the officer's instructions, the company had a reasonable excuse for having mistakenly believed that accuracy was more important than promptness in submitting its returns. *Rok Crete Units Co Ltd*, LON/87/690 (VTD 2660).

[**18.502**] Similar decisions were reached in *Goldfinch Blinds Ltd*, LON/87/821 (VTD 2671); *Auto-Factors Ltd*, LON/88/38 (VTD 3055); *Carmichael Jennifer May Ltd*, LON/88/409 (VTD 3159); *MSK (Insulation Services) Ltd*, LON/89/723Z (VTD 4198); *K Eyre*, LON/89/996Y (VTD 5200); *McGrath Brothers (Engineering) Ltd*, BEL/90/23X (VTD 5551) and *Harbury Estates Ltd*, MAN/90/1111 (VTD 8851).

Company withholding returns pending visit from VAT officer

[**18.503**] A company which operated a public house appealed against two default surcharges, contending that it had deliberately withheld returns because it had received two incorrect assessments from Customs, had been unable to resolve the situation by telephone, and had decided to withhold subsequent returns until a VAT officer could visit the public house to clarify its liability. The tribunal accepted the company's evidence and allowed its appeal, finding that there had been 'a catalogue of errors and incompetence' in the way in which Customs had handled the company's affairs and that 'the facts of this appeal are wholly exceptional'. The tribunal found that the controlling director was 'baffled' by Customs' demands for tax and interest, and had not received 'any meaningful reply' to a letter or repeated telephone calls. The tribunal observed that 'we do not condone the late rendering of returns but in our view there are obligations on both sides. Taxable persons are obliged to render their returns on time but we are also of the view that Customs and Excise have a duty of good administration. In this wholly exceptional appeal we do consider that there was a reasonable excuse.' *RO Somerton Ltd*, LON/03/1167 (VTD 18809).

Trader suffering poor eyesight—offer to submit estimated returns

[**18.504**] A trader suffered a torn retina and an ulcerated cornea, and had to undergo four laser treatments and three operations. He was off work for a total of more than five months, and was unable to do much paperwork for more than a year because of poor eyesight. He telephoned Customs' National Advice Service, and offered to submit estimated returns, but was told not to do so. He failed to submit four VAT returns and the Commissioners imposed default surcharges. The tribunal allowed the trader's appeal, holding that prolonged illness would not by itself have constituted a reasonable excuse for the non-submission of the returns, but that in the circumstances the National Advice Service should have accepted his offer to submit estimated returns, and that there was therefore a reasonable excuse for the defaults. *M Readman*, LON/04/208 (VTD 18862).

Cases where the appellant was unsuccessful

Appellant expecting control visit by VAT officer

[18.505] A trader appealed against a default surcharge, contending that he had delayed submitting his return because he was expecting a control visit by a VAT officer and wished to check that the return was correct. The tribunal dismissed his appeal, holding that this did not constitute a reasonable excuse. *T Norman*, MAN/88/543 (VTD 3257).

[18.506] Similar decisions were reached in *Cloudmead Ltd*, LON/88/943 (VTD 3290); *S Hampson*, LON/88/447Z (VTD 3402); *Gilberts Motors Ltd*, LON/88/916Z (VTD 3424); *The Commercials Trading Co Ltd*, LON/89/924Z (VTD 3962); *Soft Solutions Ltd*, LON/89/1113X (VTD 4793); *HJ Michaels*, LON/89/313 (VTD 4958); *South Wales Industrial Valve Services Ltd*, LON/90/10X (VTD 5222); *Rentexit Ltd (t/a Leadair Technical & Refrigeration)*, MAN/92/1731 (VTD 10335); *JA Rainford*, MAN/93/437 (VTD 11011); *Derby Plating Services Ltd*, MAN/93/545 (VTD 11352, 12018); *Hi-Life Promotions Ltd*, LON/94/1622P (VTD 13033); *JK Hunter*, EDN/94/88 (VTD 13099); *Bulgin Powersource plc*, MAN/95/2414 (VTD 13915); *Vinhispania Ltd*, LON/97/288 (VTD 14939); *Insite Associates Ltd*, LON/03/107 (VTD 19102) and *Darvill*, **52.370** PENALTIES: MISDECLARATION.

Doubt as to liability of supplies

[18.507] A roofing contractor contended that he had a reasonable excuse for the late submission of several returns, because it was not always clear whether his work was standard-rated or zero-rated. The tribunal dismissed his appeal, holding that this was not a reasonable excuse. *EP Basnett (t/a EB Roofing Services)*, MAN/89/205 (VTD 3795).

[18.508] Similar decisions were reached in *Faststar Ltd*, LON/89/1645 (VTD 4707); *Chasekey Personnel Ltd*, EDN/92/4 (VTD 9101) and *Diamond Investigations Ltd*, EDN/97/91 (VTD 15176).

[18.509] A trader appealed against several default surcharges, contending that he had a reasonable excuse because he had been unsure as to how to account for tax on disbursements. The tribunal dismissed his appeal, observing that 'the law is clearly stated in the case of *Rowe & Maw* (see **62.52** SUPPLY), of which the appellant was made aware', and holding that the circumstances did not constitute a reasonable excuse. *DJ Wilson*, LON/98/180 (VTD 15919).

[18.510] A trader appealed against a default surcharge, contending that he had a reasonable excuse because he had been uncertain as to whether he had to account for VAT on a supply in the Republic of Ireland. The tribunal dismissed his appeal, holding that this was not a reasonable excuse. *M McAleer (t/a McAleer Projects)*, LON/03/642 (VTD 18365).

Company wishing to claim bad debt relief and delaying return

[18.511] A company appealed against a default surcharge, contending that it had delayed submitting the relevant return because it had wished to claim bad debt relief and had been unable to contact its accountant. The tribunal dismissed the appeal, holding that the circumstances did not constitute a reasonable excuse. *Smith & Choyce Ltd*, LON/92/174Z (VTD 7817).

[18.512] A similar decision was reached in *Transam Ltd*, LON/95/2483 (VTD 13987).

Payment by credit transfer or BACS

Cases where the appellant was successful

Payment by credit transfer—application of extended time limit

[18.513] In a Scottish case, a company submitted its return for the period ending 28 February 1999 before the due date of 31 March. It paid the tax by credit transfer from its account with the Bank of Scotland, and initiated the payment on 1 April. However, the payment was not received by the Commissioners until 8 April, and a default surcharge was imposed. The company appealed, contending that the payment had been initiated within the seven-day extended time limit. The company also queried the position with the Bank of Scotland, which stated in reply that 'the nature of the transaction requires the transfer of funds from Scotland to England. The clearing cycles in either countries is (*sic*) two working days but cross-border transactions require an extra day making it three working days.' The tribunal accepted the company's evidence and allowed the appeal, describing the letter from the Bank of Scotland as 'quite extraordinary' and holding that, since the payment had been initiated within the extended time limit, the circumstances constituted a reasonable excuse. *Rowan Timber Supplies (Scotland) Ltd*, EDN/99/118 (VTD 16305).

[18.514] A similar decision was reached in *The Park Hotel*, EDN/00/135 (VTD 16959).

[18.515] In another Scottish case, a company initiated a credit transfer payment on 5 November 1997, but the Commissioners did not receive the payment from the company's bank until 10 November. The Commissioners imposed a default surcharge but the tribunal allowed the company's appeal, holding that the circumstances constituted a reasonable excuse. *Hydril UK Ltd*, EDN/99/166 (VTD 16508).

[18.516] Similar decisions were reached in *Dewar Associates Ltd*, EDN/04/35 (VTD 18748) and *Nigel Lowe Consulting Ltd (and related appeal)*, [2009] UKFTT 130 (TC), TC00098.

[18.517] The decisions in *Rowan Timber Supplies (Scotland) Ltd*, **18.513** above, and *Hydril UK Ltd*, **18.515** above, were applied in a subsequent Scottish case where the tribunal chairman held that it was 'contrary to the public interest that Scots should be penalised because of the extra day which the transfer might take, simply because of banking arrangements'. The chairman commented that 'all payments require to be made to the Bank of England. English traders have an advantage in that they can without exception instruct a credit transfer two days ahead of the delayed due date for payment in the sure and certain knowledge that 48 hours later it will show up in the Respondents' account. Scottish traders cannot be sure this instruction will be implemented as quickly.' The chairman held that it was 'not appropriate for the respondents to insist that the Scottish taxpayer should be required to perform his banking instruction differently from an English taxpayer'. *KRG Precision Ltd*, EDN/01/66 (VTD 17414).

[18.518] An appeal was allowed in another Scottish case where a company had initiated a payment by credit transfer on Thursday 3 January 2002 (which was the first working day after the New Year holiday). The tribunal held that it was reasonable to expect that the Commissioners would receive the payment on Monday 7 January 2002. *Pegasus Flooring Co Ltd*, EDN/02/43 (VTD 17708).

[18.519] A similar decision was reached in *The Murdie Partnership Ltd*, EDN/02/60 (VTD 17786).

[18.520] A company which paid its VAT by credit transfer had consistently initiated payment on the last day of the seven-day extended period, so that the Commissioners did not receive payment until after the time limit had expired. Nevertheless, the Commissioners did not impose surcharges until June 2000, when they imposed a surcharge for the period ending 30 April 2000. The company appealed, contending that the Commissioners' failure to impose surcharges for previous periods had led it to assume that its practice of initiating the payment within the seven-day period was acceptable. The tribunal allowed the appeal, holding that the circumstances constituted a reasonable excuse, since it was reasonable for the company 'to have relied on the consistent practice of the Commissioners'. The tribunal noted that the failure to impose surcharges previously had been attributable to a fault in the Commissioners' computer, and observed that the Commissioners 'should have warned the taxpayer that their computer problems had been cured so that, for the future, the full rigour of the penalty regime would be imposed'. *Renlon Ltd*, [2000] VATDR 442 (VTD 16987).

[18.521] The decision in *Renlon Ltd*, 18.512 above, was applied in the similar subsequent case of *CK Formwork Ltd*, LON/00/854 & LON/01/811 (VTD 17791). (*Note*. Appeals against earlier surcharges, where the reason for non-payment was shortage of funds, were dismissed.)

[18.522] A company which paid its VAT by credit transfer had consistently initiated payment on the penultimate day of the seven-day extended period (ie initiating the payment for the period ending 30 September 2000 on 6 November). The Commissioners received the company's payments for the periods ending 30 September and 31 December 2000 on 8 November and 8 February respectively, and imposed a default surcharge. The company appealed, contending that since its bank had debited its account within the seven-day extended time limit, it had a reasonable excuse for believing that it had made payment within the extended time limit. The tribunal accepted the company's evidence and allowed the appeal, holding that the circumstances constituted a reasonable excuse. *Wood Auto Supplies Ltd*, MAN/01/271 (VTD 17356).

[18.523] A company which paid its VAT by credit transfer appealed against a default surcharge, contending that it had a reasonable excuse because it had asked its bank to initiate payment within the seven-day extended time limit, but the bank had failed to do so. The tribunal accepted the company's evidence and allowed its appeal, finding that the delay was caused by 'a processing error' by the bank and holding that this constituted a reasonable excuse. The tribunal chairman (Mr. Oliver) commented that Customs 'have not given any further indication as to what in their view the reasonable competent business-man would have done in the circumstances' and speculated that 'perhaps the reasonable competent businessman would threaten his bank with legal action if it ever failed to process a VAT payment properly.' *H Griffiths Engineering Ltd*, LON/04/2299 (VTD 19098).

[18.524] A company paid its VAT by bank giro credit transfer. It submitted the relevant transfer form to its bank on 6 December 1994. Customs did not receive the payment until 8 December, and imposed a default surcharge. The tribunal allowed the company's appeal, holding that the wording of the notes on the form VAT100 were misleading, so that the company had a reasonable excuse. The tribunal chairman (Mr. Johnson) expressed the view that the notes should 'be rewritten to make clear that, in reality, taxpayers have only about an extra four calendar days to make payment if by Bank Giro'. It was unhelpful for the notes 'to bracket Bank Giro payments under the same "bullet-point" as automated payment methods such as BACS and CHAPS which result in paperless transfers to Customs' account. Indeed there is a difference between the speed of these other two methods, in that I understand that whilst BACS can take three days, CHAPS is a same-day transfer method. Bank Giro, for its part, is an old-fashioned method that normally involves the use of cheques and so is not a fully electronic method.' *Benjamin Clowes Ltd*, MAN/05/169 (VTD 19164, VTD 19165).

[18.525] A company paid its VAT by credit transfer (CHAPS). It instructed its bank to make such a payment on 7 January 2005. However, the bank failed to do so, and Customs imposed a default surcharge. The tribunal allowed the company's appeal, holding that the bank's failure to implement the company's instruction constituted a reasonable excuse. *HHT Ltd*, MAN/05/184 (VTD 19169).

[18.526] Similar decisions were reached in *Magma Bars Ltd*, MAN/07/196 (VTD 20329) and *Teamspirit Holdings Ltd*, LON/07/651 (VTD 20337).

[18.527] On 7 May 2008 a company instructed its bank to pay its VAT liability for the period ending 31 March 2008 to Customs via CHAPS. The bank did not make the payment until the following day, and Customs imposed a default surcharge. The company appealed, contending that it had a reasonable excuse because the bank had previously advised it that it would process all such requests on the same day if they were received by 4pm, and that it had made the request in question at 3.51pm. The tribunal accepted the company's evidence and allowed the appeal, finding that the company had 'relied on email advice from the bank which we consider that a reasonable businessman would have relied on'. *Rodcom Europe Ltd*, LON/08/1672 (VTD 20874).

[18.528] An appeal was allowed in a case where the tribunal found that a trader's bank had made a payment by BACS (thus taking three days to clear) rather than CHAPS. The tribunal found that neither the bank nor the VAT office had explained the difference to the trader's bookkeeper, and held that this constituted a reasonable excuse. *L Buck (t/a Idealogic)*, MAN/06/880 (VTD 20082).

Payment by credit transfer—effect of bank holiday

[18.529] A company, which was in financial difficulties, paid its VAT by credit transfer. It asked its bank for its liability for the period ending 31 March 2001 to be paid by credit transfer on 7 May 2001. However, since that date was a bank holiday, the bank did not make the payment until the following day. The Commissioners imposed a default surcharge but the tribunal allowed the company's appeal, observing that the company had written to its local VAT office on 27 April stating that it would make the payment in this way. The tribunal found that the company had made a 'genuine error' in overlooking that 7 May was a bank holiday, and held that, in view of the letter which the company had written to its VAT office, there was a reasonable excuse for the late payment. The tribunal held that if the company's manager 'had not written to Customs some ten days earlier specifically stating the date then there would be no excuse. The fault would be fundamental. However, she did take the trouble to write to Customs and it was reasonable for her to assume that Customs would take note of what she had said and spot that payment was to be made on a Bank Holiday and draw her attention to this error.' *Avonwave Ltd (t/a Gatewood Joinery)*, LON/01/624 (VTD 17509).

[18.530] Similar decisions were reached in *The Craiglands Hotel Ltd*, MAN/02/471 (VTD 17931) and *Sawley Security Ltd*, MAN/07/548 (VTD 20282). (*Note.* Compare *Digit Digital Experience Ltd*, **18.546** below, and *Liquatek Ltd*, **18.547** below, where similar circumstances were held not to constitute a reasonable excuse.)

VAT paid by electronic transfer but credited to incorrect Customs' account

[18.531] A trader paid his VAT for the period ending 30 November 2001 by electronic transfer. However his bank credited his payment to sort code 10-70-90 (Customs' Head Office Collection Account) rather than to the correct Customs' sort code of 10-00-00 (as shown in the VAT Guide). Customs returned the money from their Head Office Collection Account to the trader's bank, and imposed a default surcharge. The trader appealed, contending that the circumstances constituted a reasonable excuse. The tribunal accepted this contention and allowed his appeal, commenting that 'a software programme should be put in place, if it is not already in place, for redirecting the monies if necessary, in order to obviate the rejection of such payments altogether'. *AF Somji (t/a Akber & Co)*, MAN/02/555 (VTD 18443).

Bank's website not working—whether a reasonable excuse

[18.532] A company appealed against a default surcharge, contending that it had a reasonable excuse because it had attempted to pay by electronic transfer within the extended seven-day period, but its bank's website had not been working. The tribunal accepted the company's evidence and allowed the appeal. *Hope Barton Owners Association Ltd*, LON/07/1111 (VTD 20410).

Payment via Bank of England

[18.533] A barrister (C) paid his quarterly VAT liability by cash at the Bank of England on 6 October 2009, together with an HMRC bank giro credit slip. HMRC processed the credit slip on 9 October, and imposed a default surcharge. The First-Tier Tribunal allowed C's appeal, holding that C 'had a reasonable expectation, backed up by his understanding of the banking law and practice, that the payment effected by him on 6 October would be received by HMRC by the due date (7 October 2009).' *D Clark v HMRC*, [2011] UKFTT 256 (TC), TC01120.

Problems with HMRC server

[18.534] See *Kwik Move UK Ltd*, **18.78** above.

Company operating 'Faster Payments System'

[18.535] A company (R), which paid its VAT liability by electronic transfer, appealed against a default surcharge for the period ending March 2011, contending that it had paid its liability on Saturday 7 May 2011 using the 'Faster Payments System', and its bookkeeper had assumed that HMRC would receive the payments on the same day, which was within the extended seven-day time limit. The tribunal dismissed the appeal. Judge Blewitt observed that R had been 'clearly advised that payments must take account of weekends and bank holidays', and that R could not 'have had any reasonable expectation that the payment would be received on time'. *Red Contractors Ltd v HMRC*, [2011] UKFTT 788 (TC), TC01622.

Cases where the appellant was partly successful

Company operating Payments on Account Scheme under VATA 1994, s 28

[18.536] A company which was required to operate the Payments on Account Scheme under *VATA 1994, s 28* made its payments by credit transfer after the due date. Customs imposed default surcharges and the company appealed, contending that it had a reasonable excuse because it had not been aware that the seven-day extension for credit transfer payments was not available to companies within the Payments on Account Scheme. The tribunal allowed the appeal in part, holding that there was a reasonable excuse for the first default but not for subsequent defaults. *Promanex Group Ltd*, MAN/05/793 (VTD 19500).

Company operating 'Faster Payments System'

[18.537] A company (P), which paid its VAT liability by electronic transfer, appealed against default surcharges for the periods ending December 2010 and March 2011, contending that it had paid its liability on 6 February 2011 and 6 May 2011 using the 'Faster Payments System', and had assumed that HMRC would receive the payments within the extended seven-day time limit. The tribunal allowed the appeal in part, finding that in November 2010 HMRC had sent a letter and information sheet stating that 'HMRC is currently unable to accept Faster Payments'. Judge Berner held that, in view of this statement, there was no reasonable excuse for P's assumption that the payment which it made on 6 February would be received by HMRC within the time limit. However, the use of the word 'currently' implied that 'this was a state of affairs that was liable to change', and since HMRC had not told P that the payment made on 6 February had been received late, there was a reasonable excuse for

P's belief that the payment made on 6 May would be received within the extended time limit. *Palmun Ltd v HMRC*, [2011] UKFTT 738 (TC), TC01575.

Cases where the appellant was unsuccessful

Payment by credit transfer—misunderstanding of extended time limit

[18.538] A company paid its VAT liability by credit transfer. Its payment for the quarter ending 30 June 1993 was not received by Customs until 8 July 1993, and a default surcharge was imposed. The company appealed, contending that it had a reasonable excuse because it had given the bank transfer slip to its bank (which was not one of the four main 'clearing' banks) on 6 July, and had believed that this constituted payment within the extended seven-day time limit allowed by the Commissioners. The tribunal dismissed the appeal, holding that the circumstances did not constitute a reasonable excuse, since a 'reasonable competent businessman using the bank giro credit system and seeking to effect payment within a shorter period than two days should make sure that this is possible under the particular banking procedures used by him'. *Slough Motor Co*, LON/93/2450P (VTD 11818).

[18.539] The decision in *Slough Motor Co*, **18.538** above, was applied in a similar subsequent case in which the extended due date was Monday 7 August 1995, and the company had initiated payment on Friday 4 August 1995. The tribunal specifically declined to follow the decision in *Barney & Freeman*, **18.451** above. *Wingate Electrical plc*, LON/95/3067P (VTD 14078).

[18.540] The decisions in *Slough Motor Co*, **18.538** above, and *Whitport plc*, **18.63** above, were applied in the similar subsequent case of *AL Currie & Brown*, LON/96/1359 (VTD 14678).

[18.541] Similar decisions were reached in *Pan Graphics Industrial Ltd*, LON/94/2529 (VTD 13126); *Consolidated Holdings Ltd*, MAN/95/107 & MAN/96/220 (VTD 13875, 14352); *Cell Ltd*, LON/95/3005 (VTD 13942); *Hydewood Ltd*, LON/96/1944 (VTD 14828); *Jayhard Ltd*, LON/97/720 (VTD 15306); *J & S Joiners & Builders (Paisley) Ltd*, EDN/00/109 (VTD 16892); *Ronald D Rawcliffe Ltd*, MAN/00/708 (VTD 17118); *Automotive Parts Distributions Ltd*, LON/01/221 (VTD 17261); *H & V Commissioning Services*, EDN/01/81 (VTD 17461); *Tarvet Electronics Ltd*, EDN/01/53 (VTD 17463); *PNW Computer Services Ltd*, LON/01/1100 (VTD 17731); *GD & AY Donald*, EDN/01/213 (VTD 17894); *Owan Bebb A'I Gwmni*, MAN/02/711 (VTD 18047); *Cibenze Services plc*, LON/07/768 (VTD 20637); *The Funky End*, [2009] UKFTT 110 (TC), TC00078; *Headlam (Floorcovering Distributor) Ltd*, **18.64** above; *Maranello Concessionaires Ltd*, **18.210** above, and *Paragon Business Products Ltd*, **18.459** above.

Payment by BACS—misunderstanding of extended time limit

[18.542] A company paid its VAT liability by electronic transfer under the Bankers Automated Clearing System (BACS). Its payment for the period ending 31 July 2002 was not received until 9 September. Customs imposed a default surcharge and the company appealed, contending that it had a reasonable excuse because it had initiated the payment within the seven-day extended period. The tribunal rejected this contention and dismissed the appeal, holding that the payment had to be received within the seven-day extended period and that there was no reasonable excuse. *AZ Cleaning Services (South West) Ltd*, LON/02/1025 (VTD 18208).

[18.543] Similar decisions were reached in *Seymour Hunter Ltd*, LON/03/334 (VTD 18284); *MH Ruse*, LON/03/167 (VTD 18522); *JM Adkin*, EDN/04/13 (VTD 18645); *Anrich North West Ltd*, MAN/04/758 (VTD 18996); *Gunlab Ltd*, LON/04/2275 (VTD 19026); *Betterweigh Leicester*, MAN/05/705 (VTD 19551); *SP Wound Components Ltd*, LON/06/570 (VTD 19836); *Magna Kansei Ltd*, MAN/06/206 (VTD 19905); *NA & Mrs FAF Newman*, [2007] VATDR 276 (VTD 20006); *E Goozeberry Ltd*, LON/07/090 (VTD 20088); *The Joint Post Ltd*, LON/06/1287 (VTD 20089); *RA Heard*, LON/07/058 (VTD 20102); *Iconeyewear Distribution Ltd*, MAN/07/229 (VTD 20213); *Airmaster Southern Ltd*, LON/07/265 (VTD 20335); *M Harrington & M Jones (t/a The Station)*, LON/07/379 (VTD 20336); *Vital Touch Ltd*, LON/07/770 (VTD 20409); *Stikatak Ltd*, LON/07/1212 (VTD 20471), *Karakusevic Carson LLP*, LON/07/1383 (VTD 20550); *Wolfe Ware Ltd*, LON/08/2026 (VTD 20941, VTD 20954); *ADM Glass Ltd*, [2011] UKFTT 339 (TC), TC01199, and *CV Staff Services Ltd*, [2011] UKFTT 384 (TC), TC01239.

Payment by CHAPS—misunderstanding of extended time limit

[18.544] A company (V) paid its VAT by electronic CHAPS transfer. It initiated its payment for the period ending 31 January 2008 on 7 February 2008, but did not do so until after 3pm which was the cut-off time for same-day CHAPS transfers. Customs imposed a penalty and the tribunal dismissed V's appeal, holding that the circumstances did not constitute a reasonable excuse. *Vinalith Ltd*, LON/08/532 (VTD 20696).

[18.545] Similar decisions were reached in *Datapoint Global Services Ltd*,LON/08/207 (VTD 20971) and *The Depot Ltd*, FTT [2009] UKFTT 51 (TC),TC00030.

Payment by credit transfer—effect of bank holiday

[18.546] A company paid its VAT by credit transfer. It asked its bank for its liability for the period ending 31 March 2001 to be paid by credit transfer on 7 May 2001. However, since that date was a bank holiday, the bank did not make the payment until the following day. The Commissioners imposed a default surcharge and the tribunal dismissed the company's appeal. *Digit Digital Experience Ltd*, LON/01/924 (VTD 17553).

[18.547] Similar decisions were reached in *Liquatek Ltd*, LON/02/586 (VTD 17912); *ACL Engineering Ltd*, LON/01/1016 (VTD 18788); *Thamesview Estate Agents Ltd*, LON/07/1352 (VTD 20572); *The Public Relations Co Ltd*, MAN/06/8057 (VTD 20676) and *Dudman Group Ltd*, FTT [2009] UKFTT 52 (TC),TC00031.

Company operating Payments on Account Scheme under VATA 1994, s 28

[18.548] A company (S) had an annual VAT liability of more than £2,000,000, and was therefore required to operate the Payments on Account Scheme under *VATA 1994, s 28*. In 2004 Customs wrote to S, informing it that 'businesses in the Payment on Account Scheme are not entitled to the seven-day extension to due date for payments by credit transfer'. Initially S complied with this letter, but it made one payment late in 2005 and made two payments late in early 2006. Customs imposed default surcharges. S appealed, contending that it had a reasonable excuse because its group finance director had left in December 2005 and his successor had not been aware that the seven-day extension for credit transfer payments was not available to companies within the Payments on Account Scheme. The tribunal reviewed the evidence in detail and dismissed the appeal, holding that the circumstances did not constitute a reasonable excuse. *Sapphire Retail Fund Ltd*, LON/06/1219 (VTD 20232).

[18.549] A similar decision was reached in *LVG Ltd*, LON/07/1928 (VTD 20938).

Other cases

Cases where the appellant was successful

Burglary

[18.550] In a case where the appellant's business premises had been burgled and set on fire, the tribunal held that this constituted a reasonable excuse for a late return. *R Collyer*, MAN/87/314 (VTD 2628).

[18.551] A burglary at a company's premises was held to constitute a reasonable excuse for a late return in *Parkgate Quarries Ltd*, BEL/88/40 (VTD 3712); *Cirrus Reynolds & Co Ltd*, MAN/89/929 (VTD 4951); *Ricocrest Ltd*, LON/88/379Z (VTD 5179); *Knight Guard Security Ltd*, LON/90/1565X (VTD 5788); *C & C Engineering (WGC) Ltd*, LON/91/1207X (VTD 6605); *Pennington Lee Ltd*, MAN/91/518 (VTD 6625) and *MM Skip Hire Ltd*, LON/94/121 (VTD 12528).

Fire at premises

[18.552] A company suffered a serious fire in April 1988, damaging its records and causing considerable disruption. It had to move to temporary premises, and was unable to submit its returns for the periods ending 31 March and 30 June 1988 until August. The Commissioners imposed a default surcharge but the tribunal allowed the company's appeal, holding that the circumstances constituted a reasonable excuse. *Philip Law Ltd*, LON/88/1177Y (VTD 3466).

[18.553] Similar decisions were reached in *Mobile Radio Ltd*, LON/89/425X (VTD 3994); *Ernest William (Drums) Ltd*, LON/88/827Y (VTD 4278); *WE Cary Ltd*, MAN/90/197 (VTD 5056); *PC Clarke*, LON/95/904 (VTD 13728); *Himalaya Carpets Ltd*, LON/97/140 (VTD 14892) and *Firm of Brandy's*, EDN/01/03 (VTD 17250).

Cash-flow difficulties resulting from fire

[18.554] See *Baronshire Engineering Ltd*, **18.338** above, and *Forgeville Ltd*, **18.339** above.

Flooding at premises

[18.555] In a case where a firm's premises had been flooded, the tribunal held that this constituted a reasonable excuse for the late submission of a return. *Motorways Auto Spares*, LON/89/780X (VTD 4045).

Premises damaged by gales

[18.556] A trader submitted a VAT return six days late and a default surcharge was imposed. He appealed, contending that he had a reasonable excuse because his premises had been damaged by gales and he had had to spend considerable time repairing the roof of the premises. The tribunal allowed the appeal, holding that this constituted a reasonable excuse. *J Stickland*, LON/90/1596X (VTD 5971).

Premises damaged by bombs

[18.557] In a case where a company's premises had been damaged by bomb attacks, the tribunal held that this constituted a reasonable excuse for two late returns. *CSC Electrix Ltd*, LON/98/902 (VTD 15956).

Change of business premises

[18.558] A change of business premises was held to constitute a reasonable excuse in *Computer Presentations Ltd*, MAN/88/190 (VTD 3039); *Kingston Craftsmen (1981) Ltd*, MAN/89/229 (VTD 3838); *Wagstaffe Ellis & Associates*, MAN/90/315 (VTD 5115); *GL Owen (t/a New Product Research & Development)*, LON/90/1131 (VTD 5363); *City Industries Ltd*, LON/91/270Z (VTD 6097); *KCP Computer Services Ltd*, LON/92/1187Y (VTD 8877); *C & S Cladding Ltd*, LON/93/862 (VTD 11102); *William O'Hanlon & Co Ltd*, MAN/93/1346 (VTD 12309); *Gamefishing Publications Ltd*, EDN/94/39 (VTD 12553); *Anozinc Ltd*, MAN/94/564 (VTD 12695); *Cresthaven Contractors Ltd*, LON/94/1308 (VTD 12845); *Pavigres-Wich Ltd*, LON/94/2925P (VTD 13414) and *KJ Owen*, LON/01/564 (VTD 17970).

Sudden termination of partnership

[18.559] P and C operated a garage in partnership. On 22 August 1990 C informed P that, because of 'domestic difficulties' with his wife, his assets had been frozen and he therefore had to withdraw from the partnership. P wished to continue the business, and therefore had to raise sufficient cash to purchase C's share in it. The tribunal held that the circumstances constituted a reasonable excuse for the late submission of the partnership return for the period ending 31 July 1990. *PM Power & DG Clark*, LON/90/1812Y (VTD 6120).

Dispute between partners

[18.560] In a case where the facts are not fully set out in the decision, a dispute arose between the two members of a partnership, which resulted in formal arbitration. All cheques were under the control of the arbitrator and had to be signed by both partners. One of the partners was unco-operative, and the partnership repeatedly paid its VAT after the due date. The Commissioners imposed a default surcharge but the tribunal allowed the partnership's appeal, finding that the senior partner 'would have paid the tax on time' but was prevented from doing so by the arbitrator and the other partner, and holding that this constituted a reasonable excuse. *Stanley Long & Partners*, LON/02/354 (VTD 17812).

Dispute between directors

[18.561] In a case where the facts are not fully set out in the decision, the tribunal held that 'a bitter and long-standing conflict' between a company's only two directors constituted a reasonable excuse for a late return. *Croydon Power & Light Ltd*, LON/95/587P (VTD 13296).

Litigation with major client

[18.562] A sole trader became involved in litigation with his major client. The tribunal held that the disruption and stress resulting from this constituted a reasonable excuse for the late submission of a return. *TM O'Callaghan*, LON/90/1068Y (VTD 5981).

Exceptional workload

[18.563] Exceptional pressure of work was held to constitute a reasonable excuse in *Blackburn & District Group Training Association Ltd*, MAN/87/493 (VTD 2735); *WJ Mullen*, BEL/88/6 (VTD 3374); *Foster Cars (Rotherham) Ltd*, MAN/89/45 (VTD 3586); *Calderprint*, MAN/89/807 (VTD 4541); *Composite Technics Ltd*, LON/89/1760 (VTD 4683); *PC Adams*, LON/90/1602Y (VTD 5665); *NSR Gee*, LON/90/1192Z (VTD 5687); *Southern Groundworks*, LON/90/1731Z (VTD 5970); *See Europe Ltd*, LON/91/1614Z (VTD 6926); *D Molyneux*, LON/92/1499P (VTD 9265); *Churchill Express (London) Ltd*, LON/92/1720 (VTD 9726); *Briggs 'Palm Shoes' Ltd*, MAN/92/541 (VTD 9840); *TK Colgate (t/a Shrewsbury English School)*, MAN/92/1671 (VTD 10329); *PJ McMahon*, LON/92/3114 (VTD 11308); *Sandmar Technologies Ltd*, LON/93/1559P (VTD 11326); *F Duval (t/a L'Ecluse Restaurant)*, LON/93/2622P (VTD 12082) and *HS & HK Sagar (t/a AMR Pipeline Products Co)*, MAN/94/423 (VTD 12692).

Industrial action by Customs staff

[18.564] A company which imported timber operated a deferred payment system, the import formalities for which were handled by different import agents. The company found that the import agents' documents were often inaccurate, and considered it advisable to check these against a computer statement produced monthly by the VAT Central Unit. The tribunal held that delays in issuing this statement, arising from industrial action by Customs staff, constituted a reasonable excuse for a late return. *Chandler Forest Products Ltd*, LON/87/620 (VTD 2612).

VAT officer demanding immediate payment of assessed tax

[18.565] A company's managing director went abroad on 14 February 1991 for two weeks' holiday. He entrusted the company's sales clerk with the task of completing the company's return for the period ending 31 January, and left her a signed cheque made payable to the Commissioners but with the amount left blank. On 15 February the company received a letter from its local VAT office, giving details of errors discovered following a control visit in the previous week, and an assessment charging tax in respect of these errors. A week later, a VAT officer called with bailiffs demanding payment of the tax charged by the assessment. The sales clerk gave the VAT officer the cheque which the director had intended to accompany the January return. Consequently, the tax shown in that return could not be paid until the first week in March, after the director had returned from holiday. The Commissioners imposed a default surcharge but the tribunal allowed the company's appeal, criticising the VAT office for its conduct in threatening to levy distraint within a few days of the issue of the assessment, and holding that the circumstances constituted a reasonable excuse for the company's inability to pay the liability shown in its January return by the due date. *Direct Valeting Ltd*, MAN/91/1149 (VTD 7118).

Concessionary practice previously agreed by Commissioners

[18.566] A partnership traded as printers and stationers. In December 1972 the Commissioners had agreed in writing that it could adopt a concessionary practice whereby, in cases where a tax invoice was issued not later than six weeks after the end of the month in which goods were delivered, the date on which the invoice was issued could be treated as the tax point. The partnership consistently submitted its returns two weeks late. It incurred a default surcharge and appealed, contending that the terms of the concessionary practice had led the partners to believe that late returns were acceptable. The tribunal accepted this contention and allowed the appeal. *Bernard & Smith*, LON/87/683 (VTD 2607).

[18.567] A company consistently submitted returns six weeks after the end of its accounting period. It appealed against a default surcharge, contending that in 1974 a VAT officer had authorised it to submit its returns in this way. The tribunal accepted this evidence and allowed the appeal, holding that the circumstances constituted a reasonable excuse. *T & H Collard Ltd*, LON/87/692 (VTD 2654).

Local VAT office refusing to accept hand-delivered return

[18.568] A company appealed against a surcharge for the period ending 30 September 1991, contending that one of its directors had visited the Chesterfield VAT office in the late afternoon of 30 October to deliver the return by hand, but had been instructed to post the return to the VAT Central Unit in Southend. The tribunal accepted the company's evidence and allowed the appeal. *Light Wire Ltd*, MAN/92/115 (VTD 7967).

[18.569] A similar decision was reached in *R & MR Hatfield*, LON/92/1891P (VTD 11677).

Industrial action by Post Office staff

[18.570] Because of industrial action by Post Office staff, letterboxes in the Wythenshawe area were sealed for most of September 1988, and a company operating in that area was unable to post its VAT return. The tribunal allowed its appeal against a default surcharge, holding that the closure of the letterboxes constituted a reasonable excuse. *Ernest Lee (Electrical Services) Ltd*, MAN/89/67 (VTD 3584).

[18.571] A similar decision was reached in *Geoffrey Davis (Menswear) Ltd*, LON/94/521P (VTD 12576). (*Note*. An appeal against a subsequent surcharge was dismissed—see 18.372 above.)

Industrial action by Post Office staff—delay in receiving invoices

[18.572] See *Social Surveys (Gallup Poll) Ltd*, 18.255 above, and *Mercuri Urval Ltd*, 18.256 above.

Cash-flow problems following industrial action by Post Office staff

[18.573] See *A Lockett & Co Ltd*, 18.334 above, and the cases noted at 18.335 above.

Postage of return delayed by gale

[18.574] A married couple carried on a farming and haulage business in a remote and heavily wooded part of Devon, two miles from the nearest post box. On 30 January 1990 some trees in the area were blown down by a gale, blocking several roads. Because of this, the couple were unable to post their return for the period ending 31 December 1989 at their usual post box. They arranged for a young woman who worked for them to post the return at a different post box, near to her home. The return was eventually posted in the early evening, after the last collection from the box in question. The tribunal held that the circumstances constituted a reasonable excuse for the late delivery of the return. *PR & NA Hoskin (t/a Parsons & Son)*, LON/90/715Z (VTD 5306).

Hotel proprietor—application for deregistration

[18.575] The owner of a hotel suffered from ill-health and handed over the running of the hotel to his son in June 1990. Neither he nor his son submitted any VAT returns thereafter. The Commissioners imposed default surcharges and the owner appealed, contending that he had applied for deregistration in June 1990 when he had handed over the running of the hotel to his son. The Commissioners gave evidence that they had never received the application for deregistration. The tribunal accepted the hotelier's evidence and allowed his appeal, finding that he had applied for deregistration and holding that, since his turnover was below the appropriate threshold and he had genuinely believed that he was no longer registered, he had a reasonable excuse for not having submitted the returns in question. *AF Lasrado*, LON/93/296P (VTD 10656).

Other cases

[18.576] There have been a small number of other cases turning on very unusual facts in which tribunals have found that the particular circumstances have constituted a reasonable excuse, but where the nature of the case is such that it is of little if any value as a precedent. In the interests of space, such cases have been omitted from this book. For such cases reported up to 31 December 1993, see Tolley's VAT Cases 1994.

Cases where the appellant was unsuccessful

Appellant facing criminal charges

[18.577] An accountant appealed against several default surcharges, contending that he had a reasonable excuse because during the period in question he had been involved in a prolonged criminal investigation and had been indicted for theft by the Crown Prosecution Service. The tribunal dismissed the accountant's appeal, holding that this did not constitute a reasonable excuse. *GAW Sprosson*, LON/93/2578P (VTD 12073).

Effects of fire

[18.578] A company suffered from a serious fire on 16 August 1987. It submitted its return for the period ending 30 September 1987 after the due date, and a default surcharge was imposed. The company appealed, contending that the effects of the fire constituted a reasonable excuse. The tribunal dismissed the appeal, holding that the period between the fire and the due date of the return was long enough for the company to have attended to its VAT affairs. *John Pargeter & Sons Ltd*, MAN/88/435 (VTD 3318).

[18.579] Similar decisions were reached in *R Booth (t/a Discovery Trading Co)*, MAN/94/755 (VTD 12778) and *Food Concepts International Ltd*, LON/05/1201 (VTD 19484).

Flooding at premises

[18.580] A company appealed against four default surcharges, contending that it had a reasonable excuse because there had been several floods in one of its shops. The tribunal dismissed the appeal, observing that 'the floods had been occurring for some years' and holding that this was not a reasonable excuse. *Buxhall Ltd*, LON/06/848 (VTD 20075).

Effects of robbery

[18.581] There was a robbery at a partnership's premises in November 1986. The Commissioners accepted that the disruption caused by this constituted a reasonable excuse for the late submission of the return for the period ending 31 December 1986. One of the partners refused to work at the premises again after the robbery. The tribunal held that her refusal to work at the premises did not constitute a reasonable excuse for six further defaults. *G Ross & S Metcalfe*, MAN/89/1062 (VTD 4835).

Dyslexia

[18.582] A builder, who was dyslexic, submitted four VAT returns late. The tribunal rejected his contention that his dyslexia constituted a reasonable excuse. *JCNT Taylor*, MAN/88/839 (VTD 3408).

[18.583] Dyslexia was also held not to constitute a reasonable excuse in *NJ Fisher*, MAN/92/1397 (VTD 11238).

Change of address

[18.584] In a case where a trader was preparing to move house, and had packed his records away in boxes in anticipation of the move, the tribunal held that this did not constitute a reasonable excuse. *AG Fishwick*, MAN/88/874 (VTD 3642).

[18.585] A trader's change of address was held not to constitute a reasonable excuse in *MK McMullan*, LON/89/1754Y (VTD 4917); *MD Rowley*, LON/89/1779 (VTD 5089); *Dr MEC Randle*, MAN/92/379 (VTD 9000); *A Gibb (t/a Business Post Fife)*, EDN/93/104 (VTD 11166); *K Elliott (t/a Harbourne Engineering)*, LON/98/988 (VTD 16010); *JM Sheldrake*, LON/99/6 (VTD 16119) and *GN & Mrs AV Harrid (t/a Tex Cars Chauffeur Hire)*, LON/03/3123 (VTD 18132).

Change of business premises

[18.586] The change of a company's premises was held not to constitute a reasonable excuse in *Hall Garage*, LON/88/1018Z (VTD 3749); *Aviss Holdings Ltd*, LON/89/751Z (VTD 3982); *Birchwatt Productions Ltd*, LON/89/1011 (VTD 4182); *Network Data Ltd*, LON/89/676Y (VTD 4393); *CBA Enterprises Ltd*, MAN/89/883 (VTD 4741); *Interhouse Ltd*, LON/90/32X (VTD 4782); *Makebrite Ltd*, MAN/90/222 (VTD 5490); *Young Street Management Services Ltd*, EDN/90/194 (VTD 5711); *CW Aberdeen*, MAN/91/801 (VTD 7027); *Magill Business Associates Ltd*, MAN/91/516 (VTD 7855); *JFD Cartons Ltd*, MAN/92/1692 (VTD 10293); *Soundvision Ltd*, LON/94/2098P (VTD 12977); *Taylor Construction*, LON/94/3126P (VTD 13269); *Euromech Ltd*, LON/00/772 (VTD 17429); *Martin Weitz Associates Ltd*, LON/02/391 (VTD 17941), and *R Datoo & Others (t/a The Datoo Partnership)*, [2011] UKFTT 595 (TC), TC01438.

Cash-flow problems following change of premises

[18.587] See *Performance Print Ltd*, **18.369** above.

Reliance on director

[18.588] Reliance on a company director was held not to constitute a reasonable excuse in *True Engineers Ltd*, LON/89/591Z (VTD 4032); *Alpha Numeric Ltd*, LON/89/1448 (VTD 5519); *SC Campbell (Plastics) Ltd*, MAN/90/1081 (VTD 6086); *P & A Fencing & Sheds Ltd*, MAN/91/19 (VTD 6089); *Maltby Motors Ltd*, MAN/91/968 (VTD 7026); *LJ Harvey & Associates (Bournemouth) Ltd*, LON/92/3263P (VTD 10389); *Normaco Ltd*, LON/93/2137 (VTD 11821); *SC Driver (Opticians) Ltd*, LON/94/278P (VTD 12410); *Beatwood Ltd (t/a Royals of London)*, LON/95/83P (VTD 13229) and *Letchworth Polishing & Plating Co Ltd*, LON/95/902P (VTD 13675).

Reliance on accountant

[18.589] A company appealed against a number of default surcharges, contending that it had a reasonable excuse because its accountant (who was an employee of the company) had submitted the returns in question after the due date and had concealed the surcharges from the directors. The tribunal dismissed the appeal, holding that the circumstances did not constitute a reasonable excuse, and the QB upheld this decision. The tribunal had been entitled to find that the reason for the late payment was the dilatoriness of the accountant. The fact that the accountant was an employee of the company did not take him outside the definition of 'any other person' for the purposes of *VATA 1994, s 71(1)(b)*, and the effect of *s 71(1)(b)* was that the circumstances could not constitute a reasonable excuse. Macpherson J observed that, when the 1985 Finance Bill (which introduced what is now *VATA 1994, s 71*) was being debated, the Minister responsible had stated that 'if all one had to do to have a reasonable excuse was to find an accountant who would delay everything, there would be easy pickings to be made'. *Profile Security Services Ltd v C & E Commrs*, QB [1996] STC 808.

[18.590] The decision in *Profile Security Services Ltd*, **18.589** above, was applied in the similar subsequent cases of *Young Construction (London) Ltd*, LON/96/1027 (VTD 14565); *Olympiad Signs Ltd*, LON/96/1029 (VTD 14566); *Corps of Commissionaires Management Ltd*, LON/96/872 (VTD 14593) and *Europlex Technologies (UK) Ltd*, LON/01/1287 (VTD 18042).

[18.591] A company appealed against a default surcharge, contending that it had a reasonable excuse because it had relied on its accountant, who had been dilatory. The tribunal dismissed the appeal, applying *Harris*, **51.88** PENALTIES: FAILURE TO NOTIFY. *Jenkinson*, **51.83** PENALTIES: FAILURE TO NOTIFY, was distinguished because in that case the accountant had deliberately given the appellant false information, whereas in the case under appeal the accountant had not been guilty of any misrepresentation. *Global Security Services Ltd*, EDN/89/91 (VTD 4035).

[18.592] Reliance on accountants has been held not to constitute a reasonable excuse in very many other cases. In the interests of space, such cases are not reported individually in this book. For a list of such cases reported up to 31 October 1990, see Tolley's VAT Cases 1991.

Reliance on secretary

[18.593] A company appealed against a default surcharge, contending that it had a reasonable excuse because its managing director had delegated the company's VAT affairs to the company secretary, who had transpired to be inefficient and had subsequently been dismissed. The tribunal dismissed the appeal, holding that the inefficiency of the company secretary did not constitute a reasonable excuse. *Polarstar Ltd*, LON/96/623 (VTD 14445).

[18.594] There have been a large number of cases in which reliance on a secretary has been held not to be a reasonable excuse. In the interests of space, such cases are not summarised individually in this book. For a list of such cases reported up to and including 31 December 1995, see Tolley's VAT Cases 1996.

Reliance on treasurer

[18.595] Reliance on the treasurer of a golf club was held not to be a reasonable excuse in *Poulton Park Club Ltd*, MAN/89/1005 (VTD 4653).

[18.596] Reliance on the treasurer of a rugby club was held not to constitute a reasonable excuse in *Crowborough Rugby Football Club Ltd*, LON/90/1676Z (VTD 6023).

Reliance on employee

[18.597] There have been a very large number of cases in which reliance on an employee has been held not to be a reasonable excuse. In the interests of space, such cases are not summarised individually in this book. For a list of such cases decided up to 31 December 1995, see Tolley's VAT Cases 1996.

Reliance on bookkeeper

[18.598] Reliance on a bookkeeper has been held not to constitute a reasonable excuse in a very large number of cases, which appear to raise no point of general importance. In the interests of space, such cases are not summarised individually in this book. For a list of such cases decided up to 31 December 1993, see Tolley's VAT Cases 1994.

Reliance on wife

[18.599] In a case where the wife of a partner had forgotten to submit a return, the tribunal held that this did not constitute a reasonable excuse. *Nealeplan*, LON/88/1215Z (VTD 3457).

[18.600] Reliance on the wife of a sole trader was held not to constitute a reasonable excuse in *R Swain*, MAN/90/351 (VTD 5286); *AJ Howe-Davies (t/a D & B Contracts)*, LON/90/1240 (VTD 5609); *M Shalloe*, MAN/90/1036 (VTD 6234); *D Hickford*, EDN/91/126 (VTD 6290); *CV Weedon*, LON/92/2908P (VTD 10181); *PG Davies*, LON/93/1886P (VTD 11456) and *Wynd Consulting*, LON/96/1756 (VTD 14773).

Club treasurer unaware of issue of surcharge liability notice

[18.601] A golf club had submitted two returns after the due dates and had been issued with a surcharge liability notice. A new treasurer took office in late 1987 and was unaware of the issue of the notice. He submitted the return for the period ending 31 March 1988 after the due date and the Commissioners imposed a default surcharge. The tribunal dismissed the club's appeal, holding that it was the club's responsibility to ensure that the new treasurer was aware of the issue of the notice. *Stourbridge Golf Club Ltd*, MAN/88/658 (VTD 3359).

[18.602] See also *Rotherham Borough Council Employees Sports & Social Club*, 18.80 above, in which the fact that a new club treasurer was not told that his predecessor had received a surcharge liability notice was held not to constitute a reasonable excuse.

Company accountant not aware of surcharge liability notice

[18.603] A company appointed a new accountant in September 1988. It had previously received a surcharge liability notice, but the managing director did not tell the accountant this. When a subsequent return was submitted after the due date, the Commissioners imposed a default surcharge. The tribunal dismissed the company's appeal, holding that, since the company had received and been aware of the issue of the notice, it was the company's responsibility to inform its accountant. *John Hilditch Plant Hire*, LON/89/732X (VTD 4151).

Company director unaware of surcharge liability notice

[18.604] A company appealed against a default surcharge, contending that its previous bookkeeper had not told the managing director (who was her father) that the company had received a surcharge liability notice. The tribunal dismissed the appeal, holding that the circumstances did not constitute a reasonable excuse. *Surecliff Ltd*, LON/92/188X (VTD 8922).

Cheque accidentally not submitted with return

[18.605] In a case where the person whose responsibility it was to submit a VAT return accidentally omitted to enclose the necessary cheque, the tribunal held that this was not a reasonable excuse. *Brecon Brewery Ltd*, LON/87/862 (VTD 3053).

[18.606] Similar decisions have been reached in a large number of subsequent cases. In the interests of space, such cases are not summarised individually in this book. For a list of such cases decided up to 31 December 2009, see Tolley's VAT Cases 2010.

[18.607] In a case where a company contended that it had submitted a cheque with the return, but a VAT officer gave evidence that there was no cheque enclosed in the envelope containing the return, the tribunal found that the cheque had not been sent and held that the company did not have a reasonable excuse. *Camden (Hardchrome) Ltd*, MAN/89/123 (VTD 3724).

[18.608] Similar decisions were reached in *GA Mackay*, EDN/90/174 (VTD 5547); *Brockholes Electrics Co Ltd*, LON/91/1171 (VTD 6519); *RK Midda*, LON/92/254Y (VTD 8951) and *TL Smart (t/a On Tour Catering)*, LON/92/2476P (VTD 10303).

Chequebook not available

[18.609] A trader appealed against a default surcharge, contending that he could not have paid his VAT on time because he had run out of blank cheques and his bank had not supplied him with a new chequebook. The tribunal dismissed his appeal, holding that this was not a reasonable excuse. *C Beckett*, MAN/90/30 (VTD 4766).

[18.610] Similar decisions were reached in *Barking Vehicle Rentals Ltd*, LON/90/169Y (VTD 4934); *JA Armstrong*, MAN/90/350 (VTD 5262); *Lynben Ltd*, EDN/91/299 (VTD 7291) and *City Shredding Services Ltd*, LON/92/1447P (VTD 9329).

Difficulty in posting return

[18.611] A company appealed against a default surcharge, contending that it had a reasonable excuse for having posted the return late, because its directors did not have a car and the nearest post-box was three miles away. The tribunal dismissed the appeal, holding that this did not constitute a reasonable excuse. *Webbro Ltd*, MAN/92/380 (VTD 8999).

[18.612] A company appealed against a default surcharge, contending that it had a reasonable excuse for having posted the return late, because one of its employees had intended to deliver the return to its local VAT office on the due date, but had been delayed by traffic congestion and had eventually posted the return instead. The tribunal dismissed the appeal, holding that this did not constitute a reasonable excuse. *New Concept Ltd*, EDN/97/71 (VTD 15174).

Other cases

[18.613] There have been a large number of unsuccessful appeals which appear to raise no point of general importance but where appellants have contended that the surcharge has been unjust. In the interests of space, such cases are not reported individually in this book.

Material defaults (VATA 1994, s 59(8))

[18.614] A company paid its VAT for the periods ending July 2004, October 2004 and January 2005 after the due date. Customs imposed default surcharges. The company did not appeal. It also paid its VAT for the periods ending July 2005 and July 2006 after the due date, although its VAT for the intervening periods was on time. Customs again imposed surcharges. The company appealed against the surcharge for the period ending July 2006 (which was at the rate of 15%), contending that it had had a reasonable excuse for the period ending October 2004 (because its office manager had been ill and absent from work), although it had failed to appeal at the time of that default. The tribunal accepted this contention, finding that there was a reasonable excuse for the period ending October 2004 and holding that that could be taken into account because it was a 'default which is material to the surcharge', within *VATA 1994, s 59(8)*. Applying *dicta* in *Dow Chemical Company Ltd*, 18.38 above, 'where a taxable person establishes the defence of reasonable excuse under *VATA 1994, s 59(7)*, the *subsection* itself appears to contemplate that the specified percentages for subsequent defaults will be adjusted accordingly'. The tribunal concluded that 'the effect of *section 59(7)* and *(8)* is that because the appellant had a reasonable excuse for the 10/04 default, the default surcharge for the 07/06 default is to be computed as if the 10/04 default had not happened'. *Aardvark Excavations Ltd*, LON/07/545 (VTD 20468).

[18.615] The decision in *Aardvark Excavations Ltd*, 18.614 above, was applied in the similar subsequent cases of *Central Cleaning Contractors Ltd*, LON/08/436 (VTD 20869) and *RP Griffin & DM Griffin v HMRC*, [2010] UKFTT 220 (TC), TC00521.

Validity of the surcharge

Principle of 'proportionality'

[18.616] A YMCA appealed against a default surcharge, contending that the imposition of the surcharge was contrary to the legal principle of 'proportionality'. The tribunal rejected this contention and dismissed the appeal, applying the principles laid down in *W Emmett & Son Ltd*, 52.452 PENALTIES: MISDECLARATION, and observing that 'a national revenue department may well feel that default must be legislated against with even more vigour than mistakes'. *The Central Young Men's Christian Association*, LON/92/1179X (VTD 9318).

[18.617] Similar decisions, applying *W Emmett & Son Ltd*, 52.452 PENALTIES: MISDECLARATION, and *dicta* of Simon Brown J in *P & O Ferries*, 52.453 PENALTIES: MISDECLARATION, were reached in *Impetus Engineering Co*

(International) Ltd, MAN/92/669 (VTD 10596); *JF Bower (t/a Bean Bower & Co)*, [1995] VATDR 294 (VTD 13224); *Finaplan Ltd*, MAN/93/478 & 796 (VTD 13224); *Advanced Security Installations Ltd*, LON/96/447 (VTD 14297) and *Universal Display Fittings Co Ltd*, LON/98/463 (VTD 15838).

[18.618] A company appealed against a default surcharge, contending firstly that it had a reasonable excuse, and alternatively that the imposition of the surcharge contravened the legal principle of 'proportionality'. The tribunal rejected the first contention, holding that there was no reasonable excuse for the defaults, but held a further three-day hearing to consider the subject of 'proportionality' in more detail. The tribunal reviewed the relevant case law in detail and dismissed the appeal. The tribunal observed that 'a system of penalties is necessary to ensure compliance' and that 'given that some 12 to 14 per cent of the 1.7 million registered traders still default in any one year, a system of surcharges is necessary'. The tribunal expressed concern that there was no power to mitigate default surcharges, although *FA 1993* had given both the Commissioners and the tribunal powers to mitigate penalties. The tribunal commented that 'we find the justifications for the absence of a power to mitigate to be less than convincing'. However, 'the necessity for an automatic scheme without mitigation is not merely a matter of the judgment of the tribunal or court. The authorities make it clear that the legislature has a wide margin of appreciation when framing implementation policies in the area of taxation.' Furthermore, the surcharges did not contravene the European Convention on Human Rights, applying *dicta* in *Gasus Dosier- und Fördertechnik GmbH v Netherlands*, ECHR Case 15375/89; 20 EHRR 403. *Greengate Furniture Ltd*, [2003] VATDR 178 (VTD 18280).

[18.619] The decision in *Greengate Furniture Ltd*, **18.618** above, was applied and approved in the similar subsequent cases of *Market & Opinion Research International Ltd*, LON/03/569 (VTD 18422); *Steel Services (Great Yarmouth) Ltd*, LON/04/1896 (VTD 19575); *Sony Ericsson Mobile Communications AB*, LON/07/372 (VTD 20513); *H5 Hotels Ltd*, LON/07/1899 (VTD 20662); *DJW Penny*, LON/x (VTD 20813); *Eastwell Manor Ltd*, [2011] UKFTT 293 (TC), TC01155; *Saint-Gobain Building Distribution Ltd*, [2011] UKFTT 461 (TC), TC01311, and *Eco-Hygiene Ltd*, [2011] UKFTT 754 (TC), TC01591.

[18.620] A company with a substantial turnover submitted a return one day late. HMRC imposed a surcharge of £131,881 (at the rate of 5% of the VAT due). The company appealed, contending that the surcharge contravened the legal principle of 'proportionality'. The tribunal accepted this contention and allowed the appeal. Judge Bishopp held that it was 'unimaginable' that such a high penalty would be imposed 'if the penalty were not determined mechanically but by a court or tribunal with the power to set any monetary penalty it chose without statutory constraint'. There was a 'public interest in the prompt payment of taxes', but the surcharge imposed here was clearly disproportionate. Applying the principles laid down by the ECJ in *Louloudakis v Greece*, CJEC Case C-262/99, 12 July 2001 unreported, a high penalty was 'compatible with the principle of proportionality only in so far as it is made necessary by overriding requirements of enforcement and prevention, when the gravity of the infringement is taken into account'. *Enersys Holdings UK Ltd v HMRC*, FTT [2010] SFTD 387; [2010] UKFTT 20 (TC), TC00335.

[18.621] A company (T) paid its VAT liability for the period ending 30 June 2009 one day late. HMRC imposed a surcharge of £4,260. T appealed, contending that the surcharge was disproportionate. Judge Redston accepted this contention and allowed the appeal, applying the decision in *Enersys Holdings UK Ltd*, **18.620** above, and distinguishing the earlier decision in *Greengate Furniture Ltd*, **18.618** above. *Total Technology (Engineering) Ltd v HMRC*, [2011] UKFTT 473 (TC), TC01323. (*Note.* HMRC have appealed to the Upper Tribunal against this decision.)

Customs' discretion not to impose surcharge

[18.622] Three associated companies appealed against eighteen default surcharges, contending that they were invalid because the Commissioners had imposed them automatically without considering the exercise of their discretion under what is now *VATA 1994, s 76*. The tribunal dismissed the appeals, holding that the surcharge assessments were valid, since in the circumstances of the case in question there was 'no possibility that their discretion would have been exercised otherwise than to impose the surcharges'. The QB upheld this decision. Judge J specifically disapproved *obiter dicta* of the tribunal chairman in *Food Engineering Ltd*, **52.454** PENALTIES: MISDECLARATION, and the decision reached by Miss Gort in *Tamdown Ltd*, **52.456** PENALTIES: MISDECLARATION. Judge J held that the right of appeal to a VAT tribunal provided for by what is now *VATA 1994, s 83* was confined to an appeal against the liability to surcharge or against the amount of the surcharge. There was no right to appeal against the Commissioners' discretionary power whether or not to make a surcharge assessment. The remedy against any improper exercise of the Commissioners' discretionary power to impose a surcharge would be an application for judicial review. On the facts of this case, the decision to impose the surcharges was inevitable. *Dollar Land (Feltham) Ltd v C & E Commrs (and associated appeals)*, QB [1995] STC 414.

[18.623] The QB decision in *Dollar Land (Feltham) Ltd*, **18.622** above, was applied in the subsequent similar cases of *Mrs AM Rogers (t/a Quality Records)*, LON/95/2970 (VTD 13991) and *Stafford & Worcester Property Co Ltd*, MAN/98/880 (VTD 16302).

19

Drugs, Medicines, Aids for the Handicapped, etc.

The cases in this chapter are arranged under the following headings.

Supplies of goods by registered practitioner (VATA 1994, Sch 8, Group 12, Items 1, 1A) — 19.1

Supplies to handicapped people (VATA 1994, Sch 8, Group 12, Items 2, 2A, 3)

Definition of 'domestic use' (*VATA 1994, Sch 8, Group 12, Item 2(a)*) — 19.9

Medical or surgical appliances (*VATA 1994, Sch 8, Group 12, Item 2(a)*) — 19.10

Adjustable beds designed for invalids (*VATA 1994, Sch 8, Group 12, Item 2(b)*) — 19.13

Motor vehicles (*VATA 1994, Sch 8, Group 12, Items 2(f), 2A*) — 19.16

Whether equipment and appliances 'designed solely for use by a handicapped person' (*VATA 1994, Sch 8, Group 12, Item 2(g)*) — 19.24

Parts and accessories (*VATA 1994, Sch 8, Group 12, Item 2(h)*) — 19.70

Services of adapting goods for a handicapped person (*VATA 1994, Sch 8, Group 12, Item 3*) — 19.74

Supplies of widening doorways, etc. (VATA 1994, Sch 8, Group 12, Items 8, 9) — 19.76

Supplies of bathrooms, washrooms, etc. (VATA 1994, Sch 8, Group 12, Items 10–12) — 19.86

Supplies of lifts (VATA 1994, Sch 8, Group 12, Items 16–18) — 19.95

NOTE

The scope of *VATA 1994, Sch 8, Group 12* was significantly restricted by the amendments made by the *VAT (Drugs, Medicines and Aids for the Handicapped) Order 1997 (SI 1997/2744)*, which came into force on 1 January 1998. Cases relating to periods before 1998 should be read in the light of these provisions.

Supplies of goods by registered practitioner (VATA 1994, Sch 8, Group 12, Items 1, 1A)

Supply on prescription of lotion to patients at clinics

[19.1] A company, the controlling director of which was a registered pharmacist, manufactured a pharmaceutical product, minoxidil, which was made into a lotion for the treatment of alopecia and was only available on prescription. It supplied this lotion to three clinics which specialised in such treatment, and did not account for VAT on these supplies. The Commissioners issued assessments charging tax on them, considering that the company was making supplies of goods to the clinics, and that these supplies did not qualify for zero-rating. The company appealed, contending that it was making its supplies to the patients and that the supplies should be zero-rated under what is now *VATA 1994, Sch 8, Group 12, Item 1*. The tribunal accepted this contention and allowed the appeal, holding on the evidence that the lotion remained the company's property until it was dispensed to the patients, that the company was supplying the lotion to the patients rather than to the clinic, and that the payments from the clinic qualified for zero-rating. *Parsons Green Ltd*, [1990] VATTR 194 (VTD 5044). (*Note*. See now, however, *VATA 1994, Sch 8, Group 12, Note 5A*, introduced by *VAT (Drugs, Medicines and Aids for the Handicapped) Order 1997 (SI 1997/2744)*, with effect from 1 January 1998.)

Provision of drugs from hospital dispensary—whether within Item 1

[19.2] A company operated a private hospital. It supplied patients with drugs in the course of their treatment. It did not account for VAT in respect of these drugs, considering that the supply was zero-rated under what is now *VATA 1994, Sch 8, Group 12, Item 1*. The Commissioners issued a ruling that the supplies of drugs were not eligible for zero-rating, but were exempt supplies by virtue of what is now *VATA 1994, Sch 9, Group 7, Item 4*. The tribunal allowed the company's appeal, holding on the evidence that the drugs were prescribed by an 'appropriate medical practitioner' within *Medicines Act 1968, s 67(2)(a)*, and were a separate zero-rated supply, rather than merely a part of a composite exempt supply of care in a hospital. The CA upheld this decision (by a 2-1 majority, Kennedy LJ dissenting). Millett LJ held that, for VAT purposes, the Commissioners could treat as separate transactions what the contracting parties had treated as a single supply, but the Commissioners could not join together what the contracting parties had treated as separate. The supply of drugs was a separate supply of goods which qualified for zero-rating. *Wellington Private Hospital Ltd v C & E Commrs*, CA [1997] STC 445. (*Notes*. (1) See now, however, *VATA 1994, Sch 8, Group 12, Note 5A*, introduced by *VAT (Drugs, Medicines and Aids for the Handicapped) Order 1997 (SI 1997/2744)*, with effect from 1 January 1998. (2) For another issue in the tribunal appeal in this case, not taken to the QB, see **46.120** PARTIAL EXEMPTION. (3) The *dicta* of Millett LJ in this case should now be read in the light of the subsequent CJEC decision in *Card Protection Plan Ltd*, **22.324** EUROPEAN COMMUNITY LAW, where the CJEC held that 'a supply which comprises a single service from an economic point of view should not be artificially split'.)

[19.3] Similar decisions were reached in two cases which were heard in the QB and CA with *Wellington Private Hospital Ltd*, **19.2** above. *C & E Commrs v British United Provident Association Ltd (No 1); C & E Commrs v St Martins Hospital Ltd*, CA [1997] STC 445. (*Note*. For another issue in the *British United Provident Association Ltd* case, see **19.12** below.)

Supply on prescription of primrose oil products

[**19.4**] A company supplied primrose oil products. The Commissioners issued a ruling that the supply of these products, when dispensed by a registered pharmacist on the prescription of a doctor, failed to qualify for zero-rating under what is now *VATA 1994, Sch 8, Group 12, Item 1* on the grounds that the products had 'no demonstrable medicinal properties'. (The products were not available under the National Health Service, but were sometimes prescribed by private medical practitioners.) The company appealed, contending that the products were useful for patients suffering from multiple sclerosis, arthritis and pre-menstrual tension, and qualified for zero-rating under *Group 12, Item 1* when prescribed by a doctor and dispensed by a pharmacist. The tribunal allowed the appeal, holding that 'goods' for the purposes of *Group 12, Item 1* included 'pharmaceutical products normally used for health care, prevention of diseases, and treatment for medical purposes properly prescribed by a doctor (or other person mentioned in *Item 1*), and dispensed by a registered pharmacist'. The products in dispute were pharmaceutical products, so that their supply qualified for zero-rating. *Bio Oil Research Ltd*, MAN/92/1320 (VTD 12252).

Sales of Viagra

[**19.5**] An individual (T) was registered for VAT as a trader in 'health products'. He advertised Viagra on the internet, and passed the orders which he received from customers to a doctor (S) who issued private prescriptions. Before March 2001 S sent the completed prescriptions to an independent pharmacist. From March 2001, S no longer used the pharmacist's services, but used a different supplier enabling him to supply the Viagra directly to the customers. T did not account for VAT on his supplies. Customs accepted that the supplies before March 2001 qualified for zero-rating under *VATA 1994, Sch 8, Group 12, Item 1* as they were made by a registered pharmacist. However they issued an assessment on the basis that the supplies after March 2001 failed to qualify for zero-rating. The tribunal upheld the assessment and dismissed T's appeal, observing that T was acting as an agent in his own name, within *VATA 1994, s 47(2A)*, and was required to account for output tax. *PW Tomlinson*, MAN/06/035 (VTD 20059). (*Note.* Costs were awarded to Customs.)

Drugs personally administered by nurse at patient's home

[**19.6**] A company (H) arranged for nurses to visit patients to administer drugs that had been prescribed for them. It treated its supplies as zero-rated, and reclaimed the related input tax. Customs issued a ruling that the effect of the HL decision in *Dr Beynon & Partners*, **19.8** below, was that H was making exempt supplies of medical services, and thus was not entitled to credit for the related input tax. The tribunal allowed H's appeal, distinguishing *Beynon* on the grounds that in that case 'the determining characteristic of the supply was the doctor's service of consultation, diagnosis and prescription, to which the dispensing and administration of the drug were ancillary or subordinate'. In the present case, by contrast, the tribunal held that 'the necessity of a nurse does not override the patient's underlying requirement, namely the drug'. *Healthcare at Home Ltd*, [2007] VATDR 511 (VTD 20379).

Drugs personally administered by NHS doctor—whether zero-rated

[19.7] In 1997 the Commissioners issued a ruling that drugs and other medical items personally administered by a general practitioner working in the NHS formed part of a single exempt supply of medical care, so that the related input tax was not recoverable. A partnership of doctors appealed, contending that the supplies of drugs which were personally administered by a NHS doctor (for example, by injection) were supplies of goods which qualified for zero-rating under *VATA 1994, Sch 8, Group 12, Item 1A*. The tribunal accepted this contention and allowed the appeal. *Drs Woodings, Rees, Crossthwaite & Jones*, [1999] VATDR 294 (VTD 16175). (*Note*. See now, however, the subsequent HL decision in *Dr Beynon & Partners*, 19.8 below.)

[19.8] In a case where the facts were similar to those in *Drs Woodings, Rees, Crossthwaite & Jones*, 19.7 above, the CA allowed the partnership's appeal but the HL reversed this decision. Lord Hoffmann held that, applying the principles laid down by the CJEC in *Card Protection Plan Ltd*, 22.324 EUROPEAN COMMUNITY LAW, there was a single exempt supply of services. He observed that 'the level of generality which corresponds with social and economic reality is to regard the transaction as the patient's visit to the doctor for treatment and not to split it into smaller units'. Accordingly, the partnership was not entitled to reclaim the related input tax. *C & E Commrs v Dr Beynon & Partners*, HL 2004, [2005] STC 55; [2004] UKHL 53; [2004] 4 All ER 1091. (*Note*. For the Commissioners' practice following this decision, see Business Brief 1/2005, issued on 19 January 2005.)

Supplies to handicapped people (VATA 1994, Sch 8, Group 12, Items 2, 2A, 3)

Definition of 'domestic use' (VATA 1994, Sch 8, Group 12, Item 2)

[19.9] In a purchase tax case concerning the liability of electric heating pads and blankets, Cassels J held that 'domestic' should be construed as referring to 'the house or the home'. He observed that 'a great variety of articles go to make a home, not because they are necessary, but because they are calculated to contribute to the comfort and well-being of people in the home. Such articles may be said to be of a kind used for domestic purposes. The fact that any one of these articles may be used for medical purposes does not prevent its being an article of a kind used for domestic purposes.' *Attorney-General v Milliwatt Ltd*, KB [1948] 1 All ER 331.

Medical or surgical appliances (VATA 1994, Sch 8, Group 12, Item 2(a))

'Airbaths' supplied to hospitals

[19.10] A company designed 'airbaths', which were intended to relieve pains in the neck and upper back by directing underwater currents of hot air at the appropriate parts of the body. It supplied these to hospitals, and did not account for VAT on these supplies. The Commissioners issued a ruling that they were liable to VAT, and the company appealed, contending that they should be zero-rated under what is now *VATA 1994, Sch 8, Group 12, Item 2(a)*. The tribunal dismissed the company's appeal, holding that the airbaths were neither 'medical or surgical appliances' within *Item 2(a)* nor 'designed solely for use by a handicapped person within *Item 2(g)*'. *Aquakraft Ltd*, MAN/85/350 (VTD 2215).

Transcutaneous electrical nerve stimulators—whether within Item 2(a)

[19.11] A company supplied transcutaneous electrical nerve stimulators, which were intended to relieve pain by applying electrical currents to the skin through surface electrodes. It did not account for VAT on its supplies, treating them as zero-rated. The Commissioners issued a ruling that the supplies of the stimulators did not qualify for zero-rating, and the company appealed. The tribunal allowed the appeal, holding on the evidence that the stimulators had been 'designed solely for use by chronic pain sufferers' and 'solely for the relief of a severe abnormality or a severe injury', and were thus within what is now *VATA 1994, Sch 8, Group 12, Item 2(a)*. (The tribunal observed that any sales to individuals who were not within the definition of 'a handicapped person' would not qualify for zero-rating.) *Neen Design Ltd*, LON/93/1586A (VTD 11782). (*Note.* For the Commissioners' practice following this decision, see Business Brief 4/94, issued on 21 February 1994.)

Supplies of prostheses—whether within Sch 8, Group 12, Item 2(a)

[19.12] A company which operated a number of hospitals did not account for tax on supplies of prostheses (manufactured parts designed to replace or supplement natural components of the human body, such as hip joints and heart valves), but reclaimed the input tax relating to such supplies. The Commissioners issued a ruling that the supply of prostheses was an integral part of a composite supply of medical care, which was exempt from VAT, so that the related input tax was not recoverable. The company appealed, contending that the supplies of prostheses were separate supplies which qualified for zero-rating under what is now *VATA 1994, Sch 8, Group 12, Item 2(a)*, and that the services relating to the supplies of hip replacements qualified for zero-rating under what is now *VATA 1994, Sch 8, Group 12, Item 7*. The tribunal allowed the company's appeal in part, holding that the replacement hip joints fell within *Group 12, Item 2(a)* and that the services involved in the supply of replacement hip joints qualified for zero-rating under *Group 12, Item 7*, but that apparatus used for splint lumbro-sacral fusion, and plates used for osteotomy, were not designed 'solely for the relief of a severe abnormality or severe injury', and thus failed to qualify for zero-rating. The CA upheld this decision (by a 2-1 majority, Kennedy LJ dissenting). Millett LJ held that, for

VAT purposes, the Commissioners could treat as separate transactions what the contracting parties had treated as a single supply, but the Commissioners could not join together what the contracting parties had treated as separate. The supply of prostheses was a separate supply of goods which qualified for zero-rating under *Item 2(a)*, and the services involved in implanting them qualified for zero-rating under *Item 7*. *British United Provident Association Ltd v C & E Commrs (and cross-appeal)*, CA [1997] STC 445. (*Notes*. (1) See now, however, *VATA 1994, Sch 8, Group 12, Note 5B*, introduced by *VAT (Drugs, Medicines and Aids for the Handicapped) Order 1997 (SI 1997/2744)*, with effect from 1 January 1998. (2) For another issue in this case, see **19.3** above. For subsequent developments, see **22.230** EUROPEAN COMMUNITY LAW.)

Adjustable beds designed for invalids (VATA 1994, Sch 8, Group 12, Item 2(b))

Electromagnetic mattress, pillow and machine

[19.13] See *Back In Health Ltd*, **19.53** below, and *Made To Measure*, **19.54** below.

Adjustable beds—whether within Sch 8, Group 12, Item 2(b)

[19.14] A company manufactured physiotherapy products, including adjustable beds. The beds were of unusually strong construction, adjustable in height, and included two cycloidal vibrator massage units which were embedded in the mattress. The Commissioners issued a ruling that the beds did not qualify for zero-rating under what is now *VATA 1994, Sch 8, Group 12, Item 2(b)*, on the grounds that they were not 'designed for invalids'. The company appealed, contending that the beds were designed for invalids, and the fact that they could also be used by people who were not invalids was not conclusive. The tribunal allowed the appeal, holding on the evidence that the beds were not 'designed for normal sleep and rest' but were 'designed for a special purpose' and were 'designed for invalids'. Accordingly they qualified for zero-rating. *Niagara Holdings Ltd*, [1993] VATTR 503 (VTD 11400).

[19.15] A company imported adjustable beds from Germany. The Commissioners issued a ruling that the supplies of the beds did not qualify for zero-rating under *VATA 1994, Sch 8, Group 12, Item 2(b)*, on the grounds that they were suitable for able-bodied people and were not designed specifically for disabled customers. The company appealed, contending that the beds were designed for invalids, and the fact that they could also be used by people who were not invalids was not conclusive. The tribunal accepted this contention and allowed the appeal, holding on the evidence that 'the bed was specifically designed for people who are less than able'. The chairman observed that 'whilst the promotional literature is not specific in stating that the bed is designed for invalids, it is clear from all the features incorporated in the design that it is so suitable' and found that it was the intention of the manufacturers 'to produce a bed which was suitable for people who were temporarily in a state of invalidity, or suffering from permanent minor disabilities'. *Hulsta Furniture (UK) Ltd*, LON/98/936 (VTD 16289).

Motor vehicles (VATA 1994, Sch 8, Group 12, Items 2(f), 2A)

Motor vehicle supplied to paraplegic

[19.16] A paraplegic reclaimed input tax on the purchase of a motor car with an automatic gearbox and a special grab handle fitted to the driver's door. The Commissioners rejected the claim, and the paraplegic appealed. The tribunal dismissed his appeal, finding on the evidence that the car in question was not 'designed or substantially adapted for the carriage of a person in a wheelchair', and holding that it was therefore outside what is now *VATA 1994, Sch 8, Group 12, Item 2(f)* and did not qualify for zero-rating. *JG Oliver*, MAN/92/1065 (VTD 10579).

[19.17] A similar decision was reached in *AM Horstead*, MAN/05/858 (VTD 19697).

[19.18] In a Scottish case, a company (C) supplied seven motor vehicles (all of which were adapted Land Rovers or Range Rovers) to handicapped people, and treated the supplies as zero-rated. HMRC issued an assessment charging tax on the basis that the supplies did not meet the conditions of *Sch 8, Group 12, Item 2A*. The tribunal reviewed the evidence in detail and allowed C's appeal against this decision, finding that C 'had obtained sufficient evidence of eligibility'. *Croall Bryson & Co Ltd v HMRC*, [2011] UKFTT 494 (TC), TC01341.

[19.18A] A family partnership treated its supplies of an adapted Land Rover, and a Range Rover with a steering wheel spinner, to handicapped people as zero-rated. HMRC issued an assessment charging tax on the basis that the supplies did not meet the conditions of Sch 8, Group 12, Item 2A. The tribunal reviewed the evidence in detail and allowed the partnership's appeal. *DG & CD Bunning (t/a Stafford Land Rover) v HMRC*, [2012] UKFTT 32 (TC), TC01730.

Acquisition of car from Netherlands

[19.19] A woman (P), who lived in the UK and had to use a wheelchair, purchased a left-hand drive Chrysler car from the Netherlands. The Commissioners issued a ruling that VAT was due on the acquisition (although they accepted that subsequent adaptation work qualified for zero-rating). P appealed, contending that she had had to buy a left-hand drive car for her own safety, as it was dangerous for her to get out of the right-hand side of a car in a wheelchair, and that her initial acquisition of the car should also be treated as zero-rated. The tribunal dismissed her appeal, observing that 'to qualify for zero-rating, the motor vehicle must have been substantially and permanently adapted for the carriage of a person in a wheelchair'. In this case, however, 'the adaptation of the car had not been begun' when P acquired it. *EM Pantekoek*, LON/00/533 (VTD 17765).

Car adapted for handicapped person but supplied to finance company

[19.20] A company (B), which traded as a car dealer, agreed to sell a car which had been specially modified for use by a handicapped person (P), who normally used a wheelchair. It did not account for VAT on the supply. The Commissioners discovered that the supply had actually been made to a hire-purchase company, rather than to P. They therefore issued an assessment charging tax on the supply. The tribunal upheld the assessment and dismissed B's appeal, observing that B could recover the assessed tax by issuing a 'VAT-only invoice' to the hire-purchase company. *Bentley & Bentley Ltd*, MAN/03/794 (VTD 18917).

Motor caravan

[19.21] A company which designed and built motor caravans supplied a motor caravan with a door 30 inches wide, designed to accommodate a wheelchair, and a ramp to enable the wheelchair to be loaded. The Commissioners issued a ruling that the caravan did not qualify for zero-rating, on the basis that it was capable of carrying more than five persons other than the wheelchair passenger, and thus was not within what is now *VATA 1994, Sch 8, Group 12, Item 2(f)*. The company appealed. The tribunal allowed the appeal, finding on the evidence that the vehicle was 'not designed or adapted to carry more than five persons apart from the person in the wheelchair'. *Emperor Enterprises Ltd*, LON/93/803 (VTD 11038). (*Note.* The relevant limit has subsequently been increased from five persons to eleven persons—see *Item 2(f)* as amended by *SI 2001/754* with effect from 1 April 2001.)

[19.22] A company did not account for tax on the sale of a motor caravan to a handicapped person. The Commissioners issued an assessment charging tax on the sale, and the company appealed, contending that it should be treated as zero-rated under what is now *VATA 1994, Sch 8, Group 12, Item 2(f)*. The tribunal rejected this contention and dismissed the appeal, holding on the evidence that, although the caravan had been purchased by a handicapped person, it had not been 'designed or substantially and permanently adapted for the carriage of a person in a wheelchair or on a stretcher', so that the conditions of *Item 2(f)* were not satisfied. *St Andrew's Motor Homes Ltd*, EDN/96/5 (VTD 14100). (*Note.* The tribunal also rejected a contention by the company that the Commissioners were personally barred from raising the assessment—see **2.121** APPEALS.)

[19.23] An individual (H) purchased a motor caravan described as a Holiday Rambler Vacationer for the use of his father, who was confined to a wheelchair. The Commissioners issued a ruling that VAT was chargeable on the supply. H appealed, contending that the caravan had been fitted with special ramps to enable his father to use it, and therefore qualified for zero-rating under *VATA 1994, Sch 8, Group 12, Item 2A*. The tribunal accepted this contention and allowed the appeal, holding on the evidence that the fitting of the ramps meant that the caravan had been 'substantially and permanently adapted' to carry a person in a wheelchair. *Q Hylands*, LON/03/050 (VTD 18560).

Whether equipment and appliances 'designed solely for use by a handicapped person' (VATA 1994, Sch 8, Group 12, Item 2(g))

Cases held to qualify for zero-rating

Bath equipment for handicapped children

[19.24] A company designed and supplied bath equipment intended for handicapped children. The Commissioners issued a ruling that the equipment was not eligible for zero-rating, since it could also be used by children who were not handicapped. The tribunal allowed the company's appeal, holding on the evidence that the equipment was 'designed solely for use by a handicapped person', and qualified for zero-rating under what is now *VATA 1994, Sch 8, Group 12, Item 2(g)*. *Kirton Designs Ltd*, LON/86/641 (VTD 2374). (*Note.* The tribunal also held that two types of chair, designed for elderly people, failed to qualify for zero-rating.)

Kitchen sink

[19.25] The tribunal held that a specially-designed 'rise and fall' sink was designed solely for use by a handicapped person and was thus zero-rated under what is now *VATA 1994, Sch 8, Group 12, Item 2(g)*. *WN Heaton & Son Ltd*, MAN/86/336 (VTD 2397).

Fitted kitchen for handicapped person—whether supply zero-rated

[19.26] A company supplied fitted kitchens. It provided a range of such kitchens which were specially designed to be suitable for disabled people. The Commissioners issued a ruling that the kitchens did not qualify for zero-rating, on the grounds that they were suitable for use by people who were not handicapped. The company appealed, accepting that some of the kitchen units (such as an oven, a hob and an extractor fan) failed to qualify for zero-rating, but contending that certain units were specifically designed for people in wheelchairs, and thus were within *Group 12, Item 2(g)*. The tribunal accepted this contention and allowed the appeal. On the evidence, several of the kitchen units stood on a high and deeply-recessed plinth, which was designed 'solely for use by a handicapped person'. The sink facing, a special knee-face hob unit, and wall cupboards with internal pull-out drop-down fittings, also qualified for zero-rating. *Softley Ltd (t/a Softley Kitchens)*, LON/96/1810 (VTD 15034). (*Note.* For the Commissioners' practice following this decision, see Customs' VAT Manual, Part 7, chapter 12, para 23.4. The Commissioners state that 'suppliers of mass production kitchen equipment cannot benefit from zero-rating, even if that equipment might be of more use to disabled people than others'.)

High-density foam mattress and pillow

[19.27] A company manufactured high-density foam mattresses and pillows. The Commissioners issued a ruling that the supplies of these items did not qualify for zero-rating, on the basis that they were not 'designed solely for use by a handicapped person'. The company appealed, contending that the items were designed solely for use by people who were chronically sick and were therefore within the definition of 'handicapped person' in *VATA 1994, Sch 8, Group 12, Note 3*. The tribunal allowed the company's appeal. Applying *dicta* of Lord Grantchester in *Kirton Designs Ltd*, 19.24 above, the tribunal should 'apply a subjective test and consider what was in the mind of the designer'. On the evidence, the foam and the mattress had been designed 'solely for the use of those suffering long-term pain'. The foam had a strong odour, which made it 'most unlikely that it would be purchased by anyone who does not suffer from long-term pain or pressure sores'. The fact that the mattress could, in principle, be used by a normal person was not conclusive. Furthermore, 'long-term pain and pressure sores' were 'within the meaning of "chronically sick" because the conditions last a long time, and are not soon over, and those suffering from the conditions are ill, or unhealthy, or suffering from an ailment'. *Tempur Pedic (UK) Ltd*, LON/95/458A (VTD 13744).

[19.28] The decision in *Tempur Pedic (UK) Ltd*, **19.27** above, was applied in a similar subsequent case where the tribunal held that supplies of bespoke mattresses for handicapped people qualified for zero-rating. *Pure Independence (UK) Ltd v HMRC*, [2011] UKFTT 611 (TC), TC01454.

Products designed for sufferers from house dust allergy

[19.29] A company marketed a number of products which were designed for people who were allergic to house dust. The Commissioners accepted that a nebuliser qualified for zero-rating under *VATA 1994, Sch 8, Group 12, Item 2*. However, they ruled that the other products — bedding covers, a vacuum cleaner, a dehumidifier, a medication system, and an anti-allergen system — failed to qualify for zero-rating. The company appealed, contending that all five products were equipment and appliances 'designed solely for use by a handicapped person', within *Item 2(g)*. The tribunal accepted the company's evidence and allowed the appeal, finding that the products were specifically designed for people who suffered from allergy to house dust to such an extent that they were 'chronically sick', within *Group 12, Note 3. Medivac Healthcare Ltd*, LON/99/1271 (VTD 16829).

Radiator safety covers

[19.30] A company supplied radiator safety cabinets to a charity which operated nursing homes for the elderly. The Commissioners issued a ruling that these supplies were standard-rated. The company appealed, contending that the cabinets were specifically designed 'to protect people handicapped by age and confusion as well as by physical disabilities', and qualified for zero-rating under *VATA 1994, Sch 8, Group 12, Item 2(g)*. The tribunal accepted this contention and allowed the company's appeal. *Joulesave Emes Ltd*, MAN/99/462 (VTD 17115).

Air filtration system

[19.31] A woman (S) who suffered from 'multiple allergies' arranged for the installation of an air filtration system. Customs issued a ruling that VAT was chargeable on the supply. S appealed, contending that the filtration system was specially designed to filter pesticides and exhaust fumes from the air, and should therefore be treated as qualifying for zero-rating under *VATA 1994, Sch 8, Group 12, Item 2(g)*. The tribunal accepted this contention and allowed her appeal. *B Symons*, LON/04/1141 (VTD 19174).

Computer system supplied to handicapped student

[19.32] A student, who was accepted as being a 'handicapped person' within *VATA 1994, Sch 8, Group 12, Note 3*, ordered a new computer system. The Commissioners issued a ruling that only certain parts of the system qualified for zero-rating, within *VATA 1994, Sch 8, Group 12, Item 2(g)*. The tribunal allowed the student's appeal, holding on the evidence that the system had to be viewed as a single supply and that it was 'designed solely for use by a handicapped person'. *WM Hall*, LON/00/463 (VTD 16989).

Aircraft adapted for use by disabled people

[19.33] The British Disabled Flying Association is a registered charity, which was formed in 1994 with the aim of allowing 'disabled persons' to enjoy 'opportunities in aviation'. It purchased two light aircraft, and immediately arranged for them to be adapted for use by disabled people. HMRC issued a ruling that VAT was chargeable on the supply of the aircraft. The BDFA appealed, contending that the supply, and its subsequent expenditure on adapting, repairing and maintaining the aircraft, qualified for zero-rating under *Sch 8, Group 12, Item 2(g)*. The tribunal accepted this contention and allowed the appeal. Judge Geraint Jones held that the fact that the aircraft had not originally been manufactured for the use of handicapped people was not conclusive, since *Item 2(g)* applied 'to equipment designed solely for the use by a handicapped person regardless of when it became so designed'. There was 'no good reason, either as a matter of statutory construction or common sense, for an item not to be designed solely for use by a handicapped person simply because a factory manufactured item, not so designed, has then been subject to modifications to make it designed for use by handicapped person'. *Item 2(g)* should be construed as referring to 'the quality of the item as used by the handicapped person, not the quality of that item when it left the factory'. *The British Disabled Flying Association v HMRC*, [2011] UKFTT 743 (TC), TC01580.

Cases where the appellant was partly successful

Conversion and refurbishing of buildings at centre for treating epilepsy

[19.34] A registered charity provided residential assessment, treatment and care for sufferers from epilepsy. It occupied a 170-acre site, and incurred expenditure on refurbishing and improving its facilities. The Commissioners issued a ruling that the expenditure was not eligible for zero-rating, and the charity appealed, contending that much of the expenditure should be treated as zero-rated. The tribunal allowed the appeal in part, holding that the installation of a specially-designed heating system, enabling water to be circulated at lower temperatures than normal in order to reduce the risk of burning if a patient were to fall against them, qualified for zero-rating under what is now *VATA 1994, Sch 8, Group 12, Item 2(g)*. However, expenditure on woollen carpets, purchased to protect patients from scorching when falling as a result of an epileptic seizure, did not qualify for zero-rating since the carpets were not specifically designed for the use of the handicapped. Similarly, changing facilities at a sports hall did not qualify for zero-rating, since they were 'no different to what may be found in a sports hall elsewhere', and a physiotherapy unit and gymnasium also failed to qualify for zero-rating. *The David Lewis Centre*, MAN/92/69 (VTD 10860). (*Notes.* (1) For other issues in this case, taken to the QB, see **11.8** CHARITIES. (2) The Commissioners did not appeal against the tribunal decision that the heating system qualified for zero-rating, but have subsequently stated that they do not accept that the ruling 'is an authority for zero-rating supplies of low surface temperature radiators to eligible charities or disabled people'—see Customs' VAT Manual, Part 7, chapter 12, para 25.1.1.)

Hydrotherapy pool at school for disabled

[19.35] A registered charity arranged for the installation of a hydrotherapy pool at a school which it ran for disabled children. The Commissioners issued a ruling that output tax was chargeable on the relevant supplies. The charity appealed, contending that the supplies qualified for zero-rating under what is now *VATA 1994, Sch 8, Group 12*. The tribunal allowed the appeal in part, holding on the evidence that the pool itself, and the 'environmental control system', were designed solely for use by the handicapped and qualified for zero-rating, but that the supply of the building housing the pool did not qualify for zero-rating. *Boys' and Girls' Welfare Society*, MAN/96/1041 (VTD 15274). (*Note.* For another issue in this case, see **19.89** below.)

Hydrotherapy pool for disabled person

[19.36] A married couple arranged for a construction company to supply and install a hydrotherapy pool at their home for the use of the wife, who was disabled. The Commissioners issued a ruling that the effect of the contract was that the company was supplying standard-rated construction services. The company and the couple appealed. The tribunal allowed their appeals in part, holding that the supply of the pool and its enclosure qualified for zero-rating but that some of the work which was carried out at the site failed to qualify for zero-rating. *Robin Ellis Contracts Ltd; CD & JMR Dent*, LON/03/222 (VTD 18500).

Ergonomic chairs

[19.37] A company manufactured four types of ergonomic chairs, designed for elderly and infirm people, and marketed to hospitals, nursing homes and residential care homes. The Commissioners accepted that two of the four types of chair were 'designed solely for use by a handicapped person' and therefore qualified for zero-rating, but issued a ruling that the other types of chair failed to qualify. The company appealed. The tribunal reviewed the evidence in detail and allowed the appeal in part, holding that one of the chairs qualified for zero-rating and that the remaining chair failed to qualify when supplied on its own, but did qualify when supplied with specific accessories, including a 'pressure relief' seat cushion designed to relieve pressure on the sacrum or an inflatable lumbar support. *The Kirton Healthcare Group Ltd*, LON/00/498 (VTD 17062). (*Note.* See also *Lonie*, **19.66** below, where the tribunal held that a chair with an electrically operated reclining back rest failed to qualify for zero-rating.)

'Tapping rails' to help the 'visually impaired'

[19.38] A charity operated a centre for disabled people. It arranged for substantial refurbishment of the building which it occupied. It claimed that various items of work should be treated as zero-rated under *VATA 1994, Sch 8, Group 12*. The tribunal held that the installation of special 'tapping rails', which had been installed on footpaths for the use of the 'visually impaired', qualified for zero-rating under *Group 12, Item 2(g)*. However, the remainder of the work (including a new front gate, new carpets, new radiators and substantial work on the kitchen), failed to qualify for zero-rating. *Vassall Centre Trust*, LON/01/581 (VTD 17891).

Cases held not to qualify for zero-rating

Overbed tables

[19.39] A hospital purchased a number of specially-designed overbed tables which could be adjusted by one hand or foot. Customs issued a ruling that VAT was chargeable on the tables, and the hospital appealed. The tribunal dismissed the appeal, holding that the tables were not zero-rated since they were not 'designed solely for use by a handicapped person'. The tribunal observed that the tables were 'eminently practical and convenient for all sorts of hospital patients and (were) not designed with a particular class in mind'. *The Princess Louise Scottish Hospital*, [1983] VATTR 191 (VTD 1412).

'Airbaths' supplied to hospitals

[19.40] See *Aquakraft Ltd*, **19.10** above.

Jacuzzi—electricity charges

[19.41] A disabled person (T) purchased a jacuzzi, which was zero-rated under *VATA 1994, Sch 8, Group 12, Item 2(g)*. T wrote to Customs, asking that the cost of the electricity needed to operate the jacuzzi should be also treated as zero-rated. Customs rejected this request and the tribunal dismissed T's appeal, holding that there was 'no provision in the legislation for the zero-rating of electricity', which had been correctly charged to VAT at the reduced rate of 5%. *AJ Townsend*, LON/02/331 (VTD 18327).

Alterations to kitchen

[19.42] A householder, whose wife and son were both registered as disabled, had work carried out on his kitchen to make it easier for them to use. The work included altering two doors, supplying new cupboards and fitting electric points. He claimed that the work should be treated as zero-rated. The Commissioners rejected his claim and the tribunal dismissed his appeal, holding that none of the equipment was 'designed solely for use by a handicapped person'. *D Bell*, LON/83/147 (VTD 1480).

[19.43] Two handicapped persons purchased a bungalow and arranged for certain work to be done to the kitchen. Customs issued a ruling that the work did not qualify for zero-rating, and the tribunal dismissed the purchasers' appeal. *AC Bruce & ML Hull*, LON/86/315 (VTD 2248).

Architect's services

[19.44] An architect was employed to design the conversion of a house for the use of a handicapped person. The tribunal held that the architect's services did not qualify for zero-rating. *Dr AN Strachan*, MAN/86/155 (VTD 2165).

Surveyors' services

[19.45] The decision in *Strachan*, **19.44** above, was applied in a similar case where a firm of surveyors had failed to account for VAT on services relating to work carried out for a County Council in relation to accommodation for the handicapped. The tribunal held that the surveyors' services did not qualify for zero-rating. *Hewitt Overall Associates*, LON/92/536Z (VTD 9374).

Extension to house

[19.46] Extensions to a house occupied by a handicapped person were held not to qualify for zero-rating in *JA Gow (t/a Falkirk Building Co)*, EDN/88/2 (VTD 2983); *Cheverton Construction Ltd*, LON/88/164 (VTD 3254) and *KWS & BK Panesar (t/a KSP Builders and Panesar Building & Plumbers' Merchants)*, MAN/98/420 (VTD 16143).

[19.47] A married couple arranged for an extension to their house to contain a renal dialysis unit, since the husband was suffering from a condition which required renal haemodialysis treatment two or three times each week. Customs accepted that the provision of the renal dialysis unit, and the provision of a lavatory in the extension, qualified for zero-rating under what is now *VATA 1994, Sch 8, Group 12, Items 2(g)* and *10* respectively. However, they issued a ruling that the goods and services supplied in the building of the extension did not qualify for zero-rating. The wife appealed, contending that the proportion of the cost which was attributable to the room containing the dialysis unit should be treated as zero-rated. The tribunal rejected this contention and dismissed her appeal. *Mrs LJ Brailsford*, MAN/95/562 (VTD 13472).

Decking for balcony

[19.48] A married woman was confined to a wheelchair. Her husband ordered some timber decking to enable her to be wheeled from their living-room to the adjacent balcony. He claimed a refund of the tax on the decking and other materials used in the construction. HMRC rejected the claim and he appealed, contending that it should be treated as zero-rated under *VATA 1994, Sch 8, Group 12, Item 2(g)*. The tribunal rejected this contention and dismissed his appeal, holding that 'the decking is not equipment or an appliance'. *A Bokor v HMRC*, [2009] UKFTT 322 (TC), TC00265.

Air conditioning units

[19.49] A woman who suffered from multiple sclerosis purchased two air conditioning units and reclaimed input tax. Customs rejected her claim and the tribunal dismissed her appeal, holding that the units were not eligible for zero-rating since they were not 'designed solely for use by a handicapped person'. *E Simmons*, LON/90/1557Z (VTD 6622).

Air purifier

[19.50] A disabled woman purchased an air purifier. The tribunal held that the purifier did not qualify for zero-rating, since it was not 'designed solely for use by a handicapped person'. *BO Symons*, LON/02/8294 (VTD 18534).

Sloping writing board

[19.51] A company manufactured a magnetic sloping writing board, called the 'Posturite Board', which was designed to reduce neck and back pain when writing and reading. It did not account for VAT on supplies of the board. Customs issued a ruling that the supplies were standard-rated, and the tribunal dismissed the company's appeal, holding that the board was not designed solely for use by handicapped people. *Posturite (UK) Ltd*, LON/91/2723Z (VTD 7848).

Covered walkways at college for disabled

[19.52] A registered charity operated a college providing training and education for the disabled. It engaged a contractor to construct covered walkways at the college. Customs issued a ruling that the work was standard-rated. The tribunal dismissed the college's appeal, holding that the walkways did not qualify for zero-rating under *Group 12, Item 2(g)* since they were not 'designed solely for use by a handicapped person'. *Portland College*, MAN/92/226 (VTD 9815). (*Note.* The tribunal also held that the walkways failed to qualify for zero-rating under *Group 12, Item 8*—see **19.77** below.)

Electromagnetic mattress, pillow and Kenkobio machine

[19.53] A company (B) imported and distributed electromagnetic mattresses, pillows, and 'Kenkobio' machines (which were designed to reduce pain by introducing an electromagnetic field to the affected part of the body). It did not account for VAT on the sales of these items. Customs issued a ruling that the supplies did not qualify for zero-rating, and the tribunal dismissed B's appeal, holding that the items in question were not designed solely for use by handicapped people. *Back In Health Ltd*, MAN/91/1139 (VTD 10003).

[19.54] A similar decision was reached in *Made To Measure v HMRC*, [2011] UKFTT 154 (TC), TC01028.

Central heating system

[19.55] An individual (D), whose daughter who suffered from cystic fibrosis, reclaimed input tax on the purchase of a central heating system. Customs rejected the claim and the tribunal dismissed D's appeal, holding that the system was not 'designed solely for use by a handicapped person'. *P Drummond*, EDN/94/177 (VTD 13100).

[19.56] A similar decision was reached in *DJ Page*, LON/00/654 (VTD 17142).

[19.57] A charity operated a residential care home for elderly people. It arranged for the installation of a new heating system. Customs issued a ruling that the relevant supplies were standard-rated. The tribunal dismissed the charity's appeal, holding that the system was not 'designed solely for use by a handicapped person'. *Cheltenham Old People's Housing Society Ltd*, LON/02/651 (VTD 18795).

Supplies of pesticide sprays

[19.58] A company manufactured aerosol pesticide sprays, designed to kill dust mites. It supplied the sprays to pharmacists for sale to asthmatics or sufferers from eczema. Customs issued a ruling that output tax was chargeable on the supply of the sprays. The tribunal dismissed the company's appeal, holding that not all sufferers from asthma could be described as 'chronically sick or disabled' within *Group 12, Note 3*. Accordingly, the sprays were not 'designed solely for use by a handicapped person', and thus failed to qualify for zero-rating. *GD Searle & Co Ltd*, LON/94/1290A (VTD 13439).

Single-seat golf buggies

[19.59] A partnership manufactured single-seat golf buggies, which it marketed for sale to elderly golfers. It did not account for output tax on the sale of the buggies, and the Commissioners issued an assessment. The partnership appealed, contending that the buggies should be treated as zero-rated. The tribunal rejected this contention, holding that the buggies 'were not, viewed as a whole, designed solely for the use of handicapped persons'. *Foxer Industries*, LON/95/1452A (VTD 13817). (*Note.* For a subsequent appeal by the same partnership, see **19.74** below.)

[19.60] The decision in *Foxer Industries*, **19.59** above, was applied in the similar subsequent case of *CF Leisure Mobility Ltd*, LON/99/1063 (VTD 16790).

'Mobility scooters'

[19.61] A company manufactured 'mobility scooters'. Customs issued a ruling that VAT was chargeable on their sale. The tribunal dismissed the company's appeal, holding that the scooters were not 'designed solely for use by a handicapped person'. *Leisure Karts (UK) Ltd*, MAN/05/054 (VTD 19403).

Shelter for electric vehicle

[19.62] A charity arranged for the construction of a shelter for an electric vehicle at the home of a disabled person. Customs issued a ruling that VAT was payable on the work. The tribunal dismissed the charity's appeal, holding that the work failed to qualify for zero-rating. *SSAFA Forces Help*, LON/06/291 (VTD 19832).

Fire escape

[19.63] A charity operated a hotel which provided accommodation for people suffering from arthritis, and for people caring for them. It arranged for the construction of a fire escape. Customs issued a ruling that output tax was chargeable on the work. The tribunal dismissed the charity's appeal, holding that the fire escape did not qualify for zero-rating, since it was not 'designed solely for use by a handicapped person'. *Arthritis Care*, LON/95/2611A (VTD 13974).

Remote-controlled garage doors

[19.64] A householder (L) purchased some remote-controlled garage doors. The supplier charged VAT on the sale. L appealed to the tribunal, contending that the supply should be treated as zero-rated. The tribunal rejected this contention and dismissed the appeal, holding that the doors were not 'designed solely for use by a handicapped person'. *A Livingstone*, EDN/01/183 (VTD 17642).

Automatic curtain system

[19.65] A householder (R), who was a tetraplegic, purchased an automatic curtain system enabling him to open and close his curtains by remote control. The supplier charged VAT on the sale. L appealed to the tribunal, contending that the supply should be treated as zero-rated. The tribunal rejected this contention and dismissed the appeal, holding that the equipment was not 'designed solely for use by a handicapped person'. *GF Ridgeon*, LON/01/153 (VTD 17749).

Chair

[19.66] A woman purchased a chair with an electrically operated reclining back rest, on which VAT was charged. She appealed to the tribunal, contending that the chair should have been treated as zero-rated. The tribunal rejected this contention and dismissed her appeal. *SR Lonie*, MAN/06/285 (VTD 19901).

Orthotics

[19.67] A company (B) supplied orthotics to NHS trusts. The orthotics were custom-made for individual patients. B did not account for output tax on the supplies. Customs issued an assessment and B appealed, contending that the supplies should be treated as zero-rated. The tribunal rejected this contention and dismissed the appeal, holding that the relevant supplies were to the trusts rather than to the individual patients. The tribunal also observed that B had not shown that the recipients were within the definition of 'handicapped persons'. *Benefoot UK Ltd*, LON/98/942 (VTD 17022).

Incontinence pads ordered by nursing homes

[19.68] A company (F) did not account for VAT on the sale of incontinence pads to people living in registered residential or nursing homes. Customs issued an assessment charging tax on these sales, and F appealed, contending that they should be treated as zero-rated. The tribunal rejected this contention and dismissed the appeal, holding that the effect of *Group 12, Notes 5B* and *5D* was that the sales were specifically excluded from zero-rating. *First Medical Ltd*, MAN/00/061 (VTD 17847).

Metal holders for badges

[19.69] An individual sold metal holders, designed to be used for housing the badges which indicated that people who were registered as disabled were entitled to ignore certain parking restrictions. Customs issued a ruling that he was required to account for VAT on his supplies. He appealed, contending that they should be treated as zero-rated. The tribunal rejected this contention and dismissed the appeal, finding that the metal holders were not 'an "appliance" designed solely for the use of the handicapped'. *A Arnold*, MAN/05/581 (VTD 19511).

Parts and accessories (VATA 1994, Sch 8, Group 12, Item 2(h))

Overbed tables

[19.70] See *The Princess Louise Scottish Hospital*, 19.39 above.

Electric generator

[19.71] A young girl suffered from severe asthma and needed to use a nebuliser several times a day. Her father purchased an electric generator to power the nebuliser. The Commissioners issued a ruling that VAT was chargeable on the supply, and he appealed, contending that the generator should be treated as zero-rated under what is now *VATA 1994, Sch 8, Group 12, Item 2(h)*. The tribunal rejected this contention and dismissed his appeal, holding on the evidence that the generator was not 'designed solely for use by a handicapped person'. *I Mills*, LON/85/33 (VTD 1893).

[19.72] A similar decision was reached in *AC Wesley*, LON/92/407Y (VTD 9074).

Batteries for use in invalid scooters and wheelchairs

[19.73] A charity purchased a number of batteries for use in invalid scooters and wheelchairs. The Commissioners issued a ruling that VAT was chargeable on the supply of the batteries. The charity appealed, contending that the supply should be treated as zero-rated under *VATA 1994, Sch 8, Group 12, Item 2(h)*. The tribunal rejected this contention and dismissed the charity's appeal. *Poole Shopmobility*, LON/98/1486 (VTD 16290). (*Note.* For another issue in this case, see **11.18** CHARITIES.)

Services of adapting goods for a handicapped person (VATA 1994, Sch 8, Group 12, Item 3)

Adapted golf buggies

[19.74] A partnership manufactured single-seat golf buggies for elderly golfers. Following the decision noted at **19.59** above, in which the tribunal held that the buggies did not qualify for zero-rating under *VATA 1994, Sch 8, Group 12, Item 2(g)*, the partnership claimed that work done in adapting some of the buggies for specific customers should be treated as qualifying for zero-rating under *Item 3*. The partnership claimed that 21 supplies should be treated as within this provision. The tribunal found that only 9 of the 21 customers in question were within the definition of a 'handicapped person' in *Note 3*. In one of these cases, the modifications to the basic design were so fundamental that the entire buggy should be treated as zero-rated under *Item 2(g)*. In the other eight cases, an appropriate proportion of the price (fixed by the tribunal at 13.4% of the total) should be treated as zero-rated under *Item 3*. *Foxer Industries*, LON/95/1452 (VTD 14469).

Work at properties owned by housing trust

[19.75] A company carried out work at properties which were owned by a housing trust (which was not a charity) and were occupied by handicapped people. It did not account for tax on the work. The Commissioners issued an assessment and the company appealed, contending that the services were within *VATA 1994, 8 Sch, Group 12, Item 3*. The tribunal rejected this contention and dismissed the appeal, holding on the evidence that the relevant supplies had been made to the housing trust rather than to the tenants, so that they failed to qualify for zero-rating. *Cross Electrical & Building Services Ltd*, MAN/99/1070 (VTD 16954).

Supplies of widening doorways, etc. (VATA 1994, Sch 8, Group 12, Items 8, 9)

Widening of doorways at house inherited by handicapped person

[19.76] A handicapped woman inherited a house from her mother and incurred expenditure on widening the ground-floor doorways to make the house suitable for her occupation. However, before the work could be completed, the woman decided that she wanted to sell the house. The Commissioners issued an assessment charging tax on the work. The tribunal upheld the assessment, holding that the work in question was not eligible for zero-rating under what is now *VATA 1994, Sch 8, Group 12, Item 8*, since the woman had never occupied the house as her private residence. *PA Macrae*, LON/90/1734Z (VTD 7849).

Covered walkways erected at college for disabled

[19.77] In the case noted at **19.52** above, a registered charity, which operated a college providing training and education for the disabled, engaged a contractor to construct covered walkways at the college. The Commissioners issued a ruling that output tax was chargeable on the work, and the college appealed, contending *inter alia* that the work should be treated as zero-rated under what is now *VATA 1994, Sch 8, Group 12, Item 8*. The tribunal rejected this contention and dismissed the appeal. *Portland College*, MAN/92/226 (VTD 9815).

Installation of new patio doors and internal doors

[19.78] A handicapped person, who was confined to a wheelchair, purchased a bungalow. Some of the internal doors were too small to accommodate his wheelchair, and he arranged for a builder to undertake substantial alterations to the bungalow. A new entrance hall, suitable for entry in a wheelchair, was built. A new shower-room and bathroom were installed, and wider internal doorways were provided. A new kitchen was installed, the lounge window was replaced by sliding patio doors, and the level of the ground outside these doors was raised to enable the wheelchair to pass through them. A new car port was built. The Commissioners accepted that the building of the new entrance hall qualified for zero-rating under what is now *VATA 1994, Sch 8, Group 12, Item 8*, and that the new shower-room qualified for zero-rating under what is now *VATA 1994, Sch 8, Group 12, Item 10*. However, they issued a ruling that the remainder of the work was standard-rated. The builder appealed. The tribunal allowed the appeal in part, holding that the installation of the new internal doorways and the raising of the ground outside the patio doors qualified for zero-rating under *Item 8*, and the new bathroom qualified for zero-rating under *Item 10*. However, the new kitchen, patio doors, and car port were not eligible for zero-rating. *DJ Avis (t/a Property Alterations)*, LON/92/1663 (VTD 10664).

Installation of French doors and adjoining windows

[19.79] A married woman was confined to a wheelchair. Her husband arranged for the installation of a new wide front door, two pairs of French 'low threshold' doors, and three adjoining windows, at the cottage where they lived. The Commissioners accepted that the new front door qualified for zero-rating under *VATA 1994, Sch 8, Group 12, Item 8*, but ruled that the supply of the other two doors, and of the windows, was standard-rated. The husband appealed. The tribunal reviewed the evidence in detail and dismissed the appeal with regard to one of the French doors and two of the windows, holding that the work did not qualify for zero-rating under *Group 12*. However, the tribunal adjourned the appeal with regard to the dining-room door and adjoining window for further argument on the application of *VAT Notice 701/7 (August 2002 edition), para 6.5*. The tribunal observed that there appeared to be 'no statutory footing' for the paragraph in question. *LA Dennison*, LON/03/399 (VTD 18619).

[19.80] Following the decision noted at **19.79** above, the tribunal held a further hearing and dismissed the appeal, holding that the installation of the door and window failed to qualify for zero-rating. The tribunal held that the Commissioners had erred in treating the relevant construction work as qualifying for zero-rating. The tribunal expressed the hope that the Commissioners would 'honour the concession already granted', but held that it would be wrong to 'compound the error' by treating the supply of the door and window as zero-rated. *LA Dennison (No 2)*, LON/03/399 (VTD 18733).

Extension to room used as access to bedroom

[19.81] A handicapped person reclaimed input tax on work done at his residence. The work included the extension of a bedroom which was adjacent to the bedroom he slept in, and which he used as a means of access to his bedroom on occasions when a lift, which was his normal means of access to his bedroom, was not working. Customs issued a ruling that this part of the work did not qualify for zero-rating. The tribunal allowed the claimant's appeal, holding that the bedroom in question, although it was principally used as a bedroom, also qualified as a 'passage' for the purpose of what is now *VATA 1994, Sch 8, Group 12, Item 8*. Accordingly the work qualified for zero-rating. *BH Cannings-Knight*, LON/92/2256A (VTD 11291). (*Note.* Customs consider that 'the particulars of this case were unique'. For their interpretation of this decision, see Customs' VAT Manual, Part 7, chapter 12, para 11.7.)

Supply of building materials to handicapped person

[19.82] A barrister, who suffered from multiple sclerosis and was a 'handicapped person' within what is now *VATA 1994, Sch 8, Group 12, Note 3*, arranged for two builders to carry out construction work at his home. It was accepted that the builders' services qualified for zero-rating under what is now *VATA 1994, Sch 8, Group 12, Item 8*. The barrister also purchased certain building materials. The Commissioners issued a ruling that these materials did not qualify for zero-rating, since they had not been supplied by the builders who had supplied the construction services. The barrister appealed, contending that the materials had been supplied in connection with the supplies of construction services, that the fact that they were supplied by a different supplier was not conclusive, and that they qualified for zero-rating under *Sch 8, Group 12, Item 13*. The tribunal accepted this contention and allowed the appeal. *G Flather*, LON/93/1832 (VTD 11960). (*Note.* Where building services are zero-rated under *VATA 1994, Sch 8, Group 5, Item 2*, any materials supplied in connection with those services can be zero-rated under *Item 3* only if supplied by the same person. However, there is no similar provision in *VATA 1994, Sch 8, Group 12, Item 13*.)

Widening of doorways, etc. at tennis club used by charity

[19.83] A tennis club allowed its premises to be used by a charity for the disabled. To enable disabled people to use the premises, various doorways were widened, access ramps were built, and special WCs and showers were installed in the changing rooms. The club paid for the work and was subsequently reimbursed by the charity. The Commissioners issued a ruling that the work in question was standard-rated, as the relevant supplies had been made to the club rather than to the charity. The trustee of the charity (who was also the secretary of the club) appealed, contending that the work should be treated as qualifying for zero-rating under what is now *VATA 1994, Sch 8, Group 12*. The tribunal rejected this contention and dismissed the appeal. Since the relevant supplies had not been made to the charity, they failed to qualify for zero-rating. *DM Brand (as Trustee of Racket Sports for Children with Special Needs)*, LON/95/2751 (VTD 14080).

Supply of conservatory at home of handicapped person

[19.84] A married couple arranged for the construction of a conservatory at the rear of their house. The husband suffered from severe arthritis and was confined to a wheelchair. The couple reclaimed VAT on the construction of the conservatory. The Commissioners agreed to refund VAT on the widening of the existing doorway from the house to the conservatory, and on the construction of two ramps, but refused to refund the remainder on the basis that it failed to qualify for zero-rating. The wife appealed, contending that the supply of the conservatory should be treated as zero-rated. The tribunal rejected this contention and held that only the construction of the ramps and the widening of the doorway qualified for zero-rating. *GV Johnson*, MAN/99/864 (VTD 16672).

Widening of church gateway for handicapped people

[19.85] A church committee arranged for the construction of new gates, and the widening of the gateway. The Commissioners issued a ruling that VAT was payable on the work. The chairman of the committee lodged an appeal, contending that the work had been carried out to enable handicapped people to be driven to the door of the church, whereas previously there had been no vehicular access and it had been necessary to walk 300 yards from the road, and that the work should be treated as zero-rated under *VATA 1994, Sch 8, Group 12, Item 9*. The tribunal dismissed the appeal, holding that the gates could not be treated as a 'doorway' and that *Item 9* implied 'entry into the building itself', so that the work failed to qualify for zero-rating. *R Johnson (Chairman of Shalden Millennium Committee)*, LON/01/759 (VTD 17897; VTD 18670).

Supplies of bathrooms, washrooms, etc. (VATA 1994, Sch 8, Group 12, Items 10–12)

NOTE

VATA 1994, Sch 8, Group 12, Item 11 was substituted by the VAT *(Charities and Aids for the Handicapped) Order 2000 (SI 2000/805)* with effect from 1 April 2000. The cases in this section should be read in the light of this change.

Bathroom and lavatory at annexe to house for handicapped person

[**19.86**] A company extended a building by adding an annexe designed for the use of a handicapped person. The annexe included a specially-designed bathroom and lavatory. The company did not account for VAT on the work. The Commissioners accepted that 30% of the work in question was zero-rated, as being attributable to the supply of the bathroom and lavatory, but issued an assessment charging tax on the remaining 70%. The tribunal upheld the assessment and dismissed the company's appeal. *Heathill Developments Ltd*, LON/87/30 (VTD 2412).

[**19.87**] See also *Brailsford*, **19.47** above, and *Avis*, **19.78** above.

Hot water system of residential home

[**19.88**] A home for the disabled provided accommodation for 25 residents. It updated the hot water system by installing thermostatic control valves. The Commissioners accepted that such work was zero-rated in so far as it related to bathrooms and lavatories, but issued a ruling that it was standard-rated in so far as it related to washbasins and showers in the residents' bedrooms. The home appealed, contending that the bedrooms should be regarded as washrooms for the purpose of what is now *VATA 1994, Sch 8, Group 12, Item 11*, since the residents used them for washing as well as for sleeping in. The tribunal rejected this contention and dismissed the appeal, holding that a washroom was a room which primarily provided washing facilities, whereas the rooms in question primarily provided sleeping facilities. *Mid-Derbyshire Cheshire Home*, MAN/89/546 (VTD 4512). (*Note.* See also *Sch 8, Group 12, Note 5K*, introduced by the VAT *(Charities and Aids for the Handicapped) Order 2000 (SI 2000/805)* with effect from 1 April 2000. *Note 5K* defines a 'washroom' as 'a room that contains a lavatory or washbasin (or both) but does not contain a bath or a shower or cooking, sleeping or laundry facilities'.)

Special radiators in residential unit for disabled children

[19.89] A registered charity operated a residential unit for disabled children. It arranged for the installation of new radiators with a low surface temperature. The Commissioners issued a ruling that output tax was chargeable on the supply of the radiators, and the charity appealed, contending that they should be treated as zero-rated under what is now *VATA 1994, Sch 8, Group 12*. The tribunal allowed the appeal in part, holding that the radiators did not qualify for zero-rating under *Item 2(g)*, since such radiators were not 'designed solely for use by a handicapped person', but that they qualified for zero-rating under what is now *Item 11* where they were installed in bathrooms, washrooms or lavatories. *Boys' and Girls' Welfare Society*, MAN/96/1041 (VTD 15274). (*Note*. For another issue in this case, see **19.35** above.)

Renovation of shower-room used by handicapped woman

[19.90] A woman, who was accepted as being a 'handicapped person' within what is now *VATA 1994, Sch 8, Group 12*, occupied a house with a shower-room on the first floor. She had the roof and window of the shower-room replaced, and had a new central heating system fitted. She appealed against the Commissioners' decision that this work did not qualify for zero-rating. The tribunal dismissed her appeal. The conversion of a bathroom into a shower-room was within the scope of *Group 12, Item 10*, but the additional work at issue in this case was not. It was necessary because the house was not in a good state of repair, rather than because the appellant was a handicapped person. *J Drury*, LON/90/1398Y (VTD 6030).

Construction of new corridor and bathrooms in nursing home

[19.91] A charity operated a nursing home. It arranged for the construction of en-suite bathrooms for the use of people who were handicapped. These facilities extended into space which had previously formed a corridor, and a new corridor was constructed outside the existing walls. Customs agreed that the construction of the en-suite bathrooms qualified for zero-rating, but ruled that the construction of the new corridor was standard-rated. The charity appealed. The tribunal dismissed the appeal, holding that the construction of the corridor failed to qualify for zero-rating under *VATA 1994, Sch 8, Group 12, Item 11*. The tribunal noted that *Notice 701/7, para 6.5* appeared to indicate that the work qualified for zero-rating. However, the tribunal held that this was an extra-statutory concession, and that it had no jurisdiction over Customs' failure to operate an extra-statutory concession. *Lady Nuffield Home*, LON/04/248 (VTD 19123).

Construction of extension including washrooms for charity

[19.92] A builder constructed an extension, including two changing-rooms and two washrooms, at a sports hall used by a registered charity. The extension was also designed to allow wheelchair-users to enter the sports hall. The builder treated the work as zero-rated. The Commissioners issued an assessment charging tax on the basis that only the 26% of the work attributable to the washrooms qualified for zero-rating under *VATA 1994, Sch 8, Group 12, Item 12*. The builder appealed. The tribunal reviewed the evidence in detail and upheld the assessment in principle but directed that 35% of the work in question should be treated as zero-rated. *WB Evans (t/a BSEC)*, MAN/03/475 (VTD 18432). (*Note*. The tribunal also held that the extension was not an 'annexe' and did not qualify for zero-rating under *VATA 1994, Sch 8, Group 5*.)

Community Amateur Sports Club—whether a charity

[19.93] A registered community amateur sports club arranged for the installation of a new toilet block, including toilets which were specially adapted for the use of disabled people. It claimed a refund of VAT on this work, contending that it should be treated as zero-rated under *VATA 1994, Sch 8, Group 12, Item 12*. Customs rejected the claim on the grounds that the club was not a charity. The tribunal dismissed the club's appeal, observing that CASCs were not 'subject to the strict supervision accorded to charities' and holding that 'there is no logical reason why such clubs should be entitled to the same VAT reliefs as a charity'. *E Jacobs (Batchwood Hall Bowling Club)*, LON/06/331 (VTD 19797).

Installation of WCs and shower at tennis club used by charity

[19.94] See *Brand*, 19.83 above.

Supplies of lifts (VATA 1994, Sch 8, Group 12, Items 16–18)

Supplies of lifts to unregistered nursing home

[19.95] The proprietor of an unregistered nursing home arranged for the installation of a lift. The Commissioners issued a ruling that output tax was chargeable on the supply, and she appealed, contending that the supply should be zero-rated because all the residents of the nursing home were chronically sick or disabled. The tribunal dismissed her appeal, holding that the supply failed to qualify for zero-rating because the supply had been made to the proprietor, who was 'neither a handicapped person or a charity'. *KA Conroy*, LON/85/115 (VTD 1916). (*Notes*. (1) The case was decided on the provisions of *VATA 1983* as originally enacted, prior to the introduction of what is now *VATA 1994, Sch 8, Group 12, Items 16–18*, which date from 1986. However, *Items 16–18* only provide for the zero-rating of lifts where the supply is made to a handicapped person or a charity, so that the decision remains relevant to *Items 16–18*. (2) The tribunal also held that the supply failed to qualify for zero-rating under *VATA 1983* on the grounds that the lift had not been 'designed solely for use by a handicapped person'. The decision on this point has been overtaken by the introduction of *Items 16–18*.)

[19.96] A similar decision was reached in *Brian Perkins & Co Ltd*, LON/88/952Y (VTD 3885).

Installation of lift at building occupied by Student Union

[19.97] A Student Union occupied premises on four floors of the university campus. An external lift was installed to enable disabled students to have access to the top two floors. The Commissioners issued a ruling that the installation of the lift was standard-rated. The Union appealed, contending that it should be treated as zero-rated under *VATA 1994, Sch 8, Group 12, Item 17*. The tribunal dismissed the appeal, holding that, since the Student Union premises existed 'to provide facilities for students generally both to the able-bodied and the handicapped', it could not be 'properly described as a "day-centre" within the ordinary use of the term' and thus failed to qualify for zero-rating. *Union of Students of the University of Warwick*, [1995] VATDR 219 (VTD 13821).

Installation of lift at art gallery

[19.98] A charity installed a lift at an art gallery which it operated. The Commissioners issued a ruling that output tax was chargeable on the installation. The charity appealed, contending that the lift should be treated as zero-rated under *VATA 1994, Sch 8, Group 12, Item 17*. The tribunal dismissed the appeal, holding that the gallery was not within the definition of a 'day-centre', so that the lift failed to qualify for zero-rating. The tribunal observed that 'had Parliament intended to zero-rate lifts provided for the handicapped, this could have been done without restricting the provision to day-centres provided by a charity'. *Aspex Visual Arts Trust*, LON/97/683 (VTD 16419). (*Note*. The tribunal also held that the lift was not a 'chair lift' within *Item 2(d)*.)

Architects' services relating to installation of lift at care home

[19.99] A charity arranged for the installation of lifts in two care homes for the elderly. Customs accepted that the actual installation of the lifts qualified for zero-rating under *VATA 1994, Sch 8, Group 12, Item 17*, but issued a ruling that the services supplied by architects in designing the lifts failed to qualify. The charity appealed, contending that the architects' services were 'services necessarily performed in the installation of a lift for the purpose of facilitating the movement of handicapped persons', within *Item 17*, and qualified for zero-rating. The tribunal accepted this contention and allowed the appeal, finding that 'the lift manufacturer required the appellant to approve technical designs and assure the installer of the structural capability of the building and adequacy of power supplies, all of which required professional advice that the appellant was unable to provide on its own'. The tribunal observed that 'since installing a lift is a complicated and potentially dangerous process, there is no reason to suppose that Parliament impliedly intended to exclude architects' services' from the scope of zero-rating. *Friends of the Elderly*, [2008] VATDR 169 (VTD 20597).

20

EC Directive 2006/112/EC

The cases in this chapter are arranged under the following headings.

Scope of the Directive (Articles 1–4)	**20.1**
Taxable persons (Articles 9–13)	**20.5**
Taxable transactions (Articles 14–30)	
Supplies of goods (*Articles 14–19*)	**20.11**
Intra-Community acquisitions of goods (*Articles 20–23*)	**20.18**
Supplies of services (*Articles 24–29*)	**20.19**
Importation of goods (*Article 30*)	**20.23**
Place of taxable transactions (Articles 31–61)	
Place of supply of goods (*Articles 31–39*)	**20.24**
Place of supply of services (*Articles 43–59*)	**20.26**
Place of importation of goods (*Articles 60–61*)	**20.42**
Chargeable event (Articles 62–71)	
Supplies of goods or services (*Articles 63–67*)	**20.43**
Importations of goods (*Articles 70–71*)	**20.44**
Taxable amount (Articles 72–92)	
Supplies of goods or services (*Articles 73–82*)	**20.45**
Miscellaneous provisions (*Articles 90–92*)	**20.51**
Rates (Articles 93–130)	
Structure and level of rates (*Articles 96–105*)	**20.52**
Special transitional provisions (*Articles 109–122*)	**20.61**
Exemptions (Articles 131–166)	
General provisions (*Article 131*)	**20.63**
Activities in the public interest (*Articles 132–134*)	**20.64**
Exemptions for other activities (*Articles 135–137*)	**20.78**
Exemptions for intra-Community transactions (*Articles 138–142*)	**20.93**
Exemptions on exportation (*Articles 146–147*)	**20.95**
Exemptions related to international transport (*Articles 148–150*)	**20.96**
Transactions treated as exports (*Articles 151–152*)	**20.102**
Transactions relating to international trade (*Articles 154–166*)	**20.103**
Deductions (Articles 167–192)	
Origin and scope of right of deduction (*Articles 167–172*)	**20.104**
Proportional deduction (*Articles 173–175*)	**20.107**
Restrictions on the right of deduction (*Articles 176–177*)	**20.110**
Exercise of the right of deduction (*Articles 178–183*)	**20.112**
Adjustment of deductions (*Articles 184–192*)	**20.117**
Obligations of taxable persons, etc. (Articles 193–280)	
Obligation to pay (*Articles 193–212*)	**20.120**
Invoicing (*Articles 217–240*)	**20.122**
Returns (*Articles 250–261*)	**20.123**
Special schemes (Articles 281–369)	
Small enterprises (*Articles 281–294*)	**20.125**
Flat-rate scheme for farmers (*Articles 295–305*)	**20.128**
Special scheme for travel agents (*Articles 306–310*)	**20.129**
Second-hand goods, works of art, etc. (*Articles 311–343*)	**20.132**

Derogations (Articles 370–396)
Derogations applying until adoption of definitive arrangements
(*Articles 370–393*) 20.134
Derogations subject to authorisation (*Articles 394–396*) 20.135
Miscellaneous (Articles 397–401)
VAT Committee (*Article 398*) 20.137
Other taxes, duties and charges (*Article 401*) 20.138

NOTE

On 28 November 2006 the EU Council of Ministers agreed a revised *Directive 2006/112/EC*. This came into force on 1 January 2007. It replaced the previous *EC First VAT Directive* and the *EC Sixth VAT Directive (Directive 77/388/EEC)*. HMRC explained that 'the new Directive does not change EC or UK VAT law. The only impact on businesses is that they will now have an EC VAT law text that they should find easier to access and simpler to understand. The material has been extensively reorganised to provide a much simpler and clearer structure with additional headings and sub-headings and a significant reduction in confusing cross-references. As it will take some time to amend references to the current *Sixth VAT Directive* in UK VAT law and Public Notices, businesses will need to familiarise themselves with the provisions of the new principal VAT Directive. To help with this task, at *Annex XII* of the new Directive, there is a correlation table that lists all the *Sixth VAT Directive* articles and their equivalent in the new Directive. On this issue it should be noted that any references made in UK law to the repealed *First* and *Sixth VAT Directives* must be construed as references to the new Directive and thus read in accordance with the correlation table.' See Business Brief 22/06, issued on 11 December 2006.

For cases concerning the earlier *VAT Directives*, see 22 EUROPEAN COMMUNITY LAW.

Scope of the Directive (Articles 1–4)

Article 2(1)(a)—supplies of goods for consideration

[20.1] See *Mol v Inspecteur der Invoerrechten en Accijnzen*, 22.81 EUROPEAN COMMUNITY LAW; *R v Goodwin & Unstead*, 22.82 EUROPEAN COMMUNITY LAW; *British American Tobacco International Ltd v Belgian State*, 22.88 EUROPEAN COMMUNITY LAW; *Finanzamt Ülzen v Armbrecht*, 22.93 EUROPEAN COMMUNITY LAW; *Bakcsi v Finanzamt Fürstenfeldbruck*, 22.94 EUROPEAN COMMUNITY LAW, and *EC Commission v Finland*, 22.96 EUROPEAN COMMUNITY LAW.

Article 2(1)(b)—intra-Community acquisitions

[20.2] See *Patterson*, 23.25 EUROPEAN COMMUNITY: SINGLE MARKET.

Article 2(1)(c)—supplies of services for consideration

[20.3] See *Staatssecretaris van Financiën v Cooperatieve Vereniging 'Cooperatieve Aardappelenbewaarplaats GA'*, 22.78 EUROPEAN COMMUNITY LAW; *Staatssecretaris van Financiën v Hong Kong Trade Development Council*, 22.79 EUROPEAN COMMUNITY LAW; *Apple & Pear Development Council v C & E Commrs*, 22.80 EUROPEAN COMMUNITY LAW; *Staatssecretaris van*

Financiën v Coffeeshop 'Siberië' vof, **22.83** EUROPEAN COMMUNITY LAW; *Tolsma v Inspecteur der Omzetbelasting Leeuwarden*, **22.84** EUROPEAN COMMUNITY LAW; *Town & County Factors Ltd v C & E Commrs*, **22.85** EUROPEAN COMMUNITY LAW; *Société Thermale d'Eugénie-les-Bains v Ministère de l'Économie, des Finances et de l'Industrie*, **22.86** EUROPEAN COMMUNITY LAW; *C & E Commrs v First National Bank of Chicago*, **22.89** EUROPEAN COMMUNITY LAW; *KapHag Renditefonds 35 Spreecenter Berlin-Hellersdorf 3 Tanche GbR v Finanzamt Charlottenburg*, **22.90** EUROPEAN COMMUNITY LAW, and *Kretztechnik AG v Finanzamt Linz*, **22.91** EUROPEAN COMMUNITY LAW.

Article 2(1)(d)—importations of goods

[20.4] See *Einberger v Hauptzollamt Freiburg (No 2)*, **22.99** EUROPEAN COMMUNITY LAW; *Tullihallitus v Salumets & Others*, **22.100** EUROPEAN COMMUNITY LAW; *Witzemann v Hauptzollamt München-Mitte*, **22.101** EUROPEAN COMMUNITY LAW, and *EC Commission v Kingdom of Spain*, **22.102** EUROPEAN COMMUNITY LAW.

Taxable persons (Articles 9–13)

Article 9(1)—'taxable person' and 'economic activity'

[20.5] In two Polish cases which were heard together, the ECJ held that the supply of land designated for development was subject to VAT 'irrespective of whether the transaction is carried out on a continuing basis or whether the person who effected the supply carries out an activity of a producer, a trader or a person supplying services, to the extent that that transaction does not constitute the mere exercise of the right of ownership by its holder'. However, 'a natural person who carried out an agricultural activity on land that was reclassified, following a change to urban management plans which occurred for reasons beyond his control, as land designated for development' could not be regarded as a taxable person 'when he begins to sell that land if those sales fall within the scope of the management of the private property of that person. If, on the other hand, that person takes active steps, for the purpose of concluding those sales, to market property by mobilising resources similar to those deployed by a producer, a trader or a person supplying services', then he 'must be regarded as carrying out an economic activity within the meaning of that article and must, therefore, be regarded as a taxable person for value added tax'. Whether the person concerned was a flat-rate farmer within *Article 295* was irrelevant. *Slaby v Minister Finansów*, ECJ Case C-180/10; *Kuc v Dyrektor Izby Skarbowej w Warszawie*, ECJ Case C-181/10; [2011] STC 2230.

[20.6] See also *DA Rompelman & EA Rompelman-van-Deelen v Minister van Financiën*, **22.103** EUROPEAN COMMUNITY LAW; *I/S Fini H v Skatteministeriet*, **22.105** EUROPEAN COMMUNITY LAW; *Polysar Investments Netherlands BV v Inspecteur der Invoerrechten en Accijnzen*, **22.106** EUROPEAN

COMMUNITY LAW; *Banque Bruxelles Lambert SA v Belgian State*, 22.107 EUROPEAN COMMUNITY LAW; *Staatssecretaris van Financiën v Heerma*, 22.108 EUROPEAN COMMUNITY LAW; *WM van Tiem v Staatssecretaris van Financiën*, 22.109 EUROPEAN COMMUNITY LAW; *Intercommunale voor Zeewaterontzilting (in liquidation) v Belgian State*, 22.110 EUROPEAN COMMUNITY LAW; *The Wellcome Trust Ltd v C & E Commrs*, 22.111 EUROPEAN COMMUNITY LAW; *Harnas & Helm CV v Staatssecretaris van Financiën*, 22.112 EUROPEAN COMMUNITY LAW; *Cibo Participations SA v Directeur régional des impôts du Nord-Pas-de-Calais*, 22.113 EUROPEAN COMMUNITY LAW; *Enkler v Finanzamt Homburg*, 22.114 EUROPEAN COMMUNITY LAW; *Optigen Ltd v C & E Commrs*, 22.115 EUROPEAN COMMUNITY LAW, and *University of Huddersfield Higher Education Corporation v C & E Commrs*, 22.116 EUROPEAN COMMUNITY LAW.

Article 11—associated persons

[20.7] See *Van der Steen v Inspecteur van de Belastingdienst*, 22.124 EUROPEAN COMMUNITY LAW; *Barclays Bank plc*, 32.15 GROUPS OF COMPANIES; *Osman*, 57.39 REGISTRATION, and *Shamrock Leasing Ltd*, 62.505 SUPPLY.

Article 12—occasional transactions

[20.8] See *Kerrutt & Another v Finanzamt Mönchengladbach-Mitte*, 22.121 EUROPEAN COMMUNITY LAW; *Finanzamt Goslar v Breitsohl*, 22.122 EUROPEAN COMMUNITY LAW, and *Gemeente Emmen v Belastingdienst Grote Ondernemingen*, 22.123 EUROPEAN COMMUNITY LAW.

Article 13—public authorities

[20.9] In the Republic of Ireland, the State and local authorities were treated as taxable persons only where the Minister for Finance had made a specific order to that effect. The EC Commission applied to the ECJ for a ruling that this contravened the requirements of *Article 13* of *Directive 2006/112/EC*. The ECJ granted the ruling requested, holding that Ireland had failed to fulfil its obligations under the Directive. *EC Commission v Republic of Ireland*, ECJ Case C-554/07; 16 July 2009 unreported.

[20.10] See also *Wakefield College v HMRC*, 15.100 CONSTRUCTION OF BUILDINGS; *EC Commission v Netherlands*; 22.127 EUROPEAN COMMUNITY LAW; *Ufficio Distrettuale delle Imposte Dirette di Fiorenzuola d'Arda v Comune di Carpaneto Piacentino*, 22.129 EUROPEAN COMMUNITY LAW; *Comune di Carpaneto Piacentino & Others v Ufficio Provinciale Imposta sul Valore Aggiunto di Piacenza*, 22.130 EUROPEAN COMMUNITY LAW; *Ayuntamiento de Sevilla v Recaudadores de las Zonas Primera y Segunda*, 22.131 EUROPEAN COMMUNITY LAW; *Finanzamt Augsburg-Stadt v Marktgemeinde Welden*, 22.133 EUROPEAN COMMUNITY LAW; *Commission of the European Communities v United Kingdom*, 22.134 EUROPEAN COMMUNITY LAW; *Commission of the European Communities v France*, 22.135 EUROPEAN COMMUNITY LAW; *Commission of the European Communities v Netherlands*, 22.136 EUROPEAN COMMUNITY LAW; *Fazenda Pública v Câmara Municipal do Porto*, 22.137 EUROPEAN COMMUNITY LAW; *Isle of Wight Council v HMRC (No 2)*, 22.138 EUROPEAN COMMUNITY LAW; *Finanzamt Eisleben v Feuerbestattungsverein Halle eV*, 22.139 EUROPEAN COMMUNITY LAW; *The Lord Mayor & Citizens of* *the City of Westminster*, 22.143 EUROPEAN COMMUNITY LAW; *Isle of Wight Council (No 4)*, 22.144 EUROPEAN COMMUNITY LAW; *Metropolitan Borough of Wirral*, 22.145 EUROPEAN COMMUNITY LAW; *Rhondda Cynon Taff County Borough Council*, 22.146 EUROPEAN COMMUNITY LAW; *Stirling Council*, 22.147 EUROPEAN COMMUNITY LAW; *City of London Corporation*, 22.148 EUROPEAN COMMUNITY LAW, and *Chancellor, Masters & Scholars of the University of Cambridge*, 30.11 FUEL AND POWER.

Taxable transactions (Articles 14–30)

Supplies of goods (Articles 14–19)

Article 14(1)—disposals of tangible property

[20.11] See *Staatssecretaris van Financiën v Shipping & Forwarding Enterprise (SAFE) BV*, 22.151 EUROPEAN COMMUNITY LAW, and *Auto Lease Holland BV v Bundesamt für Finanzen*, 22.152 EUROPEAN COMMUNITY LAW.

Article 14(2)(c)—transfers under commission contracts

[20.12] See *Express Medicare Ltd*, 1.78 AGENTS.

Article 15(2)—interests and rights in immovable property

[20.13] See *Stichting Goed Wonen v Staatssecretaris van Financiën (No 1)*, 22.156 EUROPEAN COMMUNITY LAW.

Article 16—private use of business assets

[20.14] See *Kuwait Petroleum (GB) Ltd v C & E Commrs (Nos 1 and 2)*, 22.158 and 22.159 EUROPEAN COMMUNITY LAW; *Finanzamt Burgdorf v Fischer*, 22.160 EUROPEAN COMMUNITY LAW; *Finanzamt Düsseldorf-Mettman v Brandenstein*, 22.161 EUROPEAN COMMUNITY LAW, and *de Jong v Staatssecretaris van Financiën*, 22.163 EUROPEAN COMMUNITY LAW.

Article 17—transfer of own goods between Member States

[20.15] See *Centrax Ltd*, 23.33 EUROPEAN COMMUNITY: SINGLE MARKET.

Article 18—self-supplies of goods

[20.16] See *Robert Gordon's College v C & E Commrs*, 22.165 EUROPEAN COMMUNITY LAW.

Article 19—transfer of 'totality of assets'

[20.17] See *Spijkers v Gevroeders Benedik Abattoir CV*, 22.166 EUROPEAN COMMUNITY LAW; *Zita Modes Sàrl v Administration de l'enregistrement et des domaines*, 22.167 EUROPEAN COMMUNITY LAW, and *Finanzamt Offenbach am Main-Land v Faxworld Vorgründungsgesellschaft Peter Hünninghausen und Wolfgang Klein GbR*, 22.168 EUROPEAN COMMUNITY LAW.

Intra-Community acquisitions of goods (Articles 20–23)

[20.18] An individual (X), who was resident in Sweden, decided to purchase a sailing boat in the UK and use it for recreational purposes in the UK for a few months before sailing it to Sweden. The Swedish tax authority issued a preliminary ruling that X would be treated as making an intra-Community acquisition of a new means of transport and would be required to account for VAT in Sweden. X appealed, contending that he should not be required to pay Swedish VAT because, by the time when the boat entered Swedish waters, he would have used it for more than three months and sailed it for more than 100 hours. The case was referred to the ECJ for a ruling on the interpretation of *Article 20* of *Directive 2006/112/EC*. The ECJ found in favour of the Swedish tax authority, observing that the case 'illustrates how the principle of taxation in the Member State of destination would not be observed if a specific time period were imposed during which the transport of the goods in question to the purchaser must be commenced or completed. If X's interpretation, to the effect that there is a strict time period during which the transport of the goods in question must be commenced, were to be upheld, it would suffice for X to delay the transport of the goods concerned to the Member State of destination in order to mask the intra-Community nature of the transaction or alter the allocation of authority to tax so that a Member State other than the Member State of destination had the authority to tax the transaction. In either case, the Kingdom of Sweden would be deprived of its tax revenue. Consequently, the classification of a transaction as an intra-Community supply or acquisition cannot be made contingent on observance of a specific time period during which the transport of the goods supplied or acquired must be commenced or completed.' Where a case involved the acquisition of a new means of transport, 'the determination of the intra-Community nature of the transaction must be made through an overall assessment of all the objective circumstances and the purchaser's intentions, provided that it is supported by objective evidence which make it possible to identify the Member State in which final use of the goods concerned is envisaged'. The ECJ also held that the assessment of whether a 'means of transport' should be treated as 'new' must be made 'at the time of the supply of the goods in question by the vendor to the purchaser'. *X v Skatteverket*, ECJ Case C-84/09; [2011] STC 189.

Supplies of services (Articles 24–29)

Article 24

[20.19] See *Van Dijk's Boekhuis BV v Staatssecretaris van Financiën*, 22.171 EUROPEAN COMMUNITY LAW; *Mohr v Finanzamt Bad Segeberg*, 22.172 EUROPEAN COMMUNITY LAW; *Landboden-Agrardienste GmbH & Co KG v Finanzamt Calau*, 22.173 EUROPEAN COMMUNITY LAW; *Faaborg-Gelting Linien A/S v Finanzamt Flensburg*, 22.174 EUROPEAN COMMUNITY LAW, and *Levob Verzekeringen BV v Staatssecretaris van Financien*, 22.176 EUROPEAN COMMUNITY LAW.

Article 26—treatment of non-business use of goods as supply of services

[20.20] A charity operated an art gallery, which was not a business activity since it did not charge for admission. It also made taxable supplies including sales from a shop and the hire of parts of its premises. It had opted to tax its premises. It arranged for the refurbishment of an extension to the gallery. It claimed a repayment of some of the input tax incurred on the refurbishment. Customs accepted that some of the work qualified for zero-rating and that some of the tax was deductible since it related to an area which would be used for standard-rated supplies of catering. However they rejected part of the claim. The charity appealed, contending that the disputed tax was reclaimable by virtue of the decision in *Lennartz v Finanzamt München III*, **22.456** EUROPEAN COMMUNITY LAW. The tribunal accepted this contention and allowed the appeal. The tribunal specifically rejected Customs' contention that the *Lennartz* principle only applied where a new asset was acquired, and held that the *Lennartz* principle also applied 'when a taxable person carries out substantial reconstruction work to an existing building but the work falls short of creating an entirely new building'. The tribunal expressed the view that 'the reconstruction of the existing listed building in the present case may well cost more than if the existing building had been demolished and the planned building had been erected from scratch'. The tribunal held that 'it would be wholly unrealistic to treat the construction work otherwise than as the acquisition of capital goods', and that 'the exclusion of the construction work in the present case would conflict with the principle of fiscal neutrality which is inherent in the common system of VAT'. *Whitechapel Art Gallery (No 2)*, [2008] VATDR 530 (VTD 20720).

[20.21] See also *Kühne v Finanzamt München III*, **22.179** EUROPEAN COMMUNITY LAW; *Finanzamt München III v Mohsche*, **22.181** EUROPEAN COMMUNITY LAW; *Seeling v Finanzamt Starnberg*, **22.182** EUROPEAN COMMUNITY LAW; *Charles & Charles-Tijmens v Staatssecretaris van Financiën*, **22.183** EUROPEAN COMMUNITY LAW; *Julius Fillibeck Söhne GmbH & Co KG v Finanzamt Neustadt*, **22.184** EUROPEAN COMMUNITY LAW; *Hotel Scandic Gasaback AB v Riksskatteverket*, **22.185** EUROPEAN COMMUNITY LAW; *Danfoss A/S v Skatteministeriet*, **22.186** EUROPEAN COMMUNITY LAW; *Vereniging Noordelijke Land-en Tuinbouw Organisatie v Staatssecretaris van Financiën*, **22.187** EUROPEAN COMMUNITY LAW; *Lennartz v Finanzamt München III*, **22.456** EUROPEAN COMMUNITY LAW, and *Kingfisher Events Ltd v HMRC*, **67.132** VALUATION.

Article 27—self-supplies of services

[20.22] See *Robert Gordon's College v C & E Commrs*, **22.165** EUROPEAN COMMUNITY LAW.

Importation of goods (Article 30)

[20.23] See *Van der Kooy v Staatssecretaris van Financiën*, **22.191** EUROPEAN COMMUNITY LAW.

Place of taxable transactions (Articles 31–61)

Place of supply of goods (Articles 31–39)

Supplies of goods with transport (Articles 32–36)

[20.24] See *Azo-Maschinenfabrik Adolf Zimmerman GmbH (No 2)*, **22.193** EUROPEAN COMMUNITY LAW.

Supplies of goods on ships, aircraft or trains (Article 37)

[20.25] See *Köhler v Finanzamt Düsseldorf-Nord*, **22.195** EUROPEAN COMMUNITY LAW.

Place of supply of services (Articles 43–59)

NOTE

The cases in this section should be read in the light of the changes which were implemented by *Directive 2008/8/EC* with effect from 1 January 2010. For an outline of the changes, see the article by Mike Lambourne in Tax Journal, Issue 938, 16 June 2008.

General rule (Article 43)

Article 43—'place where supplier has established his business'

[20.26] See *Cookies World Vertriebsgesellschaft mbH iL v Finanzlandesdirektion für Tirol*, **22.203** EUROPEAN COMMUNITY LAW, and *Maatschap MJM Linthorst & Others v Inspecteur der Belastingdienst/Ondernemingen Roermond*, **22.205** EUROPEAN COMMUNITY LAW.

Article 43—definition of 'fixed establishment'

[20.27] See *Berkholz v Finanzamt Hamburg-Mitte-Altstadt*, **22.198** EUROPEAN COMMUNITY LAW; *ARO Lease BV v Inspecteur der Belastingdienst Grote Ondernemingen Amsterdam*, **22.199** EUROPEAN COMMUNITY LAW; *Lease Plan Luxembourg SA v Belgium*, **22.200** EUROPEAN COMMUNITY LAW, and *Ministero dell'Economia e delle Finanze v FCE Bank plc*, **22.201** EUROPEAN COMMUNITY LAW.

Supplies of services of intermediaries (Article 44)

[20.28] See *Staatssecretaris van Financiën v Lipjes*, **22.515** EUROPEAN COMMUNITY LAW.

Supplies of services connected with immovable property (Article 45)

Sales of fishing permits

[20.29] See *Heger Rudi GmbH v Finanzamt Graz-Stadt*, **22.206** EUROPEAN COMMUNITY LAW.

Holiday accommodation

[20.30] See *RCI Europe Ltd v HMRC*, 22.207 EUROPEAN COMMUNITY LAW.

Supplies of transport (Articles 46–51)

Article 46

[20.31] See *Trans Tirreno Express SpA v Ufficio Provinciale IVA*, 22.209 EUROPEAN COMMUNITY LAW; *EC Commission v French Republic*, 22.210 EUROPEAN COMMUNITY LAW; *EC Commission v Hellenic Republic*, 22.211 EUROPEAN COMMUNITY LAW, and *Reisebüro Binder GmbH v Finanzamt Stuttgart-Körperschaften*, 22.212 EUROPEAN COMMUNITY LAW.

Supplies of services at place of performance (Articles 53–54)

Article 54(a)—services relating to entertainment

[20.32] See *Dudda v Finanzamt Bergisch Gladbach*, 22.214 EUROPEAN COMMUNITY LAW; *RAL (Channel Islands) Ltd v C & E Commrs*, 22.215 EUROPEAN COMMUNITY LAW, and *Burrows*, 62.523 SUPPLY.

Article 54(a)—services relating to 'similar activities'

[20.33] See *Ministre de l'Économie, des Finances et de l'Industrie v Gillan Beach Ltd*, 22.216 EUROPEAN COMMUNITY LAW.

Supplies of miscellaneous services (Article 59)

Article 59(b)*—advertising services

[20.34] A Polish company supplied temporary stands for clients who wished to advertise their services at fairs and exhibitions. Many of its clients were established outside Poland. The Polish tax authority issued a ruling that the company's services should be treated as taking place where they were physically performed. The company appealed, contending that it was supplying advertising services, within what is now *Article 59(b)* of *Directive 2006/112/EC*. The case was referred to the ECJ, which found in favour of the company, holding that 'a supply of services consisting of the design, temporary provision and, where necessary, the transportation and assembly of a fair or exhibition stand for clients presenting their goods or services at fairs and exhibitions' was within *Article 59(b)* 'where that stand is designed or used for purposes of advertising'. The ECJ also held that such a supply would fall within what is now *Article 54(a)* where a stand was 'designed and provided for a specific fair or exhibition on a cultural, artistic, sporting, scientific, educational, entertainment or similar theme, or where that stand corresponds to a model in respect of which the organiser of a specific fair or exhibition has prescribed the form, size, material composition or visual appearance'. *Inter-Mark Group sp. z o.o. sp. komandytowa v Minister Finansów*, ECJ Case C-530/09; 27 October 2011 unreported.

[20.35] See also *EC Commission v French Republic*, 22.218 EUROPEAN COMMUNITY LAW; *EC Commission v Kingdom of Spain*, 22.219 EUROPEAN COMMUNITY LAW; *Syndicat des Producteurs Indépendants v Ministère de* *l'Économie, des Finances et de l'Industrie*, **22.220** EUROPEAN COMMUNITY LAW, and *Design Concept SA v Flanders Expo SA*, **22.221** EUROPEAN COMMUNITY LAW.

Article 59(c)*—services of consultants

[20.36] A Swedish foundation (K), which carried out business activities and non-business activities, wished to receive consultancy services from a Danish supplier. It asked the tax authority for a preliminary ruling as to how these supplies would be treated for VAT. The tax authority ruled that K would be treated as receiving them in its capacity as a taxable person. K appealed, and the case was referred to the ECJ, which ruled in favour of the tax authority, holding that what is now *Article 59(c)* of *Directive 2006/112/EC* 'must be interpreted as meaning that where the customer for consultancy services supplied by a taxable person established in another Member State carries out both an economic activity and an activity which falls outside the scope of those directives, that customer is to be regarded as a taxable person even where the supply is used solely for the purposes of the latter activity'. *Kollektivavtalstiftelsen TRR Trygghetsrådet v Skatteverket*, ECJ Case C-291/07; [2009] STC 526.

[20.37] See also *Zurich Insurance Company*, **62.506** SUPPLY.

Article 59(c)*—services of engineers

[20.38] See *Levob Verzekeringen BV v Staatssecretaris van Financien*, **22.176** EUROPEAN COMMUNITY LAW.

Services of arbitrator—whether within Article 59(c)*

[20.39] See *Von Hoffmann v Finanzamt Trier*, **22.223** EUROPEAN COMMUNITY LAW.

Article 59(g)*—definition of 'means of transport'

[20.40] See *Hauptzollamt Frankfurt am Main-Ost v Deutsche Olivetti GmbH*, **22.226** EUROPEAN COMMUNITY LAW, and *Hamann v Finanzamt Hamburg-Eimsbuttel*, **22.227** EUROPEAN COMMUNITY LAW.

Article 59(i)*—telecommunications services

[20.41] See *HMRC v IDT Card Services Ireland Ltd*, **67.172** VALUATION.

Place of importation of goods (Articles 60–61)

Article 61

[20.42] See *Liberexim BV v Staatssecretaris van Financien*, **22.192** EUROPEAN COMMUNITY LAW.

Chargeable event (Articles 62–71)

Supplies of goods or services (Articles 63–67)

Article 66—derogation for transactions to be chargeable on payment

[20.43] See *Ufficio IVA di Trapani v Italittica SpA*, **22.229** EUROPEAN COMMUNITY LAW, and *BUPA Hospitals Ltd v C & E Commrs*, **22.230** EUROPEAN COMMUNITY LAW.

Importations of goods (Articles 70–71)

[20.44] See *Pezzullo Molini Pastifici Mangimifici SpA v Ministero delle Finanze*, **22.231** EUROPEAN COMMUNITY LAW.

Taxable amount (Articles 72–92)

Supplies of goods or services (Articles 73–82)

Article 73—definition of 'consideration'

[20.45] See *BAZ Bausystem AG v Finanzamt München für Körperschaften*, **22.232** EUROPEAN COMMUNITY LAW; *Naturally Yours Cosmetics Ltd v C & E Commrs (No 2)*, **22.233** EUROPEAN COMMUNITY LAW; *Empire Stores Ltd v C & E Commrs*, **22.234** EUROPEAN COMMUNITY LAW; *Elida Gibbs Ltd v C & E Commrs*, **22.235** EUROPEAN COMMUNITY LAW; *Argos Distributors Ltd v C & E Commrs*, **22.236** EUROPEAN COMMUNITY LAW; *EC Commission v Federal Republic of Germany*, **22.237** EUROPEAN COMMUNITY LAW; *Chaussures Bally SA v Belgian Ministry of Finance*, **22.238** EUROPEAN COMMUNITY LAW; *HJ Glawe Spiel und Unterhaltungsgeräte Aufstellungsgesellschaft mbH & Co KG v Finanzamt Hamburg-Barmbek-Uhlenhorst*, **22.239** EUROPEAN COMMUNITY LAW; *Town & County Factors Ltd v C & E Commrs*, **22.240** EUROPEAN COMMUNITY LAW; *EC Commission v French Republic*, **22.241** EUROPEAN COMMUNITY LAW; *C & E Commrs v Primback Ltd*, **22.242** EUROPEAN COMMUNITY LAW; *Bertelsmann AG v Finanzamt Wiedenbrück*, **22.243** EUROPEAN COMMUNITY LAW, and *Yorkshire Co-Operatives Ltd v C & E Commrs*, **22.244** EUROPEAN COMMUNITY LAW.

Article 73—definition of 'subsidies directly linked to the price'

[20.46] See *Office des Produits Wallons ASBL v Belgium*, **22.246** EUROPEAN COMMUNITY LAW; *Keeping Newcastle Warm v C & E Commrs*, **22.247** EUROPEAN COMMUNITY LAW, and *EC Commission v Italy*, **22.248** EUROPEAN COMMUNITY LAW.

Article 75—cost of providing services

[20.47] See *Wollny & Wollny v Finanzamt Landshut*, **22.249** EUROPEAN COMMUNITY LAW.

Article 78—factors to be included in taxable amount

[20.48] In a Portuguese case, the ECJ held that a vehicle tax (imposto sobre veículos) fell within *Article 78(a)* of *Directive 2006/112/EC*, and therefore had to be included in the 'taxable amount' for VAT purposes. *Lidl & Companhia v Fazenda Pública*, ECJ Case C-106/10; [2011] STC 1979.

Article 79(b)—price discounts and rebates

[20.49] See *Boots Co plc v C & E Commrs*, 22.251 EUROPEAN COMMUNITY LAW; *Co-Operative Retail Services Ltd*, 22.252 EUROPEAN COMMUNITY LAW, and *Freemans plc v C & E Commrs*, 22.253 EUROPEAN COMMUNITY LAW.

Article 79(c)—repayment of expenditure incurred on behalf of customer

[20.50] See *De Danske Bilimportører v Skatteministeriet*, 22.255 EUROPEAN COMMUNITY LAW; *Trustees of the Nell Gwynn House Maintenance Fund*, 62.36 SUPPLY; *Barratt Goff & Tomlinson v HMRC*, 62.61 SUPPLY, and *Clowance Owners Club Ltd*, 62.71 SUPPLY.

Article 80—taxation of open market value

[20.50A] In a Bulgarian case where the tax authority considered that properties had been sold to a connected company at an inflated value, Advocate-General Sharpston expressed the Opinion that Article 80(1) of Directive 2006/12/EC comprised 'an exhaustive list of the circumstances in which a Member State may levy VAT on a transaction on the basis of its open market value rather than of the consideration actually paid'. The provisions did not 'authorise a Member State to take such an approach where the supplier or customer, as the case may be, has a full right of deduction'. A national provision which required VAT to be levied on the basis of open market value in all cases where the parties were connected was incompatible with Article 80(1) of Directive 2006/112, 'at least to the extent that it covers cases where the relevant party to the transaction has a full right of deduction'. *ADSITS Balkan & Sea Properties v Direktor na Direktsia Obzhalvane i upravlenie na izpalnenieto* (and related appeal), ECJ Case C-621/10; 26 January 2012 unreported.

Miscellaneous provisions (Articles 90–92)

Article 90—reduction of taxable amount

[20.51] Polish VAT legislation provided that a supplier could only reduce the taxable amount, in accordance with the national provisions deriving from Article 90(1) of Directive 2006/112/EC, if the purchaser had acknowledged receipt of an invoice correcting the taxable amount. A Polish company, which had not received such acknowledgments from some of its customers, took court proceedings seeking a declaration that this requirement contravened EC law. The Warsaw Administrative Court found in favour of the company, but the Supreme Administrative Court referred the case to the ECJ for a preliminary ruling. The ECJ held that 'the principles of VAT neutrality and proportionality do not, in principle, preclude such a requirement. However, where it is impossible or excessively difficult for the taxable person who is a supplier of goods or services to obtain such acknowledgment of receipt within a reasonable period of time, he cannot be denied the opportunity of establishing, by other means, before the national tax authorities, first, that he has taken all the steps necessary in the circumstances of the case to satisfy himself that the purchaser of the goods or services is in possession of the correcting invoice and is aware of it and, second, that the transaction in question was in fact carried out in accordance with the conditions set out in the correcting invoice.' *Minister Finansów v Kraft Foods Polska SA*, ECJ Case C-588/10; 26 January 2012 unreported.

[20.51A] See also*Times Right Marketing Ltd*, 4.32 BAD DEBT RELIEF; *Goldsmiths (Jewellers) Ltd v C & E Commrs*, 22.258 EUROPEAN COMMUNITY LAW; *Kuwait Petroleum (GB) Ltd v C & E Commrs (No 2)*, 22.259 EUROPEAN COMMUNITY LAW, and *Total UK Ltd v HMRC*, 22.260 EUROPEAN COMMUNITY LAW.

Rates (Articles 93–130)

Structure and level of rates (Articles 96–105)

Reduced rates (Articles 98–101)

Reduced rate on legal services

[20.52] France applied a reduced rate of VAT to certain services provided by lawyers, where they were funded in whole or part through legal aid from the State. The EC Commission applied to the ECJ for a ruling that this contravened *Articles 96* and *98(2)* of *Directive 2006/112/EC*. The ECJ found in favour of the Commission. *EC Commission v French Republic (No 15)*, ECJ Case C-492/08; 17 June 2010 unreported.

Reduced rate on undertakers' services

[20.53] France applied a reduced rate of VAT to certain services supplied by undertakers, including the transport of the body of the deceased, and the provision of hearses of mourners. The EC Commission applied to the ECJ for a ruling that this contravened *Articles 96* and *98(2)* of *Directive 2006/112/EC*. The ECJ rejected the application, holding that 'the transportation of a body by vehicle constitutes a concrete and specific element in the supply of services by undertakers', and that the reduced rate was authorised by *Annex III(16)* of the *Directive*. Furthermore, 'the application of a reduced rate to the transportation of a body by vehicle' did not 'infringe the principle of fiscal neutrality inherent in the common system of VAT'. *EC Commission v French Republic (No 16)*, ECJ Case C-94/09; 6 May 2010 unreported.

Reduced rate on import of animals

[20.54] The Netherlands applied a reduced rate of VAT to the supply of certain live animals, including horses, which were 'not normally intended for the preparation or production of foodstuffs for human or animal consumption'. The EC Commission applied to the ECJ for a ruling that this contravened *Articles 98* and *99(1)* of *Directive 2006/112/EC*. The ECJ granted the declaration. *EC Commission v Kingdom of the Netherlands*, ECJ Case C-41/09; 3 March 2011 unreported.

Reduced rate on babies' clothing and children's footwear

[20.55] Poland applied a reduced VAT rate of 7% to supplies of babies' clothing and children's footwear. The EC Commission applied to the ECJ for a ruling that this contravened *Article 98* of *Directive 2006/112/EC*. The ECJ granted the declaration. *EC Commission v Kingdom of Poland*, ECJ Case C-49/09; 28 October 2010 unreported.

Reduced rate on motorway tolls

[20.56] See *EC Commission v Kingdom of Spain*, **22.262** EUROPEAN COMMUNITY LAW.

Reduced rate on wine

[20.57] See *EC Commission v Portuguese Republic*, **22.264** EUROPEAN COMMUNITY LAW.

Reduced rate on musical performances

[20.58] See *EC Commission v Federal Republic of Germany*, **22.265** EUROPEAN COMMUNITY LAW.

Reduced rate on auctioneers' commission

[20.59] See *EC Commission v United Kingdom (No 5)*, **22.266** EUROPEAN COMMUNITY LAW.

Particular provisions (Articles 102–105)

Article 102—supplies of gas and electricity

[20.60] See *EC Commission v French Republic*, **22.269** EUROPEAN COMMUNITY LAW.

Special transitional provisions (Articles 109–122)

Article 110

[20.61] See *EC Commission v United Kingdom (No 2)*, **22.505** EUROPEAN COMMUNITY LAW; *EC Commission v French Republic*, **22.506** EUROPEAN COMMUNITY LAW, and *Talacre Beach Caravan Sales Ltd v C & E Commrs*, **22.507** EUROPEAN COMMUNITY LAW.

Article 118

[20.62] See *Adam v Administration de l'enregistrement et des domaines*, **22.509** EUROPEAN COMMUNITY LAW.

Exemptions (Articles 131–166)

General provisions (Article 131)

Unauthorised national exemptions

[20.63] See *EC Commission v Italian Republic*, 22.270 EUROPEAN COMMU-NITY LAW, and *EC Commission v United Kingdom*, 22.271 EUROPEAN COMMUNITY LAW.

Activities in the public interest (Articles 132–134)

Article 132(1)(a)—public postal services

[20.64] See *R (oao TNT Post UK Ltd) v HMRC*, 22.272 EUROPEAN COMMUNITY LAW.

Article 132(1)(b)—hospital and medical care

[20.65] A company (F) collected, tested, processed and stored umbilical cord blood stem cells for future therapeutic use. Initially HMRC accepted that F's supplies of collection and testing qualified for exemption under *VATA 1994, Sch 9, Group 7, Item 8*. However they subsequently issued a ruling that F was making supplies of storage services, on which VAT was chargeable. F appealed, contending that it was making single composite supplies of medical care which qualified for exemption under *Article 132(1)(b)* or *(c)* of *Directive 2006/112/EC*. The tribunal directed that the case should be referred to the ECJ for rulings on the interpretation of *Article 132(1)(b)* and *(c)* of the *Directive*. The ECJ held that 'where activities consisting in the dispatch of a kit for collecting blood from the umbilical cord of newborn children and in the testing and processing of that blood and, where appropriate, in the storage of stem cells contained in it for possible future therapeutic use, are intended only to ensure that a particular resource will be available for medical treatment in the uncertain event that treatment becomes necessary but not, as such, to diagnose, treat or cure diseases or health disorders, such activities, whether taken together or separately, do not come within the concept of "hospital and medical care" in *Article 132(1)(b)*' or within the 'provision of medical care' in *Article 132(1)(c)*. The concept of activities 'closely related' to 'hospital and medical care' did not cover 'activities, such as those in question in the main proceedings, consisting in the dispatch of a kit for collecting blood from the umbilical cord of newborn children and in the testing and processing of that blood and, where appropriate, in the storage of stem cells contained in it for possible future therapeutic use to which those activities are merely potentially related and which has not been performed, commenced or yet envisaged'.*Future Health Technologies Ltd v HMRC*, ECJ Case C-86/09; [2010] STC 1836.

[20.66] See also *EC Commission v French Republic*, 22.273 EUROPEAN COMMUNITY LAW; *Ulster Independent Clinic Ltd*, 22.274 EUROPEAN COMMU-NITY LAW; *Diagnostiko & Therapeftiko Kentro Athinon-Ygeia AE v Ipourgos*

Ikonomikon, 22.275 EUROPEAN COMMUNITY LAW, and *L.u.P. GmbH v Finanzamt Bochum-Mitte*, 22.276 EUROPEAN COMMUNITY LAW.

Article 132(1)(c)—medical care by medical professionals

[20.67] See *Dotter v Willimaier (aka D v W)*, 22.279 EUROPEAN COMMUNITY LAW; *Christoph-Dornier-Stiftung für Klinische Psychologie v Finanzamt Gießen*, 22.280 EUROPEAN COMMUNITY LAW; *Unterpertinger v Pensionsversicherungsanstalt der Arbeiter*, 22.281 EUROPEAN COMMUNITY LAW; *d'Ambrumenil v C & E Commrs (Nos 1 and 2)*, 22.282 and 22.283 EUROPEAN COMMUNITY LAW, and *Solleveld v Staatssecretaris van Financiën*, 22.284 EUROPEAN COMMUNITY LAW.

Article 132(1)(e)—services supplied by dental technicians

[20.68] See *Administration de l'enregistrement et des domaines v Eurodental Sàrl*, 22.288 EUROPEAN COMMUNITY LAW, and *VDP Dental Laboratory NV v Staatssecretaris van Financiën*, 22.289 EUROPEAN COMMUNITY LAW.

Article 132(1)(f)—services supplied by 'independent groups of persons'

[20.69] See *Stichting Uitvoering Financiële Acties (SUFA) v Staatssecretaris van Financiën*, 22.290 EUROPEAN COMMUNITY LAW.

Article 132(1)(g)—supplies 'linked to welfare and social security'

[20.70] See *Yoga for Health Foundation v C & E Commrs*, 22.293 EUROPEAN COMMUNITY LAW; *International Bible Students' Association v C & E Commrs*, 22.294 EUROPEAN COMMUNITY LAW; *Central YMCA*, 22.295 EUROPEAN COMMUNITY LAW; *Bulthuis-Griffioen v Inspector der Omzetbelasting*, 22.297 EUROPEAN COMMUNITY LAW; *J & M Gregg v C & E Commrs*, 22.298 EUROPEAN COMMUNITY LAW; *Ambulanter Pflegedienst Kügler GmbH v Finanzamt fur Körperschaften*, 22.299 EUROPEAN COMMUNITY LAW; *Kingscrest Associates Ltd & Montecello Ltd (t/a Kingscrest Residential Care Homes) v C & E Commrs (No 2)*, 22.300 EUROPEAN COMMUNITY LAW, and *Staatssecretaris van Financiën v Stichting Kinderopvang Enschede*, 22.301 EUROPEAN COMMUNITY LAW.

Article 132(1)(i)—education

[20.71] See *EC Commission v Federal Republic of Germany*, 22.303 EUROPEAN COMMUNITY LAW, and *Stichting Regionaal Opleidingen Centrum Noord-Kennemerland/West-Friesland (Horizon College) v Staatssecretaris van Financiën*, 22.304 EUROPEAN COMMUNITY LAW.

Article 132(1)(j)—private tuition

[20.72] See *HMRC v Empowerment Enterprises Ltd*, 22.306 EUROPEAN COMMUNITY LAW, and *Haderer v Finanzamt Wilmersdorf*, 22.307 EUROPEAN COMMUNITY LAW.

Article 132(1)(l)—supplies by 'non-profit-making organisations'

[20.73] See *Institute of the Motor Industry v C & E Commrs*, 22.310 EUROPEAN COMMUNITY LAW, and *The Expert Witness Institute v C & E Commrs*, 22.311 EUROPEAN COMMUNITY LAW.

Article 132(1)(m)—services closely linked to sport or physical education

[20.74] For many years a company which operated a golf club accounted for VAT on 'green fees' from non-members, in accordance with Customs' interpretation of the law and with the VAT tribunal decision in *Keswick Golf Club (and related appeals)*, [1998] VATDR 267 (VTD 15493). However in 2009 it submitted a repayment claim on the grounds that it should have treated its green fees as exempt under *Article 132(1)(m)* of *Directive 2006/112/EC*. HMRC rejected the claim but the tribunal allowed the company's appeal. Judge Bishopp specifically declined to follow his own previous decision in *Keswick Golf Club*. He held that the exclusion of supplies to non-members from the scope of the exemption in *VATA 1994, Sch 9, Group 10, Item 3* was 'not capable of properly achieving the objective of *art 133(d)* of the *Principal VAT Directive*' and therefore did not 'correctly implement its terms'. He specifically rejected HMRC's contention that the exclusion was authorised by *Article 134(b)*. Accordingly the UK legislation was invalid, and the company's supplies qualified for exemption. *Bridport & West Dorset Golf Club Ltd v HMRC*, [2011] UKFTT 354 (TC), TC01214. (*Notes*. (1) Judge Bishopp gave the parties leave to apply for a further hearing to consider the possible application of the three-year time limit for repayments, and whether any interest due to the company should be compounded. (2) HMRC have appealed to the Upper Tribunal against this decision. For their practice pending the hearing of the appeal, see HMRC Brief 30/11, issued on 27 July 2011.)

[20.75] See also *EC Commission v Spain*, 22.313 EUROPEAN COMMUNITY LAW; *Stockholm Lindöpark AB v Sweden*, 22.314 EUROPEAN COMMUNITY LAW, and *Kennemer Golf & Country Club v Staatssecretaris van Financien*, 22.315 EUROPEAN COMMUNITY LAW.

Article 132(1)(n)—cultural services

[20.76] See *Hoffmann*, 22.318 EUROPEAN COMMUNITY LAW, and *Fylkesskattesjefen v Diamond GoGo Bar*, 22.319 EUROPEAN COMMUNITY LAW.

Articles 133, 134—restrictions on exemptions

[20.77] See *Bridport & West Dorset Golf Club Ltd v HMRC*, 20.74 above; *C & E Commrs v The Zoological Society of London*, 22.321 EUROPEAN COMMUNITY LAW, and *Ball*, 22.322 EUROPEAN COMMUNITY LAW.

Exemptions for other activities (Articles 135–137)

Article 135(1)(a)—insurance transactions

[20.78] See *Card Protection Plan Ltd v C & E Commrs*, 22.324 EUROPEAN COMMUNITY LAW; *Försäkringsaktiebolaget Skandia*, 22.325 EUROPEAN COMMUNITY LAW; *Assurandør-Societetet (on behalf of Taksatorringen) v Skatteministeriet*, 22.326 EUROPEAN COMMUNITY LAW; *Staatssecretaris van Financiën v Arthur Andersen & Co*, 22.327 EUROPEAN COMMUNITY LAW; *JCM Beheer BV v Staatssecretaris van Financiën*, 22.328 EUROPEAN COMMUNITY LAW; *EC Commission v Hellenic Republic*, 22.329 EUROPEAN COMMUNITY LAW, and *Leadx*, 38.32 INSURANCE.

Article 135(1)(b)—granting and negotiation of credit

[20.79] See *U Becker v Finanzamt Münster-Innenstadt*, 22.352 EUROPEAN COMMUNITY LAW; *RA Grendel GmbH v Finanzamt für Körperschaften Hamburg*, 22.353 EUROPEAN COMMUNITY LAW; *Muys en De Winter's Bouw-en Aannemingsbedriff BV v Staatssecretaris van Financiën*, 22.354 EUROPEAN COMMUNITY LAW, and *Leadx*, 38.32 INSURANCE.

Article 135(1)(c)—credit guarantees

[20.80] See *Velvet & Steel Immobilien und Handels GmbH v Finanzamt Hamburg-Eimsbüttel*, 22.355 EUROPEAN COMMUNITY LAW.

Article 135(1)(d)—transactions concerning payments, transfers, etc.

[20.81] A company (B) made supplies in connection with the establishment and supervision of individual voluntary arrangements for consumers who had fallen into financial difficulties. HMRC issued a ruling that the company (P) which was the representative member of B's VAT group was required to account for VAT on its supplies. P appealed, contending that it was making supplies of financial services concerned with debts, which qualified for exemption under *Article 135(1)(d)* of *EC Directive 2006/112/EC*. The tribunal accepted this contention and allowed the appeal. Judge Berner held that B's services were 'related to a financial transaction which has as its purpose both a change in the legal and financial situation of the debtor and creditors, and the alteration and/or extinguishment of their respective rights and obligations in relation to those debts'. *Paymex Ltd v HMRC*, [2011] UKFTT 350 (TC); [2011] SFTD 1028, TC01210. (*Note.* For HMRC's practice following this decision, see HMRC Brief 27/11, issued on 19 July 2011, and HMRC Brief 35/11, issued on 20 September 2011.)

[20.82] See also *C & E Commrs v Electronic Data Systems Ltd*, 22.361 EUROPEAN COMMUNITY LAW, and *Finanzamt Groß-Gerau v MKG-Kraftfahrzeuge-Factoring GmbH*, 22.364 EUROPEAN COMMUNITY LAW.

Article 135(1)(f)—transactions in shares and securities

[20.83] See *Sparekassernes Datacenter v Skatteministeriet*, 22.357 EUROPEAN COMMUNITY LAW; *C & E Commrs v CSC Financial Services Ltd (aka Continuum (Europe) Ltd)*, 22.360 EUROPEAN COMMUNITY LAW, and *Skatteverket v AB SKF*, 22.366 EUROPEAN COMMUNITY LAW.

Article 135(1)(g)—management of special investment funds

[20.84] A company (C) provided fund management services to several companies which administered defined-benefit occupational pension schemes. C accounted for VAT on its supplies on the basis that the recipients did not qualify for exemption under *VATA 1994, Sch 9, Group 5*. Following the ECJ decision in *JP Morgan Fleming Claverhouse Investment Trust plc v HMRC*, 22.369 EUROPEAN COMMUNITY LAW, C submitted a repayment claim, contending that its supplies qualified for exemption under EC law. HMRC rejected the claim. The recipient companies appealed to the First-Tier Tribunal, contending that they qualified as 'special investment funds' within *Article 135(1)(g)* of *EC Directive 2006/112/EC*. The tribunal referred the case to the ECJ for a ruling on several questions, including the question of whether the reference to 'special investment funds' in *Article 135(1)(g)* was 'capable of including an occupational pension scheme established by an employer that is intended to provide pension benefits to employees and/or a common investment fund in which the assets of several such pension schemes are pooled for investment purposes'. *Wheels Common Investment Fund Trustees Ltd v HMRC (and related appeals)*, [2011] UKFTT 534 (TC); [2011] SFTD 1025; TC01381. (*Note.* The ECJ has registered the case as Case C-424/11.)

[20.85] See also *Abbey National plc v C & E Commrs (No 2)*, **22.368** EUROPEAN COMMUNITY LAW, and *JP Morgan Fleming Claverhouse Investment Trust plc v HMRC*, **22.369** EUROPEAN COMMUNITY LAW.

Article 135(1)(i)—betting, lotteries, etc.

[20.86] In a German case, a company appealed against the imposition of VAT on takings from gaming machines, contending that they qualified for exemption under *Article 135(1)(i)* of *Directive 2006/112/EC*. The case was referred to the ECJ, which found in favour of the tax authority, holding that *Article 135(1)(i)* 'must be interpreted as meaning that the exercise of the discretionary power of the Member States to fix conditions and limitations on the exemption from value added tax provided for by that provision allows those States to exempt from that tax only certain forms of gambling'. *Leo-Libera GmbH v Finanzamt Buchholz in der Nordheide*, ECJ Case C-58/09; [2010] STC 1950.

[20.87] See also *Fischer v Finanzamt Donaueschingen*, **22.371** EUROPEAN COMMUNITY LAW; *Finanzamt Gladbeck v Linneweber*, **22.372** EUROPEAN COMMUNITY LAW; *Finanzamt Herne-West v Akritidis*, **22.373** EUROPEAN COMMUNITY LAW; *United Utilities plc v C & E Commrs*, **22.374** EUROPEAN COMMUNITY LAW, and *The Rank Group plc*, **22.375** EUROPEAN COMMUNITY LAW.

Article 135(1)(i)—supplies of land other than building land

[20.88] See *Gemeente Emmen v Belastingdienst Grote Ondernemingen*, **22.123** EUROPEAN COMMUNITY LAW, and *Norbury Developments Ltd*, **22.511** EUROPEAN COMMUNITY LAW.

Article 135(1)(l)—leasing or letting of immovable property

[20.89] See *Lubbock Fine & Co v C & E Commrs*, **22.333** EUROPEAN COMMUNITY LAW; *C & E Commrs v Cantor Fitzgerald International*, **22.334** EUROPEAN COMMUNITY LAW; *Mirror Group plc v C & E Commrs*, **22.335** EUROPEAN COMMUNITY LAW; *Maierhofer v Finanzamt Augsburg-Land*, **22.337** EUROPEAN COMMUNITY LAW; *Sinclair Collis Ltd v C & E Commrs*, **22.340** EUROPEAN COMMUNITY LAW, and *Belgian State v Temco Europe SA*, **22.341** EUROPEAN COMMUNITY LAW.

Article 135(2)—exclusions from immovable property exemption

[20.90] See *Skatteministeriet v Henriksen*, **22.332** EUROPEAN COMMUNITY LAW; *EC Commission v French Republic*, **22.336** EUROPEAN COMMUNITY LAW; *Blasi v Finanzamt München I*, **22.338** EUROPEAN COMMUNITY LAW; *J Amengual Far v M Amengual Far*, **22.339** EUROPEAN COMMUNITY LAW; *Fonden*

Marselisborg Lystbådehavn v Skatteministeriet, 22.342 EUROPEAN COMMU-
NITY LAW, and *Aquarium Entertainments Ltd,* 22.345 EUROPEAN COMMUNITY
LAW.

Article 136—goods used for exempted activities

[20.91] See *EC Commission v Italian Republic,* 22.349 EUROPEAN COMMU-
NITY LAW, and *Jyske Finans A/S v Skatteministeriet,* 22.350 EUROPEAN
COMMUNITY LAW.

Article 137—option for taxation

[20.92] See *Belgocodex SA v Belgium,* 22.380 EUROPEAN COMMUNITY LAW;
*Administration de L'Enregistrement et des Domaines v Vermietungsgesell-
schaft Objekt Kirchberg SARL,* 22.381 EUROPEAN COMMUNITY LAW, and
Turn-und Sportunion Waldburg v Finanzlandesdirektion für Oberösterreich,
22.382 EUROPEAN COMMUNITY LAW.

Exemptions for intra-Community transactions (Articles 138–142)

Supplies of goods (Articles 138–139)

[20.93] See *EMAG Handel Eder OHG v Finanzlandesdirektion für Kärnten,*
22.517 EUROPEAN COMMUNITY LAW; *Teleos plc & Others v C & E Commrs,*
22.518 EUROPEAN COMMUNITY LAW; *Collée v Finanzamt Limburg an der
Lahn,* 22.519 EUROPEAN COMMUNITY LAW, and *Twoh International BV
v Staatssecretaris van Financiën,* 22.521 EUROPEAN COMMUNITY LAW.

Intra-Community acquisitions of goods (Articles 140–141)

[20.94] See *Ministère Public & Ministry of Finance v Profant,* 22.384
EUROPEAN COMMUNITY LAW; *Ministère Public & Ministre des Finances du
Royaume de Belgique v Ledoux,* 22.385 EUROPEAN COMMUNITY LAW, and
EC Commission v Italian Republic, 22.386 EUROPEAN COMMUNITY LAW.

Exemptions on exportation (Articles 146–147)

[20.95] See *Lange v Finanzamt Fürstenfeldbruck,* 22.387 EUROPEAN COM-
MUNITY LAW.

Exemptions related to international transport (Articles 148–150)

Article 148(a)—supplies for fuelling and provisioning vessels used at sea

[20.96] See *Staatssecretaris van Financiën v Velker International Oil Co Ltd
NV,* 22.389 EUROPEAN COMMUNITY LAW, and *Elmeka NE v Ipourgos
Ikonomikon,* 22.390 EUROPEAN COMMUNITY LAW.

Article 148(c)—supplies relating to seagoing ships

[20.97] See *Navicon SA v Administración del Estado,* 22.391 EUROPEAN
COMMUNITY LAW.

Article 148(d)—supplies of services to meet needs of ships

[20.98] The RNLI incurred expenditure on alterations, improvements, repairs and maintenance to its lifeboat stations, and on the dredging of harbours and the maintenance of cliff hoists. It claimed a refund of the input tax it had incurred on such expenditure. HMRC rejected the claim and the RNLI appealed, contending that the expenditure was on supplies to meet the needs of its lifeboats which qualified for zero-rating by virtue of *Article 148(d)* of *Directive 2006/112/EC*. The tribunal reviewed the evidence in detail and allowed the appeal in part, observing that 'the needs of a lifeboat are different from those of other vessels because they are intended for the special purpose of being able to set out at very short notice in all weather'. The tribunal held that alterations and modifications to lifeboat stations qualified for zero-rating where they allowed 'the speedy or speedier launch of the boat' or where they enabled a lifeboat 'to be housed in a station in which it could not otherwise properly be housed'. However, repairs to lifeboat stations did not meet direct needs of the lifeboats except where the repairs were 'necessary to ensure the speedy launch of the boat from the station'. The dredging of lifeboat channels qualified for zero-rating, as did the maintenance of slipways 'to the extent that lack of such maintenance would delay the boat's speedy progress to the sea' and 'the maintenance of hoists, winches and other equipment whose purpose is to get the boat into the water'. However the stabilisation of cliffs above lifeboat stations and the maintenance of gangways did not qualify for zero-rating. *Royal National Lifeboat Institution v HMRC*, [2009] SFTD 55; [2009] UKFTT 39 (TC); TC00017.

[20.99] See also *Berkholz v Finanzamt Hamburg-Mitte-Altstadt*, 22.394 EUROPEAN COMMUNITY LAW.

Article 148(e)—supplies for fuelling and provisioning aircraft

[20.100] See *Cimber Air A/S v Skatteministeriet*, 22.393 EUROPEAN COMMUNITY LAW.

Article 148(g)—supplies of services to meet needs of aircraft

[20.101] See *Société Internationale de Télécommunications Aeronatiques (No 2)*, 66.45 TRANSPORT.

Transactions treated as exports (Articles 151–152)

Article 151(1)(c)

[20.102] A UK company supplied 'ship decommissioning services' to the US Navy. HMRC issued a ruling that it was required to account for VAT on these supplies. The company appealed, contending that they qualified for exemption under *Article 151(1)(c)* of *EC Directive 2006/112/EC*. The First-Tier Tribunal accepted this contention but the Upper Tribunal directed that the case should be referred to the ECJ. The tribunal observed that it was not 'possible to discover an evident purpose in the wording of *Article 151(1)(c)*', and that the English language version of that Article differed from the French and Spanish versions. *HMRC v Able UK Ltd*, UT [2011] STC 1110. (*Note*. The ECJ has registered the case as Case C-225/11.)

Transactions relating to international trade (Articles 154–166)

Article 158

[20.103] See *Eurotunnel SA & Others v SeaFrance*, **22.524** EUROPEAN COMMUNITY LAW.

Deductions (Articles 167–192)

Origin and scope of right of deduction (Articles 167–172)

[20.104] In a Hungarian case, the ECJ held that *Article 167* of *Directive 2006/112/EC* 'must be interpreted as precluding national legislation or practice whereby the national authorities deny to a taxable person the right to deduct from the VAT which he is liable to pay the VAT due or paid in respect of services supplied to him on the grounds that the initial invoice, in the possession of the taxable person when the deduction is made, contained an incorrect completion date for the supply of services and the numbering of the subsequently corrected invoice and the credit note cancelling the initial invoice were not sequential, if the material conditions governing deduction are satisfied and, before the tax authority concerned has made a decision, the taxable person has submitted to the tax authority a corrected invoice stating the correct date on which that supply of services was completed, even though the numbering of that invoice and the credit note cancelling the initial invoice are not sequential.' *Pannon Gép Centrum v APEH Központi Hivatal Hatósági Főosztály Dél-dunántúli Kihelyezett Hatósági Osztály*, ECJ Case C-368/09; [2010] STC 2400.

[20.105] In another Hungarian case, the ECJ held that *Articles 167* and *168* of *Directive 2006/112/EC* 'must be interpreted as precluding the retroactive application of national legislation which, in the context of a reverse charge regime, makes the deduction of value added tax relating to construction works conditional upon the amendment of invoices for those services and the submission of a supplementary, amending tax declaration, while the tax authority concerned has all the information necessary to establish that the taxable person is, as the recipient of the supply of services at issue, liable to value added tax, and to ascertain the amount of tax deductible'. *Uszodaépítő Kft v APEH Központi Hivatal Hatósági Főosztály*, ECJ Case C-392/09; 30 September 2010 unreported.

[20.106] See *EC Commission v French Republic*, **22.397** EUROPEAN COMMUNITY LAW; *Grundstückgemeinschaft Schloßstraße GbR v Finanzamt Paderborn*, **22.398** EUROPEAN COMMUNITY LAW; *BLP Group plc v C & E Commrs*, **22.399** EUROPEAN COMMUNITY LAW; *C & E Commrs v Midland Bank plc*, **22.400** EUROPEAN COMMUNITY LAW; *Gabalfrisa SL & Others v Agencia Estatal de Administración Tributaria*, **22.401** EUROPEAN COMMUNITY LAW; *Leesportfeuille 'Intiem' CV v Staatssecretaris van Financiën*, **22.402** EUROPEAN COMMUNITY LAW; *EC Commission v Kingdom of the Netherlands*, **22.403** EUROPEAN COMMUNITY LAW; *EC Commission v United Kingdom (No 4)*, **22.404** EUROPEAN COMMUNITY LAW; *Belgium v Ghent Coal Terminal NV*,

22.406 EUROPEAN COMMUNITY LAW; *Investrand BV v Staatsecretaris van Financiën*, 22.408 EUROPEAN COMMUNITY LAW; *Genius Holding BV v Staatssecretaris van Financiën*, 22.413 EUROPEAN COMMUNITY LAW; *Schmeink & Cofreth AG & Co KG v Finanzamt Borken*, 22.414 EUROPEAN COMMUNITY LAW; *Kittel v Belgian State*, 22.415 EUROPEAN COMMUNITY LAW, and *Lennartz v Finanzamt München III*, 22.456 EUROPEAN COMMUNITY LAW.

Proportional deduction (Articles 173–175)

Article 173

[20.107] See *Finanzamt Ülzen v Armbrecht*, 22.405 EUROPEAN COMMUNITY LAW; *Finanzamt Bergisch Gladbach v HE*, 22.407 EUROPEAN COMMUNITY LAW; *Abbey National plc v C & E Commrs*, 22.419 EUROPEAN COMMUNITY LAW, and *Securenta Göttinger Immobilienanlagen und Vermögensmanagement AG v Finanzamt Göttingen*, 22.420 EUROPEAN COMMUNITY LAW.

Article 174(1)

[20.108] See *Sofitam SA (aka Satam SA) v Ministre du Budget*, 22.443 EUROPEAN COMMUNITY LAW; *António Jorge Lda v Fazenda Pública*, 22.444 EUROPEAN COMMUNITY LAW; *Royal Bank of Scotland Group plc v HMRC (No 6)*, 22.445 EUROPEAN COMMUNITY LAW; *EC Commission v Kingdom of Spain*, 22.449 EUROPEAN COMMUNITY LAW, and *EC Commission v French Republic*, 22.450 EUROPEAN COMMUNITY LAW.

Article 174(2)

[20.109] See *Régie Dauphinoise-Cabinet A Forest Sarl v Ministre du Budget*, 22.446 EUROPEAN COMMUNITY LAW; *Floridienne SA v Belgian State*, 22.447 EUROPEAN COMMUNITY LAW, and *Empresa de Desenvolvimento Mineiro SGPS v Fazenda Pública*, 22.448 EUROPEAN COMMUNITY LAW.

Restrictions on the right of deduction (Articles 176–177)

Article 176—non-business expenditure

[20.110] See *EC Commission v French Republic (No 12)*, 22.409 EUROPEAN COMMUNITY LAW; *EC Commission v French Republic (No 4)*, 22.422 EUROPEAN COMMUNITY LAW; *EC Commission v French Republic (No 10)*, 22.423 EUROPEAN COMMUNITY LAW; *Royscot Leasing Ltd v C & E Commrs*, 22.424 EUROPEAN COMMUNITY LAW, and *Danfoss A/S v Skatteministeriet*, 22.425 EUROPEAN COMMUNITY LAW.

Article 177—capital goods

[20.111] See *Verbond van Nederlandse Ondernemingen v Inspecteur der Invoerrechten en Accijnzen*, 22.432 EUROPEAN COMMUNITY LAW; *Metropol Treuhand WirtschaftstreuhandgmbH v Finanzlandesdirektion für Steinmark*, 22.433 EUROPEAN COMMUNITY LAW, and *Stradasfalti Srl v Agenzia delle Entrate Ufficio di Trento*, 22.434 EUROPEAN COMMUNITY LAW.

Exercise of the right of deduction (Articles 178–183)

Article 179

[20.112] See *Terra Baubedarf-Handel GmbH v Finanzamt Osterholz-Scharmbeck*, 22.437 EUROPEAN COMMUNITY LAW.

Article 180

[20.113] See *Douros*, 46.222 PARTIAL EXEMPTION, and *Local Authorities Mutual Investment Trust v C & E Commrs*, 48.5 PAYMENT OF TAX.

Article 183

[20.114] In a Bulgarian case, the ECJ held that *Article 183* of *Directive 2006/112/EC* precluded 'national legislation which provides, with retrospective effect, for the extension of the period within which excess value added tax is to be refunded, in so far as that legislation deprives the taxable person of the right enjoyed before the entry into force of the legislation to obtain default interest on the sum to be refunded'. It also precluded 'national legislation under which the normal period for refunding excess valued added tax, at the expiry of which default interest is payable on the sum to be refunded, is extended where a tax investigation is instigated, the effect of the extension being that such interest is payable only from the date on which the investigation is completed, the excess having already been carried forward during the three tax periods following that in which it arose'. However, *Article 183* did not preclude a 'normal period' of 45 days, and did not preclude VAT refunds from being made by set-off against other liabilities. *Enel Maritsa Iztok 3AD v Direktor Obzhalvane i upravlenie na izpalnenieto NAP*, ECJ Case C-107/10; 12 May 2011 unreported.

[20.115] Hungarian legislation provided that where a taxable person had an 'excess' of input tax within *Article 183* of *Directive 2006/112/EC*, but part of that excess related to transactions where the taxable person had not actually paid the supplier the full amount for the purchase in question, the taxable person could be required to carry the excess forward to the following tax year instead of receiving a refund. The European Commission applied to the ECJ for a ruling that this went beyond what was permitted by *Article 183*. The ECJ granted the declaration, holding that Hungary had failed to fulfil its obligations under the *Directive*. *European Commission v Republic of Hungary*, ECJ Case C-274/10; 28 July 2011 unreported.

[20.116] See also *Garage Molenheide BVBA & Others v Belgian State*, 22.439 EUROPEAN COMMUNITY LAW; *Sosnowska v Dyrektor Izby Skarbowej we Wroclawiu Osrodek Zamiejscowy w Walbrzychu*, 22.440 EUROPEAN COMMUNITY LAW, and *EC Commission v Italian Republic*, 22.442 EUROPEAN COMMUNITY LAW.

Adjustment of deductions (Articles 184–192)

Article 184

[20.117] See *Waterschap Zeeuws Vlaanderen v Staatssecretaris van Financiën*, 22.454 EUROPEAN COMMUNITY LAW.

Article 187—adjustments for capital goods

[**20.118**] See *Lennartz v Finanzamt München III*, 22.456 EUROPEAN COMMUNITY LAW; *Gemeente Leusden v Staatssecretaris van Financien*, 22.457 EUROPEAN COMMUNITY LAW, and *Uudenkaupungin kaupunki v Lounais-Suomen Verovirasto*, 22.458 EUROPEAN COMMUNITY LAW.

Article 188—capital goods supplied during adjustment period

[**20.119**] See *Centralan Property Ltd v C & E Commrs*, 22.459 EUROPEAN COMMUNITY LAW.

Obligations of taxable persons, etc. (Articles 193–280)

Obligation to pay (Articles 193–212)

Persons liable for payment of VAT (Articles 193–205)

[**20.120**] See *Finanzamt Osnabrück-Land v Langhorst*, 22.460 EUROPEAN COMMUNITY LAW; *Finanzamt Gummersbach v Bockemühl*, 22.461 EUROPEAN COMMUNITY LAW; *Elliniko Dimosio (Greek State) v Karageorgou & Others*, 22.464 EUROPEAN COMMUNITY LAW, and *Federation of Technological Industries v C & E Commrs and Attorney-General*, 22.466 EUROPEAN COMMUNITY LAW.

Payment arrangements (Articles 206–212)

[**20.121**] See *M Balocchi v Ministero delle Finanze dello Stato*, 22.476 EUROPEAN COMMUNITY LAW.

Invoicing (Articles 217–240)

[**20.122**] See *L Jorion (née Jeunehomme) & Société Anonyme d'Etude et de Gestion Immobilière 'EGI' v Belgian State*, 22.470 EUROPEAN COMMUNITY LAW, and *Reisdorf v Finanzamt Köln-West*, 22.472 EUROPEAN COMMUNITY LAW.

Returns (Articles 250–261)

[**20.123**] In *Prudential Assurance Co Ltd (No 5)*, 3.118 ASSESSMENT, the tribunal held that *Article 252 of Directive 2006/112/EC* did not prevent Customs from issuing a return covering a period of 34 months on a company which had previously failed to register for VAT.

[**20.124**] See also *Areva T & D Protection et Controle v HMRC*, 45.5 OVERSEAS TRADERS, and *R (oao BMW AG) v HMRC*, 59.4 RETURNS.

Special schemes (Articles 281-369)

Small enterprises (Articles 281-294)

Simplified procedures for charging and collection (Article 281)

[20.125] See *EC Commission v Republic of Austria*, 22.479 EUROPEAN COMMUNITY LAW.

Exemptions or graduated relief (Articles 282-292)

Article 283

[20.126] A woman (S) who lived in Germany received income from letting an apartment in Austria. Her Austrian income fell below the threshold for the 'small undertakings exemption', and she was not liable to VAT in Germany. However, the Austrian tax authority refused to grant her exemption on the grounds that she was not resident in Austria. She appealed, and the Austrian tribunal referred the case to the ECJ for a ruling on the interpretation of *Article 283* of *Directive 2006/112/EC*. The ECJ upheld the Austrian provisions, holding that 'at this stage in the evolution of the VAT system, the objective which consists in guaranteeing the effectiveness of fiscal supervision in order to combat fraud, tax evasion and possible abuse and the objective of the scheme for small undertakings, which is to support the competitiveness of such undertakings, justify, first, limiting the applicability of the VAT exemption to the activities of small undertakings established in the territory of the Member State in which the VAT is due and, second, the annual turnover generated to be taken into account being that generated in the Member State in which the undertaking is established'. *I Schmelz v Finanzamt Waldviertel*, ECJ Case C-97/09; [2011] STC 88.

Article 290

[20.127] See *Eastwood Care Homes (Ilkeston) Ltd*, 32.7 GROUPS OF COMPANIES.

Flat-rate scheme for farmers (Articles 295-305)

[20.128] See *EC Commission v Italian Republic*, 22.482 EUROPEAN COMMUNITY LAW; *Finanzamt Rendsburg v Harbs*, 22.483 EUROPEAN COMMUNITY LAW, and *Finanzamt Arnsberg v Stadt Sundern*, 22.484 EUROPEAN COMMUNITY LAW.

Special scheme for travel agents (Articles 306-310)

Article 306

[20.129] See *Beheersmaatschappij Van Ginkel Waddinxveen BV & Others v Inspecteur der Omzetbelasting Utrecht*, 22.485 EUROPEAN COMMUNITY LAW; *EC Commission v Federal Republic of Germany*, 22.486 EUROPEAN COMMUNITY LAW; *TP Madgett & RM Baldwin (t/a Howden Court Hotel) v C & E Commrs*, 22.487 EUROPEAN COMMUNITY LAW; *MyTravel plc (aka*

Airtours plc) v C & E Commrs (No 1), **22.488** EUROPEAN COMMUNITY LAW, and *Finanzamt Heidelberg v IST Internationale Sprach- und Studienreisen GmbH*, **22.489** EUROPEAN COMMUNITY LAW.

Article 307—definition of 'fixed establishment'

[20.130] See *C & E Commrs v DFDS A/S*, **22.492** EUROPEAN COMMUNITY LAW.

Article 308—definition of 'taxable amount'

[20.131] See *C & E Commrs v First Choice Holidays plc*, **22.493** EUROPEAN COMMUNITY LAW.

Second-hand goods, works of art, etc. (Articles 311–343)

[20.132] In a Bulgarian case, the ECJ held that *Article 314* of *Directive 2006/112/EC* 'must be interpreted as meaning that the margin scheme is not applicable to supplies of goods such as spare parts for motor vehicles, which the taxable dealer himself imported into the European Union under the normal value-added tax scheme'. *Article 320* of the Directive precluded 'a national provision which provides for the deferral, until the subsequent supply under the normal value added tax scheme, of the right of the taxable dealer to deduct value added tax paid on importation of goods other than works of art, collectors' items or antiques'. *Direktsia Obzhalvane i upravlenie na izpalnenieto Varna v Auto Nikolovi OOD*, ECJ Case C-203/10; [2011] STC 1307.

[20.133] See also *Förvaltnings AB Stenholmen v Riksskatteverket*, **22.494** EUROPEAN COMMUNITY LAW.

Derogations (Articles 370–396)

Derogations applying until adoption of definitive arrangements (Articles 370–393)

Article 371

[20.134] See *Norbury Developments Ltd v C & E Commrs*, **22.511** EUROPEAN COMMUNITY LAW, and *Idéal Tourisme SA v Belgium*, **22.512** EUROPEAN COMMUNITY LAW.

Derogations subject to authorisation (Articles 394–396)

Article 394

[20.135] See *Direct Cosmetics Ltd v C & E Commrs (Nos 1 and 2)*, **22.496** and **22.497** EUROPEAN COMMUNITY LAW; *EC Commission v Kingdom of Belgium*, **22.498** EUROPEAN COMMUNITY LAW, and *Finanzamt Bergisch Gladbach v Skripalle*, **22.500** EUROPEAN COMMUNITY LAW.

Article 395

[20.136] See *Ampafrance SA v Directeur des Services Fiscaux de Maine-et-Loire*, 22.501 EUROPEAN COMMUNITY LAW, and *Finanzamt Sulingen v Sudholz*, 22.502 EUROPEAN COMMUNITY LAW.

Miscellaneous (Articles 397–401)

VAT Committee (Article 398)

[20.137] See *Metropol Treuhand WirtschaftstreuhandgmbH v Finanzlandesdirektion für Steinmark*, 22.433 EUROPEAN COMMUNITY LAW, and *Stradasfalti Srl v Agenzia delle Entrate Ufficio di Trento*, 22.434 EUROPEAN COMMUNITY LAW.

Other taxes, duties and charges (Article 401)

[20.138] See *Bergandi v Directeur Général des Impôts*, 22.526 EUROPEAN COMMUNITY LAW; *Dansk Denkavit ApS & Others v Skatteministeriet*, 22.527 EUROPEAN COMMUNITY LAW; *Pelzl & Others v Steiermärkische Landesregierung & Others*, 22.528 EUROPEAN COMMUNITY LAW, and *GIL Insurance Ltd v C & E Commrs*, 22.529 EUROPEAN COMMUNITY LAW.

21

Education

The cases are arranged under the following headings.

Provision of education by an 'eligible body' (VATA 1994, Sch 9, Group 6, Item 1(a))	21.1
The provision of research (VATA 1994, Sch 9, Group 6, Item 1(b))	21.21
Vocational training (VATA 1994, Sch 9, Group 6, Items 1(c), 5, 5A)	21.23
Private tuition (VATA 1994, Sch 9, Group 6, Item 2)	21.30
Examination services (VATA 1994, Sch 9, Group 6, Item 3)	21.43
Incidental goods and services (VATA 1994, Sch 9, Group 6, Item 4)	21.44
Youth club facilities (VATA 1994, Sch 9, Group 6, Item 6)	21.49

NOTE

VATA 1994, Sch 9, Group 6 derives from VATA 1983, Sch 6, Group 6, which was substituted by the VAT (Education) Order 1994 (SI 1994/1188), with effect from 1 August 1994. Many of the cases in this chapter were heard under the previous wording of VATA 1983, Sch 6, Group 6, and should be read in the light of this change.

Provision of education by an 'eligible body' (VATA 1994, Sch 9, Group 6, Item 1(a))

NOTE

Before 1 August 1994, Item 1 referred to the provision of education by a 'school, eligible institution or university'. The cases in this section should be read in the light of this change.

Tuition at university

[21.1] A barrister (C) gave tuition to law students at Cambridge University. He did not account for VAT on the fees he received from the colleges. The Customs issued a ruling that VAT was chargeable on the fees, but the tribunal allowed C's appeal, holding that he was acting as an employee of the colleges, so that the fees were exempt under what is now VATA 1994, Sch 9, Group 6, Item 1. CI Cant, [1976] VATTR 237 (VTD 317).

[21.2] A partnership of four musicians gave lectures, seminars and tutorials at Cambridge and Glasgow Universities. The musicians did not account for VAT on their fees for these services, and Customs issued an assessment on the partnership. The partnership appealed, contending that the services were exempt from VAT. The tribunal allowed the appeal, holding that the relevant services were supplied to the students by the two universities, and that the universities had procured the partnership to provide the tuition as agents of the universities. Accordingly the services were exempt under what is now *Sch 9, Group 6, Item 1*. *Alberni String Quartet*, [1990] VATTR 166 (VTD 5024).

Open University courses—whether BBC supplying education

[21.3] The BBC invoiced the Open University in respect of expenditure which it incurred in broadcasting television and radio programmes relating to Open University courses. Customs issued a ruling that VAT was chargeable on the amounts invoiced. The Open University lodged an appeal, contending that the amounts should be treated as exempt from VAT. The tribunal dismissed the appeal, holding that the services of the BBC did not qualify for exemption, since the BBC was not itself providing education. *The Open University*, [1982] VATTR 29 (VTD 1196).

Unregistered school

[21.4] A former schoolteacher opened a nursery school in the basement of her home. She also began teaching English to foreign children living in London. However, the Department of Education and Science refused to register her school. She did not account for VAT on the fees which she received, and Customs issued an assessment on them. The tribunal dismissed her appeal, holding that the fees did not qualify for exemption. *JG Barker*, [1984] VATTR 147 (VTD 1671).

School visits to cavern

[21.5] A company (B) owned a cavern, to which school groups were admitted at reduced rates. B did not account for VAT on the amounts it received from school parties and Customs issued an assessment on them. B appealed, holding that the relevant supplies should be treated as exempt under what is now *Sch 9, Group 6*. The tribunal dismissed the appeal, holding that, although the school visits were instructional, they did not qualify as education 'of a kind provided by a school or university', since each visit lasted for only one hour, and was equivalent to a single lesson rather than to a course of instruction. *Buxton & District Civic Association Ltd*, MAN/87/385 (VTD 3380).

Zoological society

[21.6] A zoological society, which operated a large zoo, accounted for output tax on its admission charges, but subsequently submitted a repayment claim, contending that it should have treated these charges as consideration for exempt supplies of education. Customs rejected the claim and the QB dismissed the society's appeal. Carnwath J held that the fact that, in a 1959 rating case (*North of England Zoological Society v Chester Rural District Council*, CA [1959] 1 WLR 773; [1959] 3 All ER 116), the CA had held that the society had the advancement of education as an object, and conducted the zoo as an 'educational undertaking', was not conclusive. Although the society's supplies had an educational content, they were essentially recreational. The VAT legislation was 'referring to education in the sense of a course or class or lesson of instruction, rather than the broader sense in which that expression was used by the Court of Appeal in the 1959 case'. *North of England Zoological Society v C & E Commrs*, QB [1999] STC 1027.

Supplies by university to limited company

[21.7] A university had entered into various contracts for the provision of expert opinion and advice to commercial undertakings. It arranged for the incorporation of a wholly-owned subsidiary company (L) to deal with such supplies. It subsequently entered into an agreement for the provision of training in nursing and midwifery to the Scottish Executive. Under the contract, the university agreed to provide staff and administrative services to L, which then made the supplies of training to the Executive. The university reclaimed input tax in relation to its supplies to L. Customs rejected the claim on the basis that, despite the interposition of L, the 'commercial reality' was that the university was making exempt supplies of education. The CS unanimously upheld Customs' ruling. Lord Penrose held that what the university 'supplied to (L) falls properly to be characterised as a provision of education, just as much as did the supply the university made to the Scottish Executive prior to the arrangements with (L)'. *HMRC v The Board of Governors of the Robert Gordon University*, CS [2008] STC 1890; [2008] CSIH 22.

School operating insurance-type scheme for refund of fees

[21.8] A private school operated a scheme whereby fees could be refunded if pupils were unable to attend classes because of illness or accident. It charged parents for joining the scheme. Customs issued a ruling that VAT was payable on these charges. The school appealed, contending that they should be treated as part of its exempt supplies of education. The Ch D accepted this contention and allowed the appeal, applying the principles laid down by the ECJ in *Levob Verzekeringen BV v Staatssecretaris van Financien*, **22.176** EUROPEAN COMMUNITY LAW. Henderson J held that 'there can be no doubt that the educational services provided by the school come within the exemption for education, and the scheme is merely concerned with the means by which participating parents pay for those services'. Consequently, 'when a parent participates in the scheme there is still a single supply to him of educational services by the school'. *Birkdale School Sheffield v HMRC*, Ch D [2008] STC 2002; [2008] EWHC 409 (Ch).

Definition of 'eligible body'

[21.9] A charity provided educational courses for foreign students. Its income exceeded its expenditure by a substantial margin, the surplus being retained with a view to subsequent expansion. Customs registered the trust for VAT, considering that it was not eligible for exemption under the legislation then in force because it was making profits. The trust appealed, contending that the courses were provided 'otherwise than for profit' and thus were exempt from VAT, so that it was not required to be registered. The tribunal allowed the trust's appeal, holding that there was no profit motive as the surplus created had to be applied for charitable purposes. The CA upheld this decision. Sir Nicholas Browne-Wilkinson VC held that the words 'otherwise than for profit' 'refer to the objects for which an organisation is established and not to the budgeting policy being pursued for the time being by the organisation in question'. *C & E Commrs v Bell Concord Educational Trust Ltd*, CA [1989] STC 264; [1989] 2 All ER 217; [1989] 1 CMLR 845.

[21.10] The decision in *Bell Concord Educational Trust Ltd*, **21.9** above, was applied in a subsequent case where a university provided courses in English as a foreign language. The tribunal held that, in considering whether payments received for supplies exceeded the costs of making those supplies, indirect costs could be taken into account and it should consider the position over a period of time rather than on a year-to-year basis. *The University of Edinburgh*, EDN/92/196 (VTD 10936).

[21.11] A company provided degree-level education to overseas students. Successful students were awarded degrees from the University of Lincolnshire and Humberside. The company initially accounted for VAT on its supplies, but subsequently claimed a repayment on the basis that it should have treated them as exempt. Customs rejected the claim on the basis that the company was not an 'eligible body' within *Sch 9, Group 6, Item 1*. The company appealed, contending that it should be treated as a college of the University of Lincolnshire and Humberside, and was therefore part of an 'eligible body' within *Note 1(b)*. The tribunal accepted this contention and allowed the appeal, and the Ch D upheld this decision. Burton J held that the company could be regarded as a 'college of a university'. The fact that it was not 'governed by public law' was not conclusive. *School of Finance and Management (London) Ltd v C & E Commrs*, Ch D [2001] STC 1690.

[21.12] The decision in *Bell Concord Educational Trust Ltd*, **21.9** above, was distinguished in a subsequent case where a company which operated an accountancy college appealed against registration, contending that all its supplies were exempt. The tribunal rejected this contention and dismissed the appeal, finding that the company had paid remuneration to its directors and holding that this amounted to a distribution of profit for the purposes of *Group 6, Note 1(e)*. (The chairman commented that 'we cannot see that it makes any difference in principle that it was taken as remuneration and not as dividend'.) *North London College of Accountancy Ltd*, LON/95/417A (VTD 14054).

[21.13] A sole trader (C) operated a language school. Customs issued a ruling that, except where he taught English as a foreign language, he was required to account for output tax on his supplies. (Customs accepted that the teaching of English as a foreign language qualified for exemption by virtue of *Group 6, Note 1(f)*.) C appealed, contending that his supplies should be treated as exempt under *Article 13A1(i)* or *(j)* of the *EC Sixth Directive*. The tribunal rejected this contention and dismissed his appeal. (The tribunal expressed the opinion that 'the Commissioners have wrongly exercised the discretion given under *Article 13* by exempting the teaching of English as a foreign language, but that does not mean that there is an obligation upon them to exempt the appellant'.) *JE Cooke (t/a Surrey Language Centre)*, [2002] VATDR 357 (VTD 17691).

[21.14] A company (C) provided driving tuition. The Customs issued a ruling that it was required to account for tax on its supplies. C appealed, contending that its supplies were 'education' and should be treated as exempt from VAT. The tribunal rejected this contention and dismissed the appeal, holding that the effect of *Group 6, Note 1(e)* was that C was not an 'eligible body'. *Cornwall Training Ltd*, LON/96/1275 (VTD 17745). (*Note*. The tribunal also held that C's supplies were 'in the course or furtherance of a business'.)

[21.15] Customs issued a ruling that a company (J) was required to account for VAT on supplies of tuition. J appealed, contending that its supplies should be treated as exempt. The tribunal rejected this contention and dismissed the appeal, holding that J was not an 'eligible body'. *John Page Empowerment Enterprises Ltd*, EDN/04/22 (VTD 18820).

[21.16] A company (H) which operated a riding school failed to register for VAT. Customs issued a notice of compulsory registration and H appealed, contending that its supplies should be treated as exempt. The tribunal rejected this contention and dismissed the appeal, holding that the effect of *VATA 1994, Sch 9, Group 6, Note 1(e)* was that H was not an 'eligible body'. *Hangleton Farm Education Ltd*, LON/03/1147 (VTD 19001).

[21.17] A company supplied educational courses to fee-paying students on a university campus. Customs issued a ruling that the company was not an 'eligible body' and was required to account for output tax. The company appealed, contending that because it had entered into a 'recognition agreement' with the university, it should be treated as a college of that university and thus as an 'eligible body'. The tribunal accepted this contention and allowed the appeal. *HIBT Ltd (t/a Hertfordshire International College of Business and Technology)*, LON/05/1029 (VTD 19978).

[21.18] A company (T) provided training in information technology. It failed to register for VAT. HMRC issued a ruling that it was required to register and T appealed, contending that it should be treated as an 'eligible body' within *VATA 1994, Sch 9, Group 6, Item 1*. The tribunal rejected this contention and dismissed the appeal, finding that T had paid its directors significant remuneration and holding that the effect of *VATA 1994, Sch 9, Group 6, Note 1(e)* was that T was not an 'eligible body'. *Trans Medium Ltd (t/a Connectivity) v HMRC*, [2009] UKFTT 243 (TC), TC00192.

Students Union

[21.19] A Students Union operated a shop from which it made various supplies, including soft drinks, to students. It lodged a repayment claim, contending that it had wrongly accounted for output tax on certain supplies which qualified for exemption. Customs rejected the claim on the basis that the Union was not an 'eligible body' within *Sch 9, Group 6, Item 1*. The Union appealed, contending that it was 'an integral part of the University', and was therefore part of an 'eligible body' by virtue of *Note 1(b)*. The CA rejected this contention and dismissed the Union's appeal. Peter Gibson LJ held that, in view of the terms of the University's Charter, the University and the Union were 'distinct entities'. The Union was not an integral part of the University, and was not an 'eligible body'. *C & E Commrs v University of Leicester Students Union*, CA 2001, [2002] STC 147; [2001] EWCA Civ 1972.

Residential courses in English as a foreign language

[21.20] A company (P), which was accepted as being within *Sch 9, Group 6, Note 1(f)*, organised English courses for overseas students. Most of the courses were residential, although in some cases students stayed with English families. P treated its supplies as exempt. Customs issued an assessment charging tax on the basis that the effect of *Group 6, Note 2* was that some of P's supplies did not qualify for exemption. P appealed, contending that its supplies should be treated as an integral part of the provision of education by an eligible body, and as exempt. The CA accepted this contention and allowed the appeal. Schiemann LJ held that *Group 6* should be construed in accordance with *Article 13A1* of the *EC Sixth Directive*. Accordingly, *Note 2* should not be construed in such a way as to exclude supplies which were 'closely related' to the teaching of English as a foreign language. P's supplies of catering and accommodation, and of various types of excursions, were 'closely related to the supply of the teaching of English as a foreign language' and were exempt from VAT. *C & E Commrs v Pilgrims Language Courses Ltd (and cross-appeal)*, CA [1999] STC 874. (*Note.* For Customs' practice following this decision, see Business Brief 18/99, issued on 18 August 1999.)

The provision of research (VATA 1994, Sch 9, Group 6, Item 1(b))

[21.21] A charitable institution, based in York, operated a fund to help families who were caring for severely handicapped children. The fund's data was kept on a computer operated by the University of York. The University invoiced the charity for a proportion of the salaries of the staff who updated the database, but did not charge VAT on the invoices. The Commissioners issued an assessment charging output tax. The charity appealed, contending that the supplies should be treated as exempt under what is now *VATA 1994, Sch 9, Group 6, Item 1(b)*, as the provision of research by an eligible body. The tribunal accepted this contention and allowed the appeal, holding on the evidence that the database was 'a valuable research resource' of statistical data for use in the sphere of social studies. The Commissioners appealed to the QB, which remitted the case for further findings of fact. The tribunal heard further evidence and found that there were a series of contracts between the charity and the university and that it was an obligation of each of the contracts that the University would maintain and update the database, and would produce 'applied information'. The tribunal expressed the opinion that the supplies 'constituted the provision of education or research (and) did not constitute the provision of welfare or social security services'. *Joseph Rowntree Foundation*, MAN/92/537 (VTD 14534). (*Note.* There was no further hearing of the appeal by the QB. It is understood that the Commissioners accepted the tribunal's findings and agreed to withdraw the assessment.)

University research—whether exemption authorised by EC law

[21.22] See *EC Commission v Federal Republic of Germany*, 22.303 EUROPEAN COMMUNITY LAW.

Vocational training (VATA 1994, Sch 9, Group 6, Items 1(c), 5, 5A)

Company director providing lectures for MSC

[21.23] A company provided courses of lectures for the Manpower Services Commission. It was accepted that the supplies by the company were exempt under VAT under what is now *VATA 1994, Sch 9, Group 6*. The company paid its principal director for providing the lectures. The director issued invoices to the company for his services, on the basis that in giving the lectures he was acting on his own account and not as an official or employee of the company. He did not charge VAT on the invoices, and the Commissioners issued an assessment on the amounts in question. The tribunal dismissed the director's appeal, holding that although the director was supplying lecturing services to the company, these supplies by themselves did not qualify as 'training'. *AD Knowles*, MAN/87/471 (VTD 3393).

Services of YTS trainees

[21.24] A company, limited by guarantee, was established as a non-profit-making body to act as an agent for the Manpower Services Commission. It placed trainees with local employers. The employers contracted to make payments to the company every four weeks, as contributions towards training. The Commissioners issued an assessment on these payments. The company appealed, contending that they were exempt under what is now *VATA 1994, Sch 9, Group 6*. The tribunal dismissed the appeal, holding that the supplies which the company made to the trainees were exempt under what is now *VATA 1994, Sch 9, Group 6*, but that the supplies which the company made to the employers were a provision of the trainees' services, which did not qualify for exemption. *North-West Leicestershire Youth Training Scheme Ltd*, [1989] VATTR 321 (VTD 4476). (*Note.* For the award of costs in this case, see 2.402 APPEALS.)

[21.25] The decision in *North-West Leicestershire Youth Training Scheme*, 21.24 above, was applied in the similar subsequent case of *Lite Ltd*, MAN/97/264 (VTD 15223).

Supplies to businesses under Employment and Training Act 1973

[21.26] A company supplied services to new businesses under agreements with a local Training and Enterprise Council, in accordance with the *Employment and Training Act 1973*. The Commissioners issued a ruling that output tax was chargeable on the supplies. The company appealed, contending that it was making supplies of vocational training, which qualified for exemption under *VATA 1994, Sch 9, Group 6, Item 1(c)*. The tribunal accepted this contention and allowed the appeal. *Harrogate Business Development Centre Ltd*, [1998] VATDR 466 (VTD 15565).

Supplies of services to Training and Enterprise Councils

[21.27] A company was incorporated by a Metropolitan Borough Council and two Training and Enterprise Councils. It supplied management services to the Training and Enterprise Councils. The actual training was subcontracted to commercial bodies which acted as training providers. The company reclaimed input tax, but the Commissioners rejected the claim, on the basis that its supplies constituted 'vocational training', and thus were exempt from VAT under *VATA 1994, Sch 9, Group 6, Item 1(c)*. The tribunal allowed the company's appeal, holding that it was supplying standard-rated management services. Accordingly the company was entitled to reclaim input tax. *Doncaster Skillshop Ltd*, MAN/99/724 (VTD 17433).

Supplies of GCSE and A level courses—whether vocational training

[21.28] A company, which was not an 'eligible body' within *VATA 1994, Sch 9, Group 6, Item 1*, advertised GCSE and A level courses in collaboration with three colleges of further education. Under the scheme, the company advertised for students, who enrolled with one of the three colleges and worked from home with materials supplied by the company, under the supervision of a tutor provided by the company. The colleges received funding from the Further Education Funding Council, and paid the company 79% of the funds relating to the company's students. The company did not account for output tax on the amounts which it received from the colleges. The Commissioners issued an assessment charging tax on these, and the company appealed, contending that they should be treated as exempt under *VATA 1994, Sch 9, Group 6, Item 5*. The tribunal rejected this contention and dismissed the appeal, holding that 'for a course to be vocational training', it must 'constitute training or retraining for a *specific* trade, profession or employment', and finding that GCSE and A level courses were not within the definition of 'vocational training'. *Oxford Open Learning (Systems) Ltd*, LON/98/1478 (VTD 16160). (*Note*. For a subsequent appeal involving the same company, see **5.66** BOOKS, ETC.)

Supply of electronic 'distance learning' packages

[21.29] A partnership (C) supplied software packages to students at further education colleges. Until 2004, it accounted for VAT on its supplies. In 2004 its accountants formed the opinion that C's supplies qualified for exemption under *VATA 1994, Sch 9, Group 6, Item 5A*. C therefore submitted a large repayment claim, backdated to October 2001. Customs rejected the claim but the tribunal allowed C's appeal, holding on the evidence that C's coursework did 'not merely consist of a supply of goods or services relating to education' but that C's supplies 'had to be characterised as services essential to education'. They were far more than 'the mere provision of electronic textbooks'. The provision of distance learning was 'a part of education which qualifies for exemption from VAT'. *Creating Careers*, [2006] VATDR 46 (VTD 19509).

Private tuition (VATA 1994, Sch 9, Group 6, Item 2)

Whether 'a subject ordinarily taught in a school or university'

[21.30] An individual (P) provided courses in motorcycle instruction. He did not account for output tax on his fees. The Commissioners issued assessments, and he appealed, contending that his supplies should be treated as exempt supplies of education. The tribunal allowed his appeal, applying *dicta* of Lord Hailsham in *CIR v McMullen*, HL 1980, 54 TC 413, and holding that education was not confined to 'formal instruction in the classroom'. *TK Phillips (t/a Bristol Motorcycle Training Centre)*, [1992] VATTR 77 (VTD 7444). (*Note*. It is doubtful whether the supplies would qualify for exemption under the current legislation. The case was decided under the pre-1994 legislation, which allowed exemption for 'education of a kind provided by a school'. The chairman accepted that motorcycle instruction was 'education of a kind provided by a school', but it seems questionable whether it could be regarded as 'a subject ordinarily taught in a school or university', as now required by *Item 2*.)

[21.31] The proprietor of a driving school did not account for VAT on his supplies. Customs issued a ruling that VAT was chargeable, and the proprietor appealed, contending that they should be treated as exempt under *VATA 1994, Sch 9, Group 6, Item 2*. The tribunal rejected this contention and dismissed his appeal, holding that driving was not 'a subject ordinarily taught in a school or university'. *JMC Smith (t/a Qualified School of Motoring)*, MAN/06/166 (VTD 20275). (*Note*. The tribunal also held that the proprietor was required to account for tax on the full amount of the consideration, including any amounts retained by instructors working for him.)

[21.32] An experienced English teacher became interested in a process, originating in California, whereby pupils with reading difficulties caused by sciotopic sensitivity syndrome were cured by the use of glasses with coloured lenses. She began acting as a consultant and, after publicity on local television, her turnover increased to above the registration threshold. On the advice of her accountant, she charged tax on her supplies. However, she subsequently formed the opinion that they should be exempt under what is now *VATA 1994, Sch 9, Group 6*. The Commissioners issued a ruling that they were standard-rated, and she appealed. The tribunal dismissed her appeal, holding that her supplies were not within *Group 6*, since they could not be described as 'tuition in subjects which are normally taught in the course of education provided by a school or university'. *AE Wright*, LON/92/1468A (VTD 10408).

[21.33] A company, limited by guarantee, was formed to encourage dancing. It organised tests for ballroom dancers under the age of 16. It did not account for VAT on these, and the Commissioners issued a ruling that they were liable to VAT at the standard rate. The company appealed, contending that they were exempt from VAT under what is now *VATA 1994, Sch 9, Group 6*. The tribunal allowed the appeal, applying the tribunal decision in *Phillips*, **21.30** above, and holding that the teaching of ballroom dancing was within the definition of 'education of a kind provided by a school'. The fact that dancing had a 'recreational element' did not mean that the tests in question were excluded from exemption. *Allied Dancing Association Ltd*, [1993] VATTR 405 (VTD 10777). (*Notes.* (1) For another issue in this case, see **64.1** TRADE UNIONS, PROFESSIONAL AND PUBLIC INTEREST BODIES. (2) It is very doubtful whether the supplies would qualify for exemption under the current legislation. The supplier was not an 'eligible body' within *Note 1*. The case was decided under the pre-1994 legislation, which allowed exemption for 'education of a kind provided by a school'. Although the chairman regarded ballroom dancing as 'education of a kind provided by a school', it seems questionable whether it could be regarded as 'a subject ordinarily taught in a school or university', as now required by *Item 2*. Customs state in their VAT Manual, Part 7, chapter 24, para 5.4 that they 'do not accept' the tribunal's decision.)

[21.34] A teacher offered tuition in 'transcendental meditation'. Customs issued a ruling that he was required to account for VAT on his supplies. He appealed, contending that they should be treated as exempt. The tribunal rejected this contention and dismissed his appeal, holding that transcendental meditation was not 'a subject ordinarily taught in a school or university'. *C Beckley (t/a The College of Meditation)*, LON/05/389 (VTD 19860).

Whether appellant providing 'tuition'

[21.35] HMRC issued a ruling that a woman (H) who provided nutritional therapy was required to register for VAT. She appealed, contending that her supplies should be treated as exempt under *VATA 1994, Sch 9, Group 6, Item 2*. The tribunal rejected this contention and dismissed her appeal, holding that H's activities 'fall into the category of consultation/analysis and advisory as distinct from private tuition'. *Mrs R Holmes v HMRC*, [2011] UKFTT 347 (TC), TC01207.

Whether teacher 'acting independently of an employer'

[21.36] A qualified teacher taught mathematics in accordance with a method devised by a private company, with which she had entered into a licence agreement and to which she paid 50% of her fees. She did not account for VAT on her fees, and the Commissioners issued an assessment charging tax on them. She appealed, contending that her services were exempt under what is now *VATA 1994, Sch 9, Group 6*. The tribunal allowed her appeal, holding that, despite her obligations to the company which had devised the method by which she taught, she was providing private tuition and 'acting independently of any employer or organisation'. Accordingly, her supplies qualified for exemption. *V Ellicott*, LON/92/3017A (VTD 11472).

[**21.37**] The proprietor of a tutorial institute provided tuition in cranio-sacral therapy to healthcare practitioners, physiotherapists and massage therapists. He provided 60% of the tuition himself, but arranged for other tutors to provide the remaining 40%. The Commissioners issued a ruling that, where he was not carrying out the tuition himself, he was required to account for output tax on the supplies, on the basis that the tutors were not 'acting independently of any employer or organisation'. The tribunal upheld the Commissioners' ruling and dismissed the proprietor's appeal, holding that 'supplies given via paid lecturers in subjects which the appellant himself was not qualified to teach cannot in any reasonable way be described as a supply of private tuition by an individual teacher acting independently of an employer'. *J Page (t/a Upledger Institute)*, EDN/99/144 (VTD 16650). (*Note.* Customs accepted that cranio-sacral therapy was 'a subject ordinarily taught in a school or university'..)

[**21.38**] A tutor offered GCSE tuition in several subjects. In some cases he undertook the tuition himself, but in some cases he employed other tutors. The Commissioners issued a ruling that, where he was not carrying out the tuition himself, he was required to account for output tax on the supplies, on the basis that the tutors were not 'acting independently of any employer or organisation'. The tribunal upheld the Commissioners' ruling and dismissed the proprietor's appeal. *B Graham (t/a Excel Tutoring Services)*, LON/98/213 (VTD 16814).

[**21.39**] Two women operated a riding school in partnership. They offered riding tuition to customers. Some of these lessons were provided by the partners themselves. The Commissioners accepted that such lessons were exempt under *VATA 1994, Sch 9, Group 6, Item 2*. However, other lessons were provided by trainee riding instructors. The Commissioners issued a ruling that such lessons failed to qualify for exemption, because the trainee instructors were not 'acting independently of an employer', as required by *Item 2*. The partners appealed, contending that the lessons should be treated as if they had been given by the partners themselves, and as exempt. The tribunal rejected this contention and dismissed the appeal. *JA & SL Charles*, LON/01/1242 (VTD 17922).

Partnerships—ballroom dancing tuition

[**21.40**] Two partnerships provided tuition in ballroom dancing. The Commissioners issued assessments charging tax on them. The partnerships appealed, contending that the tuition qualified for exemption under *VATA 1994, Sch 9, Group 6, Item 2*. The tribunal accepted this contention and allowed the appeals. The fact that the teachers were members of partnerships did not alter the fact that the tuition was provided by an 'individual teacher' within *Item 2*. *C & E Clarke; A & H Clarke*, LON/96/1446 (VTD 15201). (*Note.* For the Commissioners' practice following this decision, see Business Brief 1/98, issued on 7 January 1998.)

Private tuition—Article 13A1(j) of EC Sixth Directive

[21.41] A partnership provided golf tuition. HMRC accepted that, where such tuition was given by one of the partners, it qualified for exemption under *VATA 1994, Sch 9, Group 6, Item 2*. However, they issued a ruling that VAT was chargeable where the tuition was given by an employee. The partnership appealed, contending that this distinction violated the principle of fiscal neutrality. The tribunal rejected this contention and dismissed the appeal, holding that the distinction was justified by *Article 13A1(j)* of the *EC Sixth Directive*, which restricted the exemption to 'tuition given privately'. *Marcus Webb Golf Professional v HMRC*, [2009] UKFTT 388 (TC), TC00323 (*Note*. HMRC apparently accepted that golf was 'a subject ordinarily taught in a school or university', within *Item 2*.)

[21.42] See also *HMRC v Empowerment Enterprises Ltd*, **22.306** EUROPEAN COMMUNITY LAW, and *Haderer v Finanzamt Wilmersdorf*, **22.307** EUROPEAN COMMUNITY LAW.

Examination services (VATA 1994, Sch 9, Group 6, Item 3)

Supply of IT services to examination board

[21.43] A company (R) supplied IT services to an examination board. Customs issued a ruling that R was required to account for VAT on these supplies. R appealed, contending that they should be treated as exempt under *VATA 1994, Sch 9, Group 6, Item 3*. The tribunal rejected this contention and dismissed R's appeal, holding that the supplies failed to qualify for exemption. The tribunal observed that 'the software drivers of the appellant's supplies consisted of applications, such as databases, workflow management, electronic imaging and web services, which were the mainstays of IT support systems cutting across a wide range of businesses.' Furthermore, R 'was not responsible for setting the curriculum, devising exam questions, establishing marking schemes and standards of marking, monitoring the performance of examiners, and the validation and accreditation of exams'. R's supplies were 'IT services not closely related to education' and 'did not have the character of examination services'. *RM Education plc* , LON/06/857 (VTD 20911).

Incidental goods and services (VATA 1994, Sch 9, Group 6, Item 4)

Sale of batteries

[21.44] A trader did not account for VAT on batteries which he sold to students. The Commissioners issued an assessment and the trader appealed, contending that the supplies were exempt by virtue of what is now *VATA*

1994, Sch 9, Group 6, Item 4. The tribunal dismissed his appeal, holding that the supplies did not qualify for exemption. *WH Saint,* LON/81/112 (VTD 1147).

Supplies of conference facilities to eligible bodies

[21.45] A trust operated a large house, which had previously been used as a convent. It provided conference facilities and accommodation to a variety of organisations, many of which were religious or charitable bodies. The Commissioners issued a ruling that these supplies were standard-rated. The trust appealed, contending that where the supplies were made to an organisation which was an 'eligible body' within *VATA 1994, Sch 9, Group 6, Note 1,* its supplies should be treated as exempt either under *Group 6, Item 4* or under *Article 13A1(i)* of the *EC Sixth Directive.* The tribunal rejected this contention and dismissed the appeal, holding that the supplies failed to qualify for exemption under *Group 6, Item 4* because that provision only exempted supplies to an eligible body which was making a 'principal supply'. On the evidence here, the recipients of the trust's supplies did not make any onward supplies for consideration which could qualify as 'principal supplies'. The tribunal also held that the condition that there must be an onward exempt supply was in accordance with the *EC Sixth Directive,* since 'in looking at the *Sixth Directive* one must not just look at *Article 13* but must also take account of the provisions of *Article 2* and also of *Article 4'. Article 2* provided that 'it is the supply of goods or services effected for consideration which is subject to value added tax, and this governs the United Kingdom requirement that there should be a supply. The fact that under *Article 4* a "taxable person" is defined as a person who independently carries out any "economic activity" does not in the tribunal's view displace the requirement in *Article 2* that the supply of goods or services shall be effected for a consideration since *Article 4* refers back to *Article 2'. Glenfall House Trust,* LON/99/308 (VTD 16657). (*Note.* For the Commissioners' practice, see *Notice No 701/30, para 6.4,* which states that 'if you are under contract to provide closely related goods and services (including conference facilities) to another eligible body rather than direct to its pupils, etc., these supplies are exempt only if the body receiving them makes supplies of education in the course or furtherance of business'.)

Supplies by Students Union—whether within Item 4

[21.46] See *University of Leicester Students Union,* **21.19** above.

School photographs—whether supplied by school

[21.47] See *H Tempest Ltd,* **67.27** VALUATION.

Supply of facilities at school premises to photographers

[21.48] See *Lancashire County Council,* **62.367** SUPPLY.

Youth club facilities (VATA 1994, Sch 9, Group 6, Item 6)

World Association of Girl Guides

[21.49] The World Association of Girl Guides and Girl Scouts reclaimed input tax in respect of payments which it received from its affiliated organisations. The Commissioners issued a ruling that the Association's services were exempt from VAT under what is now *VATA 1994, Sch 9, Group 6, Item 6*, so that the Association was not entitled to reclaim input tax. The Association appealed. The tribunal allowed the appeal, holding that the Association was not itself an 'association of youth clubs' within what is now *VATA 1994, Sch 9, Group 6, Item 6*, although its constituent members were associations of youth clubs. Although references to an organisation within *Sch 9, Group 9* specifically included an association of organisations falling within it, there was no such provision in relation to *Sch 9, Group 6*. Accordingly the Association's supplies were not exempt and it was entitled to reclaim input tax. *World Association of Girl Guides and Girl Scouts*, [1984] VATTR 28 (VTD 1611).

Local YMCA

[21.50] The Commissioners formed the opinion that a YMCA which carried on religious and sporting activities was not a 'youth club' within what is now *VATA 1994, Sch 9, Group 6*, and issued an assessment on its income. The tribunal allowed the YMCA's appeal, holding that a 'youth club' was an organisation that provided recreational, educational, social or cultural activities for members who were mainly, but not necessarily exclusively, under 21 years of age, and finding that the appellant YMCA was within this definition. *Hastings & Rother YMCA*, LON/86/388 (VTD 2329).

National Council of YMCAs—supplies of facilities to non-members

[21.51] The National Council of YMCAs administered five 'day camps', which were made available to both members and non-members. The Commissioners issued assessments on the basis that the supply of these facilities to non-members was liable to VAT. The Council appealed, contending that such supplies were exempt under what is now *VATA 1994, Sch 9, Group 6, Item 6*. (It was common ground that the supplies to members were exempt under this provision.) The tribunal allowed the Council's appeal, holding that once it was established that the facilities in question were provided by a youth club or association of youth clubs, and were available to members, the provision of those facilities remained an exempt supply even where, as here, the facilities had also been provided to non-members. *National Council of YMCAs Inc*, [1990] VATTR 68 (VTD 5160). (*Note*. For subsequent developments in this case, see **48.140** and **48.144** PAYMENT OF TAX.)

Gymnastic club

[21.52] A company which operated a gymnastic club appealed against the Commissioners' decision that it was not a 'youth club' within what is now *VATA 1994, Sch 9, Group 6, Item 6*. The tribunal dismissed the company's appeal, finding that the company was not recognised as charitable and that the club provided income for its directors, rather than being organised on a non-profit-making basis. *International Gymnastic School Ltd*, LON/91/186X (VTD 6550).

Junior section of golf club

[21.53] A members' golf club operated a 'junior section'. The Commissioners issued a ruling that VAT was chargeable on the subscriptions from members of the 'junior section'. The club appealed, contending that the 'junior section' should be treated as a youth club within what is now *VATA 1994, Sch 9, Group 6, Item 6*. The tribunal rejected this contention and dismissed the appeal, disapproving a statement in *VAT Leaflet No 701/35/84*, and holding that the exemption in *Item 6* could not be extended to a youth or junior section of a senior club. *Haggs Castle Golf Club*, EDN/95/164 (VTD 13653). (*Note. Leaflet No 701/35/84* has since been superseded by *Leaflet No 701/35/95*.)

22

European Community Law

The cases in this chapter are arranged under the following headings.

EC Treaty	**22.1**
EC Directives—general principles	**22.12**
Status of ECJ decisions	**22.39**
Time limits	**22.43**
The principle of 'abuse'	
ECJ decisions	**22.58**
UK court and tribunal decisions	**22.65**
EC Sixth VAT Directive (77/388/EEC)	
Scope of the Directive (*Article 2*)	**22.78**
Taxable persons (*Article 4*)	**22.103**
Taxable transactions (*Articles 5–7*)	**22.151**
Place of taxable transactions (*Articles 8, 9*)	**22.193**
Chargeable event (*Article 10*)	**22.229**
Taxable amount (*Article 11*)	**22.232**
Rates (*Article 12*)	**22.262**
Exemptions (*Articles 13–16*)	**22.270**
Deductions (*Articles 17–20*)	**22.397**
Persons liable for payment of tax (*Article 21*)	**22.460**
Obligations of persons liable for payment (*Articles 22, 23*)	**22.469**
Special schemes (*Articles 24–26a*)	**22.479**
Simplification procedures (*Article 27*)	**22.496**
Transitional provisions (*Articles 28–28o*)	**22.505**
Value Added Tax Committee (*Article 29*)	**22.525**
Taxes other than turnover taxes (*Article 33*)	**22.526**
EC Eighth VAT Directive (79/1072/EEC)	**22.531**
EC Thirteenth VAT Directive (86/560/EEC)	**22.545**
Miscellaneous	**22.548**

NOTE

The first significant steps towards the present-day European Union were taken in 1951, when the European Coal & Steel Community (ECSC) was established by the Treaty of Paris. This was followed by the establishment of the Council of Ministers and of the European Court of Justice. In 1957 the Treaties of Rome established the European Atomic Energy Community (EAEC) and the European Economic Community (EEC). The UK joined all three Communities with effect from 1 January 1973, following the *European Communities Act 1972*. In February 1992 the UK Government signed the Treaty on European Union (also known as the Maastricht Treaty), which made significant amendments to the EEC Treaty. These included changing the title of the Community from the 'European Economic Community' to the 'European Community', and changing the name of the Council from the 'Council of the European Communities' to the 'Council of the European Union'. The EC Treaty was further amended by the Treaty of Amsterdam, which was signed in October 1997, came into effect on 1 May 1999, and has had the effect, inter alia, of renumbering the articles of the EC Treaty. In *Proceedings of the Court of Justice & the Court of First Instance of the EC 31/98*, the ECJ note that 'this could create some confusion in the mind of the user between the version of an article before the entry into force of the Amsterdam Treaty and that subsequent to that date . . . the Court has therefore decided, in the interests of clarity and consistency, to implement a uniform system of citation of the provisions of the four treaties

(ECSC, Euratom, EC, EU) in the judgments of the Court and the Opinions of the Advocates-General. Thus, as from the entry into force of the Amsterdam Treaty, references to the provisions of the treaties are to consist of an Arabic numeral designating the article plus two designating the treaty, for example "*Article 2 EC*".' See also the Press Release reported at 1999 STI 1618 and [1999] All ER (EC) 481.

For cases concerning *Directive 2006/112/EC*, which came into force on 1 January 2007, see **20** EC DIRECTIVE 2006/112/EC. For cases concerning the European Convention for the Protection of Human Rights, see **34** HUMAN RIGHTS.

EC Treaty

EC Treaty, Article 234EC—whether case to be referred to ECJ*

[22.1] In a 1974 case, concerning a dispute between French companies which produced champagne and two English companies which produced cider, the French companies requested the case to be referred to the ECJ under what is now *Article 234EC(2)* of the *EC Treaty*. The QB refused to refer the case, and the CA upheld this decision. Lord Denning observed that the effect of *Article 234EC(3)** was that the House of Lords was required to refer questions of European law to the ECJ, since there was 'no judicial remedy under national law' against decisions of the HL. However, the High Court and Court of Appeal fell under *Article 234EC(2)** rather than *Article 234EC(3)**. The effect of *Article 234EC(2)** was that a national court may request the Court of Justice to give a ruling, but it was not required to do so, since 'the cases which get to the House of Lords are substantial cases of the first importance' whereas 'the points in the lower courts may not be worth troubling the European Court about'. Stephenson LJ observed that *Article 234EC(2)** 'confers a power', whereas *Article 234EC(3)** 'imposes an obligation'. *HP Bulmer Ltd & Another v J Bollinger SA & Others*, CA [1974] Ch 401; [1974] 2 All ER 1226.

[22.2] In a 1980 case concerning the import of pornographic material, Lord Diplock stated that English judges should not 'be too ready to hold that, because the meaning of the English text (which is one of six of equal authority) seems plain to them, no question of interpretation can be involved'. *R v Henn & Darby*, HL 1980, [1981] AC 850; [1980] 2 All ER 166. (*Note*. This was the first case which the HL referred to the ECJ for a preliminary ruling.)

[22.3] In an Italian case, the ECJ held that a case should be referred under *Article 234EC(3)** unless the national court considered that the question was 'acte claire', i.e. that the correct application of Community law was 'so obvious as to leave no scope for any reasonable doubt as to the manner in which the question raised is to be resolved'. *Srl CILFIT and Lanificio di Gavardo SpA v Ministro della Sanita*, ECJ Case 283/81; [1982] ECR 3415; [1983] 1 CMLR 472.

[22.4] The decision in *Srl CILFIT and Lanificio di Gavardo SpA v Ministro della Sanita*, **22.3** above, was applied by the QB in *Conoco Ltd*, **2.313** APPEALS, and by the CA in *HMRC v IDT Card Services Ireland Ltd*, **62.546** SUPPLY.

[22.5] However, in a subsequent German case, Advocate-General Jacobs held that it was not 'appropriate, or indeed possible, for the Court to continue to respond fully to all references which, through the creativity of lawyers and judges, are couched in terms of interpretation, even though the reference might in a particular case be better characterised as concerning the application of the law rather than its interpretation'. *Wiener SI GmbH v Hauptzollamt Emmerich*, ECJ Case C-338/95; [1997] 1 ECR 6495; [1998] 1 CMLR 1110.

[22.6] The decision in *Wiener SI GmbH v Hauptzollamt Emmerich*, 22.5 above, was applied in a subsequent customs duty case where the QB upheld the tribunal decision in favour of the appellant company, and rejected the Commissioners' contention that the case should be referred to the ECJ. Dyson J observed that 'there is no indication in the *CILFIT* judgment that the doctrine of "acte claire" has any application other than to references by a court of last instance under (*Article 234EC(3)**)', and stated that 'it is preferable for a court falling outside (*Article 234EC(3)**) not to use this phrase'. *Dicta* of Lord Denning in *HP Bulmer Ltd & Another v J Bollinger SA & Others*, 22.1 above, applied. *C & E Commrs v Anchor Foods Ltd*, QB 1998, [1999] VATDR 425.

[22.7] The decision in *Wiener SI GmbH v Hauptzollamt Emmerich*, 22.5 above, was applied by the CA in the case noted at **27.51** FINANCE, rejecting the company's application to refer the case to the ECJ. *Trinity Mirror plc (aka Mirror Group Newspapers Ltd) v C & E Commrs*, CA [2001] STC 192.

EC Treaty, Article 87EC—State aid*

[22.8] The CA held that differential rates of insurance premium tax, introduced by *FA 1997*, constituted a 'state aid' within the meaning of what is now *Article 87EC* of the *EC Treaty*, and should therefore have been notified to the EC Commission in accordance with what is now *Article 88EC*. *R v C & E Commrs (ex p. Lunn Poly Ltd and Another)*, CA [1999] STC 350.

[22.9] The Spanish province of Guipuzcoa created tax concessions for investments in new fixed assets above a certain value. The EC Commission issued a provisional decision that the concessions constituted a 'state aid' within *Article 87EC* of the *EC Treaty*. Guipuzcoa applied to the ECJ for annulment of the decision, contending that the measures should not be treated as an unlawful state aid, and that the Commission was misusing its powers. The ECJ rejected this contention and dismissed the application, observing that the Commission's decision was 'merely provisional', and holding that it was reasonable for the Commission to express the provisional view that 'the tax measures at issue, which *de facto* restrict the grant of the tax credit to undertakings with significant financial resources, offer an appreciable advantage to the beneficiaries of that tax concession in relation to their competitors'. *Territorio Historico de Guipuzcoa, Diputacion Foral de Guipuzcoa & Others v EC Commission*, ECJ Case T-269/99; [2002] All ER (D) 337 (Oct).

[22.10] A similar decision was reached in *Territorio Historico de Alava, Diputacion Foral de Alava & Others v EC Commission*, ECJ Case T-346/99; [2002] All ER (D) 338 (Oct).

[22.11] In Austria, supplies by medical practitioners were exempted from VAT from 1997. As a transitional measure, Austrian law provided that long-term medical services which were in progress at 1 January 1997 were exempt from output tax, but that medical practitioners were entitled to retain input tax already claimed in respect of capital assets which were used in providing such services. An Austrian dentist appealed against the rejection of a claim to input tax under this provision. The case was referred to the ECJ, which held that the relevant Austrian law constituted a 'state aid' within what is now *Article 87EC* of the *EC Treaty*. *Heiser v Finanzamt Innsbruck*, ECJ Case C-172/03; [2005] All ER (D) 66 (Mar).

EC Directives—general principles

EC Directives—whether directly applicable

[22.12] In the case noted at **22.352** below, the ECJ held that 'wherever the provisions of a Directive appear, as far as their subject matter is concerned, to be unconditional and sufficiently precise', their provisions may 'be relied upon as against any national provision which is incompatible with the Directive or in so far as the provisions define rights which individuals are able to assert against the state'. *U Becker v Finanzamt Münster-Innenstadt*, ECJ Case 8/81; [1982] ECR 53; [1982] 1 CMLR 499.

[22.13] In a German case, the ECJ held that what is now *Article 10EC* of the *EC Treaty* obliged Member States to 'take all appropriate measures' to ensure that their Treaty obligations were fulfilled. The Court ruled that the 'fidelity clause' contained in *Article 10 EC* applied not only to the national legislature but also to national courts as organs of the State. Therefore, national judges were obliged to interpret national law so as to give effect to provisions of Community law, thus giving Community law indirect effect via an interpretation of national provisions. The principle of indirect effect applies whether or not the Community law in question is capable of direct effect. *Von Colson v Land Nordrhein-Westfalen*, ECJ Case 14/83; [1984] ECR 1891.

[22.14] In a case concerning unequal treatment of men and women by a health authority, the ECJ held that a directive could be relied on against a state authority acting as an employer. *Marshall v Southampton & South-West Hampshire Health Authority*, ECJ Case 152/84; [1986] ECR 723; [1986] 1 CMLR 688; [1986] 2 All ER 584.

[22.15] In a Spanish case, the ECJ held that 'in applying national law, whether the provisions in question were adopted before or after the directive, the national court called upon to interpret it is required to do so, as far as possible, in the light of the wording and the purpose of the directive in order to achieve the result pursued by the latter'. *Marleasing SA v La Comercial Internacional de Alimentacion SA*, ECJ Case C-106/89; [1990] 1 ECR 4135.

[22.16] In a case concerning unequal treatment of men and women by a statutory corporation, the ECJ held that a directive was directly applicable 'against a body, whatever its legal form, which had been made responsible, pursuant to a measure adopted by the State, for providing a public service under the control of the State and has for that purpose special powers beyond those which result from the normal rules applicable in relations between individuals'. *Foster & Others v British Gas plc*, ECJ Case C-188/89; [1990] ECR 3313; [1990] 3 All ER 897.

[22.17] In a German case, where a directive had been transposed into German law in 1995, the ECJ held that from the date on which the directive was transposed, individuals could no longer rely on the provisions of the directive 'unless the national implementing measures are incorrect or inadequate in the light of the directive'. *Kampelmann & Others v Landschaftsverband Westfalen-Lippe & Others*, ECJ Cases C-253/96 & C-258/96; [1997] 1 ECR 2771.

[22.18] See also *Defrenne v Sabena*, 22.39 below; *Lord Mayor & Citizens of the City of Westminster*, 22.143 below; *Yoga for Health Foundation*, 22.293 below; *International Bible Students Association*, 22.294 below, and the cases noted at 22.353 below.

[22.19] In an Italian case, the ECJ held that a Member State which had failed to implement the provisions of a directive could not rely on the terms of the directive against individuals. *Pubblico Ministero v Ratti*, ECJ Case 148/78; [1979] ECR 1629; [1980] 1 CMLR 96.

[22.20] In an Italian case concerning a consumer protection directive which not had been implemented in Italian law, the ECJ held that, since directives did not have direct effect against private entities, consumers could not derive rights against traders from the directive. *F Dori v Recreb Srl*, ECJ Case C-91/92; [1994] 1 ECR 3325; [1994] 1 CMLR 665; [1995] All ER (EC) 1.

Primacy of EC Directives over national legislation

[22.21] In a 1964 case, the ECJ held that 'the EEC Treaty has created its own legal system which, on the entry into force of the Treaty, became an integral part of the legal systems of the Member States and which their courts are bound to apply. By creating a Community of unlimited duration, having its own institutions, its own personality, its own legal capacity and capacity of representation on the international plane and, more particularly, real powers stemming from a limitation of sovereignty or a transfer of powers from the States to the Community, the Member States have limited their sovereign rights, albeit within limited fields, and have thus created a body of law which binds both their nationals and themselves.' The transfer by the States 'from their domestic legal system to the Community legal system of the rights and obligations arising under the Treaty carries with it a permanent limitation of their sovereign rights, against which a subsequent unilateral act incompatible with the concept of the Community cannot prevail.' *Costa v ENEL*, ECJ Case 6/64; [1964] ECR 585; [1964] CMLR 425.

[22.22] In a 1978 case, the ECJ held that 'a national court which is called upon, within the limits of its jurisdiction, to apply provisions of Community law, is under a duty to give full effect to those provisions, if necessary refusing of its own motion to apply any conflicting provision of national legislation, even if adopted subsequently, and it is not necessary for the court to request or await the prior setting aside of such provisions by legislative or other constitutional means'. *Amministrazione delle Finanze dello Stato v Simmenthal SpA*, ECJ Case 106/77; [1978] ECR 629; [1978] 3 CMLR 263.

[22.23] The decision in *Amministrazione delle Finanze dello Stato v Simmenthal SpA*, 22.22 above, was applied by the VAT tribunal in *Merseyside Cablevision Ltd*, **36.554** INPUT TAX, where the tribunal held that 'the law of the European Economic Community' prevailed over 'any contrary provision in national law'.

[22.24] However, in the subsequent case noted at **62.476** SUPPLY, the tribunal held, applying *dicta* of Lord Templeman in *Duke v GEC Reliance Ltd*, HL [1988] 1 AC 718; [1988] 1 All ER 626, that the *European Communities Act 1972* does not 'enable or constrain a British court to distort the meaning of a British statute in order to enforce against an individual a Community directive which has no direct effect between individuals'. Further, 'there is no rule of law compelling, or enabling, any court to construe a pre-existing statute of the United Kingdom in order to comply with a Directive subsequent in time, where the legislature or executive of the United Kingdom has not implemented that Directive'. *George Kuikka Ltd*, [1990] VATTR 185 (VTD 5037).

[22.25] Similarly, in the case noted at **29.174** FOOD, the tribunal chairman held that 'the principles of European law . . . do not, in my view, inhibit or constrain a court here into adopting an unnecessarily narrow interpretation of the statutory provisions in order to limit the scope of relief'. *McCormick (UK) plc*, 2LON/97/1193 (VTD 15202).

[22.26] In a 1990 UK case, concerning regulations issued under the *Merchant Shipping Act 1988*, the ECJ held that a national court was required to set aside a rule of national law which it considered was the sole obstacle preventing it from granting interim relief in a case concerning Community law. *Factortame Ltd & Others v Secretary of State for Transport (No 2)*, ECJ Case C-213/89; [1990] 1 ECR 2433; [1990] 3 CMLR 375; [1991] 1 All ER 70.

[22.27] In a 1993 case, the CA held that 'the fact that a national court, in considering a case on the basis of national legislation implementing a directive but where the directive itself is not directly pleaded, did not refer to the relevant case law of the European Court on the directive, is a factor which contributes to a finding that the judgment is unreliable and should be quashed'. *Wren v Eastbourne Borough Council*, CA [1993] 3 CMLR 166.

Whether Parliament can repeal European Communities Act

[22.28] In a non-tax case, Laws LJ held that 'Parliament cannot bind its successors by stipulating against repeal, wholly or partly, of the *European Communities Act*. It cannot stipulate as to the manner and form of any subsequent legislation. It cannot stipulate against implied repeal any more than it can stipulate against express repeal. Thus there is nothing in the *European Communities Act* which allows the Court of Justice, or any other institutions of the EU, to touch or qualify the conditions of Parliament's legislative supremacy in the United Kingdom. Not because the legislature chose not to allow it; because by our law it could not allow it. That being so, the legislative and judicial institutions of the EU cannot intrude upon those conditions. The British Parliament has not the authority to authorise any such thing. Being sovereign, it cannot abandon its sovereignty. Accordingly there are no circumstances in which the jurisprudence of the Court of Justice can elevate Community Law to a status within the corpus of English domestic law to which it could not aspire by any route of English law itself.' *Thoburn v Sunderland City Council (and related appeals)*, QB [2002] EWHC 195 (Admin).

[22.29] In a direct tax case, an appellant contended that the UK Parliament had acted illegally when it ceded sovereignty to the EC by passing the *European Communities Act 1972*. The First-Tier Tribunal rejected this contention and dismissed his appeal. Aleksander J held that 'Parliament cannot fetter itself, and Parliament remains free to repeal the *European Communities Act* and withdraw from the EU'. *IK Bell v HMRC*, FTT [2009] UKFTT 270 (TC), TC00216

State liability to pay damages for failure to implement Directive

[22.30] In an Italian case, the ECJ held that the Italian government was liable to pay compensation to employees of an insolvent company, who had suffered financial loss through Italy's failure to implement a directive guaranteeing such employees their arrears of wages. *Francovich v Italian State*, ECJ Case C-6/90; [1991] 1 ECR 5357; [1993] 2 CMLR 66. (*Note*. For the procedure to be adopted in the UK in seeking to apply the principles laid down in this case, see *R v Secretary of State for Employment (ex p. Equal Opportunities Commission)*, **22.36** below.)

[22.31] The principles laid down in *Francovich v Italian State*, **22.30** above, were applied in two subsequent cases in which national legislation was held to be contrary to EC law. The ECJ ruled that 'the principle that Member States are obliged to make good damage caused to individuals by breaches of Community law attributable to the state is applicable where the national legislature was responsible for the breach in question'. *Brasserie du Pêcheur SA v Federal Republic of Germany; R v Secretary of State for Transport (ex p. Factortame Ltd & Others) (No 3)*, ECJ Cases C-46/93, C-48/93; [1996] 1 ECR 1029; [1996] 1 CMLR 889; [1996] 2 WLR 506; [1996] All ER (EC) 301.

[22.32] The decisions in *Brasserie du Pêcheur SA v Federal Republic of Germany; R v Secretary of State for Transport (ex p. Factortame Ltd & Others) (No 3)*, **22.31** above, were applied in the subsequent case of *R v Ministry of Agriculture, Fisheries & Food (ex p. Hedley Lomas (Ireland) Ltd*, ECJ Case C-5/94; [1996] 1 ECR 2553; [1996] 2 CMLR 391; [1996] All ER (EC) 493.

[22.33] In a case concerning claims for compensation by German residents following the insolvency of two German tour operators, the ECJ held that 'failure to take any measure to transpose a directive in order to achieve the result it prescribes within the period laid down for that purpose constitutes *per se* a serious breach of Community law and consequently gives rise to a right of reparation for individuals suffering injury if the right prescribed by the directive entails the grant to individuals of rights whose content is identifiable, and a causal link exists between the breach of the state's obligation and the loss and damage suffered'. *Dillenkofer & Others v Federal Republic of Germany*, ECJ Case C-178/94, C-179/94; [1996] 1 ECR 4845; [1996] 3 CMLR 469; [1996] All ER (EC) 917.

[22.34] The decisions in *Brasserie du Pêcheur SA v Federal Republic of Germany; R v Secretary of State for Transport (ex p. Factortame Ltd & Others) (No 3)*, 22.31 above, were distinguished in a case in which the ECJ held that a breach of *Directive 90/435/EEC* was not sufficiently serious to give rise to a claim to compensation. *R v HM Treasury (ex p. British Telecommunications plc)*, ECJ Case C-392/93; [1996] 1 ECR 1631; [1996] 2 CMLR 217; [1996] 3 WLR 303; [1996] All ER (EC) 401.

[22.35] A similar decision was reached in *Denkavit International BV & Others v Bundesamt für Finanzen*, ECJ Case C-283/94; [1996] STC 1445; [1996] 1 ECR 5063.

[22.36] In a case in which the HL held that certain provisions of the *Employment Protection (Consolidation) Act 1978* were incompatible with what is now *Article 141EC* of the *EC Treaty*, Lord Keith of Kinkel observed that 'if there is any individual who believes that he or she has a good claim to compensation under the *Francovich* principle, it is the Attorney-General who would be defendant in any proceedings directed to enforcing it'. *R v Secretary of State for Employment (ex p. Equal Opportunities Commission)*, HL [1994] 1 All ER 910.

EEC First VAT Directive

[22.37] See *First National Telecom Services Ltd*, 36.660 INPUT TAX.

EEC Second VAT Directive

[22.38] See *General Motors Acceptance Corporation (UK) plc (No 3)*, 48.64 PAYMENT OF TAX.

Status of ECJ decisions

Application of ECJ decisions—whether retrospective

[22.39] In a Belgian case concerning what is now *Article 141EC* of the *EC Treaty* (which lays down the principle 'that men and women should receive equal pay for equal work'), the ECJ held that, although *Article 141EC** had direct effect, its decision could not have retrospective effect for periods prior to the date of the judgment, except with regard to those who had 'already brought legal proceedings or made an equivalent claim'. The ECJ observed that 'important considerations of legal certainty affecting all the interests involved, both public and private, make it impossible in principle to reopen the question as regards the past'. *Defrenne v SA Belge de Navigation Aerienne Sabena*, ECJ Case 43/75; [1976] ECR 455; [1976] 2 CMLR 98; [1981] 1 All ER 122.

[22.40] The decision in *Defrenne v Sabena*, **22.39** above, was applied in a subsequent case concerning occupational pension schemes. The ECJ held that 'overriding considerations of legal certainty preclude legal situations which have exhausted all their effects in the past from being called into question where this might upset retroactively the financial balance of many contracted-out pension schemes'. Accordingly, *Article 141EC** of the *Treaty* 'may not be relied on in order to claim entitlement to a pension, with effect from a date prior to that of this judgment, except in the case of workers or those claiming under them who have before that date initiated legal proceedings or raised an equivalent claim under the applicable national law'. *Barber v Guardian Royal Exchange Assurance Group*, ECJ Case 262/88; [1990] 1 ECR 1889; [1990] 2 CMLR 513; [1990] 2 All ER 660.

[22.41] The decisions in *Defrenne v Sabena*, **22.39** above, and *Barber v Guardian Royal Exchange Assurance Group*, **22.40** above, were distinguished in the case noted at **22.527** below. The ECJ held that, since the EC Commission had warned the Danish government that the levy in question appeared to be a breach of Community law, it was inappropriate to limit the temporal scope of the judgment. *Dansk Denkavit ApS & Others v Skatteministeriet*, ECJ Case C-200/90; [1992] 1 ECR 2217; [1994] 2 CMLR 377; [1994] STC 482.

[22.42] The decision in *Dansk Denkavit ApS & Others v Skatteministeriet*, **22.41** above, was applied in a subsequent case in which the ECJ held that 'the financial consequences which might ensue for a government owing to the unlawfulness of a tax have never justified in themselves limiting the effects of a judgment of the Court'. To limit the effects of a judgment 'solely on the basis of such considerations would considerably diminish the judicial protection of the rights which taxpayers have under Community fiscal legislation'. *Roders BV & Others v Inspecteur der Invoerrechten en Accijnzen*, ECJ Case C-367/93; [1995] 1 ECR 2229.

Time limits

Validity of time limit imposed by national law

[22.43] In a German case, the ECJ held that 'the right conferred by Community law must be exercised before the national court in accordance with the conditions laid down by national rules'. The laying down of time limits 'with regard to actions of a fiscal procedure is an application of the fundamental principle of legal certainty protecting both the taxpayer and the administration concerned'. *Rewe-Zentralfinanz eG & Rewe-Zentral AG v Landwirtschafts-kammer für das Saarland*, ECJ Case 33/76; [1976] ECR 1989; [1977] 1 CMLR 533.

[22.44] In a French case, the ECJ held that 'a national legislature may not, subsequent to a judgment of the Court from which it follows that certain legislation is incompatible with the *EC Treaty*, adopt a procedural rule which specifically reduces the possibilities of bringing proceedings for recovery of taxes which were wrongly levied under that legislation'. *Deville v Administration des Impôts*, ECJ Case 240/87; [1988] ECR 3513; [1989] 3 CMLR 611.

[22.45] In an Irish case, a national time limit for claiming a social security benefit was held to be invalid, since the time limit in question 'had the result of depriving the applicant of any opportunity whatever to rely on her right to equal treatment under the directive'. *Emmott v Minister for Social Welfare & Another*, ECJ Case C-208/90; [1991] 1 ECR 4269; [1991] 3 CMLR 894.

[22.46] The decision in *Emmott v Minister for Social Welfare & Another*, 22.45 above, was distinguished in a subsequent Netherlands case in which a national law, under which payment of arrears of benefits was restricted to a maximum period of twelve months, was held to be valid. *Steenhorst-Neerings v Bestuur van de Bedrijfsvereniging voor Detailhandel, Ambachten en Huisvrouwen*, ECJ Case C-338/91; [1993] 1 ECR 5475; [1995] 3 CMLR 323.

[22.47] The decision in *Steenhorst-Neerings v Bestuur van de Bedriffsvereniging voor Detailhandel, Ambachten en Huisvrouwen*, 22.46 above, was applied in the similar subsequent case of *Johnson v Chief Adjudication Officer (No 2)*, ECJ Case C-410/92; [1994] 1 ECR 5483; [1994] 1 CMLR 725; [1995] All ER (EC) 258.

[22.48] In a Belgian case, a partnership had appealed against a charge to tax. During the proceedings, it sought to raise an alternative contention based on what is now *Article 43EC* of the *EC Treaty*. The Belgian Court of Appeal held that, under Belgian law, this contention could not be considered on the grounds that it had been raised outside the 60-day time limit laid down by the Belgian Tax Code, and referred the case to the ECJ to consider whether the relevant provision was compatible with Community law. The ECJ held that the time limit was invalid under Community law, and directed that the substantive question of whether the charge to tax was compatible with the *EC Treaty* should be considered by the Belgian court. *SCS Peterbroeck Van Campenhout & Cie v Belgium*, ECJ Case C-312/93; [1995] 1 ECR 4599; [1996] 1 CMLR 793; [1996] All ER (EC) 242.

[22.49] In a Danish case in which a five-year limitation period was held to be reasonable, the ECJ observed that 'the setting of reasonable limitation periods for bringing proceedings is compatible with Community law. Such periods cannot be regarded as rendering virtually impossible or excessively difficult the exercise of rights conferred by Community law, even if the expiry of those periods necessarily entails the dismissal, in whole or in part, of the action brought'. *Fantask A/S & Others v Industriministeriet*, ECJ Case C-188/95; [1998] 1 CMLR 473; [1998] All ER (EC) 1.

[22.50] In an Italian case, the ECJ held that 'the fact that the Court has given a preliminary ruling interpreting a provision of Community law without limiting the temporal effects of its judgment does not affect the right of a Member State to impose a time-limit under national law within which, on penalty of being barred, proceedings for repayment of charges levied in breach of that provision must be commenced. Community law does not prohibit a Member State from resisting actions for repayment of charges levied in breach of Community law by relying on a time-limit under national law of three years.' *Edilizia Industriale Siderurgica Srl v Ministero delle Finanze*, ECJ Case C-231/96; [1998] 1 ECR 4951.

[22.51] A similar decision was reached in *Aprile Srl v Amministrazione delle Finanze dello Stato*, ECJ Case C-228/96, 17 November 1998 unreported.

[22.52] In a similar French case, the ECJ held that 'for reparation of loss or damage the conditions relating to time-limits laid down by national law must not be less favourable than those relating to similar domestic claims (principle of equivalence) and must not be so framed as to make it virtually impossible or excessively difficult to obtain reparation (principle of effectiveness)'. *Roquette Frères SA v Direction des Services Fiscaux du Pas-de-Calais*, ECJ Case C-88/99; [2000] All ER (D) 2008.

[22.53] In a Belgian case, the ECJ held that 'in the absence of Community rules governing a matter, it is for the domestic legal system of each Member State to lay down the detailed procedural rules governing actions for safeguarding rights which individuals derive from the effect of Community law'. Furthermore, 'the position of the VAT authorities cannot be compared with that of a taxable person. The authorities do not have the information necessary to determine the amount of the tax chargeable and the deductions to be made until, at the earliest, the day when the return referred to in *Article 22(4)* of the *Sixth Directive* is made'. In the case of an inaccurate or incomplete return, 'it is therefore only from that time that the authorities can start to recover the unpaid tax. Thus, the fact that the five-year limitation period begins to run as against the tax authorities on the date on which the return should in principle be made, whereas an individual may exercise his right to deduction only within a period of five years as from the date on which that right arose, is not such as to infringe the principle of equality.' *Société Financière d'Investissements SPRL (SFI) v Belgian State*, ECJ Case C-85/97; [2000] STC 164.

[22.54] In an Italian case, the ECJ held that 'the principle of effectiveness does not preclude national rules governing the recovery of sums paid but not due, under which the time-limits for a civil law action for recovery of sums paid but not due, brought by the recipient of services against the supplier, a taxable person for the purposes of VAT, are more generous than the specific time-limits for a fiscal law action for a tax refund, brought by the supplier against the tax authority, provided that it is possible for that taxable person effectively to claim reimbursement of the VAT from the tax authority. That condition is not satisfied where the application of such rules has the effect of totally depriving the taxable person of the right to obtain from the tax authority a refund of the VAT paid but not due, which the taxable person has himself had to pay back to the recipient of his services.' *Banca Antoniana Popolare Veneta SpA v Ministero dell'Economia e delle Finanze*, ECJ Case C-427/10; 15 December 2011 unreported.

Retrospective introduction of three-year time limit

[22.55] Following the decision in the case noted at **48.38** PAYMENT OF TAX, the appellant company submitted three repayment claims, covering the entire period from the introduction of VAT in 1973 during which it had wrongly treated certain supplies of teacakes as standard-rated rather than zero-rated, and covering a period beginning in 1991 during which it had wrongly accounted for output tax on the face value of gift vouchers, rather than on the 'subjective value' as determined by the ECJ in *Argos Distributors Ltd*, **22.228** below. The Commissioners only agreed to repay the sums which had been paid within three years of the relevant repayment claim, in accordance with the provisions of *VATA 1994, s 80(4)* as substituted by *FA 1997, s 47*. The company appealed, contending that *VATA 1994, s 80(4)* (as substituted by *FA 1997*) should be held to be invalid under European law. The tribunal rejected this contention and dismissed the appeal, but the CA directed that the case should be referred to the ECJ for a ruling 'on whether it is compatible with Community law to enforce legislation which removes with retrospective effect a right under national law to reclaim VAT, which right has existed unexercised for more than three years'. The ECJ ruled that 'whilst national legislation reducing the period within which repayment of sums collected in breach of Community law may be sought is not incompatible with the principle of effectiveness, it is subject to the condition not only that the new limitation period is reasonable but also that the new legislation includes transitional arrangements allowing an adequate period after the enactment of the legislation for lodging the claims for repayment which persons were entitled to submit under the original legislation. Such transitional arrangements are necessary where the immediate application to those claims of a limitation period shorter than that which was previously in force would have the effect of retroactively depriving some individuals of their right to repayment, or of allowing them too short a period for asserting that right.' Accordingly, the UK legislation was unlawful. *Marks & Spencer plc v C & E Commrs (No 4)*, ECJ Case C-62/00; [2002] STC 1036; [2003] 2 WLR 665. (*Notes.* (1) For a preliminary issue in this case, see **2.27** APPEALS. (2) For subsequent developments, see **22.56** below.)

[22.56] Following the ECJ decision reported at **22.55** above, the company's appeal was referred back to the CA. The CA allowed the appeal with regard to the output tax on gift vouchers, holding that the company had a right to repayment under Community law, which could not be curtailed by the retrospective introduction of a national time limit without adequate transitional arrangements. However, the CA dismissed the company's appeal with regard to the supplies of teacakes. The company appealed to the HL, contending that the UK legislation concerning 'unjust enrichment' discriminated against 'payment traders' by comparison with 'repayment traders'. (The company was a 'payment trader' because it made significant sales of standard-rated goods such as clothing, whereas some of its competitors were 'repayment traders' because the great majority of their supplies were zero-rated.) The HL directed that the case should be referred back to the ECJ for further rulings. The ECJ upheld the company's contentions, holding that where a Member State 'has maintained in its national legislation an exemption with refund of input tax in respect of certain specified supplies but has mistakenly interpreted its national legislation, with the consequence that certain supplies benefiting from exemption with refund of input tax under its national legislation have been subject to tax at the standard rate, the general principles of Community law, including that of fiscal neutrality, apply so as to give a trader who has made such supplies a right to recover the sums mistakenly charged in respect of them. Although the principles of equal treatment and fiscal neutrality apply in principle to the case in the main proceedings, an infringement of those principles is not constituted merely by the fact that a refusal to make repayment was based on the unjust enrichment of the taxable person concerned. By contrast, the principle of fiscal neutrality precludes the concept of unjust enrichment from being applied only to taxable persons such as "payment traders" (taxable persons for whom, in a given prescribed accounting period, the output tax collected exceeds the input tax) and not to taxable persons such as "repayment traders" (taxable persons whose position is the inverse of that of payment traders), in so far as those taxable persons have marketed similar goods. It will be for the national court to determine whether that is the position in the present case. Furthermore, the general principle of equal treatment, the infringement of which may be established, in matters relating to tax, by discrimination affecting traders who are not necessarily in competition with each other but are nevertheless in a similar situation in other respects, precludes discrimination between "payment traders" and "repayment traders", which is not objectively justified.' This principle was 'not affected where there is evidence that a trader who has been refused repayment of value added tax which was wrongly levied has not suffered any financial loss or disadvantage'. It was for the national court 'to draw any conclusions with respect to the past from the infringement of the principle of equal treatment' in accordance with 'the principle of equal treatment and the principle that it must ensure that the remedies which it grants are not contrary to Community law'. *Marks & Spencer plc v C & E Commrs (No 5),* ECJ Case C-309/06; [2008] STC 1408. (*Note.* Following the ECJ decision, the HL formally allowed the company's appeal—[2009] STC 452; [2009] UKHL 8; [2009] 1 All ER 939.)

Retrospective shortening of time limit

[22.57] In an Italian case, the ECJ held that 'Community law precludes the retroactive application of a time-limit that is shorter and, as the case may be, more restrictive for the claimant than the period for initiating proceedings that was previously applicable to claims for the recovery of national taxes contrary to Community law where no adequate transitional period is provided during which claims relating to sums paid before the entry into force of the legislation introducing the new time-limit may still be brought within the old period. Where a limitation period of five years is replaced with a time-limit of three years, a transitional period of 90 days must be regarded as insufficient and six months must be regarded as the minimum period required to ensure that the exercise of rights of recovery is not rendered excessively difficult.' *Grundig Italiana SpA v Ministero delle Finanze,* ECJ Case C-255/00; [2003] All ER (EC) 176.

The principle of 'abuse'

ECJ decisions

[22.58] In a German case, an insolvent company assigned certain claims to its director, who used the assignment to obtained export refunds which were fraudulent. The ECJ held that the assignment of the claims was 'abusive'. *DEKA Getreideprodukte GmbH & Co KG iL v EEC*, ECJ Case C-250/78; [1983] ECR 421.

[22.59] A German company had obtained refunds on the basis that it had exported certain goods to a Swiss company. However, the German authorities subsequently discovered that the goods had been transported back to Germany by the same means of transport. The German authorities demanded repayment of the sums which had been refunded. The company appealed, and the case was referred to the ECJ, which held that 'a Community exporter can forfeit his right to payment of a non-differentiated export refund if (*a*) the product in respect of which the export refund was paid, and which is sold to a purchaser established in a non-member country, is, immediately after its release for home use in that non-member country, transported back to the Community under the external Community transit procedure and is there released for home use on payment of import duties, without any infringement being established and (*b*) that operation constitutes an abuse on the part of that Community exporter. A finding that there is an abuse presupposes an intention to obtain an advantage from the Community rules by creating artificially the conditions for obtaining it.' *Emsland-Stärke GmbH v Hauptzollamt Hamburg-Jonas*, ECJ Case C-110/99; [2001] All ER (D) 34 (Jan).

[22.60] A bank (H) wished to construct a number of 'call centres'. If it had arranged for this itself, most of the input tax would have been attributed to its exempt supplies and would have been irrecoverable. It therefore granted a leasehold interest in the relevant sites to an associated company (L), which was not a member of its VAT group. L then arranged for another associated company (C) to carry out the work. C engaged builders to undertake the construction. C reclaimed input tax on the amounts charged by the builders and charged output tax to L, which reclaimed these amounts as input tax. Customs rejected the claims and the tribunal referred the case to the ECJ for a ruling on whether the doctrine of 'abuse of rights' should 'operate to disallow the appellants their claims for recovery of or relief for input tax arising from the implementation of the relevant transactions'. Advocate-General Poiares Maduro observed that 'a person who relies upon the literal meaning of a Community law provision to claim a right that runs counter to its purposes does not deserve to have that right upheld. In such circumstances, the legal provision at issue must be interpreted, contrary to its literal meaning, as actually not conferring the right.' Tax law should not 'become a sort of legal "wild-west" in which virtually every sort of opportunistic behaviour has to be tolerated so long as it conforms with a strict formalistic interpretation of the relevant tax provisions and the legislature has not expressly taken measures to prevent such behaviour.' The ECJ held that 'the application of Community legislation cannot be extended to cover abusive practices by economic operators, that is to say transactions carried out not in the context of normal commercial operations, but solely for the purpose of wrongfully obtaining advantages provided for by Community law. That principle of prohibiting abusive practices also applies to the sphere of VAT.' It was 'for the national court to verify in accordance with the rules of evidence of national law, provided that the effectiveness of Community law is not undermined, whether action constituting such an abusive practice has taken place'. Accordingly, 'the *Sixth Directive* must be interpreted as precluding any right of a taxable person to deduct input VAT where the transactions from which that right derives constitute an abusive practice'. Transactions involved in an abusive practice 'must be redefined so as to re-establish the situation that would have prevailed in the absence of the transactions constituting that abusive practice. In that regard, the tax authorities are entitled to demand, with retroactive effect, repayment of the amounts deducted in relation to each transaction whenever they find that the right to deduct has been exercised abusively.' *Halifax plc v C & E Commrs (and related appeals)*, ECJ Case C-255/02; [2006] STC 919; [2006] 2 WLR 90. (*Note*. For Customs' practice following this decision, see Business Brief 2/2006, issued on 27 February 2006. The companies subsequently withdrew their appeals: see HMRC Brief 30/2007, issued on 28 March 2007.)

[22.61] A company (W) purchased some assets, which it leased to another company (S), which in turn leased them to two companies (CM and CA) which were associated with W but were part of a separate VAT group making exempt supplies of insurance. W reclaimed input tax on the purchase of the assets. HMRC formed the opinion that the transactions were an 'abuse', and issued assessments to recover some of the input tax which W had reclaimed. The tribunal allowed W's appeal, holding that nothing in the *Sixth Directive* precluded a trader from leasing an asset to be used for exempt activities, thus spreading the burden of irrecoverable input tax. The Ch D upheld this decision but the CA referred the case to the ECJ for a ruling on whether the adoption of an asset leasing structure gave rise to a 'tax advantage' within the Halifax principle, whether this was an 'abusive practice' within the Halifax principle, and if it was an 'abusive practice', what should be the appropriate redefinition. The ECJ held that a 'tax advantage accruing from an undertaking's recourse to asset leasing transactions, such as those at issue in the main proceedings, instead of the outright purchase of those assets' did not contravene the *Sixth Directive* 'provided that the contractual terms of those transactions, particularly those concerned with setting the level of rentals, correspond to arm's length terms and that the involvement of an intermediate third party company in those transactions is not such as to preclude the application of those provisions, a matter which it is for the national court to determine. The fact that the undertaking does not engage in leasing transactions in the context of its normal commercial operations is irrelevant in that regard. If certain contractual terms of the leasing transactions at issue in the main proceedings, and/or the intervention of an intermediate third party company in those transactions, constituted an abusive practice, those transactions must be redefined so as to re-establish the situation that would have prevailed in the absence of the elements of those contractual terms which were abusive and/or in the absence of the intervention of that company.' *HMRC v Weald Leasing Ltd*, ECJ Case C-103/09; [2011] STC 596.

[22.62] The Italian tax authorities issued a substantial assessment, and imposed penalties, on the basis that certain leasing transactions involving associated companies constituted an 'abuse', in that 'the consideration paid by the customer for the leasing arrangement had been artificially divided to reduce the taxable amount, as the role of lessor was split'. The case was referred to the ECJ for a ruling on whether there was 'an abuse of rights (or of legal form), with the consequent loss of Community own revenue accruing from value added tax, where contracts for leasing arrangements, financing, insurance and intermediation contracts are concluded separately with the effect that only the consideration paid in respect of the grant of the right to use the goods is subject to VAT, whereas a single contract of leasing in accordance with the practice and interpretation of national case-law would include the financing and would therefore make the whole of the consideration subject to VAT'. The ECJ held that 'there can be a finding of an abusive practice when the accrual of a tax advantage constitutes the principal aim of the transaction or transactions at issue' and that 'when a transaction involves the supply of a number of services, the question arises whether it should be considered to be a single transaction or as several individual and independent supplies of services requiring separate assessment.' It was for the national court to determine whether 'the evidence put before the court discloses the characteristics of a single transaction'. The court could 'take into account that the anticipated result is the accrual of a tax advantage linked to the exemption' and that 'that result would appear to be contrary to the objective of *Article 11A1* of the *Sixth Directive*, namely the taxation of everything which constitutes consideration received or to be received from the customer'. *Ministero dell'Economia e delle Finanze v Part Service Srl*, ECJ Case C-425/06; [2008] STC 3132. (*Note.* Following this decision, the Italian Supreme Court reheard the appeal and held in October 2008 that the transactions at issue were abusive and that their principal aim was to seek a tax advantage.)

[22.63] In a Slovakian case, a company (T) reclaimed a substantial amount of input tax in respect of the purported purchase of a 50% co-ownership share in a patent, which had not yet been registered, from an associated company (V). V subsequently went into administration without accounting for output tax on the transaction. The tax authority rejected the claim, considering that the transaction was an 'abusive practice'. T appealed, and the case was referred to the ECJ, which held that 'a taxpayer may, in principle, claim a right of deduction of VAT paid or payable for the supply of a service, carried out for consideration, where the applicable national law permits the assignment of a share of the co-ownership of an invention which confers rights relating to the invention'. It was for the national court 'to establish, taking into account all the factual circumstances characterising the supply of the service in the case in the main proceedings, whether or not there has been an abuse of rights with regard to the right of deduction of input VAT'. *Tanoarch sro v Daňové riaditeľstvo Slovenskej republiky*, ECJ Case C-504/10; 27 October 2011 unreported.

[22.64] See also *HMRC v RBS Deutschland Holdings GmbH*, **22.418** below, and *Amministrazione dell'Economia e delle Finanze v Fallimento Olimpiclub Srl*, **22.555** below

UK court and tribunal decisions

[22.65] A group of companies engaged in a circular series of transactions, devised by a large accountancy firm, with the aim of enabling it to obtain full input tax credit on its purchase of motor cars, while only accounting for output tax on its profit margin. Under the scheme, a Republic of Ireland company (B) applied for refunds of tax charged to it by its UK parent company. Customs rejected the claims and B appealed. The tribunal dismissed the appeal, holding that the applications had been an 'abuse of rights', applying the ECJ decision in *Emsland-Stärke GmbH v Hauptzollamt Hamburg-Jonas*, **22.59** above, since there was 'an intention to obtain an advantage from the Community rules by creating artificially the conditions for obtaining it'. *Blackqueen Ltd*, LON/00/1178 (VTD 17680). (*Note.* The scheme would no longer be effective—see now *VATA 1994, Sch 3A*, inserted by *FA 2000, s 136* with effect from 20 March 2000.)

[22.66] The ECJ decision in *Emsland-Stärke GmbH v Hauptzollamt Hamburg-Jonas*, **22.59** above, was also applied in *Kingfisher plc (No 2)*, **67.164** VALUATION.

[22.67] A group of companies which carried on a banking business implemented a scheme, designed by a large accountancy firm, intended to enable it to recover input tax on the construction of office accommodation. A newly-acquired subsidiary company (D) arranged for the construction and submitted a VAT return claiming a repayment of almost £8,000,000. Customs rejected the claim on the basis that some of the transactions (including the grant of two 'car parking' licences for a small consideration) were 'an artificial device of no true economic substance' and should be disregarded for VAT. D appealed. The tribunal reviewed the evidence in detail and found that 'the two parking agreements had no real purpose other than the creation, or in reality purported creation, of taxable supplies and with them tax points'. Furthermore, the relevant 'building agreement' between D and another group company (C) had no purpose 'beyond the desire to create a large input tax claim in (D's) hands'. The creation of separate freehold and leasehold titles, both held by D, to the land in question also had no purpose 'other than that it was necessary for the tax-saving scheme' and 'was a device with no true economic purpose'. The involvement of C and D in the transactions 'had no economic purpose but was a pure tax avoidance device'. The tribunal concluded that some of the transactions which were entered into 'had no purpose other than the avoidance of tax, and were entered into for no other reason'. *Capital One Developments Ltd (No 2)*, MAN/01/624 (VTD 18642). (*Note.* For a preliminary issue in this case, see **36.651** INPUT TAX.)

[22.68] In a Scottish case, two associated companies, which were not in the same VAT group, reclaimed input tax on certain transactions relating to the construction of a new building. Customs rejected the claim on the basis that the transactions had been carried out for tax avoidance purposes and did not constitute supplies for VAT purposes. The companies involved in the transactions appealed, contending that the transactions could not be disregarded, because although they had been partly carried out for the purpose of mitigating the companies' tax liabilities, there were also commercial reasons for the transactions. The tribunal accepted this contention and allowed the appeals, finding that the series of transactions 'was not solely directed to tax avoidance' but 'did have an independent business purpose'. Accordingly, the principles laid down in *Emsland-Stärke GmbH v Hauptzollamt Hamburg-Jonas*, 22.59 above, did not apply. *RBS Property Developments; Royal Bank of Scotland Group plc (No 5)*, EDN/01/30 (VTD 17789). (*Note*. See now *VATA 1994, s 96(10B)*, introduced by *FA 2003, s 20*.)

[22.69] A UK company (NG) purchased Japanese cars from a French company (NE), which had obtained them from the Japanese manufacturer (NM). It stored the cars in a warehouse owned by an associated company (NK). NG had to account for customs duty and import VAT (under *Article 11B1* of the *EC Sixth Directive*) on 'the price actually paid or payable for the goods when sold for export to the customs territory of the Community'. It reclaimed this VAT when it sold the cars in the UK, and accounted for output tax on its sales. It subsequently began to operate a scheme under which it purported to sell the cars to UK customers while they were being transported by sea to the UK. It failed to account for VAT on these sales. HMRC issued a ruling that import VAT and customs duty was chargeable on the price actually paid by the UK customers, rather than the price at which NE had purchased the cars from NM. They issued post-clearance demands to NG and NK, which appealed. The tribunal reviewed the evidence in detail and held that the scheme was ineffective on the grounds that the companies had failed to show that the sales to the final purchasers had taken place before the cars had reached EC territory. The tribunal also held that the scheme was an 'abuse', applying the principles laid down in *Emsland-Stärke GmbH v Hauptzollamt Hamburg-Jonas*, 22.59 above. The only purpose of the scheme was to secure a tax advantage. The tribunal observed that it was 'impossible to accept that any of the customers in this case would conceivably have entered into an arrangement under which, for no personal advantage, they would buy a car at sea and make their own arrangements for its offloading from the ship, importation, registration, taxation and preparation for delivery. They each wanted a delivered car . . . The invoices from (NG) to the customers which were produced for the purpose of the scheme are consistent only with that conclusion: they show a single price for the car, with additions only for the road fund licence and first registration fee. There is no mention at all of VAT, customs duty, transport costs or (NG's) services in effecting the importation.' *Nissan Motor Manufacturing (UK) Ltd*, [2007] VATDR 1 (C236).

[22.70] A limited company (B) operated a school, which made exempt supplies of educational services. It had a wholly-owned subsidiary company (L), which made taxable supplies of clothing and books from a shop at the school. It had also established a charitable trust (T) for fund-raising purposes. B wished to arrange for the construction of a new study centre. In an attempt to gain relief for the relevant input tax, it arranged for L to purchase the relevant land from B, and to enter into the relevant building contracts. L subsequently sold the completed study centre to T, which leased it to B. Both L and T reclaimed input tax on the relevant transactions. Customs rejected the claims on the grounds that the transactions constituted an 'abuse', applying the principles laid down in *Halifax plc v C & E Commrs*, 22.60 above. L and T appealed. The tribunal reviewed the evidence in detail and dismissed the appeals, observing that as in *Halifax*, 'once all the scheme transactions had been worked through, the exempt person whose potential irrecoverable VAT initially triggered the arrangements and who originally owned the land ended up occupying the land and the buildings as tenant under a lease granted by a cooperative counterparty'. The tribunal also held that the lease by T to B 'was not an economic activity', applying the principles laid down in *C & E Commrs v Yarburgh Children's Trust*, **15.91** CONSTRUCTION OF BUILDINGS, ETC. *Lime Avenue Sales & Services Ltd; Benenden School Trust*, [2007] VATDR 55 (VTD 20140).

[22.71] A group of companies instituted a complex scheme which was intended to allow the recovery of input tax charged on repair services made under insurance policies relating to vehicle breakdown ('MBI policies'). The scheme involved the use of two Gibraltar insurance companies, one of which (V) appointed a UK company (W) to handle claims and pay the repair bills. Customs rejected the repayment claims, considering firstly that the garages which provided the repair services were making their supplies to the insured customers, rather than to W, and additionally that the scheme was an 'abuse', within the principles laid down by the ECJ in *Halifax plc v C & E Commrs*, **22.60** above. The CA unanimously accepted this contention. Lord Neuberger of Abbotsbury held that fiscal neutrality required that an insurer who provided insurance services, which were exempt from VAT in the EU, could not recover input tax attributable to those services. Thus, in transactions in the context of 'normal commercial operations' of an insurer and a claims handler, such as that embodied in the arrangements which were replaced by the scheme, the input tax attributable to the cost of repairs and parts was not recoverable. He observed that 'the whole point' of the principle laid down in *Halifax* 'is that, although each step of the scheme in question works, the overall effect of the scheme is unacceptable'. On the evidence, the sole purpose of the scheme, and in particular the creation of the 'claims handling chain' so as to include V was 'to avoid, or at any rate to minimise, any net liability to VAT'. Accordingly the companies were not entitled to the repayments which they had claimed. *WHA Ltd v HMRC; Viscount Reinsurance Co Ltd v HMRC*, CA [2007] STC 1695; [2007] EWCA Civ 728. (*Note*. For another issue in this case, see **38.27** INSURANCE.

[22.72] An accountancy firm advised a group of companies to enter into a complex scheme with the intention of only accounting for VAT on its profit on 'demonstrator cars', rather than on their full sale price. Four associated 'dealership' companies sold various 'demonstrator cars' to three associated 'captive leasing companies' under leaseback arrangements. The 'captive leasing companies' assigned the benefit of the lease agreements and the underlying cars to a Jersey bank (S) in return for a substantial 45-day loan facility. A month after these transactions, another associated company (PD) entered into an agreement with S to acquire its car hire business. This was treated as a transfer of part of S's business as a going concern, and therefore as outside the scope of VAT. PD then sold the cars to arm's length customers under the second-hand margin scheme, only accounting for VAT on its profit margin. HMRC issued assessments on the basis that the scheme was an 'abuse', applying the principles in *Halifax plc v C & E Commrs*, **22.60** above. They also imposed misdeclaration penalties. The companies appealed. The tribunal reviewed the evidence in detail and allowed the appeals, observing that the accountancy firm 'seemed to think it was selling a means of reducing VAT on demonstrator cars which also involved the provision of third party finance'. However, the subjective aim of the accountancy firm was not conclusive. The main aim of the holding company's finance director was to ensure that its 'continued funding needs were met'. Viewed objectively, the principal aim of the transactions was 'the obtaining of finance', rather than 'an abusive VAT advantage'. *Pendragon plc v HMRC (and related appeals)*, FTT 2009, [2010] SFTD 1; [2009] UKFTT 192 (TC), TC00147. (*Note*. HMRC have appealed to the Upper Tribunal against this decision. The Upper Tribunal began hearing the appeal on 10 May 2011.)

[22.73] A company (AC) operated a fitness club which made supplies to its members. Initially it accounted for VAT on its supplies. However, in 1996 it arranged for the supplies to be made by a 'non-profit-making organisation' (AH) and ceased to account for VAT. In March 2000, following the changes to *VATA 1994, Sch 9, Group 10* made by the *VAT (Sport, Sports Competitions and Physical Education) Order 1999 (SI 1999/1994)*, AC arranged for another company (AB) to take over the running of the club from AH. AC and AB entered into various agreements. Neither AC nor AB accounted for tax. Subsequently Customs issued assessments on AB. AB did not pay the tax charged, and subsequently went into liquidation. Customs also issued a ruling that, notwithstanding the interposition of AB, AC was making taxable supplies to the members of the fitness club. The Ch D upheld this ruling (reversing the tribunal decision). Roth J held that the scheme was an 'abuse', applying the principles laid down by the ECJ in *Halifax plc v C & E Commrs*, **22.60** above. He observed that the scheme 'was designed to secure for (AC) the net proceeds of the supplies by the Club free from liability to VAT. That was to be done through establishing a new company to operate the Club that would make the supplies as a non-profit making organisation without attracting VAT, and pay over all the benefit derived from those supplies to (AC) by way of a licence fee under a Turnover Licence which similarly did not attract VAT. This combination of inter-related elements was essential to the scheme. And the latter element was necessary not in order to remove (AB's) capacity to make a profit, since (AB) could have used all the net proceeds for the development of the Club facilities without losing its non-profit making status, but so as to pass the profit over to (AC) without VAT being incurred'. On the evidence, 'the scheme resulted in (AC) achieving a real benefit' which was 'properly to be regarded as a tax advantage'. Roth J also upheld HMRC's redefinition of the transactions in question, ie that the supplies should be treated as having been made by AC. He held that 'the redefinition under the Halifax principle is not designed to create a situation which can be sustained in practice. It is a purely notional device, for the purpose of assessment to tax, that may inevitably involve ignoring the terms of existing contracts.' The essential aim of the scheme was the avoidance of VAT, and 'a permissible view of what would have prevailed in the absence of those transactions is that (AB) would never have been interposed in the supply at all. The Club would have been operated by (AC), as it had been before the scheme was introduced.' *HMRC v The Atrium Club Ltd*, Ch D [2010] STC 1493; [2010] EWHC 970 (Ch).

[22.74] A financial adviser (N), who was registered for VAT, was the controlling shareholder of a Jersey company (AC), which provided loan broking services in the UK. HMRC issued an assessment on N, charging VAT of more than £10,000,000, on the basis that he should be treated as supplying the loan broking services and was liable to a 'reverse charge' under *VATA 1994, s 8(1)* in respect of advertising services supplied by another Jersey company (W). N appealed. The tribunal allowed his appeal, finding that N had established the 'loan broking operation' in Jersey rather than the UK in order to 'avoid the irrecoverable VAT on advertising costs'. However this finding did not entitle HMRC to treat N, rather than AC, as the supplier of the loan broking services or as the recipient of the advertising services. The tribunal also held that the transactions did not constitute an 'abuse'. The tribunal distinguished *WHA Ltd v HMRC*, **22.71** above (which HMRC had cited as an authority), observing that in that case 'there was a recovery of input tax whereas in this case no input tax is incurred because the supplies of advertising services were made in Jersey'. It was not 'permissible simply to compare what has been done with what could have been done' or to 'compare a structure that a trader, or group of traders, might have adopted in the past with the current structure, and to conclude that, if the current structure is more favourable for VAT purposes than the former, the current structure is in consequence contrary to the purposes of the VAT legislation'. Since the UK VAT legislation 'itself provides for the consequences of business being carried on through an establishment in a third country', it followed that 'something more than such mere establishment must be found if elements of the scheme are to be regarded as contrary to the purposes of the VAT legislation'. *P Newey (t/a Ocean Finance) v HMRC*, [2010] SFTD 836; [2010] UKFTT 183 (TC), TC00487. (*Note*. HMRC have appealed to the Upper Tribunal against this decision.)

[22.75] A company (L) owned a site which had planning permission for the construction of up to 575 residential homes subject to the condition that these homes should not be occupied as a principal place of residence. An associated company (C) provided construction services. L sold plots of land on the site under agreements whereby C agreed to build a holiday home on the plot. C did not account for tax on its supplies, treating them as zero-rated. HMRC issued assessments on both L and C, on the basis that in reality each transaction was a single supply of the grant of a major interest in leasehold holiday accommodation, which was chargeable to VAT at the standard rate. L and C appealed. The First-Tier Tribunal dismissed the appeals, holding that L and C had engaged in an 'abusive practice' which should be redefined according to the principles laid down by the ECJ in *Halifax plc*, **22.60** above, as a single supply of a holiday home from L to the customer. However the Upper Tribunal allowed the companies' appeals against this decision, observing that 'a supply of land by a landowner and a supply of construction services by an independent trader are separate supplies to be taxed as such', and holding that there were genuine commercial reasons for L and C to treat their supplies as separate. *Lower Mill Estate Ltd v HMRC (and related appeal)*, UT [2011] STC 636. (*Note*. For a preliminary issue in this case, see **2.346** APPEALS.)

[22.76] See also *Redcats (Brands) Ltd*, **5.33** BOOKS, ETC.

Method of redefinition of 'abusive' transactions

[22.77] A college of education entered into a scheme involving a wholly-owned subsidiary company (M), intended to secure the recovery of input tax on the construction and refurbishment of some buildings at its campus. HMRC considered that the scheme was an 'abuse', applying the principles laid down in *Halifax plc v C & E Commrs*, **22.60** above, and issued assessments to recover the input tax. The college and M subsequently accepted that the scheme had been an 'abuse', but proceeded with their appeal against the assessments, contending that the 'redefinition' of the relevant transactions should include credit for output tax which M had accounted for in the course of the transactions. HMRC issued a ruling that, because M had not made a claim under *VATA 1994, s 80* within the statutory time limit, it was not entitled to credit for the output tax. The First-Tier Tribunal rejected HMRC's contention on this point, holding that the application of the *Halifax* principles required that 'a taxing authority redefining an abusive arrangement must, when recovering tax for which credit has been improperly obtained, subtract from it the tax overpaid, and must not impose a penalty'. The Upper Tribunal upheld this decision. Norris J held that 'the *Halifax* principle is a rule of construction which (once an abusive transaction is identified) requires the literal text of the relevant provisions to be construed in a way that prevents the right of deduction being used artificially. The consequence of applying the principle is that the transaction may be redefined to secure that the correct tax is paid by the correct person. In that connection HMRC may assess the taxpayer in the sums correctly due (that is to repayment of the sums abusively deducted, but having subtracted therefrom any output tax for which the taxable person is not liable on the redefinition).' On the facts here, *VATA 1994, s 80* did not apply and M had not 'lost its right to have the tax it has in fact paid set against the tax now demanded from it'. *HMRC v Moorbury Ltd*, UT [2010] STC 2715.

EC Sixth VAT Directive (77/388/EEC)

NOTE

On 28 November 2006 the EU Council of Ministers agreed a revised *Directive 2006/112/EC*. This came into force on 1 January 2007. It replaces the previous *EC First VAT Directive* and the *EC Sixth VAT Directive* (*Directive 77/388/EEC*). HMRC have explained that 'the new Directive does not change EC or UK VAT law. The only impact on businesses is that they will now have an EC VAT law text that they should find easier to access and simpler to understand. The material has been extensively reorganised to provide a much simpler and clearer structure with additional headings and sub-headings and a significant reduction in confusing cross-references. As it will take some time to amend references to the current *Sixth VAT Directive* in UK VAT law and Public Notices, businesses will need to familiarise themselves with the provisions of the new principal VAT Directive. To help with this task, at Annex XII of the new Directive, there is a correlation table that lists all the *Sixth VAT Directive* articles and their equivalent in the new Directive. On this issue it should be noted that any references made in UK law to the repealed First and Sixth VAT Directives must be construed as references to the new Directive and thus read in accordance with the correlation table.' See Business Brief 22/06, issued on 11 December 2006. The cases in this section were decided on the basis of the wording of the *Sixth VAT Directive* (*Directive 77/388/EEC*).

Scope of the Directive (Article 2)

Supplies of goods or services (Article 2(1))

[22.78] A Dutch co-operative operated a cold store for the benefit of its members, who paid a storage charge, fixed annually. In 1975 and 1976 it levied no charges on its members. The Dutch authorities raised a VAT assessment on the basis that the members had received a benefit as a consequence of the failure to make a charge. The ECJ held that there was no consideration for the supply of the storage services. Consideration for a supply for VAT purposes must have a direct link with the services supplied and must be capable of being expressed in money. It followed that a provision of services for which no definite subjective consideration was received did not constitute a provision of services 'against payment'. *Staatssecretaris van Financiën v Cooperatieve Vereniging 'Cooperatieve Aardappelenbewaarplaats GA'*, ECJ Case 154/80; [1981] ECR 445; [1981] 3 CMLR 337. (*Note*. The case was argued on the provisions of the *EC Second Directive*, the relevant provisions of which were very similar to those in *Article 2* of the *EC Sixth Directive*, except that, in the English version of the *Directive*, the words 'against payment' were replaced by the words 'for consideration'. The wording of the French, German, Italian and Dutch versions remained unchanged.)

[22.79] The Hong Kong Trade Development Council was formed to promote trade between Hong Kong and other countries by providing free information and advice about the country. It was financed partly by a grant from the Hong Kong government, and partly from a levy on products imported into and exported from Hong Kong. The ECJ was asked to rule on whether it could be regarded as a taxable person. The ECJ held that the provision of services for no consideration could not be subject to VAT and, where no other activity was involved, the provider of the services could not be regarded as a taxable person, since 'services provided free of charge are different in character from taxable transactions which, within the framework of the value added tax system, presuppose the stipulation of a price or consideration'. *Staatssecretaris van Financiën v Hong Kong Trade Development Council*, ECJ Case 89/81; [1982] ECR 1277; [1983] 1 CMLR 73.

[22.80] The Apple & Pear Development Council was established in 1966 by statutory instrument. Commercial growers had to register with it and pay a compulsory annual charge, based on the area of their land. Initially Customs accepted that its activities were business activities, on which it was entitled to reclaim input tax, and that its charges to growers were outside the scope of VAT. However, in 1981 Customs issued a ruling that its activities did not constitute a business and that it was not entitled to reclaim input tax. The Council appealed, and the HL referred the case to the ECJ. The ECJ held that, for a supply of services to be for consideration within *Article 2(1)* of the *EC Sixth Directive*, there must be a direct link between the service provided and the consideration received. On the evidence, there was no relationship between the level of the benefits which individual growers obtained from the Council's services and the amount of the mandatory charges which they were obliged to pay. The compulsory annual charges did not constitute 'consideration' and the Council was not making supplies of services for consideration. *Apple & Pear Development Council v C & E Commrs*, ECJ Case 102/86; [1988] STC 221; [1988] ECR 1443; [1988] 2 CMLR 394; [1988] 2 All ER 922.

[22.81] In two Netherlands cases, the ECJ held that the illegal sale of drugs such as amphetamines or hashish was not an 'economic activity' and thus not a supply for VAT purposes. While the principle of fiscal neutrality precluded 'a generalised differentiation between lawful and unlawful transactions', supplies of narcotic drugs were outside the scope of this principle, since 'because of their very nature, they are subject to a total prohibition on their being put into circulation in all the Member States, with the exception of strictly controlled economic channels for use for medical and scientific purposes'. *Mol v Inspecteur der Invoerrechten en Accijnzen*, ECJ Case 269/86; [1988] ECR 3627; [1989] BVC 205; [1989] 3 CMLR 729; *Vereniging Happy Family Rustenburgerstrat v Inspecteur der Omzetbelasting*, ECJ Case 289/86; [1988] ECR 3655; [1989] 3 CMLR 743. (*Note.* These decisions were distinguished in the subsequent cases of *R v Goodwin & Unstead*, 22.82 below; *Staatssecretaris van Financiën v Coffeeshop 'Siberië' vof*, 22.83 below, and *Lange v Finanzamt Fürstenfeldbruck*, 22.387 below.)

[22.82] Two individuals were convicted for selling counterfeit perfume, contrary to *VATA 1994, s 72*. They appealed to the CA, contending that VAT was not chargeable on counterfeit goods. The CA directed that the case should be referred to the ECJ, which held that the supply of counterfeit perfumes was within *Article 2*, and VAT was chargeable accordingly. The principle of fiscal neutrality 'precludes a generalised differentiation between lawful and unlawful transactions, except where, because of the special characteristics of certain products, all competition between a lawful economic sector and an unlawful sector is precluded'. The decisions in *Mol v Inspecteur der Invoerrechten en Accijnzen* and *Vereniging Happy Family Rustenburgerstrat v Inspecteur der Omzetbelasting*, 22.81 above, were distinguished, on the grounds that they concerned goods 'which, because of their special characteristics, may not be placed on the market or incorporated into economic channels'. The prohibition on counterfeit products such as perfumes, however, stemmed from the fact that they infringed intellectual property rights and was 'conditional, not absolute as in the case of narcotics or counterfeit currency'. Furthermore, there was scope for competition between counterfeit perfumes and perfumes which were traded lawfully, so that counterfeit perfumes could not 'be regarded as *extra commercium*'. *R v Goodwin & Unstead*, ECJ Case C-3/97; [1998] STC 699; [1998] All ER (EC) 500.

[22.83] In a Netherlands case, the proprietor of a coffee shop hired a table to a dealer in cannabis. The proprietor did not account for output tax on the rent received from the dealer. The Netherlands authorities demanded payment, and the proprietor appealed, contending that since the sale of cannabis was illegal under Netherlands law, the rent should be treated as outside the scope of VAT. The ECJ rejected the proprietor's contentions and held that renting out a space for the sale of narcotic drugs was within the scope of the *EC Sixth Directive*. The ECJ observed that 'renting out a place intended for commercial activities is, in principle, an economic activity and therefore falls within the scope of the *Sixth Directive*. The fact that the activities pursued there constitute a criminal offence, which may make the renting unlawful, does not alter the economic character of the renting and does not prevent competition in the sector, including that between lawful and unlawful activities. Not to charge VAT thereon would undermine the fiscal neutrality of the VAT scheme.' *Staatssecretaris van Financiën v Coffeeshop 'Siberië' vof*, ECJ Case C-158/98; [1999] STC 742; [1999] All ER (EC) 560.

[22.84] In a Netherlands case, an individual who played a barrel organ on the public highway, and invited passers-by to leave donations in a tin, was assessed to output tax on his takings. He appealed, contending that his takings were outside the scope of VAT. The ECJ held that the playing of music on the public highway for which no payment was stipulated did not constitute a 'supply of . . . services effected for consideration', and VAT was not chargeable. There was no agreement between the parties, and there was also 'no necessary link between the musical service and the payments to which it gives rise'. *Tolsma v Inspecteur der Omzetbelasting Leeuwarden*, ECJ Case C-16/93; [1994] STC 509; [1994] 1 ECR 743; [1994] 2 CMLR 908.

[22.85] A company which organised 'spot-the-ball' competitions appealed against an assessment, contending that the competitions were not taxable supplies since they were not governed by a legally binding contract. The ECJ rejected the company's contentions, holding that 'a supply of services which is effected for consideration but is not based on enforceable obligations, because it has been agreed that the provider is bound in honour only to provide the services, constitutes a transaction subject to value added tax'. *Town & County Factors Ltd v C & E Commrs*, ECJ Case C-498/99; [2002] STC 1263; [2003] All ER (EC) 33. (*Note*. For another issue in this case, see **22.240** below.)

Deposits

[22.86] In a French case, the ECJ held that 'a sum paid as a deposit, in the context of a contract relating to the supply of hotel services which is subject to value added tax, is to be regarded, where the client exercises the cancellation option available to him and that sum is retained by the hotelier, as a fixed cancellation charge paid as compensation for the loss suffered as a result of client default and which has no direct connection with the supply of any service for consideration and, as such, is not subject to that tax'. *Société Thermale d'Eugénie-les-Bains v Ministère de l'Économie, des Finances et de l'Industrie*, ECJ Case C-277/05; [2008] STC 2470.

Supplies of customised software

[22.87] See *Levob Verzekeringen BV v Staatssecretaris van Financien*, **22.176** below.

Theft of goods

[22.88] In a Belgian case, a quantity of cigarettes was stolen from a warehouse. The tax authorities demanded payment of the VAT (and excise duty) from the company (N) which owned the warehouse. N paid this under protest. However, N, and the company which had owned the cigarettes (B), then took court proceedings seeking reimbursement of the VAT. The case was referred to the ECJ, which held that 'the theft of goods does not constitute a supply of goods for consideration within the meaning of *Article 2* of the *Sixth*

Directive' and therefore 'cannot as such be subject to value added tax'. *British American Tobacco International Ltd v Belgian State; Newman Shipping & Agency Co NV v Belgian State*, ECJ Case C-435/03; [2006] STC 158.

Foreign exchange credit transactions

[22.89] A bank reclaimed input tax in respect of foreign exchange credit transactions. (The transactions concerned credits opened in foreign currency, and did not involve the physical exchange of banknotes.) Customs rejected the claim on the basis that the transactions did not constitute supplies for the purposes of VAT. The bank appealed, and the QB referred the case to the ECJ. The ECJ upheld the tribunal decision that the transactions were supplies of services for consideration, observing that 'to hold that currency transactions are taxable only when effected in return for payment of a commission or specific fees' would allow a trader 'to avoid taxation if he sought to be remunerated for his services by providing for a spread between the proposed transaction rates rather than by charging such sums'. (The ECJ also held that, where no fees or commission were calculated with regard to certain specific transactions, the taxable amount was 'the net result of the transactions of the supplier of the services over a given period of time'.) *C & E Commrs v First National Bank of Chicago*, ECJ Case C-172/96; [1998] STC 850; [1998] All ER (EC) 744; [1999] 2 WLR 230. (*Note.* For Customs' practice following this decision, see Business Brief 16/98, issued on 28 July 1998, and Business Brief 24/98, issued on 2 December 1998.)

Admission of new partner to partnership

[22.90] A German partnership admitted a new partner, who made a payment of 38,000,000 marks to the partnership. The partnership reclaimed input tax on legal fees relating to this. The tax authority rejected the claim on the basis that the fees related to an exempt supply of services. The partnership appealed and the case was referred to the ECJ, which ruled that 'a partnership which admits a partner, in consideration of payment of a contribution in cash, does not effect towards that person a supply of services for consideration'. *KapHag Renditefonds 35 Spreecenter Berlin-Hellersdorf 3 Tanche GbR v Finanzamt Charlottenburg*, ECJ Case C-442/01; [2005] STC 1500. (*Note.* For Customs' practice following this decision, see Business Brief 21/2004, issued on 10 August 2004, and Business Brief 30/2004, issued on 22 November 2004.)

Issue of shares by limited company

[22.91] An Austrian company made an issue of shares. It reclaimed input tax on the related costs. The tax authority rejected the claim, on the grounds that the issue of shares was an exempt supply. The company appealed, contending that the issue of shares was not a supply and that the related input tax should be treated as part of its general overheads. The case was referred to the ECJ, which held that 'a new share issue does not constitute a transaction falling within the scope of *Article 2(1)*', and that a taxable person could deduct the input tax 'for the various supplies acquired by him in connection with a share issue, provided that all the transactions undertaken by the taxable person in the context of his economic activity constitute taxed transactions'. *Kretztechnik AG v Finanzamt Linz*, ECJ Case C-465/03; [2005] STC 1118; [2005] 1

WLR 3755. (*Note*. For HMRC's practice following this decision, see Business Brief 12/2005, issued on 15 June 2005, and Business Brief 23/2005, issued on 23 November 2005.)

Supplies of vouchers to employees

[22.92] A pharmaceutical company gave its employees face-value vouchers as part of their remuneration. HMRC issued a ruling that this was a supply of services for consideration, which was subject to VAT. The company appealed, contending that it was not making any supply of services but that it should be allowed an input tax deduction on the costs of purchasing and providing the vouchers. The tribunal referred the case to the ECJ, which rejected the company's contentions, holding that *Article 2(1)* of the *Sixth Directive* 'must be interpreted as meaning that the provision of a retail voucher by a company, which acquired that voucher at a price including value added tax, to its employees in exchange for their giving up part of their cash remuneration constitutes a supply of services effected for consideration within the meaning of that provision'. *Astra Zeneca UK Ltd v HMRC*, ECJ Case C-40/09; [2010] STC 2298. (*Note*. For HMRC's practice following this decision, see HMRC Brief 28/11, issued on 28 July 2011.)

Sale of item partly used for private purposes

[22.93] In a German case, a hotelier sold a guesthouse, part of which he had used for private purposes rather than for business purposes. He was assessed on the whole of the proceeds, and appealed, contending that he should only be required to account for tax on the proportion of the proceeds which was attributable to the part of the guesthouse which he had used for business purposes. The case was referred to the ECJ, which ruled that where a taxable person sold property, part of which he had chosen to reserve for private use, the sale of that part was outside the scope of *Article 2(1)* of the *EC Sixth Directive*. *Finanzamt Ülzen v Armbrecht*, ECJ Case C-291/92; [1995] STC 997; [1995] 1 ECR 2775; [1995] All ER (EC) 882.

[22.94] In a German case, a trader purchased a car from a private individual and used it mainly for business purposes but partly for private purposes. He subsequently sold the car and the tax authority charged VAT. He appealed and the case was referred to the ECJ, which ruled that where a taxable person used a capital item for both business and private purposes, and had incorporated that item wholly into his business assets, the sale of that item was wholly subject to VAT. The fact that the item was purchased second-hand from a non-taxable person, and that the taxable person could not therefore reclaim input tax on its purchase, was irrelevant. The ECJ also observed that a taxable person who acquired a capital item for mixed purposes 'may retain it wholly within his private assets and thereby exclude it entirely' from the VAT system. *Bakcsi v Finanzamt Fürstenfeldbruck*, ECJ Case C-415/98; [2002] STC 802; [2002] 2 WLR 1188.

Purchase of portfolio of bad debts

[22.95] In a German case, the ECJ held that 'an operator who, at his own risk, purchases defaulted debts at a price below their face value does not effect a supply of services for consideration within the meaning of *Article 2(1)* and does not carry out an economic activity falling within the scope of that directive when the difference between the face value of those debts and their purchase price reflects the actual economic value of the debts at the time of their assignment'. *Finanzamt Essen Nord-Ost v GFKL Financial Services AG*, ECJ Case C-93/10; [2012] STC 79.

National legislation exempting works of art

[22.96] Finnish legislation provided that the sale by artists of works of art was not subject to VAT. The EC Commission applied to the ECJ for a ruling that this provision was a breach of *Article 2(1)* of the *EC Sixth Directive*. The ECJ granted the declaration, holding that the transfer of a work of art was a supply of goods and that, by maintaining legislation which exempted it, Finland had failed to fulfil its obligations under *Article 2*. *EC Commission v Finland*, ECJ Case C-169/00; [2004] STC 1232.

National legislation partly exempting works of art

[22.97] See *EC Commission v United Kingdom (No 5)*, **22.266** below.

Services of land registrars

[22.98] In Spain, VAT was not charged on services supplied to autonomous communities by land registrars acting as settlement agents in charge of settlement offices of mortgage districts. The EC Commission took proceedings against Spain, contending that this was a breach of *Article 2* of the *EC Sixth Directive*. The ECJ found in favour of the Commission, holding that the relevant services fell within *Article 2* and that Spain had failed to fulfil its obligations under the *Directive*. *EC Commission v Kingdom of Spain*, ECJ Case C-154/08; 12 November 2009 unreported.

Importations of goods (Article 2(2))

Article 2(2) of EC Sixth Directive—imports of goods from outside EC

[22.99] A German woman had imported and sold quantities of morphine, although this was illegal under German law. The German authorities charged VAT on the import and sale of the morphine. She appealed, contending that there was no VAT liability on the illegal import of narcotic drugs. The ECJ upheld this contention and allowed her appeal. *Einberger v Hauptzollamt Freiburg (No 2)*, ECJ Case 294/82; [1984] ECR 1177; [1985] 1 CMLR 765.

[22.100] In a Finnish case, the ECJ held that VAT was chargeable on sales of ethyl alcohol which had been smuggled into the EU. *Einberger v Hauptzollamt Freiburg (No 2)*, **22.99** above, was distinguished on the grounds that it dealt with 'products which may not be introduced into economic channels because of their intrinsic character of illegal goods. Ethyl alcohol, however, does not have that character'. An intrinsically lawful product such as ethyl alcohol 'may not be equated with a narcotic drug'. *Tullihallitus v Salumets & Others*, ECJ Case C-455/98; [2000] All ER (D) 891.

[22.101] In a German case, the ECJ ruled that the importation of counterfeit money was outside the scope of VAT. Advocate-General Jacobs observed that 'a line must be drawn between, on the one hand, transactions that lie so clearly outside the sphere of legitimate economic activity that, instead of being taxed, they can only be the subject of criminal prosecution, and, on the other hand, transactions which though unlawful must nonetheless be taxed, if only for ensuring in the name of fiscal neutrality, that the criminal is not treated more favourably than the legitimate trader'. *Witzemann v Hauptzollamt München-Mitte*, ECJ Case C-343/89; [1993] STC 108; [1991] 1 ECR 4477.

[22.102] The Spanish government exempted the import of armaments, ammunition and equipment for military use. The European Commission brought an action under what is now *Article 226EC* of the *EC Treaty*, seeking a declaration that Spain had failed to fulfil its obligations under the *Treaty*. The ECJ accepted this contention and granted the declaration. *EC Commission v Kingdom of Spain*, ECJ Case C-414/97; 16 September 1999 unreported.

Taxable persons (Article 4)

General (Article 4(1))

Preliminary expenditure

[22.103] In a Dutch case, a couple acquired a future title to two units which were intended to be used as showrooms and which were under construction. They gave notice that the showrooms would be let to traders and that they would opt for the supply to be taxable under the provisions of Dutch law. They applied for a refund of input tax incurred before the premises had been let. The Dutch authorities rejected the claim on the grounds that the couple had not, at that time, made any taxable supplies. The couple appealed, and the case was referred to the ECJ, which ruled that a person undertaking acts preparatory to the carrying on of an economic activity qualified as a 'taxable person' within *Article 4(1)* of the *EC Sixth Directive*, and that input tax was recoverable in such circumstances. The purpose of the system whereby input tax could be deducted was to relieve a trader entirely of the burden of VAT suffered in the course of his economic activities, which included preparatory acts such as the purchase of immovable property. *DA Rompelman & EA Rompelman-van-Deelen v Minister van Financiën*, ECJ Case 268/83; [1985] ECR 655; [1985] 3 CMLR 202.

[22.104] See also *Merseyside Cablevision Ltd*, 36.554 INPUT TAX.

'Post-cessation' expenditure

[22.105] In a Danish case, the ECJ held that *Article 4* of the *EC Sixth Directive* must 'be interpreted as meaning that a person who has ceased an economic activity but who, because the lease contains a non-termination clause, continues to pay the rent and charges on the premises used for that activity is to be regarded as a taxable person within the meaning of that article and is entitled to deduct the VAT on the amounts thus paid, provided that there is a direct and immediate link between the payments made and the commercial activity and that the absence of any fraudulent or abusive intent has been established'. The ECJ also held that it would be 'abusive or fraudulent' if a taxable person 'whilst relying on the right to deduct VAT in respect of the payment of rent and charges relating to the period after the cessation of the restaurant business, continued to use the premises previously used as a restaurant as premises for purely private purposes. If the tax authorities were to conclude that the right to deduct has been exercised fraudulently or abusively, they would be entitled to demand, with retrospective effect, repayment of the amounts deducted.' *I/S Fini H v Skatteministeriet*, ECJ Case C-32/03; [2005] STC 903. (*Note.* For a subsequent case in which this decision was distinguished, see *Royal Bank of Canada Trust Corporation Ltd*, **36.647** INPUT TAX.)

Holding company—whether a 'taxable person'

[22.106] In a Dutch case, a company (P) which acted as a holding company, and did not carry on any commercial or management activity, reclaimed input tax. The Dutch authorities issued an assessment to recover the tax, considering that since the company did not carry on any commercial activity, it was not a taxable person and could not reclaim any input tax. P appealed and the case was referred to the ECJ, which held that a holding company whose sole purpose was to hold shares in other undertakings, without any direct or indirect involvement in the management of those undertakings, was not a taxable person and had no right to deduct or reclaim input tax. *Polysar Investments Netherlands BV v Inspecteur der Invoerrechten en Accijnzen*, ECJ Case C-60/90; [1991] 1 ECR 3111; [1993] STC 222. (*Note.* For the Commissioners' practice following this decision, see their News Release 59/93, issued on 10 September 1993.)

'Open-ended investment company'—whether a 'taxable person'

[22.107] In a Belgian case, the ECJ held that 'open-ended investment companies' (SICAVs), which had as their sole object 'the collective investment in transferable securities of capital raised from the public', were 'taxable persons' within *Article 4(1)* of the *EC Sixth Directive*. The ECJ also held that where services referred to in *Article 9(2)(e)* were 'supplied to such SICAVs which are established in a Member State other than that of the supplier of the services, the place where those services are provided is the place where the SICAVs have established their business'. *Banque Bruxelles Lambert SA v Belgian State*, ECJ Case C-8/03; [2004] STC 1643.

Article 4(1) of Sixth Directive—whether activity carried on 'independently'

[22.108] A married couple operated a farming business in partnership. The husband owned a shed and let it to the partnership for an annual rent. The tax authority ruled that the letting was not to be regarded as an independent economic activity, so that the husband was not a taxable person within *Article 4(1)*. The case was referred to the ECJ, which held that the fact that the husband's economic activity was confined to letting an item of tangible property to the partnership of which he was a member was immaterial to the question of whether he was acting independently. Applying *Enkler v Finanzamt Homburg*, **22.114** below, the hiring out of intangible property with a view to obtaining income therefrom on a continuing basis was an 'economic activity' within *Article 4(2)*. Accordingly, where a person's sole economic activity consisted in the letting of an item of intangible property to a company or partnership of which he was a member, the letting was to be regarded as an independent activity within the meaning of *Article 4(1)* of the *Sixth Directive*. *Staatssecretaris van Financiën v Heerma*, ECJ Case C-23/98; [2001] STC 1437.

Economic activities (Article 4(2))

[22.109] In a Dutch case, an appellant had granted a company building rights over land in return for an annual payment. He then reclaimed input tax which he had suffered on the acquisition of the property. The Dutch court referred the case to the ECJ for a ruling on whether the grant of a right of user over property was within the definition of an 'economic activity' in *Article 4(2)* of the *EC Sixth Directive*. The ECJ held that the grant of building rights over immovable property, in the form of a grant of a right of user over the property for a specified period and in return for payment, was to be regarded as an economic activity. Accordingly the input tax was reclaimable by the appellant. *WM van Tiem v Staatssecretaris van Financiën*, ECJ Case C-186/89; [1990] 1 ECR 4363; [1993] STC 91.

[22.110] In a Belgian case, a company was established with the object of developing processes for turning sea and brackish water into drinking water. It reclaimed input tax on the costs of a profitability study, but went into liquidation without beginning to trade. The Belgian tax authority issued an assessment to recover the tax which the company had reclaimed. The liquidators of the company appealed, and the case was referred to the ECJ. The ECJ held that initial investment expenditure incurred for the purposes of a business could in principle be regarded as an economic activity within *Article 4(2)* of the *EC Sixth Directive*. However, *Article 4* did not preclude a tax authority from requiring objective evidence in support of a declared intention to commence economic activities which would give rise to taxable transactions. A taxable person only acquired that status definitively if he made such a declaration in good faith. In cases of fraud or abuse, a tax authority could claim repayment retrospectively on the ground that the deductions had been made on the basis of false declarations. Accordingly, the ECJ ruled that when a tax authority had accepted that a company which had declared an intention to begin an economic activity had the status of a taxable person, the commissioning of a profitability study could be regarded as an economic activity and the company's status as a taxable person could only be withdrawn 'in cases of fraud or abuse'. *Intercommunale voor Zeewaterontzilting (in liquidation) v Belgian State*, ECJ Case C-110/94; [1996] STC 569; [1996] 1 ECR 857.

[22.111] A company, which was registered for VAT, acted as the sole trustee of a charitable trust. In 1992 it sold a large number of shares in a public company, The shares in question had been obtained by the trust in 1986, in exchange for shares which had been bequeathed to the trust in 1936. The company reclaimed input tax in respect of expenses incurred in relation to the sale of such shares to people resident outside the EC. The Commissioners rejected the claim, on the grounds that the company's investment activities did not constitute a business. The company appealed, contending that its investment activities were carried out on such a large scale that they constituted an 'economic activity' within *Article 4(2)* of the *EC Sixth Directive*. The tribunal referred the case to the ECJ, which held that the exercise of the right of ownership could not by itself be regarded as an economic activity. Neither the scale of a sale of shares, nor the employment of consultancy undertakings in connection with it, could constitute criteria for distinguishing between the activities of a private investor, which were outside the scope of VAT, and those of a larger investor. The question of whether or not the sale of shares and securities was the predominant concern of the activity in the course of which the sales took place could not affect the classification of investment activity. Accordingly, the concept of economic activities, within *Article 4(2) of the EC Sixth Directive*, did not include an activity consisting in the purchase and sale of shares and other securities by a trustee in the course of the management of a charitable trust. *The Wellcome Trust Ltd v C & E Commrs*, ECJ Case C-155/94; [1996] STC 945; [1996] 1 ECR 3013; [1996] 2 CMLR 909; [1996] All ER (EC) 589.

[22.112] In a Netherlands case, a limited partnership held shares and bonds. It reclaimed input tax which it had incurred in connection with loan transactions. The Netherlands authority rejected the claim on the basis that the partnership was not carrying on any economic activity. The partnership appealed, and the case was referred to the ECJ, which ruled that the mere acquisition and holding of bonds and the receipt of income therefrom were not to be regarded as economic activities within *Article 4(2)* of the *EC Sixth Directive. Harnas & Helm CV v Staatssecretaris van Financiën*, ECJ Case C-80/95; [1997] STC 364; [1997] 1 ECR 745; [1997] 1 CMLR 649; [1997] All ER (EC) 267.

[22.113] In a French case, a holding company, with three subsidiaries, reclaimed input tax. The French authority rejected the claim on the basis that the company was not carrying on any economic activity. The company appealed, and the case was referred to the ECJ. The ECJ held that the management of subsidiary companies could qualify as an 'economic activity' if it was accompanied by activities such as the 'performance of administrative, financial, commercial or technical services'. Costs relating to the acquisition of shares in a subsidiary company could be treated as general overhead costs. The ECJ also held that the receipt of dividends was outside the scope of VAT. *Cibo Participations SA v Directeur régional des impôts du Nord-Pas-de-Calais*, ECJ Case C-16/00; [2002] STC 160.

[22.114] In a German case, a married woman (E) was employed by her husband who carried on business as a tax consultant. In 1984 she notified the tax authority that she was beginning a business of hiring out motor caravans. She purchased a caravan, reclaimed input tax and accounted for output tax, most of which represented payments from her husband. In 1986 she notified the tax authority that she intended to use the caravan for private purposes only. Subsequently the tax authority issued an assessment on the basis that E had never been acting as a trader. E appealed and the case was referred to the ECJ for rulings on the interpretation of *Article 4(2)* and *Article 11A1(c)* of the *EC Sixth Directive*. The ECJ held that the hiring out of tangible property was an 'economic activity' within *Article 4(2)* of the *Sixth Directive* if it was 'done for the purpose of obtaining income therefrom on a continuing basis'. The question of 'whether the hiring out of tangible property such as a motor caravan is carried on with a view to obtaining income on a continuing basis' was 'for the national court to evaluate in all the circumstances of the particular case'. With regard to the calculation of the taxable amount, *Article 11A1(c)* should be interpreted as meaning that the taxable amount in respect of transactions treated as supplies of services within *Article 6(2)(a)* of the *EC Sixth Directive* must include expenses which were incurred during a period in which the goods were at the disposal of the taxable person in such a way that he could use them at any time for non-business purposes, and the proportion of the total expenses to be included must be proportionate to the ratio between the total duration of actual use of the goods and the duration of actual use for non-business purposes. *Enkler v Finanzamt Homburg*, ECJ Case C-230/94; [1996] STC 1316; [1996] 1 ECR 4517; [1997] 1 CMLR 881.

[22.115] Three companies submitted VAT returns claiming substantial repayments, on the basis that they had purchased a quantity of central processing units (CPUs) from UK traders and had sold them to traders in other EU states. The Commissioners rejected the claims on the basis that the purchases formed part of a 'carousel missing trader fraud', designed to obtain a substantial repayment of sums which had never been paid as output tax. The tribunal dismissed the companies' appeals, holding that the companies were not entitled to the repayments which they had claimed, and observing that 'a circular series of transactions comprising the carousel fraud where the goods enter and leave the UK at the same price certainly does not look like an economic transaction'. The companies appealed to the Ch D, which directed that the case should be referred to the ECJ for a ruling on the interpretation of an 'economic activity' in *Article 4* of the *EC Sixth Directive*. Advocate-General Poiares Maduro observed that 'where an activity falls within the scope of the *Sixth Directive*, that does not mean that Member States lose their power to take action against it. In fact, *Article 21* of the *Sixth Directive* gives Member States the opportunity to introduce joint and several fiscal liability. A taxable person can accordingly be held accountable for the payment of VAT due by his co-contractor, if he knew or should have known of his co-contractor's fraudulent activities. Several Member States have adopted measures of that kind against carousel fraud.' Accordingly, 'transactions forming part of a circular supply chain in which a trader misappropriates the amounts paid to it as VAT instead of accounting for those amounts to the tax authorities do not on that account cease to constitute an economic activity within the meaning of *Article 4(2)* of the *Sixth Directive*.' The ECJ observed that 'the principle of fiscal neutrality prevents there being any general distinction as between lawful and unlawful transactions. Consequently, the mere fact that conduct amounts to an offence is not sufficient to justify exemption from VAT. That exemption applies only in specific situations where, owing to the special characteristics of certain products or certain services, any competition between a lawful economic sector and an unlawful sector is precluded.' The ECJ concluded that 'transactions such as those at issue in the main proceedings, which are not themselves vitiated by value added tax fraud', constituted supplies of goods or services, and were an 'economic activity', where they fulfilled 'the objective criteria on which the definitions of those terms are based, regardless of the intention of a trader other than the taxable person concerned involved in the same chain of supply and/or the possible fraudulent nature of another transaction in the chain, prior or subsequent to the transaction carried out by that taxable person, of which that taxable person had no knowledge and no means of knowledge. The right to deduct input value added tax of a taxable person who carries out such transactions cannot be affected by the fact that in the chain of supply of which those transactions form part another prior or subsequent transaction is vitiated by value added tax fraud, without that taxable person knowing or having any means of knowing.' *Optigen Ltd v C & E Commrs*, ECJ Case C-354/03; *Fulcrum Electronics Ltd v C & E Commrs*, ECJ Case C-355/03; *Bond House Systems Ltd v C & E Commrs*, ECJ Case C-484/03; [2006] STC 419; [2006] 2 WLR 456. (*Note*. For HMRC's practice following this decision, see Business Brief 01/06, issued on 18 January 2006.)

[22.116] A university, which was partly exempt, implemented a scheme with the objective of recovering the whole of the input tax incurred in refurbishing a derelict mill (in respect of which it elected to waive exemption). The scheme involved the creation of a discretionary trust, the grant of a 20-year lease of the mill to the trust, and a leaseback by the trust to the university. The creation of the trust and the grants of the lease and underlease all took place on the same day. Customs issued an assessment on the basis that the lease and leaseback were not effective for VAT purposes (so that most of the input tax should be attributed to the university's exempt supplies). The university appealed. The tribunal referred the case to the ECJ, which held that 'the question whether the transaction concerned is carried out for the sole purpose of obtaining a tax advantage is entirely irrelevant in determining whether it constitutes a supply of goods or services and an economic activity', although 'the *Sixth Directive* precludes any right of a taxable person to deduct input VAT where the transactions from which that right derives constitute an abusive practice'. The ECJ held that the transactions in question constituted supplies of goods or services and an economic activity provided that 'they satisfy the objective criteria on which those concepts are based, even if they are carried out with the sole aim of obtaining a tax advantage, without any other economic objective'. *University of Huddersfield Higher Education Corporation v C & E Commrs*, ECJ Case C-223/03; [2006] STC 980. (*Notes*. (1) For HMRC's practice following this decision, see Business Brief 2/2006, issued on 27 February 2006. (2) For a preliminary issue in this case, see **3.93** ASSESSMENT.)

[22.117] See also *The Arts Council of Great Britain*, **7.80** BUSINESS; *Newmir plc*, **7.116** BUSINESS; *EC Commission v Netherlands*, **22.127** below; *Finanzamt Groß-Gerau v MKG-Kraftfahrzeuge-Factoring GmbH*, **22.364** below; *Park Commercial Developments plc*, **27.46** FINANCE; *Merseyside Cablevision*, **36.554** INPUT TAX, and *Norwich City Council*, **42.11** LOCAL AUTHORITIES AND STATUTORY BODIES.

Grant of telecommunications licences

[22.118] In an Austrian case, the ECJ held that *Article 4(2)* of the *EC Sixth Directive* 'is to be interpreted as meaning that the allocation, by auction by the national regulatory authority responsible for spectrum assignment, of rights such as rights to use frequencies in the electromagnetic spectrum with the aim of providing the public with mobile telecommunications services does not constitute an economic activity within the meaning of that provision and, consequently, does not fall within the scope of that directive'. *T-Mobile Austria GmbH & Others v Republic of Austria*, ECJ Case C-284/04; [2008] STC 184.

[22.119] In 2000 the Secretary of State for Trade and Industry granted five telecommunications licences, in accordance with the *Wireless Telegraphy Act 1998*. The successful companies had to pay substantial sums of money for the licences. They reclaimed input tax on the payments. Customs rejected the claims on the basis that the grant of the licences was not subject to VAT. The companies appealed. The tribunal reviewed the evidence in detail and directed that the cases should be referred to the ECJ for rulings on whether the issue of the licences was an 'economic activity' within *Article 4(2)* of the *EC Sixth Directive*. The ECJ held that 'the issuing of licences, such as third generation mobile telecommunications licences known as "UMTS", by auction by the national regulatory authority responsible for spectrum assignment of the rights to use telecommunications equipment does not constitute an economic activity within the meaning of that provision and, consequently, does not fall within the scope of that directive'. *Hutchison 3G UK Ltd & Others v C & E Commrs*, ECJ Case C-369/04; [2008] STC 218.

Political organisation

[22.120] An Austrian political organisation (SPO) reclaimed input tax incurred in relation to advertising material. The tax authority rejected the claim on the basis that SPO was not acting as a 'taxable person'. SPO appealed, and the case was referred to the ECJ for a ruling on the interpretation of *Article 4* of the *EC Sixth Directive*. The ECJ rejected SPO's contentions, holding that *Article 4* had 'to be interpreted as meaning that external advertising activities carried out by a section of a Member State's political party is not to be regarded as an economic activity'. *Sozialdemokratische Partei Österreichs Landesorganisation Kärnten v Finanzamt Klagenfurt*, ECJ Case C-267/08; [2010] STC 287.

Occasional transactions (Article 4(3))

[22.121] In a German case, the ECJ held that a transaction which consisted of a contract for the sale of land which had not been built on, and contracts for the supply of work and services in connection with the construction and supply of a building on that land, did not constitute a supply of buildings 'and land on which they stand' within the meaning of *Article 4(3)(a)* of the *EC Sixth Directive*. The supply had to be regarded as a supply of building land within *Article 4(3)(b)*. The German government was, therefore, entitled to impose VAT on the transaction. *Kerrutt & Another v Finanzamt Mönchengladbach-Mitte*, ECJ Case 73/85; [1987] BTC 5015; [1986] ECR 2219; [1987] 2 CMLR 221.

[22.122] In a German case, a woman (B) registered as a car dealer and began building work with the aim of constructing a repair workshop. However, she was unable to complete the work for financial reasons, and subsequently sold the partly completed building and the land on which it stood. She purported to waive exemption on the building but not the land, with the intention of reclaiming input tax on the building work without having to account for output tax on the sale of the land. The German tax authority ruled that an election to waive exemption could not be limited to buildings alone, and had to include the land on which the buildings stood. B appealed and the case was referred to the ECJ, which held that 'for the purposes of VAT, buildings or parts of buildings and the land on which they stand cannot be dissociated from each other'. *Article 4(3)(a)* of the *EC Sixth Directive* had to be interpreted as meaning that the option for taxation 'must relate inseparably to the buildings or parts of buildings and the land on which they stand'. *Finanzamt Goslar v Breitsohl*, ECJ Case C-400/98; [2001] STC 355. (*Note.* For HMRC's practice following this decision, see Business Brief 23/2005, issued on 5 December 2005.)

[22.123] In a Netherlands case, a local authority appealed against an assessment charging tax on a supply of land, contending that the land was not 'building land' within *Article 4(3)(b)* of the *EC Sixth Directive*, and that the supply was therefore exempt under *Article 13B(h)*. The case was referred to the ECJ for a ruling on the definition of 'building land'. The ECJ held that it was for the Member States to define the concept of 'building land' within the meaning of *Article 4(3)(b)* and *Article 13B(h)*. It was not for the court to specify what degree of improvement had to be exhibited by land which had not actually been built on in order to be categorised as within the definition of 'building land'. *Gemeente Emmen v Belastingdienst Grote Ondernemingen*, ECJ Case C-468/93; [1996] STC 496; [1996] 1 ECR 1721; [1996] All ER (EC) 372.

Employees and associated persons (Article 4(4))

Employment

[22.124] In a Netherlands case, a cleaner (S), who had initially been self-employed, established a limited company of which he was the controlling director. The tax authority issued a ruling that the services which S carried out for the company were liable to VAT. S appealed, and the case was referred to the ECJ, which held that an employee in the position of the appellant 'could not be considered to be a taxable person' within *Article 4* of the *EC Sixth Directive*. Advocate-General Sharpston observed that 'the advantages in excluding employment from the scope of VAT are obvious. If it were not excluded, every employee would have to be registered for VAT and the tax would have to be charged on all salaries. Employers making taxable supplies would admittedly be able to deduct that VAT, but there would be a considerable burden on those making exempt supplies unless a compensatory mechanism were introduced, and such a mechanism would itself be burdensome. By contrast, when employment is excluded from the scope of VAT, the cost of that employment forms part of the value added to output supplies. It is thus automatically included in the tax base when those supplies are taxed, but has no effect, in VAT terms, on exempt output supplies. In addition to a considerable saving in administrative work, the neutrality of the tax and its general application to taxable supplies are ensured. Consequently, it is not desirable that an activity which falls within the scope of a contract of employment should be treated as an independent taxable activity.' *JA van der Steen v Inspecteur van de Belastingdienst*, ECJ Case C-355/06; [2008] STC 2379.

Associated persons

[22.125] In an Italian case, two associated companies submitted a joint VAT declaration. The tax authority issued a ruling that the companies had not been associated for long enough to adopt this treatment, and issued separate assessments to each company. The companies appealed, and the case was referred to the ECJ, which held that the Italian legislation governing associated companies failed to comply with the *Sixth Directive*. The ECJ held that 'the second subparagraph of *Article 4(4)* of the *Sixth Directive* . . . is a provision which, in order to be implemented by a Member State, requires prior consultation by that State of the Advisory Committee on value added tax and the adoption of national legislation authorising persons, in particular companies, established in the territory of the country who, while legally independent, are closely bound to one another by financial, economic and organisational links, no longer to be treated as separate taxable persons for the purposes of value added tax in order to be treated as a single taxable person to whom a single value added tax identification number is allocated and, accordingly, the sole person entitled to submit value added tax declarations. It is for the national court to determine whether national legislation, such as that at issue in the main proceedings, satisfies those criteria, subject to the qualification that, where there has been no prior consultation of the Advisory Committee on value added tax, national legislation which meets those criteria constitutes legislation adopted in breach of the procedural requirement laid down in the second subparagraph of *Article 4(4)*'. The principle of fiscal neutrality did not 'preclude national legislation which simply treats taxable persons wishing to opt for a mechanism to simplify value added tax declarations and payments differently according to whether the parent company or body has held more than 50% of the share capital or stock of the persons with whom it is linked since at least the beginning of the calendar year preceding that in which the declaration was made or, on the contrary, satisfies those conditions only after that date. It is for the national court to determine whether national legislation, such as that at issue in the main proceedings, constitutes such a provision. Moreover, neither the principle prohibiting the abuse of rights nor the principle of proportionality precludes such legislation.' *Ampliscientifica Srl & Amplifin SpA v Ministero dell'Economia e delle Finanze,*ECJ Case C-162/07; [2011] STC 566.

[22.126] See also *Barclays Bank plc*, **32.15** GROUPS OF COMPANIES; *Osman*, **57.39** REGISTRATION, and *Shamrock Leasing Ltd*, **62.505** SUPPLY.

Public authorities (Article 4(5))

ECJ decisions

[22.127] The ECJ held that self-employed notaries and bailiffs were not within *Article 4(5)* of the *EC Sixth Directive*, since 'bodies governed by public law are not automatically exempted in respect of all the activities in which they engage, but only in respect of those which form part of their specific duties as public authorities'. *EC Commission v Netherlands*, ECJ Case 235/85; [1987] ECR 1471; [1988] 2 CMLR 921.

[22.128] The ECJ also held that bailiffs were not within *Article 4(5)* of the *EC Sixth Directive* in *K Mihal v Danový úrad Košice V*, ECJ Case C-456/07; 21 May 2008 unreported.

[22.129] In two Italian cases, local authorities appealed against assessments charging VAT on receipts from various transactions. The Italian courts referred the cases to the ECJ for guidance on the interpretation of *Article 4(5)* of the *EC Sixth Directive*. The ECJ held that activities pursued 'as public authorities' were those engaged in by bodies governed by public law under the special legal regime applicable to them, but did not include activities pursued by them under the same legal conditions as those applying to private traders. Bodies subject to public law should be treated as taxable persons in respect of activities which could also be engaged in by private individuals in competition against them. *Ufficio Distrettuale delle Imposte Dirette di Fiorenzuola d'Arda v Comune di Carpaneto Piacentino; Ufficio Provinciale Imposta sul Valore Aggiunto di Piacenza v Comune di Rivergaro and Others*, ECJ Case 231/87; [1989] ECR 3233; [1991] STC 205. (*Notes.* (1) For subsequent proceedings, see **22.130** below. (2) For Customs' practice following this decision, see Business Brief 10/93, issued on 26 March 1993.)

[22.130] Following the decision in the cases noted at **22.129** above, a similar case involving the same local authorities was also submitted to the ECJ. The ECJ held that bodies subject to public law should be treated as taxable persons 'in respect of activities in which they engage as public authorities where those activities may also be engaged in, in competition with them, by private individuals, in cases in which their treatment as non-taxable persons could lead to significant distortion of competition'. *Comune di Carpaneto Piacentino & Others v Ufficio Provinciale Imposta sul Valore Aggiunto di Piacenza*, ECJ Case C-4/89; [1990] 1 ECR 1869; [1990] 3 CMLR 153.

[22.131] In a Spanish case, the ECJ held that *Article 4(5)* was not applicable where a local authority entrusted the collection of taxes to independent third parties, who were treated as self-employed and remunerated on a percentage basis. Accordingly, the payments made by the local authority to the tax collectors were subject to VAT. *Ayuntamiento de Sevilla v Recaudadores de las Zonas Primera y Segunda*, ECJ Case C-202/90; [1991] 1 ECR 4247; [1993] STC 659; [1994] 1 CMLR 424.

[22.132] In Finland, legal advice services provided by legal aid offices established by the State were treated as outside the scope of VAT. The EC Commission took proceedings against Finland, contending that this was a breach of *Article 4(5)* of the *EC Sixth Directive*. The ECJ rejected the Commission's contentions, holding that 'the link between the legal aid services provided by public offices and the payment to be made by the recipients' was not 'sufficiently direct for that payment to be regarded as consideration for those services and, accordingly, for those services to be regarded as economic activities'. Therefore *Article 4(5)* did not apply. *EC Commission v Republic of Finland*, ECJ Case C-246/08; 29 October 2009 unreported.

[22.133] In a German case, a municipality reclaimed input tax on the costs of constructing a building. The tax authority rejected the claim on the basis that the municipality was exempt from VAT and was not a taxable person. The municipality appealed, and the case was referred to the ECJ, which held that *Article 4(5)* permitted Member States to treat public bodies as non-taxable persons even where they had acted in a similar manner to private traders. *Finanzamt Augsburg-Stadt v Marktgemeinde Welden*, ECJ Case C-247/95; [1997] STC 531; [1997] 1 ECR 779; [1997] All ER (EC) 665.

[22.134] The European Commission brought an action against the UK, seeking a declaration that, by failing to subject tolls to VAT, the UK had failed to fulfil its obligations under the *Sixth Directive*. The UK defended the action, contending that such tolls were exempt under *Article 4(5)*. The ECJ rejected this contention, holding that the exemption only applied where the tolls were operated directly by bodies governed by public law, and finding that 'in the United Kingdom, the activity of providing access to roads on payment of a toll is carried out in certain cases not by a body governed by public law but by traders governed by private law'. Accordingly, the ECJ held that the UK should subject tolls to VAT, and should account to the Commission for the tax which should have been levied, with interest from 1994. *EC Commission v United Kingdom*, ECJ Case C-359/97; [2000] STC 777. (*Note*. For Customs' practice following this decision, see their News Release 36/00, issued on 12 September 2000; Business Brief 15/00, issued on 21 November 2000, and Business Brief 5/01 issued on 13 March 2001.)

[22.135] Similar decisions were reached in *EC Commission v France*, ECJ Case C-276/97; 12 September 2000 unreported and *EC Commission v Ireland*, ECJ Case C-358/97; 12 September 2000 unreported.

[22.136] However, contrasting decisions were reached in two cases involving the Netherlands and Greece, where the ECJ found that the tolls in question were operated exclusively by bodies governed by public law, within *Article 4(5)* of the *Sixth Directive*. *EC Commission v Netherlands*, ECJ Case C-408/97; 12 September 2000 unreported and *EC Commission v Hellenic Republic*, ECJ Case C-260/98; 12 September 2000 unreported.

[22.137] In a Portuguese case, a city council appealed against a demand for VAT on its receipts from parking meters and car parks. The case was referred to the ECJ, which held that the council was acting a public authority, within *Article 4(5)* of the *EC Sixth Directive*. However, the council could be treated as a taxable person, since the Finance Minister of a Member State could be authorised by a national law to define 'significant distortions of competition', provided that such decisions could be reviewed by the national courts. *Fazenda Pública v Câmara Municipal do Porto*, ECJ Case C-446/98; [2001] STC 560.

[22.138] A district council had accounted for VAT on its receipts from car parks. It claimed a repayment on the basis that it should have treated these receipts as outside the scope of VAT, by virtue of *Article 4(5)* of the *EC Sixth Directive*. Customs rejected the claim and the council appealed. The Ch D referred the case to the ECJ for a ruling on the interpretation of the phrase 'significant distortions of competition'. The ECJ held that *Article 4(5)* 'is to be interpreted as meaning that the significant distortions of competition, to which the treatment as non-taxable persons of bodies governed by private law acting as public authorities would lead, must be evaluated by reference to the activity in question, as such, without such evaluation relating to any local market in particular'. The expression 'would lead to' should 'be interpreted as encompassing not only actual competition, but also potential competition, provided that the possibility of a private operator entering the relevant market is real, and not purely hypothetical'. The word 'significant' should 'be understood as meaning that the actual or potential distortions of competition must be more than negligible.' *HMRC v Isle of Wight Council (No 2) (and related appeals)*, ECJ Case C-288/07; [2008] STC 2964. (*Notes.* (1) For HMRC's practice pending this decision, see Business Brief 04/06, issued on 24 March 2006. (2) For subsequent developments in this case, see **22.144** below.)

[22.139] In a German case, a charity operated a crematorium, which was in competition with a crematorium operated by a local authority. The charity applied to the Finanzgericht (Finance Court) for a declaration that, by treating the local authority crematorium as non-taxable, the tax authority was discriminating against the private sector and was in breach of *Article 4(5)* of the *Sixth Directive*. The case was referred to the ECJ, which ruled that 'a private person who is in competition with a body governed by public law and alleges that that body is, in respect of the activities in which it engages as a public authority, treated as a non-taxable person for value added tax purposes or undertaxed is entitled to rely, before the national court, on the second subparagraph of *Article 4(5)*'. *Finanzamt Eisleben v Feuerbestattungsverein Halle eV*, ECJ Case C-430/04; [2006] STC 2043.

[22.140] In another German case, the ECJ held that 'the treatment of a milk-quota sales point as a non-taxable person in respect of activities or transactions in which it engages as a public authority, within the meaning of *Article 4(5)* of the *Sixth Directive*' could not give rise to significant distortions of competition, 'by reason of the fact that it is not faced, in a situation such as that at issue in the main proceedings, with private operators providing services which are in competition with the public services. As that finding applies in respect of all milk-quota sales points operating within a given delivery reference quantity transfer area, defined by the Member State concerned, that area constitutes the relevant geographic market for the purpose of establishing whether there are significant distortions of competition.' *Landesanstalt für Landwirtschaft v Götz*, ECJ Case C-408/06; 13 December 2007 unreported.

[22.141] In another German case, a company agreed to construct an office building and lease it to a public authority. The company opted to tax the building, and reclaimed input tax on the construction work. The tax authority rejected the claim on the basis that the lessee was within *Article 4(5)* of the *EC Sixth Directive* and was not a 'taxable person'. (The German legislation precluded the option to tax where the supply was not made to another business.) The company appealed, and the case was referred to the ECJ for a ruling on the interpretation of *Article 4(5)*. The ECJ upheld the company's contentions, holding that 'Member States must lay down an express provision in order to be able to rely on the option provided for in the fourth subparagraph of *Article 4(5)*', according to which 'specific activities of bodies governed by public law that are exempt under *Article 13* or *Article 28* of that directive are considered as activities of public authorities.' The ECJ also held that the second subparagraph of *Article 4(5)* 'must be interpreted as meaning that bodies governed by public law are to be considered taxable persons in respect of activities or transactions in which they engage as public authorities not only where their treatment as non-taxable persons under the first or fourth subparagraphs of that provision would lead to significant distortions of competition to the detriment of their private competitors, but also where it would lead to such distortions to their own detriment'. *Finanzamt Düsseldorf-Süd v SALIX Grundstücks-Vermietungsgesellschaft mbH & Co. Objekt Offenbach KG*, ECJ Case C-102/08; [2009] STC 1607.

[22.142] See also *Waterschap Zeeuws Vlaanderen v Staatssecretaris van Financiën*, **22.454** below.

UK court and tribunal decisions

[22.143] Westminster City Council managed a hostel providing accommodation to homeless men. Customs issued an assessment, charging VAT on the basis that the Council was making supplies of accommodation and catering. The Council appealed, contending that the supplies should be treated as exempt. The tribunal accepted this contention and allowed the appeal, holding that the operation of the building was exempt under *Article 4(5)* of the *EC Sixth Directive*. The accommodation provided by the Council was of such a type that the Council was clearly not supplying services in competition with proprietors of commercial hotels, inns or boarding houses. The tribunal also held that the operation of the building fell within the provisions of *Article 13A1(g)*, as the supplies were closely linked to welfare and social security work and were made by a body governed by public law. *The Lord Mayor and Citizens of the City of Westminster*, [1989] VATTR 71 (VTD 3367).

[22.144] Following the ECJ decision noted at **22.138** above, the Ch D reheard the case and remitted it to the tribunal. Rimer J held that the facts previously found by the tribunal were not sufficient to allow a decision as to whether treating the council's receipts as exempt from VAT would lead to 'significant distortions of competition'. He therefore remitted the case to the tribunal for rehearing. *HMRC v Isle of Wight Council (No 3) (and related appeals)*, Ch D [2009] STC 1098; [2009] EWHC 592 (Ch). (*Note*. Following this decision, the tribunal held a further hearing and directed that the council should be admitted to adduce further evidence in support of its contention that 'in the case of off-street car parking, cheaper pricing will not result from the tax advantage and/or that, if it does, will not affect demand'— [2010] UKFTT 264 (TC), TC00558.)

[22.145] A District Council operated an information service. It did not account for output tax on supplies of information to an urban development corporation. Customs issued an assessment charging tax on them, and the Council appealed, contending that the effect of *Article 4(5)* of the *EC Sixth Directive* was that it should not be considered a 'taxable person'. The tribunal rejected this contention and dismissed the appeal. *Article 4(5)* stated that local authorities should be considered taxable persons 'where treatment as non-taxable persons would lead to significant distortions of competition'. The tribunal held that the work in question could have been undertaken by a private organisation, and that to treat the Council as a non-taxable person 'would bear unfairly on private organisations which would be accountable for

VAT on similar work'. The Council was making supplies to the corporation for consideration, in the course or furtherance of a business, and was therefore required to account for output tax. *Metropolitan Borough of Wirral*, MAN/95/77 (VTD 14674).

[22.146] A Borough Council reclaimed input tax, under *VATA 1994, s 33*, on supplies which it received for the purpose of providing and maintaining cemeteries. Customs issued a ruling that the Council's provision and maintenance of cemeteries was a business activity, so that its supplies were exempt supplies and it was not entitled to reclaim input tax. The tribunal allowed the Council's appeal, holding that the Council provided and maintained cemeteries 'as a public authority' and thus 'was not a taxable person in respect of those activities'. Furthermore, since the great majority of cemeteries and crematoria were operated by local authorities, 'the treatment of local authorities as non-taxable persons in connection with these activities would not lead to significant distortions of competition'. *Rhondda Cynon Taff County Borough Council*, [2000] VATDR 149 (VTD 16496). (*Note.* For Customs' practice following this decision, see Business Brief 4/2000, issued on 17 March 2000.)

[22.147] A Council wanted to acquire certain land owned by the Ministry of Defence. A Territorial Army hall stood on part of the land. After negotiation the Ministry agreed to sell the land for £2,800,000, of which £1,349,999 was allocated to the construction of a new building by the Council on Ministry land to replace the Territorial Army hall. Customs issued an assessment charging tax on the £1,349,999, on the basis that it represented consideration for a supply of services by the Council. The Council appealed, contending that the effect of *Article 4(5)* of the *EC Sixth Directive* was that it should not be considered a 'taxable person'. The tribunal rejected this contention and dismissed the appeal, holding that the construction of the building was 'a matter of private law'. In constructing the building, the Council was not acting under the 'special regime applicable to public authorities'. *Stirling Council*, EDN/00/140 (VTD 17480).

[22.148] The City of London Corporation operated three schools, charging fees to the parents of most pupils. Customs issued a ruling that this was a business activity and that the Corporation was acting as a 'taxable person' within *Article 4(5)* of the *EC Sixth Directive*. The Corporation appealed, contending that it should not be treated as a taxable person, since it provided education in accordance with its obligations as a local authority, and treating it as a non-taxable person did not give rise to any significant distortion of competition. The tribunal accepted this contention and allowed the Corporation's appeal. *City of London Corporation*, [2003] VATDR 504 (VTD 17892). (*Note.* For Customs' practice following this decision, see Business Brief 11/2003, issued on 25 July 2003. They state that they 'consider that this case turned on its own unusual facts' and now accept 'that this special treatment for VAT purposes will not lead to significant distortions of competition in this particular case'.)

[22.149] A college of further education provided courses, funded by a grant from the Scottish Education Funding Council. Customs issued a ruling that this was a business activity and that the college was acting as a 'taxable person' within *Article 4(5)* of the *EC Sixth Directive*. The college appealed, contending that it should be treated as a public authority and not as a taxable person. The CS accepted this contention and allowed the appeal. Lord Clarke held that the college was a public authority and was providing the courses in question 'as an act of public administration and not as an act governed solely by the rules of private law'. *Edinburgh Telford College v HMRC*, CS [2006] STC 1291; [2006] CSIH 13. (*Notes.* (1) The House of Lords rejected an application by the company for leave to appeal against this decision. (2) See, however, the subsequent decision in *University of Cambridge*, **30.11** FUEL AND POWER, where the Ch D held that a university or college was not a 'body governed by public law'. The decision here was apparently not cited by counsel for the university in that case. The conflict between these two decisions was considered by the First-Tier Tribunal in *Wakefield College v HMRC*, **15.100** CONSTRUCTION OF BUILDINGS, where Judge Barlow applied the *University of Cambridge* decision, and declined to follow the decision in *Edinburgh Telford College* on the grounds that it was based on a concession by Customs which was incorrect in law. Judge Barlow held that the CS decision was 'authority for the proposition that a public body is acting as such when it carries out its core activities', but was 'not authority for the proposition that a further education college is a public body in the sense required'. (3) For another issue in this case, see **46.152** PARTIAL EXEMPTION.)

[22.150] See also *The Radio Authority*, **7.79** BUSINESS; *The Arts Council of Great Britain*, **7.80** BUSINESS; *Norwich City Council*, **42.11** LOCAL AUTHORITIES AND STATUTORY BODIES, and *The Royal Academy of Music*, **55.15** PROTECTED BUILDINGS.

Taxable transactions (Articles 5–7)

Supplies of goods (Article 5)

[22.151] In a Netherlands case, the ECJ held that a supply of goods could take place even without the transfer of legal ownership, although the supplier should have the right to dispose of the property in question as owner. It was the function of the national court concerned to determine, on the facts of the case, whether the transferee had obtained the right to dispose of the property in question as owner. *Staatssecretaris van Financiën v Shipping & Forwarding Enterprise (SAFE) BV*, ECJ Case 320/88; [1990] 1 ECR 285; [1991] STC 627; [1993] 3 CMLR 547.

[22.152] A Netherlands company (H) leased a number of motor vehicles to German clients. Under the lease agreements, it gave the lessees the use of a credit card to purchase fuel. H applied for a refund of German VAT on the fuel. The tax authority rejected the claim, on the basis that the fuel had been supplied by the companies which operated the petrol stations directly to the lessees. H appealed, contending that it should be treated as having received the fuel from the retail companies and as having made onward supplies to the lessees. The case was referred to the ECJ for a ruling on the interpretation of *Article 5(1)* of the *EC Sixth Directive*. The ECJ rejected H's contentions, holding that in the circumstances of the case, the lessor of a vehicle did not make any supply of fuel to the lessee, 'even if the vehicle is filled up in the name and at the expense of that lessor'. *Auto Lease Holland BV v Bundesamt für Finanzen*, ECJ Case C-185/01; [2005] STC 598.

[22.153] A company (L) operated a sales promotion scheme, intended to reward regular customers. Under the scheme, customers who purchased goods from certain retailers received 'loyalty points' which they could use to acquire further goods or services from other specified suppliers. L paid the suppliers for these goods or services, and reclaimed input tax. Customs rejected the claim on the basis that the goods and services had been supplied to the individual customers, rather than L. The CA unanimously allowed L's appeal, applying the principles laid down in *Redrow Group plc*, **36.130** INPUT TAX, but the HL referred the case to the ECJ. The ECJ held that 'payments made by the operator of the scheme concerned to redeemers who supply loyalty rewards to customers' must be regarded 'as being the consideration, paid by a third party, for a supply of goods to those customers or, as the case may be, a supply of services to them. It is, however, for the referring court to determine whether those payments also include the consideration for a supply of services corresponding to a separate service.' *HMRC v Loyalty Management Ltd*, ECJ Case C-53/09; [2010] STC 2651. (*Notes*. (1) The ECJ heard the case with *HMRC v Baxi Group Ltd*, **22.154** below. (2) In the CA, Chadwick LJ held that 'there is no reason why, in a VAT context, a supplier may not be treated as making, in the same transaction, both a supply of services to one person and a supply of different services to another person'. He concluded that 'on the facts in the present case, there is a supply of redemption services to (L) in respect of which (L) is entitled to input tax credit'. (3) For HMRC's practice pending the ECJ decision, see HMRC Brief 46/08, issued on 17 September 2008, and HMRC Brief 60/08, issued on 17 December 2008. (4) The Supreme Court is scheduled to begin rehearing the case on 24 October 2012.)

[22.154] A group of companies (B) manufactured domestic boilers and sold them to traders who installed heating systems. It launched an incentive scheme under which traders who purchased its appliances were awarded 'points', which could be redeemed for goods, described as 'gifts'. The scheme was operated by a marketing company (G). B claimed input tax on the payments which it made to G for operating the scheme. Customs rejected part of the claim on the grounds that it related to the cost of the goods. The tribunal held that B had made onward supplies of these goods and was required to account for output tax. B appealed, contending that G was making a single supply of marketing services. The Ch D accepted this contention and allowed the appeal, holding that G was making a single supply of marketing services to B, and that the relevant goods were supplied to B's customers rather than to B. Accordingly B was entitled to credit for the input tax and was not required to account for output tax. The CA upheld this decision but the HL referred the case to the ECJ. The ECJ held that 'payments made by the sponsor to the operator of the scheme concerned who supplies loyalty rewards to customers' must be regarded 'as being, in part, the consideration, paid by a third party, for a supply of goods to those customers and, in part, the consideration for a supply of services made by the operator of that scheme for the benefit of that sponsor'. *HMRC v Baxi Group Ltd*, ECJ Case C-55/09; [2010] STC 2651. (*Note.* The ECJ heard the case with *HMRC v Loyalty Management Ltd*, **22.153** above.)

Supply of food for immediate consumption—whether a supply of goods

[22.155] In a German case, a trader sold food such as sausages and chips from mobile snack bars. He accounted for VAT at a reduced rate. The tax authority issued an assessment charging VAT at the standard rate. The trader appealed, and the case was referred to the ECJ for a ruling on whether the trader should be treated as supplying goods or services. The ECJ held that, for the purpose of the *Sixth Directive*, 'the supply of food or meals freshly prepared for immediate consumption from snack stalls or mobile snack bars or in cinema foyers is a supply of goods within the meaning of *Article 5* if a qualitative examination of the entire transaction shows that the elements of supply of services preceding and accompanying the supply of the food are not predominant'. *Finanzamt Burgdorf v M Bog (and related appeals)*, ECJ Case C-497/09; [2011] STC 1221. (*Notes.* (1) The ECJ heard the case with *Fleischerei Nier GmbH & Co KG v Finanzamt Detmold*, 22.175 below. (2) For HMRC's practice following this decision, see HMRC Brief 19/11, issued on 1 April 2011.)

Article 5(3)(b) of EC Sixth Directive

[22.156] Under Netherlands law, the grant of rights over immovable property was not treated as a taxable supply where 'the total consideration plus turnover tax amounts to less than the economic value of those rights'. A housing association, which had granted a subsidiary foundation an usufructuary right over certain houses for less than their cost price, reclaimed input tax relating to the houses in question. The Netherlands tax authority issued an assessment to recover the tax, and the association appealed, contending that the restriction in question contravened *Article 5(3)(b)* of the *EC Sixth Directive*. The case was referred to the ECJ, which rejected the association's contentions, holding that *Article 5(3)(b)* did not preclude the restriction in question. *Stichting Goed Wonen v Staatssecretaris van Financiën (No 1)*, ECJ Case C-326/99; [2003] STC 1137. (*Note.* For subsequent developments in this case, see **22.550** below.)

Article 5(4)(c) of EC Sixth Directive

[22.157] See *Express Medicare Ltd*, **1.78** AGENTS.

Article 5(6) of EC Sixth Directive—private use of business assets

[22.158] An oil company distributed vouchers to customers who purchased 12 litres of petrol. When customers had collected a certain number of such vouchers, they could be exchanged for goods. The Commissioners issued a ruling that the company was liable to account for output tax on the cost of the goods it supplied in this way. The company appealed, and the case was referred to the ECJ for a ruling on the interpretation of *Article 5(6)* and *Article 11A3(b)* of the *EC Sixth Directive*. The ECJ held that the application by an oil company of goods in exchange for vouchers must be treated as a supply for consideration, within *Article 5(6)*. Advocate-General Fennelly observed that, under the company's sales promotion scheme, the goods were described as gifts, and that the amounts paid by the customers were entirely attributable to their purchases of fuel and could not be treated as consideration for the goods. The exchange of goods for the vouchers was a 'disposal free of charge', and was taxable accordingly. *Kuwait Petroleum (GB) Ltd v C & E Commrs*, ECJ Case C-48/97; [1999] STC 488; [1999] All ER (EC) 450. (*Notes.* (1) The ECJ also held that there was no 'price discount' allowed to the customer, so that *Article 11A3(b)* did not apply. (2) For the Commissioners' practice following this decision, see Business Brief 17/99, issued on 6 August 1999. (3) The company subsequently made an unsuccessful appeal to the Ch D—see **22.159** below.)

[22.159] Following the ECJ decision in *Kuwait Petroleum (GB) Ltd*, **22.158** above, the tribunal dismissed the company's appeal and the Ch D upheld this decision. Laddie J held that, in the light of the ruling by the ECJ, the tribunal was entitled to find that the redemption goods 'were supplied to customers "otherwise than for consideration" and were therefore within *Article 5(6)*'. *Kuwait Petroleum (GB) Ltd v C & E Commrs (No 2)*, Ch D 2000, [2001] STC 62. (*Note.* For another issue in this case, taken to the CA, see **22.259** below.)

[22.160] In a German case, a car dealer had reclaimed input tax in 1990 on substantial repairs to a vintage car. In 1992 he ceased trading but retained the car as a private asset. The tax authority issued an assessment to recover tax on the car. He appealed, and the case was referred to the ECJ, which held that the effect of *Article 5(6)* of the *EC Sixth Directive* was that VAT was payable on 'component parts' in respect of which input tax had been deducted (but not on the whole value of the car, since input tax had not been reclaimable on its initial purchase). The taxable amount for this purpose should be determined 'by reference to the price, at the time of the allocation, of the goods incorporated in the vehicle which constitute component parts of the goods allocated'. Furthermore, where input tax had been reclaimed and there was no output tax liability under *Article 5(6)* (for example, on extensive bodywork repairs which did not involve the addition of component parts), the input tax deducted had to be adjusted under *Article 20(1)* 'if the value of the work in question has not been entirely consumed in the context of the business activity of the taxable person before the vehicle is allocated to his private assets'. *Finanzamt Burgdorf v Fischer*, ECJ Case C-322/99; [2001] STC 1356; [2002] 2 WLR 1207.

[22.161] A similar decision was reached in another German case where a tax adviser had reclaimed input tax on a new car windscreen and catalytic converter, and had subsequently treated the car as a private vehicle rather than as a business asset. *Finanzamt Düsseldorf-Mettman v Brandenstein*, ECJ Case C-323/99; [2001] STC 1356; [2002] 2 WLR 1207. (*Note.* The case was heard in the ECJ with *Finanzamt Burgdorf v Fischer*, **22.160** above.)

[22.162] See also *Gallaher Ltd*, 67.156 VALUATION.

Article 5(6)—whether land included in business assets

[22.163] In a Dutch case, a building contractor purchased a plot of land with an existing building. He obtained planning permission to build two houses on the land. He kept one of the houses for his private use, and sold the other house. As he had reclaimed input tax on the goods and services used in the construction of the houses, he accounted for an identical amount of output tax. The Netherlands tax authority, however, took the view that there had been a single supply consisting of the land as well as the buildings, and issued an assessment charging output tax on the value of the land. The contractor appealed, contending that he had acquired the land in a private capacity, and it had never formed part of his business assets. The case was referred to the ECJ for a preliminary ruling concerning the interpretation of *Article 5(6)* of the *EC Sixth Directive.* The ECJ held that, where a taxable person acquired land solely for private use but built a dwelling on that land in the course of his business, only the house (and not the land) was to be regarded as having been a business asset applied for private use for the purposes of *Article 5(6).* The ECJ observed that the purpose of *Article 5(6)* was 'to ensure equal treatment as between a taxable person who applies goods forming part of the assets of his business for private use and an ordinary consumer who buys goods of the same type. In pursuit of that objective, that provision prevents a taxable person who has been able to deduct VAT on the purchase of goods used for his business from escaping the payment of VAT' when he transferred those goods from his business for private purposes. *P de Jong v Staatssecretaris van Financiën,* ECJ Case C-20/91; [1992] 1 ECR 2847; [1992] 3 CMLR 260; [1995] STC 727.

Article 5(6) of EC Sixth Directive—samples and gifts of small value

[22.164] A music company distributed free copies of CDs for promotional purposes. It had accounted for VAT on these, in accordance with *VATA 1994, Sch 4 para 5.* Subsequently it formed the view that the effect of *Article 5(6)* of the *EC Sixth Directive* was that it need not have accounted for VAT on these CDs. In 2003 it submitted a repayment claim for more than £1,600,000, backdated to 1987. HMRC rejected the claim on the grounds that VAT had been correctly charged on the CDs, and that most of the claim was outside the three-year time limit laid down by *VATA 1994, s 80(4).* The company appealed. The tribunal reviewed the evidence in detail and directed that the case should be referred to the ECJ for rulings on the interpretation of the last sentence of *Article 5(6)* of the *EC Sixth Directive,* including a ruling on 'the essential characteristics of a "sample"'. The ECJ held that a 'sample' was 'a specimen of a product which is intended to promote the sales of that product and which allows the characteristics and qualities of that product to be assessed without resulting in final consumption, other than where final consumption is inherent in such promotional transactions. That term cannot be limited, in a general way, by national legislation to specimens presented in a form which is not available for sale or to the first of a series of identical specimens given by a taxable person to the same recipient, unless that legislation allows account to be taken of the nature of the product represented and of the specific business context of each transaction in which those specimens are distributed'. The concept of 'gifts of small value' did not preclude national legislation 'which fixes a monetary ceiling of the order of that established by the legislation at issue in the main proceedings, namely £50, for gifts made to the same person in the course of a 12-month period or forming part of a series or succession of gifts'. However, *Article 5(6)* did preclude 'national legislation which establishes a presumption that goods constituting "gifts of small value" within the meaning that provision, distributed by a taxable person to different individuals having the same employer, are to be treated as having been made to the same person'. *EMI Group plc v HMRC,* ECJ Case C-581/08; [2010] STC 2609. (*Note.* For HMRC's practice following this decision, see HMRC Brief 51/10, issued on 9 December 2010. See the amendments made to *VATA 1994, Sch 4, para 5* by *FA 2011, s 74.*)

Article 5(7)(a) of EC Sixth Directive—self-supplies of goods

[22.165] In 1989 the UK imposed a self-supply charge on developers of non-residential buildings put to exempt use within a ten-year period. (The charge was phased out over the period to 1 March 1997 and was abolished for all new developments beginning after 28 February 1995.) While the provisions were in force, the governors of an independent school obtained planning permission to develop new playing fields on what had previously been farmland, and incorporated a subsidiary company to administer the new facilities. The school granted the company a lease of the facilities for a period of twelve years, for a premium of £187,500 and an annual rent, and the company gave the school a non-exclusive licence to use the facilities in return for an annual licence fee. The school elected to waive exemption in respect of the lease, and reclaimed the input tax charged by the contractors who had completed the development. The Commissioners formed the opinion that the school was liable to account for output tax on the full cost of construction and the value of the land under the 'self-supply' provisions. The tribunal allowed the school's appeal, and the HL upheld this decision. *Articles 5(7)* and *6(3)* of the *EC Sixth Directive* permitted a self-supply to be treated as a taxable transaction in a case in which input tax would not have been wholly deductible if the goods or services in question had been acquired from a third person. However, the self-supply provisions did not apply where the relevant goods or services were in fact acquired from a third person, and the question of whether such input tax was deductible had to be determined in the ordinary way, i.e. according to whether it could be attributed to a taxable supply. In this case, the school was using the sports ground under the terms of the licence granted by the subsidiary company, so that the charge to tax was not in accordance with the *Sixth Directive*. *Robert Gordon's College v C & E Commrs*, HL [1995] STC 1093; [1996] 1 WLR 201.

Article 5(8) of EC Sixth Directive—transfer of 'totality of assets'

[22.166] In a Dutch case, the ECJ held that there could be a transfer of a business even if there had been a cessation of trading before the date on which the transfer took place 'if the wherewithal to carry on the business, such as plant, building and employees, are available and are transferred'. The fact that there was no transfer of goodwill or existing contracts was not conclusive. *JMA Spijkers v Gevroeders Benedik Abattoir CV*, ECJ Case 24/85; [1986] ECR 1119; [1986] 2 CMLR 296.

[22.167] In a Luxembourg case, a company sold the assets of a retail clothing business. The vendor did not charge VAT, treating the transaction as the transfer of a going concern. The Luxembourg tax authority issued an assessment charging VAT, on the basis that the purchaser 'had no administrative authorisation to trade in the relevant sector'. The vendor appealed, and the case was referred to the ECJ for a ruling on the interpretation of *Article 5(8)* of the *EC Sixth Directive*. The ECJ held that when a Member State had implemented *Article 5(8)* to provide that certain transfers of assets should not be treated as supplies of goods, the provision applied 'to any transfer of a business or an independent part of an undertaking, including tangible elements and, as the case may be, intangible elements which, together, constitute an undertaking or a part of an undertaking capable of carrying on an independent economic activity. The transferee must however intend to operate the business or the part of the undertaking transferred and not simply to immediately liquidate the activity concerned and sell the stock, if any'. The restriction of the rule to 'transfers of a totality of assets where the transferee holds the authorisation for pursuit of the economic activity' in question was not authorised by *Article 5(8)*. *Zita Modes Sàrl v Administration de l'enregistrement et des domaines*, ECJ Case C-497/01; [2005] STC 1059. (*Note*. For the Commissioners' practice following this decision, see Business Brief 9/2005, issued on 4 April 2005.)

[22.168] In a German case, a partnership was formed in order 'to prepare the means necessary for the activities of a capital company'. It reclaimed input tax on its expenditure. It then transferred its assets to the newly-formed company. It did not account for output tax on the basis that the effect of *Article 5(8)* of the *EC Sixth Directive* was that the transfer was not a supply. The tax authority rejected the partnership's claim to input tax, on the basis that, since it had transferred its assets as a going concern, it was not a 'taxable person' and the expenditure had not been incurred for the purposes of 'taxable transactions'. The partnership appealed and the case was referred to the ECJ. The ECJ found in favour of the partnership, holding that 'a partnership established for the sole purpose of founding a capital company is entitled to deduct the input tax paid on supplies of goods and services where its only output transaction in the performance of its object was to effect by formal act the transfer for consideration of the supplies obtained to that company once founded'. *Finanzamt Offenbach am Main-Land v Faxworld Vorgründungsgesellschaft Peter Hünninghausen und Wolfgang Klein GbR*, ECJ Case C-137/02; [2005] STC 1192.

[22.169] In another German case, the ECJ held that *Article 5(8)* of the *EC Sixth Directive* 'must be interpreted as meaning that there is a transfer of a totality of assets, or a part thereof, for the purposes of that provision, where the stock and fittings of a retail outlet are transferred concomitantly with the conclusion of a contract of lease, to the transferee, of the premises of that outlet for an indefinite period but terminable at short notice by either party, provided that the assets transferred are sufficient for the transferee to be able to carry on an independent economic activity on a lasting basis'. *Finanzamt Lüdenscheid v Schriever*, ECJ Case C-444/10; 10 November 2011 unreported.

[22.170] See also *Peddars Way Housing Association Ltd*, **15.20** CONSTRUCTION OF BUILDINGS, ETC.; *Abbey National plc*, **22.419** below, and *Higher Education Statistics Agency Ltd*, **65.88** TRANSFERS OF GOING CONCERNS.

Supplies of services (Article 6)

[22.171] In a Netherlands case, a trader repaired school books. The tax authority issued a ruling that he was supplying services, which were chargeable to VAT at 18%. The trader appealed, contending that he was supplying goods, which were chargeable at 4%. The case was referred to the ECJ, which held that the production of goods from materials supplied by customers only took place where the contractor produced a new article, i.e. one the function of which was different from that of the materials provided. Repairs, however extensive, did not amount to the supply of goods. *Van Dijk's Boekhuis BV v Staatssecretaris van Financiën*, ECJ Case 139/84; [1985] ECR 1405; [1986] 2 CMLR 575.

[22.172] In a German case, a dairy farmer undertook to discontinue milk production and was granted a compensation payment under an EC regulation. The German tax authority issued an assessment on the basis that the compensation payment was subject to VAT. The farmer appealed, and the case was referred for a preliminary ruling on the definition of a 'supply of services' in *Article 6(1)* of the *EC Sixth Directive*. The ECJ held that the undertaking given by the farmer did not constitute a supply of services, so that the compensation was outside the scope of VAT. In compensating farmers who undertook to cease milk production, the Community did not acquire goods or services for its own use but acted in the common interest of promoting the proper functioning of the Community milk market. The farmer's undertaking did not entail any benefit, either for the Community or for the national authority, which would enable them to be considered as consumers of a service. *Mohr v Finanzamt Bad Segeberg*, ECJ Case C-215/94; [1996] STC 328; [1996] 1 ECR 959; [1996] All ER (EC) 450.

[22.173] A similar decision was reached in a subsequent case in which a German farming company had received compensation for an undertaking not to harvest at least 20% of its potato crop. The ECJ held that the undertaking did not constitute a supply of services, so that the compensation was not taxable. *Landboden-Agrardienste GmbH & Co KG v Finanzamt Calau*, ECJ Case C-384/95; [1998] STC 171.

[22.174] A Danish company provided meals on board ferries travelling between Denmark and Germany. The German authorities issued assessments on the basis that the company was making supplies of goods within *Article 5(1)* of the *EC Sixth Directive*, so that, by virtue of *Article 8(1)*, some of the supplies would be deemed to take place in Germany. The company appealed, contending that the supplies were supplies of services within *Article 6(1)*, so that, by virtue of *Article 9(1)*, the supplies were deemed to take place in Denmark, where its business was established. The case was referred to the ECJ, which upheld the company's contentions. Restaurant transactions were to be regarded as supplies of services within *Article 6(1)*, so that, by virtue of *Article 9(1)*, they were deemed to be carried out at the place where the supplier had established his business. The ECJ held that 'restaurant transactions are characterised by a cluster of features and acts, of which the provision of food is only one component and in which services largely predominate'. The ECJ observed that, applying *Berkholz v Finanzamt Hamburg-Mitte-Altstadt*, **22.198** below, the place where the supplier had established his business was the 'primary point of reference', and that regard was only to be had to another establishment from which the services were supplied if the reference to the place where the supplier had established his business did not 'lead to a rational result for tax purposes' or if it created 'a conflict with another Member State'. *Faaborg-Gelting Linien A/S v Finanzamt Flensburg*, ECJ Case C-231/94; [1996] STC 774; [1996] 1 ECR 2395; [1996] 3 CMLR 535; [1996] All ER (EC) 656. (*Note.* Despite this decision, HMRC still treat such supplies as supplies of goods which are outside the scope of UK VAT when supplied on board international or intra-EC passenger transport: see HMRC Internal Guidance V1-4, chapter 2, para 10.8.)

[22.175] In a German case, a partnership which operated a butcher's shop also provided a catering service for parties. The tax authority issued an assessment charging VAT on the basis that whole of the amount charged for the catering service was standard-rated. The partnership appealed, and the case was referred to the ECJ for a ruling on whether the partnership should be treated as supplying goods or services. The ECJ held that, 'except in cases in which a party catering service does no more than deliver standard meals without any additional elements of supply of services, or in which other special circumstances show that the supply of the food represents the predominant element of a transaction, the activities of a party catering service are supplies of services within the meaning of *Article 6*' of the *Sixth Directive*. *Fleischerei Nier GmbH & Co KG v Finanzamt Detmold*, ECJ Case C-502/09; [2011] STC 1221. (*Note.* The ECJ heard the case with *Finanzamt Burgdorf v M Bog*, 22.155 above.)

[22.176] In a Netherlands case, a company (L) arranged for customised software to be installed by a US company. The tax authority issued assessments charging VAT on the payments for the software. L appealed, and the case was referred to the ECJ, which held that the supply was a supply of services, within *Article 6(1)* of the *Directive*, and that the supply fell within *Article 9(2)(e)*, as being 'services carried out by engineers or by those which are similar to the activity of an engineer'. *Levob Verzekeringen BV v Staatssecretaris van Financiën (and related appeal)*, ECJ Case C-41/04; [2006] STC 766.

[22.177] In a French case, a company (G) supplied reprographic services, including the reproduction of original documents. It treated its supplies as supplies of services. The tax authority issued a ruling that G was making supplies of goods. G appealed, and the case was referred to the ECJ, which observed that 'reprographics activities are not limited to the mere reproduction of original documents, but involve also the selection and programming of the photocopiers, the compilation and binding of the documents and the sorting of the copies'. The ECJ held that it was for the national court 'to determine, on the basis of the importance of those services for the customer, the degree to which the original document provided by the customer was processed, the time necessary for the performance of those services and the proportion of the total cost that they represent, whether those services are liable to be regarded as transactions which, far from being only minor or ancillary, are predominant in relation to the supply of the reproduced documents, such that they constitute, over and above that mere reproduction, an aim in themselves for the recipient of those services'. *Article 5(1)* of the *Sixth Directive* 'must be interpreted as meaning that reprographics activities have the characteristics of a supply of goods to the extent that they are limited to mere reproduction of documents on materials, where the right to dispose of them has been transferred from the reprographer to the customer who ordered the copies of the original'. However, reprographic supplies were supplies of services, within *Article 6(1)*, 'where it is clear that they involve additional services liable, having regard to the importance of those services for the recipient, the time necessary to perform them, the processing required by the original documents and the proportion of the total cost that those services represent, to be predominant in relation to the supply of goods, such that they constitute an aim in themselves for the recipient thereof'. *Graphic Procédé v Ministère du Budget, des Comptes publics et de la Fonction publique*, ECJ Case C-88/09; [2010] STC 918.

[22.178] See also *Mirror Group Newspapers Ltd*, **27.51** FINANCE.

Treatment of private use of goods as supply of services

[22.179] In a German case, the taxpayer had purchased a second-hand car from a non-taxable person. The car was purchased with the intention of being used for both private and business purposes. The German tax authority charged VAT on the private use, based on the depreciation of the car and the proportion to which it was used privately. The taxpayer appealed, contending that *Article 6(2)* of the *EC Sixth Directive* only imposed a charge to output tax where the input tax had been wholly or partly deductible, and thus precluded a charge to tax where no tax had been deducted on the acquisition of the asset from a non-taxable person. The ECJ held that *Article 6(2)* was unconditional and could be relied upon by a taxpayer against any national provision which was incompatible with it. The power of Member States to derogate from the obligation to charge tax on private use of business assets did not allow them to impose tax where VAT was not wholly or partly deductible. Accordingly VAT was not chargeable in the circumstances of the case. *Kühne v Finanzamt München III*, ECJ Case 50/88; [1989] ECR 1925; [1990] STC 749; [1990] 3 CMLR 287.

[22.180] See also *Enkler v Finanzamt Homburg*, **22.114** above, and *Lennartz v Finanzamt München III*, **22.456** below.

[22.181] In a German case, an assessment was made charging VAT on the private use of a car which had been treated as a business asset. The assessment included a proportion of certain expenses relating to the use of the car, on which the owner had not reclaimed input tax. The owner appealed and the case was referred to the ECJ, which held that ancillary services relating to the private use of goods did not fall within *Article 6(2)(a)* of the *EC Sixth Directive* and, where the owner of the goods had not been able to deduct input tax in respect of such services, taxation of such private use was precluded. *Finanzamt München III v Mohsche*, ECJ Case C-193/91; [1993] 1 ECR 2615; [1997] STC 195.

[22.182] In a German case, a trader constructed a building which he used partly for business purposes and partly for residential purposes. He reclaimed the whole of the input tax on its construction on the grounds that it was a business asset, and accounted for output tax in respect of his private use of part of the building, on the lines laid down by *Lennartz v Finanzamt München III*, **22.456** below. The tax authority rejected his claim to deduct the whole of the input tax. He appealed, and the case was referred to the ECJ for guidance on the interpretation of *Articles 6(2)* and *13B(b)* of the *EC Sixth Directive*. The ECJ held that, where a taxable person 'chooses to treat capital goods used both for business and private purposes as business goods, the VAT due as input tax on the acquisition of those goods is in principle wholly and immediately deductible'. The effect of *Article 6(2)(a)* and *11A1(c)* was that the use of such capital goods for private purposes was treated as a supply of services. Accordingly, the trader was entitled to deduct the whole of the input tax and was required to account for output tax. *Article 13B(b)* had no application to 'the private use by a taxable person of part of a building which is treated as forming, in its entirety, part of the assets of his business'. *Seeling v Finanzamt Starnberg*, ECJ Case C-269/00; [2003] STC 805. (*Note*. For Customs' practice following this decision, see Business Brief 22/2003, issued on 19 November 2003.)

[22.183] In a Netherlands case, a married couple purchased a holiday bungalow. They mainly used this for letting, but also used it for private purposes. Initially they claimed, and were granted, a deduction of 87.5% of the relevant input tax. Subsequently they formed the opinion that the effect of the decision in *Lennartz v Finanzamt München III*, 22.456 below, was that they should be entitled to a deduction for the whole of the input tax. The tax authority rejected this claim, and they appealed. The case was referred to the ECJ, which held that *Article 6(2)* and *Article 17(2)(6)* 'must be interpreted as precluding national legislation such as that at issue in the main proceedings, adopted before that directive came into force, which does not make it possible for a taxable person to allocate capital goods used in part for business purposes and in part for purposes other than those of his business wholly to his business and, where appropriate, to deduct immediately and in full the value added tax due on the acquisition of those goods'. *Charles & Charles-Tijmens v Staatssecretaris van Financiën*, ECJ Case C-434/03; [2006] STC 1429. (*Note*. For HMRC's practice following this decision, see Business Brief 15/2005, issued on 9 August 2005. See also *FA 2007, s 99*, which is intended to give effect to this decision.)

Employer providing transport for employees—whether within Article 6(2)

[22.184] In a German case, a building company provided transport to enable some of its employees to travel from their homes to the sites where they were working. The case was referred to the ECJ for a ruling on whether this should be treated as a supply of services for consideration, within *Article 6(2)* of the *EC Sixth Directive*. The ECJ held that, in principle, the provision of free transport by an employer was within *Article 6(2)*, since it served the employees' private purposes and thus purposes other than those of the business. However, *Article 6(2)* did not apply when, having regard to special circumstances such as changes in the place of work and difficulty in finding other means of transport, the requirements of the business made it necessary for the employer to provide transport for employees, in which case the supply of those services was not effected for purposes other than those of the business. It was for the national court to determine whether particular circumstances made it necessary for an employer to provide such transport. *Julius Fillibeck Söhne GmbH & Co KG v Finanzamt Neustadt*, ECJ Case C-258/95; [1998] STC 513; [1998] 1 WLR 697; [1998] All ER (EC) 466.

Employer providing subsidised meals—whether within Article 6(2)

[22.185] In a Swedish case, a company provided its employees with meals in a staff canteen at below cost price. The tax authority sought to charge VAT at 25% on the cost of the meals. The company appealed, contending that VAT should only be charged on the actual amount paid by the employees. The case was referred to the ECJ, which held that *Articles 5(6)* and *6(2)* of the *EC Sixth Directive* 'must be interpreted as precluding a national rule whereby transactions in respect of which an actual consideration is paid are regarded as an application of goods or services for private use, even where that consideration is less than the cost price of the goods or services supplied'. *Hotel Scandic Gasaback AB v Riksskatteverket*, ECJ Case C-412/03; [2005] STC 1311.

Employer providing free meals—whether within Article 6(2)

[22.186] Two Danish companies provided canteen meals to business contacts and staff in the context of business meetings. The tax authority issued assessments charging tax on the basis that these meals were taxable supplies. The companies appealed, contending that the Danish legislation contravened the *EC Sixth Directive*. The case was referred to the ECJ for a ruling on the interpretation of *Article 6(2)* of the *Directive*. The ECJ held that *Article 6(2)* 'must be interpreted in such a way that, on the one hand, it does not cover the provision, free of charge, of meals in company canteens to business contacts in the course of meetings held on the company premises where objective evidence indicates – this being a matter for the referring court to determine – that those meals are provided for strictly business-related purposes. On the other hand, *Article 6(2)* applies in principle to the provision, free of charge, of meals by a company to its staff on its premises, unless – this likewise being a matter for the referring court to determine – the needs of the company, such as the need to ensure that work meetings are run smoothly and without interruptions, require the employer to ensure that meals are provided'. The ECJ observed that the provision of sandwiches to employees in meeting rooms could be treated as a supply for business purposes, since 'the personal advantage which employees derive from such provision appears to be merely accessory to the requirements of the business'. *Danfoss A/S v Skatteministeriet (and related appeal)*, ECJ Case C-371/07; [2009] STC 701. (Note. For another issue in this case, see **22.425** below.)

Article 6(2)—capital goods not used for taxable supplies

[22.187] In a Netherlands case, an agricultural organisation (V) claimed a deduction for input tax incurred in relation to the general promotion of its members' interests. The tax authority rejected the claim and the regional court dismissed V's appeal, holding that V's general promotional activities did not constitute a significant extension of V's economic activities. However the Supreme Court referred the case to the ECJ for a ruling on the interpretation of *Article 6(2)* of the *Sixth Directive*. The ECJ held that *Articles 6(2)* and *17(2)* 'must be interpreted as not being applicable to the use of goods and services allocated to the business for the purpose of transactions other than the taxable transactions of the taxable person, as the value added tax due in respect of the acquisition of those goods and services, and relating to such transactions, is not deductible'. *Vereniging Noordelijke Land-en Tuinbouw Organisatie v Staatssecretaris van Financiën,*ECJ Case C-515/07; [2009] STC 935. (Note. For HMRC's practice following this decision, see HMRC Brief 02/10, issued on 22 January 2010. See also Clause 19 and Schedule 8 to the Finance (No 2) Bill 2010. In the House of Commons Committee Debate on 26 October 2010, the Exchequer Secretary stated that 'many taxpayers in the UK have been wrongly using *Lennartz* accounting. To ensure that taxpayers do not attempt to use the decision unfairly, the changes ensure that those who have already benefited from the up-front VAT recovery afforded by *Lennartz* accounting continue to pay the VAT due back to the Exchequer.')

Article 6(3) of EC Sixth Directive—self-supplies of services

[22.188] See *Robert Gordon's College*, **22.165** above.

Article 6(4) of EC Sixth Directive—agents acting in own name

[22.189] In a Belgian case, a company operated a bookmakers' business. It paid commission to several local agents, described as 'buralistes'. It treated this commission as exempt from VAT under *Article 13B(f)* of the *EC Sixth Directive*. The tax authority issued a ruling that VAT was chargeable on the commission. The company appealed, and the case was referred to the ECJ, which found in favour of the company, holding that 'in so far as an economic operator acts in his own name, but on behalf of an undertaking carrying on a bet-taking business, in the collection of bets covered by the exemption from value added tax under *Article 13(B)(f)*, that latter undertaking is to be considered, in accordance with *Article 6(4)*, to provide that operator with a supply of bets coming under that exemption'. *État Belge v Henfling & Others (administrators of Tiercé Franco-Belge SA)*, ECJ Case C-464/10; [2011] STC 1851.

[22.190] A UK company (L) sold phonecards to distributors which were resident in other EU Member States. Those distributors then resold the phonecards to consumers. L did not account for VAT on its sales of the phonecards, on the basis that the place of supply was the Member State where the distributor was established. HMRC issued an assessment on the basis that L was required to account for VAT on the value actually received for the services which it supplied, at the point of redemption. L appealed, contending that its supply was to the distributors of the cards, who paid VAT under the reverse charge mechanism, and that the redemption of the phonecards did not involve any supply by it to the consumers. The tribunal directed that the case should be referred to the ECJ for a ruling on whether the Sixth Directive should be interpreted as meaning that L made a supply at the time of redemption as well as its supply at the time of sale, and, if so, how VAT should be applied through the chain of supply. Advocate-General Jääskinen expressed the Opinion that '*Article 6(4)* of the *Sixth VAT Directive* creates the legal fiction of two identical supplies of services provided consecutively'. That legal fiction was 'the key to resolving this case. For VAT purposes, the distributors should be considered as commission agents acting in their own names, but on behalf of (L), who is the principal'. Accordingly, 'where a taxable person ('Trader A') sells to another taxable person ('Trader B') phonecards containing information enabling their buyer ('End User C') to access and receive telecommunications services from A to the amount specified on the card (provided that A has received from B the consideration agreed between them) Trader A supplies to end user C a service consisting of a right of access to telecommunications service against prepayment'. However, the effect of *Article 6(4)* of the *Sixth Directive* was that 'if Trader B takes part in his own name but on behalf of Trader A in the supply of that service to end user C, which is for the national court to ascertain, Trader B shall for VAT purposes be considered as having received that supply of service from Trader A and as having supplied it to End User C'. *Lebara Ltd v HMRC*, ECJ Case C-520/10; 8 December 2011 unreported.

Imports (Article 7)

[22.191] In a Dutch case, the ECJ held that the entry into the Netherlands of goods coming from the Netherlands Antilles had to be regarded as entry into the EC for the purposes of applying *Article 7(1)* of the *EC Sixth Directive*. *Van der Kooy v Staatssecretaris van Financiën*, ECJ Case C-181/97; 28 January 1999 unreported.

Article 7(3) of EC Sixth Directive

[22.192] In a Netherlands case, the ECJ held that 'where goods, transported by road under the external Community transit arrangements, are placed on the Community market after a number of irregularities have been committed in respect of those goods in various Member States, the goods cease to be covered by those arrangements' for the purposes of *Article 7(3)* of the *EC Sixth Directive*. For this purpose, 'any act or omission which prevents, if only for a short time, the competent customs authority from gaining access to goods under customs supervision and from monitoring them as provided for by the Community customs provisions must be regarded as a removal of the goods in question from customs supervision'. *Liberexim BV v Staatssecretaris van Financien*, ECJ Case C-371/99; [2002] All ER (D) 178 (Jul).

Place of taxable transactions (Articles 8, 9)

Place of supply of goods (Article 8)

[22.193] A German company, not resident in the UK, had entered into a contract with a UK company to supply and install a bulk material handling system. It also appointed another UK company to act as its sales representative and to supply technical services. It claimed a refund of input tax from the UK under the *EC Eighth Directive*, contending that, under *Article 8* of the *EC Sixth Directive*, the goods should be deemed to have been supplied in Germany. The Commissioners rejected the claim and the tribunal dismissed the company's appeal. The place of supply was the site where the components of the systems were installed and commissioned. As this site was in the UK, the supply of goods was deemed to have taken place in the UK. *Azo-Maschinenfabrik Adolf Zimmerman GmbH (No 2)*, [1987] VATTR 25 (VTD 2296). (*Note*. See now *VATA 1994, s 7(3)*, deriving from *F(No 2)A 1992*.)

[22.194] Compare *George Kuikka Ltd*, 62.476 SUPPLY, in which machine tools were treated as supplied outside the UK.

[22.195] A German trader operated a boutique on board a cruise ship. The tax authority issued a ruling that her sales were taxable transactions, on the basis that the points of arrival and departure were within the EC. The trader appealed, contending that many of the sales were made when the ship had stopped at a territory outside the EC (eg Morocco or Russia), and thus were not taxable. The case was referred to the ECJ, which held that 'stops made by a ship in the ports of a third country during which passengers may leave the ship, even for a short period, are "stops in a third territory" within the meaning of *Article 8(1)'* of the *EC Sixth Directive*. Accordingly such sales were not taxable in the EC, but fell 'within the tax jurisdiction of the State in which the stop is made'. *Köhler v Finanzamt Düsseldorf-Nord*, ECJ Case C-58/04; [2006] STC 469.

[22.196] A Swedish company arranged to install an optic cable under the Baltic Sea. The tax authority issued a ruling that the place of supply was in Sweden. The company appealed, and the case was referred to the ECJ, which held that *Article 8(1)* of the *EC Sixth Directive* 'must be interpreted as meaning that the right to tax the supply and laying of a fibre-optic cable linking two Member States and sited in part outside the territory of the Community is held by each Member State pro rata according to the length of cable in its territory with regard both to the price of the cable itself and the rest of the materials and to the cost of the services relating to the laying of the cable' and that 'the supply and laying of a fibre-optic cable linking two Member States is not subject to VAT for that part of the transaction which is carried out in the exclusive economic zone, on the continental shelf and at sea'. *Aktiebolaget NN v Skatteverket*, ECJ Case C-111/05; [2008] STC 3203.

[22.197] See also *Faaborg-Gelting Linien A/S v Finanzamt Flensburg*, **22.174** above; *EMAG Handel Eder OHG v Finanzlandesdirektion für Kärnten*, **22.517** below; *Centrax Ltd*, **23.33** EUROPEAN COMMUNITY: SINGLE MARKET, and *Peninsular & Oriental Steam Navigation Co*, **62.479** SUPPLY.

Place of supply of services (Article 9)

Article 9(1)—definition of 'fixed establishment'

[22.198] A German trader installed gaming machines on two ferry boats operating between Germany and Denmark, and contended that the services provided from such machines were provided from a fixed establishment located on the ship. The ECJ ruled that 'an installation for carrying on a commercial activity, such as the operation of gaming machines, on board a ship sailing on the high seas outside the national territory may be regarded as a fixed establishment within the meaning of that provision only if the establishment entails the permanent presence of both the human and technical resources for the provision of those services and it is not appropriate to deem those services to have been provided at the place where the supplier has established his business'. *G Berkholz v Finanzamt Hamburg-Mitte-Altstadt*, ECJ Case 168/84; [1985] ECR 2251; [1985] 3 CMLR 667. (*Notes.* (1) For another issue in this case, see **22.394** below. (2) Despite this decision, HMRC still treat such supplies as outside the scope of UK VAT when supplied on board international or intra-EC passenger transport: see HMRC VAT Guidance, Part 4, chapter 2, para 10.8.)

[22.199] A leasing company, established in the Netherlands, supplied cars to customers in Belgium and stored cars with Belgian dealers. It paid VAT to the Netherlands tax authority in respect of such transactions, and submitted a repayment claim on the basis that the place of supply was in Belgium. The Netherlands tax authority rejected the claim on the basis that the company had no fixed establishment in Belgium, so that the place of supply was in the

Netherlands. The company appealed and the case was referred to the ECJ, which held that services could not be deemed to be supplied at an establishment other than the main place of business unless that establishment had a minimum degree of stability derived from the permanent presence of both the human and technical resources necessary for the provision of the services. Accordingly, a leasing company did not supply cars from a fixed establishment in another Member State if it did not have an office or any premises on which to store the cars there. *ARO Lease BV v Inspecteur der Belastingdienst Grote Ondernemingen Amsterdam*, ECJ Case C-190/95; [1997] STC 1272; [1997] 1 ECR 4383.

[22.200] A similar decision was reached in *Lease Plan Luxembourg SA v Belgium*, 22.542 below.

[22.201] A UK bank (F) had an Italian branch, which submitted a repayment claim to the Italian tax authorities. The tax authority rejected the claim, and F appealed. The case was referred to the ECJ, which held that 'a fixed establishment, which is not a legal entity distinct from the company of which it forms part, established in another Member State and to which the company supplies services, should not be treated as a taxable person by reason of the costs imputed to it in respect of those supplies'. *Ministero dell'Economia e delle Finanze v FCE Bank plc*, ECJ Case C-210/04; [2007] STC 165.

Yachts—whether 'forms of transport'

[22.202] The proprietor of a yacht charter business, operating from Kiel in Germany, appealed against the imposition of VAT on the charter of the yachts. The ECJ held that yachts hired for pleasure were 'forms of transport', with the result that, under *Article 9(1)*, the place of supply was in Germany where the business was established. *Hamann v Finanzamt Hamburg-Eimsbuttel*, ECJ Case 51/88; [1989] ECR 767; [1991] STC 193; [1990] 2 CMLR 377.

Lease of car

[22.203] An Austrian company (C) leased a car from a German company, and used it in Austria for business purposes. The German company accounted for output tax on the lease. C reclaimed this tax under the *EC Eighth Directive*. The Austrian tax authority sought to charge VAT on C's use of the car. C appealed, and the ECJ upheld C's contentions, holding that the place of supply was in Germany, and that the Austrian legislation contravened the *EC Sixth Directive*. *Cookies World Vertriebsgesellschaft mbH iL v Finanzlandes-direktion für Tirol*, ECJ Case C-155/01; [2004] STC 1386.

[22.204] See also *Faaborg-Gelting Linien A/S v Finanzamt Flensburg*, 22.174 above.

Veterinary services

[22.205] A Netherlands veterinary partnership supplied services to Belgian cattle farmers. The Netherlands required the partnership to account for output tax on the basis that the services were supplied in the Netherlands. The partnership appealed, contending that the services had been supplied in Belgium. The ECJ rejected the partnership's contention, holding that the services fell within *Article 9(1)* of the *EC Sixth Directive*, and should be treated as being supplied in the place where the partnership had established its business. *Maatschap MJM Linthorst & Others v Inspecteur der Belastingdienst/Ondernemingen Roermond*, ECJ Case C-167/95; [1997] STC 1287. (*Note*. For Customs' practice following this decision, see Business Brief 12/98, issued on 21 May 1998.)

Article 9(2)(a)

[22.206] An Austrian company (F) sold a quantity of Austrian fishing permits to a German company (H). H sold the permits to its customers, and applied to the Austrian tax authority for a refund of input tax. The authority rejected the claim on the basis that the sales were supplies 'of services connected with immovable property', within *Article 9(2)(a)* of the *EC Sixth Directive*, so that H's supplies had taken place in Austria. H appealed, contending that fishing permits were outside the scope of *Article 9(2)(a)*. The ECJ rejected H's contentions, holding that 'the transmission of the right to fish by means of a transfer of fishing permits for valuable consideration constitutes a supply of services connected with immovable property within the meaning of *Article 9(2)(a)*'. *Heger Rudi GmbH v Finanzamt Graz-Stadt*, ECJ Case C-166/05; [2008] STC 2679.

[22.207] A company (R) operated a business involving the sale and exchange of 'timeshare' holiday accommodation outside the UK. It received income from new members in the form of 'enrolment fees' and from existing members in the form of subscriptions. It also received income from 'exchange fees' which it charged for facilitating the exchange of holiday usage rights between different members of its timeshare exchange scheme. Until 2003, R accounted for VAT on its enrolment and subscription fees, and on exchange fees which related to properties within the EU (but not on exchange fees relating to properties outside the EU). From 2004, it failed to account for VAT on its income from enrolment fees and subscriptions. HMRC issued an assessment on this income, and R appealed, contending that its supplies should be treated as 'connected with immovable property', within *Article 9(2)(a)* of the *EC Sixth Directive*. (The Spanish tax authorities treated R's income as connected with immovable property to the extent that it related to properties in Spain.) The tribunal referred the case to the ECJ for a ruling on the interpretation of *Article 9(2)(a)*. The ECJ accepted R's contentions, holding that *Article 9(2)(a)* 'must be interpreted as meaning that the place where services are supplied by an association whose business consists in organising the exchange between its members of their timeshare usage rights in holiday accommodation, in return for which that association receives from its members enrolment, annual subscription and exchange fees, is the place where the property in respect of which the member concerned holds timeshare usage rights is situated'. *RCI Europe v HMRC*, ECJ Case C-37/08; [2009] STC 2407.

[22.208] A Scottish company sold 'timeshare' interests in properties in Spain. The tribunal held that the company was making standard-rated supplies of services and that the place of supply was in the UK. The company appealed to the CS, which referred the case to the ECJ for rulings on the interpretation of the *EC Sixth Directive*. The ECJ held that the supplies at issue 'must be classified at the time when the customer participating in such a scheme converts the rights he initially acquired into a service offered by that operator.

Where those rights are converted into hotel accommodation or into a right to temporarily use a property, those supplies are supplies of services connected with immovable property'. The place of supply was 'the place where the hotel or that property is situated'. The ECJ also held that, where a customer converted his timeshare rights into the right to temporarily use a property, the supply was within *Article 13B(b)*, but this did not 'prevent Member States from excluding that supply from exemption'. *Macdonald Resorts Ltd v HMRC*, ECJ Case C-270/09; [2011] STC 412.

Article 9(2)(b)—transport services

[22.209] A company (T) provided a maritime passenger and freight service between the Italian mainland and Sardinia. The Italian authority imposed VAT on its supplies, and T appealed. The ECJ rejected T's contentions, holding that *Article 9(2)(b)* of the *Sixth Directive* did not preclude a Member State from applying its VAT legislation to a transport operation between two points within its national territory even where a part of the journey took place in international waters. *Trans Tirreno Express SpA v Ufficio Provinciale IVA*, ECJ Case 283/84; [1986] ECR 231; [1986] 2 CMLR 100.

[22.210] The French government exempted from VAT transport between mainland France and Corsica. The EC Commission applied for a declaration that this was a breach of the *EC Sixth Directive*. The ECJ dismissed the application, holding that the French government was not required to impose VAT on transport between mainland France and Corsica which took place in or above international waters. *EC Commission v French Republic*, ECJ Case C-30/89; [1990] 1 ECR 691.

[22.211] The Greek government exempted sea voyages in territorial waters from VAT. The EC Commission applied to the ECJ for a declaration that this was in breach of the *EC Sixth Directive*, contending that the place of supply was entirely within Greece. The ECJ upheld this contention and granted the declaration. *EC Commission v Hellenic Republic*, ECJ Case C-331/94; [1996] STC 1168; [1996] 1 ECR 2675.

[22.212] In a German case, a company organised cross-frontier coach tours. The German tax authority charged VAT on the basis that the consideration which the company received should be apportioned between the countries concerned on the basis of the distances covered. The company appealed, contending that the time spent in the countries concerned could also be taken into account. The ECJ rejected this contention, holding that, in a case where cross-frontier transport was supplied on an all-inclusive basis, the total consideration must be allocated on a pro rata basis, having regard to the distances covered in each state. *Reisebüro Binder GmbH v Finanzamt Stuttgart-Körperschaften*, ECJ Case C-116/96; [1998] STC 604.

[22.213] See also *Faaborg-Gelting Linien A/S v Finanzamt Flensburg*, **22.174** above; *British Sky Broadcasting Ltd*, **62.489** SUPPLY; *The Chinese Channel Ltd (HK)*, **62.490** SUPPLY, and *WH Payne & Co*, **62.536** SUPPLY.

Article 9(2)(c)

[22.214] A German (D) supplied sound engineering services for concerts. The German tax authority assessed him for VAT on the whole of his turnover, even where the concerts took place outside Germany. He appealed, contending that his services were services relating to 'entertainment or similar activities', within *Article 9(2)(c)* of the *Sixth Directive*, so that the place of supply was where the services were physically carried out. The ECJ upheld D's contention, holding that, where such sound engineering services were 'a prerequisite for the performance of the principal artistic or entertainment service supplied', they were within *Article 9(2)(c)*. *Dudda v Finanzamt Bergisch Gladbach*, ECJ Case C-327/94; [1996] STC 1290; [1996] 1 ECR 4595; [1996] 3 CMLR 1063.

[22.215] A UK company had operated 127 amusement arcades in the UK. Under an avoidance scheme, devised by an accountancy firm, the machines were leased to a newly-formed Channel Islands company (C), in the same group. C did not register for UK VAT and did not account for output tax on the takings from the arcades, but claimed repayment of substantial amounts of input tax under the *EC Thirteenth Directive*. Customs rejected the repayment claims, and issued rulings that C was liable to account for output tax on the takings and was required to register for VAT. The tribunal dismissed C's appeals, finding that the amusement arcades were a 'fixed establishment'. The ECJ upheld this decision, holding that 'the supply of services consisting of enabling the public to use, for consideration, slot gaming machines installed in amusement arcades established in the territory of a Member State must be regarded as constituting entertainment or similar activities within the meaning of the first indent *of Article 9(2)(c)* (of the *Sixth Directive)*', so that 'the place where those services are supplied is the place where they are physically carried out'. *RAL (Channel Islands) Ltd v C & E Commrs (and related appeals)*, ECJ Case C-452/03; [2005] STC 1025.

[22.216] A UK company (G) organised two boat fairs in France, and claimed a refund of tax under the *EC Eighth Directive*. The French tax authority rejected the claim on the basis that the boat fairs were within *Article 9(2)(c)* of the *Sixth Directive*, so that G's supplies had taken place in France. The ECJ found in favour of the tax authority, holding that 'an inclusive service provided by an organiser to exhibitors at a fair or in an exhibition hall falls within the category of services referred to in *(Article 9(2)(c))*'. *Ministre de l'Économie, des Finances et de l'Industrie v Gillan Beach Ltd*, ECJ Case C-114/05; [2006] STC 1080.

[22.217] See also *Burrows*, **62.523** supply, and *Sugar and Spice On Tour Catering*, **62.524** supply.

Article 9(2)(e)

[22.218] The EC Commission applied for a ruling that France had applied unauthorised restrictions to the definition of 'advertising services', thus failing properly to implement the provisions of *Article 9(2)(e)* of the *EC Sixth Directive*. The ECJ granted the application, holding that a promotional activity was within the definition of an 'advertising service' if it involved 'the dissemination of a message intended to inform the public of the existence and the qualities of the product or service which is the subject matter of the activity, with a view to increasing the sales of that product or service'. *EC Commission v French Republic*, ECJ Case C-68/92; [1993] 1 ECR 5881; [1997] STC 684; [1995] 2 CMLR 1.

[22.219] Similar decisions were reached in *EC Commission v Kingdom of Spain*, ECJ Case C-73/92; [1993] 1 ECR 5997; [1997] STC 700; [1995] 2 CMLR 1 and *EC Commission v Grand Duchy of Luxembourg*, ECJ Case C-69/92; [1993] 1 ECR 5907; [1997] STC 712; [1995] 2 CMLR 1.

[22.220] The French tax authorities issued a ruling that, although producers of advertising films supplied 'advertising services' within *Article 9(2)(e)* of the *EC Sixth Directive* when they supplied their services directly to the advertisers, their supplies were outside *Article 9(2)(e)*, and therefore took place within France, when they were invoiced to advertising agencies. A group of film producers appealed, and the case was referred to the ECJ, which held that the relevant supplies were within the definition of 'advertising services' even when they were invoiced to advertising agencies, rather than to the final customer. *Syndicat des Producteurs Indépendants v Ministère de l'Économie, des Finances et de l'Industrie*, ECJ Case C-108/00; [2001] STC 523; [2001] All ER (EC) 564.

[22.221] A Luxembourg company (D) commissioned two stands at an exhibition in Ghent from a Belgian company (F). F sent an invoice, including Belgian VAT, to D. D refused to pay the VAT, contending that the relevant services were 'advertising services' within *Article 9(2)(e)* of the *EC Sixth Directive*, so that the place of supply was in Luxembourg. The ECJ upheld D's contentions, holding that *Article 9(2)(e)* 'must be interpreted as applying to advertising services supplied indirectly to the advertiser and invoiced to an intermediate customer who in turn invoices them to the advertiser. The fact that the advertiser does not produce goods or services in the price of which the cost of the advertising services may be included is not relevant for the purpose of determining the place where the services are supplied to the intermediate customer.' *Design Concept SA v Flanders Expo SA*, ECJ Case C-438/01; [2003] STC 912.

[22.222] A Polish company (K) provided services to a Cyprus company consisting of 'research and development work relating to the environment and technology, carried out by engineers'. The Polish tax authority issued a ruling that some of K's supplies were 'scientific activities', so that the place of supply for VAT purposes was Poland. K appealed, contending that its supplies were 'services of engineers' within *Article 9(2)(e)* of the *EC Sixth Directive*, so that the place of supply was in Cyprus. The case was referred to the ECJ, which upheld K's contentions, holding that where such services were supplied 'on a contract basis for the benefit of a recipient established in another Member State', they were 'services of engineers' falling within *Article 9(2)(e)*. *Kronospan Mielec sp zoo v Dyrektor Izby Skarbowej w Rzeszowie*, ECJ Case C-222/09; [2011] STC 80.

[22.223] A German professor of law acted as an arbitrator for the International Chamber of Commerce, based in France. The German tax authority charged turnover tax on the fees which the professor received. He appealed, contending that the services were within *Article 9(2)(e)* of the *EC Sixth Directive*, so that the place of supply was in France. The case was referred to the ECJ, which rejected the professor's contentions, holding that the services of an arbitrator were not within *Article 9(2)(e)*. *Von Hoffmann v Finanzamt Trier*, ECJ Case C-145/96; [1997] STC 1321; [1997] All ER (EC) 852.

[22.224] Under German law, executors' services were treated as being supplied at the fixed establishment of the supplier, in accordance with *Article 9(1)* of the *EC Sixth Directive*. The EC Commission took proceedings against Germany, claiming that executors' services should have been treated as 'services of lawyers', falling within *Article 9(2)(e)*. The ECJ rejected the Commission's contention, holding that 'the service of executing a will constitutes neither a service principally and habitually carried out by a lawyer nor a service which is similar to those carried out by a lawyer'. *EC Commission v Federal Republic of Germany (No 6)*, ECJ Case C-401/06; [2008] STC 2906.

[22.225] A German company supplied the services of self-employed lorry drivers to customers established in Italy. Its local tax office advised it that this was not a 'supply of staff' since the drivers were self-employed, and that it was required to account for VAT on the basis that the place of supply was in Germany. However the federal tax office rejected input tax claims, ruling that the company was making supplies of staff within *Article 9(2)(e)* of the *EC Sixth Directive*, so that the place of supply was in Italy where the customer was established, and that the VAT for which the company had accounted was not reclaimable. The company appealed, and the case was referred to the ECJ, which found in favour of the tax authority, holding that a 'supply of staff' within Article 9(2)(e) 'includes the supply of self-employed persons not in the employ of the trader providing the service'. *ADV Allround Vermittlungs AG v Finanzamt Hamburg-Bergedorf, ECJ Case C-218/10,*26 January 2012 unreported.

[22.226] A German company purchased goods in Hong Kong which were packed in a container and sent by sea to Hamburg and then overland to Frankfurt. The ECJ was asked for a ruling as to whether transport by container could be considered as a 'form of transport' and as excluded from *Article 9(2)(e)* of the *EC Sixth Directive*. The ECJ held that transport by a container could not be considered as a form of transport for this purpose. *Hauptzollamt Frankfurt am Main-Ost v Deutsche Olivetti GmbH*, ECJ Case C-17/89; [1990] 1 ECR 2301; [1992] 2 CMLR 859.

[22.227] See also *Kollektivavtalsstiftelsen TRR Trygghetsrådet v Skatteverket*, **20.36** EC DIRECTIVE 2006/112/EC; *Levob Verzekeringen BV v Staatssecretaris van Financien*, **22.176** above; *American Express Services Europe Ltd*, **62.484** SUPPLY; *Diversified Agency Services Ltd (aka Omnicom UK plc)*, **62.495** SUPPLY; *Austrian National Tourist Office*, **62.497** SUPPLY; *Zurich Insurance Company*, **62.506** SUPPLY; *Miller Freeman Worldwide plc*, **62.514** SUPPLY; *International Trade & Exhibitions J/V Ltd*, **62.526** SUPPLY; *BPH Equipment Ltd*, **62.543** SUPPLY, and *HMRC v IDT Card Services Ireland Ltd*, **67.172** VALUATION.

Article 9(3)

[22.228] In an Italian case concerning the place of supply of advertising services, the ECJ held that Member States could exercise the option provided in *Article 9(3)(b)* of the *EC Sixth Directive* and define the place where the services in question were supplied 'as within the Member State concerned'. If the option was exercised, 'advertising services provided by a supplier established in the European Community to a customer situated in a non-Member state, whether that customer is the final customer or an intermediate customer, are deemed to be supplied within the European Community', provided that the effective use and enjoyment of the services took place within the Member State concerned. However, 'advertising services provided by a supplier established outside the European Community for his own clients cannot be liable to VAT under *Article 9(3)(b)*', even where the supplier had acted in the capacity of an intermediate customer in respect of an earlier supply, since such a supply did not fall within the scope of *Article 9*. Furthermore, the fact that a supply of services for the purposes of *Article 9(3)(b)* was subject to VAT did not preclude a taxable person's right to a refund where he satisfied the conditions laid down in *Article 2* of the *Thirteenth Directive*. *Athesia Druck Srl v Ministero dell'Economia e delle Finanze*, ECJ Case C-1/08; [2009] STC 1334.

Chargeable event (Article 10)

Derogation for transactions to become chargeable on payment

[22.229] In an Italian case, a company had commissioned a contractor to construct a building. The contractor issued a 'proforma' invoice in 1980 but did not issue a VAT invoice until 1982. The Italian VAT office penalised the company for breaching an Italian law requiring the recipient of a 'proforma' invoice to account for the VAT due thereon. The company appealed, contending that the effect of the derogation in *Article 10(2)* of the *EC Sixth Directive* was that the VAT was not chargeable until it had paid the contractor for the building. The case was referred to the ECJ, which ruled that Member States which availed themselves of the derogation in question were not required to lay down detailed rules providing for situations where a service had been supplied but the relevant invoice had not been issued and payment had not been made. (The Advocate-General expressly considered that the relevant Italian legislation was not inconsistent with the *Directive*, but the ECJ did not issue an explicit ruling on this point.) *Ufficio IVA di Trapani v Italittica SpA*, ECJ Case C-144/94; [1995] STC 1059; [1995] 1 ECR 3653.

[22.230] In 1997 Customs announced that they intended to abolish zero-rating for drugs and prostheses supplied to hospital in-patients (see now *VATA 1994, Sch 8, Group 12, Note 5B*, introduced by *VAT (Drugs, Medicines and Aids for the Handicapped) Order 1997 (SI 1997/2744)*, with effect from 1 January 1998). A company (B), which operated a number of hospitals, adopted a 'prepayment' scheme which involved a company in its VAT group prepaying £100,000,000 plus VAT to an associated company (G) in a different VAT group, with the intention of crystallising an entitlement to input tax recovery at the time of the prepayment. Customs rejected the input tax claims, and B and G appealed. The Ch D referred the cases to the ECJ for a ruling on the interaction of *Articles 10* and *17* of the *EC Sixth Directive*. Advocate-General Poiares Maduro observed that 'the text of the second subparagraph of *Article 10(2)* refers to situations where "a payment is to be made on account before the goods are delivered or the services are performed"'. This subparagraph required that 'in order for a payment on account for goods or services to be covered by this provision, those goods or services must be specifically identified when the payment on account takes place.' The ECJ held that 'the second subparagraph of *Article 10(2)* of the *Sixth Directive*, according to which, where payments are made on account before the goods are delivered or the services are performed, VAT becomes chargeable on receipt of payment and on the amount received, constitutes a derogation from the rule laid down in the first subparagraph of that provision and, as such, must be interpreted strictly.' The ECJ concluded that prepayments of the kind at issue, 'whereby lump sums are paid for goods referred to in general terms in a list which may be altered at any time by agreement between the buyer and the seller and from which the buyer may possibly select articles, on the basis of an agreement which he may unilaterally resile from at any time, thereupon recovering the unused balance of the prepayments, do not fall within the scope of the second subparagraph of *Article 10(2)*'. *BUPA Hospitals Ltd v C & E Commrs; Goldsborough Developments Ltd v C & E Commrs*; ECJ Case C-419/02; [2006] STC 967; [2006] 2 WLR 96. (*Note.* For Customs' practice following this decision, see Business Brief 2/2006, issued on 27 February 2006.)

Article 10(3)—chargeable event on importation

[22.231] In an Italian case, a company temporarily imported a quantity of wheat from Canada in 1982 in order to process it into semolina. It re-exported the semolina but retained the by-products of the processing, which it released for consumption in 1985. The Italian authorities required payment of an agricultural levy, VAT and interest in respect of the importation of the by-products. Subsequently the company began proceedings to seek repayment of the interest, contending that the effect of *Article 10(3)* of the *Sixth Directive* was that the chargeable event had not occurred until 1985 when it released the by-products for consumption. The case was referred to the ECJ, which upheld the company's contention with regard to the interest charged on the VAT, ruling that *Article 10(3)* precluded a Member State from requiring interest on VAT for the period between temporary importation and definitive importation in respect of goods which were subject to inward processing arrangements. (However, the ECJ upheld the validity of the charge to interest on the agricultural levy.) *Pezzullo Molini Pastifici Mangimifici SpA v Ministero delle Finanze*, ECJ Case C-166/94; [1996] STC 1236; [1996] 1 ECR 331.

Taxable amount (Article 11)

'Consideration' (Article 11A1(a))

[22.232] In a German case, the ECJ held that interest awarded by a court, in respect of the late payment of taxable consideration, was not itself part of the consideration for the services in question. *BAZ Bausystem AG v Finanzamt München für Körperschaften*, ECJ Case 222/81; [1982] ECR 2527; [1982] 3 CMLR 688.

[22.233] A company which sold cosmetics supplied some of its goods to agents at greatly reduced prices. Customs issued an assessment charging output tax on the normal wholesale price of such goods. The company appealed, contending that the consideration should be treated as the amount actually paid by the agents. The tribunal referred the case to the ECJ, which held that the taxable amount included not only the monetary consideration actually paid for the product but also the value of the services provided by the agents to the company in obtaining and rewarding hostesses. The value of this service was the difference between the normal wholesale price and the amount actually paid by the agents, so that VAT was chargeable on the whole of the normal wholesale price. *Naturally Yours Cosmetics Ltd v C & E Commrs (No 2)*, ECJ Case 230/87; [1988] STC 879; [1988] ECR 6365; [1989] 1 CMLR 797.

[22.234] A company sold goods by mail order. It offered new customers, and existing customers who introduced new customers, certain goods (such as a kettle, a toaster or an iron) free of charge as inducements. Such goods were supplied after new customers had made their first order. The company accounted for VAT on the cost of the goods, and Customs issued assessments charging tax on 150% of the cost price, being their estimate of the market value of the supply. The tribunal referred the case to the ECJ, which held that the goods in question were supplied to the customers in consideration for a service, namely the introduction of a potential customer. The value of the goods was to be determined subjectively. The value in question was that attributed by the recipient of the services (i.e. the company). Accordingly the taxable amount for VAT purposes was the cost of the articles to the company. *Empire Stores Ltd v C & E Commrs*, ECJ Case C-33/93; [1994] STC 623; [1994] 1 ECR 2329; [1994] 1 CMLR 751; [1994] 2 All ER 90. (*Notes*. (1) For Customs' practice following this decision, see Business Brief 15/94, issued on 19 July 1994. (2) For a preliminary issue in this case, see **2.294** APPEALS. (3) Following the ECJ decision, the tribunal discharged the assessments— [1994] VATTR 145.)

[22.235] A company (E) operated a sales promotion scheme, entitling customers who purchased and returned three of its toothpaste cartons to a £1 refund. It claimed a repayment of output tax which it had previously accounted for, contending that the reimbursement of this money constituted a retrospective discount which reduced the consideration for its supplies. Customs rejected the claim and E appealed. The tribunal referred the case to the ECJ, which held that the 'taxable amount' within *Article 11A1(a)* of the *EC Sixth Directive* could not exceed the amount actually paid by the final consumer. Accordingly, the amounts refunded by the manufacturer had to be deducted from the original selling price in computing the taxable amount. *Elida Gibbs Ltd v C & E Commrs*, ECJ Case C-317/94; [1996] STC 1387; [1996] 1 ECR 5339; [1997] 2 WLR 477; [1997] All ER (EC) 53. (*Notes*. (1) The case was heard in the ECJ with *Argos Distributors Ltd*, **22.236** below. (2) For HMRC's practice following this decision, see Business Brief 25/96, issued on 6 December 1996, and HMRC Brief 08/07, issued on 6 February 2007.)

[22.236] A company (D) operated a retail business. It operated a voucher scheme, under which it sold vouchers at a discount to other traders for distribution to members of the public. It had consistently accounted for output tax on the face value of the vouchers, as instructed by Customs. In 1993 it formed the opinion that that it should only have been required to account for tax on the discounted amounts at which it sold the vouchers to other traders. It claimed repayment of more than £1,000,000 in tax which it considered that it had overpaid in the previous ten years. Customs rejected the claim and D appealed. The tribunal referred the case to the ECJ, which held that the consideration for the purposes of *Article 11A1(a)* was the subjective value actually received, and that the part of the consideration represented by the voucher was the sum actually obtained by the supplier from the sale of the voucher. *Argos Distributors Ltd v C & E Commrs*, ECJ Case C-288/94; [1996] STC 1359; [1996] 1 ECR 5311; [1996] 3 CMLR 569; [1997] 2 WLR 477. (*Notes*. (1) The case was heard in the ECJ with *Elida Gibbs Ltd*, 22.235 above. (2) For the Commissioners' practice following this decision, see Business Brief 25/96, issued on 6 December 1996.)

[22.237] Under German law, amounts refunded by a manufacturer to a final customer (of the type considered by the ECJ decision in *Elida Gibbs Ltd*, 22.235 above), were not treated as deductible from the consideration. Following the ECJ decision in *Elida Gibbs Ltd*, the EC Commission brought an action against Germany, seeking a declaration that it had failed to fulfil its obligations under *Article 11* of the *EC Sixth Directive*. The ECJ granted a declaration accordingly, holding that 'by not adopting the measures necessary to allow adjustment of the taxable amount of the taxable person who has effected reimbursement where money-off coupons are reimbursed', Germany had failed to fulfil its obligations under *Article 11*. *EC Commission v Federal Republic of Germany*, ECJ Case C-427/98; [2003] STC 301. (*Note*. For HMRC's practice following this decision, see HMRC Brief 08/07, issued on 6 February 2007)

[22.238] In a Belgian case, a company appealed against assessments charging output tax, contending that, where customers made payment by credit card, the amount which the credit card company retained as commission should be excluded in computing the consideration on which VAT was chargeable. The ECJ rejected this contention, holding that in a credit card transaction, the commission retained by the credit card company must be included in the consideration which was chargeable to VAT. The fact that the purchaser did not pay the agreed price directly to the supplier, but paid it to an intermediary who retained some of the payment as commission, could not change the taxable amount. *Chaussures Bally SA v Belgian Ministry of Finance*, ECJ Case C-18/92; [1993] 1 ECR 2871; [1997] STC 209.

[22.239] In a German case, a company which operated gaming machines was required to pay out as winnings 60% of all coins inserted. It only accounted for VAT on the 40% of the takings which it retained. The German tax authority issued an assessment on the basis that the company was required to account for output tax on the full amount of the takings, including the amounts which were paid out as winnings. The company appealed, and the case was referred to the ECJ, which ruled that the effect of *Article 11A1* of the *EC Sixth Directive* was that, in the case of gaming machines offering the possibility of winning, the taxable amount did not include the statutorily prescribed proportion of the total coins inserted which corresponded to the winnings paid out to players. *HJ Glawe Spiel und Unterhaltungsgeräte Aufstellungsgesellschaft mbH & Co KG v Finanzamt Hamburg-Barmbek-Uhlenhorst*, ECJ Case C-38/93; [1994] STC 543; [1994] 1 ECR 1679; [1995] 1 CMLR 70. (*Note*. For a subsequent case in which this decision was distinguished, see *Town & County Factors Ltd*, **22.240** below.)

[22.240] The decision in *HJ Glawe Spiel*, 22.239 above, was distinguished in a subsequent case involving a company (T) which organised a number of 'spot-the-ball' competitions. It initially accounted for VAT on the full amount of entry fees, but subsequently submitted a repayment claim on the basis that it should have deducted the amounts which it paid out in prizes. Customs rejected the claim and T appealed, also raising an alternative contention that the competitions should be deemed not to be taxable supplies since they were not governed by a legally binding contract (with the effect that it would only be required to account for tax on its supplies of prizes). The case was referred to the ECJ, which rejected T's contentions, holding firstly that 'a supply of services which is effected for consideration but is not based on enforceable obligations, because it has been agreed that the provider is bound in honour only to provide the services, constitutes a transaction subject to value added tax'; and secondly, that 'the full amount of the entry fees received by the organiser of a competition constitutes the taxable amount for that competition where the organiser has that amount freely at his disposal'. *Town & County Factors Ltd v C & E Commrs*, ECJ Case C-498/99; [2002] STC 1263; [2003] All ER (EC) 33. (*Note.* For a subsequent appeal involving the same company, see **5.76 BOOKS, ETC.**)

[22.241] Under French law, service charges were specifically declared not to be liable to VAT. The EC Commission applied to the ECJ for a declaration that this provision was a breach of *Article 11A1* of the *EC Sixth Directive*. The ECJ granted the declaration. *EC Commission v French Republic*, ECJ Case C-404/99; 29 March 2001 unreported.

[22.242] A company (P), which sold furniture, arranged for customers to be provided with 'interest-free credit' by a finance company. In such cases, the finance company did not pay P the full price charged to the customer, but paid a net amount after retaining a 'discount' which was equivalent to the amount that the finance company would have charged the customer for the loan at a commercial rate. In accounting for output tax on such transactions, P only included as gross takings the amount which it actually received from the finance company. Customs issued an assessment on the basis that P should have included the full amount charged to the customer in its gross takings. P appealed, contending that it should only be required to account for tax on the amount which it actually received. The HL referred the case to the ECJ, which held that, where a retail trader sold goods 'in return for payment of the advertised price which he invoices to the purchaser and which does not vary according to whether the customer pays in cash or by way of credit', the taxable amount was the full amount payable by the purchaser. *C & E Commrs v Primback Ltd*, ECJ Case C-34/99; [2001] STC 803; [2001] 1 WLR 1693; [2001] All ER (EC) 735. (*Note.* For Customs' practice following this decision, see Business Brief 11/01, issued on 21 August 2001.)

[22.243] In a German case, a company which sold books and records gave 'bonuses in kind' (including books, records and bicycles) to customers who introduced new customers. The German tax authority issued an assessment on the basis that the costs of such goods, including delivery charges, were taxable consideration within *Article 11A1(a)* of the *EC Sixth Directive*. The company appealed, contending that the delivery charges should not be treated as part of the taxable amount. The case was referred to the ECJ, which rejected the company's contentions and held that the costs of delivery of the 'bonus' goods had to be included as part of the 'taxable amount'. *Bertelsmann AG v Finanzamt Wiedenbrück*, ECJ Case C-380/99; [2001] STC 1153.

[22.244] A company (Y), which operated several retail shops, accepted vouchers issued by manufacturers as part-payment. In such cases it was reimbursed by the manufacturer and accounted for output tax on the full sale price of the goods, including the amounts for which it had accepted vouchers. Subsequently it submitted a repayment claim on the basis that the amounts for which it had been reimbursed by the manufacturers were not 'consideration' and that output tax was not due. Customs rejected the claim on the basis that the reimbursements which Y received from the manufacturers were consideration for the supplies of the goods to its customers. Y appealed, and the tribunal referred the case to the ECJ. The ECJ upheld Customs' ruling, holding that 'when, on the sale of a product, the retailer allows the final consumer to settle the sale price partly in cash and partly by means of a reduction coupon issued by the manufacturer of that product, and the manufacturer reimburses to the retailer the amount indicated on that coupon, the nominal value of that coupon must be included in the taxable amount in the hands of that retailer'. *Yorkshire Co-Operatives Ltd v C & E Commrs*, ECJ Case C-398/99; [2003] STC 234; [2003] 1 WLR 2821.

[22.245] See also *Ministero dell'Economia e delle Finanze v Part Service Srl*, **22.62** above; *First National Bank of Chicago*, **22.89** above; *Peugeot Motor Co plc*, **38.51** INSURANCE; *Medical Centre Developments Ltd*, **62.134** SUPPLY, and *Findel plc*, **67.74** VALUATION.

'Subsidies directly linked to the price'

[22.246] A Belgian agricultural association did not account for VAT on an annual subsidy. The Belgian tax authority demanded VAT on the subsidy, and the association appealed. The case was referred to the ECJ for a ruling on the interpretation of the words 'including subsidies directly linked to the price of such supplies' in *Article 11A1(a)* of the *EC Sixth Directive*. The ECJ held that these words should 'be interpreted as covering only subsidies which constitute the whole or part of the consideration for a supply of goods or services and which are paid by a third party to the seller or supplier'. It was for the national court to determine whether the subsidy in question was within this definition. *Office des Produits Wallons ASBL v Belgium*, ECJ Case C-184/00; [2003] STC 1100; [2003] All ER (EC) 747.

[22.247] A network installer, within the *Energy Efficiency Grants Regulations 1992*, received grants from the Energy Grants Action Agency in respect of energy advice which it gave to householders. It initially accounted for VAT in respect of such grants, but subsequently claimed repayment, on the basis that the grants were not consideration for any supplies. Customs rejected the claim, considering that the grants were liable to VAT. The QB referred the case to the ECJ, which held that *Article 11A1(a)* 'is to be interpreted as meaning that a sum such as that paid in the case in the main proceedings constitutes part of the consideration for the supply of services and forms part of the taxable amount'. *Keeping Newcastle Warm v C & E Commrs*, ECJ Case C-353/00; [2002] STC 943; [2002] All ER (EC) 769.

[22.248] An EC regulation provided for aid to be paid in respect of dried fodder. The EC Commission took infraction proceedings against four Member States, claiming that VAT should have been charged on such payments. The cases were referred to the ECJ, which rejected the Commission's claims, holding that the payments were outside the scope of *Article 11A1(a)* of the *EC Sixth Directive*, since they were not 'directly linked to the price of the taxable transaction' or 'paid specifically to enable the processing undertaking to supply dried fodder to a purchaser'. *EC Commission v Italy*, ECJ Case C-381/01; [2004] All ER (D) 271 (Jul); *EC Commission v Finland*, ECJ Case C-495/01; [2004] All ER (D) 265 (Jul); *EC Commission v Germany*, ECJ Case C-144/02; [2004] All ER (D) 264 (Jul); *EC Commission v Sweden*, ECJ Case C-463/02; [2004] All ER (D) 267 (Jul).

Cost of providing services (Article 11A1(c))

[22.249] In a German case, the ECJ held that *Article 11A1(c)* of the *EC Sixth Directive* 'does not preclude the taxable amount for VAT in respect of the private use of part of a building treated by a taxable person as forming, in its entirety, part of the assets of his business from being fixed at a portion of the acquisition or construction costs of the building, established in accordance with the length of the period for adjustment of deductions concerning VAT provided for in *Article 20*'. That taxable amount 'must include the costs of acquiring the land on which the building is constructed when that acquisition has been subject to VAT and the taxable person has deducted that tax.' *J & S Wollny v Finanzamt Landshut*, ECJ Case C-72/05; [2008] STC 1618.

[22.250] See also *Enkler v Finanzamt Homburg*, 22.114 above, and *Seeling v Finanzamt Starnberg*, 22.182 above.

Exclusions from taxable amount (Article 11A3)

Article 11A3(b) of EC Sixth Directive—price discounts and rebates

[22.251] A major retail company operated sales promotion schemes whereby vouchers were given on the purchase of particular goods. The vouchers could be redeemed against the purchase of other goods. The company accounted for VAT on cash received but did not account for VAT on the face value of the vouchers. The Commissioners issued an assessment charging tax on the face value of the vouchers and the company appealed, contending that the amount of the vouchers constituted a discount which could be excluded from the consideration under *Article 11A* of the *EC Sixth Directive*. The case was referred to the ECJ, which upheld the company's contention that the amount of the vouchers constituted a 'price discount or rebate allowed to the customer and accounted for at the time of supply'. Accordingly, the amount of the vouchers fell within *Article 11A3(b)* of the *EC Sixth Directive* and did not form part of the taxable consideration. *Boots Co plc v C & E Commrs*, ECJ Case 126/88; [1990] STC 387; [1990] 1 ECR 1235; [1990] 2 CMLR 731.

[22.252] A company incorporated under the *Industrial & Provident Societies Acts* made payments, which it described as 'dividends', to some of its members who had purchased goods from it. These dividends were calculated as a percentage of the aggregate amount of the members' purchases, using a credit card issued by a bank associated with the company, during a prescribed period. The company deducted the amount of these payments in accounting for VAT. Customs issued an assessment charging output tax, considering that the dividends were distributions of profit and could not be taken into account in computing the consideration. The company appealed, contending that the amounts were 'price discounts and rebates' within *Article 11A3(b)* of the *EC Sixth Directive*. The tribunal accepted this contention and allowed the appeal, holding that 'the use of the word "dividend" to describe the payments is of no significance'. The facts that the payments were deferred, and were dependent upon a contingency, did not transform them from discounts into distributions of profit. *Co-Operative Retail Services Ltd*, [1992] VATTR 60 (VTD 7527).

[22.253] A company operated a mail order business. The Commissioners issued a letter instructing it to include the full amount of all its credit sales to agents in its gross takings, without deducting the 10% discounts which it credited to the agents. In its returns for the periods ending April 1997 and July 1997, the company continued to treat the discounts which it credited to its agents as a deduction in computing its gross takings. The Commissioners issued assessments charging tax on the amounts in question, and the company appealed, contending that the Commissioners' direction contravened *Article 11A* of the *EC Sixth Directive*. The tribunal directed that the case should be referred to the ECJ for a ruling on the interpretation of *Article 11A3* and the definition of the taxable amount in the circumstances of the case. The ECJ ruled that the taxable amount was the full catalogue price. Sums which were not credited to agents until payments were made 'do not yet constitute discounts within the meaning of *Article 11A3(b)* of the *EC Sixth Directive*'. The effect of *Article 11C1* was that the discounts could only be taken into account when they were 'withdrawn or used in another way by the customer'. *Freemans plc v C & E Commrs*, ECJ Case C-86/99; [2001] STC 960; [2001] 1 WLR 1713.

[22.254] See also *Kuwait Petroleum Ltd*, **22.158** above; *Peugeot Motor Company plc (No 5)*, **67.48** VALUATION; and *Euphony Communications Ltd*, **67.58** VALUATION.

Article 11A3(c) of EC Sixth Directive—repayments of expenses

[22.255] In a Danish case, the ECJ held that the 'registration duty' included in the price of a new motor vehicle qualified as a 'repayment of expenses', within *Article 11A3(c)* of the *EC Sixth Directive*, and was not liable to VAT. *De Danske Bilimportører v Skatteministeriet*,ECJ Case C-98/05; [2006] 1 ECR 4945.

[22.256] A company operated 'timeshare' accommodation. It accounted for output tax on its management charges. Subsequently it submitted a repayment claim on the basis that these charges were 'repayments of expenses' which, by virtue of *Article 11A3(c)* of the *EC Sixth Directive*, were not liable to VAT. The tribunal reviewed the evidence in detail and allowed the appeal in part, holding that most of the charges were within *Article 11A3(c)* and were not liable to VAT, but that amounts paid to a 'sinking fund' and a 'reserve fund' were 'not expenses but a cost component of a service provided by the management company falling within the scope of VAT'. *Clowance Holdings Ltd*, EDN/99/142 (VTD 17289). (*Note.* The decision that some of the charges were within *Article 11A3(c)* was not followed, and was implicitly disapproved, by a subsequent tribunal in the case of *Clowance Owners Club Ltd*, **62.71**

SUPPLY, on the grounds that the tribunal had followed the CA decision in *Plantiflor Ltd*, **24.2** EXEMPTIONS: MISCELLANEOUS, which had subsequently been reversed by the HL.)

[22.257] See also *Trustees of the Nell Gwynn House Maintenance Fund*, **62.36** SUPPLY; *Curtis*, **62.53** SUPPLY, and *Clowance Owners Club Ltd*, **62.71** SUPPLY.

Reduction of taxable amount (Article 11C1)

[22.258] A company (G) which traded as jewellers made a supply of goods, valued at more than £200,000, to another company (R) which promised to provide advertising services to G as consideration. However, R went into liquidation without providing the full amount of the services agreed. G claimed bad debt relief in respect of the £135,000 for which services had not been provided. The Commissioners rejected the claim, on the basis that relief was only available where supplies were made for monetary consideration. G appealed, contending that it should be entitled to relief under the provisions of *Article 11C1* of the *EC Sixth Directive*. The tribunal held that the matter should be referred to the ECJ for a ruling on the interpretation of the second sentence of *Article 11C1*. The ECJ held that the derogation in *Article 11C1* did not authorise a Member State, which had enacted provisions for the refund of VAT in cases of non-payment of the consideration, to refuse such a refund for consideration in kind when it permitted such a refund for consideration in money. *Goldsmiths (Jewellers) Ltd v C & E Commrs*, ECJ Case C-330/95; [1997] STC 1073; [1997] 1 ECR 3801; [1997] 3 CMLR 520. (*Note.* Following the ECJ decision, the tribunal allowed the company's appeal—see [1997] VATDR 325. For the Commissioners' practice following the decision, see Business Brief 21/97, issued on 3 October 1997. *VATA 1994, s 36* has subsequently been amended by *FA 1998, s 23*.)

[22.259] In the case noted at **22.159** above, the company sought to raise an alternative contention, claiming that the taxable amount should be reduced under *Article 11C1* of the *EC Sixth Directive*. The tribunal and the Ch D both rejected the company's contention, and the company appealed to the CA. The CA struck out the appeal, holding that the company should have taken the point before the appeal had been referred to the ECJ. Chadwick LJ held that 'the jurisdiction of the High Court, and of this Court, to entertain appeals in respect of a decision made by a value added tax tribunal is circumscribed by statute. It cannot be conferred by the agreement or acquiescence of the parties. It would serve no purpose for this Court to express what would be, in effect, a consultative view on an issue which is not properly before it for decision.' Chadwick LJ described the appeal as 'misconceived'. *Kuwait Petroleum (GB) Ltd v C & E Commrs (No 2)*, CA [2001] STC 1568; [2001] EWCA Civ 1542.

[22.260] A company (T) sold motor fuel through a number of service stations. It operated a promotion scheme, under which it gave 'face value' gift vouchers to regular customers, entitling them to goods worth £5 at a major retailer. (It had purchased these vouchers from the retailer at a discount of about 11%.) It claimed a repayment of £1,600,000 in output tax, on the basis that the cost of providing these vouchers was a retrospective discount, within

Article 11C1 of the *EC Sixth Directive*. Customs rejected the claim and the tribunal dismissed T's appeal. The CA unanimously upheld the tribunal decision. Richards LJ held that 'the transfer of a voucher by (T) to a customer redeeming his points' did not reduce the consideration obtained by T in respect of its supplies of fuel. He observed that 'the customer who receives a voucher does not thereby receive a discount on the price of the qualifying purchases of fuel, but gets something extra for the price he paid for the fuel'. He paid the full price for the fuel, 'but sufficient purchases of fuel entitle him to a voucher that he can use for the acquisition of additional goods or services or to make a gift to charity.' *HMRC v Total UK Ltd*, CA [2007] EWCA Civ 987; [2007] All ER (D) 253 (Oct). (*Note*. The HL subsequently rejected an application by the company for leave to appeal against this decision.)

[22.261] See also *Genie Financial Services Europe Ltd*, **3.176** ASSESSMENT; *Times Right Marketing Ltd*, **4.32** BAD DEBT RELIEF; *Elida Gibbs Ltd*, **22.235** above; *Freemans plc*, **22.253** above; *British Telecommunications plc*, **40.116** INVOICES AND CREDIT NOTES; *General Motors Acceptance Corporation (UK) plc*, **59.33** RETURNS; *The Littlewoods Organisation plc*, **67.42** VALUATION; *Euphony Communications Ltd*, **67.58** VALUATION; *Jag Communications (Plymouth) Ltd*, **67.77** VALUATION, and *AEG (UK) Ltd*, **67.127** VALUATION.

Rates (Article 12)

Application of reduced rate to road tolls

[22.262] In Spain, a Royal Decree in 1997 provided that motorway tolls should be subject to VAT at a reduced rate of 7%, rather than at the standard rate of 16%. The Commission of the EC applied to the ECJ for a declaration that, in applying this reduced rate, Spain had failed to fulfil its obligations under *Article 12* of the *EC Sixth Directive*. The ECJ granted the declaration. *EC Commission v Kingdom of Spain*, ECJ Case C-83/99, 18 January 2001 unreported.

[22.263] Portugal applied a reduced VAT rate of 5% to road tolls for crossing the River Tagus at Lisbon. The Commission of the EC applied to the ECJ for a declaration that, in applying this reduced rate, Portugal had failed to fulfil its obligations under *Article 12* of the *EC Sixth Directive*. The ECJ granted the declaration. *EC Commission v Portuguese Republic*, ECJ Case C-462/05; 12 June 2008 unreported.

Application of reduced rate to wine

[22.264] In Portugal, the VAT Code (dating from 1984) provided that wine should be subject to VAT at a reduced rate of 5%, rather than at the standard rate of 17%. The Commission of the EC applied to the ECJ for a declaration that, in applying this reduced rate, Portugal had failed to fulfil its obligations under *Article 12* of the *EC Sixth Directive*. The ECJ granted the declaration. *EC Commission v Portuguese Republic*, ECJ Case C-276/98; [2001] BTC 5135.

Application of reduced rate to musical performances

[22.265] In Germany, VAT legislation provided that a reduced VAT rate of 7% applied to services supplied directly to the public by musical ensembles or for a concert organiser, and to services provided by soloists directly to the public, but that the standard rate applied to the services of soloists working for an organiser. The Commission of the EC applied to the ECJ for a declaration that Germany had failed to fulfil its obligations under *Article 12(3)(a)* of the *EC Sixth Directive*. The ECJ granted the declaration. *EC Commission v Federal Republic of Germany*, ECJ Case C-109/02; [2006] STC 1587.

Application of reduced rate to auctioneers' commission

[22.266] In the UK, *VAT (Special Provisions) Order 1995 (SI 1995/1268)*, *article 12* provided that the 'taxable amount' of imported works of art sold at auction (including the auctioneer's commission) was to be treated as 28.58% of the true price. This had the effect of providing an effective VAT rate of 5%. The EC Commission applied to the ECJ for a declaration that the UK provisions were a breach of *Articles 2(1)* and *12(3)* of the *EC Sixth Directive*, and that the reduced rate should be applied only to the import value (ie the auction price less the auctioneer's margin), while the auctioneer's commission should be charged at the standard rate. The ECJ granted the declaration, observing that the auctioneer's profit margin could not be treated as 'part of the import value', and holding that when a Member State 'makes use of the option available under *Article 16(1)* of the *Sixth Directive* by taking special measures to exempt transactions relating to goods under the arrangements for temporary importation, it must comply with all the conditions laid down by that provision'. Accordingly, the UK had failed to fulfil its obligations under the *Sixth Directive*. *EC Commission v United Kingdom (No 5)*, ECJ Case C-305/03; [2007] STC 1211. (*Note.* See now *FA 2006, s 18*.)

Connection of household to water distribution network

[22.267] In Germany, the standard rate of VAT was 16%, and the supply of water was taxable at the reduced rate of 7% (as authorised by *Article 12(3)(a)* of the *EC Sixth Directive*). An association which supplied water in Saxony also connected householders to its water distribution network. It treated such work as part of the supply of water and as liable to the reduced rate of VAT. The tax authority issued a ruling that the connection was a separate supply which was taxable at the standard rate of VAT. The association appealed, and the case was referred to the ECJ, which held that *Article 12(3)(a)* 'must be interpreted as meaning that the laying of a mains connection which consists, as in the main proceedings, in the installation of piping permitting the connection of a building's water system to the fixed water supply network forms part of water supplies'. However, there was nothing in the text of *Article 12(3)(a)* 'which requires that provision to be interpreted as meaning that the reduced rate can be charged only if it is applied to all aspects of the water supplies covered by *Annex H* to that directive, so that a selective application of the reduced rate cannot be excluded provided that no risk of distortion of competition results'. *Finanzamt Oschatz v Zweckverband zur Trinkwasserversorgung und Abwasserbeseitigung Torgau-Westelbien*, ECJ Case C-442/05; [2009] STC 1.

Article 12(3)(a)—definition of 'cinema'

[22.268] In a Belgian case, a company (E) allowed customers to watch films of their choice from individual cubicles on its premises. It accounted for VAT at the reduced rate of 6%. The tax authority issued an assessment on the basis that it should have accounted for VAT at the standard rate. E appealed, contending that it was supplying admission to a cinema, which qualified for the reduced rate under *Article 12(3)(a)* and *Annex H* of the *EC Sixth Directive*. The case was referred to the ECJ for a ruling on the definition of a 'cinema'. The ECJ rejected E's contentions, holding that 'the concept of admissions to a cinema' should be 'interpreted as meaning that it does not cover the payment made by a customer so as to be able to watch on his own one or more films, or extracts from films, in private cubicles such as those in issue in the main proceedings'. *Erotic Center BVBA v Belgische Staat*, ECJ Case C-3/09; [2010] STC 1018.

Article 12(3)(b)—standing charges for supply of gas and electricity

[22.269] France charged a reduced rate of 5.5% on standing charges for the supply of gas and electricity from the public networks, and a standard rate of 19.6% on the consumption of those two products. The Commission of the EC applied to the ECJ for a ruling that standing charges could not be treated as 'supplies of natural gas and electricity' within *Article 12(3)(b)* of the *EC Sixth Directive*. The ECJ rejected this contention and dismissed the application, holding that standing charges were 'consideration for the supply of gas and electricity'. Furthermore, the Commission had not shown that the 'selective application of the reduced rate' would breach the principle of fiscal neutrality or give rise to any risk of distortion of competition. *EC Commission v French Republic*, ECJ Case C-384/01; 8 May 2003 unreported.

Exemptions (Articles 13–16)

Unauthorised national exemptions

[22.270] The Italian government had exempted the services of veterinary surgeons from VAT. The EC Commission brought a case against the Italian government on the grounds that such an exemption did not comply with the provisions of the *EC Sixth Directive*. The ECJ held that the exemption in question was outside the terms of *Article 13* and the Italian government was in breach of its obligations under the *Directive*. *EC Commission v Italian Republic*, ECJ Case 122/87; [1988] ECR 2919; [1989] 3 CMLR 844.

[22.271] The EC Commission applied to the ECJ for a ruling that the UK had failed to fulfil its obligations under *Article 13A* of the *Sixth Directive*, in that it had exempted the supply of medicines and corrective spectacles from VAT. The ECJ granted the application, ruling that such supplies were not eligible for exemption. Advocate-General Mancini observed that 'unless the directive expressly provides otherwise, supplies of goods are not exempt from value added tax even where they are provided in connection with supplies of services that are so exempted'. *EC Commission v United Kingdom*, ECJ Case 353/85; [1988] STC 251; [1988] ECR 817. (*Note.* The UK complied with this ruling by introducing *FA 1988, s 13*. See now *VATA 1994, Sch 9, Group 7*. The supply of medicines and corrective spectacles is generally now standard-rated. However, the supply of medicines in a hospital or similar approved institution remains exempt under *VATA 1994, Sch 9, Group 7, Item 4*, and the supply of prescribed medicines by registered pharmacists is zero-rated under *VATA 1994, Sch 8, Group 12, Item 1*. The supply of opticians' services in connection with the supply of spectacles may be treated as an exempt supply of services—see *Leightons Ltd (Nos 1 and 2)*, **33.8** and **33.9** HEALTH AND WELFARE.)

Public postal services (Article 13A(1)(a))

[22.272] The UK exempted all supplies of postal services by the Royal Mail, in accordance with *Article 13A(1)(a)* of the *EC Sixth Directive*. A private postal company, which provided distribution services for business mail, applied to the QB for judicial review, contending that the UK law was unfairly discriminatory, and that its own services should receive similar treatment. The QB referred the case to the ECJ for a ruling on the interpretation of the expression 'public postal services' in *Article 13A1(a)*. The ECJ held that the reference to 'public postal services' must be interpreted as including 'operators, whether they are public or private, who undertake to provide, in a Member State, all or part of the universal postal service, as defined in *Article 3* of *Directive 97/67/EC*'. The exemption provided for in *Article 13A1(a)* 'applies to the supply by the public postal services acting as such – that is, in their capacity as an operator who undertakes to provide all or part of the universal postal service in a Member State – of services other than passenger transport and telecommunications services, and the supply of goods incidental thereto. It does not apply to supplies of services or of goods incidental thereto for which the terms have been individually negotiated.' The ECJ specifically rejected the suggestion (adopted by the Royal Mail and HMRC) that since the Royal Mail was the provider of 'public postal services' within *Article 13A1(a)*, it followed that all its postal services were exempted by that Article. The ECJ held that the exemption only applied to the services which Royal Mail supplied in its capacity as 'universal service provider' (ie its services available to the public at standardised rates). The exemption did not extend to services which the Royal Mail supplied under contracts individually negotiated with customers to meet their specific needs. *R (oao TNT Post UK Ltd) v HMRC*, ECJ Case C-357/07; [2009] STC 1438. (*Note.* See now *Clause 22* of the *Finance (No 2) Bill 2010*; HMRC Brief 65/09, issued on 15 October 2009, and HMRC Brief 19/10, issued on 31 March 2010. HMRC stated that 'UK VAT law is being amended to bring it in line with the ECJ decision.')

Hospital and medical care (Article 13A(1)(b)(c))

Article 13A1(b)—hospital and medical care (soins médicaux)

[22.273] Under French law, VAT was chargeable on fixed allowances for the taking of samples for medical analysis. The Commission of the EC applied to the ECJ for a declaration that France had failed to fulfil its obligations under *Article 13A(1)(b)* of the *Sixth Directive*. The ECJ granted the declaration. *EC Commission v French Republic*, ECJ Case C-76/99, 11 January 2001 unreported.

[22.274] A charity operated a private hospital. It arranged for outside contractors to provide laundry and waste disposal services at the hospital. The Commissioners issued a ruling that VAT was chargeable on these supplies. The charity appealed, contending that they should be treated as exempt under *Article 13A1(b)* of the *EC Sixth Directive*. The tribunal rejected this contention and dismissed the appeal, holding that the services in question were not 'closely related to the clinic's hospital and medical care activities'. *Ulster Independent Clinic Ltd*, [2004] VATDR 32 (VTD 18517).

[22.275] A Greek company supplied telephone services, and hired television sets, to hospital patients. The tax authority issued a ruling that VAT was chargeable on these supplies. The company appealed, contending that they should be treated as exempt under *Article 13A1(b)* of the *EC Sixth Directive*. The case was referred to the ECJ, which rejected the company's contentions, holding that 'the supply of telephone services and the hiring out of televisions to in-patients' did not amount to 'activities closely related to hospital and medical care'. *Diagnostiko & Therapeftiko Kentro Athinon-Ygeia AE v Ipourgos Ikonomikon*, ECJ Case C-394/04; [2006] STC 1349.

[22.276] In a German case, the ECJ held that *Article 13A1(b)* of the *EC Sixth Directive* must 'be interpreted as meaning that medical tests which have as their purpose the observation and examination of patients for prophylactic purposes, carried out, like those at issue in the main proceedings, by a laboratory governed by private law outside a centre for treatment on prescription from general practitioners, may come within the exemption provided for by that provision as medical care provided by another duly recognised establishment of a similar nature within the meaning of that provision'. *Article 13A(1)(b)* and *(2)(a)* did not 'preclude national legislation which makes the exemption of such medical tests subject to conditions which, first, do not apply to the exemption of care provided by the general practitioners who prescribed them and, second, are different from those applicable to closely related activities to medical care within the meaning of the first-mentioned provision'. *Article 13A(1)(b)* precluded national legislation 'which makes the exemption of medical tests carried out by a laboratory governed by private law outside a centre for treatment subject to the condition that they be carried out under medical supervision. However, that provision permits such legislation to make the exemption of those tests subject to the condition that at least 40% of those services must be intended for persons insured by a social security authority.' *L.u.P. GmbH v Finanzamt Bochum-Mitte*, ECJ Case C-106/05; [2008] STC 1742.

[22.277] In a Danish case, a private stem cell bank (C) was authorised to handle stem cells extracted from umbilical cord blood. The tax authority issued a ruling that C was required to account for tax on its supplies. C appealed, contending that its supplies qualified for exemption. The case was referred to the ECJ for a ruling on the interpretation of *Article 13A1(b)* of the *EC Sixth Directive*. The ECJ held that 'the concept of activities "closely related" to "hospital and medical care"', within *Article 13A1(b)*, should 'be interpreted as meaning that it does not cover activities such as those at issue in the main proceedings consisting in the collection, transportation and analysis of umbilical cord blood and the storage of stem cells contained in it, where the medical care provided in a hospital environment to which those activities are merely potentially related has not been performed, commenced or yet envisaged'. Where the services of stem cell banks were 'performed by professional medical personnel', *Article 13A1(b)* did not 'preclude the national authorities from deciding that taxable persons such as (C)' were not within the definition of 'recognised establishments of a similar nature' to hospitals, etc. It was for the national court 'to determine whether the refusal of recognition for the purposes of the exemption' complied with EU law and the principle of fiscal neutrality. *CopyGene A/S v Skatteministeriet*, ECJ Case C-262/08; [2010] STC 1799.

[22.278] See also *Gregg*, **22.298** below; *In Health Group SA*, **33.19** HEALTH AND WELFARE; *Kaul (t/a Alpha Care Services)*, **33.57** HEALTH AND WELFARE, and *Kingscrest Associates Ltd & Montecello Ltd (t/a Kingscrest Residential Care Homes) (No 1)*, **33.60** HEALTH AND WELFARE.

Article 13A1(c)—provision of medical care (soins à la personne)

[22.279] In an Austrian case, a doctor was appointed by a court to establish, on the basis of a genetic test, whether a claimant was a child of a defendant. She included VAT on the invoice which she issued to the Austrian Federal Treasury in respect of her services. The Treasury appealed, contending that the relevant services should be treated as exempt under *Article 13A1(c)* of the *EC Sixth Directive*. The case was referred to the ECJ which held that the relevant services did not qualify for exemption, on the grounds that *Article 13A1(c)* did 'not apply to services consisting, not in providing care to persons by diagnosing and treating a disease or any other health disorder, but in establishing the genetic affinity of individuals through biological tests'. *Dotter v Willimaier (aka D v W)*, ECJ Case C-384/98; [2002] STC 1200.

[22.280] A German charity provided psychotherapeutic treatment by qualified psychologists who were not doctors. The tax authority issued a ruling that VAT was chargeable on the charity's supplies. The charity appealed, contending that they should be treated as exempt under *Article 13A1(c)* of the *EC Sixth Directive*. The case was referred to the ECJ, which accepted this contention, holding that *Article 13A1(c)* included 'services provided by persons who are not doctors but who give paramedical services, such as psychotherapeutic treatment given by qualified psychologists'. *Christoph-Dornier-Stiftung für Klinische Psychologie v Finanzamt Gießen*, ECJ Case C-45/01; [2005] STC 228.

[22.281] In a German case, the ECJ held that the exemption laid down by *Article 13A(1)(c)* of the *EC Sixth Directive* 'does not apply to the services of a doctor consisting of making an expert report on a person's health in order to support or exclude a claim for payment of a disability pension. The fact that the medical expert was instructed by a court or pension insurance institution is irrelevant in that respect'. *Unterpertinger v Pensionsversicherungsanstalt der Arbeiter*, ECJ Case C-212/01; [2005] STC 678.

[22.282] A doctor had gained considerable experience in acting as an expert medical witness before various courts and tribunals, and had become an Associate of the Chartered Institute of Arbitrators. The Commissioners issued a ruling that services provided by the doctor in conducting medical examinations, paternity testing, issuing medical certificates, assessing insurance claims, and preparing medical reports for personal injury and medical negligence cases were exempt under *VATA 1994, Sch 9, Group 7, Item 1* (so that the doctor was unable to reclaim input tax relating to these services). The doctor appealed, contending that these services should be treated as taxable. The tribunal directed that the case should be referred to the ECJ to consider whether the services qualified for exemption under *Article 13A1(c)* of the *EC Sixth Directive*. The ECJ held that the exemption laid down by *Article 13A(1)(c)* applied to 'medical examinations of individuals for employers or insurance companies'; to 'the taking of blood or other bodily samples to test for the presence of viruses, infections or other diseases on behalf of employers or insurers', and to 'certification of medical fitness, for example, as to fitness to travel, where those services are intended principally to protect the health of the person concerned'. However, exemption did not apply to 'giving certificates as to a person's medical condition for purposes such as entitlement to a war pension'; to medical examinations conducted with a view to preparing medical reports regarding 'issues of liability and the quantification of damages for individuals contemplating personal injury litigation' or 'professional medical negligence for individuals contemplating litigation'; or to the preparation of medical reports, either following such examinations or 'based on medical notes without conducting a medical examination'. *PL d'Ambrumenil v C & E Commrs; Dispute Resolution Services Ltd v C & E Commrs*, ECJ Case C-307/01; [2005] STC 650; [2004] 3 WLR 174. (*Notes.* (1) For HMRC's practice following this decision, see Business Brief 29/2003, issued on 18 December 2003; HMRC Brief 06/07, issued on 30 January 2007, and VAT Information Sheet 05/2007, issued on 15 February 2007. (2) For subsequent developments in this case, see **22.283** below.)

[22.283] Following the ECJ decision noted at **22.282** above, the doctor requested a further tribunal hearing on whether he could reclaim input tax relating to medical tests and the issue of certificates of fitness. The tribunal upheld the Commissioners' contention that both these types of service were exempt, holding that 'medical testing conducted for purposes other than those of prospective employers and insurers is an exempt activity where it is intended principally to enable the prevention or detection of illness or the monitoring of the health of the person in question' and that 'the provision of a certificate of medical fitness is an exempt activity where it is intended principally to protect the health of the person concerned'. *Dr PL d'Ambrumenil; Dispute Resolution Services Ltd (No 2)*, [2004] VATDR 134 (VTD 18551; VTD 18581).

[22.284] In a Netherlands case, the tax authority ruled that the services of a psychotherapist, and of a physiotherapist who specialised in 'disturbance field diagnostics' (which involved detailed examination of the jaw and mouth) failed to qualify for exemption. The therapists appealed, and the cases were referred to the ECJ for a ruling on the interpretation of *Article 13A1(c)* of the *EC Sixth Directive*. The ECJ held that *Article 13A1(c)* 'confers on the Member States the discretion to define the paramedical professions and the medical care coming within the scope of such professions for the purpose of the exemption laid down by that provision'. National legislation which excluded the profession of psychotherapist from the definition of the paramedical professions was 'contrary to the said objective and principle only to the extent that psychotherapeutic treatments would, if carried out by psychiatrists, psychologists or any other medical or paramedical profession, be exempt from VAT, whereas, carried out by psychotherapists, they can be regarded as being of equivalent quality having regard to the professional qualifications of the latter, a matter which it is for the referring court to determine. National legislation which excludes certain specific medical care activities, such as treatments using disturbance field diagnostics, carried out by physiotherapists from the definition of that paramedical profession is contrary to the said objective and principle only to the extent that such treatments carried out in the context of the said activities would, if carried out by doctors or dentists, be exempt from VAT, whereas, carried out by physiotherapists, they can be regarded as being of equivalent quality having regard to the professional qualifications of the latter, a matter which it is for the referring court to determine.' *Solleveld v Staatssecretaris van Financiën*, ECJ Case C-443/04; *Hout van Eijnsbergen v Staatssecretaris van Financiën*, ECJ Case C-444/04; [2007] STC 71.

[22.285] A German biotechnology company extracted cells from patients' joint cartilages, multiplied them in a laboratory, and prepared them for reintegration into the patients' bodies. The tax authority issued an assessment charging VAT on such supplies, and the company appealed, contending firstly that the supplies were exempt under *Article 13A1(c)* of the *EC Sixth Directive*, and alternatively that they fell within the derogation in *Article 28b(F)*. The case was referred to the ECJ, which found in favour of the company, holding that *Article 13A1(c)* 'must be interpreted as meaning that the removal of joint cartilage cells from cartilage material taken from a human being and the subsequent multiplication of those cells for reimplantation for therapeutic purposes constitute "provision of medical care"'. Accordingly the company's supplies were exempt from VAT. *Finanzamt Leverkusen v Verigen Transplantation Service International AG*, ECJ Case C-156/09; [2011] STC 255.

[22.286] See also *E Moss Ltd*, **33.16** HEALTH AND WELFARE.

Human organs, blood and milk (Article 13A1(d))

[22.287] In a Belgian case, a trader transported human organs and samples for various hospitals and laboratories. The tax authority issued a ruling that she was required to account for tax on her supplies. She appealed, contending that they qualified for exemption under *Article 13A1(d)* of the *EC Sixth Directive*. The ECJ held in favour of the tax authority, observing that her supplies simply involved 'physically moving the goods concerned from one place to another for various hospitals and laboratories' and did not amount to a disposal of goods. Accordingly the ECJ concluded that *Article 13A1(d)* 'must be interpreted as not applying to the activity of transporting, in a self-employed capacity, human organs and samples for hospitals and laboratories'. *Belgian State v N De Fruytier*, ECJ Case C-237/09; [2010] STC 1792.

'Services supplied by dental technicians' (Article 13A1(e))

[22.288] A Luxembourg company reclaimed input tax on goods used to manufacture and repair dental prostheses from German customers. The tax authority rejected the claim on the grounds that the input tax related to exempt supplies. The company appealed, and the case was referred to the ECJ, which held that 'a transaction which is exempted from value added tax within the territory of a Member State under *Article 13A(1)(e)*' did not 'give rise to the right to deduct input value added tax pursuant to *Article 17(3)(b)* of that directive, even when it is an intra-Community transaction, and regardless of the system of value added tax applicable in the Member State of destination'. *Administration de l'enregistrement et des domaines v Eurodental Sàrl*, ECJ Case C-240/05; [2007] STC 275.

[22.289] In a Netherlands case, a company reclaimed input tax on supplies of dental prostheses which it had purchased from a laboratory and supplied to dentists based elsewhere in the EU. The tax authority issued an assessment to recover the tax. The company appealed, and the case was referred to the ECJ for a ruling on whether such supplies qualified for exemption under *Article 13A(1)(e)* of the *Sixth Directive*. The ECJ held that *Article 13A(1)(e)* 'does not apply to supplies of dental prostheses effected by an intermediary like the one in question in the main proceedings who does not have the status of dentist or dental technician, but has acquired such prostheses from a dental technician'. *VDP Dental Laboratory NV v Staatssecretaris van Financiën*, ECJ Case C-401/05; [2007] STC 474.

'Services supplied by independent groups of persons' (Article 13A1(f))

[22.290] In a Netherlands case, a charity (S) organised lotteries for another charity (A) on behalf of social and cultural organisations affiliated to A. A reimbursed the costs incurred by S. S did not account for VAT on the amounts it received from A. The Netherlands authorities charged VAT on the supplies, and S appealed, contending that they should be treated as exempt under *Article 13A1(f)* of the *EC Sixth Directive*. The ECJ ruled that the exemption only applied to independent groups of persons rendering services for their own members. Services supplied by one foundation for another foundation, where the second foundation was not a member of the first, did not qualify for the exemption. Advocate-General Mischo observed that 'any exemptions, as exceptions to the general rule that VAT is levied on all economic activity, are to be interpreted strictly and must not exceed what is expressly and clearly provided for'. *Stichting Uitvoering Financiële Acties (SUFA) v Staatssecretaris van Financiën*, ECJ Case 348/87; [1989] ECR 1737; [1991] 2 CMLR 429.

[22.291] The decision in *Stichting Uitvoering Financiële Acties (SUFA) v Staatssecretaris van Financiën*, 22.290 above, was applied in *The Regency Villas Owners Club*, **13.2** CLUBS, ASSOCIATIONS AND ORGANISATIONS, and *Peterborough Diocesan Conference & Retreat House*, **33.68** HEALTH AND WELFARE.

[22.292] A Netherlands foundation (S) was established with the object of promoting high quality nursing care. Its members were hospitals and medical insurance bodies. It provided various services to its members, most of which were accepted as being exempt from VAT. However the tax authority issued a ruling that certain services which S provided to individual members, such as the delegation of staff to chair or speak at meetings, did not qualify for exemption. S appealed, contending that the services should be treated as exempt under *Article 13A1(f)* of the *EC Sixth Directive*. The case was referred to the ECJ, which upheld S's contentions, holding that *Article 13A(1)(f)* must be interpreted as covering 'services supplied to their members by independent groups', even if those services were 'supplied to only one or several of those members'. *Stichting Centraal Begeleidingsorgaan voor de Intercollegiale Toetsing v Staatssecretaris van Financiën*, ECJ Case C-407/07; [2009] STC 869.

Services and goods 'closely linked to welfare and social security work' (Article 13A1(g))

[22.293] A registered charity, which had been established to promote the practice of yoga, owned a residential centre. It did not account for output tax on its supplies of accommodation at the centre. The Commissioners issued an assessment charging tax on the supplies, and the charity appealed, contending firstly that it was not carrying on any business and alternatively that its supplies should be treated as exempt from VAT. The QB accepted the charity's alternative contention and allowed the appeal. Applying *dicta* of Romer LJ in *Berry v St Marylebone Borough Council*, CA 1957, [1958] Ch 406; [1957] 3 All ER 677, 'the expression "social welfare" means the well-being (whether in the physical, mental or material sense) of individuals as members of society' and 'the provision of benefits which tends directly to improve the health or conditions of life of individuals comes prima facie within the expression "social welfare"'. Accordingly, the charity's aims were within the definition of 'welfare' for the purposes of *Article 13A1(g)* of the *EC Sixth Directive*, which provided that the supply of services 'closely linked to welfare' should be exempt from VAT, and which should be treated as having direct effect in the UK. *Yoga for Health Foundation v C & E Commrs*, QB [1984] STC 630; [1985] 1 CMLR 340. (*Note.* See now *VATA 1994, Sch 9 Group 7, Items 9 & 10* and *Notes 5–7*.)

[22.294] The International Bible Students' Association organised conventions to promote the teachings of the Jehovah's Witnesses. Admission to the conventions was free, but the association made profits from catering at the conventions. The Commissioners issued an assessment charging VAT on the receipts from catering. The QB allowed the association's appeal, holding that the association had been established to promote 'spiritual welfare' and that its activities were therefore exempt from VAT under *Article 13A1(g)* of the *EC Sixth Directive*. *International Bible Students' Association v C & E Commrs*, QB 1987, [1988] STC 412; [1988] 1 CMLR 491. (*Note.* See now *VATA 1994, Sch 9, Group 7, Items 9 & 10* and *Notes 5–7*.)

[22.295] A YMCA operated a club in London, which offered leisure and sporting facilities. The Commissioners issued a ruling that VAT was due on the club subscriptions, and the YMCA appealed, contending that they should be treated as exempt under *Article 13A1(g)* of the *EC Sixth Directive*. (It was accepted that the supplies did not qualify for exemption under what is now *VATA 1994, Sch 9, Group 6*.) The tribunal dismissed the appeal, holding that the club facilities were not within the definition of 'services closely linked to welfare and social security work'. On the evidence, 60% of the club's members were over 30 years of age, and paid annual subscriptions of more than £300, which was 'beyond the means of people in financial need'. Fewer than 5% of the club's members were aged 20 or less, and the club was not therefore 'designed to supplement the needs of the young'. (The tribunal also observed that sporting facilities were the subject of *Article 13A1(m)* of the *Directive*, and commented that 'a supply which is essentially a supply of sporting or physical education facilities covered by *paragraph 1(m)* will in principle be outside the scope of *paragraph 1(g)'*.) *Yoga For Health Foundation*, **22.293** above, distinguished. *Central YMCA*, [1994] VATTR 146 (VTD 12425).

[22.296] See also *Peterborough Diocesan Conference & Retreat House*, **33.68** HEALTH AND WELFARE, and *Trustees for the Macmillan Cancer Trust*, **33.70** HEALTH AND WELFARE.

[22.297] In a Dutch case, a woman operated a day nursery as a sole proprietor. She made a profit from the nursery, and used the profit to meet her living expenses. The Dutch authority issued a ruling that her supplies were taxable, and she appealed. The case was referred to the ECJ, which held that the exemption in *Article 13A1(g)* was only available to 'bodies governed by public law or other organisations', and did not apply to sole proprietors. Consequently the nursery in question did not qualify for exemption. *Bulthuis-Griffioen v Inspector der Omzetbelasting*, ECJ Case C-453/93; [1995] STC 954; [1995] 1 ECR 2341. (*Note*. This decision was not followed in the subsequent case of *Gregg*, **22.298** below.)

[22.298] A married couple operated a nursing home in partnership, with a number of employees. The Commissioners issued a ruling that they were not entitled to register for VAT, on the grounds that all their supplies were exempt from VAT under *VATA 1994, Sch 9, Group 7, Item 4*. The couple appealed, contending that they should not be treated as exempt since the exemption should be construed in accordance with *Article 13A1(b)* and *(g)* of the *EC Sixth Directive*, which confined such exemption to 'bodies governed by public law'. The tribunal referred the case to the ECJ, which held that *Article 13A1* should be 'interpreted as meaning that the terms "other duly recognised establishments of a similar nature" and "other organisations recognised as charitable by the Member State concerned"' did not exclude from that exemption 'natural persons running a business'. Accordingly the Commissioners were justified in treating the couple's supplies as exempt and declining to register them. The ECJ distinguished *Bulthuis-Griffioen v Inspector der Omzetbelasting*, **22.297** above, holding that 'the terms "establishment" and "organisation" are in principle sufficiently broad to include natural persons as well. It may be added that none of the language versions of *Article 13A* of the *Sixth Directive* include the term "legal person", which would have been clear and unambiguous, instead of the abovementioned terms. It may be inferred that, in employing those terms, the Community legislature did not intend to confine the exemptions referred to in that provision to the activities carried on by legal persons, but meant to extend the scope of those exemptions to activities carried on by individuals. It is true that the terms "establishment" and "organisation" suggest the existence of an individualised entity performing a particular function. Those conditions are, however, satisfied not only by legal persons but also by one or more natural persons running a business. That interpretation, to the effect that the terms "establishment" and "organisation" do not refer only to legal persons, is, in particular, consistent with the principle of fiscal neutrality inherent in the common system of VAT'. The principle of fiscal neutrality 'precludes, *inter alia*, economic operators carrying on the same activities from being treated differently as far as the levying of VAT is concerned. It follows that that principle would be frustrated if the possibility of relying on the benefit of the exemption provided for activities carried on by the establishments or organisations referred to in *Article 13A(1)(b)* and *(g)* was dependent on the legal form in which the taxable person carried on his activity.' *J & M Gregg v C & E Commrs*, ECJ Case C-216/97; [1999] STC 934; [1999] All ER (EC) 775. (*Note*. In the subsequent case of *Kingscrest Associates Ltd & Montecello Ltd (t/a Kingscrest Residential Care Homes)*, **33.60** HEALTH AND WELFARE, the tribunal observed that the appellants in this case had accepted the Commissioners' view that they were supplying 'medical care and closely related activities', within *Article 13A1(b)* of the *EC Sixth Directive*, and had only contended that the exemption should be confined to 'bodies governed by public law'. The decision in *Kingscrest* suggests that the appellants here should have specifically contended that their supplies were not within *Article 13A1(b)*.)

[22.299] In a German case, a company operated an 'out-patient care service'. It appealed against tax assessments, contending that its supplies should be treated as exempt under *Article 13A1* of the *Sixth Directive*. The case was referred to the ECJ, which held that 'the provision of general care and domestic help by an out-patient care service to persons in a state of physical or economic dependence amounts to the supply of services closely linked to welfare and social security work within the meaning of *Article 13A1(g)*'. It was 'for the national court to establish, in the light of all relevant factors, whether the taxable person is an organisation recognised as charitable within the meaning of the aforesaid provision'. *Ambulanter Pflegedienst Kügler GmbH v Finanzamt fur Körperschaften*, ECJ Case C-141/00; [2002] All ER (D) 40 (Sept).

[22.300] Following the decision noted at **33.60** HEALTH AND WELFARE, *VATA 1994, Sch 9, Group 7, Item 9* was substituted by the *VAT (Health and Welfare) Order (SI 2002/762)* with the intention of providing exemption for residential care homes. Following this change in the law, the Commissioners cancelled the registration of a partnership which had been established to operate residential care homes for people with learning disabilities. The partnership appealed, contending that the provisions of *Item 9* as substituted by *SI 2002/762* contravened *Article 13A1(g)(h)* of the *EC Sixth Directive*. The tribunal directed that the case should be referred to the ECJ for rulings on the interpretation of *Article 13A1* of the *EC Sixth Directive*. The ECJ held that 'private profit-making entities' could qualify as 'charitable organisations' within *Article 13A1(g)* and *(h)* of the *Sixth Directive*. It was for the national court to determine whether such entities should be recognised as charitable, having regard to the principles of equal treatment and fiscal neutrality. *Kingscrest Associates Ltd & Montecello Ltd (t/a Kingscrest Residential Care Homes) v C & E Commrs (No 2)*, ECJ Case C-498/03; [2005] STC 1547.

[22.301] In a Netherlands case, a charity acted as an intermediary to facilitate the provision of childcare services. The tax authority issued an assessment charging tax on its supplies, and the charity appealed, contending that they qualified for exemption under *Article 13A1(g)(h)* of the *EC Sixth Directive*. The case was referred to the ECJ, which held that *Article 13A1(g)(h)* 'must be interpreted as meaning that services as an intermediary between persons seeking, and persons offering, a childcare service, provided by a body governed by public law or an organisation recognised as charitable by the Member State concerned, may benefit from exemption under those provisions only where the childcare service itself meets the conditions for exemption laid down in those provisions; that service is of such a nature or quality that parents could not be assured of obtaining a service of the same value without the assistance of an intermediary service such as that which is the subject-matter of the dispute in the main proceedings; and the basic purpose of the intermediary services is not to obtain additional income for the service provider by carrying out transactions which are in direct competition with those of commercial enterprises liable for VAT'. *Staatssecretaris van Financiën v Stichting Kinderopvang Enschede*, ECJ Case C-415/04; [2007] STC 294.

Services and goods 'closely linked to the protection of children and young persons' (Article 13A1(h))

[22.302] See *Kingscrest Associates Ltd & Montecello Ltd (t/a Kingscrest Residential Care Homes) (No 2)*, **22.300** above; *Staatssecretaris van Financiën v Stichting Kinderopvang Enschede*, **22.301** above; *Prospects Care Services Ltd*, **33.59** HEALTH AND WELFARE, and *Families For Children*, **33.73** HEALTH AND WELFARE.

Education (Article 13A1(i))

[22.303] Germany exempted university research from VAT. The EC Commission applied to the ECJ for a ruling that this exemption was not authorised by *Article 13A1(i)* of the *EC Sixth Directive*, so that Germany was in breach of its obligations under *Article 2*. The ECJ granted the ruling, holding that 'the undertaking by State universities of research projects for consideration cannot be regarded as an activity closely related to university education' for the purposes of *Article 13A1(i)*. Accordingly, Germany had failed to fulfil its obligations. *EC Commission v Federal Republic of Germany*, ECJ Case C-287/00; [2002] STC 982.

[22.304] In a Netherlands case, a college seconded some of its teachers to other educational establishments. The tax authority issued an assessment charging VAT on these supplies, and the college appealed, contending that they should be treated as exempt. The case was referred to the ECJ for a ruling on the interpretation of *Article 13A1(i)* of the *EC Sixth Directive*. The ECJ held that *Article 13A1(i)* 'is to be interpreted as meaning that the expression "children's or young people's education, school or university education, vocational training or retraining" does not cover the making available, for consideration, of a teacher to an educational establishment, within the meaning of that provision, in which that teacher temporarily carries out teaching duties under the responsibility of that establishment, even if the body which makes the teacher available is itself a body governed by public law that has an educational aim, or another organisation defined by the Member State concerned as having similar objects'. *Article 13A1(i)*, read in conjunction with *Article 13A(2)* should be interpreted 'as meaning that the making available, for consideration, of a teacher to an educational establishment in which that teacher temporarily carries out teaching duties under the responsibility of that establishment, may constitute a transaction that is exempt from value added tax on the basis that it is a supply of services "closely related" to education, within the meaning of *Article 13A1(i)*, if such a teacher placement is a means of better enjoying the education deemed to be the principal service, provided, however – which it is for the national court to verify – that both that principal service and the placement which is closely related to it are provided by bodies referred to in *Article 13A1(i)*, taking into account, where appropriate, any conditions which may have been introduced by the Member State concerned pursuant to *Article 13A(2)(a)*; that placement is of a nature and quality such that, without recourse to such a service, there could be no assurance that the education provided by the host establishment and, consequently, the education from which its students benefit, would have an equivalent value; and the basic purpose of such a placement is not to obtain additional income by carrying out a transaction which is in direct competition with commercial enterprises liable for value added tax.' *Stichting Regionaal Opleidingen Centrum Noord Kennemerland / West Friesland (Horizon College) v Staatssecretaris van Financiën*, ECJ Case C-434/05; [2008] STC 2145.

[22.305] See also *Cooke*, **21.13** EDUCATION, and *Glenfall House Trust*, **21.45** EDUCATION.

Private tuition (Article 13A1(j))

[22.306] A company which provided private tuition treated its supplies as exempt. Customs issued an assessment charging tax on them, and the company appealed, contending that the supplies qualified for exemption under *Article 13A1(j)* of the *EC Sixth Directive*. The CS unanimously rejected this contention and upheld the assessment. Lord Macfadyen held that '*sub-paragraph (j)* is an example of an exemption expressed in language which, despite the principle of fiscal neutrality, makes the nature or identity of the provider of the tuition an essential element in the definition of the scope of the exemption. On a sound construction of *sub-paragraph (j)*, it applies only where the tuition is provided by a teacher acting in an individual or personal capacity, and does not apply to tuition provided by a teacher as an employee of a company or other organisation.' *HMRC v Empowerment Enterprises Ltd*, CS 2006, [2008] STC 1835; [2006] CSIH 46. (*Note*. For HMRC's practice following this decision, see HMRC Brief 10/07, issued on 7 February 2007.)

[22.307] In a German case, a freelance tutor (H) provided assistance with schoolwork at an adult education institute, and ran ceramics and pottery courses at another adult education institute. The tax authority issued a ruling that H's services were liable to VAT. He appealed, contending that they should be treated as exempt. The case was referred to the ECJ for a ruling on the interpretation of *Article 13A1(j)* of the *EC Sixth Directive*. The ECJ held that 'the activities of an individual acting in a freelance capacity, consisting of providing assistance with schoolwork and also running ceramics and pottery courses in adult education centres', could be exempted from VAT under *Article 13A(1)(j)* 'only where such activities consist of tuition given by a teacher on his own account and at his own risk, and covering school or university education. It is for the referring court to verify whether that is the case in the main proceedings.' *W Haderer v Finanzamt Wilmersdorf*, ECJ Case C-445/05; [2008] STC 2171.

[22.308] In another German case, a partnership carried on an engineering consultancy. One of the partners (E) lectured at a university. The tax authority issued a ruling that VAT was chargeable on the income which the partnership received for this. The partnership appealed, contending that it should be treated as exempt. The case was referred to the ECJ for a ruling on the interpretation of *Article 13A1(j)* of the *EC Sixth Directive*. The ECJ held that the lectures which E gave could qualify as 'tuition', but that, 'in circumstances such as those at issue in the main proceedings, a person such as (E), a partner in the claimant in the main proceedings, who performs teaching work for training courses offered by another body, cannot be regarded as having given tuition "privately" within the meaning of that provision'. *Ingenieurbüro Eulitz GbR Thomas und Marion Eulitz v Finanzamt Dresden I*, ECJ Case C-473/08; 28 January 2010 unreported.

[22.309] See also *Marcus Webb Golf Professional v HMRC*, **21.41** EDUCA-TION.

Supplies by 'non-profit-making organisations' (Article 13A1(l))

Article 13A1(l)—whether organisation's aims of 'a trade union nature'

[22.310] The Institute of the Motor Industry was established in 1920. In 1996 it applied for a ruling that its supplies should be treated as exempt from VAT under *VATA 1994, Sch 9, Group 9*. The Commissioners ruled that the Institute did not qualify for exemption, and the Institute appealed. The tribunal referred the case to the ECJ for a ruling as to whether the Institute qualified for exemption under *Article 13A1(l)* of the *EC Sixth Directive*, observing that the English-language text of this provision, referring to 'an organisation with aims of a trade-union nature', did not appear to be as wide as the French or German text. The ECJ held that 'an organisation with aims of a trade-union nature', within *Article 13A1(l)*, was 'an organisation whose main aim is to defend the collective interests of its members—whether they are workers, employers, independent professionals or traders carrying on a particular economic activity—and to represent them vis-à-vis the appropriate third parties, including the public authorities'. However, a non-profit-making organisation which aimed to promote the interests of its members could not be regarded as having objects of a trade union nature 'where that object is not put into practice by defending and representing the collective interests of its members vis-à-vis the relevant decision-makers'. It was for the national tribunal to decide whether the Institute was within the definition and qualified for exemption. With regard to the apparent differences between the different texts of *Article 13A1(l)*, the ECJ observed that 'the wording used in one language version of a Community provision cannot serve as the sole basis for the interpretation of that provision, or be made to override the other language versions'. In the event of a divergence between the language versions, 'the provision in question must be interpreted by reference to the purpose and general scheme of the rules of which it forms a part'. *Institute of the Motor Industry v C & E Commrs*, ECJ Case C-149/97; [1998] STC 1219. (*Note.* Following the ECJ decision, the tribunal dismissed the Institute's appeal, finding that its main aim was not 'supplying defence and representational services' and holding that its supplies failed to qualify for exemption—see **64.30** TRADE UNIONS, PROFESSIONAL AND PUBLIC INTEREST BODIES.)

Whether organisation's aims of 'a philanthropic or civic nature'

[22.311] The Expert Witness Institute was incorporated in 1997. It claimed that its supplies should be treated as exempt from VAT under *VATA 1994, Sch 9, Group 9* or *Article 13A1(l)* of the *EC Sixth Directive*. The Commissioners rejected the claim but the Ch D allowed the Institute's appeal and the CA upheld this decision, unanimously holding that the institute was established to support 'the proper administration of justice'. This was an aim of a civic nature, within *Article 13A1(l)*. *The Expert Witness Institute v C & E Commrs*, CA 2001, [2002] STC 42; [2001] EWCA Civ 1882; [2002] 1 WLR 1674.

[22.312] See also *Institute of Leisure and Amenity Management*, 64.18 TRADE UNIONS, PROFESSIONAL AND PUBLIC INTEREST BODIES; *British Tenpin Bowling Association*, 64.20 TRADE UNIONS, PROFESSIONAL AND PUBLIC INTEREST BODIES, and *Committee of Directors of Polytechnics*, 64.21 TRADE UNIONS, PROFESSIONAL AND PUBLIC INTEREST BODIES.

Services closely linked to sport or physical education (Article 13A1(m))

[22.313] The Spanish government exempted private sports bodies from VAT on condition that their entry fees did not exceed certain specified amounts. The European Commission brought an action against the Spanish government, seeking a declaration that this condition was not authorised by *Article 13A1(m)* of the *EC Sixth Directive*. The ECJ granted a declaration accordingly, holding that the criterion of the amount of membership fees was contrary to *Article 13A1(m)*, since it could result in a non-profit-making body being excluded from exemption, or in a profit-making body being able to benefit from it. Accordingly, the Spanish government had failed to fulfil its obligations under the *Directive*. *EC Commission v Spain*, ECJ Case C-124/96; [1998] STC 1237.

[22.314] Under Swedish law, the supply of premises or other facilities for sporting purposes was exempt from VAT. A company which operated a golf course, and which was therefore unable to reclaim input tax, appealed, contending that the relevant provisions were a breach of *Article 13A1(m)* of the *EC Sixth Directive*. The case was referred to the ECJ, which held that the exemption in *Article 13A(1)(m)* was 'specifically limited to supplies provided by non-profit-making organisations'. It therefore precluded a general exemption from applying to services supplied by profit-making organisations. The ECJ also held that the implementation of a general exemption which was not authorised by *Article 13* was 'a serious breach of Community law that can render a Member State liable in damages'. *Stockholm Lindöpark AB v Sweden*, ECJ Case C-150/99; [2001] STC 103.

[22.315] In a Netherlands case, the tax authority ruled that a golf club was aiming to make a profit and thus did not qualify for exemption under *Article 13A(1)(m)* of the *EC Sixth Directive*. The club appealed and the case was referred to the ECJ, which held that *Article 13A(1)(m)* should be 'interpreted as meaning that an organisation may be categorised as "non-profit-making" even if it systematically seeks to achieve surpluses which it then uses for the purposes of the provision of its services'. Advocate-General Jacobs defined a 'non-profit-making organisation' as 'one which does not have as its object the enrichment of natural or legal persons and which is not in fact run in such a way as to achieve or seek to achieve such enrichment; however, the fact that a body systematically aims to make a surplus which it uses for the services it supplies in the form of a facility to practise a sport does not preclude its classification as such a non-profit-making organisation'. *Kennemer Golf & Country Club v Staatssecretaris van Financien*, ECJ Case C-174/00; [2002] STC 502; [2002] 3 WLR 829; [2002] All ER (EC) 480.

[22.316] Customs issued a ruling that VAT was chargeable on affiliation fees to the English hockey association. Two affiliated clubs lodged appeals, contending that the fees qualified for exemption under *VATA 1994, Sch 9, Group 10, Item 3* or alternatively under *Article 13A1(m)* of the *EC Sixth Directive*. The tribunal accepted this contention and allowed their appeals but the Ch D directed that the case should be referred to the ECJ for a ruling on the interpretation of *Article 13A1(m)* of the *EC Sixth Directive*. The ECJ gave judgment in favour of the clubs, holding that *Article 13A1(m)* should be interpreted as including 'services supplied to corporate persons and to unincorporated associations, provided that – which it is for the national court to establish – those services are closely linked and essential to sport, that they are supplied by non-profit-making organisations and that their true beneficiaries are persons taking part in sport'. The ECJ also held that the exemption could not be limited to services supplied to individuals, since the expression 'certain services closely linked to sport' did not permit Member States 'to limit the exemption under that provision by reference to the recipients of the services in question'. *HMRC v Canterbury Hockey Club (and related appeal)*, ECJ Case C-253/07; [2008] STC 3351. (*Note*. For HMRC's practice following this decision, see HMRC Brief 15/10, issued on 29 March 2010.)

[22.317] See also *Turn-und Sportunion Waldburg v Finanzlandesdirektion für Oberösterreich*, 22.382 below; *Chard Bowling Club*, 24.34 EXEMPTIONS: MISCELLANEOUS; *Messenger Leisure Developments Ltd*, 24.42 EXEMPTIONS: MISCELLANEOUS; *Royal Pigeon Racing Association*, 24.50 EXEMPTIONS: MISCELLANEOUS, and *Sunningdale Golf Club*, 48.31 PAYMENT OF TAX.

Cultural services (Article 13A1(n))

[22.318] A German concert promoter failed to account for VAT on the fees which he paid to three singers. He was prosecuted for tax evasion, convicted by a regional court (Landgericht), and sentenced to a term of imprisonment. He appealed to the federal court (Bundesgerichtshof) against his conviction, contending that the relevant fees should be treated as exempt from VAT. The federal court referred the case to the ECJ for a ruling on the interpretation of *Article 13A(1)(n)* of the *EC Sixth Directive*. The ECJ held that *Article 13A(1)(n)* should 'be interpreted to the effect that the expression "other cultural bodies" does not exclude soloists performing individually'. The ECJ also held that the heading of *Article 13A* ('exemptions for certain activities in the public interest') 'does not, of itself, entail restrictions on the possibilities of exemption provided for by that provision'. *Hoffmann*, ECJ Case C-144/00; [2004] STC 740.

[22.319] In a Norwegian case, a club failed to account for VAT on takings from 'striptease' performances. The tax authority issued an assessment charging VAT on the takings, and the club appealed to the Tingrett (district court), contending that 'striptease' was a 'cultural service' which qualified for exemption from VAT under Norwegian law. The court accepted this contention and allowed the club's appeal. The tax authority appealed to the Lagmannsrett, which upheld the Tingrett decision, holding that 'striptease' was a 'form of dance combined with acting' and that 'most people would characterise striptease as an artistic activity'. *Fylkesskattesjefen v Diamond GoGo Bar*, Lagmannsrett 6 December 2006; Times 7.12.2006. (*Note*. Norway is not a member of the EU. The exemption for cultural services under *Article 13A1(n)* of the *EC Sixth Directive* is confined to services 'supplied by bodies governed by public law or by other cultural bodies recognised by the Member State concerned'.)

Fund-raising events (Article 13A1(o))

[22.320] See *Northern Ireland Council for Voluntary Action*, **11.32** CHARITIES.

Restrictions on exemptions (Article 13A2)

[22.321] The Zoological Society of London, a registered charity, accounted for output tax on admission charges, but subsequently submitted a claim for repayment of the tax, contending that it should have treated its supplies as exempt under *VATA 1994, Sch 9, Group 13*. The Commissioners rejected the claim on the grounds that the management and administration of the society was in the hands of paid employees, so that the society was not 'managed and administered on a voluntary basis by persons who have no direct or indirect financial interest in its activities', as required by *Group 13, Note 2(c)*. The society appealed, contending that the responsibilities for management and administration were in the hands of the members of its Council, who were in the position of trustees, and that the fact that it paid employees who performed some functions of management and administration did not prevent it from qualifying for exemption. The tribunal accepted this contention in principle, but the QB directed that the case should be referred to the ECJ for guidance on the interpretation of the words 'managed and administered on an essentially voluntary basis' in *Article 13A2(a)* of the *EC Sixth Directive*. The ECJ observed that the aim of the condition was 'to reserve the VAT exemption for bodies which do not have a commercial purpose, by requiring that the persons who participate in the management and administration of such bodies have no financial interest of their own in their results, by means of remuneration, distribution of profits or any other financial interest'. Accordingly, 'the condition requiring a body to be managed and administered on an essentially voluntary basis refers only to members of that body who are designated in accordance with its constitution to direct it at the highest level, as well as other persons who, without being designated by the constitution, in fact direct inasmuch as they take the decisions of last resort concerning the policy of that body, especially in the financial area, and carry out the higher supervisory tasks'. *C & E Commrs v The Zoological Society of London*, ECJ Case C-267/00; [2002] STC 521; [2002] All ER (EC) 465. (*Note*. For the Commissioners' revised practice following this decision, see Business Brief 28/2003, issued on 10 December 2003, and News Release 87/2003, issued on 5 January 2004.)

[22.322] The proprietor of a 'fitness club' failed to account for VAT. The Commissioners issued assessments and he appealed, contending that he was entitled to exemption under *Article 13A1(m)* of the *EC Sixth Directive*. The tribunal rejected this contention and dismissed his appeal, holding that the effect of *Article 13A2(a)* was that he was not entitled to exemption. *B Ball*, MAN/00/41 (VTD 18708).

[22.323] See also *Stichting Regionaal Opleidingen Centrum Noord-Kennemerland/West-Friesland (Horizon College) v Staatssecretaris van Financiën*, 22.304 above; *Basingstoke & District Sports Trust*, 24.32 EXEMPTIONS: MISCELLANEOUS, and *Keswick Golf Club*, 24.47 EXEMPTIONS: MISCELLANEOUS.

Insurance transactions (Article 13B(a))

[22.324] In the case noted at **38.44** INSURANCE, a company (C) operated a service whereby, in return for a payment of £16, a customer whose credit cards were lost or stolen would be indemnified up to £750 against any claim made against him in respect of loss caused by fraudulent use of the cards. C engaged an insurance broker to arrange for an appropriate insurance policy. C did not account for VAT on the payments received from customers for this service. The Commissioners issued a ruling that the payments were taxable and C appealed, contending that they should be treated as exempt under the provisions of *VATA 1983* (see the note preceding **38.34** INSURANCE), or alternatively that it should be treated as making multiple supplies so that part of the payments qualified for exemption. The HL referred the case to the ECJ for rulings as to what was the proper test to be applied in deciding whether a transaction consisted of a single composite supply or of two or more independent supplies; whether supplies of the kind made by C constituted or included 'insurance' within *Article 13B(a)* of the *EC Sixth Directive*, and whether the restriction of the exemption for insurance transactions to supplies made by authorised insurers was compatible with *Article 13B(a)* of the *EC Sixth Directive*. The ECJ held that Member States could not restrict the scope of the exemption for insurance transactions exclusively to supplies by insurers who were authorised by national law. It was for the national court to determine whether the particular transactions in this case were to be regarded as comprising two independent supplies, namely an exempt insurance supply and a taxable card registration service. The ECJ observed that 'having regard to the diversity of commercial operations, it is not possible to give exhaustive guidance on how to approach the problem correctly in all cases.' However, 'a supply which comprises a single service from an economic point of view should not be artificially split'. There was 'a single supply in particular in cases where one or more elements are to be regarded as constituting the principal service, whilst one or more elements are to be regarded, by contrast, as ancillary services which share the tax treatment of the principal service. A service must be regarded as ancillary to a principal service if it does not constitute for customers an aim in itself, but a means of better enjoying the principal service supplied'. *Card Protection Plan Ltd v C & E Commrs*, ECJ Case C-349/96; [1999] STC 270; [1999] 3 WLR 203; [1999] All ER (EC) 339. (*Note.* The HL subsequently allowed the company's appeal—see **38.44** INSURANCE.)

[22.325] In a Swedish case, an insurance company (S) undertook to run the insurance business of one of its subsidiary companies. The Swedish tax authority ruled that this was a supply of management services on which VAT was chargeable. S appealed, contending that it should be regarded as an exempt supply of insurance. The case was referred to the ECJ, which rejected S's contentions, holding that the undertaking did not qualify as an 'insurance transaction'. *Försäkringsaktiebolaget Skandia*, ECJ Case C-240/99; [2001] STC 754; [2001] 1 WLR 1617; [2001] All ER (EC) 822.

[22.326] In a Danish case, a number of insurance companies formed a company (T) to assess damage to motor vehicles on their behalf. T applied for exemption from VAT. The tax authority rejected the application, and T appealed, contending that its supplies should be treated as exempt under *Article 13B(a)* of the *EC Sixth Directive*. The case was referred to the ECJ, which rejected T's contentions, holding that 'motor vehicle damage assessments carried out, on behalf of its members, by an association whose members are insurance companies are neither insurance transactions nor services related to insurance transactions that are performed by insurance brokers or insurance agents' within *Article 13B(a)*. *Assurandør-Societetet (on behalf of Taksatorringen) v Skatteministeriet*, ECJ Case C-8/01; [2006] STC 1842. (*Note*. This decision was distinguished in the subsequent case of *JCM Beheer BV v Staatssecretaris van Financiën*, 22.328 below.)

[22.327] In a Netherlands case, the ECJ held that *Article 13B(a)* of the *EC Sixth Directive* 'must be interpreted as meaning that "back office" activities, consisting in rendering services, for payment, to an insurance company do not constitute the performance of services relating to insurance transactions carried out by an insurance broker or an insurance agent within the meaning of that provision'. Accordingly the services in question were chargeable to VAT, and failed to qualify for exemption. *Staatssecretaris van Financiën v Arthur Andersen & Co*, ECJ Case C-472/03; [2005] STC 508. (*Notes*. (1) For HMRC's practice following this decision, see Business Brief 11/2005, issued on 18 May 2005, and Business Brief 23/2005, issued on 5 December 2005. (2) This decision was distinguished in the subsequent case of *JCM Beheer BV v Staatssecretaris van Financiën*, 22.328 below.)

[22.328] In another Netherlands case, the tax authority ruled that services carried out by an insurance broker which acted as an intermediary failed to qualify for exemption. The broker appealed, and the case was referred to the ECJ. The ECJ distinguished the earlier decisions in *Assurandør-Societetet (on behalf of Taksatorringen) v Skatteministeriet*, 22.326 above, and *Staatssecretaris van Financiën v Arthur Andersen & Co*, 22.327 above, holding that although the court had considered that the activities carried on by the taxable persons in question 'did not, of their nature, constitute activities related to insurance transactions carried out by an insurance broker or an insurance agent within the meaning of *Article 13B(a)* of the *Sixth Directive*, it did not seek to analyse the relationship of those taxable persons with the insurers and the insured parties'. Accordingly, an insurance broker 'cannot be refused the benefit of the exemption provided for in *Article 13B(a)* of the *Sixth Directive* merely because it does not have a direct relationship with the insurers on whose behalf it acts indirectly'. The ECJ concluded that *Article 13B(a)* 'must be interpreted as meaning that the fact that an insurance broker or agent does not have a direct relationship with the parties to the insurance or reinsurance contract in the conclusion of which he has been instrumental, but merely an indirect relationship with them through the intermediary of another taxable person who is, himself, in a direct relationship with one of those parties, and to whom the insurance broker or agent is contractually bound does not prevent the service provided by the latter from being exempt from value added tax under that provision'. *JCM Beheer BV v Staatssecretaris van Financiën*, ECJ Case C-124/07; [2008] STC 3360.

[22.329] A Greek association provided car accident and breakdown services to its members, in return for an annual subscription. The tax authority levied VAT on these payments. The EC Commission considered that such services qualified for exemption under *Article 13B(a)* of the *EC Sixth Directive*, and applied to the ECJ for a ruling that the relevant Greek legislation contravened the *Directive*. The ECJ granted the application, holding that 'by levying value added tax on services consisting in road assistance in the event of a breakdown, the Hellenic Republic has failed to fulfil its obligations under *Article 13B(a)*'. *EC Commission v Hellenic Republic*, ECJ Case C-13/06; [2007] STC 194.

[22.330] A German company transferred 195 reinsurance contracts to an associated Swiss company. The tax authority charged VAT on the transfer, and the company appealed, contending that it should be treated as exempt. The case was referred to the ECJ, which rejected the company's contentions, holding that 'a transfer for consideration, by a company established in one Member State, to an insurance company established in a third State, of a portfolio of life reinsurance contracts, with the consequence that the transferee company assumes, with the consent of the insured persons, all the rights and obligations resulting from those contracts' did not fall within *Article 13B* of the *EC Sixth Directive*. *Swiss Re Germany Holding GmbH v Finanzamt München für Körperschaften*, ECJ Case C-242/08; [2010] STC 236.

[22.331] See also *Century Life plc*, **38.13** INSURANCE; *SOC Private Capital Ltd*, **38.15** INSURANCE, and *Agentevent Ltd*, **38.30** INSURANCE.

Leasing or letting of immovable property (Article 13B(b))

[22.332] In a Danish case, two blocks of twelve garages were constructed in conjunction with a building development comprising 37 linked houses. Some of the garages were let to residents of the development and some were let to non-residents. The case was referred to the ECJ for a ruling on whether the letting of the garages was exempt from VAT under *Article 13B(b)* of the *Sixth Directive*, as the 'letting of immovable property', or was excluded from that exemption by *Article 13B(b)(2)*, as the 'letting of premises and sites for the parking of vehicles'. The ECJ held that where the letting of parking places was 'closely linked to lettings of immovable property' which were themselves exempt from VAT under *Article 13B(b)*, such lettings could not be excluded from exemption. *Skatteministeriet v Henriksen*, ECJ Case 173/88; [1989] ECR 2763; [1990] STC 768; [1990] 3 CMLR 558.

[22.333] An accountancy partnership surrendered the lease of offices which it had occupied, and received a payment of £850,000 from the landlords for the surrender. The partnership did not account for VAT on the £850,000, and the Commissioners issued an assessment charging tax on it. The partnership appealed, contending that, by virtue of *Article 13B* of the *EC Sixth Directive*, the payment should be treated as exempt from VAT. The tribunal referred the case to the ECJ, which held that a transaction whereby a tenant surrendered his lease and returned the immovable property to his immediate landlord was within *Article 13B(b)*, and was therefore exempt from VAT. Where the rent paid under such a lease was exempt from VAT, *Article 13B* did not authorise a Member State to tax the consideration paid in respect of such a surrender. *Lubbock Fine & Co v C & E Commrs*, ECJ Case C-63/92; [1993] 1 ECR 6665; [1994] STC 101; [1994] 3 WLR 261; [1994] 3 All ER 705. (*Notes.* (1) The relevant legislation was amended by *VAT (Land) Order 1995 (SI 1995/282)* with effect from 1 March 1995. (2) For a subsequent case where this decision was distinguished, see *Cantor Fitzgerald International*, 22.334 below.)

[22.334] An unlimited company which carried on a stockbroking business took an assignment of an underlease. It received £1,500,000 from the assignor as consideration. The Commissioners issued an assessment on the basis that this consideration was taxable. The company appealed, contending that it was exempt under *Article 13B(b)* of the *EC Sixth Directive*. The QB referred the case to the ECJ, which rejected the company's contentions, distinguishing *Lubbock Fine & Co*, 22.333 above. The ECJ held that *Article 13B(b)* 'applies to the grant of leases of property but not to transactions which are merely based on the leases or are ancillary thereto'. *Article 13B(b)* did 'not exempt a supply of services which is made by a person who does not have any interest in the immovable property and which consists in the acceptance, for consideration, of an assignment of a lease of that property from the lessee'. *C & E Commrs v Cantor Fitzgerald International*, ECJ Case C-108/99; [2001] STC 1453.

[22.335] In 1993 a publishing company (M) agreed to lease five floors of a multi-storey building, with an option to lease a further four floors. The lessor paid an inducement of £12,000,000 into an escrow account, to be paid to M in instalments. The lessor also paid VAT of £2,100,000, which M accounted for as output tax. In 1994 and 1995 M exercised its option with regard to three further floors, and £1,400,000 was repaid to the lessor in 1995 in respect of M's unexercised option for the remaining floor. Subsequently M claimed repayment of the £2,100,000 from the Commissioners, contending firstly that it had accounted for this in error as it did not relate to any supply, and alternatively that the relevant supply was exempt under *Article 13B(b)* of the *EC Sixth Directive*. The tribunal rejected M's first contention, holding that the inducement of £12,000,000 was consideration for a supply of services made by M in the course of relocating its business. Both parties appealed to the QB, which referred the case to the ECJ for a ruling on the interpretation of *Article 13B(b)* of the *EC Sixth Directive*. The ECJ held that it was for the national court to ascertain whether M had made a supply of services for consideration. However, if (as the tribunal had found) there was a supply of services, it did not qualify for exemption under *Article 13B(b)*. The ECJ held that 'a person who does not initially have any interest in the immovable property and who enters into an agreement for lease of that immovable property with a landlord and/or accepts the grant of a lease of the property in return for a sum of money paid by the landlord' did not make an exempt supply within *Article 13B(b)*. Similarly, 'a person who does not initially have any interest in the immovable property and who enters into an option agreement such as the one before the national court in relation to leases of that immovable property in return for a sum of money paid by the landlord', and who subsequently 'exercises the options under the option agreement and accepts the grant of leases of the immovable property' did not make an exempt supply within *Article 13B(b)*. *Mirror Group plc v C & E Commrs*, ECJ Case C-409/98; [2001] STC 1453; [2002] 2 WLR 288. (*Notes*. (1) The case was heard in the ECJ with *Cantor Fitzgerald International*, **22.334** above. (2) For subsequent developments in this case, see **62.129** SUPPLY.)

[22.336] The French Government exempted the letting of caravans, tents and mobile homes from VAT. The European Commission applied for a declaration that this exemption went beyond the scope of *Article 13B(b)* of the *EC Sixth Directive*. The ECJ granted the declaration, holding that France had failed to fulfil its obligations under *Article 2* of the *Directive*. *EC Commission v French Republic*, ECJ Case C-60/96; [1997] 1 ECR 3827; [1999] STC 480.

[22.337] In a German case, the tax authority issued an assessment charging tax on income from letting prefabricated buildings. The lessor appealed, contending that the income should be treated as exempt under *Article 13B(b)* of the *EC Sixth Directive*. The case was referred to the ECJ, which accepted this contention, holding that 'the letting of a building constructed from prefabricated components fixed to or in the ground in such a way that they cannot be easily dismantled or easily moved constitutes a letting of immovable property for the purposes of *Article 13B(b)*'. The ECJ distinguished *EC Commission v French Republic*, **22.336** above, observing that the buildings were not mobile and could not be easily moved: they were 'erected on concrete foundations sunk into the ground', and it would take eight people ten days to dismantle them. *Maierhofer v Finanzamt Augsburg-Land*, ECJ Case C-315/00; [2003] STC 564.

[22.338] Under German law, the leasing and letting of immovable property was exempt from VAT (in accordance with *Article 13B(b)* of the *EC Sixth Directive*), but lettings for 'short-term accommodation of guests' were excluded from exemption. A woman who let property to refugee families was assessed to output tax on her income from these lettings. The letting agreements were always for periods of less than six months, but many of the refugees stayed in the accommodation for more than a year. She appealed, and the case was referred to the ECJ for a ruling on whether the provision of short-term accommodation for guests should be excluded from exemption under *Article 13B(b)(1)*, and as to the period of accommodation which could properly be regarded as short-term. The ECJ held that *Article 13B(b)(1)* provided Member States with a margin of discretion, could be construed as meaning that the provision of short-term accommodation for guests was taxable, and did not preclude taxation in respect of agreements concluded for a period of less than six months. It was for the national court to determine whether the duration stated in the letting agreement reflected the true intention of the parties. Where the letting agreement did not reflect the true intention of the parties, the actual duration of the accommodation, rather than that specified in the letting agreement, would have to be taken into consideration. *Blasi v Finanzamt München I*, ECJ Case C-346/95; [1998] STC 336; [1998] All ER (EC) 211.

[22.339] Under Spanish law, the letting of business premises was subject to VAT. A tenant appealed to the Spanish courts, contending that this infringed *Article 13B(b)* of the *EC Sixth Directive*. The case was referred to the ECJ, which held that *Article 13B(b)* allowed Member States 'to subject to VAT lettings of immovable property and, by way of exception, to exempt only lettings of immovable property to be used for dwelling purposes'. The ECJ also observed that the wording of the *Directive* 'has left the Member States wide discretion as to whether the transactions concerned are to be exempt or taxed'. *J Amengual Far v M Amengual Far*, ECJ Case C-12/98; [2002] STC 382.

[22.340] A company supplied coin-operated vending machines for cigarettes. It entered into agreements to install such machines in public houses. The Commissioners issued a ruling that the agreements constituted the grant of licences to occupy land, so that payments under the agreements were exempt from VAT and the company was unable to reclaim the related input tax. The tribunal allowed the company's appeal but the QB reversed this decision. The company appealed to the HL, which directed that the case should be referred to the ECJ for a ruling on the interpretation of the words 'the leasing or letting of immovable property' in *Article 13B(b)* of the *EC Sixth Directive*. The ECJ held that 'the grant, by the owner of premises to an owner of a cigarette vending machine, of the right to install the machine, and to operate and maintain it in the premises for a period of two years, in a place nominated by the owner of the premises, in return for a percentage of the gross profits on the sales of cigarettes and other tobacco goods in the premises, but with no rights of possession or control being granted to the owner of the machine other than those expressly set out in the agreement between the parties, does not amount to a letting of immovable property'. *Sinclair Collis Ltd v C & E Commrs*, ECJ Case C-275/01; [2003] STC 898. (*Note.* For the Commissioners' practice following this decision, see Business Brief 18/2003, issued on 30 September 2003.)

[22.341] In a Belgian case, the ECJ held that *Article 13B(b)* of the *EC Sixth Directive* 'must be interpreted as meaning that transactions by which one company, through a number of contracts, simultaneously grants associated companies a licence to occupy a single property in return for a payment set essentially on the basis of the area occupied and by which the contracts, as performed, have as their essential object the making available, in a passive manner, of premises or parts of buildings in return for a payment linked to the passage of time, are transactions comprising the "letting of immovable property"'. *Belgian State v Temco Europe SA*, ECJ Case C-284/03; [2005] STC 1451.

[22.342] In a Danish case, the ECJ held that that *Article 13B(b)* of the *EC Sixth Directive* 'must be interpreted as meaning that the concept of letting of immovable property includes the letting of both water-based mooring berths for pleasure boats and land sites for storage of boats on port land'. The ECJ also held that 'the definition of "vehicles" includes boats'. *Fonden Marselisborg Lystbådehavn v Skatteministeriet*, ECJ Case C-428/02; [2006] STC 1467.

[22.343] In an Austrian case concerning the grant of non-exclusive fishing rights, the ECJ held that *Article 13B(b)* of the *EC Sixth Directive* 'must be interpreted to mean that the grant for consideration, under a contract of let for a period of ten years, of the right to fish, by the landowner in waters owned by that person, and by the holder of fishing rights in publicly owned waters, does not constitute either a leasing or a letting of immovable property, since that grant does not confer the right to occupy the immovable property concerned and to exclude any other person from it'. *G Walderdorff v Finanzamt Waldviertel*, ECJ Case C-451/06; [2008] STC 3079.

[22.344] In an Italian case, a company was granted a concession to use some coastal warehouses, owned by the State, to store and manufacture mineral oils. The tax authorities charged VAT, and the company appealed, contending that its occupation of the property qualified for exemption. The case was referred to the ECJ, which held that *Article 13B(b)* 'must be interpreted as meaning that a legal relationship such as that at issue in the main proceedings, under which a person has been granted the right to occupy and use, including exclusively, public property, namely areas of State maritime property, for a specified period and against payment, is covered by the concept of "leasing or letting of immovable property"'. *Ministero delle Finanze v COGEP Srl*, ECJ Case C-174/06; [2008] STC 2744.

[22.345] A company had operated an aquarium for many years. In September 1990, following a visit from a local authority fire officer, it agreed to purchase fire equipment for the premises and arranged for a contractor to carry out work recommended by the fire officer. It reclaimed input tax on the supplies. In December 1990, following adverse publicity, it leased the premises to an unrelated company, and assigned the contract for the work recommended by the fire officer to the tenant. Under the lease, the purchaser was to pay £72,500 p.a. for the premises, and £40,000 p.a. for the equipment. The Commissioners issued an assessment to recover the tax on the fire equipment, on the basis that the supply of the fire equipment was part of the supply of the premises, which was exempt from VAT. The company appealed, contending that the fire equipment was the subject of a separate supply. The tribunal allowed the appeal, holding that the effect of *Article 13B(b)(3)* of the *EC Sixth Directive* was that the letting of the equipment was to be treated as a separate taxable supply. *Aquarium Entertainments Ltd*, [1994] VATTR 61 (VTD 11845).

[22.346] In a Czech case, a company owned apartment blocks, and rented the apartments to tenants. It made separate charges to its tenants for cleaning services. The tax authority issued a ruling that the company was required to account for VAT on these charges. The company appealed, contending that for VAT purposes the letting and cleaning of the apartments should be treated as a single supply which was exempt from VAT. The case was referred to the ECJ, which rejected the company's contentions, holding that, for the purposes of *Article 13B(b)* of the *Sixth Directive*, 'the letting of immovable property and the cleaning service of the common parts of the latter must, in circumstances such as those at issue in the main proceedings, be regarded as independent, mutually divisible operations, so that the said service does not fall within that provision'. *RLRE Tellmer Property sro v Finanční ředitelství v Ústí nad*

Labem, ECJ Case C-572/07; [2009] STC 2006. (*Note*. For HMRC's practice following this decision, see HMRC Brief 67/09, issued on 27 October 2009.)

[22.347] A firm of solicitors leased serviced office accommodation. Its landlords treated their supplies as exempt in accordance with HMRC's advice. The firm appealed, contending that the effect of the ECJ decision in *RLRE Tellmer Property sro v Finanční reditelství v Ústí nad Labem*, 22.346 above, was that the service charges should be treated as taxable supplies (so that it should be allowed to reclaim input tax). The tribunal directed that the case should be referred to the ECJ. *Field Fisher Waterhouse Llp v HMRC*, [2011] UKFTT 524 (TC); [2011] SFTD 1015; TC01371. (*Note*. The ECJ has registered the case as Case C-392/11.)

[22.348] See also *Seeling v Finanzamt Starnberg*, 22.182 above; *Abbey National plc (No 4)*, 41.19 LAND; *Argents Nurseries Ltd*, 41.61 LAND; *Central Capital Corporation Ltd*, 41.66 LAND; *Ashworth*, 41.127 LAND; *Colaingrove Ltd*, 41.132 LAND; *MacDonald Resorts Ltd*, 62.513 SUPPLY, and *University of Kent*, 69.7 ZERO-RATING.

Goods used for exempted activities (Article 13B(c))

[22.349] The EC Commission took proceedings against the Italian Republic for failing to implement *Article 13B(c)* of the *EC Sixth Directive*, which exempts the supplies of goods used wholly for an exempt activity, when these goods have not given rise to a right of deduction of input tax. The Italian VAT system effectively treated such supplies as being outside the scope of VAT. This did not necessarily have the same effect as exempting the supplies, for in cases where a partial exemption calculation applied, the Italian provisions resulted in a reduction in the denominator of the fraction. The ECJ held that, by enacting legislation which did not exempt from VAT supplies of goods used wholly for an exempted activity, the Italian Republic had failed to fulfil its obligations under *Article 13B(c)*. *EC Commission v Italian Republic*, ECJ Case C-45/95; [1997] STC 1062; [1997] 1 ECR 3605. (*Note*. For HMRC's interpretation of the effects of this decision, see Business Brief 24/99, issued on 25 November 1999, and HMRC Brief 43/10, issued on 12 October 2010.)

[22.350] A Danish company purchased second-hand cars, leased them to customers, and subsequently resold them. The tax authority issued an assessment charging tax on the sales. The company appealed, contending that the sales should be treated as exempt under *Article 13B(c)* of the *EC Sixth Directive*. The case was referred to the ECJ, which held that *Article 13B(c)* should be construed as precluding 'a national law which imposes VAT on transactions by which a taxable person, after having used them for the purposes of its business, resells goods on the acquisition of which, by virtue of *Article 17(6)*, VAT did not become deductible, even where that acquisition, made from taxable persons who could not declare VAT, did not, for that reason, give rise to a right to deduct'. (The ECJ also held that *Article 26a(A)(e)* should 'be construed as meaning that an undertaking which, in the normal course of its business, resells cars which it had purchased second-hand with a view to using them for the purposes of its business of sale and leaseback and for which the resale is not, at the time of the purchase of the second-hand goods, the principal objective but only its secondary objective, ancillary to that of leasing, can be considered to be a "taxable dealer" within the meaning of that provision'.) *Jyske Finans A/S v Skatteministeriet*, ECJ Case C-280/04; [2006] STC 1744.

[22.351] See also *Stafford Land Rover*, **44.168** MOTOR CARS.

Financial transactions (Article 13B(d))

[22.352] In a German case, a credit negotiator claimed exemption under *Article 13B(d)* of the *EC Sixth Directive*. The ECJ held that *Article 13B(d)* had direct effect despite the fact that it had not been implemented in German law at the relevant time. *U Becker v Finanzamt Münster-Innenstadt*, ECJ Case 8/81; [1982] ECR 53; [1982] 1 CMLR 499.

[22.353] The decision in *Becker v Finanzamt Münster-Innenstadt*, **22.352** above, was applied in *RA Grendel GmbH v Finanzamt für Körperschaften Hamburg*, ECJ Case 255/81; [1982] ECR 2301; [1983] 1 CMLR 379; *G Kloppenburg v Finanzamt Leer*, ECJ Case 70/83; [1984] ECR 1075; [1985] 1 CMLR 205 and *G Weissgerber v Finanzamt Neustadt an der Weinstraße*, ECJ Case 207/87; [1988] ECR 4433; [1991] STC 589.

[22.354] In a Dutch case, the ECJ held that a supplier who allowed a customer to defer payment in return for interest was in principle granting credit which was exempt from VAT under *Article 13B(d)* of the *EC Sixth Directive*. However, where payment was only deferred until delivery of the goods or services (as in the case which was the subject of the appeal), interest was not in fact consideration for a separate supply of credit but was part of the taxable consideration for the supply, within *Article 11A1(a)*. *Muys en De Winter's Bouw-en Aannemingsbedriff BV v Staatssecretaris van Financiën*, ECJ Case C-281/91; [1993] 1 ECR 5405; [1997] STC 665; [1995] 1 CMLR 126.

[22.355] In a German case, the ECJ held that 'the fact that a taxable person analyses the financial situation of clients canvassed by him with a view to obtaining credit for them does not preclude recognition of the service supplied as being a negotiation of credit which is exempt under *Article 13B(d)(1)*' if 'the negotiation of credit offered by that taxable person falls to be considered as the principal service to which the provision of financial advice is ancillary, in such a way that the latter shares the same tax treatment as the former. It is for the national court to determine whether that is the case in the proceedings before it. The fact that the taxable person has no contractual link with any of the parties to a credit agreement to the conclusion of which he has contributed and that he does not establish direct contact with one of those parties does not preclude that taxable person from providing a service of negotiation of credit which is exempt under *Article 13B(d)(1)*.' *V Ludwig v Finanzamt Luckenwalde*, ECJ Case C-453/05; [2008] STC 1640.

[22.356] In another German case, the ECJ held that *Article 13B(d)(2)* of the *EC Sixth Directive* 'must be interpreted as meaning that the concept of assumption of obligations excludes from the scope of that provision obligations which are non-pecuniary, such as the obligation to renovate a property'. *Velvet & Steel Immobilien und Handels GmbH v Finanzamt Hamburg-Eimsbüttel*, ECJ Case C-455/05; [2008] STC 922.

[22.357] In a Danish case, an association of savings banks provided services comprising the execution of transfers, the provision of advice on and trade in securities, and the management of deposits, purchase contracts and loans. The association claimed repayment of VAT which it had accounted for on such transactions, contending that it should have treated them as exempt. The case was referred to the ECJ for rulings on the interpretation of *Article 13B(d)* of the *EC Sixth Directive*. The ECJ held that the exemption was not restricted to transactions effected by a particular type of institution, by a particular type of legal person, or wholly or partly by electronic means or manually. It was not necessary for the service to be provided by an institution which had a legal relationship with the final customer, and the fact that a transaction covered by the provisions was actually effected by a third party, rather than by the customer's bank, did not preclude exemption. Transactions concerning transfers and payments, and services consisting of the management of deposits, purchase contracts and loans, included operations carried out by a data-handling centre if those operations were distinct in character and were specific to, and essential for, the exempt transactions. However, services which merely consisted of making information available to banks and other users did not qualify for exemption. The ECJ also held that, provided that a supply of services fulfilled the criteria for exemption and was specified in an invoice which only concerned that service, the fact that, for organisational reasons, the service was invoiced by a third party did not prevent the transaction to which it related from qualifying for exemption. *Sparekassernes Datacenter v Skatteministeriet*, ECJ Case C-2/95; [1997] STC 932; [1997] 1 ECR 3017; [1997] 3 CMLR 999; [1997] All ER (EC) 610.

[22.358] In an Italian case, the ECJ held that where the lending of money at commercial rates of interest was exempt from VAT under *Article 13B(d)(1)*, that exemption must also be applied to 'exorbitant lending' which was a criminal offence under the national criminal code. *G Curia v Ministero dell'Economia e delle Finanze & Agenzia delle Entrate*, ECJ Case C-381/09; 7 July 2010 unreported.

[22.359] In a Belgian case, the ECJ held that 'the terms "transactions, including negotiation, concerning deposit accounts and payments" used in *Article 13(B)(d)(3)*' were to be interpreted as meaning that 'they do not refer to the supply of services by an agent acting on behalf of a client which carries out the activity of accepting bets on horse races and other sporting events, consisting of acceptance by the agent of bets on behalf of the client, registration thereof, confirmation to the client, by presentation of the betting slip, that a bet was made, collection of funds, payment of winnings, sole assumption of liability as regards the client for management of the funds collected and for thefts and/or losses of money and receipt of remuneration in the form of commission from the client as remuneration for that activity'. *Tiercé Ladbroke SA v Belgian State*, ECJ Case C-231/07; 14 May 2008 unreported.

[22.360] A company (C) supplied services to a group of companies (S) which issued personal equity plans. C dealt with telephone enquiries and with replies to advertisements which S had placed, sent application forms to potential customers and checked completed application forms. The Commissioners issued a ruling that C was required to account for output tax on its supplies.

C appealed, contending that its supplies should be treated as exempt under *VATA 1994, Sch 9, Group 5, Item 7*. The tribunal accepted this contention and allowed C's appeal, but the Commissioners appealed to the QB, which directed that the case should be referred to the ECJ for a ruling on the application of *Article 13B(d)(5)* of the *EC Sixth Directive*. The ECJ held that the exemption under *Article 13B(d)(5)* for 'transactions including negotiation' did not extend to 'services limited to providing information about a financial product and, as the case may be, receiving and processing applications for subscription, without issuing them'. *C & E Commrs v CSC Financial Services Ltd (aka Continuum (Europe) Ltd)*, ECJ Case C-235/00; [2002] STC 57; [2002] 1 WLR 2200; [2002] All ER (EC) 289. (*Note. VATA 1994, Sch 9, Group 5, Item 7* was repealed by *SI 1999/594*.)

[22.361] A bank (L) arranged for a company (E) to operate a call centre on its behalf. Under the relevant contracts, E received and processed loan applications, gathered and verified information about applicants, signed loan agreements on behalf of L, and released L's funds to borrowers. The Commissioners issued a ruling that VAT was chargeable on E's supplies. E appealed, contending that its supplies qualified for exemption under *Article 13B(d)* of the *EC Sixth Directive*. The tribunal accepted this contention and allowed the appeal, and the CA unanimously upheld this decision. Jonathan Parker LJ held that 'the functional aspects of the movements of money' effected by E resulted in 'changes in the legal and financial situation of the relevant parties'. Accordingly, applying the ECJ decision in *Sparekassernes Datacenter v Skatteministeriet*, 22.357 above, E's supplies were transactions concerning transfers', and thus qualified for exemption under *Article 13B(d)(3)* of the *EC Sixth Directive*. *C & E Commrs v Electronic Data Systems Ltd*, CA [2003] STC 688; [2003] EWCA Civ 492. (*Note. The HL rejected an application by Customs for leave to appeal against this decision. For their practice following the HL decision, see Business Brief 4/04, issued on 3 February 2004.)

[22.362] A company collected fees for dentists by monthly instalments. The dentists who participated in this scheme paid the company a monthly service charge. The company treated these service charges as exempt from VAT. HMRC issued an assessment charging tax on the service charges, and the company appealed. The tribunal reviewed the evidence in detail and allowed the appeal in part, holding that the service charges were partly consideration for transfers of money, but also covered other services such as a registration facility and the use of a website, and that the fees should be apportioned. Both HMRC and the company appealed to the CA, which directed that the case should be referred to the ECJ. The ECJ found in favour of HMRC, holding that *Article 13B(d)(3)* of the *Sixth Directive* should 'be interpreted as meaning that the exemption from VAT provided for by that provision does not cover a supply of services which consist, in essence, in requesting a third party's bank to transfer to the service supplier's account, via the direct debit system, a sum due from that party to the service supplier's client, in sending to the client a statement of the sums received, in making contact with the third parties from whom the service supplier has not received payment and, finally, in giving instructions to the service supplier's bank to transfer the payments received, less the service supplier's remuneration, to the client's bank account'. *HMRC v Axa UK plc (and cross-appeal)*, ECJ Case C-175/09; [2010] STC 2825.

(*Notes.* (1) For HMRC's practice following this decision, see HMRC Brief 54/10, issued on 12 January 2011. (2) Following the ECJ decision, the CA unanimously allowed HMRC's appeal—[2011] EWCA Civ 1607.)

[22.363] A company supplied mobile telephone services. It encouraged its customers to pay by direct debit or BACS. Where they paid by another method (eg by cheque), it imposed a £3 'payment handling charge'. Initially it accounted for VAT on these charges. However in 2005 it submitted a substantial backdated repayment claim on the basis that it should have treated these charges as exempt from VAT. HMRC rejected the claim and the company appealed to the Ch D, which referred the case to the ECJ for a ruling on the scope of *Article 13B(d)* of the *EC Sixth Directive*. The ECJ rejected the company's contentions, holding that 'the additional charges invoiced by a provider of telecommunications services to its customers, where the latter pay for those services not by direct debit or by Bankers' Automated Clearing System transfer but by credit card, debit card, cheque or cash over the counter at a bank or authorised payment agent acting on behalf of that service provider, do not constitute consideration for a supply of services distinct and independent from the principal supply of services consisting in the supply of telecommunications services'. *Everything Everywhere Ltd v HMRC (aka T-Mobile UK Ltd v HMRC)*, ECJ Case C-276/09; [2011] STC 316.

[22.364] In a German case, a factoring company reclaimed input tax. The tax authority rejected the claim on the basis that factoring was not an 'economic activity'. The company appealed and the case was referred to the ECJ for a ruling on the interpretation of 'factoring' (which is excluded from exemption under the English and Swedish versions of *Article 13B(d)(3)* of the *EC Sixth Directive*, but is not specifically referred to in any of the other versions). The ECJ held that factoring was an 'economic activity', and observed that the language versions other than the Swedish and English versions were not incompatible with an interpretation under which factoring was 'among the exceptions to the exemptions provided for in *Article 13B(d)(3)* of the *Sixth Directive*'. Accordingly, 'an economic activity by which a business purchases debts, assuming the risk of the debtors' default, and, in return, invoices its clients in respect of commission, constitutes debt collection and factoring within the meaning of the final clause of *Article 13B(d)(3)* of the *Sixth Directive* and is therefore excluded from the exemption laid down by that provision'. *Finanzamt Groß-Gerau v MKG-Kraftfahrzeuge-Factoring GmbH*, ECJ Case C-305/01; [2003] STC 951; [2004] All ER (EC) 454.

[22.365] In a Finnish case, the ECJ held that the exemption from VAT under *Article 13B(d)(3)(5)* of the *EC Sixth Directive* did not include 'electronic messaging services for financial institutions'. *Nordea Pankki Suomi Oyj v Finland*, ECJ Case C-350/10; [2011] STC 1956.

[22.366] In a Swedish case, a company decided to dispose of shares in a subsidiary company and of its remaining shareholding in another company which it controlled, for the purposes of a group restructuring. It applied for a preliminary ruling on whether it would be entitled to reclaim input tax on services relating to the share disposals. The Swedish court referred the case to the ECJ for a ruling on the interpretation of *Article 13B(d)(5)* of the *Sixth Directive*. The ECJ held that a disposal of shares of the type at issue in this case was exempt from VAT under *Article 13B(d)(5)*. The ECJ also held that 'where a parent company disposes of all the shares in a wholly-owned subsidiary and of its remaining shareholding in a controlled company which was in the past wholly owned by it, and where it has supplied to those companies services that are subject to value added tax, that disposal is an economic activity'. However, where a disposal of shares was 'equivalent to the transfer of a totality of assets or part thereof of an undertaking', within *Article 5(8)* of the *Sixth Directive*, and where the Member State concerned had chosen to exercise the option provided for by that provision, then the disposal did not constitute an economic activity subject to VAT. There was a right to deduct input tax paid on services supplied for the purposes of a disposal of shares if there was 'a direct and immediate link between the costs associated with the input services and the overall economic activities of the taxable person'. It was for the national court 'to take account of all the circumstances surrounding the transactions at issue in the main proceedings and to determine whether the costs incurred are likely to be incorporated in the price of the shares sold, or if they are among only the cost components of transactions within the scope of the taxable person's economic activities'. *Skatteverket v AB SKF*, ECJ Case C-29/08; [2010] STC 419.

[22.367] In another Swedish case, the tax authority issued a ruling that VAT was chargeable on certain underwriting guarantee services supplied by a bank. The bank appealed, contending that they were exempt, and the case was referred to the ECJ. The ECJ found in favour of the bank, holding that *Article 13B(d)(5)* 'must be interpreted as meaning that the exemption from VAT laid down therein covers services supplied by a credit institution, for consideration, in the form of an underwriting guarantee to a company wishing to issue shares, where under that guarantee the credit institution undertakes to acquire any shares which are not subscribed within the period for share subscription'. *Skandinaviska Enskilda Banken AB Momsgrupp v Skatteverket*, ECJ Case C-540/09; [2011] STC 1143.

[22.368] A company (N) acted as the authorised corporate director of an open-ended investment company. It entered into management agreements with eight fund managers, under which those managers agreed to manage subdivisions of the investment company fund. The Commissioners issued a ruling that VAT was chargeable on the services supplied by the fund managers. The company which acted as the representative member of N's VAT group appealed, contending that the fact that the services were subcontracted or delegated did not prevent them from qualifying for exemption under *VATA 1994, Sch 9, Group 5, Item 10*. The case was referred to the ECJ for a ruling on the interpretation of *Article 13B(d)(6)* of the *EC Sixth Directive*. The ECJ held that 'the concept of "management" of special investment funds in *Article 13B(d)(6)*' had its own independent meaning in Community law, 'whose content the Member States may not alter'. *Article 13B(d)(6)* was to be interpreted as meaning that 'the concept of "management of special investment funds" referred to in that provision covers the services performed by a third-party manager in respect of the administrative management of the funds, if, viewed broadly, they form a distinct whole, and are specific to, and essential for, the management of those funds.' *Abbey National plc v C & E Commrs (No 2); Inscape Investment Fund v C & E Commrs*, ECJ Case C-169/04;

[2006] STC 1136. (*Note*. For HMRC's practice following this decision, see Business Brief 07/06, issued on 27 June 2006.)

[22.369] Following the decision in *Abbey National plc v C & E Commrs (No 2)*, **22.368** above, an investment trust company which managed a 'closed-ended investment fund' claimed that its supplies were exempt from VAT. Customs rejected the claim, drawing a distinction between the management of an 'open-funded' fund and a 'closed-ended' fund. The company appealed, and the tribunal referred the case to the ECJ, which held that *Article 13B(d)(6)* of the *EC Sixth Directive* 'must be interpreted as meaning that the words "special investment funds" in that provision are capable of including closed-ended investment funds, such as investment trust companies'. *Article 13B(d)(6)* allowed Member States 'a discretion in defining the funds located on their territory which are covered by the notion of "special investment funds" for the purposes of the exemption provided for by that provision. However, in the exercise of that power, the Member States must respect the objective pursued by that provision, which is to facilitate investment in securities for investors through investment undertakings, while guaranteeing the principle of fiscal neutrality from the point of view of the levying of VAT on the management of special investment funds'. The ECJ also held that *Article 13B(d)(6)* had direct effect. *JP Morgan Fleming Claverhouse Investment Trust plc v HMRC (and related appeal)*, ECJ Case C-363/05; [2008] STC 1180. (*Note*. For HMRC's practice following this decision, see HMRC Brief 58/07, issued on 22 August 2007; HMRC Brief 65/07, issued on 5 November 2007, and HMRC Brief 35/08, issued on 24 July 2008. HMRC state that they 'now accept that fund management services supplied to investment trust companies are exempt' but consider 'that the judgment does not apply to funds other than investment trust companies'.)

[22.370] See also *FDR Ltd*, 27.5 FINANCE; *Civil Service Motoring Association*, 27.19 FINANCE; *BAA plc*, 27.20 FINANCE; *Debt Management Associates Ltd*, 27.30 FINANCE; *HBOS plc*, 27.44 FINANCE; *Nightfreight plc*, 27.57 FINANCE; *Prudential Assurance Co Ltd*, 27.59 FINANCE; *Republic National Bank of New York*, 62.195 SUPPLY, and *F & I Services Ltd*, 67.162 VALUATION.

Betting, lotteries, etc. (Article 13B(f))

[22.371] In a German case, a trader operated a form of roulette without official authorisation. He was assessed to turnover tax and appealed. The case was referred to the ECJ, which held that the unlawful operation of games of chance was within the scope of the *Sixth Directive*. Applying *Lange v Finanzamt Fürstenfeldbruck*, **22.387** below, 'the principle of tax neutrality precludes a generalised distinction' from being drawn between lawful and unlawful transactions. The decisions in *Mol v Inspecteur der Invoerrechten en Accijnzen* and *Vereniging Happy Family Rustenburgerstrat v Inspecteur der Omzetbelasting*, **22.81** above, were distinguished, on the grounds that they concerned goods 'which, because of their special characteristics, may not be placed on the market or incorporated into economic channels'. However, the ECJ also held that the exemption under *Article 13B(f)* of the *Directive* could not be restricted 'solely to lawful games of chance', and that VAT could not be imposed on unlawful games of chance where the corresponding activity was exempt when 'carried on by a licensed public casino'. *Fischer v Finanzamt Donaueschingen*, ECJ Case C-283/95; [1998] STC 708; [1998] All ER (EC) 567.

[22.372] German law provided that turnover within the scope of the *Betting and Lotteries Act*, and the turnover of licensed public casinos, was exempt from VAT. However, the exemption under German law did not extend to income from gaming and entertainment machines not situated in licensed public casinos. The tax authority sought to impose VAT on a trader who had not accounted for VAT on such income. The German court referred the case to the ECJ for a ruling on the scope of *Article 13B(f)* of the *Sixth Directive*. The ECJ held that *Article 13B(f)* 'precludes national legislation which provides that the operation of all games of chance and gaming machines is exempt from VAT where it is carried out in licensed public casinos, while the operation of the same activity by traders other than those running casinos does not enjoy that exemption'. Furthermore, *Article 13B(f)* 'has direct effect in the sense that it can be relied on by an operator of games of chance or gaming machines before national courts to prevent the application of rules of national law which are inconsistent with that provision'. *Finanzamt Gladbeck v Linneweber*, ECJ Case C-453/02; [2008] STC 1069. (*Note.* For HMRC's practice following this decision, see Business Brief 20/06, issued on 9 November 2006.)

[22.373] A similar decision was reached in a case where a trader who operated a casino had not accounted for VAT on takings from card games at the casino. *Finanzamt Herne-West v Akritidis*, ECJ Case C-462/02; [2008] STC 1069.

[22.374] A company (L) operated a telephone betting service. It 'outsourced' certain services relating to the receipt of these telephone calls to another company (V). Customs issued a ruling that output tax was chargeable on V's services. The representative member of V's VAT group appealed, contending that V's services should be treated as exempt. The tribunal rejected this contentions and dismissed the appeal, holding that V was supplying 'standard-rated call centre and IT support services', but the HL referred the case to the ECJ for a ruling on the interpretation of *Article 13B(f)* of the *EC Sixth Directive*. The ECJ held that *Article 13B(f)* 'must be interpreted as meaning that the provision of call centre services to a telephone bookmaking organiser, which entails the staff of the supplier of those services accepting bets on behalf of the organiser, does not constitute a betting transaction within the meaning of that provision and cannot, therefore, qualify for the exemption from VAT laid down by that provision'. *United Utilities plc v C & E Commrs*, ECJ Case C-89/05; [2006] STC 1423.

[22.375] A company (M) supplied 'mechanised cash bingo'. HMRC issued a ruling that it was required to account for tax on these supplies. The representative member of M's VAT group (R) appealed, contending that they should be treated as exempt under *Article 13B(f)* of the *EC Sixth Directive*, and that *VATA 1994, Sch 9, Group 4, Note 1(b)* should be treated as invalid, since it made an unjustified distinction between supplies within *Gaming Act 1968, s 14* (which it treated as taxable) and supplies within *Gaming Act 1968, s 21* (which it treated as exempt). Companies in R's group also operated large numbers of 'slot machines'. The effect of *VATA 1994, Sch 9, Group 4, Note*

3 as originally enacted was that the takings from the machines were taxable under UK law, but in December 2005 the group lodged a repayment claim, contending that the provisions of *Note 3* should be treated as invalid under EC law because similar machines falling within *Gaming Act 1968, s 21* had been exempt from VAT. HMRC rejected the claim and denied the company's contention that machines within *Gaming Act 1968, s 21* were exempt. R appealed on both issues, and the CA directed that the case should be referred to the ECJ for rulings on the interpretation of *Article 13B(f)* of the *EC Sixth Directive*. The ECJ held that 'where there is a difference in treatment of two games of chance as regards the granting of an exemption' under *Article 13B(f)* of the *Sixth Directive*, 'the principle of fiscal neutrality must be interpreted as meaning that no account should be taken of the fact that those two games fall into different licensing categories and are subject to different legal regimes relating to control and regulation. In order to assess whether, in the light of the principle of fiscal neutrality, two types of slot machine are similar and require the same treatment for the purposes of value added tax it must be established whether the use of those types of machine is comparable from the point of view of the average consumer and meets the same needs of that consumer, and the matters to be taken into account in that connection are, inter alia, the minimum and maximum permitted stakes and prizes and the chances of winning. The principle of fiscal neutrality must be interpreted as meaning that a taxable person cannot claim reimbursement of the value added tax paid on certain supplies of services in reliance on a breach of that principle, where the tax authorities of the Member State concerned have, in practice, treated similar services as exempt supplies, although they were not exempt from value added tax under the relevant national legislation.' The ECJ also held that a Member State which had 'exempted from value added tax the provision of all facilities for playing games of chance, while excluding from that exemption a category of machines which meet certain criteria, may not contest a claim for reimbursement of VAT based on the breach of that principle by arguing that it responded with due diligence to the development of a new type of machine not meeting those criteria'. *HMRC v The Rank Group plc*, ECJ Case C-259/10, C-260/10; [2012] STC 23. (*Note.* For HMRC's policy following this decision, see HMRC Brief 39/11, issued on 6 December 2011. HMRC have now accepted that R's supplies of bingo are exempt, but consider that the ECJ decision 'does not provide a final determination of the domestic litigation' with regard to gaming machines.)

[22.376] See also *Feehan*, **24.20** EXEMPTIONS, and *Ryan*, **49.29** PENALTIES: CRIMINAL OFFENCES.

Commission received by bookmaker's agents

[22.377] See *État Belge v Henfling & Others*, **22.189** above.

Supplies of buildings (Article 13B(g))

[22.378] In a Netherlands case, a company sold an area of land which was occupied by two dilapidated buildings that had already been partly demolished, and were to be replaced by new buildings. The tax authority issued a ruling that the sale was exempt from VAT (and was therefore liable to 'transfer duty'). The purchaser appealed, contending that the sale was chargeable to

VAT (and was therefore not liable to 'transfer duty'). The case was referred to the ECJ, which found in favour of the purchaser, holding that the exemption from VAT provided for by *Article 13B(g)* of the *EC Sixth Directive* 'does not cover the supply of land still occupied by a dilapidated building that is to be demolished and replaced by a new building and whose demolition, paid for by the vendor, had already begun before the actual supply took place'. For VAT purposes, 'such supply and such demolition form a single transaction, given that, taken as a whole, the aim of the transactions was not to supply the existing building and the land it stands on but land that has not been built on, regardless of how far demolition of the old building had progressed at the moment the land was actually supplied'. *Don Bosco Onroerend Goed BV v Staatssecretaris van Financiën*, ECJ Case C-461/08; [2010] STC 476. (*Note.* In the UK, the supply of building land is exempt under *Directive 2006/112/EC, Article 371, Annex X Part B.*)

Supplies of land (Article 13B(h))

[22.379] See *Gemeente Emmen v Belastingdienst Grote Ondernemingen*, 22.123 above, and *Norbury Developments Ltd*, 22.511 below.

Option for taxation (Article 13C)

Option to tax letting and leasing of immovable property

[22.380] A Belgian law, enacted in 1992, allowed taxpayers to opt to tax the letting and leasing of immovable property. However, the law in question was repealed in 1994. A company which had opted to tax certain property, and had reclaimed input tax in respect of it, appealed against the rejection of its claim, contending that it had been granted an option to tax under *Article 13C* of the *Sixth Directive*, that the abolition of that option was contrary to Community law, and that the principle of legal certainty precluded the retrospective repeal of the national law in question. The case was referred to the ECJ, which held that a Member State which had granted its taxpayers the right to opt for taxation of certain lettings of immovable property, in accordance with *Article 13C*, was not precluded from subsequently abolishing that right of option and returning to 'the basic rule that leasing and letting of immovable property are exempt from tax'. It was for the national court to determine whether the retrospective repeal of the law in question was a breach of the principle of protection of legitimate expectation or of the principle of legal certainty. *Belgocodex SA v Belgium*, ECJ Case C-381/97; [2000] STC 351.

[22.381] Luxembourg VAT legislation provided an option to tax the letting and leasing of immovable property, subject to the condition that any person exercising the option had to lodge a written declaration for approval by the tax authority, and that 'in the case of a supply for a consideration, the approval must have been obtained prior to the formal completion of the official document evidencing the transaction'. A Luxembourg company submitted such a declaration in June 1993, which was approved with effect from 1 July 1993. The company subsequently reclaimed input tax for the period from January to June 1993. The tax authority rejected the claim, and the company appealed, contending that the relevant Luxembourg legislation was a breach of *Article 13C* of the *EC Sixth Directive*. The case was referred to the ECJ, which rejected the company's contentions and upheld the Luxembourg legislation, holding that *Article 13C* did not 'preclude a Member State, which has exercised the power to allow taxpayers a right of option for taxation on leasing or letting transactions of immovable property, from adopting legislation which makes full deduction of the input VAT paid conditional upon non-retroactive, prior approval of the tax authorities'. The ECJ also observed that 'the lack of retroactivity of the approval process does not make it disproportionate. On the contrary, it may be regarded as useful in order to encourage lessors to submit their declaration of option in advance'. A retroactive approval process was 'likely to produce the opposite effect by leading lessors to submit their declaration of option late' and 'would therefore be less appropriate for the purpose of ensuring the proper implementation of the exercise of the right of option and attaining the objective of legal certainty'. *Administration de L'Enregistrement et des Domaines v Vermietungsgesellschaft Objekt Kirchberg SARL*, ECJ Case C-269/03; [2005] STC 1345.

[22.382] In an Austrian case, a sports club which was exempt from VAT under *Article 13A1(m)* of the *EC Sixth Directive* elected to waive exemption in respect of the construction of an annexe to its clubhouse, so that it could reclaim the related input tax. The tax authority rejected the claim and the club appealed, contending that the relevant Austrian legislation was a breach of *Article 13C* of the *Directive*. The case was referred to the ECJ, which held that 'Member States, when giving their taxable persons the right to opt for taxation' under *Article 13C* 'may make a distinction by reference to types of transactions or groups of taxable persons provided that they observe the general objectives and principles of the Sixth Directive, in particular the principle of fiscal neutrality'. The ECJ observed that 'there may be a breach of the principle of fiscal neutrality if a sports club having as its purpose under its statute the exercise or furthering of physical education could not opt for taxation where that is possible for other taxable persons carrying out comparable activities which are therefore in competition with those of that club'. It was for the national court 'to determine whether national legislation which, by exempting generally the transactions of non-profit-making sports clubs, restricts their right to opt for taxation of leasing and letting transactions, exceeds the discretion conferred on the Member States'. *Turn-und Sportunion Waldburg v Finanzlandesdirektion für Oberösterreich*, ECJ Case C-246/04; [2006] STC 1506.

[22.383] See also *Winterthur Life UK Ltd (No 2)*, 6.7 BUILDINGS AND LAND; *Newcourt Property Fund*, 6.18 BUILDINGS AND LAND; *R Walia Opticians Ltd*, 6.46 BUILDINGS AND LAND; *Grundstückgemeinschaft Schloßstraße GbR v Finanzamt Paderborn*, 22.398 below, and *Gemeente Leusden v Staatssecretaris van Financien*, 22.457 below.

Exemptions on importation (Article 14)

Article 14 of EC Sixth Directive—exemptions on importation

[22.384] A Luxembourg national entered Belgium as a student at Liege University in 1976. In 1978 he married a French national who worked in Liege. While staying in Belgium, he used successively two cars bought and registered in Luxembourg, where VAT was paid. In 1980 the Belgian tax authorities informed him that, as he had been normally resident in Liege since his marriage, he must pay VAT on the importation of the two cars. On appeal, the ECJ ruled that the *Sixth Directive* precluded the levying of VAT by a Member State on the importation of a motor vehicle purchased in another Member State where VAT had been paid and the vehicle registered, when the vehicle was used by a national of the second Member State. A student from another Member State remains a temporary visitor for VAT purposes, regardless of any marriage, unless the couple settle in the host State in such a way as to show their intention of not returning to the Member State of origin when the studies are completed. *Ministère Public & Ministry of Finance v Profant*, ECJ Case 249/84; [1985] ECR 3237; [1986] 2 CMLR 378.

[22.385] A Belgian resident was employed in France and was provided by his employer with a car registered in France. He used the car for business and private purposes. The Belgian authorities sought to charge VAT on the importation of the car into Belgium. The ECJ held that VAT could not be charged in such circumstances. The private use of the car in Belgium constituted temporary importation, which was exempt from VAT under *Article 14* of the *EC Sixth Directive. Ministère Public & Ministre des Finances du Royaume de Belgique v Ledoux*, ECJ Case 127/86; [1988] ECR 3741; [1991] STC 553.

[22.386] The Italian government imposed VAT on the importation of free commercial samples of low value, although supplies of such samples within Italy were exempt from VAT. On an application by the EC Commission, the ECJ ruled that, by taxing such importations, the Italian government had failed to fulfil its Treaty obligations. Accordingly the imposition of VAT in such circumstances was illegal. *EC Commission v Italian Republic*, ECJ Case 257/86; [1988] ECR 3249; [1990] 3 CMLR 718; [1991] BTC 5104.

Exemption of exports (Article 15)

Article 15 of EC Sixth Directive—goods exported unlawfully

[22.387] In a German case, a trader exported information systems to countries in respect of which the Community had imposed a ban on such exports. The German authorities sought to impose VAT, and the trader appealed, contending that the exports were exempt under *Article 15* of the *EC Sixth Directive* notwithstanding the illegality of the exports. The case was referred to the ECJ which upheld the trader's contention, holding that the principle of tax neutrality precluded a generalised distinction between lawful and unlawful transactions. The decisions in *Mol v Inspecteur der Invoerrechten en Accijnzen* and *Vereniging Happy Family Rustenburgerstrat v Inspecteur der Omzetbelasting*, **22.81** above, were distinguished, on the grounds that they concerned goods 'which, because of their special characteristics, may not be placed on the market or incorporated into economic channels'. *Lange v Finanzamt Fürstenfeldbruck*, ECJ Case C-111/92; [1993] 1 ECR 4677; [1994] 1 CMLR 573; [1997] STC 564.

Article 15(2) of EC Sixth Directive

[22.388] A German company (N) had refunded considerable amounts of VAT to Polish customers in accordance with *Article 15(2)* of the *EC Sixth Directive*, before Poland joined the EU. The German tax authority discovered that some of the Polish customers had submitted falsified customs documents in support of their refund claims. They required N to pay the tax due on the transactions. N appealed, and the case was referred to the ECJ for a ruling on the interpretation of *Article 15(2)*. The ECJ held that *Article 15(2)* 'must be interpreted as not precluding a Member State from granting an exemption from value added tax on the supply of goods for export to a destination outside the European Community, where the conditions for such an exemption are not met, but the taxable person was not able to recognise – even by exercising due commercial care – that they were not met, because the export proofs provided by the purchaser had been forged'. *Netto Supermarkt GmbH & Co OHG v Finanzamt Malchin*, ECJ Case C-271/06; [2008] STC 3280.

Article 15(4)—fuelling and provisioning vessels used at sea

[22.389] In a Dutch case, a company (V) sold to another company (F) two consignments of bunker oil which were delivered to tanks rented by F and were subsequently loaded onto seagoing vessels. V did not account for VAT on the oil supplied to F, and the Dutch authorities issued an assessment charging tax on the supplies. V appealed, contending that the supplies should be treated as exempt from VAT. The Dutch court referred the case to the ECJ for a ruling on whether the exemption under *Article 15(4)* of the *EC Sixth Directive* applied only to supplies of fuel made directly to seagoing vessels, or whether it also extended to supplies made at prior stages in the marketing chain where the goods were ultimately to be used for the fuelling and provisioning of such vessels. The ECJ held that the exemption applied only to supplies of goods made to the operator of a vessel in order to be used by him for fuelling and provisioning, and could not be extended to supplies of those goods made at an earlier marketing stage. However, the supply of the goods did not have to coincide with the fuelling and provisioning, and the fact that the goods were stored after delivery and before fuelling and provisioning did not cause the benefit of the exemption to be lost. The supplies in this case, therefore, qualified for exemption. *Staatssecretaris van Financiën v Velker International Oil Co Ltd NV*, ECJ Case C-185/89; [1990] 1 ECR 2561; [1991] STC 640.

[22.390] In a Greek case, the ECJ held that *Article 15(4)(a)* of the *EC Sixth Directive* 'applies not only to vessels used on the high seas for the carriage of passengers for reward, but also to vessels used on the high seas for the purpose of commercial, industrial or fishing activity'. *Elmeka NE v Ipourgos Ikonomikon*, ECJ Case C-181/04; 14 September 2006 unreported.

Article 15(5) of EC Sixth Directive—supplies relating to seagoing vessels

[22.391] In a Spanish case, the ECJ held that *Article 15(5)* of the *EC Sixth Directive* 'must be interpreted as covering both full chartering and partial chartering of vessels used for navigation on the high seas'. It therefore precluded national legislation 'which grants the benefit of the exemption from value added tax only in the case of full chartering of such vessels.' *Navicon SA v Administración del Estado*, ECJ Case C-97/06; [2008] STC 2693.

[22.392] In a Luxembourg case, the ECJ held that *Article 15(5)* 'must be interpreted as meaning that the exemption from value added tax provided for by that provision does not apply to services consisting of making a vessel available, for reward, with a crew, to natural persons for purposes of leisure travel on the high seas'. *Administration de l'enregistrement et des domaines v Feltgen (administrator of Bacino Charter Company SA)*, ECJ Case C-116/10; [2011] STC 994.

Article 15(6)(7) of EC Sixth Directive—supplies to aircraft

[22.393] Danish VAT legislation provided that certain supplies to aircraft flying outside Denmark were exempt from VAT in accordance with *Article 15(6)(7)* of the *EC Sixth Directive*, but similar supplies to aircraft on domestic flights were taxable. A Danish airline company appealed, contending that the effect of *Article 15(6)* was that since most of its flights were to destinations outside Denmark, the relevant supplies qualified for exemption even where they related to domestic flights. The case was referred to the ECJ, which upheld the company's contentions, holding that *Article 15(6)(7)* required that 'supplies of goods and services referred to in those provisions to aircraft which operate on domestic routes but are used by airlines chiefly operating for reward on international routes are exempt from VAT. It is for the national courts to assess the extent of the international business and the extent of the non-international business of such companies. In doing so, they may take account of all information which indicates the relative importance of the type of operations concerned, in particular turnover.' *Cimber Air A/S v Skatteministeriet*, ECJ Case C-382/02; [2005] STC 547.

Article 15(8) of EC Sixth Directive

[22.394] In the case noted at **22.198** above, the ECJ held that the operation of gaming machines on board ships did not qualify for exemption under *Article 15(8)* of the *EC Sixth Directive*. The ECJ held that 'the only services exempted under *Article 15(8)* are those which are directly connected with the needs of sea-going vessels or their cargoes, that is to say services necessary for the operation of such vessels'. *G Berkholz v Finanzamt Hamburg-Mitte-Altstadt*, ECJ Case 168/84; [1985] ECR 2251; [1985] 3 CMLR 667.

Article 15(9) of EC Sixth Directive

[22.395] See *HMRC v EB Central Services Ltd*, **66.42** TRANSPORT, and *Société Internationale de Télécommunications Aeronatiques (No 2)*, **66.45** TRANSPORT.

Article 15(10) of EC Sixth Directive

[22.396] See *MEP Research Services Ltd*, **62.499** SUPPLY.

Deductions (Articles 17–20)

Right to deduct (Article 17(1)–(4))

Article 17(1)—time when right arises

[22.397] French legislation restricted the input tax deductible in respect of the construction or purchase of a leased building, where the annual rental income was less than one-fifteenth of the value of the building. The ECJ held that, where there are no provisions in Community law which permit Member States to limit a taxable person's right to deduct input tax, the full amount of the input tax could be deducted immediately. Taxable persons who had exercised their right to treat the supply of leases as taxable were entitled to deduct the relevant input tax at the time when it was incurred. *EC Commission v French Republic*, ECJ Case 50/87; [1988] ECR 4797; [1989] 1 CMLR 505.

[22.398] A German company (G) acquired development rights over building land. It elected to waive exemption in respect of the land, and reclaimed input tax on construction work. The tax authority issued assessments to recover the tax, on the basis that the possibility of waiving exemption had been withdrawn by a retrospective amendment to German law. G appealed, and the ECJ held that the effect of *Article 17* of the *EC Sixth Directive* was that input tax incurred on intended taxable supplies was deductible despite the subsequent change in the law. The ECJ observed that the right to deduct arose at the time when the deductible tax became chargeable. The ECJ held that 'in the absence of fraud or abuse', the right of deduction was 'retained even if the taxable person has been unable to use the goods or services which gave rise to a deduction in the context of taxable transactions by reason of circumstances beyond his control'. A taxable person 'is entitled immediately to deduct the VAT due or paid on the goods or services supplied with a view to the performance of the economic activities which it envisages carrying out'. The principles of the protection of legitimate expectations and of legal certainty 'preclude its being deprived retroactively of that right by a legislative amendment postdating the supply of those goods or services'. *Grundstückgemeinschaft Schloßstraße GbR v Finanzamt Paderborn* , ECJ Case C-396/98; 8 June 2000 unreported.

Article 17(2)

[22.399] A holding company (B) provided management services to a group of subsidiary trading companies. In 1991 it disposed of 95% of the shares in a subsidiary company. It was accepted that this disposal was an exempt supply. However, B reclaimed input tax in respect of professional services supplied in relation to this disposal. Customs issued an assessment to recover the tax. The tribunal dismissed B's appeal, holding that the tax was not deductible since it related entirely to the making of an exempt supply. The ECJ upheld the tribunal decision, holding that input tax was only deductible under *Article 17* of the *EC Sixth Directive* if the goods or services in question had a direct and immediate link with taxable transactions. The fact that the ultimate aim of the taxable person was the carrying out of a taxable transaction was irrelevant. *BLP Group plc v C & E Commrs*, ECJ Case C-4/94; [1995] STC 424; [1995] 1 ECR 983; [1996] 1 WLR 174; [1995] All ER (EC) 401.

[22.400] A bank, which was partly exempt, incurred legal costs in defending a claim alleging negligent misrepresentation in relation to the sale of a company. The bank's client was a US corporation, and its supplies to the client were accepted as zero-rated under the legislation then in force. The bank reclaimed the whole of the input tax relating to the claim. Customs issued assessments on the basis that the tax should be apportioned between taxable supplies and exempt supplies. The bank appealed, contending that the tax was wholly attributable to the zero-rated taxable supplies which it had made to its US client. The ECJ held that input tax was only deductible if there was a direct and immediate link between a particular input transaction and a particular output transaction. It was for the national court to apply the 'direct and immediate link' test to the facts of each particular case. A taxable person could not deduct the full amount of input tax incurred on services which had been utilised, 'not for the purpose of carrying out a deductible transaction, but in the context of activities which are no more than the consequence of making such a transaction, unless that person can show by means of objective evidence that the expenditure involved in the acquisition of such services is part of the various cost components of the output transaction'. *C & E Commrs v Midland Bank plc*, ECJ Case C-98/98; [2000] STC 501; [2000] All ER (EC) 673.

[22.401] Under Spanish law, entrepreneurs and professional practitioners setting up a business in Spain could only deduct input tax if they submitted a formal declaration and began regular business activities within a year of its submission. If those requirements were not met, repayment of input tax was withheld and could be forfeited altogether. The ECJ held that *Article 17* precluded national legislation which made the right to deduct 'conditional upon the fulfilment of certain requirements such as the submission of an express request to that effect before the tax concerned becomes due and compliance with a time limit of one year between that submission and the actual commencement of taxable transactions, and which penalises infringement of those requirements by forfeiture of the right to deduct or deferment of the exercise of that right until the time at which taxable transactions actually begin to be carried out on a regular basis'. *Gabalfrisa SL & Others v Agencia Estatal de Administración Tributaria*, ECJ Cases C-110/98 to C-147/98; [2002] STC 535.

[22.402] In a Netherlands case, petrol was supplied to a company's employees, used exclusively for the purposes of the company's business, and invoiced to the company, which reclaimed input tax. The tax authority rejected the claim on the basis that the petrol had been supplied to the employees. The ECJ ruled in favour of the company, holding that *Article 17(2)(a)* of the *EC Sixth Directive* did not prevent a taxable person from deducting VAT paid on goods which were sold to him for use in his business, albeit that the goods were actually physically delivered to his employees. Accordingly, VAT could be reclaimed by an employer in such circumstances. *Leesportfeuille 'Intiem' CV v Staatssecretaris van Financiën*, ECJ Case 165/86; [1988] ECR 1471; [1989] 2 CMLR 856.

[22.403] The EC Commission took proceedings against the Netherlands, seeking a declaration that, by allowing employers to deduct part of an allowance paid to an employee for the business use of a private car, the Netherlands had failed to fulfil its obligations under the *EC Treaty*. The ECJ granted the declaration, holding that the Netherlands legislation was a breach of *Article 17(2)(a)* of the *EC Sixth Directive*. The ECJ distinguished *Leesportfeuille 'Intiem' CV v Staatssecretaris van Financiën*, **22.402** above, on the grounds that in that case, the employer had arranged for the petrol to be supplied and had received invoices. The ECJ held that 'intervention by the Community legislature would be necessary both in order to allow in principle a right to deduct VAT on the basis of an allowance paid to an employee using his vehicle for the purposes of a taxable employer's business and in order to establish the extent of such a right and the detailed rules for its application'. *EC Commission v Kingdom of the Netherlands*, ECJ Case C-338/98; [2003] STC 1506; [2004] 1 WLR 35.

[22.404] Following the decision noted at **22.403** above, the Commission took similar proceedings against the UK. The ECJ granted the declaration sought by the Commission, observing that *SI 1991/2306* did not 'make the right to deduction which it confers subject to the condition that the fuel bought by the non-taxable person should be used for the purposes of the taxable person's taxable transactions'. Accordingly, the ECJ held that 'by granting taxable persons the right to deduct value added tax in respect of certain supplies of road fuel to non-taxable persons', contrary to *Articles 17 and 18* of the *Sixth Directive*, the UK had failed to fulfil its obligations under the *Directive*. *EC Commission v United Kingdom (No 4)*, ECJ Case C-33/03; [2005] STC 582. (*Note. SI 1991/2306* has subsequently been replaced by the *VAT (Input Tax) (Reimbursement by Employers of Employees' Business Use of Road Fuel) Regulations 2005 (SI 2005/3290)*. See Business Brief 22/2005, issued on 1 December 2005.)

[22.405] In the case noted at **22.93** above, a hotelier sold a guesthouse, part of which he had used for private purposes rather than for business purposes. The case was referred to the ECJ, which ruled that where a taxable person sold property, part of which he had chosen at the time of acquisition not to assign to his business, only the part assigned to the business was to be taken into account for the application of *Article 17(2)(a)* of the *EC Sixth Directive*. *Finanzamt Ülzen v Armbrecht*, ECJ Case C-291/92; [1995] STC 997; [1995] 1 ECR 2775.

[22.406] In a Belgian case, a company had purchased some land in 1980. It had work carried out on the land, and reclaimed input tax on these supplies. In 1983 it was required by Ghent Council to dispose of the land, without having ever used it for any taxable transactions. The Belgian government sought to recover the tax which the company had reclaimed, and the company appealed. The case was referred to the ECJ for a ruling on the interpretation of *Article 17(2)* of the *EC Sixth Directive*. The ECJ held that the right of deduction was exercisable and remained acquired where, by reason of circumstances beyond his control, the taxable person had never actually used the goods and services in question for the purposes of taxable transactions (while observing that such a supply might give rise to a subsequent adjustment under *Article 20*). *Belgium v Ghent Coal Terminal NV*, ECJ Case C-37/95; [1998] STC 260; [1998] All ER (EC) 223.

[22.407] In a German case, a part-time writer and his wife arranged for the construction of a new house, one room of which was to be used by the husband as an office. He reclaimed 12% of the input tax on the construction of the house. The tax authority rejected the claim and the husband appealed. The case was referred to the ECJ, which ruled that 'where a person purchases a house, or has a house built, in order to live in it with his family he is acting as a taxable person, and is thus entitled to make deductions under *Article 17* of the *Sixth Directive* in so far as he uses one room in that building as an office for the purposes of carrying out an economic activity'. The ECJ also held that 'where spouses forming a community by marriage purchase a capital item, part of which is used exclusively for business purposes by one of the co-owning spouses, that spouse is entitled to deduct in respect of all the input value added tax attributable to the share of the item which he uses for the purposes of his business, in so far as the amount deducted does not exceed the limits of the taxable person's interest in the co-ownership of the item'. *Finanzamt Bergisch Gladbach v HE*, ECJ Case C-25/03; [2007] STC 128.

[22.408] In a Netherlands case, the ECJ held that *Article 17(2)* of the *Sixth Directive* 'is to be interpreted as meaning that the costs for advisory services which a taxable person obtains with a view to establishing the amount of a claim forming part of his company's assets and relating to a sale of shares prior to his becoming liable to VAT do not, in the absence of evidence establishing that the exclusive reason for those services is to be found in the economic activity, within the meaning of that directive, carried out by the taxable person, have a direct and immediate link with that activity and, consequently, do not give rise to a right to deduct the VAT charged on them'. *Investrand BV v Staatsecretaris van Financiën*, ECJ Case C-435/05; [2008] STC 518.

[22.409] From 1979 to 1982, France did not permit input tax to be deducted in respect of diesel used as fuel. In 1982 it amended its General Taxation Code to provide that some such tax was deductible. However, in 1998 it again amended the Code to provide that no such tax was deductible. The EC Commission applied to the ECJ for a declaration that, by re-introducing an exclusion from the right to deduct VAT, France had failed to fulfil its obligations under *Article 17(2)* of the *EC Sixth Directive*. The ECJ accepted this contention and granted the declaration. *EC Commission v French Republic (No 12)*, ECJ Case C-40/00; [2003] STC 390.

[22.410] In a Hungarian case, the ECJ held that *Article 17(2)* of the *EC Sixth Directive* precluded 'national legislation which in the case of acquisition of goods subsidised by public funds, allow the deduction of related VAT only up to the limit of the part of the costs of that acquisition that are not subsidised'. *Parat Automotive Cabrio Textiltetőket Gyártó Kft v Adó-és Pénzügyi Ellenőrzési Hivatal Hatósági Főosztály Észak-magyarországi Kihelyezett Hatósági Osztály*, ECJ Case C-74/08; [2009] All ER (D) 215 (Apr).

[22.411] In two Netherlands cases, companies purchased goods from other Member States and sold them to customers elsewhere in the EC. The companies did not account for VAT on the acquisitions. The tax authority issued assessments. The companies appealed, and the case was referred to the ECJ for a ruling on the interpretation of *Article 17(2)* of the *EC Sixth Directive*. The ECJ observed that the goods had never actually entered the Netherlands, and held that 'in those circumstances, those transactions cannot be regarded as giving rise to a "right to deduct" within the meaning of *Article 17* of the *Sixth Directive*. Consequently, such intra-Community acquisitions cannot benefit from the general regime of deduction set out in that article.' The ECJ observed that 'the general regime for the deduction of tax, as set out in *Article 17* of the *Sixth Directive*, is not intended to replace, in a situation such as that at issue in the main proceedings, the specific regime referred to in the second subparagraph of *Article 28b(A)(2)* of that directive, which is based on the mechanism of reducing the taxable amount in order to make it possible to correct the double taxation. Furthermore, the granting of a right to deduct in such a case would risk undermining the effectiveness of the second and third subparagraphs of *Article 28b(A)(2)* of the *Sixth Directive* in view of the fact that the taxable person, having had the right to deduct in the Member State which issued the identification number, would no longer have any incentive to establish that the intra-Community acquisition in question had been taxed in the Member State of arrival of the dispatch or transport. Such a solution could ultimately jeopardise the application of the basic rule that, in the case of an intra-Community acquisition, the place of taxation is deemed to be the Member State of arrival of the dispatch or transport, that is to say, the Member State of final consumption, which is the purpose of the transitional arrangements.' Accordingly, 'a taxable person coming within the situation referred to in the first subparagraph of *Article 28b(A)(2)* does not have the right immediately to deduct the input VAT charged on an intra-Community acquisition'. *Staatssecretaris van Financiën v X*, ECJ Case C-536/08; *Staatssecretaris van Financiën v Facet Trading BV*, ECJ Case C-539/08; [2010] STC 1701.

[22.412] See also *Thorn EMI plc*, 8.30 BUSINESS ENTERTAINMENT; *Apple & Pear Development Council*, 22.80 above; *Charles & Charles-Tijmens v Staatssecretaris van Financien*, 22.183 above; *Vereniging Noordelijke Land-en Tuinbouw Organisatie v Staatssecretaris van Financiën*, 22.187 above; *Lennartz v Finanzamt München III*, 22.456 below; *Gemeente Leusden v Staatssecretaris van Financien*, 22.457 below; *Glasse Brothers*, 36.40 INPUT TAX; *St Helens School Northwood Ltd*, 46.140 PARTIAL EXEMPTION; *Cooper & Chapman (Builders) Ltd*, 46.205 PARTIAL EXEMPTION, and *North East Media Development Trust*, 48.134 PAYMENT OF TAX.

Article 17(2)(a)—tax invoiced but not properly chargeable

[22.413] A Netherlands company (G) reclaimed input tax which had been invoiced to it by two subcontractors but was not properly due. The tax authority issued an assessment to recover the tax, and G appealed. The ECJ rejected G's contentions, holding that the right to deduct could only be exercised in respect of tax which was actually due under a transaction which was subject to VAT. The right to deduct input tax did not extend to tax which was not lawfully due but was wrongly charged on an invoice. *Genius Holding BV v Staatssecretaris van Financiën*, ECJ Case 342/87; [1989] ECR 4227; [1991] STC 239.

[22.414] The decision in *Genius Holding BV v Staatssecretaris van Financiën*, 22.413 above, was applied in two subsequent German cases where traders had issued bogus invoices. The ECJ held that it was for Member States 'to lay down the procedures to apply as regards the adjustment of improperly invoiced VAT'. Adjustments could be made conditional on the issuer of the invoice having 'in sufficient time wholly eliminated the risk of any loss in tax revenues'. Advocate-General Fennelly observed that where VAT was 'mentioned erroneously or fictitiously on invoices', the issuer of the invoice in question 'must be able to establish, to the satisfaction of the relevant national tax authorities, that no loss of VAT revenue will occur'. *Schmeink & Cofreth AG & Co KG v Finanzamt Borken; Strobel v Finanzamt Esslingen*, ECJ Case C-454/98; [2000] STC 810.

[22.415] In two Belgian cases concerning alleged 'carousel' frauds, which were heard together by the ECJ, the ECJ held that 'where a recipient of a supply of goods is a taxable person who did not and could not know that the transaction concerned was connected with a fraud committed by the seller', *Article 17* (of the *EC Sixth Directive*) precluded a rule of national law under which the fact that the contract of sale was void 'causes that taxable person to lose the right to deduct the value added tax he has paid. It is irrelevant in this respect whether the fact that the contract is void is due to fraudulent evasion of value added tax or to other fraud. By contrast, where it is ascertained, having regard to objective factors, that the supply is to a taxable person who knew or should have known that, by his purchase, he was participating in a transaction connected with fraudulent evasion of value added tax, it is for the national court to refuse that taxable person entitlement to the right to deduct.' *Kittel v Belgian State*, ECJ Case C-439/04; *Belgian State v Recolta Recycling SPRL*, ECJ Case C-440/04; [2008] STC 1537.

[22.416] See also *Podium Investments Ltd, 36.662* INPUT TAX.

Article 17(3)

[22.417] In an Italian case, the ECJ held that *Article 17(3)(a)* of the *Sixth Directive* 'must be interpreted as meaning that a supplier of telecommunications services such as the one at issue in the main proceedings, which is established in the territory of a Member State, is entitled under that provision to deduct or obtain a refund in that Member State of input value added tax on telecommunications services that have been supplied to an undertaking having its principal place of business in another Member State, since such a supplier would have had that right if the services at issue had been supplied in the territory of the former Member State'. *EGN BV Filiale Italiana v Agenzia delle Entrate Ufficio di Roma 2*, ECJ Case C-377/08; [2009] STC 2544.

[22.418] A Scottish bank had a German subsidiary company (D), which was registered for UK VAT as a 'non-established taxable person'. D purchased cars in the UK, reclaimed input tax on them, and leased them to UK customers. Although the cars were situated in the UK, D treated their supply under UK VAT law as being a supply of services which took place in Germany, where D had its business establishment. The German authorities did not charge VAT on the basis that the lease of the cars was a supply of goods, made in the UK. Consequently D did not account for output tax in either Germany or the UK. In 2003 Customs issued a ruling that D was not entitled to reclaim input tax on its purchase of the cars, on the basis that 'the fact that no tax was levied takes the rentals out of the VAT system'. The tribunal allowed D's appeal, but the CS referred the case to the ECJ for a ruling on *Article 17(3)* of the *EC Sixth Directive*, and on whether the principles laid down by the ECJ in *Halifax plc v C & E Commrs*, **22.60** above, applied in the circumstances of the case. The ECJ held that *Article 17(3)(a)* 'must be interpreted as meaning that a Member State cannot refuse to allow a taxable person to deduct input value added tax paid on the acquisition of goods in that Member State, where those goods have been used for the purposes of leasing transactions carried out in another Member State, solely on the ground that the output transactions have not given rise to the payment of value added tax in the second Member State'. The principle of prohibiting 'abusive practices' did not preclude the right to deduct VAT where 'a company established in one Member State elects to have its subsidiary, established in another Member State, carry out transactions for the leasing of goods to a third company established in the first Member State, in order to avoid a situation in which value added tax is payable on the sums paid as consideration for those transactions, the transactions having been categorised in the first Member State as supplies of rental services carried out in the second Member State, and in that second Member State as supplies of goods carried out in the first Member State'. *HMRC v RBS Deutschland Holdings GmbH (No 4)*, ECJ Case C-277/09; [2011] STC 345.

Mixed transactions (Article 17(5))

[22.419] A company, which was a subsidiary member of a banking group, carried on an assurance business and held a number of properties as investments. It sold a property which it had let under a lease, and in respect of which it had elected to waive exemption. The sale of the property was treated as the transfer of part of a business as a going concern. The company which was the representative member of the group reclaimed input tax on its solicitors' fees in relation to the transfer. The Commissioners issued an assessment on the basis that, since the transfer of a going concern was not a supply for VAT purposes, the input tax in question could not be directly attributed to taxable supplies and had to be treated as residual input tax within *VAT Regulations 1995 (SI 1995/2518), reg 101(2)(d)* (see **46.40** *et seq* PARTIAL EXEMPTION). The company appealed and the QB referred the case to the ECJ for a ruling on the interpretation of *Article 17(5)* of the *EC Sixth Directive*. The ECJ ruled that where, in accordance with *Article 5(8)* of the *EC Sixth Directive*, 'the transfer of a totality of assets or part thereof is regarded as not being a supply of goods, the costs incurred by the transferor for services acquired in order to effect that transfer form part of that taxable person's overheads and thus in principle have a direct and immediate link with the whole of his economic activity'. If, therefore, the transferor 'effects both transactions in respect of which value added tax is deductible and transactions in respect of which it is not', it followed from *Article 17(5)* that he may deduct 'only that proportion of the value added tax which is attributable to the former transactions. However, if the various services acquired by the transferor in order to effect the transfer have a direct and immediate link with a clearly defined part of his economic activities, so that the costs of those services form part of the overheads of that part of the business, and all the transactions relating to that part of the business are subject to value added tax, he may deduct all the value added tax charged on his costs of acquiring those services.' *Abbey National plc v C & E Commrs*, ECJ Case C-408/98; [2001] STC 297; [2001] 1 WLR 769; [2001] All ER (EC) 385. (*Note.* For the Commissioners' practice following this decision, see Business Brief 8/01, issued on 2 July 2001.)

[22.420] A German company (G) incurred expenditure connected with the issue of shares and 'silent partnerships'. It claimed to deduct the input tax relating to the issue of 'silent partnerships'. The tax authority rejected this claim, and only agreed to allow a deduction of 45.68% of G's residual input tax. G appealed, and the case was referred to the ECJ for rulings on the interpretation of *Article 17(5)* of the *EC Sixth Directive*, and on whether an 'investment formula' or a 'transaction formula' was appropriate for the purposes of apportioning the input tax between an economic activity and a non-economic activity. The ECJ held that 'where a taxpayer simultaneously carries out economic activities, taxed or exempt, and non-economic activities outside the scope of (the *Sixth Directive*), deduction of the VAT relating to expenditure connected with the issue of shares and atypical silent partnerships is allowed only to the extent that that expenditure is attributable to the taxpayer's economic activity within the meaning of *Article 2(1)*'. The determination of the methods and criteria for apportioning input VAT between economic and non-economic activities within the meaning of the *Sixth Directive* was 'in the discretion of the Member States who, when exercising that discretion, must have regard to the aims and broad logic of that directive and, on that basis, provide for a method of calculation which objectively reflects the part of the input expenditure actually to be attributed, respectively, to those two types of activity.' *Securenta Göttinger Immobilienanlagen und Vermögensmanagement AG v Finanzamt Göttingen*, ECJ Case C-437/06; [2008] STC 3473.

[22.421] See also *The Trustees of the Victoria & Albert Museum*, **11.53** CHARITIES; *Royal Bank of Scotland Group plc v HMRC (No 6)*, **22.445** below; *Pearl Assurance plc*, **46.103** PARTIAL EXEMPTION, and *Liverpool Institute for Performing Arts*, **46.174** PARTIAL EXEMPTION.

Non-deductible tax (Article 17(6))

[22.422] Under a law dating from 1967, the French Republic did not permit input tax to be deducted in respect of vehicles designed for the transport of persons (including motor cars, motorcycles, bicycles, boats, aeroplanes and helicopters). The EC Commission applied to the ECJ for a declaration that, by denying the right to deduct VAT incurred on means of transport, the French Republic had failed to fulfil its obligations under *Article 17* of the *EC Sixth Directive*. The ECJ rejected this contention and dismissed the application, holding that the effect of *Article 17(6)* of the *Directive* was that the French Republic was entitled to retain the exclusions in question. *EC Commission v French Republic (No 4)*, ECJ Case C-43/96; [1998] STC 805; [1998] All ER (EC) 951.

[22.423] In 1993 the French Republic amended its General Taxation Code to provide that VAT was deductible on vehicles exclusively used for driving instruction. The EC Commission applied to the ECJ, seeking a declaration that, by restricting the right to deduct to cases where the relevant vehicle was exclusively used for driving instruction, the French Republic had failed to fulfil its obligations under *Article 17* of the *EC Sixth Directive*. The ECJ rejected this contention and dismissed the application, holding that the effect of *Article 17(6)* of the *Directive* was that the French Republic was entitled to retain the exclusion in question. *EC Commission v French Republic (No 10)*, ECJ Case C-345/99; [2003] STC 372.

[22.424] Two associated companies reclaimed input tax on motor cars purchased for leasing businesses. The Commissioners issued assessments to recover the tax, on the basis that the deduction of the input tax was prohibited by *Input Tax Order, Article 7*. The companies appealed, contending that *Input Tax Order, Article 7* was incompatible with the right of deduction of input tax in *Article 17* of the *EC Sixth Directive*. The tribunal dismissed the appeals, holding that the restriction was permitted under *Article 17(6)* of the *Directive*.

Until the European Council had decided what expenditure should not be eligible for an input tax deduction, Member States could retain all the exclusions provided for under their national laws. The exclusion of any deduction of input tax on motor cars did not contravene the principle of proportionality. The QB upheld this decision but the CA directed that the case should be referred to the ECJ for a ruling on whether *Input Tax Order, Article 7* was valid under European law. The ECJ held that *Article 17(6)* authorised Member States 'to retain general exclusions from the right to deduct the value added tax payable on the purchase of motor cars used by a taxable person for the purposes of his taxable transactions, even though those cars were essential tools in the business of the taxable person concerned, or those cars could not, in a specific case, be used for private purposes by the taxable person concerned'. *Royscot Leasing Ltd v C & E Commrs (and related appeals)*, ECJ Case C-305/97; [1999] STC 998; [2000] 1 WLR 1151; [1999] All ER (EC) 908.

[22.425] In the case noted at **22.186** above, the ECJ held that *Article 17(6)* of the *EC Sixth Directive* 'must be interpreted as precluding a Member State from applying, after the entry into force of the Sixth Directive, an exclusion from the right to deduct input value added tax on expenditure in respect of meals provided by company canteens free of charge to business contacts and staff in the course of work meetings, where, at the moment when the Sixth Directive entered into force, that exclusion was not actually applied to that expenditure because of an administrative practice of taxing services provided by company canteens at cost price, that is to say, the price of the raw materials plus the cost of wages for preparation and sale of the food and drinks and the administration of the canteens, in return for the right to deduct input value added tax in full'. *Danfoss A/S v Skatteministeriet (and related appeal)*, ECJ Case C-371/07; [2009] STC 701. (*Note.* For HMRC's practice following this decision, see HMRC Brief 44/10, issued on 2 November 2010.)

[22.426] A Polish company reclaimed input tax on fuel for a car which it used under a leasing contract. The tax authority rejected the claim and the company appealed, contending that the Polish legislation (which had been amended in 2005, a year after Poland had entered the EU) contravened *Article 17(6)* of the *Sixth Directive*. The case was referred to the ECJ, which held that *Article 17(6)* precluded Member States from replacing 'national provisions concerning restrictions on the right to deduct input tax on purchases of fuel for vehicles used for a taxable activity' with provisions which had 'the effect of extending the scope of those restrictions'. *Magoora sp zoo v Dyrektor Izby Skarbowej w Krakowie*, ECJ Case C-414/07; 22 December 2008 unreported.

[22.427] In an Austrian case, a woman (P) built a house which she used as a private residence, except for one small part (covering about 11% of the building), which she let for business purposes. She reclaimed the whole of the input tax on the construction of the house. The tax authority only agreed to allow a deduction of 11% of the input tax, and P appealed. The Austrian court observed that 'the full and immediate deduction of VAT on the building costs of such a mixed-use building and the subsequent imposition of VAT on the expenses pertaining to the part of the building used as a private residence, spread over 10 years, have the effect of granting the taxable person, in respect of that period, an "interest-free loan" not available to a non-taxable person'.

The court referred the case to the ECJ for a ruling on the interpretation of *Article 17* of the *Sixth Directive*. The ECJ held that 'if the taxable person chooses, when acquiring capital goods, to allocate those goods entirely to his private assets or to allocate only part of them to his business activities, no right to deduct can arise in relation to the part allocated to his private assets'. *Article 17(6)* 'must be interpreted as meaning that the derogation it contains does not apply to a provision of national law which amends legislation existing when that directive entered into force, which is based on an approach which differs from that of the previous legislation and which laid down new procedures. In that regard, it is irrelevant whether the national legislature amended the previous national legislation on the basis of a correct or incorrect interpretation of Community law.' It was for the national court to determine the scope of the national provisions in question. *Puffer v Unabhängiger Finanzsenat Außenstelle Linz*, ECJ Case C-460/07; [2009] STC 1693.

[22.428] In a Netherlands case, a company reclaimed input tax in respect of the purchase of 30 cars for use by its employees. The tax authority issued an assessment to recover the tax, on the basis that the cars were used privately as well as for business purposes. The company appealed, and the case was referred to the ECJ for a ruling on the interpretation of *Article 17(6)* of the *EC Sixth Directive*. The ECJ held that *Article 17(6)* 'must be interpreted as not precluding national legislation, enacted before the Sixth Directive entered into force, under which a taxable person may deduct value added tax paid on the acquisition of certain goods and services used partly for private purposes and partly for professional purposes not in full but only in proportion to their use for professional purposes' and 'as not precluding an amendment by a Member State, after the entry into force of that directive, to an existing exclusion from the right of deduction, designed in principle to restrict the scope of that exclusion but in respect of which it cannot be ruled out that, in an individual case in a particular tax year, the scope of that exclusion might be extended by reason of the flat-rate nature of the amended scheme'. *X Holding BV v Staatssecretaris van Financiën*, ECJ Case C-538/08; [2010] STC 1221.

[22.429] The ECJ reached a similar decision in another Netherlands case in which a company reclaimed input tax on staff entertainment. (The ECJ heard the case with *X Holding BV v Staatssecretaris van Financiën*, **22.428** above.) *Oracle Nederland BV v Inspecteur van de Belastingdienst Utrecht-Gooi*, ECJ Case C-33/09; [2010] STC 1221.

[22.430] Polish VAT legislation disallowed claims to input tax on certain services imported from territories classified as 'tax havens' (including Gibraltar, the Channel Islands and the Isle of Man). A Polish company took court proceedings, contending that this legislation contravened *Article 17(6)* of the *EC Sixth Directive*. The case was referred to the ECJ, which found in favour of the company, holding that *Article 17(6)* precluded national legislation 'which excludes in general the right to deduct input value added tax paid at the time of the purchase of imported services, the price of which is directly or indirectly paid to a person established in a State or territory classified as a "tax haven" by that national legislation'. *Oasis East sp zoo v Minister Finansów*, ECJ Case C-395/09; 30 September 2010 unreported.

[22.431] See also *Charles & Charles-Tijmens v Staatssecretaris van Finan-cien*, 22.183 above; *EC Commission v French Republic*, ECJ Case C-40/00, 22.409 above; *Uudenkaupungin kaupunki v Lounais-Suomen Verovirasto*, 22.458 below, and *Kay Quality Management Ltd*, 44.113 MOTOR CARS.

Capital goods (Article 17(7))

Article 17(7) of EC Sixth Directive—definition of 'capital goods'

[22.432] In a Dutch case, the ECJ defined 'capital goods' as 'goods used for the purposes of some business activity and distinguishable by their durable nature and their value and such that the acquisition costs are not normally treated as current expenditure but written off over several years'. *Verbond van Nederlandse Ondernemingen v Inspecteur der Invoerrechten en Accijnzen*, ECJ Case 51/76; [1977] ECR 113; [1977] 1 CMLR 413. (*Note*. The case was argued on the provisions of the *EEC Second Directive*, but the decision is clearly relevant to the *Sixth Directive*.)

Article 17(7) of EC Sixth Directive—interaction with Article 29

[22.433] In two Austrian cases, appellants had claimed that national provisions denying the right to deduct input tax on motor vehicles were a breach of *Article 17* of the *EC Sixth Directive*. The cases were referred to the ECJ for a ruling on the interpretation of the first sentence of *Article 17(7)* (which provides that 'subject to the consultation provided for in *Article 29*, each Member State may, for cyclical economic reasons, totally or partly exclude all or some capital goods or other goods from the system of deductions'). The ECJ held that *Article 17(7)* did not authorise a Member State 'to exclude goods from the system of deducting value added tax without first consulting the committee provided for in *Article 29*'. Furthermore, *Article 17(7)* did not 'authorise a Member State to adopt measures excluding goods from the system of deducting value added tax which contain no indication as to their limitation in time and/or which form part of a package of structural adjustment measures whose aim is to reduce the budget deficit and allow State debt to be repaid'. *Metropol Treuhand WirtschaftstreuhandgmbH v Finanzlandesdirektion für Steinmark; Stadler v Finanzlandesdirektion für Vorarlberg*, ECJ Case C-409/99; [2002] All ER (D) 15 (Jan).

[22.434] In an Italian case, the ECJ held that the first sentence of *Article 17(7)* 'must be interpreted as not authorising a Member State to exclude goods from the system of deducting value added tax without first consulting the Advisory Committee on value added tax established by *Article 29*'. That provision did not authorise a Member State 'to adopt measures excluding goods from the system of deducting that tax which contain no indication as to their limitation in time and/or which form part of a body of structural adjustment measures whose aim is to reduce the budget deficit and allow State debt to be repaid. In so far as an exception from the system of deductions has not been established in accordance with *Article 17(7)* of the *Sixth Directive*, the national tax authorities may not rely as against a taxable person on a provision derogating from the principle of the right to deduct value added tax set out in *Article 17(1)*.' A taxable person which had been subject to that derogating provision 'must be able to recalculate its value added tax debt in accordance with *Article 17(2)*' in so far as the goods and services had been used for the purposes of taxable transactions. *Stradasfalti Srl v Agenzia delle Entrate Ufficio di Trento*, ECJ Case C-228/05; [2007] STC 508.

Rules governing right to deduct (Article 18)

Article 18(1) of EC Sixth Directive

[22.435] An Italian company (E) failed to operate the 'reverse charge' procedure on supplies it received from shipping companies established outside Italy, mistakenly treating them as exempt. Although there was no net loss of tax, the tax authority subsequently required E to account for tax on these supplies, and did not allow any corresponding deduction, on the grounds that the time limit for claiming this had expired. The authority also imposed penalties. E appealed, and the case was referred to the ECJ, which held that *Articles 18(1)(d)* and 22 of the *Sixth Directive* 'preclude a practice whereby tax returns are reassessed and value added tax recovered which penalises misapprehension, first, of obligations arising from formalities laid down in national legislation pursuant to *Article 18(1)(d)*, and, second, of the obligations relating to accounts and tax returns under *Article 22(2)* and *(4)* respectively, such as that at issue in the main proceedings, by denying the right to deduct in the case of a reverse charge procedure'. *Ecotrade SpA v Agenzia Entrate Ufficio Genova 3*, ECJ Case C-95/07 and C-96/07; [2008] STC 2626.

[22.436] See also *Vaughan*, **40.66** INVOICES AND CREDIT NOTES.

Article 18(2) of EC Sixth Directive

[22.437] In a German case, the ECJ held that 'the first subparagraph of *Article 18(2)* of the *Sixth Directive* must be interpreted as meaning that the right to deduct must be exercised in respect of the tax period in which the two conditions required by that provision are satisfied, namely that the goods have been delivered or the services performed and that the taxable person holds the invoice or the document which, under the criteria determined by the Member State in question, may be considered to serve as an invoice'. *Terra Baubedarf-Handel GmbH v Finanzamt Osterholz-Scharmbeck*, ECJ Case C-152/02; [2005] STC 525.

Article 18(3) of EC Sixth Directive

[22.438] See *Douros*, **46.222** PARTIAL EXEMPTION, and *Local Authorities Mutual Investment Trust v C & E Commrs*, **48.5** PAYMENT OF TAX.

Article 18(4) of EC Sixth Directive

[22.439] The Belgian tax authorities refused to refund an amount of input tax reclaimed by a company, because they suspected that the company had 'engaged in fictitious circular sales which artificially created an apparent credit'. The company appealed, and the case was referred to the ECJ (together with three other appeals where the facts were similar). The ECJ ruled that the withholding of the amounts claimed was in accordance with *Article 18(4)* of the *EC Sixth Directive*. In such cases, it was for the national court to examine whether or not the measures in question, and the way in which they were applied, were proportionate. *Garage Molenheide BVBA & Others v Belgian State*, ECJ Case C-286/94; [1998] STC 126; [1998] 1 CMLR 1186; [1998] All ER (EC) 61.

[22.440] Polish tax legislation provided that repayment claims should normally be met within 60 days. However, in the first year of trading the period for making refunds was extended to 180 days, except where the 'taxable person' provided a security deposit (of about €62,000). A claimant appealed to the Polish courts, contending that the delay in making repayments contravened the *EC Treaty*. The case was referred to the ECJ, which held that *Article 18(4)* of the *EC Sixth Directive* and the principle of proportionality 'preclude national legislation, such as that at issue in the main proceedings, which, in order to allow investigations required to prevent tax evasion and avoidance, extends from 60 to 180 days, as from the date of submission of the taxable person's VAT return, the period available to the national tax office for repayment of excess VAT to a category of taxable persons, unless those persons lodge a security deposit'. Furthermore, the Polish legislation was not authorised by *Article 27(1)*. *A Sosnowska v Dyrektor Izby Skarbowej we Wroclawiu Osrodek Zamiejscowy w Walbrzychu*, ECJ Case C-25/07; 10 July 2008 unreported.

[22.441] In a Latvian case, the ECJ held that *Article 18(4)* of the *EC Sixth Directive* 'is to be interpreted as not precluding legislation of a Member State, such as that at issue in the main proceedings, which lays down a limitation period of three years in which to make an application for the refund of excess value added tax collected by, though not due to, the tax authority'. *Alstom Power Hydro v Valsts ieņēmumu dienests*, ECJ Case C-472/08; [2010] STC 777.

Article 18(4)—Member State issuing bonds instead of making refunds

[22.442] For 1992, the Italian Government declined to make refunds of VAT in accordance with *Article 18(4)* of the *Sixth Directive*, and instead issued government bonds to taxable persons whose tax position was in credit. The EC Commission applied to the ECJ for a ruling that, by declining to make refunds, Italy had failed to fulfil its obligations under the *Sixth Directive*. The ECJ granted the declaration, observing that the phrase 'according to conditions which they shall determine' gave Member States 'a certain freedom to manoeuvre in determining the conditions for the refund of excess VAT' but holding that the conditions 'must enable the taxable person, in appropriate conditions, to recover the entirety of the credit arising from that excess VAT. This implies that the refund is carried out within a reasonable period of time by a payment in liquid funds or equivalent means.' The Italian provisions were 'clearly incompatible with the system for the refund of excess VAT provided by the *Sixth Directive*'. *EC Commission v Italian Republic*, ECJ Case C-78/00; [2003] BTC 5255.

The deductible proportion (Article 19)

[22.443] In a French case, a company which had substantial income from dividends reclaimed the whole of its input tax. The French authorities issued an assessment computed on the basis that the company was only entitled to reclaim a proportion of its input tax, since the dividend income should be included in the denominator of the fraction laid down by *Article 19(1)* of the *EC Sixth Directive* as turnover in respect of which input tax was not deductible. The company appealed, contending that dividends should not be taken into account in the denominator, and the Conseil d'Etat referred the case to the ECJ. The ECJ upheld the company's contention, holding that the receipt of dividends was not within the scope of VAT, since it did not amount to consideration for any economic activity. Consequently dividends on shares were to be excluded from the denominator of the fraction laid down by *Article 19(1)* for the purposes of calculating the deductible proportion of input tax. *Sofitam SA (aka Satam SA) v Ministre du Budget*, ECJ Case C-333/91; [1993] 1 ECR 3513; [1997] STC 226.

[22.444] In a Portuguese case, the tax authority formed the opinion that a construction company had reclaimed input tax which should have been attributed to exempt supplies. The company appealed, and the case was referred to the ECJ. The ECJ held that *Article 19(1)* of the *Sixth Directive* did not permit the inclusion 'in the denominator of the fraction making it possible to calculate the deductible proportion, the value of work in progress carried out by a taxable person in the course of civil construction activity, where that value does not correspond to the supply of goods or the provision of services which has already been made by the taxable person or which has given rise to statements of account of work and/or the receipt of payments on account'. *António Jorge Lda v Fazenda Pública*, ECJ Case C-536/03; [2008] STC 2533.

[22.445] A bank had agreed a special method of attributing its input tax, under which the 'specified proportion' was to be rounded up to two decimal places. Despite this, the bank submitted computations in which it rounded up the proportion to the nearest whole number. Customs rejected the computations and the bank appealed, contending that *Article 19(1)* of the *EC Sixth Directive* required rounding up to the next whole number. The tribunal rejected this contention and dismissed the appeal, but the CS directed that the case should be referred to the ECJ for a ruling on the interpretation of *Article 19(1)*. The ECJ rejected the bank's contentions, holding that Member States were not obliged to apply the rounding up rule in the second subparagraph of *Article 19(1)* 'where the proportion of input tax deductible is calculated in accordance with one of the special methods in *(a)*, *(b)*, *(c)* or *(d)* of the third subparagraph of *Article 17(5)*'. *Royal Bank of Scotland Group plc v HMRC (No 6)*, ECJ Case C-488/07; [2009] STC 461.

[22.446] In a French case, a company which carried on a property management business invested sums which it received as advances from co-owners and lessees, and retained the interest which it received. This interest amounted to about 14% of the company's income. It reclaimed the whole of its input tax, including the input tax relating to such investments. The tax authority took the view that, because the interest was exempt from VAT under *Article 13B* of the *EC Sixth Directive*, the effect of *Article 19(2)* of the *Directive* was that only a proportion of the input tax was deductible, and that the amount of interest received should be included in the denominator of the fraction used to calculate the deductible proportion of input tax. The company appealed, contending that the transactions were 'incidental financial transactions' for the purposes of *Article 19(2)*. The case was referred to the ECJ, which ruled that the transactions were not 'incidental financial transactions' for the purposes of *Article 19(2)*, since the receipt of such interest was a 'direct, permanent and necessary extension of the taxable activity of property management companies'. Accordingly, the amount of interest received should be included in the denominator of the fraction used to calculate the deductible proportion of input tax. *Régie Dauphinoise-Cabinet A Forest Sarl v Ministre du Budget*, ECJ Case C-306/94; [1996] STC 1176; [1996] 1 ECR 3695; [1996] 3 CMLR 193.

[22.447] In a Belgian case, two holding companies received dividends and interest from trading subsidiary companies. The holding companies reclaimed the whole of their input tax. The Belgian authorities sought to recover some of the tax on the basis that it was partly attributable to the receipt of income which was exempt from VAT. The companies appealed and the case was referred to the ECJ for guidance on the interpretation of *Article 19* of the *Sixth Directive*. The ECJ held that dividends paid by a subsidiary company to a holding company were outside the scope of VAT and had to be excluded from the denominator of the fraction used to calculate the deductible proportion of input tax. Interest paid on loans to subsidiaries should be similarly excluded where the relevant loans did not constitute 'an economic activity of the holding company', within *Article 4(2)*. Whether the relevant loans were within the charge to VAT was a question to be decided by the national court, applying the principles laid down in *Régie Dauphinoise-Cabinet A Forest Sarl v Ministre du Budget*, **22.446** above. *Floridienne SA v Belgian State; Berginvest SA v Belgian State*, ECJ Case C-142/99; [2000] STC 1044; [2001] All ER (EC) 37.

[22.448] In a Portuguese case, a holding company claimed substantial repayments of input tax. The tax authority formed the opinion that the claims were excessive. The company appealed, and the case was referred to the ECJ for guidance on the interpretation of *Article 19* of the *Sixth Directive*. The ECJ held that the simple sale of shares and other securities, such as holdings in investment funds, did not constitute economic activities, and that placements in investment funds did not constitute supplies of services 'effected for consideration', so that turnover relating to such transactions should be excluded from the calculation of the deductible proportion referred to in *Articles 17* and *19*. However, the annual granting by a holding company of interest-bearing loans to companies in which it had a shareholding and placements by that holding company in bank deposits or in securities, such as Treasury notes or certificates of deposit, constituted 'economic activities carried out by a taxable person acting as such' (and were exempt from VAT under *Article 13B(d)*). In calculating the deductible proportion referred to in *Articles 17* and *19*, such transactions were to be regarded as 'incidental transactions' within the second sentence of *Article 19(2)* in so far as they involved 'only very limited use of assets or services subject to VAT'. It was for the national court to establish whether the transactions concerned in the main proceedings involved 'only very limited use of assets or services subject to VAT' and, if so, to exclude interest generated by those transactions from the denominator of the fraction used to calculate the deductible proportion. *Empresa de Desenvolvimento Mineiro SGPS v Fazenda Pública*, ECJ Case C-77/01; [2005] STC 65.

[22.449] Spanish VAT law provided that, where a taxable person carried out both taxable and non-taxable transactions, capital subsidies should 'be included in the denominator of the proportion, but they may be imputed in fifths to the tax year during which they were received and to the four following tax years. Nevertheless, capital subsidies granted in order to fund the purchase of certain goods or services, acquired in connection with transactions that are taxable and not exempted from VAT, will reduce exclusively the amount of the deduction of VAT borne or paid in respect of those transactions, to the precise extent to which they have contributed to their funding.' The EC Commission applied to the ECJ for a declaration that this contravened the *Sixth Directive*. The ECJ granted the declaration, holding that 'by providing for a deductible proportion of value added tax for taxable persons who carry out only taxable transactions, and by laying down a special rule which limits the right to deduct VAT on the purchase of goods and services which are subsidised, the Kingdom of Spain has failed to fulfil its obligations under Community law'. *EC Commission v Kingdom of Spain*, ECJ Case C-204/03; [2006] STC 1087.

[22.450] A similar decision was reached in *EC Commission v French Republic, ECJ Case C-243/03*; [2006] STC 1098.

[22.451] In a Danish case, two associated companies, which were partly exempt, leased cars and subsequently sold them. The tax authorities issued a ruling that these cars were 'capital goods used by the taxable person for the purposes of his business', within *Article 19(2)* of the *Sixth Directive*, so that the sale proceeds could not be taken into account in the calculation of the deductible proportion under *Article 19*. The companies appealed, and the case was referred to the ECJ. The ECJ found in favour of the companies, holding that *Article 19(2)* had to be interpreted as meaning that 'the notion of "capital goods used by the taxable person for the purposes of his business"' did not include vehicles which a leasing undertaking purchased with a view to 'leasing them and subsequently selling them upon termination of the respective leasing contracts, as the sale of such vehicles at the end of those contracts is an integral part of the usual business activities of that undertaking'. *Nordania Finans A/S v Skatteministeriet; BG Factoring A/S v Skatteministeriet*, ECJ Case C-98/07; [2008] STC 3314. (*Note*. For HMRC's interpretation of this decision, see HMRC Brief 43/10, issued on 12 October 2010.)

[22.452] A Danish company carried on a construction business and sold some of the buildings which it had built. The tax authority issued a ruling that the company was partly exempt and could only deduct part of its input tax. The company appealed, contending that its sales were 'incidental transactions' within *Article 19(2)* of the *Sixth Directive*. The case was referred to the ECJ, which held that *Article 19(2)* 'is to be interpreted as meaning that the sale, in the case of a building business, of buildings constructed on its own account cannot be classified as an "incidental real estate transaction" within the meaning of that provision, where that activity constitutes the direct, permanent and necessary extension of its business. In those circumstances, it is not necessary, in this case, to assess to what extent that sales activity, viewed separately, entails a use of goods and services on which value added tax is payable. The principle of fiscal neutrality cannot preclude a building business, which is required to pay value added tax on supplies relating to construction effected on its own account (self-supply), from being unable fully to deduct the value added tax relating to the general costs incurred thereby, since the turnover from the sale of buildings thus constructed is exempt from value added tax.' *NCC Construction Danmark A/S v Skatteministeriet*, ECJ Case C-174/08; [2010] STC 532.

[22.453] See also *Dean & Chapter of the Cathedral Church of St Peter*, **46.115** PARTIAL EXEMPTION.

Adjustments of deductions (Article 20)

Article 20(1) of EC Sixth Directive—adjustments of input tax

[22.454] In a Netherlands case, a water authority arranged for the construction of a sewage treatment plant. Some years later, it sold the plant to an associated foundation under a 'leaseback' arrangement. Following the sale, it claimed a substantial repayment of input tax. The tax authority rejected the claim and the water authority appealed, contending that it was entitled to an adjustment under *Article 20* of the *Sixth Directive*. The case was referred to the ECJ, which held that 'a body governed by public law which purchases capital goods as a public authority within the meaning of the first subparagraph of *Article 4(5)*' of the *Sixth Directive*, 'that is to say as a non-taxable person, and subsequently sells those goods as a taxable person, is not entitled, in respect of that sale, to a right of adjustment based on *Article 20* of that directive in order to deduct the VAT paid on the purchase of those goods'. *Waterschap Zeeuws Vlaanderen v Staatssecretaris van Financiën*, ECJ Case C-378/02; [2005] STC 1298.

[22.455] See also *Finanzamt Burgdorf v Fischer*, 22.160 above; *Belgium v Ghent Coal Terminal NV*, 22.406 above; *Tremerton Ltd*, 46.65 PARTIAL EXEMPTION; *Briararch Ltd*, 46.212 PARTIAL EXEMPTION; *Curtis Henderson Ltd*, 46.213 PARTIAL EXEMPTION, and *University of Wales College Cardiff*, 46.215 PARTIAL EXEMPTION.

Article 20(2)—adjustments of input tax on capital goods

[22.456] In a German case, a tax consultant purchased a car. Initially he used the car mainly for private purposes, and did not reclaim any input tax on the purchase. In the following year his business use of the car increased, and he reclaimed a proportion of the input tax incurred on the purchase of the car. The German tax authority refused to repay the tax, considering that the consultant should be treated as having initially bought the car wholly for private use, and that he was not entitled to reclaim any input tax on the subsequent business use of the car. The consultant appealed and the German court referred the case to the ECJ for a ruling on whether input tax could be reclaimed under *Article 20(2)* on a capital item which was not initially used for business purposes, but was used for business purposes within five years from its acquisition. The ECJ held that the question of whether input tax was deductible was to be determined solely by reference to the capacity in which the purchaser of goods was acting at the time of the purchase. *Article 20(2)* did not itself contain any provisions as to the origin of the right to deduct, but merely established the procedure for calculating adjustments to the initial deduction. Therefore, if a person purchased goods for private purposes but subsequently used them for business purposes, no input tax would be deductible. However, the immediate use of the goods for either taxable or exempt supplies was not of itself 'a condition for the application of *Article 20(2)*'. The question of whether goods had been purchased for the purposes of an 'economic activity' was a question of fact which had to be determined in the light of all the relevant circumstances. Where goods were purchased partly for the purposes of taxable business transactions and partly for private purposes, the taxable person could reclaim the whole of the input tax but would then have to account for output tax on the private use. *Lennartz v Finanzamt München III*, ECJ Case C-97/90; [1995] STC 514; [1991] 1 ECR 3795; [1993] 3 CMLR 689. (*Note*. For HMRC's current practice following this decision, see VAT Information Sheet 14/07, issued on 14 November 2007; HMRC VAT Guidance, VATPE 4700–4760, and HMRC Brief 02/10, issued on 22 January 2010.)

[22.457] In the Netherlands, the option to tax lettings of immovable property, in accordance with *Article 13C* of the *EC Sixth Directive*, was repealed in 1995. Two lessors appealed against assessments issued to recover input tax which they had claimed, contending that the assessments were a breach of the protection of legitimate expectations and legal certainty. The cases were referred to the ECJ, which held that 'the principles of the protection of legitimate expectations and legal certainty do not preclude the withdrawal by a Member State of the right to opt for taxation of lettings of immovable property which results in the adjustment of deductions made' under *Article 20* of the *Sixth Directive*. The ECJ also held that 'where a Member State withdraws the right to opt for taxation of lettings of immovable property, it must take account of the legitimate expectation of its taxable persons when determining the arrangements for implementing the legislative amendment. The repeal of legislation from which a taxable person has derived an advantage in paying less tax, without there being any abuse, cannot however, as such, breach a legitimate expectation based on Community law.' *Gemeente Leusden v Staatssecretaris van Financien*, ECJ Case C-487/01; *Holin Groep BV cs v Staatssecretaris van Financien*, ECJ Case C-7/02; [2007] STC 776.

[22.458] In a Finnish case, a local authority opted to tax two buildings which it let. It reclaimed input tax relating to restoration work which it had previously undertaken on the buildings. The tax authority rejected the claim and the local authority appealed. The case was referred to the ECJ for a ruling on the interpretation of *Article 20* of the *EC Sixth Directive*. The ECJ found in favour of the local authority, holding that *Article 20* 'requires Member States to make provision for adjustment of deductions of value added tax on capital goods' and 'must be interpreted as meaning that the adjustment provided for therein is also applicable where the capital goods were first used in non-taxable activity that was not eligible for deduction and were then used in activity subject to value added tax during the adjustment period'. The ECJ also held that *Article 17(6)* did not permit Member States 'to exclude deduction of value added tax on immovable property investments made before that right of option is exercised, where the application to exercise that option has not been made within six months of the property being brought into use'. *Uudenkaupungin kaupunki v Lounais-Suomen Verovirasto*, ECJ Case C-184/04; [2008] STC 2329.

Article 20(3)—adjustments of input tax on capital goods

[22.459] A university constructed a building in 1994. It sold it to a subsidiary company (C) and leased it back. Since the sale to C was standard-rated, the university reclaimed all the input tax which it had incurred on constructing the building. In 1996 C granted an exempt 999-year lease to another subsidiary company (H), which was not registered for VAT. C also sold the freehold to the university, three days later, for a minimal sum, and then deregistered for VAT.

The Commissioners issued an assessment on C, to recover input tax of £796,250, on the basis that the building was a 'capital item' and that C had supplied the whole of its interest in that item, so that the provisions of *VAT Regulations (SI 1995/2518), reg 115* applied. C appealed, contending that, because there had been a three-day gap between the grant of the lease to H and the subsequent sale of the freehold, the provisions of *reg 115(3)* did not apply, and that the only necessary adjustment was under *reg 115(2)*, to take account of three days of exempt supplies. The tribunal rejected this contention and dismissed the appeal (except that it reduced the assessment to £796,090 to take account of the respective values of the two transactions). However, the Ch D referred the case to the ECJ for a ruling on the interpretation of *Article 20(3)* of the *EC Sixth Directive*. The ECJ upheld the tribunal decision, holding that *Article 20(3)* should 'be interpreted as meaning that, where a 999-year lease over capital goods is granted to a person against the payment of a substantial premium and the freehold reversion in that property is transferred three days later to another person at a much lower price, and where those two transactions are inextricably linked and consist of a first transaction which is exempt and a second transaction which is taxable', the goods in question were regarded, 'until the expiry of the period of adjustment, as having been used in business activities which are presumed to be partly taxable and partly exempt in proportion to the respective values of the two transactions'. *Centralan Property Ltd v C & E Commrs*, ECJ Case C-63/04; [2006] STC 1542. (*Note.* See now *VAT Regulations (SI 1995/2518), reg 115* as subsequently amended by *VAT (Amendment) (No 3) Regulations (SI 1997/1614), reg 12*, with effect from 1 May 1997. In the Ch D, Sir Andrew Morritt V-C commented that the effect of these amendments is 'that the scheme used by (C) in this case is unlikely to be repeated'.)

Persons liable for payment of tax (Article 21)

Article 21(1) of Sixth Directive—recipient of 'credit note'

[22.460] In a German case, a farmer who was liable to account for VAT at 7% supplied pigs to livestock dealers. He subsequently received documents described as credit notes (but akin to self-billing invoices) from some of the dealers, which included VAT at 13% rather than at 7%. The farmer originally accepted the VAT liability of 13%, but subsequently sought to reduce his liability. The German tax authority resisted the claim and the case was referred to the ECJ, which held that the credit notes qualified as a 'document serving as an invoice', and that the effect of *Article 21(1)* of the *EC Sixth Directive* was that a trader who had received a credit note serving as an invoice which included an amount of VAT, and had not contested the amount included, was liable to pay the amount in question even if it was greater than the amount actually owed. *Finanzamt Osnabrück-Land v Langhorst*, ECJ Case C-141/96; [1997] STC 1357; [1997] 1 ECR 5073; [1998] 1 WLR 52; [1998] All ER (EC) 178.

Article 21(1) of Sixth Directive—'reverse charge' procedure

[22.461] In a German case, a building contractor (B) engaged some English workers through a company (J) which had a contact address in the Netherlands. J sent invoices to B in a slightly different company name, giving a London address and a UK VAT number, but not charging VAT (describing the work as zero-rated). The German tax authority formed the opinion that the work had not been carried out by the UK company whose name appeared on the invoices, and that B was liable to pay VAT on the work under the 'reverse charge' procedure. B appealed, contending firstly that he should not be held to be liable for the tax, and alternatively that if he were liable for output tax, that he should be entitled to deduct input tax under *Article 17*. The case was referred to the ECJ for a ruling on the interpretation of *Article 21(1)* of the *EC Sixth Directive*. The ECJ held that 'a taxable person liable for VAT as the recipient of goods or services is able to rely on the right to deduct contained in *Article 17(2)(a)* of the *Sixth Directive*' and that 'where the reverse charge procedure applies, a taxable person who is liable, as the recipient of services, for the VAT relating thereto in accordance with *Article 21(1)* of the *Sixth Directive* is not obliged to be in possession of an invoice drawn up in accordance with *Article 22(3)* of the *Sixth Directive* in order to be able to exercise his right to deduct'. *Finanzamt Gummersbach v Bockemühl*, ECJ Case C-90/01; [2005] STC 958.

[22.462] A German citizen (R) established an office in Austria, from which he supplied staff to Bavarian companies. He did not charge VAT on his supplies, taking the view that this should be accounted for under the 'reverse charge' procedure. The German tax authority issued a ruling that the conditions for the 'reverse charge' procedure were not satisfied, on the basis that R was not a 'taxable person established abroad', since he had retained a residence in Germany. R appealed, and the case was referred to the ECJ for a ruling on the interpretation of *Article 21(1)* of the *EC Sixth Directive*. The ECJ found in favour of R, holding that *Article 21(1)* 'must be interpreted as meaning that, in order for him to be considered a "taxable person who is not established within the territory of the country", it is sufficient that the taxable person should have established the seat of his economic activity outside that country'. *Finanzamt Deggendorf v Stoppelkamp (Raab's Administrator)*, ECJ Case C-421/10; [2011] STC 2358.

[22.463] See also *Kollektivavtalsstiftelsen TRR Trygghetsrådet v Skatteverket*, 20.36 EC DIRECTIVE 2006/112/EC.

Invoice issued by a salaried employee treating herself as self-employed

[22.464] In a Greek case, a woman was engaged to act as a translator by the Greek Ministry of Foreign Affairs. She issued invoices charging VAT, as if she were self-employed. She subsequently sought reimbursement of the VAT, claiming that she had in fact been a salaried employee and had issued the invoices in error. The Greek Administrative Court held that she was a salaried employee, and directed that the case should be referred to the ECJ for a ruling on *Article 21(1)* of the *EC Sixth Directive*. The ECJ observed that the remuneration paid to her, and to other translators in the same situation, had been 'deemed to include an amount equal to the VAT payable, with the result that the amount actually paid to them is constituted by their statutory remuneration less the amount representing the VAT'. However, the ECJ noted that it could not 'express a view on the nature of the relationship between the translators and the Ministry of Foreign Affairs' but had to 'rely on the assessment made by the national court, pursuant to which the translators perform their activity on the basis of an employer-employee relationship'. The ECJ held that 'the amount mentioned as value added tax on the invoice drawn up by a person providing services to the State may not be classified as value added tax where that person erroneously believes that he is providing those services as a self-employed person whilst in reality there is an employer-employee relationship'. Furthermore, *Article 21(1)* 'does not preclude reimbursement of an amount mentioned in error by way of value added tax on an invoice or other document serving as invoice where the services at issue are not subject to value added tax and the amount invoiced cannot therefore be classified as value added tax'. *Elliniko Dimosio (Greek State) v Karageorgou & Others*, ECJ Cases C-78/02 to C-80/02; [2006] STC 1654.

Article 21(1)(c) of EC Sixth Directive

[22.465] In a Netherlands case, a company (S) issued invoices charging VAT, which it accounted for to the tax authority. It subsequently claimed a repayment on the basis that the relevant services had not been supplied in the Netherlands. The tax authority made the repayment, but S did not issue any credit notes or pass the refund to the customer. When the tax authority discovered this, they issued a supplementary assessment. S appealed, and the case was referred to the ECJ for a ruling on the interpretation of *Article 21(1)(c)* of the *EC Sixth Directive*. The ECJ held that *Article 21(1)(c)* 'must be interpreted as meaning that turnover tax is due, in accordance with that provision, to the Member State to which the VAT mentioned on an invoice or other document serving as invoice relates, even if the transaction in question was not taxable in that Member State. It is for the national court to ascertain, taking into account all the relevant circumstances of the case, to which Member State the VAT mentioned on the invoice in question is due. In particular, the rate mentioned, the currency in which the amount to be paid is expressed, the language in which the invoice was drawn up, the content and context of the invoice at issue, the place of establishment of the issuer of that invoice and the beneficiary of the services performed, as well as their behaviour, can be relevant in that regard. The principle of fiscal neutrality does not generally preclude Member States from making the refund of VAT due in that Member State merely because it was erroneously mentioned on the invoice subject to the requirement that the taxable person have sent the beneficiary of the services performed a corrected invoice not mentioning that VAT, if the taxable person has not completely eliminated in sufficient time the risk of the loss of tax revenue.' *Staatssecretaris van Financiën v Stadeco BV*, ECJ Case C-566/07; [2009] STC 1622.

Article 21(3) of EC Sixth Directive

[22.466] *FA 2003, ss 17, 18* introduced *VATA 1994, s 77A* and amended *Sch 11 para 4*, to extend the Commissioners' powers to require security. A group of traders applied for judicial review of the legislation, contending that it contravened *Article 21* of the *EC Sixth Directive*. The CA referred the case to the ECJ for a ruling on the interpretation of *Article 21(3)*. Advocate-General Poiares Maduro observed that 'Member States are allowed to adopt measures to protect themselves against the risk of making repayments where no genuine VAT credit exists, such as rules governing the proof of the right to deduct VAT or rules specifying the information to be contained in invoices grounding a right to deduct'. The ECJ held that *Article 21(3)* 'is to be interpreted as allowing a Member State to enact legislation, such as that in issue in the main proceedings, which provides that a taxable person, to whom a supply of goods or services has been made and who knew, or had reasonable grounds to suspect, that some or all of the value added tax payable in respect of that supply, or of any previous or subsequent supply, would go unpaid, may be made jointly and severally liable, with the person who is liable, for payment of that tax. Such legislation must, however, comply with the general principles of law which form part of the Community legal order and which include, in particular, the principles of legal certainty and proportionality.' It was 'for the national court to determine whether the national legislation at issue in the main proceedings complies with the general principles of Community law'. The ECJ also held that *Article 22(8)* did not preclude a national measure which imposed a requirement to provide security on any person who was jointly and severally liable for payment of value added tax, 'pursuant to a national measure adopted on the basis of *Article 21(3)*'. *Federation of Technological Industries v C & E Commrs and Attorney-General*, ECJ Case C-384/04; [2006] STC 1483. (*Note*. In the CA ([2004] STC 1424; [2004] EWCA Civ 1020), Ward LJ had observed that 'my first impression was that it would be quite ludicrous to suggest that an *EC Directive* was so lacking in clarity that it could possibly prevent Her Majesty's Government legislating to plug a gap in the law on VAT, which was being exploited by dishonest traders to plunder billions of pounds from the Exchequer'. Dishonest trade in these goods 'must be stamped out. *Sections 17* and *18* of the *Finance Act 2003* provide ample safeguards for honest traders'. He concluded 'I encourage the Commissioners to apply the impugned law in the expectation of eventual victory in Luxembourg'.)

[22.467] In a Netherlands case, the ECJ held that *Article 21(3)* of the *EC Sixth Directive* 'must be interpreted as not authorising the Member States to provide that a warehouse-keeper other than a customs warehouse-keeper is jointly and severally liable for the value added tax which is owing on a supply of goods made for valuable consideration, and released from the warehouse, by the owner of the goods who is liable for the tax on those goods, even where the warehouse-keeper acts in good faith or where no fault or negligence can be imputed to him'. *Vlaamse Oliemaatschappij NV v FOD Financiën*, ECJ Case C-499/10; 21 December 2011 unreported.

[22.468] See also *Optigen Ltd*, 22.115 above.

Obligations of persons liable for payment (Articles 22, 23)

Tax amnesty—whether permitted by Article 22

[22.469] In December 2002 Italy enacted legislation which effectively provided for 'a general waiver of verification of taxable transactions' from 1998 to 2001, except for people who were already being investigated for alleged tax evasion. The EC Commission took proceedings in the ECJ, seeking a declaration that this contravened *Article 22* of the *EC Sixth Directive*. The ECJ granted the declaration, holding that the effect of *Article 22* was that 'every

Member State is under an obligation to take all legislative and administrative measures appropriate for ensuring collection of all the VAT due on its territory. In that regard, Member States are required to check taxable persons' returns, accounts and other relevant documents, and to calculate and collect the tax due'. The effect of the Italian legislation was that there was 'a powerful incentive to declare only part of the tax debt actually due', and that many taxable persons 'will escape once and for all their obligations to declare and to pay the amount of VAT normally payable for the tax periods falling between 1998 and 2001'. This disrupted 'the proper functioning of the common system of VAT', distorted 'the principle of fiscal neutrality', and infringed 'the obligation to ensure that VAT is collected in a uniform manner in all the Member States'. By providing for 'a general and indiscriminate waiver of verification of taxable transactions effected in a series of tax years', Italy had failed to fulfil its obligations under *Article 22* of the *Directive* and *Article 10EC* of the *EC Treaty*. *EC Commission v Italian Republic (No 7)*,ECJ Case C-132/06; 17 July 2008 unreported.

[22.470] In December 2003 Italy extended its 'tax amnesty' noted at **22.469** above to include transactions occurring in 2002. The EC Commission took further proceedings in the ECJ, seeking a declaration that this contravened *Article 22* of the *EC Sixth Directive*. The ECJ granted the declaration. *EC Commission v Italian Republic (No 8)*, ECJ Case C-174/07; 11 December 2008 unreported.

Article 22(3) of EC Sixth Directive—invoices

[22.471] In a Belgian case, a trader reclaimed input tax in respect of invoices which did not state the registration number of the supplier, the date of the supply, or the full name of the person to whom the supply was made. The ECJ held that, by virtue of *Article 22(3)(c)* of the *EC Sixth Directive*, Member States could specify the criteria with which invoices had to comply, for the correct levying of tax and the prevention of fraud. The relevant criteria should, however, be necessary for the collection of tax and its control by the tax authorities, and should not make the exercise of the right of deduction 'practically impossible or excessively difficult'. *L Jorion (née Jeunehomme) & Société Anonyme d'Etude et de Gestion Immobilière 'EGI' v Belgian State*, ECJ Case 123/87; [1988] ECR 4517.

[22.472] In a German case, an appellant failed to produce original invoices in support of a claim to input tax. The tax authority rejected his claim, and he appealed. The case was referred to the ECJ, which ruled that *Article 22(3)* of the *EC Sixth Directive* conferred on Member States the power to require production of an original invoice in order to establish the right to deduct input tax. *Reisdorf v Finanzamt Köln-West*, ECJ Case C-85/95; [1996] 1 ECR 6257; [1997] STC 180; [1997] 1 CMLR 536.

[22.473] In a Polish case, a trader (D) reclaimed input tax in respect of marketing services. The supplier of the services had not registered for VAT, although he had issued invoices documenting the services provided and specifying the tax payable. The tax authority rejected D's claim on the basis that the supplier was not a registered trader and the invoices did not give rise to a right to deduct input tax. D appealed, and the case was referred to the ECJ for a ruling on the interpretation of the *EC Sixth Directive*. The ECJ held that 'a taxable person has the right to deduct value added tax paid in respect of services supplied by another taxable person who is not registered for that tax, where the relevant invoices contain all the information required by *Article 22(3)(b)*, in particular the information needed to identify the person who drew up those invoices and to ascertain the nature of the services provided'. *Dankowski v Dyrektor Izby Skarbowej w Łodzi*, ECJ Case C-438/09; 22 December 2010 unreported.

[22.474] See also *Finanzamt Gummersbach v Bockemühl*, **22.461** above, and *Senergy (UK) Ltd*, **36.104** INPUT TAX.

Article 22(4) of EC Sixth Directive—returns

[22.475] See *Société Financière d'Investissements SPRL (SFI) v Belgian State*, **22.53** above.

Article 22(5) of EC Sixth Directive—interim payments

[22.476] In an Italian case, the ECJ held that *Article 22(5)* of the *EC Sixth Directive* authorised Member States to derogate from the rule that payment had to be made on submission of the return, and to demand interim payments. However, payment could only be demanded for transactions which had actually been carried out. An Italian provision, which required traders to pay an amount of VAT equal to 65% of the estimated total amount payable for a period which had not yet elapsed, was contrary to *Article 22(5)* of the *EC Sixth Directive*, which could be invoked by any traders required to make such payments. *M Balocchi v Ministero delle Finanze dello Stato*, ECJ Case C-10/92; [1993] 1 ECR 5105; [1997] STC 640; [1995] 1 CMLR 486.

Article 22(8)—obligations imposed by Member States

[22.477] Polish VAT law stipulated that 'taxable persons effecting sales to natural persons not engaged in economic activity' were required to 'keep records of turnover and the amount of tax due through the use of cash registers', and that taxable persons who failed to fulfil this obligation 'shall forfeit the right to reduce the amount of tax due in an amount equivalent to 30% of the amount of input tax paid on the acquisition of goods and services'. A company which had failed to use cash registers to record its turnover appealed against a reduction of its input tax, contending that the Polish legislation contravened the *EC Sixth Directive*. The case was referred to the ECJ, which found in favour of the Polish authorities, holding that the *Directive* 'does not preclude a Member State from imposing a temporary restriction on the extent of the right of taxable persons who have not complied with a formal requirement to keep accounting records of their sales to deduct input tax paid, on condition that the sanction thus provided for complies with the principle of proportionality'. *Dyrektor Izby Skarbowej w Bialymstoku v Profaktor Kulesza Frankowski Jóźwiak Orlowski sp j*, ECJ Case C-188/09; 29 July 2010 unreported.

[22.478] See *Coleman*, **2.23** APPEALS; *Ecotrade SpA v Agenzia Entrate Ufficio Genova 3*, **22.435** above; *Federation of Technological Industries v C & E Commrs and Attorney-General*, **22.466** above; *4Distribution Ltd*, **36.108** INPUT TAX and *Bjelica*, **57.89** REGISTRATION.

Special schemes (Articles 24–26a)

Article 24 of EC Sixth Directive—small undertakings

[22.479] Austrian VAT legislation provided that 'carriers who have neither a domicile (seat), place of business or usual residence in the national territory', and whose turnover was less than €22,000 in a given tax period, cold calculate their deductible VAT 'in respect of their turnover from occasional international passenger transport by motor vehicles or trailers not registered in Austria, by applying an average rate of 10% of that turnover from such activity'. The EC Commission applied to the ECJ for a declaration that this contravened the *EC Sixth Directive*. The ECJ granted the application, observing that '*Article 24(1)* of the *Sixth Directive* provides that Member States have the option "of applying simplified procedures such as flat-rate schemes for charging and collecting the tax". The wording of the provision does not show that they may exempt small undertakings totally from their obligation to pay VAT, since it permits the charging procedures merely to be simplified and makes no mention of any possibility of exempting the undertaking concerned entirely from VAT.' Accordingly, 'the concept of "simplified procedures" cannot include a total lack of charging and collecting of the tax.' *EC Commission v Republic of Austria*, ECJ Case C-128/05; [2008] STC 2610.

[22.480] See also *Byrd*, **46.224** PARTIAL EXEMPTION.

Article 24(6) of EC Sixth Directive

[22.481] See *Eastwood Care Homes (Ilkeston) Ltd*, **32.7** GROUPS OF COMPANIES.

Article 25 of EC Sixth Directive—flat-rate scheme for farmers

[22.482] In 1981 the Italian government introduced a flat-rate scheme for VAT refunds to be paid to producers of beef, pork and unconcentrated and unsweetened milk. On an application by the EC Commission, the ECJ held that the scheme contravened the provisions of the *Sixth Directive*. *EC Commission v Italian Republic*, ECJ Case 3/86; [1988] ECR 3369; [1989] 3 CMLR 748.

[22.483] In a German case, a farmer leased some of his land, plus his milk quota and 65 cows, to his son. He did not account for output tax on the letting income which he received from his son. The tax authority issued an assessment charging tax on the income from the cows and milk quota. The farmer appealed, contending that the income in question fell within the flat-rate scheme provided for by *Article 25* of the *EC Sixth Directive*. The case was referred to the ECJ, which held that *Article 25* should be 'interpreted as meaning that a farmer who has leased and/or let on a long-term basis some of the material assets of his farming business but continues to farm with the rest of his assets and who, in respect of the continued farming activity, is subject to the common flat-rate scheme provided for in *Article 25* may not treat the income from such a lease and/or letting as being taxable under that scheme. The turnover from that arrangement must be taxed under the normal scheme or, where appropriate, the simplified scheme'. *Finanzamt Rendsburg v Harbs*, ECJ Case C-321/02; [2006] STC 340.

[22.484] In a German case, the ECJ held that the grant of hunting licences by a 'flat-rate farmer' was not an 'agricultural service' within *Article 25 of the EC Sixth Directive*. *Finanzamt Arnsberg v Stadt Sundern*, ECJ Case C-43/04; 26 May 2005 unreported.

Article 26 of EC Sixth Directive—travel agents and tour operators

[22.485] In a Dutch case, the ECJ ruled that *Article 26 of the EC Sixth Directive* applied to cases where a travel agent only provided accommodation, and was not restricted to cases where transport was also provided. *Beheersmaatschappij Van Ginkel Waddinxveen BV & Others v Inspecteur der Omzetbelasting Utrecht*, ECJ Case C-163/91; [1992] 1 ECR 5723; [1996] STC 825.

[22.486] The European Commission applied for a ruling that the German Federal Republic had failed to comply with its obligations under the *EC Sixth Directive*, in that it had exempted tour operators' margins for supplies within the Community, whereas *Article 26 of the Directive* only provided for exemption in respect of supplies outside the Community. The ECJ granted the application, ruling that Germany had failed to comply with its obligations. *EC Commission v Federal Republic of Germany*, ECJ Case C-74/91; [1992] 1 ECR 5437; [1996] STC 843. (*Note*. For the Commissioners' practice following this decision, see their News Release 43/94, issued on 25 October 1994. The Tour Operators' Margin Scheme was amended with effect from 1 January 1996. See *Notice No 709/5/96*.)

[22.487] The proprietors of a hotel in Devon provided coach transport to and from the hotel for customers from Northern England. On Saturdays the coach collected customers from Leeds and certain pick-up points en route, returning to Leeds each Friday. In addition, each Tuesday the coach was used to provide customers with a sight-seeing trip around Devon. About 90% of the hotel's customers used the coach. Customs issued assessments on the basis that the hotel proprietors were acting as tour operators, within *VATA 1994, s 53(3)*, and were required to operate the Tour Operators' Margin Scheme. The proprietors appealed, contending that the basis of apportionment laid down in *Leaflet 709/5/88* was contrary to *Article 26 of the EC Sixth Directive*. The QB referred the case to the ECJ, which ruled that the proprietors were acting as 'travel agents' within *Article 26*, but that the margin scheme under *Article 26* applied solely to the services supplied by third parties. A method based on actual costs (such as the scheme imposed by *Leaflet 709/5/88*) required a series of complex sub-apportionment exercises and meant substantial additional work for the trader. A trader could not be required to calculate the part of the package corresponding to the in-house services by such a method, where it was possible to identify that part of the package on the basis of the market value of the relevant services (which, in the instant case, were the prices charged by the hotel to 'non-package' customers). *TP Madgett & RM Baldwin (t/a Howden Court Hotel) v C & E Commrs*, ECJ Cases C-308/96 & C-94/97; [1998] STC 1189. (*Notes*. (1) The tribunal subsequently allowed the proprietors' appeals against the assessments—see **63.15** TOUR OPERATORS AND TRAVEL AGENTS. (2) In the subsequent case of *MyTravel plc*, **22.488** below,

Advocate-General Léger held that he did 'not accept the interpretation of the judgment in *Madgett & Baldwin* put forward by the United Kingdom Government'.)

[22.488] A company (M) sold 'package holidays' and operated the Tour Operators' Margin Scheme. Following the ECJ decision in *Madgett & Baldwin v C & E Commrs*, 22.487 above, it submitted a repayment claim on the basis that it should be entitled to use the market value of the in-house supplies contained in the 'packages'. (A typical 'package' included bought-in supplies of standard-rated accommodation and in-house supplies of zero-rated transport.) Customs rejected the claim on the basis that M was required to use the cost-based method stipulated by *Notice 709/5/96*. M appealed. The tribunal directed that the case should be remitted to the ECJ for clarification of whether a tour operator was entitled to use a market value method to calculate the value of the in-house component of holiday packages containing both in-house and bought-in supplies. (The chairman observed that M's proposed recalculation 'inflates the amount of the package price that is attributed to zero-rated transport' but that '*Appendix H of Notice 700* accepts that apportionment by reference to market value will be accepted by the Commissioners where apportionment is necessary'.) The tribunal also observed that, even if the ECJ held that M was entitled to use market value, M's specific computation adopted an incorrect figure as market value, and so directed that if the ECJ accepted M's contentions in principle, 'the precise method of calculating market value be determined at a rehearing of the question' by a tribunal of three persons. The ECJ held that a travel agent or tour operator who had completed a VAT return under national rules 'may recalculate his value added tax liability in accordance with the method held by the Court to comply with Community law, under the conditions laid down by national law, which have to observe the principles of equivalence and effectiveness'. *Article 26* of the *EC Sixth Directive* had to be 'interpreted as meaning that a travel agent or tour operator who, in return for a package price, supplies to a traveller services bought in from third parties and in-house services must, in principle, identify the part of the package corresponding to his in-house services on the basis of their market value where that value can be established'. The 'use of the criterion of market value is not subject to the condition that it must be simpler than use of the actual cost method'. A travel agent or tour operator who, 'in return for a package price, supplies to a traveller services bought in from third parties and in-house services must, in principle, identify the part of the package corresponding to his in-house services on the basis of their market value where that value can be established, unless he can prove that, for the tax period under consideration, the method based on the criterion of actual costs accurately reflects the actual structure of the package. In addition, it is for the national tax authorities and, where appropriate, the national court or tribunal, to assess whether it is possible to identify the part of the package corresponding to the in-house services on the basis of their market value, and in this context to determine the most appropriate market.' Furthermore, a taxable person could 'in the same tax period, apply the criterion of market value to certain services and not to others where he is not able to establish the market value of those other services'. It was 'for the national tribunal to establish, in the light of the circumstances of the main proceedings, the market value of the flights supplied in the main proceedings as part of package holidays. The national tribunal may establish this market value from average values. In this context, the market based on seats sold to other tour operators may constitute the most appropriate market.' *MyTravel plc (aka Airtours plc) v C & E Commrs (No 1)*, ECJ Case C-291/03; [2005] STC 1617.

[22.489] A German company arranged language and study trips abroad, mainly to the USA, lasting for between three and ten months. The tax authority issued a ruling that its supplies were educational services which were wholly exempt from VAT, so that it was unable to reclaim any input tax. The company appealed, contending that it was supplying travel services as well as educational services. The case was referred to the ECJ for a ruling on the interpretation of *Article 26* of the *EC Sixth Directive*. The ECJ held that *Article 26* applied to a trader who offered services 'involving the organisation of language and study trips abroad and which, in consideration of the payment of an all-inclusive sum, provides in its own name to its customers a stay abroad of three to 10 months and buys in services from other taxable persons for that purpose'. *Finanzamt Heidelberg v IST Internationale Sprach- und Studienreisen GmbH*, ECJ Case C-200/04; [2006] STC 52.

[22.490] A German company (M) carried on business as a travel agent and also sold opera tickets. The tax authority issued a ruling that the special 'margin scheme' for tour operators and travel agents did not apply where M sold opera tickets without providing any travel services. M appealed, and the case was referred to the ECJ, which found in favour of the tax authority, holding that *Article 26* of the *Sixth Directive* 'is to be interpreted as not applying to the sale by a travel agent of opera tickets in isolation, without the provision of a travel service'. *Minerva Kulturreisen GmbH v Finanzamt Freital*, ECJ Case C-31/10; [2011] STC 532.

[22.491] See also *Aer Lingus plc*, **63.2** TOUR OPERATORS AND TRAVEL AGENTS, and *Independent Coach Travel (Wholesaling) Ltd*, **63.3** TOUR OPERATORS AND TRAVEL AGENTS.

Article 26(2) of EC Sixth Directive—definition of 'fixed establishment'

[22.492] A Danish company (D), which carried on a travel business, established a UK subsidiary company (L) to act as an agent. Under the agency agreement, L received a commission of 19% on all package tours which it sold on behalf of D. L accounted for VAT on this commission, but D did not account for VAT on its profit on such sales. The Commissioners issued a ruling that D was required to register for UK VAT, and that where L sold package tours on behalf of D, D was required to account for UK VAT on its margin. D appealed, contending that it was not liable to UK VAT since it did not have a fixed establishment in the UK. The QB referred the case to the ECJ for a ruling on the interpretation of the term 'fixed establishment' in *Article 26(2)* of the *EC Sixth Directive*. The ECJ ruled that, in such a case, it was necessary to ascertain whether the subsidiary company was independent of the tour operator and to verify whether its establishment was of a requisite minimum size in terms of human and technical resources. On the facts found by the tribunal, particularly with regard to the number of D's employees established in the UK, it was clear that D did 'display the features of a fixed establishment' in the UK. *C & E Commrs v DFDS A/S*, ECJ Case C-260/95; [1997] STC 384; [1997] 1 ECR 1005; [1997] 1 WLR 1037; [1997] All ER (EC) 342. (*Note*. For the Commissioners' practice following this decision, see Business Brief 12/98, issued on 21 May 1998.)

Article 26(2)—'total amount to be paid by the traveller'

[22.493] A company (F), within the Tour Operators' Margin Scheme, sold holidays through travel agents. It paid the agents commission (usually 10%) on sales. In some cases agents arranged sales at cheaper prices than those published in F's brochures. In such cases the agents still had to pay F the full brochure price, thereby effectively reducing their commission. Initially F accounted for VAT on the basis that the sum 'paid or payable', within *article 7* of the *VAT (Tour Operators) Order 1987 (SI 1987/1806)* was its brochure price. Subsequently it submitted a repayment claim on the basis that the sum 'paid or payable' was the price actually paid by the customer, excluding the amount paid by the travel agent. The Commissioners rejected the claim and F appealed. The CA directed that the case should be referred to the ECJ for guidance on the interpretation of the phrase 'the total amount to be paid by the traveller' in *Article 26(2)* of the *EC Sixth Directive*. The ECJ held that 'the total amount to be paid by the traveller' had to be interpreted as including the additional amount that 'a travel agent, acting as an intermediary on behalf of a tour operator', had to 'pay to the tour operator on top of the price paid by the traveller and which corresponds in amount to the discount given by the travel agent to the traveller on the price of the holiday stated in the tour operator's brochure'. *C & E Commrs v First Choice Holidays plc*, ECJ Case C-149/01; [2003] STC 934; [2003] All ER (EC) 705. (*Notes*. (1) Following the ECJ decision, the CA held a further hearing and determined the appeal in favour of the Commissioners—see **63.11** TOUR OPERATORS' MARGIN SCHEME. (2) For HMRC's practice following this decision, see Business Brief 08/06, issued on 7 July 2006.)

Article 26a of EC Sixth Directive—second-hand goods

[22.494] A Swedish company purchased young horses from private individuals, trained them so that they could be used for riding, and then sold them. The tax authority ruled that the company was required to account for VAT on the full sale price of the horses. The company appealed, contending that the horses should be classified as 'second-hand goods', within *Article 26a* of the *EC Sixth Directive*, so that it should only be required to account for tax on its profit margin. The case was referred to the ECJ, which observed that animals were 'tangible property within the meaning of *Article 5* of the *Sixth Directive*' and that 'nothing in *Article 26a* of the *Sixth Directive* indicates that the special arrangements applicable to the supply of second-hand goods do not apply to the supply of animals such as horses'. Therefore, the ECJ ruled that '*Article 26a* of the *Sixth Directive* must be interpreted as meaning that live animals may be considered to be second-hand goods within the meaning of that provision' and that 'an animal bought from a private individual (other than the breeder) which is sold on after training for a specific use may be considered to be second-hand goods'. *Förvaltnings AB Stenholmen v Riksskatteverket*, ECJ Case C-320/02; [2004] STC 1041; [2004] All ER (EC) 870.

[22.495] See also *Jyske Finans A/S v Skatteministeriet*, 22.350 above; *Peugeot Motor Co plc*, **44.68** MOTOR CARS; *Angus MacKinnon Ltd*, **44.73** MOTOR CARS, and *Stafford Land Rover*, **44.168** MOTOR CARS.

Simplification procedures (Article 27)

Article 27 of EC Sixth Directive—special measures for derogation

[22.496] In December 1977 the UK Government notified the European Commission of various special measures which it wished to retain under *Article 27* of the *EC Sixth Directive*. These included *FA 1972, Sch 3 para 2* (the precursor of what is now *VATA 1994, Sch 6 para 2*). However, in 1981 the provision in question was amended by *FA 1981, s 14*. The UK Government did not notify this amendment to the Commission. Subsequently a company, to which the Commissioners had issued a direction under *FA 1972, Sch 3* requiring it to account for tax on the open market value of goods supplied to agents, appealed against the direction, contending that it was invalid. The ECJ held that the amended provision was invalid, so that the UK was not authorised to depart from the provision in *Article 11* of the *Directive* that the taxable amount in respect of a supply should be the consideration received by the supplier. Furthermore, the ECJ held that *Article 11* had direct effect and could be invoked by the appellant company to claim rights not enacted in UK legislation. *Direct Cosmetics Ltd v C & E Commrs*, ECJ Case 5/84; [1985] STC 479; [1985] ECR 617; [1985] 2 CMLR 145. (*Note*. The UK Government subsequently obtained a derogation from the Council of the European Communities authorising *VATA 1983, Sch 4 para 3* (which is now *VATA 1994, Sch 6 para 2*). For a subsequent case in which the validity of the derogation was upheld, see **22.497** below.)

[22.497] Acting under the derogation issued by the Council of the European Communities following the case noted at **22.496** above, the Commissioners issued directions under what is now *VATA 1994, Sch 6 para 2* to the company involved in that case and to a company which sold school photographs through the agency of the school's head teachers. The companies appealed, contending that the direction was ultra vires and outside the scope of the *EC Sixth Directive*, since *Article 27* only permitted derogation for the purpose of preventing tax evasion or avoidance. The tribunal referred the cases to the ECJ for a ruling on the validity of the direction. The ECJ ruled that the derogation issued by the Council of the European Communities and the direction issued by the Commissioners were valid. *Article 27(1)* of the *Sixth Directive* was not confined to situations where there was a deliberate intention to avoid tax, but included business arrangements undertaken for genuine commercial reasons, if the effect of such arrangements was that tax was avoided. The ECJ observed that the reference in *Article 27* to 'tax avoidance' indicated that 'the legislature intended to introduce a new element in relation to the pre-existing concept of tax evasion. The element lies in the inherently objective nature of tax avoidance; intention on the part of the taxpayer, which constitutes an essential element of evasion, is not required as a condition for the existence of avoidance.' *Direct Cosmetics Ltd v C & E Commrs (No 2); Laughtons Photographs Ltd v C & E Commrs*, ECJ Case 138/86; [1988] STC 540; [1988] ECR 3937.

[22.498] Belgian VAT law provided for the use of catalogue prices as a minimum taxable amount for charging VAT on the supply and importation of new cars, and notified these provisions to the EC Commission as a special measure under *Article 27(5)* of the *EC Sixth Directive*. On an application by the EC Commission, the ECJ held that the use of catalogue prices did not constitute a valid derogation from the provisions of *Article 11*, as they were too general in nature and were disproportionate to the need to prevent tax evasion or avoidance. *EC Commission v Kingdom of Belgium*, ECJ Case 324/82; [1984] ECR 1861; [1985] 1 CMLR 364.

[22.499] In 1977 the Belgian government notified the EC Commission that Belgian VAT legislation provided that 'the VAT that is due when manufactured tobacco products are imported and supplied is payable at the same time as excise duty, when the manufacturer or importer purchases the tax labels. No VAT is charged at later stages, but naturally no deduction can be made. All sales of manufactured tobacco products must be invoiced inclusive of VAT.' Notwithstanding this provision, a company (V) subsequently reclaimed input tax in respect of supplies of manufactured tobacco which it had made to another company. The tax authority rejected the claim, and V appealed, contending that the Belgian VAT legislation went beyond what was permitted by *Article 27* of the *EC Sixth Directive*. The case was referred to the ECJ, which rejected V's contentions, holding that the Directive 'must be interpreted as not precluding national legislation, such as that at issue in the main proceedings, which, by providing, for the purposes of simplifying the procedure for charging value added tax and of combating tax evasion or avoidance in regard to manufactured tobacco, for the levying of that tax by means of tax labels, in a single charge and at source, from the manufacturer or importer of those products, excludes intermediate suppliers operating at a subsequent stage in the supply chain from the right to obtain reimbursement of value added tax in the event of non-payment by the purchaser of the price for those products'. *Vandoorne NV v Belgische Staat*, ECJ Case C-489/09; 27 January 2011 unreported.

[22.500] German law provided that, for certain supplies between associated persons, the cost of the supply was to be the 'taxable amount'. A landlord, who let a number of properties to a company owned by his wife and son, appealed against an assessment issued on this basis, and the case was referred to the ECJ for a ruling on whether the relevant provision was authorised by *Article 27* of the *EC Sixth Directive*. The ECJ held that the provision was not covered by *Article 27*, since it was not confined to what was 'strictly necessary to deal with the risk of tax evasion or avoidance'. *EC Commission v Kingdom of Belgium*, 22.498 above, applied. (The ECJ observed that rents were often set at a low level for social or political reasons, whereas building costs were generally high, and that there was nothing to prevent a provision formulated in general or abstract terms from excluding cases in which the agreed rent was lower than the amount normally necessary to amortise building costs but was in accordance with normal market rent.) *Finanzamt Bergisch Gladbach v Skripalle*, ECJ Case C-63/96; [1997] STC 1035; [1997] 1 ECR 2847.

[22.501] In 1989 the EC Council issued a Decision under *Article 27(1)* of the *EC Sixth Directive*, authorising the French Republic to apply a measure derogating from *Article 17(6)* of the *Directive*, and excluding the deduction of input tax on accommodation, food, hospitality and entertainment. In subsequent proceedings, two French companies contended that the Council Decision was invalid. The case was referred to the ECJ, which held that the Council Decision was invalid because it was 'not compatible with the principle of proportionality' which was 'part of the general principles of Community law'. The Decision authorised the French Republic 'to deny traders the right to deduct the VAT charged on expenditure which they are able to show to be strictly of a business nature'. National legislation 'which excludes from the right to deduct VAT expenditure in respect of accommodation, hospitality, food and entertainment without making any provision for the taxable person to demonstrate the absence of tax evasion or avoidance in order to take advantage of the right of deduction is not a means proportionate to the objective of combating tax evasion and avoidance'. *Ampafrance SA v Directeur des Services Fiscaux de Maine-et-Loire*, ECJ Case C-177/99; *Sanofi Synthelabo v Directeur des Services Fiscaux du Val-de-Marne*, ECJ Case C-181/99; [2002] BTC 5520.

[22.502] In February 2000 the EC Council issued a Decision under *Article 27(1)* of the *EC Sixth Directive*, authorising the Federal Republic of Germany to apply a measure derogating from *Article 17(2)* of the *Directive*, 'to limit to 50% the right to deduct the VAT charged on expenditure on vehicles not used exclusively for business purposes and not to treat as supplies of services for consideration the use for private purposes of vehicles belonging to a taxable person's business'. The derogation was backdated to 1 April 1999. In subsequent proceedings, a German trader contended that the derogation was invalid. The case was referred to the ECJ, which held that the article in the Decision which provided for the derogation to have retrospective effect was invalid, since it infringed 'the principle of the protection of legitimate expectations'. However the substantive article in the Decision was not invalid, in view of 'the difficulty for the taxable person of establishing in advance the proportions of private and business use to which his vehicle will be put, the difficulty, for verification purposes, of proving precisely what use is made of the vehicle, and the discovery of irregularities in almost all cases where verification is carried out'. The 50% limit was 'reasonable' and observed 'the principle of proportionality'. *Finanzamt Sulingen v Sudholz*, ECJ Case C-17/01; [2005] STC 747.

[22.503] In 1993, a Spanish company (C) sold a number of service stations to an associated company for less than their market value. The tax authority issued an assessment charging tax on the sale in accordance with the Spanish VAT legislation then in force (which dated from 1992). C appealed, contending that the Spanish legislation did not comply with *Article 11A* of the *Sixth Directive* and was not authorised by *Article 27*. The case was referred to the ECJ, which held that the Sixth Directive 'must be interpreted as precluding a Member State from applying to transactions, such as those in the main proceedings, effected between connected parties having agreed a price which is patently lower than the open market price, a rule for determining the taxable amount other than the general rule laid down in *Article 11A(1)(a)* of that directive, by extending the scope of the rules for determining the taxable amount on the application of goods and services for private use by a taxable person, within the meaning of *Articles 5(6)* and *6(2)* of that directive, when the procedure provided for in Article 27 of that directive to obtain authorisation for such derogation from that general rule has not been followed by that Member State'. *Campsa Estaciones de Servicio SA v Administración del Estado*, ECJ Case C-285/10; [2011] STC 1603. (*Note.* Spain subsequently obtained a relevant derogation in 2006.)

[22.504] See also *British American Tobacco International Ltd v Belgian State*, **22.88** above; *Sosnowska v Dyrektor Izby Skarbowej we Wroclawiu Osrodek Zamiejscowy w Walbrzychu*, **22.440** above; *Kimber*, **44.143** MOTOR CARS; *Next plc*, **58.28** RETAILERS' SPECIAL SCHEMES; *Grattan plc*, **58.29** RETAILERS' SPECIAL SCHEMES, and *RBS Leasing & Services (No 1) Ltd*, **67.2** VALUATION.

Transitional provisions (Articles 28–28o)

Article 28 of EC Sixth Directive

[22.505] The Commission of the European Communities applied to the ECJ for a ruling that the UK had failed to fulfil its obligations under *Article 28* of the *EC Sixth Directive* in that it had applied a zero rate of tax to several types of supplies which were not eligible for zero-rating under the *Directive*. The ECJ allowed the application in part. It ruled that the supply of sewerage services and water to industry; the supply of news services to undertakings such as banks and insurance companies; the supply of fuel and power; the construction of buildings—other than local authority housing—and of civil engineering; and the supply of protective boots and helmets were not eligible for zero-rating and should be charged to a positive rate of tax. However, it ruled that the zero-rating of animal feeding stuffs, seeds or other means of propagation of plants used for human and animal foodstuffs, and live animals which yielded food for human consumption was within the terms of the *Directive*. *EC Commission v United Kingdom (No 2)*, ECJ Case 416/85; [1988] STC 456; [1988] ECR 3127. (*Note.* The UK introduced the required changes in *FA 1989*, which restricted the scope of *VATA 1983, Sch 5*. See *VATA 1994, Sch 8* for the current zero-rating provisions.)

Article 28(2) of EC Sixth Directive

[22.506] In 1989 France enacted legislation whereby the rate of VAT on certain medicinal products (those reimbursable under the social security system) was reduced to 2.1%. Subsequently the EC Commission applied to the ECJ for a ruling that this contravened the *EC Sixth Directive*. The ECJ rejected the application, and held that the rate in question was authorised by *Article 28(2)* of the *Directive*. The rate had been in force on 1 January 1991 and was in accordance with Community law, as required by *Article 28(2)(a)*. On the evidence, the rate did not infringe the principle of fiscal neutrality, and had been introduced 'for clearly defined social reasons and for the benefit of the final consumer'. *EC Commission v French Republic*, ECJ Case C-481/98; [2001] STC 919.

[22.507] A company which operated a caravan site sold a number of caravans. Initially it accepted that part of the consideration for the caravans should be attributed to standard-rated removable contents, as laid down in

Notice 701/20/96. Subsequently it submitted a repayment claim on the basis that the effect of the ECJ decision in *Card Protection Plan*, 22.324 above, was that it was making a single zero-rated supply. Customs rejected the claim and the tribunal dismissed the company's appeal, holding that 'the fact that a single supply is made does not, of itself, preclude the different tax treatment of various components of the consideration'. On the evidence, the 'consideration attributable to those items supplied which fall within (*VATA 1994, Sch 8, Group 9, Note (a)*) is taxable at the standard rate'. The company appealed to the CA, which referred the case to the ECJ for a ruling on the interpretation of *Article 28(2)(a)* of the *EC Sixth Directive*. The ECJ upheld the tribunal decision, holding that 'the fact that specific goods are counted as a single supply', including both a principal item which was 'subject to an exemption with refund of the tax paid within the meaning of *Article 28(2)(a)* of the *Sixth Directive*' and items which were excluded from the scope of that exemption, 'does not prevent the Member State concerned from levying VAT at the standard rate on the supply of those excluded items.' *Talacre Beach Caravan Sales Ltd v C & E Commrs*, ECJ Case C-251/05; [2006] STC 1671.

[22.508] See also *Marks & Spencer plc v C & E Commrs (No 5)*, 22.56 above.

Article 28(2) and Annex F2—definition of 'liberal professions'

[22.509] Under the transitional provisions of *Article 28(2)(e)* of the *EC Sixth Directive*, Luxembourg was authorised to apply a reduced rate of VAT to certain supplies of goods and supplies, including the 'liberal professions'. A woman who acted as a managing agent of a number of buildings claimed that she was entitled to be taxed at this reduced rate of 12%, rather than at the standard Luxembourg rate of 15%. The tax authority rejected her claim and she appealed. The case was referred to the ECJ for guidance on the definition of 'liberal professions' (see *Annex F2* of the *Sixth Directive*). The ECJ held that it was for each Member State to determine and define the transactions which qualified for a reduced rate under *Article 28(2)(e)*. The 'liberal professions' referred to in *Annex F2* were 'activities which involve a marked intellectual character, require a high-level qualification and are usually subject to clear and strict professional regulation. In the exercise of such an activity, the personal element is of special importance and such exercise always involves a large measure of independence in the accomplishment of the professional activities.' *Adam v Administration de l'enregistrement et des domaines*, ECJ Case C-267/99; [2003] BTC 5240.

[22.510] See also *Mohammed*, 62.500 SUPPLY.

Article 28(3) of EC Sixth Directive

[22.511] A company contracted to purchase some land. It obtained planning permission to build on the land, and sold the land at a profit. It reclaimed input tax on the purchase of the land. The Commissioners issued an assessment to recover the tax, since the land was exempt from VAT under what is now *VATA 1994, Sch 9, Group 1, Item 1*. The company appealed, contending that the relevant provisions of *VATA* were inconsistent with *Article 13B(h)* of the *EC Sixth Directive*, since the land in question was 'building land' and *Article 13B(h)* provided for the exemption of land 'other than building land'. The tribunal found that the land was 'building land', and referred the ECJ for a ruling on whether the relevant provisions of *VATA*, which exempted the supply of 'building land', were authorised by the transitional provisions of *Article 28(3)(b)* of the *Directive*. The ECJ held that a Member State was entitled to exempt the supply of building land under *Article 28(3)(b)* of the *EC Sixth Directive*, even though there had been some changes to the relevant exemption provisions since the adoption of the *Directive*. The decision in *EC Commission v Federal Republic of Germany*, **22.486** above, was distinguished. The ECJ observed that whilst *Article 28(3)(b)* 'precludes the introduction of new exemptions or the extension of the scope of existing exemptions following the entry of the *Sixth Directive*, it does not prevent a reduction of those exemptions, since their abolition constitutes the objective pursued by *Article 28(4)* of the *Sixth Directive*'. *Norbury Developments Ltd v C & E Commrs*, ECJ Case C-136/97; [1999] STC 511; [1999] All ER (EC) 436.

[22.512] In a Belgian case, a company supplied international coach transport, which was taxed at 6%. It appealed to the ECJ, contending that it was inequitable for Belgium to treat international air transport as exempt from VAT but to charge VAT on international coach transport. The ECJ rejected this contention, holding that the effect of *Article 28(3)(b)* of the *EC Sixth Directive* was that Member States were entitled to exempt international air transport. The ECJ observed that 'it is for the Community legislature to establish the definitive Community system of exemptions from VAT and thereby to bring about the progressive harmonisation of national VAT laws'. The Community principle of equal treatment did not preclude national legislation 'which on the one hand, in accordance with *Article 28(3)(b)* of the *Sixth Directive*, continues to exempt international passenger transport by air, and on the other hand taxes international passenger transport by coach'. *Idéal Tourisme SA v Belgium*, ECJ Case C-36/99; [2001] STC 1386.

Article 28a(1)(b)—transitional arrangements for means of transport

[22.513] See *Patterson*, **23.25** EUROPEAN COMMUNITY: SINGLE MARKET.

Article 28a(5)(b)—transfer of own goods between Member States

[22.514] See *Centrax Ltd*, **23.33** EUROPEAN COMMUNITY: SINGLE MARKET.

Article 28b of EC Sixth Directive—place of transactions

[22.515] A broker, who lived in the Netherlands, arranged for two yachts, located in France, to be sold by French vendors to Netherlands purchasers. He did not account for VAT on his commission. The Netherlands tax authority sought to charge VAT and he appealed, contending that the place of supply was in France. The case was referred to the ECJ for a ruling on the interpretation of *Article 28b* of the *EC Sixth Directive*. The ECJ held that the supplies were within *Article 28b(E)*, which included supplies to private individuals as well as supplies to taxable persons (with the result that the place of supply was in France, where the yachts were located). *Staatssecretaris van Financiën v Lipjes*, ECJ Case C-68/03; [2004] STC 1592.

[22.516] See also *Staatssecretaris van Financiën v X*, **22.411** above, and *Richmond Cars Ltd*, **44.69** MOTOR CARS.

Article 28c—transitional arrangements for exemptions

[22.517] An Austrian company (K) acquired quantities of metals from suppliers in Italy and the Netherlands, and sold them to another Austrian company (E). K did not itself take delivery of the metals, but instructed its suppliers to deliver the metals directly to E, or to Austrian customers to whom E had resold the metals. K charged Austrian VAT on its sales of the metals to E. E reclaimed this as input tax. The tax authority rejected the claims on the grounds that K should not have charged Austrian VAT on its supplies to E, since the relevant transactions had taken place in Italy or the Netherlands. E appealed, contending that K had supplied the metals in Austria. The case was referred to the ECJ, which held that the supplies to K were exempted under *Article 28c* of the *Sixth Directive*, but that the supplies from K to E took place in Austria. The ECJ ruled that 'where two successive supplies of the same goods, effected for consideration between taxable persons acting as such, gives rise to a single intra-Community dispatch or a single intra-Community transport of those goods, that dispatch or transport can be ascribed to only one of the two supplies, which alone will be exempted from tax under the first paragraph of *Article 28c(A)(a)*'. The ECJ also ruled that 'only the place of the supply which gives rise to dispatch or intra-Community transport of goods is determined in accordance with *Article 8(1)(a)* of the *Sixth Directive*'. That place was 'deemed to be in the Member State of the departure of that dispatch or transport. The place of the other supply is determined in accordance with *Article 8(1)(b)* of that directive; that place is deemed to be either in the Member State of departure or in the Member State of arrival of that dispatch or transport, according to whether that supply is the first or the second of the two successive supplies.' *EMAG Handel Eder OHG v Finanzlandesdirektion für Kärnten*, ECJ Case C-245/04; [2007] STC 1461.

[22.518] A number of companies reclaimed input tax on the basis that they had supplied quantities of mobile telephones to a Spanish company, such supplies being zero-rated by *VATA 1994, s 30(8)*. The Commissioners discovered that the CMR documents supplied by the Spanish company contained false information, and formed the opinion that the telephones had never left the UK. They therefore issued assessments to recover the input tax which the companies had claimed. The companies applied for judicial review, contending *inter alia* that *VATA 1994, s 30* did not fully implement the mandatory exemption provided by *Article 28c* of the *EC Sixth Directive*, and that they had not known that the telephones had not left the UK. Moses J reviewed the evidence in detail and found that 'the Commissioners were entitled to conclude that the mobile phones had not been removed from the United Kingdom'. He directed that the case should be referred to the ECJ for a ruling as to whether goods must actually be removed from the Member State of origin to the Member State of destination before the supplier could treat them as qualifying for exemption under *Article 28c*. The ECJ held that *Article 28c(A)(a)* was 'to be interpreted as meaning that the intra-Community acquisition of goods is effected and the exemption of the intra-Community supply of goods becomes applicable only when the right to dispose of the goods as owner has been transferred to the purchaser and the supplier establishes that those goods have been dispatched or transported to another Member State and that, as a result of that dispatch or that transport, they have physically left the territory of the Member State of supply'. The tax authorities could not demand tax from a supplier who had acted in good faith and was not involved in tax evasion 'provided that the supplier took every reasonable measure in his power to ensure that the intra-Community supply he was effecting did not lead to his participation in such evasion. The fact that the purchaser made a declaration concerning intra-Community acquisition, such as that in question in the main proceedings, to the tax authorities of the Member State of destination may constitute additional evidence tending to establish that the goods have actually left the territory of the Member State of supply, but it does not constitute conclusive proof for the purposes of the exemption from value added tax of an intra-Community supply.' *Teleos plc & Others v C & E Commrs*, ECJ Case C-409/04; [2008] STC 706. (*Notes*. (1) For HMRC's practice following this decision, see VAT Information Sheet 13/2007, issued on 28 September 2007, and HMRC Brief 61/07, issued on 10 October 2007. (2) For another issue in this case, see **36.654** INPUT TAX.)

[22.519] In a German case, the tax authority accepted that a German trader (C) had sold some cars to a Belgian dealer, but refused to treat the supply as exempt on the grounds that C had 'failed to produce in good time the accounting evidence required under national law'. C appealed, and the case was referred to the ECJ, which held that *Article 28c(A)(a)* 'must be interpreted as precluding the refusal by the tax authority of a Member State to allow an intra-Community supply – which actually took place – to be exempt from value added tax solely on the ground that the evidence of such a supply was not produced in good time. When examining the right of exemption from value added tax in relation to such a supply, the referring court should take into account the fact that the taxable person initially knowingly concealed the fact that an intra-Community supply had occurred only if there is a risk of a loss in tax revenues and that risk has not been wholly eliminated by the taxable person in question.' *A Collée v Finanzamt Limburg an der Lahn*, ECJ Case C-146/05; [2008] STC 757.

[22.520] In another German case, a Portuguese citizen (R) managed a German company trading in luxury cars. From 2002, R manipulated the company's accounts by drafting false invoices from fictitious purchasers to allow his Portuguese distributors to commit VAT fraud, by concealing the names of their final purchasers. All of the transactions were declared in Germany as intra-Community supplies and therefore as exempt from VAT in Germany. The fictitious purchasers were all registered in Portugal for VAT; some had consented to the use of their name and VAT registration number while others were unaware of it. R was convicted of tax evasion and sentenced to three years' imprisonment. He appealed, contending that there had been a genuine intra-Community supply and that the transactions were exempt from VAT. The German court referred the case to the ECJ for a ruling on whether exemption could be denied where there had been a physical delivery of goods but where it was established that the vendor knew that he had participated in a transaction involving VAT fraud, or had taken steps to conceal the true identity of the purchaser to enable him or a third party to commit VAT fraud. The ECJ rejected R's contentions, holding that where an intra-Community supply of goods had actually taken place, but when, at the time of supply, the supplier had concealed the identity of the true purchaser in order to enable the latter to evade payment of VAT, the Member State of departure could 'refuse to allow an exemption in respect of that transaction'. *R v Generalbundesanwalt beim Bundesgerichtshof*, ECJ Case C-285/09; [2011] STC 138.

[22.521] In a Netherlands case, the ECJ held that a supplier who claimed exemption must furnish the proof that the conditions for exemption are fulfilled. The ECJ also held that *Article 28c(A)(a)* 'does not require the tax authorities of the Member State of dispatch or transport on an intra-Community supply of goods to request information from the authorities of the destination Member State alleged by the supplier'. *Twoh International BV v Staatssecretaris van Financien*, ECJ Case C-184/05; [2008] STC 740.

[22.522] A Netherlands company (E) sold quantities of tyres to two Belgian companies (M and V), which resold them to another Belgian company (B). M and V collected the tyres from E's warehouse in the Netherlands and delivered them directly to B. E did not account for VAT on its sales, treating them as exempt under *Article 28c(A)* of the *EC Sixth Directive*. The Netherlands tax authority issued assessments on E, charging tax on the basis that the supplies failed to qualify for exemption. E appealed, and the case was referred to the ECJ for a ruling on the interpretation of *Article 28c*. The ECJ held that 'when goods are the subject of two successive supplies between different taxable persons acting as such, but of a single intra-Community transport, the determination of the transaction to which that transport should be ascribed' (i.e. the supply by E or the supplies by M and V) 'must be conducted in the light of an overall assessment of all the circumstances of the case in order to establish which of those two supplies fulfils all the conditions relating to an intra-Community supply'. In the cases in question, where M and V had obtained the right to dispose of the goods as owner in the Netherlands, had expressed their intention to transport the goods to Belgium, and had produced their Belgian VAT numbers, 'the intra-Community transport should be ascribed to the first supply, on condition that the right to dispose of the goods as owner has been transferred to the second person acquiring the goods in the Member State of destination of the intra-Community transport'. It was for the Netherlands court to establish whether that condition had been fulfilled. *Euro Tyre Holding BV v Staatssecretaris van Financiën*, ECJ Case C-430/09; [2011] STC 798.

[22.523] See also *FEA Briggs Ltd*, **23.1** EUROPEAN COMMUNITY: SINGLE MARKET; *JP Commodities Ltd*, **23.4** EUROPEAN COMMUNITY: SINGLE MARKET; *Appleyard Vehicle Contracts Ltd*, **23.21** EUROPEAN COMMUNITY: SINGLE MARKET; *Centrax Ltd*, **23.33** EUROPEAN COMMUNITY: SINGLE MARKET; *Starmill UK Ltd*, **23.35** EUROPEAN COMMUNITY: SINGLE MARKET, and *Atlantic Electronics Ltd*, **23.36** EUROPEAN COMMUNITY: SINGLE MARKET.

Article 28k of EC Sixth Directive

[22.524] A group of companies (E) which operated the Channel Tunnel terminals brought proceedings before the French courts challenging the validity of *Article 28k* of the *EC Directive* (and the similar *Directive* relating to excise duty). The ECJ held that the validity of provisions in Directives could be challenged before a national court, even though the person mounting the challenge had not brought an action for annulment of the relevant provisions under what is now *Article 230EC* of the *EC Treaty*, but held that the applicant had not shown that the provisions of *Article 28k* were invalid. *Eurotunnel SA & Others v SeaFrance*, ECJ Case C-408/95; [1998] BTC 5200.

Value Added Tax Committee (Article 29)

Article 17(7) of EC Sixth Directive—interaction with Article 29

[22.525] See *Metropol Treuhand WirtschaftstreuhandgmbH v Finanzlandesdirektion für Steinmark*, **22.433** above, and *Stradasfalti Srl v Agenzia delle Entrate Ufficio di Trento*, **22.434** above.

Taxes other than turnover taxes (Article 33)

Tax on gaming machines—whether permissible under Article 33

[22.526] In a French case, a trader appealed against an assessment to a tax imposed on the operation of automatic gaming machines, contending that the tax was a tax on turnover and was not permissible under *Article 33* of the *EC Sixth Directive*. The ECJ rejected this contention, holding that, since the tax was assessed solely on the basis of the machine being placed 'at the disposal of the public, without in fact taking account of the revenue which could be generated thereby', it could not be regarded as a turnover tax. The tax was also not incompatible with what is now *Article 90EC* of the *EC Treaty*. *Bergandi v Directeur Général des Impôts*, ECJ Case 252/86; [1988] ECR 1343; [1991] STC 529; [1989] 2 CMLR 933.

Danish employment levy—whether permissible under Article 33

[22.527] In a Danish case, the ECJ held that an 'employment levy', which had been introduced with effect from 1988, was a turnover tax and was not permissible under *Article 33* of the *EC Sixth Directive*. *Dansk Denkavit ApS & Others v Skatteministeriet*, ECJ Case C-200/90; [1992] 1 ECR 2217; [1994] STC 482; [1994] 2 CMLR 377. (*Note.* For another issue in this case, see **22.41** above.)

Austrian tax on tourism—whether permissible under Article 33

[22.528] Three Austrian states imposed charges on all traders in their territory which had an economic interest in tourism. Several traders appealed, contending that the charges were not permissible under *Article 33* of the *EC Sixth Directive*. The ECJ rejected this contention, holding that the charges were not precluded by the *Directive*. The charges were 'not passed on to the final consumer in a manner characteristic of VAT' and were 'not levied on commercial transactions in a manner comparable to VAT'. *Pelzl & Others v Steiermärkische Landesregierung & Others*, ECJ Cases C-338/97, C-344/97 & C-390/97; 8 June 1999 unreported.

Higher rate of IPT—whether permissible under Article 33

[22.529] A number of UK companies applied for a declaration that the higher rate of insurance premium tax contravened *Article 33* of the *EC Sixth Directive*. The case was referred to the ECJ, which rejected the companies' contentions, holding that the tax was compatible with *Article 33*, was not precluded by *Article 13(B)(a)* of the *Directive*, and did not require a derogation under *Article 27* of the *Directive*. *GIL Insurance Ltd v C & E Commrs (and related appeals)*, ECJ Case C-308/01; [2004] STC 961.

Article 33—other cases

[22.530] There have been a number of other cases concerning *Article 33* of the *EC Sixth Directive*, which turn on the particular facts of the tax in question. In the interests of space, such cases are not summarised individually in this book.

EC Eighth VAT Directive (79/1072/EEC)

Article 1 of Eighth Directive

[22.531] The Italian tax authorities required taxable persons established in other Member States, but with a fixed establishment in Italy, to obtain VAT refunds through the procedure laid down by the *EC Eighth Directive*, rather than through the normal deduction procedure laid down by the *Sixth Directive*. The EC Commission applied to the ECJ for a ruling that this contravened *Article 1* of the *Eighth Directive*, contending that this provided that 'a foreign taxpayer who has a fixed establishment in Italy and who engages in commercial transactions in Italy from that establishment, must be able to use the normal deduction mechanism provided for in the *Sixth Directive*, even if some commercial transactions are effected directly from the place in which that person is principally established'. The ECJ accepted the Commission's contentions and granted a ruling accordingly. *EC Commission v Italian Republic*, ECJ Case C-244/08; 16 July 2009 unreported.

Article 2 of Eighth Directive

[22.532] An Italian bank, which was partly exempt, made a repayment claim under the *Eighth Directive* for input tax incurred in France. The French authorities rejected the claim and the case was referred to the ECJ, which held that *Article 2* of the *Eighth Directive* must be interpreted as granting taxable persons which were partly exempt a right to 'partial refund'. By virtue of *Article 5*, the refundable amount should be calculated 'first, by determining which transactions give rise to a right to deduction in the Member State of establishment and, second, by taking account solely of the transactions which would also give rise a right of deduction in the Member State of refund if they were carried out there and of the expenses giving rise to a right to deduction in the latter State'. *Ministre du Budget v Société Monte Dei Paschi Di Siena*, ECJ Case C-136/99; [2001] STC 1029.

[22.533] The EC Commission brought an action against France, seeking a declaration that, by refusing VAT to taxable persons not established in France, in cases where those taxable persons had subcontracted part of their work to a taxable person established in France, that country had failed to fulfil its obligations under *Article 2* of the *Eighth Directive*. The ECJ granted the application only in relation to waste disposal services. The ECJ declared that 'by refusing to refund to taxable persons established in a Member State other than the French Republic, who are holders of a main contract for a composite supply of services relating to waste disposal, the value added tax which they have been required to pay to the French State in cases where they have subcontracted part of the work covered by such a contract to a taxable person established in France, the French Republic has failed to fulfil its obligations'. *EC Commission v French Republic*, ECJ Case C-429/97; [2001] STC 156.

[22.534] A UK insurance company (P) transferred its general insurance business to a Swiss insurance company (W) which had a business establishment in the EU, but did not itself intend to carry on insurance business in the UK, and which in turn transferred the business to an associated Bermuda company. W claimed a refund of tax under *Article 2* of the *EC Eighth Directive*. Customs rejected the claim, on the basis that the transaction constituted the transfer of a going concern, and that the effect of *Article 9(2)* of the *EC Sixth Directive* was that the place of supply of the goodwill was outside the UK. W appealed. The tribunal allowed the appeal, holding that the transaction did not constitute the transfer of a going concern under the *VAT (Special Provisions) Order*, since W 'had no intention of carrying on the same general insurance business as (P) had done'. Furthermore, the supply did not fall within *Article 9(2)(e)* of the *Sixth Directive*, so that the place of supply was where P was established, which was in the UK. The tribunal observed that those responsible for drafting the *Eighth Directive* had 'clearly not considered the possibility, which arises in this appeal, that there are exempt supplies treated as made in the State but that input tax incurred in that State is attributable to supplies outside the State on which input tax is fully recoverable'. The tribunal held that the fact that W was making exempt supplies of reinsurance services did not prevent it from qualifying for a refund under the *Eighth Directive*, which had direct effect in the UK. *Winterthur Swiss Insurance Company*, [2006] VATDR 375 (VTD 19411).

[22.535] An Italian company provided advertising and marketing services to a German company (R), and charged VAT. R paid the VAT, but considered that it had been charged in error because the effect of *Article 9(2)(e)* of the *Sixth Directive* was the supplies should be deemed to have taken place in Germany. R applied to the Italian tax authority for a refund. The tax authority rejected the claim, and R appealed. The case was referred to the ECJ, which held that *Articles 2* and *5* of the *EC Eighth Directive* 'must be interpreted as meaning that value added tax that is not due and has been invoiced in error to the beneficiary of the services and paid to the tax authorities of the Member State where those services were supplied, is not refundable under those provisions'. The principles of neutrality, effectiveness and non-discrimination 'do not preclude national legislation, such as that at issue in the main proceedings, according to which only the supplier may seek reimbursement of the sums unduly paid as value added tax to the tax authorities and the recipient of the services may bring a civil law action against that supplier for recovery of the sums paid but not due.' *Reemtsma Cigarettenfabriken GmbH v Ministero delle Finanze*, ECJ Case C-35/05; [2008] STC 3448.

[22.536] See also *Cookies World Vertriebsgesellschaft mbH iL v Finanzlandesdirektion für Tirol*, **22.203** above; *Rudi Heger GmbH v Finanzamt Graz-Stadt*, **22.206** above, and *Ministre de l'Économie, des Finances et de l'Industrie v Gillan Beach Ltd*, **22.216** above.

Article 3 of Eighth Directive

[22.537] A lawyer established in Belgium hired a car, to be used for the purposes of his profession, from a Netherlands company. Lawyers' services were exempt from VAT in Belgium under the transitional provisions of *Article 28* of the *Sixth Directive*. The lawyer applied to the Netherlands tax authority for a refund of the VAT charged to him on the hire of the car. The Netherlands authority rejected the claim, as the lawyer did not have a certificate of the type required by *Article 3* of the *Eighth Directive*. (Since the lawyer's services were exempt in Belgium, the Belgian authorities had not issued him with such a certificate.) The lawyer appealed and the case was referred to the ECJ, which ruled that the lawyer was not entitled to a refund. Since the lawyer benefited from an exemption granted by the Belgian authorities, he was not entitled to a certificate of the type required by *Article 3* of the *Eighth Directive*. He was therefore not entitled to a refund of VAT charged on services supplied to him in another Member State in which he was not established. *Debouche v Inspecteur der Invoerrechten en Accijnzen Rijswijk*, ECJ Case C-302/93; [1996] STC 1406; [1996] 1 ECR 4495; [1997] 2 CMLR 511.

[22.538] In a German case, the ECJ held that applications for a refund under *Article 3(a)* of the *Eighth Directive* 'must, in principle, be accompanied by the original invoices or import documents establishing the amount of VAT in respect of which is a refund is sought'. However, Member States could provide for a duplicate invoice or import document to be used as proof of entitlement to a refund, 'provided that the transaction which led to the refund occurred and there is no risk of further applications for a refund'. *Société Générale des Grandes Sources d'Eaux Minérales Françaises v Bundesamt für Finanzen*, ECJ Case C-361/96; [1998] STC 981.

[22.539] A Swiss company established a subsidiary company (P) with a registered office in Luxembourg. P reclaimed German VAT. The German tax authorities rejected the claims on the grounds that P did not have a business address in Luxembourg. P appealed, and the case was referred to the ECJ for a ruling on the interpretation of *Article 3* of the *Eighth Directive*. the ECJ held that, where Member States had 'doubts as to the economic reality of the establishment' from which an applicant claimed to be operating, they were not precluded 'from verifying that reality by having recourse to the administrative measures made available for that purpose by Community legislation on VAT'. The ECJ also held that 'the place of a company's business is the place where the essential decisions concerning its general management are taken and where the functions of its central administration are exercised'. *Planzer Luxembourg Sàrl v Bundeszentralamt für Steuern*, ECJ Case C-73/06; [2008] STC 1113.

Article 5 of Eighth Directive

[22.540] See *Ministre du Budget v Société Monte Dei Paschi Di Siena*, **22.531** above, and *Reemtsma Cigarettenfabriken GmbH v Ministero delle Finanze*, **22.535** above.

Article 7(1) of Eighth Directive

[22.541] See *Nova Stamps AB*, **23.30** EUROPEAN COMMUNITY: SINGLE MARKET, and *Areva T & D Protection et Controle v HMRC*, **45.5** OVERSEAS TRADERS.

Article 7(4) of Eighth Directive

[22.542] In a Belgian case, the ECJ held that it was contrary to what is now *Article 49EC* of the *EC Treaty* for national rules to provide that taxable persons not established in a Member State, who applied for a refund of VAT but were not reimbursed within the six-month period laid down by *Article 7(4)* of the *Eighth Directive*, were entitled to interest only from such time as notice to pay was served on that Member State, and at a lower rate than that applied to the interest paid to taxable persons established in the territory of that State. *Lease Plan Luxembourg SA v Belgium*, ECJ Case C-390/96; [1998] STC 628. (*Note*. For another issue in this case, see **22.200** above.)

[22.543] See also *Blackqueen Ltd*, **22.65** above.

Annex A to Eighth Directive—interpretation of 'signature'

[22.544] A Netherlands company claimed a refund of German VAT under the *Eighth Directive*. The relevant claim was signed by the company's lawyers, rather than by the company itself. The tax authority rejected the claim on the grounds that the application did not 'bear the trader's own signature', as required by the relevant German legislation. The company appealed, contending that the effect of *Annex A* of the *EC Eighth Directive* was that a signature by a company's authorised agent should be held to be sufficient. The case was referred to the ECJ, which upheld the company's contentions, holding that the 'signature' of an application for a VAT refund, as referred to in *Annex A* of the *EC Eighth Directive*, was 'a Community law notion which must be interpreted uniformly to the effect that such a refund application need not necessarily be signed by the taxable person in person and that the signature of an agent may be sufficient for those purposes'. *Yaesu Europe BV v Bundeszentralamt für Steuern*, ECJ Case C-433/08; [2010] STC 809.

EC Thirteenth VAT Directive (86/560/EEC)

[22.545] A Czech company reclaimed German input tax which it had incurred in 2002 (before the Czech Republic joined the EC). The tax authority rejected the claim, and the company appealed. The case was referred to the ECJ for a ruling on the interpretation of *Article 2(2)* of the *EC Thirteenth*

VAT Directive. The ECJ held that *Article 2(2)* 'must be interpreted as meaning that the 'third States' referred to in that provision include all third States and that that provision is without prejudice to the ability and the responsibility of the Member States to comply with their obligations under international agreements such as the General Agreement on Trade in Services'. *Řízení Letového Provozu CR sp v Bundesamt für Finanzen,* ECJ Case C-335/05; [2007] STC 1509.

[22.546] The EC Commission formed the opinion that by denying recovery of input tax in respect of certain insurance and financial transactions carried out by taxable persons not established in the EC, the United Kingdom had failed to comply with its obligations under *Article 2(1)* of the *EC Thirteenth VAT Directive.* It therefore took infraction proceedings in the ECJ. The ECJ rejected the Commission's contentions, finding that the UK legislation 'complies with the clear and precise wording of *Article 2(1)* of the *Thirteenth Directive'.* The ECJ ordered the Commission to pay the costs. *EC Commission v United Kingdom (No 7),* ECJ Case C-582/08; [2010] STC 2364.

[22.547] See also *Jack Camp Productions,* **25.7** EXPORTS; *CR Investments SRO,* **45.1** OVERSEAS TRADERS, and *Viscount Reinsurance,* **45.2** OVERSEAS TRADERS.

Miscellaneous

The principle of 'legal certainty'

[22.548] In a French case, the ECJ held that 'rules imposing charges on the taxpayer must be clear and precise so that he may know without ambiguity what are his rights and obligations and may take steps accordingly'. *Administration des Douanes v Société Anonyme Gondrand Freres,* ECJ Case 169/80; [1981] ECR 1931.

[22.549] In a (non-VAT) case which the German government brought against the European Commission, the ECJ held that 'Community legislation must be certain and its application foreseeable by those subject to it. That requirement of legal certainty must be observed all the more strictly in the case of rules liable to entail financial consequences, in order that those concerned may know precisely the extent of the obligations which they impose on them'. *Germany v EC Commission,* ECJ Case C-332/85; [1985] ECR 5143.

[22.550] In the case noted at **22.156** above, the ECJ held that the *Sixth Directive* did not preclude a Netherlands provision whereby the grant of rights over immovable property was not treated as a taxable supply where 'the total consideration plus turnover tax amounts to less than the economic value of those rights'. The housing association sought a further hearing of its appeal, contending that an amendment to the relevant Netherlands legislation contravened the principles of the protection of legitimate expectations and legal certainty. The case was again referred to the ECJ, which held that 'the principles of the protection of legitimate expectations and legal certainty do not preclude a Member State, on an exceptional basis and in order to avoid the large-scale use, during the legislative process, of contrived financial arrangements intended to minimise the burden of value added tax that an amending law is specifically designed to combat, from giving that law retroactive effect when, in circumstances such as those in the main proceedings, economic operators carrying out economic transactions such as those referred to by the law were warned of the impending adoption of that law and of the retroactive effect envisaged in a way that enabled them to understand the consequences of the legislative amendment planned for the transactions they carry out. When that law exempts an economic transaction in respect of immovable property previously subject to value added tax, it may have the effect of revoking a value added tax adjustment made on account of the exercise, when immovable property was used for a transaction regarded at that time as taxable, of a right to deduct value added tax paid in respect of the supply of that immovable property.' *Stichting Goed Wonen v Staatssecretaris van Financiën (No 2)*, ECJ Case C-376/02; [2006] STC 833.

[22.551] See *Barber v Guardian Royal Exchange Assurance Group*, **22.40** above.

The principle of legitimate expectation

[22.552] In the 1986 case of *JP Company Registrations Ltd*, LON/86/302 (VTD 2249), the VAT Tribunal held that, where a company formation agent supplied copies of a company's Memorandum and Articles of Association, the supply qualified for zero-rating. Following this decision, Customs' VAT Manual, para 9.5.4 advised officers that such supplies could be zero-rated. Following the ECJ decision in *Card Protection Plan Ltd v C & E Commrs*, **22.324** above, Customs revised their policy on multiple supplies, but failed to amend VAT Manual, para 9.5.4 until 2005. In the 2006 case of *Company Registrations Online Ltd*, **5.41** BOOKS, ETC., a subsequent VAT Tribunal specifically declined to follow the 1986 decision in *JP Company Registrations Ltd*, and upheld HMRC's contention that, in the light of the decision in *Card Protection Plan Ltd*, there was a single composite supply which failed to qualify for zero-rating. In a subsequent case where the facts were similar, a company contended that, because the relevant section of Customs' VAT Manual had not been altered until 2005, it had a legitimate expectation that its supplies qualified for zero-rating notwithstanding the decisions in *Card Protection Plan Ltd* and *Company Registrations Online Ltd*. The tribunal rejected this contention and dismissed the appeal, applying the principles laid down by Lord Woolf in *R v North & East Devon Health Authority (ex p. Coughlan)*, CA [2001] 1 QB 213. *Hanover Company Services Ltd v HMRC*, [2010] SFTD 1047; [2010] UKFTT 256 (TC), TC00550.

[22.553] A trader (N) registered for VAT in 2009. In his first return, he reclaimed input tax on services which he had received more than six months before the date of registration. HMRC rejected the claim by virtue of *VAT Regulations, reg 111* (see the cases noted at **36.591** *et seq* INPUT TAX and **46.221** *et seq* PARTIAL EXEMPTION). N appealed, contending that he had previously telephoned HMRC's National Advice Service and had been told that that there was a three-year period for reclaiming input tax. The tribunal accepted N's evidence and allowed his appeal. Judge Brooks held that the

National Advice Service had given N a 'legitimate expectation' that he could reclaim the tax in question. *A Noor v HMRC,* [2011] UKFTT 349 (TC), TC01209. (*Note.* HMRC have appealed to the Upper Tribunal against this decision. The Upper Tribunal is scheduled to begin hearing the appeal on 9 December 2011.)

[22.554] See also *CGI Group (Europe) Ltd v HMRC (No 1),* **2.296** APPEALS; *Oxfam v HMRC,* **11.51** CHARITIES; *Belgocodex SA v Belgium,* **22.380** above; *Grundstückgemeinschaft Schloßstraße GbR v Finanzamt Paderborn,* **22.398** above; *Gemeente Leusden v Staatssecretaris van Financien,* **22.457** above, and *Finanzamt Sulingen v Sudholz,* **22.502** above.

The principle of res judicata

[22.555] In an Italian case, a limited company (O) transferred the administration of a sports complex to a non-profit-making body in December 1985. The tax authority subsequently formed the opinion that this was designed to avoid VAT and was an 'abusive practice'. They issued assessments on O for 1988 to 1991. O appealed, contending that the effect of a previous court decision relating to 1987 was that the transfer was effective for VAT purposes. The case was referred to the ECJ for a ruling on the application of the '*res judicata*' principle, as laid down in Italian law. The ECJ rejected the company's contentions, holding that 'if the principle of *res judicata* were to be applied in that manner, the effect would be that, if ever the judicial decision that had become final were based on an interpretation of the Community rules concerning abusive practice in the field of VAT which was at odds with Community law, those rules would continue to be misapplied for each new tax year, without it being possible to rectify the interpretation. In those circumstances, it must be held that such extensive obstacles to the effective application of the Community rules on VAT cannot reasonably be regarded as justified in the interests of legal certainty and must therefore be considered to be contrary to the principle of effectiveness.' Community law precluded the application of a national provision 'in a VAT dispute relating to a tax year for which no final judicial decision has yet been delivered, to the extent that it would prevent the national court seised of that dispute from taking into consideration the rules of Community law concerning abusive practice in the field of VAT'. *Amministrazione dell'Economia e delle Finanze v Fallimento Olimpiclub Srl,* ECJ Case C-2/08; 3 September 2009 unreported.

Recovery of charges levied in breach of Community law

[22.556] In an Italian case, the ECJ held that the Italian government was not entitled to withhold repayment of charges which had been levied contrary to Community law. *Amministrazione delle Finanze dello Stato v San Giorgio SpA,* ECJ Case C-199/82; [1983] ECR 3513; [1985] 2 CMLR 658.

[22.557] The decision in *Amministrazione delle Finanze dello Stato v San Giorgio SpA,* **22.556** above, was applied in a subsequent Italian case in which the ECJ held that Community law precluded a Member State from making repayment of taxes, which had been levied contrary to Community law, 'subject to a condition, such as the requirement that such duties or taxes have not been passed on to third parties, which the plaintiff must show he has satisfied'. *Dilexport Srl v Amministrazione delle Finanze dello Stato*, ECJ Case C-343/96; [2000] All ER (EC) 600.

Claim to repayment of VAT levied in breach of EC law

[22.558] In a case where the ECJ held that a Greek law restricting the reclaim of input tax was incompatible with the *EC Sixth Directive*, the appellant company claimed that it should be refunded the tax which it had incurred since 1987 (when the relevant law came into force). The ECJ accepted the company's claim, holding that 'a taxable person may claim, with retroactive effect from the date on which the arrangements at issue came into force, a refund of VAT paid without being due'. *BP Supergas Anonimos Etairia Geniki Emporiki-Viomichaniki kai Antiprossopeion v Greece*, ECJ Case C-62/93; [1995] STC 805; [1995] 1 ECR 1883; [1995] All ER (EC) 684.

Repayment claim refused on grounds of 'unjust enrichment'

[22.559] In 1992 the ECJ issued a ruling that certain dock dues which had been imposed in the French overseas departments had been in breach of Community law. The relevant importers claimed repayment of the charges in question, but the French authorities rejected the claim on the grounds that, since the charges had been passed on to the purchasers of the goods sold, repayment to the importers would lead to 'unjust enrichment'. The case was referred to the ECJ, which ruled that a Member State could resist repayment to traders of charges levied in breach of Community law only where it was established that the charge had been borne in its entirety by another person and that reimbursement of the trader would constitute unjust enrichment. It was for the national courts to determine, in the light of the facts in each case, whether those conditions had been satisfied. Furthermore, where an illegally levied charge had been passed on to the purchaser, it was for the national courts to determine whether its illegal levying had caused damage to the trader to the extent that enrichment would not be 'unjust'. *Société Comateb & Others v Directeur Général des Douanes et droits indirects*, ECJ Case C-192/95; [1997] STC 1006; [1997] 1 ECR 165; [1997] 2 CMLR 649.

[22.560] In 1988 Denmark introduced a business tax known as the 'arbejdsmarkedsbidrag'. The ECJ subsequently ruled that this was illegal (see *Dansk Denkavit v Skatteministeriet*, 22.527 above), and several companies claimed reimbursement. The Danish authorities rejected the claims on the grounds that repayment would lead to 'unjust enrichment'. Four companies appealed, and the case was referred to the ECJ, which held that 'the rules of European Union law on recovery of sums wrongly paid must be interpreted to the effect that recovery of sums wrongly paid can give rise to unjust enrichment only when the amounts wrongly paid by a taxpayer under a tax levied in a Member State in breach of European Union law have been passed on direct to the purchaser. Consequently, European Union law precludes a Member State from refusing reimbursement of a tax wrongfully levied on the ground that the amounts wrongly paid by the taxpayer have been set off by a saving made as a result of the concomitant abolition of other levies, since such a set-off cannot be regarded, from the point of view of European Union law, as an unjust enrichment as regards that tax.' *Lady & Kid A/S v Skatteministeriet (and related appeals)*, ECJ Case C-398/01; 6 September 2011 unreported.

Validity of VAT 'amnesty'

[22.561] See *EC Commission v Italian Republic (No 7)*, **22.469** above.

Rounding of amounts in VAT calculation

[22.562] In a Netherlands case, the ECJ held that 'in the absence of specific Community legislation, it is for Member States to decide on the rules and methods of rounding amounts of the tax on added value, but those States must, when making that decision, observe the principles under-pinning the common system of that tax, in particular the principles of fiscal neutrality and proportionality. Community law, as it now stands, entails no specific obligation for Member States to permit taxable persons to round down per item the amount of the tax on added value.' *Fiscale eenheid Koninklijke Ahold NV v Staatssecretaris van Financiën*, ECJ Case C-484/06; [2009] STC 45.

[22.563] A company which operated a large number of public houses operated a policy of 'rounding down' its VAT liability. Customs issued a ruling that it was required to account for VAT in accordance with their published guidelines, as approved by the tribunal in *Topps Tiles plc*, **40.83** INVOICES AND CREDIT NOTES. The company appealed, and the tribunal referred the case to the ECJ. The ECJ rejected the company's contentions, holding that 'Commu-nity law, as it currently stands, contains no specific requirement concerning the method of rounding amounts of value added tax. In the absence of spe-cific Community legislation, it is for Member States to decide on the rules and methods for rounding amounts of value added tax, although those States must, when so deciding, observe the principles underpinning the common system of that tax, particularly the principles of fiscal neutrality and proportionality. In particular, Community law, first, does not preclude the application of a national rule which requires an amount of value added tax to be rounded up whenever the fraction of the smallest unit of currency concerned is at or above 0.50, and, second, does not require that taxable persons be allowed to round down any amount of value added tax which includes a fraction of the smallest unit of national currency. In a sale at a price inclusive of value added tax, in the absence of specific Community legislation, each Member State is obliged to determine, within the limits of Community law, in particular in compliance with the principles of fiscal neutrality and proportionality, the level at which the rounding of an amount of value added tax which includes a fraction of the smallest unit of national currency may or must occur. In view of the fact that traders who calculate the price of their sales of goods and services inclusive of value added tax are in a different situation to those effecting that same type of transactions at prices exclusive of value added tax, the former cannot invoke the principle of fiscal neutrality in order to claim the right also to round down, at line level and basket level, the amounts of value added tax due.' *JD Wetherspoon plc v HMRC*, ECJ Case C-302/07; [2009] STC 1022.

Whether interest may be compounded

[22.563A] Several retail companies claimed a repayment of VAT on the basis that commission which they paid to agents should have been treated as a discount. HMRC accepted the claims in principle (while disputing the amounts of the claims), and made repayments with interest under VATA 1994, s 78. The companies took court proceedings in the QB, contending that the effect of the HL decision in *CIR v Sempra Metals Ltd*, HL [2007] STC 1559 was they were entitled to compound interest. The Ch D heard the companies' claims and directed that the case should be referred to the ECJ for guidance on whether VATA 1994, ss 78 and 80 were compatible with European law. (Vos J expressed the view that the statutory regime for the payment of simple interest on overpayments should exclude any other common law remedies for claiming interest under domestic law, that EU law did not require the payment of compound interest, and that even if compound interest were required under EU law, the time for lodging claims was limited to six years from the date of the overpayment. He observed that 'the outcome of the trial, on the assumption that my provisional views are endorsed by the ECJ, would be that the claimants would fail on all their claims for the use value of the overpayments, having been already paid what is due to them under section 78'.) Advocate-General Trstenjak expressed the Opinion that 'a taxable person who has overpaid VAT which was collected by the Member State contrary to the requirements of EU VAT legislation has a right to reimbursement of the VAT collected in breach of EU law and a right to payment of interest on the principal sum to be reimbursed. The question whether the interest on the principal sum to be reimbursed is to be paid on the basis of a system of 'simple interest' or a system of 'compound interest' concerns the detailed rules governing the interest claim stemming from European Union law, which are to be determined by the Member States in accordance with the principles of effectiveness and equivalence. If the referring court should conclude that the detailed rules governing payment of interest on VAT collected in breach of EU law at issue in the main proceedings are less favourable than the detailed rules governing similar domestic interest claims and that there is therefore a breach of the principle of equivalence, it is obliged to interpret and apply the national rules in such a way that interest is paid on the VAT collected in breach of EU law in accordance with the more favourable rules which apply to similar domestic claims.' *Littlewoods Retail Ltd v HMRC (and related applications) (No 2)*, ECJ Case C-591/10; 12 January 2012 unreported. (Note. For a preliminary issue in this case, see 2.213appeals.)

Directive 77/799/EEC—whether applicable to Gibraltar

[22.564] The EC Commission took proceedings against the UK, seeking a declaration that by failing to apply the VAT and excise duty provisions of *Directive 77/799/EEC* to Gibraltar, the UK had failed to fulfil its obligations under the *EC Treaty*. The ECJ granted the declaration, holding that *Directive 77/799/EEC* was not one of 'the acts on the harmonisation of legislation of Member States concerning turnover taxes', within the meaning of *Article 28* of the *Act of Accession 1972*. Accordingly *Directive 77/799/EEC* applied to Gibraltar. *EC Commission v United Kingdom (No 6)*, ECJ Case C-349/03; [2006] STC 1944.

Validity of EC Regulation 1798/2003

[22.565] The EC Commission applied to the ECJ for the annulment of *EC Regulation 1798/2003*, contending that it had not been validly adopted and should be treated as void. The ECJ rejected this contention and dismissed the Commission's application. *EC Commission v EU Council*, ECJ Case C-533/03; [2007] STC 1121.

Application of EC Regulation 1798/2003

[22.566] Customs formed the opinion that a company (S) had engaged in a 'carousel fraud'. They issued an assessment, which S failed to pay, and subsequently took winding-up proceedings. S went into liquidation, and the liquidator began proceedings against S's controlling director and a Spanish company (T) with which S had traded. T defended the proceedings, contending as a preliminary point that the liquidator's use in evidence of material which derived from the Spanish tax authorities contravened *EC Regulation 1798/2003*. The Ch D rejected this contention, holding that in the circumstances of the case 'the factors are overwhelmingly in favour of allowing the claimants to rely upon the evidence provided full disclosure of the material is obtained'. Peter Smith J observed that 'the overwhelming creditor is HMRC for the VAT' and 'the present claim is to recover indirectly the VAT that is due to HMRC which (S) received but failed to account for'. *Silversafe Ltd (in liquidation) v Hood & Others*, Ch D 2006, [2007] STC 871; [2006] EWHC 1849(Ch).

Community Customs Code—import of contact lenses from Jersey

[22.567] See *Dollond & Aitchison Ltd v C & E Commrs*, 35.24 IMPORTS.

23

European Union: Single Market

The cases in this chapter are arranged under the following headings.
Zero-rating of specified exports (VATA 1994, s 30(8))   **23.1**
Miscellaneous   **23.23**

Zero-rating of specified exports (VATA 1994, s 30(8))

Whether customer was taxable person in other Member State

[23.1] A company sold two tables to a customer who claimed to be registered for VAT in the Netherlands. The company did not account for output tax on the sale. The Commissioners issued an assessment charging tax and the company appealed, contending that the sale should be treated as zero-rated. The tribunal dismissed the appeal, holding that the transaction did not qualify for zero-rating because the company had not complied with the conditions of *Notice No 703*, which were authorised by what is now *VATA 1994, s 30(8)* and *VAT Regulations 1995 (SI 1995/2518), reg 134*. The tribunal also observed that the conditions thus imposed were authorised by *Article 28c* of the *EC Sixth Directive. FEA Briggs Ltd*, LON/94/1156A (VTD 12804). (*Note. Notice No 703* has subsequently been replaced by *Notice No 725*.)

[23.2] A similar decision was reached in *Red Giant Promotions Ltd*, MAN/97/647 (VTD 15667). (*Note*. The company appealed to the QB, but was not represented at the hearing of the appeal, which was duly dismissed—QB 17 June 1999 unreported.)

[23.3] A company (D) did not account for tax on the sale of a Ford rally car to a customer in Spain. HMRC issued an assessment charging tax on the sale. D appealed, contending that the customer was a taxable person and that it had complied with the conditions of *VAT Regulations 1995 (SI 1995/2518), reg 134*. The tribunal reviewed the evidence in detail, accepted this contention and allowed the appeal, finding that the car had been sold to a company (V) which was a 'taxable person' in Spain, and observing that the fact that V had attempted 'to conceal that ownership from the Spanish tax authorities' was not conclusive. *Dom Buckley IRS Ltd v HMRC*, [2011] UKFTT 5 (TC), TC00882.

Goods delivered to unregistered purchaser in Belgium

[23.4] A UK company (J) transported some goods to Belgium. The purchaser was not registered for VAT in Belgium. Nevertheless J treated the supply as zero-rated, and reclaimed input tax without accounting for output tax. When HMRC discovered this, they issued a ruling that J was required to account for output tax on the supplies. J appealed, contending that the conditions of

Notice No 725 were invalid and that because its customer had a registered address in Gibraltar, it should be entitled to treat the supplies as zero-rated. The tribunal rejected these contentions and dismissed the appeal, and the Ch D upheld this decision. Briggs J held that the conditions laid down by *Notice No 725* were authorised by *Article 28c* of the *EC Sixth Directive. JP Commodities Ltd v HMRC*, Ch D 2007, [2008] STC 816; [2007] EWHC 2474 (Ch).

Goods sold to deregistered Spanish purchaser

[23.5] A UK company (C) sold some goods to a Spanish trader, which had previously been registered for VAT, but had been deregistered before the supplies in question. C treated the supplies as zero-rated, and Customs issued an assessment charging tax on them. C appealed, contending that it had complied with *Notice No 725, para 3.7*, which stated that a trader would not be required to account for output tax where it had 'taken all reasonable steps' to ensure that its customer was registered for VAT. The tribunal reviewed the evidence in detail, upheld the assessment and dismissed C's appeal, observing that 'there is much which gives rise to concern about the legitimacy of the transactions'. C's managing director had failed 'to make diligent and timely enquiries' and his conduct had been 'casual and superficial'. Accordingly, the conditions of *VATA 1994, s 30(8)* and *VAT Regulations (SI 1995/2518), reg 134* were not satisfied. *Choudhary Trading Co Ltd*, MAN/06/436 (VTD 20251).

[23.6] Similar decisions were reached in *Maine Distribution Ltd (Nos 1 & 2)*, MAN/06/611 (VTD 20284, VTD 20823).

Goods sold to deregistered Irish purchaser

[23.7] In 2002 a Northern Ireland company (D) sold five vehicles to a Republic of Ireland company (J), which had previously been registered for VAT, but had been deregistered in 1996. D treated the supplies as zero-rated, and Customs issued an assessment charging tax on them. D appealed, contending that it had 'taken all reasonable steps' to ensure that J was registered for VAT. The tribunal rejected this contention and dismissed the appeal, finding that although D checked some of its customers' VAT numbers on an annual basis, it had not checked J's number since before April 1996. Accordingly D had not 'taken all reasonable steps' to ensure that J was registered for VAT in the Republic of Ireland. *Dennison Commercials Ltd*, LON/05/423 (VTD 20334).

Goods sold to deregistered Polish purchaser

[23.8] A UK company (L) sold a machine to a Polish company, and did not account for tax on the sale. HMRC discovered that the purchaser had been deregistered, and that there was no evidence that the machine had been transported to Poland. They therefore issued an assessment charging tax on the sale. The tribunal upheld the assessment and dismissed L's appeal, finding that there was no 'evidence of what happened to the machine after it left the appellant's yard'. Accordingly the sale failed to qualify for zero-rating. *Littler Machinery Ltd v HMRC*, [2009] UKFTT 131 (TC), TC00099.

Whether goods removed from UK

[23.9] A trader (K) did not account for output tax on the sale of a quantity of clothing. The Commissioners issued an assessment charging tax on the sale, and K appealed, contending that the goods had been sold to a German trader and should be treated as zero-rated under *VATA 1994, s 30*. The tribunal dismissed the appeal, holding that K had failed to comply with the conditions laid down by *Notice No 703*, and that there was no clear evidence that the goods in question had been removed from the UK. *G Kaur*, MAN/94/1407 (VTD 13537).

[23.10] A similar decision was reached in *AR Vig (t/a One by One Fashions)*, MAN/96/137 (VTD 14504). (*Note*. A subsequent appeal against a misdeclaration penalty was also dismissed—see **52.206** PENALTIES: MISDECLARATION.)

[23.11] Similar decisions, applying *dicta* of Lord Denning in *Henry Moss of London Ltd*, **25.1** EXPORTS, were reached in *Ornamental Design plc*, MAN/97/360 (VTD 15364); *SR Talbot (t/a SRT Labels)*, MAN/98/279 (VTD 15774); *North West Cash & Carry Ltd*, MAN/01/377 (VTD 18177) and *Crestar Global Ltd*, EDN/06/68 (VTD 20258).

[23.12] Similar decisions were reached in *R Kumar*, MAN/99/233 (VTD 16893); *MTR & MKR Malik (t/a Attractions)*, MAN/99/917 (VTD 17021); *SCSI-Com Ltd*, MAN/01/551 (VTD 17644); *Best Selling Ltd*, LON/01/556 (VTD 17766) and *3D Micro Ltd*, LON/00/1262 (VTD 18907).

[23.13] A VAT officer formed the opinion that a company had not obtained sufficient evidence, as required by *Notice No 703*, to justify treating a number of supplies as zero-rated. The officer examined a sample of 234 supplies, and ascertained that 80 of these — i.e. 34% of the sample — did not have a certificate of shipment. He therefore issued an assessment charging tax of more than £500,000, on the assumption that 34% of the supplies which the company had treated as zero-rated did not qualify for zero-rating. The company appealed, contending that there was sufficient evidence to show that the goods had been removed from the UK. The tribunal accepted this contention and allowed the company's appeal, holding on the evidence that 'the package of documents provided in each stockist's file, when it contains evidence of payment for identified goods dispatched to a named stockist in the EU, together with the customer's order, any relevant correspondence, the invoice, the "picking list", and the packing list' constituted 'sufficient evidence of removal of the goods in question from the UK for the purposes of *paragraph 8.7 of Notice 703*'. The tribunal held that it was not essential for the company to have produced certificates of shipment since, by virtue of *paragraph 8.7 of Notice 703*, 'the production of certificates of shipment are (*sic*) not the sole requirement for demonstrating removal of goods from the UK to an EU customer'. *Harriet's House Ltd*, LON/99/35 (VTD 16315). (*Note*. *Notice No 703* has subsequently been replaced by *Notice No 725*.)

[23.14] A company (N) reclaimed input tax of more than £1,000,000 in respect of purported transactions in mobile telephones, which it claimed to have sold to a Portuguese customer and sent to an address in the Netherlands. Customs subsequently discovered that the Netherlands address was a domestic property without storage facilities, and that the alleged recipient of the goods had been convicted of VAT fraud in the Netherlands. They formed the opinion that the transport documents (CMRs) had been falsified, and issued an assessment to recover the tax that N had reclaimed. The tribunal reviewed the evidence in detail and dismissed N's appeal, finding that N's evidence was 'vague and inconsistent' and that 'it should have been perfectly plain that the transactions into which it was entering were likely to be dubious, if not more'. Applying the principles laid down by the CJEC in *Teleos plc v C & E Commrs*, **22.518** EUROPEAN COMMUNITY LAW, the tax authorities could not demand tax from a supplier who had acted in good faith and was not involved in tax evasion 'provided that the supplier took every reasonable measure in his power to ensure that the intra-Community supply he was effecting did not lead to his participation in such evasion'. On the evidence, N had not taken 'every reasonable measure to avoid becoming involved in fraudulent transactions', and had not shown that the telephones, in respect of which it had reclaimed input tax, had actually left the UK. The Ch D upheld this decision. Arnold J held that the tribunal had been entitled to find that N had not established that the goods had been removed from the UK. *N2J Ltd v HMRC*, Ch D [2009] STC 2193; [2009] EWHC 1596 (Ch).

[23.15] A similar decision, also applying the principles laid down by the CJEC in *Teleos plc v C & E Commrs*, **22.518** EUROPEAN COMMUNITY LAW, was reached in *Integral Resources (UK) Ltd v HMRC*, [2010] UKFTT 167 (TC), TC00472.

[23.16] A Northern Ireland car dealer failed to account for VAT on the sale of several vehicles. HMRC issued an assessment charging tax on them. The dealer appealed, contending that the sales should be treated as zero-rated since he had sold the vehicles to customers from the Republic of Ireland. The tribunal dismissed the appeal, observing that zero-rating only applied where such vehicles were sold to business customers who were registered for VAT in the Republic. The dealer had failed to produce the evidence required by *Notice No 725*, which was authorised by *VAT Regulations 1995, reg 134*. Furthermore, most of the alleged customers had denied ever receiving the vehicles. *E McNulty v HMRC*, [2009] UKFTT 111 (TC), TC00079.

[23.17] A company (W) claimed substantial repayments of VAT on the basis that it had purchased goods from a registered UK trader and sold them to a Spanish customer. HMRC received information indicating that the goods had never been delivered to Spain. They issued an assessment charging output tax on the basis that W's supplies did not qualify for zero-rating. They subsequently also issued an alternative assessment to recover the input tax which W had claimed. W appealed against both assessments. The tribunal reviewed the evidence in detail and found that 'a proportion of the goods existed but some were not exported' and that W's managing director 'knew or ought to have known something untoward was taking place'. The tribunal allowed W's appeal against the input tax assessment but dismissed its appeal against the output tax assessment, holding that it had been made to the best of the Commissioners' judgment. *Westone Wholesale Ltd v HMRC (No 2)*, [2009] UKFTT 218 (TC), TC00168. (*Note*. For a preliminary issue in this case, see **3.133** ASSESSMENT.)

[23.18] A Northern Ireland trader claimed that he had made 47 zero-rated supplies of goods to a Spanish company. HMRC issued assessments on the basis that the goods had never left the UK and thus did not qualify for zero-rating. The trader appealed, contending that he had complied with the requirements of *VAT Regulations, reg 134*. The tribunal reviewed the evidence in detail and found on the balance of probabilities that the goods in question had 'never reached Spain' and had been 'diverted after they left the appellant's premises'. The tribunal allowed the trader's appeal with regard to the first four of the 47 transactions, finding that with regard to these transactions he had taken 'every precaution reasonably required', applying the principles laid down by the CJEC in *Teleos plc v C & E Commrs*, **22.518** EUROPEAN COMMUNITY LAW. However the tribunal dismissed the appeal with regard to the remaining 43 transactions, finding that the trader 'did not take the necessary precautions reasonably required of the circumstances of that particular transaction' and 'did not hold satisfactory documentation for the overwhelming majority of the supplies made'. *B MacMahon (t/a Irish Cottage Trading Co) v HMRC*, [2009] UKFTT 304 (TC), TC00248.

Sale to unregistered customer in Republic of Ireland

[23.19] In January 1993 a company sold a van to a resident of the Republic of Ireland, and did not account for VAT. The purchaser was not registered for VAT, and the Commissioners issued a ruling that the company was required to account for output tax. The tribunal dismissed the company's appeal. *Somerset Car Sales Ltd*, LON/93/1581 (VTD 11986).

[23.20] The decision in *Somerset Car Sales Ltd*, **23.19** above, was applied in a similar subsequent case in which a company sold three lorries to a resident of the Republic of Ireland, who was not registered for VAT. *T Naughton Ltd*, MAN/99/815 (VTD 16702).

[23.21] A UK company failed to account for VAT on the sale of 256 motor vehicles. Customs issued an assessment charging tax on the sales. The company appealed, contending that the vehicles had been sold to a customer in the Irish Republic. The tribunal reviewed the evidence in detail and dismissed the appeal, finding that the customer's VAT registration had been cancelled in 2001, and that the number given by the customer contained too many digits. Since this could have been ascertained by a simple check, it followed that the UK company had failed to meet the conditions of *VAT Regulations, reg 134* or to take the 'reasonable steps' laid down by *Notice No 725, para 4.11*. The tribunal also held that the conditions laid down by *Notice No 725* were authorised by *Article 28c* of the *EC Sixth Directive*. *Appleyard Vehicle Contracts Ltd*, MAN/06/576 (VTD 20891).

Sales to unregistered customers in Germany

[23.22] A clothing retailer (C) was registered for VAT in the UK. He sometimes travelled to Germany, where he was not registered, and made sales from trade stands at agricultural shows there. Until 2008 he accounted for UK VAT on these sales, but in 2008 he submitted a repayment claim on the basis that he should not have accounted for VAT on his sales in Germany. HMRC rejected his claim and he appealed, contending that he should have treated his sales in Germany as zero-rated. The tribunal rejected this contention and dismissed his appeal. Judge Mitting observed that, when C travelled with his goods to Germany, there was a deemed supply on the removal of the goods from the UK. Since C was only registered for VAT in the UK, this was a standard-rated supply. Accordingly C should have accounted for VAT on the cost price when he removed the goods from the UK, rather than on the sale price when he sold the goods to German customers. *M Cudworth (t/a Cudworth of Norden) v HMRC*, [2011] UKFTT 312 (TC), TC01173.

Miscellaneous

Acquisition of car—application of VATA 1994, s 10

[23.23] A British army officer, who was stationed in Germany, purchased a car in Germany on 6 June 1994, having paid a deposit on 6 May. In September 1994 he was posted to the UK, and he arranged for the car to be transported to the UK on 4 September. The Commissioners charged VAT on the transfer of the car, on the basis that it was a 'new means of transport', so that VAT was chargeable under *VATA 1994, s 10*. The tribunal dismissed the officer's appeal, holding that the car was a 'new means of transport', within the definition in *VATA 1994, s 95(3)*, because less than three months had elapsed since its first entry into service. The fact that the officer had paid a deposit more than three months before the car was transported to the UK was not relevant. *PJI Lane*, LON/95/2071A (VTD 13583). (*Note. VATA 1994, s 95(3)* has subsequently been amended, increasing the relevant period from three months to six months.)

[23.24] In November 1994 a British officer, serving in Germany, purchased a car for the use of his wife. In July 1995, while he was still in Germany, he purchased a Saab car for his own use. In September 1995 he and his wife returned to the UK. The Commissioners issued a ruling that VAT was chargeable on the transfer of the Saab to the UK. The officer appealed, contending that he should be given the benefit of an extra-statutory concession (TR/60/205/1) so that tax should not be charged. The tribunal rejected this contention and dismissed the appeal. The relevant concession contained a clause providing that 'no more than one motor vehicle, vessel or aircraft per entitled person may be relieved of tax under the concession in any period of twelve months'. Since the Saab was the second car which the officer had purchased within twelve months, he had been unable to register it with British Forces Germany and the concession did not apply. *RB Howard-Williams*, LON/96/238 (VTD 14474).

[23.25] A British citizen (P) worked in Germany from June 1991 to December 1993. Shortly before his return to the UK, he purchased a car in Germany, having paid VAT at the German rate of 15%. On his return to the UK, the Commissioners informed him that he would have to pay VAT on the car at the UK rate of 17.5%. He appealed. The tribunal dismissed his appeal, holding that the car was a 'new means of transport', within what is now *VATA 1994, s 95(3)*, when P brought it into the UK. Furthermore, the provisions of *s 95(3)* were in accordance with *Article 28a(1)(b)* of the *EC Sixth Directive*. *RM Patterson*, LON/94/611A (VTD 13669).

[23.26] Similar decisions were reached in *MF Jones*, LON/00/1137 (VTD 17512) and *I Feltham*, [2011] UKFTT 612 (TC), TC01455.

[23.27] See *Pantekoek*, **19.19** DRUGS, MEDICINES, AIDS FOR THE HANDI-CAPPED, ETC; *Richmond Cars Ltd*, **44.69** MOTOR CARS, and the cases noted at **44.70** to **44.76** MOTOR CARS.

Failure to account for tax on acquisitions from other EU State

[23.28] A UK company (M) acquired large quantities of toilet paper from an Italian company (O). O did not charge VAT on the transactions, because M had used its UK VAT registration number. M did not account for VAT on the acquisitions. HMRC issued an assessment charging UK VAT on the acquisitions. M appealed, contending firstly that no VAT should be due because the goods had never entered the UK, and alternatively that if it was required to account for output tax on the acquisitions, it should also be allowed a deduction for a corresponding amount of input tax. The tribunal rejected these contentions and dismissed M's appeal, holding that the effect of *VATA 1994, s 13(3)* was that the goods had to be treated as acquired in the UK, since M had made use of a registration number which it had been assigned 'for the purposes of VAT in the United Kingdom'. Furthermore, M was not entitled to a deduction for input tax because it had not shown what had happened to the goods. It appeared that the goods had been transported to Spain, but there was no evidence that they had been sold to a registered trader. M had claimed that it had sold the goods to a company resident in the British Virgin Islands, but had not provided adequate evidence of this. Judge Walters observed that 'for the prevention of abuse of the VAT system certain obligations of proof are put upon taxable persons as a condition of their being able to benefit from VAT relieving provisions, and it is the responsibility of a taxable person to provide objective proof to meet those obligations. In this case the appellant has failed in that responsibility.' *Mexcom Ltd v HMRC*, [2010] UKFTT 163 (TC), TC00468.

[23.29] See also *West*, **28.17** FLAT-RATE SCHEME.

Time limit for repayment claim—VAT Regulations, reg 179

[23.30] In May 1997 a Swedish company submitted a claim, under the *EC Eighth Directive*, for the repayment of VAT which had been charged in 1995. The Commissioners rejected the claim on the basis that it had been made outside the six-month time limit of *VAT Regulations 1995 (SI 1995/2518), reg 179(1)*. The company appealed. The tribunal dismissed the appeal, holding that the time limit was mandatory and was in accordance with *Article 7(1)* of the *EC Eighth Directive*. *Nova Stamps AB*, LON/97/964 (VTD 15304).

[23.31] The decision in *Nova Stamps AB*, **23.30** above, was applied in the similar subsequent cases of *B Lunkowsky*, LON/06/038 (VTD 19572) and *Megaink Sro*, [2010] UKFTT 257 (TC), TC00551.

[23.32] A similar decision was reached in *Digi Systems (Ireland) Ltd*, [2009] UKFTT 183 (TC), TC00138.

Whether assessments compatible with Sixth Directive

[23.33] A UK company carried on the business of manufacturing, repairing and maintaining gas turbine generators. It sold its turbines to customers throughout the EU, and maintained turbines which it had installed. It transported a quantity of goods (parts to be used for maintenance) from the UK to Italy. The Commissioners issued assessments on the basis that the removal of goods from the UK gave rise to a deemed supply under *Sch 4 para 6(1)*, on which the company was required to account for output tax. The company appealed, contending that the effect of *Article 28a(5)(b)* of the *EC Sixth Directive* was that the transport of the goods should not be treated as a supply for consideration, since it had been undertaken for the purpose of a supply under the conditions laid down by *Article 8(1)(a)*. The tribunal accepted this contention and allowed the appeal, On the evidence, 'the parts were transported to Italy for the purposes of their subsequent installation and assembly by or on behalf of the appellant within the first indent of *Article 28a(5)(b)*, so that there is no deemed supply under the *Directive*'. The tribunal observed that what is now *VATA 1994, s 7(3)(b)* 'must be interpreted in accordance with the *Directive*, or, if this is impossible, it must be disapplied. Either way, the appellant succeeds.' Furthermore, even if there had been a deemed supply, the condition laid down by *Notice No 725, para 2.4*, that a trader removing his own goods from the UK must be registered for VAT in the country of destination or account for UK VAT on the transfer, was unreasonable, and was not authorised by *Article 28c(A)* of the *EC Sixth Directive*. *Article 28c* authorised Member States to lay down conditions 'for the purpose of ensuring the correct and straightforward application of the exemptions provided for' and 'preventing any evasion, avoidance or abuse'. However, the conditions could not 'be used as a method of ensuring the registration requirements in the other Member State', could not 'be used merely to ensure the integrity of the Single Market', and could not 'be imposed to counteract the fact that registration may not be obligatory in another Member State. The integrity of the Single Market is the responsibility of the (EC) Commission.' *Centrax Ltd*, [1998] VATDR 369 (VTD 15743). (*Note*. For the Commissioners' practice following this decision, see Business Brief 22/99, issued on 13 October 1999. The Commissioners state that 'because of the uncertain position regarding retrospective VAT registration in Italy, Customs have agreed that Centrax can exceptionally zero-rate transfers of their own goods from the UK to Italy using their VAT registration number in Italy, even though they were not registered in Italy at the time the transfers took place.')

Article 28C of EC Sixth Directive

[23.34] See *Teleos plc v C & E Commrs*, 22.518 EUROPEAN COMMUNITY LAW.

[23.35] A company reclaimed input tax on the basis that it had supplied large quantities of mobile telephones to a Spanish company, such supplies being zero-rated by *VATA 1994, s 30(8)*. The Commissioners discovered that the CMR documents supplied by the Spanish company contained false information, and formed the opinion that the telephones had never left the UK. They therefore issued assessments to recover the input tax which the company had claimed. The company appealed, contending firstly that the goods had left the UK, and alternatively that *VATA 1994, s 30* did not fully implement the mandatory exemption provided by *Article 28c* of the *EC Sixth Directive*. The tribunal rejected the company's first contention, accepting Customs' evidence that 'the fact that the Spanish company sold the telephones on the same day to other United Kingdom companies made it improbable that the telephones had been removed from the United Kingdom'. The tribunal directed that the appeal should be stood over to determine the company's alternative contention after the CJEC decision in *Teleos plc*, 22.518 EUROPEAN COMMUNITY LAW. *Starmill UK Ltd*, LON/02/1031 (VTD 18720). (*Note.* There was no further public hearing of the appeal.)

[23.36] A company reclaimed input tax on the basis that it had supplied large quantities of mobile telephones to a Spanish company, such supplies being zero-rated by *VATA 1994, s 30(8)*. Customs discovered that the CMR documents supplied by the Spanish company contained false information, and formed the opinion that the telephones had never left the UK. They therefore issued assessments to recover the input tax which the company had claimed. The company appealed, contending that the goods had left the UK. The tribunal rejected this contention, finding that the CMRs for each of the disputed supplies 'contained false particulars about the details of the carrier, the place of destination for the goods and the vehicle registration'. Accordingly, the company had failed to satisfy the tribunal 'on the balance of probabilities' that the mobile phones were removed from the United Kingdom. The tribunal directed that the appeal should be stood over pending the CJEC decision in *Teleos plc*, 22.518 EUROPEAN COMMUNITY LAW. *Atlantic Electronics Ltd*, LON/02/1141 (VTD 19256) (*Note.* There was no further public hearing of the appeal.).

Penalty for failure to submit EC Sales Statement

[23.37] See *Sloan Electronics Ltd*, 53.1 PENALTIES: REGULATORY PROVISIONS, and the cases noted at 53.2 to 53.17 PENALTIES: REGULATORY PROVISIONS.

UK company reclaiming French VAT as input tax

[23.38] See *British Iberian International Transport Ltd*, 36.665 INPUT TAX, and *Normal Films Ltd*, 36.666 INPUT TAX.

UK company reclaiming German VAT as input tax

[23.39] See *Trenchard Management Ltd*, **36.668** INPUT TAX.

24

Exemptions: Miscellaneous

The cases in this chapter are arranged under the following headings.

Group 3—Postal services	**24.1**
Group 4—Betting, gaming and lotteries	**24.10**
Group 8—Burial and cremation	**24.27**
Group 10—Sport, sports competitions and physical education	
Right to enter competitions (*VATA 1994, Sch 9, Group 10, Items 1, 2*)	**24.31**
Services 'closely linked with and essential to sport' (*VATA 1994, Sch 9, Group 10, Item 3*)	**24.32**

CROSS-REFERENCES

For cases falling within *VATA 1994, Sch 9, Group 1* (Land), see **41** LAND. For cases falling within *VATA 1994, Sch 9, Group 2* (Insurance), see **38** INSURANCE. For cases falling within *VATA 1994, Sch 9, Group 5* (Finance), see **27** FINANCE. For cases falling within *VATA 1994, Sch 9, Group 6* (Education), see **21** EDUCATION. For cases falling within *VATA 1994, Sch 9, Group 7* (Health and welfare), see **33** HEALTH AND WELFARE. For cases falling within *VATA 1994, Sch 9, Group 9* (Trade unions, professional and public interest bodies) see **64** TRADE UNIONS, PROFESSIONAL AND PUBLIC INTEREST BODIES. For cases falling within *VATA 1994, Sch 9, Group 12* (Fund-raising events by charities and other qualifying bodies), see **11** CHARITIES. For cases falling within *VATA 1994, Sch 9, Group 13* (Cultural services), see **16** CULTURAL SERVICES. For cases falling within *VATA 1994, Sch 9, Group 15* (Investment gold), see **31** GOLD. For exemptions under the *EC Sixth Directive*, see **22.270** *et seq.* EUROPEAN COMMUNITY LAW.

Group 3—Postal services

Additional charge for postage and packing—whether exempt

[24.1] A married couple supplied mounted wedding photographs. Where the photographs were to be posted to the customer, an additional charge was made varying with the number of photographs. In accounting for tax, the couple deducted 10% in arriving at their gross takings to cover the postal charge which they considered should be exempt. The Commissioners issued an assessment charging tax on the amount deducted. The tribunal dismissed the couple's appeal, holding that the additional charge did not qualify for exemption under what is now *VATA 1994, Sch 9, Group 3*. *Mr & Mrs WHG Swinger*, LON/77/127 (VTD 414).

[24.2] A company (P) supplied plant bulbs by mail order. It arranged for the bulbs to be delivered by Parcelforce. It charged its customers £2.50 for this, and paid £1.63 to Parcelforce, retaining the balance. It only accounted for output tax on the amounts which it retained, and failed to account for tax on the amounts which it passed on to Parcelforce. The Commissioners issued a ruling that P was required to account for output tax on the full amount paid by the customers. P appealed, contending that the delivery of the bulbs was a separate supply, made by Parcelforce, which qualified for exemption under *VATA 1994, Sch 9, Group 3*. The HL rejected this contention and upheld the Commissioners' ruling (by a 4-1 majority, Lord Mackay dissenting). Lord Slynn held that there was a single supply of delivered bulbs. The arrangements for delivery were 'ancillary to the making available of the bulbs'. Lord Millett held that 'the sum which the customer paid to (P) was paid as consideration for the supply which (P) made to the customer'. Accordingly P was liable to account for output tax on the payments of £1.63 to Parcelforce. *C & E Commrs v Plantiflor Ltd*, HL [2002] STC 1132; [2002] UKHL 33; [2002] 1 WLR 2287. (*Note*. For the Commissioners' practice following this decision, see Business Brief 23/2002, issued on 20 August 2002.)

[24.3] The HL decision in *Plantiflor Ltd*, 24.2 above, was applied in the similar subsequent case of *IG Coates*, MAN/07/379 (VTD 20682).

[24.4] A partnership supplied clothing by mail order. In accounting for VAT, it deducted the amounts which it paid for postage from the taxable consideration. Customs issued a ruling that the partnership was required to account for output tax on the full amount paid by the customers. The partnership appealed, contending that the postal charges should be treated as consideration for a separate exempt supply. The tribunal rejected this contention and dismissed the appeal, applying the HL decision in *Plantiflor Ltd*, 24.2 above. The Ch D upheld the tribunal decision. *Osborne's Big Man Shop v HMRC*, Ch D 2006, [2007] STC 586; [2006] EWHC 3172(Ch).

Goods sent by post—postage charged to customer

[24.5] A company sold goods by post. It invoiced customers for the net price plus the cost of the postage, and the goods were not despatched until the invoiced amount had been received. The company accounted for tax only on the price of the goods, treating the amount received for postage as exempt under what is now *VATA 1994, Sch 9, Group 3, Item 1*. The Commissioners issued an assessment on the basis that the company was liable to account for tax on the amount received for postage. The tribunal dismissed the company's appeal, holding that the amounts in question failed to qualify for exemption. Applying the principles laid down in *Rowe & Maw*, 62.52 SUPPLY, the company supplied the service of procuring the Post Office to deliver the goods in consideration of the payment from the customer of an amount equal to the charge made by the Post Office. *BSN (Import & Export) Ltd*, [1980] VATTR 177 (VTD 998).

[24.6] The decision in *BSN (Import & Export) Ltd*, 24.5 above, was applied in the similar case of *Basebuy Ltd*, LON/93/1080A (VTD 12088).

[24.7] A similar decision was reached in *SR Morris (t/a Two Plus Two)*, LON/03/1007 (VTD 18621).

Supply of books by mail order to 'club members'

[24.8] See *The Leisure Circle Ltd*, 5.21 BOOKS, ETC., and *Book Club Associates*, 5.22 BOOKS, ETC.

Interpretation of EC Sixth Directive, Article 13A(1)(a)

[24.9] See *R (oao TNT Post UK Ltd) v HMRC*, **22.272** EUROPEAN COMMUNITY LAW.

Group 4—Betting, gaming and lotteries

Provision of bingo facilities by club

[24.10] A members' club organised bingo sessions. Participants paid separate amounts in respect of, or for, entrance fees, jackpot participation fees, bingo boards and jackpot cards. The club did not register for VAT. The Commissioners issued a ruling that the club was required to register, accepting that the supply of the boards and cards was exempt under what is now *VATA 1994, Sch 9, Group 4, Item 1*, but treating the entrance fees and jackpot participation fees as within *Note 1(a)(b)* and standard-rated, so that the club's taxable turnover exceeded the registration threshold. The club appealed, contending that, in arriving at the taxable takings, the percentage of its takings which was set aside for jackpot prizes should be deducted. The tribunal rejected this contention and dismissed the appeal. *Fakenham Conservative Association Bingo Club*, LON S/73/164 (VTD 76). (*Note*. Compare the subsequent decision in *WMT Entertainments Ltd*, **24.12** below.)

[24.11] A members' club provided various forms of live entertainment and regular bingo sessions. On the evenings on which both live entertainment and bingo were provided, members wishing to play bingo were charged amounts varying from 10p to 65p. The club appealed against an assessment on these receipts, contending that they were consideration for the provision of bingo within the exemption of what is now *VATA 1994, Sch 9, Group 4, Item 1*. The QB held that the payments by members were partly for the bingo facilities (exempt) and partly for the live entertainment (taxable) and should be apportioned accordingly, and remitted the case to the tribunal to consider the apportionment. *Tynewydd Labour Working Men's Club & Institute Ltd v C & E Commrs*, [1979] STC 570. (*Note*. The tribunal directed an apportionment of 15% to bingo and 85% to the live entertainment—see **67.115** VALUATION.)

[24.12] A company operated a number of bingo clubs. It sold books of bingo cards to customers at 6p per book. It retained some of these fees, the remainder being distributed as prize money. (Customers were also required to pay stake money of £1.80, one-sixth of which was distributed as prize money.) The company only accounted for VAT on the amounts which it retained, and the Commissioners issued an assessment on the basis that it should also have accounted for VAT on the amounts distributed as prizes. The company appealed, contending that these amounts were exempt under what is now *VATA 1994, Sch 9, Group 4*. The tribunal accepted this contention and allowed the appeal. The amounts which the company retained were excluded from exemption by *Sch 9, Group 4, Note 1(b)*, but the amounts which it distributed as prize money were not within *Note 1(b)* and therefore qualified for exemption under *Sch 9, Group 4, Item 1. WMT Entertainments Ltd*, MAN/91/282 (VTD 9385). (*Note*. Compare *Fakenham Conservative Association Bingo Club*, **24.10** above, which was not referred to in this decision.)

Mechanised cash bingo

[24.13] See *HMRC v The Rank Group plc*, **22.375** EUROPEAN COMMUNITY LAW.

Payments to take part in card games returnable as winnings

[24.14] A company operated a casino and organised card games. It did not account for tax on its takings from the card games. The Commissioners issued an assessment charging tax on them, and the club appealed, contending that the takings were not taxable because all the payments were returned to the players in the form of winnings, and that it regarded the games as 'loss leaders' in relation to its other activities. The tribunal upheld the assessment and dismissed the company's appeal, holding that the payments from the members were to enable them to participate in the game, and were therefore excluded from exemption by what is now *Sch 9, Group 4, Note 1(b)*. *Rum Runner Casino Ltd*, MAN/80/33 (VTD 1036).

Payments for use of card room

[24.15] A partnership operated a proprietary social club, which included a card room. It charged club members £1.80 per hour for the use of this room. It did not account for output tax on these charges, treating them as exempt. The Commissioners issued a ruling that output tax was chargeable on the payments, and the partnership appealed. The tribunal allowed the appeal, holding on the evidence that the payments were for the right to use the club's facilities, rather than for the right to play a particular game. The card games were organised by the members themselves, rather than by the partnership. Accordingly, the payments were exempt under *VATA 1994, Sch 9, Group 4, Item 1* and were not excluded from exemption by *Note 1(b)*. *Rum Runner Casino Ltd*, **24.14** above, distinguished. *WG Lee & N Sarrafan (t/a The Regal Sporting Club)*, LON/97/940 (VTD 15563).

Shooting gallery—whether a provision of a game of chance

[24.16] A partnership ran shooting galleries at Blackpool. In return for 35p a customer was allowed four or five shots (the number dependent on the range) with a 0.22 inch calibre rifle at a cardboard target, and was given a prize if he completely obliterated the white bull's-eye. The bull's-eye was 0.312 inch in diameter. The Commissioners issued an assessment charging tax on the partnership's receipts. The partnership appealed, contending that the gallery was a 'game of chance' within *VATA 1994, Sch 9, Group 4, Item 1*, and giving evidence of two experts, of whom one had obliterated the bull's-eye in only two out of 25 attempts, while the other had had no successful attempts. On average, there was about one success in 600 by members of the public. The tribunal accepted the partners' evidence and allowed the appeal, holding on the evidence that, while simply placing four shots in the bull's-eye required skill, it would require superlative skill to eliminate the element of chance in completely obliterating the bull's-eye. (The tribunal stressed that the decision was based on the particular facts and was not to be taken as applying to all forms of small-bore rifle shooting.) *W & D Grantham*, MAN/79/102 (VTD 853). (*Note. Gaming Act 1968, s 52*—see *Group 4, Note 2*—provides, *inter alia*, that 'game of chance' includes a game of chance and skill combined and that in determining 'whether a game which is played otherwise than against one or more other players is a game of chance and skill combined, the possibility of superlative skill eliminating the element of chance shall be disregarded'.)

Provision of casino accommodation on cruise ship

[24.17] A company (S) carried on business as a casino operator. It entered into an agreement with a company operating cruise ships (P & O) whereby P & O granted to it the exclusive right to operate gaming on its cruise ships in return for 50% of the gross profits from such gaming. The Commissioners issued a ruling that the rights which P & O granted to S amounted to the granting of a licence or concession to operate certain games of chance, which was a supply of services taxable at the standard rate. S appealed, contending that what P & O supplied to it under the agreement were facilities for the playing of games of chance, and that these facilities were exempt under what is now *VATA 1994, Sch 9, Group 4, Item 1*. The tribunal allowed S's appeal, holding that the right granted by P & O to S constituted the provision of a facility for playing a game of chance and was therefore exempt. *J Seven Ltd*, [1986] VATTR 42 (VTD 2024).

Takings from gaming machines

[24.18] A trader failed to account for tax on takings from gaming machines located in pubs and clubs. The Commissioners issued an assessment charging tax on them, and the trader appealed, contending that they should be treated as exempt under *Group 4, Item 2* as the granting of a right to take part in a lottery. The tribunal rejected this contention and dismissed his appeal, holding that the machines were not 'lotteries' and the takings were excluded from exemption by *Group 4, Note 1(d)*. *G McCann (t/a Ulster Video Amusements)*, [1987] VATTR 101 (VTD 2401).

[24.19] See also *HMRC v The Rank Group plc*, **22.375** EUROPEAN COMMUNITY LAW, and the CA decision in *R v Ryan*, **49.29** PENALTIES: CRIMINAL OFFENCES.

Video poker machines

[24.20] The Commissioners issued assessments charging output tax on the owner of a number of 'video poker' machines. The owner appealed, contending that the takings should be treated as exempt from VAT under what is now *VATA 1994, Sch 9, Group 4*. The tribunal dismissed his appeal, holding that the takings were excluded from exemption by *Group 4, Note 1(d)*, and that this exclusion was not inconsistent with *Article 13B(f)* of the *EC Sixth Directive*, since the relevant exemption was 'subject to conditions and limitations laid down by each Member State'. The QB upheld the tribunal decision, applying *Ryan,* **49.29** PENALTIES: CRIMINAL OFFENCES, and *HJ Glawe Spiel,* **22.240** EUROPEAN COMMUNITY LAW. *MJ Feehan v C & E Commrs*, QB 1994, [1995] STC 75. (*Note.* For another issue in this case, not taken to the QB, see **2.122** APPEALS.)

Hire of machines for sorting roulette chips—whether within Item 1

[24.21] A company which operated casinos owned a number of machines designed for sorting roulette chips, and let these on hire. It did not account for VAT on its takings from the hire of these machines, considering that they were exempt from VAT under what is now *VATA 1994, Sch 9, Group 4, Item 1*. The Commissioners issued an assessment charging tax on the takings in question, on the basis that the machines were not used as an intrinsic or essential part of the playing of the game of roulette. The QB upheld the assessment, holding that the payments did not qualify for exemption. Schiemann J held that *Item 1* merely excluded gambling itself from the scope of VAT, and did not have the effect of requiring the exemption of supplies of equipment such as roulette wheels or sorting machines which were to be used for subsequent gambling. *C & E Commrs v Annabel's Casino Ltd*, QB 1994, [1995] STC 225. (*Note.* For another issue in this case, not taken to the QB, see **46.75** PARTIAL EXEMPTION.)

Horse-racing betting game

[24.22] A company operated a betting game whereby customers could bet, on a premium-rate telephone line, on one racehorse each day for a period of 24 days. Customers had to register by telephone before competing, each registration lasting about six minutes. Each telephone call was treated as a £1 bet, and any customer who accumulated £100 or more in winnings in a 24-day period won a special bonus. The company reclaimed input tax on its costs, and the Commissioners issued an assessment to recover the tax, considering that the company's supplies were exempt from VAT under *VATA 1994, Sch 9, Group 4*. The company appealed, contending that the telephone registration services should be treated as separate taxable supplies. The tribunal rejected this contention and dismissed the company's appeal, holding that the company was making a single supply of providing facilities for betting. The registration of the customers was 'an integral part of the game and hence of the provision of betting facilities'. *Logic Ltd*, LON/95/2634 (VTD 13934).

Electronic lottery vending machine

[24.23] A company supplied electronic lottery ticket vending machines to members' clubs. HMRC issued a ruling that the receipts from the machines were taxable supplies on which VAT was chargeable. The company appealed, contending that they qualified for exemption under *VATA 1994, Sch 9, Group*

4. The tribunal accepted this contention and allowed the appeal, holding that the machine was a 'gaming machine' within *Group 4, Note 1(d)* and that the relevant supplies fell within *Group 4, Item 2*. The tribunal specifically declined to follow the 1987 decision in *McCann*, **24.18** above. *Oasis Technologies (UK) Ltd v HMRC*, [2010] UKFTT 292 (TC), TC00581. (*Note*. For HMRC's practice following this decision, see HMRC Brief 01/11, issued on 19 January 2011.)

Outsourced services for telephone betting

[24.24] See *United Utilities plc v C & E Commrs*, **22.370** EUROPEAN COMMUNITY LAW.

Supplies by company to betting syndicate

[24.25] A company (R) placed bets on sporting events on behalf of a betting syndicate. Many, but not all, of the members of the syndicate were shareholders in R. HMRC issued a ruling that R was required to account for VAT on its supplies to the syndicate. R appealed, contending that its supplies should be treated as exempt under *VATA 1994, Sch 9, Group 4, Item 1*. The tribunal rejected this contention and dismissed the appeal. Judge Connell observed that R was 'the agent of the syndicate, not an agent of the bookmaker or betting exchange which took the risk of the bets'. He held that 'the provision of betting facilities has to be characterised by the assumption of risk. A service of a administrative or mechanical nature such as that provided by (R), not involving the risk of loss clearly does not amount to the provision of betting facilities.' Accordingly R's services failed to qualify for exemption. *Rating Report Ltd v HMRC*, [2011] UKFTT 721 (TC), TC01558.

Group 8—Burial and cremation

Clearing of old burial ground

[24.26] A property developer had planning permission to build a shopping complex on an area partly owned by a Borough Council. The Council arranged for a company to clear a burial ground which formed part of the area. The company reclaimed input tax on the basis that the work was zero-rated civil engineering work within *VATA 1983, Sch 5* as then in force. The Commissioners rejected the claim, considering that the work was exempt under what is now *VATA 1994, Sch 9, Group 8, Item 1*. The tribunal allowed the company's appeal in part, holding that the work was not civil engineering work but was also not the 'disposal of the remains of the dead' within *VATA 1994, Sch 9, Group 8, Item 1*, since the normal meaning of these words confined the exemption to services supplied by undertakers as such and to cremation services. The company was supplying 'very specialised services of clearing a burial ground or cemetery'. The tribunal therefore held that the work was neither zero-rated nor exempt, but standard-rated. Accordingly the company was entitled to reclaim input tax but was required to account for output tax on the consideration it received. *UFD Ltd*, [1981] VATTR 199 (VTD 1172).

Funeral directors—storage of cadavers and use of chapel of rest

[24.27] A partnership which carried on business as funeral directors stored cadavers for other firms, and allowed such firms to use its chapel of rest. The Commissioners issued a ruling that these supplies were exempt from VAT under *VATA 1994, Sch 9, Group 8, Item 2*, so that the partnership could not reclaim the related input tax. The tribunal dismissed the partnership's appeal, observing that the services were 'directly involved in and concerned with the burial of the dead'. The tribunal distinguished *Network Insurance Brokers Ltd*, 24.28 below, and *Co-Operative Wholesale Society Ltd*, 24.29 below, noting that those cases 'were concerned with financial arrangements rather than physical arrangements'. *CJ Williams' Funeral Service of Telford*, [1999] VATDR 318 (VTD 16261).

Insurance broker—services relating to hospital fund

[24.28] A company (N), which carried on business as a registered insurance broker, supplied services to a hospital fund which provided a funeral benefit for its members. It received commission from the fund, but did not account for output tax on the commission. The Commissioners issued an assessment charging tax on the commission and N appealed, contending that the commission should be treated as exempt under *VATA 1994, Sch 9, Group 8, Item 2*. The tribunal rejected this contention and dismissed the appeal, and the QB upheld this decision. The words 'arrangements for or in connection with the disposal of the remains of the dead' in *Item 2* should be construed in accordance with *Annex F* of the *EC Sixth Directive*, i.e. as relating to cremation services or services of the kind supplied by undertakers. Accordingly, the supplies made by N failed to qualify for exemption. *Network Insurance Brokers Ltd v C & E Commrs*, QB [1998] STC 742.

Payment to funeral directors relating to funeral benefit scheme

[24.29] A major company (C) had agreed to provide funeral services to members of an insurance fund, charging a fee of £6 per member. Subsequently the company (L) which operated the fund decided that it wished to extend the choice of funeral directors providing such services for its members. The agreement was revised and, under the revised agreement, L paid C annual compensation of £1.25 for each of its members. C did not account for output tax on these payments, treating them as exempt under *VATA 1994, Sch 9, Group 8, Item 2*. The Commissioners issued an assessment on the basis that the payments failed to qualify for exemption. C appealed, contending that it was making a single supply of services and that the whole of the consideration which it received should be treated as exempt. The tribunal rejected this contention and dismissed the appeal, holding that the compensation payments were not made 'for or in connection with the disposal of the remains of the dead', as required by *Item 2*. The QB and CA upheld this decision. Simon Brown LJ held that, whereas the consideration of £6 per member paid under the original agreement was accepted as relating to exempt supplies, the additional consideration of £1.25 per member related to separate supplies which did not qualify for exemption. Where C itself provided funeral services, its supplies were accepted as exempt, but where funeral services were supplied by other funeral directors, C's services were not exempt. *Co-Operative Wholesale Society Ltd v C & E Commrs (No 3)*, CA [2000] STC 727.

Administration fee for operating 'funeral plan'

[24.30] A company (F) sold 'funeral plans', enabling customers to choose a funeral and pay for it in advance. Under the terms of the plan, F lodged most of the payment which it received from the customers with trustees, to meet the eventual cost of the funeral. However it retained £65 as an 'administration fee'. HMRC issued a ruling that F was required to account for VAT on these administration fees. F appealed, contending that they should be treated as exempt under *VATA 1994, Sch 9, Group 8, Item 2*. The tribunal accepted this contention and allowed the appeal, holding that the fact that F did 'not itself dispose of the remains of the dead' was not conclusive. F was making a single composite supply and was acting as an independent principal. The tribunal distinguished the earlier decisions in *Network Insurance Brokers Ltd v C & E Commrs*, **24.28** above, and *Co-Operative Wholesale Society Ltd v C & E Commrs (No 3)*, **24.29** above, on the basis that the companies in those case were acting as intermediaries rather than as the principal contractor. *Funeral Planning Services Ltd*, LON/05/480 (VTD 19975).

Group 10—Sport, sports competitions and physical education

NOTE

VATA 1994, Sch 9, Group 10 was substantially amended by the *VAT (Sport, Sports Competitions and Physical Education) Order 1999 (SI 1999/1994)*, with effect from 1 January 2000. The Order substituted references to 'an eligible body' for the previous references to 'a non-profit-making body', so that supplies which would otherwise fall to be exempt 'will only do so if they are made by an eligible body'. The cases in this section should be read in the light of the changes to the legislation.

Right to enter competitions (VATA 1994, Sch 9, Group 10, Items 1, 2)

Rugby club match fees

[24.31] A rugby union club charged its players a match fee of £2.50. These fees were used to defray the purchase of shirts and rugby balls, and to pay referees' fees. The club failed to account for output tax on the match fees, and the Commissioners issued an assessment charging tax on them. The club appealed, contending that the fees should be treated as exempt under what is now *VATA 1994, Sch 9, Group 10*. The tribunal rejected this contention and dismissed the appeal, holding that the match fees did not qualify for exemption, regardless of whether they related to league matches or to friendly matches. The club's friendly matches were not within the definition of 'competitions', and with regard to the league matches, the match fees were not consideration for any 'grant' by the club to its players within the scope of *Group 10*. *Wimborne Rugby Football Club*, LON/89/755Y (VTD 4547).

Services 'closely linked with and essential to sport' (VATA 1994, Sch 9, Group 10, Item 3)

Cases held to qualify for exemption

Admission to sports centre

[24.32] A charitable trust operated a sports centre. It sold 'privilege cards', which granted the holders free admission to the centre, and the use of certain facilities (such as a swimming pool) at a reduced rate. Adults were required to pay £29.95 for such cards, and there were reduced rates for students and pensioners. It charged for admission to individuals who did not hold privilege cards. It did not account for output tax on such payments, treating them as exempt under *Group 10, Item 3*. Customs issued a ruling that the trust was required to account for output tax on payments from individuals who did not hold privilege cards, on the grounds that the privilege cards were a membership scheme and that the effect of *Item 3* was that payments from non-members did not qualify for exemption. The trust appealed, contending firstly that the privilege cards did not amount to a membership scheme, and alternatively that the provision in *Item 3* excluding payments by non-members from exemption was not in accordance with *Article 13A2(b)* of the *EC Sixth Directive*. The tribunal accepted the first contention and allowed the appeal, holding that the privilege cards did not amount to a membership scheme, since the concept of a 'membership scheme' involved 'an element of participation or belonging which is absent in the present case'. *Basingstoke & District Sports Trust Ltd*, [1995] VATDR 405 (VTD 13347). (*Note.* For Customs' practice following this decision, see Business Brief 3/96, issued on 16 February 1996.)

Golf club

[24.33] The Commissioners issued a ruling that a limited company which operated a golf club was not within the definition of a 'non-profit-making body', so that its supplies did not qualify for exemption under *Group 10, Item 3 as originally enacted*. The club appealed, contending that, although it had been founded as a proprietary club, the holding company which had originally owned it had sold it and it was now managed as a members' club. The tribunal reviewed the evidence in detail and allowed the appeal. The facts that the club paid significant sums in rent to the company which owned its course, and paid management fees to a management company, did not necessarily take it outside the definition of a 'non-profit-making body', since 'income is not profit'. On the evidence, the tribunal was satisfied that any surplus which remained after paying the club's overheads (which included rent and management fees) would be 'used in the improvement of the club's facilities'. Accordingly, the club was within the definition of a 'non-profit-making body', and its supplies to its members qualified for exemption. *Chobham Golf Club*, [1997] VATDR 36 (VTD 14867). (*Notes*. (1) Customs appealed to the High Court against this decision (see Business Brief 18/97, issued on 22 August 1997) but subsequently withdrew their appeal—see Business Brief 18/98, issued on 11 September 1998. (2) See the note at the head of this section with regard to the *VAT (Sport, Sports Competitions & Physical Education) Order 1999 (SI 1999/1994)*.)

Bowling club—payments from members for casual play

[24.34] A bowling club registered for VAT from September 1994. In its first VAT return, it treated fees charged to its members for competitions as exempt under *VATA 1994, Sch 9, Group 10* but treated all fees received for casual play (whether received from members or non-members) as standard-rated. This resulted in the club's exempt input tax being less than the *de minimis* limits, and to the club reclaiming more than £6,800 in input tax. A VAT officer visited the club and formed the opinion that the return was incorrect because fees received from members for casual play should have been treated as exempt, with the result that the exempt input tax exceeded the *de minimis* limits and the repayment actually due to the club was only £1,036. Customs issued a ruling accordingly, and the club appealed, contending that casual play was not 'closely linked and essential to sport'. The tribunal dismissed the appeal, holding that the services which the club provided to enable casual play were 'closely linked with and essential to sport', and were therefore exempt from VAT under *VATA 1994, Sch 9, Group 10, Item 3*. The tribunal also held that the terms of *Item 3* were not inconsistent with *Article 13A1(m)* of the *EC Sixth Directive*. *Chard Bowling Club*, LON/95/1121 (VTD 13575). (*Note*. See the note at the head of this section with regard to the *VAT (Sport, Sports Competitions & Physical Education) Order 1999 (SI 1999/1994)*.)

Hockey clubs—affiliation fees to national hockey association

[24.35] See *HMRC v Canterbury Hockey Club*, 22.316 EUROPEAN COMMUNITY LAW.

Yacht club—whether berthing fees exempt from VAT

[24.36] A yacht club did not account for VAT on berthing fees which it received from its members. Customs issued an assessment charging tax on such fees, and the club appealed, contending that they qualified for exemption under *VATA 1994, Sch 9, Group 10, Item 3*. The tribunal allowed the appeal, holding that the yacht club's members were people 'taking part in sport' and that the berthing fees were paid for services which were 'closely linked with and essential to sport'. *Swansea Yacht & Sub Aqua Club*, [1996] VATDR 89 (VTD 13938). (*Note*. See the note at the head of this section with regard to the *VAT (Sport, Sports Competitions & Physical Education) Order 1999 (SI 1999/1994)*.)

Flying club hiring aircraft to members

[24.37] A flying club hired aircraft to its members. Customs accepted that the hirings were an exempt supply by virtue of *VATA 1994, Sch 9, Group 10, Item*

3. However the club reclaimed input tax on its purchase of aircraft fuel. The Commissioners issued an assessment to recover the tax, and the club appealed, contending that it was making onward supplies of fuel to its members, which should be treated as a separate taxable supply. The tribunal rejected this contention and dismissed the club's appeal, holding that it was making a single exempt supply of aircraft hire. *Sherburn Aero Club Ltd*, MAN/03/55 (VTD 18540).

Company established to 'promote sporting shooting'

[24.38] A company was established to 'act as a representative national body for all sporting shooting' and to 'promote and safeguard sporting shooting'. It charged its members subscriptions, and did not account for VAT. HMRC accepted that part of the subscriptions qualified for zero-rating as attributable to the supply of zero-rated magazines, and that part was exempt as relating to the supply of insurance, but issued an assessment charging tax on the remainder of the subscriptions. The company appealed, contending that its supplies should be treated as exempt from VAT under *VATA 1994, Sch 9, Group 10, Item 3*. The tribunal initially dismissed the appeal, but the Ch D remitted the case for rehearing in the light of the subsequent ECJ decision in *HMRC v Canterbury Hockey Club*, **22.316** EUROPEAN COMMUNITY LAW. The tribunal reheard the case and allowed the appeal, holding on the evidence that the supplies were 'closely linked with the sport of shooting', and therefore qualified for exemption. *The British Association for Shooting & Conservation Ltd v HMRC (No 2)*, [2010] SFTD 993; [2010] UKFTT 268 (TC), TC00562.

[24.39] See also *Bowcombe Shoot v HMRC*, **2.491** APPEALS.

Cases held to be partly exempt

Yacht club—whether subscriptions entirely exempt from VAT

[24.40] A yacht club offered two classes of membership. Ordinary members paid a subscription of £430 p.a. but approximately 7% of members paid a reduced rate of £178 plus VAT, which enabled them to use the clubhouse but not to compete in yachting events. The club did not account for VAT on the subscriptions paid by ordinary members, treating them as exempt. Customs issued a ruling that part of the subscriptions should be attributed to a taxable supply of clubhouse facilities which did not qualify for exemption. The club appealed, contending that it was making a single supply of services closely linked to sport. The tribunal rejected this contention and dismissed the appeal, holding on the evidence that the club was making separate supplies of sporting facilities and clubhouse facilities. The clubhouse facilities were not incidental to the sporting facilities, since they could be 'characterised as supplies of all the facilities of a substantial free-standing London club capable of being enjoyed to the exclusion of the sporting facilities', as was shown by the 7% of members who paid a reduced subscription which did not entitle them to use the sporting facilities. *Royal Thames Yacht Club*, LON/94/1469 & 2081 (VTD 14046). (*Note.* See the note at the head of this section with regard to the *VAT (Sport, Sports Competitions & Physical Education) Order 1999 (SI 1999/1994)*.)

Cases held not to qualify for exemption

Limited company—whether a 'non-profit-making body'

[24.41] A group of companies operated a number of hotels, some of which included leisure facilities. It transferred the operation of these facilities to a newly-formed subsidiary company (D). D failed to account for output tax on its supplies. Customs issued assessments charging tax of more than £7,000,000. D appealed, contending that the supplies should be treated as exempt. The tribunal rejected this contention and dismissed the appeal, holding on the evidence that D was not a 'non-profit-making body', since it was 'part of a commercial organisation whose purpose is to make profits for its shareholders'. The tribunal observed that 'the purpose of the value added tax exemption is for organisations acting in the public interest and whose activities are directed to non-commercial purposes'. D was not 'an organisation acting in the public interest' and it had 'commercial purposes'. Accordingly its supplies failed to qualify for exemption. *De Vere Golf & Leisure Ltd; De Vere Group plc*, LON/01/055 & 058 (VTD 18078). (*Notes.* (1) Costs were awarded to Customs. (2) Customs had also imposed misdeclaration penalties. The appeals against the penalties were adjourned for further argument. There has been no further public hearing of the appeals.)

[24.42] A limited company (M) operated three golf courses. It charged subscriptions to people who wished to use the courses, and did not account for output tax on these subscriptions. Customs issued assessments charging tax, and M appealed, contending that its supplies should be treated as exempt. The tribunal rejected this contention and dismissed the appeal, observing that M had made loans to its parent company, and holding on the evidence that it was not a 'non-profit-making body' since it had no business purpose independent of its parent company, and there had been 'a *de facto* distribution of profits'. The Ch D and CA unanimously upheld this decision. On the evidence, the tribunal had been entitled to find that M was neither 'a non-profit making organisation for the purposes of *Article 13A(1)(m)* of the *Sixth Directive* or a non-profit making body for the purposes of *Group 10* of *Schedule 9*'. Arden LJ observed that M was 'part of a commercial group of companies' and that the aim of the group 'was to make profits for its members'. *Messenger Leisure Developments Ltd v HMRC*, CA [2005] STC 1078; [2005] EWCA Civ 648. (*Note.* The HL subsequently rejected an application by the company for leave to appeal against the CA decision. See Business Brief 22/2005, issued on 1 December 2005. HMRC state that 'it is now clear that any company which is precluded from distributing profit, but whose function is nevertheless to create VAT exemption in the context of a wider commercial undertaking, is not a non-profit making body for VAT purposes. It follows that such a company is not entitled to claim the VAT exemption which is directed at such bodies.')

[24.43] The decision in *Messenger Leisure Developments Ltd v HMRC*, 24.42 above, was applied by the tribunal in the subsequent case of *The Atrium Club Ltd*, 22.73 supply, where the tribunal held that supplies made by a company which operated a fitness club failed to qualify for exemption.

[24.44] A family partnership had operated a golf club. It transferred the operation of the club to two limited companies (while retaining ownership of the course). Customs issued a ruling that the companies were required to register for VAT. The partnership and the companies appealed, contending that the companies were not required to register because their supplies were exempt. The tribunal rejected this contention and dismissed the appeal, finding that the partnership's 'sole motivation in setting up the companies was to secure savings in VAT payments'. The senior partner 'made the decisions for the companies', and the companies 'made surpluses which were transferred to the partnership through expenditure adjustments, rent and management service charges'. Accordingly the companies were not 'eligible bodies' within *Sch 9, Group 10. South Herefordshire Golf Club (and related appeals)*, LON/02/131 (VTD 19653). (*Notes.* (1) The tribunal also held that the partnership was required to account for VAT on supplies of staff to the companies. (2) An application for costs was dismissed—see **2.365** APPEALS.)

[24.45] The decision in *South Herefordshire Golf Club*, 24.44 above, was applied in a similar subsequent case in which the tribunal found that 'as a matter of reality and substance' the relevant supplies to customers continued to be made by the appellant partnership, rather than by two companies which the partners and incorporated. *Mrs P Barnett & Mrs L Read (t/a Burghill Valley Golf Club)*, FTT June 2009, TC00087.

[24.46] See also *Lumar Developments Ltd*, **52.231** PENALTIES: MISDECLARA-TION.

Golf club—supplies to non-members

[24.47] See *Bridport & West Dorset Golf Club Ltd v HMRC*, **20.74** EC DIRECTIVE 2006/112/EC.

Golf club—grant of licence to another club

[24.48] A golf club (C) granted another club (V) a licence to play golf on its course (but not to use its clubhouse). C charged VAT on the amounts payable. V appealed to the tribunal, contending that the supplies should be treated as exempt. The tribunal rejected this contention and dismissed the appeal, holding that the supplies failed to qualify for exemption under *VATA 1994, Sch 9, Group 1* because the licence was not exclusive, and failed to qualify for exemption under *Sch 9, Group 10, Item 3* because the supplies were to an unincorporated association, rather than to individuals, and because the members of V were not members of C. *Copthorne Village Golf Club*, LON/01/300 (VTD 17426). (*Notes.* (1) The appellant club was represented by one of its members. Compare *Abbotsley Golf & Squash Club Ltd*, **41.159** LAND, where a licence to occupy a golf course was held to be exempt under *Sch 9, Group 1* even though it was not exclusive, applying *dicta* of Lord Templeman in *Street v Mountford*, HL [1985] 1 AC 809; [1985] 2 All ER 289. The decision in *Copthorne Village Golf Club* fails to refer to the HL decision in *Street v Mountford* or to the tribunal decision in *Abbotsley Golf & Squash Club Ltd*, so that the decision on the scope of *Sch 9, Group 1* appears to be of doubtful authority. (2) See the note at the head of this section with regard to the *VAT (Sport, Sports Competitions & Physical Education) Order 1999 (SI 1999/1994).)*

Golf club—non-refundable fee for place on membership waiting list

[**24.49**] A members' golf club had a waiting list of more than 18 months for membership. It required prospective members to pay a non-refundable fee of £20 for a place on this list. This fee was deducted from the first subscription if membership was subsequently taken up. The club did not account for VAT on these fees, treating them as exempt. Customs issued a ruling that VAT was chargeable on the fees. The tribunal dismissed the club's appeal, holding that the payment was 'consideration for the right to be on the waiting list, and as such standard-rated'. *Milnathort Golf Club Ltd*, EDN/98/139 (VTD 15816). (*Note*. See the note at the head of this section with regard to the *VAT (Sport, Sports Competitions & Physical Education) Order 1999 (SI 1999/1994)*.)

Pigeon racing—whether a sport

[**24.50**] Customs issued a ruling that pigeon racing did not qualify for exemption under *VATA 1994, Sch 9, Group 10, Item 3*. The Royal Pigeon Racing Association appealed against the ruling. The tribunal dismissed the appeal, holding that to qualify for exemption under *Group 10, Item 3* 'the individual must be taking part in the sport, which we interpret to the main sporting activity and not some ancillary activity'. Pigeon racing did not qualify for exemption because the only relevant physical activities were undertaken by the pigeons, rather than by their owners. Applying *dicta* of the CJEC in *Stichting Uitvoering Financiele Acties (SUFA) v Staatssecretaris van Financien*, 22.290 EUROPEAN COMMUNITY LAW, the scope of any exemption contained in the *EC Sixth Directive* had to be 'interpreted strictly'. *Royal Pigeon Racing Association*, LON/94/2910A (VTD 14006). (*Note*. See the note at the head of this section with regard to the *VAT (Sport, Sports Competitions & Physical Education) Order 1999 (SI 1999/1994)*.)

Supplies of accommodation at Windermere

[**24.51**] A company owned 18 units of timeshare accommodation at Windermere. It did not account for output tax on the subscriptions which its shareholders paid. Customs issued a ruling that the subscriptions were taxable, and the company appealed, contending that they should be treated as exempt under *Group 10, Item 3*, since its shareholders paid their subscriptions for the purpose of using the sporting facilities at Windermere. The tribunal dismissed the appeal, holding that the subscriptions failed to qualify for exemption, since the supplies were not 'services closely linked with and essential to sport'. *Quaysiders Club Ltd*, MAN/00/726 (VTD 17204). (*Note*. See the note at the head of this section with regard to the *VAT (Sport, Sports Competitions & Physical Education) Order 1999 (SI 1999/1994)*.)

Coin-operated pool tables

[**24.52**] A company had installed two coin-operated pool tables in a building used by a students' union, and accounted for tax on the takings. It subsequently submitted a repayment claim, contending that the supplies were exempt under *VATA 1994, Sch 9, Group 10, Item 3*. Customs rejected the claim and the tribunal dismissed the company's appeal, holding that the takings did not qualify for exemption since the supplies were made by the company, which was not an 'eligible body' as defined in *Sch 9, Group 10, Note 2A*. *Amusement Solutions Ltd*, MAN/08/102 (VTD 20838).

25

Exports

The cases in this chapter are arranged under the following headings.

Notice No 703	**25.1**
Retail export schemes (Notice No 704)	**25.16**
Miscellaneous	**25.27**

NOTE

This chapter covers cases concerning exports of goods outside the European Community. For cases concerning transactions within the Community, see **23** EUROPEAN COMMUNITY: SINGLE MARKET.

Notice No 703

Whether requirements of Notice No 703 unreasonable

[25.1] Two companies traded as clothing wholesalers, with substantial export sales. They failed to provide the evidence of export called for by *Notice No 703* in respect of a number of cases where they had treated goods as exported. The Commissioners issued assessments on the basis that the companies were required to account for output tax on such sales. The companies appealed, contending that the relevant sales were made 'over-the-counter', the customers had claimed that the goods were for export, and they had handed the customers a form C273 as required by *Notice No 703* but had not received the forms back from the customers duly stamped with confirmation of export. The tribunal dismissed the companies' appeals and the CA upheld this decision. Lord Denning observed that 'the Commissioners were entitled to impose very strict conditions for being satisfied. Unless there were strict conditions, value added tax could be evaded very easily.' Accordingly, 'it was necessary for the Commissioners to devise machinery to prevent people from getting out of paying value added tax'. The machinery was 'just about as good as could be devised to stop evasion'. Templeman LJ observed that the trader 'could bring pressure to bear on the customer by requiring payment by the customer of the whole or part of the appropriate VAT as a deposit until the certificate (C273) is produced'. *Henry Moss of London Ltd v C & E Commrs; The London Mob (Great Portland Street) Ltd v C & E Commrs*, CA 1980, [1981] STC 139; [1981] 2 All ER 86.

[25.2] A trader reclaimed input tax in respect of 155 water filters, claiming that they had been exported to Nigeria. The Commissioners rejected the claim, as the trader had not produced the evidence of export required by *Notice No 703*. The tribunal dismissed the appeal, holding that there was 'nothing unreasonable in the conditions required to prove export as set out in *Notice*

No 703'. JA Fashanu, LON/94/2897 (VTD 13137). (*Note*. For another issue in this case, see **40.43** INVOICES AND CREDIT NOTES.)

[25.3] A company (M) supplied goods to an export house in June 1994. The goods were exported to Libya eight weeks later. The Commissioners issued an assessment charging tax on the supply, on the grounds that the goods had not been exported within one month of the supply as required by *Notice No 703*. M appealed, accepting that it had not complied with this requirement but contending that the requirement in question was unreasonable. The tribunal dismissed the appeal, holding that it had no jurisdiction to consider whether the requirements were unreasonable, and that their validity could only be challenged by judicial review. *Henry Moss of London Ltd*, **25.1** above, applied. *Megalith Ltd*, LON/96/1505 (VTD 15207).

[25.4] The decision in *Henry Moss of London Ltd*, **25.1** above, has been applied in a large number of similar cases. In the interests of space, such cases are not reported individually in this book. For a list of such cases decided up to 31 December 1993, see Tolley's VAT Cases 1994.

Whether requirements of Notice No 703 complied with

[25.5] A company treated the sale of twelve cars as zero-rated exports, but did not produce documentary evidence that the cars had been exported. Customs issued a ruling that the sales did not qualify for zero-rating. The company appealed, contending that each of the customers had overseas addresses and had exported the cars themselves. The tribunal dismissed the appeal, finding that the company had failed to comply with the requirements of *Notice No 703*, issued in accordance with what is now *VAT Regulations 1995 (SI 1995/2518), reg 129*, so that the sales failed to qualify for zero-rating. *Robbins of Putney Ltd*, LON/77/20 (VTD 610).

[25.6] A trader sold some contact lenses and accessories to a doctor who was resident in Bombay. As the trader's husband was shortly travelling to Bombay by air, she arranged for him to take the goods with him for delivery to the Bombay customer. Some three weeks before her husband travelled, the trader wrote to the local VAT office for information as to the evidence required for zero-rating exported goods, but was not told of the requirements until after the goods had been exported. As a result she was not able to produce a form C273 to verify the exportation. The Commissioners issued a ruling that the supply of the goods did not qualify for zero-rating, and the trader appealed. The tribunal dismissed the appeal, finding that it was satisfied from the evidence that the goods had been exported, but holding (by a 2-1 majority) that the supply could not be zero-rated since the requirements of *Notice No 703*, issued in accordance with what is now *VAT Regulations 1995 (SI 1995/2518), reg 129*, had not been complied with. *AA Sadri (t/a Hutosh Commercial)*, LON/78/265 (VTD 694).

[25.7] A company sold lengths of cloth used for Nigerian national costume. The sales were mostly to Nigerians who came to the company's London premises to select and pay for the goods. Usually the company arranged the transport of the goods to Nigeria but sometimes the customer made his own arrangements. At the relevant period, Nigeria had banned the import of textiles. Accordingly, at the instigation of the customers, the goods were misdescribed on the packages containing them, and the company arranged that they were also misdescribed in the relevant carriage and export documentation. There was no misdescription in the company's own books and invoices. On discovering the discrepancies between the invoices and the documentation, the Commissioners considered that there was no satisfactory evidence that the goods had been exported and issued assessments charging tax on them. There were 133 disputed supplies. The tribunal held on the evidence that 128 of the supplies were zero-rated and reduced the assessment from £165,958 to £3,291. *Middlesex Textiles Ltd*, [1979] VATTR 239 (VTD 866).

[25.8] A company (S) supplied goods to another company (V) for export to Libya, and treated the goods as zero-rated. The Commissioners requested evidence that the goods had been exported. S produced a bill of lading and eight airway bills, but the descriptions in these bills could not be related to any of the goods invoiced. The Commissioners were not satisfied that the goods had been exported and issued an assessment charging tax on them. The tribunal upheld the assessment and dismissed S's appeal, holding that S had not produced sufficient documentary evidence to satisfy the Commissioners, acting reasonably, that the goods which it had supplied to V had been exported. *Stockton Plant & Equipment Ltd*, [1986] VATTR 94 (VTD 2093).

[25.9] A company failed to account for VAT on items of thermal clothing, considering that they should be zero-rated as they had been supplied to members of the Forces serving overseas. The Commissioners issued assessments on the basis that the supplies in question did not qualify for zero-rating as there was insufficient proof of export. The company appealed against the assessments and the tribunal allowed the appeal in part, finding that it was satisfied that four of the invoices in question related to goods in respect of which proof of export had been provided, but that the company had not proved that goods specified in other invoices had been exported. *Kingdom Sports Ltd*, [1991] VATTR 55 (VTD 5442).

[25.10] A company agreed to convert a Ford Escort into a rally car for £79,000, which the purchaser paid in September 2002. It did not account for VAT on the supply. Customs issued a ruling that VAT was due on the supply, and the company appealed, contending that the supply should be zero-rated because the purchaser intended to use the car in Kenya. The tribunal dismissed the company's appeal, finding that the supply had taken place in 2002 but the car had not been shipped to Kenya until October 2003. This was outside the three-month time limit laid down by *Notice No 703*. Accordingly the supply failed to qualify for zero-rating. *Historic Motorsport Ltd*, MAN/04/399 (VTD 19048).

[25.11] A trader (C) did not account for VAT on ten supplies of goods, treating them as zero-rated exports. HMRC issued an assessment charging tax on the supplies, on the basis that C had failed to provide the proof of export required by Notice No 703. C appealed. The tribunal reviewed the evidence in detail and allowed the appeal in respect of two of the supplies but dismissed it in respect of the other eight, and directed that the assessment should be reduced accordingly. *M Cohen v HMRC*, [2010] UKFTT 631 (TC), TC00870.

[25.12] Appeals have been dismissed in a large number of cases in which tribunals have held that the requirements of *Notice No 703* have not been complied with. In the interests of space, such cases are not reported individually in this book. For a list of such cases decided up to 31 December 1993, see Tolley's VAT Cases 1994.

[25.13] See also the cases noted at **52.204** to **52.211** PENALTIES: MISDECLARATION.

Goods sold at auction

[25.14] An antique dealer failed to account for output tax on goods sold at auction. The Commissioners issued an assessment charging tax on the sales, and the dealer appealed, producing a letter from the auctioneers stating that the goods had been sold to overseas buyers. The tribunal dismissed his appeal, applying *dicta* of Lord Denning in *Henry Moss of London Ltd*, **25.1** above, and holding that the sales did not qualify for zero-rating since the dealer had not produced the evidence of export required by *Notice No 703*, issued in accordance with what is now *VAT Regulations 1995 (SI 1995/2518), reg 129*. The chairman observed that 'if the auction houses are unable or unwilling to produce the necessary material for the sales to be zero-rated, that is a matter between them and the seller'. *JV Cambridge*, LON/90/151 (VTD 5104).

Misdescription of goods allegedly exported

[25.15] A company failed to account for output tax on supplies of silver to Bangladesh. In the export documentation, the silver was described as lead solder. The Commissioners issued an assessment charging output tax on the supplies, on the basis that they did not qualify for zero-rating since the documentation did not clearly identify the goods in question, as required by *Notice No 703*. The company appealed, contending that the goods had been wrongly described to reduce the risk of theft in transit. The tribunal dismissed the appeal, holding that the requirement in *Notice No 703* that the appellant should hold proof of export which clearly identifies the goods was clearly authorised by *Article 15* of the *EC Sixth Directive*. The appellant company did not hold such proof and thus the supplies did not qualify for zero-rating. *G McKenzie & Co Ltd*, LON/92/2015 (VTD 12949). (*Note.* For a preliminary issue in this case, see **2.21** APPEALS.)

Retail export schemes (Notice No 704)

[25.16] A company sold some fur skins to a customer who paid for them by a draft on an external US dollar account. An employee of the company travelled with the skins and the customer to Heathrow Airport, where the customer had booked a flight to America. They were delayed en route to the airport and the customer took the skins with him as luggage, without producing them to a Customs officer as required by what is now *VAT Regulations 1995 (SI 1995/2518), reg 131(1)*. The Commissioners issued a ruling that the company was required to account for output tax on the sale.

The tribunal dismissed the company's appeal, holding that the Commissioners had to be satisfied that the statutory conditions had been met. If the conditions were not complied with, the Commissioners had no jurisdiction to waive the tax. *Randall Bros. (Furs) Ltd*, LON/75/163 (VTD 210).

[25.17] A UK resident (J) visited an Edinburgh jeweller's shop with his fiancée, a US citizen, and purchased a ring for her. Shortly afterwards she flew to the USA, taking the ring with her. J claimed a refund of the VAT charged on the sale of the ring. The Commissioners rejected the claim and the tribunal dismissed J's appeal. The ring had been supplied to J, who was a UK citizen, and not to his fiancée. Furthermore, even if the supply had been to his fiancée, she had not complied with the conditions laid down by *Notice No 704*, not having produced the ring to a Customs officer on exportation. *P Johnstone*, EDN/75/16 (VTD 211).

[25.18] An individual (G) emigrated from the UK to New Zealand in March 1977, travelling by air. Shortly before he left, he bought a new motorcycle from a retailer. It was delivered to his home untaxed and without registration plates, and was later shipped to New Zealand with his household and personal effects. The Commissioners refused to refund the VAT on the motorcycle, and G appealed. The tribunal dismissed his appeal, holding that it had not been exported by the retailer and it was not within the personal retail export schemes, as it had been supplied to G at his home in the UK and not directly to the ship in which it was exported. Further, a motorcycle did not qualify as 'goods' within the schemes, as under what is now *VAT Regulations 1995 (SI 1995/2518), reg 117(4)*, the term does not include motor vehicles. *GJ Alden*, LON/77/255 (VTD 461).

[25.19] A company sold 18 fur coats and stoles to a Japanese customer, who wished to travel to Japan by air next day with the furs. The company therefore attempted to deal with the sale under the 'over-the-counter' retail export scheme. The customer was given possession of the furs with a form VAT 414 completed on behalf of the company as prescribed in *Notice No 704* (as then in force). However, the customer did not obtain the necessary certification. The company treated the sale as zero-rated. The Commissioners issued an assessment on the basis that the sale did not qualify for zero-rating. The tribunal dismissed the company's appeal, holding that although the furs had been exported, they were not capable of being dealt with under the retail export schemes since they were too bulky and numerous to be carried in the purchaser's hand luggage. They should have been dealt with in accordance with the relevant provisions of *Notice No 703*, which had not been complied with. *Helgor Furs Ltd*, LON/78/339 (VTD 728). (*Note.* Form VAT 414 has subsequently been replaced by form VAT 407.)

[25.20] An appeal was dismissed in a case where a company failed to obtain the evidence of exportation required by *Notice No 704*. *Miss Worth Ltd*, LON/83/328 (VTD 1623).

[25.21] Similar decisions were reached in *P Gandesha*, LON/89/588Z (VTD 5111) and *M Vojtisek (t/a TV & Hi-Fi Studio)*, LON/94/311A (VTD 12905).

[25.22] A company treated various sales as zero-rated under the Retail Export Scheme. The Commissioners issued an assessment on the basis that the goods did not qualify for treatment under the Retail Export Scheme, since the purchaser had acquired them for business purposes. The tribunal upheld the assessment and dismissed the company's appeal, observing that the company's director 'had not read *Notices 704* or *703*' and that 'the burden is on the appellant of convincing us, on a balance of probabilities, that the Commissioners' assessment is wrong'. *GK Electrical UK Ltd*, MAN/87/198 (VTD 2861). (*Note*. Goods exported for business purposes may only be dealt with under the Retail Export Scheme if their value does not exceed £600—see *Notice No 704*.)

[25.23] An appeal was dismissed in a case where the tribunal found that forms VAT 407 submitted by a company had not been stamped or signed by a Customs officer as required by what is now *VAT Regulations 1995 (SI 1995/2518), reg 131(1)*. *East London Fancy Goods Ltd*, LON/89/1203X (VTD 5542).

[25.24] A similar decision was reached in *HJF Enterprises Ltd*, LON/94/70A (VTD 13788).

[25.25] An individual (C) purchased a computer from an Eire company, which was registered as an overseas trader in the UK. He reclaimed the VAT charged on the purchase. The Commissioners rejected the claim and C appealed, contending that he intended to export the computer to Botswana. The tribunal dismissed his appeal, holding that the conditions laid down by *Notice No 704* had not been fulfilled, since C had taken delivery of the computer in the UK. *A Coxshall*, EDN/96/32 (VTD 14317).

[25.26] See also *Richmond Design Interiors Ltd*, 50.82 PENALTIES: EVASION OF TAX.

Miscellaneous

VATA 1994, s 30(6)—company by which goods exported

[25.27] A large group of companies had a significant export trade. It formed a subsidiary export company (E), to which all goods produced by the group and intended for export could be sold, so that E would effect the sales to the overseas buyers. E could, therefore, submit monthly returns rather than quarterly returns, with consequent cash-flow advantages. E was duly registered for VAT in 1980 and rendered monthly returns. In January 1989 the Commissioners wrote to E stating that they had reviewed its operations and considered that the goods which the group exported were not genuinely supplied to E by the other group companies, but were supplied directly to the overseas buyers, so that E was not entitled to reclaim input tax. The QB allowed E's appeal against this decision. Roch J observed that the legislation showed 'a clear intention on the part of Parliament that a wide interpretation should be given to the provisions of the *Act* so that any transaction for a consideration will be either the supply of goods or a supply of services if the supplier is registered for VAT'. *Philips Exports Ltd v C & E Commrs*, QB [1990] STC 508.

[25.28] A company (G) carried on business as an importer and distributor of pharmaceutical and other products. It received orders from Poland for a large quantity of body sprays. The orders in question were passed to G by another company (L) which acted as a broker. G ordered these items from independent manufacturers, and arranged for the manufacturers to send them directly to a seaport. G did not account for VAT on the supply of the goods, treating them as zero-rated exports. The Commissioners issued assessments on the basis that G had supplied the goods to L, that only L was entitled to treat its services in relation to the supply of the goods as zero-rated, and that G should have treated its supplies as standard-rated. G appealed, contending that it had exported the goods in question, and that L was acting as its agent. The tribunal accepted G's evidence and allowed the appeal, holding that L was acting as G's agent and that G had exported the goods for the purpose of what is now *VATA 1994, s 30(6)*. *Geistlich Sons Ltd*, MAN/93/383 (VTD 11468).

VATA 1994, Sch 8, Group 13, Item 3—definition of 'patterns'

[25.29] A company supplied overseas customers with internegatives, to be used for the production of motion picture bulk release prints. The Commissioners issued an assessment charging output tax on the supplies. The company appealed, contending that the internegatives were within the definition of 'patterns' for the purposes of *VATA 1994, Sch 8, Group 13, Item 3*, so that the supplies qualified for zero-rating. The tribunal rejected this contention and dismissed the appeal, holding that the internegatives were not within the definition of 'patterns'. *Technicolor Ltd*, LON/96/898 (VTD 14871).

VAT Regulations, reg 129—recipient of export resident in UK

[25.30] A businessman (M) had been resident in the UK since 1997. In 2006 he purchased a house in Mauritius. In June 2007 he purchased items of furniture and other goods, which were delivered to his house in Sussex. Between 10 and 14 August 2007 he arranged for these purchases to be shipped to Mauritius. On 31 August he and his family left the UK in order to live full-time in Mauritius. He claimed a refund of VAT on the purchases. HMRC rejected the claim and M appealed, contending that since the goods had been sent to Mauritius, they should be treated as zero-rated exports. The tribunal rejected this contention and dismissed his appeal. The tribunal observed that *VAT Regulations 1995, reg 129(1)* required that to qualify for zero-rating, goods must be exported to 'a person not resident in the United Kingdom'. At the time when he purchased the goods, M was still resident in the United Kingdom. *TD Martin-Jenkins v HMRC*, [2009] SFTD 192; [2009] UKFTT 99 (TC), TC00067.

Claim for refund of tax—requirements of VAT Regulations, reg 191

[25.31] An American company claimed a repayment of VAT in respect of goods exported to it. Customs rejected the claim on the grounds that the company had not submitted a 'certificate of status', as required by *VAT*

Regulations 1995 (SI 1995/2518), reg 191(1)(b), within the statutory time limit. The tribunal dismissed the company's appeal against this decision. *Arm Inc*, LON/06/922 (VTD 20238).

Claim for refund of tax lodged outside time limit

[25.32] A company resident and carrying on business in the Cayman Islands, and not carrying on business in the UK, claimed a repayment of VAT in respect of goods exported to it. The Commissioners refused the claim, as it had been made outside the six-month time limit laid down by what is now *VAT Regulations 1995 (SI 1995/2518), reg 192*. The tribunal dismissed the company's appeal, observing that the time limit was in accordance with the provisions of the *EC Thirteenth Directive. Jack Camp Productions*, LON/90/1539X (VTD 6261).

[25.33] A similar decision was reached in an appeal brought by a Norwegian company. *Oceanteam Power & Umbilical ASA v HMRC*, [2009] UKFTT 361 (TC), TC00299.

Export of telephone cards to collectors

[25.34] A trader sold British Telecom phonecards to collectors of such cards who were resident abroad. He did not account for VAT on such exports, treating the supplies as zero-rated. The Commissioners issued a ruling that the export of the cards had to be treated as a supply of services rather than of goods, and thus, where the cards still contained any credits which could be used to make telephone calls, were not eligible for zero-rating. The tribunal upheld the Commissioners' ruling. *R Farrow*, LON/91/1665Y (VTD 10612).

Export of boat—application of Extra-Statutory Concession 4.1

[25.35] A boatbuilder failed to account for VAT on the sale of a boat. The Commissioners issued an assessment charging tax on the sale. The builder appealed, contending that the sale should have been treated as zero-rated under what is now *Extra-Statutory Concession 4.1*, since he had originally arranged to sell the boat to a customer who had intended to sail it outside the UK, but the customer was unable to complete the purchase for financial reasons, and he had subsequently exported the boat to a Norwegian. The tribunal allowed the appeal, finding that the evidence was 'sufficient to establish on the balance of probabilities' that the boat would have been exported within the seven-day time limit if the customer had not fallen into financial difficulties. *Extra-Statutory Concession 4.1** did not require that the boat should actually be exported within seven days of its delivery, but to the customer *intending* that it should be exported. The tribunal held that it could consider the application of the concession, since 'the effect of what is now (*VATA 1994, s 84(10)**) is to allow the tribunal to review whether, as a matter of fact, the taxpayer has acted in accordance with guidelines prescribed by the Commissioners in the exercise of a discretion conferred on them, but not to review the laying down of the guidelines or requirements themselves'. *RW Shepherd*, [1994] VATTR 47 (VTD 11753).

Goods supplied from vending machines at airports

[25.36] A company supplied goods such as condoms and sanitary towels from vending machines in airport buildings which were used by passengers awaiting departure. The Commissioners issued a ruling that it was liable to account for output tax on such supplies. The company appealed, contending that some of the supplies in question should be treated as zero-rated exports. The tribunal dismissed the appeal, observing that some of the goods might be purchased by airport staff rather than by passengers, and holding that the supplies did not qualify for zero-rating. *Mates Vending Ltd*, [1995] VATDR 266 (VTD 13429).

Bank supplying credit to customers exporting goods

[25.37] A major bank claimed a VAT repayment of more than £14,000,000, computed on the basis that where it supplied credit to customers who exported goods, the supplies of credit should be treated as directly linked to the exports of the goods, and as giving rise to a right of deduction or refund of income tax under *VAT (Input Tax) (Specified Supplies) Order 1999 (SI 1999/3121), article 3*. Customs rejected the claim and the tribunal dismissed the bank's appeal, holding that the *Order* only gave a right of deduction where the relevant transactions were 'directly linked to the export of goods to a place outside the Member States'. *Barclays Bank plc (No 7)*, LON/04/848 (VTD 19302).

Charity reclaiming input tax relating to transactions outside UK

[25.38] See *International Planned Parenthood Federation*, 11.55 CHARITIES.

26

Farming

The cases in this chapter are arranged under the following headings.

Flat-rate scheme for farmers (VATA 1994, s 54)   **26.1**
Miscellaneous   **26.3**

Flat-rate scheme for farmers (VATA 1994, s 54)

Appeal against cancellation of certificate

[26.1] A married couple farmed land in the Isles of Scilly, as tenants of the Duchy of Cornwall. They grew and sold bulbs and flowers, and let holiday accommodation. They also bought and resold flowers from other growers. They had registered for VAT from 1987. In 1995 they applied for a flat-rate farming certificate, which was granted. In 1997 the Commissioners cancelled the certificate, considering that the couple were not eligible for the scheme because at least 20% of the flowers which they sold were bought from other growers, rather than grown on their own farm, and their total income from resale of such flowers and supplies of holiday accommodation exceeded the registration threshold. The couple appealed. The tribunal allowed the appeal, finding that the couple had 'made full disclosure of their activities', including 'matters like packaging, plant food and postage, and the holiday lets'. The tribunal held that the buying and selling of cut flowers were not separate parts of the couple's business, and held that 'as the bought-in flowers are mixed in with the flowers actually grown by the appellant on his (*sic*) own ground, there is no way in which the bought-in flowers can be described as a separate business, isolated from the appellant's own production, and excised from it in such a way as to treat that as a separate business of a florist or a dealer in flowers'. The couple carried on a business which qualified as 'growing of fruit and vegetables, flowers and ornamental plants' within *VAT (Flat-Rate Scheme for Farmers) (Designated Activities) Order 1992 (SI 1992/3220)*. Applying *TP Madgett & RM Baldwin (t/a Howden Court Hotel) v C & E Commrs*, **22.487** EUROPEAN COMMUNITY LAW, 'a farmer who buys in a certain amount of produce with the intention of incorporating it with his own produce either for reasons of quality or to make it easier to sell his produce, to render it attractive or to present it to customers in the most propitious way, is carrying out activities ancillary to those of a farmer'. Those ancillary activities 'cannot, unless they reach a significant proportion, be considered separately, treated in isolation, or taken to characterise the main supply.' *A & H Julian*, LON/97/1241 (VTD 16532).

Article 25 of EC Sixth Directive

[26.2] See *EC Commission v Italian Republic*, **22.482** EUROPEAN COMMU-NITY LAW, and *Finanzamt Rendsburg v Harbs*, **22.483** EUROPEAN COMMUNITY LAW.

Miscellaneous

Input tax on renovation of farmhouse

[26.3] For cases where input tax was apportioned, see **36.283** to **36.292** INPUT TAX. For unsuccessful appeals against the disallowance of input tax, see **36.303** to **36.307** INPUT TAX. For appeals concerning the application of *VATA 1994, s 24(3)* to farming businesses, see *RS & EM Wright Ltd*, **36.333** INPUT TAX, and *FJ Meaden Ltd*, **36.335** INPUT TAX.

27

Finance

The cases in this chapter are arranged under the following headings.

Dealings with money (VATA 1994, Sch 9, Group 5, Item 1)	**27.1**
Granting of credit (VATA 1994, Sch 9, Group 5, Item 2)	**27.10**
The provision of instalment credit finance (VATA 1994, Sch 9, Group 5, Items 3, 4)	**27.15**
Intermediary services (VATA 1994, Sch 9, Group 5, Item 5)	
Cases held to qualify for exemption	**27.18**
Cases held to be partly exempt	**27.35**
Cases held not to qualify for exemption	**27.38**
Dealings with securities (VATA 1994, Sch 9, Group 5, Item 6)	**27.46**
Arrangements for dealings with securities (VATA 1994, Sch 9, Group 5, Item 7)	**27.56**
Operation of current, deposit or savings accounts (VATA 1994, Sch 9, Group 5, Item 8)	**27.58**
Management of authorised unit trust scheme (VATA 1994, Sch 9, Group 5, Item 9)	**27.59**
Management of scheme property of open-ended investment company (VATA 1994, Sch 9, Group 5, Item 10)	**27.60**
Supplies relating to credit or charge cards (VATA 1994, Sch 9, Group 5, Note 4)	**27.61**
Miscellaneous	**27.65**

NOTE

There have been several changes to the scope of the exemption for financial services in recent years. See the *VAT (Finance) Order 2003 (SI 2003/1568)*, and the *VAT (Finance) (No 2) Order 2003 (SI 2003/1569)*, introduced with effect from 1 August 2003. The cases in this chapter should be read in the light of the changes in the legislation.

Dealings with money (VATA 1994, Sch 9, Group 5, Item 1)

Transport of cash

[27.1] The Commissioners issued a ruling that the services provided by Securicor, in transporting cash between bank branches, were chargeable to output tax at the standard rate. A bank which used Securicor's services appealed, contending that the services should be treated as exempt under what is now *VATA 1994, Sch 9, Group 5, Item 1*. The tribunal dismissed the appeal, holding that 'dealing with money' connoted 'a financial transaction or operation', and not simply the handling of money. *Williams & Glyn's Bank Ltd*, [1974] VATTR 262 (VTD 118). (*Note.* For the status of the bank as appellant, see **2.54** APPEALS.)

Building society—restocking of automated cash machines

[27.2] A building society operated about 750 automated cash machines at various sites. It arranged for Securicor to restock the machines with cash on a daily basis, collecting the required cash from the building society's bank. Securicor accounted for VAT on the charges which it made to the building society for this service. The society appealed, contending that the supply should be treated as exempt under what is now *VATA 1994, Sch 9, Group 5*. The tribunal dismissed the appeal, holding that the services did not qualify for exemption because the money remained the property of the building society throughout the operation, so that 'in no part of this cycle is there any dealing with money as money', and Securicor's services 'could just as well relate to any other goods which might be counted, packed, delivered, collected and reconciled'. *Nationwide Anglia Building Society*, [1994] VATTR 30 (VTD 11826).

'Swipe fees' paid for use of automated cash machines

[27.3] A company (C) agreed with a bank that it would seek suitable sites for automated cash machines (usually at shops). It received commission for each site that it found, and also received a 'swipe fee' of 15p for each occasion on which the machine was used. It accounted for VAT on the commission, but did not account for VAT on the 'swipe fees'. Customs issued an assessment charging tax on them, and C appealed, contending that they should be treated as exempt under *VATA 1994, Sch 9, Group 5*. The tribunal rejected this contention and dismissed the appeal, finding that C 'takes no part in the operation of the ATM machine and does not issue money'. Accordingly its supplies failed to qualify for exemption. *Concept Direct Ltd*, MAN/05/715 (VTD 19721).

Issue of bank notes from automated cash machines

[27.4] A Scottish bank was authorised to issue its own bank notes, which it issued from automated cash machines. The Commissioners issued a ruling that the issue of banknotes was exempt under *VATA 1994, Sch 9, Group 5, Item 1*. The bank appealed, contending that the issue of its own notes should be treated as zero-rated, and that the 'reciprocity fees', which it received from other banks whose customers had used its machines to withdraw cash, were consideration for zero-rated supplies (so that it was entitled to reclaim the relevant input tax). The tribunal rejected this contention and dismissed the appeal, holding that 'what was specifically and essentially supplied in consideration of the reciprocity fee was the service of providing the customers of counterparty banks with the facility to obtain money'. Furthermore, it was 'significant that the reciprocity fee is transaction-based and bears no relation to the cash dispensed'. It was 'difficult to argue that the reciprocity fee is consideration payable by a counterparty bank for the issue of bank notes when it is not related to the value of the transaction'. The bank appealed to the CS, which unanimously upheld the tribunal decision. Lord Gill observed that 'the system is established for the mutual benefit of the participating banks' and that 'the flat-rate basis of the reciprocity fee is a logical reflection of the fact that the appellant provides a service to the counterparty bank which is in essence the same whatever the value of the transaction, or the type, number or denominations of the notes dispensed'. *Royal Bank of Scotland Group plc v C & E Commrs*, CS [2002] STC 575.

Credit card services—whether exempt transfers of money

[27.5] A company (F) provided credit card services for a number of banks. The Commissioners issued a ruling that F was required to account for output tax on its supplies. F appealed, contending that its supplies should be treated as transfers of money which were exempt from VAT under *VATA 1994, Sch 9, Group 5, Item 1*. The tribunal accepted this contention and allowed the appeal in principle (subject to a further hearing with regard 'to whether other supplies are properly to be regarded as part of the principal supply or as ancillary thereto or are independent'). The CA upheld the tribunal decision, holding that the tribunal was entitled to conclude that there was 'a single or core supply'. These supplies were within *Article 13B(d)(3)* of the *EC Sixth Directive* and therefore qualified for exemption, applying the principles in *Sparekassernes Datacenter v Skatteministeriet*, 22.357 EUROPEAN COMMUNITY LAW. *C & E Commrs v FDR Ltd*, CA [2000] STC 672. (*Notes.* (1) The case was decided on the wording of *VATA 1994, Sch 9, Group 5* before the introduction of *Notes 2A, 2B*, which were introduced by *VAT (Finance) Order 1999 (SI 1999/594)* with effect from 10 March 1999. The change to the legislation was intended to clarify that 'third party credit management is not exempt'. However, the judgment of Laws LJ suggests that, notwithstanding this change to the UK legislation, the company's supplies would still be held to be exempt from VAT by virtue of *Article 13B(d)(3)* of the *EC Sixth Directive*. Compare *Becker v Finanzamt Münster-Innenstadt*, 22.352 EUROPEAN COMMUNITY LAW. (2) For the Commissioners' practice following this decision, see Business Brief 10/01, issued on 16 July 2001, and Business Brief 10/03, issued on 24 July 2003. See now, for supplies of services after 31 July 2003, the *VAT (Finance) Order 2003 (SI 2003/1568)*, which is intended to redefine the scope of the exemption for supplies consisting of credit management. *Article 2*, which removes *Note 2B*, is intended 'to mean that a relevant supply of financial services will be taxed or exempted according to its overall character instead of by reference to the presence or absence of a service listed in *Note 2B*'.)

Mobile telephone services—'payment handling charge'

[27.6] See *Everything Everywhere Ltd v HMRC*, 22.363 EUROPEAN COMMUNITY LAW.

Unsecured bonds issued by incorporated members' club

[27.7] In the case noted at **13.31** CLUBS, ASSOCIATIONS AND ORGANISATIONS, the tribunal defined a 'security for money' as 'a document under seal or under hand at a consideration containing a covenant, promise or undertaking to pay a sum of money'. The tribunal held that 'a document to be such a "security for money" does not have to be either "marketable" or "transferable" or "negotiable"'. *Dyrham Park Country Club Ltd*, [1978] VATTR 244 (VTD 700).

Voucher—whether a 'security for money'

[27.8] In the case noted at 67.152 VALUATION, a company (P) issued vouchers which could be exchanged for goods of a retail value equal to the face value of the voucher. The Ch D held that each voucher was a 'security for money' within *VATA 1994, Sch 9, Group 5, Item 1*, and that the supplies which P made to K were therefore exempt from VAT. *Kingfisher plc v C & E Commrs*, Ch D [2000] STC 992.

Management of foreign currency elements of multi-currency loan

[27.9] A company (E) offered clients what it described as a 'multi-currency debt management programme, with the objectives of reducing the size of a client's debt by borrowing in currencies which fall in value against sterling, and reducing the cost of servicing the debt, by borrowing in currencies which have a lower interest rate than sterling'. HMRC issued a ruling that E was required to account for VAT on its supplies. E appealed, contending that they qualified for exemption under *VATA 1994, Sch 9, Group 5, Item 1*. The tribunal accepted this contention and allowed the appeal, finding that the essence of what E was supplying was 'the exchange of one currency for another'. *The ECU Group plc v HMRC*, [2010] SFTD 1108; , TC00585.

Granting of credit (VATA 1994, Sch 9, Group 5, Item 2)

Subscription paid by taxi drivers—whether a supply of credit

[27.10] In the case noted at 51.53 PENALTIES: FAILURE TO NOTIFY, a company was established to provide premises and a communications network for taxi drivers. The drivers paid a weekly subscription of £20. The company appealed against an assessment, contending that the subscriptions should be treated as consideration for a supply of credit which qualified for exemption under *VATA 1994, Sch 9, Group 5, Item 2*. The tribunal rejected this contention and dismissed the appeal. The tribunal observed that 'the contention that this arrangement constituted a credit facility did not arise until the appellant's representatives consulted their new accountants' and that the appellant's constitution 'gives no power for credit facilities to be given to members'. The tribunal held that 'credit implies a sum of money being given to a person which must be repaid. There is no question of repayment in these circumstances except in the rare instance when a credit card payment is not met and the driver concerned has to repay the advance he received in that respect.' The tribunal concluded that 'the evidence points conclusively to the £20 fee being attributable to a variety of items including the running expenses for the office premises'. Applying the principles laid down by the ECJ in *Card Protection*

Plan Ltd, **22.324** EUROPEAN COMMUNITY LAW, there was 'a single, composite supply of radio and telecommunications services designed to assist the appellant's members in operating their sole trading taxi businesses'. *A1 Rushmoor Radio Taxis Ltd*, LON/x (VTD 17634).

Retail sales—customers paying by credit or debit card

[27.11] A major retail company (D) entered into a scheme, devised by a large accountancy firm, in an attempt to reduce its VAT liability where customers paid by credit or debit card. Under the scheme, D only accounted for VAT on 97.5% of the amount paid by the customers, and paid the remaining 2.5% to a wholly-owned subsidiary company (C). Customs issued an assessment charging tax on the full amount paid by the customers, and D appealed, contending that C was supplying 'card handling' services, which were exempt from VAT under *VATA 1994, Sch 9, Group 5*, and that it was entitled to attribute 2.5% of the consideration paid by the customers to this exempt supply. The tribunal rejected this contention and dismissed the appeal, finding that C was 'an inactive wholly-owned subsidiary of (D) "endowed" by its parent with bare responsibilities which it discharges solely through the agency of its parent and which enable it to make considerable profit'. The tribunal chairman observed that customers had to pay the same price whether they paid by cash, credit card or debit card, and expressed the view that 'why the customer copy of the till slip did not split out the fee for card handling on the one hand and the price for the goods on the other' could only be answered 'by the conclusion that the less the customer knew about the scheme the better'. The CA unanimously upheld the tribunal decision. Mance LJ held that there was a single contract between D and the customer, under which D was 'the supplier to its card-using customers of goods (or in some cases services) for a consideration consisting of the whole 100% payable by such customers on any such transaction'. Accordingly the whole of the amount paid by the customer was consideration for the taxable supply of goods, and none of it could be attributed to a separate exempt supply of credit. *HMRC v Debenhams Retail plc*, CA [2005] STC 1155; [2005] EWCA Civ 892. (*Note.* The HL rejected an application by the company for leave to appeal against this decision.)

Finance company offering credit to customers of retailer

[27.12] A company (H) which sold windows arranged with a finance company to provide credit to its customers. In accounting for output tax, it deducted the commission which the finance company retained. The Commissioners issued an assessment charging tax on the full sale price, and H appealed, contending that the finance company was making a separate supply of credit which qualified for exemption under *VATA 1994, Sch 9, Group 5, Item 2*. The tribunal rejected this contention and dismissed the appeal, holding that any supply of credit was ancillary to the supply of goods, applying the principles laid down by the ECJ in *Primback Ltd*, **22.242** EUROPEAN COMMUNITY LAW. Furthermore, the amounts which the finance company retained as commission were not separately disclosed to the customer, as required by *Group 5, Note 3. HPAS Ltd (t/a Safestyle UK)*, MAN/03/57 (VTD 18701).

Health club subscriptions

[27.13] A couple operated two health clubs. Some members paid annual subscriptions and others paid monthly subscriptions. The couple only accounted for VAT on 70% of the monthly subscriptions. In 1998 Customs issued a ruling that VAT was chargeable on the whole of the monthly subscriptions. In 2003 the couple lodged a late appeal against the ruling, contending that 30% of the monthly subscriptions should be treated as consideration for an exempt supply of finance. The tribunal rejected this contention and dismissed the appeal. *PD & G Taylor (t/a Riverside Sports & Leisure Club) (No 2)*, LON/03/570 (VTD 19354). (*Note.* At a separate hearing, the tribunal also dismissed an appeal against a penalty under *VATA 1994, s 60*—see 50.83 PENALTIES: EVASION OF TAX.)

Article 13B(d) of EC Sixth Directive

[27.14] See the cases noted at 22.352 to 22.361 EUROPEAN COMMUNITY LAW.

The provision of instalment credit finance (VATA 1994, Sch 9, Group 5, Items 3, 4)

Provision of finance for lease purchase agreements

[27.15] A finance company provided finance for the purchase of vehicles under lease-purchase agreements. It did not separately identify the finance charge, but quoted customers the purchase price and the number and amount of instalments. It did not account for VAT on the amount which represented the finance charge, treating this as exempt under what is now *VATA 1994, Sch 9, Group 5*. The Commissioners considered that, since the amount of the finance charge was not separately quoted, the full amount paid was liable to VAT at the standard rate, and issued an assessment accordingly. The tribunal allowed the company's appeal. The amount of the finance charge could be ascertained by a simple calculation. Since the company's customers were all businesses, a specific statement of the separate charge was not as important as it would be in a consumer credit transaction. The charges were within *Group 5, Item 3* and qualified for exemption. *Freight Transport Leasing Ltd*, [1991] VATTR 142 (VTD 5578). (*Note.* For subsequent developments in this case, 2.385 and 2.396 APPEALS.)

Sale of motor vehicles by hire-purchase 'option fee'

[27.16] A company sold motor vehicles by hire-purchase. It charged customers 'option fees', and accounted for output tax on these fees. In 1996 it submitted a repayment claim on the basis that the 'option fees' should have been treated as exempt from VAT under *VATA 1994, Sch 9, Group 5*. The Commissioners rejected the claim, considering that the 'option fees' were taxable consideration paid by the customers for the option to purchase the vehicles. The company appealed. The tribunal dismissed the appeal, holding that 'it is plain on the face of (the) agreements that the payment is for the option'. What was being supplied was 'the right to secure, if the necessary conditions are fulfilled, ownership of the car which throughout is the ultimate objective of the agreement'. *General Motors Acceptance Corporation (UK) plc*, [1999] VATDR 456 (VTD 16137).

Sale of motor vehicles by hire-purchase—'administration fee'

[27.17] A company provided finance for customers who wished to buy motor vehicles by hire-purchase. It charged customers 'administration fees', and accounted for output tax on these fees. In 1998 it submitted a repayment claim on the basis that the 'administration fees' should have been treated as exempt from VAT under *VATA 1994, Sch 9, Group 5*. The Commissioners rejected the claim, considering that the 'administration fees' related to the supply of the vehicles as well as to the supply of credit, and therefore failed to qualify for exemption. The company appealed. The tribunal allowed the appeal, holding that the company had provided the customers with 'the facility of instalment credit finance' within *Group 5, Item 3*, for a separate charge which was disclosed to the customer. On the evidence, the tribunal held that the company 'distances itself from the actual sale of the car' and the administration fees were 'in no way related to transfer of title'. The decision in *General Motors Acceptance Corporation (UK) plc*, **27.16** above, was distinguished. *Wagon Finance Ltd*, LON/98/215 (VTD 16288). (*Note*. For the Commissioners' practice following this decision, see Business Brief 27/99, issued on 21 December 1999.)

Intermediary services (VATA 1994, Sch 9, Group 5, Item 5)

NOTE

VATA 1994, Sch 9, Group 5, Item 5 was substituted by the *VAT (Finance) Order 1999 (SI 1999/594)*, with effect from 10 March 1999. Cases relating to periods before March 1999 should be read in the light of the changes in the legislation.

Cases held to qualify for exemption

Trade association acting as clearing house for members

[27.18] A federation of retailers (B) acted as a 'clearing house' for its members, who sent it monthly statements received from their suppliers, with cheques for the total amounts payable. B paid the suppliers the amounts due, making a small charge to its members for each statement dealt with. It did not account for output tax on these charges. Customs issued a ruling that the charges were taxable, and B appealed, contending that they should be treated as exempt under what is now *Sch 9, Group 5, Item 5*. The tribunal accepted this contention and allowed the appeal. *British Hardware Federation*, [1975] VATTR 172 (VTD 216).

Commission received by company for encouraging use of credit cards

[27.19] A company limited by guarantee operated a credit card scheme, whereby it encouraged its members to use a credit card issued by a bank, and received commission from the bank. It did not account for output tax on the commission which it received. Customs issued an assessment charging tax on the commission, and the company appealed, contending that the commission should be treated as exempt from VAT under *Sch 9, Group 5, Item 5*. The tribunal accepted this contention and allowed the company's appeal, and the CA upheld this decision. On the facts found by the tribunal, the arrangement between the company and the bank was an arrangement for the granting of credit to the company's members. The commission had been received as consideration for the 'making of arrangements' for 'the granting of any credit', and therefore qualified for exemption. *C & E Commrs v Civil Service Motoring Association*, CA 1997, [1998] STC 111. (*Note.* See the note at the head of this section with regard to the substitution of *Item 5* by *SI 1999/594*. In *BAA plc*, 27.20 below, Etherton J observed that, despite the changes in the UK legislation, the decision here remained a binding authority on the interpretation of *Article 13B(d)* of the *EC Sixth Directive*.)

[27.20] A company (B) operated a number of airports. It owned a subsidiary company, which entered into an agreement with a bank (S) under which B provided S with information concerning potential credit card customers. In return S paid B a fixed commission for each customer who used such a credit card, together with a percentage of the value of any transaction conducted with the card. Customs issued a ruling that VAT was chargeable on the amounts payable by S to B. B appealed, contending that it was supplying 'intermediary services' which qualified for exemption under *Sch 9, Group 5, Item 5*. The tribunal accepted this contention and allowed B's appeal, and the Ch D and CA upheld this decision. Sir Andrew Morritt V-C held that the activities carried out by B's subsidiary were within the definition of 'negotiation of credit' for the purposes of *Article 13B(d)* of the *EC Sixth Directive*, and qualified for exemption as 'intermediary services'. *BAA plc v C & E Commrs*, CA 2002, [2003] STC 35; [2002] EWCA Civ 1814. (*Notes.* (1) The CA heard the case with *Institute of Directors*, **27.22** below. (2) For the Commissioners' practice following this decision, see Business Brief 18/2003, issued on 30 September 2003.)

[27.21] The decision in *BAA plc v C & E Commrs*, 27.20 above, was applied in the similar subsequent case of *Prudential Assurance Company Ltd (No 2)*, LON/02/983 (VTD 19364).

Commission received by association for encouraging use of credit cards

[27.22] The Institute of Directors agreed with a bank that it would offer and market a credit card to its members. The bank paid the Institute commission. Initially the Institute accounted for output tax on the commission. However, following the decision in *Civil Service Motoring Association*, **27.19** above, it claimed a refund on the grounds that the commission should have been treated as exempt under *Sch 9, Group 5, Item 5*. Customs rejected the claim, on the basis that the services which the Institute had supplied to the bank were 'of a marketing and product development nature', and did not qualify for exemption. The CA allowed the Institute's appeal, holding that the supplies made by the Institute were within the definition of 'negotiation of credit' for the purposes of *Article 13B(d)* of the *EC Sixth Directive*, and qualified for exemption as 'intermediary services'. *Institute of Directors v C & E Commrs*, CA 2002, [2003] STC 35; [2002] EWCA Civ 1814. (*Note*. The CA heard the case with *BAA plc*, **27.20** above.)

Company charging fees for advance cinema bookings

[27.23] A company (B) arranged advance bookings for cinema seats by telephone or the internet. It charged an administration fee of 50p per ticket. Customs issued a ruling that these fees were standard-rated. B appealed, contending *inter alia* that it was supplying 'intermediary services' which qualified for exemption under *Sch 9, Group 5, Item 5* and *Article 13B(d)* of the *EC Sixth Directive*. The Ch D accepted this contention and allowed the appeal, and the CA unanimously upheld this decision. B's services involved transmitting credit or debit information, including security details and authorisation codes. They had 'the effect of transferring funds and did entail changes in the legal and financial situation'. *Bookit Ltd v HMRC*, CA [2006] STC 1367; [2006] EWCA Civ 550. (*Note*. For HMRC's revised practice following this decision, see Business Brief 18/2006, issued on 30 October 2006.)

[27.24] In a Scottish case where the facts were similar to *Bookit Ltd*, **27.23** above, the CS allowed the company's appeal, holding that the 'booking fee' was 'consideration of the facility of booking by credit card or debit card', and qualified for exemption. *Scottish Exhibition Centre Ltd v HMRC*, CS 2006, [2008] STC 967; [2006] CSIH 42.

Banking services

[27.25] Securicor provided a credit checking service and a money-changing service for customers of a bank. It collected and opened sealed cash containers from the customers, and advised the bank of the amounts contained. Customs issued a ruling that VAT was chargeable on these services. The bank which received the services appealed, contending that they should be treated as exempt under what is now *Sch 9, Group 5, Item 5*. The tribunal allowed the appeal, holding that the services in question were 'services which were normally performed by the bank as an integral part of its banking activities', and qualified for exemption. *Barclays Bank plc*, [1988] VATTR 23 (VTD 2622). (*Note*. See now, however, the note at the head of this section with regard to the substitution of *Item 5* by *SI 1999/594*.)

Services relating to hire-purchase arrangements for sale of cars

[27.26] A company (V), which was a member of a major group of companies in the motor industry, provided hire-purchase facilities in connection with the sale of cars manufactured by its group. It arranged for another company (L), which was a member of a major banking group, to provide various services relating to the 'necessary support functions', including making recommendations as to whether hire-purchase applications should be accepted or rejected. Customs issued a ruling that the services which L supplied to V were taxable. L appealed, contending that its services qualified for exemption under *Sch 9, Group 5, Item 5*. The tribunal accepted this contention and allowed L's appeal, and the QB upheld this decision. On the evidence, L was making a single composite supply of services which qualified as 'the making of arrangements' for 'the granting of any credit'. *C & E Commrs v Lloyds TSB Group Ltd; C & E Commrs v Volkswagen Financial Services (UK) Ltd*, QB [1998] STC 528. (*Note.* See now, however, the note at the head of this section with regard to the substitution of *Item 5* by *SI 1999/594*.)

Company arranging for provision of mortgage advice

[27.27] A company (S) provided financial services. It operated several websites with the aim of introducing customers who required mortgage advice to authorised brokers. Customs issued a ruling that it was required to account for VAT on the commission which it received from the brokers. S appealed, contending that it was providing intermediary services which qualified for exemption under *VATA 1994, Sch 9, Group 5*. The tribunal accepted this contention and allowed the appeal. *Smarter Money Ltd*, [2006] VATDR 296 (VTD 19632).

Submission of financial reports to lending institutions

[27.28] A financier registered for VAT in 1988. A VAT officer formed the opinion that he was not entitled to registration, since all his supplies were exempt. The trader appealed, contending that, although most of his supplies were exempt from VAT, he also supplied financial reports to lending institutions on behalf of clients, and these supplies were taxable. The tribunal dismissed the appeal, holding that, since the financial reports were prepared for the purpose of obtaining loans for the trader's clients, they were exempt under what is now *Sch 9, Group 5, Item 5*. *DP Devoti (t/a Belmont Associates)*, MAN/92/374 (VTD 11868).

Contract for procurement of business finance

[27.29] A company was incorporated with the object of helping businesses to raise finance. It charged clients an application fee of 0.1% of the amount of finance required, and a funding fee of 1% of the amount of finance obtained. It accepted that the 1% funding fees related to exempt supplies, but reclaimed input tax on the basis that the initial application fee related to a taxable supply of financial consultancy. Customs formed the opinion that both fees related to exempt supplies, and issued an assessment to recover the input tax which the company had reclaimed. The tribunal dismissed the company's appeal, holding that there was 'one contract for a service of making arrangements for an advance', and that the entire service was exempt from VAT under what is now *VATA 1994, Sch 9, Group 5*. *Lindum Resources Ltd*, MAN/93/784 (VTD 12445).

Company collecting money from debtors and making payment to creditors

[27.30] A company (D) carried on a debt management service, negotiating with creditors on behalf of debtors, collecting instalment payments from the debtors and passing them to the creditors. Customs issued a ruling that its supplies were liable to VAT. The tribunal allowed D's appeal, holding that it was supplying intermediary services in relation to the granting of credit. The tribunal held that 'the creditor who grants his debtor some indulgence' was 'granting him credit, even if it is additional credit'. Accordingly D's supplies qualified for exemption under *Sch 9, Group 5, Item 5*. *Debt Management Associates Ltd*, MAN/01/631 (VTD 17880). (*Note*. For Customs' revised practice following this decision, see Business Brief 30/2003, issued on 24 December 2003.)

'Debt management' services

[27.31] A couple carried on business in partnership, providing 'debt management services'. They reclaimed input tax. Customs rejected the claim on the basis that the inputs related to exempt supplies. The tribunal dismissed the couple's appeal against this decision. *DG & LM Cooper*, MAN/04/191 (VTD 19179).

[27.32] See also *Paymex Ltd v HMRC*, **20.81** EC DIRECTIVE 2006/112/EC.

Loan broker passing details of debtors to associated company

[27.33] A company (F) carried on business as a loan broker. It passed details of unsuccessful applicants to an associated company (G) which offered debt management services. HMRC issued a ruling that F was required to account for tax on its supplies to G. F appealed, contending that its supplies were 'intermediary services' which qualified for exemption under *VATA 1994, Sch 9, Group 5, Item 5*. The tribunal accepted this contention and allowed the appeal. *Friendly Loans Ltd v HMRC*, FTT 2009, [2010] SFTD 96; [2009] UKFTT 247 (TC), TC00196.

Commission relating to units in unit trust

[27.34] A limited partnership (G) engaged a partnership (J) which carried on business as an estate agency, to find a purchaser for a property in London. Before J had found a purchaser, G transferred the property to a Jersey unit trust, with the intention of avoiding stamp duty land tax. J subsequently introduced a prospective purchaser, who bought the units in the Jersey unit trust. J did not account for output tax on its commission, treating its supply as exempt. HMRC issued an assessment charging tax on the basis that the commission related to a taxable supply of estate agency services. The tribunal allowed J's appeal, holding that J had been acting as an intermediary and that its supply qualified for exemption under *VATA 1994, Sch 9, Group 5, Item 5*. *Joiner Cummings v HMRC*, [2010] UKFTT 606 (TC), TC00847.

Cases held to be partly exempt

Interest received by solicitors

[27.35] A firm of solicitors kept two clients' general bank deposit accounts, and also kept a building society account in the names of the partners, into which the undistributed profits of the firm were deposited. Customs issued an assessment to recover part of the input tax which the firm had reclaimed, considering that the interest which it received was consideration for exempt supplies of financial services, to which part of the firm's input tax should be attributed. The tribunal allowed the firm's appeal in part, holding that the deposits in the building society account were allocations of profit already earned, so that the interest on that account was not consideration for any supply by the firm, but that the interest received on the clients' accounts was consideration for exempt supplies, since the making of deposits in these accounts was an integral part of the manner in which the firm carried on its business. *Hedges & Mercer*, [1976] VATTR 146 (VTD 271).

Company operating fuel card schemes

[27.36] A company (H) operated five fuel card schemes. Customs issued a ruling that the card fees and service charges paid by cardholders, and the amounts which H received from retailers, were consideration for exempt supplies of financial services (with the result that it was not entitled to reclaim the relevant input tax). H appealed, contending that the fuel cards were agency cards rather than charge cards or credit cards and that its supplies were taxable rather than exempt. The tribunal reviewed the evidence in detail and allowed H's appeal in part, holding that in the case of three of the schemes (principally concerning supplies of fuel for heavy goods vehicles, but also including a scheme under which the cardholder had to present his card to the retailer before receiving the fuel), H purchased the fuel from the retailers and made taxable supplies of the fuel to the cardholders. However, in the case of the two standard schemes, the retailers were supplying fuel directly to the cardholders, so that H was making exempt supplies of financial services. *The Harpur Group Ltd*, [1994] VATTR 180 (VTD 12001). (*Note*. For the Commissioners' practice following this decision, see Business Brief 25/94, issued on 16 December 1994, and Customs' VAT Manual, Part 3, Chapter 2, para 2.12.)

Company collecting fees for dentists

[27.37] See *HMRC v Axa UK plc*, 22.362 EUROPEAN COMMUNITY LAW.

Cases held not to qualify for exemption

Partnership acting as financial investigator for bank

[27.38] A partnership acted as a financial investigator for a bank, checking and verifying the credentials of proposed assignees of the bank and ensuring that notice of assignment was given to debtors. It did not account for output tax on the fees which it received. The Commissioners issued an assessment charging tax on them, and the partnership appealed, contending that they should be treated as exempt under what is now *VATA 1994, Sch 9, Group 5*. The tribunal rejected this contention and dismissed the appeal [LON/85/326Z (VTD 4580)]. The partnership appealed to the QB, which upheld the tribunal decision. *Minster Associates v C & E Commrs*, QB 2 April 1992 unreported.

Estate agents arranging for provision of financial advice to clients

[27.39] A firm of estate agents entered into arrangements with a financial company and a firm of solicitors to provide financial advice to clients. The estate agents provided an office for the use of the advisor. The advisors received commission from institutions to whom they introduced clients, and paid a proportion of this commission to the estate agents. The estate agents did not account for tax on this commission. The Commissioners issued assessments charging tax on this, and the estate agents appealed. The tribunal dismissed the appeal, holding that the facilities which the estate agents provided did not amount to 'the making of arrangements'. *Wright Manley Ltd*, MAN/92/466; *Wright & Partners*, MAN/92/467 (VTD 10295).

[27.40] The decision in *Wright Manley Ltd*, **27.39** above, was applied in the similar subsequent case of *Cheshire Trafford Estates Ltd*, MAN/97/839 (VTD 15495).

Marketing services

[27.41] A company carried on a business of providing financial advice. It assisted a merchant bank to launch a new investment trust, and did not account for output tax on the fee paid to it by the merchant bank. Customs issued an assessment charging tax on the payment, and the company appealed, contending that the payment should be treated as exempt under what is now *VATA 1994, Sch 9, Group 5*. The tribunal dismissed the appeal, finding that the company's activities were 'of a promotional and marketing nature'. *Hargreaves Lansdown Asset Management Ltd*, LON/93/547A (VTD 12030).

Sales of discount vouchers by car dealers

[27.42] In the case noted at **67.162** VALUATION, the QB held that the sale of books of discount vouchers by car dealers did not qualify for exemption under *Sch 9, Group 5, Item 5*. *F & I Services Ltd v C & E Commrs*, QB [2000] STC 364.

Administrative services relating to mortgage transactions

[27.43] A company (L) provided various administrative services relating to mortgage transactions. Customs issued a ruling that it was required to account for VAT on its supplies. The representative member of L's group appealed, contending that it was providing intermediary services which qualified for exemption under *VATA 1994, Sch 9, Group 5*. The tribunal reviewed the evidence in detail, rejected this contention and dismissed the appeal, finding that L was making 'a single composite supply of management, administration, auditing and IT services' which failed to qualify for exemption. *Morpheus 2002 Ltd*, [2006] VATDR 428 (VTD 19854).

Debt collection services

[27.44] Following the issue of Business Brief 30/2003, a major bank requested Customs to issue a ruling about the VAT liability of certain supplies relating to debt collection. Customs issued a ruling that the supplies were subject to VAT. The bank appealed, contending that they should be treated as exempt. The tribunal rejected this contention and dismissed the appeal, finding that the relevant services were 'debt recovery' rather than debt negotiation'. The CS unanimously upheld this decision. Lord Nimmo Smith observed that the bank's principal objective was 'to recover as much of the crystallised debt as possible', and that 'the essential aim or dominant purpose of the service supplied' was 'debt recovery'. Accordingly the supplies failed to qualify for exemption. *HBOS plc v HMRC*, CS 2008, [2009] STC 486; [2008] CSIH 69.

[27.45] A UK bank arranged for a South African company (D) to undertake certain negotiations with credit card customers who had fallen into arrears.

Customs issued a ruling that D's services were standard-rated debt collection, so that the bank was liable to account for VAT on them under the 'reverse charge' provisions of *VATA 1994, s 8*. The tribunal upheld Customs' ruling and dismissed the bank's appeal, observing that the 'essential aim' of D's services was debt collection, and holding that ' if D gives a customer more time to pay this is done as part of the process of recovering the debt; it is not a transaction whose essential aim is to grant credit to the customer'. *Barclays Bank plc (No 8)*, [2008] VATDR 107 (VTD 20528).

Dealings with securities (VATA 1994, Sch 9, Group 5, Item 6)

Input tax relating to raising of share capital

[27.46] A company was incorporated in 1984. Its directors intended that it should purchase land for development, erect office buildings thereon, and dispose of the freeholds of the new office premises. It raised capital under the Business Expansion Scheme, and reclaimed input tax on services made to it by a licensed share dealer which helped it to raise this capital. The Commissioners raised an assessment to recover the input tax, on the basis that the dealer's services had been supplied in connection with the issue of the company's shares, which was an exempt supply. The company appealed, contending that the input tax should be treated as deductible because it had been incurred for the purpose of future trading activities. The tribunal dismissed the appeal, distinguishing *Rompelman*, 22.103 EUROPEAN COMMUNITY LAW, and *Merseyside Cablevision*, 36.554 INPUT TAX. The expenditure in this case was laid out 'in order to obtain the services of professional men in connection with issuing shares in the company for the purpose of raising capital'. It could 'not be regarded as expenditure preparatory to the carrying on of an economic activity of the sort mentioned in *Article 4(2)*' of the *EC Sixth Directive*. *Park Commercial Developments plc*, [1990] VATTR 99 (VTD 4892).

Reorganisation of share capital

[27.47] A company which was incorporated in 1980, and which operated a flying club, reorganised its share capital in 1984 and 1986. In 1984 it redeemed loan stock and replaced it, pound for pound, with ordinary shares; and in 1986 it made a rights issue under which each existing shareholder was given the right to subscribe £1 for a further ordinary £1 share. The Commissioners issued an assessment on the basis that the subscription monies provided by the shareholders were paid for the supply of services and were liable to VAT at the standard rate. The company appealed, contending that the supplies should be treated as exempt under what is now *VATA 1994, Sch 9, Group 5, Item 6*. The tribunal allowed the company's appeal, holding on the evidence that the additional subscriptions did not confer additional benefits or facilities. Both transactions were simply issues of shares and were therefore exempt supplies. *Oldbus Ltd*, LON/89/1657 (VTD 5119).

[27.48] A company reclaimed input tax in respect of fees paid to an investment bank in respect of a rights issue of shares. The Commissioners issued an assessment to recover the tax, considering that it related to an exempt supply. The tribunal upheld the assessment and dismissed the company's appeal. *MBS plc*, LON/88/1396X (VTD 7542).

[27.49] A similar decision was reached in *Celtic plc*, EDN/96/47; *Celtic Football & Athletic Co Ltd*, EDN/96/48 (VTD 14898).

[27.50] A public company, which was the representative member of a trading group, financed the acquisition of another company by a substantial share issue. It reclaimed input tax in respect of expenditure relating to the share issue. The Commissioners rejected the claim, on the grounds that the issue of the shares was an exempt supply. The company appealed, contending that the input tax should be treated as deductible since the share issue was not itself a supply and that the purpose of the share issue was to facilitate its trading activities, in the course of which it made taxable supplies. The tribunal dismissed the appeal, holding that the share issue was an exempt supply and that the expenditure in question was directly attributable to this exempt supply. *Swallowfield plc*, [1992] VATTR 212 (VTD 8865).

[27.51] A company reclaimed input tax on professional fees relating to an issue of additional shares, to raise finance for its business. The Commissioners issued an assessment to recover the tax relating to the share issue where the shares were sold to people resident in the EU. (It was accepted that the company was entitled to reclaim input tax relating to sales of shares to people resident outside the EU.) The company appealed, contending that the input tax should be treated as deductible since the issue of a company's own shares was not itself a supply and the purpose of the share issue was to facilitate its trading activities, in the course of which it made taxable supplies. The tribunal dismissed the appeal, and the QB and CA upheld this decision. The issue of a company's shares was a supply of services within *Article 6(1)* of the *EC Sixth Directive*. The supply was exempt from VAT and the expenditure in question was directly attributable to this exempt supply, so that the input tax in question was not deductible. The fact that the supply did not involve any depletion of the company's resources was not conclusive. *Trinity Mirror plc (aka Mirror Group Newspapers Ltd) v C & E Commrs*, CA [2001] STC 192; [2001] EWCA Civ 65. (*Note.* See now, however, the subsequent CJEC decision in *Kretztechnik AG v Finanzamt Linz*, **22.91** EUROPEAN COMMUNITY LAW.)

[27.52] A company was incorporated in March 2000. In May 2000 its shares were floated on the Official List of the Stock Exchange. It reclaimed input tax on professional fees relating to the company flotation. The Commissioners rejected the claim on the basis that the issue of shares was an exempt supply. The company appealed, contending that the invoices related to a mixture of taxable and exempt supplies, and that the input tax should be allowed as a deduction. The tribunal rejected this contention and dismissed the company's appeal, distinguishing *BLP Group plc*, **22.399** EUROPEAN COMMUNITY LAW, and *RAP Group plc*, **46.42** PARTIAL EXEMPTION, and holding that the company had failed to show that the services in question 'were used for taxable supplies as well as the exempt supply of the issue of shares'. *Actinic plc*,

LON/01/933 (VTD 18044). (*Note*. For the Commissioners' revised practice following this decision, see Business Brief 30/2003, issued on 24 December 2003.)

Golf club—sale of debentures to members

[27.53] A limited company (H) was incorporated to operate a golf club. It required most members (other than junior members or social members) to purchase debentures in it. The Commissioners issued a ruling that the sale of the debentures constituted a taxable supply of services. H appealed, contending that the sales should be treated as exempt from VAT under *VATA 1994, Sch 9, Group 5, Item 6*. The tribunal rejected this contention and dismissed the appeal, holding that the act of purchasing a debenture represented 'non-monetary consideration for the supply of services, namely the grant of membership rights'. *Harleyford Golf Club Ltd (No 1)*, LON/95/3076 (VTD 14466). (*Notes*. (1) For the valuation of the supplies, see **67.142** VALUATION. (2) HMRC subsequently accepted that with effect from August 2001, H should be treated as making a single exempt supply. They repaid output tax from 2003 to 2006, but rejected a claim to repay output tax from 2001 to 2003 on the grounds that H had not made a quantified claim within the statutory time limit. The tribunal rejected an application by H to make a late appeal against this decision—[2011] UKFTT 634 (TC), TC01476.)

Rugby Football Union—issue of debentures

[27.54] The Rugby Football Union (RFU) raised money by issuing 75-year non-interest-bearing debentures. Purchasers of these debentures were given the right to purchase tickets for RFU matches at Twickenham for 10 years. The Commissioners issued a ruling that part of the purchase price should be attributed to the taxable supply of the right to watch matches. The RFU appealed, contending that it was making a single exempt supply. The tribunal accepted this contention and allowed the appeal, holding that the whole of the amount paid by the purchasers related to the exempt supply of debentures. *Rugby Football Union*, [2003] VATDR 45 (VTD 18075).

Initial charge for managed personal equity plan

[27.55] A company managed personal equity plans. It levied initial charges to new clients. In cases where the shares contained in the plan were selected by the client, the Commissioners accepted that the charges were exempt from VAT under *VATA 1994, Sch 9, Group 5, Item 6*. However, in the majority of cases where the shares contained in the plan were selected by the company, the Commissioners ruled that the charges failed to qualify for exemption. The CS allowed the company's appeal (reversing the tribunal decision). On the evidence, the initial charge was applicable to both the self-selected plans and to the managed plans. Since the charges were identical, and it was accepted that the initial charges for the self-selected plans qualified for exemption, the initial charges for the managed plan were also for the purchase of securities, and qualified for exemption. *Ivory & Sime Trustlink Ltd v C & E Commrs*, CS

[1998] STC 597. (*Note.* For the Commissioners' practice following this decision, see Business Brief 7/99, issued on 23 March 1999.)

Arrangements for dealings with securities (VATA 1994, Sch 9, Group 5, Item 7)

NOTE

VATA 1994, Sch 9, Group 5, Item 7 was revoked by the *VAT (Finance) Order 1999 (SI 1999/594)*, with effect from 10 March 1999. See now *Item 5*, as substituted by *SI 1999/594*, which refers to the 'provision of intermediary services in relation to', rather than to 'the making of arrangements for' any transactions within *Item 6*, and restricts the exemption to services provided 'by a person acting in an intermediary capacity', as defined by *Item 5A*. The cases in this section are now, therefore, primarily of historical interest, but may still be of some relevance to the provisions now contained in *Item 5*.

Services relating to personal equity plans

[27.56] See *CSC Financial Services Ltd*, 22.360 EUROPEAN COMMUNITY LAW.

Accountants' services relating to flotation of shares

[27.57] A company which traded as a haulage contractor wished to increase its capital by flotation on the London Stock Exchange. It arranged a firm of accountants to prepare some reports in relation to the flotation. The accountants charged output tax on its supplies of these services, and the company reclaimed input tax on the supplies. The Commissioners rejected the claim, on the basis that the services had not been supplied for the purposes of the company's business. The company and the accountants then claimed that the services should have been treated as exempt under *VATA 1994, Sch 9, Group 5, Item 7*, so that no VAT was due on the supplies. The Commissioners rejected this claim and issued a ruling that the accountants' services were standard-rated. The company appealed. The tribunal upheld the Commissioners' ruling and dismissed the company's appeal, holding that the accountants' services constituted the provision of financial information and failed to qualify for exemption, either under *Group 5, Item 7* or under *Article 13B(d)(5)* of the *EC Sixth Directive. Nightfreight plc*, MAN/97/747 (VTD 15479).

Operation of current, deposit or savings accounts (VATA 1994, Sch 9, Group 5, Item 8)

Provision of special cheques and credit slip forms

[27.58] A bank provided certain customers with special cheques and credit slip forms. It reclaimed input tax on the cost of producing these items. The Commissioners rejected the claim on the basis that the provision of these items was an integral part of the bank's supply of services, which was exempt under *VATA 1994, Sch 9, Group 5, Item 8*. The bank appealed. The tribunal allowed the appeal, holding that the special cheques were 'supplied as a separate supply of goods and are not ancillary to the exempt supply of services'. The tribunal held that 'there is no dominant supply of an exempt nature into which it can be argued successfully (that) the special cheques can be embodied for fiscal purposes. It is their aspect as goods which perform an advertising or information-conveying function which makes customers pay the cost of obtaining the special cheques'. *National Westminster Bank plc (No 3)*, [2002] VATDR 414 (VTD 17687).

Management of authorised unit trust scheme (VATA 1994, Sch 9, Group 5, Item 9)

[27.59] A company (P), which was a member of a VAT group, operated 25 'authorised unit trust schemes', within *Financial Services Act 1986, s 207(1)*. It subcontracted the investment management of 11 of the schemes to companies outside its VAT group. The Commissioners issued a ruling that these services did not qualify for exemption under *VATA 1994, Sch 9, Group 5*, since they were not supplied by 'the operator of the scheme', as required by *Item 9 as originally enacted*. P appealed, contending that the restriction in *Item 9* was not in accordance with *Article 13B(d)(6)* of the *EC Sixth Directive*, and that its supplies qualified for exemption under the *Directive*. The tribunal accepted this contention and allowed P's appeal, holding that *Article 13B(d)(6)* 'is not limited in any way as to function or its provider and in particular is not limited to the person operating a special investment fund'. Accordingly, it was 'not legitimate to restrict the exemption accorded to a management function provided by one particular person, i.e. the operator'. Applying *Becker v Finanzamt Münster-Innenstadt*, **22.352** EUROPEAN COMMUNITY LAW, the supplies qualified for exemption under the *Directive* 'regardless of the purported restriction imposed by *VATA 1994, Sch 9, Group 5, Item 9*'. *Prudential Assurance Co Ltd*, EDN/00/37 (VTD 17030). (*Notes.* (1) The Commissioners announced in Business Brief 6/2001, issued on 18 April 2001, that they had appealed against this decision. However, it is understood that they subsequently withdrew their appeal. (2) *VATA 1994, Sch 9, Group 5, Item 9* has subsequently been amended by the *VAT (Finance) (No 2) Order 2003 (SI 2003/1569)*, introduced with effect from 1 August 2003 to delete the restriction of this exemption to supplies by the operator of the scheme. The Commissioners' interpretation of the revised legislation is set out in Business Brief 10/03, issued on 24 July 2003.)

Management of scheme property of open-ended investment company (VATA 1994, Sch 9, Group 5, Item 10)

Whether subcontracted supplies qualify for exemption

[27.60] See *Abbey National plc*, 22.368 EUROPEAN COMMUNITY LAW.

Supplies relating to credit or charge cards (VATA 1994, Sch 9, Group 5, Note 4)

Money retained as commission by companies issuing charge cards

[27.61] Two companies issued charge cards, which could be used by customers for making payments to retailers. When the companies made the necessary payments to the retailers, they retained certain sums as commission. Customs issued assessments on the basis that this commission constituted consideration for supplies of financial services, which were exempt from VAT under what is now *VATA 1994, Sch 9, Group 5, Note 4*, with the result that the companies were subject to the partial exemption provisions and their deductible input tax had to be restricted accordingly. The CA upheld the assessments, holding that the companies were making exempt supplies and that the commission which they retained constituted consideration for these supplies. *C & E Commrs v Diners Club Ltd; C & E Commrs v Cardholders Services Ltd*, [1989] STC 407; [1989] 2 All ER 385.

[27.62] The decision in *Diners Club Ltd*, 27.61 above, was applied in a subsequent case where a retail company (T) had deducted amounts charged to it by the issuers of credit cards in accounting for VAT on sales by credit card. The Commissioners issued an assessment to charge tax on the full amount of the sales, and the tribunal dismissed the company's appeal. T was making taxable supplies of goods to its customers. The exempt supplies of credit were made by the companies which issued the credit cards, rather than by T. *Thayers Ltd, LON/91/1081 (VTD 7541)*.

Commission received for encouraging use of credit cards

[27.63] See *Civil Service Motoring Association*, 27.19 above; *BAA plc*, 27.20 above; *Prudential Assurance Company Ltd (No 2)*, 27.21 above, and *Institute of Directors*, 27.22 above.

Credit card services—whether exempt transfers of money

[27.64] See *C & E Commrs v FDR Ltd*, 27.5 above.

Miscellaneous

Bank dealing in foreign currency bank notes—whether a supply

[27.65] See *Republic National Bank of New York*, 62.195 SUPPLY.

Forex transactions not involving actual banknotes

[27.66] See *The First National Bank of Chicago*, 22.89 EUROPEAN COMMUNITY LAW.

Bank—application of special partial exemption method

[27.67] See *The Governor and Company of the Bank of Scotland*, 46.158 PARTIAL EXEMPTION.

Granting of credit—whether exempt under EC Sixth Directive

[27.68] See *Electronic Data Systems Ltd*, 22.361 EUROPEAN COMMUNITY LAW.

28

Flat-Rate Scheme (VATA 1994, s 26B)

The cases in this chapter are arranged under the following headings.
Relevant supplies and turnover (VATA 1994, s 26B(2))   **28.1**
Regulatory provisions (VAT Regulations, regs 55A-55V)   **28.3**
Miscellaneous   **28.21**

NOTE

     For cases concerning the flat-rate scheme for farmers (*VATA 1994, s 54*), see **26** FARMING.

Relevant supplies and turnover (VATA 1994, s 26B(2))

VATA 1994, s 26B(2)(c)—computation of relevant turnover

[28.1] A couple who operated a small brewery applied to use the flat-rate scheme under *VATA 1994, s 26B*. The Commissioners rejected their application on the grounds that their turnover exceeded the statutory threshold laid down by *VAT Regulations 1995, reg 55L*. They appealed, contending that the Commissioners' calculation was incorrect because it included excise duty which should have been excluded from the 'relevant turnover'. The tribunal rejected this contention and dismissed the appeal, holding that 'the excise duty chargeable is part of the consideration received by the appellant and VAT is chargeable in the ordinary way as on persons not subject to the flat-rate scheme when ascertaining turnover'. Similarly, 'when ascertaining a person's relevant turnover, the turnover must include excise duty. The purpose of the flat-rate scheme is to relieve certain small traders from the paperwork involved in the normal scheme; it is not to exclude goods from VAT.' *G & D Oldershaw (t/a Oldershaw Brewery)*, MAN/04/386 (VTD 19011).

VATA 1994, s 26B(2)(c)—computation of relevant turnover

[28.2] A company (F), which provided specialist electronic analysis services, was registered for VAT and operated the flat-rate scheme. HMRC issued an assessment charging tax on the basis that bank interest which it had received formed part of its 'relevant turnover' for the purpose of computing its liability under the scheme. F appealed, contending that the interest was 'incidental, non-business investment income' which should not be included as 'relevant turnover'. The tribunal accepted this contention and allowed the appeal. Sir Stephen Oliver held that 'the supply made when a person places money with another for a period of time in return for interest is a prime example of the type of supply that is, depending on the circumstances, capable of falling on either side of the line. That "activity" will at one end of the range be pure business as where a bank or a company with a group "treasury" function makes its mainstream profit from lending at interest. At the other end of the range is the private individual who places and keeps cash on deposit; there could be no question of such a person carrying out an economic activity.' On the facts here, F's decision to keep funds on deposit at its bank was not part of its 'core business' and was not a 'direct, permanent and necessary extension' of that business, so that the interest was outside the scope of VAT. *Fanfield Ltd v HMRC (and related appeal)*, [2011] UKFTT 42 (TC); [2011] SFTD 324, TC00919.

Regulatory provisions (VAT Regulations, regs 55A–55V)

Reg 55B(1)—application for retrospective operation

[28.3] A self-employed lorry driver registered for VAT from October 2001. His father, who was an accountant, looked after his tax affairs. In 2006 he submitted an application to operate the flat-rate scheme under *VATA 1994, s 26B*, backdated to the inception of the scheme in April 2002. Customs agreed to allow him to operate the scheme with effect from 1 March 2006, but rejected the application to backdate his operation of the scheme to 2002. The driver appealed. The tribunal allowed his appeal, holding on the evidence that Customs' decision had been unreasonable, within *VATA 1994, s 84(ZA)*. The tribunal observed that Customs' VAT Guidance stated (at chapter 6, para 2.3) that 'the scheme should be encouraged' and (at para 3.3) that 'the regulations contain a power to agree a start date earlier than the date of application so long as the business is not ineligible under the flat rate scheme rules at the time of the proposed start date. This discretion should be exercised in the applicant's favour to encourage take-up of the scheme.' *CJ Anderson*, [2007] VATDR 137 (VTD 20255). (*Note.* The decision here was disapproved by the Ch D in the subsequent case of *HMRC v Burke*, 28.4 below.)

[28.4] A freelance journalist (B) registered for VAT in 1989. In February 2008 he applied to use the flat-rate scheme under *VATA 1994, s 26B*, backdated to October 2004 when he had been visited by a VAT officer who had failed to advise him about the possibility of using the scheme. Customs rejected the application to backdate his operation of the scheme, and he appealed. The tribunal allowed the appeal in part, but the Ch D reversed this decision. Henderson J observed that *VATA 1994, s 84(4ZA)* 'confines the jurisdiction of the tribunal to allow the appeal to cases where it considers that the Commissioners could not reasonably have been satisfied that there were grounds for the decision'. He held that HMRC's policy was 'entirely rational' and 'reflects the simplification policy of the flat-rate scheme itself. If a taxpayer has already accounted for VAT in the past on the normal basis, and in accordance with the general law then in force, there is no way in which retrospective admission to the scheme can simplify the accounting exercise that he has already carried out.' On the evidence, there was 'no basis for interfering with the decision which HMRC took' and 'no material which could properly have led the tribunal to conclude that the high threshold condition for a successful appeal was satisfied'. *HMRC v DE Burke*, Ch D [2009] EWHC 2587 (Ch); [2011] STC 625.

[28.5] A trader (S) carried on a packaging business. He registered for VAT in 1990. In March 2009 he applied to join the flat-rate scheme, and asked for this to be backdated to 2003. HMRC agreed that he could join the scheme with effect from 1 January 2009, but refused to allow him to backdate his entry into the scheme to 2003. The tribunal dismissed S's appeal against this decision, applying the principles laid down by the Ch D in *HMRC v Burke*, **28.4** above. *DL Skinner (t/a DLS Packaging) v HMRC*, [2010] UKFTT 64 (TC), TC00376.

[28.6] The Ch D decision in *HMRC v Burke*, **28.4** above, was also applied in the similar subsequent cases of *SD Solutions Ltd v HMRC*, [2010] UKFTT 228 (TC), TC00529; *Murdoch UK Ltd v HMRC*, [2011] UKFTT 62 (TC), TC00940, and *Anycom Ltd v HMRC*, [2011] UKFTT 654 (TC), TC01496.

[28.7] An electronics engineer (S) registered for VAT in 2003. In November 2007 he applied to join the flat-rate scheme with retrospective effect. Initially HMRC refused to allow him to backdate his entry into the scheme. However in April 2008, after correspondence, an HMRC officer agreed to allow him to backdate his entry into the scheme to 1 April 2005. S appealed, contending that he should have been permitted to backdate his entry to the scheme to April 2002, when the scheme was introduced (even though he did not register for VAT until 2003). The tribunal rejected this contention and dismissed his appeal, observing that S could have requested entry into the flat-rate scheme well before he actually did so. *CJ Sims v HMRC*, [2010] SFTD 674; [2010] UKFTT 73 (TC), TC00386. (*Note.* The appellant appeared in person.)

Reg 55B(3)—refusal of authorisation

[28.8] A publican (G) applied to use the flat-rate scheme under *VATA 1994, s 26B*. Customs rejected his application on the grounds that G constituted a risk to the revenue, as he had failed to register for VAT on time and had also underdeclared takings. Despite not having received authorisation, G submitted returns based on the scheme. Customs issued assessments to recover the additional VAT that would have been due if G had applied the standard method for calculating VAT rather than the flat-rate scheme. G appealed against the assessments and against Customs' refusal to authorise him to use the scheme. The tribunal dismissed his appeals, holding that Customs' decision to refuse authorisation had been reasonable. The tribunal observed that G had shown a 'blatant disregard of his responsibilities in respect of income tax and VAT', and an 'inclination to remain below the respondents' radar until found out by formal enquiries into his tax affairs'. *PT Genrey*, LON/x (VTD 20929).

Reg 55E(1)—capital expenditure goods

[28.9] A company (E), which supplied administrative and consultancy services, operated the flat-rate scheme. In 2004 it built an extension to its office. It reclaimed input tax on the materials. Customs rejected the claim on the basis that the materials did not qualify as 'capital expenditure goods' within *VAT Regulations 1995 (SI 1995/2518), reg 55E(1)*. The tribunal dismissed E's appeal against this decision. The tribunal also observed that 'there are a multitude of separate invoices from separate suppliers for separate items on separate dates. No one single purchase reached the mandatory value and there can be no reason or justification in lumping them all together or in attempting to construe them as one single purchase of building materials.' *Eventful Management Ltd*, MAN/05/797 (VTD 20300).

VAT Regulations 1995, reg 55H(2)—appropriate percentage

[28.10] A company applied to join the flat-rate scheme in March 2007, stating that it was carrying on a business of accountancy. HMRC accepted the application. In February 2009 the company claimed that it should have declared its activity as 'business services not listed elsewhere' (with a lower flat-rate percentage). HMRC accepted the change with effect from 1 December 2008 but refused to allow the company to backdate the change to March 2007. The company appealed. The tribunal dismissed the appeal, observing that when the company had applied to join the scheme, its director had gone through 'a procedure of self assessment in selecting what she regarded as the appropriate sector'. Her choice had not been inappropriate, and 'the legislation relating to the flat rate scheme does not place any obligation on HMRC to backdate any change of category nor is there any provision whereby a taxpayer can insist on having a change backdated'. HMRC's refusal to backdate the change had not been unreasonable. *Archibald & Co Ltd v HMRC*, [2010] UKFTT 21 (TC), TC00336.

Application of VAT Regulations 1995, reg 55JB

[28.11] An individual (P) operated a parcel delivery service. He registered for VAT from March 2001. In July 2004 he applied to join the flat-rate scheme under *VATA 1994, s 26B*. In accounting for tax, he formed the opinion that he was entitled to the 1% reduction provided for by *VAT Regulations 1995 (SI 1995/2518), reg 55JB*. Accordingly he accounted for tax at 8% rather than 9%. Customs issued a ruling that he was not entitled to the 1% reduction under *reg 55JB*, because that reduction was only available for the first year of registration (which in P's case, would have been the year ending 28 February 2002). The tribunal upheld Customs' ruling and dismissed P's appeal. *I Phillips*, MAN/05/729 (VTD 19519).

VAT Regulations 1995, reg 55K—appropriate percentage

[28.12] A married couple operated a public house. Much of their turnover derived from sales of food. In September 2003 they joined the flat-rate scheme for small business, declaring their type of business as 'pubs' and operating the appropriate flat-rate percentage (6% before 1 January 2004 and 5.5% thereafter). For the year ending October 2003, their income from sales of drink totalled £72,353 and their income from sales of food totalled £81,450. A VAT officer discovered this at a control visit in June 2005. She issued assessments on the basis that the effect of *VAT Regulations 1995 (SI 1995/2518), reg 55K* was that the couple should have treated their business as a 'restaurant' and applied a percentage of 12%. She also imposed penalties under *VATA 1994, s 60*. The couple appealed, contending that the business was primarily a 'pub', being described as a 'public house' in their lease and in the licence authorising them to sell alcoholic drinks, and that the sale of food was ancillary to bar sales even though their income from sales of food had marginally exceeded their income from sales of drinks. The tribunal dismissed the appeal against the assessments, observing that the effect of *VATA 1994, s 84(4ZA)* was that 'whilst there is a right of appeal to the tribunal against a decision of HMRC as to the appropriate percentage or percentages applicable under the Scheme, we may not allow the appeal unless we consider that HMRC would not reasonably have been satisfied that there were grounds for the decision'. With regard to the penalties, the tribunal reviewed the evidence in detail and held that there was a reasonable excuse for the couple having applied the percentage applicable to public houses for the periods up to September 2004. However, the tribunal held that 'the excuse was exhausted at the end of September 2004 when they should have carried out a review of their projected turnover in the following year'. Accordingly the tribunal dismissed the appeals against the penalties for the periods ending December 2004 and March 2005. *Mr & Mrs Morgan (t/a The Harrow Inn)*, MAN/05/726 (VTD 19671).

[28.13] A company sold ice-cream and milkshakes from a kiosk in a public square. It joined the flat-rate scheme for small businesses, stating that its business was 'retailing food', so that the appropriate percentage was 2%. Following a visit from a HMRC officer, HMRC issued a ruling that the company was supplying catering services, so that the appropriate percentage was 12%. The company appealed, contending that it was retailing food. The tribunal accepted this contention and allowed the appeal, holding that 'no ordinary person would consider that there was a supply of catering in the ordinary meaning of the word. There is no element of service in what is done as there would be in a restaurant. There was no supply of "catering services".' *The Chilly Wizard Ice Cream Co Ltd*, LON/06/010 (VTD 19977).

[28.14] In 2003 a company began operating the flat-rate scheme. It accounted for tax on the basis that it was supplying 'business services that are not listed elsewhere', so that the appropriate percentage, under *VAT Regulations 1995 (SI 1995/2518), reg 55K*, was 11%. In 2006 Customs issued a ruling that the company was carrying on a business of management consultancy, so that the appropriate percentage was 12.5%. The tribunal upheld Customs' ruling and dismissed the company's appeal. *Ken Reid Ltd*, MAN/07/345 (VTD 20494). (*Note.* Customs had initially issued an assessment backdated to 2003, but withdrew this before the hearing on the grounds that it was unreasonable to backdate the demand.)

[28.15] In 2004 a company began operating the flat-rate scheme. It accounted for tax on the basis that it was supplying 'business services that are not listed elsewhere', so that the appropriate percentage, under *VAT Regulations 1995 (SI 1995/2518), reg 55K*, was 11%. In 2007 Customs issued a ruling that the company was carrying on a business of management consultancy, so that the appropriate percentage was 12.5%. The company appealed, contending that it was supplying the services of a 'forensic employment consultant and expert witness', which was not 'management consultancy', so that it had acted correctly in accounting for VAT at 11%. The tribunal accepted this contention and allowed the company's appeal. *Calibre Tas Ltd*, LON/07/594 (VTD 20508).

[28.16] *VAT Regulations 1995 (SI 1995/2518), reg 55K*, was amended with effect from 1 April 2004. Among other changes, the flat rate percentage for couriers was increased from 5.5% to 9%. HMRC announced the change in Business Brief 7/04, issued on 2 March 2004, and in an update to *Public Notice 733*. However a company (C) which operated a courier business continued to account for VAT at the old rate of 5.5%. When HMRC discovered this, they issued an assessment to charge tax at 9%. C appealed, contending that HMRC had failed to notify it of the increase in the relevant percentage. The tribunal rejected this contention and dismissed the appeal, accepting HMRC's evidence that it had sent C a copy of the update to Public Notice 733 in May 2004, and finding that C 'did not appreciate the significance of the documents'. *Cannon Express & Logistics Ltd*, [2009] UKFTT 116 (TC), TC00084.

Reg 55P—termination of authorisation to operate scheme

[28.17] A company (W) traded as an 'exercise club'. It operated the flat-rate scheme from January 2005. Customs subsequently discovered that W's controlling shareholders also controlled another company which leased gym equipment and owned the premises from which W traded. Accordingly, the effect of *VAT Regulations 1995 (SI 1995/2518), reg 55L* was that W was ineligible to operate the scheme. Customs therefore issued a notice of termination under *reg 55P*, backdated to January 2005, and a misdeclaration penalty (mitigated by 25% to reflect a degree of co-operation). W appealed, contending that the notice should not have been backdated. The tribunal rejected this contention and dismissed the appeals, holding that W had never been entitled to operate the scheme, that the backdating of the notice was authorised by *reg 55Q*, and that there were no grounds for any further mitigation of the penalty. *Welshback Exercise Ltd*, LON/x (VTD 20310).

[28.18] A company (R) registered for VAT from October 2007, and applied to join the flat-rate scheme. Subsequently HMRC discovered that R was providing management services to another company (B), and that R's directors held 50% of the shares in B. Accordingly, the effect of *VAT Regulations 1995 (SI 1995/2518), reg 55L* was that R was ineligible to operate the scheme. HMRC therefore issued a notice of termination under *reg 55P*, backdated to January 2005, and imposed a misdeclaration penalty. R appealed, contending that it should not be treated as being associated with B. The tribunal reviewed the evidence in detail, rejected this contention and dismissed the appeal. On the evidence, 'there were close organisational links between the companies in that they had the same shareholders'. They were 'closely bound by financial, economic and organisational links'. Accordingly, R had not been entitled to operate the flat-rate scheme. Furthermore, the effect of *reg 55Q* was that HMRC were entitled 'to backdate the termination'. The tribunal also held that there was no reasonable excuse for the consequent misdeclaration of VAT, and upheld the misdeclaration penalty in principle (while mitigating it by 25% to take account of a degree of co-operation). *RDF Management Services Ltd v HMRC*, [2010] UKFTT 74 (TC), TC00387.

Reg 55Q—application for retrospective withdrawal from scheme

[28.19] A woman (M) operated a riding school. She registered for VAT from October 2005, and applied to account for VAT under the flat-rate scheme. In 2006 she arranged for the construction of a new riding arena at the riding school. She reclaimed VAT on the construction costs. HMRC rejected most of the claim on the grounds that it related to supplies of services, and issued an assessment to recover the tax which she had reclaimed. She appealed against the assessment, and also applied to be allowed to withdraw from the flat-rate scheme with retrospective effect. HMRC rejected this application, and she appealed. The tribunal allowed her appeal, holding that HMRC had acted unreasonably. On the evidence, most of the supplies relating to the construction of the riding arena had been supplies of services, although the specific supply of the track surface had been a supply of goods on which the tax could be reclaimed, and the supply of delivery of the track should have been accepted as an incidental part of the principal supply, applying the principles laid down in *AJ & K Price*, **15.280** CONSTRUCTION OF BUILDINGS, ETC. However, the tribunal noted that the February 2004 edition of *Notice 733 (Flat Rate Scheme for Small Businesses)* 'offered no guidance on the meaning of a capital asset'. Such guidance was subsequently included in the March 2007 edition, and the tribunal noted that if such guidance had been available when M applied to join the scheme, her accountants may have realised that the scheme was not suitable for her. Furthermore, the VAT officer who had visited M in February 2007 had recognised that the scheme was not suitable, and had recommended that M 'may wish to consider leaving the flat rate scheme retrospectively from 1 July 2006, in order to claim the input tax on services relating to the new indoor riding school and any capital assets less than £2,000 in value'. HMRC's subsequent decision not to allow M to withdraw retrospectively meant that she 'was liable for £11,175 more in VAT than under normal accounting'. HMRC had 'denied a proper exercise of discretion by the officer reviewing the individual circumstances of the case'. Applying the guidelines laid down by the CA in *C & E Commrs v John Dee Ltd*, **14.31** COLLECTION AND ENFORCEMENT, HMRC's refusal to allow a retrospective withdrawal from the scheme was unreasonable. *S March v HMRC*, [2009] UKFTT 94 (TC), TC00062. (*Note*. Costs were awarded to the appellant.)

[28.20] A plumber (R) applied to join the VAT flat-rate scheme in 2004. In 2008 he formed the opinion that the effect of the scheme was that he was paying more VAT than he would have done if he had accounted for VAT in the normal way. He applied for permission to withdraw from the scheme with retrospective effect. HMRC agreed that he could withdraw from the scheme with effect from 28 May 2008 (the date of his application), but refused to allow him to backdate his withdrawal. R appealed. The tribunal dismissed his appeal, holding that HMRC's decision had not been unreasonable. Aleksander J observed that 'HMRC's policy is generally not to allow retrospective application or withdrawal from the flat-rate scheme – and that retrospective applications should only be allowed in exceptional circumstances. The mere fact that a taxpayer will pay more tax under the flat-rate scheme is not considered exceptional for these purposes.' This was 'a rational policy', since 'the flat-rate scheme is intended to provide a measure of simplification for small businesses, and is intended to be revenue neutral. The objective of the scheme is not to provide a mechanism for small businesses to pay less VAT – and this is clear from the provisions of the VAT Directive which allow member states to implement simplified VAT accounting arrangements for small businesses.' *B Reynolds v HMRC*, [2010] UKFTT 40 (TC), TC00354.

Miscellaneous

Failure to account for tax on acquisitions from other EC States

[28.21] A clothing retailer acquired a number of goods from other EC member States. She failed to declare these on her VAT return. Customs issued an assessment charging tax on them. The tribunal upheld the assessment and dismissed the trader's appeal, observing that nothing in *VAT Regulations 1995 (SI 1995/2518), regs 55A-55V* altered the requirement in *VATA 1994, s 10* 'to account for VAT on acquisitions'. Accordingly, 'a person who elects to be treated, and is authorised, as a flat rate trader remains liable to account for VAT on acquisitions and importations of goods'. *JB West (t/a West One)*, LON/05/892 (VTD 19677).

Application of VATA 1994, s 26B(5)

[28.22] A company joined the flat-rate scheme in March 2005. In June 2008 it applied to withdraw from the scheme. HMRC accepted the application, and backdated the withdrawal to 29 February 2008. The company submitted returns claiming input tax for the period in which it had been included in the flat-rate scheme. HMRC issued an assessment to recover the tax, and the company appealed, contending that the flat-rate scheme was unfair and that Notice 733 was unclear. The tribunal rejected these contentions and dismissed the appeal, observing that *VATA 1994, s 26B(5)* specifically provided that 'a participant in the flat-rate scheme shall not be entitled to credit for input tax'. The tribunal also held that Notice 733 was 'clear in its explanations and instructions' and observed that 'in cases where a person needs help or clarification, there is a helpline operated by the Commissioners which the appellant had used in the past and which could have been consulted for further clarification if in doubt as to the operation of the scheme'. *Contrast Graphic Supplies Ltd v HMRC*, [2010] UKFTT 289 (TC), TC00578.

29

Food

The cases in this chapter are arranged under the following headings.

Supplies in the course of catering (VATA 1994, Sch 8, Group 1(a))

Definition of 'catering'	**29.1**
Whether food supplied 'for consumption on the premises' (*VATA 1994, Sch 8, Group 1, Note 3(a)*)	**29.20**
Whether food supplied 'hot' (*VATA 1994, Sch 8, Group 1, Note 3(b)*)	**29.55**

Whether 'food of a kind used for human consumption' (VATA 1994, Sch 8, Group 1, General Item 1)

Cases held to qualify for zero-rating	**29.81**
Cases where the consideration was apportioned	**29.95**
Cases held not to qualify for zero-rating	**29.96**

Animal feeding stuffs (VATA 1994, Sch 8, Group 1, General Item 2)	**29.106**
Means of propagation of plants (VATA 1994, Sch 8, Group 1, General Item 3)	**29.119**
Live animals (VATA 1994, Sch 8, Group 1, General Item 4)	**29.120**
Ice cream, etc. (VATA 1994, Sch 8, Group 1, Excepted Item 1)	**29.125**

Confectionery, etc. (VATA 1994, Sch 8, Group 1, Excepted Item 2)

Cases held to qualify for zero-rating	**29.128**
Cases where the consideration was apportioned	**29.141**
Cases held not to qualify for zero-rating	**29.144**

Beverages (VATA 1994, Sch 8, Group 1, Excepted Item 4)	**29.165**
Potato crisps, etc. (VATA 1994, Sch 8, Group 1, Excepted Item 5)	**29.181**
Pet food, etc. (VATA 1994, Sch 8, Group 1, Excepted Item 6)	**29.187**

NOTE

The provisions of *VATA 1994, Sch 8, Group 1* largely derive from the *Purchase Tax Act 1963* as amended by *FA 1969*. Under that provision, certain products (including ice cream, confectionery, potato crisps and salted and roasted nuts) were taxed at a higher rate of tax (22%).

Supplies in the course of catering (VATA 1994, Sch 8, Group 1(a))

Definition of 'catering'

Sale of food from mobile vans

[29.1] Supplies of hot food from mobile vans are now standard-rated by virtue of *VATA 1994, Sch 8, Group 1, Note 3(b)*, originating from *FA 1984*.

For cases concerning whether supplies are of 'hot food', see **29.55** *et seq.* below. For sales of cold food from mobile vans, where the issue was whether the food was sold for consumption on defined 'premises' within what is now *VATA 1994, Sch 8, Group 1, Note 3(a)*, see *Cooper*, **29.27** below, and *Skilton & Gregory*, **29.47** below.

Set meals supplied by butcher

[29.2] A butcher supplied food to customers to order, on the basis of eleven menus with set meals and fixed prices. He did not account for VAT on these supplies. The Commissioners issued an assessment charging tax on them, on the basis that they were 'in the course of catering' and thus did not qualify for zero-rating. He appealed, contending that his supplies were not in the course of catering, since any catering was undertaken by the customers to whom he supplied the meals. The tribunal rejected this contention and dismissed his appeal, observing that the food which he supplied was ready for immediate consumption in individual portions, and that the supplies were linked to functions organised by the recipient. Accordingly, the supplies were in the course of catering. *RV Vodden*, MAN/84/74 (VTD 1842).

Delicatessen orders delivered to customers

[29.3] A company trading as retail grocers supplied and delivered delicatessen orders to customers. The company advertised this service as 'home party catering'. However, many of the items supplied required some further preparation before they could be served. Loaves of bread were not sent out cut, gateaux were often sent out frozen, chicken joints and cocktail sausages needed to be cooked or warmed, and coffee was supplied in the form of coffee beans. The Commissioners issued a ruling that the supplies were in the course of catering and were standard-rated. The company appealed, contending that the supplies were zero-rated. The tribunal allowed the company's appeal in part, holding that because of the additional preparation required, the actual catering for the parties was done by the customer and thus the supplies were zero-rated. However, buffet boxes supplied by the company and containing complete meals were held to be supplies in the course of catering, and standard-rated. *C Chasney Ltd*, [1989] VATTR 152 (VTD 4136).

Delicatessen orders collected by customers

[29.4] See *Wendy's Kitchen*, **29.12** below.

'Party trays' sold from delicatessen counters

[29.5] A major retail company sold a range of 'party trays' of food from its delicatessen counters. Such trays had to be ordered in advance and collected from the counter. The company did not account for output tax on its supplies of the trays, treating them as a zero-rated supply of food. The Commissioners issued an assessment charging tax on the basis that the trays were a standard-rated supply of catering, and the company appealed. The tribunal allowed the appeal, holding that the company was making supplies of food, and that the arrangement of the food on trays did not amount to 'catering'. The QB upheld this decision. There had been no delivery to, or service at, the location where the food was to be consumed. There had been no waiter service and no provision of cutlery, etc. The company would normally have no knowledge as to whether the food was for a specific event or occasion. The tribunal had been entitled to find that the supplies were not in the course of catering. *C & E Commrs v Safeway Stores plc*, QB 1996, [1997] STC 163.

'Food platters' sold from sandwich bar

[**29.6**] A company operated a sandwich bar. It sold a range of 'food platters' including sandwiches, apples, bananas, sausage rolls, scotch eggs, etc. It did not account for output tax on these supplies, treating them as zero-rated. The Commissioners issued an assessment charging tax on the basis that the food was supplied in the course of catering. The tribunal allowed the company's appeal, applying the QB decision in *Safeway Stores plc*, **29.5** above, and holding that the food was not supplied in the course of catering. *Happy Place Ltd (t/a The Munch Box)*, LON/00/1218 (VTD 17654).

Sandwiches supplied on platters

[**29.7**] A partnership operated a sandwich shop. It supplied platters of sandwiches to customers (mostly to nearby offices), and did not account for tax on such supplies, treating them as zero-rated. The Commissioners issued assessments charging tax on the supplies, on the basis that they did not qualify for zero-rating since they were within the definition of 'catering'. The partnership appealed. The tribunal allowed the appeal, holding that the arrangement of sandwiches on platters did not amount to 'catering'. *Out To Lunch*, MAN/93/1182 (VTD 13031).

[**29.8**] A similar decision was reached in a subsequent case where the tribunal held that 'there is very little difference between sandwiches sold in a bag and sandwiches sold on a platter' and that 'the delivery of the platters was a very minor part' of the business. *R & A Bardetti (t/a Obertelli Quality Sandwiches)*, LON/99/561 (VTD 16758). (*Note.* For another issue in this case, see **58.36** RETAILERS' SPECIAL SCHEMES.)

'Finger buffets' delivered to customers

[**29.9**] A married couple traded in partnership as food retailers. As part of their business, they supplied 'finger buffets' to local offices, such as accountancy firms. The cheapest type of finger buffet which they offered comprised sandwiches and fruit tarts; more expensive buffets also included pies, sausage rolls, crisps, salad, cakes, etc. Initially the couple accounted for VAT on these buffets. Subsequently, on the advice of their accountants, they submitted a repayment claim, on the basis that the supplies should have been zero-rated. The Commissioners rejected the claim, considering that the supplies were in the course of catering, and thus were excluded from zero-rating. The couple appealed. The tribunal dismissed the appeal, observing that the couple described themselves in their leaflets and brochures as 'quality outside caterers', and finding that each of the finger buffets was a supply in the course of catering. *PJ & LJ Lawson (t/a Country Fayre)*, MAN/96/5 (VTD 14903).

[**29.10**] The decision in *Lawson*, **29.9** above, was applied in a subsequent case where the facts were similar. The tribunal distinguished *Safeway Stores plc*, **29.5** above, on the grounds that the supplies in that case were not delivered to customers; and distinguished *Out To Lunch*, **29.7** above, on the grounds that that case only concerned supplies of sandwiches, whereas in the present case the appellants' menu 'included a large variety of items other than sandwiches; in particular cakes, cheeseboard and fruit, which permitted a meal rather than a snack to be provided'. *C & E Taylor (t/a Sandwich Heaven)*, MAN/98/757 (VTD 16211).

[29.11] A similar decision, also distinguishing *Safeway Stores plc*, 29.5 above, was reached in *Value Catering Ltd v HMRC (and related appeal)*, [2011] UKFTT 329 (TC); [2011] SFTD 868, TC01189.

'Finger buffets' collected by customers

[29.12] A partnership operated a catering and delicatessen business from a shop. It advertised two types of menus for finger buffets. The food provided with the finger buffets included sandwiches, rolls, sausage rolls, pies, chicken drumsticks, crisps, nuts, etc. It accounted for VAT on these finger buffets where it delivered them to its customers. However, where customers collected the buffets from the shop, the partnership did not account for tax on the supplies, treating them as zero-rated. The Commissioners issued an assessment charging tax on the basis that the finger buffets were supplied in the course of catering even when they were collected by the customers, and were excluded from zero-rating. The partnership appealed. The tribunal dismissed the appeal, holding on the evidence, including the partnership's advertising material, that the supplies were within the definition of catering. *Wendy's Kitchen*, MAN/95/1073 (VTD 15531).

[29.13] A similar decision was reached in *AC & Mrs Y Hodge (t/a Priory Kitchen)*, MAN/97/326 (VTD 16185).

Supply of sandwiches ordered by electronic mail

[29.14] A company began a service whereby office employees could order sandwiches, confectionery and drinks by electronic mail. The items which had been ordered were delivered in refrigerated vans to the office where the employees worked. The Commissioners issued a ruling that the supply of the sandwiches was made in the course of catering, and was therefore standard-rated. The company appealed. The tribunal allowed the appeal, holding that the fact that the company's promotional literature described its services as 'catering' was not conclusive. *Bergonzi*, 29.53 below, was distinguished on the grounds that in that case 'the person supplying the food was physically present on the premises of the employer'. The tribunal observed that the company's supplies were equivalent to a sandwich delivery service, and were not within the ordinary definition of 'catering'. *Emphasis Ltd*, [1995] VATDR 419 (VTD 13759).

Supply of sandwiches in hospital common room

[29.15] A partnership sold sandwiches from a hospital common room. The Commissioners issued a ruling that the supply of the sandwiches was made in the course of catering, and was therefore standard-rated. The partnership appealed. The tribunal decided to hold a preliminary hearing on the question of whether the supplies were within the general definition of catering, and, if not, hold a further hearing on whether they were deemed to be in the course of catering by virtue of *VATA 1994, Sch 8, Group 1, Note 3(a)*. At the preliminary hearing, the tribunal held that the supplies were not within the general definition of catering, leaving undecided the question of whether *Note 3(a)* applied. *A Carpenter & S Hayles (t/a Carpenter Catering) (No 1)*, LON/02/143 (VTD 17851). (*Note.* For subsequent developments in this case, see **29.30** below.)

Supplies from aircraft stand at airport

[29.16] A company sold take-away food from a large vehicle situated at an aircraft stand at an airport terminal. It accounted for output tax on its supplies of hot food, but treated its supplies of cold food as zero-rated. The Commissioners issued an assessment charging output tax on the basis that all the company's supplies were in the course of catering. The tribunal allowed the company's appeal, holding that 'the ordinary person would not regard the supplies by the appellant as being done in the course of catering'. *E & G Catering Services Ltd*, LON/97/1571 (VTD 15552).

Supplies of sandwiches in airport departure lounge

[29.17] A company sold sandwiches in airport departure lounges. It initially accounted for VAT on these sales, but subsequently submitted a repayment claim, contending that the supplies should have been treated as zero-rated. The Commissioners rejected the claim on the basis that the supplies were within the definition of 'catering'. The tribunal upheld the Commissioners' ruling and dismissed the company's appeal, and the Ch D upheld this decision as one of fact. (Peter Smith J observed that the company had not produced evidence to indicate that any purchasers had bought sandwiches in order to eat them on the aircraft, rather than in the departure lounge.) *Whitbread Group plc v C & E Commrs*, Ch D [2005] STC 539; [2005] EWHC 418 (Ch). (*Note.* For a subsequent case where this decision was distinguished, see *Pret A Manger (Europe) Ltd*, **29.32** below.)

Meals provided on aircraft

[29.18] See *British Airways plc*, **66.13** TRANSPORT.

Food supplied from trolley on train

[29.19] A company operated a non-stop train service from London Victoria to Gatwick Airport. It sold food from a trolley service on the train. The Commissioners issued a ruling that VAT was chargeable on these sales, on the basis that the food was supplied in the course of catering. The company appealed. The tribunal dismissed the appeal, holding that the supplies were within the ordinary definition of 'catering'. *Central Trains Ltd*, MAN/00/1095 (VTD 17475).

Whether food supplied 'for consumption on the premises' (VATA 1994, Sch 8, Group 1, Note 3(a))

Cases held to qualify for zero-rating

Sale of doughnuts at Ideal Home Exhibition

[29.20] A company manufactured bakery equipment, including machinery designed for the manufacture of doughnuts. It displayed this machinery at the

Ideal Home Exhibition, and gave sample doughnuts to traders who visited its stand and expressed interest in renting or buying its machines. It also sold some doughnuts to members of the public, mainly in batches of six. It did not account for VAT on these sales. The Commissioners issued an assessment charging tax on the basis that they were supplies in the course of catering and thus not eligible for zero-rating. The tribunal allowed the company's appeal, holding on the evidence that the doughnuts were not sold for consumption on the premises, since they were mostly sold in batches of six and it was unlikely that the purchasers intended to consume all six doughnuts immediately. *DCA Industries Ltd*, [1983] VATTR 317 (VTD 1544).

Sale of doughnuts from mobile vans

[29.21] In *Skilton & Gregory*, 29.47 below, the tribunal held that sales of doughnuts from mobile vans in Battersea Park were zero-rated, since 'there was no delineated area capable of constituting the premises where the consumption took place'.

Food sold from kiosks in shopping centre

[29.22] A trader operated one of six food kiosks within a shopping centre. She did not account for VAT on her supplies. The Commissioners issued an assessment charging tax on 60% of her supplies, on the basis that 60% of the food which she sold was consumed within the shopping centre, and that the shopping centre constituted the premises on which the food was supplied. The tribunal allowed the trader's appeal, holding that there was no delineated area capable of constituting 'premises' where the actual consumption of food supplied by the trader took place. The shopping centre was akin to a public thoroughfare and did not constitute 'premises'. Accordingly the supplies were not within the definition of 'catering', and were zero-rated. *M Armstrong*, [1984] VATTR 53 (VTD 1609).

[29.23] A company sold food from a kiosk in the hall of a shopping centre. It did not account for tax on its sales of cold take-away food. The Commissioners issued an assessment charging tax on such supplies. The company appealed, contending that the supplies qualified for zero-rating. The tribunal allowed the company's appeal. Although much of the food which the company sold was consumed within the shopping centre, the shopping centre was akin to a 'public thoroughfare'. The food was not supplied for consumption 'on the premises', and thus was not excluded from zero-rating. *Peek Catering Ltd*, EDN/92/162 (VTD 10628).

[29.24] A similar decision was reached in *Made To Order Ltd*, MAN/07/723 (VTD 20959).

Snack bar in office block

[29.25] A trader operated a snack bar from a room on the first floor of an office block. Most of her supplies were of sandwiches. She did not account for VAT on her supplies, and the Commissioners issued an assessment charging tax on them. She appealed, contending that, since none of the food which she supplied was consumed in the room in which the snack bar was located, the supplies were zero-rated. The tribunal allowed her appeal in part, finding that 70% of her supplies were to customers who worked in the same office block as the snack bar and that 30% were to customers from other buildings, and holding that the 70% of the supplies which were consumed within the office block were standard-rated. The trader applied for judicial review of this decision. The QB granted a declaration that the supplies were entirely zero-rated. The tribunal had erred in law in regarding the whole building as the 'premises'. The word 'premises' in what is now *VATA 1994, Sch 8, Group 1, Note 3(a)* should be construed as including only the room which the trader occupied. *R v C & E Commrs (ex p. Sims (t/a Supersonic Snacks))*, QB 1987, [1988] STC 210. (*Note.* The decision in this case was distinguished in the subsequent case of *Bergonzi*, 29.53 below, on the grounds that it related to a multi-tenanted office block to which members of the public had access.)

[29.26] A company supplied sandwiches from units in multi-occupancy office blocks. Customs issued a ruling that it was required to account for VAT on the supplies, on the basis that the whole of the relevant office blocks should be regarded as 'premises', so that the sandwiches were supplied for consumption 'on the premises'. The tribunal allowed the company's appeal, finding that some of the supplies were to customers who worked outside the specific office blocks in question, and holding that the 'premises' should be treated as the specific unit which the company occupied, rather than the whole of the office block. *QSR Ltd (t/a First Taste)*, MAN/05/059 (VTD 19528).

Sandwiches sold from tray taken around offices

[29.27] A trader sold sandwiches from a mobile van and from a tray taken around offices in an office block. The Commissioners issued an assessment on the basis that his supplies were 'in the course of catering' and were standard-rated. The tribunal allowed the trader's appeal, holding that the food was not supplied in the course of catering. Sales from a van were not intended for consumption 'on the premises', since the public thoroughfare did not amount to 'premises'; and the sales of sandwiches were not for consumption 'on the premises', since the trader did not necessarily intend the sandwiches to be consumed within the office block and the customers could, for example, have taken them to a nearby park. *M Cooper*, MAN/87/269 (VTD 2665).

[29.28] A company sold sandwiches and fruit salads at offices in the City of London. The sandwiches and salads were placed in large baskets, and each basket was given to an employee to visit a number of office blocks. Most sales took place in the reception areas of the offices. The company had accounted for VAT on more than 75% of the sandwiches which it sold, but had not accounted for VAT on any of the sales of fruit salad. The Commissioners issued an assessment charging VAT on more than 75% of the sales of fruit salad. On receiving the assessment, the company director consulted an accountant, who considered that none of the supplies should have been standard-rated. He wrote to the Commissioners accordingly, and lodged an appeal. The tribunal allowed the appeal, holding that none of the food was supplied for consumption 'on the premises', applying the QB decision in *Sims*, 29.25 above. Where the food was consumed was of no consequence to the company. Food was only supplied 'for consumption on the premises on which it is supplied' where the supplier had some right or duty to supply the food on those premises. *Zeldaline Ltd*, [1989] VATTR 191 (VTD 4388).

Sandwiches sold within hospital site

[29.29] A company trading from a room within a hospital site sold sandwiches, etc., and accounted for tax on the basis that these sales were zero-rated. The Commissioners issued an assessment on the basis that 80% of the sales were for consumption within the 'hospital site' and were therefore deemed to be supplied in the course of catering. The tribunal allowed the company's appeal, holding that the 'premises' in which the food was supplied was the room in which the company operated, rather than the whole of the 'hospital site'. Applying the QB decision in *Sims*, **29.25** above, any food consumed outside that particular room was not supplied 'for consumption on the premises'. *Ashby Catering Ltd*, MAN/89/144 & MAN/89/426 (VTD 4220).

[29.30] A partnership sold sandwiches, etc. from a counter in the common room of a hospital postgraduate centre. The Commissioners issued a ruling that the supply of the sandwiches was made in the course of catering, and was therefore standard-rated. The partnership appealed. The tribunal held that for the purpose of *VATA 1994, Sch 8, Group 1, Note 3(a)*, the 'premises' should be held to be the common room, rather than the whole of the site. Accordingly VAT was only chargeable on food which was supplied for consumption in the common room, and any food consumed outside that particular room was not supplied 'for consumption on the premises'. *A Carpenter & S Hayles (t/a Carpenter Catering) (No 2)*, LON/02/143 (VTD 18148). (*Note.* For a preliminary issue in this case, see **29.15** above.)

Sales of food within BBC Television Centre

[29.31] A company (C) supplied food from various outlets within the BBC Television Centre in West London (a large complex comprising 21 buildings on the same site). Customs issued a ruling that it was required to account for VAT on all of its supplies. C appealed, accepting that supplies of hot food were standard-rated, but contending that supplies of cold food such as sandwiches from six outlets within the site qualified for zero-rating. The tribunal accepted this contention and allowed C's appeal, holding that for the purpose of *VATA 1994, Sch 8, Group 1, Note 3(a)*, the 'premises' should be held to be the specific units from which C operated, rather than the whole of the site. The CA upheld the tribunal decision (by a 2-1 majority, Sir Charles Mantell dissenting). Mummery LJ held that 'the test of whether a supply is in the course of catering is an objective one and that the states of mind or intentions of the parties do not really assist.' On the evidence, C was 'no more making supplies of sandwiches "in the course of catering" than the supermarket chain with a section set aside in its store for the sale of sandwiches. So far as the retail customers of (C) are concerned there is no relevant catering in the course of which sandwiches are supplied to them such as to render them liable to pay VAT'. *HMRC v Compass Contract Services UK Ltd*, CA [2006] STC 1999; [2006] EWCA Civ 730. (*Note.* For HMRC's practice following this decision, see Business Brief 12/06, issued on 21 August 2006.)

Sales of cold food at airport and Channel Tunnel terminals

[29.32] A company (P) sold food from units at two airport terminals and at the Channel Tunnel terminal in Kent. Initially it accounted for VAT on these supplies, but it subsequently submitted a repayment claim on the basis that its supplies of cold food qualified for zero-rating. Customs rejected the claim but the tribunal allowed P's appeal, distinguishing the earlier decision in *Whitbread Group plc*, **29.17** above, on the grounds that 'no evidence as to takeaway was led in that case'. The tribunal held that for the purpose of *VATA 1994, Sch 8, Group 1, Note 3(a)*, the 'premises' should be held to be the specific units from which P operated, rather than the whole of the relevant terminals. *Pret A Manger (Europe) Ltd (No 2)*, LON/x (VTD 19755). (*Note.* For a previous appeal by the same company, see **29.77** below.)

Seafood sold from kiosk in public park

[29.33] A company sold seafood from a kiosk in a public park at Barry Island. The park was about 700 yards in circumference, and contained at least 20 shops or kiosks. The company did not account for VAT on these sales, considering that they were zero-rated. The Commissioners issued an assessment charging tax on the sales, considering that the park constituted 'premises' so that the sales were in the course of catering. The tribunal allowed the company's appeal, holding that the park did not constitute premises and that the supplies were zero-rated. *Fresh Sea Foods (Barry) Ltd*, [1991] VATTR 388 (VTD 6658).

Supplies of cold food from school tuck shop

[29.34] The governors of a school formed a limited company to operate the school 'tuck shop', which sold hot and cold food. The tuck shop was located within the main school building, in two rooms which had previously formed a cloakroom. The company failed to account for output tax on its sales of food. The Commissioners issued an assessment charging tax on the sales, and the company appealed, accepting that output tax was due on supplies of hot food, but contending that the supplies of cold food qualified for zero-rating, on the basis that the food was not supplied for consumption on the tuck shop premises. The tribunal accepted this contention and allowed the appeal, holding that the supplies were not within the general definition of 'catering', and also that they were not excluded from zero-rating by what is now *VATA 1994, Sch 8, Group 1, Note 3(a)*, since the 'premises' should be construed as meaning the two rooms occupied by the tuck shop itself, rather than the whole of the school building. *St Benedict Trading Ltd*, MAN/93/1375 (VTD 12915).

Supplies of cold food from kiosks at railway stations

[29.35] A company sold cold take-away food from kiosks at railway stations. The Commissioners issued a ruling that the company's sales were standard-rated, on the basis that the food was supplied for consumption on the premises at which it was supplied. The company appealed, contending that the 'premises' should be interpreted as its kiosks, rather than the whole of the railway stations in question, so that the sale of food consumed outside its kiosks should be treated as zero-rated. The tribunal allowed the appeal, holding that the fact that the kiosks were situated at railway stations was not sufficient to bring them within the general definition of 'catering', and that, from the company's point of view, it was immaterial whether the food which it supplied was to be consumed on the station at which it was sold. The 'premises' on which the food was supplied were the company's kiosks, rather than the whole of the railway stations. *Travellers Fare Ltd*, MAN/94/1190 (VTD 13482).

Supplies of cold food from canteen within defence establishment

[29.36] A partnership sold cold take-away food from a canteen at a defence establishment (a naval air station). The Commissioners issued a ruling that the partnership's sales were standard-rated, on the basis that the food was supplied for consumption on the premises at which it was supplied. The partnership appealed, contending that the 'premises' should be interpreted as its canteen, rather than the whole of the naval air station, so that its supplies qualified for zero-rating. The tribunal accepted this contention and allowed the appeal. *J Bishop & P Elcocks*, LON/01/690 (VTD 17620).

Cases held not to qualify for zero-rating

Supply of food from buffets at football ground

[29.37] A football supporters' club sold food from a number of kiosks at a football ground. It did not account for VAT on these supplies. The Commissioners issued a ruling that the supplies were standard-rated on the basis that they were for consumption on the premises on which they were supplied. The club appealed, contending that its premises were the kiosks from which the food was sold, rather than the whole football ground. The tribunal rejected this contention and dismissed the appeal against this decision, holding that the whole of the football ground constituted the 'premises'. *Bristol City Football Supporters Club*, [1975] VATTR 93 (VTD 164). (*Note*. The decision was approved by the QB in *Cope*, 29.45 below.)

[29.38] A similar decision was reached in *Parker (t/a The Roker Park Suite)*, MAN/80/58 (VTD 956).

Sale of food at working men's club

[29.39] A company which operated a restaurant obtained the right to sell food at a nearby working men's club. It did not account for VAT on these sales. The Commissioners issued an assessment charging tax on these sales and the company appealed, contending that its premises should be treated as the kitchen which it occupied, rather than the whole club. The tribunal rejected this contention and dismissed the appeal, holding that the whole of the club, including the car park, constituted the 'premises'. Accordingly the supplies were standard-rated. *Ivy Café Ltd*, MAN/76/73 (VTD 288).

Drinks supplied from vending machines

[29.40] An employees' social club operated two vending machines, dispensing hot and cold drinks, on its employers' premises. It did not account for VAT on its receipts from these machines. The Commissioners issued an assessment charging tax on the supplies. The tribunal dismissed the club's appeal, holding that the drinks were supplied 'for consumption on the premises'. *Burnham Radio Recreational & Welfare Club*, CAR/77/157 (VTD 518).

[29.41] A company operated a number of vending machines, dispensing hot and cold drinks, which were installed at various premises such as factories and garages. It did not account for VAT on its receipts from these machines. The Commissioners issued an assessment charging tax on the supplies. The tribunal dismissed the company's appeal, holding that the nature of the supplies was such that they were intended for early consumption. Accordingly they were intended 'for consumption on the premises on which they were supplied'. *Macklin Services (Vending) West Ltd*, [1979] VATTR 31 (VTD 688). (*Note.* For another issue in this case, see **3.40** ASSESSMENT.)

[29.42] An accountancy partnership operated a coin-operated vending machine which dispensed hot drinks. Each week the partners were supplied with 5p coins to obtain drinks from the machine. The partners' drawings accounts were debited accordingly. The partnership did not account for VAT on the takings from the machines. The Commissioners issued an assessment charging tax on them. The tribunal dismissed the partnership's appeal, holding that the partnership was supplying the drinks to the partners and that the supplies were in the course of catering and therefore standard-rated. *Atkins Macreadie & Co*, MAN/86/333 (VTD 2381).

[29.43] Drinks supplied from vending machines were also held to be standard-rated in *Streamline Taxis (Southampton) Ltd*, LON/85/499 (VTD 2016); *Triangle Press Ltd*, LON/92/1122Y (VTD 9648) and *Bourne*, **52.215** PENALTIES: MISDECLARATION.

Snacks supplied from vending machines

[29.44] A company sold snacks from vending machines. Initially it accounted for output tax on its supplies, but it subsequently submitted a repayment claim on the basis that it should have treated its supplies as zero-rated. HMRC rejected the claim and the tribunal dismissed the company's appeal, holding that the snacks were intended 'for consumption on the premises on which they were supplied'. *West Country Vending Service Ltd v HMRC*, [2010] UKFTT 124 (TC), TC00435.

Supplies of food from mobile stall at race meetings

[29.45] A trader sold seafood for immediate consumption from a mobile stall at race meetings. The Commissioners issued an assessment on the basis that his supplies were within the definition of 'catering' and were therefore standard-rated. He appealed, contending that they were zero-rated. The QB upheld the assessment, observing that the food was supplied for consumption at the racecourses, which were within the definition of 'premises' for the purposes of *Note 3*. Furthermore, the word 'includes' in *Note 3* was not intended to be restrictive, and 'catering' included the provision of food incidental to some other activity, such as football matches, race meetings, wedding receptions, etc. Accordingly the trader's supplies were in the course of catering. *C & E Commrs v BH Cope*, QB [1981] STC 532.

[29.46] The decision in *Cope*, 29.45 above, was followed in a case where a company supplied food and drink at a 'point-to-point' course for racehorses. The tribunal held that the company's supplies were in the course of catering and thus were standard-rated. *Q Inns Ltd*, LON/92/295Z (VTD 8929).

Sale of doughnuts from mobile vans

[29.47] A partnership sold doughnuts from mobile vans. Most of the sales took place at horse-race meetings or agricultural shows, but some took place in Battersea Park. The partnership did not account for VAT on the sales, treating them as zero-rated. The Commissioners issued an assessment charging VAT on the basis that the sales were supplies in the course of catering, and thus excluded from zero-rating. The tribunal allowed the partnership's appeal in part, holding that the sales at horse-race meetings and agricultural shows were for consumption on the premises on which they were supplied, and were therefore deemed to be supplies in the course of catering and excluded from zero-rating. However, the sales in Battersea Park were zero-rated, since 'there was no delineated area capable of constituting the premises where the consumption took place'. *Skilton & Gregory*, LON/92/662X (VTD 11723). (*Note.* An appeal against a misdeclaration penalty was allowed.)

Food sold from kiosks in shopping centre

[29.48] A company sold seafood from a kiosk in a shopping centre. The kiosk was one of a number of kiosks, all of which sold food of various types, surrounding a courtyard which had tables and chairs for almost 400 people. The company did not account for VAT on its supplies, and the Commissioners issued an assessment charging tax on them. The tribunal dismissed the company's appeal, holding that the courtyard and the kiosks together constituted 'premises', so that the supplies were of food 'for consumption on the premises on which it is supplied' and were not eligible for zero-rating. *Crownlion (Seafood) Ltd*, [1985] VATTR 188 (VTD 1924).

[29.49] A partnership sold food from a snack bar on the first floor of a shopping centre. The snack bar was adjacent to two similar kiosks. About twelve feet from the kiosks was a raised seating area containing 20 tables, each of which could seat four people. The partnership did not account for VAT on its sales of food. The Commissioners issued an assessment charging tax on the supplies, considering that the kiosks and the seating area constituted 'premises', so that the food was supplied in the course of catering and was not eligible for zero-rating. The tribunal upheld the assessment and dismissed the partnership's appeal, applying *Crownlion (Seafood) Ltd*, **29.48** above, and distinguishing *Armstrong*, **29.22** above. *Breezes Patisserie*, EDN/92/295 (VTD 10081).

Seafood sold in public houses and clubs

[29.50] A trader sold seafood in public houses and clubs. The Commissioners issued an assessment on the basis that the seafood was supplied in the course of catering and was therefore standard-rated. He appealed, contending that his supplies were zero-rated. The tribunal reduced the assessment to take account of a small number of sales made in the street, which were zero-rated, but held that the sales in public houses and clubs were within the definition of 'catering' and thus were standard-rated. *K Mowbray*, [1986] VATTR 266 (VTD 2239).

Food sold at public house

[29.51] Food sold at a public house was held to be standard-rated in *MJ Hellaby*, LON/89/715Z (VTD 4790).

Food supplied from shed in country park

[29.52] A company supplied food from a shed in a 360-acre country park. The park was private property, and members of the public had to pay for admission to the park. Where appropriate, the food was supplied in containers, but no plates were provided. There were no tables or seats near to the shed, and no food was consumed inside the shed. The company did not account for VAT on its supplies. The Commissioners issued an assessment, charging tax on the basis that the food was supplied 'in the course of catering'. The tribunal dismissed the company's appeal, holding that the country park constituted 'premises' so that the supplies were standard-rated. *Mylos of Reading (Catering & Ices) Ltd*, LON/86/575 (VTD 2538).

Snack bar in office block

[29.53] A trader operated a snack bar from two rooms on the seventh floor of an office block. The whole of the office block was occupied by a single group of companies. The trader accounted for output tax on supplies of hot food, but did not account for tax on supplies of cold food. The Commissioners issued an assessment charging tax on the supplies of cold food, on the basis that they were supplies in the course of catering and thus excluded from zero-rating. The trader appealed, contending that the supplies should be treated as zero-rated, applying the decision in *Sims*, 29.25 above. The tribunal dismissed the appeal, distinguishing *Sims* because in that case 'the licence was intended to allow the grantee to deal with the general public', whereas in the present case 'the licence was granted exclusively for the benefit of the employees of the group of companies'. Applying the principle in *Cope*, 29.45 above, the supplies of food were incidental to the business activities of the group of companies, and were thus within the definition of 'catering'. Furthermore, the whole of the seventh floor of the office block constituted the premises on which the food was supplied, so that the food was supplied for consumption on the premises, and the supplies were excluded from zero-rating by what is now *VATA 1994, Sch 8, Group 1, Note 3*. *GME Bergonzi (t/a Beppi's Buffet Service)*, LON/93/1756A (VTD 12122).

Snack bar at auction site

[29.54] A partnership operated a snack bar at a site used for car auctions, under a licence agreement with the auctioneers. The partnership did not account for VAT on food sold at the snack bar, and the Commissioners issued an assessment charging tax on the supplies. The partnership appealed, contending that the supplies should be treated as zero-rated. The tribunal dismissed the appeal, observing that the snack bar existed for the purpose of enabling food to be consumed at the auctioneers' premises. *Bramley Caterers*, MAN/90/1072 (VTD 6385).

Whether food supplied 'hot' (VATA 1994, Sch 8, Group 1, Note 3(b))

Cases held to qualify for zero-rating

Hot pies sold from baker's shop

[29.55] A company trading as bakers sold freshly-baked pies from retail shops. The final baking of such pies was carried out in the shop oven, so that they were hot at the time of sale. Some customers purchased pies to consume immediately, whereas others purchased them to take away and eat later. The Commissioners issued an assessment charging tax on some of the sales, on the basis that the pies which were eaten while hot were excluded from zero-rating. The company appealed, contending that it did not heat the pies for the purpose of enabling them to be consumed at a temperature above the ambient air temperature, but in order to produce a smell which was designed to attract customers. The QB allowed the company's appeal, holding that, on the evidence accepted by the tribunal, the pies were not within the definition of 'hot food' in what is now *VATA 1994, Sch 8, Group 1, Note 3(b)(i)*. The CA upheld this decision as one of fact. *John Pimblett & Sons Ltd v C & E Commrs*, CA 1987, [1988] STC 358.

[29.56] The decision in *John Pimblett & Sons Ltd*, 29.55 above, was applied in a subsequent case where a company sold freshly-baked pies, pasties and sausage rolls. The tribunal held that the sales were zero-rated, since the company's purpose in heating the food was that the items should be seen to be freshly-baked, rather than to enable them to be consumed at a temperature above the ambient air temperature. The fact that some of the items may have been consumed above the ambient air temperature was incidental. *Greenhalgh's Craft Bakery Ltd*, MAN/91/626 (VTD 10955). (*Note.* For another issue in this case, see 3.42 ASSESSMENT.)

[29.57] A similar decision, also applying *John Pimblett & Sons Ltd*, 29.55 above, was reached in *Three Cooks Ltd*, LON/94/2558A (VTD 13352).

Hot Cornish pasties

[29.58] A shop sold freshly-baked Cornish pasties. It was accepted that a substantial proportion of the pasties were sold at a temperature above the ambient air temperature. However, the tribunal accepted that the company's purpose was solely to sell freshly-baked pasties, and that no pasties were reheated or deliberately kept warm after baking. Accordingly, the tribunal held that the pasties were zero-rated. *Lutron Ltd*, LON/88/1148Z (VTD 3686). (*Note.* See, however, the subsequent decision in *Wallace*, 29.78 below.)

Sale of toasted bagels

[29.59] A company sold toasted bagels, for consumption off the premises. The Commissioners issued a ruling that the toasted bagels were within the definition of 'hot food' in *VATA 1994, Sch 8, Group 1, Note 3(b)(i)* so that the company was required to account for output tax on these supplies. The company appealed, contending that the purpose of toasting the bagels was to 'create a crunchy interior to the bagel and to promote freshness', rather than to enable them to be consumed at a temperature above the ambient air temperature. The tribunal accepted this contention and allowed the appeal, finding that the company's intention 'was to impart to the inner cut surface a crisp texture'. It was 'no part of their purpose to enable the bagels to be consumed at any particular time or temperature'. *Great American Bagel Factory Ltd*, LON/00/659 (VTD 17018).

Sale of toasted baguette sandwiches

[29.60] Two companies sold toasted baguette sandwiches, for consumption off the premises. The Commissioners issued a ruling that the toasted sandwiches were within the definition of 'hot food' in *VATA 1994, Sch 8, Group 1, Note 3(b)(i)* so that the companies were required to account for output tax on these supplies. The companies appealed, contending that the purpose of toasting the sandwiches was not to enable them to be eaten when warm, but 'to release the flavour of the ingredients and to make the bread crisp'. The tribunal accepted the companies' evidence and allowed the appeal, finding that 'the sandwiches were supplied at temperatures varying from lukewarm to cold', and applying the reasoning in *John Pimblett & Sons Ltd*, **29.55** above. *Tuscan Food Ltd*, LON/03/646; *Pure Atma Ltd*, LON/03/647 (VTD 18716).

'Ciabatta melts'—whether zero-rated

[29.61] A company sold 'ciabatta melts'. It initially accounted for VAT on the basis that these were within the definition of 'hot food', but subsequently submitted a repayment claim on the basis that they qualified for zero-rating. Customs rejected the claim but the tribunal allowed the company's appeal, applying the reasoning in *John Pimblett & Sons Ltd*, **29.55** above, and finding that the company's purpose in heating the products was 'to sell a tasty product rather than a hot or even a warm one'. *Ainsleys of Leeds Ltd*, MAN/05/464 (VTD 19694).

[29.62] The decision in *Ainsleys of Leeds Ltd*, **29.61** above, was applied in the similar subsequent case of *Waterfields (Leigh) Ltd*, MAN/07/1451 (VTD 20761).

Hot 'paninis'—whether zero-rated

[29.63] A trader sold hot 'paninis' (described by the tribunal as similar to Cornish pasties, but using specially baked bread rather than pastry). He initially accounted for VAT on the basis that these were within the definition of 'hot food', but subsequently submitted a repayment claim on the basis that they qualified for zero-rating. Customs rejected the claim but the tribunal allowed the trader's appeal, applying the reasoning in *John Pimblett & Sons Ltd*, **29.55** above, and holding on the evidence that 'the hot state of the "paninis" following the grilling is a consequence of the grilling: it is not one of the purposes of the grilling'. *RJ Warren (t/a WT Warren & Son) (and related appeal)*, LON/06/219 (VTD 19902). (*Note.* The decision here was not followed in the subsequent case of *Coffee Republic plc*, **29.79** below.)

Sale of roast chickens in department stores

[29.64] A company owned three large department stores. It sold many types of food, including roast chickens. It did not account for VAT on the sales of chickens, treating them as zero-rated. The Commissioners issued an assessment on the basis that the chickens were within the definition of 'hot food' in what is now *VATA 1994, Sch 8, Group 1, Note 3(b)*, and were accordingly deemed to be supplied in the course of catering and standard-rated. The tribunal allowed the company's appeal, holding on the evidence that the company's predominant purpose in keeping the chickens hot until sale was to comply with hygiene requirements. Although the chickens were still hot when sold, this was not for the purpose of enabling them to be consumed above the ambient air temperature. They were not marketed in such a way as to be eaten shortly after purchase. The tribunal commented that to eat a roast chicken 'as one would eat a pie or pasty would be an unpleasantly messy process'. *The Lewis's Group Ltd*, MAN/89/389 (VTD 4931).

Sale of cooked chicken pieces in supermarkets

[29.65] A company which operated a number of supermarkets did not account for output tax on the sale of cooked chicken pieces, treating them as zero-rated. The Commissioners issued an assessment charging tax on such supplies, on the basis that they did not qualify for zero-rating since they were hot when they were sold. The company appealed, contending that the food was not heated 'for the purposes of enabling it to be consumed at a temperature above the ambient air temperature', but in order to comply with food hygiene regulations. The tribunal accepted this contention and allowed the appeal. *Stewarts Supermarkets Ltd*, BEL/93/60A (VTD 13338).

Sale of cooked chickens and chicken pieces from take-away shop

[29.66] A trader operated two take-away food shops from which she sold chickens and chicken portions, as well as other types of foodstuffs. Where she sold chickens and chicken portions with chipped potatoes, she treated the sales as standard-rated. However, where she sold chickens or chicken portions on their own, she treated the sales as zero-rated. The Commissioners issued an estimated assessment charging tax on such sales. The trader appealed, contending that the purpose of heating the chickens was to comply with food hygiene regulations. The tribunal accepted this contention and allowed the appeal in respect of these sales, applying *Stewarts Supermarkets Ltd*, **29.65** above. *NM Holmes (t/a The Chicken Shop)*, MAN/98/355 (VTD 16264).

School meals

[29.67] A trader supplied cooked lunches to two schools. Customs issued a ruling that his supplies were standard-rated, and the trader appealed. The tribunal found that the food was supplied at a temperature of at least 65°C, but accepted the trader's evidence that the 'dominant purpose' of this 'was to comply with the *Food and Hygiene Regulations*' and that the food 'was intended for re-heating before service'. The tribunal allowed the appeal, finding that the trader's purpose in heating the food was 'to provide hygienic, freshly cooked food which was fit for consumption by children who would be vulnerable to food poisoning'. *A Leach (t/a Carlton Catering)*, LON/01/46 (VTD 17767).

Food heated to comply with hygiene regulations

[29.68] A company (D) delivered a wide range of foods including crispy duck pancakes, spring rolls, samosas, falafels, sesame prawn toasts and onion bhajis. The First-tier Tribunal upheld HMRC's ruling that these items failed to qualify for zero-rating, applying the QB decision in *Malik*, 29.72 below. However the Upper Tribunal allowed D's appeal against this decision. Proudman J held that D's purpose in heating the food had been to comply with food hygiene regulations, rather than to enable the food to be consumed at a temperature above the ambient air temperature. Accordingly, applying the principles laid down by the CA in *John Pimblett & Sons Ltd v C & E Commrs*, 29.55 above, the supplies qualified for zero-rating. *Deliverance Ltd v HMRC*, [2011] UKUT 58 (TC); [2011] STC 1049.

Cases where the consideration was apportioned

Sale of heated waffles

[29.69] A trader carried on business selling hot and cold snacks, including waffles. She treated the sale of waffles as zero-rated. The Commissioners issued an assessment charging tax on the sale of waffles, on the basis that they were within the definition of 'hot food'. The trader appealed, contending that her purpose in heating the waffles was merely to ensure that they were crisp, rather than to enable them to be consumed at a temperature above the ambient air temperature. The tribunal allowed her appeal in part, finding that only some of the waffles were still hot when they were sold, and holding that although all the waffles had been heated for consumption 'at a temperature above the ambient air temperature', only those waffles which were still above the ambient temperature when sold were excluded from zero-rating. The waffles which were no longer above the ambient air temperature at the time of sale were zero-rated. *WD Redhead*, MAN/87/167 (VTD 3201).

Cases held not to qualify for zero-rating

School meals

[29.70] A catering firm supplied cooked lunches to a school. The lunches were cooked at the firm's premises and delivered to the school by minibus. The lunches were usually delivered in aluminium trays, and were kept warm at the school on electrically-heated metal trolleys. The Commissioners issued an assessment charging VAT on the lunches, on the basis that they were a supply in the course of catering. The firm appealed, contending that the supplies should be treated as zero-rated. The tribunal dismissed the appeal. On the evidence, the lunches were hot when they left the firm's premises, having been cooked in order that they could be consumed 'at a temperature above the ambient air temperature'. *P & S Catering*, LON/90/1222Z (VTD 6382).

Hot meal delivery service

[29.71] A trader provided a meals delivery service for the elderly and disabled. He did not account for VAT on his supplies. The Commissioners issued an assessment charging tax on them, and the tribunal dismissed the trader's appeal, finding that the supplies covered by the assessment were of hot food and were therefore excluded from zero-rating. (The tribunal chairman expressed the opinion, however, that such supplies would not be excluded from zero-rating if the purpose of heating the food was solely to comply with food hygiene regulations, rather than to enable the food to be consumed at a temperature above the ambient air temperature.) *PJ Bridgewater*, LON/91/1486Y (VTD 10491).

[29.72] A trader operated a meals delivery service. Until 1994 she treated her supplies as standard-rated. Subsequently she began to treat her supplies as zero-rated, and submitted a claim for repayment of output tax which she had accounted for in 1994. The Commissioners rejected the claim on the basis that her supplies were of hot food which was excluded from zero-rating. She appealed, contending that she had only heated the food for the purpose of complying with the relevant food hygiene regulations, so that, following *obiter dicta* of the tribunal chairman in *Bridgewater*, 29.71 above, her supplies should be treated as zero-rated. The tribunal rejected this contention and dismissed her appeal, and the QB upheld this decision. On the evidence, the trader had heated the food with a dual purpose, and the tribunal had been entitled to conclude that her main purpose was to enable customers to eat the food hot if they so wished. *MA Malik v C & E Commrs*, QB [1998] STC 537.

Chip butties—whether roll containing chips may be zero-rated

[29.73] A trader operated a fish and chip shop, from which he sold 'chip butties' (consisting of hot chipped potatoes inside a cold bread roll). He treated part of the price of the chip butties as attributable to the roll, and as zero-rated. The Commissioners issued an assessment on the basis that he was supplying hot food which did not qualify for zero-rating. The tribunal dismissed the trader's appeal, holding that he was making a single supply of hot food which was entirely standard-rated. *PA Marshall (t/a Harry Ramsbottom's)*, MAN/95/692 (VTD 13766).

Baked potatoes with cold fillings—whether wholly standard-rated

[29.74] A trader sold baked jacket potatoes with a variety of fillings, some of which were cold. The Commissioners issued an assessment on the basis that his sales of potatoes, including the fillings, was standard-rated. The trader appealed, contending that he should be treated as making separate supplies of the potatoes and the fillings, and that the cold fillings should be treated as zero-rated. The tribunal rejected this contention and dismissed the appeal, holding that he was making a single supply of hot food which was entirely standard-rated. *M Rourke (t/a The Market Pantry)*, MAN/99/446 (VTD 16671).

Cold 'dips' supplied with hot food—whether wholly standard-rated

[29.75] A company sold hot food such as pizza, chicken, and potato wedges. With many of its sales, it also supplied cold 'dips' (such as chilli pepper, honey & mustard, and garlic & herb). Initially it accounted for output tax on its full sale price. Subsequently it submitted a repayment claim on the basis that some of the consideration should have been attributed to the cold 'dips' and treated as zero-rated. The Commissioners rejected the claim on the basis that the company was making single supplies of hot food which were entirely standard-rated. The tribunal dismissed the company's appeal, holding that the hot food was the 'principal element' of the supply and the dips were merely 'ancillary'. *Domino's Pizza Group Ltd (No 1)*, LON/02/527 (VTD 18010).

Hot pizzas—whether zero-rated

[29.76] A company failed to account for VAT on the sale of hot pizzas. The Commissioners issued a ruling that the pizzas were standard-rated. The company appealed, contending that the purpose of heating the pizzas was 'to attain the attributes of a freshly-baked product', rather than to enable them to be consumed at a temperature above the ambient air temperature. The tribunal dismissed the appeal, observing that the company's advertising material emphasised 'delivery while hot', and finding that 'in the context of the heating of these products the purpose must be not only so as to create an edible product, but also so as to enable them to be consumed hot'. *Domino's Pizza Group Ltd (No 2)*, LON/02/139 & 310 (VTD 18866).

Sale of heated croissants

[29.77] A company sold heated filled croissants. The Commissioners issued a ruling that the croissants were within the definition of 'hot food' so that the company was required to account for output tax on these supplies. The company appealed, contending that the purpose of heating the croissants was to keep them fresh and to prevent them from hardening, rather than to enable them to be consumed at a temperature above the ambient air temperature. The tribunal dismissed the appeal, finding that the 'application and retention of heat' was necessary 'to create attractive and palatable food'. The tribunal observed that there would be 'a degree of artificiality in separating the appellant's intention to produce food for sale which is attractive and palatable because it is "hot" and its intention to sell that food while it is attractive and palatable, but not because it is "hot". On the evidence, the company's 'predominant purpose in cooking the savoury croissants and presenting them for sale hot was "for the purposes of enabling (them) to be consumed at a temperature above the ambient air temperature"'. *Pret A Manger (Europe) Ltd*, LON/C/1423 (VTD 16246).

Hot Cornish pasties

[29.78] A trader sold hot Cornish pasties. Initially she treated these as standard-rated, but she subsequently submitted a repayment claim, contending that the effect of the CA decision in *John Pimblett & Sons Ltd*, 29.55 above, was that the pasties qualified for zero-rating. The tribunal rejected this contention and dismissed her appeal, distinguishing *John Pimblett & Sons Ltd* and finding that the trader's 'predominant purpose' was to enable the pasties to be consumed while hot. *J Wallace (t/a The Cornish Pasty)*, MAN/05/712 (VTD 19793).

Hot 'paninis' and toasted sandwiches—whether zero-rated

[29.79] A company sold hot paninis and toasted sandwiches from a chain of coffee shops. It initially accounted for VAT on the basis that these were within the definition of 'hot food', but subsequently submitted a repayment claim on the basis that they qualified for zero-rating. Customs rejected the claim and the company appealed. The tribunal dismissed the appeal, finding that the company's 'dominant purpose' in heating the products was to enable them 'to be consumed hot'. Accordingly the supplies were within the definition of 'hot food', and failed to qualify for zero-rating. *Coffee Republic plc*, LON/06/756 (VTD 20150).

[29.80] The sale of toasted sandwiches was also held to be standard-rated in the subsequent cases of *European Independent Purchasing Co Ltd*, LON/06/1028 (VTD 20697) and *Sub One Ltd (t/a Subway) (No 2)*, [2010] UKFTT 487 (TC), TC00747.

Whether 'food of a kind used for human consumption' (VATA 1994, Sch 8, Group 1, General Item 1)

Cases held to qualify for zero-rating

Ritual slaughter of animals in accordance with Jewish law

[29.81] An unincorporated association provided the services of employees to carry out the ritual slaughter of animals for human consumption in accordance with Jewish dietary law. The Commissioners issued a ruling that the association's services were liable to VAT at the standard rate. The association appealed, contending that its services should be zero-rated under what is now *VATA 1994, Sch 8, Group 1*. The tribunal accepted this contention and allowed the appeal, holding that the employees were applying a process to the animals within what is now *VATA 1994, Sch 4 para 2*, and that the supply of their services was therefore a deemed supply of the meat, within *Sch 8, Group 1, General Item 1*. *The London Board for Shechita*, [1974] VATTR 24 (VTD 52).

Paan

[29.82] A retailer sold a preparation called 'paan', which consisted of a mixture of betel nut, coconut, rose petals, sugar and honey, wrapped in betel leaves. It was intended to be chewed on the completion of a meal until the flavour had been released and swallowed, the remaining fibrous constituents being spat out. The Commissioners issued a ruling that sales of paan were standard-rated, on the basis that betel nut (the main ingredient) was a stimulant rather than a food. The retailer appealed, contending that paan should be zero-rated as food for human consumption. The tribunal allowed his appeal, finding that paan had a measurable nutritive value and holding that it was within the definition of 'food'. *GR Soni*, [1980] VATTR 9 (VTD 897).

Herbal fruit concentrate

[29.83] A company imported and sold a herbal fruit concentrate, marketed in plastic containers and described by the tribunal as a 'dark, stiff, sticky fruit paste'. Cane sugar comprised 70% of its ingredients, but the tribunal found that its taste was somewhat less sweet than most jams. It was marketed to be eaten by the spoonful, rather than by being spread on bread. The Commissioners issued a ruling that the concentrate did not constitute 'food', and thus did not qualify for zero-rating. The tribunal allowed the company's appeal, holding that the concentrate was within the definition of 'food'. (Herbal tablets sold by the same company were held not to be food, and thus to be standard-rated.) *Ayurveda Ltd*, LON/88/1372X (VTD 3860).

Chinese herbal tea prescribed by doctor

[29.84] A doctor, who was registered for VAT, operated a Chinese herbal and homeopathic clinic. She prescribed and dispensed preparations of Chinese herbal tea for some of her patients. The exact ingredients of the herbal tea varied from patient to patient. The Commissioners issued a ruling that, since the prescriptions were individually prepared for medical reasons, they were not 'food of a kind used for human consumption' and thus did not qualify for zero-rating. The doctor appealed, contending that the herbal tea preparations were within the definition of 'food' and qualified for zero-rating under *VATA 1994, Sch 8, Group 1, Overriding Item No 4*. The tribunal allowed the appeal. On the evidence, the herbal tea had 'some nutritive value' and 'people drink herbal teas as part of their normal daily diet, in many cases as a substitute for what they would otherwise drink'. The ingredients of the preparations 'were substantially the same as the ingredients of sachets of herbal teas sold commercially'. The fact that the herbal teas were prescribed by a doctor did not prevent them from constituting food. *Dr X Hua*, LON/95/2069A (VTD 13811).

Biscuits packed in tin—whether wholly zero-rated

[29.85] A company which manufactured biscuits sold tins containing four varieties of biscuits. It treated its supplies of these tins as zero-rated. The cost of the tins comprised 55% of the total cost. The Commissioners issued a ruling that the tins should be treated as a mixed supply and partly standard-rated, since the tins cost more to produce than the biscuits they contained. The tribunal allowed the company's appeal, holding that the entire supply was zero-rated. On the evidence, the packaging of the biscuits in a tin was 'both normal and necessary'. The company sought to make a profit on the biscuits, rather than on the tins, and the tins were 'designed to look as attractive as possible to sell the product with the minimum expenditure necessary for a quality product'. The fact that the tins could be used after the biscuits had been consumed was not material. The CS upheld the tribunal decision. Applying the reasoning in *British Airways plc*, 66.13 TRANSPORT, 'the tin was incidental to the biscuits, rather than the biscuits being incidental to the tin'. *C & E Commrs v United Biscuits (UK) Ltd (t/a Simmers)*, CS [1992] STC 325.

Biscuits packed in ceramic jar—whether wholly zero-rated

[29.86] The decision in *United Biscuits (UK) Ltd*, 29.85 above, was applied in a similar subsequent case in which small quantities of luxury biscuits were sold in ceramic self-sealing jars. The cost of the jars comprised 70% of the total cost. The Commissioners issued a ruling that part of the consideration was attributable to the supply of the jar and was standard-rated, but the tribunal allowed the company's appeal, holding that the whole of the consideration was attributable to the supply of biscuits and qualified for zero-rating. *Paterson Arran Ltd*, EDN/96/249 (VTD 15041).

Kits for making chocolate-flavoured lollies—whether wholly zero-rated

[29.87] A limited liability partnership (S) sold kits for making 'chocolate-flavoured lollies'. The kits comprised a plastic tray containing six moulds, twelve lolly sticks, two tubes of edible icing and two bags of chocolate-flavoured edible buttons. It treated its sales of these kits as zero-rated supplies of food. HMRC issued an assessment on the basis that the principal element of each supply was the tray and the sticks, so that the supplies were standard-rated. S appealed. The tribunal allowed the appeal, finding that it was accepted that the buttons contained no cocoa and were not within the legal definition of 'chocolate'; that the lollies were not 'ice lollies' and that the buttons and icing were not within the definition of 'confectionery'. Accordingly none of the edible components of the supply were excluded from zero-rating. On the evidence, the edible ingredients represented more than 81% of the total cost, whereas the mould and the sticks represented less than 19% of the total cost. Accordingly, the principal element of each supply was of 'food', and the mould and sticks were ancillary, so that the whole of the consideration qualified for zero-rating. *Supercook UK Llp v HMRC (and related appeal)*, [2010] UKFTT 13 (TC), TC00332.

JS4 soft roll concentrate

[29.88] A company manufactured a product known as 'JS4 soft roll concentrate', which was not itself edible but was used as an aid for the baking of soft rolls. The concentrate consisted mainly of sugar, dextrose, salt, and edible oil. Flour, water and yeast had to be added to it before baking could take place. After baking, the flour, yeast and water constituted about 95% of the soft rolls; the concentrate comprised the remaining 5%. The company did not account for VAT on sales of the concentrate, considering that it should be zero-rated. The Commissioners considered that it was not eligible for zero-rating and issued an assessment charging tax on the sales, against which the company appealed. The tribunal allowed the company's appeal and the CS upheld this decision. Zero-rating was not restricted to food which was virtually ready for human consumption in the state in which it was supplied. The words 'food of a kind used for human consumption' in what is now *VATA 1994, Sch 8, Group 1, General Item 1* reflected the fact that many foods for human consumption were retailed in a form in which they were not fit to be consumed without some further preparation. The fact that part of the preparation was carried out at a stage before the food was sold to the ultimate consumer did not prevent the ingredients from qualifying for zero-rating. *C & E Commrs v MacPhie & Co (Glenbervie) Ltd*, CS [1992] STC 886.

Sausage casings

[29.89] A company manufactured sausage casings, which were made from reconstituted collagen (a structural animal protein), with the addition of a permitted additive E460 which was designed to modify the texture and which also had the effect of aiding digestion by helping in the functioning of the bowel. The Commissioners issued a ruling that the casings were not 'food of a kind used for human consumption' and were not eligible for zero-rating. The tribunal allowed the company's appeal. The sausage casings were clearly edible and were designed to be eaten. The fact that the casings had to be incorporated into a sausage after being manufactured and being consumed did not prevent them from qualifying as 'food'. *Devro Ltd*, EDN/91/259 (VTD 7570).

Dietary supplement containing powdered gelatine

[29.90] A company sold a powder which was marketed as a dietary supplement and was intended to be mixed with water and drunk. 85% of the powder consisted of edible gelatine (also known as collagen hydrolysate); the remaining 15% consisted of vitamins, minerals, colouring and flavouring. The Commissioners issued a ruling that sales of the powder were standard-rated. The company appealed, contending that the powder was within the definition of food, and qualified for zero-rating. The tribunal accepted this contention and allowed the appeal, observing that the case was 'very finely balanced' but that the powder had a very high protein value and holding that, in view of its high 'nutritional value', it qualified as a food. *Arthro Vite Ltd*, MAN/96/1190 (VTD 14836).

Powder for making sports drinks

[29.91] A company supplied products consisting primarily of carbohydrate or creatine, in powder form, which were designed to be mixed with water and drunk by people competing in, or training for, sporting events. Initially the Commissioners accepted that these products qualified for zero-rating. However, they reviewed their policy with effect from December 1997 and issued a ruling that the products should be treated as standard-rated from that date. The company appealed, contending that, as the products consisted primarily of carbohydrate or protein, they were within the definition of 'food'. The tribunal accepted this contention and allowed the appeal, finding that the products were consumed for nutritional purposes. *VATA 1994, Sch 8, Group 1, Note 1* provided that '"food" includes drink', so that a 'drinkable substance' could be within the definition of 'food'. The tribunal observed that 'food frequently contains large amounts of water: indeed, if it did not, it might be difficult or impossible to consume'. On the evidence, the products in question were 'for the preparation of food supplements (technically, "dietary integrators")'. The 'benefit to the consumer' was 'the carbohydrate and protein, alternatively pure protein, present in the product, which the consumer takes for nourishment'. *SIS (Science in Sport) Ltd*, [2000] VATDR 194 (VTD 16555). (*Note.* For a subsequent appeal by the same company, see **29.138** below.)

NuTriVeneD powder

[29.92] A woman (R) had a young daughter who suffered from Down's Syndrome. She imported a quantity of NuTriVeneD powder (an antioxidant specially formulated for Down's Syndrome sufferers) from the USA. The Commissioners demanded customs duty and VAT. R appealed, contending that the powder was 'food', so that it was exempt from customs duty and zero-rated for VAT. The tribunal accepted this contention and allowed the appeal, observing that the powder was 'taken at each meal mixed in a fruit puree, in the way that flour or cocoa might similarly be treated', and holding that it was within the definition of food. *Mrs S Ridal*, LON/01/7038 (C149).

Bottled linseed oil.

[29.93] A partnership sold bottled unrefined linseed oil, which it described as 'culinary linseed oil' and advertised as a salad dressing. Customs issued a ruling that VAT was chargeable on these supplies. The partnership appealed, contending that linseed oil was 'food' which qualified for zero-rating. The tribunal accepted this contention and allowed the appeal, distinguishing the earlier decision in *Durwin Banks (No 1)*, **29.98** below (which had concerned capsules as well as bottles). *Durwin Banks (No 2)*, [2008] VATDR 429 (VTD 20695).

Haddock and mackerel sold to fishermen

[29.94] See *North Isles Shellfish Ltd*, **29.118** below.

Cases where the consideration was apportioned

Butter sold with dish—whether wholly zero-rated

[29.95] A company sold a 'promotional' pack comprising two packets of butter together with a butter dish. It did not account for output tax on these sales. The Commissioners issued an assessment on the basis that part of the consideration had to be attributed to the supply of the dish, which did not qualify for zero-rating. The company appealed, contending that the supply should be treated as wholly zero-rated. The tribunal rejected this contention and dismissed the appeal, distinguishing *United Biscuits (UK) Ltd*, **29.85** above. *MD Foods plc*, LON/00/899 (VTD 17080).

Cases held not to qualify for zero-rating

Abattoir services

[29.96] A borough council provided a public slaughterhouse, the running of which it shared with a company representing the principal users. The company was responsible for the killing of the animals and the processing of the carcasses, while the Council was responsible for the lairage (penning of the animals awaiting slaughter), for a cooling hall in which the carcass meat was hung before collection by the owner, and for the inspection and stamping of the meat. The Council and the company made separate charges in respect of animals brought to the abattoir. The Commissioners assessed the Council on the basis that its charges were standard-rated except in so far as they were for lairage, meat inspection and a Meat Livestock Commission levy. The Council appealed, contending that since the abattoir was used to produce food for human consumption, its supplies should be treated as zero-rated. The tribunal dismissed the appeal, holding that the Council merely provided facilities for the slaughtering and carcass processing by the company which, on the evidence, was an independent principal and not an agent or employee of the Council. *Darlington Borough Council*, [1980] VATTR 120 (VTD 961).

Cod liver oil products

[29.97] A company supplied cod liver oil and related products. The Commissioners issued a ruling that the supplies were liable to VAT at the standard rate, and the company appealed, contending that they were zero-rated under what is now *VATA 1994, Sch 8, Group 1*. The tribunal dismissed the company's appeal, holding that the supplies were not within the definition of 'food'. *Marfleet Refining Co Ltd*, [1974] VATTR 289 (VTD 129).

Linseed oil capsules

[29.98] A partnership sold linseed oil, in capsules and in half-litre bottles. The Commissioners issued a ruling that VAT was chargeable on these supplies. The partnership appealed, contending that linseed oil was 'food' which qualified for zero-rating. The tribunal rejected this contention and dismissed the appeal, holding that linseed oil was a 'supplement' and was not within the definition of 'food'. *Durwin Banks (No 1)*, LON/04/1030 (VTD 18904). (*Note.* The decision with regard to linseed oil sold in bottles rather than capsules was disapproved by a subsequent tribunal in *Durwin Banks (No 2)*, **29.93** above.)

Royal Jelly capsules

[29.99] The Commissioners issued an assessment on a company which distributed 'Royal Jelly' capsules. The company appealed, contending that the capsules were 'food' and should be zero-rated. The tribunal dismissed the appeal, holding that the capsules were not food. They were meant to be swallowed undissolved, with water, and had an unpleasant taste if retained in the mouth. *Grosvenor Commodities Ltd*, LON/90/1805X (VTD 7221). (*Note.* The tribunal also rejected a contention by the company that the Commissioners were estopped from raising the assessment. For cases concerning estoppel, see **2.109** *et seq.* APPEALS.)

Chlorella pyrenoidosa tablets

[29.100] A company sold tablets of chlorella pyrenoidosa (an edible green micro-algae which contained protein, vitamins and minerals). It did not account for output tax on its sales of these tablets, treating them as zero-rated. The Commissioners issued a ruling that the sales did not qualify for zero-rating, on the grounds that the chlorella tablets were not 'food of a kind used for human consumption'. The company appealed. The tribunal dismissed the appeal, holding that although the tablets were 'palatable', they were not within the definition of 'food'. *Nature's Balance Ltd*, LON/93/2953A (VTD 12295).

Algae tablets

[29.101] A company sold algae tablets and powdered algae. The Commissioners issued a ruling that its supplies did not qualify for zero-rating, on the grounds that algae were not 'food of a kind used for human consumption'. The tribunal dismissed the company's appeal. *Hunter Ridgeley Ltd*, LON/94/2028 (VTD 13662).

Fruit and vegetable tablets

[29.102] A company manufactured two types of tablets, called 'Juice Plus Fruit Blend Tablets' and 'Juice Plus Vegetable Blend Tablets'. They were made from juices and powders derived from various fruits and vegetables, and were approximately 1.5 cm in diameter. The Commissioners issued a ruling that the supplies of the tablets were standard-rated. The company appealed, contending that the tablets were within the definition of 'food of a kind used for human consumption' and were therefore zero-rated. The tribunal rejected this contention and dismissed the appeal, observing that 'taking the word "food" in its normally understood sense, tablets do not look like food or taste like food' and holding that 'these tablets are not food in the normal present-day meaning of the word'. *National Safety Associates of America (UK) Ltd*, LON/95/3185A (VTD 14241).

Aloe vera gel products

[29.103] A company supplied a number of products based on aloe vera gel. They were marketed in litre bottles, but customers were advised not to consume more than 110 ml twice daily, as larger doses would have a laxative effect. The Commissioners issued a ruling that the products were standard-rated, and the company appealed, contending that they should be zero-rated as 'food of a kind used for human consumption'. The tribunal rejected this contention and dismissed the appeal, holding on the evidence that none of the products had 'any nutritional value whatsoever'. *Forever Living Products Ltd*, MAN/97/907 (VTD 16263).

Laxative fruit cubes

[29.104] A company manufactured laxative fruit cubes, which contained a mixture of dried fruits such as figs and senna pods. It did not account for VAT on the sale of the cubes, considering that they were zero-rated under what is now *VATA 1994, Sch 8, Group 1*. The Commissioners issued a ruling that the cubes did not constitute food and thus were not eligible for zero-rating. The tribunal dismissed the company's appeal, finding that the cubes 'were neither sold nor bought as a form of nourishment, nor were they consumed for pleasure'. The cubes were designed 'to remedy or to prevent constipation'. They were a remedial preparation, and did not constitute 'food'. *Brewhurst Health Food Supplies*, LON/91/2488Z (VTD 8928).

Carbon dioxide and nitrogen used to provide a 'head' for beer

[29.105] A company manufactured carbon dioxide and nitrogen and sold them, stored in cylinders, to public houses to provide a 'head' for beer. The Commissioners issued a ruling that the company was required to account for VAT on its supplies. The company appealed, contending that the gas should be treated as 'food of a kind used for human consumption', and as zero-rated. The tribunal rejected this contention and dismissed the appeal, holding that neither carbon dioxide or nitrogen qualified as 'food'. *Gas & Chemicals Ltd*, MAN/02/610 (VTD 18160).

Animal feeding stuffs (VATA 1994, Sch 8, Group 1, General Item 2)

Polymer additive for cattle feed

[29.106] A company, which sold animal feeding stuffs, sold an additive for cattle feed. The additive was in the form of a powder. It was a polymer, with no significant nutritive value, and was biologically inert, but was advertised as being able to increase the nutritive value of silage by enabling the cattle to digest more of the silage. The company accounted for VAT on the basis that the additive was zero-rated, and the Commissioners issued an assessment charging VAT on the sales of the additive. The tribunal dismissed the company's appeal, holding on the evidence that the additive was not itself a nutrient and thus was not within the definition of 'animal feeding stuffs'. *Chapman & Frearson Ltd*, MAN/88/618 (VTD 4428). (*Note*. Costs were awarded to the Commissioners in connection with the appearance of an expert witness.)

Worms and maggots supplied with ornamental fish

[**29.107**] A married couple trading in partnership sold ornamental fish. With the fish they also supplied worms and maggots, which were used to feed the fish when in transit. They accepted that the ornamental fish were standard-rated, since they were not intended to be eaten, but in accounting for VAT they treated part of the consideration received as zero-rated, on the basis that it was attributable to the supply of the worms and maggots. The Commissioners issued an assessment charging tax on the whole of the amounts paid, and the tribunal dismissed the couple's appeal. The subject of each sale was the fish, rather than the worms and the maggots, and since the worms and maggots were not intended for resale, they did not qualify for zero-rating. *Pier Aquatics*, MAN/90/1019 (VTD 7063).

Maggots sold from vending machines

[**29.108**] A company sold tins of maggots from vending machines. The maggots were intended to be used by fishermen as bait. The company treated its sales of the maggots as zero-rated, and the Commissioners issued an assessment charging tax on them. The company appealed, contending that the maggots were 'animal feeding stuffs' which were zero-rated under *VATA 1994, Sch 8, Group 1, General Item 2*, since they were sold and used by fishermen to feed fish with a view to attracting them to an area where they could be caught. The tribunal rejected this contention and dismissed the appeal, holding that it was 'not the intrinsic nature of the item supplied which is relevant, but the purpose for which it is sold'. In order to determine the nature of the supply, 'the purpose of the seller has to be looked at.' The company's purpose in selling the maggots was to enable its customers to catch the fish, rather than to feed the fish. *North Isles Shellfish Ltd*, **29.118** below, was distinguished, on the basis that the bait used in that case 'was not only intended for use in catching the lobsters but was also intended to be eaten by them once captured, to sustain them prior to sale'. The QB upheld this decision. Laddie J held that 'whether or not an edible substance is animal feeding stuffs is in large part answered by the way in which it is sold or supplied'. The fact that the maggots were edible did not mean that they fell within the definition of 'animal feeding stuffs'. The maggots were 'not supplied as a foodstuff for fish' but 'for use in enticing fish towards hooks'. In view of the way in which the maggots were supplied, they did not qualify for zero-rating. *Fluff Ltd (t/a Mag-It) v C & E Commrs*, QB 2000, [2001] STC 674.

Hemp seed supplied as bait for fish

[29.109] A company supplied fishing bait to anglers. It did not account for tax on its supplies of hemp seed. The Commissioners issued an assessment charging tax on these supplies, and the company appealed, contending that the seed was 'animal feeding stuffs' and should be zero-rated under *VATA 1994, Sch 8, Group 1, General Item 2*. The tribunal rejected this contention and dismissed the company's appeal, applying the decision in *Fluff Ltd*, **29.108** above. *Eurobait Ltd*, MAN/99/614 (VTD 17252).

Whether animal food within Excepted Item No 6

[29.110] See the cases at **29.188** *et seq*. below.

Charges made by stud farm

[29.111] A farmer kept two stallions at stud. Mares served were usually kept at grass on the farm until it was considered that there had been a pregnancy. In such cases there was a single contract under which the owner of the mare paid a fixed 'service charge' of £100 plus a weekly amount for the time the mare was kept at the farm. He accounted for output tax on the service charges, but did not account for tax on the weekly charges. The Commissioners considered that the whole of the consideration was standard-rated, and assessed him accordingly. He appealed, contending that the weekly charge was for the keep of the mare and should be zero-rated as 'animal feeding stuffs'. The QB rejected this contention and upheld the assessment. Applying the test used in *British Railways Board*, **66.12** TRANSPORT, the farmer was supplying the single service of keeping the mare with everything that was involved in maintaining her 'in reasonable condition and safety'. *C & E Commrs v DD Scott*, QB 1977, [1978] STC 191.

[29.112] The decision in *Scott*, **29.111** above, was applied in the similar case of *C & E Commrs v DW & MJ Bushby*, QB 1978, [1979] STC 9.

[29.113] The decisions in *Scott*, **29.111** above, and *Bushby*, **29.112** above, were applied in the similar case of *LE Barr*, LON/96/780 (VTD 14529), and in *Banstead Manor Stud Ltd*, **39.1** INTERNATIONAL SERVICES.

Casual grazing licences

[29.114] See *JA King*, **41.41** LAND.

Supply of grass feed for horses kept at livery

[29.115] A partnership carried on a livery business. They advertised for customers to send them horses to be kept at livery. They invoiced their customers for supplies of grass to the animals, and did not account for output tax on these supplies, treating them as zero-rated. The Commissioners issued an assessment charging tax on the supplies, on the basis that the partnership was making a single standard-rated supply of the keep of animals. The tribunal allowed the partnership's appeal, distinguishing *Scott*, **29.111** above, and *Smith*, **29.117** below. The partnership did not operate a stud and, on the evidence, any additional services were undertaken as agents for the owners and thus did not affect the zero-rating of the supplies of grass. *RW & JR Fidler (t/a Holt Manor Farm Partners)*, LON/94/798A (VTD 12892).

[29.116] A similar decision, also distinguishing *Scott*, **29.111** above, and *Smith*, **29.117** below, was reached in *S & J Marczak (t/a Suzanne's Riding School)*, LON/94/1682A (VTD 13141).

Rearing and keeping of cattle

[29.117] A trader whose main activity was the rearing and keeping of other persons' heifers accounted for tax on the basis that part of the charges which he made were for a separate zero-rated supply of animal feeding stuffs. The Commissioners issued an assessment on the basis that the whole of his supplies were standard-rated. The tribunal upheld the assessment and dismissed the trader's appeal, applying *Scott*, **29.111** above, and *Bushby*, **29.112** above. *ARM Smith*, MAN/87/321 (VTD 2954).

Fish sold as lobster bait

[29.118] A company sold haddock and mackerel as lobster bait. It did not account for output tax on such sales, treating them as zero-rated animal feeding stuffs. The Commissioners issued an assessment charging output tax on the basis that the sales did not qualify for zero-rating. The company appealed. The tribunal allowed the appeal, holding on the evidence that the fish qualified for zero-rating under what is now *VATA 1994, Sch 8, Group 1, General Item 2*. The tribunal observed that 'in addition to enticing the lobster it was intended that the lobster should eat the fish as a start to and a part of the fattening process which continued whilst the lobster was in captivity. This is not a case of a poisoned bait but of supplying the animal with feeding stuff which had also assisted to entrap it'. (The tribunal also considered that the haddock and mackerel qualified for zero-rating under *General Item 1* as 'food of a kind used for human consumption', on the basis that the fish was edible and that 'the motive of the purchaser in obtaining the fish is irrelevant'.) *North Isles Shellfish Ltd*, [1995] VATDR 415 (VTD 13083). (*Note.* The tribunal's opinion that that 'the motive of the purchaser in obtaining the fish is irrelevant' was disapproved in the subsequent case of *Fluff Ltd (t/a Mag-It)*, **29.108** above, where the tribunal held that it was 'not the intrinsic nature of the item supplied which is relevant, but the purpose for which it is sold' and that 'in order to determine the nature of the supply, the purpose of the seller has to be looked at.')

Means of propagation of plants (VATA 1994, Sch 8, Group 1, General Item 3)

Kits for growing mushrooms

[29.119] A farming partnership supplied kits for growing mushrooms. Each kit comprised a bucket, a label and instruction leaflet, a growing medium infused with spawn, and peat, etc. It did not account for VAT on its supplies, treating them as zero-rated under what is now *VATA 1994, Sch 8, Group 1, General Item 3*. Customs issued an assessment charging tax on the supplies, and the partnership appealed. The tribunal allowed the appeal in part, observing that 'although it may be it would be difficult to find some other satisfactory method of containing the package, the bucket or tub is a substantial part of the cost, especially if we compare it with articles such as tins in the sales of food'. Additionally, the bucket or tub had 'an intrinsic value in that it can be used afterwards as a garden bucket'. Accordingly the tribunal held that the supplies had to be apportioned and that 40% of the consideration was standard-rated as referable to the bucket and label. The remaining 60% was attributable to the growing medium and the peat, and was zero-rated. *Cheshire Mushroom Farm*, [1974] VATTR 87 (VTD 71).

Live animals (VATA 1994, Sch 8, Group 1, General Item 4)

Koi carp

[29.120] A fish farmer sold Koi carp (an ornamental type of fish originating in Japan). He did not account for VAT on these sales. The Commissioners issued an assessment charging tax on them, and the farmer appealed, contending that sales of fish were zero-rated. The tribunal dismissed the farmer's appeal, finding that the fish in question were sold for ornamental purposes, rather than to be eaten. There was no evidence that anyone had ever eaten a Koi carp, and that the fact that, in theory, they were edible was not conclusive. They were not marketed as food, and were not within the definition of 'food of a kind used for human consumption'. *JR Chalmers*, LON/82/99 (VTD 1433).

Dinkelsbuhl carp

[29.121] A fish farmer did not account for VAT on sales of Dinkelsbuhl carp. The Commissioners issued an assessment charging tax on his sales, on the basis that the carp were sold for ornamental purposes rather than as food. The tribunal allowed the farmer's appeal, finding that eating carp was 'uncommon' but was not eccentric. The Commissioners appealed to the QB which quashed the decision and remitted the case to a new tribunal to be reheard, holding that the tribunal had misdirected itself in its reasoning. *C & E Commrs v RT Lawson-Tancred*, QB [1988] STC 326. (*Note.* There was no further public hearing of the appeal. Compare the subsequent case of *Fluff Ltd (t/a Mag-It)*, **29.108** above, where the tribunal held that it was 'not the intrinsic nature of the item supplied which is relevant, but the purpose for which it is sold' and that 'in order to determine the nature of the supply, the purpose of the seller has to be looked at.')

Trout fishery supplying right to catch edible trout

[29.122] A partnership which operated a trout fishery sold tickets which allowed customers to catch trout. It only accounted for output tax on part of the consideration. The Commissioners issued an assessment charging tax on the full amount of the ticket price, and the partnership appealed, contending that there were two separate supplies, namely a standard-rated supply of the right to fish and a zero-rated supply of the trout as food. The tribunal rejected this contention and dismissed the appeal, holding that as a matter of substance and reality all that the partnership supplied was the right to catch fish, which was a standard-rated supply. *Chalk Springs Fisheries*, LON/86/706 (VTD 2518).

[29.123] The proprietor of a trout fishery charged anglers a total cost of £9.50 for a whole day, computed as £6.50 for the privilege of fishing and £3 for the cost of fish taken. The £3 cost of fish was, however, payable whether or not the angler caught any fish. The proprietor did not account for output tax on this £3, treating it as zero-rated, and the Commissioners issued an assessment on the basis that the whole of the £9.50 was subject to tax at the standard rate. The tribunal upheld the assessment and dismissed the proprietor's appeal, applying *Chalk Springs Fisheries*, **29.122** above. *RC Haynes*, LON/87/624 (VTD 2948).

Sale of pheasants

[29.124] A trader (C) bred and sold live pheasants. He sold some baby pheasants, at a price of £5 per bird, in June and July. The purchasers kept the baby pheasants on land owned by C, and arranged for them to be fed. In October the purchasers visited C's land to shoot the pheasants. The Commissioners issued an assessment charging tax on the amounts which C received for the pheasants. He appealed, contending that the payments qualified for zero-rating under *VATA 1994, Sch 8, Group 1, General Item 4*. The tribunal accepted this contention and allowed the appeal. *NCD Carter*, EDN/00/144 (VTD 17288).

Ice cream, etc. (VATA 1994, Sch 8, Group 1, Excepted Item 1)

Frozen desserts

[29.125] A company launched a range of frozen desserts. The Commissioners issued a ruling that the desserts did not qualify for zero-rating, since they were 'similar frozen products', within *VATA 1994, Sch 8, Group 1, Excepted Item 1*. The company appealed, contending that the term 'similar frozen products' should be construed as meaning similar to 'water ices' (the immediately preceding item in *Excepted Item 1*). The tribunal rejected this contention and dismissed the appeal, holding that the term 'similar frozen products' should be construed as referring to all the items in the list preceding it, including ice cream, ice lollies and frozen yoghurt as well as water ices. The tribunal observed that, as a matter of principle, and applying a statement of Sir Ernest Gowers in *'The Complete Plain Words'*, 'commas are always put after each item in (a) series (of nouns or phrases) up to the last but one, but practice varies about putting a comma between the last one and the *and* introducing the last. Neither practice is wrong.' Accordingly, the tribunal concluded that 'no help is available in answering the question from a purely grammatical angle'. However, it appeared that 'the intention of *Excepted Item 1* is to deny zero-rating to certain iced products, be they cream-based or water-based. To achieve that result it is necessary to read *Excepted Item 1* as if it includes a comma after the phrase "water ices"'. *Ross Young Holdings Ltd*, [1996] VATDR 230 (VTD 13972).

Frozen yoghurt

[29.126] A retail company sold a product described as 'soft frozen yoghurt'. When sold, it took the form of a liquid of high viscosity, with a temperature of between –1°C and –5°C. The Commissioners issued a ruling that sales of the product were standard-rated, since the product was 'frozen yoghurt', within *VATA 1994, Sch 8, Group 1, Excepted Item 1*. The company appealed, contending that at the time of sale the product was 'a liquid of high viscosity' which could not be described as 'frozen', and therefore qualified for zero-rating. The Ch D rejected this contention and dismissed the company's appeal, holding that the product was 'frozen yoghurt' and was therefore standard-rated. Hart J held that 'frozen yoghurt' should be construed as 'yoghurt reduced to a temperature below the freezing point of water'. *Meschia's Frozen Foods v C & E Commrs*, Ch D 2000, [2001] STC 1.

[29.127] A company made wholesale supplies of frozen yoghurt to retailers. The yoghurt was supplied at a temperature of –18°C but was intended for consumption at –5°C. The Commissioners issued a ruling that sales of the product were standard-rated, since the product was 'frozen yoghurt', within *VATA 1994, Sch 8, Group 1, Excepted Item 1*. The company appealed, contending that the product was 'yoghurt unsuitable for immediate consumption when frozen', within *Sch 8, Group 1, Overriding Item 1*, and therefore qualified for zero-rating. The tribunal rejected this contention and dismissed the company's appeal, holding that the product was 'frozen yoghurt' and was therefore standard-rated. The tribunal observed that there was a distinction between food which was consumed for the purpose of nourishment and food which was consumed 'as an "amusement or entertainment". Ordinary yoghurt falls into the former category, frozen yoghurt into the latter.' At the time the yoghurt in question was supplied to retailers, it had 'passed the point of no return: the added stabilisers and emulsifiers have rendered the yoghurt unsuitable for use as "nutritional" yoghurt and stamped it indelibly with the characteristic of "amusement or entertainment" yoghurt, which can only be eaten frozen.' Furthermore, 'a yoghurt which is designed and intended to be eaten frozen, which will be eaten frozen, and which is not suitable to be eaten unfrozen, cannot be described as "unsuitable for immediate consumption when frozen" simply because it has at one point been frozen down to a temperature at which it happens to be inedible, for the purpose of supply to a customer who will not in any case be consuming it'. *Tennessee Secret (UK) Ltd*, LON/99/1328 (VTD 16945).

Confectionery, etc. (VATA 1994, Sch 8, Group 1, Excepted Item 2)

Cases held to qualify for zero-rating

Toffee apples

[29.128] In a purchase tax case, the Ch D held that toffee apples were not within the definition of 'confectionery'. Cross J observed that 'despite the toffee coating, the apple is still there as a live fruit which has not been tampered with in the same way as a dried or roasted almond or raisin that has been coated in sugar or chocolate and which is not a live fruit'. Furthermore, the fact that 'drained, glacé or crystallised fruits' were specifically included in the statutory definition of confectionery indicated that toffee apples were not to be treated as confectionery. *Candy Maid Confections Ltd & Others v C & E Commrs*, Ch D [1968] 3 All ER 773. (*Note.* The Commissioners accept that, following this decision, toffee apples are zero-rated for VAT—see Customs' VAT Manual, Part 7, chapter 1, para 8.18.8.)

Biscuits for use in ice-cream trade

[29.129] A company manufactured biscuits for the ice-cream trade, suitable for eating only in conjunction with ice-cream. Most of its sales were of wafers and cones, which were agreed to be zero-rated. However, it also manufactured 'nougat wafers', which comprised two wafer biscuits with a sandwich filling of albumen, glucose and sugar, and were lightly coated with a powder comprising sugar and skimmed milk powder. The Commissioners issued a ruling that the 'nougat wafers' were confectionery and thus were standard-rated. The tribunal allowed the company's appeal, holding that, since the products were baked, they were not within the definition of confectionery. *Boni Faccenda Ltd*, [1975] VATTR 155 (VTD 196).

Marshmallow cones

[29.130] A company sold cones (of the type commonly used to contain ice-cream) which were filled with marshmallow and which had a sugar topping. The Commissioners issued a ruling that the cones were standard-rated 'confectionery'. The tribunal allowed the company's appeal, specifically declining to follow the decision noted at **29.162** below (which concerned the same product) on the grounds that the 1975 decision in *Boni Faccenda Ltd*, **29.129** above, where nougat wafers were held to be zero-rated biscuits, had not been cited in that case. The tribunal found that the cones were 'eaten by children as if they were biscuits' and concluded that 'the man in the street' would regard the cones as biscuits 'notwithstanding the earlier tribunal decision to the contrary'. Accordingly the tribunal allowed the company's appeal. *Kathy's Kones Ltd (No 2)*, LON/96/1726 (VTD 14880). (*Note*. Following this decision, the Commissioners now accept that the product in question is zero-rated—see Customs' VAT Manual, Part 7, chapter 1, para 8.7.2. Compare, however, the subsequent decision in *Marcantonio Foods Ltd*, **29.131** below, where similar cones were held not to be 'biscuits'.)

Waffle cones lined with chocolate

[29.131] A company manufactured waffle cones, similar to ice-cream cones, but lined with chocolate. The Commissioners issued a ruling that the cones were standard-rated, on the basis that they were 'biscuits wholly or partly covered with chocolate', within *VATA 1994, Sch 8, Group 1, Excepted Item 2*. The company appealed, contending that the cones were sold as incomplete products, to be used as edible containers for desserts or ice-cream, and were not 'biscuits'. The tribunal accepted this contention and allowed the appeal. *Kathy's Kones Ltd (No 2)*, **29.130** above, was distinguished on the basis that the product in that case 'was not made for use in combination with any other food products, but was made for consumption on its own'. The tribunal held that 'one of the salient characteristics of a biscuit is that it is eaten in the hand, and in the case of a sweet biscuit, it is eaten on its own'. *Marcantonio Foods Ltd*, LON/97/602 (VTD 15486).

Diet bars

[29.132] A company imported and supplied 'diet bars', which included peanuts, bran and other ingredients, and were marketed as a slimming aid to replace meals. The Commissioners issued a ruling that the diet bars were confectionery and therefore standard-rated. The tribunal allowed the company's appeal, finding that, although the bars were edible, they were not palatable. The high cost and the taste would preclude them being eaten for pleasure. Only a negligible amount of sweetener was included. Accordingly the bars were not confectionery, and were zero-rated. *Texas Touch Dallas Diet Ltd*, [1984] VATTR 115 (VTD 1664).

'Chocolate Marzipan Walnuts'

[29.133] A company manufactured a product known as 'Chocolate Marzipan Walnuts', which had a meringue base to which was added marzipan, walnuts, buttercream and a chocolate coating. The Commissioners issued a ruling that the products were confectionery and therefore excluded from zero-rating. The company appealed, contending that the products were cakes and were therefore zero-rated. The tribunal accepted the company's contention and allowed the appeal. *Goodfellow & Steven Ltd*, EDN/87/10 (VTD 2453).

'Caramel Shortcake Slices'

[29.134] A company retailed a product named 'Caramel Shortcake Slices'. The shortcake base of this product contained 50% flour, 33% butter, and 12.5% sugar. This base constituted 52% of the product, the remaining 48%

comprising caramel and chocolate. The product was baked, and had a maximum life of 25 days. The Commissioners issued a ruling that the product constituted confectionery, and was therefore not eligible for zero-rating. The company appealed, contending that the product was a cake and was therefore zero-rated. The tribunal allowed the company's appeal, holding on the evidence that the product was a cake. *Marks & Spencer plc*, LON/88/1316Y (VTD 4510).

'Jaffa Cakes'

[29.135] A company manufactured a product known as 'Jaffa Cakes'. The product consisted of a small round piece of sponge cake, on which was a small amount of sweet orange jam, and which was entirely covered by a thin layer of chocolate. The Commissioners issued a ruling that the 'Jaffa Cakes' were biscuits covered with chocolate, falling within what is now *VATA 1994, Sch 8, Group 1, Excepted Item 2*, and were therefore standard-rated. The company appealed, contending that the 'Jaffa Cakes' were cakes rather than biscuits, and were therefore zero-rated. The tribunal accepted this contention and allowed the appeal, observing that the ingredients of the sponge part of the 'Jaffa Cake' were 'virtually the same' as the ingredients of a traditional sponge cake. The 'Jaffa Cakes' were moist and had the texture of a sponge cake, and the sponge was a substantial part of the product in bulk and texture, rather than simply a base for the jam and chocolate. *United Biscuits (UK) Ltd*, LON/91/160 (VTD 6344).

'Horlicks' and 'Lucozade' tablets

[29.136] A company manufactured 'Horlicks' and 'Lucozade' tablets. It did not account for VAT on sales of these, treating them as zero-rated. In 1991 the Commissioners issued a ruling that the tablets were not eligible for zero-rating, since they were 'sweetened prepared food which is normally eaten with the fingers' and thus within the definition of confectionery in what is now *VATA 1994, Sch 8, Group 1, Note 5*. The company appealed, contending that the tablets should not be treated as confectionery, since they were not deliberately 'sweetened'. The tribunal allowed the appeal, holding that the 'Horlicks' tablets were not 'sweetened' on the basis that, although they contained some sugar, they did not taste sweet; and that the 'Lucozade' tablets were not sweetened on the basis that they consisted primarily of maltodextrin and dextrose, which were themselves sweet food products which were not the subject of any further sweetening, whereas the reference to 'sweetened prepared food' in *Note 5* should be construed as referring to items which had been deliberately made sweeter. *Smith Kline Beecham plc*, [1993] VATTR 219 (VTD 10222).

Spherical wafers with hazelnut filling and coating

[29.137] A company manufactured two types of small spherical wafers. The wafers were filled with a soft hazelnut filling; both types were covered with chopped hazelnuts and one of the types was also covered in light meringue. Hazelnuts comprised 28% of the product, while 27% consisted of sugar, 15% was vegetable fat and 10% was vegetable oil. The products were individually wrapped, and had to be consumed within about eight months of manufacture. If they were exposed to the air, the wafers would absorb the filling and become too soft. The Commissioners issued a ruling that the products were confectionery. The company appealed, contending that the products were 'biscuits' and qualified for zero-rating. The tribunal accepted the company's contentions and allowed the company's appeal (by a 2–1 majority, with the chairman dissenting). The CA upheld the majority tribunal decision as one of fact. The tribunal had correctly determined that the question of law was whether the products were biscuits, and had correctly ruled that the word 'biscuit' should be given its ordinary meaning. Accordingly, the tribunal decision was a finding of fact which could not be overturned on appeal. Hutchison LJ observed that 'there is no ideal concept, conformity with every aspect of which is necessary before an aspiring manufacturer can call his product a biscuit. It is a question of fact in each case whether the article in question can properly and sensibly be said to be a biscuit.' *C & E Commrs v Ferrero UK Ltd*, CA [1997] STC 881.

Energy bars

[29.138] A company produced 'energy bars' which included a high percentage of fruit. The Commissioners issued a ruling that the bars constituted confectionery, and were therefore excluded from zero-rating. The tribunal allowed the company's appeal, distinguishing the previous decision in *Huczek*, **29.157** below, on the grounds that the 'energy bars' in that case included fructose and glucose polymers which had clearly been added for purposes of sweetening. In the present case, however, the manufacturing process involved the removal of some of the bars' original juices such as apple and orange juice, and their replacement by grape juice, which increased the acidity and reduced the sweetness of the bar. The bars qualified for zero-rating, since 'the main ingredient of each bar is sufficiently sweet to make it unnecessary for the bar to be sweetened'. *SIS (Science in Sport) Ltd (No 2)*, MAN/00/69 (VTD 17116). (*Note.* For a previous appeal by the same company, see **29.91** above.)

Fruit and cereal bars designed for young children

[29.139] A company sold fruit and cereal bars, designed for young children, and including oats, raisins, and fruit juice concentrates. Customs issued a ruling that the bars were confectionery, and therefore standard-rated. The company appealed, contending that the bars were not within the definition of 'sweetened prepared food', and therefore qualified for zero-rating. The tribunal accepted this contention and allowed the appeal, finding that 'none of the products contained any processed or other added sugars or similar substances'. The inclusion of fruit juice concentrates did not amount to 'sweetening', and the products were not within the definition of 'sweetened prepared food'. *Organix Brands plc*, LON/x (VTD 19134).

'Cereal bites'—whether confectionery or biscuits

[29.140] A company manufactured a product which it called 'Cereal Bites', comprising a cereal coating with a cream filling. The principal ingredient was sugar, followed by maize flour and wheat flour. The products were sold in small 30g bags. The Commissioners issued a ruling that the products were confectionery, and standard-rated. The company appealed, contending that the products were biscuits, and zero-rated. The tribunal accepted this contention and allowed the appeal, holding that 'the term "biscuit" is not to be applied only to a narrow variety of product as might have been necessary 40 or 50 years ago'. *United Biscuits (UK) Ltd (No 5)*, [2004] VATDR 201 (VTD 18596).

Cases where the consideration was apportioned

Fruit and nut mixtures

[29.141] A company manufactured packets of 'Big D Tropical Fruits and Nuts', containing a mixture of raisins, peanuts, coconut chips, banana chips and pineapple pieces. The banana chips and pineapple pieces contained added sugar. The added sugar comprised about 10% of the finished product by weight. The Commissioners issued a ruling that the product was confectionery and was standard-rated. The tribunal allowed the company's appeal in part, holding that the raisins, peanuts and coconut chips qualified for zero-rating, and that the consideration should be apportioned. *Smiths Foods Ltd*, [1983] VATTR 21 (VTD 1346). (*Note*. The Commissioners now accept that fruit and nut mixtures may be wholly zero-rated if the weight of standard-rated items (e.g. sweetened fruits, pieces of chocolate or roasted nuts) does not exceed 25% of their total net weight. See *Notice No 701/14/97, para 4.2.*)

Cereal bars distinguished from 'crunch cakes'

[29.142] A company manufactured two types of cereal bars. One type of bar was retailed as a 'Tasty Bar'; it consisted mainly of syrup (31%), vanilla rice (24%) and palm fat (18%). The other type of bar was retailed as an 'Easy Bar'; it consisted mainly of syrup (24%), oats (22%) and cornflakes (18%). The Commissioners issued a ruling that both products were confectionery, and thus were excluded from zero-rating. The company appealed, contending that both products were 'crunch cakes', within *Notice 701/14, para 2.5*, rather than confectionery, and should therefore be zero-rated. The tribunal allowed the appeal in part, holding that the 'Tasty Bar' was a cake, since it was 'crunchy rather than chewy' and should be treated as a 'crunch cake', within *Notice 701/14, para 2.5.* However, the tribunal held that the 'Easy Bar' was confectionery, since it was 'chewy and softer in texture', looked like a cereal bar when unwrapped, and was within the statutory definition of an 'item of sweetened prepared food which is normally eaten with the fingers'. *Doves Farm Foods Ltd*, LON/00/884 (VTD 17805).

Finger biscuits packaged with chocolate mousse

[29.143] A company sold chocolate mousse, packaged in a plastic container with four chocolate finger biscuits. Customs issued a ruling that the consideration had to be apportioned between the mousse (which was accepted as zero-rated) and the chocolate biscuits, which were excluded from zero-rating. The company appealed, contending that the biscuits should be treated as ancillary to the mousse, and that the whole supply should be treated as zero-rated. The tribunal rejected this contention and dismissed the appeal. *Uniq Group plc*, LON/02/751 (VTD 19125).

Cases held not to qualify for zero-rating

Sweetened popcorn

[29.144] In a purchase tax case, the QB held that sweetened popcorn was within the definition of 'confectionery'. *C & E Commrs v Clark's Cereal Products Ltd*, QB 1965, [1968] 3 All ER 778.

[29.145] A similar decision was reached in *C & E Commrs v Popcorn House Ltd*, QB 1965, [1968] 3 All ER 782.

'Chocolate Dundees'

[29.146] A company manufactured a product known as 'Chocolate Dundees', which were circular and the base of which comprised 55.5% flour, 17% fat and 19.7% sugar. They were baked, partly covered with chocolate, and individually wrapped. The Commissioners issued a ruling that the 'Chocolate Dundees' were confectionery and thus did not qualify for zero-rating. The tribunal dismissed the company's appeal, finding that the 'Chocolate Dundees' were 'biscuits wholly or partly covered with chocolate', and were therefore confectionery and standard-rated. *Adams Foods Ltd*, [1983] VATTR 280 (VTD 1514).

'Zebra Shortcake Rings and Fingers'

[29.147] A company manufactured biscuits, sold in transparent packets of five or six and known as 'Zebra Shortcake Rings' and 'Zebra Shortcake Fingers'. The top of the biscuits included thin stripes of chocolate. The chocolate comprised about 1% of the total content of the biscuits. The Commissioners issued a ruling that the products were standard-rated through being biscuits 'partly covered with chocolate'. The company appealed, contending that the chocolate was merely for decorative purposes and should not be regarded as providing a covering. The tribunal dismissed the company's appeal, holding that the fact that there was some chocolate on the biscuits meant that they were excluded from zero-rating. *North Cheshire Foods Ltd*, MAN/86/216 (VTD 2709).

Chocolate 'Tartelette'

[29.148] A company manufactured a product described as a 'tartelette', which comprised a biscuit base with a raised circumference, and a chocolate filling within this circumference. The Commissioners issued a ruling that the product was a biscuit 'partly covered with chocolate', and was therefore within the definition of 'confectionery' in *VATA 1994, Sch 8, Group 1, Excepted Item 2*, and excluded from zero-rating. The company appealed, contending that the product was 'filled' with chocolate rather than 'covered' with chocolate, and was therefore not excluded from zero-rating. The tribunal rejected this contention and dismissed the company's appeal, holding that the product was 'partly covered with chocolate'. *United Biscuits (UK) Ltd (No 4)*, MAN/02/563 (VTD 18090).

'Caramel Shortcake'

[29.149] A partnership manufactured a product known as 'Caramel Short-cake', which consisted of biscuit crumbs mixed with margarine, condensed milk, syrup and chocolate. The Commissioners issued a ruling that the product was confectionery, on the basis that it was a biscuit 'wholly or partly covered with chocolate'. The partnership appealed, contending that the product was a cake and was therefore zero-rated. The tribunal dismissed the appeal, holding that the product was not a cake and was within the definition of 'confectionery'. *In Good Taste*, EDN/88/30 (VTD 2956). (*Note.* See, however, the subsequent decision in *Marks & Spencer plc*, **29.134** above. Following that decision, the Commissioners now accept that caramel shortcake is zero-rated—see Customs' VAT Manual, Part 7, chapter 1, para 8.5.4.)

Carob-coated wafer biscuits

[29.150] A company manufactured a product consisting of thin wafer biscuits with a sweet creamy filling and a carob coating. The Commissioners issued a ruling that the product was confectionery and was not eligible for zero-rating. The tribunal dismissed the company's appeal, holding that the product was within the definition of 'confectionery'. *E Round & Son Ltd*, MAN/85/165 (VTD 2069).

[29.151] The decision in *E Round & Son Ltd*, **29.150** above, was applied in the similar case of *WH Cotterell*, MAN/89/560 (VTD 4573).

'Swedish Snowballs'

[29.152] A company manufactured a product known as 'Swedish Snowballs'. They were sweet, produced by cooking, and described as similar to marshmallow. The Commissioners issued a ruling that they were confectionery, and the tribunal upheld this decision. *Swedish Snowball Production Ltd*, MAN/86/305 (VTD 2311).

Cereal bars

[29.153] The Commissioners issued a ruling that two varieties of cereal bar were confectionery, and were therefore excluded from zero-rating. The tribunal dismissed the manufacturers' appeal, finding that the bars contained a substantial quantity of honey. Accordingly they were items of sweetened prepared food normally eaten with the fingers, within the definition of confectionery in what is now *VATA 1994, Sch 8, Group 1, Note 5*. *W Jordans (Cereals) Ltd*, LON/88/514Z (VTD 3275).

[29.154] A company manufactured a type of cereal bar which contained plant stanol ester, an ingredient designed to reduce cholesterol. The Commissioners issued a ruling that the bars were 'confectionery', and were therefore standard-rated. The company appealed, contending that because the bars contained plant stanol ester, they should not be regarded as confectionery. The tribunal rejected this contention and dismissed the appeal, holding that 'regardless of the undoubted medical benefits of the product, it falls squarely within the definition of confectionery'. *McNeil Consumer Nutritionals Ltd*, LON/01/1209 (VTD 17736).

[29.155] A company manufactured cereal bars which were marketed as being suitable for people who were allergic to gluten and wheat. The principal ingredients of the bars were ragus syrup and rice. Customs issued a ruling that the bars were standard-rated. The company appealed. The tribunal dismissed the appeal, holding that the bars were within the ordinary meaning of 'confectionery'. *Bells of Lazonby Ltd*, MAN/06/916 (VTD 20490).

[29.156] A company marketed a product named 'Crunchy Granola Bars'. The main ingredients were oats and sugar. Customs issued a ruling that they were within the definition of confectionery, and thus were standard-rated. The company appealed, contending that they should be classified as biscuits, and as zero-rated. The tribunal rejected this contention and dismissed the company's appeal, observing that 'the bars did not contain flour which was regarded as an essential ingredient for a biscuit'. *General Mills UK Ltd*, LON/07/1589 (VTD 20905).

Energy bars

[29.157] A trader imported 'energy bars' from the USA. The bars contained fructose, glucose, oat bran, brown rice, syrup, peanut butter and honey. They were marketed for sale to people competing in endurance sports such as marathons and triathlons. They were priced at £1.50 per bar. The Commissioners issued a ruling that the bars constituted confectionery, and were therefore excluded from zero-rating. The tribunal dismissed the trader's appeal, finding that the bars were 'an item of sweetened prepared food which is normally eaten with the fingers', and were thus within the definition of confectionery. *EJ Huczek*, MAN/92/507 (VTD 8850).

[29.158] A similar decision was reached in *H5 Ltd (t/a High Five)*, MAN/07/584 (VTD 20821).

'Sports nutrition' bars

[29.159] A company supplied 'sports nutrition bars', which it marketed to competitive cyclists. The bars contained oats, raisins, maltodextrin, fructose syrup, and apricot or banana. Customs issued a ruling that the bars were confectionery, and were therefore excluded from zero-rating. The company appealed, contending that the bars should be classified as 'cakes'. The tribunal rejected this contention, finding that the bars were not 'cakes'. They were 'an item of sweetened prepared food which is normally eaten with the fingers', and were thus within the definition of confectionery. *Torq Ltd*, LON/04/205 (VTD 19389).

Fruit bars

[29.160] A company manufactured three types of 'fruit bars', containing apple and strawberry; apple and blackcurrant; and mango and passion fruit. The main ingredient of each type was pulped dried fruit. Customs issued a ruling that they were 'confectionery', and therefore standard-rated. The tribunal allowed the company's appeal but the Ch D reversed this decision and remitted the case to a different tribunal for rehearing, holding that the original tribunal had made a clear error of law. Sir Andrew Morritt held that neither cooking, nor additional sweetening, was necessary in order for a product to be classified as 'confectionery'. He observed that barley sugar did not require any additional sweetener but was clearly within the definition of 'confectionery'. *HMRC v Premier Foods (Holdings) Ltd*, Ch D 2007, [2008] STC 176.

'Flapjack bars' containing oats and honey

[**29.161**] A company sold a product described as 'flapjack bars', the principal ingredients of which were honey (39.8%), oats (23.3%), sunflower seeds (13.5%) and linseed (13.5%). HMRC issued a ruling that the flapjack bars were standard-rated. The company appealed, contending that they should be treated as cakes and as qualifying for zero-rating. The tribunal rejected this contention and dismissed the appeal, holding that the product was 'confectionery' and was 'not similar to a traditional flapjack, or to a cake'. The tribunal observed that 'although the product contained oats, it did not contain any other typical ingredients of a flapjack such as butter or margarine, brown sugar or golden syrup'. *Asda Stores Ltd v HMRC*, FTT 2009, [2010] SFTD 175; [2009] UKFTT 267 (TC), TC00211.

Marshmallow cones

[**29.162**] A company sold cones (of the type commonly used to contain ice-cream) which were filled with marshmallow and which had a sugar topping. The Commissioners issued a ruling that the cones were standard-rated 'confectionery'. The tribunal dismissed the company's appeal, holding that the cones were confectionery rather than biscuits, and were therefore standard-rated. *Kathy's Kones Ltd (No 1)*, MAN/93/994 (VTD 11705). (*Note.* For a subsequent appeal by the same company, see **29.130** above. Following the subsequent decision, the Commissioners now accept that the product in question is zero-rated—see Customs' VAT Manual, Part 7, chapter 1, para 8.7.2.)

Raisins with strawberry-flavoured coating

[**29.163**] A company sold raisins with a strawberry-flavoured coating. The Commissioners issued a ruling that these raisins were 'confectionery' and therefore standard-rated. The company appealed, contending that they should be treated as zero-rated. The tribunal rejected this contention and dismissed the appeal, finding that 'sugar has been added to the coating, nothing has been done to neutralise its sweetening effect, and both the coating and the overall product are sweeter than they would have been had no sugar been added to the coating'. Accordingly the raisins were 'sweetened products' within the definition of 'confectionery', and were excluded from zero-rating. *Golden Wonder Ltd*, MAN/02/334 (VTD 18650).

'Pencil jelly' and 'fruit delights'

[**29.164**] A company manufactured two products called 'pencil jelly' and 'fruity delights'. They were contained in small sachets, marketed at young children, and intended to be eaten by squeezing the sachets directly into the mouth. The Commissioners issued a ruling that the products were within the definition of 'confectionery', and therefore excluded from zero-rating. The company appealed, contending that because the products were intended to be squeezed directly into the mouth, without the use of fingers, they were outside the definition of 'confectionery' and should be treated as zero-rated. The tribunal rejected this contention and dismissed the company's appeal, observing that children eating the products would use their fingers to squeeze the sachets, and holding that 'the phrase "sweetened prepared food which is normally eaten with the fingers" simply means such food which is not normally eaten with the assistance of a knife and fork or a spoon or some other implement such as chopsticks'. *Unibev Ltd*, EDN/03/67 (VTD 18437).

Beverages (VATA 1994, Sch 8, Group 1, Excepted Item 4)

NOTE

The scope of what is now *Excepted Item No 4* was extended by the *VAT (Beverages) Order 1993 (SI 1993/2498)*, which took effect from 1 December 1993. Before that date, *Excepted Item No 4* had referred to 'manufactured beverages', rather than simply to 'beverages'.

'Kosher' meals including fruit juice—whether entirely zero-rated

[29.165] A company supplied prepacked meals, which it certified as 'Kosher' (prepared in accordance with Jewish ecclesiastical law). It treated its supplies of these meals as entirely zero-rated. In 1987 the Commissioners issued a ruling that, as the meals contained fruit juice, which was excluded from zero-rating by what is now *VATA 1994, Sch 8, Group 1, Excepted Item 4*, the supplies were deemed to be mixed supplies and part of the consideration had to be treated as standard-rated. The tribunal dismissed the company's appeal against this decision. *Hermolis & Co Ltd*, [1989] VATTR 199 (VTD 4137).

'Bio-Light'

[29.166] A company manufactured a product named 'Bio-Light', which was an opaque brown fluid sold by chemists and health food shops. The product was packaged in small bottles, and was intended to be diluted with water before consumption. It was described in the company's advertising as 'a natural detoxifying and slimming food supplement'. The company did not account for tax on sales of the product. The Commissioners issued a ruling that the product was standard-rated, on the basis that it was a 'manufactured beverage' and was excluded from zero-rating by what is now *VATA 1994, Sch 8, Group 1, Excepted Item 4*. The company appealed, contending that the product was a food supplement which should not be treated as a 'beverage', since it was designed to be sipped slowly at intervals, and would act as a violent laxative if drunk by the glassful. The tribunal allowed the appeal, observing that the product had an unpleasant taste and would not 'be consumed for pleasure', and holding that it was not within the definition of 'beverage'. The tribunal chairman observed that a beverage was a liquid that was 'characteristically taken to increase bodily liquid levels, to slake the thirst, to fortify or to give pleasure'. *Bioconcepts Ltd*, LON/92/2852 (VTD 11287).

Drink containing water, fibre and fruit juice

[29.167] A company manufactured and distributed a drink containing water, fibrous extracts and fruit juice. The fibrous extracts comprised 20% of the total product. The drink was more expensive than standard fruit juice drinks, being priced at 69p for 250 ml. The Commissioners issued a ruling that the product was a 'beverage' and thus excluded from zero-rating. The company appealed, contending that the inclusion of significant quantities of fibre meant that the product was outside the definition of 'beverage', so that the supplies should be zero-rated. The tribunal rejected this contention and dismissed the appeal. On the evidence, 'the consistency was not that of syrup but of a slightly thickened fruit juice'. The product was packaged and marketed as a drink, and was within the definition of a 'beverage'. *Smith Kline Beecham plc*, LON/95/1704A (VTD 13674).

Tomato and carrot juices

[29.168] A company manufactured various types of fruit and vegetable juices. One of its products consisted primarily of tomato juice (89%), while the other primarily contained carrot juice (45%) and tomato juice (39%). Customs issued a ruling that these products were 'beverages' and excluded from zero-rating by *VATA 1994, Sch 8, Group 1, Excepted Item 4*. The tribunal upheld Customs' ruling and dismissed the company's appeal. (The tribunal also observed that tomatoes and red peppers were actually fruits, even though the company's advertising material described them as 'vegetables'.) *Grove Fresh Ltd*, LON/04/2306 (VTD 19241).

Liquidised fruit and vegetables

[29.169] A company manufactured products described as 'Zumo Fresh Blend', comprising liquidised fruits and vegetables, and similar in consistency to a cold soup, but sold in plastic cups, to be drunk rather than eaten with a spoon. Customs issued a ruling that these products were 'beverages' and excluded from zero-rating by *VATA 1994, Sch 8, Group 1, Excepted Item 4*. The tribunal upheld Customs' ruling and dismissed the company's appeal, holding that the products were within the definition of 'beverages'. The Ch D upheld this decision as one of fact. *Kalron Foods Ltd v HMRC*, Ch D [2007] STC 1100; [2007] EWHC 695 (Ch).

Fruit 'smoothies'

[29.170] A company marketed liquid products, made from various crushed or squeezed fruits, which it described as 'smoothies'. The products had a water content of 84%. Initially the company accounted for VAT on these sales, but it subsequently submitted a repayment claim on the basis that it should have treated them as zero-rated. HMRC rejected the claim on the basis that the products were 'beverages' and excluded from zero-rating by *VATA 1994, Sch 8, Group 1, Excepted Item 4*. The tribunal upheld Customs' ruling and dismissed the company's appeal, finding that the products had 'the consistency of a moderately thin soup' but were intended 'to be drunk from the bottle'.

Since they were intended and sold as drinks, the products were within the definition of 'beverages'. *Innocent Ltd v HMRC*, [2010] UKFTT 516 (TC); [2011] SFTD 111, TC00771. (*Note.* Costs were awarded to HMRC—see 2.358 APPEALS.)

'Shots' of concentrated liquidised fruit and vegetables

[29.171] A company manufactured products described as 'Vie shots', comprising concentrated liquidised fruit and vegetables. Customs issued a ruling that these products were 'beverages' and excluded from zero-rating by *VATA 1994, Sch 8, Group 1, Excepted Item 4*. The company appealed, contending that the products were not 'beverages', but were a means of boosting the consumer's daily fruit and vegetable intake, and qualified for zero-rating. The tribunal accepted this contention and allowed the appeal, distinguishing *Kalron Foods Ltd*, 29.169 above, on the grounds that there was 'a much lower liquid content in the Vie shot than there is in the Zumo considered in the *Kalron* case'. The tribunal found that the products were neither sold nor consumed as 'something to replace bodily fluids or to slake the thirst' and were not 'sold or consumed as something to be drunk for pleasure'. Accordingly they were not within the definition of a 'beverage'. *Unilever Bestfoods UK Ltd*, [2007] VATDR 119 (VTD 20016).

Wheatgrass juice

[29.172] A company sold wheatgrass juice. Customs issued a ruling that the product was a beverage and excluded from zero-rating by *VATA 1994, Sch 8, Group 1, Excepted Item 4*. The company appealed, contending that wheatgrass juice was a food which qualified for zero-rating. The tribunal accepted this contention and allowed the appeal, observing that the taste of the juice was 'quite unpleasant, and not the sort of thing that one might want to take in any great quantity'. *Ocean Grown UK Ltd*, LON/06/1051 (VTD 20562).

Sports drinks

[29.173] A company (G) manufactured a drink which it called 'Lucozade Sport'. It contained carbohydrates and electrolytes, and was marketed for sale to people participating in high-intensity sport and exercise. HMRC issued a ruling that G was required to account for VAT on its sales of the product. G appealed, contending that even though the product was intended to be consumed as a drink, it should be treated as food rather than as a beverage, and qualified for zero-rating. The First-Tier Tribunal rejected this contention and dismissed the appeal, holding that the product was within the definition of a beverage, and was therefore excluded from zero-rating. The tribunal specifically distinguished the decision in *SIS (Science in Sport) Ltd*, 29.91 above, observing that in that case, the tribunal had found that the powder in question was only consumed by 'athletes, sports people and others who characteristically take them for nutritional purposes', whereas in the present case, the product was drunk by a significant number of consumers 'when not engaging in sport or any exercise'. The Upper Tribunal upheld this decision.

Newey J held that the tribunal had been entitled to find that the product 'is not mainly purchased or consumed on account of its nutritional ingredients'. *GlaxoSmithKline Services Unlimited v HMRC*, [2011] UKUT 432 (TCC); [2012] STC 10.

Spices for making mulled wine

[29.174] A company sold packs of spices, designed to be used for making mulled wine. The Commissioners issued a ruling that the packs were within *VATA 1994, Sch 8, Group 1, Excepted Item No 4*, as 'products for the preparation of beverages', and were therefore standard-rated. The company appealed, contending that the packs were not within *Excepted Item No 4*, and qualified for zero-rating. The tribunal accepted this contention and allowed the appeal, holding that the words 'products for the preparation of beverages' had 'to be construed *"eiusdem generis"* with the preceding words "syrups, concentrates, essences, powders, crystals" and do not comprehend every kind of product for the preparation of beverages but only those which perform the same function as syrups, concentrates, essences, etc.' The words referred to 'something from which a beverage is made by reconstitution, dilution or infusion and not just any ingredient of the finished drink'. The spices in mulled wine did not 'fulfil anything like that kind of function.' (The chairman also observed that the principles of European law 'do not, in my view, inhibit or constrain a court here into adopting an unnecessarily narrow interpretation of the statutory provisions in order to limit the scope of relief'.) *McCormick (UK) plc*, LON/97/1193 (VTD 15202).

Fruit-flavoured 'iced tea'—whether within Overriding Item No 4

[29.175] A company manufactured four varieties of fruit-flavoured 'iced tea'. Tea powder comprised less than 2% of the products, the main ingredients of which were water, glucose syrup and citric acid. The Commissioners issued a ruling that supplies of the products were standard-rated, being excluded from zero-rating by *VATA 1994, Sch 8, Group 1, Excepted Item No 4*. The company appealed, contending that the products were within the definition of 'tea' and so were zero-rated under *VATA 1994, Sch 8, Group 1, Overriding Item No 4*. The tribunal rejected this contention and dismissed the appeal, holding that the products were not 'tea pure and simple in the ordinary use of the term'. In terms of taste and smell 'the fruit flavouring predominates over the tea'. The fact that the products were marketed as 'tea' was not conclusive. *Snapple Beverage Corporation*, LON/94/1991A (VTD 13690).

'Iced tea concentrate'—whether within Overriding Item No 4

[29.176] A company manufactured 'iced tea concentrates', which took the form of a dark brown liquid. HMRC issued a ruling that the supplies were standard-rated, being excluded from zero-rating by *VATA 1994, Sch 8, Group 1, Excepted Item No 4*. The company appealed, contending that the products were within the definition of 'tea' and so were zero-rated under *VATA 1994, Sch 8, Group 1, Overriding Item No 4*. The tribunal accepted this contention and allowed the appeal, finding that 'tea is the principal ingredient', and specifically distinguishing the earlier decision in *Snapple Beverage Corporation*, 29.175 above. *Thorncroft Ltd v HMRC*, [2011] UKFTT 694 (TC), TC01536.

'Norfolk Punch'—whether within Overriding Item No 4

[29.177] A company manufactured a beverage called 'Norfolk Punch', which contained a variety of herbs as well as substantial quantities of sugar and honey. The Commissioners issued a ruling that sales of the product were standard-rated by virtue of *VATA 1994, Sch 8, Group 1, Excepted Item No 4*. The company appealed, contending that the beverage was a 'similar product' to herbal tea, and was therefore zero-rated by virtue of *VATA 1994, Sch 8, Group 1, Overriding Item No 4*. The tribunal rejected this contention and dismissed the appeal, holding on the evidence that, although it contained a variety of herbs, the beverage was not a 'similar product' to herbal tea. The tribunal observed that the common characteristic of tea, maté and herbal teas was 'that they are drinks obtained by a straightforward process of infusing leaves, without more' and were 'not the products of a manufacturing process'. The product at issue, however, was 'the result of a fairly complicated manufacturing process involving several stages and with quite a large variety of ingredients'. *Orchid Drinks Co Ltd*, MAN/95/2419 (VTD 14222).

'Rivella'—whether within Sch 8, Group 1, Overriding Item No 6

[29.178] A company manufactured a beverage called 'Rivella', which was made from lactoserum but contained no milk protein, and could therefore be drunk by people who were allergic to cows' milk. Lactoserum comprised 35% of the beverage, while water comprised more than 50% of it. The Commissioners issued a ruling that sales of the product were standard-rated by virtue of *VATA 1994, Sch 8, Group 1, Excepted Item No 4*. The company appealed, contending that the beverage was made from extracts of milk, and was therefore zero-rated by virtue of *VATA 1994, Sch 8, Group 1, Overriding Item No 6*. The tribunal accepted this contention and allowed the appeal. *Rivella (UK) Ltd*, LON/99/562 (VTD 16382).

Powder to be added to milk—whether within Overriding Item No 6

[29.179] A company manufactured a powdered product called 'Max for Milk', which had a strawberry flavour and was intended to be dissolved into milk. Its principal ingredient was maltodextrin, but it also contained skimmed milk. Customs issued a ruling that sales of the product were standard-rated by virtue of *VATA 1994, Sch 8, Group 1, Excepted Item No 4*. The company appealed, contending that the product was a 'preparation of milk', and was therefore zero-rated by virtue of *VATA 1994, Sch 8, Group 1, Overriding Item No 6*. The tribunal accepted this contention and allowed the appeal. *R Twining & Co Ltd*, LON/06/305 (VTD 20230).

Fruit-flavoured soya milk—whether a beverage

[29.180] A company sold fruit-flavoured soya milk. Customs issued a ruling that this was standard-rated by virtue of *VATA 1994, Sch 8, Group 1, Excepted Item No 4*. The company appealed, contending firstly that the product was not within the definition of a 'beverage' and was zero-rated by virtue of being 'food' (and alternatively that if the product was deemed to be a 'beverage', it was zero-rated by virtue of *VATA 1994, Sch 8, Group 1, Overriding Item No 6*). The tribunal accepted the company's first contention and allowed the appeal, holding that that a beverage was a liquid that was characteristically taken 'to slake the thirst'. Soya milk was not a beverage because it was 'not apt to slake the thirst'. However it was within the definition of 'food' and therefore qualified for zero-rating. *Alpro Ltd*, LON/04/1205 (VTD 19911).

Potato crisps, etc. (VATA 1994, Sch 8, Group 1, Excepted Item 5)

'Corn hoops'—whether 'obtained by the swelling of cereals'

[29.181] A company manufactured a product known as 'corn hoops'. 80% of the dry content of the product was cereal-based. During cooking, the volume of the product was increased by about 33%. The Commissioners issued a ruling that the product was standard-rated, since it was 'obtained by the swelling of cereals', and was thus excluded from zero-rating by *VATA 1994, Sch 8, Group 1, Excepted Item No 5*. The tribunal allowed the company's appeal, holding on the evidence that the swelling of the product was 'an incidental consequence of the cooking'. Accordingly, the product was not within *Excepted Item No 5*, and qualified for zero-rating. *United Biscuits (UK) Ltd (No 3)*, MAN/01/60 (VTD 17391).

'Snack-a-Jack' rice and corn cakes

[29.182] A company manufactured savoury rice and corn cakes, in various flavours, under the name 'Snack-a-Jacks'. The company's marketing material indicated that the products 'could be eaten on their own or with a range of toppings'. Customs issued a ruling that the products were standard-rated. The company appealed, contending that they should be treated as zero-rated. The tribunal rejected this contention and dismissed the appeal, holding that the products were 'obtained by the swelling of cereals', and were thus excluded from zero-rating by *VATA 1994, Sch 8, Group 1, Excepted Item No 5*. The tribunal also held that the products were 'packaged for human consumption without further preparation'. The fact that some customers might add a 'topping' to give additional flavour did not mean that the products qualified for zero-rating. *Quaker Trading Ltd*, LON/05/238 (VTD 20604).

'Hula hoops' sold with barbecue sauce

[29.183] A company sold a product described as 'hula hoops', the principal ingredient of which was potato. It included sachets of barbecue sauce with some of these products. It accounted for tax where the 'hula hoops' were sold without barbecue sauce. However, it did not account for tax where the 'hula hoops' were sold with barbecue sauce. The Commissioners issued a ruling that the product was excluded from zero-rating by *VATA 1994, Sch 8, Group 1, Excepted Item No 5*. The company appealed, contending that the product was not within *Excepted Item No 5* because it was intended to be eaten with a barbecue sauce and was not intended 'for human consumption without further preparation'. The tribunal rejected this contention and dismissed the appeal. The tribunal held that simply adding barbecue sauce or 'seasoning' could not 'realistically be described as "making ready"' or as constituting 'further preparation'. On the evidence, 'the product is ready to eat without the addition of the seasoning, in that it is palatable'. The fact that the consumer 'has the choice of adding or not adding the seasoning' did not take the product outside the restriction of *Excepted Item No 5*. Accordingly the product failed to qualify for zero-rating. *United Biscuits (UK) Ltd (No 6)*, MAN/03/823 (VTD 18947).

Potato crisps sold with 'dip'—whether excluded from zero-rating

[29.184] A company sold packages containing a 100g packet of potato crisps and a 95g plastic tub of a 'dip' such as mango chutney. Customs issued a ruling that there were two separate supplies, and that the company was required to account for VAT on the part of the consideration which was attributable to the potato crisps. The company appealed, contending that the crisps should be treated as zero-rated. The tribunal rejected this contention and dismissed the appeal, holding that the crisps were excluded from zero-rating by *VATA 1994, Sch 8, Group 1, Excepted Item No 5*, since they were intended 'for human consumption without further preparation'. The fact that the crisps could be dipped in the mango chutney before being eaten did not take them outside the restriction of *Excepted Item No 5*. Accordingly the crisps failed to qualify for zero-rating. *United Biscuits (UK) Ltd (No 7)*, MAN/04/285 (VTD 19319).

'Pringles'—whether excluded from zero-rating

[29.185] A partnership manufactured a product known as 'Pringles', which contained potato flour, corn flour, wheat starch and rice flour. About 42% of the product consisted of potato, and about 33% was fat. Customs issued a ruling that they were excluded from zero-rating by *VATA 1994, Sch 8, Group 1, Excepted Item No 5*. The partnership appealed, contending that the products were not 'potato crisps' or 'similar products', and should not be excluded from zero-rating. The tribunal rejected this contention and dismissed the appeal, specifically disapproving the earlier tribunal decision in *Procter & Gamble UK (No 1)*, LON/02/896 (VTD 18381). The tribunal observed that the history of the legislation showed 'an intention by Parliament to tax food not normally bought primarily for nutrition but eaten as snacks'. On the evidence, Pringles were 'not normally purchased primarily for nutrition'. The tribunal held that Pringles were excluded from zero-rating since they were made from potato flour. The CA unanimously upheld this decision. Jacob LJ held that Pringles were 'similar to the potato crisp and made from the potato'. Toulson LJ held that there was no requirement 'that the products should be made wholly (or substantially wholly) from the potato or potato derivative'. Parliament had not 'specified a minimum percentage below which a product should not fairly or sensibly be considered to be "made from the potato"'. Mummery LJ observed that 'the "made from" question would probably be answered in a more relevant and sensible way by a child consumer of crisps than by a food scientist or a culinary pedant'. Accordingly Pringles were excluded from zero-rating. *HMRC v Procter & Gamble UK (No 2)*, CA [2009] STC 1990; [2009] EWCA Civ 407.

Wheat and potato blended savoury snacks—whether excluded from zero-rating

[29.186] A company marketed two types of savoury snacks, made from a blend of wheat and potato, and sold under the name 'Discos' and 'New Recipe Frisps'. HMRC issued a ruling that the products were excluded from zero-rating by *VATA 1994, Sch 8, Group 1, Excepted Item No 5*. The company appealed, contending that the products were not 'potato crisps' or 'similar products', and should not be excluded from zero-rating. The tribunal accepted this contention and allowed the appeal, finding that 'Discos' contained 31.17% wheat starch and 27.87% dried potato, and that 'New Recipe Frisps' contained 34.7% wheat flour and 22.56% dried potato,. On the evidence, 'the defining and essential ingredient is the wheat', so that the products were not excluded from zero-rating. *United Biscuits (UK) Ltd v HMRC (No 8)*, [2011] UKFTT 673 (TC), TC01515.

Pet food, etc. (VATA 1994, Sch 8, Group 1, Excepted Item 6)

Liver brawn sold for cats and dogs

[29.187] A couple who operated a petrol station also sold rolls of liver brawn, weighing about 2lbs each and marketed as 'dog and cat food'. The couple did not account for output tax on these supplies. The Commissioners issued an assessment on the basis that the food was pet food which was excluded from zero-rating. The couple appealed, contending that the brawn should be zero-rated because it was suitable for pigs and poultry as well as for pet dogs and cats. The tribunal dismissed the appeal, holding on the evidence that the brawn was 'obviously stocked for sale to passing motorists who would have an interest in purchasing the same for their dogs or cats' and observing that 'the nature of the packaging was appropriate for small purchases by owners of one or two pets, rather than by farmers who could be expected to purchase in bulk'. *E & J Crooks*, EDN/83/65 (VTD 1602).

1lb packs of meat—whether 'packaged pet food'

[29.188] A company sold meat, advertised as pet food, in 1lb packs. The Commissioners issued a ruling that the sales were of 'packaged pet food' and were therefore excluded from zero-rating by what is now *VATA 1994, Sch 8, Group 1, Excepted Item No 6*. The tribunal upheld this decision. *Freezerman (UK) Ltd*, LON/85/454 (VTD 2061).

Raw meat sold in plastic bags—whether 'pet food'

[29.189] A company which operated a licensed slaughterhouse sold raw meat in plastic bags. It advertised the meat as pet food, but its customers included zoos, greyhound trainers, animal experimental establishments, security organisations (for guard dogs), dog breeders, farmers (for sheep dogs), and pet shop owners as well as private individuals. The Commissioners issued an assessment charging VAT on the sales, on the basis that it was advertised as pet food and thus was excluded from zero-rating by what is now *VATA 1994, Sch 8, Group 1, Excepted Item No 6*. The tribunal allowed the company's appeal in part, observing that a pet was an animal 'which is kept primarily as an object of affection', and holding on the evidence that most of the company's supplies were not 'primarily intended for pets', but were produced and offered for sale 'as foods for animals generally' and thus were not excluded from zero-rating. The decision in *Freezerman (UK) Ltd*, 29.188 above, was not followed, and was implicitly disapproved. The appeal was adjourned for the parties to agree figures. *Popes Lane Pet Food Supplies Ltd*, [1986] VATTR 221 (VTD 2186). (*Notes*. (1) There was no further public hearing of the appeal. (2) For the Commissioners' practice following this decision, see Customs' VAT Manual, Part 7, chapter 1, para 21.2.1.)

Minced chicken—whether 'pet food'

[29.190] A company sold minced chicken, as food for animals, in 1lb and 5lb packs. It did not account for VAT, considering that the sales were zero-rated under what is now *VATA 1994, Sch 8, Group 1, General Item No 2*. The Commissioners issued an assessment on the basis that the sales were of pet food and thus excluded from zero-rating by what is now *VATA 1994, Sch 8, Group 1, Excepted Item No 6*. The company appealed, contending that most of the minced chicken was sold to owners of working dogs, including the local police force and greyhound trainers. The tribunal allowed the appeal, applying the decision in *Popes Lane Pet Food Supplies Ltd*, 29.189 above, and holding that the minced chicken was not sold as pet food, and was therefore zero-rated. *Norman Riding Poultry Farm Ltd*, [1989] VATTR 124 (VTD 3726).

Meat sold as dog food—whether 'pet food'

[29.191] A partnership sold meat as dog food from a market stall and from a nearby shop. The meat was not fit for human consumption. The partnership treated the sales of the meat as zero-rated, but the Commissioners issued an assessment on the basis that the meat was sold as pet food and was therefore standard-rated. The partnership appealed, contending that most of the meat was sold to owners of 'working dogs' such as guard dogs and greyhounds. The tribunal allowed the appeal in part, holding that all the sales from the market stall were zero-rated but that the sales from the shop should be apportioned between zero-rated sales to owners of pets and standard-rated sales to owners of working dogs. The appeal was adjourned in the hope that the parties could agree an apportionment. *LJ & H Norgate (t/a Dog's Dinner)*, LON/89/1221Z (VTD 5241). (*Note.* There was no further public hearing of the appeal.)

[29.192] A partnership sold frozen meat, intended as dog food, from a shop. Above the freezer from which the meat was sold was a handwritten notice stating 'frozen pet food'. The partnership did not account for output tax on such sales, treating them as zero-rated. The Commissioners issued a ruling that the sales should have been treated as standard-rated, on the basis that they were supplies of pet food and thus were excluded from zero-rating by what is now *VATA 1994, Sch 8, Group 1, Excepted Item 6*. The partnership appealed, contending that some of the sales were to owners of working dogs rather than to owners of pets. The tribunal held that all sales to the general public were standard-rated, since the effect of the notice by the freezer was that the food was being advertised for sale as pet food. However, some of the sales were in response to orders placed by regular customers, and in such cases the effect of the notice was 'insignificant'. The tribunal adjourned the appeal in the hope that the parties could agree an apportionment. *P Peters & K P Riddles (t/a Mill Lane Farm Shop)*, LON/94/1221 (VTD 12937). (*Note.* There was no further public hearing of the appeal.)

'Premium Mixer for Working Dogs'—whether zero-rated

[29.193] A company manufactured a product which it described as 'premium mixer for working dogs'. 73% of the product was wheat, while 9% of the product was fresh chicken. The product also contained barley, rice, molasses, bran and cod liver oil. It was dark brown in colour, rough in texture, and supplied in small bone-shaped lumps. The Commissioners issued a ruling that the product was 'biscuits and meal for cats and dogs', within *VATA 1994, Sch 8, Group 1, Excepted Item 6*, and was therefore standard-rated. The company appealed, contending that the product was not within the definition of 'biscuits and meal', and should be treated as zero-rated animal feeding stuffs, within *General Item 2*. The tribunal accepted this contention and allowed the appeal. The product was not 'meal', since meal was defined by the Shorter Oxford English Dictionary as 'the edible part of any grain and pulse (usually excluding wheat) ground to a powder'. The product was also not a biscuit, because it had 'a rough external appearance, as compared with the smoothness one associates with biscuits, and is produced in small bone-shaped lumps which are of a texture much rougher and flakier than that of biscuits'. Furthermore, 'when a dog digests the product, its gastric juices act on it and first increase its size' whereas 'biscuits simply disintegrate when they come into contact with gastric juices'. *Bambers Frozen Meats Ltd*, MAN/01/629 (VTD 17626).

Rabbit food—whether 'packaged pet food'

[29.194] The proprietor of a pet shop did not account for VAT on sales of rabbit food. Some of this food was sold in 4lb bags, while some was kept in a large container, and was only weighed and placed into a bag when requested by a customer. The Commissioners issued an assessment charging tax on these supplies, and the proprietor appealed, contending that the supplies were zero-rated. The tribunal allowed the appeal in part. On the evidence, it was accepted that the food was sold for consumption by rabbits which were kept as pets. It followed that it was excluded from zero-rating by what is now *VATA 1994, Sch 8, Group 1, Excepted Item No 6* if it was 'packaged', but was not so excluded if it was not packaged. Applying the wording in *Notice No 705/21/86*, the food could only be regarded as packaged where it had been placed into a 4lb bag prior to being sold. Putting loose food into a container at the point of sale did not constitute the packaging of that food. *B Beresford*, MAN/92/99 (VTD 9673). (*Note.* The Commissioners now accept that, since 85% of rabbits kept in the UK are reared for food, rather than kept as pets, 'rabbit food sold in any quantity is only standard-rated if it is supplied, packaged, specifically for pet rabbits'—see Customs' VAT Manual, Part 7, chapter 1, para 21.3.4.)

Ferret food—whether 'pet food'

[29.195] A company supplied packaged food for ferrets. Initially it accounted for tax on these supplies, but it subsequently submitted a repayment claim on the basis that it should have treated the supplies as zero-rated animal feeding stuffs, within *VATA 1994, Sch 8, Group 1, General Item 2*. HMRC rejected the claim on the grounds that the supplies were pet food which was excluded from zero-rating by *Group 1, Excepted Item No 6*. The tribunal dismissed the company's appeal, holding that 'ferrets can be classified generally as a pet species' notwithstanding that a minority of ferrets were kept as working ferrets (eg to catch rabbits) and not as pets. *Supreme Petfoods Ltd v HMRC*, [2011] UKFTT 19 (TC), TC00896.

Nuts sold as bird food

[29.196] A firm operated a leisure garden which contained several caged birds. It sold nuts which visitors could use to feed the birds. It did not account for output tax on its sales of these nuts. The Commissioners issued an assessment charging tax on the sales, and the firm appealed, contending that the sales should be treated as zero-rated. The tribunal dismissed the appeal, holding that the nuts were 'packaged foods (not being pet foods) for birds other than poultry or game' and were therefore excluded from zero-rating by what is now *VATA 1994, Sch 8, Group 1, Excepted Item No 6*. *Merley Bird Gardens*, LON/92/2221 (VTD 12426). (*Note.* See now *Notice 701/15/95, para 16*, and compare the subsequent decision in *Hardman*, **48.44** PAYMENT OF TAX.)

30

Fuel and Power

The cases in this chapter are arranged under the following headings.

Standard-rated supplies   30.1
Supplies qualifying for reduced rate (VATA 1994, Sch 7A,
Group 1)   30.12

NOTE

Until 31 March 1993, supplies of fuel and power were zero-rated subject to the detailed conditions laid down in *VATA 1983, Sch 5, Group 7*. This provision had been substituted by *FA 1989, s 21* in relation to supplies made on or after 1 July 1990, to restrict zero-rating to supplies for domestic use or use by a charity otherwise than in the course or furtherance of a business. Cases relating to supplies before that date should be read in the light of this change. Supplies of fuel and power for domestic and charitable use were charged at 8% from 1 April 1994 to 31 August 1997 and have been charged at 5% from 1 September 1997. See now *VATA 1994, Sch 7A, Group 1*.

Standard-Rated Supplies

Supply of cylinders for butane gas

[30.1] A company supplied butane gas through authorised dealers. The customer entered into a standard 'Cylinder Refill Authority Agreement', on completion of which, and on payment of £5, he was supplied with a cylinder. When empty, the cylinder could be exchanged for a filled one on payment of £1 (or the price for gas current at the time). The cylinders remained the property of the company. The company did not account for output tax on its receipts, treating them as zero-rated. The Commissioners issued an assessment on the basis that only £1 of the £5 was eligible for zero-rating, the remaining £4 being for the supply of services relating to the cylinder and being standard-rated. The tribunal dismissed the company's appeal, holding that the £4 related to a standard-rated supply of services. *Calor Gas Ltd*, [1973] VATTR 205 (VTD 47).

Coin-operated washing machines in launderette

[30.2] See *Mander Laundries Ltd*, **69.1** ZERO-RATING: MISCELLANEOUS.

Coin-operated special lighting in club billiards room

[30.3] A members' club had a billiards room with three tables for billiards or snooker. Those using it obtained lighting over the tables by inserting coins in a meter in the room. It did not account for output tax on the takings, treating them as zero-rated. The Commissioners issued an assessment charging tax on them and the tribunal dismissed the club's appeal, holding that the supplies were standard-rated because the cost of the electricity used was only a small proportion of the money inserted, which was paid for the supply of facilities for playing billiards or snooker. *Washwood Heath & Ward End Conservative and Unionist Club Ltd*, BIR/73/12 (VTD 50).

[30.4] A club, incorporated as a company limited by guarantee, provided its members with facilities for playing squash and lawn tennis. The squash courts and some of the lawn tennis courts were equipped with artificial lighting, operated by prepayment meters. Members using these courts paid a booking fee and a fee for using the meters, as well as inserting coins in the meters. The Commissioners issued an assessment made on the basis that the coins inserted in the meters were consideration for using the courts and chargeable at the standard rate. The company appealed, contending that the coins should be treated as payment for supplies for electricity, and as zero-rated under the legislation then in force. The tribunal rejected this contention and dismissed the appeal, holding that the payments were for the supply of the facility to enjoy the game, and that 'the availability of lighting is an integral part of the composite whole'. *St Anne's-on-Sea Lawn Tennis Club Ltd*, [1977] VATTR 229 (VTD 434).

Electricity provided in holiday accommodation

[30.5] A husband and wife who supplied self-catering holiday accommodation took over the running of a hotel. They charged their visitors for food and accommodation and, in accounting for VAT, sought to attribute part of their takings to the supply of electricity, which was zero-rated. The Commissioners raised an assessment on the basis that the supplies actually made were of food and accommodation, and were entirely standard-rated. The tribunal upheld the assessment and dismissed the couple's appeal. *Lt Col TJ & Mrs ST Pine-Coffin*, LON/83/367 (VTD 1620).

[30.6] A company provided holiday accommodation in chalets and static caravans. It charged £10 per week in respect of gas and electricity, neither of which were metered. The Commissioners assessed the company on the basis that the charge was standard-rated. The company's appeal was dismissed. The supply of the gas and electricity was provided as part of a composite supply and the charge made for it bore no relation to the amounts actually used. *Hazelwood Caravans & Chalets Ltd*, [1985] VATTR 179 (VTD 1923).

[30.7] The decision in *Hazelwood Caravans & Chalets Ltd*, 30.6 above, was followed in the similar case of *CMC (Preston) Ltd*, MAN/88/78 (VTD 3858).

Supplies of charcoal

[30.8] A married couple supplied charcoal to retailers. They failed to account for output tax on these supplies. The Commissioners issued an assessment charging tax on the supplies, and the couple appealed, contending that the supplies should be treated as zero-rated. The tribunal dismissed the appeal, holding that the supplies did not qualify for zero-rating since they were intended for resale by the recipients. Accordingly they were excluded from zero-rating by what is now *VATA 1994, Sch 7A, Group 1, Item 5(b)*. *Mr & Mrs J Wyld (t/a Wyldwood Coppice)*, LON/93/3007A (VTD 12420).

Hire of agricultural machinery including petrol

[30.9] A company carried on the business of hiring agricultural machinery, such as tractors, to farmers. Where requested, it supplied petrol with the machinery. In accounting for VAT, it treated part of the consideration which it received as being attributable to the supply of petrol and as zero-rated under the legislation then in force. The Commissioners issued an assessment on the basis that there had been a single composite supply which was entirely standard-rated. The tribunal dismissed the company's appeal, applying the principles laid down in *British Airways plc*, 66.13 TRANSPORT, and holding that the petrol was 'in substance and reality an integral part of the contract and not a separate or severable supply'. *Showtry Ltd*, EDN/92/117 (VTD 10028).

Supplies of fuel and power to university

[30.10] A university owned a subsidiary company. The company purchased supplies of fuel and power, and resupplied these to the university for use in buildings which were used as residential accommodation for students. The Commissioners issued a ruling that the supplies to the company did not qualify for the 5% reduced rate, because the company had not purchased them for a 'qualifying use', but for commercial resale. The company appealed, contending that the supplies should be treated as qualifying for the reduced rate because the final consumer (the university) would be using the supplies for a qualifying purpose. The tribunal dismissed the appeal, holding that in view of the 'history and purpose' of the legislation, 'the zero rate or the reduced rate should be restricted to supplies to the final consumer who is the person who acquired goods or services for personal use'. Accordingly, the supplies to the subsidiary company did not qualify for the reduced rate. *Oval (717) Ltd*, [2003] VATDR 581 (VTD 17875). (*Note.* See also the subsequent decision in *The Chancellor, Masters & Scholars of the University of Cambridge*, 30.11 below.)

[30.11] A university applied for a certificate under *VATA 1994, Sch 7A, Group 1*, entitling it to pay the reduced rate of VAT on the supplies of electricity which it received. Customs rejected the claim on the grounds that the university was receiving the electricity 'in the course or furtherance of a business', which was not 'qualifying use' by virtue of *Sch 7A, Group 1, Note 3*. The tribunal upheld Customs' ruling and dismissed the university's appeal, and the Ch D upheld this decision. Sir Andrew Morritt held that the university was not a 'body governed by public law' within *Article 13* of *Directive 2006/112/EC*, and that its supplies of education were 'in the course or furtherance of a business'. *The Chancellor, Masters & Scholars of the University of Cambridge*, Ch D [2009] STC 1288; [2009] EWHC 434 (Ch). (*Notes.* (1) This was the first published decision in which the tribunal discussed the provisions of *Directive 2006/112/EC*, rather than the provisions of *Directive 77/388/EEC* which preceded it. (2) For HMRC's practice following the tribunal decision, see HMRC Brief 27/08, issued on 20 May 2008.)

Supplies Qualifying for Reduced Rate (VATA 1994, Sch 7A, Group 1)

Electricity provided at site for touring caravans

[30.12] The owners of a caravan site offered the use of electricity for a standard charge of £1.50 per day. Customers had to use their own caravans, none being provided by the owners of the site. Most customers occupied the site for a week or less. Customs issued a ruling that the electricity charge was standard-rated. The company appealed, contending that it qualified for zero-rating under the legislation then in force. The tribunal accepted this contention and allowed the appeal, distinguishing *Hazelwood Caravans & Chalets Ltd*, 30.6 above, and *CMC (Preston) Ltd*, 30.7 above, on the grounds that in *Hazelwood* the accommodation was in caravans owned by the company, and in both *Hazelwood* and *CMC (Preston)* many customers stayed for long periods. The tribunal held that the electricity supplied to the caravan owners was a separate supply, rather than a notional allocation of part of an inclusive rent, and that the payments for the electricity were therefore zero-rated. *J Adams, AC Woskett & Partners*, LON/91/2182Z (VTD 9647).

Electricity provided in sheltered housing

[30.13] A housing association provided sheltered accommodation to tenants. It made a separate charge in respect of electricity used for heating. The Commissioners issued a ruling that the supplies of electricity were part of a single supply of accommodation which was exempt from VAT. The association appealed, contending that the electricity was the subject of a separate supply which was chargeable to VAT at the reduced rate of 8%. The tribunal accepted this contention and allowed the appeal, applying the principles laid down in *Adams Woskett & Partners*, **30.12** above, and observing that there was 'a long-standing practice of separate charge and indeed separate payment', rather than a single inclusive rent. *Suffolk Heritage Housing Association Ltd*, LON/94/2563 (VTD 13713).

31

Gold

Whether VATA 1994, s 55 applicable

[31.1] A gold dealer (S) had agreed to supply a company (C) with quantities of 9-carat gold, and had issued invoices accordingly, but had in some cases delivered fine gold instead of 9-carat gold. In such cases C had arranged for the gold to be converted into 9-carat gold, but S had unilaterally sent C a set of substitute invoices and credit notes, describing the supplies as being of fine gold. C had refused to accept the substitute invoices and credit notes, but S had adjusted his returns on the basis that he was not required to account for output tax on the disputed transactions. The Commissioners issued three assessments cancelling the adjustments (and also charging tax on a number of other transactions where S had failed to account for tax). S appealed, contending that the effect of what is now *VATA 1994, s 55* was that he was not required to account for tax on his supplies of fine gold to C, and that the assessments were not made to the best of the Commissioners' judgment. The tribunal rejected these contentions and upheld the assessments in principle (while reducing one of them by a small amount). The tribunal held that, as S had agreed to supply C with 9-carat gold, he was required to account for output tax on the transactions in question. The effect of the agreement between C and S was that what is now *VATA 1994, s 55* 'never had application in relation to the supplies in issue. VAT was correctly charged and paid in respect of all the supplies to (C) described as relating to 9-carat gold.' C had been entitled to refuse to accept the substitute invoices and credit notes, as 'the accounting obligation for VAT was that of (S), not that of (C)' and 'the liability to account for tax remained that of the appellant supplier'. *P Sheldon (t/a Nova Gold)*, MAN/94/282 & 621 (VTD 16551).

Whether VATA 1994, Sch 9, Group 15 applicable

[31.2] A company (L) failed to account for VAT on various supplies of gold. HMRC issued an assessment charging tax on them, and L appealed, contending that the supplies should be treated as exempt under *VATA 1994, Sch 9, Group 15, Item 1*. The tribunal rejected this contention and dismissed the appeal, holding that exemption under *Group 15* was subject to the provisions of *VAT Regulations 1995 (SI 1995/2518), reg 31A(2)(a)*, which required that a person making such a supply should 'issue an invoice in respect of the supply containing such details as may be specified in a notice published by the Commissioners'. These conditions were laid down in *Public Notice 701/21*. On the evidence, L had failed to provide the invoice details required by *Notice 701/21, para 6.4*, and had failed to keep the records required by *Notice 701/21, para 7.1*. Judge Mitting observed that 'it is incumbent upon a trader to acquaint himself with the accounting and taxation obligations appertaining to his trade. Every trader has certain legal responsibilities dependent on the type of business he is running, and ignorance of those responsibilities can be no excuse.' *Lal Jewellers Ltd v HMRC*, [2010] UKFTT 594 (TC), TC00844.

32

Groups of Companies

The cases in this chapter are arranged under the following headings.

Group registration   32.1
Avoidance schemes   32.17
Miscellaneous   32.21

NOTE

FA 1999, s 16, Sch 2 made substantial changes to the legislation concerning the VAT treatment of groups of companies, including the repeal of *VATA 1994, s 43(3)–(8)* and their replacement by *VATA 1994, ss 43A–43C*. The revised provisions took effect from 27 July 1999. Cases relating to periods before that date should be read in the light of the changes in the legislation.

Group registration

Application for group registration—statutory requirements not met

[32.1] A company applied for group registration for itself and two associated companies. None of the companies controlled either of the others but all three were controlled by the same individuals (not in partnership). The Commissioners rejected the application and the tribunal dismissed the company's appeal, holding that the companies did not meet the statutory requirements for group registration. *E Du Vergier & Co Ltd*, [1973] VATTR 11 (VTD 4).

[32.2] A similar decision was reached in an Isle of Man case involving four associated companies. *Mannin Shipping Ltd*, [1979] VATTR 83 (VTD 738).

[32.3] The British Airways Board (B) applied for a trust company (T), which administered its pension fund, to be included in its group registration. T had no share capital; it had twelve management trustees of whom B nominated six, including the chairman who had a casting vote. However B was not a member of T, and thus was not its 'holding company' within the meaning of the *Companies Act*. The Commissioners rejected the application on the grounds that T was not controlled by B, and the tribunal dismissed B's appeal. *British Airways Board; British Airways Pension Fund Trustees Ltd*, LON/x (VTD 846).

Whether group registration may be retrospective

[32.4] A group registration took effect from April 1973. In October 1973 the business of a subsidiary company, covered by the group registration, was transferred to a hitherto dormant company in the group, which was not included in the group registration. The holding company (which was the representative member of the group) discovered the omission in 1977 and asked the Commissioners to permit the group registration to operate retrospectively with regard to the omitted subsidiary. The Commissioners refused, on the ground that they had no power to admit group treatment retrospectively. The QB upheld the Commissioners' ruling. Neill J held that the discretion to admit retrospective treatment was that of the Commissioners and could not be exercised by a tribunal. *C & E Commrs v Save & Prosper Group Ltd*, QB 1978, [1979] STC 205.

[32.5] In 1982 a company applied to include a subsidiary company in its group registration with retrospective effect from 1979. The Commissioners agreed to include the subsidiary in the group registration from the date of the application, but refused to apply the application retrospectively. The tribunal dismissed the company's appeal. Applying *dicta* of Viscount Simon LC in *Charles Osenton & Co v Johnston*, HL [1941] 2 All ER 245, 'the appellate tribunal is not at liberty merely to substitute its own exercise of discretion for the discretion already exercised by the judge. In other words, appellate authorities ought not to reverse the order merely because they would themselves have exercised the original discretion, had it attached to them, in a different way.' On the evidence, the Commissioners' decision had clearly not been unreasonable. *Blue Boar Property & Investment Co Ltd*, [1984] VATTR 12 (VTD 1579).

[32.6] Similar decisions were reached in *MJ Foster Ltd*, LON/74/7 (VTD 75) and *Homecraft Manufacturing Ltd*, LON/92/986Z (VTD 9300).

Whether Commissioners entitled to cancel separate registrations

[32.7] A holding company and seven subsidiaries registered for VAT as a group with effect from 1 August 1995. Most of the subsidiaries' supplies were exempt but they all made small amounts of taxable supplies. In 1996 the group appointed new accountants, who submitted applications for five of the subsidiaries to be separately registered with effect from 1992 to July 1995, to take advantage of the *de minimis* partial exemption provisions. The applications did not indicate that the companies were already registered as part of a group, and on 2 August 1996 the Commissioners accepted them. However, on 15 August, having realised that there was already a group registration, the Commissioners cancelled the separate registrations. The companies appealed. The Ch D upheld the Commissioners' cancellation of the separate registrations. Lloyd J held that *VATA 1994, Sch 1 para 9* did not oblige the Commissioners to grant the companies separate registrations, observing that 'retrospectivity of registration under *paragraph 9* is a matter of discretion' and that 'the Commissioners cannot be compelled to allow it'. Furthermore, *Sch 1 para 9* was not inconsistent with *Article 24(6)* of the *EC Sixth Directive*. *Article 24(6)* 'requires that relevant persons be free to choose between exempt status and normal registered status'. This option was provided by *Sch 1 para 9*, and the companies had made their choice by applying for group registration. There was no reason why any company 'should be regarded as entitled to make a different choice thereafter, except for the future'. *Article 24(6)* required national legislation to allow 'a prospective choice' but did not require national legislation to allow a retrospective choice. *C & E Commrs v Eastwood Care Homes (Ilkeston) Ltd (and related appeals)*, Ch D [2001] STC 1629.

Application for company to cease to be part of group

[32.8] A subsidiary company within a group sold one of its assets after it had ceased to trade. An assessment was raised on the parent company of the group for the VAT due on the asset. The parent company appealed, contending that when the subsidiary had ceased to trade, a Customs officer had been informed on a control visit that it was no longer a member of the group, and that the statement to the officer was an application to exclude the subsidiary from the group registration. The tribunal dismissed the appeal, holding that there was no requirement to make an application in writing, but that the statement to the officer did not amount to an application to exclude the subsidiary. *Marine & General Print Holdings Ltd*, MAN/85/416 (VTD 2120).

Group registration—right of appeal

[32.9] The representative member of a group of companies (J), was wound up in April 2001, owing more than £280,000 in unpaid VAT to the Commissioners. The VAT group was deregistered from the same date. The Commissioners subsequently sought to recover the VAT from two of the associated companies (P and W) under the provisions of *VATA 1994, s 43*. The companies appealed against an assessment which had previously been raised on J (and against which J had not appealed), contending that it was excessive. The Commissioners applied for the appeal to be struck out, contending that, in the case of a group registration, only the representative member of the group had a right of appeal. The tribunal rejected this contention and dismissed the Commissioners' application, specifically disapproving the 1973 decision in *Davis Advertising Service Ltd*, 2.83 APPEALS, and holding that the right of appeal against a demand for tax should not 'be deemed to be abrogated by implication in a text which relates to group registration'. There was no justification for the Commissioners' contention that 'membership of a group for purposes of value added tax implies an abandonment of any right of appeal against demands for tax'. *J & W Waste Management Ltd; J & W Plant & Tool Hire Ltd*, [2003] VATDR 333 (VTD 18069).

Liability of members other than representative member

[32.10] P, the parent company of a group, and S, one of its subsidiaries, went into creditors' voluntary liquidation at the same time. A group registration covering both companies was in force and the Commissioners claimed tax due from P, in its capacity as representative member of the group, as a preferential debt in the winding-up of S. The liquidator of S rejected the claim and referred the matter to the High Court. The Ch D upheld the Commissioners' claim, holding that, by virtue of what is now *VATA 1994, s 43*, the tax could be claimed from the other members of the group, who were jointly and severally liable for the amounts unpaid. Accordingly, any VAT not paid by P could be claimed preferentially in the winding-up of S. *Re Nadler Enterprises Ltd*, Ch D [1980] STC 457; [1981] 1 WLR 23; [1980] 3 All ER 350.

Representative member seeking to disclaim liability

[32.11] A company (S) had been registered for VAT as the representative member of a group comprising two companies, itself and a wholly-owned subsidiary. The subsidiary went into liquidation, owing more than £33,000 in VAT, and the Commissioners issued assessments to recover this amount from S. S appealed, contending that it should not be held liable for the debt incurred by its subsidiary. The tribunal upheld the assessments and dismissed S's appeal. *Sunfine Developments Ltd*, MAN/89/931 (VTD 6124).

Group registration—prescribed accounting period

[32.12] See *Atlas Interlates Ltd*, 52.1 PENALTIES: MISDECLARATION.

Customs rejecting application to include company in group

[32.13] A large insurance company (P) entered into a joint venture with an unconnected South African company (D), and incorporated a new subsidiary (K) to carry on the joint venture. Initially K was a wholly-owned subsidiary of P, but it was agreed that D would subsequently have a 50% shareholding in K. While K was a wholly-owned subsidiary, P applied to Customs for it to be included in its VAT group. Customs rejected the application on the grounds that the delay in creating the joint venture appeared to be 'structured so as to gain a VAT advantage' and was 'part of a contrived process to avoid a substantial VAT cost'. P appealed, contending that the refusal was unreasonable. The tribunal accepted this contention and allowed the appeal, holding that the tax saving which P wished to achieve was a 'normal consequence of grouping'. The decision to refuse the grouping application was not 'necessary for the protection of the revenue', and 'the refusal of grouping was irrational'. *Prudential Assurance Company Ltd (No 3)*, [2006] VATDR 301 (VTD 19607).

Commissioners issuing direction removing company from group

[32.14] In September 1994 a were sold to an outside company (X). In 2003 the Commissioners issued a direction under *VATA 1994, s 43C* removing P from the group, on the grounds that its inclusion resulted in supplies within the group, but for the benefit of a third party (X), being disregarded for VAT purposes. P appealed. The tribunal reviewed the evidence in detail and dismissed the appeal, finding that the implementation of the scheme would lead to a loss of revenue of about £3,000,000 per year. On the evidence, the Commissioners' decision was not unreasonable. *Xansa Barclaycard Partnership Ltd*, [2004] VATDR 457 (VTD 18780).

Date on which company ceases to be treated as part of group

[32.15] On 27 February 1995 a banking company (B) gave the share capital of one of its subsidiaries (T) to a charitable trust. The Commissioners informed B that the subsidiary would be removed from B's group with effect from 1 July

1995. B appealed, contending that as a matter of law T had ceased to be a member of its group at the time of the transfer of the share capital. The CA unanimously rejected this contention and upheld the Commissioners' ruling. Sir Andrew Morritt V-C observed that there was an obligation to notify the Commissioners of any change in the constitution or ownership of a company which might necessitate the variation of the register. If the Commissioners ascertained that the relevant control had ceased, they were required to give a notice terminating the group treatment from such a date as they might specify. Group treatment did not 'begin with the onset of eligibility but with the beginning of a prescribed accounting period. The express provisions for the termination of such treatment do not provide that it should be coterminous with the cesser of eligibility either.' C & E Commrs v Barclays Bank plc, CA [2001] STC 1558; [2001] EWCA Civ 1513. (Notes. (1) The decision discusses VATA 1994, s 43(6), which was repealed with effect from 27 July 1999 by FA 1999, Sch 2. Similar provisions are, however, contained in the new VATA 1994, s 43C(3)(4). (2) The House of Lords rejected the company's application for leave to appeal against this decision. (3) For Customs' practice following this decision, see Business Brief 30/2002, issued on 19 November 2002.)

[32.16] In the case noted at 9.7 CAPITAL GOODS SCHEME, a company (U) had applied to become a member of a VAT group in July 2004. In April 2005 the university applied for U to cease to be treated as a member of its VAT group, and to backdate the degrouping to 1 August 2004. HMRC refused to backdate the degrouping, and the university appealed. The tribunal dismissed the appeal, holding that HMRC had acted reasonably in refusing to allow the degrouping to be backdated. University of Essex v HMRC, [2010] UKFTT 162 (TC), TC00467.

Avoidance schemes

Vendor companies becoming separately registered

[32.17] A group of companies adopted a scheme with the object of reducing the group's VAT liability. Two companies in the group agreed with a third company in the group to sell motor cars and other goods to that third company. 90% of the purchase price was paid in advance by the purchasing company to the two vendor companies, and was then lent back to the purchasing company by the vendor companies. At the date of the agreement, and at the time of the advance payment, all three companies were covered by a single group registration. However, the two vendor companies became separately registered for VAT before the delivery of the goods (when the remaining 10% of the price became payable). The Commissioners issued a ruling that the vendor companies should account for output tax on the whole of the purchase price. The companies appealed, contending that output tax was only payable on the amount which was paid on delivery, and that tax was not chargeable on the advance payment of 90% because, under what is now VATA 1994, s 6(4), the time of supply was when the payment was made, at which time the companies were covered by the same group registration. The

CA rejected this contention and upheld the Commissioners' rulings, and the HL dismissed the companies' appeals (by a 4-1 majority, Lord Hoffmann dissenting). Lord Nolan observed that there was nothing in *VATA* which warranted excluding the payment of 90% from the charge to VAT. Neither *Article 4(4)* of the *EC Sixth Directive*, nor what is now *VATA 1994, s 43(1)*, was 'designed to confer exemption or relief from tax. They are designed to simplify and facilitate the collection of tax by treating the representative member as if it were carrying on all the businesses of the other members as well as its own, and dealing on behalf of them all with non-members.' What is now *s 43(1)* 'may have the effect of deferring the charge to tax upon the added value of goods until they are the subject of a supply outside the group, but it does not prevent that charge'. Therefore, the liability for output tax on the full amount of the consideration, including the 90% which had been paid in advance, arose on the delivery date. *Thorn Materials Supply Ltd v C & E Commrs; Thorn Resources Ltd v C & E Commrs*, HL [1998] STC 725; [1998] 1 WLR 1106; [1998] 3 All ER 384. (*Note*. See also the anti-avoidance provisions in *VATA 1994, Sch 9A*, introduced by *FA 1996* in relation to events occurring after 28 November 1995.)

Company incurring expenditure on property for subletting

[32.18] A company (J) leased an office block, which needed substantial fitting-out work, from another company (N). Under the agreement, which was dated 14 October 1994, J agreed to undertake the fitting-out work, and N paid J £1,146,660 plus VAT as a contribution to the cost. On 25 October 1994 J sublet the office block to an associated company (M), which was the representative member of the same VAT group, for a premium of £36,500,000 and a small annual rent. M paid the premium on the same day. No tax invoice was issued, as the payment was for a supply within M's VAT group. On 26 October J applied to leave M's VAT group and set up a new VAT group. On 27 October J entered into an agreement with another associated company (P), whereby P agreed to carry out the fitting-out work on the office block. P subsequently invoiced J for £12,000,000 plus VAT in respect of this work. J paid this amount and reclaimed input tax on the payment. The Commissioners issued an assessment to recover the tax on the basis that it was not attributable to any taxable supply. J appealed, contending firstly that it was attributable to the supply which it had made to N on 14 October, and alternatively that it was attributable to the annual rent which it would receive from M. The tribunal upheld the assessment in principle, but directed that it should be reduced (from £2,069,894 to £1,898,492) to take account of the supply which J had made to N. With regard to the remainder of the tax, the tribunal held that it was attributable to the premium which M had paid J while the two companies were within the same VAT group, rather than to the future payments of rent. On the evidence, it was 'clear that (J) sought to obtain repayment of the input tax without incurring substantial related output tax'. Under *VAT Regulations 1995 (SI 1995/2518), reg 101(2)*, input tax was only directly attributable to taxable supplies if it related to goods or services which were 'used or to be used' exclusively in making taxable supplies. Under *Article 17(2)* of the *EC Sixth Directive*, input tax was deductible in so far as the goods or services were used for the purposes of taxable transactions. Accordingly, 'the fact that (J) used the services supplied to a substantial extent for the purposes of an intra-group transaction, which under *VATA 1994, s 43(1)(a)* is disregarded as an output, does not have the effect that those services are to be regarded as exclusively used in making further supplies to the same company arising from the same contract, which were and are taxable because they no longer fall to be disregarded'. *JP Morgan Trading & Finance*, [1998] VATDR 161 (VTD 15373). (*Note*. See also the anti-avoidance provisions in *VATA 1994, Sch 9A*, introduced by *FA 1996* in relation to events occurring after 28 November 1995.)

Subsidiary companies receiving substantial prepayments

[32.19] Three associated companies were members of a group for VAT purposes. While they were members of the group, they received substantial prepayments of consideration under various agreements for future services. (The prepayments amounted to about 98% of the total consideration due under the agreements.)The companies subsequently left the VAT group, although they continued to remain under the same ownership. They made substantial claims for input tax relating to supplies made to them for the purposes of performing the relevant agreements. Customs issued assessments to recover the majority of the input tax which the companies had claimed. The tribunal reviewed the evidence in detail, dismissed the appeals, and increased six of the assessments under the provisions of *VATA 1994, s 84(5)*. The tribunal held that, applying the principles laid down by Lord Nolan in *Thorn Materials Supply*, **32.17** above, 'the substantial prepayments made under the "Prepayment Supply Agreements" must be disregarded for tax purposes'. The fundamental purpose of the EC VAT legislation was 'to achieve neutrality'. Accordingly, 'there has to be a fiscal balance between the right to deduct the VAT paid on the goods and services bought in by a trader for the purposes of his business and his liability to pay VAT on the goods and services he supplies in his business and for which he bought in those goods and services. That neutrality is not achieved if the full value of VAT on inputs is available as credits while only a negligible portion of the value of the outputs to which the inputs are directly linked is taxed.' *VATA 1994, s 24(5)* should be construed 'purposively to permit a restriction of the input tax credit that can be allowed in a group exit scheme such as this to a portion that reflects that small fraction of the full acknowledged value of the services supplied that is alone subject to output tax'. Without any such restriction, the principle of neutrality would be 'significantly violated'. The Ch D upheld the tribunal decision. Park J held that, on the evidence, the relevant provision of services 'was a taxable supply to the extent of only 2%'. The remaining 98% of the services were not taxable supplies, and accordingly 'any VAT borne on the price of them is not "input tax"' within *VATA 1994, s 24*. He observed that 'when a taxable person acquired services partly for the purpose of making taxable supplies himself and partly for other purposes which are outside the VAT system, the simplest and most obvious way of dealing with the matter is to apportion the input tax borne on the purchase price and to allow the part of it apportioned to the making of taxable supplies to be deducted as input tax'. To allow the companies to recover the 'input tax' which did not relate to any taxable supplies would be 'a travesty' of the principle of tax neutrality as laid down by the CJEC in *Rompelman & Rompelman-van-Deelen v Minister van Financiën*, **22.103** EUROPEAN COMMUNITY LAW. *BUPA Purchasing Ltd & Others v C & E Commrs, Ch D* [2003] STC 1203; [2003] EWHC 1957(Ch). (*Notes.* (1) See also the anti-avoidance provisions in *VATA 1994, Sch 9A*, introduced by *FA 1996* in relation to events occurring after 28 November 1995. (2) For subsequent developments in this case, see **3.179** ASSESSMENT.)

[32.20] A company (G) was a member of a VAT group. On 25 November 1994 it received a 'prepayment' of £20,000,000 from another member of the same group, relating to the intended redevelopment of a property. Four days later G left the VAT group, although it remained under the same ownership. From 1995 to 1997 it claimed substantial repayments of input tax relating to the redevelopment. Customs issued a 'global' assessment to recover most of the tax. The Ch D upheld the assessment, applying the principles laid down in *BUPA Purchasing Ltd & Others v C & E Commrs*, **32.19** above. Sir Andrew Morritt held that the effect of *Article 17(2)* of the *EC Sixth Directive* was that 'deduction of input tax is only allowed if and to the extent that the incoming goods or services are used for the purposes of taxable output transactions'. *HMRC v Gracechurch Management Services Ltd*, Ch D 2007, [2008] STC 795; [2007] EWHC 755 (Ch). (*Note.* See also the anti-avoidance provisions in *VATA 1994, Sch 9A*, introduced by *FA 1996* in relation to events occurring after 28 November 1995.)

Miscellaneous

Interpretation of VATA 1994, s 43

[32.21] In *Thorn EMI plc*, **38.40** INSURANCE, the tribunal held that what is now *VATA 1994, s 43* 'has the effect of excluding supplies within the group from the charged tax, (but) it cannot have the effect of altering the character of a supply made to a person outside the group'. A similar decision was reached in *Canary Wharf Ltd*, **43.12** MANAGEMENT SERVICES. In *Thorn Materials Supply Ltd*, **32.17** above, Lord Nolan held that the purpose of what is now *s 43(1)* 'was to enable a group to be treated as if it were a single taxable entity'.

Services provided to holding company for benefit of pension trust

[32.22] A bank was under a continuing obligation to provide investment advisory services free of charge to a pension trust, which was not a member of the bank's group for VAT purposes. The bank paid a subsidiary company, which was a member of its VAT group, for the services to be supplied to the pension trust. The bank did not account for VAT on the services in question, considering that they had been supplied by the subsidiary to the bank, and therefore fell to be disregarded for VAT purposes by virtue of what is now *VATA 1994, s 43(1)*. The Commissioners issued an assessment on the supply, considering that the services had in effect been supplied by the subsidiary directly to the pension trust, so that the bank, as the group representative member, was required to account for VAT on the supply. The tribunal allowed the bank's appeal. On the evidence, the subsidiary company had supplied its services to the bank, and the supply therefore fell to be disregarded for VAT purposes by virtue of *s 43(1)*. The fact that the services were supplied for the ultimate benefit of the pension trust did not alter the fact that the supply by the subsidiary had been to the bank. *Midland Bank plc*, [1991] VATTR 525 (VTD 6129).

Change of representative member—validity of assessment

[32.23] Until March 1996 a company (TE) had been the representative member of a group of companies (the T group). In March 1996 a new company (TP) was incorporated and became the representative member of the group. In September the Commissioners issued an assessment to TP, charging tax on supplies made by a member of the group (TU) between October 1994 and March 1995. TP appealed, contending as a preliminary point that the assessment was invalid because it had not been the representative member of the group at the time the supplies were made. The tribunal rejected this contention and held that the assessment had been validly made. The tribunal observed that 'the Commissioners could not in law have assessed (TE) in September 1996; it no longer had any of the statutory functions or obligations of representative member of the VAT group that included (TU)'. Furthermore, 'substitution of one representative member for another within the same group registration' could not 'remove the Commissioners' power of assessment of VAT due on account of the former representative member's failure to make a complete and correct return.' Applying *dicta* of Viscount Dunedin in *Whitney v CIR*, HL 1925, 10 TC 88, when it had been determined that there was a tax liability, 'it is antecedently highly improbable that the statute should not go on to make that liability effective. A statute is designed to be workable, and the interpretation thereof by a court should be to secure that object'. *Thorn plc*, [1998] VATDR 80 (VTD 15283). (*Note*. For the substantive appeal, see **67.15** VALUATION.)

Management services within group of companies

[32.24] See *Tilling Management Services Ltd*, **43.8** MANAGEMENT SERVICES.

Services supplied to unregistered associated company

[32.25] See *Svenska International plc*, **43.20** MANAGEMENT SERVICES.

Management services—time of supply

[32.26] See *Legal & Contractual Services Ltd*, **43.1** MANAGEMENT SERVICES; *Pentex Oil Ltd*, **43.2** MANAGEMENT SERVICES; *Bishop & Knight Ltd*, **43.3** MANAGEMENT SERVICES; *Missionfine Ltd*, **43.5** MANAGEMENT SERVICES, and *Waverley Housing Management Ltd*, **43.6** MANAGEMENT SERVICES.

Payments between associated companies

[32.27] See *London Regeneration Project Services Ltd*, **43.2** MANAGEMENT SERVICES.

Retail sales paid for by credit card issued by associated company

[32.28] A group of companies traded as retailers. One of the companies in the group (T) provided a consumer credit service for use in shops owned by members of the group, and issued credit cards to customers for this purpose. The holding company (K) did not account for tax on sales paid for by the credit cards issued by T until the users of the cards had paid the amounts in question to T. The Commissioners issued assessments on the basis that K should account for tax on the basis that the time of supply was when the sale took place, as with any other credit card. K appealed, contending that sales by means of T's credit cards should be distinguished from sales by other credit cards, as the credit had been provided by one of K's subsidiary companies, rather than by an independent operator. The tribunal allowed K's appeals and the QB upheld this decision. Popplewell J held that, under what is now *VATA 1994, s 43*, K was deemed to carry on the retail businesses of its retail subsidiaries, and also T's credit business. Accordingly, K's deemed retail sales were financed by its deemed credit business, and the sales in question were 'self-financed credit sales'. As indicated in *Notice No 727 (1987 edition), para 9*, tax need not be accounted for in respect of self-financed credit sales until payment was received. *C & E Commrs v Kingfisher plc*, QB 1993, [1994] STC 63. (*Note. Notice No 727 (1987 edition)* was subsequently replaced by *Notice No 727 (1997 edition)*. The 'standard' method of accounting (under which tax on self-financed credit sales was not due until payment was received) was withdrawn with effect from 1 March 1997.)

Deduction of input tax by holding companies

[32.29] See *Polysar Investments Netherlands BV v Inspecteur der Invoerrechten en Accijnzen*, **22.106** EUROPEAN COMMUNITY LAW, and *Sofitam SA v Ministre du Budget*, **22.443** EUROPEAN COMMUNITY LAW.

Input tax on costs incurred before company joined VAT group

[32.30] In 2006 a large Spanish company (F) arranged for the incorporation of a new company (AD) with the aim of making a 'takeover bid' for another company (B), which operated several British airports. The bid was successful, and AD incurred significant costs in relation to the acquisition. After the takeover, AD joined B's VAT group. The representative member of the group (BL) claimed a deduction for input tax of more than £6,000,000 which AD had incurred in relation to the takeover. HMRC issued an assessment to recover the tax on the grounds that there was no direct and immediate link between the supplies on which this VAT was incurred and any taxable supplies made, or intended to be made, by BL's group. The Upper Tribunal upheld the assessment (reversing the First-Tier decision). Proudman J held that there was 'no direct and immediate link' between the supplies made to AD, on which the relevant VAT was incurred, and any onward taxable supplies either made by AD or attributed to AD. Accordingly the input tax was not deductible. *HMRC v BAA Ltd (and cross-appeal)*, UT [2011] UKUT 258 (TCC); [2011] STC 1791.

Group of companies—application of partial exemption

[32.31] A group of three companies, with a single VAT registration, made both taxable and exempt supplies. In 1990 the group applied for permission to use a special method of computing its deductible input tax. The Commissioners approved the use of a special method, under which the deductible portion of residual input tax was to be computed using output values. At a control visit in 1991, a VAT officer discovered that the group was calculating the deductible input tax for each of the three companies individually, and then aggregating the totals to arrive at the group liability. He considered that the group should have aggregated the companies' input tax and applied the special method to the aggregate totals, and that the effect of the group's computations was that it had overclaimed input tax of more than £26,000. The Commissioners issued an assessment to recover this tax, and the group appealed. The tribunal allowed the group's appeal, holding that nothing in what is now *VATA 1994, s 43* required the companies' input tax to be aggregated, and observing that *para 3* of *Notice No 706* directed that the businesses carried on by the members of a group were to be treated separately, with the effect that 'each company in the group individually should begin its calculation of its deductible input tax after having excluded the items listed in (*para 16*)'. *Joseph Nelson Investment Planning Ltd*, MAN/92/845 (VTD 10964).

[32.32] A group of companies carried on business as retailers and fitters of parts for motor cars. It incorporated a company to supply insurance services to their customers. The group adopted the standard method of apportioning input tax between taxable and exempt supplies. The Commissioners formed the opinion that the standard method led to the group being able to reclaim too much input tax, and issued a direction requiring the use of a special method whereby any input tax which was not directly attributable to taxable or exempt supplies should be apportioned between companies 'on the same basis that both direct and indirect costs are allocated to members by means of the group's accounting system', and that the deductible proportion of input tax should then be ascertained separately for each company. The group appealed, contending that the method directed by the Commissioners was unreasonable. The CS accepted this contention and allowed the appeal, holding that the wording of the direction was ambiguous, and it was therefore 'invalid and of no legal effect'. *Kwik-Fit (GB) Ltd v C & E Commrs*, CS 1997, [1998] STC 159.

Insolvency Act 1986, Sch 6—application of Crown preference

[32.33] Two companies (V and S) were members of the same group. In March 1991 the group incurred a substantial VAT liability in respect of a sale of land. In April 1991 V went into receivership. In June 1992 S paid the Commissioners more than £400,000 in respect of the VAT liability. Subsequently S went into liquidation. In proceedings between V and S, S sought relief in respect of V's share of the VAT, contending that it was entitled to the preference which the Commissioners would have had under *Insolvency Act 1986, Sch 6*, on the basis that any co-obligant in a joint and several obligation, who discharged the liability of any of the other co-obligants, was entitled to the benefit of all the rights which were available to the principal creditor, including the right of preference, without the need for an assignation. Lord Penrose accepted this contention, holding that an appropriate part of the total VAT liability would have fallen to be paid out of V's resources. That should be paid as if the Commissioners had demanded payment from V's receivers, as a preferential debt, in priority to V's secured creditors. Lord Penrose observed that any other result would unjustly benefit V's creditors at the expense of S's creditors. *Villaswan Ltd v Sheraton (Blythswood) Ltd*, CS 9 November 1998, Times 27.1.1999.

33

Health and Welfare

The cases in this chapter are arranged under the following headings.

Supplies of services by registered practitioners, etc. (VATA 1994, Sch 9, Group 7, Item 1)
    Cases held to be exempt   **33.1**
    Cases held to be partly exempt   **33.8**
    Cases held not to be exempt   **33.17**
Dental services (VATA 1994, Sch 9, Group 7, Item 2)   **33.32**
Provision of care, etc. in hospital or similar institution (VATA 1994, Sch 9, Group 7, Item 4)
    Cases held to be exempt   **33.39**
    Cases held to be partly exempt   **33.46**
    Cases held not to be exempt   **33.48**
Human blood, organs and tissue (VATA 1994, Sch 9, Group 7, Items 6–8)   **33.61**
Supplies of welfare services (VATA 1994, Sch 9, Group 7, Item 9)   **33.62**
Supplies of transport services (VATA 1994, Sch 9, Group 7, Item 11)   **33.76**
Imported goods (VAT (Imported Goods) Relief Order (SI 1984/746), Sch 2 Group 5)   **33.77**

Supplies of services by registered practitioners, etc. (VATA 1994, Sch 9, Group 7, Item 1)

Cases held to be exempt

Mobile chest X-ray service

[33.1] The Commissioners refused an application for registration by the proprietors of a mobile chest X-ray service, considering that the supplies in question were exempt from VAT. The proprietors appealed, contending that their supplies were excluded from exemption by what is now *VATA 1994, Sch 9, Group 7, Note 1*. The tribunal rejected this contention and dismissed their appeal, holding that they were supplying services rather than goods, and that their services were exempt under *Sch 9, Group 7, Item 1(c)*. *Cleary & Cleary (t/a Mobile X-Rays)*, LON/91/2295Y (VTD 7305).

Nursing agency

[33.2] A company which carried on business as a nursing agency registered for VAT. In 1989 the Commissioners directed that the company should be deregistered on the grounds that its supplies of nursing services were exempt under what is now *VATA 1994, Sch 9, Group 7, Item 1(d)*. The company appealed, contending that it was not making exempt supplies of nursing services, but was acting as an agent of the nurses whom it represented, and that its income arose from the placement of nursing staff, which did not qualify for exemption. The tribunal dismissed the company's appeal, holding that it was acting as a principal rather than as an agent of the nurses. On the evidence, the nurses were employed by the company under a contract of service, and the company's supplies were exempt. *Allied Medicare Nursing Services Ltd*, MAN/89/484 (VTD 5485).

[33.3] The Commissioners sought to register a woman who operated a nursing agency. She appealed, contending that she was not required to register since all her supplies were exempt. The tribunal allowed her appeal, holding that although her business was described as an agency, she carried on business as a principal, rather than simply as an agent of the nurses registered with her. The services which she supplied were nursing services and were within what is now *VATA 1994, Sch 9, Group 7, Item 1(d)*. *MG Parkinson*, LON/90/1083Y (VTD 6017).

Nursing services partly provided by unqualified staff

[33.4] A company provided nursing services to patients in their own homes. Some of the company's employees were registered nurses but others were unqualified. The company did not account for tax on these supplies, considering that they were exempt. The Commissioners issued an assessment charging tax on the basis that the supplies did not qualify for exemption, since some of the supplies were not provided by registered nurses. The tribunal allowed the company's appeal, finding that the company exercised 'a very high standard of supervision' and holding that there was 'no necessity for the supervisor and the employee to be in the same premises if ready communication is available'. On the evidence, the services were 'directly supervised' within the meaning of what is now *VATA 1994, Sch 9, Group 7, Note 2* and qualified for exemption under what is now *VATA 1994, Sch 9, Group 7, Item 1(d)*. *Elder Home Care Ltd*, EDN/93/23 (VTD 11185). (*Note.* For the Commissioners' revised interpretation of what constitutes 'direct supervision', see Customs & Excise News Release 23/96, issued on 11 April 1996.)

[33.5] See also *Take Care (Agency Services) Ltd*, **2.9** APPEALS.

Unregistered optician—whether supplies 'directly supervised'

[33.6] The Commissioners issued a ruling that supplies by an unregistered optician failed to qualify for exemption under *VATA 1994, Sch 9, Group 7, Item 1*. The optician appealed, contending that his supplies were directly supervised by a registered optician, and thus qualified for exemption by virtue of *Group 7, Note 2*. The tribunal accepted this contention and allowed the appeal, holding on the evidence that the supplies were supervised by a registered optician even though there was no explicit contract requiring the supervisor to undertake this task. The tribunal observed that 'a contract may be valuable evidence of responsibility' but that its absence did 'not prove that there is no responsibility'. On the evidence, 'supervision was an implicit term of the relationship'. *AJ Land (t/a Crown Optical Centre)*, LON/97/162 (VTD 15547).

Anti-smoking therapy

[33.7] A company supplied group therapy and training manuals to clients who wished to stop smoking tobacco. It did not account for output tax on its supplies, treating them as exempt. HMRC issued a ruling that the supplies failed to qualify for exemption under *VATA 1994, Sch 9, Group 7, Item 1* and that the company was required to account for output tax. The company appealed, contending that its supplies were within the definition of 'medical care', and were 'directly supervised' by a registered medical practitioner, so that they were exempt from VAT. The tribunal accepted this contention and allowed the appeal, specifically distinguishing the earlier decision in *Easyway Productions Ltd*, **33.27** below. *Allen Carr's Easyway (International) Ltd v HMRC*, [2009] SFTD 523; [2009] UKFTT 181 (TC), TC00136.

Cases held to be partly exempt

Dispensing of corrective spectacles

[33.8] A company carried on business as opticians. It employed eight doctors and an ophthalmic optician to provide eye tests, and also employed several dispensing opticians to dispense spectacles. The Commissioners issued a ruling that its supplies of corrective spectacles were supplies of goods which did not qualify for exemption and were standard-rated. The company appealed, contending that, in addition to providing the spectacles, it made supplies of services which were exempt under what is now *VATA 1994, Sch 9, Group 7, Item 1*. The tribunal allowed the company's appeal, holding that the primary purpose of the dispensing opticians was to advise patients, rather than merely to sell spectacles, so that the payments received by the company should be apportioned. The QB upheld the tribunal decision, holding that in substance and reality there were two distinct supplies. *C & E Commrs v Leightons Ltd (and related appeal)*, QB [1995] STC 458. (*Notes*. (1) The Commissioners initially accepted this decision, and set out their practice in Business Brief 2/99. However, they subsequently resiled from this position, on the grounds that they considered that the decision in this case was inconsistent with the subsequent CJEC decision in *Card Protection Plan Ltd*, **22.324** EUROPEAN COMMUNITY LAW. For subsequent developments, see the case reported at **33.9** below. (2) For cases concerning repayment claims following this decision, see *Green*, **48.19** PAYMENT OF TAX; *Hayward Gill & Associates Ltd*, **48.20** PAYMENT OF TAX; *CL Dyer & Co*, **48.21** PAYMENT OF TAX, and *Specsavers Optical Group*, **48.127** and **48.128** PAYMENT OF TAX.)

[33.9] Following the QB decision noted at **33.8** above, the Commissioners initially accepted that supplies of spectacles involved a taxable supply of goods and an exempt supply of services, and that payments received should be apportioned. However, in February 2001, following the CJEC decision in *Card Protection Plan Ltd*, **22.324** EUROPEAN COMMUNITY LAW, they wrote to a number of opticians, instructing them to account for output tax on dispensing services with effect from 1 June 2001. Two of the opticians appealed, contending that the QB decision had been correct in law and that the payments should be apportioned. The tribunal accepted this contention and allowed the appeals. The tribunal held that it was implicit in the CJEC decision in

EC Commission v United Kingdom, **22.271** EUROPEAN COMMUNITY LAW, that 'there can be separate exempt supplies of medical care together with standard-rated supplies of goods'. The tribunal observed that 'the VAT system would be distorted if the supply of corrective spectacles were to be treated as a single standard-rated supply as this would give no effect to the exemption, which is mandatory in the *Sixth Directive*'. The dispensing services were not simply ancillary to the supply of goods, since 'a dispensed optical appliance could not be enjoyed at all without the dispensing service'. *Leightons Ltd (No 2); Eye-Tech Opticians (No 3)*, [2001] VATDR 468 (VTD 17498). (*Note.* For the Commissioners' practice following this decision, see Business Brief 3/2002, issued on 12 February 2002. Customs state that they 'will continue to challenge the apportionment' where they consider 'that there has been manipulation'.)

[33.10] A similar decision was reached in *Visionplus Southport Ltd*, LON/01/505 (VTD 17502).

[33.11] See also *FP Whiffen Opticians*, **67.82** VALUATION; *John F Stott Ltd*, **67.83** VALUATION; *McBurney, Clelland & Boyd Ltd*, **67.84** VALUATION, and the cases noted at **67.86** VALUATION.

Dispensing of hearing aids

[33.12] A registered dispenser of hearing aids, who was registered for VAT, apportioned his takings between exempt supplies of dispensing services and taxable supplies of goods. In accounting for tax, he treated the hearing aids themselves as being supplied at cost. The Commissioners issued an assessment on the basis that he should have attributed part of his profit as attributable to his taxable supplies of goods, and had therefore treated an excessive proportion of his takings as exempt. The tribunal upheld the assessment, holding that there were two separate supplies, and that the appellant's claim that he 'charged no mark-up at all on the cost price of the hearing aids' was 'inherently improbable and unrealistic'. *B Rowe (t/a Cheshire Hearing Centre)*, [2002] VATDR 156 (VTD 17600).

Services provided by doctor

[33.13] See *d'Ambrumenil*, **22.282** and **22.283** EUROPEAN COMMUNITY LAW.

Diet clinic—appetite-suppressing drugs prescribed by doctors

[33.14] A woman (K) operated a diet clinic. At her clinic, doctors prescribed customers with drugs to suppress their appetites. K failed to register for VAT. In 2002 the Commissioners issued a ruling, backdated to 1988, that she was required to register. She appealed, contending that she was supplying medical services which were exempt from VAT under *VATA 1994, Sch 9, Group 7, Item 1*, and was not therefore required to register. The tribunal reviewed the evidence in detail and held that some of K's supplies were exempt but that some were taxable. On the evidence, initial consultation fees were for medical services and were exempt, but subsequent fees had to be apportioned between medical services, which were exempt from VAT, and supplies of drugs, which were taxable. The tribunal expressed the view that 'the simplest method of apportionment is a cost-based method, possibly involving attribution of the other costs between the different supplies and elements of supplies'. In view of the size of K's turnover, she should have been registered for VAT from October 1988. *I Kinnell (t/a Berkshire Diet Clinic)*, LON/02/222 (VTD 18073). (*Note*. It was accepted that none of the supplies of drugs qualified for zero-rating under *VATA 1994, Sch 8, Group 12, Item 1*, since K was not a pharmacist.)

Supplies of domiciliary care—whether 'directly supervised'

[33.15] A company provided domiciliary nursing care for terminally ill patients living in their own homes. It did not register for VAT, considering that its supplies were exempt. The Commissioners issued a ruling that the company's supplies failed to qualify for exemption, as they were not 'directly supervised' by a registered practitioner. The tribunal reviewed the evidence and held that, since December 1999, the company's supplies had been 'directly supervised' by a registered nurse, and therefore qualified for exemption. However, in the period from April 1999 to November 1999 the company's supplies had not been 'directly supervised', and its supplies during that period were standard-rated. *Personal Assistance UK Ltd*, MAN/00/974 (VTD 17649).

Supplies by chiropodists—whether 'directly supervised'

[33.16] A company accounted for VAT on supplies of chiropodists' services. It subsequently submitted a large repayment claim, contending that it should have treated the supplies as exempt. Customs rejected the claim on the grounds that the chiropodists in question were not registered practitioners within *VATA 1994, Sch 9, Group 7, Item 1*. The company appealed, contending that the services were directly supervised by registered practitioners, and therefore qualified for exemption under *Note 2*. The tribunal reviewed the evidence in detail and allowed the appeal in part, holding that some of the supplies qualified for exemption but that some did not. (The tribunal also held that supplies by unregistered chiropodists did not qualify for exemption under *Article 13A1(c)* of the *EC Sixth Directive*.) *E Moss Ltd*, LON/03/1048 (VTD 19510).

Cases held not to be exempt

Acupuncture supplied by registered nurse

[33.17] A state registered nurse (E) carried on an acupuncture practice from his clinic. The Commissioners contending that his supplies were exempt under what is now *VATA 1994, Sch 9, Group 7, Item 1(d)*. The tribunal dismissed his appeal, holding that although he was registered as a qualified nurse, acupuncture treatment was not within the scope of a registered nurse. The exemption of *Sch 9, Group 7, Item 1* must be construed as being limited to services supplied by persons in the specified categories in the course of their professions or vocations. The services supplied by E were not supplied in his capacity as a registered nurse. *Dr AR Evans*, [1976] VATTR 175 (VTD 285).

Company hiring radiological scanner to health authorities

[33.18] A company purchased a radiological scanner with the intention of hiring it to health authorities. It reclaimed input tax on the purchase of the scanner, but the Commissioners rejected the claim on the grounds that the company's supplies were exempt under what is now *VATA 1994, Sch 9, Group 7, Item 1*. The tribunal allowed the company's appeal against this decision, holding that the company's supplies were excluded from exemption by *Sch 9, Group 7, Note 1*, since they consisted of the letting of goods on hire. The services supplied by the radiographer who accompanied the scanner were subsidiary to the letting on hire of the scanner. *Aslan Imaging Ltd*, [1989] VATTR 54 (VTD 3286).

Company providing MRI scans to NHS trusts

[33.19] A company provided magnetic resonance imaging services ('MRI scans') to NHS trusts. It reclaimed input tax relating to its supplies. Customs issued a ruling that it was supplying 'medical care' which was exempt from VAT. The tribunal allowed the company's appeal, holding that it was supplying data which was 'potentially preparatory to diagnosis by someone else'. It was not supplying 'medical care' and its supplies were standard-rated. *In Health Group SA*, [2006] VATDR 281 (VTD 19593).

Nursing agency

[33.20] The Commissioners issued a ruling that a nursing agency was making exempt supplies as well as taxable supplies (and therefore should have applied the partial exemption provisions). The tribunal allowed the agency's appeal, declining to follow the previous decision in *Allied Medicare*, 33.2 above, on the grounds that 'although the decision does not say so in terms, the inference must be that the tribunal did not accept that the documentation in that case reflected the true position'. In the case under appeal, however, there was no reason to doubt the accuracy of the documents which treated the nurses as self-employed. On the evidence, the relationship between the agency and the nurses was 'not that of master and servant', and 'such elements of control as there may be' were 'no more than are necessary for the agent/principal relationship specified in the Conditions'. The arrangements were 'wholly lacking in many of the normal features of a contract of service'; there was no guarantee of work, no minimum hours, no holiday or sick pay, no potential redundancy payment and no continuity of work. On the evidence, the nurses were self-employed, and they themselves entered into contracts with clients of the agency. The agency was not the employer of the nurses and did not make any exempt supplies. *British Nursing Co-Operation Ltd*, LON/91/1696Y (VTD 8816).

[33.21] The decision in *British Nursing Co-Operation Ltd*, 33.20 above, was applied in a subsequent case where the facts were broadly similar, although the relevant contracts did not specifically state that the agency (R) was acting as an agent for the nurses. The Commissioners issued a ruling that R was making exempt supplies (and thus was not entitled to recover the whole of its input tax). The tribunal allowed R's appeal, holding that R was not making any exempt supplies since it supplied nurses rather than nursing services. On the evidence, and despite the ambiguity of the relevant contracts, R was merely acting as an agent for the nurses, who were supplying their services to the hospitals as independent principals. The QB upheld the tribunal decision as one of fact. Laws J observed that 'where the facts involve only two parties there is necessarily little or no room for argument over who supplies what to whom. Where there are three (or more), the position may be very different.' It should be recognised that 'in that situation the parties' contractual arrangements, even though exhaustive for the purposes of their private law obligations, may not — as indeed they need not —define and conclude issues arising as to supplies'. Where the contracts were not conclusive, 'the resolution of such issues remains a question of fact for the tribunal.' *C & E Commrs v Reed Personnel Services Ltd*, QB [1995] STC 588. (*Note*. For a subsequent appeal by an associated company, see *Reed Employment plc v HMRC*, 48.39 PAYMENT OF TAX.)

[33.22] A similar decision was reached in a subsequent case in which the Commissioners issued an assessment on the basis that a partnership which operated a nursing agency was itself supplying nursing services to clients, and that since these supplies were exempt, the partnership was not entitled to reclaim input tax. The partnership appealed, contending that it was not acting as a principal, and that its only supplies were of introduction services for which it charged commission which was standard-rated, so that it had reclaimed input tax on the correct basis. The tribunal accepted the partnership's evidence and allowed the appeal, holding that the partnership was acting as an agent of the nurses rather than as a principal. *Sheffield & Rotherham Nursing Agency*, MAN/92/414 (VTD 11279).

Commission for supply of nurses

[33.23] A company which operated a nursing agency supplied two nurses to a nursing home. The company charged VAT on its commission. The proprietor of the nursing home lodged an appeal, contending that the commission should be treated as exempt under *VATA 1994, Sch 9, Group 7, Item 1(d)*. The tribunal rejected this contention and dismissed the appeal, holding on the evidence that the company was acting as an agent and 'did not purport to provide nursing services but nurses'. It 'acted as an intermediary only and correctly charged VAT on its commission'. *Dr RA Fairburn*, LON/96/1613 (VTD 15904).

Consultant psychologist

[33.24] The Commissioners issued a ruling that a self-employed consultant psychologist was required to register for VAT. He appealed, contending that his supplies qualified for exemption under *VATA 1994, Sch 9, Group 7, Item 1*, or under *Article 13A1(c)* of the *EC Sixth Directive*. The tribunal rejected this contention and dismissed his appeal. Applying *dicta* of Hutchison J in *Barkworth v C & E Commrs*, QB [1988] STC 771, 'the Member States are given a discretion to determine whom they regard as being within the medical or paramedical professions', and 'provided they have done that, they have complied with their obligations'. *L Yusupoff*, MAN/01/899 (VTD 18152). (*Note. Barkworth* was a case in which the QB held that osteopathy did not qualify for exemption under the legislation as then in force. However, *VATA 1994, 9 Sch, Group 7, Item 1* was subsequently amended to exempt the services of an osteopath—see *Item 1(ca)*, introduced in June 1998.)

Unregistered optician—whether supplies 'directly supervised'

[33.25] The Commissioners issued a ruling that supplies by an unregistered optician failed to qualify for exemption under *VATA 1994, Sch 9, Group 7,*

Item 1. The optician appealed, contending that his supplies were directly supervised by a registered optician, and thus qualified for exemption by virtue of *Group 7, Note 2.* The tribunal rejected this contention and dismissed the appeal, distinguishing *Land,* **33.6** above. *A & S Services,* LON/97/812 (VTD 16025).

Supplies by unregistered practitioner—whether 'directly supervised'

[33.26] The Commissioners issued a ruling that supplies by a chiropractor, who was not a registered practitioner within *VATA 1994, Sch 9, Group 7, Item 1,* did not qualify for exemption. She appealed, contending that her supplies should be treated as 'directly supervised' by the registered practitioners who referred patients to her, and thus as exempt by virtue of *Group 7, Note 2.* The tribunal dismissed her appeal, holding on the evidence that the chiropractor's services were not 'directly supervised'. *C Pittam,* LON/94/1975A (VTD 13268). (*Note.* See now *VATA 1994, Sch 9, Group 7, Item 1(ca),* introduced by the *VAT (Chiropractors) Order 1999 (SI 1999/1575)* with effect from 29 June 1999. The effect of this is that supplies by a chiropractor who is registered under the *Chiropractors Act 1994* now qualify for exemption.)

Anti-smoking therapy—whether supplies 'directly supervised'

[33.27] A company supplied group therapy and training manuals to clients who wished to stop smoking tobacco. It did not account for output tax on its supplies, treating them as exempt. The Commissioners issued a ruling that the supplies failed to qualify for exemption under *VATA 1994, Sch 9, Group 7, Item 1* and that the company was required to account for output tax. The company appealed, contending that its supplies should be treated as 'directly supervised' by a registered medical practitioner, and therefore as exempt from VAT. The tribunal rejected this contention and dismissed the appeal. On the evidence, a registered medical practitioner visited the company's directors three times a year, and his services were 'of an informal advisory nature'. Accordingly, the company's supplies were not 'directly supervised' by a registered medical practitioner, as required by *Group 7, Note 2. Easyway Productions Ltd,* LON/95/2613 (VTD 14938).

Supplies of biochemical analysis—whether 'directly supervised'

[33.28] A company supplied biochemical analysis of blood and urine samples. It did not account for output tax on its supplies. The Commissioners issued assessments charging tax on them, and the company appealed, contending that they should be treated as exempt. The tribunal rejected this contention and dismissed the appeal, holding that the supplies were not 'directly supervised' by a registered medical practitioner, as required by *Group 7, Note 2. Neurotech International Ltd,* LON/02/906 (VTD 18812).

Food allergy testing

[33.29] A company operated a business of food allergy testing, on a franchise basis. It had 45 franchisees, who charged customers fees ranging from £33 to £40. Part of these fees were retained by the franchisee, and part were paid to the franchisor. The franchisor did not account for tax on its share of its fees, and the Commissioners issued an assessment charging tax on them. The company appealed, contending that the fees should be treated as exempt under *VATA 1994, Sch 9, Group 7, Item 1*. The tribunal rejected this contention and dismissed the appeal, holding firstly that the relevant tests were supplied by the franchisees, so that the fees which the franchisor received were consideration for its services to the franchisees, rather than consideration for the supply of tests to customers. The franchisees 'administered the tests, not as employees or agents of the appellant but carrying on the business in their own right'. Furthermore, the tests were not 'directly supervised' by a registered practitioner, as required by *Group 7, Note 2*. *Allergycare (Testing) Ltd*, LON/99/1338 (VTD 18026).

Company arranging for diagnostic laboratory tests

[33.30] A company (L) advertised certain diagnostic tests for female customers with health problems. L arranged for the tests in question to be carried out at a laboratory, and passed the test results to its customers. It was accepted that the supplies by the laboratory to L were exempt from VAT under *VATA 1994, Sch 9, Group 7, Item 1*. However, L failed to account for tax on its onward supplies to its customers. Customs issued an assessment charging tax on these supplies. The tribunal upheld the assessment and dismissed L's appeal, holding that the effect of *Group 7, Note 2* was that L's supplies failed to qualify for exemption. *Lifestyles Healthcare (Europe) Ltd*, LON/03/737 (VTD 19300).

Company arranging for medical treatment

[33.31] A company (H) helped employers to arrange 'swift and appropriate' medical treatments for employees who sustained a musculoskeletal injury. H treated its supplies as standard-rated, and reclaimed input tax accordingly. HMRC issued assessments to recover the input tax, on the basis that H's supplies were exempt supplies of medical care. H appealed. The tribunal allowed the appeal, holding that H was supplying a single composite service, and that since only part of that service was rendered by registered medical practitioners, H's supplies were standard-rated. *Health Response UK Ltd v HMRC*, [2010] UKFTT 123 (TC), TC00434.

Dental services (VATA 1994, Sch 9, Group 7, Item 2)

Sales by dentist to other dentists

[33.32] A dentist sold X-ray equipment to other dentists, and did not account for VAT. The Commissioners issued an assessment on the supplies, and the dentist appealed, contending that they were exempt under what is now *VATA 1994, Sch 9, Group 7, Item 2*. The tribunal dismissed his appeal, holding that the supplies did not qualify for exemption. *AW Roberts*, LON/76/175 (VTD 353).

Definition of 'dental technician'

[33.33] An individual, who was licensed by the British Institute of Surgical Technologists, manufactured crowns and bridges for dentists. He reclaimed input tax, but the Commissioners rejected his claim, considering that his supplies were exempt under what is now *VATA 1994, Sch 9, Group 7, Item 2(c)*. The tribunal dismissed his appeal, holding that he was within the definition of a 'dental technician' and was not entitled to be registered for VAT since all his supplies were exempt. *JA Bennett*, LON/79/231 (VTD 865).

Supply of 'study models' by dental technician

[33.34] A dental technician was registered for VAT. The Commissioners sought to cancel his registration on the grounds that all his supplies were exempt under *VATA 1994, Sch 9, Group 7, Item 2*. He appealed, contending that he was making supplies of 'study models', which were supplies of goods rather than supplies of services, and were therefore taxable supplies. The tribunal rejected this contention and dismissed the appeal, observing that 'the model of an individual's mouth does not instantly suggest as a matter of common sense that it is a supply of goods'. The appellant 'was applying his professional expertise to supply a service to dentists and not an item of property to dentists'. Furthermore, even if the study models were to be regarded as goods, their supply would be ancillary to the supply of services, since 'it would be wholly unrealistic to regard the study model as having any independent use, value or utility'. *F Steven (t/a City Ceramic Dental Laboratory)*, EDN/98/137 (VTD 16083).

Supplies of mouthguards—apportionment of consideration

[33.35] A company supplied mouthguards, which were intended to be used by schoolchildren participating in contact sports, and were individually customised by a dental technician. The mouthguards cost between £21.95 and £35.95. The Commissioners issued a ruling that the company was making supplies of goods which were entirely standard-rated. The company appealed, contending that part of the consideration was attributable to the services of the dental technician, which were exempt from VAT. The tribunal accepted this contention and allowed the appeal, observing that 'if a parent is prepared to pay between 11 and 18 times as much for the appellant's bespoke mouthguard as for an off-the-peg "boil and bite", it is those professional services for which he is paying the extra'. *O-Pro Ltd*, LON/99/971 (VTD 16780).

Import of dental prostheses from USA

[33.36] See *Align Technology UK Ltd*, 2.7 APPEALS.

Supply of temporary dental staff

[33.37] A woman operated a dental agency which supplied temporary dental staff to dentists. She initially accounted for VAT on her supplies, but subsequently submitted a repayment claim, covering the period from 1985 to 1996, on the basis that she should have treated them as exempt. HMRC rejected her claim and the tribunal dismissed her appeal. Judge Khan observed that 'there is nothing in the *Sixth Directive* that requires Member States to exempt supplies of staff to dentists'. *S Moher (t/a Premier Dental Agency) v HMRC*, [2011] UKFTT 286 (TC); [2011] SFTD 917, TC01148.

Article 13A1(e) of EC Sixth Directive

[33.38] See *Administration de l'enregistrement et des domaines v Eurodental Sàrl*, 22.288 EUROPEAN COMMUNITY LAW.

Provision of care, etc. in hospital or similar institution (VATA 1994, Sch 9, Group 7, Item 4)

Cases held to be exempt

Surgical belt fitted at hospital

[33.39] In the case noted at 2.58 APPEALS, a woman had purchased a surgical belt from a manufacturer, on the recommendation of her doctor. The doctor fitted the belt for her at a hospital. The tribunal held that the supply qualified for exemption under what is now *VATA 1994, 9 Sch, Group 7, Item 4. M Payton*, [1974] VATTR 140 (VTD 89).

Hospitals providing accommodation for children's mothers

[33.40] A charity ran 32 private hospitals. When young children were taken into one of the hospitals, it provided accommodation for the children's mothers as well as for the children. It made separate charges for the mothers' accommodation. Customs raised an assessment on the basis that the supplies of accommodation to the mothers were standard-rated to the extent that they related to food consumed by the mothers. The charity appealed, contending that its supplies were exempt under what is now *VATA 1994, Sch 9, Group 7, Item 4*. The tribunal allowed the appeal, holding that the provision of food and accommodation for the mother of a child patient was an exempt supply, because it was a necessary ingredient of the supply of care by the hospital for the child. *Nuffield Nursing Home Trust*, [1989] VATTR 62 (VTD 3327).

Nursing home

[33.41] The proprietor of a nursing home reclaimed input tax in respect of work carried out at the home. Customs issued an assessment to recover some of the tax, considering that the supplies made by the home were exempt under what is now *VATA 1994, Sch 9, Group 7, Item 4*. The tribunal upheld the assessment and dismissed the proprietor's appeal. *Dr A Hill*, MAN/88/888 (VTD 5658).

[33.42] A similar decision was reached in *FA Saleem*, EDN/94/169 (VTD 12995).

[33.43] See also *Gregg*, 22.298 EUROPEAN COMMUNITY LAW.

Haemodialysis services supplied under 'outsourcing' agreement

[33.44] A company (G) provided haemodialysis services under an 'outsourcing' agreement with a NHS trust. It reclaimed input tax. Customs issued a ruling that G's supplies were exempt from VAT under *VATA 1994, Sch 9, Group 7, Item 4*, so that the input tax was not recoverable. The tribunal dismissed G's appeal, holding that it was supplying 'care and medical treatment', which was exempt from VAT. *Gambro Hospital Ltd*, [2004] VATDR 21 (VTD 18588).

Company supplying services at residential children's homes

[33.45] A company was established to provide psychological services and vocational training at four residential children's homes. Customs issued a ruling that it was making taxable supplies and was required to register. The company appealed, contending that all its supplies were exempt from VAT under *VATA 1994, Sch 9, Group 7, Item 4*. The tribunal accepted this contention and allowed the appeal. On the evidence, the company was providing 'psychotherapeutic and curative treatment'. This was within the definition of 'care' for the purposes of *Item 4*. *Catholic Care Consortium Ltd*, EDN/00/185 (VTD 17315).

Cases held to be partly exempt

Company providing ancillary services at hospitals

[33.46] A company supplied services to about 45 hospitals. The services included cleaning, duties relating to patients which could be entrusted to non-nursing personnel, duties for hospital staff, and the services of telephonists and receptionists. The company did not account for VAT, treating its supplies as exempt. Customs issued a ruling that the services did not qualify for exemption under what is now *VATA 1994, Sch 9, Group 7*. The tribunal allowed the company's appeal in part, holding that services which involved personal contact with patients were exempt under *Sch 9, Group 7, Item 4*, but (by a 2-1 majority) that services which did not involve contact with patients were standard-rated. *Crothall & Co Ltd*, [1973] VATTR 20 (VTD 6). (*Note.* Customs subsequently stated that 'we no longer accept that the specific services considered by the *Crothall* decision are exempt, as the case predates the *EC Sixth Directive*, which refers to "medical care", and we cannot accept that the services in the *Crothall* decision are medical care'. See Customs' VAT Manual, Part 7, chapter 22, para 3.4(b).)

Construction of premises for use as retirement home

[33.47] A couple constructed a building with residential accommodation for six people. They reclaimed input tax on the basis that they intended to use the building as a retirement home. However, they were unable to fill the home, and offered three of the places to the local authority's Social Services Department under an Adult Placement Scheme. The other three places remained unfilled. Customs issued an assessment to recover the tax which the couple had claimed, since the accommodation under the Adult Placement Scheme was within the provision of the *Registered Homes Act 1984*, and thus was exempt from VAT.

The couple appealed, contending that they had sought to let the accommodation to tenants who did not require any degree of personal care, and any supplies to such tenants would have been taxable. The tribunal allowed the appeal in part, directing that the tax should be apportioned on the basis that the part attributable to the units of accommodation which had been taken up under the Adult Placement Scheme was attributable to exempt supplies, but that the part attributable to the other three units was attributable to intended taxable supplies. *PJ & AL Haines*, MAN/95/1275 (VTD 13834).

Cases held not to be exempt

Provision of telephones in hospital

[33.48] An organisation arranged for the provision of 33 coin-operated telephones in a large hospital. Until 1988 it did not make any profit from this, but from 1989 the amounts which it received from users of the telephones began to exceed the amounts which it paid to British Telecom. Customs issued a ruling that the organisation was required to account for VAT on its surplus takings. The organisation appealed, contending that the supply of the telephones constituted the 'provision of care' which was an exempt supply under what is now *VATA 1994, Sch 9, Group 7, Item 4*. The tribunal rejected this contention and dismissed the appeal, applying the principles laid down in *Crothall & Co Ltd*, **33.46** above, and holding that the provision of telephones was not within the definition of 'care'. *Dicta* in applied. *Poole General Hospital League of Friends*, LON/92/2204 (VTD 10621).

Drugs supplied from hospital dispensary

[33.49] See *Wellington Private Hospital*, **19.2** DRUGS, MEDICINES, AIDS FOR THE HANDICAPPED, ETC.

Provision of treatment at acupuncture clinic

[33.50] The proprietor of an acupuncture clinic appealed against registration, contending that he was providing medical treatment which should be treated as exempt from VAT. The tribunal dismissed his appeal, finding that the clinic was not a registered institution within what is now *VATA 1994, Sch 9, Group 7, Item 4*. *Dr J D'Ambrosio*, BIR/73/1 (VTD 15).

[33.51] See also *Evans*, **33.17** above.

Supply of meals to doctor in hospital dining room

[33.52] A resident doctor at Bradford Royal Infirmary regularly ate meals in the hospital dining room. As required by a ruling under what is now *VATA 1994, s 41(2)*, the hospital accounted for VAT on its income from catering. The doctor lodged an appeal, contending that the catering should be treated as exempt from VAT under what is now *VATA 1994, Sch 9, Group 7, Item 4*, on the basis that it was supplied in connection with the provision of medical treatment. The tribunal dismissed her appeal, holding that the catering did not qualify for exemption. *Dr AJ Cameron*, [1973] VATTR 177 (VTD 41).

Supply and fitting of hearing aids on hospital premises

[33.53] An individual (C) supplied audiology services and hearing aids. Customs accepted that his audiology services were exempt under what is now *VATA 1994, Sch 9, Group 7, Item 1(e)*. However, Customs considered that since this exemption was confined to services rather than goods, the supply of hearing aids (which had been exempt from VAT before the changes made by *FA 1988*) did not qualify for exemption, but was standard-rated. C appealed, contending that, although the supply of hearing aids was not itself exempt, the fitting of hearing aids should be treated as exempt under *Item 4* where it was carried out on hospital premises. The tribunal dismissed the appeal, holding that the fitting of hearing aids did not qualify as 'the provision of care or medical or surgical treatment', and accordingly was not within *Sch 9, Group 7, Item 4*. *MJ Coleman*, LON/92/1274A (VTD 10512).

Unregistered hair transplant clinic

[33.54] A company opened a hair transplant clinic in 1977. However, the clinic was not registered under the *Nursing Homes Act 1975* until 31 October 1978. Customs accepted that the supplies at the clinic after that date were exempt under what is now *VATA 1994, Sch 9, Group 7, Item 4*, but issued a ruling that the supplies before that date did not qualify for exemption. The tribunal dismissed the company's appeal against this decision. *Huntley Hair Transplants Ltd*, LON/77/414 (VTD 823).

Removal of unwanted hair—whether exempt

[33.55] A woman operated a private clinic which advertised the permanent removal of unwanted hair (by applying heat to hair follicles). She did not account for VAT on her receipts from these services. HMRC issued an assessment charging tax on them, and she appealed, contending that they were 'medical or surgical treatment' which qualified for exemption under *VATA 1994, Sch 9, Group 7, Item 4*. The tribunal rejected this contention and dismissed her appeal, finding that the appellant 'was not medically qualified to perform medical diagnoses of her clients' and had failed to show that the treatments 'were for medical and not for cosmetic purposes'. *Ms J Burke v HMRC*, [2009] UKFTT 87 (TC), TC00055.

Cosmetic treatments at premises licensed under Care Standards Act 2000

[33.56] A company operated a clinic which was licensed under the Care Standards Act 2000, and at which it carried out cosmetic treatments such as facelifts, hair removal and anti-cellulite treatment. It reclaimed input tax. HMRC issued an assessment to recover the tax on the basis that the company's supplies were exempt under *VATA 1994, Sch 9, Group 7, Item 4*. The company appealed, contending that its treatments were cosmetic, and did not qualify for exemption. The tribunal accepted this contention and allowed the appeal, observing that *Notice 701/31* stated that 'Class 3B and 4 Lasers and Intense Pulse light Source Machines are now used in many medical and cosmetic procedures carried out on the premises of approved, licensed or registered institutions. However, it should not be assumed that all treatments using this equipment are exempt from VAT.' *Ultralase Medical Aesthetics Ltd v HMRC*, [2009] SFTD 541; [2009] UKFTT 187 (TC), TC00142.

Nursing home

[33.57] The proprietor of a nursing home was registered for VAT. Customs issued a ruling that he was not entitled to be registered, on the grounds that all his supplies were exempt from VAT under what is now *VATA 1994, Sch 9, Group 7, Item 4*. The proprietor appealed, contending that he should not be treated as exempt since the exemption should be construed in accordance with *Article 13A1(b)* of the *EC Sixth Directive*, which confined such exemption to 'bodies governed by public law'. The tribunal accepted this contention and allowed the appeal, applying the ECJ decision in *Bulthuis-Griffioen v Inspector der Omzetbelasting*, **22.297** EUROPEAN COMMUNITY LAW. The chairman observed that the exemptions in *Article 13A* had to be construed strictly, and it was 'not unnatural, particularly in a European context, that exemptions which are clearly directed towards activities which are socially beneficial should, in certain cases, apply to such activities only if they are carried on by organisations rather than by individuals'. *P Kaul (t/a Alpha Care Services)*, [1996] VATDR 360 (VTD 14028). (*Note.* For Customs' practice following this decision, see Business Brief 1/97, issued on 24 January 1997.)

Unregistered retirement home

[33.58] The proprietors of a retirement home reclaimed input tax on work carried out at the home. Customs issued an assessment to recover some of the tax in question, considering that the supplies made at the home were exempt under what is now *VATA 1994, Sch 9, Group 7, Item 4*. The tribunal allowed the proprietors' appeal, finding that at the relevant time the home was not registered as a Nursing Home, and holding that none of the supplies made by the proprietors were exempt from VAT. *B & E Latimer*, EDN/90/175 (VTD 6486).

Accommodation for children in need of care

[33.59] A company provided accommodation for children in need of care, in accordance with the *Children Act 1989, s 23*. It received payment from local authorities who placed children in its care. Its turnover exceeded the registration threshold, but it failed to register for VAT. Customs issued a ruling that the company was required to register. The company appealed, contending that its supplies should be treated as exempt under *VATA 1994, Sch 9, Group 7* or under *Article 13A1(h)* of the *EC Sixth Directive*. The tribunal rejected these contentions and dismissed the appeal. The tribunal held that the supplies failed to qualify for exemption under *Group 7, Item 4*, since, construing the legislation in accordance with the *eiusdem generis* principle, *Item 4* was 'concerned with a provision of a care in a medical connotation'. The supplies also failed to qualify for exemption under *Group 7, Item 9*, since the company was not a 'charity or public body', and failed to qualify under *Article 13A1(h)* of the *EC Sixth Directive*, since the company was not 'a body governed by public law'. *Prospects Care Services Ltd*, [1997] VATDR 209 (VTD 14810). (*Note.* The decision here was distinguished, and implicitly disapproved, in the subsequent Scottish case of *Catholic Care Consortium Ltd*, **33.45** above.)

Residential care homes for people with learning disabilities

[33.60] Two companies formed a partnership to operate residential care homes for people with learning disabilities. The partnership applied for registration for VAT. Customs rejected the claim on the basis that all the partnership's supplies were exempt under *VATA 1994, Sch 9, Group 7*. The partnership appealed, contending that its supplies did not qualify for exemption and that it was entitled to be registered. The tribunal accepted this contention and allowed the appeal, holding that the partnership's supplies did not constitute 'the provision of care' within *Group 7, Item 4*, since *Item 4* 'connotes care connected with medical or surgical treatment'. The Ch D upheld this decision, observing that the care homes were 'not centres for medical treatment even in a broad sense'. *C & E Commrs v Kingscrest Associates Ltd & Montecello Ltd (t/a Kingscrest Residential Care Homes) (No 1)*, Ch D [2002] STC 490; [2002] EWHC 410 (Ch). (*Notes.* (1) See now, however, the *VAT (Health and Welfare) Order (SI 2002/762)*, introduced with effect from 21 March 2002 in order to reverse this decision. In Press Release 21/02, issued on 20 March 2002, Customs explained that the Ch D decision 'threatened to allow care homes to put VAT on top of the fees they charge their residents. The Government has therefore brought forward legislation which puts the exemption for residential care beyond doubt.' (2) For subsequent developments in this case, see **22.300** EUROPEAN COMMUNITY LAW.)

Human blood, organs and tissue (VATA 1994, Sch 9, Group 7, Items 6–8)

Recombinant Factor VIII

[33.61] A company supplied a product known as Recombinant Factor VIII to the National Health Service. The Commissioners issued a ruling that the company was required to account for output tax on these supplies. The company appealed, contending firstly that the product was 'derived from human blood' within *VATA 1994, Sch 9, Group 7, Item 7* and alternatively that it was human tissue, within *VATA 1994, Sch 9, Group 7, Item 8*. The tribunal rejected these contentions and dismissed the appeal. Types of factor VIII which were derived from human plasma were exempt from VAT under *VATA 1994, Sch 9, Group 7, Item 7*. However, the product in question was not derived from human plasma and did not qualify for exemption. The tribunal observed that it was an established principle that exemptions should be strictly construed, and held that it appeared to be the intention of the legislation 'only to exempt naturally occurring parts of the human body and not to exempt substances produced as a matter of manufacture or production'. *Baxter Healthcare Ltd*, LON/96/177 (VTD 14670).

Supplies of welfare services (VATA 1994, Sch 9, Group 7, Item 9)

NOTE

VATA 1994, Sch 9, Group 7, Item 9 was substituted by *VAT (Health and Welfare) Order (SI 2002/762)*, with effect from 21 March 2002. The cases in this section should be read in the light of the changes in the legislation.

Equipment supplied with nursery services

[33.62] A company supplied nursery management services to businesses, primarily to enable employees of such businesses to have young children cared for at or near their place of work. It was accepted that these services were exempt from VAT under what is now *VATA 1994, Sch 9, Group 7*. However, the company treated supplies of various items of equipment, installed when a new nursery unit was established, as separate standard-rated supplies. It therefore accounted for output tax on the installation of such equipment, reclaimed input tax on the purchase of the equipment, and carried out partial exemption computations in which the supplies of the equipment were treated as standard-rated. The Commissioners issued an assessment to recover the input tax, on the basis that the equipment was supplied as an integral part of an exempt supply. The company appealed, contending that the equipment was a separate standard-rated supply and that it had accounted for tax on the correct basis. The tribunal dismissed the appeal, holding that the supplies of equipment were 'an integral part of the contract to supply child care services' and thus were exempt from VAT. *Kids of Wilmslow Ltd*, MAN/93/945 (VTD 12341).

Supplies of catering in sheltered housing accommodation

[33.63] A housing association, which was a registered charity, provided sheltered housing accommodation for the elderly. Some of the accommodation included kitchen facilities, but some did not. Where the accommodation did not include kitchen facilities, the association supplied catering services to the residents (most of whom were aged 80 or over, and were considered incapable of looking after themselves). It did not account for output tax on the supplies, treating them as exempt under *VATA 1994, Sch 9, Group 7, Item 9*. The Commissioners issued a ruling that the supplies were excluded from exemption by *Note 7*, and thus were standard-rated. The association appealed, contending that the supplies should be treated as ancillary to the provision of care to the residents, so that the restriction in *Note 7* was inapplicable. The tribunal allowed the appeal, holding on the evidence that the association was providing care because its staff helped the residents with tasks such as dressing, undressing and bathing. The supply of catering was therefore ancillary to the provision of care and qualified for exemption. *Viewpoint Housing Association Ltd*, EDN/94/104 (VTD 13148).

Services for elderly people

[33.64] A housing association, which was accepted as being a charity, supplied 'home help' services to 90 elderly clients under a contract with the local District Council. Each client received an average of two hours' help each week. The Commissioners issued a ruling that it was required to account for output tax on these supplies. The association appealed, contending that the supplies should be treated as exempt under *VATA 1994, Sch 9, Group 7, Item 9*. The tribunal accepted this contention and allowed the appeal, holding on the evidence that the clients had 'major difficulty in safely carrying out some key daily living tasks' and relied on help from social services to continue to live in their own homes. Accordingly, the supplies were within the definition of 'welfare services'. *Watford & District Old People's Housing Association Ltd (t/a Watford Help In The Home Service)*, [1998] VATDR 477 (VTD 15660). (*Note*. For the Commissioners' practice following this decision, see Business Brief 24/98, issued on 2 December 1998, and Business Brief 4/99, issued on 16 February 1999.)

[33.65] A charity, which provided 'day care' services for elderly people, reclaimed input tax. Customs rejected the claim on the basis that the charity's supplies were 'welfare services' which were exempt from VAT. The charity appealed, contending that it was supplying its services to local authorities and care trusts rather than to the elderly people themselves, and that its supplies were not exempt. The tribunal rejected this contention and dismissed the charity's appeal. *Age Concern Leicestershire & Rutland*, MAN/07/711 (VTD 20762).

Supplies of unqualified nursery staff to care homes

[33.66] A company supplied unqualified nursery staff to care homes. Customs issued a ruling that it was required to account for output tax on these supplies. The company appealed, contending that the supplies should be treated as exempt under *VATA 1994, Sch 9, Group 7, Item 9*. The tribunal rejected this contention and dismissed the appeal, holding that the company was supplying staff rather than nursing services, and that these supplies failed to qualify for exemption. The tribunal noted that Customs had a policy of granting exemption with regard to supplies of registered qualified nurses, but described this as a 'concession'. *Care @ Ltd*, MAN/06/454 (VTD 20316).

'Home studies' for prospective adopters—whether exempt

[33.67] A charity, which was approved as a voluntary adoption agency, undertook 'home studies' for prospective adopters. The Commissioners issued a ruling that these supplies were standard-rated for VAT purposes. The charity appealed, contending that they should be treated as exempt under *VATA 1994, Sch 9, Group 7, Item 9*, since they were 'directly connected with the protection of children and young persons', within *Group 7, Note 6(b)*. The tribunal rejected this contention and dismissed the appeal, holding that the charity was supplying its services to the prospective adopters, 'to enable them to obtain certificates of eligibility from the Department of Health', and that the services were not 'directly connected with' the protection of the children in question. *Parents and Children Together*, LON/00/1146 (VTD 17283). (*Note*. The tribunal also held that the supplies failed to qualify for zero-rating under *VATA 1994, 8 Sch, Group 7, Item 2*—see **39.3** INTERNATIONAL SERVICES.)

Supplies by Retreat House—whether exempt under Note 6(c)

[33.68] A charity operated a Retreat House from premises in the Diocese of Peterborough. It was registered for VAT and accounted for output tax, but subsequently formed the opinion that some of its supplies of services should be treated as exempt, and lodged a retrospective claim for repayment of tax. The Commissioners rejected the claim, with the exception that they accepted that certain supplies of training qualified for exemption under what is now *VATA 1994, Sch 9, Group 6*, and that some 'retreats' which the charity organised qualified as exempt supplies of spiritual welfare under what is now *VATA 1994, Sch 9, Group 7, Item 9, Note 6(c)*. The charity appealed. The tribunal reviewed the evidence in detail and allowed the appeal in part, holding that supplies relating to a 'workshop' conducted by a psychotherapist were supplies of spiritual welfare which qualified for exemption but that the remaining supplies (including supplies of accommodation and catering) did not qualify for exemption, either under the UK legislation or under *Article 13A1* of the *EC Sixth Directive*. (The tribunal also held that, even if the supplies had been held to be exempt, the tax in question would not be repayable as the tax had been passed on to the customers and repayment would have led to 'unjust enrichment'.) *Peterborough Diocesan Conference & Retreat House*, LON/94/2078 (VTD 14081).

Holiday camps organised by religious institution—whether exempt

[33.69] A religious institution, which was a registered charity, organised a number of holiday camps for people aged from 10 to 21. It did not account for output tax on the payments which it received from people attending the camps. The Commissioners issued an assessment charging tax on them, and the charity appealed, contending that the camps were supplies of spiritual welfare which qualified for exemption under *VATA 1994, Sch 9, Group 7, Item 9, Note 6(c)*. The tribunal accepted this contention and allowed the charity's appeal. *Evangelical Movement of Wales*, [2004] VATDR 138 (VTD 18556).

Charity providing hotel accommodation for cancer patients

[33.70] A registered charity purchased a hotel and used it to provide accommodation for cancer patients and their families. The Commissioners issued a ruling that output tax was payable on the supplies of accommodation. The charity appealed, contending that it was supplying welfare services which were exempt under *VATA 1994, Sch 9, Group 7, Item 9*. The tribunal accepted this contention and allowed the appeal. The building in which the accommodation was provided was 'not a hotel in the normal sense of the word', since it was 'open only to those suffering from cancer or associated with them, only upon professional recommendations (and) only for a specific length of time', but was 'an institution providing welfare'. The tribunal held that 'the provision of accommodation and catering are ancillary to the provision of welfare', so that the supplies were not excluded from exemption by *Group 7, Note 7*. The tribunal also expressed the view that the restriction laid down by *Group 7, Note 7* was incompatible with the provisions of *Article 13A1(g)* of the *EC Sixth Directive*, which had direct effect. The tribunal observed that 'the fact that old people's homes are included in *Article 13A1(g)* and that this inclusion is, from the context, an example of what is to be included, shows that services incorporating accommodation can be exempt, without conditions that the supply of accommodation shall be ancillary to the supply of welfare services'. *Trustees for the Macmillan Cancer Trust*, [1998] VATDR 289 (VTD 15603).

Charity providing hostel accommodation for homeless

[33.71] A charity provided hostel accommodation for homeless people. It reclaimed input tax. The Commissioners issued an assessment to recover the tax, on the basis that the charity was supplying welfare services which were exempt from VAT under *VATA 1994, Sch 9, Group 7, Item 9*. The charity appealed, contending that the effect of *Group 7, Note 7* was that its supplies did not qualify for exemption. The tribunal accepted this contention and allowed the charity's appeal. On the evidence, the charity was not providing 'care, treatment or instruction'. Accordingly, the effect of *Note 7* was that its supplies did not qualify for exemption under *Item 9*. *Look Ahead Housing & Care Ltd*, LON/00/1133 (VTD 17613).

Residential care homes for people with learning disabilities

[33.72] See *Kingscrest Associates Ltd & Montecello Ltd (t/a Kingscrest Residential Care Homes) (No 2)*, **22.300** EUROPEAN COMMUNITY LAW.

Partnership supplying fostering services to local authorities

[33.73] A partnership supplied fostering services to local authorities. Customs issued a ruling that its supplies were exempt from VAT under *VATA 1994, Sch 9, Group 7, Item 9* (as substituted by *SI 2002/762*), so that it was not entitled to registration for VAT. The partnership appealed. The tribunal reviewed the evidence in detail and found that the partnership was 'a state-regulated private welfare agency' and was supplying 'welfare services' within *Group 7, Note 6(b)*. Its supplies were 'closely linked to the protection of children and young persons', within *Article 13A1(h)* of the *EC Sixth Directive*. The tribunal initially directed that the appeal should be adjourned pending the CJEC decision in *Kingscrest Associates Ltd (No 2)*, **22.300** EUROPEAN COMMUNITY LAW. At a subsequent hearing the tribunal dismissed the partnership's appeal, applying the principles laid down in *Kingscrest* and holding that the partnership's supplies were exempt from VAT. *Families For Children (No 2)*, LON/02/559 (VTD 19857).

Childcare services

[33.74] A company supplied childcare services to kindergartens and nurseries. Customs issued a ruling that it was required to account for VAT on its supplies. The company appealed, contending that its supplies qualified for exemption under *VATA 1994, Sch 9, Group 7, Item 9* (as substituted by *SI 2002/762*). The Ch D rejected this contention and upheld Customs' ruling. Hart J held that the company did not qualify as 'a state-regulated private welfare institution or agency', within *VATA 1994, Sch 9, Group 7, Item 9(b)*. The company was not 'itself making supplies of welfare services', and was not 'state-regulated' as defined in *Note 8*. *HMRC v K & L Childcare Services Ltd*, Ch D 2005, [2006] STC 18; [2005] EWHC 2414 (Ch). (*Note*. The tribunal decision names the company as 'K & L Childcare Services Ltd', but Simon's Tax Cases names it as 'K & L Childcare Service Ltd'.)

Nursery staff

[33.75] In *Eyears Ltd*, 1.46 AGENTS, the tribunal held that the provision of nursery staff did not qualify for exemption under *VATA 1994, Sch 9, Group 7, Item 9*.

Supplies of transport services (VATA 1994, Sch 9, Group 7, Item 11)

Transport of human organs, etc. for transplant operations

[33.76] A trader carried on business supplying transport services for human organs and blood for use in transplant operations, and for teams of people involved in such operations. The Commissioners issued a ruling that he was required to account for output tax on his supplies. He appealed, contending that they should be treated as exempt under *VATA 1994, Sch 9, Group 7, Item 11*. The tribunal rejected this contention and dismissed his appeal. *M Peverley (t/a Lifeline Medical Transport Service)*, MAN/97/472 (VTD 15353).

Imported goods (VAT (Imported Goods) Relief Order (SI 1984/746), Sch 2 Group 5)

Vitamin supplement imported from USA

[33.77] An individual (P) purchased a vitamin supplement from a US distributor. The Commissioners issued a ruling that VAT was chargeable on the import of the supplement. P appealed. The tribunal dismissed P's appeal, holding that the supplement was not within any of the zero-rated items listed in *VAT (Imported Goods) Relief Order (SI 1984/746), Sch 2 Group 5*. *G Painter*, MAN/00/270 (VTD 17530).

34

Human Rights

The cases in this chapter are arranged under the following headings.

Penalties and surcharges   34.1
Other cases   34.14

NOTE

The European Convention for the Protection of Human Rights was adopted in 1950, as a treaty of the Council of Europe. (This body predates, and is entirely separate from, the European Community which originates from the 1957 Treaty of Rome.) Article 1 of the First Protocol of the European Convention provides that 'every natural or legal person is entitled to the peaceful enjoyment of his possessions' but goes on to add that these provisions shall not 'in any way impair the right of a State to enforce such laws as it deems necessary to control the use of property in accordance with the general interest or to secure the payment of tax or other contributions and penalties'. The Convention is recognised as part of European Community law by article 6 of the 1997 Treaty of Amsterdam. For a discussion of the Convention and its impact on UK tax law, see the article by Philip Baker in British Tax Review 2000, pp 211–377. For a critical analysis of the practical implications for the VAT practitioner, see John Price's article in 'Taxation', 20 September 2001, pp 635–637.

Penalties and surcharges

Determination of penalty under VATA 1994, s 60

[34.1] In the case noted at **50.108** PENALTIES: EVASION OF TAX, the Commissioners had imposed a penalty under *VATA 1994, s 60* on a partnership. The penalty was originally imposed at the rate of 95% of the evaded tax. The tribunal upheld the penalty in principle, but reduced it to 75% of the evaded tax. The CA upheld the tribunal decision. The partners subsequently applied to the ECHR, contending that the imposition of the penalty was a breach of the *European Convention on Human Rights*. The ECHR rejected this contention, holding that it was 'manifestly ill-founded within the meaning of *Article 35*' of the Convention, and unanimously declared the application inadmissible. The ECHR held, *inter alia*, that 'the interests of justice did not require leading counsel to be instructed on the applicants' behalf'. Furthermore, 'in the light of the circumstances of the present case seen as a whole', there was 'no appearance of unfairness within the meaning of *Article 6* of the Convention'. The length of the proceedings was 'justified by complexity of the case (*sic*) and conduct of the applicants'. *Article 1 of the First Protocol* of the Convention provided that a State could 'enforce such laws as it deems necessary to control the use of property in accordance with the general interest or to secure the payment of taxes or other contributions or penalties'. Applying *Gasus Dosier- und Fördertechnik GmbH v Netherlands*, ECHR Case 15375/89; 20 EHRR 403, 'the Court will respect the legislature's assessment in such matters unless it is devoid of reasonable foundation'. *M & A Georgiou v United Kingdom*, ECHR Case 40042/98, [2001] STC 80; 3 ITLR 145.

[34.2] The Commissioners imposed a penalty under *VATA 1994, s 60* on the proprietors of a Chinese restaurant which had underdeclared takings. The partners appealed, contending *inter alia* that the delays in determining the penalty were a breach of the *European Convention on Human Rights*. The tribunal rejected this contention and dismissed the appeal, holding that the delays were not 'sufficient to have occasioned a breach of the *Convention*'. *KH & CB Mu*, LON/00/578 (VTD 17504).

[34.3] A trader appealed against a penalty under *VATA 1994, s 60*. The appeal was set down for hearing on 29 May 2002. The trader applied for the hearing to be postponed as that date was inconvenient. The Manchester Tribunal Centre accepted this request, but did not fix a new date until November 2002, when it informed the trader and the Commissioners that the appeal was being relisted for 10 March 2003. On 4 March the Tribunal Centre advised both parties that the hearing of the appeal was again being postponed. It subsequently relisted the appeal for hearing on 18 August 2003. At the hearing, the trader contended that the delays in hearing the appeal were a breach of *Article 6* of the *European Convention on Human Rights*. The tribunal reviewed the evidence and held that the delays caused by the Tribunal Centre appeared to be '*prima facie* unreasonable'. However the tribunal also observed that it appeared that the trader had not been prejudiced by the delay, and that it did not appear that the delay would 'make for an unfair hearing of the appeal in evidential terms'. The tribunal directed that the case should be listed for a further hearing. *AR Shabani*, MAN/00/48 (E482). (*Note*. There was no further public hearing of the appeal.)

[34.4] See also *Edwards*, 50.17 PENALTIES: EVASION OF TAX, and *MS Khan*, 50.89 PENALTIES: EVASION OF TAX.

Penalties under VATA 1994, s 60—whether a 'criminal charge'

[34.5] In three appeals involving penalties under *VATA 1994, s 60*, the tribunal held, as a preliminary issue, that the imposition of a penalty under *VATA 1994, s 60* gave rise to a 'criminal charge' within *Article 6* of the *European Convention on Human Rights*. The CA upheld this decision (by a 2-1 majority, Sir Martin Nourse dissenting). Potter LJ held that the effect of the ECHR decisions in *Bendenoun v France*, ECHR Case 12547/86, 18 EHRR 54 and *AP, MP and TP v Switzerland*, ECHR Case 19958/92, 26 EHRR 541 was that the penalties had to be regarded as involving a 'criminal charge' for the purposes of *Article 6*. He observed that 'it by no means follows from a conclusion that *Article 6* applies that civil penalty proceedings are, for other domestic purposes, to be regarded as criminal and, therefore, subject to those provisions of (*Police and Criminal Evidence Act 1984*) and/or the Codes produced thereunder, which relate to the investigation of crime and the conduct of criminal proceedings as defined by English law'. Furthermore, if matters were made clear to the taxpayer 'at the time when the nature and effect of the inducement procedure are also made clear to him (whether by *VAT Notice 730* or otherwise), it is difficult to see that there would be any breach of *Article 6'*. Even if *PACE 1984* were applicable, it was 'most unlikely' that a court or tribunal would rule inadmissible 'any statements made or documents produced as a result'. *C & E Commrs v GK Han & D Yau (t/a Murdishaw Supper Bar) (and related appeals)*, CA [2001] STC 1188; 3 ITLR 873; [2001] 1 WLR 2253; [2001] 4 All ER 687.

[34.6] The tribunal decision in *Han & Yau*, 34.5 above, was applied in a subsequent Scottish case in which the tribunal observed that the effects of regarding the proceedings as 'of a criminal nature' would 'create a difference in approach to evidence and its admissibility and the conduct of investigating officers in Scotland and England. The *Police and Criminal Evidence Act 1984* as applied to Customs & Excise in 1985 has no application in this country. Provisions and guidelines therein do not have the force of law so far as interviews and availability of answers to questions are concerned.' The common law of Scotland would continue to apply. *WS & CK Shek (t/a Wing Lee Carryout)*, EDN/99/219 (VTD 17047). (*Note.* For the substantive appeal, see **50.101** PENALTIES: EVASION OF TAX.)

Admissibility of evidence

[34.7] The Commissioners formed the opinion that a partnership which operated two restaurants had underdeclared takings. They imposed a penalty under *VATA 1994, s 60*. The partnership appealed, contending *inter alia* that some of the Commissioners' evidence (including a record of an interview and a telephone conversation) breached *Article 6* of the *European Convention on Human Rights* and should not be admitted. The tribunal rejected this contention, holding that the evidence was admissible in full. (The tribunal also dismissed the appeal against the penalty, holding on the evidence that the partners had acted dishonestly.) *SC Bammi & BK Dhir (t/a The Last Viceroy)*, MAN/01/261 (VTD 17660).

[34.8] See also *Qaisar*, 50.55 PENALTIES: EVASION OF TAX.

Late appeal against penalty under VATA 1994, s 60

[34.9] See *Shatliff*, 2.189 APPEALS.

Penalty attributed to director under VATA 1994, s 61

[34.10] A penalty was imposed on a company director under *VATA 1994, s 61*. The director appealed and applied for a postponement of the hearing as he was in Australia. His solicitors wrote to the tribunal claiming that it would be a breach of the *Human Rights Act 1998* to hear the appeal in the director's absence. The tribunal rejected this contention, observing that the director 'was fully aware of the hearing date and no evidence that he could not afford to be present had been given'. Furthermore, the right to a fair trial 'does not prevent a hearing in absentia if the appellant has been given notice of the hearing'. The tribunal also held that the scale of the penalty meant that the case should be treated as a criminal one for the purposes of *Article 6* of the *European Convention on Human Rights*. Accordingly, the right to a fair trial under *Article 6* meant that the tribunal was entitled to read a witness statement submitted by the director, despite the prohibition on witness statements where notice of objection is given under *VAT Tribunals Rules 1986 (SI 1986/590), rule 21(4)*. The tribunal reviewed the evidence and held that the director's conduct had constituted 'evasion', applying *R v Dealy*, **49.10** PENALTIES: CRIMINAL OFFENCES, and *dicta* of Lord Lane CJ in *R v Ghosh*, CA [1982] 3 WLR 110; [1982] 2 All ER 689. The tribunal observed that (with the exception of two small invoices) it was clear that 'the appellant knew that what he was doing or omitting would be regarded as dishonest according to the ordinary standards of reasonable and honest people'. The tribunal therefore dismissed the appeal with the exception of two invoices where it held that dishonesty had not been proved, reducing the penalty from £59,170 to £55,354. *JL Murrell*, LON/99/121 (VTD 16878).

[34.11] See also *Edwards*, **50.17** PENALTIES: EVASION OF TAX, and *Sawyer*, **50.60** PENALTIES: EVASION OF TAX.

Surcharges—whether any breach of Article 6

[34.12] In a Finnish case, the tax authorities imposed a surcharge on the proprietor of a car repair workshop who had underdeclared VAT. He applied to the ECHR for a ruling that the imposition of the surcharge contravened *Article 6* of the *European Convention on Human Rights*. The ECHR rejected this contention and dismissed his application. *Jussila v Finland*, ECHR Case 73053/01; [2009] STC 29; 9 ITLR 662.

[34.13] In a Swedish case, the tax authorities formed the opinion that a company had reclaimed input tax in respect of false invoices. They imposed surcharges on the company, and applied to the court for the company's assets to be sequestered. The Supreme Administrative Court found in favour of the tax authority, finding that 'there was a considerable risk that the applicant company would try to shirk responsibility for the debt', and sequestered the company's assets. The company applied to the ECHR for a ruling that the imposition of the surcharges, and the sequestration of its assets, contravened *Article 6* of the *European Convention on Human Rights*. The ECHR rejected this contention and dismissed the application. *Plat Ror Och vets Service i Norden AB & Others v Sweden*, ECHR Case 12637/05; [2009] ECHR 1015.

Other cases

Delay in determining appeals

[34.14] In the case noted at **2.127** APPEALS, the Ch D held that the delays in determining the trader's liability did not involve any breach of *Article 6* of the *European Convention on Human Rights*. Patten J observed that 'the delay attributable to a new appeal from the 1998 assessment as opposed to the re-hearing ordered by Carnwath J is relatively minor'. *A Bennett v C & E Commrs (No 2)*, Ch D [2001] STC 137.

[34.15] The tribunal reached a similar decision in the excise duty case of *K Morris & Others*, [2006] VATDR 263 (E894).

Appeal procedure—whether compatible with Convention

[34.16] In a number of appeals which were heard together as 'test cases', the tribunal held that the VAT appeal procedure was compatible with *Article 6(1)* of the *European Convention on Human Rights*. *N Ali & S Begum (t/a Shapla Tandoori Restaurant) (and other appeals)*, [2002] VATDR 71 (VTD 17681). (*Notes.* (1) The tribunal also held that the majority ECHR decision in *Ferrazzini v Italy*, ECHR Case 44759/98, [2001] STC 1314 was 'not applicable' to UK VAT, since 'there is no place in the laws of any part of the United Kingdom for a "public law" relationship, distinct from civil law rights and obligations, between taxpayer (*sic*) and the tax authorities'. (2) The tribunal also held that default surcharges, misdeclaration penalties and penalties for failure to notify liability did not constitute a 'criminal charge' for the purposes of *Article 6(1).*)

VATA 1994, s 84(3)—whether any breach of Article 6

[34.17] See *B O'Brien v HMRC*, 2.135 APPEALS.

SI 1986/590, rule 7(1)—whether compatible with HRA 1998

[34.18] See *Patel*, 2.150 APPEALS.

Admissibility of tape-recorded interviews in evidence

[34.19] See *Sharland*, 2.290 APPEALS.

Witness summons—whether any breach of Article 6

[34.20] See *Home Or Away Ltd*, 2.301 APPEALS.

Search of partner's home—whether any breach of Article 8

[34.21] See *R (oao Paul da Costa & Co) v Thames Magistrates' Court*, 14.95 COLLECTION AND ENFORCEMENT.

Joint liability of partners—whether any breach of Convention

[34.22] See *Yarl Wines*, 50.11 PENALTIES: EVASION OF TAX.

Retrospective change of legislation

[34.23] In a Moldovan case, a company appealed against a VAT liability, contending that the relevant supplies were exempt under the legislation then in force. In 2002 the Moldovan Supreme Court found in favour of the company.

In October 2005 the Moldovan Parliament amended the relevant legislation. In November 2005 the Moldovan Tax Inspectorate applied for review of the 2002 Supreme Court decision, contending that the amendment to the legislation should have retrospective effect. Later that month the Moldovan Supreme Court accepted the Inspectorate's application and quashed its previous judgment. The company applied to the ECHR, contending that the quashing of the previous decision, to give effect to a retrospective change in legislation, was a breach of the *European Convention on Human Rights*. The ECHR granted the company's application, holding that the judgment of November 2005 had violated *Article 6* of the Convention and *Article 1 of the First Protocol. Agurdino Srl v Moldova*, ECHR Case 7359/06; [2012] STC 1.

Failure to implement EC Directive

[34.24] *Article 13B(a)* of the *EC Sixth Directive* exempted insurance and insurance-related transactions from VAT with effect from 1 January 1978. France failed to implement this Directive, and continued to charge VAT on such transactions. On 30 June 1978 the *EC Ninth Directive (78/583)* gave France until 1 January 1979 in which to implement *Article 13B(a)*. A French company claimed reimbursement of the tax which it had been charged from 1 January 1978 to 30 June 1978, contending that the *Ninth Directive* did not have retrospective effect so that, under EC law, the transactions were exempt from 1 January 1978 to 30 June 1978. The French authorities rejected the claim and the Conseil d'Etat dismissed the company's appeal. The company then applied to the ECHR, contending that the decision of the Conseil d'Etat contravened *Article 1 of the First Protocol of the European Convention on Human Rights*. The ECHR allowed the company's application, holding that there was no justification for 'the Conseil d'Etat's refusal to give effect to a directly applicable provision of Community law'. The decision breached the company's 'right to the peaceful enjoyment of its possessions'. The interference was 'disproportionate', since 'both the negation of the applicant company's claim against the State and the absence of domestic procedures affording a sufficient remedy to ensure the protection of the applicant company's right to the peaceful enjoyment of its possessions upset the fair balance that must be maintained between the demands of the general interest of the community and the requirements of the protection of the individual's fundamental rights'. *SA Dangeville v France*, ECHR Case 36677/97; [2003] STC 771; 5 ITLR 604.

[34.25] A similar decision was reached in *SA Cabinet Diot v France*, ECHR Case 49217/99; *SA Gras Savoye v France*, ECHR Case 49218/99; 22 July 2003 unreported.

Assessments charging tax on exports

[34.26] In an Ukrainian case, a company had failed to comply with the statutory conditions required in order to treat assessments as zero-rated. The VAT authority therefore issued assessments charging tax on the relevant transactions. The Ukrainian courts dismissed the company's appeals, and the company applied to the ECHR, contending that the imposition of VAT in such circumstances contravened *Article 1 of the First Protocol of the Euro-*

pean Convention on Human Rights. The ECHR rejected this contention and dismissed the application. On the evidence, the Ukrainian courts had been entitled to find that the company had 'failed to prove that it had actually exported any goods outside the customs territory of Ukraine' and that 'a "fair balance" was struck between the applicant's interests and the general interests of Ukrainian society'. *Masa Invest Group plc v Ukraine*, ECHR Case 3540/03; 8 ITLR 262.

Disallowance of claim to input tax

[34.27] In a Bulgarian case, a company (B) claimed a deduction for input tax on a purchase of goods. The tax authority subsequently discovered that the supplier had failed to account for output tax on the transaction, and issued an assessment to recover the tax which B had claimed. B appealed, but its appeal was dismissed by the Bulgarian Supreme Administrative Court. B then applied to the ECHR for a ruling that the disallowance of its claim to input tax constituted a breach of *Article 1* of the *First Protocol of the European Convention on Human Rights*. The ECHR reviewed the evidence in detail and granted the application, holding that 'in so far as the applicant company had complied fully and in time with the VAT rules set by the State, had no means of enforcing compliance by its supplier and had no knowledge of the latter's failure to do so, it could justifiably expect to be allowed to benefit from one of the principal rules of the VAT system of taxation by being allowed to deduct the input VAT it had paid to its supplier'. The ECHR held that 'if the national authorities, in the absence of any indication of direct involvement by an individual or entity in fraudulent abuse of a VAT chain of supply, or knowledge thereof, nevertheless penalise the fully compliant recipient of a VAT-taxable supply for the actions or inactions of a supplier over which it has no control and in relation to which it has no means of monitoring or securing compliance, they are going beyond what is reasonable and are upsetting the fair balance that must be maintained between the demands of the general interest of the community and the requirements of the protection of the right of property'. The ECHR held that B 'should not have been required to bear the full consequences of its supplier's failure to discharge its VAT reporting obligations in timely fashion, by being refused the right to deduct the input VAT and, as a result, being ordered to pay the VAT a second time, plus interest'. This had 'amounted to an excessive individual burden on the applicant company which upset the fair balance that must be maintained between the demands of the general interest of the community and the requirements of the protection of the right of property'. The ECHR awarded pecuniary damages of €1,953. *Bulves AD v Bulgaria*, ECHR Case 3991/03; [2009] STC 1161.

[34.28] The decision in *Bulves AD v Bulgaria*, **34.27** above, was applied in the similar subsequent case of *Business Support Centre v Bulgaria*, ECHR Case 6689/03; 18 March 2010 unreported.

VAT fraud investigation: detention of suspects

[34.29] In a Slovak case, two individuals were arrested in February 2002 during an investigation of a suspected large-scale VAT fraud, and were remanded in custody. In October 2004 they were also indicted for murder. They were subsequently convicted and sentenced to substantial terms of imprisonment. While in prison, they applied to the ECHR, contending that the length of time during which they had been detained in custody was a breach of the European Convention on Human Rights. The ECHR rejected their applications, describing their complaint as 'manifestly ill-founded'. *Pokrivka v Slovakia*, ECHR Case 35933/06; *Sitta v Slovakia*, ECHR Case 48144/06; 26 October 2010 unreported.

VAT fraud investigation: length of proceedings

[34.30] In an Austrian case, the tax authorities formed the opinion that a company director (M) had been involved in carousel fraud. He was questioned in August and September 1995, was indicted in March 2000, and was convicted in September 2002. He was sentenced to two years' imprisonment. He appealed to the Austrian Supreme Court, which dismissed his appeal in April 2005 and increased his sentence to three years' imprisonment. He served two years and six months in prison before being released on probation. Following his release he applied to the ECHR for a ruling that the length of the proceedings had been a breach of *Article 6(1)* of the European Convention on Human Rights. The ECHR accepted this contention, observing that the proceedings had begun when he was questioned in August 1995 and ended when the Supreme Court reached its decision in April 2005. The ECHR awarded M token damages of €8,000. *Meidl v Austria*, ECHR Case 33951/05; 12 April 2011 unreported.

35

Imports

The cases in this chapter are arranged under the following headings.

Imports from outside EU (VATA 1994, ss 15-17)   35.1
Value of imported goods (VATA 1994, s 21)   35.20
Miscellaneous   35.23

GENERAL NOTE

This chapter deals with the provisions applying to importations of goods into the UK from outside the Member States of the European Union.

Imports from outside EU (VATA 1994, ss 15–17)

Import of motor car

[35.1] An individual (M) imported a Porsche from the USA into the UK. The Commissioners issued a ruling that VAT was chargeable on the import. The tribunal upheld the Commissioners' ruling and dismissed M's appeal. *N Murray*, LON/97/677 (VTD 15149).

[35.2] A similar decision was reached in a case where a civil servant had imported a car from Cyprus, which was not part of the EU at the time in question. The tribunal observed that Cyprus was not part of the European Union and that 'the British Sovereign base area in Cyprus forms no part of the territory of the European Union for the purpose of value added tax'. *M Dullaghan*, [2000] VATDR 188 (VTD 16407). (*Note.* Cyprus subsequently joined the EU with effect from 1 May 2004.)

Import VAT certificates—duplicated claim for input tax

[35.3] See the cases noted at 52.153 PENALTIES: MISDECLARATION to 52.156 PENALTIES: MISDECLARATION, and those noted at 52.169 PENALTIES: MISDECLARATION to 52.171 PENALTIES: MISDECLARATION.

Import certificates—delay in issuing GSP certificate

[35.4] See *John Lanham Watts (Carpets) Ltd*, 52.154 PENALTIES: MISDECLARATION.

Certificates wrongly made out to associated company

[35.5] See *Rosedew Ltd*, 52.157 PENALTIES: MISDECLARATION, and the cases noted at 52.158 PENALTIES: MISDECLARATION.

Input tax assessed on importation—premature reclaim

[35.6] See *Ericsons Fashions Ltd*, 52.163 PENALTIES: MISDECLARATION.

Input tax reclaimed before receipt of certificate

[35.7] See *Quay Marine Ltd*, 52.164 PENALTIES: MISDECLARATION, and *Analog & Numeric Devices Ltd*, 52.165 PENALTIES: MISDECLARATION.

Imported goods—Customs repaying tax to agent in error

[35.8] A company (M) imported a machine valued at about £370,000. It provided a banker's draft for the VAT of £55,000, which was made payable to Customs and was handed to the VAT office in Portsmouth, where it was credited to the account of the company (E) which M had nominated to act as its import agent for this transaction. When the machine arrived at Portsmouth, the VAT officer dealing with the import wrongly charged VAT of only £14,000. The remaining £41,000 of the £55,000 paid by M, which Customs had credited to an account in E's name, was later reclaimed by, and repaid to, E without reference to M. Subsequently M claimed credit for the whole of the £55,000 as input tax, but Customs only allowed credit for the £14,000 which had been charged at the time of the import. Meanwhile E had gone into liquidation without accounting for the balance of £41,000. The tribunal allowed M's appeal. The chairman observed that 'the problem which has arisen here stems entirely from the oversight of the officer of Customs' and considered that 'as a matter of justice, the loss caused by the default of E should in this case be borne by the Commissioners rather than by the appellant'. The full amount of the VAT properly due had been paid by M to Customs by a banker's draft. It was not M's fault that Customs had, under a private arrangement with the agent, credited the money to the agent's account and subsequently allowed the agent to withdraw the money, when it should have been clear that the money did not belong to the agent, but was money provided by M as principal for the purpose of paying VAT. *Mills Marketing Services Ltd*, LON/89/1180Y (VTD 4861).

Tax not paid by import agent

[35.9] A company (M) traded as importers of steel wool. It used the services of an import agent. The agent sent M invoices for six shipments of imported goods, and M paid the invoiced amounts to the agent. However, the agent went into liquidation without accounting for the tax to Customs. M reclaimed input tax in respect of the transactions, and Customs issued an assessment to recover the tax. The tribunal dismissed M's appeal, holding that the agent had been an agent of M, rather than an agent of Customs. The fact that M had paid the money to the agent did not amount to payment to Customs, and the fact that the agent had been approved did not amount to an authority to receive moneys on behalf of Customs. M did not hold a C79 certificate in respect of the transactions in question, and Customs had not authorised M to reclaim input tax thereon. *The Metallic Wool Co Ltd*, LON/94/1062A (VTD 13495).

[35.10] The decision in *The Metallic Wool Co Ltd*, 35.9 above, was applied in the similar subsequent case of *Leather Fashions Ltd*, LON/93/2319 (VTD 15016). (*Note*. An appeal against a misdeclaration penalty was, however, allowed.)

[35.11] See also *James*, 52.161 PENALTIES: MISDECLARATION.

Import of goods—time at which input tax reclaimable

[35.12] A company (C) imported computer parts. It paid the VAT due each month by direct debit, and reclaimed the amounts in question as input tax. In April 1991 the standard rate of VAT was increased from 15% to 17.5%. However, as a result of a programming error in its accounts computer, C continued to account for VAT at the old rate of 15%. It discovered the error at the beginning of June, notified Customs, and submitted a form C305 indicating the underpayments for April and May 1991 together with a cheque for the amount in question. Customs acknowledged receipt of the C305 on 21 June. On 27 June C submitted its May return, in which it reclaimed the amounts shown on the C305 as input tax. Customs considered that, since the C305 had only been submitted in June, the tax should have been reclaimed in C's June return, rather than in the May return. They therefore issued an assessment, including a charge to default interest for one month. C appealed, contending that, since the tax related to goods which had been imported in April and May, and had been paid before submission of the May return, it had been entitled to reclaim the input tax in its May return. The tribunal accepted this contention and allowed the appeal, holding that, since Customs had acknowledged the C305, C had been entitled to reclaim the amounts as input tax by virtue of what is now *VAT Regulations 1995 (SI 1995/2158), reg 29(2)*. *Compaq Computer Manufacturing Ltd*, EDN/92/126 (VTD 10354).

Input tax reclaimed without certificate

[35.13] See *Vin-Dotco (UK) Ltd*, 52.172 PENALTIES: MISDECLARATION.

Input tax reclaimed by import agent

[35.14] A company (C) carried on business as freight forwarders and shipping agents. It paid VAT due on certain imports of goods by its clients, in order to obtain an Entry Acceptance device enabling the goods to be cleared without lodging manual documents. After Customs had issued forms C79, C reclaimed the tax as input tax. The Commissioners issued an assessment to recover the tax, considering that it was not deductible since the goods had not been imported for the purpose of C's business, as required by what is now *VATA 1994, s 24(1)(b)*. The tribunal upheld the assessment and dismissed C's appeal. *Cavenco Ltd*, LON/93/540A (VTD 11700).

[35.15] In a case where the facts were unusual and in dispute, a VAT officer discovered that a Portuguese company had exported some goods to a UK company (M), but had mistakenly issued the relevant form C79 to a trader (S) who had previously acted as M's import agent, but was no longer acting as such. S had reclaimed the relevant input tax, and the Commissioners issued an assessment to recover the tax from S, and allowed M to reclaim the tax even though it did not hold the C79. The tribunal upheld the assessment and dismissed S's appeal, finding that S had 'not been wholly candid with the Commissioners or, for that matter, with this tribunal'. *B Shokrollahi (t/a BS Mondial)*, MAN/94/526 (VTD 13781).

Import agent claiming bad debt relief

[35.16] See *Prestige Freight*, **4.24** BAD DEBT RELIEF.

Whether goods imported as agent or as principal

[35.17] A company resident outside the EU, which carried on a clothing business, appointed a woman resident in the UK (W) as a representative. She took orders for the company's clothing from UK retailers, and faxed these to the company. In many cases, the retailers were treated as the importers of the clothing. However, in some cases the retailers refused to be treated as the importers, and W was treated as the importer. She was registered for VAT and accounted for the tax due on importation. She reclaimed this as input tax. The amount was initially repaid to her, but the Commissioners subsequently formed the opinion that W was acting as an agent and that the repayment had been made in error, and issued an assessment to recover the tax. W appealed, contending that she had been acting as an independent principal and was entitled to credit for the input tax. The tribunal dismissed her appeal, holding on the evidence that she had been acting as an agent and was not entitled to credit for the input tax. *Angela Walker*, LON/92/1339A (VTD 12421).

VATA 1994, s 15(1)(c)—whether goods located in UK

[35.18] A company (P) despatched two consignments of cigarettes, originating in the USA, from the UK to Spain, under the Community transit procedure laid down by *Commission Regulation 2454/93*. The cigarettes did not arrive at their destination. The Commissioners issued a ruling that P had imported the cigarettes into the UK, so that VAT was chargeable on them. The tribunal allowed P's appeal, holding that the conditions of *VATA 1994, s 15(1)(c)* were not satisfied, since the Commissioners had not shown that the goods were located in the UK at the time when the Community customs debt was incurred. The Ch D upheld this decision. *PSL Freight Ltd v C & E Commrs*, Ch D [2001] BTC 5437. (*Note.* The Ch D also allowed P's appeal against a charge to customs duty.)

VATA 1994, s 15(1)(c)—goods imported from USA via Germany

[35.19] A woman (S) ordered some items via the internet, as presents for her daughter. She was charged VAT when the packages were delivered. She claimed repayment of the VAT. HMRC rejected the claim on the basis that the packages had been imported from the USA. She appealed, contending that she had received the goods from Germany, so that she should not have to pay VAT. The tribunal dismissed the appeal, finding on the evidence that the packages had been despatched from the US to Germany and had 'first arrived in the EU in Germany when they were taken into Customs control and whence they were sent to the UK'. The effect of *VATA 1994, s 15(1)(c)* was that 'any customs debt would be incurred on the goods in the packages when released into free circulation in the UK'. Accordingly the goods were to be treated as imported for the purposes of *VATA 1994, s 1*, and VAT had been correctly charged. *Mrs S Sheftz v HMRC*, [2009] UKFTT 316 (TC), TC00260.

Value of imported goods (VATA 1994, s 21)

Claim that original valuation excessive

[35.20] An individual (M) purchased a quantity of gemstones from a Canadian company for £52,318. He paid VAT of £8,879 in accordance with *VATA 1994, s 1*. Subsequently he formed the opinion that the gemstones were only worth about £11,000. He submitted a claim for part of the VAT which he had paid on their importation to be refunded to him. The Commissioners rejected the claim and he appealed. The tribunal dismissed his appeal, holding that the original valuation had been in accordance with *VATA 1994, s 21*, which required the gemstones to be valued for VAT purposes at the amount which M had actually paid to the vendors. *AJ Maden*, [1996] VATDR 449 (VTD 14603).

VATA 1994, s 21(5)—definition of 'collector's piece'

[35.21] In a customs duty case, an individual imported a Rolex watch which had been manufactured in 1945. He claimed that this was a 'collector's piece' within *VATA 1994, s 21(5)*, so that VAT was only due on 28.58% of its true value (so that the effective rate of VAT was 5%). The Commissioners rejected his claim and the tribunal dismissed his appeal, holding that the watch was 'not of historical interest' and was therefore not within the definition of a 'collector's piece'. *RJ Caddey*, LON/01/7061 (C154).

[35.22] See also *Pressland*, **60.10** SECOND-HAND GOODS.

Miscellaneous

Import of car—conditions of SI 1992/3193

[35.23] An individual (P) moved to Jersey in May 1997. In June 1998, while resident in Jersey, he purchased a Mitsubishi car. In October 1998 he returned to the UK and imported the car. The Commissioners issued a ruling that VAT was chargeable on the value of the car. P appealed. The tribunal dismissed his appeal, observing that although *Customs & Excise Duties (Personal Reliefs for Goods Permanently Imported) Order 1992 (SI 1992/3193)* provided for

VAT not to be chargeable on property imported by someone transferring his 'normal residence' into the UK, *article 11(1)(c)* laid down the condition that the property had been in his possession 'for a period of at least six months before its importation'. P had owned the car for less than six months before moving to the UK, so the effect of *article 11(1)(c)* was that no relief was due. (The tribunal also observed that it had no jurisdiction to consider the Commissioners' refusal to apply Extra-Statutory Concession 5.6—see **2.92** APPEALS.) *GP Powell*, MAN/00/134 (VTD 17380).

Supplies of contact lenses

[35.24] A group of companies (D) carried on business in the UK as opticians. One company in the group (J) was incorporated in Jersey (which is not part of the EC for VAT purposes). From July 1999 to June 2001 D arranged for contact lenses, prescribed to UK customers, to be supplied by J. Customs issued a ruling that J was making single supplies of goods, and that D was required to account for UK VAT. D appealed, contending that J was making separate supplies of goods and services, that the supplies of goods were exempt from VAT because they were worth less than the £18 limit of *VAT (Imported Goods) Relief Order (SI 1984/746), Sch 2 Group 8 Item 8*, and that the UK companies in its group were acting as agents for J. The tribunal reviewed the evidence in detail and directed that the case should be referred to the CJEC, holding that 'Jersey's hybrid status within the Community raises the question of whether it is appropriate in the instant case to apply the principles laid down by the CJEC in the case of *Card Protection Plan Ltd*' (see **22.324** EUROPEAN COMMUNITY LAW). The CJEC rejected D's contentions, holding that *Article 29* of the *Community Customs Code* must be interpreted as meaning that 'payment for the supply of specified services, such as examination, consultation or aftercare required in connection with contact lenses, and for specified goods, consisting of those lenses, the cleaning solutions and the soaking cases, constitutes as a whole the "transaction value" within the meaning of *Article 29* of the *Customs Code* and is, therefore, dutiable.' Furthermore, the principles laid down in *Card Protection Plan Ltd* 'cannot be used directly to determine the elements of the transaction to be taken into account for the purposes of applying *Article 29* of the *Customs Code*'. *Dollond & Aitchison Ltd v C & E Commrs*, CJEC Case C-491/04; 23 February 2006 unreported.

[35.25] See also *Painter*, **33.77** HEALTH AND WELFARE.

VAT Regulations 1995, reg 121A—SIVA

[35.26] In October 2003 a company was granted authorisation to use the 'Simplified Import VAT Accounting Scheme', without providing security. Subsequently the company made two payments of VAT after the due date, and in July 2004 Customs revoked the authorisation. The tribunal reviewed the evidence in detail, observed that there had been a reasonable excuse for one of the late payments, and held that 'officers making decisions of this kind must look beyond the mere fact of a default, and decide whether that default, with any other material information, can properly lead to the conclusion that the trader's continuing use of a SIVA approval represents a risk to the revenue.

That was not done here.' The tribunal directed that Customs should carry out a further review of the decision to revoke the SIVA authorisation. *Martin Yaffe International Ltd*, [2005] VATDR 495 (C197).

[35.27] A company (N) had been granted authorisation to use the 'Simplified Import VAT Accounting Scheme'. However it exceeded the agreed limits for the scheme on six occasions between August 2006 and April 2007. Customs therefore withdrew their authorisation for N to use the scheme. N appealed. The tribunal reviewed the evidence in detail and dismissed the appeal, distinguishing the earlier decision in *Martin Yaffe International Ltd*, **35.26** above. The tribunal held that Customs had been entitled to conclude that N's business represented 'a risk to the revenue', since 'there was an insufficient guarantee to cover the liability'. *Newstar Jeans Co Ltd*, MAN/07/7042 (C264).

[35.28] A company applied for permission to use the 'Simplified Import VAT Accounting Scheme'. HMRC rejected the application on the grounds that the company's net assets were less than its average VAT liability, so that there was a risk that the VAT might not be paid if the company ceased to trade. The tribunal dismissed the company's appeal against this decision. *IC Blue Ltd*, FTT [2009] UKFTT 40 (TC); TC00018.

36

Input Tax

The cases in this chapter are arranged under the following headings.

Whether supplies made to the appellant

Motoring expenses	**36.1**
Accommodation	**36.14**
Associated companies	**36.18**
Leasing	**36.30**
Legal costs	**36.40**
Expenditure on premises	**36.66**
Circular transactions and 'carousel fraud'	**36.77**
Sham transactions	**36.123**
Miscellaneous	**36.128**

Whether supplies used for the purposes of the business

Luxuries, amusements and entertainments (*VATA 1994, s 84(4)*)	**36.169**
Motoring expenses	**36.173**
Clothing	**36.184**
Legal costs—civil cases	**36.193**
Legal costs—criminal cases	**36.230**
Renovation and acquisition of premises—sole traders	**36.243**
Renovation and acquisition of premises—partnerships	**36.277**
Expenses of employees or agents	**36.310**
Domestic accommodation for directors (*VATA 1994, s 24(3)*)	**36.330**
Horse racing	**36.341**
Show jumping and other equine activities	**36.385**
Powerboat racing	**36.403**
Motor racing and rallying	**36.410**
Yachting	**36.441**
Aircraft	**36.463**
Personalised vehicle numberplates	**36.468**
Associated companies	**36.491**
Promotion of tourism	**36.498**
Subpostmasters	**36.501**
Miscellaneous	**36.504**

Whether supplies intended for use in future business

Cases where the appellant was successful	**36.554**
Cases where the appellant was partly successful	**36.567**
Cases where the appellant was unsuccessful	**36.568**

Pre-registration input tax	**36.589**
Advance payments	**36.620**
Compensation and damages payments	**36.637**
Post-cessation input tax	**36.643**
Disputed repayment claims	**36.648**
Other matters	**36.662**

NOTE

For cases concerning the disallowance of input tax under *Input Tax Order 1992, Article 5*, see 8 BUSINESS ENTERTAINMENT. For cases concerning *Input Tax Order 1992, Article 6*, see 15 CONSTRUCTION OF BUILDINGS, ETC. For cases concerning *Input Tax Order 1992, Article 7*, see 44 MOTOR CARS. For cases concerning the evidence required to support a claim to input tax, see 40 INVOICES AND CREDIT NOTES.

Whether supplies made to the appellant

Motoring expenses

Whether petrol supplied to company or to agents

[36.1] A company which sold clothing appointed a number of self-employed agents on a commission basis. The agents had to undertake extensive travelling, for which they used their own cars. They were allowed to deduct the amounts spent on petrol from the amounts they collected for the company, on condition that they provided the company with invoices from the garages, made out in the company's name. The company reclaimed input tax on the amounts in question, and the Commissioners issued an assessment to recover the tax. The tribunal dismissed the company's appeal. On the evidence, the agents were independent contractors rather than employees. Accordingly, the petrol had been supplied to the agents rather than to the company, and the company was not entitled to reclaim the input tax. *Berbrooke Fashions*, [1977] VATTR 168 (VTD 426).

[36.2] The decision in *Berbrooke Fashions*, 36.1 above, was applied in the similar cases of *S & U Stores Ltd*, BIR/76/89 (VTD 726) and *Holywell International (Engineering) Ltd*, MAN/83/90 (VTD 1470).

[36.3] Similar decisions were reached in *James Trevor Ltd*, LON/83/5 (VTD 1425) and *Fairway Lubricants Ltd*, LON/83/161 (VTD 1577).

Whether petrol supplied to contractor or to subcontractors

[36.4] A partnership which operated a dairy business sold milk to the public by means of regular deliveries from vans to householders. It engaged van drivers as self-employed subcontractors with contractual responsibilities to deliver regular orders to customers, collect the sums owing and pay them to the partnership. The partnership gave the van drivers money to pay for their petrol, which was to be purchased from one of a selected number of garages. The partnership reclaimed input tax in respect of the fuel purchased by the van drivers, and the Commissioners issued an assessment to recover the tax. The tribunal dismissed the partnership's appeal, holding that the petrol was supplied to the van drivers rather than to the partnership, so that the partnership was not entitled to credit for the input tax. *R Wiseman & Sons*, [1984] VATTR 168 (VTD 1691).

[36.5] A similar decision, applying *Berbrooke Fashions Ltd*, **36.1** above, was reached in *BC Allum*, LON/93/1452A (VTD 12646).

Mileage allowances to employees

[36.6] A company which retailed clothing employed 175 salesmen. It agreed with their trade union that each of them should receive a weekly allowance to cover the cost of six gallons of petrol. No record was kept of the employees' actual mileage. The company reclaimed input tax in respect of these payments and the Commissioners issued an assessment to recover the tax. The tribunal dismissed the company's appeal, accepting evidence that the allowance covered only part of the actual expenditure, but holding that the petrol had been supplied to the employees as individuals rather than to the company, so that the company could not reclaim input tax. *Stirlings (Glasgow) Ltd*, [1982] VATTR 116 (VTD 1232). (*Note.* For the treatment of 'mileage allowances', see now *Notice 700/64/07, para 8.7.*)

[36.7] A company provided senior employees with cars. The employees were allowed to use the cars privately, and were responsible for buying petrol. They were paid a mileage allowance calculated according to a fixed formula per mile travelled from the managers' homes to sites and back, with a reduction of twelve miles per day to represent private mileage. The company reclaimed input tax on the mileage allowances. The Commissioners issued an assessment to recover the tax claimed in respect of the journeys between the employees' homes and the sites at which they worked. The tribunal dismissed the company's appeal, holding that the supplies of petrol were made to the employees and not to the company. (However, the tribunal observed that if the petrol were to be treated as being supplied to the company, input tax would be reclaimable in respect of the whole of the mileage allowances paid, since they were paid for the purpose of the company's business. Because the managers had no normal workplace, the journeys from their homes to the sites were for business purposes. It also followed that, if the petrol were to be treated as being supplied to the company, it could not be expected to account for output tax in respect of either the petrol itself or the mileage allowances, since there would be neither any transfer of the petrol nor any private use of it.) *McLean Homes Midland Ltd*, MAN/89/363 (VTD 5010). (*Notes.* (1) Following this decision, the assessment under appeal was reduced from £20,819 to £7,566 by agreement. For a subsequent application for costs, see **2.406** APPEALS. (2) See also the note following *Stirlings (Glasgow) Ltd*, **36.6** above.)

[36.8] The decision in *McLean Homes Midland Ltd*, **36.7** above, was applied in a subsequent case where the tribunal held that petrol had been supplied to the employees of a company rather than to the company itself, and that the company was therefore not entitled to reclaim any input tax in respect of the petrol in question. *Klockner Ferromatik Desma Ltd*, MAN/90/144 (VTD 7061). (*Note.* See the note following *Stirlings (Glasgow) Ltd*, **36.6** above.)

City Council—mileage allowances to employees

[36.9] See *Leicester City Council*, **42.23** LOCAL AUTHORITIES AND STATUTORY BODIES.

Mileage allowances paid to self-employed care workers

[36.10] A married couple operated a business, registered as an employment agency, providing care services to local authorities and private individuals. They paid mileage allowances to the care workers, and reclaimed input tax on the allowances. The Commissioners rejected the claim on the basis that the couple were acting as agents for the care workers, rather than as an independent principal, that the care workers were self-employed, and that the payment of their travelling expenses was the responsibility of the clients. The husband appealed, contending that the care workers should be treated as employees and that the couple were acting as an independent principal. The tribunal rejected this contention and dismissed the appeal, holding that the couple were 'acting merely as agent for the care workers'. (The tribunal observed that, if the care workers had been employees, the couple would have been obliged to account for output tax on the full amount which they charged to the clients, rather than only on their commission.) *AJ Wood*, LON/01/177 (VTD 17518).

Input tax reclaimed on car leased on behalf of associated company

[36.11] A company (W) leased a car for the benefit of an associated company (J). W paid the first five instalments and was reimbursed by J, which paid the next nine instalments. The lease was then reassigned to J, which reclaimed input tax in respect of the fourteen instalments which had been paid while the car was leased to W. The Commissioners disallowed the claim since the supply had been made to W rather than to J. The tribunal upheld the Commissioners' decision and dismissed J's appeal. *Johanson Ltd*, MAN/84/200 (VTD 1730).

Input tax reclaimed on termination of lease of car

[36.12] A company (T) leased a car from a finance company (M). Under the leasing agreement, which was to last for three years, the car remained the property of M. T subsequently decided to end the lease after only one year, and in accordance with the terms of the agreement, M required payment of £10,726 plus VAT of £1,609, totalling £12,335. T ascertained from a car dealer (S) that the car was only worth £10,000, and arranged that S should purchase the car from M for a nominal price of £12,335, of which £2,335 would be reimbursed to S by T. T then reclaimed the VAT of £1,609 as input tax and appealed against the Commissioners' rejection of the claim. The tribunal dismissed T's appeal. The car had been sold to S rather than to T, and since the car had not been supplied to T, T was not entitled to reclaim the input tax. *Telequick Ltd*, MAN/90/318 (VTD 5319).

Land Rover purchased by employee—tax reclaimed by employer

[36.13] A foreman employed by a construction company purchased a Land Rover. The company reclaimed input tax on the purchase and the Commissioners issued an assessment to recover the tax. The tribunal dismissed the company's appeal, holding that as the supply was made to the employee rather than to the company, the company was not entitled to reclaim input tax. *Binof Construction Ltd*, MAN/90/105 (VTD 5113).

Accommodation

Accommodation supplied to employees of company installing machinery

[36.14] A company (B) contracted with a Dutch company to purchase a brickmaking machine. It was agreed that the machine would be installed by engineers employed by the Dutch company, and that B would arrange and pay for the engineers' board and accommodation. B reclaimed the input tax on the supplies of accommodation, and the Commissioners issued an assessment to recover the tax, considering that the accommodation had been supplied to the engineers rather than to B. The tribunal dismissed B's appeal, holding that the accommodation had been supplied to B by the hotel and by B to the engineers, so that although B was entitled to credit for input tax on the accommodation supplied by the hotel, it was liable to account for a corresponding amount of output tax on the supply by it to the engineers. *Ibstock Building Products Ltd*, [1987] VATTR 1 (VTD 2304). (*Note.* For a case in which this decision was distinguished with regard to output tax, see *Stormseal (UPVC) Window Co Ltd*, **62.286** SUPPLY.)

Accommodation supplied for lecturers at conferences

[36.15] An institute which organised conferences provided overnight accommodation, in the hotels where the conferences were held, for any lecturer who required it. The institute reclaimed input tax on the accommodation and the Commissioners issued an assessment to recover the tax, against which the institute appealed. The tribunal dismissed the appeal, holding that the accommodation was supplied by the hotel directly to the lecturers rather than to the institute. (Input tax was also disallowed on refreshments supplied to the lecturers on the grounds that they were business entertainment.) *Institute of Purchasing & Supply*, [1987] VATTR 207 (VTD 2533).

Accommodation provided for tennis players by club

[36.16] A tennis club organised an annual tournament and provided bed and breakfast accommodation at a hotel for the top eight seeded players in the men's and ladies' singles. The accommodation was booked by the club, but the hotel made the bills out to the players, who paid the bills and presented them to the club for reimbursement. The club reclaimed input tax on the basis that the hotel had supplied the accommodation to it. The Commissioners issued an assessment to recover the tax, contending that the hotels made the supplies directly to the players rather than to the club. The club appealed. The tribunal held that the hotel supplied the accommodation to the club rather than to the players, applying *Ibstock Building Products Ltd*, **36.14** above, and distinguishing *Institute of Purchasing & Supply*, **36.15** above. The fact that the bills were made out to the players, rather than to the club, was a matter of administrative convenience only, and did not affect the legal nature of the supplies. An alternative contention by the Commissioners, that the rooms were provided for the purpose of business entertainment, was also rejected by the tribunal. The essence of entertainment was that it was provided free to the recipient, applying *Celtic Football & Athletic Club*, **8.35** BUSINESS ENTERTAINMENT. However, the tribunal upheld a third contention for the Commissioners, that having received supplies from the hotel the club had made those supplies to the players, and thus, although the club could reclaim the input tax on the supplies by the hotel, it had to account for a corresponding amount of output tax on the supplies deemed to have been made by it to the players. *Northern Lawn Tennis Club*, [1989] VATTR 1 (VTD 3528).

Employer reimbursing accommodation for employees

[36.17] An insurance company (which was partly exempt) required some of its employees to travel on business. The employees sometimes had to reserve and pay for overnight hotel accommodation. The company reimbursed them for this, and reclaimed input tax. The Commissioners rejected the claim and the tribunal dismissed the company's appeal. The tribunal held that, where the accommodation in question was reserved by the company, it was supplied to the company and the input tax formed part of the company's residual input tax, to be apportioned between taxable and exempt supplies. However, where the accommodation was reserved by the employees, it was supplied by the hotels to the employees and the company was not entitled to reclaim input tax. Furthermore, the company was not itself making any supplies of accommodation to the employees. *Co-Operative Insurance Society Ltd*, [1997] VATDR 65 (VTD 14862). (*Note*. For the Commissioners' practice following this decision, see Business Brief 16/97, issued on 21 July 1997.)

Associated companies

Partnership reclaiming input tax relating to associated company

[36.18] A married couple traded in partnership as producers of slides and computer graphics. The husband (L) was also one of two directors of a company which traded from the same premises. The partnership had invested approximately £60,000 in the company. However, a serious dispute arose between L and his co-director, as a result of which L instructed solicitors to apply for an order appointing a receiver for the company. An accountant agreed to act as receiver on condition that L indemnified him for any costs incurred as receiver which the company was unable to meet. L accepted this condition, and the accountant was duly appointed as receiver of the company. He discovered that L's co-director had been acting fraudulently and had used the company's funds for his personal purposes. The receiver invoiced the company for his professional fees, which the partnership paid in accordance with the indemnity agreement which L had previously entered into. The partnership reclaimed input tax in respect of the amounts paid. The Commissioners issued an assessment to recover the tax, considering that the relevant services had been supplied to the company rather than to the partnership. The tribunal dismissed the partnership's appeal, holding that the receiver's services had not been supplied to the partnership, so that the partnership was not entitled to reclaim the relevant input tax. *M & RJ Lister*, LON/92/1336 (VTD 9972).

Input tax reclaimed on supplies to associated company

[36.19] A company (S) purchased some tooling equipment, on which it reclaimed input tax. It subsequently suffered financial difficulties, transferred its business as a going concern to an associated company (R) and went into liquidation. R's controlling director persuaded the companies which had supplied S with the tooling equipment to issue credit notes to S and to issue fresh invoices to R. R then reclaimed input tax. When the Commissioners discovered what had happened, they issued an assessment to recover the tax. The tribunal dismissed R's appeal, holding that the relevant supplies had been made to S rather than to R, that the credit notes were ineffective and that the replacement invoices were false. *Realm Defence Industries Ltd*, LON/98/799 (VTD 16831). (*Note.* The tribunal awarded costs of £2,000 to the Commissioners.)

[36.20] A company (W) suffered financial difficulties and became insolvent, owing money to its internet service provider (U). An associated company (C) wished to use the software formerly used by W, and paid some of the amounts which W owed to U. C reclaimed input tax on these payments. The Commissioners rejected the claim on the basis that the payments related to supplies made to W, rather than to C, and that C had not produced any invoices in support of the claim. The tribunal upheld the Commissioners' ruling and dismissed C's appeal. *ASR Consultants Ltd*, MAN/03/034 (VTD 18600).

[36.21] A manufacturing company (J) reclaimed input tax on various supplies of materials. It subsequently went into voluntary liquidation. Its parent company (S) submitted a voluntary disclosure, claiming that it was entitled to credit for the input tax because the supplies had been made to it rather than to J. Customs rejected the claim and the tribunal dismissed S's appeal, holding on the evidence that the supplies had been made to J and that S was not entitled to credit for the input tax. *Selbix Ltd*, LON/06/1120 (VTD 20473).

[36.22] A company (R) acted as an agent for an associated company (S), which was registered in the Turks & Caicos Islands and was not registered for VAT in the UK. R reclaimed input tax on several invoices relating to a property in London which was owned by S. Customs rejected the claims on the grounds that the relevant supplies had actually been made to S rather than to R. The tribunal reviewed the evidence in detail and dismissed R's appeal, finding that 'in substance and reality the appellant was interposed to make contracts with third party suppliers as agent for (S)'. *Rental Concepts Ltd*, LON/06/1562 (VTD 20692).

[36.23] See also *Collins*, 40.25 INVOICES AND CREDIT NOTES; *Tortoise Factory Units Ltd*, 40.26 INVOICES AND CREDIT NOTES, and *Gavacan*, 40.26 INVOICES AND CREDIT NOTES.

Whether supplies made to appellant company or to shareholders

[36.24] A petroleum company (S) reclaimed input tax on substantial items of expenditure which it described as 'investor relations expenses'. Customs rejected the claim on the basis that the supplies had actually been made to, or for the benefit of, the associated companies which held a controlling shareholding in S. The tribunal reviewed the evidence in detail and allowed S's appeal in part, holding that most of the supplies had been made to S but that some of the supplies had been made to one of its shareholders. The tribunal also held that although most of the supplies had been received for the purposes of S's business, some of the services had been 'principally directed simply to securing compliance by (the shareholding companies) with their obligations'. Furthermore, some of the services had been incurred for the benefit of companies which were not members of S's VAT group. Accordingly the tribunal directed that the tax should be apportioned. *Shell International Petroleum Co Ltd*, [2005] VATDR 503 (VTD 19345).

Purported supply between associated companies

[36.25] A company (C) was in financial difficulties. Its controlling director had incorporated a further company (M). He arranged for C to issue M with an invoice charging £298,500 plus VAT in respect of his services. M reclaimed input tax (of more than £52,000) in respect of this invoice. C did not account for the output tax, and was subsequently dissolved. The Commissioners rejected M's claim for repayment of the input tax, and the tribunal dismissed M's appeal, observing that the director had not shown that the invoice 'related to any supply of services from C to M for a consideration of £298,500 or any other agreed consideration', and that the director's evidence as to the reasons for the invoice showed a 'lack of credibility'. *Morston Properties Ltd (No 2)*, LON/97/1107 (VTD 15444).

[36.26] The appellant company (M) in the case noted at **36.25** above issued seven invoices to another company (U) incorporated by its controlling director, purporting to charge VAT of more than £69,000. Most of this related to the director's services, while some related to the sale of assets. U reclaimed this amount as input tax, while M ceased trading, owing more than £54,000 in unpaid VAT. The Commissioners rejected U's repayment claim, and the tribunal dismissed U's appeal. With regard to the purported transfers of assets, the tribunal found that, in the case of the majority of the items, there was no evidence of any actual supply. In the case of the three remaining items (a printer, some printer toner and some bookmarks) the purported transfer was at a price at least 50% more than M had been charged for them. The tribunal observed that 'since each of those three items was an everyday item whose second-hand value must have been less than its original value, we are unable to accept that the supplies were genuine taxable supplies to (U)'. With regard to the invoice in respect of the director's purported services, the tribunal was 'unable to accept that the single invoice raised by (M) represented genuine supplies of services' and found that M 'did not make a genuine taxable supply of services to (U)'. *United Society of Poets Ltd*, LON/98/182 (VTD 15772). (*Note.* The tribunal awarded costs of £500 to the Commissioners, finding that the appeal was 'frivolous in nature'.)

[36.27] A company (K) was in financial difficulties. It invoiced an associated company (L) for goods which it had sold to third parties. L reclaimed input tax in respect of these invoices, although K did not account for output tax (and subsequently went into voluntary liquidation). When the Commissioners discovered what had happened, they issued an assessment to recover the tax which L had reclaimed. The tribunal upheld the assessment and dismissed L's appeal, holding on the evidence that K had made no supplies to L, so that L was unable to reclaim the input tax shown on the invoices. *Lady Di (London) Ltd*, LON/00/1217 (VTD 17618).

[36.28] In a case where the facts were complex, an engineer (L), and three companies with which he was associated, reclaimed input tax in respect of purported transactions between themselves, and alleged purchases from an associated Isle of Man company which was not registered for VAT. HMRC rejected the claims on the basis that 'there were no genuine trades' but 'merely the creation of invoices within the group of businesses all of which were controlled by (L)'. L and the companies appealed. The tribunal reviewed the evidence in detail and dismissed the appeals, observing inter alia that the way in which the companies' shareholdings had been structured contravened *Companies Act 2006, s 136*, and finding that there was no 'evidence of any genuine trading transactions with anyone other than other entities in the business structure through which (L) conducts his business affairs'. *APS-Centriline Ltd v HMRC (and related appeals)*, [2009] UKFTT 149 (TC), TC00117.

Purported transfer of goods from company to associated partnership

[36.29] A company (K) was in financial difficulties, and the Commissioners began distraint proceedings against it. Bailiffs visited K's premises in May 1995, and sought to distrain on five motor vehicles and five items of plant and machinery. K's directors produced an invoice purporting to show that the assets in question had been sold two months earlier to an associated partnership comprising K's controlling shareholders. The Commissioners did not accept the validity of the sale, but did not execute the distraint. Although the invoice produced by K's directors indicated that it had charged VAT of £13,000 on the sale of the goods in question to the partnership, K did not pay this to the Commissioners as output tax. Subsequently an associated company (L) reclaimed the amount in question as input tax in its return for the period ending October 1996. The Commissioners rejected the claim and L appealed, contending that it had purchased the goods in question from the partnership on 25 October 1996, for the same price as the partnership had paid to K. (K had ceased trading in November 1996 and went into voluntary liquidation.) The tribunal dismissed L's appeal, holding on the evidence that it was not satisfied that 'any sale of the assets ever took place'. There was 'no dispute that no cash or cheque for the purchase price and VAT was ever paid by (L) to the partnership on 25 October 1996 and it is clear that no such payment has ever been made subsequently. The VAT returns of the partnership for the period ending 31 May 1996 to 28 February 1997 show that the partnership was not trading during these periods and no input or output tax nor supplies are recorded.' On the evidence, 'there was never any intention that (L) should pay any money to the partnership for the assets and no payment has been made'. The entries in L's books were 'paper entries' and did not 'evidence or record a genuine sale of the assets.' *LMB Holdings Ltd*, MAN/97/382 (VTD 15739). (*Note.* Costs were awarded to the Commissioners.)

Leasing

Cases where the appellant was successful

Whether lease supplied to solicitors' partnership or to company

[36.30] A firm of solicitors, with a view to future expansion, leased premises which were larger than they required, and sublet part of the premises. They incorporated a company for the purpose of holding the lease and assigning the subleases. They reclaimed input tax in respect of their expenditure on the lease. The Commissioners issued an assessment to recover the tax, on the basis that the relevant supply had been made to the company rather than to the partnership. The tribunal allowed the partnership's appeal, holding that in substance the supply had been made to the partnership for the purpose of the partnership's business. *Bird Semple & Crawford Herron*, [1986] VATTR 218 (VTD 2171).

[36.31] A similar decision was reached in *Lester Aldridge*, [2004] VATDR 292 (VTD 18864).

Supplies under finance lease

[36.32] A company (C) supplied reprographic and office equipment. Many of its customers used finance leases to finance their purchases. In some cases, the equipment which C supplied became obsolescent before the end of the term of the lease. In four cases, C made payments to the leasing company to arrange the early termination of the leases. The leasing companies issued invoices to C, which reclaimed input tax on the payments. HMRC rejected the claims on the basis that the supplies had actually been made to the customer which had entered into the finance leases, rather than to C. C appealed. The tribunal allowed the appeal, holding that in making the payments C was 'discharging its own liability, being a liability assumed in the course of its business of making taxable supplies of equipment'. *Canotec Ltd v HMRC*, [2011] UKFTT 661 (TC), TC01503.

Cases where the appellant was unsuccessful

Whether supplies made to landlord or to leaseholder

[36.33] A company agreed to purchase the premises which it occupied, but was unable to proceed with the purchase for financial reasons. The landlords agreed to release the company from the contract on condition that the company paid the landlords' costs. The landlords were not registered for VAT, and the company reclaimed the input tax on the costs. The Commissioners rejected the claim and the tribunal dismissed the company's appeal, holding that the legal services had been supplied to the landlords and not to the company. *WJ Brown Toys Ltd*, MAN/83/333 (VTD 1684).

[36.34] A photographer reclaimed input tax in respect of repairs and improvements to premises which he occupied. The Commissioners issued an assessment to recover the tax, considering that the supplies in question had been made to the landlord of the premises rather than to the photographer. The tribunal upheld the assessment and dismissed the photographer's appeal. *LA Barnett*, LON/88/753 (VTD 3245).

[36.35] A company which held a tenancy of part of a building also acted as the managing agent of that building. It reclaimed input tax on expenditure relating to the management of the building. The Commissioners issued an assessment to recover the tax, on the basis that the relevant supplies had been made to the landlord, rather than to the company. The tribunal upheld the assessment and dismissed the company's appeal. *WS Atkins (Services) Ltd*, LON/92/1872 (VTD 10131).

Payments made by guarantor of leases following default by tenant

[36.36] In 1986 a company (V) acquired a subsidiary (G). G acquired a number of leasehold properties. The landlords required V to guarantee that G would meet its obligations with regard to the leases. In 1988 V sold its shareholding in G to an unrelated company (C), but V continued to be bound by its guarantees. In 1991 C went into receivership. The landlords claimed substantial sums from V under the guarantees. In cases where the landlords had waived exemption under the leases, the claims included VAT. V reclaimed input tax in respect of its payments to the landlords. The Commissioners rejected the claim, on the grounds that the payments were not consideration for any supplies made to V. The tribunal dismissed V's appeal, holding that the landlords had made supplies to G rather than to V. Although V had paid consideration in respect of these supplies, it was not the recipient of the supplies and was therefore not entitled to reclaim input tax. *Vivat Holdings plc*, [1995] VATDR 348 (VTD 13568).

[36.37] A similar decision was reached in a case where an accountant had been a shareholder in a company which occupied rented premises, and had issued a guarantee to the landlord in respect of the rent. The company failed to pay the rent, and the accountant was called upon to pay the unpaid rent in accordance with the guarantee. The tribunal held that the accountant was not entitled to reclaim input tax on the payment. *F Cable*, EDN/94/269 (VTD 13845).

[36.38] A similar decision was reached in a case where a company (K) had accepted the assignment of a lease under conditions whereby it indemnified the assignor against default. Nine months later K assigned the lease to an unrelated company (F) which subsequently defaulted and went into liquidation. The lessor demanded and obtained payment of arrears of rent from the company (T) which had acted as surety under the original underlease, and T in turn demanded payment from K. K appealed to the tribunal, contending that the original lessee was entitled to credit for input tax on the payment which T had made to the lessor (so that its liability under the indemnity agreement would be reduced accordingly). The tribunal dismissed the appeal, holding that the relevant supplies were made to F, rather than to the original lessee, which was not entitled to input tax thereon. The chairman observed that it was a 'basic principle that it is the recipient of the supply who obtains the credit regardless of whether it is he who provides the consideration'. *Kenwood Appliances Ltd*, [1996] VATDR 127 (VTD 13876). (*Note.* The Commissioners accepted that K had sufficient *locus standi* to lodge an appeal. Compare the cases at **2.52** to **2.57** APPEALS.)

Whether sunbeds supplied by vendor to leasing company or to lessee

[36.39] A company (T) sold sunbeds. In cases where customers wished to acquire sunbeds under a leasing agreement, rather than by outright purchase, it delivered the sunbed to the customer but transferred the ownership of the sunbed to a leasing company. In such cases it paid the initial amount of rent due by the customer to the leasing company under the leasing agreement, and reclaimed input tax in respect of such payments. The Commissioners issued an assessment to recover this tax, considering that the effect of the agreement was that T sold the sunbed to the leasing company rather than to the ultimate customer, but that in paying the initial rent it was paying a liability of the customer, and that since it had made no supply to the customer, it was not entitled to reclaim input tax in respect of its payment of the customer's initial rental liability. The tribunal upheld the assessment and dismissed T's appeal. *Tantol Ltd*, MAN/91/430 (VTD 10013).

Legal costs

Cases where the appellant was successful

Legal services supplied to farming partnership

[36.40] Two brothers who were in partnership as farmers held the tenancy of their farm jointly with their father. The father took no part in the partnership's farming activities. The partners and their father purchased the freehold of the farm. They subsequently sold this farm and purchased another farm. The partners reclaimed input tax in respect of services supplied to them by two firms of land agents and a firm of solicitors in connection with these transactions. The Commissioners issued an assessment to recover the tax, considering that as the partners had owned the farms jointly with their father who was not a partner, the services were not strictly attributable to the partnership. The tribunal allowed the brother's appeal, finding that the VAT officer who had raised the assessment had acted under a misapprehension, and holding that each of the supplies was a supply to the taxable persons, the two brothers, even though the supplies were also made to their father. *Article 17(2)(a)* of the *EC Sixth Directive* made it clear that the important requirement was that the supply in question was used for the purposes of the taxable transactions of the taxable person. *Glasse Brothers*, [1989] VATTR 143 (VTD 3716).

Parent company requiring solicitors to investigate affairs of subsidiary

[36.41] A company (C), which was registered for VAT, had a subsidiary company (L), which was not registered. C's directors became concerned about the way in which one of L's directors was acting, and engaged a firm of solicitors to undertake a confidential investigation of L's affairs. C reclaimed the input tax in respect of the solicitors' services, although the relevant invoice had been made out to L rather than to C. The Commissioners issued an assessment to recover the tax, considering that the services in question had actually been supplied to L, and that since L was not registered for VAT, the tax was not reclaimable. The tribunal allowed C's appeal against the assessment, finding that the invoice had been made out in L's name in error and holding that the services had actually been supplied to C and had been supplied for the protection of C's business. *Crompton Enterprises Ltd*, [1992] VATTR 321 (VTD 7866).

Cases where the appellant was partly successful

Legal costs of sale of hotel equipment

[36.42] A farmer (J) also operated a hotel, which he leased from a company. He had a 25% shareholding in the company, and was one of the three directors. The hotel was sold in 1988. J reclaimed input tax on legal costs incurred in connection with the sale of the hotel. The Commissioners issued an assessment to recover the tax, considering that, since the hotel was owned by the company rather than by J, the legal costs had not been incurred in connection with J's business. J appealed, contending that he should be entitled to reclaim input tax since he had been treated as carrying on the business of the hotel and had accounted for tax accordingly, and that the hotel equipment and a staff bungalow in the hotel grounds were owned by him personally rather than by the company. The tribunal allowed J's appeal in part, holding that the legal costs incurred in connection with the sale of the hotel freehold were incurred by the company but that the legal costs incurred in connection with the sale of the hotel equipment and the staff bungalow were incurred by J himself for the purpose of a business which he had operated. The tribunal apportioned the total input tax shown on the relevant invoices and directed that 27.8% of the total input tax should be treated as allowable. *RJ Jones*, LON/89/1302Y (VTD 5701).

Cases where the appellant was unsuccessful

Employee prosecuted for causing death by dangerous driving

[36.43] A family company (J) employed D, the son of its managing director, and provided him with a car. J paid for the insurance for the car, for both business and private use. In February 2002 D consumed a quantity of alcohol before driving the car home. He collided with another car. The driver of that car, and a passenger in D's car, were killed. D was charged with two counts of causing death by dangerous driving. He pleaded guilty, and was sentenced to four year's imprisonment. The insurance company arranged for D's defence, and paid the solicitors their fees net of VAT. J paid the VAT, and reclaimed it as input tax. Customs rejected the claim on the basis that the solicitors' services had not been supplied to J. The Ch D upheld Customs' ruling. Lindsay J held that the solicitors had supplied their services to the insurance company, rather than to J. *HMRC v Jeancharm Ltd (t/a Beaver International)*, Ch D [2005] STC 918; [2005] EWHC 839(Ch).

Legal costs relating to breach of covenant

[36.44] A husband and wife carried on business in partnership. They acquired the lease of a commercial building. In 1982 the freeholders of the property took them to Court for breach of their repairing covenants under the lease. The couple lost the action and were ordered to pay costs to the freeholders. They reclaimed input tax on the costs and the Commissioners issued an assessment to recover the tax. The tribunal dismissed the couple's appeal, finding that the costs were in respect of supplies of legal services made to the freeholders, and holding that the lessees were not entitled to reclaim the input tax thereon. *JG & MV Potton*, LON/87/592 (VTD 2882).

Unsuccessful legal action

[36.45] A trader (T) who carried on business as a market gardener had previously been director of a company which was in liquidation. He began legal actions against the liquidator of the company and against a firm of solicitors. His actions were dismissed by the High Court which ordered him to pay the defendants' costs. He reclaimed the VAT on the costs as input tax and the Commissioners issued an assessment to recover the tax. The tribunal dismissed his appeal, holding that the relevant supplies had been made to the defendants, rather than to T, so that the input tax was not deductible. The QB upheld this decision. *NO Turner (t/a Turner Agricultural) v C & E Commrs*, QB [1992] STC 621. (*Note.* For another issue in this case, see **36.534** below.)

[36.46] The decision in *Turner*, **36.45** above, was applied in the similar subsequent cases of *KC & HM Barnes (t/a Sidlesham Common Carriage Company)*, LON/95/2983A (VTD 14090); *M Olivant*, MAN/97/344 (VTD 15422); *Dow-Nell Construction Co Ltd*, LON/99/1336 (VTD 16871); *DJ Jones*, LON/02/775 (VTD 19570), and *Iliffe*, **36.308** below.

[36.47] A firm of architects took legal action against a client. The client won the case and the firm was ordered to pay his costs, totalling more than £60,000. The firm reclaimed input tax on these costs. The Commissioners rejected the claim, as the legal services in question had been supplied to the successful client rather than to the firm. The tribunal dismissed the firm's appeal against this decision, applying *Francis Jackson Homes Ltd*, **36.52** below. *Nye Saunders & Partners*, LON/93/1318A (VTD 11384).

[36.48] The decision in *Nye Saunders & Partners*, **36.47** above, was applied in the similar subsequent case of *R Carr*, MAN/97/327 (VTD 15411).

[36.49] Similar decisions were reached in *EG Davey (t/a EG Davey & Co)*, LON/95/527A (VTD 13538) and *K Tulsidas & MK Bhatt (t/a Amazon International)*, MAN/98/770 (VTD 16335).

[36.50] A trader failed to pay a bill of £1,300 from her solicitors. The solicitors took legal action against her, and she was ordered to pay the fees and the legal costs. She appealed, but subsequently withdrew her appeal and agreed to pay the solicitors £23,000 in full settlement. She reclaimed input tax on this payment. The Commissioners rejected the claim and she appealed. The tribunal dismissed her appeal, applying *Turner*, **36.45** above. *AC Slot*, LON/94/1089 (VTD 15076). (*Note.* For another issue in this case, see **41.144** LAND.)

Legal fees relating to transfer of share capital

[36.51] A company (B) wished to acquire the share capital of another company (G). G's owners insisted that B should pay all legal fees relating to the transaction. B reclaimed input tax on the vendors' legal fees and the Commissioners issued an assessment to recover the tax. The tribunal dismissed B's appeal, holding that the solicitors had supplied their services to the vendors of G's shares, rather than to G or B. *Brucegate Ltd*, MAN/89/761(VTD 4903).

Solicitors' fees on sale of land

[36.52] A company purchased some land for development, and agreed to pay the solicitors' fees incurred by the vendors. It reclaimed the input tax on these fees, and the Commissioners issued an assessment to recover the tax, since the solicitors had supplied their services to the vendors rather than to the company. The tribunal upheld the assessment and dismissed the company's appeal. *Francis Jackson Homes Ltd*, LON/90/1228Z (VTD 6352).

Legal costs relating to abortive purchase of premises

[36.53] See *WJ Brown Toys Ltd*, 36.33 above.

Legal costs—whether supplied to partnership or to individual partner

[36.54] A partnership was dissolved in 1986 and one of the partners continued in business as a sole trader. He incurred legal and accountancy fees in the course of a dispute with his former partner, and reclaimed the VAT on the fees as input tax. The Commissioners issued an assessment to recover the tax and he appealed, contending that the expenditure had been incurred to protect his business reputation. The tribunal dismissed his appeal, holding that the expenditure was incurred in the course of the partnership business and that the partnership was a separate entity from the appellant's own business. *GG Ingram (t/a Ingram & Co)*, MAN/89/30 (VTD 4605).

[36.55] A partnership which provided services to publishers traded from a room in a house owned by the principal partner. The partner decided to sell the freehold of the house to raise finance, and the partnership reclaimed input tax on the legal costs incurred. The Commissioners issued an assessment to recover the tax, considering that the supply had not been made to the partnership and that the costs had not been directly incurred for the purposes of the partnership's business. The tribunal dismissed the partnership's appeal, applying *Rushgreen Builders Ltd*, 36.150 below. The partnership had not had any interest in the property, and had not incurred the expenditure in question. The supplies had been made to the individual partner rather than to the partnership. *Rock Lambert*, LON/90/1544Y (VTD 6637).

[36.56] Two relatives traded in partnership. In 1986 one of the partners (T) was injured in a road traffic accident. He took legal proceedings, which were not settled until 1995 (by which time the partnership had ceased to be registered). He reclaimed input tax on his solicitors' costs. The Commissioners rejected the claim on the basis that the solicitors' services had been supplied to T as an individual, rather than to the partnership. The tribunal dismissed T's appeal, applying *Rock Lambert*, 36.55 above. *KW Taylor*, MAN/96/21 (VTD 14244).

[36.57] A two-person partnership ceased trading and deregistered in January 1990. Subsequently one of the partners (S) formed the opinion that the other partner had been defrauding him. He engaged a solicitor to undertake enquiries, and reclaimed input tax on the solicitor's fees. The Commissioners rejected his claim and he appealed. The tribunal dismissed his appeal, holding that the tax was not deductible since the services in question had been supplied to S as an individual, rather than to the partnership. *B Stone*, LON/94/37 (VTD 12442).

[36.58] Two individuals, S and P, registered for VAT as a partnership from 1 January 1998. In November 1997, before they had registered, they had provided consultancy services to an accountancy partnership (G). They issued individual invoices for these services. G did not pay for the services, and S and P incurred solicitors' costs. They reclaimed input tax on these costs on their partnership VAT returns. The Commissioners issued an assessment to recover the tax, and S appealed. The tribunal dismissed the appeal and the Ch D upheld this decision. Jacob J observed that, on the facts found by the tribunal, S and P were suing on individual contracts, rather than as a partnership. *J Sherman & S Perilly v C & E Commrs*, Ch D [2001] STC 733.

[36.59] A family farming partnership reclaimed input tax on legal costs. The Commissioners issued an assessment to recover the tax, on the basis that the services had been made to the senior partner as an individual, rather than to the partnership, and did not relate to the partnership's business. The tribunal upheld the assessment and dismissed the partnership's appeal. *Wainbody Estates*, LON/99/1293 (VTD 18732).

[36.60] Three people had carried on business in partnership. The partnership was dissolved in 2002. One of the partners (L) took legal proceedings against his two former partners. He reclaimed input tax of more than £40,000 in respect of legal and professional fees. Customs rejected the claim and L appealed. The tribunal dismissed the appeal, holding that L had incurred the expenditure in a personal capacity and that the supplies were not made for the purposes of the partnership business. *G Langran*, LON/x (VTD 20969).

Legal services supplied to company director

[36.61] A publishing company reclaimed input tax in respect of legal costs. Customs discovered that the relevant invoices were addressed to the company's principal director, and related to legal action brought against him by the executors of his late father's estate. They issued an assessment to recover the tax on the basis that the supplies had not been made to the company. The tribunal upheld the assessment and dismissed the company's appeal. *Zenith Publishing Ltd*, LON/06/1349 (VTD 20973).

Legal costs relating to liquidation of associated company

[36.62] A company (D) reclaimed input tax on legal costs relating to the liquidation of an associated company (C). Customs rejected the claim on the basis that the relevant services had been supplied to C rather than to D. The tribunal dismissed D's appeal against this decision. *DIY Conservatory Centre Ltd*, MAN/04/791 (VTD 19290).

Legal costs relating to 'corporate restructuring'

[36.63] A group of companies had suffered financial difficulties. Two banks arranged for a firm of solicitors (C) to supply services to them in regard to a 'corporate restructuring' of the group. It invoiced these services to the banks. However, the representative member of the group (T) sought to reclaim some of the input tax, contending that it had paid the banks in relation to the restructuring, and should be treated as the recipient of some of C's services. Customs rejected the claim and the tribunal dismissed T's appeal. *Telent plc*, [2007] VATDR 81 (VTD 19967).

Transfer of employer's pension funds—legal advice provided for employees

[36.64] See *The Plessey Co Ltd*, **54.10** PENSION FUNDS.

Council paying solicitors' fees for prospective adopters

[36.65] See *London Borough of Camden*, **42.5** LOCAL AUTHORITIES AND STATUTORY BODIES.

Expenditure on premises

Cases where the appellant was successful

Whether supplies made to managing agent or freeholders

[36.66] An estate agent (S) acted as manager of a block of flats. He was informed by the local authority that urgent work should be carried out on the flats, and arranged for contractors to undertake the required work. However, the freeholders and leaseholders of the flats refused to accept liability for the work, contending that there had been a contravention of *Landlord and Tenant Act, s 20*. S therefore paid the contractors himself, and reclaimed the relevant input tax. The Commissioners issued an assessment to recover the tax, considering that the supply had been made to the freeholders of the flats, rather than to S, and that S was acting as an agent rather than as a principal. The tribunal allowed the appeal, holding that the supply had been made to S, who had 'accepted the obligations of principal to the contract'. The payment had been made to protect the reputation of S's business and the input tax was deductible. *GHJA Scott (t/a Chancellor & Sons)*, LON/90/1637Y (VTD 6922).

Repairs to bomb-damaged building—whether supplies made to tenant

[36.67] A major insurance company carried on business from premises in London, which it leased. The premises were badly damaged by IRA bombs, and the insurance company arranged for repairs and improvements to be carried out. The repairs were estimated to cost almost £18,000,000, and the proposed improvements were estimated to cost more than £12,000,000. The insurance company reclaimed input tax on the repairs. The Commissioners rejected the claim on the basis that the relevant supplies should be treated as having been made to the landlord, rather than to the insurance company which had effectively been acting as the landlord's agent. The insurance company appealed, contending that, in arranging for the repair work, it had acted as an independent principal. The tribunal accepted this contention and allowed the appeal. *Commercial Union Assurance Co plc*, LON/95/2756 (VTD 14195). (*Note*. The tribunal also held that a payment of £5,250,000 by the landlord to the insurance company, made as a contribution to the cost of the improvement works, represented consideration for a taxable supply of services by the insurance company to the landlord.)

Construction of farm building—whether supply made to landlord or tenant

[36.68] A tenant farmer reclaimed input tax on the construction of a grain store at the farm. The grain store cost £57,894 plus VAT. The landlord paid £57,000 and the tenant paid the balance. The Commissioners discovered that most of the cost had been met by the landlord of the farm, and issued an assessment to recover the tax. The tenant appealed. The tribunal allowed the appeal. On the evidence, the landlord had been 'under no legal or contractual obligation' to pay the £57,000. The tenant had been responsible for the erection of the building, and would be entitled to remove it under the *Agricultural Holdings Act 1986*. Accordingly, he was entitled to credit for the input tax. *JA Nichols*, MAN/96/33 (VTD 14521).

Input tax reclaimed on supplies for property development

[36.69] See *Hamstead Holdings Ltd*, 1.30 AGENTS, and *Drexlodge Ltd*, 1.50 AGENTS.

Cases where the appellant was unsuccessful

Whether supplies made to surveyor or to clients

[36.70] A surveyor supervised the work of an extension to clients' premises. When the work was nearly complete, a defect was discovered. The clients required that this be put right, but the builders who were constructing the extension went into liquidation. The clients had the work carried out by another company at a cost of £7,423, including VAT of £550. They claimed damages from the surveyor, who paid them the amount in full and also paid the clients' legal costs of £1,188 including VAT of £88. The surveyor reclaimed the £638 as input tax and the Commissioners issued an assessment to recover this amount. The tribunal dismissed the surveyor's appeal, holding that the relevant supplies were clearly made to the clients rather than to the surveyor. *ME Coster*, LON/80/394 (VTD 1057).

Remedial work on house—input tax reclaimed by original builder

[36.71] A couple, who had purchased a house from the company which had built it, discovered several structural defects and arranged for another firm of builders to remedy these. They claimed the costs of this work from the company which had built the house. The matter was referred to arbitration and the company was ordered to pay the couple more than £20,000 as compensation. The company reclaimed input tax in respect of some of the remedial work for which the purchasers had paid. The Commissioners rejected the claim on the grounds that the relevant supplies had been made to the couple who had purchased the house, rather than to the company. The tribunal upheld the Commissioners' decision and dismissed the company's appeal. *D & K Builders & Sons (Ampthill) Ltd*, LON/88/1046Z (VTD 4287).

Surveyors' fees—whether supplied to lender or to borrower

[36.72] A company (H) carried on the business of restoring old buildings and reconstructing them for residential use. It borrowed money from a finance company. The finance company arranged for surveyors to inspect the work which H had done before making stage payments, and deducted the amount of the surveyors' fees from the amounts it paid to H. H reclaimed input tax in respect of the surveyors' fees, and the Commissioners issued an assessment to recover the tax, considering that the relevant supplies had been made to the finance company, rather than to H. The tribunal upheld the assessment and dismissed H's appeal. *Heritage Venture Enterprises Ltd*, MAN/92/559 (VTD 10741).

Whether services supplied to company or to bank

[36.73] A building company (P) obtained a bank loan in order to convert a property into residential units. The bank instructed a firm of surveyors to monitor the progress of the work. The bank paid the surveyors' fees and charged these, plus certain solicitors' fees, to P. P reclaimed input tax on these amounts. When the Commissioners discovered this, they issued an assessment to recover the tax. The tribunal dismissed P's appeal, holding that the relevant services had been supplied to the bank, rather than to P. *Poladon Ltd*, MAN/99/1022 (VTD 16825).

Construction of classroom block at college

[36.74] In 1993 an institute of further education incorporated a wholly-owned subsidiary company (L), to undertake commercial activities. In 2001 the institute decided to arrange for the construction of a new classroom block. L reclaimed the input tax on the construction. HMRC issued assessments to recover the tax, on the basis that the relevant supplies had been made to the institute (most of whose supplies were exempt) rather than to L. L appealed, contending inter alia that there had been a novation of the relevant contracts. The tribunal reviewed the evidence in detail, rejected this contention, and dismissed the appeal. Judge Bishopp J observed that 'the evidence supporting an effective novation, critical to the company's case, was almost non-existent'. Furthermore, although L had ordered and paid for certain supplies of equipment, those supplies were 'incidental to the main purpose of the building, that is the teaching of engineering courses by the institute'. The institute was 'the only body in occupation of the building, in any real sense of the term'. The Upper Tribunal upheld this decision as one of fact. Briggs J observed that 'from start to finish, the arrangement was to be (and was) that the institute should be in control, through its employed staff, of the whole of the conduct of the educational activities within the building'. *Grimsby College Enterprises Ltd v HMRC*, UT [2010] SFTD 2009.

Customer reclaiming input tax in respect of invoices made out to contractor

[36.75] See *Barnes*, 40.23 INVOICES AND CREDIT NOTES.

Work carried out to comply with Clean Air Act 1956

[36.76] See *Doncaster Borough Council*, 42.2 LOCAL AUTHORITIES AND STATUTORY BODIES.

Circular transactions and 'carousel fraud'

Cases where the appellant was successful

Dealing in computer processing units

[36.77] In two of the three cases referred to the CJEC and reported at 22.115 EUROPEAN COMMUNITY LAW, Customs had specifically accepted at the tribunal hearing that the company reclaiming input tax was 'an innocent party' (so that on the basis of the CJEC decision, the companies would be entitled to reclaim the input tax). *Optigen Ltd*, LON/02/961 & 965 (VTD 18112); *Fulcrum Trading Co (UK) Ltd (in liquidation)*, LON/02/1010; LON/03/35 & 189 (VTD 18113).

[36.78] A company (C) reclaimed input tax on the purchase of a large quantity of computer processing units. HMRC rejected the claim on the basis that the transactions were connected to MTIC fraud. C appealed, contending that it had not known of this, and had entered the transactions in good faith.

The tribunal accepted C's evidence and allowed its appeal. *Crucial Components Ltd v HMRC*, [2011] UKFTT 690 (TC), TC01532.

Dealing in computer chips

[36.79] A company reclaimed input tax in respect of the purchase of substantial quantities of computer chips. Customs rejected the claim on the basis that the supplies were not 'economic transactions', but formed part of a 'carousel fraud'. The tribunal reviewed the evidence in detail and allowed the company's appeal, finding that the disputed invoices should be taken at 'face value' and as relating to genuine supplies. The tribunal observed that 'we would not be surprised if the transactions we have seen were part of carousel frauds with the chips ultimately going back to the supplier, but there is no evidence of this and accordingly we do not find that the transactions were not commercial on this basis'. *Med Trading Ltd*, LON/02/481 (VTD 19355).

[36.80] Two associated companies reclaimed input tax in respect of various transactions, mostly involving the purchase of quantities of computer chips. HMRC rejected part of the claims on the grounds that 25 of the transactions were connected to MTIC fraud. The tribunal allowed the companies' appeals. Judge Kempster held that it was reasonable for the companies' principal director 'to hold the belief that the circumstances in which the disputed transactions took place were unconnected to fraudulent evasion of VAT'. *Express Computers UK Ltd v HMRC (and related appeal)*, [2011] UKFTT 572 (TC), TC01415.

Dealing in mobile telephones

[36.81] A company reclaimed input tax in respect of the purchase of a substantial quantity of mobile telephones. Customs rejected the claim on the basis that the supplies were not 'economic transactions', but formed part of a 'carousel fraud'. The tribunal reviewed the evidence in detail and allowed the company's appeal, finding that Customs had not shown, on the balance of probabilities, that the relevant transactions were 'carousel frauds'. *Aircall Export Ltd*, LON/04/1351 (VTD 19185).

[36.82] A company (U) reclaimed input tax on the purchase of a consignment of 2500 mobile telephones, which it had sold to a Spanish trader (T). Customs rejected the claim on the grounds that the transactions formed part of a 'carousel fraud'. U appealed, contending that it had engaged in the transactions in good faith. The tribunal reviewed the evidence in detail and allowed U's appeal, applying the principles laid down by the CJEC in *Optigen Ltd*, **22.115** EUROPEAN COMMUNITY LAW. The tribunal found that the transactions had been circular, and that T had originally sold the telephones to a company which purported to be, but was not, registered for VAT in the UK. There had been 'a carousel of transactions designed to obtain by deception' the amount which the unregistered company had described as VAT. On the evidence, 'the only plausible conclusion to be drawn is that there was a circular series designed and executed for fraudulent purposes'. However, Customs had not produced any evidence to show 'any complicity by (U) in the organisation of the carousel, nor any actual knowledge on its part that elsewhere in the series there was fraudulent activity'. *Ultracell (UK) Ltd*, MAN/03/364 (VTD

19508). (*Note.* Customs had successfully taken proceedings against the Spanish company involved in the fraud—see **49.30** PENALTIES: CRIMINAL OFFENCES.)

[36.83] A company (L) reclaimed input tax of more than £2,000,000 relating to 14 transactions in consignments of mobile telephones. Customs rejected the claim on the basis that the transactions formed part of a 'missing trader intra-Community fraud'. L appealed, contending that it had engaged in the transactions in good faith. The tribunal reviewed the evidence in detail and allowed L's appeal, applying the principles laid down by the CJEC in *Optigen Ltd*, **22.115** EUROPEAN COMMUNITY LAW, and holding that L 'could not have known of the fraud'. The Ch D upheld this decision as one of fact. *HMRC v Livewire Telecom Ltd*, Ch D [2009] STC 643; [2009] EWHC 15 (Ch). (*Note.* The Ch D heard the case with *Olympia Technology Ltd (No 4)*, **36.98** below.)

[36.84] A company (R) reclaimed input tax of £99,750 in relation to a supply of 2,500 Nokia mobile telephones. Customs rejected the claim on the basis that the transactions formed part of a 'carousel fraud'. The tribunal reviewed the evidence in detail and allowed R's appeal, finding that R had 'proved on the balance of probabilities that it received a supply' of 2,500 Nokia phones, and had intended to make an onward supply of them to a purchaser in the Netherlands. The evidence suggested that the phones had been diverted in the UK as part of 'a fraud committed by others', and that R was 'an unwitting party'. Since R had purchased the phones with the intention of making an onward supply, it was entitled to credit for the input tax under *VATA 1994, s 26. Ross Pharmacy Ltd*, LON/04/744 (VTD 20634).

[36.85] A company (B) reclaimed substantial amounts of input tax in relation to transactions in mobile telephones. HMRC rejected the claim on the grounds that the transactions formed part of a 'missing trader intra-Community fraud'. B appealed, contending that it was not aware that the transactions were fraudulent. The tribunal accepted B's evidence and allowed the appeal (with the exception of two invoices where B had failed to pay the VAT charged). HMRC appealed to the Ch D, which directed that the case should be remitted to the tribunal for rehearing. The tribunal heard further argument and confirmed its earlier decision (by a 2-1 majority, Judge Demack dissenting). The Upper Tribunal upheld the majority decision as one of fact. *Brayfal Ltd v HMRC (No 4)*, UT [2011] STC 1338. (*Notes.* (1) For a preliminary issue in this case, see **2.285** APPEALS. (2) For the award of costs, see **2.416** APPEALS. (3) For another appeal by the same company, see **59.5** RETURNS.)

[36.86] A company reclaimed substantial amounts of input tax in relation to transactions in mobile telephones. Customs rejected the claim on the grounds that the transactions formed part of a 'missing trader intra-Community fraud'. The company appealed, contending that it was not aware that any of the transactions were fraudulent. The tribunal reviewed the evidence in detail, accepted this contention, and allowed the appeals, finding that some of the transactions formed part of a chain in which there was a tax loss attributable to fraud, but that the company 'had taken all available proportionate steps to ensure on the balance of probabilities that there was no connection with persons or transactions involved in VAT fraud'. *Our Communications Ltd*, LON/06/830 (and related appeals) (VTD 20903).

[36.87] A company (B) claimed an input tax repayment of more than £1,000,000, relating to transactions in mobile telephones. HMRC rejected the claim on the grounds that B ought to have known that the relevant transactions were connected to MTIC fraud. B appealed, contending that it had carried out adequate 'due diligence' on its supplier. The tribunal rejected this contention, finding that B's due diligence 'was not rigorous, copious or comprehensive'. However the Ch D allowed B's appeal and the CA upheld this decision. Moses LJ held that 'the tribunal's findings were insufficient to establish that (B) ought to have known that by its past purchases it was participating in transactions which were connected with fraudulent evasion of VAT'. He observed that 'the ultimate question is not whether the trader exercised due diligence but rather whether he should have known that the only reasonable explanation for the circumstances in which his transaction took place was that it was connected to fraudulent evasion of VAT'. *Blue Sphere Global Ltd v HMRC (No 2)*, CA [2010] STC 1436; [2010] EWCA Civ 517. (*Notes.* (1) For a preliminary issue in this case, see **2.165** APPEALS. (2) For the award of costs, see **2.483** APPEALS. (3) The CA heard the case with *Calltell Telecom Ltd v HMRC*, **36.105** below; *Opto Telelinks (Europe) Ltd v HMRC (No 2)*, **36.105** below, and *Mobilx Ltd (in administration) v HMRC (No 2)*, **36.119** below.)

[36.88] A company reclaimed input tax of more than £8,000,000 in respect of 33 purchases of mobile telephones. HMRC rejected the claims on the grounds that the company should have known that the transactions were connected with the fraudulent evasion of VAT. The tribunal reviewed the evidence in detail and allowed the company's appeal, finding that HMRC had failed to prove that 'the only reasonable explanation' for the purchases was that they were connected with fraud, or that either the company or its managing director knew that the transactions were connected with fraud. *Emblaze Mobility Solutions Ltd v HMRC*, [2010] UKFTT 410 (TC), TC00680.

[36.90] A similar decision was reached in a subsequent case where Judge Poole found that HMRC had not shown that the appellant company 'either did know or should have known that the only reasonable explanation for the transactions the subject of these appeals was that they were connected with fraudulent evasion of VAT'. *The Hira Co Ltd v HMRC*, [2011] UKFTT 450 (TC), TC01302.

[36.90A] A similar decision was reached in a case where Judge Cornwell-Kelly found that 'the objective evidence cannot lead to a finding that the appellant should have known that the only reasonable explanation of matters was that its trading was connected to fraud'. *HT Purser Ltd v HMRC*, [2011] UKFTT 860 (TC), TC01694.

Purchases of platinum

[36.91] A company reclaimed input tax on the purchase of three platinum bars, which it subsequently sold to an Italian company. Customs issued an assessment to recover the tax, on the basis that the transactions formed part of a 'carousel fraud'. The company appealed, contending that it had engaged in the transactions in good faith, and had itself been a victim of the fraud because it had not received payment from the Italian purchaser. The tribunal accepted the company's evidence and allowed its appeal. *Leogem Ltd*, MAN/x (VTD 19829).

Disposable alcohol test strips

[36.92] A company (M) carried on the business of supplying laboratory equipment and medical products. In 2006 it reclaimed input tax of £83,000 in respect of the purchase of 10,000 disposable alcohol test strips, which it sold to a French company on the same day. HMRC rejected the claim on the basis that it appeared that the purchase and sale formed part of an MTIC fraud. M appealed, contending that it had not known that the transactions were connected to fraud. The tribunal accepted M's evidence and allowed the appeal, finding that M 'could not afford to hold, and finance, a stock of test strips, and it was never its intention to effect anything other than a matched deal. These facts of a matched deal, probably effected on one day, would have arisen both in an honest and in a fraudulent transaction.' Judge Nowlan held that 'HMRC has failed to show, on the balance of probabilities, that the appellant had means of knowledge, or that it ought to have known, that there could be no other reasonable explanation for its transaction than that it was connected with fraudulent evasion of VAT'. *Masstech Ltd v HMRC*, [2010] UKFTT 386 (TC), TC00668.

Other cases

[36.93] In a case where the facts are not fully set out in the decision, a company reclaimed input tax of more than £500,000. The Commissioners rejected the claim on the basis that the transactions formed part of a 'carousel fraud'. The tribunal allowed the company's appeal, finding that it was 'not prepared to draw the necessary inferences' from the evidence submitted by the Commissioners. *Totel Distribution Ltd (No 1)*, MAN/04/028 (VTD 18956). (*Note.* A subsequent appeal by the same company was dismissed—see **36.121** below.)

Cases where the appellant was partly successful (or the case was adjourned)

Internet access cards

[36.94] A company reclaimed input tax on the purchase of a large quantity of 'internet access cards', which granted access to a pornographic website. It did not account for output tax on the disposal of the cards, informing the Commissioners that it had sold them to a Danish company. The Commissioners rejected the claim on the basis that the purchases formed part of a 'carousel missing trader fraud', designed to obtain a substantial repayment of sums which had never been paid as output tax. The tribunal reviewed the evidence in detail and directed that the hearing of the appeals should be adjourned pending the CJEC decision in *Optigen Ltd*, **22.115** EUROPEAN COMMUNITY LAW. *Hindforce Ltd*, LON/04/241 (VTD 18920). (*Note.* There was no further public hearing of the appeal.)

Dealing in mobile telephones

[36.95] A company (D) was incorporated in 2001. It conducted only 'minimal activities' until late 2003, when it began dealing in mobile telephones. It reclaimed input tax in respect of 145 transactions. Customs rejected the majority of the claim (relating to more than £15,000,000 in VAT) on the basis that the purchases formed part of a 'carousel missing trader fraud', designed to obtain a substantial repayment of sums which had never been paid as output tax. The tribunal reviewed the evidence in detail, allowed D's appeal in respect of five transactions, and partly allowed the appeal in respect of two more transactions. With regard to the other transactions, the tribunal noted that D's principal director seemed to remember 'little about the details of individual deals, even the unusual ones, although some involved considerable amounts of money, and considerable potential profits', and it was in some cases 'only a few months since he helped agree those deals'. The tribunal found that the director's 'inability to answer specific detailed questions raised, rather than answered, questions'. Furthermore, 'in some deals the documentation did not suggest the level of safeguard that (one) would expect to find when large sums of money were moved to third parties in genuine arm's length circumstances, especially when those movements occurred across national and currency frontiers'. With regard to some of the transactions, the tribunal found that there was 'no profitable, or potentially profitable, activity taking place other than that of moving the goods through VAT frontiers. It does not regard that as an economic activity.' The relevant goods 'were moving not so much round in a rapid circle that might fairly compare with a carousel but back and forth while the title to the goods went round a longer circuit that did not have any obvious commercial basis'. The paperwork and payments 'followed behind both the oral agreements and the movements of goods without that apparently causing any undue concern to any of the counterparties'. The evidence of some of the transactions showed 'prices being altered after the sales had been concluded both up the chain and down the chain'. There appeared to be no 'source of that added value but from national VAT authorities'. The tribunal was 'satisfied that there was no genuine economic activity' in many of the deals. The tribunal directed that the hearing of the appeals should be adjourned pending the CJEC decision in *Optigen Ltd*, **22.115** EUROPEAN COMMUNITY LAW. *Dragon Futures Ltd (No 2)*, LON/04/1461 (and related appeals) (VTD 19186). (*Note.* For subsequent developments in this case, see **36.115** below.)

[36.96] A similar decision was reached in *Deluni Mobile Ltd (No 2)*, MAN/04/465 (VTD 19301). (*Note.* There was no further public hearing of the appeal.)

[36.97] A company (R) reclaimed substantial amounts of input tax in relation to 46 alleged transactions in mobile telephones. Customs rejected the claim on the grounds that the transactions formed part of a 'missing trader intra-Community fraud'. R appealed, contending that it was not aware that the transactions were fraudulent. The tribunal reviewed the evidence in detail and allowed R's appeal with regard to one transaction, finding that the telephones had been manufactured in China and that Customs had produced 'no direct evidence of an importation from the EU'. However the tribunal dismissed R's appeal with regard to the other 45 transactions. The tribunal found that

R's controlling director was not 'a reliable witness', that the alleged transactions were 'wholly artificial', and that the director's actions 'were not those of a man who was concerned that he was operating in an area which he knew to be rife with fraud; the very best that could be said of his behaviour was that he closed his eyes to those aspects which were unwelcome to him'. The tribunal also held that R was not entitled to credit for any tax actually paid by 'buffer traders', since the effect of the CJEC decision in *Kittel v Belgian State*, **22.415** EUROPEAN COMMUNITY LAW, was that 'a trader with the requisite knowledge who enters into a transaction of the kind under consideration forfeits the entire right to deduct regardless of the measure of the tax lost, a desirable outcome as a means of discouraging fraud'. The Ch D upheld the tribunal decision as one of fact, applying the principles laid down in *Edwards v Bairstow & Harrison*, HL 1955, 36 TC 207. *Red 12 Trading Ltd v HMRC*, Ch D 2009, [2010] STC 589; [2009] EWHC 2563 (Ch).

[36.98] A company reclaimed substantial amounts of input tax in relation to transactions in mobile telephones. Customs rejected the claim on the grounds that the transactions formed part of a 'missing trader intra-Community fraud'. The company appealed, contending that it was not aware that any of the transactions were fraudulent. The tribunal reviewed the evidence in detail and accepted this contention, finding that the controlling director of the appellant company was 'naive and gullible', and was 'the ideal person for a "puppet master" to involve in fraud' since 'a person with his experience would not have known that there was fraud in the deal chains'. Customs appealed to the Ch D, which directed that the case should be remitted to the tribunal for rehearing. Lewison J held that 'in applying the test of what ought to have been known by a director with the knowledge, skill and experience of the particular director concerned', the tribunal had erred in law. It had 'applied a lower standard than that which would have been appropriate to support a finding of constructive knowledge' and had been 'wrong to water down the requirement that the taxable person must take every precaution reasonably required. The test does not require the taxable person to take every possible precaution: merely every precaution reasonably required. This test gives the tribunal sufficient flexibility to decide, on particular facts, that a suggested precaution would have gone beyond what could reasonably have been expected.' *HMRC v Olympia Technology Ltd (No 4)*, Ch D [2009] STC 643; [2009] EWHC 15 (Ch). (*Note.* The Ch D heard the appeal with *Livewire Telecom Ltd*, **36.83** above.)

[36.99] Following the Ch D decision noted at **36.98** above, the tribunal reheard the appeal and allowed the appeal in principle with regard to seven transactions but dismissed it with regard to eight transactions. The tribunal noted that the CA would soon be hearing HMRC's appeal against the Ch D decision in *Blue Sphere Global Ltd v HMRC (No 2)*, **36.87** above, and gave both parties leave to seek a further hearing on specific points of law following the CA decision in that case. *Olympia Technology Ltd v HMRC (No 5)*, [2010] UKFTT 45 (TC), TC00358.

[36.100] A company (M) reclaimed input tax of more than £800,000 in relation to seven transactions in mobile telephones. HMRC rejected the claim on the grounds that it that the transactions were connected to MTIC fraud. M appealed. The tribunal reviewed the evidence in detail and allowed the appeal with regard to three transactions but dismissed it with regard to the other four transactions. *My Secrets Ltd v HMRC*, [2011] UKFTT 72 (TC), TC00950.

Cases where the appellant was unsuccessful

Dealing in computer processing units

[36.101] In one of the three cases referred to the CJEC and noted at **22.115** EUROPEAN COMMUNITY LAW, the tribunal expressed serious doubts about the *bona fides* of the company's claim. The tribunal observed that the company (B) had not adequately explained 'why it preferred to sell, not within the UK, but by export to Ireland—simultaneously increasing both the cost of carriage and its exposure to risk'. The tribunal noted that 16 of the 27 purchases were from the same company (V), which was controlled by a young woman aged only 21, to whom B's technical director (C) had lent £500,000 at a low rate of interest. The tribunal observed that it was 'puzzling that (C) should lend money to someone else in order that she could set up a business in direct competition with his own'. A further nine of the purchases were from a company (S). In each of these cases, the CPUs which B purchased from S were sold by B to an Irish company (F) and were subsequently resold, directly or indirectly, to a UK company (R) which failed to account for output tax and which had subsequently been compulsorily deregistered, owing about £17,000,000 to Customs. The tribunal observed that there was a 'pattern of general circularity' about the transactions. Furthermore, it was 'inconsistent with legitimate trading activity that in every single case in which (B) bought chips from (S), it sold them to (F). Conversely, in no case in which it bought chips from (V) did it sell them to (F).' On the evidence, it was 'an irresistible conclusion that the deals were orchestrated'. The tribunal commented that 'if the transactions were entirely genuine we could expect to see, at the least, a few acquisitions of chips from (V) sold on to (F) as well as some sales of chips sourced from (S) to customers other than (F), and we would expect to find some differences in the profit margin (B) was able to achieve'. The tribunal found that there was 'copious evidence of imprudence and of the appellant's directors having failed to ask themselves obvious questions'. *Bond House Systems Ltd*, [2003] VATDR 210 (VTD 18100). (*Notes*. (1) For Customs' reaction to the tribunal decision, see News Release 23/03, issued on 30 April 2003. (2) There was no further public hearing of the appeal. The appellant company subsequently went into liquidation.)

Dealing in CPUs—criminal conviction for 'carousel fraud'

[36.102] See *R v May*, **49.19** PENALTIES: CRIMINAL OFFENCES.

Dealing in computer parts—criminal conviction for 'carousel fraud'

[36.103] See *R v Hashash*, **49.13** PENALTIES: CRIMINAL OFFENCES.

Purported supplies of golf clubs

[36.104] A company (S) reclaimed input tax of more than £1,000,000, relating to supplies of golf clubs, which it claimed to have purchased from a UK company and sold to a Spanish company. Customs rejected the claim on the basis that the transactions formed part of a 'carousel fraud'. The tribunal reviewed the evidence in detail and dismissed S's appeal, finding that 'the quantity and value of the clubs represented on the invoices' was 'incompatible with the size of the European market'. The tribunal observed that S had 'paid out some £640,000 of its investors' capital on the very first deal before any of the contractual paperwork had been put in place, and without taking advantage of any contractual requirement that its customer make a payment on confirmation of its order'. The tribunal found that neither of S's controlling directors were 'credible witnesses' and that 'the manner in which subsequent deals were cancelled without there being any penalty to (S) or any other party, and without there apparently being any concern to enforce the relevant terms and conditions indicates that there was no *bona fide* trade'. None of the invoices produced by S gave a 'description sufficient to identify the goods', as required by *SI 1005/2518, reg 14(1)(g)* and/or the quantity of those goods, as required by *reg 14(1)(h)*. The invoices also failed to satisfy the requirements of *Article 22(3)(b)* of the *EC Sixth Directive. Senergy (UK) Ltd*, LON/05/131 (VTD 19727).

Dealing in mobile telephones

[36.105] Two associated companies reclaimed input tax of more than £18,000,000 in respect of purported transactions in mobile telephones. HMRC rejected the claims on the basis that the alleged transactions formed part of a 'carousel fraud'. The companies appealed. The tribunal reviewed the evidence in detail and dismissed the appeals (except for tax of £86,000 relating to one purchase of telephones which HMRC had accepted as genuine during the course of the hearing). The tribunal concluded that the companies' controlling director 'knew that the appellants were engaged in transactions whose purpose was the commission of a fraud on the Commissioners. The appellants' creation and assembly of the documentation relating to each deal into which they entered and their due diligence were designed only to persuade the Commissioners that they were legitimate traders. The transactions between the two appellants had no true purpose other than to shift their respective VAT liabilities and repayment claims. Every one of the transactions, including those described as contra-trading, had as its objective the defrauding of the Commissioners.' The Ch D and CA unanimously upheld this decision. Floyd J held that the tribunal was entitled to find that the companies and their controlling director 'were well aware that the appellants were dealing in goods which were being used as the instrument of fraud, and the transactions in which they were themselves engaged were arranged for no other purpose'. Moses LJ held that this was 'a paradigm of a case where the traders knew of the connection between the transactions in which they were involved and VAT fraud'. *Calltell Telecom Ltd v HMRC; Opto Telelinks (Europe) Ltd v HMRC (No 2)*, CA [2010] STC 1436; [2010] EWCA Civ 517. (*Notes.* (1) The tribunal awarded costs to Customs. (2) For another issue in this case, see **2.369** APPEALS. (3) The CA heard the cases with *HMRC v Blue Sphere Global Ltd*, **36.87** above, and *Mobilx Ltd (in administration) v HMRC (No 2)*, **36.119** below.)

[36.106] A company (E) reclaimed substantial amounts of input tax in relation to transactions in mobile telephones, which it claimed to have sold to a Luxembourg trader. Customs rejected the claim on the grounds that the transactions formed part of a 'missing trader intra-Community fraud'. The tribunal reviewed the evidence in detail and dismissed E's appeal. The tribunal concluded that E's controlling director 'did not give truthful evidence' and that 'he did know when entering into the five transactions that they were part of a fraudulent chain'. *Europeans Ltd (No 2)*, LON/07/811 (VTD 20883). (*Notes.* (1) The company appealed to the High Court, but failed to pursue the appeal, which was subsequently struck out—Ch D 8 May 2009 unreported. (2) For a preliminary issue in this case, see **2.272** APPEALS. For the award of costs, see **2.371** APPEALS.)

[36.107] A company (M) reclaimed input tax of more than £5,000,000 in relation to transactions in mobile telephones. HMRC rejected the claim on the grounds that the transactions formed part of a 'missing trader intra-Community fraud'. The tribunal reviewed the evidence in detail and dismissed M's appeal, finding that the transactions in question were fraudulent. M's controlling director was 'a highly intelligent man and a very experienced businessman'. On the evidence, the tribunal was satisfied that M 'knew that the transactions were connected with fraud'. The Ch D upheld the tribunal decision as one of fact. Briggs J held that the tribunal was entitled to find that M's 'due diligence processes' were 'an elaborate sham'. He concluded that 'the primary findings amount to a whole series of alarm bells which would have caused any honest and reasonable trader in (M's) position to ask the most searching questions about the propriety of the transactions in which it was engaged and, in the light of what is now known about those transactions, M could not possibly have obtained satisfactory answers to its inquiries'. *Megtian Ltd v HMRC (No 1)*, Ch D [2010] STC 840; [2010] EWHC 18 (Ch). (*Note.* The Ch D noted that the CA would soon be hearing HMRC's appeal against the Ch D decision in *Blue Sphere Global Ltd v HMRC (No 2)*, **36.87** above, and gave M leave to seek a further hearing on specific points of law following the CA decision in that case.)

[36.108] A company reclaimed input tax relating to transactions in mobile telephones. HMRC rejected the claim on the grounds that the transactions formed part of a 'missing trader intra-Community fraud'. The company appealed, contending as a preliminary point that HMRC's policy of applying an 'extended verification' to transactions in mobile telephones was unfairly discriminatory, and was not authorised by *Article 22(8)* of the EC Sixth Directive. The tribunal heard this issue at a preliminary hearing and rejected the company's contentions, holding that 'the "obligations" referred to in *Article 22(8)* are obligations inherent in the operation of VAT by taxable persons, principally the obligations relating to invoices and returns'. Applying the principles laid down by Lightman J in *R (oao UK Tradecorp Ltd) v C & E Commrs*, **36.652** below, 'there is no right to refund, and no right to a refund is triggered, unless the right to deduct is exercised in respect of taxes actually due'. HMRC's investigations were 'the appropriate means to verify whether or not there exists a valid claim to deduction. Until the claim is accepted or established, there is no right to payment.' *4Distribution Ltd*, LON/07/1765 (VTD 20931).

[36.109] Following the decision noted at **36.108** above, the tribunal held a further hearing at which it reviewed the evidence in detail and dismissed the company's appeal, finding that the company's purchases were 'connected with fraudulent evasion of VAT' and that the company 'actually knew that by the purchases in issue, it was participating in transactions connected with fraudulent evasion of VAT'. *4Distribution Ltd v HMRC (No 2)*, [2009] UKFTT 242 (TC), TC00191. (*Note*. Costs were awarded to HMRC.)

[36.110] A company reclaimed input tax of more than £350,000 relating to transactions in mobile telephones. HMRC rejected the claim on the grounds that the transactions formed part of a 'missing trader intra-Community fraud'. The company appealed. The tribunal reviewed the evidence in detail and dismissed the appeal, finding that the company's controlling director 'acted dishonestly in engaging in the three transactions in question in this appeal'. *PD Concepts Ltd v HMRC*, [2009] SFTD 353; [2009] UKFTT 127 (TC), TC00095.

[36.111] A company (L) reclaimed input tax in respect of eight transactions in mobile telephones which it claimed to have exported to other EU states. HMRC rejected the claim on the grounds that the transactions formed part of an 'MTIC fraud'. The tribunal reviewed the evidence in detail and dismissed L's appeal, finding that L's director was 'an unconvincing witness' and that L 'must have known that its purchases were connected with the fraudulent evasion of VAT'. *Late Editions Ltd v HMRC*, [2009] SFTD 488; [2009] UKFTT 166 (TC), TC00128. (*Note*. The company appealed to the Upper Tribunal against this decision, but the Upper Tribunal struck out the appeal after the company failed to comply with directions.)

[36.112] A company (R) reclaimed input tax of more than £2,000,000 relating to alleged transactions in mobile telephones and CPUs. HMRC rejected the claim on the basis that the transactions formed part of a 'missing trader intra-Community fraud'. The First-Tier Tribunal dismissed R's appeal, finding that R knew that the transactions were connected with fraud. The Upper Tribunal upheld this decision as one of fact. *Regent Commodities Ltd v HMRC*, UT [2011] UKUT 259 (TCC); [2011] STC 1964.

[36.113] Similar decisions were reached in *Quality Import Export Ltd*, [2010] UKFTT 47 (TC), TC00360; *VIP (Scotland) Ltd v HMRC*, [2010] UKFTT 63 (TC), TC00375; *Pharmaquim Ltd v HMRC*, [2010] UKFTT 279 (TC), TC00568; *Mobile Export 365 Ltd v HMRC (No 4)*, [2010] UKFTT 367 (TC), TC00649; *Shelford (IT) Ltd v HMRC*, [2010] UKFTT 367 (TC), TC00649; *NG International Ltd v HMRC*, [2010] UKFTT 417 (TC), TC00687; *Radarbeam Ltd v HMRC*, [2010] UKFTT 431 (TC), TC00699; *Telement Ltd v HMRC*, [2010] UKFTT 470 (TC), TC00732; *Third Generation Communication Ltd v HMRC*, [2010] UKFTT 486 (TC), TC00746; *Excel RTI Solutions Ltd v HMRC*, [2010] UKFTT 519 (TC), TC00774; *Procomm Consultancy Ltd v HMRC*, [2010] UKFTT 561 (TC), TC00812; *G Comms Ltd v HMRC*, [2010] UKFTT 605 (TC), TC00846; *Eyedial Ltd v HMRC*, [2011] UKFTT 47 (TC), TC00924; *Cell Trading (UK) Ltd v HMRC*, FTT February 2011, TC00936; *Eurostar Telecom Ltd v HMRC*, [2011] UKFTT 75 (TC), TC00953; *Abbey (Manchester) Ltd v HMRC*, [2011] UKFTT 90 (TC), TC00967; *Maximum Networks Ltd v HMRC*, [2011] UKFTT 93 (TC), TC00970; *Root 89 Ltd v HMRC*, [2011] UKFTT 94 (TC), TC00971; *Euro Quest Trading Ltd v HMRC*, [2011] UKFTT 145 (TC), TC01019; *Mynt Ltd v HMRC*, [2011] UKFTT 162 (TC), TC01031; *Network Euro Ltd v HMRC*, [2011] UKFTT 255 (TC), TC01119; *Greystone International Ltd v HMRC*, [2011] UKFTT 321 (TC), TC01181; *Edgeskill Ltd v*

HMRC, [2011] UKFTT 393 (TC), TC01248; *Business Management Concepts Ltd v HMRC*, [2011] UKFTT 520 (TC), TC01367; *AR Communications & Electronics Ltd v HMRC*, [2011] UKFTT 637 (TC), TC01479; *Earthshine Ltd v HMRC (No 3)*, [2011] UKFTT 667 (TC), TC01509, and *Option NTC Ltd v HMRC*, [2011] UKFTT 768 (TC), TC01605 and *Crotek Ltd v HMRC (and related appeal)*, [2011] UKFTT 836 (TC), TC01672.

[36.113A] A company (G) reclaimed input tax of £176,000 in respect of the purchase of a quantity of mobile telephones. HMRC rejected the claim on the grounds that the transaction was connected with MTIC fraud. The First-Tier Tribunal allowed G's appeal (TC00682), finding that an individual (M) who had acted as an agent for G knew that the transaction formed part of a fraud, but holding that M's knowledge could not be imputed to G. However the Upper Tribunal reversed this decision and upheld HMRC's rejection of the claim. Warren J held that, on the evidence, M's knowledge of the fraud should be attributed to G, applying the principles laid down by the Privy Council in Meridian *Global Funds Management Asia v Securities Commission. HMRC v Greener Solutions Ltd*, UT [2012] UKUT 18 (TCC).

[36.114] See also *Ace Telecom Ltd*, 57.16 REGISTRATION, and *Innova Inc (UK) Ltd*, 57.148 REGISTRATION.

Whether appellant should have been aware of 'carousel fraud'

[36.115] Following the decision noted at **36.95** above, the CJEC delivered its decisions in *Optigen Ltd*, **22.115** EUROPEAN COMMUNITY LAW, and *Kittel v Belgian State*, **22.415** EUROPEAN COMMUNITY LAW. At the resumption of the hearing of its appeals, D asked the tribunal for a preliminary decision on the interpretation of the CJEC decisions, and on whether the applicable test was objective or subjective. The tribunal held that 'the "means of knowing" are to be tested objectively'. The taxable person 'must be judged by both the level of actual knowledge and the actions taken, or not taken, to acquire knowledge at the time of entry into the commitment that gives rise to the input tax. Hindsight cannot be used.' The taxable person 'must make a proportionate response to information actually known that indicates fraud. That knowledge is not restricted to the immediate context of the supplier or purchaser of relevant goods to or from the taxable person. It includes knowledge of fraud "in the market" for the goods in question, as well as knowledge in the public domain or otherwise actually known of fraud by a specific trader. It includes information about all known counterparties in the web of transactions of which the contract forms part, and counterparties that can be identified on proportionate enquiry made within the limits imposed by market confidentiality. The taxable person must take proportionate steps to use all means reasonably available to increase actual knowledge. For example, in these appeals, the tribunal saw the use of: checks on the validity of value added tax registration numbers; checks on customs stamps on goods going through a customs inspection; checks with and about individual suppliers and customers, including checks with national registration institutions; checks with credit agencies and inspection agencies, including checks on the IMEI numbers of telephones; use of appropriate terms of contract. Where an initial enquiry gives rise to information suggesting the need for further enquiry, the test is reapplied to assess the need for that further enquiry. What is proportionate and reasonable is a matter of fact, and involves balancing actual cost and the opportunity cost of personal effort against risk.' The tribunal must ask whether the taxable person has, 'at the time of entering a transaction involving payment of value added tax by or to that person, and taking into account the actual knowledge of the taxable person at that time (including knowledge acquired from any enquiry or investigation), taken all proportionate steps available to it to ensure that, on the balance of probabilities, no aspect of the transaction is connected with any other party involved in, or any other transaction involving, fraud on the public revenue through the value added tax system?' *Dragon Futures Ltd (No 3)*, [2006] VATDR 348 (VTD 19831). (*Note.* The appeal was subsequently dismissed—see **36.116** below.)

[36.116] Following the decision noted at **36.115** above, the tribunal held a further hearing at which it reviewed the evidence in detail and dismissed all the company's appeals, finding that the company should have been aware that the transactions were fraudulent. *Dragon Futures Ltd (No 4)*, LON/04/1461 (and related appeals) (VTD 20868).

[36.117] A company (E) reclaimed substantial amounts of input tax relating to alleged transactions in computer processing units. HMRC rejected the claim and the First-Tier Tribunal dismissed E's appeal, applying the principles laid down in *Kittel v Belgian State*, **22.415** EUROPEAN COMMUNITY LAW, and *Dragon Futures Ltd (No 3)*, **36.115** above. The Upper Tribunal upheld this decision. Arnold J held that 'there was evidence before the Tribunal from which it was entitled to conclude that (E) had actual knowledge that its purchases were connected with the fraudulent evasion of VAT'. *Euro Stock Shop Ltd v HMRC*, UT [2010] STC 2454; [2010] UKUT 259 (TCC).

[36.118] A company (H) reclaimed input tax in respect of 28 transactions in mobile telephones which it claimed to have exported to other EU states. Customs rejected the claim on the grounds that the transactions formed part of a 'carousel fraud'. The tribunal reviewed the evidence in detail and held that, in respect of 26 of the 28 transactions, H 'should have known that those transactions were connected with the fraudulent evasion of VAT'. Accordingly H was only entitled to credit for tax which had been 'actually paid by the buffer traders' (ie the companies which had been interposed in the chain between the fraudulent traders and H itself). *Honeyfone Ltd*, LON/07/404 (VTD 20667). (*Notes.* (1) Customs were awarded 75% of their costs. (2) The tribunal's decision that the appellant was entitled to credit for any tax actually paid by 'buffer traders' was criticised by a subsequent tribunal in *Red 12 Trading Ltd*, **36.97** above, where the tribunal held that the effect of the ECJ decision in *Kittel v Belgian State*, **22.415** EUROPEAN COMMUNITY LAW, was that 'a trader with the requisite knowledge who enters into a transaction of the kind under consideration forfeits the entire right to deduct regardless of the measure of the tax lost, a desirable outcome as a means of discouraging fraud'.)

[36.119] A company (M) reclaimed input tax of more than £7,000,000 relating to purported transactions in computer chips. HMRC rejected the claim on the basis that the transactions formed part of a 'carousel fraud'. The tribunal reviewed the evidence in detail and dismissed M's appeal, applying the principles laid down by the ECJ in *Kittel v Belgian State*, **22.415** EUROPEAN

COMMUNITY LAW. The tribunal found that M 'was not wholly candid with its own advisers, and consequently with HMCE', and that the honesty of one of M's directors and another of its shareholders was 'questionable'. The tribunal also criticised the accountant (H) who had acted as M's VAT adviser, commenting that 'it may be that PwC could not tell a client to cease trading; (H) was reluctant to accept even that they might advise him to do so'. The Ch D and CA unanimously upheld the tribunal decision. Moses LJ held that the 'correct question' was whether M 'should have known that its transactions were connected with fraud'. On the evidence, 'the primary facts found by the Tribunal did establish that the only reasonable explanation for the transactions in respect of which (M) claimed repayment of input tax' was 'their connection with fraudulent evasion of VAT'. *Mobilx Ltd (in administration) v HMRC (No 2)*, CA [2010] STC 1436; [2010] EWCA Civ 517. (*Notes.* (1) The CA heard the case with *HMRC v Blue Sphere Global Ltd*, **36.87** above; *Calltell Telecom Ltd v HMRC*, **36.105** above, and *Opto Telelinks (Europe) Ltd v HMRC (No 2)*, **36.105** above. (2) The Supreme Court dismissed the company's application for leave to appeal against this decision.)

[36.120] The principles laid down in *Mobilx Ltd (in administration) v HMRC (No 2)*, **36.119** above, were applied in the similar subsequent cases of *S & I Electronics plc v HMRC*, [2009] SFTD 241; [2009] UKFTT 108 (TC), TC00076; *Phonepoint Communications Ltd v HMRC*, [2010] UKFTT 452 (TC), TC00717; *Manatlantic Ltd v HMRC*, [2011] UKFTT 527 (TC), TC01374; *Fusion Electronics Ltd v HMRC*, [2011] UKFTT 529 (TC), TC01376; *Midland Mortgages Ltd v HMRC*, [2011] UKFTT 631 (TC), TC01473, *Annova Ltd v HMRC*, [2011] UKFTT 742 (TC), TC01579; *Bays Revert Ltd v HMRC*, [2012] UKFTT 43 (TC), TC01741; *Davis & Dann Ltd v HMRC*, [2012] UKFTT 55 (TC), TC01752; and *Precis 1080 Ltd v HMRC*, [2012] UKFTT 55 (TC), TC01752.

[36.120A] A similar decision was reached in a case where the Upper Tribunal held that the First-Tier Tribunal had been entitled to find that the appellant company should have known 'that the transactions in question were connected with VAT fraud'. *A One Distribution (UK) Ltd v HMRC*, [2011] UKUT 496 (TCC).

[36.121] Similar decisions were reached in *Life Enterprises Ltd v HMRC*, [2009] UKFTT 340 (TC), TC00281; *Powa (Jersey) Ltd v HMRC*, [2009] UKFTT 360 (TC), TC00298; *MBC Trading Ltd v HMRC (and related appeal)*, [2009] UKFTT 372 (TC), TC00310; *Next Generation International Ltd v HMRC*, [2010] UKFTT 46 (TC), TC00359; *PCCI Ltd v HMRC*, [2010] UKFTT 65 (TC), TC00377; *Blada Ltd v HMRC*, [2010] UKFTT 131 (TC), TC00440; *Roma II Ltd v HMRC*, [2010] UKFTT 243 (TC), TC00540; *Han Ali Ltd v HMRC*, [2010] UKFTT 351 (TC), TC00633;TC00704; *Eurosel Ltd v HMRC*, [2010] UKFTT 451 (TC), TC00716; *Gillex (UK) Ltd v HMRC*, [2010] UKFTT 517 (TC), TC00772; *Xentric Ltd v HMRC (No 2)*, [2010] UKFTT 620 (TC), TC00862; *Pars Technology Ltd v HMRC*, [2011] UKFTT 9 (TC), TC00886; *Mayfair Executive Ltd v HMRC*, [2011] UKFTT 148 (TC), TC01022; *Totel Distribution Ltd v HMRC (No 2)*, [2011] UKFTT 217 (TC), TC01082; *Deandrake Ltd v HMRC*, [2011] UKFTT 250 (TC), TC01114; *Sceptre Services Ltd v HMRC (No 3)*, [2011] UKFTT 265 (TC), TC01127; *Active Infotech Ltd v*

HMRC, [2011] UKFTT 328 (TC), TC01188; *Flashpoint Technology Ltd v HMRC*, [2011] UKFTT 353 (TC), TC01213; *Digi Trade Ltd v HMRC*, [2011] UKFTT 566 (TC), TC01411; *Ixes (UK) Ltd v HMRC*, [2011] UKFTT 586 (TC), TC01429; *JP Commodities Ltd v HMRC (No 2)*, [2011] UKFTT 622 (TC), TC01464; *Coracle Ventures Ltd v HMRC*, [2011] UKFTT 630 (TC), TC01472; *Martem Ltd v HMRC*, [2011] UKFTT 641 (TC), TC01483; *Bliss Trading Ltd v HMRC*, [2011] UKFTT 740 (TC), TC01577; *Matrix Europe Ltd v HMRC*, [2011] UKFTT 792 (TC), TC01628 and *DI & GI Electronics Ltd*,[2011] UKFTT 825 (TC), TC01661.

Other cases

[36.122] See also *R (oao UK Tradecorp Ltd) v C & E Commrs*, **36.652** below; the cases noted at **36.653** below, and *Rioni Ltd v HMRC*, **36.656** below.

Sham transactions

Company reclaiming input tax on purported purchases of platinum

[36.123] A company (P) had submitted a VAT return for the period ending January 2004 claiming a VAT repayment of £58,000, which Customs repaid. It submitted a return for the period ending March 2004, claiming a repayment of more than £700,000 in respect of purported purchases of platinum, which it claimed to have exported to China. Customs rejected the claim on the basis that the relevant transactions were a 'sham'. The tribunal reviewed the evidence in detail and dismissed P's appeal. The tribunal observed that purchase invoices which P had produced bore the VAT registration number of British Gas. The transactions appeared to be fraudulent, and intended solely to obtain a large repayment of VAT. When the transactions were considered as a whole, there was no evidence of any extrinsic profit being made by the participants in the deals. It appeared that 'the entirety of the transactions were driven by the benefit to be derived by the participants from the putative VAT credit and not from any extrinsic commercial profitability'. The tribunal also found that the goods which P had exported 'were not in fact platinum alloy'. The tribunal also found that P's controlling director 'seemed to have no idea of the necessity for integrity in business, particularly with regard to financial conduct. His website told a pack of lies about the company's trading activities and was misleading about its personnel.' The director's lack of probity meant that the tribunal was 'quite unable to accept his word that he had all times believed that he was trading in platinum alloy and in any event the evidence all points away from this conclusion.' His behaviour was 'not the behaviour of an innocent dupe caught up in someone else's fraud'. *Plasma Trading Ltd (No 2)*, LON/04/1187 & LON/05/122 (VTD 19499). (*Note.* For a preliminary issue in this case, see **2.134** APPEALS.)

Dealing in computer software—whether transactions a 'sham'

[36.124] A trader (D) reclaimed input tax in respect of two purchases of substantial quantities of computer software, which he exported to a Canadian customer. Customs rejected the claim on the basis that the transactions were a 'sham', and that no supplies had been made to D. The tribunal reviewed the evidence in detail and allowed D's appeal, finding that it was satisfied that D 'had in fact bought two consignments of computer software and had then immediately exported them'. The tribunal expressed the view that D 'knew nothing at all about the commodity dealt in', and appeared to have been 'tutored for a small role in a transaction where he should appear to be conducting a trading transaction'. However, any finding that the transactions were 'shams' would involve finding that D was 'guilty of some degree of fraud'. The tribunal was unable to 'reach a conclusion along those lines when (Customs) never contended that he was a knowing party to any fraud, and never asked one question in cross-examination that broached this subject'. The Ch D upheld this decision as one of fact. Briggs J held that 'if serious allegations, in particular allegations of dishonesty, are to be made against a party who is called as a witness they must be both fairly and squarely pleaded, and fairly and squarely put to that witness in cross-examination'. On the evidence, 'it was for the tribunal to balance the probabilities and improbabilities of the competing analyses, and to attribute such weight to each factor in that balance as they reasonably thought fit'. *HMRC v N Dempster (t/a Boulevard)*, Ch D [2008] STC 2079; [2008] EWHC 63(Ch).

Invoices for future marketing services-whether shams.

[36.125] See *FPV Ltd*, 40.48 INVOICES AND CREDIT NOTES.

Invoices for alleged supply of consultancy services.

[36.126] See *Bodyguard Workwear Ltd*, 62.51 SUPPLY.

Invoices for supplies of gold described by issuer as 'shams'

[36.127] See *Sandell*, 62.174 SUPPLY.

Miscellaneous

Cases where the appellant was successful

Whether central heating boiler supplied to claimant

[36.128] An individual (M) was building a house for his own use. He arranged for the plumbing to be done by L, who was not registered for VAT, and who was area representative for a company (W) from which he could obtain central heating equipment at a special discount. It was agreed that L should obtain the central heating boiler and associated equipment for the house from W, but that L should keep his special discount. L therefore charged M the full price of the boiler and equipment plus the VAT of £14.87 he had paid W on the discounted price. M reclaimed the £14.87 under what is now *VATA 1994, s 35*, but the Commissioners rejected the claim on the basis that the supply had been made to L rather than to M. The tribunal allowed M's appeal, holding on the evidence that L had bought the boiler and equipment as an agent for M, who was therefore entitled to the refund. *MB Murden*, LON/75/173 (VTD 207).

Chamber of Commerce operating training scheme

[36.129] A Chamber of Commerce operated a training scheme for employees under a contract with the Manpower Services Commission. It reclaimed input tax in respect of expenditure which it incurred in connection with the training. Customs refused to allow the claim, considering that the supplies in question were made to the individual trainees, the Commission or the employers. The tribunal allowed the Chamber's appeal, holding that the supplies were made to the Chamber, which was under a contractual obligation both to the Commission and to the employers. *Aberdeen Chamber of Commerce*, EDN/88/115 (VTD 3622).

Housebuilding company arranging house sales for prospective purchasers

[36.130] A group of housebuilding companies instituted a scheme for prospective purchasers of its houses, whereby it nominated an estate agent to sell the houses already owned by such purchasers, and paid the agents' fees. The scheme was instituted because most prospective purchasers could not proceed with a purchase until they had found a buyer for their existing homes. The group reclaimed input tax on the fees which it paid to the estate agents. The Commissioners issued an assessment to recover the tax, considering that the supplies were made to the owners of the houses, rather than to the company. The representative member of the group appealed, contending that it was acting as a joint principal and was a joint recipient of the supply, so that it was entitled to reclaim the input tax. The tribunal accepted this contention and allowed the appeal, holding on the evidence that the agents' services were provided both to the company and to the potential purchaser. The CA reversed this decision but the HL unanimously allowed the company's appeal and restored the decision of the tribunal. Applying the principles laid down in *Belgium v Ghent Coal Terminal NV*, 22.406 EUROPEAN COMMUNITY LAW, the supplies had been 'received in connection with the business activities of the taxable person, for the purpose of being incorporated within its economic activities'. Lord Hope observed that 'the fact that someone else—in this case, the prospective purchaser—also received a service as part of the same transaction does not deprive the person who instructed the service and who has had to pay for it of the benefit of the deduction'. *C & E Commrs v Redrow Group plc*, HL [1999] STC 161; [1999] 1 WLR 408; [1999] 2 All ER 1. (*Note*. For the Commissioners' practice following this decision, see Business Brief 27/99, issued on 21 December 1999. The Commissioners took the view that the decision only applies 'where there is a claim to input tax credit by a taxable person who has commissioned the goods or services and contracted with the supplier for them', and that the decision 'has no relevance to circumstances where a third party is simply meeting the costs of another'. See, however, the subsequent tribunal decision in *British Airways plc (No 3)*, **36.131** below.)

Meals provided for delayed airline passengers—whether supplied to airline

[36.131] A company which operated an airline made arrangements whereby passengers whose flights were delayed for more than two hours were given meal vouchers which could be exchanged for food up to a specified value at a number of restaurants at the airport. It paid the restaurant the amount shown on the vouchers, and reclaimed input tax on the amounts which it paid.

The Commissioners issued a ruling that the company was not entitled to credit for the input tax, on the grounds that the restaurants were supplying the food directly to the passengers rather than to the company. The company appealed, contending that the restaurants should be treated as supplying the food to the company, and that the company was making onward supplies of the food to the passengers which would be zero-rated as part of the overall supply of transport. The tribunal allowed the company's appeal, applying *dicta* of Lord Hope in *Redrow Group plc*, 36.130 above, and declining to follow the previous tribunal decision in *British Airways plc (No 2)*, 36.155 below, on the grounds that it was inconsistent with the HL decision in *Redrow*. *British Airways plc (No 3)*, [2000] VATDR 74 (VTD 16446).

Repairs to repossessed motor coach—whether supply made to vendor

[36.132] A company traded as motor distributors. In 1987 it sold a coach under a hire-purchase agreement. In 1990 the purchaser failed to make the required payments, and the company sought to repossess the coach. The company had some difficulty in tracing the coach, but eventually discovered that it had been damaged in an accident. It reclaimed input tax on repairs to the coach. The Commissioners issued an assessment to recover the tax, on the basis that the repairs had been supplied to the purchaser of the coach, rather than to the company. The tribunal allowed the company's appeal, holding on the evidence that the company 'had at no time parted with the ownership of the vehicle', and that it was entitled to reclaim the input tax. *Blythswood Motors Ltd*, EDN/95/325 (VTD 14203).

Purchase of vehicle—conditional sale agreement in name of trader's son

[36.133] A trader (B) carried on a vehicle hire business. He wished to purchase an 8-seat motor vehicle, and applied to a finance company for credit. However, the company rejected his application. His son then applied to the same company for credit and was accepted. The vehicle was registered in B's name and B made the monthly repayments to the finance company. B reclaimed input tax on the purchase, but the Commissioners rejected the claim on the grounds that the conditional sale agreement was in the name of B's son, rather than in the name of B himself. The tribunal allowed B's appeal, observing that in the particular circumstances it was required 'to look at all the facts and not just at the formal agreement between (the finance company) and (B's son)'. Applying *dicta* of Laws J in *Reed Personnel Services Ltd*, 33.21 HEALTH AND WELFARE, 'contractual documents determining the private law obligations of the parties involved do not necessarily conclude the issue for VAT'. The fact that the relevant documents were addressed to B's son was not conclusive. *JR Beagley*, LON/96/1001 (VTD 15107). (*Note.* For another issue in this case, see 65.28 TRANSFERS OF GOING CONCERNS.)

Retailer reimbursing independent concessionaires for discounts

[36.134] A company (B) operated a number of retail department stores. It allowed independent concessionaires to operate within its premises, in return for a licence fee based on turnover. It operated a 'storecard' (in-house credit card) scheme, under which discounts were allowed to customers. The discounts applied to purchases from B's concessionaires as well as to purchases from B itself. B reimbursed the concessionaires and reclaimed input tax on these reimbursements. The Commissioners issued a ruling that B was not entitled to make adjustments in respect of purchases from B's concessionaires, on the basis that the payments were consideration for the original supply of goods to the customer. B appealed. The tribunal allowed the appeal, holding that the payments which B made to the concessionaires were consideration for supplies of services by the concessionaires to B, being the concessionaires' agreement to accept the 'storecard' and give the relevant discount. Accordingly, VAT was chargeable on the supply, the valuation of which was the amount of the discount, and B was entitled to treat that VAT as its input tax. *JE Beale plc*, LON/97/1096 (VTD 15920).

Company operating sales promotion scheme

[**36.135**] See *HMRC v Loyalty Management UK Ltd*, **22.153** EUROPEAN COMMUNITY LAW, and *HMRC v Baxi Group Ltd*, **22.154** EUROPEAN COMMUNITY LAW.

Professional fees—whether supplied to company or to investors

[**36.136**] Two shareholders acquired a company (M) with the intention of using it to provide certain supplies to the telecommunications industry. They sought assistance from outside investors, and commissioned a major accountancy firm to provide a report as to M's likely profitability. M reclaimed input tax on the fees charged by the accountancy firm, and on other professional fees charged by two firms of consultants and by a second accountancy firm. The Commissioners rejected the claim on the basis that the professional services had been supplied to the outside investors, rather than to M. M appealed. The tribunal allowed M's appeal, applying the principles laid down in *Redrow Group plc*, **36.130** above, and holding that the services were supplied to M. The tribunal held that 'the exact contractual relationship concluded by the professional advisers does not necessarily determine the identity of the party to whom the supply is made'. M was 'the prime beneficiary', and any benefits received by the outside investors were 'incidental'. *Mono Global Ltd*, EDN/03/66 (VTD 18559).

Cases where the appellant was partly successful

Whether supplies made to company or to controlling shareholder

[**36.137**] An individual (R) purchased a 44-ton vessel in 1961 which he and his wife used for pleasure cruising. Following his retirement, he purchased a larger vessel in 1972 and, early in 1973, lent both vessels to a company (S) which he had incorporated to carry on the business of chartering them. The company, which was wholly owned by R and his wife, paid nothing for the loan but undertook to keep the vessels in good and seaworthy condition. The second vessel was overhauled in 1974 at a cost of £12,579 including VAT of £932. The invoice was addressed to 'R Esq, S Ltd', and R paid the bill himself. R then repossessed the ship and sold it through agents who charged a commission of £1,250 including VAT of £250. The company reclaimed both the £932 and the £250 as input tax and appealed against an assessment to recover these amounts. The tribunal dismissed the appeal with regard to the £250, finding that the sale had been by R and not by the company, but allowed the appeal with regard to the £932, finding that the repairs had been carried out on behalf of the company. *Setar Lines Ltd*, LON/76/155 (VTD 316).

Football club—payments to footballers' agents

[36.138] A professional football club reclaimed input tax on payments which it made to footballers' agents in connection with contract negotiations and transfers of players between clubs. Customs issued assessments to recover the tax on the basis that the agents had supplied their services to the individual players, rather than to the club. The tribunal dismissed the club's appeal, but the Ch D remitted the case for a rehearing, finding that the original tribunal chairman appeared to have misunderstood some of the evidence and misinterpreted the reference to 'exclusive agents' in some of the players' contracts. *Newcastle United plc v HMRC*, Ch D [2007] STC 1330; [2007] EWHC 612 (Ch). (*Note*. There was no further public hearing of the appeal.)

[36.139] In another case where a professional football club reclaimed input tax on payments to footballers' agents, the tribunal reviewed the evidence relating to 14 specific transactions in detail. The tribunal found that in ten of these transactions, the agent's services were supplied to the individual player and not to the club, so that input tax was not deductible in respect of those transactions. However, in respect of the other four transactions, the tribunal found that the agent was supplying services to the club, so that input tax was deductible. The tribunal therefore allowed the club's appeal in part. *Birmingham City Football Club plc*, [2007] VATDR 149 (VTD 20151). (*Note*. The tribunal awarded the club 25% of its costs.)

Cases where the appellant was unsuccessful

Whether supplies made to partnership or individual partner

[36.140] A firm of chartered accountants reclaimed input tax in respect of a caravan which had been purchased by one of the partners. The Commissioners issued an assessment to recover the tax and the firm appealed, contending that the caravan was used for the purpose of the firm's business. The tribunal dismissed the appeal, holding that the 'taxable person' was the partnership, and that, as the caravan had been supplied to one of the individual partners rather than to the partnership itself, the partnership was not entitled to reclaim the input tax. *Smith Wheeler & Hay*, LON/81/331 (VTD 1208).

[36.141] A partnership traded from premises which were leased by one of the partners. The partnership reclaimed input tax on the rent payable to the landlord under the lease. The Commissioners issued an assessment to recover the tax, on the grounds that the relevant supplies were made to the partner rather than to the partnership. The tribunal upheld the assessment and dismissed the partnership's appeal. *Fantasia (Knutsford)*, MAN/93/15 (VTD 12515).

[36.142] An appeal was dismissed in a case where a joiner had reclaimed input tax relating to an unregistered partnership of which he was a member. *MJ White*, LON/93/2368 (VTD 12360).

[36.143] A similar decision was reached in *S Grange*, MAN/96/456 (VTD 15706).

[36.144] See also *Ingram*, 36.54 above; *Stone*, 36.57 above, and *Mills*, 36.205 below.

Whether supply made to company or to director

[36.145] A company reclaimed input tax in respect of a franchise fee which its managing director had paid before the company was incorporated. The Commissioners rejected the claim and the tribunal dismissed the company's appeal, holding that the supply was made to the director as an individual rather than to the company. *Foxmead Services (Northern) Ltd*, MAN/83/296 (VTD 1625).

[36.146] Similar decisions were reached in *Bleyer Hair Clinic Ltd*, MAN/84/279 (VTD 1947); *Goodpass Ltd*, LON/95/1749 (VTD 14088); *Mowco Ltd*, EDN/98/29 (VTD 15657); *Associated Concrete Repairs Ltd*, LON/98/827 (VTD 15963) and *Edgley Management Ltd*, LON/98/1315 (VTD 17410).

[36.147] An appeal was dismissed in a case where a sole trader reclaimed input tax on a supply made to a company of which he had been a director. *PM Herbert*, LON/86/425 (VTD 2350).

[36.148] A doctor (R), whose supplies of medical services were exempt, registered for VAT on the basis that he would be supplying services such as acupuncture which did not qualify for exemption. He reclaimed input tax on construction work at his surgery, although the relevant invoices were addressed to a company, which was not registered for VAT, of which he was the controlling director. Customs issued assessments to recover the tax on the basis that the supplies had been made to the company rather than to R. The tribunal upheld the assessments and dismissed R's appeal. *Dr KC Ray*, MAN/06/003 (VTD 20516).

[36.149] See also *Collins*, 40.25 INVOICES AND CREDIT NOTES, and *Gavacan*, 40.26 INVOICES AND CREDIT NOTES.

Sale of house owned by company director

[36.150] The principal director of a building company sold his house to raise finance for the company, which reclaimed input tax on the commission paid by the director to the estate agent. The Commissioners issued an assessment to recover the tax and the tribunal dismissed the company's appeal, holding that the services had been supplied to the director rather than to the company. *Rushgreen Builders Ltd*, LON/87/116 (VTD 2470).

[36.151] The principal director of a property company, which had a large overdraft, obtained a second mortgage on his private residence as security against the overdraft. Subsequently the bank decided to call in the overdraft and required the director to sell the house. The company reclaimed input tax on the solicitors' fees and agents' fees relating to the sale. The Commissioners issued an assessment to recover the tax, on the basis that the relevant supplies were made to the director rather than to the company. The company appealed, contending that the input tax should be treated as deductible since the proceeds of the sale had been applied for the purposes of the business. The tribunal dismissed the company's appeal, observing that 'the critical question is whether the services were rendered to the business'. The services here had been rendered to the director rather than to the company. *WH Blatch Investments Ltd*, LON/95/918A (VTD 13727).

Input tax reclaimed in respect of goods supplied to winners of bingo prizes

[36.152] A company (J) carried on the business of an amusement arcade. It issued vouchers with a face value of £1 each to winners at bingo. The winners could use the vouchers for the purchase of goods from J or from a nearby firm (C), or could exchange them for vouchers issued by another company (A). J reimbursed C for the vouchers which C accepted at face value, and reclaimed input tax in respect of the goods which the winners of the vouchers had purchased from C. The Commissioners issued an assessment to recover the tax, considering that the goods were supplied by C to the winners of the vouchers rather than to J. The tribunal upheld the assessment and dismissed J's appeal. *Jomast Trading & Development Ltd*, [1984] VATTR 219 (VTD 1735).

[36.153] See also *Sooner Foods Ltd*, **62.363** SUPPLY.

Lunches provided for students at language school

[36.154] A company operated a language school. It paid students a lunch allowance of £17, with which the students bought lunch at a nearby restaurant for themselves and for their tutor. The students gave receipted bills to the school, which reclaimed input tax thereon. The Commissioners issued an assessment to recover the tax, considering that the lunches were supplied to the students, rather than to the school. The tribunal accepted this contention and dismissed the company's appeal. *Butler Question Method School of Languages Ltd*, LON/90/223Y (VTD 5677). (*Note.* An appeal against an estimated assessment on undeclared takings was also dismissed.)

Meals provided for delayed airline passengers

[36.155] A company which operated an airline made arrangements whereby passengers whose flights were delayed for more than two hours were given meal vouchers which could be exchanged for food up to a specified value at a number of restaurants at the airport. It paid the restaurant the amount shown on the vouchers, and reclaimed input tax on the amounts which it paid. The Commissioners issued a ruling that the company was not entitled to credit for the input tax, on the grounds that the restaurants were supplying the food directly to the passengers rather than to the company. The company appealed, contending that the restaurants should be treated as supplying the food to the company, and that the company was making onward supplies of the food to the passengers which would be zero-rated as part of the overall supply of transport. The tribunal dismissed the appeal, holding that the food was supplied directly by the restaurants to the passengers. The decision in *P & O European Ferries*, **36.230** below, was distinguished on the grounds that it related to supplies of services, whereas the supplies made by the restaurants were supplies of goods. The QB upheld the tribunal decision as one of fact. *British Airways plc v C & E Commrs (No 2)*, QB [1996] STC 1127. (*Note.* See now, however, the subsequent decision in *British Airways plc (No 3)*, **36.131** above.)

Input tax reclaimed by company managing pop group

[36.156] See *World Chief Ltd*, **1.13** AGENTS.

Input tax claimed on purchase of paper

[36.157] See *LS & A International Ltd*, **1.14** AGENTS.

Goods purchased by partnership—input tax reclaimed by single partner

[36.158] A sole trader reclaimed input tax in respect of goods which he had purchased while carrying on a previous business in partnership with his wife. The Commissioners issued an assessment to recover the tax, considering that the two businesses were unconnected. The tribunal dismissed the trader's appeal. Although registration related to persons rather than businesses, two or more persons carrying on business together were regarded as being separate from one of those persons carrying on business on his or her own account. *Dicta* of May J in *Glassborow*, **57.1** REGISTRATION, applied. *JR Michaelis*, LON/90/925Z (VTD 5734).

Trust employing accountants to provide services to investment trust

[36.159] In a case where the facts were complex and unusual, a trust established by will, and registered for VAT, supplied management and investment services to related trusts. From 1987 it managed an investment trust, which was not registered for VAT, and employed accountants to provide services to that trust. It reclaimed input tax in respect of the accountants' fees. The Commissioners issued an assessment to recover the tax, considering that the accountants' services had been supplied to the investment trust and not to the management trust. The tribunal upheld the assessment and dismissed the trust's appeal, applying the principles laid down in *Apple & Pear Development Council*, **22.80** EUROPEAN COMMUNITY LAW. *Sir Alexander MacRobert Memorial Trust*, [1990] VATTR 56 (VTD 5125).

Pension funds defrayed by employer—whether input tax reclaimable

[36.160] See *Linotype & Machinery Ltd*, **54.2** PENSION FUNDS; *Talbot Motor Co Ltd*, **54.3** PENSION FUNDS, and *Ultimate Advisory Services Ltd*, **54.4** PENSION FUNDS.

Whether supplies made to appellant or to appellant's bank

[36.161] A company requested a substantial increase in its overdraft facility from its bank. The bank requested a detailed report from the company's accountants. The accountants submitted their report to the bank but sent invoices to the company rather than to the bank. The company reclaimed input tax in respect of these invoices. The Commissioners rejected the claim and the tribunal dismissed the company's appeal, holding on the evidence that the accountants had supplied their services to the bank rather than to the company. *Eagle Trust plc*, MAN/93/1125 (VTD 12871).

[36.162] See also *Poladon Ltd*, **36.73** above, and *Dalesid Ltd*, **40.22** INVOICES AND CREDIT NOTES.

Whether supplies made to company or to creditors

[36.163] A large holiday company suffered financial difficulties, and agreed that a major accountancy firm (P) should liaise on its behalf with its banks, bondholders and other creditors, and prepare a detailed report on its financial status. The company reclaimed input tax in respect of the relevant supplies. HMRC issued assessments to recover the tax, on the basis that the supplies had actually been made to the company's creditors, rather than to the company itself. The Upper Tribunal upheld the assessments, distinguishing *C & E Commrs v Redrow Group plc*, **36.130** above, and finding that the company's creditors had 'first approached (P), and contracted for the work and therefore authorised it'. *HMRC v Airtours Holiday Transport Ltd*, UT [2010] UKUT 404 (TCC); [2011] STC 239.

Public house transferred as going concern

[36.164] The business of a public house was transferred as a going concern from one company (H) to another company (S) in March 1991. H went into liquidation in April 1991. A wholesaler who had supplied drinks to the public house began proceedings against two individuals in respect of money allegedly owed to it for drinks supplied before the transfer of the business. The court gave judgment in favour of the wholesaler, and ordered the named individuals to pay the wholesaler £65,000. The liquidator of H reclaimed input tax in respect of the payment, and S also reclaimed input tax in respect of the same payment. The Commissioners accepted the liquidator's claim and rejected the claim by S, which appealed. The tribunal dismissed the appeal, holding that S was not entitled to credit for the input tax since it had not carried on the business at the material time (and also noting that it did not hold an invoice in support of its claim). *A Hughes & Sons Ltd (t/a The Derby House)*, LON/94/2419 (VTD 13504). (*Note.* The relationship between the individuals and the companies is not made clear in the decision, but it is assumed that the individuals had been directors of both the companies concerned.)

Novation of hire-purchase agreement

[36.165] A company (S) claimed input tax on the novation of a hire-purchase agreement. Customs rejected the claim on the basis that the deed of novation did not create a supply for VAT services. The tribunal upheld Customs' ruling and dismissed the company's appeal. *Swan Plant Ltd*, MAN/07/1399 (VTD 20759).

[36.166] The decision in *Swan Plant Ltd*, **36.165** above, was applied in the similar subsequent case of *Scotts Group Ltd*, MAN/06/179 (VTD 20924).

Purported 'childcare licence'

[36.167] In 2006 a company registered for VAT, on the basis that it was carrying on business as a wholesaler. In 2007 it submitted a return claiming a repayment, including a deduction of £13,125 in respect of the alleged supply of a 'childcare licence' for £75,000. HMRC rejected the claim on the basis that this was a 'contrived transaction' which was not a genuine supply. The tribunal dismissed the company's appeal, finding that the purported licence 'was nothing more than a collection of word processed documentation which might be of use to a provider of child care. There were no contracts, no franchise agreement, no name of goodwill.' There were 'clear reasons to doubt the genuineness of the transactions'. *1-4 All Ltd v HMRC*, [2010] UKFTT 91 (TC), TC00402.

Other cases

[36.168] There have been a number of other cases, which appear to raise no point of general interest, in which appeals against the disallowance of input tax have been dismissed on the grounds that the relevant supply had not been made to the appellant. In the interests of space, such cases are not summarised individually in this book.

Whether supplies used for the purposes of the business

NOTE

In the cases below the issue is whether the supplies were for use in the existing business. Where the issue is whether the supplies were for the purposes of a future business or business activity, see 36.554 *et seq* below. See also, for accounting periods beginning after 27 July 1993, *VATA 1994, s 84(4)*, deriving from *FA 1993, s 46*. This provides that a tribunal can only allow an appeal against the disallowance of input tax on a 'luxury, amusement or entertainment' where the tribunal considers that the Commissioners 'could not reasonably have made' the determination which is the subject of the appeal. Cases relating to periods before the enactment of *FA 1993* should be read in the light of this change.

Luxuries, amusements and entertainments (VATA 1994, s 84(4))

Tennis club subscription for controlling director

[36.169] A company which supplied lecturing services reclaimed input tax on a subscription to a tennis club for its controlling director. The Commissioners rejected the claim on the ground that the expenditure had not been incurred for the purpose of the company's business. The tribunal dismissed the company's appeal, holding that 'the expenditure was not directly referable to the purpose of the business' and that it was not satisfied that the benefit of the company was 'the real purpose in the mind of (the director)' when he incurred the expenditure. Furthermore, the subscription was a 'luxury, amusement or entertainment' within what is now *VATA 1994, s 84(4)*. *John Price Business Courses Ltd*, [1995] VATDR 106 (VTD 13135).

Personalised vehicle numberplates—whether a 'luxury'

[36.170] In *College Street Market Gardens*, 36.485 below, the tribunal held that personalised vehicle numberplates were a 'luxury' within *VATA 1994, s 84(4)*.

Family partnership—purchase of racing car

[36.171] A family partnership carried on business as monumental masons. In January 1994 they purchased a racing car at a cost of £19,000 and reclaimed the input tax thereon. The Commissioners issued an assessment to recover the tax, considering that the car had not been purchased for the purposes of the business, but for the personal pleasure of one of the partners (M), and that the car was a 'luxury, amusement or entertainment', within what is now *VATA 1994, s 84(4)*. The partnership appealed, contending that the car had been purchased for advertising purposes. In 1994 M had driven the car in a competition, sponsored by Dunlop Rover, which comprised twelve races, and this had attracted publicity for the partnership in local newspapers and on local radio. The car had been sold in early 1995. The tribunal accepted the partnership's evidence and allowed the appeal. Applying *dicta* in *Ian Flockton Developments Ltd*, 36.341 below, the tribunal was satisfied that the car had been purchased for advertising purposes. Furthermore, the tribunal held that the car was not a 'luxury, amusement or entertainment', so that *s 84(4)* did not apply. The tribunal chairman also observed that, even if the car were deemed to fall within *s 84(4)*, the assessment would have been unreasonable on the grounds that the VAT officer responsible for it had not attempted to interview any of the partners. *Myatt & Leason*, [1995] VATDR 440 (VTD 13780).

Christmas party for employees—whether within VATA 1994, s 84(4)

[36.172] In *Ernst & Young*, 8.43 BUSINESS ENTERTAINMENT, the tribunal held that expenditure on a Christmas party for employees (who were required to make a contribution towards the cost) did not fall within *VATA 1994, s 84(4)*.

Motoring expenses

Motoring expenses—whether petrol supplied to appellant

[36.173] See *Berbrooke Fashions*, 36.1 above, and the cases noted at 36.2 above to 36.8 above.

Use of car for transport of employees

[36.174] The proprietors of a hairdressing salon reclaimed input tax on petrol and the Commissioners issued an assessment to recover the tax. The partners appealed, giving evidence that their employees were sometimes required to work in the evenings and, when this happened, the cars were used to drive the employees home. The tribunal held that the tax in respect of these journeys was deductible, and reduced the assessment accordingly. *E & S Blyth-Palk (t/a John Baxter Hair Fashions)*, LON/78/295 (VTD 718).

Rental payments for car no longer used in business

[36.175] Two individuals (S and H) had operated a restaurant in partnership. The partnership had leased a car, which was used by S partly for partnership purposes and partly for private purposes. S left the partnership and agreed with H that he would retain possession of the car, and that H would pay the rental payments on the car for the remaining 13 months of the lease. H reclaimed input tax on these payments. The Commissioners issued an assessment to recover the tax and the tribunal dismissed H's appeal. The tax was not deductible since the car was no longer used for the purposes of the business. H's motive for making the rental payments was to obtain S's share of the ownership of the restaurant. *Mrs Hague*, LON/81/262 (VTD 1159).

Accountancy partnership—accessories fitted to partner's car

[36.176] An accountancy partnership reclaimed input tax on accessories which had been fitted to a car owned by one of the partners, and used partly for partnership purposes and partly for private purposes. The Commissioners issued an assessment to recover the tax, and the partnership appealed. The tribunal directed that the tax should be apportioned. *Broadhead Peel & Co*, [1984] VATTR 195 (VTD 1737).

Repairs to car used by hotelier

[36.177] A hotelier reclaimed input tax on repairs to a car. The Commissioners issued an assessment to recover part of the tax, considering that the car was partly used for private purposes and that the cost should be apportioned accordingly. The tribunal allowed the appeal in part, finding that the private use of the car was very slight and holding that 95% of the tax was allowable. *WG Tregenza*, LON/85/130 (VTD 1907).

Repairs to vintage car used for advertising purposes

[36.178] A company dealt in 'classic' cars. It used a Lagonda car (a racing car built before World War II) for promotional purposes, although the car was actually owned by its managing director rather than the company. The car was driven in a long-distance race in Italy, and subsequently required repairs. The company reclaimed input tax on the cost of the repairs. The Commissioners issued an assessment to recover the tax but the tribunal allowed the company's appeal, holding on the evidence that the expenditure had been incurred in order to promote the company's business. *Terry Cohn Ltd*, LON/97/311 (VTD 15962).

Management consultancy partnership—upgrading of Aston Martin

[36.179] A partnership carried on a management consultancy business. It reclaimed input tax on the upgrading of an engine of an Aston Martin motor car. The car was approximately ten months old, had originally cost £145,000 and had covered 6,054 miles. The upgrading of the engine cost £50,000, and enabled the car to travel at 175 miles per hour. The Commissioners rejected the claim on the basis that the work seemed 'to have been commissioned to enhance performance rather than to effect repair and maintenance'. The partnership appealed, contending that the tax should be treated as deductible since the car was driven for business purposes. The tribunal dismissed the appeal, holding that 'there is no obvious and clear association between the business of a management consultancy and the expenditure on upgrading, as opposed to repairing an engine, simply to achieve driving speeds grossly in excess of permitted speed limits'. Accordingly, the tribunal held that the expenditure was not for the purposes of the partnership's business. *Trade Development Associates*, LON/94/347A & 419A (VTD 12699).

Transporter partly used privately

[36.180] The tribunal directed that input tax should be apportioned in a case where a trader purchased a transporter partly for business purposes and partly for private purposes. *LVJ Brooks*, LON/84/29 (VTD 1722).

Motoring offences—legal costs

[36.181] See *Scott*, 36.235 below, and *Child*, 36.236 below.

Employer paying for 'driver training' of employees' spouses and partners

[36.182] A group of companies provided its employees with cars. It required the employees to attend 'driver training' courses, and paid the costs of this. It allowed its employees to nominate one additional driver for the cars which it provided (such nominees normally being the employees' spouse or partner). It paid for these nominated drivers to attend 'driver training' courses. It reclaimed input tax on the payments made for the 'driver training' courses. The Commissioners accepted that this input tax was deductible where it related to the group's employees themselves, but issued an assessment to recover the tax relating to the nominated drivers who were not employed by the group. The representative member of the group appealed, contending that the expenditure had been incurred for commercial reasons. The tribunal dismissed the appeal, holding that the expenditure had not been incurred for the purposes of the group's business. *BMW Financial Services (GB) Ltd*, LON/01/1230 (VTD 17913).

Renovation of old vans

[36.183] A company reclaimed input tax on the renovation of two old vans, which were painted in pre-war livery and taken to local rallies. The vans did not bear the company's name, but a notice was displayed at the rallies indicating that they were sponsored by the company. The Commissioners issued an assessment to recover the tax and the company appealed, contending that the expenditure had been incurred for the purpose of advertising its business. The tribunal dismissed the company's appeal, finding that the expenditure had been incurred to enable the controlling director 'to enjoy his hobby of restoring old vans'. *Ron Miller Ltd*, LON/90/1191Z (VTD 5827). (*Note.* For another issue in this appeal, see **62.472** SUPPLY.)

Clothing

Formal clothing purchased by barrister—whether input tax deductible

[36.184] A new barrister reclaimed input tax on the purchase of two dark three-piece suits, three white tunic shirts, twelve detachable collars, two pairs of black shoes, several pairs of black socks and a suitcase. The Commissioners issued an assessment to recover the tax, considering that the clothing had not been purchased exclusively for professional purposes, since it could also be worn privately. The barrister appealed, contending that he had purchased the items in question for appearing in court, since the Bar Council required such clothing to be worn in court, and that before becoming a barrister he had habitually worn two-piece suits, coloured socks and brown shoes, which were not acceptable for court wear. The tribunal allowed his appeal in part, holding that the three tunic shirts and detachable collars, and one of the two three-piece suits, could be regarded as having been purchased for professional purposes. However, the tax on the second suit and on the shoes, socks and suitcase was not allowable. *EM Alexander*, [1976] VATTR 107 (VTD 251).

Fur coat purchased by authoress

[36.185] An authoress and scriptwriter decided to travel to New York in 1979 to attempt to gain a lucrative literary contract. Shortly before her departure she bought a mink coat for £4,950. She reclaimed the VAT on this as input tax. The Commissioners issued an assessment to recover the tax, considering that the coat had been purchased for private purposes rather than for professional purposes. She appealed, contending that her main purpose in buying the coat had been to impress the people that she would be meeting in New York and thus to improve her chances of gaining the literary contract. The tribunal held that the coat had been partly purchased for professional purposes and partly for private purposes, so that the cost should be apportioned. The appeal was adjourned in the hope that the parties could agree an apportionment. *RA Sisson*, LON/80/310 (VTD 1056). (*Note.* There was no further public hearing of the appeal. See now *VATA 1994, s 84(4)*, deriving from *FA 1993, s 46.*)

Art consultant—whether clothing purchased for business purposes

[36.186] An art consultant reclaimed input tax on the purchase of items of clothing costing more than £8,500. The Commissioners issued an assessment to recover the tax, considering that the clothing had not been purchased for the purposes of her business. She appealed, contending that she had purchased the clothing in question 'to cultivate a professional image drawing prospective clients' attention to herself'. The tribunal dismissed her appeal, holding that she had 'failed to establish' that the expenditure was incurred for the purposes of her business, within *VATA 1994, s 24(1)*). *Alexander*, 36.184 above, was distinguished since the clothing there had been purchased to comply with the rules of the Bar Council. *Sisson*, 36.185 above, was distinguished since the fur coat there had been found to have been purchased for the purpose of attempting to obtain one specific contract. *BJ Brown*, LON/91/1681 (VTD 6552).

Retailers—input tax reclaimed on suits worn while working

[36.187] In the case noted at **1.6** AGENTS, two retailers had reclaimed input tax on the cost of suits which they wore while working. The tribunal held that 'to dress well in order to conform with the standards of a particular lifestyle' was not a business expense, and that the tax was not deductible. *JK Hill & SJ Mansell (t/a JK Hill & Co)*, LON/86/472 (VTD 2379).

Electrician—input tax reclaimed on suits worn while working

[36.188] An electrician reclaimed input tax on suits which he wore at work. The Commissioners issued an assessment to recover the tax and he appealed, contending that he often had to work in dirty conditions and therefore did not wear the clothing in question when not at work. The tribunal held that 75% of the tax in question was allowable. *PR Younghusband*, LON/91/913Y (VTD 7443).

Architect—input tax reclaimed on suits worn while working

[36.189] An architect reclaimed input tax on the cost of suits which he wore while working. The Commissioners issued an assessment to recover the tax and the tribunal dismissed the architect's appeal, applying the decision in *Hill & Mansell*, **36.187** above. *W Richards*, MAN/92/324 (VTD 11674). (*Note.* For another issue in this case, see **8.2** BUSINESS ENTERTAINMENT.)

Actor—whether clothing purchased for business purposes

[36.190] An actor, who worked mainly as an 'extra' in television and films, reclaimed input tax on items of clothing such as dress suits. The Commissioners issued an assessment to recover 50% of the tax in cases where the clothing was also suitable for private wear. The actor appealed, contending that he had purchased the clothing for the purpose of his work as an actor and had not worn it privately, so that the whole of the tax should be deducted. The tribunal allowed his appeal, applying *Ian Flockton Developments Ltd*, **36.341** below, and *Lennartz*, **22.456** EUROPEAN COMMUNITY LAW. On the evidence, the actor's sole intention in buying the clothing was to wear it while acting. The Commissioners had not shown that the clothing had actually been worn privately, and the fact that it could be worn privately did not prevent the tax from being deductible. *J Pearce*, LON/91/1638Y (VTD 7860). (*Note.* For another issue in this case, see **36.549** below.)

Clothing purchased by company for wear by principal director

[36.191] A company carried on a management consultancy business from the home of its principal director. It purchased a number of items of clothing and jewellery to be worn by the director. These items included a pair of black leather boots and a sapphire mink jacket. The company reclaimed input tax on these items and the Commissioners issued an assessment to recover the tax, considering that the expenditure had not been incurred for the purpose of the company's business. The company appealed, contending that the clothing served the purpose of the company's business since, when its director attended meetings, she should be 'dressed in such a way that people would have confidence in her judgment'. The tribunal dismissed the appeal, holding that the company had not established that the clothing and jewellery in question had been purchased for business purposes. *PJ Stone Ltd*, LON/86/396 (VTD 2241).

Wig purchased by professional musician

[36.192] A professional jazz musician reclaimed input tax on the purchase of a wig. The Commissioners issued an assessment to recover the tax, considering that he had purchased the wig for private purposes rather than for professional purposes. He appealed, contending that he had always worn his hair long and had gained an 'image' as having a thick head of hair, but that his hair had recently begun to fall out and that he needed to wear a wig to maintain his image. The tribunal allowed his appeal. Applying *Ian Flockton Developments Ltd*, **36.341** below, the tribunal was satisfied that 'on the balance of probability the object in the taxpayer's mind at the time the expenditure was incurred was that the goods and services in question were to be used for the purpose of the business'. *JM Collie*, LON/90/1328X (VTD 6144). (*Note.* See now, however, *VATA 1994, s 84(4)*, deriving from *FA 1993, s 46*.)

Legal costs—civil cases

Cases where the appellant was successful

Legal services supplied to farming partnership

[36.193] See *Glasse Brothers*, 36.40 above.

Legal costs incurred by company in investigating affairs of subsidiary

[36.194] See *Crompton Enterprises Ltd*, 36.41 above.

Equine chiropractor

[36.195] An equine chiropractor (W) practised from premises which were subject to an 'agricultural condition', whereby they had to be occupied by a person 'wholly or principally employed in agriculture'. The local council issued a ruling that W's work did not comply with this condition, and took enforcement proceedings. W incurred legal costs in instructing solicitors to defend the proceedings and to seek the removal of the 'agricultural condition'. He was unsuccessful, and subsequently sold the premises in question. He reclaimed the input tax on the costs. The Commissioners issued an assessment to recover some of the tax, on the basis that the expenditure had been partly incurred for private purposes. The tribunal allowed W's appeal, holding that 'there was a clear nexus between the incurring of the expenditure on the relevant services and the purposes of the appellant's business as a chiropractor'. Accordingly, the whole of the input tax was deductible. *M Windsor*, MAN/95/2208 (VTD 14185).

Acquisition of minority shareholding in supplier—input tax on legal fees

[36.196] A limited partnership, which carried on a property management business, decided to acquire a minority shareholding in a company which supplied it with insurance services. It reclaimed input tax on the legal fees relating to the acquisition. Customs rejected the claim on the basis that the acquisition was an investment. The tribunal allowed the partnership's appeal, holding on the evidence that there was a direct and immediate link with the partnership's activities, so that the expenditure had been incurred for the purpose of the partnership's business. *Maybeck Llp*, MAN/05/78 (VTD 19898).

Bank—whether legal costs partly attributable to exempt supplies

[36.197] See *Midland Bank plc*, 22.400 EUROPEAN COMMUNITY LAW.

Cases where the appellant was partly successful

Surveyor—legal action against former partners

[36.198] A dispute arose between the members of a partnership of quantity surveyors. One of them (M) took legal proceedings against the other partners, who responded by expelling him from the partnership. The action was subsequently settled. M began a sole practice and reclaimed the input tax on the legal costs he had incurred in his action against his former partners. The Commissioners rejected the claim, and he appealed. The tribunal allowed his appeal in part, holding that the tax relating to expenditure incurred after he had begun his sole practice was reclaimable, since it had been incurred to protect his professional reputation, but that the tax relating to the recovery of his capital from the partnership was not reclaimable. *BP McCallum,* [1980] VATTR 79 (VTD 945).

Consultant—costs of libel action and discharge from bankruptcy

[36.199] A consultant reclaimed input tax in respect of legal costs incurred in obtaining his discharge from bankruptcy, in conducting a libel action, and in being represented before a Parliamentary Commission of Enquiry. The Commissioners rejected his claim and he appealed. The tribunal allowed his appeal in part, holding that tax was not reclaimable in respect of his discharge from bankruptcy or of the Parliamentary Commission of Enquiry, but that tax was deductible in respect of his successful conduct of the libel action, since this had affected his integrity in a business capacity. *WG Stern,* LON/84/416 (VTD 1970).

Company—costs of libel action

[36.200] The directors of a company which operated a health spa began libel actions against a magazine. The company was awarded damages of £7,500 and the directors were awarded damages totalling £90,000 as individuals. The company reclaimed the input tax incurred in respect of the directors' legal costs as well as that incurred in respect of its own costs. (It appears that the bill of costs did not distinguish between those referable to the company's action and those referable to the directors' actions.) The tribunal held that the directors' main purpose in incurring the expenditure had been to clear their own reputations, and that only 25% of the tax in question was allowable. *Ormac (No 49) Ltd,* EDN/90/185 (VTD 6537).

Sole trader—former cohabitee claiming to be a partner—legal costs

[36.201] An electrician (C) registered for VAT, as a sole trader, in 1984. In 1985 he began cohabiting with a woman (P). Their relationship deteriorated, and in 1991 C left their house. P took possession of his van, and C took legal proceedings against her to recover it. During the proceedings, P claimed that she should be treated as a 50% partner in the business. The proceedings were eventually settled in 1996, and P was ordered to return the van to C. C reclaimed input tax on his legal costs. The Commissioners rejected the claim, on the basis that the expenditure primarily related to a domestic dispute. C appealed. The tribunal allowed his appeal in part, holding on the evidence that one-third of the tax was deductible. *D Clark (t/a Clark Electrical Services),* MAN/98/679 (VTD 15927).

Cases where the appellant was unsuccessful

Legal costs relating to breach of covenant

[36.202] See *Potton,* 36.43 above.

Legal costs of application for judicial review

[36.203] An import and export dealer (J), who was registered for VAT, had a brother who was an undischarged bankrupt. J employed his brother to export engines to Egypt, paying his remuneration from an overseas source into an overseas bank account, with a view to keeping it out of the reach of IS's trustee in bankruptcy. Subsequently the brother was arrested and charged with five offences under *CEMA 1979, s 68(2)*. He was committed for trial and was granted bail, subject to a surety of £100,000 which J provided. While on bail, the brother went to the USA and did not return to the UK. The Court made an estreatment order for the surety of £100,000, and J applied for judicial review. His application was dismissed, and he paid the £100,000. He had to pay costs to his solicitors, and reclaimed the VAT thereon as input tax. The Commissioners issued an assessment to recover the tax, considering that the expenditure had been incurred for personal reasons rather than for business reasons. The tribunal upheld the Commissioners' contentions and dismissed J's appeal. *JH Smalley*, MAN/88/657 (VTD 3894). (*Note.* For a subsequent appeal by the same appellant, see **36.228** below.)

Legal costs of civil action concerning land purchase

[36.204] A firm of scrap dealers purchased the freehold of a site. They had previously occupied part of the site as tenants. Seven other tenants issued a writ against the firm, claiming that it had previously arranged to share part of the land with them, and seeking a share of the profits from the land. The firm reclaimed input tax on legal costs incurred in resisting this action. The Commissioners rejected the claim and the tribunal dismissed the firm's appeal, holding that expenditure arising from a dispute about the ownership of land did not qualify as expenditure for the purpose of the firm's business. *Shaw Lane Estates*, MAN/88/680 (VTD 4420).

Legal fees relating to partnership dispute

[36.205] A trader (M) had previously been in a partnership trading as garage proprietors. The partnership included his ex-wife. She withdrew from the partnership in 1974 and they were divorced the following year. Under the divorce agreement M was required to pay his ex-wife an amount in respect of her share in the partnership. There were delays in valuing the amount due, but in 1987 the couple agreed that M should pay her £5,000 in full and final settlement of her claims. M's solicitors charged him £2,500 for work done in respect of the partnership dispute. Meanwhile, in 1983 the partnership had been dissolved and M had registered for VAT as a sole trader, selling wine. He reclaimed input tax on the solicitors' fees and the Commissioners issued an assessment to recover the tax. The tribunal dismissed M's appeal, holding that the solicitors' services had not been rendered to M for the purpose of his business as a wine retailer. *C Mills*, LON/89/1423Y (VTD 4864).

[36.206] A registered trader had been in partnership with his wife until the marriage broke down, from when he continued his business as a sole trader. The couple were divorced, and the ex-wife made an application under the *Married Women's Property Act 1882, s 17*. The trader was ordered to pay costs of more than £55,000 to his ex-wife. He reclaimed input tax on the costs and the Commissioners issued an assessment to recover the tax. The tribunal dismissed the trader's appeal, holding that the relevant supplies had not been made for the purpose of the trader's business. *K Lister*, MAN/93/1079 (VTD 13044). (*Note.* An appeal against a misdeclaration penalty was, however, allowed.)

Legal fees relating to dispute between shareholders

[36.207] 66% of the shares in a company (C) were held by its principal shareholder. Another shareholder, who owned 25% of the shares, filed a winding-up petition in the High Court, contending that 'the affairs of the company had been and were continuing to be conducted in a manner which was unfairly prejudicial to his interests as a minority shareholder'. Following a hearing in the Court of Appeal, the proceedings were eventually settled by a negotiated agreement. C reclaimed substantial amounts of input tax on legal fees relating to the dispute. Customs rejected part of the claim on the grounds that it related to services supplied to the individual shareholders, rather than to C. The tribunal upheld Customs' ruling and dismissed C's appeal. *City of Belfast Warehousing Ltd*, LON/06/020 (VTD 20196).

Legal fees relating to action against former directors

[36.208] A company (D) registered for VAT in 2001, but failed to account for any output tax between 2002 and 2004. During this period it took legal proceedings against two of its former directors, alleging breach of fiduciary duty and misappropriation of funds. The court gave judgment for D, and the former directors were ordered to pay costs and damages. D reclaimed input tax on its legal fees. HMRC issued an assessment to recover the tax, on the basis that it did not relate to any taxable supplies. D appealed. The tribunal dismissed the appeal, finding that D was not trading during the period to which the legal fees related, and holding that 'the litigation was not for the purpose of (D's) economic activities' and that the costs had 'no direct and immediate link to its economic activities'. *Denbrae Ltd v HMRC*, [2010] UKFTT 195 (TC), TC00497.

Legal fees relating to transfer of share capital

[36.209] A company (F) carried on the business of manufacturing refractory fibre products. Its controlling shareholders entered into negotiations for the sale of their shares to another company, but were unable to agree satisfactory terms. During the course of the negotiations, the shareholders consulted accountants and solicitors, who charged F for their work. F reclaimed input tax on this expenditure, and the Commissioners issued an assessment to recover the tax. The tribunal dismissed F's appeal, holding that the expenditure had not been incurred for the purpose of F's business. *Ash Fibre Processors Ltd*, MAN/93/568 (VTD 12201).

[36.210] See also *Brucegate Ltd*, **36.51** above.

Legal costs incurred by director of insolvent company

[36.211] An individual (H), who carried on business as a self-employed consultant, was appointed as managing director of a company. He resigned his directorship in May 1988, and the company went into liquidation later in that year. In 1991 the Department of Trade and Industry applied for an order under *Company Directors Disqualification Act 1986, s 6* barring H from acting as a company director. He successfully opposed the application, and reclaimed input tax on his legal costs. The Commissioners rejected the claim, on the basis that the expenditure did not relate to H's consultancy business. The tribunal dismissed H's appeal, applying the principles laid down in *Rosner*, **36.232** below. *AJ Handyside (t/a Stratagem International)*, LON/94/1226A (VTD 13182).

[36.212] The decision in *Handyside*, **36.211** above, was applied in the similar subsequent cases of *ML Keam*, LON/99/897 (VTD 16685) and *R Redgrove*, LON/99/911 (VTD 16817).

Solicitor's fees on transfer of deeds of house

[36.213] A builder who had been divorced from his wife arranged for a solicitor to transfer the title deeds of his home from joint names to his sole name. He reclaimed input tax on the solicitor's fees and appealed against an assessment to recover the tax, contending that the house was a business asset as he had used it as security for a bank loan. The tribunal dismissed his appeal against the assessment, applying the decision in *Dean*, **36.531** below, and finding that the house was predominantly a private residence rather than a business asset. *SD Jordan*, LON/90/1692Y (VTD 5071).

Legal costs on sale of property owned by partner

[36.214] See *Rock Lambert*, **36.55** above.

Solicitor's fees on transfer of land

[36.215] See *Francis Jackson Homes Ltd*, **36.52** above.

Legal costs of defending action for repossession of house

[36.216] A trader borrowed money from a bank to purchase a house. She defaulted on the loans and the bank began proceedings to repossess the house. The trader reclaimed input tax on the costs which she incurred in defending the proceedings. The Commissioners issued an assessment to recover the tax, considering that the expenditure had been incurred for personal reasons rather than for business purposes. The trader appealed, contending that the tax should be treated as deductible since she ran her business from the house. The tribunal dismissed her appeal, holding that the expenditure had been incurred for personal purposes and that the tax was not deductible. *S McLeod (t/a Sally McLeod Associates)*, LON/94/1080A (VTD 12886).

Legal costs of defending claim by former wife

[36.217] A farmer (S) divorced his wife in 1997. She took legal proceedings claiming ancillary relief against a number of his assets. S incurred substantial legal costs in resisting the claim, and reclaimed input tax on these. The Commissioners rejected the claim, and S appealed, contending that the tax should be treated as deductible because the majority of the assets which his ex-wife had claimed were used for the purposes of his business. The tribunal dismissed his appeal, holding that 'the payments were, in truth, personal payments made by the appellant as an individual in order to protect and retain as many of his assets as he could. The mere fact that those assets included assets used in his business activities which would be adversely affected by a successful claim is not sufficient to establish the required nexus between the expenditure and the purposes of the businesses.' *GA Swinbank*, MAN/01/94 (VTD 18192).

Legal costs incurred by company in relation to director's previous business

[36.218] A company reclaimed input tax in respect of legal costs which its principal director had incurred in the course of a dispute with his previous company, having been dismissed from his directorship with that company. The Commissioners issued an assessment to recover the tax and the tribunal dismissed the company's appeal, holding that the legal costs had clearly not been incurred for the purpose of the appellant company's business. *Morgan Automation Ltd*, LON/90/396X (VTD 5539).

[36.219] A company (R) sold leisurewear. Its principal director (L) had previously been director of another company (B) which had gone into liquidation. L considered that the reason for B's liquidation was that its finance director had withdrawn funds without authorisation, and that B's bank had been negligent in that it had cleared cheques which only bore the signature of the finance director, although the bank mandate required a second signature. The Official Receiver declined to take legal action against the bank, so L arranged for R to pay £1 to the Receiver in return for the Receiver assigning B's right of action against the bank and the finance director. Following this assignment, R and B issued a writ against the bank claiming substantial damages. Subsequently the bank agreed to pay R £168,000, plus costs, in settlement of the claims. R reclaimed input tax on its costs, but the Commissioners rejected the claim on the basis that the expenditure had not been incurred for the purpose of R's business. The tribunal dismissed R's appeal, holding that 'it is not possible to identify the services which were the subject of the legal fees charged to (R) as the cost component of any taxable transaction of that company'. *Rushcombe Ltd*, LON/96/847 (VTD 14727).

Legal fees in respect of work done before registration

[36.220] See *Charles-Greed*, **36.608** below.

Legal costs of defending action against former employer

[36.221] An individual (M) had been managing director of a company dealing in men's clothing. In 1989 he left that company and registered for VAT as a self-employed marketing consultant. He was paid £36,000 by his former employer, and also retained a BMW car valued at £12,000. The company demanded the return of the car. M refused to return the car and his former employer obtained judgment against him in the Westminster County Court. M reclaimed input tax in respect of his solicitor's fees in defending the action. The Commissioners issued an assessment to recover the tax and the tribunal dismissed M's appeal, holding that the expenditure had not been incurred for the purposes of his business. *HD Marks*, LON/92/2951A (VTD 11381).

Legal costs of taking action against former employer

[36.222] An individual (O) was dismissed from his employment after borrowing £40 from his employer's petty cash. He was unable to find another job, and began self-employment as a management consultant. He registered for VAT. He took legal action against his former employer in an industrial tribunal, and reclaimed input tax on his legal costs. The Commissioners rejected his claim, on the basis that the expenditure had not been incurred for the purpose of his business. The tribunal dismissed his appeal, holding that the expenditure had been incurred for personal purposes rather than for the purposes of O's management consultancy business. *P Oldfield*, MAN/93/955 (VTD 12233).

Legal costs of civil action following car accident

[36.223] A builder (D) was injured in a car accident. He took a civil action against the other driver, and was awarded damages. However, as the damages awarded were less than the amount which the other driver had offered before the hearing, D had to pay a substantial proportion of his legal costs. He reclaimed input tax on these. The Commissioners issued an assessment to recover the tax, considering that the expenditure had not been incurred for the purposes of D's business. The tribunal dismissed D's appeal. Applying the QB decision in *Rosner*, 36.232 below, the tribunal held that input tax could only be deducted if the expenditure was 'directly referable to what the business is in fact doing'. The expenditure here was of benefit to D's business, but was not 'directly referable to the business of building'. Accordingly the tax was not deductible. *CB Dureau (No 2)*, LON/96/987 (VTD 14643).

Legal costs of unsuccessful civil action

[36.224] See *Nye Saunders & Partners*, **36.47** above, and *Davey*, **36.49** above.

Legal costs of realising investments

[36.225] A partnership carried on business as wholesalers and retailers of clothing, textiles and household goods. The partnership purchased a 10% interest in a residential property, as an investment. Subsequently the ownership of this property was transferred to a non-resident company, and the partnership took legal action against the couple who had held the 90% interest in the property. Meanwhile, in 1989 the partnership sold its wholesale business, and in 1990 it closed its retail shop. The partnership's action concerning the investment property was settled out of court, and the partnership reclaimed input tax on its solicitors' charges. The Commissioners issued an assessment to recover the tax, considering that the expenditure had not been incurred for the purpose of the partnership's business. The partnership appealed, contending firstly that it was carrying on a business of investing its surplus funds, and alternatively that the expenditure was incurred for the purpose of recovering money which was to be used for the purposes of its clothing business. The tribunal dismissed the appeal, holding on the evidence that the partners 'did not conduct their investment activities in such a manner that they amounted to a business' and that the funds which were recovered were not used, or intended to be used, for the purposes of the clothing business. *Kuchick Trading*, MAN/91/1190 (VTD 12131).

[36.226] A retailer purchased a 50% shareholding in a nursing home. A dispute arose between him and the other shareholders, and he consulted a solicitor. He reclaimed input tax on the solicitor's fees. The Commissioners issued an assessment to recover the tax, considering that the expenditure had not been incurred for the purpose of the retailer's business. The tribunal dismissed the retailer's appeal, holding that the shareholding was 'a personal investment rather than a business activity', and that there was no 'real connection or nexus between the legal services and the purposes of the business'. *R Anwar*, MAN/93/1524 (VTD 12748).

[36.227] An agricultural contractor (W) suffered financial difficulties, and had to realise many of his assets. He reclaimed input tax on the legal costs incurred. HMRC issued an assessment to recover the tax, and the tribunal dismissed W's appeal, observing that 'the fact that (W's) agricultural business may have benefitted from the services does not necessarily mean that those services were supplied for the purpose of the business'. *NAJ Walley v HMRC*, [2011] UKFTT 120 (TC), TC00996. (*Note.* The tribunal also upheld a misdeclaration penalty, mitigated by 50%.)

Dormant business—legal action against bank

[36.228] An individual (S) had carried on a small export business from 1985 to 1998. He submitted no VAT returns between 1998 and 2009, when he submitted a return reclaiming input tax on legal fees relating to a dispute with his bank. HMRC rejected the claim and the tribunal dismissed S's appeal, finding that the legal fees had not been incurred for the purpose of any business. *Dr JH Smalley v HMRC*, [2011] UKFTT 134 (TC), TC01008. (*Note.* For a previous appeal by the same appellant, see **36.203** above.)

Transfer of employer's pension funds—legal advice for employees

[36.229] See *The Plessey Co Ltd*, 54.10 PENSION FUNDS.

Legal costs—criminal cases

Cases where the appellant was successful

Legal costs of company employees charged with manslaughter

[36.230] A company operated a number of ferries across the English Channel. One of its ferries sailed from Zeebrugge with its doors open, and capsized. More than 190 people died, and the company and seven of its employees were charged with manslaughter. The company spent about £3,500,000 on the defence of the employees, and reclaimed the input tax incurred on this. The Commissioners issued an assessment to recover the tax, considering that the expenditure had not been incurred for the purpose of the company's business. The tribunal allowed the company's appeal, holding that the conviction of any of the employees 'would have caused severe damage to the public perception of the company's business'. The tribunal held that the expenditure had been incurred for the purposes of the company's business, notwithstanding that it had also had the effect of benefiting the individual employees. *P & O European Ferries (Dover) Ltd*, [1992] VATTR 221 (VTD 7846). (*Note.* The Commissioners consider that this decision 'was based on the very particular and unusual facts' and 'most apparently similar cases can be distinguished on the facts'. See Customs' VAT Manual, Part 13, para 7.3.)

Legal costs incurred by gold dealer in defending criminal charges

[36.231] A gold dealer was arrested and charged with offences under *CEMA 1979, s 170(1)(a)* concerning the evasion of Customs duties on gold which he had purchased from another registered dealer. He was acquitted and reclaimed input tax on his legal costs. The Commissioners rejected the claim on the basis that the expenditure had been incurred for a 'personal reason rather than for a business reason'. The tribunal allowed the dealer's appeal, observing that 'the activities described in the indictment were all steps taken in the normal course of (the dealer's) carrying on of his gold dealing business', and distinguishing *Rosner*, **36.232** below. It was not alleged that the dealer 'had in any way been involved in smuggling in the sense of knowingly importing gold with intent to defraud Her Majesty of duty'. If he had been charged with a smuggling offence under *s 170(1)(b)*, 'his legal expenses might not have been deductible'. *SR Brooks*, LON/94/412A (VTD 12754).

Cases where the appellant was unsuccessful

Legal costs of sole trader charged with criminal offence

[36.232] The proprietor of a private educational establishment was convicted of conspiracy to defraud, in relation to the provision of false information under the *Immigration Act 1971* and in assisting overseas visitors to the UK in making false representations about whether they were genuine students. He was fined and ordered to pay the costs of the prosecution. He also paid the costs of an appeal by one of his students, and incurred legal costs in negotiating with Customs for a compounded penalty to avoid criminal proceedings regarding evasion of VAT. He reclaimed input tax in respect of the legal costs incurred, and the Commissioners issued an assessment to recover the tax, considering that the expenditure had not been incurred for the purposes of the business. The proprietor appealed, contending that the expenditure had been incurred for the purpose of his business, since he had been liable to imprisonment and if he had been imprisoned for any length of time his business may have been forced to close. The QB upheld the assessment, holding that the fact that the business had benefited from the expenditure was not conclusive, since 'there must be a real connection, a nexus between the expenditure and the business'. On the evidence, there was no clear nexus between the expenditure in question and the business. Accordingly, the expenditure in question had not been incurred for the purpose of the business and none of the tax was deductible. *C & E Commrs v FW Rosner*, QB 1993, [1994] STC 228.

[36.233] In *Spillane*, 3.53 ASSESSMENT, the QB held that VAT on legal fees, incurred by a sole trader in defending proceedings for committal to prison for contempt of court, was not deductible as input tax.

[36.234] A similar decision was reached in *RN Scott*, MAN/92/1244 (VTD 11574).

Legal costs of farmer charged with motoring offence

[36.235] A farmer was prosecuted for reckless driving. He reclaimed input tax in respect of his solicitors' and counsel's fees. The Commissioners rejected his claim and the tribunal dismissed his appeal, holding that the expenditure had not been incurred for the purpose of his business. *RN Scott*, MAN/86/96 (VTD 2302). (*Note.* For a subsequent appeal by the same appellant, see **36.234** above.)

Legal costs of estate agent charged with motoring offence

[36.236] An estate agent was charged with driving when under the influence of alcohol, and refusing to take a breathalyser test. He reclaimed input tax in respect of legal costs incurred in defending himself. The Commissioners issued an assessment to recover the tax, considering that the expenditure had been incurred for personal reasons rather than for business reasons. The tribunal dismissed the estate agent's appeal, applying *Scott,* **36.235** above. 'The criminal offence of failing to take a breath test to ascertain the content of alcohol in the appellant's blood had no connection to a supply of goods or services used for the purpose of the appellant's business'. *GM Child (t/a Child & Co),* LON/90/1239X (VTD 6827). (*Note.* For another issue in this case, see **44.140** MOTOR CARS.)

Legal costs of surveyor charged with motoring offence

[36.237] A surveyor was convicted of driving with excessive alcohol and was disqualified from driving for three years. He reclaimed input tax on his legal costs. The Commissioners rejected the claim and the tribunal dismissed the surveyor's appeal, applying *dicta* in *Rosner,* **36.232** above. *VW Evans,* LON/96/1271 (VTD 14662).

Legal costs of company director charged with criminal offence

[36.238] A company carried on a grocery business, including a supermarket. In the course of its business it acquired and sold a quantity of confectionery, in relation to which W, its managing director and principal shareholder, was later charged with handling stolen property. He was convicted and served six months in prison. At his request, the solicitors who had handled his defence invoiced the company for the legal costs incurred. The company paid these and reclaimed the VAT thereon as input tax. The Commissioners issued an assessment to recover the tax and the tribunal dismissed the company's appeal. The legal services had been rendered to W personally and not to the company. The expenditure might have had the effect of benefiting the business, but it was not incurred for the purpose of the business. *Wallman Foods Ltd,* MAN/83/41 (VTD 1411).

[36.239] The managing director of a company was charged with corruption in relation to the acquisition of stock by the company. He was acquitted and the company reclaimed input tax in respect of the costs of his defence. The Commissioners rejected the claim and the tribunal dismissed the company's appeal. The charges were brought against the director personally. The expenditure had benefited the company's business but had not been incurred for the purpose of the company's business and accordingly the input tax was not deductible. *Britwood Toys Ltd,* LON/86/280 (VTD 2263).

[36.240] A company carried on business as a building contractor and property developer. In 1985 the company and its principal director were charged with obtaining money from the National Coal Board by deception, by falsely representing that the company had completed work for the Board when this was not the case. The Board also began civil proceedings against the director. The company reclaimed input tax in respect of the costs of defending the actions. The Commissioners agreed to allow the tax in respect of the civil action, but only agreed to allow 50% of the tax in respect of the criminal proceedings. The tribunal dismissed the company's appeal against this decision, holding that the company had not shown that more than 50% of the costs could be regarded as having been incurred for business purposes. (The tribunal also held that, as the company was partly exempt, the tax in question should be apportioned between taxable and exempt supplies.) *Dennis Rye Ltd*, MAN/88/764 (VTD 4545). (*Note*. For a subsequent appeal by the same company, see **46.83** PARTIAL EXEMPTION.)

[36.241] The director of a computer software company was charged with assaulting a British Rail employee, and was convicted. The company reclaimed input tax on the costs of his defence. The Commissioners issued an assessment to recover the tax, and the tribunal dismissed the company's appeal. *LHA Ltd*, LON/93/924A (VTD 11911). (*Note*. For another issue in this case, see **36.563** below.)

[36.242] An individual (M) had been the principal director of a company (T) which had gone into liquidation. The company's affairs were investigated by the Serious Fraud Office, and M was charged with fraudulent trading, contrary to *Companies Act 1985, s 458*. M was also chairman of another company (K) which had been incorporated to develop a power station. K paid substantial legal fees in defending M against the charges of fraudulent trading, and reclaimed input tax on these fees. The Commissioners rejected the claim, considering that the expenditure had not been incurred for the purpose of K's business. The tribunal dismissed K's appeal, applying the QB decision in *Rosner*, **36.232** above. The fact that the expenditure had benefited K was not conclusive. On the evidence, the legal services could not 'properly be said to have been used for the purposes of the business of the company'. *Kingsnorth Developments Ltd*, LON/93/1616 (VTD 12544).

Renovation and acquisition of premises—sole traders

Cases where the appellant was successful

Shopkeeper

[36.243] A shopkeeper lived above the shop from which he traded. He reclaimed input tax incurred on renovating the premises, and the Commissioners issued an assessment to recover the tax. The tribunal allowed his appeal, finding that the expenditure related to the retail shop and holding that the whole of the tax was allowable. *JPR Hampton*, MAN/86/93 (VTD 2196).

Grocer—renovation of kitchen used for take-away food business

[36.244] A grocer traded from two adjoining cottages, using the upper floor of one of them as living accommodation. He began to offer sandwiches and hot take-away food for sale, and renovated the kitchen of one of the cottages. He reclaimed the input tax on the relevant expenditure, but the Commissioners issued an assessment to recover the tax, considering that the use of the equipment was domestic rather than commercial. The tribunal allowed the grocer's appeal, holding on the evidence that the element of private use was insignificant and that the expenditure had been incurred for business purposes. *PA Farley*, MAN/87/208 (VTD 2567).

Farmer—erection of conservatory for use as office

[36.245] A farmer reclaimed input tax on the erection of a conservatory at her house. The Commissioners issued an assessment to recover the tax, and the farmer appealed, contending that the conservatory had been erected to be used as an office, so that the input tax should be treated as deductible in full. The tribunal accepted the farmer's evidence and allowed her appeal. *MA Murray*, EDN/95/172 (VTD 13907).

Cases where the appellant was partly successful

Fish farmer

[36.246] A fish farmer owned five ponds, covering 3 acres, in land of 48 acres. The only accommodation at the farm was a prefabricated bungalow, which was nearing the end of its life. He built a new bungalow to replace the existing one, and reclaimed input tax on the expenditure. The Commissioners issued an assessment to recover the tax but the tribunal allowed his appeal in part, holding that in view of his need to live near the fish ponds, 50% of the tax was deductible. *D Mears*, [1981] VATTR 99 (VTD 1095). (*Note*. The tribunal rejected an alternative contention by the appellant, that the work was within what is now *VATA 1994, s 35*. For cases concerning *s 35*, see **15 CONSTRUCTION OF BUILDINGS, ETC.**)

Farmer

[36.247] A farmer owned an estate of 2,000 acres, and lived in a mansion on the estate. Part of the estate was used as a caravan site. The administration of the estate, including the farming and the caravan site, was carried on from the mansion. The farmer reclaimed input tax in respect of extensive repairs to the mansion. The tribunal held that the expenditure had been incurred partly for business purposes and partly for private purposes, and held that 60% of the tax in question was deductible. *Sir Ian MacDonald of Sleat*, [1981] VATTR 223 (VTD 1179). (*Note*. See now Business Brief 18/96, issued on 27 August 1996, for guidelines which have been agreed with the National Farmers' Union regarding input tax claims for repairs and renovations to farmhouses.)

[36.248] A farmer renovated a bungalow, which had previously been vacant, to use as a home for his family and as a base from which he could run his farming business. He reclaimed the input tax incurred on the renovation. The Commissioners considered that the work had primarily been incurred for private purposes rather than business purposes, and issued an assessment to recover 80% of the tax in question. The farmer appealed. The tribunal reviewed the evidence in detail and found that half the total expenditure had been incurred for private purposes and half had been incurred for dual purposes. Of the half that had been incurred for dual purposes, 60% should be apportioned to the business, with the result that 30% of the total input tax should be treated as allowable. The assessment was reduced accordingly. *RJ Blomfield*, MAN/90/592 (VTD 5759). (*Note*. See also the note following *Sir Ian MacDonald of Sleat*, **36.247** above.)

[36.249] A sheep farmer reclaimed input tax on the restoration of a farm house. The Commissioners issued an assessment to recover the tax, on the basis that the expenditure had been incurred for private purposes rather than for the purposes of the farmer's business. The farmer appealed. The tribunal allowed the appeal in part, finding that the expenditure had been incurred for a dual purpose and holding that 40% of the tax was allowable. *MS Riches*, [1994] VATTR 401 (VTD 12210). (*Notes*. (1) An alternative contention by the appellant, that the work qualified for zero-rating under what is now *VATA 1994, Sch 8 Group 5*, was rejected by the tribunal. Compare the cases noted at **15.187** to **15.214** CONSTRUCTION OF BUILDINGS, ETC. (2) An appeal against a misdeclaration penalty was allowed. (3) See also the note following *Sir Ian MacDonald of Sleat*, **36.247** above.)

Car dealer

[36.250] A car dealer purchased and renovated a run-down property. He used it as his family home and ran his business from one room. He reclaimed the input tax on the renovation work, and the Commissioners issued an assessment to recover the tax. The tribunal allowed his appeal in part, holding that one-eighth of the tax was attributable to the business and was deductible. *RJ Ferguson*, MAN/83/198 (VTD 1578).

Solicitor

[36.251] A solicitor reclaimed input tax on the purchase of some materials for the construction of a house, one room of which he intended to use as an office. The Commissioners rejected the claim, and the solicitor appealed. The tribunal held that the expenditure had primarily been incurred for personal purposes, and that only 5% of the tax was deductible. *PF Bilton*, MAN/86/162 (VTD 2324).

Stud proprietor—refurbishment of house partly used for business purposes

[36.252] The proprietor of a stud in Oxfordshire had to visit Newmarket frequently to take his mares to be covered by stallions there, to meet clients, and to buy and sell horses at auction. He leased a small house in Newmarket to stay in overnight, and reclaimed input tax on the expenditure incurred in refurbishing it. The Commissioners issued an assessment to recover the tax, considering that the expenditure had been incurred for personal reasons rather than for business reasons. The tribunal allowed the proprietor's appeal in part, holding that his primary purpose was 'to provide himself with a place where he could do business with his customers on the many occasions when, in connection with that business, he needed to go to Newmarket'. However, since the house was partly used for business entertainment, the tribunal held that only 50% of the tax in question was deductible. *TD Rootes (t/a The Shutford Stud)*, LON/91/339X (VTD 6808).

Subpostmaster and general retailer

[36.253] A subpostmaster and general retailer refurbished his premises. The work included the creation of an office downstairs and a bedroom and bathroom upstairs. He reclaimed input tax on the refurbishment. The Commissioners rejected his claim, considering that the expenditure had not been incurred for the purpose of his retail business. The tribunal allowed his appeal in part, finding that the work had partly been incurred in order to provide better storage facilities for the business, but had also partly been incurred for the purpose of his office as a subpostmaster and partly with the intention of letting or selling the upper floor of the premises. The tribunal directed that the input tax should be apportioned. *JJ Gartland*, MAN/90/877 (VTD 7331).

Forester

[36.254] The owner of a forest in Ulster, who was registered for VAT, reclaimed input tax on the construction of storage buildings on his estate, and on the construction of a driveway leading to his house and to the storage buildings. (Previously, access to the house had been by means of a road which crossed land owned by the National Trust.) The Commissioners issued an assessment to recover the tax, considering that the expenditure had been incurred for private purposes, rather than for the purpose of administering the forest which he owned. He appealed, contending that the buildings had been constructed for the purpose of storing business assets, and that the driveway had been constructed to avoid the need to cross National Trust land. The tribunal allowed his appeal in part, holding that 50% of the expenditure on the storage buildings and on a part of the driveway leading to those buildings, and 25% of the expenditure on the remainder of the driveway, had been incurred for business purposes. *Earl of Belmore*, BEL/92/13X (VTD 9775).

Haulage contractor

[36.255] A haulage contractor reclaimed input tax on the building of a two-storey extension at the rear of his home. The Commissioners issued an assessment to recover the tax and he appealed, contending that he had built the extension to provide himself with an office. Initially he had used the lower part of the extension as his office, but subsequently he had rearranged the ground floor so that a room at the front of his house (which had previously been a lounge) became his office and the new room became a dining-room. The tribunal allowed his appeal in part, accepting that the lower floor of the extension had been built with the intention of being used as an office, finding that two-thirds of the expenditure was attributable to the lower floor, and holding that two-thirds of the disputed tax was allowable. *J Bryant*, LON/90/1588A (VTD 11212).

Ceramic designer

[36.256] A ceramic designer, who worked from home, reclaimed input tax on the construction of an extension to her home. The Commissioners issued an assessment to recover 45% of the tax, on the basis that the expenditure had been incurred for private purposes as well as for business purposes. The tribunal allowed the designer's appeal in part, finding that the business purpose was the primary purpose but that the desire to improve the value of her home was a subsidiary purpose, and holding that 80% of the tax was deductible. *J Willingale*, LON/93/2325A (VTD 12029).

Plant hire contractor

[36.257] The proprietor of a plant hire business reclaimed input tax on the renovation of a farmhouse. The Commissioners issued an assessment to recover the tax, considering that the expenditure had been incurred for domestic purposes rather than for business purposes. The proprietor appealed, contending that the expenditure had been incurred for the purpose of providing accommodation for his daughter and son-in-law, and that since his son-in-law was employed by him in the business, the tax was deductible. The tribunal held that the expenditure had been incurred for a dual purpose but that the domestic purpose was the primary purpose, and held that 10% of the tax was deductible. *LG Cook (t/a Ellon Plant Hire)*, EDN/93/216 (VTD 12302).

Cases where the appellant was unsuccessful

Doctor

[36.258] A doctor built a house on land which he owned and reclaimed input tax on the materials used. The Commissioners issued an assessment to recover the tax and the tribunal dismissed the doctor's appeal, holding that the supply of the materials was not for the purposes of his business. *Dr M Davies*, CAR/75/162 (VTD 219). (*Note*. The relevant supplies were before the introduction of what is now *VATA 1994, s 35*. See **15** CONSTRUCTION OF BUILDINGS, ETC. for cases concerning this provision.)

Fisherman

[36.259] A fisherman reclaimed input tax on expenditure incurred in renovating the barn where he and his family lived. The Commissioners issued an assessment to recover the tax on this expenditure and the tribunal dismissed his appeal. *DC Bean*, CAR/76/163 (VTD 339).

Builder

[36.260] A builder purchased an old blacksmith's forge to convert into a house for his own occupation, and reclaimed input tax on building materials relating to this work. The Commissioners issued an assessment to recover the tax, and the tribunal dismissed his appeal, holding that the materials had not been supplied for the purposes of his business. *TDO Jones (t/a Evan Jones & Son)*, CAR/76/75 (VTD 365).

[36.261] A builder, who had previously lived in a caravan, converted a barn for him and his family to live in. He reclaimed input tax on the materials used, and the Commissioners issued an assessment to recover the tax. The tribunal dismissed his appeal against the assessment, holding that the barn had not been converted for the purposes of his business. *W Ball*, MAN/88/821 (VTD 3865).

[36.262] An appeal was dismissed in a subsequent case where a builder had reclaimed input tax in respect of materials used to renovate two houses which he and his wife used as private residences. *RD Elton*, LON/92/2058A (VTD 11590).

Publican

[36.263] A publican reclaimed input tax on redecorating and carpeting the living accommodation on the upper floor of the public house. The Commissioners issued an assessment to recover the tax and the tribunal dismissed his appeal, holding that the expenditure had not been incurred for business purposes. *RTG Britton*, MAN/77/39 (VTD 445).

Coal merchant

[36.264] A coal merchant purchased a disused quarry and five Victorian cottages nearby. He used the quarry as his business premises. He renovated five of the cottages and reclaimed input tax in respect of the materials used for the renovation. The Commissioners issued an assessment to recover the tax, against which he appealed. The tribunal dismissed his appeal, holding that the cottages were not assets of his business and had not been renovated for the purpose of his business. *SJ Johnson*, MAN/82/185 (VTD 1367).

Architect

[36.265] An architect reclaimed input tax on expenditure incurred in renovating an office building of which he was the joint owner. The Commissioners issued an assessment to recover the tax, considering that he had purchased an interest in the building as an investment, so that the expenditure had not been incurred for the purpose of his profession. The tribunal upheld the assessment and dismissed the architect's appeal. *DT Morgan-Jones*, LON/83/173 (VTD 1340).

[36.266] An architect reclaimed input tax on materials used in renovating his house. The Commissioners issued an assessment to recover the tax and the tribunal dismissed the architect's appeal. *CR Butterworth*, LON/82/240 (VTD 1395).

Accountant

[36.267] An accountant reclaimed input tax on alterations carried out at the house which he and his wife occupied. The Commissioners issued an assessment to recover the tax and the tribunal dismissed the accountant's appeal. *CR Groom*, MAN/83/244 (VTD 1630).

Actor

[36.268] An actor lived in London but frequently worked in Manchester. He purchased and renovated a house in Manchester so that he could stay there when necessary in preference to a hotel. The Commissioners issued an assessment to recover the tax and the tribunal dismissed the actor's appeal, holding that the expenditure had been incurred for personal reasons rather than for the purposes of his profession. *K Farrington*, LON/86/230 (VTD 2177).

Furniture dealer

[36.269] A furniture dealer reclaimed input tax on the renovation of a flat which he occupied, including the purchase of kitchen and bathroom fittings. The Commissioners issued an assessment to recover the tax and the tribunal dismissed his appeal, holding that there was no connection between his occupation of the flat and his furniture business. *DB Bray*, LON/90/326 (VTD 5538).

Bookseller

[36.270] A bookseller lived at Westcliff-on-Sea, where he had a shop, and also owned a warehouse at Burton-on-Trent. He purchased two houses, one in

London and one in Burton-on-Trent, and reclaimed input tax on renovation work at the houses. The Commissioners issued an assessment to recover the tax and the tribunal dismissed the bookseller's appeal, holding that the houses had been purchased for personal reasons, rather than for the purposes of the business. *JR Hodgkins (t/a Clifton Books)*, LON/90/1514Y (VTD 6496).

Surveyor

[36.271] A chartered surveyor, who was a paraplegic, converted two barns into a cottage. He reclaimed the input tax incurred on the work, and the Commissioners issued an assessment to recover the tax. He appealed, contending that the expenditure had been incurred for business purposes as he needed the active assistance of someone living nearby. He gave evidence that he had intended the cottage to be used as accommodation for his son, who was aged 19 and living at home. However, at the relevant time the cottage was let on short-term tenancies. The tribunal dismissed the surveyor's appeal, holding on the evidence that the renovation of the cottage had not been carried out for the purposes of his business. *ACH Bond*, LON/89/1246Y (VTD 4722).

Conversion of houseboat

[36.272] The owner of a large houseboat undertook conversion work on it so that it could be used to provide bed and breakfast accommodation. He reclaimed the whole of the input tax incurred on the work. The Commissioners issued an assessment to recover 50% of the tax, since the owner was living in the houseboat and it appeared that he would continue to use half of the houseboat for his own occupation. The tribunal upheld the assessment and dismissed the owner's appeal. *C Pollock*, LON/91/195 (VTD 6638). (*Note*. The appellant also contended that the work was within what is now *VATA 1994, s 35*, but the tribunal rejected this contention since the houseboat was not a building and he was converting it rather than constructing it. For cases concerning *s 35*, see **15 CONSTRUCTION OF BUILDINGS, ETC.**)

Farmer—repair to farmhouse roof

[36.273] A farmer incurred expenditure on repairs to the roof of his farmhouse, and reclaimed the whole of the input tax. The Commissioners issued an assessment to recover 30% of the tax, considering that the expenditure had been partly incurred for private purposes, so that only a proportion of the tax was deductible. The farmer appealed, contending that the effect of *Article 17* of the *EC Sixth Directive*, as interpreted in *Lennartz v Finanzamt München*, **22.456 EUROPEAN COMMUNITY LAW**, was that the whole of the input tax should be treated as deductible. The tribunal dismissed his appeal, holding that the principle in *Lennartz* only applied to supplies of goods and that the subsequent private use of such goods was treated as a supply of services on which output tax was chargeable. However, the farmhouse was immovable property rather than goods, and the use of the farmhouse for private purposes could not be treated as a taxable supply of services. Since the input tax was not paid wholly for the purposes of actual or deemed taxable transactions, it followed that the decision in *Lennartz* was distinguishable and only a proportion of the input tax was deductible. *WD Hurd*, [1995] VATDR 128 (VTD 12985). (*Note*. The case was heard by the tribunal with *F & M Mounty & Sons*, 36.307 below.)

Caterer

[36.274] A married woman carried on a small catering business from her home. She reclaimed the whole of the input tax on the refurbishment of the kitchen. The Commissioners issued an assessment to recover 80% of the tax, considering that the kitchen was primarily used to prepare meals for the trader's family. She appealed, contending that the whole of the tax should be treated as allowable because the kitchen had to meet the standards set by the Health and Safety Inspectorate. The tribunal dismissed her appeal, finding that she had 'not discharged the burden of proof' that the purpose of the work was to comply with these standards. *E Gent (t/a Elizabeth Corke Catering)*, MAN/96/54 (VTD 14438).

Haulage contractor

[36.275] A haulage contractor reclaimed input tax relating to the building of an extension at the bungalow where he lived. The Commissioners issued an assessment to recover the tax, considering that it had not been incurred for the purposes of his business. The tribunal upheld the assessment and dismissed the contractor's appeal. *BCW Bushell*, LON/96/411 (VTD 15094).

Project manager

[36.276] A self-employed project manager (L) reclaimed VAT on the refurbishment of a private property owned by his partner. Customs issued an assessment to recover the tax, on the basis that the expenditure had not been incurred for the purpose of L's business. The tribunal upheld the assessment and dismissed L's appeal. *AI Linward*, LON/07/1525 (VTD 20942).

Renovation and acquisition of premises—partnerships

Cases where the appellant was successful

Family farming partnership—conversion of cowshed into cottage

[36.277] A married couple who carried on a farming business in partnership renovated an old cowshed, converting it into a cottage for the husband's mother to live in. The couple reclaimed input tax on the materials used in the renovation and the Commissioners issued an assessment to recover the tax. The couple appealed, contending that the tax should be treated as deductible since the mother did some agricultural work for them. The tribunal allowed the couple's appeal, holding on the evidence that their principal purpose had been to enable the husband's mother to continue to work for them on the farm. *CSJ & DJ Whitfield*, LON/88/452 (VTD 3506).

Family farming partnership—renovation of farmhouse

[36.278] A family farming partnership farmed a substantial area of land including three farms, each of which had a farmhouse. One of the farmhouses was occupied by the senior partner (D), the second was occupied by an employee, and the third, which was owned by D rather than by the partnership, was in very poor condition. D decided to renovate it. The work was paid for by the partnership, which reclaimed the input tax. The Commissioners issued an assessment to recover the tax, considering that the work had been carried out for D's private purposes rather than for the purposes of the partnership. The tribunal allowed the partnership's appeal, holding on the evidence that the farmhouse had been renovated to be used as a business asset of the partnership. *D Dyball & Son*, LON/89/1449X (VTD 4863).

Retailers—whether premises purchased for business or for letting

[36.279] A married couple traded in partnership, selling bicycles and perambulators from a retail shop. In 1979 they acquired the adjacent premises, which were in poor condition. They renovated the premises and converted the first floor into offices, some of which they used for storage. They reclaimed input tax on the materials used. The Commissioners issued an assessment to recover the tax, considering that the work had not been carried out for the purposes of the couple's retail business and that the renovated premises were probably intended for letting. The tribunal allowed the couple's appeal, finding that the original premises were crowded and congested, and that expansion was an 'attractive proposition'. *JF & SD Pank*, MAN/89/805 (VTD 4930).

Hotel owned and managed by married couple—enlargement of hotel

[36.280] A married couple owned and managed a hotel which contained 19 bedrooms. They occupied one of the bedrooms and their daughter occupied another bedroom, the remaining 17 being let to guests. They arranged for the building of an extension, and the bedrooms which they had previously occupied were subsequently let to guests. They reclaimed the input tax incurred in building the extension. The Commissioners issued an assessment to recover the tax, considering that the work had been undertaken to provide the couple with better living accommodation, rather than for the purposes of the business. The tribunal allowed the couple's appeal, holding on the evidence that the extension had been built for the purpose of the hotel business although it had also had the effect of improving the proprietors' living accommodation. *JA & GL Perez*, LON/90/988Z (VTD 6758).

Partnership carrying on property development business

[36.281] A married couple carried on a property development business in partnership. They reclaimed input tax on the building of a two-storey extension at their house. The extension comprised one room which was used as an office, together with a kitchen, a bathroom, and two upstairs rooms which could be used as bedrooms or for office purposes. The Commissioners issued an assessment to recover 50% of the tax, on the basis that the expenditure was partly for private purposes. The couple appealed, contending that the whole of the expenditure had been incurred for business purposes, and that both the upstairs rooms had been used as offices. The tribunal accepted the couple's evidence and allowed the appeal. *DLR & Mrs LM Chiplen*, LON/93/1458A (VTD 12280). (*Note.* The assessment under appeal also covered a duplicated claim to input tax, in respect of which the appeal was dismissed.)

Building partnership

[36.282] A married couple traded in partnership as builders. In 1990 they purchased a mill which had planning permission for conversion into a private house. They reclaimed input tax on the purchase and subsequent conversion work. In 1992 they moved into the mill. In 1994 the Commissioners issued an assessment to recover the tax, on the basis that the mill had been purchased to be used as their private residence. The couple appealed, contending that they had intended to sell the mill at a profit and were still hoping to do so, having instructed three different estate agents. The tribunal accepted the couple's evidence and allowed their appeal. *GM & JA Storrie*, MAN/95/1929 (VTD 14543).

Cases where the appellant was partly successful

Family farming partnership—conversion of oasthouse into farmhouse

[36.283] A family farming partnership converted an oasthouse for use as a farmhouse, and reclaimed the input tax on the work. The Commissioners issued an assessment to recover the tax, and the partnership appealed. The tribunal allowed the appeal in part, directing that the tax in question should be apportioned. *K & D Chapman*, LON/81/213 (VTD 1209).

Family farming partnership—conversion of mill into dwelling-house

[36.284] A family farming partnership, consisting of a married couple and their son and his wife, converted a mill into a dwelling-house for the two senior partners. The partnership reclaimed the input tax on this work and the Commissioners issued an assessment to recover the tax, considering that it had been undertaken for private purposes rather than for business purposes. The tribunal allowed the partnership's appeal in part, holding that 50% of the tax was allowable. *Herrod-Taylor & Co*, LON/83/143 (VTD 1475).

Family farming partnership—conversion of barn into dwelling-house

[36.285] A family farming partnership reclaimed input tax in respect of the conversion of a barn into a dwelling-house for one of the partners and his wife. The Commissioners issued an assessment to recover the tax, considering that the expenditure had been incurred for domestic purposes rather than private purposes. The partnership appealed, contending that the purpose of the work had been to enable the relevant partner, who had suffered a stroke and was unable to walk long distances, to live in close proximity to the farm. The tribunal allowed the appeal in part, finding that the work had a dual purpose, of which the business purpose was the dominant purpose, and holding that 70% of the tax in question was allowable. *W Cupit & Sons*, MAN/89/891 (VTD 5403).

Family farming partnership—conversion of granary into dwelling-house

[36.286] A family farming partnership comprised a married couple and their son. The partnership converted an old granary into a dwelling-house for the son and his fiancée, and reclaimed the input tax thereon. The Commissioners issued an assessment to recover the tax, considering that the work had been undertaken for domestic reasons rather than for the purposes of the business. The partnership appealed, contending that the work had been undertaken for business purposes since it was essential that the son should live on the farm. The tribunal held that the work had been undertaken with a dual purpose and adjourned the hearing in the hope that the parties could agree on an apportionment of the tax. *J & B Stanwix & Son*, MAN/90/772 (VTD 6347). (*Note.* There was no further public hearing of the appeal.)

Family farming partnership—renovation of farmhouse and cottage

[36.287] A family farming partnership owned a large farmhouse and a number of cottages. The active partners lived in the farmhouse. The partnership incurred expenditure on renovating the farmhouse and one of the cottages, and reclaimed the input tax on this expenditure. The Commissioners issued an assessment to recover 70% of the tax on the farmhouse and the whole of the tax on the cottage. The tribunal allowed the partnership's appeal in part, holding that the tax in respect of the cottage was wholly allowable, since it was intended that it should be occupied by employees, but upheld the Commissioners' decision to allow only 30% of the tax in respect of the farmhouse. *J Korner & Others*, EDN/85/73 (VTD 2008). (*Note.* See now Business Brief 18/96, issued on 27 August 1996, for guidelines which have been agreed with the National Farmers' Union regarding input tax claims for repairs and renovations to farmhouses.)

[36.288] A family farming partnership incurred expenditure in renovating and extending their farmhouse. The extension comprised 2,063 square feet, of which 1,290 were accepted as relating entirely to living accommodation. The partnership reclaimed $^{773}/_2$ of the total input tax, and the Commissioners issued an assessment to recover most of this, considering that only 10% of the total tax was deductible. The tribunal reviewed the evidence in detail and allowed the appeal in part, holding that 20% of the total tax was deductible. *PM & JB Paice*, LON/92/1007Y (VTD 9649). (*Notes.* (1) An appeal against a misdeclaration penalty was allowed. (2) See also the note following *Korner & Others*, 36.287 above.)

[36.289] A married couple carried on a livestock farming business from a hill farm not suitable for arable crops. The husband was also a partner in a nearby firm of surveyors. They incurred expenditure on renovating the farmhouse, which was described as 'an imposing period house with landscaped gardens' resembling 'a country mansion'. They reclaimed one-third of the input tax on this expenditure. The Commissioners considered that only 10% of the tax in question should be allowed, and issued an assessment to recover the balance. The tribunal allowed the couple's appeal in part, holding on the evidence that 20% of the input tax was deductible. (An appeal against the disallowance of input tax incurred on resurfacing the driveway was dismissed.) *ATB & Mrs SDL Jones*, LON/92/1763A (VTD 11410). (*Notes.* (1) For another issue in this case, see **36.392** below. (2) See also the note following *Korner & Others*, 36.287 above.)

Family farming partnership—installation of security system in farmhouse

[36.290] A family farming partnership reclaimed input tax in respect of the installation of a security system in the farmhouse. The Commissioners issued an assessment to recover the tax but the tribunal allowed the partnership's appeal in part, holding that 40% of the tax in question was allowable. *The Grange Farm*, LON/86/680 (VTD 2344). (*Note.* See now the note following *Korner & Others*, 36.287 above.)

Family farming partnership—renovation of cottage

[36.291] A family farming partnership restored an old cottage adjoining the farmhouse. Immediately after the restoration the cottage was occupied by one of the partners, but it was subsequently occupied by an employee. The partnership reclaimed the input tax on the work. The Commissioners issued an assessment to recover the tax but the tribunal allowed the partnership's appeal in part, holding that 70% of the tax in question was allowable. *ACS Eccles & Co*, EDN/85/71 (VTD 2057). (*Note.* See now the note following *Korner & Others*, **36.287** above.)

[36.292] A similar decision was arrived at in a subsequent case where the tribunal allowed 70% of the input tax on the cost of renovating and extending a cottage close to the main farmhouse. *WJL Greig & Son*, EDN/88/56 (VTD 2918). (*Note.* See now the note following *Korner & Others*, **36.287** above.)

Grocery partnership

[36.293] A grocery partnership reclaimed input tax in respect of building materials which were partly used for business purposes and partly for private purposes. The Commissioners issued an assessment to recover the tax. The tribunal allowed the partnership's appeal in part, holding that 50% of the tax in question was allowable. *AS Purewal & Others*, MAN/85/119 (VTD 2055).

Lighthouse open to viewing by public and used as private residence

[36.294] A retired naval commander and his wife had carried on a business of buying and selling pictures. In 1984 the husband bought a derelict lighthouse, and spent three years restoring it. In 1986 they closed their business of buying and selling pictures, and in 1987 they opened the lighthouse for viewing by the public in return for admission fees. They also used the lighthouse as their private residence. They reclaimed input tax on the materials used in renovating the lighthouse, and the Commissioners issued an assessment to recover the tax. The tribunal held that the expenditure had been incurred for a dual purpose and that 40% of the tax was allowable, applying *Ian Flockton Developments Ltd*, **36.341** below. *Waterford Galleries*, LON/88/896X (VTD 3448).

Hotel owned and managed by married couple—conversion of outbuildings

[36.295] A married couple purchased a hotel in 1987. They incurred expenditure in converting outbuildings into residential accommodation, and reclaimed input tax on this. The Commissioners discovered that the accommodation in question was occupied by the couple's widowed mothers, who had contributed to the cost of the work, and issued an assessment to recover the tax. The couple appealed, contending that, since their mothers worked for them at the hotel, the expenditure had been incurred for business reasons and the tax was deductible. The tribunal allowed the appeal in part, holding that the expenditure had been incurred for a dual purpose and that one-third of the tax was deductible, applying *Ian Flockton Developments Ltd*, **36.341** below. *BG & PL Menheneott*, MAN/92/90 (VTD 10542).

Renovation of bungalow adjacent to hotel

[**36.296**] A married couple had purchased a hotel in Godalming in 1983. In 1986 they also purchased a bungalow in grounds adjoining the hotel. They used the bungalow as their private residence. In April 1988 they installed a new kitchen in the bungalow. However, in May 1988 they purchased another hotel some distance away, and on 1 September they left the Godalming hotel to live in the new hotel. Between August 1988 and February 1989 they arranged for the construction of a two-storey extension to the bungalow at the Godalming hotel. This bungalow was initially occupied by hotel employees, but in December 1989 they sold it. The couple reclaimed input tax on the kitchen and the extension, and the Commissioners issued an assessment to recover the tax, considering that the expenditure had not been incurred for business purposes. The tribunal allowed the couple's appeal in part, holding that the tax on the kitchen was deductible since at that time the partners were living in the bungalow and were doing so for the purpose of running the business. However, the tax on the extension was not deductible, because at the time the expenditure was incurred the couple had left the Godalming hotel, and since the subsequent sale of the bungalow was an exempt supply, the extension had never been used for the making of taxable supplies. *Mr & Mrs M Cummings (t/a Inn On The Lake)*, LON/91/1170 (VTD 8891).

Design consultants reclaiming input tax on conservatory

[**36.297**] An unmarried couple carried on business as design consultants from the cottage where they lived. They reclaimed input tax on the supply of a conservatory at the cottage, and the Commissioners issued an assessment to recover the tax, considering that the expenditure had not been incurred for business purposes. The couple appealed, contending that the conservatory was used as a showroom and for meetings with clients. The tribunal allowed the appeal in part, holding on the evidence that 60% of the tax on the conservatory was deductible. *B Muir & G Edwards (t/a Muir-McGill Associates)*, LON/91/1684X (VTD 7469).

Solicitors' partnership—swimming pool constructed in grounds

[**36.298**] See *Willcox & Co*, 36.521 below.

Cases where the appellant was unsuccessful

Building partnership—materials for house built for partner

[**36.299**] A partnership which carried on a construction business reclaimed input tax in respect of materials used in building a house for one of the partners. Most of the work was done by the partner concerned. The Commissioners issued an assessment to recover the tax and the tribunal dismissed the partnership's appeal. *RGB Contractors*, LON/74/70 (VTD 133).

Family retail partnership—purchase of property

[**36.300**] A family partnership, which carried on a retail business, reclaimed input tax on the purchase of a property. The Commissioners rejected the claim and the tribunal dismissed the partnership's appeal, finding that 'it is not established that the property was purchased as a business asset' and that, even if it was, 'it was purchased by way of an investment and not for the purpose of obtaining income therefrom'. *T, EC, PT & A Worthington (t/a Conochies)*, EDN/98/128 (VTD 16228).

Garage built at partners' residence

[36.301] A married couple trading in partnership reclaimed input tax on a garage built at their residence. The Commissioners issued an assessment to recover the tax and the tribunal dismissed the couple's appeal, holding on the evidence that the garage was not used for business purposes. *DF & A Everett*, MAN/83/252 (VTD 1606).

[36.302] A similar decision was reached in *Mr & Mrs G Vitzthum (t/a Leeds Wine Services)*, MAN/92/1505 (VTD 11076).

Family farming partnership—renovation of castle

[36.303] A married couple who owned a livestock farm lived in a seventeenth-century castle, from which they administered the farm. They reclaimed input tax on renovation of part of the castle. The Commissioners issued an assessment to recover 90% of the tax, considering that the work had primarily been undertaken for domestic reasons. The tribunal upheld the assessment and dismissed the couple's appeal. *CMM & ISMM Crichton*, EDN/87/105 (VTD 2748). (*Note.* See now the note following *Korner & Others*, **36.287** above.)

Family farming partnership—renovation of farmhouse

[36.304] A married couple purchased 1,500 acres of farmland, including an old nine-bedroomed house which was a protected building. The house was in disrepair, and they had it renovated at a cost of more than £1,000,000. They reclaimed 30% of the input tax relating to this expenditure. The Commissioners issued an assessment to recover two-thirds of the amount reclaimed, considering that only 10% of the expenditure could be regarded as having been for the purposes of their business activities (which included occasional lettings for shooting weekends as well as the administration of the farm). The tribunal upheld the assessment and dismissed the couple's appeal. *RF & RJ Macaire*, LON/92/1139Z (VTD 10741). (*Note.* See now the note following *Korner & Others*, **36.287** above.)

[36.305] A family partnership reclaimed input tax on a payment made to a firm of quantity surveyors in connection with the renovation of the farmhouse. The Commissioners issued an assessment to recover 50% of the tax, on the basis that the expenditure had been partly incurred for private purposes. The tribunal dismissed the partnership's appeal. The chairman observed that Customs had been 'very generous indeed' in agreeing an apportionment of 50%. *CJ, JD & EN Aplin*, LON/95/1943 (VTD 14660). (*Note.* See now the note following *Korner & Others*, **36.287** above.)

Family farming partnership—conversion of coach-house into residence

[36.306] A family farming partnership arranged for the conversion of a coach-house into a dwelling-house for one of the partners. The partnership reclaimed 40% of the input tax relating to this work. The Commissioners only agreed to repay 10% of the tax in question. The tribunal upheld the Commissioners' decision and dismissed the partnership's appeal. *DM Walthall & LD Crisp*, LON/98/519 (VTD 15979).

Farming partnership—repair to farmhouse roof

[36.307] A family farming partnership incurred expenditure on repairs to the roof of a house which was occupied by one of the partners, and reclaimed the whole of the input tax. The Commissioners only agreed to repay 18% of the tax, considering that the expenditure had been primarily incurred for private purposes, so that only a proportion of the tax was deductible. The partnership appealed, contending that the effect of *Article 17* of the *EC Sixth Directive* as interpreted in *Lennartz v Finanzamt München*, **22.456** EUROPEAN COMMUNITY LAW, was that the whole of the input tax should be treated as deductible. The tribunal dismissed the appeal, holding that the principle in *Lennartz* only applied to supplies of goods and that the subsequent private use of such goods was treated as a supply of services on which output tax was chargeable. However, the farmhouse was immovable property rather than goods, and the use of the farmhouse for private purposes could not be treated as a taxable supply of services. Since the input tax was not paid wholly for the purposes of actual or deemed taxable transactions, it followed that the decision in *Lennartz* was distinguishable and only a proportion of the input tax was deductible. *F & M Mounty & Sons*, [1995] VATDR 128 (VTD 12985). (*Notes*. (1) The case was heard by the tribunal with *Hurd*, **36.273** above. (2) See also the note following *Korner & Others*, **36.287** above.)

Subpostmasters—rethatching of roof

[36.308] A married couple operated a sub-post office from an extension to their house. They arranged for the rethatching of their house roof, and reclaimed input tax on this work. The Commissioners issued an assessment to recover the tax, on the basis that the expenditure had been incurred for domestic reasons rather than for business reasons. The tribunal upheld the assessment and dismissed the couple's appeal. *M & J Iliffe (t/a Otterton Post Office)*, LON/99/1251 (VTD 18446). (*Note*. For another issue in this case, see **36.46** above.)

Partnership providing consultancy services—acquisition of property

[36.309] See *RMSG*, **52.353** PENALTIES: MISDECLARATION.

Expenses by or on behalf of employees or agents

CROSS-REFERENCE

For the liability to output tax in respect of supplies to employees (including company cars), see **62.1** *et seq.* SUPPLY.

Expenditure incurred on employees' pension funds

[36.310] See the cases noted at **54.1** to **54.7** PENSION FUNDS.

Hotel bills of employees on subsistence allowances

[36.311] A BBC employee was absent from home for four nights in the course of his duties. He received a flat-rate subsistence allowance from the BBC. His actual outlay included hotel expenses of £8.80, including VAT of 80p, for which he obtained a tax invoice. The BBC reclaimed the 80p as input tax. The Commissioners rejected the claim and the tribunal dismissed the BBC's appeal. Although the hotel accommodation had been supplied to the employee for the purposes of the BBC's business, it had not been supplied to the BBC within the meaning of what is now *VATA 1994, s 24(1)*. *British Broadcasting Corporation*, [1974] VATTR 100 (VTD 73).

Fixed allowances to employees to cover subsistence and petrol

[36.312] The decision in *British Broadcasting Corporation*, 36.311 above, was applied in another case in which a company paid its travellers fixed amounts for their expenditure on subsistence and petrol and reclaimed one-eleventh of the amounts so paid as input tax (the standard rate was then 10%). The Commissioners issued an assessment to recover the tax and the tribunal dismissed the company's appeal. *Ledamaster Ltd*, BIR/76/121 (VTD 344).

Company reimbursing petrol expenditure of self-employed representative

[36.313] See *Berbrooke Fashions*, 36.1 above, and the cases noted at 36.2 and 36.3 above.

Mileage allowances to employees

[36.314] See *Stirlings (Glasgow) Ltd*, 36.6 above; *McLean Homes Midland Ltd*, 36.7 above, and *Klockner Ferromatik Desma Ltd*, 36.8 above.

Use of car for transport of employees

[36.315] See *Blyth-Palk*, 36.174 above.

Employer paying for 'driver training' of employees' spouses and partners

[36.316] See *BMW Financial Services (GB) Ltd*, 36.182 above.

Personalised numberplates for managing director's car

[36.317] See *Ava Knit Ltd*, 36.477 below; *B J Kershaw Transport Ltd*, 36.478 below; *Empire Contracts Ltd*, 36.479 below; *Quality Care Homes Ltd*, 36.480 below; *Industrial Doors (Scotland) Ltd*, 36.480 below; *The Redington Design Co Ltd*, 36.480 below, and *NEP Group Ltd*, 52.348 PENALTIES: MISDECLARATION.

Land Rover purchased by employee—reclaimed by employer

[36.318] See *Binof Construction Ltd*, 36.13 above.

Clothing purchased by company for wear by principal director

[36.319] See *PJ Stone Ltd*, 36.191 above.

Refurbishment of houses provided for Cathedral vergers

[36.320] The Dean and Chapter of Hereford Cathedral were registered for VAT since they operated a restaurant and shop at the Cathedral, and also staged exhibitions for which visitors were charged admission. They incurred expenditure in refurbishing two houses which were situated in the Cathedral cloisters, built in 1472, and were used as residences for the Cathedral's two vergers. They reclaimed input tax on the refurbishment. The Commissioners rejected the claim, considering that the tax was not reclaimable since the Cathedral's religious and spiritual activities were not business activities, the provision of domestic accommodation for clergy and other officers was 'essentially a non-business use', and the expenditure had not been incurred for the purpose of the Cathedral's business activities. The Cathedral appealed, contending that the whole of the input tax should be treated as deductible. The tribunal allowed the appeal in part, finding that 'in the modern Cathedral the business activities constitute a significant part of the overall purpose for which a Cathedral exists'. The cost of maintaining the Cathedral could not be met 'without the finance guaranteed by secular or business activities'. The tribunal held, on the evidence, that the 'relative importance' of the business activities and the religious activities was equal, so that 50% of the tax in question was deductible. *The Dean & Chapter of Hereford Cathedral*, [1994] VATTR 159 (VTD 11737). (*Note.* For a case concerning similar expenditure on houses occupied by the Dean and Canons of a Cathedral, see *Dean & Chapter of Bristol Cathedral*, 36.552 below.)

Marketing company—renovation of house owned by directors

[36.321] A marketing company arranged for the renovation of a house which was owned by its two directors, and reclaimed input tax on the work. The Commissioners issued an assessment to recover the tax, and the tribunal dismissed the company's appeal, holding that the work had not been undertaken for the purposes of the company's business, so that the effect of *VATA 1994, s 24(1)* was that the tax was not deductible. *Durnell Marketing Ltd*, LON/01/677 (VTD 17813).

Bed and breakfast supplied to employees

[36.322] A company carried on the business of leasing amplification and lighting equipment for the popular music business. It had four full-time employees who maintained its equipment. When the equipment was on hire, they travelled with it to set it up, operate it, and dismantle it. The company paid for the employees' bed and breakfast when on tour, and reclaimed the input tax. The Commissioners issued an assessment to recover the tax and the company appealed. The tribunal allowed the company's appeal, holding that the supplies were made to the company and were for the purpose of the company's business. *Power Leasing Ltd*, [1984] VATTR 104 (VTD 1661).

Removal expenses

[36.323] A company had carried on business as a supplier of industrial electronic instruments from premises in Lincolnshire. It became insolvent and went into liquidation. The liquidator sold the shares to an individual (F) who had previously worked in London. F became the company's controlling director and moved the company's base from Lincolnshire to Peterborough. He moved his private address from London to Uppingham to be nearer the company's premises. The company reclaimed input tax on the removal expenses. The Commissioners issued an assessment to recover input tax relating to F's change of address. The tribunal allowed the company's appeal, holding on the evidence that the expenditure had been incurred for the purposes of the company's business, rather than for F's personal purposes. *SSL Ltd*, LON/87/254 (VTD 2478). (*Note*. The case was decided prior to the enactment of what is now *VATA 1994, s 24(3)*, but remains an authority on the allowability of removal expenses, particularly in view of the subsequent decision in *Michael Sellers & Co Ltd*, **36.339** below, where the tribunal held that *s 24(3)* did not apply to removal expenses.)

[36.324] A similar decision was reached in *Riftmain Ltd*, LON/87/828 (VTD 2819).

Legal costs of director charged with criminal offence

[36.325] See *Wallman Foods Ltd*, **36.238** above.

Legal costs of employees charged with manslaughter

[36.326] See *P & O European Ferries (Dover) Ltd*, **36.230** above.

Swimming pool constructed for use of employees of firm of solicitors

[36.327] See *Willcox & Co*, **36.521** below.

Carpets purchased for directors' house

[36.328] A farming company reclaimed input tax on the purchase of carpets for use in the farmhouse, where its directors lived. The Commissioners issued an assessment to recover the tax, considering that the expenditure had not been incurred for the purposes of the company's business. The tribunal dismissed the company's appeal. *GI Hadfield & Son Ltd*, MAN/90/1075 (VTD 6421).

Furniture purchased for directors' house

[36.329] An appeal was dismissed in a case where a company had reclaimed input tax in respect of furniture purchased for its directors' private residence. *Setlode Ltd*, LON/91/2223 (VTD 7765).

Domestic accommodation for directors (VATA 1994, s 24(3))

NOTE

VATA 1994, s 24(3), deriving from *FA 1990*, provides that input tax is not deductible in respect of goods or services supplied to or imported by a company and used, or to be used, in connection with the provision of accommodation by the company where the accommodation is used, or to be used, by a director of the company or by a person connected with a director of the company. Cases relating to periods before the enactment of *FA 1990* have been omitted. It should be noted that *VATA 1994, s 24(3)* only applies where it is the company which provides the accommodation. Cases where the accommodation is owned by the directors personally do not appear to fall within s *24(3)*, but the input tax would normally be non-deductible by virtue of s 24(1): see, for example, *Durnell Marketing Ltd*, **36.321** above; *GI Hadfield & Son Ltd*, **36.328** above, and *Setlode Ltd*, **36.329** above.

Double glazing

[36.330] A company reclaimed input tax on the cost of installing double glazing at the residence of its controlling directors, one room of which was used as an office. The Commissioners issued an assessment to recover five-sixths of the tax, considering that the expenditure fell within what is now *VATA 1994, s 24(3)*. The tribunal upheld the assessment and dismissed the company's appeal. *Newland Technical Services Ltd*, LON/92/1255A (VTD 9294). (*Note.* For other issues in this case, see **40.80** INVOICES AND CREDIT NOTES and **52.94** PENALTIES: MISDECLARATION.)

Conversion of premises—lease to director at low rent

[36.331] A family company which traded as builders' merchants reclaimed input tax on the conversion of part of its premises to provide residential accommodation for one of its directors. The Commissioners issued an assessment to recover the tax, and the company appealed, contending that it was leasing the accommodation to the director and should be allowed to reclaim the input tax. The tribunal rejected this contention and dismissed the appeal, observing that the lease was at a low rent and holding that the effect of *VATA 1994, s 24(3)* was that the tax was not deductible. *FD Todd & Sons Ltd*, MAN/96/724 (VTD 14731).

Short-term accommodation in Scotland

[36.332] A company, the registered office of which was in Surrey, carried on an oil consultancy business. It purchased two weeks' time-share accommodation in Scotland, about 40 miles from Aberdeen, and reclaimed input tax on the purchase. The Commissioners issued an assessment to recover the tax, considering that the accommodation had been purchased as holiday accommodation for the company's directors. The company appealed, contending that it had been purchased for business reasons, to be used for meetings with clients. The tribunal held that the accommodation had been purchased for a dual purpose, and that 25% of the tax in question was deductible, applying *Ian Flockton Developments Ltd*, **36.341** below. *Suregrove Ltd*, LON/92/571X (VTD 10740).

Farming company—expenditure on farmhouse

[36.333] A company which operated a farming business incurred expenditure on converting two derelict cottages into a farmhouse. It reclaimed input tax on the work. The Commissioners rejected the claim, considering that the effect of what is now *VATA 1994, s 24(3)* was that the tax was not deductible. The tribunal allowed the company's appeal in part, finding that the farmhouse was primarily used as domestic accommodation for the company's directors but that a small part of the expenditure related to the conversion of a pigsty into an office, and holding that 10% of the tax was deductible. *RS & EM Wright Ltd*, MAN/94/220 (VTD 12984).

[36.334] A company which operated a farming business incurred expenditure on extending and improving a cottage which was occupied by its managing director (C). It reclaimed input tax on the work. The Commissioners rejected the claim, considering that the effect of what is now *VATA 1994, s 24(3)* was that the tax was not deductible. The tribunal allowed the company's appeal in part, finding that the farmhouse was primarily used as domestic accommodation for C and his family but holding that 30% of the tax was deductible. *Quex Park Estates Ltd v HMRC*, [2010] UKFTT 126 (TC), TC00437.

Family farming company—renovation of bungalow

[36.335] A family farming company was controlled by a married couple. The company owned a bungalow, which had been occupied by an employee but had subsequently become vacant. The couple's son, who was an employee of the company, married in 1990. The company renovated the bungalow to enable him to occupy it. The company reclaimed input tax on this expenditure. The Commissioners issued an assessment to recover the tax, on the basis that the effect of what is now *VATA 1994, s 24(3)* was that the tax was not deductible, since the son was 'a person connected with a director of the company'. The company appealed. The tribunal allowed the appeal in part, holding that the expenditure had been incurred for a dual purpose and that 50% of the tax should be treated as deductible. *FJ Meaden Ltd*, LON/94/1766A (VTD 13215). (*Note.* The Commissioners did not appeal against this decision, but state in Customs' VAT Manual, Part 13, para 14.7 that they 'do not agree with the apportionment method adopted' and instruct their officers that they 'should allow apportionment only using the objective method taken by the tribunal in *RS & EM Wright Ltd*' (see **36.333** above).)

Property development company—repairs to house occupied by directors

[36.336] A company which carried on a property development business reclaimed input tax on repairs to a house occupied by its directors and their family. The Commissioners issued an assessment to recover the tax and the company appealed, contending that a proportion of the tax should be treated as deductible since two of the rooms in the house were used entirely for the company's business. The tribunal allowed the appeal in part, finding that one of the rooms was used wholly for business purposes and that a second room was used partly for business purposes, and holding that 5% of the input tax in question should be treated as deductible. *Wellright Ltd*, MAN/96/303 (VTD 14646).

Company in bloodstock industry—renovation of house

[36.337] A company, which was a member of a group, carried on the business of breeding and training thoroughbred racehorses. It owned a large house, which was used by the company chairman as a residence and for business meetings. It incurred expenditure on refurbishing the house, and reclaimed input tax on the work. The Commissioners issued an assessment on the basis that none of the tax relating to the upper floor was deductible, and that only 20% of the tax relating to the ground floor was deductible. (This was computed on the basis that, in 1995/96, the house was used for business purposes on 64 days.) The representative member of the group appealed, accepting that the tax relating to the upper floor was not deductible, but contending that 61.5% of the tax relating to the ground floor should be allowed as a deduction (on the basis that the house had been used for business purposes on 64 days and for non-business purposes on 40 days, ignoring days when the house was not used at all). The tribunal rejected this contention and dismissed the appeal, observing that, while there was 'a legitimate business element in this case', whenever the chairman stayed overnight 'he was using the accommodation including the group floor for domestic purposes', and that 'it would be unrealistic to treat every waking hour which he spent at (the house) as devoted to business'. The Commissioners' allowance of 20% of the expenditure 'was adopted in an effort to be fair and reasonable, avoiding troublesome calculations'. *Sangster Group Ltd*, LON/97/394 (VTD 15544).

Garage provided for director

[36.338] A company which supplied engineering services received planning permission for the construction of a double garage in the grounds of the house which its controlling director owned and occupied. The ownership of the plot on which the garage was built was transferred by the director to the company. The garage was used to house a car which the company owned, and which the director drove mainly but not exclusively for business purposes. The company reclaimed input tax on the construction of the garage. The Commissioners issued an assessment to recover the tax, on the basis that the effect of what is now *VATA 1994, s 24(3)* was that the tax was not deductible. The tribunal allowed the company's appeal in part, holding that the provision of the garage fell within *s 24(3)* and that the tax should be apportioned. (The tribunal rejected the Commissioners' contention that the use of the garage for business purposes was a breach of the relevant planning permission and that the tax was therefore not deductible.) On the evidence, the tribunal held that 85% of the use of the garage was for business purposes, so that 85% of the input tax was deductible. *Giffenbond Ltd*, MAN/94/1238 (VTD 13481).

Removal expenses—whether within VATA 1994, s 24(3)*

[36.339] A company carried on a financial consultancy business from the home of its controlling director. The director and the company moved from Yorkshire to Peterborough and reclaimed input tax on the removal expenses. The Commissioners issued an assessment to recover 90% of the tax, on the basis that 90% of the use of the property was for domestic purposes and that what is now *VATA 1994, s 24(3)* applied. The company appealed, contending that the move had been for business reasons rather than for domestic reasons. The tribunal accepted the company's evidence and allowed the appeal, holding that *VATA 1994, s 24(3)** did not apply. *Michael Sellers & Co Ltd*, LON/92/574X unreported. (*Note*. This decision appears not to have been publicly released by the Tribunal Centre, but is cited in Customs' VAT Manual, Part 13, para 14.6.)

Flat used partly for business purposes and partly by directors

[36.340] A company which supplied accountancy services had its main office in Perthshire, where its directors lived, but also leased a flat in Edinburgh which was used by the company's principal director and by some of its employees while meeting clients in Edinburgh. The company reclaimed input tax relating to the flat. HMRC issued an assessment to recover the tax, on the basis that since it was sometimes occupied by one of the company's directors,

VATA 1994, s 24(3) applied. The company appealed. The tribunal allowed the appeal in part, observing that VAT Notice 700 (2002 edition), para 12.2.2 stated 'if the accommodation is used partly for business purposes (for example if you use a room for meetings or as your office) then you can reclaim as input tax part of the VAT charged'. The tribunal directed that the input tax should be apportioned, and remitted the case in the hope that the parties could agree the appropriate apportionment. *Roderick Gunkel & Associates Ltd v HMRC*, [2009] UKFTT 308 (TC), TC00252.

Horse racing

NOTE

The cases listed below are those where input tax has been reclaimed on the basis that the purpose of owning racehorses has been to advertise an existing business activity. For cases where it has been contended that the ownership of horses constitutes a business activity in its own right, see *7.57 et seq*. BUSINESS. See also *VATA 1994, s 84(4)*, deriving from *FA 1993*. This provides that a tribunal can only allow an appeal against the disallowance of input tax relating to a 'luxury, amusement or entertainment' where the tribunal considers that the Commissioners 'could not reasonably have made' the determination which is the subject of the appeal. Cases relating to periods before the enactment of *FA 1993* should be read in the light of this change.

Cases where the appellant was successful

Company manufacturing plastic storage tanks

[36.341] A company which manufactured plastic storage tanks reclaimed input tax on the training and upkeep of a racehorse. The Commissioners issued an assessment to recover the tax and the company appealed, contending that it had purchased the horse for promotional purposes. The principal director gave evidence that this was the sole object which he had in mind when he decided to buy the horse. The tribunal upheld the assessment, accepting the director's evidence but holding that it should apply an objective test and that the company 'ought not to have had any commercial belief that the purchase and running of the racehorse could have been for the purpose of its business'. The QB allowed the company's appeal against this decision, holding that the tribunal had been wrong to substitute an objective test for the test of what was actually in the mind of the witness at the time of the expenditure. On the facts found by the tribunal, the company's sole object in buying the horse was to promote its business. Stuart-Smith J observed that this finding was 'a surprising one', but held that it was a finding of fact with which the court could not interfere. *Ian Flockton Developments Ltd v C & E Commrs*, QB [1987] STC 394. (*Note.* The decision here conflicts with the established case law relating to direct tax, where the HL has held that the conscious motive of the taxpayer at the time of the expenditure is not conclusive; see the judgment of Lord Brightman in *Mallalieu v Drummond*, HL [1983] STC 665. However, Customs did not take the case further, and the decision here has been followed by tribunals in many subsequent cases. For the Commissioners' interpretation of the decision, see Customs' VAT Manual, Part 13, para 4.5. See also the note at the head of this section with regard to the effect of *VATA 1994, s 84(4)*.)

Shirt manufacturing company

[36.342] A company which carried on business as designers and manufacturers of shirts purchased seven racehorses and reclaimed input tax on their purchase. The horses were given names which were identifiable with the company's shirts. The Commissioners issued an assessment to recover the tax and the company appealed, contending that the horses had been purchased for the purpose of advertising its business. The tribunal accepted this contention and allowed the appeal. *Hillingdon Shirt Co Ltd*, MAN/78/26 (VTD 678).

Farming partnership

[36.343] A farming partnership reclaimed input tax on the upkeep of racehorses, some of which it had bred. The Commissioners issued an assessment to recover the tax and the partnership appealed, contending that the expenditure had been incurred for the purpose of advertising a caravan site which the partners owned. The tribunal accepted the partners' evidence and allowed the appeal. *AE House & Son*, LON/85/373 (VTD 2620). (*Note.* For an appeal by an associated company, heard with this case, see **41.124** LAND.)

Engineering company

[36.344] A company which carried on an engineering business reclaimed input tax on the upkeep of three racehorses. The Commissioners issued an assessment to recover the tax, considering that the expenditure had not been incurred for the purposes of the company's business, but for the pleasure of the company's managing director (who owned a stud farm). The tribunal allowed the company's appeal, holding on the evidence that the expenditure had been incurred for promotional purposes. The earlier decision in *Bridge Book Co Ltd*, **36.373** below, was distinguished because in that case horse racing was the main recreational activity of the director concerned. *Skeltools Ltd*, LON/80/63 (VTD 968).

[36.345] A similar decision was reached in a subsequent case also involving an engineering company. *GW Martin & Co Ltd*, LON/82/263 (VTD 1390). (*Note.* For the award of costs in this case, see **2.467** APPEALS.)

[36.346] In another case where an engineering company had reclaimed input tax on expenditure incurred in keeping racehorses, the tribunal allowed the company's appeal against an assessment issued to recover the tax in question, applying *Ian Flockton Developments Ltd*, **36.341** above. On the evidence, the tribunal was satisfied that the managing director's purpose in purchasing and running the racehorses was to promote the company's business. *J Martin Engineers (Wishaw) Ltd*, EDN/90/206 (VTD 6667).

Heating engineering company

[36.347] A company which carried on a heating engineering business reclaimed input tax on the upkeep of a racehorse. The Commissioners issued an assessment to recover the tax but the tribunal allowed the company's appeal. On the evidence, none of the directors had had any previous material interest in horse racing, and the tribunal was satisfied that the horse had been run for the purpose of advertising the company's business. *A & E Mechanical Services Ltd*, MAN/80/47 (VTD 1069).

Company owning public house

[36.348] A company acquired a public house in Glasgow in 1977, changing its name to 'The Captain's Rest'. The company acquired three racehorses, the first of which it named 'Captain's Rest', and the third of which it named 'Restless Captain'. The company reclaimed input tax on the upkeep of the racehorses and the Commissioners issued an assessment to recover the tax. The company appealed, submitting evidence that the horses had attracted interest and enthusiasm among customers. The annual turnover of the pub had increased from £55,000 in 1977 to £260,000 in 1980. The tribunal allowed the company's appeal, holding on the evidence that the horses had been acquired for the purpose of promoting the company's business. *Demor Investments Ltd*, [1981] VATTR 66 (VTD 1091).

Housebuilding company

[36.349] A company which carried on business as housebuilders reclaimed input tax on the purchase of three racehorses, which it named Mr Sinclair, Major Sinclair and Miss Sinclair. The Commissioners issued an assessment to recover the tax and the company appealed, contending that it had acquired the horses for the purpose of promoting its business. The tribunal allowed the company's appeal, holding that the fact that the names given to the horses were closely connected to the company's name indicated that they had been purchased for advertising purposes. *Sinclair Developments Ltd*, MAN/82/127 (VTD 1466).

[36.350] An appeal was allowed in a case where a small building company based in Wantage had purchased a 50% share in a racehorse, and reclaimed input tax on the upkeep of the horse. The tribunal held that, since there were several stables in the Wantage area, the acquisition of a horse could reasonably be considered to have been for the purpose of promoting the company's business. *C & P Building & Welding (Wantage) Ltd*, LON/85/466 (VTD 2062).

Builders' merchants

[36.351] A company trading as builders' merchants reclaimed input tax on the upkeep of a racehorse. The Commissioners issued an assessment to recover the tax, considering that the horse had been purchased for the recreational interest of one of the directors, who had previously owned a racehorse of her own. The company appealed, contending that the purpose of the expenditure had been to promote its business. The tribunal accepted the company's evidence and allowed the appeal. *Wenlock Building Centre Ltd*, MAN/90/1136 (VTD 10893).

Company selling cleaning materials

[36.352] A company which sold cleaning materials, principally to restaurants and licensed premises, reclaimed input tax on the upkeep of several racehorses. The Commissioners issued an assessment to recover the tax but the tribunal allowed the company's appeal, holding on the evidence that the expenditure had been incurred for the purpose of promoting the company's business. *EL Davis & Co Ltd*, LON/83/76 (VTD 1477).

Company selling glassware

[**36.353**] An appeal was allowed in a case where a company which sold glassware to restaurants and licensed premises had reclaimed input tax on the upkeep of racehorses. *Dickins Ltd*, LON/83/77 (VTD 1477). (*Note.* The case was heard with *EL Davis & Co Ltd*, 36.352 above.)

Company manufacturing packaging

[**36.354**] A company which carried on business as a manufacturer of packaging materials reclaimed input tax on the purchase of some racehorses. The Commissioners issued an assessment to recover the tax and the company appealed, contending that the horses had been purchased for promotional purposes and that by attending meetings where the horses raced, it had obtained additional customers. The tribunal accepted the company's evidence and allowed the appeal. *AJ Bingley Ltd*, LON/83/333 (VTD 1597).

Shopfitting company

[**36.355**] A company which carried on business as shopfitters reclaimed input tax on the purchase of racehorses. The Commissioners issued an assessment to recover the tax and the company appealed, contending that it had purchased the horses in the hope of obtaining additional customers in the brewing industry. The tribunal accepted the company's evidence and allowed the appeal. *William Cowan & Son Ltd*, EDN/84/74 (VTD 1792).

Retail furniture company

[**36.356**] A company which sold furniture by retail reclaimed input tax on the purchase and upkeep of several racehorses. Some of the horses had names which reflected the company's name, and the horseblankets were used to advertise the company's business. In addition, the company sent 70,000 customers a racing calendar with a covering letter encouraging them to follow its horses and make further purchases from the company, and stating that if a customer bet 50p on one of the company's horses, that sum would be deducted from any bill paid by the customer in one of its shops. The Commissioners issued an assessment to recover the tax but the tribunal allowed the company's appeal, holding that the horses had been raced for the purpose of promoting the company's business. *J Boardmans Ltd*, MAN/84/293 (VTD 2025).

Haulage contractors

[**36.357**] A company which carried on business as haulage contractors reclaimed input tax on the upkeep of racehorses. The Commissioners issued an assessment to recover the tax but the tribunal allowed the company's appeal, holding on the evidence that the expenditure had been incurred for the purpose of promoting the company's business. *Brian Yeardley Continental Ltd*, MAN/85/225 (VTD 2035).

Printing company

[**36.358**] A company which carried on a printing business purchased a 50% share in a racehorse and reclaimed input tax on the upkeep of the horse. The horse's blanket was used to advertise the company's name at races, and advertisements were placed in local papers to emphasise the link between the company and the horse. The Commissioners issued an assessment to recover the tax but the tribunal allowed the company's appeal, holding on the evidence that the expenditure had been incurred for the purpose of promoting the company's business. *Hickling & Squires Ltd*, MAN/86/80 (VTD 2287).

[36.359] A similar decision was reached in a subsequent case where a printing company had reclaimed input tax on the purchase and upkeep of racehorses. *Alito Colour Ltd*, LON/91/1268X (VTD 7504).

Sports equipment retailers

[36.360] A company which carried on business as a retailer of sports equipment purchased a racehorse, and reclaimed input tax on the upkeep of the horse. Photographs and newspaper cuttings of the horse were used for publicity on the shop premises. The Commissioners issued an assessment to recover the tax but the tribunal allowed the company's appeal, holding on the evidence that the horse had been purchased for the purpose of advertising the company's business. *Solihull Sports Services Ltd*, MAN/86/408 (VTD 2713).

Nightclub owner

[36.361] The owner of a nightclub reclaimed input tax in respect of expenditure incurred on a racehorse. The Commissioners issued an assessment to recover the tax and he appealed, contending that the horse was used to advertise the business. The nightclub was called the 'King of Clubs', and the horse was named 'KC's Dancer'. The tribunal allowed his appeal, applying *Ian Flockton Developments Ltd*, 36.341 above, and holding that the expenditure had been incurred for the purpose of promoting the nightclub. *P Holder*, LON/91/509Z (VTD 6446).

Interior decorating company

[36.362] A company which carried on an interior decorating business reclaimed input tax on the purchase and upkeep of a racehorse. The horse had competed in several races, but had never finished higher than eighth. The Commissioners issued an assessment to recover the tax, considering that the racehorse had not been acquired for the purpose of the company's business. The tribunal allowed the company's appeal. On the evidence, one of the company's directors also owned racehorses privately, and, partly because of her contacts, more than half of the company's trade came from within racing circles. The tribunal was satisfied that the company's intention in purchasing the horse was to promote its business. *Beckett & Graham Ltd*, LON/90/1162Z (VTD 6878).

Quarrying company

[36.363] A company which operated five chalk and limestone quarries reclaimed input tax on the training and upkeep of a racehorse. The Commissioners issued an assessment to recover the tax, considering that the expenditure had not been incurred for the purpose of the company's business. The company appealed, contending that one of its quarries was located in an area of North Yorkshire which was well-known for the training of racehorses, and there were nine racing stables within two miles of the quarry. It wished to exploit land adjoining the existing quarry, for which it would need planning permission, and was concerned at the possibility of the racehorse trainers objecting to an application for such permission. Accordingly, the company had purchased the horse for the purpose of promoting its goodwill among the racing fraternity. The tribunal allowed the appeal, applying *Ian Flockton Developments Ltd*, 36.341 above, and observing that, since the quarry had an annual turnover of £1 million, expenditure of £5,000 on a racehorse was 'well within any tolerance limits' of promoting the goodwill of the company. *Fenstone (Quarries) Ltd*, MAN/91/423 (VTD 7236).

Cases where the appellant was partly successful

Company promoting work of sportswriter

[36.364] A company was incorporated to promote the work of its controlling director, who was a professional sportswriter who had written two books about horse racing. It purchased a part-share in a racehorse, and reclaimed input tax on its purchase and upkeep. It also reclaimed input tax on the upkeep of racehorses which were part-owned by its controlling director. The Commissioners issued an assessment to recover the tax, and the company appealed, contending that the expenditure had been incurred for the purpose of promoting its director's reputation among people interested in horse racing. The tribunal reviewed the evidence in detail and allowed the appeal in part, holding that the input tax attributable to the racehorse which was part-owned by the company was allowable, but the input tax attributable to the horses which were part-owned by the director as an individual was not allowable. *Sportswords Ltd*, MAN/90/278 (VTD 11178).

Company operating holiday centre

[36.365] A family company which owned and operated a 'holiday centre' in Devon purchased ten racehorses between 1989 and 1991, and reclaimed input tax on their purchase and upkeep. In October 1991 the horses were sold to an associated company which operated a stud farm. Following a control visit in 1993, the Commissioners issued assessments to recover some of the tax, considering that the expenditure had not been wholly incurred for the purposes of the company's business, but had been partly incurred for the personal pleasure of the company's directors. The company appealed, contending that the expenditure had been incurred for advertising purposes and that the incidental personal enjoyment of the directors was irrelevant. The tribunal reviewed the evidence in detail and allowed the appeal in full with regard to the period up to October 1990 (during which time four horses had been purchased). With regard to the period from November 1990 to October 1991, the tribunal found that by October 1990 it was apparent that the use of the racehorses for advertising had not been profitable, and that the directors had decided to operate a stud farm. The tribunal granted the company liberty to apply for a further hearing to consider whether any of the expenditure between November 1990 and October 1991 inclusive had been incurred for business purposes. *Kingsley Holidays Ltd*, LON/94/2241 (VTD 13487). (*Note.* There was no further public hearing of the appeal.)

Cases where the appellant was unsuccessful

Music publishing company

[36.366] A music publishing company purchased six racehorses and re-claimed input tax on their purchase. The Commissioners issued an assessment to recover the tax, considering that the horses had been purchased for the purposes of the company's managing director, who was a bloodstock dealer. The company appealed, contending that the horses had been purchased for the purposes of its business. The tribunal dismissed the appeal and the QB upheld the decision. *Ashtree Holdings Ltd v C & E Commrs*, QB [1979] STC 818.

Car auctioneering company

[36.367] A company which carried on a car auctioneering business pur-chased two racehorses and reclaimed input tax on their purchase and upkeep. The Commissioners issued an assessment to recover the tax and the company appealed, contending that the horses had been acquired for advertising purposes. The tribunal dismissed the appeal, holding on the evidence that the horses had been purchased to facilitate the entertainment of customers at race meetings. Accordingly, the expenditure constituted business entertainment and the tax was not deductible by virtue of what is now *Input Tax Order, Article 5. British Car Auctions Ltd*, [1978] VATTR 56 (VTD 522).

Housebuilding company

[36.368] A company which carried on a housebuilding business purchased three racehorses and reclaimed input tax on their upkeep. The Commissioners issued an assessment to recover the tax and the company appealed, contending that the horses had been purchased for the purpose of advertising its business. The tribunal dismissed the appeal, holding that there was insufficient connec-tion between the company's business and the racing activities to justify the deduction of the tax. There was no evidence to suggest that any purchasers of houses built by the company had been influenced by its horse racing activities. *Tallishire Ltd*, [1979] VATTR 180 (VTD 834).

[36.369] A company based in Oldham, which carried on a housebuilding business, reclaimed input tax on the purchase and upkeep of a horse which it named 'Miss Oldham'. The Commissioners issued an assessment to recover the tax and the tribunal dismissed the company's appeal, holding on the evidence that the horse had not been used to promote the company, since its name did not reflect the company's name and there was no evidence of any connection between the company's customers and the horse racing. *Que-ghan Construction Co Ltd*, MAN/83/171 (VTD 1538).

[36.370] Similar decisions were reached in *Robertson Robertson Construc-tion Co*, EDN/85/124 (VTD 2071) and *RV Young Ltd*, 52.352 PENALTIES: MISDECLARATION.

Builder

[36.371] A builder reclaimed input tax on the purchase and upkeep of two racehorses. The Commissioners issued an assessment to recover the tax and the tribunal dismissed his appeal, holding that the expenditure had not been incurred for business purposes. *J Dayani*, LON/88/489Y (VTD 3491).

Metal-dealing company

[36.372] A company which carried on a metal-dealing business reclaimed input tax on the upkeep of a racehorse (which had died after running in five races). The Commissioners issued an assessment to recover the tax and the tribunal dismissed the company's appeal, holding that the company had not proved that the expenditure had been for the purposes of its business. *MSS (North West) Ltd*, [1980] VATTR 29 (VTD 882).

Bookselling company

[36.373] An appeal was dismissed in a case where a company which carried on the business of buying and selling 'remaindered' paperback books had reclaimed input tax on the purchase and upkeep of racehorses. *The Bridge Book Co Ltd*, LON/80/18 (VTD 935).

Professional singer

[36.374] A professional singer became interested in horse racing and purchased several racehorses. She reclaimed input tax on the upkeep of the horses and the Commissioners issued an assessment to recover the tax. The tribunal dismissed her appeal, holding that she had not acquired the horses for the purpose of her profession as a singer. *D Squires*, LON/82/165 (VTD 1436).

Tool-manufacturing company

[36.375] A company which carried on a business of tool manufacturing leased a number of racehorses from its chairman, who had bred horses for several years. The company reclaimed input tax on the upkeep of the horses and the Commissioners issued an assessment to recover the tax. The tribunal dismissed the company's appeal, holding that the horse racing had been undertaken for the purposes of conferring a benefit on the chairman. *Metal Woods Ltd*, LON/83/15 (VTD 1473).

Contract cleaner

[36.376] The proprietor of a contract cleaning business reclaimed input tax on the purchase and upkeep of two racehorses, named 'Glynfield Portion' and 'Glynfield Cleaner'. The Commissioners issued an assessment to recover the tax and the tribunal dismissed the proprietor's appeal, holding that he had not satisfied it that the horses had been acquired for the purpose of promoting his business. *C Reid (t/a Glynfield Cleaning Contractors)*, MAN/83/141 (VTD 1543).

Farmer

[36.377] A farmer reclaimed input tax on the purchase and upkeep of several racehorses. The Commissioners issued an assessment to recover the tax and the tribunal dismissed the farmer's appeal, holding that the racehorses had not been purchased for the purposes of his business. *TN Bailey*, LON/83/79 (VTD 1587).

Company manufacturing footwear

[36.378] A company which manufactured slippers purchased several racehorses and reclaimed input tax on their purchase and upkeep. The Commissioners issued an assessment to recover the tax and the tribunal dismissed the company's appeal, holding on the evidence that the horses had not been purchased to promote the company's business, to which they bore no relation, but had been purchased because of the principal director's interest in horse racing. *H Lister (Slippers) Ltd*, MAN/83/237 (VTD 1747).

Accountant

[36.379] An accountant reclaimed input tax on the upkeep of several racehorses. The Commissioners issued an assessment to recover the tax, considering that the expenditure had not been incurred for the purposes of his practice. He appealed, contending that the expenditure had been incurred for promotional purposes. The tribunal dismissed his appeal, finding that there was no evidence that the horses had been used for advertising purposes, and holding that they had been used as an adjunct to business entertainment, so that the input tax was not deductible. *T Dyer*, EDN/90/89 (VTD 5356).

Engineering company

[36.380] An engineering company purchased a one-eighth share in each of four racehorses, and reclaimed input tax thereon. The Commissioners issued an assessment to recover the tax, considering that the expenditure had not been incurred for business purposes. The company appealed, contending that the expenditure had been incurred for the purpose of advertising its business. One of the four horses was registered with the Jockey Club in the name of the company's secretary; the other three were registered in the names of people unconnected with the company. The tribunal dismissed the company's appeal, finding that the company derived 'no advertising benefits whatsoever' from its ownership of the shares in the horses. *EW Ambrose Ltd*, MAN/90/548 (VTD 5766).

[36.381] A company carrying on the business of construction and civil engineering reclaimed input tax on the purchase and upkeep of two racehorses. The Commissioners issued an assessment to recover the tax, considering that the horses had not been purchased for the purpose of the company's business. The company appealed, contending that the horses had been purchased for advertising purposes. The tribunal dismissed the company's appeal, observing that the horses' names did not reflect the company's name and holding that 'no ordinary businessman would have incurred this expenditure on racehorses and their upkeep as part of his business expenditure'. On the evidence, 'the expenditure was not the result of a considered commercial decision'. *Heyrod Construction Ltd*, MAN/91/1256 (VTD 7882).

Company manufacturing plastics

[36.382] A company which manufactured plastic products reclaimed input tax on the upkeep of racehorses. The Commissioners issued an assessment to recover the tax and the company appealed, contending that the horses had been purchased for the purpose of advertising its business. The tribunal dismissed the company's appeal, holding on the evidence that the horses had been purchased as a 'private recreational interest' of the controlling director. *Sheet & Roll Convertors Ltd*, LON/92/119 (VTD 7991B).

Printing company

[36.383] A printing company named Mayspark reclaimed input tax on the purchase and upkeep of a racehorse, which it named 'Mayspark Lad'. The Commissioners issued an assessment to recover the tax, considering that the expenditure had not been incurred for the purposes of the company's business. The company appealed, contending that the horse had been purchased for advertising purposes. The tribunal dismissed the appeal, holding that, despite its name, the horse was not in fact used to advertise the company's business. The tribunal observed that 'the use of the name Mayspark Lad is the only feature of any real value' to the company's case, but found that 'even here nothing was done in the way of advertising to associate Mayspark Lad in the minds of racegoers with (the company's) printing business'. *Mayspark Ltd*, LON/94/1339 (VTD 13152).

Company owning and racing horses—whether carrying on a business

[36.384] See *Guinea Grill Stakes Ltd*, **7.61** BUSINESS.

Show jumping and other equine activities

Manufacturing company—purchase of horse and horsebox

[36.385] A company carried on business as a dealer in horse carcasses and manufacturer of meat products, bone meals, tallows and animal oils. Its principal product was named 'Sterilox'. It purchased a luxury horse box, costing £50,000, on which the name 'Sterilox' was prominently displayed, and subsequently purchased a horse, which it named 'Sterilox Bay Grange', and which it entered in show-jumping events. It reclaimed input tax on the horse and the horsebox, and the Commissioners issued an assessment to recover the tax, considering that the expenditure had been incurred for the pleasure of the company's directors, rather than for the purpose of the company's business. The tribunal allowed the company's appeal, holding on the evidence that the horse and the horsebox had been acquired for the purpose of advertising the company's business. *A Hughes & Son (Skellingthorpe) Ltd*, MAN/81/206 (VTD 1301).

Accountant

[36.386] An accountant reclaimed input tax on the purchase and upkeep of a pony which he had entered in show-jumping events. The Commissioners issued an assessment to recover the tax, and the accountant appealed, contending that he had purchased it to advertise his business. The tribunal dismissed his appeal, holding on the evidence that the pony had been purchased for the benefit of his daughters. *M Lake*, LON/82/393 (VTD 1388).

Tomato-dealing company

[36.387] A tomato-dealing company reclaimed input tax on the upkeep of horses for show-jumping and three-day events. The Commissioners issued an assessment to recover the tax but the tribunal allowed the company's appeal, holding on the evidence that the horses had been acquired to publicise the company's business. *Van Heyningen Brothers Ltd*, LON/83/201 (VTD 1675).

Management company

[36.388] A company managed a number of housing associations and marketed the houses to young couples. It reclaimed input tax on the purchase and upkeep of show-jumping horses. The Commissioners issued an assessment to recover the tax but the tribunal allowed the company's appeal, holding on the evidence that the company's show-jumping activities had been undertaken for advertising purposes. *Management Services Ltd*, LON/86/631 (VTD 2503).

Company manufacturing marine equipment

[36.389] A company carried on business as a manufacturer of marine equipment such as chains and mooring systems. It reclaimed input tax on the purchase and upkeep of six show-jumping horses. The Commissioners issued an assessment to recover the tax, considering that the expenditure had not been incurred for the purposes of the company's business. The tribunal allowed the appeal, holding on the evidence that the director had intended the horses to be used to advertise the company. *Griffin-Woodhouse Ltd*, MAN/91/977 (VTD 8942). (*Note.* An appeal against a misdeclaration penalty was also allowed.)

Partnership selling wall coverings

[36.390] A married couple traded in partnership, selling wall coverings. Their daughter competed in dressage events, and the partners reclaimed input tax in respect of expenditure on the horses which she rode in these events. The Commissioners issued an assessment to recover the tax, considering that the expenditure had been incurred for family reasons rather than for the purposes of the business. The tribunal upheld the assessment and dismissed the couple's appeal. *Mr & Mrs BJ Hooton (t/a BJH Supplies & Services)*, LON/92/1645 (VTD 10118).

Company trading as air conditioning engineers

[36.391] A company which carried on business as air conditioning engineers reclaimed input tax on the purchase of a trailer for transporting horses. The trailer was used for transporting two horses to dressage events, where they were ridden by the daughter of the company's controlling director. The Commissioners issued an assessment to recover the tax, considering that the expenditure had been incurred for the personal pleasure of the company's principal director. The company appealed, contending that the trailer had been purchased for the purpose of advertising its business. The tribunal accepted the company's evidence and allowed the appeal. *Delta House Installations Ltd*, LON/93/2521 (VTD 12151).

Equestrian centre at farm—purchase of expenditure

[36.392] A married couple owned a large farm. They incurred expenditure on establishing equestrian facilities at the farm, including stables and fences for jumping tuition, and reclaimed input tax on this expenditure. The Commissioners issued an assessment to recover the tax, considering that the expenditure had been incurred for the purpose of benefiting the couple's daughter, who was a keen rider. The couple appealed, contending that the equestrian centre was 'a legitimate diversification enterprise' designed to increase their income from the farm. The tribunal allowed the appeal in part, finding that the expenditure had been incurred for a dual purpose and that the desire to assist the couple's daughter was 'the main element in the decision', and holding that 30% of the input tax was allowable. *ATB & SDL Jones*, LON/92/1763A (VTD 11410). (*Note.* For another issue in this case, see **36.289** above.)

Farm horses also used for hunting

[36.393] A family farming company reclaimed input tax on the upkeep of three horses which were used for hunting by the company's principal director and his daughter. The Commissioners issued an assessment to recover the tax, and the company appealed. The tribunal concluded that the horses were used partly for business purposes and partly for private purposes, and directed that the assessment should be recomputed on the basis that input tax should be allowed for the maintenance and feeding of one horse. *JC & NC Ward Ltd*, LON/83/8 (VTD 1416).

Input tax reclaimed on horses used by company director for hunting

[36.394] A company carried on business as a dealer in second-hand vehicles, primarily Land Rovers and Range Rovers. It reclaimed input tax on the purchase and upkeep of horses which its director used for hunting. The Commissioners issued an assessment to recover the tax, considering that the horses had not been used for the purposes of the company's business. The company appealed, contending that it had bought the horses for the purpose of enabling it 'to make and maintain contact with current and potential customers'. The tribunal dismissed the appeal. The director had been involved in hunting from an early age, and it was his principal recreation. On the evidence, less than 2% of the company's turnover was attributable to hunting contacts. The fact that the expenditure may have resulted in an incidental benefit for the business did not mean that it had been incurred for the purpose of the business. *Walter E Sturgess & Sons Ltd*, MAN/90/615 (VTD 9009).

Horses purchased by engineering company

[36.395] See *K & K Thorogood Ltd*, **36.571** below.

Company incorporated to breed horses—purchase of colt

[36.396] See *Guest Leasing & Bloodstock Co Ltd*, **7.60** BUSINESS.

Horse boxes used by trader's family

[36.397] A trader reclaimed input tax on the purchase of three horse boxes. The Commissioners issued an assessment to recover the tax and the trader appealed, contending that they had been purchased for advertising purposes. The tribunal dismissed his appeal, finding that they had been purchased for the private purposes of the trader and his family, who rode horses and ponies as a hobby. The QB upheld this decision as one of fact. *MA Lenihan v C & E Commrs*, QB [1992] STC 478. (*Note.* For another issue in this case, see **62.75** SUPPLY.)

Horse box used by trader's son

[36.398] A publican reclaimed input tax on the purchase of a horse box, which was used by his son who competed in show-jumping events. The Commissioners issued an assessment to recover the tax and the publican appealed, contending that he had purchased the horse box for the purpose of advertising his business. The tribunal dismissed the appeal, holding on the evidence that the publican had not shown 'on a balance of probability' that the expenditure had been incurred for the purposes of his business. *P McCourt (t/a The Millstone Inn)*, MAN/96/136 (VTD 14452).

Horse box used by director's daughter

[36.399] A company reclaimed input tax on the purchase of a horse box. The Commissioners rejected the claim and the tribunal dismissed the company's appeal, finding that the horse box had been purchased in order to transport horses owned by the managing director's daughter to show-jumping events. *Harveys & Co (Clothing) Ltd*, MAN/87/381 (VTD 3166).

Horse box used by director's son

[36.400] A company trading as wholesale suppliers of fruit and vegetables reclaimed input tax on the lease of a horse box. The Commissioners issued an assessment to recover the tax, considering that the horse box had not been acquired for the purpose of the company's business, but to provide transport for the managing director's son, who was an English international show-jumper. The company appealed, contending that the horse box had been acquired for advertising purposes. The tribunal held that the horse box had been acquired with a dual purpose and the tax should be apportioned by virtue of what is now *VATA 1994, s 24(5)*. The tribunal held, on the evidence, that 20% of the tax in question was deductible. *Freshgro (Bicester) Ltd*, LON/91/321Y (VTD 7250, 7832).

Whether horse breeding activities of individual a business

[36.401] See *Prenn*, 7.57 BUSINESS, *Creber*, 7.65 BUSINESS, and *Thornton*, 7.66 BUSINESS.

Whether company carrying on a business of horsebreeding

[36.402] See *Guest Leasing & Bloodstock Co Ltd*, 7.60 BUSINESS, and the cases noted at 7.67 to 7.69 BUSINESS.

Powerboat racing

[36.403] A company, which carried on a business of cleaning industrial premises, reclaimed input tax on powerboat racing. The Commissioners issued an assessment to recover the tax but the tribunal allowed the company's appeal, holding on the evidence that the expenditure had been incurred for advertising purposes. *20th Century Cleaning & Maintenance Co Ltd*, LON/78/89 (VTD 838). (*Note.* See now, however, *VATA 1994, s 84(4)*, deriving from *FA 1993, s 46*.)

[36.404] A firm of estate agents claimed a deduction for input tax incurred on powerboat racing, contending that the expenditure was incurred for the purpose of advertising their business. The Commissioners issued an assessment to disallow the deduction, considering that the powerboat racing was a hobby of one of the partners. The tribunal held on the evidence that the boat was used to promote the firm's business and allowed the firm's appeal, applying *Ian Flockton Developments Ltd*, 36.341 above. *Hamptons*, LON/88/861Y (VTD 3883). (*Note.* See now, however, *VATA 1994, s 84(4)*, deriving from *FA 1993, s 46*. The Paymaster-General singled out this case in the Finance Bill Committee on 8 June 1993, observing that the firm's appeal 'would not succeed under the law as it shall be rewritten. It is right to rewrite the law so as not to permit such a case to take place and succeed before a tribunal.')

[36.405] A self-employed gas engineer reclaimed input tax in respect of the purchase of a powerboat, which he used for racing. The Commissioners issued an assessment to recover the tax, considering that the boat had been purchased partly for private purposes and partly to be used for business entertainment. The engineer appealed, contending that he had purchased the boat for advertising purposes. The tribunal dismissed the appeal, holding on the evidence that the boat had been purchased to be used for business entertainment, so that the tax was not deductible. *C Denby*, MAN/92/238 (VTD 9668).

Motorboat purchased by bakery partnership

[36.406] A partnership which owned a bakery business purchased a motorboat and reclaimed the input tax. The Commissioners issued an assessment to recover the tax and the partnership appealed, contending that the boat had been purchased for advertising purposes. The tribunal dismissed the appeal, holding on the evidence that the boat had been purchased for private use. *Motcombe Bakeries*, LON/86/54 (VTD 2216).

Boat acquired by engineering company—whether input tax deductible

[36.407] See *Diesel Generating (Tetbury) Ltd*, 36.537 below.

Motorboat purchased by married couple for restoration and resale

[36.408] See *Cavner*, 36.561 below.

Motorboat—whether purchased for future chartering business

[36.409] See *Castle*, 36.582 below.

Motor racing and rallying

NOTE

The cases in this section should be read in the light of *VATA 1994, s 84(4)*, originating from *FA 1993, s 46*. This section, which took effect for accounting periods beginning after 27 July 1993, provides that a tribunal can only allow an appeal against the disallowance relating to a 'luxury, amusement or entertainment' where the tribunal considers that the Commissioners 'could not reasonably have made' the determination which is the subject of the appeal. Cases relating to accounting periods beginning before 28 July 1993 should be read in the light of this change.

Cases where the appellant was successful

Motor racing—metal dealers

[36.410] A partnership carried on the business of dealing in metals. One of the partners (S) was a New Zealander who had been a successful amateur motor racing driver. He competed in several televised races, and actively sought sponsorship for his motor racing. The partnership advertised on the car which S raced, and paid for some of the expenditure incurred in running the car. It reclaimed input tax on this expenditure. The Commissioners issued an assessment to recover the tax, considering that the expenditure had not been incurred for business purposes, but the tribunal allowed the partnership's appeal. *Atlas Marketing*, LON/85/27 (VTD 1905).

Motor racing—company supplying amusement machines

[36.411] A company supplied electronic amusement machines. Its market consisted of people who distributed amusement machines or who controlled premises where amusement machines were commonly to be found. It purchased a Formula Ford racing car and reclaimed the input tax thereon. The Commissioners issued an assessment to recover the tax and the company appealed, contending that the expenditure had been incurred for advertising purposes. The tribunal accepted the company's evidence and allowed the appeal. *Terropol Ltd*, MAN/86/237 (VTD 3021).

Motor racing—company manufacturing downhole tools for oil industry

[36.412] A company carried on the business of manufacturing specialist downhole tools for the oil industry. It reclaimed input tax on expenditure incurred in running a Ferrari 308 racing car, which was driven by its controlling director. The Commissioners issued an assessment to recover the tax, considering that the expenditure had not been incurred for the purposes of the company's business. The company appealed, contending that the expenditure had been incurred for advertising purposes. The tribunal accepted the company's evidence and allowed the appeal, applying *Ian Flockton Developments Ltd*, **36.341** above. *Petroline Wireline Services Ltd*, EDN/92/29 (VTD 9200).

Motor racing—company providing TV production consultancy services

[36.413] A company was incorporated to provide consultancy services with regard to the production of television programmes and videos. Its controlling director was an amateur motor racing driver. The company purchased a 1964 Lotus racing car and spent £100,000 on restoring it. It reclaimed the relevant input tax. The Commissioners issued an assessment to recover the tax, considering that the expenditure had been incurred for the personal pleasure of the director, rather than for the purposes of the company's business. The company appealed, contending that the expenditure had been incurred for advertising purposes. The tribunal accepted the company's evidence and allowed the appeal. *Richard Drewitt Productions Ltd*, LON/93/2A (VTD 11999).

Motor racing—company hiring drape curtains

[36.414] A company carried on the business of hiring out drape curtains to the organisers of large exhibitions, trade shows and concerts. It reclaimed input tax on the purchase and maintenance of a racing car. At first the car was driven by the company's principal director, but he was not very successful and a more experienced driver was subsequently engaged. The Commissioners rejected the claim, considering that the expenditure had been incurred for the personal pleasure of the company's principal director. The company appealed, contending that the expenditure had been incurred for advertising purposes. The tribunal accepted the company's evidence and allowed the appeal, applying *Ian Flockton (Developments) Ltd*, 36.341 above, and distinguishing *Fenwick Builders Ltd*, 36.425 below. *Acrejean Ltd*, LON/93/1774A (VTD 12262).

Motor racing—monumental masons

[36.415] See *Myatt & Leason*, 36.171 above.

Motor rallying

[36.416] The managing director of a plant hire company was also a successful rally driver, who had won a national championship. The company reclaimed input tax on the purchase of a rally car which the director drove in races and which displayed the company's name. The Commissioners issued an assessment to recover the tax and the company appealed, contending that the car had been purchased for the purpose of advertising its business. The tribunal allowed the company's appeal, applying *Ian Flockton Developments Ltd*, 36.341 above. *Steve Hill (Plant Hire) Ltd*, LON/90/725X (VTD 5507).

[36.417] In a Northern Ireland case, a company carried on a business of 'the supply and laying of conducting media for the utilities industry'. It reclaimed input tax on the purchase of two rally cars, which the company's managing director drove in races and which displayed the company's name. Customs issued an assessment to recover the tax, on the basis that the expenditure had been incurred for the personal pleasure of the director, rather than for the purposes of the company's business. The company appealed, contending that it had purchased the cars for the purpose of advertising its business. The tribunal accepted the company's evidence and allowed the appeal. *KPL Contracts Ltd*, LON/04/1605 (VTD 19629).

Kart racing

[36.418] A company reclaimed input tax relating to the purchase and maintenance of a kart. The kart was raced by the company's managing director, and the company's name was painted on the kart. The Commissioners issued an assessment to recover the tax and the company appealed. The tribunal allowed the appeal, holding on the evidence that the kart had been purchased and raced for the purpose of promoting the company's business. *NCS Northern Communications Systems Ltd*, MAN/87/310 (VTD 4242).

Motorcycle racing—transport firm

[36.419] A married couple operated a transport business in partnership. They reclaimed input tax relating to motorcycle racing. The Commissioners issued an assessment to recover the tax and they appealed, contending that the expenditure had been incurred for advertising purposes. The tribunal accepted their evidence and allowed their appeal. *JA & IA Miller (t/a Miller Transport)*, BEL/85/14 (VTD 2041).

Cases where the appellant was partly successful

Motor racing—braid manufacturing company

[36.420] The principal director of a company which manufactured braid was a former motor racing driver. In 1984 he resumed motor racing after several years in retirement. The company reclaimed input tax on its director's motor racing activities and the Commissioners issued an assessment to recover the tax. The company appealed, contending that its director had resumed motor racing with the object of promoting the company. The tribunal found that the motor racing had a dual purpose and held that 45% of the disputed tax was deductible. *TD Reid (Braids) Ltd*, BEL/89/30 (VTD 4638).

Motor racing—sand extraction company

[36.421] A company carried on the business of sand extraction. Its managing director was a motor racing driver, and the company reclaimed input tax on his motor racing activities. The Commissioners issued an assessment to recover the tax, considering that the expenditure had been incurred for the personal pleasure of the director, rather than for the purposes of the company's business. The tribunal held that the expenditure had been incurred for a dual purpose, observing that it was doubtful whether 'an ordinary businessman with a business in a defined location would have spent 41% of his advertising budget on motor racing, most of which took place outside the area'. The tribunal directed that the input tax should be apportioned, and adjourned the appeal in the hope that the parties could reach agreement on an apportionment. *Chambers (Homefield Sandpit) Ltd*, LON/92/276X (VTD 9012). (*Notes.* (1) There was no further public hearing of the appeal. (2) An appeal against a misdeclaration penalty was dismissed—see **52.356** PENALTIES: MISDECLARATION.)

Motor rallying—grocery company

[36.422] A grocery company reclaimed input tax on expenditure incurred in motor rallying. The Commissioners issued an assessment to recover the tax and the company appealed, contending that the expenditure had been incurred for the purpose of advertising its business. The tribunal allowed the appeal in part, holding that one-third of the expenditure in question was allowable. *Lurgan Cash & Carry*, BEL/84/4 (VTD 1738).

Hot-rod racing—car repair business

[36.423] The proprietor of a car repair business took part in hot-rod racing and reclaimed input tax relating to this. The Commissioners issued an assessment to recover the tax and he appealed, contending that the expenditure was for advertising purposes. The tribunal allowed his appeal in part, holding that the expenditure had a dual purpose and that 70% of the tax was deductible. *L Dallas*, BEL/87/16 (VTD 3620).

Cases where the appellant was unsuccessful

Motor racing—building company—whether for promotional purposes

[36.424] The appellant company carried on business as a building contractor. Its employees included B, the son-in-law of H, its managing director. B was an enthusiastic motor racing driver and, through him, H became very interested in motor racing. The directors decided to acquire a car to be raced by B in the company's name and deducted the tax on its expenses of racing the car in its returns. The appeal was against an assessment withdrawing the deduction. The tribunal dismissed the appeal, holding that the company had acquired the car firstly to take part in motor racing activities as to which B and H had become enthusiastic, and secondly to enhance their personal prestige and, incidentally, that of the company. In the circumstances of the case it was unrealistic to say that the car had been raced for the purposes of the company's business. *Hubbard & Houghton Ltd*, LON/80/314 (VTD 1028).

[**36.425**] A building company reclaimed input tax on expenditure incurred in racing two motor cars which were driven by its managing director. The Commissioners issued an assessment to recover the tax, considering that the expenditure had not been incurred for business purposes. The company appealed, contending that the motor racing had had the effect of advertising its business. The tribunal dismissed the appeal, finding that the motor racing had been a hobby 'with a "spin-off" in the form of business contacts' and holding that the input tax was not deductible. *Fenwick Builders Ltd*, LON/90/928Z (VTD 5801).

Motor racing—aviation company

[**36.426**] A company which carried on an air taxi business claimed to deduct input tax on motor racing activities. Its appeal against an assessment withdrawing the deduction was dismissed. The tribunal held that, although the motor racing activity was begun with the object of promoting the name of the company and attracting additional business, there was never a reasonable chance of it being successful in this objective. *Renco Aviation Ltd*, LON/83/203 (VTD 1646).

Motor racing—trader selling caravans and second-hand cars

[**36.427**] A sole trader (S) carried on business selling caravans and second-hand cars. He was also a successful saloon car racing driver. At meetings where he raced saloon cars, he displayed a trailer advertising his business. The Commissioners accepted that this expenditure was incurred for business purposes and that the input tax was deductible. In 1999 S was given the opportunity to hire a Tyrell Formula 1 car and enter it in a race. He placed 6th out of 32 entrants in the race, and reclaimed input tax on the hire of the Tyrell. The Commissioners rejected the claim on the basis that he had incurred this expenditure for personal purposes rather than business purposes. S appealed. The tribunal dismissed the appeal, observing that although S had placed a logo on the Tyrell advertising his business, this was too small to be read at distance and was therefore not an effective advertisement. S had only entered one Formula 1 race and there was 'no credible oral evidence' that this was part of any 'promotional campaign'. The chairman observed that 'to qualify as a legitimate business expense' would require more 'than just displaying the company logo on the side of the vehicle'. *L Stacey (t/a LJ Motors)*, MAN/01/097 (VTD 17538).

Motor racing—sunbed manufacturers

[36.428] See *Paine Leisure Products Ltd*, **8.13** BUSINESS ENTERTAINMENT.

Renovation of March racing car—whether for business purposes

[36.429] A company, which was a member of a group of companies which dealt in expensive cars such as BMWs, Mercedes and Porsches, purchased a March racing car which was in need of extensive renovation, and reclaimed input tax on this expenditure. The Commissioners issued an assessment to recover the tax, considering that the company had purchased the car so that it could be raced by the controlling director of the group for his own pleasure, and had not been purchased for business purposes. The company appealed, contending that the car had been purchased for advertising and promotional purposes. The tribunal dismissed the appeal, finding that the racing of the car 'was unattended by any form of promotion of the group and its business' and that the group had previously engaged in motor racing but that this 'had produced very little in the way of sales'. On the evidence, the company had not shown that the car had been purchased for promotional purposes. *PLR Ltd*, LON/91/1379 (VTD 9501).

Motor rallying—whether for purposes of wife's motor-dealing business

[36.430] A married woman (T) was a dealer in motor cars and equipment. However, although the business was in her name the running of it was largely left to her husband, an undischarged bankrupt, who was a well-known motor rally driver. She claimed input tax on some of her husband's rally expenses. The expenses, some of which were invoiced to her in her business name, were mainly the cost of tyres when not donated by sponsors of her husband's rally driving. He had received over £15,000 from sponsors and also some amounts from the sale of used tyres, but none of this had gone into the appellant's business account. He had circulated potential sponsors but the circulars had not mentioned his wife's business. On this and other evidence the tribunal held that the disputed tax related to supplies for the personal activities of the husband and was not incurred for the purposes of the wife's business. The appeal was dismissed and costs were awarded to the Commissioners. *A Thompson (t/a AY Cars)*, MAN/80/115 (VTD 1043).

Motor rallying—building company

[36.431] The appellant company carried on business as building contractors. It sought to claim input tax on the purchase of and cost of maintenance of two rally cars. The Commissioners disallowed the claim on the basis that the cars were not rallied for the purpose of the business, and issued an assessment to recover the tax. The company's appeal was dismissed. *John McMillan & Son Ltd*, BEL/83/11 (VTD 1610).

Motor rallying—coal merchants

[36.432] A married couple and their son traded in partnership as coal merchants. The son was also a keen rally driver. The partnership name was displayed on the front and sides of his rally car, and the partnership paid for all repairs and spare parts for the car. The partnership reclaimed the input tax on this expenditure, and the Commissioners issued an assessment to recover the tax, considering that the expenditure had not been incurred for the purpose of the partnership's business. The tribunal upheld the assessment and dismissed the partnership's appeal. *RH Pearson & Sons*, EDN/91/154 (VTD 7287).

Motor rallying—jeweller

[**36.433**] An appeal was dismissed in a case where a jeweller, who was also a keen motor rally driver, had reclaimed input tax which was attributable to his rally driving. *JR Joannides*, MAN/91/1338 (VTD 11373). (*Note*. For another issue in this case, see **62.478** SUPPLY.)

Drag-car racing—whether part of business activities

[**36.434**] A company carried on business as a builder and developer. It incurred input tax on the import of components for a drag-racing car, which was raced by the son of the managing director, who won various championships. The company logo appeared on the car. The Commissioners disallowed the input tax and the company appealed, contending that the input tax was incurred for the purpose of its business. The tribunal dismissed the appeal, holding that, whilst the company was carrying on two separate activities of building and drag-racing, on the facts the drag-racing activity did not form part of the business activities of the company. *W & J Barrs Ltd*, LON/87/409 (VTD 2564).

Motorcycle racing

[**36.435**] A company which traded in a wide variety of goods reclaimed input tax on expenditure incurred in motorcycle racing. The Commissioners issued an assessment to recover the tax and the tribunal dismissed the company's appeal. *Fundmain Ltd*, MAN/82/135 (VTD 1493).

Motorcycles purchased by electrical dealers

[**36.436**] A married couple who sold electrical accessories reclaimed input tax on the purchase of motorcycles. The Commissioners issued an assessment to recover the tax and the tribunal dismissed the couple's appeal. *Mr & Mrs CA Eadon (t/a Motaelectrics)*, MAN/84/29 (VTD 1692).

Motorcycle purchased by design company

[**36.437**] A design company reclaimed input tax on the purchase of a motorcycle and spare parts. The Commissioners issued an assessment to recover the tax and the tribunal dismissed the company's appeal. *R & M Baker Ltd (t/a Castle Designs)*, MAN/83/339 (VTD 1695).

Motorcycle purchased by clothing shop

[**36.438**] A clothing shop reclaimed input tax on the purchase of a motorcycle used for competing in moto-cross events. The Commissioners issued an assessment to recover the tax and the tribunal dismissed the company's appeal. *C & W Clothiers Ltd*, MAN/84/163 (VTD 1756).

Motorcycle racing—manufacturing company

[**36.439**] A small manufacturing company reclaimed input tax relating to motorcycle racing. The motorcycle in question was ridden by a nephew of the company secretary. The Commissioners issued an assessment to recover the tax and the tribunal dismissed the company's appeal. *TLV (Manufacturing) Ltd*, MAN/85/298 (VTD 2058).

Motorcycle—numberplate dealers

[36.440] The proprietor of a business which sold motorcar and motorcycle numberplates reclaimed input tax on the purchase of a racing motorcycle by her son. The Commissioners issued an assessment to recover the tax and the tribunal dismissed her appeal. *PD Wood (No 2)*, LON/89/1112X (VTD 4644).

Yachting

Manufacturing company

[36.441] A company which manufactured industrial doors reclaimed input tax on the purchase of a yacht. The Commissioners issued an assessment to recover the tax, considering that the yacht had been purchased for the personal pleasure of the company's managing director. The company appealed, contending that the yacht had been purchased for advertising purposes. The tribunal held that the yacht had been purchased for a dual purpose but that the principal purpose was for the pleasure of the director, and that only a proportion of the input tax was deductible. The tribunal adjourned the appeal for the parties to consider the apportionment. *Freelance Door Services Ltd*, MAN/82/183 (VTD 1384). (*Notes.* (1) There was no further public hearing of the appeal. (2) See now *VATA 1994, s 84(4)*, originating from *FA 1993, s 46*.)

Car sales company

[36.442] A company which dealt in cars reclaimed input tax on the purchase of a yacht. The Commissioners issued an assessment to recover the tax and the tribunal dismissed the company's appeal, holding that the yacht had not been purchased for business purposes. *Omega Cars Ltd*, MAN/82/48 (VTD 1528).

[36.443] A similar decision was reached in *Hill & Son (Manor Park) Ltd*, LON/83/416 (VTD 1629).

Dairy produce company

[36.444] A company which sold dairy produce reclaimed input tax on a 51ft racing yacht which cost more than £140,000. The company's managing director skippered the yacht in races. The company reclaimed input tax on the yacht and the Commissioners issued an assessment to recover the tax. The tribunal dismissed the company's appeal, holding on the evidence that the yacht had not been acquired for business purposes. *Ernest George Ltd*, LON/83/354 (VTD 1760).

Machine tool company

[36.445] A company dealing in machine tools reclaimed input tax on the purchase of a yacht. The Commissioners refused to repay the tax, considering that the yacht had not been acquired for business purposes. The company appealed, contending that the yacht had been acquired to provide an 'upmarket setting' for meetings with potential customers, and had regularly been used for that purpose. The tribunal allowed the appeal in part, holding on the evidence that the yacht was used partly for business purposes and partly for private recreational purposes, and that 50% of the tax in question was deductible. *Tower Steel (Holdings) Ltd*, LON/89/1839X (VTD 5029). (*Note.* See now, however, *VATA 1994, s 84(4)*, deriving from *FA 1993, s 46*.)

Company repairing car engines

[36.446] A company which carried on a business of repairing car engines purchased a yacht from its managing director, and then purchased a second yacht, using the first yacht as part-exchange. The company reclaimed input tax on the purchase of the second yacht. The Commissioners issued an assessment to recover the tax and the company appealed, contending that it had acquired the yacht for research purposes and that it hoped to diversify its business into repairing yacht engines. The tribunal dismissed the appeal, holding on the evidence that this research was remote from the company's existing business and that the yacht had primarily been acquired for recreational purposes. *GL Motor Services Ltd*, LON/87/245 (VTD 2413).

Company carrying on consultancy business

[36.447] A company which carried on a consultancy business reclaimed input tax on the repair and refurbishment of a large yacht. Customs issued an assessment to recover the tax, on the basis that the expenditure had not been incurred for the purpose of the company's business. The tribunal upheld the assessment and dismissed the company's appeal. *Independent Thinking Ltd*, LON/08/927 (VTD 20884).

Farming company—whether yacht purchased for chartering

[36.448] See *Rainheath Ltd*, 7.35 BUSINESS.

Mobile crane hire company—whether yacht purchased for chartering

[36.449] See *RF Henfrey (Midlands) Ltd*, 7.36 BUSINESS.

Accountant—whether yacht purchased for chartering

[36.450] See *Evans*, 7.37 BUSINESS.

Hotel proprietors—whether yacht purchased for chartering

[36.451] See *Westbourne Hotel*, 7.38 BUSINESS.

Plant hire company—whether yacht purchased for chartering

[36.452] See *Trexagrove Ltd*, 7.39 BUSINESS.

Leasing company—whether yacht purchased for chartering

[36.453] See *Petros Leasing Ltd*, 7.40 BUSINESS, and *CR King & Partners (Holdings) Ltd*, 7.41 BUSINESS.

Property development company—whether yacht purchased for chartering

[36.454] See *Silicon Valley Estates Ltd*, 7.42 BUSINESS.

Property company—whether yacht purchased for chartering

[36.455] See *Warwest Holdings Ltd*, 36.584 below.

Waste disposal company—whether yacht purchased for chartering

[36.456] See *City Centre Commercials Ltd*, 36.585 below.

Mining company—whether yacht purchased for chartering

[36.457] See *DS Supplies Ltd*, 7.43 BUSINESS.

Married couple—whether yacht purchased for chartering

[36.458] See *Berwick*, 7.45 BUSINESS.

Family partnership—whether yacht purchased for chartering

[36.459] See *McDonald*, 7.46 BUSINESS.

New company—whether yacht purchased for chartering

[36.460] See *Furness Vale Yacht Hire Ltd*, 36.543 below.

Financial consultant—whether yacht purchased for chartering

[36.461] See *Milner*, 36.564 below.

Building contractors—whether yacht purchased for business

[36.462] See *Penjen Ltd*, 36.575 below.

Aircraft

Kitchen equipment company

[36.463] A company which supplied kitchen equipment reclaimed input tax on the purchase and restoration of an aircraft. The Commissioners issued an assessment to recover the tax, considering that the expenditure had not been incurred for the purpose of the company's business. The company appealed, contending that the aircraft had been acquired for advertising purposes. The tribunal rejected this contention and dismissed the appeal. *Spoils Kitchen Reject Shops Ltd*, LON/86/157 (VTD 2200).

Heating engineers

[36.464] A partnership which carried on business as heating engineers reclaimed input tax on the purchase of an aircraft. The partnership name was painted on the wings in letters 50cm high. The Commissioners issued an assessment to recover the tax and the partners appealed, contending that they had purchased the aircraft for business purposes. The tribunal dismissed the appeal. On the evidence, the aircraft was not used in the business, and the 'visual impact' of the partnership name on the wings when the aircraft was flying at 1000 feet was negligible. *IM & PA Munster (t/a M & M Heating Services)*, MAN/91/867 (VTD 7961).

Computer consultancy company

[36.465] A company which carried on a computer consultancy business reclaimed input tax on the purchase of a microlight aircraft. The Commissioners rejected the claim, considering that the aircraft had not been purchased for business purposes, and the company appealed, contending that the aircraft had been purchased for advertising purposes. The tribunal dismissed the company's appeal, finding that the aircraft had been purchased for the pleasure of the company's managing director, and holding that the input tax was not deductible. *Eddystone Computers Ltd*, LON/92/3036A (VTD 11018).

Property company

[36.466] A property company reclaimed input tax on the purchase of an aircraft and a helicopter. The Commissioners issued an assessment to recover the tax, considering that the expenditure had not been incurred for business purposes. The tribunal allowed the company's appeal in part, finding on the evidence that the aircraft had been purchased for the purpose of flying between the sites of its properties and for viewing potential properties, but that the helicopter had been purchased for private purposes. *Key Properties Ltd*, LON/92/2266A (VTD 11778). (*Note*. For other issues in this case, see **41.122** LAND and **52.281** PENALTIES: MISDECLARATION.)

Company operating garage

[36.467] A company which owned a garage reclaimed input tax on the maintenance and running costs of an aircraft. The Commissioners issued an assessment to recover the tax, considering that the expenditure had been incurred for the personal pleasure of the company's controlling director. The company appealed, contending that the aircraft had been purchased for advertising purposes. The tribunal upheld the assessment and dismissed the company's appeal. *Willpower Garage Ltd*, MAN/91/1269 (VTD 12114).

Personalised vehicle numberplates

Cases where the appellant was successful

Sole trader

[36.468] A haulage contractor, whose initials were MWA, reclaimed input tax on the purchase of a personalised numberplate bearing the registration 'MWA 2'. He affixed the numberplate to a car, which he used 75% for business purposes and 25% privately. The Commissioners issued an assessment to recover the tax, but the tribunal allowed the contractor's appeal, applying *Ian Flockton Developments Ltd*, 36.341 above, and holding that it was satisfied that he had purchased the numberplate for the purpose of advertising his business. *MW Alexander*, LON/91/1191Z (VTD 7208). (*Note*. See now, however, *VATA 1994, s 84(4)*, originating from *FA 1993, s 46*.)

[36.469] A management consultant (S) purchased a vehicle numberplate '100 S' for £4,400. He fixed the numberplate to a Range Rover which he drove for business purposes, and reclaimed input tax on the purchase. The Commissioners rejected the claim, and S appealed, contending that he had purchased the numberplate as an investment and to disguise the age of the Range Rover. The tribunal chairman (Miss Gort, sitting alone) accepted his evidence and allowed his appeal, applying *dicta* in *Ian Flockton Developments Ltd*, **36.341** above, and holding that the numberplate was not a 'luxury', so that the provisions of *VATA 1994, s 84(4)* did not apply. *MJ Shaw (t/a Shaw Associates)*, LON/97/277 (VTD 15099). (*Notes*. (1) The decision in this case was not followed, and was implicitly disapproved, by a subsequent tribunal in *Marinello*, **36.489** below, on the grounds that Miss Gort had not referred to the decision in *Rosner*, **36.232** above, where the QB had held that there must be 'a nexus between the expenditure and the business'. (2) Compare the decision in *College Street Market Gardens*, **36.485** below, in which the tribunal held that personalised vehicle numberplates were within the definition of a 'luxury' for the purposes of *VATA 1994, s 84(4)*.)

Publican

[36.470] A publican reclaimed input tax of £256 on the purchase of a personalised numberplate 'H 002 PER', which reflected his surname. Customs rejected the claim on the basis that the expenditure had been incurred for personal reasons. H appealed, contending that he had purchased the number-plate to advertise his business, which was in a very small village and depended on attracting custom from outside the village. The tribunal accepted H's evidence and allowed his appeal, finding that H was commonly known by his surname and that 'the number chosen was readily identifiable-unlike many "cherished" numbers that are often cryptic uses of initials of the owners'. The tribunal also observed that 'the sum involved was modest' and 'the number was purchased from the DVLA website at the going price, rather than from a private source'. *C Hooper*, LON/x (VTD 19276). (*Note*. Compare *College Street Market Gardens*, **36.485** below, in which the tribunal held that personalised vehicle numberplates were within the definition of a 'luxury' for the purposes of *VATA 1994, s 84(4)*. The decision in *Hooper* discusses *VATA 1994, s 24(1)*, but fails to refer to either *s 84(4)* or to the earlier decision in *College Street Market Gardens*.)

Partnership

[36.471] A partnership operated a supermarket under the name 'Sunner & Son'. It purchased a personalised numberplate '7 SUN' at a cost of £6,300. The numberplate was affixed to a Sierra 2.9 litre car which was owned by one of the partners, and which was normally parked outside the supermarket. The partnership reclaimed input tax on the purchase. The Commissioners issued an assessment to recover the tax, and the partnership appealed, contending that the numberplate had been purchased for advertising purposes. The tribunal accepted the partnership's evidence and allowed the appeal. *Sunner & Sons*, MAN/91/1205 (VTD 8857). (*Note*. See now, however, *VATA 1994, s 84(4)*, originating from *FA 1993, s 46*.)

Limited company

[36.472] A company carried on a business of selling, renting and repairing televisions and video recorders. In 1992 it purchased a numberplate '3 TV' and fixed it to a Lexus car which was driven by its controlling director. Later in the year it purchased a numberplate '9 TV' and fixed it to a Rover car which was driven by the director's wife, who worked for the company on a part-time basis. It reclaimed the input tax on these numberplates. The Commissioners issued an assessment to recover the tax, on the basis that the expenditure had not been incurred for the purposes of the business. The company appealed, contending that the expenditure had been incurred for advertising purposes. The tribunal allowed the appeal, observing that the initials 'TV' referred to the company's trade rather than to the initials of the director, and that if the director had wished to purchase such numberplates for his own prestige or vanity, he would have purchased numberplates bearing his own initials. *Hamlet's (Radio & TV) Ltd*, MAN/93/1285 (VTD 12716).

[36.473] A group of companies carried on a business of providing financial and advisory services. It purchased a numberplate '1 FAS', which it affixed to a BMW which was driven by the group's managing director, and reclaimed input tax on the purchase. The Commissioners issued an assessment to recover the tax, considering that the expenditure had not been incurred for the purpose of the group's business. The holding company appealed, contending that the numberplate had been purchased for advertising purposes and that '1 FAS' was intended to stand for 'Independent Financial Advisory Services'. The tribunal accepted the company's evidence and allowed the appeal, observing that 'the initials are not associated with the name of the managing director himself'. *New Mansion Pension Managers Ltd*, MAN/94/1866 (VTD 13527).

[36.474] A company which sold electrical equipment purchased a numberplate '1 OO' for £300,000 plus VAT. It reclaimed the VAT as input tax. HMRC rejected the claim on the grounds that the company had not purchased the numberplate for the purposes of its business. The company appealed, contending that it had purchased the numberplate with the intention of reselling it at a profit. The tribunal accepted the company's evidence and allowed the appeal. *David Jacobs UK Ltd (in liquidation) v HMRC*, [2009] UKFTT 106 (TC), TC00074.

Cases where the appellant was partly successful

[36.475] A car dealer bought a personalised car numberplate, 'LEW 1S', for £36,000 plus VAT, and reclaimed the relevant input tax. The Commissioners issued an assessment to recover the tax, on the basis that he had not purchased the numberplate for the purposes of his business. The dealer appealed, contending that he had purchased the numberplate as an investment, to resell it at a profit in the future, and also for advertising purposes. The tribunal allowed the appeal in part, finding that the numberplate had been partly purchased for advertising purposes, partly for resale, and partly for personal enjoyment, and held that 75% of the tax was deductible. *RA Lewis*, MAN/91/1348 (VTD 9845). (*Note.* See now, however, *VATA 1994, s 84(4)*, originating from *FA 1993, s 46*.)

[36.476] A chartered surveyor, whose initials were 'MJD', reclaimed input tax on the purchase of a personalised numberplate 'MJD2'. The Commissioners rejected the claim and the surveyor appealed. The tribunal held that, since the initials reflected the surveyor's trading name, 25% of the tax was deductible. *MJ Dant*, LON/94/318 (VTD 16043).

Cases where the appellant was unsuccessful

Limited company

[36.477] A company which manufactured women's clothing reclaimed input tax on the purchase of a personalised numberplate '714 ROD' for its managing director's car. The initials did not reflect the company's name, but were chosen because the director's Christian name was Rodney. The Commissioners issued an assessment to recover the tax and the tribunal dismissed the company's appeal, holding that the numberplate was not acquired for the purposes of the company's business, but for the personal pleasure of the director. *Ava Knit Ltd*, MAN/82/219 (VTD 1461).

[36.478] A company which carried on a transport business reclaimed input tax on the purchase of a personalised numberplate 'BK 4'. The company was named after its controlling director, and the initials reflected those of the director. The Commissioners issued an assessment to recover the tax and the tribunal dismissed the company's appeal, finding that the relationship between the numberplate and the company was so tenuous that the plate could not reasonably be expected to serve the object of promoting the company. *BJ Kershaw Transport Ltd*, MAN/84/229 (VTD 1785).

[36.479] An appeal was dismissed in another case where a company reclaimed input tax on a personalised numberplate bearing the initials of the company's managing director. The initials (GJW) were not reflected in the company's name. The tribunal held that the numberplate had not been purchased for the purpose of promoting the company's business. *Empire Contracts Ltd*, MAN/90/937 (VTD 7200).

[36.480] Similar decisions were reached in *Quality Care Homes Ltd*, MAN/91/302 (VTD 7391); *Industrial Doors (Scotland) Ltd*, EDN/94/26 (VTD 12656), and *The Redington Design Co Ltd*, LON/98/1432 (VTD 12656).

[36.481] A company which operated amusement arcades reclaimed input tax in respect of two personalised numberplates. The numberplates bore the letters 'LC', which were the initials of the son and daughter-in-law of the managing director, and were attached to cars driven by the son and daughter-in-law. The Commissioners issued an assessment to recover the tax and the tribunal dismissed the company's appeal, observing that the numberplates did not reflect the company's name and finding that the company's 'predominant motive' was to give the director's son and daughter-in-law 'the pleasure of driving cars with their initials displayed on the numberplates'. *Stardust Leisure Ltd*, LON/92/1248A (VTD 9740).

[36.482] A company reclaimed input tax on the purchase of a personalised numberplate '3 MB' bearing the initials of the company's managing director, which were not reflected in the company's name. The numberplate was fixed to a Bentley car, costing more than £100,000, which was driven by the managing director. The Commissioners rejected the claim and the tribunal dismissed the company's appeal, holding that it was 'difficult to accept that (the director) really believed that the numberplate would genuinely benefit the business'. *Welbeck Video plc*, LON/93/162A (VTD 11383).

[36.483] A company which dealt in electrical goods purchased a personalised numberplate 'FEL 1X' at a cost of more than £50,000. The company was named after its managing director, and the initials reflected the director's name. The company fixed the numberplate to a Mercedes which the director drove, and reclaimed input tax on the purchase. The Commissioners issued an assessment to recover the tax, and the company appealed. The tribunal dismissed the appeal, holding that there was 'no clear nexus between the expenditure on the numberplate and the business itself'. *Felix Quinn Enterprises Ltd*, EDN/93/171 (VTD 12411).

[36.484] See also *NEP Group Ltd*, **52.348** PENALTIES: MISDECLARATION.

Partnership

[36.485] A family partnership which operated a market gardening business reclaimed input tax on the purchase of four personalised numberplates. The numberplates reflected the initials of the individual partners, but did not reflect the trading name of the partnership. The Commissioners issued an assessment to recover the tax, and the tribunal dismissed the partnership's appeal, finding that the numberplates had been 'purchased out of a natural pride in the partners' own evident individual success and that the use of these numbers would enhance their own individual images'. *College Street Market Gardens*, LON/95/2712 (VTD 14118). (*Note.* The tribunal also held that the numberplates were within the definition of a 'luxury', so that, by virtue of *VATA 1994, s 84(4)*, it would only have allowed the appeal if the Commissioners' decision had been unreasonable.)

[36.486] Similar decisions were reached in *Engineering Quality Consultants*, EDN/99/190 (VTD 16634) and *SN Fitzgerald & DP Robinson (t/a Autozone)*, LON/x (VTD 18168).

Accountant

[36.487] A chartered accountant, whose initials were ENJ, reclaimed input tax on the purchase of a numberplate bearing the registration 'ENJ 8'. The Commissioners rejected the claim and the tribunal dismissed his appeal. The test of whether expenditure was incurred for business purposes was a subjective test, applying *Ian Flockton Developments Ltd*, **36.341** above. However, the tribunal did 'not believe that his motive in buying the number was as a business purpose' and considered that his subjective motive was 'more likely to have been to possess a personalised number personally which could do the practice no harm'. *EN Jones*, MAN/90/15 (VTD 5023).

Printer

[36.488] A printer, whose Christian name was David, purchased a personalised numberplate 'DAV 10' at a cost of £38,775. He fixed the numberplate to a BMW, and reclaimed input tax on the purchase. The Commissioners issued an assessment to recover the tax, and the tribunal dismissed the printer's appeal, holding that 'the standards and thinking of the ordinary businessman in the position of the appellant' made it 'improbable that the acquisition of the numberplate was for the purposes of the business'. *D Philips*, EDN/92/3 (VTD 7883). (*Note.* For another issue in this case, see **52.327** PENALTIES: MISDECLARATION.)

Publican

[36.489] A publican, who also had a number of other business interests, reclaimed input tax on the purchase of a personalised numberplate 'PEM 1'. (The publican's initials were 'PEM'.) The Commissioners issued an assessment to recover the tax, on the basis that he had purchased the numberplate for personal reasons rather than for business reasons. The tribunal dismissed the publican's appeal. Applying *dicta* of the QB in *Rosner*, 36.232 above, there had to be 'a nexus between the expenditure and the business'. On the evidence, 'there was no real nexus between the number on the numberplates and any of (the publican's) businesses'. The tribunal specifically declined to follow the decision in *Shaw*, 36.469 above, on the basis that the chairman in that case had failed to refer to the QB decision in *Rosner*. *PE Marinello*, EDN/98/119 (VTD 15915).

Haulage contractor

[36.490] See *Windsor*, 52.349 PENALTIES: MISDECLARATION.

Associated companies

Whether expenditure incurred for business of subsidiary or parent

[36.491] A leasing company (F) was a subsidiary of a banking company (C), which was itself the subsidiary of a US banking company. A large proportion of C's supplies were exempt from VAT, so that it could reclaim less than half of its input tax, whereas F could reclaim the whole of its input tax. F purchased some computer equipment which it leased to C for a period of eight years, and reclaimed the input tax incurred on the purchase. The Commissioners issued an assessment to recover the tax, considering that the equipment had not been purchased for the purposes of F's business. The tribunal allowed F's appeal, holding that the transactions were not a sham and that the input tax was deductible. *Friary Leasing Ltd*, LON/88/1026Z (VTD 3893). (*Note. VATA 1994, s 44* now provides that there is a deemed self-supply where a going concern is transferred to a partly exempt group.)

Enterprise Zone Trust established by property development company

[36.492] A company (V) which carried on the business of property development established an Enterprise Zone Trust to promote the sale of units in a shopping precinct which it was developing in an Enterprise Zone in the West Midlands. V reclaimed input tax on the expenditure incurred in establishing the Trust. The Commissioners issued an assessment to recover the tax, considering that, since the Trust was a separate legal entity, the expenditure was not directly for the purpose of V's business, although it would have the effect of benefiting V's business. The tribunal allowed V's appeal. Applying *Ian Flockton Developments Ltd*, 36.341 above, 'the sole purpose of incurring the expenditure was for the more advantageous and efficient way of carrying on (V's) business'. *V & P Midlands Ltd*, MAN/90/520 (VTD 7589).

[36.493] A similar decision was reached in *Property Enterprise Managers Ltd*, LON/91/234Z (VTD 7711).

Repairs to boats hired to associated company

[36.494] A married couple carried on a computer consultancy business in partnership, and were registered for VAT. They purchased three boats, and hired them to a company which they controlled. The company advertised the boats as holiday accommodation, but attracted very few customers, and traded at a loss. In 1988 the partnership had invoiced the company for the use of the boats, but, because of the company's financial difficulties, it did not issue any more invoices to the company until 1991. In the meantime the partnership undertook repairs to the boats, and reclaimed input tax. The Commissioners issued an assessment to recover the tax, considering that, because the partnership was not invoicing the company for the hire of the boats, the hire of the boats to the company did not amount to a business activity. The tribunal allowed the partners' appeal, holding that the hire of the boats was a business despite the temporary cessation of payment by the company, so that the partnership was entitled to credit for the relevant input tax. *JR & S Purdue*, [1994] VATTR 387 (VTD 11779).

Antique furniture leased to tenant of associated company

[36.495] A company (J), which was not registered for VAT, owned business premises which it leased to an unrelated company (V). V owed J rent of £5,250. The principal director of J also controlled another company (R), which operated a public house and was registered for VAT. The director arranged for R to purchase some antique furniture from V for £5,250, and lease the furniture back to V. The £5,250 was lent by J to R, paid by R to V for the furniture, and finally paid by V to J as arrears of rent, so that effectively it travelled in a circle. R reclaimed input tax on the furniture, and the Commissioners issued an assessment to recover the tax, considering that R had not purchased the furniture for the purpose of its business. The tribunal dismissed R's appeal, finding that it was satisfied that R's intention 'at the time when the expenditure was incurred on the furniture was not that the furniture should be used for the purposes of its business'. (The tribunal also observed that, although it was not necessary to apply the principle laid down in *Furniss v Dawson*, HL [1984] STC 153 to the facts here, it was clear that 'the *Furniss v Dawson* principle could apply to cases relating to the recovery of input tax'.) *Raceshine Ltd*, MAN/91/1135 (VTD 7688). (*Note.* An appeal against a misdeclaration penalty was also dismissed.)

Company reclaiming input tax on items used by associated company

[36.496] A company (P) reclaimed input tax on the lease of two cars, and on certain IT equipment and furniture. Customs formed the opinion that these items had not been used by P, but had been purchased for use by an associated company (D) which was in financial difficulties and had subsequently gone into administration. They therefore issued assessments to recover the tax. The tribunal reviewed the evidence in detail and dismissed P's appeal, finding that 'the goods were purchased by (P) not for the purpose of or in furtherance of its business but in order that they would be available for use by (D) without (D) having to pay for the goods or for the use of them'. *Platinum Acquisitions Ltd*, MAN/06/845 (VTD 20514).

Company refurbishing accommodation for associated charity

[36.497] A trading company covenanted all its profits to a charity for the homeless. It incurred expenditure in refurbishing a property for the homeless, and reclaimed the input tax on this work. The Commissioners issued an assessment to recover the tax, considering that the expenditure had been incurred for the purposes of the charity, rather than for the purpose of the company's business. The tribunal dismissed the company's appeal, holding on the evidence that the refurbishing of the accommodation was 'for the purpose of carrying out the objectives of the charity'. *Emmaus Ltd*, LON/93/699A (VTD 11679).

Promotion of tourism

Tourist board

[36.498] The Netherlands Tourist Bureau, which had been established by the Netherlands Government as a non-profit-making organisation to encourage people to visit the Netherlands, operated a branch in London. The branch was registered for VAT in 1989 under the name of the Netherlands Board of Tourism, and reclaimed the whole of its input tax. In March 1994 the Commissioners issued a ruling that only part of the input tax incurred by the Board was attributable to supplies made for business purposes, and that the remainder of the tax related to supplies made to the Netherlands Government and was not deductible. The Board appealed, contending firstly that all its supplies were made to commercial sponsors, and alternatively that those supplies which were not made to commercial sponsors were made to its parent Bureau in the course of its business. The tribunal allowed the appeal, accepting the Board's alternative contention and holding that those supplies which were not made to commercial sponsors were made through the Bureau to the Netherlands Government and were made in the course of the Board's business. *Netherlands Board of Tourism*, LON/94/607A (VTD 12935).

[36.499] The London branch of the Austrian National Tourist Office (ANTO) reclaimed the whole of its input tax. The Commissioners issued a ruling that only part of the input tax was deductible, and that part of the tax related to supplies made to the Austrian Federal Government (and the Federal States) which were essentially 'the activities of a government agency', and was not deductible. The tribunal allowed ANTO's appeal, holding that ANTO was carrying on a business for VAT purposes and that the whole of its input tax was deductible. The decision in *Turespaña*, **36.500** below, was distinguished on the grounds that the Spanish government had a degree of control over Turespaña, whereas ANTO could not 'be regarded as part of the Austrian Government even in the widest sense'. *Austrian National Tourist Office*, LON/96/674 (VTD 15561). (*Note.* For another issue in this case, see **62.497** SUPPLY.)

[36.500] Turespaña (T) was established as a statutory body to encourage tourists to visit Spain. It claimed credit for input tax on supplies of advertising services. (For the obligation on the supplier of these services to account for output tax, see *Diversified Agency Services Ltd*, **62.495** SUPPLY.) The Commissioners rejected the claim, considering that, although T was carrying on a business for VAT purposes in that it made supplies of exhibition facilities to third parties, the promotion of tourism by a statutory body was not an economic activity or a business for the purposes of VAT law. T appealed, contending that the grants which it received from the Spanish Government represented consideration for the supplies which it made to that Government. The tribunal dismissed the appeal, holding on the evidence that 'in carrying out its activities (T) was discharging its statutory duties'. Its activities were controlled by the Spanish Government, and were 'far removed from the usual concept of supplies'. *Netherlands Board of Tourism*, 36.498 above, was distinguished on the grounds that 75% of the income of the appellant in that case was commercially generated. *Turespaña*, LON/96/002 (VTD 14568). (*Note.* The decision here was distinguished in the subsequent case of *Austrian National Tourist Office*, 36.499 above, on the grounds that the Spanish government had a degree of control over Turespaña, whereas the Austrian National Tourist Office could not 'be regarded as part of the Austrian Government even in the widest sense'.)

Subpostmasters

Payment to secure appointment of partner as sub-postmaster

[36.501] In the case noted at 7.104 BUSINESS, a member of a retail partnership applied to run a sub-post office. He was required to pay Post Office Counters Ltd £88,560, including VAT of £13,189. The partnership reclaimed input tax on this payment. The Commissioners rejected the claim and the tribunal dismissed the partnership's appeal, holding that, although the partner had applied to run the sub-post office in order to expand the partnership retail business, the expenditure could not be apportioned and none of the input tax was deductible. *H & V Patel (No 2)*, LON/94/2821 (VTD 15328).

[36.502] The decision in *Patel*, 36.501 above, was applied in the similar subsequent cases of *JH & H Pugh*, LON/95/654 (VTD 16034); *N & S Chauhan*, MAN/00/724 (VTD 17160) and *D & S Mayariya (t/a Oaktree Lane Selly Oak Post Office & Stores)*, 52.331 PENALTIES: MISDECLARATION.

Retailers also acting as subpostmasters—purchase of security screen

[36.503] A couple traded from a retail shop which included a sub-post office. They reclaimed input tax on the purchase of a Post Office counter and security screen. Customs issued an assessment to recover the tax, on the basis that the expenditure had been incurred for the purposes of the sub-post office rather than of the couple's retail business. The tribunal upheld the assessment and dismissed the couple's appeal. *R & ME Taylor (t/a Chew Magna Post Office)*, LON/05/366 (VTD 19740).

Miscellaneous

Cases where the appellant was successful

Provision of Christmas street lighting by Chamber of Commerce

[36.504] A Chamber of Commerce organised a festival of street lighting each Christmas. It reclaimed input tax on the relevant expenditure. The Commissioners rejected the claim but the tribunal allowed the Chamber's appeal, holding that the expenditure had been incurred for the purpose of promoting the trade of the members of the Chamber. *Sittingbourne Milton & District Chamber of Commerce*, LON/76/178 (VTD 341).

Radios purchased by broadcaster

[36.505] A broadcaster and writer (H) reclaimed input tax on the purchase of a transistor radio and a car radio. The Commissioners issued an assessment to recover the tax, considering that the radios had been purchased for private purposes rather than professional purposes. H appealed, contending that he had purchased the radios to listen to rival broadcasters. The tribunal accepted his evidence and allowed his appeal. *R Hough*, LON/77/106 (VTD 488).

Computer—whether purchased for business purposes

[36.506] A trader who had carried on business as a general builders' merchant, and also supplied management services, purchased a computer for £13,000 and reclaimed input tax on the purchase. The Commissioners issued an assessment to recover the tax but the tribunal allowed the trader's appeal, holding on the evidence that the computer had been purchased for business purposes rather than for private purposes. *EA Kilburn*, MAN/87/277 (VTD 3937). (*Note.* For another issue in this case, see **62.190** SUPPLY. For a subsequent application for costs, see **2.401** APPEALS.)

Actor joining health club

[36.507] An actor joined a health club, and reclaimed input tax on his entrance fee and subscriptions. The Commissioners issued an assessment to recover the tax, considering that the expenditure had been incurred for private purposes since membership of such a club was not 'essential to the acting profession'. The actor appealed, contending that he had joined the club for the purpose of undertaking a specific role in a television series, which required him to portray a character with a high level of physical fitness. In the series he was filmed swimming underwater, running, and weight training. The tribunal allowed his appeal, applying *Ian Flockton Developments Ltd*, **36.341** above, and holding on the evidence that he had joined the club to serve the purposes of his profession. *A Anholt*, [1989] VATTR 297 (VTD 4215). (*Note.* See now, however, *VATA 1994, s 84(4)*, originating from *FA 1993, s 46.*)

Purchase of typesetting machines—whether for business purposes

[36.508] A company had for many years been engaged in manufacturing typesetting machines and related software, but sold this business in 1984. It continued to receive investment income, while an associated company provided financial services, mainly to companies engaged in typesetting. In the following year the company incurred expenditure in refurbishing three old typesetting machines of historic interest, and reclaimed the input tax on this expenditure. The Commissioners issued an assessment to recover the tax, considering that the machines had been refurbished as a personal hobby of the principal director, rather than for the purpose of the company's business. The tribunal allowed the company's appeal, holding on the evidence that the purchase and refurbishment of the old machines had been undertaken for the purpose of publicising the group's business of providing finance for the purchase of typesetting machines. *M & H Whittaker & Son Ltd*, MAN/88/174 (VTD 3554).

Renovation of property owned by transport company

[36.509] A company carried on the business of road transport and haulage, and had also bought and sold property. In 1986 it purchased land close to a garage which it owned. The land contained a bungalow, which the company's managing director occupied, and a row of pigsties. The company converted the pigsties into stables and reclaimed the input tax on this work. The Commissioners issued an assessment to recover the tax, considering that the expenditure had not been incurred for the purpose of the company's business. The company appealed, contending that the expenditure had been incurred to make the land more attractive to a developer. The tribunal allowed the appeal, holding that the company's business should be regarded as including property development as well as road transport and haulage. *Philip Drakard Trading Ltd*, LON/89/1473X (VTD 5030). (*Note.* For another issue in this case, taken to the QB, see **62.107** SUPPLY.)

Landscaping work at company's premises—whether input tax deductible

[36.510] A company carried on the business of providing architectural services. In 1987 it acquired new premises, which included a courtyard which was 'no more than a mud patch'. It incurred expenditure on landscaping the courtyard, erecting banking and installing steps and brickwork, and reclaimed input tax on this work. The Commissioners issued an assessment to recover the tax, considering that the work had been undertaken with a view to improving the property's resale value, rather than for the purpose of the company's business. The company appealed, contending that the work was needed because staff had to cross the courtyard, and because they had wanted to make the courtyard 'an attractive feature of the property which would impress clients'. The tribunal allowed the company's appeal, holding that the expenditure had been incurred for business purposes. *Thorpe Architecture Ltd*, LON/91/391 (VTD 6955).

Golf club—improvements to clubhouse

[36.511] A golf club leased its clubhouse from a limited company, most of the shares in which were held by members of the club. The club undertook extensive improvements to the clubhouse and reclaimed the input tax thereon. The Commissioners issued an assessment to recover the tax, considering that the work had been carried out to benefit the company which owned the premises, rather than for the purposes of the club's business. The tribunal allowed the club's appeal, finding that the club's 'sole intention in carrying out the improvements was to improve the facilities for members and the appellants' business'. *Burntisland Golf Club*, EDN/91/10 (VTD 6340).

Limited company occupying premises in property owned by director

[36.512] A property development company carried on business from leased premises in the grounds of a large property owned by its managing director. It reclaimed input tax on the refurbishment of an old pond and fountain in the grounds. The Commissioners issued an assessment to recover 50% of the tax, on the basis that the expenditure had been partly incurred for the personal pleasure of the director, and was not wholly for business purposes. The company appealed, contending that it had refurbished the pond to make it more attractive and thus to improve the company's image, and that it had reduced the size of the fountain to provide a larger turning circle for visiting lorries. The tribunal accepted the company's evidence and allowed the appeal, applying the principles in *Ian Flockton Developments Ltd*, **36.341** above. *Dysart Developments Ltd*, MAN/00/1032 (VTD 17333).

Expenditure on demolition of company's previous premises

[36.513] A small engineering company, controlled by a married couple, moved to new premises. Its directors decided that they would have to sell the company's previous premises (the freehold of which was owned by the directors rather than by the company) to raise funds. They considered that the sheds and outbuildings at its previous site reduced the resale value of the site, and the company incurred expenditure in demolishing them. It reclaimed input tax on this expenditure. The Commissioners issued an assessment to recover the tax, considering that the expenditure had not been incurred for the purposes of the company's business, but for the financial benefit of the directors. The tribunal allowed the company's appeal, finding that the company had paid for the expenditure in order to enable more money to be injected into the company, and holding that although the directors' loan account with the company would be increased by the amount injected, the expenditure had still been incurred for the purpose of the company's business. *AW Mills Engineering Ltd*, LON/94/2757A (VTD 13196).

Expenditure by owner of Scottish estate

[36.514] In 1993 a company director (F) acquired a large estate in a remote part of the Scottish highlands, which was inaccessible by road (and only accessible by boat from a large loch). The previous owner had been registered for VAT, and the transfer was treated as the transfer of a going concern. Because of its remote location, the Post Office did not deliver mail to the estate, and paid F to deliver mail, which he usually collected twice per week from the nearest town post office. F reclaimed input tax on expenses relating to the distribution of the mail, and also reclaimed input tax on expenses relating to the sale of venison from deer carcasses. In 2008 HMRC issued assessments disallowing this input tax on the grounds that the expenditure was not related to any economic activity. F appealed. The tribunal allowed his appeal. Judge Reid reviewed the discussion of whether an activity is a business in De Voil Indirect Tax Service, paras V2.201 and V2.202. He held that both the sale of venison, and the delivery of post to the estate, were supplies for consideration in the course or furtherance of a business, so that the input tax was deductible. *MZ De Ferranti v HMRC*, [2011] UKFTT 435 (TC), TC01288.

Dogs—whether used for business purposes as guard dogs

[36.515] A company carried on a computer graphics and printing business from the home of its controlling shareholder. It purchased two dogs, one of which subsequently gave birth to a litter of five puppies, three of which the director gave away and two of which he kept. The company reclaimed input tax on the upkeep of the dogs. The Commissioners issued an assessment to recover the tax, considering that the dogs were primarily kept as pets and that it would not have been necessary to keep more than one dog as a guard dog. The company appealed, contending that the dogs had been kept as guard dogs. The tribunal accepted the company's evidence and allowed the appeal, applying *Ian Flockton Developments Ltd*, **36.341** above. *Music View Ltd*, LON/91/2191 (VTD 9122).

Marketing consultant—expenditure on maintaining pilot's licence

[36.516] A marketing consultant (K), who was a qualified helicopter pilot, had owned a helicopter which he had used for business travel. However, because of a decline in his turnover, he decided that he could not afford the cost of running the helicopter, and sold it in 1990. He retained his licence as a pilot, and reclaimed input tax on his licence fees in 1991 and 1992. The Commissioners issued an assessment to recover the tax, considering that since K no longer owned a helicopter, the cost of maintaining his licence had not been incurred for the purpose of his consultancy business. K appealed, contending that he hoped that his turnover would increase and that he would again be able to afford a helicopter for business travel. If he had not maintained his licence, he would have had to incur substantial retraining costs before he could be granted a new one. The tribunal accepted K's evidence and allowed his appeal, holding that it was satisfied that at the time the expenditure was incurred, K had decided to retain his licence in the belief that he would require it for the purpose of his business. *CJ Kent (t/a Market Integration)*, LON/94/2886A (VTD 13214).

Company purchasing mailing lists

[36.517] A company (D) reclaimed input tax on the purchase of mailing lists, which it used to make onward supplies to charities for fundraising purposes. HMRC rejected the claim but the tribunal allowed D's appeal. Judge Tildesley held that there was 'no legal basis for denying the VAT credit for input tax'. *Different Kettle Ltd v HMRC*, [2011] UKFTT 540 (TC), TC01387.

Cases where the appellant was partly successful

Burglar alarm

[36.518] An appeal was allowed in part in a case where the appellant, who carried on business from his home, had reclaimed input tax on the installation of a burglar alarm after he had been burgled on two occasions. The tribunal held that 50% of the tax in question was allowable. *A Kitson*, MAN/85/239 (VTD 2030). (*Note.* The nature of the appellant's business is not stated in the decision.)

Heating equipment

[36.519] A business consultant, who worked from home, reclaimed input tax on the purchase of Aga heating equipment. The Commissioners considered that only 22% of the tax was deductible, since the house comprised nine rooms and only two of these were used for business purposes. The tribunal allowed the appeal in part, finding that the heater was kept on for 24 hours per day and that the appellant worked for up to 55 hours per week, and holding that 30% of the tax should be treated as deductible. The tribunal observed that 'to base the apportionment entirely upon the number of rooms in use for business purposes, without regard to the actual use of the heating system, is unrealistic'. *MF Phipps*, [1996] VATDR 241 (VTD 13839).

Club subscriptions

[36.520] Two solicitors in partnership in Belfast reclaimed input tax on subscriptions to the Ulster Reform Club. The Commissioners issued an assessment to recover the tax, considering that the expenditure had been incurred for private purposes rather than for professional purposes. The solicitors appealed. The tribunal allowed the appeal in part, holding that the tax should be apportioned. *KEG Morrow & AE Wells*, BEL/86/4 (VTD 2424).

Swimming pool constructed in grounds of solicitors' practice

[36.521] The principal partner in a firm of solicitors owned a large house in Norfolk, eight miles outside Norwich, in 6.5 acres of grounds. A building in the grounds, which had originally been a coach house, was used as the firm's offices. The firm paid no rent to the partner for its occupation of the building. The firm reclaimed input tax on the construction of a swimming pool in the grounds of the partner's house. The Commissioners issued a ruling that the tax was not reclaimable, considering that the expenditure had been incurred for the personal pleasure of the partner and his family. The firm appealed, contending that the pool had been built for the benefit of its staff, since it had experienced difficulty in recruiting staff and had decided that 'in an attempt to make the work conditions more congenial, some recreation facilities should be provided to compensate for the isolation and lack of amenities in the immediate surrounding area'. The pool was used by employees with 'very little restriction', and changing rooms had been provided for their use. The tribunal allowed the appeal in part, holding that the partner's main purpose in deciding to build the pool was to provide a valuable benefit for the firm's employees, but that since the pool was also used by the partner and his family, and was built on land owned by them, the tax should be apportioned. The tribunal ruled that 35% of the tax in question was allowable. *Willcox & Co*, [1992] VATTR 472 (VTD 8813). (*Note.* See now, however, *VATA 1994, s 84(4)*, originating from *FA 1993, s 46*.)

Swimming pool constructed by farmer

[36.522] See *Nielsen*, 36.567 below.

Farmer—expenditure on shooting

[36.523] An underwriter (B) purchased a farm in 1994. The main activity of the farm was breeding cattle. Between 1995 and 1999 B advertised pheasant shooting at the farm, but although he obtained some income from this, it was not profitable. In 2001 and 2002 B made several visits to a shoot in Kent, and reclaimed input tax on this. The Commissioners issued assessments to recover the tax, on the basis that B had incurred the expenditure for personal pleasure, rather than for business purposes. B appealed, contending that he had incurred the expenditure 'for the purpose of researching the way in which a large, commercially successful, shoot operates, to see if he could operate a shoot on his farm and over neighbouring land in a similarly commercially successful way'. The tribunal allowed his appeal in part, holding that the expenditure on the two visits in 2001 had been incurred for research purposes, so that the input tax on these was deductible, but that the expenditure on six further visits in 2002 had been incurred for personal pleasure, so that the input tax on these was not deductible. *RF Bailey (t/a Llancillo Hall Farm)*, LON/03/527 (VTD 18719).

Video cassette recorder

[36.524] A company carried on a design consultancy business from the home of its principal director. It reclaimed input tax on the purchase of a video cassette recorder. The Commissioners issued an assessment to recover the tax, and the company appealed. Prior to the hearing, the company had failed to give the Commissioners any details of the way in which the recorder was used for business purposes, but at the tribunal hearing the director gave evidence that it was used to record technical programmes while he was away from home, and that it was not normally used privately, since he already owned a VCR which was attached to a different set which he and his family used for private viewing. The tribunal held on the evidence that 50% of the tax was deductible. *Remlock Design Ltd*, LON/92/1124Y (VTD 9146). (*Notes*. (1) For another issue in this case, see **36.570** below. (2) For the award of costs, see **2.410** APPEALS. (3) Compare *Cobb's Croft Service Station Ltd*, **36.568** below, and *Smith*, **36.569** below, in which input tax on video cassette recorders was held not to be deductible.)

Projectors and photocopier

[36.525] A company (K) registered for VAT as an importer of copper. It reclaimed input tax on the purchase of two projectors, which were used by an associated company (M), and a photocopier. Customs discovered that K had not received any income in return for letting M use the projectors, and issued an assessment to recover the tax, on the basis that the expenditure had not been incurred for the purpose of K's business. K appealed. The tribunal reviewed the evidence in detail and dismissed the appeal with regard to the projectors, finding that the evidence given by K's controlling director was 'unreliable'. However the tribunal allowed the appeal with regard to the photocopier, finding that K had used it for the purposes of its business. *KDP(UK) Ltd*, MAN/x (VTD 20659).

Motor cruiser—whether input tax to be apportioned

[36.526] A trader purchased a motor cruiser which he let on charter during the summer. He reclaimed the whole of the input tax on the purchase. The Commissioners issued an assessment to recover 5% of the tax, on the basis that the trader sometimes used the cruiser privately. The tribunal upheld the assessment, finding that one of the reasons why the trader had purchased the cruiser 'was so that he could get some personal enjoyment and use of it', and holding that 5% could not 'be regarded as an excessive disallowance'. *HA Lovejoy (t/a HRS Recoveries)*, LON/93/2754 (VTD 12835). (*Note.* For another issue in this case, see **41.14** LAND.)

Rolex watches

[36.527] Two brothers carried on business in partnership as plumbing and heating engineers. They purchased two Rolex watches at a cost of £1,350 each, and reclaimed input tax on the purchase. The Commissioners issued an assessment to recover the tax, and the partners appealed, contending that the watches had been purchased for their reliability, durability and ability to withstand heat, vibration and humidity. The tribunal allowed the appeal in part, holding that some of the input tax should be allowed since the partners needed watches to measure gas flows, but that the partners had not shown that 'these extravagant watches were to be solely used for the purposes of the business' and it appeared that they had largely been purchased 'for their investment purposes and/or as status symbols'. The tribunal held that only 25% of the input tax was deductible. *Trigg's Plumbing & Heating*, LON/95/2614 (VTD 14142).

Company publishing religious books—expenditure on radio broadcasts

[36.528] A company (B) published religious books. It incurred expenditure on radio broadcasts, and reclaimed input tax on this. Customs issued an assessment to recover the tax on the basis that the broadcasts had primarily been used to propagate the religious views of B's principal director, rather than for the purposes of B's business. The tribunal allowed B's appeal in part, finding that the broadcasts had partly been used to 'promote the publications available from' B, and holding on the evidence that 45% of the input tax was deductible. *Amana Books Ltd*, LON/05/136 (VTD 19541).

Input tax reclaimed by charities—apportionment of input tax

[36.529] See the cases noted at **11.39** *et seq.* CHARITIES.

Cases where the appellant was unsuccessful

Family farming partnership—tuition of partner as pilot

[36.530] A farming partnership comprised a married couple and their two sons. The partnership paid for one of the sons to have flying lessons, and reclaimed input tax on the fees, although they did not own an aircraft. The Commissioners issued an assessment to recover the tax and the partnership appealed, contending that they had incurred the expenditure because they considered that at some time in the future they might need an aircraft for crop-spraying and for business travel. The tribunal dismissed the appeal, holding that the expenditure had not been incurred for the purposes of the farming business. *GWM Warner & Others*, LON/82/324 (VTD 1402).

Estate agent's charges on sale of property

[36.531] A married couple took over the tenancy of a public house. To finance improvements, they sold their existing house and bought a smaller one.

They reclaimed input tax in respect of the estate agent's charges. The Commissioners issued an assessment to recover the tax, and the couple appealed. The tribunal dismissed the appeal, holding that the agent's services had been supplied to the couple as owners of their house, rather than as publicans. *Mr & Mrs AF Dean*, LON/83/137 (VTD 1455).

[36.532] The decision in *Dean*, **36.531** above, was applied in the similar case of *DL Jones*, LON/93/585A (VTD 11430). (*Note*. For another issue in this case, see **52.202** PENALTIES: MISDECLARATION.)

[36.533] See also *Rushgreen Builders Ltd*, **36.150** above.

Surveyor's fees

[36.534] A local council proposed to make a compulsory purchase order in respect of a house owned by a market gardener. He considered that the council were undervaluing his house, and consulted a surveyor. He reclaimed input tax in respect of the surveyor's fees. The Commissioners issued an assessment to recover the tax, and the tribunal dismissed the appeal, holding that the expenditure had not been incurred for the purpose of the gardener's business. The QB upheld the tribunal decision. *NO Turner (t/a Turner Agricultural) v C & E Commrs*, QB [1992] STC 621. (*Note*. For another issue in this case, see **36.45** above.)

Music publishing company—hire of studios

[36.535] A company carried on the business of manufacturing and selling records of popular music. It reclaimed input tax on the hire of two recording studios for the use of a specific group which was under contract to it. The Commissioners rejected the claim on the grounds that the studios in question had been hired for the purposes of the group's business, rather than for the company's business, and the company's role had been the provision of finance. The tribunal upheld the assessment and dismissed the company's appeal. *The Bacon Empire (Publishing) Ltd*, LON/83/464 (VTD 1688).

Lunch

[36.536] A sole trader reclaimed input tax on the cost of lunch while he was working. The Commissioners issued an assessment to recover the tax and the tribunal dismissed the trader's appeal, applying *dicta* of Lord Davey in *Strong & Co of Romsey Ltd v Woodifield*, HL 1906, 5 TC 215. *DG Mutch*, MAN/87/109 (VTD 2559).

Engineering company—whether boat acquired for business purposes

[36.537] The managing director of an engineering company purchased a boat which had been damaged by fire and had it refurbished by the company. The company reclaimed input tax on this expenditure, and the Commissioners issued an assessment to recover the tax. The tribunal dismissed the company's appeal, holding that the company had not shown any connection between the expenditure in question and its business. *Diesel Generating (Tetbury) Ltd*, LON/87/165 (VTD 2702).

Computer consultancy company—whether boat used for business purposes

[36.538] A company which carried on a computer consultancy business reclaimed input tax on the repair and maintenance of a boat. The Commissioners issued an assessment to recover the tax and the company appealed, contending that the boat was used as an office and as a venue for business meetings. The tribunal dismissed the appeal, finding that the boat was primarily used for private purposes and holding that the company had failed to produce sufficient evidence to justify the allowance of any of the input tax. *Parker Bond Ltd*, MAN/94/504 (VTD 13160).

Farmer—purchase of shotguns

[36.539] A farmer purchased two Purdy shotguns at a cost of £34,000, and reclaimed input tax on their purchase. The Commissioners rejected the claim and the tribunal dismissed the farmer's appeal, holding on the evidence that the farmer had failed to prove that the guns had been acquired for the purposes of his business. *JD Leavesly*, MAN/88/95 (VTD 2987).

Kitchen equipment—whether acquired for publican's business

[36.540] A publican reclaimed input tax in respect of the purchase of kitchen equipment. The catering at the public house was carried on by his wife, and was treated as a separate business for tax and VAT purposes. The turnover of the wife's catering business was below the VAT registration threshold. The Commissioners issued an assessment to recover the tax, considering that the kitchen equipment had been purchased for the wife's catering business rather than for the publican's own business, and that since the wife did not account for output tax on her sales of food, input tax could not be reclaimed on the equipment purchased for her use. The tribunal upheld the assessment and dismissed the publican's appeal. *MJ Scott*, LON/88/1447Z (VTD 4257).

Cigarettes purchased by accountant—whether for business purposes

[36.541] An accountant reclaimed input tax on the purchase of quantities of cigarettes. The Commissioners issued an assessment to recover the tax and he appealed, contending that he had purchased the cigarettes in order to give them to his employees and customers, for the purposes of maintaining the goodwill of his practice. The tribunal dismissed his appeal, holding on the evidence that the cigarettes had not been supplied for the purposes of his business. *AG Fine*, MAN/89/304 (VTD 4977).

Music centre

[36.542] A company reclaimed input tax on the purchase of a music centre, which was installed in a house which the company owned and where its principal director lived. The Commissioners issued an assessment to recover the tax and the tribunal dismissed the company's appeal, holding that the music centre had not been purchased for the purpose of the company's business. *The Gourmet Sandwich Ltd*, MAN/90/428 (VTD 5505).

Building materials—whether purchased for purposes of company or director

[36.543] A company was incorporated by a retired builder (R) to provide management services for an associated design company, and for any other associated companies with which he might subsequently become involved. R arranged for two builders to erect an extension at a client's residence. The management company purchased the materials to be used for the extension, and reclaimed the input tax thereon. R was paid an agency fee for arranging the transaction. The Commissioners rejected the company's claim, considering that the building materials had not been purchased for the purpose of the management company's business. The tribunal upheld this decision and dismissed the company's appeal. *S Robertson (Management) Ltd*, LON/90/251Y (VTD 5597).

Oil painting

[36.544] A company carried on business as a retailer of confectionery and cigarettes. It reclaimed input tax on the purchase of an oil painting, which had cost £4,950 and which was kept at the home of its managing director. The Commissioners issued an assessment to recover the tax, considering that the expenditure had not been incurred for the purposes of the company's business. The company appealed, contending that it intended to display the painting in a new boardroom, which had not been completed at the time of the hearing, and that it had been purchased to impress visitors to the boardroom. The tribunal dismissed the appeal, finding that the painting had not been purchased for the purpose of the company's business. *Cough & Candy Ltd*, MAN/90/724 (VTD 5952).

Antique train sets

[36.545] A company which carried on the business of supplying lighting equipment purchased four antique train sets, at a total cost of more than £16,000, and reclaimed input tax on the purchase. The Commissioners issued an assessment to recover the tax and the tribunal dismissed the company's appeal, finding that the train sets had not been purchased for the purpose of the company's business. *Leadstar Ltd*, LON/91/1596 (VTD 7153).

Furniture sold by tenant to landlord

[36.546] A married couple were registered for VAT as proprietors of a property management business. They owned the freehold of a hotel, which was let to a company of which they were shareholders and directors. The company suffered financial difficulties and the local authority threatened distraint proceedings for non-payment of rates. In September 1991 the company sold the couple the furniture of the hotel for £35,000 (expressed as being inclusive of VAT). The couple paid the company a cheque for £35,000, and the company then paid the couple a cheque for £29,900 in respect of arrears of rent. The couple reclaimed input tax in respect of the payment of £35,000. The Commissioners issued an assessment to recover the tax, on the basis that the transaction had not been carried out for the purpose of the couple's business. The tribunal dismissed the couple's appeal, noting that the company had not accounted for output tax on the purported sale and holding on the evidence that there had been no actual supply of the furniture. Furthermore, even if there had been a supply, the supply would not have been for the purpose of the couple's business, since 'the business of the appellants was the management of property and the leasing of services and it was not suggested to us how that purpose could be served by the acquisition of furniture in a hotel belonging to their tenants'. The purpose of the transaction 'was to safeguard the hotel business and sell it on as a going concern'. *Dr & Mrs P Frost*, EDN/94/151 (VTD 13045).

Military vehicle—whether purchased for advertising purposes

[36.547] A company, which traded in surplus nuts and bolts, reclaimed input tax on the purchase of a military vehicle (a Vickers-Armstrong self-propelled gun). The Commissioners rejected the claim on the basis that the vehicle had not been purchased for the purposes of the company's business. The company appealed, contending that the vehicle had been purchased for advertising purposes. The tribunal reviewed the evidence and dismissed the appeal, observing that the company's controlling director had conducted a high-profile publicity campaign against his local council, and finding that he used the vehicle 'for the purposes of private campaigns' and had not purchased it with the aim of promoting the company's business. *Worldwide Surplus Supplies Ltd*, LON/98/833 (VTD 16198).

Farming company—purchase of old traction engine

[36.548] A farming company reclaimed input tax on the purchase of an old traction engine. The Commissioners issued an assessment to recover the tax, on the basis that the expenditure had not been incurred for the purpose of the company's business, but because one of the directors had an interest in old traction engines. The tribunal dismissed the company's appeal. *F Machin & Sons Ltd*, MAN/01/280 (VTD 17906).

Jacuzzi purchased by actor

[36.549] An actor reclaimed input tax on the purchase of a jacuzzi. The Commissioners issued an assessment to recover the tax, considering that it had not been purchased for the purposes of his profession. He appealed, contending that he had suffered from back trouble and had purchased the jacuzzi in the hope that it would help him to return to work more quickly. The tribunal dismissed the appeal, holding that his objective 'in seeking to return to health and fitness' must have 'been that of any normal person. The measures he took to return to health and fitness were no different to those which other private individuals take'. *J Pearce*, LON/91/1638Y (VTD 7860). (*Note.* For another issue in this case, see **36.173** above.)

Computer equipment purchased by accountant

[36.550] An accountant was also a shareholder and director of a company which sold computer systems. In 1990 the accountant purchased some items of computer equipment for the company, and reclaimed input tax on these items. The company went into liquidation in February 1991. When the Commissioners discovered what had happened, they issued an assessment to recover the input tax. The tribunal dismissed the accountant's appeal, holding that he had not purchased the equipment for the purpose of his accountancy practice. *L Ramm (t/a Ramm Louis & Co)*, LON/92/2465A (VTD 11242).

Religious cassettes

[36.551] A company which operated a travel agency reclaimed input tax on the purchase of some audiocassettes, which propagated the 'Sai Madhura' religious teachings of Sai-Christ of Canada, Incorporated. The Commissioners issued an assessment to recover the tax. The tribunal dismissed the company's appeal, holding that the cassettes had not been purchased for the purpose of the company's business. *Jet Across Ltd*, MAN/94/18 (VTD 12541, 13526).

Refurbishment of houses occupied by Cathedral Dean and Canons

[36.552] The Dean and Chapter of Bristol Cathedral were registered for VAT since they operated a shop and refectory at the Cathedral. They reclaimed input tax on the refurbishment of the houses occupied by the Dean and the three Canons. The Commissioners only agreed to allow 25% of the tax in question. The tribunal upheld the Commissioners' ruling and dismissed the Dean's appeal. *Dean & Chapter of Bristol Cathedral*, LON/96/126 (VTD 14591). (*Note.* For a case concerning similar expenditure on houses occupied by Cathedral vergers, see *Dean & Chapter of Hereford Cathedral*, 36.320 above.)

Input tax reclaimed by import agent

[36.553] See *Cavenco Ltd*, 35.14 IMPORTS.

Whether supplies intended for use in future business

Cases where the appellant was successful

Cable television company—pre-trading expenditure

[36.554] In 1982 a company (M) was incorporated to carry on the business of supplying cable television in the Merseyside area. It incurred considerable preliminary expenditure, and applied to be registered for VAT to enable it to reclaim input tax on this. Initially the Commissioners refused to register the company on the grounds that it was not trading. Subsequently M supplied consultancy services to another associated company, and renewed its application for registration. It was registered in December 1983, the registration being backdated to May 1982 at its request. In January 1984 it submitted its first VAT return, covering the period from May 1982 to 31 December 1983, and reclaiming more than £33,000 as input tax. In August 1985 the Commissioners formally rejected the claim, ruling that M was not entitled to be registered under the legislation then in force (*VATA 1983, Sch 1*) and that the registration should be treated as void since M was not making taxable supplies. The tribunal allowed M's appeal against this decision. Applying *Amministrazione delle Finanze dello Stato v Simmenthal SpA*, 22.22 EUROPEAN COMMUNITY LAW, the law of the European Economic Community 'prevails over any contrary provision in national law'. Under *Article 4* of the *EC Sixth Directive*, any person carrying on an economic activity was a 'taxable person'. If goods or services were supplied to him by another taxable person, and he used those goods or services for the purposes of his taxable transactions, he was entitled to deduct the tax he had suffered on the supplies made to him from the tax for which he was accountable on the supplies made by him. Applying *Rompelman & Another v Minister van Financien*, 22.103 EUROPEAN COMMUNITY LAW, a person who carried on activities which were preparatory to the carrying on of an economic activity was to be treated as a person carrying on that economic activity. M had had a fixed and continuing intention to operate a cable television service, which qualified it as a 'taxable person' within *Article 4(1)* of the *EC Sixth Directive*. The fact that, under the UK legislation then in force, M was not entitled to be registered for VAT, did not alter the fact that, under Community law, it was a taxable person and was entitled to credit for the input tax it had suffered. *Merseyside Cablevision Ltd*, [1987] VATTR 134 (VTD 2419). (*Notes.* (1) The relevant provisions of *VATA 1983, Sch 1* were subsequently amended by *FA 1988.* (2) For a case in which this decision was distinguished, see *Park Commercial Developments plc*, **27.46** FINANCE.)

Property development

[36.555] A partnership was formed to develop an estate. It acquired the freehold of the land, obtained planning permission, widened roads, and installed drainage, gas and electricity. It reclaimed input tax on the professional expenses incurred. Subsequently it sold 75% of the land on the estate to a company carrying on the business of property development. The Commissioners issued an assessment to recover the input tax which the company had previously reclaimed, considering that, in view of the sale of the land, the expenditure could not be attributed to any taxable supplies. The company appealed, contending that the input tax was correctly reclaimable since its activities had been undertaken with the intention of making taxable supplies, and that the sale of the land constituted the transfer of a part of the business as a going concern. The tribunal accepted the partnership's evidence and allowed the appeal. The fact that, at the time of the sale, the partnership had not made any supplies in respect of the land was not conclusive. *The Golden Oak Partnership*, LON/90/958Z (VTD 7212). (*Note.* For a subsequent case in which this decision was distinguished, see *Gulf Trading & Management Ltd*, **46.208** PARTIAL EXEMPTION.)

[36.556] A company (B) carried on a business of property development. It became interested in a site at Ayr, and reclaimed input tax on speculative costs relating to a project to develop it. It had to abandon the project because it was unable to obtain planning permission for the proposed development, and consequently never acquired the land. The Commissioners issued an assessment to recover the tax on the basis that it could not be attributed to a taxable supply. B appealed. The tribunal reviewed the evidence in detail and allowed the appeal, holding that 'throughout the period when the speculative costs were incurred, it was (B's) intention, had the project proceeded, to elect to waive the statutory exemption in terms of (*VATA 1994, Sch 10 para 2*) and make taxable supplies in respect of the land. Any ordinary and prudent businessman would, in the circumstances, have formed the same intention. The absence of making of such an election in the course of incurring such speculative costs does not necessarily negate that intention.' Accordingly B was 'entitled to deduct the input tax incurred in respect of these speculative costs'. *Beaverbank Properties Ltd*, [2003] VATDR 538 (VTD 18099). (*Note.* For the Commissioners' revised policy following this decision, see Business Brief 14/2004, issued on 17 May 2004.)

[36.557] A car dealer (M), who was registered for VAT, reclaimed input tax on the renovation of a residential property which was in poor condition, having been repossessed. The Commissioners issued an assessment to recover the tax, on the basis that the property development 'could not properly be regarded as a business transaction'. M appealed, contending that he had purchased and renovated the property in order to sell it at a profit, and that he 'was now intending to spend less of his time on motor dealing and more on property development'. The tribunal accepted this contention and allowed his appeal. *BJ Middleton*, MAN/96/1150 (VTD 17985). (*Note.* For another issue in this case, see **44.84** MOTOR CARS.)

Landowner

[36.558] In 1988 a landowner (H) applied for registration as an 'intending trader', and informed the Commissioners that he intended to begin selling timber in 1990. The Commissioners accepted the application, and allowed him to make provisional claims for repayment of input tax. However, such repayment claims were expressed to be 'subject to the condition, provided for by (*VATA 1994, s 25(6)**), that the Commissioners may require you, on request, to refund all or any of the input tax claimed, if you do not make taxable supplies by way of business, or if in respect of input tax claimed prior to a period in which taxable supplies in the course of business are made, that input tax is not commensurate with the related output tax'. H reclaimed input tax of £2,290. However, in March 1990 he sold the land, and in September 1990 the Commissioners issued an assessment to recover the input tax which H had reclaimed. H appealed, contending that the conditions attached to his original registration were invalid. The tribunal allowed the appeal, holding that the conditions were 'discriminatory and unenforceable'. Applying *Rompelman & Another v Minister van Financien*, **22.103** EUROPEAN COMMUNITY LAW, acts which were preparatory to commercial exploitation were 'to be considered as an economic activity'. The expenditure incurred by H had been incurred for the purpose of an economic activity notwithstanding that H had never made any taxable supplies. The sale of the land had constituted the transfer of a business as a going concern, so that the purchaser of the land would have to account for output tax in due course. *ACS Hordern*, [1992] VATTR 382 (VTD 8941). (*Note.* Compare the subsequent decision in *Wilson*, **36.578** below, in which the tribunal held that conditions imposed under *VATA 1994, s 25(6)** were valid. For a case in which the sale of land was held not to constitute the transfer of a going concern, see *Gulf Trading & Management Ltd*, **46.208** PARTIAL EXEMPTION.)

[36.559] See also *Belgium v Ghent Coal Terminal NV*, **22.406** EUROPEAN COMMUNITY LAW.

Restoration of patrol boats for exhibition and hire

[36.560] A consultant reclaimed input tax on the costs of restoring several old naval patrol boats, which he had purchased with a view to exhibiting and hiring them out. The Commissioners rejected the claim but the tribunal allowed his appeal, holding on the evidence that he had purchased the craft for the purpose of a future business and that the input tax was deductible. *WG Haydon-Baillie*, [1986] VATTR 79 (VTD 2072).

Motorboat purchased by married couple for restoration and resale

[36.561] A married couple traded in partnership as dealers in cars and mobile homes. In 1990 they purchased an expensive motorboat and reclaimed the input tax on the purchase. The Commissioners issued an assessment to recover the tax, considering that the motorboat had been purchased for private pleasure, rather than for business purposes. The couple appealed, contending that they had intended to restore the motorboat and sell it at a profit. They had advertised it for sale in yachting magazines, but had not received an acceptable offer. The tribunal allowed the appeal, holding on the evidence that the couple had purchased the boat for the purpose of an intended business of dealing in boats. *SB & JM Cavner*, LON/91/1212 (VTD 7714). (*Note.* See now, however, *VATA 1994, s 84(4)*, deriving from *FA 1993, s 46*.)

Yacht—whether purchased for future chartering business

[36.562] A company registered for VAT with effect from 1 August 1990. In its first return it reclaimed input tax on the purchase of a yacht. In October 1993 the Commissioners issued an assessment to recover the tax, on the basis that the yacht was not being used for business purposes. The company appealed, contending that it had purchased the yacht for the purpose of chartering it to an associated engineering company, for the purpose of entertaining customers. However, the engineering company had subsequently been hit by financial difficulties, and had not made use of the yacht until May 1994. The tribunal accepted the company's evidence and allowed the appeal, finding that it was satisfied that it remained the company's purpose to use the yacht for future chartering. The chairman observed that 'although to a suspicious mind the dates of the invoice and the charter were ominously close to the date of the hearing, I am satisfied that the purpose of the charter, both from the appellant's and the engineering company's points of view, were genuine'. *Furness Vale Yacht Hire Ltd*, MAN/94/16 (VTD 12628). (*Note.* Compare the subsequent decision in *Warwest Holdings Ltd*, **36.584** below, in which this case was distinguished.)

Vintage cars—whether purchased for future business

[36.563] A computer software company reclaimed input tax on the restoration of four vintage cars. The Commissioners issued an assessment to recover the tax, considering that the cars had not been purchased for business purposes, and the company appealed. The tribunal allowed the appeal, holding that the cars had been purchased as an investment, for the purpose of being sold at a profit, so that the input tax was deductible. *LHA Ltd*, LON/93/924A (VTD 11911). (*Note.* For another issue in this case, see **36.241** above.)

[36.564] A similar decision was reached in a subsequent case where a company had purchased three vintage cars and had reclaimed the input tax thereon. The tribunal accepted the company's evidence and held that the input tax was deductible. *Tarrakarn Ltd*, [1996] VATDR 516 (VTD 14279).

Restoration of vintage car—whether for purposes of future business

[36.565] An individual (H) registered for VAT as an 'intending trader' in 1989. In 1990 and 1991 he reclaimed input tax on the restoration of a vintage

Jaguar car. Following a control visit in 1995 the Commissioners became aware that H had never accounted for output tax and appeared never to have made any taxable supplies. They therefore issued an assessment to recover the input tax which H had reclaimed on the repairs to the car. H appealed, contending that he had arranged for the repairs with the intention of using the car for chauffeuring foreign tourists on conducted tours of historic sites in Devon and Cornwall, but that he had not yet completed the necessary accommodation although he hoped to do so in 1997. The tribunal accepted H's evidence and allowed his appeal. On the evidence, the tribunal was satisfied that, at the time the expenditure was incurred, H intended to use the car for business purposes. The tribunal held that 'the time at which the relevant intention of the taxpayer is to be ascertained was the time at which the relevant expenditure was incurred'. *JH Halsey*, [1996] VATDR 508 (VTD 14313).

Surveyor—arbitration proceedings to resolve dispute with former partners

[36.566] Disputes arose between the partners in a firm of surveyors. One of the partners (H) issued a writ seeking the dissolution of the partnership. The other partners responded by issuing a notice expelling him from the partnership. The matter was referred to arbitration. The arbitrator upheld the expulsion notice, but H was allowed to retain certain clients (which, under the partnership deed, he would not have been permitted to do). H subsequently registered for VAT as a consultant. In his first return he reclaimed input tax relating to the arbitration proceedings. The Commissioners issued an assessment to recover the tax but the tribunal allowed H's appeal, holding on the evidence that there was a clear nexus between the arbitration proceedings and H's subsequent consultancy business. The chairman observed that, as a direct result of pursuing the arbitration proceedings, H had been able to continue working with clients whom he might otherwise have lost. *P Hartridge (t/a Hartridge Consultancy)*, MAN/97/1158 (VTD 15553).

Cases where the appellant was partly successful

Swimming pool constructed by farmer

[36.567] In 1989 a farmer built a swimming pool in the grounds of his house. He reclaimed the input tax on this work. The Commissioners issued an assessment to recover the tax, considering that it had been incurred for private purposes, and as an investment to improve the value of his property, rather than for business purposes. The farmer appealed, contending that the swimming pool had been built for the purpose of a future business activity, and that in 1992 he had begun to open it to paying guests on six days each week, having been unable to do so earlier because of difficulties with planning permission and with dehumidification. The tribunal allowed the appeal in part, finding on the evidence that the work had been undertaken for a dual purpose but that the predominant purpose was for the purpose of a future business activity, and holding that 75% of the tax was deductible. *J Nielsen*, LON/92/2874A (VTD 11852).

Cases where the appellant was unsuccessful

Video recorder—whether purchased for future business

[36.568] A company which operated a service station reclaimed input tax on a video recorder. The Commissioners issued an assessment to recover the tax and the company appealed, contending that the video recorder had been purchased for use in future business activities. The tribunal dismissed the appeal, holding on the evidence that the company had not shown that the recorder was to be used for business purposes. *Cobb's Croft Service Station Ltd*, [1976] VATTR 170 (VTD 269).

[36.569] A similar decision was reached in a case where an electrical engineer purchased a video recorder and reclaimed the input tax, contending that he was considering setting up a new business as a wedding photographer. *DA Smith*, MAN/84/40 (VTD 1830).

Yamaha keyboard—whether purchased for future business

[36.570] A company which carried on a design consultancy business from the home of its principal director reclaimed input tax on the purchase of a Yamaha keyboard. The Commissioners issued an assessment to recover the tax and the company appealed, contending that the keyboard had been purchased so that the controlling director's son could write musical software for a computer 'with a view to developing this as a business proposition'. The tribunal dismissed the appeal, holding on the evidence that the keyboard had not been purchased for the purposes of any future business activity. *Remlock Design Ltd*, LON/92/1124Y (VTD 9146). (*Notes.* (1) For another issue in this case, see **36.524** above. (2) For the award of costs, see **2.410** APPEALS.)

Horses purchased by engineering company—whether for future business

[36.571] A company was incorporated in 1976 to carry on an engineering business. In 1977 and 1978 it purchased two horses. From 1979 the company's income from engineering declined substantially. In 1980 the company's Memorandum of Association was amended to include references to horse breeding, training and riding instruction. In 1981 the company rented some land on which it built stables, and in December 1982 the daughter of the couple who controlled the company qualified as an intermediate riding instructor. The company reclaimed income tax on its equine activities. The Commissioners issued an assessment to recover the tax in question (covering the period from December 1976 to August 1981), considering that the expenditure had not been incurred for business purposes, but for the personal enjoyment of the directors and their daughter. The company appealed, contending that it had purchased the horses with the intention of beginning a business of horse breeding and riding instruction. The tribunal dismissed the appeal, holding on the evidence that the company had not carried on any such business until December 1982. During the period covered by the assessment, the company's equine activities had not involved the making of taxable supplies. The tribunal held that 'in commencing a new business, there may be a period of gestation prior to the making of taxable supplies' but 'it must be contemplated that taxable supplies be made in the reasonably foreseeable future, in the course of or furtherance of the business'. Accordingly the input tax was not deductible. *K & K Thorogood Ltd*, LON/82/318 (VTD 1595).

Refurbishment of stables—whether for purpose of future livery business

[36.572] An individual, who had been registered as a shopkeeper but had subsequently sold his shop, reclaimed input tax on the refurbishment of some stables which he had purchased. The Commissioners issued an assessment to recover the tax, considering that he was not carrying on a business. He appealed, contending that he had purchased the stables with a view to setting up a livery stable to be run as a business. The tribunal dismissed his appeal, holding that he had not purchased the stables for the purposes of any future business, but to further his own interest in horses. *R McLintock*, EDN/85/94 (VTD 2102).

Construction company—expenditure on farm

[36.573] A construction company reclaimed input tax on expenditure on a farm which its managing director had purchased. The Commissioners issued an assessment to recover the tax and the company appealed, contending that the farm had been purchased with a view to diversification of its business. The tribunal dismissed the appeal. *F Jones & Sons (Cheltenham) Ltd*, LON/88/1078Y (VTD 4511).

Farming company—renovation of house—whether for future business

[36.574] A company which carried on a farming business incurred substantial expenditure on renovating a large house on its land, which it had not previously used for business purposes, and reclaimed input tax on the work. It subsequently sold the house, and the Commissioners issued an assessment to recover the input tax, on the basis that the sale of the renovated house was exempt from VAT. The company appealed, contending that it had incurred the expenditure with the intention of using the house for a future business of making supplies of accommodation to people interested in shooting or fishing, but, because of financial difficulties attributed to economic recession and an increase in interest rates, it had subsequently changed its intention and had sold the house instead. The tribunal dismissed the appeal, holding on the evidence that the company had failed to establish that it had incurred the expenditure in question for the purpose of making taxable supplies. *Stockton Park (Leisure) Ltd*, LON/95/1658A (VTD 14548). (*Note*. The tribunal also rejected an alternative contention by the company that the work on the farmhouse should be treated as zero-rated construction. The tribunal held that the work amounted to the reconstruction of an existing building rather than the construction of a new building.)

Building contractors—whether yacht purchased for future business

[36.575] A company which had carried on business as a building contractor reclaimed input tax on the refitting of a 21-foot yacht, which was owned by one of its directors. The Commissioners issued an assessment to recover the tax, considering that the expenditure had not been incurred for business purposes. The company appealed, contending that it intended to carry on the business of shipbuilding and repairing. The tribunal dismissed the appeal, finding that the yacht had been refitted for the benefit and private purposes of the controlling director, and that there was no evidence that the company intended to carry on a business of shipbuilding. *Penjen Ltd*, LON/89/1167X (VTD 5882).

Purchase of helicopter—whether for future business

[36.576] A property developer, who was registered for VAT, reclaimed input tax on the purchase of a helicopter. The Commissioners issued an assessment to recover the tax and he appealed, contending that he had intended to use the helicopter for a prospective business of setting up a helicopter flying school, and that when this proved impractical he had begun leasing the helicopter. The tribunal dismissed his appeal, holding that no ordinary businessman would have purchased a helicopter in such circumstances. *RB Payne*, LON/90/1576X (VTD 9211). (*Note.* For another issue in this case, see **7.74** BUSINESS.)

Tuition as helicopter pilot—whether for future business

[36.577] The proprietor of a road haulage business reclaimed input tax on the cost of lessons in flying a helicopter. The Commissioners issued an assessment to recover the tax, and the proprietor appealed, contending that he had incurred the expenditure in the hope of starting a new business of helicopter transport. The tribunal reviewed the evidence and dismissed the appeal, holding that it was satisfied that the proprietor wished to become a commercial helicopter pilot, but observing that 'he will find it difficult to put in the necessary hours' and that 'even if he does put in the hours and he does get qualified, it is not immediately clear what business he is likely to run'. *J English*, MAN/98/7 (VTD 15879).

Input tax reclaimed by 'intending trader'—no taxable supplies made

[36.578] In October 1989 an individual (W) applied to be registered for VAT as a freelance pilot. The Commissioners accepted his application 'subject to the condition, provided for by (*VATA 1994, s 25(6)**), that the Commissioners may require you, on request, to refund all or any of the input tax claimed, if you do not make taxable supplies by way of business'. In fact W never made any taxable supplies, and in November 1990 he applied to be deregistered. The Commissioners issued an assessment to recover the input tax which he had reclaimed while he had been registered. The tribunal dismissed W's appeal, holding that the Commissioners were entitled 'to require in their discretion a refund of all or any of the input tax claimed, on the ground that the appellant had not made taxable supplies by way of business'. *K Wilson*, EDN/92/341 (VTD 12042).

[36.579] A similar decision was reached in a case where the tribunal found that the appellant had failed to provide any evidence that he had actually made any taxable supplies. *J Green (t/a CMOS)*, EDN/05/31 (VTD 19265).

Development company—input tax relating to raising of share capital

[36.580] See *Park Commercial Developments plc*, **27.46** FINANCE.

Development company—expenditure on property let on short-term leases

[36.581] See the cases at 46.13 to 46.16 PARTIAL EXEMPTION.

Motorboat—whether purchased for future chartering business

[36.582] A builder reclaimed input tax on the purchase of a motorboat. The Commissioners issued an assessment to recover the tax and he appealed, contending that he had purchased the boat with the intention of setting up a future chartering business. The tribunal dismissed the appeal, finding that the builder had failed to produce sufficient evidence in support of his claim. *LD Castle (t/a Langford Building Supplies)*, LON/94/604A (VTD 12813).

Financial consultant—whether yacht purchased for future business

[36.583] In 1990 a financial consultant (M), who was employed as the chief executive of a large company, ordered a luxury yacht at a cost of £200,000. The yacht was delivered in 1991. In February 1992 M left the company which had employed him and became self-employed as a financial consultant. He registered for VAT from September 1992. In 1993 he reclaimed input tax in respect of the running costs of the yacht. The Commissioners rejected the claim on the grounds that the yacht had been purchased for private purposes rather than for business purposes. He appealed, contending that since the delivery of the yacht, he had intended to use it for chartering. He had received income from chartering totalling £1,800 up to the end of 1994, and of £5,000 in 1995. (The running costs of the yacht amounted to some £1,500 per year.) He also submitted a belated claim for input tax on the purchase of the yacht, contending that it should be treated as deductible by virtue of the principles laid down in *Lennartz v Finanzamt München III*, 22.456 EUROPEAN COMMUNITY LAW. The tribunal rejected this contention and dismissed M's appeal. On the evidence, at the time when M had decided to purchase the yacht, he had done so with the intention of using it for his own enjoyment. His subsequent decision that he would have to charter the yacht 'was not part of the purpose of the expenditure; it was an exercise in damage limitation'. The tribunal chairman also observed that, although M had received income of £6,800 from chartering by the time of the hearing, 'no business yet exists'. *KJ Milner*, LON/95/1949 (VTD 13648).

Property company—whether yacht purchased for future business

[36.584] In 1992 a property company purchased a yacht from an associated company at a cost of £117,500, and reclaimed input tax on the purchase. The Commissioners issued an assessment to recover the tax, on the basis that the yacht had not been purchased for business purposes. The company appealed, contending that the yacht had been purchased with the intention of being used for chartering, although this had not materialised and the yacht had eventually been sold at a loss in 1995. The tribunal reviewed the evidence in detail and dismissed the appeal, observing that there was 'no obvious and clear association between the taxpayer company's business and the expenditure concerned' and holding that the company had failed to prove that the expenditure had been incurred for business purposes. *Warwest Holdings Ltd*, LON/93/2972 (VTD 14114).

Waste disposal company—whether yacht purchased for future business

[36.585] A company (C) which carried on a waste disposal business reclaimed input tax on the purchase of a yacht. Customs issued an assessment to recover the tax. C appealed, contending that the yacht had been purchased for a future chartering business. The tribunal rejected this contention and dismissed the appeal, finding that the relevant insurance policy provided that the yacht 'could only be used for private and pleasure purposes and (was) not to be let out on hire or charter'. *City Centre Commercials Ltd*, MAN/05/266 (VTD 20166).

Married couple—whether yacht purchased for future chartering business

[36.586] See *Berwick*, 7.45 BUSINESS.

'Motor home'—whether purchased for future business

[36.587] A company, which carried on business making moulding for the plastics industry, purchased a 'motor home' in August 1999 for about £50,000, and reclaimed input tax on the purchase. The Commissioners issued an assessment to recover the tax, on the basis that it had been purchased for the personal use of the company's controlling director. The company appealed, contending that it had been purchased with the aim of starting a business of selling such homes at a profit. The tribunal rejected this contention and dismissed the appeal, observing that the motor home had been sold at a loss in April 2001 and commenting that 'we do not find it credible' that a successful businessman 'would pay £50,000 for a totally different business without making some investigations for which records could be produced about such matters as the potential for discounts on purchase'. The overall impression was that of 'a private purchase paid for by the appellant company'. *Pinnacle Tooling Ltd*, LON/02/913 (VTD 18271).

Refurbishment of premises—whether for purposes of future business

[36.588] A company had sold vacuum cleaners from premises which it leased, but ceased trading in 2001. It subsequently claimed a repayment of tax relating to the refurbishment of the premises. Customs rejected the claim, and the company appealed, contending that it had incurred the expenditure with the aim of opening an 'executive sauna' with massage facilities, but had subsequently decided to relinquish the lease of the premises. The tribunal dismissed the company's appeal, finding that there was no evidence that it had intended 'to carry on the sauna and massage business'. *South Wales Home Care Ltd*, LON/03/637 (VTD 19170).

Pre-registration input tax

Purchases of stock

[36.589] An ice-cream salesman, who had traded for some time before registering for VAT, reclaimed input tax on supplies made to him before registration. Customs rejected his claim and the tribunal dismissed his appeal.

There was no evidence that the supplies in question were still in his possession when he registered, and it was reasonable to assume that most of the stock would have been sold to customers. He had not been asked to account for output tax on supplies before registration and he could not reclaim input tax on purchases before registration. *M Allard*, [1984] VATTR 157 (VTD 1566).

Shopfitting

[36.590] Supplies of goods by opticians, which had previously been exempt, became taxable from September 1988. A company (R) which owned several opticians' shops registered for VAT, and reclaimed input tax on expenditure which it had incurred on refurbishing and fitting out several shops. Customs issued an assessment to recover the tax relating to expenditure incurred more than six months before the date of registration, considering that the supplies were supplies of services and that the tax was not recoverable as R had only made exempt supplies at the relevant time. R appealed, contending that the supplies were compound supplies, comprising both goods and services, and that the input tax attributable to the goods themselves was deductible. The QB accepted this contention, holding that part of the input tax related to supplies of goods and was deductible. *Rayner & Keeler Ltd v C & E Commrs*, QB [1994] STC 724.

[36.591] The decision in *Rayner & Keeler Ltd*, 36.590 above, was distinguished in a subsequent case in which the proprietors of a small shop which sold greeting cards reclaimed input tax in respect of shopfitting services carried out more than six months before they registered for VAT. Customs rejected the claim on the basis that the relevant supplies were supplies of services, so that the effect of what is now *VAT Regulations 1995, reg 111(2)* was that the input tax was not deductible. The tribunal dismissed the proprietors' appeal, holding that the supplies amounted to 'an elaborate decoration of a room' and had to be treated as supplies of services. *MEJ Burgess & AP Holmes (t/a Cards'N Cuddles)*, LON/96/292 (VTD 14475).

[36.592] A family partnership began trading in October 2001, selling retail clothing. It registered for VAT from 30 April 2002 and reclaimed input tax in respect of the 'fitting out' of its shop. Customs rejected the claim on the basis that the relevant supplies were supplies of services, so that since the time of supply was more than six months before the partnership's registration, the input tax was not deductible. The partnership appealed, contending that the relevant supplies had involved supplies of goods (including mirrors, a service counter, a seat, brackets to hold shoes on display, wall brackets on which to hang clothes, security fencing used for decoration, light fittings, various mannequins, signage, a display cabinet, and changing booths with curtains). The tribunal accepted the partnership's evidence and allowed the appeal, holding that there was a single supply of goods, so that the input tax was deductible. *G, J & B Miller*, MAN/03/559 (VTD 18630).

Hairdressing salon

[36.593] A company began trading as a hairdressing salon in September 2009 and registered for VAT from June 2010. In its first return, it reclaimed input tax on various expenses incurred in fitting out the salon. HMRC rejected the claim on the basis that the tax related to supplies of services, so that since the time of supply was more than six months before the company's registration, the input tax was not deductible. The tribunal allowed the appeal in part, applying the principles in *Miller*, **36.592** above, and holding that two of the disputed invoices related to supplies of goods on which the tax was deductible, but that the third invoice related to a supply of services on which the tax was not deductible. *Sassoon Bury Ltd v HMRC*, [2011] UKFTT 797 (TC), TC01633.

Restaurant

[36.594] An appeal was dismissed in a case in which a partnership which operated an inn and restaurant had reclaimed input tax on supplies relating to the refurbishment of the restaurant, made more than six months before its registration. *Portnacraig Inn & Restaurant*, EDN/93/44 (VTD 11528).

[36.595] A company which operated a restaurant reclaimed input tax on expenditure incurred in 'fitting out' the restaurant, although the supplies had been made more than six months before the date of registration. Customs rejected the claim on the grounds that the relevant supplies were supplies of services and that the input tax was not deductible. The tribunal dismissed the company's appeal. *Oriental Delicacy Ltd*, EDN/04/147 (VTD 19129).

[36.596] Similar decisions were reached in *Chilli Club Restaurant Ltd*, EDN/06/65 (VTD 20043) and *K & M Lai (t/a the Rice Bowl)*, LON/06/698 (VTD 20531).

Construction services

[36.597] A rugby club registered for VAT from September 1999. In its first return, it reclaimed input tax on the construction of a new clubhouse. The Commissioners rejected the claim on the basis that it related to services which had been supplied between September 1997 and March 1998, more than six months before the club had registered for VAT, so that the effect of *VAT Regulations 1995, reg 111(2)(d)* was that the input tax was not deductible. The club appealed, contending that the construction of the clubhouse should be treated as a supply of goods, so that *reg 111(2)(d)* did not apply. The tribunal rejected this contention and dismissed the appeal, holding on the evidence that 'the supply of the clubhouse was clearly a supply of services'. *Perranporth Rugby Football Club*, LON/00/689 (VTD 17422).

[36.598] An appeal was dismissed in a case where the trustees of a Methodist church reclaimed input tax on construction services supplied more than six months before the date of registration. The tribunal observed that 'the essential feature of the transaction was the provision of altered, enlarged and refurbished premises'. There was 'nothing in the construction contract providing for any distinct supply of goods'. (The tribunal also held that *VAT Regulations 1995, reg 111(2)(d)* was authorised by *Article 18(3)* of the *EC Sixth Directive*.) *The Trustees of Park Avenue Methodist Church*, LON/99/812 (VTD 17443).

[36.599] A similar decision was reached in *Glamorgan Prestige Developments Ltd v HMRC*, [2010] UKFTT 237 (TC), TC00536.

[**36.600**] A company constructed a 'crazy golf' course, and reclaimed input tax on supplies received more than six months before the date of registration. HMRC rejected the claim on the basis that the supplies were of construction services. The company appealed, contending that some of the input tax should be treated as relating to supplies of materials rather than supplies of services. The tribunal rejected this contention and dismissed the appeal, applying the principles laid down in *Card Protection Plan Ltd*, **22.324** EUROPEAN COMMU-NITY LAW. *Crazy Farm Golf Course Ltd v HMRC*, [2010] UKFTT 307 (TC), TC00594.

Covering of mares

[**36.601**] A horse-breeding company registered for VAT in 1992. In its first return, it reclaimed input tax on fees which it had paid to the owners of stallions which had covered its mares between 1987 and 1991. Customs rejected the claim, on the grounds that the tax related to pre-registration supplies of services. The company appealed, contending that it related to supplies of semen which should be treated as supplies of goods. The tribunal rejected this contention and dismissed the company's appeal. *Bristol Bloodstock Ltd*, LON/93/436A (VTD 11955).

Research and development study

[**36.602**] A company registered for VAT in July 1991. It reclaimed input tax in respect of supplies which it had received more than six months before its date of registration. The supplies in question related to a research and development study concerning the development of two pieces of electronic equipment. Customs rejected the claim, on the basis that the supplies were supplies of services so that the tax was not deductible by virtue of what is now *VAT Regulations 1995, reg 111(2)(d)*. The tribunal dismissed the company's appeal, holding on the evidence that the company had received a single supply of services and was not entitled to credit for the disputed input tax. *Aegis Technology Ltd*, LON/94/2916A (VTD 13588).

Payment to patent agents

[**36.603**] A partnership registered for VAT from April 1998. It reclaimed input tax in respect of supplies from patent agents from June 1996 to June 1997. Customs issued an assessment to recover the tax, on the basis that the invoices related to supplies of services, so that the tax was not recoverable. The partnership appealed, contending that the payments related to patent and trademark registrations which should be treated as goods. The tribunal rejected this contention, holding that the supplies were of services so that the input tax was not reclaimable. *H Parker & M Hornsby (t/a Water Two)*, MAN/98/746 (VTD 16225).

Deregistered trader re-registering for VAT and claiming input tax

[**36.604**] A furniture maker had deregistered, and had accounted for output tax of £893 on the machinery and equipment which he held at the date of deregistration, in accordance with *VATA 1994, Sch 4 para 8*. He subsequently re-registered and claimed the £893 as input tax. Customs rejected the claim and he appealed, contending that he should be entitled to credit for the £893 as he still held the machinery and equipment in question. The tribunal dismissed the appeal, observing that 'once it is appreciated that a purchase of the equipment by the appellant from an unregistered trader, who in fact passed on all or part of the tax he himself suffered on purchase, would not entitle the appellant to input tax credit, it is less surprising if he receives no credit in the circumstances in the present case'. *D Haugh*, LON/97/171 (VTD 15055).

Input tax on leased vans

[36.605] A trader registered for VAT in January 1991. Since 1988 he had leased two vans, and he reclaimed the total input tax incurred under the lease agreements. Customs agreed to allow the total input tax incurred in the six months immediately before his registration, but refused to allow the input tax incurred before that time. The tribunal dismissed the trader's appeal. *RL Windeatt*, LON/91/750Z (VTD 6571).

Computer services

[36.606] An appeal was dismissed in a case where a builder reclaimed input tax on supplies of computer services dating from more than six months before he registered for VAT. *B Woodcock*, LON/91/1711X (VTD 7459).

[36.607] A similar decision was reached in a case where the tribunal specifically held that supplies of computer software were supplies of services, rejecting the appellant company's contention that since the software was supplied on CDs, it should be treated as a supply of goods. *Pet Street Ltd v HMRC*, [2010] UKFTT 149 (TC), TC00455.

Solicitors' fees

[36.608] An appeal was dismissed in a case where an architect registered for VAT in 1990 and reclaimed input tax in respect of solicitors' fees relating to work which he had completed in 1983. *P Charles-Greed*, LON/91/1958 (VTD 7790).

[36.609] See also *Sherman & Perilly*, 36.58 above.

Reclaim of input tax relating to outputs made before registration

[36.610] A company was incorporated in 1993 to organise a three-day conference which was to run from 29 April 1994 until 1 May 1994. It received most of the fees for the conference by 31 March 1994. It registered for VAT on 14 April 1994. In its first return it reclaimed input tax relating to customers who had paid their fees before 14 April, although it did not account for output tax on such fees. Customs issued an assessment to recover the tax which related to customers who had paid before 14 April. The tribunal dismissed the company's appeal. The company was not a 'taxable person' before 14 April

1994, since it was neither registered, nor required to be registered, for VAT. Accordingly, it was not entitled to credit for the relevant input tax. Applying *dicta* of Mustill LJ in *Neuvale Ltd*, **46.17** PARTIAL EXEMPTION, 'tax on inputs should be set off against tax on the outputs to which the inputs related, and against nothing else'. *Perth Junior Chamber Conferences 1994 Ltd*, EDN/94/323 (VTD 13450).

[36.611] A builder reclaimed input tax on materials which he had purchased more than six months before registration, and which had been the subject of onward supplies made before his registration. Customs rejected his claim and the tribunal dismissed his appeal. *HE Morgan (t/a Hayden Trading Co)*, LON/97/471 (VTD 15177).

[36.612] A building company registered for VAT from 1 October 1994. At that time it was supplying building services to a nursing home. It had received payments on account totalling £54,000 between July and September 1994, and received a further £25,000 in November 1994. It had arranged for some of the work to be done by a subcontractor, to whom it paid £11,750 in September 1994 (including VAT of £1,750) and £57,000 (also including VAT) between October and December 1994. In its first return, for the two months ending 30 November 1994, it accounted for output tax on the £25,000 which it had received in that month, and reclaimed input tax of £8,000 on payments which it had made to the subcontractor, thereby claiming a repayment. Customs only agreed to allow input tax of £3,234, rejecting the balance of the claim on the grounds that it related to supplies made before the company had registered. The company appealed, accepting that it was not entitled to reclaim input tax on the payment which it had made in September, since it was not then a 'taxable person' within the definition in *VATA 1994, s 24*, but contending that it should be entitled to input tax on all the payments which it had made in October and November, since it was a taxable person at the time of making the payments. The tribunal rejected this contention and dismissed the appeal, holding that *VATA 1994, s 24* should be interpreted as restricting the definition of 'input tax' to tax on supplies made to a taxable person who was also a taxable person when he used those supplies. The disputed supplies received by the company 'were the cost components of supplies made by the appellant which were not chargeable to tax'. They were 'effectively outside the VAT system' and did not 'confer a right to deduct input tax'. The QB upheld the tribunal decision. The relevant inputs related to supplies that were made before the company became a taxable person and which were not subject to output tax. *Schemepanel Trading Ltd v C & E Commrs*, QB [1996] STC 871.

[36.613] The decision in *Schemepanel Trading Ltd*, **36.612** above, was applied in the similar subsequent case of *Southill Sawmills Ltd*, **52.128** PENALTIES: MISDECLARATION.

Rent

[36.614] A trader registered for VAT with effect from 1 December 2001. In her first return, she reclaimed input tax on the rent which she had paid for the period from 1 August 2001 to 30 November 2001. Customs rejected the claim on the grounds that it related to pre-registration supplies. She appealed, contending that the tax should be treated as deductible under *VAT Regulations 1995, reg 111(1)(a)*. The tribunal accepted this contention and allowed her appeal, observing that the trader was only making taxable supplies and holding that the rent was attributable to the continuing business, rather than solely attributable to pre-registration supplies. The tribunal chairman observed that 'some of the purposes for which the premises were used before registration were the holding of stock for sale after registration and generally developing and promoting the business both before and after the date of registration. At first sight, an apportionment might be expected but the regulation makes no provision for it.' *D Jerzynek*, MAN/03/452 (VTD 18767).

Claim under VAT Regulations, reg 111(1)(b)

[36.615] A company was incorporated on 23 February 2006 to carry on a business of property development. It was registered for VAT with effect from 30 April. In its first return, it claimed input tax relating to expenditure which its controlling director had incurred before the company was incorporated. HMRC rejected the claim and the company appealed, contending that the tax should be treated as deductible under *VAT Regulations 1995, reg 111(1)(b)*. The tribunal reviewed the evidence in detail and rejected this contention, holding that *reg 111(1)(b)* required that for pre-incorporation expenditure to be treated as deductible, the expenditure must have been incurred 'for the company'. It was 'not remotely sufficient that an individual incurs costs, and then later decides to form a company. The situation contemplated by this regulation is that one of the people likely to be involved with the formation of a company incurs the costs on the basis that it is incurring costs "for the company" which is about to be incorporated. It is not sufficient for an individual to be incurring building costs with a view to selling a house or to letting it, and then later to form the intention to put the property development role into a company.' On the evidence, it appeared that 'the actual decision to operate through a company was not made until 22 February'. Accordingly, the expenditure which the director had incurred prior to that date had not been incurred 'for the company'. (However, the tribunal allowed the company's appeal with regard to certain expenditure incurred between 23 February and 30 April, holding that HMRC were not justified in rejecting the company's claims for that period.) *Oaks Pavilion Ltd v HMRC*, FTT August 2009, TC00145.

Input tax reclaimed by 'partly exempt' traders

[36.616] See *Douros*, 46.222 PARTIAL EXEMPTION; *Byrd*, 46.224 PARTIAL EXEMPTION, and *Jolly Tots Ltd*, 46.225 PARTIAL EXEMPTION.

Expenditure incurred when business exempt and unregistered

[36.617] See *Reading & Crabtree*, 46.227 PARTIAL EXEMPTION, and the cases noted at 46.228 PARTIAL EXEMPTION.

Other cases

[36.618] An appeal was dismissed in a case where a trader had reclaimed input tax on supplies of services received more than six months before registering for VAT. *IF Dunham*, MAN/94/468 (VTD 13359).

[36.619] Similar decisions were reached in *T Zaman*, MAN/03/376 (VTD 18647); *GDI Game Domain International plc*, LON/08/1150 (VTD 20962) and *Argyll Developments Ltd*, **46.226** PARTIAL EXEMPTION.

Advance payments

Advance payment—goods not supplied

[36.620] A company which sold pine beds made an advance payment of £12,000 to one of its suppliers. It treated this amount as tax-inclusive and reclaimed the 'VAT fraction' as input tax. However, it did not receive any goods from the supplier to whom it had made the payment. When the Commissioners discovered what had happened, they issued an assessment to recover the tax. The tribunal upheld the assessment and dismissed the company's appeal. *Weldons (West One) Ltd*, LON/80/196 (VTD 984).

[36.621] Similar decisions were reached in *P Hansen*, LON/80/439 (VTD 1154); *T Smith*, LON/80/440 (VTD 1155); *JA McCall*, BEL/83/7 (VTD 1588); *F McSorley*, BEL/85/7 (VTD 1938); *Ronton Haulage Ltd*, LON/86/420 (VTD 2234); *IMO Precision Controls Ltd*, LON/91/1360X (VTD 7948); *Rodeo Catering Ltd*, LON/91/2218Z (VTD 11870) and *Ham Enterprises Ltd*, **52.95** PENALTIES: MISDECLARATION.

[36.622] A company (T) ordered nine yachts and paid deposits which included VAT. Shortly afterwards, the supplier went into liquidation and the yachts were never delivered. T reclaimed input tax on the deposits. The Commissioners issued an assessment to recover the tax and the tribunal dismissed T's appeal, applying the principles laid down in *Howard*, **36.630** below, and holding that input tax could not be reclaimed as no supply had taken place. *Theotrue Holdings Ltd*, [1983] VATTR 88 (VTD 1358).

[36.623] The decision in *Theotrue Holdings Ltd*, **36.622** above, was applied in the similar cases of *JL Laycock*, MAN/85/133 (VTD 1887); *Monks & Sons*, LON/92/2630A (VTD 10401) and *W Puddifer (Junior) Ltd*, [1996] VATDR 237 (VTD 13898).

[36.624] A company paid for a supply of fertiliser. Only part of the fertiliser was delivered, as the supplier went into liquidation before completing the supply. The company reclaimed input tax in respect of the whole payment, and the Commissioners issued an assessment to recover the tax relating to the fertiliser which had not been delivered. The tribunal dismissed the company's appeal, holding that the company was not entitled to reclaim tax on a supply that had not taken place. *Northern Counties Co-Operative Enterprises Ltd*, [1986] VATTR 250 (VTD 2238).

[36.625] A jewellery manufacturer paid for a quantity of bullion, but never received the supply. He reclaimed input tax on the payment and appealed against the Commissioners' rejection of the claim. The tribunal allowed his appeal, observing that the value of the bullion was such that the supplier was clearly liable to be registered, and holding that as the manufacturer had undoubtedly made the payment in question, he was entitled to credit for the input tax. *DN Greenall*, MAN/85/114 (VTD 2362). (*Note.* Compare the subsequent QB decision in *Pennystar Ltd*, 36.627 below.)

[36.626] A similar decision was reached in a case where a company which operated a wholesale business ordered and paid for a substantial quantity of goods, but never received them. The Commissioners issued an assessment to recover the tax but the tribunal allowed the company's appeal. *Tom Wilson (Tobacco) Ltd*, MAN/98/466 (VTD 16437). (*Note.* The decision fails to refer to the QB decision in *Pennystar Ltd*, 36.627 below, or to any of the tribunal decisions noted at 36.620 to 36.624 above, and must therefore be regarded as of doubtful authority.)

[36.627] A company reclaimed input tax of £11,910 on a payment for some computers which were not in fact delivered. The Commissioners rejected the claim and the company appealed. The QB upheld the Commissioners' ruling, holding that the property in the computers had never passed and there had been no supply. Accordingly the company was not entitled to input tax. *C & E Commrs v Pennystar Ltd*, QB 1995, [1996] STC 163.

[36.628] The decisions in *Theotrue Holdings Ltd*, 36.622 above, and *Pennystar Ltd*, 36.627 above, were applied in the similar subsequent cases of *Birchview Ltd*, MAN/96/1326; *Birchview*, MAN/96/1327 (VTD 15275).

[36.629] The decision in *Pennystar Ltd*, 36.627 above, was also applied in the similar subsequent case of *Icon Construction Services Ltd*, LON/99/59 (VTD 16416).

Payment to fraudulent trader for purchase of non-existent goods

[36.630] A trader paid amounts, including VAT, to purchase some containers. He was given what purported to be VAT invoices, and reclaimed the VAT as input tax. However, the supplier, which was the subject of police investigation, did not deliver the containers and did not pay the VAT to the Commissioners. The Commissioners issued an assessment to recover the tax and the tribunal dismissed the trader's appeal, finding on the evidence that the containers had never existed. Applying the principles laid down by Griffiths J in *Oliver*, 62.168 SUPPLY, there could be no taxable supply of non-existent goods, and it followed that there could be no deduction of input tax in respect of a non-existent supply. *P Howard*, LON/80/457 (VTD 1106).

[36.631] M, the proprietor of a business leasing heavy goods vehicles, agreed to purchase two lorries and six refrigerated trailers from a partnership comprising a father (JA) and son (A), and lease them back to the partnership. M paid for the vehicles in February and May 1986, and leased them back to the partnership as agreed. In December 1986 the partnership offered to repurchase the vehicles and this was also agreed, the leasing agreements being terminated. However, the partnership did not pay for the vehicles, and, on the same day that the vehicles were sold to the partnership, one of the partners (JA) was murdered. Five months later, the surviving partner (A) was arrested on a charge of incitement to murder his father. It transpired that he had been involved in several fraudulent transactions, and that the eight vehicles, which the partnership had purported to sell to, and repurchase from, M, had never existed. M began proceedings against the partnership, but these proved difficult since one partner was dead and the other was awaiting trial for incitement to murder him. The surviving partner (A) was the sole executor of the deceased partner's will, but could not obtain probate and was believed to have dissipated much of the estate without bothering with the formalities of probate. When the Commissioners discovered what had happened, they issued assessments on M, disallowing the input tax claimed in respect of the purchases of the eight vehicles, on the grounds that the vehicles had never existed and there could not be a supply of a non-existent vehicle. M appealed to the tribunal which upheld the assessment, applying *Howard*, **36.630** above, and *Theotrue Holdings Ltd*, **36.622** above. *MS Munn*, [1989] VATTR 11 (VTD 3296).

[36.632] A similar decision was reached in a subsequent case where an insurance company (N) had entered into an agreement with two other companies (C and W) to purchase eight electric generators from, and lease them back to, those companies. N reclaimed input tax on the generators. C and W subsequently went into liquidation and the Commissioners discovered that the generators had never existed. The tribunal dismissed N's appeal against an assessment issued to recover the input tax. *Norwich Union Life Insurance Society*, LON/90/1809 (VTD 7205).

[36.633] A similar decision was reached in a case where a company had reclaimed input tax in respect of the purported purchase of video equipment from a company whose controlling director had subsequently been convicted of conspiracy to defraud. The equipment had never been delivered to the appellant company, and the tribunal found that there was no evidence that it had ever existed. The tribunal held that the appellant company was not entitled to credit for input tax in respect of non-existent supplies. *Alvabond Ltd*, LON/90/429A (VTD 10598).

[36.634] A similar decision was reached in a case where a company (H) claimed input tax in respect of goods which it had purchased from another company (X) and resold to a Spanish company without taking delivery of them. The tribunal reviewed the evidence in detail and found that X 'was clearly defrauding Customs' and that H had failed to provide evidence 'on the balance of probabilities that the goods in fact existed'. *House of Goodness Ltd*, LON/05/1034 (VTD 19880).

Amount paid to fraudulent trader for purchase of goods

[36.635] A finance company (N) entered into six agreements with another company (H) under which N was to provide funds to enable H to purchase items of equipment for use in its business. Under the agreements, ownership of the equipment was to be transferred from a supplier (M) to N and N was to lease the equipment back to H. N reclaimed input tax on the payments which it made under the agreement (and accounted for output tax on the leasing payments which it received from H). In fact M did not own or supply any equipment, and H did not purchase any new equipment with the funds which N had paid, although the equipment described in the invoices produced in M's name corresponded with equipment which H was already using under previous lease-purchase agreements with other finance companies. H subsequently went into receivership and N discovered that the equipment which H was using in its business was owned by finance companies, so that N was unable to establish title to any of the equipment. When the Commissioners discovered what had happened, they issued an assessment to recover the input tax in question. The tribunal upheld the assessment and dismissed N's appeal, holding on the evidence that the equipment in question had never been supplied to N. At the time of the purported supplies, all the equipment which H was using was owned by other finance companies. The company from which H had claimed to have purchased the equipment was 'a business sham of no substance' and the relevant invoices 'were wholly fictitious' and had been 'prepared to enable the directors of (H) to obtain finance based on fictitious purchases of equipment'. The tribunal observed that 'it is beside the point that equipment might have existed at the premises of (H) which, with the application of false serial numbers, conformed to the descriptions in the documents produced as invoices'. *Norfolk & Suffolk Finance Ltd*, LON/97/894 (VTD 15288).

Deposit paid for purchase of land—contracts never completed

[36.636] A property company (B) entered into a contract for the purchase of some land at a price of £13.5 million (excluding VAT). It paid a deposit of £1,350,000 to the vendors' solicitors, who provided a postdated invoice showing the total VAT to be charged and the amount due on completion. The contract was never completed, partly because B did not have sufficient funds to proceed. Accordingly, B forfeited its deposit. However, B reclaimed input tax on the proposed purchase. The Commissioners rejected the claim, and B appealed. The tribunal dismissed the appeal, holding that the postdated invoice did not entitle B to reclaim the input tax, and that there had been no supply of the land. *Broadwell Land plc*, [1993] VATTR 346 (VTD 10521) (*Note.* The decision here was approved by the CA in *BJ Rice & Associates*, 62.456 SUPPLY.)

Compensation and damages payments

Payment of damages to customer—whether tax reclaimable

[36.637] A company which dealt in scrap metal repeatedly made short deliveries to one of its customers. When the customer discovered this, it threatened to take legal action, and the company paid £223,500 as damages in an out-of-court settlement. The company reclaimed tax on this payment.

The Commissioners rejected the claim, considering that the payment was outside the scope of VAT. The tribunal dismissed the company's appeal. *Whites Metal Co*, LON/86/686 (VTD 2400).

[**36.638**] A company (H) which operated a wholesale business was sued by one of its suppliers. The case went to the County Court, which gave judgment for the supplier and ordered H to pay the supplier £12,300. H reclaimed input tax on this payment. The Commissioners rejected the claim, considering that the payment constituted damages or compensation and was outside the scope of VAT. The tribunal dismissed H's appeal, holding that the payment did not relate to any taxable supply and that the Court Order was 'by way of compensation or damages (which) is outside the scope of VAT'. *Hometex Trading Ltd*, MAN/94/741 (VTD 13012).

Input tax reclaimed on settlement payment to solicitors

[**36.639**] See *Slot*, 36.50 above.

Input tax reclaimed on compensation payment to lessor

[**36.640**] In April 1990 a company (F) entered into a 'finance lease' of an expensive printing machine. In December 1990 F went into receivership, and the lease was terminated. The lessors claimed substantial compensation, and their claim was upheld by the Court of Session. F reclaimed input tax on the compensation payment. The Commissioners rejected the claim, and F appealed. The tribunal dismissed the appeal, holding that the termination of the lease was not a supply of services. Since the lessor had not supplied any services in return for the compensation payment, the payment was outside the scope of VAT. *Financial & General Print Ltd*, LON/95/1281A (VTD 13795).

[**36.641**] A company (C) made a payment of £2,000,000 to another company (H) in February 1991. C considered that this payment should be treated as inclusive of VAT. However, H considered that the payment was outside the scope of VAT, and did not issue a VAT invoice. C reclaimed input tax in respect of the payment in its return for the period ending June 1991. The Commissioners initially accepted C's claim, and issued an assessment on H charging output tax on the payment, but H's appeal was allowed by a tribunal (see *Holiday Inns (UK) Ltd*, **62.142** SUPPLY). In 1993 the Commissioners issued an assessment on C to recover the input tax which C had claimed. The tribunal allowed C's appeal, disapproving and declining to follow the previous decision in *Holiday Inns (UK) Ltd*, on the grounds that it was inconsistent with the subsequent CJEC decision in *Lubbock Fine & Co*, **22.333** EUROPEAN COMMUNITY LAW. The tribunal held that the payment was consideration for a supply of services, and that C was entitled to reclaim the input tax even though H had not issued a VAT invoice, and despite the fact that the previous tribunal had held that H was not required to account for output tax on the payment. The tribunal held that 'the right to deduct is not limited to the case where output tax has been paid but also extends to the case where it is payable' and that 'the recipient of a supply can claim input tax even though the supplier fails to account for the output tax in his return or becomes insolvent before the output tax is paid'. *Croydon Hotel & Leisure Co Ltd*, [1997] VATDR 245

(VTD 14920). (*Notes*. (1) For a preliminary issue in this case, see **3.43** ASSESSMENT. (2) Compare *Financial & General Print Ltd*, **36.640** above, which was not referred to in this decision. (3) For the corporation tax treatment of the payment, see *Croydon Hotel & Leisure Co Ltd v Bowen*, Sp C [1996] STC (SCD) 466.)

[36.642] In 1990 a trader (H) took a 20-year lease of a public house. This proved much less profitable than he anticipated. He closed the business in 1995 and returned the premises to the lessor in 1997. The lessor took legal proceedings, claiming dilapidations of more than £76,000 and arrears of rent. H counterclaimed that he had been induced to enter the lease as a result of misrepresentation by the lessor. The proceedings were subsequently settled by consent, with neither party making any payment. Despite this, H reclaimed input tax on the amount which the lessor had charged for dilapidations. The Commissioners rejected the claim and the tribunal dismissed H's appeal. Firstly, H had never received a VAT invoice in respect of the dilapidations. Secondly, the chairman observed that 'no amount was ever paid by the appellant for dilapidations, he agreed to waive his own claim for damages for loss of profit and misrepresentation and in those circumstances no money ever changed hands and therefore there was nothing on which value added tax could properly be imposed'. *KR Howes*, [2001] VATDR 263 (VTD 17196).

Post-cessation input tax

[36.643] A retail shopkeeper had entered into a long-term contract for the hire to him of various shop fittings including a counter and shelving. He closed the business in March 1973 but had to continue paying the hire charges until September 1973. He reclaimed input tax in respect of the hire charges paid from April to September. The Commissioners rejected his claim on the grounds that he was not carrying on any business at that time. The tribunal dismissed his appeal against this decision. *PT Miles*, LON/73/87 (VTD 33).

[36.644] A company which owned a factory ceased to trade. Subsequently it decided to let the factory, and had work carried out on it to make it suitable for letting. It reclaimed input tax in respect of this work and the Commissioners issued an assessment to recover the tax. The tribunal dismissed the company's appeal, holding that the company had not incurred the expenditure for the purpose of any business. *GA Hurley Ltd*, MAN/88/538 (VTD 3510).

[36.645] A married couple who had operated a hotel closed it in October 1990. They then renovated the building with the intention of reopening it as a registered residential home (which would be exempt from VAT). They reclaimed input tax incurred in the renovation on a return relating to the hotel business. On discovering what had happened, the Commissioners issued an assessment to recover the tax. The tribunal dismissed the couple's appeal, holding that since the hotel business had ceased before the renovation, the input tax was not reclaimable. *G & C Brown*, EDN/91/266 (VTD 7430).

[36.646] A married couple had operated a carpet business in partnership, but the wife withdrew from the partnership in February 1993 and the husband continued to operate the business as a sole proprietor, continuing to use the partnership registration number. Subsequently he reclaimed input tax on the renovation of some flats which were jointly owned by him and his wife. The Commissioners issued an assessment to recover the tax, and the tribunal dismissed his appeal, holding that he could not reclaim the tax since it related to a partnership activity but the partnership had ceased to trade and was no longer registered for VAT. (The chairman also noted that it appeared that the expenditure had been incurred for the purpose of making supplies of accommodation which would be exempt from VAT.) *AT Sinnett*, MAN/95/2671 (VTD 14201).

Enterprise Zone Property Unit Trust

[36.647] A company operated an Enterprise Zone Property Unit Trust. In 1994 it acquired the freehold of a retail warehouse. It received rental income from the tenants, and accounted for VAT. In May 2003 it granted a lease of the warehouse, and ceased to make taxable supplies. However it continued to reclaim input tax on supplies of services made by its trustee, manager, registrar and auditor after it ceased to make taxable supplies. Customs issued an assessment to recover the tax and the company appealed, contending that the effect of the CJEC decision in *I/S Fini H v Skatteministeriet*, **22.105** EUROPEAN COMMUNITY LAW, was that it was entitled to reclaim the input tax. The tribunal rejected this contention and dismissed the appeal, distinguishing *I/S Fini H v Skatteministeriet* on the basis that in that case 'the taxpayer's obligation to pay the rent stemmed from a contractual requirement under a lease entered into for the purposes of carrying out his taxable activities'. The company in that case had 'had no legal entitlement to terminate the lease before the expiry of its term' and had 'had to continue to pay the rent and charges for associated services during the period over which his restaurant business was wound up'. In the present case, however, 'the appellant's payments for the disputed supplies were voluntary which it chose to make to obtain the benefit of certain tax advantages'. The relevant supplies were not 'cost components of the appellant's business of letting an enterprise zone property'. *Royal Bank of Canada Trust Corporation Ltd*, LON/07/581 (VTD 20520).

Disputed repayment claims

Repayment of input tax—accuracy of claim in doubt

[36.648] A company made a claim for repayment of a substantial amount of input tax. The Commissioners withheld repayment, since the company and its principal director were under investigation for purporting to make exports of goods which had allegedly never taken place. The company applied for judicial review, contending that the Commissioners were obliged to repay the amount claimed prior to any further investigations. The QB dismissed the application, holding that the Commissioners were not obliged to repay excess input tax claimed where they had grounds for suspecting the accuracy of the claim. The Commissioners were entitled to a reasonable opportunity to investigate such a claim, and the delay in this case had not reached unreasonable proportions. *R v C & E Commrs (ex p. Strangewood Ltd)*, QB [1987] STC 502.

[36.649] The decision in *R v C & E Commrs (ex p. Strangewood Ltd)*, 36.648 above, was applied in *Pennine Carpets Ltd*, 65.48 TRANSFERS OF GOING CONCERNS.

[36.650] The QB reached a similar decision in a subsequent case where the Commissioners were investigating an alleged fraud concerning a company which exported beer and wine to France. The company had claimed repayment of more than £200,000, while the Commissioners had issued assessments charging tax of more than £1,400,000, on the basis that the company had overclaimed input tax. Keene J observed that the company had been used 'as an apparently unnecessary middleman' and that there seemed 'little commercial sense' in its involvement unless there was 'a fraudulent intent to achieve a sufficiently complex structure of companies as to enable drawback to be improperly claimed. No credible explanation has been provided to this court for this trading structure on a legitimate basis'. The Commissioners had 'evidence of prolonged wholesale fraud' and there was 'nothing unnecessary about the (Commissioners') requirements for greater verification of claims in the circumstances which have arisen'. It would clearly be premature for the court to make a declaration in favour of the company, when its appeals against the assessments had not yet been heard by the tribunal. *R v C & E Commrs (ex p. Lacara Ltd)*, QB 30 March 1998, 1998 STI 576. (*Note*. In 1999 the Commissioners were granted summary judgment against the company in respect of unpaid excise duty of more than £8,000,000. The QB dismissed the company's appeal against the judgment— QB 11 October 1999 unreported.)

[36.651] In the case noted at **22.67** EUROPEAN COMMUNITY LAW, a company claimed a repayment of input tax of almost £8,000,000. The Commissioners rejected the claim, on the basis that they considered that the purported supplies were not effective for VAT purposes. In July 2001 the company appealed. The tribunal arranged to hear the appeal in May 2002. In the meantime, the company applied to the Ch D for an interim repayment under *Civil Procedure Rules (SI 1998/3132), rule 25.1*. The Ch D rejected the application. Neuberger J held that there was no reason for the court to grant an interim payment. The company's appeal before the tribunal was awaiting hearing. The Commissioners' decision to refuse payment was not unreasonable. There was 'no evidence of particular need, let alone urgency, on the part of the claimants', and the Commissioners had not contributed to 'any delay as far as the appeal procedure is concerned'. *Capital One Developments Ltd v C & E Commrs (No 1)*, Ch D [2002] STC 479; [2002] EWHC 197(Ch).

[36.652] A company (T) claimed substantial amounts of input tax on the basis that it had purchased goods in the UK and had exported them to destinations outside the EU. The Commissioners withheld repayment pending enquiries into the validity of the transactions. T applied for judicial review. The QB dismissed the application. Lightman J observed that the goods in which T had traded were 'often used as the ostensible subject matter of artificial transactions carried out by missing traders involved in "missing trader inter-community fraud".' Furthermore, T had delayed the Commissioners' enquiries by failing to provide requested information. The Commissioners were 'entitled to take a reasonable time to investigate claims prior to authorising deductions and repayments'. The availability and exercise of their powers of investigation were 'essential to maintain the fiscal neutrality of VAT and prevent refunds being made to parties not entitled to them.' It was ' incumbent on the taxpayer to satisfy the Commissioners of his entitlement to a deduction. Fiscal neutrality requires that this should be so and that repayments should not be made to taxable persons who have or show no such entitlement.' *R (oao UK Tradecorp Ltd) v C & E Commrs*, QB 2004, [2005] STC 138; [2004] EWHC 2515 (Admin).

[36.653] Similar decisions were reached in four applications, heard together, where companies had reclaimed substantial input tax in relation to alleged transactions in mobile telephones. *R (oao Just Fabulous (UK) Ltd) v HMRC*, QB 2007, [2008] STC 2123; [2007] EWHC 521 (Admin); *R (oao Evolution Export Trading Ltd) v HMRC*, QB 2007, [2008] STC 2123; [2007] EWHC 521 (Admin); *R (oao Greystone Export Trading Ltd) v HMRC*, QB 2007, [2008] STC 2123; [2007] EWHC 521 (Admin) and *R (oao Brayfal Ltd) v HMRC*, QB 2007, [2008] STC 2123; [2007] EWHC 521 (Admin).

[36.654] In the case noted at **22.518** EUROPEAN COMMUNITY LAW, where a number of companies had claimed substantial repayments of input tax, the QB referred the case to the CJEC. One of the companies (T) subsequently applied for an interim repayment of 50% of its original claims. The QB rejected this application and the CA unanimously dismissed T's appeal, holding that while the courts had power to order an interim repayment where it was appropriate, T was not entitled to such a repayment. Dyson LJ noted that T had continued to pay substantial dividends and unusually high directors' remuneration, and to make interest-free loans to its directors. *R (oao Teleos plc) v C & E Commrs (No 2)*, CA [2005] STC 1471; [2005] EWCA Civ 200; [2005] 1 WLR 3007. (*Note*. Costs were awarded to the Commissioners.)

[36.655] An application for an interim payment was also rejected in *Megantic Services Ltd v HMRC (No 1)*, QB [2006] EWHC 3232 (Admin). (*Note*. For subsequent developments in this case, see **2.287** APPEALS and **48.107** PAYMENT OF TAX.)

[36.656] A company (R) reclaimed input tax of more than £3,000,000, relating to supplies of mobile telephones. Customs began enquiries into the claim, considering that it was likely that the transactions may have formed part of a 'carousel fraud'. R began proceedings against Customs in the QB, claiming immediate repayment. At an initial hearing, Seymour J declined to order an immediate repayment, but directed that there should be a further hearing of R's claim. *Rioni Ltd v HMRC*, QB 7 June 2007, Tax Journal 25.6.2007.

[36.657] A company which traded in mobile telephones made several substantial repayment claims. HMRC rejected the claims on the grounds that it appeared that the transactions were connected with MTIC fraud. The company appealed. In July 2008 the Manchester tribunal allowed one of the appeals, covering the period to May 2006, on the grounds that HMRC had failed to comply with a direction by the tribunal, and ordered HMRC to credit the company with £12,957,628. HMRC set £10,556,324 against other amounts which they considered to be owed by the company. In November 2008 HMRC made a net repayment of £2,401,304. The company took proceedings in the Ch D, contending that HMRC had not been entitled to make the set-off. The Ch D rejected this contention and found in favour of HMRC. Simon J held that 'the effect of the Tribunal's decision allowing the appeal was not that the Tribunal gave judgment for a sum to be paid within a certain period, as a civil court might do. Its decision had the effect of allowing the appeal against the Commissioners' decision that credit for input tax was to be denied, so that amounts which the Commissioners had excluded from account should be brought into account. In effect, the Commissioners were required to credit the claimant with input tax of £12.95m, and they did so.' HMRC had been 'entitled to amend and adjust the claimant's VAT returns'. and to set the input tax credit against assessments which were under appeal. Applying *dicta* of Mummery LJ in *Cozens v C & E Commrs*, **2.193** APPEALS, the amount assessed was 'recoverable as a debt due to the Crown' and 'remains a debt due, until that assessment is successfully appealed to the Tribunal.' *Infinity Distribution Ltd v HMRC*, Ch D [2010] STC 2258; [2010] EWHC 1393 (Ch).

[36.658] A company applied for a VAT repayment of more than £1,000,000. HMRC rejected the claim on the basis that it appeared that the transactions were connected to MTIC fraud. The company appealed. While the appeal was pending, the company applied to the tribunal for an interim repayment of £60,000. The tribunal rejected the application. Judge Mosedale held that 'ordering HMRC to repay the whole or part of the claimed input tax now would be to pre-judge the subject of the appeal'. *Aleena Electronics Ltd v HMRC*, [2011] UKFTT 608 (TC), TC01451.

[36.659] See also *Tricell UK Ltd*, **2.13** APPEALS; *Evolink Ltd*, **2.13** APPEALS; *F Options Ltd*, **2.14** APPEALS; *Mobile Export 365 Ltd v HMRC*, **2.165** APPEALS; *R (oao Indigo Global Trading Ltd) v HMRC*, **2.493** APPEALS; the cases noted at **36.77** to **36.122** above, and *Abercromby Motor Group Ltd (No 2)*, **48.25** PAYMENT OF TAX.

Input tax relating to supplies of phonecards

[36.660] A company (F) reclaimed substantial amounts of input tax relating to supplies of Irish phonecards, which it purchased from Irish companies for less than their face value and sold to UK retailers at a profit (but still at a price below the face value of the phonecards). Customs rejected the claim on the basis that F's onward supplies of phonecards were outside the scope of UK VAT and were not taxable supplies. F appealed. The tribunal allowed the appeal, specifically disapproving the earlier decision in *J & E Oluwatyi (t/a Lizjohn & Associates)*, LON/02/370 (VTD 18089). The tribunal held that 'the transactions with which this case is concerned are supplies in the ordinary sense of that word and they are done for a consideration'. The principles of VAT required that 'the appellant should be entitled to deduct input tax on its overheads.' The tribunal commented that 'if the rules about valuation of supplies of vouchers means that the output tax on the final supply was less than it would have been if the vouchers had always been sold at or above their full face value, we do not regard that as relevant to the recovery of input tax in earlier stages in the chain.' *First National Telecom Services Ltd,* LON/04/270 (VTD 19681).

Input tax reclaimed on supplies of 'laundered' rebated fuel

[36.661] A company (H), which carried on a haulage business and was a member of a VAT group, reclaimed input tax in respect of the purchase of substantial quantities of fuel. Customs discovered that the fuel in question was 'laundered' rebated fuel, which it was illegal to use in road vehicles, and that the VAT numbers shown on the invoices belonged to deregistered companies. Customs issued assessments to recover the input tax. The representative member of H's VAT group appealed. The tribunal reviewed the evidence in detail and dismissed the appeal, finding that the evidence given by H's director was 'largely untruthful' and that H had 'failed to exercise sufficient care and judgment to ensure that it received genuine taxable supplies of fuel from taxable persons'. Applying *dicta* of Advocate-General Jacobs in *Finanzamt Gummersbach v Bockemühl,* **22.461** EUROPEAN COMMUNITY LAW, the invoices were 'invalid as failing materially to describe the supplies made'. The tribunal specifically disapproved the 1994 decision in *Ellen Garage (Oldham) Ltd,* **40.11** INVOICES AND CREDIT NOTES. Applying the principles laid down by the CJEC in *Kittel v Belgian State,* **22.415** EUROPEAN COMMUNITY LAW, 'a taxable person who knew or should have known that by making a purchase he was taking part in a transaction connected with the fraudulent evasion of VAT must be regarded as a participant in that fraud'. H had 'failed to take every precaution which could reasonably be required of it to ensure that its transactions were not connected with fraud'. Accordingly, H had lost the right to deduct the VAT it paid on the fuel it bought 'as being a party to the fraudulent evasion of VAT'. *Hargreaves (UK) plc,* MAN/03/729 (VTD 20382).

Other matters

Tax properly chargeable differing from tax charged by contractor

[36.662] A company arranged with a firm of contractors for the conversion of two houses into flats. The bill submitted by the contractors included £2,250 in respect of input tax. However some of the work was zero-rated, so that the tax properly chargeable was only £1,023. Shortly after the conversion was completed, the contractors went into liquidation. The company claimed a deduction for the input tax charged of £2,250, and the Commissioners would only allow a deduction of £1,023. The tribunal accepted the Commissioners' contention and dismissed the company's appeal, holding that the 'tax' of what is now *VATA 1994, s 24(1)* is the tax properly chargeable, if different from that charged. *Podium Investments Ltd,* [1977] VATTR 121 (VTD 314).

[36.663] See also *Genius Holding BV v Staatssecretaris van Financien,* **22.413** EUROPEAN COMMUNITY LAW.

Input tax reclaimed in respect of stolen goods

[36.664] A demolition contractor reclaimed input tax in respect of the purchase of an item of equipment which had been stolen. The item was later repossessed by the police and returned to its rightful owner. The Commissioners issued an assessment to recover the tax and the tribunal dismissed the contractor's appeal, holding that there was no right to reclaim input tax in respect of stolen goods. *CR Hudson (t/a 21st Century Demolition & Plant Hire)*, MAN/91/1016 (VTD 9666).

Goods supplied in France but paid for in the UK

[36.665] A company (B), which carried on international haulage work, had an arrangement with an international fuel company (S) under which S supplied diesel fuel to B's vehicles while they were travelling in France. S provided B with monthly invoices showing the gross costs of those supplies in French currency, including French VAT (TVA). B reclaimed input tax, at the UK rate of 15%, on the sterling equivalent of the amounts in question. The Commissioners issued an assessment to recover the tax, and the tribunal dismissed B's appeal, holding that credit for input tax was limited to UK VAT charged on a supply made in the UK. *British Iberian International Transport Ltd*, LON/85/654 (VTD 2101). (*Note.* The appellant had used the *EC Eighth Directive* to recover TVA paid in France for a period subsequent to that covered by the assessment, but the French authorities had refused a late claim under that provision for the period of the assessment as being out of time.)

[36.666] A claim to deduct TVA as input tax was also rejected in *Normal Films Ltd*, LON/97/1031 (VTD 15558).

[36.667] An appeal was dismissed in another case where a UK company (D) had reclaimed input tax on supplies of goods which had taken place in France, although the supplier had also been a UK company. The supplier had initially issued a VAT invoice, but had subsequently realised its mistake and had issued a credit note. The tribunal held that, since the place of supply was in France, D was not entitled to reclaim UK input tax on the supplies in question. *Duffy & Carr Group plc*, LON/93/1525A (VTD 11728).

UK trader reclaiming German VAT as input tax

[36.668] A UK company (T) imported six cars from Germany. It did not inform the vendors that it was registered for UK VAT, so that they charged German VAT on the sales. T resold five of the cars in the UK. In its VAT returns, it set the German VAT which it had paid against the output tax due on the UK sales. The Commissioners issued an assessment to recover the tax. The tribunal upheld the assessment and dismissed T's appeal. *Trenchard Management Ltd*, LON/00/1196 (VTD 17517).

[36.669] A similar decision was reached in *R & D Loach (t/a Micronet Showroom)*, MAN/x (VTD 19560).

Yacht moored in Greece—input tax reclaimed by UK purchaser

[36.670] A UK company purchased a yacht from an associated company. At the time of the purchase the yacht was moored in Greece. However, the purchaser reclaimed input tax on the yacht. The Commissioners issued an assessment to recover the tax and the tribunal dismissed the company's appeal. Since the yacht was moored in Greece, the supply had taken place outside the UK and was not subject to UK VAT. *Da Conti International Ltd*, LON/90/444Z (VTD 6215).

Self-billing

[36.671] See the cases noted at **40.56** to **40.60** INVOICES AND CREDIT NOTES.

VATA 1994, s 26A—disallowance of input tax

[36.672] A group of companies received a substantial invoice from BT, including VAT of more than £680,000. The representative member of the group (P) reclaimed this as input tax. However the group never paid this amount to BT. The company to which the invoice was addressed subsequently went into liquidation, and BT subsequently issued a credit note. When Customs discovered what had happened, they issued an assessment to recover the tax which P had reclaimed. The tribunal upheld the assessment and dismissed P's appeal, finding that P's controlling director 'knew that there never would or could be payment of the sum demanded by BT whether it contained VAT or not' and that 'retention of the said VAT money might well be said to involve dishonesty.' *Power TV Ltd*, EDN/07/17 (VTD 20565). (*Note.* The tribunal awarded costs to Customs, finding that there was 'neither logic, substance, merit or equity in the position adopted by the appellant'.)

[36.673] A company (D) submitted a VAT return claiming a substantial repayment. HMRC began an enquiry and rejected part of the claim on the grounds that D had provided no evidence that it had actually paid the invoices, so that the effect of *VATA 1994, s 26A* was that the tax was not deductible. D appealed. The tribunal reviewed the evidence and dismissed D's appeal. *Daytona Surf Ltd v HMRC*, [2011] UKFTT 383 (TC), TC01238. (*Note.* D had also claimed input tax on supplies from unregistered traders: an appeal against the disallowance of these claims was also dismissed.)

Credit note received for tax already deducted as input tax

[36.674] See *Silvermere Golf and Equestrian Centre Ltd*, **40.102** INVOICES AND CREDIT NOTES, and the cases noted at **40.103** to **40.106** INVOICES AND CREDIT NOTES.

Repossession of goods under conditional sale

[36.675] A company (L) arranged to purchase a number of commercial vehicles from another company (V). The vehicles were supplied under contracts of conditional sale which provided that V would retain their ownership until L had paid for them in full. V accounted for VAT on the delivery of the vehicles, and L reclaimed the VAT as input tax. Subsequently, before the vehicles had been fully paid for, L went into receivership. V repossessed the vehicles and gave the receivers a credit note for an amount which included the VAT paid. The receivers applied to the Ch D for directions as to whether the VAT in question constituted a preferential debt. The Commissioners contended that, since the original sale had been conditional, L had only had a conditional entitlement to reclaim the input tax, so that the tax should rank as a preferential debt. The Ch D rejected this contention. The delivery of the goods by V was admitted to have been a supply. There were no grounds 'on which a delivery of goods pursuant to a contract which contains a title retention clause, and which constitutes a supply in respect of which VAT has become due within the clear terms of the legislation, can later be said not to constitute a supply because the goods are repossessed by the vendor'. (Accordingly, since the input tax related to a transaction which had taken place more than twelve months before the date of the receivership, the VAT was not a preferential debt.) *Re Liverpool Commercial Vehicles Ltd*, Ch D [1984] BCLC 587. (*Note.* For the Commissioners' practice following this decision, see their Press Notice No 931 dated 3 August 1984.)

Post-receivership input tax set against pre-receivership liabilities

[36.676] The joint receivers and managers of a company sought judicial review of the Commissioners' decision not to repay the excess of input tax over output tax generated by the company since the receivership, but to set the excess input tax against pre-receivership output tax liabilities. The QB dismissed the application, holding that the Commissioners were entitled to make the set-off. *R v C & E Commrs (ex p. Richmond & another)*, QB 1988, [1989] STC 429.

Estimated assessment to correct alleged overclaim of input tax

[36.677] See *WM Low & Co plc*, 3.28 ASSESSMENT.

Issue of shares to UK company acting as nominee for non-resident

[36.678] In 1999 a company made an issue of shares. 29.7% of the shares were issued to persons belonging in the EU, so that the relevant supply was exempt from VAT under *VATA 1994, Sch 9, Group 5, Item 6*. 33.7% of the shares were issued to persons belonging outside the EU, while 36.6% of the shares were issued to a UK company which acted as a nominee for persons belonging outside the UK. The company reclaimed input tax on professional fees incurred in connection with the latter two categories. The tribunal held that the input tax in relation to the 33.7% of shares which had been issued directly to non-EU residents was deductible by virtue of *VAT (Input Tax) (Specified Supplies) Order 1999 (SI 1999/3121), article 3*. However, the input tax in relation to the 36.6% of shares which had been issued to a UK nominee company was not deductible, since 'in the case of nominees, the VAT legislation does not permit "looking through" to the underlying beneficial owner'. *Water Hall Group plc*, [2003] VATDR 257 (VTD 18007). (*Note*. For the Commissioners' practice following this decision, see Business Brief 2/2005, issued on 10 February 2005, and Business Brief 21/2005, issued on 23 November 2005. In Business Brief 2/2005, Customs stated that 'there are doubts as to both the correctness and extent of application of the *Water Hall* decision' (*sic*). They also stated that 'any business that appears to be attempting artificial exploitation of *Water Hall* to recover VAT on share issue costs will be challenged robustly by Customs'. In Business Brief 21/2005, HMRC stated that 'the question of who is making or receiving the supply no longer arises' following the CJEC decision in *Kretztechnik AG v Finanzamt Linz*, **22.91** EUROPEAN COMMUNITY LAW.)

Goods paid for in US dollars—correct exchange rate for input tax

[36.679] A UK company purchased goods from a US company with a place of business in the UK. The invoices stated the value of the goods and the VAT thereon, both in UK currency and in US dollars. The company was required to pay for the goods in dollars, and did so. By the time that payment was made, the value of the pound had declined against the dollar. The company claimed as its input tax the tax fraction of the amounts it actually paid to purchase the dollars. The Commissioners considered that the input tax actually due was the amount stated in sterling on the invoice, and issued an assessment to recover the balance. The tribunal dismissed the company's appeal. The tax stated in sterling on the invoices was the tax for which the company was entitled to credit. *Advansys plc*, MAN/88/870 (VTD 4427).

Arrangement between retail company and finance company

[36.680] A company (E) carried on business as a retailer of domestic electrical appliances. Many of its sales were on a hire-purchase basis, in co-operation with a finance company which was granted an option over the appliances until the customer had paid for them in full. E agreed with the finance company concerned that, if customers defaulted, it would pay any amount outstanding under the agreement in return for reclaiming the option. E then took steps to repossess the goods from the customers. E reclaimed input tax on the appliances concerned. The Commissioners issued an assessment to recover the tax, considering that, in the absence of a formal assignation of the finance company's rights, E was not entitled to reclaim input tax. The tribunal allowed E's appeal, holding that the terms of the agreement were sufficient to constitute a supply even in cases where E had not established either physical possession or legal ownership of the goods. *Excell Consumer Industries Ltd*, [1985] VATTR 94 (VTD 1865).

Claim to assign repayment of input tax

[36.681] An accountant submitted a client's return showing a repayment due of £389. With the return he submitted a written request that £258 of the repayment should be repaid to him, rather than to the client. However, the Commissioners sent the £389 to the client. Subsequently the accountant withheld the sum of £258 from his own return. The Commissioners levied distraint to recover this amount from him, and he then lodged an appeal to the tribunal, contending that the input tax had been assigned to him. The tribunal dismissed his appeal, holding that the written request submitted by the accountant did not constitute a formal assignment of the repayment. *NS Daws*, MAN/91/957 (VTD 7643).

Payments for telecommunications licences

[36.682] See *Hutchison 3G UK Ltd & Others v C & E Commrs*, **22.150** EUROPEAN COMMUNITY LAW.

Input tax reclaimed by unregistered claimant

[36.683] See *Wayment*, **2.59** APPEALS, and *Whitehouse*, **2.60** APPEALS.

37

Insolvency

The cases in this chapter are arranged under the following headings.

Company liquidation and receivership   **37.1**
Bankruptcy and personal insolvency   **37.21**

Company liquidation and receivership

Winding-up order made against company—assessments under appeal

[37.1] Customs discovered that a company and an associated partnership had failed to account for tax on substantial supplies of mobile telephones. They issued assessments charging tax of more than £4,000,000. The company and the partnership appealed. Before the appeals had been heard by the VAT tribunal, the Commissioners presented winding-up petitions. The company and partnership applied to the Ch D for the petitions to be struck out, contending that it would not be proper to make a winding-up order while the appeal remained undetermined. The Ch D rejected this contention, dismissed the applications, and made a winding-up order in respect of the company. Evans-Lombe J observed that it would not be appropriate to make a winding-up order if it appeared 'that the company on its appeal to the VAT tribunal stood a reasonable chance of succeeding with that appeal'. However, on the evidence, the appeals did not stand 'a reasonable chance of success'. If the company liquidator were to take the view that there was 'a reasonable case to present on appeal to the VAT tribunals then it will be his duty to do so. If he succeeds, he will find himself in control of what is a solvent company. It will be his duty to apply to the court in the interim for a stay of the winding-up proceedings.' However, on the evidence, this appeared 'to be highly unlikely'. *C & E Commrs v D & D Marketing (UK) Ltd; C & E Commrs v D & D Marketing*; Ch D [2002] EWHC 660 (Ch).

[37.2] The decision in *C & E Commrs v D & D Marketing (UK) Ltd*, 37.1 above, was applied in a subsequent case where Customs had issued assessments on the basis that a company had failed to account for VAT and excise duty on substantial sales of alcohol. Customs also presented a winding-up petition. Lawrence Collins J observed that the effect of *VATA 1994, s 73(9)* was that 'the debt is due and may be recovered unless and until the tribunal decides that it is not due in whole or in part'. On the evidence, he held that the company was liable for the duty and was 'plainly insolvent'. He therefore made a winding-up order against the company. *C & E Commrs v Anglo-German Breweries Ltd*, Ch D [2002] EWHC 2458 (Ch). (*Note.* For subsequent developments in this case, see *Forrester v Hooper*, **2.510** APPEALS.)

[37.3] The decision in *C & E Commrs v Anglo-German Breweries Ltd*, 37.2 above, was applied in the similar subsequent case of *C & E Commrs v Arena Corporation Ltd*, Ch D [2003] EWHC 3032 (Ch).

Application for rescission of winding-up order

[37.4] The Commissioners had presented a petition for the winding-up of a company which owed substantial amounts of VAT and excise duty. The company went into liquidation (and the liquidator began legal proceedings against the company's controlling director, alleging that he had been involved in the fraudulent evasion of the payment of VAT and excise duties). The director applied for the winding-up order to be rescinded. The Ch D dismissed this application. Lawrence Collins J observed that the application had 'been presented in a misleading way', and that the company was 'hopelessly insolvent'. Some of the director's evidence was 'utterly implausible', and there was no evidence to justify the rescission of the winding-up order. *H Bhanderi v C & E Commrs (re Turnstem Ltd)*, Ch D [2004] EWHC 1765 (Ch); [2005] 1 BCLC 388. (*Note.* For subsequent developments in this case, see **2.74** APPEALS.)

Provisional liquidator—Insolvency Act 1986, s 135

[37.5] An individual was appointed provisional liquidator of a company, under *Insolvency Act 1986, s 135*, in September 1997, on an application by Customs. The liquidation was completed in March 1998 by the sale of the business as a going concern. The company had continued to trade, under the liquidator's supervision, in the interim period, and made sales in respect of which it was liable to pay VAT. The liquidator applied to the Ch D for directions with regard to his liability to account for the VAT, and to whether he could deduct his expenses. The Ch D held that the liquidator was under a duty to ensure that tax was accounted for, in its entirety, to the revenue authorities. This duty took priority to the liquidator's claim for expenses which he had incurred under *Insolvency Rules 1986 (SI 1986/1925), rule 4.218. Re Grey Marlin Ltd*, Ch D [1999] 3 All ER 429.

[37.6] HMRC formed the opinion that a company (R) had been involved in significant MTIC fraud. They presented a winding-up petition and applied to the Ch D for the appointment of a provisional liquidator. Peter Smith J granted the application. Floyd J subsequently revoked the appointment but the CA unanimously reversed this decision and restored the appointment. Rimer LJ observed that 'in cases in which there are real questions as to the integrity of the company's management and as to the quality of its accounting and record-keeping function, it will be an important part of a liquidator's function to ensure that he obtains control of its books and records so that he can engage in all necessary investigations of its transactions. These will or may include investigations of those who have been managing the company with a view to considering the bringing of claims against them; and the consideration of whether any of the company's directors ought to be the subject of a report to the Secretary of State to the effect that it appears to the liquidator that they were unfit to be concerned in the management of a company. Such a report might then lead to an application to the court for their disqualification. If there is any risk that, pending the hearing of the petition, records may be lost or destroyed, that will also found the basis for the appointment of a provisional liquidator, who will be able immediately to secure them and commence his own inquiries into the affairs of the company and the conduct of its management.' The evidence here provided 'ample grounds justifying the maintenance' of the appointment of a provisional liquidator. *HMRC v Rochdale Drinks Distributors Ltd*, CA [2011] EWCA Civ 1116.

Former director applying for costs against provisional liquidator

[37.7] See *Forrester v Hooper*, 2.510 APPEALS.

Company in liquidation—liquidators' obligation to pay VAT

[37.8] A company (M) sold a substantial property for almost £4,000,000. It failed to account for VAT on the sale. Customs took winding-up proceedings, and a winding-up order was made against M. There was one other creditor (another company). The liquidators discovered that M's accountant (F) had misappropriated the funds which should have been used to pay the VAT. They recovered some money from F, and applied to the Ch D for directions as to how this was to be distributed. The Ch D directed that the money should be paid to Customs, applying the principles laid down by Lord Wilberforce in *Barclays Bank Ltd v Quistclose Investments Ltd*, HL [1970] AC 567. *Freeman & Another v C & E Commrs (re Margaretta Ltd)*, Ch D [2005] STC 610.

Bank realising debts to pay floating charge

[37.9] In 1999 a company gave a bank a floating charge over its assets. In July and August 2002 it sold some of its business and assets to two subsidiaries. In September 2002 the company went into voluntary liquidation, owing VAT to Customs. The bank subsequently realised some of the debts which the company had transferred to its subsidiaries. The company liquidators issued an originating summons asking the court to determine whether the relevant assets were subject to the floating charge, and whether the bank was required to apply the sale proceeds to the preferential creditors in priority to the floating charge. The Ch D reviewed the evidence in detail and made a declaration that most of the amount realised was within *Companies Act 1985, s 196*, but that certain amounts which the bank had realised from book debts assigned to it by the subsidiaries were not subject to the floating charge. Both the bank and Customs appealed to the CA, which unanimously set the declaration aside and remitted the case for a further hearing. Sir John Chadwick held that 'there is a real prospect that the Commissioners will succeed in establishing that (*Companies Act 1985, s 196*) and (*Insolvency Act 1986, s 175*) have application to the facts of this case'. *Re Oval 1742 Ltd; C & E Commrs v Royal Bank of Scotland plc*, CA [2007] EWCA Civ 1262.

Company in receivership—receiver's obligation to pay VAT

[37.10] In 1972 a company issued a debenture in favour of a bank, creating a floating charge over the whole of its undertaking. In 1974, under the terms of the debenture, the bank appointed a receiver. The company continued to trade, and charged VAT on the supplies which it made. The receiver issued an originating summons for a declaration as to whether he was obliged to pay Customs the VAT which he had collected, or whether he was entitled instead to pay it to the bank under the terms of the debenture. Brightman J held that the receiver was obliged to pay the VAT to Customs. He would be committing a criminal offence if he failed to do so, and had no right to pay the money to the bank instead. *Re John Willment (Ashford) Ltd*, Ch D 1978, [1979] STC 286. (*Note*. The *Rules of the Supreme Court 1965 (SI 1965/1776)* refer to the use of an 'originating summons'. With effect from 26 April 1999, these rules were largely replaced by the *Civil Procedure Rules 1998 (SI 1998/3132)*, which refer instead to 'alternative procedure'.)

[37.11] The decision in *Re John Willment (Ashford) Ltd*, 37.10 above, was approved by the CA in a similar subsequent case where there were fixed charges over specific assets, rather than a floating charge over the whole of the company's undertaking. The company's receiver collected rent from properties in respect of which the company had elected to waive exemption. The CA held that the receiver was obliged to pay Customs the VAT on the rents under *Law of Property Act 1925, s 109(8)*. Nourse LJ observed that the receiver owed duties to the company as well as to the bank, and was obliged to protect the company against the potentially serious consequences of failing to account to Customs for the tax in question. *Sargent v C & E Commrs*, CA [1995] STC 399; [1995] 1 WLR 821.

Company in receivership—application for repayment of VAT

[37.12] A company (Q), which was a member of a VAT group, sold cars which were manufactured by an unrelated company (F). In 2002 Q went into receivership. It held a number of cars for which it had not paid F. In accordance with provisions in the relevant 'supply agreement', F reclaimed the cars and issued credit notes. Q's receivers subsequently submitted a claim for repayment of input tax in respect of these cars. Customs rejected the claim and the representative member of Q's VAT group appealed, contending that the credit notes should not have been treated as effective for VAT purposes, and that F should have claimed bad debt relief instead. The VAT Tribunal rejected this contention and dismissed the appeal, but the CA remitted the case to the First-Tier Tribunal, which reviewed the evidence and allowed the appeal, holding (by the casting vote of Judge Nowlan) that there had been no agreement between Q and F for the rescission of the original supplies of cars. *Brunel Motor Co Ltd v HMRC*, [2011] UKFTT 589 (TC), TC01432.

Insolvency Act 1986, s 423—amendment of claim

[37.13] HMRC were undertaking an enquiry into a complex series of transactions which appeared to constitute MTIC fraud. They lodged a claim under *Insolvency Act 1986, s 423* against a company (C) which they considered had acted as a 'buffer trader' in the chain, on the basis that it had entered into certain transactions by which it transferred £10,000,000 to a settlement (B) with a Gibraltar trustee, 'for the purposes of putting assets beyond the reach of the Commissioners'. HMRC subsequently applied to amend their particulars of claim, on the basis that the transfers had not been made directly to the settlement, but to a British Virgin Islands company which was wholly owned by B's trustee. C opposed the application but the Ch D granted it. David Richards J observed that 'the detail of the way in which HMRC put their case has changed with successive draft amendments, but the heart of the case has remained unaltered'. In the circumstances of the case, it was 'right to give HMRC permission to amend the particulars of claim'. *HMRC v Cellcom Ltd (aka HMRC v N Begum & Others)*, Ch D [2010] EWHC 1799 (Ch).

VATA 1994, Sch 11 para 2(12)*—deemed supply

[**37.14**] See *Edgewater Motel Ltd v New Zealand Commissioner of Inland Revenue*, **14.114** COLLECTION AND ENFORCEMENT.

Company in receivership—goods subsequently repossessed

[**37.15**] See *Re Liverpool Commercial Vehicles Ltd*, **36.675** INPUT TAX.

Set-off of Crown debts

[**37.16**] In February 1975 an order was made for the compulsory winding-up of a company. At the date of winding-up, the company owed £4,726 to the Inland Revenue and £951 to the DHSS. It was also owed £4,055 by Customs in respect of reclaimable input tax. The Commissioners repaid £3,651 of this before becoming aware of the other Crown debts. They then requested the liquidator to set the amount repaid against the other Crown debts in accordance with the *Bankruptcy Act 1914, s 31*. The liquidator refused to comply with this request and Customs began proceedings for the recovery of the £3,651. The Ch D gave judgment for Customs, applying the decision in *Re DH Curtis (Builders) Ltd*, Ch D [1978] 2 All ER 183, and holding that *s 31* applied to debts due to and from the Crown immediately before the commencement of the winding-up. The £3,651 had been paid by mistake and was recoverable in law. *Re Cushla Ltd*, Ch D [1979] STC 615; [1979] 3 All ER 415. (*Note. Bankruptcy Act 1914, s 31* was repealed by *Insolvency Act 1985*. See now *Insolvency Act 1986, s 323*.)

[**37.17**] A company went into liquidation, owing money to three Government departments but having overpaid £7,185 of VAT. Customs allocated this amount to the other Government departments. The liquidator objected to this set-off and rejected a proof of debt lodged by the Department of Trade and Industry. The HL gave judgment for the DTI, applying the Ch D decision in *Re DH Curtis (Builders) Ltd*, Ch D [1978] 2 All ER 183, and holding that Customs had been entitled to make the set-off. Lord Hope of Craighead held that 'the Crown is acting both as debtor and as creditor in the same capacity.

The claims to the sums in question on either side are claims due to and owed by the Crown in its own right.' *Secretary of State for Trade & Industry v Frid*, HL [2004] UKHL 24; [2004] All ER (D) 180 (May).

Continuous supplies of services—effect of liquidation

[37.18] A company which had made continuous supplies of construction services, within *regulation 90* of the *VAT Regulations 1995 (SI 1995/2518)*, went into liquidation. The liquidator failed to account for payments which he received on behalf of the company, and the Commissioners issued an assessment charging tax on them. The tribunal dismissed the liquidator's appeal, holding that since the company had never issued VAT invoices in respect of the services in question, output tax was chargeable when payment was received. *Glenshane Construction Services Ltd (in liquidation)*, LON/95/2061 (VTD 14160).

Group registration—liability of members

[37.19] See *Re Nadler Enterprises Ltd*, 32.10 GROUPS OF COMPANIES.

Insolvency Act 1986, Sch 6—application of Crown preference

[37.20] See *Villaswan Ltd v Sheraton (Blythswood) Ltd*, 32.33 GROUPS OF COMPANIES.

Bankruptcy and personal insolvency

Insolvency Act 1986, s 271—whether offer unreasonably refused

[37.21] A barrister failed to charge VAT on his invoices. He was prosecuted and convicted of fraudulently cheating the public revenue of £140,000 in unpaid VAT. Customs subsequently served a bankruptcy petition. The Registrar made a bankruptcy order against the barrister. The barrister appealed, contending that he had made an offer to secure the debt by offering a charge over a property which he and his wife owned, and that Customs' rejection of the offer was unreasonable, within *Insolvency Act 1986, s 271(3)*. The Ch D rejected this contention and dismissed the barrister's appeal. Lightman J noted that the property in question was already subject to a mortgage, and was occupied by the barrister's mother-in-law. He held that 'the test of unreasonableness is whether a reasonable creditor in the position of the petitioning creditor and in the light of the actual history as disclosed to the court could have reached the conclusion that the petitioning creditor reached. There may be a range of reasonable positions on the part of the hypothetical reasonable creditors and a rejection of an offer by the petitioner is only to be categorised as unreasonable if no reasonable creditor would have refused the offer and accordingly the refusal is beyond the range of reasonable responses to it.' He observed that the proposed charge 'was a second charge and the enforcement of a second charge creates far greater problems for a creditor than the enforcement of a first charge'. Furthermore, the charge 'was not to be enforceable until the later of the death of the mother-in-law or the sale of the property by the mother-in-law. It was, accordingly, postponed until the indefinite future and in respect of this period the interest rate payable was not a commercial rate but fixed at 5%.' Accordingly, 'the hypothetical reasonable creditor' would have been likely to object to the terms proposed, and to have considered that 'a bankruptcy would have secured a better return'. *C & E Commrs v Dougall*, Ch D 2000, [2001] BPIR 269.

Statutory demand—Insolvency Act 1986, s 375(1)

[37.22] A father and son who traded in partnership failed to pay a VAT assessment. Customs made a statutory demand against the son. He applied to have the statutory demand set aside. His application was rejected, and he applied to another district judge under *Insolvency Act 1986, s 375(1)*. The district judge dismissed the application, and he appealed to the Ch D. The Ch D dismissed the appeal, holding on the evidence that the district judge had properly exercised his discretion. *Re A Debtor (No 8 of 1997), The Debtor v C & E Commrs*, Ch D 30 November 1998 unreported.

[37.23] Applications to set aside a statutory demand were also dismissed in *MR Khan v C & E Commrs*, CA 3 May 2000 unreported, and *Cozens*, **2.193** APPEALS.

Application for annulment of bankruptcy order

[37.24] A solicitor failed to pay the VAT which she had shown as due on her VAT returns. HMRC applied for a bankruptcy order, which was duly granted. The solicitor subsequently applied for the order to be annulled, contending that her returns had been incorrect as many of her supplies had been to asylum-seekers who were not resident in the UK, so that by virtue of the *VAT (Place of Supply of Services) Order (SI 1992/3121)*, the supplies were deemed to take place outside the UK and she should not have accounted for VAT on them. The Chief Registrar rejected the solicitor's application and the CA unanimously upheld this decision. Sir Andrew Morritt held that 'the bankruptcy court does not usurp the jurisdiction of the VAT Tribunal by itself enquiring into matters within the statutory jurisdiction of the latter'. He observed that 'it cannot seriously be suggested that in cases where a complete and correct return has been made there is no liability for the amount shown by the taxable person to be due. It is at the least an admission of a statutory liability for VAT. The returns submitted by the applicant clearly established the liabilities on which the statutory demand and bankruptcy order were based.' Accordingly, 'it must follow that the legal consequences of the original returns and the unsatisfied statutory demand remain notwithstanding the assertions of the applicant'. *HMRC v M Chamberlin*, CA [2011] EWCA Civ 271; [2011] STC 1237. (*Note.* The Supreme Court has dismissed the solicitor's application for leave to appeal against this decision.)

Partnership debt—validity of statutory demand

[37.25] See *Jamieson*, 47.70 PARTNERSHIP.

Partnership debt—validity of bankruptcy order

[37.26] See *Schooler*, 47.69 PARTNERSHIP.

Trader's wife concealing statutory demand from husband

[37.27] A married couple traded in partnership. Customs served a statutory demand on a retailer in respect of unpaid VAT. The retailer's wife concealed this demand from her husband, and a bankruptcy order was made against him. He subsequently applied for the order to be rescinded, on the grounds that he had been unaware of the proceedings as his wife had concealed the relevant correspondence. The order was rescinded by consent, and a district judge ordered the couple to pay Customs' costs. The Ch D and CA unanimously upheld this decision. Chadwick LJ held that 'the service of the statutory demand by putting it through the letterbox was a reasonable way of effecting service in the circumstances of this case'. Although the statutory demand related solely to the husband, the district judge had been entitled to conclude that his wife 'had acted irrationally or irresponsibly in failing to bring to her husband's attention documents which she knew were important'. He also observed that 'it is important to keep in mind the statutory obligations in respect of VAT that are imposed upon a trader. The obligations of the trader are to make returns and to keep records available for inspection. Those obligations include the provision of a registration address at which the trader can be contacted.' It had been H's responsibility to ensure that documents delivered to his premises 'came to his attention or were dealt with by someone under his authority'. *Housiaux & Housiaux v C & E Commrs*, CA [2003] EWCA Civ 257; [2003] BPIR 858.

Trader declared bankrupt—subsequent claim for damages

[37.28] A retailer (C) failed to pay VAT to Customs, and they presented a bankruptcy petition in February 1992. C made an agreement with them that the bankruptcy proceedings should be adjourned on condition that he made certain payments. He submitted three postdated cheques. Shortly afterwards, his chequebook was stolen. He cancelled all the cheques drawn on that chequebook and provided Customs with substitute cheques. Customs presented one of the original cheques for payment as well as one of the substitute cheques. The bank did not honour the original cheque and in May 1992 Customs resumed the bankruptcy proceedings. C was declared bankrupt on 26 May. The order was annulled on 5 June, and C subsequently took proceedings against Customs, claiming substantial damages. The QB reviewed the evidence in detail and awarded nominal damages of £2 only. Seymour J observed that on the evidence, it was accepted that Customs had acted in breach of the agreement. However, there was no evidence that the making of the bankruptcy order had prevented C from obtaining subsequent employment. He had obtained employment prior to being made bankrupt, and had lost this employment, not as a result of his bankruptcy, but because of his 'failure to achieve sales targets'. He had not shown that he had suffered any loss as a result of the order, and was therefore only entitled to nominal damages. C appealed to the CA, contending that the judgment of Seymour J should be declared a nullity because he was only a circuit judge and, although he was authorised by *Supreme Court Act 1981, s 68*, he was not authorised by *Supreme Court Act 1981, s 9(1)* to sit as a judge of the High Court. The CA dismissed the appeal, holding that Seymour J was 'well qualified to sit' and was a *de facto* judge of the High Court. Sedley LJ observed that the judgment which Seymour J had delivered was 'of high quality and legally impeccable'. *EJ Coppard v C & E Commrs*, CA [2003] EWCA Civ 511; [2003] 2 WLR 1618; [2003] 3 All ER 351.

Appeal by undischarged bankrupt

[37.29] An individual who had been made bankrupt lodged a late appeal against an assessment issued before the date of bankruptcy. The tribunal adjourned the appeal, holding that the bankrupt had no *locus standi*, and that it was for his trustee in bankruptcy to decide whether an appeal should be lodged. *DT Hunt*, [1992] VATTR 255 (VTD 10147).

Supplies by undischarged bankrupt

[37.30] A consulting engineer (S) was made bankrupt in 1981 but continued to carry on business. He appealed against an assessment, contending that he could not be held to be trading while he was an undischarged bankrupt. The tribunal rejected this contention and dismissed his appeal. The fact that S was trading in breach of the law of bankruptcy did not alter the fact that he was trading. He had remained a legal person and continued to offer and supply his services as an independent principal. *JE Scally*, [1989] VATTR 245 (VTD 4592).

Husband declared bankrupt and transferring business to wife

[37.31] An electrical contractor (T) was declared bankrupt in March 1998. He applied for annulment of the bankruptcy order, and, with the consent of the Official Receiver, he arranged for his wife to carry on his business in the interim. The bankruptcy order was annulled in July 1998 and T then resumed control of the business. Subsequently Customs issued an assessment on the basis that, notwithstanding the bankruptcy order, T had continued to carry on the business during his bankruptcy and was liable to account for tax on the supplies made during that period. T appealed, contending that the relevant supplies had been made by his wife. The tribunal accepted this contention and allowed the appeal. The tribunal observed that it would have been 'theoretically possible' for T to have continued in business if he had met the requirements of *Insolvency Act 1986*, and that he would also have been liable for VAT if he had 'made supplies in breach of the law'. However, on the evidence, he had arranged for the business to be carried on by his wife. *C Thomas*, [2001] VATDR 307 (VTD 17127). (*Note.* The tribunal chairman

(Mr. Wallace) also expressed the view that Customs' attempts to treat the relevant arrangements as 'ineffective for VAT could be regarded as an attempt to apply the principles in *WT Ramsay Ltd v CIR*, HL [1981] STC 174 into VAT law' and stated that this 'would seem to run counter to' the CA decision in the 1989 case of *Faith Construction Ltd*, **62.423** SUPPLY. However, these comments are *obiter*, since Customs' representative did not refer to *Ramsay*, and Mr. Wallace's *dicta* on this point fail to refer to the 1992 case of *Raceshine Ltd*, **36.495** INPUT TAX, where the tribunal had held that the *Ramsay* principle did apply to VAT. In the 1998 case of *Thorn Materials Supply Ltd*, **32.17** GROUPS OF COMPANIES, Lord Nolan held that the application of the *Ramsay* principle to VAT raised 'novel issues of great importance and complexity, both in our national and in Community law' and that 'it would be undesirable to embark upon them until a case arises when it is necessary to do so.')

Business transferred as going concern following bankruptcy

[37.32] A furniture retailer became bankrupt in April 1994. The business was transferred, as a going concern, to a limited company seven days later. Following the transfer, the company failed to account for output tax on supplies of furniture for which deposits had been received before the bankruptcy of the previous proprietor and the transfer of the business. Customs issued an assessment charging output tax, and the company appealed, contending that the liability should be treated as that of the transferor's trustee in bankruptcy. The tribunal rejected this contention and dismissed the appeal, holding that there were two separate tax points. The tax point in respect of the deposit was the time when the deposit was taken. However, the tax point in respect of the balance of the price was the time when the furniture was delivered or the time when payment was made. *Camford Ltd (t/a The Cotswold Collection)*, LON/95/221A (VTD 13339).

Bankruptcy—whether excuse for non-registration

[37.33] See *Ambrose*, **51.137** PENALTIES: FAILURE TO NOTIFY.

Legal costs of discharge from bankruptcy

[37.34] See *Stern*, **36.199** INPUT TAX.

Insolvency of customers—whether a supply

[37.35] See the cases noted at **62.190** to **62.191** SUPPLY.

38

Insurance

The cases are arranged under the following headings.

The provision of insurance and reinsurance (VATA 1994, Sch 9, Group 2, Item 1)   **38.1**

Services of an insurance intermediary (VATA 1994, Sch 9, Group 2, Item 4)

     Cases held to qualify for exemption   **38.13**

     Cases held to be partly exempt   **38.26**

     Cases held not to qualify for exemption   **38.27**

Superseded legislation   **38.34**

NOTE

VATA 1994, Sch 9, Group 2 was substituted by *FA 1997, s 38* with effect from 19 March 1997, and was significantly amended by the *VAT (Insurance) Order 2004 (SI 2004/3083)* with effect from 1 January 2005. The changes enacted by *FA 1997* were intended to make it 'more difficult to avoid VAT when insurance is supplied with other goods and services'. The cases in this chapter should be read in the light of the changes in the legislation.

The provision of insurance and reinsurance (VATA 1994, Sch 9, Group 2, Item 1)

Provision of hired cars

[38.1] A company carried on a car hire business and had arranged insurance for its cars with a recognised insurer. In accounting for output tax, it treated part of the consideration which it received from its customers as attributable to an exempt supply of insurance. The Commissioners issued an assessment charging output tax on the whole of the consideration, and the tribunal dismissed the company's appeal, holding that the company was making a single supply of the hire of the car. The only supply of insurance was made by the insurance company to the car hire company, rather than by the car hire company to the customer. *CJ Kiff Ltd*, [1981] VATTR 88 (VTD 1084).

[38.2] Similar decisions were reached in *AJ Turner*, MAN/85/105 (VTD 1965); *Kings Lynn Motor Co Ltd*, LON/90/50Y (VTD 5312); *CA Vine (t/a Cornish Car Hire)*, LON/91/1104Z (VTD 7467); *R Stratton (t/a SRG Hire)*, LON/97/1510 (VTD 16879) and *Motor & Legal Group Ltd*, **62.469** SUPPLY.

[38.3] In a case where the facts were similar to those in *CJ Kiff Ltd*, 38.1 above, a car hire company had initially accounted for VAT on the payments it received from its customers, but subsequently claimed a repayment on the grounds that part of the consideration should be attributed to exempt supplies

---

of insurance. Customs rejected the claim but the tribunal allowed the company's appeal, holding that the effect of the policy was that the company was providing 'insurance cover for its customers', rather than simply supplying 'insured vehicles to its customers'. Accordingly the tribunal held that the company's supplies qualified for exemption. *Global Self Drive Ltd*, [2005] VATDR 284 (VTD 19162). (*Notes*. (1) The tribunal decision fails to refer to *CJ Kiff Ltd*, **38.1** above, or to any of the cases noted at **38.2** above. (2) The tribunal also held that the repayment would not lead to 'unjust enrichment'. (3) The decision here was not followed in the subsequent case of *OM Properties Investment Co Ltd v HMRC*, **38.12** below.)

Provision of motor insurance

[38.4] A company which supplied motor insurance reclaimed the whole of its input tax. The Commissioners issued an assessment to recover the tax, on the basis that it related to exempt supplies of insurance. The tribunal upheld the assessment and dismissed the company's appeal. *International Warranty Co (UK) Ltd*, EDN/85/28 (VTD 1934).

[38.5] A company which owned a garage allowed some of its employees to drive its cars privately. It extended its insurance cover accordingly and made deductions from its employees' wages. The Commissioners issued an assessment on the basis that the company had made its employees a standard-rated supply of the right to use its cars. The company appealed, contending that the deductions from its employees' salaries were for insurance and should therefore be treated as exempt under what is now *VATA 1994, Sch 9, Group 2*. The tribunal dismissed the appeal, holding that the insurance was supplied to the company and not to the employees, and that the money recovered from the employees did not qualify for exemption. On the evidence, what was supplied to the employees 'was not the insurance cover nor the making of arrangements by the appellant company for extended insurance cover, but the right to use the cars for private and pleasure purposes for the consideration which was measured by the cost of the extended insurance cover'. *T & B Garage (Wimbledon)*, LON/89/803Z (VTD 4613).

Valuation of car for insurance purposes

[38.6] A company carried on business as an insurance broker and arranged for the provision of motor insurance. It valued cars which were to be the subject of such insurance, and charged clients a fee of £8 for determining the agreed value. The Commissioners issued a ruling that these valuation fees were chargeable to VAT at the standard rate, and the company appealed, contending that they formed part of the consideration for a supply of insurance, and should be treated as exempt from VAT under what is now *VATA 1994, Sch 9, Group 2*. The tribunal allowed the company's appeal, applying *British Railways Board*, **66.12** TRANSPORT, and *British Airways plc*, **66.13** TRANSPORT, and distinguishing *Dogbreeders Associates*, **38.41** below. 'The determination of the agreed value was an integral part of the provision of the particular insurance policies.' *Lancaster Insurance Services Ltd*, LON/90/607X (VTD 5455).

Goods sold by 'party plan' system—insurance for distributors

[38.7] A company sold pottery and ceramics on a 'party plan' system, through distributors whom it provided with kits of goods. It required its distributors to pay two-thirds of the retail value of any goods which were broken or stolen. In 1982 it began a scheme whereby the distributors could insure themselves against such thefts and breakages, in return for payments of 50p per week. It did not account for VAT on these payments, and the Commissioners issued a ruling that they were standard-rated. The company appealed, contending that the payments should be treated as exempt from VAT under what is now *VATA 1994, Sch 9, Group 2, Item 1*. The tribunal dismissed the appeal, holding that the services supplied by the company did not qualify for exemption. *John E Buck & Co Ltd*, LON/83/208 (VTD 1525).

Insurance of television sets

[38.8] Two groups of companies let television sets on hire. With each of the groups, the sets were let on hire by one subsidiary company, and another subsidiary provided insurance. 70% of the total consideration was allocated to the rental subsidiary, the other 30% being allocated to the insurance subsidiary. The groups did not account for output tax on the amounts allocated to the insurance subsidiaries, treating them as exempt from VAT. The Commissioners issued assessments charging output tax on the full amounts of the payments, on the basis that there was a single composite supply which did not qualify for exemption. The groups appealed. The tribunal allowed the appeals, holding that there were two separate supplies in each case. The rental subsidiaries supplied the service of letting the goods on hire, and the insurance subsidiaries supplied insurance. The payments for insurance qualified for exemption under what is now *VATA 1994, Sch 9, Group 2, Item 1. Thorn EMI plc; Granada plc*, [1993] VATTR 94 (VTD 9782).

Video hire business

[38.9] A couple operated a video hire business in partnership. They made an annual charge of £2 to each of their customers in order to cover damage to videocassettes. They did not account for output tax on this charge. The Commissioners issued an assessment charging tax on it, and the couple appealed, contending that it was for a supply of insurance which should be treated as exempt. The tribunal rejected this contention and dismissed the appeal, holding that and the charges did not qualify for exemption. *K & V Peters*, LON/95/2904 (VTD 14328).

Personal pension schemes

[38.10] A group of companies operated two personal pension schemes. The Commissioners issued a ruling that VAT should be charged at the standard rate on the services which the group supplied in connection with the schemes. The representative member of the group appealed, contending that the supplies qualified for exemption under *VATA 1994, Sch 9, Group 2, Item 1*. The tribunal accepted this contention and allowed the appeal. On the evidence, the services in question were not simply trust administration services. The schemes embodied insurance contracts, and 'were part and parcel of the provision of insurance'. *Winterthur Life UK Ltd*, LON/96/1787 (VTD 14935).

Storage insurance

[38.11] An individual (L) arranged with a removal and storage contractor for his personal possessions to be placed in storage. He requested insurance cover, for which the contractor charged £97.50 plus VAT. L wrote to the Commissioners querying why VAT should be charged on the insurance. The Commissioners issued a ruling that VAT was chargeable since the contractor was not an authorised insurer, as required by the legislation then in force. L appealed. The tribunal allowed his appeal, holding on the evidence that L was insured with an authorised insurer under the storage contractor's policy, and that the contractor should be treated as L's agent for this purpose. The tribunal held that it was 'not strictly necessary that there should be any correlation between the amount paid by customer to contractor on the one hand and the amount paid by contractor to insurer on the other'. The correct analysis of the arrangements embodied in the master policy as between the insurer and the contractor was that 'the insurer, in consideration of the annual premium, undertakes to keep open and unrevoked an offer to grant insurance cover to any customer of (the contractor) up to the stated limit of the insurer's liability.' *AA Lee*, LON/97/446 (VTD 15205). (*Note. VATA 1994, Sch 9, Group 2, Item 1 has subsequently been amended by SI 2004/3083 with effect from 1 January 2005, so that exemption is no longer restricted to insurers who are authorised by the Financial Services Authority.*)

Letting of commercial premises

[38.12] A company (OM) let several commercial properties to tenants. It had opted to tax the properties, but treated part of the payments it received as exempt from VAT. HMRC issued an assessment charging tax on the basis that the supplies failed to qualify for exemption. OM appealed, contending that it had a 'block insurance policy' and that part of the consideration should be treated as attributable to exempt supplies of insurance, applying the principles laid down in *Global Self Drive Ltd*, **38.3** above. The tribunal rejected this contention and dismissed the appeal, holding that OM's policy failed to meet the requirements of a 'block insurance policy'. On the evidence, there was no contract between OM and the insurer which allowed OM to 'effect insurance cover'. OM had not 'procured any form of insurance cover for the tenant' and there was 'no relationship between the insurer and the tenant'. *OM Properties Investment Co Ltd v HMRC*, [2010] UKFTT 494 (TC), TC00752.

Services of an insurance intermediary (VATA 1994, Sch 9, Group 2, Item 4)

Cases held to qualify for exemption

Insurance agent reviewing pension policies for mis-selling

[38.13] A company (L) had sold a number of personal pension policies between 1988 and 1994. The Securities Investment Board and Personal Investment Authority required all such policies to be reviewed to determine whether there had been any mis-selling. L arranged for another company (C) to undertake this review. C did not account for output tax on these supplies. The Commissioners issued an assessment charging tax on them, and C appealed, contending that they should be treated as exempt under *VATA 1994, Sch 9, Group 2, Item 4*. The QB accepted this contention and allowed the appeal, and the CA upheld this decision. Jacob J held that the supplies fell within *Article 13B(a)* of the *EC Sixth Directive*. The fact that the services were not supplied by L itself, but by C acting on its behalf, did not prevent them from qualifying for exemption. The services were not merely ancillary, but were 'a vital part of the administration of the contracts'. *Century Life plc v C & E Commrs*, CA 2000, [2001] STC 38. (*Note*. For the Commissioners' practice following this decision, see Business Brief 3/01, issued on 20 February 2001.)

Management of self-administered personal pension scheme

[38.14] A company (P) provided management services to another company (S), concerning the management of a self-administered personal pension scheme. The Commissioners issued a ruling that VAT was chargeable on P's supplies. The representative member of P's VAT group appealed, contending that the supplies qualified for exemption under *VATA 1994, Sch 9, Group 2, Item 4*, since they were the provision by an insurance agent 'of any of the services of an insurance intermediary'. The tribunal accepted this contention and allowed the appeal, holding on the evidence that P qualified as an 'insurance agent'. *Winterthur Life UK Ltd (No 3)*, LON/98/1339 (VTD 17572).

Company supplying services to Lloyd's underwriters

[38.15] A company acted as a members' agent for Lloyd's underwriters. The Commissioners issued a ruling that its supplies were standard-rated. The company appealed, contending that its supplies should be treated as exempt under *VATA 1994, Sch 9, Group 2, Item 4*. The tribunal allowed the appeal, holding that the supplies of insurance were made by the underwriting members (rather than by the syndicates). The company was acting as an agent of the underwriting members, and was therefore an 'insurance agent' within *Group 2, Item 4* and *Article 13B(a)* of the *EC Sixth Directive*. Its supplies were 'services related to insurance transactions', and therefore qualified for exemption. *SOC Private Capital Ltd*, [2002] VATDR 179 (VTD 17747).

Company selling insurance by telephone

[38.16] A company (T) acted on behalf of an insurance company (L), selling insurance policies by telephone. The Commissioners issued a ruling that T was required to account for tax on its supplies to L. T appealed, contending that its supplies should be treated as exempt under *VATA 1994, Sch 9, Group 2, Item 4*. The tribunal accepted this contention and allowed the appeal, holding on the evidence that T was acting as an 'insurance agent' and was not simply supplying promotional services. *Teletech UK Ltd*, [2004] VATDR 44 (VTD 18080). (*Note.* For the Commissioners' revised practice following this case, see Business Brief 7/03, issued on 30 June 2003. Customs state that they accept that call centre services relating to insurance qualify for exemption 'where the call centre is able to put the insurer on risk at the point of sale without referral back to the insurer'. For a case where this provision was held not to apply, see *R (oao Software Solutions Partners Ltd) v HMRC*, **38.31** below.)

Company providing telephone helpline services

[38.17] A company (C) agreed with an insurance company (D) that it would provide telephone helpline services to D's customers. It did not account for tax on the payments which it received from D, treating them as exempt. The Commissioners issued an assessment charging tax on them, and C appealed. The tribunal allowed the appeal, holding that C should be treated as an 'insurance agent' and was acting as an 'insurance intermediary'. Accordingly, its supplies qualified for exemption under *VATA 1994, Sch 9, Group 2, Item 4*. *C & V (Advice Line) Services Ltd*, [2001] VATDR 446 (VTD 17310).

Insurance offered by furniture retailer

[38.18] A company (C) sold furniture. It offered 'fabric protection insurance cover' to purchasers of certain types of furniture. It was a precondition of the cover that the furniture in question was treated with a certain chemical which reduced the effect of staining. C treated the insurance premiums as exempt from VAT under *VATA 1994, Sch 9, Group 2, Item 4*. The Commissioners issued assessments charging tax on the premiums, on the basis that they should be treated as standard-rated additional payments for the chemical treatment of the furniture. The tribunal allowed C's appeal, holding that the premiums qualified for exemption. *Claytons Upholstery Ltd*, MAN/00/777 (VTD 18253).

Insurance provided with sale of car

[38.19] A company (L) which traded as a car dealer submitted a claim for repayment of tax relating to supplies of insurance on the cars which it sold. Customs rejected the claim on the basis that the supply of insurance was ancillary to the supply of the car, applying the principles laid down by the Ch D in *Peugeot Motor Co plc v C & E Commrs*, **38.51** below. L appealed. The tribunal reviewed the evidence in detail and allowed the appeal, distinguishing *Peugeot Motor Co plc* because the insurance in that case was provided free, whereas in the transactions arranged by L, the customer was required to pay £564 for the insurance. Accordingly, there was a separate supply of insurance which qualified for exemption. The tribunal also held that L qualified as an 'insurance agent' for the purposes of *VATA 1994, Sch 9, Group 2, Item 4*.

Lindsay Cars Ltd, [2005] VATDR 21 (VTD 18970). (*Note*. The decision here was distinguished in the subsequent case of *Ford Motor Co Ltd v HMRC (No 2)*, 38.29 below.)

Professional association—whether an 'insurance intermediary'

[38.20] A professional association (R) required its members to have professional indemnity insurance. It encouraged its members to take insurance with a specific company (M). M paid commission to R. In 2001 Customs issued a ruling that these payments qualified for exemption. In 2007 they reversed this and issued a ruling that the payments failed to qualify for exemption. R appealed, contending that it was acting as an 'insurance intermediary'. The tribunal accepted this contention and allowed R's appeal. *Royal Incorporation of Architects in Scotland*, EDN/07/06 (VTD 20252).

Company dealing with health questionnaires for life insurance

[38.21] A company (M) provided services to life assurance companies, relating to the completion of health questionnaires by potential customers. Customs issued a ruling that M was required to account for output tax on its supplies. M appealed, contending that they qualified for exemption under *VATA, Sch 9, Group 2, Item 4*. The tribunal accepted this contention and allowed M's appeal, holding that M was 'an insurance agent acting as an intermediary'. *Morganash Ltd*, MAN/05/749 (VTD 19777).

Warranty insurance for double glazing

[38.22] A company supplied and installed double glazing and related products. It arranged warranty insurance, and treated such supplies as exempt from VAT under *VATA 1994, Sch 9, Group 2, Item 4*. The Commissioners issued an assessment charging tax on the supplies, on the basis that the 'relevant requirements' of *Sch 9, Group 2, Notes 4* and *5* were not fulfilled. The company appealed. The tribunal reviewed the evidence in detail and held that the company's supplies made between January 1997 and June 1998 failed to qualify for exemption on the grounds that the company's documentation failed to meet the requirements of *Note 5*, since the specific amount of the premium was not stated. The HL allowed the company's appeal (by a 4-1 majority, Lord Slynn dissenting). Lord Hoffmann held that *Group 2, Note 5* was 'concerned to identify the information which the document must disclose rather than to specify any form of language or typography'. He considered that 'it would seem capriciously fastidious for Parliament to insist that the information must be communicated in self-contained form and without requiring the reader to have any knowledge of arithmetic'. All that was necessary was that 'the allocation should be unequivocally stated in the document. It need not be stated in any particular form.' *CR Smith Glaziers (Dunfermline) Ltd v C & E Commrs*, HL [2003] STC 419; [2003] UKHL 7; [2003] 1 WLR 656; [2003] 1 All ER 801. (*Notes*. (1) The tribunal allowed the company's appeal in part with regard to the period ending 31 December 1996, holding that the company's supplies qualified for exemption before the changes to *Group 2* introduced by *FA 1997*. However, the tribunal held that supplies under a transitional arrangement which the company had adopted in cases where contracts had been agreed before December 1996, but services had not yet been completed, failed to qualify for exemption on the grounds that it was the company, rather than the customer, which had absorbed the extra costs of arranging the insurance. (2) The company had altered the form of its contracts with effect from July 1998, and it was accepted that the contracts from July 1998 met the requirements of *Notes 4* and *5*.)

Company operating website to introduce customers to insurers

[38.23] A company operated a website, by which prospective customers were provided with a 'comparison service' for insurance cover from various insurers. It received commission from the insurers to whom it introduced clients. It treated its supplies as exempt from VAT under *VATA 1994, Sch 9, Group 2*, and did not register or account for VAT. HMRC issued a ruling that the company was not within the definition of an 'insurance agent', so that it was required to register for VAT and account for output tax on its supplies. The company appealed, contending that it was acting as an 'insurance intermediary' and that its supplies qualified for exemption under *Group 2, Item 4*. The Ch D accepted this contention and allowed the appeal, and the CA unanimously upheld this decision. Etherton LJ held that the company was 'providing services which were characteristic of an insurance broker or agent, and which were vital to the process of introducing those seeking insurance with insurers'. Accordingly, its supplies qualified for exemption. *HMRC v Insurancewide.com Services Ltd*, CA [2010] STC 1572; [2010] EWCA Civ 422. (*Notes.* (1) HMRC had also imposed a misdeclaration penalty. The tribunal allowed the company's appeal against the penalty, holding that the company had a reasonable excuse for having treated its supplies as exempt, since 'the matters in issue (were) very technical' and the 'plethora of authorities' showed that 'it was not a straightforward case'. (2) For HMRC's practice following the CA decision, see HMRC Brief 31/10, issued on 3 August 2010.)

[38.24] A company (T) operated a website which contained an area for customers to seek quotations for car insurance. It received commission from another company (B) which was authorised by the Financial Services Authority as an insurance intermediary, to which T introduced such customers. HMRC issued a ruling that T was required to account for VAT on the commission which it received from B. The representative member of T's group appealed, contending that T qualified as an 'insurance intermediary' and that its supplies were exempt under *VATA 1994, Sch 9, Group 2, Item 4*. The tribunal accepted this contention and allowed the appeal, and the Ch D and CA upheld this decision. *HMRC v Trader Media Group Ltd*, CA [2010] STC 1572; [2010] EWCA Civ 422. (*Note.* The Ch D and CA heard the case with *HMRC v Insurancewide.com Services Ltd*, **38.23** above.)

Supplies by bank to insurance company

[38.25] A bank formed a subsidiary company to provide insurance products to customers of the Post Office. The bank paid commission to the Post Office for introducing potential customers. The bank was not itself an authorised insurer, and referred the customers to an unrelated company (J), which in turn arranged for a panel of insurers to quote for the customers' business. It was accepted that the services which the bank provided to J qualified for exemption as the services of an insurance intermediary, within *VATA 1994, Sch 9, Group*

2, *Item 4*. Initially these arrangements did not provide profitable for either the bank or the Post Office, and the bank subsequently decided to select a specific insurance company (N) as a 'primary insurer' with the opportunity to undercut any quotes provided by other members of the panel of insurers. N paid commission to the bank. Customs issued a ruling that VAT was chargeable on these payments, and the bank appealed, contending that they qualified for exemption under *Item 4*. The tribunal accepted this contention and allowed the appeal, holding on the evidence that N was paying for 'the continued existence of the whole intermediary structure that is the panel, albeit in a refigured form'. The bank was 'assisting in bringing about a contract of insurance'. Its supplies to N were 'exempt services of an insurance intermediary'. *The Governor & Company of the Bank of Ireland*, [2008] VATDR 352 (VTD 20824).

Cases held to be partly exempt

Whether company making separate supplies of claims handling services

[38.26] An insurance company (W) took over a business which had been based in Exeter, and moved it to Birmingham. None of the previous staff were willing to move to Birmingham, and W had to recruit new staff, who needed to be trained. It arranged for another company (P) to provide claims management, claims handling and training services. P did not account for tax on the services, treating them as exempt. The Commissioners issued assessments on the basis that P was making a composite supply which included training services, and did not qualify for exemption. The representative member of P's VAT group appealed, contending that the services constituted 'the provision of assistance in the administration and performance of (insurance) contracts, including the handling of claims', and were therefore exempt by virtue of *VATA 1994, Sch 9, Group 2, Note 1(c)*. The tribunal reviewed the evidence in detail and allowed the appeal in part, holding that P was making separate supplies of training services, which were subject to VAT, and claims handling services, which qualified for exemption. The tribunal observed that 'to identify a composite transaction in a way that deprives its major part of the exemption otherwise applicable under the *Sixth Directive* and the *VAT Act* is to distort the functioning of the VAT system. Just as a single service should not be artificially split in a way which distorts the system, so also separate services should not be artificially aggregated.' *Equitable Life Assurance Society*, [2003] VATDR 523 (VTD 18072).

Cases held not to qualify for exemption

Motor vehicle insurance—supplies to Gibraltar insurance company

[38.27] In the case noted at **22.71** EUROPEAN COMMUNITY LAW, a group of companies instituted a complex scheme which was intended to allow the recovery of input tax charged on repair services made under insurance policies relating to vehicle breakdown ('MBI policies'). The scheme involved the use of two Gibraltar insurance companies, one of which (V) appointed a UK company (W) to handle claims and pay the repair bills. The Commissioners rejected the repayment claims, and W appealed, contending *inter alia* that its supplies to V were exempt under *VATA 1994, Sch 9, Group 2, Item 4*, so that it was not required to account for output tax. The CA unanimously rejected this contention, holding that W's supplies failed to qualify for exemption. Neuberger LJ held that *Item 4* 'does not extend to the cost of paying out the claim or the direct cost of satisfying the claim'. He observed that 'the conclusion that, in footing the garage bills, (W) is not providing an exempt service to (V)' appeared to be 'consistent with the structure of the VAT system'. To treat the supplies as exempt 'would mean that the otherwise irrecoverable VAT (ie, in this case that payable to the garage) could be rendered recoverable as input tax where there is an insurer outside the Community simply by the insurer creating a captive agent within the Community which would have the obligation to pay the garage invoice'. *C & E Commrs v WHA Ltd; C & E Commrs v Viscount Reinsurance Co Ltd*, CA [2004] STC 1081; [2004] EWCA Civ 559.

Hire of motor vehicles

[38.28] A partnership hired a number of motor vehicles to customers. In accounting for VAT, they treated part of the consideration which they received as relating to the insurance of the vehicles, and as exempt. The Commissioners issued an assessment on the basis that the consideration was standard-rated, and the partnership appealed. The tribunal dismissed the appeal, holding that the partnership did not qualify as an 'insurance intermediary' within *VATA 1994, Sch 9, Group 2, Item 4, Note 1*, since the relevant insurance policy named the partnership, rather than the customer, as the insured party. The tribunal observed that 'it is the appellants who are in a contractual relationship with the insurance company, not the drivers. As such the appellants cannot broker a contract between the insurers and the insured because they themselves are the insured.' Additionally, the partnership was not making separate supplies, but was making a single standard-rated supply of an insured motor vehicle. *GM Craddock & BM Walker (t/a Warwick Garages)*, MAN/99/111 (VTD 16513).

Insurance provided with sale of car

[38.29] A company (F) which traded as a car dealer provided free insurance cover as part of a sales promotion scheme. It claimed a repayment of VAT attributable to the insurance. Customs rejected the claim and the tribunal, Ch D and CA unanimously dismissed F's appeal. Sir Andrew Morritt held that 'there was no separate supply of insurance services and no consideration attributable to any such supply'. *Ford Motor Co Ltd v HMRC (No 2)*, CA 2007, [2008] STC 1016; [2007] EWCA Civ 1730. (*Note*. The HL rejected the company's application for leave to appeal against this decision.)

Company selling health insurance products

[38.30] A company (L) sold health insurance products for an insurance company (W), using a number of 'sales agents' who were treated as self-employed and were paid commission. The Commissioners issued a ruling that L's supplies to W were standard-rated. L appealed, contending that its supplies qualified for exemption under *VATA 1994, Sch 9, Group 2, Item 4* or *Article 13B(a)* of the *EC Sixth Directive*. The tribunal rejected this contention and dismissed the appeal, holding on the evidence that L 'was not acting in an intermediary capacity' and that L 'stood outside the relationship between (W) and the person who was or might be seeking insurance' although it was 'responsible for ensuring that there were trained sales advisers who could fulfil that role'. To qualify for exemption, 'a close connection needs to be demonstrated between the service performed by the insurance broker or insurance agent and the provision of insurance by the insurance company to its customers. All sorts of things provided by an insurance broker or agent to an insurance company may assist in the provision of insurance but still be in reality only incidental to such provision.' *Agentevent Ltd*, LON/00/1331 (VTD 17764).

Computer services

[38.31] A company (S) supplied computer hardware and software for the insurance industry. Customs issued a ruling that VAT was chargeable on its supplies. S applied for judicial review, contending that the effect of Business Brief 7/03 was that the supplies should be treated as exempt. The QB rejected this contention and dismissed the application, finding that S had not shown that any insurers had appointed it as an agent, either to make binding offers on their behalf, or 'to give an acceptance on their behalf of offers made by brokers'. *R (oao Software Solutions Partners Ltd) v HMRC*, QB [2007] EWHC 971 (Admin).

[38.32] A company (L) operated internet-based telecommunication and data services to insurance brokers 'in order to provide a facility for the trading of loan and insurance leads'. Customs issued a ruling that it was required to account for tax on its supplies. L appealed, contending that its supplies should be treated as exempt under *VATA 1994, Sch 9, Group 2, Item 4* or *Article 135(1)* of *EC Directive 2006/112/EC*. The tribunal rejected this contention and dismissed the appeal, finding that 'the nature of the appellant's supplies had nothing to do with the granting or negotiation of credit'. Furthermore, L was 'not an insurance agent or broker', and 'had no relationship with the insurer or the insured'. *Leadx*, MAN/07/1190 (VTD 20904).

UK company transferring business to overseas company

[38.33] In January 2002 a UK insurance company (P) entered into a series of agreements under which it sold its general insurance business to a Swiss insurance company (W). In February 2002 W novated its rights under the agreements to an associated Bermuda company. In 2003 the Bermuda company novated the rights to a company which was a subsidiary of a Scottish bank (R). R paid commission to P, primarily as a result of the renewal of general insurance policies which had been in place before P sold its general insurance business to W. Customs issued a ruling that VAT was chargeable on the commission. R appealed, contending that the commission related to services of an insurance intermediary which qualified for exemption. The VAT tribunal rejected this contention and dismissed the appeal, holding that P was not acting as an insurance broker or agent, since it was not introducing the parties to the contract and was not carrying out 'work preparatory to the conclusion of contracts of insurance'. The Ch D upheld this decision. Mann J held that 'for a person to qualify as a broker there must be more than some mechanical or quasi-mechanical act of reference as between the would-be insured and the insurer'. On the evidence, there was 'nothing at all akin to the sort of approach that a customer makes to a broker'. *Royal Bank of Scotland Group plc v HMRC (No 8)*, Ch D [2012] EWHC 9 (Ch). (Note. At an earlier hearing, the tribunal had held the transfer from P to W did not constitute the transfer of a going concern: see *Winterthur Swiss Insurance Company*, 22.534 EUROPEAN COMMUNITY LAW.)

Superseded legislation

NOTE

   VATA 1983, Sch 6, Group 2 became *VATA 1994, Sch 9, Group 2*, which was substituted by *FA 1997, s 38* with effect from 19 March 1997. What had been *Group 2, Item 3*, providing for exemption for 'the making of arrangements for the provision of any insurance or reinsurance', was not re-enacted in the substituted legislation. Accordingly, the cases summarised in the following paragraphs do not necessarily qualify for exemption under the current legislation. Some of the cases may, however, remain of interest as illustrating matters of general principle with regard to the treatment of insurance for VAT purposes.

Pensions insurance provided by financial adviser

[38.34] A chartered accountant (F) also carried on business as a financial adviser. He worked in close association with another individual (S), who had special knowledge and experience of pensions insurance. They shared commissions received from brokers for pensions insurance effected as a result of their work. Customs issued assessments on the basis that F's share of these commissions was standard-rated. F appealed, contending that the transactions constituted the making of arrangements for the provision of insurance and were exempt from VAT under the legislation then in force. The tribunal accepted this contention and allowed the appeal. *D Ford (t/a Donald Ford Financial Services)*, [1987] VATTR 130 (VTD 2432).

Sale of second-hand cars—breakdown insurance

[38.35] A partnership which sold second-hand cars offered its purchasers an insurance policy against mechanical breakdown for a cost of £250. It treated such payments as exempt from VAT. Customs issued an assessment charging tax on them, and the partnership appealed. The tribunal allowed the appeal, holding that the payments qualified for exemption under the legislation then in force. *HB & DD Geddes*, LON/88/681 (VTD 3378).

[38.36] The decision in *Geddes*, 38.35 above, was distinguished in a subsequent case where a dealer who sold sports cars attributed a large proportion of the sale price of such cars to insurance warranties, and did not account for output tax on the amounts attributed to the warranties. In a case where an MG which had been bought for £2,650 was sold for £3,895, the dealer attributed £1,045 of this price to the warranty, and only accounted for output tax on £200 (i.e. £2,850, being the price after deducting the amount attributed to the warranty, minus the purchase price of £2,650). The maximum claim under the warranty was normally £250. Customs issued assessments on the basis that, since the normal price of such a warranty was £82, only that amount could be treated as being for an exempt supply. The tribunal dismissed the dealer's appeal, finding that 'the whole process of fixing the warranty price was a sham. The figure attributed on the invoices by (the dealer) to the warranty bears no relationship whatsoever either to the amount charged by insurers or to the part played by (the dealer) in arranging the insurance'. (The tribunal also observed that, to the extent that any supplies were exempt under what is now *VATA 1994, Sch 9, Group 2*, the partial exemption rules would apply and require a restriction of input tax, although the dealer had made no such adjustment.) *G Charlesworth (t/a Centurions)*, LON/91/2150 (VTD 9015). (*Note.* See also *Notice No 711, para 19* and Business Brief 7/94, issued on 7 March 1994.)

[38.37] See also *Brisbane*, 50.58 PENALTIES: EVASION OF TAX.

[38.38] A company trading as car dealers arranged for insurance to be provided by an associated insurance company. It charged customers £950 for such insurance. It treated the whole of this £950 as exempt from VAT, but only passed £80 to the insurance company, retaining £870 as commission. Customs issued assessments charging output tax on the basis that only the cost of £80 was attributable to insurance. The tribunal held that the company's returns were incorrect and that Customs were entitled to apportion the price of £950. (However, the tribunal allowed the company's appeal, holding on the evidence that the officer responsible for the assessment had not acted to the best of his judgment.) *North East Garages Ltd*, MAN/96/63 (VTD 15734). (*Note.* For another issue in this case, taken to the QB, see **2.367** APPEALS.)

Letting of holiday cottages—insurance against cancellation

[38.39] A company let holiday cottages. It charged customers an obligatory cancellation insurance premium, and took out relevant insurance policies with an authorised insurer. In accounting for tax, it treated the amounts which it charged its customers for insurance as exempt for VAT. Customs issued a ruling that the company was making a single composite supply which did not qualify for exemption. The tribunal allowed the company's appeal, holding that there were two separate supplies and that the supply of insurance was exempt under the legislation then in force. *Rosemoor Holdings Ltd*, LON/88/1275Z (VTD 4068).

Insurance premiums paid with taxable rent

[38.40] A company owned a property which it let to tenants, and in respect of which it had elected to waive exemption. It insured the property, and required its tenants to pay it a specified proportion of the insurance premiums as rent. It did not account for output tax on such payments, treating them as a separate supply of exempt insurance. Customs issued an assessment charging output tax on the payments, on the basis that they were payments of rent in respect of which the company had elected to waive exemption. The tribunal dismissed the company's appeal, holding that the company had 'made a single supply consisting of the grant of a legal estate in land' and that 'the provisions of the lease relating to insurance cannot realistically be extricated from the lease and considered separately'. The tribunal also held that the premiums were not paid as disbursements for the tenants, since there was 'no element of agency'. *Globe Equities Ltd*, [1995] VATDR 472 (VTD 13105).

Retainer paid by insurance broker to partnership

[38.41] A husband and wife partnership advertised dogs for sale, acting as an intermediary between dogbreeders and members of the public. They received commission and annual retainers from the breeders to whom they introduced buyers. They also encouraged purchasers of dogs to take out insurance with an insurance broker, and received an annual retainer from the broker. They did not account for VAT on this retainer, and Customs issued a ruling that it was standard-rated. The tribunal dismissed the partnership's appeal, holding that the insurance arrangements were made by the broker rather than by the partnership, and that the retainer did not qualify for exemption. *Dogbreeders Associates*, [1989] VATTR 317 (VTD 4295).

Insurance provided by commercial removal service

[38.42] M, the proprietor of a commercial removal service, offered customers insurance against loss or damage of goods being moved. More than 90% of his customers requested this insurance cover, the usual charge for which was 8% of the value of the insured goods. M himself took out a policy with an established insurance company. Customs issued an assessment charging tax on the amounts paid for the insurance, and the tribunal dismissed M's appeal, finding that M provided the insurance himself. This supply was not within *VATA 1983, Sch 6, Group 2, Item 3*, since that only applied where an intermediary made arrangements for a third party to provide insurance, rather than where a principal provided insurance himself. *EJ Mooney (t/a Company Moves)*, [1990] VATTR 50 (VTD 4667).

[38.43] The decision in *Mooney (t/a Company Moves)*, 38.42 above, was distinguished in three subsequent appeals, heard together, in which the tribunal found that the customers were parties to the insurance contracts and had rights against the insurance companies under the contracts. Accordingly the relevant supplies were directly related to the making of arrangements for the provision of insurance, and were exempt from VAT under the legislation then in force. *Robinsons Removals (Cleveland) Ltd*, MAN/92/1644; *E Pearson & Sons (Teesside) Ltd*, MAN/92/1710; *KW Devereux & Sons*, MAN/92/1301 (VTD 11187).

Insurance against loss of credit cards

[38.44] A company (C) operated a service whereby, in return for a payment of £16, a customer whose credit cards were lost or stolen would be indemnified up to £750 against any claim made against him in respect of loss caused by fraudulent use of the cards. C engaged an insurance broker to arrange for an appropriate insurance policy. C did not account for VAT on the payments received from customers for this service. The Commissioners issued a ruling that the payments were taxable and C appealed, contending that they should be treated as exempt under the provisions of *VATA 1983*. The HL referred the case to the CJEC (see **22.324** EUROPEAN COMMUNITY LAW), which held that Member States could not restrict the scope of the exemption for insurance transactions exclusively to supplies by insurers who were authorised by national law. It was for the national court to determine whether the particular transactions in this case were to be regarded as comprising two independent supplies, namely an exempt insurance supply and a taxable card registration service. The HL reconsidered the case in the light of the rulings by the CJEC, and allowed C's appeal, holding that C was making supplies of insurance which qualified for exemption under *VATA 1983*. Lord Slynn observed that 'the essential feature of the scheme' was 'a provision of insurance cover against loss arising from the misuse of credit cards or other documents'. *Card Protection Plan Ltd v C & E Commrs*, HL [2001] STC 174; [2001] UKHL 4; [2001] 2 WLR 329; [2001] 2 All ER 143. (*Note.* For the Commissioners' practice following this decision, see Business Brief 2/2001, issued on 15 February 2001, and Business Brief 34/2004, issued on 15 December 2004.)

Direct marketing by insurance broker

[38.45] A company which carried on business as an insurance broker undertook direct marketing to potential customers. It received commission from other companies in the same group when customers took out policies with one of the group companies. Customs issued a ruling that the direct marketing services were standard-rated, and the company appealed, contending that they should be treated as exempt under the legislation then in force. The tribunal allowed the appeal, holding that the direct marketing consisted of 'services related to insurance transactions'. *Barclays Bank plc*, [1991] VATTR 466 (VTD 6469). (*Note.* See now, however, *VATA 1994, Sch 9, Group 2, Note 7*, introduced with effect from 19 March 1997.)

Pension fund trustees—contributions invested in insurance policies

[38.46] A company acted as trustee and administrator of a number of pension schemes. It invested the contributions paid by members of the schemes in insurance policies. It did not account for VAT on the fees which it received for this, and Customs issued a ruling that they were standard-rated. The tribunal dismissed the company's appeal, holding that the company was trading as a principal and was the person receiving the benefits of the insurance, rather than the provider of the insurance. It was making a single composite supply of trusteeship and administrative services, which did not qualify for exemption. *Federated Pensions Services Ltd*, [1992] VATTR 358 (VTD 8932).

Company formed by insurance brokers

[38.47] A number of insurance brokers established a limited company (C) to devise new insurance products and to conduct negotiations with insurers for the underwriting of such products. C did not account for VAT on its supplies. Customs issued a ruling that the supplies were standard-rated, and C appealed, contending that the supplies should be treated as exempt under the legislation then in force. The tribunal accepted this contention and allowed the appeal. *Countrywide Insurance Marketing Ltd*, [1993] VATTR 277 (VTD 11443). (*Note.* See now, however, *VATA 1994, Sch 9, Group 2, Note 7*, introduced with effect from 19 March 1997.)

Arrangements for provision of travel insurance

[38.48] A company (C) acted as an advertising agent for ferry operators. It also arranged travel insurance for the ferry operators with an insurance company. It received commission from the insurance company, and did not account for VAT on this, considering that it was exempt. Customs issued on the basis that the commission did not qualify for exemption, since C did not itself make any arrangements with the customers of the ferry operators. The tribunal allowed C's appeal, holding that its services qualified for exemption under the legislation then in force. *Curtis Edington & Say Ltd*, LON/93/1651A (VTD 11699). (*Note.* For Customs' practice following this decision, see News Release 52/94, issued on 15 December 1994. See also *VATA 1994, Sch 9, Group 2, Note 7*, introduced with effect from 19 March 1997.)

Insurance of central heating systems

[38.49] A company (D) carried on business as heating engineers, installing and maintaining domestic central heating systems. It operated a service plan in conjunction with a leading insurance company, whereby it charged customers an annual fee of £99 and paid £54 of this to the insurance company, which then issued insurance certificates indemnifying the customers against any charges in the event of the equipment breaking down within twelve months. D treated the whole of the £99 as exempt from VAT. Customs issued a ruling that only the £54 paid to the insurance company was exempt. D appealed. The tribunal allowed the appeal in part, holding that the £54 paid to the insurance company was wholly exempt, and that a proportion of the £45 which D retained should also be attributed to the making of arrangements for the supply of insurance, and thus as qualifying for exemption. The tribunal chairman expressed the opinion that, on the evidence, £67.50 should be treated as exempt and £31.50 as taxable. *Domestic Service Care Ltd*, MAN/93/163 (VTD 11869).

Exclusivity payment by insurance company

[38.50] A company (H) received a payment from an insurance company (E) in return for granting E the exclusive right to provide insurance to its members. H did not account for output tax on the payment. Customs issued an assessment, and H appealed, contending firstly that it had not made any supply to E, and alternatively that the payment was exempt from VAT under the legislation then in force. The tribunal rejected these contentions and dismissed

H's appeal, holding that the payment was consideration for a supply of services which did not qualify for exemption. *The British Horse Society Ltd*, MAN/98/736 (VTD 16204).

Sale of cars—whether a separate supply of insurance

[38.51] Two associated companies, which carried on business as car dealers, submitted claims for substantial repayments of output tax. The Commissioners repaid a small percentage of the amount claimed by one of the companies, but rejected the bulk of the claims, most of which related to supplies of 'free insurance' (i.e. insurance supplied to purchasers of cars for no extra charge). The Ch D dismissed the companies' appeals. Blackburne J held that there was a single supply and that the insurance element of the supply was ancillary to the supply of the car. Accordingly, the companies were required to account for VAT on the full invoice price. *Peugeot Motor Co plc v C & E Commrs; Citroen UK Ltd v C & E Commrs*, Ch D [2003] STC 1438; [2003] EWHC 2304 (Ch).

Estate agents arranging for provision of financial advice to clients

[38.52] See *Wright Manley Ltd*, 27.39 FINANCE.

39

International Services

The cases in this chapter are arranged under the following headings.

Zero-rating (VATA 1994, Sch 8, Group 7)   39.1
Reverse charge on services received from abroad (VATA 1994,
s 8, Sch 5)   39.4

NOTE

With effect from 1 January 1993, revised provisions covering the place of supply of services were introduced by the *VAT (Place of Supply of Services) Order 1992 (SI 1992/3121)*, and *VATA 1983, Sch 5, Group 9* was substituted by the *VAT (International Services & Transport) Order 1992 (SI 1992/3223)*. The current zero-rating provisions are contained in *VATA 1994, Sch 8, Group 7*. Many supplies which would have been treated as zero-rated before 1 January 1993 are now treated as taking place outside the UK, and thus outside the scope of UK VAT.

Zero-rating (VATA 1994, Sch 8, Group 7)

Stud fees paid for servicing of mare

[39.1] A company which owned a stud farm in the UK arranged for a mare, which was owned by a non-resident, to be serviced by a stallion at the stud. The company did not account for VAT on the consideration paid by the owner of the mare, treating it as wholly zero-rated under what is now *VATA 1994, Sch 8, Group 7, Item 1*. The Commissioners issued an assessment charging tax on part of the consideration, on the basis that it was attributable to the keep of the mare and did not qualify for zero-rating. The tribunal allowed the company's appeal, holding that there was a single supply of the servicing of the mare. The mare constituted 'goods' and the stallion's services constituted 'work carried out' within what is now *Item 1*, so that the whole of the consideration qualified for zero-rating. *Banstead Manor Stud Ltd*, [1979] VATTR 154 (VTD 816).

Diplomatic services—whether within Group 7, Item 2

[39.2] A company owned and maintained properties which were used as the official residences of the Bophutatswana Government in the UK. The premises were used to encourage tourism and investment in Bophutatswana by UK residents. The company did not account for tax on the consideration paid by the Bophutatswana Government, and the Commissioners issued an assessment charging output tax. The company appealed, contending that its services consisted of the making of arrangements for supplies of tourism and financial services which would take place in Bophutatswana, and were therefore zero-rated under what is now what is now *VATA 1994, Sch 8, Group 7, Item 2*. The tribunal dismissed the appeal, holding that the company was providing 'a single supply of services of the sort that would be supplied by an accredited diplomatic mission', but the QB remitted the case to the tribunal for rehearing, holding that the company was making multiple supplies which the tribunal had wrongly treated as a single supply. The CA upheld the QB decision, holding that it was essential to analyse the individual supplies of goods and services in order to determine how the money paid by the Bophutatswana Government should be apportioned between them. *Bophutatswana National Commercial Corporation Ltd v C & E Commrs*, CA [1993] STC 702. (*Note*. There was no further public hearing of the appeal.)

Charity assisting adoption of children from outside UK

[39.3] In the case noted at **33.67** HEALTH AND WELFARE, a charity undertook 'home studies' to help parents resident in the UK obtain permission to adopt children from outside the UK. The Commissioners issued a ruling that the charity's services were standard-rated. The charity appealed, contending that they should be treated as zero-rated under *VATA 1994, Sch 8, Group 7, Item 2(c)*. The tribunal rejected this contention and dismissed the appeal, observing that such supplies would only qualify for zero-rating if they consisted of the making of arrangements for a supply outside the EC, whereas the relevant supplies here took place inside the UK, where the parents were resident. *Parents and Children Together*, LON/00/1146 (VTD 17283).

Reverse charge on services received from abroad (VATA 1994, s 8, Sch 5)

VATA 1994, Sch 5 para 2—definition of 'advertising services'

[39.4] In 1991 and 1992 a trader distributed envelopes, containing information about a lottery, for a Netherlands company. He did not account for tax on his receipts for these services. The Commissioners issued an assessment charging tax on them, and he appealed, contending that his services were within the definition of 'advertising services' (and were thus zero-rated under the legislation then in force). The tribunal dismissed his appeal, holding that he was supplying 'distribution and delivery services', rather than advertising services. *P Lawrence (t/a PLC)*, LON/94/1233A (VTD 13092).

[39.5] See also *Austrian National Tourist Office*, **62.497** SUPPLY; *Miller Freeman Worldwide plc*, **62.514** SUPPLY; *International Trade & Exhibitions J/V Ltd*, **62.526** SUPPLY, and *John Village Automotive Ltd*, **62.527** SUPPLY.

Validity of VAT (Place of Supply of Services) Order

[39.6] See *Diversified Agency Services Ltd*, **62.495** SUPPLY.

VATA 1994, Sch 5 para 3—services of consultants

[39.7] A French company acquired a UK subsidiary, and supplied management services relating to 'new consolidation systems' and 'group structure re-organisation'. The Commissioners issued an assessment on the basis that the services were 'services of consultants', within *VATA 1994, Sch 5 para 3*, so that the UK subsidiary was liable to account for tax under the 'reverse charge' provisions of *VATA 1994, s 8*. The company appealed, contending that the relevant supplies were not 'services of consultants' and that the place of supply was in France, so that there should be no liability to UK VAT. The tribunal rejected this contention and dismissed the appeal, holding on the evidence that the relevant services were 'of a strategic, rather than a clerical or administrative nature', and were therefore 'services of consultants', within *Sch 5 para 3*. *Vision Express Ltd*, MAN/99/719 (VTD 16848).

[39.8] A trader supplied production services to customers in the film industry. He agreed to supply some photographs to a US company, to be used as advertising material. He did not account for tax on this supply. The Commissioners issued a ruling that the supply was taxable in the UK, and he appealed, contending that he was acting as a 'consultant', within *VATA 1994, Sch 5 para 3*, so that the place of supply was in the USA, where the recipient belonged. The tribunal accepted this contention and allowed H's appeal, holding that 'film directors and producers are clearly within the term "consultants" and "consultancy services"'. *I Hopkins*, EDN/01/201 (VTD 18572).

[39.9] See also *MEP Research Services Ltd*, **62.499** SUPPLY; *Mohammed*, **62.500** SUPPLY; *Zurich Insurance Company*, **62.506** SUPPLY, and *Cuthbert*, **62.533** SUPPLY.

VATA 1994, Sch 5 para 3—engineering services

[39.10] See *Hutchvision Hong Kong Ltd*, **62.488** SUPPLY.

VATA 1994, Sch 5 para 3—services of lawyers

[39.11] A company (M) acted as a professional body for doctors and dentists. It provided support to its members when they faced legal claims against them. Most of its supplies were exempt from VAT. In some cases, it paid for legal services provided outside the UK. It did not account for VAT on these supplies. In January 2008 HMRC issued a ruling, backdated for three years, that M was required to account for VAT on these services under *VATA 1994, s 8*. M applied for judicial review, contending that the ruling should not have been backdated, as it had been told in 1998 that it did need to account for VAT on these supplies. The QB dismissed the application for judicial review. Sales J accepted HMRC's contention that the advice which Customs had given in 1998 was not binding because M had not 'presented the full relevant facts'. *R (oao Medical Protection Society Ltd) v HMRC*, QB 2009, [2010] STC 555; [2009] EWHC 2780 (Admin).

VATA 1994, Sch 5 para 3—services of accountants

[39.12] See *WH Payne & Co*, 62.536 SUPPLY.

VATA 1994, Sch 5 para 3—data processing

[39.13] See *Talent & Production Services Ltd*, 62.531 SUPPLY, and *Laurentian Management Services Ltd*, 62.532 SUPPLY.

VATA 1994, Sch 5 para 3—supplies of information

[39.14] See *AC Tours v HMRC*, 62.498 SUPPLY.

VATA 1994, Sch 5 para 3—exclusion of services relating to land

[39.15] See *Brodrick Wright & Strong Ltd*, 62.510 SUPPLY, *Mechanical Engineering Consultants Ltd*, 62.511 SUPPLY, and *Aspen Advisory Services Ltd*, 62.513 SUPPLY.

Payroll services—whether within VATA 1994, Sch 5 para 3

[39.16] See *Fairpay Ltd*, 62.486 SUPPLY.

VATA 1994, Sch 5 para 5—definition of 'financial services'

[39.17] See *Gardner Lohman Ltd*, 62.538 SUPPLY, and *Culverpalm Ltd*, 62.539 SUPPLY.

VATA 1994, Sch 5 para 6—definition of 'supplies of staff'

[39.18] See *Strollmoor Ltd*, 62.482 SUPPLY, and *American Institute of Foreign Study (UK) Ltd*, 62.541 SUPPLY.

VATA 1994, Sch 5 para 7—'goods other than means of transport'

[39.19] See *BPH Equipment Ltd*, 62.543 SUPPLY.

40

Invoices and Credit Notes

The cases in this chapter are arranged under the following headings.

Whether documents to be treated as VAT invoices (VAT Regulations 1995, reg 14)

General principles	**40.1**
Documents held to constitute valid invoices	**40.3**
Documents held not to constitute valid invoices	**40.21**

Input tax reclaimed without invoices (VAT Regulations 1995, reg 29)

Cases where the appellant was successful	**40.62**
Cases where the appellant was unsuccessful	**40.69**

Rounding of VAT on invoices | **40.82**

Credit notes

Whether credit note effective for VAT purposes	**40.85**
Miscellaneous	**40.107**

Whether documents to be treated as VAT invoices (VAT Regulations 1995, reg 14)

General principles

Incomplete invoices

[40.1] See *Jeunehomme v Belgian State*, 22.471 EUROPEAN COMMUNITY LAW.

Invoices issued in names of deregistered companies

[40.2] See *Phillips v HMRC*, 62.349 SUPPLY.

Documents held to constitute valid invoices

Invoices issued one day prior to receivership—whether valid

[40.3] A company issued a set of invoices to British Telecom on 15 September 1992. It went into receivership on the following day, and subsequently went into liquidation. The Commissioners formed the opinion that, because British Telecom operated a 'self-billing' system, the invoices were not effective, and that the supplies in question had not taken place until after the company had gone into receivership, so that the tax chargeable was recoverable from the receivers. The company appealed, contending that the invoices were genuine, so that the tax was recoverable as a debt in the liquidation. The tribunal accepted this contention and allowed the appeal. The tribunal chairman (Mr. de Voil, sitting alone) stated that the self-billing procedure was 'a gross violation of the integrity of the VAT system' and 'a dangerous procedure' which 'should be strictly controlled and policed'. The fact that a customer operated a 'self-billing' system did not oblige a supplier to refrain from issuing a normal invoice. *UDL Construction plc (in administrative receivership and compulsory liquidation)*, [1995] VATDR 396 (VTD 13714).

Invoices prepared by customer on behalf of supplier

[40.4] A company (W) carried on business as steel constructional engineers. It agreed that a newly formed company (B) should do work for it as a subcontractor. The agreement was with M who held himself out as a director of B. B was registered for VAT but had no stationery or invoices of its own and, at M's request, W had duplicate invoices printed for B. The work done by B was costed and agreed weekly. An employee of W then prepared a duplicate invoice for B showing the amount due inclusive of VAT, paid this amount to M and retained the top copy of the invoice. The Commissioners refused to accept the invoices as evidence of the tax borne for input tax purposes, and assessed W for the tax on the ground that this was a case of 'self-billing' for which the company had not obtained the Commissioners' approval as was required by what is now *VAT Regulations 1995 (SI 1995/2518), reg 13*. The tribunal allowed W's appeal. Although the tribunal accepted the evidence for the Commissioners that B had not accounted for the tax and could not now be traced, it also accepted W's evidence as to what took place. This was not a case of 'self-billing' as the invoices had been printed and prepared on behalf of B. *Weldstruct Ltd*, [1977] VATTR 101 (VTD 374). (*Note*. Compare the cases noted at **40.56** to **40.60** below.)

[40.5] A similar decision was reached in *Ocean Leisure International Ltd*, MAN/94/147 (VTD 13169).

Invoices issued in wrong name

[40.6] A wholesaler (B) wished to obtain a credit account with a manufacturing company (G Ltd) but was unable to do so. G's products were in great demand and B arranged with some of G's sales representatives that goods which he required should be ordered in the name of, and invoiced and delivered to, an existing customer. The representative then collected the goods with the invoice and delivered them to B who handed the representative a cheque drawn in favour of G Ltd. It was stated that a number of wholesalers, unable to open an account with G, had entered into similar arrangements. B deducted the tax on the invoices as input tax and appealed against an assessment withdrawing the deduction. The tribunal allowed the appeal, holding that the goods had been supplied to B and the invoices were valid tax invoices. *AL Booth*, [1977] VATTR 133 (VTD 385).

[40.7] A sole trader reclaimed input tax in respect of invoices made out to a company of which he was a director, and which had a similar name to his trading name. The Commissioners issued an assessment to recover the tax but the tribunal allowed the trader's appeal, holding on the evidence that the invoices related to supplies made to the trader, that the incorrect insertion of the company's name on the invoices was a clerical error by the supplier, and that in the circumstances it would be unreasonable to reject the trader's claim to input tax. *JE Morgan (t/a Wishmore Morgan Investments)*, LON/86/165 (VTD 2150).

[40.8] See also *Hamstead Holdings Ltd*, 1.30 AGENTS, and *Crompton Enterprises Ltd*, 36.41 INPUT TAX.

Invoices bearing false VAT number

[40.9] A company (M) purchased two items of heavy earth-moving equipment and deducted input tax on the purchases. The invoices bore fictitious VAT numbers and the addresses stated on the invoices were false. The Commissioners therefore disallowed the input tax claimed on the purchases. The tribunal allowed M's appeal, holding that the vendors were clearly taxable persons since the value of the items in question was in excess of the registration limits. On the evidence, M was held not to be in any way party to the false invoices. *Morshan Contractors Ltd*, MAN/84/202 (VTD 1861). (*Note*. A subsequent tribunal specifically declined to follow this decision in *Pride & Leisure Ltd*, 40.28 below.)

[40.10] The proprietor of an off-licence reclaimed input tax in respect of invoices which bore a false VAT number and did not show the name or address of the supplier. The Commissioners issued an assessment to recover the tax, and the trader appealed, contending that the invoices recorded genuine transactions. At the hearing of the appeal the trader produced copies of delivery notes relating to the transactions, together with his chequebook stubs and copies of his bank statements. He stated in evidence that he had contacted the supplier who had refused to provide signed invoices, and that he was no longer dealing with the supplier in question. The tribunal allowed the appeal, finding that the invoices recorded genuine transactions and holding that the trader was entitled to credit for the input tax. *GN Chavda (t/a Hare Wines)*, LON/92/97 (VTD 9895).

[40.11] A company engaged a contractor to erect a building comprising four industrial units. Payment was made in cash on a weekly basis, and at the completion of the work the contractor issued an invoice showing a total charge of £33,100 plus VAT of £4,965. The company paid the balance due, and reclaimed the £4,965 as input tax. The Commissioners discovered that the registration number on the invoice was false and that the contractor was not registered for VAT. They therefore rejected the company's input tax claim. The company appealed. The tribunal allowed the appeal, holding that since the contractor's turnover clearly exceeded the registration threshold of *Sch 1 para 1*, he was a 'taxable person' and the company was entitled to credit for the input tax. *Ellen Garage (Oldham) Ltd*, [1994] VATTR 392 (VTD 12407). (*Note*. The tribunal's reasoning was specifically disapproved in the subsequent cases of *Hargreaves (UK) plc*, 36.661 INPUT TAX, and *Ahmed*, 40.37 below. In *Ahmed*, the tribunal held that 'the only way in which a taxpayer can claim a deduction for input tax is to satisfy specific evidential requirements which have built in to them a measure of discretion conferred on the Commissioners'.)

Authenticity of invoices disputed

[40.12] The Commissioners issued an assessment to recover input tax reclaimed by a company (S) trading as a coin dealer. The trader who had issued the invoices had been registered in a false name, and had been convicted and fined for this. The Commissioners formed the view that S was a party to the deception, and that the invoices were not authentic. The tribunal allowed

S's appeal, holding that the Commissioners had not proved that S was implicated in any deception. *Stewart Ward (Coins) Ltd*, LON/85/548 (VTD 2108, 2134). (*Notes.* (1) For a preliminary application in this case, see **2.224** APPEALS. (2) *Dicta* of the tribunal were disapproved by a subsequent tribunal in *Halil*, **2.235** APPEALS.)

[40.13] Two companies (L and C) reclaimed input tax in respect of substantial purchases of precious metals from a sole trader (F). F had previously been registered for VAT, but had changed his address without notifying the Commissioners, and his registration had been cancelled. He had issued VAT invoices in respect of the transactions, but had not accounted for the VAT, and had subsequently been convicted for cheating the public revenue and sentenced to two years' imprisonment. The Commissioners formed the opinion that the directors of L and C had been aware that F did not intend to account for VAT on the transactions, and had been involved in a conspiracy to cheat the public revenue. They were convicted and their convictions were upheld by the CA (see **49.28** PENALTIES: CRIMINAL OFFENCES). The Commissioners issued assessments to recover the input tax which L and C had reclaimed. L and C appealed, contending that the invoices recorded transactions which had actually taken place and that they were entitled to credit for the input tax even though F had not in fact paid the VAT to the Commissioners. The tribunal allowed the appeals, finding that the transactions had actually taken place and that F had been a taxable person at the time of the transactions, even though his registration had wrongly been cancelled. VAT was therefore chargeable on the transactions, and L and C were entitled to credit for the input tax. *Libdale Ltd; Clycol Precious Metals Ltd*, [1993] VATTR 425 (VTD 11543).

[40.14] A partnership (R) arranged for a local building firm to refurbish its bar and restaurant premises. It claimed input tax of £21,334 in respect of the work. Customs subsequently discovered that the building firm had only accounted for VAT of £14,149. R produced a document issued by the building firm, which gave the firm's VAT number, but did not include the word 'invoice'. The building firm informed Customs that this document had been an estimate rather than an invoice. Customs therefore issued an assessment to recover the balance of the input tax which R had claimed. R appealed. The tribunal reviewed the evidence in detail and allowed the appeal, finding that R had paid the disputed amounts to the building firm, and holding that the disputed document should be treated as a valid VAT invoice even though it did not include the word 'invoice'. *The Orange Rooms*, LON/04/970 (VTD 19133).

[40.15] A company (M) registered for VAT with effect from 1 May 2007. In its first return, it reclaimed input tax in respect of supplies allegedly made by three different suppliers, none of which had accounted for VAT. HMRC rejected the claim on the basis that there was no evidence that the supplies had actually taken place, and that M had failed to produce the evidence required by a direction under *VAT Regulations, reg 29(2)*. M appealed. The tribunal reviewed the evidence in detail and dismissed the appeal with regard to two of the three suppliers, finding that the purported supplies 'never took place'. However the tribunal allowed the appeal with regard to the supplies made by the other supplier (B), finding that these supplies had taken place and that HMRC's purported direction under *reg 29(2)* was ineffective. Judge Poole held that 'the fact that (B) itself may not have accounted for the VAT is of no relevance, in the absence of evidence that the Appellant knew or ought to have known that the VAT due to HMRC from (B) would go unpaid as a result of fraud'. He also held that it was not 'open to HMRC to give directions pursuant to the proviso to *regulation 29(2)* after the event', since 'the whole scheme of VAT is that a right of deduction of input tax arises when the deductible input tax becomes chargeable'. *Maliha Group Ltd v HMRC*, [2011] UKFTT 10 (TC), TC00887.

[40.16] See also *Tom Wilson (Tobacco) Ltd*, 36.626 INPUT TAX, and *Faith Clothing Ltd*, 52.365 PENALTIES: MISDECLARATION.

Self-billing—subcontractor producing false registration certificate

[40.17] A company reclaimed input tax on payments made to a subcontractor under a self-billing arrangement. The subcontractor had produced a false registration certificate and did not account for the tax. The Commissioners rejected the claim but the tribunal allowed the company's appeal, holding that the tax was allowable since the subcontractor was a 'taxable person'. *Deeds Ltd*, LON/82/20 (VTD 1500). (*Note.* For another issue in this case, see 2.278 APPEALS.)

Invoice issued by deregistered supplier

[40.18] A trader (P) reclaimed input tax of £1,750 on the purchase of a vehicle. The supplier had previously been registered for VAT, but had subsequently deregistered. No VAT number was shown on the invoice, although P had obtained the supplier's old VAT number. The Commissioners issued an assessment to recover the tax, but the tribunal (Mr. Porter, sitting alone) allowed P's appeal, holding that the Commissioners ought to have exercised their discretion to treat the invoice as a VAT invoice. *T Postlethwaite (t/a TP Transport)*, MAN/96/930 (VTD 14925). (*Note.* No other cases were cited in the decision. With regard to supplies received from deregistered traders, compare *Direct Drilling*, 40.35 below; *Ahmed*, 40.37 below, and the cases noted at 40.36 below. With regard to the nature of the tribunal's jurisdiction, compare the QB decision in *Kohanzad*, 40.71 below. With regard to the Commissioners' power to require production of an original invoice, see also *Reisdorf v Finanzamt Köln-West*, 22.472 EUROPEAN COMMUNITY LAW.)

[40.19] A company (L) which operated a recycling business reclaimed input tax of more than £1,200,000 relating to several invoices purportedly issued by deregistered traders, which had been the subject of investigations relating to MTIC fraud. HMRC rejected the claims and L appealed. The tribunal allowed the appeal, finding that the goods referred to in the invoices had genuinely existed and that the supplies had actually taken place. Judge Porter held that HMRC should have exercised their discretion to accept the invoices as valid. *London Wiper Co Ltd v HMRC*, [2011] UKFTT 445 (TC), TC01298.

Company failing to reclaim input tax within three-year time limit

[40.20] See *Innings Telecom Europe Ltd*, 62.416 SUPPLY.

Documents held not to constitute valid invoices

Contractor reclaiming input tax on invoices made out to customer

[40.21] A kitchen fitter arranged for a retailer to supply kitchen units to his customers. The retailer sold the units directly to the customers and invoiced them accordingly. The fitter retrieved the invoices from the customers and reclaimed input tax on them. Customs issued an assessment to recover the tax. The tribunal dismissed the fitter's appeal, holding that the goods had been supplied to the customers rather than to the fitter, and that he was not entitled to reclaim the input tax. *M Perks*, MAN/82/228 (VTD 1556).

[40.22] A construction company (D) had agreed to carry out certain services for a bank which had granted it a loan facility. D reclaimed input tax in respect of six invoices made out to the bank. Three of these were issued by surveyors, one by a firm of valuers, and two by a firm of solicitors. Customs issued an assessment to recover the tax. D appealed, contending that it had paid for the supplies in question and that the bank was acting as its agent. The tribunal dismissed the appeal, holding that there was no evidence that the bank had agreed to act as an agent. Since the invoices were made out to the bank, D had no right to reclaim the input tax in question. *Dalesid Ltd*, LON/90/1941 (VTD 9147).

Customer reclaiming input tax on invoices made out to contractor

[40.23] A married couple arranged for an unregistered builder to convert a barn into living accommodation. They subsequently reclaimed input tax in respect of some invoices which were made out to the builder. Customs rejected the claim and they appealed to the tribunal. The tribunal dismissed the appeal, holding that the supplies of goods in question had been made to the builder, so that the couple were not entitled to reclaim the tax. *Mr & Mrs Barnes*, MAN/05/077 (VTD 19407).

[40.24] A hairdresser (B) arranged for an unregistered trader (C) to refurbish his salon. He subsequently reclaimed input tax in respect of invoices which were addressed to C. Customs issued an assessment to recover the tax, and B appealed. The tribunal dismissed the appeal, holding that the relevant supplies had been made to C, so that B was not entitled to reclaim the tax. *K Bradshaw*, MAN/06/898 (VTD 20498). (*Note.* Costs were awarded to Customs.)

Invoices made out to associated company

[40.25] An appeal was dismissed in a case where a sole trader reclaimed input tax in respect of invoices made out to an associated company. The tribunal observed that 'although the particulars listed are onerous, there are sound reasons why claims for input tax should be supported by proper documentation. The name and address of the person to whom goods or services are supplied is of considerable importance'. *A Collins (t/a Inta Colour Brochures)*, LON/90/937X (VTD 6491).

[40.26] Similar decisions were reached in *Tortoise Factory Units Ltd*, LON/89/712 (VTD 4932); *JW Gavacan*, LON/94/2776A (VTD 13670), and *Herbert*, **36.147** INPUT TAX.

Invoice bearing false VAT number

[40.27] A trader reclaimed input tax in respect of two invoices bearing false VAT numbers and issued in the names of unregistered traders. The Commissioners issued an assessment to recover the tax and the tribunal dismissed the trader's appeal. *FP Spain*, MAN/83/147 (VTD 1555).

[40.28] A similar decision was reached in a subsequent case where the tribunal observed that 'a request for payments in cash in the course of a substantial contract would have put any trader on enquiry' and observed that the company's 'failure to obtain a proper tax invoice from a properly registered trader (if this was the position of the contractor)' seemed 'remarkable'. *Pride & Leisure Ltd*, MAN/91/212 (VTD 6911).

[40.29] Similar decisions have been reached in a large number of subsequent cases. In the interests of space, such cases are not summarised individually in this book. For a list of such cases decided up to 31 December 2003, see Tolley's VAT Cases 2004.

Transfer of going concern

[40.30] A trader (J) purchased a retail video business as a going concern for £18,000. The vendor's solicitors advised J that the price included VAT. J therefore reclaimed the VAT fraction of the purchase price as input tax. Customs rejected the claim and J appealed, accepting that the business had been transferred as a going concern but contending that she should be allowed to reclaim the VAT which she had been charged by the vendor, and citing as authority a passage in the 'British VAT Reporter' (published by CCH). The tribunal rejected this contention and dismissed J's appeal, criticising the 'British VAT Reporter'. The chairman commented that the passage which J had cited as authority 'appears to me to contain a degree of misunderstanding', since 'if the vendor purports to charge VAT the sum paid is not, in fact, VAT, because the transaction is not one which attracts VAT'. Furthermore, the letter from the vendor's solicitors was not an invoice for VAT purposes. *KK Jalf*, MAN/90/260 (VTD 5767).

Purported supply between associated companies

[40.31] See *Morston Properties Ltd (No 2)*, 36.25 INPUT TAX, and the cases noted at 36.26 INPUT TAX to 36.28 INPUT TAX.

Purported transfer of goods from company to associated partnership

[40.32] See *LMB Holdings Ltd*, 36.29 INPUT TAX.

Invoices issued as part of 'carousel fraud'

[40.33] See *Senergy (UK) Ltd*, 36.104 INPUT TAX.

Purported transfer of goods from company to controlling director

[40.34] See *Corke*, 46.233 PARTIAL EXEMPTION.

Deregistered supplier

[40.35] A partnership (D) reclaimed input tax of £1,200 on the basis of an invoice issued by a deregistered partnership (M). Customs issued an assessment to recover the tax. The tribunal dismissed D's appeal, observing that the £1,200 was not VAT, but was in effect a premium charged by M, and that D's remedy was against M rather than against Customs. *Direct Drilling*, LON/93/401A (VTD 11071).

[40.36] Similar decisions were reached in *A Hussain (t/a Villa Bombay)*, LON/93/1853 (VTD 11961); *J McGowan*, MAN/87/143 (VTD 11967); *RN Gray (t/a RN Gray & Co)*, LON/93/1520A (VTD 12661); *Kellpak Ltd*, EDN/95/283 (VTD 14018); *Sundial International plc*, MAN/97/549 (VTD 16698); *Vickers Reynolds & Co (Lye) Ltd*, MAN/99/1088 (VTD 16965); *B & B Packaging*, LON/04/913 (VTD 18792) and *R Patel (t/a AF Fashions)*, MAN/03/214 (VTD 19246).

[40.37] A trader reclaimed input tax on invoices issued by a deregistered supplier. Customs rejected the claim. The tribunal allowed the trader's appeal in part, finding that the first two invoices had been issued before the supplier had been deregistered. However the tribunal dismissed the appeal with regard to subsequent invoices, holding that the fact that the supplier had remained a 'taxable person' was not conclusive, and that Customs were entitled to 'require some corroborative documents or other similar evidence of the specific transactions entered into'. The tribunal specifically disapproved the 1994 decision in *Ellen Garage (Oldham) Ltd*, **40.11** above, and held that 'the only way in which a taxpayer can claim a deduction for input tax is to satisfy specific evidential requirements which have built in to them a measure of discretion conferred on the Commissioners'. *M Ahmed (t/a New Touch)*, LON/04/1840 (VTD 20119).

[40.38] The decision in *Ahmed*, **40.37** above, was applied in the similar subsequent case of *Hurstbourne Properties Ltd v HMRC*, [2010] UKFTT 38 (TC), TC00352.

[40.39] See also *Bodyguard Workwear Ltd*, **62.51** SUPPLY.

Invoices in names of insolvent companies

[40.40] A clothing manufacturer reclaimed input tax in respect of alleged purchases from six companies which had been registered for VAT, but had become insolvent and had ceased trading. The Commissioners issued an assessment to recover the tax, and the tribunal dismissed the manufacturer's appeal. *Y Ali (t/a HAR Fashions)*, LON/00/805 (VTD 17814).

[40.41] Similar decisions were reached in *Agentmode Ltd*, LON/01/66 (VTD 18024, VTD 18101); *Platinum Clothing Ltd*, LON/03/1201 (VTD 19144); *Steel Windows Co Ltd*, MAN/04.291 (VTD 19158); *Retro (Scotland) Ltd*, EDN/04/163 (VTD 19529); *Base Interactive Ltd*, [2007] VATDR 463 (VTD 20437), and *Justrading Ltd*, [2009] UKFTT 105 (TC), TC00073.

Unregistered supplier

[40.42] A company (C) reclaimed input tax on the basis of three invoices issued by a company which was not registered for VAT. The three invoices all included the words 'VAT number applied for', but the supplier had never registered for VAT and subsequently ceased trading without accounting for the tax. Customs issued an assessment to recover the tax and the tribunal dismissed C's appeal. *Active Clothing Ltd*, MAN/92/1714 (VTD 11363).

[40.43] Similar decisions were reached in *Dynamic Construction Ltd*, MAN/93/730 (VTD 12079); *JA Fashanu*, LON/94/2897 (VTD 13137); *JD Ogilvie (t/a O & D Consultants)*, LON/96/611 (VTD 14536) and *Goodluck Employment Services Ltd*, LON/05/440 (VTD 19766).

Invoices bearing word 'proforma'

[40.44] 'Proforma' invoices were held not to be valid tax invoices in *Harlech Estates Ltd*, MAN/90/986 (VTD 9548); *Northern 4 x 4 Centre Ltd*, MAN/06/42 (VTD 19811); *Ford Fuels Ltd*, **52.82** PENALTIES: MISDECLARA-TION; *South Caernarvon Creameries Ltd*, **52.122** PENALTIES: MISDECLARA-TION, and the cases noted at **52.123** PENALTIES: MISDECLARATION.

Application for payment not intended to constitute tax invoice

[40.45] See *ABB Power Ltd*, **62.414** SUPPLY, and *Finch*, **62.415** SUPPLY.

Purchases from retailers

[40.46] A company (M) purchased goods from local retailers, and reclaimed input tax on the evidence of till receipts. Customs issued an assessment to recover the tax and the tribunal dismissed M's appeal. *Mancumi & Sons Ltd*, LON/81/365 (VTD 1213).

[40.47] A similar decision was reached in *SMS Stores Ltd*, MAN/00/3895 (VTD 17226).

Sham invoices

[40.48] A company (M), which operated the Cash Accounting Scheme, issued an invoice to an associated company (F) in respect of future marketing services of more than £410,000. F, which did not operate the Cash Accounting Scheme, reclaimed input tax in respect of the amount charged on the invoice. Customs rejected the claim and the tribunal dismissed F's appeal, finding that there was 'very serious doubt that there was any possibility' of F ever being able to pay the amount charged by the invoice, and holding on the evidence that the 'arrangements between (M) and (F) were no more than a sham'. *FPV Ltd*, MAN/97/828 (VTD 15666). (*Note.* For another issue in this case, see **10.6** CASH ACCOUNTING SCHEME.)

Invoices described by issuer as fraudulent

[40.49] See *Sandell*, **62.174** SUPPLY.

Requirements of VAT Regulations, reg 14(1)(e)

[40.50] A company (B) which operated a 'cash and carry' warehouse reclaimed input tax of more than £150,000 in respect of purchases of drinks. Customs discovered that the relevant invoices were addressed to other businesses, rather than to B. They issued an assessment on the basis that the invoices failed to meet the requirements of *VAT Regulations 1995, reg 14(1)(e)*. B appealed, contending that the businesses named on the invoices had made the purchases on its behalf. The tribunal dismissed the appeal, applying the principles laid down by the CJEC in *Reisdorf v Finanzamt Köln-West*, **22.472** EUROPEAN COMMUNITY LAW. *Baba Cash & Carry Ltd*, LON/04/2315 (VTD 20416).

Requirements of VAT Regulations, reg 14(1)(g)

[40.51] A company (P) reclaimed input tax of more than £1,500,000 in respect of the purported purchase of large quantities of CPUs. Customs formed the opinion that the invoices which P held did not represent genuine transactions, and rejected the claim on the grounds that the invoices failed to meet the requirements of *VAT Regulations 1995, reg 14(1)(g)*. The tribunal reviewed the evidence in detail and dismissed P's appeal, finding that 'the deals into which (P) entered' did not involve 'what the invoices showed them as involving' and holding that the invoices were invalid 'since they did not give a "description sufficient to identify the goods", as required by *Regulation 14(1)(g)*'. *Pexum Ltd*, MAN/05/004 (VTD 20083).

[40.52] Similar decisions were reached in *F1 Promotions Ltd v HMRC*, [2010] UKFTT 159 (TC), TC00464 and *A1 Construction (Derby) Ltd v HMRC*, [2011] UKFTT 178 (TC), TC01047.

[40.53] A company (P) reclaimed input tax on the purported purchase of 480 Sony camcorders. HMRC rejected the claim on the basis that the relevant invoices failed to meet the requirements of *VAT Regulations 1995, reg 14(1)(g)*. The tribunal reviewed the evidence in detail and dismissed P's appeal, observing that 'from the figures provided by Sony UK in July 2003, Sony shipped 1,450 DCR-IP220 and DCr-IP220E camcorders throughout the world, including 370 to Europe. The appellant purported to purchase 480 of such camcorders on 21 July 2003 which represents over 33% of Sony's total worldwide shipment and over 129% of Sony's European shipments in that month. This creates problems of credibility and how a small business recently established could have acquired such great market share of worldwide and European markets in camcorders.' The tribunal also noted that the purchases 'form part of a supply chain leading to traders who had hijacked VAT numbers and defaulted on their liabilities to account for VAT on the supply of the goods in question. The companies through which the purchases are conducted, normally called "buffer" traders, lead to a missing trader who has imported the goods from another EC country and then fraudulently defaulted on the output tax due to the Commissioners.' Although HMRC had not alleged that P was aware of the fraud, the evidence indicated that P 'did not receive the supplies described on the invoices' and that 'the claimed supplies were not made'. *Plazadome Ltd v HMRC*, [2009] UKFTT 229 (TC), TC00179.

[40.54] A similar decision was reached in *Premier Joint Ventures Ltd v HMRC*, FTT [2010] UKFTT 135 (TC), TC00444.

'Invoice' claiming compensation for faulty goods

[40.55] A company (G) supplied another company (M) with a quantity of material for manufacturing wetsuits. M paid £20,700 plus VAT. Subsequently M discovered that the material was not waterproof. M issued G with a purported invoice, reclaiming £21,100 and the VAT. G reclaimed the VAT as input tax. Customs issued an assessment to recover the tax. The tribunal dismissed G's appeal, holding that the purported invoice did not relate to any taxable supply, and that the payment of compensation was outside the scope of VAT. *Galaxy Equipment (Europe) Ltd*, MAN/91/1457 (VTD 11415).

'Self-billing' invoices

[40.56] A company (C) issued a 'self-billing' invoice on behalf of a trader who had been deregistered. Customs issued an assessment to recover the tax. The tribunal dismissed C's appeal, holding that one of the conditions for the approval of the self-billing method had not been satisfied, so that the invoice was not effective. *Credit Ancillary Services Ltd*, [1986] VATTR 204 (VTD 2172).

[40.57] Similar decisions were reached in *Shani Fashion Industries Ltd*, LON/92/1483A (VTD 9789); *MJ Gleeson plc*, LON/94/1868A (VTD 13332); *British Teleflower Service Ltd*, [1995] VATDR 356 (VTD 13756) and *Outis Ltd*, LON/x (VTD 14864).

[40.58] An appeal was dismissed in a case where a company reclaimed input tax on the basis of 'self-billing' invoices, although it had not been authorised to operate a self-billing system. *Midland Plant & Scaffolding Ltd*, MAN/93/260 (VTD 11603).

[40.59] Similar decisions were reached in *MP Lonergan*, LON/95/639A (VTD 13305) and *D Spencer*, MAN/04/004 (VTD 19416).

[40.60] See also the cases noted at **52.275** to **52.277** PENALTIES: MISDECLA-RATION; *Beveridge*, **52.426** PENALTIES: MISDECLARATION, and the cases noted at **62.559** to **62.562** SUPPLY.

Associated partnerships—circular transactions

[40.61] See *CAL Ingot Manufacturers*, **52.367** PENALTIES: MISDECLARATION.

Input tax reclaimed without invoices (VAT Regulations 1995, reg 29)

Cases where the appellant was successful

Invoices destroyed accidentally

[40.62] A trader failed to produce invoices in support of a claim to input tax. The Commissioners issued an assessment to recover the tax, and the trader appealed, contending that the invoices had been accidentally burnt. The tribunal accepted the trader's evidence and allowed the appeal. *JJ Newman*, LON/79/32 (VTD 781, VTD 903). (*Note.* See now, however, the subsequent case of *Reisdorf v Finanzamt Köln-West*, **22.472** EUROPEAN COMMUNITY LAW, in which the CJEC ruled that *Article 22(3)* of the *EC Sixth Directive* conferred on Member States the power to require production of an original invoice in order to establish the right to deduct input tax.)

[40.63] A similar decision was reached in *Kleen Technologies International Ltd*, LON/80/66 (VTD 970). (*Note.* For the award of costs in this case, see **2.465** APPEALS.)

Invoices lost

[40.64] A partnership appealed against an assessment withdrawing an input tax credit, contending that the relevant tax invoices had been lost when one of the partners moved house, and hence were not available for inspection by a VAT officer on a subsequent normal control visit. The details had been entered in the firm's VAT book and these entries had been checked in detail by the firm's accountant, to whom the receipts and invoices had been produced. The tribunal allowed the appeal, holding that Customs had acted unreasonably in refusing to accept the firm's audited records, on the ground only that the original documentation was no longer available. *C Read & D Smith*, [1982] VATTR 12 (VTD 1188). (*Note.* See now, however, the note following *Newman*, 40.62 above.)

[40.65] The decision in *Read & Smith*, 40.64 above, was applied in the similar case of *D Wright*, LON/93/2720A (VTD 12451).

[40.66] At a control visit in December 1994, VAT officer discovered that a farmer did not hold invoices relating to input tax which he had claimed from 1992 to July 1994, and issued an assessment to recover the tax in question. The farmer appealed, contending that he had lost the invoices when he had changed his address in August 1994. The tribunal accepted his evidence and allowed the appeal for the periods from 1992 to June 1994, finding that at the time he had claimed the input tax, the farmer had held invoices as required by *Article 18(1)* of the *EC Sixth Directive*. The fact that he had subsequently lost the invoices did not deny him the right to reclaim the tax. *Kohanzad*, 40.71 below, was distinguished on the grounds that the tribunal there had not been satisfied that the claimant had ever possessed the invoices which he had claimed to have lost. The tribunal held that 'the issue whether, at the time of claiming the deduction of input tax, the appellant held the required documents (here invoices) is a question of fact to be determined by the tribunal on the evidence, the burden of proof being on the appellant'. If the assessing officer formed the view that 'the requisite documents were not in fact held at the relevant time, then he must go on to consider the exercise of the discretion under (*VAT Regulations 1995, reg 29**) to allow other documentary evidence if there was such evidence. However, the fact that, on appeal against the exercise of that discretion, an appellant must show that the Commissioners did not act reasonably, does not affect the fact that on the prior issue of whether he did hold the documents the tribunal has a full appellate jurisdiction.' (The appeal was dismissed with regard to the input tax relating to July 1994, on the grounds that the farmer had already lost the invoices at the time he had submitted the relevant return.) *MS Vaughan*, [1996] VATDR 95 (VTD 14050). (*Note.* See now the note following *Newman*, 40.62 above.)

Unregistered supplier—no invoice issued

[40.67] A company took delivery of a machine called a Yamazaki Machining Centre, for which it paid £122,500, plus purported VAT of £18,375, by banker's draft. The vendor failed to supply a VAT invoice, although it had previously been agreed that the price was inclusive of VAT. The company reclaimed the £18,375 as input tax. The Commissioners refused to allow the claim on the ground that no VAT invoice had been obtained and the machine had not been supplied by a taxable person. The tribunal allowed the company's appeal, holding on the evidence that the machine had been supplied by a taxable person and that the input tax was therefore allowable notwithstanding that an invoice had not been obtained. *Syston Tooling & Design Ltd*, MAN/89/119 (VTD 4553).

[40.68] See also *Angus MacKinnon Ltd*, **44.73** MOTOR CARS.

Cases where the appellant was unsuccessful

Invoices not produced by claimant

[40.69] The Commissioners discovered that a trader had reclaimed input tax without holding supporting invoices, and issued an assessment to recover the tax. The tribunal dismissed the trader's appeal, observing that 'the Commissioners have a discretion whether or not to accept evidence other than tax invoices' but holding that, on the evidence, the Commissioners had been justified in refusing to accept the claims in question. *S Montalbano*, LON/85/591 (VTD 2113). (*Note.* The decision in this case was approved by the QB in *Kohanzad*, **40.71** below.)

[40.70] The decision in *Montalbano*, **40.69** above, was applied in the similar cases of *Floyde Brothers*, LON/89/1530 (VTD 6765) and *DH Morgan*, LON/90/367X (VTD 6805).

[40.71] The Commissioners issued estimated assessments on a jeweller after Customs officers had discovered quantities of undeclared gold and Kruger-rands in his car. The jeweller appealed, contending that the assessments should be reduced to allow input tax on his purchases of the gold and Krugerrands in question. However, he failed to produce purchase invoices. The tribunal dismissed his appeal and the QB upheld this decision. Where an appellant failed to produce invoices, the Commissioners had a discretion as to whether to allow credit for input tax. Where they declined to allow such credit, the tribunal had a supervisory jurisdiction, the burden of proof being on the appellant to show that the Commissioners had acted unreasonably. On the evidence, the Commissioners had acted reasonably in rejecting the jeweller's claim. *A Kohanzad v C & E Commrs*, QB [1994] STC 967.

[40.72] Similar decisions were reached in *Miss Charlie Ltd*, LON/90/361 (VTD 9301); *C Glinski (t/a Redcliffe Precious Metals)*, LON/92/2752A & LON/93/169 (VTD 11300); *WFS Metals Ltd*, MAN/93/914 (VTD 12293;)*Templegate Accounting Services Ltd*, LON/96/43 (VTD 14446); *PJ & AJ Nicholas (t/a A & P Scaffolding)*, LON/98/894 (VTD 15898), and *Howes*, **36.642** INPUT TAX.

[40.73] The decision in *Kohanzad*, **40.71** above, was applied in a subsequent case in which the tribunal held that its jurisdiction in such appeals was supervisory rather than appellate. *Richmond Resources Ltd (in liquidation)*, LON/94/1496A (VTD 13435).

[40.74] Similar decisions, also applying *Kohanzad*, **40.71** above, were reached in *Sparrow (UK) Ltd*, LON/99/1085 (VTD 16642); *N O'Driscoll*,

LON/99/1265 (VTD 16941); *K Pharro (t/a KP Building Services)*, LON/00/648 (VTD 17041) and *Balmoral Ltd (No 2)*; MAN/05/768 (VTD 20677).

[40.75] The Commissioners discovered that a trader had reclaimed input tax without holding supporting invoices, and issued an assessment to recover the tax. The trader appealed, contending that he could not produce the invoices as his accountant was holding them as security for unpaid fees. The tribunal dismissed the appeal, holding that the trader had not produced evidence to justify the claim. *HR Jalota*, MAN/87/206 (VTD 2684). (*Note*. For an explanation of the circumstances in which an accountant may retain a client's records as security for unpaid fees, see *Woodworth v Conroy*, CA [1996] 1 All ER 107. The Ch D has held that the effect of *Companies Act 1985, s 221* is that an accountant cannot retain a company's sales invoices— see *DTC (CTC) Ltd v Gary Sargent & Co*, Ch D [1996] BCC 290.)

Invoices allegedly stolen

[40.76] A married couple traded in partnership as clothing retailers. The Commissioners discovered that they had reclaimed input tax without supporting invoices. They issued an assessment to recover this tax, and the partners appealed, contending that the invoices had been stolen from their car. The tribunal dismissed their appeal, observing that this was the second occasion on which the partners had claimed that records had been stolen and finding that the officer had reason for suspecting that the theft 'could have been invented for the purpose of avoiding production of the VAT records'. The tribunal chairman observed that 'the Commissioners should act in a way which will protect the revenue; they are a public body dispensing and receiving public money and they are accountable for that. For them to pay out money to an individual or firm when there was no evidence of entitlement to the money would be inconsistent with the discharge by them of their public duty'. *VK & Mrs U Dilawri (t/a East & West Textiles)*, MAN/91/632 (VTD 11409).

[40.77] The decision in *Dilawri*, 40.76 above, was applied in the similar subsequent cases of *JD Maloney*, LON/96/785 (VTD 14754) and *D Hudson*, MAN/97/1200 (VTD 15618).

[40.78] Similar decisions were reached in *WA Oloyede*, LON/93/1083A (VTD 11944); *Elegant Clothing (Blackburn) Ltd*, MAN/96/788 (VTD 14739), and *P Bennett & I Marshall (t/a Enerco)*, LON/00/998 (VTD 17520).

Invoices allegedly destroyed

[40.79] The Commissioners discovered that a trader had reclaimed input tax without holding supporting invoices, and issued an assessment to recover the tax. The trader appealed, contending that the invoices had been destroyed when his premises were flooded. The tribunal dismissed his appeal, holding that the Commissioners had not acted unreasonably in refusing to accept his claims. *JC Horton*, LON/90/837Z (VTD 7258).

Invoices not issued by supplier

[40.80] A company (N) reclaimed input tax in respect of a payment which it had made to a company which supplied registration marks, although it had received neither the registration mark in question nor a tax invoice. The Commissioners issued an assessment to recover the tax and the tribunal dismissed N's appeal, holding that although what is now *VAT Regulations 1995 (SI 1995/2518), reg 29* gave the Commissioners the right to accept claims for input tax without supporting invoices, the tribunal's jurisdiction in such cases was supervisory rather than appellate, and the Commissioners had not acted unreasonably in this case. *Newland Technical Services Ltd*, LON/92/1255A (VTD 9294). (*Note.* For other issues in this case, see **36.330** INPUT TAX and **52.94** PENALTIES: MISDECLARATION.)

Other cases

[40.81] There are a large number of other cases, which appear to raise no point of general importance, in which appeals against the disallowance of input tax have been dismissed on the grounds that the appellant has failed to provide sufficient evidence in support of the claim. In the interests of space, such cases are not included in this book.

Rounding of VAT on invoices

[40.82] A company which operated a hotel adopted a policy of rounding down fractions of a penny in respect of individual items included in invoices. The Commissioners issued an assessment on the basis that the company was only entitled to round down the total amount of tax included on any invoice, rather than individual items included within that invoice. The tribunal upheld the assessment and dismissed the company's appeal. *Catchlord Ltd*, [1985] VATTR 238 (VTD 1966).

[40.83] A retail company had accounted for VAT by rounding each invoice up or down to the nearest penny. In 2003 it adopted a policy of 'rounding down' each individual item within the invoice. Customs issued assessments on the basis that this method was incorrect, and had resulted in an underdeclaration of VAT. The tribunal upheld the assessments in principle, holding that 'the tax payable is not calculated exclusively by reference to individual supplies but by reference to all supplies in an accounting period'. Rounding only down 'will guarantee a wrong result in all cases whereas rounding both up and down will achieve as close to a perfect result as is possible.' Accordingly, the tax should have been accounted for 'with mathematical rounding both up and down'. *Topps Tiles plc*, [2006] VATDR 480 (VTD 19751).

[40.84] See also *Fiscale eenheid Koninklijke Ahold NV v Staatssecretaris van Financiën*, **22.562** EUROPEAN COMMUNITY LAW, and *JD Wetherspoon plc*, **22.563** EUROPEAN COMMUNITY LAW.

Credit notes

Whether credit note effective for VAT purposes

[40.85] A company (B) invoiced its parent company (U) for an amount described as 'service charges' including VAT. In accounting for its tax, U treated as input tax the whole of the tax on the amounts invoiced to it. In fact, most of the supplies made by U were exempt, so that it was entitled to deduct only a proportion of the tax. On discovering this, the Commissioners issued an assessment to recover input tax overdeducted up to March 1974. Thereupon B issued credit notes to U cancelling the service charges from April 1973 to October 1975, and took credit for the tax on the charges cancelled in its subsequent returns. The Commissioners considered that the credit notes were not valid for VAT purposes, and issued an assessment to recover the tax, against which B appealed. The tribunal allowed the appeal in part, holding that, to the extent that the 'service charges' represented payments to employees, B was acting as an agent for U and not as an independent principal, and that the credit notes were effective in respect of this outlay. Insofar as the service charge was for rent, rates and overheads of the head office building, there had been a taxable supply by B and the credit notes were ineffective. The tribunal held that a credit note was only effective for VAT purposes if it had been 'issued *bona fide* in order to correct a genuine mistake or overcharge, or to give a proper credit'. (The ascertainment of the figures was left for agreement by the parties.) *British United Shoe Machinery Co Ltd*, [1977] VATTR 187 (VTD 463).

[40.86] A firm of architects and surveyors invoiced a company for work carried out, and accounted for output tax of £373. However, the company subsequently went into liquidation without paying the amount invoiced. In July 1974 the firm thereupon issued a credit note for the amount invoiced and deducted the £373 in its next return. The Commissioners issued an assessment to recover the £373 and the tribunal dismissed the firm's appeal. Applying *dicta* in *British United Shoe Machinery Co Ltd*, **40.85** above, the credit note had not been issued in order to correct a genuine mistake or overcharge, and was therefore ineffective for VAT purposes. *Peter Cripwell & Associates*, CAR/78/131 (VTD 660).

[40.87] In 1980 a company (M) sold a machine to another company (E) for £45,910 plus VAT of £6,886, issuing a tax invoice for this amount. Under the terms of the sale, the whole of the VAT plus 20% of the £45,910 was payable on delivery of the machine, the remaining 80% carrying interest and being payable in instalments. E paid the deposit, the VAT and the first instalment, but failed to pay subsequent instalments and M repossessed the machine. E was then in receivership, and M sent the receiver a purported credit note for the amount originally invoiced, together with a purported invoice for £27,055 (including VAT of £3,122), for E's use of the machine. M submitted a VAT return which included the £3,122 as output tax and deducted the £6,886 as input tax. The Commissioners issued an assessment to recover the difference of £3,764, and the tribunal dismissed M's appeal, holding that the 'credit note' was not effective for tax purposes. *Mannesmann Demag Hamilton Ltd*, [1983] VATTR 156 (VTD 1437).

[40.88] A company (S) sold commercial vehicles to a finance company for subsequent resale to customers under hire-purchase agreements. The invoices which S issued to the finance company showed an inflated sale price (overvaluing old vehicles taken in part-exchange in order to meet the finance company's requirement for a minimum deposit). Subsequently S issued credit notes to the customers under the hire-purchase agreements, to correct the overcharge. The Commissioners issued an assessment on the basis that S was obliged to account for output tax on the full amount shown on the invoices which it had issued to the finance company. S appealed. The tribunal dismissed the appeal, holding that the supply had been to the finance company, not to the customer, and that the credit notes were not effective for VAT purposes. *Sheepcote Commercial (Vehicles) Ltd*, LON/86/334 (VTD 2378).

[40.89] The decision in *Sheepcote Commercial (Vehicles) Ltd*, **40.88** above, was applied in the similar subsequent case of *Senator Marketing Ltd*, LON/90/79Y (VTD 5598).

[40.90] A similar decision was reached in *Howletts (Autocare) Ltd*, MAN/94/483 (VTD 14467). (*Note*. Costs were awarded to the Commissioners.)

[40.91] A similar decision was reached in a case in which a company (F) trading as a car dealer agreed discounts with customers who purchased cars under hire-purchase agreements whereby legal ownership of the cars passed to the finance company involved in the transaction, but issued invoices to the finance company showing the gross undiscounted price and treating the discount as a deposit. F subsequently issued credit notes to the customers, and the Commissioners issued an assessment on the basis that the credit notes were ineffective for VAT purposes. The tribunal dismissed F's appeal, holding that the credit notes were ineffective since they had been issued to the customer whereas the relevant supply had been made to the finance company. *First County Garages Ltd*, LON/95/2962 (VTD 14417).

[40.92] There have been a large number of other cases where purported credit notes have been held to be ineffective for VAT purposes. In the interests of space, such cases are not listed individually in this book. For a list of such cases decided up to 31 December 2005, see Tolley's VAT Cases 2006. For cases where misdeclaration penalties were imposed, see *Engineering Building Services*, **52.251** PENALTIES: MISDECLARATION, and the cases noted at **52.252** PENALTIES: MISDECLARATION.

[40.93] In a case where the facts were complex, a number of credit notes had been issued in respect of management charges raised between associated companies for the use of capital. The Commissioners issued an assessment on the basis that the credit notes were not effective for VAT purposes. The tribunal reviewed the evidence in detail and allowed the company's appeal in part. *Laurence Scott Ltd*, [1986] VATTR 1 (VTD 2004).

[40.94] In 1979 a company issued invoices for fees including VAT of £4,960.49. The customer did not pay the fees and the company began legal proceedings. The proceedings were dismissed in 1987. The company then issued a credit note and reclaimed the VAT in its next quarterly return. The Commissioners issued an assessment to recover the tax, considering that the credit note had not been issued bona fide. The tribunal allowed the company's appeal, holding on the evidence that the money had not been due to the company in the first place. The credit note had been correctly issued to correct a genuine overcharge. *Cobojo Ltd*, MAN/89/746 (VTD 4055).

[40.95] A company which installed security alarm systems, under agreements which provided for continuing hire and maintenance of the systems, issued credit notes in cases where customers had left their premises without paying for the hire or maintenance. The Commissioners issued an assessment in respect of such credit notes, considering that they had been issued to write off bad debts and were not effective for VAT purposes. The company appealed. The tribunal allowed the company's appeal, holding that in cases where customers had left the premises it seemed reasonable to suppose that the systems in question would not have been hired or maintained. Accordingly, the credit notes had been issued in good faith and were effective for VAT purposes. *Securicor Granley Systems Ltd*, [1990] VATTR 9 (VTD 4575).

[40.96] The decision in *Securicor Granley Systems Ltd*, **40.95** above, was applied in a case where a company which fitted baby seats in cars had contracted to refund the price of the seat to any customers who returned the seat and the receipt after the fourth birthday of the child for whose use it was fitted. Where these conditions were fulfilled, the company issued credit notes. The tribunal held that there was a single transaction and that the credit notes had been issued in good faith and were effective for VAT purposes. *Kwik Fit (GB) Ltd*, [1992] VATTR 427 (VTD 9383). (*Note.* The tribunal's finding that there was a single transaction was questioned, and implicitly disapproved, in the subsequent case of *SJ Phillips Ltd*, **40.101** below.)

[40.97] A company in the motor trade offered customers a comprehensive repair service whereby it undertook to repair damaged cars and provided a substitute vehicle for the customer's use while his own vehicle was being repaired. The substitute car was provided without charge to the customer, but the company instructed the customer's solicitors to include in the relevant claim the amount of hire charges which it would otherwise have required the customer to pay. When the repairs had been completed, the customer was required to return the hire car and reclaim his own. An invoice was prepared for the amount of the hire charges, including VAT, and sent to the solicitors. Where the amount recovered was less than the amount included in the invoice (e.g. where the customer had been guilty of contributory negligence) the company prepared a credit note for the amount of the difference. The credit note was not sent to the solicitors, but was taken into account in computing the company's VAT liability. The Commissioners issued an assessment to recover the tax which was the subject of the credit notes, considering that they were not effective for VAT purposes and that the company should have claimed bad debt relief instead. The tribunal allowed the company's appeal in part, holding that the credit notes were valid in cases where it was subsequently agreed that the rate of charge was excessive. However, where the amount paid was less than the amount invoiced because of the customer's contributory negligence, or where the amount invoiced was reduced because the period of hire was subsequently agreed to have been excessive, the customer remained nominally liable to the company for the invoiced amount and the company should have claimed bad debt relief instead of issuing a credit note. Similarly, where the company had issued a credit note because it could not recover the invoiced amount from the third party, the credit note was not effective and the company should have claimed bad debt relief instead. *Barras (Garages) Ltd*, MAN/91/268 (VTD 6913).

[40.98] In a case where the facts were unusual, the tribunal held that two credit notes had been correctly issued, since the companies to whom they had been issued had not reclaimed the tax in question as input tax. *The Friary Electrical Co Ltd*, LON/91/2145 (VTD 7554). (*Note*. An appeal against a misdeclaration penalty was also allowed.)

[40.99] A married couple carried on an investment business in partnership, and were also directors of a limited company carrying on a similar business. Both the partnership and the company were registered for VAT. In 2006 the company sold two properties at a substantial profit. The couple wished to transfer this profit to the partnership, and arranged for the partnership to issue an invoice of £525,000 plus VAT in respect of 'management charges'. The partnership accounted for the VAT as output tax, and the company reclaimed it as input tax. Subsequently HMRC discovered that the company had made exempt supplies in respect of these properties, and issued a ruling that the company could not reclaim the input tax. Following this ruling, the partnership issued a credit note in respect of the 'management charges'. HMRC issued an assessment to recover the tax on the basis that the credit note was not effective for VAT purposes. The partnership appealed. The tribunal allowed the appeal, finding that a 'management charge' of £525,000 was 'completely disproportionate', that the couple had intended 'that the £525,000 should be released to the partnership as a dividend and by way of distribution of profits made on the sale of the properties', and that 'no taxable supply occurred'. *D & JE Newett (t/a Stirling Investments) v HMRC*, [2010] UKFTT 61 (TC), TC00374.

[40.100] See also *Lamdec Ltd*, 2.200 APPEALS; *Dixons Group plc*, **67.126** VALUATION, and *AEG (UK) Ltd*, **67.127** VALUATION.

Retail jewellers—treatment of credit notes

[40.101] A company traded as retail jewellers. It had a policy of allowing a customer to return an item, and issued such customers with a credit note which the customer could use to obtain another item of equivalent or greater value. The Commissioners issued a ruling that the original sale, and the company's subsequent acceptance of the credit note, were two separate supplies for VAT purposes. The company appealed, contending that it was entitled to treat the issue of the credit note as the cancellation of the original transaction. The tribunal reviewed the evidence in detail and dismissed the appeal in principle, holding that the company could only treat the transactions as a single transaction where there was a clear oral agreement between the company and the customer 'that the item can be returned, effectively as rejected, because it is not liked by the intended recipient'. However, in the majority of cases, there was no such oral agreement, and the issue of the credit note was 'a discretionary policy adopted by the company as a matter of goodwill', which was a separate transaction. *SJ Phillips Ltd*, LON/01/36 (VTD 17717). (*Note*. The tribunal gave the company three months 'to apply for a further hearing to give evidence that specific credit notes already in dispute' met the conditions for a valid credit note cancelling the first supply'. However, there was no further hearing of the appeal.)

Disputed credit note issued by supplier

[40.102] A company (G) supplied goods and services to another company (S) in 1974 and 1975. It invoiced S for the supply for an amount including VAT of £7,393. G duly accounted for this as output tax, and S deducted it as input tax. In 1978 Customs changed their practice and accepted that the relevant supplies should have been zero-rated. They allowed G to reclaim the £7,393, and G issued a credit note for that amount. However, S did not receive the credit note and was not aware of the credit until told of it by VAT officers at a meeting in January 1980. Meanwhile there had been court proceedings between G and S, as a result of which the credit note was 'commercially worthless'. Customs issued an assessment on S for the period ending 31 January 1980, seeking to recover the £7,393. The tribunal allowed the appeal, finding that S had never received the original credit note and holding that it was entitled to credit for the £7,393 and was 'under no duty to action this so-called credit note' which was 'of little or no commercial value'. *Silvermere Golf & Equestrian Centre Ltd*, [1981] VATTR 106 (VTD 1122). (*Note. Notice No 700, para 7.1* states that any VAT adjustment arising from the receipt of a credit or debit note 'must be made in the VAT account for the period in which you enter the adjustment in your business accounts'.)

[40.103] The decision in *Silvermere Golf & Equestrian Centre Ltd*, 40.102 above, was applied in a similar subsequent case where the Commissioners had issued an assessment to recover input tax which a company had deducted on receipt of an invoice, for which the supplier had purportedly issued a subsequent credit note. The tribunal found that the company had never received the credit note in question, and allowed its appeal against the assessment. *Highsize Ltd*, LON/90/945Y (VTD 7098).

[40.104] For a case in which a credit note issued by the receivers of a company was held to have been wrongly issued, and to be worthless, see *Wade*, **48.16** PAYMENT OF TAX.

[40.105] A VAT officer discovered that a company (R) had issued a credit note in respect of an alleged discount to one of its trade customers (W). However, W had not reduced his input tax to reflect the credit note. Customs issued an assessment on W to recover the tax. W appealed, contending that the credit note did not relate to his purchases from R, but related to wages which R had credited to his wife, whose name had appeared in R's wages records. The tribunal reviewed the evidence in detail, accepted this contention, and allowed W's appeal, finding that the 'so-called credit note' had not been issued 'to give (W) any credit', but 'to prevent (R) having to account for national insurance and PAYE tax on a fictitious salary'. *SE Adams (t/a Windows by Wise)*, LON/04/1613 (VTD 19218).

[40.106] For a case in which a credit note was held to have been correctly issued, so that the recipient was not entitled to credit for the relevant input tax, see *Brunel Motor Co Ltd*, **37.12** INSOLVENCY.

Miscellaneous

VAT Regulations 1995, reg 38—whether any decrease in consideration

[40.107] A company (M) had supplied goods to another company (S). S went into receivership, owing M more than £15,000. M repossessed goods to the value of this debt. In its return for the period ending December 1991, M deducted the output tax relating to the repossessed goods. The Commissioners issued an assessment to recover the tax, and M appealed, contending that the repossession amounted to a 'decrease in consideration' within what is now *VAT Regulations 1995 (SI 1995/2518), reg 38*. The tribunal dismissed M's appeal, holding that the repossession did not amount to a decrease in consideration. *Morley Electronic Fire Systems Ltd*, MAN/92/1119 (VTD 10957).

[40.108] A company made sales of bottled mineral water, on which it accounted for VAT. Following the introduction of the *VAT (Beverages) Order 1993 (SI 1993/2498)* with effect from 1 December 1993, it became aware that, although all such supplies were standard-rated after that date, some of its supplies could have been treated as zero-rated before that date, as the supplies were of natural mineral water which was not 'manufactured' and was not therefore excluded from zero-rating by the law previously in force. At first the Commissioners rejected the company's claim that any of the supplies had qualified for zero-rating, and the company had to lodge a formal appeal against a ruling that the sales had been standard-rated, but in September 1996, before the appeal had been heard by a tribunal, the Commissioners accepted the company's claim. In the meantime, the company agreed with three of its customers (all major retailers) that it would issue them with credit notes for the sums charged as VAT, together with invoices for approximately 85% of the sums as additional consideration for the original supplies. (The effect of this scheme was that the company would recover approximately 85% of the overpaid VAT and the customers would recover approximately 15%.) In its return for the period ending October 1996, the company reclaimed VAT of more than £2,000,000. The Commissioners considered that the effect of the three-year cap introduced by a Budget Resolution under *Provisional Collection of Taxes Act 1968* (and subsequently enacted by *FA 1997*) was that more than £926,000 of the amount claimed was not repayable. They therefore made a repayment of approximately £1,100,000. The company appealed, contending that its transactions with its customers constituted decreases in consideration for the original supplies, within *VAT Regulations 1995 (SI 1995/2518), reg 24*, so that it had been entitled to adjust its VAT account under *reg 38* and the balance of £926,000 was repayable accordingly. The tribunal rejected this contention and dismissed the appeal. Applying *dicta* of Lord Hope in *McMaster Scotland Stores Ltd*, **48.42** PAYMENT OF TAX, what is now *reg 38* 'is concerned only with the making of adjustments to the VAT account to reflect an increase or a decrease in consideration which includes an amount of tax chargeable on the supply'. The tribunal held that the consideration for the supplies in this case 'did not include an amount of VAT, with the consequence that the procedure under *regulation 38* is not available to the appellant and the appellant's claim fails'. The only way in which the company could claim repayment was under *VATA 1994, s 80. The Robinson Group of Companies Ltd*, MAN/97/348 (VTD 16081).

[40.109] A company (G) sold cars under hire-purchase agreements. In some cases, customers defaulted on the agreement, and G repossessed the cars and sold them for less than the original sale price. It claimed a VAT adjustment on the basis that there had been a decrease in consideration, within *VAT Regulations 1995 (SI 1995/2518), reg 38*. The Commissioners rejected the claim, considering firstly that the transaction was not within *reg 38*, and that G should have claimed bad debt relief under *VATA 1994, s 36*; and secondly that G had not submitted a credit note, as required by *reg 38*. The tribunal allowed G's appeal, holding that the transaction was an 'adjustment in the course of business', within *reg 38*, and that G had submitted sufficient documentation, since 'the overall effect of the relevant documents taken together has the same effect as a credit note would have had'. The Ch D upheld the tribunal decision. Field J held that *Article 11C1* of the *EC Sixth Directive* drew a distinction between a situation of 'refusal or total or partial non-payment' and a situation 'where the price is reduced'. The facts here fell within the latter category. The consideration for the supply had been reduced so that relief was due under *reg 38*. Furthermore, *VAT Regulations 1995, reg 24* did not require G 'to issue a document to the hirer post-termination setting out the decrease in the consideration. Instead, as the tribunal found, there must be a document that comes into being at or after the time of the decrease in the consideration and which by some means records the acceptance by both parties that the event triggering the decrease has occurred. Moreover, that document taken on its own or with others must disclose the reduced price, although there is no requirement that the documents relied on as evidencing the decrease are served on the hirer.' The decrease in consideration on which G relied for the purpose of adjusting its VAT account 'satisfied the definition of "decrease in consideration"' set out in *reg 24*. *C & E Commrs v General Motors Acceptance Corporation (UK) plc*, Ch D [2004] STC 577; [2004] EWHC 192 (Ch). (*Notes*. (1) For Customs' policy following this decision, see VAT Information Sheet 5/04, issued on 6 May 2004. See also *VAT (Special Provisions) (Amendment) Order 2006 (SI 2006/869)*, which came into force on 13 April 2006. (2) For other issues in this case, see **44.53** MOTOR CARS and **59.33** RETURNS. For subsequent developments, see **48.64** PAYMENT OF TAX.)

[40.110] A company (S) manufactured windows and doors. In some cases it installed sample windows and doors at customers' premises for promotional purposes. In such cases it issued invoices, but did not always pursue the customer for payment. In 2003 it decided that it should not have accounted for VAT where the customer had not paid for the installation, and deducted the unpaid VAT in its output tax computation. When HMRC discovered this, they issued an assessment to recover the output tax shown on the invoices which S had issued. S appealed, contending that there had been a decrease in consideration, within *VAT Regulations 1995 (SI 1995/2518), reg 38*. The tribunal rejected this contention and dismissed the appeal. The tribunal specifically distinguished the Ch D decision in *C & E Commrs v General Motors Acceptance Corporation (UK) plc*, **40.109** above (which S had cited as an authority), observing that S had failed to communicate with its customers and holding that 'there has to be some form of communication with the customer for what was being done to be accepted by both parties'. S had failed to meet the requirements of reg 38. *Starglaze Windows & Conservatories Ltd v HMRC*, [2010] UKFTT 119 (TC), TC00430.

[40.111] A company (C) operated bingo clubs, at which customers competed for cash prizes. Until 2007 it calculated its VAT liability on the 'game by game basis'. In February 2007 HMRC issued Business Brief 07/07, stating that VAT liability should be calculated on the 'session basis'. Following this, C recalculated its liability and formed the opinion that it had overdeclared VAT. It made an adjustment under *VAT Regulations 1995, reg 38*, covering the period from 1996, in its return for the period ending December 2009. HMRC rejected the adjustment, and C appealed. The tribunal allowed the appeal. Judge Reid held that Business Brief 07/07 had required VAT to be calculated on a session basis, and that this had been a change in policy. The change fell within the scope of *VAT Regulations, reg 38*. The 'internal credit note' which C had issued complied with *reg 38*, since 'it was not essential that the document passed from issuer (sic) to the person receiving the credit'. *Carlton Clubs plc v HMRC*, [2011] UKFTT 542 (TC); [2011] SFTD 1209, TC01389.

[40.112] Following an outbreak of 'foot and mouth' disease, a county council was required to supply services to the Department of Environment, Food and Rural Affairs (DEFRA). DEFRA failed to pay the full amount which the council had invoiced. The council began High Court proceedings against DEFRA. The proceedings were settled by mediation, under which the council agreed to accept a reduced amount in settlement. Since the council had accounted for VAT on the full amount which it had originally invoiced, it submitted a voluntary disclosure seeking to recover the amount which it had overpaid. HMRC rejected the claim on the grounds that it had been made outside the statutory time limit, but the First-Tier Tribunal allowed the council's appeal, holding that there had been a 'decrease in consideration', within *VAT Regulations (SI 1995/2518), reg 38(1)(b)*. Judge Demack was very critical of the HMRC officer who had rejected the council's claim, finding that his witness statement had contained an allegation 'without any evidence whatsoever to support such a statement', and had been 'totally unjustified'. *Cumbria County Council v HMRC*, [2011] UKFTT 621 (TC), TC01463.

[40.113] See also *Genie Financial Services Europe Ltd*, 3.176 ASSESSMENT; *McMaster Scotland Stores Ltd*, 48.42 PAYMENT OF TAX, and *Copson*, 59.28 RETURNS.

VAT Regulations 1995, reg 38(1A)—three-year time limit for adjustments

[40.114] During September and October 1994 a company (B) accounted for output tax of £86,000 on payments which it received from another company (S). In December 1994 S wrote to B rescinding the relevant contract. B took legal proceedings against S, claiming damages for breach of contract. In January 1998 the High Court gave judgment for S and ordered B to repay the sums which it had received. In January 2001 B issued a credit note and claimed repayment of the £86,000. The Commissioners rejected the claim on the basis that the credit note had been issued outside the three-year time limit laid down by *VAT Regulations 1995 (SI 1995/2518), reg 38(1A)*. The tribunal dismissed B's appeal, holding that the three-year limitation period was reasonable. *Burnham Logistics Ltd*, LON/01/1213 (VTD 18005).

[40.115] See also *General Motors Acceptance Corporation (UK) plc*, 59.33
RETURNS.

Decrease in consideration—whether credit note must be issued

[40.116] A company made refunds to some of its customers in some cases
where the goods which it had supplied did not meet the customers' expectations. It accounted for output tax on the basis that it could reduce the amount
of the supply by the amount of the refund, although it did not always issue a
credit note. The Commissioners issued a ruling that the company could only
reduce the amount of the supply, as shown on the invoice, where it issued a
credit note in accordance with the *VAT Regulations*. The company appealed,
contending that the effect of *Article 11C1* of the *EC Sixth Directive* was that
it was entitled to treat the taxable amount as being reduced by the amount of
the refund even where it did not issue a credit note. The tribunal rejected this
contention and dismissed the company's appeal. *Article 11C1* provided that
the taxable amount was to be reduced 'under conditions which shall be
determined by the Member States'. The relevant conditions were laid down in
regulation 38 of the *VAT Regulations 1995*, which had to be read in
conjunction with the definition of a 'decrease in consideration' in *regulation 24*. The tribunal observed that 'to suggest that increases or decreases in
consideration could be effective for VAT purposes without any credit note or
other similar document changing the amount of consideration in the original
invoice does run counter to the scheme both of the *Sixth Directive*' and 'the
national primary legislation which requires accounting for value added tax to
be on the basis of invoices'. *British Telecommunications plc*, LON/95/3145
(VTD 14669).

Treatment of credit note in partial exemption computation

[40.117] The London International Financial Futures Exchange (LIFFE)
became partly exempt with effect from January 1990, following the enactment
of what is now *VATA 1994, Sch 9, Group 5, Item 7*. It agreed a special 'direct
attribution' method of calculating its deductible input tax. In its return, it
treated a credit note, which it had received in respect of computer systems and
equipment which it had ordered before it became partly exempt, as reducing
the amount of input tax wholly attributable to exempt supplies. The Commissioners issued an assessment to recover this tax, and the tribunal dismissed
LIFFE's appeal, holding that the credit note should not have been treated as
reducing the amount of input tax wholly attributable to exempt supplies, since
it related to supplies made before the start of the period for which the
calculation of deductible input tax had to be made. *London International
Financial Futures Exchange (Administration & Management)*, [1993] VATTR
474 (VTD 11611). (*Note*. The appeal also concerned construction services
supplied to LIFFE by an associated company, in respect of which the tribunal
allowed LIFFE's appeal, holding that these services were wholly attributable to
taxable supplies.)

Article 21(1)(c) of Sixth Directive—appeal by recipient of credit note

[40.118] See *Finanzamt Osnabrück-Land v Langhorst*, 22.460 EUROPEAN
COMMUNITY LAW.

Car manufacturers and car dealers—treatment of credit notes

[40.119] See *Abercromby Motor Group Ltd*, 48.24 PAYMENT OF TAX.

Delay in processing credit notes—effect of VAT Regulations, reg 34*

[40.120] See *Copson*, 59.28 RETURNS.

41

Land

The cases in this chapter are arranged under the following headings.

Whether a licence to occupy land (VATA 1994, Sch 9, Group 1, Item 1)

General	**41.1**
Surrenders of leases	**41.63**
Club subscriptions	**41.70**
Hairdressing and massage salons	**41.73**

Hotel accommodation, etc. (VATA 1994, Sch 9, Group 1, Item 1(d))	**41.96**
Holiday accommodation (VATA 1994, Sch 9, Group 1, Item 1(e))	**41.116**
Caravan facilities (VATA 1994, Sch 9, Group 1, Item 1(f))	**41.128**
Parking facilities (VATA 1994, Sch 9, Group 1, Item 1(h))	**41.136**
Mooring facilities, etc. (VATA 1994, Sch 9, Group 1, Item 1(k))	**41.149**
Sports grounds, etc. (VATA 1994, Sch 9, Group 1, Item 1(l))	**41.153**
Facilities for playing sport (VATA 1994, Sch 9, Group 1, Item 1(m))	**41.156**
Miscellaneous	**41.163**

NOTE

The cases in this chapter are those dealing with *VATA 1994, Sch 9, Group 1*. For cases dealing with *VATA 1994, Sch 10*, see 6 BUILDINGS AND LAND. For cases dealing with *VATA 1994, Sch 7A, Groups 6 and 7*, see 56 REDUCED-RATE SUPPLIES: MISCELLANEOUS. For cases dealing with *VATA 1994, Sch 8, Group 5*, see 15 CONSTRUCTION OF BUILDINGS. For cases dealing with *VATA 1994, Sch 8, Group 6*, see 55 PROTECTED BUILDINGS.

Whether a licence to occupy land (VATA 1994, Sch 9, Group 1, Item 1)

General

Cases held to be exempt

Concession to operate shops at airport

[41.1] Under an agreement with the British Airports Authority, a company operated two shops at Heathrow Airport. It paid the BAA a percentage of its turnover. Customs issued a ruling that the agreement granted a licence to occupy land, so that the BAA's input tax had to be apportioned accordingly. The tribunal dismissed the BAA's appeal, and the CA upheld this decision. Scarman LJ observed that 'the court is under an obligation to look at the substance of the agreement and to reach a conclusion as to its nature quite irrespective of its form, or the language in which the agreement is embodied'. The true nature of the agreement was that 'it is a licence to occupy the two shops—i.e. land'. *British Airports Authority v C & E Commrs (No 1)*, CA 1976, [1977] STC 36; [1977] 1 WLR 302; [1977] 1 All ER 497.

Licence to produce play in theatre

[41.2] A company (T) granted another company a licence to produce a play in a theatre. Customs issued a ruling that the licence was a licence to occupy land within what is now *VATA 1994, Sch 9, Group 1*, so that T's input tax had to be apportioned. The tribunal dismissed T's appeal against this decision. *Theatres Consolidated Ltd*, [1975] VATTR 13 (VTD 141).

Part of premises sublet—rents paid direct to head lessor

[41.3] A partnership leased certain premises, most of which it sublet to three associated companies. These companies paid their rents direct to the head lessor. Customs issued an assessment on the basis that the partnership had granted the companies licences to occupy land, which were exempt from VAT, so that the partnership's input tax had to be apportioned. The tribunal upheld the assessment. *Star Automatics*, BIR/75/117 (VTD 311).

Receipts linked with rental payments for market sites

[41.4] A company which operated markets and fairs experienced difficulties in trading on Sundays because of the *Shops Act 1950*. It therefore established a club to carry out Sunday trading. The club received payments from traders who occupied sites provided by the company. The tribunal held that these payments were consideration for licences to occupy land, and exempt from VAT. *Wendy Fair Market Club*, LON/77/400 (VTD 679). (*Note*. For other matters in this case, see **2.455** APPEALS.)

Letting of market stall for one day

[41.5] A Borough Council controlled various markets and fairs. It let two market stalls for periods of one day only. The Council did not account for VAT on its receipts from these lettings, treating them as exempt. Customs issued an assessment charging tax on the basis that the short duration of the lettings prevented them from qualifying for exemption. The tribunal allowed the Council's appeal, holding that the stallholders had been granted licences to occupy land, and that the short duration of the licences was immaterial. *Tameside Metropolitan Borough Council*, [1979] VATTR 93 (VTD 733).

Serviced office accommodation

[41.6] A company supplied serviced office accommodation. The services in question included cleaning and the services of a telephone switchboard. Customs issued a ruling that the supplies in question were a licence to occupy land, so that the consideration was exempt from VAT and the company was not able to reclaim the related input tax. The tribunal dismissed the company's appeal. *Business Enterprises (UK) Ltd*, [1988] VATTR 160 (VTD 3161).

[41.7] Supplies of serviced office accommodation were also held to be exempt from VAT in *Birchforest Ltd*, MAN/90/1063 (VTD 6046); *Grovewood (1998) Ltd*, LON/00/660 (VTD 17125); *Trustees of the Lyndon David Hollinshead SIPP (and related appeals)*, [2009] UKFTT 92 (TC), TC00060, and *WS Atkins (Services) Ltd*, **36.35** INPUT TAX.

Licence giving non-exclusive occupation of office

[41.8] A firm of chartered accountants formed a limited company to provide investment advice. The company operated from a room in the firm's office, and paid rent to the firm. However, the company did not have exclusive occupation of the room, since it was also used at times by the firm. The firm did not account for output tax on the rental payments from the company, treating them as exempt. Customs issued an assessment charging tax on the payments. The tribunal allowed the firm's appeal, holding that the supply was of a licence to occupy land and qualified for exemption even though the licence did not grant exclusive occupation. *Altman Blane & Co*, LON/93/740 (VTD 12381). (*Note*. For another issue in this case, see **62.26** SUPPLY.)

Golf club—transfer of business

[41.9] A company (T), which owned a golf club, had registered for VAT in 1989. In 1998 it undertook a transaction, devised by a tax consultancy firm, whereby it transferred part of its business to a newly-formed non-profit-making body (C). The transfer was treated as the transfer of a going concern, and was intended to take advantage of the exemption in *VATA 1994, Sch 9, Group 10, Item 3* (so that C would not be required to account for output tax). Following the transfer, T submitted a return claiming a repayment of input tax. Customs rejected the claim and issued a ruling that T had granted C a licence to occupy land, which was exempt under *Sch 9, Group 1*. The tribunal dismissed T's appeal. *Tall Pines Golf & Leisure Co Ltd*, LON/99/266 (VTD 16538).

Licences to occupy school building

[41.10] A partnership (D) constructed a building for a preparatory school. It granted the partnership which operated the school a licence to use the building. It granted a similar licence to a separate partnership, which operated an 'assisted places scheme' to allow some pupils to attend the school. Customs issued a ruling that D had granted licences to occupy land (so that its supplies were exempt and it was unable to reclaim input tax). D appealed, contending that since neither of the licences was exclusive, neither of them constituted a 'licence to occupy land'. The tribunal rejected this contention and dismissed D's appeal. *Holmwood House School Developments*, LON/02/88 (VTD 18130).

Installation of amusement machines in leisure club

[41.11] The proprietor of a business which supplied amusement machines paid £15,000 to a leisure club at a holiday resort for the right to install a number of machines in a room at the club. He reclaimed input tax in respect of this payment. Customs issued an assessment to recover the tax, considering that the payment was for a licence to occupy land and was exempt from VAT. The tribunal dismissed the proprietor's appeal. *A Higgins*, MAN/90/748 (VTD 6205).

Installation of coin-operated telephones in hospitals

[41.12] British Telecom (BT) paid commission to the owners of hospital sites for the right to install coin-operated telephones at the hospitals. BT charged itself VAT on self-billing invoices and reclaimed it as input tax. Customs issued an assessment to recover the tax, on the basis that it related to licences to occupy land, which were exempt from VAT. The tribunal dismissed BT's appeal. *British Telecommunications plc*, LON/96/1135 (VTD 16244).

Payment made under Tomlin order to settle dispute over land

[41.13] A partnership (G) had occupied a farm for many years without paying rent to the company (L) which owned the freehold. L began legal action against G, which defended the proceedings, contending that L's claim was barred by the *Limitation Act 1939*. The dispute was settled by a 'Tomlin order', under which L paid G £450,000 for relinquishing its claim to the land. Customs issued an assessment charging VAT on this. G appealed, contending that it related to a licence to occupy land and was therefore exempt from VAT. The tribunal accepted this contention and allowed the appeal. *JE Greves & Son*, [1993] VATTR 127 (VTD 9777).

Payment for occupation of part of vehicle workshop

[41.14] A trader operated a vehicle recovery service. He allowed an unrelated partnership, which operated a repair business, to occupy part of his workshop in return for payment. He did not account for tax on the amounts which he received from the partnership. Customs issued an assessment charging tax on the payments, and the trader appealed, contending that they were for a licence to occupy land and thus were exempt. The tribunal allowed the appeal, holding on the evidence that he had granted a licence to occupy a part of the premises, rather than merely a licence to use the workshop facilities. *HA Lovejoy (t/a HRS Recoveries)*, LON/93/2754 (VTD 12835). (*Note.* For another issue in this case, see **36.526** INPUT TAX.)

Rent for stables

[41.15] A trader (W) owned stables with accommodation for 74 horses. He received rent from owners of horses which were kept at the stables. He did not account for VAT on the rent, treating it as exempt. Customs issued an assessment on the basis that, because W also supplied additional services such as feeding and watering, the rent failed to qualify for exemption. The tribunal allowed W's appeal, holding that W was making an exempt supply of land, and that any additional services were merely ancillary to it. *J Window*, [2001] VATDR 252 (VTD 17186). (*Note.* For Customs' practice following this decision, see Business Brief 21/2001, issued on 21 December 2001.)

Pitch fees for 'park homes' at caravan site

[41.16] See *Stonecliff Caravan Park*, **15.153** CONSTRUCTION OF DWELLINGS, ETC.

Refurbishment of restaurant prior to grant of licence

[41.17] See *Sheffield Co-Operative Society Ltd*, **46.22** PARTIAL EXEMPTION.

Refurbishment of houses prior to sale

[41.18] A housing association refurbished a number of houses and sold them. It reclaimed input tax on the refurbishment. The Commissioners issued an assessment to recover the tax and the tribunal dismissed the association's appeal, holding that the input tax related to exempt supplies. *Maritime Housing Association Ltd*, MAN/98/402 (VTD 16232).

Bank entering into leaseback agreement with company

[41.19] A bank held a large number of freehold and leasehold properties. It sold some of these to an unconnected company (M) which leased them back to the bank. The bank was unable to assign some short leases to M without the consent of the landlords. In the absence of such consents, the bank entered into an agreement whereby it assigned to M the 'economic benefits and burdens' of the leases. The bank remained in occupation of the premises, and paid a fee to M which was similar to the rent which would have been charged under a formal leaseback. Customs issued rulings that M was making a standard-rated supply of agency and property management services to the bank, that rents payable to the bank by sub-tenants remained the property of the bank, and that when the sub-tenants made such payments to M, they were consideration for standard-rated supplies of agency and property management services made by M to the bank. The bank appealed, contending that the supply which it received from M was exempt (and secondly that the supplies to the sub-tenants were made by M, rather than by the bank). The tribunal reviewed the evidence in detail and rejected the bank's first contention, holding that M's supply to the bank was a standard-rated supply of agency and property management services which did not qualify for exemption. (However the tribunal accepted the bank's second contention, holding that the effect of what is now *VATA 1994, Sch 10 para 40(1)* was that following the agreement, the exempt supplies to the sub-tenants were to be treated as having been made by M, and that the payments by the sub-tenants did not represent consideration for the standard-rated supplies which M made to the bank.) The CA unanimously upheld the tribunal decision. Jonathan Parker LJ held that 'a right of occupation is an essential and fundamental element of a transaction of leasing or letting for the purposes of *Article 13B(b)*' of the *EC Sixth Directive*. Since M had 'acquired no right of occupation of the properties', its supply to the bank was not a supply of 'leasing or letting' and was not exempt from VAT. *HMRC v Abbey National plc (No 4)*, CA [2006] STC 1961; [2006] EWCA Civ 886.

City Council transferring houses to housing association

[41.20] See *South Liverpool Housing Ltd*, 42.21 LOCAL AUTHORITIES AND STATUTORY BODIES.

Contract between landowner and development company

[41.21] A company (B) owned some properties which it wished to redevelop and sell. It entered into a development agreement with another company (L). Under the contract, L carried out substantial work on the properties and received part of the sale proceeds. Customs issued an assessment charging tax on L's share of the sale proceeds, on the basis that they represented consideration for standard-rated construction services. L appealed, contending that it had acquired an interest in the land under the development contract and that its share of the sale proceeds was consideration for an exempt supply of land. The tribunal accepted this contention and allowed L's appeal, and the Ch D upheld this decision. Blackburne J held that the tribunal had been entitled to find that there had been 'a joint venture between the parties', rather than 'a simple supply of construction services'. *C & E Commrs v Latchmere Properties Ltd*, Ch D [2005] STC 731; [2005] EWHC 133 (Ch).

Sale of plots of land with facility to connect to service utilities

[41.22] A partnership sold plots of land with facilities to connect to service utilities. It treated its sales as exempt. Customs issued a ruling that the effect of the utility connections was part of the consideration was standard-rated. The tribunal allowed the partnership's appeal, holding that there was a single supply of land which qualified for exemption. *D & S Virtue (t/a Lammermuir Game Services)*, [2007] VATDR 308 (VTD 20259). (*Notes.* (1) For HMRC's revised practice following this decision, see HMRC Brief 64/07, issued on 17 October 2007. HMRC state that they now accept that 'the supply of a serviced building plot of land is a single exempt supply of land by the landowner'. (2) For another issue in this case, see **15.178** CONSTRUCTION OF BUILDINGS.)

Storage facilities

[41.23] A trader (F) provided storage facilities in the form of 184 large metal containers which were kept on a site which he owned. HMRC issued a ruling that he was required to account for VAT on his receipts. The tribunal allowed F's appeal, holding that he was providing a licence to occupy land, which was exempt from VAT. *D Finnamore (t/a Hanbridge Storage Services) v HMRC*, [2011] UKFTT 216 (TC); [2011] SFTD 551, TC01081. (*Note.* HMRC have appealed to the Upper Tribunal against this decision.)

[41.24] The decision in *Finnamore*, 41.23 above, was applied in the similar subsequent case of *UK Storage Company (SW) Ltd v HMRC*, [2011] UKFTT 549 (TC); [2011] SFTD 1233, TC01394. (*Note.* HMRC have appealed to the Upper Tribunal against this decision.)

'Reverse consideration' on sale of freehold property

[41.25] A company (B) owned the freehold of a large building. It granted another company (L) a 51-year lease on the property. Subsequently it received an offer for the freehold of the property from another company (A), which also wished to take over the lease. L demanded payment of £2,460,500 as compensation for relinquishing the lease. A considered that this price was excessive, and only agreed to proceed with the transaction after receiving a 'reverse consideration' of £370,500 from B. B reclaimed input tax on this payment. Customs rejected the claim and the tribunal dismissed B's appeal, holding that the 'reverse consideration' should be attributed to the sale of the freehold, which was an exempt supply. *Brammer plc*, MAN/90/123 (VTD 6420).

Cases held to be partly exempt

Serviced office accommodation

[41.26] A company supplied serviced office accommodation, including the handling of mail and the provision of a telephone answering service. The tribunal held that, although part of the consideration paid by the company's tenants was for the grant of licences to occupy land, the services of mail handling and telephone answering were taxable supplies. Accordingly the consideration paid by the company's tenants had to be apportioned. *Sovereign Street Workplace Ltd*, MAN/91/403 (VTD 9550).

[**41.27**] A company leased a building, which it divided into office accommodation and let to tenants. It charged tenants a rent of £55 per square foot, treating £15 of this as attributable to an exempt supply of land, and £40 as attributable to taxable supplies of services such as cleaning, maintenance, electricity and insurance. It reclaimed input tax in respect of the furniture which it installed in the building, and on amounts paid in respect of cleaning the offices. The Commissioners issued an assessment to recover the input tax, considering that it was attributable to exempt supplies. The company appealed. The tribunal allowed the appeal in part, holding that the company was making multiple supplies and that the consideration paid by the tenants had to be apportioned. The tribunal held that, since the offices could have been let unfurnished, the whole of the input tax on the furniture was attributable to taxable supplies, and was reclaimable in full, but that 'the totality of the cleaning services supplied to the appellant are used in making exempt supplies of the premises, and so the input tax is not deductible'. *First Base Properties Ltd*, LON/93/3122A (VTD 11598).

[**41.28**] A statutory corporation, established under the *Housing Act 1988*, leased part of its premises to a housing association. Under the agreement, the association would occupy the premises rent-free for the first two years but would pay a market rent thereafter. The association also agreed to pay a service charge equal to the cost of the provision of various specified services including 50 telephones and a photocopying service. The Commissioners issued a ruling that the service charge was part of a single exempt supply of the leased premises. The corporation appealed, contending that the provision of the telephones and the photocopying service was a separate taxable supply. The tribunal allowed the appeal in part, holding that the provision of the telephones was part of the exempt supply of the premises, since 'it is an essential feature of a serviced office that telephones are provided'. However, the photocopying service was a separate taxable supply, since 'it is not an essential feature of a serviced office that the provision of the property should include a photocopying service as part of the rent'. On the evidence, the service in question was 'not merely the ability to use photocopying equipment' but was 'the provision by the appellant of a collection and return service including carrying out the copying and binding'. It was 'concerned with the facilitation of the administration of (the tenant's) business, whereas the tenancy agreement is concerned with the provision of a place of business'. *Tower Hamlets Housing Action Trust*, LON/00/1306 (VTD 17308).

Licence to trade from retail shops

[**41.29**] A group of companies owned a number of retail shops. It entered into agreements whereby licensees could trade from two of the shops. The licensees were required to pay fixed fortnightly sums to the group, and to stock products supplied by the group, and were entitled to keep all profits. The group incurred expenditure in respect of these shops, and reclaimed the relevant input tax.

The Commissioners issued an assessment to recover the tax, on the basis that the expenditure related to the grant of licences to occupy land, which were exempt from VAT. The representative company appealed, contending that it had granted trading rights, and that these grants were standard-rated. The tribunal allowed the appeal in part, holding on the evidence that the licensees 'received much more than a mere licence to occupy land', and that 'as a matter of economics a substantial proportion of the consideration must have been attributable to the trading rights'. The tribunal directed that the tax should be apportioned. *Cullens Holdings plc*, LON/93/1179 (VTD 12376).

Alexandra Palace

[41.30] See *Haringey Borough Council*, **42.1** LOCAL AUTHORITIES AND STATUTORY BODIES.

Cases held not to be exempt

Right to take car on harbour property

[41.31] Harbour Trustees charged motorists for access to quays or jetties. They did not account for tax on the toll receipts. Customs issued an assessment and the Trustees appealed, contending that the tolls were exempt. The tribunal dismissed the appeal, holding that the tolls did not qualify for exemption. *Mevagissey Harbour Trustees*, BIR/74/14 (VTD 111).

Grant of facilities at airport

[41.32] The British Airports Authority granted a company the right to supply goods at Gatwick Airport, in return for a percentage of the company's gross takings. Customs issued a ruling that the agreement gave the company a right over land, so that the company's payments to the Authority were exempt from VAT. The Authority appealed, contending that the agreement did not amount to a licence to occupy land, so that it was entitled to reclaim input tax. The tribunal allowed the Authority's appeal, holding that the right to pass through a control point at an airport did not amount to 'an interest in or right over land'. *British Airports Authority (No 2)*, [1975] VATTR 43 (VTD 146). (*Note*. For another issue in this case, see **66.47** TRANSPORT.)

[41.33] A similar decision was reached in a case where the British Airports Authority granted an airline company the use of certain 'transfer desks' at Heathrow Airport. The tribunal held that the grant was not of an interest over land, so that the payments were not exempt from VAT. *British Airports Authority (No 3)*, LON/74/153 (VTD 147).

Licence giving non-exclusive occupation of golf course

[41.34] A married couple operated a golf course. They granted a members' club a non-exclusive licence to use the course at certain times. They did not account for tax on the payments they received from the club, treating them as exempt. HMRC issued an assessment charging tax on the payments, on the basis that the payments were for the supply of a service rather than for a supply of land. The couple appealed. The tribunal dismissed their appeal, holding on the evidence that the 'economic purpose of the relationship between the parties' was to provide the club with 'rights to use the golf course, rather than to occupy it'. *J & M Gillan (t/a Gracehill Golf Course) v HMRC*, [2010] UKFTT 8 (TC), TC00327.

[41.35] See also *Copthorne Village Golf Club*, **24.48** EXEMPTIONS: MISCEL-LANEOUS.

Provision of rest room for taxi drivers

[41.36] A partnership operated a taxi business. Its drivers used their own vehicles, and paid the partnership £20 per week for the use of radio equipment and a rest room at the business premises while awaiting calls. The partnership did not account for VAT on these payments, and appealed against an assessment on them, contending that part of the payments should be treated as rent for the use of the rest room, and thus exempt from VAT. The tribunal dismissed the appeal, holding that the use of the room was not a licence to occupy land and did not qualify for exemption. *Ferris & Budd (t/a Z Cars)*, BIR/76/194 (VTD 412).

[41.37] A similar decision was reached in *Parker Radio Cars (Sutton Coldfield) Ltd*, MAN/87/25 (VTD 2504).

Payments by driving instructors for use of driving school offices

[41.38] A similar decision was reached in a case where self-employed driving instructors made weekly payments to a driving school in return for the use of an office. *CW & JA Garner*, LON/83/61 (VTD 1476).

Purported leases held to be shams

[41.39] A company owned a golf driving range. In 2004 it entered into agreements, purporting to be leases, under which the range was to be operated by various individuals (including a professional golfer and two relatives of the company's controlling shareholder). The identity of the lessee changed every three months. HMRC issued assessments on the basis that, notwithstanding the purported leases, the company was continuing to operate the driving range and was required to account for tax on the takings. The tribunal upheld the assessments, observing that 'the arrangement by which the purported lessees rotate every three months is designed to avoid their exceeding the VAT registration threshold' and holding on the evidence that the purported leases were 'shams'. The agreements were not leases but were 'means by which the appellant delegated the day to day running of its own business'. The company was making supplies to customers of the driving range, and was required to account for tax accordingly. *Rotherham Golf Academy Ltd v HMRC*, [2009] UKFTT 57 (TC), TC00036.

Payments by dance tutors to dance club proprietors

[41.40] See *Lait & Lait*, **62.347** SUPPLY.

Casual grazing licences

[41.41] A farmer owned two fields which were suitable for grazing. He grazed his own animals on them and, from time to time, allowed other people to place horses or ponies in the fields in return for weekly payments. He did not account for tax on these payments. Customs issued an assessment charging tax on them, and the farmer appealed, contending that the payments were exempt. The tribunal rejected this contention and dismissed his appeal, holding that the grazing facilities did not amount to licences to occupy land and thus did not qualify for exemption. *JA King*, [1980] VATTR 60 (VTD 933). (*Note.* The tribunal also held that the supply could not be treated as a zero-rated supply of animal feeding stuffs.)

Kennels

[41.42] A company supplied kennel facilities. Initially it accounted for VAT on its supplies, but subsequently lodged a repayment claim. Customs rejected the claim and the company appealed, contending that it was making exempt supplies of land. The tribunal rejected this contention and dismissed the appeal. *Leander International Pet Foods Ltd (t/a Arden Grange)*, LON/02/575 (VTD 18870).

Promotion of concerts at halls owned by Council

[41.43] The Greater London Council owned several concert halls, and granted licences to promoters to stage public performances at the halls. In several cases, it agreed to provide stewards and to supply admission tickets. It did not account for VAT on the fees it received from the promoters, treating them as exempt. Customs issued an assessment on the basis that the provision of stewards and of admission tickets was a separate supply which did not qualify for exemption. The tribunal upheld the assessment in principle, directing that the amounts which the GLC received should be apportioned between taxable and exempt supplies. (However, in a case where the GLC acted as co-promoter, the tribunal held that there was no supply by the GLC to the promoter, and the GLC was only liable to account for VAT on the supplies it made to the public.) *Greater London Council*, [1982] VATTR 94 (VTD 1224).

Management of ice rink

[41.44] See *Saturn Leisure Ltd*, 52.228 PENALTIES: MISDECLARATION.

Antique fair in hotel room

[41.45] A trader organised and promoted antique fairs which were held in hotels or public houses. She charged other traders for the right to use tables at the fairs, and also charged the public for admission. She did not account for VAT on her receipts from traders. Customs issued an assessment charging tax on them and she appealed, contending that the receipts were exempt. The tribunal dismissed her appeal, holding that the provision of tables did not amount to a licence to occupy land, so that the receipts did not qualify for exemption. *WB Enever*, LON/83/220 (VTD 1537). (*Note.* The tribunal also held that the supplies were excluded from exemption by *FA 1972, Sch 5, Group 1, Item 1(g)*. This exclusion was repealed by *FA 1989*, but the supplies would still not qualify for exemption through not being held to be for a licence to occupy land.)

Payments from associated company for use of office facilities

[41.46] A company (U), which provided financial services, owned the office from which it operated. It had two associated companies, which operated from the same premises and which also provided financial services. One of these companies paid U £3,500 p.a. for the use of its facilities. U did not account for tax on these payments, and Customs issued an assessment charging tax on them. U appealed, contending that the payments should be treated as exempt. The tribunal dismissed the appeal, holding that U had not granted its associated company a licence to occupy any land, and that the payments were made under 'an informal arrangement to share facilities' which did not qualify for exemption. *Ultimate Advisory Services Ltd (No 1)*, MAN/91/1488 (VTD 9523). (*Note*. For another issue in this case, see **54.4** PENSION FUNDS.)

[41.47] A company (P), which provided accountancy services, allowed three associated companies to use its offices. Each of these three companies was controlled by one of P's directors. P did not account for VAT on the payments it received from the companies, treating them as exempt. Customs issued an assessment charging tax on the payments. The tribunal upheld the assessment and dismissed P's appeal, finding that P 'was sharing all its office facilities in some measure with the companies', rather than simply granting a right to occupy land. *Pethericks & Gillard Ltd*, LON/07/610 (VTD 20564).

Installation of amusement machines in public houses

[41.48] A company which owned several public houses arranged for coin-operated amusement machines to be installed therein, in return for payments from the owners of the machines. Customs formed the opinion that, by allowing the owners of the machines to install them on the premises, the company had granted the owners licences to occupy land, with the result that the company was making exempt supplies as well as taxable supplies and could only reclaim a proportion of its input tax. They therefore issued an assessment to recover some of the input tax which the company had reclaimed. The tribunal allowed the company's appeal against the assessment, holding that none of the agreements granted a licence to occupy land. *The Wolverhampton & Dudley Breweries plc*, [1990] VATTR 131 (VTD 5351).

Installation of cigarette vending machines in public houses

[41.49] See *Sinclair Collis Ltd*, **22.340** EUROPEAN COMMUNITY LAW.

Grant of facilities for crane to pass through airspace

[41.50] A property developer paid a surveyor for permission to swing a tower crane above the surveyor's premises. The surveyor did not account for output tax on this payment, and Customs issued an assessment charging tax. The surveyor appealed, contending that the payment related to a licence to occupy land, and should be treated as exempt. The tribunal dismissed the appeal, holding that the agreement gave the developer the right to pass through the surveyor's airspace, rather than to occupy the airspace. *RH Carter (t/a Protheroe Carter & Eason Ltd)*, LON/93/93A (VTD 12047).

Payments for use of stand at exhibition

[41.51] The Swiss National Tourist Office (SNTO) hired a stand at an exhibition. It used part of the stand itself, and sublet the remainder of the stand to a number of Swiss organisations or businesses. It reclaimed input tax on its payment to the exhibition organisers. The Commissioners issued an assessment to recover the tax, on the basis that the supplies made by the SNTO were grants of a licence to occupy land, which was exempt from VAT. The SNTO appealed. The tribunal allowed the appeal, holding that 'the real substance of the supply' was 'the right to full participation in the Switzerland stand'. The entitlement to use facilities such as a meeting and storage room, and to be included in a catalogue which was produced by the exhibition organisers, was 'just as important as the right to occupy the table and chairs and the space where they were situated'. The supplies 'went far beyond licences to occupy land'. *Swiss National Tourist Office*, LON/94/223A (VTD 13192).

[41.52] See also *International Trade & Exhibitions J/V Ltd*, 62.526 SUPPLY.

Concession to sell goods from retail shop

[41.53] A shoe retailer (L) allowed a watch retailer (J) to sell watches from his shop, receiving 12.5% of J's turnover as consideration. L did not account for output tax on the payments which he received from J, treating them as exempt. Customs issued an assessment charging tax on the payments, and L appealed, contending that he had granted J a licence to occupy land. The tribunal rejected this contention and dismissed the appeal. On the evidence, L had not granted J 'a clearly defined area or site'. J had the right to install two display units and to display his watches in one of the shop windows, but the remainder of the shop was shared. The payments which J made were not rent, but were 'for use of facilities at the premises according to user'. *PJ Lamb (t/a Footloose)*, MAN/96/1232 (VTD 15136). (*Note*. For Customs' practice following this decision, see Business Brief 25/97, issued on 10 November 1997.)

Charity granting non-exclusive licences to wholly-owned subsidiaries

[41.54] See *Mount Edgcumbe Hospice Ltd*, 11.54 CHARITIES.

Commission retained by property management agents

[41.55] A company carried on the business of managing residential property for landlords. It did not account for output tax on its commission. Customs issued an assessment, and the company appealed, contending that the payments should be treated as exempt. The tribunal rejected this contention and dismissed the appeal. The company was a manager rather than a tenant, so that its commission did not qualify for exemption. *Peter Anthony Estates Ltd*, MAN/94/653 (VTD 13250).

Service charges

[41.56] Under a lease, the leaseholders were obliged to keep their properties in 'good order and repair'. The landlords reserved the right to appoint a factor to ensure that this was done. The landlords subsequently appointed such a factor, and VAT was imposed on the service charges. One of the leaseholders appealed, contending that the service charges should be treated as exempt. The tribunal rejected this contention and dismissed the appeal, holding that the charges did not qualify for exemption because they were not part of the original supply of land. The tribunal also noted that the charges did not fall within the scope of what is now Extra-Statutory Concession 3.18, holding that the charges were not mandatory in the sense required by the concession, since there was 'a distinction between the obligations on the proprietors to maintain the property (which were mandatory) and the method by which the proprietors chose to implement those obligations. The proprietors were not required to appoint a factor — the Owners' Association could make some other arrangement to deal with their obligations.' *J Devine*, EDN/97/97 (VTD 15312).

[41.57] Domestic service charges, paid to trustees appointed under an agreement between a freeholder and a lessor, were held not to qualify for exemption in *Trustees of the Nell Gwynn House Maintenance Fund*, **62.36** SUPPLY. (*Note.* The relevant supplies took place before the introduction of what is now Extra-Statutory Concession 3.18. It appears that the supplies might now fall within the scope of the concession, but compare *Devine*, **41.56** above.)

Hire of country house for wedding ceremonies

[41.58] A company owned a country house, in 40 acres of grounds. The house was licensed for wedding ceremonies under the *Marriage Act 1994*. The company did not account for tax on the payments which it received for letting the house for wedding ceremonies. Customs issued a ruling that the company was required to account for tax on its receipts. The tribunal dismissed the company's appeal, observing that it 'was not seeking to make a separate supply of the licence to use (the house); it was seeking to make a composite supply of what is termed wedding functions'. These included catering and other services such as musical entertainment. *Leez Priory*, LON/02/181 (VTD 18185). (*Note.* The tribunal also held that even if the company had been granting a licence to occupy land, its supplies would have been excluded from exemption by *Sch 9, Group 1, Item 1(d)*. See **41.96** to **41.114** below for cases concerning this provision.)

[41.59] Similar decisions were reached in *Chewton Glen Hotels Ltd*, LON/06/855 (VTD 20686) and *Best Images Ltd*, [2010] UKFTT 175 (TC), TC00480.

Children's parties at converted barn

[41.60] A woman (B) operated a children's nursery in a converted barn. She also organised children's parties in the barn, charging £7.95 per child (with a minimum charge of £100 per party). Initially she accounted for VAT on her receipts from these parties. Subsequently she submitted a repayment claim on the basis that she should have treated her supplies as exempt. The Upper Tribunal upheld HMRC's rejection of the claim. Roth J held that B was making a single supply which failed to qualify for exemption. *HMRC v D Bryce (t/a The Barn)*, UT [2011] STC 903; [2010] UKUT 26 (TCC).

Metal frames with polythene coverings to protect plants

[41.61] A company leased some large metal frames with polythene coverings, fixed to the ground and designed to protect growing plants. It reclaimed input tax on the supplies. Customs rejected the claim on the basis that they formed part of an exempt supply of land. The company appealed, contending that they were separate supplies. The tribunal accepted this contention and allowed the appeal, holding that the supplies were of 'permanently installed equipment and machinery', which was specifically excluded from exemption by *Article 13B(b)* of the *EC Sixth Directive. Argents Nurseries Ltd*, LON/04/1069 (VTD 20045).

Transfer of commercial building less than three years old

[41.62] See *Trade Only Plant Sales Ltd*, **62.116** SUPPLY.

Surrenders of leases

Cases held to be exempt

Payment by landlord for surrender of lease—EC Sixth Directive

[41.63] See *Lubbock Fine & Co*, **22.333** EUROPEAN COMMUNITY LAW.

Payment for assignment of lease—EC Sixth Directive

[41.64] See *Cantor Fitzgerald International*, **22.334** EUROPEAN COMMUNITY LAW, and *Mirror Group plc*, **22.335** EUROPEAN COMMUNITY LAW.

Payment by tenant to landlord for surrender of onerous lease

[41.65] A company (M) which carried on a consultancy business, and also dealt in shares, occupied leased premises, part of which it sublet. Its landlord had elected to waive exemption on the rent which M paid. However, M had not elected to waive exemption on the rent it received from its subtenant. M decided that it wished to terminate the lease before its expiry, and paid a 'reverse premium' of £67,500 to its landlord. It treated this premium as relating to an exempt supply of land. The Commissioners issued an assessment on the basis that, since the landlord had elected to waive exemption in respect of the premises, the payment did not qualify for exemption. The tribunal allowed M's appeal, holding that by surrendering its lease, M had made an exempt supply of land to the landlord. *Marbourne Ltd*, LON/93/590A (VTD 12670). (*Notes*. (1) For the Commissioners' practice following this decision, see Business Brief 18/95, issued on 4 September 1995. The Commissioners initially appealed to the High Court, contending that it must be the person receiving payment, the landlord, who made the supply in question. However, the Commissioners did not pursue the appeal, because the company had ceased trading and would not have been represented before the High Court, and because they considered that the correct legal principle was established in the subsequent case of *Central Capital Corporation Ltd*, **41.66** below, where the tribunal held that the relevant supply of land was made by the landlord rather than by the tenant. A similar decision was reached in *AA Insurance Services Ltd*, **41.67** below. For a more detailed analysis, see British Tax Review 1998, p 596. The writer (the late Hugh McKay) comments that the *Marbourne* decision was 'the right end result but the wrong reasoning'. (2) The case also concerned the operation of the partial exemption provisions prior to their substitution by *SI 1992/3102*. The decision here was largely in favour of Customs, but does not appear to be directly relevant to the current provisions. The company had reclaimed the whole of its input tax, and an appeal against a misdeclaration penalty was dismissed—see **52.344** PENALTIES: MISDECLARATION.)

[41.66] In another case concerning a 'reverse surrender', the tribunal declined to follow the decision in *Marbourne Ltd*, **41.65** above, and held that the relevant supply of land was made by the landlord rather than by the tenant. However, the tribunal held that the payment made by the tenant was exempt from VAT. The tenant was the recipient of the supply, and, applying *Williams & Glyns Bank Ltd*, **2.54** APPEALS, had a right of appeal against the Commissioners' decision that the supply was taxable. Applying the CJEC decision in *Lubbock Fine & Co*, **22.333** EUROPEAN COMMUNITY LAW, the supply by the landlord qualified for exemption under *Article 13B(b)* of the *EC Sixth Directive*. Since the original grant of the lease was not taxable, the subsequent 'reverse surrender' of that lease was also not taxable. *Central Capital Corporation Ltd*, MAN/94/2393 (VTD 13319). (*Note*. For the Commissioners' practice following this decision, see Business Brief 18/95, issued on 4 September 1995.)

[41.67] A similar decision was reached in a case where a tenant company wished to surrender its lease, and the landlord agreed to accept the surrender on condition that the tenant paid a premium of £120,000 plus VAT. The tenant reclaimed input tax on this payment. The Commissioners rejected the claim and the tribunal dismissed the tenant's appeal, holding that the relevant supply was made by the landlord and was exempt from VAT, so that the tenant was not entitled to recover input tax. *AA Insurance Services Ltd*, [1999] VATDR 361 (VTD 16117).

Cases held to be partly exempt

Payment made partly for surrender and partly as inducement

[41.68] A cricket club had leased a site which had development potential. The trust which owned the site wished to develop it as a supermarket. The local council would only grant planning permission if the trust and the development company entered into an agreement with the club under *Town and Country Planning Act 1971, s 52*, whereby the club would be provided with a new site. The trust agreed to pay the club £70,000 for the surrender of the existing lease and the development company agreed to pay the club £110,000 in return for the club surrendering the existing lease and entering into the agreement under *Town and Country Planning Act 1971, s 52*. The Commissioners issued an assessment charging tax on the payment of £110,000. The club appealed, contending that the payment should be treated as exempt from VAT. The tribunal allowed the appeal in part, finding that 'there were two distinct requirements made of the club' and holding that half of the payment was attributable to the surrender of the existing lease and was exempt from VAT, applying *Lubbock Fine & Co*, **22.333** EUROPEAN COMMUNITY LAW, but that the other half was paid as an inducement to enter into the agreement under the

Town and Country Planning Act and was standard-rated, applying *Neville Russell*, **62.127** SUPPLY. *Grantham Cricket Club*, MAN/93/457 (VTD 12287, 12863). (*Note*. For subsequent developments in this case, see **48.33** PAYMENT OF TAX.)

Cases held not to be exempt

Payment for surrender of lease

[41.69] In December 1987 a company (C) purchased the headlease of a building which was used as office accommodation. The building was let to a tenant until June 1989, when C paid the tenant £36,000 as an inducement to surrender its sublease. C sold the headlease in July 1989. In its next return, C reclaimed input tax on the payment it had made to the tenant. The Commissioners issued an assessment to recover the tax, considering that the payment related to the transfer of an interest in land, which was exempt from VAT under what is now *VATA 1994, Sch 9, Group 1*. The tribunal upheld the assessment and dismissed C's appeal, applying *Brasplern (Group Services) Ltd*, **46.13** PARTIAL EXEMPTION, and *Rentorn Ltd*, **46.14** PARTIAL EXEMPTION. *Cedar Court Business Centre Ltd*, LON/91/1132 (VTD 6976). (*Note*. Compare *Lubbock Fine*, **22.333** EUROPEAN COMMUNITY LAW.)

Club subscriptions

Golf club subscription

[41.70] A golf club used a course which was on common land, in accordance with a licence granted by the local authority. The club held the freehold of the clubhouse which was on land adjoining the course. It appealed against an assessment charging tax on members' subscriptions, contending that they should be treated as exempt under what is now *VATA 1994, Sch 9, Group 1, Item 1*. The tribunal rejected this contention and dismissed the appeal, holding that the members received 'a bag of mixed services which cannot readily be severed from each other'. *Banstead Downs Golf Club*, [1974] VATTR 219 (VTD 229).

Tennis and croquet club subscriptions

[41.71] An unincorporated members' club owned land including tennis courts and croquet lawns. It failed to account for output tax on its subscriptions. The Commissioners issued an assessment on the club secretary, charging tax on them. The secretary appealed, contending that they should be treated as exempt under what is now *VATA 1994, Sch 9, Group 1, Item 1*. The QB rejected this contention and dismissed the appeal. The subscriptions entitled members to the privilege of entering the grounds rather than to a share in the beneficial ownership of the club property. A 'right over land' must be interpreted as a legal or equitable interest, and it was impossible to say that members had a licence to occupy any part of the club's premises. *Trewby (Hurlingham Club) v C & E Commrs*, QB [1976] STC 122; [1976] 1 WLR 932; [1976] 2 All ER 199.

Holiday club—increased subscriptions

[41.72] A holiday club occupied land under a sublease. It decided to purchase the headlease of the land, and increased its subscriptions to meet this. It failed to account for tax on its increased subscriptions, and the Commissioners issued an assessment charging VAT. The club appealed, contending that the increase should be treated as exempt under what is now *VATA 1994, Sch 9, Group 1, Item 1*. The QB rejected this contention and upheld the assessment, holding that the additional payments were subscriptions rather than rent or premiums for a licence to occupy land. *C & E Commrs v Little Spain Club*, QB 1978, [1979] STC 170.

Hairdressing and massage salons

Cases held to be exempt

[41.73] A hairdresser (Q) owned two salons, one for men and one for women, in the same town. He found that he was losing money at the men's salon. He dismissed his three employees but offered them the right to continue their profession on a self-employed basis, using the same chair, washbasin and cupboard as before, and paying him a fixed weekly payment. They accepted this offer, and made regular payments to Q as agreed. Q did not account for VAT on these payments, and the Commissioners issued an assessment charging tax on them. Q appealed, contending that the payments were exempt under what is now *VATA 1994, Sch 9, Group 1*. The tribunal allowed Q's appeal, holding that he had granted his ex-employees a licence to occupy land. *R Quaife*, LON/82/305 (VTD 1394). (*Note*. See now, however, the subsequent decision in *HMRC v Denyer*, **41.90** below, where the Ch D held that the fact that a stylist was allotted a specific chair did not mean that the supply constituted a licence to occupy land.)

[41.74] A similar decision was reached in *M Bullimore*, MAN/86/154 (VTD 2626).

[41.75] A couple who owned a number of hairdressing salons did not account for tax on part of the amounts which they received from the stylists who worked at the salons. The Commissioners issued assessments charging tax on the payments, and the couple appealed, contending that the payments were for licences to occupy land and should be treated as exempt under what is now *VATA 1994, Sch 9, Group 1*. The tribunal reviewed the evidence and allowed the appeal in part, holding that the agreements in force from September 1991, which restricted each of the stylists to a specific area of the salon, constituted licences to occupy land and the payments thereunder qualified for exemption. (However, the agreements in force prior to September 1991, which did not provide for any specific interest in the premises, did not qualify for exemption.) *GG & Mrs HK Daniels (t/a Group Montage)*, MAN/91/572 (VTD 12014). (*Note*. The Commissioners announced that they had appealed to the High Court against this decision—see Business Brief 16/94, issued on 25 July 1994—but subsequently withdrew the appeal because, at the hearing, their representative 'had accepted that the agreements used accurately reflected what actually happened in the salon, i.e. that the stylists were genuinely restricted to a particular area of the salon'. See

Customs' VAT Manual, Part 8, para 5.14.2. Customs state that 'it would be most unusual for the business to be carried on in this way', and that if 'the stylists, juniors under their direction, or their clients move outside the designated area', the *Group Montage* decision is 'irrelevant'.)

[41.76] A married couple, who were registered for VAT, granted two hairstylists a licence to operate a hairdressing salon. The couple treated the payments they received from the stylists as exempt from VAT. Customs issued an assessments charging tax on the payments, and the couple appealed. The tribunal allowed the appeal, finding that the couple played no part in the management of the salon and treated it simply as an investment. The tribunal held that 'the arrangements between the partners and the two stylists had many of the features of a furnished letting'. The stylists 'were between them occupying the entire salon as licensees', and the landlords 'were passive investors who on rare occasions exercised their rights of inspection'. Applying the CJEC decision in *Belgian State v Temco Europe SA*, **22.341** EUROPEAN COMMUNITY LAW, this was 'a leasing or letting of immovable property' which qualified for exemption. *MJ Taylor's Executors & Mrs P Taylor*, LON/99/1240 (VTD 20323).

Cases held not to be exempt

[41.77] A partnership owned a hairdressing salon with eight chairs. They allowed two other hairdressers to use the premises in return for weekly payments. They did not account for VAT on these payments, and the Commissioners issued an assessment charging tax on them. The partnership appealed, contending that the payments were exempt under what is now *VATA 1994, Sch 9, Group 1*. The tribunal dismissed the appeal, holding that the arrangements did not amount to licences to occupy land. *N & J Price*, LON/83/47 (VTD 1443).

[41.78] A married couple, who had operated a hairdressing salon in partnership, incorporated a number of companies. Each stylist who worked at the salon was employed by one of the companies, and the couple gave each company the right to use specified chairs and washbasins. The couple did not account for VAT on the payments they received from the companies, and the Commissioners issued an assessment charging tax on them. The tribunal dismissed the couple's appeal, holding that they had not granted the companies licences to occupy land. *PM & Mrs P Field (t/a Paul Field Hair & Beauty Salon)*, LON/84/569 (VTD 2047).

[41.79] The proprietor of a hairdressing salon let two chairs in the salon to one of the hairdressers. He did not account for tax on these payments, and appealed against the Commissioners' ruling that they were taxable, contending that they were exempt under what is now *VATA 1994, Sch 9, Group 1*. The tribunal dismissed his appeal, holding that he had granted the hairdresser facilities which did not amount to a licence to occupy land and did not qualify for exemption. *M Genc*, [1988] VATTR 16 (VTD 2595). (*Note.* For another issue in this case, see **51.8** PENALTIES: FAILURE TO NOTIFY.)

[41.80] In the case noted at **62.258** SUPPLY, the Commissioners refused to accept a salon proprietor's contention that the payments which he received from the stylists qualified for exemption under what is now *VATA 1994, Sch*

9, *Group 1*. The tribunal dismissed the proprietor's appeal, holding that the payments were for the use of the 'general facilities of the salon' and were 'certainly not a licence to occupy exclusively or in company with others any land, but a mere incident or ingredient of what is in substance a business facility'. *ME Hosmer*, LON/89/1851 (VTD 7313).

[41.81] A similar decision was reached in *Characters (Hairdressers) Ltd*, MAN/96/919 (VTD 15351).

[41.82] A company which owned a hairdressing salon allowed its directors to use one of the chairs at the salon. It did not account for output tax in respect of this use, although it accounted for tax on amounts received from other self-employed stylists. The Commissioners issued an assessment charging tax on the basis that, since the company treated the directors as self-employed and did not account for tax on their takings, it had made a deemed supply of the use of the chair and should have accounted for VAT thereon under what is now *VATA 1994, s 19(3)*. The company appealed, contending that the supply in question was a licence to occupy land which was exempt from VAT. The tribunal dismissed the appeal, applying *Genc*, **41.79** above, and holding that the terms under which the directors made use of the chair did not constitute a licence to occupy land. *Biburtry Ltd*, LON/92/2243A (VTD 10615).

[41.83] In the case noted at **62.271** SUPPLY, self-employed hairstylists working at a salon paid the proprietor 57% of their gross takings. The proprietor only accounted for tax on 10% of the gross takings, treating the other 47% as being for a licence to occupy land, and exempt. The Commissioners issued a ruling that the payments did not qualify for exemption. The tribunal dismissed the proprietor's appeal, finding that 'although the individual stylists did have their own chair, they did not necessarily use that chair and the chairs generally were interchangeable within the salon', so that there was not 'a total exclusive use of an allocated space'. Accordingly, the proprietor had not granted the stylists a licence to occupy land, and the payments did not qualify for exemption. *A Winder (t/a Anthony & Patricia)*, MAN/92/1653 (VTD 11784).

[41.84] A similar decision was reached in a case in which the tribunal held that 'what the stylist obtained was the right to practise her vocation as a hairdresser, using the general facilities of the salon. The occupation, albeit exclusive, of two chairs (was) a mere incident or ingredient in what was in substance the use of business facilities.' *W Walker (t/a Ziska)*, EDN/92/334 (VTD 11825).

[41.85] An appeal was dismissed in a case where the tribunal held that the supplies which a company operating a hairdressing salon made to each of its stylists were single supplies of services and that any licence to occupy land was 'ancillary or incidental'. The chairman observed that 'the licences are economically useless without the other elements, the most important of which are services of the juniors and the use of the wash basins and the dryers'. It followed that 'as a matter of common sense there were single supplies'. *Simon Harris Hair Design Ltd*, [1996] VATDR 177 (VTD 13939). (*Note*. For the Commissioners' practice following this decision, see Business Brief 13/96, issued on 1 July 1996.)

[41.86] A company operated a hairdressing salon for self-employed stylists. It received payments from stylists in respect of the use of chairs and washbasins, and did not account for tax on these payments. The Commissioners accepted that the use of separate cubicles or rooms amounted to a licence to occupy land, but issued an assessment charging tax on the payments which were made in respect of chairs and washbasins in the main hairdressing area. The company appealed, contending that these payments were also consideration for a licence to occupy land, and were exempt from VAT. The tribunal rejected this contention and dismissed the appeal, applying the principles laid down in *Simon Harris Hair Design Ltd*, **41.85** above. The tribunal held that the supply of washbasins was 'an integral part of a hairdressing business' and did not qualify for exemption. While the provision of chairs and mirrors could amount to a licence to occupy land, the use of the chair and mirror was 'subsumed into the hairdressing business', so that 'that licence cannot be considered to be dissociable from the other services supplied in relation to the hairdressing business in the general area of the salon'. Accordingly the supplies were standard-rated. *Herbert of Liverpool (Hair Design) Ltd*, MAN/97/754 (VTD 15949).

[41.87] A similar decision, also applying *Simon Harris Hair Design Ltd*, **41.85** above, was reached in *George*, **57.91** REGISTRATION.

[41.88] The decision in *Simon Harris Hair Design Ltd*, **41.85** above, was also applied in a subsequent case where the tribunal held that the salon proprietors had made 'a single composite supply of the right to carry on a business of hairdressing by providing a package of hairdressing facilities'. Applying the CJEC decision in *Card Protection Plan Ltd*, **22.324** EUROPEAN COMMU-NITY LAW, 'a supply which comprises a single service from an economic point of view should not be artificially split'. Accordingly, the proprietors' supplies were wholly standard-rated. *LW & A Broadley (t/a Professional Haircare)*, LON/99/1073 (VTD 16643). (*Note.* For subsequent developments in this case, see **2.125** APPEALS.)

[41.89] Similar decisions, also applying the principles laid down in *Card Protection Plan Ltd*, **22.324** EUROPEAN COMMUNITY LAW, were reached in *Mr Francis Ltd*, EDN/99/163 (VTD 16804); *Q & M Olivieri*, LON/99/956 (VTD 16991); *SV Cranmer*, LON/95/3120 (VTD 17037); *DR Kirkman*, MAN/99/958 (VTD 17651); *WE Mallinson & M Woodbridge (t/a the Hair Team)*, MAN/99/644 (VTD 19087); and *LJ Mould (t/a Leon Jaimes Hair Fashions)*, MAN/02/041 (VTD 19087).

[41.90] A hairdresser (D) allowed other hairstylists to trade from his salon. He failed to register for VAT. Customs issued a notice of compulsory registration, and imposed a penalty for failure to register. D appealed, contending that the payments he received from the other stylists should be treated as exempt, so that his turnover was below the statutory threshold. The tribunal accepted this contention but the Ch D reversed this decision. Briggs J held that the supply which D made to the stylists was not simply a letting of immovable property, since the stylists' business of the stylists 'needed to be conducted not merely on the exclusively allocated part of the premises, but within the salon as a whole, in particular by use of the wash basins and the waiting area. Looked at in the round, the package in this case was the supply to the stylist of all the facilities requisite for the carrying on by him or her of the business of a hairdresser, including importantly the provision of an exclusive chair and allocated area, but including significantly also the facilities shared in common within the salon as a whole.' *HMRC v CJ Denyer*, Ch D 2007, [2008] STC 633; [2007] EWHC 2750 (Ch). (*Note*. The tribunal subsequently allowed D's appeal against the penalty—see **51.33** PENALTIES: FAILURE TO NOTIFY.)

[41.91] The proprietor of a hairdressing salon charged stylists working at the salon two distinct amounts, one expressed as a 'licence fee' for the right to use a specific chair and area of floor space, and one expressed as a 'service charge' for the right to use the general salon facilities. Customs issued a ruling that the proprietor was required to register for VAT, on the basis that both the 'licence fees' and the 'service charges' were taxable, so that the proprietor's turnover exceeded the statutory threshold. The proprietor appealed, contending that the 'licence fees' should be treated as exempt. The tribunal rejected this contention and dismissed the appeal, applying the principles laid down in *Card Protection Plan Ltd*, **22.324** EUROPEAN COMMUNITY LAW, and holding that the proprietor was making a single standard-rated supply of the right to use the facilities at the salon. The Ch D upheld this decision. Blackburne J held that the tribunal had been entitled to conclude that 'there was a single indivisible economic supply which it would be artificial to split'. The exemption under *Sch 9, Group 1, Item 1* did not 'extend to a licence to occupy land which is but one element of a package of supplies made by the taxpayer/lessor to his customer in consideration of a payment or payments by that customer where the supplies in question are commercial in nature or are best understood as the provision of a service and not simply as the making available of property'. *A Holland (t/a The Studio Hair Company) v HMRC*, Ch D 2008, [2009] STC 150; [2008] EWHC 2621 (Ch).

[41.92] A similar decision was reached in a case concerning a company, which the Ch D heard with *Holland*, **41.91** above. *Vigdor Ltd (t/a Michael Jane)*, Ch D 2008, [2009] STC 150; [2008] EWHC 2621 (Ch).

[41.93] A similar decision was reached in a case where the tribunal applied the principles laid down in *Holland*, **41.91** above, and specifically distinguished the decision in *Taylor's Executors*, **41.76** above. *Ms A Glen-Jones (t/a Sophisticuts) v HMRC*, [2011] UKFTT 141 (TC), TC01015.

[41.94] See also *Hopkins*, **51.69** PENALTIES: FAILURE TO NOTIFY; *Mantio*, **51.70** PENALTIES: FAILURE TO NOTIFY; *Howe*, **51.70** PENALTIES: FAILURE TO NOTIFY; and *Jamieson*, **52.407** PENALTIES: MISDECLARATION.

Massage salon—hire of rooms to masseuses

[41.95] A partnership operated a 'massage salon' in Manchester, charging customers £40 for admission. The premises included rooms equipped with double beds and bedlinen, to allow the masseuses to provide services described by the tribunal as 'of a different nature from those of pure massage'. The partnership charged masseuses £110 per day for the rent of such rooms, and provided security, cash handling, storage and changing facilities. The partnership did not register for VAT. Customs issued a ruling that the partnership was required to account for VAT on the rental payments which it received from the masseuses. The partnership appealed, contending that it was making exempt supplies of a licence to occupy land. The tribunal rejected the contention and dismissed the appeal, and the Ch D upheld this decision. Warren J held that 'the over-arching single supply is not to be treated as a supply of a licence to occupy land. The description which reflects economic and social reality is a supply of massage parlour services, one element of which is the provision of the room.' *Byrom, Kane & Kane (t/a Salon 24) v HMRC*, Ch D [2006] STC 992; [2006] EWHC 111 (Ch).

Hotel accommodation, etc. (VATA 1994, Sch 9, Group 1, Item 1(d))

University hall of residence

[41.96] The Commissioners sought to register a hall of residence at Manchester University, considering that the fees paid by the resident students were excluded from exemption by what is now *VATA 1994, Sch 9, Group 1, Item 1(d)*. The tribunal allowed the hall's appeal, holding that the hall was not a 'similar establishment' to a boarding house and was thus not excluded from exemption under *Sch 9, Group 1*. The tribunal observed that the hall placed 'emphasis on the living of a corporate, as opposed to an individual, existence while in residence'. Such emphasis was 'entirely foreign to life in a hotel or boarding house'. *J McMurray (a Governor of Allen Hall)*, [1973] VATTR 161 (VTD 39). (*Note.* The tribunal also considered that the supplies should be exempted under the then equivalent of *VATA 1994, Sch 9, Group 6*.)

Accommodation for overseas students

[41.97] A registered charity provided accommodation, in four buildings in London, for overseas students. The Commissioners issued a ruling that the charity was required to account for VAT on the fees which it received, on the basis that the buildings were a 'similar establishment' to a boarding house so that the fees were excluded from exemption by *VATA 1994, Sch 9, Group 1, Item 1(d)*. The tribunal allowed the charity's appeal, holding that the buildings were not a 'similar establishment' to a boarding house and accordingly the fees were not excluded from exemption. The tribunal observed that the 'predominant characteristic' of a hotel, inn or boarding house was 'the offer of use of accommodation for gain'. The charity was offering accommodation as part of its purpose of helping overseas students and improving international relations. Because most of the students remained in the UK for several years, they were not 'visitors or travellers' within the definition in *Sch 9, Group 1, Note 9*. *International Student House*, LON/95/3142 (VTD 14420).

[41.98] A company provided accommodation for students from US universities, who visited the UK for an average period of 15 weeks. The Commissioners issued an assessment on the fees which the company received, on the basis that the relevant accommodation was a 'similar establishment' to a boarding house so that the fees were excluded from exemption by *VATA 1994,*

Sch 9, Group 1, Item 1(d). The tribunal upheld the assessment and dismissed the company's appeal, holding that the students in question were 'visitors or travellers' within the definition in *Sch 9, Group 1, Note 9*. The tribunal distinguished *International Student House*, **41.97** above, on the grounds that the charity in that case had been providing a 'communal or corporate atmosphere' and that the students there were normally remaining in the UK for a period of several years. *Acorn Management Services Ltd*, LON/00/534 (VTD 17338).

Accommodation at Buddhist centre

[41.99] A registered charity, established to propagate the teachings of a 13th century Buddhist sage, owned a substantial property set in 80 acres of land, which it used as a base for residential courses. It reclaimed input tax on expenditure relating to the property. The Commissioners rejected the claim and issued a ruling that the supplies of accommodation were exempt under *VATA 1994, Sch 9, Group 1*. The charity appealed, contending that the supplies should be treated as excluded from exemption by *Item 1(d)*. The tribunal rejected this contention and dismissed the appeal, holding on the evidence that the property was used as a religious centre and was not 'an establishment with a function similar to a hotel'. *Soka Gakkai International UK*, LON/95/2554 (VTD 14175).

Hostel for homeless and unemployed

[41.100] A company owned a large property in London, where it provided 'bed and breakfast' accommodation for about 260 homeless and unemployed people. Most residents stayed for six months or more, and relied on financial support from the DHSS. The company did not account for VAT on the charges which it made for the accommodation. The Commissioners issued an assessment on the amounts charged, and the company appealed, contending that its supplies were exempt under what is now *VATA 1994, Sch 9, Group 1*. The tribunal dismissed the appeal, holding that the supplies were excluded from exemption by *Sch 9, Group 1, Item 1(d)*. *Namecourt Ltd*, [1984] VATTR 22 (VTD 1560).

[41.101] A company (N) operated a hostel for homeless people. It did not account for VAT on the charges which it made for the accommodation. The Commissioners issued an assessment on the amounts charged, and N appealed, contending that its supplies were exempt under what is now *VATA 1994, Sch 9, Group 1*. The tribunal dismissed the appeal, applying *Namecourt Ltd*, **41.100** above, and distinguishing *Dinaro Ltd*, **41.102** below, as the company there 'only accepted those persons who had mental health problems coming mainly from psychiatric institutions' and provided 'a higher degree of care and supervision'. Accordingly, N's supplies were excluded from exemption by *Sch 9, Group 1, Item 1(d)*. *North East Direct Access Ltd*, MAN/x (VTD 18267).

[41.102] A company owned a lodge which was used to provide supervised residential accommodation for people with mental health problems. The Commissioners issued a ruling that it was required to account for tax on its supplies of accommodation at the lodge, on the basis that the lodge was a 'similar establishment' to a boarding house so that the fees were excluded from exemption by *VATA 1994, Sch 9, Group 1, Item 1(d)*. The company appealed, contending that the lodge was not a 'similar establishment' so that the exclusion in *Item 1(d)* did not apply and its supplies qualified for exemption. The tribunal accepted this contention and allowed the appeal, observing that most of the residents at the lodge stayed for lengthy periods, 'receiving constant supervision and frequent attention'. The lodge only accepted people with 'mental problems coming mainly from psychiatric institutions upon their release to the outside world'. Most of the residents received disability living allowance. Accordingly, the lodge was not a 'similar establishment' to a boarding house. *Dinaro Ltd (t/a Fairway Lodge)*, LON/99/855 (VTD 17148).

Serviced accommodation

[41.103] An individual (M) purchased a building which was divided into flats but was in need of renovation. He renovated the flats and let them on a long-stay basis. He registered for VAT and reclaimed the input tax he had incurred. The Commissioners rejected his claim, considering that his supplies were exempt under what is now *VATA 1994, Sch 9, Group 1*. He appealed, contending that he intended to convert the flats into a hotel and that the supplies were excluded from exemption by *Sch 9, Group 1, Item 1(d)*. The tribunal dismissed his appeal, holding that the flats were not a 'similar establishment' to a hotel and that he was granting licences to occupy land, which were exempt from VAT. *BL Mills*, LON/84/91 (VTD 1686).

[41.104] Similar decisions were reached in *Asington Ltd*, EDN/02/176 (VTD 18171) and *GR & JM Holding*, LON/05/341 (VTD 19573).

Guest-house for permanent residents

[41.105] The owner of a guest-house, providing 'bed and breakfast' accommodation, failed to account for VAT on her receipts. The Commissioners issued an assessment and she appealed, contending that her supplies were exempt and that the guest-house was not similar to a hotel because she regarded her customers as permanent residents. The tribunal dismissed her appeal, holding that the guest-house was a 'similar establishment' to a boarding house and that the supplies were therefore excluded from exemption by what is now *VATA 1994, Sch 9, Group 1, Item 1(d)*. *HD Paddon*, LON/85/132 (VTD 1987).

Long-term accommodation in boarding house

[41.106] The proprietor of a boarding house failed to account for VAT on payments received from long-term residents. The Commissioners issued an assessment to recover the tax, against which she appealed. The tribunal dismissed her appeal, holding that the accommodation was excluded from exemption by what is now *VATA 1994, Sch 9, Group 1, Item 1(d)*. The QB upheld this decision. *Mrs RI McGrath v C & E Commrs*, QB [1992] STC 371.

Board and lodging in flats above restaurant

[41.107] The proprietor of a restaurant provided board and lodging in flats above the restaurant, but did not account for output tax on these supplies. The Commissioners issued an assessment charging tax on the receipts and the tribunal dismissed the proprietor's appeal, holding that the supplies were excluded from exemption by *VATA 1994, Sch 9, Group 1, Item 1(d)*. *AT Hussain (t/a Al Ameer)*, MAN/97/508 (VTD 15668).

Deposits for hotel accommodation—whether within Item 1(d)

[41.108] A company which owned a hotel failed to account for VAT on deposits. The Commissioners issued an assessment and the company appealed, contending that the deposits were exempt under what is now *VATA 1994, Sch 9, Group 1*. The tribunal dismissed the appeal, holding that the deposits were excluded from exemption by what is now *VATA 1994, Sch 9, Group 1, Item 1(d)*. *Camilla Enterprises Ltd*, EDN/92/247 (VTD 10426).

Building in London—whether a 'similar establishment' to a hotel

[41.109] A company owned the leasehold of a large building in London, which was divided into 74 rooms. These rooms were let to tenants, in many cases to companies. Initially the company accounted for tax under the 'reduced value' provisions of *VATA 1994, Sch 6 para 9*, although these provisions did not apply where the accommodation was provided to companies and was not occupied by the same individual for at least 28 days. When the Commissioners discovered this, they issued an assessment charging VAT at the standard rate on such lettings. The company appealed, contending that the building was not a 'similar establishment' to a hotel, so that the lettings were not excluded from exemption by what is now *VATA 1994, Sch 9, Group 1, Item 1(d)*, and the income should have been treated as exempt. The tribunal rejected this contention and dismissed the appeal, holding that the building was a 'similar establishment' to a hotel and that the income was excluded from exemption by *Item 1(d)*. *BJ Group Ltd*, LON/02/246 (VTD 18234).

Hire of rooms for wedding receptions—whether within Item 1(d)

[41.110] A hotelier did not account for VAT on the hire of rooms for wedding receptions. The Commissioners issued a ruling that VAT was chargeable on these supplies, on the basis that they were 'for the purpose of a supply of catering' and were therefore excluded from exemption by what is now *VATA 1994, Sch 9, Group 1, Item 1(d)*. The hotelier appealed. The tribunal chairman held that 'the fact that the bar is open in the evening to function guests' did not necessarily mean that the function room was provided for the purpose of a supply of catering. However, the burden of proof was on the appellant to show 'that the function room was not provided for the purpose of a supply of catering', and that 'so far no clear evidence of the purpose has been produced. As matters stand I do not find the facts sufficiently clear to reach any conclusion on the assessment. It may be that on some occasions the room was used in the evening for the purpose of a supply of catering and on some occasions any catering was not the substantial purpose.' The tribunal therefore adjourned the appeal for further argument. *S Packford*, LON/93/234A (VTD 11626). (*Note.* There was no further public hearing of the appeal. It is understood that Customs subsequently accepted that some of the hire charges were exempt, on the basis that 'catering was not the substantial purpose' of the hiring. Compare, however, the subsequent cases of *Willerby Manor Hotels Ltd*, **41.112** below, and *Blendhome Ltd*, **41.113** below. The decision here was not followed in *Willerby Manor Hotels*, on the grounds that it was inconsistent with the CJEC decision in *Card Protection Plan Ltd*, **22.324** EUROPEAN COMMUNITY LAW.)

[41.111] The hire of rooms for wedding receptions was held to be excluded from exemption by *VATA 1994, Sch 9, Group 1, Item 1(d)* in *Seamill Hydro*, 1998 (unreported). (*Note.* This decision has not been publicly released by the Tribunal Centre, but was cited as an authority by a subsequent tribunal in *Blendhome Ltd*, **41.113** below.)

[41.112] A company did not account for VAT on the hire of rooms for evening wedding receptions. The Commissioners issued a ruling that VAT was chargeable on these supplies, on the basis that they were 'for the purpose of a supply of catering' and were therefore excluded from exemption by what is now *VATA 1994, Sch 9, Group 1, Item 1(d)*. The company appealed, contending that the hire of rooms was a separate supply which qualified for exemption, applying *Packford*, **41.110** above. The tribunal rejected this contention and dismissed the appeal, declining to follow *Packford* on the grounds that it had been decided before the CJEC decision in *Card Protection Plan Ltd*, **22.324** EUROPEAN COMMUNITY LAW. The tribunal held that 'the hire of a function room for an evening reception is a supply ancillary to those of wedding reception facilities and is integral to the reception arrangements: it is a means of better enjoying the principal service supplied'. Accordingly, the company had 'made a composite supply of a standard-rated package of wedding reception facilities, the main ingredient in which was a supply of catering'. *Willerby Manor Hotels Ltd*, MAN/99/871 (VTD 16673).

Wedding reception at hotel—'exclusivity fee'

[41.113] A company which operated a hotel charged customers an 'exclusivity fee' of £900 entitling the guests at wedding receptions to the exclusive use of the hotel and its grounds. The Commissioners issued a ruling that the 'exclusivity fees' were paid 'for the purpose of a supply of catering' and were therefore excluded from exemption by *VATA 1994, Sch 9, Group 1, Item 1(d)*. The company appealed, contending that the 'exclusivity fees' were paid for the right of exclusive occupation of land, which should be treated as exempt from VAT. The tribunal rejected this contention and dismissed the appeal. Applying *dicta* of the CJEC in *Card Protection Plan Ltd*, **22.324** EUROPEAN COMMUNITY LAW, the 'exclusivity fee' was a 'means of better enjoying the principal service supplied'. It followed that the fees were paid 'for the purpose of a supply of catering' and were therefore excluded from exemption. *Blendhome Ltd (t/a Stanhill Court Hotel)*, LON/98/866 (VTD 16048).

Hire of country house for wedding ceremonies

[41.114] A company owned a large country house, which it hired for weddings, wedding receptions and other functions. It did not account for VAT on its income from hiring the property, treating it as exempt. HMRC issued an assessment on the basis that the property was a 'similar establishment' to a hotel, and that the supplies were excluded from exemption by *VATA 1994, Sch 9, Group 1, Item 1(d)*. They also imposed a misdeclaration penalty. The company appealed. The tribunal dismissed the appeal against the assessment, holding that the property was within *Item 1(d)*. (However the tribunal allowed the company's appeal against the misdeclaration penalty, holding that the company had a 'reasonable excuse' for having treated its supplies as exempt, since its director had telephoned HMRC's National Advice Line in 2004 and had been given the impression that the supplies would be exempt.) *Acrylux Ltd v HMRC*, [2009] SFTD 763; [2009] UKFTT 223 (TC), TC00173.

[41.115] See also *Leez Priory*, 41.58 above, and *Chewton Glen Hotels Ltd*, 41.59 above.

Holiday accommodation (VATA 1994, Sch 9, Group 1, Item 1(e))

Short lettings of furnished flats

[41.116] A married couple owned a house in Highgate comprising three furnished flats. One of the flats was let under a controlled tenancy. The other two were let for short periods. The couple registered with the English Tourist Board and advertised the flats as 'fully furnished holiday accommodation'. They did not account for VAT on the rent from the flats and the Commissioners issued an assessment charging tax on the rents, on the basis that they were excluded from exemption by what is now *VATA 1994, Sch 9, Group 1, Item 1(e)*. The couple appealed, contending that they had only advertised the flats as holiday accommodation in order to ensure that the tenancies would not be controlled, and that at least half of their lettings were not to holidaymakers. The tribunal dismissed their appeal, holding that, as the flats were advertised as holiday accommodation, the rents were excluded from exemption. *RW & B Sheppard*, [1977] VATTR 272 (VTD 481).

[41.117] Three flats located above a grocery shop, and advertised as holiday accommodation, were held to be excluded from exemption by what is now *VATA 1994, Sch 9, Group 1, Item 1(e)* in *VWS Morgan*, CAR/77/437 (VTD 633).

'Time-share' holiday accommodation

[41.118] A company built a number of houses on an estate. It sold 'holiday certificates', entitling the purchaser to occupy one of the houses for up to twelve weeks each year. It did not account for VAT on these sales. The Commissioners issued an assessment charging tax on them, and the company appealed, contending that they should be treated as exempt from VAT. The tribunal dismissed the appeal, holding that the sales were excluded from exemption by what is now *VATA 1994, Sch 9, Group 1, Item 1(e)*. *American Real Estate (Scotland) Ltd*, [1980] VATTR 80 (VTD 947).

[41.119] A couple converted a barn in Cornwall into holiday accommodation. They sold nine weekly units in the accommodation, giving each purchaser the right to occupy it for a specified week for a period of 25 years. The freehold of the property was conveyed to a bank as a trustee, to be sold after 25 years. Each purchaser of a 'time-share' unit was invited to make an additional payment of £350 to purchase a 2% interest in the sale proceeds. Seven of the nine purchasers did so. The couple did not account for VAT on their receipts and the Commissioners issued an assessment. The tribunal dismissed the couple's appeal, holding that the supplies were excluded from exemption by what is now *VATA 1994, Sch 9, Group 1, Item 1(e)*. *P & V Cretney*, [1983] VATTR 271 (VTD 1503).

[41.120] A company owned a number of cottages in Devon. It gave its shareholders the right to one week's holiday each year in one of the cottages for a period of 25 years. It advertised some of its shares for sale, at a price which depended on the cottage and time of year chosen by the shareholder. The Commissioners issued a ruling that the company was carrying on a business of supplying holiday accommodation and was required to be registered for VAT. The company appealed, contending that the only supplies which it made were of shares, which were exempt from VAT. The tribunal dismissed the appeal, observing that an intending shareholder reading the company's prospectus would be bound to notice the different subscription rates charged for the shares. The tribunal held that the amount paid by shareholders should be apportioned, with £1 being attributed to the exempt supply of a share and the balance being attributed to the taxable supply of holiday accommodation. *Court Barton Property plc*, [1985] VATTR 148 (VTD 1903).

[41.121] The time-sharing of a yacht was held to be standard-rated in *Oathplan Ltd*, [1982] VATTR 195 (VTD 1299).

[41.122] A company reclaimed input tax on the purchase of a property. The Commissioners issued an assessment to recover the tax on the basis that the property had been purchased for the purpose of making exempt supplies. The company appealed, contending that it had purchased the property 'for commercial use'. The tribunal dismissed the company's appeal, finding that the company had stated that it intended refurbishing the property with the intention of letting it as timeshare accommodation, and observing that such supplies would be exempt from VAT. (Since the building was not a 'new' building as defined by what is now *Group 1, Note 4*, the effect of *Group 1, Note 12* was that the exclusion in *Item 1(e)* would not apply—although this is not explicitly stated in the decision.) The tribunal also observed that 'it is for the appellant to show that the input tax for which he claims credit relates to taxable supplies made or to be made by him in the course or furtherance of his business, and, in respect of a provisional deduction of input tax, that no part of the input tax relates to goods or services used or to be used by him in making exempt supplies'. *Key Properties Ltd*, LON/92/2266A (VTD 11778). (*Note*. For other issues in this case, see **36.466** INPUT TAX and **52.281** PENALTIES: MISDECLARATION.)

[41.123] A company which had sold timeshare licences repurchased some of the licences from a bank which had taken over the licences after the original purchasers had defaulted. The company reclaimed input tax in respect of the repurchases. The Commissioners issued an assessment to recover the tax, considering that the repurchases were exempt from VAT under what is now *VATA 1994, Sch 9, Group 1*. The tribunal dismissed the company's appeal, holding that the repurchases were exempt and that the effect of *Group 1, Note 12* was that the exclusion in *Item 1(e)* did not apply. *Interlude Houses Ltd*, EDN/94/65 (VTD 12877).

[41.124] See also *RCI Europe Ltd*, **22.207** EUROPEAN COMMUNITY LAW.

Flats advertised for holiday use but subsequently leased

[41.125] See *Cooper & Chapman (Builders) Ltd*, **46.195** PARTIAL EXEMP-TION.

Beach huts

[41.126] A borough council did not account for VAT on income received from letting beach huts. The Commissioners issued a ruling that the income was liable to VAT on the basis that it was excluded from exemption by what is now *VATA 1994, Sch 9, Group 1, Item 1(e)*. The tribunal upheld the Commissioners' ruling and dismissed the council's appeal. 'Holiday accommodation' was not restricted to residential accommodation. The huts were capable of being used for cooking, eating, shelter, changing clothes and a variety of other uses. Accordingly they were within the definition of 'holiday accommodation'. *Poole Borough Council*, [1992] VATTR 88 (VTD 7180).

Lease of house precluding occupation in February of each year

[41.127] In 1988 a married couple were assigned a 98-year lease of a riverside property in Cambridgeshire. Under the lease, the lessees were not permitted to occupy the property during the month of February. Since they had no other residence, they spent each February with their daughter in Germany. Following amendments to *VATA 1983* by *SI 1990/2553*, the company which owned the freehold charged the couple VAT on the ground rent and service charge. The couple objected, and the Commissioners issued a formal ruling that the payments were standard-rated because of the covenant prohibiting residence throughout the year, which had the effect that the lease fell within what is now *VATA 1994, Sch 8 Group 5, Note 7* and *VATA 1994, Sch 9, Group 1, Note 11*. The wife appealed, contending that the restrictions imposed by *SI 1990/2053* were not in accordance with *Article 13B* of the *EC Sixth Directive*. The tribunal accepted this contention and allowed the appeal, observing that *Article 13B(b)* excluded 'the provision of accommodation in holiday camps or on sites developed for use as camping sites'. It was accepted that the property in question was not situated in a holiday camp. The terms of *SI 1990/2053* were outside the scope of *Article 13B*, and the introduction of what is now *VATA 1994, Sch 9, Group 1, Note 11* 'was an excessive exercise of the power given by *Article 13B(b)*'. It had led to the appellant suffering an inequality of treatment as compared with lessees who were free to occupy their homes throughout the year. Applying *dicta* of the CJEC in *Groupment des Hauts Fourneaux et Acieres Belges v High Authority of the European Coal and Steel Community*, CJEC [1958] ECSC 245, such inequality of treatment was not objectively justifiable and was therefore 'arbitrary, discriminatory and illegal'. *BA Ashworth*, [1994] VATTR 275 (VTD 12924).

Caravan facilities (VATA 1994, Sch 9, Group 1, Item 1(f))

Storage

[41.128] Winter storage of caravans was held not to be exempt from VAT in *MP & CM Warner*, MAN/86/385 (VTD 2409).

[41.129] A similar decision was reached in *Unity Farm Holiday Centre Ltd*, LON/87/145 (VTD 2620). (*Notes*. (1) For an appeal by an associated partnership, heard with this case, see **36.343** INPUT TAX. (2) The tribunal chairman also expressed the opinion, as *obiter dicta*, that caravans were not 'vehicles'. This opinion was not followed in the subsequent cases of *DH Commercials (Leasing) Ltd*, **41.143** below, or *Newall*, **41.144** below, and was specifically disapproved in the subsequent case of *Hopcraft*, **41.144** below.)

Seasonal pitches for caravans

[41.130] A caravan site was only open from 1 March to 31 October in each year, this being a condition of the relevant planning permission. The proprietors of the site did not account for output tax on receipts from licences to occupy the site for periods extending for more than one year, treating the receipts as exempt. The Commissioners issued an assessment on the basis that the receipts were excluded from exemption by what is now *VATA 1994, Sch 9, Group 1, Item 1(f)* and *Note 14*, and thus were standard-rated. The proprietors appealed. The tribunal dismissed the appeal, holding that the effect of what is now *Note 14(b)* was that the licences were for seasonal pitches and thus were excluded from exemption. *T & M Smith*, MAN/94/45 (VTD 13052).

[41.131] A similar decision was reached in a case where a caravan site was closed in January of each year. The tribunal held that the company which owned the site was supplying 'seasonal pitches' which were excluded from exemption. *Ticklock Ltd v HMRC*, [2010] UKFTT 284 (TC), TC00573.

[41.132] A company operated 22 caravan parks. It let a large number of pitches to caravan owners. It was a condition of the lettings that the owners could not use the caravans as a permanent address and could not stay overnight from December to February. The Commissioners issued rulings that the company's receipts were taxable, being excluded from exemption by *VATA 1994, Sch 9, Group 1, Item 1(f)* and *Note 14*. The company appealed, contending that this restriction was a breach of *Article 13B* of the *EC Sixth Directive*. The tribunal, Ch D and CA all rejected this contention and dismissed the appeal. Arden LJ held that 'the exclusion of such property from the lettings exemption is consistent with the rationale of the exemption', and that 'a Member State is entitled to have regard to its own economic conditions, and to take into account the differences between different sorts of immovable property'. *Colaingrove Ltd v C & E Commrs*, CA [2004] STC 712; [2004] EWCA Civ 146.

[41.133] In *DH Commercials (Leasing) Ltd*, **41.143** below, the tribunal chairman held that for the provision of a pitch for a caravan to fall within *Sch 9, Group 1, Item 1(f)*, it must 'necessarily be on a site where at some stage in the year', the caravan 'must be available for human habitation'.

Pitches for caravans—whether within Sch 9, Group 1, Note 14

[41.134] A company (T) owned a large caravan site with room for more than 300 caravans. The licence agreements provided that, in accordance with the relevant planning permission, caravans could not be occupied during February of each year. T initially treated its receipts as taxable, but subsequently submitted a repayment claim on the basis that it should have treated them as exempt. Customs rejected the claim and T appealed, contending that it no longer enforced the restriction on occupation of the site during February. The tribunal allowed the appeal but the Ch D reversed this decision and restored Customs' ruling. David Richards J held that the effect of *Town and Country Planning Act 1990, s 171B(3)* was that the local authority had still had the power to enforce the original planning permission which prevented occupation during February. The fact that T had allowed some owners to breach that condition did not prevent *VATA 1994, Sch 9, Group 1, Note 14* from applying. Accordingly the receipts did not qualify for exemption. *HMRC v Tallington Lakes Ltd*, Ch D 2007, [2008] STC 2734; [2007] EWHC 1955(Ch).

Caravan sites—whether input tax reclaimable

[41.135] See *Stonecliff Caravan Park*, **69.6** ZERO-RATING: MISCELLANEOUS.

Parking facilities (VATA 1994, Sch 9, Group 1, Item 1(h))

[41.136] An individual rented a garage for £4 per month plus VAT. He lodged an appeal against the charge to VAT, contending that he had been granted a right over land, which was exempt from VAT. The tribunal dismissed his appeal, holding that 'garage facilities are for present purposes no different to parking facilities'. The tribunal observed that 'in English parlance, "garage" implies walls and a roof, but a car can be parked in a garage just as it can be parked in a yard.' Accordingly the supply was excluded from exemption by what is now *VATA 1994, Sch 9, Group 1, Item 1(h)*. *AJ Dowse*, LON/73/102 (VTD 46).

[41.137] The decision in *Dowse*, **41.136** above, was applied in the similar cases of *F Bondi*, LON/75/70 (VTD 173) and *LO Clarke*, CAR/77/29 (VTD 457).

[41.138] An individual who leased three garages appealed against the charge to VAT, contending that he had been granted rights over land, which were exempt from VAT, and that the exclusion of 'parking facilities' did not apply, since he was using the garages for storage purposes. The tribunal rejected this contention and dismissed his appeal, holding that the garages were within the definition of 'parking facilities', so that 'there was an express grant of the facility for parking a vehicle'. Accordingly the leases were excluded from exemption by what is now *VATA 1994, Sch 9, Group 1, Item 1(h)*. *GG Wilson*, [1977] VATTR 225 (VTD 428).

[41.139] A company (H) owned a cinema with an adjacent plot of land which it used as a car park for its employees and customers. On the other side of the car park was a supermarket. H granted a licence to the company which owned the supermarket, allowing that company's employees and customers to use the car park. Under the licence, H received payments from the supermarket. H did not account for VAT on these payments, and the Commissioners issued an assessment charging tax on them. The tribunal dismissed H's appeal, holding that the payments were excluded from exemption by what is now *VATA 1994, Sch 9, Group 1, Item 1(h)*. *Henley Picture House Ltd*, BIR/79/107 (VTD 895).

[41.140] A company which carried on business as motor vehicle auctioneers charged customers for parking vehicles which they wished to sell. The Commissioners issued an assessment on the basis that the payments by the customers were liable to VAT, and the tribunal dismissed the company's appeal. *Inter City Motor Auctions Ltd*, EDN/86/83 (VTD 2319).

[41.141] The lease of two parking spaces was held to be within *VATA 1994, Sch 9, Group 1, Item 1(h)*, and thus excluded from exemption, in *Internoms Ltd*, LON/98/1112 (VTD 16527).

[41.142] A company owned a number of lock-up garages and converted stables, which it leased. Where lessees had indicated that they wished to use the garages for storage, the company did not account for tax on the payments received under the leases, considering that they were exempt under what is now *VATA 1994, Sch 9, Group 1*. The Commissioners issued an assessment charging tax on the payments, considering that they constituted parking facilities which were excluded from exemption by *Sch 9, Group 1, Item 1(h)*. The CS upheld the assessment. Where lock-up garages were let, the plain implication was that facilities had been granted for parking a vehicle. Moreover, even if, before entering the lease, the parties had agreed that the purpose of the letting was domestic storage, the terms of the lease did not preclude the lessee from using the facilities for parking a vehicle. Accordingly, where an unqualified lease of a lock-up garage was granted, the necessary implication was that there had been a grant of facilities for parking a vehicle. *C & E Commrs v Trinity Factoring Services Ltd*, CS [1994] STC 504.

[41.143] A company provided storage facilities for caravans. It did not account for output tax on its receipts. The Commissioners issued a ruling that the receipts were liable to VAT, and the company appealed, contending that they should be treated as exempt under *VATA 1994, Sch 9, Group 1*. The tribunal dismissed the appeal, holding that the company was supplying parking facilities, which were excluded from exemption by *Group 1, Item 1(h)*. *DH Commercials (Leasing) Ltd*, MAN/95/2125 (VTD 14115). (*Note.* The tribunal also held that the supplies did not fall within *Item 1(f)*—see **41.133** above.)

[41.144] The decision in *DH Commercials (Leasing) Ltd*, **41.143** above, was applied in the similar subsequent cases of *AC Slot*, LON/94/1089 (VTD 15076); *A & A Newall*, MAN/01/887 (VTD 18074) and *B Hopcraft*, LON/01/1325 (VTD 18590).

[41.145] A company granted an associated partnership a lease of an area of land. The partnership used the land as a car park, and accounted for VAT on its receipts. However, the company did not account for tax on the amounts which the partnership paid it under the lease. The Commissioners issued an assessment charging tax on them, on the basis that they were excluded from exemption by *VATA 1994, Sch 9, Group 1, Item 1(h)*. The Ch D upheld the assessment. Sir Andrew Morritt V-C observed that it was clear that the land had been used for car parking facilities for at least five years, and that clearly meant that the land had been let for parking facilities, within *Group 1, Item 1(h)*. *C & E Commrs v Venuebest Ltd*, Ch D 2002, [2003] STC 433; [2002] EWHC 2870 (Ch).

[41.146] The proprietor of a basketball club leased some land from a City Council, and sublet the land to a football club. He did not account for VAT on the rent which he received from the football club, treating it as exempt. The Commissioners issued an assessment charging tax on the rent, on the basis that the land was used as 'parking facilities', and the rent was therefore excluded from exemption by *VATA 1994, Sch 9, Group 1, Item 1(h)*. The proprietor appealed, contending that the land was not used as parking facilities, but as a means of access to and from the ground for spectators and for service vehicles (such as ambulances, fire engines and police cars). The tribunal accepted his evidence and allowed his appeal. *KT Routledge*, MAN/03/999 (VTD 18395).

[41.147] A company (C) leased 97 residential apartments and 22 car parking spaces. It did not account for VAT on the income from leasing the car parking spaces. HMRC issued an assessment charging tax on this income, and the representative member of C's VAT group appealed, contending that the leases of the apartments and the car parking spaces should be treated as an a 'single economic transaction'. The tribunal rejected this contention and dismissed the appeal, holding that the leasing of the car parking spaces was a separate standard-rated supply. *Civilscent Ltd v HMRC*, [2009] SFTD 233; [2009] UKFTT 102 (TC), TC00070.

[41.148] See also *Skatteministeriet v Henriksen*, **22.332** EUROPEAN COMMUNITY LAW.

Mooring facilities, etc. (VATA 1994, Sch 9, Group 1, Item 1(k))

Provision of berth

[41.149] An individual held a licence to berth a boat at a wharf on the River Wey. He was charged £120 plus VAT, and lodged an appeal against the charge to VAT, contending that he had been granted a right over land, which was exempt from VAT. The tribunal dismissed his appeal, holding that the supply was excluded from exemption by what is now *VATA 1994, Sch 9, Group 1, Item 1(k)*. *JW Fisher*, LON/75/47 (VTD 179).

[41.150] A company owned land alongside the River Thames. It built a creek leading from the river, and allowed members of the public to moor boats at specified plots of land alongside the creek. It did not account for VAT on the amounts which it charged for the facilities. The Commissioners issued an assessment charging tax on them, and the company appealed, contending that it had granted rights over land, which should be treated as exempt from VAT. The tribunal dismissed the company's appeal, holding that the supplies were excluded from exemption by what is now *VATA 1994, Sch 9, Group 1, Item 1(k)*. *Strand Ship Building Co Ltd*, LON/84/74 (VTD 1651).

[41.151] A similar decision was reached in *Threshfield Motors Ltd*, MAN/98/305 (VTD 16699).

[41.152] A married couple, who lived on a yacht moored at a quay on the River Medina, appealed against the imposition of VAT on the mooring fees, contending that they should be treated as exempt from VAT. The tribunal dismissed the couple's appeal, holding that the fees were specifically excluded from exemption by what is now *VATA 1994, Sch 9, Group 1, Item 1(k)*. *DM & PJ Roberts*, [1992] VATTR 30 (VTD 7516). (*Note*. The tribunal also held that, although it was accepted that the couple lived on the yacht, the yacht was not a 'houseboat' for the purposes of *VATA 1994, Sch 8 Group 9*—see **69.12** ZERO-RATING: MISCELLANEOUS.)

Sports grounds, etc. (VATA 1994, Sch 9, Group 1, Item 1(l))

Admission to rugby league ground

[41.153] A rugby league club did not account for VAT on amounts paid by spectators for admission to its home matches. The Commissioners issued an assessment on the payments and the club appealed, contending that they were exempt from VAT. The tribunal dismissed the club's appeal, holding that 'there is a distinction between a licence to occupy land and a licence generally in respect of, or relating to, land'. The spectators had 'at most an ambulatory right' and 'no dominant tenement'. Accordingly the payments did not qualify for exemption. *Rochdale Hornets Football Club Ltd*, [1975] VATTR 71 (VTD

161). (*Note.* The case also concerned zero-rating provisions in *FA 1972, Sch 4, Group 5*, which was repealed with effect from 1 May 1985.)

Admission to rugby union ground

[41.154] See *Clwb Rygbi Nant Conwy*, **13.8** CLUBS, ASSOCIATIONS AND ORGANISATIONS.

Executive boxes at football ground

[41.155] A football club granted seasonal licences of executive boxes at its ground. In accounting for VAT, it treated 97.36% of the consideration as attributable to an exempt licence to occupy land, and 2.64% as being excluded from exemption by *VATA 1994, Sch 9, Group 1, Item 1(l)*. The Commissioners issued an assessment charging tax on the basis that 98% of the consideration was excluded from exemption by *VATA 1994, Sch 9, Group 1, Item 1(l)*. The club appealed, contending that the ground was only used for football matches for 96 hours per year, whereas its licencees could use the boxes for 3,640 hours per year (i.e. 364 days at 10 hours per day), so that on a time basis, only 2.64% of the consideration should be treated as being within *Item 1(l)*. The tribunal rejected this contention and dismissed the appeal, subject to an adjustment to the assessments so that some of the consideration could be attributed to the provision of light refreshments on match days. In principle, the exception in *Item 1(l)* should be interpreted as operating only when a box was actually available to view a football match, since the purpose of the provision was 'to tax entertainment'. However, on the evidence, although some licensees made limited use of their boxes on days other than match days, others used them only to watch matches. The value of the right to use a box for 'a given unit of time for a period whilst a match was taking place was much greater than that outside such a period'. The club's calculations were wrong in principle since they 'ignored the issue of value'. The Commissioners had acted fairly and reasonably in treating 98% of the consideration as falling within *Item 1(l)*. *Southend United Football Club*, [1997] VATDR 202 (VTD 15109).

Facilities for playing sport (VATA 1994, Sch 9, Group 1, Item 1(m))

Supply of football ground for international match

[41.156] The company which owned Hampden Park allowed the Scottish Football Association to use it for international matches. The Commissioners issued a ruling that the supplies of the use of Hampden Park constituted licences to occupy land, which were exempt from VAT, so that the company's input tax had to be apportioned. The company appealed, contending that the supply amounted to the granting of facilities for playing sport, which was excluded from exemption by what is now *VATA 1994, Sch 9, Group 1, Item 1(m)*, and thus was standard-rated. The tribunal allowed the company's appeal, holding that the presence of paying spectators did not prevent the facilities from falling within *Item 1(m)*. *Queens Park Football Club Ltd*, [1988] VATTR 76 (VTD 2776).

Use of rugby union ground

[41.157] See *Clwb Rygbi Nant Conwy*, **13.8** CLUBS, ASSOCIATIONS AND ORGANISATIONS.

Grant of licence to occupy land for teaching golf

[41.158] A golf club professional (J) granted assistant professionals licences to use a practice range at the club for teaching people how to swing a golf club. He did not account for tax on the money which he received from the assistant professionals, treating them as exempt from VAT. The Commissioners issued assessments charging tax on J's receipts on the basis that they were excluded from exemption by *VATA 1994, Sch 9, Group 1, Item 1(m)*. The tribunal upheld the assessments and dismissed J's appeal. Applying *Skatteministeriet v Henriksen*, **22.332** EUROPEAN COMMUNITY LAW, exemptions were to be construed narrowly and exceptions to exemptions were to be construed widely. The practice area was within the curtilage of the golf course and should be treated as a facility for playing sport, within *Item 1(m)*. *LH Johnson*, LON/97/9 (VTD 14955).

Grant of non-exclusive licence to occupy golf courses

[41.159] A company (G) which owned two golf courses granted a golf club a non-exclusive licence to occupy its courses, receiving a licence fee of £280,000. G did not account for output tax on this fee, treating it as being consideration for a licence to occupy land and thus as exempt from VAT. The Commissioners issued an assessment on the basis that the payment was taxable, considering that it was excluded from exemption by *VATA 1994, Sch 9, Group 1, Item 1(m)*, as being 'the grant of facilities for playing any sport'. The tribunal allowed G's appeal, holding that the fact that the licence was not exclusive did not prevent it from constituting a 'licence to occupy land', within *Item 1*. Applying *dicta* of Lord Templeman in *Street v Mountford*, HL [1985] 1 AC 809; [1985] 2 All ER 289, exclusivity of occupation was an essential condition of a tenancy but was not an essential condition of a licence. The chairman observed that 'what distinguishes a tenancy from a licence is that the former grants a legal right to exclusive possession of the land for a particular period'. The chairman declined to follow *dicta* in *Mount Edgcumbe Hospice Ltd*, **11.54** CHARITIES (which the Commissioners had cited as an authority), observing that the issue in the appeal of *Mount Edgcumbe* was 'not similar to that in the present case'. The tribunal also held that *VATA 1994, Sch 9, Group 1, Item 1(m)* did not apply, since G had granted the club 'a licence to occupy land, not facilities for playing any sport or participating in any physical recreation'. The club had occupied the land for the purpose of granting such facilities to its members, but what G had granted the club was simply a licence to occupy land. The chairman observed that 'the licence envisaged that the club would occupy the property for use as a golf course and club, but that object of the licence is not the grant of the facilities which would be created after the grant. It would be a distortion of language to say that (G) was granting facilities for playing sport or participating in physical recreation to the club.' *Abbotsley Golf & Squash Club Ltd*, [1997] VATDR 355 (VTD 15042). (*Notes.* (1) For the Commissioners' practice following this decision, see Business Brief 25/97, issued on 10 November 1997, and Business Brief 22/98, issued on 3 November 1998. For their subsequent interpretation of what constitutes a licence to occupy land, see Business Brief 21/99, issued on 7 September 1999, and *Amendment 3 (October 1999)* to *Notice 742: Land and Property.* (2) The decisions in *Mount Edgcumbe Hospice Ltd* and *Abbotsley Golf & Squash Club Ltd* were reached by the same tribunal chairman (Mr. Heim), although his reasoning in the latter case appears to contradict his reasoning in the previous case on the question of the taxability of the licences. For a fuller analysis, see the memorandum by the VAT Practitioners' Group published in the Tax Journal, 8 March 1999.)

Letting of hockey pitches—whether within Item 1(m)

[41.160] A sports club granted a hockey association a licence to use some artificial hockey pitches between 8.00am and 9.30pm each day. (The relevant planning permission stipulated that the floodlights could not be used after 9.30pm.) It reclaimed input tax relating to the supply. Customs issued a ruling that the supply was exempt. The club appealed, contending that it was excluded from exemption by *VATA 1994, Sch 9, Group 1, Item 1(m)*. The tribunal accepted this contention and allowed the appeal, observing that *Note 16(a)* did not apply because the grant was not for 'a continuous period of use exceeding 24 hours' and that *Note 16(b)* did not apply because the interval between each period was ten and a half hours (ie 'less than one day'). *Polo Farm Sports Club (No 2)*, [2007] VATDR 44 (VTD 20105).

Hire of gymnasium to gymnastic clubs—whether within Item 1(m)

[41.161] A registered charity was established to build and own a gymnasium, to be used by local gymnastic clubs and other organisations. Initially it accounted for output tax on its income from letting the gymnasium to clubs, but in 1996 its treasurer wrote to the VAT office, asking for the income to be treated as exempt. The Commissioners rejected the claim and issued a ruling that the supplies were standard-rated. The tribunal dismissed the charity's appeal, holding that the supplies were excluded from exemption under *Group 1* by *Item 1(m)*. The tribunal observed that *Note 16* did not apply because none of the gymnastic clubs had exclusive use of the facilities, as required by *Note 16(b)(iv)*. (The tribunal also observed that the supplies were not exempt under *Group 10, Item 3* because they were not made to individuals.) *Colchester School of Gymnastics*, LON/97/1172 (VTD 15370).

Hire of room to dancing school—whether within Item 1(m)

[41.162] A couple operated a dancing school in partnership. They hired a room for their classes. The Commissioners issued a ruling that the hire of the room was standard-rated, being facilities for 'participating in any physical recreation', and thus excluded from exemption by *VATA 1994, Sch 9, Group 1, Item 1(m)*. The couple appealed, contending that they should be treated as operating a 'school' within *Note 16(b)(v)*, so that the hire was not excluded from exemption. The tribunal rejected this contention and dismissed their appeal, holding that their 'school of dancing' was 'not a school within the meaning of the *Note*'. *P & B Pritchard*, MAN/x (VTD 18019).

Miscellaneous

Whether Group 1, Item 1 consistent with EC Sixth Directive

[41.163] See *Norbury Developments Ltd*, **22.511** EUROPEAN COMMUNITY LAW.

42

Local Authorities and Statutory Bodies

The cases in this chapter are arranged under the following headings.

Refunds of VAT (VATA 1994, s 33)   42.1
Miscellaneous   42.11

Refunds of VAT (VATA 1994, s 33)

Rebuilding of Alexandra Palace—whether input tax reclaimable

[42.1] In 1980 most of Alexandra Palace was destroyed by fire. Between 1985 and 1990 Haringey Borough Council, which was the trustee of the Palace, reclaimed input tax incurred in rebuilding it. Customs initially accepted the repayment claims, but in December 1990 they issued an assessment to recover much of the tax, considering that a significant proportion of the expenditure was attributable to the hire of the Palace as an exhibition centre, and that such supplies were exempt from VAT under what is now *VATA 1994, Sch 9 Group 1*. The Council appealed, contending firstly that it had incurred the expenditure in the course of its statutory duties under the *Alexandra Park & Palace (Public Purposes) Act 1900*, so that the whole of the tax was reclaimable under what is now *VATA 1994, s 33(1)*, and alternatively that any input tax attributable to exempt supplies was 'an insignificant proportion' of the total tax, and should therefore be refunded under *VATA 1994, s 33(2)*. The QB rejected the Council's first contention, holding that the business purpose could not be treated as irrelevant or incidental, but accepted the Council's second contention, holding that the Council had been justified in treating the proportion of its input tax attributable to exempt supplies as insignificant. On the facts found by the tribunal, no more than 8% of the total expenditure related to exempt supplies, and this was within the definition of 'insignificant'. Furthermore, Customs had made the initial repayments on a lawful basis, and there had been no misrepresentation by the Council. The opinions which had led the Commissioners to make refunds between 1985 and 1990 'were ones which they were entitled to form'. It was not open to Customs to resile from their initial acceptance that the exempt input tax could be treated as insignificant. *Mayor & Burgesses of the London Borough of Haringey v C & E Commrs (and cross-appeal)*, QB [1995] STC 830. (*Note.* For Customs' practice following this decision, see Business Brief 11/95, issued on 2 June 1995, and Notice No 749, paras 4.4 and 4.5.)

Grants made by Council for work in reducing smoke emissions

[42.2] A Borough Council declared parts of its district as 'smoke control areas' under the *Clean Air Act 1956*, and made grants to householders who arranged for contractors to carry out specified work with the aim of reducing smoke emissions. The Department of the Environment reimbursed 57% of the amounts which the Council paid. The Council had to bear the remaining 43% of the cost itself, and reclaimed the input tax included in the contractors' charges. Customs rejected the claim, on the grounds that the supplies were made to the householders rather than to the Council. The Council appealed, contending that the tax should be treated as reclaimable under what is now *VATA 1994, s 33.* The tribunal dismissed the appeal, holding that the Council could not reclaim the input tax since it was 'not involved in the transactions between any of the householders who obtained grants from it and the contractors who carried out the grant-aided works'. *Doncaster Borough Council*, MAN/93/1157 (VTD 12458).

Home improvement grants made by Council

[42.3] A District Council made grants, under the *Housing Grants Construction and Regeneration Act 1996*, to help householders to renovate their properties. The Council reclaimed input tax on the amounts charged by the contractors which carried out the necessary work. Customs rejected the claim, on the grounds that the supplies were made to the individual householders rather than to the Council. The Council appealed, contending that the tax should be treated as reclaimable under *VATA 1994, s 33.* The tribunal rejected this contention and dismissed the appeal, holding that the contractors were not making any supplies to the Council. The Ch D upheld this decision. Sir Andrew Morritt V-C held that the relevant payments were made by the householders, with the Council merely acting as their agent. Furthermore, the payment of a grant did not give the Council any right against the contractors. *Ashfield District Council v C & E Commrs*, Ch D [2001] STC 1706.

Grant made by Council to establish community arts centre

[42.4] A borough council agreed to help to establish a community arts centre. It leased a site to a company which had been formed to operate the centre. Under the lease agreement, the council agreed to arrange for substantial building work at the site, for which the company agreed to make a contribution of £130,000. The council reclaimed input tax on the building work. Customs issued an assessment to recover the tax, on the basis that it was attributable to an exempt supply. The council appealed, contending that it should be treated as reclaimable under *VATA 1994, s 33.* The tribunal rejected this contention and dismissed the appeal, holding that the lease was 'a business transaction' so that the tax was not within *s 33(1)(b).* The Ch D upheld this decision. Patten J held that a refund under *s 33* was only available where a local authority could demonstrate that the relevant input tax related to an inward supply of services which was not made for the purpose of any business carried on by the authority. Applying the CJEC decision in *Ufficio Distrettuale delle Imposte Dirette di Fiorenzuola d'Arda v Comune di Carpaneto Piacentino*, **22.129** EUROPEAN COMMUNITY LAW, the determining factor was 'whether the transaction itself is governed by the ordinary rules of private law' or whether it took effect under 'a special legal regime applicable to local authorities'. The tribunal had been entitled to conclude that the grant of the lease 'was a business transaction and created a business relationship between the parties'. *West Devon District Council v C & E Commrs*, Ch D [2001] STC 1282. (*Note*. The Ch D also held that the assessment was in accordance with *VATA 1994, s 73*.)

Council paying solicitors' fees for prospective adopters

[42.5] A borough council ran an adoption service, as required by the *Adoption Act 1976*. It arranged for a child, whose natural parents were Catholics, to be adopted by a Jewish couple. The natural parents objected, and legal proceedings followed. The council paid the solicitors' fees of the prospective adopters, and reclaimed input tax on these fees. Customs rejected the claim, on the grounds that the supplies were made to the prospective adopters rather than to the council. The council appealed, contending that the tax should be treated as reclaimable under what is now *VATA 1994, s 33*. The tribunal rejected this contention and dismissed the appeal, holding that the solicitors had supplied their services to the prospective adopters, rather than to the council. *London Borough of Camden*, LON/00/906 (VTD 17211).

Statutory repair work carried on by City Council

[42.6] Under the *Housing (Scotland) Act 1987*, Glasgow City Council repaired a number of buildings where the owners had failed to comply with statutory repair notices. Initially it accounted for VAT on the amounts which it charged to the owners in respect of this work. In 1996 it submitted a claim for a substantial repayment, on the basis that the repair work was not supplied in the course of any business and was not liable to VAT. Customs rejected the claim, and the Council appealed. The tribunal allowed the appeal, holding that, in exercising its statutory authority, the Council was not making any supply of services within the scope of *VATA 1994*. The tribunal observed that 'the whole procedure has a compulsory flavour about it which points away from the consensual element present in most circumstances where a supply occurs'. *Apple & Pear Development Council*, **22.80** EUROPEAN COMMUNITY LAW, applied. Furthermore, the works could not 'properly be described as being carried out in the course or furtherance of a business'. *Glasgow City Council*, [1998] VATDR 407 (VTD 15491). (*Notes*. (1) For the Commissioners' practice following this decision, see Business Brief 19/98, issued on 15 September 1998. (2) For subsequent developments in this case, see **48.55** PAYMENT OF TAX.)

Conservators of Ashdown Forest—whether a 'local authority'

[42.7] Under the *Ashdown Forest Act 1974*, the Conservators of Ashdown Forest were established to regulate and manage an area of land in East Sussex. In 1988 they registered for VAT, and were treated as a 'local authority' within what is now *VATA 1994, s 33(3)*. However in 2000 Customs reconsidered the position and informed the Conservators that they were not entitled to be treated as a 'local authority'. The Conservators appealed. The tribunal dismissed the appeal, holding firstly that the Conservators were not carrying on 'business activities', and secondly that *VATA 1994, s 83* did 'not provide a statutory right of appeal against a ruling from the Commissioners where they have decided (*sic*) the body does not come within (*VATA 1994, s 33*)'. The tribunal held that 'that is a question for judicial review'. *Conservators of Ashdown Forest*, LON/03/359 (VTD 18796).

VATA 1994, s 33(3)(f)—definition of 'police authority'

[42.8] The *Police Act 1997* established a Service Authority for the National Crime Squad (NCS), with responsibility for investigating and preventing major criminal activities, and a National Criminal Intelligence Service (NCIS) to provide tactical and strategic intelligence on major organised crime. NCS and NCIS claimed refunds of VAT under *VATA 1994, s 33*. The Treasury rejected the claims on the basis that neither NCS nor NCIS qualified as a 'police authority' within *VATA 1994, s 33(3)(f)*. NCS and NCIS applied for judicial review. The QB dismissed the applications, holding that NCS and NCIS were not police authorities within *Police Act 1996, s 101(1)* and therefore were also not police authorities for the purposes of *VATA 1994, s 33(3)(f)*. Furthermore, the Treasury had been entitled not to make an order treating them as specified bodies within *s 33(3)(k)*. Applying *dicta* of Sir Thomas Bingham MR in *R v Ministry of Defence (ex p. Smith)*, CA 1995, [1996] QB 517; [1996] 1 All ER 257, 'the court may not interfere with the exercise of an administrative discretion on substantive grounds save where the court is satisfied that the decision is unreasonable in the sense that it is beyond the range of responses open to a reasonable decision-maker'. *R v HM Treasury & Another (ex p. Service Authority for the National Crime Squad and Others)*, QB [2000] STC 638.

Police Authority—claim for refund of VAT on purchase of cars

[42.9] A police authority made a claim, under *VATA 1994, s 33(1)*, for a refund of VAT paid on the purchase of new motor cars. Customs rejected the claim, on the basis that the effect of the *VAT (Input Tax) Order 1992 (SI 1992/3222), article 7* was that the tax was not repayable. The authority applied for judicial review. The QB and CA rejected the application and upheld the Commissioners' ruling. Aldous LJ held that the effect of *VATA 1994, s 33(6)* was that *article 7* of the *Input Tax Order*, which was made in accordance with *VATA 1994, s 25(7)*, applied to refund claims under *s 33(1)*. Accordingly, the authority was not entitled to a refund of the tax in question. *R v C & E Commrs (ex p. Greater Manchester Police Authority)*, CA [2001] STC 406; [2001] EWCA Civ 213.

VATA 1994, s 80(4)—whether applicable to claims under s 33

[42.10] See *R (oao Cardiff County Council) v C & E Commrs*, **48.53** PAYMENT OF TAX.

Miscellaneous

Advertising facilities supplied by Council in return for sponsorship

[42.11] A City Council, which was registered for VAT in accordance with what is now *VATA 1994, s 42*, granted advertising facilities to commercial sponsors of various campaigns organised by the Council, including a child safety campaign and an anti-smoking campaign. However, the Council did not account for tax on the sponsorship payments which it received. Customs issued an assessment charging tax on the payments, and the Council appealed, contending that it had not made the supplies in question 'in the course or furtherance of a business', so that output tax was not chargeable. The tribunal dismissed the appeal, holding that the Council 'were carrying on business activities as the means of performing their statutory functions'. Furthermore, the supplies were 'economic activities' within *Article 4(2)* of the *EC Sixth Directive*, and were not excluded from VAT by *Article 4(5)* of the *Directive*, since the supplies to the sponsors were 'under the same legal conditions as those that apply to private traders'. *Norwich City Council*, LON/93/1950A (VTD 11822).

Supplies of information by District Council

[42.12] See *Metropolitan Borough of Wirral*, **22.145** EUROPEAN COMMUNITY LAW.

Provision and maintenance of cemeteries by Borough Council

[42.13] See *Rhondda Cynon Taff County Borough Council*, **22.146** EUROPEAN COMMUNITY LAW.

Council constructing replacement building for Ministry of Defence

[42.14] See *Stirling Council*, **22.147** EUROPEAN COMMUNITY LAW.

Corporation—provision of education at fee-paying schools

[42.15] See *City of London Corporation*, **22.148** EUROPEAN COMMUNITY LAW.

College of further education—whether acting as a 'taxable person'

[42.16] See *Edinburgh Telford College v HMRC*, **22.149** EUROPEAN COMMUNITY LAW.

Application of Article 4(5) of EC Sixth Directive—other cases

[42.17] See the cases noted at **22.127** to **22.144** EUROPEAN COMMUNITY LAW.

Payments by local authority to charity

[42.18] A County Council made grants to a registered charity which ran workshops providing work experience for the physically and mentally handicapped. The charity reclaimed input tax on the construction of a new workshop. The Commissioners rejected the claim on the grounds that the workshop was not used for making taxable supplies. The charity appealed, contending that the grants which it received from the Council represented consideration for supplies to the Council. The tribunal dismissed the appeal, holding that the charity was making its supplies to the individual disabled persons for no consideration, and that the grants from the Council were donations which were outside the scope of VAT. *Trustees of the Bowthorpe Community Trust*, LON/94/1276A (VTD 12978).

[42.19] A district council made substantial payments to a charitable trust which organised a music festival. In return the trust agreed to provide 'a varied programme of high quality music events' including 'events which appeal to young people'. Customs issued a ruling that the payments were grants which were outside the scope of VAT. The charity appealed, contending that the payments were consideration for supplies of services (so that it could reclaim input tax relating to the festival). The tribunal accepted this contention and allowed the appeal, finding that 'the key issue is the satisfaction of the provisions in the service level agreements which do not permit the Trust a completely free hand'. *Bath Festivals Trust Ltd*, LON/06/511 (VTD 20840).

Registered charities operating sports centres for local authorities

[42.20] Three local authorities established 'leisure trusts', which were registered charities, to operate sports centres which the authorities owned. The council made payments to the charities. The charities reclaimed input tax on these grants. Customs rejected the claims on the basis that the charities were only making exempt supplies to the members of the public who used the sports centres, and that the payments from the local authorities were donations which were outside the scope of VAT. The tribunal allowed the charities' appeals, observing that the local authorities were under a statutory duty to provide leisure facilities, and holding that the charities were supplying services to the local authorities. The payments by the local authorities were consideration for these supplies, and the charities were entitled to reclaim input tax accordingly. *Edinburgh Leisure (and related appeals)*, [2004] VATDR 394 (VTD 18784). (*Note.* For Customs' practice following this decision, see Business Brief 1/2005, issued on 19 January 2005.)

City Council transferring houses to housing association

[42.21] Liverpool City Council transferred a large stock of houses to a housing association, which was a 'registered social landlord' under *Housing Act 1996*. Many of the houses were in poor condition. The housing association reclaimed input tax on the necessary repairs. Customs rejected the claim on the basis that the tax was attributable to the exempt supplies of accommodation which the association was making to its tenants. The tribunal upheld Customs' contentions and dismissed the association's appeal. *South Liverpool Housing Ltd*, MAN/00/423 (VTD 18750).

[**42.22**] The decision in *South Liverpool Housing Ltd*, **42.21** above, was applied in the similar subsequent case of *LHA-ASRA Group Ltd v HMRC*, [2010] UKFTT 177 (TC), TC00482.

City Council—mileage allowances to employees

[**42.23**] A City Council paid 'mileage allowances' to employees who used their private motor cars for official activities (both 'business activities' and 'non-business activities'). It reclaimed input tax on these allowances, on the basis laid down by the National Joint Council for Local Government Service (NJC). In April 2001 it notified the Commissioners that it wished to change the basis for reclaiming input tax from the NJC rates to the more generous AA rates, retrospectively. It submitted a repayment claim covering the three years ending April 2001. Customs rejected the claim to a backdated repayment, and the Council appealed. The tribunal dismissed the Council's appeal, observing that the reimbursement of input tax relating to the Council's non-business activities was a concession by Customs, and the tribunal had no jurisdiction over the operation of a concession. With regard to the mileage allowances for business activities, the tribunal held that 'it is not open to the appellant to pay one sum to its officers in respect of fuel pursuant to the NJC agreement and then to seek to reclaim another higher amount by way of input VAT'. The Council's claim was 'not simply an attempt to seek to correct errors or provide actual figures for previously estimated figures', but to substitute figures 'which they were not entitled by law to do'. *Leicester City Council*, MAN/01/532 (VTD 18108).

Council 'leisure cards'

[**42.24**] A Council operated a number of leisure facilities including sports centres and swimming pools. It sold 'leisure cards' entitling holders to use these facilities. Customs issued a ruling that it was required to account for tax on the sale of these cards. The council appealed, contending that as some of the relevant facilities qualified for exemption, a percentage of the consideration (which it estimated as 13.37%) should be treated as exempt. The tribunal rejected this contention and dismissed the appeal, holding that the council was making a single standard-rated supply of a right to receive services. The CS unanimously upheld the tribunal decision. Lord Penrose held that 'the legal relationship governing the cardholders' use of the facilities is created on payment' and was 'the provision of a contractual right to use the appellants' facilities'. *The Highland Council v HMRC*, CS 2007, [2008] STC 1280; [2007] CSIH 36. (*Note.* For HMRC's practice following this decision, see HMRC Brief 50/07, issued on 13 July 2007.)

Company operating CCTV for District Council

[**42.25**] See *North Lanarkshire CCTV Ltd*, **7.98** BUSINESS.

VATA 1994, s 33A—delay in meeting repayment claim

[42.26] See *National Galleries of Scotland*, **48.83** PAYMENT OF TAX.

Statutory bodies—whether carrying on a business

[42.27] See *National Water Council*, **7.2** BUSINESS; *The Radio Authority*, **7.79** BUSINESS; *The Arts Council of Great Britain*, **7.80** BUSINESS, and *Apple & Pear Development Council*, **22.80** EUROPEAN COMMUNITY LAW.

Statutory bodies—application of partial exemption provisions

[42.28] See *Scottish Homes*, **46.53** and **46.156** PARTIAL EXEMPTION.

43

Management Services

The cases in this chapter are arranged under the following headings
Time of supply   **43.1**
Other cases   **43.8**

Time of supply

[43.1] A company (L) and two subsidiaries were registered as a group of companies with effect from November 1982. L did not account for tax on management charges which its subsidiaries paid after the group registration, but which related to services performed before the group registration. The Commissioners issued an assessment charging tax on the payments but the tribunal allowed L's appeal, holding that the time of supply was the date of payment. *Legal & Contractual Services Ltd*, [1984] VATTR 85 (VTD 1649).

[43.2] A holding company made supplies to two subsidiary companies, the value of which was recorded by credit and debit entries in the companies' books. The tribunal held that the supplies were within what is now *VAT Regulations 1995 (SI 1995/2518), reg 90(1)*, and that the time of supply was when the entries were made in the companies' books, on the grounds that 'payment may be made by offsetting a debt owed against a debt due, e.g. by journal transfer between purchase and sales ledger accounts, or by making a credit entry in an inter-company current account having a debit balance' and that the time of payment was 'the date on which the appropriate entry is made in the accounting records'. *Pentex Oil Ltd*, EDN/91/140 (VTD 7989, 7991). (*Note*. The tribunal allowed the company's appeal against a misdeclaration penalty, holding that the circumstances constituted a reasonable excuse.)

[43.3] The decision in *Pentex Oil Ltd*, **43.2** above, was applied in the similar subsequent case of *Bishop & Knight Ltd*, LON/92/256 (VTD 9315).

[43.4] A similar decision was reached in *First Class Communications (Sales) Ltd*, LON/05/1063 (VTD 19950).

[43.5] A company's accounts for the year ending 30 September 1990 were signed by the directors on 7 January 1991. The accounts included management charges from an associated company, but the company did not account for tax on this. The Commissioners issued an assessment and imposed a misdeclaration penalty. The company appealed, contending that the tax point should have been treated as 1 July 1991 (when the accounts were adopted by the shareholders at the company's Annual General Meeting), rather than 7 January 1991. The tribunal dismissed the company's appeals, holding that the time of supply was 7 January. *Missionfine Ltd (t/a GT Air Services)*, MAN/92/293 (VTD 10331).

[43.6] A company (W) managed a number of properties for an associated company (T). Between March 1992 and October 1992 W did not issue any invoices for management charges to T, and also did not pay any of the rents it had collected to T. The Commissioners issued a ruling that, by retaining the rents instead of paying them to T, W had effectively held them as payment for its supplies of management services, so that the effect of what is now *regulation 90(1)* of the *VAT Regulations 1995* was that VAT became chargeable at that time. The tribunal allowed W's appeal, holding that the withholding of the rents did not amount to payment for the management services which W supplied to T, and that 'receipt of rent by authorised agents of a principal could not amount to payment of the agent's fee'. *Waverley Housing Management Ltd*, EDN/93/105 (VTD 11765).

[43.7] See also *Cater Clark Ltd*, **52.113** PENALTIES: MISDECLARATION.

Other cases

Management services within a group of companies

[43.8] A company (T) provided management services for the operating companies of a large group. It took this function over from the parent company on the introduction of VAT. It charged for its services insofar as they related to property or were legal services (as to which there was no dispute) but made no charge for its other services and consequently incurred substantial losses in providing them. It therefore arranged with the parent company that it would surrender its corporation tax losses to other companies in the group as 'group relief' under what is now *Income and Corporation Taxes Act 1988, s 402* in return for payments as permitted by that legislation. This arrangement was embodied in a formal agreement between T and the parent company. T did not account for tax on the payments and the Commissioners issued an assessment charging tax on them. The QB upheld the assessment, holding that T was supplying services for consideration. *C & E Commrs v Tilling Management Services Ltd*, QB 1978, [1979] STC 365.

Company going into liquidation

[43.9] In November 1993 a company (E), which was in financial difficulties and owed more than £10,000 in unpaid VAT, issued an invoice for management services to a subsidiary company (W). E issued further such invoices in February 1994 and March 1994, but failed to account for the output tax shown on the invoices. In April 1994 E went into liquidation. W reclaimed the input tax shown on the three invoices. The Commissioners rejected the claim and W appealed, contending that the assessment was unfair, since in 1987 the Commissioners had accepted that E had supplied management services to W, and had issued an assessment charging output tax on that basis. The tribunal rejected this contention and dismissed W's appeal, holding on the evidence that it was not satisfied that E had made any supplies of management services in 1993 or 1994. Furthermore, 'the Commissioners were fully entitled to reconsider the management charges in a situation where no output tax would be recoverable because of (E's) liquidation'. *The Withies Inn Ltd*, LON/95/1778 (VTD 14257).

[43.10] A company (E) issued an invoice for 'administration charges' to an associated company (D). D reclaimed input tax on the invoice, but E went into liquidation without accounting for output tax. When the Commissioners discovered this, they issued an assessment to recover the tax which D had reclaimed. The tribunal upheld the assessment and dismissed D's appeal, holding on the evidence that E had not made any supplies to D. *Warmfield Developments Ltd*, MAN/99/577 (VTD 16953).

[43.11] A partnership reclaimed input tax in respect of management services supplied to it by an associated company which had subsequently ceased trading and gone into liquidation. Customs issued an assessment to recover the tax, on the basis that the partnership 'had failed to provide sufficient evidence that the management services had in fact been supplied'. The partnership appealed. The tribunal accepted the partnership's evidence and allowed the appeal, finding 'on the balance of probabilities' that the company had supplied management services to the partnership during the period in question. *Tower Cleaners*, LON/06/710 (VTD 20333).

Whether services supplied to headlessee or underlessees

[43.12] A company (C) held the head lease of an industrial estate, most of the buildings in which were let to tenants on underleases. A management company was joined as a party to the underleases, and covenanted to provide various services such as repairs and maintenance. The Commissioners issued a ruling that the management company was supplying its services to C as the headlessee, that C was then making the supplies to the underlessees as part of an exempt supply of an interest in land, and that where the management company was in the same VAT group as C, the effect of the group registration was that there was a single exempt supply. C appealed, contending firstly that the management company was making its supplies directly to the underlessees, and secondly that the group registration did not have the effect of changing the character of a supply from a taxable supply of services to an exempt supply of goods. The tribunal accepted both these contentions and allowed the appeal. The effect of 'the wording and the structure of the underlease' was that the management company was making the disputed supplies of services directly to the underlessees. Some of the supplies conferred a benefit on the headlessee, but they were 'of their nature services to be used and paid for by' the underlessee. Furthermore, *VATA 1994, s 43* did not have the effect of 'transforming a standard-rated supply of services into an exempt supply of goods'. *Canary Wharf Ltd*, [1996] VATDR 323 (VTD 14513).

Provision of employees' services

[43.13] See the cases noted at **62.19** to **62.50** SUPPLY.

Management services—set-offs

[43.14] An accountancy partnership held all the shares in an unlimited company which provided certain financial services for the partnership's clients. The partnership and the company occupied the same premises and used the same staff, who were employed and paid by the company, which periodically invoiced the partnership for a proportion of the salaries with a set-off being made for overhead expenses borne by the partnership and attributable to the company, and for a management fee representing work done by the partners for the company. In November 1975 the company issued an invoice to the partnership for £66,218, computed on the basis that staff salaries paid by the company and attributable to the partnership totalled £93,858, from which were deducted overhead expenses of £22,640 borne by the partnership and attributable to the company, and a management fee of £5,000 charged by the partnership to the company. The Commissioners issued assessments on the basis that the company had made taxable supplies to the partnership of £93,858, and that the partnership had made taxable supplies to the company of £27,640. The partnership and the company appealed, contending that they should only be required to account for VAT on the net amount of £66,218. The tribunal rejected this contention and dismissed the appeals. *Smith & Williamson; Smith & Williamson Securities*, [1976] VATTR 215 (VTD 281).

Management services—whether credit notes effective

[43.15] See *Laurence Scott Ltd*, 40.93 INVOICES AND CREDIT NOTES.

Payments between associated companies

[43.16] In a case where the facts were complex and unusual, a subsidiary company (H) which manufactured and sold engineering products had made various payments to its holding company. The holding company had charged VAT in respect of these payments, and H reclaimed the VAT as input tax. The Commissioners formed the opinion that some of the payments related to the provision of finance by the holding company, which was an exempt supply, and that some were advance payments of pension contributions, with the result that not all the payments were liable to VAT and H was not entitled to reclaim the full amounts of input tax shown on the invoices. They issued assessments to recover some of the tax, and H appealed, contending that the payments were for a single supply of management services, which was wholly standard-rated. The tribunal rejected this contention and upheld the assessments, holding that the payments were in respect of multiple supplies, some of which were exempt and some of which were standard-rated. *TS Harrison & Sons Ltd*, MAN/91/1178 (VTD 11043).

[43.17] A company (P) set up a subsidiary company (L) to provide management services. P made regular payments to L, which did not account for output tax on these. The Commissioners issued assessments charging tax on the payments, on the basis that they represented consideration for management services. L appealed, contending that the payments were loans, and had been made solely for the purpose of keeping its bank account in credit. The tribunal accepted L's evidence and allowed the appeal, finding that the payments 'were not payments on account of management charges, but were in reality made for the purpose of maintaining (L's) account in credit'. *London Regeneration Project Services Ltd*, LON/92/1442A (VTD 12062).

[43.18] A similar decision was reached in *Glengate KG Properties Ltd*, LON/95/2520A (VTD 14239).

Payment received by publishing company

[43.19] A company published a number of magazines. It did not account for output tax on payments it received from the editor of three magazines. The Commissioners issued assessments on the basis that the payments represented consideration for taxable supplies of management services. The company appealed, contending that the payments should be treated as a distribution of profits and as outside the scope of VAT. The tribunal rejected this contention and dismissed the appeal, holding that the payments represented consideration for supplies of services. *JRL Newsletters Ltd*, LON/95/2758 (VTD 14394).

Management services supplied to unregistered company

[43.20] A Swedish bank owned a UK subsidiary company (S), which was registered for VAT. S supplied management services to the London branch of the bank, which was not registered for VAT. It was accepted that these services were 'continuous supplies of services', within what is now *VAT Regulations 1995 (SI 1995/2518), reg 90*. S reclaimed input tax on its related expenditure. In August 1991, before any invoice had been raised or any payment made for the services, the London branch was registered for VAT and joined the VAT group of which S was the representative member. The Commissioners issued an assessment to recover the input tax which S had reclaimed, and S appealed. The tribunal upheld the assessment, holding that the Commissioners were entitled to recover the tax under what is now *VAT Regulations 1995, reg 107*. The CA upheld this decision and the HL dismissed S's appeal (by a 4-1 majority, Lord Lloyd dissenting). Where there was a continuous supply of services, no supply was treated as having been made until there had been a payment or the issue of an invoice. The effect of the entry of the London branch into the VAT group was that S had claimed credit for intended supplies which, under VAT law, had never taken place. The CJEC decision in *Belgium v Ghent Coal Terminal NV*, 22.406 EUROPEAN COMMUNITY LAW (which S had cited as an authority) was distinguished, on the grounds that 'it related to circumstances where the taxable person could not make the intended supply because of circumstances outside its control', whereas 'in the present case the bringing of London Branch into the group was not by reason of circumstances beyond the control of (S) but was made with the concurrence of (S)'. The relevant supplies, for which S had received credit, had to be considered as having been appropriated for use in making exempt supplies to third parties. S was therefore required to account for tax accordingly. Lord Hope observed that 'the guiding principle as to relief for input tax as against output tax is that of fiscal neutrality' and that 'the various statutory rules which must be applied in this case have produced a result which is consistent with that principle'. *Svenska International plc v C & E Commrs*, HL [1999] STC 406; [1999] 1 WLR 769; [1999] 2 All ER 906. (*Note.* See also the anti-avoidance provisions in *VATA 1994, Sch 9A*, introduced by *FA 1996* in relation to events occurring after 28 November 1995.)

Management services supplied to unregistered investors

[43.21] See *Kingsley-Smith*, **2.61** APPEALS.

44

Motor Cars

The cases in this chapter are arranged under the following headings.

The definition of 'motor car' (Cars Order, Article 2)

Vehicles held to be motor cars	**44.1**
Vehicles held not to be motor cars	**44.36**
Treatment of specific transactions (Cars Order, Article 4)	**44.53**
Self-supplies (Cars Order, Article 5)	**44.55**
Relief for second-hand motor cars (Cars Order, Article 8)	
Whether conditions of Notice No 718 complied with (*Article 8(1)*)	**44.60**
Whether car is a 'used motor car' (*Article 8(1)*)	**44.66**
Whether acquisition within *Article 8(2)*	**44.68**
Computation of profit margin (*Article 8(5)*)	**44.77**
Disallowance of input tax (Input Tax Order, Article 7)	
General principles	**44.97**
Whether car intended for use 'exclusively for the purposes of a business' (*Article 7(2E)(2G)*)	**44.106**
Fuel for private use (VATA 1994, ss 56, 57)	**44.140**
Miscellaneous	**44.154**

NOTE

In this chapter a reference to the Cars Order is to the *VAT (Cars) Order 1992 (SI 1992/3122)*. A reference to the Input Tax Order is to the *VAT (Input Tax) Order 1992 (SI 1992/3222)*.

The definition of 'motor car' (Cars Order, Article 2)

NOTE

'Motor car' is defined in the *Cars Order (SI 1992/3122)*, *Article 2* and in the *Input Tax Order (SI 1992/3222)*, *Article 2*. The definitions are relevant in relation to, inter alia, both the margin scheme for second-hand motor cars (*Cars Order, Article 8*) and the disallowance of input tax (*Input Tax Order, Article 7*). The definitions were amended with effect from 1 December 1999. The cases in this section (most of which are input tax cases) should be read in the light of these changes. Customs issued guidance on their definition of a 'motor car' in Business Brief 16/04, issued on 9 June 2004. However, this guidance was implicitly disapproved by the tribunal in the subsequent case of *Vauxhall Motors Ltd*, 44.48 below.

Vehicles held to be motor cars

Modified Land Rover

[44.1] A company sold a Land Rover which its previous owner had fitted with a hard top body with side windows and upholstered seats, to enable it to be used to transport his daughters to gymkhanas. Customs issued an assessment charging output tax, on the basis that the vehicle was not a 'motor car'. The tribunal allowed the company's appeal, holding that the Land Rover had been converted into a 'motor car'. *Chartcliff Ltd*, [1976] VATTR 165 (VTD 262). (*Note*. For another issue in this case, see **44.36** below. For an application for costs, see **2.461** APPEALS.)

[44.2] A landscape gardener reclaimed input tax on the purchase of a Land Rover, which had been modified by the addition of a metal canopy with two side windows, and was registered as a heavy goods vehicle. Customs issued an assessment on the basis that this modification had converted the vehicle into a motor car, so that the input tax was not deductible. The tribunal upheld the assessment and dismissed the gardener's appeal. *MCF Wigley*, MAN/91/776 (VTD 7300).

Ford Escort

[44.3] A company which imported cars from Europe claimed credit for input tax incurred on the purchase of a Continental version of a Ford Escort. Customs rejected the claim and the QB dismissed the company's appeal, holding that the car was a 'motor vehicle of a kind normally used on public roads'. *Withers of Winsford Ltd v C & E Commrs*, QB [1988] STC 431.

[44.4] The tribunal held that a Ford Escort, the rear seats of which could be folded away, was within the definition of a 'motor car'. *RC Lucia*, LON/90/1536 (VTD 5776).

Tipping truck with accommodation for employees

[44.5] A firm which traded as roofing contractors purchased a Volkswagen 'LT 35' tipping truck which had, as well as the usual driver's cab with room for one passenger, a second roofed cab behind the driver's cab with room for three more passengers, with side doors with windows and a window at the back. Customs issued a ruling that the vehicle was a motor car as defined in the *Cars Order, Article 2*. The tribunal dismissed the company's appeal. *Weatherproof Flat Roofing (Plymouth) Ltd*, LON/81/351 (VTD 1240).

Estate car

[44.6] The tribunal held that a Ford Granada estate car, used by a builder mainly for the purposes of his business, was within the definition of a 'motor car'. *MC Gardner*, LON/78/23 (VTD 588).

[44.7] Similar decisions were reached in *R Howarth*, CAR/77/451 (VTD 632); *FW Chattin*, LON/82/38 (VTD 1226); *JT Thomson*, EDN/82/13 (VTD 1300); *LS Scargill*, MAN/82/122 (VTD 1420); *GA Security Systems Ltd*, MAN/83/212 (VTD 1527) and *Direct Link Couriers (Bristol) Ltd*, LON/85/481 (VTD 2105).

[44.8] A company purchased three estate cars and removed the rear seats. It reclaimed input tax on the three cars. Customs issued an assessment to recover the tax, and the company appealed, contending that by removing the rear seats, it had taken the vehicles outside the definition of 'motor car', so that the input tax was deductible. The tribunal dismissed the appeal, holding that, despite the removal of the rear seats, the vehicles remained within the definition of 'motor cars'. *County Telecommunications Systems Ltd*, LON/92/1357A (VTD 10224).

Chevrolet K10

[44.9] A contractor reclaimed input tax on a Chevrolet K10 Blazer. Customs rejected the claim on the basis that the vehicle was within the definition of a 'motor car'. The tribunal dismissed the contractor's appeal. *D Yarlett*, LON/83/194 (VTD 1490).

Volkswagen pick-up truck

[44.10] A company reclaimed input tax on a Volkswagen long-wheelbase pick-up truck which had, to the rear of the driver's seat, roofed accommodation which was fitted with side windows. Customs rejected the claim on the basis that the vehicle was within the definition of a 'motor car'. The tribunal dismissed the company's appeal. *Readings & Headley Ltd*, LON/83/193 (VTD 1535).

Toyota Hiace van

[44.11] A trader reclaimed input tax in respect of a Toyota Hiace van, fitted with side windows, which was taxed and insured as a commercial vehicle. Customs rejected the claim, considering that the vehicle was within the definition of a 'motor car' by virtue of *Cars Order, Article 2(b)*. The tribunal dismissed the trader's appeal. *TW Knapp*, LON/79/55 (VTD 778).

Toyota Previa

[44.12] A partnership which sold pine furniture purchased a Toyota Previa, registered as a commercial vehicle. The partners removed the middle and rear rows of seats and used it for delivering furniture. They reclaimed input tax on the purchase. Customs issued an assessment to recover the tax, considering that, despite the removal of the seats, the vehicle was still within the definition of a 'motor car'. The tribunal upheld the assessment and dismissed the partnership's appeal. *Gorringe Pine*, LON/95/2239A (VTD 14036).

[44.13] A similar decision was reached in *RC Kenney & BJ Stiles (t/a AD Fine Art)*, LON/94/726 (VTD 14969).

Toyota Spacecruiser

[44.14] A partnership which manufactured women's clothing reclaimed input tax on the purchase of a Toyota Spacecruiser. Customs issued an assessment to recover the tax, on the basis that the vehicle was a 'motor car'. The partners appealed, contending that because they had removed the rear seats of the vehicle and inserted a hanging rail which was used for transporting clothes, the vehicle was no longer a 'motor car'. The tribunal rejected this contention and dismissed the appeal, holding that 'the removal of the rear seats and the insertion of the hanging rail were temporary modifications' and the vehicle remained a 'motor car'. *Mr & Mrs M Gohil (t/a Gohil Fashions)*, LON/97/1124 (VTD 15435).

Toyota Hilux

[44.15] A company leased a Toyota Hilux and reclaimed input tax on the leasing payments. Customs issued an assessment to recover 50% of the tax, on the basis that the vehicle was a 'motor car'. The tribunal dismissed the company's appeal. *Western Waste Management Ltd*, LON/01/1198 (VTD 17428).

Modified Datsun pick-up

[44.16] A company had acquired a Datsun 120Y pick-up, modified by the addition of a detachable hard top superstructure with two side windows and a hatchback, fitted to the rear of the driver's seat, and having a headroom of between three and four feet and no seats or seating accommodation. Customs issued a ruling that the vehicle was within the definition of a 'motor car', since the roofed accommodation brought it within *Cars Order, Article 2(b)*. The company appealed, contending that 'roofed accommodation' should be construed as referring solely to accommodation for passengers, as distinct from freight. The tribunal rejected this contention and dismissed the company's appeal. *HKS Coachworks Ltd*, MAN/81/64 (VTD 1124). (*Note.* The decision here was disapproved by the CA in *R v C & E Commrs (ex p. Nissan UK Ltd)*, **44.40** below.)

Range Rover

[44.17] The tribunal held that a Range Rover, which had been modified by the anchoring of the back seat, was within the definition of a 'motor car'. *HJ Berry & Sons Ltd*, MAN/82/113 (VTD 1324).

[44.18] A trader who carried on a mobile catering business purchased two Range Rovers. He registered them as heavy goods vehicles and reclaimed input tax on their purchase. Customs rejected the claim and he appealed. The QB upheld Customs' decision, holding that although the vehicles had been registered as heavy goods vehicles, they remained motor cars for VAT purposes. *C & E Commrs v Jeynes (t/a Midland International (Hire) Caterers)*, QB 1983, [1984] STC 30.

[44.19] A Range Rover was also held to be a 'motor car' in *John Slough of London*, LON/82/289 (VTD 1427).

Modified jeep

[44.20] The tribunal held that a jeep pick-up, with accommodation behind the driver with plastic windows at the sides and back and a canvas roof fitted over a roll bar, was within the definition of a motor car. *PT Jones*, LON/82/360 (VTD 1401).

[44.21] A trader reclaimed input tax on the purchase of a Suzuki jeep, which had been modified by the fitting of a rear seat, although it had no rear window. Customs issued an assessment to recover the tax, considering that the jeep had been 'adapted solely or mainly for the carriage of passengers', and thus qualified as a motor car for the purposes of the *Cars Order*. The tribunal upheld this decision. *S Compton (t/a Stan Compton Electrical Engineers & Contractors)*, LON/92/1762A (VTD 10259).

Commercial vehicle modified by restoration of rear bench seat

[44.22] A trader (B) had purchased a vehicle which had been converted for commercial purposes by replacing the rear side windows with metal sheets and by removing the rear bench seat. B decided to sell the vehicle and, before doing so, restored the rear seat by rebolting it back into its original position. Customs raised an assessment on the basis that, by doing this, he had reconverted the vehicle back into a motor car. The tribunal dismissed B's appeal, holding that by securely fixing the rear seat, he had adapted the vehicle so that it could be used solely or mainly for the carriage of passengers. *K Barbour*, EDN/87/39 (VTD 2651).

Converted Citroen van

[44.23] A partnership which operated a bookshop purchased a Citroen van and reclaimed input tax. Subsequently the partnership modified the van by fitting windows behind the driver's seat. Customs issued an assessment on the basis that this amounted to a conversion of the vehicle into a motor car, which was a self-supply, so that the partnership had to reclaim the input tax reclaimed on the purchase of the van. The tribunal upheld the assessment. *Browsers Bookshop*, LON/88/47 (VTD 2837).

Mercedes van

[44.24] A furniture manufacturer reclaimed input tax on the purchase of a Mercedes van, which had two passenger seats behind the driver, and had windows on either side of the van behind the driver's seat. Customs issued an assessment to recover the tax, considering that the vehicle qualified as a car for VAT purposes, so that the input tax was not deductible. The tribunal dismissed the trader's appeal. *T Stead*, EDN/91/145 (VTD 6650).

Daihatsu Fourtrak Estate

[44.25] A company purchased a Daihatsu Fourtrak Estate, and reclaimed the input tax. Customs issued an assessment to recover the tax, considering that the Daihatsu was a 'motor car'. The company appealed, contending that the input tax should be allowed because it had purchased the Daihatsu for the purpose of towing a trailer which it used to carry expensive cars such as Ferraris. The tribunal dismissed the appeal, holding that the Daihatsu was a 'motor car' and that the input tax was not deductible. *Specialised Cars Ltd*, MAN/93/370 (VTD 11123).

[44.26] A similar decision was reached in *DR Metson & Partners*, LON/92/3193 (VTD 11218).

Suzuki Vitara Sport

[44.27] A grocer reclaimed input tax on the purchase of a Suzuki Vitara Sport. Customs issued an assessment to recover the tax, on the basis that the vehicle was a 'motor car'. The tribunal dismissed the grocer's appeal, holding that the Suzuki was within *Cars Order, Article 2(b)*. *W McAdam*, EDN/94/382 (VTD 13286).

[44.28] A Suzuki Vitara was also held to be within the definition of a 'motor car' in *MA Lock (t/a MAL Carpenters & Joiners)*, LON/95/2942A (VTD 14427).

Isuzu pick-up

[44.29] A registered trader reclaimed input tax on the purchase of a Isuzu two-axle rigid body pick-up motor vehicle. Customs issued an assessment to recover the tax, considering that the Isuzu was a 'motor car', so that the tax was not deductible. The trader appealed, contending that the Isuzu was not within the definition of a 'motor car', since it could carry twelve people (five, including the driver, in the cab, and seven in the rear). The tribunal rejected this contention and dismissed the appeal, holding on the evidence that the Isuzu was not 'suitable' for carrying more than six people, and was within the definition of a 'motor car'. *BC Kunz (t/a Wharfedale Finance Co)*, MAN/94/2546 (VTD 13514).

[44.30] An Isuzu pick-up was also held to be a 'motor car' in *Hague Farms Ltd*, LON/95/1930 (VTD 13722); *CP & EA O'Dell (t/a CP Motors)*, MAN/94/242 (VTD 13802); *DJF & PE Lamb (t/a D & R Services)*, MAN/94/1108 (VTD 13802); *DJ & Mrs SA Banwell*, LON/95/2352A (VTD 13944) and *PAJ Eccleston*, MAN/98/539 (VTD 16037).

Mitsubishi pick-up

[44.31] A Mitsubishi double-cab L200 pick-up was held to be a 'motor car' in *FWK Howells (t/a Buckingham Commercial Motor Co)*, LON/97/809 (VTD 16488).

Volkswagen Caravelle

[44.32] A partnership reclaimed input tax on a Volkswagen Caravelle, the rear seats of which were easily removable so that it could be used to carry goods. Customs rejected the claim and the tribunal dismissed the partnership's appeal. *Intercraft UK Romania*, LON/95/1947A (VTD 13707).

Rally car

[44.33] An engineer built a rally car and reclaimed input tax on the materials. Customs rejected the claim, ruling that the car was a 'motor car' within *Cars Order, Article 2*. The tribunal upheld Customs' ruling and dismissed the engineer's appeal. *D Appleby*, LON/95/2936 (VTD 14580).

Fiat Scuba

[44.34] A company reclaimed input tax on a Fiat Scuba. Customs rejected the claim, ruling that the Scuba was a 'motor car' within *Cars Order, Article 2*. The tribunal upheld Customs' ruling and dismissed the company's appeal. *Twin Cleaning Contractors Ltd*, MAN/06/833 (VTD 20624).

Vauxhall Monterey

[44.35] A four-wheel drive Vauxhall Monterey was held to be a 'motor car' in *Anglia Building & Decorating Contractors*, 52.343 PENALTIES: MISDECLARATION.

Vehicles held not to be motor cars

Van fitted with benches

[44.36] The company in the case noted at 44.1 above sold a standard 15 cwt Ford van purchased from a builder, who had fitted it with wooden benches. It had no side windows. The company did not account for output tax on the sale, and the Commissioners issued an assessment charging output tax. The company appealed, contending that the vehicle was a 'motor car' within *Cars Order, Article 2*. The tribunal rejected this contention, holding that the van was not a 'motor car'. As it was not clear whether the company could deduct input tax in respect of the van, the appeal was adjourned to enable the parties to agree as to the amount to which the assessment should be reduced. *Chartcliff Ltd*, [1976] VATTR 165 (VTD 262). (*Note*. For subsequent proceedings in this appeal as to costs, see **2.461** APPEALS. It was stated during those proceedings that it had been agreed that input tax was allowable and the assessment was reduced to nil.)

Hearses—whether within Cars Order, Article 2(vi)*

[44.37] A second-hand car dealer sold eight second-hand funeral hearses. The Commissioners issued a ruling that the hearses were 'constructed for a special purpose' within *Cars Order, Article 2(vi)**, and thus could not be dealt with under the margin scheme for second-hand cars. The tribunal dismissed the trader's appeal against this decision. *KP Davies*, CAR/79/65 (VTD 831).

Pick-up truck with attached canopy—whether a 'motor car'

[44.38] The proprietor of an engineering business purchased a pick-up truck. To protect goods from the weather and from thieves, he bought a fibreglass canopy which covered the whole of the load-carrying part of the truck and extended over the roof of the driver's cab. It was attached to the truck with clips, hooked onto hooks riveted to the side of the truck. The canopy could be removed quickly and easily, and the trader frequently used the truck without the canopy. The Commissioners issued an assessment on the basis that, by attaching the canopy to the truck, the trader had converted the truck into a motor car within the *Cars Order* and thus incurred liability to VAT. The tribunal allowed the trader's appeal, holding that, to amount to a conversion, some degree of permanence was required which was absent in this case. *KM Batty*, MAN/86/122 (VTD 2199).

Toyota Land Cruisers converted into recovery vehicles

[44.39] A trader purchased two Toyota Land Cruisers and converted them for use as recovery vehicles by welding onto them a trailer with the necessary equipment for vehicle recovery. He reclaimed input tax on their purchase. The Commissioners rejected the claim, considering that the vehicles were within the definition of 'motor cars'. The tribunal allowed the trader's appeal, holding that the converted vehicles did not fall within the definition of a 'motor car' by virtue of *Cars Order, Article 2(vi)**, as they were 'vehicles constructed for a special purpose other than the carriage of persons'. *H Lovejoy (t/a HRS Recoveries)*, LON/86/743 (VTD 2488).

Nissan pick-up truck—roofed accommodation not suitable for passengers

[44.40] In a case concerning provisions in the *Car Tax Act 1983* similar to *VAT (Cars) Order, Article 2(b)*, the CA held that 'accommodation' should be construed as referring only to accommodation for human passengers, rather than for freight. The CA specifically disapproved the earlier decision in *HKS Coachworks Ltd*, **44.16** above. *R v C & E Commrs (ex p. Nissan UK Ltd)*, CA 1987, [1988] BTC 8003. (*Note*. The decision in this case was applied in *John Beharrell Ltd*, **44.47** below.)

Converted Transit van

[44.41] A company which operated a detective agency purchased a Transit van and adapted it for the purpose of undertaking static surveillance work. The items that were fitted to the van included a long seat which could also be used as a bed, a frame to take a portable cooker, a sink, a wardrobe, a table which could be used as a desk, a radio aerial, an access ladder for the roof and reinforcement of the roof, and thermal and acoustic insulation. Dark glass was fitted to the windows and there were several other additional small alterations. The company disposed of the vehicle in 1984, and did not account for VAT on the disposal of the vehicle. The Commissioners issued an assessment charging output tax, and the company appealed, contending that the vehicle was a motor car, so that, as the selling price was less than the deemed acquisition price, no tax was chargeable. The tribunal rejected this contention and dismissed the appeal, holding that the vehicle had been converted from a van into a caravan and had never been a motor car. *Burgess Detective Agency Ltd*, MAN/87/333 (VTD 2685).

[44.42] A company purchased two Ford Transit vans, which it adapted by inserting rear seats large enough for two or three people. The seats were made of heavy duty plastic and were not upholstered, and the vans had no rear windows, handrails or seat belts. The company reclaimed input tax on the vans, and the Commissioners issued an assessment to recover the tax, considering that the insertion of the rear seats meant that the vans had been converted into cars for the purpose of the *Cars Order*. The company appealed, contending that the vans were mainly used for the transport of goods, which were usually placed on the rear seat. The tribunal allowed the company's appeal, holding that despite the installation of the seats, the vehicles were still not 'motor cars' within *Cars Order, Article 2*. *Chichester Plant Contractors Ltd*, LON/90/372Y (VTD 6575).

Land Rover fitted with two folding seats

[44.43] A farming partnership purchased a Land Rover with two folding seats in the rear. The Commissioners considered that the addition of these seats meant that the vehicle had been 'adapted solely or mainly for the carriage of passengers' within *Cars Order, Article 2*, so that the input tax was not allowable. The partnership appealed, contending that the rear seats were seldom used and were very uncomfortable in view of the hard rear suspension and the absence of armrests. The tribunal accepted this contention and allowed the appeal, distinguishing *Chartcliff Ltd*, **44.1** above. The changes made to the vehicle were relatively minor and the additional seating was 'anything but luxurious' and had been 'designed to have the least effect possible on the load carrying capacity'. The main use of the vehicle was clearly not the carriage of passengers. *Bolinge Hill Farm*, LON/89/1071Z (VTD 4217).

Daihatsu Fourtrak vehicles

[44.44] A company purchased two Daihatsu Fourtrak Commercial Hard Tops. Each vehicle had been equipped with two folding rear seats, described by the tribunal as 'of an insubstantial nature'. The company claimed a deduction for the input tax incurred on their purchase. The Commissioners issued an assessment to recover the tax, considering that the vehicles were 'motor cars' within the meaning of *Cars Order, Article 2.* The company appealed, contending that the vehicles in question were not motor cars, since they were not constructed 'solely or mainly for the carriage of passengers'. The tribunal allowed the appeal, holding that the vehicles were not motor cars since the seating was of a 'very rudimentary nature' and 'most uncomfortable for passengers on anything but the shortest of journeys'. *AL Yeoman Ltd,* EDN/89/104 (VTD 4470). (*Note.* For a subsequent case in which a Daihatsu Fourtrak was held to be a 'motor car', see *Specialised Cars Ltd,* **44.25** above.)

Land Rover with rear seats removed

[44.45] A sole trader in the construction industry had purchased a 12-seat Land Rover from which he had removed the two rear bench seats. He reclaimed the input tax on the purchase, and the Commissioners issued an assessment to recover the tax, considering that the removal of the rear seats had converted the Land Rover from a commercial vehicle into a 'motor car'. The tribunal allowed the trader's appeal against the assessment. Despite the removal of the rear bench seats, the vehicle remained suitable for carrying twelve people and had not been converted into a 'motor car'. *P Oddonetto,* LON/89/1566X (VTD 5208).

Land Rover with small window inserted

[44.46] A writer, who was registered for VAT, purchased a Land Rover and modified it by inserting a half-size window in the nearside rear panel. The Commissioners issued an assessment on the basis that, by doing so, he had converted the Land Rover into a motor car, so that there was a deemed self-supply on which output tax was chargeable. The tribunal allowed the writer's appeal, holding that the vehicle was not adapted 'solely or mainly for the carriage of passengers'. Applying *R v C & E Commrs (ex p. Nissan UK Ltd),* **44.40** above, the roofed space to the rear of the driver's seat did not amount to 'accommodation' within the meaning of *Cars Order, Article 2(b).* On the evidence, the vehicle was intended solely for the appellant's use in making expeditions to remote parts of Africa, and was within *Article 2(vi)*.* *TH Sheppard,* LON/95/2269A (VTD 13815).

Peugeot vans—whether converted into cars

[44.47] A company which carried on business as an installer of air-conditioning equipment purchased a number of Peugeot 205 and 305 vans. It modified the vehicles by adding a window on each side, behind the driver's seat. The modifications were carried out for safety reasons, to improve visibility. The Commissioners considered that the modification amounted to the conversion of the vehicles into cars, so that there was a deemed self-supply of the vehicles, and issued an assessment to recover the input tax which the company had reclaimed on their purchase. The tribunal allowed the company's appeal, holding that the 'accommodation available behind the driver's seat in the vehicles as modified could not realistically be described as reasonably suitable for the carriage of passengers'. Applying *R v C & E Commrs (ex p. Nissan UK Ltd),* **44.40** above, it did not constitute 'accommodation' for the purpose of the *Cars Order,* and the vehicles continued to be vans rather than cars. *John Beharrell Ltd,* [1991] VATTR 497 (VTD 6530).

Vauxhall Combo Crew van

[44.48] Customs issued a ruling that the Vauxhall Combo Crew van was within the definition of a motor car for VAT purposes. The company which manufactured the van appealed, contending that it was not within the definition of a motor car, since it was not 'constructed or adapted solely or mainly for the carriage of passengers'. The tribunal accepted this contention and allowed the company's appeal, holding that the van was 'a commercial vehicle' and the fact that it contained three folding rear seats did not have the effect of taking it within the statutory definition of a 'car'. *Vauxhall Motors Ltd*, LON/04/1230 (VTD 19425).

Toyota Hilux Double Cab—whether within Cars Order, Article 2(i)

[44.49] A partnership which carried on a farming business reclaimed input tax on the purchase of a converted Toyota Hilux Double Cab pick-up truck. The Commissioners issued an assessment to recover the tax, considering that the vehicle was within the definition of a 'motor car'. The partnership appealed, contending that the vehicle was suitable for carrying twelve persons and thus was excluded from the definition of a motor car by *Cars Order, Article 2(i)*. The tribunal examined the vehicle and allowed the company's appeal, observing that it could carry twelve people for short journeys if most of the passengers were young, and holding that the input tax was allowable. The tribunal observed that the fact that the vehicle was not suitable for transporting elderly people or handicapped people, or for long journeys, was not conclusive. *W Hamilton & Son*, LON/96/1434 (VTD 14812). (*Note.* The decision here was not followed in the subsequent case of *Western Waste Management Ltd*, **44.15** above, where the tribunal held that a Toyota Hilux was a car.)

Euromega Isuzu—whether within Cars Order, Article 2(iv)

[44.50] A company claimed input tax on the purchase of three Euromega Isuzu vehicles. Customs issued an assessment to recover the tax, on the basis that the vehicles were 'motor cars' within *Cars Order, Article 2*. The company appealed, contending that the vehicles were not 'motor cars', since they were covered by the exclusion in *Cars Order, Article 2(iv)*, being 'vehicles constructed to carry a payload of one tonne or more'. The tribunal accepted this contention and allowed the company's appeal. *P & C Morris Catering Group Ltd*, MAN/04/545 (VTD 19245).

Pick-up truck—whether within Cars Order, Article 2(vi)*

[44.51] The proprietor of a plant hire business purchased a Ford 250 pick-up truck and undertook certain conversion work to make it more suitable for his business. He reclaimed input tax on the vehicle. The Commissioners issued an assessment to recover the tax, considering that the vehicle was within the statutory definition of a 'motor car'. The tribunal allowed the trader's appeal, holding on the evidence that the vehicle was within the exclusion in *Cars Order, Article 2(vi)**, being 'constructed for a special purpose other than the carriage of persons and having no other accommodation for carrying persons than such as is incidental to that purpose'. *KV Barnard*, LON/95/2629 (VTD 13865).

Lamborghini Murcielago sports car

[44.52] A company reclaimed input tax on the purchase of a Lamborghini Murcielago two-seater sports car. Customs rejected the claim on the basis that the Lamborghini was a 'motor car', within *Cars Order, Article 2*. The company appealed, contending that the Lamborghini was not a 'motor vehicle of a kind normally used on public roads', since its suspension 'was programmed solely for track use'. The tribunal accepted this contention and allowed the appeal. *Sixth Gear Experience Ltd*, MAN/08/234 (VTD 20890). (*Note.* The tribunal awarded the company 75% of its costs—see **2.381** APPEALS.)

Treatment of specific transactions (Cars Order, Article 4)

Whether cars 'repossessed' within Cars Order, Article 4(1)

[44.53] A company (G) sold cars under hire-purchase agreements. In some cases, customers voluntarily returned the cars before the end of the agreement. G then sold the cars. The Commissioners issued a ruling that G was required to account for output tax on the onward sale of the car. G appealed, contending that it had repossessed the car under the terms of a finance agreement, within *VAT (Cars) Order, article 4(1)*, so that no VAT was due. The tribunal accepted this contention and allowed G's appeal, holding that the term 'repossessed' was 'not to be construed as referring only to the situation where the finance company in question has retaken possession of the motor car following a default on the part of the hirer' but was 'equally applicable to all situations where "under the terms of the finance agreement" the finance company has resumed possession of the motor car to the exclusion of the hirer'. The Ch D upheld the tribunal decision. Field J held that *article 4(1)* applied 'where the reseller has regained possession of the car in accordance with the terms of the finance agreement, whether or not there has been a breach by the hirer and whether or not the finance company has had actively to exercise a contractual right to take the car back'. All of G's hire purchase agreements provided that the hirer had to return the car to G if the agreement was terminated before payment of the cash price. Therefore, wherever G sold a car following a consensual termination, the resale was within *article 4(1)(a)* even if the car was voluntarily returned. *C & E Commrs v General Motors Acceptance Corporation (UK) plc*, Ch D [2004] STC 577; [2004] EWHC 192 (Ch). (*Notes.* (1) For the Commissioners' policy following this decision, see VAT Information Sheet 5/04, issued on 6 May 2004. See also *VAT (Special Provisions) (Amendment) Order 2006 (SI 2006/869)*, which came into force on 13 April 2006. (2) For other issues in this case, see **40.109** INVOICES AND CREDIT NOTES and **59.33** RETURNS.)

Interpretation of Cars Order, Article 4(1)(a)

[44.54] A company (M) claimed a repayment of VAT relating to supplies of cars under hire-purchase agreements, where the cars were repossessed before all the instalments had been paid. HMRC made a repayment, with an offset for output tax which it considered that M should have accounted for on the subsequent sale of the cars, on the grounds that the 'same condition' requirement of *VAT (Cars) Order, Article 4(1)(a)* had not been satisfied. M appealed. The tribunal issued a preliminary decision in principle, holding that HMRC were entitled in principle to make the set-off and giving guidance on the question of whether a car was disposed of 'in the same condition as it was when repossessed'. Judge Wallace held that 'the phrase "same condition" must be qualified by an epithet such as "substantially" or "materially"'. The 'beating out of a substantial dent' would be a change to the condition of a car, but 'the touching up of a minor scratch without respraying' would not. The tribunal observed that 'it would be anomalous if minor work to make a car roadworthy and compliant with the construction and use legislation, such as replacing defective windscreen wipers or bulbs, excluded a de-supply and still more anomalous if inflating a tyre to correct the pressure did so'. In principle, work taking not more than two hours and costing not more than £50 in respect of parts could be ignored on de minimis grounds. The tribunal adjourned the appeal in the hope that the parties could reach agreement on figures in the light of this guidance. *Masterlease Ltd v HMRC*, [2010] SFTD 1243; [2010] UKFTT 339 (TC), TC00621.

Self-supplies (Cars Order, Article 5)

Whether a self-supply

[44.55] A car dealer built a car for himself, out of new and second-hand components, at a cost of £1,300. After running it for 3,000 miles, he sold it for £1,995. The Commissioners issued an assessment on the basis that there had been a self-supply of the car within *Cars Order, Article 5*. The tribunal upheld the assessment and dismissed the trader's appeal. *EG Nicol*, MAN/77/322 (VTD 571).

[44.56] The standard rate of VAT was increased from 8% to 15% with effect from 18 June 1979. A company which dealt in cars ordered a number of new V-registration cars (which could not be used on the roads before 1 August 1979). It accounted for tax on the basis that it had made a deemed self-supply of these cars before 18 June 1979. The Commissioners issued an assessment on the basis that there had been no supply of the cars until after 31 July, so that tax was chargeable at 15% on the supply of the cars. The tribunal upheld the assessment and dismissed the company's appeal. *A & B Motors (Newton-le-Willows) Ltd*, [1981] VATTR 29 (VTD 1024).

[44.57] A car-dealing company held a large number of cars on a sale or return basis, under which they remained the property of the manufacturer until it decided to purchase them. On 11 June 1979 the Chancellor of the Exchequer announced that the standard rate of VAT would be increased from 8% to 15% with effect from 18 June. During the intervening week, the company earmarked 33 of the cars which it held as demonstration cars, making the necessary entries in its stock records and authorising the manufacturer to debit it with the price of the cars. The Commissioners issued an assessment on the basis that there had been no supply of the cars until after 18 June. The tribunal allowed the company's appeal, holding that there had been a self-supply before that date. *Arnold Clark Automobiles Ltd (and associated appeals)*, EDN/80/52-55 (VTD 1058).

[44.58] In another case where a car-dealing company held cars on a sale or return basis, and elected to purchase some of them shortly before 18 June 1979, the tribunal upheld the Commissioners' ruling that there had been no self-supply of the cars. On the evidence, the cars were not used as demonstration vehicles but were sold to customers after 18 June. *Hall Park Garage Ltd*, LON/81/194 (VTD 1185).

Whether car used for research or development

[44.59] A company which manufactured cars built a prototype, which it exhibited and also lent to the publishers of a specialist magazine so that they could write an article about it. The Commissioners issued an assessment on the basis that there had been a self-supply of the car. The company appealed, contending that the car was 'used solely for the purpose of research and development' so that, by virtue of *Cars Order, Article 5(3)*, there had been no self-supply. The tribunal accepted the company's evidence and allowed the appeal, observing that 'a significant feature of the article' was that 'whereas there are a number of features and aspects of which the author expresses his approval, there are at the same time an equal or even greater number of criticisms'. The tribunal observed that 'informed criticism of this nature, from a person such as a motoring journalist who may be expected to know what may appeal to, or irritate, the ordinary member of the public, is precisely what the developer of a car would wish to have pointed out to him for the purposes of research and development'. *Lea-Francis Cars Ltd*, MAN/81/113 (VTD 1166).

Relief for second-hand motor cars (Cars Order, Article 8)

Whether conditions of Notice No 718 complied with (Article 8(1))

[44.60] A car dealer failed to produce records to comply with the requirements specified in what is now *Notice No 718* for the 'margin scheme' for second-hand car dealers. The Commissioners issued an assessment in which the output tax was taken to be that on the full amount of the dealer's sales. The dealer appealed, contending that the assessment had not been made to the best of the Commissioners' judgment as it had not taken into account his purchases of used cars. The tribunal rejected this contention and dismissed the appeal, holding that, as the dealer had not complied with the statutory requirements so as to bring himself within the protection of the margin scheme, the Commissioners had no alternative but to charge tax on the full amount. *DA Pody*, LON/75/124 (VTD 217).

[44.61] A second-hand car dealer was liable to be registered from 1 April 1973, but did not apply for registration until July 1975, whereupon he was registered with effect from 1 April 1973. He made a return for the period from 1 April 1973 to 31 December 1975 declaring tax due of £721, calculated under the margin scheme. The Commissioners considered that throughout the period his records did not comply with the requirements of what is now *Notice No 718* and issued an assessment charging tax on the full amount of his supplies. The tribunal upheld the assessment and dismissed the dealer's appeal. *DE Chappell*, [1977] VATTR 94 (VTD 352).

[44.62] A second-hand car dealer accounted for tax under the 'margin scheme' but had not maintained the records specified by what is now *Notice No 718* and had not issued sales invoices. The Commissioners issued an assessment charging tax on the full amount of his supplies. The tribunal upheld the assessment and dismissed the dealer's appeal. *H Nixon*, [1980] VATTR 66 (VTD 973).

[44.63] Similar decisions were reached in *I Jones*, CAR/75/186 (VTD 232); *Charles Oliver Enterprises Ltd*, MAN/76/67 (VTD 268); *C Parker*, MAN/76/54 (VTD 292); *H Kitchen*, LON/77/66 (VTD 397); *Hughes Bros*, CAR/77/155 (VTD 450); *EJ Parish*, LON/77/283 (VTD 474); *TL Penfold*, CAR/77/174 (VTD 524); *J Smith (t/a Morecambe Used Car Centre)*, MAN/77/243 (VTD 554); *LW & PE Kirkwood*, MAN/77/135 & 136 (VTD 564); *JJ Woodward*, LON/77/247 (VTD 569); *PS Gabrielson*, CAR/77/22 (VTD 606); *RA Watson*, LON/78/115 (VTD 758); *RS & DE Swanson*, MAN/80/29 (VTD 959); *McNally & Waite (t/a Macray Motor Bodies)*, MAN/80/169 & 170 (VTD 1109); *AD Motors (Woodford)*, LON/83/31 (VTD 1449); *Nelsons of Newark Ltd*, MAN/84/91 (VTD 1751); *MK Sadiq*, LON/85/565 (VTD 2160); *CL Howarth*, LON/86/75 (VTD 2363); *J Roberts*, MAN/87/161 (VTD 2555); *Bordergem Ltd*, MAN/88/38 (VTD 2887); *K Tork (t/a KT Motors)*, LON/90/744 (VTD 7013); *Atlas Economy Hire Ltd*, LON/06/1020 (VTD 20472) and *A Thornhill (t/a Motormill)*, LON/07/1766 (VTD 20858).

[44.64] A partnership dealing in second-hand cars failed to keep the records required by what is now *Notice No 718*. The Commissioners issued an assessment charging tax of more than £30,000, and the partnership appealed, contending that the amount demanded was inequitable. The tribunal dismissed the appeal, finding that the records kept were inadequate and holding that the Commissioners had not acted unreasonably. *GP, D & A Bardsley (t/a Bardsley Car Sales)*, [1984] VATTR 171 (VTD 1718).

[44.65] The decision in *Bardsley*, **44.64** above, was applied in the similar cases of *JW Donaldson*, EDN/88/179 (VTD 3668); *WG McCalden*, LON/88/1332 (VTD 4216); *RM Lane*, MAN/88/28 (VTD 5038) and *Sellhire Autos Ltd*, MAN/92/1098 (VTD 10568).

Whether car is a 'used motor car' (Article 8(1))

Sale of car already registered by dealer—whether a sale of a used car

[44.66] A company which traded as a car dealer appealed against an assessment charging tax on the full sale price of some cars which it had sold, contending that the cars should be treated as used cars and dealt with under the margin scheme. The tribunal dismissed the appeal, applying *Morris Motors Ltd v Lilley*, Ch D [1959] All ER 737 and holding that the cars were new cars rather than used cars, so that the margin scheme was inapplicable. *Lincoln Street Motors (Birmingham) Ltd*, [1981] VATTR 120 (VTD 1100).

[44.67] The decision in *Lincoln Street Motors (Birmingham) Ltd*, 44.66 above, was applied in the similar cases of *Queensborough Motors*, EDN/81/39 (VTD 1139); *Ashmall & Parkinson Ltd*, MAN/82/245 (VTD 1387) and *Finglands Travel Agency Ltd*, MAN/82/232 (VTD 1447).

Whether acquisition within Article 8(2)

Sale of cars purchased from finance company

[44.68] A company (P) manufactured and imported motor cars. By an agreement with a finance company (M), it sold certain cars to M to be leased to handicapped persons for a period of at least three years. When the leases expired, M repossessed the cars and sold them back to P. Both the lease by M and the sale back to P qualified for zero-rating under *VATA 1994, Sch 8 Group 12*. P subsequently resold the cars on the open market and accounted for tax under the margin scheme. The Commissioners issued a ruling that the sales of the cars could not be dealt with under the margin scheme, on the basis that a zero-rated supply was not 'a supply in respect of which no VAT was chargeable', within *Article 8(2)* of the *Cars Order*. P appealed, contending that its acquisition of the cars, being zero-rated, was within *Article 8(2)* of the *Order*, so that it was entitled to use the margin scheme. The tribunal accepted this contention and allowed P's appeal, observing that, although *Article 26a* of the *EC Sixth Directive* indicated 'circumstances in which a taxable dealer may tax his profit margin rather than the full value of the supply', the Commissioners could not 'rely on the *Sixth Directive* to require a narrower interpretation of *Article 8(2)(a)* than it would otherwise be given, so that they cannot claim that it should be interpreted to exclude matters other than those referred to in *Article 26a(B)*'. It was 'quite plain from *article 8* that it is intended to apply in circumstances other than those for which *Article 26a(B)* makes provision'. *Peugeot Motor Co plc*, [1998] VATDR 1 (VTD 15314). (*Note.* For the effect of *Article 26a* of the *EC Sixth Directive*, see also *Stafford Land Rover*, 44.168 below.)

Cars imported from Republic of Ireland—whether purchased from dealer

[44.69] A company (R) sold cars which had been imported from the Republic of Ireland. It accounted for tax under the margin scheme. The Commissioners issued an assessment on the basis that R had obtained the cars in Ireland from an Irish dealer, and should have accounted for tax on the full sale price of the cars. R appealed, contending that it had obtained the cars from a private individual (in order to comply with regulations issued by the DETR). The tribunal rejected this contention and dismissed the appeal. On the evidence, R had obtained the cars in the Republic of Ireland from a dealer. This was not a supply in the UK, and was therefore not within *Article 8(2)* of the *Cars Order*. The purported transactions whereby R claimed to have obtained the cars from a private individual were 'documented but unreal'. They 'were shams and so "nothings" for all tax purposes'. The tribunal also held that, for the purpose of *Article 28b* of the *EC Sixth Directive*, the place of acquisition of the cars by R 'must be the United Kingdom because that is where the transportation to (R) ended'. (The tribunal also observed that the assessments had been issued on the basis that R was entitled to deduct the 'acquisition VAT properly chargeable'.) *Richmond Cars Ltd*, [2000] VATDR 388 (VTD 16942).

Cars purchased from Republic of Ireland dealer

[44.70] A car dealer purchased a number of Japanese cars from a dealer in the Republic of Ireland. The invoices for the purchases did not show any VAT but stated 'total @ zero VAT'. When the dealer sold the cars, she only accounted for tax on her profit. The Commissioners issued an assessment on the basis that she should have accounted for tax on the sale price. She appealed, contending that she should be allowed to account for tax under the margin scheme. The tribunal rejected this contention and dismissed her appeal, holding that her acquisition of the cars was not within *Article 8(2)* of the *Cars Order*. The tribunal observed that she had taken possession of the cars 'pursuant to a supply and that supply was taxable because the supply is a necessary component of the acquisition which is taxable'. The appellant could only have sold the cars under the margin scheme if Irish tax had been charged on the margin. A person knowledgeable about VAT could have deduced that the Irish dealer could not have imported the cars and sold them to someone outside Ireland under the Irish margin scheme. *Mrs EJ Wood*, LON/00/199 (VTD 17256).

[44.71] The decision in *Wood*, 44.70 above, was applied in the similar subsequent cases of *PJ Martin (t/a Martin Motors)*, LON/00/1282 (VTD 17809) and *L Phipps*, LON/03/106 (VTD 19352).

[44.72] Similar decisions were reached in *Bonusclass Ltd*, MAN/99/619 (VTD 17528); *ST McCarthy (t/a Autoelec)*, LON/00/1172 (VTD 18166) and *GE Mallon (t/a Phoenix Agency Services)*, LON/01/1054 (VTD 18222).

[44.73] A UK company (M) purchased 79 Japanese cars from a dealer (J) which was based in the Republic of Ireland, but also carried on business in the UK. When M sold the cars, it accounted for tax under the margin scheme. The Commissioners issued an assessment on the basis that M was not entitled to account for tax under the margin scheme and should have accounted for tax on the full sale price. The tribunal reviewed the evidence in detail and upheld the assessment in part. The tribunal accepted that J had imported all the cars in question into the UK. However, M was only entitled to use the margin scheme if J had also been entitled to use the margin scheme. On the evidence, since J had imported the cars from Japan into the EU, J had incurred a VAT liability on importation, should have accounted for acquisition tax when the cars were moved from Ireland to the UK, and was entitled to credit for input tax on an onward taxable supply. Accordingly, J had not been entitled to use the margin scheme, and the effect of *Article 8(2)* of the *Cars Order* was that M was also not entitled to use the margin scheme. With regard to J's dealings in the cars, the tribunal observed that *Article 26a(B)(2)* of the *EC Sixth Directive* limited the margin scheme to goods acquired within the European Community. The tribunal also observed that J had not registered for UK VAT until November 1998, although it had apparently been liable to register before that date, and had made its first sales to M in October 1998. The tribunal observed that the assessment should be adjusted since M was entitled to credit for the input tax fraction of the purchase price of the cars which it had obtained from J at a time when J was not, but should have been, registered. The fact that M did not hold any invoices in respect of these purchases did not extinguish its right to input tax, applying the decision in *Ellen Garage (Oldham) Ltd*, **40.11** INVOICES AND CREDIT NOTES. However, the tribunal also held that M was not entitled for credit in respect of its purchases from J after J had registered for UK VAT, since J could have provided VAT invoices but M had failed to obtain any. *Angus MacKinnon Ltd*, MAN/99/959 (VTD 18015).

[44.74] See also *Ball*, 52.174 PENALTIES: MISDECLARATION.

Cars purchased from Netherlands dealer—whether within Article 8(2)

[44.75] The decision in *Wood*, 44.70 above, was applied in a subsequent case where a car dealer had purchased a number of second-hand cars from a dealer in the Netherlands. The tribunal held that the dealer was not entitled to account for tax on these cars under the margin scheme. *PC Butcher (t/a Ashley Motor Services)*, LON/00/492 (VTD 17423).

Cars purchased from German dealer—whether within Article 8(2)

[44.76] A car dealer purchased three new Porsche cars in Germany, using a roundabout method involving two Malaysian companies. When he sold the cars, he accounted for tax under the margin scheme. The Commissioners issued an assessment on the basis that he was not entitled to use the scheme. He appealed, contending that he had routed the purchase through the Malaysian companies because the manufacturer would have objected to the cars being sold to a non-franchised dealer, and that he had paid German VAT which he was unable to recover, so that the assessments would result in double taxation. The tribunal dismissed his appeal, observing that there was no evidence that he had tried to recover the German VAT. The cars were not within *Article 8* of the *Cars Order* and the dealer was not entitled to use the margin scheme. *B Connors*, LON/01/486 (VTD 17666).

Computation of profit margin (Article 8(5))

Price at which car obtained (Article 8(5)(a))

Whether expenses of sale deductible

[44.77] A second-hand car dealer (T), who bought and sold his vehicles at auctions, operated the margin scheme. He claimed that, in arriving at the consideration received for car sales, the commission, entry fee and indemnity fee which he paid to the auctioneer should be deducted. The Commissioners rejected this claim and he appealed. The tribunal dismissed his appeal, observing that 'in general, VAT is chargeable on the full value of second-hand goods sold by a taxable person. So that if (T) is dissatisfied with the scheme as set out in *Notice 711* he can always turn his back on the scheme, and carry on business and account for tax in the usual way, outside the scheme, on all supplies made by him.' The tribunal observed that 'the scheme is advantageous to him in his trade. The normal rules of accountability for VAT would be disadvantageous to him. Having chosen the scheme for the conduct of a transaction, he must adhere to it in the form in which it is; not in the form in which he would like it to be.' *CG Todd*, LEE/74/31 (VTD 130).

Whether costs of restoration deductible

[44.78] A contention that expenditure incurred in restoring second-hand cars should be taken into account for the purposes of the margin scheme was rejected in *J Robertson*, EDN/84/106 (VTD 1797).

[44.79] Similar decisions were reached in *Peter Oates Ltd*, LON/87/543 (VTD 2576); *PPG Publishing Ltd*, LON/88/92 (VTD 3047); *E Barnett (t/a Barnett Motor Services)*, MAN/90/948 (VTD 6868) and *JPS Doyle*, LON/94/2550A (VTD 13742).

Sales of repossessed cars by hire-purchase finance company

[44.80] A company (D) financed hire-purchase agreements for cars sold by dealers. Sometimes it repossessed cars from defaulting purchasers, which were then sold in the open market as second-hand vehicles. The Commissioners issued an assessment charging tax on the full amount received on the sale of certain repossessed cars. D appealed, contending that the sales should be treated under the margin scheme, and that for the purposes of the *Cars Order*, its acquisition cost was the original purchase price paid to the dealer. The tribunal rejected this contention and dismissed the appeal. On payment of the purchase price to the dealer, D acquired the ownership of the car, followed immediately by a transfer of possession to the hirer which, by virtue of what is now *VATA 1994, Sch 4 para 1(2)(b)*, was an onward supply of the car to the hirer as goods. The amount paid to the dealer was wholly exhausted as consideration for the onward supply to the hirer, and could not be used as a base for establishing the consideration for the acquisition of the car on repossession. Accordingly, whether or not the sale of the car fell to be dealt with under the margin scheme, the consideration on repossession was nil and tax was chargeable on the full amount realised on its sale. *Darlington Finance Ltd*, [1982] VATTR 233 (VTD 1337).

Cars purchased from company which owed amounts to finance company

[44.81] A company (D) purchased 23 vehicles from another company (E). E had acquired the vehicles under conditional sale agreements from a finance company (F), whereby legal title to the cars remained with F. In February 1990 E went into liquidation, having failed to pay F the full amounts which it owed in respect of the vehicles. F demanded payment of the outstanding balance from D, which paid F £32,000 in settlement of its claim. In the meantime D had sold the vehicles to customers, paying VAT of £3,050 under the margin scheme. Following its payment of £32,000 to F, D reclaimed the VAT of

£3,050 from the Commissioners, on the basis that it had sold the cars at a loss and should not have accounted for any VAT in respect of the sales. The Commissioners rejected the claim, and D appealed. The tribunal allowed D's appeal, holding that the £32,000 formed part of the consideration paid by D for the vehicles. Accordingly, D had sold the cars for less than their cost of acquisition, and the effect of what is now *Article 8* of the *Cars Order* was that the sales gave rise to no VAT liability. *Daron Motors Ltd*, LON/92/3165 (VTD 11695).

Owner of vintage car registering for VAT

[44.82] An individual (D), who had purchased a vintage Bentley car for £500 in 1966, was made redundant from his employment in 1985. He decided to go into business as a restorer and supplier of vintage cars, and registered for VAT accordingly. He issued himself with a VAT invoice purporting to show that he had sold the Bentley to his business for £35,000, and reclaimed input tax accordingly. The Commissioners issued an assessment on the basis that the car had been acquired for £500 rather than for £35,000. The tribunal upheld the assessment and dismissed D's appeal. *GK Dodds*, [1989] VATTR 98 (VTD 3383).

Price at which car sold (Article 8(5)(b))

Amount of consideration for car sold with allowance for car traded in

[44.83] Two companies offered for sale second-hand cars at fixed prices, stating that the customer would be given a minimum of £1,500 for any car he 'traded in', with no reservations as to the true value of that car. The offer prices for the cars to be sold were inflated by sums which, it was hoped, would prevent losses on the deals. On a sale, the customer was given an invoice showing the sale price and also a credit note for the traded-in car. Subsequently the companies adjusted the credit notes to allocate the amount to show what they considered to be the true value of the traded-in car, and treated the difference between this and the amount actually credited to the customer as a 'special trade-in offer'. The traded-in car was taken into stock at its true value and the 'special trade-in offer' was deducted from the sale price of the car sold to the customer, in accounting for tax under the margin scheme. The Commissioners issued assessments on the basis that the sale price was the price agreed with, and invoiced to, the customer. The tribunal upheld the assessments and dismissed the companies' appeals. *James A Laidlaw (Edinburgh) Ltd; James A Laidlaw (Dunfermline) Ltd*, EDN/82/41 & 42 (VTD 1376).

[44.84] Similar decisions were reached in *Stuart & Co (Motors) Ltd*, [1984] VATTR 207 (VTD 1753); *RF Taylor*, MAN/87/279 (VTD 2841); *W Milligan & Sons*, MAN/87/342 (VTD 4297); *PV Coventry (t/a Vincent James of Bath)*, LON/91/1450X (VTD 9617) and *BJ Middleton*, MAN/96/1150 (VTD 17985).

[44.85] A company (L) traded as a car dealer. It accepted second-hand cars in part-exchange on the basis that the relevant transaction could be cancelled by the customer within 30 days. However, if the car taken in part-exchange had been sold, the customer was not entitled to a refund of the nominal part-exchange price stated on the order form, but to a lower 'trade value'. Initially L accounted for VAT on the basis of the sale prices shown on the order forms. However, it subsequently submitted a repayment claim on the basis that the sale price should be adjusted to reflect the 'trade value', rather than the sale price agreed with the customer. The Commissioners rejected the claim and the tribunal dismissed L's appeal, holding on the evidence that 'the price attributed to the part-exchange cars on sales of (L's) cars to customers was the price shown on the order forms and the invoices'. The Ch D, CA and HL all upheld this decision. Lord Walker of Gestingthorpe observed that the CJEC had consistently held that non-monetary consideration should be 'quantified by finding the appropriate monetary equivalent'. He held that the 'subjective value' was 'in a straightforward case, the value which the parties to the contract have themselves recognised in the course of their dealings, and have in that way attributed to goods or services which amount to non-monetary consideration'. In the present case, 'there was formal documentation bearing directly on the issue of attribution'. The tribunal had correctly treated the part-exchange price as the monetary equivalent. *Lex Services plc v C & E Commrs*, HL 2003, [2004] STC 73; [2003] UKHL 67; [2004] 1 WLR 1; [2004] 1 All ER 434.

[44.86] A company (H) which traded as a car dealer, and accepted second-hand cars in part-exchange for the cars which it sold, issued vouchers described as 'Purchase Plus discount notes' in an attempt to encourage sales without having to overvalue the part-exchanged car. Thus, for example, if the company was offering a car for sale for £20,000, and the customer was only willing to pay £18,000 and a second-hand car valued at £1,500, H issued a 'Purchase Plus voucher' for the balance of £500. The Commissioner issued a ruling that, in such a case, the voucher had a value of £500 so that the sale price of the car was £20,000. H appealed, contending that the voucher had no monetary value for the purposes of *VATA 1994, s 19*, so that the sale price of the car was £19,500. The Ch D accepted this contention and allowed the appeal, and the CA upheld this decision. Chadwick LJ held that 'the purpose of the "Purchase Plus" voucher scheme' was 'to make it clear that there is no overvaluation of the part exchange car. The over-allowance is provided through the issue of the "Purchase Plus" voucher. The fact that finance companies are prepared to treat the face value of the voucher as part of the deposit paid by the customer for the purposes of satisfying the requirements of their borrowing ratios provides no answer to the question "what monetary equivalent is to be ascribed to the part-exchange car?". That question is answered by identifying the value which the parties to the relevant transaction (in this context, the supply of the replacement car) have given to the part-exchange car'. Ward LJ held that the voucher 'was simply a piece of paper which enabled the deal to be done a true price which made both supplier and customer happy', and that its monetary equivalent was 'nil'. *Hartwell plc v C & E Commrs*, CA [2003] STC 396; [2003] EWCA Civ 130. (*Notes.* (1) For another issue in this case, see **67.167** VALUATION. (2) This case was distinguished in the subsequent HL decision in *Lex Services plc*, **44.85** above. Lord Walker of Gestingthorpe observed that H had 'decided to adopt a scheme which explicitly made a different attribution of value'.)

[44.87] An appeal was dismissed in a case where a car dealer had failed to account for output tax on the value of second-hand cars which he had accepted in part-exchange. *G Duncan v HMRC*, [2010] UKFTT 95 (TC), TC00406.

Disposal of taxicab licences—whether separate from disposal of taxi

[44.88] Until 31 March 1983, the Commissioners treated the sale of taxicab licences as outside the scope of VAT. After that date the Commissioners treated them as part of the sale of the taxicabs. The change in treatment was notified to the National Federation of Taxicab Associations and subsequently published in *Notice 700/25/84*. A company which disposed of one taxicab in 1986 and another in 1987 did not account for VAT on the sale of the licences. The Commissioners issued an assessment to recover the tax and the tribunal dismissed the company's appeal. *Associated Cab Co Ltd*, MAN/88/97 (VTD 3394).

[44.89] A partnership sold two cars, to which it had transferred hackney carriage licences permitting them to be used as taxis in Cambridge. It contended that in computing the margin, there should be deducted not only the original cost of the cars but also an amount in respect of the licences. The tribunal rejected this contention and dismissed the appeal, holding that there was a single supply and the fact that the company had improved the value of the vehicles by attaching the licences to them was not relevant for the purposes of the margin scheme. *GT Collins & Son*, LON/88/3134 (VTD 3738).

[44.90] The decisions in *Associated Cab Co*, **44.88** above, and *GT Collins & Son*, **44.89** above, were followed in a similar subsequent case in which an appeal against an assessment charging tax on the sale of a taxicab was dismissed. *SS Natt*, MAN/91/9 (VTD 6999).

Road fund licences sold with second-hand cars

[44.91] A company sold second-hand cars. Where a car did not have a valid road fund licence at the time of sale, the company undertook to obtain a licence on behalf of the customer. The Commissioners issued an assessment on the basis that the sale of the cars included the sale of the licences, and that VAT should be charged on the whole supply. The tribunal allowed the company's appeal, holding that the payments for road fund licences were not part of the consideration for the company's supplies. *DE Siviter (Motors) Ltd*, MAN/88/458 (VTD 3556).

[44.92] Similar decisions were reached in *Cromford Hill Motor Sales*, MAN/97/1095 (VTD 16152) and *John Wilson Cars Ltd*, MAN/99/514 (VTD 16655).

[44.93] The decision in *Cromford Hill Sales*, **44.92** above, was distinguished in a subsequent case in which the tribunal held on the evidence that the appellant company was making a single supply of a car with a road fund licence, and was required to account for tax on the full amounts paid by its customers, in accordance with *Notice No 718*. *C Hesketh & Sons Ltd*, MAN/99/823 (VTD 16963).

[44.94] A similar decision was reached in *Autolease (UK) Ltd*, MAN/04/695 (VTD 19136).

MOT certificates supplied with second-hand cars

[44.95] A company which sold second-hand cars obtained one-year MOT certificates for the cars which it supplied. It attributed part of the consideration which it received to its supply of the MOT certificates, and did not account for output tax on this. The Commissioners issued an assessment on the basis that the company was making a single supply of a car with a MOT (as laid down in *Notice No 718*), and was required to include the amount attributed to the MOT certificates as part of the consideration for the purposes of the second-hand margin scheme. The tribunal upheld the assessment and dismissed the company's appeal. On the evidence, the company was 'selling the MOT-tested car to the customer for a single price which covers both the gross price of the car plus the charge for the test'. *Family Car Centre Ltd*, LON/98/1237 (VTD 16141).

[44.96] The decision in *Family Car Centre Ltd*, 44.95 above, was applied in the similar subsequent cases of *Depot Corner Car Sales*, MAN/99/945 (VTD 16907) and *RH Hotchkiss (t/a Roger Herbert Hotchkiss Car Sales)*, MAN/00/809 (VTD 17207).

Disallowance of input tax (Input Tax Order, Article 7)

NOTE

Input Tax Order, Article 7 was amended by VAT (Input Tax) (Amendment) (No 3) Order 1995 (SI 1995/1666) with effect from 1 August 1995, and further amended by the VAT (Input Tax) (Amendment) Order 1999 (SI 1999/2930) with effect from 1 March 2000. The cases in this section should be read in the light of the changes in the legislation.

General principles

Whether Input Tax Order, Article 7 in accordance with EC law

[44.97] See *Royscot Leasing Ltd*, 22.424 EUROPEAN COMMUNITY LAW.

Delivery charges

[44.98] A car was supplied to a company at an agreed price plus a delivery charge of £47.50. The company appealed against the Commissioners' decision that the tax on the delivery charge was not allowable as input tax. The tribunal dismissed the appeal, holding that the delivery charge was in substance and reality part of the consideration for the supply of the car and not a separate charge for the service of delivery. *Wimpey Construction UK Ltd*, [1979] VATTR 174 (VTD 808).

[44.99] A company purchased substantial numbers of cars directly from the manufacturers. The manufacturers arranged for the cars to be delivered by a transport company, which made a separate charge for this service. The company reclaimed input tax on the delivery charges. The Commissioners rejected the claim and the company appealed, contending that the delivery charge was consideration for a separate supply, on which it was entitled to reclaim input tax. The HL rejected this contention and upheld the Commissioners' ruling. Lord Slynn observed that 'if the transaction is looked at as a matter of commercial reality there was one contract for a delivered car: it is artificial to split the various parts of the transaction into different supplies for VAT purposes. What (the company) wanted was a delivered car; the delivery was incidental or ancillary to the supply of the car and it was only on or after delivery that property in the car passed.' *C & E Commrs v British Telecommunications plc*, HL [1999] STC 758; [1999] 1 WLR 1376; [1999] 3 All ER 961. (*Note*. For the Commissioners' practice following this decision, see Business Brief 17/99, issued on 6 August 1999.)

Towbar fitted as optional extra

[44.100] A salesman used a caravan, towed by his car, for exhibiting and selling the Encyclopaedia Britannica. He purchased a new car and had a tow bar fitted as an optional extra. He reclaimed input tax on the towbar. The Commissioners issued an assessment to recover the tax and the tribunal dismissed the salesman's appeal. Applying the principles established by *British Railways Board v C & E Commrs*, **66.12** TRANSPORT, there had been a single supply of a motor car fitted with a tow bar. *AC Turmeau*, LON/81/164 (VTD 1135).

'Car kit' supplied with car

[44.101] A company which had ordered a new car also ordered a 'car kit', comprising side skirts and a boot lid spoiler, to be added to the car. The kit was invoiced separately from the car, and the company reclaimed input tax on the kit. The Commissioners issued an assessment to recover the tax, considering that the kit formed part of the car when it was delivered, so that the tax was not deductible by virtue of what is now *Article 7* of the *Input Tax Order*. The tribunal dismissed the company's appeal, holding that the company had been supplied with a motor car, and that the fact that the kit was invoiced separately did not alter the fact that the input tax was not deductible. *A Thompson & Sons Ltd*, MAN/91/982 (VTD 7833).

Police Authority—claim for refund of VAT on purchase of motor cars

[44.102] See *R v C & E Commrs (ex p. Greater Manchester Police Authority)*, **42.8** LOCAL AUTHORITIES.

Disallowance of input tax—other cases

[44.103] There are a number of cases in which claims to input tax on the purchase of motor cars have been dismissed. In the interests of space, such cases are not summarised individually in this book. For the imposition of penalties in such cases, see **52.341** to **52.343** PENALTIES: MISDECLARATION.

Whether cars supplied on letting on hire before 1 August 1995

[44.104] *Article 7* of the *VAT (Input Tax) Order 1992 (SI 1992/3222)* was substantially amended by *SI 1995/1666* with effect from 1 August 1995. Following the changes, a leasing company (B) reclaimed input tax on six cars. The Commissioners formed the opinion that the tax was not recoverable, on the basis that B's customer had entered into a prepayment agreement with an associated company, the effect of which was that the cars had been supplied on a letting on hire prior to 1 August 1995, so that, by virtue of *Article 7(2C)*, they were not 'qualifying motor cars' within *Article 7(2A)* and the tax was not deductible. B appealed, contending that none of the cars had been supplied before 1 August 1995. The tribunal accepted this contention and allowed the appeal, and the CA upheld this decision. Pill LJ observed that none of the cars had been identified before 1 August 1995 and that B had neither made nor received payments, nor issued invoices, before that date. He held that the fact that B's customer had, before 1 August, entered into a prepayment agreement with an associated company to make an onward supply of the cars in question was not conclusive, since B was not associated with the customer and was not a party to the customer's transaction. Pill LJ expressed the view that the purpose of *Article 7(2C)* was 'to prevent *the same* taxable person, by letting before 1 August and purchasing on or after that date, from obtaining the benefit of both regimes'. *BRS Automotive Ltd v C & E Commrs*, CA [1998] STC 1210. (*Note.* See, however, the *VAT (Input Tax) (Amendment) Order 1998 (SI 1998/2767)*, which reverses the effect of this decision. The purpose of the amendment was to ensure 'that the 50% restriction on input tax recovery will apply as Parliament intended to all leased business cars also used for private motoring'. See Customs' News Release 28/98, issued on 12 November 1998, and Business Brief 25/98, issued on 16 December 1998. The Financial Secretary to the Treasury described the scheme adopted by B's customer as a 'blatant avoidance scheme marketed by some of the leading accountants'.)

Whether car acquired exclusively for 'self-drive hire'

[44.105] A company (R) provided cars to the owners of vehicles which had been damaged in accidents, while their cars were being repaired. It reclaimed input tax on the purchase of a Bentley. HMRC rejected the claim on the basis that it appeared that the car had not been purchased with the sole intention of being used in R's business. The tribunal reviewed the evidence and dismissed R's appeal, finding that it had failed to show 'that it is entitled to the input tax credit it has claimed'. *Ravenfield Ltd v HMRC*, [2010] UKFTT 359 (TC), TC00641.

Whether car intended for use 'exclusively for the purposes of a business' (Article 7(2E)(2G))

Cases where the appellant was unsuccessful

[44.106] A farmer reclaimed input tax on the purchase of a Daihatsu 4-track vehicle. The Commissioners rejected the claim, and the farmer appealed, contending that he intended to use the vehicle exclusively for business purposes, within *Input Tax Order, Article 7(2E)*. The tribunal dismissed the appeal, accepting that the farmer's subjective intention was to use the vehicle exclusively for business purposes, but holding on the evidence that the vehicle was available for private use within *Input Tax Order, Article 7(2G)*, so that the farmer was not entitled to reclaim the input tax. The tribunal chairman (Mr. Lightman) observed that 'it is verging on the impossible that someone who acquires a motor vehicle which is freely usable on the roads for private use would not, at that time, have it at the back of his mind that it might be so usable, and that he could therefore so make it available to himself or others. In other words, he must, in such circumstances, be treated as intending that it be available, at least to himself, for private use.' *GDG Jones (t/a Jones & Son)*, LON/96/357 (VTD 14535). (*Note.* The decision here has been followed in a large number of subsequent cases. However, *obiter dicta* of the tribunal chairman were disapproved by a subsequent tribunal in the case of *Martinez*, **44.109** below, where Mr. Wallace expressed the view that Mr. Lightman's use of the word 'must' was inappropriate, and that the presumption was rebuttable, albeit with difficulty.)

[**44.107**] The decision in *GDG Jones*, **44.106** above, was applied in a similar subsequent case in which the tribunal specifically declined to follow the decisions in *Lowe*, **44.126** below, and *Grace*, **44.128** below. *LP & CG Brown*, MAN/97/337 (VTD 16109).

[**44.108**] A similar decision, again applying *GDG Jones*, **44.106** above, and specifically declining to follow the decisions in *Lowe*, **44.126** below, and *Grace*, **44.128** below, was reached in *JA Heath (t/a Heath Private & Commercial Vehicles)*, MAN/99/63 (VTD 16212).

[**44.109**] A car dealer reclaimed input tax on the purchase of a four-wheel drive Nissan Terano. The Commissioners issued an assessment to recover the tax and the dealer appealed, contending that he had bought the Terano for the purpose of towing vehicles. The tribunal dismissed his appeal, accepting that this was the dealer's main purpose, but holding on the evidence that he had not shown 'that he did not intend to make it available for private use even in an emergency'. The tribunal chairman (Mr. Wallace) observed that 'the fact that a vehicle is insured for private use, and is kept at the trader's home, is likely to cause a tribunal to approach evidence and submissions that it is intended to be used only for business with circumspection'. *L Martinez*, [1999] VATDR 267 (VTD 16320).

[**44.110**] A trader, who lived in Central London, carried on the business of supplying and servicing vending machines in public houses. He reclaimed input tax on the purchase of a Lamborghini. The Commissioners rejected the claim on the basis that the Lamborghini was available for private use. The CA unanimously dismissed the trader's appeal. Peter Gibson LJ observed that 'the intention specified in (*Input Tax Order, Article 7(2E)(a)*), viz. to use, is not synonymous with the intention specified in *para (2G)(b)*, viz. to make available for use, nor does an intention to use a car exclusively for business purposes exclude the possibility of an intention to make the car available for private use'. Where an individual trader acquired a car, 'the very fact of his deliberate acquisition of the car whereby he makes himself the owner of the car and controller of it means that at least ordinarily he must intend to make it available to himself for private use, even if he never intends to use it privately'. On the evidence, the result of the trader's 'deliberate action in acquiring the car and obtaining insurance permitting private use was to make the car available to himself for private use' and 'he must be taken to have intended that result in the absence of evidence to the contrary, even if he did not intend to use the car privately'. Accordingly, the effect of *Article 7(2G)* was that the tax was not deductible. *CM Upton (t/a Fagomatic) v C & E Commrs*, CA [2002] EWCA Civ 520; [2002] STC 640.

[44.111] In a Scottish case, a sole trader reclaimed input tax on the purchase of a Mitsubishi Shogun. The Commissioners rejected the claim and he appealed, contending that he used the Shogun solely for business purposes, as he used another car (which was owned by his fiancée) for private motoring. The Shogun was equipped as a 'mobile office and workshop', with a laptop computer with printing and email facilities. The tribunal accepted the trader's evidence and allowed his appeal but the CS unanimously reversed this decision. Lord Osborne approved the reasoning of the CA in *Upton*, **44.110** above. He held that, while the wording of *Input Tax Order, Article 7* was 'somewhat difficult to follow', it was clear that '*paragraphs (2E) and (2G)* are quite distinct and are couched in significantly different language'. The effect of *Article 7(2G)* was that 'where a motor vehicle is acquired by a sole trader', that vehicle 'will indeed have been made available to that person for private use, unless effective steps are taken to render the vehicle incapable of such use by that person'. *C & E Commrs v CH Skellett (t/a Vidcom Computer Services)*, CS 2003, [2004] STC 201.

[44.112] The decision in *Skellett*, **44.111** above, was applied in a subsequent Scottish case where the tribunal chairman (Mr.Coutts) observed that it was 'virtually impossible' for a sole trader to satisfy the exclusivity test. *W Beattie*, EDN/04/129 (VTD 18979).

[44.113] A company claimed input tax on the purchase of a Hyundai car. The Commissioners rejected the claim on the basis that the effect of *Input Tax Order, Article 7(2G)* was that the tax was not deductible. The company appealed, contending that *Article 7(2G)* contravened the *EC Sixth Directive*. The tribunal rejected this contention and dismissed the company's appeal, holding that *Article 7(2G)* was authorised by *Article 17(6) of the EC Sixth Directive*. *Kay Quality Management Ltd*, LON/01/939 (VTD 18373).

[44.114] Between March 1997 and September 1998 an accountant reclaimed input tax on the purchase of six cars, three of which he sold in the same period (accounting for output tax on the sale). The Commissioners issued an assessment to recover the tax, considering that the cars were available for private use and that the effect of *Input Tax Order, Article 7(2G)* was that the input tax was not deductible. The accountant appealed, contending that the six cars were intended exclusively for business use because he already owned other cars which he could use privately. The tribunal dismissed the accountant's appeal, applying the principles in *Upton*, **44.110** above, and holding on the evidence that 'all six cars were made available for private use'. The Ch D upheld this decision as one of fact. *HAS Thompson (t/a HAS Thompson & Co) v C & E Commrs (No 2)*, Ch D [2005] STC 1777; [2005] EWHC 342 (Ch).

[44.115] A married couple owned and operated a hotel. The husband (R) purchased a Toyota Previa, and reclaimed input tax on the purchase. The Commissioners issued an assessment to recover the tax, on the basis that the effect of *Input Tax Order, Article 7(2G)* was that the tax was not deductible. The Ch D upheld the assessment, applying the CA decision in *Upton*, **44.110** above. Lloyd J held that 'the correct test in law' was that 'the taxable person does intend to make the car available for his own private use unless, at the time of acquisition, he intends to take effective steps to exclude the necessary consequence of availability which would follow from his ownership of the car'. *C & E Commrs v PJ Robbins*, Ch D 2004, [2005] STC 1103; [2004] EWHC 3373 (Ch).

[44.116] A farmer purchased a BMW X5 station wagon, powered by petrol, for private use, and a similar vehicle, but with a diesel engine, for use on his farm. He reclaimed input tax on the purchase of the latter vehicle. Customs issued an assessment to recover the tax, and he appealed, contending that he had purchased the diesel X5 solely for use on his farm, 'to provide the high torque necessary for towing'. The Ch D upheld the assessment, applying the CA decision in *Upton*, **44.110** above. Lindsay J observed that the effect of the legislation was that a sole trader was 'put at a disadvantage to his competitors or colleagues who have organised themselves as companies albeit even only one man companies'. *HMRC v PJR Shaw*, Ch D 2006, [2007] STC 1525; [2006] EWHC 3699 (Ch).

[44.117] There have been a large number of other cases, both before and after the CA decision in *Upton*, in which tribunals have rejected claims for input tax on cars. In the interests of space, such cases have not been summarised individually in this book. For lists of such decisions issued up to and including 31 December 2001, see Tolley's VAT Cases 2002.

Leasing of car to company director—whether at undervalue

[44.118] A company which operated an employment agency reclaimed input tax on the purchase of a Mercedes. The Commissioners issued an assessment to recover the tax, and the company appealed, contending that it should be entitled to reclaim the tax since it was hiring the Mercedes to its managing director. The tribunal rejected this contention and dismissed the appeal, holding on the evidence that it was not satisfied that the letting of the Mercedes had been under a legally binding agreement, and furthermore that it was not satisfied that the hiring 'was intended to be on commercial terms'. Accordingly, the effect of *Article 7(2G)* of the *Input Tax Order* was that the tax was not deductible. *Orin Engineering (UK) Ltd*, LON/97/163 (VTD 15254).

Leasing of car to associated company—Input Tax Order, Article 7(2G)

[44.119] A woman (N), who operated a car leasing business, purchased a Mercedes and leased it to a company of which she and her husband were directors. She reclaimed input tax on the purchase. The Commissioners rejected the claim, on the basis that the Mercedes had been leased 'for a consideration which is less than that which would be payable in money if it were a commercial transaction conducted at arm's length', so the effect of *Article 7(2G)* of the *Input Tax Order* was that the tax was not deductible. The tribunal upheld the Commissioners' decision and dismissed N's appeal. *Mrs ACS Nightingale (t/a Arrowe Rental)*, LON/96/1955 (VTD 17750).

Leasing of car to associated partnership—Input Tax Order, Article 7(2G)

[44.120] A company provided consultancy and car leasing services. Its company secretary had previously been a partner in an accountancy firm, for whom he still worked. In 1999 the company purchased a BMW and leased it to the firm. The company reclaimed input tax on the purchase. The Commissioners rejected the claim, on the basis that the BMW had been leased 'for a consideration which is less than that which would be payable in money if it were a commercial transaction conducted at arm's length', so the effect of *Article 7(2G)* of the *Input Tax Order* was that the tax was not deductible. The tribunal upheld the Commissioners' decision and dismissed the company's appeal. *M Barton Consultancy Ltd*, LON/00/865 (VTD 18233).

Leasing of Rolls Royce—application of Input Tax Order, Article 7(2G)

[44.121] A company (C) owned five hotels. It leased one of these to another company (E), the controlling director of which had previously been employed by C as the hotel manager. C also leased a Rolls-Royce car to E. This car was made available to customers who booked large wedding receptions at the hotel. In 1998 the original Rolls Royce became unroadworthy. C purchased a replacement for £85,000, and leased it to E. C reclaimed input tax on the purchase. The Commissioners issued an assessment to recover the tax, on the basis that the Rolls Royce had been leased 'for a consideration which is less than that which would be payable in money if it were a commercial transaction conducted at arm's length', so the effect of *Article 7(2G)* of the *Input Tax Order* was that the tax was not deductible. The tribunal dismissed C's appeal, observing that the new Rolls-Royce had cost 'over nine times more than the sum obtained for the Rolls-Royce it replaced'. If the lease had been a commercial transaction, that increase would have been 'reflected in an increase in the rental figure commensurate with the sum involved'. On the evidence, this 'was not a commercial transaction conducted at arm's length'. The Ch D upheld the tribunal decision. Lawrence Collins J observed that 'a purely commercial arm's length approach would have led the appellant to provide the cheapest possible car consistent with its obligation to maintain and replace the inventory, including a Rolls-Royce suitable for the wedding requirements of the hotel'. The company applied to the CA for leave to appeal against this decision. The CA rejected the application. Waller LJ observed that 'the requirement is not that there should actually be a commercial transaction conducted at arm's length; the question is whether the value of the consideration intended would be equivalent to what would apply on the market'. On the evidence, the tribunal and the Ch D 'were entitled to come to the conclusion that they did'. *Crown & Cushion Hotel (Chipping Norton) Ltd v C & E Commrs*, CA [2004] STC 1212; [2004] EWCA Civ 516.

Leasing of Mercedes cars—application of Input Tax Order, Article 7(2G)

[44.122] A leasing company purchased a Mercedes for £97,000 and leased it to an individual (apparently a friend of the managing director) for £167 per month. It purchased a second Mercedes for £37,000 and leased it to its company secretary for £221 per month. It reclaimed input tax on the purchase of both cars. The Commissioners rejected the claims on the basis that the cars had been leased 'for a consideration which is less than that which would be payable in money if it were a commercial transaction conducted at arm's length', so the effect of *Article 7(2G)* of the *Input Tax Order* was that the tax was not deductible. The tribunal dismissed the company's appeal against this decision. *ACL Leasing & Finance Ltd*, LON/03/586 (VTD 18808). (*Note.* Costs of £600 were awarded to the Commissioners.)

[44.123] See also *West Midlands Motors Ltd*, 52.447 PENALTIES: MISDECLA-RATION.

Cases where the appellant was partly successful

[44.124] In a Scottish case, a company which carried on a printing business reclaimed input tax on the purchase of a Daewoo Nexia and a Toyota Previa. The Commissioners issued an assessment to recover the tax, and the company appealed. The tribunal reviewed the evidence and allowed the appeal in respect of the Daewoo, noting that this had been issued to the company's sales representative, who already had a private car and had been instructed not to use the Daewoo for private motoring. Accordingly, the tribunal held that the company had demonstrated that 'its intention at the time of purchase was that this vehicle was for business use only'. However, the tribunal dismissed the appeal in respect of the Toyota, finding that there had been some private use of this vehicle. *Neil MacLeod (Prints & Enterprises) Ltd*, EDN/00/151 (VTD 17144). (*Note*. See now, however, the subsequent CA decision in *Upton*, **44.110** above.)

Cases where the appellant was successful

NOTE

The cases noted at **44.125** to **44.134** below were all decided before the CA decision in *Upton*, **44.110** above, and should all now be read in the light of the decision in *Upton*.

[44.125] An accountant, who owned three cars, purchased a further four cars and reclaimed input tax on their purchase. The Commissioners issued an assessment to recover the tax, considering that they were available for private use and that the effect of *Input Tax Order, Article 7(2G)* was that the input tax was not deductible. The accountant appealed, contending that the cars were intended exclusively for business use because he already owned three cars which he could use privately, and he had insured the four cars in dispute for business use only. The tribunal accepted the accountant's evidence and allowed his appeal. *HAS Thompson (No 1)*, LON/96/357 (VTD 14777). (*Note*. The decision was not followed in a subsequent appeal by the same accountant, heard after the CA decision in *Upton*, **44.110** above—see *Thompson (No 2)*, **44.114** above.)

[44.126] A trader carried on business as a breeder and supplier of game birds (pheasants). He reclaimed input tax on the purchase of a Nissan Patrol. The Commissioners rejected the claim, on the basis that the vehicle was available for private use, so that the effect of *Input Tax Order, Article 7(2G)* was that the input tax was not deductible. The trader appealed, contending that the Nissan was intended exclusively for business use, and that he had purchased it because he needed a large four-wheel drive vehicle which could be used for towing a trailer. He already owned two other vehicles, one of which was a saloon which he used for private journeys. The tribunal accepted the trader's evidence and allowed the appeal. The tribunal chairman (Mr. Lawson, sitting alone) distinguished *Jones*, **44.106** above, holding that that case relied on 'inference', whereas in the present case it was clear from the trader's evidence 'that he intended from the outset to use the vehicle exclusively for business purposes' and 'never intended or needed to use the vehicle for private purposes'. *SF Lowe*, LON/97/225 (VTD 15124). (*Note*. The decision here was not followed, and was implicitly disapproved, in the subsequent cases of *Brown*, **44.107** above, and *Heath*, **44.108** above.)

[44.127] A partnership of three people carried on business as licensed artificial inseminators. The partnership reclaimed input tax on the purchase of three Citroen cars. The Commissioners rejected the claim, considering that the cars were 'available for private use', within *Input Tax Order, Article 7(2G)*. The partnership appealed, contending that the effect of the licences issued by the Ministry of Agriculture, Fisheries and Food, under which the business operated, was that the cars could not be used privately. Under the licences, the cars were treated as part of the store where the company kept its stocks of semen. The boots of the cars contained canisters of liquid nitrogen, at a temperature of –150°C, in which flasks containing semen were kept while the partners were visiting farmers whose cattle were on heat and ready for insemination. The partners owned their own cars which they used for all their private motoring including travel to and from the partnership premises. The tribunal accepted the partnership's evidence and allowed the appeal. *Southern UK Breeders*, LON/97/598 (VTD 15303).

[44.128] A trader (G), who lived at Crawley, operated catering facilities at go-kart tracks at Crawley and Eastleigh. He reclaimed input tax on the purchase of an estate car. The Commissioners issued an assessment to recover the tax. G appealed, contending that he had purchased and used the estate car solely for the purposes of his business, as he owned another car which he used for private motoring. The tribunal chairman (Miss Gort, sitting alone) accepted G's evidence and allowed the appeal. *I Grace*, [1998] VATDR 86 (VTD 15323). (*Note*. The decision here was not followed, and was implicitly disapproved, in the subsequent cases of *Brown*, **44.107** above, and *Heath*, **44.108** above.)

[44.129] The decision in *Grace*, **44.128** above, was applied in a similar subsequent case in which a caterer had reclaimed input tax on the purchase of a jeep, which he used for delivering food to various sites. The tribunal chairman (Mr. Heim) noted that the trader had specifically requested that the vehicle should be insured for business purposes only, and that he had other vehicles which he could use for private motoring. *JC Aldam (t/a John Charles Associates)*, [1998] VATDR 425 (VTD 15851).

[44.130] A similar decision, also applying *Grace*, **44.128** above, was reached in a Scottish case where a couple who carried on business as foresters and farmers had reclaimed input tax on a Toyota four-wheel drive dual-cab pick-up. *R & HM Swailes*, EDN/98/169 (VTD 16069).

[44.131] An appeal was allowed in another Scottish case where the tribunal chairman (Mrs. Pritchard) accepted the trader's evidence that he had purchased a Ford Mondeo for business purposes only, as he had the use of another vehicle for private motoring. *J Berry (t/a Automotive Management Services)*, EDN/00/1 (VTD 16664).

[44.132] A similar decision was reached in a case where a steel fixer, who already owned a Vauxhall Cavalier which he used privately, reclaimed input tax on a Land Rover Discovery, which he used for transporting steel on a trailer. *GJ Henderson*, MAN/99/433 (VTD 17294).

Isuzu modified by removal of rear seats

[44.133] In a Scottish case, a couple who carried on business as forestry contractors reclaimed input tax on a Isuzu, from which they had removed the rear seats. The Commissioners issued an assessment to recover the tax and the couple appealed, contending that they had arranged for the removal of the rear seats so that they could use the Isuzu for business purposes, and they already had two cars which they used privately. The tribunal allowed the couple's appeal, distinguishing the Ch D decision in *Upton*, **44.**110 above, and observing that 'the fact that steps were taken so to alter the configuration of the vehicle as to make it, apart from the rear windows, the same as a van', together with the expressed intention of use and the actual use, 'negative by the actions taken an intention to make available for private use' (*sic*). *C & S Paterson*, EDN/01/49 (VTD 17323). (*Note.* See now, however, the subsequent CA decision in *Upton*, **44.**110 above.)

Mitsubishi L200 pick-up

[44.134] In another Scottish case, a family partnership reclaimed input tax on the purchase of a Mitsubishi L200 pick-up. The Commissioners rejected the claim and the partnership appealed, contending that it had been purchased and used solely for business purposes and had never been made available for private use, as the partners already had cars which they used privately. The tribunal accepted the partnership's evidence and allowed the appeal, applying *Paterson*, **44.**133 above, and distinguishing the Ch D decision in *Upton*, **44.**110 above. *AF Ross & Sons*, EDN/01/140 (VTD 17525). (*Note.* See now, however, the subsequent CA decision in *Upton*, **44.**110 above.)

Range Rover and Jaguar purchased by demolition company

[44.135] A company which operated a demolition business, and had an annual turnover of more than £10,000,000, reclaimed input tax on the purchase of a Range Rover and a Jaguar. The Commissioners rejected the claim and the company appealed, contending that the vehicles had been purchased and used solely for business purposes and had never been made available for private use. The Range Rover was designed as a mobile office; it was equipped with a fax machine, and was used for overnight work on railway sites. The Jaguar had been purchased to collect important clients from a railway station and take them to meetings. The company's directors and managers were not allowed to use the Jaguar for private motoring; it had only travelled 10,000 miles in 18 months, and each journey had been recorded in a notebook. The directors all owned expensive sports cars which they used privately. The tribunal accepted the company's evidence and allowed the appeal, distinguishing the CA decision in *Upton*, **44.**110 above. *Squibb & Davies (Demolition) Ltd*, LON/01/653 (VTD 17829).

Company maintaining alarm systems—vehicles provided for employees

[44.136] A company carried on a business of installing and maintaining alarm systems at industrial and commercial premises. It employed a number of security guards, and provided them with cars. It reclaimed input tax on the cars. The Commissioners rejected the claim on the basis that the cars were available for private use. The company appealed, contending that it prohibited private use by the employees, all of whom had their own cars which they used privately. The tribunal accepted the company's evidence and allowed the appeal. *Masterguard Security Services Ltd*, MAN/02/169 (VTD 18631).

Company trading as retail jewellers—Ford Ka provided for employees

[44.137] A company carried on business as a retail jeweller, with four shops in different locations. It reclaimed input tax on the purchase of a Ford Ka. Customs rejected the claim on the basis that the Ka was available for private use by the company's employees. The company appealed, contending that it prohibited private use, and that the car was used for transporting stock. The tribunal accepted the company's evidence and allowed the appeal. *Peter Jackson (Jewellers) Ltd*, MAN/05/615 (VTD 19474).

Mercedes made available to director who was not a shareholder

[44.138] A family company, which carried on a consultancy business, purchased a Mercedes for the use of its managing director (P), who was a family member but not himself a shareholder in the company, and was required to do a substantial amount of driving on company business. The company reclaimed input tax on the Mercedes. Customs rejected the claim on the basis that the effect of *Input Tax Order, Article 7(2G)* was that the input tax was not deductible. The company appealed, contending that it had minuted a resolution that the car was for business use only, and that P (who lived only 50 yards from the company's premises) had another car which he used privately. The tribunal accepted the company's evidence and allowed the appeal, holding that the effect of the company's resolution was that there was 'a legal embargo on private use of the motor car'. Customs appealed to the CA, which upheld the tribunal decision as one of fact. Arden LJ held that there was 'no reason why a car cannot be made unavailable for private use by suitable contractual restraints, that is effective restraints'. Applying the principles laid down in *Lee v Lee's Air Farming Ltd*, PC [1961] AC 12, 'a company can enter into a binding employment contract with its sole director'. On the evidence, the tribunal had been entitled to find that the company had complied with the requirements of *Article 7(2G)*. *C & E Commrs v Elm Milk Ltd*, CA [2006] STC 792; [2006] EWCA Civ 164.

Leasing of cars—whether at undervalue

[44.139] A company (T) purchased three cars for leasing and reclaimed input tax on the purchase. One of the cars was leased to an associated company (H) and the other two were leased to a company (R) which operated a golf centre. The Commissioners issued an assessment to recover the tax on the basis that T had intended to lease the cars for less than a commercial value, so that the effect of *Input Tax Order, Article 7(2G)* was that the cars should not be held to have been purchased for business purposes. T appealed, contending that the transactions met the test of commerciality and that *Article 7(2G)* did not apply to them. The tribunal accepted this contention and allowed the appeal. With regard to the cars which had been leased to R, the tribunal noted that R was not associated with T but that the leases in question had been entered into as a result of a 'personal friendship' between one of T's directors and a 'person connected with' R. However, although the rental payments under the leases were less than would be expected in an arm's length transaction, T had also received interest-free loans from the lessees, and the effect of this was that T would receive 'a reasonable commercial rate of return for its participation in the transaction'. Accordingly it was entitled to reclaim input tax on its purchase of the cars. *Tamburello Ltd*, [1996] VATDR 268 (VTD 14305). (*Note.* An alternative contention by T, that *Article 7(2G)* should be disregarded as being incompatible with *Article 17* of the *EC Sixth Directive*, was rejected by the tribunal.)

Fuel for private use (VATA 1994, ss 56, 57)

Sole trader

[44.140] An estate agent failed to account for tax on petrol used for private motoring, although he had reclaimed input tax on the petrol in question. The Commissioners issued an assessment to charge tax on the basis of the scale charges laid down by what is now *VATA 1994, s 57*. The tribunal upheld the assessment and dismissed the estate agent's appeal. *GM Child (t/a Child & Co)*, LON/90/1239X (VTD 6827). (*Note.* For another issue in this case, see **36.236** INPUT TAX.)

[44.141] Similar decisions were reached in *BA Hicks*, LON/92/1799P & 2075P (VTD 11215); *ME Conway*, LON/93/612A (VTD 11725); *RNM Anderson*, EDN/93/32 (VTD 11776); *R Desouza*, LON/93/400A (VTD 11819); *JA Bowles (t/a Oakey Bros Butchers)*, LON/93/2202 (VTD 12422); *AF Sanders*, MAN/94/2289 (VTD 13423); *RM Bevan*, MAN/95/2491 (VTD 14016); *WS Thayer*, LON/95/2533 (VTD 14382); *MI Gross (t/a AME Engineering Services)*, MAN/96/19 (VTD 14454); *DV Birch (t/a Robert Gibbons & Son)*, MAN/98/210 (VTD 15762); *SJ Mower*, LON/00/1157 (VTD 17210); *W Milward*, MAN/02/342 (VTD 18442), *SJ Jeffries (t/a Stu's Fruit & Convenience Store)*, [2011] UKFTT 724 (TC), TC01561 , and *G King*, [2012] UKFTT 64 (TC), TC01761.

[44.142] A trader (P) owned three cars, two of which were used solely for business. The third car, a Mercedes, was used for business and private mileage, but P failed to account for output tax on the basis of *VATA 1994, s 57*. The Commissioners issued an assessment charging tax on the scale charge and P appealed, contending that 95% of the mileage was business mileage and that when he had used the car for private purposes he had judged the length of the journey, topped the vehicle up with fuel to cover the private use and paid for that fuel privately. The tribunal dismissed P's appeal, observing that there was no evidence to substantiate the amount of private use. There was no way of showing that fuel for private use had not been paid for out of business funds. The chairman cast doubt on the claimed 5% private use as the mileage it represented was very low, and observed that 'that doubt could only be displaced by contemporary log entries'. *G Phillips*, LON/93/2934A (VTD 12184).

[44.143] A similar decision was reached in a case where the tribunal held that the provisions of what is now *VATA 1994, s 56(1)* were within the powers granted by the relevant derogation issued by the Council of the European Communities *(86/356/EEC)*. *M Kimber*, LON/92/944Y (VTD 10469).

[44.144] The decision in *Kimber*, **44.143** above, was applied in the similar subsequent case of *SJ Prosser*, MAN/97/1050 (VTD 15461).

Sole trader—fuel found to be used exclusively for business

[44.145] Customs issued an assessment on an architect, charging tax under *VATA 1994, ss 56, 57* in respect of the use of an Audi car. The architect appealed, contending that the car and all the fuel had been used exclusively for the purposes of his business (as he used a car owned by his wife for all private motoring). The tribunal accepted his evidence and allowed his appeal. The tribunal observed that the input tax on the car was not deductible, because the car was available for private use, even though it had not actually been used privately. However, since there had been no private mileage, there was no liability to output tax under *VATA 1994, ss 56, 57*. *NL Lewis (t/a Care Design)*, LON/04/841 (VTD 19210).

[44.146] A similar decision was reached in *P Worsfold*, EDN/06/44 (VTD 19968).

Partnership—fuel supplied to partners

[44.147] A partnership which operated a hotel paid for petrol which the partners used for private motoring, but did not account for output tax in respect of the petrol, although it had previously reclaimed input tax on the purchase of the petrol. The Commissioners issued an assessment charging output tax on the basis of the scale charges laid down by what is now *VATA 1994, s 57*. The tribunal dismissed the partnership's appeal, holding that, in the absence of a detailed record of private and business mileage, the adoption of the scale charges was mandatory. *Playden Oasts Hotel*, LON/90/1648Z (VTD 6468).

[44.148] Similar decisions were reached in *Harry Friar Partnership*, LON/92/1059X (VTD 9395); *Brown & Rochester*, MAN/92/633 (VTD 9751); *RD & EC Spicer (t/a Sands Executive)*, LON/94/1370A (VTD 13858) and *Seddon Investments*, MAN/97/1086 (VTD 15679).

Fuel supplied to employees

[44.149] A company failed to account for VAT on petrol supplied to its employees, and the Commissioners issued an assessment computed in accordance with the scale charges laid down by what is now *VATA 1994, s 57*. The tribunal upheld the assessment and dismissed the company's appeal. On the evidence, the company paid for the petrol used by some of its employees in travelling between their homes and the company's office. This was private mileage rather than business mileage, and the company was, therefore, obliged to account for VAT thereon. *Magor Products Engineering Ltd*, MAN/90/612 (VTD 6532).

[44.150] A similar decision was reached in *Rapide Security & Surveillance Ltd*, MAN/06/667 (VTD 20198).

[44.151] See also the cases noted at **52.293** PENALTIES: MISDECLARATION.

[44.152] An appeal was allowed in a case where the tribunal accepted the evidence of the appellant company that it only reimbursed business mileage and did not reimburse any private mileage. The tribunal chairman observed that the requirement (in what is now *Notice No 700/64/96, para 3(d)*) 'that there be detailed records was not a statutory requirement'. *Timewade Ltd*, LON/94/316 (VTD 12786). (*Note*. The tribunal noted that the company had been dilatory in replying to the Commissioners' enquiries, and only awarded the company 50% of its costs.)

[44.153] The Commissioners assessed a company which operated a garage, charging output tax under *VATA 1994, ss 56, 57* in respect of two cars which the company owned. The tribunal allowed the company's appeal in part, finding that one of the cars was not used for private purposes, but that output tax was chargeable in respect of one of the cars which was driven by the company's managing director. The chairman observed that it was 'improbable that (the director's) purchases of petrol were so accurate that he could be sure that he paid for all private use of this car'. *Deans Ltd*, LON/94/1792A (VTD 13935).

Miscellaneous

Valuation of new cars supplied under hire-purchase agreements

[44.154] A car-dealing company (N) made arrangements with finance companies to enable it to sell cars by hire-purchase, and accepted second-hand cars from its customers in part-exchange, treating the part-exchange value as the deposit required by the finance companies. Since the finance companies required a minimum deposit before they would agree to make loans to the customers, N frequently offered to inflate the allowance which it offered for the used cars which it took in part-exchange. To maintain its profit levels, it inflated the nominal sale price of the cars which it was selling to the finance companies by a similar amount (a practice known as 'bumping'). However, it only accounted for output tax on what it considered to be the true value of the cars, rather than on their inflated price. The Commissioners issued an assessment on the basis that output tax was chargeable on the price shown in the hire-purchase agreement with the finance company. The tribunal upheld the assessment and dismissed N's appeal. As a matter of law, N was supplying the cars to the finance companies. Accordingly, there was 'no room for any other value than that attributed by the parties in the document sent or which is prepared for the purposes of the finance house'. The chairman observed that 'that analysis removes the necessity to have regard to a wholly artificial, if not dishonest, method of securing finance. If, in order to do so, the appellants have manipulated figures, then they can scarcely complain if a value they have promulgated for a vehicle for their own purposes is accepted as its value for the particular transaction.' As a matter of principle, the appellants should not be entitled to benefit from a 'false attribution of value'. The CS upheld the tribunal decision. Earlsferry LJ held that the 'central question' was the value which the parties to the supply treated as the consideration. On the evidence, the only value which could be attributed to the transaction was the amount stated in the finance documents. *North Anderson Cars Ltd v C & E Commrs*, CS [1999] STC 902.

[44.155] A group of companies manufactured cars and sold them under hire-purchase agreements. The manufacturing company introduced a bonus scheme under which it paid monthly sums, on behalf of the customer, to the hire-purchase company (which was in the same VAT group). In accounting for VAT, the company treated these bonus payments as deductible from the consideration. Customs issued a ruling that the payments were not deductible, and the representative member of the group appealed. The tribunal reviewed the evidence in detail and allowed the appeal, applying the principles laid down in *Elida Gibbs Ltd*, **22.235** EUROPEAN COMMUNITY LAW. *Ford Motor Co Ltd (No 3)*, LON/05/936 (VTD 20028). (*Note.* For a preliminary issue in this case, see **2.8** APPEALS.)

Valuation of second-hand cars supplied to finance company

[44.156] A company (S), which traded as a car dealer, supplied second-hand cars to a finance company (C). Under the relevant agreements, the full purchase price payable by C to S was shown on an invoice. However, S was required to pay C a specified 'subsidy payment', representing the finance charges payable by the customers who would purchase the cars from C. C paid S a net payment, ie the purchase price reduced by the subsidy payment. The Commissioners issued a ruling that S was required to account for VAT on the full purchase price. S appealed, contending that the 'subsidy payment' was a discount, and it should only be required to account for tax on the amounts actually paid by C. The tribunal accepted this contention and allowed the appeal, holding that the taxable amount was 'the money actually received by (S) from (C)'. *A & D Stevenson (Trading) Ltd*, [2003] VATDR 82 (VTD 17979).

Buying and selling cars—whether a hobby or a business

[44.157] See *Adams*, **7.88** BUSINESS.

Treatment of car expenses of employees or agents

[44.158] See the cases noted at **36.1** to **36.13** INPUT TAX.

DVLA fees on sale of personalised vehicle numberplates

[44.159] A trader (C) sold personalised vehicle numberplates. When a registration number was transferred from one owner or vehicle to another, the Driver and Vehicle Licensing Agency charged a fee of £80. C recharged these fees to his customers, but did not account for VAT on them. The Commissioners issued an assessment on the basis that, where C sold a numberplate to a customer (acting as a principal rather than as an agent), he was required to account for VAT on the full sale price, including the £80 DVLA fee. The tribunal upheld the assessment and dismissed C's appeal, observing that C was making a 'standard-rated supply of a cherished number' and that the whole of the supply was standard-rated. *B Chapman*, MAN/00/262 (VTD 17932).

Personalised vehicle numberplates—whether input tax deductible

[44.160] See the cases noted at **36.468** *et seq.* INPUT TAX.

Company cars

[44.161] For whether the provision of a company car may constitute a taxable supply, see the cases noted at **62.1** to **62.7** SUPPLY.

Fees for arranging Ministry of Transport vehicle tests

[44.162] A garage proprietor (W) was not authorised by the Department of Transport to carry out Ministry of Transport vehicle tests. He therefore arranged for such tests to be carried out at approved garages, charging his customers the test fee plus an additional amount for arranging the test. He did not account for output tax on these charges. The Commissioners issued assessments charging output tax, on the basis that only test fees charged to customers separately as disbursements were outside the scope of VAT, as stipulated in Business Brief 21/96. The tribunal dismissed W's appeal, holding that as a matter of law he was required to charge output tax on the fees. However, the chairman commented that the assessment of the fees was 'a particularly harsh decision by the Commissioners' and that 'it was incumbent upon the Commissioners to inform taxpayers such as (W) in the plainest and simplest of terms precisely what the changes they made on 1 November 1996 meant to them. I appreciate that the Commissioners cannot spell out in detail every change in practice but, where a change affects a particularly vulnerable group of people, something more should be done to help them than simply to issue Notes with VAT returns and say that a Business Brief is available further to explain changes made.' *MA Ward (t/a Acorn Garage)*, MAN/98/507 (VTD 15875).

[44.163] The decision in *Ward*, **44.162** above, was applied in a similar subsequent case where the tribunal held that 'a payment cannot be regarded as a "disbursement" unless it was made by the payer in the capacity of an agent. The fact that the agent, ie the appellant, in this case was receiving a discount, or secret profit, precludes it from being an agent in law'. *Waterhouse Ltd*, LON/x (VTD 17483).

[44.164] Similar decisions were reached in *Chandlers Garage Holdings Ltd,* LON/99/271 (VTD 16610); *D Gillespie Ltd,* MAN/01/453 (VTD 17492); *AL Davis & Co,* LON/01/399 (VTD 17802); *Genuine Car Services,* LON/02/757 (VTD 18141); *Keswick Motor Co Ltd,* MAN/03/700 (VTD 18831); *P Benning (t/a PB Cars),* LON/05/891 (VTD 19557) and *RM Smith (t/a Smiths Auto Services),* MAN/00/056 (VTD 19702).

[44.165] The decisions in *D Gillespie Ltd,* 44.164 above, and *AL Davis & Co,* 44.164 above, were not followed in a subsequent Scottish case where a trader (D), who was not authorised by the Department of Transport to carry out Ministry of Transport vehicle tests, arranged for such tests to be carried out at approved garages. He charged the customers £44 for each test, paying £35 of this to the approved garage and retaining £9 himself. Customs issued an assessment on the basis that he was required to account for output tax on the full amounts which he charged. The tribunal allowed D's appeal, holding that only the £9 which the trader retained was liable to VAT. The tribunal expressed the view that the amount which D paid to the approved garage should not 'be deemed or regarded as part of the appellant's overall supply. The terms of the invoice do not reflect the involvement of the testing station as an independent party, but the customers were aware of this. We appreciate that our approach runs contrary to *Notice 700, section 25.1.1* and the suggested requirement that a disbursement should be itemised separately on the taxpayer's invoice. It does not, of course, have the force of law, and in our view the commentary there and in the case law cited does not pay sufficient regard to the legal monopoly of approved testing stations in relation to the conduct of MoT vehicle tests.' *G Duncan (t/a G Duncan Motor Services),* [2007] VATDR 114 (VTD 20100).

[44.166] The decision in *Duncan,* 44.165 above, was approved and applied in the subsequent English case of *MP Jamieson (t/a Martin Jamieson Motor Repairs),* LON/06/1248 (VTD 20269).

[44.167] Similar decisions were reached in *KJ & Mrs SJ Lower,* [2008] VATDR 199 (VTD 20567) and *CJW Denton (t/a Denton Auto Repairs),* LON/07/1708 (VTD 20627).

Second-hand cars—effect of Article 26a(B) of EC Sixth Directive

[44.168] A married couple who traded in partnership as car dealers had accounted for tax under the margin scheme. Subsequently they submitted a repayment claim on the basis that their supplies should have been treated as exempt from VAT. The Commissioners rejected the claim and the tribunal dismissed the couple's appeal, holding that the margin scheme was authorised by *Article 26a(B)* of the *EC Sixth Directive.* When the couple received second-hand cars from customers in part-exchange deals, the supplies by the customers were exempt from VAT under *Article 13B(c),* applying *EC Commission v Italian Republic,* 22.349 EUROPEAN COMMUNITY LAW. However, when the couple supplied cars to customers, the exemption in *Article 13B(c)* did not apply and they were required to account for tax on their profit margin. *Stafford Land Rover,* [1999] VATDR 471 (VTD 16388).

Partnership selling taxis to drivers on hire-purchase basis

[**44.169**] A partnership which operated a taxi business purchased suitable vehicles and sold them to the drivers on a hire-purchase basis. The drivers were required to pay the partnership £50 per week, of which £30 was treated as being for 'maintenance and repairs' and £20 was treated as an instalment of the purchase price. The partnership failed to account for VAT on these payments. Customs issued an assessment charging tax on them. The tribunal upheld the assessment and dismissed the partnership's appeal. *Club Taxis*, MAN/06/470 (VTD 20179).

Motor cars previously used for demonstration purposes

[**44.170**] See *JDL Ltd*, 46.98 PARTIAL EXEMPTION.

Vintage cars—whether 'collector's pieces of historical interest'

[**44.171**] See *Barnfinds Ltd*, 60.11 SECOND-HAND GOODS.

'Security deposit' for lease of expensive car

[**44.172**] See *Cross Border Lease Management Ltd*, 62.453 SUPPLY.

45

Overseas Traders

The cases in this chapter are arranged under the following headings.

Repayments of VAT (VATA 1994, s 39)	45.1
Other cases	45.9

Repayments of VAT (VATA 1994, s 39)

Whether supplies made for business purposes

[45.1] A company established in the Czech Republic (which was not part of the EC at the relevant time) claimed repayments of VAT under *VATA 1994, s 39* and the *EC Thirteenth Directive*. The Commissioners rejected part of the claims on the grounds that they related to 'day-to-day living expenses which are not directly business-related', and that, in several cases, the claims were not supported by invoices. The tribunal dismissed the company's appeal, finding that the relevant supplies appeared to have been made directly to the company's representatives, rather than to the company itself. Furthermore, it appeared that the supplies had been made for the personal benefit of the representatives, rather than for the purposes of the company's business. *CR Investments SRO*, LON/97/1201-1204 (VTD 15474).

[45.2] A Delaware company was incorporated in 1999. It entered into a 15-year lease of premises in London, but ceased trading in 2001. A Californian corporation (S) had guaranteed the rent under the lease. In 2004 S paid the lessor £1,500,000 plus VAT in order to be released from its guarantee. S reclaimed the VAT under *VAT Regulations 1995 (SI 1995/2518), reg 186*. HMRC rejected the claim on the basis that they were not satisfied that S was carrying on a business. S appealed. The Upper Tribunal allowed the appeal (reversing the decision of the First-Tier Tribunal). Sir Stephen Oliver held that 'the only requirement under *regulation 186* is that the VAT would be "input tax" if the trader was a taxable person in the UK. If that requirement is satisfied, all of the VAT is recoverable.' On the evidence, the payment which S had made to the lessor was incurred for the purposes of its business, and the VAT would have been input tax if S had been a taxable person in the UK. *SRI International v HMRC*, UT [2011] UKUT 240 (TCC); [2011] STC 1614.

Repayment claim by Gibraltar company

[45.3] See *Viscount Reinsurance Ltd*, 22.71 EUROPEAN COMMUNITY LAW.

Repayment claims—time limit for claim

[45.4] In September 1994 a Jersey company claimed a substantial repayment of VAT under what is now *VATA 1994, s 39*. The Commissioners rejected the claim on the grounds that it had been made outside the statutory six-month time limit laid down by what is now *VAT Regulations 1995 (SI 1995/2518), reg 192*. The tribunal dismissed the company's appeal against this decision. Applying *dicta* of Lord Lane in *JH Corbitt (Numismatists) Ltd*, **60.1** SECOND-HAND GOODS, and of Neill LJ in *John Dee Ltd*, **14.31** COLLECTION AND ENFORCEMENT, the tribunal had no 'jurisdiction to review the exercise by Customs & Excise of any discretion it may have in its management of the collection and refund of VAT'. *Jersey Telecoms*, LON/95/1965 (VTD 13940).

[45.5] In four appeals which were heard together, HMRC had rejected repayment claims on the basis that the necessary documentation had not been submitted within the statutory time limits. The claimants appealed to the tribunal, contending that the rejection of their claims violated the European principle of 'fiscal neutrality'. The tribunal rejected this contention and dismissed all four appeals. Sir Stephen Oliver observed that '*paragraph 7(1)* of the *Eighth Directive* sets down a specific time frame for the submission of non-domestic traders for refunds of VAT. That time frame is different from the one provided for domestic traders by *Article 252* of the *VAT Directive*. This is explicable because domestic traders make regular tax returns at the end of each tax period and have the right to make corrections in later returns under, for example, *regulation 34* of the *VAT Regulations*. The regime for non-domestic applicants is different. They have a much longer time over which to make their application. This is because they may only be making infrequent and possibly one-off requests for refunds.' Accordingly, 'different rules apply to domestic and non-domestic applications for refunds of VAT, because the situations of the two are different. The policies of HMRC towards domestic traders on the one hand and non-domestic applicants on the other reflect a different rule expressly provided for in the relevant Directives, and in the circumstances any differences between the two cannot, we think, be said to infringe the principle of non-discrimination.' There had been no breach of the principle of 'fiscal neutrality'. *Areva T & D Protection et Controle v HMRC (and related appeals)*, FTT [2010] UKFTT 134 (TC), TC00443.

[45.6] An American businessman (S) applied for a repayment of VAT under *VAT Regulations, regs 185-196*. HMRC rejected the claim on the basis that it had been lodged outside the time limit. The tribunal dismissed S's appeal against this decision. *RH Smith (t/a Robert H Smith Investments & Consulting) v HMRC*, [2011] UKFTT 576 (TC), TC01419.

[45.7] See also *Jack Camp Productions*, **25.32** EXPORTS, and *Oceanteam Power & Umbilical ASA*, **25.33** EXPORTS.

German company purchasing cars for leasing in UK

[45.8] See *HMRC v RBS Deutschland Holdings GmbH (No 4)*, **22.418** EUROPEAN COMMUNITY LAW.

Other cases

Whether Canadian company had a business establishment in the UK

[45.9] A company registered in Canada, which sold dartboards in Canada, owned a property in Lancashire. Its directors visited the UK occasionally, and purchased goods for resale in Canada. However, the company made no sales in the UK. It had registered for VAT in 1976. In 1988 it made a VAT repayment claim. The Commissioners formed the opinion that the company should not have been registered for VAT in the UK, and refused to repay the amount claimed. Subsequently they cancelled the company's registration. The company appealed, contending that it had a business establishment in the UK, and was therefore entitled to be registered under what is now *VATA 1994, Sch 1 para 10*. The tribunal allowed the company's appeal. The company's directors used the Lancashire property as a base when visiting the UK to purchase goods. The fact that the property was not continuously occupied did not prevent it from constituting a 'business establishment' in the UK. (The tribunal also held that its jurisdiction in the case was appellate rather than merely supervisory.) *The Source Enterprise Ltd*, MAN/91/450 (VTD 7881).

Whether German company supplying goods in UK or Germany

[45.10] See *Azo-Maschinenfabrik Adolf Zimmerman GmbH (No 2)*, **22.193** EUROPEAN COMMUNITY LAW.

46

Partial Exemption

The cases in this chapter are arranged under the following headings.

Non-business input tax (VAT Regulations 1995, reg 100) 46.1

Attribution of input tax to taxable supplies (VAT Regulations 1995, reg 101)

    Input tax held to be used 'exclusively in making taxable supplies' (*Regulation 101(2)(b)*) 46.2

    Input tax held to be used 'exclusively in making exempt supplies' (*Regulation 101(2)(c)*) 46.13

    Input tax held to be used 'in making both taxable and exempt supplies' (*Regulation 101(2)(d)*) 46.40

    Input tax in respect of 'capital goods' (*Regulation 101(3)(a)*) 46.97

    Input tax held to be used for 'incidental supplies' (*Regulation 101(3)(b)*) 46.99

Special methods (VAT Regulations 1995, reg 102)

    Approval or direction of special method (*Regulation 102(1)*) 46.102

    Termination of special method (*Regulation 102(3)*) 46.113

    Date from which special method effective (*Regulation 102(4)*) 46.128

    Notice overriding special method (*Regulations 102A–102C*) 46.131

    Customs refusing application for special method 46.134

    Universities and colleges 46.145

    Miscellaneous 46.153

Attribution of input tax to foreign and specified supplies (VAT Regulations 1995, reg 103) 46.173

Attribution of input tax on self-supplies (VAT Regulations 1995, reg 104) 46.182

Treatment of input tax attributable to exempt supplies as being attributable to taxable supplies (VAT Regulations 1995, reg 106) 46.183

Adjustments of attributions (VAT Regulations 1995, regs 107–110)

    Whether *Regulation 107* applicable 46.194

    Whether *Regulation 107B* applicable 46.201

    Whether *Regulation 108* applicable 46.205

    Whether *Regulation 109* applicable 46.212

Exceptional claims for VAT relief (VAT Regulations 1995, reg 111) 46.221

GENERAL NOTE

The law concerning the deduction of tax by partly exempt persons was substantially amended from 1 April 1987, and there were further changes with effect from 1 April 1992. See now *VATA 1994, ss 14, 15* and *VAT Regulations 1995 (SI 1995/2518), regs 99–111.*

Non-business input tax (VAT Regulations 1995, reg 100)

College of further education

[46.1] A college of further education was partly exempt, making some taxable supplies and some exempt supplies of educational services. It also provided free education for a number of students aged under 19. This was treated as outside the scope of VAT. However, in its returns, the college reclaimed input tax relating to these services. The Commissioners issued an assessment to recover the tax, on the basis that the relevant goods or services were not 'used or to be used for the purposes of any business' within *VATA 1994, s 24(1)*, so that the effect of *VAT Regulations 1995 (SI 1995/2518), reg 100* was that the input tax was not deductible. The tribunal upheld the assessments and dismissed the college's appeal. *North East Worcestershire College*, MAN/98/717 (VTD 16665).

Attribution of input tax to taxable supplies (VAT Regulations 1995, reg 101)

Input tax held to be used 'exclusively in making taxable supplies' (Regulation 101(2)(b))

Museum admitting school parties free of charge

[46.2] In 1989 the Imperial War Museum began charging visitors admission, but continued to allow free admission to school parties, and to other visitors at restricted times. It reclaimed the whole of its input tax. In 1991 the Commissioners formed the opinion that, in allowing some visitors free admission, the Museum was making 'non-taxable supplies', and that not all of its input tax was deductible. They concluded that only 85% of the Museum's input tax was deductible, and issued an assessment to recover the remaining 15%. The Museum appealed, contending that all its input tax was deductible. The tribunal allowed the appeal. The running of the Museum amounted to a business. The general overheads incurred by the Museum were used for the purpose of making taxable supplies. The Museum did not make any exempt supplies, and the fact that some visitors were admitted free of charge did not alter the fact that all the Museum's supplies were taxable. Thus the whole of the input tax was incurred for the purpose of making taxable supplies, even though it was not exclusively used for this purpose. *Whitechapel Art Gallery*, 11.46 CHARITIES, was distinguished since in that case the free art displays had been separate from the gallery's business activities. On the facts here, there was a single business activity of running the exhibition area of the Museum. Applying what is now *VAT Regulations 1995 (SI 1995/2518), reg 101*, all of the input tax fell to be attributed to this activity, and therefore all the input tax was deductible. *Imperial War Museum*, [1992] VATTR 346 (VTD 9097).

Dental association

[46.3] The British Dental Association, which was partly exempt, gave free membership to dental students. HMRC issued a ruling that this was a 'non-business activity', and that part of the association's input tax should be allocated to this and treated as disallowable. The association appealed. The tribunal allowed the appeal, applying the principles laid down in *Imperial War Museum*, **46.2** above. The tribunal held that 'the provision of free membership to dental students is a provision within the compass of the appellant's one business' and that 'there is no VAT principle, either in the Directives or in UK law, that requires a provision of free services, inherently made in the course of the undertaking of the one business, and given on very sensible commercial grounds, as requiring any disallowance of input tax'. *British Dental Association v HMRC*, [2010] SFTD 757; [2010] UKFTT 176 (TC), TC00481.

Property let for one week and subsequently sold

[46.4] In 1987, a company acquired a lease of a flat in London, with the intention of letting it as holiday accommodation. It incurred expenditure on refurbishing the flat, and advertised it as holiday accommodation for overseas visitors. However, it only attracted one customer, who occupied the flat for a week in 1988, paying £500 plus VAT. Subsequently the company sold the flat to one of its directors for £190,000. Since this sale was an exempt supply, the Commissioners considered that most of the input tax which the company had reclaimed should be attributed to this exempt supply, and issued assessments to recover $^{1900}/_{1905}$ of the tax. The company appealed, contending that since it had incurred the expenditure with the intention of making taxable supplies, and the whole of the flat had been the subject of a taxable supply, it was entitled to credit for the whole of the input tax. The tribunal accepted this contention and allowed the appeal, distinguishing *Briararch Ltd*, **46.212** below, and *Cooper & Chapman (Builders) Ltd*, **46.205** below. *Pembridge Estates Ltd*, LON/90/1803X (VTD 9606). (*Note.* The decision here was not followed in the subsequent case of *Key*, **46.21** below.)

Input tax on legal fees—whether to be attributed to taxable supply

[46.5] An insurance company, which was partly exempt, resisted a claim under a policy which it had entered into, claiming that the other party had been guilty of misrepresentation. It incurred legal fees in resisting the claim, which was eventually settled by a compromise agreement. The company reclaimed the full amount of the input tax relating to the fees in question. The Commissioners issued an assessment to recover part of the tax, considering that the expenditure was a general overhead of the business and should be treated as residual input tax, to be apportioned. The company appealed, contending that the input tax was entirely recoverable since it related to the supply of a zero-rated policy. The tribunal allowed the company's appeal, holding that the legal services had been used in the making of the taxable supply, rather than merely as a consequence of having made the supply, and accordingly the whole of the input tax was deductible. The QB upheld this decision. Auld J held that the legal services were causally connected with the making of the payment of the claim if and when it was made, and were therefore used 'exclusively in making taxable supplies'. *C & E Commrs v*

Deutsche Ruck UK Reinsurance Co Ltd, QB [1995] STC 495. (*Notes*. (1) For the Commissioners' practice following this decision, see Business Brief 6/95, issued on 28 March 1995. (2) The expression 'residual tax' does not appear in the *VAT Regulations 1995 (SI 1995/2518)*. but is used in Customs' Notice 706, which contains guidance on the operation of *VAT Regulations, reg 101*.)

Bank—whether legal costs wholly attributable to taxable supplies

[46.6] See *C & E Commrs v Midland Bank plc*, **22.400** EUROPEAN COMMU- NITY LAW.

Bank—acquisition of leasing companies

[46.7] A bank, which was partly exempt, had operated an equipment leasing business for several years. In 1987 this business had suffered losses. In 1990 and 1991 the bank acquired the share capital of three existing leasing companies. It took over the leasing businesses formerly operated by these companies, which became dormant subsidiaries. The bank reclaimed input tax on fees which it paid to solicitors and brokers relating to the acquisition of the companies. The Commissioners issued an assessment to recover some 28% of the tax, considering that it was partly attributable to exempt supplies. The bank appealed, contending that all the input tax should be treated as reclaimable, since it had acquired the companies for the purpose of making taxable supplies. The tribunal accepted this contention and allowed the bank's appeal, holding that there was 'no need to distinguish between the share purchases and the subsequent purchases of the businesses'. The CA upheld this decision. On the evidence, the tribunal had been entitled to find that there was a direct link between the acquisitions and the making of taxable supplies. *C & E Commrs v UBAF Bank Ltd*, CA [1996] STC 372. (*Note*. For the Commissioners' practice following this decision, see Business Brief 7/96, issued on 3 May 1996.)

Tourist board—installation of improved internet site

[46.8] A tourist board was partly exempt. It arranged for the installation of an improved internet site. Initially it treated the relevant input tax as residual input tax, but subsequently it submitted a repayment claim on the basis that it should have been attributed to taxable supplies. The Commissioners rejected the claim and the board appealed. The tribunal allowed the appeal in principle (subject to agreement as to figures), holding on the evidence that the expenditure had been incurred 'for the primary purpose of making taxable supplies, i.e. the booking service for which a charge is made'. *Scottish Tourist Board*, EDN/00/46 (VTD 16883).

Golf club—refurbishment of clubhouse kitchen and bar

[46.9] A golf club, which was partly exempt, arranged for the refurbishment of the kitchen and bar in its clubhouse, and reclaimed the relevant input tax. The Commissioners issued an assessment on the basis that the tax should have been treated as residual tax, and apportioned between the club's taxable and exempt supplies. The club appealed, contending that the input tax was entirely attributable to the taxable supplies which it made from the bar and kitchen. The tribunal accepted this contention and allowed the appeal. *Milnathort Golf Club*, EDN/02/109 (VTD 17889).

Property management company

[46.10] A property management company, with three offices, employed about 80 staff. One of the offices had a separate department of three staff which dealt with insurance business (acting as an insurance intermediary). Customs issued an assessment on the basis that the company had incorrectly treated too much of its input tax as attributable to its taxable supplies. The company appealed, contending that its returns were correct. The tribunal accepted the company's evidence and allowed the appeal, finding that the property management business and the insurance business were 'separate economic activities', and holding that it was 'incorrect as a matter of generality to regard property management costs as a cost component of insurance intermediary services'. *Ross & Liddell Ltd*, EDN/03/124 (VTD 19559)

Nursing agency—whether subject to partial exemption provisions

[46.11] See *British Nursing Co-Operation Ltd*, 33.20 HEALTH AND WELFARE.

College supplying free prospectuses

[46.12] See *West Herts College*, 62.114 SUPPLY.

Input tax held to be used 'exclusively in making exempt supplies' (Regulation 101(2)(c))

Expenditure on premises

Short-term lease of building pending sale

[46.13] A company was unable to sell a building which it had constructed, and therefore let it on a short-term lease. The Commissioners issued an assessment to recover the input tax which the company had claimed, considering that it should be attributed to the lease, which was an exempt supply. The company appealed, contending that the input tax should be allowed since it intended to sell the building, and any sale would be a taxable (zero-rated) supply. The tribunal dismissed the appeal, holding that the company had made an exempt supply and the input tax had to be attributed to that supply. *Brasplern (Group Services) Ltd*, MAN/83/223 (VTD 1558).

[46.14] The decision in *Brasplern (Group Services) Ltd*, 46.13 above, was applied in the similar subsequent case of *Rentorn Ltd*, EDN/88/105 (VTD 3334). (*Note*. This case was distinguished in *Curtis Henderson Ltd*, 46.213 below. Compare also *Briararch Ltd*, 46.212 below.)

Conversion of property let on short-term leases

[46.15] A company was registered as an intending trader with effect from August 1980. It converted a large house, which its managing director had purchased, into two self-contained units, and reclaimed the input tax incurred. It also reclaimed input tax incurred in building four houses. However, it did not make any taxable supplies, but let the properties on short-term leases. Accordingly, as the only supplies made were exempt from VAT, the Commissioners issued assessments to recover the tax. The tribunal upheld the assessments and dismissed the company's appeal, holding that the Commissioners were entitled to reject claims for input tax where no taxable supply was made within a reasonable period. *Fishguard Bay Developments Ltd*, LON/87/625X (VTD 3225, VTD 4549).

[46.16] A property development company purchased a building and converted it into a number of self-contained flats or apartments, which it let on short-term leases. It reclaimed input tax on the work. The Commissioners issued an assessment to recover the tax on the basis that the expenditure should be attributed to the leases, which were exempt supplies. The tribunal dismissed the company's appeal, finding that the building had not been used for taxable supplies and that the company had not proved that it had any intention of using the building for taxable supplies. *Celahurst Ltd*, LON/92/257 (VTD 13502). (*Note.* An appeal against a misdeclaration penalty was also dismissed.)

Refurbishment costs incurred against future exempt supplies

[46.17] Two companies reclaimed input tax on expenditure incurred in refurbishing a property to be used as offices and warehouses. The Commissioners issued assessments to recover the tax, as the expenditure related to future exempt supplies. The tribunal dismissed the companies' appeals and the CA upheld this decision. Mustill LJ observed that 'tax on inputs should be set off against tax on the outputs to which the inputs related, and against nothing else'. The leasing of the property would be an exempt supply, and the tax incurred for the purpose of making exempt supplies could not be deducted as input tax. *Neuvale Ltd v C & E Commrs; Frambeck Ltd v C & E Commrs*, CA [1989] STC 395. (*Note.* The claims related to periods before 1 April 1987. *VATA 1983, s 15* was amended by *FA 1987, s 12*, to specifically limit credit for input tax to input tax attributable to taxable supplies made, or to be made, by the taxable person. See now *VATA 1994, s 26*.)

[46.18] The decision in *Neuvale Ltd*, 46.17 above, was applied in a subsequent case where a company had reclaimed input tax which the tribunal found to have been wholly attributable to the making of exempt supplies. *Montague Burton Developments Ltd*, LON/90/1551Z (VTD 10090).

Premises leased after refurbishment

[46.19] A company purchased business premises and reclaimed input tax on their refurbishment. Subsequently it granted a lease of part of the premises to an associated partnership. The Commissioners issued an assessment to recover the input tax, on the basis that it should be attributed to the supply of the lease, which was exempt from VAT under what is now *VATA 1994, Sch 9, Group 1*. The tribunal upheld the assessment and dismissed the company's appeal. *North West Business Centres Ltd*, MAN/89/768 (VTD 4594).

[46.20] Similar decisions were reached in *Wigan Metropolitan Development Co (Investment) Ltd*, MAN/89/591 (VTD 4993); *The Really Useful Group plc*, LON/91/136Y (VTD 6578), and *St James Court Hotel Ltd*, LON/00/1003 (VTD 17487).

Refurbishment work undertaken for purpose of exempt supply

[46.21] A property developer (K) converted a barn into a house, with the intention of selling it. It was accepted that the sale would be exempt from VAT under the legislation then in force. However, before selling the converted house, K used it to make four short-term supplies of bed and breakfast accommodation. He accounted for output tax on these supplies, and reclaimed input tax on the refurbishment. The Commissioners issued an assessment to recover the tax, and K appealed, contending that the input tax should be attributed to the taxable supplies which he had actually made. The tribunal rejected this contention and dismissed his appeal, finding on the evidence that it was satisfied that he had incurred the expenditure for the purpose of making an exempt supply, and holding that he was not entitled to recover the tax in question. Applying the principles laid down in *Briararch Ltd*, **46.212** below, and *Curtis Henderson Ltd*, **46.213** below, where input tax was incurred with the intention of making 'a supply of a particular nature', the tax should be attributed on the basis of that intended supply, 'notwithstanding that for a short time he made a supply of a different nature before making the intended supply'. *WEH Key*, MAN/97/480 (VTD 15354, 15794). (*Note*. The conversion of a barn into a house would normally now qualify for zero-rating. See Tolley's Value Added Tax.)

Costs of refurbishing department store restaurant

[46.22] A company, which was partly exempt, operated a department store which contained a restaurant. It decided to refurbish the restaurant and grant a licence to an independent operator, in order to attract more customers to the store. The restaurant was extensively refurbished and a licence was subsequently granted. The company reclaimed the whole of the input tax incurred on the cost of the refurbishment. The Commissioners issued assessments to recover the tax, considering that it was directly related to the grant of the licence, which was an exempt supply. The company appealed, contending that the input tax should be attributed to taxable supplies because its intention in incurring the expenditure had been to attract more customers to the department store. The tribunal dismissed the company's appeal, holding that the company's motive of improving its trade was not to be confused with the objective purpose of the expenditure, which had to be treated as directly attributable to the exempt supply. *Sheffield Co-Operative Society Ltd*, [1987] VATTR 216 (VTD 2549).

Costs of refurbishing Masonic temple

[46.23] A company owned a building which was used as a Masonic temple. It let the building to several Masonic Lodges, these lettings being exempt from VAT. The building also contained a bar, where drinks were sold, these sales being standard-rated supplies for VAT purposes. The company incurred expenditure on refurbishing the building and reclaimed the relevant input tax. The Commissioners issued an assessment to recover the tax, on the basis that the expenditure was directly attributable to the lettings which were exempt supplies. The company appealed, contending that the expenditure was partly attributable to its standard-rated supplies of drinks, so that the expenditure should be apportioned. The tribunal dismissed the appeal, holding that the expenditure was directly attributable to the exempt supplies. *Ashwell House (St Albans) Ltd*, LON/93/2757A (VTD 12483).

Company operating parks for 'mobile homes'

[46.24] A company operated six residential parks for 'mobile homes'. Its business comprised the sale of some such homes, the letting or licensing of the pitches on which the mobile homes were situated, and the performance of work for the occupiers of such homes. The 'pitch fees' were accepted as being exempt from VAT (compare *Stonecliff Caravan Park*, **15.153** CONSTRUCTION OF BUILDINGS, ETC.) and the company was therefore partly exempt. In accounting for tax, it treated input tax relating to the maintenance and improvement of its parks as relating to both taxable and exempt supplies, and as apportionable. It also reclaimed input tax on its purchase of building materials relating to the siting of new park homes (such as concrete bases and pipework for the connection of services). The Commissioners issued an assessment on the basis that both these categories of input tax were solely attributable to the grant of exempt licences to occupy land, and thus the tax was not recoverable. The company appealed. The QB upheld the assessment, holding that all the expenditure in question should be attributed to the land on which the mobile homes stood, rather than to the mobile homes themselves. The pitch fees which the company received under the agreements were wholly exempt from VAT, and thus all the relevant input tax was attributable to exempt supplies. *C & E Commrs v Harpcombe Ltd*, QB [1996] STC 726.

[46.25] The decision in *Harpcombe Ltd*, **46.24** above, was applied in the similar subsequent case of *Tingdene Developments Ltd*, LON/99/274 (VTD 16546).

Standard-rated purchase of property—exempt sale to housing association

[46.26] In February 2002 a company (S) purchased some land, with the intention of obtaining planning permission for the construction of flats on the land and then selling the land to a housing association. VAT was charged on this transaction, because the vendor had elected to waive exemption in respect of the land. Two months later S agreed to sell the land to a housing association, under a contract whereby it agreed to build 24 flats on the land. It treated the sale as exempt, but treated the input tax on its purchase of the land as partly attributable to taxable supplies of building work. Subsequently the Commissioners issued an assessment on the basis that the tax was wholly attributable to S's resale of the land, which was an exempt supply. The CA unanimously upheld the assessment, holding that the input tax on the cost of buying the land was not a 'cost component' of the contract for the development of the land. Jacob LJ observed that 'there is nothing about the development contract as such which makes the land purchase and sale essential. If the housing association had already owned the land or had bought it from some third party, the inputs of the development contract would have been just the costs of carrying it out. The fact that there were commercially linked land transactions does not mean that those transactions are directly linked to the costs of the development contract. One would not say that the cost of buying the land was a cost of the development contract itself. It follows that the input tax on that cost is not a cost of the contract.' *C & E Commrs v Southern Primary Housing Association Ltd*, CA 2003, [2004] STC 209; [2003] EWCA Civ 1662.

[46.27] In April 2001 a company (G) purchased a three-year lease of an office block, together with an option to purchase the freehold. It elected to waive exemption in respect of the property. In March 2002 it exercised its option to purchase the freehold for £420,000 plus VAT of £73,500. On the same day it sold the property to a housing association for £460,000. The sale was exempt from VAT. G reclaimed input tax on the purchase. The Commissioners rejected the claim on the basis that the tax was solely attributable to the exempt sale of the property. The tribunal dismissed G's appeal. *Goldmax Resources Ltd*, LON/01/1138 (VTD 18219).

Legal costs of aborted purchase of property

[46.28] A property investment company (L) entered into negotiations to purchase a building which had previously been used by a bank. The vendors subsequently sold the building to a brewery. L reclaimed input tax on its legal costs. The Commissioners rejected the claim and the tribunal dismissed L's appeal, holding that the input tax was not reclaimable, because it related to an abortive exempt supply and could not be related to any taxable supply. *London & Exmoor Estates Ltd*, LON/x (VTD 16707).

Effect of change in rating of supply

[46.29] In 1987 a building company (H) granted a lease of a commercial property which it had constructed to a bank. The lease was zero-rated under the legislation then in force. From 1 April 1989, such leases became exempt from VAT. Subsequently H incurred legal costs in defending certain claims relating to its construction work. It reclaimed input tax on these costs. The Commissioners rejected the claim, since the lease was exempt from VAT at the time the expenditure was incurred. H appealed, contending that since the lease had been zero-rated when it was entered into, the input tax should be treated as relating to a taxable supply rather than to an exempt supply. The tribunal rejected this contention and dismissed the appeal, holding that 'the supplies of services representing the input tax in issue in this appeal (were) not so closely identifiable with the original supply as to remain unaffected by the legislation reclassifying the entire class of transaction from zero-rated to exempt supplies'. *HDG Harbour Development Group Ltd*, LON/90/1482Y (VTD 9386).

[46.30] See also *Martins Properties (Chelsea) Ltd*, **46.220** below.

NHBC—supplies by builders under insurance policy

[46.31] The National House Building Council (N) maintained a register of builders, and operated an insurance policy which provided cover for home-owners in respect of defects in houses constructed by builders who were registered with N. Under the policy, N arranged for remedial work to be carried out by other 'third party' builders. It reclaimed input tax on these supplies. HMRC rejected the claim on the basis that the remedial supplies were solely attributable to exempt supplies of insurance which N made to the relevant homeowners. The tribunal upheld HMRC's ruling and dismissed N's appeal. *National House Building Council v HMRC*, [2010] UKFTT 326 (TC), TC00611.

Miscellaneous

Equipment purchased by opticians

[46.32] A firm of opticians purchased four items of equipment: a frame heater, a slit lamp, a keratometer, and a field analyser. The firm treated the input tax as residual input tax, to be apportioned between exempt supplies and taxable supplies. The Commissioners issued a ruling that the input tax was wholly attributable to exempt supplies of services. The tribunal dismissed the firm's appeal against this decision. *Vision Aid Centre*, MAN/00/1026 (VTD 17298).

Advertising services—whether input tax attributable to exempt supplies

[46.33] An agricultural college reclaimed input tax relating to advertising services. The Commissioners rejected the claim on the basis that the tax was wholly attributable to exempt supplies of education. The college appealed, contending that the tax should be treated as residual, and apportioned between taxable and exempt supplies. The tribunal rejected this contention and dismissed the appeal, holding on the evidence that the advertising services had 'a direct and immediate link with the provision of the exempt supply of education to students'. *Royal Agricultural College*, LON/00/1017 (VTD 17508).

Supplies of car cleaning products—whether ancillary to supply of insurance

[46.34] A company supplied 'an insurance-backed protection treatment for motor vehicles'. It was accepted that its supplies were exempt from VAT under *VATA 1994, Sch 9, Group 2*. It provided some customers with cleaning products for their cars, and reclaimed input tax on the cost of these. HMRC issued a ruling that the products were ancillary to the company's exempt supplies of insurance, so that the input tax was not deductible. The company appealed, contending that the cleaning products were free gifts and that it should be entitled to deduct input tax on their cost. The tribunal rejected this contention and dismissed the company's appeal in principle, holding that the cleaning products were 'an ancillary supply' for 'promoting the better enjoyment of the basic insurance-based car protection plan'. (The tribunal commented that many of the facts were 'not made clear to us during the hearing' and gave the company leave to apply for a further hearing.) *Insured Vehicle Coatings Ltd v HMRC*, [2009] UKFTT 97 (TC), TC00065.

Professional fees in connection with disposal of farm

[46.35] A woman (P) reclaimed input tax on professional fees relating to the disposal of a farm, which was an exempt supply. HMRC issued an assessment to recover the tax, and the tribunal dismissed P's appeal. Judge Brooks held that there was 'a direct and immediate link' between the relevant professional services and the exempt supply. *Mrs LA Parkhouse v HMRC*, [2011] UKFTT 677 (TC), TC01519.

Professional fees in connection with disposal of shares

[46.36] See *BLP Group plc*, **22.399** EUROPEAN COMMUNITY LAW.

Professional fees in connection with reorganisation of share capital

[46.37] See *MBS plc*, 27.48 FINANCE; *Celtic plc*, 27.49 FINANCE; *Swallowfield plc*, 27.50 FINANCE, and *Mirror Group Newspapers Ltd*, 27.51 FINANCE.

Professional fees in connection with company flotation

[46.38] See *Actinic plc*, 27.52 FINANCE.

Zoological society accepted as making exempt supplies—claim for input tax

[46.39] See *Twycross Zoo East Midland Zoological Society*, 16.4 CULTURAL SERVICES.

Input tax held to be used 'in making both taxable and exempt supplies' (Regulation 101(2)(d))

Professional fees

Fees incurred in connection with share issue and bank loan

[46.40] A building company raised additional capital by making a share issue and by obtaining a bank loan. It received professional advice from accountants and solicitors in connection with this, and reclaimed input tax on the fees. The Commissioners issued an assessment to recover the tax, considering that it related to exempt supplies and was not therefore deductible. The company appealed, contending that the need for the services was partly attributable to the taxable supplies made by the company, and that the input tax should therefore be apportioned between taxable and exempt supplies. The tribunal allowed the appeal in part, holding that the accountants' services were partly used in connection with the making of exempt supplies (the issue of shares) and partly with the making of taxable supplies, but that the solicitors' services were wholly used in connection with exempt supplies. *Banner Management Ltd*, [1991] VATTR 254 (VTD 5678).

Professional fees incurred in connection with management buy-out

[46.41] A company incurred lawyers' and accountants' fees in connection with a management buy-out, including arranging a loan and an overdraft facility. It reclaimed the whole of the input tax on these fees. The Commissioners issued a ruling that the input tax was not deductible, since it related to exempt supplies of shares and loan stock. The company appealed, contending that the whole of the input tax was deductible since the professional fees had been incurred in connection with the company's general business intentions of making taxable supplies, rather than exclusively in the making of exempt supplies. The tribunal allowed the appeal, holding that the issue of shares and loan stock was 'purely incidental' to the company's trading objectives and that the professional fees partly related to the loan and overdraft facility. Accordingly, the supplies of professional services were 'for mixed use' and fell within what is now *VAT Regulations 1995 (SI 1995/2518), reg 101(2)(d)*. (Since the overwhelming majority of the company's supplies were taxable, it followed that the whole of the input tax was deductible.) *Edgemond Group Ltd*, MAN/93/35 (VTD 11620). (*Notes.* (1) The Commissioners initially appealed to the High Court against this decision, but subsequently withdrew their appeal. (2) The decision here was distinguished in the subsequent case of *RAP Group plc*, **46.42** below.)

Fees incurred in connection with share issue and management services

[46.42] A company (R) acquired the share capital of another company (W). Each of W's shareholders was issued one new ordinary share in R, plus a warrant, in exchange for each 130 ordinary shares in W. R reclaimed input tax on professional fees paid to stockbrokers, accountants and solicitors relating to this transaction. The Commissioners issued a ruling that the input tax was used 'exclusively in making exempt supplies' within *VAT Regulations, reg 101(2)(c)*. R appealed, contending that the fees related to its supplies of management services to W, so that the tax should be apportioned under *reg 101(2)(d)*. The Ch D allowed the appeal in part, holding on the evidence that the services supplied by the stockbrokers and the accountants related entirely to the share issue, which was an exempt supply. However, the solicitors' services were not 'limited to the issue of shares' but had been partly used for the purposes of making taxable supplies, so that the tax shown on the invoice from the solicitors should be apportioned. *RAP Group plc v C & E Commrs*, Ch D [2000] STC 980.

Fees in connection with acquisition of subsidiary company

[46.43] A company (L), which was partly exempt, acquired the share capital of a company which traded as a professional football club (F). L treated input tax on professional fees connected to the acquisition (from six different firms of advisers) as residual tax, within *VAT Regulations, reg 101(2)(d)*. The Commissioners issued an assessment on the basis that the tax was wholly attributable to the exempt supply of shares. L appealed, contending that it had acquired F for the purpose of making taxable supplies of management services to it, and that the input tax should therefore be apportioned. The tribunal accepted this contention and allowed the appeal in part, holding on the evidence that, with respect to four of the six firms, the relevant supplies had been used 'partly for the exempt transaction and partly for the general purposes of the business', so that the relevant input tax fell to be treated as residual input tax. However, the tribunal held that the supplies by the remaining two suppliers had been 'exclusively used in making exempt supplies', so that the relevant tax was not deductible. *Southampton Leisure Holdings plc*, [2002] VATDR 235 (VTD 17716). (*Note.* For the Commissioners' practice following this decision, see Business Brief 23/2002, issued on 20 August 2002.)

Issue of shares and listing on Alternative Investment Market

[46.44] A property company reclaimed input tax on professional fees relating to an issue of shares and to the listing of its shares on the London Stock Exchange Alternative Investment Market. The Commissioners issued a ruling that the input tax was used 'exclusively in making exempt supplies' within *VAT Regulations, reg 101(2)(c)*. The company appealed, contending that the fees relating to the listing on the Alternative Investment Market were partly attributable to making future taxable supplies, so that the tax should be apportioned under *reg 101(2)(d)*. The tribunal accepted this contention and allowed the appeal, holding that 'the AIM listing was in part for the general business purposes of the appellants and was not an essential element of the issue of shares'. The expenditure had 'a dual purpose'. *Halladale Group plc*, [2003] VATDR 551 (VTD 18218). (*Note.* For the Commissioners' revised practice following this decision, see Business Brief 30/2003, issued on 24 December 2003.)

Solicitors' fees incurred in transfer of part of business

[46.45] See *Abbey National plc*, **22.419** EUROPEAN COMMUNITY LAW.

Expenditure on premises

Tourist village

[46.46] A company (C) owned a village which it sought to preserve in an unspoilt condition, as an attraction to tourists, who were charged for admission. C reclaimed input tax on the refurbishment of cottages which it let to tenants. Customs issued an assessment to recover the tax, considering that the expenditure was wholly attributable to the exempt letting of the cottages. The tribunal allowed C's appeal in part, holding that some of the work had been undertaken to make the village more attractive to tourists, i.e. for the purpose of taxable supplies. *Clovelly Estate Co Ltd*, [1991] VATTR 351 (VTD 6353).

Mortgage broker

[46.47] A company which traded as a mortgage broker and estate agent reclaimed input tax on alterations to its premises. Customs issued an assessment on the basis that most of the tax was attributable to exempt supplies. The tribunal upheld the assessment in principle but reduced it in amount, holding that 29% of the tax in question was deductible. *Ace Estates Ltd*, LON/90/255Y (VTD 6216).

Workshops let to tenants

[46.48] A married couple purchased an old pottery. They occupied part of it for an antiques business, and let several workshops on short-term tenancies. They reclaimed input tax in respect of building work at the premises. Customs issued an assessment to recover 80% of the tax. The tribunal allowed the couple's appeal in part, holding that 40% of the tax was attributable to taxable supplies. *Mr & Mrs Buckley (t/a Wheelcraft Centre & Original Homes)*, LON/90/943Y (VTD 7150).

Part of premises intended to be used as residential accommodation

[46.49] A company (C) obtained planning permission to convert part of its premises into residential flats, intending to lease or sell them. Before the conversion was completed, the premises were damaged by workmen who were replacing the main sewer. C reclaimed the whole of the input tax on the repair work. Customs issued an assessment on the basis that 55% of the expenditure was attributable to exempt supplies (the sale or lease of flats). The tribunal upheld the assessment. *Circa Ltd*, LON/92/113Z (VTD 9908).

Part of premises leased to finance company

[46.50] A trader reclaimed input tax on refurbishing a café. Customs discovered that the upper floor of the property was let to a finance company. They issued an assessment to recover one-third of the input tax. The tribunal upheld the assessment. *S McElroy (t/a Boundary Café)*, MAN/92/564 (VTD 10540).

Purchase of premises by partly exempt charity

[46.51] A charity (B) registered for VAT in May 1991, and elected to waive exemption on its existing premises. In June 1991 it purchased new premises from a development company, and assigned its interest in its old premises to the same company. In its return for the period ending June 1991, B accounted for output tax on the disposal of its old premises, and reclaimed input tax in respect of its new premises, claiming a substantial net repayment. It subsequently applied to be deregistered with effect from July 1991. Customs issued a ruling that B was not entitled to credit for the input tax in question, and B appealed. The tribunal allowed the appeal in part, holding that a proportion of the input tax should be apportioned to B's management activities and was therefore deductible. *Bristol Churches Housing Association*, LON/91/2008Z (VTD 10515).

Refurbishment of premises

[46.52] A company which carried on business as a stockbroker and financial adviser acquired new premises, and reclaimed the whole of the input tax on their refurbishment. Customs rejected the claim, considering that the tax was partly attributable to exempt supplies. The tribunal dismissed the company's appeal. *Fox-Pitt Kelton Ltd*, LON/93/1296A (VTD 11556).

[46.53] The *Housing (Scotland) Act 1988* established a statutory body (S) for the purpose of providing housing and promoting the provision of housing. It took over a stock of about 75,000 houses. During the next ten years it sold about 25,000 of these and transferred about 40,000 to housing associations. In 1999 it submitted a retrospective reclaim of input tax relating to the refurbishment of some of the properties which it let to tenants. Customs rejected the claim, on the basis that the input tax was wholly attributable to exempt supplies. S appealed, contending that it was entitled to apportion the tax because although it was currently letting the houses in question, it hoped to sell some of them in due course. The tribunal accepted this contention and allowed the appeal in principle (subject to agreement as to figures). *Scottish Homes (No 2)*, EDN/99/126 (VTD 16644).

Office premises no longer needed for business purposes

[46.54] A company (H) leased a five-storey building, with the intention of using it for business purposes. In 1990 it vacated two of the floors, which remained unoccupied for about two years before being let to tenants. In 1993 H elected to waive exemption in respect of the rents. It continued to reclaim input tax incurred in respect of the whole of the premises. Customs issued an assessment to recover input tax from 1991 to February 1993, on the basis that it was attributable to exempt supplies. H appealed, contending that the input tax attributable to the vacant periods should be treated as residual. The tribunal accepted this contention and allowed the appeal, finding that H had retained the two floors 'exclusively for the purpose of making taxable supplies and not carrying out any other activity', so that 'the vacant periods should be treated as residual'. *Harper Collins Publishers Ltd*, EDN/92/219 (VTD 12040).

Conversion of hotel into residential home

[46.55] A married couple owned a hotel. They purchased a large house adjoining the hotel, with the intention of converting the two buildings into one and using them as a residential home. They reclaimed input tax in respect of the conversion work. Customs issued an assessment to recover the tax, on the basis that since the provision of care in the residential home was exempt from VAT, the tax should be attributed to exempt supplies. The couple appealed, contending that the tax should be apportioned since they had continued to accept guests at the hotel during the conversion. The tribunal accepted this contention and allowed the appeal in part. *JJ & BM Gallagher*, MAN/91/118 (VTD 12140).

Exempt supplies preceding taxable supplies

[46.56] A partnership which carried on a management consultancy business reclaimed input tax on the construction of a self-contained flat. Customs discovered that the flat was let on an assured shorthold tenancy, and issued an assessment to recover the tax, on the basis that the expenditure related to exempt supplies. The partnership appealed, contending that the tax should be apportioned since, at the time the expenditure was incurred, it had intended to use the flat to make serviced supplies of accommodation which would be excluded from exemption. The tribunal accepted the partnership's evidence and allowed the appeal. *Richard Haynes Associates*, LON/92/2597 (VTD 12300).

[46.57] See also *C & E Commrs v University of Wales College Cardiff*, 46.215 below, and *Royal & Sun Alliance Insurance Group plc*, 46.216 below.

Property company

[46.58] Customs issued assessments on a property company which had failed to operate the partial exemption provisions correctly. The company appealed, contending that some of the input tax which Customs had apportioned should have been directly attributed to taxable supplies. The tribunal upheld the assessments and the QB dismissed the company's appeal. Laws J observed that it was frequently impossible to discover the exact or literal extent to which 'mixed use' supplies were used in the making of taxable supplies. The company had failed to produce 'facts or figures to demonstrate the extent to which mixed use supplies had been deployed for the making of taxable supplies'. *Dwyer Property Ltd v C & E Commrs*, QB [1995] STC 1035.

Nursing home

[46.59] A company which operated a nursing home arranged for the construction of an extension, and reclaimed the whole of its input tax. Customs issued an assessment to recover part of the tax. The tribunal upheld the assessment. *The Laurels Nursing Home Ltd*, MAN/96/1065 (VTD 15259). (*Note*. An appeal against a misdeclaration penalty was subsequently allowed—see 52.312 PENALTIES: MISDECLARATION.)

Construction of college building—contract for maintenance services

[46.60] A company was formed in 1999 to construct a building for a college. The college leased the land to the company, which granted a sublease back to the college. The company also contracted to provide maintenance services. It reclaimed part of the input tax incurred on the construction. Customs issued a ruling that the input tax was solely attributable to an exempt supply of a building, and was not recoverable. The company appealed, contending that since it had contracted to provide maintenance services, the input tax was attributable to both taxable and exempt supplies, and should be treated as residual. The tribunal accepted this contention and allowed the company's appeal, holding that there was a 'necessary direct and immediate link' between the construction costs and the 25-year maintenance contract. *West Lothian College SPV Ltd*, EDN/02/58 (VTD 18133).

Effect of election to waive exemption

[46.61] A college arranged for the construction of two buildings to be used for conferences. It formed a subsidiary company to conduct the conference activities, and elected to waive exemption in respect of the rent paid by the subsidiary. In applying the partial exemption provisions, it treated this input tax as attributable to taxable supplies. Customs formed the opinion that the input tax relating to the buildings should be excluded from the partial exemption calculation, and issued an assessment to recover some of the tax. The tribunal upheld the assessment with regard to the periods preceding the election, but discharged the assessment with regard to the periods subsequent to the election, holding that the expenditure was used for the purpose of making taxable supplies following the election to waive exemption. *Cliff College*, MAN/92/695 (VTD 12000).

[46.62] In May 1997 a property company elected to waive exemption in respect of its stock of properties. The company reclaimed input tax on the basis that the election should be treated as retrospective, so that its exempt input tax for the period ending April 1997 was *de minimis*. Customs issued an assessment on the basis that the election could not have retrospective effect and that the relevant input tax had to be apportioned. The tribunal upheld the assessment and dismissed the company's appeal. *Hellesdon Developments Ltd*, LON/99/354 (VTD 16833). (*Note*. The tribunal also held that certain correspondence between the company and Customs did not amount to the agreement of a special method.)

Rent paid on properties subject to election to waive exemption

[46.63] See *R Walia Opticians Ltd*, 6.46 BUILDINGS AND LAND.

Office rent

[46.64] A company made supplies of financial services, which were exempt from VAT, and business consultancy services, which were standard-rated. It had two offices, one of which it rented. It reclaimed the whole of the input tax on the rent. Customs issued an assessment on the basis that the tax had to be apportioned between the company's taxable and exempt supplies. The tribunal upheld the assessment and dismissed the company's appeal. *Charles Dominic Ltd*, LON/02/215 (VTD 17830).

Bowling club constructing clubhouse

[46.65] A bowling club, which was partly exempt, arranged for the construction of a clubhouse. For the year ending March 1996, it had adopted the standard method of attribution and had treated 25% of the relevant input tax as attributable to taxable supplies. In June 1996 it wrote to its VAT office, estimating that, following the opening of a bar in the clubhouse, 56% of its supplies would be taxable, and requesting 56% of its residual input tax to be treated as attributable to taxable supplies. Customs rejected the claim, on the grounds that there was nothing in *VAT Regulations 1995 (SI 1995/2518), reg 101* which permitted estimation of expected future supplies. The tribunal dismissed the club's appeal, holding that the wording of *reg 101* allowed 'no room for any interpretation that would replace sales made in the period by estimated sales to be made at some later date'. *Chard Bowling Club*, [1997] VATDR 375 (VTD 15114). (*Note.* For another issue in this case, see **46.130** below.)

Golf club

[46.66] A golf club, which was partly exempt, constructed an extension to its clubhouse. Customs issued a ruling that the relevant input tax should be treated as residual, and apportioned between taxable and exempt supplies. The club appealed, contending that the relevant input tax should be treated as wholly attributable to taxable supplies. The tribunal dismissed the club's appeal, finding that the extension had sometimes been used 'for holding various meetings and for fund-raising events'. Accordingly it was not used wholly for taxable supplies, and the input tax had to be apportioned. *Elsham Golf Club Ltd*, MAN/00/795 (VTD 18107).

[46.67] A golf club, which was partly exempt, refurbished its clubhouse and reclaimed the whole of the input tax. HMRC issued an assessment to recover part of the tax, and the club appealed. The tribunal dismissed the appeal, holding that the input tax had to be apportioned between taxable and exempt supplies. *Bridgnorth Golf Club v HMRC*, [2009] UKFTT 126 (TC), TC00094.

Extension to greyhound stadium

[46.68] A company which operated a greyhound stadium reclaimed the whole of the input tax on the construction of an extension at the stadium. Customs issued an assessment on the basis that the relevant input tax should be treated as residual, and apportioned between taxable and exempt supplies. The tribunal upheld the assessment. *Leeside Leisure Ltd*, LON/03/165 (VTD 18688).

Rugby club—construction of new pitch

[46.69] A rugby club, which was partly exempt, arranged for the construction of a new pitch. HMRC issued a ruling that the relevant input tax was wholly attributable to exempt supplies. The club appealed, contending that the tax should be treated as residual, as it was partly attributable to taxable supplies of advertising facilities. The tribunal accepted this contention and allowed the appeal. *Cirencester Rugby Football Club v HMRC*, [2010] UKFTT 453 (TC), TC00718. (*Note.* The tribunal also allowed the club's appeal against a misdeclaration penalty.)

Extension to amusement arcade

[46.70] The proprietor of an amusement arcade made exempt supplies of bingo as well as taxable supplies from gaming and amusement machines. He reclaimed input tax on the construction of an extension. Customs issued an assessment to recover part of the tax, on the basis that the extension was to be used for both taxable and exempt supplies, so that the tax had to be apportioned under *VAT Regulations, reg 101(2)(d)*. The tribunal upheld the assessment and dismissed the trader's appeal. *LJ Mulhearn (t/a Sandancer Amusements)*, MAN/04/691 (VTD 19188).

Interaction of partial exemption provisions and 'capital items' scheme

[46.71] See *Witney Golf Club*, 9.5 CAPITAL GOODS SCHEME.

Self-supplies

Building society reclaiming input tax in respect of deemed self-supply

[46.72] A building society, most of whose supplies were exempt, made a small number of taxable supplies such as the provision of services to its staff. The total value of its taxable supplies was approximately 0.25% of the total value of all its supplies. The society also produced a large amount of printed material, mostly for internal use. This printed material was a deemed self-supply for VAT purposes, and the society accounted for output tax accordingly. It reclaimed input tax on the whole value of this self-supplied stationery. Customs rejected the claim, since not all the stationery was used in connection with taxable supplies, so that the deductible input tax was only that proportion of the relevant total input tax which corresponded with the proportion of taxable supplies to total supplies. The tribunal dismissed the society's appeal. The society had suffered VAT on a large proportion of the value of the printed matter which it had produced, but this was clearly in accordance with the intention of the legislation, since if VAT was not paid on such self-supplies, businesses producing printed matter for their own commercial use might gain a commercial advantage. *The National & Provincial Building Society*, MAN/90/694 (VTD 6293). (*Note.* See also *VAT Regulations 1995 (SI 1995/2518), reg 104*, which provides that where a person makes a supply to himself, 'the input tax on that supply shall not be allowable as attributable to that supply'.)

Miscellaneous

Annual motor rally

[46.73] A company (M) was incorporated to organise an annual motor rally. It received taxable income from sponsorship and exempt income from entry fees, which was exempt from VAT. M reclaimed input tax on its expenditure in organising the rally. The Isle of Man Treasury issued an assessment to recover the tax, considering that the costs of organising the rally should be set against the entry fees, which were exempt from VAT. The tribunal allowed M's appeal, holding that the sponsorship was received for the specific purpose of organising the rally. The rally was the subject of a supply to the sponsors as well as to the competitors, and the appropriate proportion of the input tax was, therefore, deductible. *Manx International Rally Ltd v The Isle of Man Treasury*, MAN/91/196 (VTD 6711).

Partnership operating caravan site

[46.74] A partnership (R) operated a caravan site. The letting of caravans on the site was exempt from VAT, but R also had taxable income from a shop and from letting six seasonal pitches. R reclaimed input tax on a new water main. Customs issued an assessment on the basis that 80% of the expenditure should be treated as attributable to exempt supplies, so that only 20% of the input tax was deductible. The tribunal allowed the appeal in part, holding that 30% of the tax was deductible. *RBF & NJ Morris (t/a Roundstone Caravan Depot)*, LON/92/2346A (VTD 11092).

Purchase of helicopter

[46.75] A group of companies operated casinos in four cities in the UK. The group's income from gambling in the casinos was exempt from VAT, but the group also received taxable income from gaming machines, vending machines and bar sales. It was permitted to treat 16% of its general input tax as being attributable to exempt supplies. The group purchased a helicopter, which was used for transporting company directors and officers from one city to another to supervise the casinos. The group reclaimed the whole of the input tax attributable to the helicopter (and accounted for output tax on its sale two years later). At a subsequent control visit, a VAT officer formed the opinion that the company should only have reclaimed 16% of the input tax, since the helicopter had been purchased for the purpose of supervising the whole of the group's business activities, which included exempt supplies as well as taxable supplies. Customs therefore issued an assessment to recover 84% of the input tax in question. The tribunal upheld the assessment. *Annabel's Casino Ltd*, MAN/92/1037 (VTD 10859). (*Note.* For another issue in this case, see **24.21** EXEMPTIONS: MISCELLANEOUS.)

Building society advertising

[46.76] A building society incurred expenditure on television advertisements. It accounted for input tax on the basis that the relevant input tax was residual input tax which should be apportioned between its taxable and exempt supplies. Customs issued a ruling that the relevant input tax should be treated as wholly attributable to exempt supplies. The tribunal allowed the society's appeal, holding that as the advertisements were not advertising specific products, the input tax was residual and fell to be apportioned. *Britannia Building Society*, MAN/96/174 (VTD 14886).

[46.77] A building society owned a number of subsidiaries which traded as estate agents and advertised houses for sale in local newspapers. In the group VAT returns, the society treated the costs of advertising as attributable to the taxable sales of the properties. HMRC issued a ruling that the expenditure was partly attributable to the society's exempt supplies. The society appealed. The tribunal allowed the appeal in part, observing that some of the advertisements included 'strap lines' which mentioned the availability of mortgage services, and holding that the costs of those advertisements had to be treated as attributable to both taxable and exempt services. However, where advertisements did not include any reference to mortgage services, but simply advertised houses for sale, then the cost of those advertisements was wholly attributable to taxable supplies. *Skipton Building Society v HMRC*, FTT August 2009, TC00146.

Partly exempt charity—machinery and packaging materials

[46.78] A registered charity had been incorporated to provide work for psychiatric patients. It made taxable supplies of packaging to commercial customers and exempt supplies of training to its clients. It reclaimed input tax on purchases of machinery and packaging materials. Customs issued a ruling that this input tax was used in making both taxable and exempt supplies, so that only a proportion of the input tax was reclaimable. The charity appealed, contending that the tax should be wholly attributed to its taxable supplies. The tribunal rejected this contention and dismissed the appeal. *Reading Industrial Therapy Organisation Ltd*, LON/96/1545 (VTD 15132).

Change in partial exemption rules—method of attribution

[46.79] A butcher (P) purchased a property in June 1986. Between July 1986 and April 1987 he redeveloped it in order to be able to let it. The relevant materials and services were all supplied before 1 April 1987 (when the rules regarding attribution of input tax between taxable supplies and exempt supplies were amended) but some of them were not paid for until after that date. P reclaimed input tax on the basis that the old rules for attributing input tax applied. However, Customs issued an assessment to recover some of the tax, considering that, as the input tax had not been reclaimed until after March 1987, the new method of attribution applied (so that some of the tax was attributable to exempt supplies). The tribunal allowed P's appeal, holding that as the time of supply was before April 1987 the old rules for attributing input tax applied. *V Perna*, [1990] VATTR 106 (VTD 5017).

Bank reclaiming input tax on assignments of debts

[46.80] A bank had loaned large sums of money to a number of South American countries. The debtors were unable to keep up the interest payments. The bank assigned a number of the debts either for cash or for other debts. In 1988 it adjusted its calculations of input tax in respect of some of the debts which it had assigned. Customs issued an assessment to recover the tax. The bank appealed, contending that the assignments were not exempt supplies and should be taken into account in determining the percentage of its costs which related to taxable service charge income. The tribunal accepted this contention and allowed the bank's appeal. *Barclays Bank plc*, [1991] VATTR 115 (VTD 5616).

Treatment of credit note

[46.81] See *London International Financial Futures Exchange*, **40.117** IN-VOICES AND CREDIT NOTES.

Insurance broker

[46.82] A company which traded as an insurance broker, but also made some taxable supplies, registered for VAT and reclaimed the whole of its input tax, without operating the partial exemption provisions. Customs formed the opinion that the tax should have been apportioned and that most of it should have been attributed to exempt supplies. They therefore issued an assessment to recover most of the tax. The tribunal dismissed the company's appeal. *Credit Risk Management Ltd*, MAN/94/416 (VTD 12971).

Property development company

[46.83] A company which carried on business as a builder and property developer, and was partly exempt, purchased two sites for future development. It included the input tax on these purchases in calculating its deductible input tax under the (pre-1992) standard method as then in force. Customs formed the opinion that the inclusion of these purchases had distorted the input tax calculation and produced an unfair result. They recalculated the apportionment without reference to the acquisition of the two sites and issued an assessment, against which the company appealed. The QB upheld the assessment. The standard method in force at the relevant time did not prescribe the manner of ascertaining the relative extent to which supplies were to be used. However, the method used had to achieve a fair and reasonable attribution of the tax paid on the inputs. The attribution arising from the company's calculation was distortive, unfair and unreasonable. *C & E Commrs v Dennis Rye Ltd*, QB 1995, [1996] STC 27.

Company supplying advertising facilities and financial services

[46.84] A company acted as a financial intermediary, and supplied advertising facilities to various banks. It reclaimed input tax on the hiring of space at venues such as airports and motorway service stations. Customs issued a ruling that the relevant tax had been incurred for the dual purpose of making taxable supplies of advertising facilities and exempt supplies of financial services, and should therefore be apportioned. The company appealed, contending that the tax should be treated as wholly attributable to its taxable supplies of advertising facilities. The tribunal rejected this contention and dismissed the appeal. *ODM Ltd*, LON/00/1024 (VTD 17484).

Company supplying mobile telephones and receiving insurance commission

[46.85] A company (D) advertised mobile telephones. It received commission from the airtime service providers (ASPs) to whom it introduced customers. It also encouraged customers to take out insurance policies, and received commission from the insurers, which was accepted as exempt from VAT. It reclaimed input tax on expenditure relating to its advertising services. Customs ruled that the tax was partly attributable to its exempt supplies of insurance services. D appealed, contending that the tax should be treated as wholly attributable to the taxable supplies which it made to the ASPs. The tribunal rejected this contention and dismissed the appeal, holding that 'the input tax on costs of advertising taxable phones with exempt insurance is directly and immediately linked to both the exempt and taxable supplies'. The Ch D and CA unanimously upheld this decision. *Dial-a-Phone Ltd v C & E Commrs*, CA [2004] STC 987; [2004] EWCA Civ 603.

University—supplies of staff to hospital trusts

[46.86] A university supplied the services of some of its staff to hospital trusts. Customs issued an assessment to recover input tax which the university had claimed. The university appealed, contending that its supplies of staff to hospital trusts were taxable rather than exempt, and that the assessment did not provide a fair apportionment of its residual input tax between its business and non-business activities. The tribunal accepted these contentions and allowed the appeal, holding that 'the supply of staff is standard-rated and requires to be treated as taxable income in the appellant's partial exemption calculations'. The tribunal also held that Customs' assessment had been computed on an incorrect basis, holding that 'the first stage in arriving at a basis for calculation has to be an apportionment between business and non-business activity'. With regard to the apportionment of the residual input tax, the tribunal held that 'the adoption in this instance of a tax-based as opposed to income-based calculation would be both fair and reasonable'. The tribunal observed that the amount of tax which could be attributed was 'susceptible of calculation, and it does not seem irrational to adopt a proportion disclosed over the university's whole activities as between business and non-business activities and apply that to the residual tax which cannot be specifically attributed'. *University Court of the University of Glasgow (No 3)*, [2005] VATDR 198 (VTD 19052). (*Note.* For Customs' practice following this decision, see Business Brief 13/05, issued on 4 July 2005.)

Company operating theatre

[46.87] A company (M) operated a theatre. It engaged production companies to stage performances at the theatre. Prior to the CJEC decision in *The Zoological Society of London*, 22.321 EUROPEAN COMMUNITY LAW, these performances had been treated as taxable. Following that decision, Customs accepted that the sales of tickets for these performances qualified for exemption. However, in accounting for VAT, M treated the input tax on the payments which it made to these production companies as 'residual', and reclaimed a percentage of the tax in question. Customs issued a ruling that the input tax was solely attributable to exempt supplies, so that none of the input tax was reclaimable. The Ch D allowed M's appeal and the CA unanimously upheld this decision. Carnwath LJ held that the production services had a 'direct and immediate link' to M's taxable supplies of programme sales as well as to its exempt supplies. Accordingly M was entitled to treat the relevant input tax as 'residual'. *HMRC v Mayflower Theatre Trust Ltd*, CA [2007] STC 880; [2007] EWCA Civ 116. (*Note.* For HMRC's practice following this decision, see HMRC Brief 45/07, issued on 15 June 2007.)

Opera company

[46.88] An opera company reclaimed input tax relating to the production costs of operatic performances. HMRC issued an assessment to recover the tax on the basis that it was exclusively attributable to the company's exempt supplies of operatic performances. The company appealed, contending that the expenditure was partly attributable to taxable supplies of sponsorship rights and sales of CDs, and therefore fell within *VAT Regulations, reg 101(2)(d)*. The tribunal accepted this contention and allowed the appeal, holding on the evidence that the grants of sponsorship rights were a means by which the company exploited its productions for reward, and that the production costs were not exclusively linked to the exempt supplies of tickets. *Garsington Opera Ltd v HMRC*, [2009] UKFTT 77 (TC), TC00045. (Note. For HMRC's practice following this decision, see HMRC Brief 65/09, published on 14 October 2009.)

Medical partnership—motoring expenses

[46.89] A medical partnership, which was partly exempt, reclaimed input tax on motoring expenses. Customs issued assessments on the basis that the relevant supplies were 'non-attributable supplies', so that the partnership was only able to reclaim the appropriate proportion of the tax. The tribunal upheld the assessments and dismissed the partners' appeal. *KUR Joy & PB Rao*, MAN/720 (VTD 19568).

Licensed betting offices

[46.90] A group of companies operated a large number of betting offices, which contained gaming machines as well as facilities for 'over-the-counter' betting. The group paid for the broadcast of racing and sporting information at the offices. The representative member (T) reclaimed a proportion of the relevant input tax, on the basis that these supplies were attributable to both taxable and exempt supplies. Customs issued assessments on the basis that they were wholly attributable to exempt supplies of 'over-the-counter' betting. The tribunal allowed T's appeal, finding that the existence of the broadcasting service 'attracted people to use gaming machines in addition to OTC betting'. *Town & County Factors Ltd (No 3)*, LON/04/791 (VTD 19616). (*Note.* For HMRC's practice following this decision, see Business Brief 17/2006, issued on 19 October 2006.)

[46.91] The decision in *Town & County Factors Ltd (No 3)*, 46.90 above, was applied in a similar subsequent case in which the tribunal specifically criticised HMRC's interpretation of that decision, as set out in Business Brief 17/2006. *Cheshire Racing Ltd*, [2007] VATDR 345 (VTD 20283). (*Note.* For HMRC's practice following this decision, see HMRC Brief 01/08, issued on 3 January 2008. HMRC state that they now accept that 'SIS services have a direct and immediate link to gaming machine supplies made by bookmakers as the SIS provides commentary relevant to those machines'.)

Trade union producing in-house magazine

[46.92] See *Public & Commercial Services Union*, **3.166** ASSESSMENT.

Professional association

[46.93] A professional association received membership subscriptions which were accepted as exempt from VAT by virtue of *VATA 1994, Sch 9, Group 9, Item 1*. It also received taxable income relating to publications. It claimed that it should be entitled to recover the majority of its input tax. Customs accepted that the association was within ESC 3.35 and was entitled to recover some of its input tax, but rejected the specific claim on the grounds that it attributed too much input tax to the association's taxable supplies. The association appealed. The tribunal reviewed the evidence in detail and adjourned the appeal in the hope that the parties could 'agree the relevant values'. *Institute of Biomedical Science*, LON/07/359 (VTD 20609).

[46.94] See also *Royal College of Anaesthetists*, **13.20** CLUBS, ASSOCIATIONS AND ORGANISATIONS.

Whether company making taxable supplies of director's services

[46.95] See *Goodshelter Holdings Ltd*, **62.48** SUPPLY.

Exclusion of capital expenditure

[46.96] A building society submitted a repayment claim in which, in computing the repayable fraction of its residual input tax, it excluded capital expenditure from the denominator but not from the numerator. Customs rejected the claim on the grounds that capital expenditure should be excluded from both the numerator and the denominator. The tribunal dismissed the society's appeal, observing that 'the object of excluding capital goods from the fraction is to exclude the value of inputs whose inclusion would distort the results of the calculation'. *Derbyshire Building Society*, MAN/95/2311 (VTD 14026).

Input tax in respect of 'capital goods' (Regulation 101(3)(a))

Sale of land

[46.97] Trustees who administered an estate sold some land which was needed for the construction of a by-pass. They reclaimed input tax relating to the sale. The Commissioners issued an assessment to recover the tax, on the basis that it was attributable to a 'supply of capital goods', within *VAT Regulations 1995 (SI 1995/2518), reg 101(3)(a)*. The tribunal upheld the assessment and dismissed the trustees' appeal, holding that it was clear that 'the land constituted a capital asset of the business'. *Trustees of the Whitbread Harrowden Settlement (and related appeals)*, LON/99/1091 (VTD 16781). (*Note*. A misdeclaration penalty was upheld in principle but mitigated by 25%—see **52.423** PENALTIES: MISDECLARATION.)

Motor cars previously used for demonstration purposes

[46.98] A company (J) which traded as a car dealer disposed of cars which had previously been used for demonstration purposes. By virtue of *Input Tax Order 1992 (SI 1992/3222), Article 7(1)*, it was unable to claim input tax on its acquisition of these cars. However, under *Article 7(4)* as originally enacted, it was required to account for output tax on any profit margin. Following the CJEC decision in *EC Commission v Italian Republic*, **22.349** EUROPEAN COMMUNITY LAW, the Commissioners accepted that *Article 7(4)* contravened the *EC Sixth Directive*, and announced (in Business Brief 23/97) that they would accept repayment claims. J duly submitted such a claim. The Commissioners issued a ruling that the effect of the disposals was that J was subject to the partial exemption provisions, so that not all the tax was repayable. J appealed, contending that the cars had been 'capital goods', within *VAT Regulations 1995 (SI 1995/2518), reg 101(3)(a)*, and that, since it had made no other relevant exempt supplies, no partial exemption calculation was required. The tribunal accepted this contention and allowed the appeal, and the Ch D upheld this decision. Lawrence Collins J observed that there was no general statutory definition of 'capital goods'. The cars were 'of substantial durability and value compared with other articles used in the management and day-to-day running of the business, and were depreciated in the management accounts'. Accordingly, the tribunal was entitled to find that they were 'capital goods'. *JDL Ltd v C & E Commrs*, Ch D 2001, [2002] STC 1. (*Note. Article 7(4) of the Input Tax Order 1992 was revoked by the VAT (Input Tax) (Amendment) Order 1999 (SI 1999/2930) with effect from 1 March 2000.)*

Input tax held to be used for 'incidental supplies' (Regulation 101(3)(b))

Partly exempt holding company—input tax on share disposals

[46.99] A company (H) was the holding company of a group of companies in the construction industry, and was partly exempt. In 1985 it reclaimed input tax incurred in respect of share disposals and of a rights issue of its shares. In calculating the deductible proportion of its input tax, it ignored money it had received for the sale of a minority holding of shares in another public company (B). The Commissioners considered that H had reclaimed an excessive proportion of its input tax, and issued an assessment to recover part of the tax. The tribunal allowed H's appeal in part, holding on the evidence that H was an active industrial holding company and was not a passive investment company. Accordingly, the sale of its minority shareholding in B was incidental to its business, so that what is now *VAT Regulations 1995 (SI 1995/2518), reg 101(3)(b)* applied, and the proceeds of the sale fell to be excluded from the partial exemption calculation. The tribunal chairman observed that 'the ordinary everyday meaning of "incidental" is "occurring or liable to occur in fortuitous or subordinate conjunction with"'. The QB upheld this decision. H was not carrying on a business similar to an investment company, and the sale of its holding of shares in B was incidental to its business. *C & E Commrs v CH Beazer (Holdings) plc*, QB [1989] STC 549.

Trading in shares—whether 'incidental' to company's main activities

[46.100] A property company, which was partly exempt, began trading in shares. Customs issued an assessment on the basis that these transaction should be included in the company's partial exemption computation. The company appealed, contending that its share transactions were 'incidental' to its main activities, and, by virtue of *VAT Regulations 1995 (SI 1995/2518), reg 101(3)(b)*, should be excluded from its partial exemption computation. The tribunal reviewed the evidence in detail, rejected this contention, and dismissed the appeal. The tribunal held that the company had 'diversified into handling the shares as a second activity and not as an incidental activity tied in with the property development and rental'. *Rightacres Ltd*, LON/03/125 (VTD 19140).

Financial transactions—whether 'incidental' to company's main activities

[46.101] See *Régie Dauphinoise-Cabinet A Forest Sarl v Ministre du Budget*, **22.446** EUROPEAN COMMUNITY LAW, and *Empresa de Desenvolvimento Mineiro SGPS v Fazenda Pública*, **22.448** EUROPEAN COMMUNITY LAW.

Special methods (VAT Regulations 1995, reg 102)

Approval or direction of special method (Regulation 102(1))

Whether special method agreed by Commissioners

[46.102] A group of companies made both taxable and exempt supplies, but had reclaimed input tax on all supplies received. The Commissioners threatened criminal proceedings to recover the tax which had been wrongly reclaimed. In December 1978 the companies sent the Commissioners a cheque for £13,456, which was the VAT due based on a calculation using a special method (the 'Stanlor' method) approved under the *VAT (General) Regulations* as then in force. The Commissioners cashed the cheque and the group continued to use the method in question without having formally agreed this with the Commissioners. In May 1980 the Commissioners wrote to the representative company (S) instructing it not to use the Stanlor method. S did not comply with this instruction, and the Commissioners issued an assessment to recover the input tax which S had reclaimed. The tribunal allowed S's appeal with regard to the period up to May 1980, holding that the Commissioners had implicitly approved the group's use of the Stanlor method in December 1978, but dismissed S's appeal with regard to the period after May 1980, holding that S should not have continued to use the Stanlor method after it had been instructed not to do so. The QB upheld this decision, holding that the Commissioners' letter of May 1980 was a valid notice under what is now *VAT Regulations 1995 (SI 1995/2518), reg 102(3)*. *S & U Stores plc v C & E Commrs*, QB [1985] STC 506.

[46.103] A life assurance company, which was partly exempt, submitted a substantial repayment claim covering a period of almost six years. The Commissioners rejected the claim on the basis that the company's returns had been made in accordance with its agreed special partial exemption method. (The method in question excluded the values of taxable supplies of properties and securities, on the basis that the inclusion of such figures would distort the calculation.) The company appealed, contending firstly that the method which it had initially adopted had never been 'approved or directed' by the Commissioners, within *VAT Regulations 1995 (SI 1995/2518), reg 102(1)*, and alternatively that, if the method had been 'approved or directed', that approval or direction was invalid under *Article 17(5)* of the *EC Sixth Directive*. The tribunal rejected these contentions and dismissed the appeal. On the evidence, the company was, at all relevant times, 'calculating its residual input tax by a method which excluded from the numerator and the denominator of the partial exemption fraction the values of both all supplies of securities and all supplies of property'. This method had been approved by the local VAT office.

Furthermore, the use of the method in question was authorised by *Article 17(5)(c)* of the *Sixth Directive*. *Pearl Assurance plc*, LON/98/428 (VTD 15960).

[46.104] In the case noted at **46.62** above, the tribunal held that certain correspondence between the company and the Commissioners did not amount to the agreement of a special method. *Hellesdon Developments Ltd*, LON/99/354 (VTD 16833).

[46.105] A similar decision was reached in *Claim 13 plc*, LON/03/191 (VTD 19122).

[46.106] A charitable trust operated a school. Most of the trustees' supplies were therefore exempt from VAT, but they also made a number of taxable supplies. The trustees registered for VAT with effect from April 1973. Between then and May 1974 they entered into correspondence with the Commissioners concerning their right to reclaim input tax. Following this correspondence, the trustees only reclaimed input tax which was specifically attributable to taxable supplies. Subsequently the trustees consulted an accountancy firm, which considered that the trustees should also have been permitted to reclaim a proportion of residual input tax, and submitted a claim for repayment of more than £140,000. The Commissioners rejected the claim, on the basis that the correspondence in May 1974 amounted to the formal agreement of a special method for attributing input tax, and that this special method could not be altered retrospectively. The trustees appealed, contending that they had never specifically applied to use a special method and that the correspondence did not constitute a formal agreement to adopt a special method. The tribunal accepted this contention and allowed the trustees' appeal in principle, holding on the evidence that the arrangement which was made was 'simply an arrangement whereby the appellants reclaimed input tax on taxable supplies and what has happened is that the appellants did not actually seek to make any apportionment at all of input tax which arose in respect of both taxable and exempt supplies'. The question of apportioning input tax between taxable and non-taxable or exempt supplies 'was simply not addressed'. Accordingly, the arrangement could not 'purport to restrict the right of the appellants to seek to use the UK equivalent of the pro rata rule and seek to apportion input tax between the taxable and non-taxable supplies'. *Ampleforth Abbey Trust*, MAN/97/21 (VTD 15763).

[46.107] A company (D) sold furniture, and also made some exempt supplies. In 1986 it requested permission to use a special method of attributing its input tax. HMRC replied agreeing to the use of a special method under which overheads were to be apportioned using the 'standard fraction', in broadly the same way as was to become the standard method of attribution from 1992. However from 1987 D did not apportion overheads in this manner, and did not disallow any input tax relating to 'general overheads'. Customs did not query the company's returns, possibly because D's exempt input tax was below the de minimis limits. In 2006 HMRC formed the opinion that D's returns were incorrect, and issued assessments on the basis that it had reclaimed input tax which should have been treated as attributable to exempt supplies. D appealed, contending that a Customs officer had agreed the manner in which it was attributing its input tax. The tribunal reviewed the evidence in detail and allowed the appeal in principle, finding that D had received significant exempt income from 1987 onwards, but holding that D's financial controller had been entitled to assume that 'HMRC were happy with (D's) treatment of exempt inputs' because 'a reasonably competent officer would have been aware of the exempt income and would have considered whether input VAT should be blocked'. HMRC had had sufficient knowledge to have realised that D's exempt input tax was not being computed in accordance with either the 'applicable standard method' or with the special method which Customs had proposed in 1986. On the evidence, Customs had allowed D's method of attribution before 1992, and that method therefore became an approved special method when the applicable regulations were amended in 1992. Accordingly D had submitted its returns in accordance with an 'approved special method'. (The tribunal also held that D's advertisements were directly related to its taxable sales of furniture, but that inputs related to D's stores, factories and head office were residual.) *DFS Furniture Co Ltd v HMRC (No 3)*, [2010] SFTD 195; [2009] UKFTT 204 (TC), TC00157.

Whether company entitled to revert to previous special method

[46.108] A company (J) provided financial services, of which some were standard-rated and some were exempt. In 1981 it agreed a special method with the Commissioners for calculating its deductible input tax. In early 1986 the Commissioners agreed a method of attributing the input tax of partly exempt finance companies with the Finance Houses Association. This method differed from that used by J, and at a subsequent control visit a VAT officer ascertained that, for the year ending 31 May 1986, J would be able to deduct more input tax if it used the method adopted by the Finance Houses Association than if it continued to adopt the method which it had used in 1981. J agreed to use the method adopted by the Finance Houses Association, and its VAT liability for the year ending 31 May 1986 was calculated accordingly. However, in December 1986 J changed its accountant, and the new accountant reverted to the previous special method which J had used from 1981 to the year ending 31 May 1985. The Commissioners did not discover this until the company's next control visit in early 1989. The VAT officer who carried out the visit ascertained that, for the periods from June 1987 to November 1988, J had accounted for a lesser amount of tax than would have been the case if it had continued to use the special method adopted by the Finance Houses Association. The Commissioners issued an assessment calculated on the basis that J should have continued to use the latter method. The tribunal dismissed J's appeal, finding that there had been an agreement in 1986 that J should use the method adopted by the Finance Houses Association, and holding that J was not entitled to revert to its previous method unilaterally. *Julian Hodge Bank Ltd*, LON/92/232 (VTD 10197).

Special method verbally agreed by VAT officer

[46.109] A property company registered for VAT with effect from October 1993. It made exempt supplies to residential tenants and standard-rated supplies to commercial tenants. In its first return it reclaimed part of the input tax relating to service charges, attributing the relevant input tax by reference to floor area rather than by reference to the relative value of its taxable and exempt supplies, and also reclaimed the whole of the input tax relating to professional expenses for the acquisition of its property. A VAT officer visited the company in February 1994 and agreed that the company could apportion its input tax on the basis of floor area, rather than by reference to the relative value of its taxable and exempt supplies. He did not query the reclaim of input tax attributable to acquisition costs at his visit, but did so subsequently, in a letter dated June 1994, informing the company that this input tax should also be apportioned. In August 1994 the Commissioners issued an assessment to recover that part of the input tax which they considered should be attributed to exempt supplies. The company appealed, accepting in principle that the input tax relating to the acquisition expenses should be apportioned, but contending that it had only intended its special method of attributing input tax by reference to floor area to apply to its service charge inputs, and that it should be allowed to use the standard method of apportioning the input tax relating to the acquisition expenses. The tribunal accepted this contention and directed that the assessment should be recomputed using the standard method of apportionment. On the evidence, the correspondence could not 'be construed as constituting or evidencing approval of a special method of apportionment which included the acquisition inputs'. The Commissioners did not wish the 'floor area' method of apportionment to apply solely to the service charges input tax (which was relatively small) and the company had not agreed to such a special method applying to the whole of its input tax. Accordingly, the whole of the company's input tax should be apportioned using the standard method of attribution under what is now *VAT Regulations 1995 (SI 1995/2518), reg 101. Trustcorp Ltd*, LON/95/1054 (VTD 13779).

Customs directing use of special method—whether unreasonable

[46.110] The Dean and Chapter of Liverpool Cathedral were registered for VAT, and received both taxable and exempt income. They had agreed a method of apportioning their input tax with the local VAT office. In 1995 the Commissioners agreed a system of apportioning residual input tax with a representative body known as the Churches Main Committee. In 1996 the Commissioners issued a direction that the Cathedral should cease using its existing method of apportionment, and should adopt the method agreed with the Churches Main Committee, under which 65% of its residual input tax would be recoverable. The Cathedral appealed, contending that the direction was unreasonable, since, unlike most cathedrals, it had elected to waive exemption in respect of the cathedral building, and should therefore be entitled to apportion more than 65% of its residual input tax to taxable supplies. The tribunal accepted this contention and allowed the Cathedral's appeal. *Dean & Chapter of the Cathedral Church of Christ*, MAN/x (15068).

Company applying for change to agreed special method

[46.111] In 1989 a company, which provided funeral services and which was therefore partly exempt, had agreed a special method of apportioning its input tax with the Commissioners. This agreed special method was based on the company's outputs, and resulted in about 8% of the company's residual input tax being treated as recoverable. In 1996 the company applied for an amendment to the special method which would change the base of two of the calculations from outputs to inputs, and would have the result in about 22% of its residual input tax being treated as recoverable. The Commissioners rejected the claim on the basis that the changes 'would not produce a fair and reasonable attribution of residual input tax', since 'the funeral parlour operating expenses essentially relate to what is a core exempt supply' whereas there was 'relatively high value input tax in catering, flowers and obituary notices'. The tribunal reviewed the evidence and dismissed the company's appeal, holding that the company's suggested method of attribution was 'unfair and unreasonable in principle'. *Co-Operative Wholesale Society Ltd (No 2)*, MAN/96/1059 (VTD 15633).

Whether special method void for unfairness

[46.112] A company had agreed a special method with the Commissioners. The Commissioners discovered that the company had apparently reclaimed more input tax than it was entitled to, and issued an assessment accordingly. The company appealed, contending that the special method was unfair and should be treated as void. The tribunal rejected this contention and dismissed the appeal. *Dennis Rye Ltd*, MAN/97/120 (VTD 15848).

Termination of special method (Regulation 102(3))

Letter from Customs terminating special method—whether a valid notice

[46.113] In 1994 a university had agreed a special method of attributing its input tax with the Commissioners. In 1997 the Commissioners issued a letter ordering the university to cease using this special method, and to claim only 10% of its relevant input tax pending agreement on a new method (which the Commissioners stated would be backdated). The university initially accepted this, but there was no progress in agreeing a new method, and in 2001 the university lodged a repayment claim on the basis of the special method agreed in 1994. The Commissioners rejected the claim and the university appealed, contending that because the Commissioners had not directed a fair and reasonable replacement method of attribution, the letter ordering it to cease using its existing special method was not a valid notice under *VAT Regulations 1995 (SI 1995/2518), reg 102(3)*. The tribunal reviewed the evidence in detail, accepted this contention and allowed the appeal, holding that 'the Commissioners cannot withdraw approval of a particular special method if the result is to force the university to use a less satisfactory method'. On the evidence, the Customs officers who were dealing with the university's affairs had been 'unreasonable and unfair' in failing to consider the university's proposals for a replacement special method. Accordingly 'the special method agreed in 1994 continues in operation'. *University of Exeter*, MAN/02/399 (VTD 18117).

[46.114] See also *S & U Stores plc*, 46.102 above.

Whether Cathedral entitled to terminate special method unilaterally

[46.115] A cathedral owned a shop, at which a variety of goods were sold to tourists. It also ran a school which charged fees to pupils, these fees being exempt from VAT. In 1984 the Commissioners authorised a special method for attributing the cathedral's input tax. The required calculation was based on income levels, and grants and donations which the cathedral received were included in the computation of the denominator. The cathedral initially operated the special method, but subsequently formed the view that the result of including grants and donations in the computation was that too little of its input tax was being attributed to taxable supplies, and unilaterally ceased to operate the special method. The Commissioners issued an assessment on the basis that the cathedral should have continued to operate the special method. The tribunal dismissed the cathedral's appeal, holding that it had not been entitled to stop using the special method without the agreement of the Commissioners. The tribunal also observed that the inclusion of grants and donations in the computation was in accordance with *Article 19* of the *EC Sixth Directive*. *Dean & Chapter of the Cathedral Church of St Peter*, LON/87/832X (VTD 3591).

Whether change of method may be retrospective

[46.116] In 1984 a company began using a special 'direct attribution' method of apportioning its input tax between taxable and exempt supplies. Following a control visit in 1991, it realised that it would have been to its advantage to have reverted to the standard method of attribution as amended with effect from 1 April 1987. The Commissioners agreed to allow it to change to the standard method and to backdate the change to 1 April 1990, but refused to allow it to recompute its input tax in accordance with the special method for the period from April 1987 to March 1990. The tribunal dismissed the company's appeal against this decision. *PL Schofield Ltd*, MAN/91/878 (VTD 7736).

[46.117] A company carried on the businesses of building and of property management. In 1976 it received permission to adopt a special method of calculating its deductible input tax. In 1985 it received the Commissioners' agreement to a change in the method of apportioning its input tax. In 1990 its accountant formed the view that this method had led to insufficient input tax being treated as deductible, and submitted a claim for repayment of tax, computed on the basis that the standard method of apportionment should have been used with effect from 1 April 1987. The Commissioners refused to accept a retrospective claim and the company appealed. The tribunal dismissed the appeal, holding that the Commissioners had not acted unreasonably in refusing to accept a retrospective claim. *T Clark & Son Ltd*, LON/91/239Z (VTD 8933).

[46.118] A similar decision was reached in a subsequent case where the tribunal held, applying *dicta* of Neill LJ in *John Dee Ltd*, 14.31 COLLECTION AND ENFORCEMENT, and of the tribunal chairman in *BMW (GB) Ltd*, 46.123 below, that its jurisdiction was limited to deciding whether the Commissioners' decision was a reasonable one. On the evidence, the Commissioners had not acted unreasonably in refusing to accept a retrospective claim. *The Chartered Society of Physiotherapy*, LON/97/185 (VTD 15108). (*Note.* Dicta of the tribunal chairman with regard to the tribunal's jurisdiction were disapproved by a subsequent tribunal in *University of Exeter*, **46.113** above, and by the Ch D in *Banbury Visionplus Ltd*, **46.126** below.)

[46.119] A college, which was partly exempt, had agreed a special method with the Commissioners. It subsequently formed the opinion that the method was unfair, as other colleges were not adopting a similar method of attributing their input tax. The college therefore lodged an appeal, contending that it had only agreed to the special method on the understanding that other colleges would be using a similar method, and that it should be therefore allowed to recompute its input tax for the previous seven accounting periods. The tribunal rejected this contention and dismissed the appeal. On the evidence, the college had agreed a special method and there had been no misrepresentation by Customs. Accordingly, the college could not recompute its input tax retrospectively. *James Watt College*, EDN/98/6 & 7 (VTD 15916).

[46.120] A company which operated a private hospital, and made both taxable and exempt supplies, began to operate a special method for the apportionment of its input tax with effect from its accounting period ending 31 May 1987. It had not received written permission to adopt this special method, but its records were inspected by VAT officers in December 1987 and again in 1988. It continued to adopt this special method for all its returns up to and including May 1989. On the advice of its accountants, it unilaterally reverted to the standard method for subsequent returns. The Commissioners refused to accept this change for the periods up to and including 31 August 1991 (the returns for which were submitted late). The company's accountants also calculated that, as a result of having adopted the special method, the input tax which it had reclaimed for the periods from 1 March 1987 to 31 May 1989 was £157,000 less than would have been the case if it had adopted the standard method. It submitted a retrospective claim for this amount, which the Commissioners rejected. The company appealed, contending that since it had never requested nor received permission to use a special method, all its returns should have been submitted using the standard method. The tribunal allowed the appeal in part, finding that, since the company's use of the special method for the periods from 1 March 1987 to 30 November 1987 had not been approved by the Commissioners, it was entitled to use the standard method for those periods. However, when the company had been visited by VAT officers in December 1987, its use of the special method had been approved and permitted. Accordingly, after having received this permission, the company was not entitled to revert to the standard method until its accounting period ending in November 1991. *The Wellington Private Hospital Ltd*, LON/92/2284 (VTD 10627B). (*Note.* For another issue in this case, taken to the QB, see **19.2** DRUGS, MEDICINES, AIDS FOR THE HANDICAPPED, ETC.)

[46.121] The decision in *Wellington Private Hospital*, 46.120 above, was applied in the similar case of *BMW Finance (GB) Ltd*, EDN/94/71 (VTD 13131). (*Note.* For a subsequent 'partial exemption' appeal by an associated company, see **46.123** below.)

Customs directing termination of special method

[46.122] Two associated companies which administered pension funds owned a number of properties, some of which produced taxable income and some produced exempt income. In 1991 the companies had agreed special methods for attributing their input tax. In 1995 the Commissioners issued directions terminating the special methods and requiring the companies to adopt the standard method of attribution. The companies appealed, contending that the adoption of the standard method would be unreasonable. The tribunal accepted this contention and allowed the appeals. Applying *dicta* of the CA in *John Dee Ltd*, **14.31** COLLECTION AND ENFORCEMENT, the tribunal's jurisdiction was appellate rather than merely supervisory. The enabling provision for the relevant regulations was *VATA 1994, s 26(3)*, which provided that the regulations should be for the purpose of 'securing a fair and reasonable attribution of input tax'. On the evidence, the 1991 methods were 'unsatisfactory' but the adoption of the standard method would be 'even more unsatisfactory in that it was likely to lead to greater distortions'. The Commissioners could reasonably have directed the use of an alternative special method, such as one based on the rental values of the relevant properties. However, they had not done so. Since the standard method was less satisfactory than the 1991 schemes, the directions were flawed in that they did not achieve an attribution which was more fair and reasonable. *Merchant Navy Officers Pension Fund Trustees Ltd; Merchant Navy Ratings Pension Fund Trustees Ltd*, LON/95/2944 (VTD 14262).

[46.123] A company (B) was the representative member of a large VAT group, which made both taxable and exempt supplies. It had used a special method of attributing its input tax, which was very similar to the standard method as it was based on the values of supplies made. However, the Commissioners had not formally approved this method (which, because it included the values of cars sold under hire-purchase agreements, had yielded a recovery rate of 93% of input tax in 1994, and 84% in 1995). In April 1996 the Commissioners issued a direction that this method should be terminated, and that a new special method, based on the method agreed with the Finance Houses Association and described in *Notice No 700/57/95*, should be adopted. B appealed, contending that the proposed method did not give a fair and reasonable attribution of input tax because it ignored the fact that taxable leasing supplies involved more overheads than exempt hire-purchase supplies. The tribunal dismissed the appeal, holding that the method which B had adopted prior to the direction had not secured a fair and reasonable attribution of input tax. Where a car was sold under a hire-purchase agreement, the costs which B incurred related to the exempt provision of finance, rather than to the taxable sale of the cars. The Commissioners had 'acted reasonably in seeking to alter the method used'. Although it was accepted that a leasing transaction was more complex than a hire-purchase transaction, B's proposals for taking this into account could not be objectively verified 'without unreasonable effort'. Accordingly, the Commissioners' direction had been reasonable. *BMW (GB) Ltd*, LON/96/733 (VTD 14823). (*Note.* The tribunal held that it had a limited supervisory jurisdiction rather than a full appellate jurisdiction. Its reasoning on this point was subsequently disapproved by the Ch D in *Banbury Visionplus Ltd*, **46.126** below.)

[46.124] A similar decision was reached in a case in which the Commissioners had issued a direction terminating a special method used by a bowling club and requiring the club to use the standard method. The tribunal held that the Commissioners' direction was reasonable, distinguishing *Merchant Navy Officers Pension Fund Trustees*, **46.122** above. *Glasgow Indoor Bowling Club*, EDN/96/75 (VTD 14889).

[46.125] A similar decision, also distinguishing *Merchant Navy Officers Pension Fund Trustees*, **46.122** above, was reached in *Cliff College Outreach*, MAN/00/516 (VTD 17301).

[46.126] Customs had agreed that several companies which carried on business as opticians, and were partly exempt, could use special methods for attributing their input tax, based on floor area. In 2004 Customs issued directions terminating the special methods, and requiring the companies to use the standard method of attributing their input tax. The companies appealed, contending that the directions were unreasonable. The tribunal reviewed the evidence in detail, rejected this contention, and dismissed the appeals, observing that less than half of the companies' taxable inputs related to property, and that less than half the floor area was specifically allocated to either taxable or exempt supplies. The Ch D upheld the tribunal decision, holding that the tribunal had been entitled to conclude that the standard method achieved 'a fair and reasonable attribution of input tax', whereas the special methods did not. *Banbury Visionplus Ltd v HMRC (and related appeals)*, Ch D [2006] STC 1568; [2006] EWHC 1024 (Ch). (*Note*. Etherton J also held that the tribunal had a full appellate jurisdiction rather than a limited supervisory jurisdiction, specifically disapproving the earlier tribunal decision in *BMW (GB) Ltd*, **46.123** above.)

[46.127] See also *MBNA Europe Bank Ltd*, **46.181** below.

Date from which special method effective (Regulation 102(4))

Whether special method may be backdated

[46.128] At a meeting on 26 February 1988 between a VAT officer and a company which was partly exempt, a special method for attributing the company's input tax was agreed. However, the company failed to account for input tax in accordance with the agreement. When the Commissioners discovered this, they issued an assessment in accordance with the special method, covering the period from 1 April 1987 to 31 March 1989. The tribunal allowed the company's appeal in part, holding that the Commissioners could not insist on the use of the special method for any period prior to 26 February 1988. *North British Housing Association Ltd*, MAN/91/45 (VTD 7195).

[46.129] A bank, which was partly exempt and had agreed a special method of calculating its deductible input tax, went into liquidation in February 1991. It ceased to trade but the liquidator incurred input tax. The liquidator formed the opinion that the existing special method had been to the bank's detriment as the percentage of deductible input tax had been unreasonably low. In April 1992 the accountants acting for the liquidator wrote to the local VAT office proposing a new special method. The Commissioners agreed to the revised method being used with effect from 1 April 1992, but refused to allow the revised method to be backdated. The liquidator appealed, contending that the revised method should be used retrospectively for the period from 1 July 1991 to 31 March 1992. The tribunal dismissed the liquidator's appeal, holding that the Commissioners had not acted unreasonably in refusing to allow the revised special method to be backdated. *AJ Barrett (as provisional liquidator for Rafidain Bank)*, LON/92/2732A (VTD 11016).

[46.130] A bowling club applied for permission to adopt a special method of attributing its input tax with retrospective effect, to take account of an anticipated future increase in the proportion of its taxable supplies. The Commissioners rejected the application and the tribunal dismissed the club's appeal. Applying *dicta* in *BMW (GB) Ltd*, **46.123** above, the tribunal's jurisdiction was limited to deciding whether the Commissioners' decision was a reasonable one. On the evidence, the Commissioners had not acted unreasonably in refusing to accept a retrospective claim. *Chard Bowling Club (No 2)*, [1997] VATDR 375 (VTD 15114). (*Note.* For another issue in this case, see **46.65** above.)

Notice overriding special method (Regulations 102A–102C)

Notice by Customs under Reg 102A

[46.131] In 2001 Customs agreed that a company (V) which traded as a retail optician could use a special partial exemption method based on floor space. Subsequently Customs formed the opinion that this had led to V reclaiming excessive amounts of input tax, and in 2005 they served an override notice under *VAT Regulations 1995 (SI 1995/2518), reg 102A*. V appealed. The tribunal dismissed the appeal, observing that similar special methods had been criticised by the tribunal and the Ch D in *Banbury Visionplus Ltd*, **46.126** above, and *Optika Ltd*, **46.137** below. The tribunal commented that it was impossible to precisely identify 'the areas of the stores which are used for exempt, taxable and mixed purposes', since 'a member of (V's) staff engaged in selling a frame into which dispensed lenses are to be fitted is, throughout the process, simultaneously selling taxable goods and making an exempt supply of dispensing services. The two are inextricably mixed in that the one is of no value without the other.' It was 'impossible to conclude that, when the customer is in the display area but not at a dispensing desk, the dispenser is making a wholly taxable supply of a frame, but when the customer sits at the dispensing desk the dispenser is making a mixed supply'. The fact that V had chosen to trade from open-plan stores had 'by its nature the result that only a modest part of each store can properly be regarded as used for exclusively taxable or exclusively exempt supplies'. The display area was used for both taxable and exempt supplies, and the only area which was exclusively used for taxable supplies was V's laboratory. Furthermore, there was no ambiguity in the wording of the override notice. The tribunal also dismissed an appeal against an assessment issued to recover input tax which V had overclaimed. The Ch D upheld the tribunal decisions on both issues. McCombe J held that there was 'no ground on which to fault the tribunal's finding as a matter of law'. *Vision Express (UK) Ltd*, Ch D 2009, [2010] STC 742; [2009] EWHC 3245 (Ch). (Note. The CA has granted the company leave to appeal against this decision—[2010] EWCA Civ 972.

Notice by appellant under Reg 102C

[46.132] A university, which was partly exempt, had agreed a special method of attributing its input tax. In 2004 the university sent a letter to HMRC, expressed as being a 'special method override notice' under *VAT Regulations 1995 (SI 1995/2518), reg 102C*. HMRC responded with a letter requiring the university to determine the amount of deductible VAT using its agreed special method and the amount of deductible VAT 'in accordance with the use or intended use of purchases', and to account for 'any difference between these amounts as a Notice correction'. HMRC also stated that they 'neither approve nor reject' the university's calculations, but would 'accept any calculation, providing the result fairly and reasonably reflects the use or intended use of purchases in making taxable supplies'. Following subsequent correspondence, the university applied to the tribunal for a preliminary ruling on the effect of *regulation 102C*, contending that the requirement to determine deductible VAT in accordance with usage only applied to the matters referred to in the university's letter, rather than to any aspect of the special method. The tribunal rejected the university's contentions, holding that 'the reasons given in support of a taxpayer's override notice do not limit the scope or nature of the necessary calculation of input tax deductible after the existing special method has been overridden. That is because *regulation 102B* is, on the face of it, specific and can only be interpreted as meaning that the taxpayer is required to make a calculation under the special method ("the attribution" referred to in *reg 102B(1)(a)*) and then to make a calculation ("an attribution" referred to in *reg 102B(1)(b)*) and then to account for the difference between the two.' The tribunal also held that 'the status of the reasons for the override notice are also plain on the face of *reg 102C*. They are only required and only have effect to satisfy or fail to satisfy the Commissioners that the existing method should be overridden on the ground that the existing method does not produce a fair and reasonable result. Once the Commissioners are so satisfied, *reg 102B* takes over as far as the calculation is concerned. If the Commissioners refuse to agree the override, the taxpayer has a right of appeal under *section 83(c)* of the *VAT Act* or, as here, pursuant to an assessment being issued. It is also open to the taxpayer to seek approval of a new special method incorporating the reasons.' Accordingly, 'the true construction of *reg 102C* is that reasons stated in support of an application for approval of an override notice do not entitle the taxpayer, when making a calculation under *reg 102B* following the approval, to make it only in accordance with the matters mentioned in the notice or its reasons'. *Loughborough University v HMRC*, [2009] SFTD 200; [2009] UKFTT 91 (TC), TC00059.

[46.133] In 1998 a university college, which was partly exempt, had agreed a special method of attributing its input tax. It subsequently formed the opinion that this method did not give sufficient credit for input tax which it had incurred. In 2003 it proposed an alternative special method, which HMRC rejected. In 2004 the college sent a letter to HMRC, expressed as being a 'special method override notice' under *VAT Regulations 1995 (SI 1995/2518), reg 102C*. HMRC accepted the notice, and the college then submitted a repayment claim for £147,000. HMRC rejected the claim and the college appealed. The tribunal reviewed the evidence in detail and observed that 'the college had material activities which were funded, broadly, by the endowment income of the college and which were not concerned with the making of supplies for consideration'. It held, inter alia, that the provision of free meals to Fellows of the college 'was not used in making any economic supply by the college'. The tribunal dismissed the college's appeal against HMRC's refusal to agree its proposed special method, holding that the college's proposed method was 'unfair and unreasonable'. With regard to the override notice, the tribunal rejected the college's calculation, but held that the appeal should be adjourned rather than dismissed. The tribunal held that '*regulation 102C* requires a complete revisiting of the input tax calculated on the basis of use'. It held that the evidence submitted by the college did not permit the tribunal 'to make a precise calculation'. The tribunal provided specific guidelines with regard to the input tax attributable to the college's guestrooms, kitchens and lunchrooms. *St John's College Oxford v HMRC*, [2010] UKFTT 113 (TC), TC00424.

Customs refusing application for special method

[46.134] An estate agent, who was partly exempt, reclaimed the whole of his input tax. The Commissioners issued an assessment to recover part of the tax. The assessment was computed using the standard method of attributing input tax. The estate agent appealed, contending that the standard method was inequitable and that the Commissioners should have allowed him to use a special method. The tribunal rejected this contention and dismissed his appeal. *JG Whitelaw*, EDN/89/28 (VTD 4299).

[46.135] A company operated a licensed casino. Most of its income was exempt from VAT, but it also operated a bar and a dining room, from which it made some standard-rated supplies. The company applied to the Commissioners for permission to use a special method for attributing its input tax on the basis of floor area. The Commissioners rejected the application on the grounds that it would lead to an excessive amount of input tax being attributed to taxable supplies (since the parts of the premises used for gambling were relatively small compared with the parts used for dining and drinking). The tribunal dismissed the appeal, finding that only about 1% of the company's supplies were taxable and that 'the catering activities by themselves are not conducted with a view to profit', whereas under the company's proposed special method, 'up to 55%' of its input tax would be recoverable. *Aspinall's Club Ltd*, LON/99/540 (VTD 17797).

[46.136] A group of companies operated eleven UK casinos, which included bar and restaurant facilities. It applied for permission to use a special 'floor-based' partial exemption method for apportioning its input tax. HMRC rejected the claim and the representative member of the group appealed. The First-Tier Tribunal allowed the appeal, finding that 'the food and beverage supplies made by the appellant are made from defined and measurable parts of the appellant's premises, and specifically distinguishing the earlier decision in *Aspinall's Club Ltd*, **46.135** above, on the grounds that in that case the tribunal had found that 'the catering activities were not conducted for profit'. In the present case, however, the catering activities were 'businesses in their own right' and were 'not merely ancillary to the gaming business'. The Upper Tribunal and the CA unanimously upheld this decision. Etherton LJ held that a 'fair and reasonable' attribution of input tax must include an assessment 'of the real economic use of the asset, that is to say having regard to economic reality, in the light of the observable terms and features of the taxpayer's business'. The tribunal had been entitled to find that 'the catering activity was carried on as a business in its own right by the respondent and with a view to profit'. *HMRC v London Clubs Management Ltd* , CA [2011] EWCA Civ 1323.

[46.137] A company carried on business as an optician. It applied to use a special 'partial exemption' method for attributing its input tax on the basis of floor space. The Commissioners rejected the application on the grounds that it would lead to an excessive amount of input tax being attributed to taxable supplies. The tribunal dismissed the company's appeal, holding that there did not appear to be 'any distortion in the standard method'. However, the method which the company had proposed lacked any 'direct connexion between recovery and the purpose of the inputs' and would not have 'produced a fair and reasonable recovery'. The tribunal chairman expressed the view that 'methods based on floor area are seldom fair and reasonable'. *Optika Ltd*, LON/00/1281 (VTD 18627). (*Note.* For the Commissioners' practice following this decision, see Business Brief 34/2004, issued on 15 December 2004.)

[46.138] In a Scottish case where the facts were similar, the tribunal reached a similar decision, but expressed the view that it had a limited supervisory jurisdiction rather than a full appellate jurisdiction. The company appealed to the CS, which remitted the case to the tribunal, holding that the tribunal had a full appellate jurisdiction. The tribunal reheard the case and observed that 'in valuing floor area the feature of zoning proposed as a feature of the PESM, i.e. attribution of higher values to certain floor areas in accordance with valuation practice, has been disapproved by other tribunals'. However the tribunal held that there was 'merit in other aspects of the proposed PESM', and that the 'aspect of zoning' was 'severable from the proposed scheme and could be removed without damaging it in principle'. The tribunal observed that with regard to one specific retail outlet, this would produce a recoverable percentage of 21.17% (as opposed to 47.39% under the company's original proposal, or 8.49% under the standard method). *DCM (Optical Holdings) Ltd v HMRC*, [2010] SFTD 1204; [2010] UKFTT 393 (TC), TC00675, TC00675A. (*Note.* HMRC have appealed to the Upper Tribunal against this decision.)

[46.139] A company received taxable income from the sale of kitchens, and exempt income in the form of commission from finance companies. It applied to the Commissioners for permission to use a special method for attributing its input tax on the basis of costs rather than outputs. The Commissioners rejected the application. The tribunal dismissed the company's appeal, holding that the method which the company had proposed 'was inherently ambiguous because it failed clearly to identify which particular costs could be attributed to taxable and exempt supplies respectively'. *Living Design (Home Improvements) Ltd*, EDN/02/12 & 95 (VTD 17874).

[46.140] A school constructed a sports complex. It incorporated a subsidiary company, to which it granted a licence to use the complex outside school hours. The school registered for VAT, in the hope of reclaiming some of the VAT incurred on the building of the complex. It applied to Customs for permission to use a special method for apportioning the input tax on the construction of the complex by reference to the hours of use of the complex by the school and the subsidiary company (which would have resulted in 54% of the tax being attributed to taxable supplies). Customs rejected the application and the tribunal dismissed the school's appeal, observing that *Article 17(2)* of the *Sixth Directive* required that 'supplies to the taxable person claiming to deduct the VAT charged on them be used by that taxable person for the purposes of *his* taxable transactions'. The tribunal held that 'a method that brings the use by a third party trader for the purposes of that third party's taxable business into the apportionment calculation' would 'go beyond what is authorized.' The Ch D upheld the tribunal decision. Warren J held that the standard method produced 'an allocation which is more fair and reasonable than the school's proposed special method'. Since the standard method produced a result which did not differ substantially from the extent to which the goods or services were used by the school in making taxable supplies, there were no grounds for applying a 'standard method override' under *regulation 107B*. *St Helen's School Northwood Ltd v HMRC*, Ch D 2006, [2007] STC 633; [2006] EWHC 3306 (Ch).

[46.141] A golf club which had constructed a large extension to its clubhouse applied to Customs for permission to use a special 'floor-based' method for apportioning its input tax. Customs rejected the claim and the club appealed. The tribunal dismissed the appeal, finding that none of the clubhouse was used for wholly taxable activities and only a small area (a changing-room) was wholly exempt in use. On the evidence, the club had failed to demonstrate that its proposed method would lead to a fair apportionment. However the tribunal chairman (Mr. Coutts) specifically disapproved *obiter dicta* of the London tribunal in *Optika Ltd*, **46.137** above, and expressed the view that 'it should be possible to formulate into an agreement some ascertainable modification to the mathematical floor area based percentage to reflect the realities and achieve fairness'. *Auchterarder Golf Club*, EDN/06/28 (VTD 19907).

[46.142] A partnership which operated a physiotherapy clinic applied to Customs for permission to use a special 'floor-based' method for apportioning its input tax. Customs rejected the claim and the partnership appealed. The tribunal dismissed the appeal, observing that the partnership's proposals would achieve 'something over a 70% level of recovery when half the building is used to make exempt supplies. Further, the area used to make exempt supplies produces considerably more income and turnover and seemingly costs than the rest of the building'. The partnership's proposed method 'did not achieve a fair and reasonable attribution and was not a reasonable method'. *Farnham Physiotherapy & Sports Clinic*, LON/05/1108 (VTD 20004).

[46.143] A company, which advertised 'home improvements', received commission from finance companies to whom it introduced some of its customers. It was therefore partly exempt, and applied to Customs for permission to use a special method for apportioning its input tax. Customs rejected the claim and the company appealed. The tribunal reviewed the evidence in detail and dismissed the appeal, finding that the company's proposed method involved an 'element of double counting' and therefore did not produce 'a fair and reasonable attribution'. *Laura Anderson Ltd*, MAN/07/952 (VTD 20743).

[46.144] A company, which provided investment management services and was partly exempt, had used the standard method of apportioning its input tax, under which it recovered about 20% of its residual input tax. It applied to Customs for permission to use a special method which took account of its expenditure rather than its turnover, and under which more than 50% of its residual input tax would be recoverable. Customs rejected the application and the tribunal dismissed the company's appeal, holding on the evidence that the standard method produced a result which was more 'fair and reasonable' than the company's proposed special method. *McInroy & Wood Ltd*, EDN/07/130 (VTD 20780).

Universities and colleges

University

[46.145] The value of the exempt outputs of a university is much greater than the value of its taxable outputs. Since 1973 Customs have therefore approved special arrangements for universities, whereby each activity giving rise to an output tax liability may be dealt with separately. (The arrangements in force from 1973 to 1997 were agreed with the Committee of Vice-Chancellors and Principals, and were known as the 'CVCP Guidelines'.) In 1990 Edinburgh University made a claim for repayment of residual input tax attributable to its computer services department. Customs refused to repay the tax, considering that the agreed special method did not allow a claim for residual input tax. The tribunal allowed the University's appeal, holding that it was entitled to reclaim the residual input tax and that its failure to have done so previously was an error which it was 'now entitled to have put right'. *The University of Edinburgh*, EDN/91/55 (VTD 6569).

[46.146] A similar decision was reached in *The University of Sussex*, LON/98/851 (VTD 16221). (*Note.* For subsequent developments in this case, see **48.2 PAYMENT OF TAX**.)

[46.147] In 1994 a university, which was partly exempt, applied to use a special method for attributing its input tax. Customs agreed to this. In 1998 Customs formed the opinion that the university was attributing too much input tax to taxable supplies, because, in computing the denominator of its partial exemption fraction, it had used consolidated accounts, so that supplies which the university made to two subsidiary companies were reflected in computing the numerator but not in the denominator. The university agreed to change the method with effect from August 1998 but refused to change its claims for periods ending before that date. Customs issued assessments covering the period from 1994 to 1998. The tribunal allowed the university's appeal, finding that the university had submitted consolidated accounts in 1994 when it had requested to use a special method, and that 'the Commissioners either knew or ought to have known that the appellant was using consolidated accounts to derive the total income figure to be used in the partial exemption calculation'. *University of Bristol*, LON/00/293 (VTD 17316).

[46.148] A university had agreed a special method for attributing its input tax. It applied to amend the special method by allowing separate accounting for a specific sports facility. Customs rejected the application on the grounds that it would not produce a 'fair and reasonable apportionment', noting that the university had other sports facilities and considering that 'if sports facilities were to be sectioned off the other sports facilities of the University should be within that section'. The university appealed. The tribunal dismissed its appeal, holding that its jurisdiction was supervisory rather than appellate, and that Customs' decision had been reasonable. The tribunal held that it was 'neither fair nor reasonable to "cherry-pick"' a specific sports facility 'as being the place where input tax recovery might be made to obtain that benefit while ignoring the university's general activities within the sector'. *University Court of the University of Glasgow (No 4)*, EDN/02/11 (VTD 19885). (*Notes.* (1) The appeal was heard in September 2002, and the tribunal chairman released the decision to the parties in October 2002, but the Tribunal Centre did not publish it until December 2006. (2) In the subsequent case of *DCM (Optical Holdings) Ltd v HMRC*, **46.138** above, the CS held that the tribunal's jurisdiction in such cases was appellate rather than merely supervisory. The Ch D had reached a similar decision in *Banbury Visionplus Ltd*, **46.126** above.)

University colleges

[46.149] Two Oxford colleges had reclaimed input tax in accordance with a special method based on the guidelines which Customs had agreed with the Committee of Vice-Chancellors and Principals (the 'CVCP Guidelines'). This allowed them to reclaim input tax relating to catering, bar sales, and outside conferences (described by the tribunal as 'three formulaic tunnels'). Subsequently the colleges submitted further claims for repayment of input tax. Customs rejected these claims and the colleges appealed. The tribunal reviewed the evidence in detail and allowed the appeals in principle, finding that 'the colleges did engage in activities outside the formulaic tunnels. No input tax was recovered in respect of all or many of those activities. The colleges are entitled under the special method to recover that tax.' However, the colleges were not entitled to any further repayment of tax relating to their outside conferences. The tribunal adjourned the appeals in the hope that the parties could 'agree the amounts involved'. *Wadham College Oxford; Merton College Oxford*, [2007] VATDR 177 (VTD 20233). (*Note.* For HMRC's practice following this decision, see HMRC Brief 34/08, issued on 24 July 2008.)

[46.150] A Cambridge college had reclaimed input tax in accordance with the 'CVCP Guidelines' (see **46.145** and **46.149** above). In 2003 it submitted a further repayment claim, backdated to 1973, relating to capital expenditure. HMRC rejected the claim on the grounds that the CVCP method had already granted relief for the tax. The tribunal dismissed the college's appeal. Sir Stephen Oliver observed that 'save in certain specific areas (such as the capital goods scheme), the VAT code makes no distinction, in either the output tax or the input tax provisions, between capital and revenue expenditure'. Accordingly the agreed CVCP method covered capital expenditure as well as revenue expenditure. (The college also appealed against an assessment which HMRC had issued in 2007 to recover input tax which the college had reclaimed in 2006. The tribunal held that this assessment had been issued within the statutory time limit, and that the college had no 'legitimate expectation' to the contrary.) *Master & Fellows of St Mary Magdalene College in the University of Cambridge v HMRC*, [2011] UKFTT 680 (TC), TC01522.

[46.151] A London college (U) made zero-rated supplies of scientific equipment. It submitted a repayment claim for 2002 and 2003 on the basis that the effect of this was that it was entitled to deduct a proportion of its residual input tax. Customs rejected the claim on the basis that U's computation had included goods which it donated, although such donations had no value for partial exemption purposes. U appealed. The appeal was settled by an agreement under *VATA 1994, s 85*, under which 'the numerator and denominator of the fraction in the appellant's partial exemption special method calculation shall include the value of the specific supplies of the goods to the extent that it is established that those supplies were properly zero-rated'. The value of the zero-rated goods was to be determined in accordance with *VATA 1994, Sch 6 para 6(2)(c)*. Following this agreement, U submitted a further repayment claim, on the agreed basis, for 2004. Customs again rejected the claim but the tribunal allowed U's appeal. The tribunal chairman (Mr. Clark) held that an appeal under *VATA 1994, s 83(e)* was not 'necessarily tied to a particular period. The appeal may be brought in the context of a decision which covers a specific period, but the principle may well be relevant to the continuing basis for the calculation of the taxable person's allowable input tax.' Having accepted U's claim for 2003, Customs should have applied the same principles when considering the corresponding claim for 2004. The agreement under *VATA 1994, s 85* fell 'within the narrow category of agreements which can found an application to stay proceedings on the ground of issue estoppel'. Accordingly, Customs were precluded from arguing that' zero-rated supplies made by (U) are excluded from the numerator and denominator of the fraction used in (U's) partial exemption special method'. The tribunal specifically declined to follow the HL decision in the corporation tax case of *MacNiven v Westmoreland Investments Ltd*, HL [2001] STC 237, in which the HL held that an agreement under *TMA, s 54* only covered the assessments which had been the subject of the relevant appeal, and did not bind the Revenue for subsequent years. The tribunal also distinguished the earlier decision in *Société Internationale de Télécommunications Aeronautiques (No 2)*, 2.124 APPEALS, on the grounds that 'the application of a partial exemption special method is not "unalterable", and so its continuation does not raise questions of inequity between one trader and others making similar supplies'. *University College London*, [2008] VATDR 409 (VTD 20664).

College—construction of new campus

[46.152] A college of further education reclaimed input tax on the construction of a new campus. Customs issued a ruling that it was only entitled to reclaim 10% of the input tax, since it had agreed a special method of attributing its input tax, which treated 10% of its business income as taxable and 90% as exempt. (It was accepted that 80% of the college's income was 'non-business income'.) The tribunal allowed the college's appeal and Customs appealed to the CS. The college subsequently agreed a revised special method with Customs, and the CS determined the appeal accordingly. *HMRC v Edinburgh Telford College*, CS [2006] CSIH 13. (*Notes*. (1) The tribunal chairman (Mr. Coutts) had expressed the view that the effect of the CJEC decision in *Lennartz v Finanzamt München III*, **22.456** EUROPEAN COMMUNITY LAW, was that the college was 'entitled to recover the whole input tax of the construction costs of its building and to account for the output tax on its non-business use as a deemed supply over a 20-year period'. The CS reversed this decision. (2) For another issue in this case, see **22.149** EUROPEAN COMMUNITY LAW.)

Miscellaneous

Holding company—supplies by subsidiary

[46.153] A holding company had agreed a special method of attributing input tax. Under the agreement one of its subsidiaries, which supplied taxable services to a customer outside the group, was treated as fully taxable, so that its input tax was wholly deductible. Subsequently the subsidiary began making supplies to other members of the group. Customs considered that, since these supplies were not subject to VAT, the subsidiary's input tax should be restricted accordingly. They therefore issued an assessment to recover some of the subsidiary's input tax. The holding company appealed, contending that the wording of the agreed special method required that all the subsidiary's input tax should be treated as allowable, even though some of its supplies were no longer subject to VAT. The tribunal accepted this contention and allowed the company's appeal. *Fidelity International Management Holdings Ltd*, LON/91/1915 (VTD 7323).

Group of companies

[46.154] See *Joseph Nelson Investment Planning Ltd*, 32.31 GROUPS OF COMPANIES, and *Kwik-Fit (GB) Ltd*, 32.32 GROUPS OF COMPANIES.

Refurbishment of premises

[46.155] A company which made taxable supplies also made exempt dealings in securities and let part of its premises to tenants, so that it was partly exempt. It had agreed a special method of apportioning its input tax, by which tax relating to the 'general management and general upkeep of the structure and common areas of the premises' was to be apportioned on the basis of the percentage of the total floor space which it occupied, but any remaining input tax was to be deductible in full. It undertook substantial refurbishment of the premises, and reclaimed the whole of the input tax on this. Customs issued an assessment to recover part of the tax, considering that it should have been apportioned under the special method. The company appealed, contending that, in view of the scale of the refurbishment, the expenditure was not within the definition of 'general upkeep' of the premises, and therefore fell within the definition of 'remaining input tax' and was deductible in full. The tribunal accepted this contention and allowed the appeal. *Louis Dreyfus & Co Ltd*, LON/90/236Z (VTD 10795).

Statutory body—non-business activities

[46.156] The *Housing (Scotland) Act 1988* established a statutory body (S) for the purpose of providing housing and promoting the provision of housing. Until June 1990, S was entitled to reclaim input tax on non-business activities under what is now *VATA 1994, s 33*. From July 1990 S lost this status and became partly exempt. Its accountants subsequently applied for permission to operate a special method of calculating its deductible input tax. Customs replied approving an alternative method subject to the exclusion of 'the value of any goods or services not supplied by way of business'. In 1993 Customs discovered that S had been treating its distribution of grants to housing associations as a business activity and reclaiming a proportion of the input tax relating to this. Customs considered that the provision of grants to housing associations was not a business activity, and issued an assessment to recover some of the input tax which S had reclaimed. The tribunal dismissed S's appeal, observing that Customs had directed that 'non-business supplies must be excluded' from the partial exemption calculations, and holding that Customs were entitled to treat the provision of grants as a non-business activity. *Scottish Homes*, EDN/94/138 (VTD 13292). (*Note.* For a subsequent appeal by the same association, see **46.53** above.)

Bank—definition of 'significant change in business'

[46.157] A bank, which was partly exempt, had agreed a special method of calculating its deductible input tax. The agreement stipulated that any significant change in the bank's business must be notified. In 1986 the bank made zero-rated supplies of gold bullion totalling more than £395 million. Customs rejected the bank's input tax claim, considering that the supplies of bullion constituted a significant change in the bank's business. The tribunal allowed the bank's appeal, holding on the evidence that the supplies in question did not amount to a significant change in the bank's business. *Union Bank of Switzerland*, [1987] VATTR 221 (VTD 2551).

Bank—service charge income

[46.158] A group of companies which carried on a retail banking business had agreed a special method, under which the total percentage of input tax recoverable would be sum of the percentage of costs relating to lending income, multiplied by the product of the group's taxable lending income divided by the total of its taxable and exempt lending income, and the percentage of costs relating to service charge income, multiplied by the product of the group's taxable service charge income divided by the total of its taxable and exempt service charge income. Subsequently Customs discovered that, for some periods, the costs which the group was treating as attributable to service charge income exceeded the service charge income itself. They issued an assessment to recover some of the input tax which the group had reclaimed. The group appealed, contending that it had operated the special method correctly, and that the reason that the service charge income was less than the associated costs was that a large number of its customers kept their accounts in credit and were provided with free banking facilities. The tribunal accepted this contention and allowed the group's appeal, holding that the free banking facilities should be treated as being supplies for consideration, so that the bank was entitled to reclaim the relevant input tax. *The Governor and Company of the Bank of Scotland*, EDN/94/114 (VTD 13854).

Bank—assignment of 'receivables' to Jersey company

[46.159] A bank (C), which operated a credit card business, was partly exempt and operated a special method for calculating its deductible input tax. It assigned a large number of present and future debts ('receivables') to a newly-incorporated Jersey company (L). In its return, it treated this as a taxable supply, and claimed a refund of more than £11,000,000 in input tax. Customs rejected the claim on the grounds (*inter alia*) that the assignment was not a supply, but was simply the granting of security for a loan, and that C's return was incorrect as it had wrongly excluded its exempt supplies to its cardholders from its partial exemption calculations. The tribunal reviewed the evidence in detail and dismissed C's appeal. The tribunal observed that L was not a 'free agent' and that its 'role was pre-ordained by (C)'. L, and another Jersey company involved in the transactions, were 'no more than (C's) instruments' and could not 'act independently. The two Jersey companies could 'do only what (C) requires them to do'. On the evidence, 'the assignment of the receivables was an assignment by way of security and not an assignment by way of sale'. Furthermore, 'the value of (C's) supplies to its customers are to be included in the calculation of its recoverable residual input tax', and 'its exclusion of that value was wrong'. *Capital One Bank (Europe) plc*, MAN/03/628 (VTD 19238). (*Notes.* (1) At a subsequent hearing, the tribunal awarded costs to Customs (VTD 19556). (2) Some of the tribunal's reasoning was subsequently disapproved by the Ch D in *MBNA Europe Bank Ltd v HMRC*, **46.181** below.)

[46.160] In the case noted at **46.181** below, Briggs J held that assignments of receivables to a Jersey trustee did not constitute supplies. *MBNA Europe Bank Ltd v HMRC*, Ch D [2006] STC 2089; [2006] EWHC 2326 (Ch).

Bank—rounding of residual input tax

[46.161] See *Royal Bank of Scotland Group plc v HMRC (No 6)*, **22.445** EUROPEAN COMMUNITY LAW.

Bank—Customs' powers to review basis of computation

[46.162] See *Lloyds TSB Group plc (No 2)*, **14.92** COLLECTION AND ENFORCEMENT

Finance company—special method involving 'transaction count'

[46.163] A finance company (S), which was partly exempt, operated a special method which stated, *inter alia*, that 'the taxable percentage applied to VAT directly attributable to sales and new business administration costs should be calculated by using a transaction method of taxable new deals created in the tax period over all new deals created in the tax period'. S treated hire-purchase transactions as wholly exempt, so that they were included in the denominator of the appropriate fraction, but not in the numerator. Subsequently it formed the opinion that a hire-purchase transaction should have been treated as both a taxable deal (the hiring of goods) and an exempt deal (credit finance), and lodged a backdated repayment claim accordingly. Customs rejected the claim on the basis that, because a hire-purchase transaction was not wholly taxable, it did not qualify as a 'taxable deal'. The tribunal allowed S's appeal, holding that it was entitled to treat a hire purchase transaction as two deals (i.e. included once in the numerator and twice in the denominator) in arriving at the appropriate fraction. *Sovereign Finance plc*, MAN/97/778 (VTD 16237).

Input tax on currency transactions

[46.164] A company, established in the British Virgin Islands, operated a number of 'bureaux de change' in the UK. In 1993 Customs wrote to the company, specifying the terms of a special partial exemption method for calculating its recoverable input tax. Under the method, the input tax relating to overheads was to be recovered by reference to customers' domicile, on a transaction count basis. Initially the company accounted for tax on the basis that 38% of the residual input tax was recoverable, on the basis that 38% of its transactions were with customers domiciled outside the EU. Subsequently the company formed the opinion that it should be allowed to reclaim more than 38% of its residual input tax, and lodged a retrospective repayment claim, computed on the basis that 45% of the currency which it received for exchange was non-EU currency. Customs rejected the claim and the tribunal dismissed the company's appeal, observing that the currency presented by a customer 'need not represent the country of domicile'. On the evidence, the tribunal held that the company had 'not established that the transaction count method was in any way wrong' and had 'not shown that the calculations based on the currency method invalidate that original method'. *Chequepoint (UK) Ltd*, LON/98/1543 (VTD 16754).

Hire purchase transactions—application to change special method

[46.165] A group of companies had agreed a special partial exemption method for calculating its recoverable input tax. Some of the companies in the group engaged in hire-purchase transactions, and the special method treated 15% of general business overheads as attributable to instalment credit business (and thus as exempt and irrecoverable). The group formed the opinion that this was unreasonable, and applied for the method to be changed to a 'transaction-based approach'. Customs rejected the claim and the representative member of the group appealed. The tribunal allowed the appeal but the CS unanimously reversed this decision. Lord Penrose held that the principal company had failed to analyse its overheads in such a way as to identify those which were attributable to instalment credit business. He observed that 'the fair and reasonable allocation of overhead expenditure across the several activities of any commercial company would appear to be an essential element of financial control. To fail to institute and maintain a system for allocating general overheads in pricing products, or in accounting for distribution and sale, might in some circumstances call in question the management of the business'. The tribunal had failed to examine the overhead expenditure in sufficient detail, and had provided 'no explanation of the basis of its decision'. *HMRC v Royal Bank of Scotland Group plc (No 7)*, CS [2008] STC 3301; [2008] CSIH 49. (*Note.* For HMRC's practice pending the CS decision, see HMRC Brief 31/2007, issued on 30 March 2007.)

Sales of vehicles under hire-purchase agreements

[46.166] A company (V), which sold motor vehicles under hire-purchase agreements, had agreed a special partial exemption method for calculating its recoverable input tax. It attributed part of its residual input tax to its taxable supplies of goods, and part to its exempt supplies of finance, using a 'transaction count' method. HMRC issued an assessment on the basis that V had failed to comply with the guidelines in HMRC Brief 82/09, and that some of the input tax should have been treated as wholly attributable to exempt supplies. The tribunal allowed V's appeal, implicitly disapproving HMRC Brief 82/09. Judge Berner held that 'any method that has the effect of treating the overhead costs as solely cost components of a particular element, or elements, of the transactions, to the exclusion of another element, or other elements, cannot be fair and reasonable'. *Volkswagen Financial Services*

(UK) Ltd v HMRC, [2011] UKFTT 556 (TC), TC01401. (*Note.* HMRC have appealed to the Upper Tribunal against this decision.)

Investment trust—treatment of 'stock-lending' transactions

[46.167] An investment trust agreed a special partial exemption method in 1988. In 1997 it began to carry out 'stock-lending' transactions. Customs issued a ruling that the value of the exempt supplies should be treated as including the open market values of the stocks lent, as laid down by *Notice No 701/44*. The trust appealed, contending that the value of the relevant supplies was simply the amounts paid to it for the transactions in question. The tribunal accepted this contention and allowed the appeal, finding that 'the only trading benefit obtained by the appellants was their fee' and holding that it would 'be wholly artificial and unreal to attempt to attribute a consideration based upon the whole value of shares which were transferred for a temporary purpose'. *Scottish Eastern Investment Trust plc*, EDN/99/211 (VTD 16882).

Political party

[46.168] In 1978 the Commissioners and the Labour Party agreed a special formula for apportioning the Party's input tax. In 1998 the Party claimed a substantial repayment of input tax. Customs rejected the claim on the basis that the formula agreed in 1978 'related only to the apportionment of input tax as between business and non-business supplies and did not relate to the attribution of input tax as between taxable and exempt supplies'. The tribunal allowed the Party's appeal, finding that 'the agreed formula did not relate only to the apportionment as between business and non-business supplies but also related to the attribution of input tax as between taxable and exempt supplies'. *The Labour Party*, [2001] VATDR 39 (VTD 17034).

Charity

[46.169] In 2001 a charity agreed a special method of attributing its 'residual' input tax, specifically including tax on repairs to certain care homes which it operated. In 2003 the charity submitted a retrospective claim for 62.5% of such input tax to be treated as deductible. Customs rejected the claim on the basis that it did not accord with the special method which had been agreed in 2001. The tribunal dismissed the charity's appeal. *Sue Ryder Care*, LON/03/1035 (VTD 18826).

[46.170] See also *Hospitality Training Foundation*, **11.50** CHARITIES.

Whether special method invalidated by ECJ decision

[46.171] In 2002 a company (M) agreed a special partial exemption method with Customs. In 2009 it submitted a backdated repayment claim on the basis that the effect of the ECJ decision in *Nordania Finans A/S v Skatteministeriet*, **22.451** EUROPEAN COMMUNITY LAW, was that supplies arising from the disposal of leased goods should have been included in the calculation. The tribunal rejected this contention and dismissed the appeal, accepting HMRC's contentions that the Nordania decision concerned Danish legislation giving effect to *Article 19* of the *Sixth VAT Directive* (rather than *Article 17(5)*) and had no direct application to the UK, and that the special method continued until it was varied or replaced by agreement. Judge Avery Jones observed that if M wished to change its special method, it could serve a notice under *VAT Regulations, reg 102C. Mercedes-Benz Financial Services Ltd v HMRC*, [2010] UKFTT 332 (TC), TC00617.

Application of 'three-year cap' to special partial exemption method

[46.172] A group of companies, which was partly exempt, had agreed an 'interim' special method of attributing its input tax. In 2006 it submitted a repayment claim relating to input tax incurred from April 2001 to October 2002. Customs rejected the claim on the basis that it was outside the three-year time limit imposed by *VAT Regulations 1995 (SI 1995/2518), reg 29(1A)*. The representative member of the group appealed, contending that *reg 29(1A)* should not be treated as applying to 'partial exemption' cases. The tribunal rejected this contention and dismissed the appeal, observing that 'the wording of *regulation 29(1A)* is mandatory in terms', and that there was no indication 'that its operation does not extend to partial exemption'. *Morgan Stanley UK Group*, LON/06/549 (VTD 20424).

Attribution of input tax to foreign and specified supplies (VAT Regulations 1995, reg 103)

Japanese horse racing

[46.173] A Japanese corporation was established to promote Japanese horse racing. It established an office in the UK, and registered for UK VAT under what is now *VATA 1994, Sch 1 para 10*. It reclaimed the whole of the input tax incurred in respect of its London office, on the basis that it was attributable to supplies which would be taxable supplies if they were made in the UK. The Commissioners rejected the claim and issued a ruling that most of the tax had to be attributed to supplies of betting facilities which would have been exempt from UK VAT under what is now *VATA 1994, Sch 9, Group 4*. The tribunal allowed the corporation's appeal, finding that none of the supplies made by the UK office were attributable to betting activities, and holding that the return had been made in accordance with what is now *VAT Regulations 1995 (SI 1995/2518), reg 103. Japan Racing Association*, LON/93/1830A (VTD 11489).

Advertising services supplied to German company

[46.174] An educational institute (L) did not begin accepting students (thereby making exempt supplies of educational services) until 1995, but in 1993 it had entered into a sponsorship agreement with a German company (G), whereby G made substantial payments to L in return for advertising and publicity services. It was accepted that the effect of the *VAT (Place of Supply of Services) Order 1992 (SI 1992/3121), article 16* was that the place of supply of these services was in Germany. The Commissioners issued a ruling that these supplies were not to be treated as taxable supplies for the purposes of the partial exemption provisions, but should be apportioned in accordance with what is now *VAT Regulations 1995 (SI 1995/2518), reg 103*. L appealed, contending that, even though the supplies were deemed to be made outside the UK, they should be treated as taxable supplies in the denominator of the fraction prescribed by what is now *VAT Regulations 1995 (SI 1995/2518), reg 101(2)(d)* (so that it was able to reclaim all its input tax in 1993 and 1994, and a substantial proportion of its input tax in 1995). The HL unanimously rejected this contention and dismissed the company's appeal. Lord Slynn of Hadley observed that what is now *regulation 103* 'provides a separate code for determining the amount of input tax relevant to the making of out-of-country supplies'. Lord Scott of Foscote observed that the provisions of what is now *regulation 103* were authorised by *Article 17(5)(c)* of the EC *Sixth Directive*. *Liverpool Institute for Performing Arts (aka The Liverpool School of Performing Arts) v C & E Commrs*, HL [2001] STC 891; [2001] UKHL 28; [2001] 1 WLR 1187. (*Note.* For the Commissioners' practice following this decision, see Business Brief 12/01, issued on 11 September 2001.)

Audit fees covering issue of shares outside EU

[46.175] A company (E), which operated an airline business, made an initial public offering of shares. About 23.65% of the shares were issued to investors located outside the EU. E's auditors charged it £1,866,000, plus VAT of £326,577. E claimed that the whole of this VAT should be treated as residual input tax, and as recoverable under *VAT Regulations 1995 (SI 1995/2518), reg 101*. The Commissioners rejected the claim, holding that the tax should be apportioned under *regulation 103*. E appealed. The tribunal reviewed the evidence in detail and dismissed E's appeal in principle, holding that 'the correct approach is to treat the *regulation 103(2)* attribution method as an exclusive, self-contained code for the attribution of input tax falling within it'. The relevant input tax should be 'attributed to taxable supplies to the extent that the services were used for the purposes of making taxable supplies (ie the audit element) and to supplies treated as taxable supplies to the extent that the services were used for the purposes of the issue of shares to persons outside the EU. To the extent that the services were used for the purposes of supplying shares in the UK (exempt), and within the EU but outside the UK (outside the scope), the input tax is not recoverable.' *EasyJet plc*, [2003] VATDR 559 (VTD 18230). (*Note. Regulation 103(2)* has subsequently been replaced by *regulation 103B*: see *VAT (Amendment) (No 4) Regulations 2004 (SI 2004/3140)*. However, the change does not appear to affect the relevance of the decision in this case.)

Professional fees incurred by 'placing agent'

[46.176] A company (N) acted as a 'placing agent' in connection with a share issue by an Irish company. It reclaimed the whole of its related input tax. Customs only agreed to repay part of the tax, on the basis that it was partly attributable to exempt supplies. The tribunal upheld Customs' ruling and dismissed N's appeal, holding that Customs' apportionment was in accordance with *VAT Regulations 1995 (SI 1995/2518), reg 103*. *NDF Administration Ltd*, LON/01/319 (VTD 18301). (*Note.* The tribunal also held that the company was not entitled to any repayment supplement—see **48.91** PAYMENT OF TAX.)

Sale of securities outside EU

[46.177] A financial institution (N) sold securities outside the EU. In its partial exemption calculations, it included the value of such securities as if they were taxable supplies, and reclaimed input tax accordingly. The Commissioners issued assessments on the basis that the input tax on goods or services which were partly used in making 'specified supplies' (i.e. supplies outside the EU with a right to recover input tax) should have been calculated by estimating the percentage of employees engaged in dealings with securities, then applying that percentage to the amount of residual input tax, and then reducing that amount by a further percentage, calculated by reference to the values of 'specified supplies' in relation to the value of total supplies of dealing in securities. N appealed. The tribunal reviewed the evidence in detail and allowed N's appeal, holding that 'the attribution of inputs to different types of supply on the basis of actual use can, in some circumstances, be impossible or impractical in which case any other method will only approximate to actual use and has to be estimated or assumed. The method used must be fair and reasonable; should have the merit of simplicity; must be reasonable for the trader to operate (and) must not involve disproportionate or unreasonable resources'. The assessments were 'unsustainable', since 'it was not reasonable to expect that the residual input tax would be incurred by each of the appellant's locations in approximately the same proportion as staff numbers'. The tribunal held that 'this is a case where the attribution of inputs to different types of supply on the basis of actual use is impossible or impractical and we have to accept that any other method will only be approximate to actual use and has to be estimated or assumed. The values-based method is as good as any.' (The tribunal also held that the assessments had been made outside the statutory time limit.) *National Provident Institution*, [2005] VATDR 297 (VTD 18944). (*Note.* For HMRC's practice following this decision, see Business Brief 14/05, issued on 28 July 2005. They state that they 'decided not to appeal because the decision was made on the facts of the case' but 'consider that sales of securities will normally be distortive when they are included with other sorts of supply in a combined values-based calculation'. See now, however, the subsequent decision in *Lincoln Assurance Ltd*, **46.178** below.)

[46.178] A life assurance company (L) sold securities outside the EU. Customs issued a ruling that the values of the securities which L sold should not be included in the fraction used under its partial exemption method to determine the deductible proportion of its residual input tax. L appealed. The tribunal allowed the appeal. The tribunal observed that Customs considered that 'a values-based method did not reflect the use of the supplies made to the appellant because few, if any, of those supplies were consumed directly in making specified supplies'. The tribunal rejected Customs' contentions, observing that a 'values-based' method had 'the important merit of simplicity'. L's proposed method of attributing its residual inputs to 'specified supplies' was 'a rationally fair method that corresponds with the use of those inputs'. Accordingly, the tribunal concluded that 'the attribution of input tax to specified supplies under *regulation 103* may, in this case, be made by reference to the proportion which the value of specified supplies bore to the value of total supplies'. *Lincoln Assurance Ltd (No 2)*, LON/00/752 (VTD 20619).

Customs' powers to conclude agreement for attributing supplies

[46.179] A company (R) had agreed a special 'partial exemption' method with the Commissioners in 1999. It subsequently submitted claims for repayment of significant amounts of input tax, relating to 'out-of-country' supplies within *VAT Regulations 1995 (SI 1995/2518), reg 103*. The Commissioners rejected the claims on the grounds that the agreement which had been reached in 1999 covered the attribution of 'out-of-country' supplies as well as UK supplies, and that R's repayment claims did not accord with the agreement. R appealed, contending that the agreement should only be construed as relating to supplies within the UK, and should not be treated as relating to 'out-of-country' supplies. The tribunal held that 'out-of-country' supplies could not be dealt with under a partial exemption special method, but had to be dealt with in accordance with *reg 103*. However, the Commissioners were authorised by *VATA 1994, Sch 11 para 1* to conclude agreements as to the manner of attributing residual input tax on 'out-of-country' supplies. The Commissioners were, therefore, empowered to enter into a single agreement with R, 'dealing both with the residual input tax on out-of-country supplies and a PESM under *regulation 102*'. The 1999 letter had provided for a valid value-based method of attributing *regulation 103* supplies. (The appeal was adjourned for further argument.) *Royal & Sun Alliance plc*, MAN/03/109 (VTD 18842). (*Note.* There has been no further public hearing of the appeal.)

Life assurance company—supplies within reg 103

[46.180] In 2001 a life assurance company had agreed a special partial exemption method with Customs. In 2005 and 2006 it submitted large repayment claims, relating to 'out-of-country' supplies within *VAT Regulations 1995 (SI 1995/2518), reg 103*. Customs rejected the claims on the basis that they did not produce a 'fair and reasonable recovery'. The tribunal allowed the company's appeal in principle, finding that the claims were in accordance with the terms of the agreed special method and holding that the agreed method remained in force until it was formally terminated. The tribunal also observed that Customs were 'entitled to verify the claims not only arithmetically but individually' and allowed Customs 'a period of six months from the publication of this decision to identify any areas of dispute'. *Standard Life Assurance Co*, [2007] VATDR 356 (VTD 20355).

Customs' power to terminate agreement for attributing supplies

[46.181] A bank (M), which was partly exempt, had agreed a special method of attributing its residual input tax under *regulation 102*, and had also reached an agreement under *regulation 103* for attributing residual input tax on 'out-of-country' supplies. M assigned some of its receivables to a Jersey trustee. In June 2003 Customs terminated the agreements under *regulations 102* and *103*, on the grounds that they gave an unfair result because they wrongly excluded the value of exempt supplies to M's 'securitised cardholders' from the denominator of the 'partial exemption' fraction. However, M initially continued to submit its returns in accordance with the previously agreed methods, and also submitted a claim for repayment of more than £8,000,000 in input tax, backdated to April 2000. Customs rejected the claim, and subsequently issued assessments covering the periods from July 2003 to December 2004. The tribunal dismissed M's appeal, observing that M's taxable supplies were less than 0.01% of its total supplies, but it had claimed a recovery rate of 24% of its input tax. Accordingly, 'the agreed method did not produce a fair and reasonable attribution', and Customs had been entitled to withdraw it. The tribunal also upheld the assessments in principle. M appealed to the Ch D, which reviewed the evidence in detail and allowed M's appeal in part, holding that Customs had been entitled to terminate the agreed special method, but that the assessments were excessive and that Customs and the tribunal had treated certain transactions (relating to the servicing of designated customers' accounts) incorrectly. Briggs J held that there was 'no reason why, in circumstances where a single business activity constitutes a supply of a service to two different persons who each pay separately for what they receive, the inputs incurred in carrying out the single activity should be wholly attributable to the supply to one of them. The fact that the supply to one consists of the performance of a promise to go on making a continuing supply to the other may be relevant to the fair and reasonable apportionment of the inputs as between each supply, but it does not justify the *a priori* conclusion that no part of the inputs can be attributed to the supply to the promisee.' *MBNA Europe Bank Ltd v HMRC*, Ch D [2006] STC 2089; [2006] EWHC 2326 (Ch).

Attribution of input tax on self-supplies (VAT Regulations 1995, reg 104)

Building society—self-supplies of stationery

[46.182] A building society, which was partly exempt, had operated a special method on the lines agreed by the Building Societies Association and laid down in *Notice No 700/57/95*. It sought to modify the method and proposed that inputs should be attributed to taxable supplies on the basis of the time spent by its staff in connection with the making of taxable supplies, including time spent by its printing staff in producing stationery. The Commissioners refused to accept that time spent by the printing staff ought to be included, and the society appealed. The tribunal rejected the society's claim, holding that the effect of *VAT Regulations 1995, reg 104* was that the Commissioners were 'acting properly in refusing to allow a method which treats the input tax on self-supplies of stationery, however calculated, as attributable to taxable supplies'. *Leeds & Holbeck Building Society*, MAN/96/670 (VTD 15356). (*Note*. The appeal also concerned the validity of *VATA 1994, s 80(4)*, in respect of which the appeal was adjourned pending the hearing of the substantive appeal in *Marks & Spencer plc*, 22.55 EUROPEAN COMMUNITY LAW. There was no further public hearing of the appeal.)

Treatment of input tax attributable to exempt supplies as being attributable to taxable supplies (VAT Regulations 1995, reg 106)

Interpretation of de minimis limits

[46.183] A partnership, which was partly exempt, used a special direct attribution method. Its annual adjustment period for this purpose ended on 30 April 1987. New partial exemption regulations were introduced with effect from 1 April 1987, but the partnership contended that the old *de minimis* rules should be treated as applying to it for the whole of the period to 30 April 1987. The Commissioners issued a ruling that the old rules could only be applied in considering the period up to 31 March 1987, and that the new method laid down by *SI 1987/510* should be applied to the partnership's input tax for April 1987. The tribunal upheld the Commissioners' ruling and dismissed the partnership's appeal, holding that there was 'nothing in either *FA 1987* or *SI 1987/510* that expressly or by necessary implication extends the life of the old *de minimis* rules' beyond 31 March 1987. *BC & ME Risby*, LON/90/1300Y (VTD 6544). (*Note.* The regulations introduced by *SI 1987 No 510* were themselves subsequently substituted by *SI 1992/645*. The *de minimis* rules are now contained in *VAT Regulations 1995 (SI 1995/2518), reg 106*.)

[46.184] A partnership became liable to register for VAT from October 1986, but did not actually do so until October 1988. Its first VAT return covered the 31 months from October 1986 to April 1989. Until October 1988, all its activities related to taxable supplies, but from October 1988 it began work on converting a barn, the disposal of which would be an exempt supply. The partnership reclaimed input tax of £2,030 attributable to the work on the barn, but the Commissioners refused to repay the tax, considering that it was not recoverable since it related to an exempt supply. The partnership appealed, contending that, since the tax in question was less than £3,000, it was within the *de minimis* limit of £100 per month prescribed by the *VAT (General) Regulations* as then in force. (The Commissioners considered that the tax in question could only be averaged over the twelve months ending on 30 April 1989, and therefore exceeded the *de minimis* limit.) The tribunal accepted the partnership's contention and allowed the appeal. By issuing the partnership with a return covering the period from October 1986 to April 1989, the Commissioners had established the whole of that period as the 'prescribed accounting period' for the purposes of what is now *VAT Regulations 1995 (SI 1995/2518), reg 99(1)(b)*. *JR Williams & RJS Wallis*, LON/91/300Z (VTD 7286). (*Note.* This case was distinguished in the subsequent cases of *Eltham Park Insurance Brokers Ltd*, **46.189** below, and *Dr Dunn & Others*, **46.191** below.)

[46.185] A company reclaimed input tax of £797 in its return for the period ending 31 March 1990, although the invoice was dated July 1989. The input tax related to an exempt supply, and the Commissioners issued an assessment to recover the tax, since the company's total input tax for the period ending 30 September 1989 (when the invoice was issued) exceeded the *de minimis* limits. The company appealed, contending that the input tax should be allowed since its input tax for the period ending 31 March 1990 did not exceed the *de minimis* limits. The tribunal dismissed the appeal, holding that the reference to an accounting period in what is now *VAT Regulations 1995 (SI 1995/2518), reg 106* was 'to the period in which the supply to which the tax relates was made, rather than to the period in which it was claimed'. *Trevor Toys Ltd*, LON/91/1760Y (VTD 7805).

[46.186] The decision in *Trevor Toys Ltd*, **46.185** above, was applied in the similar subsequent case of *Dayrich Bookmakers*, MAN/96/153 (VTD 15492).

[46.187] A company which operated a swimming pool made both taxable and exempt supplies. The input tax attributable to its exempt supplies was usually within the *de minimis* limits, with the result that it was able to reclaim the whole of its input tax. However, in 1991 it had to replace the sand filters at the pool. Because of this expenditure, its input tax for that year was much greater than usual, and the input tax attributable to exempt supplies exceeded the *de minimis* limits for the first time. The Commissioners restricted the deductible input tax accordingly, and the company appealed, contending that, since the sand filters were capital expenditure which had to be paid for out of reserves rather than out of current profits, the input tax relating to them should be spread over a five-year period. The tribunal rejected this contention and dismissed the appeal, holding that there was nothing in the *VAT Regulations* which permitted input tax to be spread in this way. *Chester Swimming Association*, MAN/91/900 (VTD 10969).

[46.188] A company reclaimed the whole of its input tax for a three-month period, although its exempt input tax for that period was more than the *de minimis* limit laid down by what is now *VAT Regulations 1995 (SI 1995/2518), reg 106*. The Commissioners issued an assessment to recover the tax and the company appealed, contending that its input tax for the quarterly period in question should be aggregated with the previous quarter, since the effect of aggregating the two quarters was to bring the exempt input tax below the *de minimis* limit. The tribunal dismissed the appeal, holding that the exempt input tax could not be averaged in this way, and that the reference in *regulation 106(1)** to 'any longer period' was to a period ending on 31 March, as laid down by *regulation 99**. *Polo Farm Sports Club*, LON/93/909A & LON/93/1225P (VTD 11386). (*Note.* An appeal against a misdeclaration penalty was, however, allowed.)

[46.189] A similar decision was reached in a subsequent case in which the tribunal found that a partly exempt company which had registered retrospectively had wrongly informed the Newry VAT office that its exempt input tax was more than 50% of its total input tax, although this was not in fact the case. The tribunal held that the company was not entitled to adopt a non-standard tax year (for the purpose of manipulating the transitional *de minimis* limits) without the approval of the Commissioners. *Eltham Park Insurance Brokers Ltd*, LON/96/108 (VTD 14306).

[46.190] A company, which made both exempt and taxable supplies, registered for VAT with effect from 1992. For the period ending 31 May 1993, its exempt input tax was within the *de minimis* limits, so that it was able to reclaim all its input tax. However, for the two years ending 31 May 1995 its exempt input tax exceeded the *de minimis* limits. Nevertheless, it reclaimed the whole of its input tax for those years, and the Commissioners issued an assessment to recover the tax attributable to exempt supplies. The company appealed, contending that, for the purposes of what is now *VAT Regulations 1995, reg 99(1)(d)*, the 34 months from 1 August 1992 to 31 May 1995 should be treated as the company's 'tax year' (thus bringing the exempt input tax within the *de minimis* limit). The tribunal rejected this contention and dismissed the appeal, holding that the effect of *VAT Regulations 1995, reg 99(1)(d)* was that the Commissioners had a discretion whether or not to extend the period to be treated as the 'tax year', and that their refusal to exercise this discretion in this case was not unreasonable. *Yorkhurst Ltd*, MAN/95/2757 (VTD 14458).

[46.191] A medical partnership registered for VAT from 1 January 1994. Its first accounting period ended on 28 February 1994, but its accounting dates were then amended, at its request, so that its second accounting period ended on 30 June 1994. Following a control visit, the Commissioners issued an assessment on the basis that the partnership had overclaimed input tax for the year ending 31 March 1995, by reclaiming input tax which was attributable to exempt supplies and failing to observe the *de minimis* limits. The partnership appealed, contending that because of its change of accounting dates, its first 'tax year' for the purposes of what is now *VAT Regulations 1995, reg 99(1)(d)* was the year beginning on 1 April 1995. The tribunal rejected this contention and dismissed the appeal. On a proper interpretation of what is now *VAT Regulations 1995, reg 99(1)(d)*, the partnership's first 'tax year' was the year beginning on 1 April 1994. Their total exempt input tax for that year exceeded the *de minimis* limits. *Dr Dunn & Others*, LON/96/620 (VTD 14788).

[46.192] A family farming partnership had some exempt income from properties which it rented. In March 2000 one of its partners (E) incurred certain expenditure on its behalf by credit card, relating to exempt supplies. The partnership did not reimburse E until after 31 March 2000. In its return for the period ended 31 March 2000, it treated all its input tax as relating to taxable supplies, on the basis that its input tax directly attributable to exempt supplies for the year ending 31 March 2000 was £7464 (omitting the tax relating to the expenditure for which it had delayed reimbursing E), and was thus below the *de minimis* limit of £7500 in *VAT Regulations 1995, reg 106*. The Commissioners issued an assessment on the basis that the input tax relating to the expenditure which E had incurred should have been included in the calculation, so that the tax attributable to exempt supplies exceeded the *de minimis* limit of *reg 106*, and some of it was not recoverable. The partnership appealed, contending that the expenditure which E had incurred in March 2000 should be treated as relating to the following tax year, being the year in which it was reimbursed, rather than the year in which it was incurred. The tribunal rejected this contention and dismissed the partnership's appeal, holding that the credit card purchases made by E were payments made by the partnership in its partial exemption year to 31 March 2000. Accordingly, the partnership's exempt input tax exceeded the *de minimis* limits, and it was required to operate the partial exemption provisions. *The Little Bradley Farm Partnership*, LON/02/773 (VTD 18420).

[46.193] See also *Camden Motors (Holdings) Ltd*, 46.202 below.

Adjustments of attributions (VAT Regulations 1995, regs 107–110)

Whether Regulation 107 applicable

Short-term lease of premises purchased for taxable purposes

[46.194] A company carried on a business of providing management and marketing services. In July 1991 it purchased a freehold property, and reclaimed input tax on the purchase and refurbishment of the property. In August 1992 it granted a two-year lease of part of the premises. In January 1993 it elected to waive exemption in respect of the lease. The Commissioners formed the opinion that some of the input tax which the company had reclaimed should be attributed to the exempt supplies which it had made between August 1992 and December 1992, and issued an assessment for the period ending November 1992 to recover part of the tax (£4,120). The company appealed, contending firstly that, at the time of purchase, it had intended to use the whole of the property for the purpose of its taxable business activities, but had subsequently been obliged to lease part of the property because it had been unable to dispose of its previous premises; and also contending that the £4,120 input tax which the Commissioners had sought to recover was within the *de minimis* limits of what is now *VAT Regulations 1995, reg 106*. The tribunal accepted these contentions and allowed the appeal, holding that the initial reclaim of input tax had been in accordance with the decision in *Briararch Ltd*, 46.212 below. The effect of what is now *VAT Regulations 1995, reg 107* was that the initial attribution did not fall to be adjusted until the end of the company's tax year in May 1993, and *reg 108(2)* did not require the attribution to be adjusted in the November 1992 return. With regard to the period ending May 1993, the *de minimis* limits of what is now *VAT Regulations 1995, reg 106* applied, so that, again, no adjustment was required. (The tribunal also held that *VATA 1994, Sch 10 para 3(9)** did not empower the Commissioners to require a retrospective amendment to the November 1992 return as a condition of accepting the election to waive exemption.) *The Island Trading Co Ltd*, [1996] VATDR 245 (VTD 13838).

Initial taxable supplies followed by exempt supplies—effect of reg 107

[46.195] A company registered for VAT in 1996, with the object of building and selling nurseries. It began building a nursery in early 1997, with the intention of selling it. Since the sale of the nursery would be a taxable supply, the company reclaimed the relevant input tax. However, it found that it was unable to sell the nursery, and in November 1997 it began to operate the nursery itself. It continued to reclaim input tax on construction work. When the Commissioners discovered this, they issued an assessment to recover input tax which the company had reclaimed from September 1997 to August 1998, on the basis that, in operating the nursery, the company was making exempt supplies, and the input tax was attributable to these exempt supplies. The tribunal dismissed the company's appeal, holding that the assessment was in accordance with the provisions of *VAT Regulations 1995, reg 107*. *Kiddicare Ltd*, MAN/00/480 (VTD 17349).

Adjustment under reg 107—effect of regulation 99

[46.196] A company's accounting periods ended in February. May, August and November. It made no taxable supplies during the twelve months ending in May 1999, but reclaimed input tax for that year. The Commissioners issued an assessment to recover the tax, and the company appealed, contending that the tax should be attributed to taxable supplies which it had made in May 2000. The tribunal rejected this contention and dismissed the appeal, observing that the effect of *VAT Regulations 1995, reg 107* and *reg 99(1)(d)* was that 'a trader such as the appellant in this case, making occasional rather than frequent taxable supplies as well as exempt supplies, may determine whether he is entitled to credit for the input tax he incurs on a year-by-year rather than quarter-by-quarter basis, but those years must be tax years rather than any 12-month period he chooses'. The effect of *reg 99(1)(d)* was that the company's 'tax year' ran from 1 June to 31 May, so that the input tax for the year ending May 1999 could not be attributed to taxable supplies for the year ending May 2000. *CEB Ltd*, MAN/00/273 (VTD 17054).

Request to adjust attribution of input tax retrospectively

[46.197] A company with political objectives derived some income from non-business activities, including donations. It was partly exempt, and operated a special method of attributing its input tax. In its returns for 1994 and 1995, it treated some of its subscription income as outside the scope of VAT, and failed to reclaim the relevant input tax. In 1998 it submitted two 'voluntary disclosures' seeking to correct its annual adjustments for 1994 and 1995 in order to reclaim the tax. The Commissioners rejected the claim on the basis that such errors could only be corrected through the special procedures laid down by *VAT Regulations 1995 (SI 1995/2518), regs 34* and *35*. The company appealed. The tribunal dismissed the appeal, holding that 'we cannot accept that *regulation 107* applies to the present situation. Our principal reason is that *regulation 107* is concerned exclusively with annual adjustments of attributions of input tax to taxable supplies.' The tribunal held that *reg 107* 'has no bearing on the antecedent question of whether the tax incurred by the taxable person is or is not input tax'. That was covered by *VATA 1994, s 24(5)* and by the agreed method designed to determine what 'tax incurred' was referable to a person's business. Furthermore, 'neither the special method nor *regulation 107* makes any reference to error correction either through the annual adjustment or at all'. By contrast, *regs 34* and *35* provided 'a specific mechanism for correcting errors'. The tribunal held that 'the presence of such specific mandatory provisions for correcting errors' removed 'any necessity for incorporation of error correction into the special method of a taxable person'. *Greenpeace Ltd*, LON/99/532 (VTD 16681).

VAT Regulations 1995, reg 107(1)(c)—failure to make annual adjustment

[46.198] An appeal was dismissed in a case where the tribunal found that a college, which was partly exempt, had failed to make the annual adjustment required by *VAT Regulations 1995, reg 107(1)(c)*. (The tribunal also found that the Commissioners and the college had agreed that its 'tax year', as defined in *reg 99(1)(d)*, should begin on 1 August, in order to coincide with the academic year.) *Ruskin College*, LON/99/443 (VTD 16726).

[46.199] See also *Tse*, 3.97 ASSESSMENT.

Management services supplied to unregistered company

[46.200] See *Svenska International plc*, 43.20 MANAGEMENT SERVICES.

Whether Regulation 107B applicable

[46.201] A bowling club received taxable income from catering and sales of drinks, and was therefore partly exempt. It decided to construct an indoor bowling rink as an annexe to its existing clubhouse. It reclaimed part of the input tax on the construction, using the standard 'partial exemption' method for attributing its input tax. Customs issued an assessment to recover much of the tax, applying a 'standard method override' under *VAT Regulations 1995 (SI 1995/2518), reg 107B*. The club appealed. The tribunal reviewed the evidence in detail and allowed the club's appeal, finding that 'the difference in the level of input tax recoverable using the standard method as compared to the standard method override' was £35,438 (rather than £59,187 as in Customs' assessment). Since the difference was less than the £50,000 limit laid down by *reg 107C*, it followed that *reg 107B* did not apply. The tribunal also observed that 'the reason for the introduction of the override was the targeting of aggressive tax avoidance. It was conceded that this description did not apply to the appellant's activities. They were a bowling club attempting to provide social and leisure facilities in a somewhat deprived area of Dunfermline and were run on a substantially voluntary basis by dedicated office bearers in a wholly commendable enterprise'. *Abbeyview Bowling Club*, EDN/07/69 (VTD 20661).

[46.202] A company (C) which sold cars also obtained commission relating to financial products, and was therefore partly exempt. It operated the standard method of attributing its input tax. Customs issued an assessment to recover some of the tax, applying a 'standard method override' under *VAT Regulations 1995 (SI 1995/2518), reg 107B*. C appealed, contending that it satisfied the *de minimis* limits of *reg 106*, and accordingly the 'standard method override' could not be applied. The tribunal accepted this contention and allowed the appeal, holding that the standard method gave 'a fair result', and there was no justification for applying a 'standard method override'. *Camden Motors (Holdings) Ltd*, [2008] VATDR 245 (VTD 20674). (*Note.* This decision was disapproved by Judge Tildesley in the subsequent case of *HJ Banks & Co Ltd v HMRC*, 46.203 below. He held that the chairman's decision showed 'a misunderstanding of the various stages in the process which formed the trigger for the application of *regulation 107B*' and had 'missed out the step of examining the *de minimis* limits with reference to *regulation 107B* and jumped to the attribution under *regulation 107(1)(a)*'.)

[46.203] A company, which used the standard partial exemption method for attributing its input tax, reclaimed input tax on the purchase of some land and two commercial buildings. It sold both the commercial buildings, one of the sales being taxable and the other being exempt. It constructed nine flats on the remaining land. It reclaimed the whole of the input tax on the purchase. HMRC formed the opinion that the company's attribution of input tax did not fairly reflect the use to which the land and buildings were put, and issued an assessment on the basis that a 'standard method override' under *VAT Regulations 1995 (SI 1995/2518), reg 107B* should be applied. The company appealed. The tribunal reviewed the evidence in detail and dismissed the appeal. Judge Tildesley held that 'potential adjustments to the attribution of input tax must be carried out before the de minimis limit is applied so as to ensure a fair and reasonable attribution of input tax to taxable supplies. The statutory method override affects the attribution of input tax to taxable supplies.' He specifically disapproved the earlier decision in *Camden Motors (Holdings) Ltd*, **46.202** above, holding that the decision in that case showed 'a misunderstanding of the various stages in the process which formed the trigger for the application of *regulation 107B*'. On the evidence here, 'the site area apportionment gave a representative measure of the extent to which the land was used for taxable supplies'. *HJ Banks & Co Ltd v HMRC*, [2010] UKFTT 33 (TC), TC00347.

[46.204] See also *The Funding Corporation Ltd*, **2.481** APPEALS; *Turbine Motor Works Ltd*, **9.6** CAPITAL GOODS SCHEME, and *St Helens School Northwood Ltd*, **46.140** above.

Whether Regulation 108 applicable

Flats advertised as holiday accommodation but subsequently leased

[46.205] A company (C) converted a large house at Richmond-on-Thames into ten self-contained furnished flats. It advertised these flats as holiday accommodation for people visiting London. Some of the flats were thus occupied between December 1988 (when the conversion was completed) and February 1989. In February 1989 C received an offer from a US company to enter into a lease of the whole building so that the flats could be used to house the US company's employees. C reclaimed the whole of the input tax incurred on the conversion. The Commissioners issued an assessment to recover part of the tax, considering that it related to the supply of a lease which was exempt from VAT. C appealed, contending that the whole of the conversion work had been undertaken for the purpose of providing holiday accommodation, which was a taxable supply. The tribunal rejected C's contentions, holding that each floor of the building had to be considered separately, and that the input tax should be apportioned between that charged on supplies used for the making of taxable supplies of holiday accommodation, and that charged on supplies used for the supply of the tenancy to the US company. The QB upheld this decision. There was 'no causative nexus between the publication of the advertisement of holiday flats and the letting of the whole building for some quite different purpose'. The company had made a supply which was not a supply of holiday accommodation and thus not excluded from exemption. Furthermore, the relevant provisions of the *VAT Regulations* were in accordance with *Article 17* of the *EC Sixth Directive*, which permitted the amount of input tax provisionally treated as deductible to be subject to a subsequent adjustment on the basis of actual use. *Cooper & Chapman (Builders) Ltd v C & E Commrs*, QB 1992, [1993] STC 1.

Exempt sale of land six months after purchase

[46.206] A company purchased some land in January 1990. The vendor had elected to waive exemption, so that the purchase price included VAT of £105,000, which the company reclaimed as input tax. Six months later the company sold the land without electing to waive exemption. The Commissioners issued an assessment for the period ending 31 January 1990 to recover the input tax, on the basis that it was attributable to an exempt supply. The company appealed, contending that when it had purchased the land, it had intended to build a warehouse and use the land for taxable supplies, but it had subsequently decided that it could not afford the cost of construction. The Commissioners thereupon withdrew the assessment and issued an assessment for the same amount for the period ending 31 July 1990, on the basis that the effect of what is now *VAT Regulations 1995 (SI 1995/2518), reg 108* was that the company should have adjusted its claim to input tax when it submitted its return for the period in which the sale was made. The tribunal upheld this assessment and dismissed the company's appeal. *Franco F'Lli Ltd*, LON/91/242X (VTD 13153).

[46.207] Similar decisions were reached in the Isle of Man cases of *Old Chelsea Properties Ltd v Isle of Man Treasury*, MAN/96/850; *Villiers Group plc v Isle of Man Treasury*, MAN/96/851 (VTD 15230).

[46.208] A company purchased a plot of land in 1998. It reclaimed input tax on professional fees relating to plans for building houses on the land. However, it subsequently sold the land without developing it. The Commissioners issued an assessment on the basis that the input tax had to be attributed to the exempt sale of the land, in accordance with *VAT Regulations 1995 (SI 1995/2518), reg 108*. The company appealed, contending that its sale of the land was the transfer of a going concern, rather than an exempt supply. The tribunal rejected this contention and dismissed the appeal, observing that 'the land was not being actively developed when it was sold'. Accordingly, the sale of the land was an exempt supply, rather than the transfer of a going concern, and the company was obliged to adjust its input tax under *reg 108*. *Golden Oak Partnership*, **36.555** INPUT TAX, was distinguished, on the grounds that the partnership in that case had 'carried out substantial infrastructural works' and the land there 'was in the course of active development' when it was sold. *Gulf Trading & Management Ltd*, LON/99/842 (VTD 16847).

[46.209] A company purchased some land with the intention of developing it. The vendor had elected to waive exemption, so that the purchase price included VAT, which the company reclaimed as input tax. Subsequently it received an offer from a housing association, and agreed to sell the land to the association under a contract whereby it agreed to construct a number of flats on the land. The Commissioners issued an assessment on the basis that the whole of the input tax which the company had reclaimed should be attributed to the exempt sale of the land, in accordance with *VAT Regulations 1995 (SI 1995/2518), reg 108*. The company appealed, contending that, because it had agreed to make zero-rated supplies of construction services to the housing association, only part of the input tax was attributable to the exempt sale of the land, and part was attributable to the zero-rated supplies of construction services. The tribunal accepted this contention and allowed the appeal, and the Ch D upheld this decision. Lightman J held that the tribunal was entitled to conclude that the company had used the site to make taxable supplies of building services as well as the exempt resale of the land. *C & E Commrs v Wiggett Construction Ltd*, Ch D [2001] STC 933. (*Note.* Compare the subsequent CA decision in *Southern Primary Housing Ltd*, 46.26 above.)

Exempt supply of redeveloped property—whether reg 108 applicable

[46.210] In 1995 a company (T) purchased a property with the intention of redeveloping it as residential accommodation. It obtained the necessary planning permission, and reclaimed input tax on services supplied by planning consultants, engineers, surveyors, etc. relating to the proposed redevelopment. However, it was unable to raise the necessary finance to proceed with the redevelopment, and in May 1996 it made an exempt supply of the site (with the benefit of the planning permission) to a Jersey company. The Commissioners issued an assessment to recover the input tax which T had reclaimed. The tribunal dismissed T's appeal, holding that the effect of *VAT Regulations 1995 (SI 1995/2518), reg 108* was that the input tax had to be attributed to the exempt supply which T had actually made, rather than to the taxable supply which it had originally intended to make. The provisions of *regulation 108* were consistent with *Article 20(1)* of the *EC Sixth Directive*. The wording of *Article 20(1)* was wide enough 'to include a change of intention which results in a change of the VAT status of a transaction from taxable to exempt'. The QB upheld this decision. Carnwath J observed that there had been a change in 'the factors used to determine the amount to be deducted', within *Article 20(1)(b)*. The tribunal had been entitled to find that there had been a sufficient direct and immediate link between the supplies which T received and the supply which it made for the input tax to be reattributed from the intended taxable supply to the actual exempt supply. *Tremerton Ltd v C & E Commrs*, QB [1999] STC 1039.

'Intending trader' subsequently making exempt supplies

[46.211] A company registered for VAT in 1996, stating that it intended to supply counselling services. It failed to attract any clients, and in 1997 it began letting rooms at its premises. The Commissioners issued an assessment to recover input tax which the company had reclaimed from 1996 to 1999. The tribunal reviewed the evidence in detail and upheld the assessment in principle (subject to agreement as to figures), holding that, from 1996 to October 1997, the company 'was entitled to be registered as an intending trader' but that from November 1997 this was no longer the case. Accordingly *VAT Regulations 1995 (SI 1995/2518), reg 108* applied and the company was obliged to repay the input tax. *Infinite Mind Ltd*, LON/99/1349 (VTD 16980).

Whether Regulation 109 applicable

Grant of short tenancy pending sale of major interest in building

[46.212] A company (B) restored a listed building with the intention of selling a leasehold interest in it. However, it was unable to find a lessee who would accept a long lease, and therefore granted a four-year tenancy to provide it with temporary rental income. It reclaimed the whole of the input tax incurred on the restoration. The Commissioners issued an assessment to recover the tax, considering that it should be wholly attributed to the four-year tenancy, which was an exempt supply. B appealed, contending that it remained its intention to sell a long lease, which would be a taxable supply, and that the input tax should therefore be apportioned between the exempt supply and the future taxable supply. The tribunal allowed B's appeal, holding that, since the Commissioners had accepted B's evidence that it intended to make a taxable supply of a 25-year lease in the building, it followed that $^{25}/_{29}$ of the input tax which B had incurred related to this future taxable supply and was therefore deductible. The QB upheld the tribunal decision. The regulations envisaged that input tax should be apportioned in such cases, and such an apportionment was in accordance with *Article 20* of the *EC Sixth Directive*. *C & E Commrs v Briararch Ltd*, QB [1992] STC 732. (*Notes.* (1) The case was heard in the QB with *Curtis Henderson Ltd*, **46.213** below. (2) For Customs' practice following this decision, see Business Brief 15/92, issued on 5 October 1992. For their current practice, see VAT Information Sheet 07/08, issued on 15 September 2008.)

[46.213] A development company built a house with the intention of selling it, and reclaimed the input tax incurred on its construction. The house was completed in April 1989. The company was unable to sell the house, and in August 1990 the house was let on a short lease. The tenant remained in occupation for nine months, and the house was subsequently sold in September 1990. When the Commissioners became aware of the letting of the house, they issued an assessment to recover the input tax that had been repaid to the company. The company appealed, contending that it was entitled to credit for the input tax. The tribunal allowed the appeal in part, holding that the tax should be apportioned, applying *Briararch Ltd*, **46.212** above, and distinguishing *Rentorn Ltd*, **46.14** above. The QB upheld the tribunal decision. The regulations envisaged that input tax should be apportioned in such cases, and such an apportionment was in accordance with *Article 20* of the *EC Sixth Directive*. *C & E Commrs v Curtis Henderson Ltd*, QB [1992] STC 732. (*Notes.* (1) The case was heard in the QB with *Briararch Ltd*, **46.212** above. (2) For Customs' practice following this decision, see Business Brief 15/92, issued on 5 October 1992. For their current practice, see VAT Information Sheet 07/08, issued on 15 September 2008.)

Transfer of freehold of airport—receipt of rental income

[46.214] In October 1988 a company (F) acquired the freehold of Eastleigh Airport, which had previously been owned by a Jersey company. Both before and after the acquisition, the airport was leased to the British Airports Authority. In March 1989, F sold a 50% interest in the airport to another company (R) for £30 million. F and R applied for planning permission to develop the airport as a 'business park'. F reclaimed the input tax on fees which it had incurred in respect of its acquisition of the airport. The Commissioners issued an assessment to recover the tax, since the rental income which F received in respect of the airport was exempt from VAT. F appealed, contending that it intended to make taxable supplies in the future, and that the input tax should be apportioned to take account of this. The tribunal held that the input tax should be apportioned, applying *Briararch Ltd*, 46.212 above, and *Curtis Henderson Ltd*, 46.213 above. In making the apportionment, residual input tax which could not be directly apportioned to either exempt or taxable supplies should be apportioned on the basis that the proposed 'business park' development had a value of £35 million and that the rest of the airport had a value of £15 million. *Findhelp Ltd*, [1991] VATTR 341 (VTD 6431, VTD 7015).

University buildings—adjustment of attribution

[46.215] A university constructed two buildings. It began to use the buildings, in making exempt supplies of educational services, in October 1990. In April 1992, on the advice of its accountants, it leased the buildings to an associated company for a 20-year period, and elected to waive exemption. In its return for the period ending 31 July 1992, it reclaimed 93% of the input tax on the construction of the buildings. The Commissioners issued an assessment to recover part of the tax, considering that since 51% of the university's income for the year ending July 1990 had been standard-rated, only 51% of the input tax was allowable. The university appealed, contending that 93% of the input tax on the first building (and 97% of the tax on the second building) should be treated as deductible since, on a time-apportionment basis, the buildings had been used for exempt supplies for no more than 18 months and were to be used for taxable supplies for at least 20 years. The QB rejected this contention and upheld the assessment. Carnwath J held that the effect of the company's contentions would be that adjustments to recoverable input tax could be made without any time limit as long as a building existed. Such a result would lead to an unacceptable degree of uncertainty, and was contrary to the spirit of the *EC Sixth Directive*, which contemplated a capital goods adjustment period of not more than ten years. The provisions of the *VAT Regulations* permitted specific adjustments for a period of up to six years, and were in accordance with *Article 20* of the *EC Sixth Directive*, which permitted Member States to lay down procedures as to the input tax to be allowed. *C & E Commrs v University of Wales College Cardiff*, QB [1995] STC 611.

Option to tax property—subsequent claim under VAT reg 109

[46.216] A group of insurance companies held the leasehold of a number of properties. The group had originally used the properties for the purposes of its insurance business, but subsequently vacated them, and decided to sublet them. In 1995 it opted to tax the properties. It subsequently claimed a repayment of input tax incurred on rents and service charges relating to the properties prior to the election, while they were vacant, although it had initially attributed this input tax to exempt supplies. The Commissioners rejected the claim and the representative member of the group (RSA) appealed, contending that it was entitled to make an adjustment under *VAT Regulations 1995 (SI 1995/2518), reg 109*. The tribunal rejected this contention and dismissed the appeal, finding that the input tax in dispute related to a period when R was actively seeking to sublet the properties, and holding that any such supplies would be exempt, because R had not elected to waive exemption at the relevant time. The Ch D reversed the tribunal decision but the HL restored it (by a 3-2 majority, Lord Woolf and Lord Clyde dissenting). Lord Hoffmann observed that in order to come within *regulation 109*, 'RSA must have first had an intention to use the inputs in supplying exempt sub-leases and then used them, or formed an intention to use them, in supplying taxable sub-leases'. On the evidence, RSA 'was not carrying on an economic activity for the purpose of making taxable outputs'. Applying the principles in *Belgium v Ghent Coal Terminal NV*, 22.406 EUROPEAN COMMUNITY LAW, 'just as a failure to make taxable supplies does not destroy a right of deduction, so a failure to make exempt supplies does not create one'. RSA were in the same position as someone 'who decided to change from an activity which involved making exempt supplies to a different activity making taxable supplies. If there are still inputs around from the previous activity which can be used in the new taxable activity, like a building which has been constructed for exempt letting and is then used, after an election, for taxable letting, the taxpayer will be entitled to an adjustment', but 'he cannot rewrite history'. Lord Walker of Gestingthorpe observed that 'it is an inescapable consequence of the general structure of VAT that a trader who makes partially exempt and partially taxable supplies (or who switches from exempt to taxable supplies) cannot expect precisely the same treatment as one who makes taxable supplies throughout. That would be pressing the principle of fiscal neutrality too far.' *C & E Commrs v Royal & Sun Alliance Insurance Group plc*, HL [2003] STC 832; UKHL 29; [2003] 1 WLR 1387; [2003] 2 All ER 1073. (*Note*. For the Commissioners' practice following this decision, see Business Brief 14/2004, issued on 17 May 2004.)

[46.217] In 1988 a charity (W), which undertook medical research, purchased a building, which it opted to tax. Initially it did not reclaim any input tax on the purchase. In 1999 it began demolishing the building, and in 2001 it began constructing a new building on the site. In 2003 W submitted a claim under *VAT Regulations 1995 (SI 1995/2518), reg 109* for repayment of some of the input tax on the purchase. Customs rejected the claim on the grounds that W had originally acquired the building for non-business purposes, and that the claim had been made outside the statutory three-year time limit. W appealed. The tribunal reviewed the evidence in detail and allowed the appeal in part, holding that W was entitled to reclaim input tax under *reg 109* to the extent to which there had been a change of intended use of the land within three years of the claim. The tribunal found that W had originally purchased the building 'to meet its own needs for more office space, and therefore the use would be a mixture of non-business, business and exempt, there being no direct evidence as to the proportions of such use'. W had been entitled to make a claim in 2003 'to recover input tax in respect of the proportion of its supplies that initially were attributed to exempt supplies but which subsequently became taxable supplies, albeit it had never specifically identified which were those supplies'. The tribunal also observed that W could have made an earlier claim for full recovery of input tax, applying the CJEC decision in *Lennartz v Finanzamt München III*, 22.456 EUROPEAN COMMUNITY LAW, but that the effect of the 'three-year cap' was that it was now too late to make such a claim. *The Wellcome Trust (No 4)*, [2008] VATDR 509 (VTD 20731).

Bank reclaiming input tax on obsolete stationery

[46.218] A banking company, which was partly exempt, had a large quantity of stationery which became obsolete. It supplied this to a scrap paper merchant to be destroyed. It reclaimed input tax in respect of the stationery. The Commissioners issued an assessment to recover the tax. The bank appealed, contending that it should be entitled to recover the tax under *VAT Regulations 1995 (SI 1995/2518), reg 109*. The tribunal rejected this contention and dismissed the appeal. *Nationwide Building Society*, **61.1** SELF-SUPPLY, was distinguished, on the grounds that it related to a building society which had printed its own stationery, whereas the bank here purchased printed stationery. On the evidence, the bank could not prove 'in connection with any particular supply, what provisional attribution was made, and what was the final use of each of the items in any particular supply'. In the absence of such proof, 'the Commissioners could not reasonably be satisfied that (the bank) was entitled to adjust under *regulation 109*'. Furthermore, *reg 109* did not apply because each supply of stationery to the bank was a single composite supply, and the bank had 'simply used some of the goods comprised in the supply for a different taxable supply from the one originally intended'. *Halifax plc*, MAN/98/282 (VTD 16697).

Company transferring development project to subsidiary

[46.219] In 2006 a company (C), which was incorporated under the *Friendly and Industrial Provident Societies Act 1968* and was a registered social landlord, set up a wholly-owned subsidiary company (V). C then transferred various development projects to V, and reclaimed input tax on professional services which it had commissioned before the transfer. Customs rejected the claim but the Ch D allowed C's appeal. Sales J held that C's assignment of the benefit of its contracts relating to the construction projects was a supply of services. Since it was not exempt, it was a taxable supply to which *VAT Regulations 1995 (SI 1995/2518), reg 109* applied. *Community Housing Association Ltd*, Ch D [2009] STC 1324; [2009] EWHC 455 (Ch). (*Note.* For HMRC's practice following this decision, see HMRC Brief 57/09, issued on 4 September 2009.)

Construction work—change in rating of supplies

[46.220] In 1994 a construction company incurred expenditure on the construction of penthouse apartments to be let on long leases. Such supplies were exempt under the legislation then in force, but became zero-rated from 1 March 1995, following the *VAT (Construction of Buildings) Order 1995 (SI 1995/280)*. In June 1995 the company submitted a claim for the input tax to be attributed to taxable supplies. The Commissioners rejected the claim and the tribunal dismissed the company's appeal, holding that 'a change of law cannot affect prior attributions of input tax'. *Martin's Properties (Chelsea) Ltd*, LON/95/2945A (VTD 14092).

Exceptional claims for VAT relief (VAT Regulations 1995, reg 111)

NOTE

With regard to the Commissioners' interpretation of what is now *VAT Regulations 1995 (SI 1995/2518), reg 111*, see Business Brief 30/93, issued on 24 September 1993.

Effect of change in partial exemption rules

[46.221] A company registered for VAT with effect from 1 April 1987. In its first return, it reclaimed input tax which it had incurred before registration, in accordance with what is now *VAT Regulations 1995 (SI 1995/2518), reg 111*. The company was partly exempt, and calculated the deductible amount of the input tax in question under the partial exemption rules in force up to 31 March 1987. The Commissioners formed the opinion that, since the company had not registered for VAT until 1 April 1987, it should have calculated its deductible input tax under the revised rules introduced from that date, and calculated the repayable amount accordingly. The tribunal dismissed the company's appeal against this decision, holding that, since there had been no entitlement to reclaim the relevant input tax until after the change in the input tax rules on 1 April 1987, it followed that the deductible input tax had to be calculated under the rules in force from that date. *St George's Home Co Ltd*, MAN/90/876 (VTD 10213).

Input tax reclaimed on pre-registration supplies

[46.222] A trader who provided financial services registered for VAT from April 1993. Most of his supplies were exempt from VAT but he also made a few taxable supplies. He reclaimed input tax on office equipment which he had purchased between 1988 and 1992. The Commissioners rejected his claim and he appealed, contending that the input tax should be treated as deductible under what is now *VAT Regulations 1995 (SI 1995/2518), reg 111*. The tribunal dismissed his appeal, holding that the office equipment had been almost exclusively used for making exempt supplies and that, since he had not reclaimed the tax at the time it became chargeable, the effect of *Article 18(3)* of the *EC Sixth Directive* was that the Commissioners had a discretion as to whether to allow the claim to input tax. The tribunal chairman observed that *regulation 111** did not specify how the pre-registration inputs of a partly exempt trader should be treated, and held that the Commissioners' policy of using a direct attribution method for all such claims was justified, since 'partial exemption involves complicated calculations which are not appropriate to unregistered traders who may not have kept the right records for the purpose'. (The chairman also commented that 'this case is what might be termed the pre-registration toothbrush trick but applied to the financial services industry'.) *T Douros (t/a Olympic Financial Services)*, LON/93/2523A (VTD 12454).

[46.223] The decision in *Douros*, **46.222** above, was applied in the similar subsequent case of *M Jenkins (t/a Lifetime Financial Services)*, LON/96/3072 (VTD 14784).

[46.224] An insurance broker also supplied photocopying and fax facilities. His turnover from his insurance brokerage, which was accepted as being exempt from VAT, exceeded £60,000 per annum. His receipts from photo-copying and fax facilities were between £500 and £600 per annum. He registered for VAT with effect from April 1992. In his first return he reclaimed input tax on various items of office equipment which he had purchased since September 1987. The Commissioners rejected the claim, on the basis that what is now *VAT Regulations 1995 (SI 1995/2518), reg 111* only permitted the claiming of pre-registration input tax which had been incurred for the purposes of making taxable supplies. The broker appealed, contending that the combined effect of *regs 106** and *111** was that the tax should be treated as deductible. The tribunal dismissed the appeal, applying *dicta* in *Douros*, **46.222** above, and holding that *regulation 111** was 'a free-standing provision notwithstanding that it is to be found in (*Part XIV**) of the (*VAT Regulations**)'. The Commissioners' exercise of their discretion not to allow the input tax had not been unreasonable, and did not contravene *Article 18* of the *EC Sixth Directive*. The broker had been 'a taxable person for the purposes of the *Sixth Directive* before he became a taxable person for the purposes of *VATA*'. His right to deduct input tax in accordance with *Article 17* of the *Sixth Directive* had arisen 'when the supplies to him were used for the purposes of his taxable transactions'. At that time he had chosen to be treated as exempt from tax under *Article 24*. Accordingly, the effect of *Article 24(5)* was that he was not entitled to deduct the tax in question. The tribunal observed that 'it is consistent with the *Sixth Directive* and the observations in *Rompelman* (see **22.103** EUROPEAN COMMUNITY LAW) for the Commissioners to restrict credit to so much of the tax claimed as can be demonstrated to have been used for the purposes of his taxable transactions'. *GN Byrd (t/a GN Byrd & Co)*, MAN/93/1433 (VTD 12675).

[46.225] A company which operated a nursery school registered for VAT from August 1993. Most of its supplies were exempt from VAT. However, it also supplied swimming lessons, sold sweatshirts, and hired its premises for children's parties. These supplies were accepted as taxable. In its first return it reclaimed input tax on supplies which it had received before registration. The Commissioners rejected the claim, on the basis that pre-registration input tax was only reclaimable if it was directly attributable to taxable supplies. The company appealed, contending that the tax should be treated as deductible under what is now *VAT Regulations 1995 (SI 1995/2518), reg 111*. The tribunal dismissed the appeal, applying *Douros*, **46.222** above. *Jolly Tots Ltd*, MAN/93/1356 (VTD 13087).

[46.226] A company was incorporated in September 2006 and registered for VAT from August 2007. In January 2008 it opted to tax a property it was developing, and submitted a return reclaiming input tax for the period between its incorporation and its registration. HMRC only agreed to allow it to reclaim input tax relating to services supplied in the six months prior to its registration, in accordance with *VAT Regulations 1995 (SI 1995/2518), reg 111*. The company applied for judicial review, contending that HMRC should have granted an extra-statutory remission, as referred to in *VAT Notice 742A, para 9.4*. The CS rejected this contention and dismissed the application. Lord Woolman observed that *Notice 742A, para 9.4* applied only where a trader had 'become registered for VAT as a result of opting to tax'. This was not the case here, as the company had registered before opting to tax. There was nothing irrational in HMRC's rejection of the claim. *Argyll Developments Ltd v HMRC*, CS [2009] STC 2698; [2009] CSOH 131.

Previously exempt business becoming liable to VAT

[46.227] A nursing home opened in April 1991 but was unsuccessful. In May 1992 the proprietors ceased to use the building as a nursing home and opened it as a licensed hotel. In October 1992 they registered for VAT. They reclaimed input tax on expenditure which they had incurred while the building was used as a nursing home. The Commissioners rejected the claim and the proprietors appealed, contending that the input tax should be treated as deductible under what is now *VAT Regulations 1995 (SI 1995/2518), reg 111*. The tribunal dismissed the appeal, holding that the tax was not deductible since it had been used for the purpose of making exempt supplies and there had been no intention to make taxable supplies at the time the expenditure was incurred. *R Reading & R Crabtree (t/a Mostyn Lodge Hotel)*, MAN/93/1353 (VTD 12756).

[46.228] Similar decisions were reached in *Gulland Properties*, LON/95/370A (VTD 13955) and *Wilf Gilbert (Staffs) Ltd*, MAN/06/540 (VTD 20170).

Rent paid prior to registration

[46.229] See *Jerzynek*, 36.614 INPUT TAX.

VAT Regulations 1995, reg 111*— jurisdiction of tribunal

[46.230] See *Barar & Barar (t/a Turret House Rest Home)*, 2.12 APPEALS, and *Noor v HMRC*, 22.553 EUROPEAN COMMUNITY LAW.

Interpretation of VAT Regulations 1995, reg 111(1)(b).

[46.231] See *Oaks Pavilion Ltd*, 36.615 INPUT TAX.

Effect of VAT Regulations 1995, reg 111(2)*

[46.232] See *Burgess & Holmes*, 36.591 INPUT TAX; *Perranporth Rugby Football Club*, 36.597 INPUT TAX; *Trustees of Park Avenue Methodist Church*, 36.598 INPUT TAX; *Glamorgan Prestige Developments Ltd*, 36.599 INPUT TAX; *Crazy Farm Golf Course Ltd*, 36.600 INPUT TAX, and *Aegis Technology Ltd*, 36.602 INPUT TAX.

Application of VAT Regulations 1995, reg 111(3)*

[46.233] A trader registered for VAT in 1995. He reclaimed input tax under *VAT Regulations 1995 (SI 1995/2518), reg 111* in respect of an invoice purportedly issued by a company he controlled, which had ceased trading (and had been struck off of the Register of Companies six days before the date of the invoice). The Commissioners rejected the claim and the tribunal dismissed the trader's appeal. *Reg 111(3)* provided that a claim had to be supported by 'invoices and other evidence'. The Commissioners had to be satisfied that the company had made a supply to the trader for consideration. The trader had failed to provide 'satisfactory evidence' of the purported supply. *NR Corke*, LON/98/1125 (VTD 16832).

VAT Regulations 1995, reg 111(5)—claim after deregistration

[46.234] A couple who operated a nursing home deregistered for VAT, and subsequently submitted a claim for repayment of input tax relating to professional advice. The Commissioners rejected the claim on the basis that the tax in question was attributable to the general overheads of the business, rather than to taxable supplies. The tribunal dismissed the couple's appeal against this decision. *Mr & Mrs L Jones*, MAN/97/1027 (VTD 15595).

47

Partnership

The cases in this chapter are arranged under the following headings.

Partnership assessments	**47.1**
Partnership appeals	**47.12**
Partnership registration	**47.13**
Whether a partnership exists	
Cases held to constitute a partnership	**47.17**
Cases held not to constitute a partnership	**47.41**
Associated partnerships	**47.65**
Miscellaneous	**47.69**

Partnership assessments

Assessment issued in partnership name

[47.1] A restaurant was registered for VAT as a partnership of three people. A control visit took place in November 1986 and the VAT officer was told by the partnership's accountant that one of the partners had left. The VAT office wrote to the partner in question but received no reply. Subsequently an assessment was raised on the partnership, in the partnership name, charging tax on undeclared takings. The partnership did not dispute the amount of the assessment, but lodged an appeal, contending that the assessment was invalid because it was issued in the partnership name and a partnership was not an entity in English law. The tribunal rejected this contention and dismissed the appeal. The partnership here was at fault in not having notified the Commissioners of the partnership change in writing, as required by what is now *VAT Regulations 1995 (SI 1995/2518), reg 4*. The issue of an assessment in the partnership name was in accordance with the requirements of what is now *VATA 1994, s 45*. The tribunal specifically declined to follow *obiter dicta* of Glidewell J in *Evans & Others*, QB 1981, [1982] STC 342 (which the appellants had cited as an authority), observing that the relevant legislation had been amended by *FA 1982* to reverse the effect of that decision. *The Bengal Brasserie*, [1991] VATTR 210 (VTD 5925).

[47.2] An assessment in a partnership name was held to be valid, notwithstanding a change in the members of the partnership, in *Eleanor Cleaning Services*, LON/93/652 (VTD 11353) and *DE Barber & PA Bayly (t/a The Pitts Head)*, LON/00/259 (VTD 17856).

[47.3] Similar decisions, applying *The Bengal Brasserie*, 47.1 above, were reached in *JE, JH & AG Jones (t/a S Jones & Son)*, LON/93/2663A (VTD 13308) and *Oysters Fish Bar*, MAN/96/1256 (VTD 16203).

Partnership changing trading name during period of assessment

[47.4] A partnership failed to submit VAT returns, and Customs issued assessments. The partnership appealed, contending that the assessment was invalid because it had changed its trading name during the period covered by the assessment, and the assessment only gave the later trading name. The tribunal rejected this contention and dismissed the appeal, and the Ch D upheld this decision. Blackburne J held that 'whether persons carrying on a partnership business are registered under the *VATA* or the registration under that Act is of the firm in which the partners are trading, the liability for VAT is that of the individual members of the firm subject to apportionment under *s 45(5)* where appropriate'. *VATA 1994, s 45(1)* was 'permissive and procedural only. It does not affect the liability to VAT of the individuals trading from time to time in partnership under that or any other name'. *C Scrace & E Keeshan v HMRC*, Ch D 2006, [2007] STC 269; [2006] EWHC 2646 (Ch).

Assessment issued in names of declared partners—whether valid

[47.5] A married couple (Mr & Mrs P) carried on a property business, and were registered for VAT. They held the lease of a restaurant. In June 2001 they granted two individuals (Q and B) a licence to operate the restaurant. In January 2002 Q submitted a VAT registration form stating that the restaurant was being operated by a partnership of four people (himself, B, and Mr & Mrs P). All these four people signed the relevant form VAT2. Difficulties arose between Q and B, and in April 2002 they signed an agreement providing that B would operate the restaurant and would take the whole of the profits after paying a salary of £1,000 to Q. Mr & Mrs P were not parties to this agreement, and none of the four declared partners notified Customs of a change in the partnership. B's accountant submitted a VAT return for the period ending 30 April 2002, claiming a repayment of VAT. However, B subsequently left the country without arranging for any more VAT returns, and the restaurant was temporarily closed. In 2003 Customs issued an estimated assessment covering the periods from May 2002 to October 2002, addressed to the four declared partners who had signed the form VAT2. Three of these (Q and Mr & Mrs P) lodged appeals, contending that the original partnership had ceased in April 2002, and that during the period of the assessment the restaurant had actually been operated by B, who should be treated as liable for the VAT. The tribunal found that despite the contents of the form VAT2, the effect of the June 2001 agreement was that the restaurant had been operated by a partnership of two people (Q and B), and that 'there was never a partnership agreement involving Mr & Mrs P'. The Ch D held that, on the tribunal's findings of fact, the assessment was ineffective against the two people (Mr & Mrs P) who were not in fact partners, but was valid and enforceable against the two actual partners (Q and B). Patten J held that 'a registration under *s 45(1)* is only effective to include in the collection of individuals registered under the partnership name those who were at the relevant time carrying on business in partnership within the meaning of *s 45(1)*. Only a "person" who makes taxable supplies may be registered', and 'the inclusion of non-partners on form VAT2 is of no effect in relation to other individuals. The registration can only take effect in relation to those on the form who are partners and can therefore constitute a taxable person for VAT purposes.' Furthermore, the tribunal had been entitled to find that Q was a partner in the business. *HMRC v K Pal, R Pal, E Quillen Alonso & HB El Bouacheri (t/a Tapas Bar Cerveceria)*, Ch D 2006, [2008] STC 2442; [2006] EWHC 2016 (Ch).

Change of partnership—old partner continuing in new partnership

[47.6] A partnership which operated a Chinese restaurant decided to sell it as a going concern. The purchaser decided to take one of the old partners into partnership with him. The Commissioners issued an assessment on the basis that there had been no sale of the business, merely a change of partners. The tribunal allowed the new partners' appeal, holding that the new partnership was a separate entity so that a new registration number should have been issued. *Hoi Shan Chinese Restaurant*, LON/86/299 (VTD 2368).

Dissolution of partnership—one partner continuing business

[47.7] A partnership which operated a dry-cleaning business registered for VAT from 1985. The partnership originally comprised three people. One of them resigned in 1986 and another (M) resigned in October 1998. The remaining partner (H) continued to trade from the same premises. He did not notify the Commissioners of the dissolution of the partnership, but submitted returns showing no tax due. On 13 October 1999 a VAT officer visited the premises. H told him that the partnership had been dissolved and that he was now operating as a sole trader. However, the Commissioners did not cancel the partnership's registration. In 2002 another VAT officer visited the premises. He took the view that, because the Commissioners had not received written confirmation that the partnership had been dissolved, it should be treated as continuing. He therefore arranged for the issue of assessments, in the partnership name, covering the three years from 1 September 1999 to 31 August 2002, charging tax of over £21,000. H appealed. The tribunal observed that the effect of *Partnership Act 1890, s 36(1)* was that 'where a person deals with a firm after a change in its constitution, he is entitled to treat all apparent members of the old firm as still being members of the firm until he has notice of the change'. Accordingly the tribunal held that the assessment was valid with regard to the period from 1 September to 12 October 1999, but was invalid with regard to the period from 13 October 1999 onwards. *TAZ Hussein & M Asim (t/a Pressing Dry Cleaners)*, [2003] VATDR 440 (VTD 18341).

[47.8] Two people (M and U) operated a restaurant in partnership, and were registered for VAT. In November 1998 the partnership was dissolved, and the restaurant was transferred to M as a going concern. Neither M nor U notified the Commissioners of the change within 30 days, as required by *VAT Regulations 1995, reg 5(2)*, but M completed forms VAT 1 and VAT 68 in June 1999. M had completed VAT returns for the periods ending June 1999 under the partnership registration number. On receipt of the form VAT 1, the Commissioners issued him with a new registration number, which he used for his returns for the periods ending in September and December. However M's accountant subsequently agreed with a VAT officer that M could continue to use the previous registration number. Subsequently the Commissioners issued assessments on M on the basis that he had underdeclared his takings. He appealed, contending as a preliminary point that the assessments were invalid because he should not have been allowed to continue using the partnership registration number. The tribunal rejected this contention and held that the assessments were valid. Applying the decision in *L Reich & Sons Ltd*, 57.218 REGISTRATION, 'the allocation of a registration number is a matter which falls within the administrative discretion of the Commissioners'. *D Miah (No 2)*, MAN/01/675 (VTD 18387). *(Note. For a preliminary issue in this case, see 2.258 APPEALS.)*

Assessment of penalty under VATA 1994, s 60

[47.9] See *Akbar & Others*, 50.7 PENALTIES: EVASION OF TAX; *Standard Tandoori Nepalese Restaurant*, 50.8 PENALTIES: EVASION OF TAX; *Islam & Others*, 50.9 PENALTIES: EVASION OF TAX, and *Santi Bag Restaurant*, 50.99 PENALTIES: EVASION OF TAX.

Whether husband and wife trading in partnership—penalty on wife

[47.10] See *Segger*, 50.10 PENALTIES: EVASION OF TAX.

Penalty imposed on partnership—form VAT 292 not received

[47.11] See *Yarl Wines*, 50.11 PENALTIES: EVASION OF TAX.

Partnership appeals

Appeal delayed by illness of partner

[47.12] See *Hornby*, 2.191 APPEALS.

Partnership registration

Separate businesses carried on by the same partners

[47.13] In the case noted at 57.1 REGISTRATION, the QB held that where the same individuals carried on more than one business in partnership, they were only entitled to one registration. May J held that the requirement (in *VATA 1994, s 45**) that a registration may be in the partnership name was 'permissive and procedural only, and once a firm name has been registered, the effect of the registration is as though the names of all the individuals trading under that name from time to time were recorded'. *C & E Commrs v MJ & BJ Glassborow*, QB [1974] STC 142; [1975] QB 465; [1974] 1 All ER 1041.

[47.14] See also the cases noted at 57.2 to 57.4 REGISTRATION.

Limited partnerships—whether entitled to separate registrations

[47.15] Two individuals each practised as a patent agent on his own, one in Middlesex and the other in Kent. Each was registered for VAT. In order to protect their respective practices should either die or be incapacitated, they had (in 1972) entered into reciprocal arrangements under which each formed a partnership with the other as a limited partner. The limited partner contributed £250 as capital but drew no profits and took no part in the management of the practice. The partnership was to terminate on the death or incapacity of the general partner, but the limited partner was then required to offer his services to the business for up to six months so as to preserve the goodwill pending sale. In 1979 the Commissioners issued a ruling that the two businesses should be covered by the same registration (in the name of either firm). The choice between the two firms was left to the two individuals, who appealed against the decision. The tribunal allowed their appeals, distinguishing *Glassborow*, 57.1 REGISTRATION, on the grounds that it related to general partnerships. Lord Grantchester held that a limited partner, taking no part in the management of the business, could not be said to have made taxable supplies in the course of that business. Furthermore, he did not carry on the business in partnership 'within the meaning and intent' of what is now *VATA 1994, s 45(1)*, so that since each of the limited partnerships was carried on by a different active partner, each was entitled to a separate registration. *H Saunders; TG Sorrell*, [1980] VATTR 53 (VTD 913).

Partnership name wrongly recorded on registration certificate

[47.16] The Commissioners discovered that a partnership which operated a taxi business had failed to register for VAT. The partners' names were Razaq and Bashir, but because of a clerical error by a VAT officer, the registration certificate which the Commissioners issued wrongly stated their names as Razaq and Shabir (although the partnership trading name was correctly stated). The Commissioners subsequently issued a 'global' assessment covering the period from 1 November 1994 to 30 November 1998. The partnership appealed. The tribunal held that the registration certificate was invalid, observing that the error in recording the name was 'not a mere spelling error or transposition of letters' but was an error which 'goes to the very root of the certificate'. The effect of *VAT Regulations, reg 25(1)* was that the partnership was required to be registered from 1 November 1994, and was required to make quarterly returns from that date even though there was no valid certificate of registration. However, since there was no valid certificate of registration, the effect of *VATA 1994, s 73* was that 'the Commissioners' power to assess is restricted to assessing accounting period by accounting period, i.e. in the present case quarter by quarter, in the overall period during which a taxable person should have made returns: they cannot make a valid global assessment for that overall period'. *M Razaq & M Bashir (t/a Streamline Taxis)*, [2002] VATDR 92 (VTD 17537).

Whether a partnership exists

Cases held to constitute a partnership

Country club

[47.17] Customs issued an assessment on a country club in Cornwall which had been registered for VAT as a partnership between two individuals, L and C. C appealed, contending that she was not a partner and that L was the sole proprietor. It was accepted that the club had been run by L as the sole proprietor until 1975, when C moved to the club. Later that year L moved to the USA, although he told C that he intended to return in the near future. The club's bank account remained in L's sole name, but C had authority to sign cheques. C had told a VAT officer in 1976 that she was in partnership with L, and the club had been registered accordingly. C had also signed form VAT2 as a partner. At the hearing C produced a letter from L, who was still in the USA, stating that he had never taken her into partnership in the club. The tribunal dismissed C's appeal, finding that she had acted as a partner in her dealings with Customs, and had been responsible for the operation of the club since late 1975 when L had left the country. The fact that L and C had subsequently claimed not to be in partnership was not conclusive. On the evidence, C had been in partnership with L in running the business of the club. *B Leighton-Jones & A Craig (t/a Saddletramps)*, CAR/77/231 (VTD 597).

Husband and wife—whether trading in partnership

[47.18] A married woman (W) registered for VAT in 1979 as the proprietor of a shop. The shop did not prove successful, and in 1983 she and her husband also opened a café. They did not register for VAT, on the basis that the café was a separate business and that the takings were below the registration threshold. The Commissioners issued an assessment on W charging tax on the café takings. W appealed, contending that although she was the sole proprietor of the shop, the café was a separate business which she ran in partnership with her husband. The tribunal accepted this contention and allowed her appeal. *JM & MC Wade v Isle of Man Finance Board*, MAN/85/273 (VTD 2022). (*Note.* Customs might now have recourse to a direction under *VATA 1994, Sch 1 para 2*. For cases concerning this provision, see **57.35** *et seq.* REGISTRATION.)

[47.19] A married couple purchased a shop as a going concern in 1988. Their takings were lower than they had anticipated, and in 1991 the husband purchased a car hire business with money he had received on being made redundant from a previous employment. They submitted accounts to the Inland Revenue indicating that both the shop and the car hire business were run as a partnership (with the husband being allocated most of the profit from the car hire business, and the profits and losses of the shop being split equally). The couple did not register for VAT, and in 1998 the Commissioners issued a notice of compulsory registration. The couple appealed, contending that, notwithstanding the accounts which they had submitted to the Inland Revenue, the car hire business was actually being run by the husband as a sole trader while the shop was run by the wife as a sole trader. The tribunal rejected this contention and dismissed the appeal, observing that they had signed the accounts as partners and that 'the accounts are more likely to have shown the true position'. *CD & MD Gow*, LON/99/28 (VTD 16272).

[47.20] A married woman was registered for VAT as the proprietor of a public house. She was subsequently declared bankrupt. The Commissioners formed the opinion that the public house had in fact been operated by the woman and her husband in partnership. They issued an amended certificate of registration and an assessment accordingly. The couple appealed, contending that the wife had run the public house as a sole trader with her husband acting as an employee. The tribunal rejected this contention and dismissed the appeal, holding on the evidence that the couple had traded in partnership. *R & Mrs J Wilson (t/a Mountain View Hotel)*, MAN/98/639 (VTD 16404).

[47.21] A married couple, who traded from a café at a seaside resort, did not register for VAT. Customs issued a retrospective notice of compulsory registration. The couple appealed, contending that the husband was operating the café as a sole trader while the sale of ice creams for consumption off the premises was a separate business, carried on by the wife as a sole trader. The tribunal rejected this contention, holding on the evidence that the couple were trading in partnership. *PC & VL Leonidas*, [2000] VATDR 207 (VTD 16588). (*Note*. For other issues in this case, see **51.31** PENALTIES: FAILURE TO NOTIFY and **59.15** RETURNS.)

[47.22] The Commissioners discovered that a married couple who carried on a taxi business had not registered for VAT. They issued a notice of compulsory registration. The couple appealed, contending that each of them were trading separately as the proprietor of a different business (with the result that their turnover was below the threshold). The tribunal reviewed the evidence in detail, rejected this contention, and dismissed the appeal. *DP & C Hughes*, MAN/01/148 (VTD 17700).

[47.23] A married couple operated a sandwich bar and bistro from the same premises. They did not register for VAT. Customs issued a ruling that the couple were running a single business. The couple appealed, contending that the husband was operating the sandwich bar and the wife was running the bistro as a separate business. The tribunal rejected this contention and dismissed the couple's appeal. *D Harris (t/a Fellows Sandwich Bar); Mrs M Harris (t/a Fellows Bistro)*, MAN/x (VTD 20235).

Family members—whether operating restaurant in partnership

[47.24] In 2001 a company registered for VAT on the basis that it was carrying on a restaurant business, succeeding another company which had been struck off the Register of Companies. Customs formed the impression that the restaurant was in fact being operated by four members of the same family (a married couple and their two children), carrying on business in partnership. They issued a notice of compulsory registration. The family members appealed. The tribunal reviewed the evidence in detail and dismissed the appeal, finding that 'all four partners were in business as a partnership throughout the period'. The tribunal observed that substantial sums had been 'diverted from the business to pay for purely personal expenditure of (the) family'. The net profits of the business were shared by the four family members, rather than by the purported company director, who was a kitchen worker with 'very limited command of English'. The tribunal held that 'the companies were a mere sham and not the source of control of the business' and 'the companies were a device to disguise the true ownership of the business by the (M) family'. On the evidence, although the husband acted as the 'senior partner', it was clear that 'his wife and children each exercised and participated in the management and control of the partnership business'. The tribunal also observed that 'our understanding of the concept of the Asian family' was that it 'tends to approximate in many respects to the legal definition of partnership'. *A, A, A & R Miah (t/a the Raj Restaurant) (No 1)*, EDN/03/03 (VTD 19465). (*Note.* For subsequent developments in this case, see **3.144** ASSESSMENT.)

Unmarried couple—whether trading in partnership

[47.25] An individual (K) owned a car hire business and a small shop. He failed to register for VAT, and the Commissioners issued an assessment on the takings of both these businesses. The assessment also charged tax on the sale of plants and gardening equipment from the same premises as the car hire business. K appealed, contending that the sale of plants and gardening equipment was a separate business, which he carried on in partnership with the woman with whom he was living. The tribunal accepted this contention and allowed the appeal in respect of the sale of plants and gardening equipment. *WE Kenny (t/a Scruples)*, LON/85/150 (VTD 2039). (*Note.* For another issue in this case, see **47.58** below.)

Husband and wife partnership—whether wife also A sole trader

[47.26] A married couple who operated a public house did not account for VAT on supplies of catering and accommodation. The Commissioners issued an assessment charging tax on them, and the couple appealed, contending that these supplies were a separate business carried on by the wife. The tribunal reviewed the evidence in detail, rejected this contention and dismissed the appeal. Applying *dicta* of Lord Lindley (see *Lindley & Banks on Partnership, 17th edition, para 16.28*), a partner was 'not allowed in transacting the partnership affairs, to carry on for his own sole benefit any separate trade or business which, were it not for his connection with the partnership, he would not have been in a position to carry on. Bound to do his best for the firm, he is not at liberty to labour for himself to their detriment; and if his connection with the firm enables him to acquire gain, he cannot appropriate that gain to himself on the pretence that it arose from a separate transaction with which the firm had nothing to do.' Accordingly, the use of the public house for catering and accommodation was a partnership activity 'unless the partners arrived at a clearly defined commercial arrangement whereunder (the wife) alone were to benefit from them'. On the evidence, 'there was no arrangement in this case operating to separate the catering and accommodation activities from the rest of the activities of the public house'. *J & Mrs SF Smith (t/a The Salmon Tail)*, MAN/99/213 (VTD 16190).

[47.27] Similar decisions were reached in *AE & Mrs ME Fraser*, LON/99/453 (VTD 16761); *J & A Smith (t/a Ty Gwyn Hotel)*, MAN/01/065 (VTD 17406) and *JNE & SA Ashcroft*, MAN/00/55 (VTD 17476).

[47.28] A married couple were registered for VAT as proprietors of a car hire business. The Commissioners discovered that they had not accounted for VAT on contract work, and issued an assessment charging tax. The couple appealed, contending that the contract work was a separate business, carried on by the wife as a sole trader. The tribunal rejected this contention and dismissed the appeal, holding on the evidence that 'there was in reality only one business'. *W & B Brough (t/a Chaddy Cars)*, MAN/98/702 (VTD 16700).

Catering at public house

[47.29] See *Potts*, 62.296 SUPPLY, and *Allen*, 62.299 SUPPLY.

Catering at hotel

[47.30] See *Albert*, 62.301 SUPPLY.

Whether supplies made by partnership or by individual partner

[47.31] A partnership operated a retail shop. One of the partners had previously been a graphic designer, and he issued a number of invoices in his own name in respect of such work. The income from this work was paid into the partnership bank account, but the partnership did not account for output tax on it. The Commissioners issued an assessment charging tax on it, and the tribunal dismissed the partnership's appeal, holding on the evidence that the supplies had been made by the partnership. The chairman observed that 'the critical and decisive factor' was 'the inclusion of the proceeds in the partnership accounts as income of the partnership'. *W & J Tang (t/a Ziploc)*, MAN/97/1123 (VTD 15426).

[47.32] A married couple operated a general store and off-licence in partnership. The Commissioners discovered that they had not accounted for output tax on wholesale supplies of alcoholic drinks to other traders. They issued an assessment charging tax on these supplies. The couple appealed, contending that the wholesale supplies had been made by the husband as an individual, rather than by the partnership. The tribunal rejected this contention and dismissed the appeal. The tribunal observed that when someone enters into the relationship of partnership, 'one voluntarily surrenders certain rights, including the right, if such it be, not to suffer the consequences of another person's actions. A partner who, for whatever reason, does not keep herself informed as to what her partner is doing cannot be heard to complain of the consequences.' *M & N Singh (t/a The Food Palace & Wine King)*, LON/98/1064 (VTD 16378).

Partnership operating restaurant—kitchen also used for take-away sales

[47.33] A married couple registered for VAT as proprietors of a restaurant. They also used the restaurant kitchen to prepare take-away food, which was sold from adjacent premises. They did not account for VAT on the take-away sales. The Commissioners issued an assessment, and the couple appealed, contending that the take-away business was operated by a three-person partnership which also included one of their uncles (L). The tribunal rejected this contention and dismissed the appeal. *P & A Yung (t/a Chilli Restaurant & Hong Kong Food)*, LON/00/90 (VTD 16695).

Florists

[47.34] Two individuals (R and K) were registered for VAT in partnership as the proprietors of a newsagency and a florists' shop. The Commissioners issued an assessment to the partnership on the basis that the takings of the florists' shop had been underdeclared. One of the partners (K) lodged an appeal, contending that, although he continued to be a partner in the newsagency, he had ceased to be a partner in the florists' shop, which was being run by R as a sole proprietor. The tribunal reviewed the evidence, rejected this contention, and dismissed the appeal. *K Khan*, EDN/02/9 (VTD 17790).

Sale of pianos

[47.35] A married couple carried on business in partnership, selling pianos, and were registered for VAT. Customs discovered that there appeared to have been a significant number of unrecorded sales, and issued assessments charging tax on these. The couple appealed, contending that these sales had in fact been made by a number of associated companies which they controlled and which were not registered for VAT. The tribunal rejected this contention and dismissed the appeals in principle (while adjusting the amounts of some of the assessments), finding that 'there was a single business being carried on by the partnership together with all the companies' and that 'together Mr and Mrs (W) and the companies were carrying on the business of buying and selling pianos, whether new or second-hand, or on commission, as a partnership'. The Ch D upheld this decision as one of fact. *MA & AJ Wild v HMRC*, Ch D 2008, [2009] STC 566; [2008] EWHC 3401 (Ch).

Builders

[47.36] See *Malin & Malin*, 51.30 PENALTIES: FAILURE TO NOTIFY.

Industrial cleaning business

[47.37] See *Cutler*, 51.62 PENALTIES: FAILURE TO NOTIFY.

Hairdressers

[47.38] See *Sumner & Kiddle*, 51.63 PENALTIES: FAILURE TO NOTIFY; *Hooper & Hooper*, 51.64 PENALTIES: FAILURE TO NOTIFY, and *Bear & Hill*, 57.197 REGISTRATION.

Partnership carrying on property development business

[47.39] See *Fengate Developments*, 62.342 SUPPLY.

Other cases

[47.40] There are a number of other cases, which appear to raise no point of general importance, in which the tribunal has held that a partnership has existed. Such cases turn entirely on their own facts and, in the interests of space, are not summarised individually in this book.

Cases held not to constitute a partnership

Health club—whether operated as a partnership

[47.41] The proprietor of a health club failed to account for output tax on income from aerobics classes at the club. The Commissioners issued an assessment charging tax on them, and he appealed, contending that the aerobics was a separate business which he carried on in partnership with his father (who had lent him money to help finance the club). The tribunal rejected this contention and upheld the assessment, observing that there was no written partnership agreement and that the proprietor's father 'played no part in the conduct or management of the aerobics activities'. The QB upheld this decision as one of fact. *RJ Burrell (t/a The Firm) v C & E Commrs*, QB [1997] STC 1413.

Husband and wife partnership—wife also held to be a sole trader.

[47.42] A married couple operated a public house in partnership. They did not account for output tax on receipts from catering at the public house, and the Commissioners issued an assessment charging tax on these receipts. The couple appealed, contending that the catering was a separate business, carried on by the wife as a sole trader, and that VAT was not chargeable because these receipts were below the limits of *Sch 1 para 1*. The tribunal accepted the couple's evidence and allowed their appeal, holding that the catering was a separate business. *P & V Marner*, MAN/77/140 (VTD 443). (*Notes.* (1) The Commissioners might now have recourse to a direction under *VATA 1994, Sch 1 para 2*. For cases concerning this provision, see **57.35** *et seq.* REGISTRATION. (2) The decision here was not followed, and was implicitly disapproved, in the subsequent case of *Smith & Smith*, **47.26** above. See also the cases noted at **47.27** above; *Brown*, **62.297** SUPPLY; *Davies*, **62.298** SUPPLY, and *Allen (t/a The Shovel)*, **62.299** SUPPLY.)

Husband and wife partnership—husband also held to be a sole trader

[47.43] An individual (R) registered for VAT in 1973 as the proprietor of a retail shop. In 1981 a small amusement arcade was opened at the same premises. R reclaimed input tax on the purchase of the amusement machines, but did not account for output tax on the takings from them. The Commissioners discovered this at a control visit in 1983. They also discovered that accounts had been drawn up showing that the shop was operated by a partnership of R and his wife, rather than by R as a sole trader. They therefore registered the couple as a partnership, and issued an assessment to recover the tax on the purchase of the machines. R appealed, contending that, notwithstanding the accounts, he remained the sole proprietor of the shop, and that he had purchased the machines personally and had subsequently hired them to a separate partnership business comprising himself and his wife, the turnover of which was below the VAT registration threshold. The tribunal reviewed the evidence in detail, rejected R's contentions, and dismissed the appeal. The tribunal held that the shop was run by R and his wife in partnership; that R was the sole proprietor of the amusement arcade, and that the couple had not purchased the amusement machines for the purpose of the retail shop business. The tribunal observed that the purported rental of the machines was 'an afterthought'. Accordingly the couple were not entitled to reclaim input tax on the purchase. *RD & SL Jackson (t/a B & S Fancy Goods)*, LON/85/70 (VTD 1959).

[47.44] See also *Parker & Parker*, 57.207 REGISTRATION.

Husband and wife—whether trading in partnership

[47.45] In the case noted at 7.51 BUSINESS, a married couple purchased an old stable and coach-house with the intention of converting it into a dwelling-house. The tribunal held that the couple were not carrying on a business in partnership and were not entitled to reclaim input tax on the conversion. *GWH Kelly*, EDN/77/43 (VTD 598).

[47.46] In 1973 a married couple purchased a newsagents' shop, and were registered for VAT accordingly. In 1977 the husband began a shopfitting business, which occupied him for at least 40 hours per week. His wife kept the books and records for this business, but there was no formal partnership agreement, and the couple did not account for tax on this income. In 1980 the couple separated. Subsequently the Commissioners issued a ruling that the husband had been operating the shopfitting business as a sole trader from 1977 to 1980, and should be registered as such. He appealed, contending that he and his wife had carried on the shopfitting business in partnership. The tribunal rejected this contention and dismissed his appeal, holding that his wife had assisted him under an informal domestic arrangement which fell short of being a partnership. *VJ Britton*, [1986] VATTR 209 (VTD 2173).

[47.47] A management consultant, who was registered for VAT, owned a flat which was let as holiday accommodation. He did not account for output tax on his income from this, and the Commissioners issued an assessment. He appealed, contending that the letting of the flat should be treated as a partnership between him and his wife. The tribunal dismissed his appeal, finding that he had not produced evidence to show that his wife took any part in the management of the business. The fact that he had paid some of the rental income to his wife was not conclusive. *AG Pole*, LON/94/2467A (VTD 13225).

[47.48] A married couple, and their son and daughter-in-law, had traded in partnership as potters. Following disagreements, the couple left the partnership in 1997. Their son and daughter-in-law continued the previous business. The couple continued to work as potters, and the Commissioners issued a ruling that they were trading as a two-person partnership and were therefore required to register. The couple appealed, contending that they were working as individuals and carrying on separate businesses, with the turnover of each being below the registration threshold. The tribunal accepted their evidence and allowed the appeal. *D & M Townsend*, LON/00/349-350 (VTD 17081).

[47.49] An individual (K) registered for VAT as an ice-cream salesman, but did not account for VAT on his sales. Customs issued assessments and he appealed, contending that the shop from which the business was based was run by him and his wife in partnership, but that when he sold ice-cream from a mobile van, he was acting as a sole trader (so that the turnover of both businesses was below the threshold). The tribunal rejected this contention and dismissed the appeal, holding that there was 'only one business'. K was the sole proprietor of the shop and was required to account for VAT on the sales from both the shop and the van. *SN Khan*, MAN/04/374 (VTD 19513). (*Note.* Costs were awarded to Customs.)

Fairground entertainments—whether family trading in partnership

[47.50] A married couple and their daughter all operated various fairground entertainments. None of them were registered for VAT. The Commissioners issued a notice of compulsory registration on the basis that the couple and their daughter were trading together in partnership. They appealed, contending that each of them was sole proprietor of at least one of the entertainments, while one of the entertainments was operated by the husband and wife in partnership, and a 'ghost train' was operated by the wife and her daughter in partnership. The tribunal accepted their evidence and allowed the appeal. *JJ, BB & S O'Connor*, MAN/81/12 (VTD 1170). (*Note.* The Commissioners might now have recourse to a direction under *VATA 1994, Sch 1 para 2*. For a similar case where such a direction was upheld, see *Evans*, 57.59 REGISTRATION. For other cases concerning this provision, see 57.35 *et seq.* REGISTRATION.)

Car hire business—whether carried on in partnership

[47.51] A trader (B) operated a car hire business. He used four different trading names, and had a separate telephone number for each of these branches of the business. In 1978 he sold the rights to use three of the telephones and the related trading name, and granted each of the purchasers the right to use six car radios. Following these sales, B and the three purchasers used the same office and shared certain overheads. The Commissioners issued an assessment on the basis that the effect of these arrangements was that B had in fact traded in partnership with the three purchasers. He appealed, contending that he had genuinely disposed of the relevant parts of his business, was not in partnership with the purchasers, and was no longer required to be registered. The tribunal accepted his evidence and allowed his appeal, holding that the fact that the four traders shared certain overheads did not mean that they were trading in partnership. *T Blomfield*, LON/81/130 (VTD 1177).

Hairdresser—alleged partnership with sons

[47.52] The Commissioners registered a hairdresser on the basis that he was the proprietor of two salons. He appealed, contending that he was only the sole proprietor of one of the salons, and that he was operating the second salon in partnership with his three sons, all of whom were below the age of 18. The tribunal rejected this contention and dismissed his appeal, finding that he was the sole proprietor of both salons, and observing that 'the existence of a partnership requires a consensus between the partners' which was entirely lacking in this case. *JP Bridgeman*, MAN/81/162 (VTD 1206).

Carpenter and musician—alleged partnership with sons

[47.53] The Commissioners discovered that a carpenter, who was registered for VAT, was also working as a part-time jazz musician. They issued an assessment charging VAT on his income from this source. He appealed, contending that he had set up his jazz band as a partnership with his children (one of whom was aged 17, while the other two were under seven years old). The tribunal rejected this contention and dismissed his appeal, finding that, although he paid some of his income into bank accounts in his children's names, he was the sole proprietor of the jazz band and was required to account for VAT on these takings. *RW Kirby*, LON/89/1130Z (VTD 5092).

Joint venture agreement—whether a partnership

[47.54] A company (S) carried on a management consultancy business and also engaged in property development. It did not account for tax on its receipts from property development and the Commissioners issued an assessment. S appealed, contending that its receipts were remuneration for joint ventures which amounted to a partnership. The tribunal dismissed S's appeal, holding that participation in joint venture agreements did not amount to a partnership. The fact that S had only received a specified percentage of the total profits was not conclusive. The essential requirements of a partnership were not fulfilled. S had agreed to supervise the work carried out and this was a taxable supply of services. *Strathearn Gordon Associates Ltd*, [1985] VATTR 79 (VTD 1884).

[47.55] A company (K) carried on the business of property development. It received commission of £125,000 from a larger company (L) with which it had made a profit-sharing agreement, but did not account for VAT on this. The Commissioners issued an assessment and K appealed, contending that it had been in partnership with L. The tribunal dismissed K's appeal, holding that although it had entered into a profit-sharing agreement with L, and had supplied services to L, this did not amount to a partnership. *Keydon Estates Ltd*, LON/88/1225X (VTD 4471).

[47.56] A company (F) carried on the business of property development. It entered into a joint venture agreement with a larger company (C) under which it was to receive £75,000 plus 5% of the profits of the venture. It did not account for VAT on its receipts under the agreement, and the Commissioners issued an assessment. F appealed, contending that the agreement amounted to a partnership. The tribunal dismissed F's appeal, applying *Strathearn Gordon Associates*, **47.54** above, and *Keydon Estates Ltd*, **47.55** above, and holding that the agreement did not amount to a partnership. *Fivegrange Ltd*, LON/89/1631Y (VTD 5338).

[47.57] The decisions in *Strathearn Gordon Associates*, **47.54** above, *Keydon Estates Ltd*, **47.55** above, and *Fivegrange Ltd*, **47.56** above, were applied in the similar subsequent cases of *Forestmead Ltd*, LON/98/219 (VTD 15852); *Thorstone Developments Ltd*, LON/01/007 (VTD 17821) and *Private & Confidential Ltd*, FTT [2009] UKFTT 59 (TC), TC00038.

Retail shop—whether shop manager a partner or employee

[47.58] In the case noted at **47.25** above, the owner of a small shop had failed to register for VAT. The Commissioners issued an assessment charging tax on the shop takings. He appealed, contending that he was operating the shop in partnership with the woman whom he had appointed as shop manager. The tribunal rejected this contention and upheld the assessment, holding that the manager was an employee rather than a partner. The tribunal observed that she was paid a fixed salary and 'had no right to share in either the profits or the capital of the business'. *WE Kenny (t/a Scruples)*, LON/85/150 (VTD 2039).

Hairdressers—whether trading in partnership

[47.59] Four women carried on business as hairdressers from a salon in Blackpool. The Commissioners issued a notice of compulsory registration on the basis that they were trading in partnership. They appealed, contending that they were trading as individuals and not as a partnership, and were not required to register as their individual turnover was below the registration threshold in each case. The tribunal accepted this contention and allowed their appeal. On the evidence, the business had 'very little passing or casual trade' and each hairdresser had 'her own established clientele which she has built up over the years'. Customers were 'not attracted to the salon but to the individual stylist by word of mouth and recommendation'. The hairdressers were each conducting their own business from shared premises, and the fact that they shared certain overheads did not mean that they were trading in partnership. *C Hunter, A Kiernan, M Wigglesworth & LA Wright*, MAN/99/376 (VTD 16558).

Public house—whether publican and caterer trading in partnership

[47.60] A publican arranged for a friend to provide catering at the public house. The caterer was not registered for VAT. The publican was registered, but did not account for VAT on the receipts from catering. The Commissioners issued a ruling that the publican and the caterer were trading in partnership. They appealed. The tribunal allowed their appeal, holding on the evidence that they were not trading in partnership; there were two separate businesses and the catering business was not liable for VAT. *GM Prottey (t/a The Lord Nelson) & MW Brampton*, MAN/99/367 (VTD 16730).

Fish and chip shop and mobile van

[47.61] See *Insley & Clayton*, **62.309** SUPPLY.

Bookmakers—alleged partnership

[47.62] See *SP Graham Ltd & Others*, **57.105** REGISTRATION.

Father and son operating cleaning businesses from same premises

[47.63] See *James*, **57.211** REGISTRATION.

Other cases

[47.64] There are a number of other cases, which appear to raise no point of general importance, in which the tribunal has held that a partnership has not existed. Such cases turn entirely on their own facts and, in the interests of space, are not summarised individually in this book.

Associated partnerships

Adjacent take-away restaurants

[47.65] See *Plummer*, 57.205 REGISTRATION.

Associated partnerships operating hotel and holiday flats

[47.66] See *Hodges*, 57.209 REGISTRATION.

Associated partnerships supplying carpentry services

[47.67] See *RE & RL Newton*, 62.369 SUPPLY.

Waste disposal and skip hire—whether a single business

[47.68] See *Skelton Waste Disposal*, 62.370 SUPPLY.

Miscellaneous

Partnership debt—bankruptcy order against one partner

[47.69] A married couple operated a wine business in partnership. There was no formal partnership deed. The partnership failed to account for substantial amounts of VAT, and the Commissioners served statutory demands on both partners. The husband made an individual voluntary arrangement with his creditors under *Insolvency Act 1986, Part VIII*. However the wife's creditors rejected a similar proposal, and in March 1994 the wife (who was engaged in matrimonial proceedings against her husband) was declared bankrupt. The CA dismissed her appeal against the order. *Article 15(3) of the Insolvent Partnerships Order 1986* expressly dispensed with any need to couple the presentation of a bankruptcy petition with a petition to wind up the partnership. A creditor could rely on an admitted or indisputable debt, including one established by an unsatisfied statutory demand, as a proper basis for a bankruptcy petition. The joint debt of a partner was a debt owed by that partner for the purposes of *Insolvency Act 1986, s 267(1)*. The fact that one member of a partnership had entered into an individual voluntary arrangement did not protect other members of the partnership from enforcement by a partnership creditor against their separate estates. *VGM Schooler v C & E Commrs*, CA 20 July 1995 unreported.

Partnership debt—statutory demand against one partner

[47.70] A married couple operated a public house in partnership. In August 1999 the marriage broke down and the wife left her husband. In February 2000 she notified the Commissioners that the partnership had been dissolved. In January 2001 the Commissioners served a statutory demand on her for unpaid VAT of almost £20,000, covering the periods from June 1999 to February 2000. She applied for the demand to be set aside, contending that the partnership had ceased in August 1999 so that the demands for subsequent periods were invalid. The Ch D rejected this contention and upheld the demand, holding that the effect of *VATA 1994, s 45(2)* was that, for the purposes of VAT, the partnership was deemed to have continued until the Commissioners were notified of its dissolution. The purpose of *s 45(2)* was 'plainly to place the onus of notifying the Commissioners of a change in partnership firmly on the partners'. Furthermore, this was 'eminently sensible', since 'those who know that a partnership has been dissolved are the partners. Neither the Commissioners nor anyone else dealing with the partnership will know of the dissolution until they have received notification of the dissolution.' The tribunal commented that it would 'be strange if it were otherwise, as partners could then avoid liability by the simple expedient of asserting the dissolution of the partnership. Those dealing with the partnership have no way of knowing that the partnership had been dissolved until they had been notified of that fact.' *C & E Commrs v Jamieson*, Ch D 2001, [2002] STC 1418.

Partnership debt—joint and several liability of partners

[47.71] A partnership was dissolved in 1995 and deregistered. Its accountants subsequently informed the Commissioners that the partnership owed £3,738 in unpaid VAT. The Commissioners issued an assessment accordingly. One of the partners appealed. The tribunal dismissed the appeal, observing that 'as they were partners in the business, both are responsible for any debt incurred whilst partners'. *SR Foster*, LON/00/710 (VTD 17241).

Retirement of partner—subsequent VAT repayment to partnership

[47.72] From 1985 to 1992 two individuals (H and S) traded in partnership as opticians. In 1992 H retired. Subsequently S submitted a claim to Customs for repayment of overpaid VAT, and in January 1996 Customs made a substantial repayment. H took proceedings against S, claiming that he was entitled to a share of the part of the VAT repayment relating to the period when the business had been carried on in partnership. The QB accepted this contention and gave judgment for H, holding that the terms of the partnership deed did not bar H from his right to a share in the repayment. *Hawthorn v Smallcorn*, Ch D [1998] STC 591.

Supplies by partnership to individual partner

[47.73] See *Border Flying Co*, 7.48 BUSINESS, and *RGB Contractors*, 36.299 INPUT TAX.

Partner's caravan partly used for business purposes

[47.74] See *Smith Wheeler & Hay*, 36.140 INPUT TAX.

Retention of leased car by outgoing partner

[47.75] See *Mrs Hague*, 36.175 INPUT TAX.

Partnership Act business—whether a business for VAT purposes

[47.76] See *Three H Aircraft Hire*, 7.7 BUSINESS.

Family farming partnership—second dwelling-house on farm

[47.77] See *Herrod-Taylor & Co*, 36.284 INPUT TAX.

Whether partnership temporarily discontinued

[47.78] See *Barnett & Larsen*, 52.303 PENALTIES: MISDECLARATION.

Payment by new partner for admission to partnership

[47.79] See *KapHag Renditefonds 35 Spreecenter Berlin-Hellersdorf 3 Tanche GbR v Finanzamt Charlottenburg*, 22.90 EUROPEAN COMMUNITY LAW.

48

Payment of Tax

The cases in this chapter are arranged under the following headings.

Payment of VAT and credit for input tax (VATA 1994, s 25)   **48.1**
Repayment of tax (VATA 1994, s 80)
    Recovery of overpaid VAT *(VATA 1994, s 80(1))*   **48.16**
    Unjust enrichment *(VATA 1994, s 80(3))*   **48.28**
    Three-year time limit *(VATA 1994, s 80(4))*   **48.50**
    'Clawback' assessments *(VATA 1994, s 80(4A))*   **48.76**
    Calculation of claim *(VATA 1994, s 80(6))*   **48.81**
Repayment supplement (VATA 1994, s 79)
    Conditions for supplement *(VATA 1994, s 79(2))*   **48.82**
    Periods to be left out of account *(VATA 1994, s 79(3))*   **48.85**
    Period of inquiry *(VATA 1994, s 79(4))*   **48.97**
    Miscellaneous   **48.109**
Interest payable in cases of official error (VATA 1994, s 78)
    Whether any official error   **48.114**
    Computation of interest   **48.140**
Miscellaneous   **48.148**

Payment of VAT and credit for input tax (VATA 1994, s 25)

Application of VATA 1994, s 25

[48.1] On the introduction of VAT, the Royal College of Obstetricians and Gynaecologists did not apply for registration, on the basis that its supplies were predominantly exempt. In 1995 its advisers became aware that it would have been to the College's advantage to register for VAT, as it had made taxable supplies and would have been able to recover significant amounts of input tax. It thereupon applied for registration in October 1995. The Commissioners accepted the application and issued a VAT return covering the period from 1 April 1973 to 31 December 1995. In January 1996 the College submitted the return, claiming a repayment of more than £640,000. On 18 July 1996 the Paymaster-General stated in Parliament that legislation was to be included in the 1997 Finance Bill to introduce a three-year limit for retrospective repayment claims with retrospective effect from 18 July 1996. Following this announcement, the Commissioners wrote to the College stating that they were only willing to repay £47,454. The College lodged an appeal against this ruling. The Commissioners applied for the appeal to be struck out, contending that the tribunal had no jurisdiction. The tribunal rejected this application, holding that there was a dispute concerning 'the amount of input tax which may be credited', within *VATA 1994, s 83(c)*. The tribunal also allowed the College's appeal, observing that *VATA 1994* 'provides for no specified time within which, and no precise date by which, the Commissioners are required to make a payment found to be due from them to a taxpayer under *s 25*', but holding that the Commissioners had no 'discretion to delay or defer such a payment' and that *s 25* 'envisages that the Commissioners will diligently, expeditiously and scrupulously deal with any claim by a taxpayer'. *Royal College of Obstetricians and Gynaecologists*, MAN/96/967 (VTD 14558). (*Note*. For a subsequent application for judicial review, see *R v C & E Commrs (ex p. Kay & Co Ltd and Others)*, **48.50** below.)

Claim under VAT Regulations 1995, reg 29 as originally enacted

[48.2] Following the decision noted at **46.146** PARTIAL EXEMPTION, the university claimed a repayment of tax dating back to 1973. The claim was lodged in November 1996. The Commissioners only agreed to repay tax within the three-year time limit laid down by *VATA 1994, s 80(4)*. The university appealed, contending that the claim had been lodged under *VAT Regulations 1995 (SI 1995/2518), reg 29*, so that *VATA 1994, s 80(4)* did not apply. The Ch D accepted this contention and allowed the appeal. Neuberger J held that the university's failure to claim input tax at the earliest time did not mean that it had overpaid money to the Commissioners. Accordingly the claim was not within *VATA 1994, s 80*. Under the wording of *reg 29* as in force at the relevant time, the Commissioners should have accepted the claim as valid. The CA unanimously upheld this decision. Auld LJ held that the Commissioners were not entitled to reject the claim, since it 'was not in breach of any reasonable administrative or procedural requirements'. *C & E Commrs v University of Sussex*, CA 2003, [2004] STC 1; [2003] EWCA Civ 1448. (*Notes*. (1) *VAT Regulations, reg 29* was subsequently amended by *VAT (Amendment) Regulations 1997 (SI 1997/1086)*, to introduce a three-year 'cap' with effect from 1 May 1997. For cases concerning *VAT Regulations 1995 (SI 1995/2518), reg 29(1A)*, see **48.3** to **48.6** below. (2) The case was heard in the CA with *Marks & Spencer plc (No 5)*, **22.56** EUROPEAN COMMUNITY LAW.)

Late claim to input tax—application of reg 29(1A)

[48.3] In late 1999 a company discovered that it had failed to claim input tax on an invoice dated January 1996. It reclaimed the tax in its return for the period ending 31 January 2000. The Commissioners rejected the claim on the basis that the claim was outside the three-year time limit imposed by *VAT Regulations 1995 (SI 1995/2518), reg 29(1A)*. The tribunal dismissed the company's appeal. *Plastic Developments Ltd*, MAN/00/914 (VTD 17416).

[48.4] Similar decisions were reached in *MJG Garlick (t/a John Moreton Photography)*, LON/01/818 (VTD 17672); *Knowles Food Services Ltd*, EDN/01/166 (VTD 17674); *James Paget Industries Ltd*, MAN/03/041 (VTD 18436); *Westland Horticulture Ltd*, LON/02/263 (VTD 18686); *Constructive Solutions (Contracts) Ltd*, MAN/04/053 (VTD 18930); *The Wine Portfolio Company Ltd*, LON/01/095 (VTD 19058); *Trademarque Tools Ltd*, MAN/06/720 (VTD 20308), and *Morgan Stanley UK Group*, **46.172** PARTIAL EXEMPTION.

[48.5] In November 2001 an investment trust claimed a substantial repayment of VAT relating to the period from February 1998 to August 1998. The Commissioners rejected the claim on the basis that it was outside the three-year time limit laid down by *VAT Regulations 1995 (SI 1995/2518), reg 29(1A)*. The trust appealed, contending that *reg 29(1A)* was invalid under European law. The Ch D rejected this contention and dismissed the appeal. *Local Authorities Mutual Investment Trust v C & E Commrs*, Ch D 2003, [2004] STC 246; [2003] EWHC 2766 (Ch). (*Note.* See now, however, the HL decisions in *Fleming*, 48.6 below, and *Condé Nast Publications Ltd*, 48.7 below.)

[48.6] In October 2000 a trader (F) reclaimed input tax in respect of three cars which he had purchased in 1989 and 1990. Customs rejected the claim on the basis that it was outside the three-year time limit laid down by *VAT Regulations 1995 (SI 1995/2518), reg 29(1A)*. F appealed, contending that the time limit should be treated as invalid under European Community law, since there had been no 'transitional period', as required by the CJEC decision in *Marks & Spencer plc*, 22.55 EUROPEAN COMMUNITY LAW. The CA unanimously accepted this contention and allowed F's appeal, and the HL unanimously upheld this decision. Lord Hope of Craighead held that 'it is for Parliament or the Commissioners, if they choose to do so by means of an announcement disseminated to all taxpayers, to introduce prospectively an adequate transitional period. Until that is done the three-year time limit must be disapplied in the case of all claims for the deduction of input tax that had accrued before the introduction of the time limit.' Lord Neuberger of Abbotsbury held that there was 'no difference in principle or practice between a case where there is an inadequate transitional period and one where there is no transitional period'. *HMRC v M Fleming (t/a Bodycraft)*, HL [2008] STC 324; [2008] UKHL 2; [2008] 1 All ER 1061. (*Notes.* (1) The HL heard the appeal with *Condé Nast Publications Ltd*, 48.7 below. (2) For HMRC's practice following this decision, see HMRC Brief 07/08, issued on 20 February 2008. See also *FA 2008, s 121*.)

[48.7] In June 2003 a company (C) claimed a repayment of input tax relating to staff entertainment, backdated to April 1973. Customs rejected the majority of the claim on the basis that it was outside the three-year time limit laid down by *VAT Regulations 1995 (SI 1995/2518), reg 29(1A)* and the practice laid down by Business Brief 22/2002, in which Customs had stated that they would allow repayments where taxpayers 'can demonstrate that they discovered the error before 31 March 1997'. C appealed, contending that the three-year time limit should be treated as invalid under European Community law. The CA accepted this contention and allowed the appeal, and the HL upheld this decision (by a 4-1 majority, Lord Walker of Gestingthorpe dissenting). Lord Neuberger of Abbotsbury held that Customs' Business Briefs 22/2002 and 27/2002 'both limited the concession to a very narrow group of those with accrued rights at the date the time limit in *regulation 29(1A)* was introduced'. It would not 'be reasonable to hold that a person who had an accrued right has fairly been given an opportunity of making a claim, when the Commissioners, the relevant organ of the executive arm of government, was officially announcing that, if such a claim were made, it would not be allowed.' Furthermore, the Business Briefs had not 'been sufficiently widely disseminated to make it right to conclude that all potential claimants should be treated as having had sufficient notice of the period of disapplication'. Lord Scott of Foscote held that 'Business Briefs published by the Commissioners can properly be regarded as published pursuant to the Commissioners' management powers but are not a means enabling the Commissioners to amend the VAT regime made by primary and secondary legislation'. *HMRC v Condé Nast Publications Ltd*, HL [2008] STC 324; [2008] UKHL 2; [2008] 1 All ER 1061. (*Note.* The HL heard the appeal with *Fleming*, **48.6** above.)

[48.8] The decision in *Fleming*, **48.6** above, was applied in the similar subsequent cases of *Seymour Caravan Sales Ltd*, LON/05/158 (VTD 19869) and *Alberto-Culver (UK) Ltd*, [2011] UKFTT 832 (TC), TC01668.

[48.9] In a Scottish case where the facts were broadly similar, the CS adjourned the appeal pending the final decision in *HMRC v Scottish Equitable plc*, **48.57** below. *National Galleries of Scotland (No 3)*, [2007] VATDR 234 (VTD 20253).

[48.10] In April 1997 a company incurred substantial amounts of input tax in respect of professional fees relating to a proposed merger. It only claimed a small part of these fees as input tax in its return for the period ending 30 June 1997. Customs formed the opinion that none of the tax was deductible, and in October 1997 they issued an assessment to recover the tax which the company had claimed. The company paid the tax charged by the assessment. In 2005, following the CJEC decision in *Kretztechnik AG v Finanzamt Linz*, **22.91** EUROPEAN COMMUNITY LAW, the company formed the opinion that it should have been allowed to reclaim the whole of the tax. Customs rejected the claim on the basis that it had been made outside the statutory three-year time limit. The company appealed, contending that the three-year time limit should be treated as invalid under European Community law. The tribunal dismissed the company's appeal, distinguishing the HL decision in *Fleming*, **48.6** above, on the basis that the trader in that case had a pre-existing right to input tax at 30 April 1997 which could not be extinguished by the introduction of the three-year time limit with effect from 1 May. In this case, however, the company only acquired a 'meaningful and exercisable right' at the end of its quarterly accounting period on 30 June 1997, and did not have a 'pre-existing claim' at 30 April 1997, immediately before the introduction of the three-year time limit. Accordingly the effect of *regulation 29(1A)* was that the tax could not be claimed outside the three-year time limit. *Cable & Wireless plc v HMRC*, [2009] VATDR 538; [2009] UKFTT 32 (TC), TC00004.

Whether repayment claim made within three-year time limit

[48.11] In June 2002 a company submitted a repayment claim relating to the period ending February 2000. It did not receive any acknowledgment, and did not pursue the claim until May 2003. The Commissioners replied that they had no record of receiving the claim which the company claimed to have submitted in 2002, and rejected the claim on the basis that it had not been lodged until May 2003, which was outside the statutory three-year time limit. The company appealed. The tribunal accepted the company's evidence and allowed the appeal, finding that it was satisfied that the company had posted its claim in June 2002. It appeared that the claim had been lost in the post. However, the claim had been made when it had been posted, which was within the three-year time limit. The tribunal observed that 'the essence of entrusting a claim to the Post Office is that once the letter is in the hands of the Post Office it is, so far as the taxpayer is concerned, beyond recall and in that sense has been made'. The tribunal declined to follow the case of *W Timms & Son (Builders) Ltd*, **59.10** RETURNS (which the Commissioners had cited as an authority) on the grounds that it 'concerned the use of the word "received" in the relevant statutory provision and that it was a case in which it was proved that the relevant return was *not* received by the specified time'. *Quintain Estates Development plc*, [2005] VATDR 123 (VTD 18877).

[48.12] In a Scottish case, a charity claimed a repayment of input tax covering the period from 1973 to 1995. Customs rejected the claim on the basis that it had not been made until September 1998, which was outside the three-year time limit laid down by *VAT Regulations 1995 (SI 1995/2518), reg 29(1A)*. The trust appealed, contending that it had made an initial unquantified claim by letter in December 1996, before the introduction of *reg 29(1A)*. The tribunal accepted this contention and allowed the appeal, holding that the letter of December 1996 was 'an unquantified claim' in which the charity sought 'to obtain refund of either an agreed amount or an arguable amount of input tax'. *National Galleries of Scotland (No 2)*, EDN/04/115 (VTD 19372). (*Notes.* (1) The chairman (Mr. Coutts) also expressed the view that the three-year time limit laid down by *VAT Regulations 1995 (SI 1995/2518), reg 29(1A)* did not comply with the CJEC decision in *Grundig Italiana SpA v Ministero delle Finanze*, **22.57** EUROPEAN COMMUNITY LAW, and that 'unless and until the legislation is amended or modified by the only appropriate body to do so, the capping provision in *regulation 29(1A)* cannot be relied on'. However Mr. Coutts' views on this issue were subsequently disapproved by the CS in *HMRC v Scottish Equitable plc*, **48.57** below. (2) For a subsequent appeal by the same company, see **48.9** above.)

[48.13] A couple operated a public house. They ceased trading in late 2005 and submitted a repayment claim in October 2006. In October 2007 HMRC rejected the claim on the basis that the couple had not provided sufficient information. In March 2008 the couple's accountant resubmitted the claim with an accompanying schedule and all relevant invoices. HMRC repaid part of the tax claimed, but disallowed the input tax shown on all invoices prior to 21 April 2005, on the grounds that 'the date of the invoice must be taken from the date an acceptable claim is received'. The couple appealed. The tribunal allowed their appeal, holding that the letter of 31 March 2008 was a continuation of the claim originally submitted in October 2006, that the decision to reject the claim was 'quite unacceptable and oppressive', and that all the input tax claimed was within the three-year time limit. The tribunal commented that 'the appellants have been treated entirely unreasonably by the respondents'. *J & J Dixon v HMRC*, [2010] UKFTT 281 (TC), TC00570.

Interaction of VATA 1994, s 25 and VATA 1994, s 80(4)

[48.14] See also *Royal Bank of Scotland Group plc*, **48.54** below, and *BICC plc*, **48.59** below.

Claim for repayment of input tax—accuracy of claim in doubt

[48.15] See the cases noted at 36.648 to 36.651 INPUT TAX.

Repayment of tax (VATA 1994, s 80)

NOTE

VATA 1994, s 80, which lays down the conditions under which a taxable person may claim recovery of overpaid VAT, was amended by *FA 1997, ss 46, 47*. *VATA 1994, s 80(3A)–(3C)*, which are intended to provide that a taxable person may not claim repayment if he does not intend to pass the repayment to his customers, were introduced by *FA 1997, s 46* with effect from 19 March 1997. *VATA 1994, s 80(4)* was amended by *FA 1997, s 47* to introduce a three-year time limit for retrospective repayment claims with effect from 18 July 1996. Cases relating to periods before 19 March 1997 should be read in the light of the changes in the legislation.

Recovery of overpaid VAT (VATA 1994, s 80(1))

Goods supplied to building firm and resold to purchaser of bungalow

[48.16] In 1988 an individual (W), who was not registered for VAT, purchased a new bungalow from a building firm. He also ordered a number of wardrobes, which were supplied to the building firm by a company (S) and installed in the bungalow. S went into receivership in April 1993. The accountancy firm which was appointed as receivers considered that the wardrobes could have been treated as zero-rated, and issued a purported credit note to the builders, observing in a covering letter that the credit note had no commercial value since there were no funds to pay unsecured creditors. In December 1993 W wrote to the Commissioners applying for a refund of the tax charged on the supply of the wardrobes under what is now *VATA 1994, s 80*. The Commissioners rejected the claim and he appealed to a tribunal. The tribunal dismissed his appeal, holding that he was not entitled to a repayment of tax since S had supplied the wardrobes to the building firm, rather than to W. W was not a person who had 'paid an amount to the Commissioners' within *s 80(1)*, and thus he had no right to claim repayment. (The tribunal also held that the wardrobes in question had been correctly treated as standard-rated, distinguishing *McLean Homes Midland Ltd*, 15.226 CONSTRUCTION OF BUILDINGS, ETC., and observed that the receivers had misunderstood the relevant law and had been wrong to issue the purported credit note.) *SH Wade*, MAN/94/642 (VTD 13164).

Business transferred as going concern—claim by transferee

[48.17] See *Shendish Manor Ltd*, 65.118 TRANSFERS OF GOING CONCERNS.

Output tax wrongly charged on surrender of lease

[48.18] In February 1991 a company (E) paid another company (G) £17,250, including VAT of £2,250, in relation to the surrender of a lease. G subsequently went into receivership. Following the CJEC decision in *Lubbock Fine & Co*, 22.333 EUROPEAN COMMUNITY LAW, E formed the opinion that the surrender should have been treated as exempt. It claimed repayment of the £2,250 from the Commissioners. The Commissioners rejected the claim on the grounds that the tax had been accounted for by G rather than E, and that they had no power to refund the tax to anyone other than G. The tribunal dismissed E's appeal, holding that the claim was outside the scope of *VATA 1994, s 80*. *Aberdeen Estates Ltd*, EDN/94/235 (VTD 13622).

Repayment claim by optician

[48.19] Prior to May 1995, the Commissioners treated the sale of spectacles by opticians as a single standard-rated supply. In August 1993, a tribunal held that, while the sale of spectacles was taxable, the services supplied by the optician who dispensed the spectacles was a separate supply which qualified for exemption. The Commissioners appealed against this decision, but it was upheld by the QB in March 1995 (see *Leightons Ltd*, **33.8** HEALTH AND WELFARE). In May 1995 the Commissioners announced that they had accepted the QB decision and would accept repayment claims on certain conditions (see Business Brief 8/95). Meanwhile, in January 1994, an optician who had apportioned his takings between exempt and taxable supplies until February 1993, but had accounted for tax on the whole of his takings from March 1993 to November 1993 in accordance with the Commissioners' instructions, submitted a repayment claim, backdated to August 1988. In the claim, he apportioned his takings on the basis that he had sold spectacles at a 33% mark-up, and that the remainder of his output tax (approximately 30%) related to his exempt supplies of dispensing services. The Commissioners rejected the claim, considering firstly that the repayment should be restricted to the nine-month period from March to November 1993, and secondly that the method of apportionment used in the claim was unacceptable. The optician appealed. The tribunal allowed the appeal in part, finding that the optician's returns for the periods from March 1993 had been submitted on a provisional basis, and holding firstly that the method of valuation used in the claim was acceptable and secondly that the optician was entitled to repayment of the amount claimed for the period from March 1993 to May 1995. (However, the tribunal rejected the claim for the period from August 1988 to February 1993, finding that the returns for those periods had not been provisional and that the method of apportionment used in those returns had also been acceptable.) *MWJ Green*, LON/96/321 (VTD 14844). (*Note.* For the Commissioners' current practice with regard to the apportionment of opticians' income, see Business Brief 2/99, issued on 13 January 1999.)

[48.20] In July 1994, following the tribunal decision in *Leightons Ltd*, **33.8** HEALTH AND WELFARE, a company trading as opticians submitted a repayment claim. In March 1995, following the QB decision in that case, the Commissioners accepted the claim, and in June 1995 they repaid the company £258,000 plus interest. The company then wrote to the Commissioners, stating that its initial claim had been 'based on information produced by the industry prior to Business Brief 31A/93' and 'did not include contact lens dispensing fees'. In April 1996 the company submitted a second repayment claim, based on the 'full cost apportionment method' set out in Business Brief 8/95. The Commissioners rejected this claim on the basis that 'in order for a further claim to be entertained, there must have been an indication, at the time the first claim was submitted, that this was a provisional or interim claim' but there had been no such indication 'that the records were unsatisfactory or likely to produce an inaccurate reflection of the dispensing element'. The company appealed, contending that the initial claim had been submitted in order 'not to be prejudiced by any time limit which might be applicable to a claim for a refund' and that, at the relevant time, 'there was no authoritative information as to how any overpayment should be calculated'. The tribunal accepted this contention and allowed the company's appeal, observing that 'there is nothing on the face of s 80 which in terms provides that only one claim may be made. If the claimant can show that tax has been overpaid, *prima facie* there is a liability on the Commissioners to repay it.' The initial claim did not give rise to *res judicata*, since 'there has been no adjudication on the claim by an independent authority'. There had been no specific agreement to calculate the amount of the overpaid tax by use of the method put forward in the initial claim, since 'what took place in fact took place pursuant to the provisions of a statute and it is inappropriate to seek to regard what occurred as amounting to a contract or binding agreement between the parties'. The company was not estopped from recalculating the amount of the overpayment, since it was 'impossible to see what detriment the Commissioners have suffered'. The initial repayment had not been 'made in reliance on any representation but in pursuance of the statutory obligation under s 80(1)'. *Hayward Gill & Associates Ltd*, [1998] VATDR 352 (VTD 15635). (*Notes.* (1) For the Commissioners' current practice with regard to the apportionment of opticians' income, see Business Brief 2/99, issued on 13 January 1999. (2) The decision in this case was distinguished in the subsequent case of *CL Dyer & Co*, 48.21 below.)

[48.21] The decision in *Hayward Gill & Associates*, **48.20** above, was distinguished in a subsequent case in which a partnership trading as opticians made an initial repayment claim in December 1993 and a subsequent claim, computed on a different basis, in September 1996. The tribunal held on the evidence that 'in no way can the method used to formulate the second claim be described as an "accurate" claim'. Customs had 'allowed themselves to be persuaded by the professional bodies representing opticians that they could in defined circumstances accept an apportionment based upon the cost-plus method in order to dispose of the past'. However, it was 'inherently impossible (except by accident) that a method relying on the mark-up on sundries' (such as contact lens solutions with specific 'sell-by' dates) would 'correctly identify the element in the price paid for spectacles that is attributable to the "hardware"'. The tribunal was 'not persuaded that the original claim did not produce a fair and reasonable attribution' and was satisfied that 'the second claim certainly did not produce one that was more fair and reasonable'. *CL Dyer & Co*, LON/97/1013 (VTD 16053).

[48.22] In 1996, following the QB decision in *Leightons Ltd*, **33.8** HEALTH AND WELFARE, a partnership trading as opticians made a repayment claim on the basis set out in Business Brief 19/95. The Commissioners accepted this claim and made the repayment. In August 1997 the partnership made a further claim, computed on the basis that its standard-rated sales of spectacles should be treated as having been made at a 25% mark-up, and that the remainder of its output tax should be treated as relating to exempt supplies of dispensing services. The Commissioners rejected this claim and the tribunal dismissed the partnership's appeal, holding on the evidence that many of the partnership's sales had been made at a mark-up of more than 25%. *G Langrick & DG Coe*, MAN/x (VTD 18205).

[48.23] See also *Specsavers Optical Group*, **48.127** below, and *FP Whiffen Opticians*, **67.82** VALUATION.

Companies trading as car dealers—bonuses from manufacturers

[48.24] In a Scottish case, two companies which traded as motor dealers submitted claims for the repayment of output tax which they had wrongly accounted for on the receipt of 'demonstrator bonuses' from manufacturers, but which should have been treated as discounts on the sale price of the cars, applying the CJEC decision in *Elida Gibbs Ltd*, **22.235** EUROPEAN COMMUNITY LAW. Customs accepted part of the claims, but rejected part of the claims on the grounds that the companies had not submitted adequate documentary evidence, and also rejected part of the claims on the grounds that the bonuses had been paid by credit note, so that the claim related to input tax rather than output tax and was outside the three-year time limit laid down by *VAT Regulations 1995 (SI 1995/2518), reg 29(1A)*. The tribunal reviewed the evidence in detail and allowed the appeals in part, holding that the companies had not produced evidence to support the amount of the claims, but accepting the companies' contention that the claims related to output tax even where a credit note had been issued. The tribunal held that 'the tax remains properly classified as output tax. The issue of a credit note in this context' was 'no more than an accounting mechanism' whereby 'the manufacturer and dealer organised how they were to pay and be paid the bonus'. *Abercromby Motor Group Ltd; Linn Motor Group Ltd (No 1)*, EDN/04/41 (VTD 19015). (*Note.* The tribunal chairman (Mr. Coutts) also expressed the view that the three-year time limit laid down by *VAT Regulations 1995 (SI 1995/2518), reg 29(1A)* did not comply with the CJEC decision in *Grundig Italiana SpA v Ministero delle Finanze*, **22.57** EUROPEAN COMMUNITY LAW. However Mr. Coutts' views on this issue were subsequently disapproved by the CS in *HMRC v Scottish Equitable plc*, **48.57** below.)

[48.25] Following the CA decision in *Fleming*, **48.6** above, Customs wrote to the companies in the case noted at **48.24** above, accepting that a repayment was due, but stating that they still required verification of the amount sought. The companies applied to the tribunal, which declined to order an immediate repayment, holding that Customs had a 'duty to review the quantum' of the claims and that '"verification" means more than checking sums. It involves a demonstration of the truth or correctness of the claim'. *Abercromby Motor Group Ltd; Linn Motor Group Ltd (No 2)*, EDN/06/34 (VTD 20092).

Car dealers—claim for repayment of tax attributable to free insurance

[48.26] See *Peugeot Motor Co plc v C & E Commrs (and related appeal)*, **38.52** INSURANCE.

Supplies wrongly treated as exempt in partial exemption computation

[48.27] A bank supplied certain services to open-ended investment companies. The Commissioners had treated these supplies as taxable, since they failed to qualify for exemption under the provisions of *VATA 1994, Sch 9, Group 5* as in force at the relevant time. Following the tribunal decisions in *Prudential Assurance Co Ltd*, 27.59 FINANCE, and *Abbey National plc*, 22.368 EUROPEAN COMMUNITY LAW, the Commissioners accepted that the provisions of *Group 5* did not comply with *Article 13B(d)* of the *EC Sixth Directive*, and that the supplies qualified for exemption under EC law. The bank claimed a repayment of more than £448,000, being the total VAT which it had charged to its customers in respect of the relevant supplies. The Commissioners issued a ruling that the repayable amount was the £137,000 which the bank had actually paid as VAT, ie after deducting the relevant input tax of £311,000. The tribunal upheld the Commissioners' ruling and dismissed the bank's appeal. The tribunal observed that, for the purposes of *VATA 1994, s 80(1)*, 'it is not possible to repay an amount greater than the amount paid. The concept of repayment necessarily involves prior payment.' Applying the principles laid down in *Sunningdale Golf Club*, 48.31 below, 'the appellant cannot take the benefit of direct effect without the burden'. *Barclays Bank plc*, LON/02/815 (VTD 18410).

Unjust enrichment (*VATA 1994, s 80(3)*)

Cases where the appellant was unsuccessful

[48.28] Two companies went into voluntary liquidation and were deregistered. Subsequently the companies' liquidator discovered that the companies had accounted for VAT on some supplies which had qualified for zero-rating. In May 1992 he submitted repayment claims in respect of these supplies. The Commissioners rejected the claims, considering that the repayment would result in unjust enrichment, as the liquidator did not intend to pass the benefit of the repayment back to the customers. The liquidator appealed, contending that there would be no unjust enrichment since the funds would be distributed to the company's creditors. The tribunal dismissed the appeals, holding that, under the principles of natural justice, if the Commissioners were to repay the money to the liquidator, the liquidator should repay the money to the customers who had actually paid the VAT to the company. Since the liquidator was not proposing to refund the money to the original customers, but to distribute it in accordance with insolvency law, any repayment would result in 'unjust enrichment'. *Creative Facility Ltd*, MAN/92/1157; *Oblique Press Ltd*, MAN/92/1158 (VTD 10891).

[48.29] A married couple were registered for VAT as the proprietors of a hotel and some holiday chalets. In April 1990 they signed a deed of partnership whereby one of their sons was accepted as a partner in the hotel business, but not in the chalet business. They did not notify the Commissioners of this change, and continued to account for VAT in respect of both businesses under the same registration number. In December 1992 they submitted a claim for repayment of the output tax for which they had accounted in respect of the chalet business, on the basis that the turnover of that business, if treated separately, was below the registration threshold. The Commissioners rejected the claim, considering that the effect of what is now *VATA 1994, s 80* was that no repayment was due. The tribunal dismissed the couple's appeal, holding that, since the couple did not intend to repay the VAT to the customers to whom they had originally charged it, any repayment to the couple would result in 'unjust enrichment'. *P & E Daynes*, EDN/93/16 (VTD 10988).

[48.30] A similar decision was reached in *Peterborough Diocesan Conference & Retreat House*, 33.68 HEALTH AND WELFARE.

[48.31] A golf club registered for VAT from 1973. For all its accounting periods until 1 April 1994, it accounted for output tax on its membership subscriptions as taxable supplies, and was allowed credit for input tax. On 1 April 1994 its membership subscriptions became exempt following the introduction of what is now *VATA 1994, Sch 9, Group 10* by *SI 1994/687*. This was intended to give effect to *Article 13A1(m)* of the *EC Sixth Directive*, which the UK should have implemented by 1 January 1990. Accordingly, under EC law, the requirement for the club to account for output tax was unlawful with effect from 1 January 1990. The club submitted a repayment claim, as invited by the Commissioners' News Release dated 10 March 1994. The Commissioners made a net repayment of the amount of wrongly-paid output tax reduced by the amount of input tax for which credit had been allowed. Subsequently the club submitted a further claim for the amount of the input tax. The Commissioners rejected the claim and the club appealed. The tribunal dismissed the appeal, holding that the club 'would be unjustly enriched if repaid an amount which has already been credited to or received by them as input tax'. Applying *Becker v Finanzamt Münster-Innenstadt*, 22.352 EUROPEAN COMMUNITY LAW, 'an individual who relies on the (*Sixth*) *Directive* as the source of his Community law right to exemption for his supplies must accept that this carries with it the corresponding disqualification of relief for input tax on goods and services used in making those supplies'. The club could not 'invoke *Article 13A1(m)* and claim exemption in isolation; it must accept as a concomitant "disadvantage", in asserting its Community law right to exemption, that deduction for input tax is not available'. The tribunal observed that 'where there is a net liability to output tax, it will never be appropriate for a taxable person to be "repaid" input tax by the Commissioners, since full credit for that input tax will already have been given. The most that they could ever be required to repay will be what has actually been paid over to them, namely the "gross" amount of output tax less the input tax properly recoverable against that tax by way of credit or deduction'. *Sunningdale Golf Club*, [1997] VATDR 79 (VTD 14899).

[48.32] The principles laid down in *Sunningdale Golf Club*, 48.31 above, were applied in a subsequent case in which the tribunal dismissed an appeal by a company which operated a residential home. *Benridge Care Homes Ltd v HMRC*, [2010] UKFTT 493 (TC), TC00751.

[48.33] A trust had paid a cricket club £70,000 as consideration for surrendering a lease. The club accounted for VAT (of £10,500) on this. However, following the decisions in *Lubbock Fine & Co*, 22.333 EUROPEAN COMMUNITY LAW, and *Grantham Cricket Club*, 41.68 LAND, the club formed the opinion that the payment should have been treated as exempt, and claimed repayment of the £10,500 from the Commissioners. The Commissioners rejected the claim under *VATA 1994, s 80(3)*, on the basis that repayment would unjustly enrich the club. The club appealed. The tribunal dismissed the appeal, holding on the evidence that the repayment would be unjust, since the

VAT had been borne by the landlord and repayment would mean that the club 'would be in receipt of funds it would not have had in the first place and which it never expected to retain'. *Grantham Cricket Club (No 2)*, MAN/97/465 (VTD 15527).

[48.34] A company sold standard forms of contract documents, principally relating to building contracts. In 1994 the Commissioners issued a ruling that sales of such documents did not qualify for zero-rating. Subsequently the Commissioners accepted that most of the documents qualified for zero-rating under *VATA 1994, Sch 8, Group 3, Item 1*. The company submitted a claim for repayment of tax on such supplies. The Commissioners agreed to pay a small percentage of the claim (slightly under 10%), but refused to repay the balance, on the grounds that the VAT had been borne by the company's customers and that repaying it to the company would lead to 'unjust enrichment'. The company appealed, contending that, since it had covenanted to pay its profits to the Royal Institute of British Architects, which was a registered charity, it would not be unjustly enriched by the repayment. The tribunal rejected this contention and dismissed the company's appeal, observing that 'this structure, whereby a charity puts its taxable trading activities into a separate trading company, which undertakes to make an annual payment back to the charity of profits, is a common one'. The fact that the company would not retain the repayment was the voluntary decision of the company, and was 'a very different type of obligation to that under the law of receivership or liquidation'. *RIBA Publications*, [1999] VATDR 230 (VTD 15983).

[48.35] Before July 1997, the Commissioners had treated 'manufacturers' bonuses', paid by car manufacturers in relation to leasing transactions, as consideration for taxable supplies of services. In Business Brief 16/97, issued following the CJEC decision in *Elida Gibbs Ltd*, 22.235 EUROPEAN COMMUNITY LAW, the Commissioners announced that they would treat such bonuses as discounts on the purchase price of cars. Subsequently a company (L), which had received a large number of such bonuses and had accounted for output tax on them, submitted a repayment claim. The Commissioners rejected the claim on the basis that it would lead to the 'unjust enrichment' of L and its VAT group, contrary to *VATA 1994, s 80(3)*. The representative member of the group appealed. The tribunal allowed the appeal but the Ch D reversed this decision and upheld the Commissioners' rejection of the claim. Jacob J held that 'the only reasonable inference from the evidence placed before the tribunal is that those who bore the loss caused by the wrongful treatment of manufacturers' bonuses were (L's) customers, not (L). For (L) to be repaid the tax would be unjust enrichment.' The fact that other VAT offices had accepted similar claims by some of L's rivals, without raising the question of unjust enrichment, was not within the jurisdiction of the tribunal. Furthermore, 'just because a tax gatherer makes a blunder which favours some taxpayers by way of a windfall does not mean that he should perpetuate the blunder in favour of others. A number of wrongs do not necessarily make a right. The interests of the general community are involved — taxpayers collectively have an interest that tax properly due should be collected, and that there should not be repayments to people who are not entitled to them.' *C & E Commrs v National Westminster Bank plc*, Ch D [2003] STC 1072; [2003] EWHC 1822 (Ch).

[48.36] A woman (C) operated a riding school and livery yard. She accounted for VAT on her livery supplies. Subsequently she formed the opinion that these supplies should have been treated as exempt, and submitted a repayment claim. The Commissioners rejected the claim on the basis that it appeared that C had agreed to let her accountants keep 20% of the proposed repayment, instead of repaying it to the original customers, so that repayment would lead to 'unjust enrichment', contrary to *VATA 1994, s 80(3)*. The tribunal accepted this contention and dismissed C's appeal. *PA Cowdy (t/a Berriewood Farm)*, MAN/03/153 (VTD 18599).

[48.37] HMRC presented a winding-up petition against a football club which had failed to pay its VAT liabilities. The club applied for the petition to be struck out, contending that it should not have been required to account for VAT on fees which it had received for the transfer of some of its players' registrations, since these should be treated as compensation and as outside the scope of VAT. The Ch D rejected this contention and dismissed the club's application. Newey J held that the club had failed to show that VAT was not payable on transfer fees, but that even if this were so, it would not reduce the club's liabilities to HMRC, since the club would be obliged to pass any repayment onto the clubs which had purchased the registrations. *Portsmouth City Football Club Ltd v HMRC*, Ch D [2010] EWHC 75 (Ch); [2011] STC 683. (*Note*. The club subsequently entered a company voluntary arrangement with its creditors: for subsequent proceedings, see Ch D [2010] EWHC 2013 (Ch).)

Cases where the appellant was partly successful

[48.38] A major retail company submitted two claims for repayment of substantial amounts of VAT. One of the claims related to sales of boys' socks for shoe sizes 4 to 7, which the company had treated as standard-rated until May 1995, although the Commissioners had accepted that they qualified for zero-rating from April 1994. The tribunal allowed the company's appeal with regard to this claim, observing that the company had not reduced its prices when it began to treat the socks as zero-rated, and holding on the evidence that the VAT had been absorbed by the company. The other claim related to sales of chocolate-covered teacakes, which the company had treated as standard-rated from 1973 until 1994, when the Commissioners accepted that they qualified for zero-rating. The Commissioners agreed to repay 10% of the amount claimed, but rejected the balance of the claim on the grounds that repayment would 'unjustly enrich' the company, contrary to *VATA 1994, s 80(3)*. The tribunal dismissed the company's appeal with regard to this claim, observing that the company had reduced its prices when it began to treat the teacakes as zero-rated, and holding on the evidence that the balance of the VAT had been passed on to the purchasers of the teacakes. The company appealed to the CA, which upheld the tribunal decision. The tribunal had been entitled to find on the evidence that the burden of VAT had been passed on to the company's customers, and that its imposition had caused no loss of profit. *Marks & Spencer plc v C & E Commrs*, CA 1999, [2000] STC 16. (*Notes.* (1) See now, however, *VATA 1994, s 80(3A)–(3C)*, introduced by *FA 1997, s 46* with effect from 19 March 1997 (2) For another issue in this case, taken to the CJEC, see **22.55** EUROPEAN COMMUNITY LAW. For subsequent developments, see **22.56** EUROPEAN COMMUNITY LAW.)

[48.39] A company (R) which operated an employment agency had accounted for VAT on the whole of its receipts from its clients. In 1997 it submitted a substantial repayment claim, covering the period since 1991, on the grounds that it should only have accounted for VAT on its commission. In 2003, following the ECJ decision in *Marks & Spencer plc v C & E Commrs (No 4)*, **22.55** EUROPEAN COMMUNITY LAW, Customs made a repayment. R made a further claim, dating back to 1973, seeking to recover output tax relating to supplies to clients which were wholly or partly exempt or were not registered for VAT. Customs rejected this claim and R appealed. In March 2009, following the ECJ decision in *Marks & Spencer plc v C & E Commrs (No 5)*, **22.56** EUROPEAN COMMUNITY LAW, and while its appeal was pending, R made two additional repayment claims in respect of supplies to clients who were taxable (and thus were able to recover output tax in full). HMRC rejected these claims on the grounds that they would lead to unjust enrichment. The First-Tier Tribunal held a preliminary hearing in 2011 and allowed R's appeal in principle with regard to the 2003 claim, accepting R's contention that it should only have accounted for VAT on its commission. Judge Berner held that 'the proper analysis of the nature of (R's) supply to its clients does not depend on whether (R) was acting in a particular case as principal or as agent'. However, with regard to the claims which R had made in 2009, the tribunal upheld HMRC's contention that these had been new claims rather than amendments to the claim made in 2003, with the result that HMRC was entitled to rely on the defence of unjust enrichment. *Reed Employment Ltd v HMRC (No 3)*, [2011] UKFTT 200 (TC); [2011] SFTD 720, TC01069. (*Notes.* (1) For HMRC's practice following this decision, see HMRC Brief 32/11, issued on 24 August 2011. (2) For a preliminary issue in this case, see **2.166** APPEALS.)

Cases where the appellant was successful

[48.40] A company carried on business as a dealer in car registration numberplates. In many such transactions, it acted on an agency basis, keeping registers of clients who wished to sell particular plates and of clients who wished to buy particular plates, and introducing the clients to each other in return for commission. The company accounted for VAT on the commission which it received. In May 1990 the Commissioners issued a ruling that the company was acting as a principal, rather than as an agent, in respect of such transactions, and should therefore account for VAT on the full sale price, rather than only on its commission. The company appealed, and in December 1991 the Commissioners belatedly accepted that the company was acting as an agent, and withdrew the disputed ruling. During the period for which the ruling was in force, however, the company had accounted for output tax on the full sale price in accordance with the ruling. Following the withdrawal of the ruling, the company submitted a claim for repayment of the amount which it had paid in accordance with the Commissioners' ruling, and which it would not have had to pay if the Commissioners had accepted that it was only liable to account for VAT on its commission. The Commissioners rejected the claim, considering that it would lead to the 'unjust enrichment' of the company, within what is now *VATA 1994, s 80(3)*. The tribunal allowed the company's appeal, finding that the company had lost potential customers through being forced to account for VAT on the full sale price, and holding that 'far from being enriched by repayment from the respondents, the appellants are no more than compensated for the loss of commission which they suffered'. *Tayside Numbers Ltd*, [1992] VATTR 406 (VTD 8874). (*Note*. See now, however, *VATA 1994, s 80(3A)–(3C)*, introduced by *FA 1997, s 46* with effect from 19 March 1997.)

[48.41] A partnership carried on business as a dealer in vehicle numberplates. In most of its transactions it acted as an agent, but in some cases it acted as an independent principal. For the year to 31 July 1990, it had accounted for output tax as if it had been acting as a principal in all its transactions. In 1995 it submitted a claim for repayment of the amount overpaid. The Commissioners rejected the claim on the basis that it would lead to 'unjust enrichment', and the partnership appealed. The tribunal allowed the appeal in principle, holding on the evidence that the partnership had suffered a loss of business as a result of having set its selling prices at VAT-inclusive amounts. (However, the tribunal also found that the claim submitted was excessive, holding that 'the VAT which the partnership should have accounted for in respect of a transaction should be calculated on the basis that the VAT-inclusive commission was equal to the difference between the amount paid by the partnership to the seller and the total amount paid by the purchaser inclusive of VAT but net of the DVLA fee'.) *SJ & CA Frampton (t/a Framptons)*, LON/95/2438 (VTD 14065). (*Note*. See the note following *Tayside Numbers Ltd*, **48.40** above.)

[48.42] A company owned seven department stores, parts of which it rented to tenants. In 1990 it informed the tenants that it had opted to tax the property, and following the option it accounted for output tax on the rents. In December 1992 the company went into receivership. The receivers discovered that the company had failed to notify Customs of the option, and formed the opinion that the option was invalid under what is now *VATA 1994, Sch 10 para 20*. They issued credit notes to the tenants, and reclaimed the output tax from Customs. Customs rejected the claim, considering that the credit notes did not comply with what is now *VAT Regulations 1995 (SI 1995/2518), reg 38*, and that, since the company was in liquidation, the tax should not be repaid on the grounds that to do so would result in 'unjust enrichment' within what is now *VATA 1994, s 80(3)*. The receivers appealed. The tribunal allowed the appeal, holding that the repayment would not result in unjust enrichment. The CS upheld this decision, holding that, although that the credit notes did not comply with what is now *reg 38**, the tax was correctly repayable under what is now *VATA 1994, s 80*. Lord Hope held that, although the repayment would result in the company's enrichment, the question of whether that enrichment was 'unjust' was 'a question of fact and degree which ought to be left to the decision of the tribunal, subject to review only where it can be shown that that decision was erroneous in point of law or on the facts was wholly unsustainable'. In the present case, the tribunal had been entitled to conclude that the company's enrichment would not be 'unjust'. *C & E Commrs v McMaster Scotland Stores Ltd (in receivership)*, CS [1995] STC 846. (*Note*. See now *VATA 1994, s 80(3A)–(3C)*, introduced by *FA 1997, s 46* with effect from 19 March 1997.)

[48.43] Until 1990 a building society accounted for VAT on fees which it received from its customers for producing title deeds. In 1990 the Commissioners issued a ruling that VAT was not chargeable on such fees. The society submitted a claim for repayment of the VAT for which it had accounted on such fees between 1979 and 1989. The Commissioners rejected the claim on the grounds that the repayment would 'unjustly enrich' the society, contrary to *VATA 1994, s 80(3)*, since the fees would not be returned to the society's customers. The tribunal allowed the society's appeal, holding that the repayment would not lead to unjust enrichment under the legislation then in force, on the grounds that the society had not reduced the fees after the ruling that VAT was not chargeable, but had retained the same fees and had increased its profit margins. *National & Provincial Building Society*, [1996] VATDR 153 (VTD 14017). (*Note.* See now, however, *VATA 1994, s 80(3A)–(3C)*, introduced by *FA 1997, s 46* with effect from 19 March 1997.)

[48.44] A trader (H) sold nuts, intended as bird food for wild birds, from a market stall. On the instructions of her local VAT office, she accounted for output tax on her sales. In 1995 the Commissioners issued a revised statement (see *Notice 701/15/95, para 16*) following which they accepted that H's sales qualified for zero-rating, since they were neither 'pet food' nor 'packaged'. H then submitted a claim for repayment of the tax for which she had accounted since 1974. The Commissioners rejected the claim on the basis that it would 'unjustly enrich' H, contrary to *VATA 1994, s 80(3)*. H appealed. The tribunal allowed her appeal in principle (subject to agreement on figures), holding on the evidence that the repayment would not 'unjustly enrich' H, since she had not fixed her prices by reference to the rate of VAT, and had not increased her prices when the VAT rate had increased in 1979 and 1991. *DA Hardman*, MAN/92/1424 (VTD 14045). (*Note.* See now, however, *VATA 1994, s 80(3A)–(3C)*, introduced by *FA 1997, s 46* with effect from 19 March 1997.)

[48.45] A married couple operated a 'shooting school', providing tuition in various types of shooting and charging customers £60 per hour. Initially they accounted for output tax on all their supplies, but subsequently ascertained that supplies to individual customers qualified for exemption under *VATA 1994, Sch 9, Group 6, Item 2*. The couple submitted a claim for the repayment of output tax, but the Commissioners rejected the claim on the basis that it would 'unjustly enrich' the couple. The tribunal allowed the couple's appeal, holding on the evidence that 'the prices were set at the level the market would bear' and that the couple 'were charging amounts that would have been charged even if they had realised that some of the supplies were exempt'. *Mr & Mrs J King (t/a Barbury Shooting School)*, LON/02/228 (VTD 17822). (*Note.* For a subsequent application for costs, see **2.391** APPEALS.)

[48.46] A company which operated a theatre accounted for VAT on its receipts. Following the CJEC decision in *Zoological Society of London*, **22.322** EUROPEAN COMMUNITY LAW, it submitted a repayment claim on the grounds that it should have treated its supplies as exempt. The Commissioners made a small repayment, but rejected the majority of claim on the basis that it would lead to the 'unjust enrichment' of the company, contrary to *VATA 1994, s 80(3)*. The tribunal reviewed the evidence in detail and allowed the company's appeal, finding that the company did not have VAT in mind when it fixed the prices for its performances. On the evidence, there were 'cases in which, the show being likely to attract large audiences, the ticket prices could be set at a fairly high level', but there were 'others when the ticket price needed to be set at a low level in order to attract an adequate audience'. These considerations 'far outweighed the inclusion of VAT as a determining factor. In other words, the VAT was passed on in only the most incidental of senses, and in reality because, as the law was understood at the time, the appellant had no means by which it could not include an element of VAT within its ticket prices.' *Newcastle Theatre Royal Trust Ltd*, MAN/03/758 (VTD 18952).

[48.47] A similar decision was reached in *Northampton Theatres Trust Ltd*, [2006] VATDR 27 (VTD 19485).

[48.48] In *Debt Management Associates Ltd*, 27.30 FINANCE, the tribunal held that debt management services were exempt from VAT. Following this decision, a company which supplied similar services claimed repayment of more than £5,000,000 in VAT. Customs agreed to repay some of the amount claimed, but rejected the remainder of the claim on the basis that it would 'unjustly enrich' the company, contrary to *VATA 1994, s 80(3)*. The Ch D allowed the company's appeal and the CA unanimously upheld this decision. Lloyd LJ held that 'a taxpayer who has paid tax which was not due has a primary right to be repaid the amount of that tax'. On the evidence, Customs' 'defence of unjust enrichment to the repayment claim cannot be made out in full or in part'. *Baines & Ernst Ltd v HMRC*, CA [2006] STC 1632; [2006] EWCA Civ 1040. (*Note.* For a preliminary issue in this case, see **2.160** APPEALS.)

[48.49] For other cases in which it was held that repayment would not lead to 'unjust enrichment', see *Lamdec Ltd*, **2.200** APPEALS; *Global Self Drive Ltd*, **38.3** INSURANCE, and *Norman Allen Group Travel*, **63.4** TOUR OPERATORS AND TRAVEL AGENTS.

Three-year time limit (VATA 1994, s 80(4))

Applications for judicial review

[48.50] Following the decision in *Next plc*, **58.28** RETAILERS' SPECIAL SCHEMES, two associated companies which sold goods by mail order lodged substantial repayment claims under *VATA 1994, s 80*. On 18 July 1996 the Paymaster-General stated in Parliament that legislation was to be included in the 1997 Finance Bill to introduce a three-year limit for retrospective repayment claims, and to amend the law on unjust enrichment, with retrospective effect from 18 July 1996. Following this announcement, Customs wrote to the companies to inform them that, although the amount of the claim was agreed, they would 'not be making a repayment of the claim as it relates to prescribed accounting periods of more than three years before the claim was made'. The companies appealed. The tribunal allowed the appeals, holding that it was implicit from *s 79* that Customs were 'expected to make payment in most cases within a period of 30 days'. The *Tribunal Rules* did not confer power on the tribunal to direct Customs to make payments, but if Customs were dilatory in making repayments, the proper remedy would be judicial review. The companies then applied to the QB for judicial review of Customs' refusal to make the repayments. The QB granted the applications, holding that

Customs had no power to defer payment of a claim once it had been established as well-founded. Keene J observed that Customs' policy document 'proceeded on the basis that the legislation would be passed'. It was not simply 'suggesting that claims should be deferred until Parliament had expressed its will one way or the other. In so doing, it was to that extent an unlawful and *ultra vires* policy.' The Commissioners were entitled to check the validity of any claim. However, they did 'not have a discretion to defer payment of sums due from them to the taxpayer, once a claim by the latter has been established as well-founded'. In the cases in question, the amount of the claims had been agreed, and the applicants were entitled to payment of the outstanding sums without further delay. *R v C & E Commrs (ex p. Kay & Co Ltd and Others)*, QB [1996] STC 1500. (*Notes.* (1) See now *VATA 1994, s 80(4)* as amended by *FA 1997, s 47*. (2) For a preliminary issue in this case, see **2.29** APPEALS.)

[48.51] A company registered for VAT with effect from 1987, and accounted for output tax. In 1995 its accountants submitted a repayment claim on the basis that it was not in fact making any taxable supplies. On 2 December 1996, following the QB decision in *R v C & E Commrs (ex p. Kay & Co Ltd and Others)*, **48.50** above, the tribunal directed Customs to make the repayment claimed. Customs made the repayment in January 1997. Meanwhile, on 4 December 1996, the House of Commons had passed a Budget Resolution under *Provisional Collection of Taxes Act 1968*, imposing a three-year time limit on repayment claims by means of an amendment to *VATA 1994, s 80(4)*. In May 1997, following the confirmation of the retrospective three-year time limit by *FA 1997, s 47*, Customs issued an assessment to recover the part of the refund which was outside the three-year time limit. The company applied for judicial review. The CA granted the application. Rix LJ held that the introduction of the retrospective three-year time limit did not 'permit the Commissioners to use their new clawback powers so as to override a judicial decision which pre-dates 4 December 1996'. *R v C & E Commrs (ex p. Building Societies Ombudsman Co Ltd)*, CA [2000] STC 892. (*Note.* For Customs' revised practice following this decision, see Business Brief 3/01, issued on 20 February 2001.)

[48.52] Because of an error in its accounting software, a major company made substantial overpayments of VAT over a period of eleven years. It did not discover the error until September 2003. Customs agreed to repay the VAT overpaid within the three-year limitation period of *VATA 1994, s 80(4)*, but refused to repay the overpayments for the preceding eight years on the grounds that the claim had been made outside the statutory time limit. The company applied for judicial review. The QB dismissed its application. Lightman J awarded costs to Customs on the indemnity basis, finding that the company had failed 'to lend proper attention to the factual basis on which the application was made'. *R (oao British Telecommunications plc) v HMRC*, QB [2005] STC 1148; [2005] EWHC 1043 (Admin). (*Note.* The company appealed to the CA, which referred the case to the CJEC. The CJEC initially registered the case as *Case C-185/06*, but the President subsequently removed the Case from the register: see the Official Journal, 25 August 2007, p 24.)

VATA 1994, s 80(4)—whether applicable to claims under VATA 1994, s 33

[48.53] A city council submitted VAT returns which included claims for refunds of tax under *VATA 1994, s 33*. Between 1991 and February 2000, it wrongly accounted for tax in respect of certain notional fees relating to its 'grant agency', so that the repayments which it received from Customs were less than the amounts to which it would otherwise have been entitled. In March 2000, having discovered the errors, it submitted a repayment claim, backdated to 1991. Customs repaid the amounts claimed from April 1997 to February 2000, but rejected the claims for periods before April 1997 on the basis that they were time-barred by virtue of *VATA 1994, s 80(4)*. The council applied for judicial review, contending that *VATA 1994, s 80(4)* should not be treated as applying to claims under *s 33*. The CA unanimously rejected this contention and dismissed the application. Schiemann LJ held that Customs had met the claims which the council had made under *s 33*, and that, under common law principles, the council was not entitled to make a further claim under that *section*. The claim which the council had lodged in March 2000 fell under *s 80*, so that the restriction of *s 80(4)* applied. *R (oao Cardiff City Council) v C & E Commrs*, CA 2003, [2004] STC 356; [2003] EWCA Civ 1456. (*Note*. Although the decision on the facts of the case was unanimous, Arden LJ and Scott-Baker LJ specifically disagreed on the interpretation of *VATA 1994, s 81(3)*.)

Scottish appeals

[48.54] A company submitted a claim for repayment of input tax. Customs rejected the claim on the basis that it had been made outside the three-year time limit laid down by *VATA 1994, s 80(4)* (as substituted by *FA 1997*). The company appealed, contending that *s 80(4)* should be treated as only applying to output tax and not to input tax. The tribunal accepted this contention and allowed the appeal, specifically declining to follow the English decision in *BICC plc*, 48.59 below, and holding that the provisions of *s 80(4)* were 'inapplicable to a claim for input tax underclaimed in error'. *The Royal Bank of Scotland Group plc*, [1999] VATDR 122 (VTD 16035). (*Notes*. (1) The tribunal's reasoning was disapproved by the Ch D in *University of Sussex*, 48.2 above. (2) See now *VAT Regulations (SI 1995/2518) regs 29(1A)* and *34(1A)(1B)*, introduced with effect from 1 May 1997 by *VAT (Amendment) Regulations 1997 (SI 1997/1086)*.)

[48.55] Following the decision noted at 42.6 LOCAL AUTHORITIES, Customs repaid more than £22,000,000, plus interest of more than £12,000,000, to Glasgow City Council. The council claimed further repayments covering periods from May 1988 to January 1992. Customs rejected the claim on the basis that they were outside the three-year time limit laid down by *VATA 1994, s 80(4)*. The tribunal reviewed the evidence in detail and allowed the appeal in part, holding that the 'capping' provisions, as in force at the relevant time, applied to 'payment traders only (i.e.) to taxable persons who have paid more sums by way of VAT than they have deducted from VAT otherwise due by virtue of input tax or refunds'. *Glasgow City Council*, EDN/97/33 (VTD 16613). (*Note*. See now *VAT Regulations (SI 1995/2518) regs 29(1A)* and *34(1A)(1B)*, introduced with effect from 1 May 1997 by *SI 1997 No 1086*, under which 'repayment traders' are also now subject to the 'three-year cap'.')

[48.56] In 2003 a group of companies submitted repayment claims relating to the profit on sales of demonstration cars, which should have been treated as exempt from VAT, applying the CJEC decision in *EC Commission v Italian Republic*, **22.349** EUROPEAN COMMUNITY LAW. Customs rejected the claims on the grounds that they were outside the three-year time limit laid down by *VATA 1994, s 80(4)*. The representative member of the group appealed. The tribunal allowed the appeal, finding that the conditions of Business Brief 22/2002 were satisfied, and that the group was entitled to repayment. The tribunal observed that 'the doctrine of effectiveness should apply to support a taxpayer in maintaining this right to claim repayment over an extended period'. This principle 'directs that such rights should not be rendered virtually impossible or excessively difficult to pursue'. *John Clark (Holdings) Ltd*, EDN/05/25 (VTD 19327). (*Note*. For the status of Business Brief 22/2002, see now the HL judgments in *HMRC v Condé Nast Publications Ltd*, **48.7** above.)

[48.57] In a Scottish case, a company (S) submitted a repayment claim in September 2002, relating to tax which it had paid between January 1995 and January 1998 in respect of services that should have been treated as exempt following the CA decision in *Century Life plc*, **38.13** INSURANCE. HMRC rejected the claim on the basis that it had been made outside the three-year time limit of *VATA 1994, s 80*. S appealed, contending that *s 80(4)* should be treated as invalid because it failed to provide for a transitional period, as required by the CJEC decision in *Grundig Italiana SpA v Ministero delle Finanze*, **22.57** EUROPEAN COMMUNITY LAW. The tribunal accepted this contention and allowed the appeal, but the CS reversed this decision with regard to accounting periods ending after 30 April 1996, holding that the failure to provide for a transitional period did not render the three-year time limit invalid. *HMRC v Scottish Equitable plc*, CS 2 July 2009 unreported. (*Notes*. (1) At the time of writing, the full text of the CS decision is not available. Compare *HMRC v Fleming*, **48.6** above. (2) For HMRC's practice following this decision, see HMRC Brief 41/09, issued on 17 July 2009. HMRC consider that the effect of FA 2008, s 121 is that 'all VAT claims are now capped at four years, or back to 1 April 2006, whichever is the shorter'.)

[48.58] See also *National Galleries of Scotland (No 3)*, **48.9** above, and *Abercromby Motor Group Ltd*, **48.24** above.

English appeals

Validity of VATA 1994, s 80(4) as substituted by FA 1997

[48.59] In April 1997 a company, which was partly exempt, submitted a claim for repayment of VAT which it had paid during 1992, considering that it had wrongly attributed some of its input tax to exempt supplies. Customs rejected the claim on the basis that it had been made outside the three-year time limit laid down by *VATA 1994, s 80(4)* (as substituted by *FA 1997*). The company appealed, contending firstly that as the overpayment related to underclaimed input tax, it was outside the scope of *VATA 1994, s 80(4)*, and alternatively that *VATA 1994, s 80(4)* should be held to be invalid under European law. The tribunal rejected the company's first contention, holding that *VATA 1994, s 80(4)* applied to the claim, so that the tax was not repayable under UK law. *BICC plc*, [1998] VATDR 224 (VTD 15324). (*Notes*. (1) The tribunal directed that the appeal should be stood over pending a further hearing on the question of whether *s 80(4)* violated European law. There was no further public hearing of the appeal. See, however, the subsequent decision in *Marks & Spencer plc*, **22.55** EUROPEAN COMMUNITY LAW. (2) See also the subsequent QB decision in *University of Sussex*, **48.2** above, where Neuberger J held that a claim for repayment of input tax had been lodged under *VAT Regulations 1995 (SI 1995/2518), reg 29*, so that *VATA 1994, s 80(4)* did not apply.)

[48.60] The decision in *BICC plc*, **48.59** above, was applied in the similar subsequent case of *JB & PA Haigh*, MAN/97/1214 (VTD 15835).

[48.61] In 2000 Customs accepted that a college was an 'eligible body' under *VATA 1994, Sch 9, Group 6, Note 1(e)*, so that its supplies were exempt. The college subsequently claimed a repayment of VAT which it had paid on its supplies, backdated to 1990. Customs agreed to repay the VAT from July 1997, but rejected the claim for earlier periods, on the grounds that it had been made outside the three-year time limit laid down by *VATA 1994, s 80(4)* (as substituted by *FA 1997*). The company appealed, contending that *VATA 1994, s 80(4)* should be held to be invalid under European law. The tribunal accepted this contention and allowed the appeal, applying the CA decision in *Fleming*, **48.6** above. *Church of Scientology Religious Education College Inc*, LON/01/390 (VTD 19673). (*Note*. The Ch D dismissed an application by HMRC to lodge a late appeal to against this decision—see **2.175** APPEALS.)

Application of VATA 1994, s 80(4) as substituted by FA 1997

[48.62] A members' club provided snooker and billiards facilities to its members. It registered for VAT from 1973. In April 1994 the *VAT (Sport, Physical Education and Fundraising Events) Order* provided that 'sporting activities' should be exempt from VAT (see now *VATA 1994, Sch 9, Group 10*). With regard to non-profit-making organisations, the exemption was backdated to January 1990. In May 1996 one of the club's trustees wrote to Customs, applying for its subscriptions to be treated as exempt from VAT. Customs requested further information, which the club provided, and on 18 July Customs wrote to the club accepting that the club was 'able to claim exemption on membership fees and the income from snooker and billiards'. However, on the same day, the Paymaster-General announced in Parliament that legislation was to be included in the 1997 Finance Bill to introduce a three-year limit for retrospective repayment claims, with retrospective effect. The club formally claimed repayment in August 1996, and Customs made the repayment claimed. Following the enactment of *FA 1997*, they wrote to the club demanding the return of the repayment relating to periods from January 1990 to August 1993. The club repaid the amount demanded, but lodged an appeal to the tribunal. The tribunal observed that, if Customs had 'responded sooner to the appellant's letter of 31 May 1996, and again to its letter of 8 July 1996, the appellant's claim would have been made in time'. Customs had 'received a windfall by virtue of the fact that the appellant failed to understand the specific niceties of the law in time to make a claim in proper form for a repayment for which he was entitled at the time he first realised his position in May 1996'. The tribunal directed that the case should be 'referred back to the Commissioners for them to consider whether or not it would be appropriate in the circumstances of this case to exercise their discretion in the appellant's favour'. *The Union Club Seaford*, LON/98/1567 (VTD 17442).

[48.63] Tribunals dismissed claims for repayment, which had been made outside the three-year time limit of *VATA 1994, s 80(4)*, in *University of Liverpool*, MAN/96/728 (VTD 16769); *DG & SE Hamer*, MAN/01/718 (VTD 17669); *Mrs BD Hedley (t/a Birtle Riding Centre)*, MAN/01/484 (VTD 18250); *BE Cox*, MAN/03/530 (VTD 18709, VTD 18990); *SS Gandhum*, LON/04/237 (VTD 18848); *J Parker*, LON/03/1197 (VTD 18853); *BG Patel*, LON/05/397 (VTD 19634); *I & CJ Van Colle (t/a GVC Optometrists)*, LON/06/991 (VTD 20332); *Instamech Ltd*, LON/07/1135 (VTD 20596); *K Mowbray (t/a Maypole Self-Service Station)*, MAN/07/608 (VTD 20620); *A Russell Heating*, MAN/07/754 (VTD 20681); *J Koundakjian*, [2009] UKFTT 89 (TC), TC00057; *M Hutchinson (t/a Clifton Fisheries)*, [2009] UKFTT 252 (TC), TC00200; *Botanical Catering Ltd*, [2009] UKFTT 265 (TC), TC00212; *I Dear*, [2010] UKFTT 111 (TC), TC00422; *McGee Associates*, [2010] UKFTT 144 (TC), TC00450; *ED Yelland*, [2010] UKFTT 340 (TC), TC00622; *Nathaniel & Co (Solicitors)*, [2010] UKFTT 472 (TC), TC00734; *Mobile Motoring Maintenance Ltd*, [2011] UKFTT 6 (TC), TC00883; *HC Motors Ltd*, [2011] UKFTT 129 (TC), TC01003; *Wilsons of Rathkenny Ltd*, [2011] UKFTT 406 (TC), TC01261; *GF Mercer Ltd*, [2011] UKFTT 539 (TC), TC01386; *AG Byrt*, [2011] UKFTT 600 (TC), TC01443, and *B Corvi (t/a A & B Corvi Seaside Cafe)*, [2011] UKFTT 758 (TC), TC01595.

[48.64] In 2002 a company claimed a repayment of VAT which it claimed to have overpaid between 1973 and 1996. Customs rejected the claim on the basis that it had been made outside the three-year time limit of *VATA 1994, s 80(4)*. The company appealed, contending firstly that *s 80(4)* did not apply because it was entitled to make adjustments under what is now *VAT Regulations 1995 (SI 1995/2518), reg 38* (see **40.109** INVOICES AND CREDIT NOTES), and alternatively that *s 80(4)* was invalid under EC law because it did not provide for a transitional period. The tribunal reviewed the evidence in detail and rejected the company's first contention with regard to the period after 1990 (when what is now *reg 38* came into force), holding that *'regulation 38* is mandatory and does require adjustment to the VAT account in the period when the business accounts reflect the change'. The failure to make timeous adjustments had 'resulted in overpayments and *section 80* therefore applies to the claims'. However, before 1990 there had been 'no statutory mechanism in domestic law for adjustment'. The tribunal also held that the company's rights under EC law did not extend back beyond 1 January 1978 when the *EC Sixth Directive* came into force, holding that the *EEC Second VAT Directive* which applied from 1973 to 1977 did not have direct effect. However, the effect of the CA decision in *Fleming v C & E Commrs*, **48.6** above, was that *s 80(4)* was invalid for 1978 onwards, since there was 'no difference in principle between reducing the time limit under *section 80(4)* without transitional relief and introducing the time limit in *regulation 29(1A)* of the *VAT Regulations 1995* with which *Fleming* was concerned'. The tribunal observed that 'our decisions on the above issues do not determine the appeal because they do not cover the amount of VAT repayable, which have not (*sic*) been verified by Customs'. *General Motors Acceptance Corporation (UK) plc (No 3)*, LON/02/806 (VTD 19989).

Long delay in submission of returns claiming repayments

[48.65] Between January 1997 and April 1998 a company failed to submit several VAT returns, and Customs issued estimated assessments. Between September 1997 and June 1998 the company paid the tax charged by the assessments. In September and November 2001 the company belatedly submitted returns showing VAT liability of less than the amounts which had been assessed, and claimed repayments accordingly. Customs rejected the repayment claims on the basis that they had been made outside the three-year time limit of *VATA 1994, s 80(4)*. The tribunal dismissed the company's appeal against this decision. *Bissell Homecare (Overseas) Inc*, LON/02/904 (VTD 18217).

Date on which repayment claim made

[48.66] Until March 1993, Customs required motor traders to account for VAT on the surrender value of the road fund licences of second-hand vehicles. From March 1993 they accepted that traders were not required to account for tax on these licences, and were entitled to a refund of tax which they had paid. They published this policy in *Notice 700/59/94*. At a control visit in 1998, a company asked the VAT officer conducting the visit why it had never received such a repayment, and produced a copy of a form which it claimed to have submitted in July 1994. The officer ascertained that there was no record of receipt of a claim, and Customs subsequently issued a ruling that the effect of *VATA 1994, s 80(4)* (as substituted by *FA 1997*) was that no repayment could now be made. The company appealed. The tribunal accepted the company's evidence that it had submitted a claim form in July 1994, and allowed the claim for repayment of the tax overpaid from August 1991 to July 1994. *Olivers of Hull Ltd*, MAN/00/396 (VTD 17434).

[48.67] A partnership had failed to make returns for the periods from 1 April to 31 December 2001, and from 1 October 2002 to 30 September 2003. Customs issued estimated assessments, which the partnership paid. The partnership subsequently submitted returns claiming repayments. Customs rejected the claims on the grounds that they had not been made until April 2007, so that they were outside the three-year time limit. The partnership appealed, contending that it had submitted the returns on 28 February 2006, so that part of the claim was inside the three-year time limit. The tribunal accepted the partnership's evidence and allowed the appeal with regard to the periods from 1 October 2002 to September 2003, as the returns had been submitted within three years of the issue of the assessments for those periods. (The tribunal also observed that the decision in *Fleming*, 48.6 above, did not apply because the claims were 'all made in relation to overpaid tax for prescribed accounting periods that occurred long after the introduction of the three-year cap'.) *Warren Bradley Estates, LON/07/972 (VTD 20672)*.

Interaction of VATA 1994, s 80(4) and Business Brief 22/2002

[48.68] For the status of Business Brief 22/2002, see now *HMRC v Condé Nast Publications Ltd*, 48.7 above. The cases noted at **48.69** to **48.74** below should be read in the light of this decision.

[48.69] A partnership (M) provided dancing tuition. It accounted for VAT on its receipts. In January 1998, following the tribunal decision in *Clarke*, **21.40**

EDUCATION, Customs issued Business Brief 1/98, accepting that supplies of private tuition by partnerships qualified for exemption under the *Sixth Directive*. In July 1998 M submitted a claim for the refund of the VAT which it had paid. Customs accepted the claim with regard to the period from May 1995, but rejected the claim for earlier periods on the grounds that it was outside the three-year time limit laid down by *VATA 1994, s 80(4)*. In August 2002, following the CJEC decision in *Marks & Spencer plc*, **22.55** EUROPEAN COMMUNITY LAW, Customs issued Business Brief 22/2002, stating that they would give retrospective effect 'to a transitional regime for when the three-year time limit was introduced in 1996 to allow taxpayers to make claims that they ought to have been able to make at the time' and that they would allow repayments where taxpayers 'can demonstrate that they discovered the error before 31 March 1997'. Following this, M renewed its claim for repayment of the VAT it had paid prior to May 1995, stating that it had become aware in 1996 that an appeal was pending in the *Clarke* case and that it had formed the opinion that its supplies qualified for exemption under EC law, although it had not made a formal claim until after Customs had responded to the *Clarke* decision. Customs again rejected the claim and M appealed. The tribunal accepted M's evidence and allowed the appeal, finding that M had been aware that 'there was an error in the Commissioners' interpretation of the EC law with regard to partnerships' before 31 March 1997. Accordingly the conditions of Business Brief 22/2002 were satisfied, and M was 'entitled to rely on the wording of the Business Brief and to claim repayment of all the money paid to the Customs since January 1978'. *The Marguerita Hoare School of Dancing*, LON/98/1304 (VTD 18906).

[48.70] In June 2003 a partnership which carried on business as a motor dealer submitted a repayment claim covering the periods from 1973 to 1996. Part of this claim related to output tax which it had wrongly accounted for on the receipt of 'demonstrator bonuses' from manufacturers, but which should have been treated as discounts on the sale price of the car, applying the CJEC decision in *Elida Gibbs Ltd*, **22.235** EUROPEAN COMMUNITY LAW. The remainder of the claim related to the profit on sales of demonstration cars, which should have been treated as exempt from VAT, applying the CJEC decision in *EC Commission v Italian Republic*, **22.349** EUROPEAN COMMUNITY LAW. Customs rejected the claim on the grounds that it was outside the three-year time limit laid down by *VATA 1994, s 80(4)*. The partnership appealed. The tribunal allowed the appeal in part, finding that the provisions of Business Brief 22/2002 were satisfied with regard to the claim relating to the profit on sales of demonstration cars. However, the tribunal dismissed the appeal with regard to the 'demonstrator bonuses', finding that the provisions of Business Brief 22/2002 were not satisfied with regard to that claim. *F Troop & Son*, MAN/04/79 (VTD 18957).

[48.71] In another case relating to the sale of demonstration cars, Customs rejected a repayment claim but the tribunal allowed the company's appeal, finding that the company 'would have made a claim in 1997, had there had been a proper transitional period'. *Bristol Street Group Ltd*, LON/04/1189 (VTD 19398).

[48.72] A similar decision was reached in *Marshall Motor Group Ltd*, LON/04/1811 (VTD 19828).

[48.73] In June 2003 a company submitted a repayment claim, backdated to March 1978, relating to the sales of demonstration cars, which should have been treated as exempt from VAT, applying the CJEC decision in *EC Commission v Italian Republic*, **22.349** EUROPEAN COMMUNITY LAW. Customs rejected the claim and the company appealed, contending that its claim should be allowed by virtue of Business Briefs 22/2002 and 27/2002. The tribunal reviewed the evidence in detail, rejected this contention, and dismissed the company's appeal, finding that it appeared that the company had initially decided that 'the expense and effect of the partial exemption recalculation' was not worthwhile, and had only decided to make a claim after the Ch D decision in *JDL Ltd*, **46.98** PARTIAL EXEMPTION. Accordingly the company had not shown 'that, on the balance of probabilities, had UK law permitted it to make such a claim before 30 June 1997, it would have made such a claim'. *Anglia Regional Co-Operative Society Ltd*, [2005] VATDR 100 (VTD 18991).

[48.74] Similar decisions were reached in *Robert Smith & Sons Ltd*, MAN/04/249 (VTD 19010); *Rye Mill Garage Ltd*, LON/04/1035 (VTD 19060) and *Halsall Riding & Livery Centre*, MAN/04/798 (VTD 19342).

Application of VATA 1994, s 80(4ZA)

[48.75] A company which operated a chain of health and fitness centres submitted a repayment claim, relating to overpaid output tax, on 31 May 2007, including its period ending April 2004. Customs rejected the claim for this period on the grounds that it had been made outside the three-year time limit laid down by *VATA 1994, s 80(4ZA)*, introduced by *FA 2005*. The company appealed, contending that the effect of the HL decision in *HMRC v Fleming*, **48.6** above, was that *s 80(4ZA)* should be held to be invalid. The tribunal rejected this contention and dismissed the appeal, distinguishing *Fleming* on the grounds that that case had concerned 'an entirely different situation'. The *Fleming* case 'concerned a considerable reduction having been made in the time limits from six to three years. The outcome of the *Fleming* case was that the absence of a transitional period for the reduction of the time limit for deduction of input tax pursuant to *regulation 29(1A)* contravened the principle of effectiveness with the result that no transitional period has yet expired. The facts of the current appeal are quite different.' The tribunal held that the absence of a transitional period for *s 80(4ZA)* did not contravene the principles of equivalence or effectiveness, since 'the purpose of the changes brought in by the *Finance Act 2005* was to ensure equality between repayment traders and payment traders in respect of the defence of unjust enrichment. There was no need for a transitional period because there was no directly effective right to be unjustly enriched. Accordingly there was no right to bring Community law into play in that respect. The change introduced by *section 80(4ZA)* was not to the period of limitation but as to how it was calculated', and 'the change in the calculation did not make it excessively difficult or virtually impossible for the appellant to exercise a right conferred by Community law.' *LA Leisure Ltd*, MAN/07/791 (VTD 20648).

'Clawback' assessments (VATA 1994, s 80(4A))

Whether assessment settled by agreement under VATA 1994, s 85

[48.76] A company (D) sold furniture and arranged interest-free credit for customers. Initially, it accounted for VAT on the full purchase price. However, following a CA decision in April 1996, it submitted a repayment claim on the basis that it should not have accounted for output tax on the commission which it paid to the finance company. (The CA decision in question was subsequently overruled by the CJEC and HL—see *Primback Ltd*, **22.242** EUROPEAN COMMUNITY LAW.) The Commissioners accepted that, on the basis of the CA decision, D would be entitled to a repayment. However, they informed D that they would defer the repayment relating to periods prior to April 1993, pending the retrospective introduction of a three-year 'cap'. D lodged a formal appeal with the tribunal. Following the QB decision in *R v C & E Commrs (ex p. Kay & Co Ltd)*, **48.50** above, the Commissioners made the repayment in December 1996. However, they informed D that, following the anticipated enactment of subsequent amendments to the legislation (see the amendments made to *VATA 1994, s 80* by *FA 1997*), they would require repayment of the amount repaid. Following receipt of the repayment, D wrote to the tribunal in January 1997 to state that its claim had been met and it wished to withdraw its appeal. Following the introduction of *VATA 1994, s 80(4A)* by *FA 1997*, the Commissioners issued a 'clawback' assessment in April 1997 to recover £6,200,000. D paid the amount in question in June 1997. However, following the CA decision in *R v C & E Commrs (ex p. Building Societies Ombudsman Co Ltd)*, **48.51** above, D claimed repayment of the amount charged by the assessment. The Commissioners rejected the claim and D applied for judicial review, contending that its appeal had been settled by agreement, within *VATA 1994, s 85*, and that the Commissioners were, therefore, not entitled to issue the assessment. The QB accepted this contention and granted the application, but the CA unanimously reversed this decision, holding on the evidence that, following the decision in *Kay & Co*, the Commissioners had unilaterally reversed their policy of deferring repayments. On the evidence, there had not been any agreement within *s 85*. (The CA directed that the hearing of the substantive appeal should be adjourned pending the CA decision in *Marks & Spencer plc*, **22.55** EUROPEAN COMMUNITY LAW.) *C & E Commrs v DFS Furniture Co plc (No 1)*, CA 2002, [2003] STC 1; [2002] EWCA Civ 1708. (*Note.* For subsequent developments in this case, see **3.111** ASSESSMENT.)

Assessments issued following HL reversal of CA decision

[48.77] A company (B) sold furniture and arranged interest-free credit for customers. Initially, it accounted for VAT on the full purchase price. However, following a CA decision in April 1996, it submitted a repayment claim on the basis that it should not have accounted for output tax on the commission which it paid to the finance company. The Commissioners had received significant numbers of such claims, and had issued Business Brief 15/96, stating that they had appealed to the HL, and that while they would make repayments pending the HL decision, they would seek to recover the repayments with interest if the HL reversed the CA decision. In 2001 the CA decision was overruled by the HL—see *Primback Ltd*, **22.242** EUROPEAN COMMUNITY LAW.

Following this, the Commissioners issued assessments to B to recover the amounts of the repayments. The tribunal upheld the assessments and dismissed B's appeal. *Bremen Fitted Furniture Ltd*, EDN/01/182 (VTD 17676).

[48.78] Following the tribunal decision reported at **38.51** INSURANCE, the Commissioners made a repayment of slightly over £300,000 to the appellant company. Following the HL decision in *Primback Ltd*, **22.242** EUROPEAN COMMUNITY LAW, they issued a 'clawback' assessment under *VATA 1994, s 80(4A)*. The company appealed, contending that the effect of the tribunal decision was that the subsequent assessment was invalid. The tribunal rejected this contention and dismissed the appeal, holding that the previous tribunal decision (by Mr. Wallace) did not determine 'the amount which (the Commissioners) were liable at that time to repay' within *s 80(4B)*. The tribunal noted that Mr. Wallace's decision 'neither allows nor dismisses the appeals, either wholly in part. It makes no directions as to what the next steps are to be. It states certain conclusions on the law.' Accordingly the decision did not 'determine the repayment liability of the Commissioners', but simply decided 'as a matter of principle, that the sales by group dealers to consumers were within the scope of the *Primback* decision'. *Peugeot Motor Co plc (No 4)*, LON/01/1279 (VTD 18059). (*Note.* The Ch D subsequently allowed the Commissioners' appeal against the tribunal decision in the case noted at **38.51** INSURANCE.)

[48.79] For another case where assessments under *VATA 1994, s 80(4A)* were held to be valid, see *Laura Ashley*, **3.44** ASSESSMENT.

VATA 1994, s 80(4C)—time limit for 'clawback' assessments

[48.80] See *DFS Furniture Co plc*, **3.111** ASSESSMENT.

Calculation of claim (VATA 1994, s 80(6))

Gaming machine takings

[48.81] A company operated gaming machines. Small prizes were paid out in cash but larger prizes were paid in tokens, which customers could exchange for gift vouchers. The company did not keep any record of the tokens which it placed in the machines, but the directors subsequently realised that this resulted in an overdeclaration of VAT, since the tokens which were replaced in the machines represented amounts won by the customers which, applying the principles in *HJ Glawe Spiel und Unterhaltungsgeräte Aufstellungsgesellschaft mbH & Co KG v Finanzamt Hamburg-Barmbek-Uhlenhorst*, **22.240** EUROPEAN COMMUNITY LAW, did not form part of the company's turnover. The company therefore submitted a repayment claim on the basis that the amounts of tokens exchanged for vouchers should have been excluded from its turnover. The Commissioners rejected the claim on the basis that some of the tokens which were exchanged for vouchers did not represent prizes paid out by the machines, but were refunds of amounts which customers had previously paid for tokens. The tribunal reviewed the evidence and held that 'the only just solution would be to allow a proportion of the amount claimed', and directed that 50% of the amount claimed should be repaid. *Morris Amusements Ltd*, EDN/97/197 (VTD 15829).

Repayment supplement (VATA 1994, s 79)

Conditions for supplement (VATA 1994, s 79(2))

Whether repayment instruction 'issued' by Commissioners—s 79(2)(b)

[48.82] A return claiming a repayment of VAT was received by the VAT Central Unit on 10 November 1989. According to the records kept at the Central Unit, a payable order was authorised for issue to the claimant on the same day. However, the order was not received by the claimant, nor was it cashed by any other person. On 5 January 1990 the claimant telephoned his local VAT office to complain that he had not received the repayment. The original payable order was cancelled, and a replacement order was sent on 24 January. No repayment supplement was included. The Commissioners refused to pay any repayment supplement, and informed the claimant that supplement was not due since the repayment had been made within 30 days of receiving his telephone call on 5 January. The claimant appealed, contending that repayment supplement was due since the repayment had not been issued within 30 days of the receipt of his return on 10 November. He also gave evidence that he had telephoned the local VAT office in November and December, to state that the repayment had not been received. The tribunal accepted the claimant's evidence and allowed the appeal. The Commissioners had not proved, on the balance of probabilities, that the payable order authorised on 10 November had actually been sent to the claimant. The instruction that a repayment should be made had not therefore been 'issued' as required by what is now *VATA 1994, s 79(2)(b)*. *AA Aston*, [1991] VATTR 170 (VTD 5955).

[48.83] A charity within *VATA 1994, s 33A* submitted returns claiming VAT repayments for the periods ending in March and June 2002. The Commissioners accepted the returns, but set the repayments against two unpaid assessments for previous periods, against which the charity had appealed. The charity's appeals against these assessments were allowed in September 2002, and the Commissioners authorised a repayment by bank giro in October 2002. The charity claimed repayment supplement under *VATA 1994, s 79*. The Commissioners rejected the claim, and the charity appealed. The tribunal allowed the appeal, finding that the officer responsible for rejecting the claim had failed to take account of the fact that the charity was entitled to a repayment under *VATA 1994, s 33A*. Additionally, the Commissioners had treated an internal set-off as if it were a written repayment instruction, within *VATA 1994, s 79(2)(b)*. The tribunal held that the repayments which were accepted as due to the charity should not have been set against the assessments which were under appeal, and commented that the VAT officers responsible for the decision did not understand 'the precise legal position of set-off'. The Commissioners had not issued a written instruction directing a refund during the relevant period, as required by *VATA 1994, s 79(2)(b)*. *National Galleries of Scotland (No 1)*, EDN/03/47 (VTD 18413). (*Note.* The tribunal also awarded interest to the charity under *VATA 1994, s 78* and *s 84(8)*, commenting that 'repayment supplement and interest are not mutually exclusive', and that 'the repayment supplement is intended as a penalty regime running alongside the interest regime, equiparating it with the taxpayers' position on accountability'.)

Excessive repayment claim—effect of VATA 1994, s 79(2)(c)

[48.84] A company submitted a return claiming a repayment of £3,095. The Commissioners ascertained that £1,176 of this amount was not supported by an invoice, and only repaid £1,919. They refused to pay any repayment supplement on the grounds that the repayment claimed had exceeded the repayment due by more than the limits laid down in what is now *VATA 1994, s 79(2)(c)*. The tribunal dismissed the company's appeal against this decision. *Trent Manor Farms*, LON/93/1523A (VTD 11216).

Periods to be left out of account (VATA 1994, s 79(3))

[48.85] A company's return for the period ending 30 September 1988 showed a repayment due. On 15 November 1988 the Commissioners queried the figures in the return. Initially the company refused to co-operate with the Commissioners, but on 23 December the company telephoned its local VAT office and made an appointment for an officer to visit its premises on 3 January 1989. The company satisfied the Commissioners that the return was correct, and on 5 January the Commissioners authorised a repayment. The company claimed a repayment supplement, as the Commissioners had failed to repay the VAT within 30 days of the receipt of the return. The Commissioners issued a ruling that no repayment supplement was due by virtue of what is now *VATA 1994, s 79(3)(a)*, which provides that, in calculating the thirty days, no account should be taken of the period for the raising and answering of any reasonable enquiry relating to the return. The company appealed, contending that the enquiry was not 'reasonable'. The tribunal dismissed the appeal, holding that there was nothing unreasonable in the Commissioners' decision to make an enquiry. *Kitsfern Ltd*, [1989] VATTR 312 (VTD 4472).

[48.86] A company (O) had traded for several years and, because most of its supplies were zero-rated, had regularly received repayments of VAT. In June 1989 it applied for group registration for itself and for its new parent company. It was allocated a new registration number, and the Commissioners instructed it that its next return should cover the period from 1 May 1989 to 30 September 1989. The completed return was received by the Commissioners on 18 October, and showed a repayment due of more than £20,000. The repayment was not received until 29 November and the company claimed a repayment supplement. The Commissioners refused the claim, considering that what is now *VATA 1994, s 79(3)* applied, as they had had to make enquiries before authorising the repayment, and accordingly a VAT officer had visited the company on 14 November. The company appealed, contending that the Commissioners' enquiries had not been reasonable. The tribunal dismissed the company's appeal, holding that the enquiries had been reasonable. *Olive Tree Press Ltd*, LON/90/186X (VTD 5349).

[48.87] A company's return for April 1990, claiming a repayment of tax, was received by the Chester VAT office on 4 June. It was forwarded by the Chester office to the VAT Central Unit, which processed it on 14 June. The Central

Unit computer indicated that the repayment which had been claimed required investigation. The case was referred back to the Chester office, and a control visit was arranged for 4 July. At the visit, the VAT officer was satisfied that the repayment was due. The company claimed a repayment supplement, which the Commissioners refused, considering that what is now *VATA 1994, s 79(3)(a)* applied. The tribunal allowed the company's appeal, holding that the Commissioners' enquiries had been reasonable but that, on the evidence, the Commissioners had not actually informed the company of the nature of their enquiries until the visit on 4 July. The only time which could properly be left out of account for the purposes of what is now *VATA 1994, s 79(3)* was two days; i.e. the day on which the queries were made and answered, plus one day for the officer to make her report. It followed that repayment supplement was due. The Commissioners appealed to the QB, which upheld the tribunal decision. *C & E Commrs v L Rowland & Co (Retail) Ltd*, QB [1992] STC 647. (*Note.* See now, however, *VATA 1994, s 79(4)*, deriving from *F(No 2)A 1992, s 15*.)

[48.88] A company submitted a return for November 1989 claiming a repayment of more than £210,000. This was primarily due to reclaiming input tax on development work at its premises. The return was received by the Commissioners on 5 January 1990, and on 26 January the local VAT office telephoned the company to request an appointment to verify the return. The director responsible for the return was not available, and a VAT officer visited the company without an appointment three days later. The director was unable to see him, and the officer sent the company a letter requesting further information. The company stated in evidence that it never received that letter. Following a reminder, a visit was arranged for 20 March and repayment was authorised on that date. The Commissioners refused to pay repayment supplement, considering that what is now *VATA 1994, s 79(3)* applied, and that in computing the 30-day period laid down in *VATA 1994, s 79(2)*, the period from 26 January to 20 March should be left out of account. The tribunal dismissed the company's appeal against this decision. The Commissioners' enquiries were reasonable. On the evidence, the tribunal was not satisfied that the company had not received the Commissioners' letter of 29 January. *The Wren Group Ltd*, LON/90/1553Z (VTD 5998).

[48.89] A company submitted a return for June 1990 claiming a repayment of more than £470,000. The return was received by the VAT Central Unit on 9 July. On 18 July the case was referred to the Westminster VAT office to verify the repayment. The relevant notification was not received by the Westminster office until 23 July. The company was telephoned on 26 July, and a visit was arranged for 31 July. After considering the case further, the Westminster office authorised the repayment on 10 August. The repayment was issued on 14 August, and the company received it on 17 August. The company claimed a repayment supplement. The Commissioners rejected the claim, considering that no supplement was due, by virtue of what is now *VATA 1994, s 79(3)*. The company appealed, contending that the Commissioners' enquiries had not been raised with them until 31 July, and had been answered by them on that date, so that one day was the only time which, by virtue of *VATA 1994, s 79(3)*, should be left out of account in computing the 30-day period of *VATA 1994, s 79(2)(b)*. The tribunal allowed the appeal, holding that the Commissioners' enquiries had effectively begun on 26 July, when the company had been telephoned (rather than on 9 July, as contended by the Commissioners, or on 31 July, as contended by the company). The enquiries had been fully answered at the meeting on 31 July. Therefore, the only time that fell to be left out of account, by virtue of *VATA 1994, s 79(3)*, in computing the 30-day period of *VATA 1994, s 79(2)(b)*, was the six days from 26 July to 31 July inclusive. *Kitsfern Ltd*, **48.85** above, was distinguished, as in that case the company had failed to co-operate with the Commissioners, whereas the company here had co-operated with the Commissioners' enquiries. *Five Oaks Properties Ltd*, LON/90/1674 (VTD 6085). (*Note.* See now, however, *VATA 1994, s 79(4)*, deriving from *F(No 2)A 1992, s 15*.)

[48.90] In October 1998 a partnership submitted a return claiming a repayment of more than £1,000,000. On 9 November the Chester VAT office issued a letter rejecting the bulk of the claim. Subsequently the Commissioners agreed that the claim was correct, and made a repayment of interest under *VATA 1994, s 78*, covering the period from 13 November 1998 to 1 February 1999. The interest paid was £16,580. The partnership claimed that it was entitled to a repayment supplement of £66,980 under *VATA 1994, s 79*. The Commissioners rejected the claim and the partnership appealed. The tribunal allowed the appeal, holding that the conditions of *VATA 1994, s 79(2)* were satisfied. The Commissioners' enquiries had been raised on 26 October and had been answered by 9 November. The Commissioners had failed to issue a written instruction within the relevant period. With regard to the repayment already made under *VATA 1994, s 78*, the tribunal held that 'the intention of the legislation would not permit a *s 79* payment without deducting any lesser relevant *s 78* payment already made', and 'the mechanics of this is achieved through the operation of *s 78A*'. Accordingly, the partnership was 'entitled to the repayment supplement which it is claiming, but pursuant to *s 78A* it is obliged to repay the interest payment already made pursuant to *s 78*'. *THI Leisure Two Partnership*, LON/99/373 (VTD 16876).

[48.91] In the case noted at **46.176** PARTIAL EXEMPTION, the tribunal held that the effect of *VATA 1994, s 79(3)* was that the appellant company was not entitled to any repayment supplement, holding that throughout the period in question 'reasonable inquiries were being raised, and answered evasively, sometimes self-contradictorily, and in some cases not at all'. *NDF Administration Ltd*, LON/01/319 (VTD 18301).

[48.92] In November 2003 a company (O) submitted a VAT return claiming repayment of £806,202. Customs received the return on 10 November, and decided to investigate the claim in detail. On 12 November they arranged to visit the company. Between December 2003 and April 2004 they made repayments to O totalling £612,508. They issued a ruling that the balance of £193,704 was not repayable. O appealed. In May 2005, shortly before the hearing of the appeal, Customs accepted that the £193,704 was due, and paid O that amount, with repayment supplement. O proceeded with its appeal to the tribunal, contending that it should also receive repayment supplement with regard to the earlier repayments. The tribunal rejected this contention and dismissed the appeal, holding that *VATA 1994, s 79* should be construed 'as recognizing part payments and part refunds of the VAT credit for the particular period, taking the VAT credit as a single amount. Thus where by the end of the prescribed period, extended because the clock has stopped to enable reasonable inquiries to be made, a part payment has (as here) been made to a taxable person, the amount of that part payment earns no repayment supplement.' Furthermore, Customs' inquiries had been 'reasonable', as required by *s 79(3)(a)*. The period to be left out of account, by virtue of *s 79(3)*, ran from 12 November 2003 (when Customs notified O that they were beginning an enquiry) to 30 March 2004 (when they had received 'a complete answer' to their enquiries). Therefore the repayments of £612,508 had all been made within the statutory 'relevant period'. *Olympia Technology Ltd (No 2), LON/05/596 (VTD 19647)*. (*Notes*. (1) Costs were awarded to Customs. (2) For a preliminary issue in this case, see **2.515** APPEALS. (3) For a subsequent appeal by the same company, see **2.15** APPEALS.)

[48.93] A company which dealt in mobile telephones submitted three VAT returns claiming repayments. Customs decided to investigate the claims in detail, but eventually agreed that repayments were due. The company claimed repayment supplement, as Customs had failed to repay the VAT within 30 days of the receipt of the return. Customs issued a ruling that no repayment supplement was due by virtue of what is now *VATA 1994, s 79(3)(a)*, which provides that, in calculating the thirty days, no account should be taken of the period for the raising and answering of any reasonable enquiry relating to the return. The company appealed, contending that the enquiries had not been 'reasonable'. The tribunal reviewed the evidence in detail and dismissed the appeals with regard to two of the returns, holding that Customs' enquiries had been reasonable. However the tribunal allowed the company's appeal with regard to the other return, holding that the initial enquiry had been reasonable but finding that it had been answered on 30 December 2004 whereas the repayment had not been made until 15 February 2005. Since this period exceeded 30 days, it followed that repayment supplement was due in respect of this period. *Cellular Solutions (T Wells) Ltd, LON/05/268 (VTD 19903)*.

[48.94] In April 2006 a company (B) submitted a return claiming a repayment of VAT. HMRC received the return on 25 April and made enquiries. An HMRC officer authorised the repayment on 27 June, and on 29 June HMRC made the repayment by direct transfer to B's account with Barclays Bank. However B had closed that account (apparently without notifying HMRC) and Barclays returned the money to HMRC on 30 June. HMRC then asked B for details of its current bank account. B provided these details on 7 July, and HMRC then made the repayment to that account. B claimed repayment supplement, on the basis that the repayment had not been made within the statutory time limit. HMRC rejected the claim on the basis that the repayment had been made within the time limit as extended by *VATA 1994, s 79(3)* to allow for reasonable enquiries, and that the repayment made on 29 June satisfied the requirements of *s 79* even though B had closed the relevant bank account. The tribunal reviewed the evidence in detail and dismissed B's appeal, holding that 36 days should be left out of account by virtue of *s 79(3)* and that the repayment on 29 June constituted 'a written instruction directing the making of the payment or refund' for the purposes of *s 79(2)(b)*. This was the last day of the relevant 30-day period for the purposes of *s 79(2A)*, and therefore no repayment supplement was due. *Beast in the Heart Films (UK) Ltd, [2009] UKFTT 230 (TC), TC00180*.

[48.95] In 2002 a company (M) which dealt in mobile telephones submitted a VAT return claiming a substantial repayment. Customs were concerned that the relevant transactions may have formed part of a MTIC fraud, and began an enquiry into M's return. However in February 2003 they decided to make the repayment. M claimed repayment supplement. Customs rejected the claim and the tribunal dismissed M's appeal, holding that Customs' enquiries had been reasonable. Judge Gort observed that 'at no stage was there any unnecessary delay by the Commissioners in pursuing enquiries which we consider to be entirely reasonable in the circumstances of a potential MTIC fraud' and 'at no stage had the Commissioners received a complete answer to the enquiries which they were in our judgment legitimately making'. *Major Micros Ltd (in liquidation) v HMRC*, [2010] UKFTT 105 (TC), TC00417.

[48.96] See also the cases noted at **48.97** to **48.108** below.

Period of inquiry (VATA 1994, s 79(4))

[48.97] On 16 February 1995 a company submitted a return claiming a repayment of £221,000 (which was attributable to the purchase of a new site). This was received by the VAT Central Unit at Southend on 17 February. The Central Unit referred the claim to a specialist office at Liverpool. On 13 March the Liverpool office referred the claim to the company's local VAT office at Uxbridge. That office telephoned the company on 16 March and confirmed that the repayment claim was correct. The Liverpool office received the report from the Uxbridge office on 20 March. It approved the repayment claim on 21 March, and the repayment was credited to the company's bank account on 24 March. The company subsequently claimed a repayment supplement on the grounds that the repayment had not been made within 30 days of the receipt of the return. The Commissioners rejected the claim, considering that the effect of *VATA 1994, s 79(4)* was that the period from 16 March to 20 March should be left out of account, and that the payment had been authorised on 21 March, which was within the 30-day period as extended by *s 79(3)*. The company appealed, contending that the Commissioners' inquiry had been answered on 16 March, the date on which it was raised, so that only one day should be left out of account in computing the 30-day period. The tribunal rejected this contention and dismissed the company's appeal. By virtue of *VATA 1994, s 79(4)*, the period to be left out of account ended with the date on which the Commissioners satisfied themselves that they had received a complete answer to their inquiry. The tribunal held that this date was 20 March (the date on which the Liverpool office was satisfied) rather than 16 March (the date on which the Uxbridge office was satisfied). Accordingly, the repayment had been made within the extended 30-day period and no supplement was due. (The tribunal declined to follow the decision in *Five Oaks Properties Ltd*, **48.89** above, on the grounds that that case had been decided before the enactment of *VATA 1994, s 79(4)*.) *Watford Timber Co Ltd*, LON/96/1223 (VTD 14756).

[48.98] A company submitted a return for the period ending 30 September 2000, claiming a repayment of £25,137. The Commissioners received the return on 3 November. On 22 November they wrote to the company requesting further information. The company received the letter on 30 November and immediately faxed a list of the relevant invoices. On 8 December a VAT officer telephoned the company to ask for copies of some of the invoices. The company faxed these the same day, and the Commissioners authorised the repayment on 14 December. The company claimed a repayment supplement, on the grounds that the repayment had been made outside the 30-day period of *VATA 1994, s 79*. The tribunal observed that, since the company paid any VAT due by credit transfer, the due date for the receipt of its return was 7 November rather than 31 October, so that the requirements of *s 79(2)(a)* had been met. On the evidence, it had been reasonable for the Commissioners to make enquiries. However, applying *dicta* in *Watford Timber Co Ltd*, **48.97** above, 'if an enquiry is to be reasonable it must at least set up reasonable deadlines, and compliance with those deadlines must be followed up reasonably. Furthermore, the enquiry must be made reasonably promptly.' The tribunal observed that 'bearing in mind that the appellants are evidently well organised and efficient, we would assess the time required for a credibility check of this nature to be eleven days at the outside.' In this case, there had been 'too much slippage on the part of the Customs & Excise'. Parliament had given the Commissioners 'only 30 days in which to process repayment claims. In limited circumstances the period is extended; but any extension must be within the spirit of *section 79*, which demands expedition on the Commissioners' part.' The period to be left out of account, by virtue of *s 79(4)*, should not exceed eleven days. *Refrigeration Spares (Manchester) Ltd*, LON/01/276 (VTD 17603). (*Note.* For a subsequent application for costs, see **2.471** APPEALS.)

[48.99] An appeal against the refusal of repayment supplement was dismissed in a case where the tribunal found that the Commissioners had raised an enquiry at a control visit in June 1990 and that the company had not answered the enquiry until a subsequent visit in July 1991. *Tary Cash & Carry Ltd*, LON/92/1419P (VTD 11850).

[48.100] A partnership submitted a return, claiming a substantial VAT repayment. The Commissioners received the return on 22 June 2001. On 3 July 2001 they wrote to the partnership seeking further information. The partnership supplied the Commissioners with some information on 11 July, and wrote to the Commissioners on 25 July 2001. The Commissioners received this letter on 26 July, and authorised the repayment on 31 July. The partnership subsequently claimed a repayment supplement on the grounds that the repayment had not been made within 30 days of the receipt of the return. The Commissioners rejected the claim and the tribunal dismissed the partnership's appeal, holding that the effect of *VATA 1994, s 79(4)* was that the period from 3 July to 26 July should be left out of account, so that the payment had been authorised within the 30-day period as extended by *s 79(3)*. *The Thornfield Redditch Limited Partnership*, MAN/02/456 (VTD 17997).

[48.101] A company which dealt in mobile telephones and accessories submitted a return for the period ending 30 June 2002, claiming a repayment of more than £1,700,000. The Commissioners received the return on 1 July 2002. On 11 July the Commissioners informed the company that repayment would be withheld pending further enquiries. On 17 July a VAT officer contacted the company to arrange a visit, which took place on 19 July. The officer was not satisfied that the company had proof that certain goods had been despatched from the UK, and the Commissioners made further enquiries, considering that the company may have engaged in circular transactions (of the type concerned in *Optigen Ltd*, **22.115** EUROPEAN COMMUNITY LAW). On 2 September a senior VAT officer concluded that 'there was no clear evidence of impropriety', and later that day the Commissioners authorised the repayment. The company subsequently claimed a repayment supplement on the grounds that the repayment had not been made within 30 days of the receipt of the return. The Commissioners rejected the claim and the tribunal dismissed the partnership's appeal, observing that 'the inquiry started and remained a reasonable inquiry', and holding that the effect of *VATA 1994, s 79(4)* was that the period from 11 July to 2 September should be left out of account, so that the payment had been authorised within the 30-day period as extended by *s 79(3)*. *Purple International Ltd*, LON/02/1139 (VTD 18243).

[48.102] A company submitted a return for the period ending 30 September 2003, claiming a repayment. The Commissioners received the return on 23 October. They took no action until 17 November, when a VAT officer telephoned the company and left a message asking for the company's accountant to telephone him. The accountant apparently did not receive this message, and the officer telephoned again on 26 November. He arranged to visit the company on 4 December. At the visit, he agreed that repayment was due. The repayment was authorised on 8 December (and the company received it on 11 December). The company claimed repayment supplement, on the grounds that the repayment had been made outside the 30-day period of *VATA 1994, s 79*. The Commissioners rejected the claim on the basis that the period from 17 November to 4 December should be left out of account by virtue of *VATA 1994, s 79(4)*, so that the repayment had been authorised within the 30-day period as extended by *s 79(3)*. The company appealed, contending that it was unreasonable to leave the period from 17 November to 26 November out of account, since the officer had not left a clear message for its accountant indicating that he was querying the return, and had made no further attempt to contact the accountant until nine days later. The tribunal accepted this contention and allowed the company's appeal. *Lookers Ellesmere Port Ltd*, MAN/04/078 (VTD 18770).

[48.103] A company submitted a return for the period ending February 2004, claiming a large repayment. Customs received the return on 19 March, and a VAT officer telephoned the company on 5 April. She visited the company on 16 April and agreed that repayment was due. The repayment was made on 22 April. The company claimed a repayment supplement. Customs rejected the claim and the company appealed, contending that the delay between Customs receiving the return on 19 March and an officer visiting the company on 16 April was unreasonable. The tribunal rejected this contention and dismissed the appeal, observing that the period of enquiry included the Easter holiday and finding that 'in the context of a holiday period, it had been reasonably carried out'. *McGreevy Construction Ltd*, LON/04/1572 (VTD 19877).

[48.104] A company which dealt in mobile telephones submitted a return for the period ending October 2004, claiming a repayment of more than £1,200,000. Customs received the return on 5 November. On 25 November a Customs officer visited the company to collect certain documents in support of the claim. Customs subsequently made further enquiries but later agreed that a repayment was due. The company claimed repayment supplement. Customs rejected the claim and the tribunal dismissed the company's appeal, holding that the effect of *VATA 1994, s 79(4)* was that the period from 25 November to the conclusion of the enquiry should be left out of account. *S & I Electronics plc*, LON/05/682 (VTD 20078).

[48.105] A bank submitted a return for the period ending 31 March 2004, claiming a repayment of £2,343,905. Customs received the return on 7 May. On 25 May a Customs officer telephoned the bank with questions about the return. On 28 May the bank provided the requested information. The officer dealing with the return was on leave from 29 May to 6 June. He began examining the information on 7 June. On 14 June Customs agreed to repay £2,208,670, and formally authorised this repayment on 16 June (i.e. 41 days after receiving the return). They subsequently agreed that the repayable amount was £2,276,548. The bank claimed repayment supplement. Customs rejected the claim but the tribunal allowed the bank's appeal, finding that the bank had provided all the necessary information on 28 May, so that only the four days from 25 May to 28 May should be left out of account by virtue of *VATA 1994, s 79(4)*. The chairman (Mr. Bishopp) observed that 'the obligation of processing a return within 30 days is not imposed on an individual officer, but on the Commissioners. If they are to avoid being required to pay repayment supplement, they must devote sufficient resources to the processing of returns in that timescale.' *Alliance & Leicester plc*, [2007] VATDR 240 (VTD 20094).

[48.106] A company submitted a VAT return for October 2003, claiming a repayment. HMRC decided to begin an enquiry into the return. On 14 November a HMRC officer telephoned the company and arranged to visit it on 24 November to discuss the return. On 8 December the officer decided to authorise the repayment, which the company received on 9 December. The company claimed repayment supplement. HMRC rejected the claim and the tribunal dismissed the company's appeal, holding that the enquiry had been reasonable and that the effect of *VATA 1994, s 79(4)* was that the 25 days from 14 November to 8 December should be left out of account, so that the payment had been authorised within the 30-day period as extended by *s 79(3)*. *Future Components Ltd v HMRC*, [2010] UKFTT 101 (TC), TC00412.

[48.107] A company (M) submitted a VAT return for April 2004, claiming a repayment. HMRC made the repayment on 29 June. M claimed repayment supplement. HMRC rejected the claim and the tribunal dismissed M's appeal, finding that HMRC had received the return on 25 May, and that the effect of *VATA 1994, s 79(4)* was that the period from 7 June to 22 June should be left out of account, so that the payment had been authorised within the 30-day period as extended by *s 79(3)*. (The tribunal also dismissed similar appeals for subsequent periods.) *Megantic Services Ltd v HMRC (No 3)*, [2010] UKFTT 125 (TC), TC00436. (*Note.* For a previous appeal by the same company, see **2.287** APPEALS.)

[48.108] A company submitted a VAT return, claiming a repayment, on 16 March 2006. HMRC queried the return with the company but authorised the repayment on 10 May. The company claimed repayment supplement.

HMRC rejected the claim but the tribunal allowed the company's appeal, applying the principles laid down in *Alliance & Leicester plc*, **48.105** above. On the evidence, the tribunal held that the period to be left out of account by virtue of *VATA 1994, s 79(4)* was the eleven days from 11 April to 21 April, so that the repayment had been made after the 30-day period as extended by *s 79(3)*. *Raptor Commerce Ltd v HMRC*, [2010] UKFTT 620 (TC), TC00620.

Miscellaneous

Company claiming repayment—return containing errors

[48.109] A company submitted a return claiming a repayment of VAT of more than £18 million. The Commissioners discovered that there were errors in the return, and raised detailed enquiries with the company. The company formally claimed a repayment supplement on the basis of the figures in the return, notwithstanding the errors which the Commissioners had discovered. The Commissioners refused to make a provisional repayment and the company appealed, contending that the Commissioners were obliged to make a repayment on the basis of the figures in the return subject to any errors which were discovered within 30 days. The tribunal dismissed the appeal, holding that what is now *VATA 1994, s 79* did not confer an automatic right to repayment supplement in such circumstances. Where the amount to be repaid was in dispute, no repayment supplement was due until the amount was agreed by the Commissioners or determined by the tribunal. *British Steel Exports Ltd*, LON/90/385Z & LON/91/2481Z (VTD 7562).

Interaction of VATA 1994, ss 78 and 79

[48.110] See *Kohanzad & Kohanzad*, **48.132** below.

Interaction of VATA 1994, ss 79 and 84

[48.111] See *Bank Austria Trade Services Gesellschaft mbH*, **2.528** APPEALS.

Whether return made

[48.112] See *W Timms & Son (Builders) Ltd*, **59.10** RETURNS.

Whether claim withdrawn

[48.113] See *Computer Equipment Investors Ltd*, **59.36** RETURNS.

Interest payable in cases of official error (VATA 1994, s 78)

NOTE

VATA 1994, s 78(11), introduced by *FA 1997, s 47*, lays down a three-year limit for retrospective repayment claims with effect from 18 July 1996. Cases relating to periods before the enactment of *FA 1997* should be read in the light of this change. For the relationship between *VATA 1994, s 78* and *VATA 1994, s 79*, see *THI Leisure Two Partnership*, **48.90** above.

Whether any official error

Cases where the appellant was unsuccessful

Delay in reclaiming input tax

[48.114] A company with its head office in the USA established a subsidiary company in the UK, to provide banking services and support facilities for branches and subsidiary companies in Europe and Asia. The UK company was entitled to reclaim input tax in accordance with the *VAT (General) Regulations 1985*. In August 1991 it submitted a claim for repayment of input tax, backdated to 1986. It also submitted a claim to interest under what is now *VATA 1994, s 78(1)*, backdated to June 1988. The Commissioners repaid the input tax but rejected the company's claim to interest. The tribunal dismissed the company's appeal, observing that its claim to credit for input tax had not been presented until August 1991. Much of the delay in quantifying the claim appeared to have resulted from the fact that the company's tax manager had left the company in the summer of 1989, and had not been replaced. *American Express Bank Ltd*, LON/92/1165Z (VTD 9748).

[48.115] A similar decision was reached in a case where a tourist agency had initially reclaimed only part of its input tax, but had subsequently claimed a repayment of tax on the basis of the decision in *Netherlands Board of Tourism*, 36.498 INPUT TAX. The tribunal reviewed the evidence in detail and held that the 'true cause of the failure to claim input tax in full' was 'the decision taken by (the appellant) and its professional advisers not to pursue the view which they had formed that its activities were covered by the *Netherlands* decision'. *Switzerland Tourism*, LON/99/007 (VTD 17068).

[48.116] A partnership discovered that it had overpaid tax through failing to claim all the input tax to which it was entitled. It applied for an award of interest under what is now *VATA 1994, s 78(1)*, contending that the underclaim should have been identified by a VAT officer on a control visit. The Commissioners rejected the claim to interest and the tribunal dismissed the partnership's appeal. *Newton Newton*, MAN/92/1160 (VTD 11372).

Incorrect information from company auditors

[48.117] A VAT officer made a control visit to a company in March 1992. The company's director showed the officer a letter from the company's auditors, indicating that it had appeared that the company had failed to account for VAT of £3,150 on a payment from Esso. The company completed a form VAT 652 disclosing this, and paid the tax in question. In August 1992 the company's bookkeepers discovered that the £3,150 had already been accounted for in July 1990. The VAT officer verified that this was correct, and the company deducted the overpayment of £3,150 from its return for October 1992. The company submitted a claim to interest under what is now *VATA 1994, s 78(1)*. The Commissioners rejected the claim and the tribunal dismissed the company's appeal. *Rogers Torbay Ltd*, LON/93/835 (VTD 11389).

Time limit for claim

[48.118] A married couple traded as distributors of Tupperware. They had a number of 'sub-distributors', who retained a percentage of the takings as commission. The couple accounted for VAT on the full amounts paid by the purchasers of the goods, including the amounts retained by the sub-distributors, in accordance with advice given to such distributors by the Commissioners. However, in October 1984 the CA held (in *Potter*, **1.91** AGENTS) that such distributors were only required to account for VAT on the amounts which they received from the sub-distributors, and were not required to account for VAT on the amounts retained by the sub-distributors. In October 1989, following the HL decision in *Fine Arts Developments plc*, **59.23** RETURNS, the Commissioners made repayments to the distributors affected, but without interest. In 1991, following the enactment of what is now *VATA 1994, s 78* (introduced by *FA 1991*) the couple submitted a claim for interest on the repayment. The Commissioners rejected the claim and the tribunal dismissed the couple's appeal, holding that 'the error in assessing the proper relationship between distributors and dealers for its implications for VAT was authoritatively found to exist in the judgment of the appeal of *Potter* on 26 October 1984'. The claim to interest was 'barred by the terms of (*VATA 1994, s 78(11)**)'. *Mr & Mrs P Bonanni*, LON/92/1485A (VTD 11823).

[48.119] Similar decisions were reached in *A & D Keen*, LON/92/1400A (VTD 11824) and *M & R Davidson*, EDN/94/148 (VTD 12908).

Overdeclaration of output tax

[48.120] A company overdeclared output tax in its return for the period ending 31 August 1991. This was discovered at a control visit in April 1992. The officer who made the control visit requested further information, which the company supplied in May, and the sum was repaid in June. The company submitted a claim to interest under *VATA 1994, s 78**. The Commissioners rejected the claim and the tribunal dismissed the company's appeal, holding on the evidence that 'the error was entirely that of the appellant company'. *Alba Motor Homes Ltd*, EDN/93/191 (VTD 12853). (*Note.* An appeal against a default surcharge was also dismissed.)

[48.121] Similar decisions were reached in *Thomas M Devon & Co*, EDN/94/142 (VTD 13098) and *MB Champion*, LON/95/56A (VTD 13307).

[48.122] A company accounted for tax, under the 'reverse charge' provisions, on management charges levied by its parent company, which was resident outside the UK. Following a change of accountants, it subsequently reclaimed the tax, on the basis that the services in question were not 'relevant services' within *VATA 1994, Sch 5*, so that the 'reverse charge' provisions did not apply. The Commissioners accepted the repayment claim and the company submitted a claim to be repaid interest under *VATA 1994, s 78*. The Commissioners rejected the claim to interest and the tribunal dismissed the company's appeal, holding that the overpayment was not due to an error on the part of the Commissioners and was therefore not within the scope of *s 78(1)*. *Avco Trust plc*, LON/x (VTD 16251).

Estimated assessment—whether any 'official error'

[48.123] In August 1988 the Commissioners issued an estimated assessment charging tax of more than £34,000 on a motor dealer for the periods ending March 1987. The dealer submitted returns claiming repayments for the periods ending June 1988 and September 1988. The Commissioners set the repayments against the tax assessed for the previous periods. In November 1990 the dealer closed his business, and the Commissioners were unable to enforce payment of the unpaid tax. In 1993, following information from the dealer's accountants, the Commissioners withdrew the assessment. In February 1994 they repaid the tax for the periods ending June and September 1988. The dealer submitted a claim to interest under what is now *VATA 1994, s 78*. The Commissioners rejected the claim and the tribunal dismissed the dealer's appeal. On the evidence, there had been reasonable grounds for the Commissioners' having issued the estimated assessment in August 1988. The true cause of the delay in repaying the tax was 'the failure by (the dealer) or of those acting for him to provide that information which, had it been provided timeously, would have obviated the need for an assessment or led to its early withdrawal'. *AD Wheeler (t/a Wheeler Motor Co)*, LON/95/1780A (VTD 13617).

[48.124] The decision in *Wheeler*, **48.123** above, was applied in the similar subsequent case of *Alan Glaves International Ltd*, MAN/99/29 (VTD 16151).

Use of inappropriate Retail Scheme

[48.125] A company registered for VAT in 1973 and operated a Retail Scheme. In 1991 a VAT officer visited the company and discovered that it was making wholesale supplies as well as retail supplies, and informed the company that it should not use a Retail Scheme for wholesale supplies. Subsequently the company's directors formed the opinion that the result of having operated Scheme G was that it had paid more tax than was necessary, and submitted a claim for repayment of more than £100,000, together with interest. The Commissioners rejected the claim and the tribunal dismissed the company's appeal, observing that the company 'had the benefit of professional advice from the commencement of VAT' and holding that 'any claim for interest under (*VATA 1994, s 78*) is barred by the provisions of (*s 78(11)*)'. *RJN Creighton Ltd*, BEL/93/57 (VTD 12395).

[48.126] A married couple who owned a village shop accounted for tax under Retail Scheme D from 1989 to 1995. Since part of their business consisted of the sale of home-made cakes, they were not in fact eligible to use Scheme D. In 1995 they applied to make a retrospective change to Scheme F. The Commissioners accepted the application and subsequently made a repayment to the couple. The couple then applied for interest on the repayment. The Commissioners rejected the claim and the tribunal dismissed the couple's appeal, finding on the evidence that there had been 'no error on the part of the Commissioners'. *JL & PA Peart (t/a The Border Reiver)*, MAN/96/433 (VTD 14672). (*Note.* Retrospective changes of retail scheme are only allowed in exceptional cases, and the maximum period of recalculation is now three years.)

Opticians—percentage of output tax to be treated as exempt

[48.127] Prior to May 1995, the Commissioners treated the sale of spectacles by opticians as a single standard-rated supply. In August 1993, a tribunal held that, while the sale of spectacles was taxable, the services supplied by the optician who dispensed the spectacles was a separate supply which qualified for exemption. The Commissioners appealed against this decision, but it was upheld by the QB in March 1995 (see *Leightons Ltd,* **33.8** HEALTH AND WELFARE). In May 1995 the Commissioners announced that they had accepted the QB decision and would accept repayment claims on certain conditions (see Business Brief 8/95). A group of companies lodged such a claim, and in December 1995, the Commissioners agreed that a percentage of the group's takings should be treated as exempt. In September 1998 they agreed that a higher percentage of the group's takings should be treated as exempt with regard to future supplies, but rejected the group's request for the increased percentage to be applied retrospectively. In April 1999 the group submitted a repayment claim on the basis that the increased percentage should be backdated to January 1996. The Commissioners rejected the claim, and subsequently made a repayment covering the period from January 1998 to September 1999. The group applied for interest. The Commissioners rejected the application and the tribunal dismissed the group's appeal, holding that there had been no error on the part of the Commissioners, and 'there was no delay attributable to the Commissioners in dealing with the repayments'. *Specsavers Optical Group,* [2003] VATDR 268 (VTD 18025). (*Note.* Costs were awarded to the Commissioners.)

[48.128] The tribunal reached a similar decision in a subsequent appeal by the same group. *Specsavers Optical Group (No 2),* [2003] VATDR 268 (VTD 18186).

Assessment issued to recover input tax—whether any 'official error'

[48.129] In 1985 a trader (G) reclaimed input tax relating to the renovation and extension of a cottage. A VAT officer formed the opinion that this work had not been carried out for the purpose of G's business, and the Commissioners issued an assessment to recover the tax. G appealed, but, on the advice of his solicitor, subsequently withdrew the appeal and paid the tax. In 1995 another VAT officer visited G and discovered that, from 1990, he had been letting the cottage as holiday accommodation, but had not been accounting for tax on this income. He arranged for the issue of an assessment charging output tax on this income. G complained that it was unfair that he should have to pay output tax on this income when his previous claim for input tax had been disallowed. The Commissioners accepted that, since the cottage was being used for business purposes, the input tax should be repaid. However, they refused to pay interest. The tribunal dismissed G's appeal, finding that it was not 'conceivable that (the officer) would have acted in the way he did if (G) had said that the intended use of the cottage was for holiday lets'. *RJ Gynn,* LON/97/595 (VTD 15360).

[48.130] A charity reclaimed input tax of more than £200,000 for the period ending 30 June 2006. HMRC formed the opinion that the claim was excessive, and issued an assessment to recover some of the tax. In July 2008, following correspondence with the charity's accountants, HMRC agreed to repay some of the disputed tax. The charity claimed interest under *VATA 1994, s 78.* HMRC rejected the claim and the tribunal dismissed the charity's appeal, finding that there had been no 'official error' and observing that the repayment was late because the charity had been dilatory in responding to enquiries from HMRC. *Walk The Walk in Action Ltd v HMRC*, [2009] UKFTT 186 (TC), TC00141.

Attribution of input tax between exempt and zero-rated income

[48.131] In 1978 the Institute of Bankers agreed with the Commissioners that its subscription income should be treated as exempt from VAT under what is now *VATA 1994, Sch 9, Group 9*. Subsequently one of the Institute's employees wrote to the Commissioners, requesting permission to treat a large proportion of the subscription income as attributable to the supply of a zero-rated journal to its members, and to apportion its input tax accordingly. However, in 1980 the Institute's principal finance officer informed the Commissioners that, as it did 'not in any way wish to imperil the exempt status of members' subscriptions', it 'would prefer to leave the present arrangements undisturbed rather than court any such risk'. In 1992 the Institute engaged a new accountant, who formed the opinion that part of the subscription income should be treated as attributable to its zero-rated supplies. In 1993 he wrote to the Commissioners submitting repayment claims. The Commissioners accepted the claims and made the requested repayment. In 1997 the Institute submitted a claim for interest under *VATA 1994, s 78*. The Commissioners rejected the claim on the basis that there had been no 'official error'. The tribunal dismissed the Institute's appeal against this decision, finding that the Institute's principal finance officer had decided in 1980 that it would not be in its interests to attribute part of its income to zero-rated supplies. Since the Institute had 'decided its position', there had not been 'a relevant error on the part of the Commissioners'. *The Chartered Institute of Bankers*, LON/97/1598 (VTD 15648).

Interaction of VATA 1994, ss 78 and 79

[48.132] A partnership claimed a repayment of more than £94,000 input tax. Customs initially rejected the claim, but subsequently agreed that the partnership was entitled to a lesser repayment of £26,000. Customs also paid repayment supplement under *VATA 1994, s 79*. The partnership claimed that it should also be entitled to a payment of interest under *VATA 1994, s 78*. Customs rejected this claim and the tribunal dismissed the partnership's appeal, holding that the effect of *VATA 1994, s 78(2)* was that interest was not payable 'on an amount which falls to be increased by a supplement under *section 79*'. *R & N Kohanzad*, MAN/01/849 (VTD 19013).

Cases where the appellant was partly successful

Input tax wholly attributed to exempt supplies—whether any 'official error'

[48.133] Fifteen associated housebuilding companies (not comprising a VAT group) operated a scheme for prospective purchasers of their houses whereby they agreed to acquire the purchaser's existing house in part-exchange. From 1981 to 1996 they treated the input tax attributable to such acquisitions as wholly attributable to exempt supplies. In 1996 they formed the opinion that part of the tax could have been attributed to their zero-rated supplies of new houses, and submitted repayment claims accordingly, which the Commissioners accepted. The companies then claimed interest under *VATA 1994, s 78*.

The Commissioners rejected the claim to interest on the basis that there had been no 'official error' within *s 78*. The companies appealed. The tribunal reviewed the evidence in detail and dismissed fourteen of the appeals, while allowing the appeal by one company on the basis of a specific letter which it had received from the Nottingham VAT office in 1985. (The letter was only produced on the morning of the hearing, and the Commissioners accepted that it gave erroneous advice, falling within the scope of *s 78*.) The tribunal observed that each of the companies was a separate entity for VAT purposes, and 'each should have dealt with its own VAT affairs'. *Barratt Homes Ltd (and associated appeals)*, MAN/99/250 (VTD 16533).

Cases where the appellant was successful

Input tax apportioned to take account of non-business use

[48.134] In May 1987 a charity submitted a return claiming a repayment of input tax of more than £25,000. The Commissioners formed the opinion that some of the input tax was not directly related to business activities and should therefore be apportioned in accordance with what is now *VATA 1994, s 24(5)* (see **11.39** *et seq*. CHARITIES). In 1991 the CJEC gave judgment in the case of *Lennartz v Finanzamt München*, **22.456** EUROPEAN COMMUNITY LAW. The charity's accountants formed the opinion that, in the light of this decision, the charity should have been permitted to reclaim the whole of the input tax in question. The Commissioners accepted this and repaid the input tax, and the charity made a claim for interest under what is now *VATA 1994, s 78*. The Commissioners rejected the claim to interest, and the charity appealed. The tribunal allowed the appeal, holding that what is now *VATA 1994, s 24(5)* was inconsistent with *Article 17* of the *EC Sixth Directive* as interpreted in *Lennartz*. The Commissioners' correspondence to the company in 1987 had been based on an erroneous interpretation of the law, and this error had led to the company failing to claim credit for input tax to which it had in fact been entitled. *North East Media Development Trust Ltd*, MAN/94/448 (VTD 13104). (*Note*. For subsequent developments, see **48.142** and **48.143** below.)

Failure to claim input tax on disposals of shares outside EC

[48.135] A company which managed a pension fund disposed of various shares on markets outside the EC. In 1987 a VAT officer informed the company that such disposals were exempt supplies, so that the input tax on associated expenses was not deductible, and the company was no longer entitled to be registered. The company followed the officer's advice, and duly deregistered. In 1995 the company engaged a firm of accountants to review its VAT affairs. The accountants realised that the company was making disposals which qualified for zero-rating until the end of 1992, and thereafter were outside the scope of VAT but with the right of recovery of input tax. As a result of this, the company re-registered and reclaimed input tax relating to the supplies in question, backdated to 1987. The Commissioners repaid the tax in question, but refused to pay any interest. The company appealed, contending that it was entitled to interest under *VATA 1994, s 78*. The tribunal accepted this contention and allowed the appeal. On the evidence, the tribunal found that the officer had been 'supplied with complete and correct information and documents by (the company), so that he was provided with everything necessary to enable him properly to consider whether any of the company's transactions in securities qualified for zero-rating'. The officer 'should have known, or should have realised, that typically a pension fund, and particularly one of an international company with its main base outside the UK as in this case, would have made share sales to persons overseas, and that the input VAT on expenses relating thereto qualified for zero-rating'. The tribunal observed that it was essential that, before Customs' officers give definitive advice, they should 'be sure they understand the reality of the situation with which they are dealing, and give rulings according with that reality'. The company's failure to claim its input tax at the appropriate time was attributable to the incorrect information given by the VAT officer who had visited the company. *CGI Pension Trust Ltd*, MAN/98/85 (VTD 15926).

Retail Scheme—overdeclaration of tax—whether any official error

[48.136] A retailer, who had overdeclared tax in respect of newspaper delivery charges, claimed a repayment. The Commissioners repaid tax of £13,900, but refused to repay any interest. The trader appealed, contending that she had been misled by a VAT officer and was entitled to interest under *VATA 1994, s 78*. The CS accepted this contention and allowed her appeal (reversing the tribunal decision). Lord Macfadyen held that, on the evidence, it was accepted that the scheme proposed and adopted by the trader was an adaptation of what is now Direct Calculation Scheme 1. However, the officer whom the trader had consulted had been under the impression that the trader was adopting an apportionment scheme. The advice given by the officer had been incomplete and misleading, and the only reasonable conclusion on the evidence was that the trader was entitled to interest under *VATA 1994, s 78*. *Mrs ID Mathieson v C & E Commrs*, CS [1999] STC 835.

Output tax accounted for on exempt supplies—whether any 'official error'

[48.137] A religious organisation ran educational courses from its premises. Until early 1994 it accounted for output tax on these supplies. In 1994 it engaged a tax consultant who ascertained that these courses should have been treated as exempt and claimed repayment of the overdeclared tax together with interest under what is now *VATA 1994, s 78**. The Commissioners accepted the claim for repayment of output tax but rejected the claim to payment of interest on the grounds that there had not been any 'official error'. The organisation appealed, contending that the Commissioners' *Leaflet 701/30/87* was misleading as it had not reflected the changes enacted by the *VAT (Education) Order 1987 (SI 1987 No 1259)*, and that it had been misled at a control visit by a VAT officer who had given it the impression that it should account for output tax on the supplies in question. The tribunal accepted this contention and allowed the appeal. *Wydale Hall*, MAN/94/687 (VTD 14273). (*Note. Leaflet 701/30/87* has subsequently been superseded by *Leaflet 701/30/97*.)

Mail order business—assessments on discounts credited to agents

[48.138] In the case noted at 22.253 EUROPEAN COMMUNITY LAW, a company which operated a mail order business had computed its gross takings in accordance with the standard method in force until 28 February 1997. On 27 February 1997 the Commissioners issued a letter withdrawing this method, and instructing the company to include in gross takings the full amount of all credit sales to agents, without deducting the 10% discounts which it credited to the agents. In its subsequent returns, the company continued to treat the discounts which it credited to its agents as a deduction in computing its gross takings. The Commissioners issued assessments charging tax on the basis that no adjustments for discounts on agents' own purchases could be given until the goods were paid and the discounts claimed, and that commission not yet paid to agents could not be used to reduce the figure of gross takings used to calculate output tax. Following the CA decision in *R v C & E Commrs (ex p. Littlewoods Home Shopping Group Ltd)*, **58.39** RETAILERS' SPECIAL SCHEMES, an assessment which the Commissioners had issued in January 1998 was substantially reduced to take account of that decision. The company claimed repayment together with interest under *VATA 1994, s 78*. The Commissioners rejected the claim to interest, and the company appealed. The tribunal reviewed the evidence in detail and allowed the appeal, finding that the assessment had been excessive and that the officer responsible for raising it had failed to inform the company of the detailed basis on which it had been raised. There had been 'an official error' in the way in which the assessment was raised. *Freemans plc (No 2)*, LON/99/435 (VTD 17019).

Interaction of VATA 1994, ss 78 and 79

[48.139] See *National Galleries of Scotland*, 48.83 above.

Computation of interest

[48.140] The successful appellant association in the case noted at **21.51** EDUCATION applied for an award of interest under what is now *VATA 1994, s 78*. The Commissioners made a payment of interest of £75,655, computed in accordance with the rates laid down by *SI 1991/1754*. The association appealed to the tribunal, contending that the interest should have been compounded. The tribunal rejected this contention and dismissed the appeal, holding that there was no statutory provision for compounding the award of interest under *VATA 1994, s 78*. *National Council of YMCAs Inc*, [1993] VATTR 299 (VTD 10537). (*Note.* For a subsequent unsuccessful application by the association, see **48.144** below.)

[48.141] The proprietors of a hotel submitted a return for the period ending 30 September 1990, claiming a repayment of £1,924. On 15 November a VAT officer made a control visit to the hotel. He formed the opinion that only £691 should be repaid, and that the proprietors were liable to a misdeclaration penalty of £369. The Commissioners repaid the balance of £322 to the proprietors on 29 November 1990. Following representations by the proprietors, the penalty was withdrawn and the sum of £369 was repaid to them on 4 April 1991. Following a further control visit on 27 September 1991, the Commissioners accepted that the original repayment claim had been correct and that the VAT officer had been wrong to refuse it. The balance of £1,233, together with interest of £119, was repaid to the proprietors in October 1991. The proprietors complained that the interest paid to them was inadequate, and in February 1992 the Commissioners made a payment of interest of £151 under what is now *VATA 1994, s 78*. The proprietors appealed to the tribunal, contending that they were entitled to a more substantial payment. The tribunal allowed their appeal in part, holding that the rates of interest were fixed by statutory instrument (*SI 1991/1754*) and could not be altered, but finding that the Commissioners' computation of interest had only begun on 29 December 1990, whereas the commencement date should have been 29 November 1990. The tribunal chairman noted that 'the appellants are out of pocket to the extent that the Commissioners' error cost them interest on their bank account which exceeded the interest payable by the Commissioners', and recommended 'that the Commissioners consider making an ex gratia payment to the appellants'. *S & DE Jarman*, MAN/92/632 (VTD 11637).

[48.142] Following the decision in the case noted at **48.134** above, the company claimed interest on the whole of the input tax which the Commissioners had wrongly refused to repay. The Commissioners considered that interest should only be payable on the excess of the input tax over the output tax which the company would have had to pay if the principles in *Lennartz v Finanzamt München*, **22.456** EUROPEAN COMMUNITY LAW, had been adopted. They applied to the tribunal for clarification of the amount of interest payable. The tribunal upheld the Commissioners' contention, holding that 'interest should be computed upon an amount equal to the input tax net of the output tax underpaid'. Interest should be computed on this amount from the date determined under what is now *VATA 1994, s 78(5)* to the date on which the Commissioners authorised the relevant repayment. *North East Media Development Trust Ltd*, [1995] VATDR 240 (VTD 13425). (*Note*. For subsequent developments in this case, see **48.143** below.)

[48.143] Following the decision in the case noted at **48.142** above, the Commissioners repaid interest of £19,000 to the company. The Commissioners calculated the interest on the basis that interest ceased to run in December 1993, when they repaid the disputed input tax. However, the Commissioners did not repay the interest until 1995. The company applied to the tribunal for a ruling that it was entitled to interest on the £19,000 from December 1993 until the date on which it was actually paid. The tribunal accepted this contention and directed that a further payment of interest should be made to the company. The chairman observed that, applying *Hunt v RM Douglas (Roofing) Ltd*, HL [1990] 1 AC 398, 'a person to whom money is due is not to be deprived of his interest simply because the paying party is unable to calculate the amount to which he is entitled'. There was 'nothing offensive in the notion that the Commissioners should pay interest upon interest'. The Commissioners should have repaid the £19,000 in December 1993 but had not done so, with the result that the company had been deprived of the use of its money. *North East Media Development Trust Ltd (No 3)*, [1996] VATDR 396 (VTD 14416). (*Note*. See now, however, *VATA 1994, s 78(1A)*, introduced by *FA 1997, s 44* with retrospective effect.)

Computation of interest—application of VATA 1994, s 78(1A)

[48.144] The Commissioners repaid interest of £75,655 to the successful appellant association in the case noted at **21.51** EDUCATION. The association subsequently applied for a further payment of interest on the lines of the payment made in *North East Media Development Trust Ltd (No 3)*, **48.143**

above. The tribunal dismissed the application, declining to follow the decision in *North East Media Development Trust Ltd (No 3)* because of the subsequent enactment, with retrospective effect, of *VATA 1994, s 78(1A)*. The effect of *s 78(1A)(b)* was that interest under *s 78* was not payable on interest. *National Council of YMCAs*, LON/97/797 (VTD 15247).

Repayment claim—effect of VATA 1994, s 78(2)

[48.145] A trader's first VAT return claimed a substantial repayment of VAT. The Commissioners made enquiries into the return before agreeing that a repayment was due. They made the repayment in two stages, and agreed to pay repayment supplement under *VATA 1994, s 79*. The trader also submitted a claim for interest under *VATA 1994, s 78* in respect of the second repayment. The Commissioners rejected the claim on the basis that *VATA 1994, s 78(2)* applied. The tribunal dismissed the trader's appeal against this decision. *DR Davidson*, EDN/04/40 (VTD 18721).

Car dealers—application of Limitation Act 1980, s 32

[48.146] Two companies which traded as motor dealers submitted claims for the repayment of output tax which they had wrongly accounted for from 1973 to 1996 on sales of 'demonstrator cars' on which input tax had been 'blocked' and which should have been treated as exempt (applying the CJEC decision in *EC Commission v Italian Republic*, 22.349 EUROPEAN COMMUNITY LAW) and on payments from manufacturers which should have been treated as discounts on the sale price of the cars (applying the CJEC decision in *Elida Gibbs Ltd*, 22.235 EUROPEAN COMMUNITY LAW). Customs made the repayments, together with simple interest under *VATA 1994, s 78*. The companies appealed, contending that the effect of the HL decision in *CIR v Sempra Metals Ltd*, HL [2007] STC 1559 was they were entitled to compound interest. The Ch D and the CA unanimously dismissed the appeals, holding that the effect of *Limitation Act 1980, s 32(1)(c)* was that the companies' restitutionary claims were out of time. Etherton LJ expressed the view that the question of whether interest should be compounded should be referred to the CJEC in an appropriate case. *FJ Chalke Ltd v HMRC (and related appeal)*, CA [2010] STC 1640; [2010] EWCA Civ 313.

Whether interest payable under VATA 1994, s 78 or VATA 1994, s 84

[48.147] See *Peoples Bathgate & Livingston Ltd*, 2.526 APPEALS; *Seaton Sands Ltd & Others*, 2.527 APPEALS, and *Bank Austria Trade Services Gesellschaft mbH*, 2.528 APPEALS.

Miscellaneous

Customs mistakenly making repayment to company's bank

[48.148] A company was entitled to a VAT refund of £46,000. The company wrote to the Commissioners asking them to make the repayment to its solicitors, rather than to its bank, as it was 'experiencing difficulties' with its bank. Despite this letter, the Commissioners mistakenly made the repayment to the company's bank. The company lodged a complaint and the Commissioners correctly repaid the money to the company's solicitors. The Commissioners asked the bank to repay the £46,000. The bank refused to do so, and the Commissioners took proceedings against the bank. The Ch D gave judgment for the Commissioners, holding that the bank was not entitled to retain the money. In transferring the £46,000 to the bank, the Commissioners had been making a tender of the amount which they owed to the company. The company had rejected that method of tendering the debt, and the Commissioners had accepted that refusal. Accordingly, the Commissioners were entitled to reclaim the money from the bank. *C & E Commrs v National Westminster Bank plc*, Ch D [2002] EWHC 2204 (Ch); [2003] 1 All ER (Comm).

Whether overpaid tax may be set against current tax due

[48.149] See *Fine Art Developments plc*, 59.23 RETURNS.

Payment by credit transfer

[48.150] See *Matilot Ltd*, 18.60 DEFAULT SURCHARGE.

VATA 1994, s 28—payments on account

[48.151] See *Premier Despatch Ltd*, **18.463** DEFAULT SURCHARGE, and *Sapphire Retail Fund Ltd*, **18.548** DEFAULT SURCHARGE.

VATA 1994, s 81—set-off of credits

[48.152] A trader (L) submitted three claims for repayment of input tax. HMRC set the input tax against output tax which L owed, under *VATA 1994, s 81(3)*. L appealed. The tribunal dismissed the appeal, holding that the set-off was authorised by *s 81(3)*, and observing that set-offs under *s 81(3)* did not appear to be an appealable matter under *VATA 1994, s 83*. *M Lancaster (t/a Airport Cars) v HMRC (No 2)*, [2010] UKFTT 559 (TC), TC00810.

[48.153] A company had submitted a number of incorrect returns in which it underdeclared VAT. In its return for November 2000, it purported to unilaterally correct these underdeclarations by restricting its claim to input tax. However, it failed to notify the Commissioners by way of voluntary disclosure. In July 2002 a VAT officer examined the company's returns and discovered a number of errors, including both underdeclarations and overdeclarations, with a net overdeclaration. Following this, the Commissioners made a net repayment to the company. The company appealed, contending that the Commissioners should not have restricted the repayment to take account of underdeclarations in 1998 and 1999. The tribunal rejected this contention and dismissed the appeal, observing that the company had failed to make any disclosure to the Commissioners in November 2000 when it discovered the underdeclarations. The effect of *VATA 1994, s 81(3A)* was that the Commissioners were entitled to take these underdeclarations into account in calculating the repayment due to the company. *Laing The Jeweller Ltd*, EDN/03/97 (VTD 18841).

[48.154] A company (B) which was a registered charity, and operated a theatre, had accounted for VAT on supplies which qualified for exemption as 'cultural services'. In 2007 it submitted a claim for repayment covering the period from 1990 to 1996. HMRC rejected the claim on the grounds that for 2000 and 2001 B had reclaimed substantial input tax on the refurbishment of its theatre, which should have been attributed to exempt supplies, and that the effect of *VATA 1994, s 81(3A)* was that the previous underclaim of input tax should be set against the subsequent overclaim. The tribunal accepted this contention and dismissed the appeal. *Birmingham Hippodrome Theatre Trust Ltd v HMRC*, [2011] UKFTT 117 (TC); [2011] SFTD 473; TC00993. (*Note.* HMRC raised an alternative contention that the claim was 'abusive'. The tribunal rejected this contention, distinguishing the ECJ decision in *DEKA Getreideprodukte GmbH & Co KG iL v EEC*, 22.58 EUROPEAN COMMUNITY LAW, which HMRC had cited as an authority.)

[48.155] See also *Infinity Distribution Ltd v HMRC*, 36.657 INPUT TAX; *R v C & E Commrs (ex p. Richmond & another)*, 36.676 INPUT TAX, and *R (oao Cardiff City Council) v C & E Commrs*, 48.53 above.

Commissioners' right of set-off

[48.156] For other cases concerning the Commissioners' right of set-off, see *Re Cushla Ltd*, 37.16 INSOLVENCY, and *Secretary of State for Trade & Industry v Frid*, 37.17 INSOLVENCY.

VATA 1994, Sch 11 para 2(12)*—deemed supply under Sch 4 para 7*

[48.157] See *Edgewater Motel Ltd v New Zealand Commissioner of Inland Revenue*, 14.114 COLLECTION AND ENFORCEMENT.

Application of VATA 1994, Sch 11 para 5

[48.158] See *International Language Centres Ltd*, 3.41 ASSESSMENT.

Assessment to recover unpaid tax—jurisdiction of tribunal

[48.159] See *Goldenberg*, 2.50 APPEALS.

Customs' powers under VAT Regulations 1995, reg 40

[48.160] See *Caro*, 18.446 DEFAULT SURCHARGE, and *Starlite (Chandeliers) Ltd*, 18.448 DEFAULT SURCHARGE.

49

Penalties: Criminal Offences

The cases in this chapter are arranged under the following headings.

Offences under VATA 1994, s 72   49.1
Offences under Proceeds of Crime Act 2002   49.18
Common law offences   49.25

Offences under VATA 1994, s 72

Failure to register—whether taking steps to evade tax

[49.1] A trader who had failed to register for VAT was convicted for 'being knowingly concerned in, or in the taking of steps with a view to the fraudulent evasion of tax', contrary to what is now *VATA 1994, s 72(1)*. He appealed, contending that inaction did not amount to 'the taking of steps'. The CA rejected this contention and dismissed his appeal. *R v McCarthy*, CA Criminal Division [1981] STC 298.

[49.2] A similar decision was reached in *R v Fairclough*, CA Criminal Division 25 October 1982 unreported.

Indictment under VATA 1994, s 72—whether void for duplicity

[49.3] A defendant was convicted of conduct involving the commission of offences under what is now *VATA 1994, s 72(1)* and *(3)*, contrary to *s 72(8)*. He appealed, contending that the indictment was void for duplicity. The CA rejected this contention and dismissed his appeal, holding that *VATA 1994, s 72(8)* could embrace the commission of numerous offences, which, if the details were known, could have been charged individually under *s 72(1)* and *(3)*. *R v Asif*, CA Criminal Division 1985, 82 Cr AR 123; [1985] CLR 679.

[49.4] The decision in *R v Asif*, 49.3 above, was applied in a similar case in which the CA upheld the convictions of two partners in a restaurant business. The CA observed that, while it was preferable for an indictment to charge a defendant with a particular offence under what is now *VATA 1994, s 72(1)* or *(3)*, the provisions of *s 72(8)* covered a case where a 'deficiency was so striking that it was possible to say that a fraud had been perpetrated but impossible to say how it was done'. *R v KA Choudhury; R v J Uddin*, CA Criminal Division [1996] STC 1163.

Indictment under VATA 1994, s 72—whether defective

[49.5] A woman was convicted of conduct involving the commission of offences under *VATA 1994, s 72*, in that she had made claims for refunds of VAT to which she was not entitled, and had furnished or made use of forms

VAT 407 on which false Customs stamps had been applied. She appealed, contending that the indictment was defective in that it failed to make any specific reference to fraudulent intent or intent to deceive. The CA rejected this contention and dismissed her appeal, holding that the jury had been correctly directed and that there had been no miscarriage of justice. *R v Ike*, CA Criminal Division 1995, [1996] STC 391.

Amendment of indictment under VATA 1994, s 72—whether unfair

[49.6] An individual (S) was charged with offences under *VATA 1994, s 72*, comprising the understatement of output tax and the submission of false claims to input tax. He indicated that he was prepared to plead guilty to the charge relating to input tax, but not to the charge relating to output tax. The Crown therefore applied to amend the indictment so as to split the single count into two separate counts, one relating to input tax and one relating to output tax. The trial judge accepted the application, and S appealed to the CA, contending that the amendment was unfair. The CA rejected this contention and dismissed his appeal, holding that there were good reasons for the amendment and that the amended indictment was not defective. *R v Stanley*, CA Criminal Division 17 September 1998, Times 8.12.1998.

Whether Customs' officers' notebooks admissible in evidence

[49.7] VAT officers formed the opinion that the proprietors of a fish and chip shop had been underdeclaring VAT. Two officers observed the shop, recording the numbers of people entering it. The proprietors were convicted of fraudulent evasion of VAT. They appealed to the CA, contending that there had been an irregularity in the course of the trial and that the notebooks kept by the VAT officers who had conducted the observations should not have been admitted in evidence. The CA allowed the appeals, holding that the notebooks were inadmissible, and that the VAT officers should not have been allowed to refer to the notebooks to refresh their memories of what had happened. *R v Kelsey* 1981, 74 Cr App R 213, was distinguished since in that case the police officer's notebook which was admitted as evidence had been checked by an observer at the time the relevant entry was made, whereas in the present case there had been no check on the accuracy of what each of the VAT officers had written down. The prosecution had admitted that there were some errors and omissions in the notebooks. Nolan LJ described the prosecution evidence as 'fundamentally flawed'. *R v Eleftheriou & Another*, CA Criminal Division [1993] BTC 257.

Whether offences to be tried summarily or on indictment

[49.8] A trader was charged under what is now *VATA 1994, s 72* with being knowingly concerned in the fraudulent evasion of VAT, in that he had been controlling director of a company which had used an obsolete VAT registration number and charged customers output tax of £193,000 but had not paid this to the Commissioners. The local magistrates decided to deal with the case by way of summary proceedings. The Commissioners sought judicial review of the magistrates' decision, contending that, since the maximum penalty by way of summary proceedings was six months' imprisonment, the magistrates' decision was perverse and the case should be tried on indictment. The QB held that the magistrates' decision was unreasonable, since in the absence of mitigating factors or unusual circumstances, a sentence of more than six months' imprisonment might be expected where an amount of almost £200,000 was involved. The case should therefore be tried on indictment. *R v Northampton Magistrates' Court (ex p. C & E Commrs)*, QB [1994] BVC 111.

[49.9] An accountant was charged with fraudulent conduct after submitting a claim for repayment of VAT by a company for which he acted, although the company did not hold an invoice in support of the claim. The local magistrates ruled that the case should be dealt with by summary proceedings and the Commissioners sought judicial review of their decision. The QB granted the Commissioners' application and remitted the case to a different panel of magistrates for them to reconsider the case, applying *dicta* of Schiemann J in *R v Northampton Magistrates' Court (ex p. C & E Commrs)*, **49.8** above. *R v Flax Bourton Magistrates' Court (ex p. C & E Commrs)*, QB 29 January 1996, Times 6.2.1996.

Fraudulent evasion of VAT—definition of 'evasion'

[49.10] A company director was convicted of four counts of being knowingly concerned in the fraudulent evasion of VAT. He appealed, contending that his conduct did not amount to 'evasion' since he had not intended to permanently deprive Customs of the VAT due, but had refrained from submitting VAT returns while the company was trading at a loss. The CA dismissed his appeal, holding that deliberate non-payment of tax was within the definition of 'evasion', and that the prosecution did not have to prove that the defendant intended to permanently deprive Customs of the VAT in question. *R v JC Dealy*, CA Criminal Division 1994, [1995] STC 217: [1995] 1 WLR 658.

Fraudulent evasion of VAT—conviction upheld

[49.11] A partner in a scrap metal business was convicted of fraudulent evasion of VAT after Customs officers had discovered that purchase invoices from unregistered suppliers, which did not include any VAT, had been destroyed, and that input tax had been reclaimed on the basis of false invoices. The CA dismissed the partner's appeal against his conviction. *R v Collier*, CA Criminal Division 26 March 1997, 1997 STI 474.

Evasion of VAT—conviction for unlawful supply of steroids

[49.12] Two defendants were convicted for fraudulent evasion of VAT, in that they had failed to account for output tax on supplies of anabolic steroids. They appealed to the CA, contending that since their supplies had been unlawful under *Medicines Act 1968*, no VAT was due on them, and that this question should have been referred to the CJEC. The CA rejected this contention and dismissed their appeal, applying the principles laid down by the CJEC in *R v*

Goodwin & Unstead, **22.82** EUROPEAN COMMUNITY LAW. Under the principle of fiscal neutrality, unlawful supplies were subject to VAT except where, because of the special characteristics of certain goods, all competition between a lawful and an unlawful economic sector was precluded. *R v C & J Citrone*, CA Criminal Division 1998, [1999] STC 29.

Fraudulent evasion of VAT—'missing trader fraud'

[49.13] An individual (H) was convicted of the fraudulent evasion of VAT after Customs officers had produced evidence indicating that he had been involved in a 'missing trader fraud' involving the sale and purchase of computers and computer parts between different EU countries. He was sentenced to five years' imprisonment, and at a subsequent hearing the judge imposed a confiscation order of £177,453. H appealed, contending that 'missing trader fraud' was not an economic activity and therefore he should not have been convicted for fraudulent evasion of VAT. The CA unanimously rejected this contention and upheld the conviction and the confiscation order. Simon J held that the effect of the CJEC decision in *Optigen Ltd*, **22.115** EUROPEAN COMMUNITY LAW, was that 'so long as the trade itself is lawful, there is economic activity irrespective of whether any particular trader is acting fraudulently or otherwise'. In the present case, 'there were invoices and delivery notes which were evidence of the sale and of the transfer of title in goods (computers and computer parts) which are traded legitimately. Furthermore, money transfers were made as part of these sale and purchase transactions. Viewed objectively, the transactions to which the appellant and his company were parties constituted supplies of goods by a taxable person acting as such and economic activities within the meaning of Sixth Directive, and were therefore subject to VAT.' *R v Hashash*, CA Criminal Division 2006, [2008] STC 1158; [2006] EWCA Crim 2518.

Fraudulent evasion of VAT—appropriate sentence

[49.14] The controlling director of a number of companies which sold double glazing was convicted of fraudulent evasion of VAT. At the Crown Court, he was sentenced to 12 month's imprisonment. He appealed to the CA. The CA upheld the conviction and held that the offence 'passes the custody threshold and that the imposition of an immediate custodial sentence was correct'. However, the CA reduced the sentence to six months' imprisonment. *R v Quigley*, CA [2002] BTC 5518; [2002] EWCA Crim 2148.

[49.15] A barrister (W) submitted a VAT return claiming a repayment of £17,500,000. He claimed that this related to the purchase of aircraft engines which he had subsequently exported. Customs began an investigation and found that the relevant purchase and sale invoices had been produced on W's computer. The company from which he claimed to have purchased the engines stated that it had never had any dealings with him. W was convicted of fraud and sentenced to five years' imprisonment. Taylor J described the claim as 'an audacious attempt to obtain a large sum of money by fabricating evidence'. *RCPO v Wilmot*, Southwark Crown Court 1 July 2008 unreported.

Prosecution not proceeded with—claim for damages

[49.16] Customs officers formed the opinion that a company (T) had been involved in a VAT 'carousel fraud' relating to transactions in mobile telephones. They arrested T's controlling director (S) and another individual (C), whom S had told Customs was T's secretary. They charged both S and C with offences under *VATA 1994, s 72(8)*. Customs subsequently began proceedings against S, who fled the country before his trial. However, Customs did not take further proceedings against C, who denied that he had acted as secretary of T, and described himself as an 'independent selling agent' acting on behalf of T. C subsequently took proceedings against Customs, claiming damages for wrongful arrest. The CA unanimously dismissed his claim, holding that it had been 'entirely reasonable' for the Customs officers to have formed the opinion that C had known that T was involved in VAT fraud. There had been sufficient evidence to justify charging C with an offence under *s 72(8)*. *Coudrat v C & E Commrs*, CA [2005] STC 1006; [2005] EWCA Civ 616.

Conviction for supply of counterfeit goods

[49.17] See *R v Goodwin & Unstead*, 22.82 EUROPEAN COMMUNITY LAW.

Offences under Proceeds of Crime Act 2002

[49.18] An individual (C) was prosecuted for allegedly being involved in a carousel fraud involving transactions in computer chips. He was acquitted at the Blackfriars Crown Court, where he gave evidence that he had not known that the transactions formed part of an attempted fraud, although he accepted that he had done business with fraudsters. Despite his acquittal, the Assets Recovery Agency took proceedings against him under the *Proceeds of Crime Act 2002*, applying the guidelines laid down by the ECJ in *Kittel v Belgian State*, 22.415 EUROPEAN COMMUNITY LAW, and alleging that although, applying the criminal burden of proof beyond reasonable doubt, the jury had found no proof that C had known of the fraud, he had the 'means of knowledge' ('pouvait avoir connaissance') to render him liable under the civil burden of proof on the balance of probabilities. C agreed to pay more than £12,000,000 to the Assets Recovery Agency and more than £6,000,000 to the Republic of Ireland Criminal Assets Bureau. *Director of Assets Recovery Agency v D Creaven*, QB [2005] EWHC 2726 (Admin); Times 4.10.2006.

POCA 2002, s 6—amount of confiscation order

[49.19] Customs formed the opinion that a company director (M) had been involved in 'carousel fraud', involving purported transactions in computer processing units. He pleaded guilty to conspiracy to cheat the revenue, and was sentenced to five years' imprisonment (subsequently reduced to four years on appeal). The court also imposed a confiscation order of more than £3,000,000 under *Proceeds of Crime Act 2002, s 6*. M appealed against the confiscation order. The HL unanimously dismissed his appeal, observing that 'the sum which the appellant, jointly with others, was found to have fraudulently obtained from HM Customs & Excise was, in law, as much his as if he had acted alone. That conclusion leads ineluctably to the further conclusions that he benefited from his offending, and benefited to an extent substantially greater than the confiscation order made against him'. The order made was 'less than his realisable assets. It is entirely consistent with the legitimate objects of the legislation, and it requires, that he be ordered to pay such sum, which involves no injustice or lack of proportionality.' R v May, HL 2008, [2009] STC 852; [2008] UKHL 28.

[49.20] Three company directors were convicted of cheating the public revenue following their participation in a VAT carousel fraud. The court imposed a confiscation order of more than £4,000,000 against one of the directors, and imposed orders for lesser amounts against the other directors, to reflect 'the lower amount of their realisable property'. The directors appealed to the CA. The CA dismissed the appeals, applying the HL decision in R v May, **49.19** above. David Richards LJ held that the judge had been entitled to conclude 'that the sums obtained from the onward sales of the goods were obtained "in connection with" the commission of the relevant offence', and that 'each of the appellants had benefited from his relevant criminal conduct'. R v Sangha & Others, CA Criminal Division 2008, [2009] STC 570; [2008] EWCA Crim 2562.

[49.21] Following an investigation into a VAT MTIC fraud, a company director (T) was convicted of conspiracy to cheat the public revenue, cheating the public revenue, and fraudulent trading. The Guildford Crown Court imposed a confiscation order of £5,320,420. T appealed to the CA, which dismissed his appeal, applying the principles laid down in R v May, **49.19** above. Stanley Burnton LJ observed that T had obtained a 'pecuniary advantage by reason of the evasion of the VAT liability'. Accordingly he must be treated 'as having received a sum of money equal in value to that VAT liability'. R v Takkar, CA [2011] EWCA Crim 646; [2011] 3 All ER 340.

[49.22] Following an investigation into a VAT MTIC fraud, two defendants were convicted of conspiracy to cheat the public revenue. The Northampton Crown Court imposed confiscation orders of £3,668,990 against each of them. They appealed to the CA, contending that the amounts of the orders were excessive, and that the amount of their realisable assets was less than the amount by which they had benefited from the fraud. The CA rejected this contention and dismissed their appeals, applying the principles laid down in R v May, **49.19** above, and holding that the Crown Court had been entitled to find that the defendants had not proved that the amount of their realisable assets was as low as they had claimed. R v McIntosh; R v Marsden, CA [2011] EWCA Crim 1501; [2011] STC 2349.

Scope of confiscation order

[49.23] Following the HL decision noted at **49.19** above, the RCPO sought to treat a flat in London as one of M's 'realisable assets' for the purposes of the confiscation order. M opposed the claim, contending that the flat was owned by a limited company (L) and that it should not be treated as a 'realisable asset' since it had not been purchased by the 'proceeds of crime'. The QB gave judgment for the RCPO, holding that the flat was 'relevant realisable property' of M, but the CA allowed L's appeal against this decision. Etherton LJ held that the QB's conclusion 'that the flat was the realisable property of (M)' was 'unsustainable on the evidence'. *Larkfield Ltd v RCPO (aka RCPO v May & Others)*, CA [2010] STC 1506; [2010] EWCA Civ 521.

[49.24] An individual (P) was convicted of two counts of cheating the public revenue in relation to a VAT MTIC fraud. He was sentenced to eight years' imprisonment. The court also made a confiscation order requiring him to pay more than £1,400,000. The court also granted the RCPO a receivership order in respect of a property in London which P had occupied and used for the purposes of the fraud. Another individual (L) lodged an appeal to the CA, contending that he was the legal and beneficial owner of the property in question, and that the order relating to the property should be lifted. The CA reviewed the evidence in detail and unanimously dismissed L's appeal. Rix LJ held that 'once a confiscation order has been made against a defendant in respect of the value of identified realisable property, it is possible to speak of such property as being realisable property (as it has been adjudicated to be as between the RCPO and the defendant) even though it is still open for third parties to vindicate their own interests in such property by proving that it is not realisable property or that the defendant's interest in it is less than total'. He also observed that the property had been occupied by squatters, so that it had been reasonable to appoint a receiver 'to protect the value of the property'. *S Lamb v RCPO (aka RCPO v Pigott)*, CA [2010] STC 1190; [2010] EWCA Civ 285.

Common law offences

Common law offence of cheating public revenue

[49.25] The director of a company was convicted of cheating the public revenue by failing to account for VAT on sales of gold. The CA dismissed his appeal against conviction, holding that *Theft Act 1968, s 32(1)* retains the common law offence of cheating the public revenue even though other statutory offences (e.g. under what is now *VATA 1994, s 72*) might be in point. Drake J held that 'the common law offence of cheating does not necessarily require a false representation, either by words or conduct. Cheating can include any form of fraudulent conduct which results in diverting money from the revenue and in depriving the revenue of money to which it is entitled.' *R v Mavji*, CA Criminal Division [1986] STC 508.

[49.26] The proprietor of a business dealing in motor vehicles was convicted of cheating the public revenue by charging VAT to customers while not being registered, and not accounting to the Commissioners for the tax charged. The CA dismissed his appeal against conviction, holding that *Theft Act 1968, s 32(1)* retained the common law offence of cheating the public revenue notwithstanding that other statutory offences might be relevant. The CA also held that the common law offence of cheating the Revenue was satisfied by omission, and a positive act of deception was not required. *R v Redford*, CA Criminal Division [1988] STC 845.

[49.27] A company director was charged with cheating the public revenue by submitting VAT returns claiming a net repayment of £4,000,000, based on fraudulent invoices. She was convicted, and was sentenced to five and a half years' imprisonment. The CA unanimously dismissed her appeal against her conviction, holding that there were no grounds for interfering with the verdict of the jury. *R v E Matthews*, CA Criminal Division [2008] STC 1999; [2008] EWCA Crim 423.

[49.28] Convictions for cheating the public revenue were also upheld in *R v Fisher*, CA Criminal Division 21 March 1989, 1989 STI 269; *R v Hooper*, CA Criminal Division 21 March 1989, 1989 STI 269; and *Dougall*, 37.21 INSOLVENCY.

[49.29] Three individuals, who had failed to account for VAT on takings from gaming machines, were convicted of cheating the public revenue. They appealed, contending that the takings should be treated as exempt under *Article 13B(f)* of the *EC Sixth Directive*. The CA rejected this contention and dismissed their appeals, holding that *Article 13B(f)* did not require all forms of gambling to be exempt from VAT, since Member States were authorised to limit the scope of the exemption. Accordingly, the restriction laid down by what is now *VATA 1994, Sch 9 Group 4, Note 1(d)* was not incompatible with the *Sixth Directive*. *R v E Ryan (and related appeals)*, CA Criminal Division [1994] STC 446.

Common law offence of conspiracy to cheat the public revenue

[49.30] Customs formed the opinion that a Spanish company (T) had been involved in a series of carousel frauds in relation to the sale of mobile telephones from Spain to the UK. They took proceedings against T, claiming damages for conspiracy to cheat the public revenue. The QB gave judgment for Customs, and the HL upheld this decision (by a 3-2 majority, Lord Hope and Lord Neuberger dissenting). Lord Scott of Foscote described the transactions as a 'charade' and 'a fraudulent scheme designed to extract by deception money from the Revenue'. The statutory provisions relating to VAT did not 'provide protection against tort claims for those who by fraudulent schemes succeed in extracting money from the Commissioners'. Lord Walker of Gestingthorpe observed that the case concerned 'illegal, fraudulent tax evasion which is costing the Exchequer more than a billion pounds a year. Indeed it is worse than evasion: it is the fraudulent extraction of money from the Exchequer.' Lord Mance held that 'there would be an evident lacuna if the law did not respond to this situation by recognising a civil liability', and that 'the wrongful extraction of the money from the Commissioners by deceit involved unlawful means and a sufficiently actionable wrong to justify a civil claim in conspiracy.' Customs were entitled 'to take common law action in respect of a successful conspiracy which abstracts monies en route to the Commissioners or which prevents the Commissioners from recovering from others what is due from such others to the Commissioners.' There was 'no incongruity in their and the public's interests being in this respect protected by a common law action for conspiracy'. The claim was 'not for the VAT due or for repayment of the VAT credit, it is for damages in respect of loss suffered by the Commissioners due to a successful conspiracy to manipulate the VAT system.' Accordingly there was 'nothing in the statutory scheme to preclude the Commissioners' pursuit of a common law claim for conspiracy against (T)'. *HMRC v Total Network SL*, HL [2008] STC 644; [2008] UKHL 19; [2008] 2 All ER 413.

[49.31] See also *Feehan*, **2.122** APPEALS.

Conviction for cheating the revenue—appropriate sentence

[49.32] A company director (B) was convicted by a jury of cheating the revenue of £1,200,000 in unpaid VAT. Sentencing was adjourned. At the subsequent sentencing hearing, B's lawyer contended that there had been an overpayment of VAT by an associated company, so that B should not be imprisoned. Anthony King J rejected this contention and sentenced B to three and a half years in prison. On the evidence placed before the jury, B had 'deliberately evaded paying tax that he knew was due' and was guilty of a 'very serious cheat'. Any new evidence could only be considered by the Court of Appeal. The Crown Court had to pass sentence in accordance with established legal procedure. *RCPO v P Bowles*, Oxford Crown Court 7 December 2009, Times 9.12.2009.

50

Penalties: Evasion of Tax

The cases in this chapter are arranged under the following headings.

Computation of the penalty	**50.1**
The assessment of the penalty (VATA 1994, s 76)	**50.3**
Liability of directors (VATA 1994, s 61)	
Cases where the appellant was unsuccessful	**50.13**
Cases where the penalty was increased by the tribunal	**50.44**
Cases where the appellant was partly successful	**50.45**
Cases where the appellant was successful	**50.62**
Other cases	
Cases where the appellant was unsuccessful	**50.67**
Cases where the penalty was increased by the tribunal	**50.93**
Cases where the penalty was reduced by the tribunal (VATA 1994, s 70)	**50.95**
Cases where the appellant was successful	**50.131**
Miscellaneous	**50.156**

NOTE

See now *FA 2007, Sch 24*, which proposes to replace *VATA 1994, ss 60, 61* with effect from a date to be appointed by statutory instrument.

Computation of the penalty

Penalty imposed on unregistered trader

[50.1] A company traded without being registered for VAT. The Commissioners imposed a penalty of £46,000 under what is now *VATA 1994, s 60*, attributed to the controlling director under *VATA 1994, s 61*. Both the company and the director appealed, contending that they were not liable to any penalty under *VATA 1994, s 60* since, in the absence of returns, there had not been any false claims or understatements. The CA rejected this contention and dismissed the appeals. It had clearly been the intention of Parliament that *VATA 1994, s 60** should be capable of applying to cases of non-registration. *VATA 1994, s 60(3)** provided 'a formula for the calculation of the statutory maximum in those cases where the method of tax evasion is a fraudulent understatement of output tax or overstatement of input tax' but 'was not intended to provide a formula where the method of evasion was not to register or make declarations at all'. Peter Gibson LJ observed that 'the dishonest omission by a person to register for VAT or, having registered, to make a return', fell within *VATA 1994, s 60(1)**. The provisions of *VATA 1994, s 60(3)* had 'no application to a case of non-registration or an omission by a registered person to make a return'. In such a case, 'the amount of the penalty is equal to the amount of tax evaded by that person's conduct'. *CS Stevenson v C & E Commrs (and related appeal)*, CA [1996] STC 1096.

[50.2] The CA reached a similar decision in the subsequent case of *MS Khan*, 50.89 below.

The assessment of the penalty (VATA 1994, s 76)

Whether notice must apportion penalty to specific periods

[50.3] The Commissioners imposed a penalty of £65,000 on a company under what is now *VATA 1994, s 60*, covering 18 prescribed accounting periods. The company had had three directors during the period in question, but the Commissioners attributed the whole of the penalty to one director (B) under *VATA 1994, s 61*, and notified B of the liability without specifically apportioning the penalty to the particular accounting periods. The CA dismissed B's appeal, holding that both the assessment and its notification were valid. The legislation did not require the Commissioners to carry out, or notify, any unnecessary calculations, and it was not necessary to refer to individual quarterly figures within the overall period to which the penalty related. *N Bassimeh v C & E Commrs*, CA 1996, [1997] STC 33. (*Note.* The CA also held that, where directors had collaborated in a company's dishonest conduct, each director was *prima facie* responsible for the whole penalty. The decision here was not followed by a subsequent tribunal in *Sawyer*, 50.60 below, on the grounds that it was inconsistent with the *Human Rights Act 1998*.)

[50.4] In a subsequent case where the facts were similar, but the Commissioners' representative failed to draw the CA decision in *Bassimeh*, 50.3 above, to the tribunal's attention, the tribunal allowed the trader's appeal against the penalty. The tribunal chairman (Mr. Bishopp) expressed the view that the effect of *VATA 1994, s 76* was that 'the notification, as well as the assessment itself, must be made by reference to prescribed accounting periods'. *DB Brundrit*, MAN/00/582 (VTD 17952). (*Note.* For another issue in this case, see 50.88 below.)

Whether penalty properly notified to company directors

[50.5] The Commissioners imposed a penalty under what is now *VATA 1994, s 60* on a company which manufactured women's clothing, on the grounds that it had reclaimed input tax in respect of false invoices. They sought to recover half of the penalty from the company's controlling directors under what is now *VATA 1994, s 61*. The directors appealed, contending that the penalty had not been properly notified. The tribunal chairman (Mr. Miller, sitting alone) accepted this contention and allowed the appeals. It was 'an antecedent step to the portion of the basic penalty being recoverable from the named officer as his liability that there is service of a notice under (*s 61**), which must mean a valid notice'. There was no prescribed form of notice, but it was essential that the notice should show the amount of the basic penalty and that it should state that the Commissioners propose to recover from the officer to whom the notice was addressed 'the portion of the penalty which is specified in the notice'. The fact that the notices did not set out separate amounts in respect of each relevant accounting period did not render them defective. However, the notices did not inform the appellants what portion of the penalty it was proposed to recover from each of them and, because they failed to do this, the notices were defective. The chairman observed that 'it would have been the easiest of things for the Commissioners to have stated the portion which they proposed to recover from the appellants', and held that 'each appellant had to be told in the notice addressed to him the precise portion of the penalty which the Commissioners proposed to recover from him'. The chairman commented that 'this may seem a very technical point, but imposition of tax and penalties depend upon the requirements prescribed by Parliament being satisfied'. *MK & ME Nazif*, LON/92/70P (VTD 13616).

[50.6] The Commissioners imposed a penalty under *VATA 1994, s 60* on a company which had failed to account for VAT on certain supplies, and apportioned the whole of the penalty to the company's controlling director under *VATA 1994, s 61*. They issued a notice, addressed to the company for the attention of the director, and subsequently issued a further notice, similarly addressed, reducing the amount of the penalty. The company and the director appealed, contending as a preliminary point that the notices were defectively worded and should be held to be invalid, since each of the notices had been addressed to both the company and the director. The tribunal rejected this contention, holding that each of the notices had been validly served and observing that although the notices 'could have been more satisfactorily worded, each of them sufficiently stated the matters specified in *s 61(2)*'. The tribunal held that, for the purposes of *s 61(1)*, 'one notice will suffice, provided that both parties (i.e. the company and the director) receive it'. The QB upheld this decision. Keene J held that a *s 61* notice did not have to be in any particular form, or use any particular wording. The notice had sufficiently identified the director, and had been properly served both on the company and on the director. *Nidderdale Building Ltd v C & E Commrs; J Lofthouse v C & E Commrs*, QB [1997] STC 800.

Penalty assessed on partnership—validity of assessment

[50.7] The Commissioners imposed a penalty under *VATA 1994, s 60* on a partnership. The partners appealed, contending as a preliminary point that separate assessments should have been raised on each of the partners individually, and that a penalty assessment on the partnership was invalid. The tribunal rejected this contention and upheld the validity of the penalty, holding that a penalty assessment under *s 60* 'can be validly made against several persons together, whether the dishonest conduct alleged is alleged to have been that of all of them together or is alleged to have been that of one or more of them in circumstances where the liability for the penalty is imposed on all of them'. The tribunal declined to follow *obiter dicta* of Glidewell J in *Evans & Others*, QB 1981, [1982] STC 342 (which the appellants had cited as an authority), observing that the relevant legislation had been amended by *FA 1982* to reverse the effect of that decision. *GK, RK, GK, M, FB & KG Akbar* *(t/a Mumtaz Paan House)*, [1998] VATDR 52 (VTD 15386). (*Note.* The substantive appeal was subsequently dismissed—see **50.72** below.)

[50.8] The decision in *Akbar (t/a Mumtaz Paan House)*, **50.7** above, was applied in the similar subsequent case of *Standard Tandoori Nepalese Restaurant*, LON/97/535 (VTD 16458). (*Note.* For the award of costs in this case, see **2.420** APPEALS.)

[50.9] Five partners operated a restaurant. The Commissioners formed the opinion that the partnership had been underdeclaring its takings, and imposed a penalty, at the rate of 90% of the evaded tax, under *VATA 1994, s 60*. The partnership appealed, contending *inter alia* that not all of the partners had been involved in any evasion, and that only specific partners should be held liable to any penalty. The tribunal rejected this contention and dismissed the appeal, holding that the issue of a penalty assessment to a partnership was authorised by *s 60*. The tribunal held that 'the words "a person does an act" and "his conduct involves dishonesty" are as much applicable to an individual or a legal person as they are to individuals or other persons carrying on business in common with a view to profit whose relationship constitutes a partnership. The partners act through each other and they are each jointly and severally liable for each other's conduct, where that conduct occurs in the course of the partnership business.' The tribunal held that the word 'person' in *s 60* was 'clearly not limited to individuals', but also included companies and partnerships. (The tribunal also found that, although only two of the five partners had been involved in the record-keeping, the other three partners had been in the business for such a long time that 'they must have known that a VAT fraud was going on, even though they may not have known precisely what form it was taking'. The tribunal held on the evidence that 'the Commissioners have proved dishonest evasion on the part of the appellants in relation to all the relevant accounting periods', and that there were no grounds for reducing the penalty.) *N Islam & Others (t/a India Garden Tandoori Restaurant)*, LON/98/1557 (VTD 17834).

Whether husband and wife trading in partnership

[50.10] A plant hire business was registered for VAT from 1987. The form VAT 1 described the business as being carried on by a married couple in partnership. However, it was only signed by the husband. In 1999 the Commissioners formed the opinion that the business had been evading tax by improperly treating certain supplies as zero-rated. They issued assessments, followed by a penalty. In May 2001 the husband was made bankrupt. The wife appealed against the penalty. The tribunal reviewed the evidence in detail and allowed her appeal, finding that the husband had acted dishonestly but that, although the husband had described the business as a partnership, there was no proof that the wife 'was in truth her husband's partner'. The tribunal distinguished the decisions in *Akbar & Others (t/a Mumtaz Paan House)*, **50.7** above, and *Islam & Others (t/a India Garden Tandoori Restaurant)*, **50.9** above. The tribunal held that 'it is clear from those authorities that an inactive or "sleeping" partner is no less liable to a penalty', notwithstanding 'his or her lack of direct involvement in the dishonest conduct for the purpose of tax evasion'. However, in this case, the tribunal held that to dismiss the appeal would produce 'a danger of a miscarriage of justice'. The tribunal therefore allowed her appeal against the penalty. *Mrs GA Segger*, MAN/01/358 (VTD 18673).

Penalty imposed on partnership—form VAT 292 not received

[50.11] A partnership of three people operated an off-licence from 1992 to 31 October 1994, when one of the partners (K) left. In March 1995 the partnership submitted a form VAT 2, showing that K had retired and that the wives of the two continuing partners had been admitted to the partnership from 1 November 1994. Subsequently a Customs officer discovered that the takings recorded in the partnership's record books exceeded those declared on the partnership VAT returns. The Commissioners issued assessments, and imposed penalties under *VATA 1994, s 60*, mitigated by 30%. The tribunal reviewed the evidence in detail and dismissed the partnership's appeals. The tribunal found that the partnership had not received a form VAT 292 which had been intended to notify the assessment, but held that the effect of *Partnership Act 1890, s 16* was that a letter which had been sent to one of the partners constituted sufficient notification of the penalty assessment, within *VATA 1994, s 76(1)*. The tribunal also held that the effect of *VATA 1994, s 45(2)* was that K should be treated as having remained as a partner until March 1995, and that the effect of *s 45(3)* was that the penalty assessment should be treated as having been served on him. Furthermore, the tribunal held that the joint liability of partners under *Partnership Act 1890, s 12* was not incompatible with the European Convention on Human Rights. The tribunal held that there were no grounds for reducing the assessments, and that the mitigation of 30% was 'generous'. *Yarl Wines*, LON/00/861 (VTD 17846).

Part of underdeclaration not validly assessed—effect on penalty

[50.12] Customs formed the opinion that the proprietor of an Indian restaurant had made substantial underdeclarations of takings. In April 1999 they issued an assessment for the periods from August 1997 to December 1998, charging tax of £25,788. In May 1999 they issued an assessment for the year ending July 1997, charging tax of £6,972. They subsequently formed the opinion that this assessment was inadequate, and purported to increase it to £14,284. They also imposed a penalty of £36,062 (mitigated by 10% to take account of co-operation). The proprietor appealed. Prior to the hearing, Customs accepted that their purported increase in the May 1999 assessment was not valid, so that only £32,760 of VAT had been validly assessed. However, they contended that as there had been underdeclarations giving rise to a liability of £40,072, it remained appropriate to impose a penalty of £36,062. The tribunal accepted this contention and upheld the penalty, finding that the proprietor had been dishonest and had underdeclared tax of £40,072. The chairman observed that *VATA 1994, s 60* 'does not stipulate that there has to be an assessment of tax but that a trader is liable to a penalty equal to the amount of tax evaded. We have already found that there was a suppression or evasion of that amount in that period and we accept the penalty should reflect this.' The CA unanimously upheld the tribunal decision. Arden LJ held that 'the correct interpretation of *section 60* is that a penalty may be assessed on the basis that a larger amount of VAT was due than that finally determined as between the taxpayer and the Commissioners'. There was 'no basis for reading into *sec 60* a requirement that the amount of the penalty be fixed only by reference to the amount of the VAT finally determined to be due'. *HMRC v L Ali (t/a Vakas Balti)*, CA 2006, [2007] STC 618; [2006] EWCA Civ 1572. (*Note.* This decision was distinguished in the subsequent case of *HMRC v BUPA Purchasing Ltd (No 2)*, **3.179** ASSESSMENT. Arden LJ observed that the court 'did not have in mind the situation' where 'the Commissioners have sought to amend the input tax and output tax on which the computation of the amount due was based.')

Liability of directors (VATA 1994, s 61)

Cases where the appellant was unsuccessful

[50.13] The Commissioners imposed a penalty, reduced by 50% to take account of co-operation, on a company which had carried on business as a building contractor, and which had made returns in which its output tax was understated and its input tax was overstated. The penalty was attributed to the company's controlling director under *VATA 1994, s 61*. The tribunal dismissed the director's appeal, holding that 'if a return contains a misstatement, and the person who makes the return has no honest belief in the truth of the statement (and in particular, if he makes the statement recklessly, not caring whether it is true or false), that is dishonesty according to the ordinary standards of reasonable and honest people'. *PG Howroyd*, MAN/88/841 (VTD 5582).

[50.14] The decision in *Howroyd*, **50.13** above, was applied in the similar subsequent case of *DG Cohen*, MAN/98/325 (VTD 16074). (*Note.* The tribunal also upheld the validity of the underlying assessment on the company—see **3.103** ASSESSMENT.)

[50.15] The Commissioners imposed a penalty, mitigated by 50%, on a civil engineering company which had failed to account for output tax and had subsequently ceased trading. They sought to recover the whole of the penalty from the controlling director under what is now *VATA 1994, s 61*, on the grounds that the penalty was wholly attributable to his dishonesty. The tribunal dismissed the director's appeal, holding on the evidence that the director had acted dishonestly and that the fact that he had not withdrawn the evaded tax from the company was not a ground for waiving the penalty. *I Turnbull*, LON/92/1257A (VTD 9903).

[50.16] A similar decision was reached in *B Reeve*, LON/93/2422P (VTD 12430).

[50.17] A company went into liquidation without accounting for output tax on the sale of a boat. The Commissioners imposed a penalty on the company, under *VATA 1994, s 60*, in September 1992. In May 1993 they issued a notice under *VATA 1994, s 61*, attributing the penalty to the company's controlling director. The director appealed, contending that the delay of eight months was a breach of *Article 6(3)(a)* of the *European Convention on Human Rights*. The tribunal rejected this contention and dismissed the appeal. *CW Edwards*, LON/93/2423 (VTD 16245).

[50.18] Following an investigation into the garment trade, the Commissioners formed the opinion that a company (M) had reclaimed input tax in respect of false invoices, issued in the names of five non-existent traders. A handwriting expert gave evidence that the invoices were written by two individuals in the garment trade who had been convicted of offences under what is now *VATA 1994, s 72*. The Commissioners issued assessments to recover the tax, imposed penalties under what is now *VATA 1994, s 60*, and issued notices under *VATA 1994, s 61* that the penalties should be recovered from M's controlling director. M and the director appealed, and the director claimed in evidence that the invoices represented genuine supplies. The tribunal dismissed the appeals, holding on the evidence that the Commissioners had proved 'to a high degree of probability' that the director had acted dishonestly, and that the 'limited co-operation' given by the director did not justify any mitigation. *Moda Ltd*, LON/91/205 & 1925; *D Costa*, LON/91/1926 (VTD 10761).

[50.19] An appeal against a penalty under what is now *VATA 1994, s 60* and a direction under *VATA 1994, s 61* was dismissed in another case where a company in the rag trade had reclaimed input tax in respect of false invoices. *A Kocaman*, LON/92/3382A (VTD 11730).

[50.20] Similar decisions were reached in *Fox v HMRC*, Ch D 11 May 2006 unreported; *H Kirbas*, LON/91/2528X (VTD 12329); *BS Bhambra*, LON/96/1732 (VTD 15503); *I Hadjigeorgiou*, LON/98/937 (VTD 18246); *A Gibbs*, LON/x (VTD 18270); *H D'Jan*, LON/03/669 (VTD 19045); *TF Jackson (No 2)*, LON/02/1044 (VTD 19225); *AP Gallucci*, LON/03/322 (VTD 19830) and *R Armsarmah*, LON/99/750 (VTD 19988).

[50.21] An appeal was dismissed in a case where the tribunal found that the manager of a company had deliberately created false 'self-billing' invoices and reclaimed input tax accordingly. *S Hillas*, MAN/92/1603 (VTD 12630).

[50.22] The Commissioners imposed a penalty under what is now *VATA 1994, s 60* (at the rate of 50% of the evaded tax) on a company which had reclaimed input tax on the basis of false invoices. They issued notices under what is now *VATA 1994, s 61* to recover the penalty from the company's two directors, 50% of the penalty being apportioned to each director. One of the directors appealed, contending that the dishonesty had been perpetrated by his fellow-director. The tribunal dismissed his appeal, observing that he had signed the return in question and finding that 'he was well aware at the time he signed the return that it overstated (the company's) entitlement to a refund of input tax and that he had knowingly closed his eyes to its falsity'. *P Robinson*, MAN/93/745 (VTD 12325).

[50.23] The Commissioners discovered that the controlling director of a company in the construction industry had altered VAT-exclusive invoices issued by suppliers in respect of work which was zero-rated, and had reclaimed input tax on the supplies. They imposed a penalty under what is now *VATA 1994, s 60* and issued a notice under what is now *VATA 1994, s 61*, attributing the penalty to the director. (The penalty was mitigated by 35% to take account of co-operation.) The company and the director appealed. The tribunal upheld the penalty and dismissed the appeals. *Isfa Management Ltd; AQ Mohammed*, MAN/94/987 (VTD 14999). (*Note.* Costs of £1,000 were awarded to the Commissioners.)

[50.24] An appeal against a notice under what is now *VATA 1994, s 61* was dismissed in a case where the tribunal found that a company, which had operated a restaurant and had subsequently gone into liquidation, had underdeclared takings. *M Khan (Jesmond Tandoori Takeaway Ltd)*, MAN/91/210 (VTD 12336).

[50.25] Similar decisions were reached in *D Cheung*, LON/01/837 (VTD 18276) and *M Aslam*, MAN/x (VTD 18775).

[50.26] A similar decision was reached in a case where a company had failed to account for tax on sales of second-hand cars. *Bugmile Ltd*, MAN/93/485 (VTD 12574).

[50.27] A similar decision was reached in a case where a company which operated a nightclub had underdeclared its takings, and the Commissioners had attributed the whole of the penalty to the controlling director. *Hamore Ltd*; JA Stott, MAN/96/374 (VTD 15061).

[50.28] In the case noted at **50.70** below, the Commissioners imposed a penalty on a company which operated a restaurant. They issued a notice under *VATA 1994, s 61* directing that the penalty should be attributed to the company's principal director. The tribunal upheld the notice, holding that the standard of proof was the normal civil standard of the balance of probabilities. The director appealed to the CS, contending that the tribunal should have held that the standard of proof was the criminal standard of 'beyond reasonable doubt'. The CS rejected this contention and dismissed the appeal, holding that it was clear that Parliament had intended the standard of proof for penalties under *ss 60* and *61* to be the normal civil standard of the balance of probabilities. *SA Chowdhury v C & E Commrs*, CS 1997, [1998] STC 293.

[50.29] The Commissioners imposed a penalty, reduced by 75% to take account of co-operation, on a company in the 'rag trade' which had failed to register for VAT and had subsequently ceased trading. They sought to recover the whole of the penalty from the company's controlling director, under *VATA 1994, s 61*. The tribunal upheld the penalty and dismissed the director's appeal. Applying *dicta* of Lord Lane CJ in *R v Ghosh*, CA [1982] 3 WLR 110; [1982] 2 All ER 689, 'it is dishonest for a defendant to act in a way which he knows ordinary people consider to be dishonest even if he asserts or genuinely believes that he is morally justified in acting as he did'. *K Georghiou*, LON/96/1193 (VTD 14970).

[50.30] A similar decision was reached in *SA Malik*, LON/00/19 (VTD 18091).

[50.31] The Commissioners imposed a penalty, mitigated by 50%, on a company in the construction industry which had failed to account for output tax on a substantial invoice, and had subsequently ceased trading. They sought to recover 50% of the penalty from the company's sole director and 50% from the company secretary. The director appealed, contending that he had not been dishonest and that the VAT returns were the responsibility of the company secretary. The tribunal rejected this contention and dismissed his appeal, holding on the evidence that the company's conduct 'was in part attributable to the dishonesty of the appellant', that he had 'an equal responsibility' and that 50% of the penalty should be recovered from him. *JJ Kelly*, LON/97/1609 (VTD 15637). (*Note.* Costs were awarded to the Commissioners.)

[50.32] The Commissioners imposed a penalty, mitigated by 50%, on a company in the construction industry which had failed to account for output tax on a substantial invoice, and had subsequently deregistered. They sought to recover 50% of the penalty from the company secretary. He appealed, contending that he had not acted dishonestly. The tribunal rejected this contention and dismissed his appeal, finding that the 'allegation of dishonesty' was 'proved to the requisite standard'. *G Bland*, LON/99/1035 (VTD 17395).

[50.33] A similar decision was reached in *MJ Kirkham*, MAN/98/838 (VTD 18640).

[50.34] Three companies which manufactured clothing failed to account for VAT and went into liquidation. All three companies were run by the same family, with the mother and daughter acting as directors and the father (N) acting as an employee. The Commissioners imposed penalties, mitigated by 10%. 50% of the penalties were attributed to N and the remaining 50% were attributed to the directors. They appealed, contending, *inter alia*, that the dishonesty was largely attributable to N, who was the head of the family, and that the directors were merely carrying out N's instructions. The tribunal dismissed the appeals, holding on the evidence that, although the directors 'may not have known every detail of the companies' businesses', they knew the purpose 'of withholding the returns and payments of VAT'. Accordingly, the directors 'ought to bear an equal responsibility'. *A & T Neocli; F Darker*, MAN/95/2377 (VTD 15771).

[50.35] The Commissioners imposed a penalty, reduced by 75% to take account of co-operation, on a company which had failed to submit VAT returns and had failed to appeal against estimated assessments which were inadequate. They sought to recover the whole of the penalty from the company's controlling director, under *VATA 1994, s 61*. The tribunal upheld the penalty and dismissed the director's appeal, applying *dicta* of Lord Lane CJ in *R v Ghosh*, CA [1982] 3 WLR 110; [1982] 2 All ER 689 (see **50.29** above). *NCS Associates Ltd; JC Gymer*, LON/98/952 (VTD 16007).

[50.36] Similar decisions were reached in *TE Woods*, MAN/01/236 (VTD 18049); *P Barrowcliffe*, MAN/01/406 (VTD 18855), and *R Littley*, [2010] UKFTT 616 (TC), TC00858.

[50.37] The Commissioners imposed a penalty, reduced by 75% to take account of co-operation, on a company which had substantially overclaimed input tax. They sought to recover the whole of the penalty from the company's controlling director, under *VATA 1994, s 61*. The tribunal upheld the penalty and dismissed the director's appeal, applying *dicta* of Lord Lane CJ in *R v Ghosh*, CA [1982] 3 WLR 110; [1982] 2 All ER 689 (see **50.29** above). *RV Casselson*, MAN/95/2512 (VTD 17164).

[50.38] A company ordered some equipment from a supplier. It received an invoice from the supplier. It failed to pay the amount shown on the invoice to the supplier, but reclaimed the input tax shown on the invoice. Subsequently the company cancelled the order, and the supplier issued a credit note. However, the company did not make any adjustment in its VAT returns. When the Commissioners discovered what had happened, they imposed a penalty (mitigated by 45% to take account of co-operation). They sought to recover the penalty from the company's controlling director. He appealed. The tribunal dismissed the appeal, holding that 'the retention of the monies to which the company was no longer entitled' was 'conduct involving dishonesty'. *MJ Campbell*, EDN/01/45 (VTD 17425).

[50.39] The Commissioners imposed a penalty, mitigated by 65%, on the director of a company which had made two incorrect claims for bad debt relief. The tribunal dismissed the director's appeal, observing that the director was a chartered accountant and finding that the claims had been made dishonestly. *TAN Thomson*, EDN/01/62 (VTD 17489).

[50.40] The Commissioners discovered that a company, which had gone into voluntary liquidation, had reclaimed input tax on a property which was owned and occupied by its controlling director. They imposed a penalty, mitigated by 65%, and sought to recover the penalty from the director under *VATA 1994, s 61*. The tribunal upheld the penalty and dismissed the director's appeal, observing that the director's accountant had told him that he would not be able to recover the VAT, and holding that the director had acted dishonestly. *W Taylor*, LON/00/930 (VTD 18298).

[50.41] Customs discovered that a company, which had gone into liquidation, had failed to account for tax on supplies to associated companies, and had reclaimed input tax on the basis of invoices with false VAT numbers. They imposed a penalty, mitigated by 30%, and sought to recover the penalty from the company's controlling director under *VATA 1994, s 61*. The tribunal upheld the penalty and dismissed the director's appeal, finding that the director had acted dishonestly. *J Thornton*, EDN/05/105 (VTD 20719).

[50.42] HMRC imposed a penalty, mitigated by 80%, on a company which had overclaimed input tax and had ceased trading. They sought to attribute the whole of the penalty to one of the company's five directors (G). G appealed, contending that the penalty 'should be split equally between all directors'. The tribunal rejected this contention and dismissed G's appeal, observing that HMRC had mitigated the penalty by 80% to take account of disclosure and co-operation from the other four directors. *G Giles*, [2009] UKFTT 109 (TC), TC00077.

[50.43] See also *Bassimeh*, 50.3 above.

Cases where the penalty was increased by the tribunal

[50.44] The Commissioners imposed a penalty on a company which had failed to account for output tax. The penalty was attributed to the company's controlling director, and was mitigated by 75% to take account of co-operation. The director appealed, contending that the underdeclaration was attributable to an employee who had subsequently been dismissed. (The employee had sued the company for unfair dismissal, but the Industrial Tribunal had rejected the claim, finding that the contract of employment was 'tainted with illegality' since the director and employee had 'connived in paying (the employee) a net salary of £1,000 per month in such a way that involved a loss of tax to the Revenue'.) The tribunal rejected the director's contentions and dismissed his appeal. The tribunal also directed that the level of mitigation of the penalty should be reduced from 75% to 65% of the tax since, in the course of his appeal, the director had 'contradicted in large measure what he had already said to HM Customs & Excise, on the basis of which co-operation he had been accorded a 75% mitigation'. The tribunal held that it should exercise its discretion under *VATA 1994, s 70(2)* to cancel or reduce the mitigation of a penalty 'where the time of the tribunal is taken up contradicting material, on the basis of which a generous mitigation was accorded to the appellant'. *WA Tanner (Redland Auto Service Centre Ltd)*, LON/96/1701 (VTD 15691). (*Note.* Costs were awarded to the Commissioners.)

Cases where the appellant was partly successful

[50.45] The Commissioners imposed a penalty on a company, with three directors, which had evaded tax. The investigating officers accepted a statement by one of the directors that he was not involved in the evasion, and apportioned the penalty among the other two directors under what is now *VATA 1994, s 61*. One of these directors appealed, contending that he should only be liable for one-third of the total penalty, as all three directors were involved in the evasion. The tribunal accepted this contention on the evidence and reduced the director's share of the penalty accordingly. *JC Lock*, LON/92/273 (VTD 9720).

[50.46] The Commissioners formed the opinion that a company which operated an Indian restaurant had failed to account for tax on more than one-third of its takings. They imposed a penalty under what is now *VATA 1994, s 60* and sought to recover the penalty from two of the three directors under what is now *VATA 1994, s 61*. The tribunal reviewed the evidence in detail and upheld the penalty on one of the directors, finding that he was 'personally involved in the suppression of takings', but discharged the penalty on the second director, finding that there was no evidence that he was also involved, and considering it possible that he might have been defrauded by his co-director. (The tribunal also found that there was no evidence that the first director had been guilty of dishonest conduct in return periods prior to 1989, when VAT officers had begun investigating the restaurant.) *JU Ahmed & JA Wahab*, LON/90/1889 (VTD 10120).

[50.47] The Commissioners imposed a penalty under *VATA 1994, s 60* on a company (G) which had failed to submit VAT returns and had paid the tax charged by estimated assessments which significantly understated the true liability. The company subsequently went into liquidation and the Commissioners assessed the penalty on the company's two directors under *VATA 1994, s 61*. The tribunal reviewed the evidence in detail and upheld the penalty on the company's principal director but allowed the appeal by the other director, finding that although he knew that Customs 'were not being paid promptly (which is wrong but not dishonest), we are satisfied that he did not know that the true extent of (G's) liability was being concealed'. *J Wood & P Riley*, MAN/04/557 (VTD 18743).

[50.48] The Commissioners imposed a penalty under what is now *VATA 1994, s 60* on a company in the garment trade, which had reclaimed input tax on the basis of invoices issued in the name of a company which had been deregistered three years previously. The Commissioners sought to apportion the penalty to the company secretary and his son under the provisions of what is now *VATA 1994, s 61*. The tribunal reviewed the evidence in detail and upheld the penalty on the company secretary, finding that his evidence was 'untrue and that he acted dishonestly in claiming input relief'. However, the tribunal allowed the appeal by the secretary's son, holding that the Commissioners had failed to establish that the dishonest conduct was partly attributable to him. *M & F Bolukbasi*, LON/91/2689 (VTD 11293).

[50.49] The Commissioners imposed a penalty under what is now *VATA 1994, s 60* on a company in the rag trade, which had reclaimed input tax in respect of false invoices issued in the names of three dormant companies, and had subsequently gone into liquidation. (The supplier of the invoices had been convicted in criminal proceedings, and had been sentenced to 18 months' imprisonment.) They sought to recover the penalty from the company's controlling director under what is now *VATA 1994, s 61*. The tribunal reviewed the evidence in detail and upheld the penalty in respect of the majority of the invoices, but held that it had not been proved that the invoices issued in the name of the third company were not genuine. The assessment and penalty were reduced accordingly. The tribunal also held that there were no grounds for mitigating the penalty. *C Celikyay*, LON/91/2695Z (VTD 11491).

[50.50] A VAT officer discovered that a company which operated a confectionery business had underdeclared tax. The company's controlling director admitted that he had understated the company's output tax liability, and stated that he had done so because of the company's cash-flow problems. The Commissioners imposed a penalty under what is now *VATA 1994, s 60*, computed at the rate of 50% of the tax allegedly evaded, and issued a notice under what is now *VATA 1994, s 61* to recover the penalty from the director. (The company had subsequently gone into liquidation.) The tribunal upheld the penalty and the notice in principle, holding that a 'general intention to pay at some uncertain date' did not constitute a defence, applying *Corbyn v Saunders*, QB [1978] 1 WLR 400; [1978] 2 All ER 697. However, the tribunal reduced the amount charged in respect of one return period. *K Gold*, LON/92/318Y (VTD 11939).

[50.51] The Commissioners imposed a penalty under *VATA 1994, s 60* on a company which sold electrical goods, and issued a notice under *VATA 1994, s 61* apportioning the penalty to the company's managing director. The penalty was computed at the rate of 80% of the tax allegedly evaded. The tribunal upheld the penalty in principle, but found that the assessments on which the penalty was based were excessive, and reduced them to 80% of the amount originally charged. The tribunal held that the reduction of 20% in the penalty was 'adequate in all the circumstances', and upheld the notice apportioning the penalty to the director, holding on the evidence that the evasion of tax was attributable to the dishonesty of the director. (The tribunal also held that, applying the CS decision in *First Indian Cavalry Club Ltd*, 50.70 below, the standard of proof was the normal civil standard of 'the balance of probabilities'.) *Best Electrical Factors Ltd; IJ Davis*, MAN/96/1021, 1173 & 1174 (VTD 15508).

[50.52] The Commissioners imposed a penalty under what is now *VATA 1994, s 60*, mitigated by 50%, on a development company which had reclaimed input tax on the basis of invoices which had been altered by the company's controlling director to treat the invoiced sums as inclusive of VAT. They sought to recover the whole of the penalty from the controlling director under what is now *VATA 1994, s 61*. The director appealed, contending that he should be liable for half of the total penalty, since his co-director had been equally involved in the evasion. The tribunal upheld the penalty in principle, holding that the company had acted dishonestly, but accepted that both directors had been involved in the evasion and directed that only half the penalty should be apportioned to the controlling director. *AJF Tottey*, LON/93/1014P (VTD 12149). (*Note.* Compare, however, the subsequent CA decision in *Bassimeh*, 50.3 above, where it was held that, where directors had collaborated in a company's dishonest conduct, each director was *prima facie* responsible for the whole penalty.)

Penalty imposed in respect of more than one return

[50.53] The Commissioners imposed a penalty under what is now *VATA 1994, s 60* on a company which had reclaimed input tax in respect of false invoices and had subsequently ceased trading. They also imposed a penalty in respect of an earlier return in which the company had reclaimed input tax in respect of what the Commissioners considered to be expenditure not relating to any business activity. The whole of the penalty was apportioned to the controlling director, and the Commissioners made no reduction for mitigation. The tribunal upheld the penalty in respect of the false invoices, finding that the controlling director was responsible for the return in question, but allowed the appeal in respect of the earlier return, finding that the Commissioners had not proved 'that the return was despatched without any genuine belief that the claim to credit for input tax which it contained was or would in due course be justifiable'. The tribunal also directed that the penalty in respect of the false invoices should be mitigated by 25% to take account of co-operation. (The tribunal observed that the mitigation was limited because the director's 'professed ignorance of what had been done made it more difficult for the Commissioners to ascertain the facts'.) *Checkstatus Ltd; PJ Fitzpatrick*, [1996] VATDR 81 (VTD 13168, 13893).

[50.54] A company failed to appeal against four estimated assessments which understated its liability to VAT, and subsequently ceased trading. When Customs discovered this, they imposed a penalty under *VATA 1994, s 60*, mitigated by 55% to take account of co-operation. They attributed the penalty to the company's controlling director and to her husband (who was not formally a director of the company but was described as its 'sales and marketing manager'). They appealed, contending that they had relied on their financial consultant. The tribunal reviewed the evidence in detail and allowed their appeals against the penalty for the first two periods, holding that it was reasonable for the couple to have believed that the consultant was dealing with the company's VAT. The tribunal upheld the penalty in principle with regard to the last two periods, holding that there was no reasonable excuse for their failure to deal with the VAT liability. However, the tribunal directed that the penalty should be mitigated by 65% rather than 55%. *I & L Quinton*, MAN/03/101 & 102 (VTD 19117).

Penalty imposed in respect of both input and output tax

[50.55] The Commissioners formed the opinion that a company (K) had submitted returns which were incorrect in four ways: firstly that it had claimed input tax on the basis that it had purchased plant for more than £100,000 whereas the true consideration was only £27,500; secondly that it had reclaimed input tax in respect of a number of fictitious invoices; thirdly that it had wrongly failed to account for output tax on a leaseback transaction; and fourthly that it had wrongly failed to account for output tax on five sales to another company (C). They imposed a penalty under *VATA 1994, s 60*. K had subsequently gone into liquidation, and the penalty was apportioned to K's controlling director (Q), and was mitigated by 10% to take account of a degree of co-operation. Q appealed, contending with regard to output tax that K's bookkeeper had accidentally failed to include the output tax in respect of the leaseback transaction, and that K had not issued the five invoices in respect of which C had reclaimed input tax. The tribunal reviewed the evidence in detail and upheld the penalty in so far as it related to input tax, but accepted Q's evidence with regard to output tax and discharged the penalty in so far as it related to output tax. The result was that the penalty was reduced from £31,734 to £21,824. Q appealed to the Ch D, contending *inter alia* that the tribunal hearing had been unfair because he had had to represent himself, and should have been given legal aid. The Ch D rejected this contention and upheld the tribunal decision. *MS Qaisar v C & E Commrs*, Ch D 2004, [2005] STC 119; [2004] EWHC 506 (Ch). (*Notes.* (1) The appellant appeared in person. (2) For a preliminary issue in this case, see **2.283** APPEALS.)

Mitigation of penalty attributed to company director

[50.56] The Commissioners imposed a penalty under *VATA 1994, s 60* on a company in the construction industry which had failed to account for output tax and had subsequently ceased trading. The penalty was imposed at the rate of 90% of the evaded tax, and was attributed to the company's controlling director under *VATA 1994, s 61*. The tribunal upheld the penalty in principle, applying *dicta* of Lord Lane CJ in *R v Ghosh*, CA [1982] 3 WLR 110; [1982] 2 All ER 689 (see **50.29** above). However, the tribunal reduced the amount of the penalty from 90% to 65% of the evaded tax to take account of co-operation. *Brentwood Construction & Development Ltd; A Cowley*, MAN/97/1175 & MAN/98/182 (VTD 16073).

[50.57] A similar decision, also applying *dicta* of Lord Lane CJ in *R v Ghosh*, CA [1982] 3 WLR 110; [1982] 2 All ER 689 (see **50.29** above), was reached in a case where a company had failed to appeal against inadequate estimated assessments. The tribunal upheld the penalty in principle, finding that the company and its controlling director had acted dishonestly. However, the tribunal reduced the amount of the penalty from 45% to 35% of the evaded tax to take account of co-operation. The tribunal also observed that the company had been assessed to default surcharges in respect of the same accounting periods, and directed that the penalty should be reduced by the amount of the surcharges. *F Thornber*, MAN/98/65 (VTD 16235).

[50.58] The Commissioners discovered that a company which traded as a car dealer had treated part of its takings as attributable to the sale of warranties which were exempt from VAT. They formed the opinion that the transactions in question did not qualify for exemption. They issued an assessment covering the period from June 1993 to February 1996, and imposed a penalty under *VATA 1994, s 60*, at the rate of 55% of the evaded tax. The penalty was attributed to the company's controlling director under *VATA 1994, s 61*. The director appealed, contending *inter alia* that 'the manipulation of the selling price' had not begun until March 1994. The tribunal accepted this contention and allowed the appeal to that extent. With regard to the period from March 1994 to February 1996, the tribunal upheld the penalty in principle, but reduced it from 55% to 50% of the evaded tax. *GT Brisbane*, MAN/97/281 (VTD 16691).

[50.59] Customs formed the opinion that a company which manufactured clothing had claimed input tax in respect of false invoices. They imposed a misdeclaration penalty of £113,720. Since the company had ceased trading, they attributed the penalty to the company's controlling director under *VATA 1994, s 61*. The director appealed, contending firstly that the supplies had been genuine and additionally that the penalty should be mitigated. The tribunal reviewed the evidence in detail and allowed the appeal in part, holding that invoices in the name of one supplier were false but that Customs had not discharged the onus of proving that invoices in the name of another supplier were false. The tribunal noted that £15,682 of the penalty related to an underdeclaration which had been declared by the company's accountant, and directed that this part of the penalty should be mitigated by 80% to take account of the disclosure. The tribunal directed that the remainder of the penalty should be mitigated by 10% to take account of a degree of co-operation. The result was that the total penalty on the company was reduced from £113,720 to £42,122. The tribunal also directed that only 90% of the penalty should be attributed to the controlling director, finding that the dishonest conduct giving rise to the attempted evasion was 'substantially attributable to him' but that the company's accountant should 'bear or share some of the responsibility for the company's conduct'. *KJ Abedin (director of M & S London Ltd)*, LON/02/314 (VTD 19149).

Penalty attributed to director—effect of Human Rights Act 1998

[50.60] Customs imposed a penalty under *VATA 1994, s 60* on a company which had claimed input tax in respect of false invoices. The penalty was imposed at the rate of 70% of the evaded tax. The company had four equal shareholders, three of whom acted as directors. Customs sought to collect the whole of the penalty from one of the directors (S). The tribunal upheld the penalty in principle, but directed that the penalty attributed to S should be reduced by 75% (ie from 70% to 17.5% of the evaded tax), to take account of the culpability of the other shareholders in the company. The tribunal declined to follow the principles laid down by the CA in *Bassimeh*, 50.3 above, on the grounds that that decision predated, and was inconsistent with, the *Human Rights Act 1998*. *D Sawyer*, LON/03/317 (VTD 19035).

[50.61] See also *Murrell*, 34.10 HUMAN RIGHTS, and *Edwards*, 50.17 above.

Cases where the appellant was successful

[50.62] The Commissioners imposed a penalty under what is now *VATA 1994, s 60* on a company in the construction industry which had failed to issue invoices or account for VAT on various contracts carried out for associated companies, and which had subsequently ceased to trade. The penalty was assessed on the company's controlling director under what is now *VATA 1994, s 61*. The director appealed, contending that he had not acted dishonestly and that invoices had not been issued because the companies in question were all suffering financial difficulties. The tribunal allowed the appeal, observing that the director's 'conduct in this matter left a great deal to be desired', but holding that 'the crucial question which we have to decide is whether the Commissioners have satisfied us that that conduct was for the purpose of dishonestly evading tax'. Applying *Khawaja v Secretary of State for the Home Department*, HL [1983] 1 All ER 765, the tribunal 'should not be satisfied with anything less than probability of a high degree' and 'we do not find the case put against (the appellant) proved to that standard'. *A Canton*, LON/92/2482 (VTD 11485).

[50.63] A company (L) was incorporated on 6 March 1992 and began to trade as a scrap metal merchant. It registered for VAT and, in its first return (for the period ending 30 April 1992), claimed a repayment of slightly more than £2,000. It did not submit any subsequent returns. When L was incorporated, it had one director (C), but on 20 July 1992 he was replaced by his father (M), who had been released from prison on 19 March. On 30 September 1992 Customs officers searched L's premises and formed the opinion that it had been involved in a VAT fraud. The Commissioners subsequently imposed a penalty under *VATA 1994, s 60*, mitigated by 50%. They attributed the penalty to M. (C had been convicted on a charge of fraud, unrelated to L, and had been sentenced to five years' imprisonment.) M appealed, contending that he had not been involved in the underdeclaration. The tribunal reviewed the evidence in detail and allowed M's appeal. The tribunal was satisfied that the company had reclaimed input tax in respect of false invoices, but found that 'there were no false invoices after he (M) formally became a director'. M's release from prison had been unexpected. It appeared that L had been set up by C 'as a vehicle for an input tax fraud'. However, the Customs officer responsible for attributing the penalty to M had apparently assumed that C had set the company up for M to run when he came out of prison. The tribunal found that this supposition was 'very unlikely', and held that the question of whether M 'knew about the mechanics of false invoicing remains unproven'. There was insufficient evidence to justify an inference that M 'was wholly or partly responsible for being deliberately involved with the false invoices'. *CR Matthews*, LON/95/1039 (VTD 15935).

[50.64] A company (M) was incorporated in 1994 and began trading in August 1995. It did not register for VAT until January 1996. During the intervening period, it used the VAT number of an associated company (B), which had been registered for VAT for several years. One of M's directors (C) was also a director of B, but the other director (W) was not. However, it failed to account for the tax charged. The Commissioners discovered this in July 1996, and imposed a penalty under *VATA 1994, s 60*, mitigated by 75%. The mitigated penalty was apportioned equally between C and W. W appealed, contending that he had not acted dishonestly, as he had repeatedly asked his co-director to sort out the VAT position, and had believed that the two companies would be covered by some form of group registration. The tribunal accepted W's evidence and allowed his appeal, holding that the Commissioners had not proved that W had acted dishonestly, since 'he had been taking steps from August 1995 through to July 1996 to regularise the position', including 'regularly attempting to persuade (C) to regularise the situation'. The tribunal accepted that W 'genuinely believed' that M could use B's VAT number, and while such ignorance would not amount to a 'reasonable excuse', W was not guilty of 'intentional or reckless dishonesty'. *WJ Ward*, LON/97/1350 (VTD 15713). (*Note.* The tribunal chairman (Miss Gort) also expressed the view that *VATA 1994, s 60* did not cover amounts 'attributable to VAT', within *VATA 1994, s 67(1)(c)*, and observed that the Commissioners could have taken steps to recover the tax under *Sch 11 para 5*. However, Miss Gort's suggestion that *VATA 1994, s 60* should not include amounts within *VATA 1994, s 67* appears to be of doubtful authority, as her decision here fails to refer to the CA decision in *Stevenson*, 50.1 above, where the CA unanimously held that *VATA 1994, s 60* was capable of applying to offences under *VATA 1994, s 67*.)

[50.65] The Commissioners formed the opinion that a company which manufactured clothing, using subcontractors, had reclaimed input tax in respect of false invoices. They imposed a penalty, mitigated by 80%, which they attributed to the company's controlling director (V). He appealed. The tribunal reviewed the evidence in detail and allowed V's appeal, holding that there was 'clear evidence of dishonesty on the part of the subcontractors' but 'that is not itself evidence against (V)'. The tribunal commented that 'payment by cash seems to be the norm in this industry' and that 'the case of dishonesty against (V) is really one of association with dishonest subcontractors. We are not prepared to find guilt by association'. The tribunal concluded that the Commissioners had not 'proved their case against him to a sufficient standard'. *Postproof Ltd; D Vitouladitis*, LON/02/996 (VTD 18547).

Acceptance of inadequate estimated assessment

[50.66] A company which was in financial difficulties failed to submit VAT returns, and paid an estimated assessment which was less than its true liability.. When Customs discovered this, they imposed penalties under *VATA 1994, s 60*, which they attributed to the company's managing director under *VATA 1994, s 61*. The director appealed, contending that he had not acted dishonestly. The tribunal accepted the director's evidence and allowed the appeal. The tribunal strongly criticised two Customs officers who had interviewed the director, finding that an interview had been 'aggressively conducted, in a hectoring, insistent manner' and that 'excessive persuasion was sought to be applied, and the atmosphere in which the interview was conducted was one of undue pressure exerted upon an unrepresented layman not versed in VAT matters'. The tribunal commented that 'the manner in which this interview was conducted' was 'entirely unacceptable. We are very surprised that so little regard was paid to the elementary safeguards that exist in this country to ensure the fairness of such interviews and the reliability of such replies as may be given by the interviewee.' *A Suhail*, MAN/00/864 (and related appeal) (VTD 19448).

Other cases

Cases where the appellant was unsuccessful

Alteration of purchase invoices

[50.67] A couple engaged contractors to carry out reconstruction works to a castle which they owned. The castle was a protected building and the works were zero-rated. The contractors sent ten invoices to the couple, four of which made no reference to VAT and the other six of which stated that no VAT was due. The husband altered each of the invoices by adding VAT in his own handwriting, but did not pay any VAT to the contractors. The couple submitted a VAT return claiming repayment of the amounts which the husband had inserted on the invoices. When Customs discovered this, they issued a penalty assessment. The tribunal upheld the penalty, finding that the couple had acted dishonestly in deliberately acquiring payments to which they knew they were not entitled. *DC & LM Leslie*, EDN/88/121 (VTD 3294).

Underdeclaration of takings

[50.68] The tribunal upheld two assessments on a restaurant which had suppressed purchases and substantially underdeclared takings. The tribunal also upheld a civil penalty, finding that the proprietors of the restaurant had consistently and dishonestly submitted incorrect returns with the intention of evading tax. Applying *dicta* of Lord Bridge in *Khawaja v Secretary of State for the Home Department*, HL [1983] 1 All ER 765, 'the civil standard of proof by a preponderance of probability will suffice, always provided that, in view of the gravity of the charge of fraud which has to be made out and of the consequences which will follow if it is, the court should not be satisfied with anything less than probability of a high degree'. *Gandhi Tandoori Restaurant*, [1989] VATTR 39 (VTD 3303).

[50.69] The decision in *Gandhi Tandoori Restaurant*, 50.68 above, has been applied in a large number of subsequent appeals in which appeals against penalties under what is now *VATA 1994, s 60* have been dismissed. In the interests of space, such cases are not listed individually in this book.

[50.70] Customs formed the opinion that a company which operated a restaurant was underdeclaring its takings, and imposed a penalty. The tribunal upheld the penalty (in a slightly reduced amount), holding that the standard of proof was the normal civil standard of the balance of probabilities. The company appealed to the CS, contending that the standard of proof should be the criminal standard of 'beyond reasonable doubt'. The CS rejected this contention and dismissed the appeal, holding that the standard of proof for penalties under *VATA 1994, s 60* was the normal civil standard of the balance of probabilities. The CS specifically declined to apply *obiter dicta* of Lord Jauncey in the direct tax case of *CIR v Ruffle*, CS [1979] SC 371. *First Indian Cavalry Club Ltd v C & E Commrs*, CS 1997, [1998] STC 293. (*Note.* The penalty was attributed to the controlling director under *VATA 1994, s 61*—see **50.28** above.)

[50.71] The decision in *First Indian Cavalry Club Ltd*, 50.70 above, was applied in the similar subsequent cases of *C Antoniou (t/a Cosmos Patisserie)*, LON/96/958 (VTD 15781); *S Ahmed & SA Haque (t/a Taj Tandoori Restaurant)*, LON/96/1714 (16262) and *ME Ismail*, LON/99/69 (VTD 16423).

[50.72] The decisions in *First Indian Cavalry Club Ltd*, 50.70 above, and *Antoniou*, 50.71 above, were applied in a subsequent case in which the tribunal upheld a penalty under *VATA 1994, s 60*, which Customs had mitigated by 5%. The tribunal found that there were no grounds for any further reduction in the penalty, since 'the evidence points to the appellants having done everything in their power to frustrate the Commissioners in so determining that liability'. The tribunal also specifically disapproved *dicta* of the tribunal chairman in *Nandera*, 50.149 below, on the grounds that they were inconsistent with the principles laid down by Lord Lane CJ in *R v Ghosh*, CA [1982] 2 All ER 689 (see **50.29** above). The QB upheld the tribunal decision. Dyson J held that, in considering mitigation, Customs were entitled to take into account all relevant matters up to the date on which the penalty was assessed, including the conduct of the appeal against any relevant assessment. *GK, RK, GK, M, FB & KG Akbar (t/a Mumtaz Paan House)*, QB [2000] STC 237. (*Notes.* (1) For a preliminary issue in this case, see **50.7** above. (2) The CA dismissed the partners' application for leave to appeal against this decision—CA 22 June 2000 unreported.)

[50.73] The QB decision in *Akbar*, 50.72 above, was applied in the similar subsequent case of *PA Ellinas*, MAN/94/1980 (VTD 16576).

[50.74] The principles laid down in *R v Ghosh*, CA [1982] 2 All ER 689 (see **50.29** above) were also applied in the subsequent cases of *Metrogold Ltd*, MAN/91/30 (12002); *RW & J Hodgson*, MAN/96/1350 (VTD 15165); *Bourne Vehicle Hire Ltd*, LON/97/711 (VTD 15267); *Maharani Restaurant*, LON/96/830 & 858 (VTD 16537) and *MA Uddin & A Bari (t/a Ringmer Tandoori Restaurant)*, LON/98/624 (VTD 19043).

[50.75] The Ch D upheld a penalty under *VATA 1994, s 60* in *Hindle*, 3.12 ASSESSMENT.

[50.76] There have been a large number of other cases, which appear to raise no point of general importance, in which appeals against penalties under what is now *VATA 1994, s 60*, in respect of underdeclarations of output tax, have been dismissed. In the interests of space, such cases are not reported individually in this book.

Sale of milk quotas

[50.77] Customs imposed a penalty under what is now *VATA 1994, s 60* on a family farming partnership which had failed to account for VAT on sales of milk quotas. The tribunal dismissed the partnership's appeal, applying *dicta* of the CS in *Mullan v Anderson*, CS [1993] SLT 835, to the effect that the standard of proof in civil cases was 'a balance of probabilities', rather than 'a high degree of probability'. The evidence here was 'sufficient to establish the (Commissioners') case on a balance of probabilities'. *Norman Wood & Sons*, EDN/92/15 (VTD 10558).

[50.78] Customs imposed a penalty under what is now *VATA 1994, s 60* on a farmer who had failed to account for VAT on sales of milk quota, but had submitted returns declaring no output tax liability but claiming repayments of input tax. The farmer appealed, contending that he had not acted dishonestly, but had delayed declaring the tax due because of financial difficulties. The tribunal dismissed his appeal and upheld the penalty, applying *dicta* of Lord Lane CJ in *R v Ghosh*, CA [1982] 2 All ER 689 (see **50.29** above), that 'it is dishonest for a defendant to act in a way which he knows ordinary people consider to be dishonest even if he asserts or genuinely believes that he is morally justified in acting as he did'. *MH Wright*, LON/91/1605 (VTD 10760).

Input tax claimed in respect of fictitious invoices

[50.79] Customs imposed a penalty under what is now *VATA 1994, s 60* on a company which sold clothing, after discovering that it had claimed input tax in respect of purported invoices totalling £88,000, issued in the name of a non-existent company and bearing a false registration number. The tribunal dismissed the company's appeal, finding that the purported invoices had been created 'in order to reclaim the input tax shown on them'. The input tax claim had been made 'for the purpose of evading tax, and this conduct involved dishonesty'. There were no grounds for reducing the amount of the penalty. *D & J Singh (t/a Sandhu Brothers)*, MAN/91/1019 (VTD 9387).

[50.80] A company reclaimed input tax of £86,625 in respect of the purported purchase of 500 alarms. HMRC formed the opinion that the relevant invoice had been manufactured by the company's controlling director (R). They imposed a penalty under *VATA 1994, s 60*, mitigated by 15% to take account of a degree of co-operation. The company appealed. The tribunal reviewed the evidence in detail and dismissed the appeal, finding that the invoice was a 'clumsy forgery' and that R had deliberately given evidence which he knew to be 'an untruth'. It had been 'dishonest to seek an input tax credit for a supply which the appellant knew had not been made, on the basis of a document which it must have known did not represent a real supply'. There were no grounds for any further mitigation of the penalty. *Activ8 Alarms Ltd v HMRC*, [2010] UKFTT 48 (TC), TC00361.

Input tax claimed without supporting invoices

[50.81] A builder submitted several returns claiming repayments of VAT. When Customs began investigating his affairs, he failed to provide invoices in support of the returns. Customs imposed a penalty under *VATA 1994, s 60*, mitigated by 5%. The builder appealed. The tribunal dismissed the appeal, finding that the builder had been 'deliberately evasive and dishonest' and had been fortunate 'to avoid being prosecuted'. *G Potts (t/a Landmark)*, MAN/96/725 (VTD 18467). (*Note*. Costs of £2,500 were awarded to Customs.)

Supplies wrongly treated as zero-rated

[50.82] A company (R) which supplied interior design services issued six invoices relating to a flat in Kensington. The customer submitted forms VAT 407, stamped by the Ministry of Works in Bahrain, certifying that the goods which R had supplied would be exported. R treated the supplies as zero-rated exports. A VAT officer discovered that the supplies were of furniture and soft furnishings which had been delivered to the flat, and which did not appear appropriate for personal export. Customs issued an assessment to charge output tax on the supplies, and also imposed penalties under *VATA 1994, s 60*. The tribunal upheld the penalties, holding that R had not complied with the requirements of *VATA 1994, s 30(8)*, so that the supplies did not qualify for zero-rating. The tribunal found that R's director was not 'a truthful or credible witness'. The tribunal was 'satisfied to a high degree of probability' that the director 'knew that the goods had not been exported and that they were still in the flat'. She knew that 'ordinary people would regard it as dishonest to refund the value added tax to a customer who had not exported the goods', and she had therefore acted dishonestly. *Richmond Design Interiors Ltd*, LON/95/99P (VTD 13549).

Supplies wrongly treated as exempt

[50.83] A couple operated two health clubs. Some members paid annual subscriptions and others paid monthly subscriptions. The couple only accounted for VAT on 70% of the monthly subscriptions. In 1998 Customs issued a ruling that VAT was chargeable on the whole of the monthly subscriptions. The couple ignored the ruling and continued to treat 30% of the monthly subscriptions as exempt. In 2000 Customs imposed a penalty under *VATA 1994, s 60*, mitigated by 65% to take account of co-operation. The tribunal dismissed the couple's appeal, observing that the managing partner (T) had 'received a ruling from the Commissioners, which was repeated twice, and which he ignored'. As a result, 'the appellants obtained a substantial financial advantage'. On the evidence, T 'knew that the appellants were not entitled to that advantage, but nonetheless continued to obtain it'. His actions 'were dishonest according to the standards of reasonable and honest persons'. *PD & G Taylor (t/a Riverside Sports & Leisure Club)*, LON/00/1387 (VTD 18056). (*Note*. For a subsequent unsuccessful appeal by the same couple, see **27.12** FINANCE.)

Persistent underdeclaration

[50.84] In 1993 a company informed Customs that it had underdeclared VAT by more than £100,000 over a period of ten years. The company co-operated in ascertaining the amount of the underdeclaration, and Customs imposed a penalty under *VATA 1994, s 60* at the rate of 25% of the assessed tax. The company appealed, contending that the penalty should be mitigated still further. The tribunal rejected this contention and dismissed the appeal. The chairman observed that the statutory provisions 'make it clear that the tribunals have the power both to reduce and to increase the amount of mitigation allowed by the Commissioners'. This was 'not a case in which the power of the tribunal is limited to quashing the decision if it is satisfied that it was made incorrectly', but was 'one in which the tribunal can exercise a fresh discretion'. On the evidence, the chairman also observed that 'I doubt whether I would have thought it appropriate to mitigate this penalty by as much as 75%' and held that 'it is not appropriate to mitigate the penalty any more than the Commissioners have already done'. However, the amount of the penalty would not be increased, since 'that power should be exercised cautiously, and only in the clearest cases when the tribunal is satisfied that the level of mitigation allowed by the Commissioners is manifestly too generous'. Any sanction 'upon the frivolous or vexatious appellant should be effected by means of an order for costs, and not by means of an increase in the penalty'. *James Ashworth Waterfoot (Successors) Ltd*, [1996] VATDR 66 (VTD 13851).

[50.85] The decision in *James Ashworth Waterfoot (Successors) Ltd*, 50.84 above, was applied in the similar subsequent case of *RA Tabner*, MAN/98/141 (VTD 16155).

[50.86] A company (E) dismissed its managing director and its company secretary after its accountants discovered significant financial irregularities. HMRC subsequently formed the opinion that E had underdeclared VAT by more than £13,000,000. They issued assessments, and imposed a penalty of £2,700,000 under *VATA 1994, s 60* (mitigated by 80%). E appealed, contending inter alia that the penalty should be mitigated by more than 80%. The tribunal reviewed the evidence in detail, rejected this contention and upheld the penalty in principle, reducing it by £36,000 and holding that there were no grounds for any further mitigation. *ERF Ltd v HMRC*, [2010] UKFTT 238 (TC), TC00537.

Acceptance of inadequate estimated assessment

[50.87] A trader (S) who operated a printing business failed to submit a return for the period ending January 1999. Customs issued an estimated assessment, charging tax of £9,686, which he paid. Subsequently a VAT officer ascertained that his true liability for the period had been £49,711. Customs imposed a penalty under *VATA 1994, s 60*. S appealed, contending that he had not acted dishonestly, but had deliberately deferred payment to ease cash-flow problems, and that Customs should have imposed a penalty under *VATA 1994, s 63*. The tribunal dismissed S's appeal, holding that he had adopted 'a course of conduct that the ordinary person would regard as dishonest'. The fact that he did not have sufficient funds to meet his actual liability 'does not exculpate him'. On the evidence, S's conduct 'amounted to the dishonest evasion of tax'. *G Storey*, LON/99/1132 (VTD 17793).

[50.88] Similar decisions were reached in *JF Lavelle*, MAN/01/464 (VTD 18023); *J Blackwell*, MAN/02/759 (VTD 18523); *P Conlon*, LON/06/308 (VTD 20877), and *Brundrit*, 50.4 above.

Penalty under VATA 1994, s 60—European Convention on Human Rights

[50.89] A trader (K) who operated a dry-cleaning business failed to register for VAT. The Commissioners discovered that his turnover was above the statutory threshold, and imposed a penalty under *VATA 1994, s 60* (mitigated by 25% to allow for a degree of co-operation). The tribunal upheld the penalty, finding that K had acted dishonestly. K appealed to the CA, contending *inter alia* that the accountant who had represented him before the tribunal had been incompetent, and that the proceedings had therefore constituted a breach of *Article 6* of the *European Convention on Human Rights*. The CA unanimously rejected this contention and dismissed the appeal. Carnwath LJ held that 'there was ample material to support a *prima facie* case that there had been evasion of tax, and that this had been both intentional and dishonest'. Buxton LJ observed that K 'was represented throughout by an accredited member of a profession that holds itself out as competent to act before VAT tribunals'. The tribunal 'would need to tread carefully before giving the taxpayer advice on the basis' that 'his professional representation was incompetent'. *MS Khan (t/a Greyhound Dry Cleaners) v C & E Commrs*, CA [2006] STC 1167; [2006] EWCA Civ 89.

[50.90] See also *Mu & Mu*, 34.2 HUMAN RIGHTS, and *Bammi & Dhir (t/a The Last Viceroy)*, 34.7 HUMAN RIGHTS.

Failure to register—penalty under VATA 1994, s 60

[50.91] See *Stevenson*, 50.1 above, and *Khan*, 50.89 above.

Trader deregistering while turnover above threshold

[50.92] A trader who operated a cleaning business registered for VAT in October 1995. Seven months later he applied to be deregistered, stating that he had ceased trading. Customs accepted this application, but subsequently discovered that he had continued to trade with a turnover above the registration threshold. They imposed a penalty under *VATA 1994, s 60*. The tribunal upheld the penalty and dismissed the trader's appeal. *G Watson (t/a Watson Cleaning Contractors)*, LON/03/319 (VTD 18811).

Cases where the penalty was increased by the tribunal

[50.93] The Commissioners imposed a penalty under *VATA 1994, s 60*, at the rate of 25% of the evaded tax, on a trader who carried on business as a tyre dealer. The trader appealed, contending that he had not acted dishonestly. The tribunal rejected this contention and directed that the penalty should be increased to 50% of the evaded tax, observing that neither the trader nor his accountant had co-operated with the Commissioners, and holding that 'in reducing the penalty to the 25% level, the Commissioners acted with a generosity that was totally unjustified'. *K Lee (t/a Euro Impex)*, MAN/95/1391 & 1459 (VTD 15427).

[50.94] A VAT officer discovered that a trader (E), who carried on a business of supplying and installing security systems, and was not registered for VAT, had two separate account books. A red book contained the figures which he had declared to the Inland Revenue, and a blue book contained significantly higher figures. The Commissioners formed the opinion that the figures in the blue book were the true record of his takings. They issued a notice of compulsory registration and assessments charging VAT on the takings shown in the blue book, and imposed a penalty under *VATA 1994, s 60*. The penalty was imposed at the rate of 20% of the evaded tax to allow for the co-operation which E had shown to the VAT officers. E appealed against the assessments and penalty, contending that the figures shown in the blue book were 'estimates which were given to prospective customers' and that his actual takings were 'far lower'. The tribunal reviewed the evidence and rejected this contention, observing that there was no reason 'why any taxpayer should maintain private records showing figures different from those in public records, other than for the purpose of tax evasion', and finding that the figures in the blue book were E's true takings. The tribunal observed that the penalty had been reduced to 20% on the basis of E's admission at interview 'that the figures contained in the blue book were the true ones'. However, he had subsequently withdrawn this admission 'so that it was necessary for his appeal to proceed to a full hearing'. Accordingly, mitigation of 80% was no longer appropriate. The tribunal directed that the penalty should be increased to 50% of the evaded tax. *M Eggleton*, MAN/00/687 (VTD 18287). (*Note.* Costs of £1,000 were awarded to the Commissioners.)

Cases where the penalty was reduced by the tribunal (VATA 1994, s 70)

Penalty reduced to 95%

[50.95] The tribunal reduced a penalty on a publican from 100% to 95% of the evaded tax to take account of a degree of co-operation. *JT Egan*, MAN/91/11 (VTD 7528). (*Note.* An appeal against an estimated assessment was dismissed.)

[50.96] A penalty was also reduced from 100% to 95% in *Sahib Restaurant Ltd*, MAN/00/1096 (VTD 20264).

Penalty reduced to 90%

[50.97] Customs imposed a penalty on a clothing manufacturer after discovering that he had failed to account for VAT on a large number of adults' sweatshirts and T-shirts, incorrectly treating them as zero-rated children's clothing. The tribunal upheld the penalty in principle but reduced it from 100% to 90% to take account of co-operation. *AU Khan*, MAN/89/823 (VTD 6450). (*Note.* An appeal against an estimated assessment was also dismissed.)

[50.98] The tribunal reduced a penalty on a partnership, which had reclaimed input tax on the basis of false invoices, from 95% to 90% to take account of co-operation. *M & ZP Akhtar (t/a Ruwaz Knitwear)*, MAN/98/767 (VTD 17824).

Penalty reduced to 85%

[50.99] A penalty was reduced to 85% of the evaded tax in a case where the tribunal found that one of two partners in a restaurant was guilty of dishonest conduct and that the other partner was innocent. (The tribunal also observed that the effect of *Partnership Act 1890, s 10* was that both partners were jointly and severally liable for the penalty, even though only one of them had acted dishonestly.) *Santi Bag Restaurant*, MAN/93/1177 (VTD 13114).

[50.100] Customs formed the opinion that the proprietor of a fish and chip shop had understated his takings. They issued an estimated assessment and imposed a misdeclaration penalty. The tribunal reviewed the evidence in detail and upheld the penalty in principle but mitigated it by 15% to take account of co-operation. The proprietor appealed to the Ch D, which upheld the tribunal decision. Lewison J held that the tribunal had been entitled to find that the proprietor had been dishonest. *M Arif (t/a Trinity Fisheries) v HMRC*, Ch D [2006] STC 1989; [2006] EWHC 1262 (Ch). (*Note.* For a preliminary issue in this case, see **2.305** APPEALS.)

[50.101] A penalty was also reduced to 85% of the evaded tax in *WS & CK Shek (t/a Wing Lee Carryout)*, EDN/99/219 (VTD 17247).

Penalty reduced to 80%

[50.102] The tribunal reduced a penalty on a partnership which operated two cafés from 100% to 80% to take account of the partners' co-operation. *Café Da Vinci & Da Vinci Too*, EDN/90/132 (VTD 7298). (*Note.* For a subsequent application for costs, see **2.409** APPEALS.)

[50.103] Customs imposed a penalty under what is now *VATA 1994, s 60* on the proprietor of a kebab shop who had not registered for VAT, although his turnover had exceeded the statutory threshold. The penalty was computed at the rate of 90% of the evaded tax, covering the period from 1 July 1986 to 31 July 1989. The tribunal reviewed the evidence in detail and found that, while the trader's turnover had exceeded the threshold throughout the period in question, his failure to register could not be proved to be dishonest with regard for the period from July 1986 to 31 March 1988. For the period beginning on 1 April 1988, however, his turnover had exceeded the threshold by such an amount that the 'inescapable conclusion' was that his conduct had been dishonest. Accordingly the penalties were correctly imposed for the period from 1 April 1988 to 31 July 1989. With regard to the computation of the penalty, the tribunal held that the appropriate rate was 80% of the evaded tax, to take account of a degree of co-operation. *K Sedat (t/a Sherry's Kebab & Burger Bar)*, LON/90/1780Y (VTD 9566).

[50.104] Penalties were reduced to 80% of the evaded tax in *HC Yeung (t/a Yeung's Garden)*, LON/99/429 (VTD 17574); *KL Cheung (t/a K Yuen Chinese Takeaway)*, LON/99/280 (VTD 17635); *VS Kudhail*, MAN/96/1260 (VTD 18161) and *D Miah (t/a Village Tandoori)*, MAN/01/675 (VTD 19084, VTD 19085).

Penalty reduced to 75%

[50.105] The tribunal reduced a penalty on the proprietors of a fish and chip shop to 75% of the evaded tax to take account of co-operation. *AR & A Smith (t/a Ginger's Fish & Chip Shop)*, EDN/90/32 (VTD 5694).

[50.106] Customs imposed a penalty on a partnership operating a restaurant, which had only declared about 50% of its takings. The penalty was calculated at the rate of 90% of the evaded tax. The tribunal upheld the penalty in principle, but reduced it to 75% of the tax to take account of a 'degree of co-operation' by the principal partner. *The Nawab Tandoori Restaurant*, LON/89/1829Z (VTD 6636).

[50.107] A similar decision was reached in *SS Alam & SU Ahmed (t/a Anarkali Tandoori Restaurant)*, MAN/95/572 (VTD 14584).

[50.108] Customs imposed a penalty on a couple who operated a fish and chip shop. The penalty was imposed at the rate of 95% of the evaded tax. The tribunal upheld the penalty in principle, but reduced it to 75% of the evaded tax. The CA dismissed the couple's appeal against this decision, holding that the penalty had been validly imposed and that the reduction of 25% was sufficient. *M & A Georgiou (t/a Mario's Chippery) v C & E Commrs*, CA [1996] STC 463. (*Note.* For another issue in this case, see **3.6** ASSESSMENT. For a subsequent unsuccessful application to the ECHR, see **34.1** HUMAN RIGHTS.)

Penalty reduced to 70%

[50.109] The tribunal reduced a penalty on the proprietors of a Chinese restaurant from 85% to 70% of the evaded tax to take account of co-operation. *WC & LT Wan*, MAN/91/1502 (VTD 10107).

Penalty reduced to 65%

[50.110] The tribunal reduced a penalty on the proprietor of a Chinese takeaway from 90% to 65% of the evaded tax to take account of co-operation. *Mrs M Tai (t/a North Bersted Chinese Takeaway)*, LON/99/448 (VTD 16451).

Penalty reduced to 60%

[50.111] A retired police officer and his wife operated a café in partnership. Customs discovered that the couple had wrongly treated a number of supplies as zero-rated, and imposed a penalty under *VATA 1994, s 60*, at the rate of 90% of the evaded tax. The tribunal upheld the penalty in principle but reduced it to 60% of the evaded tax. The partnership appealed to the QB, which upheld the tribunal decision. Carnwath J held that 'in most cases it is a straightforward jury question whether there has been dishonesty'. On the evidence, the tribunal had been entitled to conclude that the husband had pursued a dishonest system of calculating the partnership's zero-rated sales. *B & D Stuttard (t/a De Wynns Coffee House) v C & E Commrs*, QB [2000] STC 342.

[50.112] Customs imposed a penalty on a couple who operated a fish and chip shop, and had underdeclared takings and had wrongly treated a number of supplies as zero-rated. The penalty was imposed at the rate of 65% of the evaded tax. The tribunal upheld the penalty in principle but reduced it to 60% of the evaded tax relating to the overstatement of zero-rated sales (while maintaining it at 65% in respect of underdeclared takings). *SS & MK Mann (t/a Chaucer Fish Bar)*, LON/98/1318 (VTD 16442).

Penalty reduced to 55%

[50.113] The tribunal reduced a penalty on the proprietor of a restaurant from 80% to 55% of the evaded tax to take account of co-operation. *P Pang (t/a Lafite's)*, EDN/91/20 (VTD 7065).

Penalty reduced to 50%

[50.114] Customs imposed a penalty under what is now *VATA 1994, s 60* on the proprietor of a Greek restaurant. The penalty was computed at the rate of 75% of the tax allegedly evaded. The proprietor appealed, contending that the assessment was excessive and that, since he had co-operated with Customs, the penalty should be reduced to 50% of the culpable tax. The tribunal accepted these contentions, holding that the assessment was justified on the evidence but that the allowance for wastage should be increased and that 5% of the sales should be treated as of cold take-away food, and that the penalty should be reduced to 50% to take account of the appellant's co-operation. *JO Kyriacou (t/a Niki Taverna)*, LON/92/2098A (VTD 11537). (*Note.* A subsequent application by the appellant for costs was rejected—see **2.412** APPEALS.)

[50.115] Penalties on restaurant proprietors were reduced from 90% to 50% of the evaded tax in *JHK Fu*, MAN/90/579 & MAN/91/331 (VTD 11718) and *Stevie's Restaurant Ltd*, EDN/93/123 & 160 (VTD 12349).

[50.116] A penalty was reduced from 80% to 50% of the evaded tax in *J Allen-Fletcher*, MAN/92/807 (VTD 12898).

Penalty reduced to 40%

[50.117] A penalty was reduced from 65% to 40% of the evaded tax in *J Marquez (t/a Kwick Chick Barbecue)*, MAN/95/1844 (VTD 15767).

[50.118] A penalty was reduced from 60% to 40% of the evaded tax in *Oriental Kitchen*, MAN/94/481 (VTD 13736).

[50.119] A penalty was reduced from 45% to 40% of the evaded tax in *Zen Internet Ltd*, MAN/00/178 (VTD 18563).

Penalty reduced to 35%

[50.120] A penalty was reduced from 65% to 35% of the evaded tax in *MS Amiji*, MAN/96/754 (VTD 16552).

Penalty reduced to 30%

[50.121] A penalty was reduced from 45% to 30% of the evaded tax in *CJ Christon (t/a Christon Davies Advertising)*, MAN/01/725 (VTD 17953).

[50.122] A penalty was reduced from 35% to 30% of the evaded tax in *MA & DJ Collinson (t/a Megazone)*, LON/98/21 (VTD 15942).

Penalty reduced to 25%

[50.123] A penalty was reduced from 40% to 25% of the evaded tax in *AJ & R Jepp*, MAN/03/036 (VTD 19065).

[50.124] A penalty was reduced from 30% to 25% of the evaded tax in *Evans Brothers (Glass & Glazing) Ltd*, LON/95/3190 (VTD 14333).

Penalty reduced to 20%

[50.125] A penalty was reduced from 30% to 20% of the evaded tax in a case where a company had failed to account for output tax on the sale of seven coaches under a leaseback agreement. *Staffordian Travel Ltd*, MAN/96/1044 (VTD 15135).

[50.126] A trader failed to submit six successive VAT returns. Customs issued estimated assessments which were inadequate. When they discovered that the tax due was substantially greater than that charged by the assessments, they imposed a penalty (mitigated to 25% of the evaded tax to take account of co-operation). The tribunal upheld the penalty in principle, finding that the trader's 'conduct was dishonest by the standards of the reasonable and honest person, and he knew this'. However, the tribunal reduced the penalty to 20% of the evaded tax. *RK Johnson*, LON/98/231 (VTD 15868).

[50.127] The tribunal reduced a penalty on a partnership which sold take-away food, and which had underdeclared its output tax, from 40% to 20% of the evaded tax to take account of co-operation. *CT, C & P Ellinas (t/a Hunts Cross Supper Bar)*, MAN/97/193 (VTD 16105). (*Note.* For a preliminary issue in this case, see **2.282** APPEALS.)

Penalty reduced to 17.5%

[50.128] In a Scottish case, Customs imposed a penalty, at the rate of 20% of the evaded tax, on a small company which had withheld its VAT because of cash-flow difficulties. The tribunal noted that the penalty 'would be 20% of the value of the company', and directed that it should be reduced to 17.5% of the evaded tax. *Central Blasting & Painting Ltd*, EDN/03/39 (VTD 18294).

Penalty reduced to 15%

[50.129] A sole trader submitted nil returns for the two years ending October 1992. He was questioned about this at a control visit in April 1994, and told the VAT officer that he had not worked during that period because of injuries sustained in a fall. In July 1994, at an interview which had been arranged at his request, he admitted that he had done some work during this period and provided Customs with full information about the underdeclarations. The evaded tax totalled £7,741, and Customs imposed a penalty, mitigated by 80% to take account of co-operation. The trader appealed, contending that the penalty should be mitigated still further. The tribunal accepted this contention, holding that, since the disclosure was 'full and unprompted', the penalty should be reduced by 85%. *AR Carter*, LON/95/2763P (VTD 14217).

Penalty imposed in respect of more than one period

[50.130] A partnership began trading in 1981, registered for VAT in 1986, and deregistered in 1991. Customs subsequently formed the opinion that the partnership should never have deregistered, and imposed a penalty under *VATA 1994, s 60*, covering the period from 1991 to January 1998. The tribunal reviewed the evidence in detail and found that the partnership turnover had significantly exceeded the registration threshold in the year ending April 1994, but had only slightly exceeded the threshold in the two previous years. The tribunal held that the partners had acted dishonestly in failing to reregister from 1994 onwards, applying the principles laid down in *R v Ghosh*, CA [1982] 2 All ER 689 (see **50.29** above). However, Customs had not proved that the partners had been dishonest when they deregistered in 1991, or in remaining deregistered in 1992 and 1993. The tribunal directed that the penalty should be reduced accordingly. The tribunal observed that although dishonesty had not been proved for the earlier period, 'it does not follow that the penalty as a whole must fail. The effect of our decision is to restrict the recoverable penalty to that portion which has been charged in respect of the period from early 1994 to January 1998. This part of the penalty has been validly charged and cannot be struck down.' *C & H Prebble (t/a Monks Kitchen)*, LON/98/1327 (VTD 16631, VTD 19331). (*Note.* The tribunal subsequently dismissed an application by one of the partners to set this decision aside (VTD 19722).)

Cases where the appellant was successful

Undeclared output tax

[50.131] A farmer (P) sold milk quotas for more than £150,000, but failed to account for VAT on these sales. He submitted a VAT return claiming a repayment. Customs imposed a penalty under what is now *VATA 1994, s 60(1)*. The tribunal allowed P's appeal, holding that Customs had to prove deliberate dishonesty 'to a high degree of probability'. On the evidence, P was clearly guilty of great negligence, but the tribunal was 'unable to make a finding of deliberate tax evasion'. *IW Parker*, [1989] VATTR 258 (VTD 4473). (*Note.* Compare, with regard to the standard of proof, the subsequent case of *Norman Wood & Sons*, **50.77** above, where the tribunal held, applying *dicta* of the CS in *Mullan v Anderson*, CS [1993] SLT 835, that the standard of proof in civil cases was 'a balance of probabilities', rather than 'a high degree of probability'.)

[50.132] Customs imposed a penalty on the proprietors of a shop which sold hot and cold food for consumption on and off the premises, and had only accounted for VAT on 9% of their total sales. The tribunal found that the proprietors' returns were incorrect, and upheld an estimated assessment issued by Customs. However, the tribunal allowed the proprietors' appeal against the penalty, holding that the onus was on Customs 'to establish on a high degree of probability that (the proprietors) deliberately and dishonestly evaded the tax due'. The tribunal did not regard it as 'highly probable that (the active partner) was deliberately dishonest'. *MAG & G Morga*, EDN/89/31 (VTD 4905).

[50.133] An engineer (M), who was not registered for VAT, issued invoices on which he charged VAT to his customers, although no registration number was shown. When Customs discovered this, M admitted that he should have registered for VAT, and stated that he had intended to register, but had not done so because of cash-flow difficulties caused by some of his customers failing to pay him. He had kept full records, which he produced to the VAT officers who interviewed him, and denied any intention of defrauding Customs. Customs imposed a penalty, but the tribunal allowed M's appeal, finding that 'he was not guilty of any dishonest intention' and that 'he eventually intended to account for the tax'. There was 'no evidence of any device or attempt to conceal the transactions of which he was engaged; his records were ready for inspection and accepted as accurate; and his disclosure of the factual background was frank and consistent throughout'. *R McDivitt*, EDN/89/210 (VTD 5203). (*Note.* Compare, however, the subsequent decision in *Wright*, 50.78 above.)

[50.134] Customs imposed a penalty on a partner in a building firm, after discovering that receipts had been issued in his name in respect of cash sales which had not been included in the partnership records. The partner appealed, contending that he had not made any unrecorded sales and that he had not issued the receipts in question. The tribunal allowed his appeal, holding that Customs had not proved that the partner had made any of the purported cash sales in respect of which the receipts had been issued. *JH Martin*, LON/89/927X (VTD 5543).

[50.135] The tribunal dismissed an appeal against an estimated assessment on a pizza restaurant, but allowed an appeal against a penalty under what is now *VATA 1994, s 60*. The tribunal was satisfied on the evidence that the restaurant proprietor had underdeclared his takings, but was not satisfied that this was deliberate or dishonest. On the evidence, 'the underdeclaration might very possibly have been caused innocently', either by 'the failure of the appellant's staff to see that all bills were properly recorded at the cash desk or by his slipshod methods of keeping his records'. *B Gallo*, MAN/88/478 (VTD 7686).

[50.136] Similar decisions were reached in *NM & HN Patel*, MAN/92/1722 (VTD 11635); *CL Copeland*, MAN/91/1554 (VTD 13325); *KW Lam (t/a Dragon Inn Chinese Restaurant)*, MAN/96/244 (VTD 14974); *The Mild Seven Chinese Takeaway*, MAN/97/600 (VTD 16962); *H Kudmany (t/a The Kasbah)*, LON/98/1264 (VTD 17198) and *MA Matin*, LON/00/708 (VTD 17441).

[50.137] Customs imposed a penalty on a married couple who operated an Indian restaurant. The tribunal allowed the appeal, holding that Customs had not discharged the burden of proof required by *VATA 1994, s 60(7)*. *Moti Mahal Indian Restaurant*, [1992] VATTR 188 (VTD 9375). (*Note. Obiter dicta* of the tribunal were disapproved by the QB in the subsequent case of *Dollar Land (Feltham) Ltd*, **18.622** DEFAULT SURCHARGE.)

[50.138] Similar decisions were reached in *CS Leung (t/a Driffield Tasty House)*, MAN/94/86 (VTD 13862); *SW & XM Li (t/a Summer Palace Restaurant)*, MAN/95/1321 (VTD 15133); *HS & KK Ahluwalia (t/a Kings Headlines)*, LON/96/501 (VTD 15258); *K & H Nicolaides*, MAN/95/2201 (VTD 15355) and *B & A Heaton (t/a Freshmaid Sandwiches Take Away)*, MAN/97/313 (VTD 16661).

[50.139] Customs formed the opinion that a firm of clothing manufacturers had wrongly treated sales of clothing as zero-rated. They issued an estimated assessment and imposed a penalty under what is now *VATA 1994, s 60*. The tribunal dismissed the firm's appeal against the assessment, but allowed the appeal against the penalty, holding that the 'evidence does not irresistibly lead to an inference to dishonesty', since the errors could have been attributable to 'gross carelessness'. *Hytex Clothing*, MAN/91/1214 (VTD 10700).

[50.140] Similar decisions were reached in *BH Taylor*, LON/93/774P (VTD 12061) and *Baltex Clothing Manufacturers*, MAN/92/108 (VTD 12606).

[50.141] An appeal against a penalty was allowed in another case where the appellant company contended that an underdeclaration of tax was attributable to carelessness and overwork, rather than dishonesty. The tribunal held that Customs had 'failed to discharge the burden of proof' that the company's conduct had been dishonest. *Smith & Byford Ltd*, [1996] VATDR 386 (VTD 14512).

[50.142] A similar decision was reached in *I Denizli & N Karaca*, LON/96/239 (VTD 14644).

[50.143] Customs issued estimated assessments on a couple who sold Indian clothing and silk, after discovering that their records indicated that they had been trading at a gross loss for some periods. They also imposed a penalty. The couple appealed against the penalty, contending that they had not acted dishonestly. The tribunal allowed their appeal, finding that Customs had not proved to 'a high degree of probability' that the couple had acted dishonestly. *Shazia Fashion Fabrics*, LON/92/22 (VTD 11020).

[50.144] Customs imposed a penalty on a partnership which operated a fish and chip shop, after a VAT officer had discovered that the records of a company which supplied the partnership showed transactions which did not appear in the partnership's records, and had concluded that the partnership had underdeclared its takings. The partnership appealed, contending that the supplier's records were incorrect and that it had not received the supplies which the supplier claimed to have made. The tribunal accepted the partnership's evidence and allowed the appeal, finding that the disputed supplies had not been made to the appellant partnership, but had in reality been made to unregistered traders. *G, A & C Andreucci (t/a Joe's Chip Shop)*, EDN/92/260 & EDN/93/107 (VTD 11223).

[50.145] A similar decision was reached in *CC Mann*, LON/96/462 & 1574 (VTD 15182).

[50.146] A company trading as car dealers purchased a number of cars for the purpose of hiring them to customers, and reclaimed input tax. It subsequently sold 88 of the cars (of which 36 had actually been used as hire cars and 52 had not). It accounted for output tax under the margin scheme for second-hand cars, rather than on their full sale price. When Customs discovered this, they imposed a penalty under *VATA 1994, s 60*. The company appealed, accepting that its returns had been incorrect but contending that it had made a 'genuine error'. The tribunal accepted this contention and allowed the appeal. *Brown & Frewer Ltd*, MAN/96/1199 (VTD 15209).

[50.147] See also *Freer*, 62.79 SUPPLY.

[50.148] Customs imposed a penalty on a company which operated an aviation business, after discovering that it failed to account for VAT on some of its income. The company appealed against the penalty, contending that it had not acted dishonestly but that the director who had completed the return had not received the necessary information from his co-director. The tribunal accepted this contention and allowed the appeal. *Airspeed Aviation Ltd*, MAN/91/1358 (VTD 11544).

'Self-billing' invoices—failure to account for tax

[50.149] Customs imposed a penalty on a clothing manufacturer who had failed to account for VAT on 'self-billing' invoices issued by one of the retailers to whom he supplied clothing. The manufacturer appealed against the penalty, contending that he had not understood the self-billing system and had not deliberately intended to evade tax. The tribunal allowed the appeal, holding that 'the standard of proof required to establish dishonesty must be a very high degree of probability, not a mere balance of probabilities'. On the evidence, there was a 'reasonable possibility' that the manufacturer's failure to account for tax on the 'self-billing' invoices had been the result of misunderstanding and carelessness, rather than deliberate dishonesty. *KS Nandera*, MAN/91/123 (VTD 7880). (*Note. Dicta* of the tribunal chairman were disapproved by a subsequent tribunal in *Akbar (t/a Mumtaz Paan House)*, **50.72** above. The chairman here applied a subjective definition of 'dishonesty', whereas in other cases tribunals have applied an objective test, in accordance with the principles laid down by Lord Lane CJ in *R v Ghosh*, CA [1982] 2 All ER 689 (see **50.29** above).)

Alleged overclaim of input tax

[50.150] A publican (D) reclaimed input tax on the refurbishment of his public house. Most of the work was carried out by a partnership, which issued the publican with an invoice charging VAT. D paid the invoice and reclaimed the VAT as input tax. However, the partnership was not registered for VAT and the VAT number shown on the invoice had never been allocated. Customs therefore rejected the claim, and a VAT officer subsequently interviewed the D and formed the opinion that he had known that the invoice in question was fictitious. Customs imposed a penalty and the D appealed, contending that he had paid the amount to the partnership in good faith, and had assumed that the partners must have been registered for VAT. The tribunal accepted his evidence and allowed the appeal. *R Dickinson*, MAN/89/199 (VTD 6309).

[50.151] Customs formed the opinion that a trader (C) had reclaimed input tax on the basis of four false invoices. They issued an assessment to recover the tax, and imposed a penalty. C appealed, contending that the invoices were genuine. The tribunal reviewed the evidence in detail, finding that two of the invoices represented genuine supplies, upholding the assessment in respect of the other two invoices, and allowing C's appeal against the penalty, on the grounds that Customs had 'failed to show' that C had been responsible for producing the two invoices in question. *R Crompton*, MAN/92/765 (VTD 12033).

[50.152] A married couple operated a hotel in partnership. They reclaimed input tax in respect of building work allegedly done at the hotel by a company which the husband controlled. Most of the work was carried out in 1992, but the invoice was not issued until April 1993, at which time the company was in financial difficulties. The company went into receivership shortly afterwards without accounting for the output tax shown on the invoice. Customs formed the opinion that the invoice overstated the cost of the work, and that the price of the work had been artificially inflated for tax reasons. They rejected the claim to input tax, and imposed a penalty. The tribunal allowed the partnership's appeal against the penalty. On the evidence, it was satisfied that the invoice was issued in April 1993 'because the appointment of the receivers was imminent and (the husband) was about to lose control of the situation'. However, it was satisfied that the invoice represented supplies which the company had made to the partnership, and that the work 'was of the value claimed'. *CJ & K Snape (t/a The Homelea Hotel)*, LON/94/645P (VTD 13465).

[50.153] A company (K) which sold motor cars reclaimed input tax on four invoices from its accountant (D), described as being for consultancy services, and relating to a scheme which D had devised to minimise CGT liability on a property which K owned. D was subsequently investigated by the Inland Revenue and was convicted and imprisoned. Customs subsequently imposed a penalty on the basis that K had acted dishonestly in reclaiming the input tax shown on the invoices. K appealed, contending that it had not acted dishonestly and that it had in fact lost about £100,000 as a result of D's dishonesty. The tribunal accepted K's evidence and allowed the appeal, observing that 'although the scheme was subsequently seen to be a scam, it was not one which was devised in order that the Inland Revenue or Customs & Excise should be defrauded by the appellant, but was one which in the event ended with the appellant itself being defrauded by (D)'. *Keith Motors (Christchurch) Ltd*, LON/00/813 (VTD 17592).

Failure to register—Customs imposing penalty under VATA 1994, s 60

[50.154] A sole trader (E) carried on an equestrian business, providing livery, riding lessons and riding holidays. In 1983 Customs advised him that he was 'no longer liable or entitled to be registered', and cancelled his registration. In 1998 he applied to be re-registered. Customs subsequently formed the opinion that he should have re-registered with effect from 1990 rather than 1998. They imposed a penalty under *VATA 1994, s 60* (rather than under *s 67*). E appealed, contending that he had not acted dishonestly. The tribunal accepted his evidence and allowed his appeal, observing that some of his supplies (eg riding lessons) qualified for exemption for VAT, that Customs had treated E's livery activities as exempt when they deregistered him in 1983, and subsequently changed their interpretation again in 2001 when they issued a Business Brief accepting that livery activities were exempt. The tribunal found that an interview at which a VAT officer had accused E of dishonesty 'was premature because one cannot sensibly investigate dishonesty in not registering without previously settling any liability issues that affect the date of registration' and that 'the way the interview was conducted was unfair' because E had not been told that his accountant could accompany him. *CK Ellis*, LON/01/223 (VTD 18279).

[50.155] Customs imposed a penalty under *VATA 1994, s 60* on the proprietor of a pizza restaurant (B), who had failed to register for VAT. B appealed, contending that he had not acted dishonestly because the landlord had been attempting to regain possession of the premises. The tribunal accepted this contention and allowed B's appeal, holding that 'the failure to register was inexcusable; but this does not establish dishonesty on (B's) part in the relevant sense. Because of the continuing uncertainty as to (B's) tenancy', the tribunal was 'not satisfied that he acted dishonestly in omitting to register and in continuing to trade while unregistered'. *M Bornoosh*, LON/02/347 (VTD 18493). (*Note*. An appeal against a subsequent penalty under *VATA 1994, s 61*, for a period where B had carried on business as a controlling director of a limited company, was dismissed.)

Miscellaneous

Penalty under VATA 1994, s 60—effect of Human Rights Act 1998

[50.156] See *Patel*, 2.150 APPEALS; *Nene Packaging Ltd*, 2.170 APPEALS; *Sharland*, 2.290 APPEALS; *Mu & Mu*, 34.2 HUMAN RIGHTS; *Han & Yau*, 34.5 HUMAN RIGHTS, and *Bammi & Dhir (t/a The Last Viceroy)*, 34.7 HUMAN RIGHTS.

51

Penalties: Failure to Notify, etc

The cases in this chapter are arranged under the following headings.

Definition of 'relevant VAT' (VATA 1994, s 67(1))   **51.1**
Date from which penalty commences (VATA 1994, s 67(3))   **51.5**
Date on which penalty ceases (VATA 1994, s 67(3))   **51.9**
Whether a reasonable excuse (VATA 1994, s 67(8); FA 2008, Sch 41 para 20)
    Illness or bereavement   **51.13**
    Liability uncertain   **51.21**
    Reliance on third party (VATA 1994, s 71(1)(b))   **51.83**
    Miscellaneous   **51.103**
Unauthorised issue of invoices (VATA 1994, s 67(1)(c); FA 2008, Sch 41 para 2)   **51.139**
Mitigation of penalties (VATA 1994, s 70; FA 2008, Sch 41 paras 12, 13)
    Cases where the penalty was mitigated by the tribunal   **51.146**
    Cases where the penalty was mitigated by the Commissioners   **51.174**
    Cases where the penalty was not mitigated   **51.181**

Definition of 'relevant VAT' (VATA 1994, s 67(1))

[51.1] A trader became liable to register on 1 August 1987 but did not do so until 8 December. The Commissioners imposed a penalty calculated at the rate of 30% of the tax due for the period from 1 August to 8 December, and he appealed, contending that the penalty should only be applied to the tax for the period from 1 August until 31 October, since if he had been registered, the tax for the period from 1 November to 8 December would not have been payable until 29 February 1988. The tribunal rejected this contention and dismissed his appeal. The tax for which he was 'liable' included tax on supplies made between the date on which he should have registered and the date on which he in fact did so, even though he was not required to pay the tax in question until after the date on which he notified the Commissioners. *WJ Corthine*, [1988] VATTR 90 (VTD 3012). (*Note.* The penalty would now only be 5% of the relevant tax—see *VATA 1994, s 67(4)*.)

Appellant failing to apply for deregistration

[51.2] In the case noted at 57.128 REGISTRATION, a trader's turnover exceeded the registration threshold in 1987 but dropped below the deregistration threshold in 1990. The Commissioners imposed a penalty covering the whole period from November 1987 to 16 August 1990 (the date on which he had notified the VAT office that he had previously been liable to register). He appealed, contending that the penalty should cease to run with effect from

March 1990, when he could have applied for deregistration. The tribunal rejected this contention and dismissed his appeal. *RR Bissmire*, LON/90/1563X (VTD 7303).

Penalty where assessment issued to collect outstanding tax

[51.3] A trader became liable to register in 1975 but did not do so until 1987. The Commissioners imposed a penalty under what is now *VATA 1994, s 67* and also issued an assessment covering the period in question. The trader appealed, contending that a penalty under what is now *VATA 1994, s 67* should not be imposed where the Commissioners had issued an assessment to collect the outstanding tax in respect of which the penalty had been imposed. The tribunal dismissed the appeal and the QB upheld this decision. Leonard J held that there was 'nothing in the legislation which supports the proposition that penalty and assessment are alternative processes' and observing that it was 'inevitable that the tax lost should be the yardstick by which both are measured'. *V Bjellica (t/a Eddy's Domestic Appliances) v C & E Commrs*, QB [1993] STC 730. (*Note.* For another issue in this case, taken to the CA, see **57.89** REGISTRATION.)

Assessment not made to 'best judgment'—whether any 'relevant VAT'

[51.4] In February 1997 the Commissioners issued a ruling that the proprietor of a shop selling take-away food had been liable to register for VAT from July 1990. They issued a notice of compulsory registration and an estimated assessment covering the period from July 1990 to January 1997, charging tax of £92,000. They also imposed a penalty of £12,800 for failure to notify. The trader appealed, contending that the assessment was excessive because most of his sales were zero-rated (and that this was a reasonable excuse for his failure to register). The tribunal reviewed the evidence in detail and held that the trader had become liable to register in October 1990, and that there was no reasonable excuse for his failure to do so. However, the tribunal also held that the estimated assessment had not been made to the best of the Commissioners' judgment, and held that 'because the assessment has fallen', the civil penalty assessed by the Commissioners must also fall. The tribunal held that there was 'no relevant VAT' for the purposes of *VATA 1994, s 67(1)*, and also held that it had no jurisdiction to impose the £50 penalty referred to in *s 67(1)*. *D Barrett (t/a The Carib Takeaway)*, LON/678 (VTD 15389).

Date from which penalty commences (VATA 1994, s 67(3))

[51.5] A trader became liable to register from 21 July 1985, but did not do so until 23 December 1985. The Commissioners imposed a penalty under *FA 1985, s 15* (now *VATA 1994, s 67*) and he appealed, contending that *FA 1985, s 15* created a single offence, which in his case had occurred before 25 July 1985 when the relevant provisions came into force. The tribunal dismissed his appeal, holding that *FA 1985, s 15* created a continuous offence rather than a single offence. Since the failure to register had continued at the time when the provisions of *FA 1985, s 15* came into force, the penalty should be calculated from that date. *JF Gale*, [1986] VATTR 185 (VTD 2138).

[51.6] A similar decision was reached in *Kelvingold Ltd*, LON/86/180 (VTD 2110).

[51.7] A trader became liable to register in July 1984 but did not do so until May 1986. The Commissioners imposed a penalty under what is now *VATA 1994, s 67* and he appealed, raising the same contention as the appellant in *Gale*, **51.5** above. The Ch D rejected this contention and upheld the penalty, holding that what is now *VATA 1994, s 67* recognised a continuing obligation to notify a liability to register and that there was no presumption against retrospection. *C & E Commrs v Shingleton*, Ch D 1987, [1988] STC 190.

[51.8] The Ch D decision in *Shingleton*, **51.7** above, was followed in *Genc*, **41.79** LAND, and *Typeflow Ltd*, LON/88/808 (VTD 3264).

Date on which penalty ceases (VATA 1994, s 67(3))

Claim of earlier notification

[51.9] An actor became liable to register for VAT in August 1985. He did not notify the Commissioners of this until July 1987, and they imposed a penalty under what is now *VATA 1994, s 67*. He appealed, contending that he had submitted an application for registration in May 1986, so that the penalty should only be calculated to that time. The tribunal dismissed his appeal, finding on the evidence that the Commissioners had not been notified of his liability to register until July 1987. *PS Dean*, LON/89/795Z (VTD 4314).

[51.10] Similar decisions were reached in *S & SJ Hayes*, MAN/89/352 (VTD 4693); *RP Lambourne*, LON/89/1324 (VTD 4771); *A Patel (t/a Swami Stores)*, LON/89/1002Y (VTD 4912); *FJ Kwiatkowski*, LON/90/1250Z (VTD 5457); *Ryan Evans Ltd*, LON/90/637X (VTD 5682); *Country Manor Manufacturing Ltd*, LON/91/1413X (VTD 6518) and *Betar Aluminium Fixings Ltd*, MAN/92/1151 (VTD 9432).

[51.11] A trader became liable to register for VAT in March 1983, but did not do so. He visited his local VAT office in June 1984 to apply for registration. A VAT officer helped him to complete a form VAT 1, but he heard nothing further from the office. At first he did not pursue the matter, but eventually he visited the office again. By this time the officer to whom he had previously spoken had left. (The VAT office had no record of this second visit and the trader could not recall its date.) He was still not registered after this second visit, and visited the office for a third time in June 1986. The Commissioners then imposed a penalty under what is now *VATA 1994, s 67*. The tribunal allowed the trader's appeal, finding that the trader had notified the Commissioners of his liability to register in June 1984. *RV McLaren*, MAN/89/393 (VTD 4117).

[51.12] A Northern Ireland company (M) was incorporated in December 2007. It became liable to register for VAT from July 2008. In July 2009 HMRC imposed a penalty under *VATA 1994, s 67*, on the basis that they had not received a form VAT1 until May 2009. M appealed, contending that it had sent a form VAT1 to the Wolverhampton VAT office in April 2008, had sent a further letter to that office in September 2008, and had made several telephone calls before submitting a second form VAT1 in April 2009. The tribunal accepted M's evidence and allowed its appeal. Judge Hennessey noted that HMRC had written to M's accountants, in response to a complaint about another client, stating that 'the telephone lines into the registration team have been limited due to the amount of calls they have been receiving. The high volume of calls experienced is hampering the caseworkers in processing the registration applications, thus delaying the issue of VAT registration numbers.' He also noted that a JVCC meeting in October 2008 had discussed problems at the Wolverhampton VAT office, and that HMRC had acknowledged that 'its handling of telephone calls had been unsatisfactory and further confirmed that the registration centre had been unable to handle the volume of applications submitted. There was an unequivocal acceptance that its service had been poor.' *McMullen Holdings Ltd v HMRC*, [2011] UKFTT 327 (TC), TC01187.

Whether a reasonable excuse (VATA 1994, s 67(8); FA 2008, Sch 41 para 20)

Illness or bereavement

Cases where the appellant was successful

Illness of wife

[51.13] A trader, whose wife acted as his bookkeeper, appealed against a penalty under what is now *VATA 1994, s 67*, giving evidence that his wife had been ill, and thus had been unable to keep his books up to date. He had therefore been unaware that his turnover had exceeded the registration threshold. The tribunal allowed the appeal, holding that the circumstances constituted a reasonable excuse. *J Warnock*, EDN/90/106 (VTD 5396).

[51.14] An engineer became liable to register for VAT from April 1988, but did not do so until May 1991. The Commissioners imposed a penalty under what is now *VATA 1994, s 67* and he appealed, contending that he had a reasonable excuse because in March 1988 his wife had been diagnosed as having cervical cancer, and he had required medical and psychiatric treatment for stress. In 1991 he and his wife had divorced. The tribunal allowed his appeal, holding that the circumstances constituted a reasonable excuse for his failure to register. *N McPherson*, LON/92/144Z (VTD 9580).

Illness of company director

[51.15] A company appealed against a penalty under what is now *VATA 1994, s 67*, contending that it had a reasonable excuse because at the relevant time the controlling director and his wife had both suffered from illness, the director's mother had died, and their landlord had attempted to evict them from their house. The tribunal allowed the appeal, holding that the circumstances constituted a reasonable excuse for the company's failure to register. *RHS Structural Engineering Ltd*, LON/91/2036Z (VTD 7354).

Illness of bookkeeper

[51.16] A florist became liable to register for VAT in April 1986, but did not do so until April 1990, and a penalty under what is now *VATA 1994, s 67* was imposed. The florist appealed, contending that she had a reasonable excuse because her bookkeeper had sent a form VAT 1 to the local VAT office in December 1987, and had failed to follow this up because she had been ill and had spent several periods in hospital. A photocopy of the form VAT 1 was produced in evidence. The Commissioners gave evidence that the form VAT 1 had never been received. The tribunal allowed the appeal in part, upholding the penalty for the period from April 1986 to December 1987, but holding that there was a reasonable excuse for the period from December 1987 to April 1990. The chairman observed that the prolonged failure to follow up an application for registration would not normally constitute a reasonable excuse, applying *dicta* in *Hislop*, **51.104** below, and *Pacey Rogers & Co*, **51.123** below, and disapproving *obiter dicta* of the tribunal chairman in *Selwyn*, **51.103** below. However, the prolonged illness of the bookkeeper did constitute a reasonable excuse for the failure to follow up the application which had been sent in December 1987. *CD Tomkins (t/a Options)*, MAN/90/995 (VTD 11738).

Death of partner

[51.17] A married couple purchased a riding stable in February 1989. The vendors had not been registered for VAT, since their turnover had been below the statutory threshold. In August 1989 the husband, who had been worried about the couple's finances, committed suicide. His widow continued to run the stable as a sole proprietor. Her husband's affairs were in a 'terrible state', and it took her several months to straighten them out. She did not register for VAT until August 1990 and the Commissioners imposed a penalty under what is now *VATA 1994, s 67*. The tribunal allowed her appeal, holding that the circumstances of her husband's suicide and the ensuing difficulties constituted a reasonable excuse. *P Ford (t/a Children's Riding Stables)*, MAN/91/109 (VTD 6855).

Cases where the appellant was unsuccessful

Injury to partner

[51.18] A married couple ran a café in partnership. They became liable to register for VAT in July 1986 but did not do so. In September 1986 the husband fell off a bridge and seriously injured his back. He remained in hospital for several months. The partnership did not apply for registration until August 1988 and the Commissioners imposed a penalty under what is now *VATA 1994, s 67*. The couple appealed, contending that the husband's injury was a reasonable excuse. The tribunal dismissed the appeal, observing that the couple had become liable to register two months before the injury occurred. *DB & JP Blake*, MAN/88/862 (VTD 3515).

Solicitor suffering miscarriage

[51.19] A female solicitor became liable to register for VAT in January 1987, but did not do so until September 1988. The Commissioners imposed a penalty under what is now *VATA 1994, s 67* and she appealed, contending that she had a reasonable excuse because she had hoped to conceive and stop working, but that although she had become pregnant, she had suffered a miscarriage in August 1987. The tribunal dismissed her appeal, observing that both her pregnancy and her miscarriage had occurred after she had become liable to register and thus could not constitute a reasonable excuse. *CDA From*, LON/90/1621X (VTD 5605).

Illness of bookkeeper

[51.20] A contractor (C) became liable to register in December 1991 but did not do so until June 1994. The Commissioners imposed a penalty and C appealed, contending firstly that he had a reasonable excuse because his father, who had acted as his bookkeeper, had been ill with cancer at the relevant time, and secondly that the penalty should be mitigated. The tribunal dismissed the appeal, observing that C had been incorrectly issuing invoices with a registration number which related to a business previously carried on by his father, and holding that, in view of the length of time for which the situation had continued, there was no reasonable excuse for C's failure to register. (The tribunal also held that, in view of the serious nature of the default, the penalty should not be mitigated.) *AJP Cheek (t/a Swanley Contractors)*, LON/95/1302P (VTD 13456).

Liability uncertain

Cases where the appellant was successful

Computation of turnover uncertain

[51.21] A freelance journalist became liable to register for VAT from 1987, but did not do so until 1991. The Commissioners imposed a penalty under what is now *VATA 1994, s 67*, and he appealed, contending that he had a reasonable excuse because part of his income consisted of reimbursements of expenses which he had incurred abroad, and he had not realised that this should have been included in his turnover for VAT purposes. The tribunal allowed his appeal in part, holding on the evidence that he had a reasonable excuse for failing to register before November 1989, but not for his continuing failure thereafter. *P Nichols*, LON/92/657 (VTD 9304).

[51.22] Similar decisions were reached in *A Garrett*, LON/92/3089P (VTD 10798) and *JFE Tyrrel*, LON/93/166A (VTD 11984).

[51.23] A curtain manufacturer became liable to register for VAT in January 1989, but did not do so until June 1989. The Commissioners imposed a penalty under what is now *VATA 1994, s 67*. She appealed, contending that she had a reasonable excuse because her turnover in the quarter ending December 1988 had included an advance payment from a major customer, and she had regarded this as a loan and had not realised that it formed part of her turnover. The tribunal allowed her appeal, holding that the circumstances constituted a reasonable excuse. *M Nield (t/a Soft Options)*, MAN/92/137 (10677).

[51.24] A medical partnership became liable to register for VAT in 1990, after the building of a new surgery which was a deemed self-supply under the legislation then in force. They failed to register, and the Commissioners imposed a penalty but the tribunal allowed the partners' appeal, holding that they had a reasonable excuse for not having realised that the effect of the construction of their new surgery was that they should have registered for VAT. *Dr Lock & Partners*, LON/93/771 (VTD 10946).

Death of bookkeeper—turnover uncertain

[51.25] An appeal was allowed in a case where a partnership gave evidence that its bookkeeper had died while its books were in her possession, and that the partners had been unable to recover the books for six months, and thus had not realised that their turnover had exceeded the threshold. *AM Autos*, LON/89/442 (VTD 3698).

Illness of bookkeeper

[51.26] See *Warnock*, 51.13 above.

Contractor using subcontract labour

[51.27] A ceiling fitter arranged for himself and three colleagues to carry out some work for a company. He did not register for VAT, and the Commissioners imposed a penalty under what is now *VATA 1994, s 67*. He appealed, contending that he had not realised that his three colleagues would be treated as his subcontractors and that the amounts he paid to them would be treated as part of his turnover for VAT purposes. The tribunal allowed his appeal, holding that the circumstances constituted a reasonable excuse. *P Bailey*, LON/88/200 (VTD 2851).

[51.28] Similar decisions were reached in *WG Hubbard*, LON/88/207 (VTD 2913); *WA Scott*, LON/88/315 (VTD 2938, 4208); *SR Ling*, LON/88/262 (VTD 3099); *L Dugdale & Son*, MAN/90/713 (VTD 5431); *K Kavanagh*, LON/90/1113X (VTD 6409); *JG Wallace*, LON/92/178Z (VTD 7487) and *G Gillespie*, EDN/93/202 (VTD 11504).

Band leader receiving payments for band of musicians

[51.29] A musician (K) organised a band, comprising himself and three other musicians, to play at a holiday camp. K received the payments for the band, and paid the other three musicians at Musicians' Union rates. The amounts paid to K exceeded the registration threshold but the amounts retained by him after making payments to the other musicians were below the threshold. He did not register for VAT and the Commissioners imposed a penalty under what is now *VATA 1994, s 67*. K appealed against the penalty, contending that he had a reasonable excuse because he had not realised that the amounts which he paid to the other musicians formed part of his turnover for VAT purposes. The tribunal allowed his appeal, holding that the circumstances constituted a reasonable excuse. *BJ Kirkby*, LON/91/375Y (VTD 6545).

Dispute over existence of partnership

[51.30] Two brothers traded as builders. They each had their own premises, and each had accounts drawn up as if they were trading as individuals. However, in 1987 they began advertising under a partnership name, and in 1988 they took out a joint public liability insurance policy. They subsequently obtained several contracts from the local council, and registered for VAT as a partnership in 1989. The Commissioners imposed a penalty on the basis that they should have registered as a partnership in 1988, when they had taken out their joint insurance policy. The brothers appealed, contending that, until 1989, they had regarded themselves as being sole traders rather than a partnership. The tribunal held that the brothers had been trading in partnership from 1988, but allowed their appeal against the penalty, holding that the complexity of the relevant law constituted a reasonable excuse. *J & E Malin*, LON/91/2224 (VTD 10085).

[51.31] The decision in *Malin*, 51.30 above, was applied in *Leonidas*, 47.21 PARTNERSHIP, where the tribunal held that a married couple had been trading in partnership but had a reasonable excuse for regarding themselves as sole traders.

Hairdressing salon—amounts retained by stylists

[51.32] The proprietor of a hairdressing salon became liable to register for VAT in 1988, but failed to do so. The Commissioners imposed a penalty under what is now *VATA 1994, s 67*. The proprietor appealed, contending firstly that the amounts retained by the stylists should not be treated as forming part of her turnover, and alternatively that she had a reasonable excuse for not treating them as part of her turnover. The tribunal held that the relevant services were supplied to customers by the salon proprietor, rather than by the employees. However, since the proprietor had acted in good faith, there was a reasonable excuse for her failure to register. *B Harrison*, LON/91/880 (VTD 12351). (*Note.* Compare *Hopkins*, 51.69 below, and *Mantio*, 51.70 below, where similar circumstances were held not to constitute a reasonable excuse.)

[51.33] In the case noted at 41.90 LAND, a hairdresser (D) allowed other hairstylists to trade from his salon. He failed to register for VAT. Customs issued a notice of compulsory registration, and imposed a penalty for failure to register. The Ch D held that D was required to account for VAT on the amounts which the stylists retained. However the tribunal allowed D's appeal against the penalty, holding that the circumstances constituted a reasonable excuse. *C Denyer (No 2)*, LON/06/758 (VTD 20691). (*Note.* Compare *Hopkins*, 51.69 PENALTIES: FAILURE TO NOTIFY, and *Mantio*, 51.70 PENAL-TIES: FAILURE TO NOTIFY, neither of which was cited in this decision.)

Computation of turnover—misleading advice from VAT office

[51.34] A builder appealed against a penalty for late registration, contending that he had a reasonable excuse because he had telephoned his local VAT Advice Centre, which had told him that for the purposes of the registration threshold, each year of trading would be treated separately, and had failed to explain that his turnover needed to be monitored on a 'rolling year' basis. The tribunal accepted his evidence and allowed his appeal, holding that the misleading advice constituted a reasonable excuse. *A Edwards*, LON/00/246 (VTD 16849).

Belief that supplies exempt

[51.35] An orthodontist became liable to register for VAT from 1984 but did not do so. The Commissioners imposed a penalty under what is now *VATA 1994, s 67*, and he appealed, contending that he had a reasonable excuse because he had been advised that his supplies were exempt. The tribunal accepted his evidence and allowed his appeal. *G Davies*, LON/86/174 (VTD 2126).

[51.36] Two associated partnerships operated chiropractic clinics. They became liable to register for VAT in 1986 and 1987 respectively, but did not do so until 1992. The Commissioners imposed penalties under what is now *VATA 1994, s 67* and the partnerships appealed, contending that they had a reasonable excuse because they had believed that their supplies were exempt from VAT, and that this had been confirmed by a telephone call to the Newcastle VAT office. The tribunal allowed the appeals in part, holding that the partnerships had a reasonable excuse for their failure to register before May 1991, but that since the partnerships had consulted accountants in the spring of 1991, there was no excuse for the continuing failure to register thereafter. *Dr KP & P Burns (t/a North Ferriby Chiropractic Clinic)*, MAN/92/987; *Dr KP & Mrs LM Burns (t/a Sheffield Clinic of Complementary Medicine)*, MAN/93/401 (VTD 12046).

Belief that supplies zero-rated

[51.37] An appeal was allowed in a case where the tribunal accepted a writer's evidence that he had assumed that his supplies were outside the scope of VAT, and held that this constituted a reasonable excuse. *JD Waugh*, MAN/90/274 (VTD 5344, 6206).

[51.38] Similar decisions were reached in *P Palliser*, LON/91/1120 (VTD 6262); *PJ Doyle*, LON/92/17Y (VTD 8811); *K Sharpe*, MAN/91/924 (VTD 8914) and *GM Neville & MR Clark (t/a Trueline Interiors)*, LON/92/3238P (VTD 10350).

School operating 'tuck shop' and selling tickets for school play

[51.39] A school operated a 'tuck shop' under the control of the bursar, who had previously been the school secretary. In 1987 the school also sold tickets for a school play, with the result that its turnover exceeded the threshold for registration. The school did not register until 1991. The Commissioners imposed a penalty but the tribunal allowed the school's appeal, holding that it had a reasonable excuse for having failed to register previously. The tribunal observed that although the supplies at the tuck shop were clearly made by the school, it was accepted that supplies of education were, for VAT purposes, made by the local education authority, and it was at least arguable that the school play should not be deemed to be supplied by the school as principal, but as agent for the local education authority. *St Benedict's School*, MAN/91/950 (VTD 7235).

Sales of timber

[51.40] A solicitor and his wife bought an area of woodland in 1988. In 1989 they sold a large quantity of timber. They did not register for VAT, and the Commissioners imposed a penalty under what is now *VATA 1994, s 67*. They appealed, contending that they had assumed that the sales of timber were outside the scope of VAT. The tribunal allowed their appeal, holding that ignorance of the primary law relating to VAT was not a reasonable excuse, but ignorance of the detailed provisions of VAT law could constitute a reasonable excuse. *MJ & KE Prior*, LON/92/432Y (VTD 7978).

Charity receiving grants

[51.41] An appeal was allowed in a case where a charity contended that it had a reasonable excuse because it had not realised that grants which it received were liable to VAT. The tribunal allowed the appeal, holding that this 'was not a simple matter of primary law governing VAT'. *Standing Conference of Voluntary Organisations for People with a Learning Disability in Wales*, LON/01/419 (VTD 17827).

[51.42] A similar decision was reached in *Trustees of Langley House Trust*, LON/06/537 (VTD 19749).

Subcontractors claiming to be employees

[51.43] The Commissioners imposed penalties under what is now *VATA 1994, s 67* on three painters, working for the same company, who had not registered for VAT. They appealed, contending firstly that they should be treated as employees rather than as self-employed, and alternatively that the circumstances constituted a reasonable excuse for their failure to register. The tribunal rejected the appellants' first contention, finding that they were self-employed and were not employees, but held that they had a reasonable excuse for having incorrectly assumed that they were not required to register for VAT. *SJ Geary*, LON/86/395; *G Jackson*, LON/86/530; *C Pook*, LON/86/394 (VTD 2314).

[51.44] Similar decisions were reached in *S Butler*, MAN/87/119 & 185 (VTD 3067); *WJS Gillard*, LON/90/141Z (5040); *PG Hughes*, LON/90/55X (VTD 5223); *JA Bell*, BEL/91/61X (VTD 7411); *M & GA Stone*, LON/91/427X (VTD 7798); *MB Beardshaw*, MAN/91/1316 (VTD 9245) and *KS Brown*, LON/92/2063P (VTD 9614).

Salesman claiming to be employee

[51.45] A salesman was granted a franchise to act as an agent, on a commission-only basis, for a company selling windows, doors and conservatories. He failed to register for VAT, and the Commissioners imposed a penalty under what is now *VATA 1994, s 67*. The tribunal allowed his appeal, holding that the wording of the agreement between him and the company constituted a reasonable excuse. *JAJ Dickson*, MAN/87/218 (VTD 2560).

[51.46] A similar decision was reached in *BF James*, LON/90/153X (VTD 5078).

Actor claiming to be employee

[51.47] An appeal was allowed in a case where the tribunal held that a Swedish actor, who had accepted a part in a musical in London, had a reasonable excuse for having believed that he was an employee. *BTG Korberg*, LON/88/553 (VTD 2966).

Place of supply uncertain

[51.48] A Dutch subsidiary of a UK company sold goods which had been manufactured in the UK. Some of its sales were to UK customers, and it became liable to register for VAT in 1991, but did not do so until the following year. The Commissioners imposed a penalty under what is now *VATA 1994, s 67* and the company appealed, contending that it had a reasonable excuse because it had believed that its supplies took place in the Netherlands and were outside the scope of UK VAT. The tribunal allowed the appeal, holding that the circumstances constituted a reasonable excuse. *HMG Europe BV*, EDN/92/251 (VTD 9814).

Uncertainty of time of supply of services

[51.49] An architect became liable to register in 1989 but did not do so until 1990. He appealed, contending that he had believed that the tax point for his supplies was either the time he received payment or the time he issued invoices, whereas the Commissioners had treated the time of supply as being the time when the services were actually performed. The tribunal allowed his appeal, holding that the Commissioners were correct in treating the time of performance as the tax point, but that the complexity of the law constituted a reasonable excuse. *AM Weldon-Hollingworth*, LON/94/592A (VTD 13248).

Cases where the appellant was unsuccessful

Ignorance of VAT

[51.50] A freelance model became liable to register for VAT in 1985, but did not do so until 1986. The Commissioners imposed a penalty under what is now *VATA 1994, s 67* and she appealed, contending that she had no knowledge of VAT and was unaware that her income exceeded the registration limits. The tribunal dismissed her appeal, holding that her ignorance of the law could not constitute a reasonable excuse. The QB upheld this decision, observing that VAT was 'now well enough established in our daily commerce that anyone, however inexperienced, ought to recognise the need to become acquainted with its basic requirements when embarking upon a career'. *Jo-Ann Neal v C & E Commrs*, QB 1987, [1988] STC 131.

[51.51] The decision in *Jo-Ann Neal*, 51.50 above, has been applied in a large number of subsequent cases in which appeals against penalties under what is now *VATA 1994, s 67* have been dismissed. Such cases appear to raise no point of general importance, and, in the interests of space, are not reported individually in this book. For a list of such cases decided up to 31 December 1993, see Tolley's VAT Cases 1994.

Belief that activities not constituting a 'business'

[51.52] An unincorporated association was established to organise a conference. It became liable to register for VAT in September 1985 but did not do so until March 1987, after the conference had taken place. The Commissioners imposed a penalty under what is now *VATA 1994, s 67*. The tribunal dismissed the association's appeal, holding that the circumstances did not constitute a reasonable excuse. *First International Conference on Emergency Medicine*, MAN/88/218 (VTD 2881).

[51.53] A similar decision was reached in *A1 Rushmoor Radio Taxis Ltd*, 27.10 FINANCE.

Separate businesses operated by sole trader

[51.54] A trader who operated two separate businesses failed to register for VAT. The combined turnover of the businesses exceeded the registration threshold and the Commissioners imposed a penalty under what is now *VATA 1994, s 67*. The tribunal dismissed the trader's appeal, holding that his failure to seek advice on the position meant that the circumstances could not constitute a reasonable excuse. *BW Dawson*, LON/90/216X (VTD 5216).

[51.55] Similar decisions were reached in *J Boggeln (t/a Divine Fireplaces)*, LON/03/886 (VTD 18965) and *J Yarlett v HMRC*, [2011] UKFTT 253 (TC), TC01117.

Turnover uncertain

[51.56] A film production manager appealed against a penalty under what is now *VATA 1994, s 67*, contending that although he was aware that his supplies had exceeded the quarterly threshold then in force, he was not certain whether they would exceed the annual threshold. The tribunal dismissed his appeal, holding that he should have registered as soon as his supplies exceeded the quarterly threshold. *WF Shephard*, LON/86/318 (VTD 2232).

[51.57] Similar decisions were reached in *Spurtrade Ltd*, LON/86/725Z (VTD 2290); *Managerial Problem Solving Ltd*, LON/88/331 (VTD 2826); *PK Cruse*, LON/90/750X (VTD 5975); *G Wisker*, LON/91/2585A (VTD 9716) and *LR Thorne*, LON/92/2982P (VTD 10051, 10175).

[51.58] A self-employed salesman, who sold goods produced by a limited company, appealed against a penalty under what is now *VATA 1994, s 67*, contending that he had a reasonable excuse in that he had not been certain whether his turnover consisted of his total sales or of his commission only, and that the company which produced the goods which he sold had not given him adequate advice. The tribunal dismissed his appeal, holding that the circumstances did not constitute a reasonable excuse. *JG Smith*, MAN/87/189 (VTD 2917).

[51.59] A barrister appealed against a penalty under what is now *VATA 1994, s 67*, contending that he had a reasonable excuse as he was uncertain as to the amount of his turnover. The tribunal rejected this contention and dismissed his appeal. *MA Syed*, LON/88/1077X (VTD 3534).

[51.60] Similar decisions were reached in *KA Metzger*, LON/89/1534X (VTD 5304); *GW Baxter*, EDN/92/124 (VTD 9152); *N Slater*, LON/92/1541A (VTD 9865); *Norman Adams Artists & Potters*, LON/92/1457 (VTD 9964); *P Newby (t/a Peter Newby & Co)*, MAN/92/898

(VTD 10395); *DN Mawhinney*, BEL/92/86 (VTD 10475); *GC Barrie*, MAN/93/89 (VTD 11470); *PB Abrook*, LON/93/1827P (VTD 11473); *NP Scott-Dickinson & AF Nunn*, LON/92/3173A (VTD 11859) and *Gent*, 51.160 below.

[51.61] See also *Savannah Landscapes & Building Services*, 51.177 below; *Optimum Personnel Evaluation (Operations) Ltd*, 57.12 REGISTRATION, and *Sullivan*, 57.168 REGISTRATION.

Dispute over existence of partnership

[51.62] The Commissioners discovered that an industrial cleaning business had not been registered for VAT. After enquiries, they formed the opinion that it had been carried on by two relatives (BC and OC) in partnership. They imposed a penalty under *VATA 1994, s 67*. BC appealed, contending that he was only an employee and that the business had actually been carried on by OC and his wife. The tribunal reviewed the evidence, rejected this contention and dismissed the appeal, finding that BC had been a partner and holding that there was no reasonable excuse for the failure to register. *BV Cutler*, LON/00/240 (VTD 17149).

[51.63] A similar decision was reached in a case where two hair stylists failed to register for VAT. *TJ Sumner & PS Kiddle (t/a Extravaganza Hair Workshop)*, LON/00/280 (VTD 17784). (*Note.* The tribunal held that the penalty should be mitigated by 75% to take account of co-operation.)

[51.64] HMRC formed the opinion that a married couple, who were not registered for VAT, were carrying on two hairdressing businesses in partnership, and were required to be registered. They imposed a penalty for failure to register. The tribunal upheld the penalty in principle, holding that there was no reasonable excuse for the failure to register, but directed that the penalty should be mitigated to take account of co-operation. *JA & LA Hooper*, LON/07/094, TC00042.

Partnership claiming that some supplies made by one partner as individual

[51.65] In the case noted at 57.197 REGISTRATION, the Commissioners imposed a penalty on a partnership which had treated some of its supplies as being made by one of the partners as a sole trader. The tribunal dismissed the partnership's appeal, holding that the circumstances did not constitute a reasonable excuse. *P Bear & S Hill*, MAN/98/554 (VTD 17215).

Illiteracy

[51.66] A trader became liable to register for VAT in January 1983, but did not do so until December 1988. The Commissioners imposed a penalty under what is now *VATA 1994, s 67* and he appealed, contending that he had a reasonable excuse because he was illiterate and had believed that his turnover was below the registration threshold. The tribunal dismissed his appeal. *D Searle*, LON/90/1407Z (VTD 5900).

Contractor using subcontract labour

[51.67] An engineer, working as a contractor with one subcontractor, appealed against a penalty under what is now *VATA 1994, s 67*, contending that he had a reasonable excuse because he had not realised that the amounts he had paid to his subcontractor formed part of his turnover for VAT purposes. The tribunal dismissed his appeal, holding that ignorance of the law was not a reasonable excuse. *AD Morris*, LON/88/852X (VTD 3456).

[51.68] Similar decisions were reached in *SG Pinder*, MAN/88/909 (VTD 3582); *AS Worboys*, LON/88/408Y (VTD 3866) and *LP Marsh*, LON/92/135Y (VTD 9810).

Hairdressing salon

[51.69] A partnership which operated a hairdressing salon became liable to register for VAT from February 1988, but failed to do so. The Commissioners imposed a penalty under what is now *VATA 1994, s 67*. The partners appealed, contending that they had a reasonable excuse for their failure to register because their accountant had led them to believe that the amounts which were retained by the hairstylists who worked for them did not form part of their turnover for VAT purposes. The tribunal dismissed the appeal, finding that the partners had attempted to rely on a 'flimsy avoidance scheme' and that the circumstances did not constitute a reasonable excuse. *GD & M Hopkins (t/a Marianne's Hair Salon)*, LON/93/1969 (VTD 11587).

[51.70] Similar decisions were reached in *S Mantio (t/a Zazzera Hair Salon)*, LON/99/1150 (VTD 17190) and *M Howe*, [2009] UKFTT 73 (TC), TC00041.

Belief that supplies exempt

[51.71] The Commissioners imposed a penalty under what is now *VATA 1994, s 67* on two partners who sold videotapes on commission. They appealed, contending that they had a reasonable excuse because they had been wrongly advised by their accountant that commission was exempt from VAT. The tribunal dismissed their appeal, holding that this was not a reasonable excuse. *RFS Phillips & Another*, LON/88/314 (VTD 2829).

[51.72] A private hospital, which made standard-rated supplies as well as exempt supplies, appealed against a penalty under what is now *VATA 1994, s 67*, contending that uncertainty as to the liability of its supplies constituted a reasonable excuse. The tribunal rejected this contention and dismissed the appeal. *Warwickshire Private Hospital*, MAN/88/863 (VTD 3531).

[51.73] An educational college appealed against a penalty under what is now *VATA 1994, s 67*, contending that it had a reasonable excuse because it had believed that its supplies were exempt. The tribunal dismissed the appeal, finding that the college's supplies did not qualify for exemption and holding that the college had no reasonable excuse for having failed to ascertain this. *Metro College of English*, LON/93/1465P (VTD 11312).

Belief that supplies zero-rated

[51.74] A bricklayer failed to register for VAT and the Commissioners imposed a penalty under what is now *VATA 1994, s 67*. He appealed, contending that he had believed that his supplies were zero-rated. The tribunal dismissed his appeal, holding that this was not a 'reasonable excuse'. *D Farrow*, LON/91/1051X (VTD 6410).

[51.75] Similar decisions were reached in *Revelstar Ltd*, LON/91/1036 (VTD 6734); *K W Paterson*, LON/91/1224Z (VTD 7423); *KJ Hopkins*, LON/92/654 (VTD 8890); *CS Bruce*, LON/93/2380A (VTD 11861); *KA Wales*, MAN/94/24 (VTD 12561) and *Barrett*, **51.4** above.

[51.76] A consultant became liable to register for VAT in 1985, but did not do so until 1987. The Commissioners imposed a penalty under what is now *VATA 1994, s 67*. He appealed, contending that many of his supplies were zero-rated under *VATA 1983, Sch 5, Group 9*, and he had assumed that they could be ignored in considering whether he was liable to register. The tribunal dismissed his appeal, holding that he should have read *Notice No 700* with greater care and should have sought advice from his local VAT office. *DA Smith*, LON/90/1212Y (VTD 6598).

[51.77] A similar decision was reached in *T Haycock*, LON/91/162Y (VTD 6850).

Consultant claiming to be an employee

[51.78] An appeal was dismissed in a case where a consultant, who had previously worked as an employee for the same company, contended that he had not realised the implications of the consultancy agreement. The tribunal held that the circumstances did not constitute a reasonable excuse. *NJR Kay*, MAN/87/74 (VTD 2373).

[51.79] A similar decision was reached in *Scott*, **57.184** REGISTRATION.

Self-employed salesman claiming to be an employee

[51.80] An appeal was dismissed in a case where a salesman, working for a single company on a self-employed basis, contended that he had believed that he was an employee and therefore not liable to register for VAT. *T Lowrie*, LON/90/763 (VTD 5965).

[51.81] Similar decisions were reached in *ME Smith*, LON/90/887Y (VTD 6921); *Osborn*, **51.153** below, and *Sullivan*, **57.185** REGISTRATION.

Contractor claiming to be an employee

[51.82] An appeal against a penalty was dismissed in a case where a contractor contended that he had believed that he was an employee and had not realised that he was required to register for VAT. The tribunal held that the circumstances did not constitute a reasonable excuse. *J Divers*, MAN/93/185 (VTD 12525).

Reliance on third party (VATA 1994, s 71(1)(b))

Cases where the appellant was successful

Misrepresentation by acquaintance

[51.83] J, who had previously been an employee, began self-employment in May 1987. He sought advice concerning VAT from G, an acquaintance whom he had met while travelling to work by train. G had told J that he was a qualified accountant, and promised J that he would arrange his registration for

VAT. In May 1987 he gave J a registration number, which J used on his invoices. In September 1987 J telephoned his local VAT office to enquire why he had not received a VAT return. It transpired that the number which G had given to J was not an official registration number, and G had not registered J for VAT. J subsequently discovered that G was not in fact a qualified accountant. The Commissioners imposed a penalty on J under what is now *VATA 1994, s 67*, and J appealed, contending that he had a reasonable excuse because he had genuinely believed that he was registered. The tribunal allowed J's appeal, applying *dicta* in *Bowen*, **18.103** DEFAULT SURCHARGE, and distinguishing *Neal*, **51.50** above. Merely delegating a task to a third party was not a reasonable excuse, but in this case J had actually been given what he believed to be a registration number, and G's misrepresentations did amount to a reasonable excuse. *KE Jenkinson*, [1988] VATTR 45 (VTD 2688).

Misleading advice from former partner

[51.84] Two brothers (R and ID) had carried on business together in partnership. They dissolved the partnership in July 1985 and ID continued as a sole trader. R, who had been the senior partner, told ID and their accountant that he had notified the VAT office that ID was continuing the business, although in fact he had not done so. ID gradually became concerned that he was not receiving VAT forms, and consulted an accountant in June 1986, as a result of which he registered for VAT in July 1986. The Commissioners imposed a penalty under what is now *VATA 1994, s 67*, but the tribunal allowed ID's appeal, finding that he had genuinely believed that he remained registered despite his brother's resignation from the partnership, and holding that he therefore had a reasonable excuse. *I W Dale*, LON/87/562 (VTD 3385). (*Note.* For the award of costs in this case, see **2.384** APPEALS.)

[51.85] Two individuals (R and S) began a double-glazing business in partnership in July 1988. They completed and signed a VAT registration form, and R told S that he would send the form to the VAT office. Six months later R flew to Africa with a female companion, having withdrawn all the money from the partnership's bank account. S subsequently discovered that R had never sent the VAT registration form to the VAT office. He was unable to contact R, and carried on the double-glazing business as sole proprietor. The Commissioners imposed a penalty on him under what is now *VATA 1994, s 67*. He appealed, contending that he had a reasonable excuse in that R had told him that the registration form had been submitted. The tribunal allowed his appeal, observing that both S and the Commissioners had been defrauded by R, and holding that S had a reasonable excuse for his failure to register. *DB Smith*, LON/90/1094X (VTD 5561).

Misleading advice from bookkeeper

[51.86] In a case where a sole trader had received misleading advice from a qualified bookkeeper, and had subsequently dispensed with the bookkeeper's services and appointed an accountant, the tribunal held that this constituted a reasonable excuse, applying *Jenkinson*, **51.83** above. *PAF Parker*, MAN/89/120 (VTD 3810).

Appellant misled by accountant

[51.87] The Commissioners imposed a penalty under what is now *VATA 1994, s 67* on a subcontractor who had become liable to register in November 1989 but had failed to do so. The subcontractor appealed, contending that he had a reasonable excuse because he had completed a form VAT 1 and had given it to his accountant. He had subsequently asked the accountant for his registration number on several occasions, and the accountant had indicated that he was waiting for a reply from the Commissioners. In 1991 the accountant disappeared without leaving a forwarding address, and the sub-contractor discovered that the Commissioners had never received the VAT 1 and that the Inland Revenue had not received his accounts. The tribunal allowed the appeal, holding that the accountant's misrepresentations consti-tuted a reasonable excuse. *GW Chapman*, [1992] VATTR 402 (VTD 7843). (*Note*. Compare the QB decision in *Harris*, **51.88** below, which was not referred to in this decision. The tribunal decision in *Chapman* was specifically disapproved by a subsequent tribunal in *Roebuck*, **51.92** below, on the grounds that it was inconsistent with the QB decision in *Harris*, which should have been treated as a binding precedent.)

Cases where the appellant was unsuccessful

Reliance on accountant

[51.88] A married couple should have registered for VAT in March 1987 but did not do so until March 1988. The Commissioners imposed a penalty under what is now *VATA 1994, s 67* and the couple appealed, contending that they had a reasonable excuse in that their accountant had told them that it was not necessary to register. The QB upheld the penalty, holding that what is now *VATA 1994, s 71(1)(b)* prevented reliance on an accountant from constituting a reasonable excuse. *C & E Commrs v D & DA Harris*, QB [1989] STC 907.

[51.89] The QB decision in *Harris*, **51.88** above, was followed in *KJ Graham*, MAN/89/656 (VTD 4350); *B & S Tomlinson*, MAN/89/93 (VTD 4351); *Uncles the Original Pawnbrokers Ltd*, MAN/89/811 (VTD 4437); *Beaumont English Language Centre*, LON/89/1834Z (VTD 4907); *Trioport Ltd*, LON/90/160Y (VTD 4923); *PW Willert*, MAN/89/525 (VTD 4970); *J Powell*, MAN/90/593 (VTD 5261); *B Endersby*, LON/90/603 (VTD 5754); *FM Peach*, MAN/91/884 (VTD 6499); *JF Spokes*, LON/92/1658P (VTD 10191) and *C Hadley*, LON/92/512 (VTD 10663).

[51.90] In a similar case where a partnership's solicitor contended that *Jenkinson*, **51.83** above, should be applied, the tribunal distinguished *Jenkin-son* because in that case the agent had given the trader a purported registration number, although the number given turned out to be false. In the case under appeal the partners had not asked their accountant what their registration number was, and their reliance on a dilatory accountant was precluded from constituting a reasonable excuse by what is now *VATA 1994, s 71(1)(b)*. *RM Joinery & Double Glazing, MAN/88/533 (VTD 3658)*.

[51.91] A similar decision, applying *Harris*, **51.88** above, and distinguishing *Jenkinson*, **51.83** above, was reached in a case where a trader had been wrongly advised by his accountant that he was not liable to register. *GS Davies*, LON/90/249X (VTD 5182).

[51.92] The QB decision in *Harris*, **51.88** above, was also followed in a subsequent case in which the tribunal decision in *Chapman*, **51.87** above, was specifically disapproved as being inconsistent with the QB decision in *Harris*. *JB Roebuck*, MAN/92/1189 (VTD 10171).

[51.93] In a case where the appellant had been told by a firm of chartered accountants that VAT was only payable on net earnings (rather than on gross turnover), the tribunal held that the inaccuracy of the advice could not constitute a reasonable excuse. *Lt Col RH Stafford*, LON/88/961 (VTD 3472).

[51.94] There have been a very large number of other cases where reliance on an accountant has been held not to constitute a reasonable excuse. In the interests of space, such cases are not summarised individually in this book. For a list of such cases decided up to 31 December 1994, see Tolley's VAT Cases 1995.

Reliance on manager

[51.95] A company appealed against a penalty under what is now *VATA 1994, s 67*, contending that it had relied on its manager to comply with the requirements for registration, but that the manager had been dismissed following the discovery of cash discrepancies, and that he had not notified the Commissioners of the company's liability to register. The tribunal dismissed the appeal, holding that what is now *VATA 1994, s 71(1)(b)* prevented this from constituting a reasonable excuse. *Vinetay Ltd*, EDN/86/68 (VTD 2230).

Reliance on secretary

[51.96] Reliance on a secretary was held not to be a reasonable excuse in *RJ Harrison*, LON/89/1152Y (VTD 4908).

Reliance on club treasurer

[51.97] An operatic society had at one time been registered for VAT, but had subsequently deregistered because its turnover was below the then statutory threshold. It became liable to re-register in 1987 but did not do so until 1990. The Commissioners imposed a penalty under what is now *VATA 1994, s 67* and the society appealed, contending that it had a reasonable excuse because its treasurer had not realised that it needed to register for VAT. The tribunal dismissed the society's appeal, holding that reliance on the society's treasurer did not constitute a reasonable excuse. *Canterbury Amateur Operatic Society*, LON/90/1575Y (VTD 5709).

Reliance on bookkeeper

[51.98] Reliance on a company's bookkeeper was held not to constitute a reasonable excuse in *Earlswood Environmental Systems Ltd*, MAN/87/416 (VTD 2605).

Reliance on wife

[51.99] A builder appealed against a penalty under what is now *VATA 1994, s 67*, contending that he had relied on his wife who acted as his bookkeeper.

The tribunal dismissed his appeal, holding that this did not constitute a reasonable excuse. *GA Brannan (t/a G Brannan Builders)*, LON/90/1828Z (VTD 5939).

Shop operated under franchise agreement—reliance on franchisor

[51.100] A newsagent operated a shop under a franchise agreement. He was accepted as self-employed for income tax and national insurance purposes, but did not register for VAT, and a penalty under what is now *VATA 1994, s 67* was imposed. He appealed, contending that the company which had granted him the franchise had advised him that it was not necessary for him to register. The tribunal dismissed his appeal, holding that the misleading advice given could not constitute a reasonable excuse. *FW Greer*, MAN/90/914 (VTD 6070).

Reliance on Inland Revenue

[51.101] A self-employed computer programmer became liable to register for VAT not later than 1 February 1988 (on the basis of turnover for the year ended 31 December 1987), but did not do so until June 1990. The Commissioners imposed a penalty under what is now *VATA 1994, s 67* and he appealed, contending that he had a reasonable excuse because in March 1989 he had asked the Inland Revenue for advice on VAT. He had repeated this request in January 1990 but without success. The tribunal dismissed his appeal, holding that the appellant was clearly ignorant of basic VAT law, and such ignorance could not constitute a reasonable excuse. Furthermore, he had made no enquiry whatsoever until almost fourteen months after he had become liable to register, and had not followed up this enquiry for ten months, whereas in *Hislop*, **51.104** below, the tribunal had regarded five months as being the longest delay that could be considered excusable in following up an application. *JA Farrington*, LON/90/1338Y (VTD 5456).

Director in prison

[51.102] A company became liable to register for VAT at a time when its principal director was in prison. During his imprisonment he had left the management of the company in the hands of his brother, who was not a director. The tribunal dismissed the appeal, holding that this amounted to reliance on a third party, which was specifically precluded from constituting a reasonable excuse by what is now *VATA 1994, s 71(1)(b)*. *Cosmogen Ltd*, LON/88/74 (VTD 3347).

Miscellaneous

Cases where the appellant was successful

Registration form posted but not received by VAT office

[51.103] A self-employed film editor became liable to register for VAT in December 1984. His accountant submitted a registration form in April 1985. However, the Commissioners did not receive the form, and subsequently imposed a penalty under what is now *VATA 1994, s 67* for failure to register by 25 July 1985 (when the relevant provisions came into force). The editor appealed, contending firstly that the submission of the form constituted notification, and alternatively that he had a reasonable excuse for not being registered because he had completed the appropriate form. The tribunal accepted the second contention and allowed the appeal. The postage of a form VAT 1 did not of itself constitute notification of liability to register. *Aikman v White*, **59.8** RETURNS, was distinguished because it related to the furnishing of returns rather than to the notification of liability to register. In the case of notification of liability to register, the Post Office was an agent of both parties, but this agency was an agency to carry and not an agency to receive information. However, the editor had 'done everything that was reasonably required of him', and therefore had a reasonable excuse for failing to notify his liability to register. *L Selwyn*, [1986] VATTR 142 (VTD 2135). (*Note. Dicta* of the tribunal chairman were disapproved by a subsequent tribunal in *Tomkins*, **51.16** above.)

[51.104] Similar decisions were reached in *Celtic Trading (Midlands)*, MAN/86/118 (VTD 2194); *B Birks*, MAN/86/64 (VTD 2201); *MP Hislop (t/a Dorchester Productions)*, LON/86/583 (VTD 2258); *Z & C Savva*, MAN/87/153 (VTD 2561); *Timeplas Ltd*, LON/87/369 (VTD 2570); *Cobrabrook Ltd*, LON/88/969 (VTD 3185); *M Ali (t/a The Candy Bar)*, EDN/88/156 (VTD 3441) and *Beverley Video*, BEL/88/46 (VTD 3550).

Commissioners failing to provide registration form

[51.105] A trader became liable to register for VAT on 1 September 1985. His brother-in-law telephoned the local VAT office in September, November and December to request a registration form. However, the office did not send a form until December. The trader submitted the completed form later that month, but the Commissioners imposed a penalty under what is now *VATA 1994, s 67*. The tribunal allowed the trader's appeal, holding that the Commissioners' failure to provide a registration form constituted a reasonable excuse. *S Zaveri (t/a The Paper Shop)*, [1986] VATTR 133 (VTD 2121).

[51.106] The decision in *Zaveri*, **51.105** above, was applied in the similar case of *J Brennan*, LON/92/505Z (VTD 11657).

[51.107] Similar decisions were reached in *DS Nolan*, LON/86/712 (VTD 2283); *GK Millar & JD Turner (t/a Britannia Wine Bar)*, LON/87/82 (VTD 2389); *Y Lucky & Another (t/a Le Bistenoo)*, LON/87/858 (VTD 2701); *P Alexandrou*, LON/88/244 (VTD 2944); *Russguild Ltd*, MAN/88/610 (VTD 3321); *SJ Cutting*, LON/88/1048Y (VTD 3443); *GJ & GM Flanaghan*, MAN/89/999 (VTD 4648); *R Kelly*, MAN/90/266 (VTD 5026); *Hollies Discount Furniture Centre Ltd*, MAN/90/277 (VTD 5243); *J Marchant*, LON/93/1226P (VTD 11026) and *HW Lloyd*, LON/92/3206 (VTD 11307).

[51.108] A partnership telephoned a local VAT office in April 1988 to notify its liability to VAT. No form VAT 1 was received, and the partnership made a further telephone request in June. The VAT office had no record of the previous call, and sent a form VAT 1 which the partnership returned later that month. The Commissioners imposed a penalty under what is now *VATA 1994, s 67* but the tribunal allowed the partnership's appeal, holding that the delay of less than two months in following up the earlier call was not unreasonable. *Ventnor Towers Hotel*, LON/89/386X (VTD 4537).

Mistaken belief that registration already in force

[51.109] The shares of a newly-formed company were sold by company formation agents to an individual who became the company's principal director. On the invoice from the company formation agents was typed 'with compliments VAT No 241 1563 95'. The director assumed that this was the company's registration number, whereas it was in fact the number of the company formation agents, who had not registered the new company for VAT. The tribunal allowed the company's appeal against a penalty under what is now *VATA 1994, s 67*, finding that the director had been misled by the invoice and had genuinely believed that the company had been registered by the formation agency. *Electric Tool Repair Ltd*, [1986] VATTR 257 (VTD 2208).

[51.110] The tenant of a public house walked out after a disagreement with the brewery. A married couple took over the tenancy on a temporary basis. Because they had only taken over the tenancy temporarily, the husband continued to work full-time for his previous employers. The couple did not register for VAT. The Commissioners imposed a penalty under what is now *VATA 1994, s 67* and the couple appealed, contending that they had assumed that they would simply take over the existing registration. The tribunal allowed the couple's appeal, holding that the circumstances constituted a reasonable excuse. *Mr & Mrs J Daltry*, MAN/86/261 (VTD 2277). (*Note.* Compare *James*, **51.128** below, in which similar circumstances were held not to constitute a reasonable excuse.)

[51.111] The shares of a company (B) had been purchased by its directors from a company formation agency. B's directors did not realise that it had not been registered for VAT by the agency. One of them telephoned the firm of accountants they had appointed and asked for B's registration number. The partner dealing with B's affairs was on holiday, and the director spoke to a woman employed by the firm, who gave him a registration number. Unknown to the director, the number given to him by the woman was the registration number of the accountants' firm. Subsequently B's directors had letterheads printed showing the number as if it were B's own. The accountants did not discover this until the end of B's first accounting period. They then notified the Commissioners, who imposed a penalty under what is now *VATA 1994, s 67*, against which B appealed. The tribunal allowed B's appeal, finding that B's directors had acted in the genuine belief that it was registered and holding that the circumstances constituted a reasonable excuse for B's failure to register. *Beaublade Ltd*, MAN/88/374 (VTD 3066).

[51.112] A trader had been registered for VAT in 1982, but had subsequently ceased self-employment, and his registration had been cancelled. He resumed self-employment in November 1987 and visited the Dudley VAT office to ask if he could use his old VAT registration number. He was advised by a VAT officer that this would be acceptable. However, the officer in question kept no record of his visit and did not ask him to complete an application form. Subsequently the Commissioners imposed a penalty under what is now *VATA 1994, s 67*. The tribunal allowed the trader's appeal, holding that the incorrect advice given by the VAT officer had led him to believe that his old registration would remain in force. *A Hill*, MAN/89/464 (VTD 4973).

Director not aware of company's deregistration

[51.113] A company was formed in 1982 and was registered for VAT. Later that year the principal director went abroad and left his accountant in charge of the company. The accountant deregistered the company. The director returned to the UK in 1985 and the company resumed making taxable supplies in September 1985. The accountant did not tell the principal director that the company had been deregistered, and the director did not become aware that this was so until the Commissioners advised him of it in January 1986. The Commissioners imposed a penalty under what is now *VATA 1994, s 67*, but the tribunal allowed the company's appeal, finding that the director was unaware that the company had been deregistered in his absence. *Standoak Ltd*, LON/86/500 (VTD 2250).

[51.114] A similar decision was reached in a case where a company had been dormant for some time before recommencing business, and the Commissioners had deregistered it, but the director gave evidence that he had not received notification of the deregistration. *Folknoll Ltd*, LON/89/20Y (VTD 4022).

Deafness

[51.115] An appellant contended that he had a reasonable excuse for failure to register because he was profoundly deaf and had great difficulty in communicating. He had difficulty in reading and could only communicate with his accountant through an interpreter. The tribunal allowed his appeal, holding that, as the 'normal sources of enquiry' were not open to him, he had a reasonable excuse for late registration. *CW Mason*, MAN/88/861 (VTD 3517).

Increase in turnover following redundancy of wife

[51.116] A subcontractor (K), whose turnover was below the VAT registration threshold, was married to a woman with a salary of about £30,000 p.a. However, she was unexpectedly made redundant in February 1991. Following her redundancy, K had to work substantially longer hours in order to meet their financial commitments. His turnover therefore increased, and he became liable to register for VAT from August 1991, but did not do so until 1992. The Commissioners imposed a penalty under what is now *VATA 1994, s 67*, but the tribunal allowed K's appeal, holding that the exceptional workload following the redundancy of K's wife constituted a reasonable excuse. *A Kear*, LON/92/2605P (VTD 9896).

Marriage breakdown

[51.117] A woman became liable to register for VAT in July 1986, but did not do so until April 1990. The Commissioners imposed a penalty under what is now *VATA 1994, s 67* and she appealed, contending that she had a reasonable excuse because her husband had been an alcoholic and had been violent towards her, and she had to work very long hours which had led to her turnover exceeding the registration threshold by a small amount. The marriage had finally broken down in the autumn of 1989 when her husband left her, and she had subsequently consulted an accountant. The tribunal allowed the appeal, finding that throughout the period in question the appellant 'was grossly overworked, intimidated and suffering acute stress as a result of her business responsibilities and domestic problems'. Since her turnover had 'only marginally exceeded the statutory limits', the circumstances constituted a reasonable excuse. *J Braes (t/a Aquarius)*, EDN/93/155 (VTD 11951).

Sole trader taking wife into partnership

[51.118] The proprietor of a haulage business took his wife and son into partnership with him. The partnership did not apply for registration and the Commissioners imposed a penalty under what is now *VATA 1994, s 67*. The partners appealed, contending that they had a reasonable excuse because they had not realised that they had to apply for a separate registration instead of using the registration number previously allocated to the husband. The tribunal allowed the appeal, holding that the circumstances constituted a reasonable excuse. *Peter Jones & Son*, MAN/88/309 (VTD 2990).

[51.119] A similar decision was reached in *JA & J Wright (t/a Euro-Dec)*, MAN/89/105 (VTD 3540).

Dissolution of partnership—one partner continuing as sole trader

[51.120] A husband and wife had traded in partnership as hairdressers. The marriage broke down and the wife ceased working in the business in June 1988. Draft accounts to 30 June 1988 were prepared in October, and the husband notified the Commissioners that the partnership had ceased and that he was continuing in business as a sole trader. The Commissioners imposed a penalty under what is now *VATA 1994, s 67*, on the basis that he should have notified this in July. He appealed, contending that he had a reasonable excuse because he had hoped that his wife would change her mind, and that he had not realised that he could not continue to use the partnership's existing registration number. The tribunal allowed his appeal, holding that, in the circumstances, his uncertainty about the future of his marriage constituted a reasonable excuse. *MJ Lewis*, MAN/89/526 (VTD 4150).

Partners initially intending to trade through limited company

[51.121] The two directors of a limited company, which operated a number of public houses and was registered for VAT, sought to purchase a licensed restaurant. Initially they intended that the company would acquire and operate the restaurant. However, they were only able to raise sufficient capital as individuals rather than through the company. They therefore purchased the restaurant as a partnership and traded as such. They became liable to register for VAT in November 1985 but did not do so until June 1986, and the Commissioners imposed a penalty under what is now *VATA 1994, s 67*. The tribunal allowed the partners' appeal, accepting that at the time they began to operate the restaurant, they still hoped to transfer it to their company, and holding that, although the case was 'near the borderline', their conduct in awaiting the outcome of negotiations was not unreasonable. *PHV Hutchings & JH Liggett (t/a Cashlandoo Inn)*, [1987] VATTR 58 (VTD 2313).

Cases where the appellant was unsuccessful

Failure to follow up preliminary enquiry

[51.122] A company, aware that it might be liable to register for VAT, wrote to its local VAT office but received no reply. It did not pursue the matter until five months after its initial enquiry. The Commissioners imposed a penalty under what is now *VATA 1994, s 67* and the tribunal dismissed the company's appeal, holding that the delay of five months in following up the enquiry meant that the circumstances did not amount to a reasonable excuse. *Barmor Engineering Ltd*, LON/86/305 (VTD 2214).

[51.123] Similar decisions were reached in *P Roberts & D Brooke*, MAN/86/189 (VTD 2153); *R Jones*, LON/86/270 (VTD 2182); *SL Martin*, LON/86/494 (VTD 2224); *Pacey Rogers & Co*, LON/87/13 (VTD 2308); *GC Molyneux*, MAN/88/609 (VTD 3322); *DJI Electrical Services Ltd*, LON/88/1059X (VTD 3671); *BS Watkins*, LON/89/1136X (VTD 4668); *PH Leighton & JP Henry (t/a Lacy's Wine Bar)*, BEL/92/20X (VTD 9793); *London Brick Company King's Dyke Social Club*, LON/92/2462A (VTD 10387); *Soul Jazz Records*, LON/93/1093P (VTD 11066); *Mr & Mrs F Raywood*, LON/93/2031 (VTD 11945); *PA Heron*, LON/95/847 (VTD 13529B) and *R Sheikh*, EDN/98/84 (VTD 15684).

Pressure of work

[51.124] A company appealed against a penalty under what is now *VATA 1994, s 67*, contending that its directors had overlooked the need for registration because of pressure of work. The tribunal dismissed the appeal, holding that this was not a reasonable excuse. *Pepper Personnel Ltd*, LON/86/424 (VTD 2175).

[51.125] There have been many other cases in which tribunals have held that pressure of work does not constitute a reasonable excuse for failure to register. In the interests of space, such cases are not listed individually in this book.

Formation of accountancy partnership

[51.126] A firm of chartered accountants was established on 1 October 1985. Each of the partners had been registered for VAT as a sole practitioner, but they did not register as a partnership until February 1986. The Commissioners imposed a penalty under what is now *VATA 1994, s 67*. The tribunal dismissed the firm's appeal, holding that there was no excuse for its failure to register at the appropriate time. *Beaton Snelling & Co*, LON/86/459 (VTD 2206).

Former partner continuing business as sole trader

[51.127] A restaurant had previously been run by two people in partnership. One of the partners left the country and the other continued to trade as sole proprietor. The partnership had been registered for VAT but the remaining partner did not notify the Commissioners that he had continued to trade as a sole proprietor. The tribunal dismissed his appeal against a penalty under what is now *VATA 1994, s 67*, holding that there was no reasonable excuse for his failure to make the required notification. *SH Liakat (t/a Banaras Tandoori Restaurant)*, LON/88/940 (VTD 3300).

Business acquired as going concern

[51.128] A publican took over a public house which had previously been registered for VAT. He did not notify the Commissioners, and they imposed a penalty under what is now *VATA 1994, s 67*. He appealed, contending that he had a reasonable excuse as he had assumed that the existing registration would be transferred to him. The tribunal dismissed his appeal, holding that his grounds for appeal amounted to ignorance of the law, which was not a reasonable excuse. *GA James*, LON/86/363 (VTD 2207).

[51.129] Similar decisions were reached in *Bistro Inns Ltd*, LON/97/1476 (VTD 15613); *R Cuthbert*, EDN/99/61 (VTD 16518); *Presentway Ltd*, MAN/98/861 (VTD 17383); *Elgar Hotel Worcester Ltd*, MAN/05/475 (VTD 19579); *M Haque*, LON/06/214 (VTD 20296) and *Ali*, **51.164** below.

[51.130] A company which had operated an engineering business, and was registered for VAT, ceased trading on 30 April 1997. A new company, with the same controlling director, took over the business from 1 May 1997, but did not register for VAT. When the Commissioners discovered this, they imposed a penalty under *VATA 1994, s 67*. The company appealed, contending that it had begun a new business and that there had not been any transfer of the previous company's business. The tribunal rejected this contention and dismissed the appeal. *Denholmegate Engineering Ltd*, MAN/00/127 (VTD 17350).

[51.131] Similar decisions were reached in *A Aslanbeigi & M Kanani (t/a Cuccina)*, MAN/02/264 (VTD 18382) and *A Hamid*, LON/03/723 (VTD 18802).

Dyslexia

[51.132] A partnership appealed against a penalty under what is now *VATA 1994, s 67*, contending that it had a reasonable excuse because one of the partners was dyslexic and misread the annual threshold for registration as £25,000 when in fact it was £20,500. The tribunal dismissed the partnership's appeal, holding that this was not a reasonable excuse. *JE & JB Fletcher*, MAN/87/39 (VTD 2356).

[51.133] Dyslexia was also held not to be a reasonable excuse in *EP McKay*, LON/88/988Z (VTD 3406).

Marriage breakdown

[51.134] A plumber appealed against a penalty under what is now *VATA 1994, s 67*, contending that he had a reasonable excuse because his marriage had broken down. The tribunal dismissed his appeal, holding that this was not a reasonable excuse. *CJ Talbot*, LON/89/759Y (VTD 4807).

[51.135] A similar decision was reached in *A Veitch (t/a Pine Products)*, EDN/94/4 (VTD 11963).

Wife giving birth

[51.136] A taxi driver became liable to register for VAT in January 1989 but did not do so until March 1990. The Commissioners imposed a penalty under what is now *VATA 1994, s 67* and he appealed, contending that he had a reasonable excuse as his wife, who acted as his bookkeeper, had given birth to a daughter in February 1989. The tribunal dismissed his appeal, holding that this did not constitute a reasonable excuse. *M Hazell*, LON/90/1018Z (VTD 5574).

Bankruptcy

[51.137] The tribunal held that the fact that a trader had been an undischarged bankrupt throughout the period of his liability to register did not constitute a reasonable excuse. *CH Ambrose*, LON/86/711 (VTD 2303).

Other cases

[51.138] There have been a large number of unsuccessful appeals which appear to raise no point of general importance, but where appellants have claimed that the penalty imposed has been unjust. In the interests of space, such cases are not reported individually in this book.

Unauthorised issue of invoices (VATA 1994, s 67(1)(c); FA 2008, Sch 41 para 2)

[51.139] A company was incorporated on 11 June 1979 and registered for VAT from 9 July 1979. On 7 September 1985, the managing director wrote to the Commissioners stating that he was resident in the Netherlands and that all VAT forms should be sent to the Netherlands. The Commissioners issued notices cancelling the company's registration and exempting it from registering for VAT in the UK. In January 1987 the managing director and his wife, who was a co-director and the company secretary, returned to the UK. The company entered into a contract for services in London, and issued a VAT invoice. The Commissioners imposed a penalty under what is now *VATA 1994, s 67(1)(c)* for the unauthorised issue of a VAT invoice. The tribunal allowed the company's appeal, finding that there had been no malicious intent but that the directors had been confused as to the legal consequences of their return to the UK, and holding that this constituted a reasonable excuse. *Countgold Ltd*, MAN/88/155 (VTD 2894).

[51.140] An appeal against a penalty under what is now *VATA 1994, s 67(1)(c)* was dismissed in a case where a trader had issued unauthorised invoices before applying for registration. The tribunal accepted that the trader had intended to register and subsequently to pay the tax charged by the invoice, but held that the circumstances did not constitute a reasonable excuse. *J Scott-Martin (t/a SM Harris)*, LON/92/1109Z (VTD 8954).

[51.141] A builder registered for VAT in 1982 but deregistered in 1992. In 1996 and 1997 he issued eleven invoices purporting to charge VAT, although he was no longer registered. When the Commissioners discovered this, they imposed a penalty under *VATA 1994, s 67(1)(c)*. The tribunal dismissed the builder's appeal, holding that there was no reasonable excuse and no grounds for mitigation. *GE Alm*, LON/98/961 (VTD 15863). (*Note.* For another issue in this case, see **2.46** APPEALS.)

[51.142] The proprietor of a business, who had not been registered for VAT, died and the business was taken over by his son. The son did not register for VAT, but issued invoices charging VAT, and the Commissioners imposed a penalty under what is now *VATA 1994, s 67(1)(c)*. The tribunal allowed the son's appeal, holding that since he had succeeded to the business with no knowledge of the details of the business, or of business matters generally, he had a reasonable excuse for having issued the invoices in question. *A Kulka (t/a Kulka Models)*, MAN/92/1246 (VTD 9753).

[51.143] A company was incorporated in February 1996, as a non-profit-making organisation limited by guarantee. It did not register for VAT, but issued three invoices to its sole customer. The invoices purported to charge VAT. When the Commissioners discovered this, they imposed a penalty under *VATA 1994, s 67(1)(c)*. The company appealed. The tribunal upheld the penalty in principle, holding that there was no reasonable excuse, but directed that the penalty should be mitigated by 50% in view of the fact that the company was a non-profit-making organisation. *Global Trade Centre Ltd*, LON/96/1559 (VTD 14866).

[51.144] Two individuals began trading in partnership as car repairers. They did not register for VAT, but issued invoices purporting to charge VAT. When the Commissioners discovered this, they imposed a penalty under *VATA 1994, s 67(1)(c)*. One of the partners appealed. The tribunal dismissed the appeal, holding that there was no reasonable excuse and no grounds for mitigating the penalty. *TJ Pratt*, LON/00/129 (VTD 17718).

[51.145] Customs discovered that a married couple had issued invoices in the name of companies which were not registered for VAT. At the relevant time, the husband had been disqualified from acting as a director under *Company Directors Disqualification Act 1986*. Customs imposed a penalty under *VATA 1997, s 67(1)(c)*. The tribunal reviewed the evidence in detail, upheld the penalty and dismissed the couple's appeal. *S & Mrs R Chatha*, MAN/05/701 (VTD 20135).

Mitigation of penalties (VATA 1994, s 70; FA 2008, Sch 41 paras 12, 13)

Cases where the penalty was mitigated by the tribunal

Penalty mitigated by 10%

[51.146] In the case noted at 57.198 REGISTRATION, a penalty was upheld in principle but mitigated by 10% to take account of a limited degree of co-operation. *VA Noades*, LON/00/210 (VTD 17152).

Penalty mitigated by 23%

[51.147] The Commissioners imposed a penalty of £1,297 on the proprietor of a guest house, who had failed to register for VAT. The tribunal upheld the penalty in principle, but observed that the proprietor had had a 'very stressful period' and reduced it to £1,000. *G Abel (t/a Abel Guest House)*, EDN/01/55 (VTD 17409).

Penalty mitigated by 30%

[51.148] A penalty under what is now *VATA 1994, s 67* was mitigated by 30% in a case where the tribunal observed that it could take into account the fact that the trader had been unable to get credit for input tax, and that 'this was not a case where a trader gained a competitive advantage against others who had registered'. *MB Cohen*, [1994] VATTR 290 (VTD 12732).

Penalty mitigated by 40%

[51.149] The Commissioners imposed a penalty under what is now *VATA 1994, s 67* on a trader who had become liable to register for VAT from 1 January 1993 but had failed to notify his liability until 13 January 1994. The tribunal held that the trader had no reasonable excuse, but considered whether the penalty should be mitigated under what is now *VATA 1994, s 70*. The tribunal observed that, in considering mitigation, 'essentially the question is one of how far the taxpayer is to blame for the defaults. If he is wholly blameworthy, the full penalty will be the proper amount; otherwise there may be a case for a reduction'. On the evidence, the trader's turnover 'went through the registration threshold progressively. It was the result of increments to his earnings and may not have been immediately apparent.' Furthermore, the appellant had 'wasted little time in putting things right after he realised that he should probably have registered. He engaged and paid an accountant to investigate his personal liability.' The tribunal mitigated the penalty by 40%. *TR Jordan*, [1994] VATTR 286 (VTD 12616).

[51.150] A penalty was mitigated by 40% in a case where the tribunal took into account the fact that the appellant's income was 'somewhat erratic'. *RJ Dodd (t/a Able Machines)*, MAN/94/511 (VTD 12856).

[51.151] Penalties were mitigated by 40%, to take account of co-operation, in *L Ringer*, MAN/06/792 (VTD 20060) and *D Taylor*, LON/06/977 (VTD 20099).

Penalty mitigated by 44%

[51.152] A company failed to register for VAT within the prescribed period. HMRC imposed a penalty, which they mitigated by 25%. The tribunal upheld the penalty in principle, but expressed the opinion that it was harsh that the penalty was charged at 10% rather than 5%. In view of this, the tribunal reduced the penalty from £2515 to £1886 (ie allowing total mitigation of about 44%). *ALH Interiors Ltd v HMRC*, [2009] UKFTT 234 (TC), TC00183.

Penalty mitigated by 50%

[51.153] A self-employed salesman, who worked on a commission basis for a single company, became liable to register in May 1988 but did not do so until October 1990. The Commissioners imposed a penalty for late registration. He appealed, contending that he had a reasonable excuse because he had assumed that he could be treated as an employee, and had telephoned the Reading VAT office in 1988. The tribunal held that the circumstances did not constitute a reasonable excuse, because the appellant should have sought professional advice or should have written to the VAT office rather than telephoning them. However, since the appellant had made a voluntary telephone call to the VAT office, and there had been no attempt to evade registration, the tribunal directed that the penalty should be mitigated by 50%. *GA Osborn*, LON/94/3450 (VTD 13254).

[51.154] A penalty was mitigated by 50%, to take account of co-operation, in *CM Broadbent*, MAN/98/244 (VTD 15809).

[51.155] The Commissioners imposed a penalty on the proprietors of a dry-cleaning business who had become liable to register for VAT from 31 July 1988 but had failed to do so. The proprietors appealed, contending that they had a reasonable excuse because they had believed that their turnover was below the registration limits. The tribunal rejected this contention, finding that the proprietors should have been registered from 31 July 1988 to 20 March 1991 and holding that there was no reasonable excuse for their failure to do so. However, the tribunal directed that the penalty should be mitigated by 50% to take account of the facts that the proprietors had not previously been in business, that their turnover had been below the registration limits when they took over the business, and that they had co-operated with the Commissioners. *T & L Mehmet (t/a Leyla Dry Cleaners)*, LON/96/464 & 468 (VTD 14473).

[51.156] A penalty was mitigated by 50% in a case where the tribunal found that a trader's turnover had exceeded the annual registration threshold by only £952. *AA Abdullah (t/a Aladdin's Cave Kebab House)*, MAN/99/1116 (VTD 16774).

[51.157] A penalty was mitigated by 50% in a case where the tribunal found that a trader's failure to register was attributable to 'lack of action' by his accountant. *AP Lombardelli (t/a Century 21 Lombard Estates)*, LON/00/799 (VTD 17016).

[51.158] A trader became liable to register in December 1999 but failed to do so until December 2000, after his accountants had discovered that his turnover had exceeded the registration threshold. The Commissioners imposed a penalty of £436 under *VATA 1994, s 67*. The tribunal upheld the penalty in principle but mitigated it by 50% since 'the trader applied for registration when told by his accountants that he should do so (this is not a case in which the Commissioners have registered him compulsorily following an investigation)'. *ME Loftus*, MAN/03/397 (VTD 18435).

[51.159] A penalty was also mitigated by 50% in *Global Trade Centre Ltd*, 51.143 above.

Penalty mitigated by 55%

[51.160] The wife of a publican provided catering at her husband's public house. The Commissioners accepted that the catering was a separate business for VAT purposes. In March 1991 a VAT officer discovered that the wife's turnover had exceeded the VAT registration threshold. It was subsequently discovered that she should have registered with effect from August 1988. The Commissioners imposed a penalty of £2,771. The tribunal held that there was no reasonable excuse for the failure to register, since the wife had relied on her accountant, but directed that, since she had young children to look after, and had not tried to mislead the Commissioners, the penalty should be reduced to £1,250 (a reduction of slightly under 55%). *L Gent*, LON/95/82 (VTD 13227).

[51.161] A penalty was mitigated by 55%, to take account of co-operation, in *Cobra Consultancy Ltd*, LON/01/1232 (VTD 17615).

Penalty mitigated by 70%

[51.162] The Commissioners imposed a penalty under *VATA 1994, s 67*, mitigated by 50% to take account of co-operation. The tribunal upheld the penalty in principle but increased the mitigation to 70% to reflect the fact that the trader's 'failure to register in time was attributable to the advice she had received from her accountant'. *Mrs S Woods*, LON/04/2344 (VTD 19024).

[51.163] A penalty was mitigated by 70%, to take account of co-operation, in *WW Brydon*, EDN/08/86 (VTD 20740).

Penalty mitigated by 71%

[51.164] The Commissioners imposed a penalty of £1,760 on a trader who had acquired a takeaway restaurant as a going concern, and had failed to register for VAT. The tribunal upheld the penalty in principle, but reduced it to £500, observing that the trader was not 'greatly to blame', since it was clear that his solicitors 'did not understand that they were dealing with the transfer of a going concern with all that that implied for VAT purposes'. *A Ali*, MAN/99/398 (VTD 17565).

Penalty mitigated by 75%

[51.165] In the case noted at **51.53** above, the tribunal mitigated the penalty by 75% to take account of co-operation. *A1 Rushmoor Radio Taxis Ltd*, LON/x (VTD 17634).

[51.166] A similar decision, also mitigating the penalty by 75%, was reached in the case noted at **51.62** above. *TJ Sumner & PS Kiddle (t/a Extravaganza Hair Workshop)*, LON/00/280 (VTD 17784).

Penalty mitigated by 90%

[51.167] The Commissioners imposed a penalty on a sole trader who had failed to register. The tribunal upheld the penalty in principle, holding that there was no reasonable excuse for the failure to register. However, the tribunal directed that the penalty should be mitigated by 90% to take account of the fact that the trader's turnover had only exceeded the registration threshold for a period of three months and had then fallen to below the threshold. *J Barnard (t/a Baron Security)*, LON/96/128 (VTD 14206).

[51.168] A company became liable to register from 1 May 2005 but did not submit form VAT 1 until 27 May. Customs imposed a penalty of £494. The tribunal upheld the penalty in principle but reduced it to £50. *Ryebank Ltd*, MAN/06/766 (VTD 20212).

Penalty mitigated by 100%

[51.169] In November 1997 a VAT officer visited an unregistered trader and formed the opinion that he had become liable to register from November 1995. In July 1998, after having consulted an accountant, the trader applied for registration. In July 1999 the Commissioners formally registered him, and in December 1999 they imposed a penalty covering the period from November 1995 to July 1998. The tribunal held that there was no reasonable excuse for the trader's failure to register, applying *Neal*, 51.50 above, but held that, since the Commissioners had 'delayed inordinately', the penalty should be mitigated to nil. *SJ Whereat*, LON/99/937 (VTD 16751).

[51.170] The Commissioners imposed a penalty on a milliner, who had failed to register for VAT although her turnover had narrowly exceeded the threshold. She appealed, contending that she had had to cease trading and had suffered a 'breakdown'. The tribunal mitigated the penalty in full. *P Durrant*, LON/00/827 (VTD 17430).

[51.171] Customs imposed a penalty on an electrical subcontractor (P), who had become liable to register in 2003 but failed to do so until 2005. The tribunal directed that the penalty should be mitigated in full, finding that P had 'supplied the information about the value of his supplies promptly with no intention to disguise the values' and that Customs had also imposed a misdeclaration penalty 'derived from the same facts as the late notification penalty'. *CP Parsons*, LON/06/318 (VTD 20033).

[51.172] A shop which sold hot Balti take-away food was sold in 2001. The vendor was registered for VAT but the purchaser (S) failed to register. A Customs officer visited the premises in 2005. Following this, Customs issued a ruling that the business had been transferred as a going concern, and imposed a penalty for failure to register. S appealed, contending that he had not known that the vendor had been registered for VAT. The tribunal held that the business had been transferred as a going concern. However the tribunal criticised Customs for failing to communicate with S before 2005, and directed that the penalty should be mitigated in full. *SZ Ahmed*, LON/06/611 (VTD 20187).

[51.173] A woman (E) traded as a retailer from October 1997 until April 2008, without registering for VAT. Her income tax returns suggested that her income had exceeded the VAT registration threshold. In 2009 HMRC issued a ruling that E had been liable to register for VAT from January 2002. They issued an assessment and imposed a penalty. E appealed. The tribunal upheld the assessment and found that there was no reasonable excuse for E's failure to register. However the tribunal but directed that the penalty should be reduced to nil. Judge Blewitt expressed the view that 'the delay by HMRC in contacting the appellant' was 'excessive and without justification'. *Mrs S Evans v HMRC*, [2011] UKFTT 464 (TC), TC01314.

Cases where the penalty was mitigated by the Commissioners

[51.174] The Commissioners imposed a penalty on a woman who had failed to register. They mitigated the penalty by 50%, the grounds for mitigation being that the woman had been harassed and assaulted by her former partner. She appealed, contending that the penalty should be mitigated still further. The tribunal dismissed her appeal, holding that 'the 50% mitigation already allowed is fair and reasonable and that there would be no justification for any increase'. *K Doherty*, EDN/94/459 (VTD 13075).

[51.175] A trader became liable to register for VAT in January 1988 but did not do so until September 1993. He appealed, contending that the penalty should be mitigated because his wife who had acted as his bookkeeper had been ill, he had been unable to afford an accountant until 1993, and during the period in question he had been acting as a director of a boatbuilding company which had been in serious financial difficulties. The Commissioners mitigated the penalty by 50% and the tribunal upheld their decision, applying *dicta* in *Jordan*, **51.149** above. (The tribunal also held that the trader did not have a 'reasonable excuse' for his failure to register.) *EM Vann*, LON/95/1612P (VTD 13581).

[51.176] A similar decision, also applying *dicta* in *Jordan*, **51.149** above, was reached in a case where the tribunal found that a self-employed minibus driver was suffering from 'acute shyness and a difficulty in leaving his home'. The Commissioners mitigated the penalty by 50%, to take account of 'the age, experience and level of education of the trader, and the fact that Customs were notified promptly of (his) requirement to be registered once it was discovered'. The tribunal held that no further mitigation was appropriate. *H Haines*, LON/95/2494 (VTD 13986).

[51.177] The Commissioners imposed a penalty, mitigated by 50%, on a partnership which had failed to notify its liability to register. The partnership appealed, contending that it had a reasonable excuse because the partners had believed that the registration threshold applied to each individual partner, rather than to the partnership. The tribunal dismissed the appeal, holding that there was no reasonable excuse for the failure to register, and that the 50% mitigation which the Commissioners had allowed was 'fair and reasonable'. *Savannah Landscapes & Building Services*, MAN/02/433 (VTD 17883).

[51.178] Customs imposed a penalty, mitigated by 50%, on a sole trader (C) who carried on business as a self-employed plumbing and heating engineer since 1970, and had become liable to register for VAT from December 2000 but had failed to do so. He appealed, contending that the penalty should be discharged because he had traded for many years with a turnover below the VAT threshold, had not realised that he was liable to register, and had co-operated fully with Customs. The tribunal upheld the penalty, holding that there was no reasonable excuse and that 50% was 'an appropriately high level of mitigation'. *SLE Condon*, LON/06/817 (VTD 19837).

[51.179] Customs issued a penalty, mitigated by 25%, on a trader who had become liable to register from August 2002 but had failed to notify them until September 2005. The tribunal upheld the penalty, holding that there was no reasonable excuse and no grounds for any further mitigation. *J Snaddon*, MAN/06/600 (VTD 19964).

[51.180] HMRC imposed a penalty, mitigated by 50%, on a sole trader who had become liable to register in February 2007 but had failed to notify HMRC until October 2009. The tribunal upheld the penalty, holding that there was no reasonable excuse and no grounds for any further mitigation. *B McAdam (t/a Brian McAdam Plumbing & Heating) v HMRC*, [2011] UKFTT 22 (TC), TC00899.

Cases where the penalty was not mitigated

[51.181] A builder became liable to register for VAT in February 1989 but did not do so until after he was visited by a VAT officer in August 1994. The Commissioners imposed a penalty and the builder appealed, contending that the penalty should be mitigated since he had co-operated in establishing his turnover for the period in question. The tribunal dismissed his appeal, observing that 'that kind of co-operation is in a different category from the concept of "full co-operation" in the context of a (*VATA 1994, s 60**) case, and carries very much less weight'. *Cohen*, **51.148** above, was distinguished on the grounds that many of the builder's customers were not registered for VAT, so that 'some advantage would have accrued to the appellant as a result of his not charging VAT to his customers, whilst the disadvantage of being unable to claim input tax may have been small'. On the evidence, the builder was 'wholly to blame for the defaults and the full penalty is the proper amount'. *FD Snow*, LON/94/2178 (VTD 13283).

[51.182] A similar decision, also distinguishing *Cohen*, **51.148** above, was reached in *JS Upson*, LON/94/2742 (VTD 13350).

[51.183] In July 1994 the Commissioners imposed a penalty on a partnership which operated a taxi business and which had become liable to register for VAT in 1990 but had failed to do so. The partners appealed, contending that the penalty should be mitigated because they had relied on an accountant and that the amount of such penalties had subsequently been reduced by *FA 1995*. The tribunal dismissed the appeal, observing that 'neither partner made any attempt to assist with the investigations; in fact they went out of their way to be obtuse'. *P Khan & M Parvez (t/a On Time Cars)*, MAN/96/179 (VTD 14293).

[51.184] A chartered accountant became liable to register for VAT in 1983 but failed to do so. His turnover dropped to below the registration threshold in 1991 but he became liable to register again in 1992. He again failed to notify the Commissioners. The Commissioners discovered this in 1995, and in January 1996 they imposed penalties under *VATA 1994, s 67*. The tribunal dismissed the accountant's appeal, holding on the evidence that there was no reasonable excuse and no grounds for mitigation. *MYH Murat*, LON/96/295 (VTD 14759). (*Note.* For another issue in this case, taken to the QB, see **3.164** ASSESSMENT.)

Illness of bookkeeper

[51.185] See *Cheek (t/a Swanley Contractors)*, **51.20** above.

52

Penalties: Misdeclaration and Errors

The cases in this chapter are arranged under the following headings.

Definition of 'prescribed accounting period' (VATA 1994, s 63(1))	**52.1**
Whether a return has been 'made' (VATA 1994, s 63(1)(a))	**52.2**
Inadequate estimated assessment (VATA 1994, s 63(1)(b); FA 2007, Sch 24 para 2)	
Cases where the appellant was successful	**52.5**
Cases where the appellant was unsuccessful	**52.12**
Definition of 'tax which would have been lost' (VATA 1994, s 63(2))	**52.24**
Whether return corrected by subsequent return (VATA 1994, s 63(8))	**52.27**
Whether a 'reasonable excuse' (VATA 1994, s 63(10)(a))	
Clerical errors	**52.31**
Misunderstanding of the time of supply	**52.81**
Imports and acquisitions	**52.147**
Supplies incorrectly treated as zero-rated	**52.175**
Supplies incorrectly treated as exempt	**52.220**
Incorrect claims for bad debt relief	**52.232**
Credit notes—incorrect treatment	**52.244**
Failure to account for output tax—other cases	**52.253**
Incorrect input tax claims—other cases	**52.311**
Miscellaneous	**52.368**
Whether error 'voluntarily disclosed' (VATA 1994, s 63(10)(b))	**52.377**
Mitigation of penalties (VATA 1994, s 70)	
Cases where the penalty was mitigated by the tribunal	**52.392**
Cases where the penalty was mitigated by the Commissioners	**52.435**
Cases where the penalty was not mitigated	**52.445**
Penalties for errors: amount of penalty (FA 2007, Sch 24 paras 4–12)	**52.449**
Validity of the penalty	**52.452**

NOTE

The misdeclaration penalty was originally introduced by *FA 1985, s 14*. There were substantial changes to the provisions during the succeeding years, with significant changes being made by *FA 1994, s 45*. The legislation was consolidated in *VATA 1994, ss 63, 64*. However, this consolidated legislation was replaced by *FA 2007, Sch 24*, which refers to penalties for errors, rather than to penalties for misdeclarations. The provisions of *FA 2007* have various commencement dates ranging from 1 April 2008 to 1 April 2009: see Tolley's Value Added Tax for details. The cases in this chapter should be read in the light of the changes in the legislation.

Definition of prescribed accounting period (VATA 1994, s 63(1))

[52.1] A company had been registered for VAT since 1984, with monthly accounting periods. On 20 March 1991 it applied to be included in a VAT group. In April 1991 it submitted a return for the period ending 31 March 1991, in which it overclaimed input tax by more than £35,000. The Commissioners imposed a misdeclaration penalty and the company appealed, contending that the penalty was not valid because the effect of its application for group registration was that the period in question was no longer a 'prescribed accounting period'. The tribunal dismissed the appeal. The Commissioners had not authorised the group registration until June 1991. Being treated as a member of a group did not absolve a company joining the group from its liability to be registered under what is now *VATA 1994, Sch 1*. At the time when the return in question was made, the company had been required to submit a return for the period ending 31 March, which was therefore a 'prescribed accounting period' as laid down by what is now *regulation 25* of the *VAT Regulations (SI 1995/2518)*. *Atlas Interlates Ltd*, MAN/91/1468 (VTD 7904).

Whether a return has been 'made' (VATA 1994, s 63(1)(a))

Whether return a 'nullity'

[52.2] A county council's return for April 1991 included a negative figure for output tax. It was accepted that this resulted from an error by a clerical officer in making an incorrect subtraction from the cumulative figure of output tax indicated by the council's computer. The Commissioners imposed a misdeclaration penalty. The tribunal allowed the council's appeal, holding that 'the mistake was so fundamentally wrong that the April return was not, in the opinion of the tribunal, "made" for the purposes of (*VATA 1994, Sch 11 para 2(1)**) and (*VAT Regulations 1995, reg 25**)'. The return had to be treated as a nullity, and since no return had been made, no penalty under what is now *VATA 1994, s 63* was due. *Gwent County Council*, LON/90/1389X (VTD 6153). (*Note.* The decision in this case was disapproved by the QB in *Nomura Properties Management Services Ltd*, **52.4** below.)

[52.3] The principal director of a company also carried on a farming business in partnership with his wife. The Commissioners sent a return to the company, but the director's wife inadvertently completed the return as if it related to the partnership. This resulted in a lower VAT liability being declared than would have been the case if the return had been correctly completed. When the Commissioners discovered this, they imposed a misdeclaration penalty on the company. The tribunal allowed the company's appeal, holding that the director 'was not acting in the course of his duties, nor was he purporting to do so, when he mistakenly used the appellant's return form as the means of supplying the figures for his own partnership farming business'. The company could 'not be said to have furnished a return showing the tax payable by, and other information in respect of, it and containing the requisite declaration'. *Tannington Growers (1984) Ltd*, [1992] VATTR 135 (VTD 6877).

[52.4] A company submitted a return in which the value of outputs was included in Box 1 instead of Box 4; the value of inputs was included in Box 5 rather than Box 2; the amounts of output tax and input tax were entered in Boxes 4 and 5 instead of Boxes 1 and 2; and in Box 3 was entered the excess of inputs over outputs, rather than the excess of input tax over output tax. This resulted in the return claiming a repayment of £218,718, whereas the repayment actually due was £32,808. The Commissioners imposed a penalty under what is now *VATA 1994, s 63*. The company appealed, contending that the return should be treated as a 'nullity'. The QB rejected this contention and upheld the penalty. An inaccurate return was still a return and a penalty arose as a result. Furthermore, the penalty was not invalidated by the subsequent correction of the return. The QB specifically disapproved the tribunal decision in *Gwent County Council*, 52.2 above. *C & E Commrs v Nomura Properties Management Services Ltd*, QB [1994] STC 461.

Inadequate estimated assessment (VATA 1994, s 63(1)(b); FA 2007 Sch 24 para 2)

Cases where the appellant was successful

[52.5] The Commissioners had not received a trader's return for the period ending 31 July 1990 by the due date of 31 August. They therefore issued an estimated assessment charging tax of £2 and imposed a default surcharge of £30 (the statutory minimum). In February 1991 a VAT officer discovered that the amount of tax actually due for the period in question was £9,670. The Commissioners therefore imposed a penalty under what is now *VATA 1994, s 63(1)(b)*. The trader appealed, contending that he had delivered the return by hand to the Maidenhead VAT office in September 1990. The Commissioners denied receiving the return. The tribunal allowed the trader's appeal, finding on the balance of probabilities that the trader had delivered the return and that it had been lost at the VAT office, and holding that by delivering the return the trader had taken 'all such steps as are reasonable to draw the understatement to the attention of the Commissioners'. *PM Carr (t/a P & L Packaging)*, LON/91/1561X (VTD 6726). (*Note*. For other cases where the Commissioners have denied receiving a return but tribunals have accepted appellants' evidence that the return has been delivered by hand to a VAT office, see **18.50** and **18.51** DEFAULT SURCHARGE.)

[52.6] The decision in *Carr*, 52.5 above, was applied in a subsequent case where an appellant gave evidence that his bookkeeper had posted the return in question to the local VAT office. The tribunal did not consider that 'Parliament intended that a penalty should apply in a case such as this where a return was lost in the post'. *KR Meads*, LON/91/1677Z (VTD 7283).

[52.7] In a case where the facts are not fully recorded in the decision, the tribunal accepted that a company had a reasonable excuse for not having realised that an estimated assessment was inadequate, and allowed the company's appeal against a penalty under what is now *VATA 1994, s 63(1)(b)*. *Southwest Blasting Ltd*, LON/92/2210 (VTD 9657).

[52.8] An appeal was allowed in a case where the tribunal held that the notice of assessment had been defective, in that it had not included a specific statement that the return for the relevant period had not been received. *HG Jones & Associates*, LON/92/3141 (VTD 10399).

Bookkeeper suffering stress following pregnancy of common-law wife

[52.9] An appeal was allowed in a case where the tribunal found that a company's bookkeeper had not notified the directors that an estimated assessment was inadequate because he was suffering from stress following the pregnancy of his common-law wife, and held that this constituted a reasonable excuse. *Acquisitions (Fireplaces) Ltd*, LON/92/2516 (VTD 10097).

Prolonged illness of partner

[52.10] A married couple operated a public house. The husband suffered prolonged illness, and their VAT affairs fell into arrears. The Commissioners issued estimated assessments which were subsequently discovered to be inadequate. Accordingly the Commissioners imposed penalties under what is now *VATA 1994, s 63(1)(b)*. The tribunal allowed the couple's appeals against the penalties, holding that the husband's illness constituted a reasonable excuse. *DN & JF Thomas*, LON/92/2005 (VTD 11040).

Computer malfunction

[52.11] A company appealed against a penalty under what is now *VATA 1994, s 63(1)(b)*, contending that it had a reasonable excuse because its computer had been erratic and unreliable, and its officers had not known what its true VAT liability was. The tribunal accepted the company's evidence and allowed the appeal. *Physical Distribution Services Ltd*, LON/93/2538P (VTD 12069).

Cases where the appellant was unsuccessful

[52.12] A company failed to submit its return for the period ending 31 August 1990. The Commissioners issued an estimated assessment charging VAT of 23,000, which the company paid. In November 1990 a control visit took place and the VAT officer discovered that the assessment had been inadequate. A further assessment was issued and a penalty under what is now *VATA 1994, s 63(1)(b)* was imposed. The company appealed, contending that it had a reasonable excuse because its accountant, who had begun working for the company on 13 August, had proved to be incompetent and had been dismissed in November. The tribunal dismissed the appeal, holding on the evidence that the company's finance director had been negligent in not supervising the accountant's work and in not ensuring that the relevant return was submitted. *New Western (Panels) Ltd*, MAN/91/317 (VTD 6990).

[52.13] The proprietors of a hotel failed to submit a VAT return for the period ending 30 September 1990. The Commissioners issued an estimated assessment charging tax of £6,350. The proprietors did not appeal. Subsequently the Commissioners discovered that the true liability for the period was almost £25,000. They therefore imposed a penalty under what is now *VATA 1994, s 63(1)(b)*. The proprietors appealed, contending that they had not appealed since they had assumed that the estimated assessment was 'about right'. The tribunal dismissed the appeal, holding that the principal partner 'should have been aware from his knowledge of his turnover' that the assessment was a 'gross underestimate'. *Muirtown Motel*, EDN/91/313 (VTD 7431).

[52.14] A similar decision was reached in *C Stevenson*, EDN/91/308 (VTD 7598).

[52.15] In a case where the proprietor of a Chinese restaurant could not understand English and relied on his son to deal with official correspondence, the tribunal held that there was no reasonable excuse for the acceptance of inadequate estimated assessments. *YY Wong*, MAN/91/860 (VTD 7591).

[52.16] A company failed to appeal against an inadequate estimated assessment, and a penalty under what is now *VATA 1994, s 63(1)(b)* was subsequently imposed. The company appealed against the penalty, contending that it had a reasonable excuse for not having checked the estimated assessment because of pressure of work following a change of premises. The tribunal dismissed the appeal, holding that the circumstances did not constitute a reasonable excuse. *Leckwith Engineering Ltd*, LON/92/88Z (VTD 7702).

[52.17] An appeal was dismissed in a case where a company with a VAT liability of £32,000 failed to appeal against an estimated assessment of £1,420, and contended that it had had difficulty in balancing its books for the period in question. *Spinnaker MDC Ltd*, LON/92/266Z (VTD 7841).

[52.18] A company failed to submit four successive returns. The Commissioners issued estimated assessments, which the company paid. Subsequently the Commissioners ascertained that the estimated assessments were inadequate, and imposed penalties under what is now *VATA 1994, s 63(1)(b)*. The company appealed, contending that it had a reasonable excuse because its bookkeeper had suffered from prolonged illness. The tribunal dismissed the appeal, holding that in view of the prolonged nature of the bookkeeper's illness, the company should have taken steps to keep its affairs up to date. *Social Workline Ltd*, LON/92/2746P (VTD 10351). (*Note*. Appeals against default surcharges were also dismissed.)

[52.19] A company failed to submit a number of returns and the Commissioners imposed estimated assessments which subsequently transpired to be inadequate. They therefore imposed penalties under *VATA 1994, s 63(1)(b)*. The company appealed, contending that the penalties should be waived because the Commissioners should have exercised their discretion not to impose them. The tribunal dismissed the appeal, applying *dicta* of Judge J in *Dollar Land (Feltham) Ltd*, **18.622** DEFAULT SURCHARGE. *Dicksmith Properties Ltd*, LON/94/1789P (VTD 13136).

[52.20] The Commissioners did not receive a company's return for the period ending August 1995, and issued an estimated assessment charging tax of £958.

Subsequently they discovered that the company's tax liability for that period had been more than £39,000. They imposed a penalty under *VATA 1994, s 63(1)(b)*. The company appealed, contending that it had a reasonable excuse because it had posted the return in question. The tribunal rejected this contention and dismissed the appeal, finding on the evidence that the company's postal arrangements were 'casual and inefficient' and, on the balance of probabilities, the return had never been posted. Accordingly there was no reasonable excuse. *Yorkshire Rural Investments Ltd*, MAN/96/614 (VTD 15083).

[52.21] Appeals against penalties under what is now *VATA 1994, s 63(1)(b)* were also dismissed in *TR Cawthorne*, LON/91/2249Z (VTD 7877); *PRG Whatling*, LON/92/1435P (VTD 9322); *JR Bridges (t/a Plastering Contractors Ltd)*, LON/91/2490P (VTD 9653); *Davies & Davies Ltd*, LON/92/444Z (VTD 9692); *JE Hewitt*, MAN/92/128 (VTD 9910); *J Eftekhari*, MAN/91/1448 (VTD 10271); *ACP Technical Services Ltd*, MAN/92/131 (VTD 10332); *Apex Denim & Fabric Finishers*, MAN/93/166 (VTD 10989); *Systemplay Ltd*, MAN/93/325 (VTD 11030); *A Ansari (t/a Northside House Hotel)*, LON/93/735 (VTD 11093); *KRG Designs Ltd*, MAN/93/307 (VTD 11348); *A Mohammed*, EDN/97/199 (VTD 15438); *K & A Uddin (t/a Sangam Balti House)*, MAN/99/254 (VTD 16337); *Aura Trading Ltd*, MAN/99/912 (VTD 16534); *Wilson Boyle (Development) Ltd*, EDN/00/119 (VTD 17029); *S Miah (t/a Agra Indian Restaurant)*, MAN/01/208 (VTD 17450); *SS & AK Nagra*, MAN/06/347 (VTD 19849); *J Saunders-Pederson (t/a Advanced Information Systems UK)*, **52.430** below, and *Citistar (UK) Ltd*, **52.431** below.

[52.22] For a case involving the acceptance of an inadequate estimated assessment, where a penalty was imposed under *VATA 1994, s 60* rather than *VATA 1994, s 63(1)(b)*, see *Storey*, **50.87** PENALTIES: EVASION OF TAX.

Penalty under FA 2007, Sch 24 para 2

[52.23] A company (L) submitted five returns after the due date, and HMRC issued estimated assessments which were less than L's true liability. When HMRC discovered this, they imposed penalties under *FA 2007, Sch 24*. The penalties were mitigated by 75% in respect of the first two periods, by 40% in respect of the next two periods, and by 30% in respect of the final period. The tribunal dismissed L's appeal against the penalties. *Littlemoss Preservation Ltd v HMRC*, [2011] UKFTT 692 (TC), TC01534. (*Note*. For another issue in this case, see **18.349** DEFAULT SURCHARGE.)

Definition of 'tax which would have been lost' (VATA 1994, s 63(2))

Whether tax 'lost'

[52.24] In the case noted at **52.34** below, a company contended that the penalty was invalid because the tax in respect of which it had been imposed had been only temporarily lost to the Commissioners, since its auditors would have discovered the error in due course. The tribunal rejected this contention, applying the principles laid down in *Knight v CIR*, CA [1974] STC 156 and *R v Holborn Commrs (ex p. Rind Settlement Trustees)*, QB [1974] STC 567, and holding that 'tax lost' could include 'tax delayed'. *Fritz Bender Metals (UK) Ltd*, [1991] VATTR 80 (VTD 5426).

[52.25] A partnership failed to account for output tax of £2,400, and the Commissioners imposed a misdeclaration penalty. The partnership appealed, contending that the tax in question had not been 'lost' since it would have been declared in its next return. The tribunal rejected this contention and dismissed the appeal, applying *dicta* of Lord Widgery in *R v Holborn Commrs (ex p. Rind Settlement Trustees)*, QB [1974] STC 567 (TTC 6.5). *A Oliver & Sons*, EDN/90/180 (VTD 5953).

[52.26] Similar decisions were reached in *Pursol Ltd*, EDN/90/188 (VTD 5721); *ACC American Car Centre Ltd*, LON/90/1847Y (VTD 5883); *Livebrace Ltd*, MAN/90/973 (VTD 5957); *Swithland Motors plc*, MAN/90/943 (VTD 6125); *BES Holdings Ltd*, LON/91/559Y (VTD 6405); *Blue Boar Computers Ltd*, LON/91/997 (VTD 6416); *Poloco SA*, LON/91/929 (VTD 6565) and *Sweetmate Ltd*, LON/90/1667Y (VTD 6676).

Whether return corrected by subsequent return (VATA 1994, s 63(8))

Corrected return sent after error discovered by VAT officer

[52.27] A company submitted a return for the period ending 30 June 1990 which included a misdeclaration attributable to a clerical error. The return was received by the VAT Central Unit on 17 July 1990, and the error was discovered almost immediately by a VAT officer on a control visit. Following the visit, the company's director sent a replacement return which corrected the original return. The Commissioners imposed a misdeclaration penalty and the company appealed, contending that the first return should be treated as having been superseded by the second return. The tribunal dismissed the appeal, holding that the initial misdeclaration could not be rendered ineffective by sending an amended return after the error had been discovered. *Masterscore Ltd*, MAN/90/746 (VTD 5611).

[52.28] Similar decisions were reached in *PCC (Agriculture) Ltd*, MAN/91/585 (VTD 9034); *Stalwart Environmental Services Ltd*, 52.50 below, and *Ridgeway*, 52.88 below.

[52.29] A similar decision was reached in a subsequent case where a return for the period ending October 1990 contained a duplication of input tax, and a VAT officer discovered this at a control visit on 27 November. On 28 November the company submitted a corrected return by fax to the VAT Central Unit. (The company had not informed either the Central Unit or the VAT officer that it proposed to do this.) The Commissioners imposed a misdeclaration penalty, and the tribunal dismissed the company's appeal, holding that the original incorrect return 'did not cease to be a return on a further return being submitted'. *Oddbins Ltd*, LON/91/648Y (VTD 9011).

[52.30] A company submitted a return for the period ending 30 June 1990 in which it reclaimed input tax in respect of an invoice issued in March 1990, which had already been included in its previous return. The error was discovered at a control visit on 31 July 1990. The officer conducting the visit warned the company that a misdeclaration penalty would arise. The company's managing director telephoned the VAT Central Unit, stating that an error had been discovered but not stating that a control visit was in progress, and arranged to send a corrected return by fax. Nevertheless, the Commissioners imposed a penalty in respect of the original return. The company appealed, contending that the amended return should be treated as correcting the original return. The tribunal allowed the company's appeal, holding that 'in the circumstances the Commissioners are estopped from treating the original return as valid'. The tribunal observed that where 'the Commissioners represent to a taxable person that they will give him the opportunity of formally declaring that a return which he has made is to be treated as ineffective, and the taxable person acts on the representation', there was 'nothing in law to prevent the representation from creating a binding estoppel, notwithstanding that the Commissioners thereafter refuse to give him the opportunity which they had promised him'. It followed that the original return should be treated as ineffective and that the faxed return should be treated as the effective return. *Masterscore Ltd*, 52.27 above, was distinguished on the grounds that in that case there had been no such arrangement between the company and the VAT Central Unit as had occurred in the instant case. *AB Gee of Ripley Ltd*, [1991] VATTR 217 (VTD 5948). (*Note.* For cases concerning estoppel, see **2.109** to **2.121** APPEALS.)

Whether a 'reasonable excuse' (VATA 1994, s 63(10)(a))

Clerical errors

Cases where the appellant was successful

Misdeclaration following malfunction of computer

[52.31] A company submitted a VAT return for April 1990 in which it claimed a repayment of more than £114,000. A VAT officer visited the company and discovered that it had included input tax of £70,653 relating to invoices for services supplied in May. Customs therefore imposed a penalty. The company appealed, contending that the error followed the installation of a new computer on 1 April. The company's accounts manager had been absent on study leave for two weeks in early May, and his assistant had been absent unexpectedly on sick leave for three weeks at the same time. On their return they faced a backlog of work and did not notice that, because of a fault in programming the computer, the printout from which they prepared the April return included a large number of invoices relating to May. The tribunal allowed the appeal, holding that, applying the standpoint of 'a reasonable conscientious businessman', there was a reasonable excuse for the misdeclaration. *Appropriate Technology Ltd*, [1991] VATTR 226 (VTD 5696).

[52.32] The decision in *Appropriate Technology Ltd*, **52.31** above, was applied in the similar cases of *Zonner Industries Ltd*, LON/90/1722Y (VTD 6031); *JJH (Building Developments) Ltd*, LON/91/649Y (VTD 6651); *Hare Wines Ltd*, LON/91/1376Z (VTD 6721); *Arco British Ltd*, LON/91/1406 (VTD 7041); *Holmen Paper AB*, LON/91/2379X (VTD 7628); *Thanet District Council*, LON/92/770Z (VTD 9308) and *Godiva Bearings (Southern) Ltd*, LON/92/2172 (VTD 9778). (*Note.* For cases where the malfunction of a computer was held not to be a reasonable excuse, see **52.57** and **52.58** below.)

[52.33] Computer malfunction was also held to constitute a reasonable excuse for a misdeclaration in *Warehouse & Interior Design Ltd*, LON/90/1718X (VTD 5893); *Trident Exhibitions Ltd*, LON/90/1912Z (VTD 6028); *J & V Printing Services Ltd*, MAN/91/5 (VTD 6136); *Good Marriott & Hursthouse Ltd*, MAN/91/553 (VTD 6633); *F Hurley & Sons Ltd*, LON/91/1056X (VTD 6719); *The Midland Repetition Co Ltd*, MAN/91/57 (VTD 6869); *Peter Turner Associates*, LON/91/1438 (VTD 6896) and *JC Merrett (Builders) Ltd*, LON/92/83 (VTD 10279).

Company bookkeeper receiving medication

[52.34] A company submitted an incorrect return, in which the amount of output tax in Box 1 was understated by £17,175 and the amount of input tax in Box 2 was overstated by £20,000. Customs discovered the error at a control visit, and imposed a penalty. The company appealed, contending that the errors were clerical errors by its bookkeeper, who had been receiving medication for high blood pressure, which had caused side-effects of lethargy, fatigue and decreased concentration. The company had not been aware that the bookkeeper was receiving medical treatment until after the errors had been discovered. The tribunal allowed the company's appeal, holding that although reliance on a bookkeeper could not of itself constitute a reasonable excuse, the tribunal was entitled to examine the reason for the bookkeeper's errors. On the evidence, 'the mistakes from which the inaccuracy resulted were caused by the drugs as opposed to simple human error'. *Fritz Bender Metals (UK) Ltd*, [1991] VATTR 80 (VTD 5426). (*Note.* For another issue in this case, see **52.24** above.)

[52.35] The decision in *Fritz Bender Metals (UK) Ltd*, **52.34** above, was applied in the similar cases of *Tecnomare (UK) Ltd*, LON/91/732Y (VTD 6329); *Hayter Brothers Ltd*, LON/91/2581X (VTD 9378) and *Timark Warehousing Ltd*, MAN/92/1127 (VTD 10360).

[52.36] Similar decisions were reached in *Peter Scott (Printers) Ltd*, MAN/91/552 (VTD 6356) and *K Malin*, LON/91/2015X (VTD 7623).

Appellant partly blind

[52.37] An appeal was allowed in a case where a man who was visually handicapped had gone into business as a retailer, but the business had been unsuccessful and had closed after five months, and both the VAT returns which he had submitted had contained clerical errors. The tribunal held that the circumstances constituted a reasonable excuse. *S Lancaster*, LON/92/1288P (VTD 9261).

Illness of appellant

[52.38] An appeal was allowed in a case where a sole trader gave evidence that he was recovering from a heart bypass operation at the time when he submitted a return which underdeclared output tax, and that he would have noticed the error had it not been for his ill-health. The tribunal held that the circumstances constituted a reasonable excuse. *RL Curley (t/a Scan Print Services)*, LON/93/233P (VTD 10691).

Illness of employee

[52.39] The illness of the employee responsible for the submission of the relevant return was held to constitute a reasonable excuse for a misdeclaration in *Kenkay Ltd*, LON/91/1480X (VTD 6923); *Anti-Sonics Ltd*, MAN/91/218 (VTD 7196); *A & M Insulations Ltd*, MAN/91/839 (VTD 7498); *Wright & Son (Building Contractors) Ltd*, MAN/91/1652 (VTD 10055); *Southcombe Brothers Ltd*, LON/91/745Z (VTD 10151); *JH Palmer & Sons*, LON/92/2470P (VTD 10230); *Guardian Building Services*, MAN/91/1060 (VTD 11050); *AOC International Ltd*, EDN/93/31 (VTD 11139); *Artistic Ironworkers Supplies Ltd*, MAN/93/502 (VTD 11228); *Allman Holdings Ltd*, LON/93/1694 (VTD 11285) and *Food Engineering Ltd*, 52.454 below.

Illness of employee—clerical error by inexperienced substitute

[52.40] A company submitted a return in which it overclaimed input tax. Customs imposed a misdeclaration penalty. The company appealed, contending that at the time the return was submitted, its bookkeeper had been unable to work for two weeks through illness, and the employee who prepared the return in her place had inadvertently carried forward input tax from the previous period. The tribunal allowed the company's appeal, holding that the circumstances constituted a reasonable excuse. *Draxtech Ltd*, LON/91/962X (VTD 6432).

[52.41] Similar decisions were reached in *Robeda Ltd*, LON/91/1435Z (VTD 7781); *Burley Estates Ltd*, LON/92/30X (VTD 7937); *HA & DB Kitchin Ltd*, LON/92/1410P (VTD 9513) and *Alan Franks Group*, MAN/92/211 (VTD 10146).

Death of employee

[52.42] A company's bookkeeper died in March 1990. A replacement was appointed, and prepared the company's returns for the periods ending June and September 1990. However, in the September return, the new bookkeeper reclaimed input tax on an invoice which had already been included in the June return. Customs imposed a misdeclaration penalty. The tribunal allowed the company's appeal, holding that the disruption caused by the bookkeeper's death constituted a reasonable excuse. *Coxhill Electronics Ltd*, LON/91/675 (VTD 6433).

[52.43] Similar decisions were reached in *Charnwood Holdings Ltd*, LON/91/276 (VTD 7056) and *Communications Consultants Ltd*, LON/91/2526X (VTD 8973).

Change of bookkeeper

[52.44] An appeal was allowed in a case where a company had changed its bookkeeper shortly before the due date of a return, and attributed an error in dealing with management charges to the fact that the new bookkeeper had found her predecessor's working papers 'impossible to follow'. The tribunal held that the circumstances constituted a reasonable excuse. *Stanhope Properties plc*, LON/91/1539X (VTD 6971).

[52.45] A change of bookkeeper was also held to constitute a reasonable excuse for a misdeclaration in *C Maguire (t/a TC Autos)*, BEL/90/47X (VTD 7056) and *Standen Ltd*, LON/93/669 (VTD 10785).

Bereavement of employee

[52.46] A company appealed against a misdeclaration penalty, contending that it had a reasonable excuse because the employee responsible for the return had suffered from a bereavement shortly before completing the return. The tribunal allowed the appeal, holding that the circumstances constituted a reasonable excuse. *Danish Firma Center plc*, LON/91/442Z (VTD 6196).

Terminal illness of partner's father

[52.47] A married couple carried on business in partnership. The wife was responsible for the completion of the VAT returns. She submitted a return in which she overclaimed input tax, and Customs imposed a misdeclaration penalty. The partners appealed, contending that the wife had been suffering from severe strain because her father was terminally ill. The tribunal allowed the appeal, holding that this constituted a reasonable excuse. *ED & M Middleton*, MAN/91/33 (VTD 6208).

Exceptional workload

[52.48] A company carried on business as travel agents. It decided to change its trading name after a large agency with a similar name went into liquidation with adverse publicity. The change of the company's trading name necessitated considerable extra work. During this period the company submitted a VAT return in which it reclaimed input tax on invoices made out to an associated company. Customs imposed a misdeclaration penalty, but the tribunal allowed the company's appeal, holding that the 'sudden and disconcerting pressure' of additional work constituted a reasonable excuse. *Zenith Holdings Ltd*, LON/90/884Z (VTD 6032).

[52.49] There have been a small number of other cases in which exceptional pressure of work has been held to constitute a reasonable excuse for a misdeclaration. In the interests of space, such cases have not been summarised individually in this book. For a list of such cases decided up to 31 December 1996, see Tolley's VAT Cases 1997.

Contract with local authority—lack of co-operation by local authority staff

[52.50] In October 1990 a company which carried on a refuse collection business entered into a contract with Harrow Borough Council. Under the contract, the Council would pay it each month in arrear, and the company agreed not to issue invoices until the work done had been valued. Many of the Council staff objected to the refuse collection being carried out by a private company, so that the procedures for valuing the work fell behind schedule. The company's general manager advised its accountant that it was unlikely to issue any invoices for its return period ending November 1990. On 6 December, the accountant submitted a return showing no output tax due. However, despite the statement made by the manager, the company did issue an invoice at the end of November. A VAT officer discovered this at a control visit on 21 December and drew it to the attention of the accountant, who issued a corrected return with a cheque for the VAT payable. Customs imposed a misdeclaration penalty, but the tribunal allowed the company's appeal, holding that, in view of the lack of co-operation the company had suffered from the Council's staff, the circumstances constituted a reasonable excuse. *Stalwart Environmental Services Ltd*, LON/91/791Y (VTD 7179). (*Note.* The tribunal rejected an alternative contention by the company that the penalty should be discharged by virtue of what is now *VATA 1994, s 63(8)*—see **52.28** above.)

Isolated clerical error

[52.51] There have been a number of cases in which an isolated clerical error has been held to constitute a reasonable excuse. In the interests of space, such cases are not summarised individually in this book. For a list of such cases decided up to 31 December 1996, see Tolley's VAT Cases 1997.

Misreading of dates on return form

[52.52] An appeal was allowed in a case where a company's first return was issued for the period ending 30 November 1990, with a due date of 31 December 1990, but the company's controlling director included its transactions for December 1990 and stated in evidence that he had misread the return. *GC Parts Ltd*, LON/91/2248Z (VTD 7545).

Mistaken belief that underdeclaration corrected by subsequent assessment

[52.53] In July 1990 a VAT officer made a control visit to a company and discovered that certain sales had been omitted from its returns. He issued an assessment to recover the tax due for the period omitted from the return for the period ending March 1990. The company paid the tax charged. In June 1991 a second control visit took place by a different officer, who discovered that some sales had been omitted from the company's return for the period ending June 1990. Customs imposed a penalty and the company appealed, contending that it had a reasonable excuse because its directors had assumed that the errors had been included in the assessment which had been issued following the previous control visit. The tribunal allowed the appeal, holding that the fact that the officer had seen the June 1990 records at the July 1990 visit made it reasonable for the company to have assumed that the errors in the June 1990 return would have been corrected by the assessment issued immediately afterwards. *People Products Ltd*, MAN/91/1080 (VTD 7379).

Duplicate invoices issued by contractor

[52.54] In a case where a contractor issued duplicate invoices in respect of the same transaction, and the customer reclaimed input tax in respect of both invoices, the tribunal held that the circumstances constituted a reasonable excuse. *WH Clarkson & Son*, MAN/91/1564 (VTD 7479). (*Note.* Compare *McLaughlin*, 52.77 below, in which the receipt of duplicate invoices was held not to be a reasonable excuse.)

[52.55] A similar decision was reached in *Manchester Young Men's Christian Association*, MAN/91/255 (VTD 9215).

Duplicate payment made to contractor

[52.56] In October 1990 a district council made two payments to one contractor in respect of the same invoice. The contractor only banked one of the cheques, and returned the duplicate cheque in early November. However, in its October VAT return the council reclaimed input tax in respect of both cheques. When the Commissioners discovered this, they imposed a misdeclaration penalty. The tribunal allowed the council's appeal, holding that since the council had actually issued two cheques there was a reasonable excuse for the misdeclaration. *Vale of White Horse District Council*, LON/91/587Y (VTD 6924).

Cases where the appellant was unsuccessful

Reliance on computer

[52.57] The Commissioners imposed a misdeclaration penalty on a firm which had underdeclared its output tax by £4,606. The firm appealed, contending that it had a reasonable excuse because its computer had failed to account for VAT on sales at one of the firm's shops. The tribunal dismissed the firm's appeal, holding that what is now *VATA 1994, s 71(1)(b)* precluded reliance on a computer programmer from constituting a reasonable excuse. *City Cycles*, EDN/90/199 (VTD 5699).

[52.58] Computer errors were also held not to constitute a reasonable excuse in *Cheyne Motors Ltd*, LON/90/1799 (VTD 5854); *London Borough of Camden*, LON/90/1592X (VTD 6123); *Bristol Street Motors (Bromley) Ltd*, LON/91/153 (VTD 6381); *Blyth Valley Borough Council*, MAN/91/414 (VTD 6417); *Hancock & Wood Ltd*, MAN/91/544 (VTD 6691); *PJ Hall*, LON/90/1892X (VTD 6722); *Spelthorne Borough Council*, LON/91/1475X (VTD 6958); *Kubota (UK) Ltd*, LON/90/1309Y (VTD 6960); *Campus Martius Ltd*, MAN/91/756 (VTD 7199); *Jordans Plumbing Merchants Ltd*, LON/91/1817 (VTD 7822); *Apple Contractors (Northern) Ltd*, MAN/91/1264 (VTD 7853); *JMD Group plc*, LON/92/483X (VTD 9129); *Bruce Miller & Co*, EDN/92/158 (VTD 9402); *NS Dajani (t/a Lancashire Marketing Consultants)*, MAN/92/1701 (VTD 10861) and *Dunelm (Castle Homes) Ltd*, 52.410 below.

Clerical error by bookkeeper

[52.59] The Commissioners imposed a misdeclaration penalty on a borough council which had claimed a repayment of VAT for April 1990 which exceeded the amount actually due by more than £50,000, as a result of a clerical error by a member of staff who had accidentally included on the return the input tax relating to the first two weeks in May. The tribunal dismissed the council's appeal, holding that, although the error was a 'mere accident', it did not constitute a reasonable excuse. *Taunton Deane Borough Council*, LON/90/1225Z (VTD 5545). (*Note.* For another issue in this case, see **52.377** below.)

[52.60] The decision in *Taunton Deane Borough Council*, **52.59** above, was applied in the similar cases of *EA Chiverton Ltd*, LON/90/1397 (VTD 6130); *Whitehead & Wood Ltd*, MAN/91/232 (VTD 6341); *Waterlink Distribution Ltd*, LON/91/2611X (VTD 7913) and *Tong Garden Centre plc*, MAN/93/1056 (VTD 12103).

[52.61] A company failed to charge VAT on an invoice of £39,060. The error was discovered on a control visit after the company had claimed a repayment of more than £10,000. The Commissioners imposed a misdeclaration penalty and the company appealed, contending that it had a reasonable excuse because its bookkeeper had accidentally forgotten to include any VAT on the invoice. The tribunal dismissed the company's appeal, holding that what is now *VATA 1994, s 71(1)* prevented this from being a reasonable excuse. *Victoria Alloys (UK) Ltd*, [1991] VATTR 163 (VTD 5608).

[52.62] A similar decision was reached in *Scanland Agencies Ltd*, MAN/91/37 (VTD 6648).

[52.63] The decision in *Victoria Alloys (UK) Ltd*, **52.61** above, was applied in a subsequent case where the tribunal held that there was no reasonable excuse for a clerical error which caused a company to claim a repayment of £173,000 when the correct figure was £18,000. *Cavendish Constructors plc*, LON/91/5901 (VTD 6957).

[52.64] A police authority submitted a VAT return claiming a repayment of tax. The return included a claim for input tax of £104,204 in respect of a cheque made payable to British Telecom. However, the cheque had been cancelled and a replacement issued for a slightly smaller amount. The tax of £97,257 included in the second cheque was also included on the return, which therefore overclaimed input tax by £104,204. The Commissioners discovered the error on a control visit, and imposed a misdeclaration penalty. The authority appealed, contending that the inclusion of the amount of the first cheque in the return was a clerical error by one of its staff. The tribunal dismissed the appeal. The chairman stated that he was 'amazed that the authority adopted a system which allowed such an elementary mistake to pass undetected at the time of origin'. The management 'was aware of the frailty of the system yet it allowed the verification procedure to be given a low priority'. The authority's chief accountant had 'been aware of certain problems for several months yet a simple weekly check was not performed'. The circumstances did not constitute a reasonable excuse for the error. *Merseyside Police Authority*, [1991] VATTR 152 (VTD 5654).

[52.65] In July 1989 a borough council, which submitted monthly returns, sought permission from the Commissioners to estimate part of its deductible input tax. The Commissioners agreed to this request, and allowed the council to reclaim an estimated amount of £123,000 in its next return. In December the Commissioners wrote to the Council again, requesting it to review the figure of £123,000, which it had continued to carry forward as an estimated credit, and ascertain the average amount of input tax due for the previous six months. The council's accountant computed this average as £113,000. In the return for January 1990 she claimed estimated input tax of £113,000 accordingly, but also continued to claim credit for the original estimate of £123,000. The VAT office discovered the error and explained the position. The next three returns were computed on an acceptable basis, but in the May 1990 return the council's accountant again claimed credit for a cumulative figure of two months' input tax. The Commissioners imposed a misdeclaration penalty. The council appealed, contending that the complexity of the estimation procedure, and pressure of work caused by the introduction of the community charge (or 'poll tax'), constituted a reasonable excuse. The tribunal dismissed the council's appeal. On the evidence, the system had been explained to the council's accountant after the detection of the error in the January return, and subsequent returns had been correctly completed. It should have been clear to the accountant, or to her supervisors, that the May return was incorrect. Pressure of work might, in certain circumstances, excuse 'minor clerical errors', but it could not excuse a fundamental error of the type which had occurred in this case. *Havant Borough Council*, LON/90/1360Y (VTD 6080).

[52.66] A company submitted a return in which it overstated its input tax by £37,000, so that it claimed a repayment of £30,000 instead of declaring a liability of £7,000. The Commissioners imposed a misdeclaration penalty and the company appealed, contending that it had a reasonable excuse because the return had been completed by an inexperienced member of staff who had only been employed for one month, and the company secretary had been too busy to check the return. The tribunal dismissed the appeal, holding that what is now *VATA 1994, s 71(1)(b)* 'applies equally to the maker of the original mistake, the compiler of the return, and anyone whose job it may have been to check the figures'. The QB upheld this decision. The fact that a mistake had been made by an employee need not prevent the tribunal from looking behind the fact of the mistake to the reason for the mistake, applying the principle laid down in *Salevon Ltd*, **18.312** DEFAULT SURCHARGE. However, on the evidence here, the misdeclaration arose from a simple human error which could have been discovered if the figures had been checked. The unavoidable conclusion was that there was no reasonable excuse for the misdeclaration. *Frank Galliers Ltd v C & E Commrs*, QB 1992, [1993] STC 284.

[52.67] There are a very large number of other cases in which clerical errors by bookkeepers or employees have been held not to constitute a reasonable excuse. In the interests of space, such cases are not listed individually in this book. For a list of such cases decided up to 31 December 1993, see Tolley's VAT Cases 1994.

Absence of employee through illness

[52.68] See *South Caernarvon Creameries Ltd*, **52.122** below.

Clerical error by accountant

[52.69] Clerical errors by accountants were held not to constitute a reasonable excuse in *Elanders (UK) Ltd*, MAN/91/63 (VTD 6137); *W Mayne-Flower*, MAN/91/641 (VTD 6513); *Progenitive Chemicals Ltd*, EDN/91/171 (VTD 6591); *Americana Europe Ltd*, EDN/91/232 (VTD 6712); *Imagebase Technology Ltd*, LON/91/1230Z (VTD 6720); *Golden Cloud Solarium*, LON/91/1110Z (VTD 6761); *KM Muir (t/a Ken Muir Nurseries)*, LON/91/1611Z (VTD 6830); *Shoot Super Soccer Ltd*, EDN/91/90 (VTD 6882); *Holman Kelly Paper Co Ltd*, LON/91/951Z (VTD 6899); *Broadside Colours & Chemicals Ltd*, MAN/91/807 (VTD 6994); *JE Smallman*, MAN/91/58 (VTD 7228); *Lam Watson & Woods*, LON/91/2001 (VTD 7307); *Resincrest Ltd*, LON/91/2168X (VTD 7310); *Bidco Impex Ltd*, MAN/91/540 (VTD 7406); *D Carey*, LON/91/2393 (VTD 7619); *R Caira (t/a The Ambassador Leisure Club)*, EDN/91/130 (VTD 7625); *Coller Paper Co Ltd*, LON/92/60X (VTD 7890); *R Eggleton*, LON/92/546X (VTD 7932); *RG Francis*, LON/92/596Z (VTD 9063); *Pet-Reks Southern Ltd*, LON/92/1364P (VTD 9070); *Boz Ltd*, LON/92/1520P (VTD 9353); *Eversleigh Investments & Property Co Ltd*, LON/92/1784 (VTD 9646); *Gleeds Chartered Quantity Surveyors*, LON/92/2219P (VTD 9770, 10069); *Tex Holdings plc*, LON/92/3117 (VTD 10416); *MBS Rüter Fassadenbau GmbH*, LON/92/3258P (VTD 10472) and *AB Transport*, MAN/94/53 (VTD 12481).

[52.70] A shopkeeper was sentenced to a term of imprisonment in January 1991. His accountant submitted his VAT return for the period ending 31 December 1990. The return overclaimed input tax, and the Commissioners imposed a misdeclaration penalty. The shopkeeper appealed, contending that he had a reasonable excuse because he would have been able to check the return had it not been for his imprisonment. The tribunal dismissed the appeal, holding that what is now *VATA 1994, s 71(1)(b)* precluded the circumstances from constituting a reasonable excuse. *AJ Whitehead*, MAN/92/1468 (VTD 10696).

Clerical error by director

[52.71] A company reclaimed input tax twice in respect of the same transaction, and the Commissioners imposed a misdeclaration penalty. The company appealed, contending that this was an innocent clerical error by a director. The tribunal dismissed the appeal, holding that an innocent mistake could not of itself constitute a reasonable excuse without further extenuating circumstances. *M Holt (Manchester) Ltd*, MAN/91/6 (VTD 6312).

[52.72] Clerical errors by directors were also held not to constitute a reasonable excuse in *Turmeaus Ltd*, MAN/90/969 (VTD 6052); *Integrated Furniture System Ltd*, LON/91/421 (VTD 6549); *Landowner Liquid Fertilisers Ltd*, MAN/91/615 (VTD 6692); *The Art Store (British Isles) Ltd*, MAN/91/1094 (VTD 6938); *Duvan Estates Ltd*, LON/91/804 (VTD 7040) *Geoffery Clarke Grain Co Ltd*, LON/91/1251Z (VTD 7142); *Morgan Brothers (Mid-Wales) Ltd*, MAN/91/1247 (VTD 8913); *Bornfleet Forwarding Ltd*, LON/92/1509P (VTD 9704); *Fast Technology Ltd*, LON/92/2114A (VTD 9974); *School Book Fairs (GB) Ltd*, LON/93/422P (VTD 10553); *D & M Electro Plating Ltd*, MAN/92/1421 (VTD 10966); *AG Tisdall & Co Ltd*, LON/93/1914P (VTD 11521) and *Manyee UK Ltd*, **52.437** below.

Deliberate clerical error by managing director suffering from illness

[52.73] The Commissioners discovered that a company had failed to account for VAT of more than £30,000 in respect of the sale of property, although the amount had been paid by the customer. The amount in question had been paid into an account in the names of the managing director and his wife, rather than into the company account. The Commissioners imposed a misdeclaration penalty and the company appealed, contending that it had a reasonable excuse because the managing director had been ill at the relevant time. The tribunal dismissed the appeal, observing that 'there was a deliberate understatement of outputs' and that 'no taxpayer who had a responsible attitude to his duties as a taxpayer, and who conscientiously sought to ensure that his returns were accurate, would make a deliberate understatement of outputs'. *Amspray Ltd (t/a Champion Tools & Supplies)*, MAN/93/225 (VTD 10888).

Clerical error by partner

[52.74] Clerical errors by partners were held not to constitute a reasonable excuse in *Messrs WB Erskine*, EDN/91/136 (VTD 6310); *The Main Pine Company*, MAN/91/305 (VTD 6384); *RWJB & GH Pryce*, BEL/91/4 (VTD 6398); *Sutton Kitchens*, LON/91/2147Y (VTD 7432); *Good Roofing (Devon)*, LON/91/2414Y (VTD 7845); *Tudor Hotel & Restaurant*, MAN/92/554 (VTD 9683); *A & M Soni*, MAN/92/938 (VTD 9919) and *JW & MJ Whitefield & AJ & JA Osbourne*, LON/93/714P (VTD 10926).

Clerical error by appellant

[52.75] Clerical errors by the appellant were held not to constitute a reasonable excuse in *D Malloch*, EDN/91/22 (VTD 5811); *A Frost*, EDN/90/216 (VTD 5813); *J Doherty*, LON/91/28X (VTD 6609); *RJ Bird*, LON/91/37X (VTD 6715); *GM Harris*, LON/92/851Y (VTD 9069); *GF Bateman*, MAN/91/1678 (VTD 9344); *KA Terry (t/a Advanced Laboratory Techniques)*, LON/92/2541P (VTD 9803); *M Bott (t/a Clothesline)*, EDN/92/225 (VTD 10267); *A Reid*, EDN/92/353 (VTD 10403) and *K Round (t/a Circle Interiors)*, MAN/93/203 (VTD 10844).

Marriage breakdown—whether excuse for clerical error in return

[52.76] A trader appealed against a penalty imposed in respect of a duplicated claim for input tax, contending that he had a reasonable excuse because he had been suffering from stress following the breakdown of his marriage. The tribunal dismissed his appeal, holding that this was not a reasonable excuse. *JD Pauline*, MAN/93/500 (VTD 11029).

Duplicate invoices issued by supplier

[52.77] In a case where an oil company issued duplicate invoices to a garage proprietor in respect of the same transaction, and the proprietor reclaimed input tax in respect of both invoices, the tribunal dismissed the proprietor's appeal, holding that the circumstances did not constitute a reasonable excuse. *R McLaughlin*, BEL/91/62 (VTD 7514).

Supplies to associated partnership—failure to account for tax

[52.78] An appeal was dismissed in a case where a company had failed to account for VAT on supplies to an associated partnership with a similar name, and contended that this was attributable to a clerical error. The tribunal held that the circumstances did not constitute a reasonable excuse. *Auto-Plas (International) Ltd*, LON/91/2350X (VTD 8860).

[52.79] See also *Michael Rogers Ltd*, 52.284 below.

Sale to associated company—failure to account for tax

[52.80] See *Precious Metal Industries (Wales) Ltd*, 52.282 below, and the cases noted at 52.283 below.

Misunderstanding of the time of supply

Cases where the appellant was successful

Input tax reclaimed prematurely

[52.81] A company reclaimed input tax on two proforma invoices. The tribunal held that the company had a reasonable excuse for believing that the date shown on the 'proforma' invoices was the time of supply. *Enterprise Safety Coaches Ltd*, [1991] VATTR 74 (VTD 5391). (*Note.* The reasoning in this case was disapproved by a subsequent tribunal in *GB Capital Ltd*, 52.344 below.)

[52.82] Similar decisions were reached in *Joe Pole Construction Co Ltd*, MAN/91/392 (VTD 7101); *Ford Fuels Ltd*, LON/91/20Y (VTD 7213) and *The Austin Company of UK Ltd*, LON/91/1990X (VTD 7981).

[52.83] A company arranged to purchase a coach under a leasing agreement. It reclaimed the whole of the input tax due under the agreement at the time when it made the first payment. The Commissioners imposed a misdeclaration penalty. The company appealed, contending that its bookkeeper had mistakenly treated the agreement as a hire-purchase agreement. The tribunal allowed the appeal, holding that the circumstances constituted a reasonable excuse. *Chartercoach Holidays Ltd*, LON/93/1464P (VTD 11193).

[52.84] A company reclaimed input tax on the basis of an architect's certificate dated 29 June 1990, although the contractor had not issued the relevant tax invoice until 2 July and the company had paid the amount due on 6 July. The Commissioners imposed a misdeclaration penalty but the tribunal held that the circumstances constituted a reasonable excuse. *The Clean Car Company Ltd*, [1991] VATTR 234 (VTD 5695).

[52.85] Similar decisions were reached in *Banbridge District Enterprises Ltd*, BEL/91/20X (VTD 6406); *Fielder & Sons (Enfield) Ltd*, LON/91/1647Z (VTD 7017); *Crosstyle plc*, LON/91/257Y (VTD 7169); *Sprowston Hall Hotel Ltd*, LON/91/255Y (VTD 7253); *Coventry Motors & Sundries Co Ltd*, MAN/91/104 (VTD 7378); *NCC Developments Ltd*, LON/91/2137X (VTD 7388) and *Mitchells of Hailsham Ltd*, LON/91/1806X (VTD 9862).

[52.86] A company reclaimed input tax on the basis of an application for payment dated 27 September, although the contractor did not issue a VAT invoice until 11 October. The tribunal held that the circumstances constituted a reasonable excuse. *TS International Freight Forwarders Ltd*, MAN/91/399 (VTD 7080).

[52.87] Similar decisions were reached in *Equiname Ltd*, MAN/91/609 (VTD 7592) and *Wyndley Nurseries Ltd*, MAN/91/970 (VTD 10269).

[52.88] A trader ordered, and paid for, some materials in June 1990. He reclaimed the input tax in his return for the period ending 30 June, although he had not yet received the materials or the invoice. The Commissioners imposed a misdeclaration penalty but the tribunal held that the trader had a reasonable excuse for the premature claim. *PJ Ridgeway*, MAN/90/664 (VTD 6140). (*Note.* For another issue in this case, see **52.28** above.)

[52.89] Similar decisions were reached in *Wisebeck Construction Ltd*, LON/91/1020Z (VTD 6612) and *M Farrey*, MAN/91/478 (VTD 6709).

[52.90] A company received a large quantity of fuel from Texaco on 28 September 1990 and reclaimed the relevant input tax in its return for the period ending 30 September, although Texaco had not issued the invoice until 4 October. The Commissioners imposed a misdeclaration penalty but the tribunal held that the circumstances constituted a reasonable excuse. *Croft Fuels Ltd*, MAN/91/630 (VTD 6644).

[52.91] Similar decisions were reached in *Jones Executive Coaches Ltd*, MAN/90/1110 (VTD 6870) and *Z Hussain (t/a Zabar Hosiery)*, MAN/91/634 (VTD 6895).

[52.92] An company trading as a car dealer entered into contracts in July 1990 for the delivery of some H-registration cars which could not legally be delivered until August. The company reclaimed the relevant input tax in the period ending 31 July. The tribunal held that it had a reasonable excuse for the premature claim. *Olympian Automotive Ltd*, LON/91/1048Z (VTD 7141).

[52.93] A trader agreed to purchase two tractors by four annual instalments. He received an invoice for the 1990 instalment in April and reclaimed the relevant input tax in his return for that period, although he did not pay the invoice until September. The tribunal held that there was a reasonable excuse for the premature claim. *MR Hampden-Smith*, LON/91/790 (VTD 7468).

[52.94] In the case noted at **40.80** INVOICES AND CREDIT NOTES, a company reclaimed input tax in respect of a payment made to a supplier which went into liquidation shortly afterwards without supplying either the goods paid for or an invoice for them. The tribunal held that there was a reasonable excuse for the misdeclaration. *Newland Technical Services Ltd*, LON/92/1255A (VTD 9294). (*Note.* For another issue in this case, see **36.330** INPUT TAX.)

[52.95] A similar decision was reached in *Ham Enterprises Ltd*, EDN/06/66 (VTD 19908).

[52.96] A firm of solicitors paid its annual contributions to the Solicitors Indemnity Fund in two instalments, due on 1 September and 1 March. In August 1991 the Fund sent the firm an invoice for its 1991/92 contributions. The firm reclaimed input tax in respect of both instalments in its return for the period ending 31 August 1991. The Commissioners imposed a misdeclaration penalty, since, by virtue of what is now *VAT Regulations 1995 (SI 1995/2518), reg 90(2)*, the tax was not reclaimable until the due dates for payment. The tribunal held that there was a reasonable excuse for the premature claim. *The Simkins Partnership*, LON/92/1553 (VTD 9705).

[52.97] A trader who operated the Cash Accounting Scheme reclaimed input tax by reference to the dates on which he received invoices, rather than the dates on which he made payment. The Commissioners imposed a misdeclaration penalty but the tribunal held that the circumstances constituted a reasonable excuse. *BD Cake*, MAN/91/1068 (VTD 10272).

Imports—input tax reclaimed prematurely

[52.98] See the cases noted at **52.147** to **52.162** below.

Delay in reclaiming input tax

[52.99] An appeal was allowed in a case where a company had delayed reclaiming input tax on certain invoices until the end of its accounting year, although the invoices had been issued in previous accounting periods. *Color-lam Ltd*, LON/92/895Z (VTD 9412).

Misleading invoices issued by finance company

[52.100] A company leased two vehicles from a finance company. The invoices issued by the finance company included the total rental, including VAT, payable in respect of twelve monthly instalments from May 1990 to April 1991. The company reclaimed this total figure of VAT as input tax in its return for the period ending June 1990. The Commissioners imposed a penalty but the tribunal held that there was a reasonable excuse for the misdeclaration. *Wrights International Leather Ltd*, BEL/91/10 (VTD 6399).

Input tax reclaimed on supplies before registration

[52.101] A trader reclaimed input tax on supplies he had received before registration. The Commissioners imposed a misdeclaration penalty. The tribunal allowed the trader's appeal in part, observing that, under what is now *VAT Regulations 1995 (SI 1995/2518), reg 111*, the Commissioners had discretion to allow credit for input tax on supplies received before registration. *DW Wyck*, LON/91/845X (VTD 6619). (*Note.* For another issue in this case, see **52.342** below.)

Delay in accounting for output tax

[52.102] A company supplied goods to an associated company. It issued a single invoice, at the end of each accounting year, for the goods supplied in that year. The Commissioners imposed a misdeclaration penalty on the basis that the company should have accounted for tax at the time the goods were removed, as required by what is now *VATA 1994, s 6(2)*. The tribunal allowed the company's appeal, holding that the circumstances constituted a reasonable excuse. *Jamestown Concrete Co Ltd*, EDN/91/3 (VTD 5722).

[52.103] The decision in *Jamestown Concrete Co Ltd*, **52.102** above, was applied in the similar subsequent case of *KCT Holdings Ltd*, MAN/03/403 (VTD 18734B).

[52.104] A golf club professional (Q) accounted for VAT at the time when he received payment, rather than when he issued invoices. The Commissioners imposed a misdeclaration penalty but the tribunal held that Q had a reasonable excuse. *AD Quarterman*, MAN/90/1056 (VTD 6200).

[52.105] Similar decisions were reached in *Watson Norrie Ltd*, MAN/91/31 (VTD 6248); *Tal Ltd*, BEL/90/56X (VTD 6397); *The Parr Partnership*, EDN/91/177 (VTD 6733); *PT Garrett & Sons (Contractors) Ltd*, LON/91/1028X (VTD 7073); *H James Builders (Wolverhampton) Ltd*, MAN/91/213 (VTD 7102); *JC Lewis Partnership*, LON/91/1954X (VTD 7368); *Ryebank Heating Ltd*, MAN/91/1371 (VTD 7405); *Avonline Communications (Bristol) Ltd*, LON/90/1504X (VTD 9204); *V Brice*, LON/92/1387P (VTD 9721) and *P Zimmatore*, LON/92/1008A (VTD 10376).

[52.106] A partnership had a contract with a local council, which insisted upon paying the partnership in twelve monthly instalments. The partnership did not include the VAT in the invoices for the instalments, but, after receiving payment from the council, issued further invoices charging VAT on the amounts paid. The Commissioners imposed a penalty but the tribunal held that the circumstances constituted a reasonable excuse. *D & J Nuttall*, MAN/91/444 (VTD 6343).

[52.107] A contractor did not account for VAT on payments for work in progress. The Commissioners imposed a penalty but the tribunal held that there was a reasonable excuse for the misdeclaration. *RM Bridgeman (t/a Bridgeman Building & Public Works Contractors)*, LON/91/611 (VTD 6563).

[52.108] Similar decisions were reached in *Hill Welsh*, LON/91/1510 (VTD 6828); *A Kane*, LON/92/993X (VTD 9784); *McKean Smith & Co Ltd*, MAN/91/1151 (VTD 10334); *GN Mellor*, MAN/92/626 (VTD 10703) and *PH Hardwill*, LON/93/2582 (VTD 13958).

[52.109] A company (G) which submitted monthly returns contracted to sell 15 trailers to a customer. Nine of the trailers were delivered in August, but the delivery of the other six was delayed until 3 September. G declared the output tax in its September return. The Commissioners imposed a penalty on the basis that G should have accounted for tax on the first nine trailers in its August return. G appealed, contending that there had been a single contract to supply 15 trailers, so that it had assumed that the tax point was 3 September. The tribunal held that the circumstances constituted a reasonable excuse. *GB Express Ltd*, LON/91/1167Z (VTD 6822).

Failure to account for VAT at time of receipt of deposits

[52.110] A company which supplied interior furnishings did not account for VAT when it received deposits. The Commissioners imposed a misdeclaration penalty but the tribunal held that the company had a reasonable excuse, observing that *Notice No 700* stated that 'some types of deposit are not consideration for a supply and their receipt does not create a tax point'. *Colson & Kay Ltd*, MAN/91/59 (VTD 6148). (*Note.* For whether VAT is chargeable at the time a deposit is received, see the cases noted at **62.417** to **62.464** SUPPLY.)

[52.111] Similar decisions were reached in *Jelson Holdings Ltd*, MAN/91/551 (VTD 6682); *Mr & Mrs I Foster*, MAN/91/493 (VTD 6787); *Inspection Equipment Ltd*, LON/92/278X (VTD 10237); *Simplelink Ltd (t/a Homecare Exteriors)*, LON/93/801A (VTD 11593) and *Rivers Machinery Ltd*, **62.449** SUPPLY.

Advance payments—failure to account for tax

[52.112] A company was established to set up an indoor bowls centre. In order to finance the building of the centre, it offered life membership in return for a payment of £500. In its first VAT return, it did not account for output tax on such payments. The Commissioners imposed a misdeclaration penalty but the tribunal held that the circumstances constituted a reasonable excuse. *Bournemouth Indoor Bowls Centre Ltd*, LON/96/766 (VTD 14335B).

Continuous supplies of services—delay in accounting for tax

[52.113] A company (C) failed to account for tax on supplies to an associated company. Customs imposed a misdeclaration penalty (mitigated by 80%). C appealed. The tribunal allowed C's appeal, finding that the supplies appeared to be within *VAT Regulations 1995 (SI 1995/2518), reg 90(1)* and that there was 'some uncertainty as to whether the mere accrual of the charge gave rise to a VAT liability'. Accordingly the circumstances constituted a reasonable excuse. *Cater Clark Ltd*, LON/07/1059 (VTD 20546).

[52.114] See also *Pentex Oil Ltd*, **43.2** MANAGEMENT SERVICES; *Bishop & Knight Ltd*, **43.3** MANAGEMENT SERVICES, and *Halpern & Woolf*, **62.468** SUPPLY.

Continuous supplies of services—business transferred as going concern

[52.115] A company sold a holiday caravan park to a partnership as a going concern. The company had accounted for output tax on the site fees on a receipts basis, since it had been making continuous supplies of services. The partnership failed to account for output tax in respect of fees which had been due before the transfer but not collected until after the transfer. The Commissioners imposed a misdeclaration penalty but the tribunal held that the circumstances constituted a reasonable excuse. *Marine Caravan Park*, MAN/92/231 (VTD 12342).

Invoices issued prematurely and subsequently cancelled

[52.116] A company (S) carried on the business of servicing and repairing office equipment. Towards the end of the guarantee period of equipment it had supplied, it wrote to its customers offering to extend the guarantee for 12 months for a fixed sum, and enclosing invoices which included VAT. When customers did not respond to the letter, S telephoned them, and where the customer indicated that it did not wish to extend the guarantee, S treated the invoices as cancelled and did not account for output tax. The Commissioners imposed a misdeclaration penalty but the tribunal held that the circumstances constituted a reasonable excuse. *SET (Services) Ltd*, LON/91/2245Z (VTD 7420).

Application for payment not intended as tax invoice

[52.117] See *ABB Power Ltd*, **62.414** SUPPLY.

Cases where the appellant was unsuccessful

Input tax reclaimed prematurely

[52.118] A company (B) submitted a VAT return for May 1990 claiming a repayment of tax. The return included input tax relating to hire-purchase transactions. The goods which were the subject of the transactions were collected by B in May, but the hire-purchase company did not issue the VAT invoices until June. The Commissioners imposed a misdeclaration penalty, and the tribunal dismissed B's appeal. The time of supply for VAT purposes was in June 1990 when the invoices were issued, and the circumstances did not constitute a reasonable excuse. *Bulkhaul Ltd*, MAN/90/792 (VTD 5725).

[52.119] A company which owned a hotel incurred expenditure on reconstruction work. The work was completed in May 1990, but the contractor did not issue a VAT invoice until 13 June 1990. However, the company reclaimed the input tax shown on the invoice in its return for May 1990. The Commissioners imposed a misdeclaration penalty and the tribunal dismissed the company's appeal, holding that the circumstances did not constitute a reasonable excuse. *Cawley Hotels & Leisure Ltd*, EDN/90/213 (VTD 5812).

[52.120] A company reclaimed input tax in its return for the period ending 30 June 1990 in respect of construction work for which it held an architect's certificate dated June 1990, but the relevant VAT invoice was dated 16 July. When the Commissioners discovered this, they imposed a misdeclaration penalty. The tribunal dismissed the company's appeal. On the evidence, the company's bookkeeper had known that the sum in question could not be claimed as input tax 'unless it was supported by a tax invoice which had been issued during the relevant accounting period', but had failed to check whether the invoice had been issued at the appropriate time. *Pepis (Marina) Ltd*, MAN/91/794 (VTD 5879).

[52.121] Similar decisions were reached in *Breese Brick Ltd*, LON/90/1117X (VTD 6009) and *Robert S Monk Ltd*, 52.409 below.

[52.122] An appeal was dismissed in a case where a company had reclaimed input tax in respect of two documents described as 'proforma invoices', which were not VAT invoices. *South Caernarvon Creameries Ltd*, MAN/90/727 (VTD 6230). (*Note.* An alternative contention by the company, that it had a reasonable excuse because of the long-term illness of an employee who might have noticed the error, was also rejected.)

[52.123] Similar decisions were reached in *Kirklees Developments Ltd*, MAN/91/417 (VTD 6785); *Floris Merchandise Ltd*, MAN/91/496 (VTD 7437) and *Triton Properties Ltd*, LON/91/1168Z (VTD 7492).

[52.124] An appeal was dismissed in a case where a company reclaimed input tax in respect of an amount it had paid to a solicitor as a stakeholder. *Stonehills Television Ltd*, MAN/91/1516 (VTD 8993).

[52.125] There was also held to be no reasonable excuse for the premature reclaim of input tax in *Harrison Meillam Construction Ltd*, MAN/90/900 (VTD 5875); *ACH Transport Ltd*, LON/90/1475X (VTD 6006); *Farnglobe Ltd (t/a Tooto's The Club)*, LON/91/905X (VTD 6582); *CHA Ltd*,

LON/91/1044Z (VTD 6618); *B Mullan & Son (Contractors) Ltd*, BEL/91/58 (VTD 6833); *GPC Properties Ltd*, LON/91/342 (VTD 7044); *HJ Surgenor*, BEL/91/30X (VTD 7223); *Vedilux Ltd*, LON/91/1497Z (VTD 7252); *Springvale EPS Ltd*, BEL/91/67 (VTD 7421); *Walker Navigation*, MAN/91/1356 (VTD 7775); *Rouse Kent Ltd*, LON/91/1593X (VTD 8862); *Paradise Forum Ltd*, MAN/91/216 (VTD 8885); *Chartridge Construction Ltd*, LON/92/2043P (VTD 9449); *Brechin Motor Co Ltd*, EDN/92/228 (VTD 9525); *Pierre Leon Ltd*, LON/91/1180X (VTD 9794); *Tritin Ltd*, LON/91/1513Y (VTD 10254); *Simon Macczak Transport*, MAN/91/849 (VTD 10887) and *Armstrong*, 52.417 below.

Company operating Cash Accounting Scheme but reclaiming input tax before paying invoices

[52.126] A company which operated the Cash Accounting Scheme reclaimed input tax in respect of invoices which it had received but had not paid. When the Commissioners discovered this, they imposed a misdeclaration penalty. The tribunal dismissed the company's appeal, holding that there was no reasonable excuse for the company's premature claim. *Training Technology International Ltd*, LON/91/291Z (VTD 6727).

[52.127] Similar decisions were reached in *SSY Research Services Ltd*, LON/91/2364Z (VTD 7306); *Coastal Design*, MAN/92/24 (VTD 9001) and *RLO Fyffe*, EDN/92/112 (VTD 9686).

Input tax reclaimed on pre-registration supplies

[52.128] A company reclaimed input tax relating to supplies made more than six months before it had registered for VAT. The Commissioners issued an assessment to recover the tax, and also imposed a misdeclaration penalty. The tribunal dismissed the company's appeal. Applying the QB decision in *Schemepanel Ltd*, **36.612** INPUT TAX, 'input tax cannot be credited to the extent that it is referable to pre-registration supplies'. Furthermore, there was no reasonable excuse for the misdeclaration. *Southill Sawmills Ltd*, LON/98/322 (VTD 17337).

[52.129] A similar decision was reached in *Monevate Services Ltd*, MAN/06/208 (VTD 19965).

Delay in accounting for output tax—whether a reasonable excuse

[52.130] An opera singer received payments from opera companies which did not include VAT, and had to issue invoices to recover the VAT due. He accounted for the VAT when he received it from the opera companies, rather than when he received the fees themselves. When the Commissioners discovered this, they imposed a misdeclaration penalty. The singer appealed, contending that his misunderstanding of the correct accounting procedure constituted a reasonable excuse. The tribunal dismissed his appeal, holding that the circumstances did not constitute a reasonable excuse. *A Shore*, LON/90/1649 (VTD 5799).

[52.131] A similar decision was reached in a case involving a company trading as a building subcontractor, where the main contractor made payments which were exclusive of VAT and the company had to issue additional invoices to recover the VAT. The tribunal held that the company should have sought advice from its local VAT office, from an accountant, or from other companies in the construction industry. *Talon Holdings Ltd*, LON/91/658Z (VTD 6897).

[52.132] The decision in *Talon Holdings Ltd*, **52.131** above, was applied in the similar case of *Nivek Holdings Ltd*, LON/91/670 (VTD 7383).

[52.133] A company registered for VAT from 1 May 1990. It was required to submit a return covering the month to 31 May 1990. During this period it issued one invoice on 29 May. However, it submitted a return showing no output tax liability. The Commissioners imposed a misdeclaration penalty and the company appealed, contending that it had submitted the incorrect return to avoid incurring a default surcharge. The tribunal dismissed the appeal, holding that this was not a reasonable excuse. *Markdome Ltd*, LON/90/1761Z (VTD 6007).

[52.134] An appeal was dismissed in a case where a building contractor had failed to account for VAT on stage payments for which he had issued invoices. *TJ Ditchfield v The Isle of Man Treasury*, MAN/91/173 (VTD 6533).

[52.135] A company which was carrying on the business of property development agreed to develop a site and sell it to an insurance company for 13,000,000. In August 1990 it issued an invoice for the sale of four office blocks at the site. The invoice charged VAT, but the company did not include the VAT in its return for the period ending 31 August. The Commissioners imposed a misdeclaration penalty and the company appealed, contending that it had not intended the invoices to be VAT invoices and that the tribunal should apply the principles in *Watson Norrie Ltd*, **52.105** above. The tribunal dismissed the appeal, observing that 'although the facts in *Watson Norrie Ltd* bear some resemblance to those in this case it is not binding on us; in any event in reasonable excuse cases the facts are crucial'. On the evidence, there was no reasonable excuse for the company's failure to account for the VAT shown on the invoice in question. *Western Road Properties Ltd*, LON/91/867Z (VTD 7304).

[52.136] Failure to account for tax on 'progress payments' was also held not to be a reasonable excuse in *Regis Commercial Property*, LON/91/121 (VTD 6617); *Feal & Oats*, LON/91/1101 (VTD 6706); *Trevalyn Estates Ltd*, MAN/90/398 (VTD 6749); *Cindason*, MAN/90/399 (VTD 6749); *Marshall Brown Aluminium Ltd*, EDN/91/111 (VTD 6853); *The Window Glazing Consultancy*, LON/91/142 (VTD 6982); *Poyser & Holmes*, MAN/91/639 (VTD 7059); *North Scene Video Ltd*, EDN/91/255 (VTD 7136); *SM & E Properties Ltd*, MAN/91/616 (VTD 7140); *P Burke Construction Ltd*, LON/91/1670Y (VTD 7222); *Carter Morris Roofing Ltd*, MAN/91/1171 (VTD 7229); *K Rose (t/a KJ Rose Building Services)*, LON/92/879X (VTD 7694); *Hookcroft Ltd*, LON/91/725 (VTD 8870); *Acoustiolox Suspended Ceilings*, LON/91/2713Y (VTD 9049); *DC Burdett*, LON/92/2279 (VTD 9695); *Reverse Osmosis Systems Ltd*, MAN/92/821 (VTD 10436); *WSJ (Contractors) Ltd*, MAN/93/36 (VTD 11602) and *J Tolley (t/a WH Tolley & Son)*, LON/93/2056P (VTD 11627).

[52.137] An appeal was dismissed in a case where a company received a substantial payment for sale of property on 23 October 1990, but dated the relevant VAT invoice 2 November, and did not include the VAT in question in its return for the period ending 31 October. *D & M Builders (Hamilton) Ltd*, EDN/91/210 (VTD 6713).

[52.138] Similar decisions were reached in *Nightingale Holdings*, 52.400 below, and *Park Industrial & Commercial Holdings Ltd*, 52.400 below.

[52.139] An appeal was dismissed in a case where a company had failed to account for VAT in respect of invoices it had issued which remained unpaid. *Renaissance Bronzes Ltd*, LON/91/341Y (VTD 6849).

[52.140] Similar decisions were reached in *JR Kircher*, LON/91/1075Z (VTD 7352); *RJ Wheeler*, LON/91/1995Y (VTD 7366); *Hastings Borough Council*, LON/92/1112X (VTD 8934); *CB Dureau*, LON/92/36X (VTD 9355); *Meldreth Construction Ltd*, LON/92/1136Z (VTD 9418); *Oceana Holdings plc*, LON/92/2359 (VTD 9961); *AR Waller & Associates*, LON/92/3402P (VTD 10297); *Arrowfinch*, LON/92/3340 (VTD 10413); *William Johnson & Sons (Contractors) Ltd*, MAN/93/164 (VTD 11028) and *Tru-Form Sheet Metal Ltd*, 62.88 SUPPLY.

Management charges—delay in accounting for output tax

[52.141] See *Missionfine Ltd*, 43.5 MANAGEMENT SERVICES.

Failure to account for VAT on deposits

[52.142] An appeal was dismissed in a case where a company had failed to account for VAT on the receipt of a large deposit. The tribunal held that, since the company was used to receiving deposits, and in many cases issued invoices for deposits, there was no reasonable excuse for its failure to account for VAT. *Cleco Ltd*, MAN/91/361 (VTD 7084).

[52.143] A partnership which organised jazz festivals failed to account for VAT on deposits, and the Commissioners imposed misdeclaration penalties. The partnership appealed, contending that it had a reasonable excuse because the partners had assumed that they did not have to account for VAT on deposits until the time when the festivals took place. The tribunal dismissed the appeal, finding that the principal partner was 'a competent and intelligent businessman', but had not 'made any significant efforts to get any help or advice on how to prepare his returns' and had not 'made any serious attempt to understand the *General Notice*'. *Don Aldridge Associates*, LON/93/713P (VTD 11452).

Failure to account for tax on advance payments

[52.144] A partnership which manufactured vehicles received an advance payment on 26 October 1990 in respect of a vehicle which it had agreed to manufacture in the following quarter. The partnership did not account for tax on the payment in its return for the period ending 31 October 1990. The Commissioners imposed a misdeclaration penalty and the tribunal dismissed the partnership's appeal, holding that the time of supply for VAT purposes was 26 October 1990 and there was no reasonable excuse for the failure to account for tax. *Marquiss of Scotland*, EDN/91/256 (VTD 7161).

[52.145] An appeal was dismissed in a case where a company which organised music concerts failed to account for output tax on advance payments. *Regular Music Ltd*, EDN/98/46 (VTD 15571).

Failure to account for tax on advance royalties

[52.146] A company failed to account for tax on advance royalties. The Commissioners imposed a misdeclaration penalty and the company appealed, contending firstly that the payments should be regarded as loans which did not give rise to any VAT liability, and alternatively that it had a reasonable excuse for not having regarded them as giving rise to a liability. The tribunal dismissed the company's appeal, finding that the payments were clearly described as advance royalties in the relevant contract, and holding that there was no reasonable excuse for the company's failure to account for tax on them. *Software One Ltd*, LON/92/1904A (VTD 11090).

Imports and acquisitions

Cases where the appellant was successful

Imports—input tax reclaimed prematurely

[52.147] A company traded as an importer of goods, using an agent to deal with the payment of duty and VAT. On 30 September 1990 it was telephoned by its agent, who requested a cheque for duty of £1,150 and VAT of £3,922. The cheque was sent on that day and the company reclaimed the VAT as input tax in its return for the period ending 30 September 1990. However, the agent did not issue an invoice until 2 October. When the Commissioners discovered this, they imposed a misdeclaration penalty. The tribunal allowed the company's appeal. Although the tax point for the transaction was 2 October, the fact that the company had sent a cheque for the VAT in question on 30 September meant that it had a reasonable excuse for having believed that that date had been the tax point. *Pennine Industrial Equipment Ltd*, MAN/91/390 (VTD 6512).

[52.148] A similar decision was reached in *Sealjet UK Ltd*, LON/91/1098Y (VTD 6683).

[52.149] An appeal against a misdeclaration penalty was allowed in a case where a company purchased goods from an agent of an overseas manufacturer, and the bill of lading in respect of the goods was dated 25 September 1990 but the VAT invoice was dated 8 October. *Senit Steels Ltd*, LON/91/1358X (VTD 6898).

[52.150] An appeal was allowed in a case where a double-glazing manufacturer reclaimed input tax in respect of goods he had imported and for which he had received invoices from the supplier but had not received import certificates from Customs. *MRW Richardson*, MAN/90/961 (VTD 6937).

[52.151] Similar decisions were reached in *European Computer Centre Ltd*, LON/91/2131X (VTD 7220) and *Severnside Machinery Ltd*, MAN/91/1546 (VTD 10828).

[52.152] A company imported a production machine from the USA. The machine arrived in the UK on 30 November 1990 but did not clear Customs until 1 December. The company reclaimed input tax on the machine in its return for the period ending 30 November. The Commissioners imposed a misdeclaration penalty but the tribunal allowed the company's appeal, holding that the circumstances constituted a reasonable excuse. *DCB Mouldings*, EDN/91/35 (VTD 7522).

Import VAT certificates—effect of change in arrangements

[52.153] The Commissioners introduced new arrangements for import VAT certificates with effect from 1 October 1990 (see *VAT Notes No 2 (1990)*). Previously, import certificates had been produced weekly and distributed via shipping agents. Under the new arrangements, the weekly certificates were replaced by a single monthly certificate to be issued direct to importers. A company which imported textiles received both a weekly certificate and a monthly certificate in respect of the same transactions, and reclaimed input tax in respect of both certificates. When the Commissioners discovered this, they imposed a misdeclaration penalty. The company appealed, contending that it had not received a copy of either *VAT Notes No 2 (1990)* or of a VAT information sheet entitled *Import VAT Certificates* which explained the change of arrangements. The tribunal held that, since the company had not been aware of the new arrangements, the duplication of import certificates constituted a reasonable excuse for the duplicated claim to input tax. (There was, however, held to be no reasonable excuse for other misdeclarations on the same return.) *Rose Household Textiles Ltd*, MAN/91/973 (VTD 7105).

[52.154] The Commissioners introduced new arrangements for import VAT certificates with effect from 1 October 1990, under which weekly certificates distributed via shipping agents were replaced by monthly certificates issued direct to importers (see *VAT Notes No 2 (1990)*). A company which imported carpets had not received its certificate for October 1990 by 23 November, and felt obliged to complete its October return on that date without the certificate. In the return it reclaimed input tax in respect of goods which had been received by its agent on 31 October, and for which it had paid import duty, but for which the agent had subsequently issued a GSP exemption certificate on 8 November. The Commissioners imposed a misdeclaration penalty, since the issue of the GSP certificate confirmed that the transaction was exempt from VAT, and the import duty which had been paid in error had subsequently been repaid. The company appealed, contending that the inclusion of the amount in the return had been a genuine error, which would not have occurred but for the delay in receiving the October certificate from the Commissioners. The tribunal allowed the company's appeal, holding that the circumstances constituted a reasonable excuse. *John Lanham Watts (Carpets) Ltd*, MAN/91/763 (VTD 8846).

Import VAT certificates—no deferment account operated

[52.155] A company was incorporated in 1991 to import goods from the Netherlands for distribution to retailers in the UK. It did not have a deferment account, and paid VAT on its imports to a freight company on receipt of an invoice. In its VAT return for the period ending 31 May 1991, which was prepared by its accountants, it included the input tax shown on its certificate for May, although it did not pay the amount shown on that certificate until early June, after receiving an invoice from the freight company. Its next VAT return was prepared by its company secretary, who prepared the return from the invoices received in the period, and thus included the amount shown on the May certificate, although this had already been included in the previous return. The Commissioners imposed a misdeclaration penalty and the company appealed, contending that it had a reasonable excuse because the company secretary had made an innocent error, and that its local VAT office had failed to reply to a request to open a deferment account. The tribunal allowed the appeal, holding that 'the duplication of the figures on the VAT certificates and the invoices received from the freight company' was 'a source of understandable confusion' which constituted a reasonable excuse. *Eltraco (UK) Ltd*, LON/92/731Y (VTD 9089).

Import VAT certificates—payment entered by Customs on wrong C79

[52.156] A company which made substantial imports of goods paid £4,200 to Customs by bankers' draft in May 1991. The amount of the draft was entered into the company's records for that month. The payment was not included in the company's C79 certificate issued by Customs on 12 June 1991 covering payments in May 1991. However, it was included on a subsequent C79 issued by Customs on 12 July, covering payments in June 1991. Following receipt of this C79, the company entered the amount of the payment in its records for June. Since the payment had been entered in its records for two successive months, the company made a duplicated claim for input tax. The Commissioners imposed a misdeclaration penalty, and the company appealed, contending that it had a reasonable excuse because it had never previously found it necessary to reconcile its records of payments with the C79 certificates. The tribunal allowed the appeal, finding that 'the error by Customs & Excise, in entering the amount in the wrong C79, was a contributory factor to the second entry of that sum in the appellant's accounts', and holding that the circumstances therefore constituted a reasonable excuse. *Plastic Protection Ltd*, LON/92/583Y (VTD 9259). (*Note.* For another issue in this case, see 52.240 below.)

Import VAT certificates wrongly made out to associated company

[52.157] A company (R) imported goods from China. It used the services of an import agent. This agent also acted for E, a company associated with R. During the period ending 30 September 1990, the agent mistakenly issued certificates to E in respect of goods imported by R. R reclaimed the input tax shown on these certificates, and the Commissioners imposed a misdeclaration penalty. The tribunal allowed R's appeal, observing that there had been no loss of tax, and holding that the agent's error constituted a reasonable excuse for the misdeclaration. *Rosedew Ltd*, LON/92/514X (VTD 9619).

[52.158] Similar decisions were reached in *Arendal Smelterwork AS*, LON/93/1599P (VTD 11427) and *Downey Ltd*, LON/93/361P (VTD 11862).

Input tax incorrectly reclaimed by company acting as import agent

[52.159] A Japanese company had established a UK subsidiary (T) to sell its products in the UK. T reclaimed input tax in respect of supplies which were invoiced and delivered to its principal UK customer. The Commissioners imposed a misdeclaration penalty, since the tax should have been reclaimed by the customer rather than by T. T appealed, contending that its misunderstanding of the provisions was a reasonable excuse. The tribunal allowed the appeal, holding that this was 'neither a deliberate nor a careless error but an error based on a genuine misunderstanding' and that the circumstances constituted a reasonable excuse. *Taito (Europe) Corporation Ltd*, LON/91/396 (VTD 7758).

[52.160] Similar decisions were reached in *CP Textiles*, MAN/92/352 (VTD 11031) and *Cauillez (UK) Ltd*, MAN/92/353 (VTD 11031).

Input tax reclaimed but tax not paid to Commissioners by import agent

[52.161] A trader imported goods, using the services of a company which acted as an import agent. He received an invoice from the company dated 27 April 1990, and paid the amount in question to the company. He reclaimed the amount he had paid as input tax in his return for the period ending 31 May 1990. However, the company was suffering financial difficulties, and had not paid the tax to the Commissioners. (The company had subsequently gone into liquidation.) When the Commissioners discovered that the trader had reclaimed the tax without holding a valid certificate C79, they imposed a misdeclaration penalty. The trader appealed, contending that since he had received an invoice from the import agent, and had paid the amount demanded to the agent, he had a reasonable excuse for his premature claim. The tribunal accepted this contention and allowed the appeal against the penalty, holding that the circumstances constituted a reasonable excuse for the incorrect claim. *MP James*, LON/92/1312A (VTD 10474). (*Note.* An appeal against a subsequent penalty was dismissed.)

[52.162] A similar decision was reached in *Leather Fashions Ltd*, 35.10 IMPORTS.

Cases where the appellant was unsuccessful

Input tax assessed on importation and reclaimed before assessment paid

[52.163] A company imported clothing from Asia for resale in the UK. It paid commission to a US company under an agency agreement, but did not account for VAT on such commission. When the Commissioners discovered this, they issued an assessment charging tax on these payments. With the assessment was a covering letter stating 'subject to the normal rules you may claim the amount of VAT paid in box 2 of your VAT return only when you have received from Customs the VAT copy of the post-clearance demand note (form C18) after processing by Customs'. Despite this instruction, the company reclaimed the amount as input tax before it had paid the assessment. The Commissioners imposed a misdeclaration penalty, and the tribunal dismissed the company's appeal, holding that there was no reasonable excuse for the incorrect claim. *Ericsons Fashions Ltd*, LON/90/1880Z (VTD 6241).

Input tax reclaimed before import VAT certificate received

[52.164] An appeal was dismissed in a case where a company reclaimed input tax on imported goods in its return for the period ending 31 December 1990, although the goods in question had not cleared Customs until 11 January

1991. (The company had sent a cheque as payment for the goods on 23 December 1990.) The tribunal held that, as the company was aware that it should not claim input tax on imported goods without holding a certificate, there was no reasonable excuse for the premature claim. *Quay Marine Ltd*, LON/91/668X (VTD 9054).

[52.165] A similar decision was reached in *Analog & Numeric Devices Ltd*, MAN/91/550 (VTD 9340). (*Note.* For another issue in this case, see 52.455 below.)

Customs duty reclaimed as input tax

[52.166] A company which manufactured clothing imported materials from overseas. It paid customs duty on the import of such materials, and reclaimed the duty as input tax. When the Commissioners discovered this, they imposed a misdeclaration penalty. The tribunal dismissed the company's appeal, holding that there was no reasonable excuse for the incorrect claim. *Leofabs Ltd*, MAN/91/401 (VTD 6632).

[52.167] Similar decisions were reached in *NGF 90 (Gateshead) Ltd*, MAN/92/666 (VTD 9816) and *Anglo Persian Emporium Trading Co Ltd*, [2010] UKFTT 296 (TC), TC00584.

Input tax reclaimed on supply made to import agents

[52.168] An appeal was dismissed in a case where a trader who had imported four haulage vehicles from a French company reclaimed input tax in respect of an invoice made out to his import agents. The tribunal held that the appellant was at fault through not having followed the guidelines in *para 15* of *VAT Notice No 702* (subsequently updated by *Notice No 702/94*) and that the circumstances did not constitute a reasonable excuse. *PJ Robinson*, MAN/91/1107 (VTD 7145).

Deferment limit exceeded—duplicated claim for input tax

[52.169] A company which manufactured flexible hosing imported certain items and had adopted the deferment scheme. Its agreed deferment limit was £3,000, but it exceeded this limit in the accounting periods ending 31 July 1990 and 31 October 1990. Because it had exceeded its deferment limit, it was required to pay invoices which had been raised by its freight forwarders for the duty and VAT attributable to certain imports and was unable, so far as those imports were concerned, to avail itself of the deferment scheme. It made a duplicated claim for input tax in respect of the amounts shown on the freight forwarders' invoices. The Commissioners imposed a misdeclaration penalty, and the company appealed, contending that the unusual nature of the invoices concerned constituted a reasonable excuse. The tribunal rejected this contention and dismissed the appeal, holding that the director who was responsible for the company's returns had not 'acted with the standard of care which is reasonably to be expected', and that there was no reasonable excuse for the duplicated claim. *Arctrend Ltd*, MAN/91/1294 (VTD 10011).

[52.170] A similar decision was reached in *Barnett Gray Ltd*, LON/93/879P (VTD 11155).

[52.171] There was also held to be no reasonable excuse for duplicated input tax claims in respect of imports in *Strong (UK) Ltd*, LON/93/772 (VTD 10799).

Input tax reclaimed on imported goods—no certificate held

[52.172] An appeal was dismissed in a case where a company had reclaimed input tax on imported goods without holding a certificate as required by what is now *VATA 1994, s 24(6)(a)*. *Vin-Dotco (UK) Ltd*, MAN/92/935 (VTD 11346).

Acquisition of vehicle from Republic of Ireland—failure to account for tax

[52.173] A partnership which carried on business in Northern Ireland acquired a new BMW motor vehicle from the Irish Republic. The partnership signed a form VAT 414, stating that it would account for VAT on the acquisition. However, it failed to do so. When the Commissioners discovered this, they imposed a misdeclaration penalty. The tribunal upheld the penalty and dismissed the partnership's appeal. *KS & P*, LON/01/273 (VTD 17548).

[52.174] A car dealer imported a number of Japanese cars from Ireland. He did not declare them as imports when they entered the UK, and he sold them in the UK under the margin scheme. When the Commissioners discovered this, they imposed a misdeclaration penalty. The tribunal upheld the penalty, holding that there was no reasonable excuse for the misdeclaration. *W Ball*, MAN/01/170 (VTD 17648). (*Note.* The tribunal mitigated the penalty by 66%: see **52.408** below.)

Supplies incorrectly treated as zero-rated

Cases where the appellant was successful

Misunderstanding of VATA 1994, Sch 8, Group 8*

[52.175] A company carried on business as a subcontractor in the ship-repairing industry. In 1990 it undertook the painting of two new ships. It did not account for VAT on this work, considering that the work was zero-rated under what is now *VATA 1994, Sch 8, Group 8*. The Commissioners imposed a misdeclaration penalty and the company appealed, contending that it had made an innocent error which constituted a reasonable excuse. The tribunal accepted this contention and allowed the appeal. *Nor-Clean Ltd*, [1991] VATTR 239 (VTD 5954).

Misunderstanding of VATA 1994, Sch 8, Group 6*

[52.176] A construction company was carrying out work on a listed building. The work was inspected monthly by an architect employed by the customer. After each inspection the architect issued an RIBA certificate, which was not a VAT invoice but which indicated the amount of VAT payable on the work carried out. In June 1990 the architect issued a certificate for work carried out to the value of £36,171, but stating that only £5,425 of this was subject to VAT. The company issued an invoice accordingly. However the Commissioners subsequently ascertained that the whole of the £36,171 should have been treated as standard-rated, so that the company should have charged VAT of £5,425 rather than £814. They therefore imposed a misdeclaration penalty. The tribunal allowed the company's appeal against the penalty, holding that, in view of the information on the architect's certificate, the company had a reasonable excuse for having assumed that most of the work in question was zero-rated. *Shelston (Construction) Ltd*, LON/91/934X (VTD 6616).

[52.177] A builder undertook the substantial reconstruction of an old house (No. 7 Albany Villas) in a conservation area. He did not account for VAT on the work. The Commissioners ascertained that the building was not listed as a protected building (although Nos. 2–5 Albany Buildings were protected) and that VAT should have been charged on the work. They imposed a misdeclaration penalty. The builder appealed, accepting that the work should have been standard-rated but contending that he had a reasonable excuse since he had previously worked on No. 2 Albany Villas which was a protected building, and that the detailed planning restrictions which had been imposed because the building was in a conservation area had led him to believe that No. 7 was also a protected building. The tribunal allowed his appeal, holding that the circumstances constituted a reasonable excuse. *BA Lowe (t/a BA Lowe Construction)*, LON/91/838Z (VTD 6806).

[52.178] A trader did not account for tax on the construction of a building within the curtilage of a protected building, but separate from it. The Commissioners imposed a misdeclaration penalty and the trader appealed, contending that he had a reasonable excuse because he had believed that the work was zero-rated. The tribunal allowed his appeal, holding that the circumstances constituted a reasonable excuse. *BK Sergeant*, LON/92/874X (VTD 9039).

[52.179] A company failed to account for VAT in respect of work carried out on a listed building. The Commissioners ascertained that the work did not qualify for zero-rating, and imposed a misdeclaration penalty. The company appealed against the penalty, contending that it had a reasonable excuse since the contractor for whom it had carried out the work had advised it that it was zero-rated. The tribunal allowed the appeal, holding that the circumstances constituted a reasonable excuse. *E Coules & Son Ltd*, LON/92/976Y (VTD 9608).

[52.180] A similar decision was reached in *P Lewsey*, LON/93/711 (VTD 10784).

*Misunderstanding of VATA 1994, Sch 8, Group 5**

[52.181] A company agreed to install a new heating and lighting system in a parish church. It did not charge VAT, having been advised by the main contractor that the work was zero-rated since the church was accepted as a charity. The Commissioners ruled that, since the company was undertaking the work for the main contractor, rather than making supplies directly to the charity, it should have charged and accounted for VAT, and imposed a misdeclaration penalty. The tribunal allowed the company's appeal, holding that the circumstances constituted a reasonable excuse. *Ian Fraser & Partners Ltd*, EDN/91/115 (VTD 6931).

[52.182] The decision in *Ian Fraser & Partners Ltd*, **52.181** above, was applied in the similar case of *Taylor & Fraser Ltd*, EDN/92/163 (VTD 8977).

[52.183] A similar decision was reached in *T McRandal*, LON/92/2102 (VTD 9860).

[52.184] A bricklayer failed to account for VAT in respect of work carried out in building extensions to a church and to a nursing home. The Commissioners imposed a misdeclaration penalty and the bricklayer appealed, contending that he had a reasonable excuse as he had assumed that the work was zero-rated. The tribunal allowed his appeal, holding that the circumstances constituted a reasonable excuse. *M Inger*, MAN/91/1524 (VTD 9522).

[52.185] A builder failed to account for VAT in respect of scaffolding work at an old people's home, and of the installation of ramps for disabled students at a school. The Commissioners imposed a misdeclaration penalty and the builder appealed, contending that he had a reasonable excuse as he had assumed that the work was zero-rated. The tribunal allowed his appeal, holding that the circumstances constituted a reasonable excuse. *DM Stratford*, LON/91/2681Y (VTD 9621). (*Note.* For another issue in this case, see **17.2** DEFAULT INTEREST.)

[52.186] An appeal against a misdeclaration penalty was allowed in a case where a builder, who had only recently registered for VAT, failed to account for VAT on the construction of a clubhouse at a golf course, and on extensions to houses. The tribunal held that the circumstances constituted a reasonable excuse. *PJ Bowen*, LON/92/3399A (VTD 11167).

[52.187] A building company failed to account for VAT on work carried out in extending a church. The Commissioners imposed misdeclaration penalties and the company appealed, contending that it had a reasonable excuse because its director had been told by a surveyor that the work was zero-rated. The tribunal allowed the company's appeal, holding that the misleading advice from the surveyor constituted a reasonable excuse for the misdeclaration. *Lacy Simmons Ltd*, LON/93/1000P (VTD 11211).

[52.188] The decision in *Lacy Simmons Ltd*, **52.187** above, was applied in the similar subsequent case of *Partridge Homes Ltd*, LON/97/1279 (VTD 15289).

[52.189] An appeal against a penalty was allowed in a case where a partnership failed to charge VAT on the installation of a built-in kitchen, and contended that it had a reasonable excuse since the partners had assumed that the work was zero-rated. *DA Phillips & Sons*, LON/91/523Y (VTD 7006).

[52.190] A similar decision was reached in *David Morris Homes Ltd*, MAN/91/330 (VTD 7081).

[52.191] A company undertook excavation work for the London Borough of Islington. The Borough Council advised the company that some of the work in question was zero-rated. A VAT officer on a control visit formed the opinion that the work should have been standard-rated, and asked the company for evidence that the work qualified for zero-rating in view of the changes implemented by *FA 1989*. Neither the company nor the Council produced such evidence, and the Commissioners imposed a misdeclaration penalty. The tribunal allowed the company's appeal, holding that in view of the information provided by the Council, the company had a reasonable excuse for having incorrectly treated the work as zero-rated. *Walsh Brothers (Tunnelling) Ltd*, LON/91/1451 (VTD 7186).

[52.192] A similar decision was reached in *Bomanite (Southeast)*, LON/95/2478 (VTD 13745).

[52.193] A company undertook to construct a workshop for a registered charity. It did not charge VAT on the work, considering that it was zero-rated. However, the Commissioners ascertained that the new workshop was linked to an existing building by a covered walkway, so that the work was not eligible for zero-rating. They imposed a misdeclaration penalty. The tribunal allowed the company's appeal against the penalty, holding that the circumstances constituted a reasonable excuse. *DJ Trimming Ltd*, LON/91/1327 (VTD 7733).

[52.194] A local authority arranged for a company to construct an overflow chamber to alleviate flooding on a housing estate. The local authority advised the company that the work would be zero-rated, and the company did not account for VAT. The Commissioners ascertained that the work was not eligible for zero-rating, and imposed a misdeclaration penalty. The company appealed, contending that in view of the advice given by the local authority, it had a reasonable excuse for not having accounted for VAT. The tribunal allowed the appeal, holding that the circumstances constituted a reasonable excuse. *Barhale Construction plc*, [1992] VATTR 409 (VTD 9137).

[52.195] A scaffolder erected and dismantled scaffolding for the use of building contractors. He did not account for tax on the consideration which he received. The Commissioners issued an assessment charging tax on the consideration, on the basis that, by leaving the scaffolding on the site, he was supplying a standard-rated service to the contractors. They also imposed a misdeclaration penalty. The scaffolder appealed. The tribunal held that the scaffolder was supplying standard-rated services, but allowed his appeal against the penalty, holding that the complexity of the law constituted a reasonable excuse. *PJ Guntert (t/a Abingdon Scaffolding Co)*, LON/92/2183 (VTD 10604). (*Notes.* (1) For the award of costs in this case, see **2.419** APPEALS. (2) For a more recent case in which supplies of scaffolding services were held to be zero-rated, see *GT Scaffolding Ltd*, **15.177** CONSTRUCTION OF BUILDINGS, ETC.)

[52.196] A builder failed to account for VAT on progress payments received for the construction of a sports pavilion. The Commissioners imposed a misdeclaration penalty, and the builder appealed, contending that he had a reasonable excuse as he had been misled by his former accountant and had believed that the work was zero-rated. The tribunal accepted the builder's evidence and allowed the appeal. *Colin Maynard Builders*, LON/93/295P (VTD 10895).

[52.197] A builder failed to account for output tax on the construction of a swimming pool complex in the grounds of an existing house. The Commissioners imposed a misdeclaration penalty and the builder appealed, contending that he had a reasonable excuse because he had believed that the work qualified for zero-rating. The tribunal allowed the appeal, holding that he had a reasonable excuse for the misdeclaration. *C Hall*, LON/92/1194 (VTD 14131).

[52.198] See also *Derby YMCA*, **15.217** CONSTRUCTION OF BUILDINGS, ETC.

Customs not satisfied that conditions for zero-rating complied with

[52.199] An appeal was allowed in a case where a company had treated certain supplies of goods to India as zero-rated, but had been unable to produce copy bills of lading which the Commissioners had required as proof of export. The tribunal was satisfied that the goods had been exported, and held that the company had a reasonable excuse for having zero-rated them despite not having the necessary evidence of export. *TC Plastics (Manchester) Ltd*, MAN/91/1426 (VTD 7684).

[52.200] A similar decision was reached in *Roopers Export Sales Ltd*, LON/92/2896P (VTD 10801).

[52.201] A company sold some machinery to a Pakistani and did not account for VAT on the sale, treating it as zero-rated. The Commissioners discovered that the purchaser also had an address in Rochdale, and imposed a misdeclaration penalty. The company appealed. The tribunal held that the transaction did not qualify for zero-rating since the purchaser had a business address in the UK, but allowed the appeal against the penalty, holding that the company had a reasonable excuse for having mistakenly treated the sale as zero-rated. *Print On Time (Pontefract) Ltd*, MAN/93/417 (VTD 11458).

Misunderstanding of VATA 1994, Sch 8, Group 3*

[52.202] A graphic designer (J) failed to account for VAT on the provision of artwork for the production of a booklet, and the Commissioners imposed a misdeclaration penalty. J appealed, contending that he had a reasonable excuse because he had assumed that the artwork would be zero-rated. The tribunal allowed his appeal, holding that the circumstances constituted a reasonable excuse. *DL Jones*, LON/93/585A (VTD 11430). (*Note.* For another issue in this case, see **36.532** INPUT TAX.)

Misunderstanding of VATA 1994, Sch 8, Group 1*

[52.203] See *Skilton & Gregory*, **29.47** FOOD.

Cases where the appellant was unsuccessful

Exports—conditions of VATA 1994, s 30(6) not satisfied

[52.204] An appeal was dismissed in a case where a company had failed to charge VAT on goods invoiced to an overseas company but delivered to an address in London, and contended that it had assumed that the goods would be zero-rated. The tribunal held that the company was at fault in not having referred to the *VAT Guide*. *Dynic (UK) Ltd*, LON/91/2043X (VTD 7412).

[52.205] A similar decision was reached in a subsequent case where the tribunal held that the company's evidence failed to show that identifiable goods had been removed from the UK, or that the documentation related to any of the invoices in respect of which the penalties had been imposed. *Dallas Knitwear (Manchester) Ltd*, MAN/96/407 & 660 (VTD 14653).

[52.206] The decision in *Dallas Knitwear (Manchester) Ltd*, **52.205** above, was applied in a similar subsequent case in which an appeal against a misdeclaration penalty was dismissed. The tribunal observed that the appellant had an annual turnover of some 6,000,000, and held that there was no reasonable excuse. (The tribunal also held that there were no grounds for mitigating the penalty.) *AR Vig (t/a One by One Fashions)*, MAN/96/137 (VTD 14837).

[52.207] A similar decision was reached in a case where a company had failed to account for VAT on the sale of three helicopters, and contended that they had been exported. *MW Helicopters Ltd*, LON/00/49 (VTD 16888).

[52.208] A similar decision was reached in a case where a company had failed to account for VAT on the supply of a large quantity of computer chips, and contended that they had been exported to the Republic of Ireland. *Mercer Associates Ltd*, LON/03/217 (VTD 18779).

[52.209] A company based in England failed to account for VAT on goods which it supplied to a Welsh branch of an American company. The Commissioners imposed a misdeclaration penalty, and the company appealed, contending that it had a reasonable excuse because it had believed that the goods could be described as exports and were therefore zero-rated. The tribunal dismissed the appeal, holding that there was no reasonable excuse for having treated the transactions as exports. *JW Froelich (UK) Ltd*, LON/91/1667Y (VTD 10193).

[52.210] A company sold a machine which was intended to be exported to Australia. It issued an invoice to an export house on 13 April 1992. The machine was actually exported on 30 May 1992. The company did not account for output tax on the invoice which it issued, treating the sale as zero-rated. The Commissioners issued an assessment charging tax on the sale, since the conditions laid down under what is now *VATA 1994, s 30(6)* and *VAT Regulations 1995 (SI 1995/2518)* had not been satisfied. They also imposed a misdeclaration penalty. The company appealed. The tribunal dismissed the appeals, holding that the sale did not qualify for zero-rating and that there was no reasonable excuse for the company's failure to account for output tax on the sale. *Butler Newall Ltd*, MAN/93/1004 (VTD 12292).

[52.211] In the case noted at **1.76** AGENTS, the tribunal held that there was no reasonable excuse for a company's failure to account for tax on a supply within *VATA 1994, s 47(2A)*. The tribunal held that 'an experienced trader taking part in a normal transaction of sale by auction has an obligation to be aware of the law regarding value added tax on such sale and the existence of the deeming provision. Its complications, and its possible inconveniences, do not afford a reasonable excuse for the misdeclaration.' *Bashir Mohamed Ltd*, LON/99/188 (VTD 16762).

Misunderstanding of VATA 1994, Sch 8, Group 1*

[52.212] A trader sold hot food from a transit van. He did not account for VAT on such sales and the Commissioners imposed a misdeclaration penalty.

He appealed, contending that his accountants had not told him that his sales were liable to VAT. The tribunal dismissed his appeal, holding that the circumstances did not constitute a reasonable excuse. *S Lamming*, LON/91/1045Z (VTD 6635).

[52.213] An appeal was dismissed in a case where a restaurant proprietor had failed to account for VAT on sales of hot take-away food. *M Siddique*, MAN/91/918 (VTD 9244).

[52.214] An appeal was dismissed in a case where the tribunal found that a partnership, which operated a restaurant selling take-away food as well as food for consumption on the premises, had treated an excessively high percentage of its sales as zero-rated. *Hounslow Sweet Centre*, LON/92/271X (VTD 10026). (*Note.* For a preliminary application in this case, see **2.231** APPEALS.)

[52.215] A trader (B) failed to account for output tax on supplies of beverages from vending machines. The Commissioners imposed a misdeclaration penalty, and B appealed, contending firstly that he was making zero-rated supplies to the company on whose premises the machines were sited, and that that company was making onward supplies to the consumers, and alternatively that he had a reasonable excuse because he had assumed that his supplies qualified for zero-rating. The tribunal rejected these contentions and dismissed B's appeal, holding that he was making standard-rated supplies to the consumers and that there was no reasonable excuse for his failure to account for tax. (The tribunal also held that there were no grounds for mitigating the penalty.) *SA Bourne*, LON/96/1973 (VTD 16023).

Misunderstanding of VATA 1994, Sch 8, Group 5*

[52.216] An appeal was dismissed in a case where, in the period ending September 1990, a partnership trading as building contractors had failed to charge VAT on extensions to houses. The work in question would have been zero-rated before 1984 under *VATA 1983, Sch 5 Group 8* (the predecessor of *VATA 1994, Sch 8, Group 5*), and the principal partner gave evidence that he was unaware of the change in the law. The tribunal held that this was not a reasonable excuse. *Alan Wright & Partners*, MAN/91/54 (VTD 6114).

[52.217] Similar decisions were reached in *GJ Bennett & Co (Builders) Ltd*, MAN/90/1003 (VTD 6457); *Bolton Consultants Ltd*, LON/91/1147X (VTD 6611); *H Turner & Sons (Construction) Ltd*, LON/91/1589Z (VTD 6657); *Matrec Ltd*, MAN/91/667 (VTD 6693); *Premier Aluminium & Glass Ltd*, LON/91/758X (VTD 6831); *Ashe Construction Southern Ltd*, LON/91/723X (VTD 7075); *MG Lineham (t/a MG Lineham Homes & Improvements)*, LON/91/1671Z (VTD 7410); *T & GA Russell*, MAN/91/1434 (VTD 7534); *Swaffer Truscott Ltd*, LON/91/1948 (VTD 7780); *Italpaving Ltd*, LON/92/398 (VTD 7807); *Fida Interiors Ltd*, EDN/92/138 (VTD 8907); *Nationwide Roofing Co*, LON/92/566Z (VTD 9861); *R & F Building Services*, MAN/92/1143 (VTD 11083) and *BE Roose*, LON/92/3166 (VTD 12350).

Misunderstanding of VATA 1994, Sch 8, Group 6*

[52.218] An appeal was dismissed in a case where a company had failed to account for output tax in respect of work carried out on a listed building, although the work did not qualify for zero-rating under what is now *VATA 1994, Sch 8, Group 6* since the building was used as an office and not as a residence. *DJ Trimming Ltd*, LON/91/1327 (VTD 7733). (*Note.* For another issue in this case, see **52.193** above.)

Misunderstanding of VATA 1994, Sch 8, Group 10*

[52.219] See *Premiair Charter Ltd*, **52.404** below.

Supplies incorrectly treated as exempt

Cases where the appellant was successful

Misunderstanding of VATA 1994, Sch 9, Group 1

[52.220] A company purchased some land, this purchase being exempt from VAT under what is now *VATA 1994, Sch 9, Group 1*. It constructed two industrial buildings on the land. It sold one of the buildings, with the land on which it stood, to an associated company. It did not account for tax on the sale, and the Commissioners imposed a misdeclaration penalty. The company appealed, contending that it had a reasonable excuse for not having accounted for tax since it had assumed that, because its purchase of the land had been exempt from VAT, its sale of the land would also be exempt. The tribunal allowed the appeal, observing that this was a 'borderline case' but holding that, since the transaction 'involved both an understanding of the law of real property and of the way in which land and buildings are to be dealt with in VAT law', the circumstances constituted a reasonable excuse for the failure to account for tax. *Prior Diesel Ltd*, LON/93/2820 (VTD 10306).

[52.221] See also *Acrylux Ltd*, **41.114** LAND.

Election to waive exemption—failure to account for output tax

[52.222] In March 1990 a company elected to waive exemption in respect of a property it owned and occupied. In December 1991 it sold the property without accounting for output tax. The Commissioners imposed a misdeclaration penalty. The company appealed, contending that it had a reasonable excuse because it had undergone a change of ownership and its finance director, who had suffered from illness, had forgotten the election. The tribunal allowed the appeal, describing the election as 'an insignificant event' and holding that the circumstances constituted a reasonable excuse. *Lynton Tool & Die Ltd*, LON/93/1206 (VTD 11288). (*Note.* Compare *Satnam Investments Ltd*, **52.224** below, *Black Eagle Ltd*, **52.225** below, *Embleton Ltd*, **52.225** below, and *Fairhome Ltd*, **52.226** below, in all of which there was held to be no reasonable excuse for a failure to account for output tax following an election to waive exemption.)

Misunderstanding of VATA 1994, Sch 9, Group 2

[52.223] See *Insurancewide.com Services Ltd v HMRC*, **38.23** INSURANCE.

Cases where the appellant was unsuccessful

Election to waive exemption—failure to account for tax

[52.224] A company made an election to waive exemption in respect of property which it owned. However, it failed to account for VAT on the rents it received in respect of the property. The Commissioners imposed a misdeclaration penalty and the tribunal dismissed the company's appeal, holding that there was no reasonable excuse for the failure. *Satnam Investments Ltd*, LON/91/1039 (VTD 6746).

[52.225] Similar decisions were reached in *Black Eagle Ltd*, MAN/91/1325 (VTD 7682) and *Embleton Ltd*, LON/93/3034P (VTD 12897).

[52.226] A company sold a property in respect of which it had lodged an election to waive exemption, but failed to account for output tax on the sale. The Commissioners imposed a misdeclaration penalty and the tribunal dismissed the company's appeal, holding that there was no reasonable excuse for the company's failure to account for tax. *Fairhome Ltd*, LON/93/500P (VTD 11314).

Misunderstanding of VATA 1994, Sch 9, Group 1

[52.227] An appeal was dismissed in a case where a company had failed to account for VAT on the sale of a property which it had built, and contended that it had assumed that the sale would be exempt under what is now *VATA 1994, Sch 9, Group 1*. The tribunal held that since the company was carrying on business as a developer of commercial property, it should have sought professional advice. The company appeared to have been ignorant of the basic liability of the supplies which it made. Applying *Neal*, 51.50 PENALTIES: FAILURE TO NOTIFY, this ignorance could not constitute a reasonable excuse. *Cotel Developments Ltd*, LON/92/243X (VTD 9149).

[52.228] A company managed an ice rink under an agreement with a local council. It did not account for VAT on its takings. Customs imposed a misdeclaration penalty, and the company appealed, contending that it had believed that its supplies could be treated as exempt. The tribunal dismissed the appeal, finding that the company had attempted to implement 'a complex avoidance scheme' but that 'those implementing the scheme did not understand the legal effect of the agreements'. The tribunal described the company's principal director as 'a most unsatisfactory witness'. The tribunal held that the supplies failed to qualify for exemption and that there was no reasonable excuse and no grounds for mitigating the penalty. *Saturn Leisure Ltd*, LON/05/532 (VTD 20185).

[52.229] See also *Jamieson*, 52.407 below.

Misunderstanding of VATA 1994, Sch 9, Group 6

[52.230] An appeal against a misdeclaration penalty was dismissed in a case where a college failed to account for output tax on fees which it received from students for educational services, although the relevant supplies failed to qualify for exemption under *VATA 1983, Sch 6, Group 6* (the predecessor of *VATA 1994, Sch 9, Group 6*). The tribunal found that the college's proprietor and accountant had 'behaved irresponsibly having recklessly given themselves the benefit of the doubt', and held that there was no reasonable excuse for the college's failure to account for output tax on the fees in question. *London International College*, LON/92/907 (VTD 10886).

Incorrect claim to exemption under VATA 1994, Sch 9, Group 10

[52.231] A company (L) operated a golf club. From 1992 to 1999 it accounted for VAT. It then ceased accounting for VAT. Customs issued assessments and a misdeclaration penalty (which they subsequently mitigated by 50%). L appealed, contending that it had transferred the operation of the club to a separate non-profit-making company (B), so that the supplies qualified for exemption under *VATA 1994, Sch 9, Group 10*. The tribunal reviewed the evidence in detail, rejected this contention and dismissed the appeal, finding that B 'did not have the resources nor the means to supply a fully functional golf course to the members of the golf club'. On the evidence, L had 'continued to supply the golfers with the premises, a working golf course, staff, machinery, fertilisers, sand, flags, agronomist, competition trophies and catering'. Accordingly L had remained liable to account for VAT. Furthermore, there was no reasonable excuse for the failure to account for tax. *Lumar Developments Ltd*, MAN/x (VTD 19729).

Incorrect claims for bad debt relief

Cases where the appellant was successful

[52.232] In November 1990 a company claimed bad debt relief in respect of eight debts where the customer had ceased trading. However, one of the companies was not formally in liquidation, so that under the law then in force no relief was due. When the Commissioners discovered this, they imposed a misdeclaration penalty. The tribunal allowed the company's appeal against the penalty. Ignorance of general VAT law was not a reasonable excuse, but the detailed rules concerning bad debt relief were complex, and the claim would have been allowed if the supply had been made after 31 March 1991, when the law was changed by the *VAT (Refunds for Bad Debts) Regulations (SI 1991/371)*. The tribunal chairman observed that she did 'not consider that Parliament, when legislating for serious misdeclaration penalties, intended that these penalties would be applied in circumstances such as these'. *Vision Computer Products Ltd*, LON/91/1511Y (VTD 7072). (*Note.* The decision in this case was disapproved by a subsequent tribunal in *Ramm Contract Furnishing (Northern) Ltd*, 52.239 below, where the tribunal observed that 'we cannot accept that the application of the basic provisions for bad debt relief was so complex as to afford (the appellant) a reasonable excuse for making a premature claim for bad debt relief'.)

[52.233] In April 1991 a company claimed bad debt relief in respect of debts which had been incurred in 1987. The Commissioners disallowed the claim, as the company had been unable to submit the evidence of insolvency required by *VATA 1983, s 22* and the supplies had taken place before the revised provisions of *FA 1990, s 11* came into force. They also imposed a misdeclaration penalty. The company appealed against the penalty, contending that it had a reasonable excuse for having made the incorrect claim, since its director had wrongly assumed that the provisions of *FA 1990, s 11* were retrospective. The tribunal allowed the appeal, holding that the circumstances constituted a reasonable excuse. (There was, however, held to be no reasonable excuse for other misdeclarations on the return in question.) *James Yorke (Holdings) Ltd*, LON/92/1121Y (VTD 9583).

[52.234] A company (D) carried on business as paper merchants. In November 1991 one of its customers went into liquidation, owing it £62,000. D claimed bad debt relief in respect of this in its return for the period ending March 1992. The Commissioners imposed a misdeclaration penalty, since the claim had been made before the expiry of the one-year time limit laid down by *FA 1990, s 11* (as amended by *FA 1991, s 15*). D appealed, contending that it had a reasonable excuse because it had been unaware of the changes to the rules for bad debt relief made by *FA 1990*, and that, since the customer was formally in liquidation, the claim would have been allowable under the previous provisions of *VATA 1983, s 22*. The tribunal allowed the appeal, observing that in cases of insolvencies, the 1990 changes had made the law 'much harsher' and that the rules had been changed in 'an unexpected and irrational way', and holding that D's ignorance of the relevant changes in the legislation constituted a reasonable excuse. *David John (Papers) Ltd*, LON/92/2762 (VTD 10084).

[52.235] A similar decision was reached in *Leberl Advertising Ltd*, LON/92/3234P (VTD 10599).

[52.236] A company (T) which carried on business as shipping and freight forwarding agents paid tax on behalf of a customer. The customer failed to reimburse T for the payment, and subsequently went into liquidation. T claimed bad debt relief, but the Commissioners rejected the claim, since T had not made any supply. The Commissioners also imposed a misdeclaration penalty, but the tribunal allowed T's appeal against the penalty, holding that the circumstances constituted a reasonable excuse. *Toga Freight Services (UK) Ltd*, LON/91/2170X (VTD 9906).

Cases where the appellant was unsuccessful

[52.237] A trader supplied satellite dishes to a company in which he had a 50% shareholding. The company then sold the dishes to members of the public. Subsequently, the company went into voluntary liquidation. The trader reclaimed bad debt relief of more than 12,000 in respect of supplies which he claimed to have made to the company, although he had no VAT invoices in support of this claim. When the Commissioners discovered this, they imposed a misdeclaration penalty. The tribunal dismissed the trader's appeal, holding that the circumstances did not constitute a reasonable excuse for reclaiming bad debt relief without supporting invoices. *JD Spellar (t/a Allied Satellite Systems)*, LON/91/813X (VTD 6829).

[52.238] A company (M) operating the 'self-billing' system did a substantial amount of work for a company (J). J went into liquidation owing M £86,000. M had accounted for tax on a VAT invoice issued by J, showing a VAT liability of £1,765. No other outstanding VAT invoices had been issued by J, and M had not accounted for any other unpaid VAT. Although M had only paid VAT of £1,765 to Customs, it claimed bad debt relief of £12,980. When the Commissioners discovered this, they imposed a misdeclaration penalty in respect of the false claim. The tribunal dismissed M's appeal. There was no reasonable excuse for reclaiming amounts as bad debt relief where no VAT had ever been accounted for on such amounts in the first place. *Magright Ltd*, LON/91/275X (VTD 6925).

[52.239] An appeal was dismissed in a case where a company had claimed bad debt relief without holding a liquidator's certificate as required by the legislation then in force. The tribunal declined to follow the decision in *Vision Computer Products Ltd*, **52.232** above, observing that 'we cannot accept that the application of the basic provisions for bad debt relief was so complex as to afford (the appellant) a reasonable excuse for making a premature claim for bad debt relief'. *Ramm Contract Furnishing (Northern) Ltd*, MAN/91/1127 (VTD 9098). (*Note.* The law relating to bad debt relief was subsequently amended by *FA 1991*. See now *VATA 1994, s 36.*)

[52.240] An appeal was dismissed in a case where a company had claimed bad debt relief before the expiry of the one-year period laid down by *FA 1991, s 15*. *Plastic Protection Ltd*, LON/92/583Y (VTD 9259). (*Notes.* (1) For another issue in this case, see **52.156** above. (2) The one-year period has subsequently been reduced to six months—see *VATA 1994, s 36(1)(c)*.)

[52.241] Similar decisions were reached in *Highview Ltd*, LON/92/1680 (VTD 9564); *Post Form Products Ltd*, LON/92/757X (VTD 9767); *Trade Direct Ltd*, MAN/92/1391 (VTD 10142); *Kernot Cases & Cartons Ltd*, MAN/93/1082 (VTD 11564), and *Digva*, **52.428** below.

Failure to comply with VAT Regulations, reg 166A

[52.242] A company claimed bad debt relief without notifying the relevant customer, as required by *VAT Regulations 1995 (SI 1995/2518), reg 166A*. When the Commissioners discovered this, they imposed a misdeclaration penalty (mitigated by 50%). The company appealed, contending that it had not been aware of the relevant requirements. The tribunal dismissed the appeal, holding that this was not a reasonable excuse, since a 'reasonable and conscientious finance director' would have sought a copy of the relevant Customs' Notice. (The tribunal also held that no further mitigation was appropriate.) *Fort Vale Engineering Ltd*, MAN/00/714 (VTD 17456).

[52.243] See also *Cooper*, **52.429** below.

Credit notes—incorrect treatment

Cases where the appellant was successful

Return wrongly amended to take account of subsequent credit note

[52.244] A company issued an invoice on 30 June 1990 including VAT of £1,508. On 21 July 1990 a credit note was issued cancelling the invoice. The company's VAT return for the period ending 30 June 1990 was prepared by its accountant and included the tax on the invoice in question. When the company's managing director received the completed return from the accountant, he amended the return to exclude the £1,508. The Commissioners imposed a misdeclaration penalty, and the company appealed, contending that it had a reasonable excuse for the error, because its director had genuinely believed that there was no need to account for VAT on the invoice since it had subsequently been cancelled. The tribunal allowed the appeal. The return should have included the tax of £1,508 and the credit note should have been taken into account in the following return. However, the director's belief that the return should be amended, to take account of the subsequent credit note, was not unreasonable. *NCJ Electrical Ltd*, MAN/91/224 (VTD 6383).

Delay in receiving credit note from finance company

[52.245] A building company leased an excavator from a finance company. In April 1990 the agreement was cancelled, and a similar agreement was entered into in respect of another similar machine. The finance company issued a credit note for rebate of rentals due under the first agreement, stating that the tax point was April 1990, and that the building company should account for the VAT shown on the credit note. However, the building company did not receive the credit note until August 1990, and did not account for the VAT in question until its return for the period ending August 1990. When the Commissioners discovered this, they imposed a misdeclaration penalty, as the tax should have been accounted for in the company's return for the period ending May 1990. The tribunal allowed the company's appeal, holding that the delay in receiving the credit note from the finance company constituted a reasonable excuse. *GJ Bennett & Co (Builders) Ltd*, MAN/90/1003 (VTD 6457). (*Note.* For other issues in this case, see **52.217** above and **52.378** below.)

Credit note prepared to cancel invoice but not issued to customer

[52.246] A small company (M) agreed to supply three lifeboats to a large company (H) which was constructing an oil platform. 10% of the agreed price was paid as a deposit. It was agreed that a further 80% should be paid after H had taken delivery of the boats and confirmed their acceptability, and that the final 10% should be paid after M had provided a warranty bond. The boats were completed in October 1990, and M issued an invoice for 80% of the price, although H had not yet confirmed their acceptability. On 3 November H advised M that it did not consider the boats to be of an acceptable standard, and would not pay the invoice. M then prepared a credit note, which it backdated to 31 October. The credit note was mistakenly not issued, although it was entered in M's records. On 12 November H advised M that it had decided that the boats were acceptable after all, and would pay the invoice. M prepared a second invoice to reverse the effect of the credit note in its records, but, since it had discovered that it had not issued the credit note to H, it did not issue the second invoice to H. In preparing its VAT return for the period ending 31 October, M did not include the output tax charged on the first invoice, treating it as having been cancelled by the credit note dated 31 October. When the Commissioners discovered that the output tax had not been included in the return, they imposed a misdeclaration penalty. The company appealed, contending that it had believed that the first invoice should not be treated as effective since at the time it was issued H had not accepted the lifeboats and the amount charged was not due under the terms of the contract. The tribunal allowed the appeal. On the evidence, the tax should have been accounted for in the October return, since the invoice had been issued in that period but the credit note had not. However, applying dicta in *The Clean Car Co Ltd*, **52.84** above, the company 'ought not to be blamed for taking the view that' the tax point was November rather than October. *Offshore Marine Engineering Ltd*, MAN/91/712 (VTD 6840).

Validity of credit notes disputed by Commissioners

[52.247] A company (P) was carrying out building work for a customer. The customer ran into financial difficulties and could not continue to pay for the work. P issued the customer with credit notes for £202,800 plus VAT. The Commissioners took the view that the credit notes were not effective for VAT purposes (see the cases noted at **40.85** *et seq.* INVOICES AND CREDIT NOTES), and imposed a misdeclaration penalty. The tribunal allowed the company's appeal against the penalty, observing that 'the validity of the credit notes in these circumstances is a difficult item over which an ordinary conscientious businessman might well make a mistake'. *Portal Contracting Ltd*, LON/92/1458A (VTD 10234).

[52.248] See also *The Friary Electrical Co Ltd*, **40.98** INVOICES AND CREDIT NOTES.

Cases where the appellant was unsuccessful

Failure to account for tax shown on credit note

[52.249] An appeal against a misdeclaration penalty was dismissed in a case where a company had failed to account for tax shown on a credit note. *V Tech Electronics Ltd*, LON/91/139Y (VTD 6677).

[52.250] Similar decisions were reached in *Scomark Engineering Ltd*, MAN/91/826 (VTD 9104) and *Meadow Contracts Group plc*, LON/92/98X (VTD 9431).

Credit note not effective for VAT—failure to account for tax

[52.251] A company (E) was carrying out work on an office development for a client. It issued an invoice for £357,000 plus VAT. The client disputed the amount of the invoice, and E issued a credit note for the amount. Subsequently E began litigation against the client. In the meantime E did not account for tax on the invoice. The Commissioners formed the opinion that the purpose of the credit note had not been to correct a mistake or error, but to avoid liability to VAT, so that the credit note was not effective for VAT purposes. They imposed a misdeclaration penalty. The tribunal dismissed E's appeal, holding that there was no reasonable excuse for E's failure to account for tax on the invoice in question. *Engineering Building Services Ltd*, LON/92/2552A (VTD 10875). (*Note.* For whether a credit note is effective for VAT purposes, see the cases at **40.85** to **40.96** INVOICES AND CREDIT NOTES.)

[52.252] Similar decisions were reached in *Vaughans of Dudley's Ltd*, MAN/92/1292 (VTD 11374) and *Bartram Planned Preventative Maintenance Ltd*, MAN/93/473 (VTD 12418).

Failure to account for output tax—other cases

Cases where the appellant was successful

Payment received following insurance claim for damaged goods

[52.253] A company which manufactured paper took delivery of two consignments of pulp which were subsequently found to have been contaminated. The company lodged a claim with its insurers. Subsequently it received payment from a salvage association acting on behalf of the insurance company. It did not account for VAT on this payment. Following a control visit by a VAT officer, the company accepted that the payment was taxable since it related to the sale of the damaged pulp by the salvage association. The Commissioners imposed a misdeclaration penalty and the company appealed, contending that until the control visit, it had believed that the payment was not liable to VAT. The tribunal allowed the company's appeal, holding that the circumstances constituted a reasonable excuse. *Caledonian Paper plc*, EDN/91/74 (VTD 6139).

Incorrect operation of self-billing system

[52.254] A company (R) worked on a building project as a subcontractor for another company (W), which operated a self-billing system. W issued to R a 'self-billing' invoice for £73,720 in respect of work done by R. No VAT was included on the invoice, although the work was standard-rated and VAT should have been charged. The Commissioners imposed a misdeclaration penalty but the tribunal allowed R's appeal, holding that the inaccuracy of the invoice issued by W was a reasonable excuse for R's failure to account for the VAT in question. *RC Frame Erectors Ltd*, LON/91/1535X (VTD 7042). (*Note.* Compare the cases noted at 52.275 to 52.277 below, in which similar circumstances were held not to constitute a reasonable excuse.)

[52.255] A similar decision was reached in *AE Pipework Services Ltd*, MAN/92/1257 (VTD 10724).

Failure to account for tax on management charges

[52.256] A partnership issued invoices to an associated company in respect of management charges, but did not account for VAT in respect of these. The Commissioners imposed a misdeclaration penalty and the partnership appealed, contending that it had a reasonable excuse because it had not realised that the management charges were liable to VAT, and there had been no loss of revenue as the company had not reclaimed any input tax. The tribunal held that the circumstances constituted a reasonable excuse. *Ardmore Direct*, BEL/90/50X (VTD 7055). (*Note.* Compare *Mr Builder (1987) Ltd*, 52.280 below, and the cases noted at 52.281 below.)

[52.257] Similar decisions were reached in *Rawlings Bros (GS) Ltd*, MAN/91/1183 (VTD 7533); *AM Proos & Sons Ltd*, MAN/90/932 (VTD 7717, 7734); *Scorpio Marine Enterprises Ltd*, LON/92/1178X (VTD 9121); *Diacutt Concrete Drilling Services Ltd*, LON/92/934X (VTD 9728); *Cargo Express (UK) Ltd*, LON/92/1798 (VTD 9779); *Robert Matthews Ltd*, LON/92/2561 (VTD 9801); *Adcon Holdings Ltd*, MAN/92/1407 (VTD 10324) and *Plantation Wharf Management Ltd*, LON/93/1484P (VTD 12755).

Failure to account for output tax on amounts invoiced for supplies of staff

[52.258] A company operated a retail newsagency. Some of its shops also housed sub-post offices. In such shops, it appointed one of its directors as the nominal subpostmaster and provided employees to carry out the running of the sub-post offices. The nominal subpostmaster was paid a salary by the Post Office, which was accepted as being outside the scope of VAT (see *Rickarby*, 7.103 BUSINESS). He paid this to the company, which paid his salary and the salaries of its employees who actually worked in the sub-post offices. The company did not account for output tax on the amounts which it paid to such staff. The Commissioners issued an assessment charging output tax on the deemed supplies of staff, and imposed a misdeclaration penalty. The company accepted the assessment, but appealed against the penalty, contending that the complexity of the arrangements constituted a reasonable excuse. The tribunal accepted this contention and allowed the appeal. *United News Shops (Holdings) Ltd*, MAN/92/1394 (VTD 12321).

Council acting as agent for water authority—effect of Water Act 1989

[52.259] A borough council acted as agent for its local water authority. It submitted claims for reimbursement to the authority. Prior to the *Water Act 1989*, the council had not been required to charge VAT on the supply of its services to the water authority. However, after the passing of the *Water Act*, the water authority became a limited company (instead of a statutory body), so that the council was required to charge VAT on such supplies. The council did not appreciate the significance of this, and failed to charge VAT on its supplies in the two months following the privatisation of the water authority. The Commissioners imposed a misdeclaration penalty, but the tribunal allowed the council's appeal, holding that the circumstances constituted a reasonable excuse. *Chesterfield Borough Council*, MAN/91/808 (VTD 7104).

[52.260] The decision in *Chesterfield Borough Council*, 52.259 above, was applied in the similar case of *Wyre Borough Council*, MAN/91/1391 (VTD 8880).

[52.261] A similar decision was reached in *Eden District Council*, MAN/92/1061 (VTD 10245).

Misunderstanding of place of supply

[52.262] A consulting engineer supplied services to a Belgian company in relation to the supply of furnaces used for water treatment. He did not charge or account for VAT. The Commissioners ruled that his services were excluded from zero-rating, since they were 'services relating to land' within what is now *VATA 1994, Sch 5 para 3*, and imposed a misdeclaration penalty. The engineer appealed, contending that he had a reasonable excuse for believing that the supplies were zero-rated. The tribunal allowed the appeal, holding that the circumstances constituted a reasonable excuse. *DC Day*, LON/91/2492 (VTD 7764).

Reverse premium—failure to account for tax

[52.263] The Commissioners imposed a misdeclaration penalty on a company which had failed to account for tax on a reverse premium. The company appealed, contending that it had a reasonable excuse because its financial controller had not realised that the payment was liable to VAT. The tribunal allowed the appeal, holding that the circumstances constituted a reasonable excuse. *Anacomp Ltd*, LON/92/322Z (VTD 7824).

[52.264] A similar decision was reached in *Silver Knight Exhibitions Ltd*, MAN/92/1826 (VTD 10569).

Supplies at hairdressing salon

[52.265] In the case noted at **62.260** SUPPLY, the proprietor of a hairdressing salon had only accounted for VAT in respect of the 60% of the gross takings which he retained, and did not account for VAT on the 40% of the takings which he paid to the stylists. The Commissioners imposed a misdeclaration penalty, but the tribunal allowed the proprietor's appeal against the penalty. On the evidence, the supplies to customers were made by the salon proprietor, and he should have accounted for VAT on the full amount of the takings. However, his belief that he only needed to account for VAT on the takings which he retained was not unreasonable, and thus there was a reasonable excuse for his failure to account for VAT. *DL Freer*, LON/91/1069Y (VTD 7648). (*Note.* Compare the subsequent case of *S Taylor (Machine Tools) Ltd*, **52.297** below, where similar circumstances were held not to constitute a reasonable excuse.)

Separate businesses operated by sole trader

[52.266] A self-employed hairdresser had not been registered for VAT, as his turnover had consistently been below the registration threshold. In 1989 he began a separate business of selling water purifiers. He hoped that his turnover in this business would exceed the threshold, and therefore registered for VAT. However, he did not account for VAT on his income from hairdressing, and the Commissioners imposed a misdeclaration penalty. He appealed, contending that he had a reasonable excuse because he had only intended to register in respect of his business of selling water purifiers, and had not realised that the effect of this was that he would also have to account for VAT on his hairdressing income. The tribunal allowed his appeal against the penalty, holding that although he should have accounted for VAT on his hairdressing supplies, his ignorance of the need to do so constituted a reasonable excuse. *AD Laurie (t/a Betterwater Systems)*, LON/91/1899X (VTD 7889). (*Note.* Compare *Bobacre Ltd (t/a Geary Drive Hire)*, **52.299** below, and *Ezzi-Irani*, **52.300** below. For cases in which it was held that a registration covers more than one business, see **57.1** *et seq.* REGISTRATION. For a case in which it was held that ignorance of this principle was not a reasonable excuse for failure to register, see *Dawson*, **51.54** PENALTIES: FAILURE TO NOTIFY.)

[52.267] A similar decision was reached in *R Gallo (t/a The Fun Pub)*, EDN/93/36 (VTD 11502).

Failure to account for VAT on rents collected by assignee

[52.268] A company (C) leased computer equipment to customers. It purchased such equipment from suppliers, and, after leasing the equipment, it sold it to a finance company (F) and agreed to repurchase the equipment from F on a hire-purchase basis. It executed deeds of assignment whereby it assigned to

F the rents receivable under the leases. Following the execution of these deeds, C did not account for VAT on the payments which its customers made to F as its assignee. The Commissioners ruled that, despite the assignments, C remained legally responsible for invoicing and for accounting for VAT, and imposed a misdeclaration penalty. C appealed, contending that it had a reasonable excuse since it had assumed that F was responsible for the VAT. The tribunal allowed the appeal against the penalty, holding that the circumstances constituted a reasonable excuse. *Capital Computers Ltd*, LON/92/561Z (VTD 9095).

Failure to account for tax on disposal of part of business

[52.269] A company (J) which manufactured and sold household consumer products disposed of a blow moulding business. It did not account for VAT on the disposal, and the Commissioners imposed a misdeclaration penalty. J appealed, contending that it had regarded the disposal as the transfer of a business as a going concern, on which output tax was not chargeable. The tribunal allowed the appeal, holding that it had not been unreasonable for J to have treated the disposal as the transfer of a going concern. *Jeyes Ltd*, LON/92/1277P (VTD 10513).

[52.270] In May 1991 a trader purchased 15 public houses, all of which were let to tenants, from a brewery. The purchase was treated as the transfer of a going concern, so that no tax was charged. The trader elected to waive exemption in respect of the properties, so that the rents were chargeable to tax. Later in 1991 he sold one of the houses to the tenant, and did not account for output tax on the transfer. The Commissioners imposed a misdeclaration penalty, and the trader appealed, contending that he had assumed that the sale could be treated as the transfer of a going concern, on which no tax was due. The tribunal allowed the appeal, holding that the circumstances constituted a reasonable excuse. *EQ Melville*, EDN/92/253 (VTD 10548).

[52.271] A building company owned three properties, in respect of which it had elected to waive exemption. It sold two of these properties to tenants in September 1991, and sold the other property in December 1991. It did not account for output tax on these sales. The Commissioners imposed misdeclaration penalties and the partnership appealed, contending that it had a reasonable excuse because the partners had assumed that the sale of the properties constituted the transfer of a business as a going concern. The tribunal allowed the appeals, holding that the circumstances constituted a reasonable excuse. *Spencer & Harrison*, MAN/93/138 (VTD 10697).

Stolen takings—failure to account for tax

[52.272] A VAT officer on a control visit formed the opinion that a trader who sold garden furniture had underdeclared his takings. Following the officer's visit, the Commissioners issued an estimated assessment and imposed a misdeclaration penalty. The trader appealed, contending that the discrepancy was attributable to takings which had been stolen. The tribunal dismissed the trader's appeal against the assessment, applying the principle in *Benton*, **62.382** SUPPLY. However, the tribunal allowed the appeal against the penalty, holding that the circumstances constituted a reasonable excuse. *DF Venton*, LON/92/1859A (VTD 10526).

Customer in liquidation after work carried out but before invoice sent

[52.273] A trader carried out work for a company which went into liquidation before he had submitted an invoice for the work done. The trader did not account for tax on the work in question, and the Commissioners imposed a misdeclaration penalty. The tribunal allowed the trader's appeal against the penalty, holding that the circumstances constituted a reasonable excuse. *C Dillon*, MAN/92/1565 (VTD 10681).

Sale of capital assets to finance company

[52.274] A coach operator had had to arrange an overdraft in order to finance the building of some new coaches. She sold the completed coaches to a finance company but failed to account for output tax on the sale. The Commissioners imposed a misdeclaration penalty but the tribunal allowed the trader's appeal, holding that since this was the first time she had entered into transactions of this nature, the circumstances constituted a reasonable excuse. *A Jones (t/a Jones Motors of Ynysybwl)*, LON/98/235 (VTD 15861).

Cases where the appellant was unsuccessful

Incorrect operation of self-billing system

[52.275] An engineering company (A) acted as subcontractor for another company (R), which operated a 'self-billing' system. R provided A with remittance advices intended to show the net amount due to A and the amount of VAT due in respect of that amount. However, the advices received by A did not show any VAT details, and A did not account for VAT on the payments from R. When the Commissioners discovered this, they imposed a misdeclaration penalty. A appealed, contending that it had a reasonable excuse because the misdeclaration resulted from R's failure to operate the 'self-billing' system correctly. The tribunal dismissed A's appeal. The operation of the 'self-billing' system 'did not shift the responsibility for accounting for the VAT' from A to R, and reliance on R was in any event precluded from constituting a reasonable excuse by *VATA 1994, s 71(1)(b)*. *Alpha Engineering Services Ltd*, LON/90/1978Y (VTD 5775).

[52.276] The decision in *Alpha Engineering Systems Ltd*, 52.275 above, was applied in the similar case of *Clover Asphalte (IOM) Ltd v The Isle of Man Treasury*, MAN/91/342 (VTD 6645).

[52.277] Similar decisions were reached in *C & S Glaziers (North Wales) Ltd*, MAN/91/40 (VTD 6247); *Red Barn Contracting Ltd*, MAN/90/1094 (VTD 6294); *Yazaki (UK) Ltd*, LON/91/776Z (VTD 7128); *Specialist Rainwater Services Ltd*, LON/91/2548Z (VTD 7732); *General Metals (Glasgow) Ltd*, EDN/92/224 (VTD 9399); *Overburn Properties Ltd*, EDN/92/323 (VTD 9966); *Throston Ltd*, MAN/93/991 (VTD 11770), and *Beveridge*, 52.426 below.

Incorrect operation of flat-rate scheme for small businesses

[52.278] See *Mr & Mrs Morgan (t/a The Harrow Inn)*, **28.12** FLAT-RATE SCHEME.

Company operating flat-rate scheme although not eligible to do so

[52.279] See *Welshback Exercise Ltd*, **28.17** FLAT-RATE SCHEME, and *RDF Management Services Ltd*, **28.18** FLAT-RATE SCHEME.

Failure to account for tax on management charges

[52.280] An appeal against a misdeclaration penalty was dismissed in a case where a company had failed to account for tax on management charges. *Mr Builder (1987) Ltd*, MAN/91/319 (VTD 6265).

[52.281] Similar decisions were reached in *Euroweb Ltd*, LON/91/1672Z (VTD 6843); *Gardith Construction Ltd*, LON/91/1348Z (VTD 6959); *M & N Dwek & Co Ltd*, MAN/91/989 (VTD 7082); *Trina Ltd*, LON/91/1928 (VTD 7713); *Cleshar Contract Services Ltd*, LON/91/1641Z (VTD 8803); *WM Ayrton & Co (Holdings) Ltd*, MAN/92/188 (VTD 9195); *Pet-Reks (Southern) Ltd*, LON/92/1364P (VTD 9347); *PR Mitchell Ltd*, LON/92/1708P (VTD 9394); *Minstead House Care Management Ltd*, LON/91/2315X (VTD 9506); *Michael Cooney & Co Ltd*, MAN/92/433 (VTD 9627); *Blake Paper Ltd*, LON/92/2155 (VTD 9829); *Temple Avenue Finance Ltd*, LON/92/2669P (VTD 9965); *Omega Design & Marketing Ltd*, MAN/92/848 (VTD 10004); *West London Air Conditioning Ltd*, LON/93/705P (VTD 10797); *Churchill Radio Cars Ltd*, LON/92/2899A (VTD 11658); *Slouand Ltd*, MAN/93/438 (VTD 11701); *Key Properties Ltd*, LON/92/2266A (VTD 11778); *NEP Group Ltd*, **52.348** below and *Mission-fine Ltd*, **43.5** MANAGEMENT SERVICES.

Supply to associated company—failure to account for tax

[52.282] An appeal against a misdeclaration penalty was dismissed in a case where a company had failed to account for VAT on a sale to an associated company. *Precious Metal Industries (Wales) Ltd*, LON/91/2712 (VTD 7750).

[52.283] Similar decisions were reached in *Mart Play Ltd*, LON/91/2080X (VTD 9046); *RC & CH Hunt*, LON/92/619Y (VTD 9135); *Deeside Welding Co*, MAN/91/910 (VTD 9238); *William Youngs & Son (Farms) Ltd*, LON/92/1510P (VTD 9660); *Arrowin Ltd*, MAN/91/1341 (VTD 10575); *Irish Roofing Felts Ltd*, BEL/93/27 (VTD 11425); *LEP Luma Ltd*, LON/93/1167P (VTD 11490); *Euromer Stevedores Ltd*, MAN/91/1111 (VTD 11755); *I Loftus & Son Ltd*, LON/93/1346 (VTD 12678); *Antrobus Farm Ltd*, MAN/98/258 (VTD 16029); *London & Newcastle Holdings plc*, LON/99/850 (VTD 16402); *Roundhouse Work Ltd*, LON/02/711 (VTD 18595) and *I & N Martin*, **52.394** below.

Supplies to associated partnership—failure to account for tax

[52.284] A company failed to account for VAT on supplies to an associated partnership. The Commissioners imposed a misdeclaration penalty and the company appealed, contending that it had not realised that the supplies were liable to VAT. The tribunal dismissed the appeal, holding that there was no reasonable excuse for the company's failure to account for tax, and that the fact that the partnership could have reclaimed the appropriate input tax was irrelevant. *Michael Rogers Ltd*, LON/91/2454Z (VTD 9157).

[52.285] Similar decisions were reached in *R Baker*, MAN/93/915 (VTD 11634) and *TRS Cabinet Co Ltd*, MAN/91/1640 (VTD 11750).

[52.286] See also *Auto-Plas (International) Ltd*, **52.78** above.

Supply by partnership to retiring partner—failure to account for tax

[52.287] A partnership transferred a vehicle valued at £18,000 to a retiring partner, and failed to account for output tax. The Commissioners imposed a misdeclaration penalty and the tribunal dismissed the partnership's appeal, holding that there was no reasonable excuse for the failure to account for tax. *Coombes Transport*, MAN/92/1462 (VTD 11275).

Supply by company to director—failure to account for tax

[52.288] See *Thimbleby Farms Ltd v HMRC*, **67.133** VALUATION.

Failure to account for output tax on sale of property

[52.289] A trader failed to account for output tax on a sale of land which he had opted to tax, and on which he had previously reclaimed input tax. Customs imposed a misdeclaration penalty and the tribunal dismissed the trader's appeal. *R Sadler (t/a Warmfield Group)*, MAN/07/1106 (VTD 20893). (*Note*. For another issue in this case, see **52.390** below.)

[52.290] See also *Porters End Estates Ltd*, **52.399** below; the cases noted at **52.400** and **52.401** below, and *Ellis*, **52.440** below.

Failure to account for output tax on deregistration

[52.291] A company (M) had registered for VAT in 2002. It cancelled its registration in 2009, but failed to account for output tax as required by *VATA 1994, Sch 4 para 8*. HMRC imposed a penalty under *FA 2007, Sch 24*, and the tribunal dismissed M's appeal. *Mollan & Co Ltd*, [2010] UKFTT 578 (TC), TC00828.

Failure to account for tax on lease premium

[52.292] An appeal against a misdeclaration penalty was dismissed in a case where a solicitor had failed to account for output tax on the receipt of a premium for the grant of a lease. *WT Stockler*, LON/96/288 (VTD 15350).

Private use of fuel

[52.293] Failure to account for tax on petrol used privately was held not to constitute a reasonable excuse in *Claremont Construction (London) Ltd*, LON/91/1301Y (VTD 7016) and *Property & Investment Centre Ltd*, LON/93/2037P (VTD 11686).

Failure to account for tax on profit on sale of car

[52.294] In 1988 a company purchased a rare Ferrari car for £315,000. In April 1990 it sold the car for £700,000. It failed to account for VAT on its profit. The Commissioners imposed a misdeclaration penalty and the tribunal dismissed the company's appeal, holding that there was no reasonable excuse for the company's failure to seek advice on the tax consequences of the sale. *T Baden Hardstaff Ltd*, MAN/90/808 (VTD 7230).

Sales made as agent—failure to account for tax on commission

[52.295] A farmer acted as an agent for a landowner, selling grain on behalf of the landowner and retaining 25% of the sale price as his commission. He failed to account for VAT on the sums which he retained, and the Commissioners imposed a misdeclaration penalty. The tribunal dismissed the farmer's appeal, holding that there was no reasonable excuse for the failure to account for tax. *P Forster*, LON/92/1047Z (VTD 9367).

Commission

[52.296] Failure to account for tax on commission was held not to constitute a reasonable excuse in *ND Lieder*, LON/92/2308A (VTD 10400); *Alcatel Business Systems Ltd*, LON/92/2398 (VTD 11411) and *Merlin HC Ltd*, **1.100** AGENTS.

Supplies at hairdressing salon

[52.297] A company which operated hairdressing salons only accounted for output tax on the amounts which it retained, and did not account for tax on the amounts which were retained by the stylists. The Commissioners imposed a misdeclaration penalty. The company appealed, contending firstly that it should only be required to account for tax on the amounts which it retained, and alternatively that it had a reasonable excuse for having believed that it was only required to account for tax on these amounts. The tribunal dismissed the appeal, holding on the evidence that the supplies were made by the company, rather than by the individual stylists, and that there was no reasonable excuse for the misdeclaration since the company 'chose to depart from the normal straightforward method of conducting its business and to enter into confused and imprecise arrangements. The complexity was of the appellant's own making.' *S Taylor (Machine Tools) Ltd*, LON/92/860A (VTD 11171).

Supplies of chauffeur-driven car hire

[52.298] A partnership provided a chauffeur-driven car hire business. It only accounted for VAT on the amounts which it retained, and did not account for VAT on the amounts which were paid to the drivers who worked for it. The Commissioners issued an assessment charging output tax on the full amounts paid by the customers, and imposed a misdeclaration penalty. The tribunal dismissed the partnership's appeal against both the assessment and the penalty, holding that the supplies were made by the partnership and that there was no reasonable excuse for the partnership's failure to account for tax on the correct basis. *Japan Executive Chauffeur*, LON/92/3128A (VTD 11836).

Company acquiring assets of separate business

[52.299] A company (B), which was registered for VAT, took over the assets of a separate business and continued to trade both under its existing trading name and under the trading name of the new business. It did not account for output tax on its income under the trading name of the second business. The Commissioners imposed a misdeclaration penalty and the tribunal dismissed the company's appeal, holding that there was no reasonable excuse for the failure to account for tax. *Bobacre Ltd (t/a Geary Drive Hire)*, MAN/94/761 (VTD 12829).

Separate businesses operated by sole trader

[52.300] A trader, who owned two shops selling take-away food, failed to account for VAT on the takings of one of the shops. When the Commissioners discovered this, they imposed a misdeclaration penalty. The trader appealed, contending that he had transferred the operation of the shop in question to his wife. The tribunal reviewed the evidence in detail, rejected this contention, and dismissed the appeal. *M Ezzi-Irani*, EDN/00/44 (VTD 17360).

Incorrect operation of Retail Scheme

[52.301] An appeal against a misdeclaration penalty was dismissed in a case where a married couple who operated a newsagency had operated their Retail Scheme incorrectly and had failed to account for tax on several items of income. *BK & U Sood (t/a Good News)*, LON/92/2435 (VTD 9950).

[52.302] Similar decisions were reached in *DK Popat*, MAN/91/684 (VTD 10452) and *AP & P Renshall (t/a Kingsway Convenience Store)*, MAN/98/1092 (VTD 16273).

Failure to comply with direction under VATA 1994, Sch 1 para 2

[52.303] The proprietors of a public house failed to account for output tax on receipts from catering, treating it as a separate business carried on by one of the partners (B) as an individual. In October 1988 the Commissioners issued a direction under what is now *VATA 1994, Sch 1 para 2*, against which the partners did not appeal. However, the partners continued not to account for tax on the catering receipts. When the Commissioners discovered this, they imposed a misdeclaration penalty. The partners appealed, contending that they had terminated the partnership on 18 March 1990 but had recommenced it on 8 April, and that they had considered that the result of the temporary termination of the partnership was that the direction under *VATA 1994, Sch 1 para 2* was no longer valid. The tribunal dismissed the partners' appeal, finding that the partnership had continued throughout the period and holding that there was no reasonable excuse for the partners' failure to account for tax. *PG Barnett & TG Larsen*, MAN/92/1585 (VTD 11056).

Underdeclaration of takings

[52.304] A VAT officer formed the opinion that a publican had underdeclared takings, and issued an estimated assessment using a mark-up calculation. Following further information from the publican's accountant, the mark-up was reduced to 55.9%, and the revised assessment was confirmed by the tribunal, applying the principles laid down in *Van Boeckel*, 3.1 ASSESSMENT. The Commissioners also imposed a misdeclaration penalty. The tribunal dismissed the publican's appeal against the penalty, holding on the evidence that there was no reasonable excuse for the failure to keep an accurate record of takings. *MA Rimmer*, LON/92/2410A (VTD 11397).

[52.305] Similar decisions were reached in *M Mahoney*, LON/93/2542A (VTD 12063); *RD Stavrinou*, LON/93/1670A (VTD 12546); *Digbeth Cash & Carry Ltd*, MAN/94/342 (VTD 13180); *H Jin-Xu (t/a Wong Kok Fish & Chips)*, MAN/98/984 (VTD 16520); *KH Yip (t/a Manie Takeaway)*, EDN/00/139 & EDN/00/150 (VTD 17163); *Cun (SQ) (t/a Kung Fung*

Takeaway), LON/04/1081 (VTD 19491); *PRC Mackay & SJ Correll (t/a The Black Horse)*, LON/06/197 (VTD 20928); *A Pouladdej*, [2010] UKFTT 592 (TC), TC00842; *McCourtie*, **3.15** ASSESSMENT, and *Sessions*, **52.392** below.

[52.306] An appeal against a misdeclaration penalty was dismissed in a case where the tribunal found that a trader had failed to account for VAT in respect of several invoices which he had issued. *C Jacobson*, MAN/92/289 (VTD 11741).

[52.307] Similar decisions were reached in *Caroline General Services Ltd*, LON/93/4911A (VTD 12048); *HS Savin*, MAN/93/662 (VTD 12104, 12873), and *DD Group Ltd*, MAN/05/612 (VTD 19405).

[52.308] An appeal against a misdeclaration penalty was dismissed in a case where the tribunal found that a trader had failed to account for VAT on the sale of large quantities of mobile telephones. *MF Mahmood (t/a Mahmood Mobile Service) v HMRC*, [2010] UKFTT 166 (TC), TC00471.

Failure to account for tax on fundraising services

[52.309] An individual (H) agreed to provide fundraising services for a charity in return for 80% of the amounts he collected. He failed to account for tax on the full amount which he received under this agreement. Customs imposed a misdeclaration penalty and the tribunal dismissed H's appeal. *T Hands*, MAN/06/602 (VTD 20788).

Failure to account for output tax on private use of assets

[52.310] See *Kingfisher Events Ltd v HMRC*, **67.132** VALUATION.

Incorrect input tax claims—other cases

Cases where the appellant was successful

Failure to apply partial exemption provisions

[52.311] A company was incorporated to sell houses and plots of land. In its first return it reclaimed the whole of its input tax. The Commissioners imposed a misdeclaration penalty, since some of the supplies related to the exempt sale of plots of land, so that the company should have restricted its input tax claims by applying the partial exemption provisions. The tribunal allowed the company's appeal, holding that the circumstances constituted a reasonable excuse. *Scotia Homes Ltd*, EDN/90/211 (VTD 6044).

[52.312] There was also held to be a reasonable excuse for failure to apply the partial exemption provisions in *Murrayfield Indoor Sports Club*, EDN/91/147 (VTD 6613); *M & P McNaughton*, MAN/91/346 (VTD 7438); *F Wright*, LON/91/1840 (VTD 7465); *Humatt Holdings Ltd*, LON/92/2292Z (VTD 10236); *PJ Robinson*, MAN/92/322 (VTD 13102); *The Laurels Nursing Home Ltd*, MAN/96/1065 (VTD 16092); *Five Steps Community Nursery*, LON/99/701 (VTD 16684); *Medialift Ltd (t/a Pitman Training Centre)*, MAN/02/101 (VTD 18468); and *Polo Farm Sports Club*, **46.188** PARTIAL EXEMPTION.

Input tax relating to exempt supply

[52.313] A hairdresser purchased a boarding house and had work carried out on it to convert it into a retirement home. His accountant advised him that he could reclaim the input tax on the conversion, and he did so. However, on a subsequent control visit, a VAT officer informed him that the supplies made by the retirement home would be exempt under what is now *VATA 1994, Sch 9, Group 7, Item 4*, and that the input tax was therefore not reclaimable. The Commissioners imposed a misdeclaration penalty, but the tribunal allowed the proprietor's appeal. Although it was not necessary to decide the point, the tribunal considered it possible that the supplies might be excluded from exemption under what is now *VATA 1994, Sch 9, Group 1, Item 1(d)*, applying *Namecourt Ltd*, **41.100** LAND. In view of the uncertainty over the status of the supplies, the proprietor had a reasonable excuse for having reclaimed the relevant input tax. *J Bowe*, MAN/91/303 (VTD 6748).

[52.314] An appeal against a misdeclaration penalty was allowed in a case where a company had reclaimed input tax in respect of repairs to premises which it let to a tenant. The tribunal held that the complexity of the legislation was a reasonable excuse for the misdeclaration. *Du Beau Ltd*, LON/91/2521X (VTD 7667).

[52.315] Similar decisions were reached in *The Communications & Leisure Group of Companies*, LON/91/1149X (VTD 7788); *ST Rafferty*, LON/92/638 (VTD 8911); *GAG Cooper*, LON/92/1633P (VTD 9719); *Abbasford Ltd (t/a Watford Electronics)*, LON/92/3200P (VTD 10229); *Terard Ltd*, LON/99/126 (VTD 16949) and *Abbeygate Holdings Ltd*, LON/00/393 (VTD 17046).

[52.316] A company had reclaimed input tax in respect of work carried out on land which it owned, and on which it had intended to build a house. However in 1991, before construction of the house had started, the company sold the site. The sale was an exempt supply, but the company failed to repay the input tax it had previously reclaimed, as required by what is now *VAT Regulations, reg 108*. The Commissioners imposed a misdeclaration penalty, and the company appealed, contending that it had a reasonable excuse since it had not been aware of the relevant regulation. The tribunal allowed the appeal, holding that the circumstances constituted a reasonable excuse. *Time (Ancient & Modern) Ltd*, LON/92/810 (VTD 8814).

[52.317] A married couple sold a farm for £1,800,000. Their solicitor charged them £300,000, plus VAT of £45,000, for his advice with regard to the sale. The couple reclaimed the £45,000 as input tax. The Commissioners imposed a misdeclaration penalty, since the sale of the farm had been an exempt supply, so that the input tax was not deductible. The tribunal allowed the couple's appeal, holding that there was a reasonable excuse for the misdeclaration. *FFJ & FK Forrest*, MAN/91/1355 (VTD 10576).

[52.318] A company purchased a public house. The vendor had elected to waive exemption, and accordingly charged output tax on the sale. The purchaser reclaimed input tax without making any election to waive exemption. The Commissioners therefore issued an assessment to recover the tax, and also imposed a misdeclaration penalty. The tribunal upheld the assessment but allowed the company's appeal against the penalty, holding that the circumstances constituted a reasonable excuse. *Maplefine Ltd*, MAN/97/1103 (VTD 15499).

[52.319] See also *John Lanham Watts (Carpets) Ltd*, 52.154 above.

Input tax reclaimed on zero-rated supply

[52.320] A farmer arranged for builders to carry out work on his farmhouse, which was a listed building. The work should have been zero-rated under what is now *VATA 1994, Sch 8, Group 6*, but the builders included VAT on their invoices. The farmer paid the VAT to the builders, and reclaimed it as input tax. The Commissioners imposed a misdeclaration penalty but the tribunal allowed the farmer's appeal, holding that he had a reasonable excuse for having reclaimed the input tax. *AS Macgregor*, LON/91/1841Y (VTD 7840).

[52.321] A members' club claimed input tax in respect of a water bill, treating the amount charged as inclusive of VAT. Since the supply was zero-rated, HMRC imposed a penalty under *FA 2007, Sch 24*. Judge Radford allowed the club's appeal, finding that the club had acted in good faith. *The Athenaeum Club v HMRC*, [2010] UKFTT 583 (TC), TC00833.

Input tax reclaimed on motor car

[52.322] A company which carried on the business of leasing motor vehicles reclaimed input tax on cars which it had purchased. The Commissioners rejected the claim and imposed a misdeclaration penalty. The company appealed against the penalty, contending that it had a reasonable excuse for reclaiming this input tax, since what is now *Notice No 700/64/96, para 35* indicated that 'if you are a car dealer—a person whose business is the selling of cars—you can reclaim VAT you are charged on unused cars imported for sale'. The company contended that its directors were justified in believing that it qualified as a 'car dealer'. The tribunal allowed the appeal. For the purposes of the case it was not necessary to decide whether the company actually qualified as a car dealer, but it was not unreasonable for the company's directors to have considered that it would qualify as a car dealer. *EP Mooney Ltd*, MAN/91/360 (VTD 6418).

[52.323] An appeal was allowed in a case where a partnership reclaimed input tax on the import of a Chevrolet car which was 'cannibalised' for spare parts. The tribunal held that the circumstances constituted a reasonable excuse. *DR Auto Repair Tech*, LON/92/220Y (VTD 7489).

[52.324] An appeal was allowed in a case where a company had reclaimed input tax on a car purchased for demonstration purposes. The tribunal held that, since the car was not purchased for resale, the company had a reasonable excuse for having reclaimed the input tax. *Top Grade Cars Ltd*, LON/91/337Z (VTD 7602).

[52.325] A couple carried on a plant hire business in partnership. They reclaimed input tax on a Land Rover. HMRC issued an assessment to recover the tax, and also imposed a misdeclaration penalty. The couple appealed, contending that the Land Rover was solely used for the purposes of their business. The tribunal dismissed their appeal against the input tax assessment, applying the CA decision in *CM Upton (t/a Fagomatic) v C & E Commrs*, **44.110** MOTOR CARS, but allowed their appeal against the penalty, holding that there was a reasonable excuse for the incorrect claim. *R & L Waddell (t/a LCD Plant Hire) v HMRC*, [2009] UKFTT 185 (TC), TC00140.

Input tax reclaimed by tour operator

[52.326] A company trading as a tour operator in South Wales failed to operate the appropriate margin scheme and submitted a return reclaiming input tax. The Commissioners imposed a misdeclaration penalty but the tribunal allowed the company's appeal, holding that there was a reasonable excuse for the misdeclaration. *City Centre Ticketline Ltd*, LON/91/1937Y (VTD 7553).

Input tax reclaimed on supply not used for business purposes

[52.327] In the case noted at **36.488** INPUT TAX, the tribunal had held that a printer was not entitled to reclaim input tax on the purchase of a personalised car numberplate. However, the tribunal allowed the printer's appeal against a misdeclaration penalty, holding that since he had been advised by his accountant that he could reclaim the tax in question, he had a reasonable excuse for having done so. *D Philips*, EDN/92/3 (VTD 7883). (*Note*. Compare *NEP Group Ltd*, **52.348** below, in which an appeal against a penalty imposed in similar circumstances was dismissed, partly on the grounds that the appellant company in that case had not sought professional advice.)

[52.328] A similar decision was reached in *Lister*, **36.206** INPUT TAX.

Input tax reclaimed on supply not wholly for business purposes

[52.329] A newsagent, who lived above the shop from which he traded, incurred expenditure on refurbishing the premises. He reclaimed input tax on the whole of the expenditure. The Commissioners ruled that only part of the tax was reclaimable, and imposed a misdeclaration penalty. The tribunal allowed the newsagent's appeal against the penalty. The Commissioners were correct in requiring the expenditure to be apportioned. However, the primary purpose of the expenditure had been to improve the business premises, so that more than half of the input tax was deductible. The newsagent had not acted unreasonably in reclaiming the whole of the tax. *B Singh*, MAN/91/987 (VTD 7584).

[52.330] A Citizens' Advice Bureau arranged for the refurbishment of its premises, and reclaimed the whole of the input tax on this. The Commissioners issued an assessment to recover part of the tax, on the basis that the building was partly used for non-business purposes, so that only a proportion of the tax was deductible. They also imposed a misdeclaration penalty. The Bureau appealed. The tribunal upheld the assessment but allowed the Bureau's appeal against the penalty, holding that the complexity of the law constituted a reasonable excuse. *Stoke-on-Trent Citizens Advice Bureau*, MAN/97/976 (VTD 17296).

Payment to secure appointment of partner as sub-postmistress

[52.331] A couple purchased a retail shop which included a sub-post office. They were required to pay Post Office Counters Ltd £13,928, including VAT of £2,074. They reclaimed input tax on this payment. Customs rejected the claim and imposed a misdeclaration penalty. The couple appealed. The tribunal held that the input tax was not deductible, applying the decision in *H & V Patel (No 2)*, **36.501** INPUT TAX. However, the tribunal allowed the appeal against the penalty, holding that their action in reclaiming the tax 'was reasonable, although wrong'. *D & S Mayariya (t/a Oaktree Lane Selly Oak Post Office & Stores)*, MAN/04/190 (VTD 19049, VTD 19078).

Input tax reclaimed on transfer of going concern

[52.332] An ice-cream salesman reclaimed input tax on the purchase of the van and stock of another salesman. The Commissioners issued an assessment to recover the tax, considering that the transaction constituted the transfer of a business as a going concern. They also imposed a misdeclaration penalty. The tribunal dismissed the salesman's appeal against the assessment, holding that the transaction did constitute the transfer of a going concern, but allowed his appeal against the penalty, holding that the circumstances constituted a reasonable excuse. *A Black*, EDN/92/58 (VTD 7919).

[52.333] See also *Mawji*, **65.49** TRANSFERS OF GOING CONCERNS.

Input tax reclaimed by associated company

[52.334] A company (O) operated a restaurant. Its directors wished to transfer the business to a new company (C), which they incorporated for this purpose. The companies' accountant asked a VAT officer whether it would be possible to transfer O's registration to C, and was told that this would be acceptable. However, before this had been done, C incurred expenditure on refurbishing the restaurant. Since C was not yet registered for VAT, O reclaimed the relevant input tax. The Commissioners imposed a misdeclaration penalty, but the tribunal allowed O's appeal, holding that the circumstances constituted a reasonable excuse. *Orbvent Ltd*, LON/91/967 (VTD 6602).

[52.335] An appeal was allowed in a case where a partnership had reclaimed input tax in respect of invoices made out to an associated company. The tribunal held that the circumstances constituted a reasonable excuse. *Gateway Leisure (Caravan Sales)*, EDN/92/85 (VTD 7943).

[52.336] Similar decisions were reached in *Long's Supermarket Ltd*, BEL/91/21X (VTD 9309) and *Leaders (North East) Ltd*, MAN/92/110 (VTD 9004).

Input tax incorrectly reclaimed by agent

[52.337] In 1990 a caravan site was flooded and 25 of the caravans were damaged. The owner of the site (N), who was registered for VAT, arranged for the necessary repairs and insurance claims. (The caravans themselves were owned by private individuals, rather than by N.) The contractors who carried out the repairs submitted invoices which included VAT, but the insurance company failed to pay the VAT shown on the invoices. N therefore paid the VAT himself, and reclaimed it as input tax. The Commissioners issued an assessment to recover the tax, since the supply had been to the insurance company rather than to N, who had in effect been acting as an agent. They also imposed a misdeclaration penalty. N appealed against the penalty, contending that he had a reasonable excuse for the incorrect claim since the insurance company had advised him that he was entitled to reclaim the VAT. The tribunal allowed his appeal against the penalty, holding that the circumstances constituted a reasonable excuse for the incorrect claim. *PC Nock*, MAN/92/157 (VTD 10169). (*Note.* For the consequences of an insurance company failing to pay a VAT liability, see also the cases noted at **4.5** to **4.8** BAD DEBTS.)

Input tax reclaimed on supply not made to claimant

[52.338] A company (C) arranged a loan from another company (S), and agreed to pay S's solicitors' fees. C reclaimed input tax on the fees in question, and the Commissioners imposed a misdeclaration penalty, since the solicitors had supplied their services to S rather than to C, so that C was not entitled to reclaim the input tax. The tribunal allowed C's appeal against the penalty, holding that the circumstances constituted a reasonable excuse. *Crux Engineering Ltd*, LON/92/179 (VTD 7706).

Cases where the appellant was unsuccessful

Input tax reclaimed on supply outside UK

[52.339] A company (J) was a UK subsidiary of a US company, and undertook a transaction in which goods were exported directly from the USA to the Netherlands, so that any VAT due would be payable to, and reclaimable from, the Dutch authorities. However, J reclaimed UK VAT on this transaction. The Commissioners imposed a misdeclaration penalty and the tribunal dismissed J's appeal. *JLG Industries (UK) Ltd*, EDN/91/13 (VTD 5814).

[52.340] See also *The Edinburgh Piano Company Ltd*, **52.415** below.

Input tax reclaimed on motor car

[52.341] A trader had reclaimed input tax on the purchase of a Land Rover. The Commissioners imposed a misdeclaration penalty and the tribunal dismissed the trader's appeal, holding that there was no reasonable excuse for the trader's failure to realise that the Land Rover was a 'car' for the purposes of the VAT legislation. *RJ Holloway*, LON/91/2578Z (VTD 7493).

[52.342] There was also held to be no reasonable excuse for reclaiming input tax on a car in *PM Birkin*, EDN/91/81 (VTD 6113); *DW Wyck*, LON/91/845X (VTD 6619); *Hardys of Telford*, MAN/91/353 (VTD 6791); *Nightingales Motors (Exmouth) Ltd*, LON/91/1032Y (VTD 6842); *KJ Hodgson*, MAN/91/326 (VTD 7138, 7159); *Page Motors (Ferndown) Ltd*, LON/91/1174 (VTD 7517); *S Travers*, EDN/92/109 (VTD 7942); *RAF Aldergrove Service Institute Fund*, BEL/91/12X (VTD 8812); *CT Finance Ltd*, MAN/91/978 (VTD 9286); *Transtrek Ltd (t/a Thropton Motor Co)*, MAN/91/785 (VTD 9749); *Nigel Sullivan Fibres Ltd*, MAN/92/169 (VTD 9842); *Maple Network Consultancy Ltd*, LON/93/6A (VTD 11488); *RG Barnes*, EDN/96/106 (VTD 14463); *BD Williams*, LON/96/1734 (VTD 15163); *Standridge Farm Ltd*, MAN/00/18 (VTD 16850); *R & LJ Lythgoe (t/a Utopia)*, MAN/x (VTD 18201); *S Evans (t/a EPS Plant & Safety Services)*, LON/03/497 (VTD 18644) and *West Midlands Motors Ltd*, **52.447** below.

[52.343] A similar decision was reached in a case where a partnership reclaimed input tax on two four-wheel drive Vauxhall Montereys. The tribunal held that the vehicles were 'cars' and there was no reasonable excuse for reclaiming input tax on them. *Anglia Building & Decorating Contractors*, MAN/00/306 (VTD 16852).

Failure to apply partial exemption provisions

[52.344] There was held to be no reasonable excuse for failure to apply the partial exemption provisions in *GB Capital Ltd*, EDN/91/31 (VTD 6138); *Palatine Hotel Ltd v The Isle of Man Treasury*, MAN/91/600 (VTD 6534); *ETS (Scotland) Ltd*, EDN/91/219 (VTD 6987); *M Ramzan*, MAN/91/1071 (VTD 7725); *Sefton I-Tec Ltd*, MAN/92/284 (VTD 7813); *Discovery Housing Association Ltd*, EDN/92/119 (VTD 8847); *Pack & Moore Builders Co Ltd*, LON/92/1202 (VTD 9130); *Ashbolt Ltd*, LON/91/2081Y (VTD 11019); *Regent Investment Fund Ltd*, EDN/92/203 (VTD 12152); *Liam Findlay Architects*, EDN/98/8 (VTD 15568); *Kidease Ltd*, LON/03/1034 (VTD 20793); *Marbourne Ltd*, 41.65 LAND, and *Trustees of the Whitbread Harrowden Settlement*, **52.423** below.

Incorrect operation of partial exemption provisions

[52.345] An appeal against a misdeclaration penalty was dismissed in a case where a company had operated the partial exemption provisions incorrectly, and thus had reclaimed more input tax than it was entitled to. *Landene Investments Ltd*, LON/92/106Y (VTD 9510).

[52.346] Similar decisions were reached in *Hexham Steeplechase Co Ltd*, MAN/92/538 (VTD 10481); *Dayrich Bookmakers*, MAN/96/153 (VTD 14638) and the cases noted at **52.421** to **52.424** below.

Input tax relating to exempt supply

[52.347] There was held to be no reasonable excuse for relating input tax relating to an exempt supply in *Bristow & Darlington Ltd*, LON/91/1126Y (VTD 6961); *Tregarn Developments Ltd*, LON/91/1815Y (VTD 7358); *South Tyne Chalets Ltd*, MAN/91/350 (VTD 7377); *Binof Construction Ltd*, MAN/91/559 (VTD 7404); *Eagle Capital Corporation Ltd*, MAN/91/1108 (VTD 7447); *Unwin Estates Ltd*, LON/91/2078X (VTD 7955); *Charles Church Spitfires Ltd*, LON/91/850X (VTD 9512); *Northumbria & Cumbria Estates Ltd*, MAN/92/1270 (VTD 10366); *Woodward & Stalder Ltd*, LON/91/1893X (VTD 10378); *Masstype Properties Ltd*, LON/92/450X (VTD 11124); *DC Smith*, LON/93/812A (VTD 11382); *Woods Place Management Ltd*, LON/93/1920A (VTD 12812); *Dinglis Property Services Ltd*, LON/97/801 (VTD 15159); *Applied Software Control Ltd*, EDN/01/144 (VTD 17675); *Spicer Kilpatrick Ltd*, EDN/03/56 (VTD 18384); *Crestbond Ltd*, **52.420** below, and *Celahurst Ltd*, **46.16** PARTIAL EXEMPTION.

Input tax reclaimed on supply not used for business purposes

[52.348] A company reclaimed input tax on the purchase of a personalised car numberplate. The Commissioners imposed a misdeclaration penalty and the tribunal dismissed the company's appeal, holding that the company should have sought professional advice on whether the tax was deductible, and there was no reasonable excuse for its failure to do so. *NEP Group Ltd*, MAN/91/418 (VTD 6751). (*Note.* For another issue in this case, see **52.281** above.)

[52.349] A similar decision was reached in *AT Windsor (t/a ATW Transport)*, LON/92/520 (VTD 11241).

[52.350] A married couple reclaimed input tax on the construction of a tennis court at their home. The Commissioners imposed a misdeclaration penalty, and the tribunal dismissed the couple's appeal. *GS & H Randhawa*, LON/91/2445Y (VTD 7704).

[52.351] A married couple who owned a retail shop reclaimed input tax on school fees for their two children and golf club membership for the husband. The Commissioners imposed a misdeclaration penalty, and the tribunal dismissed the couple's appeal. *DL & LE Cheesman (t/a Kraft E)*, LON/92/917 (VTD 10347).

[52.352] A building company reclaimed input tax on the upkeep of two racehorses. The Commissioners issued an assessment to recover the tax, on the basis that the expenditure had not been incurred for the purpose of the company's business. They also imposed a misdeclaration penalty. The tribunal dismissed the company's appeals, finding that 'there was no link between horse racing and the company's business'. On the evidence, the Commissioners 'had every justification for seeking to impose a serious misdeclaration penalty'. The company had been reckless, and had 'not satisfied the burden of proving that it had a reasonable excuse for overclaiming the input tax'. *RV Young Ltd*, LON/93/925A (VTD 12123).

[52.353] A married couple trading in partnership reclaimed input tax in respect of invoices relating to a property which was divided into three flats, one of which was owned by the husband and two of which had been purchased by a trust which the husband controlled. The Commissioners imposed a misdeclaration penalty and the tribunal dismissed the couple's appeal. *RMSG*, LON/93/723A (VTD 12520).

[52.354] There was also held to be no reasonable excuse for reclaiming input tax on items of private expenditure in *L Dewar*, EDN/92/60 (VTD 7899); *Golden Echo Productions*, MAN/93/674 (VTD 11747), and *Raceshine Ltd*, **36.495** INPUT TAX.

Input tax reclaimed on supply not wholly for business purposes

[52.355] A farming company reclaimed all the input tax incurred in respect of a farmhouse which it owned and which was occupied by its managing director. The Commissioners imposed a misdeclaration penalty on the basis that only one-third of the tax in question was allowable, the remaining two-thirds having been incurred for the personal purposes of the director. The tribunal dismissed the company's appeal. *Hazel Street Ltd*, LON/91/120X (VTD 6229).

[52.356] In the case noted at **36.421** INPUT TAX, where the tribunal had held that expenditure on motor racing was primarily incurred for private pleasure rather than for business purposes, the tribunal dismissed an appeal against a misdeclaration penalty, holding that no reasonable businessman would have claimed the whole of the input tax in question. *Chambers (Homefield Sandpit) Ltd*, LON/92/276X (VTD 9012).

[52.357] See also *Walley*, 36.227 INPUT TAX.

Input tax reclaimed on supply made to agent

[52.358] An incorporated foundation reclaimed input tax in respect of invoices which were not made out to it, but to a company which acted as its agent. The Commissioners imposed a misdeclaration penalty and the tribunal dismissed the foundation's appeal. *Dolmetsch Foundation Inc*, LON/90/1801X (VTD 5876).

Company acting as agent for overseas suppliers

[52.359] A company, which acted as an agent for overseas suppliers, reclaimed input tax in respect of supplies which had been imported on behalf of its overseas principals, although it did not recharge the necessary output tax to the overseas principals. The Commissioners imposed a misdeclaration penalty and the tribunal dismissed the company's appeal. *MB Appleton Yarns & Co*, MAN/91/916 (VTD 7083).

Input tax reclaimed on supply to associated company

[52.360] There was held to be no reasonable excuse for the reclaiming of input tax on invoices made out to an associated company in *Stockwell Carpets Ltd*, LON/92/77Y (VTD 7782).

[52.361] A similar decision was reached in a case where a sole trader reclaimed input tax in respect of invoices made out to a company of which he was the principal director. *J Johnson (t/a London Angling Supplies)*, LON/92/660A (VTD 9898).

Input tax reclaimed on electrical appliances for installation in new flats

[52.362] A builder constructed a block of flats and reclaimed input tax on electrical appliances (such as washing machines and refrigerators) which he had purchased for installation in the flats. The Commissioners rejected his claim, since the input tax was not deductible by virtue of what is now *Article 6* of the *Input Tax Order 1992*. They also imposed a misdeclaration penalty. The tribunal dismissed the builder's appeal. *JL Dart*, LON/91/2033 (VTD 9066). (*Note*. For another issue in this case, see **3.69** ASSESSMENT.)

Input tax reclaimed on transfer of business as going concern

[52.363] There was held to be no reasonable excuse for reclaiming input tax on the transfer of a going concern in *Windowmaker UPVC Ltd*, MAN/91/1206 (VTD 9939); *Magnum Craft Ltd*, LON/92/2953 (VTD 11316); *RN Banbury (t/a Creative Impressions)*, LON/96/1720 (VTD 15047) and *Ayr Pavilion Ltd*, **52.419** below.

Input tax reclaimed on basis of documents not constituting tax invoices

[52.364] A company reclaimed input tax of £11,600 on the basis of documents purporting to be invoices issued by an associated company. The associated company had gone into liquidation without accounting for the tax in question, and the invoices did not comply with the requirements of the *VAT Regulations*. The Commissioners issued an assessment to recover the tax in question, and imposed a misdeclaration penalty. The company appealed, contending that the invoices had been issued in respect of management charges. The tribunal dismissed the appeal, holding that the invoices did not constitute tax invoices, and that there was no reasonable excuse for the company having used them to reclaim the input tax, since 'the most favourable construction (of the company's) action in claiming input tax relief of the four invoices is that they were recklessly giving themselves the benefit of the doubt'. *Suitmart (UK) Ltd*, LON/92/1659A (VTD 10392).

[52.365] A company (F) reclaimed input tax in respect of clothing which it claimed to have purchased from the driver of an unmarked van. HMRC rejected the input tax claim and imposed a misdeclaration penalty. F appealed. The tribunal dismissed the appeal, holding that F had 'failed to pursue the proper verification process that it should have undertaken when being offered goods in the circumstances that prevailed here'. Furthermore, there was no reasonable excuse for the incorrect claim. *Faith Clothing Ltd*, [2008] VATDR 379 (VTD 20854).

[52.366] There have been a number of other cases in which misdeclaration penalties have been imposed on traders who have reclaimed input tax on the basis of documents not constituting tax invoices. In the interests of space, such cases are not reported individually in this book.

Associated partnerships—circular transactions

[52.367] A partnership reclaimed input tax in respect of certain invoices relating to alleged purchases from an associated partnership with different return periods. A VAT officer formed the opinion that the transactions were fictitious and that the invoices had been created for the purpose of obtaining repayments of VAT which would give the partnerships a cash-flow advantage. The Commissioners issued an assessment to recover the tax, and also imposed a misdeclaration penalty. The tribunal dismissed the partnership's appeals, holding that the assessments had been made to the best of the Commissioners' judgment, that there were reasonable grounds for regarding the invoices as fictitious, that the partnerships had not submitted evidence to prove that the transactions had actually taken place, and that there was no reasonable excuse for the partnership's incorrect claims. *CAL Ingot Manufacturers*, LON/93/816 (VTD 12298, 13069).

Miscellaneous

Cases where the appellant was successful

Error corrected before due date—whether a reasonable excuse

[52.368] Two partners took over a business of selling and hiring videotapes. They mistakenly believed that the letting on hire of videotapes was not subject to VAT, and therefore accounted for VAT only on sales, rather than on receipts from hire and sales. Their return, for the period ending 30 June 1990, was submitted on 6 July and the figures were queried by VAT Central Unit. A VAT officer visited the partners and informed them that the hiring out of videotapes was standard-rated. The partners submitted an amended return and a cheque for the tax due. The amended return and cheque were both received before the due date. However, the Commissioners imposed a misdeclaration penalty. The partners appealed, contending that they had a reasonable excuse as they had genuinely misunderstood the rating of their supplies and had shown their good faith by correcting the error before the due date. The tribunal accepted this contention and allowed their appeal. Applying *Jenkinson*, 51.83 PENALTIES: FAILURE TO NOTIFY, 'there is no overriding rule of law in relation to the words "reasonable excuse" that ignorance or mistake of law can never be an excuse'. The mistake had been put right before the due date and this was 'not an appropriate case to impose the penalty'. *T & D Kennedy*, [1991] VATTR 157 (VTD 5880).

Dishonesty of former director

[52.369] A company required one of its directors to resign after discovering that he had misappropriated company funds. Subsequently a VAT officer discovered that management charges, for which the director in question was responsible, had not been accounted for in the relevant VAT return. The Commissioners imposed a misdeclaration penalty but the tribunal allowed the company's appeal, holding that there was no reason for the continuing directors to have suspected the error, and that the circumstances constituted a reasonable excuse. *Foster Penny Ltd*, EDN/92/46 (VTD 7716).

Incorrect Retail Scheme operated

[52.370] An appeal was allowed in a case where a trader had continued to operate a Retail Scheme for which his business was no longer eligible. *JT Darvill*, LON/92/560Z (VTD 9299). (*Note.* For another issue in this case, see **18.506** DEFAULT SURCHARGE.)

Incorrect operation of Tour Operators' Margin Scheme

[52.371] A company which carried on business as a tour operator, and operated the Tour Operators' Margin Scheme, submitted a return for November 1991 in which it failed to make the annual adjustment required by the Scheme for the year ending 31 October 1991, and consequently underdeclared tax by more than 1,000,000. The Commissioners imposed a misdeclaration penalty, and the company appealed, contending that it had a reasonable excuse for its inability to make the adjustment in time. The tribunal allowed the appeal, observing that the Tour Operators' Scheme was 'a highly complicated scheme which clearly puts an additional burden on traders in that field beyond the normal requirements of the VAT system'. The company had only a short period of time to make the necessary calculations, and had submitted the necessary details to the Commissioners in February 1992, which was not unreasonable in view of the complexity of the case. Accordingly, the circumstances constituted a reasonable excuse for the misdeclaration. (The tribunal observed that 'the company would be ill-advised to suppose that the same result would necessarily be achieved in respect of a future period when the circumstances might be different'.) *Owners Abroad Group plc*, LON/92/859Y (VTD 9354).

Other cases

[52.372] There have been a small number of other cases turning on very unusual facts in which tribunals have found that the particular circumstances have constituted a reasonable excuse, but where the nature of the case is such that it is of little if any value as a precedent. In the interests of space, such cases have not been summarised individually in this book. For such cases reported up to 31 December 1995, see Tolley's VAT Cases 1996.

Cases where the appellant was unsuccessful

Return amended to deduct output tax in respect of unpaid invoice

[52.373] A trader carried out work for a customer and accounted for the relevant VAT in his return for the period ending 31 July 1990. However, the customer was in financial difficulty and did not pay for the work. The trader therefore deducted the output tax in question in his return for the period ending 31 October 1990. When the Commissioners discovered this, they imposed a misdeclaration penalty. The tribunal dismissed the trader's appeal, holding that there was no reasonable excuse for the deduction. *R Clark (t/a Norblast)*, EDN/91/181 (VTD 7043).

Wages deducted in computing tax liability

[52.374] A sole trader, who operated a business of hiring sunbeds, deducted the wages which he paid to his employees in computing his VAT liability. The Commissioners imposed a misdeclaration penalty, and the tribunal dismissed the trader's appeal, holding that there was no reasonable excuse for the misdeclaration. *W Graham (t/a Sunlover Sunbeds)*, EDN/92/303 (VTD 10148).

Company claiming to have been misdirected by VAT officer

[52.375] A company appealed against a misdeclaration penalty, contending that it had a reasonable excuse because it had been misdirected by a VAT officer. The tribunal dismissed the appeal, finding that the officer had not misdirected the company. *Albany Building Services Ltd*, EDN/92/335 (VTD 11294).

Other cases

[52.376] There have been many other cases, which appear to raise no point of general importance, in which appeals against misdeclaration penalties have been dismissed. In the interests of space, such cases are not reported individually in this book.

Whether error voluntarily disclosed (VATA 1994, s 63(10)(b))

[52.377] In the case noted at 52.59 above, the error in the return was noticed by the council's principal accountant while he was collecting papers for a VAT officer who was conducting a control visit. The council contended that the penalty should be discharged because its own accountant had brought the error to the attention of the VAT officer. The tribunal rejected this contention, finding that the error had been discovered at a time when the Commissioners were making enquiries into the council's tax affairs, so that the conditions of what is now *VATA 1994, s 63(10)(b)* were not satisfied. The tribunal held that the purpose of *s 63(10)(b)* was 'to provide a defence to a taxpayer who makes a truly voluntary disclosure; and a disclosure made under the shadow of an official review is not a voluntary disclosure as envisaged'. *Taunton Deane Borough Council*, LON/90/1225Z (VTD 5545).

[52.378] Similar decisions were reached in *Tyre Team Ltd*, LON/91/34X (VTD 6407); *Shipquay Enterprises Ltd*, BEL/91/38 (VTD 6741); *Venture Capital Ltd*, MAN/90/899 (VTD 6794); *Rhymney Valley District Council*, LON/91/722 (VTD 6939); *S Atkinson*, MAN/90/1053 (VTD 6989); *Jones & Attwood Ltd*, MAN/91/729 (VTD 7046); *Redland Timber Co Ltd*, LON/91/2217Z (VTD 7558); *Elmec (Blackburn) Ltd*, MAN/92/445 (VTD 9222); *WB Crewlyn (Electrical Contractors) Ltd*, LON/92/2608 (VTD 10027); *Holden Plant Hire Ltd*, LON/92/300X (VTD 10685); *Orchard Associates Ltd*, MAN/93/734 (11576); *Wall Colmonoy Ltd*, LON/92/1385P (13210); *Whitehead & Wood Ltd*, 52.60 above; *Tong Garden Centre plc*, 52.60 above; *Springvale EPS Ltd*, 52.125 above; *GJ Bennett & Co (Builders) Ltd*, 52.217 above, and *Thornsett Structures Ltd*, 52.397 below.

[52.379] A company appointed a new financial director in June 1990. After his appointment, he discovered that there were several errors in the company's records. When a control visit was arranged, he informed the VAT office that he had discovered two errors in previous VAT returns, and would welcome the visit, which took place in October 1990. During the visit, the VAT officer discovered further errors, in respect of which a misdeclaration penalty was imposed. The company appealed, contending that it had made a full disclosure and that the penalty should be waived under what is now *VATA 1994, s 63(10)(b)*. The tribunal dismissed the appeal, applying *dicta* in *Taunton Deane Borough Council*, 52.377 above. The fact that there were errors in the company's returns had not been disclosed until after the Commissioners had sought to arrange a control visit. Accordingly, the disclosure had not been made at a time when the company 'had no reason to believe that enquiries were being made', as required by what is now *VATA 1994, s 63(10)(b)*. Further, although the company had disclosed that there were errors in its returns, it had not supplied 'full information with respect to the inaccuracy concerned'. *Vernon Packaging Ltd*, LON/91/233Z (VTD 6360).

[52.380] The decisions in *Taunton Deane Borough Council*, 52.377 above, and *Vernon Packaging Ltd*, 52.379 above, were applied in the similar case of *Britannia Steel Ltd*, LON/92/892 (VTD 11675).

[52.381] A borough council submitted a return for May 1990 which included cumulative figures for both April and May instead of the monthly figures for May. For June 1990 it submitted a return which included the cumulative figures for April, May and June. The Commissioners queried the June return and the council's senior accountant discovered the errors. She notified the VAT office of the errors by telephone. The Commissioners imposed a misdeclaration penalty, and the council appealed, contending that it had voluntarily furnished the Commissioners with full information regarding the inaccuracies concerned, so that what is now *VATA 1994, s 63(10)(b)* applied. The tribunal accepted this contention and allowed the appeal. The fact that the voluntary disclosure had not occurred until after the Commissioners had queried the June return did not alter the fact that the council had supplied full information concerning the errors. Accordingly, this was not 'a suitable case for a penalty to be imposed'. *Tewkesbury Borough Council*, MAN/90/765 (VTD 5773).

[52.382] An appeal was allowed in a case where a company which had discovered a misdeclaration sent the Commissioners a cheque for the tax due, without providing a written explanation of the circumstances. The Commissioners, instead of asking the company for details of the payment, repaid it. A VAT officer discovered the misdeclaration at a control visit, and a penalty was imposed. The tribunal held that the penalty was not due, since the company had effectively advised the Commissioners of the misdeclaration when it had sent a cheque for the tax due, and the Commissioners should have requested further information instead of repaying the amount to the company. *Maston (Property Holding) Ltd*, LON/91/974 (VTD 6564).

[52.383] A company reclaimed input tax in respect of work carried out on developing a hotel and restaurant. Some of the invoices in question were made out to the directors, rather than in the name of the company. The directors advised the company's VAT office of this in October 1990, before a control visit took place. However, the Commissioners imposed a misdeclaration penalty. The tribunal allowed the company's appeal, holding that the company had made a voluntary disclosure within what is now *VATA 1994, s 63(10)(b)*. *Gean House Hotel Ltd*, EDN/91/164 (VTD 6687).

[52.384] On 30 September 1990 a company submitted an invoice to an associated partnership for work done. The input tax shown on the invoice was included in the partnership's return for the relevant period, but the output tax was not included in the company's return. In November a VAT officer made a control visit to the partnership and examined the invoice in question. The senior partner told the VAT officer that the output tax had not been included in the company's September return, because the company could not afford to pay the tax charged, but would be included in the following return. The Commissioners imposed a misdeclaration penalty on the company. The company appealed, contending that it had made a voluntary disclosure within what is now *VATA 1994, s 63(10)(b)*. The tribunal accepted this contention and allowed the appeal. At the time of the disclosure, the Commissioners were making enquiries into the partnership's affairs, but they were not making any enquiries into the company's affairs. *Moor Lodge Developments Ltd*, LON/91/2192X (VTD 7285). (*Note.* Compare the subsequent case of *FR Jenks (Overseas) Ltd*, 52.389 below, in which a tribunal held that the fact that a control visit had not been arranged to inspect the affairs of an appellant company, but to inspect the affairs of an associated company, did not provide a defence against the penalty, since 'the wording of (*VATA 1994, s 63(10)(b)**) does not limit its scope to formal enquiries, or those of which advance warning has been given, but include impromptu enquiries of the kind which occurred here'.)

[52.385] An appeal was allowed in a case where the tribunal accepted a company's evidence that its managing director had told a VAT officer that invoices relating to a contract with Cambridgeshire County Council had not been included in its returns, but that it had accounted for tax on the contract in question on a cash basis, since there were long delays in receiving payment from the Council. The tribunal found that 'the disclosure was made at a time when the appellant company had no reason to believe that enquiries were being made by the Commissioners into its affairs', and held that it was sufficient for the director 'to have volunteered the nature of the error and the periods in which it had occurred'. *Bekelect Ltd*, LON/92/126X (VTD 7779).

[52.386] The decision in *Bekelect Ltd*, 52.385 above, was applied in a subsequent case where the tribunal found that a company's director had made a voluntary disclosure by telephone to the local VAT office. *Knockhatch Leisure Ltd*, LON/93/14P (VTD 10518).

[52.387] A company, which was a member of a group, received a control visit by a VAT officer in November 1991. Following the visit, the officer wrote to the company in December 1991 querying five transactions with a company which was not a member of the group for VAT purposes, and a recent share issue. The company did not reply to the letter, but in January 1992 the company's accountant met the company's auditors to review its VAT affairs. The auditors ascertained that the company had failed to account for VAT on four management charges within the group of companies. In March 1992 the company wrote to its local VAT office disclosing this, and the Commissioners imposed a misdeclaration penalty. The company appealed, contending that it had made a voluntary disclosure within what is now *VATA 1994, s 63(10)*. The tribunal accepted this contention and allowed the appeal, holding that, since the question of intra-group management charges had not been discussed at the November 1991 control visit, or referred to in the VAT officer's letter of December 1991, 'the voluntary disclosure was not therefore the response of the taxpayers to (the officer's) letter'. At the time the voluntary disclosure was made, the company had no 'reason to believe that enquiries were being made into the matter of management charges within the company grouping'. *Hunter Saphir plc*, LON/92/1941 (VTD 10770).

[52.388] An individual (B), who was registered for VAT, arranged for some work to be done on his home, which was a listed building. The builder charged VAT at 17.5%, which B disputed but paid in full. Customs subsequently accepted that the work qualified for the reduced rate of 5%, and issued a ruling accordingly. However the builder failed to make the appropriate refund to B. B reclaimed the amount of tax he had overpaid as input tax on a subsequent VAT return, and explained what he had done in a covering letter. Customs imposed a misdeclaration penalty on the basis that the relevant supplies had not been made for the purposes of B's business. The tribunal allowed B's appeal against the penalty, holding that the covering letter which B had sent with his return fell within *VATA 1994, s 63(10)(b)*, in that B had 'furnished to the Commissioners full information with respect to the inaccuracy concerned'. *A Boffey*, [2008] VATDR 395 (VTD 20865).

[52.389] A company reclaimed input tax in respect of a management charge which it had paid to its holding company. A VAT officer made a control visit to the company. During the visit she also asked to see the holding company's books. While she was looking at these, one of the directors of the two companies admitted that, although the subsidiary company had reclaimed input tax in respect of the management charge, the holding company had not accounted for the relevant output tax. The Commissioners imposed a misdeclaration penalty on the holding company. The holding company appealed, contending that it had made a voluntary disclosure. The tribunal dismissed the appeal. The fact that the control visit had been arranged to inspect the records of the subsidiary company, rather than those of the holding company, was not material. Applying *dicta* in *Taunton Deane Borough Council*, 52.377 above, 'the wording of (*VATA 1994, s 63(10)(b)*) does not limit its scope to formal enquiries, or those of which advance warning has been given, but includes impromptu enquiries of the kind which occurred here'. *FR Jenks (Overseas) Ltd*, MAN/91/1142 (VTD 8858).

[52.390] In the case noted at 52.289 above, the tribunal held that a form 652 was not a 'valid voluntary disclosure', since it had been sent to the VAT Central Unit rather than to the local VAT office. *R Sadler (t/a Warmfield Group)*, MAN/07/1106 (VTD 20893).

[52.391] There have been a number of other cases in which the appellant has contended that an error has been voluntarily disclosed, but the tribunal has found that the conditions of what is now *VATA 1994, s 63(10)(b)* have not been satisfied, and has dismissed the appeal. In the interests of space, such cases are not included in this book.

Mitigation of penalties (VATA 1994, s 70)

Cases where the penalty was mitigated by the tribunal

Underdeclaration of takings

[52.392] Customs discovered that the proprietors of a public house had not declared the whole of their takings. They imposed a misdeclaration penalty of £2,391. The tribunal upheld the penalty in principle but reduced it to £2,013. *DG & C Sessions*, MAN/92/490 (VTD 13162).

[52.393] In a case where a partnership had understated its takings by £100,000, the tribunal mitigated the penalty by 50%. *DR Evans & GL Rees (t/a L & R Building Contractors)*, MAN/97/841 (VTD 15738).

Failure to account for output tax on supplies to associated company

[52.394] A penalty was mitigated by 50% in a case where a partnership transferred some of its fixed assets to an associated company, but failed to account for output tax on the transfers. *I & N Martin (t/a Beechwood Studios)*, LON/95/24P (VTD 13805).

[52.395] A penalty was mitigated by 50% in a case where a company had failed to account for output tax on supplies to subsidiary companies. *Clycan Management Ltd*, EDN/99/218 (VTD 16651).

[52.396] A similar decision was reached in *Eurocare Impex Trading Ltd*, EDN/01/127 (VTD 17516).

[52.397] A penalty was mitigated by 85% in a case where three associated companies had failed to account for output tax on certain supplies to another associated company. *Thornsett Structures Ltd (and related appeals)*, LON/x (VTD 15934).

[52.398] A partnership failed to account for output tax on supplies of services to an associated company. The tribunal observed that the company could have reclaimed the tax as input tax and directed that the penalty should be reduced to £50 (ie approximately 1.5% of the evaded tax). *R & J Morton*, LON/00/130 (VTD 17179).

Failure to account for output tax on sale of property

[52.399] A company failed to account for output tax on the sale of eleven garages. Customs imposed a misdeclaration penalty. The tribunal upheld the penalty in principle but mitigated it by 75%. *Porters End Estates Ltd*, LON/98/700 (VTD 15872).

[52.400] Similar decisions were reached in *Nightingale Holdings*, LON/132/00 (VTD 16721) and *Park Industrial & Commercial Holdings Ltd*, MAN/02/385 (VTD 17882).

[52.401] A penalty was mitigated by 66% in a case where a trader had opted to tax a property, but failed to account for output tax on its sale. *J Whitelaw (t/a Law Property & Leisure Group)*, EDN/01/191 (VTD 17640).

[52.402] In another case where a trader opted to tax a property but failed to account for tax on its sale, HMRC mitigated the penalty by 70% but the tribunal increased the mitigation to 100%, holding that 'the appellant's own behaviour was reasonable in leaving the VAT matters in the hands of the accountants who were acting for him and in taking their advice and no personal blame is involved. *J Connell*, FTT [2009] UKFTT 34 (TC); TC00003.

[52.403] A company failed to account for output tax on the sale of a property. Customs imposed a misdeclaration penalty. The tribunal upheld the penalty in principle but mitigated it by 50%. *Ultra Sport Europe Ltd Directors Retirement Benefits Scheme*, MAN/07/250 (VTD 20194).

Supplies incorrectly treated as zero-rated

[52.404] A penalty was mitigated by 75% in a case where company transported some goods from the UK to France, and failed to account for output tax. *Premiair Charter Ltd*, LON/97/252 (VTD 15129).

[52.405] A penalty was mitigated by 50% in a case where a builder had incorrectly treated supplies as zero-rated. *AB Mearns*, EDN/00/76 (VTD 16947).

[52.406] A trader sold some goods to a Spanish customer who had quoted an invalid VAT number. HMRC imposed a misdeclaration penalty. The tribunal upheld the penalty in principle, holding that the circumstances did not constitute a reasonable excuse, but mitigated the penalty by 50%. *JL Eydmann v HMRC*, [2011] UKFTT 732 (TC), TC01569.

Supplies incorrectly treated as exempt

[52.407] A penalty was mitigated by 75% in a case where a hairdresser failed to account for tax on income from letting chairs at the salon to other stylists. *H Jamieson*, EDN/98/157, 99/65 & 99/97 (VTD 16476).

Car dealer acquiring vehicles from Republic of Ireland

[52.408] In the case noted at 52.174 above, a car dealer had imported a number of Japanese cars from Ireland, had not declared them as imports when they entered the UK, and had sold them in the UK under the margin scheme. The tribunal upheld the penalty in principle but mitigated it by 66% to take account of the fact that the dealer had paid Irish VAT on the purchases. *W Ball*, MAN/01/170 (VTD 17648).

Premature claim to input tax

[52.409] A penalty was mitigated by 50% in a case where a property company claimed input tax in respect of an architect's certificate, although it had not received the relevant invoice or made the relevant payment until January 1995. *Robert S Monk Ltd*, MAN/95/2679 (VTD 14346).

Duplicated claim to input tax

[52.410] A penalty was reduced from £4,871 to £3,000 in a case where a company had duplicated a claim to input tax, and attributed this to a clerical error by its computer operator. *Dunelm (Castle Homes) Ltd*, MAN/98/824 (VTD 16052).

Overclaim of input tax

[52.411] A penalty was mitigated by 70% in a case where a company overclaimed input tax by more than £23,000 as a result of a mistake by its office manager. *R Moulding (Contractors Plant) Ltd*, MAN/x (VTD 15102).

[52.412] A penalty was mitigated by 80% in a case where the tribunal found that an overclaim of input tax was attributable to an isolated clerical error by a 'competent and diligent bookkeeper'. *Marine Electronic Services Ltd*, LON/96/1983 (VTD 15172).

[52.413] Customs discovered that a large motor company had overclaimed input tax by more than £1,800,000. They imposed a misdeclaration penalty, which they mitigated by 40%. The company appealed, contending that the mitigation was inadequate. The tribunal accepted this contention and directed that the penalty be mitigated by 90%. *Ford Motor Co Ltd (No 4)*, [2007] VATDR 475 (VTD 20315).

[52.414] A penalty was mitigated by 50% in a case where the tribunal found that a partnership had overclaimed input tax as a result of a 'clerical error'. *RMO & RCO Capper*, MAN/01/08 (VTD 18116).

[52.415] A company reclaimed input tax in respect of two purchases from Germany. Customs imposed a misdeclaration penalty. The tribunal upheld the penalty in principle but mitigated it by 20% because the wording of form VAT 100 was 'confusing'. *The Edinburgh Piano Company Ltd*, EDN/99/42 (VTD 16132).

[52.416] A penalty was mitigated by 40% in a case where a couple who operated a public house had reclaimed input tax without invoices. *N & T Foster (t/a Foster Leisure)*, MAN/97/1060 (VTD 16617).

[52.417] A penalty was mitigated by 20% in a case where a trader had reclaimed input tax in respect of advance payments for the purchase of two vehicles, but had not completed the purchase and had not obtained a VAT invoice. *W Armstrong (t/a Armstrong Stone Quarries)*, MAN/97/855 (VTD 17072).

[52.418] A company (K) agreed to purchase a substantial quantity of equipment from another company (L). L did not proceed with the sale, but K reclaimed input tax on the aborted purchase. Customs imposed a misdeclaration penalty. The tribunal upheld the penalty in principle but mitigated it by 20% to take account of co-operation. *Key Finance Ltd*, LON/03/1104 (VTD 19148).

Input tax reclaimed on transfer of going concern

[52.419] A company reclaimed input tax on the transfer of a going concern. Customs imposed a misdeclaration penalty. The tribunal upheld the penalty in principle but mitigated it from £3917 to £3000 (ie by 23.3%). *Ayr Pavilion Ltd*, EDN/04/87 & 103 (VTD 19119).

Input tax reclaimed on exempt supplies

[52.420] A company reclaimed input tax relating to exempt supplies, although the value of such supplies exceeded the *de minimis* limits. Customs imposed a penalty. The tribunal upheld the penalty in principle, but directed that it should be mitigated by one-third. *Crestbond Ltd*, LON/96/1582 (VTD 15728).

Incorrect partial exemption computation

[52.421] A golf club, which was partly exempt, overclaimed input tax as a result of an error in computing its annual adjustment. Customs imposed a misdeclaration penalty. The tribunal upheld the penalty in principle but mitigated it by 75%. *Hexham Golf Club*, MAN/97/454 (VTD 15286).

[52.422] A similar decision was reached in a subsequent case where a company which was partly exempt had reclaimed too much input tax. *Adam Smith Ltd*, EDN/99/87 (VTD 16282).

[52.423] In the case noted at 46.97 PARTIAL EXEMPTION, the tribunal upheld a penalty in principle but mitigated it by 25%. *Trustees of the Whitbread Harrowden Settlement (and related appeals)*, LON/99/1091 (VTD 16781).

[52.424] Customs imposed a misdeclaration penalty on a funeral director who had repeatedly overclaimed input tax by operating the 'partial exemption' provisions incorrectly. The tribunal upheld the penalty in principle but directed that it should be mitigated from 15% to 5% of the relevant tax. *AW Smith*, MAN/04/038 (VTD 19113).

Unclear advice by local VAT office

[52.425] A trader reclaimed input tax in respect of two transactions for which he had acted as an agent. Customs imposed a misdeclaration penalty.

The tribunal held that there was no reasonable excuse for the misdeclarations, but found that the trader had visited his local VAT office between the two transactions, and that, while the VAT officer to whom he spoke had 'tried to explain the procedures to him in a measure of detail', the position 'may not have been explained very clearly'. Accordingly, the tribunal mitigated the penalty in respect of the second transaction by 50%. *MJ Evans (t/a ATC)*, MAN/96/452 (VTD 14665).

'Self-billing' invoices

[52.426] A penalty was mitigated by 90%, to take account of co-operation, in a case where a contractor had accepted 'self-billing' invoices which did not charge VAT. *W Beveridge*, EDN/99/54 (VTD 16205).

Output tax accounted for on cash basis—input tax reclaimed on invoices

[52.427] A trader (M) accounted for output tax on the basis of payments received, but reclaimed input tax when he received invoices, rather than when he paid for the items in question. Customs imposed a misdeclaration penalty. The tribunal directed that the penalty should be mitigated in full, observing that M had been eligible to operate the cash accounting scheme, and had apparently been attempting to do so. *TPG Morrison*, EDN/97/49 (VTD 15244).

Premature claims to bad debt relief

[52.428] A penalty was mitigated by one-third, to take account of co-operation, in a case where a partnership claimed bad debt relief prematurely, before the expiry of the statutory six-month time limit. *SS & Mrs GRK Digva (t/a International Marketing)*, MAN/00/1019 (VTD 17684).

[52.429] A trader (C) claimed bad debt relief before the expiry of the statutory time limit, and failed to notify the relevant customers, as required by *VAT Regulations 1995 (SI 1995/2518), reg 166A*. Customs imposed a misdeclaration penalty. The tribunal directed that the penalty should be mitigated in full, observing that C had 'rectified the matter through a subsequent VAT return' and was no longer trading. *PA Cooper (t/a Bits of PCs)*, MAN/00/1083 (VTD 17927).

Inadequate estimated assessments

[52.430] A trader failed to appeal against a number of inadequate estimated assessments, and Customs imposed a penalty under *VATA 1994, s 63(1)(b)*. The tribunal upheld the penalty in principle but directed that it penalty should be mitigated by 30%, since the trader's accountant appeared 'to have done nothing, although it must have been clear to him that the appellant was relying upon him to do his accounts and to deal with the VAT returns'. *J Saunders-Pederson (t/a Advanced Information Systems UK)*, LON/98/222 (VTD 15675).

[52.431] A company failed to submit a VAT return, and paid the tax charged by an estimated assessment which was inadequate. Customs imposed a misdeclaration penalty. The tribunal directed that the penalty should be mitigated by 50% on the grounds that the issue of an amended certificate of registration 'may have caused some confusion'. *Citistar (UK) Ltd*, LON/04/858 (VTD 18967).

Misleading advice from accountants

[52.432] A penalty was mitigated by 50% in a case where the tribunal held that a misdeclaration was 'entirely due to wrong advice' by the company's accountants. *M & J Investment Co Ltd*, MAN/00/669 (VTD 16996).

Overseas company

[52.433] In a case where a Swedish company had failed to account for output tax on supplies in the UK, the tribunal directed that the penalty should be mitigated by 75%. *Wartsila NSD Sweden AB*, EDN/00/78 (VTD 16921).

[52.434] There have been a number of cases where the tribunal has directed that a penalty should be mitigated, but where the facts of the case are not fully set out in the tribunal decision. In the interests of space, such cases are not listed in this book.

Cases where the penalty was mitigated by the Commissioners

Customs mitigating penalty by 10%—no further mitigation appropriate

[52.435] In a case where a trader had underdeclared her tax liability as a result of a clerical error, the Commissioners imposed a misdeclaration penalty which they mitigated by 10%. The trader appealed, contending that the penalty should be mitigated further. The tribunal rejected this contention and dismissed the appeal, observing that the trader had failed to make a voluntary disclosure when her accountant had drawn the matter to her attention, and that she was 'fortunate in having received 10% mitigation'. *E Williams (t/a Memories on Video)*, LON/96/60 (VTD 14960).

Customs mitigating penalty by 25%—no further mitigation appropriate

[52.436] A property dealer (C) helped a company to arrange a property purchase. He issued an invoice to the company, charging 1,000,000 plus VAT for his services. Although he had charged VAT on the invoice, he did not pay this to Customs. When Customs discovered this, they imposed a misdeclaration penalty, which they mitigated by 25% to take account of co-operation. The tribunal upheld the penalty and dismissed C's appeal, holding that there was no reasonable excuse, that the 25% mitigation granted by Customs was generous, and that no further mitigation was appropriate. *RA Carr*, LON/07/1880 (VTD 20690).

Customs mitigating penalty by 30%—no further mitigation appropriate

[52.437] A company issued an invoice charging VAT of more than £50,000. It failed to account for output tax on this invoice. Customs discovered this at a control visit more than two years later, and imposed a misdeclaration penalty, mitigated by 30%. The company appealed, contending that the penalty should have been mitigated in full. The tribunal rejected this contention and dismissed the appeal, holding that there was no reasonable excuse for the error, and that since 'nearly two years had elapsed before the discovery of the fault', there were no grounds for increasing 'the degree of the mitigation'. *Manyee UK Ltd*, MAN/06/405 (VTD 19810).

Customs mitigating penalty by 45%—no further mitigation appropriate

[52.438] A company which had constructed a block of flats reclaimed input tax on business entertainment and failed to account for tax on 'white goods' which did not qualify for zero-rating under *VATA 1994, Sch 8, Group 5, Item 4*. Customs imposed a misdeclaration penalty, which they mitigated by 45%. The tribunal dismissed the company's appeal, holding that there was no reasonable excuse and no grounds for any further mitigation. *Waterside (Wakefield) Ltd*, MAN/07/1473 (VTD 20723).

Customs mitigating penalty by 50%—no further mitigation appropriate

[52.439] In a case where a partnership had reclaimed input tax prematurely, the Commissioners imposed a misdeclaration penalty which they mitigated by 50%. The tribunal dismissed the partnership's appeal, holding that there was no reasonable excuse and no grounds for any further mitigation. *WHD, PM & AD Hobson*, MAN/96/591 (VTD 14671).

[52.440] A partnership sold a property, in respect of which it had elected to waive exemption. The Commissioners imposed a misdeclaration penalty which they mitigated by 50%. The tribunal dismissed the partnership's appeal, holding that there was no reasonable excuse and no grounds for any further mitigation. *N, J & N Ellis*, MAN/03/567 (VTD 18460).

[52.441] A similar decision was reached in *Europa Plaza Developments Ltd*, MAN/05/259 (VTD 19196).

[52.442] In a case where the facts are not fully stated in the decision, Customs imposed a misdeclaration penalty which they mitigated by 50%. The tribunal dismissed the company's appeal, holding that 'misfeasance' by a former director was not a reasonable excuse, and that there were no grounds for any further mitigation. *Propaganda Pictures Ltd*, LON/07/1956 (VTD 20613).

Customs mitigating penalty by 55%—no further mitigation appropriate

[52.443] In a case where a restaurant proprietor had underdeclared output tax, the Commissioners imposed a misdeclaration penalty which they mitigated by 55% to take account of co-operation. The tribunal dismissed the proprietor's appeal, holding on the evidence that the mitigation allowed by the Commissioners was 'positively generous' and 'should have amply satisfied both the appellant and his advisers'. *SM Choudhury (t/a Eastcheap Tandoori)*, LON/96/1754 (VTD 15003).

[52.444] A solicitor purchased a property for £47,000. Although the transaction was exempt from VAT, he reclaimed £7,000 as input tax. HMRC imposed a misdeclaration penalty which they mitigated by 55% to take account of co-operation. The tribunal dismissed the solicitor's appeal, holding that 'no further mitigation is possible'. *AS Lambert v HMRC*, [2009] UKFTT 208 (TC), TC00161.

Cases where the penalty was not mitigated

Whether returns incorrect through incompetence or recklessness

[52.445] A sole trader appealed against three misdeclaration penalties. His accountant contended that the penalties should be mitigated on the grounds that the errors 'were the result of incompetence rather than recklessness'. The tribunal dismissed the appeal, holding that there was no reasonable excuse and finding that there were also no grounds for mitigation, since the trader's wife, who completed the returns in question, had admitted that she guessed at some of the figures which she had included. *CB Derbyshire*, MAN/94/505 (VTD 12963).

Underdeclaration of takings

[52.446] The Commissioners imposed misdeclaration penalties on the proprietor of a Chinese restaurant, after discovering that he had underdeclared takings. The proprietor appealed, contending that the penalties should be mitigated. The tribunal dismissed the appeal, holding on the evidence that there were no grounds for mitigation of the penalties. The chairman observed that 'a penalty should be mitigated only where the trader, by co-operation or remorse, or for some other similar reason, has demonstrated that it is deserved. That is plainly not the case here.' *PDJ Lee (t/a Jumbo Express)*, MAN/95/1126 & 1312 (VTD 14127).

Input tax reclaimed on purchase of cars

[52.447] A company reclaimed input tax on the purchase of a Mercedes and a Range Rover. The Commissioners issued an assessment to recover the tax, and imposed a misdeclaration penalty. The company appealed, contending that it should be entitled to reclaim the input tax because it had purchased the vehicles in order to lease them to an associated company. The tribunal dismissed the appeal, holding that the effect of *Input Tax Order, Article 7(2G)(a)* was that the tax was not deductible. Furthermore, there was no reasonable excuse for the misdeclaration and there were no grounds for mitigation, since, although the tribunal accepted 'on the balance of probabilities' that the company had acted in good faith, the effect of *VATA 1994, s 70(4)(c)* was that 'acting in good faith is specifically excluded when a tribunal considers mitigation'. *West Midlands Motors Ltd*, MAN/98/990 (VTD 16512).

Application for mitigation rejected

[52.448] Applications for penalties to be mitigated were rejected in *Hunters Hereditaments Ltd*, MAN/96/637 (VTD 14748); *K Kaur & N Singh (t/a Andy's Fish Bar)*, MAN/96/772 (VTD 14857); *European Lift Services Ltd*, LON/98/261 (VTD 15551); *J Ali & F Rahman (t/a Dilraj Indian Tandoori Takeaway)*, LON/x/294 (VTD 16277); *A & A Ali (t/a Dos Tandoori & Balti House Restaurant)*, LON/99/1220 (VTD 16803); *DJ Souter (t/a Brodie Duncan Marketing)*, EDN/03/74 (VTD 18515); *D Brown Scaffolding Ltd*, LON/07/171 (VTD 20685); *AR Vig (t/a One by One Fashions)*, **52.206** above; *Bourne*, **52.215** above, and *Dinglis Property Services Ltd*, **52.347** above.

Penalties for errors: amount of penalty (FA 2007, Sch 24 paras 4–12)

[52.449] A trader submitted a VAT repayment claiming a repayment of more than £21,000. HMRC queried the claim and the trader's accountant subsequently confirmed that the actual repayment due was £1,082. HMRC imposed a penalty under *FA 2007, Sch 24*, calculated at the rate of 15% of the potential lost revenue. The trader appealed, contending that the errors in the return were attributable to a temporary employee. The tribunal dismissed the appeal, holding that the trader had shown a 'lack of reasonable care' in completing the return. *NA Al-Faham (t/a Express Food Supplies) v HMRC*, [2010] UKFTT 466 (TC), TC00728.

[52.450] A partnership agreed to purchase a warehouse, which it opted to tax. It exchanged contracts in May 2009 but did not complete the purchase until July 2009. It reclaimed the whole of the input tax in its return for the period ending 30 June 2009. HMRC imposed a penalty under *FA 2007, Sch 24*. The penalty was imposed at the rate of 15% of the potential lost revenue to take account of the fact that the partnership had made a 'prompted disclosure'. The partnership appealed, contending that the penalty was unduly harsh. The tribunal accepted this contention and allowed the appeal in part, reducing the penalty under *Sch 24 para 11* to 7.5% of the potential lost revenue. Judge Tildesley observed that the provisions of *Sch 24* were 'more prescriptive' than the previous provisions of *VATA 1994, s 67*, and expressed the view that 'the new concepts should not be interpreted against the terms of reasonable excuse and mitigation' as applied by *VATA 1994*. In reducing the penalty to 15%, HMRC had applied the maximum reduction for prompted disclosure permitted by *Sch 24, para 10(2)*. However, Judge Tildesley held that 'the *Schedule 24* penalty regime without a provision for special circumstances does not distinguish between different categories of failures to take reasonable care and disregards aspects of the tax payer's conduct unconnected with disclosure. Further, the tax-geared element may produce an unduly harsh monetary penalty which has no relationship to the tax payer's culpability.' Accordingly, 'the provision for special circumstances enables consideration of all circumstances of the individual case except those matters specifically excluded by *paragraph 11* so as to ensure that the penalty is proportionate to the taxpayer's contravention'. On the evidence, 'the one-off nature of the transaction, and its unusually large value together with no real likelihood of tax loss constituted special circumstances for reducing the penalty. The combination of these factors produced a disproportionate monetary penalty in relation to the contravention and the appellants' culpability.' *GD & Mrs D Lewis (t/a Russell Francis Interiors) v HMRC*, [2011] UKFTT 107 (TC), TC00983.

[52.451] See also *Mollan & Co Ltd*, **52.291** above, and *The Athenaeum Club*, **52.321** above.

Validity of the penalty

Whether penalty contrary to principle of 'proportionality'

[52.452] The Commissioners imposed a misdeclaration penalty on a company which had failed to include output tax of more than £36,000 on a monthly return. The company appealed, contending that the penalty should be regarded as void since it was contrary to the legal principle of 'proportionality'. The tribunal rejected this contention and dismissed the appeal. Applying *R v Secretary of State for the Home Department (ex p. Brind)*, HL [1991] 2 WLR 588; [1991] 1 All ER 720, 'the doctrine of proportionality is not a part of the law of the United Kingdom'. It followed that 'the penalties imposed by Parliament can only be struck down if they infringe a clear principle of European law which is binding on the Government of this country'. Applying *Amsterdam Bulb v Produktsckap voor Sietegewassen*, CJEC [1977] ECR 137, the Treaty of Rome 'allows the various Member States to choose the measures which they consider appropriate' to ensure the fulfilment of the Treaty obligations. *FA 1985, s 14* had been enacted following a detailed report after considering a great deal of evidence, and it was 'clear that the UK Government considered the penalties appropriate for the purpose of enforcing the provisions of the *EC Sixth Directive* which related to the rendering and accuracy of returns'. It would be an abuse of the jurisdiction of the tribunal for it to interfere with the decision of Parliament. *W Emmett & Son Ltd*, [1991] VATTR 456 (VTD 5459, 6516).

[52.453] The tribunal decision in *W Emmett & Son Ltd*, 52.452 above, was approved by the QB in a case in which Simon Brown J observed that 'member States must inevitably have the very widest margin of appreciation for determining just what penalties are appropriate to underpin the efficient functioning of the value added tax system'; and that, while *FA 1985, s 14* was 'a blunt and heavy instrument', this was 'a feature of penalties imposed to encourage the initiation and maintenance of better procedures rather than necessarily an indication of disproportionality'. *C & E Commrs v The Peninsular & Oriental Steam Navigation Co plc (t/a P & O Ferries)*, QB [1992] STC 809. (*Note.* Another issue in this case, concerning the interpretation of *FA 1985, s 14(4)*, was taken to the CA. However, the relevant legislation was subsequently amended by *FA 1994, s 45* to reverse the effect of the CA decision, which is no longer relevant to the current legislation.)

Whether Customs acting unreasonably

[52.454] In one of the cases noted at 52.39 above, the company contended that the Commissioners had exercised their discretion unreasonably in imposing the penalty. The tribunal rejected this contention, holding that the tribunal's power of supervision in such a case was supervisory rather than appellate, and that the onus was for the appellant to establish that the Commissioners had acted unreasonably, applying the principles in *Associated Provincial Picture Houses Ltd v Wednesbury Corporation*, CA 1947, [1948] 1 KB 223; [1947] 2 All ER 680. On the evidence, it had not been unreasonable for the Commissioners to have imposed a penalty in this case, notwithstanding that the tribunal had held that the circumstances constituted a reasonable excuse for the misdeclaration in question. *Food Engineering Ltd*, [1992] VATTR 327 (VTD 7787). (*Note*. *Obiter dicta* of the tribunal chairman were subsequently disapproved by the QB in *Dollar Land (Feltham) Ltd*, **18.622** DEFAULT SURCHARGE.)

[52.455] Similar decisions, also applying *Associated Provincial Picture Houses Ltd v Wednesbury Corporation*, CA 1947, [1948] 1 KB 223; [1947] 2 All ER 680, were reached in *Pilling House Properties Ltd*, MAN/93/812 (VTD 12965) and *Analog & Numeric Devices Ltd*, **52.165** above.

[52.456] The decision in *Food Engineering Ltd*, **52.454** above, was distinguished in a subsequent case where the Commissioners had written a letter to a company stating that 'the imposition of the penalty is not at the discretion of the individual officer. A penalty is imposed automatically when a detected error fails the objective tests set out in *FA 1985, s 14*'. The VAT officer responsible for imposing the penalty stated in evidence that he had followed the Commissioners' instructions and had acted on the basis that 'if a return fails the objective tests set out in *FA 1985, s 14* then a serious misdeclaration penalty is imposed automatically unless it has been corrected in the next return'. The tribunal allowed the company's appeal, holding that the effect of what is now *VATA 1994, s 76(1)* was that the Commissioners had a discretionary power, rather than a mandatory duty, to impose a penalty, and that they were at fault in not having considered whether they should have exercised their discretion not to impose the penalty. The tribunal chairman (Miss Gort, sitting alone) made 'no finding as to whether or not there was in fact a reasonable excuse' but held that 'the fact that the Commissioners reviewed the decision to impose a penalty subsequently is of no avail to them: there is a statutory requirement that they exercise their discretion, and this must be done before imposing the penalty, not afterwards'. *Tamdown Ltd*, LON/92/2921P (VTD 10180). (*Notes*. (1) The decision in this case was specifically disapproved by the QB in the subsequent case of *Dollar Land (Feltham) Ltd*, **18.622** DEFAULT SURCHARGE. Judge J held that the right of appeal to a VAT tribunal provided for by what is now *VATA 1994, s 83* did not include a right to appeal against the Commissioners' discretionary power whether or not to make a penalty assessment. The remedy against any improper exercise of the Commissioners' discretionary power to impose a penalty would be an application for judicial review. (2) Compare the direct tax case of *Baylis v Roberts & Roberts*, Ch D [1989] STC 693, in which the Ch D held that the use of the word 'may' in tax legislation did not confer a general discretion as to whether an assessment should be raised, and that an inspector had acted correctly in considering that it was his mandatory duty to issue an assessment. Miss Gort's decision in *Tamdown* makes no reference to the Ch D decision in *Baylis v Roberts*.)

[52.457] A similar decision was reached (again by Miss Gort sitting alone) in *J Abassi*, LON/92/1053 (VTD 10411). (*Note*. See the notes following *Tamdown Ltd*, **52.456** above.)

'Period of grace'

[52.458] An appeal was allowed in a case where the tribunal observed that 'the Commissioners' practice was not to impose a penalty in the period between the end of the prescribed accounting period in which the misdeclaration occurred and the due date for furnishing the return for the subsequent period, i.e. to allow a "period of grace". In this case the Commissioners had not adhered to their policy and had raised the penalty before the expiration of the period of grace.' *UK Digital Ltd*, MAN/00/774 (VTD 17096).

53

Penalties: Sales Statements and Regulatory Provisions

The cases in this chapter are arranged under the following headings.

Failure to submit EC sales statement (VATA 1994, s 66)   **53.1**
Breaches of regulatory provisions (VATA 1994, s 69)   **53.18**

Failure to submit EC sales statements (VATA 1994, s 66)

Appeal dismissed

[53.1] The Commissioners imposed two penalties on a company under *VATA 1994, s 66* for failure to submit EC sales statements. The tribunal upheld the penalties and dismissed the company's appeal, finding that the notices had been validly served, that the company's system 'for preparing and despatching their (*sic*) EC sales statements was deficient' and that there was no reasonable excuse. *Sloan Electronics Ltd*, MAN/98/596 (VTD 16062).

[53.2] A company appealed against a penalty under *VATA 1994, s 66*, contending that the penalty notice under *s 66(2)* had not been served. The tribunal reviewed the evidence, rejected this contention, finding 'on the balance of probabilities' that the company had received the notice, and dismissed the appeal. *Autotag Ltd*, LON/00/952 (VTD 17126). (*Note.* The tribunal also dismissed appeals against subsequent penalties, holding that illness suffered by the company's accountant did not constitute a reasonable excuse.)

[53.3] The Commissioners imposed a penalty of £500, under *VATA 1994, s 66*, on a trader who had failed to submit an EC sales statement. The trader appealed, contending that the penalty was unfair and disproportionate because his supplies in the relevant quarter had only totalled £178. The tribunal dismissed his appeal, finding that the notice had been validly served and observing that there were no powers of mitigation in the case of penalties under *s 66*. *M Radford (t/a Atlantis Trading Co)*, MAN/99/88 (VTD 16243).

[53.4] A partnership submitted an EC sales statement six weeks late and the Commissioners imposed a penalty of £215 under *VATA 1994, s 66*. The partnership appealed, contending that the penalty was unfair. The tribunal rejected this contention and dismissed the appeal. *Fitch (MW) & Slade (B) (t/a Michael W Fitch Antiques)*, LON/99/1292 (VTD 16880).

[53.5] The Commissioners imposed penalties under *VATA 1994, s 66* on an antique dealer who had failed to submit an EC sales statement. The dealer appealed, contending that he had a reasonable excuse because he had not received the relevant form VAT 101. The tribunal dismissed his appeal, holding that he should have requested a copy of the form, and that 'the simple failure to obtain the form when it was easily within his power to do so does not provide the appellant with a reasonable excuse. It is the taxpayer's responsibility to complete and submit the EC sales list by the due date, just as it is his responsibility to complete and submit his VAT return.' *J Proops (t/a JP Antiques)*, LON/99/744 (VTD 16409).

[53.6] A similar decision was reached in *Beaches Ltd*, LON/97/569 (VTD 16448).

[53.7] The Commissioners imposed penalties on a company which had submitted two EC sales statements after the due date. The company appealed, contending that it had a reasonable excuse because its computer had broken down. The tribunal dismissed the appeal, holding on the evidence that the circumstances did not constitute a reasonable excuse. *CJW Manufacturing Ltd*, LON/99/727 (VTD 16417).

[53.8] An appeal was dismissed in a case where the tribunal held that 'the unsatisfactory behaviour of the person responsible for preparing the statement' was not a reasonable excuse. *Badge Sales*, LON/01/490 (VTD 17388).

[53.9] A company appealed against a penalty under *VATA 1994, s 66*, contending that it had been 'unaware of the need to submit timely EC Sales Lists'. The tribunal dismissed the appeal, holding that this was not a reasonable excuse. *Leander Shellfish Ltd*, LON/03/174 (VTD 18227).

[53.10] Appeals against penalties under *VATA 1994, s 66* were also dismissed in *St Honore Mailles (Scotland) Ltd*, EDN/04/88 (VTD 18901); *Kardi Car & Van Hire Ltd*, EDN/05/56 (VTD 19299); *TFA Box Company Ltd*, MAN/x (VTD 19771); *Millennium Nails Ltd*, MAN/06/467 (VTD 19900); *Introbond Ltd*, LON/06/1205 (VTD 19976); *G & G Boyd (t/a Boyd Motors)*, LON/06/640 (VTD 20034); *Acrol UK Ltd*, LON/07/875 (VTD 20338); *Rashmi Knitwear & Leisurewear*, MAN/07/479 (VTD 20497); *TR Shop Ltd*, LON/08/1020 (VTD 20776); *Tia (GB) Ltd*, MAN/08/944 (VTD 20861) and *Corriform Ltd*, [2010] UKFTT 52 (TC), TC00365.

Appeal allowed

[53.11] The Commissioners imposed penalties on a company which had submitted EC sales statements after the due date. The company appealed, contending that it had a reasonable excuse because it had had difficulties in obtaining correct registration numbers from customers in the Irish Republic (some of whom had cited nine-digit numbers although Irish VAT numbers contain only eight digits). Furthermore, its director had written to its VAT office in October and November 1997 asking for advice, but had not received a reply until October 1998. The tribunal allowed the appeal, holding that it was unreasonable for the Commissioners 'to have ignored (the director's) pleas for some 11 months while further penalties were imposed'. *The Decal Co Ltd*, EDN/98/194 (VTD 16274).

[53.12] A company appealed against a penalty under *VATA 1994, s 66*, contending that it had posted its sales list before the due date. The tribunal accepted the company's evidence and allowed the appeal. *Eurospray Midlands Ltd*, MAN/00/205 (VTD 16775).

[53.13] Similar decisions were reached in *SC Jebb*, LON/01/1317 (VTD 17811); *Docutex Business Solutions Ltd*, LON/03/115 (VTD 18138) and *Kedington (NI) Ltd*, LON/03/922 (VTD 18544).

[53.14] A company appealed against a penalty under *VATA 1994, s 66*, contending that the penalty notice under *s 66(2)* had not been served. The tribunal accepted this contention and allowed the appeal. *BC Shutters & Doors Ltd*, LON/07/874 (VTD 20404).

[53.15] A trader (M) failed to submit his EC sales list for the period ending 30 June 1998 by the due date. On 5 November the Commissioners sent him a reminder letter, and on 25 November they sent him a formal notice under *VATA 1994, s 66(2)* warning that, if the list was not received within 14 days, he would become liable to a penalty. M submitted the list in question within the 14-day period. On 29 January the Commissioners sent M a further warning letter, this time in respect of the EC sales list for the period ending 30 September, the due date for which had been 11 November. The Commissioners did not receive the list until March 1999, and imposed a penalty under *VATA 1994, s 66*. The tribunal allowed the trader's appeal, holding that the penalty did not comply with the requirements of *VATA 1994, s 66(3)(b)*. The effect of *s 66(3)(b)* was to authorise 'a penalty in respect of any EC sales statement the last day for the submission of which is after the service and before the expiry of the notice and in relation to which he is in default'. On 25 November 1998, when the liability notice under *s 66(2)* was issued in respect of the June list, the September list was already overdue. 'Accordingly, it was not a statement the last day for the submission of which was after the service of the notice issued on 25 November 1998.' The tribunal held that the 'only course open to the Commissioners' should have been to issue a further *s 66(2)* notice, in respect of the September list. As they had failed to do so, the penalty was invalid. *AD Moll*, LON/99/731 (VTD 17302).

[53.16] A company did not submit its EC sales statement for the period ending 30 June 1999 until 31 October 1999. The Commissioners imposed a penalty under *VATA 1994, s 66*, and the company appealed, contending that its local VAT office had allowed it to submit the return late. The tribunal accepted the company's evidence and allowed its appeal. *Allseal Gasket & Engineering Services Ltd*, MAN/00/412 (VTD 17358). (*Note*. The decision is very brief and does not set out the terms of the relevant letter or the relevant statutory provisions. Compare, however, the similar case of *Starlite (Chandeliers) Ltd*, **18.448** DEFAULT SURCHARGE.)

Penalty reduced

[53.17] A trader did not submit his EC sales statement for the period ending 30 September 2002 by the due date. The Commissioners imposed a penalty under *VATA 1994, s 66*, computed in the basis that the statement had not been submitted until February 2003. The trader appealed, contending that the penalty was excessive because he had submitted the statement with his VAT return in November 2002. The tribunal accepted the trader's evidence and directed that the penalty should be reduced accordingly. *S Maguire (t/a Skian Mhor)*, [2004] VATDR 288 (VTD 18667).

Breaches of regulatory provisions (VATA 1994, s 69)

[53.18] A company carried on the business of selling women's clothing from market stalls. Its registered office was the premises of its accountants, but on its form VAT 1 it cited its principal director's house as its business address. The Commissioners wished to carry out a control visit to inspect the company's records in accordance with what is now *VATA 1994, Sch 11 para 7*, and asked the company to make its records available at its business address. The company failed to comply with repeated requests, and the Commissioners imposed a penalty under what is now *VATA 1994, s 69*. The tribunal dismissed the company's appeal against the penalty, holding that it was not unreasonable for the Commissioners to have required to inspect the records at the business address and that there was no reasonable excuse for the company's failure to comply with the notice. *Fabco Ltd*, LON/92/1009Y (VTD 9739).

[53.19] In January 1993 a VAT officer telephoned a construction company to arrange a control visit. The company subsequently telephoned the VAT office to cancel the appointment, and also cancelled several subsequent appointments. In July the Commissioners issued a formal notice calling for the production of specified documents in accordance with what is now *VATA 1994, Sch 11 para 7(2)*. The company did not produce the documents, and in February 1994 the Commissioners issued a penalty assessment under what is now *VATA 1994, s 69*, charging a penalty of £5 per day. The company appealed, contending that it had a reasonable excuse because the documents in question were held by its accountants. The tribunal dismissed the appeal, holding that the circumstances did not constitute a reasonable excuse. The company was obliged to produce the documents at its principal place of business 'and it should have been possible to arrange for the records to be returned for one day, or longer if necessary, to enable them to be inspected'. *HEM Construction Ltd*, LON/94/489A (VTD 12449).

[53.20] The company in the case noted at **53.19** above appealed against a subsequent penalty of £500. The tribunal dismissed the appeal, holding that there was no reasonable excuse for the company's failure to produce the required documents, and awarded costs of £300 to the Commissioners. *HEM Construction Ltd (No 2)*, LON/94/1964P (VTD 13203).

[53.21] Appeals against penalties under *VATA 1994, s 69* were also dismissed in *M Safdar*, MAN/95/1612 (VTD 13646); *H, H & M Suleyman (t/a Red Rose Dry Cleaners)*, LON/95/2619 (VTD 13753); *T Dyer*, EDN/97/178 & 230 (VTD 16359) and *Lloyds TSB Group plc (No 2)*, **14.92** COLLECTION AND ENFORCEMENT.

[53.22] For a case where an appeal against a penalty under *VATA 1994, s 69* was allowed, see *University Court of the University of Glasgow (No 2)*, **14.89** COLLECTION AND ENFORCEMENT.

54

Pension Funds

The cases in this chapter are arranged under the following headings.

Input tax cases	**54.1**
Output tax cases	**54.11**

Input tax cases

Professional services supplied to employer as trustee

[54.1] The British Railways Board received professional advice from merchant bankers and others concerning its employees' pension funds, of which it was the trustee. It reclaimed the input tax charged to it on such services. The Commissioners rejected the claim but the tribunal allowed the Board's appeal and the CA upheld this decision. The management of the pension funds was one of the Board's functions as an employer and there was no justification for the Commissioners' refusal to allow the claim. *C & E Commrs v British Railways Board*, CA [1976] STC 359; [1976] 1 WLR 1036; [1976] 3 All ER 100.

Trustees' expenses defrayed by employer

[54.2] A company defrayed the expenses incurred by the trustees of a pension fund established for its employees and for employees of subsidiary companies. However the company was not itself a trustee of the fund. The company reclaimed the input tax incurred by the trustees. The Commissioners issued an assessment to recover the tax. The tribunal upheld the assessment and dismissed the company's appeal. *British Railways Board*, 54.1 above, was distinguished because in that case the employer had been a trustee of the fund. The relevant services here had been supplied to the trustees and not to the company. *Linotype & Machinery Ltd*, [1978] VATTR 123 (VTD 594).

[54.3] Similar decisions were reached in *Talbot Motor Co Ltd*, MAN/82/242 (VTD 1728) and *Rambla Properties*, LON/94/298A (VTD 13030).

[54.4] A similar decision, applying *Linotype & Machinery Ltd*, 54.2 above, and *Talbot Motor Co Ltd*, 54.3 above, was reached in *Ultimate Advisory Services Ltd (No 1)*, MAN/91/1488 (VTD 9523). (*Note.* For another issue in this case, see **41.46** LAND.)

[54.5] The decisions in *Linotype & Machinery Ltd*, 54.2 above, and *Ultimate Advisory Services Ltd (No 1)*, 54.4 above, were not followed in a subsequent case in which the a company reclaimed input tax on solicitors' fees relating to a legal action in which both the company and the pension fund trustees were parties. The Commissioners issued an assessment to recover 75% of the tax, on the basis that only 25% of the tax related to the company and the remaining 75% related to the trustees. The company appealed, contending that the previous tribunal decisions should not be followed, on the grounds that they were inconsistent with the CJEC decision in *Belgium v Ghent Coal Terminal NV*, **22.406** EUROPEAN COMMUNITY LAW, and the HL decision in *Redrow Group plc*, **36.130** INPUT TAX. The tribunal chairman (Mr. Bishopp, sitting alone) accepted this contention and allowed the appeal. *Ultimate Advisory Services Ltd (No 2)*, MAN/95/2550 (VTD 17610).

Pension funds of company established by statute

[54.6] A company was established by statute to administer a canal. It had established three pension schemes, which were administered by committees on its behalf, and appointed and paid actuaries for each of the three schemes. It reclaimed input tax on the expenses of the schemes. The Commissioners rejected the claim but the QB allowed the company's appeal. Applying *British Railways Board*, **54.1** above, the provision of pension funds was within the functions of an employer and the actuaries' advice as to the solvency of the funds had been incurred for the purpose of the company's business. *Manchester Ship Canal Co v C & E Commrs*, QB [1982] STC 351.

Company acting as trustee of pension funds

[54.7] A company was established to act as trustee of two pension funds for employees of associated companies. The companies were registered as a group for VAT, and the parent company reclaimed the input tax incurred by the company established to act as trustee of the pension funds. The Commissioners rejected the claim but the tribunal allowed the company's appeal. The services in question were deemed to have been supplied to the parent company by virtue of what is now *VATA 1994, s 43(1)(b)*, and the investment of the pension funds was within the scope of the company's business. *BOC International Ltd*, [1982] VATTR 84 (VTD 1248).

[54.8] A company (C), which was registered for VAT, acted as the trustee of a pension fund. It reclaimed input tax on supplies which it received from solicitors and actuaries. Customs rejected the claim on the grounds that 'the registered business of (C) cannot be equated with its trustee function for VAT purposes with the result that, in its role as trustee as opposed to adviser to trusts, (C) cannot deduct input tax at all in respect of expenses incurred in the fulfilment of that role unless they can be directly linked to supplies made by the trustees on behalf of the specific pension fund'. The tribunal allowed C's appeal, observing that C had correctly accounted for output tax on the services it provided in its capacity as a trustee. C made supplies to the beneficiaries of the funds by managing the fund for their benefit. The effect of *Pensions Act 1995, s 25(6)* was that the supplies which C received from solicitors and actuaries were made to it 'in its capacity as a taxable person'. Accordingly C was entitled to deduct the input tax on those services. *Capital Cranfield Trustees Ltd*, [2008] VATDR 123 (VTD 20532).

Failure to claim input tax on disposals of shares outside EC

[54.9] See *CGI Pension Trust Ltd*, **48.135** PAYMENT OF TAX.

Transfer of pension funds—legal advice for employees

[54.10] A company was taken over by a larger company and its pension funds were transferred to other pension schemes. Legal advice was provided for representatives of the employees affected by the change. The company reclaimed input tax on these legal costs. The Commissioners rejected the claim on the basis that the relevant supplies had not been made to the company. The tribunal dismissed the company's appeal. It was accepted that, if the solicitors' services had been made to the trustees of the pension funds, these would be treated as supplies to the company for VAT purposes. However, the supplies in this case had been made to independent representatives of the beneficiaries. The beneficiaries were 'clients being separately advised', and 'the advice was given to the representative beneficiaries and not to the trustees'. *The Plessey Co Ltd*, LON/94/254A (VTD 12814).

Output tax cases

Services supplied by employer to trustees

[54.11] The National Coal Board operated a contributory pension scheme for its employees. The Board was not itself a trustee of the fund, but it was responsible for the routine administration and management of the scheme. The Commissioners sought to charge tax on the services supplied by the Board for the trustees. The QB allowed the Board's appeal, holding that although the Board had provided services for the trustees, the services had not been provided for a consideration, and, by virtue of what is now *VATA 1994, s 5(2)(a)*, did not constitute a supply for VAT purposes. *National Coal Board v C & E Commrs*, QB [1982] STC 863.

Investment management of pension funds

[54.12] A company based in the UK supplied investment management services to two Irish pension funds. The Irish tax authorities issued assessments on the basis that these supplies were subject to the 'reverse charge'. The pension funds appealed, contending that the supplies were not received for the purposes of any business. The Appeal Commissioner rejected this contention and dismissed the appeals, and the High Court upheld this decision, applying the principles laid down by the CS in *C & E Commrs v Morrison's Academy Boarding Houses Association*, **7.1** BUSINESS. *Cadbury Ireland Pension Trust Ltd v Revenue Commrs (Ireland) (and related appeal)*, HC(I) [2007] IEHC 179.

55

Protected Buildings

The cases in this chapter are arranged under the following headings.

Definition of 'protected building' (VATA 1994, Sch 8, Group 6,
Note 1)   55.1
Whether a 'substantial reconstruction' (VATA 1994, Group
6, Item 1, Note 4)   55.19
Whether an 'approved alteration' (VATA 1994, Sch 8, Group 6,
Item 2, Note 6)
    Cases held to constitute an approved alteration   55.27
    Cases where the tax was apportioned   55.40
    Cases held not to constitute an approved alteration   55.52
Whether a supply of services (VATA 1994, Sch 8, Group 6,
Item 2)   55.83
Miscellaneous   55.88

NOTE

VATA 1994, Sch 8, Group 6 was substituted by the *VAT (Protected Buildings) Order 1995 (SI 1995/283)*, with effect from 1 March 1995. Cases relating to periods before March 1995 should be read in the light of the changes in the legislation.

Definition of 'protected building' (VATA 1994, Sch 8, Group 6, Note 1)

Listed building—change of use from nursing home to country club

[55.1] In 1986 planning permission was obtained for the conversion of a protected building into a nursing home. In 1988 a further application was made for conversion of the same building into a country club. Planning permission for this was granted in 1989. The contractor did not account for VAT on the conversion, and the Commissioners issued an assessment charging output tax. The contractor appealed, contending that the work should be treated as zero-rated under what is now *VATA 1994, Sch 8, Group 6*. The tribunal dismissed the appeal, holding that since the building was intended to be used as a country club, it was not 'designed to remain as or become a dwelling' or 'intended for use solely for a relevant residential purpose or a relevant charitable purpose'. Accordingly the building did not qualify as a protected building under *Sch 8, Group 6, Note 1*, and the contractor's supplies did not qualify for zero-rating. The tribunal observed that the contractor had not taken 'proper steps to verify that the supplies he was making' were 'of a description entitling him to treat them as zero-rated'. *P Butland (t/a Harrogate Site Services)*, MAN/91/193 (VTD 6531).

Conversion of barn into music room

[55.2] The owner of a 17th century barn, which stood in the grounds of the owner's house and was a listed building under the *Planning (Listed Buildings and Conservation Areas) Act 1990*, engaged a building partnership to convert the barn into a music room. The terms of the listed building consent required the barn not to be occupied as a 'separate unit of residential accommodation', but only to be occupied as an adjunct to the house in the grounds of which it stood. The partnership did not account for VAT on the work. The Commissioners issued an assessment charging output tax, and the partnership appealed, contending that the work should be zero-rated under what is now *VATA 1994, Sch 8, Group 6*. The tribunal dismissed the appeal, holding on the evidence that the barn was not 'designed to remain as or become a dwelling', and therefore did not qualify as a protected building within *Sch 8, Group 6, Note 1*. *MKM Builders*, LON/92/2421A (VTD 10511).

Conversion of barn into living accommodation—effect of Note 2(c)

[55.3] An individual (F) owned a house, which had been built in around 1780 and was a protected building. About 8 feet from the house stood a barn, which had been built in around 1730 and was a listed building. F obtained listed building consent to convert the barn into dwelling accommodation. The relevant planning permission provided that the barn conversion should 'be occupied solely for purposes incidental to the occupation and enjoyment of (the house) as a dwelling and shall not be used as a separate unit of accommodation'. The Commissioners issued a ruling that, because of this, the conditions of *VATA 1994, Sch 8, Group 6, Note 2(c)* were not satisfied and the barn did not qualify as a 'protected building' within *Group 6, Note 1*. The tribunal upheld this decision and dismissed F's appeal. *DS Ford*, LON/x (VTD 16271).

[55.4] A couple converted a barn, which stood in the grounds of a protected building, into living accommodation. The Commissioners issued a ruling that output tax was chargeable on the conversion. The couple appealed, contending that it should be treated as zero-rated under *VATA 1994, Sch 8, Group 6*. The tribunal rejected this contention and dismissed the appeal, holding that the conditions of *Group 6, Note 2(c)* were not satisfied, since the relevant planning permission prohibited the separate use or disposal of the barn. The tribunal observed that the fact that the main building 'is a domestic building and is a protected building does not mean that all the buildings within its curtilage, even if covered by the listing, are domestic buildings'. *D & L Clamp*, [1999] VATDR 520 (VTD 16422).

Conversion of oast house into living accommodation—Note 2(c)

[55.5] A married couple owned a house, which was a protected building, and a nearby oast house, which was a listed building. They obtained listed building consent to convert the oast house into living accommodation. Customs issued a ruling that output tax was chargeable on the conversion. The husband appealed, contending that it should be treated as zero-rated under *VATA 1994,*

Sch 8, Group 6. The tribunal rejected this contention and dismissed the appeal, holding that the conditions of *Group 6, Note 2(c)* were not satisfied, since the relevant planning permission prohibited the separate use or disposal of the oast house. *NP Smith*, LON/03/681 (VTD 19064).

Barn used as garage—whether within Group 6, Note 2

[55.6] A company carried out approved alterations to a protected building, including alterations to a building which had been built as a barn but was used as a garage. The Commissioners issued a ruling that the work on the barn was standard-rated. The company appealed, contending that the barn should be treated as a 'garage', within *Sch 8, Group 6, Note 2*, and that the work on it qualified for zero-rating. The tribunal accepted this contention and allowed the appeal, holding that although the barn had not originally been constructed as a 'garage', it qualified as a 'garage' for the purposes of *Group 6, Note 2*. The tribunal held that 'the word "garage" connotes only a building or shed for the storage of one or more motor vehicles'. There was 'no additional requirement that the garage must have been constructed as a garage, or that it must have been designed as a garage or have been a dedicated garage at the time of its construction. It is enough if it was built at the same time as the building designed to remain as or become the dwelling together with which it is occupied.' *Grange Builders (Quainton) Ltd*, [2005] VATDR 147 (VTD 18905). (*Note.* For Customs' practice following this decision, see Business Brief 11/2005, issued on 18 May 2005. Customs stated that they 'now accept that, provided a garage is in use as a garage before the alteration or reconstruction takes place and continues to be used as one afterwards, it is not necessary for the garage to have been constructed as a garage (ie as an enclosure for the storage of motor vehicles). It can also have been constructed as something different eg a barn.')

Conversion of outbuilding within grounds of protected building

[55.7] The owner of a listed building arranged for the conversion of a barn into living accommodation. The Commissioners issued a ruling that output tax was chargeable on the work. The owner appealed, contending that the work qualified for zero-rating on the basis that the barn was 'designed to remain as or become a dwelling', within *VATA 1994, Sch 8, Group 6, Note 2*. The tribunal accepted this contention and allowed the appeal, holding that the restriction in *Note 2(c)* did not apply, because the relevant planning permission did not prohibit the separate disposal of the dwelling. *N Hopewell-Smith*, LON/99/947 (VTD 16725). (*Note.* The decision here was disapproved in the subsequent case of *Wiseman*, 15.51 CONSTRUCTION OF BUILDINGS, ETC., on the grounds that the tribunal here had erred in regarding the two limbs of *Note 2(c)* as alternative. The tribunal in *Wiseman* held that 'Parliament undoubtedly meant by *Note 2(c)* to exclude from zero-rating any residential building which was not capable of *either* separate use *or* disposal. Both conditions have to be satisfied'. See also the subsequent HL decision in *Zielinski Baker & Partners Ltd*, 55.9 below.)

[55.8] See also *CM Lee*, 55.75 below, and *Kernahan*, 55.76 below.

[55.9] The owners of a protected building arranged for the construction of a swimming pool in the grounds, and the conversion of an outbuilding into changing rooms and a games room. Both the protected building and the outbuilding had been built in 1830. The outbuilding, which was accepted as being within the curtilage of the protected building, had only been used for residential purposes for about 12 months in 1945. The Commissioners issued a ruling that the conversion of the outbuilding failed to qualify for zero-rating, since the outbuilding was not a 'protected building'. The company which carried out the conversion appealed. The HL upheld the Commissioners' ruling (by a 4-1 majority, Lord Nicholls dissenting). Lord Hoffmann observed that 'the actual outbuilding to which the alterations in this case were made was not designed to remain as or become a dwelling house'. Lord Hope observed that 'it is only the outbuilding and not the house that is being altered, and it is the house and not the outbuilding that has been listed'. The outbuilding was not within the definition of a 'protected building', and the work on it failed to qualify for zero-rating. *C & E Commrs v Zielinski Baker & Partners Ltd*, HL [2004] STC 456; [2004] UKHL 7; [2004] 1 WLR 707; [2004] 2 All ER 141. (*Note.* For the Commissioners' practice following this decision, see Business Brief 10/2004, issued on 22 March 2004.)

[55.10] The HL decision in *Zielinski Baker & Partners Ltd*, 55.9 above, was applied in a subsequent case where the tribunal held that the conversion of a small outbuilding from a 'utility workroom' into a guest bedroom did not qualify for zero-rating. The tribunal specifically declined to follow the 1994 decision in *Forman Hardy*, 55.37 below, on the grounds that it was inconsistent with the subsequent decision in *Zielinski Baker & Partners Ltd*. *Lord and Lady Watson of Richmond*, LON/01/1210 (VTD 18903).

[55.11] The owner of a former vicarage, which was a protected building, arranged for the reconstruction of a barn in the vicarage grounds. Customs issued a ruling that VAT was chargeable on the work. The owner appealed, contending that it should be treated as an approved alteration to a protected building. The tribunal rejected this contention and dismissed the appeal, applying the HL decision in *Zielinski Baker & Partners Ltd*, 55.9 above, and observing that 'the barn was a physically separate building from the house not designed or intended for use as a separate dwelling'. The tribunal observed that 'the only way that the barn could attract zero-rating would be if it was designed to become and became a dwelling on completion of the works'. On the evidence, this was not the case. *E King*, LON/04/1086 (VTD 19208).

[55.12] The owner of a protected building obtained listed building consent for a cottage, within the curtilage of the protected building, to be converted into a five-bedroomed house. The relevant planning permission provided that the house 'shall only be used for purposes either incidental or ancillary to the residential use' of the protected building. HMRC issued a ruling that tax was chargeable on the conversion. The owner appealed, contending that the work should be treated as a zero-rated approved alteration to a protected building. The Upper Tribunal rejected this contention and upheld HMRC's ruling, holding that the planning permission prohibited 'separate use as such', so that the work failed to satisfy the conditions of *VATA 1994, Sch 8, Group 6, Note 2(c)*. The Upper Tribunal specifically disapproved the earlier decision of the

VAT Tribunal in *Dr RW Nicholson*, LON/04/1033 (VTD 19412). *HMRC v S Lunn*, UT 2009, [2010] STC 493; [2009] UKUT 244 (TCC).

Weir—whether a 'building'

[55.13] A registered charity, which was not registered for VAT, owned a weir, which was a scheduled monument and was listed as a building of special historic interest under *Town and Country Planning Act 1971, s 54*. During 2009 and 2010 the charity restored the weir, and reclaimed VAT on the work. HMRC rejected the claim on the basis that the weir was not within the definition of a 'building' for VAT purposes. The tribunal dismissed the charity's appeal against this decision. *Calver Weir Restoration Project v HMRC*, [2011] UKFTT 460 (TC); [2011] SFTD 1001, TC01310.

Home for rehabilitation of people suffering brain injuries

[55.14] See *General Healthcare Group Ltd*, 15.73 CONSTRUCTION OF BUILDINGS, ETC.

Whether building to be used 'for relevant charitable purpose'

[55.15] The Royal Academy of Music arranged for a contractor to carry out reconstruction work on a listed building which it used as a concert hall. It applied for a certificate that the work qualified for zero-rating. The Commissioners rejected the claim on the basis that the building was not 'intended for use solely for a relevant residential purpose or a relevant charitable purpose', as required by *VATA 1994, Sch 8, Group 6, Note 1*, but was intended to be used for business purposes. The Academy appealed, contending that it was not carrying on a business, and that the effect of *Article 4(5)* of the *EC Sixth Directive* was that it should not be treated as a 'taxable person'. The tribunal dismissed the appeal, holding that the Academy was carrying on a business activity. The fact that its objects were charitable or philanthropic was not conclusive. Furthermore, the Academy was not a 'public authority', and was not 'governed by public law', so that *Article 4(5)* was not applicable. *Royal Academy of Music*, [1994] VATTR 105 (VTD 11871).

[55.16] A charity used premises on the first floor of a listed building to run a sports and fitness centre. It arranged for substantial refurbishment of the premises. The Commissioners issued a ruling that VAT was chargeable on the work. The charity appealed, contending that the work should be zero-rated under *VATA 1994, Sch 8, Group 6*, on the basis that the building was intended for use solely for a 'relevant charitable purpose'. The tribunal rejected this contention and dismissed the appeal, and the CA upheld this decision. On the evidence, the use of the building was not 'similar to the use of a village hall in providing social or recreational facilities for a local community'. Sir John Vinelott held that the conditions of what is now *VATA 1994, Sch 8, Group 5, Note 6(b)* were only satisfied 'where a local community is the final consumer in respect of the supply of the services' in the sense that 'the local community is the user of the services (through a body of trustees or a management committee acting on its behalf) and in which the only economic activity is one in which they participate directly'. *C & E Commrs v Jubilee Hall Recreation Centre Ltd*, CA 1998, [1999] STC 381.

[55.17] A charity occupied a listed building, from which it provided residential care for blind ex-servicemen. It arranged for substantial refurbishment of the building. The Commissioners issued a ruling that VAT was chargeable on the work. The charity appealed, contending that the building was 'intended for use solely for a relevant residential purpose or a relevant charitable purpose', so that it was a 'protected building' within the definition in *VATA 1994, Sch 8, Group 6, Note 1*, and the work should be zero-rated. The tribunal rejected this contention and dismissed the appeal, holding on the evidence that the building failed to qualify as a 'protected building', and the work in question was standard-rated. *St Dunstan's*, [2003] VATDR 634 (VTD 17896). (*Note.* The charity appealed to the Ch D, where the appeal was allowed by consent without a formal hearing, on the basis of additional evidence which had not been included in the tribunal decision.)

Insufficient evidence

[55.18] An appeal was dismissed in a case where the appellant company failed to submit evidence that the building in question was a 'protected building' within the definition laid down by *VATA 1994, 8 Sch, Group 6, Note 1*. *DM Builders (Chichester) Ltd*, LON/91/778 (VTD 7618).

Whether a 'substantial reconstruction' (VATA 1994, Sch 8, Group 6, Item 1, Note 4)

[55.19] A company purchased a listed building which was in very poor condition, with the intention of refurbishing and selling it. It reclaimed input tax on the basis that it had carried out a 'substantial reconstruction' of the property, so that the sale would be zero-rated under *VATA 1994, Sch 8, Group 6*. The Commissioners rejected the claim on the basis that the work did not amount to a 'substantial reconstruction', so that the sale of the building would be exempt. The company appealed. The tribunal reviewed the evidence in detail and allowed the appeal, finding that when the company purchased the building, it was 'a ruin, unfit for habitation despite the vendor remaining in occupation'. On the evidence, 'the property was substantially reconstructed within the ordinary everyday meaning of that expression'. Furthermore, the work met the requirements of *Group 6, Note 4(a)*. The tribunal commented that 'the supplies comprising the work on the roof' amounted to 'supplies in the course of an approved alteration even though a number of individual elements of that work might be described as repairs to particular parts of the roof and its timbers'. *Lordsregal Ltd*, LON/01/1243 (VTD 18535).

[55.20] A charity operated a boarding school. It owned a listed building which was used as a boarding house, and which was in need of renovation. In an attempt to recover the VAT on such work, the college granted a long lease of the building to a subsidiary company (E) in July 2005. E arranged for contractors to carry out substantial work at the boarding house. In March

2006, shortly before the completion of the work, E leased the boarding house back to the charity. E then reclaimed the input tax on the construction. HMRC rejected the claim, considering that the work had not amounted to a substantial reconstruction of the boarding house. E appealed. The tribunal reviewed the evidence in detail and allowed E's appeal in principle, holding that the work did amount to a 'substantial reconstruction'. (The tribunal noted that HMRC's decision, against which E had appealed, only concerned the question of whether there had been a 'substantial reconstruction'. The tribunal noted that the parties had not agreed as to whether the work met the other requirements of Group 6, Note 4, and specifically rejected E's contention that HMRC should be deemed to have conceded this point. The tribunal directed that there should be a further hearing if the parties were unable to agree this issue.) *Cheltenham College Enterprises Ltd v HMRC*, [2010] SFTD 696; [2010] UKFTT 118 (TC), TC00429.

Renovation

[55.21] A property developer bought two protected buildings, which he renovated and sold. He did not account for tax on the sale, but reclaimed input tax on the work. The Commissioners rejected the claim, considering that the sale of the properties was exempt from VAT. He appealed, contending that the work was zero-rated under what is now *VATA 1994, Sch 8, Group 6*. The tribunal dismissed his appeal, holding on the evidence that the work was 'a minor enlargement of the building and a modernisation of its interior'. This did not amount to 'substantial reconstruction'. *D Barraclough*, LON/86/699 (VTD 2529).

[55.22] A building contractor obtained permission for the 'renovation of the roof, repositioning of the back door, provision of first floor bathroom and reflooring on ground floor' of a protected building. He carried out the work in question and sold the building. The Commissioners issued a ruling that the sale was exempt and he appealed, contending that it should be zero-rated under what is now *VATA 1994, Sch 8, Group 6*. The tribunal dismissed his appeal, holding that the work did not amount to 'substantial reconstruction'. *TR Bates*, LON/87/623 (VTD 2925).

[55.23] The owner of a Grade II listed building had it restored at a cost of £900,000. He reclaimed the input tax incurred, and then sold the building. The Commissioners issued an assessment to recover the tax, on the basis that the sale was an exempt supply. The vendor appealed, contending that the sale should be treated as zero-rated under what is now *VATA 1994, Sch 8, Group 6*. The tribunal dismissed the appeal, holding that the work in question did not amount to 'substantial reconstruction', so that the sale did not qualify for zero-rating. *ADJ Lee*, LON/90/93X (VTD 5887).

[55.24] A company which owned a protected building obtained permission for alterations to the building including underpinning, rewiring, repointing and overhauling of the roof. It reclaimed input tax on the work. The Commissioners issued an assessment to recover the tax, and the company appealed, contending that the work should be zero-rated under what is now *VATA 1994, Sch 8, Group 6*. The tribunal dismissed the appeal, holding that the work did not amount to 'substantial reconstruction', since there had been 'no material reconstruction of the building looked at as a whole'. *Vivodean Ltd*, EDN/90/134 (VTD 6538).

[55.25] The addition of a two-storey extension to a dilapidated farmhouse, which was a Grade II listed building, was held not to constitute 'substantial reconstruction' in *NB Church (t/a Milton Antique Restoration)*, LON/92/2751 (VTD 12427).

[55.26] A company purchased a listed building which had been unoccupied for a long time, and was in poor condition. It obtained listed building consent for the demolition of a small part of the building, the construction of a small extension, and an internal reorganisation of the rooms. It then sold the building, treating the sale as zero-rated. The Commissioners issued an assessment charging tax on the sale, and the company appealed, contending that the work had constituted a 'substantial reconstruction'. The tribunal rejected this contention and dismissed the appeal, holding that the work constituted a 'minor enlargement of the building and a modernisation of its interior', and did not amount to 'reconstruction'. *Southlong East Midlands Ltd*, LON/03/789 (VTD 18943).

Whether an 'approved alteration' (VATA 1994, Sch 8, Group 6, Item 2, Note 6)

Cases held to constitute an approved alteration

Replacement of roof

[55.27] The owner of a protected building obtained consent for replacement of the roof, which was of slate. The Commissioners issued a ruling that the work did not qualify for zero-rating, on the basis that it was 'repair or maintenance' and was excluded from zero-rating by what is now *VATA 1994, Sch 8, Group 6, Note 6*. The tribunal allowed the owner's appeal, holding that the works were 'works of alteration', rather than 'repair or maintenance', and qualified for zero-rating. Applying *dicta* of Lord Diplock in *C & E Commrs v Viva Gas Appliances*, 56.10 REDUCED-RATE SUPPLIES, 'alteration' should be construed as including 'any work upon the fabric of the building except that which is so slight or trivial as to attract the application of the *de minimis* rule'. *CN Evans*, MAN/88/587 (VTD 4415). (*Note.* Compare the subsequent decisions in *The Vicar and Parochial Church Council of St Petroc Minor*, 55.54 below; *Meanwell Construction Co Ltd*, 55.57 below, and *Windflower Housing Association*, 55.59 below. In *The Vicar and Parochial Church Council of St Petroc Minor* the tribunal specifically declined to apply *dicta* of Lord Diplock in *Viva Gas*, observing that in that case the word 'alteration' was used 'in a context which no longer appears in (*VATA 1994*). That contextual interpretation is therefore of no help now.')

[55.28] A company rethatched the roofs of two listed buildings, and did not account for output tax on the work. The Commissioners issued an assessment charging tax, and the company appealed, contending that the work constituted 'approved alterations' which qualified for zero-rating. The tribunal accepted this contention and allowed the appeal. In each case, the roof had previously been thatched with straw, whereas the company had used reeds, which altered the appearance of the roofs. Furthermore, neither of the roofs had been in specific need of repair, and the work went beyond 'repair or maintenance'. *Dodson Bros. (Thatchers) Ltd*, [1995] VATDR 514 (VTD 13734).

[55.29] A parish church council arranged for the replacement of the existing church roof with a new roof made of lead. The Commissioners issued a ruling that the work constituted 'repair or maintenance', so that output tax was chargeable. The church council appealed, contending that the work was an 'approved alteration' and qualified for zero-rating. The tribunal accepted this contention and allowed the appeal. *Parochial Church Council of St Andrew's Church Eakring*, MAN/97/368 (VTD 15320).

Replacement of guttering

[55.30] The guttering of a church was replaced in order to improve drainage from the church roof. The new guttering was laid onto new soles, sloping in a different direction to the old soles and leading to new exit chutes. The Commissioners issued a ruling that the work did not qualify for zero-rating under what is now *VATA 1994, Sch 8, Group 6*, on the basis that it constituted 'repair or maintenance'. The church council appealed. The tribunal reviewed the evidence in detail and allowed the appeal in principle, holding that the replacement of the gutter was an alteration, rather than repair or maintenance. (The appeal was adjourned to consider the apportionment of the time spent by the contractors between this work and other work which did not qualify for zero-rating.) *All Saints Church (Tilsworth) Parochial Church Council*, [1993] VATTR 315 (VTD 10490). (*Note.* There was no further public hearing of the appeal.)

[55.31] The owner of a protected building obtained listed building consent for the removal of some lead guttering and its replacement by an extra layer of slates. The contractor charged VAT on the work. The owner applied to Customs for a ruling that the work should be treated as zero-rated. Customs rejected his claim but the tribunal allowed his appeal, holding that the work was an 'approved alteration' and not simply 'repair and maintenance'. *D Starr*, MAN/05/043 (VTD 19176).

Insertion of additional floor timbers

[55.32] A protected building was converted from a nursing home into a residential home. Additional floor timbers were inserted in the course of the work. The Commissioners issued an assessment charging output tax on the company which had carried out the work. The company appealed, contending that the work should be zero-rated under what is now *VATA 1994, Sch 8, Group 6*. The tribunal allowed the company's appeal, holding that, since the timbers were 'part of the fabric', the work was an alteration, and was not merely 'repair or maintenance'. *Davencroft Brickwork Ltd*, LON/92/1688 (VTD 10692).

Installation of wardrobes

[55.33] The owner of a castle, which was a listed building, obtained listed building consent for certain internal alterations. The work included the installation of new wardrobes along the wall of a bedroom. The Commissioners issued a ruling that this work did not qualify for zero-rating. The tribunal allowed the owner's appeal, applying the principles laid down by the HL in *C & E Commrs v Viva Gas Appliances*, **56.10** REDUCED-RATE SUPPLIES, and holding that the work materially affected 'the structure of the building and the fabric of the building beyond what could be termed *de minimis*'. The tribunal observed that 'the purpose of the zero-rating provisions for protected buildings appears to be to encourage their preservation and continued viability and to recognise the fact that work on such buildings when permitted by planning authorities may generally be more costly than work on non-listed buildings'. *EC Owen*, LON/03/462 (VTD 18660).

Installation of slab mirrors

[55.34] A company (N) obtained listed consent to convert a row of Georgian buildings from offices into houses. It arranged for a subcontractor (C) to install slab mirrors in the houses. C did not account for tax on its supplies. Customs issued an assessment charging tax on them, and C appealed, contending that they should be zero-rated. The tribunal accepted this contention and allowed the appeal, finding that the slab mirrors were 'permanent features which effectively formed part of the fabric of the buildings and very much in keeping with restoring the Georgian buildings to their former glory. They were not mirrors as usually understood as pieces of furniture that could be re-arranged and moved around the property.' Accordingly they formed part of an 'approved alteration' of the buildings, and qualified for zero-rating. *Chamelon Mirrors Ltd*, MAN/x (VTD 20640).

Installation of lighting in church

[55.35] A vicar arranged for the installation of a new lighting system in his church, which was a protected building. The Commissioners issued a ruling that VAT was chargeable on the work. The vicar appealed, contending that the work constituted an 'approved alteration'. The tribunal accepted this contention and allowed the appeal. Applying *Holy Trinity Church (Heath Town Wolverhampton) Parochial Church Council*, **55.45** below, the installation of new lighting was within the definition of an 'alteration'. On the evidence, the work here was 'a one-off in the sense of exceptional expenditure' and could not be 'categorised as repair or maintenance'. *All Saints with St Nicholas Church Icklesham*, LON/x (VTD 16321). (*Note.* For the Commissioners' revised policy on mains wiring, following this case, see Business Brief 7/2000, issued on 18 May 2000.)

Damp-proofing and insulation

[55.36] An individual (C) purchased a large house, which was a protected building. He arranged for damp-proofing and insulation work to be carried out on the property. Customs issued a ruling that VAT was chargeable on the work, on the basis that it constituted 'repair or maintenance', which was excluded from zero-rating. C appealed, contending that the work constituted an approved alteration, which qualified for zero-rating. The tribunal accepted this contention and allowed the appeal, holding on the evidence that 'this was entirely new work resulting in improvement to the buildings' and 'was not undertaken in the ordinary course of property management to keep up the building'. *DH Carr*, LON/03/715 (VTD 19267). (*Note.* The tribunal also held that C was not entitled to registration for VAT, since he was not making or intending to make any taxable supplies.)

Alterations to outbuilding within grounds of protected building

[55.37] The owner of a listed building obtained listed building consent for alterations to a secondary building which was within the curtilage of the listed building but was separated from it by a driveway which was 18 foot wide. The Commissioners issued a ruling that the work did not qualify for zero-rating, on the basis that the secondary building did not form part of the protected building. The owner appealed, contending that the outbuilding should be treated as part of the listed building since it was used as a games room and effectively formed part of his private residence. The tribunal accepted this contention and allowed the appeal. *N Forman Hardy*, [1994] VATTR 302 (VTD 12776). (*Note.* See now, however, the subsequent HL decision in *Zielinski Baker & Partners Ltd*, 55.9 above. In the subsequent case of *Lord and Lady Watson of Richmond*, 55.10 above, the tribunal held that the effect of the *Zielinski Baker* decision was 'that the decision of the tribunal in the *Forman Hardy* case can no longer stand as authority'.)

[55.38] A trader purchased a farmhouse, which was a protected building, with the aim of converting it into a nursing home. He obtained listed building consent to convert the farmhouse into a nursing home, and to convert some redundant agricultural buildings, which stood in the grounds of the home, into flats and an office to be used in conjunction with the home. The partnership which carried out the work treated it as zero-rated. The Commissioners issued an assessment on the basis that the work relating to the office did not qualify for zero-rating. The partnership appealed. The tribunal allowed the appeal, holding that, although the office did not contain any sleeping accommodation, 'residential accommodation clearly includes a number of ancillary matters without which the building or institution could not properly function. In the present case it was expedient to house the administration side in a separate building, rather than to have some of the old people sleeping in one building and some in another'. *Hill Ash Developments*, [2000] VATDR 366 (VTD 16747).

Indoor swimming pool connected to protected building by walkway

[55.39] The owner of a farmhouse, which was a listed building, arranged for the construction of an indoor swimming pool, connected to the farmhouse by a covered walkway. The Commissioners issued a ruling that the restriction in what is now *VATA 1994, Sch 8, Group 6, Note 10* applied, so that the work was standard-rated. The owner appealed, contending that the work was an approved alteration to the farmhouse, which was a protected building, so that the work should be treated as zero-rated under *Sch 8, Group 6*. The tribunal allowed the appeal, holding that the swimming pool was part of the protected building, so that the restriction in *Sch 8, Group 6, Note 10* did not apply and the work was an alteration of the protected building which qualified for zero-rating. The QB upheld the tribunal decision as one of fact. *C & E Commrs v M Arbib*, QB [1995] STC 490.

Cases where the tax was apportioned

Replacement of roof

[55.40] The owner of a protected building obtained permission for the replacement of the roof, which was made of stone slates and comprised 14 pitches. The builder who carried out the work treated it as zero-rated. The Commissioners issued an assessment charging tax on the work, on the basis that it was 'repair or maintenance' which did not qualify for zero-rating. The builder appealed, contending that the work was an 'alteration' because it had been necessary to raise some of the valleys and alter the pitches, and to demolish an unsafe chimney and roof over three skylights. The tribunal allowed the appeal in part, holding that 'the work of replacing or renewing a tile comes within the definition of repair and maintenance' but that 'the work of changing the height of the ridges and the pitches of the roof slopes as well as increasing the height of the valleys does not come within the term "repair and maintenance"'. Furthermore, the removal of the chimney did not qualify for zero-rating, since it was not covered by the listed building consent. The tribunal directed that the expenditure should be apportioned. *CN Foley*, LON/94/2772A (VTD 13496).

[55.41] The owner of a protected building obtained listed building consent to cover the roof with stone tiles. The contractor responsible for the work did not account for output tax on it, treating it as zero-rated. The Commissioners issued an assessment charging tax on the basis that the work was 'repair or maintenance' which did not qualify for zero-rating, and the contractor appealed. The tribunal reviewed the evidence in detail and allowed the appeal in part. On the evidence, approximately 65% of the roof area had been in need of repair, and the re-roofing of this section was 'repair or maintenance' which did not qualify for zero-rating. However, the remaining 35% of the roof had been in good condition, and the re-roofing of this section was not within the definition of 'repair or maintenance' and therefore qualified for zero-rating. *NF Rhodes*, MAN/96/9 (VTD 14533).

Repairs and alteration to roof

[55.42] A company carried out substantial work on a church, which was a protected building. This included attaching steelwork to the main trusses, strapping purlins onto the gable end, and inserting wooden braces in the roof structure. The tribunal held that attaching steelwork to the main trusses was a repair and was standard-rated, but that strapping purlins onto the gable end and inserting wooden braces in the roof structure were 'alterations' and were zero-rated. *Randall Orchard Holdings Ltd*, MAN/02/406 (VTD 18046). (*Note*. Costs were awarded to the company.)

Rebuilding of external walls—replacement of roof

[55.43] A building company obtained listed building consent for the 'refurbishment' of a dilapidated 16th century farmhouse. The work included the rebuilding of the external walls and the replacement of the roof. The company did not account for output tax on the work, treating it as zero-rated. The Commissioners issued an assessment charging tax on the basis that the work constituted 'repair and maintenance' and failed to qualify for zero-rating. The tribunal allowed the company's appeal in part, holding on the evidence that the rebuilding of the external walls and the insertion of a new window constituted an 'approved alteration'. However, applying the QB decision in *Windflower Housing Association*, 55.59 below, the replacement of the roof was 'repair and maintenance' which failed to qualify for zero-rating. The fitting of new gutters and of new external gates, the construction of a new garage, the laying of new pavings and the landscaping of the grounds also failed to qualify for zero-rating. *Logmoor Ltd*, MAN/95/2750 (VTD 14733).

Internal alterations including installation of septic tank and damp-proofing

[55.44] A married couple purchased a listed building, which was in a run-down condition, and obtained listed building consent for various internal alterations, including the lowering of some windows, the replacement of a door with a window, the construction of various partitions, and the installation of a septic tank. The work which was eventually carried out was more extensive than the work for which listed building consent had been obtained. The Commissioners accepted that the lowering of windows and the replacement of a door with a window were approved alterations which qualified for zero-rating, but ruled that the remainder of the work did not qualify. The couple appealed, contending that 25 further items of work (including the installation of the septic tank, the installation of damp-proofing, the replacement of a staircase, the relocation of a fireplace and the lowering of a ceiling) should be treated as qualifying for zero-rating. The tribunal reviewed the evidence in detail and allowed the appeal in part, holding that seven of the 25 items (including the installation of the septic tank, and the removal and erection of various partitions) qualified for zero-rating, but that the remaining 18 items did not. Of the items which failed to qualify, some (including the installation of damp-proofing and the replacement of a staircase) were within the definition of 'repair and maintenance', while others (including the relocation of a fireplace and the lowering of a ceiling) were not covered by the grant of listed building consent and thus did not meet the requirements of *Sch 8, Group 6, Note 6(c)*. *Mr & Mrs MP Wells*, MAN/96/11 (VTD 15169).

Installation of lighting in church

[55.45] A parochial church council arranged for the installation of a new lighting system in the church, which was a protected building. The Commissioners issued a ruling that VAT was chargeable on the work. The church council appealed, contending that the work constituted an 'approved alteration'. The tribunal reviewed the evidence in detail and allowed the appeal in part, holding that the installation of new lighting was within the definition of an 'alteration' but that much of the work was within the definition of 'repair and maintenance' and thus failed to qualify for zero-rating. *Holy Trinity Church (Heath Town Wolverhampton) Parochial Church Council*, MAN/94/1910 (VTD 13652).

New drainage system

[55.46] A company owned a 21-acre estate which included a Grade II listed building. The sewage treatment plant at the estate was found to be inadequate. It obtained planning permission and listed building consent for a new sewage treatment plant. The Commissioners issued a ruling that output tax was chargeable on the cost of the plant, since it constituted 'repair or maintenance' rather than an 'approved alteration' within what is now *VATA 1994, Sch 8, Group 6*. The company appealed, contending that the work qualified for zero-rating. The tribunal allowed the appeal in part, holding that the work 'went far beyond mere repair or maintenance' but finding that part of the work related to three cottages on the estate which were not a part of the listed building. The tribunal directed that the tax should be apportioned accordingly. *Walsingham College (Yorkshire Properties) Ltd*, [1995] VATDR 141 (VTD 13223).

Erection of railings around church

[55.47] A contractor erected railings around a churchyard. On the northern part of the site, the railings were fixed to the top of the churchyard wall, but on the southern part of the site they were free-standing with a small gap where they reached the church. The church was a protected building, and listed building consent had been obtained for the work. The contractor did not account for output tax on the work, treating it as zero-rated. The Commissioners issued an assessment charging tax on the work, and he appealed, contending that it was an 'approved alteration'. The tribunal allowed the appeal in part. The churchyard wall formed part of the protected building, and the erection of railings on top of this wall was within the definition of an 'approved alteration'. However, an approved alteration 'must touch the fabric of the building', so that the erection of free-standing railings around the southern part of the site did not qualify for zero-rating. *RG Powell (t/a Anwick Agricultural Engineers)*, MAN/96/284 (VTD 14520). (*Note*. The tribunal decision that the erection of railings qualified for zero-rating was questioned by Laddie J in the subsequent case of *Tinsley*, **55.62** below. He held that the decision 'must now be seriously in doubt' following the HL decision in *Zielinski Baker & Partners Ltd*, **55.9** above.)

Construction of boundary wall

[55.48] The owner of a 16th century cottage, which was a protected building, obtained listed building consent for the replacement of a boundary fence by a wall. He reclaimed input tax on the cost of the wall. The Commissioners rejected the claim on the basis that the construction of the wall did not qualify as an approved alteration to a building. He appealed. The tribunal allowed the appeal in part, holding on the evidence that a short section of the wall, which was linked to the cottage by a 'timber-boxing' arrangement, qualified for zero-rating on the basis that it should 'be considered as part of the cottage'. However, the effect of *VATA 1994, Sch 8, Group 6, Note 10* was that the remainder of the wall did not qualify for zero-rating. *C Mason*, MAN/99/109 (VTD 16250).(*Note*. The tribunal decision that part of the work qualified for zero-rating was questioned by Laddie J in the subsequent case of *Tinsley*, **55.62** below. He held that the decision 'must now be seriously in doubt' following the HL decision in *Zielinski Baker & Partners Ltd*, **55.9** above.)

Construction of new retaining wall and drainage system

[55.49] The owner of an 18th century house, which was a protected building, arranged for the construction of a new retaining wall and a new drainage system. The Commissioners issued a ruling that the work was standard-rated. She appealed, contending that it should be treated as an 'approved alteration' and as zero-rated under *VATA 1994, Sch 8, Group 6*. The tribunal reviewed the evidence in detail and allowed her appeal in part, holding that the construction of the wall was zero-rated. Applying the principles laid down in *Walsingham College (Yorkshire Properties) Ltd*, 55.46 above, the part of the drainage system extending from the house to a 'perforated land drain' qualified for zero-rating on the grounds that it was an 'integral part of the house', but the remainder of the drainage failed to qualify for zero-rating. *Mrs AW Adams*, LON/02/340 (VTD 18054).

Construction of greenhouse, stables and swimming pool

[55.50] The owner of a protected building, which dated from the 15th century, obtained listed building consent for various alterations to the building. The Commissioners accepted that the work which was carried out on the building itself qualified for zero-rating. However, they issued a ruling that the construction of a greenhouse attached to the protected building, and of stables and a swimming pool enclosure in the grounds of the building did not qualify for zero-rating. The owner appealed. The tribunal allowed the appeal in part, holding that the construction of the greenhouse was an 'approved alteration' and thus qualified for zero-rating, but that the construction of the stables and the swimming pool enclosure did not qualify. On the evidence, the greenhouse was not a separate building, since it was 'attached to and integrated with the two pre-existing walls' of the protected building. However, the swimming pool enclosure was not sufficiently attached to the protected building to amount to an alteration to that building, and the stables were also a separate building, the construction of which was excluded from zero-rating by what is now *VATA 1994, 8 Sch, Group 6, Note 10*. *CW Mann*, LON/95/2066 (VTD 14004).

Rebuilding of swimming pool and construction of link to house

[55.51] The owner of a protected building obtained listed building consent for the rebuilding of a swimming pool enclosure and the construction of a 'pedestrian link' to the house. Customs issued a ruling that VAT was chargeable on the work. The company which carried out the work appealed, contending that it qualified for zero-rating. The tribunal reviewed the evidence in detail and allowed the appeal in part, holding that the effect of *VATA 1994, 8 Sch, Group 6, Note 10* was that the rebuilding of 'the swimming pool complex' failed to qualify for zero-rating. The tribunal held that 'a building which is essentially separate from the protected building cannot be taken outside *Note 10* by some link back to the protected building' and found that 'the pool complex is a separate building albeit one which is physically linked to the house by the passage'. However, the tribunal held that the construction of the passage between the swimming pool and the house did qualify for zero-rating as an 'approved alteration' to the house, within *Group 6, Item 2*. *Collins & Beckett Ltd*, LON/04/100 (VTD 19212).

Cases held not to constitute an approved alteration

Rebuilding of wall

[55.52] The owner of a Grade II listed building demolished and rebuilt part of the boundary wall. The tribunal held that the work did not qualify as an 'approved alteration', since the owner had not obtained the formal consent required by what is now *VATA 1994, Sch 8, Group 6, Note 6(c)*. *J Hollier*, LON/87/456 (VTD 3758).

Partial rebuilding of walls

[55.53] The owner of a protected building obtained listed building consent for the partial rebuilding of the front main wall. The tribunal held that the work was 'repair or maintenance', which was excluded from zero-rating by what is now *VATA 1994, Sch 8, Group 6, Note 6*. The tribunal observed that 'it is difficult for repair and maintenance not to involve some element of alteration, but it was not alteration for the sake of alteration or for any other reason apart from the more effective repair and maintenance of the building'. If the most effective way to repair or maintain a building was 'by employing modern methods which involve the use of different building materials', the element of alteration involved 'does not prevent the work from being essentially a work of repair and maintenance and therefore not eligible for zero-rating.' *Dr NDF Browne*, LON/93/480A (VTD 11388).

[55.54] A similar decision was reached in a subsequent case in which the tribunal specifically declined to apply *dicta* of Lord Diplock in *C & E Commrs v Viva Gas Appliances*, 56.10 REDUCED-RATE SUPPLIES, observing that in that case the word 'alteration' was used 'in a context which no longer appears in (*VATA 1994*). That contextual interpretation is therefore of no help now.' On the evidence, the tribunal held that 'to the extent that there may be an element of alteration it is incidental, resulting from the carrying out of the maintenance work'. *The Vicar and Parochial Church Council of St Petroc Minor*, LON/98/1381 (VTD 16450).

Strengthening of walls

[55.55] The owner of two protected buildings arranged for the rear walls of the buildings, which were unstable, to be strengthened by the injection of certain chemicals. The tribunal held that the work amounted to 'repair or maintenance' and was therefore excluded from zero-rating by what is now *VATA 1994, Sch 8, Group 6, Note 6*. *B Cheeseman*, LON/89/1344Z (VTD 5133).

Replacement of roof

[55.56] The owner of a protected building obtained permission to reconvert it from three flats to a single dwelling. He also reslated the roof with natural slate, replacing the existing mixture of slate and asbestos. He reclaimed the input tax relating to the reslating of the roof. The Commissioners rejected the claim, since this work was not referred to in the application for listed building consent, so that it did not constitute an 'approved alteration'. The tribunal dismissed the owner's appeal, holding that 'an "approved alteration" for the purposes of zero-rating requires written consent of the appropriate authority and oral consent, even if proved, would not be sufficient'. *N Brice*, LON/91/708Y (VTD 6376).

[55.57] A construction company obtained listed building consent to replace the roof of a protected building. The tribunal held that the work constituted 'repair or maintenance' and was excluded from zero-rating by what is now *VATA 1994, Sch 8, Group 6, Note 6. Meanwell Construction Co Ltd*, MAN/91/1225 (VTD 10726).

[55.58] Similar decisions were reached in *A Wanklin (Haresfield Court Tenants Association)*, LON/06/432 (VTD 20133) and *GGN Builders Ltd*, [2010] UKFTT 184 (TC), TC00488.

[55.59] A housing association, which owned a Grade II listed building, obtained listed building consent for the improvement of the roof structure. The existing cast lead was removed and wooden divisions were erected to support a new rolled lead covering. The length of the parapet gutters was reduced, and the roof plane was raised. The Commissioners issued a ruling that the work was standard-rated, on the basis that it constituted 'repair or maintenance'. The association appealed, contending that the work was an 'approved alteration' and should be treated as zero-rated. The QB rejected this contention and upheld the Commissioners' ruling. Ognall J held that the work was within the definition of 'repair or maintenance', and thus did not qualify for zero-rating. The raising of the roof plane was an alteration, but since it was an integral part of wider works of repair or maintenance, it fell to be treated likewise. *C & E Commrs v Windflower Housing Association*, QB [1995] STC 860.

[55.60] The owners of a protected building, which had had a thatched straw roof, obtained listed building consent to rethatch the roof with reeds. The tribunal held that the work was 'repair or maintenance' which did not qualify for zero-rating. *SH & VS Kain*, LON/93/2588A (VTD 12331).

[55.61] A listed building was badly damaged by fire. The roof had to be replaced and part of the exterior walls had to be rebuilt. The builder who carried out this work treated it as zero-rated. The Commissioners issued an assessment on the basis that it did not qualify for zero-rating, and the builder appealed, contending that the whole of the work should be treated as approved alterations and as zero-rated under what is now *VATA 1994, Sch 8, Group 6*. The QB rejected this contention, holding that the work did not qualify for zero-rating under *Group 6* (but remitted the case to a new tribunal to consider whether they qualified for zero-rating under *Group 5*). Moses J observed that what is now *VATA 1994, Sch 8, Group 6* excluded works of reconstruction, except where they could be described as an alteration which was not repair or maintenance. *C & E Commrs v CR Morrish*, QB [1998] STC 954.

Construction of terrace

[55.62] The owner of a large house, which was a protected building, obtained listed building consent for the construction of a terrace, which adjoined the house. Customs issued a ruling that VAT was chargeable on the work. The owner appealed, contending that the work was an 'approved alteration' and therefore zero-rated. The tribunal accepted this contention but the Ch D reversed this decision and upheld Customs' ruling. Laddie J held that the only reasonable conclusion on the evidence was that the alterations had been made to the garden rather than to the house. 'Furthermore, the work carried out in the garden left it as part of the garden which was not designed to remain as or to become a dwelling'. Accordingly the supplies failed to qualify for zero-rating. *HMRC v AC Tinsley*, Ch D [2005] STC 1612; [2005] EWHC 1508 (Ch).

Replacement of stone balcony

[55.63] A company replaced a stone balcony at an old hotel which was a protected building. Customs issued a ruling that VAT was chargeable on the work. The company appealed, contending that it was an 'approved alteration' which qualified for zero-rating. The tribunal rejected this contention and dismissed the appeal, holding that the work was 'repair or maintenance' which was excluded from zero-rating. *Metropole (Folkestone) Ltd*, LON/05/914 (VTD 19917).

Improvement of windows

[55.64] A company patented and supplied a perimeter sealing system for sliding sash windows. The system was installed in a number of listed buildings. The tribunal held that the installation of the system constituted 'repair or maintenance', which did not qualify for zero-rating. *Ventrolla Ltd*, MAN/92/1825 (VTD 12045).

[55.65] The owner of a listed building arranged for the original sash windows to be replaced by double-glazed sash windows. The tribunal upheld the Commissioners' ruling that this was 'repair or maintenance', and failed to qualify for zero-rating. *B Moore*, EDN/03/85 (VTD 18653).

Removal of asbestos

[55.66] The owner of a protected building engaged a contractor to carry out substantial work on the building, including the removal of asbestos. The tribunal held that, since the work did not affect the character of the building, it constituted 'repair or maintenance' which was excluded from zero-rating by *Sch 8, Group 6, Note 6. RW Gibbs*, LON/89/1681X (VTD 5596).

Painting of exterior of listed building

[55.67] A company applied two coats of masonry paint to the exterior of a listed building, and did not account for output tax on this work. The tribunal held that the work was 'repair or maintenance', which was excluded from zero-rating by *VATA 1994, Sch 8, Group 6, Note 6. Wrencon Ltd*, LON/95/264 (VTD 13968).

Redecoration of church—whether an 'alteration'

[55.68] The priest of a Catholic church arranged for the church to be redecorated in its original Victorian style. The tribunal held that the services of the contractors who had carried out the redecoration were standard-rated, since the work did not amount to an 'alteration'. Applying *dicta* of Lord

Roskill in *ACT Construction Ltd*, **56.9** REDUCED-RATE SUPPLIES, an 'alteration' must be construed as a 'structural alteration'. *St Anne's Catholic Church*, [1994] VATTR 102 (VTD 11783).

Internal alterations

[55.69] The owner of a listed building had obtained consent for the construction of three dormer windows and 'minor alterations'. The work was carried out by a contractor, but the owner also arranged for a friend (R) to supply kitchen and bathroom fittings, tiles, wallpaper and curtains. The tribunal held that R's supplies did not qualify for zero-rating. *R Irving (t/a Rosemary Irving Contracts)*, LON/96/912 (VTD 15188).

Refitting of kitchen

[55.70] The tribunal held that the refitting of a kitchen in a listed building failed to qualify for zero-rating. *Mr & Mrs T Horlick*, LON/01/1234 (VTD 17977).

Construction of garage within curtilage of protected building

[55.71] The owner of a protected building obtained planning permission to erect a double garage within its curtilage. The garage was physically separate from the rest of the building. The tribunal held that the work did not qualify for zero-rating, since the garage was a separate building and the work constituted the construction of a new building rather than an alteration to the existing building. *JH Bradfield*, [1991] VATTR 22 (VTD 5339).

[55.72] Similar decisions were reached in *CA Orme*, LON/92/1885 (VTD 9975); *DL Wilson*, LON/97/1651 (VTD 15803) and *Sherlock & Neal Ltd*, LON/04/64 (VTD 18793).

[55.73] The decision in *Orme*, 55.72 above, was applied in the similar case of *PVR Nicholls*, LON/93/1041A (VTD 11115).

Construction of shed within grounds of protected building

[55.74] An old rectory, standing in 16 acres of land with a walled garden and outbuildings, was a protected building. Its owner obtained listed building consent for the construction within its grounds, and attached to an existing garden wall, of a building to comprise a garage, a workshop, and changing rooms for a swimming pool. The tribunal held that the work constituted the construction of a new building, rather than the alteration of the existing rectory. *K & G Levell*, LON/89/896X (VTD 6202).

Conversion of outbuilding within grounds of protected building

[55.75] The owner of a protected building obtained planning permission for the conversion of an outbuilding, which was within the curtilage of the protected building and about 20 feet away from it, into a study. The tribunal held that the outbuilding was 'not an integral part of the main house', so that the work was not an alteration to the protected building. (The tribunal also observed that the outbuilding was not itself a 'protected building', since it was not a dwelling either before or after the work in question.) *CM Lee*, LON/92/980 (VTD 10662).

[55.76] The decision in *Lee*, 55.75 above, was applied in a similar subsequent case in which *Forman Hardy*, 55.37 above, was distinguished. The tribunal observed that 'the provision of study/office accommodation and secure garaging was not enough to make (the outbuilding) an integral part of the main house'. *AJ & L Kernahan*, LON/97/307 (VTD 15203).

[55.77] See also *Ford*, 55.3 above, and *Clamp*, 55.4 above.

Construction of swimming pool in grounds of protected building

[55.78] The owner of a protected building arranged for the construction of a swimming pool complex within the curtilage of the existing building. The tribunal held that the work did not qualify for zero-rating, since the swimming pool complex was not 'integral to the house'. *Dr A Heijn*, LON/96/1338 (VTD 15562).

Construction of car park in grounds of listed building

[55.79] A builder constructed a car park in the grounds of a listed building. The tribunal held that the work did not qualify for zero-rating. *MD Plumb*, LON/94/2040A (VTD 13621).

Listed building consent obtained retrospectively

[55.80] A building company carried out alterations to a protected building. The work was completed in 1995, but the relevant listed building consent was not granted until January 1996. The Commissioners issued a ruling that the work failed to qualify for zero-rating. The tribunal dismissed the company's appeal, holding that there were 'no grounds for reading the words of *Note* 6 as incorporating retrospective approvals'. *Alan Roper & Sons Ltd*, MAN/96/1169 (VTD 15260).

Listed building consent not obtained

[55.81] The owner of a protected building arranged for the construction of a new drainage system. The local authority advised him that the work did not require listed building consent, as it was under the ground. The owner applied for a refund of the VAT charged by the contractor. Customs rejected the claim, and the owner appealed, contending that the work should be treated as a zero-rated alteration to a protected building. The tribunal rejected this contention and dismissed the appeal, holding that 'in order for works to a listed building to qualify for zero-rating, listed building consent for the works must be granted by the local planning authority before the works are undertaken'. The tribunal chairman (Mr. Huggins) held that there should be 'no relaxation of this rule for whatever reason and it must be strictly applied in accordance with the statutory provision'. *Dr DT Haigh*, LON/07/588 (VTD 20934).

[55.82] See also *Hollier*, 55.52 above, and *Brice*, 55.56 above. There have been a number of other cases in which appeals have been dismissed on the grounds that the appellant has not obtained the formal listed building consent required by what is now *VATA 1994, Sch 8, Group 6, Note 6(c)*. In the interests of space, such cases are not reported individually in this book.

Whether a supply of services (VATA 1994, Sch 8, Group 6, Item 2)

Materials purchased by owner of protected building

[55.83] A builder owned a Grade II listed building, which he used as his business address. He reclaimed input tax relating to materials which he had used in altering the building. The Commissioners rejected the claim and the tribunal dismissed his appeal, holding that there had been no supply of services as required by what is now *VATA 1994, Sch 8, Group 6, Item 2*. The tribunal observed that there was no provision in *Group 6* for zero-rating supplies of goods, and such goods could be zero-rated under *Group 5, Item 4* only if there were a supply of services within *Group 6*. *P Robinson*, MAN/89/131 (VTD 4063). (*Note.* For subsequent developments in this case, see **2.317** APPEALS.)

[55.84] A couple who owned a protected building obtained planning permission and listed building consent for alterations to it. They purchased the necessary materials and arranged for four workmen to carry out the work. They reclaimed input tax on the cost of the materials which they had purchased. The Commissioners rejected the claim, and the couple appealed, contending that the materials should be treated as zero-rated. The tribunal rejected this contention and dismissed the appeal, holding that materials were only zero-rated under what is now *VATA 1994, Sch 8, Group 5, Item 4* if they were supplied by a supplier of services within *Sch 8, Group 6, Item 2*, which was not the case here. *A & A Goddard*, LON/93/1655A (VTD 11983).

[55.85] A similar decision was reached in *R Barugh*, MAN/03/759 (VTD 18725).

Conservatories, roof timbers and fire doors

[55.86] See *Jeffs*, **15.252** CONSTRUCTION OF BUILDINGS, ETC.

Installation of kitchen in protected building

[55.87] The owner of a protected building obtained permission for approved alterations including the installation of a modern kitchen. He purchased kitchen units from a supplier (M), which arranged for the necessary measurement and design work. The actual fitting of the units was undertaken by a carpenter who was engaged by the owner of the building, rather than by M. The Commissioners issued a ruling that the supply of the kitchen units was a standard-rated supply of goods. The owner appealed, contending that M had also supplied services within what is now *VATA 1994, Sch 8, Group 6, Item 2*, so that the goods qualified for zero-rating under what is now *VATA 1994, Sch 8, Group 5, Item 4*. The tribunal allowed the appeal, holding on the evidence that M had supplied the services of visiting and measuring the site, designing the kitchen, and manufacturing non-standard parts. The tribunal chairman observed that '"services" in (*Sch 8**) is not limited to the service of fitting the goods on site'. *PW Cook*, LON/93/1952A (VTD 12571).

Miscellaneous

Whether work may be zero-rated retrospectively

[55.88] A contractor carried out work on a protected building. His accountant issued invoices on his behalf charging VAT on the work. The customer disputed the amount charged, and a surveyor was consulted. The surveyor pointed out that the work qualified for zero-rating, and, at his suggestion, the contractor issued revised invoices which did not charge VAT. The Commissioners issued an assessment charging tax on the work, and the contractor appealed. At the hearing the Commissioners accepted that the work qualified for zero-rating, but contended that it could not be zero-rated retrospectively. The tribunal allowed the contractor's appeal, holding that the effect of what is now *VATA 1994, s 30* was that no tax was chargeable on the supplies in question. *A Kleanthous (t/a AK Building Services)*, LON/92/389Z (VTD 9504).

Purchase of heaters for installation in protected building

[55.89] A parochial church council arranged for the installation of a new heating system in the church, which was a protected building. It purchased the heaters from the manufacturer, and arranged for them to be installed by a contractor. The Commissioners accepted that the work was an approved alteration, and that the contractor's services qualified for zero-rating under *VATA 1994, Sch 8, Group 6, Item 2*. However, they issued a ruling that the purchase of the heaters failed to qualify for zero-rating because they had not been supplied by the contractor, as required by *Group 6, Item 3*. The tribunal upheld the Commissioners' ruling and dismissed the council's appeal, commenting that it was unfortunate that 'by arranging its supply in this fashion it has deprived itself of the benefit of zero-rating the heaters' but that 'that is the inescapable consequence of the arrangement it has made'. *Seaton Parochial Church Council*, MAN/04/045 (VTD 18742).

Protected building temporarily used as private residence

[55.90] An individual (M) reclaimed input tax on the renovation of a protected building. The Commissioners rejected the claim on the grounds that M had lived in the house for three and a half years while the work was being carried out. M appealed, contending that he had only occupied the house on a temporary basis, and had not intended to occupy it as a permanent residence. The tribunal accepted M's evidence and allowed the appeal in part, holding that the tax should be apportioned on a time basis, the denominator being 20 years and the input tax relating to the proportion of those 20 years in which M had occupied the house not being recoverable. Accordingly 82.5% of the input tax was deductible. *I Mason*, MAN/92/1308 (VTD 12406).

56

Reduced-rate Supplies: Miscellaneous

The cases in this chapter are arranged under the following headings.

Group 2—Energy-saving materials   56.1
Group 5—Children's car seats   56.2
Group 6—Residential conversions   56.3
Group 7—Residential renovations and alterations   56.8

CROSS-REFERENCE

For the reduced rate under *VATA 1994, Sch 7A, Group 1*, see 30 FUEL AND POWER.

Group 2—Energy-saving materials

[56.1] A company manufactured and supplied energy-saving materials for installation in buildings. It supplied lightweight hollow building blocks, made of moulded expanded polystyrene, which were used to form walls. Following correspondence, the Commissioners accepted that the installation of these blocks, in residential accommodation or a building intended for a relevant charitable purpose, attracted VAT at the reduced rate of 5% under *VATA 1994, Sch 7A, Group 2*. The company claimed that, where it carried out such work in the course of an extension or alteration, the whole of the work covered by the relevant contract should be treated as qualifying for the reduced rate. The Commissioners rejected this claim, and the company appealed. The tribunal dismissed the company's appeal, holding that the blocks were simply '"insulation for walls", etc, like any other insulation, such as cavity-wall in-filling'. Where the blocks were 'installed as part of an entire contract for construction, the dominant purpose of the contract will be the building that results. The dominant purpose will not be the insulation provided by the system.' The purchaser 'wants a building first and foremost, and that is indeed what he gets'. For the building to be 'a solid structure, permanent and weatherproof' would normally be more important than the quality of the insulation. *Beco Products Ltd; BAG Building Contractors*, MAN/01/04 (VTD 18638).

Group 5—Children's car seats

Definition of 'children's car seats'

[56.2] A company operated a number of 'holiday parks'. It allowed customers to hire trailers, designed to be attached to bicycles and to allow young children to be towed behind a bicycle ridden by a parent. Initially it accounted for VAT on the hire of these trailers. However it subsequently submitted a repayment claim on the basis that the hire qualified for the reduced rate of 5% under *VATA 1994, Sch 7A, Group 5*. Customs rejected the claim and the tribunal dismissed the company's appeal, observing that 'in modern English usage, the word "car", when used without any qualifying adjective, is synonymous with "motor car"'. Accordingly the trailers did not qualify as 'children's car seats'. The tribunal also observed that 'either the bicycle and trailer, together, form the vehicle, in which case *Note 2(b)* is not satisfied, or alternatively the bicycle alone is the vehicle, in which case *Note 2(a)* cannot be satisfied.' Furthermore, 'the purpose of *Note 1(1)(b)* is to extend the reduced rate to supplies, together, of a safety seat and related wheeled framework (supplies which the Appellant does not make), but not to change the concept of a safety seat'. *Center Parcs (UK) Group plc*, MAN/05/741 (VTD 19848).

Group 6—Residential conversions

VATA 1994, Sch 7A, Group 6—whether a 'residential conversion'

[56.3] An individual (M) converted a stable wing and an upstairs flat, which formed part of a mid-Victorian manor house, into a single dwelling. He claimed that the work should be treated as liable to the reduced rate of 5% under *VATA 1994, Sch 7A, Group 6*. The Commissioners rejected the claim on the basis that the premises contained a single-household dwelling both before and after the work, so that the work was not a 'changed number of dwellings conversion' within *Sch 7A, Group 6, Note 2(1)*. M appealed, contending that before the conversion, the flat was not 'self-contained living accommodation', within *Group 6, Note 4(3)*. The tribunal rejected this contention and dismissed M's appeal, finding that 'before the conversion work there was a dwelling on the first floor' and that this dwelling was 'self-contained'. Accordingly, the work was not a 'changed number of dwellings conversion' within *Sch 7A, Group 6, Note 2(1)*, and did not qualify for the reduced rate. *P Monoprio*, LON/01/1149 (VTD 17806).

[56.4] A company arranged for the refurbishment of some student halls of residence which it owned. HMRC issued a ruling that VAT was chargeable on the refurbishment at the standard rate. The company appealed. contending that the work should be treated as a 'changed number of dwellings conversion' within *VATA 1994, Sch 7A, Group 6, Note 2(1)*. The tribunal rejected this contention and dismissed the appeal, holding that the halls of residence continued to constitute 'residential accommodation for students' within *Sch 7A, Group 6, Note 6*, and the work was therefore standard-rated. *Opal Carleton Ltd v HMRC*, [2010] UKFTT 353 (TC), TC00635.

Definition of 'residential conversion'—Sch 7A, Group 6, Note 3

[56.5] A registered charity owned two interconnecting six-storey terraced houses, which were divided into six flats. It arranged for the houses to be converted into four flats. The Commissioners accepted that the work on five storeys of the building qualified for VAT at the reduced rate of 5% under

VATA 1994, Sch 7A, Group 6. However they issued a ruling that the effect of *Group 6, Note 3* was that the work on the second floor did not qualify for the reduced rate, because that floor remained a 'single household dwelling' before and after the conversion. The charity appealed. The tribunal upheld the Commissioners' ruling and dismissed the charity's appeal, observing that 'it is not apparent from the statute what the social policy is' but holding that 'there must be some limitation on the meaning of "part" in that it must have some minimum size'. In construing *Group 6, Note 3(3)*, 'any relevant part of the premises must be capable of being identified by reference to physical boundaries, normally walls, floors and ceilings after the conversion; a notional line in the middle of a room would not suffice'. On the evidence, the second-floor apartment had to be viewed as a 'part' of the building. Since it contained a single dwelling both before and after the conversion, it followed that the work on the second floor failed to qualify for the reduced rate. *Wellcome Trust*, [2003] VATDR 572(VTD 18417).

Services supplied by unregistered subcontractors

[56.6] A company (L) arranged for a former nursing home to be converted into a number of single-household dwellings. L provided the materials and arranged for unregistered subcontractors to carry out the necessary work. The Commissioners issued a ruling that L's supplies were standard-rated. L appealed, contending that its supplies should be treated as qualifying for the reduced rate under *VATA 1994, Sch 7A, Group 6*. The tribunal rejected this contention and dismissed the appeal, observing that *Group 6, Item 1* only applied to a supply of building materials by a person who was 'supplying qualifying services related to the conversion'. The tribunal held that 'the supplies of materials and the services must go together. In the instant case the suppliers of materials and the services were separate.' The tribunal also observed that 'the supply of services from non-registered contractors meant that they were received equivalent to zero-rated'. *Lincoln Oak Co Ltd*, MAN/03/176 (VTD 18503).

Claimant paying standard rate of VAT to contractors

[56.7] A woman (L) arranged for contractors to convert a barn into two holiday lettings. The contractors charged VAT at the standard rate of 17.5%. L formed the opinion that the work was a residential conversion which qualified for VAT at the reduced rate of 5%. However, instead of querying this with the contractors, she paid the standard rate of VAT to the contractors and then claimed a refund of 12.5% from Customs. Customs rejected the claim and L appealed. The tribunal dismissed her appeal, holding that she had 'no direct recourse' against Customs and that 'the appropriate rate is a matter for negotiation with the contractor'. *C Legge*, EDN/08/152 (VTD 20964).

Group 7—Residential renovations and alterations

VATA 1994, Sch 7A, Group 7—definition of 'alteration'

[56.8] In a case concerning zero-rating provisions in *FA 1972*, which were subsequently repealed by *FA 1984*, Neill J held that an 'alteration' should be defined as 'an alteration of the building and therefore one which involves some structural alteration'. *C & E Commrs v Morrison Dunbar Ltd; C & E Commrs v Mecca Ltd (and cross-appeal)*, QB 1978, [1979] STC 406. (*Note.* The case related to the conversion of a cinema into a bingo hall, which would be standard-rated under the current legislation.)

[56.9] The QB decision in *C & E Commrs v Morrison Dunbar Ltd*, 56.8 above, was approved by the HL in a subsequent case where Lord Roskill held that an 'alteration' must be construed as a 'structural alteration'. *ACT Construction Ltd v C & E Commrs*, HL 1981, [1982] STC 25; [1981] 1 WLR 1542; [1982] 1 All ER 84.

[56.10] However, in a subsequent case which also concerned the zero-rating provisions of *FA 1972*, Lord Diplock held that 'alteration' should be construed as including 'any work on the fabric of the building except that which is so slight or trivial as to attract the application of the *de minimis* rule'. *C & E Commrs v Viva Gas Appliances Ltd*, HL [1983] STC 819; [1983] 1 WLR 1445. (*Note.* The extent to which the tribunals will apply the *dicta* of Lord Diplock with regard to cases concerning *VATA 1994, Sch 7A, Group 7* is currently unclear. In *The Vicar and Parochial Church Council of St Petroc Minor*, 55.54 PROTECTED BUILDINGS, the tribunal specifically declined to apply Lord Diplock's *dicta* in *Viva Gas* to a case concerning *VATA 1994, Sch 8, Group 6*, observing that in *Viva Gas* the word 'alteration' was used 'in a context which no longer appears in (*VATA 1994*). That contextual interpretation is therefore of no help now.' However in the subsequent case of *Owen*, 55.33 PROTECTED BUILDINGS, a different tribunal chairman did apply Lord Diplock's *dicta* in *Viva Gas* to a case concerning *VATA 1994, Sch 8, Group 6*, holding that 'except so far as it is affected by (*Sch 8, Group 5, Note 22*) the *Viva Gas* case is still good law and is binding upon us'.)

57

Registration

The cases in this chapter are arranged under the following headings.

Liability to be registered (VATA 1994, Sch 1 para 1)

Whether registration covers more than one business	**57.1**
Registration on basis of future turnover (*VATA 1994, Sch 1 para 1(1)(b)*)	**57.12**
Business transferred as going concern (*VATA 1994, Sch 1 para 1(2)*)	**57.17**
Subsequent decline in turnover (*VATA 1994, Sch 1 para 1(3)*)	**57.20**
Disregard of previous registration (*VATA 1994, Sch 1 para 1(4)*)	**57.33**
Capital assets (*VATA 1994, Sch 1 para 1(7)*)	**57.34**

Registration of associated persons as a single taxable person (VATA 1994, Sch 1 para 2)

Cases where the direction was upheld	**57.35**
Cases where the appellant was successful	**57.64**

Notification of liability and registration (VATA 1994, Sch 1 para 5)	**57.82**
Entitlement to be registered (VATA 1994, Sch 1 paras 9, 10)	**57.101**

Cancellation of registration (VATA 1994, Sch 1 para 13)

Requests for cancellation of registration (*VATA 1994, Sch 1 para 13(1)*)	**57.120**
Registration cancelled by Commissioners (*VATA 1994, Sch 1 para 13(2)*)	**57.144**

Exemption from registration (VATA 1994, Sch 1 para 14)	**57.167**

The person(s) by whom the business is carried on

Cases where the appellant was unsuccessful	**57.170**
Cases where the appellant was successful	**57.202**
Miscellaneous	**57.218**

NOTE

The provisions concerning registration are contained in *VATA 1994, Sch 1*. There were substantial changes to the legislation between 1983 and 1994, with particularly significant changes being effected by *FA 1988* and *FA 1990*. For details of the current legislation, see Tolley's Value Added Tax. In this chapter, summaries of cases relating to periods before the enactment of *VATA 1994* should be read in the light of subsequent changes in the law. For penalties imposed for failure to register, see **51** PENALTIES: FAILURE TO NOTIFY. For cases concerning the registration of groups of companies, see **32** GROUPS OF COMPANIES. For cases concerning partnership registration, see **47.13** PARTNERSHIP et seq. For cases concerning the provisions of *Sch 1 para 1(2)*, where the question at issue is whether a business has been transferred as a going concern, see **65.90** to **65.107** TRANSFERS OF GOING CONCERNS.

Liability to be registered (VATA 1994, Sch 1 para 1)

Whether registration covers more than one business

Partnership operating separate businesses

[57.1] A married couple carried on two separate businesses in partnership, with different trading names, one as estate agents and the other as land developers. They applied or two separate registrations. The Commissioners rejected the claim on the basis that they were entitled to only one registration. The couple appealed, contending that they were entitled to a separate registration for each trading name. The QB rejected this contention and upheld the Commissioners' ruling. May J held that 'the scheme of the *Act* is to register "persons" as accountable for VAT, not the business or businesses which they may carry on. Further, the necessary corollary of this conclusion and approach to the *Act* is that any one person is entitled to only one registration'. *C & E Commrs v MJ & BJ Glassborow*, QB [1974] STC 142; [1975] QB 465; [1974] 1 All ER 1041.

[57.2] Four people carried on a business in partnership and were registered in the partnership name from August 1973. The business did not flourish and two of the partners left in November 1973. The two remaining partners notified the VAT office of the change and continued to carry on the business, although with a low turnover. They had throughout carried on in partnership an entirely separate business, the takings of which were well below the threshold of *Sch 1 para 1*, and in respect of which they had not applied for registration. The Commissioners issued an assessment for the year to 30 November 1974 covering both businesses. The partners appealed, contending that they should not be required to account for tax on the takings from their original business. The tribunal rejected this contention and dismissed the appeal, holding that the retirement of the two partners in November 1973 meant that the August 1973 registration thereafter covered both businesses. *J & E Harris*, CAR/76/220 (VTD 373).

[57.3] A married couple, who carried on a dealing business in partnership and were registered for VAT, also operated a guest-house. They did not account for output tax on the takings from the guest-house, and the Commissioners issued an assessment charging tax on them. They appealed, contending that the guest-house should be treated as a separate entity and that the turnover of the guest-house was below the registration threshold. The tribunal dismissed the appeal, holding that the partnership registration covered the guest-house as well as the dealing business. *CAM & P Humphreys (t/a Wilmington Trading Co)*, LON/93/1871A (VTD 13007).

[57.4] A partnership operated a motor repair business, the turnover of which was below the registration threshold. In July 1991 they registered for VAT in respect of a second business of the supply of toner cartridges for photocopiers and printers. They duly accounted for VAT in respect of their takings from this business, but did not account for VAT on their takings from their motor repair business. The Commissioners issued an assessment charging tax on the takings from that business, and the tribunal dismissed the partnership's appeal. *K & G Taylor*, LON/95/657A (VTD 13475).

[57.5] A partnership, which was registered for VAT, carried on a joinery business. The partners also provided building services under a different trading name, and using a separate bank account. They did not account for tax on these takings. The Commissioners issued an assessment charging tax on them, and the tribunal dismissed the partnership's appeal. *Clarke Street Joinery (t/a Clarke Street Building Services)*, MAN/99/816 (VTD 16805).

Sole trader operating more than one business

[57.6] A married woman was registered from 1 April 1973 in respect of a taxi business. The Commissioners discovered that she was also carrying on a separate business as ladies' hairdresser which had not been disclosed in her returns, and assessed her for the period from April 1973 to 31 December 1975 for the tax on the takings from the hairdressing business. She appealed, contending that her takings from hairdressing were below the then registration threshold. The tribunal upheld the assessment and dismissed her appeal. Applying the QB decision in *Glassborow*, 57.1 above, her registration covered both businesses. *M Padmore*, MAN/76/163 (VTD 345).

[57.7] Similar decisions, also applying *Glassborow*, 57.1 above, were reached in *Scanes*, LON/76/209 (VTD 347); *N & M Basran*, MAN/82/151 (VTD 1312); *MD Podbury (t/a Moordown Graphics)*, LON/85/43 (VTD 1906); *R Glendinning*, LON/89/107Y (VTD 5245); *LF Callaghan*, LON/90/1627X (VTD 6445); *D Richardson*, MAN/91/1219 (VTD 8849); *AM Steele*, LON/92/400 (VTD 9017); *WD Allen*, LON/92/1592A (VTD 11000); *B Stratton*, MAN/94/1175 (VTD 13185); *JD & J Harley (t/a The Treasure Chest)*, LON/95/499 (VTD 13533); *M & TEJ Hollosi*, LON/95/1348A (VTD 13757); *R Knight*, LON/95/2136A (VTD 13769); *K Fitton*, MAN/95/1040 (VTD 13844); *JD Lovejoy (t/a Crumbs)*, MAN/95/2723 (VTD 14370); *JJ Duffy*, LON/x (VTD 15343); *A Bishop*, MAN/00/964 (VTD 17267); *GA Mulligan*, LON/02/149 (VTD 17895); *HW Thomas*, LON/03/639 (VTD 18680); *S Hare (t/a Ican Finance)*, [2011] UKFTT 81 (TC), TC00958; *Walker*, 7.17 BUSINESS; *Dawson*, 51.54 PENALTIES: FAILURE TO NOTIFY; *Boggeln*, 51.55 PENALTIES: FAILURE TO NOTIFY, and *Yarlett*, 51.55 PENALTIES: FAILURE TO NOTIFY.

Partners also acting as directors of limited companies

[57.8] Two individuals operated a dry-cleaning business in partnership. They were also directors of three limited companies, each of which operated a dry-cleaning business at different premises. Neither the partnership, nor any of the companies, were registered for VAT. The Commissioners issued a notice of compulsory registration to the partnership, backdated to January 1996. The partnership appealed, contending that its turnover was below the registration threshold, so that it was not required to register for VAT. The Commissioners defended the notice on the basis that the four businesses 'constituted supplies made by a single taxable person for the purposes of (*VATA 1994, ss 3, 4*)'. The officer responsible for the notice gave evidence that 'she had not considered issuing a direction under *paragraph 2* of *VATA 1994, Schedule 1* related to the artificial separating of business activities, as she considered that there had only ever been one business'. The tribunal allowed the partnership's appeal. The tribunal observed that 'the majority of cases involving separation of business activities have been in connection with directions made by (the) Commissioners under (*Sch 1 para 2*)'. Those cases had involved 'a consideration of whether activities are closely bound to one another by financial, economic and organisational links'. They involved 'different considerations to the issues in the present appeal which relate to *paragraph 1* of *Schedule 1.*' On the evidence, the tribunal held that there were four separate businesses, and the Commissioners had 'acted unreasonably in treating the activities as one business carried on by one taxable person'. *S Garton & J Davies (t/a The Dolly Tub)*, MAN/98/927 (VTD 16260).

Business changed—whether old registration continues

[57.9] A trader had been registered as a dairy roundsman from 1 April 1973. In June 1973 he began a new business as a ladies' hairdresser, giving up his dairy roundsman's business a few days later. He informed the VAT office of his change of business, but did not state that his takings as a hairdresser would be substantially below the threshold limit of *Sch 1 para 1* (then £5,000). He failed to account for output tax on the takings of his hairdressing business. The Commissioners issued an assessment charging tax on them, and the tribunal dismissed the trader's appeal. Applying the QB decision in *Glassborow*, 57.1 above, the original registration covered the hairdressing business. *C Wiper*, LEE/74/57A (VTD 152).

[57.10] A similar decision was reached in a case where a trader who had carried on business as a wholesaler ceased this business and began working as a self-employed taxi driver. *H Zemmel*, LON/77/298 (VTD 498).

[57.11] A married woman had carried on a guest-house until her death in October 1974. The takings from the guest-house were below the threshold of *Sch 1 para 1*, and she had not been registered for VAT. Following her death, her husband, who was registered as a coal merchant, took over the guest-house. He transferred his previous business to his daughter in March 1975 but did not inform the Commissioners of the change and he did not make any returns in respect of the guest-house business. On discovering the position, the Commissioners issued an assessment charging tax on the takings of the guest-house. He appealed. The tribunal upheld the assessment and dismissed his appeal, holding that his registration covered the guest-house business as well as the business he had originally carried on. *WA Renton*, EDN/79/12 (VTD 870).

Registration on basis of future turnover (VATA 1994, Sch 1 para 1(1)(b))

NOTE

The 'future turnover' test under what is now *VATA 1994, Sch 1 para 1(1)(b)* was significantly amended with effect from March 1990. A trader is now only required to register under *Sch 1 para 1(1)(b)* if there are reasonable grounds for believing that his turnover will exceed the registration threshold in the next 30 days, rather than (as previously) in the next twelve months. The practical effect of this is, as stated in Customs' Press Notice dated 20 March 1990, that the 'future turnover' test which applied from 1973 to 1989 no longer applies to most new or expanding businesses. The cases noted at **57.12** to **57.14** below relate to periods before 21 March 1990.

[57.12] A company which operated a recruitment agency applied for registration in January 1986. The Commissioners formed the opinion that it should have been registered from 1 September 1985, when it had taken over a number of clients from another company, under what is now *Sch 1 para 1(1)(b)*. They imposed a penalty. The company appealed, contending that on 1 September 1985 there were reasonable grounds for considering that its turnover would not exceed the threshold of *Sch 1 para 1(1)(b)* (which was then £19,500) within the next twelve months. The tribunal reviewed the evidence in detail, rejected this contention and dismissed the company's appeal. Lord Grantchester observed that the test under *Sch 1 para 1(1)(b)* was an 'objective test' and 'involves a consideration of the question whether, on balance, taking all the relevant factors into consideration, it was more reasonable to believe that the value of the taxable supplies would exceed the stipulated amount rather than fall short thereof'. On the evidence, Lord Grantchester held that, at 1 September 1985, 'it would have been reasonable to believe that the value of the appellant's taxable supplies in the year then beginning' would exceed £19,500. *Optimum Personnel Evaluation (Operations) Ltd*, LON/86/620 (VTD 2334).

[57.13] The proprietor of a dry-cleaning business was registered for VAT in March 1996 after the Commissioners had formed the opinion that his turnover exceeded the registration threshold under what is now *VATA 1994, Sch 1 para 1(1)(a)*. The registration was backdated to 11 March 1990. The proprietor appealed, contending that he had not been liable to register. The tribunal reviewed the evidence and concluded that the proprietor had been liable to register under the 'future turnover' test of what is now *VATA 1994, Sch 1 para 1(1)(b)*. (The tribunal observed that 'it seems likely' that the proprietor had also been liable to register under the 'historic turnover' test of *Sch 1 para 1(1)(a)*, as the Commissioners had contended, but did not state this as a firm conclusion.) The proprietor appealed to the QB, which remitted the case to a new tribunal for rehearing, holding that the previous tribunal had erred in law in its interpretation of *Sch 1 para 1(1)(b)*. Carnwath J held that the test applied by Lord Grantchester in *Optimum Personnel Evaluation (Operations) Ltd*, **57.12** above, was 'understandable and capable of application to a particular point in time, at which there is some identifiable change in the nature or scale of the business' but was 'practically unworkable if it is applied not to a specific date defined by external circumstances, but on a rolling basis from day to day'. Applying the CJEC decision in *Administration des Douanes v Société Anonyme Gondrand Freres*, **22.80** EUROPEAN COMMUNITY LAW, 'rules imposing charges on the taxpayer must be clear and precise so that he may know without ambiguity what are his rights and obligations and may take steps accordingly'. Accordingly, the principle of legal certainty 'requires the implication of some objectively definable criterion for bringing *subparagraph (b)* into play'. The tribunal had failed to make a firm finding that the proprietor was liable to register under *Sch 1 para 1(1)(a)*. Its statement that 'it seems likely' that he had done so was 'an incidental observation, rather than an alternative basis for the decision'. Accordingly the case should be remitted to a new tribunal for a rehearing. *A Bennett v C & E Commrs*, QB [1999] STC 248. (*Note.* For other issues in this case, see **2.127** APPEALS and **3.21** ASSESSMENT.)

[57.14] The Commissioners issued a ruling that the proprietor of a taxi business was required to register for VAT from 6 July 1988 under the provisions of what is now *Sch 1 para 1(1)(b)*. The proprietor appealed. The tribunal reviewed the evidence in detail and allowed the appeal, finding that 'given the condition and nature of the business which the appellant took over, and his evidence, which we accept, about its development, we do not believe that, looked at objectively, there were reasonable ground (*sic*) for believing that the appellant's rental income would reach the stipulated threshold within his first year of trading beginning on 6 July 1988'. *M Nawaz (t/a Elvis Private Hire)*, MAN/94/224 (VTD 16017).

[57.15] See also *Prudential Assurance Co Ltd (No 5)*, 3.118 ASSESSMENT.

Application for voluntary registration—whether Sch 1 para 1(1)(b) applicable

[57.16] A company applied for registration for VAT, stating that it intended to trade in mobile telephones. Customs rejected the claim on the basis that the company had not produced 'satisfactory evidence' of an 'intent to trade'. The company appealed. The tribunal allowed the appeal, holding that Customs 'must register a person who becomes liable to registration by virtue of *paragraph 1(1)(b)* (of *VATA 1994, Sch 1*) and notifies them of that liability: they have no discretion in the matter'. (The tribunal also held that the company would be entitled to registration under *Sch 1, para 9*.) The tribunal observed that 'it is implicit in the respondents' case that (the company's) proposed trade in mobile telephones would not be an economic activity', and held on the evidence that the company 'had carried out preparatory acts attributable to the economic activity of trading in mobile telephones'. *Ace Telecom Ltd*, MAN/04/324 (VTD 19214).

Business transferred as going concern (VATA 1994, Sch 1 para 1(2))

[57.17] For cases concerning the provisions of *Sch 1 para 1(2)*, where the question at issue is whether a business has been transferred as a going concern, see **65.90** to **65.107** TRANSFERS OF GOING CONCERNS.

Application for retrospective cancellation of registration

[57.18] A trader took over a business as a going concern in April 1992, and registered for VAT from that date. However, his turnover never exceeded the threshold of *Sch 1 para 1*, and in September 1992 he applied for his registration to be cancelled. The Commissioners agreed to cancel his registration with effect from 1 October 1992, but refused to backdate the cancellation, and issued an assessment charging output tax on the supplies which he had made between 1 April and 30 September. The tribunal dismissed the trader's appeal, holding that the effect of what is now *VATA 1994, Sch 1 para 13* was that a valid registration could only be cancelled from the date on which an application for cancellation was made, or from an agreed later date, and that registration could not be cancelled retrospectively. *JD Rana*, LON/92/3295A (VTD 11842).

[57.19] Similar decisions were reached in *SM Alexander*, LON/94/570A (VTD 12810); *Mrs S Oldfield (t/a Merchant's Bistro)*, MAN/01/031 (VTD 17352); *J Zhiren (t/a Captain's Catch Restaurant)*, LON/01/664 (VTD 17785) and *S & H Clarke*, MAN/04/088 (VTD 18859).

Subsequent decline in turnover (VATA 1994, Sch 1 para 1(3))

Whether evidence that future supplies would not exceed threshold

[57.20] In the case noted at **51.56** PENALTIES: FAILURE TO NOTIFY, Lord Grantchester held that the exception in what is now *Sch 1 para 1(3)* 'can only be sought to be relied upon by a trader, where he has not applied to the Commissioners at the right time to consider all the relevant circumstances, if the value of his taxable supplies in the year did not exceed the relevant amount and he establishes that no reasonable body of Commissioners at the relevant time could have come to any conclusion other than that his taxable supplies in the year would not exceed the relevant amount'. *WF Shephard*, LON/86/318 (VTD 2232).

[57.21] A similar decision was reached in *DE Cannon*, LON/84/350 (VTD 2486).

[57.22] A subcontractor became liable to register from June 1990, but did not do so. The Commissioners did not discover this until February 1991, by which time he had ceased working, as the contractor for which he worked had ceased trading and subsequently went into liquidation. His turnover for the period from 1 June 1990 to 10 February 1991 was below the threshold laid down by *Sch 1 para 1(3)*. The tribunal chairman (Miss Plumptre, sitting alone) held that he could not be required to register retrospectively. *R Fawson*, LON/92/1350A (VTD 9724). (*Note*. No other cases were cited in this decision, which was subsequently disapproved by the Ch D in *Gray*, 57.28 below.)

[57.23] An individual (G), who was registered for VAT, ran a dry-cleaning business, which consisted of a small retail unit and a number of agency contracts with hotels and similar businesses. In July 1993 G sold the retail unit and some of the agency contracts to another individual (H). At the time of the transfer, H was operating an existing dry-cleaning agency business in partnership with his wife. The Commissioners issued a ruling that H should be registered for VAT by virtue of *Sch 1 para 1(2)* with effect from the date of transfer. H appealed. The tribunal allowed his appeal, accepting that the business had been acquired as a going concern, within *Sch 1 para 1(2)*, but holding on the evidence that the Commissioners should have accepted H's contention that his turnover in the 12 months following the transfer would not exceed the then threshold in *Sch 1 para 1(3)*. The tribunal held that, notwithstanding the wording of *Sch 1 para 1(3)*, it had an appellate jurisdiction in considering an appeal against registration. Applying *dicta* in *JH Corbitt (Numismatists) Ltd*, **60.1** SECOND-HAND GOODS, the officer responsible for the relevant decisions (and who did not give evidence to the tribunal) had acted unreasonably in taking the partnership turnover into account when concluding that H should be required to register. *A Hare (t/a Imperial Dry Cleaners)*, MAN/95/2347 (VTD 14202). (*Note*. Compare the subsequent decision in *Timur & Timur*, 57.25 below, in which the tribunal held that its jurisdiction under *Sch 1 para 1(3)* was only supervisory.)

[57.24] The owner of a minicab business, who was registered for VAT, transferred it, as a going concern, to a partnership comprising his wife and son. His accountant advised the Commissioners that the owner had ceased trading, but did not advise them that the business had been transferred. Accordingly the business was deregistered with the effect from the date of the transfer. Subsequently the Commissioners discovered that the business had continued to trade, and issued an assessment on the basis that *Sch 1 para 1(2)* applied. The partners appealed, contending that following the transfer, their turnover had declined to below the registration threshold and that the effect of *Sch 1 para 1(3)* was that they should not be required to account for tax. The tribunal rejected this contention and dismissed the appeal. It was accepted that the partners' turnover had in fact declined to below the registration threshold, but there were no grounds on which the Commissioners could be expected, at the date of the transfer, to have believed that this would be the case. Applying *dicta* of Lord Grantchester in *WF Shephard*, 57.20 above, the exception in what is now *Sch 1 para 1(3)* 'can only be sought to be relied upon by a trader, where he has not applied to the Commissioners at the right time to consider all the relevant circumstances', if he 'establishes that no reasonable body of Commissioners *at the relevant time* could have come to any conclusion other than that his taxable supplies in the year would not exceed the relevant amount'. The decision in *Fawson*, 57.22 above, was specifically disapproved, on the grounds that the chairman in that case had not referred to the previous decisions in *Shephard*, 57.20 above, or *Cannon*, 57.21 above. *RJ & J Nash*, MAN/96/1132 (VTD 14944). (*Note.* The decision here was approved by the Ch D in *Gray*, 57.28 below.)

[57.25] The decision in *Nash & Nash*, 57.24 above, was applied in a similar subsequent case in which the tribunal held that it had a supervisory jurisdiction and could not substitute its own discretion or decision for that of the Commissioners, provided that the Commissioners' decision was reasonable. *Dicta* in *JH Corbitt (Numismatists) Ltd*, **60.1** SECOND-HAND SCHEMES, applied. On the evidence, the Commissioners had acted reasonably in not being satisfied that the appellants' turnover would not fall below the threshold of *Sch 1 para 1(3)*. *B & J Timur (t/a Istanbul Kebab House)*, LON/97/319 (VTD 15305). (*Note.* An appeal against a penalty for failure to notify was also dismissed.)

[57.26] Similar decisions, also applying *Nash & Nash*, 57.24 above, were reached in *D Harry (t/a Principal Financial Associates)*, LON/97/1322 (VTD 15747) and *M & EJ Burr (t/a Penny's Place)*, LON/x (VTD 16866).

[57.27] A similar decision was reached in the Scottish case of *Mrs N Raza*, EDN/00/118 (VTD 17084).

[57.28] In February 1997 a VAT officer discovered that a building contractor (G) had become liable to register from September 1996. The Commissioners issued a notice of registration and imposed a penalty. G appealed, contending that his turnover would not exceed the threshold in future periods, because he had arranged for some work to be carried on by a registered company which he controlled. The tribunal dismissed his appeal, holding on the evidence that the Commissioners had acted reasonably in not being satisfied that G's turn-over would fall below the threshold. The Ch D upheld this decision. Ferris J held that the effect of *Sch 1 para 1(3)* was that 'a VAT tribunal, or this court itself, can only interfere with the decision if it is shown that the decision is one which no reasonable body of Commissioners could reach'. Where a trader registered late, 'the Commissioners must give effect to *para 1(3)* by considering the case as at the date from which registration would otherwise take effect and, by looking forward, asking themselves whether they are or are not satisfied that turnover will not exceed the threshold amount'. *JG Gray (t/a William Gray & Son) v C & E Commrs*, Ch D [2000] STC 880.

[57.29] The Ch D decision in *Gray*, 57.28 above, was applied in the similar subsequent cases of *Jabat Ltd*, LON/04/133 (VTD 18752); *T Malik*, MAN/99/747 (VTD 18891); *NP Drury*, FTT [2009] UKFTT 50 (TC), TC00029, and *RV Evans (t/a Britannia Services)*, [2011] UKFTT 439 (TC), TC01292.

[57.30] A married couple who operated a hotel failed to register for VAT. HMRC formed the opinion that they had been required to register from 1997 and issued an assessment covering the period from May 1997 to November 2005. The couple appealed, contending that their turnover had fallen below the registration threshold from April 2005 and that the period from April to November 2005 should be excluded from the assessment. The tribunal rejected this contention and dismissed the appeal, holding that 'HMRC were justifiably not satisfied that the period between April and November 2005 was not a time when the appellants would be subject to a requirement to be registered'. *Mr & Mrs D Robbie (t/a Dunlaw House Hotel) v HMRC*, [2009] UKFTT 82 (TC), TC00050.

[57.31] A builder (C) traded below the VAT registration threshold from 1977 to 1997. However, in the year ending June 1997 he worked longer hours than usual to meet increased mortgage payments, and hired subcontractors for the first time, so that his turnover rose above the threshold for the first time. Customs discovered this in 2001, and issued a ruling that he was required to register retrospectively for the period from 1 August 1997 to 31 May 1998. (Customs accepted that as his turnover had subsequently declined, he was entitled to be deregistered from June 1998.) C appealed, contending that since his turnover had subsequently declined and he had ceased using subcontrac-tors, the effect of *VATA 1994, Sch 1 para 1(3)* was that he should not be required to register. The tribunal accepted this contention and allowed his appeal, finding that C's turnover for the period from 1 July 1997 to 30 June 1998 was below the statutory threshold. The tribunal held that Customs had acted unreasonably in failing to take account of the fact that C's turnover had only exceeded the threshold for a short period because of his use of subcontractors, and that by June 1997 he had decided to revert to working alone. *MJ Clements*, LON/04/1026 (VTD 19216).

[57.32] A trader (V) took over a cafe as a going concern on 1 October 2005. The vendor had been registered for VAT, and his turnover for the year ending September 2005 had been above the statutory threshold. V's takings were significantly lower than that of her predecessor, and in February 2006 she applied for her registration to be cancelled with retrospective effect. Customs rejected the application, and she appealed. The tribunal dismissed the appeal against Customs' refusal to cancel her registration retrospectively, holding that there were 'no grounds upon which the appellant's initial registration can be impeached'. However, the tribunal held on the evidence that Customs should have agreed to cancel V's registration with effect from 11 July 2006, since they had then received details of V's turnover from 1 October 2005 to 30 June 2006 which showed that she was trading with 'a turnover below the registration threshold'. The tribunal concluded that 'on the basis of the information available to the Commissioners on 11 July 2006 the only reasonable conclusion would have been that the turnover for the 12 months thereafter would have been less than the deregistration threshold'. *AM Vaughan*, LON/06/932 (VTD 20547).

Disregard of previous registration (VATA 1994, Sch 1 para 1(4))

[57.33] A trader (D) had registered for VAT from March 1993, although his turnover had not exceeded the statutory threshold. In August 1996 D informed the Commissioners that he had ceased trading, and asked for his registration to be cancelled. The Commissioners accepted this request, and informed D that his registration had been cancelled with effect from 1 September 1996. Subsequently the Commissioners received information suggesting that D was continuing to trade. In February 2000 they re-registered him with effect from 1 October 1996. D appealed, contending firstly that he was employed by a limited company, and was not a 'taxable person' for VAT purposes; and additionally that the decision to re-register him was wrong in law, because the effect of *VATA 1994, Sch 1 para 1(4)* was that the supplies he had made during the year ending 31 August 1996 should be disregarded in computing his turnover. The tribunal rejected this contention, finding that the Commissioners had not been 'satisfied that before his registration was cancelled, he had given them all the information they needed in order to determine whether to cancel the registration', so that the effect of *para 1(4)(b)* was that D's turnover prior to September 1996 should not be disregarded. D appealed to the CS, contending that the tribunal had acted unreasonably in finding that he 'had not supplied all of the information needed or requested in respect of his deregistration' and that the evidence indicated 'that the Commissioners were fully satisfied before deregistration was allowed'. The CS accepted this contention and allowed D's appeal. Lord Osborne held that since the Commissioners had agreed to cancel D's registration, it appeared that at that time, they had been satisfied that 'he had given them all the information they needed in order to determine whether to cancel the registration'. They were, therefore, not entitled to take his turnover for that period into account in subsequently deciding to re-register him from October 1996. Lord Osborne also held that the Commissioners had failed to indicate 'what precise information (they) considered that they needed in order to determine whether to cancel the previous registration which they had not been given'. He observed that since 'the basis for the respondents' decision to re-register the appellant was in issue before the tribunal', it was 'unfortunate that the precise basis for that decision was not apparently explored and was not made the subject of specific findings in fact'. *T Dyer v C & E Commrs (No 3)*, CS [2005] STC 715.

Capital assets (VATA 1994, Sch 1 para 1(7))

Sale of motor cars—whether capital assets

[57.34] A company (H) acquired a number of motor cars from its parent company and leased them to a customer for period averaging less than six months. When the leases had expired, it sold the cars back to the original dealers. It failed to register for VAT. The Commissioners discovered that its turnover had exceeded the statutory threshold, and issued a notice of compulsory registration. H appealed, contending that the cars which it had sold to the original dealers were capital assets, so that these sales should be disregarded in computing its turnover, by virtue of *VATA 1994, Sch 1 para 1(7)*. The tribunal rejected this contention and dismissed the appeal, holding on the evidence that 'the motor cars were not intended to be of a durable nature within the context of the business of the appellant'. Further-more, 'the sales of the cars were frequent and usual and did not make drastic changes in turnover for one year'. Accordingly, the cars were not 'capital assets'. *Harbig Leasing Two Ltd*, [2000] VATDR 469 (VTD 16843).

Registration of associated persons as a single taxable person (VATA 1994, Sch 1 para 2)

Cases where the direction was upheld

Associated companies operating launderettes

[57.35] A trader (C) purchased a number of launderettes which he trans-ferred to separate companies. He also operated a launderette in partnership with his wife, and another launderette in partnership with his mother-in-law. The Commissioners made directions under what is now *VATA 1994, Sch 1 para 2* that C, the two partnerships, and the various companies should be treated as a single taxable person. The tribunal upheld the directions, finding that the businesses were conducted in such a way with the specific aim of avoiding VAT. The QB dismissed C's appeal against this decision. McCowan J observed that 'anybody who carries on a business by four companies which each trade for part of the year must not be surprised if that operation arouses a strong belief in any sensible mind that he is doing that in order to avoid registering for the purposes of value added tax'. *JO Chamberlain v C & E Commrs*, QB [1989] STC 505.

[57.36] Similar decisions were reached in *I Lyons*, [1987] VATTR 187 (VTD 2451); *South West Launderettes Ltd*, LON/87/35 (VTD 2608); *B Bills, Mrs SA Bills, and Matcroft Ltd* (VTD 14715) and *Halls Dry Cleaning Co Ltd*, MAN/96/1269 (VTD 15069).

Dry-cleaning and ironing from same premises

[57.37] A couple registered for VAT as proprietors of a dry-cleaning business, which also provided ironing services. In 1998 the couple's accountant in-formed the Commissioners that he intended to treat the ironing as a separate business, operated by the husband as a sole proprietor. The Commissioners issued a direction under *VATA 1994, Sch 1 para 2* requiring the couple and the husband to be treated as a single taxable person. The tribunal upheld the direction and dismissed the couple's appeal. *I & H Jackson*, MAN/x (VTD 16001).

[57.38] A similar decision, applying *Chamberlain*, 57.35 above, and *Osman*, 57.39 below, was reached in the subsequent case of *S & C Ahmed*, LON/99/852 (VTD 16998).

Tax consultancy and accountancy services

[57.39] A tax consultant, also providing financial and accounting services, acted as a sole practitioner. His wife provided similar services, also as a sole practitioner, from the same office. Additionally he and his wife provided similar services in partnership, again from the same office, and a company controlled by him and his wife also provided similar services from the same office. The Commissioners issued a direction that all four businesses should be treated as one business under what is now *VATA 1994, Sch 1 para 2*. The tribunal upheld the direction and the consultant appealed, contending that *Sch 1 para 2** contravened European Community law. The QB rejected this contention and dismissed the appeal. Kennedy J held that *Sch 1 para 2** was authorised by *Article 4(4)* of the *EC Sixth Directive*, which allowed persons to be brought together for VAT purposes if they were 'closely bound to one another by financial, economic and organisational links'. *AB Osman v C & E Commrs*, QB [1989] STC 596.

[57.40] Similar decisions were reached in the subsequent cases of *HD Mitchell (t/a Mitchell & Co)*, LON/99/613 (VTD 16547) and *DB Jones*, MAN/99/1009 (VTD 16796).

Café and bread shop at same premises

[57.41] A trader (W) operated a café and a bread shop from the same premises. In 1985 he transferred the café to his mother. The Commissioners issued a notice directing that W and his mother should be treated as a single taxable person. The tribunal upheld the direction. *TSD & ME Williams*, LON/87/132 (VTD 2445).

Café and sandwich shop at same premises

[57.42] A company, controlled by a married couple, operated a café. It failed to register for VAT. When Customs discovered this, the directors claimed that the company's turnover was below the statutory threshold, because they treated the sale of sandwiches as a separate business which they carried on in partnership. Customs issued a notice directing that the company and the partnership should be treated as a single taxable person, and an assessment charging tax on the company. The tribunal upheld the direction and the assessment. *Mr & Mrs Sterling (t/a Sally's Sandwich Bar); The Corner Café (Tooting) Ltd*, LON/04/928 (VTD 19057).

Fish and chip shop

[57.43] A married couple, registered as a partnership, ran a take-away fish and chip shop. In 1984 they applied to be deregistered, claiming that they had decided to divide the business between them, with the wife operating the shop at lunchtime and the husband operating it in the evenings. The Commissioners issued a direction that they should be treated as a single taxable person. They appealed, contending that they had decided to divide the business because of matrimonial difficulties. The tribunal dismissed their appeal, holding that the Commissioners had been entitled to conclude that the avoidance of VAT liability was a 'main reason' for dividing the business. *T & AJ Lee*, MAN/87/252 (VTD 2640).

Hairdressers

[57.44] A hairdresser, who owned two salons, failed to account for VAT on supplies made at the salons by his wife and three other female hairdressers. The Commissioners issued a direction treating them as a single taxable person. The tribunal upheld the direction. *AS Lewis*, MAN/88/260 (VTD 3329).

Gymnasium

[57.45] A trader (S) operated a gymnasium. The premises also contained sunbeds. In 1988 S applied for deregistration, claiming that he was now only operating the gymnasium on three days a week for female customers, while his son was operating it on three days a week for male customers, and his wife was responsible for the sunbeds. The Commissioners issued a direction that S and his wife and son should be treated as a single taxable person. The tribunal upheld the direction. *M, J & P Summers*, MAN/88/513 (VTD 3498).

[57.46] A similar decision was reached in *S Gibson (t/a Miss Toner)*, EDN/94/224 (VTD 13293).

Fitness club and beauty salon at same premises

[57.47] A company operated a fitness club and was registered for VAT. One of the company's directors and his wife operated a beauty salon in partnership at the same premises. The partnership was not registered for VAT. The Commissioners issued a direction that the company and the partnership should be treated as a single taxable person. The tribunal upheld the direction. *West End Health & Fitness Club*, EDN/89/70 (VTD 4070).

Catering at public house

[57.48] The wife of a publican provided catering at the public house of which her husband was the tenant. The husband was registered for VAT, but did not account for VAT on the catering. The Commissioners issued a direction that the couple should be treated as a single taxable person. The tribunal upheld the direction. *P & R J Jervis*, MAN/88/596 (VTD 3920).

[57.49] The decision in *Jervis*, 57.48 above, was applied in the similar subsequent case of *DJ & PA Coe*, LON/92/2371A (VTD 10911).

[57.50] An unmarried couple operated a public house and were registered for VAT as a partnership. The partnership did not account for VAT on receipts from catering at the public house, treating it as a separate business operated by the female partner (T) as an individual. The Commissioners issued a direction under what is now *VATA 1994, Sch 1 para 2* that T and the partnership should be treated as a single taxable person. T appealed, contending that the catering had been treated as a separate business for the purpose of providing her with an independent source of income in case of any rift in her relationship with her partner, and not for the purpose of avoiding VAT. The tribunal dismissed her appeal and upheld the direction. *TJ Ilott*, LON/92/3384 (VTD 10942).

Catering and accommodation at public house

[57.51] A publican did not account for VAT on income from catering and accommodation at the public house, claiming that these were a separate business carried on by his wife. The Commissioners issued a direction that the couple should be treated as a single taxable person, and the tribunal dismissed the couple's appeal. *WP & DKM Spence*, EDN/90/142 (VTD 5698).

Service station and video club at same premises

[57.52] A company operated a service station. The son of one of its directors opened a video club at the same premises. The Commissioners issued a direction that the company and the club proprietor should be treated as a single taxable person. The tribunal upheld the direction. *Old Farm Service Station Ltd; L Williams*, MAN/89/56 (VTD 4261).

Manufacture and sale of model aircraft kits

[57.53] A former Customs officer (H) began a business of manufacturing and selling model aircraft kits. Some of these were exported to Germany. In June 1989 he formed a partnership with his wife. The partnership took over the existing UK business, but H continued the export business in his own name. The Commissioners issued a direction under what is now *VATA 1994, Sch 1 para 2*. The tribunal upheld the direction and dismissed H's appeal. *AD Head*, LON/90/109Y (VTD 4828).

Taxi and wedding car hire

[57.54] The proprietor of a taxi business did not account for VAT on the hire of cars for weddings, claiming that this was a separate business which he operated in partnership with his wife. The Commissioners issued a direction that the couple should be treated as a single taxable person. The tribunal upheld the direction. *A & J Harris (t/a Gribbens Taxis & Wedding Cars)*, EDN/89/211 (VTD 4882).

Ice-cream vendors

[57.55] An ice-cream vendor (G) had six ice-cream vans, one of which he drove himself, and three of which were driven by his sons, who were aged between 20 and 21. In 1991 he sold a van to each of his three sons, and applied for deregistration, claiming that his turnover would fall below the deregistration threshold. The Commissioners issued a direction that G and his sons should be treated as a single taxable person. The tribunal upheld the direction. *D Gregorio & Sons*, MAN/91/1262 (VTD 9105).

Holiday cottages and restaurant

[57.56] A married woman provided self-catering holiday accommodation from five cottages. In 1987 her husband, who had been unemployed for more than a year, opened a restaurant in a room of their own house, about 100 yards from the cottages. From 1987 to 1990 their accountant drew up combined accounts covering both the restaurant and the holiday cottages. However, for 1991 and 1992 separate accounts were prepared. In 1992 the Commissioners issued a direction that the couple should be treated as a single taxable person. The tribunal upheld the direction. *S & L Taylor*, EDN/92/115 (VTD 9125).

Restaurant and gift shop

[57.57] The proprietor of a restaurant and gift shop had registered for VAT with effect from April 1980. In 1983 he transferred the gift shop to his wife, and deregistered. In 1991 the Commissioners issued a direction that the couple should be treated as a single taxable person. The tribunal upheld the direction. *J Roy*, EDN/92/50 (VTD 9384).

Car sales and car washing at same premises

[57.58] A partnership which sold cars did not account for VAT on receipts from an automatic car wash at its premises, and treated these as accruing to the wife of one of the partners (E), although she was in full-time employment elsewhere and only visited the premises at weekends. The Commissioners issued a direction that the partnership and E should be treated as a single taxable person. The tribunal upheld the direction. *Allerton Motors*, MAN/91/903 (VTD 9427).

Fairground amusement operators

[57.59] A married couple and their son were registered for VAT as proprietors of fairground amusements. At a control visit, VAT officers discovered that they had not accounted for VAT on some of their income, but had treated it as accruing to one of the partners as an individual, to the married couple as a partnership excluding the son, or to the father and son as a partnership excluding the mother. The Commissioners issued a direction that all three partners should be treated as a single taxable person. The tribunal upheld the direction. *EM, PG & CP Evans*, LON/92/1247 (VTD 10532).

Computer supplies

[57.60] A married couple carried on business in partnership, providing services of computer programming, system analysis and related training. They were not registered for VAT. They subsequently incorporated a limited company which supplied computer hardware. The company registered for VAT. The Commissioners issued a direction that the partnership and the company should be treated as a single taxable person. The tribunal upheld the direction. *A & S Essex (t/a Essex Associates)*, LON/97/175 (VTD 15072).

Market traders—relevance of cohabitation

[57.61] A man and woman, who were not married but lived together, both sold leather goods from separate market stalls in the same market. The Commissioners issued a direction under *VATA 1994, Sch 1 para 2*. The woman appealed, contending that she was carrying on a separate business and wanted to keep her finances separate from those of the man with whom she was living. There were four independent stalls between her stall and that of her cohabitee. The tribunal reviewed the evidence and dismissed her appeal, holding that the fact that both traders had previously had broken marriages, and wished to keep their finances separate, was not conclusive. On the evidence, the two stalls 'were closely bound to one another by financial, economic and organisational links' and the Commissioners' direction had not been unreasonable. *DY Sharples*, MAN/99/164 (VTD 16234). (*Note.* For another case involving cohabitees, see *Ilott*, 57.50 above.)

Farming and bed and breakfast facilities

[57.61A] A married couple operated a farming business in partnership and also provided self-catering accommodation. HMRC discovered that the couple were not accounting for VAT on income from 'bed and breakfast' accommodation, which they treated as a separate business. They issued a direction under VATA 1994, Sch 1 para 2. The tribunal upheld the direction. *HR & Mrs JR Patrick v HMRC*, [2011] UKFTT 865 (TC), TC01699.

Car parking

[57.62] A company provided car parking facilities to contract customers. It leased the remainder of the land to an associated partnership, which provided 'pay and display' car parking. The Commissioners issued a direction under *VATA 1994, Sch 1 para 2*. The tribunal upheld the direction, holding that 'the separation of the car parking business into contract and pay and display categories was artificial'. *Venuebest Ltd (No 2)*, [2005] VATDR 92 (VTD 18863).

Failure to comply with direction under VATA 1994, Sch 1 para 2

[57.63] See *Barnett & Larsen*, 52.303 PENALTIES: MISDECLARATION.

Cases where the appellant was successful

NOTE

The provisions now contained in *VATA 1994, Sch 1 para 2* were introduced by *FA 1986*. As originally enacted, *VATA 1983, Sch 1 para 1A(2)(d)* required that the Commissioners should be satisfied that the avoidance of VAT liability was a 'main reason' for the way in which the business is organised. This requirement was abolished with effect from 19 March 1997, when the legislation was amended by *FA 1997*. The legislation now provides that a direction is valid if the avoidance of VAT is an effect of the separation of the business, rather than a reason for the separation. The cases in this section should be read in the light of the changes in the legislation.

Tea room at furniture shop

[57.64] A husband and wife owned a shop which sold furniture. The wife's parents, who were both retired, sold tea and coffee from a room at the same premises. Customs issued a direction that both couples should be treated as a single taxable person. The tribunal allowed the traders' appeal against this direction, finding that the two businesses were quite separate and holding that the tea room was not operated with a view to tax avoidance. *JT & SM Myers*, MAN/89/157 (VTD 3951).

Catering at public house

[57.65] The wife of a publican provided catering at the public house of which her husband was the tenant. The husband was registered for VAT, but he did not account for VAT on the catering. Customs issued a direction that the couple should be treated as a single taxable person, although the VAT officer responsible for the direction had not interviewed the wife. The tribunal allowed the couple's appeal against the direction, holding that there was no evidence to justify the officer's conclusion that the avoidance of VAT was the reason for the catering being operated as a separate business. *G & Mrs W Grisdale*, [1989] VATTR 162 (VTD 4069). (*Note.* This case was distinguished in *Coe*, **57.49** above. See also the note at the head of this section.)

[57.66] A company, which was registered for VAT, operated a public house, alongside a marina. The wife of the controlling director (K) provided catering at the public house, and an associated company operated a mooring business from the public house. Neither this company, nor K's wife, was registered for VAT. Customs issued a direction that the two companies and K's wife should be treated as a single taxable person. The company appealed, contending that the catering was treated as a separate business because K's wife 'had no intention of working under him'; there had been friction between them, and K had been charged with assaulting her, causing actual bodily harm. Although they were married and worked at the same premises, they had not lived together for several years, and were in the process of divorcing: K lived on a boat in the marina, while his wife and their two children lived in the public house. The tribunal accepted the company's evidence and allowed the appeal. *Mike Kiernan's Beer Tent Co Ltd (t/a Fish & Duck)*, LON/99/328 (VTD 17794; VTD 18310).

Bed and breakfast facilities at public house

[57.67] The wife of a publican provided bed and breakfast facilities at the public house of which her husband was the tenant. She paid her husband 35% of her income. The husband was registered for VAT. With regard to the bed and breakfast facilities, he accounted for VAT on the amounts which he received from his wife but not on the amounts which his wife retained. Customs issued a direction that the husband and wife should be treated as a single taxable person. The tribunal allowed the couple's appeal, finding that 'the two businesses were run separately with separate bank accounts, separate accounts for accounting purposes and separate records'. *S & AJ Trippitt*, MAN/00/249 (VTD 17340).

Catering and takeaway sandwich bar

[57.68] In 1997 a chef (P) opened a takeaway sandwich bar. In 1998 he married. Later that year he and his wife began a catering business in partnership, providing food for functions such as Masonic dinners. Subsequently Customs issued a direction that P and the partnership should be treated as a single taxable person. They appealed, contending that there were two separate businesses. The tribunal accepted this contention and allowed their appeal. *KL Pemberton (t/a The Sandwich Box Plus); KL & EM Pemberton (t/a Desmond's)*, LON/04/783 (VTD 19307).

Fencing contractors

[57.69] Two brothers and a brother-in-law operated as fencing contractors from the same premises. Customs issued a direction that all three should be treated as a single taxable person, and they appealed. The tribunal allowed their appeal, finding that, although there was a close connection between the trades of the two brothers, the business of the brother-in-law was entirely independent. The VAT officer dealing with the case had not interviewed the younger brother or the brother-in-law. He had made assumptions which were unreasonable and the notice was therefore invalid. *Thompson, Thompson & Giblin*, MAN/88/819 (VTD 4196).

Hairdressers

[57.70] Customs issued a direction that two hairdressers carrying on business at the same premises should be treated as a single taxable person. The hairdressers had previously worked for several years on a self-employed basis. In 1989 they leased new premises in their joint names. They kept separate tills, ledgers and appointment books. The tribunal allowed the hairdressers' appeal against the direction, holding on the evidence that the officer responsible for the direction had acted unreasonably in considering that the avoidance of VAT had been one of the main reasons for the hairdressers trading as individuals rather than as partners. *RJ Knights & WC Wendon*, LON/90/147 (VTD 5165).

[57.71] Two hairdressers, who had previously been employees, took a joint lease of premises which they used as a hairdressing salon. They opened a joint bank account, for payment of common liabilities, and also operated individual bank accounts. Customs issued a direction under what is now *VATA 1994, Sch 1 para 2*, and they appealed. The tribunal allowed their appeal, holding on the evidence that the avoidance of VAT was not the main reason for the hairdressers deciding to trade as individuals, rather than as partners. *W Cringan & T Watson*, EDN/91/330 (VTD 7519).

Hairdressing and beauty salon

[57.72] A married woman operated a beauty salon. Her husband owned a hairdressing salon on a different floor of the same premises. Customs issued a direction under *VATA 1994, Sch 1 para 2*, and the couple appealed. The tribunal allowed their appeal, holding on the evidence that there had always been two separate businesses and that Customs' direction was unreasonable. *G & Mrs H Francis*, [2006] VATDR 487 (VTD 19919).

Farming and pony trekking

[57.73] A farmer's first wife had begun a pony trekking business in 1981. This was treated as a separate business from the husband's farming. In 1984 the couple divorced and the husband took over the pony trekking business, which he ran alongside his farming business. He accounted for VAT on both businesses. In 1985 the farmer remarried and handed over the running of the pony trekking business to his second wife. In 1988 he formally transferred the pony trekking business to her. As the turnover of the pony trekking business was below the registration threshold, she stopped charging and accounting for

VAT. Customs issued a direction that the farmer and his wife should be treated as a single taxable person. The tribunal allowed the couple's appeal against this direction, finding that the two businesses were genuinely independent and holding that the conditions of *Sch 1 para 2* were not satisfied. *D & LM Horsman*, [1990] VATTR 151 (VTD 5401).

Farming and bed and breakfast facilities

[57.74] A farmer had been registered for VAT since 1973. His wife provided bed and breakfast facilities from the farmhouse and from a converted building adjacent to it. The Commissioners issued a direction that the couple should be treated as a single taxable person. The couple appealed, contending that the wife had wanted an independent source of income. The tribunal allowed the couple's appeal, finding that the officer responsible for the direction had acted unreasonably and that tax avoidance was not the reason for the operation of two separate businesses. *HD & DM Hundsdoerfer*, [1990] VATTR 158 (VTD 5450).

[57.75] A similar decision was reached in a case where a married couple and their son carried on a farming business in partnership, and the wife also operated a bed and breakfast business from the farmhouse. *A, D & J Forster v HMRC*, [2011] UKFTT 469 (TC), TC01319.

Bookselling and launderettes

[57.76] A trader (P) was registered for VAT from 1973 as the proprietor of a mail order bookselling business and of three launderettes. In 1991 he told Customs that he had taken his wife (whom he had married in 1988) into partnership in the bookselling business. He also told Customs that he would only continue to operate one of the launderettes, since he had transferred one of them to his wife, and had taken his son (by a previous marriage) into partnership in the third launderette. Following this, the couple continued to account for output tax in respect of the bookselling business, since its turnover remained above the registration threshold, but the couple did not account for output tax in respect of the launderettes, since the turnover of each of the launderettes, treated independently, was below the threshold. Customs issued a direction that P, his wife and the two partnerships should be treated as a single taxable person for VAT purposes. P and his wife and son appealed, contending that the main reason for the division of the business was not the avoidance of VAT, but was the desire to avoid inheritance tax and to provide P's wife with an independent source of income. The tribunal allowed the appeal, finding that P's decision to take his wife into partnership was not to avoid VAT, since the wife had been acting as a *de facto* partner since their marriage. Furthermore, since P was considerably older than his wife, it was understandable that P should have wished to transfer one of the launderettes to her, while the taking of P's son into partnership in one of the other launderettes 'clearly achieved potential inheritance tax savings'. *P, C & J Allen*, LON/93/2586A (VTD 12209).

Dry-cleaning businesses

[57.77] An individual (IR) operated a dry-cleaning business from a shop in Leigh-on-Sea. His mother (AR) operated a similar business from a shop in

Westcliff-on-Sea, and his common law wife (C) operated a similar business from a shop in Shoeburyness. All three shops used the same trading name, but had separate sets of records and separate bank accounts. Customs issued a direction that all three shops should be treated as a single taxable person. The proprietors appealed, contending that, although IR and C lived together and had three children together, they operated the shops as individuals because they wanted to maintain their independence, both having previously been divorced. The shop in Westcliff had originally been purchased by IR's father (AR's husband), who had subsequently died. The tribunal accepted the proprietors' evidence and allowed the appeals, holding that the officer responsible for the direction had not made adequate enquiries but had relied on outdated information. The tribunal observed that 'the fact that there was substantial mutual assistance between three traders who were related to one another does not necessarily mean that the businesses should properly be regarded as one'. *I Reayner, J Colegate & A Reayner*, LON/97/431 (VTD 15396).

Jewellers carrying on business from same premises

[57.78] From 1981 to 1990 two individuals (H and S) carried on business from the same premises. H sold jewellery, while S specialised in the retail sale of second-hand jewellery and antiques. In 1990 they went into partnership and registered for VAT, but in 1993 they decided to terminate the partnership, applied for deregistration, and reverted to trading separately (while continuing to operate from the same premises). In 1994 Customs issued a direction that, despite the termination of the partnership, they should be treated as a single taxable person. They appealed, contending that they had terminated the partnership because of disagreements about trading policy, particularly with regard to the purchase of second-hand jewellery for resale, and that they were searching for separate premises. They had separate bank accounts as well as a joint account which was used for meeting joint expenses. They kept separate records. The tribunal accepted their evidence and allowed their appeals, holding that the VAT officers responsible for the direction had not given sufficient weight to the reasons for terminating the partnership, and had given too much weight to the existence of a joint bank account. *J Humphrey & AG Smith (t/a Abacus Jewellery & Antiques)*, MAN/95/1133 (VTD 13561).

Trader manufacturing rocking-horses—company repairing them

[57.79] In 1988 a sole trader (M) began a business of manufacturing rocking-horses. He did not register for VAT, as his turnover was below the threshold. As his business grew, he was sometimes asked to repair old rocking-horses. In 1999 he and his wife incorporated a limited company to carry on repair and restoration work. Neither he nor the company registered for VAT. Because of M's commitments as a sole trader, much of the company's work was undertaken by subcontractors. In 2002 Customs issued a direction that M and the company should be treated as a single taxable person. M and the company appealed, contending that the company was carrying on a separate and distinct business and that there was a genuine commercial reason for the existence of the limited company. The tribunal accepted this contention and allowed the appeals. *R Mullis; Robert Mullis Restoration Services Ltd*, LON/02/814 (VTD 18501).

Whether direction under VATA 1994, Sch 1 para 2 may be retrospective

[**57.80**] On 5 June 1997 Customs issued a direction under *VATA 1994, Sch 1 para 2* on a married couple. The direction stated that it took effect from 1 June 1997. The couple appealed, contending that a direction under *Sch 1 para 2* could not be retrospective. The tribunal accepted this contention and allowed the appeals, holding that 'it is plain from the terms of (*Sch 1 para 2*) that the date on which registration takes effect must be the date of the direction or some later date specified in the direction, but not an earlier date'. The error could not be regarded as immaterial, and the direction was, therefore, invalid and ineffective. *RD & SM Elder*, EDN/97/126 & 127 (VTD 15881, VTD 15882). (*Note.* For an appeal against a subsequent direction, see 2.359 APPEALS.)

Direction under VATA 1994, Sch 1 para 2—whether correctly issued

[**57.81**] A sole trader (T) carried on a project design business. He and his wife subsequently also started a project management business in partnership. Customs issued directions under *VATA 1994, Sch 1 para 2*, purporting to direct that T and his wife should be treated as a single taxable person. However, the notice issued to T named his wife, rather than the partnership, as the 'other person' to be treated as a single taxable person. The other notice was issued to the wife, rather than to the partnership. The tribunal allowed the couple's appeals, holding that the notices were incorrectly worded and were invalid. The tribunal observed that 'we have adopted an approach of strict construction of the statutory provisions. We could in theory have taken a broader common-sense approach that glossed over the tightly worded conditions for issue of a direction under *Sch 1 para 2*. But *paragraph 1A* states that the *paragraph 2* direction is an anti-avoidance measure. The conditions for a direction and the machinery for its implementation are as much to identify the precise scope of the anti-avoidance measure as to protect the taxpayer.' The tribunal also noted that Customs' own Guidance Manual stated 'it is very important to remember that you must serve a notice of direction upon each separate business or "person" whom you are directing to register as a single taxable person ("person" here covers both natural persons – such as sole proprietors (and) partnerships – and legal persons)'. The Manual specifically stated that 'if you are directing, for example, that a sole proprietor (A), a sole proprietor (B), a partnership (C) and a limited company (D) are to register as a single taxable person, you must issue four directions, one to each of the entities or "persons"'. This applied 'even if the sole proprietors are members of the partnership or directors of the company'. *K & E Turner*, LON/02/1094 (VTD 19076).

Notification of liability and registration (VATA 1994, Sch 1 para 5)

[**57.82**] A married couple began a hairdressing business in February 1973 and became liable to register in August 1973. They failed to register and a VAT officer issued a notice of compulsory registration. The tribunal dismissed their appeal. *EF & Mrs K Norton*, LON/75/5 (VTD 151).

Sch 1 para 5(2)—date from which registration is effective

[57.83] A trader became liable to register for VAT from October 1974 but did not notify the Commissioners until January 1975. Her registration was backdated and she appealed, contending that she should not have been registered retrospectively. The tribunal dismissed her appeal, holding that the Commissioners were obliged to backdate her registration and had no discretion to waive the statutory provisions. *SJ Whitehead*, [1975] VATTR 152 (VTD 202).

[57.84] The decision in *Whitehead*, 57.83 above, was applied in the similar cases of *JR Atkinson*, CAR/76/142 (VTD 309); *P & G Dyer*, LON/77/50 (VTD 390); *GJ Jelley*, MAN/90/321 (VTD 6790); *P & F Arnaoutis (t/a Trafford Chip Shop)*, MAN/95/403 (VTD 13829); *D Kirk*, MAN/95/379 (VTD 14042) and *Lindley*, 62.169 SUPPLY.

[57.85] A sole trader, who was registered for VAT, transferred his business to a company with effect from August 1975. The company was not informed of its registration number until April 1976 and did not charge its customers VAT on its supplies in the intervening period. The Commissioners issued an assessment charging tax on the supplies in question, and the tribunal dismissed the company's appeal. *JJ Foggon Ltd*, MAN/78/164 (VTD 789).

[57.86] The decision in *JJ Foggon Ltd*, 57.85 above, was applied in a case where a trader had applied for registration on 1 October 1987 but was not informed of his registration number until 13 November, and did not charge VAT on supplies made in the intervening period. *JC Tobin*, [1991] VATTR 165 (VTD 5740).

[57.87] A similar decision was reached in *M Lucas & G Jones (t/a Mayfair Building & Roofing Services)*, LON/92/96 (VTD 10715).

[57.88] A company applied for registration from 1 October 1987. On a subsequent control visit the Commissioners discovered that the company should have been registered from 1 August rather than 1 October, and issued an assessment charging tax on the supplies made in August and September. The tribunal dismissed the company's appeal. Although the company had not been registered in August and September 1987, it was required to be registered, and its supplies in that period were taxable accordingly. *Adler Properties Ltd*, LON/89/688X (VTD 4088).

[57.89] A trader applied for registration from 1 November 1987. At a control visit in 1989, a VAT officer discovered that he should have registered from April 1975. In January 1990 the Commissioners issued a return to the trader covering the period from April 1975 to October 1987. The trader failed to complete the return, and in May 1990 the Commissioners issued an assessment covering the period in question. The trader appealed, contending that the date of registration could not be altered retrospectively. The tribunal rejected this contention and dismissed the appeal, and the CA upheld this decision. The trader had been required to be registered throughout the period covered by the return and the assessment. The Commissioners had been entitled to issue the return in question, and the assessment had been made to the best of their judgment. The validity of the assessment was not altered by the fact that the trader had subsequently transferred the business to a family partnership which used the same trading name. The obligations imposed by the Commissioners were in accordance with *Article 22* of the *EC Sixth Directive*. Neill LJ observed that '*Article 22(4)* was not intended to prevent or inhibit the collection of tax' from those who had 'continued to trade without paying tax'. *V Bjellica (t/a Eddy's Domestic Appliances) v C & E Commrs*, CA [1995] STC 329. (*Note.* An appeal against a penalty under what is now *VATA 1994, s 67* was also dismissed—see **51.3** PENALTIES: FAILURE TO NOTIFY.)

[57.90] The CA decision in *Bjellica*, 57.89 above, was applied in the similar subsequent cases of *M Yasin & M Hussain*, MAN/94/959 (VTD 15804) and *A Goni & A Ali (t/a Curry Centre Tandoori Restaurant)*, LON/98/67 (VTD 15840).

[57.91] Similar decisions were reached in *G George (t/a Top Six Hairdressing)*, LON/99/927 (VTD 16971); *M Smith*, MAN/02/246 (VTD 18393) and *B Singh (t/a BS Construction)*, [2009] UKFTT 245 (TC), TC00194.

[57.92] See also *Henderson*, **3.10** ASSESSMENT, and *Prudential Assurance Co Ltd (No 5)*, **3.118** ASSESSMENT.

Certificate of registration issued with wrong date

[57.93] A sailing club became liable to register for VAT with effect from July 1975 but did not do so until April 1977. The certificate of registration issued by the Commissioners incorrectly stated the date of registration as 20 April 1977, and subsequently the Commissioners issued a return to the club for the period from 20 April 1977 to 30 June 1977. The club submitted the return, claiming a repayment of £57. The Commissioners then discovered the error in the registration date and issued an estimated assessment for the period from 21 July 1975, together with an amended certificate of registration. The club appealed, contending that the Commissioners were bound by their first certificate of registration and that, as the club had not been called on to make a return for the period from 21 July 1975, the assessment was not authorised by what is now *VATA 1994, s 73(1)*. The tribunal rejected this contention and dismissed the appeal, holding that the Commissioners were under no obligation to issue a certificate of registration. Furthermore, the liability to make returns was laid down by what is now *VAT Regulations 1995 (SI 1995/2518), reg 25* and was absolute, notwithstanding that the requisite form on which to make the return had not been provided. *DG Oliver (for Maidstone Sailing Club)*, LON/77/359 (VTD 511).

Date from which re-registration effective

[57.94] A hairdresser, who was registered for VAT, dismissed one of his employees in May 1981. He applied for deregistration with effect from 1 June 1981, on the basis that his turnover would decline to below the deregistration threshold of what is now *Sch 1 para 4*. The Commissioners accepted his application. However, his turnover did not decline to the extent that he had anticipated, and in the following year he applied to be re-registered with effect from 1 April 1982. At a control visit in October 1982, a VAT officer ascertained that the value of the hairdresser's supplies in the year ended 30 June 1981 had exceeded the threshold in *Sch 1 para 1(1)*, so that he had been liable to re-register with effect from 10 July 1981. The Commissioners issued an assessment charging tax on the hairdresser's supplies from 10 July 1981 to 31 March 1982. The tribunal dismissed the hairdresser's appeal. *HR Short*, [1983] VATTR 94 (VTD 1408).

Whether date of registration can be amended

[57.95] A trader began to carry on business on 11 April 1990. On 29 October he submitted a form VAT1 stating that he had become liable to register from 11 April. However, he only accounted for tax from 1 November. Customs subsequently issued an assessment charging tax on his supplies from that date, and he appealed, contending that the effective date of registration should be amended to 1 November. The tribunal dismissed his appeal, finding that Customs had not acted unreasonably. *PS Bruce*, LON/93/2930 (VTD 12484).

[57.96] Similar decisions were reached in *N Ludovico & M De Martiis (t/a Paradiso Italian Restaurant)*, LON/03/630 (VTD 18620) and *L Howard*, LON/06/163 (VTD 19838). (*Note.* Compare *Rowe*, 57.97 below, which was not cited in either of these decisions.)

[57.97] A partnership which operated a restaurant kept a daily record of takings, and passed the registration threshold of *Sch 1 para 1* (which was £45,000 at the relevant time) on 7 June 1994. The partners submitted a form VAT1 notifying the Commissioners that they were required to be registered from 7 June. Subsequently their accountants advised them that, by virtue of what is now *VATA 1994, Sch 1 para 5*, their registration need not have taken effect until 1 August 1994. They applied to the Commissioners requesting that the effective date of registration be amended accordingly. The Commissioners rejected this request but the tribunal allowed the partnership's appeal, holding that the effect of what is now *VATA 1994, Sch 1 para 5(2)* was that the partnership was not required to be registered until 1 August unless it agreed to an earlier date, and the incorrect completion of the form VAT1 did not amount to such an agreement. *AJ & AE Rowe (t/a Arthur's)*, LON/95/423A (VTD 13650).

Application to backdate voluntary registration

[57.98] See *Attwater*, 57.113 below, and the cases noted at 57.114 below.

Deliberate mis-statement on form VAT1

[57.99] See *The Gables Nursing Home*, 57.118 below.

Appeals against retrospective registration

[57.100] There have been a large number of cases, which appear to raise no point of general importance, in which appeals against retrospective registration have been dismissed. In the interests of space, such cases are not listed individually in this book. For summaries of such cases decided up to 31 December 1992, see Tolley's VAT Cases 1993.

Entitlement to be registered (VATA 1994, Sch 1 paras 9, 10)

[57.101] A housing association applied for registration for VAT. Customs rejected the application on the basis that it was not making any taxable supplies. The association appealed, contending that it had given its members an option to purchase the houses in which they lived, and that when any members exercised its option, it would be making a zero-rated supply. The tribunal accepted this contention and allowed the association's appeal. *Pinetree Housing Association Ltd*, LON/83/155 (VTD 1487).

[57.102] A company was incorporated in April 1991 and applied to be registered for VAT as an 'intending trader' under the provisions of what is now *VATA 1994, Sch 1 para 9(1)*. The Commissioners rejected the application on the grounds that the company had not supplied satisfactory evidence of its intention to trade. It appeared to have done nothing other than to purchase a fax machine, and the address given on the company's application form was that of its professional advisers, rather than a business address. The company appealed, contending that it was unreasonable for the Commissioners to have rejected its assertions that it hoped to begin trading. The tribunal rejected this contention and dismissed the appeal, holding that its jurisdiction was supervisory rather than appellate, applying *JH Corbitt (Numismatists) Ltd*, **60.1** SECOND-HAND GOODS. The company had not submitted objective evidence of an intention to trade and the Commissioners had not acted unreasonably in rejecting the application. *Golden Pyramid Ltd*, LON/91/1306Y (VTD 9133).

[57.103] In 1988 a Swiss property developer purchased a site in Newcastle-upon-Tyne. In 1990 he applied for registration as an 'intending trader'. The Commissioners rejected his application. In 1992 the site which he had purchased was taken over by the Tyne & Wear Development Corporation under a compulsory purchase order, the question of compensation being referred to a tribunal. In 1993 he made a further application for registration, which the Commissioners again rejected. He appealed, contending that he wished to waive exemption in respect of the site so that he could reclaim input tax which he had incurred. The tribunal dismissed his appeal, holding that since he was no longer the owner of the site, he was no longer an 'intending trader' and was no longer entitled to registration. *L Landau*, LON/95/1944 (VTD 13644).

[57.104] In 1995 a charity, which was not registered for VAT, purchased a former hotel, which was subsequently converted and used as a residential home for the elderly (i.e. a 'relevant residential building' within *VATA 1994, Sch 8, Group 5*). In 1997 the charity applied for retrospective registration, backdated to 1995. The Commissioners refused to backdate the registration, on the basis that in 1995 the charity had neither made any taxable supplies, nor intended to do so. The charity appealed, contending that at the time when the building was being converted, it had intended to transfer a major interest (i.e. a lease of at least 21 years) in the building, and was therefore entitled to registration under *Sch 1 para 9*. The tribunal reviewed the evidence in detail and dismissed the appeal. The chairman found that he was 'not satisfied that the appellants formed an intention to grant a major interest in the property at the relevant period, July to October 1995. I am satisfied that that intention only existed and arose some time between October 1996 and April 1997. An intention is different from a hope or a discussion or a consideration. An intention implies that the mind has been directed upon or fixed upon a purpose.' *Birmingham Royal Institution for the Blind*, MAN/97/912 (VTD 16386).

[57.105] A company operated a chain of 23 bookmaking shops. It had not registered for VAT, since its supplies were exempt under what is now *VATA 1994, Sch 9, Group 4, Item 1*. In May 1995 the company's accountants submitted 23 retrospective applications for registration, backdated to April 1993, on the basis that the company had transferred each of its shops to a partnership in which it held a 95% interest, and that the partnerships had been making taxable supplies of tea and coffee to employees at the shops. The Commissioners rejected the applications, considering firstly that the alleged partnerships did not in fact exist, and alternatively that if the partnerships were deemed to exist, they were not making any taxable supplies. The company and its alleged partners appealed, contending that they were entitled to register under *VATA 1994, Sch 1 para 9*. The tribunal rejected this contention and dismissed the appeal. Under *Sch 1 para 9*, an applicant had to satisfy the Commissioners that he was making, or intending to make, taxable supplies. On the evidence presented, the Commissioners were not satisfied that the alleged partnerships were making taxable supplies, and their conclusion was 'reasonable' and 'correct in law'. There were no separate bank accounts for each partnerships, no partnership accounts, and no partners' meetings. None of the alleged partnerships owned any business assets or held bookmakers' licences. Applying *dicta* of Lord Clyde in *CIR v Williamson*, CS 1928, 14 TC 335, 'you do not constitute or create or prove a partnership by saying that there is one'. *SP Graham Ltd & Others*, LON/96/1121 (VTD 14789).

[57.106] In June 1994 an individual (D) applied for registration as an 'intending trader'. The Commissioners rejected his application, and he appealed, contending that he intended to undertake building work for a VAT-registered partnership of which he was a member, and to continue in business as a commercial building contractor. The tribunal accepted his evidence and allowed the appeal, holding that D had satisfied 'the conditions specified in the legislation' and that the Commissioners were 'required to register him'. On the evidence, the VAT officers responsible for rejecting his application had failed to 'consider the case put to them' and had 'closed their minds to the possibility that he could be carrying on business'. *JP Dewhirst*, LON/94/2414A (VTD 13793).

[57.107] A couple who owned a three-bedroomed cottage began work on converting it into two semi-detached properties. In 2010 they applied to be registered for VAT as 'intending traders'. HMRC rejected the claim on the basis that they intended to make exempt supplies. The couple appealed, contending that they were enlarging the cottage in order to create an additional dwelling, and the subsequent sale of that dwelling would be a zero-rated supply. The tribunal accepted this contention and allowed their appeal. Judge Brooks held that the work on the cottage 'consists partly of zero-rated new building and partly of an exempt supply of land (ie the part of the existing building incorporated into the new building). Accordingly the tax should be apportioned and the couple were entitled to be registered. *A & Mrs M Wright v HMRC*, [2011] UKFTT 681 (TC), TC01523.

[57.108] An individual (J) purchased a van in November 2000. He applied for VAT registration, to enable him to recover input tax on the van. The Commissioners rejected the claim on the basis that he was not carrying on any business. The tribunal dismissed J's appeal against this decision. *EH Jones*, MAN/01/326 (VTD 17558).

[57.109] A company (G) applied to be registered for VAT. Customs rejected the application on the basis that G was not making any taxable supplies. G appealed, contending that it had purchased 945 computer units and sold them to another company for a price above the VAT threshold. The tribunal accepted G's evidence and allowed its appeal. *Goldstar Distribution Ltd*, LON/06/122 (VTD 20467).

[57.110] A company (G) applied to be registered for VAT. Customs rejected the application on the basis that G was not making any taxable supplies, and that an associated company had previously been involved in MTIC fraud. G appealed, contending that it intended to carry on a business of dealing in surplus medical products. The tribunal reviewed the evidence in detail and dismissed G's appeal, finding that there was evidence that medical supplies were 'a new MTIC commodity with the strong possibility of tax risk'. The two companies from which G had stated that it intended to obtain supplies had both 'been involved in chains of transactions in which there were missing traders'. On the evidence, Customs' decision to reject G's application had been reasonable. *Global Master Ltd*, MAN/07/209 (VTD 20476). (*Note.* Costs were awarded to Customs.)

[57.111] A company (C) was incorporated in the UK. One of its two directors was a Spanish citizen: the other was a UK citizen who spent considerable time in Spain. C applied for registration for UK VAT. HMRC rejected the claim on the basis that C had not shown that it intended to carry on any business in the UK. C appealed, contending that it intended to carry on a business of buying second-hand cars in Spain and selling them to other EU countries (eg Germany and Italy) where they would command higher prices. The tribunal accepted C's evidence and allowed its appeal, observing that its intended supplies fell within *VATA 1994 Sch 1 para 10(2)*, and holding that the effect of the ECJ decision in *Rompelman & EA Rompelman-van-Deelen v Minister van Finan-ciën*, **22.103** EUROPEAN COMMUNITY LAW, was that it was entitled to registra-tion. *Car Factors Ltd v HMRC*, [2011] UKFTT 465 (TC), TC01315.

[57.112] See also *Kingscrest Associates Ltd & Montecello Ltd (t/a Kingscrest Residential Care Homes)*, **33.60** HEALTH AND WELFARE; *Carr*, **55.36** PRO-TECTED BUILDINGS; *Ace Telecom Ltd*, **57.16** above, and *22A Property Investments Ltd*, **62.199** SUPPLY.

Date from which voluntary registration effective

[57.113] In March 1997 a dentist applied to be registered for VAT with retrospective effect, to enable him to reclaim input tax for previous years. The Commissioners agreed to register him with effect from 1 April 1994, but rejected his application to backdate his registration to 1 April 1992. He appealed. The tribunal dismissed his appeal, holding that the effect of *Sch 1 para 9* was that a voluntary registration took effect 'from the day on which the request is made or from such earlier date as may be agreed'. Applying *dicta* in *John Dee Ltd*, **14.31** COLLECTION AND ENFORCEMENT, the tribunal's jurisdiction was limited to considering whether the Commissioners had acted unreasonably. On the evidence, the Commissioners' decision had not been unreasonable. *A Attwater*, MAN/97/903 (VTD 15496).

[57.114] Similar decisions, also applying *dicta* in *John Dee Ltd*, **14.31** COLLECTION AND ENFORCEMENT, were reached in *PJ & ML Edwards*, MAN/97/1084 (VTD 15533); *R & M Davis (t/a El Shaddai Private Nursing Home) (and related appeals)*, LON/98/260 (VTD 16275); *Drosden Plantruck Ltd*, [2009] UKFTT 115 (TC), TC00083; *Lead Asset Strategies (Liverpool) Ltd*, [2009] UKFTT 122 (TC), TC00090, and *IJ Middleton (t/a Freshfields)*, [2011] UKFTT 316 (TC), TC01177.

[57.115] A similar decision was reached in a case where the appellant contended that he had submitted a previous form VAT1, but had sent it to an office which had closed almost two years previously. The tribunal held, applying *dicta* in *Selwyn*, **51.103** PENALTIES: FAILURE TO NOTIFY, that 'the postage of a form VAT1 does not of itself constitute notification to the Commissioners of liability to register'. *Dr J Hill*, LON/97/1526 (VTD 15543).

Companies in group requesting backdated separate registrations

[57.116] See *Eastwood Care Homes (Ilkeston) Ltd*, **32.7** GROUPS OF COMPANIES.

Conditional registration—whether conditions valid

[57.117] See *Hordern*, **36.558** INPUT TAX, and *Wilson*, **36.578** INPUT TAX.

Incorrect statement on form VAT1

[57.118] On 1 May 1995 a nursing home was transferred from a company to a partnership. The partnership submitted a form VAT1, applying to be registered with effect from April 1992. The Commissioners initially accepted the application, and sent the partnership a VAT return covering the period from April 1992. The partnership completed the return and submitted it to the Commissioners, claiming a substantial repayment of VAT. A VAT officer visited the nursing home to verify the claim and discovered that the partnership had only begun to carry on the business on 1 May 1995. The Commissioners issued a ruling under *VAT Regulations 1995 (SI 1995 No 2518), reg 5*, that the registration should be amended so that it ran from 1 May 1995 rather than from 1992, with the result that no tax was repayable. The tribunal upheld the Commissioners' ruling and dismissed the partnership's appeal, holding on the evidence that the Commissioners had been 'misled by the untrue statement in the application for registration' and that 'having discovered the truth, they were entitled to put the matter right'. The effect of *reg 5(2)* was that the Commissioners were entitled to alter the date of registration. *The Gables Nursing Home*, MAN/97/51 (VTD 15456).

Interpretation of VATA 1994, Sch 1 para 10

[57.119] See *The Source Enterprise Ltd*, 45.9 OVERSEAS TRADERS.

Cancellation of registration (VATA 1994, Sch 1 para 13)

Requests for cancellation of registration (VATA 1994, Sch 1 para 13(1))

Anticipated future decline in turnover

[57.120] A married couple, who had recently acquired a small restaurant, registered for VAT from 1 April 1973. In June 1974 they applied for deregistration on the basis that their takings for the following year would probably be below the threshold of what is now *VATA 1994, Sch 1 para 4* (which was then £4,000). The Commissioners were not satisfied that their takings would be less than the threshold, and formally rejected the application on 10 July 1974. The tribunal dismissed the couple's appeal, noting that their takings for the year ended 31 July 1974 were £4,178 and finding that it was not clear that the takings for the year from 10 July 1974, the date of the Commissioners' decision, would be less than £4,000. *Mr & Mrs K Savva (t/a Venus Restaurant)*, LON/74/94 (VTD 127).

[57.121] A trader (D) who carried on two small businesses registered for VAT from 1 April 1973 and applied for deregistration on 30 July 1973. The Commissioners rejected this application but subsequently agreed to deregister him from 16 February 1974, the date on which he discontinued one of the businesses. D appealed, contending that he should have been allowed to deregister from July 1973. The tribunal rejected this contention and dismissed his appeal. *JF Delves (No 2)*, LEE/75/3 (VTD 157).

[57.122] An application for cancellation of registration was dismissed in a case where a trader had contended that her turnover would decline to below the registration threshold, although at the time of making the application it was still above the threshold. The tribunal held that its jurisdiction was supervisory and that the Commissioners' decision to refuse the application was not unreasonable. *N Smith (t/a The Chippy)*, MAN/93/822 (VTD 11806).

[57.123] Similar decisions were reached in *TE Darker (t/a Fig Tree Coffee Shop)*, MAN/99/413 (VTD 16620); *S Wilkes (t/a Dipton Chippy)*, MAN/99/189 (VTD 16652); *Genesis Hair & Beauty Ltd*, EDN/00/152 (VTD 17177) and *M Singh*, MAN/02/422 (VTD 18179).

Application for cancellation of registration to be retrospective

[57.124] A hairdresser closed her business on 31 January 1977 and her registration was cancelled from 1 February. The Commissioners subsequently discovered that she had underpaid £90 VAT and sought to recover this amount. She appealed, contending that, for some time before she ceased trading, her annual turnover had been below £5,000 (the then limit of *Sch 1 para 1*) and that she could have applied for the cancellation of her registration from an earlier date. The tribunal dismissed her appeal, holding that, as she had applied for her registration to be cancelled from 1 February 1977, the cancellation could not take effect retrospectively. *B Jackson (t/a Suite Sixe)*, MAN/77/20 (VTD 469).

[57.125] A married couple operated a fish and chip shop and were registered for VAT. Their turnover was less than the registration threshold and they did not account for any output tax. The Commissioners issued an assessment to charge output tax on the supplies they had made. They appealed, contending that they had assumed that, although they were registered, they did not have to charge VAT since their turnover was below the threshold, and that in the circumstances their registration should be cancelled retrospectively. The tribunal dismissed their appeal, holding that the cancellation of a registration could not be retrospective. *B & C Parker*, MAN/87/59 (VTD 2454).

[57.126] A married couple became liable to register in July 1984 but failed to do so. The Commissioners discovered this in 1988 and issued a ruling that they had been required to be registered from July 1984 to 31 December 1985 (when their turnover declined to below the threshold of what is now *Sch 1 para 4*). The partners appealed, contending that their registration should be cancelled with effect from 1 January 1985. The tribunal rejected this contention and dismissed the appeal, finding that 'there was no evidence to show that the low turnover in the last quarter of 1985 was to be foreseen'. *RE & EM Harvey*, MAN/88/938 (VTD 4899).

[57.127] A hairdresser ceased to be required to be registered with effect from 15 March 1989, when the deregistration threshold of what is now *VATA 1994, Sch 1 para 4* was increased. She applied for her registration to be cancelled with effect from June 1988. The Commissioners agreed to cancel her registration from 31 March 1989, but refused to backdate the cancellation. The tribunal dismissed her appeal against this decision. *S Gilmour*, EDN/90/57 (VTD 5305).

[57.128] A trader's turnover exceeded the threshold of *Sch 1 para 1* in 1987 but dropped below the threshold of what is now *VATA 1994, Sch 1 para 4* in 1990, so that although he remained entitled to be registered under what is now *VATA 1994, Sch 1 para 9*, he was no longer required to be registered under *Sch 1 para 1*. The tribunal rejected the trader's contention that his registration should be cancelled retrospectively, holding that 'a tribunal cannot decide a question of deregistration with the benefit of hindsight'. *RR Bissmire*, LON/90/1563X (VTD 7303). (*Note.* For another issue in this case, see **51.2** PENALTIES: FAILURE TO NOTIFY.)

[57.129] Similar decisions, also applying *Harvey*, 57.124 above, were reached in *RG Henderson (t/a La Coupe)*, EDN/95/67 (VTD 13469) and *P Constantine (t/a The Red Lion Inn)*, MAN/98/308 (VTD 15792).

[57.130] Similar decisions were reached in *Professor RM Young*, LON/91/2710X (VTD 7922); *AD Davidson*, LON/91/2056Z (VTD 9537); *M Jones*, LON/95/997 (VTD 13302); *J Dunhill*, MAN/93/964 (VTD 13313); *TR O'Driscoll (t/a Kitchenfit)*, MAN/95/2266 (VTD 14350); *S Moloney*, LON/96/1723 (VTD 14873); *C Bond Ltd*, EDN/97/75 (VTD 15515); *N & A Grogan (t/a Valet Plus)*, EDN/98/201 (VTD 16084); *Royal British Legion Drumnadrochit Branch*, EDN/00/58 (VTD 16957); *P Bedford*, LON/98/1081 (VTD 17085); *Chapeltown Baths Community Business Ltd*, MAN/01/558 (VTD 18142); *I & G Tindsley (t/a Padway Nurseries)*, MAN/03/592 (VTD 18571); *Goldcrest Transport Services Ltd*, MAN/03/822 (VTD 18722); *MP Dennett*, MAN/04/125 (VTD 18763); *K Savidge (t/a KCS Car Spa)*, LON/08/629 (VTD 20972); *Wessex Continental Travel Co Ltd*, [2010] UKFTT 36 (TC), TC00350; *P Vass*, [2010] UKFTT 208 (TC), TC00510, *Ms C James (t/a Ilkley Dress Agency)*, [2011] UKFTT 693 (TC), TC01535.

Voluntary registration before turnover reaching statutory threshold

[57.131] A partnership began to trade in April 1992. On the advice of their accountant, they registered for VAT from May 1992. However, their turnover had not reached the statutory threshold (and did not do so until December 1992). The accountant realised that the partnership need not have made its application for registration, and in June the partnership applied for cancellation of its registration. The Commissioners rejected the application, considering that deregistration was not appropriate as the partnership's turnover made it likely that the registration threshold would be exceeded within the next twelve months. The tribunal dismissed the partnership's appeal against this decision, holding that what is now *VATA 1994, Sch 1 para 13* did not enable the Commissioners 'to reverse a decision retroactively'. *M & P Stosic (t/a Dave & Sidas Fish Bar)*, MAN/92/1727 (VTD 10728).

[57.132] The decision in *Stosic*, 57.131 above, was applied in a case in which a couple purchased a Chinese restaurant in June 1992. The restaurant had previously been closed for some time, so that it was accepted that the transfer did not constitute the transfer of a going concern. However, the couple applied for registration with effect from the date on which they took over the restaurant. In August 1992 their accountant realised that they did not need to have registered from that date, and applied for the registration to be cancelled retrospectively. The Commissioners agreed to cancel the registration from the date on which they received this application, but refused to backdate the cancellation to June. The tribunal dismissed the couple's appeal against this decision, observing that the couple had been entitled to register under what is now *VATA 1994, Sch 1 para 9*, so that the application for registration was valid and effective until the subsequent application for cancellation. *Mr & Mrs Y Luong (t/a Golden Lion)*, [1994] VATTR 349 (VTD 12234).

[57.133] The decision in *Luong*, 57.132 above, was applied in the similar subsequent cases of *A Odell & M Ogden*, MAN/95/1436 (VTD 13512); *FL Lewis-Cox (t/a The Hair Emporium)*, MAN/96/120 (VTD 14349); *KW Weale*, MAN/96/212 (VTD 14654); *PE MacDonald*, EDN/01/02 (VTD 17326); *N Goodrich (t/a Uye Tours)*, LON/01/584 (VTD 17707), and *S Mills (t/a Steve Mills Advertising)*, EDN/03/16 (VTD 18292).

[57.134] Similar decisions were reached in *G McMenemy*, EDN/95/184 (VTD 13878); *Faimana Properties Ltd*, LON/96/375 (VTD 14600); *ST Oshitola*, LON/96/489 (VTD 15487); *Inward Treasure (UK) Ltd*, MAN/04/488 (VTD 19047) and *LH Fenning*, MAN/04/479 (VTD 19297).

[57.135] On 10 October 2000 a partnership applied for registration with effect from 1 November 2000, although its turnover had not then exceeded the statutory threshold. The Commissioners registered the partnership accordingly. Subsequently the partnership wrote to the Commissioners asking to be registered from 1 January 2001 (the date from which it was required to be registered under *VATA 1994, Sch 1*) rather than from 1 November 2000. The Commissioners rejected the request but the tribunal allowed the partnership's appeal, finding that the partnership had made 'mistakes in filling up the form (VAT1)'. The tribunal chairman (Mr. Walters) directed that the Commissioners should carry out a further review of the decision to reject the partnership's application for the cancellation of its original registration. *S Daniels & S Stevenson (t/a Homeforce)*, [2003] VATDR 591 (VTD 17948).

Delay by Customs in processing application

[57.136] A restaurant proprietor (M) applied for registration for VAT in July 2001, although his turnover had not then exceeded the statutory threshold. His turnover remained well below the threshold, and in July 2002 he submitted a form VAT7 applying to cancel his registration from 1 August 2002. Customs did not acknowledge the VAT7 until December 2002, when they wrote to M asking him to telephone them. After further correspondence, they agreed to cancel his registration from 1 December 2002. M appealed, contending that he should not be required to account for VAT on his supplies from 1 August to 30 November. The tribunal accepted this contention and allowed his appeal, holding that 'the appellant should have been deregistered with effect from 1 August 2002 which was the date which the appellant had actually asked for'. *L Migliore*, MAN/03/584 (VTD 18692).

Mistaken application for registration before turnover reaching threshold

[57.137] The proprietor of a Chinese restaurant registered for VAT in July 2001. In February 2002 she applied to cancel her registration, on the basis that her turnover had never exceeded the statutory threshold. The Commissioners agreed to cancel her registration from 1 March, but refused to backdate the cancellation. The tribunal allowed the proprietor's appeal, holding that the registration should be treated as void. The chairman commented that the proprietor spoke poor English and 'was clearly confused when she applied for the first registration'. The proprietor had signed a form in September 2001 which showed that her turnover was well below the statutory threshold. The tribunal held that 'given that position and the appellant's lack of grasp of the English language', the Commissioners 'could not have been satisfied that this was a voluntary request by the appellant to register for VAT purposes. Had they gone to the trouble of asking her, it would have been clear, as it is from the evidence, that she believed she had to register'. The registration was 'not a voluntary act' and 'was not properly constituted'. *YM Yeung (t/a Golden House)*, MAN/02/405 (VTD 18017).

[57.138] A company (M) was incorporated in July 2006 and began trading in November 2006. On 29 November its bookkeeper submitted an electronic form VAT1, applying for immediate voluntary registration for VAT. However M's controlling director had only intended to register for VAT from 1 March 2007. M's accountants wrote to HMRC asking them to correct their records accordingly. HMRC treated the letter as an application to amend the effective date of registration, and refused to accept it. M appealed. The tribunal allowed the appeal in part, applying the earlier decision in *Daniels & Stevenson (t/a Homeforce)*, 57.135 above. The tribunal observed that 'the average person "on the Clapham omnibus" would not be expected to know that the only way permitted by statute to change/amend an effective date of registration to some future date was to apply for the original registration to be cancelled and re-registration with the future date to take place'. The tribunal held that HMRC's decision to treat M's application as a request to amend the effective date of registration was flawed 'in that it did not take into account that effectively the Appellant was endeavouring to cancel the original registration and re-register with an effective date of registration of 1 March'. The tribunal directed that M's application should 'be reviewed by an officer or officers without any previous involvement with this appeal'. *Modified Gumball Rally Ltd (t/a Modball Ltd)*, [2009] UKFTT 250 (TC), TC00198.

Registered business acquired as going concern

[57.139] See *Rana*, 57.18 above, and the cases noted at 57.19 above.

Anticipated future change in rating of supplies

[57.140] In January 1998 an osteopathy partnership applied for cancellation of its registration, on the basis that the partners had arranged to be registered under the *Osteopaths Act 1993*, and that their supplies would subsequently become exempt under *VATA 1994, Sch 9, Group 7*. The Commissioners rejected the application, on the basis that the partnership's services were still standard-rated at the relevant time. The tribunal dismissed the partnership's appeal, holding that the Commissioners had not acted unreasonably. *RN & BA Lloyd*, MAN/98/307 (VTD 15786). (*Note. VATA 1994, Sch 9, Group 7* was amended by the *VAT (Osteopaths) Order 1998* to provide for the exemption of supplies by registered osteopaths with effect from 12 June 1998. The Commissioners agreed to backdate exemption to 9 May 1998 by extra-statutory concession.)

[57.141] A similar decision was reached in *MG Duffree*, MAN/98/231 (VTD 15793).

[57.142] The decisions in *Lloyd*, 57.140 above, and *Duffree*, 57.141 above, were applied in the similar subsequent case of *RG Wadsworth*, MAN/98/762 (VTD 16128).

Time at which application for cancellation of registration made

[57.143] A married couple had registered for VAT in February 2004, although their turnover had never exceeded the statutory threshold. They only submitted one VAT return, for the period ending May 2004. The business ceased trading in December 2005. Customs subsequently issued an assessment charging VAT for the period to the cessation of the business. The couple appealed, contending that they had applied for deregistration at the time when they submitted their return for the period ending May 2004, as that they had realised that their turnover would not exceed the threshold. The tribunal accepted their evidence and allowed the appeal. *MJ & Mrs G Casban (t/a Lounge)*, LON/06/1399 (VTD 20469).

Registration cancelled by Commissioners (VATA 1994, Sch 1 para 13(2))

Cancellation of one of two registrations—whether appealable

[57.144] A trader carried on two separate businesses and obtained separate registration numbers for each. When the Commissioners discovered this, they cancelled one of the registrations. The trader appealed. The tribunal dismissed his appeal, holding that 'the practice of the Commissioners of only registering the same individual once, even if he is carrying on more than one separate business activity, conforms with the requirements of the law'. The tribunal also held that there was no appealable matter within what is now *VATA 1994, s 83(a)*, since the remaining registration number covered both businesses. *KN Weakley*, LON/73/142 (VTD 56).

Appeal against retrospective cancellation of registration

[57.145] See *Brookes*, 2.49 APPEALS.

Group registration—appeal against cancellation of separate registration

[57.146] See *Eastwood Care Homes (Ilkeston) Ltd*, 32.7 GROUPS OF COM-PANIES.

Registration but no business carried on

[57.147] In 1995 a company purchased some land and registered for VAT under *VATA 1994, Sch 1 para 9*. It reclaimed input tax on the land. It did not make any taxable supplies and did not respond to correspondence from the Commissioners. In 1999 the Commissioners cancelled the company's registration. The company appealed, contending that it still intended to develop the land. The tribunal reviewed the evidence, rejected this contention and dismissed the appeal. Applying *Associated Provincial Picture Houses v Wednesbury Corporation, CA 1947*, [1948] 1 KB 223; [1947] 2 All ER 680, the tribunal's jurisdiction was supervisory. The Commissioners' decision had been 'entirely reasonable'. *DCM Leisure Ltd*, MAN/00/323 (VTD 16966). (*Note*. The tribunal also upheld an assessment under *Sch 4 para 8*—see **67.24** VALUATION.)

[57.148] In 2002 a company (L) registered for VAT. It subsequently failed to submit VAT returns, or to allow a VAT officer to inspect its records. The Commissioners cancelled its registration, on the basis that it was not carrying on a business. L appealed, contending that it was carrying on a business of dealing in mobile telephones. The tribunal reviewed the evidence and dismissed L's appeal, finding that the company's director (W) had attempted 'to conceal his and (L's) whereabouts from the Commissioners'. The tribunal also found that L 'appears, unwittingly, to have dealt in telephones designed to be used in Arabic-speaking countries. This disclosure evidently surprised (W), who could not explain why (L) should have bought such goods nor why it should fail — as it evidently did — to inform its customer of the unusual specification.' Furthermore, L had never made 'any effort to move the goods, either by taking them from its supplier and putting them into safe storage, or in delivering them to its customer'. The tribunal held that the Commissioners' decision to cancel L's registration was reasonable. There was 'ample evidence to support (the) view that (L) was not engaged in any genuine business venture'. On the evidence, the VAT officer 'was right to conclude that the "business" was a sham, designed to create a paper trail'. It was inconceivable that 'any legitimate businessman would buy and sell goods which, though supposedly satisfying a demand in the retail market, never moved from a warehouse, and whose existence he never verified, and that he would happily disclose to his customers the identity of his own suppliers, with the risk that he would be by-passed.' *Innova Inc (UK) Ltd*, MAN/04/1620 (VTD 18989).

[57.149] In an Isle of Man case, two associated companies registered for VAT and reclaimed input tax. The Manx Treasury rejected the claims and cancelled the companies' registrations on the basis that the companies were not carrying on any business. The companies appealed, contending that they intended to carry on a business of dealing in MP3 players. The tribunal dismissed the appeals, finding that the evidence which the companies had 'produced to support the claim of a continuing intention to trade is not merely unconvincing; it was in our view quite obviously manufactured for no other purpose than to support that claim'. *Gillamoor Ltd v Isle of Man Treasury*, MAN/07/623; *Airdre Ltd v Isle of Man Treasury*, MAN/07/624 (VTD 20591).

[57.150] In 2005 an individual (M), who was in full-time employment, registered for VAT, stating on form VAT 1 that he was carrying on a business of 'art history lecturing'. He subsequently submitted VAT returns reclaiming input tax without declaring any output tax. Following a visit by a VAT officer, Customs cancelled his registration on the basis that he 'was neither liable nor entitled to be registered'. The tribunal dismissed M's appeal, holding on the evidence that 'Customs were correct in their decision to remove (M) from the VAT register'. *J Miah*, LON/07/0127 (VTD 20684).

[57.151] In January 2008 an individual (S) registered for VAT, stating that he was carrying on a business of IT consultancy services. He subsequently submitted a return claiming a repayment of more than £190,000. Customs formed the opinion that his input tax claims were fictitious and that he was not in fact carrying on any business, and cancelled his registration. S appealed, contending that he had engaged in 'constructive accounting'. The tribunal reviewed the evidence in detail and dismissed his appeal, finding that S had engaged in 'a startlingly unsubtle raid on the Exchequer which stood no chance of succeeding', and that in reality he 'was not conducting business at all'. *KA Singh (t/a Borealis)*, LON/08/1532 (VTD 20956).

[57.152] In June 2007 an individual (G) registered for VAT. He submitted several VAT returns claiming repayments. His first return included a figure for output tax, relating to sales of some T shirts. His subsequent returns did not declare any output tax liability. In June 2008 Customs formed the opinion that

G was not carrying on any business, and cancelled his registration. The tribunal upheld Customs' ruling and dismissed G's appeal. *NN Gayle*, LON/08/1012 (VTD 20982).

[57.153] A company was incorporated in 2007 and registered for VAT later that year. In February 2008 it issued an invoice to an associated company in respect of 'sales and marketing consultancy services'. It did not issue any subsequent invoices, although it submitted VAT returns claiming repayments of input tax. HMRC subsequently formed the opinion that the company was not carrying on any business, and cancelled its registration. The tribunal upheld HMRC's ruling and dismissed the company's appeal. *Shadow Photographic Ltd v HMRC*, [2010] UKFTT 467 (TC), TC00729.

[57.154] A similar decision was reached in *System Fabricators Ltd v Director of Border Revenue*, [2011] UKFTT 436 (TC), TC01289.

[57.155] A woman (L) registered for VAT in 2004, stating that she intended to carry on a business of property development. She subsequently reclaimed input tax of more than £65,000, but did not account for any output tax. In 2008 HMRC cancelled her registration on the grounds that she was not carrying on any business, and issued assessments to recover the input tax which L had reclaimed. L appealed. The tribunal reviewed the evidence in detail and dismissed her appeal, finding that she had never carried on a business. *P Lee v HMRC*, [2010] UKFTT 520 (TC), TC00775.

[57.156] See also *Three H Aircraft Hire*, 7.7 BUSINESS; *Blandy*, 7.28 BUSINESS; *Tibbs*, 7.34 BUSINESS; *Berwick*, 7.45 BUSINESS; *McDonald*, 7.46 BUSINESS; *Kelly*, 7.51 BUSINESS; *Higson*, 7.70 BUSINESS; *Newmir plc*, 7.116 BUSINESS, and *Ladbroke (Palace Gate) Property Services Ltd*, 7.119 BUSINESS.

Cancellation of registration—whether appellant carrying on a business

[57.157] A builder (G) registered for VAT in 1973. He was made bankrupt in 2004. He completed VAT returns showing no input or output tax from July 2004 to December 2008, but in 2009 he reclaimed input tax of more than £10,000. HMRC rejected the claim on the basis that G was no longer carrying on any business, and also issued a notice cancelling his registration from 20 August 2009. G appealed, contending that he was still intending to resume his building business, and had agreed a contract to build a new house. The tribunal accepted this contention and allowed his appeal against the cancellation of his registration. Judge Walters held that although G had made no taxable supplies since 2004, he was carrying on a business in August 2009 and was intending to make supplies in the course or furtherance of that business. (He noted that some of the input tax which G had claimed did not appear to be attributable to the business, and directed that the appeal against the disallowance of input tax should be adjourned for six months in the hope that the parties could reach an agreement.) *M Gardner (t/a Gardner & Co) v HMRC*, [2011] UKFTT 470 (TC), TC01320.

[57.158] For other successful appeals against the cancellation of registration, in cases where the issue was whether the appellant was carrying on a business, see *Border Flying Co*, 7.48 BUSINESS; *Prenn*, 7.57 BUSINESS; *Jenks*, 7.75 BUSINESS; *Bird Racing (Management) Ltd*, 7.97 BUSINESS, and *Merseyside Cablevision Ltd*, 36.554 INPUT TAX.

Supplies of transport within EU

[57.159] In 1993 a Swiss company (S) registered for UK VAT, on the basis that it was making supplies of transport within the UK. In May 2005 Customs cancelled its registration on the grounds that it was not making any supplies within the UK. S appealed, contending that it was supplying 'relevant services' within *VAT (Place of Supply of Services) Order 1992 (SI 1992/3121), reg 14*. The tribunal accepted this contention and allowed the appeal. The tribunal chairman (Mr. Shipwright) observed that S had never 'ceased to be liable to be registered' within *VATA 1994, Sch 1 para 3*. He expressed the view that Customs could have cancelled S's registration with the effect from the date of registration (ie 1993) by virtue of *VATA 1994, Sch 1 para 13(3)*. However *para 13(3)* did not empower Customs to cancel the registration with effect from a subsequent date. *Satis Italsempione SA*, LON/05/715 (VTD 19683). (*Note*. Some of the statutory references in Mr. Shipwright's decision are incorrect. He refers to *paragraphs 10* and *14* of *VATA 1994, Sch 5* when he apparently intends to refer to *regulations 10* and *14* of the *VAT (Place of Supply of Services) Order 1992 (SI 1992/3121)*: there is no *paragraph 14* in *VATA 1994, Sch 5*.)

Registration but all supplies exempt from VAT

[57.160] In 1985 two people acquired premises in Hull, which had been used as bedsitting accommodation for students. They converted the premises for use as a residential home for the elderly. In December 1985 they applied for registration for VAT. In January 1986 they were registered under the *Registered Homes Act 1984*. In February 1986 the Commissioners cancelled their VAT registration, on the basis that all their supplies were exempt under what is now *VATA 1994, Sch 9, Group 7, Item 4*. The proprietors appealed, contending that the cancellation should not be retrospective (and that they should therefore be allowed to reclaim input tax on the conversion work). The tribunal rejected this contention and dismissed their appeal, holding that they had never been entitled to be registered and that their registration 'was not a valid registration'. *DR Bramley & MA Bradley*, [1987] VATTR 72 (VTD 2349).

[57.161] A similar decision was reached in *MV Wright*, LON/94/196A (VTD 12701).

[57.162] A property company (B) applied to be registered for VAT on the basis that it intended to make a zero-rated supply of a building (and wished to reclaim VAT on the conversion work). The Commissioners ascertained that the building was not a 'non-residential building' as defined in *VATA 1994, Sch 8, Group 5*, so that any supplies made by B would be exempt from VAT. They therefore cancelled B's registration under *VATA 1994, Sch 1 para 13*. The tribunal upheld the Commissioners' decision and dismissed B's appeal. *Beverley Properties Ltd*, LON/02/710 (VTD 18232).

[57.163] A similar decision was reached in *J Palfry & JD Rodzian*, MAN/03/330 (VTD 18465).

[57.164] See also *Steven*, 33.34 HEALTH AND WELFARE, and *Llanfyllin Group Practice*, 57.169 below.

Registration cancelled following sale of business

[57.165] In 1985 an individual (R) purchased some land, which he intended to develop as a timber estate. He registered for VAT as an 'intending trader', although he had not begun to make taxable supplies and was not likely to do so for some time. During the next four years he reclaimed substantial amounts of input tax. He faced financial problems, and in 1989 he sold the land to trustees. The Commissioners cancelled his registration, and issued an assessment to recover the input tax which he had reclaimed. The tribunal allowed R's appeal against the assessment. On the evidence, R had sold a quantity of stone from the land in 1987, and this was a taxable supply. Furthermore, although the sale of the land was an exempt supply, R had also sold a quantity of fertiliser to the trustees, and this too constituted a taxable supply. Since R had made two taxable supplies, the Commissioners were not entitled to require repayment of the input tax which he had previously incurred. *D Rye*, MAN/90/158 (VTD 7578).

Registration cancelled following cessation of business

[57.166] An insurance broker (T) had been registered for VAT as a partly exempt trader since 1973. At a control visit in July 1990, a VAT officer formed the impression that T had not made any taxable supplies since December 1988. T disagreed with this, contending that he had made a taxable supply in the period ending 30 June 1990. Nevertheless, the Commissioners issued an assessment to recover the input tax which T had reclaimed for the periods between 1 January 1989 and 30 June 1990. The Commissioners also cancelled T's registration with effect from 1 July 1990. In January 1991 the case was reviewed by a senior VAT officer, who decided that the disputed assessment would have to be withdrawn since T had only been deregistered with effect from July 1990. T was therefore notified that the assessment was being withdrawn. In August 1991 the Commissioners wrote to T again, requesting him to refund the input tax which had previously been assessed; and in September 1991 the Commissioners issued a further notice retrospectively cancelling T's registration for the period from 1 January 1989 to 30 June 1990. T appealed against the retrospective deregistration and the demand for tax, contending firstly that the Commissioners had acted unreasonably in renewing their demand for the tax after having withdrawn the original assessments, and additionally that he had made a taxable supply in June 1990, so that he was entitled to remain registered until 30 June 1990. The tribunal adjourned the hearing for further argument, but severely criticised the Commissioners for their handling of the case, observing that the original assessment appeared to have been withdrawn by agreement under what is now *VATA 1994, s 85*, and that the Commissioners were in effect attempting 'having lost the match, (to) move the goalposts and demand a replay'. *M Tourick (t/a RM Tourick & Co)*, LON/91/1938Y (VTD 7712). (*Note.* There was no further public hearing of the appeal.)

Exemption from registration (VATA 1994, Sch 1 para 14)

[**57.167**] The proprietor of a restaurant and 'take-away' food shop had applied to be registered for VAT, but discovered that most of her supplies were zero-rated under the legislation then in force, so that she was usually entitled to a repayment of input tax. She applied for exemption from registration under what is now *VATA 1994, Sch 1 para 14*. The Commissioners rejected her application and she appealed. The tribunal allowed her appeal against this decision, holding that it had jurisdiction to consider how the Commissioners' powers under *Sch 1 para 14* should be exercised, and that 'the test should be whether or not the grant of exemption is in the interests of the revenue'. On the evidence, the refusal of the application would be unreasonable, since 'we cannot conceive it to be in the interests of the Revenue to retain a repayment trader as a taxable person against his or her wishes'. *TK Fong*, [1978] VATTR 75 (VTD 590).

[**57.168**] A builder had registered for VAT in 1988. Following a decline in his turnover, he deregistered in September 1991. However, in February and March 1992 his turnover increased significantly as a result of a short-term contract, and he again became liable to register. However, he failed to do so. The contract in question finished at the end of March, and his monthly turnover dropped to around £3,000. In September 1992, on the advice of his accountants, he made a retrospective application for exemption from registration under what is now *VATA 1994, Sch 1 para 14*. The Commissioners rejected the application and the tribunal dismissed his appeal against this decision. In view of his turnover in February and March, the builder had become liable to register from 1 May 1992. The tribunal's jurisdiction on applications under *Sch 1 para 14* was supervisory, rather than appellate. Since the builder's turnover from April to August 1992 had continued to average £3,000 per month (at a time when the registration threshold was an annual turnover of £36,600), the Commissioners had not acted unreasonably in deciding that he should not be exempted from registration. *PT Sullivan (t/a Property Trade Services)*, LON/92/3331P (VTD 10349). (*Note.* An appeal against a penalty under what is now *VATA 1994, s 67* was also dismissed.)

[**57.169**] A medical partnership, which had not been registered from VAT, applied in 1995 for exemption from registration under *VATA 1994, Sch 1 para 14*. The Commissioners accepted the application. Subsequently, in January 1997, the partnership applied to be registered retrospectively from April 1992, and submitted a claim for repayment of input tax. The Commissioners agreed to register the partnership from January 1997, but, in view of the partnership's previous application for exemption, refused to backdate the registration to 1992, and refused to repay input tax which the partnership had incurred from April 1992 to January 1997. The tribunal dismissed the partnership's appeal, applying the decision in *Bramley & Bradley*, **57.165** above. *Llanfyllin Group Practice*, MAN/98/703 (VTD 16156).

The person by whom the business is carried on

NOTE

For cases concerning whether a business is operated in partnership, see **47.17** *et seq.* PARTNERSHIP. For cases concerning the identity of the person making specific supplies, see **62.330** *et seq.* SUPPLY.

Cases where the appellant was unsuccessful

Sale of cars

[57.170] The wife of an undischarged bankrupt carried on a small business of making car number plates. She employed her husband and son in this business. Her husband had previously been self-employed as a car dealer, and after his bankruptcy he continued to arrange for the buying and selling of cars. The wife paid for the purchase of cars for resale, and also paid for advertisements, but left the actual purchases and sales entirely to her husband. She did not account for VAT on the cars sold, and Customs issued an assessment charging tax on them. She appealed, contending that the car dealing was a separate business carried on by her husband. The tribunal rejected this contention and dismissed her appeal, holding that the wife was 'responsible for the carrying on of the business'. *PO Wood*, LON/80/317 (VTD 1037).

Hotel

[57.171] The proprietor of a small hotel failed to register for VAT. Customs issued a notice of compulsory registration, and he appealed, contending that the management of the hotel was delegated to three separate companies, one of which supplied the accommodation, one of which supplied the food, and one of which ran the bar. The tribunal rejected his contentions and dismissed his appeal. *APG McGuire*, LON/82/22 (VTD 1305).

Public house

[57.172] A company which operated a public house failed to register for VAT. Customs issued a notice of compulsory registration, and the company appealed, contending that it was merely acting as an agent for a number of Panamanian companies which operated the public house successively. The tribunal rejected the company's evidence and dismissed the appeal. *Blusins Ltd*, EDN/96/195 (VTD 15119).

Catering at public house

[57.173] See *J & S Smith*, **47.26** PARTNERSHIP; *Fraser & Fraser*, **47.27** PARTNERSHIP; *J & A Smith*, **47.27** PARTNERSHIP; *Ashcroft*, **47.27** PARTNERSHIP; *Brown*, **62.297** SUPPLY; *Davies*, **62.298** SUPPLY, and *Allen (t/a The Shovel)*, **62.299** SUPPLY.

Catering at hotel

[57.174] See *Albert*, **62.301** SUPPLY, and *Cherry*, **62.302** SUPPLY.

Manager acting for non-resident

[57.175] The owner of a property conveyancing business registered for VAT in 1983. In 1984 he emigrated to Spain and delegated the running of the business to a manager. Customs issued a notice of compulsory registration to the manager. He appealed, contending that he could not be registered since he was not the legal owner of the business. The tribunal rejected this contention and dismissed his appeal, holding that he was making supplies of conveyancing services and that Customs were entitled to register him. *RJ Culverhouse*, LON/86/125 (VTD 2130).

Restaurant

[57.176] A company which owned a hotel and restaurant applied to be deregistered on the basis that it no longer operated the restaurant. The application was accepted, but a Customs officer subsequently discovered that the restaurant business had continued. Customs issued a notice of compulsory registration to the company. The company appealed, contending that the wife of the principal director had taken over the restaurant as a separate business and that there was insufficient turnover for her to register for VAT. The tribunal dismissed the appeal, finding that the wife was not the proprietor of the business but that the restaurant had at all times been run by the company. *Waterwynch House Ltd*, LON/87/505 (VTD 2734).

[57.177] A similar decision was reached in a case where the tribunal upheld Customs' contentions that a fish and chip shop and an Indian restaurant operating from adjacent premises were both run by the same individual (U), and rejected U's contention that the Indian restaurant was a separate business operated by his common law wife. *DS Uppal (t/a Mr Chips)*, MAN/94/512 (VTD 14074).

[57.178] A trader (N) owned two restaurants, and was registered for VAT. Customs discovered that he had not accounted for VAT on the takings of one of the restaurants, and issued an assessment. N appealed, contending that he had leased that restaurant to another individual (K), and that K should be treated as responsible for the unpaid VAT. The tribunal rejected this contention and dismissed N's appeal, finding that K had been appointed to act as manager of the restaurant but that N remained liable for the VAT liability. *B Noudoost-Beni*, MAN/00/563 (VTD 17625).

[57.179] Customs issued an assessment on the registered proprietor of a restaurant. He appealed, contending that he had transferred the restaurant to another trader. The tribunal reviewed the evidence, rejected this contention, and dismissed the appeal. *M Bozdag*, LON/00/1276 (VTD 17787).

[57.180] Customs issued an assessment on a company, charging tax on the takings of a restaurant. The company appealed, contending that the restaurant had actually been operated by a former director, who had subsequently emigrated. The tribunal dismissed the appeal, finding that the company had registered for VAT and operated the restaurant. *Casa Frattini Ltd*, LON/06/1402 (VTD 20645).

Shop selling take-away food

[57.181] Customs issued an assessment on an individual (S), who had registered for VAT as the proprietor of a fish and chip shop. S appealed, contending that he had registered in error and that the business was actually carried on by his wife. The tribunal dismissed the appeal, finding that the business was carried on by S. *S Sajawal*, MAN/92/428 (VTD 10971).

[57.182] See also *Ezzi-Irani*, 52.300 PENALTIES: MISDECLARATION.

[57.183] Customs issued an assessment on a couple who had registered for VAT as the proprietors of a kebab shop. They appealed, contending that they only operated the shop on four days each week, and that for the other three days it was operated by a licencee. The tribunal rejected this contention and dismissed their appeal, finding that there was a single business which was operated by the couple. *L & A Eleftheriou (t/a Picnic Kebab House)*, MAN/99/13 (VTD 16659).

Computer consultant

[57.184] A computer engineer provided consultancy services for a company (F), charging £500 per week. In 1983 he began working for another company (T) but still continued to supply some services to F until 1984. He was treated as self-employed for income tax purposes. In 1987 Customs issued a ruling that he had been liable to register for VAT with effect from 1982. He appealed, accepting that he had become liable to register in 1982 but contending that he had ceased to be liable in 1983 because he had become an employee of T. The tribunal rejected this contention and dismissed his appeal, finding that he was self-employed and was not employed by T. *AJ Scott*, LON/87/713 (VTD 2926). (*Note.* An appeal against a penalty for failure to register was also dismissed.)

Salesman

[57.185] In 1987 an individual (S) entered into an agreement with a company (K) which sold kitchen units. The agreement stated that S was self-employed, and that 'nothing in this agreement shall be construed as giving rise to the relationship of employer and employee'. S also undertook to pay all VAT due. In 1988 S and K entered into a new agreement described as a contract of employment, which took effect on 1 July. S failed to register for VAT. Customs issued a notice of registration, and an assessment charging tax on the amounts paid before July 1988. S appealed, contending that, despite the wording of the 1987 agreement, he had in fact been an employee of K since January 1987. The tribunal rejected this contention and dismissed the appeal, finding that before July 1988 S's 'relationship with K was that of an independent contractor'. *J Sullivan*, MAN/90/94 (VTD 5881). (*Note.* An appeal against a penalty for failure to register was also dismissed.)

Individual providing services to import company

[57.186] Customs discovered that an individual (B), who was not registered for VAT, had received significant sums from a company (D) which imported drinks, and which had subsequently gone into liquidation. They issued a notice of compulsory registration to B, and an assessment charging VAT on the sums he had received. B appealed, contending that he had been an employee of D, which had paid him 'to assess the drinks market and advise (D) on purchases of stocks of drink for sale'. One of D's employees gave evidence that D had paid B to introduce it to 'missing traders', and had treated B as self-employed. The tribunal reviewed the evidence in detail and dismissed B's appeal, finding that he had been 'carrying on business on his own account' and had been required to register for VAT. *T Bashir*, LON/04/1348 (VTD 19295).

Franchise agreement

[57.187] Customs registered an individual (D) on the basis that he was operating a buffet at a railway station. He appealed, contending that he only sold food and that the sale of liquid refreshments was a separate business carried out by another trader. The tribunal dismissed the appeal, finding that the relevant franchise agreement showed that D was responsible for the sale of both food and drink. *D Duwel*, LON/88/703Y (VTD 3483).

[57.188] Customs registered an individual (E) on the basis that he was the franchisee of a warehouse, and was therefore a 'taxable person'. E appealed, contending that he was an employee rather than a franchisee. The tribunal dismissed his appeal, finding that he was acting as a franchisee and was required to be registered for VAT. *DR Evans*, LON/94/409A (VTD 13290).

Retail shops

[57.189] A married couple was registered for VAT as the proprietors of four retail shops. Customs discovered that there had been underdeclarations of takings, and issued an assessment. The couple appealed, contending that the registration had been made in error because three of the shops were run by their sons. The tribunal dismissed the appeal, finding that 'no written evidence was produced to justify the assertion that the businesses were separate and independent'. *MA Shad (Newsagents)*, EDN/94/133 (VTD 13145).

[57.190] See also *Tang & Tang (t/a Ziploc)*, **47.31** PARTNERSHIP.

Market stall

[57.191] Customs issued a notice of compulsory registration to a market trader, on the basis that his income from three market stalls exceeded the registration threshold. He appealed, contending that he only operated two of the stalls, and that the third stall was a separate business operated by his wife. The tribunal rejected this contention and dismissed his appeal, finding that all three stalls were part of his business. *L Bennett*, LON/04/2287 (VTD 19305).

Launderette

[57.192] Customs issued an assessment on a trader (S), charging tax on the takings of a launderette and a fish-and-chip shop. He appealed, accepting that he was the proprietor of the fish-and-chip shop, but contending that the launderette was operated by his wife. The tribunal rejected this contention and dismissed his appeal, finding that S was the proprietor of both businesses. *RS Sahota*, MAN/96/379 (VTD 14986).

Taxi and car hire

[57.193] See *Hughes & Hughes*, **47.22** PARTNERSHIP, and *Brough*, **47.28** PARTNERSHIP.

Hairdressing salons

[57.194] In 1996 a hairdresser (C), who had been registered for VAT since 1985, applied for his registration to be cancelled on the basis that three stylists working at his premises were working as independent contractors and were supplying their services directly to the customers. Customs rejected the application and issued assessments charging tax on the full amount of the takings, on the basis that the services at the salon were still being supplied by C, and the fact that the stylists were self-employed was not conclusive. The tribunal upheld the assessments and dismissed C's appeal. *K Colby*, MAN/98/314 (VTD 16387).

[57.195] A company which owned several hairdressing salons failed to register for VAT. Customs issued a notice of compulsory registration, and the company appealed, contending that the supplies at the salons were made by the individual hairdressers and that the income which the stylists retained did not form part of its turnover. The tribunal rejected this contention and dismissed the appeal. *SFU Barbers Ltd*, MAN/04/7012 (VTD 19851). (*Note*. The tribunal also dismissed an appeal against a notice requiring security, and awarded costs to Customs, finding that the appeal was 'without merit'.)

[57.196] See also *Jane Montgomery (Hair Stylists) Ltd*, **62.255** SUPPLY, and the cases noted at **62.256** to **62.263** SUPPLY.

Sale of hairdressing products

[57.197] Two people who operated a hairdressing salon in partnership failed to register for VAT. Customs issued a notice of compulsory registration, and the partners appealed, contending that part of the relevant turnover related to the sale of hairdressing products, which was a separate business carried on by one of the partners as a sole trader. The tribunal rejected this contention and dismissed the appeal, holding that there was a single business carried on by the partnership. *P Bear & S Hill*, MAN/98/554 (VTD 17215). (*Note*. An appeal against a penalty for failure to register was also dismissed.)

Construction services

[57.198] Customs issued a notice of compulsory registration to a trader in the construction industry. He appealed, contending that his turnover was below the registration threshold and that some of the supplies which Customs had treated as made by him had in fact been made by a limited company which he controlled. The tribunal reviewed the evidence in detail, rejected this contention, and dismissed his appeal. *VA Noades*, LON/00/210 (VTD 17152). (*Note*. For another issue in this case, see **51.146** PENALTIES: FAILURE TO NOTIFY.)

Car washing at petrol stations

[57.199] A company (G) operated several petrol stations, at two of which it offered car washing services. It did not account for tax on this income, and Customs issued an assessment. G appealed, contending that the car washing was a separate business operated by one of its directors. The tribunal rejected this contention and dismissed the appeal, applying the principles laid down in *Burrell*, **47.41** PARTNERSHIP. *Gateacre Park Motor Co Ltd*, MAN/01/873 (VTD 17921).

Wholesale florist

[57.200] In 2002 a woman (W) registered for VAT as a wholesale florist. In 2005 Customs discovered that the business appeared to have overclaimed input tax and underdeclared output tax. They issued assessments. W appealed, contending that the business was actually operated by her son. The tribunal dismissed the appeal, finding that W was the owner of the business. *Mrs E Williams (t/a Premier Flowers)*, MAN/06/416 (VTD 20639).

Letting of garages

[57.201] See *King*, 62.332 SUPPLY.

Cases where the appellant was successful

Company establishing trust—whether separate registrations required

[57.202] The British Institute of Management was formed in 1947 as a company limited by guarantee. In 1976 it established a charitable trust (the Foundation), with the Institute as its sole trustee. The Commissioners considered that the Institute's existing registration for VAT could not cover the activities of the Foundation, and issued a ruling that a separate registration was required. The tribunal allowed the Institute's appeal against this decision, holding that the activities of the Foundation were part of the activities of the Institute. Part of the Institute's services were supplied through the Foundation, and, as sole trustee, it carried on the Foundation's business in the course of its own business. *British Institute of Management (No 1)*, [1978] VATTR 101 (VTD 565).

Restaurant operated under 'franchise' agreement

[57.203] From 1979 to January 1981 two women (N and Y) operated a restaurant. In January 1981 they entered into an agreement, described as a franchise agreement, with the head waiter (M). Under the agreement, M paid N a sum varying between £350 and £400 each week, and N assisted M with the bookkeeping. In 1984 M died, having failed to account for VAT in respect of the restaurant's takings. The Commissioners issued an assessment to recover the tax from N and Y. They appealed, contending that the effect of the agreement was that M had operated the business from January 1981 until his death. The QB accepted this contention and allowed the appeal. Simon Brown J held that the agreements provided M 'with the opportunity of running the business precisely as he wished and entirely for his own benefit, albeit of course upon a substantial fixed weekly payment to (N)'. *TS & Y Nasim (t/a Yasmine Restaurant) v C & E Commrs*, QB [1987] STC 387.

Take-away restaurant—by whom operated

[57.204] A partnership, which was registered for VAT, had operated a take-away burger restaurant and a take-away Indian restaurant from adjacent premises. It sold the lease of the premises to an individual (G). Following the sale, G's son took over the burger restaurant and was registered for VAT. G's wife took over the Indian restaurant and applied for deregistration on the basis that her turnover was below the registration threshold. A VAT officer visited the premises and formed the opinion that both businesses were being run by G's son. He issued an assessment to G's son, charging output tax on the sales made from the Indian restaurant. The tribunal allowed the son's appeal, finding on the evidence that he was only operating the burger restaurant, and that the Indian restaurant was being run as a separate business by G's wife. *B Ghafoor*, LON/94/462A (VTD 13329).

Adjacent take-away restaurants—whether operated by same partnership

[57.205] In the case noted at **3.140** ASSESSMENT, a married couple had owned two adjacent shops, both of which were used as take-away restaurants. They registered for VAT from November 1998. One of the restaurants mainly sold fish and chips, while the other mainly sold chicken and kebabs. The Commissioners issued a notice of registration on the basis that the two restaurants had constituted a single business for VAT purposes since 1996, carried on by the couple and their son. They appealed, contending that from 1996 to October 1998 the son had only been a partner in the fish and chip shop and had not been a partner in the shop selling chicken and kebabs. They gave evidence that they had intended to involve their daughter in this business, but she had emigrated to Spain in 1998 and they had merged the shops following her emigration. The tribunal accepted their evidence and allowed the appeal. *DJ, J & S Plummer*, MAN/99/589 (VTD 16976).

Mexican restaurant in 'function suite' of 'traditional' restaurant

[57.206] A company (G) operated a bar and restaurant from premises in Dundee. The restaurant sold 'traditional' food. Its head chef (S) had developed an interest in Mexican food. After negotiation, he persuaded G to allow him to operate a separate Mexican restaurant, as a sole trader, from a function suite at the premises. Initially S did not register for VAT on the grounds that his turnover from the Mexican restaurant was below the registration threshold, but he registered subsequently after his turnover had increased. When the Commissioners discovered the arrangements, a VAT officer issued two letters, the first directing that the two restaurants should be treated as a 'single entity' (albeit not specifically referring to *VATA 1994, Sch 1 para 2*) and the second described as a 'notice of assessment', albeit not specifying an amount. G and S appealed. The tribunal reviewed the evidence in detail and allowed their appeals. The tribunal chairman strongly criticised the VAT officer responsible for the decisions for her ignorance of the law, describing one of the letters which she had issued as 'vexatious and unwarranted', and 'designed to distress and intimidate'. The tribunal held that 'the substance and reality showed (that) two businesses existed'. Although the arrangements between G and S were 'unusual', there was 'a normal commercial relationship which was at arm's length'. *George Kerr Enterprises Ltd; B Sinclair*, EDN/02/59 (VTD 18079).

Fish and chip shop—by whom operated

[**57.207**] A married couple opened a café in 1995, but did not register for VAT as their turnover was below the registration threshold. In 1996 the husband purchased a second-hand fryer and began to sell fish and chips. Subsequently the Commissioners registered the couple on the basis that their turnover had exceeded the threshold. They appealed, contending that the sales of fish and chips were a separate business carried on by the husband as an individual. The tribunal accepted this contention and allowed the appeal, observing that there were separate menus and separate financial arrangements. *BR & JG Parker (t/a Sea Breeze Café)*, LON/98/1284 (VTD 16350).

Catering at public house—whether separate business

[**57.208**] See *Potts*, 62.296 SUPPLY.

Associated partnerships operating hotel and holiday flats in same road

[**57.209**] In 1987 a married couple purchased a hotel. In 1994 their son and son-in-law purchased a house, divided into holiday flats, on the opposite side of the same road. The turnover of each partnership was below the registration threshold. In 1999 the Commissioners issued a ruling that the two couples formed a single partnership which was carrying on a single business for VAT purposes and should be registered accordingly. The couples appealed. The tribunal allowed their appeal, holding that there were two separate businesses. *EL, CM, KC & E Hodges*, MAN/99/941 (VTD 16983).

Associated partnerships supplying carpentry services

[**57.210**] See *RE & RL Newton*, 62.369 SUPPLY.

Father and son operating cleaning businesses from same premises

[**57.211**] A father and son had traded in partnership, operating a dry-cleaning business, from 1989 to 1992. By the end of 1992 their turnover had fallen to below the VAT deregistration threshold and they deregistered. They then decided to run separate businesses at the same premises. The father (AJ) carried on specialist cleaning work, while the son (GJ) carried on general dry-cleaning work. Subsequently the Commissioners issued a notice of compulsory registration on the basis that AJ and GJ were still carrying on a single business in partnership. They appealed. The tribunal allowed their appeal, holding on the evidence that they were carrying on separate businesses. *AC & GC James*, LON/00/29 (VTD 16988).

Engineering business

[**57.212**] The Commissioners sought to register an individual (D) whom they considered was the sole proprietor of an engineering business from 1982 to 1987. D appealed, contending that the business was operated by a limited company. The company in question had previously been owned by D and a former partner of his (B), with whom he had subsequently fallen out. Originally B and D had been registered at Companies House as the directors of the company, but Companies House had subsequently been advised by an accountant, apparently acting on behalf of B, that D had resigned and that B and Mrs B were the sole directors. However accounts had been submitted to the Inland Revenue, by a different accountant, showing that the company was trading with D and Mrs D as directors. The tribunal found that D and his wife had remained shareholders and directors of the company, and allowed D's appeal, holding that he had not carried on a business as a sole trader during the years in question. *H Demack*, MAN/89/190 (VTD 5534).

Hairdressing salons

[57.213] A married woman (F), whose husband was a chartered accountant, carried on business from an office in Edinburgh, collecting income for four companies which operated hairdressing salons, of which she was a director and in which her husband had a controlling interest. One of these companies had been temporarily struck off the register but subsequently restored with retrospective effect, and some returns lodged with the Registrar of Companies indicated that the companies were no longer trading. The Commissioners issued an assessment charging tax on the full amount of the income which she collected, on the basis that she was carrying on the business previously carried on by the companies. She appealed, contending that the companies had continued to trade, that the information supplied to the Registrar of Companies was incorrect, and that her only income was the 10% commission which she retained, which was below the VAT registration threshold. The tribunal allowed her appeal, finding (by a 2–1 majority) that the four companies had traded continuously throughout the period concerned, and holding that the income in question belonged to the individual companies rather than to F. *F Shanks*, EDN/91/308 (VTD 11015).

[57.214] See also the cases noted at **62.265** to **62.273** SUPPLY.

Car hire business—whether carried on by husband or wife

[57.215] The Commissioners discovered that a car hire business was not registered for VAT. They issued a notice of compulsory registration on an individual whom they believed to be the proprietor. He appealed, contending that he was only a driver and that the business was actually carried on by his wife. The tribunal accepted his evidence and allowed his appeal. *M Hussain*, MAN/98/900 (VTD 17217).

Taxi business—by whom carried on

[57.216] The Commissioners discovered that a taxi business was not registered for VAT. They issued a notice of compulsory registration on an individual whom they believed to be the proprietor. He appealed, contending that the business was actually carried on by his brother. The tribunal accepted his evidence and allowed his appeal. *M Shafiq*, MAN/03/360 (VTD 18815).

Counterfeit audiocassettes

[57.217] The Commissioners sought to register an individual (M) whom they considered was carrying on a business of manufacturing and selling counterfeit audiocassettes. M appealed, contending that he was an employee and was not required to be registered. The tribunal accepted his evidence and allowed his appeal. *M McGuckin*, EDN/92/345 (VTD 12659).

Miscellaneous

Whether registration number can be transferred

[57.218] A company, registered for VAT, changed its name and transferred its business to a newly formed subsidiary bearing its old name. The new company applied for registration and requested that, to enable it to use the old company's unused stationery, etc., it should be allocated the registration number of the old company which should be given a new number. The Commissioners rejected this request and the tribunal dismissed the company's appeal, holding that the allocation of numbers was within the administrative discretion of the Commissioners. *L Reich & Sons Ltd*, LON H/74/34 (VTD 97).

[57.219] Two people had carried on a catering business. One of them left and the other continued the business as a sole trader. HMRC issued him with a new registration number. He appealed, contending that he should have been allowed to continue using the same registration number. The tribunal rejected this contention and dismissed the appeal. *T Maryam v HMRC*, [2010] UKFTT 528 (TC), TC00782.

[57.220] See also *Miah*, 47.8 PARTNERSHIP.

Change of registration following direction under Sch 1 para 2

[57.221] A partnership had been registered for VAT for several years with the registration number 481 3534 48. Following the issue of a direction under *VATA 1994, Sch 1 para 2*, the Commissioners issued a notice cancelling this registration, and registering the partnership under the registration number 680 3961 19. The partnership appealed, contending that it should be permitted to continue to use the previous number. The tribunal rejected this contention and dismissed the appeal, holding that 'it was within the administrative discretion of the Commissioners to assign registration number 680 3961 19 to the appellants'. *S & M McCrindle (t/a Frisco Hair)*, EDN/00/92 (VTD 17134).

58

Retailers' Special Schemes

The cases are arranged under the following headings.

What supplies are within the schemes	58.1
Retrospective changes of scheme	58.13
Transitional matters	58.25
Gross takings	58.36
Expected selling prices	58.48
Point of Sale Scheme	58.50
Apportionment Schemes	58.53
Direct Calculation Schemes	58.55
Miscellaneous	58.60

GENERAL NOTE

The Special Schemes for retailers were substantially amended during 1997, with the 15 original retail schemes being replaced by the Point of Sale Scheme, Apportionment Schemes 1 and 2 and Direct Calculation Schemes 1 and 2. The key changes were that Schemes A and F continued in revised form as the Point of Sale Scheme; Scheme D continued in revised form as Apportionment Scheme 1; Scheme H continued in revised form as Apportionment Scheme 2; Schemes B and E continued in revised form as the Direct Calculation Scheme 1; Schemes B1 and E1 continued in revised form as the Direct Calculation Scheme 2; and Schemes B2, C, D1, G, J, J1 and J2 were withdrawn for supplies made after 31 March 1998. For details of the changes, see *Notice 727*, *Notices 727/2* to *727/5*, and Tolley's Value Added Tax. The cases in this chapter relating to periods before 1997 should be read in the light of the changes.

What supplies are within the schemes

Goods supplied to selling agents for promotional purposes

[58.1] A large mail order company operated through agents, most of whom were housewives. It sent new agents a 'free gift' of a teaset of a value not exceeding £10. The Commissioners issued assessments charging tax on the value of the teasets. The company appealed, contending firstly that the teasets were gifts within what is now *VATA 1994, Sch 4 para 5(2)(a)*, and secondly that, if the teasets were deemed to be supplies, they should be dealt with under the company's Retail Scheme. The tribunal rejected these contentions and dismissed the company's appeal, and the CA upheld this decision. The teasets were not gifts, since the agent had a contractual right to them. They were not within the Retail Schemes, and the company was obliged to account for VAT in the normal way. *GUS Merchandise Corporation Ltd v C & E Commrs*, CA [1981] STC 569; [1981] 1 WLR 1309. (*Note.* For other matters raised at the tribunal hearing but not pursued in the courts, see **2.113** APPEALS.)

Newspaper delivery charges

[58.2] A couple operated a newsagency and charged customers 6p per week for delivery. They accounted for tax under a Scheme which has since been replaced, but was similar to Apportionment Scheme 1. The Commissioners issued a ruling that the delivery charges should be taken into account in arriving at the gross takings for the purposes of the Scheme. The couple appealed, contending that the charges should be treated as zero-rated and the effect of including them as takings within the Scheme was that they would be paying tax on a zero-rated supply. The tribunal dismissed the appeal, holding that, by electing to account for tax under a Retail Scheme, the couple had elected to have their zero-rated supplies determined in accordance with that Scheme instead of by any other manner. *NG & BE Coe*, LON/75/35 (VTD 165).

[58.3] Similar decisions were reached in *PD Hayhoe*, LON/78/3 (VTD 568); *BM Coleman (t/a D & A Newsagents)*, LON/80/256 (VTD 1013); *L & R Harrison*, MAN/95/1427 (VTD 13544); *AD & JR Eckels*, MAN/97/1024 (VTD 15593) and *Fryer*, 58.21 below.

[58.4] A married couple operated a newsagency and accounted for tax under Retail Scheme H (which, in revised form, is now Apportionment Scheme 2). In accounting for tax, they did not include the charges which they made to customers for delivering newspapers. Subsequently they formed the opinion that these charges should be treated as part of the expected selling prices of the zero-rated newspapers, and in March 1994 they submitted a claim for repayment of tax which they considered that they had overdeclared as a result of failing to treat the newspaper delivery charges as attributable to zero-rated supplies. The Commissioners agreed the claim with respect to periods beginning after 1 May 1990 but rejected the claim with regard to periods from 1 December 1987 to 1 May 1990, considering that while such adjustments were permitted by *Leaflet 727/14/90* with effect from 1 May 1990, they had not been permitted by *Leaflet 727/14/87* as previously in force. The couple appealed. The tribunal allowed the appeal, holding that the effect of what the couple had done had been to increase the total of their estimated standard-rated supplies as compared with their estimated zero-rated supplies and to increase the proportion of their total takings which were to be attributed to standard-rated supplies under Scheme H. Furthermore, the Commissioners had not been justified in limiting the repayment of tax to payments made since 1 May 1990. *PK & PM Lloyd*, MAN/94/2506 (VTD 13562). (*Note.* See now, however, the three-year limit on repayment claims introduced by *FA 1997* with effect from 18 July 1996.)

[58.5] In the case noted at 48.136 PAYMENT OF TAX, Lord MacFadyen observed that, while newspaper delivery charges had to be included in gross turnover, a VAT officer should have advised the trader that the charges should also be 'included in the sum deducted as the expected selling price of zero-rated supplies'. *Mrs ID Mathieson v C & E Commrs*, CS [1999] STC 835.

Electricity stamps—whether to be included in gross takings

[58.6] A partnership traded as retailers and operated Scheme D (which, in revised form, is now Apportionment Scheme 1). It included the sale of electricity stamps, which it purchased at a 3% discount from the local Electricity Board, in its Scheme calculations. The Commissioners issued an assessment on the basis that the stamps should have been dealt with outside the Scheme, but the tribunal allowed the partnership's appeal, holding that there was nothing in the 'ordinary meaning of the words of the statute or notices' which prevented the partnership from including the relevant transactions within its calculations. *TE, M & IJ Parr*, [1985] VATTR 250 (VTD 1967). (*Note.* The Commissioners subsequently amended *Notice No 727* to require the sale of electricity stamps to be dealt with outside the Retail Schemes.)

Retail florist—amounts received from delivery service

[58.7] A retail florist accounted for tax using Retail Scheme E (which, in revised form, is now Direct Calculation Scheme 1). He received sums from a national flower delivery service, and dealt with these receipts under the Scheme. A VAT officer formed the opinion that these receipts were outside the scope of the Retail Scheme, and that the florist should have accounted for tax on them independently. He issued an assessment charging tax on these receipts. The florist appealed, contending that the flowers in question had been included in the stock of purchases from which he had calculated his liability under Scheme E, using a 20% mark-up. The tribunal allowed the florist's appeal, holding on the evidence that his returns were 'not incomplete or incorrect', so that there was no justification for the assessment. *NR Williams*, MAN/92/1756 (VTD 11361).

Subscriptions for discount cards

[58.8] A company (M) sold children's clothing and a variety of other goods. About 50% of its sales of goods were zero-rated. In 1988 it introduced a 'discount scheme' for regular customers. Customers who held a credit card issued by M could purchase a discount card for an annual subscription of £25. This card entitled them to a discount of 20% against all future credit card purchases. In 1989 the Commissioners issued a ruling that the discount card subscriptions were standard-rated. M appealed, contending that the subscriptions were 'an integral part of the consideration for the purchases subsequently made', and should be treated as part of its gross takings, to be apportioned between standard-rated goods and zero-rated goods under Retail Scheme J (which has subsequently been withdrawn). The tribunal allowed the appeal, holding that there was a direct link between the payments for the discount cards and the subsequent payments for goods. *Mothercare (UK) Ltd*, [1993] VATTR 391 (VTD 10751). (*Note.* See now *Notices No 727/3, 727/4* and *727/5* for the treatment of sales of discount vouchers and discount cards.)

Supplies to registered traders—whether within Retail Schemes

[58.9] A co-operative society operated Retail Scheme B (which, in revised form, is now Direct Calculation Scheme 1). A number of its supplies were to registered traders. The Commissioners considered that these supplies could not be dealt with within a Retail Scheme, and that, as the exclusion of such supplies meant that more than 50% of the society's takings were from zero-rated supplies, it was not eligible to use Scheme B. The society appealed, contending that supplies to other registered traders could be dealt with under a Retail Scheme, and that the inclusion of its supplies to registered traders meant that less than 50% of its takings were zero-rated, so that it remained entitled to use Scheme B. The tribunal dismissed the appeal, holding that the effect of *Notice No 727* was that supplies to registered traders had to be dealt with outside the Retail Schemes. The QB upheld this decision. *Oxford Swindon & Gloucester Society Ltd v C & E Commrs*, QB [1995] STC 583.

Hire of videos—whether within Retail Scheme

[58.10] A trader operated Retail Scheme C (which has subsequently been withdrawn). In the course of his business he hired videocassettes to customers. He treated his takings from this as being within the Scheme, with the result that he only accounted for output tax on a proportion of the takings. The Commissioners considered that the hire of videocassettes should be dealt with outside the Retail Schemes, and issued an estimated assessment to charge tax on the full amount of the receipts from video hire. The tribunal dismissed the trader's appeal, holding that the supply of videos on hire was a supply of services which was outside the scope of the Retail Schemes. *R Singh (t/a Best Buy Conventional Store)*, MAN/94/418 (VTD 13011).

Payments received for 'cheque administration services'

[58.11] A large retail company (S) operated a 'bespoke' retail scheme under *VAT Regulations 1995, reg 67*. It entered into an agreement with another company (C) which provided 'cheque administration services'. When S received cheques from customers which were not supported by a bank guarantee card, it would telephone C for guidance as to whether the cheque could be accepted. S paid C a monthly fee, plus 1.79% of the value of the cheques in question. Where C had indicated that a cheque could be accepted, but it was subsequently dishonoured on presentation, C purchased the cheque from S at its face value. S initially accounted for VAT on the amounts it received from C under this agreement (having previously deducted the amount of the dishonoured cheques from its gross takings). It subsequently submitted a repayment claim on the basis that the money it received from C was not consideration for any supply of goods. Customs rejected the claim and S appealed. The tribunal allowed the appeal, finding that 'the reason why (S) received the payments from (C) was because it made a payment to (C) of 1.79% of the value of qualifying cheques'. The sums which S had received 'were not in return for the sales to customers' and were not liable to VAT. *Selfridges Retail Ltd*, [2007] VATDR (VTD 20314).

Goods partly paid for by redemption of coupons

[58.12] A large retail company (B) operated a 'bespoke' retail scheme under *VAT Regulations 1995, reg 67*. It ran several sales promotion schemes, under which customers who spent at least £15 were given coupons entitling them to £5 off subsequent purchases. Initially B accounted for VAT on the full price of the original goods and the reduced price of the subsequent purchases. Subsequently Customs agreed that B could take the coupons into account when they were initially given to the customers, thus accounting for VAT on the reduced price of the original goods and the full price of the subsequent goods. In 2003 Customs made a repayment of more than £3,000,000 on this basis. In 2005 Customs decided to resile from this concession, and issued an assessment to recover most of the amount they had repaid in 2003. B appealed, contending that the correspondence which had preceded the 2003 repayment had been a binding amendment to the terms of its 'bespoke' retail scheme, and that Customs could not amend that agreement retrospectively. The Ch D rejected this contention and upheld the assessment, and the CA unanimously upheld this decision. Lloyd LJ held that the effect of the correspondence was that B had 'put forward a claim to the repayment of sums wrongly paid as tax which, if it had been correctly analysed, arose under *section 80* (of *VATA 1994*), and HMRC ultimately acceded to that request. It follows that it was open to HMRC to claim the return of the money under *section 80(4A)*, as it did.' *Boots Company plc v HMRC (No 2)*, CA 2009, [2010] STC 637; [2009] EWCA Civ 1396. (*Note.* The Supreme Court rejected the company's application to appeal against this decision.)

Retrospective changes of scheme

NOTE

Customs will now only allow retrospective changes of a retail scheme in exceptional cases. The maximum period for recalculation following an agreed retrospective claim is three years. See *Notice No 727, para 11*. The previous conditions, set out in *Notice No 727 (1993 edition), para 85*, under which Customs were prepared to consider recalculations for earlier years have now been withdrawn. For a case where a recalculation was accepted by the Commissioners, see *Peart & Peart*, **48.126** PAYMENT OF TAX.

Appeal dismissed

[58.13] A couple who carried on business as newsagents, tobacconists and confectioners originally operated Scheme 2 (which subsequently became Scheme G, and has since been withdrawn) but, realising that this was not to their advantage, applied in August 1973 to change to Scheme 3 (which subsequently became Scheme J, and has also since been withdrawn) with effect from 1 April 1973. The Commissioners allowed the change from 10 October 1973 but refused a retrospective change. The tribunal dismissed the couple's appeal against this decision. *P & M Summerfield*, BIR/74/24 (VTD 108).

[58.14] A retailer operated Scheme 2 (which subsequently became Scheme G, and has since been withdrawn). By November 1975 he began to suspect that he was paying too much tax, and asked a VAT officer for someone to see and advise him as quickly as possible. A VAT officer visited him in January 1976 and, without going into the matter deeply, told him that his increasing liability was probably due to the expansion in his business. The retailer then consulted a tax adviser, who wrote to the Commissioners in March 1976 asking for the liability to be recomputed under Scheme E (which, in revised form, is now Direct Calculation Scheme 1) or Scheme H (which, in revised form, is now Apportionment Scheme 2) with effect from 1 April 1975. The Commissioners agreed to allow retrospective treatment from 1 October 1975 but not from any earlier date. The retailer appealed. The tribunal dismissed his appeal, holding that he had failed to establish any special circumstances to justify his claim. *RJ Vulgar*, [1976] VATTR 197 (VTD 304).

[58.15] The decision in *Vulgar*, 58.14 above, was applied in the similar cases of *J Boden*, MAN/76/188 (VTD 377); *Brookfields*, LON/78/79 (VTD 577); *EWA Charles*, LON/77/388 (VTD 596) and *Marine Confectioners & Tobacconists Ltd*, LON/90/6X (VTD 5435).

[58.16] A trader began business as a retail newsagent and tobacconist in January 1979. His weekly turnover was within the limits of both Scheme B (which, in revised form, is now Direct Calculation Scheme 1) and Scheme G (which has subsequently been withdrawn). He elected to use Scheme G. However, in December 1979 he realised that he had made the wrong choice and should have elected to use Scheme B, under which he calculated that his liability up to September 1979 would have been £2,500 less. He applied to change to Scheme B retrospectively with effect from January 1979. The Commissioners agreed to allow him to change from October 1979 but refused to admit a retrospective change from January. The tribunal dismissed the trader's appeal, applying the principles laid down in *JH Corbitt (Numismatists) Ltd*, 60.1 SECOND-HAND GOODS, and holding that it had no jurisdiction to order the Commissioners to operate a retrospective change. *JM Patel (t/a Magsons)*, LON/80/39 (VTD 936).

[58.17] A similar decision was reached in a case where the tribunal chairman observed that a retrospective change of scheme 'could only be justified in exceptional circumstances' and 'the fact that, in retrospect, one scheme might have proved less advantageous than another scheme did not constitute exceptional circumstances. It is of course the case that one scheme may operate differently, for better or worse, as to the amount of value added tax which results, but in other respects, a scheme may be more advantageous in providing a system of accounting which is more convenient to the particular retailer concerned. It is for the retailer to choose the scheme most suited to himself in the light of his own knowledge about his own business.' *RB & MR Patel (t/a Rama Stores)*, MAN/82/152 (VTD 1392).

[58.18] The decision in *Patel & Patel (t/a Rama Stores)*, 58.17 above, was applied in the similar case of *MP & EM Dean (t/a Hartlebury Store)*, MAN/93/1320 (VTD 12116).

[58.19] Two partners carried on business as grocers, confectioners, tobacconists and newsagents from two premises, one of which was also an off-licence and the other contained a sub-post office. They chose to operate Scheme 2 (which subsequently became Scheme G, and has since been withdrawn). This resulted in their paying more VAT than if they had operated alternative schemes. They had received *Notice No 727*, issued in February 1975, warning of the possible disadvantage of Scheme G. Between 1976 and 1981 four control visits were made to the partners, during which VAT officers pointed out the unsuitability of Scheme G and advised the adoption of alternatives. The partners declined to do so until 1981 when they finally applied to change to Scheme E (which, in revised form, is now Direct Calculation Scheme 1). The Commissioners agreed to the change with effect from 1 April 1981 but refused to approve a retrospective change from 1 April 1977. The tribunal dismissed the partners' appeal against this decision, holding that although the Commissioners had a discretion to allow a retrospective change, the tribunal had no jurisdiction to consider whether that discretion should be exercised in any particular case. *RJ Withers & S Gibbs (t/a The General Stores), [1983] VATTR 323 (VTD 1553)*.

[58.20] A married couple who operated a newsagency applied to change retrospectively from Scheme D to Scheme B. The Commissioners refused to allow a retrospective change and the tribunal dismissed the couple's appeal, applying *Vulgar*, **58.14** above, and *Dean*, **58.18** above. The tribunal observed that its power in such an appeal was supervisory and it could only allow an appeal if the Commissioners' decision was unreasonable, which was not the case here. The tribunal declined to follow the decision in *Wadlewski*, **58.24** below, observing that the tribunal there had 'misconstrued the purpose of the £100 requirement' (in *Notice No 727, 1993 edition, para 85*) and holding that the fact that 'a retrospective change would result in an adjustment of tax significantly in excess of £100' did not in itself amount to 'exceptional circumstances'. The tribunal held that 'the amount of tax concerned is not to be measured by reference to the figure of £100 but, rather, to the turnover or profit of the business'. *L & J Lewis, [1996] VATDR 541 (VTD 14085)*.

[58.21] The decision in *Lewis*, **58.20** above, was applied in the similar subsequent cases of *L & P Fryer, MAN/95/1532 (VTD 14265); Mr & Mrs MAR Killingbeck, MAN/95/2452 (VTD 14592)* and *E Saleh, MAN/06/796 (VTD 20288)*.

[58.22] A similar decision was reached in a case where the tribunal held that it was 'only entitled to investigate the exercise of discretion by the Commissioners with a view to seeing if they have taken into account any matters that ought not to be taken into account, or disregarded matters that ought to have been taken into account, or have acted in a manner in which no reasonable body of Commissioners could have acted. The tribunal cannot override the decision of the Commissioners save as a judicial authority concerned to see whether they have contravened the law by acting in excess of their power'. *AC & PS Gyte, [1999] VATDR 241 (VTD 16031)*.

[58.23] Appeals against the Commissioners' refusal to allow a retrospective change of scheme were also dismissed in *R & A Powell, CAR/77/164 (VTD 601); GA & DM Lunn, MAN/83/157 (VTD 1518); LM & R Food Stores, MAN/84/222 (VTD 1936); Maystore Ltd, LON/85/391 (VTD 2096); Bryan Markwell & Co Ltd, LON/89/895 (VTD 4358); Mr & Mrs A Pollitt,*

MAN/89/160 (VTD 4463); *JE Low*, LON/90/848X (VTD 5586); *SJ West (t/a Stallard News)*, LON/90/57Z (VTD 5802); *JR Buckley*, MAN/91/793 (VTD 7644); *Garcha Group*, LON/94/241A (VTD 13130); *K, J & M Patel (t/a Dhruva Newsagents)*, LON/95/2327 (VTD 14843); *O Neilson (t/a The News Shop)*, EDN/97/63 (VTD 15197); *SS & JK Jutla*, LON/97/002 (VTD 15446); *I & J Hamilton*, EDN/97/61 (VTD 15556); *RSK Newsagents Ltd*, EDN/97/168 (VTD 15750); *P & E Waring*, MAN/97/1059 (VTD 15864); *KS Tiwana*, MAN/98/350 (VTD 16202); *E Wallace*, EDN/99/52 (VTD 16281) and *K Jamil*, MAN/99/869 (VTD 16795).

Appeal allowed

[58.24] A couple operated a grocery shop. From 1983 they accounted for tax under Retail Scheme G (which has subsequently been withdrawn). They subsequently discovered that the effect of using Retail Scheme G was that they were overpaying tax by about £8,000 per year, amounting on average to about 40% of their annual profits. They applied to change to Scheme F with retrospective effect. The Commissioners agreed that they could use Scheme F, but refused to allow a retrospective change. They issued a formal ruling to this effect in March 1994, and the couple appealed. The tribunal chairman (Mr. Heim, sitting alone) allowed the appeal, holding that the Commissioners had erred in failing to take account of the amount of the overpayments which had resulted from the couple using Scheme G, and noting that entry into Scheme G had been closed with effect from 1991 because it had been recognised that it produced overpayments of tax, although existing traders had been allowed to use it. The tribunal held that it had a supervisory jurisdiction, and that the Commissioners had exercised their discretion unreasonably by giving insufficient consideration to the 'exceptional circumstances'. *A & C Wadlewski*, LON/94/1849A (VTD 13340). (*Note.* The decision here was not followed, and was implicitly disapproved, by subsequent tribunals in *Lewis*, 58.20 above; *Fryer*, 58.21 above; *Neilson*, 58.23 above, and *Jutla*, 58.23 above.)

Transitional matters

Receipts after increase in rate from sales before the increase

[58.25] A trader sold flowers, garden produce, garden machinery and allied goods and services. Before 18 June 1979 his supplies were variously zero-rated, chargeable at the standard rate of 8%, or chargeable at the higher rate of 12.5%. He accounted for tax under Scheme F (which, in revised form, is now the Point of Sale Scheme), using the 'standard method' for arriving at his gross takings. As from 18 June 1979, the two positive rates were replaced by a single standard rate of 15%. The trader accounted for tax under the old rates in respect of takings from 18 June under agreements, etc. entered into before that date. The Commissioners issued an assessment on the basis that tax should have been accounted for by reference to the increased rate as regards all his takings from 18 June. The tribunal upheld the assessment and dismissed the trader's appeal. *AS Gandy*, LON/80/253 (VTD 1029).

[58.26] The decision in *Gandy*, 58.25 above, was applied in the similar case of *Norman Lavelle Ltd*, MAN/82/8 (VTD 1330).

[58.27] A similar decision was reached in *Wesley Barrell (Witney) Ltd*, LON/80/465 (VTD 1087).

[58.28] A company (N) which sold clothing by mail order operated Retail Scheme H (which, in revised form, is now Apportionment Scheme 2), using the 'standard method' of computing its gross takings. On 1 April 1991 the standard rate of VAT was increased from 15% to 17.5%, with the result that the VAT fraction changed from $^3/_{23}$ to $^7/_{47}$. Consequently, N was required to calculate its output tax beginning on 1 April 1991 by applying the VAT fraction of $^7/_{47}$. It did so, except in respect of its takings from self-financed credit sales entered into before 1 April 1991, on which it calculated output tax applying the old fraction of $^3/_{23}$. The Commissioners issued assessments covering the accounting periods from 1 February 1991 to 31 January 1992, charging tax on receipts after 31 March 1991 from self-financed credit sales made before 1 April 1991 at the new rate rather than at the old rate. N appealed, contending that the assessments were invalid as the requirements of *Appendix C of Notice No 727 (1993 edition)* did not conform with *Article 27* of the *EC Sixth Directive*. The tribunal accepted this contention and allowed N's appeal, and the QB upheld this decision. *C & E Commrs v Next plc*, QB [1995] STC 651. (*Notes.* (1) The decision in this case was disapproved and overruled by the CA in the subsequent case of *R v C & E Commrs (ex p. Littlewoods Home Shopping Group Ltd)*, 58.39 below. Millett LJ observed that, when the VAT rate was increased, the adoption of the 'standard method' of calculating gross takings, rather than the normal method of calculating the VAT due, would not affect the ultimate consumer, since the consumer 'is invoiced for his purchases at the time of supply for a price which is inclusive of VAT at the rate then in force. Later increases in the rate of tax before he completes payment in full do not affect the amount of the outstanding payments for which he is liable.' For the Commissioners' practice following the CA decision, see Business Brief 22/98, issued on 3 November 1998. (2) The 'standard method' of calculating gross takings was withdrawn with effect from 1 March 1997.)

[58.29] A similar decision was reached in a case which was heard in the QB with *Next plc*, 58.28 above. *C & E Commrs v Grattan plc*, QB [1995] STC 651.

Business taken over as going concern—treatment of stock

[58.30] A trader purchased an existing business, selling both standard-rated and zero-rated goods, and accounted for tax under Scheme B (which, in revised form, is now Direct Calculation Scheme 1). *Notice No 727B, para 10* explicitly stated that, in arriving at the zero-rated goods received in the first period for which the scheme is used, goods held at the beginning must not be included. However, in arriving at the liability for the first period of her business, the trader included, in the zero-rated goods, stock which she had taken over with the business. The Commissioners issued an assessment to exclude the stock from the calculation. The tribunal upheld the assessment and dismissed the trader's appeal. *AL Housden*, [1981] VATTR 217 (VTD 1178). (*Note. Notice No 727B* has since been replaced. See now *Notice No 727/5*.)

[58.31] In April 1992 a co-operative (CWS), which operated Retail Scheme B (which, in revised form, is now Direct Calculation Scheme 1), took over, as a going concern, the business of another co-operative which had operated Retail Scheme H (which, in revised form, is now Apportionment Scheme 2). It accounted for tax under Scheme B in respect of the sale of the stock it had taken over. The Commissioners considered that such stock should have been excluded from the Scheme B calculation, and that the result of including it was that CWS had underdeclared tax. They issued an assessment, against which CWS appealed. The tribunal allowed the appeal, holding that CWS had acted correctly in treating the stock taken over in its Scheme B calculation, and the QB upheld this decision. Carnwath J held that, although the effect of what is now *Article 5* of the *VAT (Special Provisions) Order* was that the transfer of goods to CWS was not to be treated as a supply, it did not follow that it should be ignored altogether. Scheme B was not confined to goods acquired through a taxable supply. The goods had been 'received for resale' and should therefore be included in the Scheme B calculation. The fact that the transferor had operated Scheme H was irrelevant. *Dicta* of the tribunal chairman in *Kelly*, 58.58 below, were disapproved. *C & E Commrs v Co-Operative Wholesale Society Ltd*, QB [1995] STC 983. (*Note*. The decision here was distinguished in the subsequent case of *Iceland Foodstores Ltd*, 58.34 below.)

[58.32] A co-operative, which used Retail Scheme B (which, in revised form, is now Direct Calculation Scheme 1), transferred its food-retailing business to an associated company, as a going concern, in two stages. The business assets of two of the foodstores were transferred in January 1996, the assets of the remaining foodstores being transferred in February 1996. For its accounting period ending in January 1996, the co-operative accounted for tax on the basis that the zero-rated stock which was included in the first transfer should be excluded from its daily gross takings, but included in the computation of 'zero-rated goods received, made or grown for resale', at its expected retail price. The Commissioners issued a ruling that the stock should have been wholly excluded from the calculations. The tribunal upheld the ruling and the CA dismissed the co-operative's appeal. Jonathan Parker J held that, since a disposal of zero-rated goods on a transfer of a business as a going concern was a sale which was not a retail sale, the transferor had not received the 'expected selling price'. Accordingly, it was necessary to make an adjustment in respect of such goods, as directed in *Notice No 727*, issued in accordance with the Commissioners' powers under *VAT Regulations 1995 (SI 1995/2518)*, *reg 67*. The 'only appropriate adjustment' was to exclude from the calculation the figure which had initially been included as the expected selling price. *United Norwest Co-Operatives Ltd v C & E Commrs*, CA [1999] STC 686. (*Note*. For another appeal relating to the transfer, heard with this case by the tribunal but not taken to the QB or CA, see *United Norwest Food Markets Ltd*, 58.55 below.)

[58.33] The decision in *United Norwest Co-Operatives Ltd*, 58.32 above, was applied in a similar subsequent case where a co-operative had transferred its business to another co-operative as a going concern, and had failed to make the adjustment required by *Notice No 727, para 22*. Lightman J observed that the operation of the scheme 'would be distorted if no adjustment were made for transfers of a going concern' and held that 'the language of *paragraph 22* is mandatory in requiring the adjustment'. *Midlands Co-Operative Society Ltd v C & E Commrs*, Ch D 2001, [2002] STC 198. (*Note. Notice No 727* has subsequently been replaced. See now *Notice 727/5/97, para 9.3*.)

[58.34] A company took over a retail business as a going concern and began to use Retail Scheme B1 (which, in revised form, is now Direct Calculation Scheme 2). In its first return, it treated the stock which had been transferred to it with the business as goods received for resale in the tax period. On this basis, it declared negative output tax of more than £9,000,000 and claimed a repayment of more than £18,000,000. The Commissioners issued a ruling that the stock should be treated as stock held at the beginning of the year, with the result that the repayment due to the company was reduced from £18,600,000 to £7,300,000. The tribunal upheld the Commissioners' ruling and dismissed the company's appeal, holding that the stock in question 'was not to be included in the calculations until the end of the year'. *Co-Operative Wholesale Society Ltd*, 58.31 above, was distinguished, firstly on the basis that it dealt with Scheme B rather than Scheme B1, and Scheme B 'required no adjustment, annual or otherwise, to allow for differences between opening and closing stock', and secondly because the appellant company in that case was already carrying on business when it received the stock in question. *Iceland Foodstores Ltd*, [1998] VATDR 498 (VTD 15833).

[58.35] A retail company (D) had a number of departments, some of which accounted for tax under Retail Scheme A (which, in revised form, is now the Point of Sale Scheme), some of which accounted for tax under Retail Scheme B (which, in revised form, is now Direct Calculation Scheme 1), and some of which accounted for tax under Retail Scheme H (which, in revised form, is now Apportionment Scheme 2). Its parent company (B), which was the representative member of the VAT group, considered that the use of Scheme H was disadvantageous, and that it would be beneficial to use Scheme B instead. A new subsidiary company (J) was incorporated and the businesses of D's departments which had used Schemes B and H were transferred to that company as a going concern. In B's next return, no adjustment was made to D's Scheme B and Scheme H calculations to take account of the stock which had been transferred to J. The Commissioners issued an assessment on the basis that, since the stock transferred to J was not a retail supply, the relevant calculations should have been adjusted by reducing the value of the zero-rated expected selling prices by the value of that stock (and effectively increasing the value attributed to standard-rated outputs for the period). B appealed. The tribunal upheld the assessment and dismissed B's appeal, observing that the stock had not been sold by retail and that the transfer had had the effect of reducing the stock available for sale by retail. The tribunal held that 'the operation of Scheme B would be distorted if no account was taken of self-supply or gratuitous supply by traders. So also would it be distorted if no adjustment were made for transfers of a going concern as those in this case.' *The Burton Group plc*, LON/96/1116 (VTD 15046). (*Notes*. (1) For another appeal relating to the transfer, heard with this case, see *Jubilee Fashions Ltd*,

58.56 below. (2) The decision was approved by the Ch D in the subsequent case of *Midlands Co-Operative Society Ltd*, **58.33** above.)

Gross takings

NOTE

The 'standard method' of calculating gross takings, which had been introduced in 1973 (and which provided that credit sales should not be included in gross takings until payments were received in respect of them), was withdrawn with effect from 1 March 1997. See *R v C & E Commrs (ex p. Littlewoods Home Shopping Group Ltd)*, **58.39** below, for a case concerning the consequences of this withdrawal.

VAT Regulations, reg 67(2)(c)—value of standard-rated supplies

[58.36] A partnership operated a snack bar. Following a visit by a Customs officer in 1996, they accounted for tax on the basis that 13% of their supplies were standard-rated and 87% were zero-rated. In 1998 a subsequent Customs officer formed the opinion that 41% of the partnership's supplies were standard-rated. He arranged for the issue of an assessment covering the periods from September 1996 to November 1998, computed on the basis that the percentage of standard-rated supplies had increased from 13% to 41% during that time. The partnership appealed, contending that the previous officer had agreed that 13% of their supplies were standard-rated and this agreement should be treated as binding until the subsequent visit. The tribunal accepted this contention and allowed the appeal, holding that the effect of *VAT Regulations 1995, reg 67(2)(c)* was that the agreement reached in 1996 was valid and could not be changed retrospectively. *R & A Bardetti (t/a Obertelli Quality Sandwiches)*, LON/99/561 (VTD 16758). (*Note.* For another issue in this case, see **29.8** FOOD.)

[58.37] In *Mithras (Wine Bars) Ltd*, **3.165** ASSESSMENTS, the tribunal held that an agreement that 30% of a company's sales were standard-rated was binding and could not be changed retrospectively.

Direction under VAT Regulations, reg 68*—whether unreasonable

[58.38] A company was incorporated to take over the trade of a retail furnishings company, which had adopted the optional method of calculating gross takings. The new company wished to adopt the 'standard method' as then in force, but the Commissioners issued a direction under what is now *VAT Regulations, reg 68*, instructing it to use the optional method of calculating gross takings. The company appealed, contending that the direction was unreasonable and that the ultimate tax liability would be the same whichever method was used, although the use of the standard method would give it a legitimate cash-flow advantage. The tribunal allowed the company's appeal, holding that the direction was unreasonable, and observing that deferment of tax under the standard method was not a tax advantage as the correct amount of tax still had to be paid. The QB upheld this decision. *C & E Commrs v J Boardmans (1980) Ltd*, QB 1985, [1986] STC 10. (*Note*. The 'standard method' of computing gross takings, as in force at the relevant time, was subsequently withdrawn—see the note preceding this section.)

Withdrawal of standard method of calculating gross takings

[58.39] A company (L) sold goods by mail order. On the introduction of VAT in 1973 the Commissioners had stated that a trader who adopted the standard method of calculating gross takings (which provided that credit sales should not be included until payments were received in respect of them), and included as gross takings payments received in respect of supplies made before the introduction of VAT, would not normally be required to account for VAT on payments due to him at the end of the last period in which he used a retail scheme. L adopted the standard method and accounted for tax accordingly. In the November 1996 Budget, the Chancellor of the Exchequer announced that the standard method would be withdrawn with effect from 1 March 1997. The Commissioners also announced that retailers who financed their own credit sales would have to account for VAT at the time of supply even if payment had not been received. L applied for judicial review, contending that the Commissioners were not entitled to withdraw the assurances they had made in 1973. The QB dismissed the application but the CA allowed L's appeal. The CA held that the cases of *Next plc*, **58.28** above, and *Grattan plc*, **58.29** above, had been 'wrongly decided and should be over-ruled'. The decision to charge output tax on outstanding balances, on the withdrawal of the 'standard method' of calculating gross takings, would result in double taxation. This would be 'neither fair nor reasonable' and would be incompatible with *Articles 11* and *12* of the *EC Sixth Directive*. The decision had 'no statutory basis', and was unlawful. *R v C & E Commrs (ex p. Littlewoods Home Shopping Group Ltd)*, CA [1998] STC 445. (*Note*. For the Commissioners' practice following this decision, see Business Brief 11/98, issued on 1 May 1998.)

Mail order business—inclusion of credit sales in gross takings

[58.40] See *Freemans plc*, **22.253** EUROPEAN COMMUNITY LAW.

Point of Sale Scheme—definition of 'takings'

[58.41] A company which operated a large number of public houses accounted for VAT under Retail Scheme A (now the Point of Sale Scheme), using the standard method of computing gross takings. It computed its takings by reference to the total cash in its tills, rather than by reference to the takings recorded on its till rolls. The Commissioners issued an assessment on the basis that the company's practice was incorrect, and had resulted in an underdeclaration of tax. (The company's declared takings over the periods assessed were £716,500,000. The Commissioners analysed a sample of the company's takings, and formed the opinion that the company's incorrect method of computing its takings led to 0.1013% of the total takings not being declared.

This percentage was then applied to the whole of the period in question, resulting in an assessment being raised on an estimated underdeclaration of £725,774.) The tribunal dismissed the company's appeal, holding that the company had been at fault in failing to account for tax on some of the takings recorded on its till rolls, and the Commissioners' extrapolation of an estimated total underdeclaration from a particular sample was reasonable in the circumstances. *Courage Ltd*, LON/92/319Y (VTD 8808).

Stock deficiency attributed to assumed thefts of cash

[58.42] A group of retail companies accounted for tax under Retail Scheme F (now the Point of Sale Scheme) and Retail Scheme J (which has now been withdrawn). The representative member of the group treated the amount recorded on the till rolls as the daily gross takings. However, the group's accounts indicated stock deficiencies of between £15,000,000 and £23,000,000 per year. This was primarily attributed to theft by customers and employees. The Commissioners formed the opinion that part of this discrepancy was attributable to theft by employees of cash which had not been recorded on the till rolls, rather than to thefts of stock. They issued assessments computed on the basis that about 27% of the stock deficiencies were attributable to thefts by employees, of which about 20% was attributable to thefts of cash, rather than to thefts of stock. The company appealed, contending as a preliminary point that the assessments had not been made to the best of the Commissioners' judgment. The tribunal rejected this contention and dismissed the appeal in principle (giving the company leave to apply for a further hearing with regard to the amount of the assessments). Applying *dicta* of Lord Donovan in *Argosy Co Ltd v Guyana Commissioner of Inland Revenue*, PC [1971] 1 WLR 514, 'once a reasonable opinion that liability exists is formed, there must necessarily be guess-work at times as to the quantum of liability'. *WH Smith Ltd*, [2000] VATDR 1 (VTD 16505).

Point of Sale Scheme—discount retained by finance company

[58.43] See *Primback Ltd*, 22.242 EUROPEAN COMMUNITY LAW.

Payments by retailer to company operating promotion scheme

[58.44] A company (C) trading as carpet retailers used Retail Scheme A (now the Point of Sale Scheme). It operated a promotion scheme, whereby customers who spent £200 or more on its carpets could apply to a travel company for a voucher. The nominal value of the voucher was half of the cost of the carpets (up to a maximum of £750), and the voucher could be redeemed against certain holidays offered by the travel company. C paid 2% of the sale price of the carpets covered by the scheme to the company which had devised the scheme (L). Initially C accounted for tax on the full amount of its receipts, but it subsequently submitted a repayment claim on the basis that it should have deducted the amounts which it paid to L. The Commissioners rejected the claim, and C appealed. The tribunal dismissed the appeal, and the QB upheld this decision. On the evidence, although the vouchers were within the definition of 'trading stamps', C had never made any delivery of the vouchers, which were supplied to customers by the travel company and never became C's property. L and the travel company were running the scheme independently, and the travel company was not acting as an agent of C. The payments which C made were calculated by reference to the value of the carpets which it sold, rather than by reference to the number of the vouchers delivered, and were not consideration for the purchase of the vouchers. Accordingly, C was not entitled to deduct the amounts which it paid to L in computing its gross takings. *Allied Carpets Group plc v C & E Commrs*, QB [1998] STC 894.

Newspaper delivery charges—inclusion in gross takings

[58.45] See *Coe*, 58.2 above, and the cases noted at 58.3 above.

Subscriptions for discount cards

[58.46] See *Mothercare (UK) Ltd*, 58.8 above.

Retail sales paid for by credit card—time of supplies

[58.47] See *Kingfisher plc*, 32.28 GROUPS OF COMPANIES.

Expected selling prices

Newspaper delivery charges—Apportionment Scheme 2

[58.48] See *Lloyd*, 58.4 above.

Business transferred as going concern

[58.49] See *The Burton Group plc*, 58.34 above.

Point of Sale scheme

Definition of 'takings'

[58.50] See *Courage Ltd*, 58.41 above.

Discount retained by finance company

[58.51] See *Primback Ltd*, 22.242 EUROPEAN COMMUNITY LAW.

Payments to company operating promotion scheme

[58.52] See *Allied Carpets Group plc*, 58.44 above.

Apportionment schemes

Mail order goods sold to agents

[58.53] A group of companies sold goods by mail order, sending copies of its catalogues to agents. Such agents received commission of 10% of the catalogue price on sales to third parties, and were credited with a discount or rebate of 10% on goods which they purchased personally. Where agents purchased goods personally, the companies accounted for VAT on the net amount paid by the agent, but where goods were sold to agents on behalf of third parties, the companies accounted for VAT on the whole of the catalogue price. Some of the goods sold were standard-rated and others zero-rated, and the companies had, by agreement with the Commissioners, operated a modified version of Retail Scheme H (which, in revised form, is now Apportionment Scheme 2). In October 1987 the group formed the opinion that it had treated a significant number of sales, which in fact had been made to agents, as having been made to third parties, and had therefore accounted for VAT on the catalogue price instead of on the net amounts paid by agents. In its return for the period ending 31 December 1987, the group increased the proportion of its sales which it treated as having been made for the agents' own use. In its return for the period ending 31 December 1988, it made a deduction for output tax which it considered that it had overdeducted in earlier periods by treating too many sales as having been made to third parties. The Commissioners accepted that, for periods after 1 January 1988, the companies could alter the proportion of its sales which they treated as being for agents' own use, but considered that the companies could not make a retrospective alteration. They therefore issued assessments on the basis that the companies should have continued to adopt the previous percentage in its return to 31 December 1987, and were not entitled to make a retrospective deduction of output tax in its return for the period ending 31 December 1988. The QB upheld both assessments. The correspondence in question showed that the companies had adopted a modified version of Retail Scheme H. The correspondence between the companies and the Commissioners constituted a series of offers to cover the ensuing three-year period, and when such offers were accepted (by the submission of the first return made on the offered basis) this acceptance was binding on the companies for the next three years. The companies appealed to the CA, which upheld the QB decision. The parties had entered into a binding agreement and the group was not entitled to resile from it. *GUS Merchandise Corporation Ltd (No 2) v C & E Commrs*, CA 1994, [1995] STC 279. (*Note.* For a preliminary issue in this case, see **2.284** APPEALS.)

Newspaper delivery charges

[58.54] See *Coe*, 58.2 above, and the cases noted at 58.3 and 58.4 above.

Direct calculation schemes

Customs refusing application to use Direct Calculation Scheme

[58.55] A company took over (in two stages) the food-retailing business of a co-operative as a going concern. The co-operative had accounted for tax using Retail Scheme B (which, in revised form, is now Direct Calculation Scheme 1). The Commissioners issued a ruling that the company was not permitted to use Scheme B, on the grounds that its use would 'distort the output tax' and would 'not give a fair and reasonable result'. The company appealed. The tribunal allowed the appeal, holding that the Commissioners' ruling was unreasonable. The decision to refuse Scheme B was 'flawed', since the officer responsible for the ruling had treated the transfers as a tax avoidance scheme, which was not the case. The tribunal held that, although the transfers brought fiscal advantages, they 'would have been carried out as they were carried out even if no fiscal advantages had existed'. The fiscal advantages of the arrangements were 'inherent in the proper and legitimate use of Scheme B'. *United Norwest Food Markets Ltd*, MAN/96/423 (VTD 14923). (*Note.* For an appeal by the transferor, heard with this appeal and dismissed, see *United Norwest Co-Operatives Ltd*, 58.32 above.)

[58.56] A retail company had a number of departments, some of which accounted for tax under Retail Scheme A (now the Point of Sale Scheme), some of which accounted for tax under Retail Scheme B (which, in revised form, is now Direct Calculation Scheme 1), and some of which accounted for tax under Retail Scheme H (which, in revised form, is now Apportionment Scheme 2). The parent company considered that the use of Scheme H was disadvantageous, and that it would be beneficial to use Scheme B instead. A new subsidiary company (J) was incorporated and the businesses of those departments which had used Schemes B and H were transferred to J as a going concern. In its first return (submitted in March 1996 and covering the period ending February 1996), J claimed a repayment of more than £3,000,000. The Commissioners repaid the amount claimed in April 1996. However, the Commissioners made a routine control visit to the companies in May 1996, and in June they issued a ruling under *VAT Regulations 1995, reg 68*, refusing J permission to use Scheme B and instructing it to resubmit its return using another Scheme. J appealed, contending firstly that the repayment made in April amounted to acceptance that J could use Scheme B, and alternatively that the refusal was unreasonable. The Commissioners accepted the first contention and allowed J's appeal, holding that 'by making an unconditional repayment the Commissioners permitted the use of Scheme B', and that 'having permitted use of the Scheme, the Commissioners were not entitled to resile from the permission with retrospective effect.' The tribunal also held that the officer responsible for the ruling had acted unreasonably, in that he had informed J that he had issued the ruling because J's return had included a figure of negative output tax. The tribunal observed that 'if he had relied on the size of the negative output tax, he could not have been criticised' but that 'reliance on the fact of negative output tax was an irrelevant matter and wrong in law'. Applying *dicta* of Lord Lane in *JH Corbitt (Numismatists) Ltd*, **60.1** SECOND-HAND GOODS, the officer had taken irrelevant matter into account. *Jubilee Fashions Ltd*, LON/96/1116 (VTD 15046). (*Note*. For an appeal by the transferor, heard with this appeal and dismissed, see *The Burton Group plc*, 58.35 above.)

Improper use of Direct Calculation Scheme

[58.57] A partnership carrying on a retail business as confectioners, tobacconists and newsagents accounted for tax under Scheme B (which, in revised form, is now Direct Calculation Scheme 1), although it was not entitled to do so as its zero-rated supplies were more than half of its total supplies. The Commissioners therefore issued assessments on the basis that the partnership should have accounted for tax under Scheme D (which has subsequently been withdrawn). The tribunal dismissed the partnership's appeal. *NG & MG Patel*, LON/87/48 & LON/87/189 (VTD 2463).

[58.58] A partnership operating Retail Scheme B (which, in revised form, is now Direct Calculation Scheme 1) included the estimated selling prices of zero-rated opening stock in estimating its zero-rated outputs for its first period of trading. The Commissioners issued an assessment on the basis that the opening zero-rated stock should not have been brought into the partnership's computation of zero-rated goods received in the period. The tribunal accepted the Commissioners' contentions and dismissed the partnership's appeal. If opening zero-rated stock were brought into a computation, closing zero-rated stock would need to be deducted. Scheme B did not provide for such adjustments, but operated on the assumption that the percentage of stock which was zero-rated remained constant. *JM & MC Kelly*, LON/87/576X (VTD 4139). (*Note*. *Dicta* of the tribunal chairman were subsequently disapproved by Carnwath J in *Co-Operative Wholesale Society Ltd*, 58.31 above.)

Direct Calculation Scheme—deduction for wastage

[58.59] In 1991 the Commissioners permitted a major retail company (T) to calculate the value of its standard-rated supplies by an adaptation of Scheme B1 (which, in revised form, is now Direct Calculation Scheme 2, and under which output tax is paid on daily gross takings minus expected zero-rated sales). In calculating the expected zero-rated sales, deductions were made for wastage. In 1993 the Commissioners formed the opinion that T had been underestimating its wastage, with the result that it had been making deductions for zero-rated sales which were too high, and thus had been underdeclaring its output tax. They issued an assessment charging tax of more than £2,500,000. T appealed, contending that it had operated the scheme in accordance with its agreement with the Commissioners, and that the assessment had not been made to the best of the Commissioners' judgment. The tribunal reviewed the evidence in detail and allowed the appeal, holding that the agreement as to how the scheme was to be operated was 'a contract binding on both sides from which one party cannot resile'. On the evidence, the Commissioners had given 'a final and unqualified assent' to T's proposals. The tribunal observed that 'once a permission has been granted, then it could be refused for the future if it was found that the scheme did not produce a fair and reasonable valuation'. However, 'a scheme which has been agreed cannot be altered retrospectively just because Customs and Excise then find that it does not produce a fair and reasonable valuation'. Furthermore, T had not made any misrepresentation of fact, and had acted 'honestly and *bona fide*'. The tribunal held that 'in entering into a retail scheme agreement, there is no wider duty of disclosure than applies under the normal law of contract'. It followed that the assessment was invalid. *Tesco plc*, [1994] VATTR 425 (VTD 12740).

Miscellaneous

Estimated assessment on trader using Retail Scheme

[58.60] See *Briggs*, 3.34 ASSESSMENT.

Company adopting Retail Scheme for wholesale supplies

[58.61] See *RJN Creighton Ltd*, 48.125 PAYMENT OF TAX.

Use of inappropriate Scheme—whether any 'official error'

[58.62] See *Peart*, 48.126 PAYMENT OF TAX, and *Mathieson*, 48.136 PAYMENT OF TAX.

59

Returns

The cases in this chapter are arranged under the following headings.

Accounting periods	**59.1**
Making of returns (VAT Regulations 1995, reg 25)	**59.8**
Correction of errors (VAT Regulations 1995, regs 34, 35)	**59.23**
Miscellaneous	**59.34**

Accounting periods

Application to use long accounting periods

[59.1] A company requested permission to use accounting periods of longer than the three months specified by what is now *VAT Regulations 1995 (SI 1995/2518), reg 25(1)*. The Commissioners rejected the request and the company appealed. The tribunal struck out the appeal, holding that there was no appealable matter within what is now *VATA 1994, s 83*. It also considered that there was no provision permitting departure from the requirements of the *Regulations. Selected Growers Ltd*, LON/73/21 (VTD 10).

Customs' decision regarding period of returns

[59.2] A company was registered with effect from 1 May 1980 and was instructed to make a return for the period to 30 September 1980, which it did. On 18 December 1980, the Commissioners wrote to the company stating that it was now considered necessary to vary the length of its first accounting period which would now be deemed to end on 30 November 1980 and that the return already made was 'of no effect'. The company applied for an extension of the period in which to appeal against this decision and the Commissioners contended as a preliminary issue that there was no appealable matter within what is now *VATA 1994, s 83(a)*. The tribunal accepted this contention and struck out the appeal, holding that 'all requirements concerning the dates on which returns shall be made are matters of the administration of the tax'. The Commissioners' letter was not 'a decision with respect to "the registration or cancellation of registration of any person"'. *Punchwell Ltd*, [1981] VATTR 93 (VTD 1085).

[59.3] A company registered for VAT on 1 May 2000. It submitted a return for the period ending 31 May, claiming a substantial repayment. The Commissioners issued a direction under *VAT Regulations 1995 (SI 1995/2518), reg 25(1)(c)* that the company's first accounting period should run from 1 May 2000 to 30 September 2000, and that its second accounting period should run from 1 October to 30 November. The company appealed. The tribunal struck out the appeal, holding that there was no appealable matter within *VATA 1994, s 83*. *Nuniv Developments Ltd*, EDN/01/77 (VTD 17424).

Application for judicial review of direction by Customs

[59.4] Three companies which exported cars had been permitted to make monthly returns. Because most of these supplies were zero-rated, they were 'repayment traders'. In 2005 and 2006 Customs issued directions requiring the companies to make quarterly returns rather than monthly returns (and to align their quarterly accounting periods with the associated companies from which they acquired the cars which they exported). The companies applied for judicial review. The QB dismissed two of the applications on the grounds that there had been undue delay in making them, but granted the application by the third company. The CA unanimously allowed Customs' appeal against this decision. Moses LJ observed that 'the system by which VAT-registered traders account for VAT may give rise to cash-flow benefits to traders at the expense of the Exchequer'. By allowing 'repayment traders' to make monthly returns, Customs were frequently in the position of having to make repayments 'before receiving output tax in respect of the supply on which input tax was charged and recovered'. Customs were given extensive power to regulate accounting periods by *Article 252* of *Directive 2006/112/EC*. They were entitled 'to distinguish between associated and non-associated companies to alleviate the cash-flow disadvantage to the Exchequer'. On the evidence, Customs' policy was 'neither unlawful nor irrational'. *R (oao BMW AG) v HMRC*, CA [2009] STC 963; [2009] EWCA Civ 77.

[59.5] From 1993 to 2007 a company (B) accounted for VAT using monthly accounting periods. It submitted some large repayment claims, and HMRC subsequently formed the opinion that it had been involved in MTIC fraud. In September 2007 they issued a ruling that B should be required to submit quarterly returns rather than monthly returns. B applied for judicial review. The QB dismissed the application. Burnett J observed that while HMRC had a discretion to allow monthly returns, it was 'entirely understandable why they have chosen not to exercise that discretion in favour of the claimant'. Inglis J held that 'the allegation that the policy as applied to the circumstances of this claimant is unlawful is not truly arguable'. *R (oao Brayfal Ltd) v HMRC (No 2)*, QB [2009] EWHC 3354 (Admin).

Return following prolonged failure to register

[59.6] See *Prudential Assurance Co Ltd (No 5)*, **3.118** ASSESSMENT; *Royal College of Obstetricians & Gynaecologists*, **48.1** PAYMENT OF TAX, and *Bjelica*, **57.89** REGISTRATION.

VATA 1994, s 77—definition of 'prescribed accounting period'

[59.7] See *Wright*, **3.108** ASSESSMENT.

Making of returns (VAT Regulations 1995, reg 25)

Whether return 'made' when posted

[59.8] A taxpayer was charged with failing to furnish a VAT return as required by what is now *VAT Regulations 1995 (SI 1995/2518), reg 25*. He had posted the return in Edinburgh in the envelope supplied, but it had not been received. The Sheriff acquitted the taxpayer, holding that he had furnished the return when he posted it. The CS dismissed the Commissioners' appeal against this decision, holding that the return had been furnished because the form instructed the taxpayer to send the return to the Controller in the envelope provided. Lord Dunpark held that the effect of this wording was that the Commissioners 'were appointing the Post Office as their agent to receive the return on their behalf'. Therefore the return was 'furnished' when it was completed and posted. *Aikman v White*, CS 1985, [1986] STC 1. (*Note.* The *VAT (General) Regulations* as in force at the relevant time used the words 'furnish' and 'furnished', whereas the *VAT Regulations 1995* use the words 'make' and 'made'. The Commissioners subsequently altered the wording of the form so that it reads 'You must ensure that the completed form and any VAT payable are received no later than the due date by the Controller'. In *W Timms & Son (Builders) Ltd*, **59.10** below, the QB distinguished this case as having been decided in the context of criminal liability, under the provisions of *VATA 1983, s 39(8)* which had subsequently been repealed. For the purposes of *FA 1985, ss 19, 20* (which have now become *VATA 1994, ss 59, 79*), the QB held that a return was furnished at the time it was received, rather than at the time it was posted. However, the decision remains relevant with regard to the making of repayment claims: see *Quintain Estates Development plc*, **48.11** PAYMENT OF TAX.)

[59.9] The decision in *Aikman v White*, **59.8** above, was followed in the English cases of *Hayman v Griffiths & Another* and *Walker v Hanby* QB [1987] STC 649. (*Note.* See now, however, the note following **59.8** above.)

[59.10] A company's return for the period ending 31 August 1987, due to be received by the Commissioners by 30 September 1987, indicated that a repayment was due. The company claimed a supplement in respect of this repayment. The Commissioners contended that no repayment supplement was due because the return was not received by them until more than thirty days after the due date. The tribunal found, on the evidence, that the return in question was posted by the company on 15 September 1987 but was not received by the Commissioners until 31 March 1988. The QB held that, on the facts found by the tribunal, repayment supplement was not due. What is now *VATA 1994, s 79(1)* required a return to be received by the Commissioners within one month of the due date. *VATA 1994, ss 59, 79*, which were related provisions and should be construed to harmonise with each other, drew a clear distinction between the despatching and the receiving of a return. The decisions in *Aikman v White*, **59.8** above, and *Hayman v Griffiths*, **59.9** above, were distinguished since they had been decided on the basis of the wording of the return forms issued at the relevant time, which had subsequently been altered, and in the wholly different context of criminal liability under *VATA*

1983, s 39(8), which had subsequently been repealed. *C & E Commrs v W Timms & Son (Builders) Ltd*, QB [1992] STC 374.

[59.11] Similar decisions, also distinguishing *Aikman v White*, 59.8 above, were reached in *Gould & Co*, LON/89/1594X (VTD 4773); and *R Jones*, LON/90/1502X (VTD 5753).

[59.12] Similar decisions were reached by tribunals in *Gale*, 51.5 PENALTIES: FAILURE TO NOTIFY, and *Selwyn*, 51.103 PENALTIES: FAILURE TO NOTIFY. In *Selwyn* the tribunal held that, while the Commissioners had appointed the Post Office as their agent, this was an agency to carry information, not an agency to receive information.

Application of VAT Regulations, reg 25(1)

[59.13] On 4 February 1997 the Commissioners issued a letter to the proprietors of a restaurant, notifying them that they were required to register for VAT with effect from 18 March 1991. In April 1997 the Commissioners issued an estimated assessment, covering the period from 18 March 1991 to 28 February 1997. The proprietors appealed, contending that they had not received a certificate of registration or a return form, and that the assessment was invalid. The Commissioners gave evidence that the relevant certificate of registration had been posted on 12 February 1997, but failed to produce a copy of this certificate, or of the return form. The tribunal accepted the proprietors' contention and allowed the appeal, finding that, because of a typing error, the certificate and return had been sent to an incorrect address and had not been received by the proprietors. The tribunal held that the registration was valid but that the assessment was not authorised by *VAT Regulations 1995 (SI 1995/2518), reg 25(1)*, since the effect of *reg 25(1)* was that assessments had to be issued for specific periods and 'if a taxable person is not registered for VAT, he must make his returns for the quarters ending with March, June, September and December'. The effect of *reg 25(1)* was that the Commissioners could have directed the proprietors to submit a return for an extended period ending in February 1997. However, on the evidence, the Commissioners had not sent either the certificate or the return form to the correct address and 'since no other act or document was argued to have notified the accounting periods to the appellants before the assessment was notified to them', it followed that 'the accounting periods were not notified to them before then, and consequently that the assessment was made in respect of an accounting period for which they had not been required to make a return'. *K & D Antoniou (t/a Sackville Fisheries)*, MAN/97/157 (VTD 17165).

Application of VAT Regulations, reg 25(1)(b)

[59.14] On 1 September 1992 a company was struck off the Register of Companies, under *Companies Act 1985, s 652*. In November 1997 the company was restored to the Register, under *Companies Act 1985, s 653*, and was deemed to have continued in operation as if it had not been struck off. The Commissioners issued a return covering the period from 2 September 1992 to 30 April 1998. The company submitted this return and claimed a repayment. The Commissioners considered that the return was incorrect, and rejected the claim and issued an assessment covering the whole of the period covered by the return. The company appealed. The tribunal dismissed the appeal, holding that the effect of *VAT Regulations 1995 (SI 1995/2518), reg 25(1)(b)* was that the period was a single prescribed accounting period. Accordingly, as the assessment covered a single accounting period, the relevant time limits ran from the end of that single accounting period. *Eastgate Christian Bookshop Ltd, LON/00/381 (VTD 16766).*

Application of VAT Regulations, reg 25(1)(c)

[59.15] In the case noted at 47.21 PARTNERSHIP, the Commissioners issued an assessment on a married couple in 1999, covering the period from 1 April 1991 to 31 August 1997. The couple appealed, contending that, because the Commissioners had not issued a direction under *VAT Regulations 1995 (SI 1995/2518), reg 25(1)(c)*, the assessment was a global assessment covering separate accounting periods and was therefore invalid through having been made outside the statutory time limit. The tribunal accepted this contention and allowed the appeal, holding that 'there was no sufficiently clear instruction to the appellants which could constitute a direction under *rule (sic) 25*'. *House*, 3.127 ASSESSMENT, was distinguished, on the grounds that, in that case, 'all relevant documents were received on the same day'. *PC & VL Leonidas*, [2000] VATDR 207 (VTD 16588).

[59.16] The Commissioners discovered that a restaurant proprietor had failed to register for VAT. At an interview in February 2000, the proprietor accepted that he should have registered from March 1999. The Commissioners formed the opinion that he had been suppressing takings, and issued a notice of compulsory registration backdated to June 1996, together with a notice of assessment covering the period from June 1996 to May 2000. The proprietor appealed. The tribunal reviewed the evidence in detail and found that the proprietor was not 'a witness of truth' and that there had been some suppression of takings, but that the assessment was excessive. The tribunal also observed 'that at no time do the Commissioners appear to have directed in accordance with *regulation 25(1)(c)* that the first return should be for a period longer than the normal period of three months laid down by *regulation 25(1)*'. The tribunal adjourned the case and requested the Commissioners 'to submit further evidence and argument on this point' (which had not been raised by the appellant, who appeared in person). *R Abbarchi*, LON/00/1138 (VTD 17444). (*Note*. There was no further public hearing of the appeal.)

[59.17] A trader (H) registered for VAT in January 1988 and deregistered on 19 July 1994. However, he continued to trade until 19 January 1998, when he transferred the business to a limited company. In November 1998 the Commissioners issued a certificate of registration with an effective date of registration of 20 July 1994, requiring H to make a return for the period from 20 July 1994 to 31 December 1998. In March 1999 they issued an assessment. H appealed, contending that the certificate of registration and the assessment were invalid. The tribunal accepted this contention and allowed the appeal, holding that *VAT Regulations 1995 (SI 1995/2518), reg 25(1)(c)* 'cannot logically cover a period when a person is not required to be registered, as was the case here'. H was not 'liable to render returns after 19 January 1998' and it was not 'open to the Commissioners to require him to be registered after that date'. *MK Hassan*, LON/98/1491 (VTD 17949).

[59.18] A retailer registered for VAT from 1 December 1997 and was required, under *VAT Regulations 1995 (SI 1995/2518), reg 25*, to make returns for the periods ending in February, May, August and November of each year. He ceased trading in 2001. Subsequently the Commissioners issued an assessment covering the six months from 1 September 2000 to 28 February 2001. The trader appealed, contending *inter alia* that the assessment was invalid because it had not been made for a prescribed accounting period as required by *regulation 25*. The tribunal accepted this contention and allowed the appeal. The tribunal chairman (Mrs Gilliland) held that 'the issue in the instant case is whether the Commissioners exercised their power under proviso (*c*) to vary the length of the period 02/01 from the prescribed accounting period of three months from 1 December 2000 to 28 February 2001 to a different prescribed accounting period of five months (*sic*) from 1 September 2000 to 28 February 2001'. *M Weston*, MAN/01/914 (VTD 18190). (*Note.* Mrs Gilliland's decision repeatedly refers to the period from 1 September 2000 to 28 February 2001 as being a period of five months, although it is in fact a period of six months, covering two prescribed quarterly accounting periods. There have been a large number of previous cases in which tribunals and the courts have held that assessments covering more than one prescribed accounting period were valid: see, for example, the 1978 CA decision in *SJ Grange Ltd*, 3.114 ASSESSMENT, and the 2003 Ch D decision in *Hindle*, 3.117 ASSESSMENT. None of these cases are referred to in Mrs Gilliland's decision, which must therefore be regarded as being of very doubtful authority.)

[59.19] Customs issued an assessment on a partnership, purporting to cover the period from 1 March 1998 to 12 September 2001 (when the partnership ceased by virtue of the death of one of the partners). The tribunal held that the assessment had been validly issued, holding that it would not have been valid unless Customs had issued a direction under *VAT Regulations 1995 (SI 1995/2518), reg 25(1)(c)*, but finding that a letter issued by Customs constituted such a direction. *B Hopcraft (No 2)*, LON/02/459 (VTD 19220).

[59.20] For another case where the Ch D held that an assessment was authorised by *VAT Regulations 1995 (SI 1995/2518), reg 25(1)(c)*, see *Hindle*, 3.117 ASSESSMENT. For a case where the CS held that an assessment was not authorised by *reg 25(1)(c)*, see *Miah*, 3.144 ASSESSMENT.

Interpretation of VAT Regulations, reg 25(5)

[59.21] In 1992 a company received a substantial interim payment of compensation from the Department of Transport in return for surrendering its interest in some land under a compulsory purchase order. It did not account for output tax on the compensation, although it had previously elected to waive exemption in respect of the land in question. In 1994 it made a voluntary disclosure of the liability, advising the Commissioners that the amount of compensation had not been finally agreed. The compensation was finally agreed in 1997. Following subsequent correspondence, the Commissioners wrote to the company in March 1998, instructing it to account for tax on the compensation on its next return, in accordance with *VAT Regulations 1995 (SI 1995/2518), reg 35*. The company refused to do so, and in August 1998 the Commissioners issued an assessment, purporting to be for the prescribed accounting period ending in May 1998, charging tax of more than £1,600,000 on the compensation. The company appealed, contending that the assessment was invalid as it had been made outside the statutory time limit. The Commissioners defended the assessment on the basis that, by virtue of *VAT Regulations 1995 (SI 1995/2518), reg 25(5)*, they had exercised their power to 'allow VAT chargeable in any period to be treated as being chargeable in such later period as they may specify'. The tribunal allowed the company's appeal, observing that the Commissioners had not made an immediate reply to the company's letter of 1994, and holding that 'there is no evidence that they put their minds to the possibility of the exercise of the *regulation 25(5)* power until they came to draft their Statement of Case.' The tribunal held that 'the interests of legal certainty (a fundamental principle of Community law which applies to VAT) require that the taxable person be told that the power has been exercised and be told precisely what his new obligations are'. On the evidence, there had not been 'an effective exercise by the Commissioners of their *regulation 25(5)* power'. Since the Commissioners had not exercised their power under *reg 25(5)*, it followed that the assessment had been issued more than three years after the end of the relevant accounting period, and it was therefore out of time. *Inchcape Management Services Ltd*, [1999] VATDR 397 (VTD 16256).

Whether tax payable where return qualified

[59.22] A company had submitted returns showing net tax payable of £43,073, qualified by a statement that they were 'subject to reserved claims for input tax on expenses'. The Commissioners rejected the claims and the company appealed. The Commissioners applied for the appeals to be struck out as the company had not paid the £43,073. The tribunal accepted this contention and struck out the appeals, holding that a return must be an unqualified one, any underpayments or overpayments being rectified in later returns. *DK Wright & Associates Ltd*, [1975] VATTR 168 (VTD 203).

Correction Of Errors (VAT Regulations 1995, regs 34, 35)

Unilateral correction of error by company

[59.23] Following a direction made by the Commissioners under what is now *VATA 1994, Sch 6 para 2* that tax should be accounted for on the open market value of goods sold, a company paid a sum of £1,399,000 in tax to the Commissioners. It subsequently transpired that, in the light of the CJEC decision in *Direct Cosmetics Ltd*, 22.496 EUROPEAN COMMUNITY LAW, the Commissioners' direction had no legal effect and was void. The Commissioners refused to repay the tax previously paid, and the company therefore deducted the amount from the amount owing on its next return. The Commissioners issued a writ for the sum concerned and applied for summary judgment under *Rules of the Supreme Court 1965* as then in force. The HL rejected the application, holding that it did not matter whether the previous error was one of law or fact, since what is now *VATA 1994, s 25* allowed the company to correct errors in previous returns. Where a taxpayer had been required to pay VAT on a basis which was subsequently held to be contrary to the law, the taxpayer was entitled to deduct the wrongly paid tax from his next return. Furthermore, the Commissioners' publications could only be construed as giving the legal right to make a deduction for a past overdeclaration made in error. *C & E Commrs v Fine Art Developments plc*, HL [1989] STC 85; [1989] 2 WLR 369; [1989] 1 All ER 502; [1989] 2 CMLR 185. (*Notes.* (1) Under *VAT Regulations 1995 (SI 1995/2518), reg 34(3)*, it is only permissible to adjust errors on a subsequent return where the net value of errors discovered does not exceed £2,000. In other cases, the VAT office must be informed in writing. (2) The *Rules of the Supreme Court 1965* have now been replaced by the *Civil Procedure Rules 1998 (SI 1998/3132)*, of which *rule 24* deals with applications for summary judgment.)

Error in original return—corrected return submitted by fax

[59.24] See *AB Gee of Ripley Ltd*, 52.30 PENALTIES: MISDECLARATION.

Unilateral 'correction' of assessment in subsequent return

[59.25] A company failed to make a VAT return, because its records had been mislaid. The Commissioners issued an estimated assessment charging tax of £3,816, which the company paid. Subsequently the company attempted to reconstruct its records and formed the view that, for the relevant period, its input tax had exceeded its output tax by £2,649. For its next accounting period it accordingly deducted the aggregate of these two amounts (£6,465) as input tax. The Commissioners issued an assessment to recover the tax. The tribunal dismissed the company's appeal against this assessment, holding that as the company had not appealed against the original assessment, it could not be entitled to adjust its next return in this manner without the Commissioners' consent. *Greenspear Products Ltd*, MAN/86/32 (VTD 2124). (*Note.* See also the note following *Fine Art Developments plc*, 59.23 above.)

Unilateral correction of errors in past returns

[59.26] A company which manufactured bone china offered its major customers a 5% discount for settlement within 30 days. It initially accounted for VAT on the full price shown in the invoices, but subsequently took the view that it should only account for tax on the actual price received. In its next return it therefore deducted an amount of £2,044 in respect of output tax allegedly overdeclared, and also deducted a further sum of £310 in respect of interest. The Commissioners issued an assessment to recover the tax, and the tribunal dismissed the company's appeal. Firstly, the company had failed to comply with the procedure for the correction of errors set out in *Notice No*

700 (as then in force). It had not issued credit notes to correct the errors on the invoices it had issued to its customers. Secondly, there was no justification for the claim to deduct a sum in respect of interest. *Springfield China Ltd*, MAN/89/180 (VTD 4546). (*Note.* See also the note following *Fine Art Developments plc*, 59.23 above.)

[59.27] For a case in which a company was held not to be entitled to make a unilateral correction to recover tax which it had allegedly overpaid, see *GUS Merchandising Corporation Ltd*, 58.53 RETAILERS' SPECIAL SCHEMES.

*Delay in processing credit notes—effect of regulation 34**

[59.28] A trader received two credit notes in 1991. However, he failed to process the notes until 1994. In his return for the period ending June 1994 he claimed credit for the tax shown by the credit notes. The Commissioners considered that the effect of what is now *VAT Regulations 1995 (SI 1995/2518), reg 38* was that the trader was no longer entitled to credit for the amounts shown on the credit notes. They therefore issued an assessment to recover the tax in question, and the trader appealed, contending that the effect of *VAT Regulations, reg 34** was that he was entitled to correct the return for the period in which he had received the credit notes. The tribunal allowed the appeal, holding that the regulations did not give a trader 'the right to process credit notes as and when he chooses' but finding that 'the original failure to process the credit notes was an accounting error which the appellant was entitled to rectify on discovery'. *J Copson (t/a Compressors & Air Equipment)*, MAN/94/833 (VTD 13335). (*Note.* See now *VAT Regulations 1995, reg 34(1A)*, inserted with effect from 1 May 1997, which imposes a three-year time limit for corrections under *reg 34*.)

VAT Regulations 1995, reg 34(1A)—time limit for adjustments

[59.29] A company (V) supplied some goods to two customers, and accounted for output tax accordingly. The customers returned the goods. However V did not adjust its VAT records until after the three-year time limit laid down by *VAT Regulations 1995 (SI 1995/2518), reg 34(1A)*. The Commissioners rejected V's claim for repayment, and the tribunal dismissed V's appeal. *Valley Chemical Co Ltd*, LON/01/705 (VTD 17989).

[59.30] Similar decisions were reached in *MML Systems*, LON/03/477 (VTD 18677) and *Enviroengineering Ltd (No 2)*, 2.26 APPEALS.

Application of VAT Regulations 1995, reg 35

[59.31] See *Inchcape Management Services Ltd*, 59.12 above.

VAT Regulations 1995, reg 38(1A)— time limit for adjustments

[59.32] See *Burnham Logistics Ltd*, 40.114 INVOICES AND CREDIT NOTES.

VAT Regulations 1995, reg 38(1A)—whether valid under EC law

[59.33] A company (G) sold cars under hire-purchase agreements. In some cases, customers defaulted on the agreement, and G repossessed the cars and sold them for less than the original sale price. It claimed a VAT adjustment on the basis that there had been a decrease in consideration, within *VAT Regulations 1995 (SI 1995/2518), reg 38*. The Commissioners issued a ruling that the effect of *reg 38(1A)* was that G was not entitled to make any adjustment where the car was returned more than three years after the start of the hire-purchase agreement. G appealed, contending that *reg 38(1A)* contravened *Article 11C1* of the *EC Sixth Directive*. The tribunal accepted this contention and allowed the appeal, holding that '*Article 11C1* has direct effect' and that 'a Member State cannot take away the right conferred by that provision'. The three-year 'cap' imposed by *reg 38(1A)* was 'a blanket limitation which has the effect of ousting the taxable person's basic right to be taxed on the consideration received by him and no more. As such, the three-year limitation on making the claim by reference to the time when the original supply is made is incompatible with *Article 11*'. *General Motors Acceptance Corporation (UK) plc*, LON/01/242 (VTD 17990). (*Note.* For other issues in this case, taken to the Ch D, see **40.109** INVOICES AND CREDIT NOTES and **44.53** MOTOR CARS.)

Miscellaneous

Return showing negative amount of output tax

[59.34] See *Gwent County Council*, **52.2** PENALTIES: MISDECLARATION.

Return submitted on form relating to different business

[59.35] See *Tannington Growers (1984) Ltd*, **52.3** PENALTIES: MISDECLARATION.

Whether part of return withdrawn

[59.36] In November 1991 a company (C) submitted a VAT return for the period ending 30 September, claiming a repayment of £324,000. The Commissioners queried the claim, £310,000 of which related to a computer which had been imported from France. C's accounts manager asked if the £310,000 relating to the computer could be 'put on hold' and the remaining £14,000 repaid to the company. The Commissioners agreed to this and repaid the £14,000. In December 1991 C transferred ownership of the computer to an associated company. In its return for the period ending 31 December, it repeated its claim for input tax on the computer, and declared a corresponding amount of output tax. The return claimed a net repayment of £1,200, which was duly repaid by the Commissioners. In March C lodged a claim for repayment supplement on the basis that the £310,000 input tax relating to the computer should have been repaid following receipt of its September return.

The Commissioners rejected the claim and the tribunal dismissed C's appeal. On the evidence, C had withdrawn the relevant claim from its September return when the Commissioners had queried it, and had subsequently claimed the relevant input tax in its December return. The tribunal observed that C could not 'have it both ways' and that 'the only basis on which (C) could lawfully claim input credit for December 1991 for the import VAT was that it had either accepted the disallowance or, which comes to the same, had withdrawn that part of the September 1991 return'. *Computer Equipment Investors Ltd*, LON/92/1161Z (VTD 10092).

VAT Regulations, reg 40—power to extend time limit

[59.37] See *Caro*, **18.446** DEFAULT SURCHARGE, and *Starlite (Chandeliers) Ltd*, **18.448** DEFAULT SURCHARGE.

Rounding of VAT on invoices

[59.38] See *Catchlord Ltd*, **40.82** INVOICES AND CREDIT NOTES, and *Topps Tiles plc*, **40.83** INVOICES AND CREDIT NOTES.

60

Second-Hand Goods

The cases in this chapter are arranged under the following headings.

Records and accounts   60.1
Works of art, etc.   60.7
Miscellaneous   60.16

NOTE

The 'margin scheme' of accounting was extended to all second-hand goods, works of art, antiques and collectors' items (except precious metals and gemstones) with effect from 1 January 1995. For a full explanation of the changes, see Tolley's Value Added Tax. For cases concerning the scheme for sales of second-hand cars, see **44.60** to **44.96** MOTOR CARS.

Records and accounts

Whether tribunal has jurisdiction to review Customs' decision

[60.1] The Commissioners issued a ruling that a company which dealt in old coins and medals could not use the 'margin scheme' on the grounds that its records did not comply with the requirements laid down under what is now *Special Provisions Order 1995, Article 12*. The company appealed, contending that the Commissioners should have exercised their discretion to permit it to use the scheme. The HL rejected this contention and dismissed the appeal, holding that the tribunal could consider whether the records complied with the statutory requirements, but where the records did not meet those requirements, the tribunal could not consider whether the Commissioners should have exercised their discretion to permit the use of the scheme. *C & E Commrs v JH Corbitt (Numismatists) Ltd, HL* [1980] STC 231; [1981] AC 22; [1980] 2 All ER 72. (*Note.* This decision was not followed in the 1992 case of *Christopher Gibbs Ltd*, **60.2** below, on the grounds that it had been decided before the enactment of what is now *VATA 1994, s 84(10)*. *Obiter dicta* of Lord Lane were subsequently disapproved by Sales J in the 2009 case of *Oxfam v HMRC*, **11.51** CHARITIES.)

[60.2] The Commissioners issued an assessment charging tax on the full sale price of two antique tables, considering that the conditions for the application of the margin scheme had not been satisfied. The tribunal held that it had jurisdiction to review the Commissioners' decision, applying *dicta* in *Bardsley*, **44.64** MOTOR CARS, and not following *JH Corbitt (Numismatists) Ltd*, **60.1** above, since that case had been decided before the enactment of what is now *VATA 1994, s 84(10)*. The tribunal reviewed the evidence in detail and held that one of the tables should have been dealt with under the margin scheme, because all the relevant details were recorded except for the purchaser's signature. Since there was no reasonable doubt that the table had been sold to the person named, the tribunal held that the need for the purchaser to sign the invoice should 'have been dispensed with'. However, in the case of the second table, the details of the purchase price had not been recorded, so that the company was obliged to account for tax on the full sale price. *Christopher Gibbs Ltd*, [1992] VATTR 376 (VTD 8981).

[60.3] A partnership which sold second-hand goods registered for VAT from 1990. In 1998 they submitted a substantial repayment claim on the basis that they should be permitted to use the global accounting scheme, provided for by *Special Provisions Order 1995, Article 13*, and to backdate their use of the scheme to 1995. The Commissioners rejected the claim on the basis that the partnership could not use the scheme retrospectively. The partnership appealed. The tribunal dismissed the appeal, holding that there was 'no discretion to allow the use of the Global Scheme where the taxpayer has not opted to use the Margin Scheme'. Furthermore, the appeal was outside the scope of *VATA 1994, s 83*, so that the tribunal had no jurisdiction to hear the appeal. *I McCord & M Alford*, LON/99/663 (VTD 17189).

Application for retrospective use of Global Accounting Scheme

[60.4] In January 2000 a company which dealt in second-hand goods began to adopt the Global Accounting Scheme. Subsequently it applied to be allowed to use the Scheme retrospectively, so as to recompute its tax liability for 1998 and 1999. The Commissioners rejected this application, and the company appealed. The tribunal dismissed the appeal, holding that the Commissioners had not acted unreasonably. *Baysouth Ltd*, MAN/01/592 (VTD 17597).

Application for retrospective use of Global Accounting Scheme

[60.5] A gold coin dealer accounted for VAT under the margin scheme for works of art, etc. where the coins were within the definition of 'collectors' pieces', or were more than 100 years old. The Commissioners discovered that his records indicated that he had sold a consignment of coins to a resident of the USA for £93,000, and another consignment to a Canadian for £181,000. The invoices recorded the name and address of the alleged purchasers, but they both denied having purchased the coins in question. The Commissioners formed the opinion that the dealer had acted fraudulently, by inventing the supposed transactions so as to avoid paying tax on supplies which did not qualify for the margin scheme. The trader appealed, contending that the transactions had been genuine, and that it appeared that the real purchasers of the antique coins had given him false names and addresses. The tribunal allowed the appeal, finding that, on the balance of probabilities, the sale to the Canadian purchaser had actually taken place despite the alleged purchaser's subsequent denial, and that the other sale had been to an unidentified American who had given a false name and address. The records complied with the requirements of the scheme, and there was no obligation on the dealer to check the identity of his customer. *MD Bord*, LON/91/2595Y (VTD 9824). (*Note.* For a preliminary issue in this case, see **2.266** APPEALS.)

Other cases

[60.6] There have been a large number of cases in which tribunals have found that a trader's records have not complied with the requirements of the margin scheme or the global accounting scheme, and have dismissed appeals against assessments charging tax on the full amount of the takings. In the interests of space, such cases are not reported individually in this book. For summaries of such cases decided up to 31 December 1993, see Tolley's VAT Cases 1994.

Works of art, etc.

Works of art sold at auction—amount of consideration

[60.7] A company sold works of art at auction. Under the relevant conditions of sale, the vendor received the 'hammer price' (the price at which the item was 'knocked down' to the buyer) less a 6% commission which was retained by the auctioneer. The buyer was also required to pay to the auctioneer a premium of 10% of the 'hammer price'. The Commissioners issued an assessment treating the buyer's premium as part of the consideration. The company appealed, contending that the consideration was the 'hammer price'. The tribunal accepted this contention and allowed the appeal. *Jocelyn Feilding Fine Arts Ltd*, [1978] VATTR 164 (VTD 652). (*Notes.* (1) For the award of costs in this case, see **2.463** APPEALS. (2) There is now an optional scheme for auctioneers acting in their own name. Where this scheme is used, the purchase price is the hammer price less the VAT-inclusive commission charged to the vendor, and the selling price is the hammer price plus the buyer's premium, including VAT.)

Definition of 'collectors' pieces'

[60.8] In two German cases, the CJEC defined 'collectors' pieces' as 'objects which possess the requisite characteristics for inclusion in a collection, that is to say pieces which are relatively rare, are not normally used for their original intention, are the subject of special transactions outside the normal trade in similar utility pieces and are of greater value'. The CJEC also held that 'collectors' pieces which evidence a significant step in the evolution of human achievements or illustrate a period of that evolution are to be regarded as being of historical or ethnographic interest'. *E Daiber v Hauptzollamt Reutlingen*, CJEC Case 200/84; [1985] ECR 3363; *Collection Guns GmbH v Hauptzollamt Koblenz*, CJEC [1985] ECR 3387. (*Note.* The cases concerned customs duty, but the decision is clearly relevant to *VATA 1994, s 21(5)*, which deals with imports of 'collectors' pieces', and *Special Provisions Order 1995, Article 12(2)(a)*, which deals with supplies of 'collectors' items'. The decision was applied in *HMRC v West*, **60.14** below, but *obiter dicta* of the Advocate-General were disapproved.)

[60.9] The decision in *Daiber v Hauptzollamt Reutlingen*, **60.8** above, was applied in the subsequent German case of *U Clees v Hauptzollamt Wuppertal*, CJEC Case C-259/97; 3 December 1998 unreported.

Antique model railway train—whether a 'collector's piece'

[60.10] An individual imported into the UK a Märklin gauge 3 model train, originally sold in 1900. The Commissioners issued a ruling that VAT was due on the importation. He appealed, contending that the train was a 'collector's piece of historical interest' so that no VAT was chargeable under the legislation then in force. The tribunal allowed his appeal, finding that the train in question was 'a special article representing a culminating period in the evolution of toy manufacture having an economic and sociological significance and representing a technological achievement in the history of that manufacture and the evolution of industry'. Accordingly it qualified as a 'collector's piece of historical interest', applying the CJEC decision in *Daiber v Hauptzollamt Reutlingen and Collection Guns GmbH v Hauptzollamt Koblenz*, 60.8 above. *D Pressland*, [1995] VATDR 432 (VTD 13059).

Vintage cars—whether 'collector's pieces'

[60.11] A company carried on a business of importing and restoring vintage sports cars. It imported a 1954 Jaguar XK 120, a 1956 Jaguar XK140, and a 1960 Jaguar XK 150. Customs issued a ruling that the cars fell under customs duty tariff classification 8703. The company appealed, contending that the cars should be treated as 'collectors' pieces of historical interest', within tariff classification 9705. The tribunal rejected this contention and dismissed the appeal, applying the CJEC decision in *Daiber v Hauptzollamt Reutlingen*, 60.8 above. *Barnfinds Ltd*, LON/05/7005 (C198).

[60.12] A company imported 23 vintage cars, including 20 Jaguars, dating from 1954 to 1967. HMRC issued a ruling that the cars fell under customs duty tariff classification 8703. The company appealed, contending that the cars should be treated as 'collectors' pieces of historical interest', within tariff classification 9705. The tribunal accepted this contention and allowed the appeal, specifically declining to follow the 2005 decision in *Barnfinds Ltd*, 60.11 above. The tribunal held that all 23 cars possessed 'a certain scarcity value', and 'illustrated a significant step in the evolution of human achievements, or a period of that evolution'. *JD Classics Holdings Ltd v HMRC*, [2010] UKFTT 259 (TC), TC00553.

Bentley S3 Continental Flying Spur— whether a 'collector's piece

[60.13] An individual (P) imported a Bentley S3 'Continental Flying Spur' motor car, manufactured in 1964, from the USA. Customs issued a ruling that this was a 'means of transport', within Tariff Classification 8703, attracting customs duty of 10% and VAT at 17.5%. P appealed, contending that the car was a 'collector's piece of historical interest', within Tariff Classification 9705. The tribunal rejected this contention and dismissed the appeal, applying the principles laid down by the CJEC in *Daiber v Hauptzollamt Reutlingen*, 60.8 above. The tribunal found that, after allowing for inflation, the car had not increased in value, and held that it was not of sufficient 'historical interest' to satisfy the principles laid down in *Daiber*. *JS Paul*, MAN/05/7044 (C210).

Ford Zephyr Mark 1— whether a 'collector's piece

[60.14] An individual (W) imported a Ford Zephyr Mark 1 motor car, manufactured in 1955, from New Zealand. Customs issued a ruling that this was a 'means of transport', within Tariff Classification 8703, attracting customs duty of 10% and VAT at 17.5%. W appealed, contending that the car was a 'collector's piece of historical interest', within Tariff Classification 9705. The tribunal accepted this contention and allowed the appeal, and the Ch D upheld this decision. Sir Andrew Park observed that Customs had adopted a policy of only treating cars as 'collector's pieces' if they had a value of at least £20,000. He held that this policy was unreasonable and arbitrary, and observed that it relied on *obiter dicta* of the Advocate-General in *Daiber v Hauptzollamt Reutlingen*, 60.8 above, which had not been adopted by the CJEC in its judgment. On the evidence, the car qualified as a 'collector's piece of historical interest', since its historical value significantly exceeded its 'utility value', i.e. the amount which someone might be willing to pay for it simply in order to use it as a car. *HMRC v P West*, Ch D [2008] EWHC 2277 (Ch).

Rolex watch—whether a 'collector's piece'

[60.15] See *Caddey*, 35.21 IMPORTS.

Miscellaneous

Special Provisions Order—whether compatible with EC law

[60.16] See *EC Commission v United Kingdom (No 5)*, 22.266 EUROPEAN COMMUNITY LAW.

Animals—whether 'second-hand goods'

[60.17] See *Förvaltnings AB Stenholmen v Riksskatteverket*, 22.494 EUROPEAN COMMUNITY LAW.

Cost of fitting out hull—whether part of cost of boat

[60.18] A company carried on a business of hiring out boats. It acquired four bare hulls, which it fitted out and commissioned. It used the hulls in its business for several years before selling them. In accounting for tax under the margin scheme, it included the cost of fitting out and commissioning the hulls as part of the cost of acquiring them. The Commissioners issued an assessment on the basis that only the actual cost of the hulls could be deducted. The tribunal dismissed the company's appeal and the QB upheld this decision. For the purposes of what is now *Special Provisions Order 1995, Article 12*, the acquisition cost was restricted to the actual cost of the hulls. *Wyvern Shipping Co Ltd v C & E Commrs*, QB 1978, [1979] STC 91.

Whether cost of insurance deductible in computing margin

[60.19] A company sold second-hand goods from a number of shops, and operated the 'margin scheme'. It paid insurance premiums to an associated Guernsey company, and treated these premiums as deductions in computing its profit margin. The Commissioners issued an assessment on the basis that the insurance premiums were not an allowable deduction. The tribunal upheld the assessment and dismissed the company's appeal, holding on the evidence that 'the cost of the insurance cannot be said to be part of the consideration for the contract'. *General Trading Stores Ltd*, LON/99/871 (VTD 17591).

Supplies of repossessed goods—Special Provisions Order, Article 4

[60.20] A company (B) sold electrical goods such as televisions, refrigerators and washing machines under hire-purchase agreements. In cases where customers could not make the necessary payments, it repossessed the goods. Where possible, it resold the goods (although some items were repossessed in such poor condition that it was impossible to resell them). Initially B accounted for output tax on such supplies. In 2003 it submitted a substantial repayment claim on the basis that it should not have accounted for output tax, on the basis that the supplies fell within *VAT (Special Provisions) Order 1995 (SI 1995/1268), article 4*, which stated that there was no supply of goods or services for VAT purposes if goods repossessed under a finance agreement were sold as 'second-hand' goods, and were 'in the same condition at the time of disposal as they were when they were repossessed or taken into possession'. HMRC rejected the majority of the claim on the grounds that B had had to undertake some repair work, so that the goods had not been 'in the same condition at the time of disposal as they were when they were repossessed or taken into possession'. B appealed. The tribunal reviewed the evidence in detail and allowed the appeal in part. The tribunal held that no VAT was due 'where, at the point of repossession of TVs or washing machines, remote control units, TV stands or washing machine water hoses were not repossessed, and the machines themselves were re-sold after mere cleaning, without any other work'. It would be 'too artificial to say that the eventual sale was, for instance, of a TV with a remote control unit, which is one single item in a different condition than it was in when it was repossessed'. In such cases, 'VAT should be accounted for in relation to the sale of a new remote control unit, TV stand or washing machine hoses for an apportioned part of the total price', but no VAT should be accounted for in relation to the second-hand item. Similarly, the replacement of batteries, fuses, washing machine filters or light bulbs in refrigerators did not prevent an item from being treated as sold 'in the same condition'. However, the replacement of a TV casing, tube or circuit board did 'change the condition of repossessed televisions', so that VAT was due on such sales. *Buy As You View Ltd v HMRC*, [2010] UKFTT 182 (TC), TC00486.

61

Self-Supply

The cases in this chapter are arranged under the following headings
Self-supplies of goods (VATA 1994, s 5(5))   **61.1**
Self-supplies of services (VATA 1994, s 5(6))   **61.8**

Note

For cases concerning the self-supply provisions of *VAT (Cars) Order, Article 5*, see **44.55** to **44.59** MOTOR CARS.

Self-supplies of goods (VATA 1994, s 5(5))

Printed stationery destroyed before use

[61.1] A building society printed its own stationery. It accounted for VAT at the time of printing, under the self-supply rules then in force. It destroyed a quantity of stationery on which it had already accounted for tax, and reclaimed the VAT in question. The Commissioners rejected the claim, considering that the deemed self-supply had taken place at the time the stationery was printed, so that the tax could not be refunded. The tribunal allowed the society's appeal, holding that there had never been any supply of the stationery, since the stationery had never been used by the society for the purpose of its business. *Nationwide Building Society*, [1993] VATTR 205 (VTD 10117). (*Note*. The self-supply rules became *Article 11* of the *VAT (Special Provisions) Order 1995 (SI 1995/1268)*, which was revoked by the *VAT (Special Provisions) Order 2002 (SI 2002/1280)* with effect from 1 June 2002.)

Self-supplies of stationery by building society

[61.2] See *Leeds & Holbeck Building Society*, **46.182** PARTIAL EXEMPTION.

Chequebooks and credit slip books—whether within Article 11

[61.3] A major bank had accounted for VAT on the basis that it had made a 'self-supply', within *Article 11* of the *VAT (Special Provisions) Order 1995 (SI 1995/1268)*, of chequebooks, credit slip books, and bank statements. Subsequently it formed the opinion that it should not have accounted for tax on these items, on the basis that, when they were sent to customers, they were 'supplied to another person' within the meaning of *Article 11(1)(a)*. The bank claimed a substantial repayment. The Commissioners rejected the claim, considering that the items were not 'supplied' within the meaning of *Article 11*, since they were supplied as part of a financial service, rather than as goods. The bank appealed. The tribunal allowed the bank's appeal, holding that the items had been 'supplied to another person' and were therefore outside the scope of the self-supply provisions. *National Westminster Bank plc (No 2)*, [2000] VATDR 484 (VTD 17000). (*Note*. See now the note following *Nationwide Building Society*, **61.1** above.)

Self-supply of advertising posters

[61.4] See *The Royal Society for the Encouragement of Arts, Manufacture & Commerce*, **11.24** CHARITIES.

Whether direction should have been withdrawn retrospectively.

[61.5] In 1973 a university examination board had applied for, and had been granted, a direction that the self-supply provisions contained in what is now *VAT (Special Provisions) Order (SI 1995/1268), Article 11* should not apply to it, on the basis that the tax attributable to its self-supplies of printed materials was negligible. Subsequently the in-house printing activities of the examination board increased in number. In 1996 its accountants applied for the declaration to be withdrawn retrospectively, and submitted a consequential claim for repayment of about £2,500,000 in input tax. The Commissioners rejected the claim, on the grounds that they could only withdraw a direction under *Article 11(2)(c)* 'from a current or future date', and could not withdraw such a direction respectively. The examination board appealed. The tribunal dismissed the appeal, holding that, although the Commissioners had a discretionary power to withdraw such a direction respectively, it was not unreasonable for them to have refused to do so in this case. The tribunal observed that, when the original direction was issued in 1973, the examination board had undertaken to notify the Commissioners of 'any change in the general pattern or volume of self-supplied printed matter', but had failed to do so. Accordingly, the Commissioners had not acted unreasonably. *University of Cambridge Local Examination Syndicate*, [1997] VATDR 245 (VTD 15015). (*Note*. See now the note following *Nationwide Building Society*, **61.1** above.)

Assets used for private purposes—whether a self-supply

[61.6] See *Broadhurst*, **62.101** SUPPLY, and *Mellor*, **62.102** SUPPLY.

Assets retained on cessation of trade—whether a self-supply

[61.7] See the cases noted at **62.103** to **62.106** SUPPLY.

Self-supplies of services (VATA 1994, s 5(6))

Self-supplies of construction services

[61.8] See *Fforestfach Medical Centre*, **6.31** BUILDINGS AND LAND; *C & E Commrs v Trustees for R & R Pension Fund*, **6.44** BUILDINGS AND LAND, and *Robert Gordon's College*, **22.165** EUROPEAN COMMUNITY LAW.

62

Supply

The cases in this chapter are arranged under the following headings.

Whether there has been a supply

Supplies to employees (including company cars)	**62.1**
Provision of employees' services and administrative services	**62.19**
Reimbursements of expenses	**62.52**
Sales of assets	**62.72**
Conditional supplies (*VATA 1994, Sch 4 para 1*)	**62.87**
Transfers of assets (*VATA 1994, Sch 4 paras 5, 8*)	**62.95**
Donations	**62.119**
Inducement payments ('reverse premiums') and rent-free periods, etc.	**62.125**
Compensation payments	**62.135**
Whether supply 'in the course or furtherance of any business' (*VATA 1994, s 4(1)*)	**62.150**
Services supplied by office-holders (*VATA 1994, s 94(4)*)	**62.163**
Miscellaneous—supplies of goods	**62.167**
Miscellaneous—supplies of services	**62.184**

By whom the supply was made

Driving tuition	**62.223**
Taxi and minicab drivers	**62.232**
Hairdressing	**62.255**
Massage and personal services	**62.274**
Supplies of accommodation	**62.284**
Supplies of catering	**62.292**
Employees—whether making supplies as individuals or on behalf of employer	**62.315**
Deemed supplies under *Sch 4 para 7*	**62.329**
Miscellaneous	**62.330**

The time of the supply (VATA 1994, s 6)

Time of supply of goods (*VATA 1994, s 6(2)*)	**62.382**
Time of performance of services (*VATA 1994, s 6(3)*)	**62.396**
Issue of invoice (*VATA 1994, s 6(4)*)	**62.411**
Receipt of payment (*VATA 1994, s 6(4)*)	**62.417**
Supplies of water, gas, etc. (*VAT Regulations 1995, reg 86*)	**62.465**
Continuous supplies of services (*VAT Regulations 1995, reg 90*)	**62.466**
Royalties and similar payments (*VAT Regulations 1995, reg 91*)	**62.472**
Supplies by barristers and advocates (*VAT Regulations 1995, reg 92*)	**62.474**
Supplies in the construction industry (*VAT Regulations 1995, reg 93*)	**62.475**

The place of the supply (VATA 1994, s 7)

Place of supply of goods	**62.476**
Place of supply of services	**62.480**

Single or multiple supplies	**62.548**
Miscellaneous matters	**62.557**

Whether there has been a supply

NOTE

In the cases under this heading it is accepted that there is a business within what is now *VATA 1994, s 94*, and the issue is whether there has been a supply in the course or furtherance of that business. For cases where the issue is whether a supply has been received for the purpose of a business (including input tax claims where Customs consider that the transactions form part of a 'carousel fraud'), see **36** INPUT TAX. For cases where the existence of a business is disputed, see **7** BUSINESS.

Supplies to employees (including company cars)

NOTE

For the deduction of input tax in respect of the expenses (including car expenses) of employees or agents, see **36.311** INPUT TAX *et seq.*

Payments by employee for private use of company car

[62.1] A company provided one of its employees with a company car. He was allowed to use the car privately, and the company deducted £4 per month from his salary to cover this. Customs issued a ruling that tax was chargeable on the supply of the car for private use, and the tribunal dismissed the company's appeal. *W & JR Watson Ltd*, [1974] VATTR 83 (VTD 67). (*Note.* The provisions concerning the VAT treatment of private motoring were changed with effect from 1 August 1995. See Tolley's Value Added Tax. Although charges for the use of a motor car remain taxable in principle, the making available of a motor car for private use is not a taxable supply if VAT was wholly excluded from credit on the purchase of the vehicle.)

[62.2] The decision in *W & JR Watson Ltd*, 62.1 above, was applied in the similar subsequent case of *William Peto & Co Ltd*, MAN/78/66 (VTD 736).

[62.3] A company provided its directors with cars and allowed them to use the cars privately. The directors paid the company for this private use. The Commissioners issued assessments charging tax on the payments and the tribunal dismissed the companies' appeals. *Mitchell Haselhurst Ltd*, [1979] VATTR 166 (VTD 812). (*Note.* See now the note following *W & JR Watson Ltd*, 62.1 above.)

[62.4] A company which carried on a brewery business supplied a large number of its employees with cars. It deducted sums from the employees' salaries to cover the private use of the cars. The Commissioners issued a ruling that VAT was chargeable on the sums in question. The company appealed, contending that, since it had not been able to deduct input tax on the purchase of the cars, no output tax should be due. The tribunal dismissed the appeal, holding that 'the input tax on the cost of the car is not sufficiently linked to the output tax on the supply as to offend the neutrality principle'. *Allied*

Lyons plc, [1994] VATTR 361 (VTD 11731). (*Note*. See now the note following *W & JR Watson Ltd*, **62.1** above.)

Employees provided with company car—reduction in salary

[62.5] A company provided some of its employees with cars. Such employees were paid less than the scale salary for their grade, the reduction in salary being calculated by reference to the price of the car. Once an employee accepted that he would receive a lower salary in return for being provided with a car, he was not permitted to revert to the normal scale salary, even if he was banned from driving. The Commissioners took the view that the reduction in salary constituted consideration paid by the employee for the provision of the car, and was therefore chargeable to VAT. The company appealed, contending that the acceptance of a reduced salary did not constitute the giving of 'consideration' for the private use of the car. The tribunal accepted this contention and allowed the appeal, applying *Goodfellow*, **62.13** below. The provision of the car was taken into account in fixing the employee's gross salary, which remained the same whether or not he actually used the car. His gross salary was the amount specified in his contract, and there was therefore no reduction of salary which could constitute 'consideration'. *Co-Operative Insurance Society Ltd*, [1992] VATTR 44 (VTD 7109). (*Note*. See now the *VAT (Treatment of Transactions) Order 1992 (SI 1992/630)*, which gives statutory effect to this decision.)

Provision of parking facility to employee

[62.6] A university charged one of its employees for the provision of a parking space. The Commissioners issued a ruling that output tax was chargeable on the amount in question. The employee appealed. The tribunal allowed the appeal, holding that the university was not providing the parking facility in the course of its business. *RA Archer (No 2)*, [1975] VATTR 1 (VTD 134).

Whether employee's car supplied by employer

[62.7] A company had introduced a complex 'private car scheme', designed to ensure that an employee would have an inducement to look after his car well. Under the scheme, the company paid 90% of the cost of the car and the employee paid the balance. When the car was replaced—generally after two years—the allowance for the old car was similarly shared. There were appropriate rules as to how the cost of running and maintaining the car was to be borne. The employee could not use the car privately for more than 10% of the total mileage except with the company's approval. The employee could negotiate the purchase of the car but the purchase invoice, car registration and insurance were in the company's name, and the make of car and the price range were defined by the company. The Commissioners issued assessments on the basis that, under the scheme, there was a taxable supply of the car to the employee. The tribunal allowed the company's appeal, holding that the arrangement resulted in joint ownership of the car and accordingly the company did not supply it to the employee. *TBS (South Wales) Ltd*, [1981] VATTR 183 (VTD 1144).

Long service awards to employees

[62.8] Two associated companies in the clothing trade customarily presented gold watches or similar articles to its employees on completing 25 years' service. The Commissioners issued a ruling that such presentations constituted a supply of goods in the course of the company's business, and that output tax was chargeable accordingly. The companies appealed, contending that the articles had not been supplied in the course of their business, since their business consisted of the supply of clothing rather than of gold watches, etc. The tribunal dismissed the appeals, holding that the articles had been supplied in the course of the companies' business. *UDS Group Ltd; UDS Tailoring Ltd*, [1977] VATTR 16 (VTD 333).

[62.9] The Commissioners issued an assessment on a bakery company, charging tax on the value of long-service awards to employees. The company appealed, contending that as the value of the presentation was part of the employee's emoluments for income tax purposes, it was not a supply in the course of the business. The tribunal rejected this contention and dismissed the appeal, and the QB upheld this decision, holding that the fact that payments in kind were treated as emoluments for income tax did not prevent them from constituting supplies within the charge to VAT. *RHM Bakeries (Northern) Ltd v C & E Commrs*, QB 1978, [1979] STC 72.

[62.10] Under a company's conditions of employment, its employees were entitled to the choice of a 'variety of gifts' on completing 25 years' service and a further gift on retiring. The Commissioners issued a ruling that tax was chargeable on the awards, and the tribunal dismissed the company's appeal. *Grants of St James's Ltd*, MAN/77/103 (VTD 427).

Receipts of canteen provided by employer

[62.11] A company provided canteen facilities for the employees at its factory. The canteen staff were paid by the company and the expenses and receipts were met out of, or paid into, the company's general funds. The company did not account for output tax on its receipts from the canteen. The Commissioners issued an assessment charging tax on them and the tribunal dismissed the company's appeal. *MB Metals Ltd*, LON/77/466 (VTD 666).

[62.12] The proprietors of a poultry farm provided a canteen for their staff. Meals were provided at cost and the canteen was run by employees of the proprietors. The proprietors appealed against an assessment charging tax on the canteen receipts, contending that they did not supply the meals. The tribunal dismissed the appeal. On the evidence, the food was purchased, prepared and cooked by one of the proprietors' employees. The proprietors were supplying the meals through the employee. *M & E Barker*, MAN/89/138 (VTD 4589).

Board and lodging provided to hotel employees—whether a supply

[62.13] The proprietors of a hotel provided board and lodging to their employees. They made deductions from their employees' wages in respect of the board and lodging. However the Commissioners sought to charge tax on the board and lodging provided to the employees, and the hoteliers appealed. The tribunal allowed their appeal, holding that the board and lodging was provided as part of the employees' remuneration and the effect of what is now *VATA 1994, Sch 6 para 10* was that the deductions made from the wages were not consideration for VAT purposes. *RW & MJ Goodfellow*, [1986] VATTR 119 (VTD 2107).

Clothing supplied to employees

[62.14] A company carried on business as a retailer of women's and children's clothing. It supplied clothing to its employees, and did not account for tax on such supplies. The Commissioners issued an assessment charging tax on the clothing in question, and the company appealed, contending that VAT should not be chargeable since the clothing was intended to be worn as a uniform. The tribunal dismissed the appeal. On the evidence, the clothing in question was suitable for everyday wear. The supply of clothing to employees was a taxable supply. The fact that the company required its employees to wear clothing from its retail stock did not mean that the supply was outside the scope of VAT. *Zoo Clothing Ltd*, LON/91/572X (VTD 9161).

Cable network connections provided to employees

[62.15] A company carried on the business of providing telecommunications and cable television services. It provided its employees with free connections to its cable television and telephone networks. The Commissioners issued an assessment charging tax on these supplies under *VAT (Supply of Services) Order 1993 (SI 1993/1507)*. The company appealed, contending that it had made the supplies for the purposes of its business, so that the provision in *article 3* of the *Order* was not satisfied. The tribunal rejected this contention and dismissed the appeal, holding that although the supplies brought some incidental benefits to the company, the company's 'relevant purpose here is the non-business purpose of providing all employees who are in a position to make use of them with the benefit of cable television and free line rental at home'. *Telecential Communications Ltd*, LON/97/321 (VTD 15361).

Provision of sports tickets to employees under staff incentive scheme

[62.16] A company (P) awarded tickets to football matches and motor races to some of its employees under a staff incentive scheme. The Commissioners issued assessments charging tax under *VAT (Supply of Services) Order 1993 (SI 1993/1507)*. P appealed, contending that it had made the supplies for the purposes of its business, so that the provision in *article 3* of the *Order* was not satisfied. The tribunal accepted this contention and allowed the appeal, finding that the scheme had 'proved successful in reducing absenteeism' and had 'encouraged the submission of ideas to improve efficiency'. On the evidence, P had 'acted for purely business reasons' and 'the personal benefit derived by (P's) employees was of secondary importance compared to the needs of its business'. *Peugeot Motor Co plc*, MAN/99/856 (VTD 16731).

In-house magazines supplied to employees

[62.17] See *The Post Office*, 62.112 below.

Supply of shooting facilities to director

[62.18] See *Thimbleby Farms Ltd v HMRC*, 67.133 VALUATION.

Provision of employees' services and administrative services

Cases held to constitute a supply

[62.19] A charitable organisation (H) presented cinema films in Children's Homes throughout the country. In this it received the co-operation of a leading cinema operator (EMI) of which one of its members was an executive. Seven projectionists were used of whom five were 'borrowed' from EMI and two were engaged by H. These two were placed on EMI's payroll and the wages and expenses of all seven were paid through the wages officer of EMI. H reimbursed EMI monthly for the amounts so paid but EMI made no further charge for its services. The Commissioners issued a ruling that the arrangement involved a taxable supply of services by EMI and that EMI should account for output tax. H appealed. The tribunal dismissed the appeal, observing that 'the concepts of consideration and profit are wholly different', and the fact that a trader made no profit on a supply did not mean that there was no consideration for it. *Heart of Variety*, [1975] VATTR 103 (VTD 168).

[62.20] A company (U) supplied a caretaker to an associated company (C). U continued to pay the caretaker's wages and charged them to C at cost plus 9.5%. The Commissioners issued a ruling that output tax was chargeable on the supply. C, which was exempt and therefore unable to reclaim input tax, appealed. The tribunal upheld the Commissioners' ruling and dismissed the appeal, holding that there had been a taxable supply. *Calabar Developments Ltd*, [1976] VATTR 1 (VTD 218).

[62.21] A company (M) sold electrical goods and also provided accounting, bookkeeping and administrative services to two wholly owned subsidiaries and to an associated company. One of the three companies was a finance company not registered, or required to be registered, for VAT. The other two were trading companies and registered. There was no group registration. M charged the other three companies for the services it supplied but did not account for output tax. The Commissioners issued an assessment charging tax on the supplies and the tribunal dismissed M's appeal, applying *Heart of Variety*, 62.19 above, and distinguishing *Processed Vegetable Growers*, 62.42 below. *Metravision (GB) Ltd*, [1977] VATTR 26 (VTD 340).

[62.22] A company (P) was one of a group of companies operating casinos throughout the country, two of which it operated itself. Among its employees were three chartered accountants who spent a considerable part of their time visiting the casinos of the group to look after their books and security arrangements and advise them generally. It also provided management services to its own subsidiaries. In its accounts it credited substantial round sum amounts charged to some casinos as management fees and consultant fees respectively. It did not account for output tax on these charges. The Commissioners issued an assessment charging tax on these supplies and the tribunal dismissed P's appeal. *Pleasurama Casinos Ltd*, LON/76/181 & 208 (VTD 357).

[62.23] The British Airways Board (BAB) provided the services of some of its employees to a subsidiary (H), which in turn supplied the services of some of the employees to a housing society, which had been formed by employees of the British Overseas Airways Corporation (BOAC) in 1947 to help BOAC employees find living accommodation within travelling distance of Heathrow Airport. BOAC had been absorbed by BAB following the *Civil Aviation Act 1971*. H reimbursed BAB the salaries of the employees in question and made a management charge to the housing society in respect of the employees who had been 'seconded' to the Society. The tribunal held that BAB was supplying the employees' services in the course of its business, and that output tax was chargeable on the supply. *British Airways Board; British Airways Housing Trust Ltd*, LON/78/191A & 191B (VTD 663).

[62.24] A company (C) owned and managed commercial property in the UK and Australia. In order to join the company pension scheme, eight individuals employed by the company's controlling shareholder or by a subsidiary company gave up their existing employments to become employees of C. They were immediately seconded to their previous employers, and the salaries which C paid to them were reimbursed to it by the employers. C did not account for output tax, and the Commissioners issued an assessment charging tax on the basis that the supply of the seconded employees was a supply in the course of C's business. The tribunal dismissed C's appeal and the QB upheld this decision. The company existed exclusively for business purposes and was created specifically to administer the controlling shareholder's business affairs. All of its activities were part of an overall scheme to further those business purposes. The particular activity of providing staff was 'interrelated to the overall objects of the company in that it is intrinsically part of a normal business activity to make pension provisions'. *Cumbrae Properties (1963) Ltd v C & E Commrs*, QB [1981] STC 799. (*Note.* For another issue in this case, see **3.72** ASSESSMENT.)

[62.25] A company (T) was the representative member of a group of companies registered for VAT. It had a subsidiary company (M) which traded as an insurance broker, all its supplies being exempt. T seconded some of its employees to M and paid their salaries. The Commissioners issued an assessment on the basis that T was making taxable supplies of its employees' services to M. T appealed, contending that it was acting as an agent and had not made any supply to M. The QB rejected this contention and upheld the assessment, and the CA dismissed T's appeal, holding on the evidence that T retained the right to direct its employees and was acting as a principal rather than as an agent. The supply of employees' services was a taxable supply. *C & E Commrs v Tarmac Roadstone Holdings Ltd*, CA [1987] STC 610.

[62.26] The CA decision in *Tarmac Roadstone Holdings Ltd*, **62.25** above, was applied in the similar cases of *International Advisory Co Ltd*, LON/93/1654 (VTD 12186); Job Creation (UK) Ltd, LON/93/1653 (VTD 12186) and *Altman Blane & Co*, **41.8** LAND.

[62.27] A group of companies operated a chain of launderettes. The Commissioners issued an assessment on the basis that cleaners who worked at the launderettes were employed by the holding company, which was making a taxable supply of their services to the subsidiary companies. The tribunal upheld the assessment and dismissed the holding company's appeal. *Launderette Investments Ltd*, MAN/86/57 (VTD 2360).

[62.28] A company (P), which was a wholly-owned subsidiary of a US company, provided management services to a number of UK companies in the same group. It did not account for output tax on sums paid to it by such companies, although some of the companies were not in the same group of companies as P for VAT purposes. The Commissioners issued an assessment charging tax on payments by companies which were not in P's VAT group, on the basis that they represented consideration for taxable supplies of administrative services. P appealed, contending that it was not supplying such services in the course or furtherance of its business. The tribunal rejected this contention and dismissed P's appeal, applying the CA decision in *Tarmac Roadstone Holdings Ltd*, **62.25** above. *PHH Europe plc*, LON/93/927A (VTD 12027).

[62.29] A company made an annual charge to a subsidiary company to cover the use of its office and the services of two of its employees. It did not account for VAT on the charges and the Commissioners issued an assessment on the basis that the company had made a taxable supply of services to its subsidiary. The tribunal upheld the assessment and dismissed the company's appeal. On the evidence, the charge was for supplies made by the company, and was not merely a reimbursement of expenses. *Marvelle Bras (London) Ltd*, LON/92/1196Z (VTD 9350).

[62.30] A printer provided the services of some of his employees to a company, and failed to account for VAT on these supplies. The Commissioners issued an assessment charging tax on the supplies, and the tribunal dismissed the printer's appeal, applying the CA decision in *Tarmac Roadstone Holdings Ltd*, **62.25** above. *SCS Beresfors (t/a Elidaprint)*, LON/92/2246A (VTD 11555).

[62.31] A company in the construction industry (W) arranged for some of its employees and subcontractors to work for an associated company. It charged these costs to the associated company, but did not account for output tax on the costs. The Commissioners issued an assessment charging tax on the basis that W had made a taxable supply of services. The tribunal upheld the assessment and dismissed W's appeal. *WJ Marston & Son Ltd*, LON/97/388 (VTD 15208).

[62.32] An association was established to provide premises and a communications network for cab drivers in the Eastbourne area. It employed an office manager and telephone operators. It registered for VAT in 1991. In 1994 it applied for deregistration, contending that it was simply acting as an agent of its members and was not making any supplies for VAT purposes. The Commissioners rejected the application, considering that the association was making supplies to its members. The tribunal dismissed the association's appeal and the CA and HL unanimously upheld this decision. Lord Slynn observed that the intention of *VATA 1994, s 94* was that 'the activities of an association should not be excluded from VAT merely because it was unincorporated and not a legal person'. For VAT purposes, an unincorporated association was a legal entity, separate from its members. On the evidence, there was a direct link between the services which the association provided and the payments which its members made. The association was supplying facilities or advantages to its members for consideration, and was required to register for VAT. *Eastbourne Town Radio Cars Association v C & E Commrs*, HL [2001] STC 606; [2001] UKHL 19; [2001] 1 WLR 794; [2001] 2 All ER 597.

[62.33] The decision in *Eastbourne Town Radio Cars Association*, 62.32 above, was applied in the similar subsequent case of *AC Newline Cabs*, LON/04/1853 (VTD 19343).

[62.34] A similar decision was reached in *A1 Rushmoor Radio Taxis Ltd*, LON/x (VTD 17634). (*Note*. For other issues in this case, see **27.10** FINANCE and **51.53** PENALTIES: FAILURE TO NOTIFY.)

[62.35] A Training and Enterprise Council supplied the services of one of its employees to a charity, which was not registered for VAT. The TEC charged output tax on the supply. The charity appealed to a tribunal, contending that output tax should not have been charged on the supply. The tribunal rejected this contention and dismissed the appeal, holding that VAT had been correctly charged. *Life Education Centre (Nottinghamshire) Ltd*, MAN/98/846 (VTD 16499).

[62.36] Three solicitors acted as the trustees of a fund for the maintenance of a large building, containing 435 luxury apartments and some commercial premises. They employed 17 staff for this purpose. They did not account for output tax on maintenance contributions which they received from tenants, or on service charges which they received from the company which held the lease of the building. The Commissioners issued an assessment charging tax on these receipts. The trustees appealed, contending that they only supplied the limited services of arranging for the employees to carry out maintenance services, for which they accepted remuneration on which they accounted for output tax, but that the maintenance services were supplied by the employees directly to the tenants. The HL rejected this contention and upheld the assessments. On the evidence, the trustees made a supply to the tenants by supplying the services of staff, thereby enhancing the enjoyment and amenity of the flats and the building as a whole. The maintenance contributions paid by tenants to the fund were consideration for the provision of services by the trustees to the tenants. Lord Slynn observed that it would 'be wrong and artificial to regard the suppliers of the services as the individual employees'. Furthermore, the contributions were part of the taxable amount, within *Article 11A1* of the *EC Sixth Directive*, and were not 'repayment for expenses' within *Article 11A3(c)* of the *EC Sixth Directive. C & E Commrs v Trustees of the Nell Gwynn House Maintenance Fund*, HL 1998, [1999] STC 79; [1999] 1 WLR 174; [1999] 1 All ER 385. (*Note.* The HL also held that the payments did not qualify for exemption under what is now *VATA 1994, Sch 9, Group 1*—see **41.57** LAND.)

[62.37] Customs formed the opinion that a housing trust was making supplies of two administrative services to two associated bodies. The trust appealed, contending that it was acting as an agent for the two bodies and was not making supplies to them. The tribunal reviewed the evidence in detail, rejected this contention and dismissed the appeal, holding that 'the correct categorisation of (the) arrangement is not as a cost-sharing system, but as a supply to one legal entity with an onward supply to two separate legal entities'. *London & Quadrant Housing Trust*, LON/03/269 (VTD 19206).

[62.38] A police authority provided the services of some of its staff to two police welfare funds. HMRC issued a ruling that the authority was required to account for VAT on these supplies of staff. The authority appealed. The tribunal dismissed the appeal, applying the CA decision in *C & E Commrs v Tarmac Roadstone Holdings Ltd*, **62.25** above. *Sussex Police Authority v HMRC*, [2009] UKFTT 188 (TC), TC00143.

[62.39] An insurance company (CS) outsourced its IT department to another company (CG). It was agreed that the relevant employees would be joint employees of CS and CG. HMRC issued an assessment to CG charging output tax on the amounts which it received from CS under the relevant agreement. CG appealed, contending firstly that the payment was outside the scope of VAT, and alternatively that it had a legitimate expectation that the effect of Notice 700/34 was that there was 'no supply of staff for VAT purposes'. The tribunal reviewed the evidence in detail, rejected these contentions and dismissed the appeal, holding that 'VAT is chargeable on the whole of the consideration'. The tribunal held that Notice 700/34 should be understood as making a distinction 'between a supply of staff of which "the determining factor is that the staff are not contractually employed by the recipient company, but come under the direction of that company"; and a supply of services where "your staff continue to operate under your own direction" which "is not a supply of staff, but is a supply of those services"'. On the facts here, the tribunal found that there was a supply of services rather than a supply of staff. *CGI Group (Europe) Ltd v HMRC (No 2)*, [2010] SFTD 1178; [2010] UKFTT 396 (TC), TC00678.

[62.40] See also *Accenture Services Ltd*, **2.347** APPEALS, and *United News Shops (Holdings) Ltd*, **52.258** PENALTIES: MISDECLARATION.

Management services within group of companies

[62.41] See *Tilling Management Services Ltd*, **43.8** MANAGEMENT SERVICES.

Cases held not to constitute a supply

[62.42] Members of the National Farmers Union set up a company to promote the interests of vegetable growers. Some of the company's employees were transferred to the NFU, to enable them to be included in the NFU pension scheme. The NFU invoiced the company for the employees' salaries. The Commissioners issued a ruling that output tax was chargeable on the amounts invoiced. The tribunal allowed the company's appeal, holding that the secondment of the employees was a 'domestic arrangement' and not a taxable supply. *Processed Vegetable Growers Association Ltd*, [1973] VATTR 87 (VTD 25). (*Note.* For a preliminary issue in this case, see **2.52** APPEALS.)

[62.43] In 1972 the Post Office agreed that one of its employees (A) should be released from his Post Office duties to work for a statutory body (CTB). The Post Office continued to pay his normal Post Office salary, etc., and also paid him additional amounts as salary from CTB. CTB reimbursed the Post Office for all its payments and also paid it an administration charge. The Commissioners issued a ruling that the amounts invoiced by the Post Office to CTB for sums due to it under the agreement were taxable. CTB appealed. The tribunal allowed the appeal in part, holding on the evidence that A was an employee of CTB in the relevant period, so that the Post Office was not supplying A's services and tax was payable only on the administration charge. *Commonwealth Telecommunications Bureau*, LON H/75/25 (VTD 189).

[62.44] The general manager of a company which operated a gaming club also managed the affairs of a subsidiary company with a similar trade. The Commissioners issued an assessment on the basis that the parent company had made a taxable supply of the manager's services to the subsidiary company. The tribunal allowed the company's appeal, holding that, as the manager received salary from the subsidiary company as well as from the parent company, there was a dual employment rather than a taxable supply. *The Midland Wheel Club Ltd*, LON/84/284 (VTD 1770).

[62.45] A charity, established to provide housing for aged mineworkers, owned office accommodation which it shared with an associated company (M). The Commissioners issued an assessment charging output tax on the payments which the charity received from M. The QB allowed the charity's appeal, holding that the only reasonable conclusion on the evidence was that the charity was acting as an agent for M and was not supplying services to M. *Durham Aged Mineworkers' Homes Association v C & E Commrs*, QB [1994] STC 553.

[62.46] An educational charity (F) owned a number of schools, which were operated by an associated charity (C). F received £1,000,000 from C, and did not account for output tax on this. The Commissioners issued an assessment charging tax on it. F appealed, contending that the payment did not represent consideration for any supply. The CA accepted this contention and allowed the appeal (by a 2-1 majority, Buxton LJ dissenting). Sir Andrew Morritt V-C held that, on the evidence, the payment was a donation. Although F had used the payment to improve the premises used by the schools which C operated, there was no direct link between the donation and the building work. Accordingly the payment did not represent consideration for supplies of services. *Church Schools Foundation Ltd v C & E Commrs*, CA [2001] STC 1661; [2001] EWCA Civ 1745.

[62.47] The Central Council of Physical Recreation (C) was established as a company limited by guarantee, to act as a consultative body for sport and recreation. It had 26 employees. It acted as the sole trustee of a registered charity (B). Both C and B were registered for VAT. Some of C's employees carried out administrative work for B, and C invoiced B for the time spent by these employees on B's business. The Commissioners issued a ruling that C was required to account for VAT on the amounts invoiced to B. C appealed, contending that it was not making any taxable supplies of services. The tribunal accepted this contention and allowed the appeal, holding that 'in using trust funds for the purpose of employing staff for (B), it is using those funds for trust purposes'. C was acting as a trustee and was 'not making a supply except to itself'. This did 'not amount to the making of a taxable supply to (B)'. The tribunal observed that the invoices which C had issued were unnecessary, since 'what (C) did was, in its capacity of trustee, to use trust monies for the purposes of the trust'. That was not a taxable supply of services. *The Central Council of Physical Recreation*, LON/00/1534 (VTD 17803).

[62.48] A company which was partly exempt appealed against an assessment, contending that it was making taxable supplies of its director's services to an associated company (and thus would be able to attribute a substantial percentage of its input tax to taxable supplies). The tribunal reviewed the evidence in detail, rejected this contention, and dismissed the company's appeal. *Goodshelter Holdings Ltd*, LON/03/1182 (VTD 19219).

[62.49] HMRC issued an assessment on a company (W) on the basis that it had failed to account for VAT on supplies of staff to associated companies which were not members of its VAT group. The representative member of W's VAT group appealed, contending that it was acting as an agent for an insurance partnership, and was not required to account for tax on the amounts paid by the companies. The tribunal accepted this contention and allowed the appeal. *Hilltop Assistance Ltd v HMRC*, [2009] UKFTT 200 (TC), TC00153.

Retail partnership operating sub-post office

[62.50] A married couple operated a retail shop in partnership. The shop included a sub-post office, the husband being the subpostmaster. They had one employee, who spent approximately 25% of her time on Post Office work. The Commissioners issued an assessment on the basis that the couple were making a deemed supply of their employee's services to the Post Office. The couple appealed. The tribunal allowed the appeal, holding on the evidence that the couple did not receive any consideration from the Post Office in respect of the work performed by their employee. The subpostmaster's remuneration was based entirely on the turnover of the sub-post office, and none of the remuneration related to staff salaries. *RA & BD Hampton (t/a Tongue Electrics)*, EDN/96/99 (VTD 15171).

Alleged supply of consultancy services

[62.51] A company (B) reclaimed substantial amounts of input tax in respect of invoices issued by another company (U), which had ceased trading without accounting for output tax. Customs issued an assessment to recover the tax on the basis that U had never actually made any supplies to B. B appealed, contending that the invoices were in respect of consultancy services and that it had agreed to outsource its directors' payroll to U. The tribunal reviewed the evidence in detail and dismissed the appeal, finding that B's evidence lacked credibility. There had been 'no correspondence between the parties' and 'no evidence of the day-to-day operation of the arrangement'. There was 'no evidence of anything happening at all until the flurry of invoices and payments in the dying stages of the arrangement'. It appeared that there had not been 'any genuine arrangement between the two parties'. On the evidence, it appeared that nothing had been 'done in the legal or factual sense to demonstrate the existence of a supply which would give (B) the right to reclaim its input tax on the invoices'. *Bodyguard Workwear Ltd*, MAN/07/1108 (VTD 20949).

Reimbursements of expenses

Solicitor's fees charged to clients—whether disbursements

[62.52] A firm of solicitors charged travelling expenses to clients as 'disbursements'. The firm did not account for tax on these charges and the Commissioners issued an assessment. The tribunal dismissed the firm's appeal and the QB upheld this decision, holding that the travelling expenses in question were a part of the whole taxable supply of legal services by the firm to the client. *Rowe & Maw v C & E Commrs*, QB [1975] STC 340; [1975] 1 WLR 1291; [1975] 2 All ER 444.

[62.53] A solicitor (C) failed to account for VAT on various items such as telegraphic transfers, copies of Land Registry documents, and fees for land and bankruptcy searches, which he billed to his clients. Customs issued an assessment charging tax on them, and C appealed, contending that they should be treated as 'disbursements' on behalf of his clients, and that he should not be required to account for VAT. The tribunal rejected this contention and dismissed C's appeal, holding that 'the supplies of telegraphic services and Land Registry documents were not disbursements since they were supplied to the appellant in his own right and not as agent of his clients'. The tribunal also observed that Customs 'as a concession will treat local authority search fees as if they are disbursements provided the actual fees are passed on to the client'. However, C 'was not passing on the actual fees for the land and bankruptcy searches but notional fees which incorporated an element for profit costs. In such circumstances the notional fees did not meet the definition of disbursement as set out in *EC Sixth Directive, Article 11A3(c)* and *Notice 700, paragraph 25.1*'. *DJ Curtis*, MAN/06/329 (VTD 20330).

Transfer fees for remittance of sums from solicitors' client account

[62.54] See *Shuttleworth & Co*, 62.340 below.

Surveyor's expenses charged to clients

[62.55] A surveyor failed to account for VAT on out-of-pocket expenses charged out to clients. The Commissioners issued an assessment charging tax on the amounts in question and the tribunal dismissed the surveyor's appeal, applying *Rowe & Maw*, 62.52 above. *BL Westbury*, LON/81/291 (VTD 1168).

[62.56] A similar decision was reached in *RK Short*, LON/89/410 (VTD 4296).

Estate agents' expenses charged to clients

[62.57] An estate agency charged clients a fixed commission of 1% and also charged in respect of 'marketing expenditure' such as advertisements, 'For Sale' boards, etc. The agency did not account for VAT on these items and the Commissioners issued an assessment charging tax on them. The tribunal dismissed the agency's appeal, applying *Rowe & Maw*, **62.52** above. *J & L Lea*, MAN/85/261 (VTD 2018).

Consultant's expenses charged out to clients

[62.58] A financial consultant charged various expenses to clients but did not account for VAT on the amounts in question. The Commissioners issued an assessment charging tax on these amounts and the tribunal dismissed the consultant's appeal, applying *Rowe & Maw*, **62.52** above. *SD McDonald*, LON/90/739Y (VTD 5313).

[62.59] Similar decisions, also applying *Rowe & Maw*, **62.52** above, were reached in *P Barron*, LON/91/345Y (VTD 6370) and *JK Nawrot*, EDN/92/250 (VTD 11775).

[62.60] A software consultant charged car parking expenses, and the costs of travelling by ferry between Scotland and Northern Ireland, to clients. However, he did not account for output tax on these amounts. The Commissioners issued an assessment charging tax on them and the tribunal dismissed the consultant's appeal, holding that 'the ferry charges and car parking charges are cost components of the consideration being charged for the appellant's services. As such they form part of the taxable amount.' *K McEwan (t/a Scotpoint)*, EDN/11/156 (VTD 17554).

Medical expenses—whether disbursements

[62.61] A partnership of solicitors did not account for VAT on fees charged by medical professionals for providing medical records and medico-legal reports for litigation purposes, treating them as disbursements. HMRC issued assessments charging VAT on the basis that the fees were consideration for supplies of legal services. The partnership appealed. The tribunal allowed the appeal, applying the principles laid down in *De Danske Bilimportører v Skatteministeriet*, **22.255** EUROPEAN COMMUNITY LAW, and specifically distinguishing the QB decision in *Rowe & Maw v C & E Commrs*, **62.52** above. *Barratt Goff & Tomlinson v HMRC*, [2011] UKFTT 71 (TC); [2011] SFTD 334, TC 00949.

Chauffeur-driven tours—chauffeur's expenses charged out to customer

[62.62] A company carried on the business of organising chauffeur-driven tours for overseas visitors, and employed about 50 chauffeurs. Each chauffeur was given a cash float for the tour to cover his food and overnight accommodation (at a flat rate) and any minor incidental expenses such as parking fees. At the end of the tour he returned the balance of the float with a statement of his expenses and the relevant bills. The company charged these amounts to the customers, but did not account for VAT on them. The Commissioners issued an assessment charging tax on the amounts in respect of food and accommodation. The tribunal dismissed the company's appeal, applying

Rowe & Maw, **62.52** above. The costs incurred by the chauffeur and billed to the customer constituted part of the consideration for the supply of services by the company. *Camelot Cars Couriers Ltd*, LON/83/152 (VTD 1474).

Transport services—payments for fuel

[62.63] A trader (L) operated a 'vehicle transportation service'. Initially he accounted for VAT on the amounts paid by his customers. Subsequently he submitted a repayment claim on the basis that some of the payments were consideration for the fuel which he used in the course of transporting the vehicles, and that he should have treated these as disbursements on which he was not required to account for VAT. HMRC rejected the claim and the tribunal dismissed L's appeal, holding that the amounts in question formed part of his taxable turnover and were subject to VAT. *WE Lafferty (t/a Bell Transport)*, [2010] UKFTT 12 (TC), TC00331.

Director's expenses charged to customer

[62.64] A company supplied the services of its managing director to a customer. It charged the customer £200 as an advance payment of its director's expenses, but did not account for VAT on this amount. The Commissioners issued an assessment charging tax on the £200 and the tribunal dismissed the company's appeal, applying the principles in *Rowe & Maw Ltd*, **62.52** above. *Glassiron Ltd*, [1989] VATTR 245 (VTD 4592). (*Note.* An appeal against a penalty under what is now *VATA 1994, s 67* was also dismissed.)

[62.65] A similar decision, also applying *Rowe & Maw*, **62.52** above, was reached in *Medical Services & Equipment (ME) Ltd*, LON/94/1702A (VTD 13077).

Subcontractor's expenses reimbursed by contractor

[62.66] A subcontractor failed to account for VAT on payments received from the contractor for whom he worked, as reimbursements of expenditure on materials and petrol. The Commissioners issued an assessment charging tax on such payments and the tribunal dismissed the subcontractor's appeal, holding that the payments were chargeable to VAT. *JT Giles*, MAN/90/475 (VTD 6789).

Art gallery proprietor

[62.67] The proprietor of an art gallery invoiced artists for 50% of various costs he incurred such as the production of catalogues and advertisements, postage, insurance, etc. He did not account for VAT on such amounts. The Commissioners issued a ruling that VAT was chargeable on them, and the proprietor appealed, contending that they should be treated as disbursements and as outside the scope of VAT. The tribunal rejected this contention and dismissed his appeal, holding that the amounts in question constituted consideration for taxable supplies of services. *DS Campbell*, LON/95/2323 (VTD 15051).

Prince of Wales Trust—reimbursed expenses

[62.68] See *Gardner*, **62.163** below.

Chartered secretary appointed as Administrator—reimbursed expenses

[62.69] A chartered secretary, who was registered for VAT, was appointed by the Secretary of State for Wales as the Independent Groundwater Complaints Administrator for the Cardiff Bay Barrage, under the *Cardiff Bay Barrage Act 1993*. She reclaimed input tax in respect of solicitors' bills and photocopying relating to this office. The Commissioners rejected the claim and she appealed. The tribunal dismissed her appeal, holding that it was not 'proper for her to charge value added tax in respect of her services as administrator, but not to charge value added tax in respect of the legal services and purchases for the office on the basis that she was the end user'. The items of expenditure had been 'incurred in the course of her work as administrator and as such should have been charged to the corporation'. *EM Lee*, LON/99/649 (VTD 16750).

Reimbursement of director's expenses

[62.70] See *Alpha International Coal Ltd*, **1.77** AGENTS.

Supplies of timeshare accommodation

[62.71] A company managed and administered timeshare accommodation at a resort in Cornwall. The Commissioners issued a ruling that it was making standard-rated supplies and was required to register and account for VAT accordingly. The company appealed, contending that many of its receipts should be treated as repayments of expenses which, by virtue of *Article 11A3(c)* of the *EC Sixth Directive*, were not taxable consideration. The tribunal reviewed the evidence in detail, rejected this contention and dismissed the appeal (except with regard to payments for TV licences, which it held to be disbursements and not liable to VAT). The tribunal found that 'except for the TV licences, none of the services represented by the itemised charges is made directly to the individual timeshare owners'. Th etribunal observed that 'in substance and reality, what the charges represent are cost components in the overall supply of managed accommodation'. The tribunal specifically declined to apply the reasoning of the Edinburgh tribunal in the earlier case of *Clowance Holdings Ltd*, **22.255** EUROPEAN COMMUNITY LAW, on the grounds that the tribunal in that case had followed the CA decision in *Plantiflor Ltd*, **24.2** EXEMPTIONS: MISCELLANEOUS, which had subsequently been reversed by the HL. *Clowance Owners Club Ltd*, LON/02/565 (VTD 18787).

Sales of assets

Sale of vans used in business

[62.72] A company sold some vans which it had used in its radio and television business. The Commissioners issued an assessment charging tax on the sales and the tribunal dismissed the company's appeal. *HB Mattia Ltd*, [1976] VATTR 33 (VTD 243).

Sale of lorry

[62.73] The decision in *HB Mattia Ltd*, **62.72** above, was applied in a subsequent case where a haulage contractor failed to account for tax on the sale of a lorry. *JE Hughes*, MAN/77/262 (VTD 552).

[62.74] A similar decision was reached in *T Naughton*, MAN/91/422 (VTD 7854).

Sale of horse boxes

[62.75] A registered trader sold two horse boxes and charged VAT on their sale. He subsequently appealed to the QB, contending that he should not have charged output tax since the sales had not been in the course of his business. The QB dismissed his appeal, holding that his case was without merit. *MA Lenihan v C & E Commrs*, QB [1992] STC 478. (*Note.* For another issue in this case, see **36.397** INPUT TAX.)

Sale of jewellery

[62.76] A retail jeweller sold some jewellery which had been owned by his wife, and did not account for VAT on the sale. The Commissioners issued an assessment charging tax on the proceeds, and he appealed, contending that the jewellery had not been sold in the course of his business. The tribunal rejected this contention and dismissed his appeal, holding that the jewellery had been sold in the furtherance of the business, so that VAT was chargeable. *JS Mittu*, MAN/82/32 (VTD 1275).

Sale of private assets to raise capital for business

[62.77] A farmer (S) had inherited a large estate from his father, but was faced with a large capital gains tax liability. He therefore decided to lease his late father's house to a rifle club. The house was let fully furnished. During the term of the lease S kept a number of valuable paintings in the house, some of these being locked away in storerooms but others being displayed in the rooms used by the club. When the lease expired S sold the house. The paintings, and a valuable stamp collection, were sold separately and the proceeds were paid into his business account as capital. The Commissioners issued an assessment charging tax on these proceeds, considering that the paintings and stamp collection had been business assets. The tribunal allowed S's appeal, observing that *Article 2* of the *EC Sixth Directive* taxes supplies 'by a taxable person acting as such', and thus implicitly excludes a supply by a taxable person in his personal capacity, and finding that the assets sold were personal assets, not connected with S's business. *RWK Stirling*, [1985] VATTR 232 (VTD 1963).

[62.78] An engineer had, for many years, collected items of machinery as a hobby. In 1990 and in 1991 he was suffering financial difficulties, and sold some of these items. He did not account for VAT on the sales, and the Commissioners issued an assessment charging tax on them. He appealed, contending that they were private transactions and should not be subject to VAT. The tribunal allowed his appeal, holding that the sales had not been supplies in the course or furtherance of any business, but that he had had 'to realise private investments or personal possessions to provide moneys to tide him over'. *MR Atkinson*, LON/93/31A (VTD 12763).

Sale of guns—whether private assets or business assets

[62.79] The Commissioners discovered that a married couple who traded in partnership as gun dealers had not accounted for tax on a significant number of sales. They issued an assessment, and imposed a penalty under *VATA 1994*, *s* 60. The partnership appealed, contending that the guns in question had been privately owned by the husband, so that the sales were private transactions which were not subject to VAT, applying the principles laid down in *Stirling*, **62.77** above. The tribunal upheld the assessment, observing that the receipts had been paid into the business bank account, and finding on the evidence that the couple had not shown that the sales were private non-business transactions. (However, the tribunal allowed the couple's appeal against the penalty, finding that the business 'was run on chaotic and negligent lines' and holding that the Commissioners had not proved, on the balance of probability, that the husband had acted dishonestly.) *DJ & Mrs AP Freer (t/a Shooting & Fishing)*, MAN/99/91 (VTD 18921).

Sale of boat previously hired out

[62.80] A registered trader failed to account for VAT on the sale of a boat which he had occasionally let on hire. The Commissioners issued an assessment charging tax on the sale of the boat, and the trader appealed, contending that no tax was due since the boat had not been a business asset. The tribunal dismissed the appeal, finding that the trader had previously described the boat as a business asset (for the purpose of reclaiming input tax) and was 'evasive in his evidence'. On the evidence, the trader had not discharged the onus of showing that the boat was not used for business purposes. *WJ Collins (t/a Triangle TVs)*, BEL/89/11 (VTD 6804).

Sale of assets after business given up

[62.81] An individual (M) had carried on business as a yacht charterer and sailing instructor, using two yachts which he had purchased for business purposes but also used privately. He had registered for VAT from April 1973 but gave up the business in November 1973 and sold the two yachts shortly afterwards. His registration was cancelled in November 1974. The Commissioners issued an assessment on the basis that tax was chargeable on the sale proceeds. The tribunal upheld the assessment and dismissed M's appeal. Although he ceased to be a taxable person on giving up his business, he was deemed to have then disposed of the yachts in the course of the business. *AJD Marshall*, [1975] VATTR 98 (VTD 166).

[62.82] A trader (W) carried on a coach hire business, using two coaches. He was registered for VAT from 1 April 1973. He sold one of the coaches in October 1973, closed the business on 10 November 1973 and was deregistered from 31 January 1974. The Commissioners issued an assessment charging output tax on the sale of the two coaches. The tribunal upheld the assessment and dismissed W's appeal. *M Wolfe (t/a Arrow Coach Services)*, LEE/75/22 (VTD 171).

Sale of shop

[62.83] A trader failed to account for output tax on the sale of a shop. The Commissioners issued an assessment and the tribunal dismissed the trader's appeal. *VAT (Special Provisions) Order, article 5(1)* did not apply since the shop's turnover was below the registration threshold and the purchaser was not a 'taxable person'. However, the vendor had been a taxable person, and he was therefore required to account for output tax. *RC Blackburn*, MAN/94/810 (VTD 13798).

Sale of fixtures and fittings on surrender of lease

[62.84] A married couple had operated a public house which they had leased from a brewery. They surrendered the lease to the brewery, which took over fixtures and fittings which the couple had installed, paying them £10,000 in cash and releasing them from a debt of £3,958. The Commissioners issued a ruling that the couple were required to account for VAT on $^7/_{47}$ of the £13,958. The tribunal dismissed the couple's appeal, holding that, in view of the terms of the agreement in question, the £13,958 was taxable consideration for the sale of the fixtures and fittings. *Mr & Mrs D Campbell*, MAN/95/1029 (VTD 14410).

Publishing company—sale of paintings used as artwork

[62.85] A publishing company sold a number of paintings which it had used as artwork, and did not account for VAT on the proceeds. The Commissioners issued an assessment charging tax on the sale, and the company appealed, contending that the sale had not been made in the course of its business. The tribunal dismissed the appeal, distinguishing *Stirling*, 62.77 above. The paintings had been bought for business purposes and the fact that they had been stored for several years did not cause them to lose their character as business assets. *Blackie & Sons Ltd*, EDN/91/274 (VTD 7632).

Sale of original painting by owner of art gallery

[62.86] See *Conlin*, 62.156 below.

Conditional supplies (VATA 1994, Sch 4 para 1)

Goods sold subject to reservation of title

[62.87] A company (V) sold goods to another company under a conditional sale agreement, whereby V retained legal ownership until the purchase price had been paid in full. The purchaser company went into receivership without paying for the goods, and had in the meantime resold some of the goods without V's approval or knowledge. The Commissioners issued an assessment on the basis that V had made a taxable supply of the goods. The tribunal upheld the assessment, holding that there had been a supply when the goods had been consigned to the purchaser and observing that 'it makes no difference that the legal title to the goods may not have passed contemporaneously with the moment of supply'. *Vernitron Ltd*, [1978] VATTR 157 (VTD 615).

[62.88] A similar decision was reached in *Tru-Form Sheet Metal Ltd*, MAN/91/998 (VTD 9240). (*Note.* An appeal against a misdeclaration penalty was also dismissed.)

[62.89] A company (T) carried on business as a supplier and installer of lighting systems. One of its customers (L) went into liquidation after paying about £56,000 for services which T had carried out under a contract to install a discotheque lighting system. By the time of the liquidation, most of the equipment had been installed, but T retained their legal ownership by virtue of a *Romalpa* clause in the contract. T had also issued another invoice, which remained unpaid, for a further £8,400. T did not account for output tax on any of the sums paid by L, and the Commissioners issued an assessment charging tax on the amounts in question. The tribunal dismissed T's appeal, holding that the system was to be treated as supplied at the time the payments were made. The QB upheld this decision. Although the contract had not been completed, the goods were in the possession of the customer, which had received the benefit of T's services. There had been a supply despite the fact that T retained the legal ownership of the system. T had issued invoices and had received payment. By virtue of what is now *VATA 1994, s 6(4)*, the time of payment was the time of supply. *Tas-Stage Ltd v C & E Commrs*, QB [1988] STC 436.

[62.90] A company (E) which supplied computer equipment agreed to sell some equipment to an Eire company, subject to the condition that it would retain title to the equipment until the customer paid for them in full. The goods were invoiced to the Eire company and were collected by a freight company which was acting as agent for the Eire company. The Eire company had intended to sell the equipment to a company registered in Hong Kong which carried on business in Switzerland. However, the necessary export licence had not been obtained, and the equipment was impounded at Manchester Airport and subsequently forfeited under *CEMA 1979, s 139, Sch 3*. The Eire company never paid for the equipment, so that E retained legal ownership of the equipment, and did not account for VAT on the sale. The Commissioners issued an assessment on the basis that there had been a taxable supply, and E appealed, contending that there had been no supply, since it had retained the ownership of the equipment. The tribunal rejected this contention and dismissed the appeal, holding that the delivery of the goods to the freight company, which was acting as agent for the Eire customer, constituted a transfer of possession of the equipment which was a supply by virtue of what is now *VATA 1994, Sch 4 para 1(2)*. *ESS International Ltd*, [1992] VATTR 336 (VTD 7771).

[62.91] See also *Re Liverpool Commercial Vehicles Ltd*, **36.675** INPUT TAX, and *Mannesmann Demag Hamilton Ltd*, **40.87** INVOICES AND CREDIT NOTES.

Provisional sale agreement not proceeded with—whether a supply

[62.92] A company (C) wished to sell a number of machines. It made a provisional agreement to sell them to an associated company (M) to which it owed more than £600,000. Under this agreement, if M was unable to sell any of the machines to an external buyer, the machines would remain the property of C. Despite this condition, C recorded the sale of the machines to M in its accounts for the year ended 30 June 1987. M was only able to sell one of the machines, and in January 1989 C issued a credit note to M in respect of the remaining machines, the provisional sale agreement being treated as cancelled. C had not accounted for VAT on the sale of the machines to M, and the Commissioners issued an assessment on the basis that the sale recorded in C's accounts had taken place and was a taxable supply. C appealed, contending that, despite the entry in its accounts, it had never transferred possession or ownership of the machines to M. The tribunal allowed C's appeal, describing the agreement as 'obscure and contradictory' and finding that there had been no sale of the machines, which had remained the property of C. 'Once the legal position is identified, the state of affairs between the parties cannot be changed by the description of the transaction by one of the parties in its accounts. The accounts were wrong; but that error cannot transform a contingent liability to pay an unascertainable amount into the receipt of payment for the purposes of (*VATA 1994, s 6(4)**).' *Creditgrade Ltd*, [1991] VATTR 87 (VTD 5390).

Charge made for booking hotel room where booking not fulfilled

[62.93] A company operated a chain of hotels. In cases where customers booked accommodation at the hotels, but failed to fulfil the booking, it levied a charge of the agreed price of the room, less the amount which would have represented VAT if the room had been occupied. (At the relevant time the VAT rate was 15%, so that the charge levied was 86.95% of the price of the room.) It did not account for VAT at such charges, and the Commissioners issued an assessment to charge tax on the amounts in question. The company appealed, contending that since the rooms had not been occupied, there had been no supply and no liability to VAT. The QB rejected this contention and upheld the assessment. The company was charging the customer for the room, whether or not the customer occupied it. Making the room available was a supply for VAT purposes. *C & E Commrs v Bass plc*, QB 1992, [1993] STC 42. (*Note.* See now, however, the subsequent CJEC decision in *Société Thermale d'Eugénie-les-Bains v Ministère de l'Économie, des Finances et de l'Industrie*, **22.86** EUROPEAN COMMUNITY LAW.)

Payment in advance of order—whether a supply

[62.94] See *Weldons (West One) Ltd*, **36.620** INPUT TAX.

Transfers of assets (VATA 1994, Sch 4 paras 5, 8)

VATA 1994, Sch 4 para 5—whether compatible with EC Sixth Directive

[62.95] See *EMI Group plc*, **22.164** EUROPEAN COMMUNITY LAW.

Mail order company—goods given to agents as incentives

[62.96] See *GUS Merchandise Corporation Ltd*, **58.1** RETAILERS' SPECIAL SCHEMES.

Goods donated to promote business

[62.97] A company which manufactured fastenings did a considerable amount of business with local boatbuilders, and donated some of its products to assist a British yacht competing in the Americas Cup. It also purchased some playground equipment and donated this to the local council. The Commissioners issued an assessment on the basis that the donation of the goods in question was a taxable supply. The tribunal dismissed the company's appeal, holding that what is now *VATA 1994, Sch 4 para 5(1)* provided that the donations were to be treated as a taxable supply. *TR Fastenings Ltd*, LON/80/290 (VTD 1016).

[62.98] A similar decision was reached in a case where a company operating a 'time-share' business provided 'gifts' to potential purchasers. The company had reclaimed input tax on the 'gifts', but had not accounted for output tax.

The tribunal dismissed the company's appeal against an assessment charging tax on the market value of the supplies. *Mitrolone Ltd*, LON/88/1335X (VTD 4301).

Free films supplied to customers by film processing company

[62.99] A company carried on the business of processing photographic films for members of the public. Most of the films which it processed were delivered by customers to retail shops such as pharmacies, from which they were collected by van drivers acting on behalf of the company. As part of a promotional scheme, the company provided customers with a free unexposed film when it returned their processed film. The Commissioners issued an assessment charging tax on the value of the free films, considering that they were supplied to the retailers and were within what is now *VATA 1994, Sch 4 para 5*. The company appealed, contending that the films were supplied to the customers rather than to the retailers, and were free gifts which fell outside *Sch 4 para 5*. The tribunal accepted the company's contention and allowed the appeal. The gift of the film was within *Sch 4 para 5(2)*, since it was a free gift which did not form part of a series of gifts to the same person and which cost the company less than £10. *United Photographic Laboratories Ltd*, LON/92/527 (VTD 10071).

Vouchers and wine given to householders by salesmen

[62.100] The proprietor of a business which sold carpet cleaning equipment provided salesmen working for him with wine and vouchers for hotel accommodation to give to householders when they visited their homes to demonstrate the equipment. The Commissioners issued an assessment on the cost of the wine and vouchers, considering that they were supplied as consideration for the right to enter the householder's premises. (The cost of the wine was 99p per bottle and the cost of the vouchers ranged from 50p to £1 each.) The proprietor appealed, contending that the wine and vouchers were gifts which were outside the scope of VAT by virtue of what is now *VATA 1994, Sch 4 para 5(2)(a)*. The tribunal allowed the proprietor's appeal. It was entirely at the salesman's discretion whether or not he gave a voucher or a bottle of wine. The customer did not obtain any contractual right to receive an item in return for allowing a salesman into his home, and he could not therefore have given consideration for the supply of such an item. *QJ Cartlidge*, LON/91/546 (VTD 7152).

Assets used for private purposes—whether a self-supply

[62.101] A married couple who traded as central heating engineers carried out work on their own house. The work was invoiced to the husband and the necessary materials were purchased from their business bank account, but they did not account for VAT. The Commissioners issued an assessment on the basis that there had been a deemed supply of materials under what is now *VATA 1994, Sch 4 para 5(1)*, and the tribunal dismissed the couple's appeal. *Mr & Mrs Broadhurst (t/a RMS Heating)*, MAN/85/157 (VTD 2007).

[62.102] A similar decision was reached in *GN Mellor*, MAN/92/626 (VTD 10703). (*Note*. For another issue in this case, see **52.108** PENALTIES: MISDECLARATION.)

Assets retained on cessation of trade—whether a self-supply

[62.103] A partnership ceased to trade and the partners retained the partnership assets. Although they had previously claimed input tax on the assets in question, they failed to account for output tax and the Commissioners issued an assessment charging tax on the basis that the partners' retention of the assets was a deemed self-supply. The tribunal upheld the assessment and dismissed the partners' appeal. *J Kerr, E Lloyd & R Flatman*, EDN/86/40 (VTD 2193).

[62.104] Similar decisions were reached in *RJ McHarg*, LON/90/1238Z (VTD 7254) and *MF Lyons (t/a Trendz Jewellery)*, LON/93/219A (VTD 12243).

[62.105] A similar decision was reached in a case where a couple who traded from a shop were evicted by their landlord for not paying their rent, and the landlord took over the traders' stock. The tribunal held that the traders were required to account for output tax on the value of the stock, observing that 'what occurred to the stock thereafter is not relevant'. *Mr & Mrs Rashid (t/a Handy Store)*, EDN/94/153 (VTD 13321).

[62.106] See also *Mendes*, 67.20 VALUATION; *Ambu-Medics Ltd*, 67.21 VALUATION, and *McCormick*, 67.22 VALUATION.

Transfer of vehicles previously held under hire-purchase agreement

[62.107] A company (P) had held two vehicles under a hire-purchase agreement. Because of financial difficulties, it could not make the payments required by the agreement. It therefore transferred the vehicles to a sole trader (M), who promised to settle the hire-purchase agreement. P's managing director indemnified the hire-purchase company against any loss. The Commissioners issued an assessment on the basis that P had supplied the vehicles to M, the consideration being the amount outstanding under the hire-purchase agreement. The tribunal dismissed P's appeal and the QB upheld this decision. Where a person paid off the settlement figure under a hire purchase agreement to a finance company, it was reasonable to conclude that he did so on behalf of the hirer, since only the hirer had the contractual right to pay the amount in question to acquire ownership. The essence of the agreement was that P would supply the vehicles to M and that M would pay the amount outstanding to the hire-purchase company. *Philip Drakard Trading Ltd v C & E Commrs*, QB [1992] STC 568. (*Note.* For another issue in this case, not taken to the QB, see 36.509 INPUT TAX.)

[62.108] A similar decision was reached in *RP Childs*, LON/90/1072 (VTD 6120).

Transfer of furniture to associated company

[62.109] A registered trader failed to account for output tax on the transfer of some items of furniture to a company which he controlled, although he had previously reclaimed input tax on the purchase of the furniture. The Commissioners issued an assessment charging output tax on the supply. The tribunal dismissed the trader's appeal and the QB upheld this decision as one of fact, applying *Edwards v Bairstow & Harrison*, HL 1955, 36 TC 207. *BJ Sandley (t/a Bemba Sandley Management Co) v C & E Commrs*, QB [1995] STC 230.

Social club providing free drinks for committee members

[62.110] A social club provided free drinks to members of its committee, each committee member being entitled to three pints of beer in return for attending committee meetings. The Commissioners issued an assessment charging output tax on the supply of these drinks. The club appealed, contending that the committee members should be treated as employees, so that there should be no output tax liability. The tribunal rejected this contention and dismissed the appeal, holding that the committee members were not employees and that the effect of what is now *VATA 1994, Sch 4 para 5* was that the club was required to account for output tax. *Glendale Social Club*, [1994] VATTR 372 (VTD 12869).

Caps presented to international footballers

[62.111] See *Scottish Football Association*, 67.13 VALUATION.

Supply of magazines to staff—whether within Sch 4 para 5(1)

[62.112] The Post Office distributed three periodical magazines to current and former employees. It reclaimed input tax on the related production costs, on the basis that it was making supplies of the magazines, within *Sch 4 para 5(1)*, which were zero-rated under *Sch 8, Group 3*. The Commissioners accepted the claim with regard to one of the magazines, but rejected the claim with regard to the other two, on the basis that the magazines were intended to 'inform employees of developments and current thinking within the Post Office business', were 'akin to the publications one finds circulating or on staff notice boards in any large organisation' and remained 'assets of the business after distribution to the employees, in the same sense as any other consumable overhead of the business such as stationery or pens'. The tribunal allowed the Post Office's appeal against this decision, holding on the evidence that the Post Office intended 'to transfer the property in each of the three magazines with which this appeal is concerned', and that there was a supply of each of the magazines on delivery. Accordingly the Post Office was entitled to reclaim the input tax in question. *The Post Office*, MAN/95/1322 (VTD 14075).

Charity supplying newsletters to donors—whether within Sch 4 para 5

[62.113] See *The Church of England Children's Society*, 11.45 CHARITIES.

College supplying free prospectuses—whether within Sch 4 para 5(1)

[62.114] A college, which was partly exempt, issued free prospectuses to local residents. It claimed that, for the purposes of its partial exemption calculation, the issue of these prospectuses should be treated as free supplies, so that their deemed value should be included in the computation of total taxable supplies and the input tax related to their design and production should be treated as attributable to taxable supplies. The Commissioners rejected the claim and the college appealed. The tribunal allowed the appeal, holding that the issue of the prospectuses was within *VATA 1994, Sch 4 para 5(1)*. The tribunal held that, although the cost of producing each prospectus was less than the £15 limit in *Sch 4 para 5(2)*, it was not excluded from *Sch 4 para 5(1)* since, on the evidence, the prospectuses were 'as a matter of course, distributed to the same local households on a regular basis'.

Accordingly, each prospectus formed 'part of a series or succession of gifts made to the person from time to time'. The Ch D upheld this decision. Hart J observed that the Commissioners accepted that the prospectuses were within the definition of 'goods'. The 'central purpose' of *Sch 4 para 5* was 'to deal with the situation where "business" goods have ceased to be such by their having been transferred into private ownership'. It was 'in broad terms, an anti-avoidance provision, deeming something to be a supply . . . which would not otherwise be a supply'. However, there was nothing in the language of *para 5(1)* which could exclude from its ambit a transfer of goods such as the prospectuses, effected for promotional purposes. The fact that, in the present case, the provisions of *para 5* operated in favour of the college was because 'the rate of output tax on the notional supply is zero, coupled with the fact that the Commissioners have not established that the goods or services, in respect of which the input tax is deductible, are used exclusively by the college for making its exempt supplies'. *C & E Commrs v West Herts College*, Ch D 2000, [2001] STC 1245. (*Note*. The £15 limit was increased to £50 with effect from 8 March 2001: see *VAT (Business Gifts of Small Value) Order 2001 (SI 2001/735)*.)

Plastic toy boxes supplied with disposable nappies

[62.115] In the case noted at **12.25** CLOTHING, the tribunal held that supplies of plastic toy boxes with disposable nappies were within *VATA 1994, Sch 4 para 5(1)*, and that the provisions of *Sch 4 para 5(2)* did not apply. *Kimberly-Clark Ltd*, LON/01/1273 (VTD 17861).

Deemed supply of commercial property—application of Sch 4 para 8

[62.116] In 1998 a company (V) purchased a commercial property. In January 2000 V transferred its business to an associated company (T) as a going concern. V retained the property, and ceased to be registered. The Commissioners issued an assessment on T, charging tax on the basis that when V ceased to be a taxable person, it was deemed to have made a supply of the property, and that since T had acquired V's business as a going concern, it was required to account for output tax on the supply under *VAT Regulations, reg 6(3)(a)*. The tribunal upheld the assessment and dismissed T's appeal, observing that the effect of *VATA 1994, Sch 9, Group 1, Item 1(a)(ii), Note 4* was that the grant of a commercial building less than three years old did not qualify for exemption. *Trade Only Plant Sales Ltd*, LON/03/593 (VTD 18847).

[62.117] See also *Mollan & Co Ltd*, **52.291** PENALTIES: MISDECLARATION AND ERRORS.

Supply of computer software licences—whether within Sch 4 para 8

[62.118] See *Rowledge*, 67.140 VALUATION.

Donations

Donations by Freemasons to Masonic Association

[62.119] The Commissioners issued an assessment on a Masonic association, charging tax on donations from Masons. The tribunal allowed the Association's appeal, holding that the donations were outside the scope of VAT since there was no relevant supply of goods or services. *Swindon Masonic Association Ltd*, [1978] VATTR 200 (VTD 682).

Donations to Masonic company for use of car park

[62.120] A Masonic company owned a large building with a car park behind it. The building included a suite of rooms which was mainly used for Masonic purposes but was sometimes let out for other functions. No charge was made for use of the car park, but some users, including a local solicitors' firm, made voluntary annual payments. The Commissioners issued an assessment on the basis that these payments were taxable consideration for parking facilities, but the tribunal allowed the company's appeal, holding that the payments were donations which were not liable to VAT. *Warwick Masonic Rooms Ltd*, BIR/79/33 (VTD 839).

Sponsorship fee received from bank—whether consideration for a supply

[62.121] A non-profit-making association organised an annual film competition. It received a sponsorship fee of £7,500 from a bank, and did not account for VAT on this. The Commissioners issued an assessment charging tax on the fee. The association appealed, contending that, as it had passed the money to the winner of the competition, VAT should not be chargeable. The tribunal dismissed the association's appeal, holding that the £7,500 was paid in respect of services in the form of advertising and publicity rights supplied to the bank, and that VAT was chargeable thereon despite the fact that the money had been earmarked for the winner of the competition. *Oxford Film Foundation*, LON/89/911Y (VTD 5031).

Rugby club—donations and sponsorship payments

[62.122] The accounts of a rugby club showed significant income under the headings of 'miscellaneous income' and 'sponsorship/donations'. Customs issued assessments on the basis that most of this represented taxable consideration for supplies made by the club. The club appealed. The tribunal reviewed the evidence in detail and allowed the appeal in part, holding that some of the income in question came from voluntary donations (including collections made at the club's home matches) which were outside the scope of VAT, but that some of the income came from commercial sponsorship or represented consideration for advertisements in the club's programmes, on which VAT was chargeable. *Rumney Rugby Football Club*, LON/04/895 (VTD 19480).

Football supporters' club—whether grant of 'founder membership' a supply for consideration

[62.123] A group of football supporters raised £32,000 to build a clubhouse. In 2001 the supporters' club was incorporated as a limited company, which granted 'founder membership' to a number of supporters who had helped to raise the £32,000. Customs issued an assessment charging tax on the basis that the grant of founder membership was a supply for consideration. The tribunal allowed the club's appeal, holding that 'for a supply to be for a consideration there must be a direct link between the supply and the consideration'. On the evidence, the donations here had been made before the supporters' club had been formed, and there was no direct link between the donations and the grant of founder membership. *Newport County AFC Social Club Ltd*, LON/05/1107 (VTD 19807).

Donations received by musician performing on public highway

[62.124] See *Tolsma v Inspecteur der Omzetbelasting Leeuwarden*, 22.84 EUROPEAN COMMUNITY LAW.

Inducement payments ('reverse premiums') and rent-free periods, etc

'Reverse premium' to assist with repair costs—whether any supply

[62.125] The landlord of a hotel granted a lease to a company, and paid a 'reverse premium' of £1.4 million to help the company repair the property. The Commissioners issued an assessment on the basis that the payment was liable to VAT. The company appealed, contending that there had been no supply. The tribunal dismissed the company's appeal, holding that the £1.4 million was consideration paid by the landlord for the company's agreement to provide more valuable benefits under the lease. *Gleneagles Hotel plc*, [1986] VATTR 196 (VTD 2152).

[62.126] For a case in which a 'reverse premium', paid in view of anticipated repair costs, was held not to be attributable to any supply for consideration, see *British Eventing Ltd v HMRC*, 6.48 BUILDINGS AND LAND.

Inducement payment by lessor to lessee—whether any supply of services

[62.127] In a similar case, a firm of chartered accountants appealed against an assessment in respect of a payment of £940,000 made to it in connection with the renewal of a lease on premises of which it held the tenancy. The £940,000 comprised three elements: £240,000 constituted a rent rebate to take into account that two floors were not required; £400,000 was an amount paid by the freeholder to enable the firm to refurbish the property; and £300,000 was paid by the freeholder as an inducement for the acceptance of the lease. The tribunal reduced the assessment to £700,000, holding that there was no supply with regard to the payment of £240,000. However, the £400,000 paid to enable the firm to refurbish the premises was consideration for a taxable supply under the principle laid down in *Gleneagles Hotel plc*, **62.125** above. The £300,000 paid as an inducement to enter into the lease, i.e. as a reverse premium, was an amount paid for the execution of the new lease and consequently, for tax purposes, represented a supply of services. *Neville Russell*, [1987] VATTR 194 (VTD 2484).

[62.128] A firm of architects received a 'reverse premium' of £340,000 from a company which had granted it a lease of two floors of a building. It did not account for VAT on this amount, and the Commissioners issued an assessment, against which the firm appealed. The tribunal dismissed the firm's appeal, holding that, by accepting an inducement to enter into the lease, the firm had made a taxable supply of services for consideration. *Hutchinson Locke & Monk*, LON/88/1028 & LON/89/1763 (VTD 5212).

[62.129] In 1993 a publishing company (M) agreed to lease five floors of a multi-storey building, with an option to lease a further four floors. The lessor paid an inducement of £12,000,000 into an escrow account, to be paid to M in instalments. The lessor also paid VAT of £2,100,000, which M accounted for as output tax. In 1994 and 1995 M exercised its option with regard to three further floors, and £1,400,000 was repaid to the lessor in 1995 in respect of M's unexercised option for the remaining floor. Subsequently M claimed repayment of the £2,100,000 from Customs, contending firstly that it had accounted for this in error as it did not relate to any supply, and alternatively that the relevant supply was exempt under *Article 13B(b)* of the *EC Sixth Directive*. The tribunal held that the inducement of £12,000,000 was consideration for a supply of services made by M in the course of relocating its business. The QB referred the case to the CJEC for a ruling on the interpretation of *Article 13B(b)* of the *EC Sixth Directive* (see **22.335** EUROPEAN COMMUNITY LAW). Following the CJEC decision, the company appealed to the Ch D, contending that the case should be remitted to the tribunal to reconsider whether there had been a supply. The Ch D rejected this contention, observing that the tribunal had already made a specific finding on this point. Accordingly the Ch D upheld the Commissioners' rejection of the company's claim for repayment. *Trinity Mirror plc (formerly Mirror Group plc) v C & E Commrs*, Ch D [2003] STC 518; [2003] EWHC 480 (Ch). (*Note.* See, however, Business Brief 12/05, issued on 15 June 2005. HMRC state that they 'now accept that lease obligations, to which tenants are normally bound, do not constitute supplies for which inducement payments on entering leases are consideration' so that 'the majority of such payments are therefore likely to be outside the scope of VAT as they are no more than inducements to tenants to take leases and to observe the obligations in them. There will be a taxable supply only where a payment is linked to benefits a tenant provides outside normal lease terms'. They state that 'this change of policy now effectively puts inducement payments on a similar VAT footing to rent-free periods, in being mainly outside the scope of VAT and only a taxable consideration when directly linked to a specific benefit supplied by a tenant to a landlord'.)

Improvements to hotel paid for by tenant—whether a supply by tenant

[62.130] A company (P) operated two hotels in the Isle of Man. The hotels were owned by P's parent company (C). P paid for alterations and improvements to the hotels. C did not reimburse P for this work, but agreed not to charge P any rent for the hotels. The Isle of Man Treasury issued an assessment on the basis that P had made taxable supplies to C and should account for VAT on the costs of the alterations and improvements. The tribunal dismissed P's appeal, applying the principles laid down in *Neville Russell*, **62.127** above. The waiver of rent by C constituted consideration for the work carried out by P. Since the transaction was not at arm's length and the consideration was non-monetary, the costs of the work carried out should be treated as the open market value of the supplies. *Port Erin Hotels v The Isle of Man Treasury*, MAN/89/722 (VTD 5045).

Repairs to premises paid for by tenant in return for rent-free occupation

[62.131] A company (R) obtained a tenancy of some premises from an associated company (S). The premises were in need of repair, and it was agreed that R would pay for the repairs in return for being allowed to occupy the premises rent-free for three years. R reclaimed the input tax on the repairs, and the Commissioners issued an assessment on the basis that the supply had been to S as the landlord, so that R was not entitled to reclaim the input tax. The tribunal held that R had made an onward supply to S and that the consideration for that supply was the right to occupy the premises rent-free for three years, so that, although R was entitled to reclaim input tax, it was required to account for a corresponding amount of output tax. *Ridgeons Bulk Ltd*, [1992] VATTR 169 (VTD 7655). (*Note.* Another issue in this case was taken to the QB, but Popplewell J's decision was subsequently overruled by the CA—see **3.179** ASSESSMENT.)

Sale of houses after refurbishment

[62.132] See *Maritime Housing Association Ltd*, **41.18** LAND.

Payments under agreement capping mortgage interest

[62.133] A partnership carried on the business of letting commercial property. It entered into an agreement with a development company for the lease of an industrial unit from the company at a peppercorn rent. Under the agreement, the partnership paid a premium of £86,000 plus VAT to the development company. The partnership had to borrow part of this amount, and under a 'mortgage-capping' agreement, the development company agreed to pay the partnership any amount by which its interest payments in the first two years after completion of the lease exceeded 12.5%. The partnership elected to waive exemption in respect of the property. During the first two years of the lease, interest rates were high, and the development company paid the partnership £2,250 under the 'mortgage-capping' agreement. The partnership did not account for tax on these payments. The Commissioners issued an assessment charging output tax on them, on the basis that the payments were equivalent to reverse premiums. The partnership appealed, contending that the payments did not constitute consideration for any supply. The tribunal accepted this contention and allowed the appeal, holding that the 'mortgage-capping' agreement was not an inducement to enter the leasing agreement, but was supplemental to that agreement and 'was part and parcel of the overall transaction'. *N Iliffe & DC Holloway*, [1993] VATTR 439 (VTD 10922).

Inducement payments to development company by health authority

[62.134] A local health authority made four payments of £49,500 each to a development company (M), under a tripartite agreement whereby M agreed to purchase a hospital site from the Department of Health, to construct surgeries for two medical practices on the site, and to grant the health authority an underlease of the surgeries. M did not account for output tax on the payments, and the Commissioners issued assessments charging tax on them. M appealed, contending that the payments did not represent consideration for a supply of services, but should be treated as grants which were outside the scope of VAT. The tribunal rejected this contention and dismissed M's appeal. On the evidence, the payments were consideration for a service supplied by M in agreeing to enter into the agreement. Furthermore, the payments were 'subsidies directly linked to the price' of the relevant supplies, and thus formed part of the taxable amount, within *Article 11A1* of the *EC Sixth Directive*. *Medical Centre Developments Ltd*, LON/95/2714 & 2860 (VTD 15601).

Compensation payments

Compensation payment following disputed bill

[62.135] An architectural partnership (H) was commissioned by a firm of contractors (G) to design a building. H sent G an interim payment application for £10,000 plus VAT of £800 (the standard rate of VAT being 8% at the relevant time). G disputed the amount demanded, and the matter was referred to solicitors. Subsequently G went into liquidation, and H received compensation of £15,000 from the intended purchaser of the building. H failed to account for output tax on this payment, and the Commissioners issued an assessment charging tax of £800, on the basis that £10,800 of the payment represented consideration for H's services, and that only the balance of £4,200 was outside the scope of VAT. The tribunal upheld the assessment and dismissed H's appeal. *Hurley Robinson Partnership*, BIR/78/231 (VTD 750).

Payment by contractor to subcontractor—whether taxable consideration

[62.136] A partnership, which carried out road resurfacing work, had acted for several years as a subcontractor for a civil engineering company (B). In 1997 B stopped providing the partnership with new work, and also failed to pay for work which the partnership had previously done. The partnership issued a writ against B, claiming payment of more than £130,000. The proceedings were eventually settled by an agreement under which B paid the partnership £115,000, expressed as including 'any liability to VAT'. The partnership failed to account for output tax on this receipt. The Commissioners issued an assessment charging tax on it, and the partnership appealed, contending that it should be treated as compensation which was outside the scope of VAT. The tribunal rejected this contention and upheld the assessment in principle, holding that 'a mere payment of compensation would be outside the scope of VAT' but that the payment here was consideration for work which the partnership had carried out. B had 'in substance and reality agreed to pay the £115,000 in respect of work which (the partnership) had carried out'. (However, the tribunal observed on reviewing the evidence that 'the assessment had probably been made for the wrong accounting period'—a point that had not been raised by the appellants. The Commissioners subsequently accepted that the assessment had been made for the wrong accounting period, and agreed to withdraw the assessment. No costs were awarded to either side.) *Mr & Mrs Garnham (t/a Pro-Mac Surfacing)*, LON/98/571 (VTD 15918).

Payment for surrender of rights to product name

[62.137] A company (C) had used a particular trading name and style of logo for some time. In 1983 it became aware that another company (U) was using a similar trading name and logo, and that this was damaging C's business. C began proceedings against U. In 1988 U paid C £30,000 in full and final settlement of C's claims, under an agreement by which C abandoned its rights to the disputed trading name and logo. The Commissioners issued an assessment charging VAT on the payment of £30,000. The tribunal dismissed C's appeal against the assessment. Under what is now *VATA 1994, s 5(2)*, 'anything which is not a supply of goods but is done for a consideration (including, if so done, the granting, assignment or surrender of any right) is a supply of services'. C had surrendered a right in return for the £30,000, which was, therefore, consideration for a deemed supply of services. *Cooper Chasney Ltd*, LON/89/1409Z (VTD 4898).

Payment received as 'out-of-court' settlement

[62.138] A broker began legal proceedings against a company (H) which traded as a travel agent, claiming that he had provided H with information concerning a number of shops which were for sale, but that H had failed to pay him the commission which had been agreed. The broker had claimed £45,000 from H, but agreed to accept £35,000 under a *Tomlin* order as an out-of-court settlement. The Commissioners issued an assessment charging tax on the £35,000, and the broker appealed. The tribunal allowed the broker's appeal, holding that, since he had not obtained judgment against H, it had not been proved that there had been any actual supply of services, and the payment included an element of compensation. The payment should be treated as being outside the scope of VAT, in accordance with the Commissioners' *Press Notice 82/87*. *L Reich*, MAN/92/454 (VTD 9548).

[62.139] A similar decision was reached in *King Engineering Ltd*, LON/02/765 (VTD 19432).

[62.140] Compare *Whites Metal Co*, 36.637 INPUT TAX.

Compensation payment for loss of consultancy—whether a taxable supply

[62.141] A consultant had provided services to a company for nine years, mainly in training its salesmen. In 1989 the company informed him that his services were no longer required, and paid him £30,000 as compensation, in return for which he agreed not to divulge information concerning the company to its competitors. He did not account for tax on this payment, and the Commissioners issued an assessment on the basis that it represented consideration for a taxable supply of services. He appealed, contending that the payment should be treated as being outside the scope of VAT. The tribunal accepted this contention and allowed his appeal. *F Penny (t/a FMS Management Services)*, LON/92/722 (VTD 10398).

Compensation payment for loss of future fees—whether a taxable supply

[62.142] A company (C) owned a hotel, which was managed by another company (H) under a written agreement. In 1991 C terminated the agreement, paying H £2,000,000 as compensation. The Commissioners issued an assessment charging tax on the payment. The tribunal allowed H's appeal, holding that the payment constituted liquidated damages for the loss of future income, and did not represent consideration for a taxable supply. *Holiday Inns (UK) Ltd*, [1993] VATTR 321 (VTD 10609). (*Note*. The decision in this case was disapproved by a subsequent tribunal in *Croydon Hotel & Leisure Co Ltd*, **36.641** INPUT TAX, on the grounds that it was inconsistent with the subsequent CJEC decision in *Lubbock Fine & Co*, **22.333** EUROPEAN COMMUNITY LAW.)

Compensation payment by tenant for termination of taxable lease

[62.143] A bank occupied a leased property. The landlord of the property had elected to waive exemption in respect of the property. The bank decided to vacate the property, and paid the landlord £597,220 as compensation. The Commissioners issued a ruling that output tax was chargeable on this payment, on the basis that it represented consideration for a taxable supply of services. The bank appealed, contending that the payment should be treated as compensation and as outside the scope of VAT. The tribunal rejected this contention and dismissed the appeal, holding on the evidence that 'the contemporaneous granting and exercise' of the option to terminate the lease amounted to a supply of services by the landlord in return for the payment made by the bank. Applying *dicta* of the tribunal in *Central Capital Corporation*, **41.66** LAND, 'what governs the taxability or otherwise of any transaction in leasehold property is whether the grant of the original lease, underlease or licence was taxable or not. If it was taxable, then all subsequent transactions based on the original contractual relationship are taxable'. *Lloyds Bank plc*, LON/95/2524 (VTD 14181).

Compensation for termination of management agreement

[62.144] An investment trust decided to terminate the contract of its manager. It paid the manager a substantial sum as compensation. It did not account for output tax on the payment. The Commissioners issued a ruling that the payment was taxable and the trust appealed, contending that the payment did not represent consideration for any supply and was outside the scope of VAT. The tribunal accepted this contention and allowed the appeal, holding on the evidence that the payment was compensation for a breach of contract, rather than consideration for the manager's rights under the contract. The decision in *Lloyds Bank plc*, **62.143** above, was distinguished on the grounds that the termination of the lease in that case was consensual. *Themis FTSE Fledgling Index Trust plc*, LON/00/501 (VTD 17039).

Compensation for surrender of handguns

[62.145] A company (P) manufactured and sold handguns. Following a shooting at a primary school in Scotland, where a number of children were killed, Parliament enacted the *Firearms (Amendment) Act 1997*, which made the possession and sale of most handguns an offence. A compensation scheme was instituted, whereby compensation was paid for the surrender of such handguns. P surrendered a substantial number of guns, and was paid more than £500,000 as compensation. The Commissioners issued an assessment charging tax on this. P appealed, contending that it had not made any supply of the guns. The tribunal rejected this contention and dismissed the appeal, holding that the surrender of each gun was a supply of goods for consideration equal to the amount of compensation. The QB upheld the tribunal decision. Moses J held that, in order to determine whether or not there had been a supply, it was necessary to identify whether there had been a consumption. However, consumption did not depend upon the question of whether the guns were acquired for further use or were to be destroyed, but upon 'the acquisition of title to the goods'. P had transferred title to the guns to the Government, which gave rise to consumption by the Government. It followed that there had been a supply of goods. The payments of compensation to P represented consideration for that supply. *Parker Hale Ltd v C & E Commrs*, QB [2000] STC 388. (*Note.* For the Commissioners' policy on compensation payments for the surrender of firearms, see Business Brief 27/97, issued on 21 November 1997.)

[62.146] The QB decision in *Parker Hale Ltd*, **62.145** above, was approved by the CA in a similar subsequent case. The CA unanimously held that the surrender of the guns was a supply of goods within *VATA 1994, Sch 4 para 1*. Laws LJ observed that there was 'plainly a legal relationship between supplier and recipient so that the payment of compensation represented consideration for the supply of the handguns'. *G Stewart & T Hammond (t/a GT Shooting) v C & E Commrs*, CA 2001, [2002] STC 255; [2001] EWCA Civ 1988.

Compensation payment for faulty goods

[62.147] See *Galaxy Equipment (Europe) Ltd*, **40.55** INVOICES AND CREDIT NOTES.

Compensation payment made by order of Court

[62.148] See *Hometex Trading Ltd*, **36.638** INPUT TAX, and *Financial & General Print Ltd*, **36.640** INPUT TAX.

Fitness club recovering payments from defaulting members—whether compensation

[62.149] A company (E) operated a chain of fitness clubs. It required new members to join for a minimum of twelve months. In some cases, members failed to make the agreed twelve payments. Such members were barred from using E's facilities within five days of failing to make an agreed payment, and E arranged for debt collection agencies to recover the outstanding amounts. Initially E accounted for VAT on these payments, on the basis that they were taxable consideration for supplies of membership services. Subsequently it submitted a repayment claim on the basis that, while it accepted that output tax was payable for the five-day period before access was barred, it should have treated the balance of the payments as non-taxable compensation for breach of contract. HMRC rejected the claim but the tribunal allowed E's appeal. Judge Khan held that the exclusion of a defaulting member from E's premises resulted in the cessation of E's supplies. Any subsequent payment did not relate directly to any supply of goods or services, and was outside the scope of VAT. *Esporta Ltd v HMRC*, [2011] UKFTT 633 (TC), TC01475.

Whether supply 'in the course or furtherance of any business' (VATA 1994, s 4(1))

NOTE

In the cases under this heading it is accepted that there is a business within what is now *VATA 1994, s 94*, and the issue is whether there has been a supply in the course or furtherance of that business. For cases where the existence of a business is disputed, see 7 BUSINESS.

Sale of sporting rights by farmer

[62.150] An individual (R) purchased a farm in March 1979 and sold sporting rights over the farmland for £12,000 in July 1980. The Commissioners issued an assessment on the basis that the sale of the sporting rights was a standard-rated supply of goods or services. The tribunal upheld the assessment and dismissed R's appeal. It was not essential for an asset to have been used for the purpose of a business for its sale to be in the course or furtherance of that business. There had been the exploitation of an asset of the farming business which, applying what is now *VATA 1994, s 94(6)*, was made in the course or furtherance of the business. Alternatively, as the purpose of the sale was to reduce the business overdraft, it followed that it was 'in furtherance' of the business. *A Ridley*, [1983] VATTR 81 (VTD 1406).

Farmer organising shooting syndicate

[62.151] A farmer, who was registered for VAT, organised a shooting syndicate on his farm. Members of the syndicate paid him subscriptions in return for the right to shoot. He did not account for output tax on these subscriptions. The Commissioners issued an assessment charging tax on them and he appealed, contending that the shooting was organised for pleasure, was not on a commercial basis, and did not constitute a business. (The Inland Revenue treated the shooting as 'hobby farming', giving rise to neither a profit nor a loss.) The tribunal dismissed the appeal, holding on the evidence that the organisation of the shooting went much farther than 'just being a particularly well-run pleasure activity'. The farmer was carrying on a business and was supplying the right to shoot in the course or furtherance of a business. *JO Williams*, LON/95/2173A (VTD 14240).

Chairman of Prince of Wales Trust

[62.152] See *Gardner*, 62.163 below.

Chartered Secretary appointed as Complaints Administrator

[62.153] See *Lee*, 62.69 above.

Paid lectures given by practising barrister

[62.154] A barrister received fees for lecturing at a course for Patent Agents, but did not account for VAT on these fees. The Commissioners issued an assessment charging tax on the fees, and the barrister appealed, contending that he had not given the lectures 'in the course or furtherance of his business'. The tribunal rejected this contention and dismissed the appeal. The barrister specialised in patent law and had been engaged to lecture at the course because of his professional expertise. Accordingly, he had undertaken the lectures in the course or furtherance of his business as a barrister, and was obliged to account for VAT on the fees. *BC Reid*, LON/93/1373A (VTD 11625).

Football club providing services to associated 'members' club

[62.155] A professional football club, which was registered for VAT, established a 'members' club', in accordance with guidelines issued by the Football League. Part of the ground was set aside for the exclusive use of members of the 'members' club'. The Commissioners issued a ruling that the club was required to account for VAT on the sums which it received from 'members'. The club appealed, contending that the supplies were not made in the course or furtherance of its business. The tribunal dismissed the appeal, holding that the benefits provided by the club to the members were taxable supplies in the course or furtherance of the club's business, within what is now *VATA 1994, s 4(1)*. (The tribunal chairman observed that what is now *VATA 1994, s 94(3)(a)* was not relevant, since the 'members' club' was not in law a true members' club, but was in fact a proprietary club run as a business by the limited liability company which owned the football club. The tribunal also held that the whole of the sums paid by members were standard-rated, rejecting the club's contention that part of the consideration should be apportioned to zero-rated supplies of a booklet and a monthly newspaper.) *Southend United Football Club*, LON/93/121A (VTD 11919).

Sale of original painting by owner of art gallery

[62.156] The owner of an art gallery, who was registered for VAT, sold an original painting for £1,500 and did not account for output tax on the sale. The Commissioners issued an assessment and the owner appealed, contending that, although he had displayed a print of the painting in his gallery, the original painting was a private asset which had been hanging in his living-room, so that he should not be required to account for tax on its sale. The tribunal rejected this contention and dismissed his appeal, holding on the evidence that the sale of the painting was 'a business transaction'. *J Conlin (t/a Cottage Art & Frames)*, EDN/01/131 (VTD 17550).

Sale of private assets to raise capital for business

[62.157] See *Stirling*, 62.77 above, and *Atkinson*, 62.78 above.

Administrative supplies to associated companies

[62.158] See *PHH Europe plc*, 62.28 above.

Institute of Chartered Accountants

[62.159] The Institute of Chartered Accountants in England and Wales is registered for VAT as an organisation providing advantages or facilities to its members, within what is now *VATA 1994, s 94(2)*. It is also a 'recognised professional body' under *Financial Services Act 1986, s 17* and *Insolvency Act 1986, s 391* and a 'recognised supervisory body' under *Companies Act 1989*, and issues certificates accordingly, authorising (or 'licensing') practitioners to carry on investment business, insolvency work and audit work. The Commissioners issued a ruling that the services supplied by the Institute in the course of its licensing activities were not supplied in the course or furtherance of a business, so that it was not required to account for output tax on them and was not entitled to reclaim input tax in respect of them. The Institute appealed, contending that its licensing functions amounted to a 'business' or an 'economic activity'. The tribunal rejected this contention and dismissed the appeal, holding that the relevant supplies were not of a kind which 'are commonly made by those who seek to make profit from them', nor were the relevant activities 'predominantly concerned with the making of taxable supplies for a consideration'. The predominant concern of the licensing activities was 'the implementation of the statutory policy of protecting the public interest through self-regulation of the relevant practitioners', and 'charging fees for investigative and monitoring services is not the predominant concern or characteristic of the activities'. The Ch D, CA and HL unanimously upheld this decision. Applying *Polysar Investments Netherlands BV v Inspecteur der Invoerrechten en Accijnzen*, **22.106** EUROPEAN COMMUNITY LAW, 'it is not enough merely to point to the fact that there is a supply of services in return for a money payment and some loose economic connection', but 'the activities must be of an "economic character"'. Lord Slynn observed that the Institute was carrying out a regulatory function, on behalf of the State, to ensure that only fit and proper persons were licensed or authorised to carry out the various activities and to monitor what they did. This was not in any real sense a trading, commercial or economic activity, and the fact that fees were charged for the grant of the licences did not convert it into one. Performing a licensing function on behalf of the State was not a 'business'. *The Institute of Chartered Accountants in England and Wales v C & E Commrs*, HL [1999] STC 398; [1999] 1 WLR 701; [1999] 2 All ER 449.

Lease and leaseback arrangement

[62.160] A father and daughter formed a partnership to operate a nursery school. They registered for VAT in April 1999. In May they took a lease of a disused barn which was owned by the father and two other members of his family, and began to convert it. In July they were advised that, because the supply of nursery care was exempt from VAT, the input tax on the conversion would be subject to the partial exemption provisions (and most of it would be irrecoverable). In October, on the advice of an accountancy firm, they leased the property back to the landlords for a nominal consideration. On the same day the landlords sublet the property back to the partnership, also for a nominal consideration, and the partnership elected to waive exemption on the property. In November the partnership claimed a repayment of input tax in respect of the conversion work. The Commissioners rejected the claim on the grounds that the work was attributable to exempt supplies, and that the grants of the subleases in October did not constitute supplies in the course or furtherance of a business. The partnership appealed, contending that its grant of the sublease to the landlords was a taxable supply, and that the input tax was fully attributable to this taxable supply. The tribunal rejected this contention and dismissed the appeal, holding that the grants of the subleases 'were not transactions effected in the course or furtherance of a business'. *J & H Laurie (t/a The Peacock Montessori Nursery)*, LON/00/42 (VTD 17219).

Work carried out for Historic Buildings and Monuments Commission

[62.161] A company (L) was constructing a new railway line. In the course of the work, it wished to arrange for the moving of a Grade II listed building. It reached an agreement with the Historic Buildings and Monuments Commission for England, under which L would pay for the building to be dismantled but not for the cost of re-erecting it elsewhere. The Historic Buildings and Monuments Commission arranged for another company (H) to carry out the relevant work. L agreed to pay H £100,000 towards the cost of the removal, although no formal contract was ever signed. H also received a grant from the Heritage Lottery Fund. H arranged for contractors to carry out the work, which turned out to be more expensive than anticipated. H reclaimed input tax on the amounts charged by the contractors. The Commissioners rejected the claim on the basis that in the absence of a formal contract, all the payments received by H were donations and it had not made any relevant supply in the course or furtherance of its business. H appealed. The tribunal allowed the appeal, holding on the evidence that there was an 'oral contract' between H and L, and that H was entitled to reclaim the relevant input tax. *Heritage of London Trust Operations Ltd*, LON/02/984 (VTD 18545).

Advertising facilities supplied by Council for sponsorship payments

[62.162] See *Norwich City Council*, 42.11 LOCAL AUTHORITIES AND STATUTORY BODIES.

Supplies by office-holders (VATA 1994, s 94(4))

Chairman of Prince of Wales Trust

[62.163] The chairman-designate of the Prince of Wales Trust, who had been employed in local government, became self-employed as a business consultant and registered for VAT. At the time he began self-employment, he had not taken up his office as chairman of the Trust, although his appointment had been confirmed in writing. As chairman of the Trust he received no salary but his expenses were reimbursed. The Commissioners issued an assessment on the basis that he had accepted this office in the course of his business and, by virtue of *VATA 1994, s 94(4)*, should have accounted for VAT on the reimbursed expenses. The tribunal allowed his appeal against the assessment, holding that he had not accepted the chairmanship of the Trust in the course of his business, as his consultancy business had not begun at the time he accepted the office. *JJ Gardner*, [1989] VATTR 132 (VTD 3687).

Partners in solicitors' firm holding various offices

[62.164] Five partners in a solicitors' firm held various offices, including acting as clerk and/or treasurer of various local charities, and as secretary and treasurer of a local law society. The Commissioners issued a ruling that the partners had accepted the offices in the course or furtherance of their profession, so that the effect of *VATA 1994, s 94(4)* was that the partnership was required to account for output tax on any payments which the solicitors received in relation to these offices. The tribunal allowed the partnership's appeal, finding that the duties involved were 'of an administrative nature such as are capable of being carried out either by professional persons or by others of proven intelligence and honesty, in both cases having a modicum of common sense and ability to deal with day to day secretarial duties'. On the evidence, 'all the appointments were made on the basis of the appointees' personal merit and/or standing in the community, as distinct from their professional expertise'. Accordingly, the partnership was not liable to account for output tax. *Oglethorpe Sturton & Gillibrand*, MAN/00/322 (VTD 17491).

[62.165] Seven partners in a solicitors' firm in Suffolk held various offices, including serving on health service trusts, acting as clerk to a body of General Commissioners, and acting as a director of a local building society. The partnership encouraged its members to accept such offices, on the grounds that it was 'beneficial for the firm to be recognised as being involved in the local community'. However, the partnership required the partners to share any fees received for such offices, since the duties involved 'took up an appreciable amount of partnership office time' and 'equity with other partners who did not hold outside positions had to be achieved'. The Commissioners issued an assessment on the basis that the partners had accepted the offices in the course or furtherance of their profession, so that the effect of *VATA 1994, s 94(4)* was that the partnership was required to account for output tax on any payments which the solicitors received in relation to these offices. The tribunal allowed the partnership's appeal with regard to six of the partners, holding that the test to be applied was 'did one or more of the solicitors accept the offices in the course or furtherance of their profession' and 'did one or more of the solicitors accept the offices in the course or furtherance of the partnership business'. The assessment could only be upheld if the answer to both questions was 'yes'. On the evidence, this test was only satisfied with regard to the partner who acted as a director of a local building society. (The tribunal observed that 'as a result of the assessment, he now receives his building society salary personally and there is a reduction in his net share of the profits accordingly. If that had occurred before the assessment was raised, then our decision in his case might have been different.') *Birketts*, [2002] VATDR 100 (VTD 17515).

[62.166] A firm of solicitors comprised two partners. One of the partners (W) accepted a post as a director of a limited company (L). This company paid the partnership £3,000 in respect of W's services. The Commissioners issued an assessment charging tax on this. The partnership appealed, contending that W was employed by L and that VAT should not be charged on the fees. The tribunal rejected this contention and dismissed the appeal, observing that 'normally a director holds an office and is not employed', and 'evidence is required to establish that he is employed'. On the evidence, W 'was acting only as a director and not as an employee'. He had accepted the directorship in the course or furtherance of his profession, within *VATA 1994, s 94(4)*, and the partnership was required to account for tax on the fees. *Bray Walker*, LON/00/264 (VTD 18339).

Miscellaneous—supplies of goods

Contract rendered void through misrepresentation by purchaser

[62.167] A company (L) which dealt in electrical goods had regularly supplied goods to a large hotel group (T). The orders were regularly placed on behalf of T by one of its employees (G). G told L that he had ceased to work for T and had set up in business on his own account. In that capacity he ordered 150 television sets from L, stating that they were for installation in T's hotels. He collected the sets and L invoiced him for them, giving him one month's credit. He did not pay for them within the month. L was unable to trace him, and notified the police. Some months later G was arrested, and was subsequently convicted of theft of the sets, having obtained them by deception through having falsely represented that they were for installation in T's hotels. L did not account for tax on the sets, and the Commissioners issued an assessment on the basis that the sets had been supplied when L issued G with an invoice. The tribunal allowed L's appeal, holding that the contract with G had been rendered void by G's deception and L's prompt notification of the facts to the police. On the evidence, the sets had been stolen by G and L had not supplied them. *Harry B Litherland & Co Ltd*, [1978] VATTR 226 (VTD 701).

Sale of stolen cars

[62.168] A second-hand car dealer sold a number of stolen cars at auction. He did not account for VAT on the sales, and the Commissioners issued an assessment charging tax on the amounts received. He appealed, contending that there had been no supply since he did not own the cars. The QB rejected this contention and upheld the assessment. The fact that the dealer had no legal title to the cars did not alter the fact that he had supplied them. Griffiths J defined supply as 'the passing of possession in goods pursuant to an agreement whereunder the supplier agrees to part and the recipient agrees to take possession'. *C & E Commrs v JRR Oliver*, QB 1979, [1980] STC 73; [1980] 1 All ER 353. (*Note.* Compare the subsequent case of *Hudson*, **36.664** INPUT TAX, in which a tribunal held that there was no right to reclaim input tax in respect of acquisitions of stolen goods.)

[62.169] The decision in *Oliver*, 62.168 above, was applied in the similar case of *D Lindley*, MAN/92/716 (VTD 12037).

Supply of waste for extraction of silver content

[62.170] A company (R) carried on the business of recovering silver from photographic waste. It had no facilities for producing refined silver, and therefore disposed of its products, comprising silver and ash with a high silver content, to another company (M) which used them with its own products to form rough silver bars for disposal to a third company (J) which traded as silver brokers and was able to produce and dispose of refined silver bars. It was only at this stage that a monetary value could be placed on the preceding supplies by R and M. M accounted for VAT on the amounts it received from J and passed to R the net amount due on it. R did not account for VAT on its supplies of swarf and ash to M, and appealed against an assessment on them. The tribunal dismissed the appeal. Any difficulty arising from the delay in ascertaining the value of the supply could have been met by a request for a direction under what is now *VATA 1994, s 6(6)*. *United Refining Co (Precious Metals) Ltd*, MAN/79/51 (VTD 1019).

Refundable deposits for goods—whether a supply

[62.171] A partnership acted as distributors for an American company. It had a large number of its own distributors, to whom it provided 'training tools', the sale of which would have been illegal under the *Fair Trading Act 1973*, in return for a refundable deposit. The deposits exceeded the cost of the tools. The Commissioners issued an assessment charging tax on the deposits and the partnership appealed, contending that the deposits did not represent consideration for a supply. The tribunal dismissed the partnership's appeal, holding that the distribution of the tools was a supply by the partnership and that the deposits were the consideration. *BJ Executive Services*, LON/85/13 (VTD 2048).

Commemorative coins issued under sales promotion scheme

[62.172] A company distributed to purchasers of its products more than 150,000 commemorative £2 coins in presentation folders under a sales promotion scheme. The Commissioners issued an assessment on the basis that the distribution constituted a standard-rated supply. The tribunal dismissed the company's appeal, holding that, for VAT purposes, the distributions were supplies of coins which were collector's pieces and were chargeable to tax. *Milk Marketing Board*, LON/87/495 (VTD 3389).

Subcontract work where materials provided by contractor

[62.173] A construction company engaged independent subcontractors to carry out specific work. All materials were invoiced to the company and all accounts were settled by the company. The Commissioners issued an assessment on the basis that the arrangements constituted a supply by the contractor to the subcontractor of the materials and plant hire, at cost, and a supply back to the contractor by the subcontractor of the finished job. The company appealed, contending that the subcontractors were supplying labour only. The tribunal allowed the company's appeal, holding that the materials were the sole responsibility of the main contractor from start to finish. *J Hopkins (Contractors) Ltd*, [1989] VATTR 107 (VTD 3511).

Invoices for supplies of gold described by issuer as 'shams'

[62.174] A taxi driver issued VAT invoices showing sales of gold to an individual who was an acquaintance of his. In accounting for tax he only accounted for output tax on a small proportion of the amount shown on the invoices he had issued to the acquaintance, and reclaimed input tax in respect of purported invoices which he subsequently admitted to be false. The Commissioners issued an assessment to require payment of the full amounts of output tax shown on the invoices issued by the taxi driver, and to recover the input tax which he had fraudulently reclaimed. The taxi driver appealed, contending that all the invoices were shams and that he had not made any actual supplies of gold, but had issued the invoices at the request of the acquaintance, who was in possession of a large quantity of gold which he had acquired illegally and in respect of which he wished to reclaim input tax. (The Commissioners had taken criminal proceedings against the acquaintance, but he had been acquitted by a jury.) The tribunal accepted the taxi driver's evidence and allowed his appeal on the grounds that the assessment had not been made to the best of the Commissioners' judgment. On the evidence, the purported transactions were 'fiscal nullities' and, notwithstanding the issue of fraudulent invoices, could not form the basis of any claims for input tax or any liability to output tax. (The tribunal also observed that the Commissioners should have assessed the acquaintance to recover the input tax shown on the invoices issued to him by the taxi driver.) *Sandell*, LON/91/1000X (VTD 9665).

Contract for supply of jewellery—goods not of required standard

[62.175] A company (B) agreed to supply another company (G) with substantial quantities of gold-plated jewellery. B purchased the jewellery from a third company (S), which imported the jewellery from Korea. G ascertained that some of the jewellery was not in fact gold-plated. It returned 60,000 items to B, and B refunded the money which G had paid for these items. B returned the items in question to S, and S paid £175,000 to B. The Commissioners issued assessments charging output tax on these payments. B appealed, contending that it had retained title to the goods, notwithstanding that S had paid it £175,000 and that the goods had been physically returned to S. The tribunal accepted this contention and allowed the appeal, finding that the terms of the agreement were such that title to the goods would not pass from B to S until it was established that G would not take any further proceedings against B. *Basdring Ltd*, MAN/92/1036 (VTD 13263).

Vendor of computer units intending to defraud Customs of VAT

[62.176] A company (T) agreed to sell some computer units to another company (M) for £770,400 plus VAT, and introduced M to a third party which would repurchase the units. T issued an invoice charging UK VAT on the sale, but asked M to make its payment for the goods outside the UK. M queried this with the Commissioners, who formed the opinion that T was involved in an attempted 'carousel fraud'. They obtained a 'freezing injunction' against T, and a winding-up petition was subsequently presented, as a result of which T went into liquidation. T's liquidator took proceedings against M, seeking payment for the computer units. M defended the proceedings, contending that because T's managing director had intended to defraud Customs, the contract was illegal and unenforceable. The QB rejected this contention and gave judgment for T. Field J held that 'not every contract entered into with the intention of committing an illegal act is illegal and unenforceable'. On the evidence, there was not 'sufficient proximity between (T's) fraudulent intention and the contract for the contract to be vitiated by illegality'. *21st Century Logistic Solutions Ltd (in liquidation) v Madysen Ltd*, QB [2004] STC 1535; [2004] EWHC 231 (QB).

Supply of counterfeit goods

[62.177] See *R v Goodwin & Unstead*, **22.82** EUROPEAN COMMUNITY LAW.

Unlawful supplies of anabolic steroids

[62.178] See *R v C & J Citrone*, 49.12 PENALTIES: EVASION OF TAX.

Purchase by partners from partnership—whether a supply

[62.179] See *Atkins Macreadie & Co*, 29.42 FOOD.

Supplies of repossessed goods—Special Provisions Order, Article 4

[62.180] See *Buy As You View Ltd v HMRC*, 60.20 SECOND-HAND GOODS.

Takings stolen—whether a supply

[62.181] See *Benton*, 62.382 below, and the cases noted at 62.383 and 62.384 below.

Whether there can be a taxable supply of non-existent goods

[62.182] See *Howard*, 36.630 INPUT TAX.

Arrangement between retailer and finance company—whether a supply

[62.183] See *Excell Consumer Industries Ltd*, 36.680 INPUT TAX.

Miscellaneous—supplies of services

Cases held to constitute a supply

Vouchers issued under incentive scheme

[62.184] A company (N) issued vouchers, with a face value of £3, to purchasers of its products. These vouchers could be redeemed for vouchers of the same face value exchangeable for goods at stores owned by another company (F). N did not account for VAT on the issue of the vouchers and the Commissioners issued an assessment on the basis that their issue was a taxable supply. The tribunal held that N made a taxable supply of services when it exchanged the vouchers for F's vouchers, and that the consideration was the face value of F's vouchers. *Normal Motor Factors Ltd*, [1978] VATTR 20 (VTD 499).

[62.185] See also the cases noted at 67.151 to 67.174 VALUATION.

Payments from manufacturer under promotion scheme

[62.186] A company, limited by guarantee, had been established as a mutual concern by companies engaged in the cash and carry trade. Its principal activity was to organise promotions of selected products in co-operation with the manufacturers. The manufacturers contributed to the costs of the promotions, and made additional payments computed by reference to the sales of the products being promoted. The company distributed such payments to its members on the basis of their sales of the products in question. The company did not account for tax on the payments from the manufacturers and appealed against an assessment charging tax on them. The tribunal dismissed the appeal, holding that the payments were consideration for a supply within what is now

VATA 1994, s 5(2)(b). *The Landmark Cash & Carry Group Ltd*, [1980] VATTR 1 (VTD 883).

Hospitality provided by manufacturer to sales staff of dealers

[62.187] A company (P) which manufactured cars devised an incentive scheme to encourage sales staff working for car dealers who sold P's cars. Staff who attained a certain number of sales received a 'double ticket' entitling them and a partner to attend a dinner-dance at a hotel, with overnight accommodation. P reclaimed input tax on the costs it incurred under the scheme, and did not account for any output tax in respect of the provision of the tickets. The Commissioners issued an assessment to recover input tax on the basis that P was supplying business entertainment, and issued an alternative assessment charging output tax on the basis that if the supplies did not constitute 'business entertainment', then P was supplying benefits in return for consideration. P appealed against both assessments. The tribunal allowed P's appeal against the input tax assessment, holding that the supplies were outside the definition of 'business entertainment' since there was 'a clear direct link between the level of sales and the reward'. However, the tribunal dismissed P's appeal against the output tax assessment, observing that 'if the preferred assessment fails, the alternative assessment must succeed'. On the evidence, 'the successful participants provided consideration for the supply to them of the right to a double ticket' and this was 'a taxable supply on which output tax is due'. *Peugeot-Citroen Automobiles Ltd*, [2004] VATDR 157 (VTD 18681).

Money received for abandoned project

[62.188] An architect failed to account for VAT on payment he had received for carrying out work for a project which had subsequently been abandoned. The Commissioners issued an assessment charging tax on the payment and he appealed, contending that the payment represented compensation and should not be treated as liable to VAT. The tribunal dismissed his appeal, holding that the payment constituted consideration. *WG Richards*, MAN/86/154 (VTD 2355).

Payment described as 'interest-free loan'

[62.189] A firm of architects performed various services relating to a potential development scheme, for which it received interim payments on which VAT was correctly accounted for. Subsequently its client informed the firm that the project might be aborted, and it would therefore be unable to make further payments. The firm protested at this and it was agreed that, in view of the work which the firm had already undertaken, the client would pay the firm £50,000, described as an 'interest-free loan', repayable on a specified date if the project was proceeded with and further payments became due. The specified date passed without any more work being carried out and without repayment of the loan being made or requested. The Commissioners issued an assessment charging VAT on the £50,000, and the tribunal dismissed the firm's appeal, holding that the payment was consideration for the services which the firm had supplied. *Shingler Risdon Associates*, LON/88/248 (VTD 2981).

Customer in liquidation—payment not received

[62.190] A trader supplied management services to a company which subsequently went into liquidation without paying for the services. Invoices were issued to the company, but the trader did not account for the VAT shown on the invoices. The Commissioners issued an assessment charging tax on the invoices, and the trader appealed, contending that the invoices had been issued in error by one of his staff without his knowledge. The tribunal dismissed his appeal, finding that either the appellant or his bookkeeper had been responsible for the issue of the invoices, which were genuine invoices for services that the trader had supplied to the company. *EA Kilburn*, MAN/87/277 (VTD 3937). (*Note.* For another issue in this case, see **36.506** INPUT TAX.)

[62.191] Similar decisions were reached in *Charles Forrington & Partners Ltd*, LON/90/358Z (VTD 5540). and *JR Nicholson*, LON/91/860 (VTD 6707).

Payphone in public house

[62.192] A publican failed to account for VAT on receipts from a 'payphone' which he had installed in the public house. The Commissioners issued an assessment charging tax on the receipts and he appealed, contending that he should not have to account for VAT since he did not make a separate charge to the customers. The tribunal dismissed the appeal, holding that the service was clearly a supply by the publican for consideration. *K Hodson*, MAN/89/606 (VTD 4709).

Payphones in launderettes

[62.193] A company which operated a number of launderettes installed payphones in the launderettes but did not account for output tax on the receipts from these. The Commissioners issued an assessment charging tax on them and the tribunal dismissed the company's appeal. *Chamberlain Domestic Services Ltd*, LON/93/2764A (VTD 12492).

Free meals provided to coach drivers

[62.194] A company which operated motorway service stations provided free meals to coach drivers in return for bringing passengers to the service stations. To claim a free meal, a driver had to be carrying at least 20 passengers, and also had to sign a book and produce his PSV licence. Drivers were also given gift stamps which could be exchanged for goods. The Commissioners issued assessments charging tax on the value of the free meals, on the basis that the company was making supplies for a consideration. The company appealed, contending that there was no taxable transaction. The tribunal dismissed the appeal, holding that the allowance of a free meal and a gift stamp constituted a supply by the company for consideration. The driver was given his free meal as consideration for bringing potential customers to the service station. *Granada Group plc*, [1991] VATTR 104 (VTD 5565). (*Note.* For the valuation of such supplies, see *Westmorland Motorway Services Ltd*, **67.143** VALUATION.)

Bank dealing in foreign currency bank notes

[62.195] The London branch of a United States bank dealt in bank notes in 150 currencies. It had no retail branches, dealing entirely with other banks and with travel agents. It was registered for VAT and had been accepted as partly exempt. However, in 1992 the Commissioners formed the opinion that the bank's supplies of notes did not constitute the making of supplies for consideration (with the result that the bank would no longer be entitled to use the partial exemption special method which had previously been agreed, and would have to restrict its input tax claims). The bank appealed, contending that the supplies of notes were made for profit and were therefore supplies of services for consideration. The tribunal allowed the bank's appeal. The provision of bank notes in one currency, in return for an undertaking to pay in another currency, was a supply for consideration. The transactions fell within *Article 13B(d)(4)* of the *EC Sixth Directive*. *Republic National Bank of New York*, [1992] VATTR 299 (VTD 7894).

Foreign exchange transactions not involving supplies of banknotes

[62.196] A company which acted as trustee of a pension fund entered into a number of foreign currency transactions with a number of banks. Customs issued a ruling that the effect of the CJEC decision in *C & E Commrs v First National Bank of Chicago*, **22.89** EUROPEAN COMMUNITY LAW, was that the company was making exempt supplies of services to the banks, and was accordingly unable to recover the related input tax. The company appealed, contending that the decision in *First National Bank of Chicago* was applicable only to banks, and did not apply 'automatically to any person entering into a foreign currency transaction with a bank'. The tribunal accepted this contention and allowed the appeal, holding that 'where it is possible to identify consideration received by a party to a foreign exchange contract which is directly related to his supply in relation to that contract, then there is a supply for a consideration for the purposes of the *Sixth Directive*'. However, when a bank entered into a foreign exchange transaction with a customer, the customer was not generally providing any service to the bank, and did not generally receive any consideration from the bank. The profit which the company had made on its transactions did not constitute 'consideration'. *Willis Pension Trustees Ltd*, [2005] VATDR 418 (VTD 19183). (*Note.* For HMRC's practice following this decision, see Business Brief 21/2005, issued on 23 November 2005, and HMRC Brief 05/07, issued on 26 January 2007.)

Transfer of rights under hire-purchase agreement

[62.197] In 1991 a trader acquired a van under a hire-purchase agreement. In 1992 he disposed of the van to a company. The company agreed to pay the amounts outstanding under the hire-purchase agreement. The trader did not account for output tax on the disposal, and the Commissioners issued an assessment, against which he appealed. The tribunal dismissed his appeal. As indicated in *Notice 700/5/85*, the transfer of rights under a hire-purchase agreement was a standard-rated supply of services, and the consideration for the supply was the amount outstanding under the hire-purchase agreement. *ME Noble*, MAN/93/1294 (VTD 12346).

Competitions under contract expressed not to be legally binding

[62.198] See *Town & County Factors Ltd*, 22.240 EUROPEAN COMMUNITY LAW.

Assignment of right to share in proceeds of litigation

[62.199] A property company (P) had acquired an option to purchase a piece of land. The owners of the land decided to sell the land to a third party, and agreed to pay P £3,100,000 for forgoing its option. However, the landowners' solicitors missed the completion date and the deal collapsed. Because of a fall in property prices, the land had to be sold at a lower price than had originally been agreed. P only received £1,900,000 for its option and began legal proceedings against the landowners' solicitors. The litigation was protracted and P entered into an agreement with an associated company (J) whereby, in return for financial support, it assigned J a right to share in the proceeds of the litigation. Subsequently P applied to register for VAT. The Commissioners rejected the application on the basis that P was not making any taxable supplies. The tribunal allowed P's appeal, holding that the assignment of a right to share in the proceeds of litigation was a taxable supply of services and the payments which P was receiving from J were consideration for that supply, so that P was entitled to register. *22A Property Investments Ltd*, MAN/96/264 (VTD 14544). (*Note.* The tribunal upheld the Commissioners' ruling that P was not entitled to make a late election to waive exemption in respect of its disposal of its option.)

Charge for abortive visit

[62.200] A telecommunications company (BT) arranged for visits by engineers to rectify faults reported by customers. The visits were arranged at times agreed with the customers. Where the engineer was unable to gain access to the premises at the agreed time, BT levied an 'abortive visit charge'. It did not account for output tax on these charges. The Commissioners issued an assessment charging tax on the basis that the charges represented consideration for taxable supplies of services. BT appealed, contending that the charges should be treated as 'liquidated damages' and as outside the scope of VAT. The tribunal rejected this contention and dismissed the appeal, holding that BT was providing a fault repair service 'from the time the fault is reported until it has been corrected'. *British Telecommunications plc*, LON/94/5730 (VTD 14830).

Deposits for hotel accommodation

[62.201] See *Société Thermale d'Eugénie-les-Bains v Ministère de l'Économie, des Finances et de l'Industrie*, 22.86 EUROPEAN COMMUNITY LAW, and *Bass plc*, 62.93 above.

Parking charges

[62.202] A company imposed parking charges on certain sites which it administered, including penalties for 'excess or improper parking'. The Commissioners issued an assessment charging output tax on such charges, and the tribunal dismissed the company's appeal. *Town & City Parking Ltd*, EDN/96/142 (VTD 15730).

[62.203] A company (V) operated a 'parking control' service for landowners. It did not account for VAT on all of the amounts which it received from motorists. HMRC issued an assessment, and V appealed, contending that the amounts in question were penalties for contraventions which should be treated as damages for trespass and as outside the scope of VAT. The tribunal rejected this contention and dismissed the appeal, specifically distinguishing the case of *Bristol City Council*, 62.214 below, which V had cited as an authority. Judge King held that 'what is being offered is a right to park in accordance with the signs without fear of an action for trespass being brought by the private landowner. Parking in one of these car parks is an acceptance of the offer and payment of the additional charges is a term of that contract not a consequence of breaching that contract.' *Vehicle Control Services Ltd v HMRC*, [2011] UKFTT 125 (TC), TC00999.

Licence fees for right to use boat on river

[62.204] The British Waterways Board issued licences allowing boat-owners to use certain rivers. It charged VAT on these licences. A boat-owner appealed to the VAT tribunal, contending that VAT should not have been charged. The tribunal rejected this contention and dismissed the appeal, holding that the Board was making supplies of services to boat-owners and had correctly charged VAT on its supplies. *SR Peters*, MAN/05/135 (VTD 19876).

Takings stolen

[62.205] See *Benton*, 62.382 below, and the cases noted at 62.383 and 62.384 below.

Fees for arranging Ministry of Transport vehicle test

[62.206] See *Ward*, 44.162 MOTOR CARS; *Waterhouse Ltd*, 44.163 MOTOR CARS, and the cases noted at **44.164** MOTOR CARS.

Statutory repair work carried on by City Council

[62.207] See *Glasgow City Council*, 42.6 LOCAL AUTHORITIES AND STATUTORY BODIES.

Contribution to cost of repairs to bomb-damaged building

[62.208] See *Commercial Union Assurance Co plc*, 36.67 INPUT TAX.

Payments from parent company to subsidiary company

[62.209] See *Tilling Management Services Ltd*, 43.8 MANAGEMENT SERVICES.

Tourist board

[62.210] See *Netherlands Board of Tourism*, 36.498 INPUT TAX, and *Austrian National Tourist Office*, 36.499 INPUT TAX.

Cases held not to constitute a supply

Cartage by fisherman—whether a supply

[62.211] A fisherman (G) owned two fishing boats operating from Harwich, manned by him, his son and two nephews. He took one-third of the net proceeds of the catch, and his son and nephews shared the remainder. He drove most of the catch to Lowestoft to be sold at auction. The auctioneers prepared a document for G in which 7.5% of the gross proceeds were treated as 'cartage' to be retained by G before sharing the net proceeds with his son and nephews. Customs issued an assessment charging VAT on the cartage but the tribunal allowed G's appeal, holding that G's son and nephews were employees and that the cartage was not a taxable supply. *FVE Good*, [1974] VATTR 256 (VTD 119).

Examination fees received by tutor from part-time employment

[62.212] A former teacher began self-employment as a tutor and registered for VAT. While a teacher, she had held a part-time employment as an examiner. She continued this work after beginning self-employment, but did not account for VAT on her examiner's salary. The Commissioners issued an assessment charging tax on the salary, but the tribunal allowed her appeal, holding that the salary was not connected with her profession as a tutor and was outside the scope of VAT. *ME Holland*, [1978] VATTR 108 (VTD 580).

Sole trader negotiating agreements with manufacturers

[62.213] A sole trader operated a bulk purchasing organisation for electrical wholesalers, who paid him a membership fee plus quarterly subscriptions. He negotiated agreements with electrical manufacturers whereby they paid him rebates calculated by reference to the volume of sales made to his subscribers. The Commissioners issued an assessment on the basis that he was making a supply to the manufacturers and that the rebates which he received constituted consideration for this supply. He appealed, contending that he was not making any supply to the manufacturers, and that the rebates belonged to his subscribers. The tribunal accepted this contention and allowed his appeal, holding that there was a direct link between the rebate received by the member and 'the supplies to the member of goods by the manufacturer'. Accordingly, the rebates were 'contingent rebates in respect of the sales of goods by the manufacturers to the members'. *Landmark Cash & Carry Group Ltd*, **62.186** above, was distinguished on the basis that in that case 'any link was broken by the particular role of that company, a separate legal entity'. *M Morris (t/a Reward)*, LON/99/796 (VTD 16846).

Excess charges for unlawful parking—whether consideration for a supply

[62.214] A City Council operated a number of car parks. It accounted for tax on its receipts from these, including the 'excess charges' which it levied for unlawful parking. Subsequently it formed the opinion that it should not have accounted for tax on the 'excess charges' and submitted a repayment claim on the basis that these should not be treated as consideration for any supply. The Commissioners rejected the claim and the Council appealed. The tribunal allowed the Council's appeal, observing that 'the level of the excess charge is such that it would probably be held to be a penalty' and holding that the excess charges were 'not consideration for a supply of parking'. *Bristol City Council*, LON/99/261 (VTD 17665). (*Note.* For the Commissioners' practice following this decision, see Business Brief 19/2002, issued on 19 July 2002. HMRC now accept that excess charges levied in Council car parks, under the *1984 Road Traffic Regulation Act*, are statutory penalties and so are outside the scope of

VAT. However, they also state that excess charges levied in private car parks remain subject to VAT; see, for example, *Town & City Parking Ltd*, **62.202** above.)

Payment for work on contaminated building site—whether any supply

[62.215] A company (N) purchased an area of land which had previously been used as a landfill site, but was close to a city centre and was considered to have development potential. N obtained planning permission for the development of accommodation on the site, conditional on the site being decontaminated. N subsequently formed the opinion that the vendor (W), from which it had purchased the site, had not revealed the full extent of the contamination. In 1999 W agreed to pay N the excess of the decontamination costs over £560,000. However W subsequently disputed the extent of the work which N considered necessary, and N had to take court proceedings against W. Eventually W paid £2,700,000 to N. The Commissioners issued an assessment charging tax on this. N appealed, contending that this was not consideration for any supply of services, and was not subject to VAT. The tribunal accepted this contention and allowed N's appeal, observing that the supply of land by W to N was exempt, and holding on the evidence that 'there was no supply of any kind by (N) to (W)'. *Navydock Ltd*, LON/02/316 (VTD 18281).

Optional service charges—whether a supply

[62.216] See *NDP Co Ltd*, **67.107** VALUATION.

Musician performing on public highway—whether supplying services

[62.217] See *Tolsma v Inspecteur der Omzetbelasting Leeuwarden*, **22.84** EUROPEAN COMMUNITY LAW.

Local authority providing grants to charity

[62.218] See *Trustees of the Bowthorpe Community Trust*, **42.18** LOCAL AUTHORITIES AND STATUTORY BODIES, and *Edinburgh Leisure*, **42.20** LOCAL AUTHORITIES AND STATUTORY BODIES.

Payments from parent company to subsidiary company

[62.219] See *London Regeneration Project Services Ltd*, **43.17** MANAGEMENT SERVICES, and *Glengate KG Properties Ltd*, **43.18** MANAGEMENT SERVICES.

Invoices issued by parent company to subsidiary company

[62.220] See *The Withies Inn Ltd*, **43.9** MANAGEMENT SERVICES.

Assignment of 'receivables' by bank—whether a supply

[62.221] See *Capital One Bank (Europe) plc*, **46.159** PARTIAL EXEMPTION.

Tourist board—whether making supplies to overseas State

[62.222] See *Turespaña*, **36.500** INPUT TAX.

By whom the supply was made

NOTE

The cases in this section concern the identity of the person making specific supplies. For cases concerning the identity of the person by whom a business is carried on, see 57.170 *et seq.* REGISTRATION.

Driving tuition

Driving school—whether tuition supplied by school or instructors

[62.223] A company carried on business as a school of motoring. It had on its books a number of instructors, and provided for each of them a dual-control car for which it paid the insurance, car tax and repairs. The instructors paid for petrol, oil and cleaning. The fees for the lessons were collected by the instructors and shared between the company and the instructor, the scale of fees being fixed at meetings between the instructors and a representative of the company. Until March 1977 these arrangements were not committed to writing, but thereafter each instructor was required to sign a document headed 'Conditions of Employment' providing, *inter alia*, for 'commission' to be paid to the instructors and including the statement: 'you are self-employed therefore it is your responsibility to pay your tax and stamp your card'. The instructors were accepted as self-employed for income tax and national insurance purposes. The tribunal held on the evidence that until March 1977 the instructors provided the tuition as independent contractors, but that thereafter they were employees of the company, giving the tuition on behalf of the company which was therefore liable to account for VAT on the full amount of the tuition fees. *New Way School of Motoring Ltd*, [1979] VATTR 57 (VTD 724).

[62.224] The decision in *New Way School of Motoring Ltd*, **62.223** above, was applied in a subsequent case in which the tribunal held that driving tuition was supplied by a partnership which operated a driving school, rather than by the instructors as individuals. *JW & MW Chalmers*, LON/82/84 (VTD 1354).

[62.225] Similar decisions were reached in *JS Phillips Ltd*, EDN/86/52 (VTD 2359); DJ Whitley, LON/87/106 (VTD 2435); *TDA (School) Ltd*, LON/89/982 (VTD 4900) and *Smith*, **21.31** EDUCATION.

[62.226] A trader (R) was the sole proprietor of four driving schools in different cities, and was the controlling director of a company which also owned a driving school. Instructors at the five schools were employed under franchise agreements, by which they were to pay the schools an agreed weekly fee and keep any remaining fees for themselves. However, in practice, the instructors paid the whole of their receipts to the schools, which then returned some of the receipts to the instructors. The Commissioners issued assessments on the basis that the driving tuition at the schools was provided by the schools. R and the company appealed, contending that the tuition was provided by the instructors rather than by the schools. The tribunal dismissed the appeals, holding on the evidence that pupils contracted for their tuition with the schools and not with individual instructors. The instructors were agents of the schools, and it was the schools which provided the tuition. *E Reeds*, MAN/84/270 & MAN/86/105; *Reeds School of Motoring (Nottingham) Ltd*, MAN/86/103 (VTD 4578).

[62.227] The decisions in *Reeds* and *Reeds School of Motoring (Nottingham) Ltd*, **62.226** above, were not followed in a subsequent case involving an associated company which provided driving tuition in a different area. Payments were made to a third company in the same ownership, rather than to the individual instructors. The tribunal chairman (Mr. Simpson, sitting alone) held on the evidence that the instructors were making supplies of driving tuition as independent principals. The company's role was 'to provide a supporting organisation by which the instructors were provided with the means to give tuition'. The chairman observed that the tight control which the appellant maintained over the instructor, 'which in earlier days might have been argued to suggest that the instructor's business was really the appellant's, is nowadays a common characteristic of franchise agreements, where the franchisor does not carry on the business in question', but instead 'licenses another to do so under a name and method of operation which are, or are intended to be, distinctive and well-known'. The third company 'was a mere depositary, notwithstanding that it was controlled by (the same directors) and that it acted on the instructions of the appellant'. *Reeds School of Motoring (Sheffield) Ltd*, MAN/92/85 (VTD 13404).

[62.228] The proprietor of a driving school appealed against a decision that he should be registered for VAT, contending that the driving tuition was provided by the individual instructors and that he was not liable to account for VAT on takings retained by the instructors. The tribunal dismissed his appeal, applying *New Way School of Motoring Ltd*, **62.223** above. The proprietor owned the cars, all of which bore the name of the driving school. Although the instructors were independent contractors, they were supplying the services of tuition on behalf of the school proprietor. The QB upheld this decision. On the evidence, the tribunal had been justified in reaching the conclusion that the tuition was supplied by the proprietor. *J Cronin (t/a Cronin's Driving School) v C & E Commrs*, QB [1991] STC 333.

[62.229] A married couple carried on a driving school in partnership. They granted franchises to a number of drivers, under which the drivers were treated as self-employed subcontractors. The instructors collected fees from pupils and paid the couple agreed amounts each week. The Commissioners issued an assessment on the basis that the couple should account for tax on the amounts retained by the instructors, considering that the driving tuition was supplied by the school rather than by the individual instructors. The couple appealed, contending that the tuition was supplied by the individual instructors. The tribunal allowed the appeal, holding that the drivers 'were genuinely in business on their own account and that they were making a supply of tuition services to the pupils'. *Mr & Mrs ABC McIver (t/a Alan's School of Motoring)*, EDN/90/28 (VTD 5315). (*Note.* The decision does not refer to *New Way School of Motoring*, **62.223** above, or to any of the cases noted at **62.224** to **62.226** above.)

[62.230] A partnership operated a driving school which provided facilities for driving instructors in return for weekly payments. The facilities consisted of a booking office, staffed by a receptionist; a waiting room for pupils; and advertising. The fees charged for driving tuition were fixed by the individual instructors, rather than by the school, and were paid to the instructors, rather than to the school. The Commissioners accepted that the instructors who used the school's facilities were self-employed, but issued an assessment on the school on the basis that the driving tuition provided by the instructors was supplied by the school. The partnership appealed, contending that the tuition was supplied by the instructors as principals. The tribunal allowed the appeal, distinguishing *Cronin*, 62.228 above, and applying *MacIver*, 62.229 above. On the evidence, there was 'no element of control or direction' and each instructor remained free 'to run his own business as he chose, while neverthe-less making use of the communal facilities provided by the appellant'. *Fleet School of Motoring*, MAN/90/1064 (VTD 7299).

[62.231] Three driving schools, operated by members of the same family, failed to account for VAT on the full amounts charged to customers. The Commissioners issued assessments charging tax on the full amounts paid, and the schools appealed, contending that the driving instructors who worked for them were independent principals, so that they were not liable to account for tax on the amounts retained by the instructors. (The instructors were accepted as self-employed, but the cars which they used were owned or leased by the driving schools, and the driving schools arranged for the insurance of the cars.) The tribunal dismissed the appeals, observing that 'the extent of the control exercised by the appellant over its instructors was considerable, and not indicative of the instructors being able to conduct their instruction of pupils as they themselves would have done so left to their own devices'. On the evidence, the instructors were supplying their services as agents of the driving schools, so that the driving schools were required to account for tax on the full amounts which customers paid. *ADI School of Motoring*, MAN/93/7; *ADI Driving School 'A'*, MAN/93/8; *ADI Driving School*, MAN/93/9 (VTD 11469).

Taxi and minicab drivers

Taxi hired to driver who provides transport on behalf of owner

[62.232] A trader (M) owned a number of taxi-cabs which he hired at fixed weekly rates to independent self-employed drivers. A term of the hire was that, if called on, the driver was to do work under long-term contracts between M and an education authority and British Rail respectively. The driver doing this work was not paid in cash but was given a signed voucher for the amount of the hire. The driver sent these vouchers to M weekly with an amount of cash which, with the amounts on the vouchers, would make up his weekly hire payment. M invoiced the authority and BR monthly for the amounts on the vouchers with an addition for VAT. Hence over a period M received from the drivers cash and vouchers, which together equalled the hire payments for the taxi. In accounting for VAT he treated his output tax as one-eleventh of the cash plus one-tenth of the amount of the vouchers (the VAT rate at the relevant time being 10%). The Commissioners issued assessments in which the output tax was taken as one-eleventh of the aggregate of the cash and the vouchers, plus one-tenth of the amount of the vouchers. M appealed, contending that he had been doubly charged on the amount of the vouchers. The tribunal dismissed the appeal, holding that there had been two separate supplies, one the hire of the taxis to the drivers and the other the supply of transport to the authority and BR. *E Mann (t/a Black & Gold Taxis)*, LEE/75/70 (VTD 204).

[62.233] A partnership operated taxis, which it hired to drivers on the basis that the drivers could retain 30% of their fares and had to pay 70% of the fares to the partnership. The partnership only accounted for tax on the 70% of the fares which it received from the drivers. The Commissioners issued an assessment on the basis that the partnership should have accounted for VAT on the full amount of the fares charged to customers. The partnership appealed, contending that the drivers were independent principals who were providing services to customers on their own account. The tribunal rejected this contention and dismissed the appeal, holding that the drivers were acting as agents of the partnership. *Hamiltax*, LON/91/1420X (VTD 8948).

[62.234] A similar decision was reached in a subsequent case in which *Triumph & Albany Car Service*, 62.240 below, was distinguished. *J Knowles (t/a Rainbow Taxis)*, MAN/95/948 (VTD 13913).

[62.235] The decisions in *Hamiltax*, 62.233 above, and *Knowles*, 62.234 above, were applied in a similar subsequent case in which *Camberwell Cars Ltd*, 62.249 below, was distinguished. The tribunal held on the evidence that the drivers were acting as agents of the proprietor, who was 'the principal in all transactions involved in his business whether account or cash'. *R Snaith (t/a English Rose Collection)*, LON/00/428 (VTD 16997).

[62.236] Similar decisions were reached in *JARS*, MAN/94/337 (VTD 13451); *BT Saxton*, LON/00/164 (VTD 17191); *B Murray (t/a Benco Taxis)*, MAN/00/1051 (VTD 17334); *Chubb Cars Ltd*, MAN/05/757 (VTD 20368), and *Japan Executive Chauffeur*, 52.298 PENALTIES: MISDECLARATION.

[62.237] A partnership owned ten taxis, which it hired to drivers. The partnership accounted for VAT in respect of its accounts customers, but failed to account to VAT in respect of cash customers. Customs issued an assessment charging tax on supplies to cash customers, and the partnership appealed, contending that the supplies to cash customers were made by the drivers as independent principals. The tribunal accepted this contention and allowed the appeal, distinguishing the decisions in *Hamiltax*, 62.233 above, and *Clark*, 62.254 below, and holding that the partnership had shown that there was 'a genuine difference in the operation of the two sides of its business'. *Gibbs Travel*, LON/03/343 (VTD 18472).

[62.238] A company (S) owned a number of taxis which it hired to drivers. Customs issued a ruling that S was required to account for VAT on the full amounts which customers paid, including the amounts which were retained by the drivers (normally 38% of the total fares). S appealed. The tribunal reviewed the evidence in detail and allowed the appeal in part. The tribunal drew a distinction between cases where customers telephoned S to book a taxi, and cases where customers hired one of S's taxis at a taxi rank. The tribunal held that in the case of 'accounts customers', and other cases where a customer telephoned S to make a booking, S was supplying the service and was required to account for VAT on the whole of the consideration, including the amounts which the driver retained. However the tribunal held that where a customer hired one of S's taxis at a taxi rank, the relevant supply was made by the driver, and S was only required to account for VAT on the consideration which it received from the drivers for the use of the taxi. The tribunal specifically distinguished the earlier decision in *Hamiltax*, 62.233 above, on the grounds that in that case 'there was no written contract between the firm and the drivers'. *Starline & Wessex Taxis Ltd*, LON/04/1096 (VTD 20294).

[62.239] A company owned several taxis, which it hired to drivers. The company accounted for VAT in respect of its accounts customers, but failed to account for VAT in respect of cash customers. HMRC issued an assessment charging tax on supplies to cash customers, and the company appealed, contending that the supplies to cash customers were made by the drivers as independent principals. The tribunal rejected this contention and dismissed the appeal, distinguishing the decision in the 2004 case of *Gibbs Travel*, 62.237 above, and finding that in relation to cash fares, the company exercised 'an implicit, if not an express, control'. Accordingly the company was acting as a principal 'for both account and cash work' so that 'VAT is due on 100% of the income generated from all fares'. *Albion Taxis Ltd v HMRC*, [2010] UKFTT 389 (TC), TC00671.

'Dial-a-taxi' agency—supplies to accounts customers

[62.240] A firm carried on a 'dial-a-taxi' agency for a number of mini-cab drivers. The drivers owned their vehicles and maintained them and provided the petrol for them. The firm advertised and generally organised the service which involved two-way radio communication between the firm and the drivers, the firm providing the radio installation. It received a fixed weekly amount from each driver who otherwise retained the full fares from customers. In accordance with their normal practice, the Commissioners accepted that the firm and the driver were agent and principal respectively and that, as the gross takings of the drivers were below the threshold limits of *Sch 1*, VAT was not chargeable on fares paid to the drivers in cash. However certain customers could, by arrangement with the firm, become 'accounts customers', and pay their fares monthly. The Commissioners issued an assessment charging tax on the amounts invoiced to the 'accounts customers', but the tribunal allowed the firm's appeal, holding on the evidence that the cash customers and the accounts customers were not distinguishable. *Triumph & Albany Car Service*, LON/80/115 (VTD 977, 1004).

[62.241] A partnership operated a 'dial-a-taxi' agency on broadly similar lines to *Triumph & Albany Car Service*, 62.240 above. Customs issued an assessment charging tax on the amounts invoiced to 'accounts customers'. The partnership appealed, contending that the relevant supplies were made by the drivers and that it was only liable to account for VAT on the flat fees it received from the drivers. The tribunal accepted this contention with regard to the majority of the 'accounts customers', but upheld the assessment with regard to services provided to the local county council. The tribunal held that 'the account work for (the) county council was of a quite different nature. There was a formal agreement with (the) council that was only consistent with the appellants acting as principal'. *DR Macey & DJ Atkins (t/a Sandwich Cars)*, LON/05/551 (VTD 20257).

[**62.242**] The decision in *Triumph & Albany Car Service*, **62.240** above, was distinguished in a subsequent case in which the tribunal upheld an assessment charging tax on the amounts invoiced to 'accounts customers'. The tribunal observed that the proprietor of the business set the fares for accounts work, allowed discounts to accounts customers, and insisted on drivers reporting for work by 6.00am if they wished to undertake accounts work. Accordingly, the tribunal held that 'the supply of services to an account customer is made by the appellant using the services of the self-employed drivers'. On the evidence, although the proprietor was acting as an agent of the drivers in respect of cash work, he was acting as an independent principal in respect of accounts work. *A Hussain (t/a Crossleys Private Hire Cars)*, MAN/99/20 (VTD 16194).

[**62.243**] The decision in *Hussain*, **62.242** above, was applied in the similar subsequent cases of *Argyle Park Taxis Ltd*, MAN/06/755 (VTD 20277) and *Bath Taxis (UK) Ltd*, LON/07/1767 (VTD 20974).

[**62.244**] A company which operated a taxi service accounted for VAT on supplies to 'accounts customers'. Subsequently it submitted a repayment claim on the basis that it should be treated as acting an agent for the drivers (as in *Triumph & Albany Car Service*, **62.240** above), rather than as an independent principal. HMRC rejected the claim and the tribunal dismissed the company's appeal. *Gemini Cars (Egham) Ltd*, LON/04/2395 (VTD 20035).

[**62.245**] A trader (C) was the proprietor of a taxi and private car hire business, and also ran a local removal and delivery service. He had two employees who acted as drivers, and also subcontracted work to a number of self-employed drivers who paid him a percentage of their takings. Some of these drivers used their own cars, while others used cars provided by C. Some customers paid in cash but others were allowed credit accounts. A VAT officer examining C's records discovered that there were a number of contra entries relating to money passing between C and the self-employed drivers, and formed the opinion that C had failed to account for VAT on some of the money credited to him from the drivers in respect of these transactions. He issued an assessment on the basis that, where credit customers were allocated to drivers who were not C's employees, C was dealing with such customers as an agent of the drivers, and was making supplies to the drivers and was liable to account for VAT on the amounts credited to him. C appealed, contending that he made all the relevant supplies to the credit customers, that his transactions with the drivers should be treated as not giving rise to any VAT liability, and that he had accounted for VAT on the correct basis. The tribunal upheld the assessment, holding that C was acting as an agent for the self-employed drivers for both cash and account customers, and finding that he 'had incorrectly dealt with the income and expenditure relating to the credit customers'. The QB upheld the tribunal decision as one of fact. *FG Carless v C & E Commrs*, QB [1993] STC 632.

[**62.246**] See also *Blanks*, **67.121** VALUATION, and *A2B Radio Cars*, **67.122** VALUATION.

Taxi company—whether director acting as principal

[**62.247**] The director of a taxi company owned a taxi which he drove himself. The Commissioners issued an assessment on the basis that the company was liable to account for tax on the hire of this taxi. The company appealed, contending that the director supplied his services as a principal and not as an agent of the company. The tribunal allowed the appeal on the grounds that the taxi in question was owned by the director and not by the company. (The company was, however, held to be liable for tax in cases where the director drove a taxi which the company owned.) *Jivelynn Ltd*, LON/80/430 (VTD 1092).

Partnership operating taxi and car hire business

[62.248] A couple operated a taxi and car hire business as a partnership. The partnership owned several taxis at the relevant time, and also used the services of a number of drivers who owned their own vehicles. The Commissioners discovered that the partnership had failed to account for VAT on the takings in respect of two cars which the partners owned, and issued an assessment charging tax on them. The partnership appealed, contending that the supplies in question had been made by the partners as individuals, rather than by the partnership. The tribunal allowed the appeal, holding on the evidence that the partners were making supplies to their customers as independent principals and that the partnership was not liable to account for tax on the takings in question. *GA & AE Kearns (t/a Victoria Cars)*, MAN/93/337 (VTD 11655).

Minicab company—supplies to cash customers

[62.249] A company operated a minicab business, using the services of drivers who owned their own cars. The company had a considerable number of accounts customers, and encouraged its drivers to undertake such work. The company accounted for VAT in respect of fares from accounts customers. However, the company did not account for VAT in cases where the drivers accepted fares from casual customers who paid cash. The Commissioners issued an assessment charging tax on such supplies, and the company appealed, contending that in such cases the relevant supply was made by the driver as an individual and not by the company. The tribunal allowed the appeal, holding on the evidence that there was 'a real distinction between the conduct of the account work and the cash work', and that the company accepted telephone enquiries from casual cash-paying customers 'on behalf of the drivers and not in furtherance of its own business'. *Camberwell Cars Ltd*, LON/92/2167A (VTD 10178). (*Notes.* (1) The decision here was distinguished in the subsequent case of *Snaith*, **62.235** above, where the drivers used cars belonging to the business proprietor. (2) *Obiter dicta* of the tribunal chairman were subsequently disapproved in a subsequent appeal involving the same company—see *Camberwell Cars Ltd (No 2)*, **67.124** VALUATION.)

Company operating cab hire business—amounts paid to 'controllers'

[62.250] A company operated a cab hire business. It engaged staff (whom it treated as self-employed) to act as controllers. The drivers paid 10% of their fares directly to the controllers. The Commissioners issued a ruling that the company was supplying the controllers' services to the drivers, so that these payments were consideration for services supplied by the company, and the company was required to account for VAT. The company appealed, contending that the relevant supplies were made by the controllers rather than by the company. The tribunal rejected this contention and dismissed the company's appeal, holding on the evidence that 'the 10% paid by the drivers to the controllers, though paid directly to the controllers, as a matter of convenience, was paid for the supply by the appellant of the services of the controllers to the drivers, who carried on a part of the appellant's business'. *Home Or Away Ltd*, LON/99/1333 (VTD 18195). (*Note.* For a preliminary issue in this case, see **2.301** APPEALS.)

[62.251] The decision in *Home Or Away Ltd*, 62.250 above, was applied in the similar subsequent case of *M Lancaster (t/a Airport Cars) v HMRC*, [2009] UKFTT 155 (TC), TC00121. (*Note.* For another appeal by the same trader, see **48.152** PAYMENT OF TAX.)

[62.252] See also *Crayford & Bexleyheath (Motors) Ltd*, 67.99 VALUATION; *Wren*, 67.100 VALUATION, and *Wharmby*, 67.101 VALUATION.

Taxi driver—whether an employee

[62.253] A taxi driver appealed against assessments on his takings, contending that he should be treated as an employee. The tribunal rejected this contention and dismissed his appeal, holding that he was self-employed and was making taxable supplies of his services. *RJ Newall*, LON/95/2715 (VTD 14109).

Taxibus service—whether drivers acting as agents or principals

[62.254] A garage proprietor obtained a licence to operate a 'taxibus' service using minibuses. He purchased a number of minibuses, which he sold to the drivers who worked for him. All the minibuses were painted in a standard livery. The drivers paid him a fixed fee of £45 per week. He only accounted for output tax on the amounts paid to him by the drivers, and did not account for tax on the amounts which the drivers retained. The Commissioners issued an assessment on the basis that the drivers were acting as his agents, and he appealed, contending that the drivers were independent principals. The tribunal dismissed his appeal, holding that 'the service must be regarded as a single enterprise'. The chairman observed that it was possible to operate a taxi service as an individual, but that it was 'not, in my judgment, possible to operate a bus service of the scale of that described to me in that fashion. No one driver alone could conceivably provide the frequency of service which is offered. The timetables make it abundantly clear that the drivers are working as a group and not as individuals'. The proprietor appealed to the QB, which upheld the tribunal decision as one of fact. *RD Clark v C & E Commrs*, QB 1995, [1996] STC 263.

Hairdressing

Supplies held to be made by salon proprietor

[62.255] A company which owned a hairdressing salon entered into a franchise agreement with three hairstylists who worked at the salon, whereby the franchisees were to be entitled to retain their individual takings but were to pay the company amounts in respect of rent, reception charges, bookkeeping charges, secretarial charges and franchise fees. The takings were entered in the salon till under a code number identifying the stylist to whom they belonged, and were paid to the stylists by the company accountant after deducting the sums due to him and to the salon under the franchise agreement. The Commissioners took the view that the supplies at the salon were still being made by the company, and issued a notice of compulsory registration, against which the company appealed. The CS upheld the notice. In such cases, it was necessary to look at the substance of what had been established, rather than at matters of form. On the evidence, there was only one business being carried on at the salon. The stylists did not act 'in ways that independent contractors would be expected to act in, for example, in advertising their business or otherwise acting independently'. Whether the stylists acted under contracts of service or contracts for services was not conclusive. The services provided by the stylists were made by the company and formed part of its turnover. *C & E Commrs v Jane Montgomery (Hair Stylists) Ltd*, CS 1993, [1994] STC 256.

[62.256] The Commissioners issued assessments on two hairdressing partnerships and an associated company, on the basis that tax had not been accounted for in respect of supplies made by hairstylists employed at salons which they operated. The partnerships and the company appealed against the assessments, contending that the hairstylists were independent contractors supplying their services directly to customers. The tribunal dismissed the appeal, following the principles laid down in *New Way School of Motoring Ltd*, **62.223** above, and holding that the stylists were engaged under contracts of service rather than under contracts for service. The proprietors of the salons provided the materials and equipment, and set the fees to be charged by the stylists. The stylists took no financial risks and had no responsibility for management. *Francis John*, EDN/85/78; *Francis John Hair Studio*, EDN/85/79; *Francis John (Saltcoats) Ltd*, EDN/85/80 (VTD 3447).

[62.257] The proprietors of two associated hairdressing salons engaged hairstylists on the basis that the stylists could retain 40% of their takings, and that the salon proprietors would keep the other 60%. The salon proprietors did not account for VAT on the amounts which were retained by stylists working at the salons, and the Commissioners issued assessments on the basis that the supplies to customers were made by the salon proprietors, who should account for VAT on the full amount of the takings. The tribunal upheld the assessments and dismissed the proprietors' appeals. *Headline*, LON/88/1392Z; *Just Hair*, LON/88/1291Y (VTD 4089).

[62.258] The decision in *Headline*, **62.257** above, was applied in a subsequent case in which the tribunal distinguished *Ashmore*, **62.268** below, and held that hairdressing services at a salon were supplied by the salon proprietor, regardless of whether the hairstylists were employees or self-employed. As in *Headline*, the salon proprietor received 60% of the gross takings, the stylist retaining 40%. There was a standard price list at the salon, although stylists could charge more than the amount shown in the list if this was agreed with the customer. The tribunal noted that the salon appeared 'physically to be a single business; one well-ordered room with seven chairs or places, nothing differentiating the employee chairs from the self-employed chairs'. *ME Hosmer*, LON/89/1851 (VTD 7313). (*Note.* For another issue in this case, see **41.80** LAND.)

[62.259] In another case involving hairstylists working at a salon, the tribunal held that the stylists were self-employed but that they were supplying their services to the salon proprietor rather than directly to the customers. Each stylist paid 55% of his or her gross takings to the proprietor, and the stylists did not have the right to a specific chair. Cheques and credit cards were made out to the salon, rather than to the stylist. On the evidence, customers at the salon were entering into contracts with the salon proprietor, rather than with the stylists. *LC Ong*, LON/91/1395 (VTD 7460).

[62.260] A similar decision was reached in another case involving hairstylists working at a salon, where the salon proprietor retained 60% of the gross takings. The stylists were treated as self-employed by the Inland Revenue. The tribunal held that 'the arrangements for the collection of the money paid by customers and the fixing of prices by (the salon proprietor) indicate that the customers contracted with (the proprietor) and not with the individual hairstylist'. *DL Freer*, LON/91/1069Y (VTD 7648). (*Note.* For another issue in this case, see **52.265** PENALTIES: MISDECLARATION.)

[62.261] The proprietor of a hairdressing salon failed to account for tax on the takings which were retained by the stylists working at the salon. The Commissioners issued assessments charging output tax and she appealed, contending that the stylists working at the salon were independent contractors who were supplying their services directly to the customers. The tribunal rejected this contention and dismissed the appeals, holding on the evidence that the stylists were not 'the prime functionaries' at the salon. The fact that the stylists were accepted as being self-employed, rather than employees, was not conclusive. *LJB Clarke (t/a Snips & Snips Hair & Beauty Salon)*, EDN/95/293 & 295 (VTD 14227).

[62.262] The proprietor of a hairdressing salon engaged a number of self-employed hairstylists on the basis that the stylists could retain 40% of their takings, and that he would keep the other 60%. He failed to account for tax on the takings which the stylists retained. The Commissioners issued a ruling that the proprietor was required to account for tax on the full amount of the takings. He appealed, contending that the stylists working at the salon were independent contractors who were supplying their services directly to the customers. The tribunal rejected this contention and dismissed the appeals, applying *dicta* in *Cronin*, **62.228** above, and distinguishing *Hooper*, **62.270** below. *G Brammer (t/a Talking Heads)*, MAN/00/935 (VTD 17761).

[62.263] A hairdresser (M) began trading in 1992. In 1993 he acquired a licence to trade from adjoining premises. He continued to operate as a men's hairdresser from his original premises, while the new premises were used as a ladies' hairdressing salon. The premises shared a common entrance, and were divided by a counter and a cabinet, rather than by a wall. M did not account for VAT on the income from the ladies' salon. The Commissioners issued an assessment charging tax on them, and M appealed, contending that the ladies' salon was a separate business operated by his wife. The tribunal rejected this contention and upheld the assessment in principle, holding on the evidence that there was a single business. The fact that there were separate tills was not conclusive. On the evidence, M's wife was not a hairdresser, and M acted as the proprietor of the ladies' section as well as of the men's section. *AY Mehmet*, LON/98/1394 & 1561 (VTD 16189).

[62.264] See also *Harrison*, 51.32 PENALTIES: FAILURE TO NOTIFY; *Hopkins (t/a Marianne's Hair Salon)*, 51.69 PENALTIES: FAILURE TO NOTIFY; *Mantio (t/a Zazzera Hair Salon)*, 51.70 PENALTIES: FAILURE TO NOTIFY; *S Taylor (Machine Tools) Ltd*, 52.297 PENALTIES: MISDECLARATION; *Colby*, 57.194 REGISTRATION, and *SFU Barbers Ltd*, 57.195 REGISTRATION.

Supplies held to be made by hairstylists as independent contractors

[62.265] A partnership and an associated company operated hairdressing salons. For some time they had treated the hairstylists working for them as employees, and had accounted for tax on the full amount of the takings at the salons. Subsequently they began to treat their senior stylists as self-employed, and ceased to account for VAT on the takings retained by the stylists. The stylists received no salary or wages from the proprietors, and were required to insure against liability to the public. They were accepted as self-employed by the Inland Revenue. The Commissioners issued assessments on the basis that the proprietors should continue to account for VAT on the full amount of the takings. The tribunal allowed the salon proprietors' appeals, applying *dicta* in *New Way School of Motoring Ltd*, 62.223 above, and holding that 'according to the weight which we give to each factor, the position is more consistent with the performance by the senior stylists of their hairdressing treatments being carried out under contracts for services rather than contracts of service'. The QB upheld this decision as one of fact. Having found that the stylists were self-employed, the tribunal was entitled to hold, on the evidence, that they supplied their services directly to the public. *C & E Commrs v MacHenrys (Hairdressers) Ltd & MacHenrys*, QB 1992, [1993] STC 170. (*Note.* It was agreed that payments by the stylists to the salon proprietors, for the use of chairs in the salon, were exempt from VAT through being for licences to occupy land, following *dicta* in *Niven*, 67.95 VALUATION. Compare the cases noted at **41.73** to **41.82** LAND.)

[62.266] A company which operated a number of hairdressing salons failed to account for tax on the amounts which were retained by self-employed stylists. The Commissioners issued a ruling that the company was required to account for tax on the full amount of the takings. The company appealed, contending that the stylists were supplying their services directly to the customers. The Ch D accepted this contention and allowed the appeal. Park J held that the contracts clearly indicated that the stylists were supplying their services directly to the customers, and there was no evidence requiring a departure from the contractual position. *Kieran Mullin Ltd v C & E Commrs*, Ch D [2003] STC 274; [2003] EWHC 4 (Ch).

[62.267] A similar decision was reached in another case where hairstylists working at a salon were accepted as self-employed by the Inland Revenue and the DSS. They received no holiday or sick pay, and their contracts were liable to be terminated at short notice, without compensation for unfair dismissal. The tribunal held that the relevant supplies were made by the stylists, rather than by the salon proprietors. On the evidence, the proprietors provided 'co-ordination rather than control'. *Mr & Mrs Giles*, LON/90/509Z (VTD 5449).

[62.268] In another case involving hairstylists working at a salon, the tribunal held that the stylists were self-employed and were supplying their services as principals, rather than as agents of the salon proprietor. The stylists, who paid 57% of their takings to the proprietor, had to obtain clients through their efforts, since clients were not introduced to them by the proprietor. The tribunal therefore allowed the proprietor's appeal against an assessment charging tax on the full amount of the stylists' takings. *P Ashmore*, LON/90/252Y (VTD 6910).

[62.269] The QB decision in *MacHenrys*, 62.265 above, was applied in a similar subsequent case in which self-employed stylists retained 40% of their gross takings, paying the remaining 60% to the salon proprietor. The tribunal held that the fact that the stylists were self-employed was not conclusive, but that, on the evidence, the self-employed stylists were 'in a position to render to the customer the entire supply which that customer received'. The stylists were supplying their services to the customers, rather than to the salon proprietor. It followed that the salon proprietor was only liable to account for tax on the amounts which he received from the stylists, and was not liable to account for tax on the amounts which the stylists retained. *JA Wragg (t/a Take 5 Hair Design)*, MAN/91/398 (VTD 10574).

[62.270] A similar decision, also applying *MacHenrys*, 62.265 above, was reached in a similar subsequent case in which self-employed stylists retained 35% of their gross takings, paying the remaining 65% to the salon proprietors. *D & S Hooper (t/a Masterclass)*, LON/99/487 (VTD 16764).

[62.271] The proprietor of a hairdressing salon applied for deregistration. The Commissioners rejected his application, on the grounds that the turnover of the salon was above the threshold for deregistration. The proprietor appealed, contending that the supplies to customers at the salon were made by the individual stylists, so that his turnover should be restricted to the amounts which he received from the stylists, rather than the full amounts paid by the customers. (The stylists, who were accepted as self-employed, paid the proprietor 57% of their gross takings.) The tribunal allowed the appeal, holding on the evidence that the stylists were supplying their services directly to the customers. *A Winder (t/a Anthony & Patricia)*, MAN/92/1653 (VTD 11784). (*Note.* For another issue in this case, see **41.83** LAND.)

[62.272] Similar decisions were reached in *P Sorisi*, LON/97/808 (VTD 15453) and *G Vasiljevic (t/a Geneve)*, LON/01/691 (VTD 17820).

[62.273] In 1995 a woman (L) took over a hairdressing business which had previously been operated by her husband. The premises included a ladies' salon, where three stylists worked, and a men's salon with one stylist (S). S kept 40% of his takings and paid 60% to L. The Commissioners issued a ruling that L was required to register for VAT from December 1996, on the basis that the whole of S's takings should be treated as part of her turnover. She appealed, contending that S was an independent contractor who supplied his services directly to his customers, and that the 40% which S retained did not form part of her turnover. The tribunal accepted this contention and allowed her appeal, observing that 'a gentlemen's hairdresser operates quite differently to a ladies' hairdressers'. *C Lyons (t/a Wayne Anthony's)*, MAN/99/338 (VTD 16791).

Massage and personal services

Services at massage parlour

[62.274] The proprietor of a sauna and massage parlour failed to register for VAT. The Commissioners issued a notice of compulsory registration and an assessment charging tax on the total takings at the salon. He appealed, contending that the massage services were supplied by the individual masseuses who worked at the salon on a self-employed basis. Customers were charged a £20 entrance fee, which included a basic massage, but were also charged between £50 and £70 for 'personal relaxation massages'. The proprietor retained the £20 entrance fees, and gave evidence that the masseuses paid him a room rental of £20 per day but retained the amounts they received for 'relaxation massages'. The Commissioners called a former masseuse as a witness. She gave evidence that there was no room rental and she was required to pay the proprietor £10 for each 'relaxation massage'. The tribunal accepted the evidence of this witness and dismissed the proprietor's appeal, finding that there was 'one unified business' and the proprietor fixed the prices charged for 'relaxation massages'. Accordingly, the proprietor was required to account for tax on the full amounts paid by customers, including the amounts which the masseuses retained. *SP Rudd (t/a Duo's Spa & Sauna)*, LON/99/1176 (VTD 16844).

[62.275] A company operated a sauna and massage parlour. Customers paid £15 for admission and also paid £50 for a 30-minute massage. Of this £50, the masseuse kept £35 and paid £15 to the company. The company only accounted for output tax on the admission charges. Customs issued an assessment on the company, charging tax on the payments for massages, including the amounts which the masseuses retained. The tribunal upheld the assessment, holding on the evidence that the masseuses were employed by the company and that the company was required to account for tax on the full amounts paid by the customers. *Sparkholme Ltd (t/a Top Class Sauna)*, LON/04/907 (VTD 19187).

[62.276] See also *Niven*, 67.95 VALUATION.

Sexual services at sauna

[62.277] A company (J) operated a sauna in Edinburgh. Customers visiting the sauna were required to pay for admission (£20 for 30 minutes or £35 for 60 minutes). After entering the sauna, a customer would be approached by a woman working at the sauna, and invited to pay her for sexual services. The prices for these varied 'according to the nature of the service and its duration'. J provided condoms for the women, and indicated that they were 'expected to provide a full adult massage to customers'. J only accounted for VAT on a percentage of the admission fees, and did not account for VAT on the additional fees paid by the customers. Customs issued an estimated assessment on the basis that J should account for VAT on the full amount of the fees paid by the customers. J appealed, contending that the women were acting as independent principals and that 'the tribunal should distinguish between the legal services provided by the appellants and services which it would be illegal for the appellants to provide'. The tribunal reviewed the evidence in detail and allowed the appeal in part, holding that J was required to account for VAT on the full amount of the admission fees, since 'the service provided to the client was entry to the premises and the opportunity to avail himself of the facilities therein'. However J was not required to account for VAT on the payments which the customers made directly to the women working at the sauna. J appealed to the CS, which upheld the tribunal decision. Lady Paton held that 'the entry fee represented payment of a consideration to the appellant for services supplied to the customer, namely access to the premises and permission to enjoy everything therein, including the lounge, refreshments, newspapers, television, the services of a hostess (with further charges being negotiated with and paid to her as necessary) and the use of a private room'. Accordingly J was 'liable to VAT on the full amount of the door money received at the sauna'. *Joppa Enterprises Ltd v HMRC*, CS [2009] STC 1279; [2009] CSIH 17.

'Escort agency'

[62.278] The Commissioners discovered that the proprietors of an escort agency had failed to register for VAT. They issued a notice of compulsory registration, and two assessments charging tax on the full amounts which the proprietors received from the customers. The proprietors appealed against the assessments, contending that they paid each escort £2 per customer, and that these amounts should not be included as part of their turnover. The tribunal dismissed their appeal, holding that the whole of the amounts paid by customers to the agency were consideration for the services which the agency provided. *Marlow & Hind*, LON/77/14 & LON/77/99 (VTD 407).

[62.279] The Commissioners discovered that a couple who operated an escort agency had not registered for VAT. They issued a notice of compulsory registration, and an assessment on the couple's takings. The assessment was computed on the basis that the couple were required to account for tax on the whole of the amounts paid by customers, including the sums which the escorts retained. The couple appealed, contending that they should only be required to account for tax on the amounts which they actually received (normally £30 per client), and should not be required to account for tax on the amounts which the escorts kept (normally £100 per client), with the result that they were not liable to register. The tribunal chairman accepted this contention, but also expressed the view that 'the appellants' business consists wholly, or at least very substantially, of the procurement of women for the purposes of their becoming common prostitutes', and that VAT should not be charged on prostitution or procurement. The Commissioners appealed to the Ch D, which reversed this decision. Jacob J observed that there were 'obvious dangers of a tribunal striking out in a wholly independent way — it is apt to fall into error'. The case was 'directly comparable' with *Staatssecretaris van Financiën v Coffeeshop 'Siberië' vof*, 22.83 EUROPEAN COMMUNITY LAW, where the CJEC had held that income from renting tables for the sale of cannabis was within the scope of VAT. Jacob J observed that 'the respondents provide the time of their escorts. That is a lawful and autonomous activity. The activities of the escorts and their customers are separable from the service of the taxpayers, just as the supply of tables for the sale of drugs and the actual sale of drugs were separable in *'Siberië'*.' Accordingly, prostitution and procurement were within the scope of VAT. Jacob J remitted the case to the tribunal to consider whether the couple's takings had in fact exceeded the registration threshold. *C & E Commrs v R & J Polok*, Ch D [2002] STC 361. (*Note.* There was no further public hearing of the appeal. The tribunal had also held that the escorts were 'independent service providers' and that the couple were acting as agents, so that the appellants were not in any event required to account for VAT on the amounts which the escorts retained. It is understood that, in view of this decision, the Commissioners subsequently accepted that the couple's takings had not exceeded the registration threshold.)

[62.280] An escort agency (P) charged clients £80 for an introduction to a young woman who was willing to act as an 'escort'. It accounted for VAT on these 'introduction fees'. Customs issued an estimated assessment on the basis that P should also have accounted for VAT on sums which customers paid to the escorts, and which the escorts retained. (Customers were generally expected to pay at least £200 to the escort as consideration for two hours of her time.) The tribunal reviewed the evidence in detail and allowed P's appeal, finding that 'it was the girls who negotiated with a customer what services she was to perform, how and where the services were to be performed, and how much the girl was to receive for those services'. The tribunal oberved that 'the very personal nature of the services makes it entirely credible that the girls would themselves fix their charges'. On the evidence, P 'never in fact knew what services a girl had performed, and how much she had been paid for those services'. Accordingly P was acting as an agent rather than as an independent principal, and was not required to account for VAT on the amounts which the escorts retained. *Portman Escort Agency*, LON/04/900 (VTD 19728).

Hostesses at night club—whether services supplied by club

[62.281] A company operated a 'gentlemen's night club' in London. On entering the club premises, a customer would be approached by a young woman, described as a 'hostess', who would invite him to come to the club's basement with her. Customers who accepted such an invitation were required to buy a bottle of champagne from the company, priced at not less than £60. They were also expected to pay a fee to the hostess in return for her company, either in cash or by credit card. The company did not account for VAT on these fees, and the Commissioners issued an assessment on the basis that the company should have charged VAT on fees which the customers had paid by credit card. The company appealed, contending that the hostesses had been supplying their services directly to the customers, and the fees were not consideration for any supply by the company. The tribunal accepted this contention and allowed the company's appeal. *Leapmagic Ltd*, LON/91/90Z (VTD 6441).

'Dance services' provided on licensed premises

[62.282] A family partnership traded from licensed premises, at which alcoholic drinks were sold and customers were entertained by 'exotic dancers'. The dancers performed 'pole dances' on a stage at the premises, and also offered individual dances to customers, in private booths, for a fee of £10 per dance. The customers paid this amount to the licensees, who retained 30% and paid the other 70% to the dancers. The Commissioners issued an assessment on the basis that the licensees were required to account for VAT on the full amounts paid by the customers, including the amounts which they paid to the dancers. The licencees appealed, contending that the services were supplied to the customers by the dancers (and that the 30% which the licencees retained represented rent for the booths). The tribunal rejected this contention and dismissed the licencees' appeal, finding that the licencees kept 'a close control and supervision of all activities conducted at their premises' and holding that they were supplying the dancers' services to the customers. (The tribunal also held that the amounts paid by the dancers did not qualify for exemption since no dancers had exclusive occupation of a booth.) *F & D Di Resta (t/a Bottoms Up)*, EDN/03/88 (VTD 18641).

[62.283] A company (S) operated six clubs, at which customers were entertained in small booths by women who danced naked or semi-naked. Customers were required to pay admission fees to S. They could ask the dancers to perform short individual dances in the booths, in return for a fee of £10 where the dancer was 'topless' and £20 where the dancer was naked. They could also ask the dancers for private conversations in the booths, in return for an agreed fee (the standard rate being £250 for an hour). The women who danced at the clubs retained the amounts which they received from the customers, but were required to pay S a fee ranging from £15 to £80 per eight-hour session, and a further fee ranging from £5 to £40 for each hour spent with a customer. (The dancers also paid tips to the club doormen and waitresses for introductions to particularly wealthy customers.) Customs issued a ruling that S was supplying entertainment services, and was required to account for VAT on the amounts paid by the customers. S appealed, contending that the dance services were provided by the individual dancers, so that it was only required to account for VAT on the admission fees and on the amounts which it received from the dancers, and was not required to account for VAT on the amounts which the customers paid to the dancers. The Ch D accepted this contention and allowed the appeal. Mann J held that S had granted the dancers a licence to carry on their 'trade or profession' at its premises, and that the dancers were supplying their services directly to the customers. *Spearmint Rhino Ventures (UK) Ltd v HMRC*, Ch D [2007] STC 1252; [2007] EWHC 613 (Ch).

Supplies of accommodation

Hotel expenses of visiting teams met by Football Association

[62.284] The Football Association organised a competition for national youth teams in accordance with regulations laid down by the Union of European Football Associations, of which it was a member. These regulations required the Association to provide accommodation for the participating teams. The Association arranged and paid for such accommodation in suitable hotels, and reclaimed the input tax thereon. The Commissioners assessed the Association on the basis that it had supplied the accommodation to the visiting teams and should account for output tax on the accommodation. The Association appealed, contending that it had not made any supply. The tribunal allowed the appeal, holding that, although the Association had paid for the accommodation, it had not made any supply of the accommodation. The supplies had been made by the hotels. The making of payment for a supply of goods or services, under an arrangement with a third party, did not constitute an onward supply of the goods or services in question. *Football Association Ltd*, [1985] VATTR 106 (VTD 1860). (*Note.* For a preliminary issue in this case, see **2.163** APPEALS.)

Accommodation supplied to students attending language school

[62.285] A language school found accommodation for many of its students. The accommodation was provided by families who lived close to the school. The school paid the families, and charged the students, for the accommodation. The amounts it charged the students exceeded the amounts it paid the families. The Commissioners issued an assessment on the basis that the school should account for VAT on the full amount of the accommodation charges which it received from the students. The school appealed, contending that it should only account for VAT on the difference between the amounts it received from the students and the amounts it paid to the families with whom the students stayed, on the grounds that the accommodation was supplied by the families and the school was merely acting as the students' agent. The Commissioners contended that the school was acting as a principal rather than an agent. The tribunal dismissed the school's appeal, holding on the evidence that the school supplied the accommodation through the agency of the families. The school was therefore liable to account for VAT on the full amounts it charged to the students. *Cicero Languages International*, LON/89/272Y (VTD 4286).

Hotel accommodation supplied for subcontractors

[62.286] Two associated companies successively carried on the business of manufacturing, supplying and fitting new and replacement windows and entrance doors. The doors and windows were installed by self-employed subcontractors. The companies arranged and paid for hotel accommodation for the subcontractors when necessary. The companies reclaimed the tax on the accommodation as input tax and the Commissioners issued assessments to recover the tax, considering that the accommodation had been supplied by the companies to the subcontractors and that the companies were therefore obliged to account for output tax on the supply. The tribunal allowed the companies' appeals, holding that although there had been a supply by the hotel to the company, it did not follow that there had been a supply by the company to the subcontractors. The accommodation was not used for the subcontractors' own purposes, but was used solely in the course of their work. *Ibstock Building Products Ltd*, **36.14** INPUT TAX, was distinguished on the grounds that the engineers in that case were engaged by the vendors rather than by the appellant. *Northern Lawn Tennis Club*, **36.16** INPUT TAX, was distinguished on the grounds that the tennis players competed in the tournaments in furtherance of their own careers, rather than simply on the club's business. *Stormseal (UPVC) Window Co Ltd; Probelook Ltd*, [1989] VATTR 303 (VTD 4538).

Supply of accommodation to tennis players by club

[62.287] See *Northern Lawn Tennis Club*, **36.16** INPUT TAX.

Accommodationprovided for employees of supplier

[62.288] See *Ibstock Building Products Ltd*, 36.14 INPUT TAX.

Supply of accommodation to visiting lecturers

[62.289] See *Institute of Purchasing and Supply*, 36.15 INPUT TAX.

Holiday accommodation—whether supplied by partnership

[62.290] A married couple purchased a farm in 1988, and registered for VAT in 1989. The farm incorporated a cottage which they let as holiday accommodation. Their VAT returns for the periods up to February 1990 included the income from letting the cottage. However, they did not include such income on subsequent returns. When the Commissioners discovered this, they issued an assessment charging tax on this income, and the couple appealed, contending that, with effect from 1 March 1990, the cottage had been operated by the wife as a sole trader, and that since the income from the cottage was below the registration threshold, she was not required to account for VAT on the income. The tribunal accepted the couple's evidence and allowed the appeal. *A & K Hurst*, EDN/92/252 (VTD 9756).

'Bed and breakfast' accommodation at public house

[62.291] A publican did not account for output tax on supplies of 'bed and breakfast' at the public house. The Commissioners issued an assessment charging tax on these supplies. The publican appealed, contending that the 'bed and breakfast' was a separate business carried on by his wife as a sole trader. The tribunal rejected this contention and dismissed the appeal, holding on the evidence that there was a single business. *A Pugh*, MAN/00/610 (VTD 17202).

Supplies of catering

Catering at public house

[62.292] The Commissioners issued an assessment on a publican which included tax on sales of food. The tribunal accepted the publican's contention that the catering was a separate business carried on by his wife, and reduced the assessment accordingly. *J Oldham*, MAN/80/240 (VTD 1113). (*Note.* The Commissioners might now have recourse to a direction under *VATA 1994, Sch 1 para 2*. For cases concerning this provision, see 57.35 *et seq.* REGISTRATION.)

[62.293] Similar decisions were reached in *TR Clark*, LON/82/338 (VTD 1370); *WD Cummins*, LON/85/45 (VTD 1985); *GE Moss (t/a The Red House)*, MAN/96/541 (VTD 14633) and *L Young*, MAN/96/387 (VTD 14987).

[62.294] A publican, who was divorced, lived with a woman (G) who was also divorced. He accounted for output tax on the bar sales, but did not account for tax on the receipts from catering at the public house. The Commissioners issued an assessment charging tax on them, and he appealed, contending that the catering was a separate business carried on by G. The tribunal accepted this contention and allowed the appeal. *R Wallace (t/a Inn House)*, LON/00/599 (VTD 17109).

[62.295] A married couple traded in partnership as publicans. They did not account for tax on receipts from catering at the public house. The Commissioners issued an assessment charging tax on the receipts from catering. They appealed, contending that the catering was a separate business carried on by their two daughters (the elder of whom was a qualified chef). The tribunal accepted their evidence and allowed their appeal. *R & GA Parson*, MAN/98/586 (VTD 17137).

[62.296] A publican did not account for VAT on receipts from catering, and the Commissioners issued an assessment charging tax on them. The publican appealed, contending that the catering was a separate business which she carried on in partnership with her mother. The tribunal accepted her evidence and allowed her appeal. *KM Potts*, MAN/99/450 (VTD 17390)

[62.297] A publican did not account for VAT on receipts from catering, and the Commissioners issued an assessment charging tax on them. The publican appealed, contending that the catering was a separate business carried on by his wife. The Inland Revenue had accepted that the catering should be treated as a separate business. The tribunal dismissed the appeal, observing that the publican's accountant had prepared a single balance sheet and that the publican had reclaimed input tax on items which were used for catering. On the evidence, the couple 'may well have intended to run the two sides of the business separately', but 'their intention was not carried into effect'. *ME Brown*, LON/92/2804A (VTD 11429).

[62.298] A similar decision was reached in *B Davies*, MAN/93/416 (VTD 12023).

[62.299] A public house was run by a partnership of four people. The partnership did not account for VAT on receipts from catering, and the Commissioners issued an assessment charging tax on them. The partnership appealed, contending that the catering was a separate business carried on by one of the partners. The Inland Revenue had accepted that the catering should be treated as a separate business. The tribunal dismissed the appeal, holding that there was a single business for VAT purposes, and observing that 'we do not know what information was supplied to the Inland Revenue or what if any inquiries were made. We however have heard evidence over a period of two days and are satisfied that there was not in fact a separate business in respect of the catering activities. In the circumstances the income tax treatment does not assist or cause us to alter the conclusion to which we have come.' *SH, HA, BP & D Allen (t/a The Shovel)*, MAN/98/808 (16906).

[62.300] For other cases where a public house was operated by a partnership, and catering was held to be part of the partnership business, see **47.26** to **47.27** PARTNERSHIP. For a case where catering at a public house was held to be a separate business from that of the partnership, see *Marner*, **47.42** PARTNERSHIP. For a case where the Commissioners accepted that catering by the wife of a publican constituted a separate business carried on by the wife, see *Gent*, **51.160** PENALTIES: FAILURE TO NOTIFY.

Catering at hotel

[62.301] A partnership operated a hotel. It did not account for VAT on catering receipts. The Commissioners issued an assessment charging tax on such receipts, and the partnership appealed, contending that the catering was a separate business carried on by one of the partners as an individual. The tribunal dismissed the appeal, holding on the evidence that the catering was a part of the partnership business. *JG & SJ Albert (t/a The Groves Hotel)*, MAN/92/1601 (VTD 11651).

[62.302] The proprietor of a hotel failed to account for VAT on receipts from catering. The Commissioners issued an assessment charging output tax and the proprietor appealed, contending that the catering was supplied by a friend of hers. The tribunal rejected this contention and dismissed her appeal. *CA Cherry*, MAN/93/150 (VTD 13861).

Catering—whether supplies made by franchisor or franchisee

[62.303] A family partnership carried on a catering business, supplying items such as hamburgers and 'hot dogs' to franchisees. The partnership accounted for tax on the basis that it was supplying food to its franchisees (so that most of its supplies were zero-rated), and that the franchisees were making the subsequent sales to the customers. The Commissioners issued an assessment, and imposed a misdeclaration penalty, on the basis that the partnership should be treated as making the standard-rated supplies of catering to the customers. The tribunal upheld the assessment but the Ch D allowed the partnership's appeal, applying the principles laid down by Park J in *Kieran Mullin Ltd*, **62.266** above. Evans-Lombe J held that the effect of the relevant contracts was that the franchisees were trading as independent principals, and there was no evidence requiring a departure from the contractual position. *Ringside Refreshments v C & E Commrs*, Ch D 2003, [2004] STC 426; [2003] EWHC 3043 (Ch). (*Note.* Although the tribunal had upheld the assessment, it allowed the partnership's appeal against the penalty, holding that the circumstances constituted a reasonable excuse for the misdeclaration.)

Restaurant—by whom operated

[62.304] See the cases noted at **57.176** to **57.179** REGISTRATION, and the cases noted at **57.203** to **57.206** REGISTRATION.

Fish and chip shop—proprietor on holiday abroad

[62.305] The proprietor of a fish-and-chip shop appealed against an assessment, contending that he had temporarily transferred the operation of his business to a tenant while he took an extended holiday in Italy. The tribunal dismissed his appeal, holding on the evidence that the proprietor remained 'the taxable person liable to account for VAT' and observing that a trader 'can make an interpersonal arrangement or contract for a third party to meet the liability, but he cannot absolve himself of his own direct statutory responsibility without fully discharging any liability in that respect'. *F Di Rienzo (t/a Franco's Fish Bar)*, EDN/98/10 (VTD 15599B).

[62.306] A married couple operated a fish and chip shop in partnership. They took a six-week holiday in Italy, and arranged for a temporary tenant to carry on the business during their absence. They did not account for output tax on the takings during this six-week period. The Commissioners issued an assessment charging tax on the takings, but the tribunal allowed the couple's appeal, distinguishing *Di Rienzo*, **62.305** above, and holding that the relevant supplies had been made by the temporary tenant. *F & M Cortellesa*, EDN/98/136 (VTD 16333).

[62.307] The decision in *Cortellesa*, **62.306** above, was applied in the similar subsequent cases of *G & M Treta (t/a The Golden Fry)*, EDN/99/119 (VTD 16690) and *G Pacitti*, EDN/98/44 (VTD 16759).

Shop selling take-away food—by whom operated

[62.308] See the cases noted at **57.181** to **57.183** REGISTRATION.

Partnership owning fish and chip shop—whether also operating van

[62.309] An unmarried couple operated a fish and chip shop in partnership, and were registered for VAT accordingly. The male partner also sold fish and chips from a mobile van, but did not account for VAT on such sales. The Commissioners issued an assessment on the basis that the van was part of the partnership business. The partnership appealed, contending that the van was a separate business which the partner carried on as a sole trader, and that the stocks for the shop and the van were kept separately. The tribunal accepted the partners' evidence and allowed the appeal, observing that the absence of a separate business bank account was inconclusive. *SR Insley & L Clayton (t/a S & L Caterers)*, MAN/95/1284 (VTD 13677).

Delivery charge for meals

[62.310] The proprietor of a take-away restaurant (H) arranged for a contractor (Y) to deliver meals to customers where customers required this. H paid Y £12 per night in return for Y making himself available, and Y also charged customers between 90p and £1.60 per delivery. The Commissioners issued an assessment on the basis that H was required to account for output tax on the amounts paid to Y. H appealed, contending that Y was an independent contractor and was making a separate supply of services. The tribunal accepted this contention and allowed the appeal, finding that, under the terms of the agreement between H and Y, the safe delivery of the meals was the responsibility of Y, rather than of H. The tribunal held on the evidence that the delivery of the order was a separate supply of services, and that the supply of delivery was made by Y, so that H was not required to account for output tax on the payments in question. *CK Ho (t/a New Lucky Ho)*, EDN/97/189 (VTD 15605). (*Note.* Compare, however, the subsequent decision in *Wong's Chinese Takeaway*, **62.311** below.)

[62.311] The decision in *Ho*, **62.310** above, was not followed in a subsequent case where a partnership which operated a Chinese takeaway restaurant charged customers £1 for delivery, and did not account for tax on this charge, which was paid directly to the driver (an employee of the partnership) who was responsible for delivery. The tribunal held that there was a single supply of a delivered meal and that the partnership was required to account for tax on the whole amount paid by the customer, including the delivery charge. *Wong's Chinese Takeaway*, MAN/02/209 (VTD 18766).

Partnership operating restaurant—kitchen also used for take-away sales

[62.312] See *Yung*, 47.33 PARTNERSHIP.

Catering at embassy

[62.313] See *Aramark Ltd*, 1.39 AGENTS.

Catering by educational charity

[62.314] See *Summer Institute of Linguistics Ltd*, 15.111 CONSTRUCTION OF BUILDINGS, ETC.

Employees—whether making supplies as individuals or on behalf of employer

Service washes at launderette

[62.315] A company owned a launderette, at which it employed part-time attendants. These attendants provided 'service washes' whereby they would process laundry left by customers. A notice on one of the launderette walls stated that the service washes were 'a private arrangement between customers and staff'. The company did not specify a set price for the service washes, which were a matter for negotiation between the attendants, and the customers, some attendants charging different rates. The attendants kept the difference between the amounts paid by customers and the amounts which they had to feed into the machines. The company did not account for VAT on the amounts retained by the attendants, and the Commissioners issued an assessment charging tax on these receipts. The company appealed, contending that the service washes were supplied by the attendants and not by the company. The tribunal accepted this contention and allowed the appeal, holding that the attendants were acting on their own account and not as agents of the company. *Ivychain Ltd*, LON/89/1601Y (VTD 5627).

Nursing services—whether supplied by nursing agency or by nurses

[62.316] A nursing agency operated a register of self-employed nurses, whom it introduced to clients. Clients paid the agency for the nurses' services, and the agency paid the nurses their fees weekly in arrear. The agency required the nurses to wear uniform and to obey certain rules of conduct (such as not wearing high-heeled shoes or nail varnish while on duty, and not smoking on duty). The Commissioners issued an assessment on the basis that the nurses were supplying their services to the agency, and that the agency was supplying those services to clients, and was obliged to account for VAT on the amounts paid by the clients. The agency appealed, contending that the nurses supplied their services directly to the clients, and that it was merely acting as an agent. The tribunal accepted this contention and allowed the appeal. The contracts which the agency entered into clearly indicated that it was acting as an agent rather than as a principal, and nothing in the rules of conduct which the agency laid down was inconsistent with its position as an agent. *BUPA Nursing Services Ltd*, MAN/92/92 (VTD 10010).

[62.317] The decision in *BUPA Nursing Services Ltd*, **62.316** above, was applied in the similar case of *South Hams Nursing Agency*, LON/94/904A (VTD 13027).

[62.318] Compare *Allied Medicare Nursing Services Ltd*, **33.2** HEALTH AND WELFARE, and *Parkinson*, **33.3** HEALTH AND WELFARE.

Food supplied at licensed club—whether supplied by club or by steward

[62.319] A licensed club employed a steward, who was required to work for 51 hours per week and was provided with accommodation. The steward was permitted to supply food to customers at the club, paying the club £5 per week for the use of the kitchen, and to keep all profits from sales of food. The club did not account for VAT on the sales of food. The Commissioners issued an assessment on the club charging tax on these supplies, and the club appealed, contending that the food was supplied by the steward as an individual, rather than by the club. The tribunal accepted this contention and allowed the appeal. On the evidence, the steward was supplying food to club members on his own account, rather than on behalf of the club. *Beckenham Constitutional Club Ltd*, LON/92/1037 (VTD 10041).

Consultancy services—whether supplied by individual or company

[62.320] An individual (P) did not register for VAT or account for VAT on consultancy fees which he received. The Commissioners issued an assessment on him charging tax on these supplies. He appealed, contending that some of the supplies had not been made by him as an individual but by a company of which he and his wife were directors, but that he had been dismissed from employment with that company in May 1989 and had made supplies as an individual after that date. The tribunal dismissed his appeal. The company had never declared P as an employee on any of its P35 returns, nor had it deducted any tax from payments made to him. He had paid Class 2 National Insurance contributions, and had issued invoices to the company for consultancy fees. He had therefore supplied the consultancy services in question as an individual, rather than as a director of the company. *R Preston*, LON/90/174Z (VTD 5702). (*Note*. The Ch D subsequently dismissed an application to make a late appeal against this decision—see **2.186** APPEALS).

Sale of commercial vehicle by company director

[62.321] The director of a company dealing in commercial vehicles bought a second-hand vehicle from a private individual and sold it at a profit. The Commissioners issued an assessment to the company charging tax on the sale. The company appealed, contending that the director had bought and sold the vehicle in a private capacity and had not been acting on behalf of the company. The tribunal accepted this contention and allowed the appeal. *Bedworth Commercials Ltd*, MAN/91/164 (VTD 7585).

Sale of second-hand electrical goods by company director

[62.322] A company dealt in specialised lighting. Because of an economic recession, its managing director had to reduce his income from the company. He began attending local auctions to buy cheap second-hand electrical goods, which he sold at a profit. As his income from such sales was below the VAT registration threshold, he did not account for VAT. The Commissioners formed the opinion that the director was acting on behalf of the company, and assessed the company on the income from these sales. The company appealed, contending that the director was acting as a private individual. The tribunal accepted this contention and allowed the appeal, holding on the evidence that the director had not made the sales in the course of the company's business, and observing that the sales were 'of a different class of goods which had been bought from a different class of supplier, made at a different time to a different class of customers in a different way'. (The tribunal chairman also observed that the Commissioners could have issued a direction under what is now *VATA 1994, Sch 1 para 2.) Southern Counties Lighting Ltd*, LON/93/564A (VTD 11438).

Painting and decorating services

[62.323] The Commissioners issued an assessment on a company which carried on a painting and decorating business. The company appealed, contending that the supplies in question had been made by its controlling director as an individual, rather than by the company. The tribunal rejected this contention and dismissed the appeal, holding on the evidence that 'the only real segregation was between work undertaken for customers who would not be concerned about paying VAT, and work for those who would. (The director's) keeping separate accounting records and preparing separate accounts were no more than an inevitable consequence of a device designed to enable the appellant to avoid charging VAT to certain of its customers. In reality, this was not a case of there being two businesses, but of two vehicles being used to carry on a single business.' *E Stringer (Paints) Ltd*, MAN/99/79 (VTD 16319).

Salesman—whether acting as individual or as employee of company

[62.324] See *Sullivan*, 57.185 REGISTRATION.

Apprentice jockeys—whether riding in races as employees of trainers

[62.325] A couple, who carried on business in partnership as racehorse trainers, arranged for apprentice and conditional jockeys, employed at their stables, to ride customers' horses in races. The Commissioners issued assessments charging output tax on the basis that the trainers were supplying the services of the apprentice and conditional jockeys to the owners of the racehorses, and should have accounted for tax accordingly. The trainers appealed, contending that, when riding in races, the apprentices should be treated as self-employed and as supplying their own services directly to the owners. The tribunal accepted this contention and allowed the appeal, but the QB remitted the case to a new tribunal for rehearing. Moses J held that it appeared that the tribunal had erred in the way in which it had analysed the relevant agreements, and had failed to have regard to the fact that apprentice and conditional jockeys were answerable to the partnership. Furthermore, the tribunal had erred in attaching weight to the fact that fully-fledged jockeys were self-employed. It did not follow that, because fully-fledged jockeys were self-employed, apprentice and conditional jockeys were also self-employed. *C & E Commrs v RJ & AS Hodges*, QB [2000] STC 262. (*Note.* There was no further public hearing of the appeal.)

Computer engineer—whether acting as individual or employee

[62.326] See *Scott*, 57.184 REGISTRATION.

Engineer—whether acting as individual or director of company

[62.327] See *Demack*, 57.213 REGISTRATION.

Supplies of counterfeit audiocassettes

[62.328] See *McGuckin*, 57.207 REGISTRATION.

Deemed supplies under Sch 4 para 7

Sale of mortgaged aircraft

[62.329] A company mortgaged an aircraft as security for a loan. The company defaulted on the loan, and the lender sold the aircraft. The Commissioners issued an assessment on the basis that the sale constituted a deemed supply by the company under *Sch 4 para 7*. The tribunal upheld the assessment and dismissed the company's appeal. *Aiseireigh Investments Ltd*, LON/97/376 (VTD 15988).

Miscellaneous

Cases where the appellant was unsuccessful

Stock car racing

[62.330] A company (P) promoted stock car race meetings at a stadium owned by another company. Customs assessed P on the basis that it was liable to account for VAT on gate receipts and car park receipts at the meetings. P appealed, contending that, since part of the receipts in question were paid to the stadium owner, it should only be liable to account for VAT on the share of the receipts which it retained. The tribunal rejected this contention and dismissed the appeal. *Mike Parker Productions Ltd*, [1976] VATTR 115 (VTD 275).

Admission to hostess bar

[62.331] A company operated a 'hostess bar' in West London. It engaged a man and a woman, on a self-employed basis, to operate the front kiosk which allowed admission to the bar. No wages were paid, but the kiosk operators were allowed to retain the whole of the admission fees which they collected. The company did not account for tax on these fees. The Commissioners issued an assessment charging tax on the fees, and the company appealed. The tribunal dismissed the appeal, holding that the entrance fee was an integral part of the supplies which the company made to customers visiting the bar. The kiosk operators were not carrying on business on their own account, but were acting on behalf of the company. *Ablefame Ltd*, LON/89/1283Z (VTD 5560).

Letting of garages purchased by plumber with money lent by wife

[62.332] A plumber, registered for VAT, purchased a number of garages with money lent to him by his wife. The garages were let to tenants. The plumber did not account for VAT on the rental income, although it was included in the accounts which his accountant submitted to the Inland Revenue. When the Commissioners discovered this, they issued an assessment charging tax on the rents. The plumber appealed, contending that the rental income should be treated as belonging to his wife, rather than to himself. The tribunal rejected this contention and dismissed his appeal. *R King*, MAN/90/496 (VTD 7201).

Fitting of kitchen furniture

[62.333] A married couple traded in partnership as suppliers of kitchen furniture. They arranged for such furniture to be fitted by self-employed fitters. They accounted for output tax on the amounts paid for the supply of the items of furniture, but did not account for output tax on the fitting charges. The Commissioners issued an assessment charging tax on these services, and the couple appealed, contending that the fitting services were supplied by the fitters as individuals, rather than on behalf of the couple. The tribunal dismissed the appeal, holding on the evidence that the couple were supplying services as well as goods. The fitters were supplying their services to the partnership, rather than directly to the customers. The couple were required to account for output tax on the full amounts paid by the customers. *I & PA Ramsay (t/a Kitchen Format)*, LON/93/949A (VTD 12393).

[62.334] A similar decision was reached in *M Wilson (t/a M & S Interiors) (and related appeals)*, MAN/01/107 (VTD 17494).

[62.335] The decision in *Ramsay*, 62.333 above, was distinguished in a subsequent case where the tribunal found that there was 'no formal contract' between a company which sold kitchen furniture and the fitters who installed it, and held that the fitters were supplying their services to the customers rather than to the company. *Fineline Bedrooms & Kitchens Ltd*, MAN/05/781 (VTD 20049).

Sale of fitted carpets—supplies of carpet fitting

[62.336] Two associated partnerships sold carpets (and one of the partners carried on a similar business as a sole trader). Many of their customers asked them to arrange for the carpets to be fitted. In such cases, the retailers arranged for the carpets to be fitted by self-employed fitters. They accounted for output tax on the amounts paid for the carpets, but did not account for output tax on the fitting charges. The Commissioners issued assessments charging tax on these charges. The retailers appealed, contending that the fitting services were supplied by the fitters as individuals. The tribunal dismissed the appeals, holding on the evidence that the fitters were supplying their services to the retailers and that the retailers were making an onward supply of those services to the customers. Accordingly the retailers were required to account for output tax on the fitting charges. *SE Lockwood (t/a Cash & Carry Carpets)*, MAN/01/427; *B & SE Lockwood (t/a Northern Carpet Group)*, MAN/01/428; *S Sharp & B Lockwood (t/a Lancashire Carpet Centre)*, MAN/01/828 (VTD 18235).

[62.337] A similar decision was reached in *JM & CE Ledger (t/a Lewis Carpets)*, LON/03/959 (VTD 18756).

Supplies of loft conversion services

[62.338] See *A1 Lofts Ltd*, **1.69** AGENTS.

Goods sold at auction following compulsory purchase of business premises

[62.339] A County Council issued a compulsory purchase order to acquire premises which were used as a drapers' shop. Following the compulsory purchase, the goods held at the shop, and the fixtures and fittings, were sold at auction. The partnership which had owned the shop did not account for output tax on the sale proceeds. The Commissioners issued an assessment, and the partnership appealed, contending that the sale had been made by the Council. The tribunal dismissed the appeal, holding on the evidence that the items had been sold by the partnership. *Iqbal Jaurah & Sons*, MAN/93/285 (VTD 12501).

Telegraphic transfer fees for payments from solicitors' client account

[62.340] A firm of solicitors arranged for money to be transferred from its client account to the client accounts of other solicitors under the Clearing Houses Automated Payments Service. Its bank charged it £25 for each such transfer, and it recharged these amounts to the appropriate clients. The firm did not account for output tax on these charges. The Commissioners issued a ruling that the firm was required to account for tax on the charges, and the firm appealed, contending that the relevant supplies were made to its clients by the bank. The tribunal dismissed the appeal, holding that the bank was supplying its services to the firm and that the firm was then making a separate supply to its clients. *Shuttleworth & Co*, [1994] VATTR 355 (VTD 12805).

Sale of plant—whether supply made by partnership or by company

[62.341] A married couple carried on a farming business in partnership and were registered for VAT. They were also the controlling directors of a company which carried on a water bottling business, using plant which the couple leased to the company. The company suffered financial difficulties and it was agreed to sell the plant, and an adjacent field containing the source of the water, to an outside purchaser. The vendors charged the purchaser VAT of £15,750 on the sale of the plant, but did not account for this to the Commissioners. Subsequently the company ceased trading, went into liquidation, and submitted a VAT return declaring the £15,750 output tax. The Commissioners issued an assessment on the partnership, on the basis that the supply of the plant had been made by the partnership rather than the company. The partners appealed, contending that the supply should be treated as having been made by the company. The tribunal rejected this contention and dismissed the appeal, holding on the evidence that the plant had been owned by the partnership and had been sold by the partnership. *D & DA Veale*, LON/95/3182A (VTD 14637).

Partnership carrying on property development business

[62.342] A married couple were registered for VAT as a partnership (F), carrying on a business of property development. The husband (D) was also a member of another partnership (P) which carried on business as potato merchants, the other member of this partnership being his first wife. F owned some land, in respect of which it had elected to waive exemption. In 1999 it agreed to transfer part of the land to P for £250,000. F did not account for output tax on this amount. The Commissioners issued an assessment charging tax on it. F appealed, contending that the transfer had been made by D's second wife to D's first wife, both acting as individuals, rather than by F. The tribunal rejected this contention and dismissed the appeal, holding that the effect of the agreement was that F had transferred the land to its two members (D and his second wife) and that D's second wife had then transferred her half of the land to D's first wife. The Ch D and CA unanimously upheld this decision as one of fact. *Fengate Developments v C & E Commrs*, CA 2004, [2005] STC 191; [2004] EWCA Civ 1591.

Partnership operating retail shop—invoices for graphic design services

[62.343] See *W & J Tang (t/a Ziploc)*, **47.31** PARTNERSHIP.

Partnership operating retail shop—undeclared wholesale supplies

[62.344] See *M & N Singh*, **47.32** PARTNERSHIP.

Admission to playground including miniature railway

[62.345] A Town Council operated a children's playground, charging £1 for admission. Included in the playground was a miniature railway, operated by a private contractor, who was not registered for VAT. The contractor paid the Council a nominal rent and received 30% of the admission fees. The Council only accounted for VAT on the net amount which it retained. The Commissioners issued an assessment on the basis that the Council should have accounted for VAT on the full amount of the admission fees. The Council appealed, contending that, with regard to the 30% which it passed on to the contractor, it was acting as an agent of the contractor. The tribunal rejected this contention and dismissed the Council's appeal, holding on the evidence that the contractor was supplying his services to the council and the council was making a single supply of the right to use the playground. Accordingly the Council was obliged to account for VAT on the full amount of the admission fees, including the amounts which it passed to the contractor. *Hemsworth Town Council*, MAN/96/1391 (VTD 14985).

Fortune-telling services

[62.346] A company advertised fortune-telling services. Customers paid £3 to enter the company's premises and paid a further fee of about £10 to the fortune-teller. The fortune-tellers retained 60% of this, paying 40% to the company. The Commissioners issued an assessment charging tax on the full amounts paid by the customers. The company appealed, contending that the fortune-tellers were supplying their services directly to the customers, so that it should not be required to account for tax on the amounts which the tellers retained. The tribunal rejected this contention and dismissed the appeal, holding that 'in substance what was being offered to the public was a supply by the company'. The fortune-tellers were supplying their services to the company and the company was then supplying those services to the public. *Infocall Universal Ltd (t/a The Psychic Centre)*, EDN/00/38 (VTD 16909).

Dance tuition—whether supplied by club proprietors or individual tutors

[62.347] The proprietors of a dance club arranged for self-employed tutors to give tuition at the club. The club proprietors fixed the hourly charge. The tutors retained 50% of the amount charged, paying 50% to the proprietors as a 'floor rent'. The proprietors only accounted for tax on the 50% which they retained. The Commissioners issued an assessment charging tax on the full amount charged to the students. The proprietors appealed, contending that the tutors were supplying their services directly to the students. The tribunal rejected this contention and dismissed the appeal, holding that the tuition was supplied by the proprietors, who were liable to account for tax on the full amounts charged. *TH & PG Lait (t/a The Lait Dance Club)*, [2001] VATDR 159 (VTD 17038). (*Note.* The tribunal also held that the 'room rent' did not qualify for exemption.)

Tree surgeon—work delegated to subcontractor

[62.348] A tree surgeon appealed against a ruling that he was required to register for VAT, contending that work which he had delegated to a subcontractor should not be treated as part of his turnover. The tribunal rejected this contention and dismissed his appeal, finding that he had negotiated the total price of the contract and invoiced the customers. Accordingly he had made the relevant supplies and was required to account for tax accordingly. *RJ Timms*, LON/03/845 (VTD 18760).

Invoices issued in names of deregistered companies

[62.349] HMRC discovered that several invoices had been issued in the names of companies which had been struck off the Register of Companies. They issued a notice of registration, and an assessment charging VAT of more than £130,000, on the basis that the relevant supplies had actually been made by the companies' controlling director (P), who was a chartered accountant. P appealed, contending that he should not be treated as a 'taxable person'. The tribunal reviewed the evidence in detail, rejected this contention and dismissed the appeal, finding that P's evidence was 'unconvincing' and that it was difficult to believe that 'a man of his experience and training failed to understand how to form, run and dissolve companies. He knew that he could not use the VAT number of a defunct company for all of the companies that he alleged he traded through.' He had chosen 'to form companies with no intention of complying with company and tax law. When a company was about to be struck off he formed another, again with no intention of being compliant. All the companies were convenient vehicles to give an aura of respectability and to confuse HMRC as to his trading activities.' In the circumstances, HMRC 'were entitled to take the view that (P) was continuing to trade in his own capacity'. *SL Phillips v HMRC*, [2010] UKFTT 262 (TC), TC00556.

Motorcycle courier service—supplies to cash customers

[62.350] See *Prontobikes Ltd*, **1.26** AGENTS.

Goods sold at auction organised by fund-raising committee

[62.351] See *The Cheltenham Countryside Race Day*, **1.42** AGENTS.

Company providing staff for clients

[62.352] See *Hays Personnel Services Ltd*, **1.45** AGENTS.

Partnership providing live-in carers—whether acting as principal or agent

[62.353] See *Clarina Live-In Care Service*, **1.48** AGENTS.

Company providing 'outsourcing service'—whether making supplies of staff

[62.354] See *Oriel Support Ltd*, **1.79** AGENTS.

Embroidery kits sold under 'party plan' system

[62.355] See *Simply Cross-stitch*, **1.94** AGENTS.

Supplies by undischarged bankrupt

[62.356] See *Scally*, **37.30** INSOLVENCY.

Business transferred as going concern following bankruptcy

[62.357] See *Camford Ltd*, **37.32** INSOLVENCY.

Whether supplies made by franchisor or franchisee

[62.358] See *Allergycare (Testing) Ltd*, **33.29** HEALTH AND WELFARE; *Duwel*, **57.187** REGISTRATION, and *Evans*, **57.188** REGISTRATION.

Canteen for employees

[62.359] See *MB Metals*, **62.11** above, and *Barker*, **62.12** above.

Cases where the appellant was successful

Partner in solicitors' firm also acting for Borough Council

[62.360] A partner in a firm of solicitors also held a part-time appointment as a solicitor to a Borough Council. The Commissioners issued a ruling that the firm should account for VAT on the solicitor's salary from the Council. The tribunal allowed the firm's appeal, holding that the contract was with the solicitor as an individual and not with the firm. *Lean & Rose*, [1974] VATTR 7 (VTD 54).

Sales of racehorses owned by syndicates

[62.361] A racehorse breeder had a one-fortieth share in two syndicates which each owned a stallion at stud, one in the UK and the other in Ireland. Each syndicate was managed by a committee on behalf of its members. Each committee, after obtaining the requisite approval of a majority of the members, sold the syndicate's stallion to a Japanese breeder to whom it was exported. The Commissioners assessed the breeder on his share of the sale proceeds. The tribunal allowed the breeder's appeal, holding that in each case the committee had supplied the stallion. The supply of the stallion in Ireland, being a supply outside the UK, was outside the scope of VAT. The stallion in the UK had been exported and its supply was accordingly zero-rated. *Sir John Astor*, [1981] VATTR 174 (VTD 1030).

House-to-house sales of goods from vans

[62.362] A firm sold domestic household goods by 'door-to-door' selling. It had a number of vans, each of which was under the charge of a 'supervisor', two of whom were partners in the firm and five of whom were treated as self-employed. The firm determined the retail price of the goods and invoiced the supervisor for 50% of this price in respect of the goods loaded on his van. The Commissioners issued an assessment on the basis that the supervisors were selling the goods on behalf of the firm, so that tax was chargeable on the full retail price. The firm accepted that this was so in respect of the two supervisors who were partners, but appealed against the assessment in respect of sales by the other supervisors, contending that the supervisors had purchased the goods from the firm and sold them on their own account. The tribunal accepted this contention and allowed the appeal to this extent, holding that, in the case of the self-employed supervisors, the firm was only liable to account for tax on the amounts invoiced to them. *Headley Enterprises*, LON/82/65 (VTD 1295).

Goods exchanged for coupons under promotional scheme

[62.363] A company (S) manufactured foodstuffs, principally crisps, and sold them to retailers. In 1975 it introduced a promotional scheme, administered by another company (G), whereby each box of crisps contained coupons, which retailers could exchange for a variety of goods. G supplied the goods requested, and issued invoices to S to cover the cost of the goods in question, plus a service charge. VAT was charged on these invoices, and S reclaimed this as input tax. The Commissioners issued assessments on the basis that S had supplied the goods to the retailers, and should account for output tax on their value. S appealed, contending that it had not made any supply of the goods, which had been supplied by G. The tribunal accepted this contention and allowed S's appeal. The Commissioners appealed to the QB, which upheld the tribunal's decision that the goods had been supplied by G, but also held that S had not been entitled to reclaim input tax on the supplies, and directed that the assessments should be amended accordingly. *C & E Commrs v Sooner Foods Ltd*, QB [1983] STC 376.

Company arranging supplies of goods to customers under incentive scheme

[62.364] See *HMRC v Baxi Group Ltd*, **22.154** EUROPEAN COMMUNITY LAW.

Feedstuffs supplied to racehorses

[62.365] A company carried on the business of training racehorses. Its controlling shareholder (R) was a farmer, who supplied feedstuffs to the company and owned a number of racehorses which the company trained. R only invoiced the company for feedstuffs consumed by horses owned by other customers and did not charge it for feedstuffs consumed by his own horses. The Commissioners issued an assessment on the basis that the company should account for output tax on the open market value of the feedstuffs it provided for the horses owned by R. The company appealed, contending that it had not made any supply of the feedstuffs in question, which had remained the property of R until consumed by the horses. The QB accepted this contention and allowed the appeal, holding that the company had only supplied training facilities and had not made any supply of the feedstuffs. *Spigot Lodge Ltd v C & E Commrs*, QB [1985] STC 255.

Sale of imported radios

[62.366] A company (O) carried on business as a haulage contractor and worked as a subcontractor for another company (L). The directors of the two companies decided to organise the importation and sale of radios from Korea. Initially the radios were imported on the basis that L was the importer, and L's VAT number was used. Subsequently O's principal director became personally involved in selling large numbers of the radios, and arranged substantial sales to UK wholesalers using L's invoices. The Commissioners assessed O in respect of the sales of the radios. O appealed, contending that it had made no supplies of the radios, and that the supplies had been made by L. The tribunal accepted this contention and allowed the appeal. *O'Reilly Transport (Newry) Ltd*, BEL/86/1 (VTD 2434).

Examination fees collected by college on behalf of examining boards

[62.367] A college of higher education was an approved centre for examinations set by boards approved by the Department of Education and Science. The college collected examination fees on behalf of the examining boards, and also charged additional fees to candidates who sat examinations at its premises. It accounted for VAT on the fees which it charged, but not on the fees which it collected on behalf of the examining boards. The Commissioners assessed the college on the fees which it collected on behalf of the boards, and the college appealed. The tribunal allowed the college's appeal, holding that the examinations were supplied by the boards rather than by the college. *City College of Higher Education Ltd*, LON/87/203 (VTD 2500).

Supply of facilities at school premises to photographers

[62.368] A company photographed schoolchildren at school premises and sold the photographs to parents. It made payments to the schools in return for the use of the school facilities. Following *dicta* of the tribunal chairman in *H Tempest Ltd (No 2)*, **67.28** VALUATION, the Commissioners took the view (set out in VAT Information Sheet 5/94) that the schools were acting as agents of the local education authorities, so that the local education authorities should account for output tax on the amounts received from the company. They issued an assessment on a County Council which had failed to account for output tax on this basis. The Council appealed, contending that the effect of the *Education Act 1993* was that the school facilities were supplied by the school governors rather than by the County Council. The tribunal accepted this contention and allowed the appeal, holding that 'while the head teacher is nominally an employee of the local education authority, in truth his authority to manage the school derives from his appointment by the governing body', and 'he does so as their representative'. *Lancashire County Council*, [1996] VATDR 550 (VTD 14655). (*Note.* For the Commissioners' practice following this decision, see Business Brief 11/97, issued on 9 May 1997, and Business Brief 21/97, issued on 3 October 1997.)

Associated partnerships supplying carpentry services

[62.369] A father and son traded in partnership, supplying carpentry services, and were registered for VAT. Because they had to account for VAT, they found it difficult to compete with unregistered traders when quoting for private individuals. In 1996 the son entered into a separate written partnership agreement with his mother, to provide carpentry services to private individuals for cash. Both partnerships kept separate records. The turnover of the registered partnership was substantially higher than that of the unregistered partnership. In 1999 a VAT officer visited the registered partnership and discovered the existence of the unregistered partnership. Following her visit, the Commissioners issued an assessment charging tax on the supplies purportedly made by the unregistered partnership, on the basis that in reality there was a single business. The registered partnership appealed, contending that there were two partnerships which carried on separate businesses. The tribunal accepted the partnership's evidence and allowed the appeal, finding that 'all customers were aware of the partnership with which they were trading'. The chairman observed that 'this is not a case where one business was separated so as to ensure that neither entity was registered' and that 'if Customs & Excise do not like the fact that there are two similar businesses, one of which is not registered, then their remedy is to make a direction under *paragraphs 1A* and 2 of *Schedule 1*'. *RE & RL Newton (t/a RE Newton)*, LON/00/84 (VTD 17222).

Waste disposal and skip hire—whether a single business

[62.370] A father and son operated a waste disposal business, including the hire of large skips to trade customers, in partnership, and were registered for VAT accordingly. Subsequently the son also began to operate a separate business, of hiring small skips to domestic customers, in partnership with his wife. This partnership was not registered for VAT. The Commissioners issued an assessment to the registered partnership, charging tax on supplies by the unregistered partnership, on the basis that there was a single business. The registered partnership appealed, contending that there were two partnerships which carried on separate businesses. The tribunal accepted the partnership's evidence and allowed the appeal. *Skelton Waste Disposal*, MAN/00/866 (VTD 17351).

Monthly magazines giving details of cable television services

[62.371] A group of companies (T) supplied cable broadcasting services to subscribers. It provided the subscribers with a monthly magazine providing details of the programmes which it broadcast. Until 1999, it treated part of the subscriptions as attributable to zero-rated supplies of the magazines. Following the decision in *British Sky Broadcasting Group plc*, 5.97 BOOKS, ETC., the Commissioners issued a ruling that the whole of the subscriptions were for standard-rated supplies of broadcasting services. T then incorporated a separate company (P) with the intention that T should supply the standard-rated broadcasting services and that P should supply the magazines. P registered for VAT, and treated its supplies of the magazines as zero-rated. The Commissioners issued a ruling that in reality the magazines were still being supplied by T (and were part of a single standard-rated supply). T and

P appealed. The CA allowed their appeals, holding on the evidence that there had been a partial novation and that the customers had become contractually bound to P. Arden LJ held that the supply of television services and the supply of a magazine could not be treated as a single supply, merely because the customer could not enter into one transaction without the other. There was no authority for the proposition that the concept of 'principal and ancillary contracts', as propounded in *Card Protection Plan Ltd*, **22.324** EUROPEAN COMMUNITY LAW, could apply where there was more than one supplier. The principle of 'economic neutrality' did not require the court to treat two separate supplies as a single supply simply because the suppliers were related parties and their supplies were linked. *Telewest Communications plc v C & E Commrs; Telewest Communications (Publications) Ltd v C & E Commrs*, CA [2005] STC 481; [2005] EWCA Civ 102.

Goods sold under 'party plan' system—by whom supplied

[62.372] See *Potter*, **1.91** AGENTS, and *Kelly*, **1.95** AGENTS.

Goods sold by 'direct selling'—whether salesmen acting as agents

[62.373] See *Betterware Products Ltd*, **1.96** AGENTS, and *Kelly*, **1.97** AGENTS.

Optional service charge in restaurant

[62.374] See *NDP Co Ltd*, **67.107** VALUATION.

Husband declared bankrupt and transferring business to wife

[62.375] See *Thomas*, **37.31** INSOLVENCY.

Sales of car numberplates—by whom supplied

[62.376] See *Wood*, **57.170** REGISTRATION.

Gaming machines in shop—by whom supplies made

[62.377] See *Bennetts of Sheffield Ltd*, **67.134** VALUATION.

Goods exported by group of companies—company by which supply made

[62.378] See *Philips Exports Ltd*, **25.27** EXPORTS.

Export of goods—more than one company involved—by whom supply made

[62.379] See *Geistlich Sons Ltd*, **25.28** EXPORTS.

Canteen for employees—by whom supplies made

[62.380] See *Notts Fire Service Messing Club*, **13.12** CLUBS, ASSOCIATIONS AND ORGANISATIONS.

Supplies of magazines to subscribers

[62.381] See *Nordic Subscription Service UK Ltd*, **5.105** BOOKS, ETC.

The time of supply (VATA 1994, s 6)

Time of supply of goods (VATA 1994, s 6(2))

Stolen takings

[62.382] A hotel proprietor appealed against an estimated assessment, contending that the underdeclared takings had been stolen by dishonest bar staff. The tribunal held that the proprietor was still liable to account for tax on the stolen takings, as the time of supply was when the goods were handed to the customer. *G Benton*, [1975] VATTR 138 (VTD 185).

[62.383] The decision in *Benton*, **62.382** above, was applied in the subsequent cases of *AJ Furby*, MAN/77/316 (VTD 622); *Townville (Wheldale) Miners Sports & Recreation Club & Institute*, MAN/78/212 (VTD 719); *West Way Garage (Bournemouth) Ltd*, LON/86/204 (VTD 2151); *CJ Huntley & RJ Brookes (t/a Brimar Guest House)*, LON/90/1237X (VTD 5847); *JP Sharp*, MAN/91/520 (VTD 6795); *Mr & Mrs AA Lewis*, LON/92/2429A (VTD 11596) and *Metrogold (Building Contractors) Ltd*, MAN/00/202 (VTD 16911) and *Moorthorpe Empire Working Men's Club*, **3.152** ASSESSMENT.

[62.384] Similar decisions were reached in *M & M Wholesale (NE) Ltd*, MAN/02/259 (VTD 18055) and *The Skelmersdale Centre Ltd*, LON/04/192 (VTD 18813).

[62.385] See also *Courage Ltd*, **58.41** RETAILERS' SPECIAL SCHEMES.

Vending machines

[62.386] The standard rate of VAT was increased from 8% to 15% with effect from 18 June 1979. A firm which operated a number of vending machines was unable to modify some of its machines in time to pass on this increase to its customers. In cases where it had been unable to alter the machines, it accounted for output tax at 8%. The Commissioners issued an assessment on a time-apportionment basis, treating the appropriate proportion of the takings as chargeable at 15%. The tribunal upheld the assessment and dismissed the firm's appeal. *Glasgow Vending Services*, LON/79/334 (VTD 943).

Supplies of coins

[62.387] On 31 March 1982 it was announced that supplies of gold coins, which had previously been exempt under *FA 1972*, were to become standard-rated from the following day. A partnership which traded as coin dealers had many customers on the day of the announcement, and had to order extra coins to meet the demand. These coins were delivered on 1 April. The partnership failed to account for output tax on coins which customers had ordered on 31 March, but which it had been unable to supply to the customers until 1 April. The Commissioners issued an assessment charging tax on these supplies (except that where a deposit had been paid on 31 March, tax was not due on the amount of the deposit). The tribunal dismissed the partnership's appeal and the QB upheld this decision. By virtue of what is now *VATA 1994, s 6(2)*, the time of supply was 1 April. *Purshotam M Pattni & Sons v C & E Commrs*, QB 1986, [1987] STC 1.

Goods sold subject to reservation of title—time of supply

[62.388] A company (V) sold bus chassis under agreements whereby it retained title until receipt of payment. The chassis were delivered to coach-builders nominated by the customers. V did not account for output tax until the completed coaches were delivered by the coachbuilders to the customers, and the Commissioners issued an assessment on the basis that the chassis were supplied when V delivered them to the coachbuilders. The tribunal upheld the assessment and dismissed V's appeal. *Volvo Trucks (GB) Ltd*, [1988] VATTR 11 (VTD 2579).

Machine tools made available for demonstration purposes

[62.389] A company manufactured machine tools which were intended to be mounted on grinding machines. It delivered some of these tools to agents of grinding wheel manufacturers for demonstration purposes. The Commissioners issued an assessment on the basis that the tools were delivered to the manufacturers on a sale or return basis, within what is now *VATA 1994, s 6(2)(c)*. The company appealed, contending that the transactions were not within *s 6(2)*. The tribunal allowed the company's appeal, finding that the tools remained the company's property and that, when a tool was delivered, it was not the expectation of either party that that particular tool would be sold to a customer, but that a customer would see the way in which the tools worked and would then order one meeting his own particular requirements. On the evidence, 'property in the goods was not intended to pass unless and until the agent by a separate act signified that he wished to buy the (tool) on show and appropriated it in order to sell it on to his buyer'. *Diaform Ltd*, LON/93/469A (VTD 11069).

Transfer of assets by trader to associated company—time of supply

[62.390] A sole trader (J), who had for many years competed in Formula 3 and Formula 3000 motor racing, developed a Formula 1 racing car. In 1990 he and his wife purchased the whole of the shares in a limited company, which he used to seek finance and sponsorship for Formula 1 motor racing. His accountant prepared draft accounts, with a journal entry indicating that, on 27 September 1990, J had transferred assets relating to the Formula 1 car to his company. The Commissioners issued an assessment, including a charge to default interest, on the basis that there had been a supply of the assets on that date. J appealed, contending that despite the journal entry, the assets had not been transferred until 1991, when the company first began to race the Formula 1 cars. The tribunal allowed the appeal, finding that the accounts were 'erroneous' and that the journal entry did not constitute a tax point, so that for VAT purposes the time of supply was in 1991. *E Jordan (t/a Eddie Jordan Racing)*, LON/92/734 (VTD 11310).

Transfer of land—time of supply

[62.391] The Cumbernauld Development Corporation, which had begun the development of the Cumbernauld area in 1956, transferred some of its remaining land to a local golf club in exchange for some land owned by the club. Under the agreement, there was no monetary consideration for either transfer, but the Corporation had to pay for work to be carried out on the golf club's course and for a new clubhouse. The Commissioners issued an assessment on the basis that the time of the supply was the date of the relevant disposition (March 1997). The Corporation appealed, contending that the supply had taken place in May 1996, when the land was made available to the club (with the result that the assessment was outside the statutory time limit). The tribunal rejected this contention and dismissed the appeal, and the CS upheld this decision. Lord Gill held that 'while the land itself was made available to the club on 1 May 1996 in the sense that the club was given the occupation and use of it, the interest of the appellant as proprietor of the *dominium utile* was not made available to the club at that date. The club had no more than a right *in personam* against the appellant to receive a conveyance in the form of a feu disposition. Meanwhile the appellant retained the major interest in the land as defined by (*VATA 1994, s 96(1)*).' Accordingly the assessment had been made within the statutory time limit. *Cumbernauld Development Corporation v C & E Commrs (No 2)*, CS [2002] STC 226. (*Note.* For the valuation of the supply, see **67.81** VALUATION.)

Retail sales paid for by credit card—time of supply

[62.392] See *Kingfisher plc*, **32.28** GROUPS OF COMPANIES.

Retail sales by mail order—whether within VATA 1994, s 6(2)(c)

[62.393] A company supplied goods by mail order. It allowed customers to make payment by instalments. Prior to the QB decisions in *Next plc*, **58.28** RETAILERS' SPECIAL SCHEMES and *Grattan plc*, **58.29** RETAILERS' SPECIAL SCHEMES, it had accounted for tax on the basis that the time of supply was the time of the first payment. Following those decisions, it submitted a repayment claim on the basis that the time of supply was the time the goods were despatched, so that, in the case of goods which had been despatched when the VAT rate was 15% but the first payment had not been made until after the rate had been increased to 17.5%, it should have accounted for VAT at 15% rather than 17.5%. The Commissioners made a provisional repayment of the amount claimed, but subsequently formed the opinion that the goods were supplied 'on approval or sale or return or similar terms', within what is now *VATA 1994, s 6(2)(c)*, and that the time of supply should be taken as 14 days after the delivery of the goods. They issued an assessment charging tax on this basis. The company appealed. The tribunal allowed the appeal, holding on the evidence that the supplies were within *s 6(2)(a)* rather than *s 6(2)(c)*. The tribunal held that *s 6(2)(c)* applied to transactions where there was no contract of sale 'unless and until the person concerned adopts or is deemed to have adopted the transaction', whereas *s 6(2)(a)* applied to transactions where there was a contract of sale but the buyer had the right to rescind the contract if he wished. Accordingly the time of supply was the date of despatch of the goods. *Littlewoods Organisation plc*, [1997] VATDR 408 (VTD 14977). (*Notes.* (1) The QB decisions in *Next plc*, **58.28** RETAILERS' SPECIAL SCHEMES and *Grattan plc*, **58.29** RETAILERS' SPECIAL SCHEMES, were subsequently disapproved by the CA in *R v C & E Commrs (ex p. Littlewoods Home Shopping Group Ltd)*, **58.39** RETAILERS' SPECIAL SCHEMES. (2) The decision here was unanimously approved by the CS in the subsequent Scottish case of *Robertson's Electrical Ltd*, **62.464** below.)

[62.394] See also *Grattan plc (No 2)*, **62.462** below, and *Compton & Woodhouse Ltd*, **62.463** below.

Retail sales by internet—whether within VATA 1994, s 6(2)(c)

[62.395] See *C & E Commrs v Robertson's Electrical Ltd*, **62.464** below.

Time of performance of services (VATA 1994, s 6(3))

Supplies of accommodation

[62.396] The proprietors of a guest-house registered for VAT with effect from June 1977. They had taken several bookings before registration for clients to stay at the guest-house after the date of registration. They did not account for output tax on such supplies. The Commissioners issued an assessment charging tax on them and the tribunal dismissed the proprietors' appeal. By virtue of what is now *VATA 1994, s 6(3)*, the accommodation was not supplied until the clients arrived at the guest-house. *E & B Palotai*, LON/78/149 (VTD 656).

[62.397] The standard rate of VAT was increased from 8% to 15% in June 1979. A company which carried on business as a tour operator continued to account for VAT at 8% on supplies which it made after the change of rate. The Commissioners issued an assessment charging tax at 15% and the company appealed, contending that the accommodation had been booked before the increase in rate and that tax should only be charged at 8%. The tribunal rejected this contention and dismissed the appeal. By virtue of what is now *VATA 1994, s 6(3)*, the time of the supply was the supply was the time when the accommodation was provided, except where an invoice had previously been issued or payment had previously been made. *Scottish Highland Hotel Group Ltd*, [1981] VATTR 146 (VTD 1115).

[62.398] For cases concerning the payment of deposits for holiday accommodation, see *Caine*, **62.441** below, and *Moonraker's Guest House Ltd*, **62.441** below.

Estate agents—fees agreed before registration

[62.399] An estate agent began trading on 24 June 1982 but did not register for VAT until 1 April 1983. He did not account for VAT on fees which had been agreed before April 1983 and the Commissioners issued an assessment charging tax on such supplies where completion took place on or after 1 April 1983. The tribunal upheld the assessment and dismissed the agent's appeal, holding that the time of supply was the date of completion. *WJ Cooke*, MAN/84/265 (VTD 1844).

[62.400] Similar decisions were reached in *Madisons*, LON/87/276 (VTD 2516); *J Calland*, MAN/87/201 & 202 (VTD 2627) and *S & J Property Centres*, MAN/00/101 (VTD 16985).

[62.401] In a case where a contract for the sale of two houses was signed on 16 February 1987, but completion did not take place until 1 July, the Commissioners issued an assessment on the basis that the estate agents' services were not supplied until completion took place (with the result that changes to the partial exemption rules which took effect from 1 April 1987 applied to the input tax in question). The tribunal upheld the assessment, applying *Madisons* and *Calland*, **62.400** above, and holding that 'where the services are performed over a period of time and there is one consideration for the services as a whole, then the "time when services are performed"' must mean 'the point in time when all the services to be supplied have been performed'. *Trustees for the Greater World Association Trust*, [1989] VATTR 91 (VTD 3401).

Supplies of double glazing

[62.402] In March 1984 the Chancellor of the Exchequer announced that building alterations, which had previously been zero-rated, would be treated as standard-rated after 31 May 1984. A company which supplied double glazing did not account for output tax in cases where it had agreed contracts before June 1984 although the relevant work was not carried out until after 31 May. The Commissioners issued an assessment charging tax on the basis that the time of supply was after 31 May so that VAT was chargeable on the work. The tribunal upheld the assessment and dismissed the company's appeal. *APD Insulations [Group] Ltd*, [1987] VATTR 36 (VTD 2292).

[62.403] For a case where the tribunal held that double glazing work had been paid for before 1 June 1984, see *Dolomite Double Glazing Ltd*, **62.422** below. For a case where the tribunal held that such work had not been paid before that date, see *Double Shield Window Co Ltd*, **62.421** below. For a case where the tribunal held that the time of supply for double glazing was the date on which the relevant invoice was issued, see *Tingley*, **62.413** below.

Building contractor—quotations issued before registration

[62.404] A building contractor registered for VAT with effect from 1 February 1989. He failed to account for VAT on a contract where he had issued a quotation in January 1989, but had not carried out the work until after 1 February. The Commissioners issued an assessment on the basis that VAT was chargeable on the contract. The tribunal dismissed the contractor's appeal. By virtue of what is now *VATA 1994, s 6(3)*, the time of supply was when the contract was carried out. *NCJ Hughes*, MAN/92/208 (VTD 8916).

[62.405] A similar decision was reached in *Chiltern Windows Ltd*, LON/93/2604A (VTD 12208).

Solicitor—delay in supplying services requested before registration but

[62.406] A solicitor registered for VAT in September 1991. He did not account for tax on services which he supplied to two clients who had given him instructions before he had registered, although the relevant services had been supplied after the date of registration. The Commissioners issued a ruling that the solicitor was obliged to account for output tax on the services supplied after registration, and the tribunal dismissed the solicitor's appeal, applying *Cooke*, **62.399** above, and *Madisons*, **62.400** above. *WN Bagshawe (t/a Bagshawes)*, LON/95/1675A (VTD 14103).

Conversion of building into flats—payment delayed for five years

[62.407] A company agreed to convert a building into five flats at a price of £72,500 plus VAT. The price was not payable until five years after completion of the work. The work was completed by November 1987, when the first tenant moved in, and all the flats were occupied by February 1988. The Commissioners issued an assessment on the basis that the supply had taken place in the company's return period ending 29 February 1988. The company appealed, contending that it had an obligation to maintain the building until the contract price became five years after completion, and that the time of supply should be treated as being the time when payment was due. The tribunal upheld the assessment in principle, holding that, by virtue of what is now *VATA 1994, s 6(3)*, the time of supply for VAT purposes was the time when the services were performed, and the Commissioners were therefore correct to assess the company on the basis that tax became chargeable in the period ending February 1988. (However, the tribunal also held that the value of the consideration should be reduced to take account of the delay in reaching the due date for payment and the possibility of the final price being reduced to allow for any defects in the work—see **67.139** VALUATION.) *Mercantile Contracts Ltd*, LON/88/786 (VTD 4357).

Commission for hotel bookings—time of supply

[62.408] A company received commission from hotels in return for introducing potential clients. It initially sent the hotels 'pro forma' invoices which did not include VAT, and subsequently issued further invoices for the VAT. It did not account for output tax until it had received payment of the second invoices from the hotels. The Commissioners issued an assessment on the basis that the company should have accounted for VAT when it introduced the clients to the hotels, in accordance with what is now *VATA 1994, s 6(3)*. The tribunal upheld the assessment and dismissed the company's appeal. *Hotel Booking Service Ltd*, LON/92/1856 (VTD 10606).

Restaurant 'discount cards'—time of supply

[62.409] Two companies issued 'discount cards' entitling the holder to obtain a price reduction on up to twelve occasions at a stated restaurant. The Commissioners issued a ruling that, by virtue of *VATA 1994, s 6(3)*, the time of supply was when the cards were consigned to the immediate recipients (marketing companies which resold the cards to the ultimate consumers). The companies appealed, contending that the time of supply should be taken as the time of payment, when the cards were actually sold to the ultimate consumer. The tribunal rejected this contention and dismissed the appeal, holding that the time of supply was 'the time when the supply of the services is performed for the consideration fixed at the time of consignment and that the time when the services of consignment are performed is when the consignee can use the services consigned to it by making a reconsignment'. *Granton Marketing Ltd; Wentwalk Ltd*, [1999] VATDR 383 (VTD 16118).

Stolen takings

[62.410] See *Benton*, **62.382** above, and the cases noted at **62.383** and **62.384** above.

Issue of invoice (VATA 1994, s 6(4))

Car dealer—date of issue of invoices

[62.411] The standard rate of VAT was increased from 8% to 15% with effect from 18 June 1979. A company which traded as a car dealer had received several orders for cars before 18 June 1979, but the cars were not ready for delivery until after that date. In such cases, the company prepared its normal triplicate invoices before 18 June and asked the prospective purchasers to confirm their agreement to the details on the invoices. It accounted for output tax at 8% on these invoices. The Commissioners issued an assessment on the basis that the company should have accounted for tax at 15%. The company appealed, contending that the invoices had been issued before 18 June 1979. The QB rejected this contention and upheld the assessment. The invoices had not been given to the prospective purchasers until after 18 June 1979, and consequently had not been 'issued' before that date. *C & E Commrs v Woolfold Motor Co Ltd*, QB [1983] STC 715.

Accountancy partnership

[62.412] An accountancy partnership did not account for output tax until it received payment for its supplies. The Commissioners issued an assessment on the basis that the partnership should have accounted for tax at the time it issued invoices. The tribunal dismissed the partnership's appeal, holding that the effect of what is now *VATA 1994, s 6(4)* was that a supply should be treated as taking place at the earlier of the time of the receipt of payment or the issue of an invoice, and not at the later of the two. *P Smith & AR Ashton*, MAN/88/333 (VTD 3317).

Invoices issued after 1 April 1991 for contracts agreed before that date

[62.413] The standard rate of VAT was increased from 15% to 17.5% with effect from 1 April 1991. A double glazing contractor had entered into contracts with customers before that date, but had not completed the work or issued an invoice. In such cases, he accounted for VAT at 15%. The Commissioners issued an assessment charging VAT at 17.5%, on the basis that the tax point was the date of issue of the invoices. The tribunal upheld the assessment and dismissed the contractor's appeal. *D Tingley (t/a Homecare Exteriors)*, LON/93/800A (VTD 11592).

Application for payment—whether an invoice for VATA 1994, s 6(4)

[62.414] A company (P) was building a power station for an associated company (L). It issued applications for progress payments in accordance with the terms of the relevant contract. It intended that these applications should not be treated as tax invoices, so that the time of the supply would be the date of receipt of the payment. However, on 30 July 1990 it issued such an application which stated that the tax point was 30 July 1990. L treated this application as a tax invoice and reclaimed input tax accordingly, but P did not account for output tax. When the Commissioners discovered what had happened, they formed the opinion that the document constituted a tax invoice, so that L had acted correctly in reclaiming input tax and P had acted wrongly in failing to account for output tax. They issued an assessment imposing a misdeclaration penalty and interest, on the basis that the time of supply was 30 July 1990. P appealed, contending that the entry of 30 July 1990 in the space marked 'tax point' was a clerical error and the document did not constitute an invoice, so that the time of supply was when L made the relevant payment, rather than when the document was issued. The tribunal accepted this contention and allowed P's appeal, holding that the document was not a tax invoice and did not have the effect of making 30 July 1990 the tax point. *ABB Power Ltd*, [1992] VATTR 491 (VTD 9373).

[62.415] The decision in *ABB Power Ltd*, 62.412 above, was applied in a subsequent case where a builder had failed to account for VAT shown on applications for payment which he had issued to customers, and the Commissioners issued an assessment treating the applications as invoices and thus as giving rise to a tax point. The tribunal allowed the trader's appeal, holding that the documents were not invoices and thus their date of issue was not to be treated as the time of supply. *SR Finch*, LON/91/1950A (VTD 10948).

[62.416] A company (T) had engaged a construction company (F) to build new premises. In May 1997 F issued an invoice to T for £47,970 plus VAT. However, T failed to reclaim the VAT as input tax until August 2000, when its auditor discovered the omission. T submitted a late repayment claim, which the Commissioners rejected on the grounds that it was outside the statutory three-year time limit. T appealed, contending that the invoice was invalid, so that the time of supply was when it had made the relevant payment, which was inside the three-year limit. The tribunal dismissed the appeal, finding that the invoice was valid so that the time of supply was the date on which the invoice was issued. *Innings Telecom Europe Ltd*, MAN/01/102 (VTD 17335).

Receipt of payment (VATA 1994, s 6(4))

Advance payments

Secretarial college

[62.417] The proprietor of a secretarial college charged its students fees in advance. The Commissioners issued an assessment on the basis that the time of supply was when the fees were received. The proprietor appealed, contending that the fees should be apportioned over the period in which the tuition was to be given. The tribunal rejected this contention and dismissed the appeal. *H Walters (t/a St George's Secretarial College)*, MAN/78/60 (VTD 602).

[62.417A] A similar decision was reached in *Bromley Training & Development Ltd v HMRC*, [2012] UKFTT 30 (TC), TC01728.

Club subscriptions

[62.418] A company which had operated a golf club went into liquidation. Members' subscriptions had been payable in advance, the members being supplied with a tax invoice. The liquidator admitted proofs of debts from members for the proportion of their subscriptions referable to the period after the beginning of the winding-up. He appealed against an assessment on the company, contending that it should be reduced by the tax relating to the subscriptions which he hoped to refund to the members. The tribunal dismissed the appeal. The letters admitting proofs of debts due to the members were not credit notes for VAT purposes, and, by virtue of what is now *VATA 1994, s 6(4)*, the supplies of services to the members were treated as having been made when the company issued tax invoices for them. *George Hamshaw (Golf Services) Ltd*, [1979] VATTR 51 (VTD 722).

[62.419] A club for former pupils of an independent school invited the parents of current pupils to make termly advance payments towards future life membership of the club. It did not account for output tax on these payments. The Commissioners issued an assessment on the basis that tax was chargeable when the payments were made. The club appealed, contending that it did not supply any services until the pupil had been elected to membership. The tribunal accepted this contention and allowed the appeal. *The Old Chigwellians' Club*, [1987] VATTR 66 (VTD 2332).

[62.420] A golf club instituted a scheme whereby members could pay part of their subscriptions in advance by monthly standing order. The Commissioners issued a ruling that VAT was chargeable when the payments were made. The tribunal dismissed the club's appeal, observing that what is now *VATA 1994, s 6(4)* provided that the supply should be treated as taking place at the time when payment was received. *East Kilbride Golf Club*, EDN/90/101 (VTD 5503).

Payment made to solicitor as stakeholder

[62.421] In March 1984 the Chancellor of the Exchequer announced that building alterations, which had previously been zero-rated, would be treated as standard-rated after 31 May 1984, but that, under transitional provisions, such work could be treated as zero-rated if it was paid for before 1 June 1984. A company which supplied double glazing instigated a scheme whereby customers who had placed orders before 1 June 1984 were encouraged to pay the agreed price for the work to its solicitors before that date. The solicitors undertook not to release the amounts to the company until the customer had confirmed in writing that he was satisfied with the work. The Commissioners issued an assessment on the basis that the payments to the solicitors did not constitute payment within what is now *VATA 1994, s 6(4)*, so that the supplies were not eligible for zero-rating. The tribunal upheld the assessment and dismissed the company's appeal. *Double Shield Window Co Ltd*, MAN/84/227 (VTD 1771).

Cost of supply lent to customer by supplier

[62.422] A double glazing company (D) had agreed to carry out work valued at £2,370 for a customer (S). S became aware that, if he paid for the work before 1 June 1984, it would be zero-rated. However, he could not afford to pay the full amount until June. He therefore asked one of D's directors if he would lend him the money for a month. The director agreed to this, and gave S a cheque for £2,370 on 29 May 1984. On 31 May S gave D a cheque for the same amount. The work was completed on 18 June. S repaid most of the loan on that date, and repaid the balance in September. The Commissioners issued an assessment on the basis that the exchange of cheques did not constitute payment, so that the time of supply was 18 June and the work was not eligible for zero-rating. The tribunal allowed D's appeal, holding that payment was made on 31 May. If S had refused to repay the loan after the work was completed, D would have had to sue him for repayment of the loan, rather than for payment for the work. *Dolomite Double Glazing Ltd*, [1985] VATTR 184 (VTD 1922).

Circular payments

[62.423] A company (D) had entered into a contract with an associated construction company (F) in 1983, whereby it was agreed that F would carry out alterations to a property for D. In March 1984 the Chancellor of the Exchequer announced that such work would be standard-rated after 31 May 1984, unless it was paid for before 1 June 1984. The principal director of D and F arranged with D's bank for it to advance the whole of the contract price so that it could pay F on 31 May. At the same time D and F entered into an agreement whereby F, having received the money in question, would lend it back to D at 6% p.a. interest, and the loan would be repaid by D as the work proceeded. On 31 May D and F exchanged cheques as agreed. The Commissioners issued an assessment charging VAT on the contract price on the basis that the exchange of cheques did not constitute payment within what is now *VATA 1994, s 6(4)* The tribunal allowed F's appeal and the CA upheld this decision. The payment made discharged D's liability under the building contract and left F with no right to sue for payment thereunder. The payment was in law a genuine contractual payment, and the court was not entitled to disregard its legal effect and treat it as something else. *C & E Commrs v Faith Construction Ltd*, CA [1989] STC 539; [1990] 1 QB 905; [1989] 2 All ER 938.

[62.424] A similar decision was reached in a case which the CA heard with *Faith Construction Ltd*, **62.423** above. *C & E Commrs v West Yorkshire Independent Hospital (Contract Services) Ltd*, CA [1989] STC 539; [1990] 1 QB 905; [1989] 2 All ER 938.

[62.425] See also *BUPA Hospitals Ltd*, **22.230** EUROPEAN COMMUNITY LAW.

Payment by cheque

[62.426] Building alterations became standard-rated after 31 May 1984, unless payment was made before 1 June 1984. A builder who was carrying out work for a customer in May 1984 received a cheque for the full amount of the work in May but did not present the cheque to his bank until June. The Commissioners issued an assessment charging tax on the work. The tribunal dismissed the builder's appeal, holding that payment did not take place until the cheque was presented. *MH Rampling*, [1986] VATTR 62 (VTD 2067).

[62.427] Similar decisions were reached in *Aldford Aluminium Products*, MAN/86/38 (VTD 2190) and *BJ Charman*, LON/86/638 (VTD 2270).

Money placed in joint account by recipient

[62.428] Building alterations became standard-rated after 31 May 1984, unless payment was made before 1 June 1984. A company instigated a scheme whereby it agreed with customers that, if they paid the full agreed price for such work before 1 June, it would place 75% of the amount paid in a building society account in the joint names of it and the customer. The Commissioners issued an assessment charging tax on the work in question and the company appealed, contending that the money placed in the joint account had been paid to it before 1 June 1984 for the purposes of what is now *VATA 1994, s 6(4)*. The tribunal accepted this contention and allowed the company's appeal, holding that although the company had voluntarily placed the money in a joint account, the payment remained the company's property. *Key Kitchens Ltd*, LON/85/228 (VTD 2261).

[62.429] The decision in *Key Kitchens Ltd*, 62.428 above, was applied in the similar case of *S Rankin (t/a RDR Construction)*, BEL/88/5 (VTD 3623).

Money paid into builder's deposit account for subsequent release

[62.430] In May 1984 a development company borrowed £600,000 from a bank to finance the refurbishment of some flats. It paid the £600,000 into a deposit account at the same bank, in the name of the building company which was to carry out the work. The money was held in the deposit account subject to the condition that it could not be transferred into the building company's current account until the work carried out had been verified by architect's certificates. None of the money was transferred in this way until after 31 May 1984, when building alterations became liable to VAT at 15%. The Commissioners issued an assessment charging tax on the work. The QB allowed the company's appeal, holding that payment had taken place before 1 June 1984 so that the work was zero-rated. The CA upheld this decision. Although the payment was made under arrangements which restricted the recipients' use of the money received, it discharged the contractual liability of the development company to the building company, and left the building company with no right to sue for payment. *C & E Commrs v Dormers Builders (London) Ltd*, CA [1989] STC 539; [1989] 2 All ER 938.

[62.431] Similar decisions were reached in *C & E Commrs v Nevisbrook Ltd*, CA [1989] STC 539; [1989] 2 All ER 938, and *DL Rhodes*, MAN/87/339 (VTD 2883).

Advance payments for time-share accommodation

[62.432] A company which constructed time-share lodges received advance payments from potential purchasers. These payments were refundable if the accommodation was not completed by a specified date. The company failed to account for tax on such payments and the Commissioners issued an assessment on the basis that tax was chargeable at the time the payment was made. The tribunal dismissed the company's appeal. *Clowance plc*, LON/87/103 (VTD 2541).

Advance payment received by vehicle manufacturers

[62.433] See *Marquiss of Scotland*, 52.145 PENALTIES: MISDECLARATION.

Advance payments for theatre bookings

[62.434] A company which operated a theatre did not account for tax on ticket sales until the time of the performance in question, even where payment had been made in advance of the performance. Money received for advance sales was kept in a deposit account until the time of the performance, at which time it was transferred to a current account and an agreed percentage was paid to the producer of the play. The Commissioners issued an assessment on the basis that the company should have accounted for tax at the time when it received payment. The company appealed, contending that since it might have to refund the money if the performance were to be cancelled, it should not be required to account for tax until the performance had actually taken place. The QB rejected this contention and upheld the assessment. The terms of the sale of the ticket did not give the customer any proprietary interest in the money paid and received for the theatre performance, so that output tax was due at the time of payment. Furthermore, even if the customers had had an equitable interest in the money paid, the payment would still be an advance payment in respect of a supply and would still give rise to output tax liability. *C & E Commrs v Richmond Theatre Management Ltd*, QB [1995] STC 257.

Advance payments for concerts

[62.435] See *Regular Music Ltd*, 52.145 PENALTIES: MISDECLARATION.

Advance payments for football matches

[62.436] A football club required all spectators to purchase tickets in advance. It sold 'season books' which contained a total of 82 numbered vouchers. 40 of these provided for admission to specific matches, 20 were for use when applying for tickets for away matches, and the remaining 22 were for use when applying for tickets for Cup matches or friendly matches. It also sold more restricted 'season books', which only provided for admission to 16 or 18 league matches. In accounting for VAT, the club treated the vouchers as falling within *VATA 1994, Sch 6 para 5*, so that it only accounted for output tax when the vouchers were presented by the purchasers on a match-by-match basis. The Commissioners issued a ruling that VAT was chargeable on the amount paid for the 'season books' at the time of their purchase, by virtue of *VATA 1994, s 6(4)*. The tribunal upheld the Commissioners' ruling and dismissed the club's appeal. *Celtic plc*, [1997] VATDR 111 (VTD 14762).

Advance royalties

[62.437] See *Software One Ltd*, 52.146 PENALTIES: MISDECLARATION.

Advance payment for construction of oil rig

[62.438] A company (T) entered into a contract to construct an oil rig for a customer. The customer made an advance payment of £800,000, and T did not account for VAT on this payment. The Commissioners issued an assessment on the basis that VAT was chargeable at the time when the £800,000 was paid. The tribunal upheld the assessment and dismissed T's appeal, holding that the payment was consideration and that, in accordance with what is now *VATA 1994, s 6(4)*, the tax point occurred when the payment was received. *THC Fabricators (UK) Ltd*, MAN/92/659 (VTD 11414).

Advance payments for landscape gardening services

[62.439] A company failed to account for tax on advance payments for landscape gardening services. The Commissioners issued an assessment charging tax on the payments, and the tribunal dismissed the company's appeal. *Landscape Management Construction Ltd*, LON/99/961 (VTD 17131).

Deposits

Sale of furniture—rate of tax increased after payment of deposit

[62.440] A company which manufactured furniture had received deposits for a number of items of furniture before 18 June 1979, but had not delivered the furniture in question. On 18 June 1979 the standard rate of VAT was increased from 8% to 15%. The company only accounted for VAT on 8% on furniture for which it had held deposits at 18 June, although the items were not delivered and paid for until after 18 June. The Commissioners issued an assessment on the basis that only the deposits could properly be treated as taxable at 8%, and that the balance of the payments in question were taxable at 15%. The tribunal dismissed the company's appeal, holding that, by virtue of what is now *VATA 1994, s 6(4)*, the tax point for the deposit was the time when it was paid, but the tax point for the remainder of the payment was when the furniture was delivered. The tribunal also held that there was a taxable supply when the deposit was paid, even if the customer did not complete the purchase. *JD Fox Ltd*, LON/80/237 (VTD 1012).

Deposits for holiday accommodation

[62.441] A couple who provided accommodation in holiday flats failed to account for VAT on deposits for such accommodation. The Commissioners issued an assessment charging tax on the deposits and the tribunal dismissed the couple's appeal. The deposit was a payment in respect of a supply, within what is now *VATA 1994, s 6(4)*. *MH & ST Caine*, LON/86/440 (VTD 2398).

(*Note.* The decision was approved by the QB in *Moonraker's Guest House Ltd*, **62.443** below.)

[62.442] A similar decision was reached in *G Thompson*, MAN/87/112 (VTD 2666).

[62.443] A company which provided holiday accommodation failed to account for VAT on deposits. The Commissioners issued an assessment charging tax on the deposits and the company appealed, contending that it regarded the deposits as fully refundable and as remaining the property of its customers. The QB rejected this contention and upheld the assessment. Whether the deposits remained the property of the payer was a question of law. On the evidence, the deposits formed part payment of the total price payable, and thus did not remain the property of the payer. *C & E Commrs v Moonraker's Guest House Ltd*, QB [1992] STC 544.

Deposits for fitted kitchen units

[62.444] A company which supplied fitted kitchen units required payment of a deposit by customers when an order was signed, but did not account for VAT on these deposits until the units were delivered. The Commissioners issued an assessment on the basis that tax should have been accounted for when the deposit was received. The tribunal dismissed the company's appeal, holding that a deposit constituted payment in respect of a supply, within what is now

VATA 1994, s 6(4). Bethway & Moss Ltd, MAN/86/331 (VTD 2667). (*Note.* The decision was approved by the QB in *Moonraker's Guest House Ltd*, **62.443** above.)

Deposits received by shopfitters

[62.445] A shopfitting firm generally took deposits of 50% of the agreed price, but did not account for tax on the deposits. The Commissioners issued an assessment on the basis that tax should have been accounted for when the deposit was received. The tribunal dismissed the firm's appeal, applying *Bethway & Moss Ltd*, **62.444** above. *Regalstar Enterprises*, LON/88/197 (VTD 3102).

Deposits received by company manufacturing sails

[62.446] A company which manufactured sails charged customers deposits, which were refundable in certain circumstances. The company did not account for VAT on the deposits, and the Commissioners issued an assessment. The tribunal dismissed the company's appeal, applying *Bethway & Moss Ltd*, **62.444** above, and *Regalstar Enterprises*, **62.445** above. *Bruce Banks Sails Ltd*, [1990] VATTR 175 (VTD 4896).

Deposits for bathroom furniture

[62.447] A company which sold bathroom furniture did not account for tax until sales were completed, although it frequently received deposits from customers. The Commissioners issued an assessment on the basis that the company should have accounted for tax when it received the deposits. The tribunal dismissed the company's appeal, applying *Regalstar Enterprises*, **62.445** above, *Bruce Banks Sails Ltd*, **62.446** above, and *Purshotam M Pattni & Sons*, **62.387** above. The deposit was a payment in respect of a supply, within what is now *VATA 1994, s 6(4)*. *Bristol Bathroom Co*, LON/89/571Z (VTD 5340).

Deposits for furniture

[62.448] A company failed to account for output tax on deposits for the supply of furniture. The Commissioners issued an assessment on the basis that the supply took place when the deposit was paid. The tribunal dismissed the company's appeal, applying *Bethway & Moss Ltd*, **62.444** above. *UNO Upholstery Superstores Ltd*, MAN/93/1493 (VTD 13036).

Deposits for machine tools

[62.449] A company which supplied machine tools failed to account for VAT on deposits. The Commissioners issued an assessment charging tax on the deposits, and the tribunal dismissed the company's appeal, applying *Bethway & Moss Ltd*, **62.444** above, and *East Kilbride Golf Club*, **62.420** above. The deposits were received in respect of taxable supplies. *Rivers Machinery Ltd*, LON/91/542X (VTD 7505). (*Note.* An appeal against a misdeclaration penalty was allowed. Compare the cases noted at **52.142** and **52.143** PENALTIES: MISDECLARATION.)

Deposits received for entertainment functions

[62.450] A trader promoted entertainment functions, for which he received deposits. He did not account for output tax on the deposits. The Commissioners issued an assessment, including a charge to default interest, on the basis that the trader should have accounted for output tax at the time of receipt of the deposits. The tribunal upheld the assessment and dismissed the trader's appeal, applying the QB decision in *Moonraker's Guest House Ltd*, 62.443 above. *MJ Kirtley (t/a Encore International)*, MAN/93/1350 (VTD 12471).

Company operating hotel—deposits received for receptions, etc

[62.451] A company operated a hotel. It failed to account for output tax on deposits received for wedding receptions and similar functions. The Commissioners issued an assessment, including a charge to default interest, on the basis that the company should have accounted for output tax at the time of receipt of the deposits. The tribunal upheld the assessment and dismissed the company's appeal, applying the QB decision in *Moonraker's Guest House Ltd*, 62.443 above. *Hollybourne Hotels Ltd*, LON/01/592 (VTD 17486).

Sale of sports cars—whether initial deposit within VATA 1994, s 6(4)

[62.452] A company had a franchise to sell Ferrari sports cars. There was a limited supply of such cars, and the company asked prospective customers to make an initial deposit of about £5,000. When a firm order was placed, the customer was asked to increase the deposit to 10% of the price of the car. The company did not account for VAT on the initial deposits, and the Commissioners issued an assessment charging tax on these. The company appealed, contending that the initial deposits did not relate to any definite supply, and that there was no tax point until a firm order was placed and a 10% deposit was received. The tribunal accepted this contention and allowed the appeal, holding that the initial deposit did not create any contractual relationship, but it was only 'an agreement to make an agreement'. *Nigel Mansell Sports Co Ltd*, LON/90/613Y (VTD 6116).

'Security deposit' for lease of expensive car

[62.453] A company purchased a Mercedes McLaren car for £300,000. It leased it to a customer for two years. The customer was required to drive the car for no more than 20,000 miles and to pay a 'security deposit' of £200,000, as well as rental payments totalling £47,999. The company accounted for output tax on the rental payments but did not account for tax on the 'security deposit'. Customs issued a ruling that it was required to account for VAT on the 'security deposit' of £200,000 when it was paid. The tribunal allowed the company's appeal, holding that 'this arrangement was, in substance, the same as an ordinary car leasing agreement by which a lessor acquires a vehicle, lets it to a customer for a certain period, and then either lets it to another customer or sells it'. *Cross Border Lease Management Ltd*, MAN/06/237 (VTD 19853).

Miscellaneous

Accountant transferring money from clients' account to working account

[62.454] An accountant transferred sums of money from his clients' account to his working account without issuing VAT invoices. The Commissioners issued an assessment on the basis that the transfer of the money constituted its receipt by the accountant and, by virtue of what is now *VATA 1994, s 6(4)*, was therefore to be treated as the time of supply. The tribunal upheld the assessment and dismissed the accountant's appeal. *MR Ghaus (t/a Ghaus & Co)*, LON/89/1217 (VTD 4999).

[62.455] A similar decision was reached in a subsequent appeal by the same accountant. *MR Ghaus (t/a Ghaus & Co)*, LON/91/950 (VTD 10419).

Tax consultants receiving payment after registration for work done earlier

[62.456] A firm of tax consultants registered for VAT in October 1986. Earlier in that year they had invoiced a client for work done, but had not received payment and eventually wrote the amount off as a bad debt. In 1991 the client contacted the firm again to ask them to carry out further work. The firm requested payment of the previous debt and the client paid the outstanding amount. The Commissioners issued a ruling that the payment was liable to VAT by virtue of what is now *VAT Regulations 1995 (SI 1995/2518), reg 90*, and the firm appealed. The CA allowed the appeal (by a 2–1 majority, Sir Ralph Gibson LJ dissenting). Staughton LJ held that since the supply had taken place before the firm had registered for VAT, it was not then a 'taxable person' within what is now *VATA 1994, s 4(1)*. The question of whether there had been a chargeable transaction had to be determined at the time when the supply was actually made, and the provisions of what is now *VATA 1994, s 6* only applied if there was a charge to tax within the ordinary meaning of *s 4(1)**. Ward LJ held that 'the fictions for determining the time of supply for accounting purposes' do not 'govern the ordinary meaning of the language in (*VATA 1994, s 4**) which make supply by a taxable person a prerequisite of liability'. What is now *VATA 1994, s 6** only determined when, rather than whether, a supply was chargeable to VAT. *Dicta* of the tribunal in *Broadwell Land plc*, 36.636 INPUT TAX, approved and applied. *BJ Rice & Associates v C & E Commrs*, CA [1996] STC 581. (*Notes.* (1) Compare, however, the subsequent HL decision in *Svenska International plc*, **43.20** MANAGEMENT SERVICES, where the HL held that there was no supply until there was an invoice or a payment. (2) For a subsequent application for costs, see **2.456** APPEALS.)

Overpayments by telephone subscribers credited to next accounts

[62.457] In cases where customers of British Telecom (BT) made overpayments, BT retained the amounts overpaid and credited them to the customers' next accounts, unless the customers requested repayment of the amounts involved. It accounted for VAT on the amounts it had invoiced, and thus did not account for any VAT on the overpayments until the issue of an invoice against which they could be set. The Commissioners issued an assessment, charging tax of more than £2,600,000, on the basis that the receipt of the overpayments constituted a tax point for VAT purposes, and that BT should have accounted for VAT accordingly. BT appealed, contending that the overpayments were accidental and did not constitute consideration for any supply. The tribunal allowed the appeal, holding that an accidental overpayment, which was paid 'under mistake of fact', 'lacked the consensual element required for consideration', and that BT could not 'convert a payment made under a mistake into consideration simply by crediting it to the customer's account'. The CA upheld this decision. Millett LJ held that, for a payment to represent consideration for a supply of services, there had to be a 'direct link' with the service provided. The inadvertent overpayment of a current debt was not a payment on account of a future liability. It was not paid on account of, or in respect of, future supplies. Under English law the recipient of an accidental overpayment was under an immediate obligation to repay it. A creditor could not appropriate a payment to a debt unless that debt was presently due and payable. There was no payment in respect of future supplies until the relevant invoice was issued. *C & E Commrs v British Telecommunications plc*, CA [1996] STC 818; [1996] 1 WLR 1309.

Unredeemed activity vouchers—time of supply

[62.458] A company supplied 'activity vouchers', giving holders the right to participate in a specific activity such as gliding, parachuting or skydiving. It accounted for output tax on its supplies of the vouchers. About 18% of the vouchers which it issued were never redeemed. In September 2000 the company submitted a repayment claim on the basis that it need not have accounted for output tax in cases where customers failed to redeem the vouchers. The Commissioners rejected the claim on the basis that the company was supplying a right to receive services, so that the effect of *VATA 1994, s 6(4)* was that the tax point was the time of payment. The tribunal upheld the Commissioners' ruling and dismissed the company's appeal. *Acorne Sports Ltd*, LON/02/254 (VTD 18009).

[62.459] A similar decision was reached in *Tayside Aviation Ltd*, EDN/02/152 (VTD 18241).

Avoidance scheme operated by group of companies—time of supply

[62.460] See *Thorn Materials Supply Ltd*, **32.17** GROUPS OF COMPANIES.

Stolen takings

[62.461] See *Benton*, **62.382** above, and the cases noted at **62.383** and **62.384** above.

Retail sales by mail order

[62.462] A company supplied goods by mail order, requiring payment in advance but allowing customers 14 days in which they could return the goods if they were dissatisfied. In accounting for VAT, the company took the view that the goods were supplied 'on approval or sale or return or similar terms', within *VATA 1994, s 6(2)(c)*, and that the time of supply should be taken as 14 days after the delivery of the goods. Customs issued an assessment on the basis that the time of supply was when payment was received, within *VATA 1994, s 6(4)*. The tribunal upheld the assessment and dismissed the company's appeal, applying the principles laid down in *Littlewoods Organisa-*

tion plc, 62.393 above, and *Robertson's Electrical Ltd*, **62.464** below. *Grattan plc (No 2)*, MAN/05/175 (VTD 19515). (*Note.* Costs were awarded to Customs.)

[62.463] The decision in *Grattan plc (No 2)*, 62.462 above, was applied in the similar subsequent case of *Compton & Woodhouse Ltd*, LON/05/1156 (VTD 20551).

Retail sales by internet

[62.464] A company sold electrical goods. It made several sales by the internet. In the case of such sales, it did not account for output tax until seven days after delivery. The Commissioners issued an assessment on the basis that the company was required to account for tax as soon as the goods were delivered. The company appealed, contending that the goods were supplied 'on approval', so that the effect of *VATA 1994, s 6(2)(c)* was that it was not required to account for tax until 'the time when it becomes certain that the supply has taken place'. The CS unanimously rejected this contention and upheld the assessment. Lord Gill held that 'the provisions relating to payment, ordering and returns' all indicated that 'the nature of the online transaction is one of outright sale'. The company's 'terms and conditions have the effect that there is a concluded sale, although it is subject to the purchaser's statutory right to annul it'. The fact that payment must be made when the order was placed indicated that *s 6(2)(c)* could not apply to the transaction. The supply took place on the making of the online payment, by virtue of *VATA 1994, s 6(4)*. *C & E Commrs v Robertson's Electrical Ltd*, CS 2005, [2007] STC 612; [2005] CSIH 75.

Supplies of water, gas, etc. (VAT Regulations 1995, reg 86)

Continuous supplies—supplier going into administration

[62.465] A company (E) made continuous supplies of gas and electricity. In October 2001 it went into administration. It entered into a 'netting agreement' with another company (M), in respect of supplies which it had made to M and received from M. In July 2002 M made a payment of £655,000 to E's administrator (P) in respect of supplies made by E under this agreement. P considered that M owed substantially more than this, but accounted for output tax on this payment in its accounting period ending 30 September 2002. In the return, P also reclaimed input tax in respect of E's transactions with M, so that the return claimed a net repayment. Customs subsequently discovered that M had reclaimed input tax of more than £6,000,000 in respect of its transactions with E. They issued an assessment on E charging output tax on the amount by which the input tax reclaimed by M exceeded the output tax which E had actually accounted for. E appealed, contending that the effect of *VAT Regulations 1995 (SI 1995/2518), reg 86* was that it was only required to account for output tax on the amount actually paid by M, and that the return had been correct. The tribunal accepted this contention and allowed E's appeal. Customs appealed to the Ch D, which disapproved the tribunal's reasoning, but dismissed Customs' appeal on the grounds that the assessment had been raised for the wrong period, and was therefore invalid. Lightman J held that the effect of the agreement between M and E was that the balance had become due on 21 February 2002. He observed that it was 'highly unsatisfactory that recovery of VAT turns upon the Commissioners determining correctly and within a limited period of time the date on which a supply (or payment) is made. The taxpayer (who is possessed of the relevant information) may not be forthcoming in disclosing his hand (as the taxpayer was not forthcoming until a late date in this case); and even when and where the facts are clear, a difficult and contentious issue of law may arise (as it does in this case). Fairness to other taxpayers who pay their tax may require steps to be taken to remove (at any rate in cases such as the present) serious (and on occasion insurmountable) hurdles to the recovery of VAT which is unquestionably due and should be paid.' *HMRC v Enron Europe Ltd*, Ch D [2006] STC 1339; [2006] EWHC 824 (Ch). (*Note.* For subsequent developments in this case, see **3.82** ASSESSMENT.)

Continuous supplies of services (VAT Regulations 1995, reg 90)

Rental payments between associated companies—time of supply

[62.466] A company (C) made regular payments of rent to an associated company (D). On 7 April 1992 the companies' directors reviewed the accounting period ending 31 December 1991, considered that the rental payments had been inadequate, and decided to charge an additional rent for that period of £6,000,000. This was entered in the companies' accounts, but the companies did not account for VAT. A VAT officer discovered this at a control visit in December 1992. Following his visit, D issued an invoice to C on 16 December for £6,000,000 plus VAT. The invoice was backdated to 30 November (to enable C to claim the VAT as input tax in its return for that period). The Commissioners issued an assessment and a misdeclaration penalty on the basis that the time of the supply had been 7 April 1992, when the companies' directors had agreed to make the payment. D appealed, contending that the time of supply was 30 November, being the date on the invoice. The tribunal held on the evidence that the payment was within what is now *VAT Regulations 1995 (SI 1995/2518), reg 90* as being for a continuous supply of services, and therefore that the time of supply was 16 December, the date on which the invoice was actually issued. The tribunal therefore allowed D's appeal, while criticising the directors' conduct in having backdated the invoice, and observing that an award of costs was inappropriate. *Diggor Gaylord Ltd; CP Holdings Ltd*, LON/93/536A (VTD 11380).

Management services—time of supply

[62.467] See *Legal & Contractual Services Ltd*, **43.1** MANAGEMENT SERVICES; *Pentex Oil Ltd*, **43.2** MANAGEMENT SERVICES; *Bishop & Knight Ltd*, **43.3** MANAGEMENT SERVICES; *Missionfine Ltd*, **43.5** MANAGEMENT SERVICES; *Waverley Housing Management Ltd*, **43.6** MANAGEMENT SERVICES; *Svenska International plc*, **43.20** MANAGEMENT SERVICES, and *Cater Clark Ltd*, **52.113** PENALTIES: MISDECLARATION.

Accountancy services—whether a continuous supply of services within regulation 90*

[62.468] An accountancy partnership (H) employed a VAT consultant, and hired his services to a number of associated partnerships. H did not issue a formal VAT invoice for the consultant's services, and did not request payment from its associated partnerships until after the end of its financial year. The Commissioners imposed a misdeclaration penalty, considering that H should have accounted for VAT when the consultant's services were supplied. H appealed, contending firstly that the consultant's services were continuous supplies within what is now *VAT Regulations 1995 (SI 1995/2518), reg 90*, and alternatively that it had a reasonable excuse for having treated the consultant's services as a continuous supply on which payment of VAT could be delayed. The tribunal held that the services were not within *reg 90*, and that the supplies had taken place at the time when the services were performed. (However, the tribunal allowed the appeal against the penalty, holding that H had a reasonable excuse for the misdeclaration.) *Halpern & Woolf*, LON/92/40Y (VTD 10072).

Car hire—time of supply

[62.469] A company (M) operated a fleet of motor cars. It agreed with another company (D) that, in return for payment from D, it would make such cars available to motorists who had lost the use of their own cars as a result of an accident. D described itself as an insurance company, but was not an authorised motor insurer, and M had a block insurance policy with an authorised insurer. The Commissioners issued a ruling that the arrangements between D and M resulted in separate supplies each time an individual vehicle was hired, with the result that there was a tax point at the end of each hire period. M appealed, contending that the effect of the arrangements was that there was a continuous supply, so that VAT was only payable when payment was received or when an invoice was issued. The tribunal allowed M's appeal, holding that there was a continuous supply and that the tax point fell to be determined under what is now *VAT Regulations 1995 (SI 1995/2518), reg 90*. *Motor & Legal Group Ltd*, MAN/93/896 (VTD 12036). (*Note.* An alternative contention by M, that part of the consideration should be treated as being for insurance and as exempt from VAT under what is now *VATA 1994, Sch 9, Group 2*, was rejected—see **38.2** INSURANCE.)

Continuous supplies—whether supplier obliged to issue invoices

[62.470] A company (F) agreed to provide another company (E) with telecommunications services, in return for specified payments. E fell into arrears with its payments. F continued to provide the relevant services, but did not issue invoices, because issuing invoices would have obliged it to account for output tax on the supplies. E subsequently went into receivership, and its receivers took proceedings against F, claiming that F was obliged to issue a VAT invoice. The Ch D rejected this contention and dismissed the proceedings, holding that E had no reasonable cause of action. Neither the specific terms of the contract, nor the *VAT Regulations*, obliged F to issue a VAT invoice for the supplies in question. *VAT Regulations, reg 13(1)* imposed a requirement to provide a VAT invoice upon a person who made a taxable supply. The making of the taxable supply must, therefore, precede, or be contemporaneous with, the arising of the obligation. Under the rules for continuous supplies of services, F only made a taxable supply to E when it received payment or issued a VAT invoice. On the evidence, it was clear that E would not make a payment in respect of the services which F supplied. (Ferris J observed that, if F had issued a VAT invoice, the receivers would not have paid the amount shown on the invoice, since F was an unsecured creditor, but would have sought credit for input tax, thereby increasing the amount payable to E's debenture-holder.) *Europhone International Ltd v Frontel Communications Ltd*, Ch D [2001] STC 1399.

Continuous supplies of services—payments received after liquidation

[62.471] See *Glenshane Construction Services Ltd (in liquidation)*, 37.18 INSOLVENCY.

Royalties and similar payments (VAT Regulations 1995, reg 91)

[62.472] A company carried on the business of supplying milk and other grocery products from two depots. It agreed to transfer the operation of one of the depots to a franchisee in return for a royalty of one penny per pint on all milk sold from that depot. The company did not account for tax on payments received under that agreement, and the Commissioners issued an assessment charging tax on such receipts. The company appealed, contending that the receipts should not be subject to VAT since they were, in effect, for the sale of milk, which was zero-rated. The tribunal dismissed the appeal, holding that tax was chargeable on the royalties by virtue of what is now *VAT Regulations 1995 (SI 1995/2518), reg 91*. *Ron Miller Ltd*, LON/90/1191Z (VTD 5827). (*Note.* For another issue in this case, see 36.183 INPUT TAX.)

[62.473] In July 2000 a company (O) was awarded 'preferred bidder' status in relation to a Home Office Private Finance Initiative project. In April 2001 it agreed to withdraw from the project in favour of another company (N), under an agreement whereby N's major shareholder (B) agreed to pay O £3,300,000 'on the completion date of the project or 36 months after the date of the closure', and agreed to indemnify O's creditors up to an agreed 'cap' of £1,255,388. The project was completed in March 2002, and in April 2002 O invoiced B for £577,931 (plus VAT) in respect of the indemnity agreement. In January 2004 it invoiced B for £3,300,000 (plus VAT). Customs formed the opinion that O should have invoiced B for a further £677,457 under the indemnity agreement. In April 2004 they issued an assessment on the basis that the tax point under the indemnity agreement had taken place at the time the services were performed, in April 2001. The company appealed, contending that the full amount of the consideration was not ascertainable at the time when it performed the service of withdrawing from the project, and that the time of supply was governed by *VAT Regulations 1995 (SI 1995/2518), reg 91*. The tribunal reviewed the evidence in detail, accepted this contention and allowed the appeal. The tribunal observed that the 'April 2001 agreements were poorly drafted' but found that 'the parties intended that a significant part of the consideration would only become payable if there was a successful close of the project which conformed with the overall expectations of the parties'. *AGP (2001) Ltd*, LON/05/276 (VTD 20020).

Supplies by barristers and advocates (VAT Regulations 1995, reg 92)

[62.474] A barrister became liable to register for VAT in May 1987, but did not do so until November 1988. He appealed against a penalty under what is now *VATA 1994, s 67*, contending that he had assumed that fees which he had received could be spread over earlier years, and that what is now *VAT Regulations 1995 (SI 1995/2518), reg 92*, which provided that services supplied by barristers were to be treated as taking place on receipt of the relevant fees, was *ultra vires*. The tribunal rejected this contention and dismissed his appeal, observing that 'a barrister who was in practice throughout the period from the introduction of VAT in 1973 until 1988 should have made himself familiar with the provisions relating to the way VAT should be accounted for to the Customs & Excise by members of the Bar'. The tribunal held that *regulation 92** was valid and properly made. (The tribunal also observed that an incorrect view of the law did not provide a barrister with a reasonable excuse for failing to register.) *JD Seal*, LON/89/1200X (VTD 4586).

Supplies in the construction industry (VAT Regulations 1995, reg 93)

[62.475] A college wished to construct three new buildings. On the advice of an accountancy firm, it entered into a complex series of transactions involving the incorporation of two subsidiary companies, one of which (D) was registered for VAT and the other (P) was not. In 1997 the college granted P a 15-year lease of the site of the development. P and D then signed an agreement for D to perform construction services on the land. In its first VAT return, D claimed a substantial repayment, declaring inputs of more than £2,700,000 and one output of £50,000 (a 'stage payment' from P). In response to an enquiry from the Commissioners, D explained that it 'had been established with a view to "drip feeding" the VAT charges so delaying tax points'. The Commissioners made the repayment claimed. In 1998 D offered P £100,000 for its leasehold (and £1 for its 'assets, liabilities and obligations'). When the Commissioners discovered this, they issued an assessment under *VAT Regulations 1995, reg 93(1)(a)* on the basis that the assignment of the lease represented the payment of non-monetary consideration. The assessment was computed on the basis that the value of the construction services supplied by D was the total costs of more than £3,300,000 which it had incurred prior to the assignment, plus 2%, minus £100,000 which it had invoiced to P (of which £50,000 had been paid). D appealed. The tribunal reviewed the evidence in detail and upheld the assessment, holding that the transfer of the lease constituted payment of non-monetary consideration for the construction services supplied by D, since there was 'the necessary direct link between the assignment of the lease and the performance of the construction services'. The tribunal observed that 'it would be absurd if accepting a cheque for a sum due for services was receipt of payment but an agreement to accept an asset in return for discharging the liability to pay the sum was not receipt of payment. The reality is that (D) took an assignment of the lease in return for paying £100,000 and discharging (P) from the liability to make any further payment for the work done by the appellant for (P). The lease was non-monetary consideration. The value attributed by the parties to the lease was the amount of the liability discharged plus £100,000. The receipt of that non-monetary consideration constituted the receipt of "payment" by the appellant within *regulation 93(1)(a)'. Cross Levels Developments Ltd*, [2004] VATDR 248 (VTD 18689).

The place of the supply (VATA 1994, s 7)

Place of supply of goods

Machine tools manufactured overseas but assembled and installed in UK

[62.476] A company traded as a selling agent on behalf of a number of overseas manufacturers of machine tools, and received commission based on the value of the machine tools ordered. The company did not account for tax on this commission, and the Commissioners issued an assessment charging output tax. The company appealed, contending that the goods were supplied outside the UK (and thus were zero-rated under the legislation then in force). The tribunal allowed the appeal, holding that, by virtue of what is now *VATA 1994, s 7(7)*, the machine tools were to be treated as supplied outside the UK. The tribunal distinguished *Azo-Maschinenfabrik Adolf Zimmerman*, **22.193** EUROPEAN COMMUNITY LAW, holding that 'there is no rule of law compelling, or enabling, any court to construe a pre-existing statute of the United Kingdom in order to comply with a Directive subsequent in time, where the legislature or executive of the United Kingdom has not implemented that Directive'. *George Kuikka Ltd*, [1990] VATTR 185 (VTD 5037).

Purchase of yacht moored in Greece—place of supply

[62.477] See *Da Conti International Ltd*, **36.670** INPUT TAX.

Whether cars sold in Germany or UK

[62.478] A jeweller sold two Peugeot cars, one to a German and one to a resident of Scotland. The Commissioners issued an assessment charging tax on the sales. The jeweller appealed, contending that the sales had taken place in Germany and were thus outside the scope of UK VAT. The tribunal accepted the jeweller's evidence and allowed the appeal. *JR Joannides*, MAN/91/1338 (VTD 11373). (*Note.* For another issue in this case, see **36.433** INPUT TAX.)

Goods sold on board ships

[62.479] A company operated a ferry from Portsmouth to Spain. It sold various goods to passengers. The Commissioners issued a ruling that VAT was chargeable on the sales, on the basis that the place of supply was the UK. The company appealed, contending that the effect of *Article 8(1)(c)* of the *EC Sixth*

Directive was that VAT should not be charged on sales made when the ferry was outside EC territorial waters. The tribunal rejected this contention and dismissed the appeal, and the QB upheld this decision. Lightman J held that *Article 8(1)(c)* was 'clear and unambiguous'. Its effect was that, in the absence of a stop in a third territory, 'in the case of goods supplied between the first point of passenger embarkation within the Community and the last point of disembarkation within the Community, the place of supply of goods shall be deemed to be the first point of passenger embarkation, and this general rule operates irrespective of the fact that in the course of the journey between the two points the ship travels through territorial waters or the high seas'. Accordingly, 'on intra-Community sailings supplies of goods made on the high seas outside the territory of Member States fall within the scope of VAT'. *Peninsular & Oriental Steam Navigation Company v C & E Commrs*, QB [2000] STC 488.

Place of supply of services

Place where supplier belongs (VATA 1994, ss 7(10), 9(2))

Accountancy services

[62.480] An accountancy firm supplied services to a company which traded in Jamaica but had its registered office in the UK. It did not account for output tax on these supplies. The Commissioners issued an assessment charging tax on them, and the firm appealed, contending that the services were supplied outside the UK and thus were zero-rated under the legislation then in force. The tribunal dismissed the appeal, holding that the company's registered office was a 'fixed establishment' for the purpose of what is now *VATA 1994, s 9(2)*. Accordingly, the place of supply was in the UK. *Binder Hamlyn*, [1983] VATTR 171 (VTD 1439).

[62.481] Similar decisions were reached in *Vincent Consultants Ltd*, [1988] VATTR 152 (VTD 3091); *Singer & Friedlander Ltd*, [1989] VATTR 27 (VTD 3274); *Chantrey Vellacott*, [1992] VATTR 138 (VTD 7311) and *A Marks (t/a Marks Cameron Davies & Co)*, LON/95/1773 (VTD 15541).

Management services

[62.482] A UK-resident company (S) was the parent company of thirteen investment companies resident in Monaco but incorporated in the UK and having their registered offices in the UK. The subsidiary companies owned property in the UK, from which they received rental income. S supplied the services of accounting and administrative staff to the investment companies, and did not account for tax on these supplies. The Commissioners issued an assessment charging tax on them, and S appealed, contending that the supplies were supplies of staff within what is now *VATA 1994, Sch 5 para 6*, so that the supplies took place outside the UK and were zero-rated under the legislation then in force. The tribunal rejected this contention and dismissed the appeal, holding that the services were general management services, rather than simply the supply of staff. Each of the investment companies had a fixed establishment in the UK for the purpose of what is now *VATA 1994, s 9(2)*, and the staff were used to administer and collect rent from properties in the UK. Accordingly, the place of supply was in the UK. *Strollmoor Ltd*, LON/90/1506X (VTD 5454).

[62.483] The company in the case noted at **62.482** above appealed against a subsequent assessment charging tax on supplies of management services to its Monaco subsidiaries. The tribunal dismissed the appeal. *Strollmoor Ltd (No 2)*, LON/94/632A (VTD 12765). (*Note*. An alternative contention by the company, that the assessment was out of time and invalid, was also rejected.)

[62.484] A UK company supplied management services for its US parent. HMRC issued an assessment on the basis that the effect of *VATA 1994, s 7(10)* was that the place of supply was in the UK. The company appealed, contending that the services should be treated as being where its customer belonged, which was in the USA. The tribunal rejected this contention and dismissed the appeal, holding that the company was making 'single indivisible economic supplies' which did not fall within *Article 9(2)(a) or (e) of the EC Sixth Directive*. The Ch D upheld this decision. Proudman J held that 'there was a single indivisible economic supply which it would be artificial to split', and that the company was undertaking 'a management function going much further than consultancy activities'. *American Express Services Europe Ltd v HMRC*, Ch D [2010] STC 1023; [2010] EWHC 120 (Ch).

[62.485] A Japanese bank incorporated a UK subsidiary (E). HMRC issued a ruling that E was required to account for VAT on its supplies to its Japanese parent. E appealed, contending that it was supplying consultancy services within *VATA 1994, Sch 5 para 3*, so that the supplies should be treated as taking place in Japan. The tribunal rejected this contention and dismissed E's appeal, holding on the evidence that E's supplies were 'an integral part of the management control process' and were not 'services of consultants or consultancy bureaux'. Accordingly the place of supply was in the UK. *Sumitomo Mitsui Banking Corporation Europe Ltd v HMRC (No 1)*, [2009] UKFTT 121 (TC), TC00089. (*Note*. The company subsequently applied for costs—see **2.504** APPEALS.)

Payroll services

[62.486] A UK company (F) supplied payroll services to a Guernsey company. It failed to account for tax on these supplies. Customs issued an assessment charging tax on them, and F appealed, contending that the supplies were within *VATA 1994, Sch 5 para 3*, so that the place of supply was in Guernsey. The tribunal rejected this contention and dismissed the appeal. *Fairpay Ltd*, LON/06/032 (VTD 20455).

'Guardianship' services to overseas parents

[62.487] A company (G) supplied 'guardianship services' to parents resident overseas whose children were being educated at schools in the UK. HMRC issued a ruling that G was required to account for VAT on these supplies. G appealed, contending that it was supplying 'services of consultants', within *VATA 1994, Sch 5 para 3*, so that the place of supply was where the parents were resident, which was outside the EC. The tribunal rejected this contention and dismissed the appeal, holding on the evidence that 'the majority of the disputed services were organisational, administrative or the provision of practical advice. They were not services that a consultant would principally and habitually supply.' *Gabbitas Educational Consultants Ltd v HMRC*, [2009] UKFTT 325 (TC), TC00268.

Television signals transmitted from UK to overseas recipient

[62.488] A Hong Kong company (H) agreed to transmit BBC World Service television to a receiving station in Hong Kong. The Commissioners issued a ruling that VAT was chargeable on these supplies. H company appealed, contending that the supplies should be treated as supplies of engineering services, within what is now *VATA 1994, Sch 5 para 3*, and as taking place outside the UK. The tribunal rejected this contention and dismissed the appeal, holding that the supplies were not within the definition of 'engineering services' and that the place of supply was where the supplier belonged, which was in the UK. *Hutchvision Hong Kong Ltd*, LON/92/2736A (VTD 10509). (*Note*. With regard to the place of supply of telecommunication services, see now *VAT (Place of Supply of Services) Order 1992 (SI 1992/3121), articles 19 and 20, introduced by SI 1997/1524.*)

[62.489] A UK company supplied satellite television broadcasts. The Commissioners issued a ruling that it was required to account for output tax on such supplies to residents of the Irish Republic and the Channel Islands. The company appealed, contending that the services were 'entertainment services', within *Article 9(2)(c)* of the *EC Sixth Directive*, and should be deemed to be supplied where they were received. The tribunal dismissed the appeal, holding that although the services could be described as 'entertainment', they were not within *Article 9(2)(c)* of the *EC Sixth Directive*, which should be construed as 'dealing with the case of the supplier of the service moving between countries'. Entertainment services 'which do not involve performance before a live audience are not covered'. Accordingly, the effect of *Article 9(1)* of the *EC Sixth Directive* was that the services were deemed to be supplied where the supplier was established, which was in the UK. *British Sky Broadcasting Ltd*, [1994] VATTR 1 (VTD 12394). (*Notes*. (1) See now the note following *Hutchvision Hong Kong Ltd*, **62.488** above. (2) The tribunal decision that 'entertainment services which do not involve performance before a live audience are not covered' was specifically disapproved by a subsequent tribunal in *Burrows*, **62.523** below)

Satellite television company—whether carrying on business in UK

[62.490] A company (H), which was incorporated in Hong Kong, provided Chinese-language satellite television programmes to subscribers in Western Europe (including the UK). It had an associated company (C) which operated from premises in the UK, and which assisted in broadcasting the satellite signals to subscribers, providing local news items and editing some of the tapes which H provided. The Commissioners issued a ruling that H was carrying on business in the UK through C as its agent, so that, by virtue of *VATA 1994, s 9(5)*, C was liable to account for output tax on the relevant supplies of broadcasting services. H appealed, contending that it was making the supplies of broadcasting services itself, that it was not carrying on business in the UK, that C was an independent principal acting as a subcontractor rather than an agent, and that by virtue of *VATA 1994, s 7(10)*, the place of supply of the services in question was in Hong Kong. The tribunal accepted H's evidence and allowed its appeal, finding that the greater part of the broadcasting business, such as the selection of programmes and the establishment of timetables, took place in Hong Kong, and holding that the relevant supplies were made from Hong Kong, where H was established. The QB upheld this decision as one of fact. Moses J observed that *Article 9* of the *EC Sixth Directive* 'requires a factual judgment as to whether the service is supplied from a fixed establishment'. *C & E Commrs v The Chinese Channel (Hong Kong) Ltd*, QB [1998] STC 347. (*Note.* For the Commissioners' practice following this decision, see Business Brief 12/98, issued on 21 May 1998.)

Gaming machines

[62.491] See *RAL (Channel Islands) Ltd*, **22.215** EUROPEAN COMMUNITY LAW.

Lease of aircraft

[62.492] A UK company leased a Cessna aircraft to a Jersey company. It did not account for output tax on the consideration, and the Commissioners issued an assessment charging tax thereon. The company appealed, contending that the place of supply was outside the EC so that no output tax was due. The tribunal dismissed the appeal, holding that the effect of what is now *VATA 1994, s 7(10)* was that the supply was to be treated as having taken place in the UK. *IDS Aircraft Ltd*, LON/93/2684 (VTD 12452).

Lease of dental equipment

[62.493] A Guernsey company (H) leased dental equipment to dentists in the UK. Customs issued assessments on the basis that the supplies had been made from a fixed establishment in the UK. The tribunal allowed H's appeal, holding on the evidence that it did not have a fixed establishment in the UK. *Healthcare Leasing Ltd*, [2007] VATDR 494 (VTD 20260).

Hire of trailers

[62.494] A Northern Ireland partnership owned some haulage trailers, which it hired to clients from the Republic of Ireland. The Commissioners issued a ruling that the supplies were liable to UK VAT. The company appealed, contending that by virtue of *VATA 1994, Sch 5 para 7*, the trailers should be treated as being supplied in the Republic of Ireland. The tribunal rejected this contention and dismissed the appeal, holding that *Sch 5* did not apply since the trailers were 'means of transport'. Accordingly, by virtue of *VATA 1994, s 7(10)*, the supplies had taken place in the UK. *Derry Brothers*, LON/00/1323 (VTD 17701).

Advertising services

[62.495] A UK company supplied advertising services to the Spanish Tourist Board. It did not account for output tax on such supplies. The Commissioners issued assessments charging tax on the company, on the basis that the Spanish Tourist Board was not receiving the supplies for the purposes of a business, so that the supplies did not meet the conditions of *Article 16(b)* of the *VAT (Place of Supply of Services) Order*, and the place of supply was therefore in the UK, where the supplier belonged. The company appealed, contending that *Article 16(b)* of the *VAT (Place of Supply of Services) Order 1992 (SI 1992/3121)* was incompatible with *Article 9(2)* of the *EC Sixth Directive*, and that the effect of *Article 9(2)(e)* of the *EC Sixth Directive* was that the supplies should be deemed to have taken place in Spain. The tribunal rejected this contention and upheld the assessments for accounting periods from 1 January 1993, holding that the Spanish Tourist Board had not received the advertising services for the purpose of any business, since it was a government body and its promotion of tourism was 'not an economic activity or a business in the VAT sense of those expressions'. Accordingly the conditions of *Article 16(b)* of the *VAT (Place of Supply of Services) Order* were not satisfied, and the services had to be treated as supplied in the UK, where the supplier was established. Furthermore, the *VAT (Place of Supply of Services) Order* was not incompatible with the *EC Sixth Directive*. The tribunal observed that 'the structure of *Article 9* of the *Directive* is to lay down as a presumptive rule that the member state of origin is to tax supplies of services made by its taxable persons, unless any of the exemptions in *paragraph 2* apply to transfer the right to tax to the member state of receipt'. The fact that the Spanish Tourist Board was registered for VAT in Spain was not conclusive, since it was a state authority within *Article 4(5)* of the *Directive*, rather than a taxable person. The QB upheld this decision. Owen J held that, for *Article 9(2)(e)* of the *Directive* to apply, it was not sufficient for a recipient of the services to be a 'taxable person', but 'he must also receive the service as one who is carrying on an economic activity so that the cost of the services is included in the price of the goods which will bring into operation the reverse charge mechanism'. *Diversified Agency Services Ltd (aka Omnicom UK plc) v C & E Commrs*, QB 1995, [1996] STC 398. (*Notes.* (1) The appeal to the tribunal also concerned periods before 1 January 1993, in respect of which the tribunal allowed the company's appeal, holding that the relevant supplies were zero-rated under the UK legislation then in force. (2) In a subsequent appeal, it was held that the Spanish Tourist Board could not reclaim input tax on the payments—see 36.552 INPUT TAX.)

[62.496] In July 1996 a UK company (B) made a prepayment of £70,000,000 to a company (W), which was in the same VAT group, for advertising services. W arranged to buy in the required services from an associated Guernsey company (P), which in turn obtained the services from an unrelated UK advertising agency. The Commissioners issued an assessment on the basis that W was established in the UK, where it had its registered office, so that B was obliged to account for VAT on the services under the 'reverse charge' procedure. B appealed, contending that W was established in Guernsey, where it carried on business, and that, because B and W were in the same VAT group, no VAT was payable under the legislation then in force. The tribunal accepted this contention and allowed the appeal, holding that 'the fact that the registered office of (W) is in the United Kingdom is not the test of the establishment of (W)', and finding that W had 'established its business in Guernsey'. *British United Provident Association Ltd*, LON/00/250 (VTD 17286). (*Note.* See now *VATA 1994, s 43(2A–2E)*, deriving from *FA 1997*.)

Promotion of tourism

[62.497] The London branch of the Austrian National Tourist Office (ANTO), which was registered for UK VAT, organised two workshops in London, at which it made supplies of services to Austrian businesses. It did not account for output tax in respect of these supplies, treating them as supplies of advertising services which, by virtue of *VAT (Place of Supply of Services) Order 1992 (SI 1992/3121), article 16*, were deemed to be supplied in Austria, where the recipients belonged. The Commissioners issued a ruling that output tax was chargeable on the supplies, on the basis that the supplies were not within the definition of 'advertising services' and that, since the supplies were made from a fixed establishment in the UK, the place of supply was in the UK, where the supplier was established. The tribunal dismissed ANTO's appeal, holding that the definition of an 'advertising service' in *EC Commission v French Republic*, 22.218 EUROPEAN COMMUNITY LAW, should be restricted to promotional activities involving the dissemination of a message 'by the person providing the service' and that ANTO's supplies were not within this definition since ANTO 'provides facilities for others to disseminate that message'. The tribunal held that it was 'apparent from the Court's judgment that what it had in contemplation was the provision, particularly by an advertising agency' of 'advertising services to include promotional activities for a particular client. That is not the case here.' *Austrian National Tourist Office*, LON/96/674 (VTD 15561). (*Note*. For another issue in this case, see **36.499** INPUT TAX.)

Hotel accommodation and tours

[62.498] A UK partnership supplied hotel accommodation and organised tours to overseas tour firms. HMRC issued a ruling that the place of supply was in the UK, where the partnership belonged. The partnership appealed, contending that part of the consideration which it received should be treated as attributable to supplies of information, falling within *VATA 1994, Sch 5 para 3*. The tribunal rejected this contention and dismissed the appeal. *AC Tours v HMRC*, [2010] UKFTT 363 (TC), TC00645.

Consultancy services supplied to MEPs

[62.499] A UK company supplied research and consultancy services to Members of the European Parliament. It did not account for tax on these supplies. The Commissioners issued a ruling that it was required to account for output tax. The company appealed, contending that since it was supplying services within *VATA 1994, Sch 5 para 3*, the place of the supply was where the recipients belonged, which was outside the UK. The tribunal rejected this contention and dismissed the appeal. It was accepted that the company's supplies were within *Sch 5 para 3*. However, the Members of the European Parliament were not receiving the supplies 'for the purpose of a business', as required by *VAT (Place of Supply of Services) Order 1992 (SI 1992/3121), article 16(b)(i)*. Accordingly, the provisions of *article 16* did not apply, and the place of the supply was where the company belonged, which was in the UK. (The tribunal also held that the supplies did not qualify for exemption under *Article 15(10)* of the *EC Sixth Directive*.) *MEP Research Services Ltd*, LON/96/1284 (VTD 16044).

Supplies of 'clairvoyancy and palmistry services'

[62.500] A registered trader (M) supplied 'clairvoyancy and palmistry services', based partly on astrological calculations. Some of his customers were resident outside EU (for example, in Pakistan or the USA). The Commissioners issued a ruling that M's supplies to these customers took place in the UK, so that he was required to account for VAT. He appealed, contending that he was supplying consultancy services within *VATA 1994, Sch 5 para 3*, so that the place of the supply was where the recipients belonged, which was outside the UK. The tribunal rejected this contention and dismissed M's appeal, holding that the reference to 'consultants' in *Sch 5 para 3* should be construed as referring specifically to members of the 'liberal professions', as referred to in *Annex F* of the *EC Sixth Directive*. Applying the CJEC decision in *Adam v Administration de l'enregistrement et des domaines*, 22.509 EUROPEAN COMMUNITY LAW, 'a "liberal profession" must have a marked intellectual character, require a high level qualification, and be subject to clear and strict professional regulation'. The tribunal observed that M was 'not an individual of marked intellectual character' and had 'no high-level qualification whatsoever', and that 'there is no regulatory body'. Accordingly his supplies did not fall within *Sch 5 para 3*, and he was required to account for VAT. *N Mohammed (t/a The Indian Palmist)*, MAN/03/20 (VTD 18397).

Sale of personalised numberplate

[62.501] An individual (H), who lived outside the EU, purchased a personalised numberplate from a UK company. The company charged VAT on the supply. H appealed to the tribunal, contending that the supply should be treated as taking place where he lived, which was outside the EU. The tribunal rejected this contention and dismissed the appeal. *T Hovan v HMRC*, [2010] UKFTT 260 (TC), TC00554. (*Note*. The appellant appeared in person.)

Place where recipient belongs (VATA 1994, s 9(3, 4))

VATA 1994, s 9(3)*—definition of 'usual place of residence'

[62.502] In a case where the substantive issue (involving the liability of certain supplies of insurance) has been overtaken by subsequent changes in the legislation, the tribunal held that US Forces personnel living in England on a three-year tour of duty had their 'usual place of residence' in the UK. During the tour of duty their houses in the USA were let, and, if they returned for training to the USA, their families remained in the UK. They could not therefore be regarded as having their usual place of residence in the USA. *USAA Ltd*, LON/92/1950A (VTD 10369).

[62.503] In August 1992 an Indian woman (H) entered the UK as an employee in domestic service. She left her employers in November 1992 and began legal proceedings against them. She remained in the UK during the proceedings, which were eventually settled in October 1996 by a consent order, under which her former employers were liable to pay her legal costs. The Commissioners issued a ruling that the place of supply was in the UK, so that VAT was chargeable on the costs. Her former employers appealed, contending that H's usual place of residence was in India so that the services were deemed to be supplied in India and UK VAT was not chargeable. The tribunal accepted this contention and allowed the appeal. The fact that H had been physically present in the UK throughout the period when the services were performed was not conclusive. *SA Razzak & MA Mishari*, [1997] VATDR 392 (VTD 15240).

Carpentry services—whether supplied in Republic of Ireland

[62.504] A carpenter (C), who lived in Greater London, had not registered for VAT on the basis that his turnover was below the statutory threshold. HMRC formed the opinion that his turnover had exceeded the threshold in 2006, and issued a ruling that he was required to register. C appealed, contending that much of the relevant work had been carried out in the Republic of Ireland, where he had stayed temporarily. The tribunal accepted his evidence and allowed his appeal. *R Carville v HMRC*, [2011] UKFTT 763 (TC), TC01600.

Overseas company admitted to UK group under extra-statutory concession

[62.505] A UK company (L) made supplies of leasing office and computer equipment to a US company (P). Although P had no business establishment in the UK, it had been accepted as a member of a UK VAT group. The Commissioners issued an assessment on L on the basis that, because P was a member of a UK VAT group, it was deemed to belong in the UK for the purpose of *VATA 1994, s 9*, so that the place of supply was in the UK and L was required to account for output tax. L appealed, contending that P belonged in the USA and that, by virtue of *VATA 1994, s 9(4)*, the place of supply was in the USA. The tribunal accepted this contention and allowed L's appeal, holding that P could only be treated as a member of the group if it was established in the UK within the meaning of *Article 4(4)* of the *EC Sixth Directive* and if *VATA 1994, s 43* was capable of being interpreted accordingly. On the evidence, P was neither established nor resident in the UK, and 'the Commissioners were not in law entitled to treat (P) as a member of a UK VAT group. The result of this is that the consequences of grouping cannot be applied when determining the place of supply which must therefore be in the USA. The grouping, which was extra-statutory, falls to be disregarded.' *Shamrock Leasing Ltd*, [1998] VATDR 323 (VTD 15719).

Consultancy services supplied to UK branch of Swiss company

[62.506] A Swiss insurance company (Z) had a large fixed establishment in the UK. It arranged for another company to supply consultancy services within *VATA 1994, Sch 5 para 3* and *Article 9(2)(e)* of the *EC Sixth Directive*, relating to new financial accounting software. Customs issued an assessment on the basis that the services had been supplied to the UK fixed establishment, so that the recipient was required to account for UK VAT under the 'reverse charge' provisions of *VATA 1994, s 8*. Z appealed, contending that the relevant services had been supplied to its head office in Switzerland, and were therefore outside the scope of UK VAT. The CA unanimously rejected this contention and dismissed the appeal. Sir Andrew Morritt held that 'on the facts found by the tribunal the only tenable outcome of the proper application of *Article 9(2)(e)* is the conclusion that the place of supply was the United Kingdom'. *Zurich Insurance Company v HMRC*, CA [2007] STC 1756; [2007] EWCA Civ 218.

Services supplied through a branch or agency (VATA 1994, s 9(5))

[62.507] The Commissioners sent a notice to a Jersey company at the York office of a UK company, which the Commissioners considered was acting as a branch or agency of the Jersey company. The Jersey company appealed against that notice. The tribunal upheld the notice and dismissed the appeal, finding that the Jersey company was 'rendering services for reward to persons having addresses in the United Kingdom through the agency of (the UK company)'. The UK company was 'an agent of the appellant in the United Kingdom whereby the appellant is to be deemed to have a business establishment there'. The UK company's office was 'the establishment most directly concerned with the supplies of the services made in the United Kingdom'. Accordingly the conditions of what is now *VATA 1994, s 9(5)(a)* were satisfied, and when a UK resident used the services of the Jersey company, the services had been supplied in the UK. *Interbet Trading Ltd (No 2)*, [1978] VATTR 235 (VTD 696).

[62.508] For a case where the QB held that the provisions of *VATA 1994, s 9(5)* did not apply, see *The Chinese Channel (Hong Kong) Ltd*, **62.490** above.

[62.509] For a case where the tribunal held that the provisions of *VATA 1994, s 9(5)* were inconsistent with *Article 9* of the *EC Sixth Directive*, see *WH Payne & Co*, **62.536** below.

Services relating to land (VAT (Place of Supply of Services) Order, article 5)

Surveyors' services—whether 'services relating to land'

[62.510] A company surveyed damage to a jetty and lock at Hull and Immingham respectively. The work was carried out for companies registered in Hong Kong and Bermuda, and the company did not account for output tax on the supplies. The Commissioners issued a ruling that output tax was chargeable. The tribunal dismissed the company's appeal, holding that the work constituted 'services relating to land', within what is now *VAT (Place of Supply of Services) Order 1992 (SI 1992/3121), Article 5*, so that the place of supply was in the UK and the work did not qualify for zero-rating. *Brodrick Wright & Strong Ltd*, LON/86/461 (VTD 2347).

Services relating to commissioning of industrial waste incinerator

[62.511] A company supplied services to a Swiss company relating to the commissioning of an industrial waste incinerator complex in Cheshire. The Commissioners issued a ruling that the services were 'services relating to land', within *VAT (Place of Supply of Services) Order 1992 (SI 1992/3121), Article 5*, so that the services should be treated as supplied in Cheshire. The company appealed, contending that the effect of *Article 9* of the *EC Sixth Directive* was that the services should be treated as supplied in Switzerland, where the recipient was established. The tribunal rejected this contention and dismissed the appeal, holding that the services were 'services relating to land', since 'it is a general rule of English law that anything affixed to land becomes part of it'. Furthermore, the waste incinerator complex was 'immovable property', so that under *Article 9(2)* of the *EC Sixth Directive* the services were also to be treated as supplied in the UK. *Mechanical Engineering Consultants Ltd*, MAN/93/1074 (VTD 13287).

Demolition of plant—whether 'services relating to land'

[62.512] A South African company purchased some second-hand plant from Scotland. A UK company arranged for the demolition and shipping of the plant. It did not account for output tax on the consideration which it received. The Commissioners issued an assessment charging tax on this. The company appealed, contending that the transaction should be treated as a zero-rated export. The tribunal rejected this contention and dismissed the appeal, holding that the company had supplied 'services relating to land', within *VAT (Place of Supply of Services) Order 1992 (SI 1992/3121), article 5*. Accordingly the supplies had taken place in Scotland, and VAT was chargeable. *McLean & Gibson (Engineers) Ltd*, EDN/01/119 (VTD 17500).

Management services supplied to Channel Islands companies

[62.513] A UK company supplied management services to two companies registered in the Channel Islands companies, in respect of properties situated in the UK which those companies owned. The Commissioners issued an assessment charging tax on the supplies. The company appealed, accepting that 25% of the fees which it charged related to specific properties in the UK, and were therefore supplies relating to UK land and thus standard-rated, but contending that the remaining 75% of its fees should be treated as relating to accountancy and bookkeeping services, in respect of which the place of supply was the Channel Islands where the recipient companies belonged. The tribunal rejected this contention and dismissed the appeal, holding on the evidence that the whole of the services in question were services relating to land, within *VAT (Place of Supply of Services) Order 1992 (SI 1992/3121), Article 5*, so that the supplies were deemed to take place in the UK. *Aspen Advisory Services Ltd*, LON/94/2773A (VTD 13489).

Provision of display space at exhibitions

[62.514] A company organised exhibitions. Before 1996, it treated its supplies of display space to exhibitors as licences to occupy land. Since it had elected to waive exemption, it accounted for tax on these supplies. Following the tribunal decision in *International Trade & Exhibitions J/V Ltd*, 62.526 below, it applied to the Commissioners for authority to treat its supplies as advertising services falling within *Article 16 of the VAT (Supply of Services) Order 1992 (SI 1992/3121)*, so that, where the recipient of the supplies belonged outside the UK, it should not be required to account for output tax. The Commissioners rejected the application and ruled that, despite the decision in *International Trade & Exhibitions J/V Ltd*, the company was granting licences to occupy land and, in view of its election to waive exemption, output tax was chargeable. The tribunal upheld the Commissioners' ruling and dismissed the company's appeal, distinguishing (and implicitly disapproving) the decision in *International Trade & Exhibitions J/V Ltd*. The tribunal held that the company was supplying 'the right to occupy space at the venue to which the exhibitor expects that the sort of customer he wants to attend will come. What he is getting, in effect, is the right to set up his stall so that his potential customers can visit him there.' The supplies were not within the definition of 'advertising services', since there was 'a legitimate distinction to be drawn between a supplier providing particular clients in the course of an advertising campaign with the means to get across a message about their products and services, and the situation here where what is provided is the opportunity in a specific location for clients to be there and do all the work of promoting themselves to those potential customers who attend the exhibition'. *Miller Freeman Worldwide plc*, [1998] VATDR 435 (VTD 15452).

Solicitors' services relating to UK property

[62.515] An individual (D), who lived in Jersey, helped a woman (H) to purchase a leasehold flat in Bristol, under an agreement whereby H would occupy the flat for her lifetime but that D would then be entitled to vacant possession and ownership of the flat. H died in 2003. D took court proceedings against her personal representative to gain possession of the flat. The solicitors who acted for D charged VAT on their services. D lodged an appeal to the VAT tribunal, contending that the services should be treated as having been supplied in Jersey, where he lived. The tribunal rejected this contention and dismissed the appeal, holding that the supplies were of 'services relating to land', so that the place of supply was in the UK. The tribunal observed that although solicitors were not specifically referred to in *VAT (Place of Supply of Services) Order, article 5*, their services were included in the *Order* as 'others involved in matters relating to land'. *KR Daunter*, LON/06/671 (VTD 20120).

Services of intermediaries (VAT (Place of Supply of Services) Order, article 13; VATA 1994, Sch 4A para 10)

[62.516] A company (F), based in the UK, was formed to help members of expensive golf clubs to play at similar clubs elsewhere in the world. It charged its subscribers an initial 'joining fee' of £27,000, plus annual fees of £2,600 pa. Customs issued a ruling that F was required to account for VAT on its supplies. F appealed, contending that it was supplying 'services of intermediaries', within *VAT (Place of Supply of Services) Order 1992 (SI 1992/3121), article 13*, so that the place of supply was where the game took place, and that 90% of the arrangements which it made were for subscribers to play at a golf club outside the UK and were therefore outside the scope of UK VAT. The tribunal accepted this contention and allowed F's appeal in principle (subject to agreement as to figures). The tribunal also observed that there were 'EC implications when arrangement services relate, as they will to quite a significant degree, to the arrangement of games of golf in France and other EC countries. Doubtless in certain circumstances, and depending on local rules and registerable limits, that could occasion liability to equivalent tax in other EC countries.' *The Finest Golf Clubs of the World Ltd*, LON/04/151 (VTD 19347).

[62.517] See also *Macdonald Resorts Ltd*, 22.208 EUROPEAN COMMUNITY LAW, in which the Edinburgh tribunal implicitly disapproved some of the reasoning in *The Finest Golf Clubs of the World Ltd*, 62.516 above.

[62.518] A Scottish company (F) was formed to provide guidance and advice to students pursuing sports scholarships in the USA. Initially HMRC accepted that, for VAT purposes, its supplies should be treated as taking place in the USA, and as outside the scope of UK VAT. However subsequently HMRC issued a ruling that the place of supply was in the UK, where F was incorporated and where its clients lived. F appealed, contending that it was an intermediary and that its supplies fell within *VATA 1994, Sch 4A para 10*, so that its supplies should be 'treated as made in the same country as the supply to which it relates', which was the USA. The tribunal accepted this contention and allowed the appeal, holding that F's supplies were within *para 10(2)*, since they were 'made to people who are not relevant business people consisting of activities intended to facilitate the making of other supplies' (ie supplies of education made by US colleges in the USA). *Firstpoint (Europe) Ltd v HMRC*, [2011] UKFTT 708 (TC), TC01545.

Use of customer's registration number (VAT (Place of Supply of Services) Order, article 14)

[62.519] A UK trader supplied transport services, beginning in France, to a UK company which was registered for VAT. He failed to account for tax on the supply and the Commissioners issued an assessment. The tribunal dismissed the trader's appeal, observing that *VAT (Place of Supply of Services) Order 1992 (SI 1992/3121), article 14* provided that where a supply of services 'consists of ancillary transport services provided in connection with the intra-Community transport of goods, and the recipient of those services makes use, for the purpose of the supply, of a registration number, then the supply shall be treated as made in the member State which issued the registration number' if the supply would otherwise be treated as taking place in a different member State. *J Blair*, EDN/00/17 (VTD 16767).

[62.520] See also *Satis Italsempione SA*, 57.159 REGISTRATION.

Services supplied where performed (VAT (Place of Supply of Services) Order, article 15)

Payment for services of jockey—whether for 'sporting services'

[62.521] An Irish trainer paid a UK company £150,000 for the right to have first claim on the services of a leading UK jockey for races outside the UK. The Commissioners issued an assessment charging VAT on the payment. The company appealed, contending that the supply was a supply of sporting services, within what is now *VAT (Place of Supply of Services) Order 1992 (SI 1992/3121), Article 15*, so that the place of supply was outside the UK. The tribunal accepted this contention and allowed the company's appeal. *Patrick Eddery Ltd*, [1986] VATTR 30 (VTD 2009).

Payment for services of motor racing driver

[62.522] A company (W) operated a Formula 1 motor racing team. It entered into an agreement with a Japanese company (T) under which certain drivers, who were contracted to T, were leased to W for a specified period, and W granted T a licence to use the drivers' image rights while they were driving for W. HMRC issued a ruling that W was making a supply of sporting services, so that the place of supply was where the services were performed, which was partly in the UK. W appealed, contending that it had made a supply of advertising services, and that the place of supply was where the recipient (T) belonged. The tribunal rejected this contention and dismissed the appeal, holding that the predominant feature of the supply was that W was providing

T's drivers with the experience of driving in its Formula One team. *Williams Grand Prix Engineering Ltd v HMRC*, [2010] UKFTT 607 (TC), TC00848.

Film actress performing on location outside UK

[62.523] A New Zealand company paid a British actress to perform in a film which was shot in New Zealand. Customs issued an assessment charging tax on the fees which the actress received. She appealed, contending that she had supplied 'cultural, artistic or entertainment services', within *Article 9(2)(c)* of the *EC Sixth Directive* (and *VAT (Place of Supply of Services) Order 1992 (SI 1992/3121), Article 15(a)*), so that the place of supply was New Zealand, where her services were performed. The tribunal accepted this contention and allowed her appeal, holding that the phrase 'cultural, artistic or entertainment services' was not restricted to live performances, and specifically disapproving *dicta* of the tribunal chairman in the 1994 case of *British Sky Broadcasting Ltd*, 62.489 above. The tribunal also observed that 'the charging of VAT on United Kingdom actors on their supplies for a film physically carried out outside the United Kingdom would prevent United Kingdom actors from competing on an equal footing with actors not based in the United Kingdom'. *S Burrows*, [2007] VATDR 478 (VTD 20454).

Supplies of catering for entertainers touring outside UK

[62.524] A UK partnership provided catering services for UK entertainers (principally singers and musicians) and their supporting technicians while touring outside the UK. The Commissioners issued a ruling that the place of supply was in the UK, where the partnership was established. The partnership appealed, contending that the supplies related to entertainment services, within *Article 9(2)(c)* of the *EC Sixth Directive* (and *VAT (Place of Supply of Services) Order 1992 (SI 1992/3121), Article 15(c)*), so that the services were supplied where they were performed. The tribunal accepted this contention and allowed the appeal. *Sugar and Spice On Tour Catering*, MAN/99/1053 (VTD 17698).

Waste disposal services

[62.525] A Republic of Ireland company carried on a demolition business. It delivered waste material (principally timber) to a Northern Ireland trader (K) who carried on a waste disposal business. K charged the company for sorting and disposing of the waste, but failed to account for VAT on his supplies. HMRC issued an assessment charging tax on them. K appealed, contending that because the waste originated in the Republic of Ireland, his supplies should be treated as being outside the scope of UK VAT. The tribunal rejected this contention and dismissed his appeal, holding that the effect of *VAT (Place of Supply of Services) Order 1992 (SI 1992/3121), Article 15(d)* was that the place of supply was in the UK. *G Kinney v HMRC*, [2009] UKFTT 273 (TC), TC00219.

Services supplied where received (VAT (Place of Supply of Services) Order, article 16)

VATA 1994, Sch 5 para 2—definition of 'advertising services'

[62.526] A UK company supplied an exhibition stand to a Georgian institute for an exhibition in Bahrain. It reclaimed input tax under *VATA 1994,* *s 26(2)(b)* on the costs of providing the stand. The Commissioners rejected the claim, considering that the supply was a 'service relating to land' which would have been an exempt supply if made in the UK, so that the company could not recover the attributable input tax. The company appealed, contending that the services were not 'relating to land' but were advertising services falling within *Article 16* of the *VAT (Supply of Services) Order 1992 (SI 1992/3121)*, and that it was entitled to recover this input tax. The tribunal accepted these contentions and allowed the appeal, holding that the service should not be treated as a 'service relating to land', since 'the right of occupation of the land at the exhibition centre' was not 'the dominant feature of the supply'. The company was supplying 'advertising services' within *Article 9(2)(e)* of the *EC Sixth Directive. International Trade & Exhibitions J/V Ltd*, [1996] VATDR 165 (VTD 14212). (*Notes.* (1) For the Commissioners' practice following this decision, see Business Brief 24/96, issued on 28 November 1996. (2) The decision in this case was not followed, and was implicitly disapproved, in the subsequent case of *Miller Freeman Worldwide plc*, 62.514 above.)

[62.527] A company operated a motor racing team. Its income was derived almost entirely from sponsorship. Some of its sponsors were established outside the EC. It did not account for tax on its payments from such sponsors, treating them as consideration for supplies of advertising services which, by virtue of *VAT (Place of Supply of Services) Order 1992 (SI 1992/3121), article 16*, were deemed to be supplied where the recipients belonged. The Commissioners issued an assessment charging tax on the basis that the company was supplying sporting services which, by virtue of *VAT (Place of Supply of Services) Order 1992 (SI 1992/3121), article 15*, should be treated as being supplied in the UK. The company appealed. The tribunal allowed the appeal, holding on the evidence that 'the overwhelmingly predominant element of the services supplied by the appellant to the sponsors was advertising' and observing that 'the fact that the publicity was to be provided by means of the appellant's taking part in a sporting event did not turn what, in our judgment, would otherwise have been beyond question a supply of advertising services into a supply of sporting services'. *John Village Automotive Ltd*, [1998] VATDR 340 (VTD 15540).

[62.528] See also *Lawrence*, **39.4** INTERNATIONAL SERVICES, and *Miller Freeman Worldwide plc*, **62.514** above.

Advertising services—validity of VAT (Place of Supply of Services) Order

[62.529] See *Diversified Agency Services Ltd*, **62.491** above.

Advertising services—whether supplied to Liechtenstein or UK

[62.530] In 1996 an organisation (G) was formed in Liechtenstein, primarily to criticise the policies adopted by the European Union. It arranged for a UK partnership (B) to supply advertisements in the UK, calling for a referendum on European issues. B sent G invoices in respect of these services, treating them as zero-rated on the basis that the place of supply was where G belonged, which was outside the EU. The Commissioners issued an assessment charging tax on B, on the basis that the advertisements had actually been supplied to a UK political party (R), so that the place of supply was in the UK. G appealed, contending that it was the recipient of the services in question, so that the supplies were therefore zero-rated. The tribunal accepted this contention and allowed the appeal, holding that B was supplying the relevant services to G, and that 'the fact that (R) may also have received a service or benefit as part of the same transaction does not alter the position'. *The Goldsmith Foundation for European Affairs*, [2000] VATDR 97 (VTD 16544).

VATA 1994, Sch 5 para 3—data processing services

[62.531] A UK company provided a US client with data relating to repeats of television programmes and advertisements, in return for payment of £15,200. It did not account for tax on this amount. The Commissioners issued an assessment charging VAT, and the company appealed, contending that the services were 'data processing', within *VATA 1994, Sch 5 para 3*, so that the place of supply was where the customer belonged, which was in the USA. The tribunal accepted this contention and allowed the appeal, observing that 'data processing' was described in *Notice No 741, para 12.4.10* as 'the application of programmed instructions on existing data which results in the production of required information'. The tribunal held that the disputed supply was 'fairly and squarely' within this definition, so that the place of supply was in the USA. *Talent & Production Services Ltd*, LON/03/732 (VTD 18654).

Data processing and related services—whether supplied in UK

[62.532] Two UK companies imported data processing and related services from a Canadian company. The Commissioners issued a ruling that the services were within *VAT (Place of Supply of Services) Order 1992 (SI 1992/3121), article 16*, and were supplied where they were received, i.e. in the UK. The companies appealed, accepting that approximately 60% of the relevant services fell within *article 16*, but contending that about 40% of the services were outside the scope of *article 16* and thus were supplied in Canada, where the supplier belonged. The tribunal accepted this contention and allowed the appeal, holding that 'the services appear to vary widely both in nature and in taxability'. *Laurentian Management Services Ltd; Lincoln Assurance Ltd*, LON/96/1017 & 1018 (VTD 16447).

VATA 1994, Sch 5 para 3—services of consultants

[62.533] A married couple organised UK tours for Japanese students on behalf of a Japanese organisation. They did not account for VAT. Customs issued an assessment charging tax on the supplies. The couple appealed, contending that they had supplied 'services of consultants', within *VATA 1994, Sch 5 para 3*, so that the effect of *VAT (Place of Supply of Services) Order 1992 (SI 1992/3121), article 16* was that the services were supplied where the recipient belonged, i.e. in Japan. The tribunal accepted this contention and allowed the appeal, finding that the tours were 'largely dependent' on the husband's 'own particular knowledge, which he has gleaned over the years as a consequence of film location work and his connections with Japan'. *J & Mrs A Cuthbert*, LON/06/453 (VTD 20466).

[62.534] See also *Vision Express Ltd*, **39.7** INTERNATIONAL SERVICES; *Hopkins*, **39.8** INTERNATIONAL SERVICES *MEP Research Services Ltd*, **62.499** above, and *Zurich Insurance Company*, **62.506** above.

VATA 1994, Sch 5 para 3—engineering services

[62.535] See *Hutchvision Hong Kong Ltd*, **62.488** above.

Accountancy services supplied to overseas companies owning UK property

[62.536] An accountancy firm supplied accountancy and taxation services to a number of overseas companies which owned properties in the UK, the properties in question being let to tenants. The firm did not account for output tax on the supplies in question. The Commissioners issued an assessment on the basis that the supplies should be treated as having taken place in the UK so that VAT was chargeable. The firm appealed, contending that the effect of *Article 9(2)(e)* of the *EC Sixth Directive* and of *VATA 1994, Sch 5 para 3* was that the services should be treated as being supplied where the recipients belonged and that the place of supply was therefore outside the UK. The tribunal allowed the appeal, holding on the evidence that the recipient companies did not have a 'fixed establishment' in the UK. *Binder Hamlyn*, **62.480** above, was distinguished on the grounds that the recipient company in that case had its registered office in the UK. The tribunal held that the fact that the companies had appointed agents to manage their UK properties was not conclusive, and that the provisions of *VATA 1994, s 9(5)*, treating a person who carries on business through a branch or agency as having a business establishment in that country, were inconsistent with *Article 9* of the *Sixth Directive* as interpreted in *Berkholz v Finanzamt Hamburg-Mitte-Altstadt*, **22.198** EUROPEAN COMMUNITY LAW. The supplies in question had taken place where the recipient companies were established, which was outside the UK. *WH Payne & Co*, [1995] VATDR 490 (VTD 13668). (*Note.* With regard to the definition of a 'fixed establishment', see the subsequent CJEC decision in *DFDS A/S*, **22.492** EUROPEAN COMMUNITY LAW. For the Commissioners' practice following the CJEC decision in *DFDS*, see Business Brief 12/98, issued on 21 May 1998.)

VATA 1994, Sch 5 para 3—exclusion of services relating to land

[62.537] See *Brodrick Wright & Strong Ltd*, **62.510** above, *Mechanical Engineering Consultants Ltd*, **62.511** above, and *Aspen Advisory Services Ltd*, **62.513** above.

VATA 1994, Sch 5 para 5—definition of 'financial services'

[62.538] A company trading as a metal broker acquired options for the purchase of a quantity of cadmium, and gave corresponding options to a client company. The company had reclaimed input tax on the amount it had paid for the options, but failed to account for tax on the amount it had received for them. The Commissioners issued an assessment charging tax on the amount received. The company appealed, contending firstly that it had made supplies of goods and that the place of supply was where the cadmium was situated, which was outside the UK, and alternatively, that if the supply was of services, that it was a supply of financial services within what is now *VATA 1994, Sch 5 para 5*, so that it was zero-rated under the legislation then in force. The tribunal rejected these contentions and dismissed the appeal, holding that the grant of an option to acquire cadmium was not a financial service within what is now *VATA 1994, Sch 5 para 5*. Lord Grantchester held that the words 'financial services' should 'be confined to services in connection with money and credit'. *Gardner Lohman Ltd*, [1981] VATTR 76 (VTD 1081).

[62.539] In a case where a company had unsuccessfully appealed against assessments on payments which a company received for property management, the tribunal held that rent collection was not a financial service within what is now *VATA 1994, Sch 5 para 5*. *Culverpalm Ltd*, [1984] VATTR 199 (VTD 1727).

[62.540] In the case noted at **64.36** TRADE UNIONS, PROFESSIONAL AND PUBLIC INTEREST BODIES, the tribunal held that a company formed to encourage the use of standard terminology in financial reports was not supplying financial services within *VATA 1994, Sch 5 para 5*. *Rixml.org Ltd*, LON/02/185 (VTD 18717).

VATA 1994, Sch 5 para 6—definition of 'supplies of staff'

[62.541] A UK company provided the services of travel couriers to two associated US companies. It did not account for tax on such supplies. The Commissioners issued an assessment charging tax of more than £150,000. The company appealed, contending that the supplies were supplies of staff, within *VATA 1994, Sch 5 para 6*, and were therefore, by virtue of *VAT (Place of Supply of Services) Order 1992 (SI 1992/3121), article 16*, deemed to take place where the recipient companies belonged, which was outside the EU. The tribunal accepted this contention and allowed the appeal, observing that it was 'more natural to describe the provision of couriers by the UK company as the supply of couriers than as the supply of courier services'. *American Institute of Foreign Study (UK) Ltd*, LON/95/898A (VTD 13886).

[62.542] See also *Seymour Limousines Ltd*, **2.488** APPEALS.

VATA 1994, Sch 5 para 7—'goods other than means of transport'

[62.543] A UK company hired cranes to a Netherlands company. The Commissioners issued an assessment on the basis that the supply was deemed to take place in the UK. The company appealed, contending that the effect of what is now *VATA 1994, Sch 5 para 7* and *VAT (Place of Supply of Services) Order 1992 (SI 1992/3121), article 16*, was that the supply was deemed to take place in the Netherlands. The tribunal accepted this contention and allowed the appeal, rejecting the Commissioners' contention that the cranes should be treated as 'means of transport'. The fact that the cranes had an engine, caterpillar tread, gearing and brakes was not sufficient to bring them within the definition of 'means of transport', since 'transport' should be construed as involving 'movement from one place to another'. The cranes were 'not intended for travelling on roads' and their 'primary function (was) not to carry goods from A to B but to position them when on site'. *BPH Equipment Ltd*, MAN/94/530 (VTD 13914).

VATA 1994, Sch 5 para 7A—Telecommunications services

[62.544] See *HMRC v IDT Card Services Ireland Ltd*, **67.172** VALUATION.

VATA 1994, Sch 5 para 7C—electronically supplied services

[62.545] A UK company (S) was registered with the Financial Services Authority as an 'electronic money institution'. It advertised an 'electronic money system' which consumers could use to make online purchases without divulging their credit or debit card details. HMRC issued a ruling that S was making supplies in the UK, where it belonged. S appealed, contending that it was providing 'electronically supplied services', within *VATA 1994, Sch 5 para 7C*, so that the services were supplied where they were received. The tribunal accepted this contention and allowed the appeal. *Smart Voucher Ltd v HMRC*, [2009] UKFTT 169 (TC), TC00131.

Supplies of right to services (VAT (Place of Supply of Services) Order, article 21)

Supplies of phonecards

[62.546] A retailer failed to account for VAT on sales of phonecards. HMRC issued an assessment charging tax on his supplies (except where VAT had been paid at source by the service provider under *VATA 1994, Sch 10A, para 3(3)*). The retailer appealed, contending that the effect of the *VAT (Place of Supply of Services) Order (SI 1992/3121), article 21(1)* was that the supplies fell to be treated as if they had been supplied where the supplier of the telecommunications service was based, and were thus outside the scope of UK VAT. The CA unanimously rejected this contention and dismissed the appeal. Etherton LJ held that the supply of the phonecards was the supply of a service, rather than simply a supply of a 'right to services'. Applying the principles laid down by Arden LJ in *HMRC v IDT Card Services Ireland Ltd*, **67.172** VALUATION, the place of supply was in the UK. *PKS Arachchige v HMRC*, CA [2010] EWCA Civ 1255; [2011] STC 33. (*Note. SI 1992/3121, article 21* was amended with effect from 1 August 2006. The amendment was intended to clarify that sales of phonecards are within the charge to UK VAT.)

[62.547] See also *Lebara Ltd v HMRC*, **22.190** EUROPEAN COMMUNITY LAW.

Single or multiple supplies

General principles

[62.548] In the case noted at **22.324** EUROPEAN COMMUNITY LAW, the ECJ held that it was for the national court to determine whether the particular transactions in dispute were to be regarded as comprising two independent supplies, namely an exempt insurance supply and a taxable card registration service. The CJEC observed that 'having regard to the diversity of commercial operations, it is not possible to give exhaustive guidance on how to approach the problem correctly in all cases.' However, 'a supply which comprises a single service from an economic point of view should not be artificially split'. There was 'a single supply in particular in cases where one or more elements are to be regarded as constituting the principal service, whilst one or more elements are to be regarded, by contrast, as ancillary services which share the tax treatment of the principal service. A service must be regarded as ancillary to a principal service if it does not constitute for customers an aim in itself, but a means of better enjoying the principal service supplied'. *Card Protection Plan Ltd v C & E Commrs*, CJEC Case C-349/96; [1999] STC 270; [1999] 3 WLR 203; [1999] All ER (EC) 339. (*Notes.* (1) The HL subsequently allowed the company's appeal, holding that it was making a single exempt supply of insurance—see **38.44** INSURANCE. (2) In the subsequent case of *Dr Beynon & Partners*, **19.8** DRUGS, MEDICINES, AIDS FOR THE HANDICAPPED ETC., Lord Hoffmann observed that counsel had referred 'to a number of cases, both in this country and in the Court of Justice, which were decided before the *Card Protection* case. Submissions were made as to whether the principles upon which those cases were decided had application to this case. Their Lordships think that there is no advantage in referring to such earlier cases and their citation in future should be discouraged. The *Card Protection* case was a restatement of principle and it should not be necessary to go back any further.')

Sale price including delivery

[62.549] A company manufactured and sold dishwashers which, at the relevant time, were chargeable to a higher rate of VAT. It treated part of the sale price as being for delivery of the dishwasher and chargeable at the standard rate. The tribunal held that the whole of the consideration was chargeable at the higher rate. *Lylybet Dishwashers (UK) Ltd*, LON/79/244 (VTD 915).

Postal computer games

[62.550] A trader (C) operated a number of postal computer games. Players had to pay a 'turn fee' of £1.80 per turn and were supplied with cards, described as 'turn cards', on which they could direct particular actions. C processed the various 'turn cards' and sent each player a computer-generated report of the results. Customs issued a ruling that VAT was chargeable on the 'turn fees'. C appealed, contending that part of the fees should be attributed to supplies of zero-rated documents. The tribunal rejected this contention and dismissed C's appeal. *KJ Cropper (t/a KJC Games)*, MAN/95/180 (VTD 13679).

[62.551] The decision in *Cropper*, 62.550 above, was applied in a similar subsequent case involving a 'fantasy football' game. The tribunal held that the whole of the consideration was standard-rated. *M & E Sports Ltd*, MAN/98/461 (VTD 16051).

'Student meals'

[62.552] A student union supplied 'student meals', comprising a sandwich, a packet of crisps and a soft drink, for £2.50. It treated this as zero-rated. Customs issued an assessment on the basis that 33% of the price was attributable to the crisps and the soft drink, and standard-rated. The union appealed, contending that it should be treated as making zero-rated supplies of sandwiches, and that the crisps and drinks were merely ancillary. The tribunal rejected this contention and dismissed the appeal. *De Montfort University Students' Union*, MAN/02/523 (VTD 18434). (*Note.* Customs accepted that the supplies were not within the definition of 'catering'.)

Food supplied with 'weight loss' services

[62.553] A company (D) advertised 'weight loss' services. It gave its customers dietary packs and 'support services' including weekly meetings. HMRC issued a ruling that D was required to account for VAT on its supplies. D appealed, contending that it was making supplies of food which qualified for zero-rating. The Ch D rejected this contention and upheld HMRC's ruling, and the CA unanimously upheld this decision. Patten LJ held that the 'support services' were 'part of a continuous programme of dieting and weight stabilisation designed to achieve the permanent reduction of the customer's weight', and were 'integral to the achievement of the customer's needs'. Accordingly D was making a single composite supply of services, which was chargeable at the standard rate. *David Baxendale Ltd v HMRC*, CA [2009] STC 2578; [2009] EWCA Civ 831.

Lease of building including plant and machinery

[62.554] A company leased a large building, including plant and machinery, to a university. It opted to tax the building. HMRC issued a ruling that it was required to account for VAT on the payments it received from the university. The university appealed, contending that part of the payments which it made should be treated as qualifying for zero-rating under *VATA 1994, Sch 8*. The tribunal rejected this contention and dismissed the appeal, holding that L was making a single supply which was standard-rated. *Queen Mary University of London v HMRC*, [2011] UKFTT 229 (TC), TC01094.

Cross-references—single supply

[62.555] In the following cases the consideration was held to cover a single supply, not apportionable: *PBK Catering Ltd*, 1.5 AGENTS (catering services supplied to charity); *International News Syndicate Ltd*, 5.3 BOOKS, ETC. (supply of manuals and course books); *International Correspondence Schools Ltd*, 5.4 BOOKS, ETC. (supply of manuals and course books); *The Leisure Circle Ltd*, 5.21 BOOKS, ETC. (supply of books including delivery); *Book Club Associates*, 5.22 BOOKS, ETC. (supply of books including delivery); *EW (Computer Training) Ltd*, 5.35 BOOKS, ETC. (computer tuition including manuals); *College of Estate Management*, 5.36 BOOKS, ETC. (educational services including study materials); *Franchise Development Services Ltd*, 5.38 BOOKS, ETC. (advisory services including instruction manual); *Games Workshop Ltd*, 5.39 BOOKS, ETC. (supplies of boxed games including books); *International Masters Publishers Ltd*, 5.40 BOOKS, ETC. (supplies of CDs including booklets); *Company Registrations Online Ltd*, 5.41 BOOKS, ETC. (services of company formation agency including Memorandum and Articles of Association); *National Business Register plc*, 5.42 BOOKS, ETC. (services of company formation agency including Memorandum and Articles of

Association); *Betty Foster (Fashion Sewing) Ltd*, 5.55 BOOKS, ETC. (dress designing kit); *Town & County Factors Ltd*, 5.76 BOOKS, ETC. (admission to greyhound stadium including programme); *Manchester United plc*, 5.77 BOOKS, ETC. (supply of hospitality package, including programme, at football match); *BNR Company Services Ltd*, 5.90 BOOKS, ETC. (supply of registering business names including registration certificate); *Weight Watchers UK Ltd*, 5.91 BOOKS, ETC (supply of weight-loss programme including leaflets and magazines); *British Sky Broadcasting plc*, 5.97 BOOKS, ETC (supply of broadcasting services including magazine); *The Angel Foundation Ltd*, 5.98 BOOKS, ETC (supply of broadcasting services including magazine); *Institute of Chartered Foresters*, 13.19 CLUBS, ASSOCIATIONS AND ORGANISATIONS (subscription including supply of magazine); *Downes Crediton Golf Club*, 13.23 CLUBS, ASSOCIATIONS AND ORGANISATIONS (entrance fee and annual subscription to golf club); *Drs Beynon & Partners*, 19.8 DRUGS, MEDICINES, AIDS FOR THE HANDICAPPED ETC. (drugs personally administered by NHS doctor); *Hall*, 19.32 DRUGS, MEDICINES, AIDS FOR THE HANDICAPPED ETC. (computer system supplied to handicapped student); *Pilgrims Language Courses Ltd*, 21.20 EDUCATION (supplies to overseas students learning English); *Primback Ltd*, 22.242 EUROPEAN COMMUNITY LAW (retailer arranging for supply of credit); *Finanzamt Oschatz v Zweckverband zur Trinkwasserversorgung und Abwasserbeseitigung Torgau-Westelbien*, 22.267 EUROPEAN COMMUNITY LAW (supply of water including connection to distribution network); *Swinger*, 24.1 EXEMPTIONS: MISCELLANEOUS (supply of photographs including delivery); *Plantiflor Ltd*, 24.2 EXEMPTIONS: MISCELLANEOUS (supply of bulbs including delivery); *BSN (Import & Export) Ltd*, 24.5 EXEMPTIONS: MISCELLANEOUS (supply of photographs including delivery); *Basebuy Ltd*, 24.6 EXEMPTIONS: MISCELLANEOUS (supply of photographs including delivery); *Morris*, 24.7 EXEMPTIONS: MISCELLANEOUS (supply of photographs including delivery); *Sherburn Aero Club Ltd*, 24.37 EXEMPTIONS: MISCELLANEOUS (flying club hiring aircraft including fuel); *Taylor & Taylor*, 27.13 FINANCE (monthly subscriptions to health club); *Marshall*, 29.73 FOOD (chip butties); *Rourke*, 29.74 FOOD (baked potatoes with cold fillings); *Domino's Pizza Group Ltd*, 29.75 FOOD (hot food including cold 'dips'); *United Biscuits (UK) Ltd*, 29.85 FOOD (biscuits sold in tins); *Paterson Arran Ltd*, 29.86 FOOD (biscuits packed in ceramic jars); *Pier Aquatics*, 29.107 FOOD (worms and maggots supplied with ornamental fish); *Scott*, 29.111 FOOD (keep of mare at stud farm); *Bushby*, 29.112 FOOD (keep of mare at stud farm); *Barr*, 29.113 FOOD (keep of mare at stud farm); *Smith*, 29.117 FOOD (rearing and keeping of cattle); *Chalk Springs Fisheries*, 29.122 FOOD (supply of right to catch fish); *Haynes*, 29.123 FOOD (supply of right to catch fish); *Pine-Coffin*, 30.5 FUEL AND POWER (electricity in holiday accommodation); *Hazelwood Caravans & Chalets Ltd*, 30.6 FUEL AND POWER (electricity in holiday accommodation); *CMC (Preston) Ltd*, 30.7 FUEL AND POWER (electricity in holiday accommodation); *Showtry Ltd*, 30.9 FUEL AND POWER (hire of agricultural machinery including petrol); *Kids of Wilmslow Ltd*, 33.62 HEALTH AND WELFARE (equipment supplied with nursery services); *Perranporth Rugby Football Club*, 36.597 INPUT TAX (construction services); *Trustees of Park Avenue Methodist Church*, 36.598 INPUT TAX (construction services); *Glamorgan Prestige Developments Ltd*, 36.599 INPUT TAX (construction services); *Crazy Farm Golf Course Ltd*, 36.600 INPUT TAX (construction services);

Lancaster Insurance Services Ltd, **38.6** INSURANCE (valuation fee charged as part of motor insurance policy); *Craddock & Walker*, **38.28** INSURANCE (supply of insured motor vehicles); *Ford Motor Co Ltd*, **38.29** INSURANCE (supply of insured motor vehicles); *Globe Equities Ltd*, **38.40** INSURANCE (insurance premiums paid as rent); *Federated Pensions Services Ltd*, **38.46** INSURANCE (company acting as pension fund trustee and administrator); *Banstead Manor Farm*, **39.1** INTERNATIONAL SERVICES (keep of mare at stud farm); *Business Enterprises (UK) Ltd*, **41.6** LAND (serviced office accommodation); *Birchforest Ltd*, **41.7** LAND (serviced office accommodation); *Grovewood (1998) Ltd*, **41.7** LAND (serviced office accommodation); *Tall Pines Golf & Leisure Co Ltd*, **41.9** LAND (licence to occupy golf course); *Window*, **41.15** LAND (rent for stables); *Virtue*, **41.22** LAND (supply of serviced land); *Banstead Downs Golf Club*, **41.70** LAND (annual subscription to golf club); *Willerby Manor Hotels Ltd*, **41.112** LAND (hire of rooms for wedding reception); *Blendhome Ltd*, **41.113** LAND (exclusivity fee in conjunction with hire of rooms for wedding reception); *Highland Council v HMRC*, **42.24** LOCAL AUTHORITIES AND STATUTORY BODIES (leisure cards giving admission to council facilities); *Wimpey Construction UK Ltd*, **44.98** MOTOR CARS (delivery charges for cars); *British Telecommunications plc*, **44.99** MOTOR CARS (delivery charges for cars); *Taylor & Taylor*, **50.83** PENALTIES: EVASION OF TAX (monthly subscriptions to health club); *Mothercare (UK) Ltd*, **58.8** RETAILERS' SPECIAL SCHEMES (discount card for use in retail clothing shop); *Southend United Football Club Ltd*, **62.155** above (club subscriptions including provision of booklet and newspapers); *Wong's Chinese Takeaway*, **62.311** above (delivery of meals); *Hemsworth Town Council*, **62.345** above (admission to playground including miniature railway); *Aspen Advisory Services Ltd*, **62.513** above (management services relating to UK properties); *British Railways Board*, **66.12** TRANSPORT (student railcard); *British Airways plc*, **66.13** TRANSPORT (air transport including catering); *Hughes*, **66.21** TRANSPORT (boat transport including catering); *Granada Group plc*, **66.36** TRANSPORT (admission to theme park including miniature railway); *Big Pit (Blaenafon) Trust Ltd*, **66.37** TRANSPORT (guided tour around disused coal mine); *Purple Parking Ltd*, **66.39** TRANSPORT (parking near airport including courtesy bus to terminal); *Computeach International Ltd*, **67.120** VALUATION (computer tuition including manuals); *Mander Laundries Ltd*, **69.1** ZERO-RATING (launderette charges). The list is not exhaustive.

Cross-references—multiple supply

[62.556] In the following cases the consideration was held to cover more than one supply and to be apportionable: *Lonsdale Travel Ltd*, **1.67** AGENTS (renovation and sale of building); *Ultratone Ltd*, **2.446** APPEALS (supplying and fitting of hearing aids); *The Rapid Results College Ltd*, **5.2** BOOKS, ETC. (textbooks supplied with correspondence course); *Rendle*, **5.5** BOOKS, ETC. (textbooks supplied with educational services); *LSA (Full Time Courses) Ltd*, **5.6** BOOKS, ETC. (study materials supplied with educational services); *Force One Training Ltd*, **5.7** BOOKS, ETC. (course books supplied with educational services); *Status Cards Ltd*, **5.9** BOOKS, ETC. (cards enabling holders to obtain discounts); *Direct Marketing Bureau*, **5.63** BOOKS, ETC. (separate supplies of design services and brochures); *Appleby Bowers*, **5.64** BOOKS, ETC. (separate supplies of promotional services and leaflets); *Jarmain*, **5.68** BOOKS, ETC. (admission to stamp fair by programme); *Thomas*, **5.69** BOOKS, ETC. (admission to greyhound stadium by programme); *Avondale Management Ltd*, **5.70** BOOKS, ETC. (admission to motorcycle championship by programme); *Charterhall Marketing Ltd*, **5.71** BOOKS, ETC. (marketing company supplying 'mail packs' including letters and leaflets); *Keesing (UK) Ltd*, **5.103** BOOKS, ETC. (free gifts supplied with magazines); *News Trade Supplies Ltd*, **5.104** BOOKS, ETC. (videotapes supplied with magazines); *Medical Aviation Services Ltd*, **11.16** CHARITIES (supply of helicopter and pilot); *Kimberly-Clark Ltd*, **12.25** CLOTHING (plastic toy boxes supplied with disposable nappies); *Tumble Tots UK Ltd*, **12.26** CLOTHING (membership of playgroup including T-shirt); *Automobile Association*, **13.17** CLUBS, ASSOCIATIONS AND ORGANISATIONS (handbook and magazine supplied as part of subscription); *Barton*, **13.18** CLUBS, ASSOCIATIONS AND ORGANISATIONS (handbook and magazine supplied as part of subscription); *Royal College of Anaesthetists*, **13.20** CLUBS, ASSOCIATIONS AND ORGANISATIONS (subscription including supply of journal); *Dyrham Park Country Club Ltd*, **13.31** CLUBS, ASSOCIATIONS AND ORGANISATIONS (bond subscribed for as condition of club membership); *Wellington Private Hospital Ltd*, **19.2** DRUGS, MEDICINES, AIDS FOR THE HANDICAPPED, ETC. (drugs provided from hospital dispensary); *Clowance Holdings Ltd*, **22.255** EUROPEAN COMMUNITY LAW (management charges paid to company operating timeshare accommodation); *Aquarium Entertainments Ltd*, **22.345** EUROPEAN COMMUNITY LAW (fire equipment leased with premises); *Tynewydd Working Men's Club*, **24.11** EXEMPTIONS: MISCELLANEOUS (entry payments covering both live entertainment and bingo); *Royal Thames Yacht Club*, **24.40** EXEMPTIONS: MISCELLANEOUS (yacht club subscriptions including sporting facilities and clubhouse facilities); *Debenhams Retail plc*, **27.11** FINANCE (retail sales paid for credit or debit card); *Thayers Ltd*, **27.62** FINANCE (retail sales paid for by credit card); *National Westminster Bank plc*, **27.58** FINANCE (provision of special cheques and credit slip forms); *MD Foods plc*, **29.95** FOOD (butter sold with dish); *Cheshire Mushroom Farm*, **29.119** FOOD (kit for growing mushrooms); *Smiths Foods Ltd*, **29.141** FOOD (packets of fruits and nuts); *Hermolis & Co Ltd*, **29.165** FOOD (Kosher meals for airlines); *Adams Woskett & Partners*, **30.12** FUEL AND POWER (electricity at caravan site); *Suffolk Heritage Housing Association Ltd*, **30.13** FUEL AND POWER (electricity in sheltered housing); *Leightons Ltd (Nos 1 & 2)*, **33.8** and **33.9** HEALTH AND WELFARE (provision of opticians' services in conjunction with supply of spectacles); *Kinnell*, **33.14** HEALTH AND WELFARE (provision of medical services and supply of appetite-suppressing drugs); *O-Pro Ltd*, **33.35** HEALTH AND WELFARE (provision of dental services in conjunction with supply of mouthguards); *Rayner & Keeler Ltd*, **36.590** INPUT TAX (refurbishment of shops including supply of furniture); *Thorn EMI plc & Granada plc*, **38.8** INSURANCE (insurance supplied with letting on hire of televisions); *Equitable Life Assurance Society*, **38.26** INSURANCE (claims handling and training services); *Bophutatswana National Commercial Corporation Ltd*, **39.2** INTERNATIONAL SERVICES (supplies of diplomatic services by company to government of Bophutatswana); *Sovereign Street Workplace Ltd*, **41.26** LAND (serviced office accommodation); *First Base Properties Ltd*, **41.27** LAND (serviced office accommodation); *Tower Hamlets Housing Action Trust*, **41.28**

LAND (serviced office accommodation); *Greater London Council*, **41.43** LAND (consideration for use of concert hall); *Court Barton Property plc*, **41.120** LAND (shares in company owning holiday accommodation); *Civilscent Ltd*, **41.147** LAND (leasing of residential apartments and car parking spaces); *TS Harrison & Sons Ltd*, **43.16** MANAGEMENT SERVICES (management and financial services); *Ho*, **62.310** above (delivery of meals); *Telewest Communications plc*, **62.371** above (supply of broadcasting services including magazine); *Laurentian Management Services Ltd*, **62.532** above (data processing and related services); *Virgin Atlantic Airways Ltd*, **66.14** TRANSPORT (chauffeur-driven car service supplied by airline company); *Virgin Atlantic Airways Ltd (No 2)*, **66.23** TRANSPORT (river transport including supplies of catering); *Durham River Trips Ltd*, **66.24** TRANSPORT (river transport including supplies of catering); *Tucker*, **66.25** TRANSPORT (river transport including supplies of catering); *Sea Containers Services Ltd*, **66.26** TRANSPORT (supplies of catering on luxury train); *Cairngorm Mountain*, **66.27** TRANSPORT (ski passes including transport on funicular railway); *El Al Airlines Ltd*, **66.38** TRANSPORT (payments to airline company for preferential facilities); *British Airports Authority (No 4)*, **66.41** TRANSPORT (payments by airline for facilities at airport). The list is not exhaustive. Where the case predates the CJEC and HL decisions in *Card Protection Plan Ltd*, **22.324** EUROPEAN COMMUNITY LAW and **38.44** INSURANCE, it should be read in the light of those decisions. For the Commissioners' views, see Business Brief 2/2001, issued on 15 February 2001.

Miscellaneous matters

VATA 1994, Sch 11 para 5(2)—recovery of tax

[62.557] See the cases noted at **14.71** to **14.74** COLLECTION AND ENFORCEMENT.

VATA 1994, s 41(2)—supplies by Government departments

[62.558] See *Cameron*, **33.52** HEALTH AND WELFARE.

'Self-billing'—responsibility of supplier for accuracy regarding VAT

[62.559] A contractor (S) was carrying out work on renovating council houses for a local authority. Some of the electrical work was carried out by the appellant company (L) as subcontractor for S. S invoiced the local authority for all work done and, with the approval of the Commissioners, operated the 'self-billing' system, under which it periodically issued payment certificates to L for the work it did. The certificates did not include VAT and L, knowing that part of its work could be standard-rated, queried this with the Commissioners. The result was that the Commissioners assessed L for the tax on its standard-rated supplies to S. There was no dispute about the figures but L was unlikely to get reimbursement of the tax from S, which had gone into liquidation. The tribunal dismissed L's appeal. The fact that 'self-billing' had been used did not absolve L from its obligation to ensure the accuracy of the payment certificates from S. *TA Landels & Sons Ltd*, MAN/78/52 (VTD 521). (*Note. VATA 1994, s 29* allows the Commissioners the discretion to collect the tax due from the recipient of the services and not the supplier where the recipient produces the tax invoice.)

[62.560] The decision in *TA Landels & Sons Ltd*, 62.559 above, was applied in the similar case of *Heath Plastering Co Ltd*, MAN/92/923 (VTD 10680).

[62.561] Similar decisions were reached in *M & D Price Bros Ltd*, BIR/78/143 (VTD 713) and *EC Shearer*, EDN/92/189 (VTD 10608).

[62.562] A company (S), which traded as a scrap metal dealer, sold a quantity of gold bullion to a dealer who purported to operate as an authorised purchaser under the 'gold scheme'. (This was a scheme operated by the Commissioners to combat fraud whereby, if the strict conditions of the scheme were complied with, the purchaser rather than the seller accounted for tax on the supply.) VAT shown on twelve invoices issued on a self-billing arrangement by the purchaser was never paid to the Commissioners. The required undertaking to pay VAT was stamped on the invoices but in no case was it signed. S had deducted the input tax and was assessed on the corresponding output tax. S appealed, contending that under the scheme the responsibility for paying the VAT should rest on the buyer rather than the seller. The tribunal dismissed the appeal, holding that the scheme did not absolve S from its statutory liability to account for the tax due. *K Squire Group Ltd*, [1985] VATTR 97 (VTD 1841).

[62.563] See also the cases noted at 52.275 to 52.278 PENALTIES: MISDECLARATION.

Validity of invoices where customer operates 'self-billing' system

[62.564] See *UDL Construction plc*, 40.3 INVOICES AND CREDIT NOTES.

63

Tour Operators and Travel Agents

The cases in this chapter are arranged under the following headings.

Definition of 'tour operator' (VATA 1994, s 53(3))   63.1
Tour Operators' Margin Scheme   63.9

Definition of 'tour operator' (VATA 1994, s 53(3))

[63.1] A company which supplied holiday accommodation in Spain failed to account for VAT. The Commissioners issued an assessment in accordance with the *VAT (Tour Operators) Order 1987 (SI 1987/1806)*. The tribunal dismissed the company's appeal, holding that the company was a 'tour operator' within what is now *VATA 1994, s 53(3)*. *Coastrider Holidays Ltd*, LON/89/1730 (VTD 5289).

[63.2] A company which traded as a tour operator reclaimed input tax in respect of hotel room bookings and car hirings used for an 'executive bonus scheme', under which passengers travelling in executive class from the Republic of Ireland to London were provided with vouchers offering one night's free hotel accommodation or 24 hours' free car hire. The Commissioners rejected the claim, considering that the tax was not deductible by virtue of the *VAT (Tour Operators) Order 1987 (SI 1987/1806)*. The tribunal dismissed the company's appeal. The company was a tour operator as defined in what is now *VATA 1994, s 53(3)*. The bookings of hotel accommodation and car hire were supplies of services within *Article 3(1)(a)* of the *VAT (Tour Operators) Order*. They were not integral or incidental to the supply of air transport. Accordingly, the input tax on those supplies was not deductible by virtue of *Article 12* of the *Order*. Furthermore, *s 53(3)* was in accordance with *Article 26* of the *EC Sixth Directive*. *Aer Lingus plc*, [1992] VATTR 438 (VTD 8893).

[63.3] A company carried on business by making block bookings of ferry crossings over the English Channel and the Irish Sea, and of hotel accommodation, and reselling these bookings to coach companies which provided Continental holidays. It did not deal directly with members of the public, and did not operate the Tour Operators' Margin Scheme. The Commissioners formed the opinion that the company should have operated the Scheme, and had underpaid tax through failing to do so, and issued an assessment accordingly. The company appealed, contending firstly that it was not within the definition of 'tour operator' in what is now *VATA 1994, s 53(3)* and that its supplies were not of a 'designated travel service' within *Article 3(1)* of the *VAT (Tour Operators) Order (SI 1987/1806)*, and alternatively that its supplies were not within *Article 26* of the *EC Sixth Directive*, which was inconsistent with the UK legislation and should be treated as having direct effect. The tribunal allowed the company's appeal, holding that the company was a 'tour operator' and was supplying 'designated travel services' within the terms of the UK legislation, but that it was not within *Article 26* of the *EC Sixth Directive*, since it did not deal with members of the public. The tribunal held, after comparing the text of the *Directive* with other language texts, that the reference to 'customers' in *Article 26(1)* should be construed as a reference to 'travellers', and that *Article 26* applied only to travel agents who dealt with travellers, and not to travel agents who acted as wholesalers making supplies to retailers. *Independent Coach Travel (Wholesaling) Ltd*, [1993] VATTR 357 (VTD 11037). (*Note.* Compare the subsequent decision in *Gulliver's Travel Agency Ltd*, **63.5** below.)

[63.4] The decision in *Independent Coach Travel (Wholesaling) Ltd*, **63.3** above, was applied in the similar subsequent case of *Norman Allen Group Travel Ltd*, [1996] VATDR 405 (VTD 14158). (*Note.* For the Commissioners' practice following this decision, see Business Brief 14/97, issued on 30 June 1997.)

[63.5] A Japanese company (G), with a place of business in the UK, made supplies to Japanese tour operators by arranging for the provision of hotel accommodation, restaurant meals, tour guides and theatre tickets for Japanese tourists visiting the UK. The Commissioners issued a ruling that G's supplies should be treated as taking place in the UK by virtue of *Article 2* of the *VAT (Tour Operators) Order*. G appealed, contending that its supplies took place outside the UK and that it was not within the *Order*, and that the *Order* was incompatible with the *EC Sixth Directive*. The tribunal reviewed the evidence in detail and allowed G's appeal in part, holding that the supplies of hotel accommodation and of tour guides were made by G, as an independent principal, in the UK, applying *Ibstock Building Products Ltd*, **36.14** INPUT TAX, and *Northern Lawn Tennis Club*, **36.16** INPUT TAX, and distinguishing *Institute of Purchasing and Supply*, **36.15** INPUT TAX, and *Football Association Ltd*, **8.36** BUSINESS ENTERTAINMENT. However, the tribunal held that with regard to the supplies of restaurant meals, G was merely supplying services and was not actually supplying the meals itself, observing that 'at no stage was it ever contemplated that G should become the owner of the roast beef or have any proprietorial interest in it' and holding that G's services were supplied at its head office in Japan rather than in the UK. With regard to the theatre tickets, G was acting as an agent for the tour operators and its supplies of agency services were made at its Japanese head office and were outside the scope of the *Order*. The tribunal distinguished *Independent Coach Travel (Wholesaling) Ltd*, **63.3** above, on the grounds that G was not supplying 'designated travel services' within *Article 3* of the *VAT (Tour Operators) Order*, and held that it was only *Article 3* of the *Order* which was *ultra vires* and ineffective. The expression 'for the benefit of travellers' covered 'supplies by wholesale providers of travel services to retail providers', so that G's supplies were within *Article 2* of the *Order*. *Gulliver's Travel Agency Ltd*, [1994] VATTR 210 (VTD 12494).

[63.6] A company arranged hotel accommodation overseas for UK customers, but did not arrange transport. It did not operate the Tour Operators' Margin Scheme. The Commissioners issued a ruling that the company was required to operate the Margin Scheme. The tribunal dismissed the company's appeal, holding that the company was within the definition of a 'travel agent' and thus was within *VATA 1994, s 53(3)*. *Beheersmaatschappij Van*

Ginkel Waddinxveen BV & Others v Inspecteur de Omzetbelasting Utrecht, **22.485** EUROPEAN COMMUNITY LAW, applied. *Hotels Abroad Ltd*, LON/93/255A (VTD 13026).

Limousine services

[63.7] In the case noted at **66.14** TRANSPORT, the Commissioners issued a ruling that an airline company, which supplied a chauffeur-driven car service to some of its passengers on international flights, was within what is now *VATA 1994, s 53*, so that the input tax in question was not deductible. The tribunal allowed the company's appeal on this point, observing that the fact that the company was supplying a bought-in transport service did not mean that it had to be treated as a 'travel agent' or 'tour operator' within what is now *VATA 1994, s 53(3)*. *Virgin Atlantic Airways Ltd*, [1993] VATTR 136 (VTD 11096).

Whether company acting as 'tour operator' or as agent

[63.8] A company (L) accounted for VAT under the Tour Operators' Margin Scheme in respect of supplies of French holiday accommodation. It subsequently submitted a repayment claim on the basis that it had been acting as an agent rather than as a 'tour operator', and should not have operated the scheme. Customs rejected the claim and the tribunal dismissed L's appeal, holding that the effect of the booking conditions in L's holiday brochures was that it was acting as a principal rather than as agent, and was required to operate the Margin Scheme. *International Life Leisure Ltd*, MAN/02/524 (VTD 19649). (*Note.* Costs were awarded to Customs.)

Tour operators' margin scheme

Definition of 'specified method'

[63.9] A VAT officer wrote to a company (J) which provided holidays for language students, attempting to explain the Tour Operators' Margin Scheme, and setting out calculations of J's VAT liability for an earlier period. However, the officer wrongly treated some of J's inputs as zero-rated, when in fact they were standard-rated. J accounted for tax on the basis set out in the officer's letter, with the result that it accounted for less tax than it should have done. A different VAT officer subsequently discovered this, and Customs issued assessments charging tax on the basis of *Leaflet No 709/5/88*. J appealed, contending as a preliminary point that the VAT officer's letter should be treated as a specified method conforming with the Tour Operators' Order (*SI 1987/1806*). The tribunal rejected this contention, holding that the VAT officer's letter did not qualify as a 'specified method'. At a subsequent hearing, J contended that certain services which it had received from local organisers, and which Customs had treated as general overheads, should be dealt with under the Scheme, thereby reducing its taxable margin. The tribunal allowed J's appeal in part, finding that 'all the services supplied by the local organisers are enjoyed unchanged and in kind by the travellers'. The local organiser 'provides the services of engaging the accommodation which is occupied by the students; she hires the halls and the local teachers and the benefit of both are enjoyed by the students'. *Jenny Braden Holidays Ltd*, LON/92/2699 & 3095 (VTD 10892, 12860). (*Notes*. (1) For an application for judicial review, see **2.330** APPEALS. (2) *Leaflet 709/5/88* has subsequently been replaced by *Notice 709/5/04*.)

Definition of 'designated travel service'

[63.10] A trader supplied weekend trips (including rail travel and hotel accommodation) and day trips by rail. For the day trips, he hired an engine and coaches from railway companies, and provided stewards and catering facilities. He accounted for tax on the basis that the day trips fell outside the Tour Operators' Margin Scheme and were zero-rated. Customs issued a ruling that the day trips were a 'designated travel service', within *VAT (Tour Operators) Order 1987 (SI 1987/1806), article 3*. The tribunal upheld Customs' ruling. *N Harvey (t/a Green Express Railtours)*, MAN/97/594 (VTD 15608).

Treatment of discounts

[63.11] In the case noted at **22.493** EUROPEAN COMMUNITY LAW, a company (F) sold holidays through travel agents. It paid the agents commission (usually 10%) on sales. In some cases agents arranged sales at cheaper prices than those published in F's brochures. In such cases the agents still had to pay F the full brochure price, thereby effectively reducing their commission. Initially F accounted for VAT on the basis that the sum 'paid or payable', within *article 7* of the *VAT (Tour Operators) Order 1987 (SI 1987/1806)* was its brochure price. Subsequently it submitted a repayment claim on the basis that the sum 'paid or payable' was the price actually paid by the customer, excluding the amount paid by the travel agent. Customs rejected the claim and F appealed. The CA referred the case to the CJEC, which held that 'the total amount to be paid by the traveller' (in *Article 26(2)* of the *EC Sixth Directive*) included any additional amount that 'a travel agent, acting as an intermediary on behalf of a tour operator', had to 'pay to the tour operator on top of the price paid by the traveller and which corresponds in amount to the discount given by the travel agent to the traveller on the price of the holiday stated in the tour operator's brochure'. Following the CJEC decision, the CA determined the appeal in favour of Customs. Rix LJ held that *Leaflet 709/5/88* should be 'construed by reference to the "charge" of £1,000, rather than the sum paid by the traveller himself of £950. Alternatively, and in effect, the phrase "your total charge to your customers" can be interpreted as meaning, by implication, "your total charge to be paid by or for the account of your customer"'. *C & E Commrs v First Choice Holidays plc*, CA [2004] STC 1407; [2004] EWCA Civ 1044. (*Notes*. (1) *Leaflet 709/5/88* has subsequently been replaced by *Notice 709/5/04*. (2) For HMRC's practice following this decision, see Business Brief 08/06, issued on 7 July 2006.)

Calculation of depreciation

[63.12] The Commissioners issued a direction to a partnership which operated a number of buses and coaches, requiring it to account for tax under the Tour Operators' Margin Scheme. The partnership appealed, contending that it should be allowed to adopt a calculation of depreciation based on replacement cost, and to include general overheads in the calculation of liability under the Scheme. The tribunal allowed the partnership's appeal in part, holding that the calculation of depreciation should be based on historic cost rather than on replacement cost, and that general overheads could not be included in the calculation of liability under the Scheme, but that costs which could be regarded 'as an indirect cost of the tour operations' (such as the provision of garage facilities) could be included in the calculation. *RA, DL & GA Whittle (t/a Go Whittle)*, [1994] VATTR 202 (VTD 12164). (*Note.* This case was distinguished—and, in part, implicitly disapproved—in the subsequent case of *Cicero Languages International*, **63.16** below.)

Cost of in-house standard-rated supplies

[63.13] A company (D) operated two hotels. Most of its customers were simply supplied with accommodation ('full paying' customers), but it also offered 'package holidays'. 'Package holiday' customers were supplied with transport to and from the hotel and coach outings to nearby places of interest. They were offered a more restricted menu than the 'full paying' customers. Customs issued an assessment on the basis that various overheads (including salaries, rates, lighting, heating and repairs) should be included as part of the cost of D's in-house standard-rated supplies. D appealed, contending firstly that overheads should not be included in the calculation of cost, and secondly that, in apportioning the cost of standard-rated in-house supplies between the 'full paying' customers and the 'package holiday' customers, an adjustment should be made to reflect 'the lower standard of supplies made to the package holiday guests'. The tribunal allowed D's appeal in part, holding that there should be 'a fair allocation of the total profit on a mixed package of margin scheme supplies and in-house supplies between those two categories of supplies so that the margin scheme supplies are only taxed on the margin and so that the in-house supplies are taxed in the usual way'. The tribunal held that a proportion of the rent, rates, water, lighting, heating and depreciation of the premises used by the package holiday guests should be treated as part of the cost of the hotel accommodation. However, management and administration salaries, repairs and maintenance, gardening expenses, insurance and various other expenses should be treated as part of the general expenses of the business, not forming part of the cost of the 'in-house' supplies. The tribunal also held that the apportionment between the 'full paying' customers and the 'package holiday' customers should be made 'by reference to the number of nights spent by each category of guests, weighted to take account of the reduced standard of accommodation available to the package holiday guests'. *The Devonshire Hotel (Torquay) Ltd*, LON/94/584A (VTD 14448). (*Note. Leaflet 709/5/88* has subsequently been replaced by *Notice 709/5/04*.)

Catering at hotel

[63.14] A hotel proprietor (M) provided coach transport to and from the hotel for some customers. He operated the Tour Operators' Margin Scheme, but treated the cost of the food which he purchased as a deduction. Customs issued an assessment on the basis that the cost of the food was not an allowable deduction. The tribunal dismissed M's appeal, holding that he was making supplies of catering. These were 'in-house supplies' which had to be excluded from the calculation of the tax due under the Margin Scheme. *M Myerscough (t/a Summerleaze Beach Hotel)*, LON/97/1183 (VTD 17583).

Hotel proprietors providing transport

[63.15] The proprietors of a hotel in Devon provided coach transport to and from the hotel for customers from Northern England. About 90% of the hotel's customers used the coach. Customs issued assessments on the basis that the hotel proprietors were required to operate the Tour Operators' Margin Scheme. The proprietors appealed, contending that the basis of apportionment laid down in *Leaflet 709/5/88* contravened *Article 26* of the *EC Sixth Directive*. The case was referred to the CJEC, which delivered a judgment in favour of the proprietors (see **22.487** EUROPEAN COMMUNITY LAW). The tribunal subsequently allowed the proprietors' appeals, holding that *Leaflet 709/5/88* 'which provided for a mandatory costs apportionment was contrary to Community Law as interpreted by the Court of Justice and was *ultra vires* the domestic legislation. On the basis of the interpretation by the Court of Justice of *Article 26* of the *Sixth Directive*, the United Kingdom was not entitled to require tour operators to apportion package prices between in-house and bought-in supplies on a costs basis. A costs basis may only be required or used where the market value of in-house supplies is not possible and where a cost apportionment accurately reflects the structure of the package. In requiring a cost apportionment under the Leaflet, the Commissioners did not comply with the Directive and acted outside their powers under domestic law.' *Madgett, Baldwin & Madgett (t/a The Howden Court Hotel) (No 2)*, [2006] VATDR 214 (VTD 19719). (*Note. Leaflet 709/5/88* has subsequently been replaced by *Notice 709/5/04*.)

Bought-in supplies of designated travel services

[63.16] A partnership which supplied educational services made a number of designated travel services, and operated the Tour Operators' Margin Scheme. In accounting for tax under the Scheme, it included as negative amounts incidental costs which were linked with bought-in supplies, such as the costs of supervising, and advertising for, accommodation to be supplied to students. Customs issued an assessment charging tax on the basis that the inclusion of such incidental costs was incorrect, and that, in the case of supplies of accommodation, the negative amounts should be limited to the amounts which the partnership actually paid host families for accommodating its students. The tribunal upheld the assessment. *Cicero Languages International*, LON/97/603 (VTD 15246).

Charges for credit card transactions

[63.17] A company which operated the Tour Operators' Margin Scheme sought to deduct charges which it paid to credit card companies for transactions by credit card. Customs issued an assessment on the basis that these charges were not allowable deductions. The company appealed, contending that the charges should be treated as a direct cost of making the relevant supplies. The tribunal rejected this contention and dismissed the company's appeal, holding that the relevant charges were an 'indirect cost' and were not deductible in the TOMS calculation. *Atlantic Holidays Ltd*, LON/05/214 (VTD 20011).

Holiday packages containing in-house and bought-in supplies

[63.18] A company (W) which provided coach tours failed to account for VAT on its 'bought-in' supplies of hotel accommodation. Customs issued an assessment under the Tour Operators' Margin Scheme. W appealed, contending firstly that it should be allowed to use National Express coach fares as a comparator in calculating the value of its in-house supplies of transport, and alternatively that it should be allowed to deduct notional rent and hire-purchase interest on the purchase of its coaches. The tribunal rejected these contentions and dismissed W's appeal. *Welsh's Coaches Ltd*, MAN/04/114 (VTD 20193).

[63.19] See also *MyTravel plc (No 1)*, **22.488** EUROPEAN COMMUNITY LAW.

Danish company—tours sold by UK subsidiary

[63.20] See *DFDS A/S*, **22.492** EUROPEAN COMMUNITY LAW.

Election for separate computation of non-EC supplies

[63.21] A company operated the Tour Operators' Margin Scheme. It formed the opinion that it would have been to its advantage if it had accounted for tax on supplies outside the EC separately, and submitted a retrospective repayment claim. Customs rejected the claim on the basis that such an election must be made in advance, and could not be retrospective. The tribunal dismissed the company's appeal and the QB upheld this decision. The scheme provided for tour operators to elect if they wished to use the 'separated supplies' method. Neither the standard method of calculation nor the 'separated supplies' method contained any inherent disadvantage for a tour operator, and the question of which method was more advantageous would depend on the particular composition of each operator's business. There was nothing unreasonable in refusing retrospective applications. *Aspro Travel Ltd v C & E Commrs*, QB 1996, [1997] STC 151.

[63.22] The decision in *Aspro Travel Ltd*, 63.21 above, was applied in the similar subsequent case of *Best Travel Ltd (in liquidation)*, LON/96/500 (VTD 15753).

[63.23] A company operated the Tour Operators' Margin Scheme, and had elected to treat its supplies outside the EC separately, but wrongly treated supplies to the Canary Islands in its computation of zero-rated EC supplies. Customs issued an assessment to correct the error. The tribunal upheld the assessment. *Elvington Ltd*, LON/96/350 (VTD 14537).

[63.24] A company operated the Tour Operators' Margin Scheme, and had elected to treat its supplies outside the EC separately. In December 1998 it applied to Customs to revoke the election and change to the standard 'worldwide' method for its financial year ending October 1998. Customs rejected the claim on the basis that a tour operator could 'only ask to do a separate calculation or revert to a single calculation' at the start of its financial year, and that 'permission will not be granted retrospectively'. The Ch D upheld Customs' ruling. Lightman J held that *Leaflet 709/5/96, para 13(c)* clearly required that notification should be given at the start of the relevant financial year. That paragraph had the force of law. *C & E Commrs v Simply Travel Ltd*, Ch D 2001, [2002] STC 194. (*Note. Leaflet 709/5/96* has subsequently been replaced by *Notice 709/5/04*.)

[63.25] The decision in *Simply Travel Ltd*, **63.24** above, was applied in the similar subsequent case of *Mytravel Group plc (No 2)*, MAN/02/426 (VTD 18940).

Failure to make annual adjustment—time limit for assessment

[63.26] See *Dunwood Travel Ltd*, **3.98** ASSESSMENT.

64

Trade Unions, Professional and Public Interest Bodies

The cases are arranged under the following headings.

Associations held to be within VATA 1994, Sch 9, Group 9
    Professional bodies (*VATA 1994, Sch 9, Group 9, Item 1(b)*)   **64.1**
    Associations for advancement of knowledge (*VATA 1994, Sch 9, Group 9, Item 1(c)*)   **64.3**
    Representative associations (*VATA 1994, Sch 9, Group 9, Item 1(d)*)   **64.8**
    Public interest bodies (*VATA 1994, Sch 9, Group 9, Item 1(e)*)   **64.9**
Associations held not to be within VATA 1994, Sch 9, Group 9   **64.12**
Miscellaneous   **64.37**

NOTE

The scope of *VATA 1994, Sch 9, Group 9* was expanded with effect from 1 December 1999 to extend exemption to subscriptions to certain bodies in the public interest, which had previously been held to be outside the scope of VAT by virtue of *VATA 1994, s 94(3)*. See *VATA 1994, Sch 9, Group 9, Item 1(e)*, introduced by the *VAT (Subscriptions to Trade Unions, Professional and Other Public Interest Bodies) Order 1999 (SI 1999/2834)*. Cases relating to periods before December 1999 should be read in the light of the changes to the legislation.

Associations held to be within VATA 1994, Sch 9, Group 9

Professional bodies (VATA 1994, Sch 9 Group 9, Item 1(b))

Association of dancing teachers

[64.1] A company, limited by guarantee, was formed to encourage dancing. The Commissioners issued a ruling that its subscriptions from dancing teachers were standard-rated, and the company appealed, contending that they were exempt from VAT by virtue of what is now *VATA 1994, Sch 9, Group 9, Item 1(b)*. The tribunal accepted the company's contention and allowed the appeal, holding that the teaching of dancing was a profession and that the association was within the definition of a professional association. *Allied Dancing Association Ltd*, [1993] VATTR 405 (10777). (*Notes.* (1) The tribunal held that the association qualified for exemption under *Item 1(c)* as well as *Item 1(b)*. The Commissioners accepted the decision with regard to *Item 1(b)*, but state in Customs' VAT Manual, Part 7, chapter 24, para 5.4 that they 'do not accept' the tribunal's decision with regard to *Item 1(c)*. (2) For another issue in this case, see **21.33** EDUCATION.)

Institute of Shipbrokers

[64.2] The Commissioners issued a ruling that the Institute of Chartered Shipbrokers was obliged to account for VAT on its members' subscriptions. The Institute appealed, contending that it was a professional association, and that its supplies were exempt from VAT under *VATA 1994, Sch 9, Group 9*. The tribunal accepted this contention and allowed the appeal, observing that shipbroking involved 'considerable expertise' and that the Institute set examinations which 'have a substantial intellectual element as well as purely practical aspects'. The Institute required 'certain standards of conduct and takes sanctions against those who fall short'. Accordingly, the Institute was within the definition of a 'professional association' in *Group 9, Item 1(b)*. *Institute of Chartered Shipbrokers*, LON/96/1743 (VTD 15033).

Associations for advancement of knowledge (VATA 1994, Sch 9, Group 9, Item 1(c))

Organic farmers

[64.3] An unincorporated association was established with the aim of promoting research into organic farming. The Commissioners issued a ruling that it was required to account for output tax on its members' subscriptions. The association appealed, contending that its supplies should be treated as exempt under what is now *VATA 1994, Sch 9, Group 9*. The tribunal accepted this contention and allowed the appeal, holding that organic farming was a science, so that the association's services came within *Group 9, Item 1(c)*, which provided exemption for associations whose primary purpose was the advancement of a particular branch of science. *British Organic Farmers*, [1988] VATTR 64 (VTD 2700).

British Association for Counselling

[64.4] The British Association for Counselling was formed in 1977, as a non-profit making organisation, with funding from the DHSS and the Home Office. By 1993 it had 11,600 individual members. It published a quarterly journal and a number of directories, organised conferences, and ran an information service. The Commissioners issued a ruling that it did not qualify for exemption under what is now *VATA 1994, Sch 9, Group 9*, on the grounds that counselling was not a profession. The Association appealed, contending that it was exempt under what is now *VATA 1994, Sch 9, Group 9, Item 1(c)*. The tribunal accepted this contention and allowed the appeal, holding that counselling was not a profession, but that the primary purpose of the Association was the advancement of a particular branch of knowledge 'connected with the past or present professions or employments of its members'. Accordingly the services which the Association supplied to its members were exempt from VAT. *The British Association for Counselling*, LON/93/1494 (VTD 11855).

Permanent Way Institution

[64.5] The Permanent Way Institution was founded in 1884 by a group of railway track inspectors, with the principal object of promoting 'the acquisition and exchange of technical and general knowledge' relating to the design, construction, inspection and maintenance of railway track. In 2001 the Commissioners issued a ruling that it was required to account for VAT on its subscriptions. The Institution appealed, contending that its primary purpose was the advancement of a particular branch of knowledge 'connected with the past or present professions or employments of its members', so that its subscriptions qualified for exemption under *VATA 1994, Sch 9, Group 9, Item 1(c)*. The tribunal accepted this contention and allowed the appeal, observing that the Institution's 'role in disseminating knowledge has, since 1996 when British Rail ceased to exist, become more important than ever, especially as Railtrack merely has overall responsibility for the permanent way and the actual work on it is carried out by major contractors who employ numerous subcontractors'. *The Permanent Way Institution*, LON/01/585 (VTD 17746).

Company established to promote use of medical information systems

[64.6] A company (E), limited by guarantee and registered as a charity, was established as a non-profit-making organisation to 'improve patient care through the better use of health information and information technology', and to support users of certain 'medical information systems'. Customs issued a ruling that it was required to account for VAT on its membership subscriptions. E appealed, contending that they should be treated as exempt from VAT under *VATA 1994, Sch 9, Group 9, Item 1(c)*. The tribunal accepted this contention and allowed the appeal, finding that E's primary purpose was 'to assist and encourage its members to acquire and utilise the knowledge, skills and tools, which enable information to be collected, managed, used and shared to support the delivery of healthcare and promote health'. This constituted 'the fostering of professional expertise' and qualified for exemption. *EMIS National User Group*, MAN/05/594 (VTD 19645).

Institute of Information Security Professionals

[64.7] The Institute of Information Security Professionals was established in 2006 with the aim of promoting 'the study and practice of Information Security and to advance knowledge, education and professionalism therein for the benefit of the public'. HMRC issued a ruling that it was required to account for VAT on its members' subscriptions. The Institute appealed, contending they should be treated as exempt from VAT under *VATA 1994, Sch 9, Group 9, Item 1(c)*. The First-Tier Tribunal accepted this contention and allowed the appeal. Gort J held that the primary purpose of the Institute was 'to advance the professionalism of information security practitioners and thereby the professionalism of the industry as a whole'. Accordingly it qualified for exemption under *Item 1(c)*. *Institute of Information Security Professionals v HMRC*, [2009] UKFTT 365 (TC), TC00303.

Representative associations (VATA 1994, Sch 9, Group 9, Item 1(d))

Association of tour operators

[64.8] An association of tour operators registered for VAT in 1991, and accounted for VAT on its membership subscriptions. In 2008 it submitted a repayment claim on the basis that it should have treated these subscriptions as exempt under *VATA 1994, Sch 9, Group 9, Item 1(d)*. HMRC rejected the claim but the tribunal allowed the association's appeal in principle (subject to agreement as to figures). Judge Kempster held that, for the purpose of *Item 1(d)*, the reference to 'the Government' should not be construed as being restricted to the UK Government. He held that exemption should 'include representations to EU institutions in relation to matters that will have effect in the UK'. On the evidence, the primary purpose of the association was within *Item 1(d)*. Furthermore, the fact that some of the association's members had joined it because of its 'networking and marketing opportunities', rather than because of its lobbying activities, did not prevent it from qualifying for exemption, since *Note 5* referred to 'the purposes of the association', rather than to the 'primary purpose' of the association. *European Tour Operators Association v HMRC*, [2011] UKFTT 88 (TC), TC00965. (*Note.* HMRC have appealed to the Upper Tribunal against this decision. The Upper Tribunal is scheduled to begin hearing the appeal on 17 May 2012.)

Public interest bodies (VATA 1994, Sch 9, Group 9, Item 1(e))

Rotary Clubs

[64.9] Rotary International (RI), an unincorporated association of Rotary Clubs in the UK, was registered for VAT in 1973. In 1988 it applied to be deregistered. The Commissioners rejected the application and RI appealed, contending that it was a body with objects of a philanthropic nature (see now *VATA 1994, Sch 9, Group 9, Item 1(e)*), and therefore should not be required to account for output tax. The tribunal accepted this contention and allowed the appeal, holding that the objects of RI were 'redolent of a desire to promote the well-being of mankind by serving one's fellow-men'. The fact that some of RI's members had joined it for 'social reasons' did not prevent it from qualifying for exemption. *Rotary International*, [1991] VATTR 177 (VTD 5946).

Game Conservancy Trust

[64.10] The Game Conservancy Trust was established in 1969 and was recognised as a charity in 1980. Its objects were, *inter alia*, 'to promote for the public benefit the conservation and study of game species, their habitats and other species associated with those habitats'. Until 1999 it accounted for VAT on its members' subscriptions. It subsequently formed the opinion that it was a body with objects of a philanthropic nature, within *VATA 1994, Sch 9, Group 9, Item 1(e)*, and applied for repayment. The Commissioners rejected the claim on the basis that the trust primarily existed to support the self-interest of its members, most of whom enjoyed shooting as a hobby. The Trust appealed. The tribunal reviewed the evidence in detail and allowed the appeal, holding that the objects of the Trust were 'directed at the promotion of the well-being of mankind' and 'serve to benefit the general community'. *The Game Conservancy Trust*, [2001] VATDR 422 (VTD 17394).

Ethical Trading Initiative

[64.11] The Ethical Trading Initiative (ETI) was established in 1998 as a company limited by guarantee, to 'promote and encourage ethical trading in order to improve conditions for workers and their communities in the supply chains of companies supplying products in the UK market'. It registered for VAT in 1999, and charged VAT on the subscriptions paid by its corporate members. In 2007 HMRC issued a ruling that these subscriptions were exempt under *VATA 1994, Sch 9, Group 9, Item 1(e)* (so that ETI's corporate members could not reclaim input tax on them). ETI appealed, contending inter alia that it should not be treated as falling within *Item 1(e)* since its objects were not 'in the public domain'. The tribunal rejected this contention and dismissed the appeal. *Ethical Trading Initiative v HMRC*, [2010] UKFTT 423 (TC), TC00690.

Associations held not to be within VATA 1994, Sch 9, Group 9

Royal Photographic Society

[64.12] The Royal Photographic Society was a company limited by guarantee established to promote the general advancement of photographic science. It had some 6,000 members. Membership was open to any person interested in photography whether or not professionally. The Commissioners issued a ruling that the Society was required to register for VAT. The Society appealed, contending that it was a professional body within what is now *VATA 1994, Sch 9, Group 9*. The tribunal rejected this contention and dismissed the appeal, holding that the Society was not within *Item 1(b)* and, although it was an association for the advancement of a particular branch of knowledge, it was not within *Item 1(c)* by virtue of *Note 4*. *Royal Photographic Society*, [1978] VATTR 191 (VTD 647).

Bookmakers' association

[64.13] A company limited by guarantee, with no share capital, had a membership of bookmakers in London and the Home Counties, each paying an annual subscription. The Commissioners issued a ruling that it was liable to account for VAT on the subscriptions it received. The company appealed, contending that its supplies were exempt under what is now *VATA 1994, Sch 9, Group 9*. The tribunal rejected this contention and dismissed the appeal, holding on the evidence that the company's main activity was advising and helping its members in their day-to-day business. This was not for the advancement of a 'branch of knowledge'. The association did nothing to foster its members' expertise and, even if it did, their expertise was not professional. *The Bookmakers' Protection Association (Southern Area) Ltd*, [1979] VATTR 215 (VTD 849).

Association of taxi-cab owners

[64.14] A company was incorporated as an association of taxi-cab proprietors. Its members paid a basic subscription of £2 per week and an optional
'radio subscription' of £11.89 per week. The most important facility it
provided was a 24-hour radio taxi service, with the loan of a radio, for those
members (nearly 90% of the total) who paid the 'radio subscription'.
The Commissioners issued an assessment charging VAT on all members'
subscriptions, and the company appealed, contending that they were exempt
under what is now *VATA 1994, Sch 9, Group 9*. The tribunal rejected this
contention and dismissed the appeal, holding that the association was not
within *Item 1(a)* as its main activity was the provision of the radio service and
in any event its members were not employees. It was also not a professional
association within *Item 1(b)*; applying the principles laid down by Du Parcq LJ
in *Carr v CIR*, CA [1944] 2 All ER 163, 'no ordinary intelligent man today
would regard the driving of a taxi cab as a profession'. *City Cabs
(Edinburgh) Ltd*, EDN/79/30 (VTD 928).

Bee farmers

[64.15] The Commissioners issued an assessment on an association of bee
farmers, charging tax on members' subscriptions. The association's treasurer
appealed, contending that its supplies were exempt under what is now *VATA
1994, Sch 9, Group 9*. The tribunal rejected this contention and dismissed the
appeal, holding that beekeeping was not 'a particular branch of knowledge'
and did not involve 'professional expertise'. On the evidence, the association
resembled a craft guild, its primary purpose being to further the commercial
interests of beekeepers. *MJ Chandler (as Treasurer of the Bee Farmers
Association)*, LON/83/248 (VTD 1565).

Cleaning contractors

[64.16] A company was established to promote 'the science of cleaning'.
The Commissioners issued a ruling that it was required to register for VAT, and
the company appealed, contending that its supplies were exempt under what
is now *VATA 1994, Sch 9, Group 9*. The tribunal rejected this contention and
dismissed the appeal, holding that cleaning could not be regarded as a
particular branch of knowledge and that those engaged in the cleaning
industry were not exercising 'professional expertise'. *The British Institute of
Cleaning Science Ltd*, LON/85/184 (VTD 1981).

National Association of Funeral Directors

[64.17] An association had been established to organise, watch over, maintain, promote and assist the rights and interests of funeral directors. The Commissioners issued a ruling that it was required to account for output tax on its
subscriptions. The Association appealed, contending that its subscriptions
were exempt from tax under what is now *VATA 1994, Sch 9, Group 9, Item
1(c)*. The tribunal rejected this contention and dismissed the appeal, holding
that, although the Association fostered expertise about the techniques of

funeral directing and related matters, funeral directors were not members of a recognised profession and accordingly the primary aim of the Association could not be for the advancement of a particular branch of knowledge or the fostering of professional expertise. *National Association of Funeral Directors*, LON/84/467 (VTD 1989).

Institute of Leisure and Amenity Management

[64.18] An institute was established in 1983 to represent people employed in the management of leisure and amenity facilities. The Commissioners issued an assessment charging tax on its subscriptions. The institute appealed, contending that it was a professional association within what is now *VATA 1994, Sch 9, Group 9*, and alternatively that its aims were of a 'civic nature' and exempt under *Article 13A1(l)* of the *EC Sixth Directive*. The tribunal rejected this contention and dismissed the appeal, and the QB upheld this decision. On the evidence, the Institute had been set up to serve the needs of a particular industry and it could not be said that the members were practising a profession. Furthermore, the expression 'of a civic nature' did not include everyday and generally expected municipal services such as parks, leisure centres and other similar facilities. *Institute of Leisure & Amenity Management v C & E Commrs*, QB [1988] STC 602; [1988] 3 CMLR 380.

Institute of Employment Consultants

[64.19] A company was established to represent and educate workers in the employment agency industry. The Commissioners issued a ruling that it was required to account for output tax on its subscriptions, and the company appealed, contending that its supplies were exempt under what is now *VATA 1994, Sch 9, Group 9*. The tribunal rejected this contention and dismissed the appeal, holding that the recruitment industry was not a recognised profession. *The Institute of Employment Consultants Ltd*, LON/86/410 (VTD 2309).

Tenpin Bowling Association

[64.20] The Commissioners issued a ruling that the British Tenpin Bowling Association was required to register for VAT. The association appealed, contending that its supplies should be treated as exempt under what is now *VATA 1994, Sch 9, Group 9* or under *Article 13A1(l)* of the *EC Sixth Directive*. The tribunal rejected these contentions and dismissed the appeal. *British Tenpin Bowling Association*, [1989] VATTR 101 (VTD 3213, 3552).

Committee of Directors of Polytechnics

[64.21] The Committee of Directors of Polytechnics was a company limited by guarantee and registered as an educational charity. The Commissioners issued a ruling that it was required to account for output tax on its subscriptions. The committee appealed, contending that its supplies should be treated as exempt under what is now *VATA 1994, Sch 9, Group 9*. The tribunal rejected this contention and dismissed the appeal, and the QB upheld this decision. The committee was not a professional association, since there was no such profession as that of being a polytechnic director. The primary purpose of the committee was not to advance a particular branch of knowledge, nor to foster professional expertise, but was to raise the standards of teaching in polytechnics. Furthermore, the aims of the committee were not aims of a civic nature within *Article 13A1(l)* of the *EC Sixth Directive*. *Committee of Directors of Polytechnics v C & E Commrs*, QB [1992] STC 873.

Association of Payroll and Superannuation Administrators

[64.22] The Commissioners issued an assessment charging tax on the subscriptions which the Association of Payroll and Superannuation Administrators received from its members. The Association appealed, contending that its subscriptions were exempt under what is now *VATA 1994, Sch 9, Group 9, Item 1(b)*. The tribunal rejected this contention and dismissed the appeal. Applying *Carr v CIR*, CA [1944] 2 All ER 163, payroll and pension administration did not constitute a 'profession'. *The Association of Payroll & Superannuation Administrators*, MAN/90/1015 (VTD 7009).

Institute of Legal Cashiers and Administrators

[64.23] The Institute of Legal Cashiers and Administrators was founded in 1978 as a non-profit-making organisation. It provided correspondence courses and arranged examinations, and had a disciplinary committee which administered a code of ethics and heard charges of incompetence or misconduct. The Commissioners issued a ruling that it did not qualify for exemption under what is now *VATA 1994, Sch 9, Group 9*. The Institute appealed, contending that it was a professional body. The tribunal rejected this contention and dismissed the appeal, holding that 'the severely technical and very constricted nature of the skill which its members acquire is inconsistent with the character of a profession as it is normally understood'. Furthermore, the purpose of the Institute was not 'the advancement of a particular branch of knowledge' since 'the phrase must have an academic connotation to some degree at least, and that in turn presupposes some element of research or reflection being characteristic of the way in which the subject in question is addressed'. *The Institute of Legal Cashiers and Administrators*, LON/93/2444A (VTD 12383).

Pensioners' organisation

[64.24] The Civil Service Pensioners' Alliance (CSPA) was established to protect the interests of retired civil servants. The Commissioners issued a ruling that it was liable to account for output tax on its subscriptions. The CSPA appealed, contending that it qualified for exemption under what is now *VATA 1994, Sch 9, Group 9* or alternatively under *Article 13A1* of the *EC Sixth Directive*. The tribunal rejected these contentions and dismissed the appeal. The CSPA was not a trade union, because it consisted of pensioners rather than workers, and was not a professional organisation. Furthermore, it was not within *Article 13A1(l)* of the *Sixth Directive*. *Civil Service Pensioners' Alliance*, [1995] VATDR 228 (VTD 13024).

[64.25] The tribunal reached a similar decision in a subsequent appeal by the same organisation. *Civil Service Pensioners' Alliance (No 2)*, MAN/03/410 (VTD 18911).

[64.26] The Commissioners issued a ruling that the National Federation of Post Office and British Telecom Pensioners was required to account for output tax on its income from members' subscriptions. The Federation appealed, contending that it had political objectives, and therefore qualified for exemption under *VATA 1994, Sch 9, Group 9, Item 1(e)*. The tribunal rejected this contention and dismissed the appeal, holding that 'a great deal of laudable effort is put into lobbying Members of Parliament and the Government about the rights of pensioners generally but this cannot be said to be a political objective'. *National Federation of Post Office and British Telecom Pensioners*, LON/01/434 (VTD 17980).

Association of reflexologists

[64.27] The Association of Reflexology was established in 1984 to promote the study of the body's reflexes as a guide to behaviour. The Commissioners issued a ruling that it was liable to account for output tax on its income from subscriptions. The Association appealed, contending that it should be treated as exempt under what is now *VATA 1994, Sch 9, Group 9*. The tribunal rejected this contention and dismissed the appeal. The tribunal found that the practice of reflexology largely consisted of 'treating particular bodily ailments and general stress carried out through massage on the soles of the feet, on the principle that specific areas of the feet relate to specific parts and organs of the body', and held that reflexology was not within the definition of a 'profession', since there was not 'sufficient general acceptance of reflexology as a subject for the practice of it to be generally regarded as a profession'. Furthermore, reflexology did not qualify as 'a particular branch of knowledge', within *Item 1(c)*. *The Association of Reflexologists*, LON/94/403A (VTD 13078).

Fund to raise money for former footballer

[64.28] See *Bailes*, **11.38** CHARITIES.

Working Men's Club

[64.29] See *Southchurch Workingmen's Club & Institute Ltd*, **13.4** CLUBS, ASSOCIATIONS AND ORGANISATIONS.

Association of workers in motor industry

[64.30] Following the decision noted at **22.310** EUROPEAN COMMUNITY LAW, the Institute for the Motor Industry applied to the tribunal for a further hearing of its claim to exemption. The tribunal dismissed the Institute's appeal, finding that the main aim of the Institute was not 'supplying defence and representational services' and holding that its supplies failed to qualify for exemption. *Institute of the Motor Industry*, [2000] VATDR 62 (VTD 16586).

Livery company

[64.31] A livery company claimed that its membership subscriptions should be treated as exempt from VAT under *VATA 1994, Sch 9, Group 9, Item 1(e)*. Customs rejected the claim and the tribunal dismissed the company's appeal, holding that the company's objects were 'not primarily in the public domain' and were not primarily 'of a patriotic, philanthropic or civil nature'. The tribunal observed that although the company had 'some objects in the public domain, it cannot be said that they are primarily in the public domain because those objects solely for the benefit of members rather than the public are too significant to be treated as incidental to the ones in the public domain'. *The Worshipful Company of Painter-Stainers*, LON/06/1304 (VTD 20668).

Motoring association

[64.32] An unincorporated association sold fuel to its members without accounting for VAT, and claimed a substantial repayment of input tax. Customs rejected the claim and issued a ruling that the association was required to account for tax on its supplies. The association appealed, contending that it should be treated as exempt from VAT under *VATA 1994, Sch 9, Group 9*. The tribunal rejected this contention and dismissed the appeal, describing the association's contentions as 'self-deluding sophistry'. *Motor Vehicle Protection Association*, EDN/07/142 (VTD 20673).

Camping and caravanning club

[64.33] A camping and caravanning club claimed a repayment of VAT on its members' subscriptions, contending that they should be treated as exempt from VAT under *VATA 1994, Sch 9, Group 9*. Customs rejected the claim and the tribunal dismissed the club's appeal, holding that the club's aims were not primarily 'of a patriotic, philanthropic or civil nature', since 'there was no evidence that camping itself promoted the well-being of mankind'. *The Camping & Caravanning Club*, MAN/x (VTD 20679).

Association of heating contractors

[64.34] The Heating and Ventilating Contractors Association registered for VAT in 1973. In 2006 it claimed a repayment of VAT on its members' subscriptions, contending that they should be treated as exempt from VAT under *VATA 1994, Sch 9, Group 9*. Customs rejected the claim and the tribunal dismissed the association's appeal, holding that the association's aims were not 'of a civic nature' and that it was not a trade union or a 'professional association'. *Heating & Ventilating Contractors' Association*, LON/07/1777 (VTD 20887).

Association of amusement park proprietors

[64.35] An association was formed in 1938 to represent proprietors of amusement parks and similar attractions. It registered for VAT from 1982. In

2008 it claimed a repayment of VAT on its members' subscriptions, contending that they should be treated as exempt from VAT under *VATA 1994, Sch 9, Group 9*. HMRC rejected the claim and the tribunal dismissed the association's appeal, finding that it was primarily a 'trade association' and holding that its subscriptions failed to qualify for exemption. *British Association of Leisure Parks, Piers & Attractions Ltd v HMRC*, [2011] UKFTT 662 (TC), TC01504.

Effect of Group 9, Note 4

[64.36] A private company was incorporated in the UK to encourage the use of RIXML (a standardised 'language' or terminology designed to be used in writing financial reports). Its members were investment banks and investment management firms. The Commissioners issued a ruling that it was required to account for VAT. The company appealed, contending that it qualified for exemption under *VATA 1994, Sch 9, Group 9, Item 1(c)*. The tribunal rejected this contention and dismissed the appeal, observing that *Group 9, Note 4* limited the scope of this exemption 'to cases where the members of the association are wholly or mainly "individuals" in the relevant profession or employment. In this case all the members are corporate bodies'. *Rixml.org Ltd*, LON/02/185 (VTD 18717). (*Note.* The tribunal also held that the company's supplies took place in the UK, where it was incorporated, rejecting the company's contention that they were within *VAT (Place of Supply of Services) Order, article 16*.)

Miscellaneous

Whether subscription partly attributable to supply of magazine

[64.37] See *Institute of Chartered Foresters*, **13.19** CLUBS, ASSOCIATIONS AND ORGANISATIONS.

65

Transfers of Going Concerns

The cases in this chapter are arranged under the following headings.

Cases held to fall within Special Provisions Order, Article 5(1)

Reclaim of input tax by purchaser	**65.1**
Output tax	**65.31**

Cases held not to fall within Special Provisions Order, Article 5(1)

Assessments to recover input tax—appellant successful	**65.38**
Vendor failing to account for output tax	**65.76**

Land and buildings (Special Provisions Order, Article 5(2))	**65.86**
Liability to register (VATA 1994, Sch 1 para 1(2))	**65.90**
Liability to account for tax (VAT Regulations 1995, reg 6)	**65.108**
Miscellaneous	**65.118**

Cases held to fall within Special Provisions Order, Article 5(1)

Reclaim of input tax by purchaser

[65.1] Two partners purchased an existing business, and reclaimed input tax on the stock. The Commissioners issued an assessment to recover the tax, and the tribunal dismissed the partners' appeal, holding that the business had been transferred as a going concern, within what is now *VAT (Special Provisions) Order (SI 1995/1268), Article 5*. *E & E Phillips*, LON/81/131 (VTD 1130).

[65.2] A partnership purchased a restaurant. Following the purchase, the restaurant was closed for eight days for redecoration. The partnership reclaimed input tax on the purchase. The tribunal rejected the claim, holding that the eight-day closure did not prevent the transferred business from being within the definition of a 'going concern'. *The Old Red Lion Restaurant*, LON/83/28 (VTD 1446).

[65.3] A similar decision was reached in a case where a public house had been closed for 2½ months before reopening. *G Draper (Marlow) Ltd*, LON/85/439 (VTD 2079).

[65.4] A company (S) purchased the plant, equipment, stock, vehicles, fixtures and fittings of an associated company (D) which had ceased to trade and subsequently went into liquidation. S reclaimed input tax on the purchase. The tribunal rejected the claim, holding that the transaction constituted the transfer of a business as a going concern, and observing that D had failed to pay the purported VAT to the Commissioners. *Shire Equip Ltd*, MAN/83/52 (VTD 1464). (*Note*. Where an amount charged as VAT has been paid to Customs, they will allow the purchaser to recover it—see Customs' VAT Manual, Part 10, chapter 2, para 3.2.)

[65.5] A similar decision was reached in *Jaymix*, LON/83/265 (VTD 1526).

[65.6] See also *Jalf*, **40.30** INVOICES AND CREDIT NOTES.

[65.7] A parachute club became insolvent and ceased to operate on 8 December 1982. On 12 January 1983 its assets were purchased by another club. The tribunal held that, despite the gap of five weeks, the transaction constituted the transfer of a business as a going concern. *Thruxton Parachute Club*, LON/84/331 (VTD 1816).

[65.8] A company took over a division of another company, paying VAT of £15,000 in respect of the stock taken over. It reclaimed the £15,000 as input tax. The tribunal rejected the claim, holding that the transaction constituted the transfer of a business as a going concern. *Advanced Business Technology Ltd*, LON/83/195 (VTD 1488).

[65.9] A company had reclaimed input tax on the purchase of five shops. The purchase agreement attributed only £1 to goodwill, the remainder of the price being attributed to the premises, fixtures and fittings and stock. The Commissioners issued an assessment to recover the tax, and the tribunal dismissed the company's appeal. *Quadrant Stationers Ltd*, LON/83/32 (VTD 1599). (*Note.* Costs were awarded to the Commissioners—see **2.353** APPEALS.)

[65.10] A couple reclaimed input tax on the purchase of a sweetshop. The Commissioners issued an assessment to recover the tax, considering that the shop had been transferred as a going concern. The tribunal upheld the assessment and dismissed the couple's appeal. Applying *dicta* of Widgery J in *Kenmir Ltd v Frizzell*, QB [1968] 1 All ER 414 (a case concerning the *Contracts of Employment Act 1963*), 'in deciding whether a transaction amounted to the transfer of a business, regard must be had to its substance rather than its form'. The 'vital consideration is whether the effect of the transaction was to put the transferee in possession of a going concern, the activities of which he could carry on without interruption.' The tribunal indicated that the conclusive factor was the transfer of the premises, observing that 'the focal point of goodwill is the premises to which persons may be expected to gravitate'. *RP & DK Agnihotri*, MAN/84/165 (VTD 1765).

[65.11] *Dicta* of Widgery J in *Kenmir Ltd v Frizzell*, QB [1968] 1 All ER 414 (see **65.10** above) have been applied in a large number of subsequent cases in which appeals against the disallowance of input tax have been dismissed. In the interests of space, such cases are not summarised individually in this book.

[65.12] A company (F) sold reproduction furniture from leased premises. It became insolvent, and another company (D) agreed to purchase the lease, fixtures, fittings and stock. D reclaimed input tax on the stock and the Commissioners issued an assessment to recover the tax, considering that the business had been transferred as a going concern. D appealed, contending that its motive had been to obtain the lease of the premises, and that its directors did not intend to continue selling reproduction furniture but intended to set up a new trade of selling fitted kitchens and bedrooms. The QB upheld the assessment. In deciding whether a business had been transferred as a going concern, the question was whether it could be carried on without interruption, not whether it would be carried on without interruption. The transactions here constituted the transfer of a business as a going concern and D's intention of changing the nature of the business in the future was irrelevant. *C & E Commrs v Dearwood Ltd*, QB [1986] STC 327. (*Note*. For a case where a Scottish tribunal specifically declined to follow this decision, see *Sawadee Restaurant*, **65.101** below. See also *Hartley Engineering Ltd*, **65.51** below.)

[65.13] The QB decision in *Dearwood Ltd*, **65.12** above, was followed in a case in which the tribunal disapproved the reasoning in *Westpark Interiors Ltd*, **65.38** below, on the grounds that *Kenmir Ltd v Frizzell* (see **65.10** above) had not been cited in that case, and that *Westpark Interiors* had applied a subjective test whereas *Kenmir Ltd v Frizzell* and *Dearwood Ltd* had laid down an objective test. *Curtain Clearance*, MAN/92/1215 (VTD 10683).

[65.14] The QB decision in *Dearwood Ltd*, **65.12** above, has been applied in a large number of subsequent cases. In the interests of space, such cases are not summarised individually in this book. For a list of such cases decided up to 31 December 2002, see Tolley's VAT Cases 2003.

[65.15] A company (A) was formed to take over a pet food shop from another company (C) which carried on business as a pet food retailer. C purported to charge A tax on the stock, fixtures and fittings which it sold to A. However C, which already had substantial VAT liabilities, did not account for the tax to the Commissioners. A reclaimed the input tax which C had purported to charge and appealed against the Commissioners' refusal to repay the amounts in question. The tribunal dismissed A's appeal, holding that what is now *Special Provisions Order, Article 5* was to be 'construed as including every transfer of a separate business as a going concern, notwithstanding that the business and assets transferred constituted only a part of the businesses of the transferor'. *Acrefirst Ltd*, [1985] VATTR 133 (VTD 1857).

[65.16] A company (C) carrying on business as ventilation engineers purchased the assets of one of the branches of another company with a similar business. C reclaimed input tax on the transfer. The Commissioners rejected the claim and the tribunal dismissed C's appeal, holding that the transaction constituted the transfer of a going concern. The tribunal observed that 'the fact that part of a business can only run if integrated into another business which has the facilities to support it' did not necessarily mean that it was 'incapable of separate operation'. *Cosalt Coolair Ltd*, MAN/85/38 (VTD 1908).

[65.17] A company carried on the business of leasing cars and computer equipment. It sold its business to another company (B), which occupied adjoining premises. B reclaimed input tax on the transaction. The Commissioners issued an assessment to recover the tax and the tribunal dismissed B's appeal, holding that the business had been transferred as a going concern. *Baltic Leasing Ltd*, [1986] VATTR 98 (VTD 2088).

[65.18] A company (F) was established as a subsidiary of a company whose business included the hiring and repairing of fork lift trucks. F purchased some of the parent company's assets, including 29 fork lift trucks. The parent company purported to charge VAT on the assets in question, but did not pay this to the Commissioners, and subsequently went into receivership. However, F reclaimed the amounts concerned as input tax, and obtained repayment from the Commissioners. On discovering what had happened, the Commissioners issued an assessment to recover the tax from F. The tribunal dismissed F's appeal, holding that the transaction constituted the transfer of a business as a going concern. *Farm Facilities (Fork Lift) Ltd*, [1987] VATTR 80 (VTD 2366). (*Note.* An alternative contention by F, that the repayment of the amounts claimed in its return meant that the Commissioners were estopped from recovering the tax, was also rejected. For cases concerning estoppel, see **2.109** APPEALS *et seq.*)

[65.19] The decision in *Farm Facilities (Fork Lift) Ltd*, **65.18** above, was applied in the similar cases of *Safety Boat Services Ltd*, EDN/91/40 (VTD 6487) and *S Scotford-Smith*, LON/95/1869 (VTD 14609).

[65.20] A company purchased a DIY shop. The shop was closed for two months before re-opening. The company reclaimed input tax but the Commissioners rejected the claim and the tribunal dismissed the company's appeal, holding that there had been the transfer of a going concern despite the two-month closure. *Montrose DIY Ltd*, EDN/87/98 (VTD 2652).

[65.21] A company purchased a petrol station as a going concern. Under a separate contract, it also purchased the vendor's stock of 22 cars, and reclaimed input tax on these. The Commissioners rejected the claim and the tribunal dismissed the company's appeal, holding that the purchase of the cars was a part of the transfer of the vendor's business as a going concern. *Fondbane Motors*, LON/87/229 (VTD 2813).

[65.22] An individual purchased a nightclub. He intended to convert the premises into a restaurant. However, he kept the nightclub open for one week before closing it. He reclaimed input tax on the purchase. The Commissioners rejected his claim and the tribunal dismissed his appeal, holding that the fact that he intended to use the premises as a restaurant did not alter the fact that he had purchased the nightclub as a going concern. *BO Jones*, MAN/90/136 (VTD 6141).

[65.23] A company (P) manufactured furniture and sold it to a company (V) with 16 retail shops. P suffered financial difficulties and transferred its manufacturing business to V. V reclaimed input tax on the purchase. The Commissioners issued an assessment to recover the tax, on the basis that V had acquired P's business as a going concern. The tribunal upheld the assessment and dismissed V's appeal, holding that the business had been transferred as a going concern despite the switch from wholesale to retail sales. *Village Collection Interiors Ltd*, LON/90/1882 (VTD 6146).

[65.24] A manufacturing company (E) purchased the plant and stock of a company (D) carrying on a similar business, and reclaimed input tax on the purchase. The Commissioners rejected the claim and the tribunal dismissed E's appeal, observing that 'where, as in this case, the purchaser by a separate contract with a third party, executed contemporaneously and also having immediate effect, has put himself in the position to be able to carry on the vendor's business, there can be a transfer of that business as a going concern'. *Augusta Extrusions Ltd*, LON/91/2298Y (VTD 8892).

[65.25] A company (H) which carried on a property investment business purchased a leasehold estate. The vendor had granted the lease a year before the sale, electing to waive exemption. H also elected to waive exemption, and reclaimed input tax on the purchase of the estate. The Commissioners rejected the claim on the basis that the sale of the estate constituted the transfer of a business as a going concern. The tribunal dismissed H's appeal, holding that the letting and management of the estate was a part of the vendor's business, consisting of the receipt of rental income. *Hallborough Properties Ltd*, MAN/92/877 (VTD 10849).

[65.26] In December 1991 an individual (L) purchased the leasehold premises, goodwill and furniture and fittings of a café. He closed the business for two days and reopened it as a 'take-away' restaurant. He reclaimed input tax on the purchase. The tribunal rejected the claim, finding that L had 'purchased all that was needed to carry on the vendors' business, the premises, the fixtures and fittings and the goodwill'. Applying *Kenmir Ltd v Frizzell* (see **65.10** above), and *Dearwood Ltd*, **65.12** above, this constituted the transfer of a going concern. *L Louca (t/a Gardner's Café)*, LON/94/930A (VTD 13186).

[65.27] In April and early May 1995 a company (F) purchased three quantities of stock, and two quantities of materials, from another company (L). On 19 May 1995 F purchased L's business as a going concern. F reclaimed input tax on the five invoices relating to the prior purchases of stock and materials. The Commissioners rejected the claim, considering that the transactions in question constituted part of the transfer of L's business. The tribunal dismissed F's appeal, holding that the transactions were 'consistent with a series of transactions comprising the transfer of a business' and that the relevant assets were intended 'to be used in carrying on the same kind of business'. *Fairmatch Ltd*, LON/95/3171A (VTD 14194).

[65.28] A trader (F) had operated a coach hire business. He sold his only coach to another trader (B), who already carried on a similar business. F then ceased to trade. B reclaimed input tax on the coach, but the tribunal rejected his claim, holding that the transaction constituted the sale of F's business as a going concern. *JR Beagley*, LON/96/1001 (VTD 15107). (*Note.* For another issue in this case, see **36.133** INPUT TAX.)

[65.29] See also *Black*, **52.332** PENALTIES: MISDECLARATION.

[65.30] There are a large number of other cases, which appear to raise no point of general importance, in which appeals against the disallowance of input tax on the transfer of a going concern have been dismissed. In the interests of space, such cases are not reported individually in this book. For a list of such cases decided up to 31 October 1990, see Tolley's VAT Cases 1991.

Output tax

Vendor failing to account for output tax—whether Article 5 applicable

[65.31] A trader operated a mobile simulator (a type of hydraulic machine which simulated the effect of various forms of travel, and which customers paid to spend short periods of time in). He sold the machine and did not account for VAT on the sale. The Commissioners issued an assessment charging output tax and the trader appealed, contending that the sale constituted the transfer of a business as a going concern. The tribunal allowed the appeal, finding that 'the business consisted solely of the simulator' and holding that it had been sold as a going concern, so that no VAT was chargeable. *A Wrenshall*, MAN/92/1031 (VTD 10963).

[65.32] A company (F) had operated a retail clothing business. It suffered financial difficulties and owed more than £90,000 to creditors. F's two managers (neither of whom were directors) offered to take over its stock and its liabilities. The stock was valued at £100,000. F did not account for VAT on this stock, and the Commissioners issued an assessment charging tax on it. F appealed, contending that its business had been transferred as a going concern, so that no VAT was chargeable. The tribunal accepted this contention and allowed the appeal. *Flashshine Ltd*, LON/92/202A (VTD 11433).

[65.33] A bank decided to outsource its cheque clearing functions to an independent company. It sold the relevant equipment to the company for more than £17,000,000. The Commissioners issued a ruling that VAT was chargeable on the sale. The bank appealed, contending that the sale was the transfer of a going concern, so that the effect of *VAT (Special Provisions) Order 1995 (SI 1995 No 1268), article 5* was that no VAT was chargeable. The tribunal accepted this contention and allowed the appeal. The tribunal observed that the principal factors were 'the transfer of the whole staff' involved in the activities in question, 'the sale or lease of the various properties in which these activities were carried out, and the supply of the equipment and intellectual property requisite to their continuing'. *Royal Bank of Scotland Group plc (No 4)*, EDN/01/105 (VTD 17637).

[65.34] A company (H) sold three hotels to another company (S). Customs issued a ruling that H was required to account for output tax on the sale. H appealed, contending that the sale was the transfer of a going concern, so that the effect of *VAT (Special Provisions) Order 1995 (SI 1995/1268), article 5* was that no VAT was chargeable. The tribunal accepted this contention and allowed the appeal, holding that H had sold the hotels as a going concern. The fact that S had subsequently entered into a 'leaseback' arrangement for financial reasons did not prevent H's sale from constituting the transfer of a going concern. *Morton Hotels Ltd*, EDN/05/37 (VTD 20039).

[65.35] In 2003 a borough council entered into a development agreement with a company (P), whereby P was to develop a site, in respect of which the council had elected to waive exemption. In 2004 the council and P entered into an agreement with a company (S) which operated a chain of supermarkets, whereby a warehouse would be constructed on the site and would be leased to S. In 2005 the council agreed to sell the freehold of the site to another company (G), subject to the existing lease to S. The council did not account for output tax on the sale of the freehold. Customs issued an assessment charging tax, and the council appealed, contending that the sale should be treated as the transfer of a going concern, so that no VAT was chargeable. The tribunal accepted this contention and allowed the appeal, finding that 'at the time of sale the appellant was carrying on an economic activity' in relation to the site. G was continuing the economic activity of obtaining rental income from the site, which had previously been carried on by the council. Accordingly the sale of the freehold constituted the transfer of a going concern. *Dartford Bor-*

ough Council, LON/06/993 (VTD 20423). (*Note*. The tribunal also strongly criticised Customs' Solicitor's Office for failing to understand 'the nature of an agreement for lease'.)

[65.36] See also *The Golden Oak Partnership*, 36.555 INPUT TAX, and *Jeyes Ltd*, 52.269 PENALTIES: MISDECLARATION.

Liability of transferee for unpaid output tax arising before date of transfer

[65.37] See the cases noted at **65.108** *et seq.* below.

Cases held not to fall within Special Provisions Order, Article 5(1)

Assessments to recover input tax—appellant successful

Retail businesses

Purchase of stock of furniture

[65.38] A company carried on business as interior designers and suppliers of furniture and furnishings. It decided to close one of its branches, and sold the stock of that branch to another company (W). W reclaimed input tax, and the Commissioners rejected the claim, considering that the business had been transferred as a going concern. The tribunal allowed W's appeal, holding that the sale of the stock of one branch which had been earmarked for closure did not amount to the transfer of a business as a going concern. *Westpark Interiors Ltd*, [1983] VATTR 289 (VTD 1534). (*Note*. The decision here was not followed, and was implicitly disapproved, in the subsequent case of *Curtain Clearance*, **65.14** above, on the grounds that the QB decision in *Kenmir Ltd v Frizzell* (see **65.10** above), which had been treated as a binding precedent in the subsequent QB case of *Dearwood Ltd*, **65.12** above, had not been cited to the tribunal, and that the tribunal had erred in applying a subjective test rather than an objective test.)

Purchase of stock of confectionery

[65.39] A confectioner purchased stock and office furniture from a business which was closing down, and reclaimed the input tax thereon. The Commissioners rejected the claim, considering that this constituted the transfer of a business as a going concern, and he appealed. The tribunal allowed his appeal, holding that the business from which he purchased the items was not transferred as a going concern. The tribunal observed that for the transfer of a business as a going concern, there must be 'a consensus between the vendor and the purchaser'. In cases where 'evidence of consensus may be lacking or suspect, the expression "transfer of a going concern" must be interpreted as meaning succession by way of continuity of the previous business, succession by itself not being conclusive'. *EJ Caunt (t/a Edward James Confectionery)*, MAN/83/160 (VTD 1561).

Purchase of stock of hi-fi equipment

[65.40] A partnership (S) traded as retailers of hi-fi equipment. It agreed to purchase from another company (H) the trading stock of a shop which H owned, which had been trading at a loss. Under the agreement, H was to retain the tenancy of the shop premises, and was to receive 25% of the shop profits. S reclaimed input tax on the stock, and the Commissioners issued an assessment to recover the tax, considering that the transaction constituted the transfer of a business as a going concern. The tribunal allowed S's appeal, holding that the transaction was not the transfer of a going concern, applying *Westpark Interiors Ltd*, **65.38** above, and *dicta* of Plowman J in *Baytrust Holdings Ltd v CIR*, Ch D [1971] 3 All ER 76 (a stamp duty case). The tribunal observed that S's occupation of the premises was unlawful, and that S would have no rights against the head landlord, although the partners might have 'some equitable rights against H'. There was no assignment of the premises, and no transfer of goodwill. On the evidence, S had previously bought stock from H, and even if S had declined to purchase the stock which was involved in the transaction, H would still have agreed to let S trade from the shop in question in return for a share of the profits. The purchase of the second-hand stock was, therefore, a normal trading transaction. *Dearwood Ltd*, **65.12** above, was distinguished because in that case the sales manager employed by the transferor was re-employed by the transferee, whereas in this case the previous shop manager was not re-employed by S. *PW Lee-Kemp & PM O'Brien (t/a Sevenoaks Hi-Fi & Video)*, LON/91/1068 (VTD 7772). (*Note.* The decision in *Westpark Interiors* was not followed, and was implicitly disapproved, in the subsequent case of *Curtain Clearance*, **65.14** above, on the grounds that the QB decision in *Kenmir Ltd v Frizzell* (see **65.10** above), which had been treated as a binding precedent in the subsequent QB case of *Dearwood Ltd*, **65.12** above, had not been cited to the tribunal, and that the tribunal had erred in applying a subjective test rather than an objective test.)

Purchase of assets of petrol station licencee

[65.41] A partnership acquired the licence of a petrol station. They purchased, from the previous licencee, two refrigerators, stocks of confectionery and groceries, and a computer. They reclaimed input tax on these items. The Commissioners issued an assessment to recover the tax, considering that the items in question had been acquired as part of the transfer of the previous licencee's business as a going concern. The tribunal allowed the partnership's appeal, finding that none of the items in question fell within the terms of operation which the licencees were required to observe. The tribunal concluded that 'either on or before the outgoing licencee vacated the property the chattels and equipment belonging to that licence were removed', so that 'the terms of the licence having been complied with, there was an interruption in the supply of sweets, groceries, ice cream and coca-cola'. The business transferred as a going concern only consisted of the sale of the motor fuel and lubricants produced by the company which owned the petrol station and granted the relevant licences. The ancillary items on which the partnership had reclaimed input tax did not form part of that transfer of a going concern. *M Ryan & M Townsend (t/a Reliables Fuel Plus)*, LON/94/512A (VTD 12806).

Purchase of stock of motor accessories from director's fiancée

[65.42] A trader (N) owned two shops, one in Thurrock and one in Ilford, selling cycles and motor accessories. He decided to sell the Ilford shop, and moved his stock of cycles to the Thurrock shop. His fiancée (J), who worked at the Ilford shop, agreed to purchase that shop's stock of motor accessories for £5,000 including VAT. The stock was duly sold to a company of which J was the controlling director. The Ilford shop then closed. N did not account for output tax on the £5,000 which the company had paid him. The company opened a shop in Romford, seven miles from the Ilford shop, with the stock of motor accessories which it had purchased, and reclaimed input tax on the basis that the £5,000 which it had paid to N was inclusive of VAT. The Commissioners rejected the claim on the basis that the transaction was the transfer of a going concern. The company appealed, contending that it had merely purchased stock, and had adopted a different trading name and sold to different customers, so that the transaction was not the transfer of a business as a going concern. The tribunal allowed the appeal, observing that 'the form of the sale was very clearly not that of the sale of a business as a going concern, but simply the sale of specific goods'. No rights or obligations were transferred, and there was no transfer of goodwill. *Bonnet To Boot Ltd*, LON/95/1273A (VTD 13466).

Purchase of stock of photocopiers

[65.43] In June 1994 a woman (G) registered for VAT as a photocopier dealer. In July 1994 she purchased a quantity of photocopiers from a company which had carried on a similar business. The company's directors had decided to cease trading and had advertised the photocopiers in 'Exchange and Mart'. G reclaimed input tax on the purchase. The Commissioners issued an assessment to recover the tax, considering that G had purchased the company's business as a going concern. The tribunal allowed G's appeal. On the evidence, G had not taken over the company's business premises, furniture, fixtures and fittings or any outstanding contracts. There had been no transfer of goodwill and G had not taken on any of the company's employees. Her purchase of the company's stock did not constitute the transfer of the company's business as a going concern. *AS Godfrey*, LON/95/2163A (VTD 14648).

Manufacturing and wholesale businesses

Purchase of plant for manufacturing furniture

[65.44] A company (C) manufactured furniture from a site in Daventry. It had an associated company (V) which sold 'self-assembly' furniture from a site in Merseyside. In 1989 both companies began suffering financial difficulties, and in late 1989 some plant was transferred from C to V. C's turnover declined substantially after the loss of this plant, and V continued to trade at a loss, so that in October 1990 the directors decided to transfer the plant back from V to C. V issued an invoice charging tax on the transfer, and C reclaimed the tax as input tax. In December 1990 V went into receivership. The receivers were unable to sell the business as a going concern, and the Merseyside premises were purchased by the holding company in March 1991. C began to trade from these premises under an 'informal licence', until they were sold to an outside purchaser in June 1991. The Commissioners issued an assessment to recover the tax which C had reclaimed on the transfer of the plant, considering that the transactions amounted to the transfer of V's business as a going concern. The tribunal allowed C's appeal, holding on the evidence that, at the time the plant was transferred, the directors still hoped that V would continue to trade, and that since the furniture produced by C differed from that produced by V, the sale of the plant did not amount to the transfer of a going concern. *Computech Development Ltd*, LON/91/2090A (VTD 9798).

[65.45] A company (S), which manufactured furniture, suffered financial difficulties and went into liquidation. Its liquidator sold some of its assets to a newly-incorporated company (B). B reclaimed input tax on the purchase. The Commissioners issued an assessment to recover the tax, on the basis that the transaction constituted the transfer of S's business as a going concern. The tribunal allowed B's appeal, holding on the evidence that S's business had ceased to exist and had not been transferred as a going concern. *Bristol Engineering & Hydraulics Ltd*, LON/97/41 (VTD 15431).

Purchase of assets of company manufacturing ladders

[65.46] A company (W) which had manufactured ladders went into liquidation in June 1985. Another company (H) agreed to purchase W's assets, in order to set up a similar business. The purchase took place in August 1985, and H began to trade in October 1985. H reclaimed input tax on the purchase, but the Commissioners rejected the claim, considering that W's business had been transferred as a going concern. The tribunal allowed H's appeal, holding that, since W had already ceased to trade and gone into liquidation, the transactions amounted to a transfer of assets rather than to the transfer of a going concern. Applying *dicta* of Sugarman J in the Australian case of *Electricity Commission (Balmain Electric Light Co)*, NSW CA [1957] SR (NSW) 100, a business would only qualify as a 'going concern' if its doors were 'open for business' and it had 'all the plant, etc, which is necessary to keep it in operation, as distinct from its being only an inert aggregation of plant'. *Hardlife Ladder Co Ltd*, LON/87/218 (VTD 2715).

Purchase of stock of clothing

[65.47] A company (C), which carried on business as manufacturers and wholesalers of leather and fur clothing, reclaimed input tax on the purchase of stock from another company (R). R had been in financial difficulties, owing C £80,000, and had made its staff redundant. Three days after the transfer of the stock, C took possession of R's premises. C also purchased some machinery from R, and re-employed some of the staff whom R had made redundant. The Commissioners rejected the input tax claim, considering that the stock had been purchased as part of the transfer of a business as a going concern. The tribunal allowed C's appeal, holding on the evidence 'that there was no consensus between the parties', either tacit or otherwise, that 'the business should be transferred as a going concern'. *C Cohen (Furriers) Ltd*, EDN/89/155 (VTD 4933).

Purchase of carpets

[65.48] A company (P) was incorporated in May 1986 to manufacture and sell carpets. Two of its three directors (M and his wife) were also directors of another company (F) which carried on a similar business; the third director was employed by F but was not a director of F. P and F shared the same office, which was owned by M and his wife. F was contractually obliged to sell through six regional agents, who also acted for other manufacturers. In August 1987 P purchased various items of machinery from F, and in September and October P purchased various items of stock from F. P reclaimed input tax in respect of the transactions. In November 1987 F dismissed its employees, all of whom were re-employed by P. In January 1988 F went into voluntary liquidation. The Commissioners issued an assessment to recover the tax, considering that the transactions constituted the transfer of a business as a going concern. The tribunal allowed P's appeal in part, holding that the transfer of the machinery fell within what is now *Article 5* of the *Special Provisions Order*, but that the sale of the items of stock did not. On the evidence, the stock had been manufactured by F's employees, and the price paid by P was reasonable. *Pennine Carpets Ltd*, MAN/88/614 (VTD 5894). (*Note.* For another issue in this case, see **36.649** INPUT TAX.)

Purchase of machine for manufacturing plastic forks

[65.49] A trader (W) carried on the business of manufacturing plastic forks by injection moulding. The forks were sold to fish and chip shops and other take-away food shops. He agreed to sell the machine and ancillary equipment to three brothers. The brothers registered for VAT as a partnership and reclaimed the input tax on the machinery. The Commissioners rejected the claim, considering that the partnership had purchased W's business as a going concern. The partnership appealed, contending that the transaction did not constitute the transfer of a business, since they had not taken over any stock or raw material, or any lists of suppliers or customers. The tribunal allowed the appeal, applying *dicta* in *Kenmir Ltd v Frizzell* (see **65.10** above), and distinguishing *Dearwood Ltd*, **65.12** above. *AK, VK & HK Mawji*, MAN/91/564 (VTD 7769, 10829). (*Note.* An appeal against a misdeclaration penalty was also allowed.)

Purchase of assets of textile company

[65.50] A company (M), which traded as textile merchants, suffered financial difficulties, and a creditor issued a winding-up petition against it. M's principal director decided to form a new company (P), which was incorporated on 7 April 1992. Two days later M sold two vehicles, some office furniture and equipment, and many items of textile products to P (these items being sold at cost, and representing 70% of M's total stock). In June 1992 a winding-up order was made against M. P reclaimed input tax on the items it had purchased from M, and the Commissioners issued an assessment to recover the tax, considering that the transactions constituted the transfer of M's business as a going concern. P appealed, contending that the transactions did not constitute the transfer of a going concern, since at the time they took place, the director still hoped that M would continue to trade, and that, whereas M's customers had been in the textile trade, he had intended P to seek customers from outside the trade, such as hotels and nursing homes. The tribunal allowed the appeal, holding on the evidence that 'there was no intention to transfer any part of a business (but) simply to sell assets in the form of certain equipment and some stock'. The QB upheld this decision. Schiemann J held that the tribunal had been entitled to take the intentions of the transferor and the transferee into account, although such intentions were not conclusive. The fact that the transferor and the transferee were controlled by the same person was also not conclusive. The tribunal decision was not inconsistent with the evidence. *C & E Commrs v Padglade Ltd*, QB [1995] STC 602.

Purchase of metal-turning machinery

[65.51] A company (P) which produced machined parts ceased to trade in December 1991, and subsequently went into liquidation. One of its shareholders incorporated a new company (H) to carry on an engineering business, and purchased P's metal-turning machinery from the liquidators. H reclaimed input tax on the machinery, and the Commissioners issued an assessment to recover the tax, considering that H had taken over part of P's business as a going concern. The tribunal allowed H's appeal, holding on the evidence that, although the businesses carried on by P and H both obtained the cutting of metal, they had nothing else in common and were 'entirely different'. The tribunal chairman (Mr. de Voil) distinguished *Dearwood Ltd*, **65.12** above, and declined to follow *Kenmir Ltd v Frizzell* (see **65.10** above), since that case had dealt with an employment law provision (*Contracts of Employment Act 1963, Sch 1 para 10(2)*), the wording of which was significantly different from the wording of *Special Provisions Order, Article 5*. The *Special Provisions Order* included the words 'where the assets are to be used by the transferee in carrying on the same kind of business'. Mr. de Voil observed that '"are to be" does not mean "could" as distinct from "would"'. The expression '"are to be" suggests an intention — presumably that of the transferee and presumably at the moment of transfer'. *Hartley Engineering Ltd*, [1994] VATTR 453 (VTD 12385). (*Note*. The decision in this case was approved in the subsequent Scottish case of *Sawadee Restaurant*, **65.101** below.)

Purchase of assets of company manufacturing nursery products

[65.52] A company (G) manufactured electrical products, including under-blankets, heating pads and baby alarms. In September 1989 it launched a range of nursery products. In October 1989 its directors acquired a newly-formed company (B) which marketed the nursery products which G manufactured. In 1991 G began to suffer financial problems, despite recruiting two new directors, one of whom lent it substantial funds. In September 1991 a creditor presented a winding-up petition. In October 1991 G agreed to sell to B the injection mould tooling for the nursery merchandise which it manufactured. In November 1991 G sold its stock of nursery products, and other items of manufacturing equipment, to B. In January 1992 G sold to B, for the nominal sum of £10, its rights and interest in the trade marks under which the nursery products were marketed. Later that month G went into liquidation. B reclaimed input tax on the various items which it had purchased from G. The Commissioners issued an assessment to recover the tax, considering that the transactions constituted the transfer of G's business as a going concern. The tribunal allowed B's appeal, holding that there was 'no evidence of any overall agreement between G and B for G to transfer its business or any part of its business to B'. *Babytec Ltd*, LON/92/3219A (VTD 12391).

Purchase of assets of company manufacturing jewellery

[65.53] A company (S), which manufactured costume jewellery, suffered financial difficulties. In March 2000 its bank froze its account, and the Revenue levied distraint on some of its assets, including its computers. It was unable to pay its employees' salaries and issued them with redundancy letters in early April. A rival company (B) then agreed to purchase some of S's remaining assets, including the primary moulds from which it produced items of jewellery. B reclaimed input tax on the purchase, but the Commissioners rejected B's claim on the basis that the transaction constituted the transfer of S's business as a going concern. The tribunal allowed B's appeal, holding that at the time of the purchase, 'there was no longer a possibility' of S's business continuing, so that the transactions amounted to a transfer of assets rather than to the transfer of a going concern. *Buckley (Jewellery) Ltd*, MAN/00/1068 (VTD 18178).

Miscellaneous

Scrapyard

[65.54] A trader had purchased scrap metal from members of the public, for his own use. He sold the scrapyard to a company (E) which began to sell the processed scrap metal to the public. E reclaimed input tax on the purchase. Customs issued an assessment to recover the tax, considering that the scrapyard had been transferred as a going concern. The tribunal allowed E's appeal, holding that the transfer was not of a going concern since E sold scrap metal to the public whereas the vendor had not done so. *Eric Ladbroke (Holbeach) Ltd*, LON/83/184 (VTD 1557).

Assets of printing company

[65.55] A company (S) reclaimed input tax on the purchase of some of the stock of a printing company, which ceased to trade after the sale. Customs rejected the claim, considering that the purchase constituted the transfer of a going concern. The tribunal allowed S's appeal, holding that since it had not taken over the whole of the vendor's stock, and had only taken on some of the employees, the purchase was a purchase of assets rather than the transfer of a going concern. *Staimer Productions Ltd*, EDN/83/68 (VTD 1605).

Vehicles

[65.56] A company (E) which carried on a haulage and removal business wished to purchase some vehicles from a company which had ceased to trade. The vendor would only agree to sell the vehicles if E also took over its other assets, i.e. its premises, plant and stock. Customs issued an assessment to recover the tax, considering that the transactions constituted the transfer of a going concern. The tribunal allowed E's appeal, holding that the sale of the assets in question did not constitute the transfer of a going concern. *Euromove International Movers Ltd*, LON/84/153 (VTD 1710).

Assets of vehicle body repairers

[65.57] An individual (L) worked as a self-employed motor mechanic from a shed owned by a company (C) which traded as vehicle body repairers. C gave him notice to leave the shed, as it was closing its business. L offered to purchase C's premises. C would only agree to sell its premises if L also purchased its other assets (some workshop equipment, a truck, some office equipment and some spare parts). L reclaimed input tax. Customs rejected the claim, considering that L had purchased C's business as a going concern. The tribunal allowed L's appeal, holding that since C had already ceased to trade, the transactions did not constitute the transfer of a going concern. *WPJ Lawson*, LON/84/164 (VTD 1749).

[65.58] A similar decision was reached in *SA Sutton (t/a Dunchurch Motor Co)*, LON/92/1229A (VTD 9987).

Quarries

[65.59] A civil engineering company wished to expand into road laying, but found it difficult to obtain materials from quarry owners. It therefore purchased the freehold of one quarry and the leasehold of another quarry, and reclaimed the input tax charged. Customs rejected the claim, considering that the quarries had been transferred as a going concern. The tribunal allowed the company's appeal, finding that the company had only wished to acquire the raw materials and had not purchased any goodwill, debtors or work in progress from the vendors. Accordingly the purchase of the quarries did not constitute the transfer of a going concern. *ICB Ltd*, BEL/84/8 (VTD 1796).

Farm equipment

[65.60] A partnership (F) ran one of three farms on an estate in Scotland. The other two farms were run by the landowner (R), who was a member of another partnership (S), which carried on a contracting business, and had become insolvent. R subsequently retired from farming, and assigned the lease of the two farms to F. F purchased various items of farm equipment from S, and reclaimed input tax on the purchase. Customs rejected the claim, considering that F had acquired S's business as a going concern. The tribunal allowed F's appeal, holding that since S was already insolvent, and F did not continue the contracting business, the transactions did not amount to the purchase of a going concern. *Auchtertyre Farmers*, EDN/87/109 (VTD 2822).

Assets of civil engineering company

[65.61] A civil engineering company (C) was in financial difficulties. In February and March 1987 it sold most of its assets to an associated company (S). In April 1987 C went into receivership and ceased trading. Its three outstanding contracts were transferred to S. S reclaimed input tax on the items it had purchased from C. Customs rejected the claim, considering that C's business had been transferred as a going concern. The tribunal allowed S's appeal, finding that when the assets were transferred, it was still hoped that C could continue trading. The transfer of C's three contracts in April 1987 had been the transfer of a going concern, but the previous transfer of assets had not been the transfer of a going concern. *Cedac Structures Ltd*, LON/88/522 (VTD 3307).

Public houses

[65.62] A brewery company (M) purchased the freehold of 98 public houses from an investment company (E), and reclaimed input tax on the purchase.

The public houses in question had previously been leased by E to another brewery company (C), which owned 50% of the shares in E, and had been sublet by C to tenants as tied houses. Customs rejected the claim, considering that the transaction constituted the transfer of a going concern. The tribunal allowed M's appeal. If the sale had been subject to the existing leases to C, it would have constituted the transfer of a business as a going concern. However, the sale was not subject to the leases to C, and following the sale, the houses were let by M directly to the tenants. The operation of the public houses had not formed a part of E's business, since E had leased them to a single customer. Accordingly, E had not transferred part of its business as a going concern. *Morland & Co plc*, [1992] VATTR 411 (VTD 8869).

[65.63] A public house, which had been run by a licensee, closed at the end of 1991. The owner of the premises repossessed them and applied for the licence to be transferred to his wife. He refurbished the premises and reopened them, under a new name, in 1992 as an 'upmarket' public house providing food as well as drinks. Customs issued a ruling that the business had been transferred as a going concern. The tribunal allowed the owner's appeal, finding that the business had been 'too moribund to deserve the description of a going concern'. *JG McLaughlin (t/a The Hip Flask)*, EDN/92/309 (VTD 10920).

Steel

[65.64] A sole trader (N) had worked as a subcontractor in the sheet metal industry for many years. From July 1990 to January 1991 he had worked for one contractor (C). However, in January 1991 C suffered financial difficulties when his main customer ceased trading. C was unable to continue paying N, and made his employees redundant. N found three companies which were willing to provide him with work, and took over premises which had, for the previous six months, been used by C. He purchased some steel from C, and reclaimed input tax on the purchase. Customs issued an assessment to recover the tax, considering that N had purchased C's business as a going concern. The tribunal allowed N's appeal, observing that C had already disposed of his equipment and premises and had made his employees redundant, and holding that the transfer of the steel from C to N did not amount to the transfer of a business. *JP Neville (t/a JP Neville Engineering)*, LON/92/2527A (VTD 10128).

Builders' skips

[65.65] A company (R) carried on business in the building industry. It owned a large quantity of skips, some of which it hired out to builders' merchants. In April 1992 one of its directors established another company (W) with a very similar name, to carry on a waste recycling business. W used an identical logo to that used by R, and took on two employees whom R had made redundant. In May W purchased 90 skips and a lorry from R, and reclaimed input tax. In July 1992 R ceased trading. Customs rejected the input tax claim, considering that the transaction constituted the transfer of part of R's business as a going concern. The tribunal allowed W's appeal, holding that the sale was simply a sale of assets, and did not amount to the transfer of R's business of skip hire. *Richards & Goldsworthy (Wales) Ltd*, LON/92/2671A (VTD 10346).

Workshop and office equipment

[65.66] A company (M) carried on the business of selling and leasing commercial vehicles. In May 1991 it purchased four vehicles and some workshop and office equipment from an associated company (P) which was in financial difficulties. It leased the equipment back to P, and reclaimed the input tax on the purchase. In July 1991 P went into liquidation. M leased the equipment to the liquidator until October, when it leased it to a third company which had been formed to take over P's former business. Customs issued an assessment on the basis that the sale constituted the transfer of P's business as a going concern. The tribunal allowed M's appeal, holding that the sale and leaseback did not amount to the transfer of a going concern. *Mohawk (Contract Hire & Leasing) Ltd*, LON/92/2031 (VTD 10998).

Machinery used for peat extraction

[65.67] A company (N) purchased some items of machinery from a sole trader (W), who had carried on the business of extracting peat for sale as fuel or compost. N reclaimed input tax on the purchase. W was made bankrupt in 1991, and N took over the lease of some land from which W had previously traded. N began the business of recycling mushroom waste on the land. Customs issued an assessment to recover the input tax which N had reclaimed, considering that the sale had constituted the transfer of W's business as a going concern. The tribunal allowed N's appeal, finding that W had ceased to trade before the transfer of the machinery, and holding that since N carried on the business of recycling mushroom waste whereas W had carried on a business of peat extraction, the sale of the machinery had not amounted to the transfer of a going concern. *Natural World Products Ltd*, BEL/92/55 (VTD 11064).

Assets of company installing and maintaining security systems

[65.68] A company (D), which had carried on a business of maintaining and installing security systems, ceased to trade. Some of its assets (comprising stock, fixtures and fittings, and a car) were transferred to another company (S), which began a similar trade on the following day. However, S did not take over D's contracts. S reclaimed input tax on the assets. Customs rejected the claim, considering that the transaction constituted the transfer of part of D's business as a going concern. S appealed, contending that as it had not taken over D's contracts, and acquired less than 30% of D's customers, the sale did not constitute the transfer of a going concern. The tribunal accepted this contention and allowed the appeal. *IHD Security Ltd*, LON/94/138A (VTD 12359).

Tanks used for transport and storage of bulk liquid

[65.69] A company (R) carried on the business of selling and leasing tanks used for the transport and storage of bulk liquid. It purchased a quantity of such tanks from another company (C), which it granted C a 20% shareholding together with £40,000 redeemable shares and £60,000 in cash. R reclaimed input tax, and Customs issued an assessment to recover the tax. R appealed, contending that it had deliberately decided not to purchase C's business as a going concern, since C had liabilities which it did not wish to take over, and that the transaction had been a sale and purchase of assets. The tribunal accepted this contention and allowed the appeal. *Riverward Ltd*, MAN/93/1055 (VTD 13094).

Assets of roofing company

[65.70] A company (S), which carried on a business of fitting flat roofs, was looking for new premises. Its directors became aware that an unrelated company (R), which carried on a business of fitting pitched roofs, had gone into receivership. The receivers were only willing to sell the premises if S also took over R's debtors, plant and machinery, and other assets. S did so, and reclaimed input tax on the purchase. Customs issued an assessment to recover the tax, considering that S had purchased R's business as a going concern. The tribunal allowed S's appeal, holding that, at the time of the invoice, there was no longer any business carried on by R 'which could be described as a going concern'. R had no work in progress, and S only fitted flat roofs whereas R had only fitted pitched roofs. S had entered into the transaction to acquire new premises, rather than to acquire a business. *Standard Flat Roofing Co Ltd*, LON/94/1461A (VTD 13151).

Assets of scaffolding partnership

[65.71] Four people had operated a scaffolding business in partnership. When the partnership dissolved, three of the partners continued to operate the business under the same trading name. The partner who had left (S) purchased some of the partnership's equipment, and three lorries. The partnership issued invoices charging VAT, which S reclaimed as input tax. Customs issued an assessment to recover the tax, on the basis that S had purchased part of the existing business as a going concern. The tribunal allowed S' appeal, holding on the evidence that the transactions were a transfer of assets rather than a transfer of a going concern. *MJ Shorter (t/a Ideal Scaffolding)*, LON/00/753 (VTD 17277).

Helicopters

[65.72] A company (R), which bought and sold helicopters, suffered financial difficulties and ceased trading, retaining two helicopters. Two years later, on the advice of its bank, it sold these to an associated company (E). E reclaimed input tax on the purchase. Customs issued an assessment to recover the tax, on the basis that E had taken over R's business as a going concern. The tribunal allowed E's appeal, holding that the helicopters were stock and their sale was not the transfer of a going concern. *R & M International Engineering Ltd*, LON/99/953 (VTD 17278).

Assets of photographic processing company

[65.73] A company (C) operated a photographic processing laboratory. It also produced and sold rubber stamps. It ceased trading after 15 months and its premises were repossessed. Its assets (including some camera equipment and 140,000 postcards) were purchased by an associated company (M). M reclaimed input tax on the purchase. Customs issued an assessment to recover the tax, considering that M had purchased C's business as a going concern. The tribunal allowed M's appeal in part, finding that C had never used most of the assets which it had sold (including the camera equipment and postcards) but had purchased them for the purpose of future trading activities, and holding that M had no intention of carrying on a business of photographic processing. Accordingly, the input tax was deductible (except for tax on 600 rolls of film and a small stock of rubber stamps, which the tribunal held constituted separate businesses which had been transferred as going concerns). *Morston Properties Ltd*, LON/97/96 (VTD 15004). (*Note.* For a subsequent appeal involving these companies, see **36.25** INPUT TAX.)

Assets of food technology company

[65.74] A company (M) had carried on a business of food testing. It sold its laboratory testing activities and assets to an unrelated company (C). It subsequently sold some of its other assets (including furniture, cars, computers and software) and the rights to a trading name, to a third company (S). Two of M's directors were also directors of S, which reclaimed input tax on the purchase. Customs rejected the claim on the basis that the purchase constituted the transfer of a business as a going concern. S appealed, contending that M had already disposed of its business as a going concern to C. The tribunal accepted this contention and allowed S's appeal. *International Supplier Auditing Ltd (t/a MNGP Food Technology)*, LON/02/741 (VTD 18111).

Transfer of insurance business

[65.75] See *Winterthur Swiss Insurance Company*, **22.534** EUROPEAN COMMUNITY LAW.

Vendor failing to account for output tax

[65.76] A company carried on the business of acquiring newsagents' shops and granting franchise agreements. In 1982 it set up a newsagency and appointed a married couple as its franchisees. In 1984 it sold the newsagency, including goodwill and fixtures and fittings, to the couple. It did not account for VAT on the sale, and the Commissioners issued an assessment. The company appealed, contending that the sale of the newsagency was the transfer of a business as a going concern, so that no output tax was due. The tribunal dismissed the appeal, holding that since the company was carrying on the business of granting franchises, the sale was a sale of business assets and did not constitute the transfer of part of its business. *Delta Newsagents Ltd*, [1986] VATTR 260 (VTD 2220).

[65.77] The proprietors of a shop sold the fixtures, fittings and goodwill of the shop for £20,000. They did not account for VAT on this amount and the Commissioners issued an assessment. They appealed, contending that the business had been sold as a going concern. The tribunal dismissed their appeal, finding that there was no evidence that the business had been sold as a going concern. *JH & M Clayton*, MAN/90/988 (VTD 6207).

[65.78] A partnership, which carried on the business of property ownership and management, sold the freehold of four industrial units to the trustees of a retirement benefit scheme, and did not account for output tax on the sale. The Commissioners issued an assessment charging tax, and the partnership appealed, contending that the sale constituted the transfer of a business as a going concern. The tribunal dismissed the appeal, holding that although the transfer was of a going concern, the transferee was not a taxable person, so that what is now *Special Provisions Order, Article 5(1)(a)(ii)* was not satisfied, and output tax should therefore have been charged. *Gould & Cullen*, [1993] VATTR 209 (VTD 10156).

[65.79] In 1992 a company (F), which had been incorporated to act as a jewellery and giftware trade association, sold the intellectual copyright in two publications, 'British Jeweller' and 'British Jeweller Year Book', to a newly-formed company, which was established as a joint venture between it and the publishing company which had been responsible for the publishing of the publications since 1989. F did not account for output tax on the sale. The Commissioners issued an assessment charging output tax, and F appealed, contending that the sale constituted the transfer of part of its business as a going concern. The tribunal dismissed the appeal, holding that the sale was not within what is now *Special Provisions Order, Article 5*, since the assets were not intended to be used by the transferee in carrying on the same kind of business as that carried on by the transferor. It was significant that F had not itself carried on a publishing business, but had only held the intellectual property rights in the publications. Accordingly the publications were business assets, rather than part of F's business. The new company 'was not put in possession of a going concern the activities of which it could carry on without interruption', and 'two different business assets coming together to create a new enterprise cannot amount to the transfer of going concerns'. *British Jewellery & Giftware Federation Ltd*, MAN/93/993 (VTD 12194).

[65.80] A public company (K) which carried on a retail business purchased a number of foodstores and transferred them to a wholly-owned subsidiary. It did not account for output tax on these transfers. The Commissioners issued an assessment charging tax on them, including a charge to interest. K appealed, contending that the transfers were outside the scope of VAT, since they constituted the transfers of going concerns. The tribunal dismissed the appeal, holding on the evidence that since K had never actually operated the foodstores, the transactions did not fall within *Article 5* of the *Special Provisions Order*. K had transferred the business assets to its subsidiary and was required to account for output tax on the transfers. *Kwik Save Group plc*, [1994] VATTR 457 (VTD 12749). (*Note.* The Commissioners accepted that the subsidiary could reclaim the VAT charged by the assessment as input tax, so that the substantive issue was K's liability to pay interest to the Commissioners which the subsidiary was unable to reclaim.)

[65.81] A partnership supplied security services. It entered into a contract with a company, under which the company took over certain security contracts (valued at £180,000) from the partnership and agreed to pay £90,000 in instalments. (The company subsequently became insolvent after paying £70,000 of this amount.) The partnership did not account for output tax on the payments which it received from the company, and the Commissioners issued assessments charging tax on them. The partnership appealed, contending that it had transferred part of its business as a going concern. The tribunal rejected this contention and dismissed the appeal, observing that contracts such as these 'do not constitute part of a business capable of separate operation'. *Derbyshire Security Services*, LON/96/384 (VTD 14809). (*Note.* An appeal against a misdeclaration penalty was also dismissed.)

[65.82] A car dealer sold his stock for £19,000. He did not account for output tax on this, and the Commissioners issued an assessment. The dealer appealed, contending that he had transferred his business as a going concern, so that the sale should not be treated as a supply. The tribunal rejected this contention and dismissed his appeal, holding that the purchaser was not a 'taxable person', so that the conditions of *Article 5* of the *Special Provisions Order* were not satisfied and output tax was due on the supply. *J Balmain (t/a Glenrothes Motor Factors)*, EDN/99/146 (VTD 16678).

[65.83] A large insurance company (P) transferred its cash collection activities to another company (F). The Commissioners issued a ruling that output tax was chargeable on the consideration paid by F. P and F appealed, contending that the transaction constituted the transfer of a going concern, so that no output tax was due on the transaction. The tribunal reviewed the evidence in detail, rejected this contention and dismissed the appeal. The tribunal observed that P carried on the business of an insurance company, whereas F carried on a business of 'collecting sums of money'. Before the transfer, P's cash collection had been an overhead of its insurance business, rather than a separate business in its own right. P had transferred part of its assets, and this transfer did not constitute the transfer of a business as a going concern. *FMCG Home Services Ltd*, LON/00/529 (VTD 18377).

Sale of property used as restaurant

[65.84] A restaurant proprietor (T) sold his restaurant. Most of the sale price was attributable to the freehold of the premises. T did not account for output tax on the sale. Customs issued an assessment charging tax on the sale of the goodwill, fixtures and fittings. T appealed, contending that the sale had constituted the transfer of a going concern. The tribunal rejected this contention and dismissed the appeal, holding that the sale was not within *VAT (Special Provisions) Order (SI 1995/1268), Article 5(1)* because T had operated the restaurant himself whereas the purchaser had rented the restaurant to a third party who operated the restaurant without owning the premises. *A Tezgel (t/a Master Chef)*, LON/06/1081 (VTD 20462).

[65.85] A company (S) owned a property, which consisted of a flat above a restaurant. S let the property to tenants, and opted to tax it. Subsequently S sold its interest in the property to the partnership which operated the restaurant. It did not charge VAT on the sale. Customs issued an assessment charging tax and S appealed, contending that the sale had constituted the transfer of a going concern. The tribunal rejected this contention and dismissed the appeal, holding that the sale was not within *VAT (Special Provisions) Order (SI 1995/1268), Article 5(1)* because S had used the property as an asset of a property letting business, whereas the purchasers were using it as an asset of a restaurant business. Applying the principles laid down in *Tezgel*, 65.84 above, there was a 'requirement that the buyer carry on the same kind of business as the transferor'. *Sydenham Commercial Property Ltd*, EDN/07/97 (VTD 20742).

Land and buildings (Special Provisions Order, Article 5(2))

[65.86] A company sold a public house, in respect of which it had elected to waive exemption. The purchaser reclaimed input tax on the basis that the effect of *Article 5(2)* of the *Special Provisions Order* was that the transfer of the land and buildings was a taxable supply. The Commissioners issued an assessment to recover part of the tax, considering firstly that 44% of the premises was used for a non-business purpose, so that that proportion of the input tax was not recoverable in any event, and secondly that part of the purchase price was attributable to a transfer of fixtures, fittings and goodwill which was not covered by the election to waive exemption, and was not therefore within *Article 5(2)* but which had been transferred as a going concern within *Article 5(1)*. The purchaser appealed, and it was agreed that the question of whether *Article 5(2)* applied should be considered at a separate preliminary hearing. The tribunal reviewed the evidence and held that the company's election extended to the whole of the land and buildings in question, on the basis that no part of the premises was 'designed as a dwelling' or consisted of 'self-contained living accommodation'. The tribunal also held that the fixtures and fittings were not part of the land and were therefore not covered by the election to waive exemption, so that the input tax which related to the fixtures and fittings was not within *Article 5(2)* and was, in principle, not deductible by virtue of *Article 5(1)* (unless the purchaser could show, at a subsequent hearing, that the business had not in fact been transferred as a going concern). However, with regard to the goodwill, while it was established that goodwill could exist as a separate intangible asset, the goodwill of this particular business was 'an attribute of the venue' and there was 'no separate goodwill in the reputation and clientele'. Accordingly, the goodwill attached to the land and was not severable from it. *AJ White*, LON/96/1964 (VTD 15388). (*Note.* The tribunal directed that the question of whether part of the premises had been purchased for a non-business purpose, and the quantification of the deductible input tax, should be considered at a separate hearing. There has as yet been no further public hearing of the appeal.)

[65.87] In December 1999 a company purchased several units on an industrial estate, which were let to tenants, and elected to waive exemption. In July 2000 it agreed to sell some of the units to a partnership for £120,000 (exclusive of VAT). The company failed to account for output tax on the sale, and the Commissioners issued an assessment. The company appealed, contending that the sale of the units should be treated as the transfer of a going concern. The tribunal rejected this contention and dismissed the appeal, holding that the effect of *Article 5(2)* of the *Special Provisions Order* was that the sale could not be treated as a transfer of a going concern, since the purchaser had not made an election to waive exemption. *Churchview Ltd*, MAN/01/762 (VTD 17919).

Special Provisions Order, Article 5(2)—definition of 'relevant date'

[65.88] A company, which was a registered charity, purchased a rented property at auction. The vendor had elected to waive exemption in respect of the property, and it was accepted that the letting of the property constituted a business. Following the exchange of contracts, the charity elected to waive exemption in respect of the property. The Commissioners issued a ruling that tax was chargeable on the transfer. (The effect of the ruling was that, by virtue of the transfer, the property became a 'capital item' within the capital goods scheme, so that if the property were to be used for exempt or non-business purposes within the following ten years, there would be a charge to tax by means of an adjustment to the initial deduction of input tax.) The charity appealed, contending that the effect of *Article 5* of the *Special Provisions Order* was that the transfer should not be treated as a supply. The tribunal rejected this contention and dismissed the appeal. The effect of *Article 5(2)* was that the transfer was to be treated as a supply, unless the transferee had elected to waive exemption 'no later than the relevant date'. The effect of *Article 5(3)* was that the relevant date was the date of the contract, rather than the date of completion. The tribunal observed that conveyancing solicitors were generally aware of the Commissioners' view that 'where it is intended that the transfer of otherwise taxable property is to be regarded as the transfer of a going concern, then the purchaser must elect prior to the tax point relating to the transfer'. The tribunal also held that the relevant legislation was not inconsistent with the *Sixth Directive*, since *Article 5(8)* of the *Directive* 'provides a specific power to Member States to take the necessary measures to prevent distortion of competition in cases where the recipient of assets is not wholly liable to tax'. The charity appealed to the QB, which upheld the tribunal decision. Moses J held that 'the relevant date is the date when the deposit was paid'. Since the charity had not made an election on or before that date, it was liable to pay output tax on the purchase. *Higher Education Statistics Agency Ltd v C & E Commrs*, QB [2000] STC 332.

Article 5(2)—whether election made before 'relevant date'

[65.89] A company, which carried on business as a 'property investor and developer', owned a large property in Sussex, in respect of which it had elected to waive exemption. On 30 August 1996 it formally agreed to sell the property to another company, for £2,475,000 exclusive of VAT. The agreement stated that the parties intended that the property should be transferred as a going concern, and that they should 'use all reasonable endeavours' to ensure that it was not treated as a supply for VAT purposes. On the previous day, the prospective purchaser had sent a letter to the Commissioners, giving notice of its election to waive exemption in respect of the property. The Commissioners received this letter on 3 September. Despite the elections, the Commissioners issued an assessment charging tax on the sale. The vendor appealed, contending that the purchaser had made an election before the 'relevant date' so that the sale should be treated as the transfer of a going concern. The tribunal accepted this contention and allowed the appeal, holding that, for the purposes of *Article 5(2)* of the *Special Provisions Order*, 'the "written notification" of the election is "given" by the "transferee" when he puts it in the post. From that moment onwards he can say with certainty to the transferor, to the Commissioners or to anyone else who might have an interest, that he has done everything in his power to make the election and to give written notification of it. Transferor and transferee can then proceed with certainty as to their respective tax positions. Whether or not relief is available to them will not depend on the vagaries of the post.' *Chalegrove Properties Ltd*, [2001] VATDR 316 (VTD 17151). (*Note*. For the Commissioners' practice following this decision, see Business Brief 11/01, issued on 21 August 2001.)

Liability to register (VATA 1994, Sch 1 para 1(2))

[65.90] The proprietor of a snooker club, who had been registered for VAT, ceased trading in November 1991. He sold the assets of the club to an individual (C) five weeks later. C registered for VAT, stating on the form VAT 1 that he had acquired the club as a going concern. However, C subsequently engaged an accountant who formed the opinion that C need not have registered for VAT, and applied for the registration to be cancelled. The Commissioners refused to cancel the registration, and C appealed, contending that he should not be required to register as his turnover had not exceeded the threshold laid down by *Sch 1 para 1(1)*. The tribunal dismissed C's appeal, holding on the evidence that the business had been transferred as a going concern despite the fact that the club had been closed for five weeks. Since the business had been transferred as a going concern, C was required by *Sch 1 para 1(2)* to register with effect from the date on which he purchased the business. *CA Curtis (t/a Green Baize Snooker)*, LON/92/2655 (VTD 11128).

[65.91] Similar decisions were reached in *L'Image Ltd and M Turner*, LON/93/2282A (VTD 12028); *S Grieco (t/a Globetrotters Fish Bar)*, EDN/94/131 (VTD 13194); *JDs*, EDN/95/182 (VTD 13703); *A & A Poullais (t/a Nightingale Café*, LON/96/73 (VTD 14140); *C Ravanfar*, LON/95/2540A (VTD 14159); *J Singh & G Kaur (t/a Denim House Clothing Co)*, MAN/96/339 (VTD 14532); *The Walnut Tree at Yalding Ltd*, LON/95/19 (VTD 14551, 15082); *DJ Whittaker (t/a Cheslyn Hay Fish Bar)*, MAN/96/182 (VTD 14585); *D Ojeh*, LON/97/213 (VTD 15369); *PA Malik*, MAN/97/1205 (VTD 15711); *C Menendez (t/a La Casona)*, MAN/98/300 (VTD 15784); *P Holland*, MAN/x (VTD 15996); *D Barnes (t/a The Haven)*, LON/98/1254 (VTD 16371); *Bootle Transfer Station Ltd*, MAN/99/1059 (VTD 17051); *SY Chau (t/a Oriental Fry)*, LON/00/1343 (VTD 17263); *K Munir (t/a Favourite Chicken)*, MAN/03/434 (VTD 18612); *S Dollard*, LON/02/1107 (VTD 18656); *Dolphin Fish Bar Ltd*, LON/04/161 (VTD 18993); *Begum Eastern Ocean Ltd*, LON/05/784 (VTD 19633); *MPH Leisure Ltd*, MAN/05/891 (VTD 19778); *D & KL Harper (t/a Tee Time Catering)*, MAN/06/363 (VTD 20176); *JW Brown*, [2009] UKFTT 359 (TC), TC00297; *James*, **51.128** PENALTIES: FAILURE TO NOTIFY; *Ahmed*, **51.172** PENALTIES: FAILURE TO NOTIFY, and the cases noted at **51.129** to **51.131** PENALTIES: FAILURE TO NOTIFY.

[65.92] The tenancy of a public house changed hands on 30 September 1993. The previous tenant had been registered for VAT, but the new tenant did not register. The Commissioners issued a ruling that he was required to register from 1 October, on the basis that he had taken over the tenancy as a going concern. The tenant appealed, contending that the tenancy had not been transferred as a going concern, because the old tenant had closed the public house for a few days before 30 September, and he had not been able to open it until a few days thereafter. The tribunal dismissed the appeal, holding that the fact that the new tenant 'wished to place the premises in better shape and thus there was a very small gap before he opened his doors does not mean that there was not a transfer of a going concern'. The tribunal also held that the fact that the two tenants sold different brands of beer was 'not relevant'. *AT Harber*, LON/94/972 (VTD 12979).

[65.93] The decision in *Harber*, 65.92 above, was applied in the similar cases of *GA & P Andrews*, MAN/94/939 (VTD 13310); *G Coward*, MAN/95/179 (VTD 13542) and *S Lagumina & A Bottiglieri (t/a La Piazza)*, LON/97/1515 (VTD 15542).

[65.94] The leasehold premises, goodwill and furnishings and equipment of an Indian restaurant were sold in October 1993. The purchaser closed the restaurant for several weeks, and reopened it as an Italian restaurant. The vendor had been registered for VAT, and the Commissioners issued a ruling that the purchaser was required to register from the date of purchase, on the basis that the restaurant had been transferred as a going concern. He appealed, contending that he had not acquired the business as a going concern, since he had changed the nature of the business. The tribunal dismissed his appeal, holding that the vendors had transferred the restaurant as a going concern. The fact that the purchaser had elected 'to close for a period of a number of weeks so that he could make all the necessary preparations to reopen in a radically different form' did not alter 'the fact that what was transferred to him was a restaurant business which enabled him to trade as such'. *H Tahmassebi (t/a Sale Pepe)*, MAN/94/197 (VTD 13177).

[65.95] The decision in *Tahmassebi*, 65.94 above, was applied in the similar subsequent case of *M Onemli, B Onemli, A Onemli & R Karadal (t/a West Kebab)*, LON/95/2989A (VTD 13983).

[65.96] Similar decisions were reached in *M Haroun (t/a Prince of Bengal Restaurant)*, MAN/95/2736 (VTD 14232); *Mr & Mrs Dulay (t/a Star Fisheries)*, MAN/98/256 (VTD 16443); *S Zargari*, MAN/00/123 (VTD 17138) and *Steliana's and Saphos Ltd*, MAN/07/036 (VTD 20387).

Conditions of Sch 1 para 1(2)(a) not satisfied

[65.97] A restaurant was transferred as a going concern on 1 July 1995. The previous proprietors had been registered for VAT, but the new proprietor did not register. The Commissioners issued a ruling that he was required to register from 1 July. He appealed, contending that he was not required to register because the previous owners' turnover during the previous year had been less than £46,000 (which was the then figure in *Sch 1 para 1(2)*). The tribunal accepted this contention and allowed the appeal, observing that the previous proprietors' turnover, as declared on their VAT returns, had been £50,980 including VAT but only £43,389 excluding VAT. The tribunal held that, by virtue of *VATA 1994, s 19(2)*, 'the value of a supply is the tax-exclusive figure. The fact that the Commissioners may have regard to the tax-inclusive figure when considering deregistration under *Sch 1 para 4* or non-registration under *Sch 1 para 1(3)* does not mean that a tax-inclusive figure is to be taken to determine the value of taxable supplies under *Sch 1 para 1(2)(a)*. The tax-inclusive figure is merely evidence which the Commissioners are entitled to consider when seeking to establish what will be a tax-exclusive figure, after deregistration or non-registration.' *M Ahmed*, MAN/96/939 (VTD 15399).

Business held not to be transferred as going concern

[65.98] A public house closed in September 1993 because the company which had operated it became insolvent. The tenancy was transferred to the former manager in December 1993. The Commissioners issued a ruling that he had acquired the public house as a going concern, so that he was required to register for VAT from December 1993. He appealed, contending that *VATA 1994, Sch 1 para 1(2)* did not apply and he was not required to register until March 1994. The tribunal accepted this contention and allowed the appeal, observing that 'the gap in trading was not associated with refurbishment and the customers might well have wondered whether as rumours go the financial difficulties experienced by one tenant might put off others', and held that the previous business which had been carried on at the premises had 'ceased entirely'. *A Hulse*, MAN/95/1726 (VTD 13896).

[65.99] Similar decisions were reached in *D Harrild*, LON/05/693 (VTD 19604); *LS Harrison*, MAN/05/604 (VTD 20392), and *T Carr (t/a The Princess Royal Public House)*, LON/07/312 (VTD 20507).

[65.100] A company operated a public house. The business included a restaurant on the upper floor of the premises. The company closed the restaurant at the end of 1995 and leased the relevant part of the premises to a woman (W), who used the premises to operate a smaller restaurant under a different trading name. This venture was not a success and W ceased trading after six months. The Commissioners issued an assessment on the basis that W had taken over part of the company's business as a going concern, and had therefore been liable to register for VAT. The tribunal allowed W's appeal, holding on the evidence that 'there was no transfer of a part of a business as a going concern'. *Mrs S Watt*, EDN/98/4 (VTD 15800).

[65.101] In a Scottish case, a Japanese restaurant, run by three people in partnership, ceased to trade on 27 April 1996. The premises re-opened as a Thai restaurant on 16 June 1996. The new business was run by a partnership of two people, one of whom had been a member of the previous partnership. The Commissioners issued a ruling that the business had been transferred as a going concern, so that the new partnership was required to register for VAT accordingly. The partnership appealed. The tribunal allowed the appeal, holding on the evidence that the business had not been transferred as a going concern. The tribunal specifically declined to follow the QB decision in *Dearwood Ltd*, **65.12** above, holding that 'the case of *Dearwood*, being a decision of a single judge in England, is not binding on a tribunal in Scotland. It has persuasive authority. However, the reasoning in it fails wholly to persuade. The test in the view of this tribunal is not whether the business "could be" carried on without interruption but is properly to be found in the words of the statute and the context of VAT legislation whether the transferred matters, if any, "are to be" carried on as a business. The trenchant criticism of *Dearwood* in *Hartley Engineering Ltd* (see **65.51** above), with which this tribunal agrees, plainly points the error of the test "could be carried on" and adverts to a consideration of the intention of the transferee as one of the matters which requires to be taken into account'. *Sawadee Restaurant*, EDN/98/43 (VTD 15933).

[65.102] The proprietor of an Italian restaurant, who was registered for VAT, died in August 2003. His executors carried on the business for one week, but then closed the restaurant. They removed some of the equipment, for use in a nearby restaurant which was owned by members of the deceased proprietor's family. The former head waiter of the restaurant (D) purchased some of the fixtures, fittings and equipment for £6,000. He negotiated a new lease with the landlord, and reopened the restaurant, under a different trading name, in October 2003. Customs issued a ruling that the restaurant had been transferred as a going concern, so that D was required to register for VAT. The tribunal allowed D's appeal, holding that what was sold 'was not a business as a going concern, but a package of assets'. *F Danielon*, MAN/04/681 (VTD 19244).

[65.103] A woman (D) had operated a restaurant from premises which she leased. She closed the restaurant on 24 December 2004 and terminated her tenancy. One of the leaseholders (S) bought some of D's crockery and opened a restaurant on the same premises on 14 January 2005. Customs issued a ruling that he had acquired the restaurant as a going concern, and was required to register accordingly. S appealed, contending that the transaction did not constitute the transfer of a going concern. The tribunal accepted this contention and allowed his appeal, finding that S had not acquired D's goodwill, stock or employees, and holding that his purchase of D's crockery did not amount to the transfer of a going concern. *N Spence*, LON/06/919 (VTD 20563).

[65.104] A hairdresser, who traded from a salon in Glasgow and was registered for VAT, suffered from ill-health and financial problems. In July 1995 his wife (W), who was not a hairdresser, took over the premises. She arranged for three stylists, one of whom had previously been employed by her husband, to work at the salon on a self-employed basis, paying her a percentage of their gross takings. Her husband also continued to work at the salon on a self-employed basis (and subsequently cancelled his VAT registration in view of the decline in his turnover). The other hairdressers who had previously been employed by her husband ceased to work at the salon. These arrangements lasted for just over a year, following which she and her husband (whose health had improved) entered into partnership and registered for VAT. Subsequently the Commissioners issued a ruling that W had taken over her husband's business as a going concern, and was therefore required to register for VAT under *Sch 1 para 1(2)*. She appealed, contending that she had not taken over her husband's business as a going concern, but had begun 'a new and separate business of property rental or facility services'. The tribunal accepted this contention and allowed her appeal. W was not herself a hairdresser, and 'the substance of her business was to provide facilities'. There had been 'a legitimate separation of (her husband's) business for administrative purposes'. On the evidence, W 'had no intention of becoming a hairdresser or of employing hairdressers. Her intention was to manage a business making available facilities to self-employed hairdressing stylists.' *E Woods*, EDN/97/111 & 122 (VTD 15485).

[65.105] A company, which carried on a flooring business from three shops, suffered financial difficulties and ceased trading. Its directors formed a partnership to carry on a similar business on a smaller scale from one of the shops. The Commissioners issued a ruling that the business had been transferred as a going concern, so that the new partnership was required to register for VAT accordingly. The partnership appealed. The tribunal allowed the appeal, holding on the evidence that the partnership had 'started a new business' and there had not been a transfer of a going concern. The tribunal observed that the partners 'started the new business because it was the only trade of which they had experience'. *R Owen & D Freeman (t/a Worcester Flooring)*, MAN/02/8098 (VTD 18539).

[65.106] A woman (W) operated a licensed restaurant in a pedestrian alley in Arbroath. This restaurant suffered financial difficulties, and closed in May 2008. W was subsequently made bankrupt. Another woman (M), who had worked as a waitress at the restaurant, persuaded the landlord to let her and a friend (C) operate a café from the same premises. The café opened five weeks after the restaurant had closed. In October 2008 M and C were visited by two HMRC officers, who persuaded them to register for VAT. Two months later their accountants wrote to HMRC seeking to revoke their registration. HMRC rejected this application on the grounds that they had acquired the café as a going concern. M and C appealed. The tribunal reviewed the evidence in detail and allowed their appeal, observing that there was a significant distinction between a licensed restaurant and a seaside café, and holding that the appellants had not acquired the café as a going concern. *A Cargill & K McWilliams (t/a Pende Café)*, [2009] UKFTT 381 (TC), TC00316. (Note. The tribunal was very critical of the HMRC officer who had conducted the initial visit, observing that he had referred in correspondence to the case of *Kenmir Ltd v Frizzell*, QB [1968] 1 All ER 414 (see **65.10** above) but, under cross-examination, he 'had no idea what the case was about'.)

Transfer of going concern—whether Sch 1 para 1(3) applicable

[65.107] See *Nash & Nash*, 57.24 REGISTRATION; *Timur*, 57.25 REGISTRATION, and the cases noted at 57.26 REGISTRATION.

Liability to account for tax (VAT Regulations 1995, reg 6)

Whether transferee liable for tax arising before date of transfer

[65.108] A married couple took over as a going concern the business of a company which they had controlled. The company's VAT affairs were in arrears, but the couple were allowed to keep the same VAT registration number on condition that they would submit a return which was outstanding, and would pay the VAT due in respect of the supplies made by the company before the date of transfer. The couple accepted these conditions but did not submit the outstanding return, and appealed against a subsequent assessment charging tax on supplies made by the company. The tribunal dismissed the appeal, finding that the couple had agreed to take over the company's liabilities and holding that the liability to furnish returns and to pay the tax due had passed from the company to the couple as partners. The QB upheld this decision, holding on the evidence that the couple had accepted liability to furnish returns and account for tax. *WH & AJ Ponsonby v C & E Commrs*, QB 1987, [1988] STC 28.

[65.109] The decision in *Ponsonby*, 65.108 above, was applied in *Bjellica*, 57.89 REGISTRATION, and in *MS Alkhatib (t/a Roxana Takeaway)*, MAN/03/390 (VTD 18514).

[65.110] In a similar case, a restaurant proprietor who had previously been in partnership with his wife was held to be personally liable for tax due in respect of the partnership, because he had taken over the liabilities in question under what is now *VAT Regulations, reg 6*. *BA Choudhury*, LON/87/16 (VTD 2490).

[65.111] In 1993 a plumber (T) transferred his business to a newly-formed limited company. In the following year he reverted to being a sole trader, and completed form VAT68, indicating that the business was being transferred as a going concern. The company failed to account for VAT on supplies which it had made, and the Commissioners sought to recover this tax from T under what is now *VAT Regulations, reg 6*. T appealed. The tribunal dismissed his appeal, holding on the evidence that the business had been transferred as a going concern and that T was liable for the outstanding tax. *CV Todd (t/a Sweeney Todd's Plumbing Squad)*, LON/95/1060 (VTD 14341).

[65.112] A similar decision was reached in a case where a plant hire company had acquired the business of a similar company as a going concern. The tribunal held that the effect of *VAT Regulations, reg 6* was that the transferee was responsible for meeting the outstanding VAT liabilities of the transferor. *Ruttle Plant (Midlands) Ltd*, MAN/02/033 (VTD 18048).

Whether public house transferred as going concern

[65.113] A publican and his wife separated in July 1987. The publican had previously been registered for VAT as a sole trader. Following the separation, the wife took over the licence and the running of the public house. She completed a form VAT 1 indicating that the business had been transferred as a going concern, and stating that she wished to retain the previous registration number. Subsequently, a VAT officer on a control visit formed the view that there had been an underdeclaration of tax, and the Commissioners issued an assessment on the wife, charging tax for periods both before and after the transfer. The wife appealed, contending that she was not liable for tax arising before the date on which she took over the business. The tribunal accepted this contention and allowed the appeal in part, finding that, despite the statement on the form VAT 1, the business had not in fact been transferred as a going concern, and holding that the assessment was not valid with regard to supplies made before the wife acquired the business from her husband. *L MacLean*, LON/89/1362 (VTD 5350). (*Note.* Compare *Ponsonby & Ponsonby*, **65.108** above, and *Choudhury*, **65.110** above, neither of which were referred to in this decision.)

Whether transferee liable for tax assessed on transferor

[65.114] A partnership operated a pet shop. It suffered financial difficulties and transferred its business as a going concern to a company of which the partners were directors. The Commissioners discovered that the partnership had overclaimed input tax and issued an assessment in July 1994. The partners were declared bankrupt and did not pay the tax charged by the assessment. In October 1994 the Commissioners withdrew the assessment on the partnership and issued an assessment on the company to recover the tax in question. The company appealed, contending that it should not be held liable for the tax in question. The tribunal accepted this contention and allowed the appeal, distinguishing *Ponsonby & Ponsonby*, **65.108** above, because in that case there had been no previous assessment. The tribunal chairman held that the relevant provisions of the *VAT Regulations* did not 'entitle the Commissioners to recover from the transferee tax on an assessment which has been validly made on the transferor and has, to borrow words from direct tax legislation, become final and conclusive'. *Pets Place (UK) Ltd*, [1996] VATDR 418 (VTD 14642).

Business transferred as going concern following bankruptcy

[65.115] See *Camford Ltd*, 37.32 INSOLVENCY.

Whether registration number can be transferred

[65.116] See *Miah*, 47.8 PARTNERSHIP.

Interaction of VAT Regulations, reg 6(3) with Sch 4 para 8

[65.117] See *Trade Only Plant Sales Ltd*, 62.116 SUPPLY.

Miscellaneous

Whether transferee can reclaim tax wrongly paid by transferor

[65.118] Between 1990 and 1993 a company (D) mistakenly accounted for VAT on certain supplies which qualified for exemption under EC law. In 1993 the company sold its business as a going concern to an individual (T). In 1994 T transferred the business to another company (S). Subsequently S claimed repayment of the tax which D had mistakenly accounted for. The Commissioners rejected the claim on the grounds that *VATA 1994, s 80(1)* restricted the claim for repayment to the taxable person who had actually paid the tax.

S appealed, contending that where there had been a transfer of a going concern, the transferee should be entitled to make a claim. The tribunal rejected this contention and dismissed the appeal, holding that even if D's registration number had been transferred (which was not the case), 'the provisions of (*VAT Regulations 1995, reg 6*) would not cover the right to make a repayment claim under *section 80*'. *Shendish Manor Ltd*, [2004] VATDR 64 (VTD 18474). (*Note.* This decision was subsequently disapproved by the Ch D in *Midlands Co-Operative Society Ltd v HMRC (No 2)*, **65.119** below.)

Transferee reclaiming tax allegedly overpaid by transferor

[65.119] A co-operative society transferred its business to another society. The societies did not elect for the transfer to be treated as the transfer of a going concern under *VATA 1994, s 49(3)* and *VAT Regulations 1995, reg 6*. Subsequently the transferee submitted a claim for the repayment of tax which it alleged that the transferor had wrongly accounted for. Customs rejected the claim but the Ch D allowed the society's appeal and the CA unanimously upheld this decision. Arden LJ held that there was nothing in the statutory provisions to prevent a person who had a claim under *VATA 1994, s 80* from assigning the benefit of that claim. The transfer of engagements between the two societies, under *Industrial and Provident Societies Act 1965, s 51(1)*, was effective to transfer the benefit of the transferor's claim. *HMRC v Midlands Co-Operative Society Ltd (No 2)*, CA [2008] STC 1803; [2008] EWCA Civ 305. (*Note.* See now, however, *FA 2008, s 133*, which has effect for assignments or transfers on or after 25 June 2008. For HMRC's explanation of the section, see HMRC Brief 31/08, issued on 26 June 2008.)

66

Transport

The cases in this chapter are arranged under the following headings.

Supply and maintenance of ships (VATA 1994, Sch 8, Group 8, Item 1)   66.1

Transport of passengers (VATA 1994, Sch 8, Group 8, Item 4)

     Cases held to qualify for zero-rating   66.12

     Cases where the consideration was apportioned   66.23

     Cases held not to qualify for zero-rating   66.30

Transport of goods (VATA 1994, Sch 8, Group 8, Item 5)   66.40

Handling services (VATA 1994, Sch 8, Group 8, Item 6)   66.41

The 'making of arrangements' (VATA 1994, Sch 8, Group 8, Item 10)   66.44

Handling or storage of goods (VATA 1994, Sch 8, Group 8, Item 11)   66.50

Supply and maintenance of ships (VATA 1994, Sch 8, Group 8, Item 1)

42-ton ketch

[66.1] Customs issued an assessment charging tax on the supply of a 42-ton, two-masted ketch. The vendor appealed, contending that it should be zero-rated under what is now *VATA 1994, Sch 8, Group 8, Item 1*. The tribunal rejected this contention and dismissed the appeal, holding that the ketch was 'designed for use for recreation or pleasure', and thus did not qualify for zero-rating. *BR Callison*, EDN/78/34 (VTD 810).

Work on tug intended as support vessel for racing yachts

[66.2] A company which carried on the business of ship-repairing undertook substantial work on a 209-ton tug, which was intended as a support vessel for British yachts competing in the America's Cup. In the event, the tug was not used for this purpose, as the company for which the work was carried out did not compete in the Cup. The company did not charge VAT on the work done, and the Commissioners issued an assessment charging tax on the amounts invoiced. The company appealed, contending that the work should be zero-rated under what is now *VATA 1994, Sch 8, Group 8, Item 1*. The tribunal rejected this contention and dismissed the appeal. The work carried out went far beyond 'repair or maintenance', and resulted in the tug becoming 'substantially more luxurious' and 'adapted to enable it to perform a different task'. Furthermore, the tug was not intended to be used for commercial activities, but was intended to be used for 'recreation or pleasure'. Accordingly, the work did not qualify for zero-rating. *A & P Appledore (Falmouth) Ltd*, [1992] VATTR 22 (VTD 7308).

Conversion of barges into houseboats—whether within Note A1(a)

[66.3] Two companies converted barges into houseboats, to be used as permanent residences but remaining capable of self-propulsion. The Commissioners issued rulings that VAT was chargeable on the work, considering that it was excluded from zero-rating by what is now *VATA 1994, Sch 8, Group 8, Note A1(a)*, on the basis that the barges were 'designed or adapted for use for recreation or pleasure'. One of the companies, and a customer of the second company, appealed. (The second company had gone into liquidation by the time the appeal was heard.) The tribunal allowed the appeals. The chairman (Miss Plumptre) observed that the barges had not originally been designed for 'recreation or pleasure' and holding that 'it stretches the ordinary meaning of the words recreation or pleasure well beyond their natural meaning to say that this encompasses a home or place of permanent habitation'. The barges remained 'ships' within *Group 8, Item 1*, and were not excluded from zero-rating by *Note A1(a)*. DG *Everett*, LON/92/1911A; *The London Tideway Harbour Co Ltd*, LON/92/1912A (VTD 11736). (*Note*. The decision here was approved by the Ch D in the subsequent case of *Stone*, **66.5** below.)

Purchase of replica barge for use as houseboat

[66.4] An individual (G) purchased a replica barge, with no cargo hold. The interior of the barge was arranged for residential use, with two bedrooms and a bathroom. The barge had an engine and was not intended to be permanently moored. Customs issued a ruling that VAT was chargeable on the supply. G appealed, contending that the barge was a 'qualifying ship' within *VATA 1994, Sch 8, Group 8, Note A1(a)*, so that its supply qualified for zero-rating. The tribunal rejected this contention and dismissed the appeal, declining to follow the earlier decision in *Everett*, **66.3** above. The tribunal chairman (Dr. Brice) held that the barge was 'designed for use for recreation or pleasure', and so was not a 'qualifying ship'. *J Grieve*, LON/06/860 (VTD 20149). (*Note*. See now, however, the subsequent Ch D decision in *Stone*, **66.5** below. Sir Andrew Park specifically disapproved Dr. Brice's decision in *Grieve*, holding that the tribunal had misdirected itself by treating the case as falling within *Article 15(5)* of the *EC Sixth Directive*, rather than *Article 28(2)* of the *Directive*.)

Purchase of barge for use as houseboat and office

[66.5] A naval officer (S) imported a barge from the Netherlands. The interior of the barge was arranged for residential use, and part of it was furnished as an office. The barge had an engine. Customs issued a ruling that VAT was chargeable on the importation. S appealed, contending that the barge was a 'qualifying ship' within *VATA 1994, Sch 8, Group 8, Note A1(a)*, so that its supply qualified for zero-rating. The tribunal accepted this contention and allowed the appeal, applying the earlier decision in *Everett*, **66.3** above. The Ch D upheld the tribunal decision. Sir Andrew Park observed that the barge had been 'designed and constructed from the outset for the purpose of being used as a family home, together with some business use'. He held that that did not constitute 'use for recreation or pleasure'. He also specifically rejected Customs' contention that *VATA 1994, Sch 8, Group 8* should be construed so as to conform with *Article 15(5)* of the *EC Sixth Directive*, observing that *Group 8, Item 1* 'was not enacted to give effect to *Article 15(5)* and indeed was enacted before *Article 15(5)* ever existed'. Furthermore, 'the *Group 8 Item 1* zero-rating was expressly permitted by *Article 28(2)* to remain in force'. Accordingly there was no liability to VAT when S imported the barge. *HMRC v Lt-Cmdr C Stone*, Ch D [2008] STC 2501; [2008] EWHC 1249 (Ch). (*Note*. For HMRC's practice following this decision, see HMRC Brief 38/09, issued on 8 July 2009. HMRC state that 'it was never the intention that UK legislation should provide for the supply of such vessels to benefit from zero-rating' and that they 'do not rule out a wider review of policy and legislation in this area. However, in the meantime, we have decided to treat Dutch barges and similar vessels that are designed and supplied for use as the permanent residence of the customer as qualifying ships and eligible for zero-rating. As vessels of less than 15 gross tons can never be zero-rated regardless of their design, the majority of narrow boats designed for permanent residential use will not meet this requirement and their supply will continue to be standard-rated.')

Conversion of barge into floating restaurant

[66.6] A trader purchased a barge, converted it into a floating restaurant moored on the River Thames, and hired it out for parties. Initially he accounted for tax on the amounts he received from customers, but he subsequently submitted a repayment claim on the basis that his supplies qualified for zero-rating. The Commissioners rejected the claim on the basis that the barge had been 'adapted for use for recreation or pleasure', so that it was no longer a 'qualifying ship' within *VATA 1994, Sch 8, Group 8, Note A1(a)*. The tribunal dismissed the trader's appeal against this decision, holding that the barge 'no longer had the basic attributes' of a ship and 'had become a floating party venue and restaurant, adapted solely for recreation and pleasure'. *MJA Halliwell*, LON/99/602 (VTD 17743).

Narrowboats for use on canals—calculation of 'gross tonnage'

[66.7] A trader (F) built several narrowboats, intended for use on canals. He treated their sale as zero-rated. Customs issued an assessment charging tax on the supplies, and F appealed, contending that the narrowboats were 'qualifying ships' within *VATA 1994, Sch 8, Group 8, Note A1(a)*, since they had a gross tonnage of not less than 15 tons (and were neither designed nor adapted for use for recreation or pleasure). The tribunal allowed F's appeal, holding that 'the tonnage of a ship is not a measure of its weight or the weight of cargo it can carry. It is a measure of the space inside the ship (or some of that space) multiplied by a numerical factor'. The tribunal noted that, at the time the relevant supplies were made, Customs' *Notice No 744C* stated that for VAT purposes, gross tonnage should be determined by multiplying the length, breadth and depth of the ship (all in metres) and multiplying this by 0.235. (In a subsequent edition, the multiplication factor had been reduced from 0.235 to 0.16.) The tribunal described the boats as 'basically box-shaped' but as having 'a "step" in the sides of the boats about 1.28 metres above the baseline which reduces the width of the boat above that point by 100 millimetres on each side'. These 'steps' were so small that they did not 'afford a safe or even a practicable means of moving from one end of a boat to the other'. Their purpose was to protect the portholes of the boat from coming into contact with jetties or lock walls. The tribunal specifically rejected Customs' contention that these 'steps' should be treated as limiting the measurement of the depth of the boat for the purposes of the tonnage calculation. Since the 'steps' were 'too narrow to afford a safe footing', they should not be treated as part of the deck, and 'the measurement should therefore be taken from the midpoint of the underside of the actual deck which is the top of the boat'. The result was that the boats in question exceeded 15 tons of tonnage and qualified for zero-rating. *RJ Fee (t/a Swiftcraft Boats)*, MAN/06/525 (VTD 20489). (*Note.* The tribunal's decision discusses the 'gross tonnage' test in considerable detail, but does not discuss the 'recreation or pleasure' test.)

Design work related to modifications of ships

[66.8] In an Isle of Man case, a company did not account for output tax on design work relating to modifications of ships. The Isle of Man Treasury issued an assessment charging tax on the work, and the company appealed, contending that it should be treated as zero-rated. The tribunal accepted this contention and allowed the appeal, holding that the design work 'forms an integral part of the modifications themselves and is zero-rated as services of the repair or maintenance of a ship'. The tribunal also held that the question of whether the supplies were made to the owners of the ships, or to their operating agents, was immaterial. *Cholerton Ltd v The Isle of Man Treasury*, MAN/94/799 (VTD 13387). (*Note.* For the Commissioners' practice following this decision, see Business Brief 5/99, issued on 24 February 1999. Customs state that they 'consider that the tribunal failed to take into account that Cholerton was contracted to supply only design services and therefore made no supply of modification services to which the design services could be integral. Accordingly, with effect from 1 July 1999, Customs will treat design services supplied in the UK as integral to the supply, modification or conversion of a qualifying ship only where a supplier specifically contracts with a customer to design *and* supply, modify or convert a qualifying ship.')

Supply of hull

[66.9] A company sold a hull to an unregistered partnership. The Commissioners issued a ruling that VAT was chargeable on the sale. The partnership appealed, contending that the sale should be treated as zero-rated under *VATA 1994, Sch 8, Group 8, Item 1*. The tribunal rejected this contention and dismissed the appeal, holding that the hull was not 'a qualifying ship' within *Item 1*. The tribunal held that a ship became a qualifying ship 'from the time when it is seaworthy or, if it is not designed to go to sea, when it is fit to navigate the waterways for which it is designed'. *QED Marine*, [2001] VATDR 534 (VTD 17336).

Group 8, Note 1—whether services supplied under charter

[66.10] A charity (P) conducted scientific studies of the River Tamar and the sea in the Plymouth area. It owned three boats, and outsourced their operation to a company (S). HMRC issued a ruling that S was required to account for VAT on the payments which it received from P. P appealed, contending that the services were supplied 'under a charter' within *VATA 1994, Sch 8, Group 8, Note 1* and qualified for zero-rating under *Group 8, Item 1*. The tribunal rejected this contention and dismissed the appeal, holding that there was a bareboat charter of the three boats by P to S, but rejecting P's contention that S had granted a 'time charter' of the boats with their crews back to P. The tribunal held that the effect of the relevant contract was that S was using the boats in its own trade, and had agreed to perform the services of collecting water, samples and specimens of marine life, and data. These services were not within *Group 8, Item 1*, and did not qualify for zero-rating. The tribunal observed that 'had the contract been drafted in a different manner, the outcome of this appeal would have been different'. *Plymouth Marine Laboratory*, [2009] UKFTT 179 (TC), TC00134.

Repair and maintenance of yachts

[66.11] See *Cirdan Sailing Trust*, **66.19** below.

Transport of passengers (VATA 1994, Sch 8, Group 8, Item 4)

NOTE

The scope of *VATA 1994, Sch 8, Group 8, Item 4* is now restricted by *Note 4A*, which was introduced by the *VAT (Transport) Order 1994 (SI 1994/3014)* with effect from 1 April 1995. Cases relating to periods before 1 April 1995 should be read in the light of this change.

Cases held to qualify for zero-rating

Payment for railcard enabling holder to travel at half-fare

[66.12] The British Railways Board instituted a scheme whereby students could travel at half-fare. Students wishing to take advantage of the scheme were required to pay £1.50 for a railcard, valid for six months. The Commissioners issued an assessment charging VAT on these supplies, and the Board appealed, contending that they should be zero-rated under what is now *VATA 1994, Sch 8, Group 8, Item 4*. The CA accepted this contention and allowed the Board's appeal. Lord Denning held that the payments of £1.50 were 'part and parcel of the payment which the student made for travelling on the railway. Just as a season ticket is payment in full in advance for travelling on the railway (whether the passenger uses it or not) so also this £1.50 is part payment in advance'. Browne LJ held that 'the transaction should be looked at as a whole, including both the issue of the card and the later taking of a ticket'.

The £1.50 'should be regarded as part payment in advance for the supply of transport by rail'. *British Railways Board v C & E Commrs*, CA [1977] STC 221; [1977] 2 All ER 873. (*Note*. Sir John Pennycuick also observed that the supply would appear to qualify for zero-rating under what is now *VATA 1994, Sch 8, Group 8, Item 10*.)

Air transport including catering—whether consideration apportionable

[66.13] A company which operated air transport services within the UK supplied passengers with free in-flight catering. The Commissioners issued an assessment on the basis that part of the price paid by the passengers should be attributed to the catering, and was therefore standard-rated. The company appealed, contending that the sums paid by the passengers were for the provision of transport and should be wholly zero-rated. The QB accepted this contention and allowed the appeal, and the CA upheld this decision, holding that the provision of in-flight catering on domestic passenger flights was an integral part of the supply of air transport, which was zero-rated. *British Airways plc v C & E Commrs (No 1)*, CA [1990] STC 643.

Chauffeur-driven car service supplied to airline passengers

[66.14] A company which operated an airline supplied a chauffeur-driven car service to some of its customers (whom it described as 'Upper Class Passengers') on international flights. It did not account for VAT in respect of these services. The Commissioners issued a ruling that the supplies of limousine services were a standard-rated supply on which VAT was chargeable. The company appealed, contending that they were a part of a single composite supply of air transport, which was zero-rated under what is now *VATA 1994, Sch 8, Group 8, Item 4*. The QB accepted this contention and allowed the company's appeal. Turner J held that the word 'place' in *Item 4* was not confined to the airport where the flight began or ended, but could mean the place where the passenger began his or her journey, i.e. his or her home. Since the company did not charge a separate price for the limousine service, it formed part of a single supply which qualified for zero-rating. *Virgin Atlantic Airways Ltd v C & E Commrs*, QB [1995] STC 341. (*Notes*. (1) For another issue in this case, not taken to the QB, see 63.7 TOUR OPERATORS AND TRAVEL AGENTS. (2) For the Commissioners' practice following this decision, see Business Brief 4/96, issued on 13 March 1996.)

[66.15] A similar decision was reached in a case which the QB heard with *Virgin Atlantic Airways Ltd*, **66.14** above. *Canadian Airlines International Ltd v C & E Commrs*, QB [1995] STC 341.

Railway ticket also giving admission to museum and engine shed

[66.16] A company operated a steam railway from Loughborough to Leicester via Quorn and Rothley, on track which had previously been owned by British Rail. It did not account for VAT on its fares, considering that they were zero-rated under what is now *VATA 1994, Sch 8, Group 8, Item 4*. In its publicity material, the company advertised the fact that, at the Loughborough terminus, there were a museum and an engine shed, which passengers could visit without any further charge. (Anyone not travelling on the railway could only visit the museum and engine shed by paying £1 for a platform ticket, although at other stations a platform ticket cost only 25p. Both parties accepted that the platform tickets were standard-rated.) The Commissioners formed the opinion that part of the amounts paid by passengers should be attributed to the right to visit the museum and engine shed, and should therefore be treated as standard-rated. The company appealed, contending that its only supply was a supply of transport which was zero-rated. The tribunal allowed the company's appeal, holding that, since the fare for travelling to Loughborough from the nearest station was the same as the fare for travelling to Leicester, Quorn or Rothley from the nearest station, none of the consideration paid by the passengers was specifically attributable to the right to visit the museum or the engine shed, and the whole of the fares were zero-rated. *Great Central Railway (1976) plc*, MAN/90/1071 (VTD 11402).

Membership fees for travel club—whether zero-rated

[66.17] A company which traded as a tour operator operated a 'travel club'. Membership of the club was only open to people who were employed by travel agents and dealt directly with the public. Members were entitled to tours, airline flights, hotel accommodation and car hire at reduced rates. The company did not account for output tax on the subscriptions which it received from its members, treating them as advance payments for zero-rated supplies of transport. The Commissioners issued a ruling that the membership fees did not qualify for zero-rating (with the exception of a small proportion which the Commissioners accepted as attributable to a zero-rated publication). The company appealed. The tribunal allowed the appeal, holding on the evidence that the whole of the membership fee was 'attributable to the supply of reduced rate travel products'. The membership card was 'an integral part of the consideration for which the travel product is supplied'. The company was acting as an independent principal, rather than as an agent. Accordingly, the membership fees qualified for zero-rating. *The UK Travel Agent Ltd*, LON/94/432A (VTD 12861).

Narrowboats—passenger capacity

[66.18] A trader provided cruising holidays along canals and navigable rivers, using two narrowboats. Only one of the narrowboats had an engine and it towed the other boat. Together the narrowboats provided sleeping accommodation for a maximum of nine guests and four crew. The trader treated his supplies of transport as zero-rated. The Commissioners accepted that the crew could be treated as 'passengers' for the purposes of *Item 4*, but issued a ruling that the supplies failed to qualify for zero-rating, on the basis that the narrowboats had to be treated individually and were not 'designed or adapted to carry not less than 12 passengers', as required by *VATA 1994, Sch 8, Group 8, Item 4(a)*. The trader appealed, contending that since twelve people (including three of the crew) could travel on either narrowboat at any time, each of the narrowboats should be treated as within *Item 4(a)* even though some of the passengers would have to transfer to the other narrowboat in order to sleep. The tribunal accepted this contention and allowed the trader's appeal, holding on the evidence that there was ample space on each of the narrowboats to transport twelve people and noting that 'the carrying capacity of each boat is greater than its capacity to provide sleeping accommodation'. The fact that neither of the narrowboats could provide sleeping accommodation for twelve people was not conclusive. *GL Ashton (t/a Country Hotel Narrowboats)*, MAN/95/1587 (VTD 14197). (*Note*. The figure in *Item 4(a)* has been reduced from twelve to ten, with effect from 1 April 2001, by the *VAT (Passenger Vehicles) Order 2001 (SI 2001/753)*.)

Yacht—passenger capacity

[66.19] A charity (C) was incorporated 'to help educate young people' by 'the provision of training and instruction in the art and craft of sailing'. It owned four yachts, which it chartered to groups of young people (supplying a crew). The Commissioners issued a ruling that C was making exempt supplies of education and sporting facilities, and issued an assessment to recover input tax which C had claimed. C appealed, contending that it was making zero-rated supplies of passenger transport. The tribunal accepted this contention and allowed the appeal, with the exception of one of the yachts, which it found was only designed to carry seven passengers, and therefore failed to meet the requirements for zero-rating under *VATA 1994, Sch 8, Group 8, Item 4(a)*. (The tribunal also held that the repair and maintenance of the yachts qualified for zero-rating as the repair and maintenance of a qualifying ship.) C appealed to the Ch D, contending that although the yacht only had berths for seven passengers, it could carry ten passengers on day trips and should be treated as qualifying for zero-rating. The Ch D rejected this contention and upheld the tribunal decision as one of fact. Park J observed that 'where a vessel is equipped with a significant number of bunks', it was 'realistic to regard the bunks as giving an indication of what the vessel is designed or adapted to do. If a vessel was designed or adapted predominantly or solely for day trips, it would be unlikely to have a considerable amount of its space occupied by bunks.' *Cirdan Sailing Trust v HMRC*, Ch D 2005, [2006] STC 185; [2005] EWHC 2999 (Ch).

Holiday cruises—whether whole consideration zero-rated

[66.20] A company supplied holiday cruises. It treated the consideration which it received for such cruises as wholly zero-rated. The Commissioners issued a ruling that the cruises were not simply a supply of transport, since the passengers also received accommodation, food and entertainment, so that not all the consideration qualified for zero-rating. The company appealed, contending that each cruise was a single supply of transport which qualified for zero-rating under *VATA 1994, Sch 8, Group 8, Item 4*, and that the services of arranging passenger transport within the EC were also zero-rated when supplied to a person registered for VAT in the UK. The tribunal allowed the appeal, holding that a holiday cruise was a single supply of the transport of passengers. 'The elements of accommodation, entertainment, catering, sightseeing, etc., which the Commissioners suggest to be a multiple supply of goods and services additional to a supply of passenger transport are in fact integral to the cruises and incidental to their main purpose.' The fact that the cruise was a journey of a 'leisurely nature' did not prevent it from constituting the supply of transport of passengers. *River Barge Holidays Ltd*, 67.114 VALUATION, was distinguished on the grounds that 'the river barge appears to have been used more as a place in which to sleep and eat than as a means of transportation'. The QB upheld this decision as one of fact. On the evidence, the tribunal was entitled to find that the main purpose of the cruise was the supply of passenger transport. *C & E Commrs v The Peninsular & Oriental Steam Navigation Co (No 2)*, QB [1996] STC 698. (*Note*. For the Commissioners' practice following this decision, see Business Brief 14/96, issued on 15 July 1996.)

River trip including catering—whether separate supplies

[66.21] A couple supplied canal boat trips on the Leeds and Liverpool Canal. They provided food for parties of 30 or more people. The Commissioners issued a ruling that, in such cases, they were making a separate standard-rated supply of catering as well as a zero-rated supply of transport. The couple appealed, contending that they were making a single supply of transport which was zero-rated. The tribunal accepted this contention and allowed the appeal, holding on the evidence that 'the substance and reality of the appellants' activities are "a day out on the river"', and that the provision of food was incidental to the supply of passenger transport. *Virgin Atlantic Airways Ltd (No 2)*, **66.23** below, was distinguished on the grounds that in that case functions such as wedding receptions and corporate entertaining were a 'primary purpose' of the hiring out of the vessel. *A & J Hughes (t/a Pennine Boat Trips of Skipton)*, MAN/97/1027 (VTD 15680). (*Notes*. (1) For the Commissioners' interpretation of this decision, see Business Brief 5/99, issued on 24 February 1999, and Business Brief 10/99, issued on 22 April 1999 following the decision in *Sea Containers Services Ltd*, **66.26** below. Customs state that they consider that the decision in *Hughes* 'is confined to that case' and 'will not accept claims seeking refunds of VAT on the basis of this decision from operators of boat trips or providers of other transport services with catering' (2) The decision in this case was distinguished, and implicitly disapproved, by subsequent tribunals in *Durham River Trips Ltd*, **66.24** below, and *Tucker*, **66.25** below.)

Narrow-gauge railway in country park

[66.22] A company operated a narrow-gauge railway in a country park in Hampshire. The railway consisted of a single loop which was slightly more than a mile in length. There were two stations, although the smaller station was only 375 yards away from the main station. The Commissioners issued a ruling that the company was required to account for output tax on its fares from the railway. The company appealed, contending that the fares qualified for zero-rating. The tribunal accepted this contention and allowed the appeal. The railway was not within *VATA 1994, Sch 8, Group 8, Note 4A* because the company did not provide any right of admission to the country park in which the railway was situated. The tribunal held that, despite the short distance between the two stations, the company was making supplies of transport which qualified for zero-rating. *Narogauge Ltd*, LON/95/1867 (VTD 14680).

Cases where the consideration was apportioned

River trip including catering—whether separate supplies

[66.23] A company operated a paddle-steamer ship which was based on the River Thames. It hired the ship out for functions such as wedding receptions and summer balls, during which catering services were supplied. In accounting for tax, the company treated part of the consideration which it received as attributable to zero-rated supplies of transport and part as attributable to standard-rated supplies of catering. The Commissioners issued an assessment on the basis that the whole of the consideration should be attributed to the standard-rated supplies of catering, and that the transport should be treated as incidental. The company appealed. The tribunal allowed the appeal, holding that 'in substance and reality' the company was making separate supplies, and the supply of transport was neither incidental to, nor a part of, the supply of catering. The fact that the passengers were transported 'to a certain degree of comfort' did not prevent the supply from qualifying as a supply of transport. *Virgin Atlantic Airways Ltd (No 2)*, LON/94/1530 (VTD 13840). (*Note.* For the Commissioners' practice following this decision, see Business Brief 14/96, issued on 15 July 1996.

[66.24] A company provided evening boat trips, including barbecues, on the River Wear, for an inclusive price of £14. It did not account for output tax on these receipts, treating them as wholly attributable to zero-rated supplies of transport. The Commissioners issued a ruling that the consideration was partly attributable to supplies of catering, and had to be apportioned. The tribunal dismissed the company's appeal, holding on the evidence that 'the passengers were not seeking merely an evening trip on the River Wear but a trip which had the separate but equally important feature of a barbecue meal'. Accordingly there were 'two separate and distinct supplies', namely 'a zero-rated transport supply and a standard-rated catering supply'. *Durham River Trips Ltd*, MAN/99/876 (VTD 17328).

[66.25] A trader provided boat trips on the Montgomery Canal, for a price of £3.50. She also provided charter trips, including food, at a price which varied from £7.95 to £12.95, depending on the type of food chosen. Initially she treated £3.50 of this as zero-rated, and accounted for VAT on the remainder of the price. However, following the tribunal decision in *Hughes (t/a Pennine Boat Trips of Skipton)*, **66.21** above, she submitted a repayment claim on the basis that she should have treated the whole consideration as zero-rated. The Commissioners rejected the claim and she appealed. The tribunal dismissed her appeal, distinguishing *Hughes* and observing that 'in the case before us the passenger chose a menu option which varied the overall price. As the journey itself did not vary, the conclusion has to be that the catering element of the trip was not ancillary but a separate feature.' *AM Tucker (t/a Montgomery Canal Cruises)*, MAN/99/921 (VTD 17329).

Rail transport including catering—whether separate supply of catering

[66.26] A company operated a luxury train, which was also available for charter within the UK. Passengers were supplied with catering. The company initially accounted for VAT on part of its receipts which was attributed to catering services. However, following the decision in *The Peninsular & Oriental Steam Navigation Co (No 2)*, **66.20** above, the company claimed a repayment on the basis that it was making single supplies of transport which qualified for zero-rating. The Commissioners accepted that, where the train was used for transport to Continental destinations such as Venice, there was a single supply of transport, but rejected the repayment claim with regard to the UK charters, considering that the company was making separate supplies of transport and catering. The tribunal dismissed the company's appeal and the QB upheld this decision. Keene J held that, as a matter of commercial reality, the provision of catering was clearly a distinct and separate supply. *Sea Containers Services Ltd v C & E Commrs*, QB 1999, [2000] STC 82. (*Note.* For the Commissioners' practice following the tribunal decision, see Business Brief 10/99, issued on 22 April 1999.)

Ski passes including transport on funicular railway

[66.27] A charity operated a funicular railway, enabling skiers to ascend a mountain by train and ski down it. It sold ski passes which included the right to transport on the railway. The Commissioners issued a ruling that the ski passes were standard-rated (although they accepted that spectator tickets, enabling spectators to descend and ascend the mountain by train, qualified for zero-rating). The charity appealed, contending that part of the consideration for the ski passes should be attributed to a separate supply of transport and treated as zero-rated. The tribunal accepted this contention and allowed the appeal, holding on the evidence that 51% of the consideration qualified for zero-rating. *Cairngorm Mountain*, EDN/01/208 (VTD 17679).

Apportionment of consideration for holiday including transport

[66.28] See *River Barge Holidays Ltd*, 67.114 VALUATION.

Rail ticket also allowing entrance to tourist attraction

[66.29] See *Aberystwyth Cliff Railway Co Ltd*, 67.117 VALUATION.

Cases held not to qualify for zero-rating

Cabinlift—passenger capacity

[66.30] A company operated a cabinlift to a scenic headland. The cabinlift comprised 41 cabins, each of which was designed to hold up to four passengers, and was hauled by a continuous cable with a device for detaching the cabins at the terminals. The Commissioners issued a ruling that the supplies made by the company did not qualify for zero-rating. The company appealed, contending that the cabinlift should be viewed as a whole for the purpose of what is now *VATA 1994, Sch 8, Group 8, Item 4(a)*, so that it was making zero-rated supplies of transport. The tribunal rejected this contention and dismissed the appeal, holding that each cabin was a separate vehicle, and that as each cabin carried fewer than twelve people, the supplies did not qualify for zero-rating. *Llandudno Cabinlift Co Ltd*, [1973] VATTR 1 (VTD 1). (*Note.* The figure in *Item 4(a)* has been reduced from twelve to ten, with effect from 1 April 2001, by the *VAT (Passenger Vehicles) Order 2001 (SI 2001/753)*.)

[66.31] The decision in *Llandudno Cabinlift Co Ltd*, 66.30 above, was applied in the similar cases of *Needles Chairlift Co Ltd*, LON/73/168 (VTD 90); *Glenshee Chairlift Co Ltd*, EDN/02/172 (VTD 18162) and *Lecht Ski Co Ltd (No 1)*, EDN/02/162 (VTD 18163).

Cable cars—passenger capacity

[66.32] A company operated a cable car system to carry passengers from a railway station to a nearby pleasure garden. The system provided twelve gondolas, each of which could carry up to six passengers. The Commissioners issued a ruling that the company's supplies did not qualify for zero-rating. The company appealed, contending that the system should be viewed as a whole for the purpose of what is now *VATA 1994, Sch 8, Group 8, Item 4(a)*, so that it was making zero-rated supplies of transport. The tribunal rejected this contention and dismissed the appeal, holding that each of the gondolas had to be regarded as a separate vehicle, and that as each gondola carried fewer than twelve people, the supplies did not qualify for zero-rating. *Heights of Abraham (Matlock Bath) Ltd*, MAN/85/51 (VTD 1914). (*Note.* See the note following *Llandudno Cabinlift Co Ltd*, **66.30** above.)

'Travelator' for skiers

[66.33] A company operated a 'travelator' (a continuous moving belt, just over 100 yards long) to enable skiers to reach the top of ski slopes. Customs issued a ruling that it was required to account for tax on the amounts it charged skiers for this service. The company appealed, contending that it should be treated as making a supply of transport which qualified for zero-rating. The tribunal rejected this contention and dismissed the appeal, holding that 'the travelator does not come within the definition of a vehicle. Its function is to take the skiers in one direction over a fixed route from one extremity of the device to the other, and not beyond. Its location is fixed where it has been installed. It is not capable of independent or relatively independent movement.' *The Lecht Ski Co Ltd (No 2)*, EDN/08/96 (VTD 20886).

'Big Dipper'—whether a form of transport

[66.34] A company operated a 'Big Dipper' at Blackpool. It did not account for VAT on its receipts from the 'Big Dipper', and the Commissioners issued an assessment charging tax on them. The company appealed, contending that the 'Big Dipper' was a form of transport so that its supplies were zero-rated. The QB rejected this contention and upheld the assessment, holding that 'transport' involved the movement of passengers from one place to another, so that the 'Big Dipper' was not a form of transport. Lord Widgery CJ observed that the essence of 'transport of passengers' was that 'the passenger is taken from A to B because he wants to be at B or because there is some purpose in being at B'. A person 'who in effect remains on one spot all the time' was not 'being transported as a passenger'. *C & E Commrs v Blackpool Pleasure Beach Co*, QB [1974] STC 138; [1974] 1 WLR 540; [1974] 1 All ER 1011.

Miniature railway in 'theme park'

[66.35] A company operated an indoor 'theme park' within a large shopping centre. The 'theme park' included carousels, dodgems, and a miniature railway track, comprising a single loop. The company charged £1 for rides on the railway (which lasted about two minutes). The Commissioners issued a ruling that output tax was chargeable on the fares, and the company appealed, contending that they should be treated as zero-rated passenger transport. The tribunal rejected this contention and dismissed the appeal. Applying *dicta* of

Lord Widgery in *Blackpool Pleasure Beach Co*, **66.34** above, the miniature railway was not within the definition of 'transport'. *Metroland Ltd*, MAN/95/2709 (VTD 14550). (*Note*. Costs were awarded to the Commissioners.)

[66.36] A company owned and operated a 200-acre 'theme park', on the site of a former colliery, in Derbyshire. The park included a lake, covering about 37 acres, and a circular railway track, of about one mile in length, which ran around the lake. Visitors to the 'theme park' paid a single entrance fee which entitled them to use the railway. The company accounted for output tax on the entrance fees, but subsequently submitted a repayment claim, contending that, for periods up to 1 April 1995 (when what is now *VATA 1994, Sch 8, Group 8, Note 4A* was introduced by *SI 1994/3014*) some of the fees should be treated as being attributable to zero-rated supplies of transport. The Commissioners rejected the claim and the tribunal dismissed the company's appeal. On the evidence, the company was making a single supply of admission to the park which was subject to VAT at the standard rate. *Granada Group plc*, MAN/95/2573 (VTD 14803).

Guided tour around disused mine including transport in miners' cage

[66.37] A company which owned a disused coal mine charged visitors £4 for a guided tour of the mine. The visitors were transported to and from the mine in a mechanically operated miners' cage, the journey taking about two minutes and the distance between the top and bottom of the shaft being about 300 feet. The Commissioners issued an assessment charging tax on the full amount charged for the guided tour, and the company appealed, contending that part of the £4 should be zero-rated as being paid for the transport to and from the bottom of the shaft. The tribunal dismissed the company's appeal, holding that the £4 was paid for the single supply of a guided tour, and that the time spent in the miners' cage was an integral part of the tour, rather than a separate supply of transport. *Big Pit (Blaenafon) Trust Ltd*, LON/90/1767 (VTD 6705).

Subscription paid by airline customers—whether zero-rated

[66.38] A company which operated an airline established a club, whereby potential customers would receive additional pre-flight and post-flight facilities in return for their subscriptions. These facilities included priority seat reservations and the use of VIP lounges at certain airports. It did not account for VAT on the club subscriptions. The Commissioners issued an assessment charging tax on these, and the company appealed, contending that the subscriptions should be treated as zero-rated under what is now *VATA 1994, Sch 8, Group 8, Item 4*. The tribunal dismissed the appeal, holding that the club subscriptions could not be regarded as an integral part of the supply of transport, and did not qualify for zero-rating. *El Al Israel Airlines Ltd*, LON/93/3037A (VTD 12750).

Transport from car park to airport—Sch 8, Group 8, Note 4A(b)

[66.39] Two companies advertised car parking facilities at airports. Some of their car parks were situated about five miles from the airport terminals. The companies therefore provided courtesy buses between the car parks and the airports. From 1995 to 2006 the companies accounted for tax on these payments. However, in 2006 they submitted repayment claims, contending that part of the consideration they received should be attributed to zero-rated supplies of transport, and that *VATA 1994, Sch 8, Group 8, Note 4A(b)* was invalid under EC law since it breached the principle of fiscal neutrality. The First-Tier Tribunal rejected the companies' contentions and dismissed the appeals, holding that the companies were making single supplies of parking facilities and that the supplies of transport were incidental. The companies appealed to the Upper Tribunal, which directed that the cases should be referred to the ECJ for guidance on the factors which should be taken into account 'when deciding whether, in circumstances such as those of the present case, a taxable person is providing a single taxable supply of parking services or two separate supplies, one of parking and one of transport of passengers'. *Airparks Services Ltd v HMRC (and related appeal)*, UT April 2011 unreported. (*Note.* The ECJ has registered the case as Case C-117/11. At the time of writing, no transcript of the Upper Tribunal decision is available.)

Transport of goods (VATA 1994, Sch 8, Group 8, Item 5)

Carriage of household goods to UK port

[66.40] An individual (B) emigrated from the UK to South Africa, and arranged for a company to collect and pack his furniture and personal effects into packing cases, and transport the cases to a quay at Southampton, alongside the ship in which he and his family were travelling to South Africa. The company accounted for VAT on its services. B lodged an appeal, contending that the services should be treated as zero-rated under what is now *VATA 1994, Sch 8, Group 8, Item 5*. The tribunal rejected this contention and dismissed his appeal. The company's services had been wholly within the UK, so that they did not qualify for zero-rating. *JD Bevington*, LON/76/85 (VTD 282).

Handling services (VATA 1994, Sch 8, Group 8, Item 6)

Facilities at airport

[66.41] The British Airports Authority granted an airline company the use of check-in desks and information desks at an airport, together with the rights to use the Authority's scales and conveyor belts for weighing and transporting passengers' luggage. The tribunal held that payments for the use of the scales and conveyor belts were zero-rated under what is now *VATA 1994, Sch 8, Group 8, Item 6*, but that payments for the use of the check-in and information desks did not qualify for zero-rating. *British Airports Authority (No 4)*, LON/74/154 (VTD 148).

[66.42] A company (E) provided facilities for the storage of luggage at three major UK airports. Customs issued rulings that VAT was chargeable on the services. E appealed, contending that they should be treated as zero-rated under *VATA 1994, Sch 8, Group 8*. The CA unanimously rejected this contention, holding that the supplies failed to qualify for zero-rating. Mummery LJ held that the relevant provisions of *VATA 1994, Sch 8, Group 8* had to be 'construed compatibly' with *Article 15* of the *EC Sixth Directive*. E's supplies did not 'meet the direct needs of aircraft or their cargoes' and were not 'directly connected' with the import or export of the passengers' luggage. Dyson LJ observed that there was 'no obligation imposed on (E) by the airports to accept only luggage that is going to be, or has been, carried on an aircraft. There is no contractual requirement on customers that they should only deposit luggage that is going to be, or has been, carried on an aircraft. There is no inevitability, or practical necessity, that luggage stored in (E's) stores has just been or will shortly be carried on an aircraft. The customer terms permit an item of luggage to be left in store for 90 days.' *HMRC v EB Central Services Ltd*, CA [2008] STC 2209; [2008] EWCA Civ 486.

Supply of hotel and taxi services for ships' crew

[66.43] A company (G) traded as a port agent, providing various services to ship-owners. It arranged hotel and taxi services for the crew of ships when the ships were delayed in port. Customs issued a ruling that it was required to account for VAT on these supplies. G appealed, contending that they should be treated as zero-rated under *VATA 1994, Sch 8, Group 8, Item 6*. The tribunal accepted this contention and allowed the appeal, holding that G was acting as an independent principal rather than an agent when it arranged to receive services from hoteliers and taxi drivers. The tribunal held that 'the concept of "handling of ships", i.e. the wording of *Item 6* of *Group 8*, is wider than that of meeting the "direct needs" of the vessel in question'. The tribunal also observed that 'it is difficult to imagine anything more directly connected to the handling of a ship than the provision of the ship's crew'. The ships in question 'would have been unable to sail without the crew and the crew would not have been available if they had not been accommodated for the duration of the delay, nor have been present at the ship if they had not been transported there'. Accordingly the services in question qualified for zero-rating. *George Hammond plc*, [2007] VATDR 383 (VTD 20353).

The 'making of arrangements' (VATA 1994, Sch 8, Group 8, Item 10)

Operation of telecommunications network for aircraft

[66.44] A Belgian company (S) operated a telecommunications network for aircraft. In 1973 the Commissioners issued a ruling that its supplies were standard-rated for VAT purposes. S appealed, contending that its supplies should be treated as zero-rated under what is now *VATA 1994, Sch 8, Group 8, Item 10*. The Commissioners accepted S's contentions and the tribunal formally allowed the appeal. *Société Internationale de Télécommunications Aeronautiques (No 1)*, LON/73/12 (VTD 19).

[66.45] Following the tribunal decision noted at **66.44** above, S continued to treat its supplies as zero-rated. However, in 1997 the Commissioners issued a further ruling that the supplies were standard-rated. S appealed, contending firstly that the supplies qualified for zero-rating under *VATA 1994, Sch 8, Group 8, Item 10*; secondly that they qualified for exemption under *Article 15(9)* of the *EC Sixth Directive*, and thirdly that the Commissioners were bound by the tribunal decision reached in 1973. The tribunal rejected these contentions and dismissed the appeal, and the Ch D upheld this decision. Sir Andrew Morritt V-C held that the supplies did not qualify for exemption, since they were not 'necessary to the operation' of the aircraft. They also failed to qualify for zero-rating, since the service provided was simply 'a means of communication and nothing more'. *Société Internationale de Télécommunications Aeronautiques v C & E Commrs (No 3)*, Ch D 2003, [2004] STC 950; [2003] EWHC 3039(Ch). (*Note.* The tribunal also held that the 1973 decision did not give rise to any estoppel—see **2.124** APPEALS. S did not take this issue to the Ch D.)

Payment for railcard enabling holder to travel at half-fare

[66.46] See *British Railways Board v C & E Commrs*, **66.12** above.

Grant of facilities at airport

[66.47] In the case noted at **41.32** LAND, the British Airports Authority granted a company the right to supply goods at Gatwick Airport, in return for a percentage of the company's gross takings. The Authority contended that its supply should be treated as zero-rated under what is now *VATA 1994, Sch 8, Group 8, Item 10*. The tribunal rejected this contention, holding that the supply failed to qualify for zero-rating. *British Airports Authority (No 2)*, [1975] VATTR 43 (VTD 146).

Flight vouchers

[66.48] A company (F) supplied and sold books of 'flight vouchers' to retailers for use in business promotion schemes. The vouchers entitled customers to claim free return flights to the USA on condition that they booked and paid for accommodation at an expensive hotel with which F had entered into an agreement. F did not account for VAT on the payments it received from retailers, and the Commissioners issued a ruling that VAT should have been charged on the payments. The tribunal allowed F's appeal against this decision. Applying *British Railways Board*, **66.12** above, the voucher was provided as part of the making of arrangements for the supply of space in an aircraft. This was a zero-rated supply under what is now *VATA 1994, Sch 8, Group 8, Item 10*. *Facthaven Incentive Marketing Ltd*, LON/90/1340Z (VTD 6443). (*Note.* A subsequent application by the Commissioners to make a late appeal against this decision was rejected—see **2.174** APPEALS.)

Grant towards purchase of buses—whether zero-rated

[66.49] A NHS trust wished to arrange for a bus service to a local hospital. It agreed to pay £330,000 to a bus company (T) as a grant towards the cost of purchasing three new buses, in return for T undertaking to operate a bus service to the hospital. T did not account for output tax on the grant and Customs issued an assessment charging tax on it. T appealed, contending that the grant should be treated as zero-rated under *VATA 1994, Sch 8, Group 8, Item 10*. The tribunal rejected this contention and dismissed the appeal, holding that 'the crucial point is that the appellant is acting as a principal with regard to the supply of transport and so cannot be an intermediary with regard to those supplies'. *Thamesdown Transport Ltd*, LON/04/1622 (VTD 19386).

Handling or storage of goods (VATA 1994, Sch 8, Group 8, Item 11)

Luggage storage facilities at airports

[66.50] See *EB Central Services Ltd*, **66.42** above.

67

Valuation

The cases in this chapter are arranged under the following headings.

Transaction between connected persons (VATA 1994, Sch 6 paras 1, 1A) — 67.1

Whether agreed price to be treated as exclusive or inclusive of VAT — 67.4

Supplies of goods

Deemed supplies under *VATA 1994, Sch 4 para 5* — 67.11

Deemed supplies under *VATA 1994, Sch 4 para 8* — 67.20

Supplies to non-taxable persons for retail sale (*VATA 1994, Sch 6 para 2*) — 67.27

Supplies of goods to agents for own use — 67.37

Whether commission deductible — 67.43

Sales of jewellery — 67.59

Sales of motor vehicles — 67.62

Miscellaneous — 67.66

Supplies of services

Prompt payment discounts (*VATA 1994, Sch 6 para 4*) — 67.88

Supplies of accommodation (*VATA 1994, Sch 6 para 9*) — 67.90

Whether commission deductible — 67.94

Sponsorship payments — 67.103

Voluntary payments — 67.106

Multiple supplies — 67.114

Car hire and minicab businesses — 67.121

Repair services — 67.126

Miscellaneous — 67.128

Face value vouchers (VATA 1994, Sch 10A)

Supplies of goods — 67.151

Supplies of services — 67.166

Transactions between connected persons (VATA 1994, Sch 6 paras 1, 1A)

Direction under VATA 1994, Sch 6 para 1—whether valid

[67.1] A company (L) was the holding company of a group. One of its subsidiaries (H) carried on an insurance business and was not registered for VAT. L carried on business as a shipping and freight-forwarding agent and was registered. In March 1980 the holding company bought a computer, in which data relating to H was stored. Although it was originally intended that data relating to other companies in the group should be similarly stored, in fact the computer was only used by H. At first L made no charge to H for the use of the computer but from 1983 L charged £300 per month plus VAT. Following a further visit in 1986, the Commissioners discovered that the computer had been used exclusively by H, and took the view that this amounted to a supply of services, the value of which was to be taken to be the full cost to L. Accordingly in April 1987 the Commissioners issued a notice to L under what is now *VATA 1994, Sch 6 para 1*, directing that the value of any supply made between 28 April 1984 and the date of the notice to any connected person for a consideration less than the open market value, should be treated as being made at the open market value, and further directing that any future supplies to connected persons should be subject to VAT at the open market value. Accompanying the direction was a letter which stated that, since the computer had been used exclusively by H, the entire tax-exclusive costs of depreciation, maintenance, manning, etc. incurred by the holding company would constitute the tax-exclusive value for VAT. L appealed, contending that the direction was void for uncertainty. The tribunal rejected this contention, holding that the direction was valid with regard to previous supplies of the use of the computer by L to H and with regard to all future supplies in relation to which the three conditions in what is now *VATA 1994, Sch 6 para 1* were satisfied (but was void with regard to any other previous supplies). *Oughtred & Harrison Ltd*, [1988] VATTR 140 (VTD 3174).

[67.2] A bank (which was partly exempt, and could only recover 10% of its input tax) sold various assets to four associated companies, which were not members of its VAT group. The companies then leased the assets back to the bank. The Commissioners issued a direction under *VATA 1994, Sch 6 para 1*. The four companies appealed, contending that the direction was invalid. The tribunal rejected this contention and dismissed the appeals. The provisions of *Sch 6 para 1* were authorised by *Article 27* of the *EC Sixth Directive*. The relevant derogation under *Article 27* covered tax avoidance as well as tax evasion. The bank had 'deliberately implemented a scheme for VAT avoidance'. The decision to issue the direction had not been unreasonable, and the leases had been made for consideration which was less than their open market value. *RBS Leasing & Services (No 1) Ltd (and related appeals)*, [2000] VATDR 33 (VTD 16569). (*Note.* For a preliminary issue in this case, see **2.51** APPEALS.)

Motor dealers—direction under VATA 1994, Sch 6 para 1A

[67.3] In 2004 a company which traded as a motor dealer entered into agreements with some of its employees, allowing them to use some of its cars for private motoring for the next ten years in return for a nominal payment of £10 each. HMRC subsequently issued a direction under *VATA 1994, Sch 6 para 1A*, directing the company to account for output tax on the market value of the deemed supply with effect from January 2005 (the date on which *Sch 6 para 1A* came into effect by virtue of *SI 2004/3104*). The company appealed, contending that the direction was not effective because the effect of the prepayment agreements was that the time of supply of the service was in 2004, before *Sch 6 para 1A* came into effect. The tribunal rejected this contention and dismissed the appeal, holding that the time of supply was governed by *VATA 1994, s 6(14)* and *SI 1995/2518, reg 81(1)*. The effect of those provisions was that the time of supply was 'the last day of the supplier's prescribed accounting period, or of each such accounting period, in which the goods are made available or used'. The tribunal observed that 'directions under *paragraph 1A(3)* can be of indefinite duration and so they may apply for longer than the nine years or so for which the appellants contend, with the consequence that the open market value must be intended to be established at different times and not once for all time at some particular point.' *Lookers Motor Group Ltd v HMRC (and related appeals)*, [2009] UKFTT 215 (TC), TC00165.

Whether agreed price to be treated as exclusive or inclusive of VAT

Work carried out by builder

[67.4] A farmer engaged a builder to supply and erect a shed and to build a stable block at his farm. He subsequently formed the opinion that he had paid the builder more than the true value of the work, and took legal proceedings against the builder in the Carlisle County Court. The court gave judgment for the farmer and ordered the builder to pay the farmer £4,367 including interest. The court held, *inter alia*, that although the builder had been entitled to charge VAT in respect of the supply of the shed, he was not entitled to add VAT to the agreed price for the stable block. The builder applied to the CA for leave to appeal against this decision, contending *inter alia* that the court had erred in law in holding that the price for the stable block should be treated as VAT-inclusive. The CA rejected this contention and dismissed the builder's application. Chadwick LJ observed that this 'was a contract under which the defendant stipulated for payment in cash, and was paid in cash'. The question of 'whether or not the price for a building contract is inclusive or exclusive of VAT must turn on the terms of the particular contract', and 'if the builder fails to make it plain to the employer (*sic*) that he is stipulating for payment of VAT in addition to the contract price, he will be left to account to the revenue for the VAT out of what he receives'. Chadwick LJ accepted that 'there may well be a custom in the construction industry that prices quoted are exclusive of VAT'. However, there was no evidence 'that, on a contract between a small builder seeking to be paid in cash and a part-time farmer, it was an implied custom that VAT would be paid on top of the cash payments'. It would appear most unlikely that 'the parties to such a transaction intended that VAT should be paid on top of the cash payments'. *Lancaster v Bird*, CA 19 November 1998 unreported.

Sale of freehold property

[67.5] A company purchased a freehold property. The supply was subject to VAT, as an election under *VATA 1994, Sch 10* (see **6.18** BUILDINGS AND LAND *et seq.*) had been made in respect of the property. The contract stated that the purchase price was £400,000 and that 'sums payable under this agreement . . . are exclusive of VAT'. The purchaser paid £400,000. The vendor demanded an additional £70,000 as VAT, and took proceedings to recover this amount. The Ch D gave judgment for the vendor. Under *VATA 1994, s 19(2)*, if a supply was for a monetary consideration, its value was to be taken to be such amount as, with the addition of VAT chargeable, was equal to the consideration. Thus, if a VAT-registered supplier simply charged £100 to a customer, while the VAT rate was 17.5%, he was obliged to treat $^7/_{47}$ of that sum as VAT, and pay it to the Commissioners. In order to obtain £100 net of VAT, the supplier would be obliged to charge £117.50 to the customer. However, where, as here, a contract specifically stated that a price was VAT-exclusive, it was commonly understood that the purchaser would have to pay the VAT in addition to the quoted price. Accordingly the purchaser was required to pay £70,000 to the vendor, which in return was required to account for that £70,000 to the Commissioners. *Hostgilt Ltd v Megahart Ltd*, Ch D 1998, [1999] STC 141.

[67.6] A company (W) sold a property to another company (V). The contract provided that the price was 'exclusive of VAT'. Both companies had assumed that the sale was exempt from VAT. However, the building was a 'new' building as defined by *VATA 1994, Sch 9, Group 1, Note 4*, so that VAT was chargeable. The Commissioners issued an assessment on W, charging tax of £107,250. W paid the tax charged, and sought to recover the tax from V. The CA gave judgment for W. Morritt LJ observed that the effect of the contract was that, if VAT was payable, the price provided by the contract was exclusive of it. *Wynn Realisations Ltd v Vogue Holdings Inc*, CA [1999] STC 524.

[67.7] See also *Jaymarke Developments Ltd v Elinacre Ltd*, 6.42 BUILDINGS AND LAND.

Lease of property—whether rent inclusive or exclusive of VAT

[67.8] In a Mauritius case, a company leased a property to a tenant. The lease agreement made no mention of VAT. The landlord added VAT to the rent. The tenant refused to pay the VAT and the landlord took legal proceedings. The Privy Council allowed the tenant's appeal, holding that under the lease agreement, the landlord had no claim on the tenant for any further payment in respect of VAT. It was the person making the supply who was liable for VAT on the value of the supply that he had made. If a supplier failed to make it plain that he required payment of VAT in addition to the contract price, he would have to account for VAT out of what he received. *Mauritius National Transport Authority v Mauritius Secondary Industry Ltd*, PC [2010] UKPC 31.

Lease of property—rent calculated by reference to 'turnover'

[67.9] In 1965 a company (D) leased some retail premises from another company (S). The relevant agreement provided that the amount of rent payable by D was partly dependent on the amount of its turnover. Following the introduction of VAT in 1973, D calculated the rent payable by reference to its VAT-inclusive turnover. Subsequently it formed the opinion that it should have calculated the rent payable by reference to its VAT-exclusive turnover. S refused to agree to this, and D applied to the High Court for a declaration that the rent should be calculated by reference to its turnover exclusive of VAT. The CA unanimously rejected this contention and gave judgment for S. Jacob LJ observed that VAT had originally been introduced to replace purchase tax, and held that there was no reason to treat 'a substitute for purchase tax which also affected ultimate prices as excluded by the words "gross amount of the total sales including services from trade". As a commercial matter, tax was included originally and is included now. It is just that the tax is levied further down the chain of supply now than it was in 1965.' Mance LJ held that it was 'clear that VAT should be regarded as a substitute for purchase tax and as part of the gross amount'. *Debenhams Retail plc v Sun Alliance & London Assurance Co Ltd*, CA [2005] STC 1443; [2005] EWCA Civ 868.

Compensation for compulsory purchase—whether VAT to be added

[67.10] The Department of the Environment purchased certain land, including the site of a sports hall. It agreed to pay compensation, including the cost of building an equivalent sports hall. A company (B), which was associated with the leaseholder of the land (S), paid contractors for the construction of a new sports hall, including VAT. It reclaimed this VAT from Customs. Subsequently Customs formed the opinion that B's services were exempt under *VATA 1994, Sch 9, Group 10*, and issued an assessment to recover the input tax. B appealed, and after correspondence, Customs withdrew the disputed assessment. In determining the compensation payable by the Department of the Environment, the Lands Tribunal held that the VAT which B had reclaimed from Customs should be excluded. S appealed to the CA, contending that the VAT should be included in the compensation, since there was a possibility that Customs might seek to reopen its contention that B's supplies were exempt. The CA unanimously rejected this contention and dismissed S's appeal. Sir Peter Gibson observed that Customs had 'repeatedly and consistently said that they would not seek to recover that tax'. Accordingly, 'the only reasonable conclusion which the Lands Tribunal could properly reach (was) that the input tax should be excluded from the compensation'. *Scout Association Trust Corporation and Others v Secretary of State for the Environment*, CA [2005] STC 1808; [2005] EWCA Civ 980.

Supplies of goods

Deemed supplies under VATA 1994, Sch 4 para 5

Valuation of deemed supply under VATA 1994, Sch 4 para 5(1)

[67.11] In March 1988 a partnership purchased two JCBs for £26,000. The JCBs were not in good condition, and after a few months they both required repairs which the partnership could not afford to pay for. They were temporarily parked in a field, but the local council demanded that they should be moved. An acquaintance of one of the partners offered to dispose of the JCBs for scrap. The partnership accepted this offer. The Commissioners issued an assessment on the basis that the JCBs had depreciated by 25% during the period in which they were owned by the partnership, and that by virtue of what is now *VATA 1994, Sch 4 para 5(1)*, the partnership should account for

VAT on their value at the time they were disposed of. The tribunal upheld the assessment in principle but reduced it in amount, holding on the evidence that the JCBs should be treated as having halved in value on account of their heavy use, and that a further £2,000 should be deducted from their value in respect of necessary repairs, so that their deemed value for VAT purposes at the date of disposal was £11,000. *CR Construction*, LON/91/2661Z (VTD 7737).

Footballers' presentation dinner—valuation of supply of trophies

[67.12] A company organised a presentation dinner for the Professional Footballers' Association. The company accounted for VAT on the price of the tickets. At the dinner various trophies, which had cost about £3,000, were presented. The Commissioners issued an assessment charging VAT on the cost of the trophies, on the basis that they had been supplied to the recipients without consideration. The company appealed, accepting that there was a deemed supply under *VATA 1994, Sch 4 para 5*, but contending that the awards of the trophies were an integral part of the dinner, and that the price of the tickets included consideration for the presentation of the trophies. The tribunal allowed the appeal, holding that the company supplied the purchasers of the tickets with the right to attend a function at which they would be given dinner and would see the presentation of the awards, the awards ceremony being an integral part of the supply. The consideration for the trophies was included in the price of the tickets, and the fact that the consideration was paid by people other than the recipients of the trophies was irrelevant, applying a *dictum* of Lord Cameron in *Lord Advocate v Largs Golf Club*, 13.6 CLUBS, ASSOCIATIONS AND ORGANISATIONS. The HL upheld this decision. The awards were made for sound commercial reasons, and their cost was borne by the diners and by the sponsors of the dinner. The fact that it was impossible to identify what part of the ticket price was consideration for the supply to the award winners was irrelevant. There was a direct link between the payment of the ticket price and the supply. *C & E Commrs v Professional Footballers' Association (Enterprises) Ltd*, HL [1993] STC 86; [1993] 1 WLR 153.

Caps presented to international footballers

[67.13] The Scottish Football Association (SFA) awarded commemorative caps to players who represented its team. The Commissioners issued an assessment on the basis that the SFA was required to account for output tax on the supply of the caps. The SFA appealed, accepting that there was a deemed supply under *VATA 1994, Sch 4 para 5*, but contending that no additional output tax was due because the consideration for the supply of the caps was part of the admission fees paid by the spectators. The tribunal accepted this contention and allowed the appeal, applying *Professional Footballers' Association (Enterprises) Ltd*, 67.12 above. *Scottish Football Association Ltd*, EDN/96/127 (VTD 14895).

Videotapes supplied free of charge to doctors

[67.14] A company produced videotapes containing programmes of interest to doctors, interspersed with advertisements of pharmaceutical products. The company distributed the videotapes to doctors free of charge, but charged the advertisers for the inclusion of their advertisements. The Commissioners considered that the tapes were supplied for no consideration, so that, by virtue of what is now *VATA 1994, Sch 6 para 6*, the company should account for VAT on the cost of producing the videotapes as well as on the payments received from the advertisers. The company appealed, accepting that there was a deemed supply under *VATA 1994, Sch 4 para 5*, but contending that the consideration it received for the videotapes comprised the sums received by it from the advertisers. The tribunal allowed the company's appeal, holding that it was not necessary for the consideration for goods or services to be paid by the actual recipient, applying *dicta* of Lord Cameron in *Lord Advocate v Largs Golf Club*, **13.6** CLUBS, ASSOCIATIONS AND ORGANISATIONS. The QB upheld the tribunal decision. The company received consideration from the advertisers in return for supplying the tapes to the doctors. The supply of the tapes was, therefore, outside the scope of *Sch 6 para 6. C & E Commrs v Telemed Ltd*, QB 1991, [1992] STC 89.

Supply of mobile telephones

[67.15] A company (T) supplied mobile telephones to customers under a promotion scheme, under which no charge was made to the customer for the supply of the telephone, provided that the customer agreed to rent a telephone line from another company (V) for a minimum period of twelve months. V paid T £190 for each new customer who entered into such an agreement under the scheme. The Commissioners issued an assessment on T, charging output tax on the cost of the telephones, on the basis that they had been supplied to the customers 'otherwise than for consideration'. T appealed, accepting that there was a deemed supply under *VATA 1994, Sch 4 para 5*, but contending that the payments which it received from V represented consideration for its supply of the telephones. The tribunal accepted this contention and allowed the appeal. There was 'a contractual link between the supply of the mobile phone to the customer and (V's) payment to (T)'. *Thorn plc*, [1998] VATDR 383 (VTD 15284). (*Notes.* (1) For a preliminary issue in this case, see **32.23** GROUPS OF COMPANIES. (2) For the Commissioners' practice following this decision, see Business Brief 23/98, issued on 17 November 1998.)

Computers supplied as competition prizes

[67.16] A company (S) carried on business as an internet service provider. It did not charge customers for the use of its services, but it received a share of the charges which its customers paid to their telephone service provider (usually British Telecom). It promoted a competition with the intention of attracting new customers, and inducing existing customers to make more use of its services. It offered computers as prizes. The Commissioners issued an assessment charging tax on the basis that the computers were gifts, within *VATA 1994, Sch 4 para 5*, so that S was required to account for output tax on their cost. The tribunal upheld the assessment and dismissed S's appeal. *Supanet Ltd*, MAN/x (VTD 17682).

Supplies of jewellery

[67.17] A company sold expensive jewellery. It occasionally rewarded regular customers by giving them an additional item of jewellery. Initially, in accordance with Customs' advice, it accounted for VAT on the cost price of the additional items as well as the agreed price of the items which the customer had ordered (so that, for example, if a customer ordered jewellery advertised at £10,000, and was also given an additional item costing £1,000, it accounted for VAT on £11,000). Subsequently it lodged a repayment claim on the basis that it should have treated the agreed price as covering both the item ordered by the customer and the additional item given to the customer (so that, in the above example, it would only have to account for VAT on £10,000). The Commissioners rejected the claim, and the company appealed. The tribunal dismissed the company's appeal, holding that the additional items given to the customers were gifts within *VATA 1994, Sch 4 para 5*. Accordingly, the effect of *VATA 1994, Sch 6 para 6* was that the company was required to account for VAT on the cost price of the additional items as well as on the original consideration agreed with the customers. *Boodle & Dunthorne Ltd*, MAN/02/761 (VTD 18429).

Valuation of deemed supply under VATA 1994, Sch 4 para 5(4)

[67.18] A company which sold cars allowed its employees to use demonstrator cars privately. It treated this as a deemed supply under *VATA 1994, Sch 4 para 5(4)* and accounted for output tax under *VATA 1994, Sch 6 para 7*. Subsequently it formed the opinion that it had overvalued the deemed supplies, and submitted a repayment claim. Customs rejected the claim and the company appealed. The tribunal reviewed the evidence in detail and dismissed the appeal, finding that the company had not provided 'satisfactory evidence to calculate the output tax properly due' and had not shown that there had been an overdeclaration of tax. The tribunal observed that it did not 'propose to provide a ruling which sets out all the factors that determine how the costs of private use of demonstrator vehicles is (*sic*) to be calculated. The function of the tribunal is not to provide tax advice.' *Caledonia Motor Group Ltd*, MAN/05/900 (VTD 20021).

VATA 1994, Sch 4 para 5—whether compatible with EC Sixth Directive

[67.19] See *EMI Group plc*, 22.164 EUROPEAN COMMUNITY LAW.

Deemed supplies under VATA 1994, Sch 4 para 8

[67.20] In June 1979 a trader had acquired an aircraft for the purposes of his business at a cost of more than £73,000, and had reclaimed input tax on the purchase. He ceased trading some months later and his registration was cancelled on 1 November 1980, at which date he still owned the aircraft. The Commissioners issued an assessment on the basis that the value of the aircraft at that time was £35,000, and that tax should be accounted for on this value under what is now *VATA 1994, Sch 4 para 8*. The tribunal upheld the assessment in principle but directed that it should be recomputed on the basis that the aircraft should be valued at £27,500. *B Mendes*, LON/81/259 (VTD 1192).

[67.21] A company which operated a private ambulance service ceased to be liable to register for VAT from 1 January 1990, when its supplies became exempt by virtue of the *VAT (Finance, Health & Welfare) Order 1989 (SI 1989/2272)*. The company owned an ambulance, purchased in 1989, on which it had reclaimed input tax. The Commissioners issued an assessment to charge tax on the deemed supply of the vehicle under what is now *VATA 1994, Sch*

4 para 8. The assessment was computed on the basis that the value of the ambulance had decreased by 30% in the period since its purchase. The tribunal upheld the assessment and dismissed the company's appeal. *Ambu-Medics Ltd*, MAN/90/447 (VTD 5697).

[67.22] A trader had registered for VAT as distributor of a product to be used for the valeting of motor vehicles. The product was not successful, and the trader deregistered with effect from 31 December 1988. At that time he had 300 unsold kits of the product. The Commissioners issued an assessment under what is now *VATA 1994, Sch 4 para 8*, considering that the stock should be valued at its cost price of £9 per item. The trader appealed, contending that the stock was unsaleable and worthless. The tribunal accepted this contention and allowed the appeal, holding that 'the value of the deemed supply must be based on the value of the goods at the time of deregistration'. *A McCormick*, [1991] VATTR 196 (VTD 5724).

[67.23] An aircraft maintenance engineer ceased trading and applied for deregistration. The Commissioners issued an assessment charging output tax on items of equipment which he held, valuing them at cost less depreciation. The trader appealed, contending that the equipment was worthless. The tribunal accepted the trader's evidence and allowed the appeal. *F Hadi (t/a Avionics Maintenance)*, EDN/96/115 (VTD 14677).

[67.24] In the case noted at **57.147** REGISTRATION, a company had purchased some land in 1995 for £100,000 plus VAT of £17,500. It failed to make any subsequent supplies, and was deregistered in 1999. The Commissioners issued an assessment charging VAT of £18,680, on the basis that the value of the land had increased by 2.2% pa. The company appealed, contending that the land had proved to be almost worthless and should be valued at only £1,250. The tribunal rejected this contention and dismissed the appeal, holding that the assessment had been made to the best of the Commissioners' judgment and observing that the company had failed to submit a professional valuation. *DCM Leisure Ltd*, MAN/00/323 (VTD 16966).

[67.25] A company purchased a property for £520,000 plus VAT of £91,000. It registered for VAT in February 1995, stating on form VAT1 that it was carrying on a business of property letting. In its first return, it reclaimed the VAT as input tax. However, it never accounted for any output tax, and in July 1997 it applied for its registration to be cancelled. The Commissioners accepted the application and issued an assessment charging VAT of £99,842 on the deemed value of the property. The tribunal upheld the assessment and dismissed the company's appeal. *Zanex Ltd*, LON/00/594 (VTD 17460). (*Note.* Costs were awarded to the Commissioners.)

[67.26] See also *Mollan & Co Ltd*, **52.291** PENALTIES: MISDECLARATION AND ERRORS.

Supplies to non-taxable persons for retail sale (VATA 1994, Sch 6 para 2)

School photographs supplied to school for sale to parents

[67.27] A company supplied school photographs. It sent these to the head teachers of schools on a sale or return basis. The company stipulated the prices at which the photographs were to be sold by the head teachers, and permitted the head teachers to retain up to 30% of the sale price. The company only accounted for VAT on the amount which it received from the teachers, and the Commissioners issued a direction under what is now *VATA 1994, Sch 6 para 2*, requiring the company to account for VAT on the price paid by the parents. The tribunal dismissed the company's appeal, holding that the sales to the parents were 'by retail', notwithstanding that the head teacher was not carrying on a business of supplying photographs. *H Tempest Ltd*, [1975] VATTR 161 (VTD 201).

[67.28] The company in the case noted at 67.27 above, and an associated company, appealed against subsequent directions under what is now *VATA 1994, Sch 6 para 2*, contending that the directions were invalid since they were making their supplies to local education authorities which were taxable persons, whereas the provisions of *Sch 6 para 2* were confined to cases where supplies were made to non-taxable persons. The tribunal accepted this contention and held that the directions were invalid in so far as they related to supplies made to schools (rather than to supplies made directly to parents), since any schools which received supplies of photographs were acting as agents of the local education authorities. *H Tempest Ltd (No 2); H Tempest (Cardiff) Ltd*, [1993] VATTR 482 (VTD 11210). (*Notes.* (1) For appeals against assessments raised on the basis that the companies were supplying photographs directly to parents, see **67.54** below. (2) For a subsequent case in which the decision here was not followed, and where it was held that the effect of the *Education Act 1993* was that schools were no longer acting as agents of local education authorities, see *Lancashire County Council*, 62.368 SUPPLY. The Commissioners now accept that the tribunal's findings in the *Tempest* case have been overtaken by the *Education Act 1993*—see Business Brief 11/97, issued on 9 May 1997.)

[67.29] See also *Laughtons Photographs Ltd*, 22.497 EUROPEAN COMMUNITY LAW.

Cosmetics supplied to agents for resale

[67.30] See *Direct Cosmetics Ltd (No 2)*, 22.497 EUROPEAN COMMUNITY LAW.

Sales of lingerie—definition of open market value

[67.31] A company supplied lingerie and 'marital aids' to women who acted as demonstrators of its products. These demonstrators were not registered for VAT, since their turnover was below the registration threshold. The demonstrators effected sales to the public by attending parties arranged by hostesses, and displaying samples of goods and copies of catalogues at the parties. After each party the demonstrators placed orders with the company by telephone, and the company supplied the goods to the demonstrators with invoices which included a 30% discount for prompt payment. In cases where the demonstrators were unable to obtain payment from customers who had ordered goods, they could return the goods to the company and would receive a credit note. In accounting for output tax, the company deducted the 30% discount from the sale price. The Commissioners issued a direction under what is now *VATA 1994, Sch 6 para 2*, requiring the company to account for tax on the market value of the goods. The company continued to account for tax as before, and the Commissioners issued an assessment charging tax on the basis that the market value of the goods was the full undiscounted price. The company appealed, contending that the market value was the discounted price. The tribunal dismissed the company's appeal, holding that the 'discount' was in fact a commission. The company was a wholesaler and the demonstrators were retailers. Consequently, the market value of the goods was the undiscounted price, and the company was obliged to account for VAT on that basis. The QB upheld this decision. The 'open market value' for the purposes of *VATA 1994, Sch 6 para 2* was the price paid by the ultimate customer to the demonstrator, not the price paid by the demonstrator to the company. *Gold Star Publications Ltd v C & E Commrs*, QB [1992] STC 365.

Whether direction under VATA 1994, Sch 6 para 2 unreasonable

[67.32] A married couple traded as distributors of Tupperware products. They sold these products through a number of sub-distributors, who were usually housewives and were not registered for VAT. The sub-distributors retained 30% of the price paid by the customers, and the distributors received the remaining 70%. The Commissioners issued a direction under what is now *VATA 1994, Sch 6 para 2*, requiring the distributors to account for VAT on the full recommended retail price paid by the customers. The distributors failed to comply with the direction, and the Commissioners issued an assessment to recover the undeclared tax. The husband lodged an appeal against the assessment, contending that the direction was unfair and unreasonable because he knew of two other Tupperware distributors who had not received directions. The tribunal dismissed the appeal. The Commissioners had a wide managerial discretion, and although it might not have been possible for them to take simultaneous steps against every trader who was avoiding tax, it did not follow that their conduct was unreasonable. *JK Moore*, [1989] VATTR 276 (VTD 4474).

[67.33] A company which carried on a mail order business sent catalogues to more than 800,000 'agents', most of whom were housewives. None of the agents were registered for VAT. Agents were allowed commission on orders taken, and in some cases were allowed to purchase goods at a price less than the normal catalogue price. Where commission was allowed, the company deducted the commission in accounting for VAT. The Commissioners issued a direction under what is now *VATA 1994, Sch 6 para 2*, requiring the company to account for tax on the open market value of the goods, and the company appealed. The HL upheld the direction, holding that the 'agents' were not strictly agents of the company, but were acting as independent principals. The fact that the company did not know whether the 'agents' were ordering its goods for resale or for their own use did not render the direction invalid. Part of the company's business consisted of supplying goods to non-taxable persons for retail sale. The direction was applicable to such supplies, and did not contravene European Community law. *Fine Art Developments plc v C & E Commrs*, HL [1996] STC 246; [1996] 1 WLR 1054; [1996] 1 All ER 888.

[67.34] A company sold an assortment of low-priced goods such as pocket calculators, manufactured overseas, through door-to-door salesmen. The goods were supplied to the salesmen on a 'sale or return' basis. The company accounted for VAT only on the amounts which it charged the salesmen, rather than on the amounts which the salesmen charged the ultimate purchasers. The Commissioners issued a direction under what is now *VATA 1994, Sch 6 para 2*, requiring the company to account for tax on the retail market value of the goods. The company appealed, contending that the direction was unreasonable, since the company did not fix a recommended retail price and frequently charged its salesmen different prices for identical goods. Most salesmen only worked for the company for less than two months, and the company had no way of knowing how much the salesmen charged the customers for the goods. The tribunal allowed the company's appeal, holding on the evidence that it was not possible for the company to ascertain the open market value of the goods which it sold. *Beckbell Ltd*, [1993] VATTR 212 (VTD 9847).

[67.35] A company (T) manufactured outdoor toys such as garden swings, climbing frames, trampolines, etc. Most of its sales were to registered traders, but it also had about 20 customers who carried on small retail businesses on a part-time basis and were not registered for VAT because their turnover was below the threshold. The Commissioners issued a direction under *VATA 1994, Sch 6 para 2* in respect of such sales, requiring T to account for output tax on the recommended retail price. T appealed, contending that the requirement was unreasonable in view of the small number of such sales. The tribunal rejected this contention and dismissed the appeal. It was arguable that occasional sales to unregistered retailers could be ignored, but in this case, T's sales to unregistered retailers exceeded £250,000 p.a., so that the direction was not unreasonable. *TP Activity Toys Ltd*, MAN/96/142 (VTD 14377).

[67.36] A company (T) imported goods from outside the UK and sold them to retailers at discounts varying from 10% to 25% from its catalogue price. Many of its customers were not registered for VAT because their turnover was below the threshold. The Commissioners issued a direction under *VATA 1994, Sch 6 para 2* in respect of sales to unregistered retailers, requiring T to account for output tax on the recommended retail price as shown in its catalogue. The tribunal upheld the direction and dismissed the company's appeal. *Traidcraft plc*, [2003] VATDR 583 (VTD 18189).

Supplies of goods to agents for own use

Value of goods supplied to hostesses under 'party plan' system

[67.37] A company sold women's and children's clothing under the 'party plan' system, under which its agents arranged meetings of potential customers in private houses to demonstrate its products and secure orders. The customer whose house was used as the venue was allowed a commission on the orders placed. She could take commission in cash, or alternatively could take goods produced by the company up to a prescribed retail price, which was considerably greater than the cash commission. Thus, in lieu of cash commission of £4.57, she could take clothing with a retail price of £11.67, paying cash for the excess if the price exceeded the £11.67. The Commissioners issued an assessment on the basis that the company should account for VAT on the retail price of goods supplied in this way. The company appealed, contending that it should only be required to account for VAT on the cash commission. The QB rejected this contention and upheld the assessment. By virtue of what is now *VATA 1994, s 19(3)*, the company was required to account for VAT on the market value of the goods, and this was equivalent to the retail price. *C & E Commrs v Pippa-Dee Parties Ltd*, QB [1981] STC 495.

[67.38] In a subsequent case where the facts were similar to those in *Pippa-Dee Parties Ltd*, 67.37 above, the appellant company contended that *Pippa-Dee Parties Ltd* should not be followed on the grounds that Ralph Gibson J had not considered the application of the *EC Sixth Directive*. The tribunal rejected this contention and dismissed the appeal, holding that output tax was chargeable on the normal retail price of the goods supplied to the agent. The CA upheld this decision. There was a direct link between the hostess's services in arranging parties and the supply of the goods to the hostess. Therefore, the supply was for a consideration 'not wholly consisting of money', within what is now *VATA 1994, s 19(3)*. On the evidence, the value of the service rendered by the agent was the difference between the normal retail price and the price actually paid. The facts that the price actually paid for the goods exceeded their cost, and that the hostess could have taken cash instead, were immaterial. *Empire Stores Ltd*, 22.234 EUROPEAN COMMUNITY LAW, was distinguished, on the grounds that the goods supplied as inducements in that case were not in the company's current catalogue and thus had no 'usual retail price'. *Rosgill Group Ltd v C & E Commrs*, CA [1997] STC 811; [1997] 3 All ER 1012.

[67.39] The Commissioners issued an assessment on a company which sold wickerwork goods under the 'party plan' system. The company appealed against the assessment, contending that, in ascertaining the 'market value' of goods it supplied to its hostesses, discounts which it gave to staff and agents should be taken into account. The tribunal dismissed the appeal, holding that the market value was the price which a member of the public would pay in a retail shop. *Churchway Crafts Ltd (No 2)*, LON/80/204 (VTD 1186).

[67.40] Two companies which sold cosmetics supplied some of their goods to agents at greatly reduced prices. The agents were expected to arrange 'party plan' sales of the companies' goods, and give the goods which they had obtained cheaply to the hostesses of the parties. The companies accounted for VAT on the price charged to the agents, and the Commissioners issued an assessment on the basis that the companies should have accounted for VAT on the normal wholesale price. The tribunal dismissed the companies' appeals, holding that the companies were required to account for tax on the market value of the goods. *Naturally Yours Cosmetics Ltd; Miss Mary of Swe-*

den Cosmetics Ltd, [1985] VATTR 159 (VTD 1921). (*Note.* For a subsequent appeal by one of the companies in this case, see **22.233** EUROPEAN COMMUNITY LAW.)

Mail order company offering goods as inducements to new customers

[67.41] See *Empire Stores Ltd*, **22.234** EUROPEAN COMMUNITY LAW.

Mail order company—supplies of goods to agents for own use

[67.42] A company sold goods by mail order, through agents. It allowed its agents commission on payments received. This commission was allowed at 10% in cash or as a part payment for goods which the agents had already ordered, or at 12.5% as a part payment for future orders. When an agent ordered goods for her own use, the company contemplated that she would earn 10% commission on those goods, and therefore treated the commission as a 10% discount on the catalogue price of the goods in question. When an agent ordered goods for customers, the company accounted for output tax on the sale price. When an agent used commission credited to her to buy further goods, the company treated the full 12.5% commission as a discount on the catalogue price. The Commissioners issued an assessment on the basis that only the standard 10% commission could be treated as deductible from the consideration for VAT purposes, and that the additional 2.5% was not deductible. The company appealed, contending that it had accounted for VAT on the correct basis. The tribunal accepted this contention and allowed the appeal, holding that if an agent applied her commission in payment for further goods, 'the whole of any reduction below the catalogue price of those goods to which she is contractually entitled must for VAT purposes be treated as a discount on the catalogue price of the goods, and it matters not what it may be called. It must therefore be excluded from the taxable amount in determining (the company's) VAT liability on its remittances for sales of further goods to the agent.' The decision in *Rosgill Group Ltd*, **67.38** above, was distinguished, on the basis that 'the transaction there concerned involved both monetary and non-monetary consideration', whereas 'in the instant case there was only monetary consideration'. The CA upheld the tribunal decision, holding that there was no direct link between the discount allowed to the agent and any services which she provided relating to the sale of goods to third parties. Accordingly, there was 'no basis for treating the provision of services as a non-monetary element in the consideration for the supply' of goods to the agent. Chadwick LJ also expressed the view that the cash commission was a price reduction within *Article 11C1* of the *EC Sixth Directive*. *The Littlewoods Organisation plc v C & E Commrs*, CA [2001] STC 1568; [2001] EWCA Civ 1542.

Whether commission deductible

Retail sales under concession with holiday camp

[67.43] A company (P), which sold toys and fancy goods, had a concession agreement with another company (L) to sell its goods in the general shop of a holiday camp controlled by L, paying L a prescribed percentage of the proceeds of such sales. The goods were sold by P's employees, but the proceeds were banked by L. L accounted to P for the net amount after deducting the agreed percentage. P accounted for tax on the net amount received from L, and appealed against an assessment made on the basis that it should have accounted for tax on the gross takings. The tribunal dismissed the appeal. The consideration for the sale of P's goods in the shop was the gross amount. The percentage deducted by L was not deductible. *P & M Marketing (UK) Ltd*, LON/82/328 (VTD 1385).

Sale of cars—interest on loan paid by vendor

[67.44] Two companies which sold cars arranged for purchasers of the cars to obtain finance from a finance company, under a scheme whereby they paid the interest on the loans by way of a deduction from the amounts payable to them by the finance company in respect of the cars. The companies only accounted for tax on the net amounts which they received from the finance company, and the Commissioners issued assessments to charge tax on the full sale price of the cars. The tribunal dismissed the companies' appeals, holding that the deduction made by the finance company as part of the arrangement with the vendors could not affect the consideration for the supply previously agreed between the vendors and the purchasers. *Grant Melrose & Tennant Ltd; Arnold Clark Automobiles Ltd (No 2)*, [1985] VATTR 90 (VTD 1858).

Sale of cars under '0% hire-purchase scheme'

[67.45] A company (N) sold cars. It arranged with the manufacturers of the cars, and with a finance company (F) associated with the manufacturers, for customers to be able to purchase the cars under a '0% hire-purchase scheme'. Under this scheme N sold the cars to F and made out invoices to F accordingly. F then entered into agreements with the purchasers of the cars for the repayment of the purchase price. The price paid by F to N was reduced by an amount described in the agreement as a 'subsidy', and N deducted this subsidy from the sale price in computing its VAT liability. The Commissioners issued an assessment on the basis that VAT was chargeable on the full sale price. The tribunal upheld the assessment and dismissed N's appeal. On the evidence, the subsidy was consideration for the services provided by F, and was not simply a discount. *North Kent Motor Company*, LON/87/633Z (VTD 3735).

Goods sold on credit—'commission' allowed to associated company

[67.46] Two associated companies, not registered as a group for VAT purposes at the relevant time, co-operated in selling goods to members of the public on credit. The goods were supplied by one of the companies (S), and credit facilities were supplied by the other company (C). Part of the consideration paid by customers was allocated to C as consideration for the supply of credit, and a further part was allocated to C as 'commission'. Thus, for example, where goods were advertised for sale at £100, and a further £35 was charged to the customer for the supply for credit, the customer would pay £135 but, in accounting for VAT, S not only deducted the £35 which was expressed to be for the supply of credit but also deducted a further £10 as 'commission' allocated to C, and only accounted for VAT on £90 of the £135 paid. The Commissioners issued a ruling that S should only have deducted the amount specifically expressed to be for the supply of credit, so that, in the above example, it should have accounted for VAT on £100 rather than on £90. S appealed, contending that it supplied the goods to C which in turn supplied them to the ultimate customers, so that it was only required to account for VAT on the net amount received after deducting the amounts allocated to C. The tribunal rejected this contention and dismissed the appeal, finding that the goods were supplied to the customers by S, so that, in accounting for VAT, S was only entitled to deduct the amount specifically attributable to the exempt supply of credit, and was not also entitled to deduct the amounts described as 'commission'. *Provident Financial plc*, MAN/91/1114 (VTD 10215).

Commission paid to finance company—whether deductible

[67.47] A company (T) which sold television products arranged with a finance company to provide credit to its customers for periods of up to twelve months. In accounting for output tax, T deducted the commission which it paid to the finance company. The Commissioners issued an assessment charging tax on the full amounts which T charged to its customers, and the tribunal dismissed T's appeal. *A5 Television Ltd*, LON/88/1358Y (VTD 12181).

[67.48] A company (P) which sold motor cars arranged for a finance company to provide credit to its customers. P submitted a claim for a large VAT repayment, contending that the payments which it made to the finance company should be deducted from the consideration which it received for the sale of the cars. Customs rejected the claim and P appealed, contending that the payments should be treated as a 'price discount or rebate' within *Article 11A3(b)* of the *EC Sixth Directive*. The tribunal rejected this contention and dismissed P's appeal, holding that 'a payment which is made in order to procure the granting of cheap, or free, credit' could not 'be treated as if it were something else, a reduction in the cost of the goods themselves'. On the evidence, the payments which P made were 'consideration for a distinct, exempt, supply of the granting of credit'. *Peugeot Motor Company plc (No 5)*, MAN/96/946 (VTD 19260).

[67.49] See also *HPAS Ltd (t/a Safestyle UK)*, 27.12 FINANCE.

Amount paid to finance company under sales promotion scheme

[67.50] A company (C) sold concrete driveways. It entered into a sales promotion scheme with a finance company (ICL), whereby it paid ICL 12.5% of the amount paid by its customers. In return, ICL supplied C with postdated cheques, payable over a five-year period, made out to the customers. C failed to account for output tax on the amounts paid by its customers which it passed to ICL. The Commissioners issued an assessment charging tax on the payments and C appealed, contending that it was acting as an agent for ICL and was not required to account for tax on these amounts. The tribunal rejected this contention and dismissed the appeal. *Classic Driveways (UK) Ltd*, MAN/97/834 (VTD 15521).

Interest-free credit granted to customers by finance company

[67.51] See *Primback Ltd*, 22.242 EUROPEAN COMMUNITY LAW.

Import of fish meal from Chile—commission paid to Chilean company

[67.52] A company (D) imported fish meal into the UK from Chile, under an agreement with a Chilean company under which it paid one-third of its commission to the Chilean company. The Commissioners assessed D on the full amount of the commission, and D appealed, contending that it should only have to account for VAT on the two-thirds share which it retained, and not on the one-third which it was obliged to pay the Chilean company. The tribunal accepted this contention and allowed the appeal. *David Geddes (Commodities) Ltd*, LON/87/573 (VTD 2664).

School photographs—whether commission to schools deductible

[67.53] A company supplied school photographs. It paid part of the price of the photographs to the headmasters of the schools as commission, and only accounted for output tax on the amounts which it retained. The Commissioners issued an assessment charging tax on the full amounts paid by the purchasers of the photographs, and the tribunal dismissed the company's appeal. *Paget*, **1.64** AGENTS, was distinguished on the grounds that the prices at which the photographs were to be sold were stipulated by the company, and most parents made their cheques payable to the company, whereas in *Paget* parents had made their cheques payable to the schools. Any bad debts were borne by the company, rather than by the schools. It followed that the company was obliged to account for VAT on the whole of the amounts paid by the parents, including the amounts which it passed to the schools as commission. *Flashlight Photography Ltd*, LON/91/207Z (VTD 9088).

[67.54] The decision in *Flashlight Photography Ltd*, 67.53 above, was applied in a similar subsequent case where *Paget*, **1.64** AGENTS, was distinguished. The tribunal held that the appellant companies was supplying photographs directly to the parents of the pupils whom it photographed, rather than to the school. Accordingly the companies were liable to account for output tax on the full amounts paid by the parents. *H Tempest Ltd (No 2); H Tempest (Cardiff) Ltd*, [1993] VATTR 482 (VTD 11210). (*Notes.* (1) The appeals were adjourned to enable the parties to consider whether the companies could reclaim input tax on amounts which it paid to the schools in return for the use of the school facilities. However, there was no further public hearing of the appeal. (2) For another issue in this case, see 67.28 above. (3) This case was decided before the enactment of the *Education Act 1993*. For the effects of that enactment, see *Lancashire County Council*, 62.368 SUPPLY. The Commissioners now accept that the tribunal's findings in the *Tempest* case have been overtaken by the *Education Act 1993*—see Business Brief 11/97, issued on 9 May 1997.)

Sales of carpets—commission paid to fitter

[67.55] A carpet retailer arranged for carpets which he sold to be fitted by a self-employed contractor, whom he paid accordingly. He claimed that the amounts which he paid to the fitter should not be treated as part of his turnover and that he should not be required to account for output tax on them. The tribunal rejected this contention and dismissed his appeal, holding on the evidence that there was a single supply of a fitted carpet and that output tax was due on the full amount paid by the customer. *T Lynam (t/a Victoria Road Carpets)*, EDN/97/53 (VTD 15585).

Mail order company—cash commission to agents

[67.56] A company (G) sold goods by mail order through agents. It paid commission to these agents. Initially it did not claim a deduction for this commission. However, following the ECJ decision in *Marks & Spencer plc v C & E Commrs (No 4)*, 22.55 EUROPEAN COMMUNITY LAW, it claimed a retrospective deduction, backdated to April 1973. HMRC accepted that the effect of *Article 11C(1)* of the *EC Sixth Directive* was that G was entitled to such a deduction for the period from 1 January 1978, but rejected G's claim for the period from 1973 to 1977 on the basis that neither the *EC Second VAT Directive* nor *FA 1972* gave G the right to make such a deduction. The tribunal referred the case to the ECJ for a ruling on the interpretation of *Article 8* of the *Second Directive. Grattan plc v HMRC (No 5)*, [2011] UKFTT 31 (TC); [2011] SFTD 297, TC00908. (*Notes.* (1) The ECJ has registered the case as Case C-310/11. (2) For another issue in this case, see **2.523** APPEALS.)

[67.57] See also *The Littlewoods Organisation plc*, **67.42** above.

Telecommunications company—cash commission to sales 'consultants'

[67.58] A company supplied telecommunications services. It made sales through a network of self-employed 'consultants'. It paid commission to consultants who introduced new customers. The Commissioners issued a ruling that the company was required to account for tax on the full amount of its turnover. The company appealed, contending that the effect of *Article 11C1* of the *EC Sixth Directive* was that it should be allowed to deduct the commission in computing its taxable turnover. The Ch D rejected this contention and upheld the Commissioners' ruling. Hart J distinguished *The Littlewoods Organisation plc*, **67.42** above, observing that the question in that case 'was whether the whole of the "taken in goods" commission should be treated as a price discount in relation to the secondary goods allowed and accounted for at the time of supply within *Article 11A3(b)* or whether it should be attributable to a non-monetary element of the total consideration'. In the present case, however, there was 'no question of the right to commission arising, in respect of a supply to a third party, as the result of a payment by the consultant'. Although the 'principle of neutrality' pointed to 'the third party commission being treated in the same way as the AOP commission', that had to 'yield to the countervailing principle that, where there has been an independent supply of goods which explain (and are directly linked to) the consideration received, that consideration constitutes a transaction for VAT purposes, separately accountable as such, rather than a post-supply discount which can be treated as reducing the taxable amount of a separate supply of services'. On the evidence, the commission paid to the consultants had to be treated 'as a payment made referable to the services supplied by the consultant in procuring them'. *C & E Commrs v Euphony Communications Ltd*, Ch D 2003, [2004] STC 301; [2003] EWHC 3008(Ch).

Sales of jewellery

[67.59] A partnership manufactured gold jewellery to customers' specifications. In some cases the customer provided pieces of old jewellery for adaptation or for re-use of the gold contained therein. The partnership charged its customers for the work done plus the cost of the gold used in excess of the gold content of the old jewellery handed in. It did not account for VAT on the value of the gold handed in for re-use. The Commissioners issued an assessment on the basis that the partnership should have accounted for VAT on the value of all the gold used in the new jewellery supplied to the customers. The tribunal allowed the partnership's appeal, holding that the partnership had accounted for tax on the correct basis. *Sharuna Jewellers*, [1979] VATTR 14 (VTD 709).

[67.60] The decision in *Sharuna Jewellers*, 67.59 above, was not followed in a subsequent case where the tribunal held that the old articles which the trader melted down became part of his trading stock, so that he was required to account for output tax on all the gold in the new item, rather than only on the excess gold. *HR Babber (t/a Ram Parkash Sunderdass & Sons)*, [1992] VATTR 268 (VTD 5958). (*Note.* For another issue in this case, see **3.62** ASSESSMENT.)

[67.61] In a case where the facts were broadly similar to those in *Sharuna Jewellers*, 67.60 above, the tribunal held that the important question was 'whether the appellants and their customers must be taken as having agreed that the new ornament be made using the gold provided by the customer but with the addition of any necessary gold or as having agreed that the old ornament be given in part exchange for a new ornament to be fashioned from no specific gold'. On the evidence, the tribunal found that 'the agreement with some customers was on the basis that their gold was to be refashioned and not mixed, but that the agreements with others was (*sic*) for part exchange'. The tribunal held that transactions where additional gold amounted to 25% or less of the finished article should be treated as refashioning, but that transactions where additional gold amounted to more than 25% of the finished article should be treated as part exchange, and directed that the assessment should be reduced accordingly. Both parties appealed to the QB, which upheld the tribunal decision as one of fact, applying *Edwards v Bairstow & Harrison*, HL 1955, 36 TC 207. *C & E Commrs v SAI Jewellers (and cross-appeal)*, QB [1996] STC 269. (*Note.* An alternative contention by the partnership, that the Commissioners were estopped from raising the assessment, was rejected by the tribunal and was not pursued in the QB. For cases concerning estoppel, see **2.109** *et seq.* APPEALS.)

Sales of motor vehicles

Valuation of new cars supplied under hire-purchase agreements

[67.62] See *North Anderson Cars Ltd*, **44.154** MOTOR CARS, and *Ford Motor Co Ltd (No 3)*, **44.155** MOTOR CARS.

Valuation of second-hand cars supplied by dealer to finance company

[67.63] See *A & D Stevenson (Trading) Ltd*, **44.156** MOTOR CARS.

Valuation of second-hand cars in part-exchange transactions

[67.64] See the cases noted at 44.83 to 44.87 MOTOR CARS.

Valuation of second-hand vans sold by hire-purchase

[67.65] A company (H) sold second-hand vans by hire-purchase. The hire-purchase company (C) required customers to pay a deposit. In cases where a customer was unable to afford a deposit, H agreed with the customer that it would enable the customer to obtain hire-purchase by increasing the price of the van and treating the price increase as if it were a deposit which the customer had paid. H only accounted for VAT on the price at which it had originally offered the van for sale. Customs issued an assessment on the basis that H was required to account for VAT on the price actually agreed with the customer and shown in the documents which H submitted to C. The tribunal upheld the assessment and dismissed H's appeal, applying the CS decision in *North Anderson Cars Ltd*, 44.154 MOTOR CARS. The tribunal observed that the legal transaction was that H was supplying the van to C, and that 'there was no suggestion that (C) was prepared to collude in any arrangement whereby payment of its minimum deposit could be circumvented'. Accordingly, the taxable consideration was the amount 'expressed as the price in the tax invoices issued to (C). In other words, the customer is not to be treated as the purchaser for the purpose of identifying the consideration in a case where the supply is, and is invoiced to, a finance company.' *Andrew Hillas Ltd*, MAN/03/435 (VTD 18671).

Miscellaneous

Repurchase of television sets

[67.66] A company sold television sets. It agreed that, if customers wished, it would repurchase the sets from them for £100 within four years. Where customers exercised this option, the company treated the £100 in question as deductible from the original consideration. Customs issued an assessment on the basis that tax remained chargeable on the original sale price. The tribunal dismissed the company's appeal, holding that 'the original sale and the subsequent repurchase were two separate transactions'. *WH Trace & Sons Ltd*, MAN/86/177 (VTD 2306).

Payments made to members of co-operative and described as 'dividends'

[67.67] See *Co-Operative Retail Services Ltd*, 22.252 EUROPEAN COMMUNITY LAW.

Unsold stock returned to supplier

[67.68] A company was unable to sell a quantity of stock and returned it to its supplier. Customs issued an assessment on the basis that the stock should be valued at cost, and that tax should be accounted for accordingly. The tribunal allowed the company's appeal, holding on the evidence that the stock was worthless at the time of its return. *Montessori Teachers Supplies Ltd*, LON/91/2421Z (VTD 8825).

[67.69] A furniture retailer, who was not registered for VAT, returned quantities of unsold furniture to the wholesaler from whom he had obtained them. Customs issued an assessment on the basis that the amounts paid by the wholesaler were consideration for a separate supply of furniture by the retailer to the wholesaler, with the result that the retailer's supplies exceeded the registration threshold and that he was required to account for output tax. The retailer appealed, contending that he had obtained the furniture on a 'sale or return' basis and that the amounts which he received from the wholesaler should be treated as deductible from the amounts which he had previously paid to the wholesaler for the furniture, rather than as consideration for a separate supply. The tribunal accepted the retailer's evidence and allowed his appeal. *K Hussain*, MAN/97/131 (VTD 15830).

Sale of furniture—part of consideration attributed to supply of insurance

[67.70] A company (C) sold furniture. It entered into a 'value-shifting' scheme intended to attribute part of the sale price to supplies of insurance which would be treated as exempt from VAT. Broadly, customers were offered a discount of 19% of the retail price on condition that they paid the 19% as an insurance premium. Almost 90% of the 'insurance premium' was returned to C as commission. Customs issued assessments on the basis that the scheme was ineffective and that C was obliged to account for VAT on the normal retail price. C appealed. The tribunal reviewed the evidence in detail at a preliminary hearing and held with regard to some of the supplies that the documentation did not create separate supplies of insurance. With regard to later supplies using more detailed documentation, the tribunal held that there were separate supplies of insurance but that C's apportionment of the consideration 'does not represent the real consideration in domestic law' and was ineffective for VAT purposes. The tribunal directed that the correct apportionment of the consideration should be considered at a further hearing. *Courts plc (No 2)*, [2004] VATDR 316 (VTD 18746). (*Notes.* (1) The appellant company subsequently went into liquidation, and there was no further public hearing of this appeal. (2) For another appeal by the same company, taken to the CA, see **3.46** ASSESSMENT.)

Repossession of goods—whether a 'decrease in consideration'

[67.71] See *Morley Electronic Fire Systems Ltd*, **40.107** INVOICES AND CREDIT NOTES.

Computer games supplied by barter

[67.72] A retailer sold computer games and accessories. He also began a scheme whereby people who had computer games which they no longer wished to use could exchange them for others at his shop. Customers were charged £5 to join this scheme, and could then, after paying a £3 handling fee, exchange games which they no longer wanted for others from a stock of old games kept by the retailer. The retailer accounted for output tax on the £5 joining fees and the £3 handling charges. Customs issued an assessment on the basis that he should also have accounted for output tax on the market value of the games which he passed to the customers under the scheme. The assessment was computed on the basis that the average value of such games was £27.50. The tribunal upheld the assessment in principle, holding that 'for tax purposes there was a supply by barter which is to be taken as a supply at open market value', but reduced the amount of the assessment, holding that the value of each of the second-hand games should be treated as £15. *TC Antoniou-Savva (t/a Game Atronics)*, LON/93/2225A (VTD 11982).

Sale of painting at auction—50% of proceeds allocated to charity

[67.73] An artist sold a painting at an auction. The sale price of the painting was £13,000, but the artist only received £6,500 of this, the remaining £6,500 being paid to the charity which had organised the auction. The artist accounted for output tax on the £6,500 which she had retained. Customs issued an assessment requiring her to account for tax on the £6,500 which had been retained by the charity. She appealed, contending that, because the bidders were aware that the charity would retain 50% of the total price, the £6,500 which the charity retained should be deemed to have been paid by the buyer of the painting, rather than by her. The tribunal accepted this contention and allowed her appeal. *E Patrick*, [1994] VATTR 247 (VTD 12354). (*Note.* The decision here was disapproved in the subsequent case of *Findel plc v HMRC*, 67.74 below.)

Company selling goods by mail order—part of proceeds donated to charity

[67.74] A company (E) sold goods by mail order. Its catalogues indicated that part of the proceeds would be donated to charity. Initially it accounted for VAT on the full amount of its takings, but it subsequently submitted a substantial repayment claim on the basis that it should not have accounted for VAT on the amounts which it passed to charity. HMRC rejected the claim, and the representative member of E's group appealed. The tribunal dismissed the appeal. Judge Demack specifically declined to follow the earlier decisions in *Patrick*, 67.73 above, or *EMAP MacLaren Ltd*, 67.105 below, and held that both cases had been wrongly decided. (With regard to the *EMAP MacLaren* case, he observed that McCullough J had applied the CA decision in *Nell Gwynn House Maintenance Fund*, 62.36 supply, which had subsequently been reversed by the HL.) He held that the consideration for VAT purposes was 'the full catalogue price'. *Findel plc v HMRC*, [2011] UKFTT 723 (TC), TC01560.

Supplies of diaries

[67.75] A number of associated companies produced diaries for various organisations such as local charities. They were entitled to sell advertising space in the diaries, and to retain the advertising revenue which they received. In 1981 Customs issued a ruling that the companies should account for output tax on the cost of producing the diaries and on a notional 30% mark-up, as well as on the advertising revenue. Initially the companies accepted this, but in 1993 they formed the opinion that they should only be required to account for tax on the advertising revenue, and claimed a repayment of tax which they considered that they had overdeclared. In 1995 Customs agreed to repay the tax relating to the notional 30% mark-up, but rejected the claim to repay the output tax on the cost of the diaries. The companies appealed, contending that the only consideration which they obtained was the revenue paid by the advertisers. The tribunal accepted this contention and allowed the appeals.

The advertising charges were the consideration for the supply of the diaries to the recipient organisations. The fact that the consideration was paid by a third party did not require any additional value to be attributed to the supplies. *Seaton Sands Ltd & Others*, LON/95/2609A (VTD 13879). (*Note.* For subsequent developments in this case, see 2.527 APPEALS.)

Supplies of videocassettes

[67.76] A trader (B) sold videocassettes for £20. However, where a customer offered a videocassette which he had previously purchased from B in part-exchange, B only charged the customer £10 for the new videocassette. Customs issued an assessment on the basis that B was required to account for output tax on the basis that the consideration for each of his supplies was £20. B appealed, contending that, where he accepted an old videocassette in part-exchange, he should only be required to account for output tax on the £10 cash payment which he received. The CA rejected this contention and upheld the assessment. On the evidence, both the trader and the customer had treated the returned videocassette as having a value of £10 (the difference between the sale price of £20 and the part-exchange price of £10). *C & E Commrs v A Bugeja*, CA [2001] STC 1568; [2001] EWCA Civ 1542.

Sales of mobile phones—subsequent 'cashback' payments

[67.77] A company sold mobile phones. It received commission from service providers in addition to the consideration which it received from the purchasers. Under a promotional scheme, it offered customers a 'cashback' payment, exceeding the price of the phone, if they remained with the relevant service provider for a specified length of time. It treated these 'cashback' payments as deductible from the consideration which it received. Customs issued an assessment on the basis that the company was not entitled to deduct the 'cashback' payments in accounting for VAT. The tribunal upheld the assessment and dismissed the company's appeal, observing that treating the cashback as a reduction in the price of the phone would resulted in a 'negative consideration'. The tribunal held that 'the promise of the cashback was a generalised inducement to enter into the two contracts (to buy the phone from the appellant, and to contract for phone services)'. It was not 'a reduction in the price of either of them'. Accordingly, the company was not entitled 'to reduce the amount of its outputs on account of the cashback'. *Jag Communications (Plymouth) Ltd*, [2007] VATDR 251 (VTD 20002). (*Note.* The tribunal also upheld the validity of the assessment under *VATA 1994, s 73(1)*.)

Sales of golf clubs

[67.78] A company (P) sold golf clubs. In 1990 the Royal & Ancient Golf Club of St Andrews declared that some of P's clubs did not comply with the Rules of Golf, so that they could not be used for competitions in the UK. P announced that it would supply a new club for £22 to anyone surrendering one of the 'illegal' clubs in part-exchange. These new clubs had a normal wholesale price of £49.99 and a normal retail price of £72. Customs issued a ruling that the 'illegal' clubs had a part-exchange value of £27.99, so that P was required to account for output tax on the normal wholesale price of £49.99. P appealed, contending that the 'illegal' clubs had no value, so that it should only be required to account for output tax on the consideration of £22 which it actually received. The tribunal accepted this contention and allowed the appeal, holding that 'the value of the non-monetary consideration involved in the present case is nil'. The CA upheld this decision. Robert Walker LJ held that, while the return of the old club was 'consideration', the tribunal had been entitled to find that 'the monetary vale of the consideration was nil'. P 'wanted the old clubs back not because they were of any value to it but simply in order to comply with its obligation to the R & A'. *C & E Commrs v Ping (Europe) Ltd*, CA [2002] STC 1186; [2002] EWCA Civ 1115.

Sale of asset partly used privately

[67.79] A trader had purchased a glider and had accepted that he was only entitled to reclaim 80% of the relevant input tax, on the basis that the glider was partly used for private purposes. Subsequently he sold the glider at a profit, and only accounted for output tax on 80% of the proceeds. Customs issued a ruling that he was required to account for output tax on the full amount of the proceeds. The tribunal dismissed the trader's appeal. *DA Smith (t/a Varcom Sailplane Computers)*, LON/95/2353 (VTD 14196).

[67.80] The decision in *Smith*, 67.79 above, was applied in a similar subsequent case involving the sale of a yacht. *D Seward*, LON/96/213 (14706).

Transfer of land

[67.81] The Cumbernauld Development Corporation transferred some of its land to a local golf club in exchange for some land owned by the club. Under the agreement, there was no monetary consideration for either transfer, but the Corporation had to pay for work to be carried out on the golf club's course and for a new clubhouse. The total cost to the Corporation was about £3,000,000, although the land which it obtained by the golf club had been valued at only £120,000. Customs issued a ruling that the supply made by the Corporation should be valued at the subjective cost of £3,000,000. The Corporation appealed, contending that the supply should be valued at £120,000, being the valuation of the land which it had received in exchange. The tribunal rejected this contention, holding that the value had to be determined subjectively, but also held that Customs' valuation was excessive, since, on the evidence, 'the costs of the additional 18 holes for the golf club would not truly form part of the subjective value for the transfer of the old club house'. The tribunal adjourned the appeal in the hope that an 'appropriate value' could be agreed. *Cumbernauld Development Corporation*, EDN/96/92 (VTD 14630). (*Note*. Following the hearing, the parties agreed that the supply should be valued at £1,505,000. For subsequent developments in this case, see **62.391** SUPPLY.)

Valuation of spectacles dispensed by optician

[67.82] An optician had submitted VAT returns on the basis that, where he sold spectacles, 50% of the sale price related to the standard-rated supply of the spectacles themselves, and that 50% related to his dispensing services, which were exempt from VAT. Customs issued an assessment charging tax of £44,000 plus interest, computed on the basis that all his turnover, with the exception of the specific eye-testing charges, should be treated as standard-rated. The optician appealed. The tribunal reviewed the evidence in detail and held that the assessment was grossly excessive. The tribunal found that 80% of the optician's time was spent on dispensing of spectacles and that 20% of his time was spent on 'overhead matters such as management and administration'. On the evidence, the goods which he had sold had a total cost of £81,538, while the total cost of the dispensing services was £80,567. On this basis, it followed that 51% of the sale price was standard-rated and that 49% was exempt. *FP Whiffen (t/a FP Whiffen Opticians)*, LON/01/1351 (VTD 18951). (*Note.* For the award of costs, see **2.415** APPEALS.)

[67.83] A company carried on business as opticians. Where it sold spectacles, it treated 20% of the sale price as relating to the standard-rated supply of the spectacles themselves, and 80% as relating to its dispensing services, which were exempt from VAT. Customs issued an assessment on the basis that 32.77% of the total consideration paid by the customers was attributable to the standard-rated supplies of spectacles. The tribunal reviewed the evidence in detail, upheld the assessment, and dismissed the company's appeal. *John F Stott Ltd*, MAN/05/516 (VTD 19406).

[67.84] A company which dispensed and sold spectacles accounted for VAT on the basis that 90% of its opticians' time was attributable to exempt supplies of dispensing services, and that only 10% of their time was attributable to the standard-rated supplies of spectacles, with the result that 46.34% of the consideration which the company received was taxable and that 53.66% was exempt. Customs issued assessments on the basis that 73.08% of the opticians' time was attributable to exempt supplies, with the result that 48.65% of the consideration which the company received was taxable and that 51.35% was exempt. The tribunal dismissed the company's appeal, observing that 'a significant portion of the professional service rendered in providing a patient with spectacles must be referable to services other than the pure dispensing function'. *McBurney, Clelland & Boyd Ltd*, EDN/07/83 (VTD 20701).

[67.85] An optician had submitted VAT returns on the basis that 40% of the consideration which he received was taxable and 60% was exempt. HMRC issued assessments on the basis that 62% of the consideration should have been treated as taxable. The tribunal reviewed the evidence in detail and allowed the optician's appeal, finding that 'HMRC failed to apply best judgment to the assessments under appeal'. *D Doris (t/a Gardiners of Denny) v HMRC (and related appeals)*, [2011] UKFTT 142 (TC), TC01016.

[67.86] See also *Green*, **48.19** PAYMENT OF TAX; *Hayward Gill & Associates Ltd*, **48.20** PAYMENT OF TAX; *CL Dyer & Co*, **48.21** PAYMENT OF TAX; *Langrick & Coe*, **48.22** PAYMENT OF TAX, and *Specsavers Optical Group*, **48.127** PAYMENT OF TAX.

Supplies paid for by issue of shares in company

[67.87] See *A-Z Electrical*, **10.12** CASH ACCOUNTING SCHEME.

Supplies of services

Prompt payment discounts (VATA 1994, Sch 6 para 4)

[67.88] A company (S) sold holidays. It offered customers discounts for prompt payment. In accounting for VAT, it failed to take account of such discounts. It subsequently submitted a repayment claim. The Commissioners agreed to refund the amounts which S had overpaid where customers actually received discounts. However S also claimed that it was entitled to a repayment in respect of cases where it had offered customers discounts, but the customers had not actually taken advantage of such discounts. The Commissioners rejected this claim and the tribunal dismissed S's appeal, observing that *VATA 1994, Sch 6 para 4(1)* provided that the consideration should be taken as 'reduced by the discount', and holding that 'the words "by the discount" can more readily be interpreted as a reference to a discount that has actually come into existence than to one that is available but may never come into existence'. Accordingly the tribunal held that *Sch 6 para 4(1)* should be construed as meaning that 'the consideration is only reduced where the discount is achieved'. *Saga Holidays Ltd*, [2005] VATDR 94 (VTD 18591).

[67.89] For a case where a purported 'discount' was held to be a commission, and outside the scope of *VATA 1994, Sch 6 para 4*, see *Gold Star Publications Ltd*, 67.31 above.

Supplies of accommodation (VATA 1994, Sch 6 para 9)

Block hotel bookings by tour operators

[67.90] Two companies each owned a hotel used by tour operators, with whom arrangements were made for advance block bookings of the hotel accommodation. The arrangements varied in detail from operator to operator, but in a typical contract, the tour operator booked 30 double and four single rooms at specified prices for the seven months to 31 October. The contract provided a 'release date' six days in advance, which enabled the operator to release rooms which would not be required for a tour due to start a week ahead. The operator was not required to make any payment for the rooms released. He made no payment in advance, and normally paid for the rooms not released after each tour. The companies accounted for VAT on the basis that the reduced rate of what is now *VATA 1994, Sch 6 para 9* applied to all the accommodation booked by the tour operators for the required four-week period, even where this accommodation was subsequently released and not occupied. The Commissioners issued an assessment on the basis that the provisions of *VATA 1994, Sch 6 para 9* applied only to the accommodation actually used. The tribunal upheld the assessment and the QB dismissed the companies' appeals. The reduced rate of *Sch 6 para 9* could only apply to accommodation actually supplied for more than four weeks. *Elga & Askar Co Ltd and Another v C & E Commrs*, QB [1983] STC 628.

Hotel accommodation supplied to US Air Force personnel

[67.91] A married couple owned and managed a hotel in Suffolk. Most of their customers were members of the US Air Force. Where they provided accommodation to US service personnel for more than four weeks, the couple only charged VAT at 3%. The Commissioners issued an assessment on the basis that the conditions for the application of the reduced rate under what is now *VATA 1994, Sch 6 para 9* were not satisfied, and that VAT should have been accounted for at 15%. The tribunal dismissed the couple's appeal, finding that the couple had not produced the evidence required to prove that the conditions of *Sch 6 para 9(1)* were satisfied. *BE & CS Rey (t/a Wood Hall Hotel & Country Club)*, LON/89/653Y (VTD 5676).

Housing association providing accommodation for refugees, etc.

[67.92] A charity (B) provided advice and assistance to refugees and people seeking asylum in the UK. It entered into an agreement with a housing association (C), whereby C would provide accommodation for refugees and asylum-seekers, in return for payments from B. In accounting for VAT, C initially failed to apply the reduced rate of *VATA 1994, Sch 6 para 9* where accommodation was provided for more than four weeks. In 2005 C submitted a repayment claim, backdated for three years. Customs rejected the claim on the basis that *Sch 6 para 9* only applied where supplies were made to an individual occupier. C appealed, contending that there was a tripartite agreement between itself, B and the occupiers, and that the supplies were within *Sch 6 para 9*. The tribunal accepted this contention and allowed the appeal, holding that 'the derogation requires the individual occupying the accommodation to stay for 4 weeks or more but does not require the payment for the room be by the same party who occupies it (*sic*) and to this extent allows payment to be made by a third party'. There was 'no requirement in the legislation that the person who receives the taxable supply of accommodation and the person physically occupying the room be the same person.' *The Afro-Caribbean Housing Association Ltd*, [2006] VATDR 124 (VTD 19450). (*Note.* For HMRC's revised practice following this decision, see Business Brief 15/06, issued on 27 September 2006.)

VATA 1994, Sch 6 para 9(2)—treatment of payments for meals

[67.93] A company operated a hotel in Northern Ireland. In accounting for output tax on income from long-stay guests, it failed to account for tax on the price it charged for breakfasts. The Commissioners issued an assessment on the basis that the price charged for breakfast was liable to VAT. The company appealed, contending that its provision of breakfast was an integral part of its provision of accommodation. The tribunal rejected this contention and dismissed the appeal, holding that there was a distinction between 'accommodation' and 'board'. 'Accommodation' had to be interpreted as 'sleeping accommodation' or as 'accommodation of rooms'. The provision of breakfast was a supply of catering, not a supply of accommodation. The payments for breakfast were therefore 'attributable to facilities other than the right to occupy the accommodation', within *VATA 1994, Sch 6 para 9(2)(a)*, and were therefore liable to VAT. *Hospitality Resource Ltd*, LON/98/582 (VTD 16526).

Whether commission deductible

Escort agency—commission paid to escorts

[67.94] See *Marlow & Hind*, 62.278 SUPPLY, and *Polok*, 62.279 SUPPLY.

Massage parlour—commission retained by masseuses

[67.95] The proprietor of a sauna and massage parlour charged customers for services provided at the parlour by masseuses. The masseuses were treated as self-employed and the proprietor paid the masseuses commission. She deducted such commissions from her takings in accounting for VAT, and the Commissioners issued an assessment to charge tax on the full fees charged to customers. The tribunal dismissed the proprietor's appeal against the assessment, holding that the proprietor should account for VAT on the full amount charged to the customers. *Y Niven*, EDN/87/62 (VTD 2591).

[67.96] See also *Rudd*, 62.274 SUPPLY, and *Sparkholme Ltd*, 62.275 SUPPLY.

'Commission' paid to Bermudan holding company

[67.97] A company (T), which was a subsidiary of a Bermudan holding company, provided coach tours in Europe from premises in London. The Bermudan company arranged for brochures describing the tours to be published and distributed, and determined the tour prices in local currencies. Payments for the tours were made to the Bermudan company, which deducted a percentage as commission and paid the balance to T. T only accounted for VAT on the net amount it received, and did not account for tax on the commission retained by the Bermudan company. The Commissioners considered that the value of the supplies for tax purposes was the price advertised in the brochures and paid by the customers. T appealed, contending that it supplied the tours to the Bermudan company which in turn supplied those tours to the actual customers. The tribunal dismissed T's appeal, holding that the tours were clearly supplied to the passengers and the Bermudan company was acting as an agent. The Bermudan company was incapable of physically enjoying the services supplied. The consideration was the amount paid by the passengers to the travel agents through whom they booked. The CA upheld this decision. The tribunal was clearly entitled, on the evidence, to regard the detailed arrangements as a facade, designed to conceal the fact that the supply was made to the passengers rather than to the Bermudan company. The consideration for the supply was the total amount paid by the passengers. The fact that T did not receive this total amount was irrelevant; it only failed to receive this amount because it had authorised the Bermudan company and other overseas companies to deduct sums as commission. *Trafalgar Tours Ltd v C & E Commrs*, CA 1989, [1990] STC 127.

Language school paying commission to overseas schools

[67.98] A company which operated a language school paid commission to overseas schools which introduced students to it. The company sought to deduct this commission from the consideration it received from the students. The tribunal held that the commission was not deductible. *Butler Question Method School of Languages Ltd*, LON/91/1239X (VTD 7178).

Company operating cab hire business—amounts paid to 'controllers'

[67.99] A company operated a cab hire business. It had about 40 drivers, who paid a fixed weekly charge of £50, described as a 'circuit fee', to the company. The company engaged staff (whom it treated as self-employed) to act as controllers, and paid them a weekly amount of £15 per driver. Initially the company accounted for tax on the full amounts which it received from the drivers, but subsequently it submitted a repayment claim on the basis that the amounts which it paid to the controllers should not have been included as part of its consideration. The Commissioners rejected the claim and the tribunal dismissed the company's appeal. The company received the 'circuit fees' as an independent principal and was obliged to account for output tax on the full amounts of the fees. *Crayford & Bexleyheath (Motors) Ltd*, LON/95/1469A (VTD 13620).

[67.100] The decision in *Crayford & Bexleyheath (Motors) Ltd*, 67.99 above, was applied in the similar subsequent case of *S Wren (t/a Blue & White Car Service)*, LON/00/27 (VTD 17024).

[67.101] A similar decision was reached in *CA Wharmby*, MAN/97/1036 (VTD 16436).

[67.102] See also *Home Or Away Ltd*, 62.250 SUPPLY, and *Lancaster*, 62.251 SUPPLY.

Sponsorship payments

Valuation of benefits supplied by charity in return for sponsorship

[67.103] A company was registered as a charity with the object of promoting drama. It issued a brochure requesting potential supporters to sponsor seats in its theatre by paying it £150. In return for their sponsorship, sponsors were entitled to priority bookings for two gala evenings, and their sponsorship was acknowledged by personalised brass plaques on the seats, and by an acknowledgement on a board in the theatre foyer. The company did not account for VAT on the sponsorship payments, and the Commissioners issued an assessment charging tax on the full amount paid. The CS upheld the assessment. The company would not have provided the goods and services in question for less than the £150 which the sponsors paid. Accordingly, the whole of the £150 was 'consideration in money' within what is now *VATA 1994, s 19(2)*, and VAT was chargeable accordingly. *C & E Commrs v Tron Theatre Ltd*, CS 1993, [1994] STC 177.

[67.104] The CS decision in *Tron Theatre Ltd*, 67.103 above, was applied in the similar subsequent case of *High Peak Theatre Trust Ltd*, MAN/95/1108 (VTD 13678).

Publishing company making cash awards to scientists

[67.105] A company (E) published a scientific periodical. It organised cash awards to scientists. The cost of the awards was met by sponsors. In return for their sponsorship, the sponsors received publicity in the periodical and tickets to attend the annual award. Customs issued a ruling that E should account for output tax on the payments from the sponsors. E appealed. The tribunal allowed the appeal and the QB upheld this decision, applying the CA decision in *Nell Gwynn House Maintenance Fund*, **62.36** SUPPLY. *C & E Commrs v EMAP MacLaren Ltd*, QB [1997] STC 490. (Note. The CA decision in *Nell Gwynn House Maintenance Fund* was subsequently reversed by the HL. In the subsequent case of *Findel plc v HMRC*, **67.74** above. Judge Demack held that, in view of the HL decision in *Nell Gwynn House Maintenance Fund*, this case had been wrongly decided.)

Voluntary payments

Tips received by taxi driver

[67.106] Tips received by the owner of a taxi were held to be chargeable to VAT, as part of the consideration paid for his services, in *P Kenealy*, LON/77/208 (VTD 466).

Optional service charge in restaurant

[67.107] A company operated a restaurant. A suggested 'service charge' was included on its menu and on bills which it gave to customers, but it was stated both on the menu and on the bills that the 'service charge' was optional. The Commissioners issued an assessment on the basis that the service charge formed part of the consideration for meals consumed. The company appealed, contending that the payments for service were voluntary. The tribunal allowed the appeal, holding that under the contract between the company and the customers there was no liability to pay anything for service. Any payments made for service were not part of the consideration for the supplies made by the company, and accordingly were not chargeable to VAT. *NDP Co Ltd*, [1988] VATTR 40 (VTD 2653).

[67.108] The decision in *NDP Co Ltd*, **67.107** above, was applied in the similar subsequent case of *JD Joyce*, LON/95/2747A (VTD 14573).

Additional ex gratia payment made more than two years after supplies

[67.109] A veterinary surgeon (P) had practised for several years without registering for VAT, although his turnover exceeded the statutory threshold. When the Commissioners discovered this, they imposed a penalty for non-registration and issued an assessment for the tax due, both of which P paid. P subsequently sought to recover VAT from some of his customers, whom he had not charged VAT during the period in which he had not been registered. One of these customers was the Department of Agriculture for Northern Ireland, which made an ex gratia payment in July 1988, representing the VAT at 15% on supplies made up to July 1986, on which VAT had not originally been charged. P did not account for VAT on the ex gratia payment. A VAT officer discovered this at a control visit in May 1989, and the Commissioners subsequently issued an assessment charging VAT on the amount P had received from the Department of Agriculture. P appealed, contending that the payment was not chargeable to VAT since it was voluntary. The tribunal dismissed P's appeal, holding that the payment related to taxable supplies which P had made to the Department, and was taxable consideration which had not previously been assessed. *AD Pottie*, BEL/90/31X (VTD 5460).

Insulation services—whether Government grants subject to VAT

[67.110] A company supplied insulation services. Where such services were supplied to people on low incomes or aged over 60, grants were paid under a scheme initiated by the Department of the Environment. The company failed to account for output tax on the grants. The Commissioners issued a ruling that the grants were taxable, and the tribunal dismissed the company's appeal, holding that the grants were consideration for the services which the company supplied. The chairman observed that there was 'the clearest possible link' between the grant and the services supplied to the customer, and that the fact that the customer did not know the amount of the grant was irrelevant. *Anglia Energy Conservation Ltd*, LON/96/1228 (VTD 14620).

[67.111] The decision in *Anglia Energy Conservation Ltd*, 67.110 above, was applied in the similar subsequent case of *Interglow Ltd*, LON/97/114 (VTD 15200).

[67.112] See also *Keeping Newcastle Warm*, 22.247 EUROPEAN COMMUNITY LAW.

Fund-raising ball—whether part of payment voluntary

[67.113] See *Glasgow's Miles Better Mid-Summer 5th Anniversary Ball*, 67.135 below.

Multiple supplies

Inclusive charge for river cruise holiday—method of apportionment

[67.114] A company provided holiday cruises on the Thames between Windsor and Oxford, using converted river barges for the purpose. The customer paid an inclusive charge to cover his cabin accommodation on the barge, meals, sightseeing tours in places called at en route and transport to and from the barge at the beginning and end of the cruise. The tribunal held that, in apportioning the consideration between cabin accommodation and catering (standard-rated) and the road and river transport (zero-rated), and the apportionment should be by reference to the cost of the supplies including overheads but disregarding capital expenditure. *River Barge Holidays Ltd*, LON/77/345 (VTD 572).

Social club providing bingo and live entertainment

[67.115] In the case noted at **24.11** EXEMPTIONS: MISCELLANEOUS, a social club provided live entertainment and bingo, for a combined admission fee. The tribunal had originally held that the consideration could not be apportioned and had to be treated as taxable in full, but the QB reversed this decision and remitted the case for reconsideration. Forbes J observed that the apportionment 'should take account of the profit element by ensuring that the part of the payment attributable to the facilities for bingo included a due proportion of the profit for the club from this part of the enterprise'. The tribunal directed that 15% of the consideration should be attributed to bingo (which was exempt from VAT) and 85% should be attributed to the taxable live entertainment. *Tynewydd Labour Working Men's Club & Institute Ltd*, [1980] VATTR 165 (VTD 1089).

Coach tours—apportionment of consideration

[67.116] A company sold coach tours which included zero-rated transport and standard-rated meals and hotel accommodation. It accounted for tax on the basis that claimed that it was charging its customers for the meals and accommodation at cost, and making all its profit on the transport supplies. The Commissioners issued an assessment on the basis that the profit should be apportioned. The tribunal upheld the assessment and dismissed the company's appeal, observing that 'in arriving at the proportion of a single price which reflects the zero-rated element and the standard-rated elements making up the whole, it is not proper for the appellant company to affect to charge a profit cost on the zero-rated supply of transport and to pass on at cost the standard-rated supplies'. *Waterhouse Coaches Ltd*, LON/82/378 (VTD 1417). (*Note.* The substantive issue has been overtaken by the introduction of the Tour Operators' Margin Scheme, but the case remains an authority on the principles of apportionment. For the Commissioners' interpretation of the decision, see Customs' VAT Manual, Part 12, chapter 2, para 3.10.)

Rail ticket also allowing entrance to tourist attraction

[67.117] A company owned and operated a funicular railway. In 1985 it also opened a tourist attraction called a 'Camera Obscura', at the top of the cliff served by the railway. It sold tickets allowing both use of the railway and entrance to the Camera Obscura. During 1988 such a combined ticket was priced at £1.65, whereas a ticket allowing use of the railway only was priced at £1, as was a ticket allowing entry to the Camera Obscura but not use of the railway. The Commissioners issued an assessment on the basis that, since travel on the railway was zero-rated but entry to the Camera Obscura was standard-rated, 50% of the amounts paid for combined tickets should be treated as liable to VAT at the standard rate. The company appealed, contending that the railway was more popular than the Camera, and that the price paid for a combined ticket should be apportioned as £1 for the railway and 65p for the Camera. At the relevant time, more than 50% of the tickets sold by the company were for the railway only, whereas fewer than 10% were for the Camera only, the remainder being combined tickets. The tribunal accepted the company's contentions and allowed the appeal, holding that the price of the combined tickets should be apportioned as £1 to the zero-rated supply of transport and only 65p to the standard-rated supply of admission to the Camera. *Aberystwyth Cliff Railway Co Ltd*, MAN/90/1102 (VTD 6449).

Programmes included with admission charge to greyhound stadium

[67.118] In the case noted at 5.69 BOOKS, ETC. (where admission to a greyhound stadium included the provision of a programme), the tribunal found that 10% of the proprietor's costs related to zero-rated supplies, and held that an uplift of 50% should be allowed for the compilation and distribution of the material. Accordingly, the tribunal directed that 15% of the appellant's supplies should be treated as zero-rated and 85% as standard-rated. *IC Thomas*, [1985] VATTR 67 (VTD 1862).

Introduction agency

[67.119] The proprietor of an introduction agency supplied clients with bulletins and a handbook, which were accepted as zero-rated. These items were not charged for separately, but formed part of the services provided in return for members' subscriptions. The Commissioners directed the proprietor to apportion her supplies on the basis of their relevant value. She appealed, contending that the apportionment should be based on the relevant cost. The tribunal allowed her appeal, holding that the Commissioners had not put forward any basis on which the value of the services could be calculated and that an apportionment between standard-rated and zero-rated services should be made by reference to the cost of supplying those services. The parties were unable to agree on the ratio to be adopted, and the proprietor applied to the tribunal for a determination of the issue. The tribunal found that 95% of the proprietor's printing costs related to zero-rated supplies, and held that an uplift of 100% should be allowed for the compilation and distribution of the material. On the evidence, the tribunal directed that 33.5% of the appellant's supplies should be treated as zero-rated and 66.5% as standard-rated. *BH Bright*, LON/88/1383X (VTD 4577). (*Note.* For a subsequent application for costs, see **2.403** APPEALS.)

Correspondence courses in computer training—amount of consideration

[67.120] A company supplied correspondence courses in computer training. The Commissioners agreed that 30% of the consideration was for manuals which qualified for zero-rating. In June 1991 the company claimed that part of the consideration was paid for examination fees, society membership fees and accommodation costs, and should be treated as disbursements which were outside the scope of VAT, thus reducing the amount of output tax payable. The Commissioners rejected the claim, and issued an assessment charging output tax on accommodation costs charged to students in 1992, on which the company had failed to account for tax. The company appealed. The tribunal dismissed the appeal, holding that the company was making a single supply of computer tuition. Output tax was chargeable on the whole of the amounts paid by the students, and the fact that the company spent some of its income on examination fees, subscriptions to professional bodies, and accommodation costs for students, did not reduce the taxable consideration. (The tribunal described the Commissioners' acceptance that 30% of the gross consideration should be treated as paid for the supply of zero-rated manuals as a 'concession'.) *Computeach International Ltd*, [1994] VATTR 237 (VTD 12115).

Car hire and minicab businesses

Minicab business—valuation of supplies of services to drivers

[67.121] A partnership operated a minicab business. The drivers who worked for it provided their own vehicles, but the partnership supplied the drivers with two-way radios and introductions to customers, and paid the drivers agreed rates for carrying accounts customers (0.05p per mile for the first 100 miles and not less than 0.65p per mile thereafter). Full-time drivers who failed to reach a 'target mileage' of 100 miles each week in relation to accounts customers were required to pay a 'penalty' of up to £70 for the use of the radio. The drivers were allowed to retain all fares received from cash customers. The partnership accounted for tax on the actual amounts which it received. The Commissioners issued an assessment on the basis that the partnership was making taxable supplies of services to the drivers, and that such services should be valued at £70 per week (i.e. the maximum amount which the partnership charged for the use of its radios). The tribunal upheld the assessment and dismissed the partnership's appeal, holding that there was a 'direct link' between the services which the partnership supplied to the drivers and the drivers' obligation either to provide driving services to the partnership or to pay the partnership cash for the use of the radios. *RJ & CA Blanks*, LON/95/3117 (VTD 14099).

[67.122] The decision in *Blanks*, 67.121 above, was distinguished in a subsequent case where a partnership which operated a minicab business using self-employed drivers had a number of accounts customers. The partnership paid the drivers 90% of the amounts which it charged the accounts customers, less a deduction which it described as a 'contract levy'. (The partnership's other source of income was payments made by the drivers for the hire of radios.) The Commissioners issued an assessment on the basis that the 'contract levy' represented consideration paid by the drivers for a supply of services by the partnership. The partnership appealed, contending that the 'contract levy' was not consideration for a supply, but was simply an amount taken into account in determining the amount payable to the drivers for the services which they provided. The tribunal accepted this contention and allowed the appeal, holding on the evidence that the consideration for the services which the partnership supplied consisted of the amounts paid by the drivers for the hire of radios. Since the partnership was receiving consideration from the drivers for the services which it provided, it followed that there were no grounds for treating the 'contract levy' as additional consideration. On the evidence, the 'contract levy' was simply 'an attempt at creating fairness between drivers who may do more or less contract work ' and its true nature was an adjustment to the 90% paid to drivers for client work. *A2B Radio Cars*, LON/96/933 (VTD 15145).

[67.123] A company (C) carried on a radio-controlled minicab business, under which it acted as an agent for a number of self-employed owner-drivers, supplying them with radio equipment, providing advertising and putting them in touch with prospective passengers. The drivers paid C for the services which it provided. The normal weekly rates were £73 for part-time drivers and £88 for full-time drivers, but these amounts were frequently reduced if C had been unable to supply sufficient work for a driver during any particular week. On occasions some of the drivers worked for a company associated with C. That company paid the drivers a mileage rate lower than usual for the first 100 miles (as in *Blanks*, 67.121 above) and in such cases, C reduced its weekly charges by a corresponding amount. C accounted for output tax on the amounts which it received from the drivers. The Commissioners issued assessments on the basis that the effect of the arrangements with the drivers who worked for the associated company was that the cash consideration did not fully reflect the value of the services which C provided, and that output tax should be charged on the normal weekly charges, without taking account of the reduction in the rates. C appealed, contending that the rates which it charged the drivers were proportionate to the amount of work which they performed for C and therefore proportionate to the extent to which they used C's services. The tribunal accepted this contention and allowed C's appeal, holding on the evidence that the cash payments 'represented the entirety of the consideration moving to (C) from the drivers for the services supplied to them by (C)'. *Computer Minicabs Ltd*, LON/97/1541 (VTD 15614).

[67.124] A company operated a minicab and courier business, primarily for accounts customers. Drivers who made fewer than 40 journeys for 'accounts customers' in any week were required to pay the company a fee ranging from £65 to £100 in respect of their use of the company radio and introductions to 'cash customers'. (Drivers who made 40 or more journeys per week for 'accounts customers' were paid a bonus of up to £20 by the company in addition to their agreed percentage of the amounts paid by the customers.) The Commissioners issued an assessment on the basis that VAT was chargeable on the full fees paid by the drivers to the company (without any deduction for amounts paid by the company to the drivers). The tribunal upheld the assessment, except in so far as it related to two vans owned by the company (for which the company deducted a weekly fee of £100 from the amounts it paid to the drivers, and the tribunal held that this £100 was not liable to VAT, since the company 'could just as easily have reduced the rate of payment by £100'). The tribunal declined to follow the previous tribunal decision in *A2B Radio Cars*, 67.122 above. *Camberwell Cars Ltd (No 2)*, LON/00/303 (VTD 17376). (*Notes.* (1) Costs were awarded to the company—see 2.503 APPEALS. (2) The decision here was disapproved in the subsequent case of *Parker Car Services*, 67.125 below, where the tribunal approved and applied the decision in *A2B Radio Cars*, 67.122 above.)

[67.125] A partnership operated a taxi business, using about 300 self-employed drivers to make supplies to 'accounts customers'. These customers made payment to the partnership, who retained part of the payment as commission and passed the balance to the drivers. HMRC formed the opinion that the partnership had failed to account for VAT on the full consideration for supplies which it made to the drivers, in return for introducing them to the accounts customers. The partnership appealed, contending that the sums in question (which it described as 'accounts work discount') did not represent consideration for any supply, but was simply a means of calculating the payments which it had to make to the drivers. The tribunal accepted this contention and allowed the appeal, applying the principles laid down in *A2B Radio Cars*, 67.122 above, and specifically declining to follow the decision in *Camberwell Cars Ltd (No 2)*, 67.124 above. *Parker Car Services v HMRC*, [2010] UKFTT 227 (TC), TC00528.

Repair services

Valuation of repairs carried out under contract

[67.126] A company (M), which was a member of a group, carried on the business of repairing electrical goods sold by other members of the group. To have goods repaired by M, the purchasers of the goods had to have taken out an insurance policy at the time of purchase. These policies were underwritten by an insurance company, which reimbursed M for repairs at an agreed rate. M accounted for tax on the amounts it received from the insurance company. However, the Commissioners formed the opinion that M was making its supplies to the purchasers of the goods, that these supplies should be valued at market value, and that the amounts which M received from the insurance company were significantly less than market value. They issued an assessment accordingly, charging tax of more than £270,000. M appealed, contending that the supplies should be valued at the rate agreed between M and the insurance company, so that there had been no underdeclaration of tax. The tribunal allowed the appeal, holding that M was making the relevant supplies to the insurance company, rather than to the purchasers of the goods. The consideration paid by the insurance company was the agreed rate of reimbursement, and there were no grounds for seeking to charge tax on the supposed market value of the work. *Dixons Group plc*, LON/91/2716Y & LON/92/2730A (VTD 9604). (*Note*. The tribunal also held that certain credit notes issued by M to the insurance company had been issued *bona fide* and were effective for tax purposes.)

Call-out charges for repairs of electrical appliances

[67.127] A company sold electrical appliances. It employed a number of engineers to repair and service these appliances. When customers requested repairs, the company charged a call-out fee of between £30 and £40 in addition to its charges for parts and labour. However, the company informed customers that the call-out charge would be refunded if they purchased a replacement appliance from the company within three months. The company accounted for VAT on the amounts of the call-out charges when they were invoiced, but deducted the VAT element of any refunds made or credit notes issued during each accounting period. The Commissioners issued an assessment on the basis that the company was obliged to account for VAT on the full amounts of the call-out charges and was not entitled to deduct the VAT element of any refunds or credit notes from the amount payable. The company appealed, contending that there was in effect a single transaction and that VAT should not be charged on any call-out charges that were subsequently refunded. The tribunal allowed the appeal, holding that the effect of *Article 11C1* of the *EC Sixth Directive* was that the taxable amount was to be reduced by the amount of the refund or credit note. *AEG (UK) Ltd*, LON/93/589A (VTD 10944).

Miscellaneous

Service charges by restaurant

[67.128] A company carried on a restaurant business. The bills rendered to customers included a 10% service charge and the total, including the service charge, was stated to be tax inclusive. The total of the service charges was paid to the waiters at the end of each day, to be shared between themselves as they agreed. In its returns the company did not account for tax on the service charges. The Commissioners issued an assessment charging tax on them and the tribunal dismissed the company's appeal. The service charge was part of the consideration paid by the customer, and the company's liability to account for the tax on this consideration could not be affected by an arrangement between the company and its employees under which part of the consideration was paid over to the employees. *Potters Lodge Restaurant Ltd*, LON/79/286 (VTD 905).

[67.129] In *EC Commission v French Republic*, 22.241 EUROPEAN COMMUNITY LAW, the CJEC held that VAT had to be imposed on service charges.

'Touring allowance' to actress

[67.130] An actress, registered for VAT, was engaged by a company to take a part in a play being taken on tour in theatres in various parts of the country. For this purpose she entered into a 'standard contract' under which the company agreed to pay her specified amounts when rehearsing for or performing in the play, together with a weekly 'touring allowance' when rehearsing or performing more than 25 miles away from her address. She did not account for tax on the 'touring allowance', and the Commissioners issued an assessment charging tax on it. The tribunal upheld the assessment and dismissed the actress's appeal. *AC Twigg*, [1983] VATTR 17 (VTD 1329).

Use of company yacht by employees

[67.131] A company purchased a yacht for use by its employees. The yacht was also used to entertain customers. The Commissioners issued an assessment to charge tax on the supply of the yacht to the employees. The running costs of the yacht, and depreciation at an annual rate of 20%, were apportioned between days when the yacht was used by employees and days when it was used to entertain customers. Thus, in a year where the yacht was used on 51 days by employees and on 9 days for entertaining customers, tax was charged on $^{51}/_{60}$ of the depreciation and running costs. The company appealed, contending that the amount charged should be $^{51}/_{365}$ of the depreciation. The QB rejected this contention and upheld the assessment. It was not permissible to avoid tax on depreciation by allocating most of the charge for depreciation to days on which the yacht was not in use. On the facts found by the tribunal, tax should be charged on $^{51}/_{60}$ of the depreciation for the year. *C & E Commrs v Teknequip Ltd*, QB [1987] STC 664.

[67.132] A similar decision was reached in a case where the tribunal observed that the charge to tax on private use was in accordance with *Article 26 of Directive 2006/112/EC*. (The tribunal also upheld a misdeclaration penalty.) *Kingfisher Events Ltd v HMRC*, [2011] UKFTT 140 (TC), TC01014.

Supplies of game shoots to company director

[67.133] A company (T) owned shooting rights over an estate. It arranged 12 commercial shoots each year, charging customers £8,000 per shoot. It also provided its controlling director (S) with 12 private shoots, in respect of which it failed to account for VAT. HMRC issued assessments and misdeclaration penalties on the basis that T should have accounted for tax on these shoots and that the monetary value was the price charged for the commercial shoots, ie £8,000 per shoot. T appealed, contending firstly that its supplies to S were not supplies for consideration, and alternatively that if they were taxable supplies, the consideration was the cost of making them, which was £1,000 per shoot.

The tribunal rejected T's first contention, holding that the supplies were made in return for S's services as a director, which constituted consideration. However the tribunal accepted T's alternative contention, finding that 'the parties had agreed the value attributed to the consideration for the game shoots supplied to (S), which was 1,000 per shoot'. The tribunal observed that 'the value of 12,000 for twelve shoots bore a reasonable correlation to the value of the services supplied by (S). The evidence showed that (S's) participation as a director was a part-time activity, which did not consume much of his time. (S) did not rely on his appointment as the appellant's director for his source of income.' The tribunal directed that the assessments should be reduced accordingly. (The tribunal upheld the misdeclaration penalties, holding that there was no reasonable excuse for T's failure to account for VAT.) *Thimbleby Farms Ltd v HMRC*, [2010] SFTD 1216; [2010] UKFTT 320 (TC), TC00607.

Gaming machines hired by company owning shop

[67.134] A company (B) owned a shop which sold fishing tackle. It hired two amusement machines for installation in the shop, under a verbal agreement whereby the company which owned the machines (S) would service and empty them, and the takings would be split equally. S treated its 50% of the takings as a hire charge, and retained a further 7.5% of the takings as VAT thereon (the rate of VAT was 15% at the relevant time). S paid this 7.5% to the Commissioners and B reclaimed it as input tax. B accounted for output tax on the 42.5% of the takings which it retained. When the Commissioners discovered this, they issued an assessment on the basis that, since B was hiring the machines from S, B was supplying the use of the machines to its customers and should have accounted for output tax on the full amount of the takings. The tribunal upheld the assessment and dismissed B's appeal. *Bennetts of Sheffield Ltd*, [1986] VATTR 253 (VTD 2219).

Fund-raising ball—whether part of ticket price not paid as 'consideration'

[67.135] An association organised a fund-raising ball. It printed application forms showing the ticket price as £50. In small print at the foot of the form it was stated that 'for VAT purposes the entrance fee is £20. The balance of £30 represents a minimum voluntary donation in aid of hospice funds.' Similar wording appeared on the tickets. The association accounted for VAT on only £20 per ticket, and the Commissioners issued an assessment on the basis that VAT was chargeable on the full price of £50. The tribunal dismissed the appeal. The statement that £30 was a 'minimum voluntary donation' indicated 'an element of compulsion'. The application forms and tickets clearly stated that the purchase price of the tickets was £50, and indicated that admission could not be obtained for less. Accordingly, the full price of £50 represented consideration for the tickets. *Glasgow's Miles Better Mid-Summer 5th Anniversary Ball*, EDN/89/95 (VTD 4460).

Removal of asbestos—whether contribution from CEGB 'consideration'

[67.136] A company agreed to purchase the Battersea Power Station from the CEGB. It also agreed to remove asbestos and asbestos-related plant from the site. The CEGB paid the company more than £2 million as a contribution towards the costs of the removal of the asbestos. The Commissioners issued an assessment charging tax on this payment, on the basis that the removal of the asbestos was a service supplied by the company and the payment represented consideration for this service. The company appealed, contending that the payment should not be regarded as consideration for VAT purposes. The QB rejected this contention and upheld the assessment. 'Consideration' meant everything which the supplier had received or was to receive from the purchaser for the relevant supply. The payment by the CEGB was directly linked to the services to be supplied by the company, and was therefore within the definition of 'consideration'. The fact that the CEGB was motivated by a sense of public duty, rather than by commercial motives, did not alter the objective nature of the supply. *C & E Commrs v Battersea Leisure Ltd*, QB [1992] STC 213.

Video hire—fines for late return of videos

[67.137] The proprietor of a video club imposed fines on customers who returned videos later than agreed. He did not account for VAT on these fines. The Commissioners issued a decision that the fines were chargeable to VAT as part of the consideration for the supply of the films. The tribunal upheld the Commissioners' decision and dismissed the trader's appeal. *JG Leigh (t/a Moor Lane Video)*, [1990] VATTR 59 (VTD 5098).

Payphones—excess coins deposited by customers

[67.138] A company provided telephone services through a number of coin-operated payphones. In some cases, customers paid more than the amount which the company charged for the calls made (e.g. by inserting a £1 coin for a call which only cost 40p). In such cases, the machines did not give the customer any change, and the company retained the full amounts paid into the machines. The Commissioners issued a ruling that the company should account for output tax on the full amounts paid by customers. The company appealed, contending that output tax was only chargeable on the amounts which it charged, and that excess payments received from customers were outside the scope of VAT. The tribunal rejected this contention and dismissed the appeal, holding that the customers had purchased 'the possibility of making telephone calls up to the amount of the coins inserted. The length of the telephone call made does not convert the credit purchased by those coins into a surplus or gift.' *New World Payphones Ltd*, LON/98/712 (VTD 15964).

Building of work—contract price not payable for five years

[67.139] In the case noted at 62.407 SUPPLY, the contract price for certain building work was not payable until five years after completion of the work. The tribunal had held that the supply took place when the work was carried out, but that the value of the consideration should be reduced to take account of the delay in reaching the due date for payment and the possibility of the final price being reduced to allow for any defects in the work. The agreed price of the work had been £72,500, but the company had to pay £5,900 to remedy defects in the work. The company had received £52,500 in the form of an interest-free loan, and the tribunal held that the balance of £20,000 should be discounted at 16% p.a. for five years, the total discount being computed as £10,844. The tribunal's decision therefore was that the original price of £72,500 should be reduced by £10,844 in respect of discounting and by

£5,900 in respect of the necessary remedial work, so that VAT was only chargeable on the balance of £55,756. *Mercantile Contracts Ltd*, LON/88/786Y (VTD 5266).

Computer software licences

[67.140] A computer software consultant (R) registered for VAT from January 1991 and deregistered in October 1991. While registered, he had purchased, and reclaimed input tax on, 50 software licences. He had only sold one of these. The Commissioners therefore issued an assessment under what is now *VATA 1994, Sch 4 para 8*, charging tax on the cost of the 49 licences which he still held at deregistration. He appealed, contending that the licences were worth substantially less than their cost, and that they should be valued at their market value. The tribunal allowed the appeal, holding that what R had purchased was 'a software program with the rights to use, make 50 copies and distribute'. Accordingly the supply to R was a supply of services, rather than a supply of goods, and *VATA 1994, Sch 4 para 8* did not apply. The tribunal also held that, even if the supply had been a supply of goods, the supply would have been valued at cost, rather than at market value. *TP Rowledge*, LON/93/237A (VTD 12590). (*Note.* See now, however, *VATA 1994, Sch 6 para 6.*)

Football club—supplies of season tickets to bondholders

[67.141] A football club wished to raise funds to finance a new stand. It issued bonds which carried no interest, but which guaranteed the holders the right to buy, or to allow a nominated person to buy, a season ticket in the new stand. It did not account for output tax on the issue of the bonds (which it treated as exempt from VAT under *VATA 1994, Sch 9, Group 5*) and accounted for output tax on the sale price of the season tickets. The Commissioners issued an assessment on the basis that the consideration for such season tickets was not solely the amount paid by the bondholders for the tickets, but included an amount representing the interest forgone by the bondholders. The club appealed, contending that the only consideration for the season tickets was the money specifically paid for them. The tribunal accepted this contention and allowed the appeal, holding that the two transactions were separate and that the interest-free loans could not be regarded as consideration for the season tickets. The tribunal observed that 'the most significant feature of the whole arrangement that, in our view, severs the subscription transaction from the subsequent season ticket purchase transaction is that subscriber and purchaser may, and as time goes by inevitably will, be different people'. *The Arsenal Football Club plc*, [1996] VATDR 5 (VTD 14011).

Golf club—sale of debentures to members

[67.142] In the case noted at 27.53 FINANCE, in which the tribunal held that the purchase of debentures in a company formed to operate a golf club represented 'non-monetary consideration for the supply of services, namely the grant of membership rights', the valuation of the consideration was in dispute. The tribunal held that the taxable amount should be taken as the interest which the company would otherwise have been obliged to pay on the amount borrowed, calculated at the minimum lending rate. The tribunal declined to follow *obiter dicta* of Cumming-Bruce LJ in *Exeter Golf & Country Club Ltd*,

13.32 CLUBS, ASSOCIATIONS AND ORGANISATIONS, on the grounds that they were inconsistent with the subsequent CJEC decisions in *Naturally Yours Cosmetics Ltd (No 2)*, **22.233** EUROPEAN COMMUNITY LAW, and *Empire Stores Ltd*, **22.234** EUROPEAN COMMUNITY LAW. *Harleyford Golf Club Ltd (No 1)*, LON/95/3076 (VTD 14466).

Free meals supplied to coach drivers

[67.143] A company operated a motorway service station. In an attempt to induce coach drivers to stop at its premises, it offered a free meal to any coach driver with at least 20 passengers who stopped at its premises for at least 30 minutes. The Commissioners issued an assessment charging tax on the normal retail price of the meals consumed by the drivers. The company appealed, contending that output tax should only be chargeable on the cost of the meals. The QB rejected this contention and upheld the assessment, and the CA dismissed the company's appeal. Applying the principles laid down by the CJEC in *Naturally Yours Cosmetics Ltd (No 2)*, **22.233** EUROPEAN COMMUNITY LAW, the crucial question was whether there was an agreement between the company and the drivers placing a monetary value on the meals. On the evidence, the parties must be taken to have attributed a specific monetary value, being the normal retail price of the meal chosen by the driver. *Empire Stores Ltd*, **22.234** EUROPEAN COMMUNITY LAW, was distinguished, on the grounds that the goods in that case were not in the company's catalogue and that no specific value had been attributed to them. *Westmorland Motorway Services Ltd v C & E Commrs*, CA [1998] STC 431.

Cable television company—inducements to new customers

[67.144] A cable television company launched a scheme whereby it offered reduced charges to new customers (£19.99 per month instead of the standard charge of £30.99 per month) who already held a satellite dish if the customers let the company remove the dish. It accounted for tax on the amounts which it actually received. The Commissioners issued assessments on the basis that the price reductions allowed to such customers were consideration for the right to remove the existing satellite dishes, so that output tax was chargeable on the amount of the standard charge. The tribunal allowed the company's appeal. In principle, the customer's undertaking to allow the company to remove his dish was part of the consideration for the supply of cable television services. However, the dishes (which were scrapped) had no monetary value to either party, so that 'no value falls to be attributed to the consideration obtained by the appellant in the form of its right to remove the customer's satellite dish'. *Telewest Communications Group Ltd*, [1996] VATDR 566 (VTD 14383).

Medical partnership leasing premises to associated partnership

[67.145] A medical partnership (D) granted a lease of a surgery, in respect of which it had elected to waive exemption, to an associated partnership (M). D received payments of rent from M. M received an allowance from the NHS in respect of the rental payments which it was required to make. D failed to account for VAT on the total amount of rent which it received from M, but only accounted for VAT on the net amount after excluding the amounts for which M was reimbursed by the NHS. Customs issued an assessment on the basis that D was required to account for VAT on the full amount of the rent.

The tribunal upheld the assessment and dismissed D's appeal. *Danebridge Group Practice*, MAN/01/552 (VTD 18610).

Barter transactions involving lease of sports fields

[67.146] A school granted a lease over some sports fields to a partnership which operated a commercial sports centre. Under the agreement, the school received a peppercorn rent and became entitled to use the facilities in the sports centre at certain defined times. The partnership subsequently transferred its business to a company (R), and also assigned R the benefit of the lease. HMRC issued assessments on R, on the basis that the transaction was a barter transaction under which R was supplying facilities at the sports centre (these supplies being taxable) in return for the initial grant of the lease was exempt. R appealed, contending firstly that there had not been a barter transaction and secondly that if there was deemed to have been a barter transaction, Customs' valuation of the supplies it was deemed to have made was excessive. The tribunal reviewed the evidence in detail and upheld the assessments in principle, holding that the transaction was a barter transaction and that 'the user rights were granted as the consideration for the lease'. The tribunal observed that 'the result would be identical if the parties had paid cash consideration in both directions for the lease and the user rights, since the service supplied by the appellant would have been taxable, and the related input would have been an exempt item'. With regard to the valuation of the supplies, the tribunal accepted Customs' contention that 'where a monetary equivalent has been established as the value of the services being provided, then when goods or services are supplied the consideration is the amount of that monetary equivalent'. However the valuation should take account of the fact that 'the school might well want to use the facilities at times when other school children would be likely to be at their respective schools and not therefore able to use the facilities, and also not at times (in other words in the evening) when third party members who might well work in the day might wish to use the facilities'. Accordingly, 'attention should be given, period by period, to the "discount adjusted" current list prices at which similar services are being provided by the appellant for those services, that the school is minded to receive from time to time'. *Riverside Sports & Leisure Ltd*, [2008] VATDR 326 (VTD 20848).

'Cashback' payments—whether deductible from consideration

[67.147] A company (E) supplied double glazing and similar home improvement services. It offered customers a 'cashback' if they took out a specific loan in order to finance their purchase. It treated these payments as discounts which were deductible from the consideration it received. HMRC issued assessments in the basis that the 'cashback' was not deductible from the stated consideration. E appealed. The tribunal reviewed the evidence in detail and allowed the appeal, holding that 'the cashback was a reduction of the price for the supply by the appellant of home improvement goods and services, and was a reduction in the taxable amount or consideration of that supply for VAT purposes'. *Everest Ltd v HMRC*, [2010] UKFTT 621 (TC); [2011] SFTD 217, TC00863.

Competitions—whether prize money deductible

[67.148] See *Town & County Factors Ltd*, 22.240 EUROPEAN COMMUNITY LAW.

Management services—set-offs between partnership and company

[67.149] See *Smith & Williamson*, 43.14 MANAGEMENT SERVICES.

Valuation of stock-lending transactions

[67.150] See *Scottish Eastern Investment Trust plc*, 46.167 PARTIAL EXEMPTION.

Face value vouchers (VATA 1994, Sch 10A)

NOTE

FA 1972, Sch 3 para 6 provided that 'where a right to receive goods or services for an amount stated on any token, stamp or voucher is granted for a consideration', the consideration should be disregarded 'except to the extent (if any) that exceeds that amount'. This provision became *VATA 1994, Sch 6 para 5*, which was repealed by *FA 2003* with effect for supplies after 8 April 2003, and was replaced by *VATA 1994, Sch 10A*. This legislation was intended to provide that 'any intermediate suppliers who sell vouchers will be liable to account for VAT on the full amount for which they sell a voucher'. The cases in this section should be read in the light of the changes in the legislation.

Supplies of goods

Vouchers exchanged for goods

[67.151] A company (P) issued vouchers which could be exchanged for goods of a retail value equal for the face value of the voucher. Where traders accepted such vouchers, P did not reimburse the full face value, but deducted 13.75% as its 'commission'. A draper who accepted such vouchers only accounted for output tax on the amounts which P reimbursed him, and the Commissioners issued an assessment charging tax on the full face value of the vouchers. The tribunal dismissed the trader's appeal and the QB upheld this decision. Lord Widgery CJ observed that customers who presented the vouchers were 'paying cash and not consideration other than cash'. *JJ Davies v C & E Commrs*, QB 1974, [1975] STC 28; [1975] 1 WLR 204; [1975] 1 All ER 309.

[67.152] In a subsequent case which concerned vouchers issued by the same company (P) as in *Davies*, **67.151** above, a large retail company (K) had accounted for tax on the full face value of P's vouchers, in accordance with the decision in *Davies*. However, K subsequently submitted a substantial repayment claim, contending that the amount (10%) deducted by P as commission should not be treated as part of its consideration. The Commissioners rejected the claim and the Ch D dismissed K's appeal, holding that P was providing a service to K, and that K benefited from being able to advertise its acceptance of P's vouchers. The decisions in *Elida Gibbs Ltd*, 22.235 EUROPEAN COMMUNITY LAW, and *Argos Distributors Ltd*, 22.236 EUROPEAN COMMUNITY

LAW, were distinguished, on the grounds that in those cases there was no third party involved, and the relevant scheme 'was that of the retailer itself'. *Kingfisher plc v C & E Commrs*, Ch D [2000] STC 992. (*Notes*. (1) The Ch D also held that the discount given by K to P on redemption of the voucher was consideration for a separate supply of services by P to K, which was exempt from VAT under *VATA 1994, Sch 9, Group 5, Item 1*. (2) This decision was approved by the CA in the subsequent case of *F & I Services Ltd*, **67.162** below. (3) For a subsequent case involving the same company, see **67.164** below.)

[67.153] A company which traded as a retailer issued vouchers to customers at the rate of £1 for every £20 worth of goods purchased. The vouchers could be redeemed against goods supplied by the company. The company did not account for VAT on the redeemed vouchers and the Commissioners issued an assessment charging tax on the market value of the goods supplied in exchange. The tribunal upheld the assessment and dismissed the company's appeal. *Body Shop Supply Services Ltd*, [1984] VATTR 233 (VTD 1752).

[67.154] Under a sales promotion scheme, a company gave free hamburgers to readers of a tabloid newspaper. The Commissioners issued an assessment on the basis that VAT was chargeable on the supply of the hamburgers. The company appealed, contending that the hamburgers were gifts. The tribunal rejected this contention, holding that the production of the completed voucher was consideration for the hamburger, applying *Chappell & Co Ltd v Nestlé Co Ltd*, HL 1959, [1960] AC 87; [1959] 2 All ER 701 (a case in which the HL held, by a 3-2 majority, that where a company manufacturing chocolate offered gramophone records at a reduced price to members of the public who submitted three wrappers from packets of its milk chocolate, the acquisition and delivery of the wrappers formed part of the consideration for the records). *McDonald's Restaurants Ltd*, LON/88/1190Y (VTD 3884). (*Note*. The appeal was adjourned to enable consideration of other issues to be deferred until the CJEC had issued its decision in *The Boots Co plc*, **22.251** EUROPEAN COMMUNITY LAW. However, there was no further public hearing of the appeal.)

[67.155] A company which sold motor fuel distributed vouchers which entitled purchasers of its fuel to discounts. Some of the company's sales were directly to the public at sites which it owned, but it also supplied some fuel to dealers who then resold the fuel to members of the public. When a dealer submitted such vouchers for redemption, the company credited the dealer with an amount equal to the face value of the voucher. In accounting for output tax, it deducted the amount of such vouchers from its gross takings. The Commissioners issued an assessment on the basis that the company should have accounted on the full amount of its takings without deducting the amounts of the vouchers. The company appealed, contending that the taxable consideration should be reduced by the amount of the vouchers. The tribunal accepted this contention and allowed the appeal, applying the CJEC decision in *Elida Gibbs Ltd*, **22.235** EUROPEAN COMMUNITY LAW. *Conoco Ltd*, [1997] VATDR 47 (VTD 14679). (*Note*. For the award of costs in this case, see **2.413** APPEALS.)

[67.156] A company which manufactured cigarettes operated a promotion scheme whereby it supplied vouchers with packets of cigarettes. When customers had collected a certain number of such vouchers, they could be exchanged for goods. The Commissioners issued a ruling that the company was liable to account for output tax on the cost of the goods it supplied in this way, and the company appealed. The tribunal dismissed the company's appeal. Applying the CJEC decision in *Kuwait Petroleum (GB) Ltd*, **22.158** EUROPEAN COMMUNITY LAW, the vouchers 'were supplied free of charge' for the purposes of *Article 5(6)* of the *EC Sixth Directive*, so that the company was required to account for output tax on the cost of the goods for which the customers exchanged the vouchers. *Gallaher Ltd*, LON/96/1928 (VTD 14827, 16395).

[67.157] A company (T), which operated a large number of supermarkets, offered 'loyalty cards' to customers, and issued vouchers to customers holding such cards who spent at least £150 per quarter in T's shops (at the rate of 1p for each £1 spent). Certain transactions with a finance company (F) and with 'third party suppliers' also qualified for vouchers, under agreements with F and the 'third party suppliers', whereby those suppliers paid agreed amounts to T. Initially T accounted for VAT by excluding the face value of the redeemed vouchers from its daily gross takings, so that only the cash received was treated as takings. Subsequently T formed the opinion that this treatment was incorrect, and that it should be permitted to deduct the value of the vouchers from its daily gross takings when they were issued, and add the value of redeemed vouchers. (This would provide T with a significant cash-flow advantage, and would permanently exclude the face value of unredeemed vouchers from its daily gross takings.) The Commissioners considered that this treatment was incorrect, and issued a ruling that the vouchers were not 'granted for a consideration' for the purposes of *VATA 1994, Sch 6 para 5*. The Ch D upheld the Commissioners' ruling and the CA unanimously dismissed T's appeal. Jonathan Parker LJ observed that, for *Sch 6 para 5* to take effect, there had to be 'a grant, for a consideration, of a right to receive goods or services for an amount stated on a token, stamp or voucher'. On the evidence, T's customers were not 'paying for a voucher or vouchers: the issue of vouchers is a subsequent, and distinct, stage in the operation of the scheme'. *C & E Commrs v Tesco plc*, CA [2003] STC 1561; [2003] EWCA Civ 1367.

[67.158] See also *Kuwait (Petroleum) Ltd*, **22.158** EUROPEAN COMMUNITY LAW; *Elida Gibbs Ltd*, **22.235** EUROPEAN COMMUNITY LAW; *Yorkshire Co-Operatives Ltd*, **22.244** EUROPEAN COMMUNITY LAW; *Boots Co plc*, **22.251** EUROPEAN COMMUNITY LAW, and *Total UK Ltd*, **22.260** EUROPEAN COMMUNITY LAW.

Promotional scheme—trading stamps obtained from petrol wholesaler

[67.159] A company (C) operated a number of petrol stations. It obtained its supplies of petrol from a wholesaler (T), which operated a promotional scheme involving the use of trading stamps. Under the scheme, C paid T an additional 0.18p per litre of fuel purchased. Until March 1994, C accounted for tax on its full daily gross takings. In its return for June 1994, it sought to recover £22,000 relating to its purchase of trading stamps from T. The Commissioners issued an assessment to recover this amount, and C appealed. The tribunal upheld the assessment and dismissed C's appeal, holding on the evidence that the payments which C had made to T were for the right to participate in a promotional scheme, rather than simply for the purchase of trading stamps.

The tribunal observed that the stamps were supplied to C 'not to dispose of much as it wished, but only to enable it to operate the scheme', and 'it handed them to customers as (T's) agent'. *Copes Service Station Ltd*, MAN/96/331 (VTD 17934).

Vouchers repurchased by issuing company after use

[67.160] A company (H) produced and sold vouchers for a limited number of large retail companies. The companies to which the vouchers were sold distributed them to members of the public, either for payment or as prizes in competitions. The Commissioners issued an assessment on the basis that the difference between the face value of the vouchers and the price at which H repurchased them constituted consideration received by H, chargeable to VAT. The QB upheld the assessment, holding that the amount of the discount forgone by the retailers constituted the consideration paid by the retailers for the services provided by H. *C & E Commrs v High Street Vouchers Ltd*, QB [1990] STC 575.

Sales of vouchers to retailers

[67.161] A company distributed vouchers with a nominal value of £5 or £10, which it sold to retailers for use in sales promotions. The company did not account for output tax on the sales of the vouchers, and the Commissioners issued an assessment charging tax on them. The QB upheld the assessment, observing that the retailers did not have any right to receive goods or services for the amounts stated on the vouchers. The right to receive goods or services was granted to the customers of the retailers to whom the vouchers were sold, rather than to the retailers themselves. *C & E Commrs v Showmarch Marketing Ltd*, QB 1993, [1994] STC 19.

Sales of vouchers by car dealers

[67.162] A company (F) sold books of vouchers to car dealers, who then passed the books of vouchers to the purchasers of second-hand cars. F accounted for output tax on the amounts which it received from the car dealers for the vouchers, but the car dealers did not account for tax on their onward supply of the vouchers to their customers. In March 1998 a local VAT officer ruled that no tax was chargeable on these onward supplies. However, the scheme came to the attention of a regional office, and in June 1998 the Commissioners withdrew the first ruling and ruled that VAT was chargeable on the sale of the vouchers. The CA dismissed F's appeal, holding that the vouchers entitled customers to a discount, but did not give them 'a right to receive goods or services'. Furthermore, the vouchers could not be treated as a prepayment, since 'the money which a customer paid to a car dealer for (the) vouchers did not reach the participating retailers in any shape or form'. *F & I Services Ltd v C & E Commrs*, CA [2001] STC 939. (*Notes.* (1) The CA also held that the vouchers were not exempt under either *VATA 1994, Sch 9, Group 5, Item 5* or *Article 13B(d)* of the *EC Sixth Directive*. See **27.18** *et seq.* FINANCE and **22.352** *et seq.* EUROPEAN COMMUNITY LAW respectively for cases concerning these provisions. (2) For the Commissioners' view of the scheme, see Business Brief 18/98, issued on 11 September 1998. (3) The company also applied for judicial review of the Commissioners' decision to withdraw their original ruling—see **2.338** APPEALS.)

Vouchers sold at discount to persons other than purchasers of goods

[67.163] See *Argos Distributors Ltd*, 22.236 EUROPEAN COMMUNITY LAW.

Vouchers sold at discount to subsidiary company not in same VAT group

[67.164] A VAT group contained five retail companies. The parent company and representative member (K) implemented a scheme, designed by a large accountancy firm, designed to take advantage of the provisions of *VATA 1994, Sch 6 para 5* as then in force, and to reduce its VAT liability on sales of vouchers. It established a wholly-owned subsidiary (F) outside its VAT group, and sold vouchers to F at a discount of 18.52%. F sold some of these vouchers to individual purchasers, through the five retail companies, at face value (paying these companies 10% commission). The purchasers could then exchange these vouchers at face value. F also sold some vouchers to corporate purchasers at a corporate discount related to the volume of vouchers sold. The Commissioners issued a ruling that when vouchers were redeemed, K was required to account for output tax on the face value of the vouchers sold to individual purchasers (and on the face value less the corporate discount in respect of vouchers sold to corporate purchasers). K appealed, contending that the 18.52% discount at which it sold the vouchers to F was effective for VAT purposes, so that it should only be required to account for output tax on 81.48% of the face value of the vouchers. The tribunal reviewed the evidence in detail, rejected this contention, and dismissed the appeal, finding that 'as a matter of commercial reality, the supply of the vouchers was made to the purchasers by the appellant. (F) did not act independently as a principal and had no power to deal with the vouchers as an independent owner'. The tribunal held that 'the consideration for the supply of goods by a retail company to a customer in exchange for a voucher is the amount paid by the purchaser of the voucher, namely the full face value of vouchers sold to individual purchasers and the face value less the corporate discount of vouchers sold to corporate purchasers'. *Kingfisher plc (No 3)*, [2004] VATDR 206 (VTD 18668). (*Notes.* (1) See now *VATA 1994, Sch 6 para 10A*. (2) The tribunal also held that the scheme which K had adopted 'amounted to an abuse of rights', within the principles laid down by the CJEC in *Emsland-Stärke GmbH v Hauptzollamt Hamburg-Jonas*, 22.59 EUROPEAN COMMUNITY LAW.)

Retailers—payments made to company operating promotion scheme

[67.165] See *Allied Carpets Group plc*, 58.44 RETAILERS' SPECIAL SCHEMES.

Supplies of services

Restaurant 'discount cards'

[67.166] Two companies issued 'discount cards', with a face value of £14.99, entitling the holder to obtain a free course on up to twelve occasions at a stated restaurant. The Commissioners issued a ruling that output tax was payable on the supplies of the cards. The CA upheld the Commissioners' ruling, observing that the discount cards conferred a right to pay a reduced price for certain supplies, but did not confer any rights to goods or services. *C & E Commrs v*

Granton Marketing Ltd; C & E Commrs v Wentwalk Ltd, CA [1996] STC 1049. (*Notes.* (1) For a subsequent case in which it was held that the 'discount cards' were not zero-rated brochures, see **5.89 BOOKS, ETC.** (2) For another subsequent case concerning the time of the supply of the vouchers, see **62.409 SUPPLY.**)

Vouchers for MOT tests

[67.167] In the case noted at **44.86 MOTOR CARS**, the CA held that the face value of vouchers for MOT tests could not be deducted from the company's taxable turnover, since there was no separate consideration for them and they were given whether the customer wanted them or not. *Hartwell plc v C & E Commrs*, CA [2003] STC 396; [2003] EWCA Civ 130.

Company operating amusement park

[67.168] A company (B) operated an amusement park, charging customers £30 (or £52 per couple) for admission to the 'rides' at the park. It issued a small number of selected pairs of customers with a voucher for another park, some distance away, operated by a company in the same VAT group. The normal price of the 'rides' at that park was £16. In accounting for VAT, it treated these as face-value vouchers within *VATA 1994, Sch 10A*, so that it only accounted for output tax on £36, instead of on the £52 which the customers had actually paid. Customs issued an assessment on the basis that the purported vouchers were not effective for VAT purposes, and that B was required to account for VAT on the £52 actually paid by the customers. The tribunal reviewed the evidence in detail and dismissed B's appeal, finding that B made no attempt to advertise the promotion, that it only provided the vouchers to selected customers, and that it deliberately intended that only a small percentage of vouchers would be redeemed. The tribunal found that B had taken 'all necessary steps to ensure that as few customers as possible knew of the availability of the discounted price'. Accordingly the vouchers were not within *VATA 1994, Sch 10A*, and B was required to account for VAT on the full £52 paid by its customers. *Blackpool Pleasure Beach (Holdings) Ltd*, MAN/04/051 (VTD 19014). (*Note.* Costs were awarded to Customs.)

'Leisure passes' entitling holder to visit various attractions

[67.169] A company (L) sold 'leisure passes', which were similar in appearance to credit cards, and entitled purchasers to visit various attractions in London without further payment. (Admission to some of these attractions, eg London Zoo, was exempt from VAT, while admission to other attractions was taxable.) Customs issued a ruling that L was required to account for tax on the full price it received from purchasers. L appealed, contending that the passes should be treated as face-value vouchers, within *VATA 1994, Sch 10A*. The tribunal rejected this contention and dismissed L's appeal, observing that *Sch 10A* applied to a voucher 'to the value of any amount stated on it or recorded in it'. The tribunal held that although the passes were within the definition of 'vouchers', they were not within the definition of 'face-value' vouchers, since 'the right to receive goods or services that the pass represents is a single right to free entry to such of the attractions as the holder chooses to visit, which should not be dissected into a series of separate rights to admission to each attraction each with its own recorded value. That single right is not "to the value of an amount stated on it or recorded in it" which implies that the holder can in a meaningful way spend up to a given value on the goods or services represented by the voucher'. The right represented by the pass 'is not, viewed realistically, that the holder has the right to visit attractions to any stated (or recorded) value; it is to visit such of the attractions he chooses.' The Ch D upheld this decision. Sir Andrew Park observed that 'the pass does represent a right to services, but it is not a right to services to the value of an amount stated on it or recorded in it', as required by *Sch 10A para 1(1)*. *Leisure Pass Group Ltd v HMRC*, Ch D [2008] STC 3340; [2008] EWHC 2158 (Ch).

[67.170] Following the decision noted at **67.169** above, the company (L) altered the design and configuration of its 'leisure passes', giving them a set maximum value which was shown on their face (and which ranged from £70 for a one-day pass to £420 for a six-day pass). Customs issued a ruling that, despite these changes, the passes were still not within the definition of a face-value voucher, within *VATA 1994, Sch 10A*. The tribunal allowed L's appeal, holding that 'the inclusion of a daily maximum value has the result that the pass represents a right to receive goods or services to the value of an amount stated on it or recorded in it'. The tribunal observed that L made 'a profit that is not liable to VAT on the difference between the amount it sells the pass for and what it pays to the attraction in respect of the use of the voucher'. However, that was the inherent result of the legislation. *Leisure Pass Group Ltd (No 2)*, LON/08/1143 (VTD 20910).

Company operating nightclubs—whether supplying face-value vouchers

[67.171] A company operated a number of nightclubs. It gave its customers vouchers, entitling them to admission at a reduced rate on subsequent visits. In accounting for VAT, it treated these as 'face-value vouchers' and deducted the amounts shown on the vouchers from its takings. Customs issued an assessment on the basis that the vouchers were not 'face-value vouchers' for VAT purposes, and that the company was required to account for VAT on the actual cash takings received. The tribunal upheld the assessment and dismissed the company's appeal, holding that there was a single contract for admission to the club, 'to which the provision of the voucher was no more than ancillary'. The customers gave no consideration for the vouchers. *Brook Leisure Holdings Ltd*, MAN/x (VTD 19156).

Telecommunications services

[67.172] A company (C), which was established in the Republic of Ireland, supplied telephone cards to UK customers. The Irish VAT authorities did not charge VAT on these supplies, on the basis that the place of supply was in the UK. The UK Commissioners issued a ruling that C was required to account for VAT. C appealed, contending that the effect of *VATA 1994, Sch 10A, para 3(3)* was that it could not be required to account for UK tax. The CA unanimously rejected this contention and upheld the Commissioners' ruling. Arden LJ held that 'the recitals in the preamble to the *Sixth Directive* make it clear that the objectives of the Directive include the avoidance of the distortion of competition by reference to the origin of goods or services and the harmonisation of the rules for VAT'. Applying the principles laid down by the CJEC in *Srl CILFIT and Lanificio di Gavardo SpA v Ministro della Sanita*, **22.3** EUROPEAN

COMMUNITY LAW, 'the court should have regard to the objectives of the legislation', since 'the objectives of a measure have a greater normative force under Community law than they would under English law'. The principle of 'avoidance of non-taxation' was a general principle of the *Sixth Directive*. One of the objectives of the *Directive* was the harmonisation of rules on turnover taxes, and the directive contained 'mandatory rules as to which supplies should be taxable and where those supplies are deemed to take place. It must follow from these provisions that one of the objectives of the directive is to prevent situations arising in which a taxable supply escapes taxation because it is not caught by the legislation of Member States.' The issue of a phonecard was a supply of telecommunications services, which was treated by the *Sixth Directive* as a supply subject to VAT. If neither the issue of phonecards for C's telecommunications services nor the supply of those services to persons within the Community was subject to VAT, the principle of 'the avoidance of non-taxation' would be infringed. It would also lead to a distortion of competition if C and its distributors were able to market C's telecommunications services without having to account for VAT. It appeared that, in enacting *VATA 1994, Sch 10A*, Parliament had not 'foreseen the particular problem that has arisen in this case'. Applying the principles laid down by the HL in *Ghaidan v Godin-Mendoza*, HL [2004] 2 AC 557, *Sch 10A* had to be interpreted in accordance with the *Sixth Directive*. This could be done by 'reading into *paragraph 3(3)* a further disapplication of the disregard in *paragraph 3(2)* to make *paragraph 3* conform to the objectives of the *Sixth Directive*'. Such an interpretation 'gives effect to the wording and purpose of the *Sixth Directive* because it implements the general principles of VAT law identified above in respect of the harmonised rule relating to the place of supply of telecommunications services, i.e. that such supply should in the case of private consumers be taxed in Ireland but in the case of registered persons such as the United Kingdom distributors be taxed in the place where such persons are established'. Pill LJ observed that 'under *Article 9(2)(e)* of the *Sixth Directive*, the place of supply of the phone cards is the United Kingdom, when they are sold to UK registered distributors'. In interpreting the relevant legislation, the courts had a 'fundamental duty arising from EU Directives to impose VAT on the supply of services'. *HMRC v IDT Card Services Ireland Ltd*, CA [2006] STC 1252; [2006] EWCA Civ 29. (*Notes*. (1) The HL rejected the company's application for leave to appeal against this decision. (2) For HMRC's practice following this decision, see Business Brief 03/06, issued on 9 March 2006, and Business Brief 07/06, issued on 27 June 2006. See also *FA 2006, s 22*.)

[67.173] See also *Arachchige*, 62.546 SUPPLY.

Vouchers for future treatments at spa

[67.174] A company operated two spas. As part of a promotion scheme, it issued vouchers, with a face value of £15, to customers who purchased treatments. These vouchers were only redeemable against future visits. It treated part of the consideration paid by the customers as attributable to these vouchers, and did not account for tax on those amounts. Customs issued an assessment on the basis that where the company issued vouchers to customers who purchased treatments, there was no consideration for the vouchers, and that the whole amount paid by the customers resulted in an immediate liability to output tax. The company appealed, contending that the vouchers were 'face-value' vouchers, which should be treated in the same way as gift vouchers which it sold, and that it should only be required to account for tax on them when they were redeemed. The tribunal rejected this contention and dismissed the appeal. The tribunal observed that less than 5% of the vouchers which the company issued were ever redeemed. Furthermore, 'the only natural meaning of the words on the vouchers, and the associated documents and information, is that a guest is to pay a single price – the price at which the package she has purchased is advertised'. On the evidence, the company entered into a single contract with each customer, and there was no separate consideration for the voucher. *Spa & Resort Operations Ltd*, MAN/06/238 (VTD 20979). (*Note.* Costs were awarded to Customs.)

Football club—sale of vouchers for admission to matches

[67.175] See *Celtic plc*, 62.420 SUPPLY.

68

Warehoused Goods and Free Zones

VATA 1994, s 18—removal of goods from warehouse

[68.1] An individual (C) purchased consignments of alcohol while they were in bonded warehouses. He was subsequently convicted of being knowingly concerned in the fraudulent evasion of duty, and sentenced to four years' imprisonment. In addition the Commissioners issued an assessment charging VAT in respect of the consignments. The tribunal upheld the assessment in principle (while reducing the amount in respect of a consignment which was still in a lorry when C was arrested). The tribunal observed that where goods were removed from a warehouse to be used in the UK, a liability to VAT arose by virtue of *VATA 1994, s 18*. The procedure for removing goods for export involved the issue of a C88 which had to be stamped at the port through which the goods were exported. C had not submitted a stamped C88 in respect of any of the goods covered by the assessment. The Commissioners had produced evidence linking C 'with the diversion of the goods to the home market'. The Ch D dismissed C's appeal against this decision. Park J held that 'there is no tenable basis on which the decision of the tribunal can be challenged'. *DL Chitolie v C & E Commrs*, Ch D [2002] STC 1532; [2002] EWHC 2323 (Ch). (*Note.* Costs were awarded to the Commissioners.)

VATA 1994, s 18—duty point on supplies of petroleum

[68.2] A UK company (E) agreed to purchase a large quantity of petroleum from a Netherlands company (O). It was agreed that the petrol would be supplied in the UK. O included VAT in its invoices to E, but failed to account for this to the Commissioners. E reclaimed input tax on the supplies. The Commissioners rejected the claim, considering that E had purchased the petroleum 'in bond' and was therefore liable to account for acquisition VAT when it removed the petroleum from the warehouse. The tribunal reviewed the evidence in detail and allowed E's appeal, finding that both E and the Commissioners had 'been the victim of a fraud' perpetrated by O, and observing that 'the question is which of the parties in this appeal should bear the loss arising from the fraud'. Under the agreement, O had been 'legally bound to deliver duty-paid product only'. E 'did not have bonded storage capacity available to it during the period in question', and 'only after (O) had paid the excise duty and accounted for VAT could the product be removed from bond and only then did title to the product pass to (E). Only when the warehouseman on production of the requisite documentation (W50) was satisfied that the excise duty had been paid and the VAT accounted for could the product be released for free circulation and delivery to the ultimate purchaser.' *Emir 8 Petroleum plc*, LON/01/203 (VTD 17400).

69

Zero-Rating: Miscellaneous

The cases in this chapter are arranged under the following headings.

Group 2—Sewerage services and water **69.1**
Group 9—Caravans and houseboats **69.5**

CROSS-REFERENCES

For zero-rating under *VATA 1994, Sch 8, Group 1*, see **29** FOOD. For zero-rating under *VATA 1994, Sch 8, Group 3*, see **5** BOOKS, ETC. For zero-rating under *VATA 1994, Sch 8, Groups 5 and 6*, see **15** CONSTRUCTION OF BUILDINGS, ETC. and **55** PROTECTED BUILDINGS. For zero-rating under *VATA 1994, Sch 8, Group 7*, see **39** INTERNATIONAL SERVICES. For zero-rating under *VATA 1994, Sch 8, Group 8*, see **66** TRANSPORT. For zero-rating under *VATA 1994, Sch 8, Group 12*, see **19** DRUGS, MEDICINES, AIDS FOR THE HANDICAPPED, ETC. For the zero-rating of exports see **25** EXPORTS. For zero-rating under *VATA 1994, Sch 8, Group 15*, see **11** CHARITIES. For zero-rating under *VATA 1994, Sch 8, Group 16*, see **12** CLOTHING.

Group 2—Sewerage services and water

Coin-operated washing machines in launderette

[69.1] A company owned a number of self-service launderettes. The Commissioners issued a ruling that the company was required to account for output tax on the full amount of its takings. The company appealed, contending that part of the charge was for the supply of water and should be treated as zero-rated under what is now *VATA 1994, Sch 8, Group 2, Item 2*. The tribunal rejected this contention and dismissed the appeal, observing that 'the customer goes to the launderette to wash dirty clothes in a washing machine. What is obtained at the end of the transaction is cleaned clothes'. This was 'the provision of a service of which the water, gas and electricity form an integral part'. Accordingly the whole of the charge was standard-rated. *Mander Laundries Ltd*, [1973] VATTR 136 (VTD 31).

Lease of land—whether a separate supply of water

[69.2] Trustees of certain land in the City of London leased several properties, used as barristers' chambers, to tenants. The trustees had opted to tax the properties. The tenants were supplied with water. In accounting for VAT, the trustees treated part of the rent paid by the tenants as attributable to a zero-rated supply of water. HMRC issued a ruling that the trustees were making a single supply of a leased property, and that none of the consideration qualified for zero-rating. The tribunal allowed the trustees' appeal. Judge Khan expressed the view that it would be 'an economic distortion' to treat 'the supply of water under a commercial lease granted by the Middle Temple to its tenants as a standard-rated supply because they receive their water, not directly from Thames Water, but through pipes established hundreds of years ago'. *The Honourable Society of Middle Temple v HMRC*, [2011] UKFTT 390 (TC); [2011] SFTD 1088, TC01245. (*Note.* HMRC have appealed to the Upper Tribunal against this decision.)

Connection of mains water supply to moored houseboat

[69.3] An individual (W) owned a houseboat. He arranged for the connection of a mains water supply to the mooring. The contractor charged VAT on the necessary work. W appealed to the tribunal, contending that it should be treated as zero-rated under *VATA 1994, Sch 8, Group 2, Item 2*. The tribunal rejected this contention and dismissed the appeal, observing that 'the supply we are concerned with is not of water, but of the work carried out to connect his houseboat to the water mains. Once that connection is made the water company will supply him with water, and such supply will be zero-rated by virtue of this provision. But the work of excavating trenches, laying pipes, connecting the pipe-line into the mains supply, testing the pipe-line and all the other work of connecting the houseboat to the water mains is not the supply of water.' *JDJ Winser*, LON/05/580 (VTD 19366).

Saline solution imported for research—whether water

[69.4] The proprietor of an acupuncture clinic imported a large number of ampoules of water described as 'distilled water', but which in fact contained a saline solution with about 0.9% of salt. The Commissioners issued a ruling that tax was chargeable on the importation, and the proprietor appealed, contending that the solution should be treated as water and should be zero-rated under what is now *VATA 1994, Sch 8, Group 2, Item 2*. The tribunal rejected this contention and dismissed the appeal, holding that the solution was not 'water'. *AJ Scott-Morley*, LON/80/297 (VTD 1097).

Group 9—Caravans and houseboats

Scanner—whether a caravan

[69.5] A company failed to account for output tax on the supply of a mobile body scanner on an articulated chassis. The Commissioners issued an assessment charging tax on the scanner, and the company appealed, contending that the scanner was a caravan and should be treated as zero-rated. The tribunal rejected this contention and dismissed the appeal, holding that the scanner was not a caravan since it was not designed for human habitation. *Elscint (GB) Ltd*, LON/83/337 (VTD 1654).

'Park homes'—whether 'caravans' within Sch 8, Group 9

[69.6] A company which owned a caravan site arranged for structures, described as 'park homes', to be erected on the site. It did not account for output tax on the sale of these 'park homes', and reclaimed the input tax attributable to their construction. The Commissioners issued an assessment to recover the tax, considering that it related to licences to occupy land, which were exempt supplies. The company appealed, contending that the sale of the 'park homes' was zero-rated under what is now either *VATA 1994, Sch 8, Group 5* or *Sch 8, Group 9*. The tribunal held firstly that the 'park homes' were buildings, but that their sale did not qualify for zero-rating under *Sch 8, Group 5* (see **15.153** CONSTRUCTION OF DWELLINGS, ETC.), and secondly that their sale qualified for zero-rating under *Sch 8, Group 9*. The fact that the 'park homes' were within the definition of a 'building' did not prevent them from being within the definition of a 'caravan', since 'the two categories are not necessarily exclusive'. *Stonecliff Caravan Park*, [1993] VATTR 464 (VTD 11097). (*Note.* The tribunal held that most of the company's input tax was attributable to exempt supplies but that the tax relating to the provision of brick skirtings was directly attributable to the sale of the 'park homes', and adjourned the hearing for the parties to reach agreement on the amount of the allowable input tax. There was no further public hearing of the appeal.)

'Lodja Sleep' units supplied to university—whether 'caravans'

[69.7] A university hired 12 'Lodja Sleep' units, to be used as temporary accommodation for students. The units, which were not designed for cooking or eating, were sited in a car park on the campus. The hirer charged VAT. The university lodged an appeal, contending that the units should be treated as 'caravans' and as zero-rated. The tribunal rejected this contention and dismissed the appeal, holding that 'in order to be equated with houses, "caravans" must provide a broad range of facilities similar to those to be found in a house'. On the evidence, the units 'did not constitute self-contained living accommodation'. Accordingly they were not 'caravans' and their supply was standard-rated. (The tribunal also held that the units 'were not sufficiently attached to the ground to render them "immovable" for the purposes of the exemption' in *Article 13B(b)* of the *EC Sixth Directive*.) *University of Kent*, [2004] VATDR 372 (VTD 18625).

Sale of caravans—apportionment of consideration

[69.8] The owner of a caravan site sold furnished caravans on the site. He did not account for output tax on the sale of the caravans, but did account for output tax on a proportion of the consideration which he treated as being for fixtures and fittings. In a case where he sold a furnished caravan (the cost of which was £26,500) for £56,000, he treated £4,400 of this as being for fixtures and fittings, and accounted for output tax accordingly. The Commissioners issued an assessment on the basis that he should have accounted for output tax on a greater proportion of the consideration (in the above example, on £6,975 rather than on £4,400), in accordance with the method laid down by *Notice 701/20/89*. The tribunal allowed the owner's appeal in part, holding that the consideration of £56,000 included an element in respect of work carried out on the site, which was zero-rated under what is now *VATA 1994, Sch 8, Group 5*, and directing that the assessment should be recomputed accordingly. The Commissioners appealed to the QB, which remitted the case to the tribunal for rehearing, finding that the tribunal had failed to consider the terms of the invoice between the owner and the purchaser. *C & E Commrs v DR Barratt*, QB [1995] STC 661. (*Notes.* (1) There was no further public hearing of the appeal. (2) *Notice 701/20/89* has subsequently been superseded by *Notice 701/20/96*.)

[69.9] A company which sold furnished caravans submitted a repayment claim on the basis that it had attributed an excessive proportion of the consideration to the standard-rated contents of the caravans. The Commissioners rejected the claim on the basis that it did not conform with the guidelines laid down in *Notice 701/20/89*. The company appealed, contending that the method of apportionment set out in the *Notice* was inappropriate, because it assumed that the manufacturers' apportionment was correct, and that the trader made the same profit margin on the removable contents as on the caravan itself. The tribunal dismissed the appeal, holding that the method of apportionment must give 'a fair and reasonable result', and finding that the method laid down in the *Notice* 'is much more likely to produce such a result than that advanced by the appellant'. *Haulfryn Estates Co Ltd*, MAN/97/244 (VTD 16145). (*Note. Notice 701/20/89* has subsequently been superseded by *Notice 701/20/96*.)

[69.10] See also *Talacre Beach Caravan Sales Ltd*, 22.507 EUROPEAN COMMUNITY LAW.

Caravan used as office—whether input tax reclaimable

[69.11] A trader reclaimed input tax on the purchase of a caravan which he used as an office, although the purchase price was exclusive of VAT. The Commissioners issued an assessment to recover the tax, considering that the caravan was zero-rated so that no input tax was reclaimable. The trader appealed, contending that the input tax should be treated as reclaimable since the caravan was purchased for business use rather than as domestic accommodation. The tribunal dismissed the appeal, holding that the caravan was within what is now *VATA 1994, Sch 8, Group 9, Item 1* and was therefore zero-rated. *MJ Rooke*, MAN/91/1566 (VTD 9819).

Yacht used as permanent residence—whether a 'houseboat'

[69.12] In the case noted at **41.152** LAND, the tribunal held that a yacht was not within the definition of a 'houseboat', even though the appellants used it as their permanent residence. *DM & PJ Roberts*, [1992] VATTR 30 (VTD 7516).

Supply of 'timeshare' interests in houseboats

[69.13] A company (C) owned a number of narrowboats which were used as holiday accommodation. It was accepted that these supplies were standard-rated. It also built a number of houseboats, and decided to sell timeshares in them. It arranged for two retailers to sell the timeshares to customers, and transferred the legal ownership of the houseboats to a nominee company. It did not account for tax on the payments which it received under the agreements. The Commissioners issued an assessment charging tax on these receipts, and C appealed, contending that it had made supplies of houseboats which were zero-rated under *VATA 1994, Sch 8, Group 9, Item 3*. The tribunal dismissed the appeal, observing that there were 'conflicting clauses in the documentation', and holding that in reality C was supplying accommodation in a houseboat, which was excluded from zero-rating by *Group 9, Note (b)*. The tribunal observed that C was entitled 'to substitute a boat or even alternative accommodation in certain circumstances', and that this demonstrated 'the limited degree of control the retailer's clients have over the boat'. *Canaltime Developments Ltd*, LON/02/0032 (VTD 18561).

Index

This index is referenced to the paragraph number.

The entries printed in bold capitals are chapter headings in the text.

A

Abattoir services, not zero-rated, 29.96
'Abuse', principle of, 22.58–22.77
    redefinition, 22.77
Accommodation,
    by whom supplied, 62.284–62.291
    directors, for, 36.330–36.340
    handicapped persons, for, 19.46, 19.47
    hospital, 33.39–33.60
    hostel, 22.143, 33.71, 41.100–41.102
    hotel, 41.96–41.115
        —time of supply, 62.93
    office, 41.46, 41.47
    overseas students, for, 41.97
    public house, 62.291
    time of supply, 62.396–62.398
    tour operators, 67.90
    to whom supplied, 36.14–36.17
    valuation of supplies, 67.90–67.93
Accountancy services, time of supply, 62.454,
    62.455
Accounting periods, 59.1–59.7
    prescribed, 3.108, 52.1
Acupuncture, whether exempt, 33.17, 33.50
Adjournments, applications for, 2.211–2.233
Advance payments,
    input tax, 36.620–36.636
    time of supply, 62.417–62.439
Advertising services,
    attribution of input tax, 46.33, 46.76,
        46.77
    definition, 22.218, 62.497, 62.514, 62.526,
        62.527
    place of supply, 62.495, 62.496
    self-supply, 11.24
AGENTS,
    acting in own name, 1.72–1.80
    definition of, 1.1
    disbursements, 1.81–1.85
    estate agents, 62.57, 62.399–62.401
    nursing agencies, 33.2–33.4

Aircraft,
    catering on, 36.131, 36.155, 66.13
    hire of, 7.7, 7.49
    purchase, whether for business purposes,
        36.463–36.467
    supplies to, 22.393
Airport,
    facilities at,
        —whether exempt, 41.1, 41.32, 41.33
        —whether zero-rated, 66.41, 66.42
Alteration,
    approved, to protected building,
        55.27–55.82
    definition, 56.8–56.10
Amnesty, whether valid, 22.469, 22.470
Animal feeding stuffs, whether zero-rated,
    29.106–29.118
Animals, live, whether zero-rated,
    29.120–29.124
Antique, whether a 'collector's piece', 60.10
'Anton Piller' order, documents held under,
    14.87, 14.88
APPEALS,
    adjournments, applications for,
        2.211–2.233
    agreement of, 2.200–2.210
    associated companies, 2.79
    associated partnerships, 2.78
    categorisation of cases, 2.148, 2.149
    champerty, 2.297
    compounding agreement, 2.206
    concessions, 2.83–2.96
    costs, award of, 2.350–2.510
    date of appealable decision, 2.32
    disclosure of documents, 2.257–2.265
    estoppel and allied matters, 2.109–2.127
    evidence,
        —admissibility, 2.277–2.290
        —public interest immunity, 2.282
    future supplies, 2.1–2.8
    groups of companies, 32.9
    grounds of appeal, 2.1–2.50

APPEALS, – *cont.*

hardship applications, 2.136–2.147, 2.446
hearing before tribunal, 2.234–2.308
illness, 2.225–2.229
interest, award of, 2.512–2.533
issue estoppel, 2.122, 2.124
judicial review, 2.328–2.349
late appeals, 2.172–2.197
notice of appeal, 2.62–2.66
proof, onus of, 2.234–2.237
res judicata, 2.71, 2.125–2.127, 22.555
settlement by agreement, 2.200–2.210
statement of case, 2.150–2.171
summons to accountant, 2.301
third party, joinder of, 2.75, 2.495
tribunal,
— decision, 2.309–2.314
— jurisdiction, 2.1–2.51, 2.83–2.108
withdrawal of, 2.71
witnesses and evidence, 2.277–2.291
Approved alterations, to protected buildings,
55.27–55.82
ASSESSMENT,
alternative, 3.132, 3.133
amount, 3.146–3.169
change of basis, 3.177–3.179
estimated, 3.1–3.39
increased after issue, 3.17, 3.168
notification of, 3.61–3.70
overpayments, 3.111, 3.112
partnerships, 47.1–47.11
supplementary, 3.110
time limit, 3.40–3.110
undated, whether valid, 3.120
validity, 3.114–3.145
Assets,
cessation of trade, 62.103–62.105,
67.20–67.26
private use of, 62.101, 62.102
sales of, 62.72–62.86, 65.76–65.80
transfers of, 62.95–62.118
Associated companies,
input tax, 36.18–36.29
payments between, 43.16, 62.466
Associated partnerships, 47.65–47.68
Associated persons,
European Community law, 22.125, 22.126
registration as single taxable person,
57.35–57.81
Associations,—see also CLUBS, ASSOCIATIONS AND
ORGANISATIONS
fund-raising associations, 13.13
residents' association, 13.1

B

BAD DEBTS,
barter transactions, 22.258
factoring agreements, 4.22, 4.23
group of companies, 4.19, 4.20
import agent, 4.24
intermediary insolvent, 4.18
'outstanding amount', 4.1–4.15
records inadequate, 4.16, 4.17
repayment of input tax, 4.31
time limit for claims, 4.25, 4.26
Bank,
assignment of receivables, 46.159, 46.181
partial exemption, 22.400, 46.7,
46.158–46.160, 46.181
service charge income, 46.158
Bankrupt,
appeal by, 37.29
supplies by, 37.30
Barristers,
criminal prosecution, 37.21
supplies by, 62.474
Betting, gaming, etc., 22.371–22.377,
24.10–24.25
bingo, 24.10–24.12
call centre services, 22.374
card games, 22.373, 24.14, 24.15
casino accommodation, 24.17
gaming machines, 24.18–24.20
horse racing, 24.22
roulette, 22.371, 24.21
shooting gallery, 24.16
Binders, whether zero-rated, 5.1, 5.25–5.28
Bingo, whether exempt, 24.10–24.12
Boats,
hire of, 7.29–7.45
second-hand, sale of, 60.18
BOOKS, ETC.,
address books, 5.44
binders, 5.1, 5.25–5.28
brochures, 5.54–5.92
charts, 5.110
children's books, 5.11–5.13
church memorial book, 5.46
cricket scorecards, 5.78
diaries, 5.17, 5.44, 5.45
dress design kits, 5.55
histographs, 5.110
information sheets, 5.82
journals, 5.93–5.108
leaflets, 5.54–5.90
mail order catalogues, 5.10, 5.33, 5.34
market research reports, 5.14
music, 5.109

BOOKS, ETC., – *cont.*
newspapers, 5.93–5.108
pamphlets, 5.54–5.92
periodicals, 5.93–5.108
photobooks, 5.24
photograph albums, 5.29
pictorial magazine, 5.95, 5.96
property guides, 5.93
recipe cards, 5.85
religious cards, 5.84
stamp fair programmes, 5.68
surname histories, 5.43
tax cards, 5.83
telecommunications manuals, 5.60
television viewing figures, 5.15
textbooks, 5.2–5.7, 5.35, 5.38
vouchers, 5.31, 5.32
Branch or agency, services supplied through, 62.507
Bridge, whether a 'building', 15.33
Brochures, whether zero-rated, 5.54–5.90
Building materials, etc., 15.221–15.260
Aga cooker, 15.236, 15.237
kitchen units, 15.253
mechanical ventilator units, 15.241
roller blinds, 15.250
soundproofing material, 15.255
Venetian blinds, 15.248, 15.249
ventilating system, 15.242, 15.243
waste disposal units, 15.246
BUILDINGS AND LAND,
beneficial interests, 6.51
construction of buildings, 15.1–15.283
—access roads, 15.180
—bridge, 15.33
—church annexe, 15.155
—church garage, 15.98
—church hall, 15.154
—community centre, 15.88, 15.89
—conversions, 15.51–15.54, 15.130–15.147
—extensions, 15.27–15.29, 19.46, 19.47
—flats, construction of, 15.160–15.164
—garage, 15.146, 15.218
—leisure centre, 15.85
—nursing homes, 15.195–15.198
—recreation centre, 15.105
—renovation, 15.25, 15.26
—site, definition of, 15.18, 15.150, 15.151
—sports hall, 15.104
—sports pavilion, 15.83, 15.84, 15.102, 15.103
—swimming pool, 15.106, 15.210, 15.239, 15.240

BUILDINGS AND LAND, – *cont.*
construction of buildings, 15.1–15.283 – *cont.*
—theatre, 15.87
demolition, 15.159, 15.212
fixtures, 15.234–15.260
leaseback agreement, 6.51
option to tax, 6.1–6.50
protected, 55.1–55.18
—change of use, 55.1
—definition, 55.1–55.18
—internal alterations, 55.69
—painting, 55.67
reconstruction of, 15.12, 15.13, 15.158, 15.211, 55.19–55.26
Burial and cremation, 24.26–24.30
BUSINESS,
Briefs (HMRC), status, 48.7
cessation of, 36.643–36.647
date of commencement, 7.107
educational activities, 7.82–7.86
entertainment, 8.1–8.48
—dinner-dances, 8.34, 8.42, 8.43
—employees, 8.42–8.44
hiring of chattels, 7.29–7.49
pictures, sale of, 7.106
statutory bodies, 7.2, 7.79, 7.80
subpostmaster, 7.103, 7.104
tourism, promotion of, 7.78
yachts,
—chartering of, 7.34–7.45, 36.583–36.585
—construction of, 7.123

C

CAPITAL GOODS,
definition, 9.3, 22.432, 46.98, 57.34
input tax adjustments, 9.5, 22.456–22.459, 46.97, 46.98
land and buildings, 9.3
leaseback transaction, 22.459
Caravans,
whether zero-rated, 69.5–69.11
Carousel fraud, 22.115, 36.77–36.122, 49.13
Cars,
accessories, 36.176
company cars, 62.1–62.7
definition of, 44.1–44.52
delivery charges, 44.98, 44.99
insurance, 38.1–38.6, 38.29, 38.51
kit supplied with car, 44.101
margin scheme, 44.60–44.96, 44.168

Cars, – *cont.*
MOT certificates, 44.95, 44.96
MOT test fees, 44.162–44.164
parking facilities, 41.136–41.148
place of supply, 62.478
restoration costs, 44.78, 44.79
road fund licences, 44.91–44.94
self-supplies, 44.55–44.59
stolen cars, sale of, 62.168, 62.169
taxicab licences, 44.88–44.90
taxis, 62.232–62.254
used cars, definition, 44.66, 44.67
valuation, 44.83–44.87, 44.154–44.156
CASH ACCOUNTING SCHEME,
assignment of debts, 10.15
input tax, evidence for claim, 10.14
termination of authorisation, 10.1–10.10
Cashback payments, 67.77, 67.147
Catering,
definition, 29.1–29.19
delicatessens, 29.3–29.5
finger buffets, 29.9–29.13
free meals or drinks, 62.194, 67.143
hot food, definition, 29.55–29.80
premises, definition, 29.20–29.54
race meetings, at, 29.45, 29.46
railway stations, at, 29.35
sandwiches, 29.7, 29.8, 29.14, 29.17,
29.27–29.30, 29.60
supplies, by whom made, 62.292–62.312
schools, in, 29.34, 29.70
Cessation of business, 36.643–36.647,
62.103–62.105, 67.20–67.26
Champerty, 2.297
CHARITIES,
goods donated for sale, 11.1, 11.2
input tax, apportionment, 11.39–11.59
medicinal products, 11.30, 11.31
'relevant goods', 11.3–11.14
theatre, construction of, 15.87
Children,
car seats, 56.2
clothing, 12.10–12.24
Cinemas, 16.11, 22.268
Circular transactions, 52.367
Civil penalties,—see PENALTIES: EVASION OF TAX;
PENALTIES: FAILURE TO NOTIFY; PENALTIES:
MISDECLARATION AND ERRORS **and** PENALTIES:
REGULATORY PROVISIONS
'Clawback' assessments, 48.76–48.80
CLOTHING AND FOOTWEAR,
children's wear, 12.10–12.24
definition, 12.1–12.9
employees, supplied to, 62.14
school uniforms, 12.20, 12.21

CLOTHING AND FOOTWEAR, – *cont.*
'young children', 12.11, 12.14
**CLUBS, ASSOCIATIONS AND
ORGANISATIONS,**
fund-raising associations, 13.13
golf club,
—subscriptions, 13.23, 13.24
—trust established by, 13.6
interest-free loans, 13.32–13.36
match fees, 13.40, 13.41
receipts, taxation of, 13.17–13.42
registration, 13.12
residents' association, 13.1
subscriptions, 13.17–13.28
COLLECTION AND ENFORCEMENT,
compounding agreement, 14.120
Crown debts, set-off of, 37.16, 37.17
distraint, 14.77–14.85
'freezing' orders, 14.111, 14.112
receivership, 37.10, 37.11, 14.101, 14.102,
36.675
recovery of VAT, 14.69–14.76
security, 14.1–14.68
Collector's piece, definition, 35.21,
60.8–60.14
Commission, 67.43–67.58, 67.95–67.102
Commissioners,
best judgment, 3.1–3.39
Business Briefs, status, 48.7
costs, application for, 2.350–2.374
Community Amateur Sports Clubs, 19.93
Concessions,
application of, 2.89–2.94
refusal to backdate, 2.88
Conditional registration, 36.558
Conditional sale agreement,
repossession of goods after, 36.675, 60.20
whether a supply, 62.87–62.94
Condoms, supplies of, 11.30
Confectionery, 29.128–29.164
biscuits for ice-creams, 29.129
caramel shortcake, 29.134, 29.149
carob-coated biscuits, 29.150, 29.151
cereal bars, whether, 29.153–29.156
diet bars, whether, 29.132
energy bars, whether, 29.138,
29.157–29.159
fruit and nut mixtures, 29.141
hazelnut wafers, 29.137
Horlicks tablets, whether, 29.136
'Jaffa Cakes', whether, 29.135
Lucozade tablets, whether, 29.136
popcorn, whether, 29.144, 29.145
'tartelettes', whether, 29.148
toffee apples, whether, 29.128

Connected persons, transactions between, 67.1–67.3
Consideration,
  amount of, 67.11–67.150
  apportionable, 62.548–62.556
  barter transactions, 67.146
  deemed supplies, 67.11–67.26
  deferred, 62.407, 67.139
  definition of, 22.78–22.85, 22.232–22.248
  mail order business, 22.234, 67.33, 67.42
  repossession of goods, 67.71
  'salary sacrifice', 62.5
  shares received as, 4.10
  'value-shifting', 67.70
  vouchers, etc. 67.151–67.175
CONSTRUCTION OF BUILDINGS, ETC.,
  access roads, 15.180
  bridge, 15.33
  building materials, etc., 15.221–15.260
  church annexe, 15.155
  church garage, 15.98
  church hall, 15.154
  community centre, 15.88, 15.89
  conversions, 15.51–15.54, 15.130–15.147
  demolition, 15.159, 15.212
  dwellings, definition, 15.35–15.66
  extensions, 15.27–15.29, 19.46, –19.47
  garages, 15.146, 15.218
  leisure centre, 15.85
  major interest, whether a grant of,
    15.148–15.153
  nursing homes, 15.195–15.198
  prefabricated bungalows, 15.35
  reconstruction work, 15.158, 15.211
  recreation centre, 15.105
  renovation, 15.25, 15.26
  scaffolding, supplies of, 15.177
  school classrooms, 15.184, 15.190
  school playgrounds, 15.189
  site, definition of, 15.18, 15.150, 15.151
  sports hall, 15.104
  sports pavilion, 15.83, 15.84, 15.102,
    15.103
  swimming pool, 15.106,15.210, 15.239,
    15.240
  theatre, 15.87
  time of supply of services, 62.475
Computer software, 22.176, 36.607, 67.140
Costs,
  amount of award, 2.375–2.420
  applications by Customs, 2.350–2.374
  Customs' practice, 2.354
  indemnity basis, 2.473–2.493
  security, 2.369, 2.370
  set-off, 2.509

Costs, – cont.
  third party, 2.371
Counterfeit goods, supply of, 22.82
Credit,
  cards, 32.28
  exemption for grant of, 22.352–22.363,
    27.10
  notes, 22.460, 40.85–40.119
Cremation, 24.26
CULTURAL SERVICES,
  definition, 22.319, 62.523
  whether exempt, 16.1–16.14, 22.318,
    22.319
  —chapel, 16.6
  —cinema, 16.11
  —museum, 16.1
  —operatic company, 16.8
  —orchestra, 16.7
  —student union, 16.9
  —zoological society, 16.2, 16.4, 22.321
Customs & Excise Commissioners,
  best judgment, 3.1–3.39
  Business Briefs, status, 48.7
  costs, application for, 2.350–2.374

D

Dancers, supplies of services, 62.282, 62.283
Deemed supply, valuation, 67.11–67.26
DEFAULT INTEREST,
  appeals, 17.1–17.5
  assessment, validity, 17.16
  calculation of interest, 17.6–17.12
  jurisdiction of tribunal, 17.1–17.3
  validity of charge, 17.13, 17.14
DEFAULT SURCHARGE,
  BACS, payment by, 18.67
  company name, change of, 18.33
  computation, 18.18–18.41
  date of posting disputed, 18.49
  'material defaults', 18.614, 18.615
  no tax due, 18.31, 18.32
  reasonable excuse, whether, 18.70–18.613
  validity of cheque, 18.28–18.30
Deferred consideration,
  time of supply, 62.407
  value of supply, 67.139
Delivery charges,
  cars, 44.98, 44.99
  meals, 62.310, 62.311
  newspapers, 58.2–58.5

Demolition, whether zero-rated, 15.159, 15.212
Dental services, 22.288, 22.289, 33.32–33.38
Deposits, 22.86, 62.93, 62.171, 62.440–62.453
  coin dealers, 62.387
  furniture, 62.447, 62.448
  hotel accommodation, 22.86, 41.108, 62.93, 62.451
  machine tool company, 62.449
  manufacturers, 62.446
  purchase not completed, 36.636
  shopfitters, 62.445
Deregistration, 57.120–57.143
Derogations, EC, 22.229, 22.496–22.504
Diaries, whether zero-rated, 5.17, 5.44, 5.45
Directors,
  domestic accommodation, 36.330–36.340
  penalties on, 50.13–50.66
Disbursements, 1.81–1.85
Discounts, 'prompt payment', 67.88
Distraint, 14.77–14.85
  levy of, effect on appeal, 2.197
Dog food, 29.187, 29.191–29.193
Domestic accommodation, 36.330–36.340
Donations, 62.119–62.122
DRUGS, MEDICINES, AIDS FOR THE HANDICAPPED, ETC.,
  bathrooms, etc., 19.86–19.94
  lifts, 19.95–19.99
  registered practitioners, 19.1–19.8
  —Viagra, 19.5
  supplies to handicapped, 19.9–19.75
  —airbath, 19.10
  —aircraft, 19.33
  —architect's services, 19.90
  —beds, adjustable, 19.14, 19.15
  —chairs, ergonomic, 19.37, 19.66
  —computer system, 19.32
  —'domestic use', 19.9
  —electric generators, 19.71, 19.72
  —extension to house, 19.46, 19.47
  —fire escape, 19.63
  —golf buggies, 19.59, 19.60, 19.74
  —hydrotherapy pool, 19.35, 19.36
  —incontinence pads, 19.68
  —kitchens, 19.42, 19.43
  —mattress, 19.27, 19.28
  —motor caravan, 19.21–19.23
  —overbed tables, 19.39
  —pesticide sprays, 19.58
  —prostheses, 19.12
  —surveyors' services, 19.45
  —writing board, 19.51

E

Economic activities, 22.109–22.119, 36.554, 36.558
EDUCATION,
  'eligible body', 21.1–21.20
  —music tuition, 21.2
  —Open University, 21.3
  —students union, 21.19
  —tuition by barrister, 21.1
  —unregistered school, 21.4
  —zoological society, 21.6
  examination services, 21.43
  private tuition, 21.30–21.41, 22.306–22.308
  research, 11.40, 11.41, 21.21, 22.303
  school photographs, 67.27–67.29, 67.53, 67.54
  vocational training, 21.23–21.29
  —distance learning, 21.29
  —YTS trainees, 21.24, 21.25
  youth club facilities, 21.49–21.53
  —Girl Guides, 21.49
  —golf club, 21.53
  —gymnastic club, 21.52
  —YMCAs, 21.50, 21.51
Electrical or gas appliances, 15.234–15.240
  Aga cooker, 15.236, 15.237
  cooker hoods, 15.234
  ovens, 15.235
  security gates, 15.238
  swimming pool covers, 15.239, 15.240
Electricity supplies,
  caravan site, at, 30.12
  sheltered housing, in, 30.13
Employees,
  canteen facilities, 62.11, 62.12
  clothing supplied to, 62.14
  company cars, 62.1–62.7
  long service awards, 62.8–62.10
  secondment of, 62.19, 62.20, 62.23–62.38
  supplies to, 62.1–62.17
'Energy-saving materials', 56.1
Entertainment services, 22.214, 22.215, 62.523
Escort agency, 62.278–62.280
Estate agency,
  expenses charged to clients, 62.57
  time of supply, 62.399–62.401
Estoppel and allied matters, 2.109–2.127
  issue estoppel, 2.122, 2.124
  Scottish appeals, 2.120, 2.121
EUROPEAN COMMUNITY LAW,
  'abuse', principle, 22.58–22.77
  —redefinition, 22.77

EUROPEAN COMMUNITY LAW, – *cont.*

advertising services, 22.218
amnesty, 22.469, 22.470
arbitration services, 22.223
associated persons, 22.125, 22.126
betting, 22.371–22.375
capital goods,
—definition, 22.432
—input tax adjustments, 22.456–22.459
chargeable event, 22.229, 22.231
cinemas, 22.268
consideration, 22.78–22.85,
  22.232–22.248
consultancy services, 20.36
counterfeit money, 22.101
Court decisions, status, 22.39–22.42
Court of Justice, 22.1–22.7
credit, 22.352–22.363
credit notes, 22.460
deductions, 22.397–22.459
derogations, 22.229, 22.496–22.504
Directives, 20, 22.12–22.38
EC Treaty, 22.1–22.11
economic activities, 22.109–22.119,
  36.554, 36.558
employment, 22.124
engineers' services, 22.176, 22.222, 22.315
exemptions, 22.270–22.396
  —aircraft, 22.393
  —buildings, 22.378
  —credit, 22.352–22.363
  —cultural services, 22.318, 22.319
  —dental technicians, 22.288, 22.289
  —education, 22.303, 22.304
  —entertainment services, 22.214,
    22.215, 62.523
  —exports, 22.387–22.396
  —human organs, 22.287
  —imports, 22.384–22.386
  —insurance, 22.324–22.327
  —medical care, 20.65, 22.273–22.285
  —private tuition, 22.306–22.308
fishing rights, 22.206
'fixed establishment', 22.198, 22.199,
  22.492
gas and electricity, 22.269
Gibraltar, 22.564
holiday accommodation, 22.207
illegal supplies of goods, 22.81, 22.82,
  22.99, 22.100
imports, 22.99–22.102, 22.191, 22.192,
  22.384–22.386
input tax, 22.397–22.459
insurance, 22.324–22.327
interim payments, 22.476

EUROPEAN COMMUNITY LAW, – *cont.*

investment company, 22.111
invoices, 22.471–22.473
legal certainty, 22.548–22.551
legitimate expectation, 22.552, 22.554
'liberal professions', 22.509
partnerships, 22.90
place of supply, 22.193–22.228
  —goods, 22.193, 22.194
  —services, 22.198–22.228
public authorities, 22.127–22.150
rates of tax, 22.262–22.269
repayments of expenses, 22.255, 22.256,
  62.36
res judicata, 22.555
rounding, 22.562
second-hand goods, 22.494
services, definition of, 22.171, 22.172,
  22.174, 22.175
share issues, 22.91
special schemes, 22.479–22.495
sporting services, 22.313–22.315
subsidies, definition, 22.246–22.248
supply, definition of, 22.78–22.85
taxable amount, 22.232–22.261
taxable persons, 22.103–22.150
taxable transactions, 22.151–22.192
time limits, 22.43–22.57
timeshare accommodation, 22.208
tour operators, 22.485–22.487
transport services, 22.209–22.213,
  22.226–22.228
travel agents, 22.485–22.487
unjust enrichment, 22.559, 22.560
veterinary services, 22.205
water, 22.267
EUROPEAN COMMUNITY:
  SINGLE MARKET,
  cars, acquisition of, 23.23–23.26
  removal of goods, 23.33
  time limits, 23.30–23.32
Evidence,
  admissibility, 2.277–2.290, 34.7, 49.7
  hearsay, 2.277, 2.278
  public interest immunity, 2.282
EXEMPTIONS,
  betting, etc., 24.10–24.25
  —bingo, 24.10–24.12
  —card games, 24.14, 24.15
  —horse racing, 24.22
  —roulette, 24.21
  —shooting gallery, 24.16
  burial and cremation, 24.26–24.30
  cultural services, 16.1–16.14, 22.318,
    22.319

EXEMPTIONS, – *cont.*
  cultural services, 16.1–16.14, 22.318,
      22.319 – *cont.*
    —chapel, 16.6
    —cinema, 16.11
    —museum, 16.1
    —operatic company, 16.8
    —orchestra, 16.7
    —student union, 16.9
    —zoological society, 16.2, 16.4, 22.321
  EC law, 22.270–22.396
  education, 21.1–21.53
  elections to waive, 6.1–6.50
  finance, 27.1–27.63
  gold, 31.2
  health and welfare, 33.1–33.77
    —acupuncture, 33.17, 33.50
    —biochemical analysis, 33.28
    —chest X-ray service, 33.1
    —cosmetic treatments, 33.55, 33.56
    —domiciliary care, 33.15
    —haemodialysis, 33.47
    —hair removal, 33.55
    —hearing aids, 33.12, 33.53
    —imported goods, 33.77
    —nursing services, 33.4
    —opticians, 33.8–33.11, 33.25
    —transport services, 33.76
  insurance, 38.1–38.52
    —car, 38.1–38.6, 38.29, 38.51
  land, 41.1–41.163
  postal services, 24.1–24.9
  spiritual welfare, 22.294
  sport, etc, 24.31–24.52
    —bowling club, 24.34
    —golf club, 24.33, 24.41–24.49
    —pigeon racing, 24.50
    —rugby club, 24.31
    —shooting, 24.38
    —sports centre, 24.32
    —yacht club, 24.36, 24.40
  surrender of leases, 22.333, 41.63–41.69
  trade unions, etc, 64.1–64.36
EXPORTS,
  airports, goods supplied at, 25.36
  auction, goods sold at, 25.14
  'certificate of status', 25.31
  Notice No 703, 25.1–25.15
  'patterns', definition, 25.29
  retail exports, 25.16–25.26
  telephone cards, 25.34
  unlawful, 22.387–22.396
Extra-statutory concessions,
  application of, 2.89–2.94

Extra-statutory concessions, – *cont.*
  exported goods, 25.35
  refusal to backdate, 2.88

F

FARMING,
  flat-rate scheme, 26.1
FINANCE,
  bank notes, issue of, 27.4
  banking services, 27.25
  cash machines, restocking of, 27.2
  dealings with money, 27.1–27.9
  debt management services, 20.81,
      27.30–27.33
  granting of credit, 27.10–27.14
  instalment credit, 27.15–27.17
  intermediary services, 27.18–27.45
  lease purchase, 27.15
  payment handling charges, 22.363
  personal equity plans, 22.360, 27.55
  securities,
    —arrangements for, 27.57
    —dealings with, 27.46–27.55
  shares, flotation of, 27.57
  transport of cash, 27.1
Fishing rights, 22.206
Fixtures, 15.221–15.260
  soundproofing material, 15.255
  ventilating system, 15.242, 15.243
  waste disposal units, 15.246
FLAT-RATE SCHEME,
  appropriate percentage, 28.12–28.16
  capital expenditure goods, 28.9
  first-year reduction, 28.11
  refusal of authorisation, 28.8
  relevant turnover, 28.1, 28.2
  retrospective application, 28.3–28.7
  termination of authorisation, 28.17, 28.18
  withdrawal from scheme, 28.19, 28.20
FOOD,
  animal feeding stuffs, 29.106–29.118
  beverages, 29.165–29.180
    —'Bio-Light', 29.166
    —carrot juice, 29.168
    —iced tea, 29.175
    —'Kosher' meals, 29.165
    —mulled wine, 29.174
    —'Norfolk Punch', 29.177
    —'Rivella', 29.178
    —soya milk, 29.180
    —sports drinks, 29.173
    —tomato juice, 29.168

FOOD, – *cont.*

beverages, 29.165–29.180 – *cont.*

—wheatgrass juice, 29.172

catering, 29.1–29.80

—hot food, 29.55–29.80

—'premises',, 29.20–29.54

—sandwiches, 29.7, 29.8, 29.14, 29.17, 29.27–29.30, 29.60

—supplied on aircraft, 66.13

—supplied on train, 29.19, 66.26

confectionery, etc., 29.128–29.164

—cereal bars, 29.153–29.156

—diet bars, 29.132

—'energy bars', 29.138, 29.157–29.159

—hazelnut wafers, 29.137

—Horlicks tablets, 29.136

—'Jaffa Cakes', 29.135

—Lucozade tablets, 29.136

—popcorn, whether, 29.144, 29.145

ice cream, 29.125–29.127

live animals, 29.120–29.124

pet food, 29.187–29.196

potato crisps, etc., 29.181–29.186

Footballers' agents, 36.138, 36.139

Fraud,

'carousel', 22.115, 36.77–36.122, 49.13

detention of suspects, 34.29

FUEL AND POWER,

charcoal, supplies of, 30.8

electricity, 30.5–30.7, 30.12, 30.13

gas cylinders, 30.1

Furniture,

definition, 15.221–15.233

G

Gaming, 24.10–24.25

machines, 24.18–24.20

services, place of supply, 22.215

Garages,

conversion of, 15.146

construction of, 15.218

letting of, 7.22, 7.23

Gas cookers, 15.236, 15.237

Gas cylinders, supplies of, 30.1

Gibraltar,

companies, 22.71

status, 22.564

Gifts,

donations, 62.119–62.122

long service awards, 62.8–62.10

Going concern, transfer of, 40.30, 65.1–65.30

penalties, 51.128–51.131, 52.269–52.271, 52.332, 52.363

GOLD,

nine-carat, 31.1

whether supplies exempt, 31.2

Golf clubs,

subscriptions, 13.23, 13.24

trust established by, 13.6

Goods,

distinguished from services, 22.171

place of supply, 22.193, 22.194

private use of, 22.179–22.183, 22.456

valuation, 67.11–67.87

Gross takings, 58.36–58.46

GROUPS OF COMPANIES,

appeals, 32.9

avoidance schemes, 32.17–32.20

bad debt relief claims, 4.19, 4.20

'degrouping', 32.14

liability of members, 32.10, 32.11

management services, 43.1–43.8, 43.16–43.18, 43.20

overseas companies, 62.505

partial exemption, 32.31, 32.32

prescribed accounting period, 52.1

registration, 32.1–32.15

—whether retrospective, 32.4–32.7

supplies within, 32.22

H

Handicapped persons,

care, provided for, 11.21–11.23

equipment, etc. for,

—airbath, 19.10

—aircraft, 19.33

—beds, adjustable, 19.14, 19.15

—chairs, ergonomic, 19.37, 19.66

—computer system, 19.32

—'domestic use', 19.9

—electric generators, 19.71, 19.72

—fire escape, 19.63

—golf buggies, 19.59, 19.60, 19.74

—hydrotherapy pool, 19.35, 19.36

—incontinence pads, 19.68

—kitchens, 19.42, 19.43

—mattress, 19.27, 19.28

—motor caravan, 19.21–19.23

—overbed tables, 19.39

—parts and accessories, 19.70–19.73

—prostheses, 19.12

Handicapped persons, – *cont.*
  equipment, etc. for, – *cont.*
    —writing board, 19.51
Hardship applications, 2.136–2.147
HEALTH AND WELFARE,
  dental services, 33.32–33.38
  imported goods, 33.77
  registered practitioners, 33.1–33.31
    —acupuncture, 33.17
    —biochemical analysis, 33.28
    —chest X-ray service, 33.1
    —diet clinic, 33.14
    —domiciliary care, 33.15
    —nursing services, 33.4
    —optician, 33.25
    —psychologist, 33.24
  transport services, 33.76
  welfare services, supplies of, 33.62–33.75
    —cancer patients, 33.70
    —childcare services, 33.74
    —home help, 33.64
    —nursery services, 33.62, 33.75
    —religious camps, 33.69
    —Retreat House, 33.68
    —services for elderly, 33.64, 33.65
Hire,
  aircraft, 7.48, 7.49
  boats, 7.29–7.45
  cars, provision of insurance, 38.1, 38.2
Hire purchase agreement, novation, 36.165, 36.166
HMRC,
  best judgment, 3.1–3.39
  Business Briefs, status, 48.7
  costs, application for, 2.350–2.374
Holding company,
  partial exemption, 46.153
  whether taxable person, 22.106
Holiday accommodation, 22.207, 41.116–41.127
Holidays,
  cruises, whether zero-rated, 66.20
  whether excuse for late return,
    —accountant, 18.233
    —appellant, 18.486, 18.487
    —bookkeeper, 18.227
    —Christmas, 18.237
    —director, 18.218
    —Easter, 18.238
    —employees, 18.235
    —office manager, 18.230
    —partner, 18.206
    —secretary, 18.220
    —treasurer, 18.221

Horse racing, 7.57–7.77, 36.341–36.384
  betting, whether exempt, 24.22
Hospitals,
  definition, 15.73–15.76, 15.81
  provision of care, 33.39–33.60
Hotel accommodation,
  by whom supplied, 1.29
  cancellation charges, 62.93
  enlargement of, 36.295
  to whom supplied, 36.14–36.17
  whether exempt, 41.96–41.115
    —guest house, 41.105
    —serviced flats, 41.103
Houseboats, 15.30–15.32, 36.272, 69.12, 69.13
HUMAN RIGHTS,
  admissibility of evidence, 34.7
  appeal procedure, 34.16
  disallowance of input tax, 34.27, 34.28
  fraud investigation, 34.29, 34.30
  penalties, 34.1–34.11
  retrospective legislation, 34.23
  surcharges, 34.12, 34.13

I

Illegal supplies,
  goods, 22.82, 22.99, 22.100, 49.12
  services, 62.279
IMPORTS,
  Community law, 22.99–22.102, 22.191, 22.192, 22.384–22.386
  contact lenses, 35.24
  simplified accounting, 35.26–35.28
  tax not paid by agent, 35.9, 35.10, 52.161, 52.162
  tax repaid in error, 35.8
  valuation, 35.20, 35.21
INPUT TAX,
  advance payments, 36.620–36.636
  apportionment, 8.28–8.34, 11.39–11.59, 36.42, 36.198–36.200, 36.246–36.257, 36.273, 36.283–36.298, 36.307, 36.420–36.423, 36.475, 36.476, 36.518–36.529, 36.567, 46.51, 48.134
  assignment of claim, 36.681
  attribution to taxable supplies, 46.2–46.101
    —bank, 22.400, 46.7
    —building society, 46.72, 46.76, 46.77
    —capital goods, 46.97, 46.98

INPUT TAX, – *cont.*
attribution to taxable supplies,
46.2–46.101 – *cont.*
—charity, 46.51, 46.78
—credit note, 40.117
—incidental supplies, 46.99–46.101
—insurance broker, 46.82
—mobile home park, 46.24, 46.25
—nursing home, 46.59
—opticians, 46.32
—tourist board, 46.8
business entertainment, 8.1–8.48
carousel fraud, 22.115, 36.77–36.122,
49.13
damages payment, 36.637, 36.638
disallowance where consideration unpaid,
36.672, 36.673
disputed repayment claims, 36.648–36.661
hire purchase agreements, novation,
36.165, 36.166
invoices destroyed, 40.62, 40.63, 40.79
invoices lost, 40.64–40.66
late claims, 48.3–48.8
legal costs, 36.40–36.65, 36.193–36.242
mileage allowances, 36.6–36.10
motor racing, 36.171, 36.410–36.429
motor rallying, 36.430–36.433
motoring expenses, 36.1–36.13,
36.173–36.183
—car accessories, 36.176
—petrol, 36.1–36.5
—repairs, 36.177, 36.178
non-business, 46.1
pension funds, 54.1–54.10
post-cessation, 36.643–36.647
pre-registration, 36.589–36.619, 52.128
—building services, 36.612
—computer services, 36.606
—hairdressing salon, 36.593
—shopfitting, 36.590–36.592
—solicitors' fees, 36.608, 36.609
—stock, 36.589
right to deduct, 22.397–22.459
self-billing, 40.56–40.60
self-supplies, attribution, 46.182
telecommunications licences, 22.118,
22.119
transfer of business, 52.332, 52.363,
65.1–65.30
unregistered claimant, 2.58–2.61
whether supplies made to appellant,
36.1–36.168
—estate agency, 36.130
—footballers' agents, 36.138, 36.139
—leasing, 36.30–36.39

INPUT TAX, – *cont.*
whether supplies made to appellant,
36.1–36.168 – *cont.*
—legal costs, 36.40–36.65
—sham invoices, 36.123
whether supplies used for purposes of
business, 36.173–36.553
—aircraft, 36.463–36.467
—boats, 36.537, 36.538
—broadcasting, 36.528
—car accessories, 36.176
—cars, 44.106–44.138
—cathedral officers, 36.320, 36.552
—clothing, 36.184–36.192
—conservatory, 36.297
—demolition work, 36.513
—double glazing, 36.330
—equestrian centre, 36.392
—farmhouse, 36.273, 36.283,
36.287–36.290, 36.304, 36.305,
36.333, 36.334
—furniture, 36.329, 36.495, 36.546
—grocers' premises, 36.184, 36.293
—horse riding, 36.390
—hunting, 36.393, 36.394
—lunch, 36.536
—motorboat, 36.561, 36.582
—pilot's licence, 36.516
—subpostmasters, 36.501–36.503
—tennis court, 52.350
—watches, 36.527
—wig, purchase of, 36.192
—yachting, 36.441–36.462, 36.562,
36.583–36.585
INSOLVENCY,
corporate, 37.1–37.20
Crown debts, set-off of, 37.16, 37.17
group registration, 37.19
personal, 37.21–37.35
provisional liquidator, 37.5, 37.6
receivership, 37.10, 37.11, 14.101, 14.102,
36.675
statutory demands, 37.22, 37.27, 47.69,
47.70
winding-up order, 37.1–37.4
INSURANCE,
cars, 38.1–38.6, 38.29, 38.51
intermediary services, 38.13–38.33
provision of, 38.1–38.12
Interest,
award of, 2.512–2.533
compounding, 2.517–2.520
default interest, 17.1–17.21
official error, 48.114–48.147
—estimated assessment, 48.123, 48.124

Interest, – *cont.*
  rates of, 2.531, 2.532
Interest-free loan, 62.189
Intermediary services, 62.516–62.518
INTERNATIONAL SERVICES,
  advertising services, 36.3, 62.497, 62.514,
    62.526
  consultancy services, 20.36, 39.7, 39.8,
    62.499, 62.500, 62.506, 62.533
  diplomatic services, 39.2
  financial services, 62.538, 62.539
  intermediary services, 62.516–62.518
  mare at stud farm, 39.1
  reverse charge, 39.4–39.19
  staff, supplies of, 22.225, 62.541
  telecommunications, 62.546, 62.547,
    67.172
  transport, definition, 62.543
  zero-rating, 39.1–39.3
Internet sales, 62.464
INVOICES AND CREDIT NOTES,
  associated companies, 40.48
  authenticity disputed, 40.12–40.14, 40.40,
    40.41, 52.364
  calculation of VAT, 40.82–40.84
  cancellation of, 52.116
  destroyed accidentally, 40.62, 40.63, 40.79
  false VAT number, 40.27–40.29
  faulty goods, 40.55
  incomplete, 22.471
  lost, 40.64–40.66
  not issued by supplier, 40.80
  'proforma', 40.44
  requirements, 22.471–22.473
  rounding of, 40.82–40.84
  self-billing, 40.56–40.60
  'shams', 36.123, 62.174
  time of issue, 62.411–62.416
  unauthorised issue, 51.139–51.145

J

Jersey company, avoidance scheme, 35.24
Joint ventures, 47.54–47.57
Journals, 5.93–5.108
Judicial review,
  applications for, 2.328–2.349
  legal costs, 36.203

K

Kitchen,
  alterations, 19.42, 19.43
  fitted, whether zero-rated, 19.26
  units, not zero-rated, 15.253

L

LAND,
  caravan facilities, 41.128–41.135
    —seasonal pitches, 41.130
  holiday accommodation, 41.116–41.127
    —beach huts, 41.126
    —furnished flats, 41.116, 41.117,
      46.205
  hotel accommodation, 41.96–41.115
    —Buddhist centre, in, 41.99
    —guest house, 41.105
    —serviced flats, 41.103
  licence to occupy, whether, 41.1–41.95
    —antique fair, 41.45
    —concert halls, 41.43
    —harbour tolls, 41.31
    —kennels, 41.42
    —market sites, 41.4, 41.5
    —massage salon, 41.95
    —office facilities, 41.46, 41.47
    —stables, 41.15
    —vehicle workshop, 41.14
  mooring facilities, 41.149–41.152
  options to tax, 6.1–6.50
  parking facilities, 41.136–41.148
  services relating to, 62.510–62.515
  sports facilities, 41.153–41.162
    —dancing, 41.162
    —football, 41.155, 41.156
    —golf, 41.158, 41.159
    —gymnastics, 41.161
    —hockey, 41.160
    —rugby, 41.153
Land Rover, whether a car, 44.1, 44.2, 44.43,
  44.45, 44.46
Late appeals, 2.172–2.197
Launderettes, 69.1
'Leaflet', definition, 5.54–5.92
  car stickers, whether, 5.72
  photographs, whether, 5.79
  story sheets, whether, 5.81

Leases,
  Community law, 22.332–22.348
  grant of, 15.149
  input tax, 36.30–36.39
  leaseback arrangements, 6.51, 22.116,
    62.160
  rectification of, 15.148
  sham, 41.39
  short-term, pending sale, 46.13, 46.14
  surrender of, 22.333, 41.63–41.69
  time-sharing, 15.149
Legal costs,
  input tax, 36.40–36.65, 36.193–36.242
LOCAL AUTHORITIES AND STATUTORY
  BODIES,
  adoption service, 42.5
  home improvement grants, 42.3
  mileage allowances, 42.23
  police authorities, 42.8, 42.9
  sports centres, 42.20
  statutory repair work, 42.6

M

MANAGEMENT SERVICES,
  place of supply, 62.513
  time of supply, 43.1–43.7
Massage parlours, 41.95, 62.274, 62.275,
    62.277, 67.95
Medicinal products, 11.30, 11.31
Mileage allowances, 36.6–36.10
  local authorities, 42.23
Misdeclaration and errors, civil penalties,
    52.1–52.458
  liability, 52.449
  mitigation, 52.392–52.448
  'period of grace', 52.458
  return, whether made, 52.2–52.4
  validity of penalty, 52.452–52.458
'Missing trader' fraud, 22.115, 36.77–36.122,
    49.13
Mitigation of penalties,
  evasion of tax, 50.67–50.154
  failure to notify, 51.146–51.185
  misdeclaration, 52.392–52.448
Mooring facilities, 41.149–41.152
MOTOR CARS,
  company cars, 62.1–62.7
  definition of, 44.1–44.52
  delivery charge, 44.98, 44.99
  insurance, 38.1–38.6, 38.29, 38.51
  margin scheme, 44.60–44.96, 44.168
  MOT certificates, 44.95, 44.96

MOTOR CARS, – cont.
  MOT test fees, 44.162–44.164
  parking facilities, 41.136–41.148
  place of supply, 62.478
  restoration costs, 44.78, 44.79
  road fund licences, 44.91–44.94
  self-supplies, 44.55–44.59
  taxicab licences, 44.88–44.90
  taxis, 62.232–62.254
  used cars, definition, 44.66, 44.67
  valuation, 44.83–44.87, 44.154–44.156
Museum,
  definition, 16.10
  whether exempt, 16.1
Music, definition, 5.109
Music tuition, whether exempt, 21.2
Musicians, registration, 1.53, 51.29

N

Newspapers,
  definition, 5.93–5.108
  delivery charges for, 58.2–58.5
Nominees, issue of shares to, 36.678
Notice of Appeal, 2.62–2.66
Notice of Assessment, 3.61–3.70, 47.1–47.8

O

Official error, 48.114–48.147
'Open-ended investment companies', 22.107
Opticians,
  attribution of input tax, 46.32
  liability of supplies, 33.8–33.10, 33.25
  repayment claims, 48.19–48.22, 48.127
  valuation of supplies, 48.19–48.22,
    48.127, 67.82–67.85
'Option to tax', 6.1–6.50
  attribution of input tax, 6.44
  building leased to charity, 6.5
  date from which effective, 6.18–6.41
  refusal of permission, 6.48
  whether ineffective, 6.1–6.11
  whether irrevocable, 6.24–6.30
  whether made, 6.24–6.41
Outsourced services, 22.374
OVERSEAS TRADERS,
  place of supply of goods, 22.193
  repayment claims, 45.1–45.8

P

Parking facilities, 41.136–41.148
PARTIAL EXEMPTION,
  adjustments, 46.194–46.220
  attribution to taxable supplies,
    46.2–46.101
    —bank, 22.400, 46.7
    —building society, 46.72, 46.76, 46.77
    —capital goods, 46.97, 46.98
    —charity, 46.51, 46.78
    —credit note, 40.117
    —incidental supplies, 46.99–46.101
    —insurance broker, 46.82
    —motor rally, 46.73
    —nursing home, 46.59
    —opticians, 46.32
    —premises, 46.46–46.71
  de minimis limits, 46.183–46.193
  foreign supplies, 46.173–46.181
  non-business input tax, 46.1
  self-supplies, 46.182
  special methods, 46.102–46.172
    —bank, 46.158–46.160, 46.181
    —holding company, 46.153
    —override, 46.131–46.133
    —residual input tax, 46.145, 46.146
    —statutory body, 46.156
    —'stock-lending', 46.167
    —termination, 46.115–46.127
    —universities and colleges,
      46.145–46.152
PARTNERSHIP,
  appeals, 47.12
  assessments, 47.1–47.11
  associated, 47.65–47.68
  bankruptcy of partner, 47.69
  change in members of, 22.90, 47.6
  fact of, 47.17–47.64, 51.30, 51.62–51.64
  joint ventures, 47.54–47.57
  penalty assessments, 50.7–50.11, 50.99
  registration, 47.15, 47.16, 57.1–57.5
  statutory demand, validity, 47.70
Passenger transport, 66.12–66.39
  'Big Dipper', 66.34
  cabinlifts, 66.30, 66.31
  cable cars, 66.32
  cruises, 66.20
  funicular railway, 66.27
  miners' cage, 66.37
  narrowboats, 66.18
  railway, 66.16
  travelator, 66.33
PAYMENT OF TAX,
  BACS, by, 18.67

PAYMENT OF TAX, – cont.
  overpayments, 48.1–48.81
  repayment supplement, 48.82–48.113,
    59.10
    —excessive claim, 48.84
  set-off, by Commissioners, 36.657, 36.676,
    48.152, 48.153
  unjust enrichment, 48.28–48.49
Payroll services, 62.486
PENALTIES: CRIMINAL OFFENCES,
  cheating the public revenue, 49.25–49.29
  common law offences, 49.25–49.32
  confiscation orders, 49.19–49.24
  conspiracy to cheat public revenue, 49.30
  'missing trader fraud', 49.13
  offences under POCA 2002, 49.18–49.24
  offences under VATA 1994, 49.1–49.17
PENALTIES: EVASION OF TAX,
  appeal successful, 50.131–50.154
  appeal unsuccessful, 50.67–50.92
  assessment of penalty, 50.3–50.12
  computation of penalty, 50.1
  directors, liability of, 50.13–50.66
  mitigation, 50.67–50.154
  notification of penalty, 50.5, 50.6
  partners, liability, 50.99
  penalty increased, 50.44, 50.93, 50.94
  penalty reduced, 50.95–50.130
PENALTIES: FAILURE TO NOTIFY,
  mitigation, 51.146–51.185
  reasonable excuse, whether, 51.13–51.138
    —bankruptcy, 51.137
    —deafness, 51.115
    —death of partner, 51.17
    —dyslexia, 51.132, 51.133
    —illiteracy, 51.66
    —illness of director, 51.15
    —illness of wife, 51.13, 51.14
    —injury to partner, 51.18
    —miscarriage, 51.19
    —overwork, 51.124, 51.125
    —reliance on wife, 51.99
    —school tuck shop, 51.39
    —timber, sales of, 51.40
    —wife giving birth, 51.136
  relevant VAT, 51.1–51.4
  unauthorised invoices, 51.139–51.145
PENALTIES: MISDECLARATION AND
  ERRORS,
  liability, 52.449
  mitigation, 52.392–52.448
  'period of grace', 52.458
  reasonable excuse, whether, 52.31–52.376
    —blind appellant, 52.37

PENALTIES: MISDECLARATION AND ER-
RORS, – *cont.*
reasonable excuse, whether, 52.31–52.376
– *cont.*
—deposits, 52.110, 52.111,
52.142–52.145
—illness of appellant, 52.38
—illness of director, 52.73
—illness of father, 52.47
—illness of partner, 52.10
—imprisonment, 52.70
—isolated error, 52.51
—overwork, 52.48, 52.49
—partner, error by, 52.74
—stolen takings, 52.272
—tennis court, 52.350
return, whether made, 52.2–52.4
validity of penalty, 52.452–52.458
PENALTIES: SALES STATEMENTS AND
REGULATORY PROVISIONS,
failure to produce records, 53.18–53.22
failure to submit EC sales statement,
53.1–53.17
PENSION FUNDS,
associated companies, 54.7
employer acting as trustee, 54.1
established by statute, 54.6
input tax, 54.1–54.10
output tax, 54.11, 54.12
transfer of funds, 54.10
Personal equity plans, 22.360, 27.55
Pet food, 29.187–29.196
bird food, whether, 29.196
dog food, whether, 29.187, 29.191, 29.192
minced chicken, whether, 29.190
Photobooks, 5.24
Photograph albums, 5.29
Photographs, school, 67.27–67.29, 67.53,
67.54
Place of supply, 22.193–22.228,
36.665–36.670, 62.476–62.547
goods, 22.193, 22.194, 36.665–36.670,
62.476–62.479
services, 22.198–22.228, 62.480–62.547
Playgroup, membership fees, 12.26
Postal services, 24.1–24.9
Potato crisps, etc., definition, 29.181–29.186
Premises,
definition of, 29.20–29.54
entry and search of, 14.93–14.96
subletting, 41.3

Profession, definition, 64.1, 64.14, 64.27
Professional bodies, 64.1, 64.2
'Prompt payment' discounts, 67.88
Proof, onus of, 2.234–2.237
'Proportionality', 18.616–18.621, 52.452,
52.453
Prostitution, 62.277, 62.279, 62.280
PROTECTED BUILDINGS,
approved alterations, 55.27–55.82
car park, in grounds of, 55.79
change of use, 55.1
definition, 55.1–55.18
drainage system, new, 55.46
gutter, replacement of, 55.30, 55.31
internal alterations, 55.69
kitchen, installation in, 55.87
lighting, installation of, 55.35, 55.45
listed building consent,
—not obtained, 55.52, 55.56, 55.81,
55.82
—retrospective, 55.80
painting, 55.67
railings, erection of, 55.47
rebuilding of walls, 55.43, 55.52, 55.54
removal of asbestos, 55.66
replacement of roof, 55.27–55.29,
55.40–55.43, 55.56–55.61
septic tank, installation, 55.44
strengthening of walls, 55.55
swimming pool, 55.39, 55.78
Public authorities, 22.127–22.150
Public interest bodies, 64.9–64.11

R

Reasonable excuse,
default surcharge, 18.70–18.613
—BACS payment, 18.542
—burglary, 18.340, 18.341, 18.550,
18.551
—business travel, 18.164,
18.202–18.205, 18.213–18.216,
18.478, 18.482–18.485
—cheque unsigned, 18.422
—death of brother, 18.102
—death of wife, 18.89
—depression, 18.121, 18.122
—director bankrupt, 18.364
—director in Court, 18.211

Reasonable excuse, – *cont.*
  default surcharge, 18.70–18.613 – *cont.*
    —director in prison, 18.174
    —divorce, 18.381, 18.489, 18.490,
      18.495, 18.496
    —dyslexia, 18.582, 18.583
    —Easter holiday, 18.238
    —fire, 18.338, 18.339, 18.552, 18.553,
      18.578, 18.579
    —flood, 18.348, 18.555, 18.580
    —holiday, 18.486, 18.487
    —honeymoon, 18.207, 18.208, 18.488
    —illness of cashier, 18.111, 18.112
    —illness of mother, 18.96
    —illness of partner, 18.95,
      18.124–18.126
    —illness of wife, 18.88, 18.99, 18.130
    —imprisonment, 18.174, 18.212,
      18.477, 18.480, 18.481
    —industrial action, 18.230, 18.255,
      18.256, 18.334, 18.335, 18.564,
      18.570, 18.571
    —labour costs, 18.368
    —loss of employee, 18.380
    —loss of manager, 18.193, 18.194
    —overwork, 18.563
    —reliance on wife, 18.599, 18.600
    —robbery, 18.581
    —staff holidays, 18.235
    —staff shortages, 18.201, 18.234
    —theft of computer, 18.76, 18.77
  failure to register, 51.13–51.138
    —bankruptcy, 51.137
    —deafness, 51.115
    —death of partner, 51.17
    —dyslexia, 51.132, 51.133
    —illiteracy, 51.66
    —illness of director, 51.15
    —illness of wife, 51.13, 51.14
    —miscarriage, 51.19
    —overwork, 51.124, 51.125
    —school tuck shop, 51.39
    —timber, sales of, 51.40
  misdeclaration, 52.31–52.376
    —blind appellant, 52.37
    —deposits, 52.110, 52.111,
      52.142–52.145
    —illness of director, 52.73
    —illness of partner, 52.10
    —imprisonment, 52.70
    —isolated error, 52.51
    —overwork, 52.48, 52.49
    —partner, error by, 52.74
    —stolen takings, 52.272
    —tennis court, 52.350

Receivership, 37.10, 37.11, 14.101, 14.102,
  36.675
Reconstruction,
  definition, 15.12, 15.13, 15.158
  whether substantial, 55.19–55.26
REDUCED-RATE SUPPLIES,
  children's car seats, 56.2
  energy-saving materials, 56.1
  fuel and power, 30.1–30.13
  residential conversions, 56.3–56.7
  residential renovations and alterations,
    56.8–56.10
REGISTRATION,
  appealable matters, 59.1–59.3
  associated persons, 57.35–57.81
    —accountancy, 57.39, 57.40
    —car hire, 57.54
    —cohabitees, 57.49, 57.61
    —computer supplies, 57.60
    —fencing contractors, 57.69
    —fish and chip shop, 57.43
    —hairdressers, 57.44, 57.70–57.72
    —health studio, 57.45, 57.46
    —ice-cream vendors, 57.55
    —jewellers, 57.78
    —launderettes, 57.35, 57.36
    —market traders, 57.61
  cancellation, 57.120–57.166
  conditional, 36.558
  future turnover, 57.12–57.16
  group, 32.1–32.15
  'intending traders', 36.558, 57.101–57.106
  number, change of, 57.221
  partnerships, 57.1–57.5
  period of returns, 59.1
  voluntary, 57.113–57.115
Repayment,
  assignment of claim, 36.681
  'certificate of status', 25.31
  errors in return, 48.109
  provisional claims, 48.19–48.22
  retrospective, whether, 22.558
  time limit for claims, 23.30–23.32, 25.32,
    48.50–48.75
Repayment supplement, 48.82–48.113, 59.10
  excessive claim, 48.84
  whether claim withdrawn, 48.113
  whether return made, 59.10
Repossession of goods, 36.675, 60.20, 67.71
Res judicata, 2.71, 2.125–2.127, 22.555
Residual input tax, 46.145, 46.146
Retail export schemes, 25.16–25.26
RETAILERS' SPECIAL SCHEMES,
  apportionment schemes, 58.53, 58.54

RETAILERS' SPECIAL SCHEMES, – *cont.*
  credit card sales, 32.28
  direct calculation schemes, 58.30–58.34, 58.55–58.59
  expected selling prices, 58.48, 58.49
  gross takings, 58.36–58.46
  Point of Sale schemes, 58.50–58.52
  Scheme A, 58.44
  Scheme B, 58.57, 58.58
  Scheme B1, 58.59
  transitional matters, 58.25–58.35
RETURNS,
  accounting periods, 59.1–59.7
  date of posting disputed, 18.49
  extended period, validity of, 57.89
  form not available, 18.465–18.476
  making of, 59.8–59.22
  period of, 59.1–59.3
  whether made, 52.2–52.4
  whether withdrawn, 59.36
Reverse premiums, 62.125–62.133
Rounding of VAT, 22.562
Royalties, 62.472

S

Sale, conditional, 62.87–62.94
Sales of assets, 62.72–62.86, 65.76–65.80
Sales promotion schemes, 22.153, 22.154, 62.172, 62.363, 67.153–67.158
Satellite TV, place of supply, 62.490
School,
  meals, whether zero-rated, 29.70
  photographs, 62.368, 67.27–67.29, 67.53, 67.54
  unregistered, not exempt, 21.4
Search warrants, 14.97–14.99
SECOND-HAND GOODS,
  art, works of, 60.7–60.15
  boats, 60.18
  EC law, 22.494
  motorcars, 44.60–44.96
  repossessed, 60.20
Security, requirement, 14.1–14.68
Self-billing, 40.56–40.60, 62.559–62.563
SELF-SUPPLY,
  advertising posters, 11.24
  assets used privately, 62.101, 62.102

SELF-SUPPLY, – *cont.*
  attribution of input tax on, 46.182
  chequebooks, 61.3
  motor cars, 44.55–44.59
  printed stationery, 61.1
Service charges, 67.107, 67.108, 67.128, 67.129
Services,
  definition, 22.171, 22.172, 22.174, 22.175
  place of supply, 22.198–22.228
  valuation, 67.88–67.150
Set-offs, Crown debts, 37.16, 37.17
Sexual services, 62.277, 62.279, 62.280
Shams,
  invoices, 36.123, 62.174
  leases, 41.39
Share issues, 22.91
Ships,
  handling services, 66.43
  lifeboats, 20.98
  qualifying, 66.1–66.11
Site, definition of, 15.18, 15.150, 15.151
Special Schemes for Retailers,
  apportionment schemes, 58.53, 58.54
  credit card sales, 32.28
  direct calculation schemes, 58.30–58.34, 58.55–58.59
  expected selling prices, 58.48, 58.49
  gross takings, 58.36–58.46
  Point of Sale schemes, 58.50–58.52
  retrospective changes, 58.13–58.24
  Scheme A, 58.44
  Scheme B, 58.57, 58.58
  Scheme B1, 58.59
  transitional matters, 58.25–58.35
Sporting services, 22.313–22.315, 62.521, 62.522, 62.527
Sports clubs,
  bowling club, 24.34
  golf club, 24.33, 24.41–24.49
  rugby club, 13.8, 24.31, 41.153, 46.69, 62.122
  yacht club, 24.36, 24.40
Sports facilities, 24.32, 41.156–41.162
  dancing, 41.162
  football, 41.156
  golf, 41.158, 41.159
  gymnastics, 41.161
  hockey, 41.160

Sports grounds, 41.153–41.155
Statements of case, 2.150–2.171
   amendment of, 2.162, 2.163
   content of, 2.167
Statutory bodies, 7.2, 7.79, 7.80, 22.80
Statutory demands, 37.22, 37.27, 47.69,
   47.70
Stock, valuation of, 67.68
Stolen takings, 62.382–62.385
Subpostmasters, input tax, 36.501–36.503
Subscriptions,
   clubs, 13.17–13.28
   discount cards, 58.8
   time of supply, 62.418–62.420
Subsidies, definition, 22.246–22.248
Subsistence allowance, 36.311, 36.312
SUPPLY,
   accommodation, 62.284–62.291,
      62.396–62.398, 67.90–67.93
   advance payments, 62.417–62.439
   advertising services, 22.218,
      62.495–62.497, 62.514, 62.526,
      62.527
   appeal by recipient of, 2.52–2.61
   assets, sales of, 62.72–62.86, 65.76–65.80
   bankrupt, supplies by, 37.30
   by whom made, 62.223–62.381
   carousel fraud, 22.115, 36.77–36.122,
      49.13
   carpet fitting, 62.336, 62.337
   cartage, 62.211
   catering, 62.292–62.312
   cheque, payment by, 62.426, 62.427
   commodities, imported, 67.52
   consideration,
      —amount, 67.11–67.150
      —apportionable, 62.548–62.556
      —barter transactions, 67.146
      —deferred, 62.407, 67.139
      —'salary sacrifice', 62.5
      —'value-shifting', 67.70
   consultancy services, 20.36, 62.58, 62.59,
      62.499, 62.500, 62.506, 62.533
   co-operative dividends, 22.252
   counterfeit goods, 22.82
   credit notes, 40.85–40.119
   currency transactions, 62.195
   dance tuition, 62.347
   dancers, 62.282, 62.283
   definition of, 22.78–22.85
   deposits, 62.171, 62.440–62.453
      —coin dealers, 62.387
      —furniture, 62.447, 62.448
      —hotel, 62.451
      —manufacturers, 62.446

SUPPLY, – cont.
   deposits, 62.171, 62.440–62.453 – cont.
      —shopfitters, 62.445
   donations, 62.119–62.122
      —Masonic, 62.119, 62.120
      —sponsorship, 62.121, 62.122
   'door-to-door' selling, 62.362, 67.34
   driving schools, 62.223–62.231
   employees' services, 62.19–62.51
   entertainment services, 62.523, 62.524
   escort agency, 62.278–62.280
   estate agency, 62.399–62.401
   examination fees, 62.212, 62.367
   expenses, reimbursed, 62.52–62.71
      —chauffeur, 62.62
      —consultant, 62.58, 62.59
      —director, 62.64
      —estate agents, 62.57
      —solicitor, 62.52, 62.53
      —subcontractor, 62.66
      —surveyor, 62.55, 62.56
   financial services, 62.538, 62.539
   foreign exchange transactions, 62.195,
      62.196
   franchise agreement, 33.29, 57.187,
      57.188, 57.203, 62.358
   gaming machines, 67.134
   goods, of, 62.167–62.183
   horse boxes, 62.75
   hotel accommodation, 62.93
   illegal,
      —goods, 22.82, 22.99, 22.100, 49.12
      —services, 62.279
   interest-free loan, 62.189
   intermediary services, 62.516–62.518
   jewellery, sale of, 62.76, 67.59–67.61
   leaseback arrangement, 62.160
   lingerie, sales of, 67.31
   liquidation, 62.190–62.191
   mail order business, 22.234, 67.33, 67.42
   massage parlour, 62.274, 62.275, 62.277
   nightclub hostesses, 62.281
   nursing services, 33.2–33.4
   office-holders, 62.163–62.166
   parking charges, 62.202, 62.203
   'party plan' sales, 67.37–67.40
   place of, 22.193–22.228, 36.665–36.670,
      62.476–62.547
      —goods, 22.193, 22.194,
         36.665–36.670, 62.476–62.479
      —services, 22.198–22.228,
         62.480–62.547
   private use of assets, 62.101, 62.102
   prostitution, 62.279, 62.280
   radios, sales of, 62.366

SUPPLY, – *cont.*
repairs, valuation of, 67.126, 67.127
royalty agreement, 62.472
salary sacrifice, 62.5
sales of assets, 62.72–62.86, 65.76–65.80
—horse boxes, 62.75
—lorry, 62.73, 62.74
—paintings, 62.85, 62.156
—vans, 62.72
sales promotion schemes, 22.154, 62.172, 62.363, 67.153–67.158
school photographs, 62.368, 67.27–67.29, 67.53, 67.54
secondment of employees, 62.19, 62.20, 62.23–62.38
services,
—definition, 22.171, 22.172, 22.174, 22.175, 62.184–62.222
—valuation, 67.88–67.150
sexual services, 62.277, 62.279, 62.280
sham invoices, 36.123, 62.174
shooting rights, 7.114, 62.151
solicitor's services, 62.360
sponsorship payments, 67.103–67.105
sporting services, 22.313–22.315, 62.521, 62.522, 62.527
staff, 62.541
stakeholder, payment to, 62.421
stationery, 61.1
stock valuation, 67.68
stolen goods, 62.168, 62.169
stolen takings, 62.382–62.385
taxi drivers, 62.232–62.254
telephone in public house, 62.192
theft of cash, 62.382–62.385
time of, 62.382–62.475
—barristers, 62.474
—deposits, 62.440–62.453
—goods, 62.382–62.395
—internet sales, 62.464
—mail order sales, 62.393, 62.462
—royalties, 62.472
—services, 62.396–62.410
—theatre bookings, 62.434
—vending machines, 62.386
tips, 67.106
to whom made, 36.1–36.168
transfers of assets, 62.95–62.118
Tupperware distributors, 67.32
valuation, 67.11–67.150
—barter transactions, 67.146
—deemed supply, 67.11–67.26
—deferred consideration, 67.139
vending machines, 62.386

SUPPLY, – *cont.*
vouchers, etc., 62.100, 62.184, 67.151–67.175
Surcharge liability notice,
appeal against, 2.43–2.45
receipt disputed, 18.1–18.3
validity of, 18.7–18.16
whether withdrawn, 18.4–18.6

T

Takings,
definition, 58.41
stolen, 58.42, 62.382–62.385
Tax avoidance,
Gibraltar companies, 22.71
groups of companies, 32.17–32.20
leaseback arrangements, 62.160
Tax evasion,
civil penalties, 50.13–50.154
criminal penalties, 49.1–49.24
Taxable person, definition, 22.103–22.106
Taxis,
drivers' association, 62.32
hired to driver, 62.232–62.234
licences, 44.88–44.90
tips received by driver, 67.106
Tea,
herbal, whether zero-rated, 29.84
iced, whether zero-rated, 29.175
Telecommunications services,
grant of licences, 22.118, 22.119
place of supply, 62.546, 62.547, 67.172
time of supply, 62.457
valuation of supply, 67.138
Theft of cash, 62.382–62.385
Time limits,
assessment, 3.40–3.110
EC law, 22.43–22.57
repayment claims, 23.30–23.32, 48.50–48.75
Time of supply, 62.382–62.475
accountancy services, 62.454, 62.455
advance payments, 62.417–62.439
barristers, 62.474
cheque, payment by, 62.426, 62.427
circular payments, 22.230, 62.423, 62.424
club subscriptions, 62.418–62.420
construction services, 62.475
continuous, 62.466–62.471
deferred consideration, 62.407
deposits, 62.440–62.453
estate agents, 62.399, 62.401

Time of supply, 62.382–62.475 – cont.
  goods, 62.382–62.395
  hotel accommodation, 62.93
  internet sales, 62.464
  invoices, issue of, 62.411–62.416
  mail order sales, 62.393, 62.462
  management services, 43.1–43.7
  royalties, 62.472
  services, 62.396–62.410
  stakeholder, payment to, 62.421
  theatre bookings, 62.434
  unredeemed vouchers, 62.458, 62.459
  vending machines, 62.386
  water, gas, etc., 62.465
Timeshare accommodation, 15.149, 22.208,
  41.118–41.123, 62.71, 62.417
Tips, 67.106
TOUR OPERATORS AND TRAVEL
  AGENTS,
  credit card charges, 63.17
  European law, 22.485–22.487
  limousine services, 63.7
  margin scheme, 63.9–63.25
  representative association, 64.8
TRADE UNIONS, PROFESSIONAL AND
  PUBLIC INTEREST BODIES,
  professional bodies, 64.1, 64.2
  public interest bodies, 64.9–64.11
  representative association, 64.8
TRANSFERS OF GOING CONCERNS,
  civil penalties, 51.128–51.131,
    52.269–52.271, 52.332, 52.363
  land and buildings, 65.86–65.89
  registration, 65.90–65.107
TRANSPORT,
  definition, 22.226–22.228, 62.543
  goods, transport of, 66.40
  handling services, 66.41–66.43
  passengers, 66.12–66.39
  —'Big Dipper', 66.34
  —cabinlifts, 66.30, 66.31
  —cable cars, 66.32
  —catering on aircraft, 66.13
  —catering on train, 66.26
  —cruises, 66.20
  —funicular railway, 66.27
  —miners' cage, 66.37
  —narrowboats, 66.18
  —railway, 66.16
  —travelator, 66.33
  place of supply, 22.209–22.213,
    22.226–22.228
  ships, qualifying, 66.1–66.11

Triangulation arrangements, 2.346
Tribunal,
  appeal, hearing of, 2.234–2.308
  decision, 2.309–2.314
  jurisdiction of, 2.1–2.51, 2.83–2.108
  rules, application of, 2.136–2.149

U

Universities and colleges,
  non-business input tax, 11.39–11.41
  partial exemption, 46.145–46.152
  research, 11.40, 11.41
  vacation lettings, 15.65, 15.66
Unjust enrichment, 22.559, 22.560,
  48.28–48.49

V

VALUATION,
  accommodation, 67.90–67.93
  agents, supplies to, 67.37–67.42
  cars, 44.83–44.87, 44.154–44.156
  cashback payments, 67.77, 67.147
  computer games, 67.72
  Co-Operative dividends, 22.252
  deemed supplies, 67.11–67.26
  deferred consideration, 67.139
  discounts, 67.88
  face value vouchers, 67.151–67.175
  gaming machines, 67.134
  goods, 67.11–67.87
  imported goods, 35.20, 35.21
  introduction agency, 67.119
  jewellery, 67.17, 67.59–67.61
  lingerie, 67.31
  mail order business, 22.234, 67.33, 67.42
  management services, 43.14
  multiple supplies, 67.114–67.120
  'prompt payment' discounts, 67.88
  repairs, 67.126, 67.127
  repossession of goods, 67.71
  school photographs, 67.27–67.29, 67.53,
    67.54
  service charges, 67.107, 67.108, 67.128,
    67.129
  services, 67.88–67.150
  shares, 10.12
  stock, 67.68
  telephone calls, 67.138
  telephones, 67.15

VALUATION, – *cont.*
  Tupperware, 67.32
  'value-shifting', 67.70
  vans, 67.65
  yacht, use of, 67.131
'Value-shifting', 67.70
Vans,
  second-hand, valuation, 67.65
  whether 'motor cars', 44.23, 44.24, 44.36,
    44.41, 44.42, 44.47
Ventilating system, 15.242, 15.243
Viagra, supplies of, 19.5
Videotapes,
  hire of, 67.137
  valuation of supply, 67.14
Vouchers, etc.,
  whether a supply, 62.184
  whether zero-rated, 5.31, 5.32

W

**WAREHOUSED GOODS AND FREE
    ZONES,**
  duty point on supplies of petroleum, 68.2
  removal of goods from warehouse, 68.1
Water,
  definition, 69.4
  supply of, 22.267, 69.1
Winding-up orders,
  application for rescission, 37.4
  validity of, 37.1–37.3
Works of art, 60.7–60.15

X

X-ray service, whether exempt, 33.1

Y

YMCA,
  supplies by, 21.51
  whether a youth club, 21.50
Yoga, whether exempt, 22.293
Youth club facilities, 21.49–21.53

Z

ZERO-RATING,
  books, etc.,
  —address books, 5.44
  —binders, 5.1, 5.25–5.28
  —brochures, 5.54–5.92
  —charts, 5.110
  —cricket scorecards, 5.78
  —diaries, 5.17, 5.44, 5.45
  —dress design kits, 5.55
  —histographs, 5.110
  —information sheets, 5.82
  —journals, 5.93–5.108
  —leaflets, 5.54–5.92
  —mail order catalogues, 5.10, 5.33,
    5.34
  —music, 5.109
  —newspapers, 5.93–5.108
  —pamphlets, 5.54–5.92
  —periodicals, 5.93–5.108
  —photobooks, 5.24
  —photograph albums, 5.29
  —pictorial magazine, 5.95, 5.96
  —property guides, 5.93
  —recipe cards, 5.85
  —religious cards, 5.84
  —surname histories, 5.43
  —tax cards, 5.83
  —textbooks, 5.2–5.7, 5.35, 5.38
  —vouchers, 5.31, 5.32
  caravans and houseboats, 69.5–69.13
  clothing and footwear, 12.1–12.24
  construction of buildings, etc.,
    15.1–15.283
  —access roads, 15.180
  —bridge, 15.33
  —church annexe, 15.155
  —church garage, 15.98
  —church hall, 15.154
  —community centre, 15.88, 15.89
  —conversions, 15.51–15.54,
    15.130–15.147
  —extensions, 15.27–15.29, 19.46, 19.47
  —garages, 15.146, 15.218
  —leisure centre, 15.85
  —recreation centre, 15.105
  —renovation, 15.25, 15.26
  —site, definition of, 15.18, 15.150,
    15.151
  —sports hall, 15.104

ZERO-RATING, – *cont.*
  construction of buildings, etc.,
    15.1–15.283 – *cont.*
    —sports pavilion, 15.83, 15.84, 15.102,
      15.103
    —swimming pool, 15.106, 15.210,
      15.239, 15.240
    —theatre, 15.87
  drugs, medicines, aids for the handicapped,
    etc., 19.1–19.99
    —lifts, 19.95–19.99
  exports, 25.1–25.26
  food, 29.1–29.196
    —beverages, 29.165–29.180
    —catering, 29.1–29.80
    —'confectionery', 29.128–29.164
    —definition of, 29.81–29.105
    —ice cream, 29.125–29.127
    —pet, 29.187–29.196

ZERO-RATING, – *cont.*
  food, 29.1–29.196 – *cont.*
    —potato crisps, etc., 29.181–29.185
  international services, 39.1–39.3
    —diplomatic services, 39.2
    —mare at stud farm, 39.1
  protected buildings, 55.1–55.90
    —definition, 55.1–55.18
  transport, 66.1–66.49
    —definition, 22.226–22.228
    —goods, 66.40
    —handling services, 66.41–66.43
    —passengers, 66.12–66.39
    —ships, 66.1–66.11
  water,
    —definition, 69.4
    —supply of, 69.1
Zoological societies, 16.2, 16.4, 21.6, 22.321